P9-EER-502

THE FACTS ON FILE ENCYCLOPEDIA OF THE 20TH CENTURY

THE FACTS ON FILE ENCYCLOPEDIA OF THE 20TH CENTURY

GENERAL EDITOR
JOHN DREXEL

New York • Oxford

The Facts On File Encyclopedia of the 20th Century

Facts On File, Inc.
460 Park Avenue South
New York NY 10016
USA

Facts On File Limited
Collins Street
Oxford OX4 1XJ
United Kingdom

Library of Congress Cataloging-in-Publication Data

The Facts on file encyclopedia of the 20th century / general editor, John Drexel.
p. cm.
Includes bibliographical references and index.
ISBN 0-8160-2461-8 :
1. History, Modern—20th century—Dictionaries. I. Drexel, John, 1954– . II. Facts on File, Inc. III. Title: Encyclopedia of the 20th century.
D419.F33 1991
909.82'03—dc20 91-21278

British CIP data available on request from Facts On File.

Jacket design by Catherine Hyman
Composition by The Maple-Vail Book Manufacturing Group
Manufactured by R. R. Donnelley
Printed in the United States of America

10 9 8 7 6 5 4 3 2 1

This book is printed on acid-free paper.

General Editor
John Drexel

Consultants
Gert H. Brieger, M.D., William H. Welch Professor of the History of Medicine, Johns Hopkins University School of Medicine

Rachel Hadas, Ph.D., poet, essayist and critic. Associate Professor of English, Rutgers University

John C. Tibbetts, Ph.D., writer, critic and broadcaster

Paul Turok, writer, critic, broadcaster and composer

Contributors
Michael Adams
Chuck Berg
Gregory D. Black
Allan Carpenter
Carole Cook
Chris Cook
John Daintith
Lora Goldman
Barbara Hanson
James John Jurinski
George C. Kohn
Molly McQuade
Sarah Mitchell
Sean Moroney
Diane Moser
John Paxton
John Pile
Karla Powell
Donna Singer
Ray Spangenburg
Harry G. Summers Jr.
Lawrence Sutin
Robert H. Taylor
John C. Tibbetts
Elizabeth Tootill
Martha Visser

Copyeditors
Paul Scaramazza
Joseph Reilly
Sue J. Lowe
Debra Manette
Raine H. Young

Editorial Assistants
James Allen
Anne M. Baxter
Katherine Bruce
Neill Bogan
Carole Campbell
Donald Chapman
Chandrika Kaul
Lisabeth MacKinlay
Douglas C. Smythe

Cartography
Dale Wiliams
Eleanora Sioretti

Photo Research
Randall Pink

Research
Sandra Dhols
Leslie Gale
David Graf

Index
Marjorie Bank

Word Processing
KV Publishing Services

Art Director
Jo Stein

Computer Graphics
Ron Monteleone

Vice President, Production
Olivia McKean

Production Manager
Michael Braunschweiger

PHOTO CREDITS

AP/Wide World Photos: 1, 2, 3, 6, 7, 8, 9 (top; bottom center), 15, 17, 22, 23 (top left; bottom right), 28, 32, 33, 35, 38, 41, 42 (top left; top right), 43, 47, 50 (top; bottom right), 51 (top center; bottom), 53 (top), 55, 56, 65, 66, 67, 68, 69, 72 (top left; bottom right), 74, 75, 77, 78 (top right), 79 (top left; bottom center), 83, 84, 85 (top left; top right), 87, 89, 91, 96, 97 (top center; bottom right), 98 (bottom), 100, 103 (bottom left; center right), 104, 106, 108 (top; bottom right), 112 (top; bottom), 113, 114, 117, 121, 122, 124 (top right), 125, 126, 127, 130, 131 (bottom), 133, 135, 136, 137, 142, 143 (bottom right), 144, 148, 152, 155, 158, 159, 160, 161, 163, 165, 166 (top left; top right), 174, 175, 176 (left), 177, 178, 179 (top left; bottom right), 180, 185 (bottom right), 186, 187, 188 (top left), 189, 191, 192 (bottom), 198, 199, 203, 206 (bottom left; bottom right), 207, 209, 210 (top; bottom right), 213, 219, 222, 223, 225, 229, 230, 233, 234, 236, 237, 238, 239, 246, 251 (bottom right), 252 (top left), 253 (top left), 254 (top left; top right), 255, 260, 263, 264 (top right), 267 (top center; bottom right), 268, 269 (bottom right), 272, 273, 274, 278, 282, 283, 284, 285 (top right), 288 (top left; bottom center), 290, 297 (bottom center; top right), 301 (top right), 302 (top; bottom left), 305, 306 (bottom right), 309 (top; bottom), 315, 320, 322, 323, 327, 332 (bottom center; top right), 333, 334 (top left; bottom), 335, 336, 337 (top left; bottom center), 338 (bottom), 349 (bottom left), 350 (left), 354, 359 (top left; bottom), 360 (top left; bottom center), 361 (top center; bottom right), 366, 372, 373, 374, 375 (bottom right), 377, 380 (top left; bottom left), 381 (top left), 383, 384 (bottom center), 386, 387, 389, 393, 394, 396, 400, 401, 403, 408 (bottom left; top center), 410 (top left; top right; bottom), 411, 413 (top right), 415, 418, 420, 421, 422 (top center), 424, 425, 426 (bottom left), 428, 432 (bottom), 433, 434 (top left; bottom left; bottom right), 436, 437, 439, 445, 446, 447, 450 (top left; bottom right), 452, 454, 455, 466 (top left; top right), 467, 477, 479, 480, 489, 490 (bottom center; top right), 492 (top left), 493, 494, 497 (top right), 502, 504, 505 (bottom left; top center), 506, 508, 510, 513 (top left; bottom center), 514, 515 (bottom), 516 (top center), 518, 525, 530 (top center; bottom), 531, 533, 539, 540, 541 (bottom left; top right), 543, 546, 549, 550, 551, 552, 553, 554, 556, 561, 562, 563, 564, 565, 571 (bottom right), 573, 578, 579, 582 (bottom left; top right), 583, 588, 589, 590, 591, 593 (top; bottom), 594, 595, 596 (top right; bottom right), 598, 599, 605 (bottom; top right), 607 (top left), 608 (top center; bottom right), 610, 612, 613, 616, 620, 622 (center left; top right; bottom), 625, 626, 630, 631 (top left; bottom center), 632 (bottom left), 635, 638, 640 (bottom center; top right), 641, 642, 643, 647, 648 (bottom center), 650 (bottom), 654 (top right), 660, 665, 669, 671 (top left), 672, 675, 677, 680 (top right), 685, 686, 688 (top left), 689, 691, 692, 693, 696, 701, 704 (bottom left), 707, 708 (top right), 709 (top center; bottom right), 710 (top left; bottom center), 711 (bottom right), 713, 714, 715, 717 (top; bottom), 719, 722, 723 (center; top right), 725, 727, 729, 731, 737, 739 (top right), 743 (bottom left; bottom right), 745, 746, 749, 750, 753, 755, 761, 764, 771, 772, 774, 781, 782, 784, 786, 787, 792 (top left; bottom right), 796, 797, 798, 807, 809 (top; bottom center), 810 (top left), 811, 813, 814, 818, 820, 826 (top right; bottom), 830 (bottom center; top right), 833, 835 (top left; bottom center), 838, 839, 843, 844, 847, 849 (top left, bottom center), 854 (bottom left; top center), 859 (bottom left; bottom right), 861, 866 (top center; bottom center), 869, 880, 883, 884 (top right; bottom), 887, 889 (top left, top right), 891, 892, 895 (top; bottom center), 897 (top left; bottom center), 898, 899, 902 (top right), 907, 914, 926, 927, 928, 931, 936 (top), 939, 943 (top left; bottom left), 946, 953, 955, 956, 960 (top left), 961, 962 (top left; bottom right), 963, 965, 975, 976, 979 (bottom left), 980, 987

The Bettmann Archive: 78 (bottom left), 131 (top left), 256, 265, 624, 668, 705, 945

British Information Services: 201

Library of Congress: 13, 29, 31, 42, 52, 54, 92, 99 (top center; bottom center), 108 (bottom left), 132 (bottom center; top right), 143 (top left), 147, 153, 170, 185 (top center), 188 (bottom), 192 (top left), 221, 253 (bottom), 264 (bottom right), 269 (top right), 275, 281, 285, 287, 294, 295 (top left; bottom center), 298, 301 (bottom left), 302 (bottom right), 306 (top left), 307, 318, 338 (top left), 340, 345 (top left; bottom right), 350 (right), 355, 356 (top center; bottom right), 363, 369, 382, 384 (top left), 385, 390, 406 (bottom left; top right), 413 (bottom left), 422 (bottom right), 426 (top right), 427, 432 (top left), 443 (bottom left; bottom right), 444 (top right), 451, 482, 492 (bottom left), 497 (top left), 499, 503, 509, 511, 515, 516 (bottom right), 526, 527, 528, 534, 535, 549, 560, 567, 569, 571 (top center), 581, 597 (bottom left; top right), 600, 602, 606, 607 (bottom right), 614, 615 (top left), 628, 632 (top left), 633, 644, 648 (top left), 650 (top left), 651, 654 (bottom left), 656, 669 (bottom right), 671 (bottom left), 674, 680 (top left), 683, 694, 708 (bottom left), 724, 734, 735 (bottom right), 736, 739 (top right), 741, 751, 754, 756, 757, 770, 773, 778, 779 (bottom left; top right), 780, 783, 788, 810 (bottom right), 821, 825 (top left; bottom right), 834, 857, 862, 875, 902 (top left), 944 (bottom left; top center), 954, 960 (right), 966, 974 (bottom right), 979 (bottom right)

NASA: 40, 364, 379, 615

National Archives: 53 (bottom), 124 (bottom), 176 (bottom right), 194, 217, 248, 251 (top left), 299, 367, 375, 381 (bottom), 431, 444 (bottom left), 456, 478, 485, 501, 523 (top; bottom), 524, 555, 576, 645, 655, 673 (top; bottom), 679, 688, 698, 704 (bottom right), 706, 711, 716, 735 (top), 740, 742, 748, 760, 766, 767, 851, 853, 857, 864, 903, 919, 936 (bottom), 937, 947, 948, 969 (top left; bottom left; top right; bottom right), 971 (top; bottom), 973, 974 (top left), 978, 988

United Nations: 559

FOREWORD

Without discounting the labors of chroniclers of earlier times, it would be safe to say that, in terms of the sheer volume of information available, the 20th century has been more fully documented than any previous century. Indeed, the latter half of the century has been dubbed "the Information Age." To an unprecedented degree, events have been overtaken by a torrent of information (and, often, misinformation); news travels around the globe in microseconds, bursts into the living room and quickly becomes assimilated into the background of everyday life. But information is not the same as insight or understanding. The encyclopedist's task is to distill what is known about a particular subject and to present its essence in a clear and concise form, neither swamping the reader in a sea of overwhelming details nor leaving him or her stranded in a desert of vague conjecture. The question that the editor, consultants and contributors have asked again and again in preparing *The Facts On File Encyclopedia of the 20th Century* is: What information will the reader want, or expect, to find on a particular subject in a single-volume encyclopedia? Or, to phrase it a little differently, what information *must* be included in a particular entry in order to give the reader a basic understanding of that subject in relation to the 20th century? And, beyond that, what information *might* be included that would help to stimulate the reader's curiosity as well as to convey the flavor of the subject in the context of the century? We have endeavored to present as much significant and useful information as can be conveyed gracefully in a concise reference format.

The story of the 20th century is perhaps best understood through the lives of the people who have shaped it. The majority of the entries are therefore biographical: writers, artists, musicians, scientists, inventors, soldiers, politicians, social activists, explorers, athletes, business people and other significant personalities are well represented. This encyclopedia gives prominence to both the movers and shakers of events, and to those whose contributions were less universal but no less indicative of the time and place in which they lived. The focus here is not simply on biographical facts, although these are given; each person is placed in the context of the 20th century, and significant accomplishments are emphasized.

There are also entries for specific events. The 20th century has seen numerous wars, disasters, incidents of terrorism and scandal, and these have been given ample coverage. In addition, well-defined political, social, intellectual, literary and artistic movements are included. On a broader scale, individual nations as well as assimilated nations, former colonies, historic regions and specific places where noteworthy events have occurred, are also given their own entries.

The reader should be aware that the length of any particular entry is not necessarily an indication of the subject's relative importance. Some subjects, including many that are obviously important or even momentous, readily lend themselves to straightforward explanation or condensation. Others, more intrinsically complex, require greater depth of detail in order to convey clearly their significance.

The Facts On File Encyclopedia of the 20th Century is a concise-entry-format reference book, not a historical survey. Therefore, it has not been our intention to include long entries on general topics; rather, we have tried to limit the coverage to specific, well-defined subjects that can be treated in a brief scope. Nevertheless, there are some broad developments so closely identified with the 20th century that they could not be ignored, and we have endeavored to give these as much coverage as space allows.

Controversy has been endemic to the 20th century, and any reference work dealing with this period cannot avoid dealing with its controversies. At the same time, the reference book must leave partisanship to others and take a stance that is scrupulously objective, dispassionate and disinterested (in that word's original meaning). Therefore, when a subject has been the focus of historic controversy, we have mentioned the controversy and stated the various conflicting positions that may exist. Likewise, when historical evidence overwhelmingly supports a particular characterization, we have reported that characterization and cited the facts that support it. However, it is not our purpose to establish a 20th-century canon; the inclusion of a particular subject is not intended to denote editorial "approval," nor is a subject's omission a sign of editorial "disapproval." In determining what specific entries to include in the book, we have relied upon the advice of our consultants and other authorities.

Every effort has been made to verify the facts recorded in this encyclopedia. Names, dates, titles and other details have been carefully checked and rechecked; in many cases where sources disagree, the contradictory claims have been resolved by our consultants or other authorities. In many cases, I have relied on my own judgment—sometimes fallible but more often, I hope, on the mark—in making final editorial decisions. Needless to say, any errors of commission or omission are entirely my responsibility.

USING THIS BOOK

The Facts On File Encyclopedia of the 20th Century includes a number of features that will make the book easy to use and will enhance the reader's pleasure in using it. Foremost among these features are the cross-references that appear within individual entries. Indicated by small capital letters, these cross-references not only alert the reader to a related entry elsewhere in the encyclopedia, but also help the reader to see the often complex but significant connections between different topics that might not otherwise be apparent.

Boldface type within an entry indicates a subsidiary entry—that is, a subject that is closely related to the main entry heading but that does not have a separate entry of its own.

Many of the entries conclude with a list of suggested books for further reading. These particular titles have been selected because of their currency, comprehensiveness and authority; many have been acknowledged by reviewers as definitive treatments of the subject.

Entries on individual nations are accompanied by chronologies, which outline important 20th-century events and give the reader a sense of historical context. The maps and photographs throughout the book complement and enhance the text.

In a work that covers so much information, the index will be particularly helpful. Naturally, it gives the reader the location of the main entry on each subject. But because many subjects are discussed not only under their headings but in other, related entries as well, it will enable the reader to find additional information on that subject in the encyclopedia. If you don't find an entry on the subject you are looking for, consult the index.

ACKNOWLEDGMENTS

Every encyclopedia is the product of a collaborative effort; this one is no different. This book would not have been possible without the contributions of many writers, researchers, scholars, editors. Yet the individual entries have not been written by committee, nor has there been an attempt to impose an artificial uniformity on the entries—such an attempt would not only have been fruitless, but it would also have a leveling effect, robbing each entry of its individual character. Rather, while following certain standard editorial guidelines and keeping in mind the needs of the reader (as outlined above), the contributors have been allowed some latitude to pursue their enthusiasms within their areas of expertise.

Much of the hard work that has gone into producing this encyclopedia has been done behind the scenes. I would personally like to acknowledge the quiet assistance and constructive criticism of a number of colleagues at Facts On File. I am grateful to Gerard Helferich, who gave me the opportunity to edit the encyclopedia and provided many valuable suggestions, and much encouragement, throughout the course of the project. Lydia Grier and Lesly Lavaud of the FOF computer services department helped solve numerous technical problems, including the conversion of hundreds of computer disks from various sources into a compatible program. Nick Bakalar, Gary Krebs, Deirdre Mullane, Paul Scaramazza, James Warren and Mark Young all gave me the benefit of their editorial experience and personal knowledge. Tom Hitchings, Marjorie Bank and the staff of the *Facts On File News Digest* provided much useful information and advice. I am especially indebted to Eleanora von Dehsen, whose immense energy, expertise and good humor proved invaluable during the complex and difficult final stages of preparing this encyclopedia for production. And to my wife, Maureen, whose constant encouragement, steady confidence and practical wisdom helped make a formidable task rather less daunting than it might otherwise have been, I owe more than I can possibly say.

John Drexel
New York City, April 16, 1991

Aachen [French: Aix-la-Chapelle]. Ancient city in the province of North Rhine-Westphalia, in northwestern Germany. Aachen was held by Allied troops (predominantly French) from the end of WORLD WAR I until 1930. It was the first major German city to fall to the Allies in WORLD WAR II.

Aalto, Alvar (1898–1976). Finnish architect and designer. Aalto is one of the most renowned of 20th-century architects. He began his career in the 1920s and soon became a leading member of the International Modern school of architecture, with projects such as the library in Vipuri, Finland (1927–1935). Aalto drew heavily upon native Finnish lumbers in his projects of this period. He also designed wooden furniture and, in 1932, invented the basic process for bent plywood furniture. After World War II, Aalto designed what most critics feel to be his finest architectural projects, most of which showed his independent creative spirit and featured curved walls and single-pitched roofs. These include the Hall of Residence at the Massachusetts Institute of Technology (1947–1949) and the Hall of Culture in Helsinki, Finland (1958).

Aarnio, Eero (1932–). Finnish interior and industrial designer trained in Helsinki at the Institute of Industrial Arts. Aarnio's best known designs are for chairs using plastics as the primary material. His Ball or Globe chair of 1960 is a sphere, open on one side to permit the occupant to move into its upholstered interior. The Gyro chair of 1968 is a round, hollowed-out form of FIBERGLASS in which seating space is a simple hollow in what appears to be a solid, flattened spherical mass.

Aaron, Henry Louis "Hank" (1934–). American baseball player. Aaron is major league baseball's all-time home run leader, with a career total of 755. He broke the record of 714, previously held by Babe RUTH, in April 1974, after a year of building pressure and anticipation. He began his career in the NEGRO LEAGUES, playing two seasons for the Indianapolis Clowns.

Hank Aaron hits number 715.

He spent most of his major league career (1954–74) with the Braves organization, playing his final year with the Milwaukee Brewers, and was named an All-Star every one of those years. Averaging 33 home runs per season, he batted in over 100 runs 15 times. In addition to his batting prowess, he was a skilled fielder, winning four Gold Gloves for his right field play. He was inducted into the Baseball Hall of Fame in 1982.

Aba. City on the Aba River in NIGERIA. Originally settled by the indigenous Ibo tribe, Aba became an administrative center for the British colonial regime in the early decades of the century. In 1929, it was the site of a notable revolt by the women of Aba in protest against British taxation policies.

Abadan. City on Abadan Island in Iran's Khuzestan province, near the northern head of the Persian Gulf. Abadan is an oil pipeline and refining center. It was a key target of Iraqi forces during the IRAN-IRAQ WAR (1980–88).

Abadan Crisis. Crisis of 1951–54, developing from the expulsion by the Iranian government of Western companies from Abadan oil refineries, and the nationalization of the Anglo-Iranian Oil Company. Rather than alleviating poverty, the resulting falling production and exports undermined the position of Premier MOSSADEQ, who was ousted. In August 1954 the oil company was placed under the control of an international consortium.

Abaiang Atoll. Coral atoll (formerly known as Charlotte Island) in Kiribati chain (formerly the Gilbert Islands) in the west-central Pacific Ocean. During WORLD WAR II, it was occupied by the Japanese from 1941 to 1943. After its conquest by American forces, it served as a base of operations for the subsequent capture of the Marshall Islands.

Abbado, Claudio (1933–). Italian conductor. Born in Milan of a musical family, Abbado graduated from the Verdi Conservatory (1955) and also studied conducting with Hans Swarowsky at the Vienna Academy. He made his conducting debut in Trieste in 1958 and debuted in the U.S. conducting the New York Philharmonic in 1963. He made his Metropolitan Opera debut in 1968, became the permanent conductor of Milan's La Scala in 1969 and was appointed its artistic director in 1977. There he instituted a number of innovations, including lengthening the season and broadening the repertoire to include such contemporary composers as Luigi DALLAPICCOLA and Luigi NONO. After the death of Herbert von KARAJAN in 1989, Abbado was appointed music director of the Berlin Philharmonic.

Abbas, Ferhat (1899–1985). Algerian political leader. Abbas' *Manifesto of the Algerian People*, published in 1943, was vital to ALGERIA's fight for independence from FRANCE. In 1958, during Algeria's war for independence, he was named president of the first provisional government declared by the National Liberation Front, a post he held until 1961. In 1962 he was elected president of the National Assembly. He resigned from that position in 1963, when he became dissatisfied with the policies of Algeria's first president, Ahmed BEN BELLA. Ben Bella had him placed under house arrest in 1964. Abbas was not officially rehabilitated until 1984.

Abbey Theatre. Dublin theatre, founded in 1904 by Annie HORNIMAN to provide a venue for Irish drama. Opened with a presentation of work by W.B. YEATS and Lady Augusta GREGORY, the theatre became home to the Irish National Dramatic Society and a focus for the IRISH LITERARY REVIVAL. In 1907 the production of J.M. SYNGE's *Playboy of the Western World* caused riots. However, despite frequent public controversy, the theatre continued to produce new works by Synge, AE, G.B. SHAW, and later Sean O'CASEY. Following World War I, the Abbey began to suffer financially, but in 1925 it received a grant from the new government of Eire, becoming the first state-subsidized theater in the English-speaking world. The theater burned down in 1951 but was rebuilt in 1966. The main Abbey Theatre continued to present largely Irish drama, while experimental works were produced in the Peacock Theatre, opened in 1925 and reopened in 1967.

Abbott, Berenice (1898–). American photographer known for a design-oriented, documentary approach. Abbott went to Paris in 1921 as an art student and, while there, became an assistant to the avant-garde photographer Man RAY. In 1925 she set up practice as a professional portrait photographer. Also during that year, she met French photographer Eugene ATGET, then an elderly and little-known commercial photographer who had, over a lifetime, documented Paris with a huge collection of photos. Abbott acquired his negatives, eventually arranging to have them sold to the MUSEUM OF MODERN ART in New York. After returning to New York in 1929, Abbott turned to documentary photography, taking on the 1935 WPA photo project known as "Changing New York." Later she worked in scientific photography and on a documentary project, "U.S. Route 1." The direct and unsentimental character of her images gave them a design-oriented quality of a kind that came to typify "modern photography." She taught at the New School in New York beginning in 1934 and continued until 1958. She was the author of several technical photography books.

Abbott, Grace (1878–1939). American social reformer. After finishing graduate work at the University of Nebraska in Lincoln, Abbott joined Jane ADDAMS at Hull House in Chicago (1908). That same year she was made director of the Immigrants' Protective League. In the period 1909–1910 her series of articles for the *Chicago Evening Post* exposed the exploitation of immigrants. She joined the faculty of the Chicago School of Civics and Philanthropy in 1910. In 1917 she became director of the child-labor division of the Children's Bureau in Washington, D.C. and administered the first child-labor law. Her subsequent moves took her to various federal and state government posts, and finally to the University of Chicago, where she was a professor of public welfare until her death. At Chicago she also edited the *Social Service Review* (1934–39). Her best known work is considered to be *The Child and the State,* in two volumes (1938).

Abbott and Costello. The comedy team of **Bud Abbott** (William Abbott, 1895–1974) and **Lou Costello** (Louis Francis Cristillo, 1906–59) enjoyed phenomenal popularity in the 1940s and early 1950s. Abbott and Costello were unsuccessful veterans of the vaudeville circuit when they met in 1931. They worked the vaudeville and burlesque theaters in the 1930s, then won national fame after appearing on the Kate SMITH radio show in 1938. Throughout the 1940s they were one of Hollywood's top box-office draws, appearing in farcical slapstick comedies. These include their phenomenally successful *Buck Privates* (1941), *Hold That Ghost* (1942), *The Naughty Nineties* (1945) (featuring the duo's famous "Who's on First?" stand-up routine) and *Abbott & Costello Meet Frankenstein* (1948). Abbott typically played the "straight man" (although he was often a con man at the same time), while Costello was his bumbling sidekick. Their comedy routines relied heavily upon mistaken identity and verbal misunderstandings, usually carried to a ridiculous extreme. Abbott and Costello appeared frequently on the live-television variety shows of the early 1950s and also had a successful TV series of their own, "The Abbott and Costello Show."

"Who's on First?"

ABC [American Broadcasting Company]. The third of the three major television broadcasting networks in the U.S., ABC was formed in 1943 when Edward J. Noble, head of Life Savers candy, purchased the so-called "Blue network" of six radio stations from NBC. ABC merged with United Paramount Theaters in 1952. While its larger rivals NBC and CBS prospered throughout the 1950s and '60s, ABC subsisted on a diet of westerns and popular melodramas but consistently remained in third place, drawing fewer viewers and losing money. The network finally came into its own in the mid-1970s, and during the 1975–76 season it beat CBS and NBC in the ratings for the first time. This success was largely due to ABC's innovative sports programs, produced by Roone ARLEDGE. Situation comedies and made-for-TV movies also featured in the network's programming. The network's news coverage increased and improved during the 1980s (again under Arledge, who had become president of ABC news). ABC and its affiliate local stations led the way in popularizing news broadcasts with light human-interest features and newsroom chat. ABC was acquired by Capital Cities Communications, Inc., in 1986; the new company was known as Capital Cities/ABC, Inc. In addition to its television and radio broadcasting interests, the company is also involved in publishing, recording and other facets of the entertainment industry.

Abdali. Located to the north of the port of ADEN, this onetime sultanate of southern Arabia was a signatory to the 1937 treaty that established Aden as a British colony. In 1967, it was annexed to Southern Yemen (now part of the Republic of YEMEN).

Abd el-Krim (1882–1963). Nationalist leader of the Rif tribes in Morocco. A public official and newspaper editor in Spanish Morocco, he was infuriated by

Spain's corrupt colonial practices. He led a small rebel force in victorious sorties against the Spanish army in 1921. During the next four years Abd el-Krim led his troops against the Spanish in a number of successful engagements, culminating in his advance into French Morocco in 1925. There he was defeated by a massive Franco-Spanish army led by Marshal PETAIN. Exiled to Reunion, he was detained there for over 20 years. In 1947 he escaped to Egypt, where he continued to encourage Arab resistance to imperialism.

Abdication Crisis. Crisis provoked in the United Kingdom in 1936 by the abdication of King Edward VIII so that he could marry the American divorcee Wallis SIMPSON. The marriage was opposed by the government of Prime Minister Stanley BALDWIN. Edward insisted on the right to marry the woman he loved; Baldwin and the British cabinet felt the marriage was constitutionally and doctrinally unsound. After efforts to create a morganatic marriage failed, Edward decided to abdicate, a decision announced in a moving radio address to the realm on December 11, 1936. Created duke of WINDSOR, he went into voluntary exile in France, marrying Mrs. Simpson there in 1937. Edward, the first British monarch to abdicate voluntarily, was succeeded by GEORGE VI.

Abdul Hamid (1842–1918). Sultan of TURKEY (1876–1909). The son of Sultan Abdul Majid, he succeeded his insane brother Murad V. During 1876–77, after the Berlin Treaty, which reduced Turkey's European territory, he ruled constitutionally, but after May 1877 he ruled as an absolute monarch. Despite some local administrative reforms in the Asiatic provinces, the sultan's ministers adamantly opposed reform, and in 1895–96 his inability to restrain irregular troops during the Armenian massacres made him notorious throughout Europe. Turkey's main European ally was now GERMANY. In 1908 the YOUNG TURKS forced Abdul Hamid to summon a parliament. An attempted counterrevolution resulted in his overthrow and exile from the capital in April 1909. (See also OTTOMAN EMPIRE.)

For further reading:

Pears, Edwin, *The Life of Abdul Hamid.* New York: Ayer, first pub. 1917.

Abdul-Jabbar, Kareem [born Ferdinand Lewis Alcindor Jr.] (1947–). American basketball player. Beginning with his years as a high school star center at Power Memorial Academy in New York City, Abdul-Jabbar dominated every court he played on. First known as Lew Alcindor, he later joined the BLACK MUSLIMS and took the name Kareem Abdul-Jabbar. During his years at UCLA (1965–68), the team won three National Collegiate Athletic Association (NCAA) championships. He turned pro with the NBA Milwaukee Bucks in 1969 and was named that season's rookie of the year. While with the Bucks, he twice led the league in scoring and game point average and led the team to a championship. In 1975 he was traded to the Los Angeles Lakers, where he would

Kareem lets go with the "skyhook" in his final NBA season (Nov. 22, 1988).

be a part of championship teams. He announced his retirement before the 1988–89 season, and was honored in every city in the league. Abdul-Jabbar finished his career with 38,387 points, eclipsing Wilt CHAMBERLAIN's record of 31,419. He has written two autobiographical books, *Giant Steps* (1985) and *Kareem* (1990).

Abdullah ibn Hussein (1882–1951). King of JORDAN. Second son of Emir Hussein and brother of King FAISAL I, he was also the king of Hejaz (1916–24). During WORLD WAR I, Abdullah was associated with T.E. LAWRENCE, and was a leader of the Arab revolt against the Ottoman Turks. His guerrilla raids isolated Turkish troops in MEDINA, in western Arabia. In 1921 Britain recognized Abdullah as emir of Transjordania—the eastern portion of the PALESTINE mandate taken from Turkey after 1918. Abdullah remained on good terms with the British, becoming king of Transjordan (renamed Jordan in 1949) when the mandate expired in 1946. After the failure of an attempt to unite Palestine under his rule in 1949, Abdullah accepted the throne of the Hashemite Kingdom of the Jordan—the eastern part of the former Palestine mandate. He was assassinated on June 20, 1951, in Jerusalem.

Abe, Kobo [Kimfusa Abe] (1924–). Japanese novelist, short story writer, dramatist, essayist. Abe received an M.D. from Tokyo University in 1948, but his first short story collection, *The Wall*, established his reputation in Japan in 1951. The most avant-garde and metaphysical author of modern Japan, Abe was influenced by DADA and SURREALISM, but he brings a scientist's point of view to his fiction. He is often compared to KAFKA and BECKETT. His greatest success both at home and abroad was the existentialist novel *Woman in the Dunes* (1962; tr. 1964), which he adapted for film. Abe also writes for radio and television. Other novels in translation include *Inter Ice Age Four* (1959; tr. 1970), *The Face of Another* (1964; tr. 1966), *The Ruined Map* (1967; tr. 1969), *The Box Man* (1973; tr. 1975) and *Secret Rendezvous* (1977; tr. 1979); his first English-language collection of stories was *Beyond the Curve* (1991).

Abel, I(orwith) W(ilbur) (1908–1987). U.S. labor leader. Abel helped found the United Steelworkers of America and served as the union's third president from 1965 to 1977. During that period union membership rose dramatically, and a strike fund of more than $85 million was amassed. Abel was instrumental in the historic 1973 no-strike agreement to end production and stockpiling swings.

Abel, John Jacob (1857–1938). American biochemist. Abel was educated at the University of Michigan, Johns Hopkins University, and at universities in Leipzig, Heidelberg, Wurzburg, Vienna, Bern and Strasbourg, where he received an M.D. in 1888. He worked briefly at the University of Michigan before being appointed in 1893 to the first chair of pharmacology at Johns Hopkins, a post he retained until his retirement in 1932. Abel had first-rate training in chemistry and was convinced that the study of molecules and atoms was as important as the observation of multicellular tissues under the microscope. He thus began by working on the chemical composition of various bodily tissues and fluids and, in 1897, succeeded in isolating a physiologically active substance from the adrenal glands, which he named epinephrine, also known as **adrenaline.**

As early as 1912 Abel formulated the idea of an artificial kidney and in 1914 isolated for the first time amino acids from the blood. He was less successful with his search (1917–24) for the pituitary hormone, as he was unaware that several hormones were involved. His 1926 announcement that he had crystallized INSULIN met with considerable skepticism, especially regarding its protein nature. This work was not generally accepted until the mid 1930s.

After his retirement Abel devoted himself to a study of the tetanus toxin.

Abell, George (1927–1983). American astronomer and cosmologist. He was known for his discovery of the **Abell Galaxy,** which was for many years considered the largest known object in the universe. His *Abell Catalogue of Clusters* (1958) was long the standard catalog of clusters of galaxies visible from the Northern Hemisphere; it was used by astronomers throughout the world. Abell helped popularize astronomy with his books, lectures and television appearances. He was also a public critic of popular claims of supernatural phenomena. He taught at the University of California for 17 years.

Abell, Kjeld (1901–1961). Danish playwright and artist. He studied economics and later worked as a commercial artist in Paris and London, resettling in Denmark in 1930 to work as a stage designer. His early works, including *Melodien der blevvock* (*The Melody That Got Lost,* 1931), wittily assailed bourgeois values and pettiness. Most notable is *Anna Sophie Hedvig* (1939), which expresses his dismay at the failure of the middle classes to rise up against FASCISM. Other works include *Dan bla pekineser* (*The Blue Pekingese,* 1954) and *Skiget* (*The Scream,* 1961). Abell's plays reject naturalism in favor of experimentalism.

Abelson, Philip Hauge (1913–). American physical chemist. Abelson was educated at Washington State College and at the University of California at Berkeley, where he obtained his Ph.D. in 1939. Apart from the war years at the Naval Research Laboratory in Washington, he spent his entire career at the Carnegie Institution, Washington. He served as the director of the geophysics laboratory from 1953 and became president of the institute in 1971. In 1940 he assisted Edwin MCMILLAN in creating the first transuranic element, neptunium, by bombarding uranium with neutrons in the Berkeley cyclotron.

Abelson next worked on separating the isotopes of uranium by thermal diffusion. Collecting sufficient uranium-235 involved Abelson in massive research and engineering projects possible only in wartime. In the Philadelphia Navy Yard, he constructed 100 or so 48-foot precision-engineered pipes through which steam was pumped. From this Abelson was able to obtain uranium enriched to 14 U-235 atoms per 1,000.

Although this was still too weak a mixture for a bomb, it was sufficiently enriched to use in other separation processes. A bigger plant was constructed at Oak Ridge, Tenn., and provided enriched material for the separation process from which came the fuel for the first ATOMIC BOMB. After the war Abelson extended the important work of Stanley MILLER on the origin of vital biological molecules. He found that amino acids could be produced from a variety of gases if carbon, nitrogen, hydrogen and oxygen were present. He was also able to show the great stability of amino acids by identifying them in 300-million-year-old fossils.

Abemana Atoll. Coral atoll (formerly known as Roger Simpson Island) in Kiribati (formerly the Gilbert Islands chain) in the west-central Pacific Ocean; site of the formal British annexation of the Gilbert Islands in 1892. Held by Japanese forces during WORLD WAR II, from 1942 to 1943, when it was captured by the American military.

Abercrombie, Lascalles (1881–1938). British poet and critic. Born in Cheshire, Abercrombie was educated at Malvern College and Manchester University. He began his career as a journalist and reviewer, publishing his first collection of verse, *Interludes in Poems,* in 1908. He became lecturer in poetry at the University of Liverpool and, eventually, Goldsmith's Reader of English at Oxford. A contributor to *Georgian Poetry,* he was admired by fellow contributor Rupert BROOKE. Abercrombie's work reflects his marvel at the rapid changes of the early 20th century. Highly regarded during his lifetime, Abercrombie has been overshadowed by the modernist poets who followed him (see MODERNISM). Other works include: *The Sale of St. Thomas* (1931), a play; *Thomas Hardy* (1912), and *Principles of Literary Criticism* (1932).

Aberdeen. Port city on the North Sea. Aberdeen serves as an administrative center for the Grampian region of Scotland, but it has also grown as an industrial hub since the commencement of oil drilling operations in the North Sea in the 1970s.

Aberfan disaster. Slide of two million tons of coal waste, mud and rocks that occurred in the Welsh village of Aberfan on the morning of October 21, 1966. Engulfing a schoolhouse, farm and 16 cottages in debris that reached a height of 45 ft., the avalanche of slag from a mountain of mine waste caused 192 deaths, 113 of them children.

Abernathy, Ralph David (1926–1990). American CIVIL RIGHTS leader. Abernathy was a top aide to the Rev. Martin Luther KING Jr. in the 1950s and 1960s. The two organized the MONTGOMERY BUS BOYCOTT (1955) after a black woman, Rosa Parks, was arrested for refusing to give up her seat to a white person. Abernathy was also a leading figure in the 1963 MARCH ON WASHINGTON. Following King's assassination in 1968, Abernathy became head of the SOUTHERN CHRISTIAN LEADERSHIP CONFERENCE, a position he held for nine years. His 1989 autobiography, *And the Walls Came Tumbling Down,* caused a storm of controversy. In the book, Abernathy alleged that King had had an adulterous affair on the night before he was killed.

Abidjan. Port city on the Gulf of Guinea in West Africa. The capital and major urban center of COTE D'IVOIRE (formerly Ivory Coast), Abidjan enjoyed its first major growth under French colonial rule during the 1920s. It became the colonial capital in 1934 and retained that status when Ivory Coast achieved independence in 1960.

ABM Treaty. The Anti-Ballistic Missile Treaty, signed by the U.S. and the Soviet Union on May 26, 1972, sought to maintain the nuclear balance of power by limiting both nations' ability to deploy anti-nuclear weapons systems. In 1967, President Lyndon JOHNSON had first suggested an ABM treaty; negotiations began at the SALT I talks in 1969, and the treaty was signed with the rest of the SALT I agreement three years later. The ABM Treaty later figured prominently in debate of the STRATEGIC DEFENSE INITIATIVE, because critics of that system contended that it was in violation of the earlier agreement.

abortion. Abortion is perhaps the most controversial moral, legal and political issue in the U.S. in the late 20th century. In technical terms, abortion is a method of preventing the birth of an unwanted child by inducing a miscarriage. Although the procedure itself is relatively simple when practiced by a qualified medical person, the issue of whether abortion is an appropriate means of ending a pregnancy is one fraught with emotional and philosophical repercussions.

Advocates of legalized abortion, who regard themselves as "pro-choice," claim that a fetus is not a person and that a woman should have the right to make her own reproductive decisions; government regulation of abortion is seen as an unconstitutional intrusion of government into a private matter. Abortion rights advocates also cite the high incidence of serious injury or death from illegal abortions performed under unsanitary conditions by unskilled abortionists. In the U.S. and Western Europe, the demand for the legalization of abortion was led by the WOMEN'S MOVEMENT in the 1960s and '70s. In asserting the right to abortion in ROE V. WADE (1973), the Supreme Court invoked the right to privacy implicit in the Constitution and affirmed earlier in GRISWOLD V. CONNECTICUT.

Opponents of abortion, mainly Roman Catholics and Protestant fundamentalists who regard themselves as "pro-life," rely largely on moral and religious arguments. Many abortion opponents believe that human life begins at the moment of conception, or at least that a fetus is more than a mere collection of tissues; in this view, abortion is therefore murder. Some opponents of abortion claim that if abortion can be justified, any means can be used to justify any end. For them, the fact that a baby is unwanted is not sufficient cause to justify abortion. Anti-abortion activists have sought to protect the rights of the unborn, but most U.S. courts ruling on the issue have ruled in favor of the woman's rights over those of the fetus. The Supreme Court decision in WEBSTER V. REPRODUCTIVE HEALTH SERVICES (1989) neither upheld nor overturned the ruling in *Roe v. Wade,* but gave states the right to regulate abortion. Subsequently, abortion again became a major issue in state and local elections.

Public opinion polls in the U.S. in the late 1980s and early '90s show that the American population is almost evenly divided over the issue. Despite the polarized views on abortion, most Americans believe that abortions should not be undertaken lightly or encouraged as a routine method of birth control; on the other hand, few believe that prohibitions on abortion should be absolute, but rather believe that exceptions may be made in cases in which the fetus is deformed, the mother's health is at risk, or of rape. Abortion laws were liberalized in the UNITED KINGDOM in 1967, and abortion is currently legal, to various degrees, in all the nations of Western Europe except IRELAND. In such communist nations as the U.S.S.R. and the People's Republic of CHINA (and in nations formerly under communist control, such as East Germany), abortion is widely practiced as a means of birth control.

Abrahams, Peter [Peter (Henry) Graham] (1919–). South African novelist and journalist. Born in Vrededorp near Johannesburg to an Ethiopian father and a mother of mixed races, Abrahams did not learn to read until he was nine, but was later educated at St. Peter's College and Teacher's Training College. He held many menial jobs and tried unsuccessfully to start a school for poor Africans. After publication of his first volume of poetry, *A Black Man Speaks of Freedom* (1940), he enlisted on a British ship and moved to England, where he worked as a journalist. He was commissioned by the British government to write *Jamaica* (1957); while researching the book he was seduced by the charm of the island and moved there. Abrahams's writing explores the problems and history of Africa, at times angrily denouncing the racism and repression of his birthplace. His other works include: *Mine Boy* (1946), *This Island Now* (1966), *The View from Coyaba* (1985), all novels; and two volumes of autobiography, *Return to Goli* (1953) and *Tell Freedom* (1954). (See also APARTHEID, SOUTH AFRICA.)

Abrams, Creighton Williams, Jr. (1914–1974). U.S. Army general; commander of U.S. forces in VIETNAM. A graduate of West Point in 1936, Abrams served as deputy to General William WESTMORELAND, then succeeded him as commander of U.S. forces in Vietnam in July 1968, when Westmoreland was named Army chief of staff. In his new position, Abrams was faced with the difficult tasks of reducing U.S troop levels and "Vietnamizing" the war; he also planned the 1970 invasion of CAMBODIA. In 1972, Abrams was named Army chief of staff.

ABSCAM. Bribery scandal that resulted in the conviction of several congressmen and a U.S. senator in 1980–81. Representative John W. Jenrette Jr. (Ohio) and Senator Harrison Williams (New Jersey), among other officials, were lured into a "sting" operation conducted by FBI agents posing as wealthy Arabs wishing to pay cash bribes in return for legislative favors. During the scandal the nightly news included film of several congressmen receiving and stuffing cash into their pockets. A congressional investigation was followed by federal prosecution. Despite pleas that they were "entrapped" by overzealous government agents, most of the participants were ultimately convicted. All of the wrongdoers either resigned or were defeated for reelection to Congress.

Abstract Art. Term applied to a dominant movement in 20th-century art that has abandoned the traditional Western aesthetic view that art should imitate the forms of nature. Instead, Abstract Art validates the analytical and imaginative creation by artists of new pictorial and sculptural realities that either drastically simplify natural forms or resort to altogether nonrepresentational geometric or random forms. The Russian painter Wassily KANDINSKY is commonly regarded as the first purely abstract painter by virtue of his 1910 geometric canvases, while the Rumanian sculptor Constantin BRANCUSI pioneered the use of abstract forms in sculpture in the subsequent decade. Another early, influential abstract painter was the Dutch artist Piet MONDRIAN, who was a member of the abstract-influenced de STIJL group formed in 1917. By the 1930s, Abstract Art had become a widely accepted form of artistic expression.

Abstract Expressionism. Emerged in New York in the late 1940s and flourished 1950s; in essence an intensification of ABSTRACT ART aesthetics. The term Abstract Expressionism was first applied to the work of the Russian painter Wassily KANDINSKY, but in general usage it refers to the works of a group of Manhattan-based painters of the postwar period, most notably Arshile Gorky, Franz KLINE, Willem DE KOONING, Jackson POLLOCK and Mark ROTHKO. Abstract Expressionism was the first American artistic movement to have a dominant influence on European painting. Its primary tenets were an emphasis on intuitive, emotional expression over prescribed technique, a denial of the classical ideal of a "finished" work of art that concealed the creative process, and a celebration of self-determined aesthetic standards. A famous form of Abstract Expressionism was the "action" paintings of Pollock, who spattered his canvases with paint to allow for free-form energy patterns in his work.

Abu Dhabi. One of the emirate states located on the west coast of the Persian Gulf. Abu Dhabi became a British protectorate in 1892. After it was granted independence in 1971, it joined six other emirates to become the UNITED ARAB EMIRATES, with the city of Abu Dhabi as capital. Abu Dhabi is the largest and most economically powerful of the emirates.

Abu Nidal [nom de guerre of Sabry al-Banna] (1937–). Palestinian terrorist. Born in Jaffa (now part of ISRAEL), he was educated at a private Palestinian school in Jerusalem. Committing himself to the cause of Palestinian liberation, he received military training in North Korea (1970). He joined the Al-Fatah party of Yasir ARAFAT, but broke with it in 1973 over policy disputes and founded the radical FATAH REVOLUTIONARY COUNCIL in 1974. Abu Nidal directed numerous terrorist attacks on Israelis, on Western targets, on moderate Arabs and on rival terrorist leaders. He vowed to kill Arafat after Arafat and the PLO publicly renounced terrorism in 1988. In 1989 he was arrested in Libya, probably at the insistence of Arab governments and the PLO, who could no longer tolerate his violent hard line.

Abu-Simbel. Archaeological dig site on the Nile River, in Egypt's Aswan province. Abu-Simbel, once a center of the ancient Nubian civilization, is the site of two sandstone temples constructed ca. 1250 B.C. These temples were rediscovered in 1812 but were subsequently threatened by the waters banked up by the ASWAN DAM. In the 1960s, UNESCO completed a rescue effort in the course of which the temples were cut out of their surrounding cliffs and reassembled on higher ground 200 feet up.

Abwehr. German intelligence agency during WORLD WAR II. Formed after the Nazis came to power in 1933, in contravention of the terms of the VERSAILLES TREATY, it became extremely powerful under the direction of Admiral Wilhelm CANARIS, who took command in 1935. The agency was active in information-gathering and counterespionage work but was rendered less efficient by the meddling of Reinhard HEYDRICH, head of the army's intelligence services. Gradually, after 1938, the Abwehr became a center of conspiracy against HITLER's regime, while still being involved in intelligence work. Heinrich HIMMLER, who also distrusted the Abwehr and its leader, was instrumental in having Canaris dismissed in 1944, and the Abwehr was absorbed into a combined intelligence service called the *Militarische Amt*.

Abzug, Bella (1920–). U.S. political leader. Bella Abzug was born in the Bronx, New York, and practiced law in New York City beginning in 1944. In the 1960s she was a founder of Women's Strike for Peace, and in 1970 she was elected to Congress as a Democrat from Manhattan. In the House, she was an outspoken advocate of welfare reform, women's rights and other liberal causes and an outspoken critic of the war in Vietnam. She resigned her congressional seat in 1976 to run for the U.S. Senate, but lost to Daniel Patrick Moynihan in the primary. After leaving office, Abzug remained active in politics and was an active supporter of the EQUAL RIGHTS AMENDMENT.

Academy Awards. Annual U.S. awards, popularly known as Oscars, bestowed by the Academy of Motion Picture Arts and Sciences upon films and film artists and technicians. The first awards ceremony, on May 16, 1929—presided over by Academy President Douglas FAIRBANKS Sr.—was a small, informal banquet where a handful of members voted several merit awards for 1927–28, including a best picture award to the aviation epic, *Wings*. Voting was soon extended to the entire membership. In 1941 the policy of using sealed envelopes was begun. Four years later national radio covered the event; and in 1953 network television broadcast

Marlee Matlin receiving Academy Award for best actress, 1987.

it nationwide. Today, the nominations are made from each of 13 art and craft branches—actors selecting actors, editors selecting editors, etc.—and the entire membership, which has held steady at 4,000, then votes by secret ballot on the final winners in all categories. Legend holds that the "Oscar" nickname comes from Bette DAVIS, who declared the figurine resembled her first husband, Harmon Oscar Nelson Jr. Each statuette—the original design is by MGM art director Cedric Gibbons—is valued at $100, but the box-office benefits to a film can be enormous. For example, when *Platoon* (1986) won several Oscars (including best picture), its box-office income exceeded $138 million in a matter of weeks. All-time winners in the Oscar sweepstakes include *Ben Hur* (1959) with 11 Oscars, John FORD with four best director Oscars and Katharine HEPBURN with three best actress Oscars. Some celebrities have refused their awards (George C. Scott in 1970 for *Patton* and Marlon BRANDO in 1972 for THE GODFATHER) and others have never won at all (GARBO, HITCHCOCK, MONROE, BARRYMORE and Cary GRANT, to name but a few). Although the academy insists that its awards honor the work and not the particular person, many critics and artists insist that it is a popularity contest.

For further reading:

Peter H. Brown, *The Real Oscar: The Story Behind the Academy Awards.* Westport: Arlington House, 1981

Academy of Sciences of the U.S.S.R. Founded in St. Petersburg in 1724 by Peter the Great as the Russian Academy of Sciences. From the Russian Revolution (1917) until 1925 it was known as the Academy of Sciences of Russia. It is the chief coordinating body for scientific research within the U.S.S.R., directing the work of over 260 scientific institutions.

Achebe, Chinua (1930–). Nigerian novelist. Born in Nigeria, he was among the first students to pursue a degree at the University College of Ibadan. He later worked for the Nigerian Broadcasting Company. He is perhaps best known for his first four novels, *Things Fall Apart* (1958), *No Longer at Ease* (1960), *Arrow of God* (1964) and *A Man of the People* (1966), which examined the clash between tradition and modern civilization. A prolific writer, his other works include *Ant Hills of the Savannah* (1988) and *Hopes and Impediments* (1989). Achebe's often angry, deft satire and his keen ear for spoken language have made him one of the most highly esteemed African writers in English.

For further reading:

Innes, C.L., *Chinua Achebe,* New York: Cambridge University Press, 1990.

Acheson, Dean (Gooderham) (1893–1971). American statesman and secretary of state (1949–53); a key figure in planning U.S. foreign policy in the immediate post-World War II period. Born in Middletown, Connecticut, Acheson attended Yale University and graduated from Harvard Law School in 1918. He was private secretary to Supreme Court Associate Justice Louis D. BRANDEIS from 1919 to 1921, afterward joining a Washington, D.C., law firm. Acheson entered government service in 1933 as undersecretary of the treasury under President ROOSEVELT. He joined the State Department in 1941, serving as assistant secretary of state until 1945, as undersecretary of state from 1945 to 1947 and as secretary of state from 1949 to 1953. Acheson was instrumental in planning and carrying out America's activist role in the postwar world and in instituting the economic and military containment of communist expansion that was to be the cornerstone of U.S. COLD WAR policy for over four decades. Consistent with this stance, he was also important in establishing the NORTH ATLANTIC TREATY ORGANIZATION (NATO). His attempts to disengage the U.S. from its commitment to the Nationalist Chinese regime drew a great deal of criticism, as did his support of American involvement and failure to achieve peace in the KOREAN WAR. In spite of his unswerving anticommunist stand, Acheson became the target of the reigning red-baiters of the 1950s, in particular, of their leader, Senator Joseph R. MCCARTHY. He left government service in 1953 but retained an unofficial role by advising Presidents John F. KENNEDY and Lyndon B. JOHNSON.

Achi Baba. Prominent high ground located at tip of European Turkey's GALLIPOLI PENINSULA. In WORLD WAR I, during the battle of Gallipoli, Achi Baba was the chief defensive location for Turkish military forces.

***Achille Lauro* hijacking.** On October 7, 1985, Palestinian terrorists hijacked an Italian cruise liner, the *Achille Lauro,* in the Mediterranean and murdered an invalid American passenger. The hijackers surrendered in Egypt on October 9 in return for safe passage to Tunis. American jets intercepted the aircraft taking the hijackers to Tunis on October 10 and forced it to land in Sicily, where the Italian authorities arrested them.

Achinese Rebellion of 1953–59. In 1953 Muslim Achinese rebels in northern Sumatra protested against the annexation of the state of Achin (Acheh; now Atjeh) to the republic of INDONESIA, formed in 1950. On September 20 Tengku Daud Beureuh, military governor of Achin before its annexation, led an open armed rebellion against the government of President SUKARNO. Achinese attacked police and army posts, attempting to obtain more arms for a full-scale rebellion. Scattered guerrilla fighting continued until a cease-fire was arranged in March 1957, when Achin was declared a separate province. Native revolts broke out on other Indonesian islands that sought more autonomy. The Achinese rebels resumed fighting, which resulted in Sukarno declaring Achin a special district with autonomy in matters of religion and local law.

Achinese War of 1873–1907. After the British recognized Dutch influence in Achin (now Atjeh), a Muslim state in northern Sumatra, the Dutch sent two expeditions to conquer the Achinese in 1873. The Achinese palace in the capital, Kutaraja, was seized. In 1903 the sultan of Achin, Muhammed Daud, concluded a treaty with the Dutch, recognizing Dutch sovereignty and relinquishing his throne. Many Achinese refused to accept Dutch rule and continued to wage war. Slowly, using a "castle strategy" (establishing fortresses for Dutch troops throughout the area), the Dutch were able to pacify the Achinese by the end of 1907.

acid rain. Precipitation (rain, snow, sleet and hail) containing acid pollutants, usually sulfuric or nitric acid. This rain has a pH of 2.4–4.5 as opposed to the 5.0 pH of unpolluted precipitation. The rain is basically an industrial phenomenon, resulting from the chemical reaction of airborne water vapor with the sulfur dioxide and nitrogen oxides contained in such pollutants as the exhaust from automobiles and the high-sulfur materials expelled from factory smokestacks. Acid rain has been a particularly disturbing environmental problem since the 1950s, polluting lakes, rivers and streams and destroying aquatic life; killing trees and plants; contaminating drinking water with acid-laced soil leachates; and eroding such manmade objects as buildings, bridges and outdoor sculpture. The problem has yet to be solved, although it has been treated by devices that reduce sulfur and nitrogen compounds in car and factory emissions, by the addition of alkaline lime to certain bodies of water and by other measures.

ACLU. See AMERICAN CIVIL LIBERTIES UNION.

Acmeists. Group of Russian poets formed in 1912 in ST. PETERSBURG in reaction to the SYMBOLISTS. The leading members were Anna AKHMATOVA, her husband Nikolai Stepanovich GUMILEV and Osip MANDELSTAM; other members included Mikhail Kuzmin and Sergei Gorodetsky. Their work was published in the journal *Apollon,* edited by Sergei Makovsky. Acmeist poetry was highly individualistic and was marked by a strong emphasis on aesthetics and form, concise imagery and direct expression. In contrast to the FUTURISTS, the Acmeists had great respect for tradition. Mandelstam described Acmeism as "a longing for world culture." The group disbanded in 1917 and its members went their separate ways.

Action Francaise. Rightist political movement in France (1899–1944). It was founded by poet and journalist Charles Maurras (1868–1952) and championed by essayist and journalist Leon DAUDET (1867–1942). Through its eponymous newspaper and through student groups, the *Camelots du Roi,* it attacked the democratic institutions of the Third Republic, supported royalism and nationalism and espoused ANTI-SEMITISM. Pope PIUS XI condemned the movement in 1926, and it was banned by the French government 10 years later. Action Francaise continued as an underground movement, surfacing to support the VICHY government during World War II. It was disbanded in 1944 when France was liberated and Maurras was sentenced to life imprisonment for collaboration.

Adamawa. Former African tribal kingdom, located near the Benue River basin. After its conquest by the British in 1901, Adamawa was divided between Britain's NIGERIA colony and the German colony of Kamerun. The German portion was conquered by Allied forces during WORLD WAR I and was placed under joint British and French mandate in 1922. (See also CAMEROON.)

Adams, Ansel (Easton) (1902–1984). American photographer. One of the most widely exhibited photographers in the U.S., Adams was best known for his majestic black-and-white landscapes of the American West. He began taking photographs at the age of 14. Adams was credited with pioneering innovations in photographic technology and helping to gain recognition for photography as a legitimate art form. In a career spanning more than 50 years, he had photographs published in more than 35 books and portfolios. He cofounded the department of photography at the MUSEUM OF MODERN ART in New York City. An avid environmentalist, Adams became the official photographer of the Sierra Club in 1928 and served as a director of the club for 37 years.

Adams, John Bertram. British nuclear physicist. Adams was considered the architect of the giant atom-smasher built in the early 1970s for the European Center for Nuclear Research (CERN). He directed the center from 1976 to 1981. Under his leadership, the laboratory discovered the W and Z particles, subatomic particles considered to be keys to the understanding of matter.

Adams, John Michael Geoffrey "Tom" (1931–1985). Barbadan politician. Adams became prime minister of BARBADOS in 1976 when his Barbados Labour Party won an election after 15 years in opposition. A staunch anticommunist and a firm ally of the U.S. in the Caribbean, he gave strong support to the U.S.-led invasion of GRENADA in October 1983. He served as prime minister until his death.

Adams, Maude [Maude Adams Kiskadden] (1872–1953). American stage actress. Daughter of the leading lady of a Salt Lake City stock company, Adams played most of the standard child roles of the day, including "Little Eva" in *Uncle Tom's Cabin,* before she was 15. Her big break came when legendary Broadway producer Charles Frohman introduced her to writer James M. BARRIE. The three collaborated on a string of sensational successes, Adams appearing in Frohman's American productions from the popular Scottish writer: as Lady Babbie in *The Little Minister* (1897); Miss Phoebe in *Quality Street* (1902); Maggie Wylie in *What Every Woman Knows* (1908); and the title role in *Peter Pan.* From opening night, November 6, 1905, to her farewell as "Pan" in 1915, Adams played the flying boy more than 1,500 times in New York and

Ansel Adams in front of his photograph "Boards and Thistles."

on tour. Onstage, she seemed a boy-girl, or a woman-child—a curious hybrid of earthy experience and elfin charm. Offstage, she had a passion for privacy, despite a string of unsuccessful suitors. At the peak of her success she was the top moneymaking star in America, averaging $20,000 a week. She retired in 1918. Perhaps her greatest tribute came from Barrie himself: "I believe you have become Peter Pan in such a magical way that my only fear is your flying clear away out of the theatre some night."

For further reading:

Robbins, Phyllis, *Maude Adams: An Intimate Portrait.* New York: G.P. Putnam's Sons, 1956.

Adams, Michael (1930–1967). U.S. test pilot; killed while making the 191st flight of the U.S.'s most famous experimental plane—the X-15. He was the only X-15 test flight fatality, with just eight more flights to go before completion of the tests. Adams, who had flown 49 combat missions in Korea, had joined the Air Force Test Pilot School at Edwards Air Force Base in California in 1962. Originally chosen to participate in the Air Force Manned Orbiting Laboratory programs, Adams chose in 1966 to fly the X-15 instead. During his final flight, Adams pushed the X-15 rocket plane to an altitude of 50.4 miles, qualifying him for U.S. Air Force astronaut wings.

Adams, Roger (1889–1971). American organic chemist. Adams studied chemistry at Harvard, where he obtained his Ph.D. in 1912, and at the University of Berlin. After working briefly at Harvard, he joined the staff of the University of Illinois in 1916 and later served as professor of organic chemistry from 1919 until his retirement in 1957. Adams was one of the most important chemists in the U.S. in the interwar period, and under him the University of Illinois became one of the leading centers of American chemistry.

Adams, Samuel A. (1934–1988). Central Intelligence Agency analyst; a codefendant in General William WESTMORELAND's libel suit against CBS Inc. A Southeast Asia expert, Adams was a consultant and major contributor to the CBS documentary "The Uncounted Enemy: A Vietnam Deception," which accused Westmoreland of conspiring to underestimate enemy troop strength in 1967. Before resigning from the CIA's VIETNAM desk in 1968, Adams expressed his belief that the Army was minimizing North Vietnamese and VIET CONG troop strength for political reasons. He first expressed his views publicly as a witness for the defense in the PENTAGON PAPERS espionage trial of Daniel Ellsberg and Anthony J. Russo, telling the court that the "facts" revealed by Ellsberg were false and therefore not state secrets.

Adams, (Llewellyn) Sherman (1899–1986). American politician. In 1952, during his second term as governor of New Hampshire, Adams played a key role in securing victory for Dwight D. EISENHOWER in that state's early presidential primary. He then served as special advisor to President Eisenhower from 1953 to 1958. In that post he wielded so much power that he came to be known as "assistant president." He resigned under fire in 1958 after a scandal in which he admitted accepting gifts, including a vicuna coat, from Bernard Goldfine, a Boston industrialist. In later years Adams operated a ski resort in his home state.

Sherman Adams, one of the most influential advisors in Eisenhower's administration.

Adams, Walter Sydney (1876–1956). American astronomer. Adams was the son of missionaries working in Syria, then part of the Ottoman Empire, who returned to the U.S. in 1885. He graduated from Dartmouth College in 1898 and obtained his A.M. from the University of Chicago in 1900. After a year in Munich he began his career in astronomy as assistant to George Hale in 1901 at the Yerkes Observatory. In 1904 he moved with Hale to the newly established Mount Wilson Observatory, where he served as assistant director from 1913 to 1923, and then as director from 1923 until his retirement in 1946. At Mount Wilson Adams was able to use first the 60–inch and, from 1917, the 100–inch reflecting telescopes in whose design and construction he had been closely associated. His early work was mainly concerned with solar spectroscopy, studying sunspots and solar rotation, but he gradually turned to stellar spectroscopy.

In 1914 he showed how it was possible to distinguish between a dwarf and a giant star merely from their spectra. He also demonstrated that it was possible to determine the luminosity—intrinsic brightness—of a star from its spectrum. This led to Adams introducing the method of spectroscopic parallax whereby a star's distance from the Earth could be estimated using the luminosity deduced from the star's spectrum. This method has been used to calculate the distance of many thousands of stars. He is better known for his work on the orbiting companion of Sirius, named Sirius B. Adams succeeded in obtaining the spectrum of Sirius B in 1915 and found it to be considerably hotter than the sun. He realized that such a hot body, just eight light-years distant, could remain invisible to the naked eye only if it was very much smaller than the Sun, no bigger in fact than the Earth. Adams had thus discovered the first known "white dwarf"—a star that has collapsed into a highly compressed object after its nuclear fuel is exhausted. If such an interpretation was correct, then Sirius B should possess a very strong gravitational field. According to EINSTEIN's general theory of RELATIVITY, this strong field should shift the wavelength of light waves emitted by it toward the red end of the spectrum. In 1924 Adams made the difficult spectroscopic observations and detected the predicted red shift, which confirmed his own account of Sirius B and provided strong evidence for general relativity.

Adana. Capital of TURKEY's Adana province, located on the Seyhan River near the Taurus Mountains. A major massacre of the Armenian populace of Turkey occurred here in 1909. In 1943, during WORLD WAR II, Winston CHURCHILL attended a conference in Adana between Allied and Turkish officials.

Addams, Charles (1912–1988). American cartoonist. Born in Westfield, N.J., and educated at Colgate University, the University of Pennsylvania, and Grand Central School of Art, he was noted for the ghoulish, gallows-humor cartoons that appeared primarily in THE NEW YORKER from 1935 onward. His work inspired a 1960s television series, "The Addams Family." Twelve collections of his morbid cartoons were published, the last of them, *Creature Comforts,* in 1982. His work was also displayed at the Metropolitan Museum of Art, the Fogg Art Museum and the Museum of the City of New York.

Addams, Jane (1860–1935). American settlement worker who won the NOBEL PRIZE for peace in 1931. After graduating from Rockford College, Addams attended Woman's Medical College in Philadelphia until failing health caused her to leave in 1882. While visiting Europe in 1887–88, she became interested in the British settlement houses. Inspired by the movement to help the urban poor, she returned and founded Hull House in Chicago in 1889. There the working poor could leave their children for care and instruction, and adults could come together for study and socialization. Jane Addams' dedication soon earned the respect and help of many Chicagoans. By 1905 she was acknowledged to have created by far the finest facilities and program for working-class education and recreation in the U.S., and the most famous settlement house in the world. Her many books, such as *Twenty Years at Hull House* (1910), helped to bring her work to public attention. She later branched out to aid the woman suffrage movement and

Jane Addams greeting young visitors at Hull House.

cause for world peace. Addams was accepted as one of the greatest women of her time.

Adderley, Julian "Cannonball" (1928–1975). American jazz musician. Adderley played alto, tenor and soprano saxophone as well as the flute. He led his own quintet and also worked with Miles DAVIS and John COLTRANE. Adderley won a Grammy Award in 1968 for his album *Mercy, Mercy.*

Addis Ababa. Capital of Ethiopia. Addis Ababa was founded in 1887 by King Menelik II and became the capital in 1896. The city was conquered by the fascist Italian forces of Benito MUSSOLINI in 1936 but was retaken by British forces in 1943, during WORLD WAR II. In 1963, it was named the headquarters of the ORGANIZATION OF AFRICAN UNITY.

Ade, George (1866–1944). U.S. playwright and humorist. Ade joined the staff of the *Chicago Record* in 1890. Eleven volumes written by Ade pointed out the follies and foibles of his peers. Many have considered his work to be a master portrait of the common man. He was especially praised for his use of the vernacular. As a playwright Ade once had three plays in New York running simultaneously. He also wrote a number of motion picture scripts. In 1936 Ade wrote the popular book, *The Old Time Saloon.*

Aden. Capital city of South Yemen (which is now a part of the Republic of YEMEN); located on the Gulf of Aden in the southwestern part of the Arabian Peninsula. Aden has served as a port linking the trade of the Indian Ocean and the Mediterranean Sea since the first millennium B.C. Captured by British forces in 1839, it was formally established as a British colony in 1935. The colonial era ended in 1967 with the independence of South Yemen.

Adenauer, Konrad (1876–1967). German statesman, first chancellor of WEST GERMANY (1949–63). Born in Cologne, Adenauer studied law at the universities of Freiburg, Munich and Bonn and became a lawyer in his native city. Elected Cologne's mayor and a member of the provincial diet from 1917 to 1933, he was a staunch opponent of HITLER and in 1933 was banned from the city, forced to flee and finally arrested by the GESTAPO. After escaping to Switzerland, he returned to Germany at the outbreak of WORLD WAR II and led a relatively uneventful life until rearrested by the Nazis in 1944. After the Allied victory, Adenauer was returned (1945) to the mayor's office in Cologne but was dismissed after the city was transferred to British military control. He founded the CHRISTIAN DEMOCRATIC UNION (CDU) in the mid-1940s, was elected president of the constituent assembly in 1948 and helped to write the new constitution for the Bonn republic. When the CDU gained a majority in the 1949 elections, Adenauer was appointed chancellor; he also served as foreign minister from 1951 to 1955. During his long tenure as chancellor he attempted to achieve reconciliation with France, relaxation of occupation laws and an end to the dismantling of German industry.

Konrad Adenauer shortly after his election as president of the West German Parliamentary Council.

Adenauer developed a thriving economy and a successful political democracy out of the wartime ruins and is widely regarded as the architect of West Germany's remarkable postwar recovery. A strong opponent of communist East Germany, he also worked to reinstate West Germany as a member of the EUROPEAN COMMUNITY. A CDU defeat in 1961 and a cabinet scandal the following year forced him to resign in 1963. Nonetheless, *Der Alte* [the old one] continued to be an influential and popular figure in West Germany until his death.

For further reading:
Cudlipp, Edythe, *Konrad Adenauer.* New York: Chelsea House, 1985.

Adige River. River that flows southeastward from the Tyrolean Alps to the Adriatic Sea. The second longest river in Italy, it was the site of a key battle in 1916, during WORLD WAR I.

Adivar, Halide Ebib (1883–1964). Turkish novelist. Adivar was educated in the U.S. and served for a time in the Anatolian nationalist army, an experience that inspired *The Daughter of Smyrna* (1922). This and Adivar's other early fiction examines the role of women in Turkish society. After living abroad for several years, Adivar wrote *The Clown and His Daughter* (1935) in English; she translated it into Turkish in 1936. Considered her most important work, the novel assesses the effects of westernization on Turkish society.

Adler, Alfred (1870–1937). Austrian psychologist. Adler achieved renown, along with Carl Gustav JUNG, as one of the rare disciples of Sigmund FREUD to emerge from Freud's shadow with a distinctive psychological theory of his own. Adler graduated from the University of Vienna Medical School in 1895. Freud invited Adler to join his psychoanalytic discussion group on the basis of an insightful review Adler had written in 1902 of a book by Freud on dream interpretation. But Adler always maintained an intellectually independent status and left the group with nine followers in 1911, establishing his own "Individualpsychologie." In *The Neurotic Constitution* (1912), Adler stressed a teleologic (goal-oriented) basis for neurotic behavior as opposed to Freud's focus on infantile sexuality. In 1925, Adler coined the term "inferiority complex" to apply to those who adapted badly to physical or other disabilities. Adler's *Understanding Human Nature* (1927) is based on a series of his lectures that drew wide audiences in both Europe and America.

Adler, Mortimer Jerome (1902–). American educator and writer. Adler, one of the most influential intellectuals of midcentury America, wrote a wide range of books and articles but is best remembered for his cofounder role (along with Robert HUTCHINS) in establishing the GREAT BOOKS PROGRAM—a 54–volume collection (1952) of the great writings of Western Civilization designed for broad educational use. Adler earned a doctorate at Columbia University in 1928, having already established himself as an opponent of the pragmatism of Columbia philosopher John Dewey. Dewey held that truth was whatever is useful to a society in a given stage of its evolution. Adler countered that certain moral and spiritual values were absolute truths and that the progressive education system fostered by pragmatism was producing a half-educated public trained for money-making but not for living the inspired Greek ideal of the "good life." In the 1940s, while teaching at the University of Chicago, Adler guided a team of scholars in the production of the Syntopicon, a synthesis of the great ideas of Western Civilization that was published along with the Great Books collection.

Adler, Peter Herman (1899–1990). U.S. conductor. As music and artistic director of the NBC Opera between 1949 and 1959, he pioneered the broadcasting of opera on U.S. television. Among the works he commissioned was Gian Carlo MENOTTI's *Amahl and the Night Visitors.* He served as music director of the Baltimore Symphony from 1959 until 1968.

Adler, Renata (1938–). American author and journalist. Born in Italy, she was educated at Bryn Mawr, the Sorbonne and Harvard, later earning a law degree from Yale. From 1962 she worked intermittently for THE NEW YORKER as a film critic and writer-reporter. She is the author of two unconventional novels, *Speedboat* (1976), an amalgamation of short, overlapping stories, and *Pitch Dark* (1983), variously described as minimalist and an "antinovel." She brought her legal training to bear in *Reckless Disregard: Westmoreland v. CBS et al.; Sharon v. Time* (1986), an examination of media ethics in two important libel cases of the 1980s. Much of the work first appeared in *The New Yorker,* which was itself embroiled in a lawsuit by CBS as a result. Adler has contributed articles and short stories to various publications under the pseudonym Brett Daniels and has also published collections of film criticism and reportage.

Adler, Samuel (1898–1979). American abstract painter, sculptor and educator. Adler was best known for his paintings and collages, which were once described as "ghostly presences and dreamlike memories." His artwork was exhibited in more than 150 national and international shows and was included in the collections of 25 public museums.

Admiralty Islands [Admiralties]. Group of islands in the Bismarck Archipelago, north of New Guinea. The Admiralty Islands were annexed by Germany to its New Guinea colony in 1884. During WORLD WAR I, the islands were seized by Australian forces and placed under Australian mandate in 1921. They were held by Japanese forces from 1942 to 1944, during WORLD WAR II; now a part of the independent Papua-New Guinea.

Adorno, Theodor [born Theodor Weisengrund] (1903–1969). German philosopher, sociologist, literary and music critic. Adorno was one of the most influential German cultural critics of his generation, along with Walter Benjamin and Georg LUKACS, with whom Adorno was often linked due to his Marxist-influenced approach to the interpretation of societal patterns and literary works. Adorno joined the renowned philosophical faculty of Frankfurt University in 1930 but emigrated from Germany to Oxford in 1933 to escape the Nazi regime. In 1938, Adorno came to America, where he formed a friendship with fellow German emigre Thomas MANN. In 1950 he returned to Frankfurt, where he headed the Institute of Social Relations from 1958 to 1959. Adorno's most famous works are *The Dialectic of Enlightenment* (1947), which argues that reason has become an instrument of totalitarian control, and *The Authoritarian Personality* (1950), a study of FASCISM. His posthumous *Collected Writings* appeared in 16 volumes (1970–1980).

Adoula, Cyrille (1921–1978). Premier of the Republic of the Congo (now ZAIRE) (1961–64). Adoula later served as ambassador to Belgium (1964–66), ambassador to the U.S. (1966–69), and as foreign minister (1969–70).

Adrenalin. See John Jacob ABEL; Thomas Renton ELLIOTT.

Adrian, Edgar Douglas [Baron Adrian of Cambridge] (1889–1977). British neurophysiologist. Adrian, a lawyer's son, studied at Cambridge University and St. Bartholomew's Hospital, London, where he obtained his M.D. in 1915. He returned to Cambridge in 1919, was appointed professor of physiology in 1937 and became the master of Trinity College in 1951, an office he retained until his retirement in 1965. He was made a peer in 1955.

Adrian's greatest contribution to neurophysiology was his work on nerve impulses. When he started his work, it was known that nerves transmit nerve impulses as signals, but little was known of the frequency and control of such impulses. The first insight into this process came from Adrian's colleague Keith Lucas, who demonstrated in 1905 that the impulse obeyed the "all-or-none" law. This asserted that below a certain threshold of stimulation a nerve does not respond. But once the threshold is reached, the nerve continues to respond by a fixed amount, however much the stimulation increases. Thus increased stimulation, although it stimulates more fibers, does not affect the magnitude of the signal itself.

It was not until 1925 that Adrian advanced beyond this position. By painstaking surgical techniques he succeeded in separating individual nerve fibers and amplifying and recording the small action potentials in them. He demonstrated how the nerve, even though it transmits an impulse of fixed strength, can still convey a complex message. He discovered that as the extension increased, so did the frequency of the nerve impulse, rising from 10 to 50 impulses per second. Thus he concluded that the message is conveyed by changes in the frequency of the discharge. For this work Adrian shared the 1932 NOBEL PRIZE for physiology or medicine with Charles Sherrington.

Adwa. Town in Ethiopia's Tigre province and site of the 1896 battle in which King Menelik II defeated invading Italian forces and preserved Ethiopia's independent status. Adwa thus became a symbol of African resistance to European colonialism. Captured by the fascist Italian forces of Benito MUSSOLINI in 1935, Adwa was subsequently liberated by British forces in 1941, during WORLD WAR II.

Ady, Endre (1877–1919). Hungarian poet, critic and journalist. Ady is generally recognized as the finest Hungarian poet of this century. He created a sensation in his native land with the appearance of his very first volume of verse, *New Poems* (1906). Ady's lyrics defied the social and poetical conventions of the era by including highly charged erotic imagery as well as scenes of intense violence. Ady was an expressionistic poet who wrote fervently of his own spiritual torment as one unable to find faith or certainty in any creed or personal relationship. The combined horror and release of death was a frequent theme in his work. English translations of Ady's verse have been issued as *Poems* (1969) and *The Explosive Country* (1977).

AE [pen name of George William Russell] (1867–1935). Irish poet, playwright and nationalist. AE (Russell's pseudonym is an abbreviation of AEON) studied art in Dublin and published his first collection of poetry, *Homeward* (1894), with the encouragement of W.B. YEATS, with whom, along with Lady GREGORY, AE later helped form the ABBEY THEATRE. AE's first play, *Deirdre,* a poetic drama, was performed at the Irish National Theatre, an early incarnation of the Abbey, in 1902. From 1905 to 1923 AE edited *The Irish Homestead,* a publication encouraging Irish culture, and from 1923 to 1930 he served as editor of *The Irish Statesman,* which advocated Irish independence. He is perhaps best known for *The Avatars* (1933), a poetic, futuristic fantasy. Other poetic works include *Midsummer Eve* (1928), *The House of the Titans* (1934) and *Selected Poems* (1935). AE also contributed political articles to various journals and was a mentor to many young Irish writers, among them Padraic COLUM and James STEPHENS.

AEG [Allgemeine Elektrizitats-Gesellschaft]. Giant German manufacturer of electrical products, founded in 1883 by Emil Rathenau. It became a significant force in the design world through its patronage of the designer and architect Peter BEHRENS in the early 20th century. Behrens designed the AEG trademark, such products as electric fans and lighting fixtures, and many brochures and other graphic materials. The AEG turbine factory he designed in Berlin is an important, pioneering work of modern architecture.

Aehrenthal, Count Alois Lexa von (1854–1912). Diplomat and politician of the Austro-Hungarian empire. He was ambassador to St. Petersburg (1898–1906) and foreign minister (1906–12). While he was foreign minister, Austria-Hungary, with German approval, annexed BOSNIA AND HERZEGOVINA (1908); this action raised the threat that Russia would make war and was one of the incidents leading to WORLD WAR I.

aerodynamic styling. Design using forms derived from the science of aerodynamics, which developed in connection with aviation and is concerned with the study of the movement of solid bodies through the air. In the 1920s and 1930s it became known that certain shapes, such as the bullet-shaped front and tapering rear typical of large dirigibles, were maximally efficient for aircraft. Such forms came to be called streamlined and were associated with concepts of MODERNISM, speed and progress. Aerodynamic forms were adopted by industrial designers for locomotives, automobiles and eventually for such illogical applications as pencil sharpeners and toasters. In recent years, a more serious interest in aerodynamics has developed in automotive design in an effort to improve fuel efficiency. Minimizing air resistance has led to many recent designs characterized by flowing shapes and smooth surfaces.

affirmative action programs. Programs implemented in the U.S. after the 1970s to encourage racial and sexual diversity in schools and workplaces in order to redress past imbalances. Although the CIVIL RIGHTS ACT OF 1964 and its amendments outlawed discriminatory hiring by most private employers and most discriminatory school and college admission policies, the results of historical discrimination remained. Affirmative action programs—some voluntary and some imposed by court order—were designed to encourage racial and sexual diversity by giving preference to minority groups and women in hiring and in college admissions. The programs were extremely controversial, and white men objected that the result was "reverse discrimination" because they were passed over despite having better qualifications than successful minority group members. The Supreme Court in a number of decisions upheld the use of affirmative action programs so long as they did not impose rigid racial or sexual quotas.

Affirmed (1975–). American thoroughbred racehorse. In 1978, Affirmed became the second half of racing's first back-to-back Triple Crown sweep, after SEATTLE SLEW took the honors in 1977. Affirmed, the top-rated two-year-old of 1977, spent much of his racing life fighting off ALYDAR, who handed the horse his only defeats in his first season. The following season, the two colts finished one-two in all three Triple Crown races. Affirmed was ridden by Steve CAUTHEN, who became the second youngest rider ever to take the Kentucky Derby. Their Belmont Stakes battle is particularly remembered as a racing classic, as the two horses were stride for stride through two-thirds of the race and finished with the third fastest time in the history of the race.

Afghan Civil War of 1928–29. Opponents to internal reforms caused a large-scale revolt in November 1928 as AMANULLAH KHAN, emir of AFGHANISTAN, attempted to modernize his country. In mid-January 1929 Amanullah abdicated in favor of his weak older brother, but an outlaw leader led a strong band to capture the Afghan capital of Kabul and proclaimed himself emir as Habibullah Ghazi. At Kandahar, Amanullah assembled an army and began a march on Kabul to retake the throne in the spring of 1929; he was defeated and fled the country. Other early claimants to the throne were also unsuccessful. General Muhammad Nadir Khan, an Afghan officer and Amanullah's cousin, organized an army after returning from Europe and marched against Habibullah, defeating him and taking Kabul in October 1929. Habibullah was captured and executed, and Khan took the throne, renaming himself Nadir Shah. With British assistance he instituted reforms, restored order and placated Amanullah's loyal followers. In 1932 he established a constitutional government.

Afghan Civil War of 1979–. The Soviet

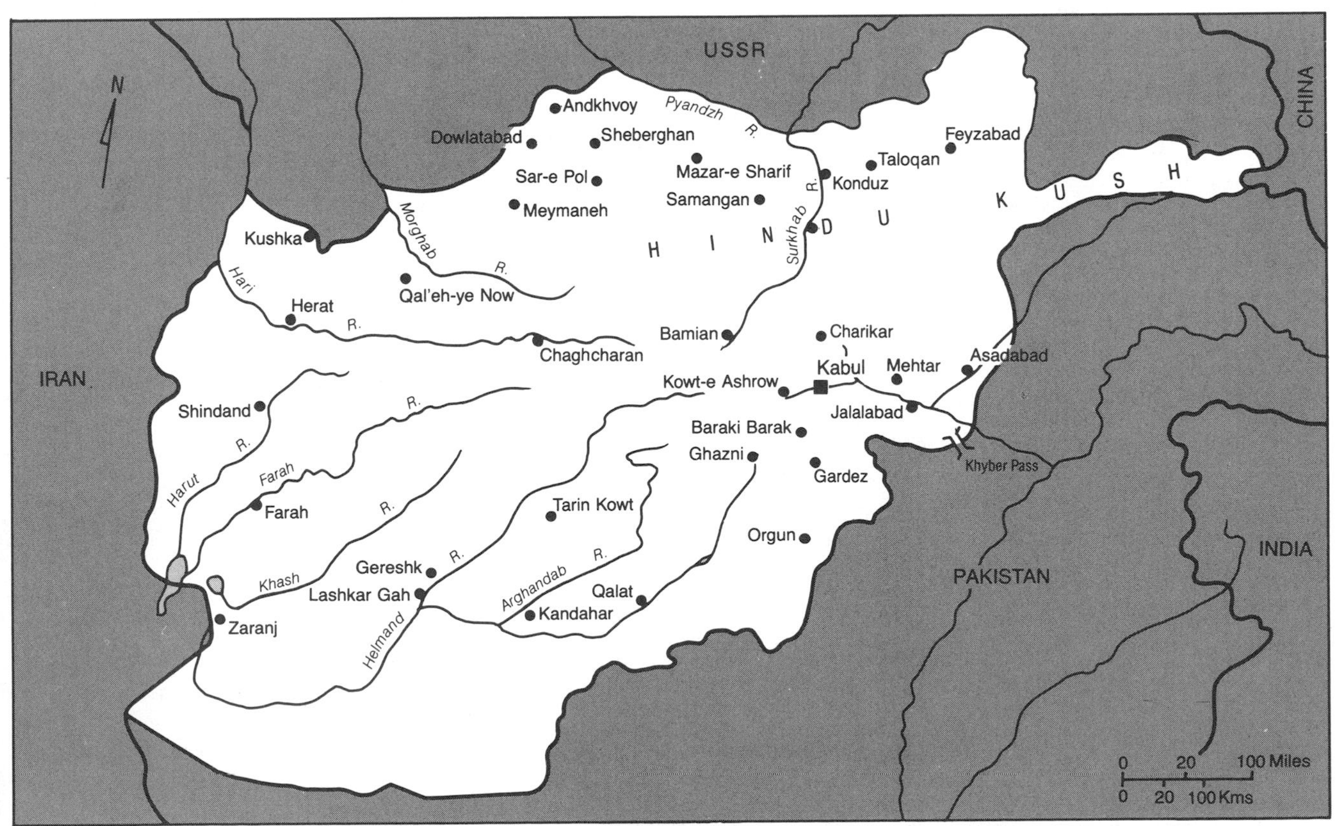

AFGHANISTAN

invasion of AFGHANISTAN in late December 1979 dramatized a momentous failure in Soviet foreign policy. When Afghanistan became a republic in 1973, the U.S.S.R. increased its efforts to make the country a buffer state against Pakistan by supporting radical political parties like the Khalq (Peoples Democratic) Party. In 1978 Khalq militants assassinated Afghanistan's first president; a Khalq leader became president but was ousted by his prime minister (September 1979), who himself was overthrown (December 27, 1979) by another leftist, Babrak Karmal, who had Soviet backing. When Karmal's attempt to impose Russianization met with armed resistance, he asked for Soviet aid to crush the opposition. Despite having modern equipment, more than 100,000 Soviet troops found it difficult to defeat the Afghan rebels, whose guerrilla tactics and sabotage confused the invaders. Ancient tribal antagonisms and linguistic differences prevented the rebels from developing a unified strategy to defeat the Soviets and the official Afghanistan army, the latter so riddled by defections that in 1984 the Kabul government was drafting 14-year-olds. The civil war, labeled by some as the Soviets' "Vietnam," embarrassed the U.S.S.R. internationally. The Soviets signed a UN-sponsored withdrawal agreement on April 14, 1988. They began to withdraw on May 15, 1988, and completed their withdrawal by early 1989. However, fighting between the rebels and Afghan government continued.

For further reading:

Urban, Mark, *War in Afghanistan*. New York: St. Martin's, 1988, rev. 1990.

Afghanistan. Country in southwestern Asia; bounded by the U.S.S.R. to its north, PAKISTAN to its south and east and IRAN to its west. With a long history of fierce resistance to outside pressures, Afghanistan remained neutral during WORLD WAR I and was recognized as an independent nation by Britain, Persia (Iran), Russia and TURKEY. AMANULLAH KHAN, a progressive monarch, took office in 1919 and oversaw the adoption of a written constitution in 1923. But Khan was overthrown in 1929, due to opposition to his efforts to westernize Afghanistan (see AFGHAN CIVIL WAR OF 1928–29). Nadir Shah, his successor, was killed in 1933. Mohammed Zahir Shah, Nadir Shah's son, continued westernization efforts. He also helped to found, in 1937, the Oriental Entente, consisting of Afghanistan, Iran, IRAQ and Turkey. Afghanistan again was neutral during WORLD WAR II. In the 1950s and 1960s, westernization efforts continued in an attempt to modernize the Afghan economy. In 1973, the monarchy was overthrown and a republican form of rule established. A pro-U.S.S.R. communist government emerged, and in 1979 Soviet troops occupied Afghanistan to strengthen that government, which had been in danger of toppling. After a decade of armed resistance to its pacification efforts, Soviet forces withdrew in 1989. But fighting has continued between the communist Afghan government and anticommunist rebel forces. (See also AFGHAN CIVIL WAR OF 1979–.)

AFGHANISTAN

1919	Independence confirmed by British.
1921	Treaty of Friendship signed with Soviet Union.
1929	British intervene to establish General Nadir Shah on throne after brigands seize Kabul.
1961	U.S. President John F. Kennedy offers to mediate border dispute with Pakistan.
1965	First Marxist party formed, People's Democratic Party of Afghanistan (PDPA).
1978	Military dictator Mohammed Daoud Khan killed in Marxist coup.
1979	Soviet troops invade to fight Muslim rebels threatening communist government; identified as major supplier of heroin to Western Europe.
1989	Last of Soviet troops are withdrawn in accordance with UN-sponsored agreement; civil strife continues.

Afinogenov, Alexander Nikolayevich (1904–1941). Russian playwright, one of the few important dramatists to emerge immediately after the Russian Revolution. *The Strange Fellow* (1928) and *Fear* (1931) were his best-known plays and dealt with the difficulties of change in a new social order. Subsequent plays—*The Distant, Greetings Spain, Mashenka* and *On the Eve*—were more acceptable politically to the regime. He was killed in a German air raid during World War II.

Aflaq, Michel (1910–1989). Syrian political leader. Together with Salah Baytar, he founded the BA'ATH movement in SYRIA in 1940. The Ba'athists, who advocated Arab nationalism and socialism, came to power in Syria in 1963 and Iraq in 1968, but a split between factions forced Aflaq to move to Iraq in 1968. He was said to have been out of the mainstream of Arab politics since that time.

AFL-CIO. See AMERICAN FEDERATION OF LABOR AND CONGRESS OF INDUSTRIAL ORGANIZATIONS.

African National Congress [ANC]. Organization formed in 1912 to promote the rights of the black people of SOUTH AFRICA. Growing out of the Native Education Association (established in Cape Colony in 1882), the ANC joined forces with representatives of the South African Indian community in 1927. Thereafter, it sought a unified, multiracial and democratic country offering full citizenship to all South Africans. The ANC adopted a strategy of passive resistance, particularly under the leadership (1952–67) of Albert LUTHULI, but was nonetheless banned by South African authorities in 1960. From then on, the organization operated underground or in exile. Maintaining its goal of total abolition of APARTHEID, the ANC was later split between those who continued to support nonviolence and militants who supported armed insurrection. After the legalization of the ANC by South African President F.W. DE KLERK and the release of its long-imprisoned leader Nelson MANDELA in 1990, the organization abandoned the threat of guerrilla warfare while orchestrating a campaign of strikes, marches, boycotts and other protests. As South Africa moved into the 1990s, it appeared that the ANC was moving toward a new identity as a viable political party.

Afyonkarahisar [Greek: Nicopolis]. Capital of Afyonkarahisar province in southern TURKEY. A longtime trade route center of Asia Minor, it was the site of a major battle during the GRECO-TURKISH WAR OF 1921–22 and was at last conquered by the Turks in 1922.

Agadir. Port city on MOROCCO's Atlantic coast, in Agadir province. In 1911, the arrival of the German warship *Panther* at Agadir triggered an intense political struggle between GERMANY and FRANCE over control of Morocco. War was averted by an agreement that ceded an interest in the Congo to Germany while establishing Morocco as a French protectorate. During WORLD WAR II, Agadir was the site of a 1942 landing by Allied forces.

Aga Khan. The hereditary title for the spiritual leader (imam) of the Ismaili sect of Shiite Muslims, whose greatest population concentration is in Africa and parts of Asia. It was first used by the imam Hassan Ali Shah in the 1800s and represents the belief that the Aga Khan is a direct descendant of Mohammad's daughter, Fatima, through the Fatimid caliphs of Egypt. **Aga Khan III** (1877–1957) worked to improve Muslim education and representation in Hindu-dominated INDIA. He helped to establish the Muslim League, which gave the impetus for the creation of the independent country of PAKISTAN. He also represented India at the LEAGUE OF NATIONS (1932; 1934–37). His grandson, Karim Al Hussaini Shah, succeeded him as Aga Khan IV in 1957 and continues to work for the welfare of his followers.

Agana. Capital of the U.S. Trust Territory of Guam in the western Pacific Ocean. Captured by Japanese invaders early in WORLD WAR II, Agana was later razed during the battle for Guam between Japan and the U.S. American forces had reconquered the entire island by August 1944.

Agee, James (1909–1955). American author. Agee was born in Tennessee and educated at Exeter and Harvard. His first poetry collection, *Permit Me Voyage*, appeared in the 1934 Yale Series of Younger Poets. In 1936 Agee and photographer Walker EVANS were commissioned to depict the lives of rural Alabama sharecroppers. The product of their observations, *Let Us Now Praise Famous Men* (1939), is a poignant, lyrical description of the American South during the GREAT DEPRESSION. Agee is perhaps best known for the loosely autobiographical novel *A Death in the Family* (1957), which examines the effect on a family of the father's death in an automobile accident, but he was a poet, film critic and screenwriter as well.

For further reading:

Agee, James, *Selected Journalism*. Knoxville: University of Tennessee Press, 1985.
Bergreen, Laurence, *James Agee: A Life*. New York: Viking Penguin, 1985.

Agent Orange. One of the terrible legacies of the VIETNAM WAR is what many veterans believe to be their contamination with the herbicide Agent Orange. The major herbicides sprayed in Vietnam were assigned code names corresponding to the color of identification bands painted on their storage drums. Agent Orange was sprayed by the U.S. Air Force in a defoliation operation called Ranch Hand from 1962 to 1970. The chemical contained minute amounts of a poisonous type of dioxin, which has been claimed to result in various health problems.

During the initial stages of light herbicide use in Vietnam, from 1962 through 1964, the most commonly used herbicides were Purple and Pink. During this period of Operation Ranch Hand, approximately 145,000 gallons of Purple and 123,000 gallons of Pink were sprayed in South Vietnam. After 1964 the most widely used herbicides were Orange, White and Blue, which rapidly replaced Purple and Pink. Heavily sprayed areas included inland forests near the DMZ; inland forests at the junction of the borders of Cambodia, Laos and South Vietnam; inland forests north and northwest of Saigon; mangrove forests on the southernmost peninsula of Vietnam; and mangrove forests along major inland shipping channels southeast of Saigon. Crop destruction missions were concentrated in northern and eastern central areas of South Vietnam. The primary use of herbicide was to kill vegetation and thereby deny cover to enemy forces. By making ambushes more difficult, Agent Orange undoubtedly saved American lives. Often confused with pesticides that were sprayed directly over U.S. installations to control malaria-carrying mosquitoes, Agent Orange was not normally sprayed directly on troops. But soldiers did come in contact with it as they moved through jungle areas that had been defoliated.

Beginning in the late 1970s, Vietnam veterans began citing dioxin as the cause of health problems ranging from skin rashes to cancer to birth defects in their children. Although dioxin has proven extremely poisonous in laboratory animals, considerable controversy still exists over its effect on humans. While not admitting any liability, chemical companies that manufactured the herbicide have agreed to establish a $180 million fund to be distributed to eligible veterans by a "special master" appointed by the U.S. District Court in Brooklyn, New York. The agreement was made in response to a class action suit by veterans. According to the terms of the settlement, a claimant "who dies or becomes totally disabled from an illness (not caused by trauma such as auto accident or gunshot wound) anytime during the period from the Vietnam war to December 31, 1994" and who meets the exposure standards will be eligible. Since the late 1970s the Veterans Administration has provided free medical tests to veterans citing health problems that they believe may be related to Agent Orange.

Agnew, Spiro T(heodore) (1918–). Vice president of the UNITED STATES (1969–73). Perhaps the most controversial U.S. vice president in the 20th century, Agnew was the son of Greek immigrants. A native of Baltimore, Md., he attended Johns Hopkins University and Baltimore Law School. After army service in World War II, he received his law degree (1947). He became active in Maryland state politics in the 1950s. Elected governor in 1966, he was the surprise choice as Richard M. NIXON's vice presidential running mate in the 1968 national elections. During the campaign Agnew established himself as a champion of law and order and a leading spokesman for the U.S. right wing. He gained particular attention for his colorful and uncompromising rhetoric as he castigated antiwar demonstrators and liberals in the news media as an "effete corps of impudent snobs." Throughout Nixon's first term and during the 1972 reelection campaign, Agnew continued his defense of the administration's VIETNAM WAR policy and his condemnation of administration opponents. Nixon and Agnew were reelected in 1972. Agnew was not implicated in the developing WATERGATE Scandal, but he soon faced his own legal troubles. In mid-1973 he was charged with having committed numerous criminal acts, including extortion and bribery, while governor of Maryland and earlier. Though protesting his innocence, he was ultimately forced to resign the vice presidency (October 10, 1973). He pleaded no contest and was fined $10,000 and sentenced to three years unsupervised probation. Disbarred and disgraced, Agnew disappeared from the political scene. Nixon chose Gerald FORD as Agnew's replacement; Ford in turn succeeded to the presidency after Nixon's resignation the following year.

Spiro T. Agnew.

Agnon, S(hmuel) Y(osef) [Halevi Czaczkes] (1880–1970). Israeli poet and novelist. Born in Galicia (then a region of Austria-Hungary, now part of Poland), he received a traditional Talmudic education and studied Jewish and Hebrew literature. He published his first poems in his teens, when he also became an active Zionist (see ZIONISM). In 1908 he moved to Jerusalem, where he published his first novel, *Agunot* (1909), from which he derived his pen name. In 1912 he moved to Berlin, where he helped found the journal *Der Jude* (*The Jew*), and where he met businessman Salman Schocken, who became his lifelong friend, patron and publisher. He later settled in Palestine. Agnon's work, written in Hebrew, is rich in folklore and fantasy. *The Bridal Suite* (1931) is the story of a poor Hasidic Jew searching for husbands and dowries for his daughters. Other works include *A Guest for the Night* (1937) and *A Simple Story* (1935). Critic Edmund WILSON was an admirer of Agnon's work and was instrumental in his nomination for the NOBEL PRIZE in literature, which Agnon received in 1966 along with Nelly SACHS. Agnon received numerous honors during his lifetime and is considered to be among the finest writers of Hebrew fiction.

Agricultural Adjustment Administration [AAA]. U.S. government agency, established as part of President Franklin D. ROOSEVELT'S NEW DEAL during the GREAT DEPRESSION. The AAA was created in May 1933, during the Roosevelt administration's first HUNDRED DAYS. It attempted to raise farm prices by lowering production of certain agricultural goods. The AAA's policy of paying farmers to grow less food was highly controversial. In 1936 the U.S. Supreme Court declared that the AAA was unconstitutional.

Aguascalientes. Capital of Aguascalientes state, Mexico. A onetime Spanish colonial center, it was the site during the MEXICAN CIVIL WAR OF 1911 of a key meeting between the revolutionary forces of Pancho VILLA, Emiliano ZAPATA and other leaders, the failed goal of which was to organize a central Mexican government and thus end the fighting.

Ahidjo, Ahmadou (1924–1989). First president of CAMEROON (1960–82). Ahidjo was elected shortly after independence and reelected four times (1965, 1970, 1975, 1980). His rule was authoritarian, but the country became self-sufficient in food. Ahidjo put down several rebellions and survived a coup attempt in 1970. A year after his resignation in 1982, he was charged with plotting against his successor, Paul Biya. He went into exile and was sentenced to death *in absentia*. Although the sentence was later commuted to indefinite detention, he never returned to Cameroon.

Ahmadabad. City in India's Gujarat state. It was a key center of support for Mohandas K. GANDHI, the nonviolent nationalist leader who was arrested there by British colonial forces in 1933.

Ahren, Uno (1897–1977). A Swedish architect and designer who was a pioneer in introducing the concepts of MODERNISM into Sweden in the 1920s. Ahren collaborated with Sven Markelius and E. Gunnar ASPLUND in buildings for the Stockholm exhibition of 1930 and was the designer of a Ford factory of 1929 and a 1930 cinema in Stockholm that were among the first major Modern works in Sweden. Ahren exerted a significant influence on the development of the style known as **Swedish Modern.**

Ahvaz. Capital of Iran's Khuzestan province, located on the Karun River. Ahvaz was a key trading center during the rise of the Islamic Arab empire in medieval times. In this century, it has emerged as an industrial and oil transport center. It was a major target of Iraqi forces during the IRAN-IRAQ WAR (1980–88).

AIDS [Acquired Immune Deficiency Syndrome]. A serious disorder that has become one of the health scourges of the late 20th century. First identified in 1981 in the U.S., AIDS affects the ability of the body's immune system to fight disease. It is caused by a retrovirus—isolated in France in 1983 and in the U.S. in 1984—that has come to be known as **HIV** (Human Immunodeficiency Virus). Researchers have speculated that AIDS may have arisen on the African continent (where it is now a leading cause of death in many countries) as a virus of monkeys or primates that has since undergone mutation. However, the nature of the genesis of AIDS, like so much about the disorder, has yet to be definitely established.

Two separate HIV viruses have been discovered that share about 40% of their genetic makeup; HIV-1 was identified in 1984 and HIV-2 the following year. Within each of these viruses there are a multiplicity of different strains. The virus has been shown to have an unusually long incubation period and, after initial introduction into the body, can lie dormant for up to 10 years in a symptom-free individual before manifesting itself. It strikes mainly at the body's disease-fighting white blood cells, particularly the T-helper cells, leaving the infected person vulnerable to a number of opportunistic infections.

The earliest sign of infection is the production of HIV antibodies, a state in which an individual is commonly known as HIV-positive. Normally, the first signs of HIV infection are several of a cluster of symptoms called ARC (AIDS-related complex). These include tiredness, fevers, night sweats, enlarged lymph glands, diarrhea and severe weight loss. In full-blown AIDS a number of previously-rare diseases tend to manifest themselves in the infected individual. These include Kaposi's sarcoma, a skin cancer characterized by bruise-like patches that spread throughout the body, and Pneumocystis carinii pneumonia, a parasitic lung infection. Among other infections often accompanying AIDS are cytomegalovirus, which often produces blindness, and diseases of the central nervous system that sometimes lead to an AIDS-related dementia.

AIDS has been shown to spread from one individual to another by contact with bodily fluids such as blood and semen. Never found to be spread by casual contact, it is passed on through sexual contact, by blood to blood transmission or from an infected mother to her unborn fetus, resulting in an AIDS-infected newborn. The AIDS virus was first detected in the U.S. and most Western countries in homosexual or bisexual men. Since the early 1980s it has spread through a large percentage of the homosexual population, especially affecting large urban areas. In the late 1980s and early 1990s, the disorder has become extremely prevalent among minority communities in large cities, spread mostly by intravenous drug use of infected needles and by sexual transmission from drug users to their partners.

After tests for the HIV virus became available in 1985, the nation's blood supply was tested and, to a very great degree, made safe. However, before testing was available, some of the blood supply was tainted and many hemophiliacs, who must use large quantities of blood products, and some recipients of blood transfusions, were infected with AIDS.

By the early 1990s, no cure for the virus had been found and, while more persons with AIDS (PWAs) are surviving for longer periods of time, the diseases brought on by the virus have invariably proved to be fatal. Promising research on a number of vaccines is in progress, but no effective vaccine has yet been discovered, although a number of medications have been found to slow the course of the disorder by treating the underlying disease and the opportunistic infections that characterize it. The former treatments include **AZT** (zidovudine, earlier called azidothymidine) and DDI; the latter group includes aerosolized pentamidine, an inhalant used to prevent symptoms of Pneumocystis carinii, several interferons and fluconizole. But with no cure for the disease found and since all treatments discovered to date merely slow its course, the best defense against AIDS has been education into its causes and avoidance of such high-risk behaviors as unprotected intercourse or needle-sharing.

New and deadly, AIDS has strained society's resources in dealing with the pandemic and raised difficult moral and social questions. Many activists advocate early education to help prevent the spread of AIDS, but school programs involving the discussion of sexual behavior and the distribution of condoms to students have generated much controversy. Movements to provide drug addicts with sterile needles have met with a similar disapproval from citizens who feel that such distribution will only condone and encourage drug use. AIDS patients have sometimes been socially stigmatized, denied care and housing and often pauperized by their disease; issues of confidentiality regarding HIV status have become extremely important.

The healthcare system has also been strained, and new types of treatment, such as increased outpatient care for the sick and hospice care for the dying, have increasingly been implemented. Dissatisfied with the slow pace of public and government reaction to the AIDS crisis, many advocacy and activist groups have been formed to educate the public and lobby for action. Research into the treatment and prevention of AIDS is likely to remain among the greatest medical challenges of the 21st century.

Aiken, Conrad (1889–1973). American poet, novelist and critic. Born into a prosperous Southern family, Aiken used an independent income to support his writing career. His early work was influenced by his Harvard classmate T.S. ELIOT, by the IMAGISM of John Gould Fletcher and by the French Symbolists (see SYMBOLISM). After graduating, he spent several years in London, where he edited the *Dial* (1916–19). He was also American correspondent of the *Atheneum* and *London Mercury* (1921–22), and London correspondent of the NEW YORKER (1933–36). A prolific writer, he produced over two dozen volumes of poetry and 10 volumes of fiction between 1914 and 1952. His *Selected Poems* won a PULITZER PRIZE in 1929; in 1950–51 he was poetry consultant at the Library of Congress; and in 1953 his *Collected Poems* won the National Book Award. His autobiography, *Ushant*, appeared in 1952.

For further reading:

Marten, Harry, *The Art of Knowing: The Poetry and Prose of Conrad Aiken*. Columbia: University of Missouri Press, 1988.

Butscher, Edward, *Poet of White Horse Vale*. Athens: University of Georgia Press, 1988.

Ailey, Alvin (1931–1989). American dancer, choreographer and ballet director. Born in Texas, Ailey discovered dance as a Los Angeles high school student. While at UCLA, he studied modern dance with Lester Horton, who became his mentor and was a prime influence, along with Katherine DUNHAM and Martha GRAHAM, on his choreographic style. After Horton's death in 1953, Ailey left for New York City to dance in the Broadway mu-

Alvin Ailey (1983).

sical *House of Flowers* with Carmen de Lavallade. He founded his own company in 1958; its first concert included *Blues Suite,* which, with his company's signature piece *Revelations* (1960) and *Cry* (1971), made his name as a choreographer who eloquently dramatized the black experience. His choreography blended elements of classical ballet, JAZZ, Afro-Caribbean dance and modern dance. In 1971 he established the Alvin Ailey American Dance Center. His company, interracial since 1963, has performed worldwide, and Ailey has also choreographed for Broadway musicals, opera and other dance companies. In 1988 he received one of the Kennedy Center Honors in recognition for his lifetime of achievement in modern dance. Ailey arguably did more than anyone else to open up opportunities for black dancers.

air conditioning. A technological means of controlling the temperature within a room or building, cooling and dehumidifying the air in order to make it comfortable for human habitation. Air conditioning is a phenomenon of life in the late 20th century, particularly in the U.S. and in affluent warm-weather countries such as Australia and Saudi Arabia; it is less common in Europe and in the Third World. Willis H. Carrier, who presented a paper on the subject to the American Society of Mechanical Engineers in 1911, is commonly considered the inventor of the air conditioner; credit is sometimes given to Stuart W. Cramer, who rigged a primitive air conditioner in 1906. Air conditioning was introduced in public buildings in the U.S. in the 1920s; by the 1960s, it had become a common feature in American homes. Although most commonly thought of strictly in terms of cooling, air conditioning is also intended to filter out impurities. However, air conditioning systems can be breeding grounds for harmful microorganisms, as with Legionnaire's disease, first identified in the 1970s. Some people feel that air conditioning is one more artificial barrier between human life and nature; the American writer Henry MILLER titled one of his books *The Air-Conditioned Nightmare* (referring to the U.S.). Nonetheless, on hot, humid summer days in city offices and apartment buildings, few would scorn this 20th-century invention.

Airflow Chrysler. Chrysler and DeSoto 1934 automobiles developed by Carl Breer with curving, streamlined forms derived from aerodynamics. Their appearance was so startlingly unlike that of other, more boxlike automotive products that public acceptance was very poor. The Airflow Chrysler has come to be considered a classic case of a consumer design ahead of its time, although later admired for being inventive and advanced.

Airstream. Brand name of the travel trailers manufactured by the firm of the same name founded by Wally Byam, an advertising executive and publisher. Byam built a trailer for his own use as a hobby in 1934. He used ALUMINUM for a streamlined unit based on aircraft technology. Its light weight and lowered air resistance were highly functional, but its striking shape and gleaming exterior finish made the Airstream trailer handsome in contrast with most competitors. Over the years since its mid-1930s introduction, various improvements and varied designs have been introduced by Airstream, but all Airstreams retain an elegantly streamlined, functional form and aluminum exterior finish.

Aisne River. River that flows northwestward from France's Argonne Forest to join with the Oise River. The Aisne served as a key battlefield line during WORLD WAR I, with major battles along its shores in 1914, 1917 and 1918. In the latter engagement, Germany launched its last major offensive from the Aisne River, only to see it decisively halted at the MARNE River.

Aitken, Sir (John William) Max(well) (1910–1985). British newspaper publisher. Born in Canada, Aitken was raised and educated in England. He joined the Royal Air Force just before the outbreak of WORLD WAR II and was a hero of the BATTLE OF BRITAIN. After the war he was a Conservative member of Parliament until 1950. Upon his father's death in 1964, he became chairman of Beaverbrook Newspapers, which included the *Daily Express,* the *Sunday Express* and London's *Evening Standard.* He held that post until 1977, when the group was sold to Trafalgar House. After the sale, Aitken stayed on as life president.

Aitken, Robert Grant (1864–1951). American astronomer. Aitken obtained his A.B. in 1887 and his A.M. in 1892 from Williams College, Mass. He began his career at the University of the Pacific, then in San Jose, as professor of mathematics from 1891 until 1895, when he joined the staff of Lick Observatory, Mount Hamilton, Calif. He remained at Lick for his entire career, serving as its director from 1930 until his retirement in 1935. Aitken did much to advance knowledge of binary stars, pairs of stars orbiting about the same point under their mutual gravitational attraction. He described over 3,000 binary systems and published in 1932 the comprehensive work *New General Catalogue of Double Stars Within 120° of the North Pole.* He also produced the standard work *The Binary Stars* (1918).

Aix-la-Chapelle. See AACHEN.

Aix-les-Bains. Town in France's Savoie department, on Lake Bourget. Founded by the Romans in 125 B.C., it has long been known for its bath spas. It was the site of a 1955 conference between French and Moroccan nationalist leaders that ultimately led to the establishment of Moroccan independence.

Ajdabiyah [Agedabia]. Town in Libya's Benghazi province, near the Gulf of Sidra. From 1919 to 1923, it was the administrative center for the emir of Cyrenaica. Occupied by fascist Italian forces in 1923, it was held by Axis partners Italy and Germany during the early stages of WORLD WAR II, until the British drove out the Afrika Korps of Erwin ROMMEL in 1942—the first victory by the Allies over Rommel.

Akers, Sir Wallace Allen (1888–1954). British industrial chemist. Akers, the son of an accountant, was educated at Oxford University. He first worked for the chemical company Brunner Mond from 1911 to 1924. After four years in Borneo with an oil company, in 1928 he returned to Brunner Mond, which had become part of ICI. From 1931 he was in charge of the Billingham Research Laboratory and from 1944 was the company director responsible for all ICI research. In WORLD WAR II Akers worked under Sir John Anderson, the government minister responsible for work on the ATOM BOMB. He was put in charge of Tube Alloys, the Ministry of Supply's front for secret nuclear work. Akers led the mission of British scientists in 1943 to the U.S. to work out details of collaboration, although he proved unacceptable to the Americans and was replaced by James CHADWICK. Akers returned to head Tube Alloys in the United Kingdom. After the war one of his main tasks was setting up the Central Research Laboratory for ICI at Welwyn near London, later named the Akers Research Laboratory. He was knighted in 1946.

Akhmadulina, Bella (1937–). Russian poet. Influenced by the Acmeists, and by Anna AKHMATOVA and Marina TSVETAEVA in particular, Akhmadulina's work has been noted for its "surprising imagery" and sense of humor as well as its ability to find significance in the most seemingly trivial things and events. Though published infrequently, she is probably best known for her collections *String* (1962) and *Music Lessons.* Akhmadulina's first marriage was to fellow poet Yevgeny YEVTUSHENKO in 1955.

Akhmatova, Anna (1889–1966). Russian poet. Considered Russia's greatest woman poet, Akhmatova belonged to the group of poets called the ACMEISTS before 1918. Her first two collections of poetry, *Evening* (1912) and *Rosary* (1914), established her reputation. She was married to fellow poet Nikolai GUMILEV (1910–1918), and his execution in 1921 by the BOLSHEVIKS stigmatized her. From 1923 to 1940 she had practically no publications, suffered from hardships, isolation and official censorship, and supported herself by doing translations. Her great work, *Poem Without a Hero* (1943), exemplifies her characteristic way of merging personal emotions and memories with important events. Other poetry collections include *In 1940* and the famous *Requiem* (1935–1940). Her complete poems were issued in 1990 in a definitive bilingual (Russian and English) edition.

For further reading:

Chukovskaya, Lydia, *Conversations with Akhmatova, Vol. 1: 1938–1941*. New York: Farrar, Straus & Giroux, 1990.

Haight, Amanda, *Anna Akhmatova: A Poetic Pilgrimage*. New York: Oxford University Press, 1976.

Akihito (1933–). Emperor of Japan (1989–); eldest son of Emperor HIROHITO and Empress Nagako. Crown Prince Akihito studied marine biology at Jakushuin University. He has traveled widely, knows English and is well versed in Western culture. He assumed imperial duties in September 1988 when his father became ill. On January 7, 1989, upon Hirohito's death, Akihito rose to the Chrysanthemum Throne and became Japan's emperor. He and his wife, the Empress Michiko, were married in 1959.

Akins, Zoe (1886–1958). American author, poet, dramatist and screenwriter. Akins won a PULITZER PRIZE in 1935 for her play *The Old Maid*. This work, along with several of her non-dramatic works, was adapted for audiences. She also wrote a screenplay based on Edna FERBER's *Showboat*. Her major poetic works are *Interpretations* (1911) and *The Hills Grow Smaller* (1937).

Aksynov, Vassily (Pavlovich) (1932–). Russian author. Aksynov was born in Kazan, U.S.S.R.; his parents were political prisoners exiled in Siberia for 18 years. He spent his youth in an orphanage for Children of Enemies of the State, was educated at the first Leningrad Medical Institute and practiced as a physician at Leningrad Hospital from 1956 to 1960. His first novel, *Zvezdnyi Bilit* (1961; translated both as *A Starry Ticket*, 1962, and as *A Ticket to the Stars*, 1963), drew comparisons to the work of J.D. SALINGER because of its exploration of the yearnings of youth, a theme he carried through in successive fiction. In 1980 Aksynov left the Soviet Union because of increasing government harassment and his frustration at his inability to get his work published there. He went to the United States, serving as writer-in-residence at the University of Southern California in 1981, George Washington University in 1982, and Goucher College in 1984, and settled in Washington, D.C. Other works include *The Island of Crimea* (1983), *The Burn* (1984), and *In Search of Melancholy Baby* (1987). Aksynov has also written short stories and a play.

Akutagawa, Ryunosuke (1892–1927). Japanese short story writer and novelist. Akutagawa was influenced by his teachers Soseki Natsume and Ogai Mori, the two greatest figures of the late-19th-century Meiji period. At Tokyo Imperial University, he specialized in English literature and published his first short stories in student magazines. These included "Rashomon," the source for Akira KUROSAWA's 1951 film masterpiece. Akutagawa's stories drew heavily on Chinese and Japanese history and ancient story books. A profound individualist with a precise and elegant style, he has been compared to both Aubrey Beardsley and Jonathan Swift. Sensitive, morose and frail in health, he committed suicide in 1927, leaving a legacy of about 150 short stories, a novel (*Kappa*) and some poems and essays.

Al-Agheila [Al-'Uqaylah, El-Agheila]. Town in Libya's Benghazi province, near the Gulf of Sidra. During WORLD WAR II, it was the site of numerous battles between Allied and Axis forces, most notably witnessing the commencement of a major Axis offensive led by Erwin ROMMEL against British forces in 1942. The town was conquered by British forces that same year.

Alameda. Port city on an island in San Francisco Bay. The first Pan-American China Clipper flight took off from Alameda in 1935. In 1938–39, the Alameda Naval Air Station, a major U.S. naval air base, was constructed there.

Alamogordo. City in the U.S. state of New Mexico, west of the Sacramento Mountains. The first test detonation of an ATOMIC BOMB took place on June 16, 1945, at the nearby White Sands Missile Range.

Alaska. Became the 49th U.S. state in 1959. Located in the far northwest of North America, Alaska was purchased by the United States from Russia for $7 million in 1867. After being governed by the U.S. Army and Navy, and as a federal agency, it was accorded formal territorial status in 1912. Successive gold strikes in 1898, 1899 and 1902 brought waves of prospectors. In 1903, a boundary dispute between the U.S., Britain and Canada led to arbitration and a favorable result for the U.S. A 1912 treaty, reflecting early environmental concern for the area, restricted seal hunting in Alaskan waters by Britain, Japan and Russia. During WORLD WAR II, Attu and Kiska Islands, in the territory's Aleutian Islands chain, were held by Japanese forces from 1942 to 1943 before reconquest by the Americans. Postwar Alaska became the site of American military bases deployed with reference to the Soviet Union—only a few miles from the tip of Alaska's Seward Peninsula. The most massive earthquake ever recorded in North America occurred in Alaska in March 1964, killing over 100 people. The 1968 discovery of major oil deposits on the Alaskan North Slope led to increased economic wealth for the state. Controversy continues between commercial and environmental interests as to just how developed the oil deposits, as well as other Alaskan natural resources, should be. In 1988 an oil tanker, the *Exxon Valdez*, ran aground in Prince William Sound, spilling 11 million gallons of crude oil that washed up on the Alaskan shoreline. This accident—the worst civilian oil spill ever—and the subsequent cleanup effort focused international attention on the state and on the environment.

Alaska Highway. Highway extending some 1,523 miles, from Dawson Creek in British Columbia, northwest to Fairbanks, Alaska; formerly known as the Alcan Highway. Built by the United States in 1942 during WORLD WAR II, it served as a strategic supply road for American forces stationed in Alaska to defend against Japanese invasion.

Alaska pipeline. Pipeline, about 800 miles long, that carries crude oil from Prudhoe Bay on the Arctic north coast of Alaska to the port of Valdez on the state's south coast. Massive petroleum deposits were discovered at Prudhoe Bay in 1968. Because Prudhoe Bay is locked in by ice for much of the year, the oil companies required a pipeline to transport the oil across Alaska to the south coast for shipment to refineries. The pipeline became a major political issue. Environmental groups opposed it, fearing that an accidental leak could contaminate Alaska's pristine environment. However, many state residents felt that the pipeline would bring new jobs and an influx of money. The pipeline was built between 1974 and 1977. (See also EXXON VALDEZ.)

Alba Iulia [Alba Julia]. Town in Romania's Transylvania; a center of Romanian nationalism in the first two decades of the century, in a region otherwise dominated by Hungarian sympathies. It was the site of the December 1, 1918, proclamation of Transylvanian and Romanian union, and of the 1922 coronation of King Ferdinand I and Queen Marie.

Albania [People's Republic of Albania]. European nation located in the Balkans and on the east shore of the Adriatic Sea; bordered to its north and east by Yugoslavia and to its south by Greece. Scholars trace the ancestry of the Albanian populace to the ancient Illyrian and Thracian peoples. The nation is naturally isolated by mountains, forests and swampland. For centuries a part of the OTTOMAN EMPIRE, Albania asserted its independence during the First BALKAN WAR in 1912. The Serbian invasion of 1913 and the intensive fighting of WORLD WAR I interrupted, and independence was not fully reestablished until the 1920s. The conservative leader Ahmed Zogu became King Zog in 1928. In 1939, at the outset of WORLD WAR II, Italy seized Albania. During the war, partisan forces led by communist leader Enver HOXHA were aided exclusively by Britain and France, leading to the postwar establishment of a European communist state free of Soviet economic or military dependence. Albania broke diplomatic relations with the U.S.S.R. in 1961 to ally itself with the more doctrinally pure communist Chinese regime. Albania remained isolated and

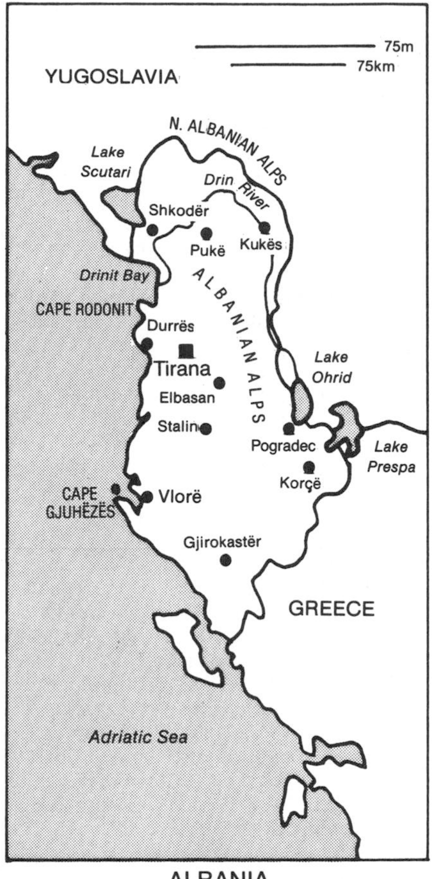

ALBANIA

ALBANIA

1912	Ottoman empire breaks up; patriots led by Ismail Quemal Bey proclaim independence for Albania.
1915	Secret Treaty of London; Allied powers prepare to divide Albania among Greece, Italy and Serbia.
1920	Partisans drive out Italians and reestablish independence.
1923	Albanian Muslims (69% of its population) declare their autonomy from outside authority.
1924	Ahmet Zogu declares himself president, begins modernization.
1928	Zogu crowns himself Zog I.
1939	Italians annex Albania; Zog flees.
1944	Communist-dominated government takes power following internal struggle.
1946	People's Republic of Albania proclaimed; Enver Hoxha consolidates dictatorial power.
1961	Hoxha breaks relations with U.S.S.R., forms alliance with China.
1969	Last Catholic church closes; all organized religious activity ended.
1982	China severs relations; Albania becomes one of the world's most isolated countries.
1985	Hoxha dies; replaced by Ramiz Alia.
1987	Tentative moves to make contact with Greece and other neighbors.
1990	Thousands protesting communist government jam foreign embassies; many are allowed to emigrate.
1991	In the face of a general strike and violent protests, Alia promises free elections, release of political prisoners and an open border.

subject to a repressive regime that frequently employed purges. However, in 1990 the communist regime announced that opposition parties would be allowed. Many Albanians began fleeing to Greece and Yugoslavia, and in early 1991 there were anti-communist demonstrations.

Albanian Uprising of 1910. A rebellion of about 8,000 Albanians in the northern part of the country beginning in March 1910. The Albanians had aided the YOUNG TURKS of the OTTOMAN EMPIRE after being promised autonomy and relief from oppressive Turkish taxation. However, once in power the Young Turks reneged and levied new taxes. The uprising spread to southeastern Albania and western Macedonia. Albanian leaders in Montenegro issued a memorandum demanding Albanian self-government. The Turkish government rejected it, and a large Turkish army crushed the uprising in June 1910.

Albanian Uprisings of 1932, 1935 and 1937. ALBANIA's King Zog I (1895–1961) faced insurrections in 1932, 1935 and 1937 from groups of liberal reformers and Marxist-oriented Muslim radicals. A dictator who ruled autocratically to preserve Albania's feudal society, Zog easily put down these relatively small and poorly planned uprisings. His punishment was lenient: only a few ringleaders were executed; minor social and administrative reforms were undertaken. Zog's rule ended on April 7, 1939, when ITALY, Albania's sole foreign support, declared Albania a protectorate and invaded, forcing Zog to flee into exile.

For further reading:
Fischer, Bernard J., *King Zog and the Struggle for Stability in Albania.* East European Quarterly, 1984.

Albee, Edward (1928–). American playwright. Albee is perhaps the best known American playwright of his generation, primarily due to the great critical and popular success of WHO'S AFRAID OF VIRGINIA WOOLF? (1962). Albee first earned recognition through his one-act play *The Zoo Story* (1959), which explores the illusions people cherish in the face of a harsher reality. Albee won Pulitzer Prizes for two subsequent dramas, *A Delicate Balance* (1966) and *Seascape* (1975). His other plays include *Tiny Alice* (1964), *Counting the Ways* (1976) and *The Man Who Had Three Arms* (1983). In 1981 he adapted the Vladimir NABOKOV novel *Lolita* for the Broadway stage.

Edward Albee outside Boston's Colonial Theater (1976).

For further reading:
Kolin, Philip C., ed., *Conversations with Edward Albee.* Jackson: University Press of Mississippi, 1988.

Albeniz, Isaac (1860–1909). Spanish composer and pianist. Born in Camprodon, Catalonia, the piano virtuoso made his piano debut at the age of four. A young adventurer, he left his home at 13, traveling to Central America, South America and the U.S., supporting himself by playing the piano. Settling in Paris in 1893, he was strongly influenced by DEBUSSY and D'INDY, and his teacher, Felipe Pedrell, interested Albeniz in the music of his native Spain. The best known of his compositions are those he wrote for the piano, with strong Spanish dance rhythms and pervasive musical references to Spanish folk themes. The most important of these is *Iberia* (1906–9), a group of 12 piano pieces. Albeniz also wrote several operas, such as *Pepita Jimenez* (1896), and a number of other vocal works.

Albers, Anni (1899–). German designer whose special interests were weaving and textile design, fields in which she was a leader in the development of a Modern, fully abstract approach. Born in Berlin, in 1922 Albers became a student at the BAUHAUS, where she met and married Josef

ALBERS. She taught with her husband at Black Mountain College in North Carolina until 1949 when she moved to New Haven. Her work as a weaver is widely respected, and she has taught and lectured in many universities in the U.S., Europe, and Japan. Her books, *On Designing* (1959) and *On Weaving* (1965), are definitive works in their area.

Albers, Josef (1888–1976). German-American painter, printmaker, designer and art theorist. Born in Bottrop, Germany, he studied in Berlin (1913–15), Essen (1916–19), Munich (1919–20) and finally at the BAUHAUS in Weimar (1920–23), where he became an instructor (in Weimar, Dessau and Berlin) from 1923 to 1930. In this period he began his experiments with optics, color and light. In 1933 he and his wife, the weaver Anni Albers, immigrated to the U.S., and he became a citizen in 1939. A popular and influential teacher, he headed the art department at Black Mountain College until 1940 and was director of the Department of Design at Yale University from 1950 to 1958. Albers' many books on color theory include the massive *Interaction of Color* (1963). His best known works, *Homage to the Square,* are a series of geometrical paintings and graphics begun in 1949 and continued until his death.

For further reading:

Weber, Nicholas F., *Josef Albers: A Retrospective.* New York: Harry N. Abrams, 1988.

Albert. Town in France's Somme department; formerly known as Ancre. During WORLD WAR I, Albert was the scene of recurrent and intensive fighting and was destroyed. It was rebuilt only to again be destroyed, in WORLD WAR II.

Albert I [King of the Belgians] (1875–1934). Succeeding his uncle, Leopold II (1835–1909), he reigned from 1909 to 1934. He was married (1900) to the Bavarian Princess Elizabeth. A courageous and popular monarch, he strongly resisted the German invasion of Belgium (1914) during WORLD WAR I. Albert spent the duration of the war commanding the nation's army, and in 1918 he headed the final Allied offensive. After the war, he supported economic reconstruction, worked to improve social conditions at home and in the BELGIAN CONGO and promoted currency reform (1926). He was killed in a mountain-climbing accident in 1934 and was succeeded by his son, LEOPOLD III.

Alberta. A Prairie province of western Canada; first linked to eastern Canada via railroad in the 1880s. In the early part of this century, Alberta was primarily a ranching center. It became a Canadian province in 1905, and subsequent waves of immigration led to a wheat farming boom. In 1935, during the GREAT DEPRESSION, the people of Alberta voted control of their government to the Social Credit Party, which attempted to transform the banking and currency systems, attempts that were declared unconstitutional. Alberta produces some 85% of Canadian gas and oil, and the process by which it shared the resultant revenues with the central government was hotly debated until a final resolution in 1981. The decline of oil prices in the late 1980s was a recessionary influence upon the Alberta economy.

Alberti, Rafael (1902–). Spanish poet and playwright. A member of the GENERATION OF 1927 in Spain, Alberti began his career as a painter but turned to poetry in 1923. His first book, *Marinero en tierra* (1925, "Sailor on Land"), won the *Premio Nacional de Literature.* His finest work, *Sobre los angeles* (1929, "About the Angels"), was abstract and difficult and showed the influence of SURREALISM. After 1931, Alberti professed Marxism. A Loyalist in the SPANISH CIVIL WAR, he went into exile in Argentina after the triumph of FRANCO, only returning to Spain in 1977. His later poetry was lyrical and spiritual. His work shows the influence of Juan Ramon JIMENEZ and the classical Spanish poets, especially Gongora.

For further reading:

Nantell, Judith, *Rafael Alberti's Poetry of the Thirties: The Poet's Public Voice.* Athens: University of Georgia Press, 1986.

Albery, Sir Donald (1914–1988). British theater manager. Albery was the chairman and manager of Wyndham Theatres Ltd. of London and supported playwrights such as Samuel BECKETT, John OSBORNE and Edward ALBEE. Besides now-standard modern works such as WAITING FOR GODOT, *A Taste of Honey,* WHO'S AFRAID OF VIRGINIA WOOLF and Graham GREENE'S *The Living Room,* he staged box office smashes such as *Oliver!* Born into a four-generation theater family, he was the first to recognize the importance of American tourists to the economic health of the West End theater.

Albright, Ivan de Lorraine (1897–1983). American painter associated with the 1930s style called MAGIC REALISM. Labeled by critics "the painter of horrors" and "the specialist in the repulsive," he was best known for his painting *The Window* and for the portraits used in a film version of Oscar Wilde's *The Picture of Dorian Gray.*

Alcatraz. U.S. island in California's San Francisco Bay. From 1859 to 1934, it was the site of an American military prison. Thereafter, it became a maximum security, civilian facility for prisoners deemed to be hard cases. After closing in 1963, the island and its prison became a popular tourist site. Alcatraz was briefly seized by American Indian activists demanding civil rights for their people.

Alcock and Brown. British aviator John William Alcock (1892–1919) and his navigator, Arthur Whitten Brown (1886–1948), made the first nonstop flight over the Atlantic Ocean, in a Vickers-Vimy biplane, on June 14, 1919. Flying from St. John's, Newfoundland, to Clifden, Ireland, the men made the historic 1,960-mile trip in 16 hours, 27 minutes. Both were knighted by King George V; one week later, Alcock was killed in an airplane crash in France.

Alcoholics Anonymous. Alcoholics Anonymous (AA) is an international, nonprofit self-help organization for alcoholics, dedicated to helping members maintain sobriety. AA was founded in 1935 by Bill Wilson, an alcoholic Wall Street worker, who built on the concepts and techniques of the nondenominational OXFORD GROUP. Wilson's book *Alcoholics Anonymous* was published in 1939, and in 1946 "the Twelve Traditions" were promulgated to formalize the organization's goals and practices. Today there are estimated to be more than one million AA members worldwide.

Aldanov, Mark [Mark Aleksandrovich Landau] (1886–1957). Russian writer. Aldanov left Russia for France in 1919 and wrote a series of books on the French revolutionary period. His essay on LENIN (1912) compared the French and RUSSIAN REVOLUTIONS. In *The Fifth Seal* (1939) he depicted the decline in revolutionary idealism that followed the Russian Revolution. Among his later works are *A Night at the Airport* (1949) and *The Escape* (1950). After 1941 he lived in the United States.

Aldeburgh. Town in Suffolk, England; the first British town to elect a woman as mayor—Dr. Elizabeth Garrett Anderson in 1908. It is also the setting for an annual classical music festival inaugurated by British composer Benjamin BRITTEN.

Alden, John G. (1884–1962). American designer of yachts and other craft, particularly known for his schooners based on traditional New England fishing boats. John Alden was a largely self-taught naval architect, although he worked for eight years for the firm of B.B. Crowninshield, a Boston specialist in Gloucester fishing schooners. After World War I he established himself as a designer of yachts as well as a dealer and marine insurance broker. By the time of his retirement in 1955, Alden had designed some 900 yachts, many of them ocean-racing schooners, ketches or yawls.

Alder, Kurt (1902–1958). German organic chemist. Alder studied chemistry in Berlin and Kiel, receiving his doctorate in 1926 under Otto DIELS. In 1928 the two discovered the chemical reaction that bears their names. Alder was professor of chemistry at Kiel (1934), chemist with I.G. Farben at Leverkusen (1936) and director of the Chemical Institute at the University of Cologne (1940). In 1950 Diels and Alder jointly received the NOBEL PRIZE for chemistry for their discovery.

Aldermaston. Town in Berkshire, England; site of the British Atomic Weapons Research Institute. In the 1950s and 1960s, it was the location of frequent nuclear weapons protest marches organized by the CAMPAIGN FOR NUCLEAR DISARMAMENT.

Aldington, Richard (1892–1962). British author. Aldington was born in Hampshire and educated at University College in London, though he did not complete a degree there. As a young imagist poet, Aldington became acquainted with Ezra POUND, Ford Maddox FORD and Hilda DOOLITTLE (HD), whom he married in 1913, while he was assistant editor of *The Egoist.* His first volume of poetry, *Images 1910–1915,* was published in 1915. WORLD

WAR I left Aldington psychologically scarred and bitter. His first novel, *Death of a Hero* (1929), depicts a frivolous young civilian, George Winterbourne, his transformation into a soldier and, finally, his death. The book's anger and graphic descriptions of the atrocities of war made an impact unmatched by his following novels, such as *The Colonel's Daughter* (1931) and *All Men are Enemies* (1933). During WORLD WAR II, Aldington moved to the U.S. where he wrote the biographies, *Wellington* (1946); *Portrait of a Genius, But . . .* (1950) about D.H. LAWRENCE; and *Lawrence of Arabia: A Biographic Enquiry* (1955), which raised hackles for its negative portrayal of T.E. LAWRENCE. He also wrote an autobiography, *Life for Life's Sake* (1941). (See also IMAGISM.)

Aldiss, Brian (1925–). British science fiction writer. Aldiss holds a secure position in the front rank of contemporary science fiction writers by virtue of his prolific output of stories, novels, critical essays and anthologies. Aldiss published his first stories in the mid-1950s; they were distinguished by their literary style and their deemphasis of strict scientific plausibility in favor of imaginative plot development. In 1962 he won a Hugo Award (the highest honor in the genre) for the "Hothouse Series" of novelettes depicting a future humanity living in the branches of a continent-wide tree. Aldiss has also won a Nebula Award and a British Science Fiction Award. Notable novels by Aldiss include *Greybeard* (1964), *Cryptozoic!* (1967), *The Malacia Tapestry* (1976) and *Helliconia Spring* (1982) and its two sequels. He has also written a compendious history of science fiction, *The Billion-Year Spree* (1973, revised 1989).

Aldrin, Edwin E. "Buzz," Jr. (1930–). U.S. astronaut. "We both landed at the same time," Buzz Aldrin would usually reply when introduced as the "second man to land on the moon." As lunar module pilot of the most famous flight in space history, Aldrin was the second human to set foot on the moon, following APOLLO 11 Commander Neil ARMSTRONG down the ladder of the lunar lander to the moon's dusty surface only 15 minutes after Armstrong's famous "small step." "Magnificent desolation" was how Aldrin described the moon's surface—without the ring of Armstrong's words. Being the second man to walk the surface of the moon was a hard act to follow, and that historic mission of July 16–24, 1969, was the restless Buzz Aldrin's last space flight.

Born in Montclair, New Jersey, he was a West Point graduate and served as a combat pilot in the KOREAN WAR, flying over 60 combat missions before returning to the U.S. to become an aide to the dean of faculty at the U.S. Air Force Academy. After three years he moved to Germany and spent the next three years as an F-100 pilot with the 36th Fighter Day Wing at Bitburg. Joining NASA in October 1963, he served as capcom (capsule communicator) for Gemini 5 and Gemini 10, making his first space flight on Gemini 12 (November 11–15, 1966), the last Gemini mission. Spending four days in space, Aldrin put in over five hours of EVA (extravehicular activity) in one of the most successful space walks of the Gemini program.

Gemini 12 and Apollo 11 were Aldrin's only space flights. Resigning from NASA in July 1971, he was appointed commander of the Test Pilot School at Edwards Air Force Base in California. It wasn't an easy time for Aldrin. He had upset some conservative NASA officials during his tour of duty there by participating in a march after the death of civil rights activist Dr. Martin Luther KING Jr. His return to the Air Force was cut short in 1972 when he suffered a nervous breakdown and retired from the service. *The Eagle Has Landed* was the name of a popular NASA motion picture detailing the historic flight of Apollo 11. He authored a 1973 autobiography, *Return to Earth*, and a 1989 book about the Apollo program, *Men from Earth*.

Aleichem, Sholom [Sholem Rabinowitz] (1859–1916). Yiddish author. Sholom Aleichem (literally, "peace be unto you") was born in the Poltava Province of the U.S.S.R., where he attended a government school. He worked intermittently at the Kiev bourse (stock exchange) but in 1903 dedicated himself solely to writing. Around this time he also co-edited a Russian anthology of Yiddish writing with Maxim GORKY. Aleichem fled the POGROMS of 1905, living in Italy from 1908 to 1914, when the advent of WORLD WAR I drove him to the U.S. He is best known for his humorous, tender short stories depicting Russian Jewish peasants. English-language editions of his works include *The Old Country* (1946), *Some Laughter Some Tears* (1968) and a novel, *The Adventures of Manahem-Mendle* (1969). The short story collection *Tevye's Daughters* (1949) was adapted as the Broadway musical *Fiddler on the Roof* (1964) and a film (1971).

Aleixandre, Vicente (1898–1984). Spanish poet. Aleixandre earned his degrees in law and business management from the University of Madrid but wrote poetry in secret. A member of the GENERATION OF 1927, he published his first book, *Ambito*, in 1928. The influence of Sigmund FREUD is evident in *Espados como labios* (1932) and *Pasion de la tierra* (1935). His intensely erotic *La destruccion o el amor* won the National Prize for literature in 1934. Because of illness, Aleixandre remained in Spain during the Civil War, but his work was banned. *Sombra del paradiso* (1944) and *Historia del corazon* (1954) concerned man's place in the universe. Later works include *En un vasto Dominio* (1962), *Poemas de la consumacion* (1968) and *Dialogos del conocimiento* (1974). He has been a major influence in Spanish poetry in the 20th century.

For further reading:

Schwartz, Kessel, *Vicente Aleixandre*. New York: Irvington, 1970.

Alekhine, Alexander Alexandrovich (1892–1946). A Russian who became a French citizen, Alekhine was world chess champion (1927–33) when he defeated Capablanca, and again from 1937 until his death.

Alekseyev, Michael Vasilyevich (1857–1918). Russian general. Alekseyev was commander in chief on the Western Front (1915) and chief of staff to Czar NICHOLAS II (1915–17) during WORLD WAR I. For a brief period after the overthrow of the czar he was chief of staff to KERENSKY. In 1918 he took the initiative to organize the White (anti-BOLSHEVIK) forces in the RUSSIAN CIVIL WAR. He died soon afterward of pneumonia.

Aleutian Islands. Archipelago extending from the ALASKA Peninsula of the U.S. to the Kamchatka Peninsula of the U.S.S.R. The Bering Sea is to the north of the Aleutians, while the Pacific Ocean is to the south. Certain of the Aleutians—Attu, Agattu, Dutch Harbor (or Unalaska) Island and Kiska—were briefly occupied or attacked by Japanese forces during WORLD WAR II. At present, the U.S. military utilizes the Aleutians for military and radar installations.

Alexander (1888–1934). King of Yugoslavia (reigned 1921–34) and son and successor of the Serbian King Peter I (1844–1921), he was a member of the Karadjordjevic family. Alexander commanded the Serbian army during World War I and, upon his father's death in 1921, became king of the newly-created Kingdom of Serbs, Croats and Slovenes, which he later renamed Yugoslavia to promote unity. Nonetheless, strife among nationalities, notably between Serbs and Croats, caused him to abolish the constitution in 1929 and assume absolute rule. While an end to his dictatorship was announced in 1931, Alexander continued to hold the reins of power, antagonizing separatist minorities. On October 9, 1934, during a state visit to France, Alexander was assassinated by a Croatian terrorist. He was succeeded by his 11-year-old son PETER II, with Prince Paul (1893–1976) acting as chief regent until 1941.

Alexander, Harold Rupert Leofric George [Viscount (1946) and 1st Earl of Tunis (1952)] (1891–1969). British general in WORLD WAR II. Educated at Harrow and Sandhurst, he was commissioned in the Irish Guard and was a decorated batallion commander in France during World War I. Between the wars (1934–38), he served as an officer in India. One of Britain's most celebrated commanders, he led the retreats at Dunkirk (1940) and Burma (1942), going on the offensive as he directed the great Allied advance across North Africa to Tunis and led the invasion of Sicily and Italy (both 1943). In 1944 he was appointed field marshal, acting as supreme Allied commander in the Mediterranean from 1944 to 1945. Alexander served as governor-general of Canada (1946–52) and as minister of defense (1952–54) in the cabinet of Sir Winston CHURCHILL.

Alexander, Samuel (1859–1938). British philosopher and essayist. Alexander is one of the few British philosophers of this century to devote his primary efforts to metaphysical questions. Alexander's magnum opus, *Space, Time and Deity* (1920), remains a basic text for philosophers interested in explaining the human perception of a space-time continuum within reality. In that work, Alexander argued that metaphysical questions—such as the existence of God or the nature of time—were nonempirical in that they were not subject to direct verification by experiment. But Alexander also insisted that the observation of human metaphysical beliefs was an empirical activity that could be aided by the experimental findings of physiological psychology, a newly emerging field that Alexander championed in British academic circles. Alexander, who was educated at Oxford and was the first Jew to win a fellowship there, taught for most of his academic career at the University of Manchester.

Alexanderson, Ernst (1878–1975). Swedish-born engineer. Alexanderson is credited as the inventor of the first home television (1927). A pioneer in the development of radio broadcasting, he was responsible for the device that first made voice communication possible (1906). Altogether he held 322 patents.

Alexandra, Queen of England (1844–1925). Queen of EDWARD VII of England. A princess of Denmark, Alexandra married Edward in 1863, when he was still Prince of Wales. On Victoria's death in 1901, Edward ascended to the throne and Alexandra became queen. A popular figure, she was known for her charitable work, and she helped to establish a military nursing service. Tolerant of her husband's many marital infidelities, Alexandra outlived the king by 13 years and was buried beside him at Windsor.

Alexandra Fedorovna (1872–1918). Empress of All the Russias. Born a princess of Hesse-Darmstadt and a granddaughter of Queen Victoria, she married (1894) NICHOLAS II of Russia. Her belief in the powers of the monk RASPUTIN to cure the young czarevich of HEMOPHILIA brought her under Rasputin's disastrous domination and encouraged her to exert an unfortunate political influence, much resented by the czar's ministers and the population at large. After the 1917 RUSSIAN REVOLUTION she was murdered along with her husband and children.

For further reading:

Massie, Robert K., *Nicholas and Alexandra*. New York: Atheneum, 1967.

Alexandretta. City and province on the Mediterranean Sea's Gulf of Iskenderun. Due to its strategic location, Alexandretta was the source of international controversy in the decades between the two world wars. The French ceded it to Syria under the Treaty of Sevres in 1920. It briefly became the independent Republic of Hatay in 1938 before being reconsolidated into TURKEY in 1939.

Alexandria Quartet, The. Four related novels by Lawrence DURRELL—*Justine* (1957), *Balthazar* (1958), *Mountolive* (1950) and *Clea* (1960)—set in Alexandria, Egypt, just before World War II. The first three books describe the same events and time period; only in *Clea* is there a regular chronological narrative. The main characters are Darley, a novelist and narrator of the first two books; Melissa, his mistress; Justine and her husband Nessim; Mountolive, the British ambassador; Pursewarden, a British intelligence agent; and Clea, an artist. All are involved with one another, often sexually. Durrell examines the shifting nature of truth by presenting the same events through different character's eyes, always with a strong dose of ambiguity. The writing is sensual and explores a common theme in Durrell's writing: the nature of love and sexuality. Alexandria is presented as decadent and corrupt, a cauldron of urbanity, ancient tradition and exotic ethnicity. *The Alexandria Quartet* shows Durrell's departure from realism and the influence of James JOYCE and Henry MILLER. While critics have argued about the work's significance, *The Alexandria Quartet* has achieved cult status among readers.

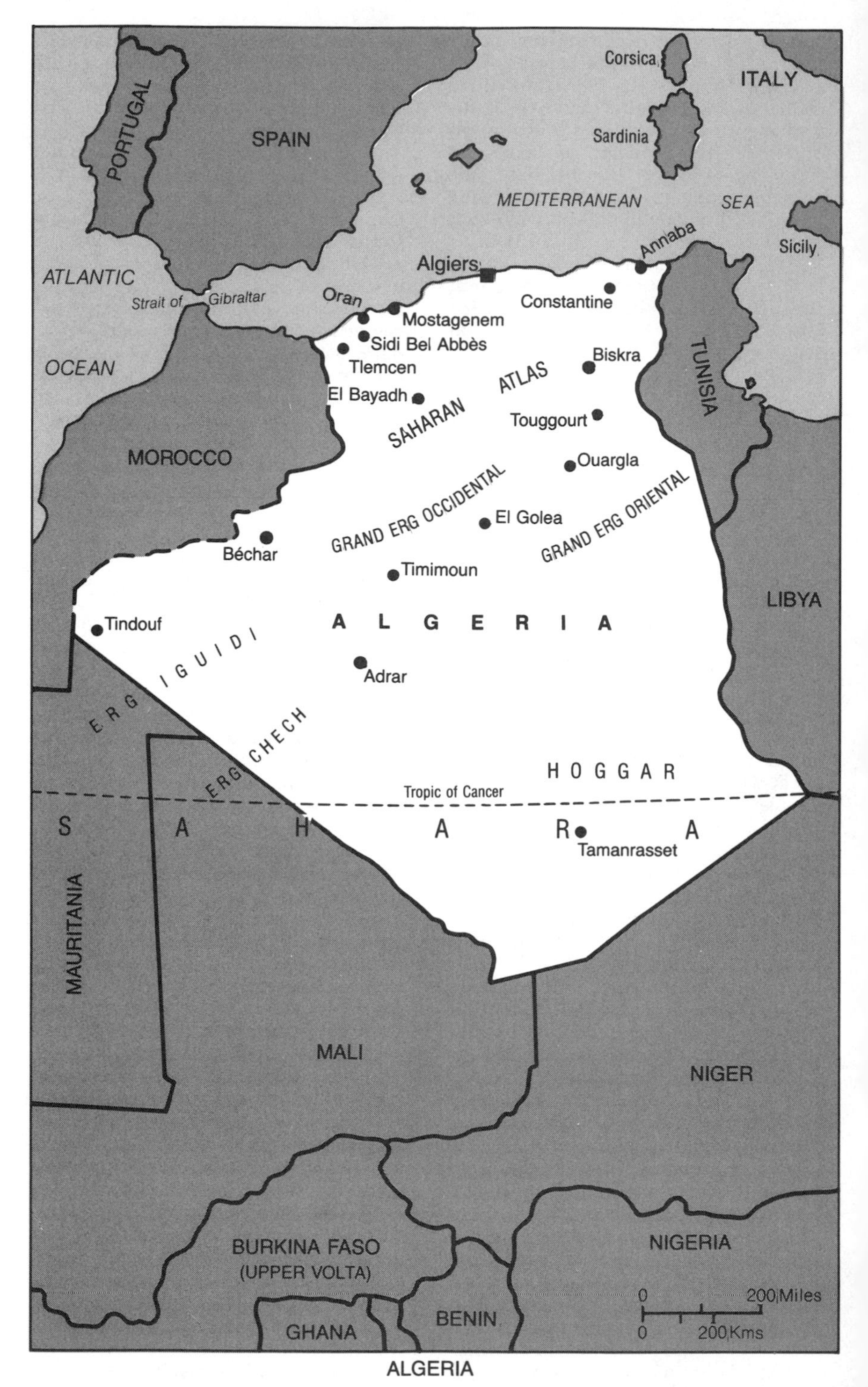

ALGERIA

Alexis [Sergei Vladimirovich Simansky] (1873–1970). Patriarch of Moscow and All Russia (1945–70). He was ordained bishop in 1913 and was archbishop (1929), metropolitan of Novgorod (1932) and metropolitan of Leningrad (1933). From about 1925 he cooperated with the Soviet authorities and secured considerable expansion of church activity as a result.

Alfonsin, Raul (1927–). President of ARGENTINA. After earning a law degree in 1950, Alfonsin joined the Radical Civic Union political party. Over the next two decades he held seats in provincial and national legislatures, but his failed attempt to assume party control from Ricardo Balbin in 1972 appeared to put his political career at an end. In 1983, however, when the military stepped down from power, after Argentina's defeat in the FALKLAND ISLANDS WAR, Alfonsin won his party's nomination and was elected president of the country. Despite assassination attempts and threatened coups, he brought many members of the preceding military governments, including three former presidents, to trial for human rights violations. In the middle to late '80s, Alfonsin imposed economic austerity measures in an attempt to reduce Argentina's crushing foreign debt. He resigned the presidency in 1989, five months before the end of his six-year term, citing the nation's loss of confidence in his ability to lead the country out of its worst economic crisis. Succeeded in the presidency by Carlos Saul Menem, Alfonsin remained leader of the RCU.

Alfonso XIII (1886–1941). King of Spain (reigned 1902–31), the posthumous son and successor of Alfonso XII; his mother, Queen Maria Christina of Hapsburg (1858–1929), was regent during his minority. In 1906 he married Princess Victoria Eugenia of Battenberg (1887–1969), a granddaughter of Britain's Queen Victoria. His early reign was beset by problems: political instability and corruption, labor disputes, Catalan separatism and the rise of socialism and ANARCHISM. Alfonso kept Spain neutral in World War I, but suffered the decline of his prestige in the 1920s, largely due to the 1922 defeat of the Spanish army in Morocco by ABD EL-KRIM. The king supported the 1923 coup d'etat of Gen. Miguel PRIMO DE RIVERA and the military dictatorship that ensued. After de Rivera was deposed in 1930 and Republicans won landslides in municipal elections, Alfonso was almost completely discredited. He left Spain in 1931, going into self-imposed exile in Italy, where he died 10 years later. There was no reigning king in Spain until the accession of Alfonso's grandson, JUAN CARLOS, in 1975.

Alfven, Hannes Olof Gosta (1908–). Swedish physicist. Alfven was educated at the University of Uppsala, where he received his Ph.D. in 1934. He served as professor of electronics at the Royal Institute of Technology, Stockholm, from 1945 until 1963 when a special chair of plasma physics was created for him. He became a professor at the University of California at San Diego in 1967. Alfven is noted for his pioneering theoretical research in the field of magnetohydrodynamics—the study of conducting fluids and their interaction with magnetic fields. This work, for which he shared the 1970 NOBEL PRIZE for physics with Louis Neel, is mainly concerned with plasmas—ionized gases containing positive and negative particles. He investigated the interactions of electrical and magnetic fields and showed theoretically that the magnetic field, under certain circumstances, can move with the plasma. In 1942 he postulated the existence of waves in plasmas; these **Alfven waves** were later observed in both liquid metals and ionized plasmas. Alfven applied his theories to the motion of particles in the Earth's magnetic field and to the properties of plasmas in stars. In 1942 and later in the 1950s he developed a theory of the origin of the solar system. This he assumed to have formed from a magnetic plasma, which condensed into small particles that clustered together into larger bodies. His work is also applicable to the properties of plasmas in experimental nuclear fusion reactors.

Algeciras. Port city in the region of Andalusia. It is Spain's southernmost Mediterranean port and was the site in 1906 of the **Algeciras Conference** that established a privileged hegemony for France and Spain in Morocco.

Algeria [Democratic and Popular Republic of Algeria]. Country in North Africa bound on the north by the Mediterranean Sea, on the east by Tunisia and Libya, on the south by Mali and Niger and on the west by Mauritania and Morocco. A French colony at the start of the century, Algeria was ruled by a French governor-general. Prior to WORLD WAR II, over one million French settlers had colonized Algeria, but after the war an anticolonial Arab nationalist movement gained strength and ultimately started a violent civil war (see ALGERIAN WAR OF 1954–62). Estimates as of 1960 placed the number of dead at 10,000 each for the French and Arab sides. The EVIAN Accords of 1962 established an independent Algeria. The government was led initially by the moderate Ben Khedda; he was soon replaced by the nationalist leader Ahmed BEN BELLA. In the following year, most of the French residents of Algeria returned to their native land (a "native land" that many of them had never seen), thereby severely disrupting the Algerian economy. In 1965 Ben Bella was deposed by his defense minister, Houari BOUMEDIENNE. Income from Algerian oil fields in the Sahara helped stabilize the country; the fields were nationalized in 1971. In 1976, a new national charter (approved by 99% of the voters) declared Algeria a socialist and Islamic state; one-party rule was also ratified. Economic problems led to riots in the late 1980s. Political parties were legalized in 1989.

Algerian-Moroccan War of 1963–64. In October 1963 Algerian and Moroccan forces began a border war after ALGERIA separated from FRANCE (see ALGERIAN WAR OF 1954–62). The French had established the shared boundary between Algeria and MOROCCO (to which France had relinquished its rights in 1956) without consulting either former possession. Demands for adjustment by Algerian president BEN BELLA were ignored. Many lives were lost before the ORGANIZATION OF AFRICAN UNITY (OAU), led by Ethiopian Emperor HAILE SELASSIE and Mali's president Modibo Keita, intervened and arranged a cease-fire (February 20, 1964). Relations between Algeria and Morocco remained strained and border clashes re-

ALGERIA

1900	Algeria gains autonomy from France.
1942	Becomes North African base for Allied armies.
1945	Nationalists kill 88 Europeans; French kill several thousand Muslims in reprisal, dampening hopes for independence.
1955	Front de Liberation National massacres dozens of settler families.
1959	(Sept. 15) After fierce fighting between French and Muslims, De Gaulle concedes that Algerian self-rule should be put to a vote.
1961-62	OAS opposes Algerian independence, launches unsuccessful coup to overthrow De Gaulle.
1962	(July 3) France recognizes new state of Algeria.
1965	Coup led by defense minister Houari Boumedienne deposes President Ben Bella.
1971	French oil and gas companies nationalized, become mainstay of economy.
1985	(Dec.) Referendum providing for some private enterprise approved.
1989	(Feb.) Referendum legalizes multiple political parties.
1990	(May 10) Led by four recently formed opposition parties, tens of thousands of Algerians march through capital to support democracy and oppose Islamic fundamentalism.

sumed in 1967. In 1976, when the Spanish Sahara (renamed Western Sahara) became independent, Algeria and Morocco began a low-key military dispute over ownership of that region.

Algerian National Movement. See Mohammed Ahmed BEN BELLA.

Algerian War of 1954–62. Algerian Muslims of the Front de Liberation National (FLN, or National Liberation Front), began open warfare against French rule in 1954. They raided French army installations and European holdings. In 1957, the French government refused to grant Algeria independence, and thousands of French troops were sent to crush the Algerian rebels. After taking office as president of France (1958), Charles DE GAULLE offered a plan of self-determination for Algeria and later sought a cease fire with Algerian rebel leaders in 1960. Raoul SALAN, a French general opposed to the plan, led an unsuccessful insurrection in Algiers in April 1961, trying to thwart Algerian independence from France. French and Algerian rebel leaders signed a cease-fire in March 1962, but Salan led the illegal Algerian Secret Army Organization (OAS) in revolt against it. Loyal French forces seized Salan, but the French-OAS war continued. On July 1, 1962, Algerians, voting in a national referendum, approved independence, and two days later France recognized Algeria's sovereignty.

Algiers. Port city and capital of Algeria, located on the Bay of Algiers; the city was conquered by the French in 1830. During WORLD WAR II, Algiers became the provisional capital in exile of the FREE FRENCH forces led by Charles DE GAULLE. After the war, it became a center of anticolonial resistance to French rule and was the site of the unsuccessful, pro-colonial putsch of General SALAN in 1958, which helped to overturn the French Fourth Republic and return De Gaulle to power (a De Gaulle who would eventually grant independence to the Arabs). (See also ALGERIAN WAR OF 1954–62.)

Algren, Nelson (1909–1981). American novelist. Born in Detroit, Mich., Algren was raised in Chicago and educated at the University of Illinois School of Journalism. During the GREAT DEPRESSION he worked as a salesman, migrant laborer and writer on the WPA Writers Project and for the Chicago Board of Health in venereal disease control. He sought out the underclass of depression-era Chicago, and his realistic writing depicts the desolation and brutality of that life. His first novel was *Somebody in Boots* (1935). He is best known for the ground-breaking *Man with the Golden Arm* (1949; filmed 1955), a novel about drug addiction that won the NATIONAL BOOK AWARD in 1950. Other work includes *Chicago: City on the Make* (1951), a prose poem; *Walk on the Wild Side* (1956; filmed 1962), and *The Last Carousel* (1973), a collection of short stories. Following WORLD WAR II, Algren traveled occasionally with Simone de BEAUVOIR and became acquainted with Jean Paul SARTRE. His work was much admired by Ernest HEMINGWAY.

For further reading:

Giles, James R. *Confronting the Horror: The Novels of Nelson Algren*. Kent, Ohio: Kent State University Press, 1989.

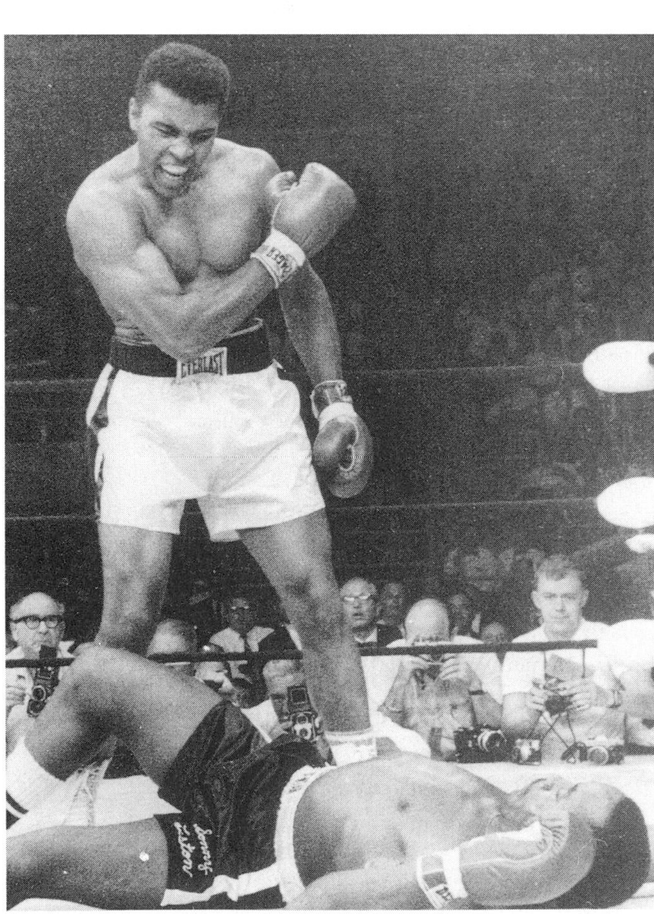

A fearsome Muhammad Ali snarls "Get up!" to a fallen Sonny Liston in their second fight (May 25, 1965).

Al-Hoceima. Port city on Morocco's Mediterranean Sea coast. In 1926, it was the site of the last major military offensive by French and Spanish troops in their successful suppression of a Moroccan independence movement. (See also RIF WAR.)

Ali, Muhammad [Cassius Clay] (1942–). U.S. boxer; burst on the boxing world in 1960, winning the amateur light heavyweight championship, the Golden Gloves heavyweight title and an Olympic gold medal. He then turned professional, taking the national heavyweight championship from Sonny Liston in 1964; he defeated Liston in a rematch the following year. A handsome and glib man, given to reciting his own poetry, he brought a sense of style to boxing. In 1967, Clay converted to the Muslim religion and took the name Muhammad Ali. Later that year, when he refused to enter U.S. military service, he was stripped of his title. He began a comeback in 1970, which led to a series of historic fights throughout the 1970s against such opponents as Joe FRAZIER and George FOREMAN, winning, losing and regaining his championship title.

Alice Springs. Town in virtual center of the Australian continent; formerly known as Stuart. From 1926 to 1931, it served as capital for the former territory of Central Australia. Presently, it is the final northern stop for the Central Australian Railway.

Aliger, Margarita Iosifovna (1915–1979). Soviet poet who was first published in 1933 but who gained fame during World War II with her patriotic poems, including "Zoya" (1942). Her poem "The Most Important Thing" (1948) caused her to be criticized by the authorities.

Al-Kuneitra. Town located in Syria's Golan Heights. Once an artillery post used for the shelling of northern Israel, it was conquered by Israeli forces during the SIX DAY WAR of 1967 and has been held by Israel since that time.

Al-Kut [Kut-El-Amara]. Iraqi town on the Tigris River, in the ancient region of Mesopotamia. During WORLD WAR I, it was captured by British forces in 1915, endured a six-month siege in 1916 and was recaptured by Turkish forces—only to be seized again by British forces in 1917, as part of the campaign by General Frederick Maude to capture Baghdad.

Allegret, Yves (1907–1987). French film director. He was a leading light of post-World War II French cinema. He made a series of starkly realistic dramas of social criticism, some of which starred Simone SIGNORET, to whom Allegret was married from 1944 to 1949. Perhaps his most notable film was *Les Orgueilleux* (*The Proud and the Beautiful*, 1953).

Allen Affair. During the early years of the Reagan administration, a scandal centering on the conduct of the president's national security affairs adviser, Richard

Woody Allen (1987).

Allen. Allen was initially accused of taking a $1,000 bribe in order to arrange an interview with Nancy Reagan, the president's wife, for a writer on a Japanese women's magazine. Although Allen at first denied any wrongdoing and argued that he had not solicited the gift and had merely "forgotten" about the money, an FBI investigation of the matter revealed a number of troubling discrepancies in Allen's personal financial dealings. Allen took a leave of absence and was eventually cleared of wrongdoing by Attorney General Edwin Meese, a close adviser of the president. Although he was cleared of any criminal charges, Allen was an embarrassment to the administration in general and to Mrs. Reagan in particular. He was forced to resign his position as national security adviser, although he continued to work in other capacities within the Reagan administration.

Allen, Edgar (1892–1943). American endocrinologist. Allen, the son of a physician, was educated at Brown University. After war service he worked at Washington University before being appointed (1923) to the chair of anatomy at the University of Missouri. In 1933 he moved to a similar post at Yale and remained there until his death.

In 1923 Allen, working with Edward Doisy, began the modern study of the sex hormones. It was widely thought that the female reproductive cycle was under the control of some substance found in the corpus luteum, the body formed in the ovary after ovulation. But Allen thought that the active ingredient was probably in the follicles surrounding the ovum. To test this he made an extract of the follicular fluid. On injection, he found it induced the physiological changes normally found only in the estrous cycle. Allen had in fact discovered estrogen, although it was only identified some six years later by Adolf BUTENANDT.

Allen, Fred [John Florence Sullivan] (1894–1956). American humorist. Allen began performing in vaudeville as "Freddy James, The World's Worst Juggler." Moving to Broadway in the early 1920s, he appeared in revues such as *The Passing Show of 1922* and *Greenwich Follies of 1924.* But it was in the 1930s on radio that Allen developed his famous laid-back, detached comic style. His show featured a hilarious segment known as "Allen's Alley," in which he played straight man to the fictional Mrs. Nussbaum, Ajax Cassidy, Senator Claghorn and Titus Moody. In the 1950s Allen was fortunate enough to capitalize on the nationwide craze for game shows and appeared regularly on the quiz program "What's My Line." The stress of the live weekly show eventually caused heart problems, and Allen collapsed on St. Patrick's Day.

Allen, Steve (1921–). American television personality, composer, pianist, comedian and social satirist, arguably the most versatile showman in the history of radio and television. Allen is best known for the creation in 1954 of the original TONIGHT SHOW, the model for various broadcast incarnations ever since. He was born in New York City to vaudeville parents and his early years were spent mostly on the road, in and out of 18 schools. He began his broadcasting career in 1942 in Phoenix, Ariz., and continued in Los Angeles after 1945 on several network radio programs. "Smile Time" and "The Steve Allen Show" helped him develop and refine the "ad lib" comedy that is his trademark. These verbal pyrotechnics, facility at the piano and utter fearlessness in front of an audience won him a national following on the NBC television airwaves. He has hosted or appeared in 20 network and/or syndicated shows, including the Peabody Award-winning "Meeting of the Minds" (1977–81). He has also recorded to date 30 music albums, authored 32 books of poetry, fiction and social commentary, written Broadway shows (*Sophie*) and appeared in movies (*The Benny Goodman Story,* 1956). THE GUINNESS BOOK OF RECORDS lists him as the most prolific composer of modern times (4,000 songs to date).

For further reading:

Steve Allen, *Mark It and Strike It: An Autobiography.* New York: Holt, Rinehart, and Winston, 1956.

Allen, Woody [Allen Stewart Konigsberg] (1935–). American film director, actor, screenplay writer and comedian; the most critically acclaimed American film director of his generation. Born in Brooklyn, New York, Allen briefly attended New York University but flunked out. He quickly moved on to comedy writing for Sid Caesar's 1950s television program "Your Show of Shows." In the early 1960s, Allen became a highly popular stand-up comedian with his persona of neurotic but articulate everyman. Turning his attention to films, Allen wrote, directed and starred in two highly successful comedies—*Take the Money and Run* (1969) and *Bananas* (1971)—that earned him financial and creative freedom. His numerous films since then have ranged from farces to intense dramas, but the best of them have successfully blended comedy and drama. These include *Annie Hall* (1977), which won that year's ACADEMY AWARD for best picture (as well as best director and best screenplay Oscars for Allen), *Manhattan* (1979), *Zelig* (1983), *The Purple Rose of Cairo* (1985), *Hannah and Her Sisters* (1986), *Crimes and Misdemeanors* (1989) and *Alice* (1990). Like the Swedish director Ingmar BERGMAN, whose films have influenced him, Allen draws upon a core group of actors who work with him from one film to the next. His collaborations (both as actor and director) with Diane Keaton and Mia Farrow have been particularly noteworthy.

For further reading:

McCann, Graham, *Woody Allen.* Cambridge, Mass.: Basil Blackwell, 1990.

Allenby, Edmund Henry Hynman [1st Viscount Allenby] (1861–1936). British general. Educated at Sandhurst, he was a cavalry officer in South Africa (1899–1902). After the outbreak of WORLD WAR I, he was stationed in France with the British Expeditionary Force (BEF), first commanding a cavalry division. As general of the Third Army (1915–17), he commanded British forces at the battle of ARRAS (1917). Posted to EGYPT in 1917, he conducted a successful cavalry campaign against the Turks, invading PALESTINE and capturing JERUSALEM in December of that year. A skilled tactician, he was victorious at the **battle of Megiddo** (Sept. 18–21, 1918), pushing the Turks back through Syria. Allenby served as high commissioner for Egypt from 1919 to 1925.

Allende Gossens, Salvador (1908–1973). President of Chile (1970–73). A Marxist democrat who served as a Chilean Socialist Party deputy from 1937 to 1945 and senator from 1945 to 1970, after three unsuccessful attempts he won the 1970 presidential election. His efforts to bring social reform by democratic means en-

Salvador Allende (1972).

countered increasing opposition and unrest, supported in part by the CIA. In 1973 he was overthrown in a military coup led by General PINOCHET and died during fighting at the presidential palace. His daughter **Isabelle Allende** is a noted novelist.

For further reading:

Davis, Nathaniel, *The Last Two Years of Salvador Allende*. Cornell, N.Y.: Cornell University Press, 1985.

Alliance. Political party in NORTHERN IRELAND, founded in 1970 by Oliver John Napier (b. 1935). Its members are moderate, mostly middle-class people—both Protestants and Catholics—opposed to sectarian violence in the region. The party enjoyed some initial success; members were elected to provincial and local offices but never to the British Parliament. Alliance hoped to play a conciliatory role and provide an alternative to the more established and extremist Northern Irish parties. However, by 1985 it seemed destined to remain a minority party.

Alliance for Progress. Program to promote the economic and social development of Latin America; proposed by President John F. KENNEDY and established at a conference at Punta del Este, Uruguay, in August 1961. Embodied in a treaty signed by the U.S. and the 19 nations of Latin America (excluding Cuba), the Alliance pledged members to coordinate their economies, to institute tax and land reform and to resist communist expansion within their borders. The initial aim of the Alliance was a 2.5% annual increase in per capita income in Latin American countries, a goal that was never reached. In all, the U.S. government spent about $100 billion on Alliance for Progress programs, which included health and education programs, housing projects and general economic development. Faced by mounting criticism during the Johnson and Nixon administrations, the Alliance ceased operation in 1974 when U.S. financial support was withdrawn.

Alliluyeva, Svetlana Iosifovna (1927–). The daughter of Josef STALIN by his second wife, Nadezhda Alliluyeva, Svetlana Alliluyeva defected to the U.S. in March 1967, at the U.S. embassy in New Delhi, India. She arrived in New York in April, saying she had come to "seek the self-expression that has been denied me for so long in Russia." Stalin's only daughter and last surviving child, she was stripped of her Soviet citizenship in December 1969. In 1973, Alliluyeva divorced her American husband, William Peters, and in November 1984, after living in Great Britain for two years, she returned, with her daughter, Olga Peters, to the Soviet Union, where she attacked Western "pseudodemocracy." Her Soviet citizenship was restored, but in April 1986 she fled to the U.S. again, returning her daughter to her boarding school in Great Britain.

"All in the Family". Long-running comedy series that changed the course of American television entertainment. From the first telecast on CBS (January 12, 1971) to the last (September 21, 1983) the address of the Archie Bunker residence in New York's Queens—704 Houser Street—was the place to be each week for millions of viewers. Producers Norman LEAR and Bud Yorkin and cast members Jean Stapleton (Edith), Carroll O'Connor (Archie), Sally Struthers (Gloria) and Rob Reiner (the "Meathead," Mike) took an obscure British TV series called "Till Death Us Do Part" and transplanted its Cockney sensibilities to Queens. The program challenged conventional values, using comedy to skewer the hypocrisies of racism and sexism as well as air out issues like abortion and homosexuality. There were two spinoffs: "Maude," based on a relative of Edith's played by Beatrice Arthur, debuted in 1972; "The Jeffersons," based on characters who lived next door, debuted three years later. In 1979, after Stapleton, Struthers and Reiner had left the program, Archie bought Kelsey's Bar, and the series continued under the title, "Archie Bunker's Place." In the words of the "All in the Family" theme song, "Those were the days."

For further reading:

Brooks, Tim, *The Complete Directory of Prime Time Network TV Shows*. New York: Ballantine, 1988.

Allison, Fran (?–1989). U.S. singer and entertainer. She was best known as the human star of the children's television program "Kukla, Fran, and Ollie" in the late 1940s and 1950s. The pioneering show, which was created by puppeteer Burr TILLSTROM in 1947, soon became one of the most popular television programs in the U.S. Allison, a former teacher, played the warm-hearted human companion to two eccentric puppets—Kukla, an earnest clown, and Ollie, a roguish dragon. The show ended in 1957 but was revived briefly on public television (1969–71) and in syndication (1975–76).

Allon, Yigal (1918–1980). Israeli military and political leader, a hero of the Jewish struggle for independence in PALESTINE. Allon held a series of cabinet posts, including deputy prime minister and foreign minister in the Labor government of Golda MEIR. He was known for his controversial peace plan put forward after the SIX-DAY WAR (1967). He proposed returning most of the WEST BANK territory to JORDAN in exchange for a narrow security strip along the Jordan River. The plan was not carried out.

"All Power to the Soviets". A slogan adopted by LENIN. In the name of the Soviets, the BOLSHEVIK Party was able to dominate the political organization of post-revolutionary Russia—the newly formed Soviet Union.

All Quiet on the Western Front. Novel by German author Erich Maria REMARQUE, filmed in 1930. First serialized in a German magazine in 1928, it tells the story of a young German soldier in WORLD WAR I who enlists in a burst of patriotic fervor but who soon awakens to the horrors of trench warfare. The book was later banned by the NAZIS because of its pacifism and was also forbidden in MUSSOLINI's Italy and in the U.S.S.R. for several years following WORLD WAR II. The intensely moving novel is considered a classic of war fiction and is studied in schools and universities. A sequel, *The Road Back*, was published in 1931.

All-Russian Congress of Soviets. The first congress of the RUSSIAN REVOLUTION met in Petrograd in June 1917 with representatives from more than 350 units from all over Russia. It appointed a central executive committee, which sat permanently in Petrograd. Some of the leaders of this committee were also leaders of the executive committee of the Petrograd Soviet, having attended the congress as delegates.

All-Russian Directory. A Russian counterrevolutionary organization consisting of five members. It was established in Omsk in September 1918. (See also RUSSIAN REVOLUTION.)

All the King's Men. Novel by Robert Penn WARREN, published in 1946. Awarded the PULITZER PRIZE in 1947, the novel portrays Willie Stark, a profligate, influence-wielding southern governor who is loosely based on former Louisiana Governor Huey LONG. The story is told from the perspective of Jack Burden, an aide to Stark, and his discovery of the identity of his father, a seemingly incorruptible judge known to him since childhood, is an important subplot. The writing vacillates between a gripping realism and poetic intensity. The film made from the book won the ACADEMY AWARD for best picture in 1949.

Al-Mechili. Town in northeastern Libya. In 1940, during WORLD WAR II, it was established as a gas depot by Britsh forces in North Africa. Captured by the Germans, it was retaken by the British in 1942.

Almond, Edward M(allory) "Ned" (1892–1979). American military officer. Almond commanded a machine-gun battalion in World War I, when he was wounded and decorated. During WORLD WAR II IN ITALY he commanded the only black combat division in the U.S. After the war he was chief of staff (1946–50) under General Douglas MACARTHUR at the Army's Far East Headquarters and the UNITED NATIONS command. During the first two years (1950–51) of the KOREAN WAR he commanded the 10th Corps. He participated in the landing at INCHON, the capture of SEOUL and the evacuation of Hungnam after the Chinese intervened on the side of the North Koreans, but returned to the U.S. in July 1951.

Alonso, Alicia [born Alicia Martinez] (1921–). Cuban ballerina and ballet director. Educated in Havana and at the School of American Ballet in New York City, she was first married to fellow dancer Fernando Alonso; now she is married to Pedro Simon. She earned an international reputation in ballet after beginning as a dancer in musical theater. Alonso joined Lincoln KIRSTEN's touring company, Ballet Caravan, in 1939, then performed regularly with AMERICAN BALLET THEATRE (1941–60) and the Ballet Russes de Monte Carlo (1955–57), as well as in concert with Andre Eglevsky, Royes Fernandez and Igor Youskevitch with whom she formed a legendary partnership. Among the roles created for her were those of the ballerina in *Theme and Variations* (1947) by George BALANCHINE and the Accused in *Fall River Legend* (1948) by Agnes DE MILLE. She was also considered one of the outstanding "Giselles" of her generation. In 1947 Alonso received Cuba's Decoration of Carlos Manuel de Cespedes, and in 1959 a Dance Magazine Award. In 1948 she established her own dance company in Cuba; with the rise of Fidel CASTRO it became known as the National Ballet of Cuba. She has also choreographed several ballets and staged ballets for other companies.

For further reading:
De Gamez, Tana, *Alicia Alonso: At Home and Abroad*. New York: Carol Publishing Group, 1970.

Alonso, Damaso (1898–1990). Spanish poet, literary critic and scholar. Alonso was a member of the so-called GENERATION OF 1927, a literary group that also included Federico Garcia LORCA and Rafael ALBERTI. Alonso's best known work appeared in the books *Pure Poems, Poems of the City* (1921), *The Sons of Anger* (1944) and *Man and God* (1955). He was also a director of the Royal Academy of the Spanish Language. In 1978 he was awarded Spain's Miguel de Cervantes Prize, considered the highest literary prize for Spanish writers.

Alpher, Ralph Asher (1921–). American physicist. Alpher studied at George Washington University, Washington, D.C., where he obtained his B.S. in 1943 and his Ph.D. in 1948. He spent the war as a physicist with the U.S. Navy's Naval Ordnance Laboratory in Washington followed by a period (1944–55) with the applied physics laboratory of Johns Hopkins University, Baltimore. In 1955 Alpher joined the staff of the General Electric Research and Development Center, Schenectady, N.Y.

At George Washington, Alpher came under the influence of the physicist George GAMOW with whom he collaborated on a number of papers. With Hans BETHE they produced a major paper on the origin of the chemical elements, sometimes called the *Alpher-Bethe-Gamow theory*, which was incorporated into Gamow's modern form of the BIG-BANG THEORY of the origin of the universe, published in 1948. In the same year Alpher and Herman published a remarkable paper in which they predicted that the big bang should have produced intense radiation that gradually lost energy as the universe expanded and by now would be characteristic of a temperature of about minus 268° C. Unlike its later independent formulation by Robert Dicke in 1964, the 1948 paper had surprisingly little impact. Alpher did approach a number of radar experts but was informed that it was then impossible to detect such radiation. When this radiation was discovered by Arno Penzias and Robert Wilson in 1964–65, a major revolution in cosmology and astrophysics began.

Alsace-Lorraine. Ancient region of eastern France bordering on Germany, Luxembourg and Switzerland. Created as a territory in 1871, it was carved from French lands by a victorious Germany in the Treaty of Frankfurt, to recognize German victories in the Franco-Prussian War. After WORLD WAR I, control of the region returned to France, but it was seized again by the Germans during WORLD WAR II. Since 1945, it has remained under French control, its area distributed among several modern French departments.

Althusser, Louis (1918–1990). French Marxist philosopher. A longtime member of the French Communist Party, he became an outspoken critic of Soviet and French communism in the 1970s. He taught at the Ecole Normale Superieure in Paris for more than three decades. A victim of manic-depression, his career virtually ended in 1980 after he strangled his wife. He was judged mentally incompetent to stand trial and was institutionalized until 1984.

Altman, Robert (1925–). American film director, best known for his irreverent views of America in the 1970s. A pilot in World War II, Altman returned to his native Kansas City, Missouri, to make industrial films. After working on the television series "Whirlybirds" and "Bonanza," he scored his first big movie success with M*A*S*H in 1970, a savage antiwar comedy about Army medics in Korea. For the next five years he averaged two films a year, presenting an unbroken string of commercially successful and critically praised hits. He satirized the western (*McCabe and Mrs. Miller*, 1971), the psychological drama (*Images*, 1972), the gangster thriller (*The Long Goodbye*, 1973) and the caper film (*California Split*, 1974). Films far more difficult to categorize during this time included an allegory about a flying boy (*Brewster McCloud*, 1970), Altman's personal favorite; a poignant story about a trio of young robbers (*Thieves Like Us*, 1974); and the masterful, densely textured *Nashville* (1975). Subsequently, he has directed a number of stage plays and a string of quirky, occasionally bewildering films, including the science fiction allegory *Quintet* (1979) and *Come Back to the Five and Dime, Jimmy Dean* (1982). Altman has said he is preoccupied in his pictures with the "flexible boundary between sanity and insanity."

For further reading:
Jacobs, Diane, *Hollywood Renaissance*. Cranbury, N.J.: A.S. Barnes, 1977.

Alto Adige. Italian term for a region of the South Tyrol, a part of the present Bolzano province. Ceded to Italy by AUSTRIA after WORLD WAR I, in the TREATY OF ST. GERMAIN (1919), this largely German-speaking area gave Italy a border on the Brenner Pass. Dissatisfaction with Italian rule by the Austrian population of the region led to agreements in 1939 and 1946 and to United Nations debate in 1960. In 1971 a new settlement backed by the INTERNATIONAL COURT OF JUSTICE at The Hague provided the region with considerable administrative and legislative autonomy, as well as with assurances of non-intervention by Austria.

aluminum. Lightweight, silvery metal refined from bauxite ore, a naturally occurring mineral. Because aluminum is lighter than steel of comparable strength, it came to be used in the construction of aircraft. It is also nonrusting (although it develops a surface oxide) and so is widely used for kitchen cookwear, household utensils, and decorative objects. Because of its recent availability and its association with aviation, it came to be associated with MODERNISM in the 1920s and 1930s.

Alvarez, A(lfred) (1929–). British critic and author. Born in London, he was educated at Corpus Christi College, Oxford, where he later served as a senior research scholar and tutor in English. He established himself as literary critic with his first book, *Stewards of Excellence* (1958). In *The Savage God* (1971) he coined the term "extremists," referring to poets such as Sylvia PLATH and Robert LOWELL, whose work explores their personal obsessions. While he helped to popularize these CONFESSIONAL POETS, he was also criticized for promoting the view that madness is necessary for creating great literature. His first novel, *Hers*, was published in 1975; a volume of poetry, *Autumn to Autumn: Selected Poems 1953–1976*, in 1976. Alvarez's eclectic non-fiction includes *Life After Marriage: People in Divorce* (1982), *The Biggest Game in Town* (1983), and *Offshore: A North Sea Journey* (1986). He contributed to THE NEW YORKER.

Alvarez, Luis (1911–1988). American scientist, winner of the 1968 NOBEL PRIZE for physics for his use of bubble chambers to detect new subatomic particles. A member of the team at Los Alamos that developed the ATOMIC BOMB, Alvarez witnessed its first use at Hiroshima in WORLD WAR II. He also supported the development of the HYDROGEN BOMB. Alvarez joined his son Walter in supporting a controversial theory holding that one or more asteroid impacts were responsible for the extinction of the dinosaurs and thousands of other species 65 million years ago.

Alwyn, William (1905–1985). British composer. Alwyn was for many years a professor of composition at London's Royal Academy of Music. In addition to writing much concert music, including five symphonies, he wrote many film scores, including those for *Odd Man Out* and *Fallen Idol*.

Alydar (1975–1990). American thoroughbred racehorse who faced off against AFFIRMED in one of the most celebrated rivalries in racing history. Alydar finished second to Affirmed in all three 1978 Triple Crown races, with the total distance between them amounting to less than two lengths. While Alydar beat Affirmed only three times in his career, he captured the public imagination with his courage and his unfaltering will to win. His post-racing career at stud has assured his place in the annals of thoroughbred history, as he sired such major stakes winners as Alysheba, Easy Goer and Strike the Gold. At the time of his death from complications following a broken leg, Alydar's offspring were approaching the $35 million mark in winnings.

Amado, Jorge (1912–). Brazilian novelist. Amado enjoys the relatively rare status of a novelist who is both lionized by critics and read avidly by a worldwide general public. Born on a plantation in northeast Brazil, Amado studied law and began his writing career as a popular proletarian novelist. *The Violent Land* (1943) is the major work of this early phase. From 1946 to 1948, Amado was elected as a communist to the Brazilian parliament; his political career ended when his Communist Party was outlawed. For the past four decades, Amado has continued to express populist themes in his fiction while transforming his style to utilize picaresque narratives full of bawdy humor and folk wisdom. His novels include *Gabriela, Cinnamon and Clove* (1958), *Dona Flor and Her Two Husbands* (1966), *Home Is the Sailor* (1968) and *Tent of Miracles* (1969).

Amahl and the Night Visitors. The first full-length opera to be presented on network television December 24, 1951. Composer Gian Carlo MENOTTI was commissioned by the NBC network in the fall of 1950 to compose an original opera. He prepared his own text, the story of a encounter between a crippled beggar boy and the Magi on the way to Bethlehem. Mr. Joyce C. HALL, founder of Hallmark Cards, Inc., of Kansas City, sponsored the project as a "thank you" to customers. Hosted by the composer and actress Sarah Churchill (daughter of Winston), the "live" telecast made television history and launched what would become known as THE HALLMARK HALL OF FAME anthology series. The program was rebroadcast on April 13, 1952. Again Churchill and Menotti hosted and the cast was repeated. (Chet Allen and Rosemary Kuhlman portrayed, respectively, Amahl and his mother; Thomas Schippers conducted.) Hallmark sponsored four other television versions including a color telecast on NBC on December 20, 1953 (the first color telecast in television history) and a remounting on December 12, 1965 with an entirely new cast—Kurt Haghjian as Amahl and Martha King as his mother. With the premiere telecast in 1951, wrote critic Olin Downes, "television, operatically speaking, has come of age."

For further reading:

Hall, Joyce C., *Amahl and the Night Visitors—When You Care Enough.* Kansas City: Hallmark Books, 1979.

Amaldi, Edoardo (1908–). Italian physicist. Amaldi graduated from the University of Rome in 1929, where he had studied under Enrico FERMI. Together with Fermi and others he discovered that fast-moving neutrons are slowed down (moderated) by substances containing hydrogen and can thus be brought to energies at which they more easily interact with nuclei. He has also contributed to the study of taumesons, hyperons and antiprotons. In 1937 he was made professor of general physics at the University of Rome, and from 1952 until 1954 he was secretary-general of the European Organization for Nuclear Research. He has also served as president of the International Union of Pure and Applied Physics (1957–60) and president of the Istituto Nazionale di Fisica Nucleare (1960–65).

Amal militia. Shiite Muslim militia in LEBANON and one of the most important political and military groups in the country. Founded in 1974, it is the military arm of the large Shiite faction originally headed by Imam Musa Sadr, who disappeared during a visit to Libya in 1978. Led by Nabih Berri and closely aligned with Syria, it existed alongside the PALESTINE LIBERATION ORGANIZATION until the Israeli invasion of Lebanon (1982), after which it became the sole militia in southern Lebanon. It was temporarily aligned with the Druze forces of Walid Jumblat. The Islamic Amal, a more militant offshoot and now a rival of the Amal with headquarters in the Bekaa Valley, was involved in a variety of terrorist attacks, including the raid on the U.S. embassy and the Marine barracks. Two other Shiite extremist groups also oppose the Amal, the HEZBOLLAH (Party of God) and the Islamic Jihad (Islamic Holy War).

Amalrik, Andrei Alekseyevich (1938–1980). Soviet writer, historian, dissident and human rights activist. During the 1960s and '70s Amalrik was a leader in the movement for intellectual and political freedom in the U.S.S.R. He was the first dissident to seek out American news correspondents in Moscow in the mid-1960s, thereby establishing a link between Soviet political dissidents and the West. Because of his beliefs he was expelled from his university (1965), harassed by the KGB and eventually exiled to Siberia (1965). In 1976 he was pressured to leave the U.S.S.R. He gained worldwide attention for his unrelenting criticism of repression and backwardness in Soviet society. His books include *Revolutionary Journey to Siberia* (1970) and *Will the Soviet Union Survive Until 1984?* (1970).

Amanullah Khan (1892–1960). King of AFGHANISTAN (1919–29). He ended British control of Afghanistan, but revolts forced him to abdicate when he tried to end the slavery of women and to introduce monogamy. (See also AFGHAN CIVIL WAR OF 1928–29.)

For further reading:

Poullada, Leon B., *Reform and Rebellion in Afghanistan, 1919–1929: King Amanullah's Failure to Modernize a Tribal Society.* Cornell, N.Y.: Cornell University Press, 1973.

Ambartsumian, Viktor Amazaspovich (1908–). Soviet astrophysicist. Ambartsumian, the son of a distinguished Armenian philologist, graduated from the University of Leningrad in 1928 and did graduate work at nearby Pulkovo Observatory from 1928 to 1931. He was professor of astrophysics from 1934 to 1946 at Leningrad and held the same post from 1947 at the State University of Yerevan in Armenia. In 1946 he organized the construction, near Yerevan, of the Byurakan Astronomical Observatory, having been appointed its director in 1944. Ambartsumian's work was mainly concerned with the evolution of stellar systems, both galaxies and smaller clusters of stars, and the processes taking place during the evolution of stars. In 1947 Ambartsumian introduced into astronomy the idea of a stellar "association." These associations are loose clusters of hot stars that lie in or near the disk-shaped plane of our galaxy. They must be young, no more than a few million years old, as the galaxy's gravitational field will tend to disperse them. Thus star formation is still going on in the galaxy. He also argued in 1955 that the idea of colliding galaxies proposed by Rudolph Minkowski and Walter BAADE to explain such radio sources as Cygnus A would not produce the required energy. Instead he proposed that the source of energy was gigantic explosions occurring in the dense central regions of galaxies.

Ambassadors, The. Novel by Henry JAMES, published in 1903. The work examines the reactions of several Americans to European mores and morals in the early 20th century. The story revolves around a young American, Chad Newsome, who is living a reputedly dissolute life in Paris, and the "ambassador" of the story, Lambert Strether, who has been sent by Chad's mother to fetch her son back. The middle-aged Strether is initially caught up in the happy atmosphere of Paris and takes Chad's side; ultimately, his loyalty to Mrs. Newsome prevails. James captured American and European "types" of the period with wit and deftness of perception. Many critics consider *The Ambassadors* to be his finest novel.

Amchitka. One of the ALEUTIAN ISLANDS, in the U.S. state of Alaska. It was the site of a U.S. Army Air Force base during WORLD WAR II. Designated for underground nuclear weaponry testing in 1967, the first test was conducted in 1971.

Amendola, Giorgio (1907–1980). Italian Communist Party leader. Amendola began his political career as a staunch opponent of Benito MUSSOLINI. He was arrested in 1932 and later exiled. During the German occupation of ITALY toward the end of WORLD WAR II, he led guerrillas against the NAZIS in northern Italy. He served in all postwar Italian parliaments up to his death. He was among party leaders who denounced the SOVIET INVASION OF CZECHOSLOVAKIA in 1956.

America First. Isolationist movement that attempted to maintain American neutrality as World War II raged in Europe and Japanese expansionism swept Asia. It was spearheaded by the America First Committee, an organization that was formed in 1940 and reached a membership of some 800,000. The group argued that the U.S. should maintain a strong defense and avoid foreign entanglements. It was abruptly disbanded after the Japanese attack on PEARL HARBOR (December 7, 1941) catapulted the U.S. into war.

American Ballet Theatre. American Ballet Theatre was founded by Richard Pleasant in New York City in 1939 with a core group of dancers and a repertory primarily from the Russian dance companies. Pleasant managed the company with dancer and heiress Lucia CHASE until resigning in 1941, whereupon his place was taken by designer Oliver Smith. Smith and Chase were succeeded by Mikhail BARYSHNIKOV (1980–89). Jane Herman took over the management in 1989. From the start, ABT was envisioned as an eclectic repository for the best dances of the Russian, English, Spanish, American and popular heritages, and as a venue for star dancers (Natalia MAKAROVA, Fernando Bujones) from all corners of the world. Though not marked by one choreographer's imprimatur, the company's general tenor and broad-based appeal were established by choreographers Antony TUDOR (*Pillar of Fire*) and Jerome ROBBINS (*Fancy Free*) during the 1940s. Today the company performs works from the classical and romantic ballet tradition by such choreographers as Agnes DE MILLE, Kenneth MACMILLAN and George BALANCHINE, as well as dances in the modern and postmodern vein by Twyla THARP, Paul TAYLOR, Mark Morris and others.

For further reading:

Arnold, Eve (photography), *Private View: Behind the Scenes with American Ballet Theatre,* with text by John Fraser. New York: Bantam, 1988.

American Broadcasting Company. See ABC.

American Civil Liberties Union [ACLU]. A U.S. public interest group founded to protect individual liberties as guaranteed by the U.S. Constitution's Bill of Rights. Although the group's espoused aims seem uncontroversial, the group has been involved in constant controversy since its founding in 1920, because of its support for controversial and often unpopular causes.

The ACLU was founded by a number of prominent Americans, including Jane ADDAMS, Roger Baldwin, Felix FRANKFURTER, Helen KELLER and Norman THOMAS. The organization has brought numerous court challenges against statutes violative of the Bill of Rights, including the famous Scopes Monkey Trial, which involved a law banning the teaching of the theory of evolution in Tennessee public schools. The ACLU has defended Jews and Nazis alike whenever individual rights are imperiled. Critics maintain that its rigid adherence to principle sometimes conflicts with common sense, but despite the criticism the organization continues as a vigorous champion of American individual rights.

American Dance Festival. An annual event since 1948, the ADF presents dance companies, choreographers, dance critics and others from the United States and abroad in a series of public performances, workshops and seminars. The festival's orginal focus was modern dance, featuring the works of Martha GRAHAM, Doris Humphrey, Jose LIMON, Alwin Nikolais, Merce CUNNINGHAM and Paul TAYLOR. Notable festival premieres included Graham's *Diversion of Angels* (1948) and Limon's *The Moor's Pavane* (1949). Not until the 1960s did the artistic agenda grow to include ethnic dance, such as that from Korea, Spain and Jamaica, as well as other dance forms. Under the direction of Charles Reinhart since 1969, the festival has grown steadily more eclectic. Though housed for many years at Connecticut College, the ADF has been based at Duke University in Durham, North Carolina, since 1978.

American Federation of Labor and Congress of Industrial Organizations (AFL-CIO). Federation of over 100 autonomous labor unions. Primarily an American body with a membership of about 13 million, it also has international members in U.S. territories, Puerto Rico, Canada and Panama. The federation was created in 1955 with the merger of the AFL, a group consisting mainly of craft unions, and the CIO, an organization of industrial unions. The history of the AFL stretches back to 1881, when a number of trade unions meeting in Pittsburgh established the Federation of Organized Trades and Labor Unions of the U.S. and Canada. The group reorganized in 1886 and changed its name to the American Federation of Labor. From its inception, the AFL was a trade union, organizing workers by their individual skills. Led by Samuel GOMPERS until his death in 1924, it acted as a lobbying group to secure labor-rights legislation, helped to organize workers and was successful in securing such benefits as a shorter working day, higher wages, workmen's compensation and laws prohibiting child labor. Led later by William GREEN and George MEANY, it became America's largest and most important labor federation.

The CIO, originally called the Committee for Industrial Organization, was formed within the AFL in 1935 to organize factory workers on an industry-wide basis. Expelled from the AFL in 1938 in a dispute over whether mass-production workers should be organized on an industrial or craft basis, it changed its name to the Congress of Industrial Organizations and elected John L. LEWIS as its head. Lewis, who served until 1940, was succeeded by Phillip MURRAY, who headed the federation until his death in 1952. The group was extremely successful in organizing large industries such as steel and automobiles.

As an antiunion climate began to prevail in the 1950s and the distinctions between craft and industrial unions were perceived as less important, the groups reunited in 1955 and elected George Meany as president. Under a 1957 antirackets provision, the AFL-CIO expelled the Teamsters Union (readmitted in 1987). Led by Walter REUTHER, the United Automobile Workers left the federation in 1968, only to reaffiliate in 1981. The AFL-CIO acts as the collective representative of labor, seeking to influence pro-labor legislation on the federal and state levels. It is active politically and has traditionally supported Democratic candidates. It assists its member unions in organizing activities and maintains a staff to handle research, information, publicity, legal affairs and various special issues such as civil rights and veterans' interests. It is also active in general social welfare and community-building areas. The AFL-CIO is governed by a convention that meets biennially. It is headed by a president, a secretary-treasurer and 33 vice presidents, who form an executive council that governs between conventions and carries out convention decisions.

American Friends Service Committee [AFSC]. A social service organization founded by Quakers in Philadelphia in 1917, it grew from opposition to WORLD WAR I. The organization proposed various methods of noncombatant service for Quakers and other conscientious objectors. The group's first chairman, philosophy professor Rufus M. Jones, established voluntary civilian work in France, much of it in hospitals, as an alternative to military service. After the war the AFSC distributed food and clothing in Germany, and in the early 1920s it worked to ameliorate famine in the U.S.S.R. Between the world wars the committee worked in four basic areas: foreign, interracial, peace and home service. In the years preceding World War II, the AFSC provided relief in the SPANISH CIVIL WAR and aided Jews persecuted by the Nazi regime. During WORLD WAR II, it administered public service camps, assisted interned Japanese-Americans and undertook relief efforts in China, France, England and other areas. In the postwar era the organization distributed food, clothing, medical supplies and other relief to refugees worldwide. The AFSC was particularly active in humanitarian programs during the KOREAN WAR and the VIETNAM WAR. In 1947 the AFSC shared the NOBEL PRIZE for peace with the British FRIENDS SERVICE COUNCIL.

American Popular Revolutionary Alliance [APRA]. Marxist political movement in Peru. (See also Victor Raul HAYA DE LA TORRE.)

American Samoa. Chain of islands that form the eastern portion of the Samoa chain in the southwest Pacific Ocean. The United States won control of them pursuant to a 1899 treaty with Germany and Great Britain. Until 1951, they were administered by the United States Navy, which also established a now defunct base at Pago Pago, the capital. Also known as Eastern Samoa, the islands presently form an unincorporated territory administered by the U.S. Department of the Interior.

American Tragedy, An. Novel by Theodore DREISER; considered to be his masterpiece, it is a pioneering psychological study of a murderer. Unlike literary precedents in Poe, Dostoevski, and CONRAD, the crime is not motivated by passion, alienation, or madness so much as by simple expedience. Clyde Griffiths murders Roberta Alden, a mill worker he has seduced, because her unexpected pregnancy threatens his courtship of a socially prominent debutante. The novel grew out of several of Dreiser's preoccupations—an absorbing interest in real-life crime stories (the murder by Chester Gillette of Grace Brown in Moose Lake, N.Y. in 1906), his growing frustration with his own loveless marriage and his readings in Sigmund FREUD and Jacques Loeb of the biological, subconscious, and mechanistic forces that work upon our lives. The book, published in 1925, became Dreiser's most successful novel, selling 25,000 copies in the first six months. Critic Joseph Wood Krutch called it the greatest book of its generation; criminal lawyer Clarence DARROW praised its "fanatical devotion to truth"; and, more recently, critic Ellen Moers in her classic study, *The Two Dreisers,* appraised it as a modern version of the Aladdin myth. Unimpressed, the city of Boston banned it. Two watered-down movie versions have appeared—a 1931 version by Josef von STERNBERG and one in 1951 by George STEVENS.

For further reading:

Ellen Moers, *An American Tragedy—The Two Dreisers.* New York: Viking Press, 1969.

American Volunteer Group. See FLYING TIGERS.

***Amethyst* Incident.** Attack on the British frigate H.M.S. *Amethyst* by Chinese communist troops on April 20, 1949. The ship was fired on while sailing up the Yangtze River with supplies for the British community in Nanking. Occurring during the final phase of the Chinese revolution, the attack was assumed to be an assertion of Chinese sovereignty over the waterway. Seventeen of the *Amethyst*'s crew were killed, 30 were wounded and the ship was detained in China. After attempts to rescue the vessel failed, the ship successfully sailed downriver, reaching the sea on July 31, 1949, an escape that was greeted with great joy in Great Britain.

Amfiteatrov, Alexander Valentinovich (1862–1938). Russian journalist. He was exiled by the czarist government for his satirical piece "The Obmanovs" (1902). In 1905 he went abroad and published *Krasni Flag,* a revolutionary magazine. On his return to Russia he became editor of the newspaper *Russkaya Svoboda* (Russian Freedom). He left Russia again after the Russian Revolution and wrote articles against the BOLSHEVIKS. His books include *Maria Luseva* (1904), *Those of the Eighties* (1907–08) and *Those of the Nineties* (1910).

Amichai, Yehuda (1924–). Israeli poet. Born in Germany, Amichai immigrated to Palestine in 1936. He served in the Israeli army during the ARAB-ISRAELI WAR OF 1948. His novel *Not of This Time, Not of That Place* (translated from the Hebrew in 1968), concerns the author's ambivalence about his citizenship and the situation of the Jewish writer. His lyrical, highly metaphoric and psalm-like poetry focuses on the themes of love, war and loss. His collections include *Songs of Jerusalem and Myself* (translated 1973) and *Amen* (translated 1977). Amichai is generally considered Israel's foremost poet.

Amiens. Capital of France's Somme department; on the Somme River. During WORLD WAR I, on the banks of the nearby Ancre River, tanks were first used successfully on a battlefield as part of an Allied campaign against German forces. It was again the site of fighting during WORLD WAR II, when it was occupied by the Germans and suffered extensive damage.

Amin, Idi (ca. 1925–). President of UGANDA (1971–79). A Moslem and a member of the Kakwa tribe, he served as a sergeant in the British colonial army and later rose in the Ugandan military to become commander in chief in 1966. That year he aided Prime Minister Milton OBOTE in the overthrow of President Kabaka Mutesa II. In 1971, while Obote was out of the country, Amin seized control and proclaimed himself president. Brutal and unpredictable, he was regarded as a buffoon by some and a monster by others. He established a dictatorship, expelled most resident Asians, feuded with neighboring African republics and was responsible for the slaughter of hundreds of thousands of Ugandans. As the Ugandan economy worsened and his abuses of power became widely known, Amin's prestige in the international community rapidly waned; he was condemned after giving haven to the Palestinian hijackers of an Israeli airliner in 1976 (see ENTEBBE RAID). In 1979 Tanzanian troops invaded Uganda and forced Amin into exile; he reportedly settled in Libya and then Saudi Arabia.

Amis, Kingsley (1922–). British author. Born in London, Amis was educated at St. John's College, Oxford, where he met Philip LARKIN. His first novel, *Lucky Jim* (1954), was a popular and critical success and earned him a reputation as one of the ANGRY YOUNG MEN. Though best known for his comic satires, such as *Take a Girl Like You* (1960), *Jake's Thing* (1978) and *The Old Devils* (1987; Booker Prize), Amis has also tried his hand at other literary genres, including detective stories (published under the pseudonym Robert Markham) that reveal his enthusiasm for author Ian FLEMING. He is an accomplished poet as well; his early verse appeared in the MOVEMENT anthology *New Lines* (1956). Like many of the Angry Young Men, Amis later embraced conservative values. His son Martin AMIS is also an author.

For further reading:

McDermott, John, *Kingsley Amis: An English Moralist.* New York: St. Martin's Press, 1989.

Amis, Martin (1949–). British author. Born in Oxford and educated there at Exeter College, Amis is the son of author Kingsley AMIS. Martin Amis's first novel *The Rachel Papers* (1973), which explores adolescent sexuality, established him as a satirist of contemporary British middle-class life. His steady output of dark, comedic fiction upholds this reputation. His works include *Money* (1984), *Success* (1987) and *London Fields* (1990). Amis also served as editorial assistant on the *Times Literary Supplement* (1972–75), assistant literary editor of *The New Statesman* and writer for the *Observer*. His literary journalism has appeared in periodicals in Britain and the U.S.

Idi Amin giving a radio address (1979).

Ammann, Othmar H. (1875–1965). Distinguished Swiss-born American structural engineer and designer of many major bridges. Othmar Ammann received his training in engineering at the Swiss Federal Polytechnical Institute before moving to the United States in 1904. Ammann designed the steel arch Bayonne Bridge over the Kill van Kull, connecting New Jersey and Staten Island with a span of 1,675 feet, with partner Allston Dana in 1927. As chief engineer for the Port of New York Authority, Ammann was in charge of the design of the George Washington Bridge (1931), the Goethals Bridge and Outerbridge Crossing (1928), the Triborough (1936), and the Bronx-Whitestone Bridge (1939). He was a consultant for the design of the Golden Gate Bridge in San Francisco (1937). As a partner in the firm of Ammann and Whitney, he was responsible for the design of the Throgs Neck (1961) and Verrazano-Narrows (1964) suspension bridges as well as many other structures, including several very wide-span airplane hangars.

Ammons, A(rchie) R(andolph) (1926–). American poet. Born on a farm near Whiteville, N.C., Ammons worked in a shipyard after high school. After World War II he graduated from Wake Forest College on the GI Bill and attended Berkeley. For eight years he was vice president of a glassware manufacturing firm in New York state. In 1953 his first poems appeared in *The Hudson Review.* In 1965, he attracted attention with *Corsons Inlet* and *Tape for the Turn of the Year,* a witty poem-diary written on adding machine tape. *Collected Poems 1951–1971* won a National Book Award in 1973, and he received the BOLLINGEN PRIZE in 1974–75. Other works include *Sphere: The*

Form of a Motion (1974), *Diversifications* (1975) and *The Snow Poems* (1977). He taught at Cornell University. Ammons is a meditative writer in the transcendentalist tradition of Emerson, Dickinson and Whitman. He writes in open, expansive forms.

Amnesty International. International organization founded by Peter Benenson, a British barrister, in 1961. It campaigns for the release of political prisoners who have neither committed nor advocated acts of violence and seeks to help their families and to improve international standards of treatment of prisoners and detainees. Based in London, it is funded entirely by private donations, has 50,000 members in 57 countries and was awarded the NOBEL PRIZE for peace in 1972.

For further reading:

Power, Jonathan, *Amnesty International.* New York: McGraw-Hill, 1981.

Amoco Cadiz. Supertanker that broke up and sank off Portsall, on France's Brittany coast, in March 1978, resulting in the spill of 68 million gallons of oil. A total of $665 million in claims were filed against Standard Oil Co. as a result of the spill, which was one of the worst on record.

"Amos and Andy". An immensely popular radio program that changed the hours and the routine of millions of American families and may have had as great an influence on the development of radio as Milton Berle's TEXACO STAR THEATER had on early television. The show swiftly became an American institution after it hit the airwaves in 1929; from then until 1951, when it moved to television, "Amos and Andy" suffered little controversy over its depiction of black stereotypes. The main radio characters—Andy Brown and Amos Jones—were created by white vaudevillians Charles Correll and Freeman Gosden, who performed on stage in "blackface." But for television, black comedians were selected for all the roles, with Alvin Childress as Amos, Spencer Williams as Andy and Tim Moore as "Kingfish," the show's key figure. That made the television show funnier and more real—and just a bit embarrassing to a newly enlightened American public. The show lasted for two seasons and, after the late 1950s, disappeared from syndication. In spite of continuing controversy over the show's dialogue humor and simple characters—actually, little different from "The Jeffersons" of the 1980s—"Amos and Andy" has continued to influence comedians and find a cult audience.

Amritsar. City in India's Punjab state; site of the central Golden Temple of the Sikhs. In 1919, it was the scene of the AMRITSAR MASSACRE, in which several hundred followers of Mohandas K. GANDHI were killed by British-commanded troops while protesting colonial abuses. In 1984, more than 300 were killed when Indian troops, in order to crush a terrorist campaign by Sikh extremists, attacked Sikhs occupying the Golden Temple. (See also GOLDEN TEMPLE MASSACRE.)

Amritsar Massacre. On April 12, 1919, in the city of Amritsar in the Punjab, INDIA, five British subjects were killed during a riot by Indian nationalists protesting antisedition measures (the Rowlatt Acts). About 10,000 unarmed Indians assembled the next day to continue the protest. Refusing to disperse, the Indians were fired upon by Gurkha troops under the command of British Brigadier General Reginald Dyer (1864–1927); 379 Indians were killed and about 1,200 wounded. Dyer then imposed martial law and ordered floggings. His actions were denounced in the British House of Commons but upheld by the House of Lords. An army council later called the massacre "an error in judgment."

For further reading:

Fein, Helen, *Imperial Crime and Punishment: The Massacre at Jallianwalla Bagh and British Judgment, 1919–1920.* Honolulu: University of Hawaii Press, 1977.

Amsterdam. Capital of the Netherlands, located at the juncture of the Amstel and Ij rivers, near the North Sea; the largest city in the country. It was occupied by German forces from 1940 to 1945, during WORLD WAR II. The Germans killed most of the Jewish population of Amsterdam (75,000 people) during that time.

Amundsen, Roald (Engelbregt Gravning) (1872–1928). Norwegian explorer who led the first expedition to reach the South Pole. Born near Oslo, Amundsen attended university and medical school but left in 1897 to join a two-year Belgian expedition to the Antarctic. From then on, the polar regions of the Earth were to haunt him, and he was to return to the frozen wastes time and time again. From 1903 to 1906 he commanded the ship *Gjoa* in the Arctic Ocean, negotiating the Northwest Passage. After long preparation to conquer the North Pole, he learned (1909) that Robert E. PEARY had reached this destination, and so Amundsen turned his attention to the South Pole. With this goal in mind, he sailed from Norway in 1910 in a ship borrowed from NANSEN, the *Fram,* racing a British expedition under Robert Falcon SCOTT. Well prepared for this venture, Amundsen used dogsleds and took a shorter overland route across Antarctica. He and four compatriots reached the South Pole on December 14, 1911. Scott reached the Pole 35 days later, but he and his men died on their return trip. After a shipboard journey along the northern coast of Europe and Asia in 1918–19, Amundsen turned to exploring by air. He and Lincoln ELLSWORTH tried unsuccessfully to fly across the North Pole in 1925. The following year, the two explorers and Italian airman General Umberto NOBILE were able to fly over the pole and to explore the northern Arctic Ocean. Two years later Nobile crashed in another dirigible, the *Italia,* and Amundsen disappeared while trying to rescue his colleague. His autobiography, *My Life as an Explorer,* was published in 1927, and he was the author and coauthor of several volumes describing his explorations.

Roald Amundsen (ca 1906).

For further reading:

Huntford, Roland, ed., *The Amundsen Photographs.* Boston: Atlantic Monthly Press/Little, Brown, 1987.

Huntford, Roland, *Scott and Amundsen: The Race to the South Pole.* New York: Putnam, 1980.

Anami, Korechika (1887–1945). Japanese general. A career officer and graduate of the Army War College, Anami held a number of posts before World War II. From 1938 to 1943 he commanded various Japanese armies in China, and in 1943 he directed operations in western New Guinea. The following year he was appointed inspector general of army aviation. As the tide of war turned against Japan in 1945, Anami became the nation's last war minister, serving in the cabinet of Kantaro Suzuki. He advocated improving his nation's bargaining posture by attacking the expected Allied invasion forces and, after the ATOMIC BOMB attack on HIROSHIMA, continued to strive for conditional rather than unconditional surrender. Certain of defeat, he committed suicide in August 1945.

anarchism. A political philosophy holding that government is evil and that it should be abolished in favor of free agreements between individuals. First formulated by ancient Greek Stoics, its modern manifestations were outlined by such philosophers as William Godwin (1756–1836) and Pierre Joseph Proudhon (1807–65). In Russia, the theory was espoused by Mikhail Bakunin (1814–76), who provided much of the violent and revolutionary tone that persisted into the 20th century. Anarchism was suppressed by the BOLSHEVIKS after the RUSSIAN REVOLUTION. In the late 19th and early 20th centuries the movement became closely associated with a series of assassinations, including those of French President Sadi-Carnot (1894), Austrian Empress Elizabeth (1898), Italian King Umberto I (1900) and U.S. President William MCKINLEY (1901). Anarchists were forbidden entry into the U.S. early in the 20th century, and some adherents of the movement such as Emma GOLDMAN were deported (1919). In Europe, anarchism was linked with syndicalism and gained considerable public support. The movement had much less currency as the 20th century progressed, after Spain's anarchists and communists clashed during the SPANISH CIVIL WAR and Soviet power grew in the 1940s. While anarchist thought was somewhat revived during the 1960s and anarchist terror resurfaced in the contemporary world in actions by such groups as West Germany's BAADER-MEINHOF, today anarchism is more important as a theoretical construct than as a political movement.

Anastasia Nikolayevna (1901–1918). Youngest daughter of Czar NICHOLAS II of Russia, murdered along with the rest of the Russian royal family at Yekaterinburg in 1918. In 1929 a German citizen named Anna ANDERSON claimed to be Anastasia; the claim continues to provoke controversy.

Anchorage. City in U.S. state of Alaska, located at the head of Cook Inlet. Founded in 1915 as a central terminal for the Alaskan railroad, the population grew considerably during WORLD WAR II after the construction of Elmendorf Air Force Base and Fort Richardson. It was the site of a severe earthquake in 1964. At present, it is a key center for oil and gas pipeline activity.

Ancona. Port city on Italy's Adriatic Sea coast; capital of Ancona province. During WORLD WAR I it was bombarded by the Austrian navy. During WORLD WAR II, it was occupied by Polish forces in 1944.

Ancre River. River in northern France that flows eastward into the SOMME River. Site of numerous battles between 1916 and 1918, during WORLD WAR I, including a 1916 Allied offensive that featured the first battlefield use of armored tanks.

Anders, William (1933–). U.S. astronaut. Aboard Apollo 8 (December 21–27, 1968) Bill Anders was one of the first three men to orbit the moon. Anders, Frank BORMAN and James LOVELL began their historic orbit on Christmas Eve 1968 after escaping from Earth orbit via NASA's Apollo workhorse, the powerful Saturn 5 rocket. Circling the moon 10 times, the crew of Apollo 8 were the first humans ever to see its far side with their own eyes. After his historic flight, Anders became executive secretary for the National Aeronautics and Space Council in 1969 and remained with the council until 1973, when he was appointed to the Atomic Energy Commission. Later serving as first chairman of the Nuclear Regulatory Commission in 1975, he left in 1976 to become U.S. ambassador to Norway. Anders left government service in 1977 to enter private industry. Apollo 8 was his only space flight.

Anderson, Anna (1901–1984). Woman who claimed to be Grand Duchess Anastasia, the youngest daughter of Czar NICHOLAS II of Russia; allegedly the only member of the Russian imperial family to survive execution by the BOLSHEVIKS in 1918. The fate of the real Anastasia (and the identity of Anna Anderson) remains one of the great non-mysteries of the 20th century. Anderson spent some 60 years trying to prove her claim. In 1967 a German court rejected her claim after she had sued the duchess of Mecklenburg for part of the imperial Russian fortune; however, the court said that its decision did not settle the identity of Anderson. The duchess contended that "Anastasia" was really one Franziska Schanzkowski, the daughter of a Polish worker. Her life was the basis of the movie *Anastasia* (1957).

Anderson, Carl David (1905–). American physicist. Anderson, the son of Swedish immigrants, was educated at the California Institute of Technology where he obtained his Ph.D. in 1930 and where he remained for his entire career, serving as professor of physics from 1939 until his retirement in 1978. Anderson was deeply involved in the discovery of two new elementary particles. In 1930 he began to study cosmic rays by photographing their tracks in a cloud chamber. He was able to determine the existence of the positron, or positive electron, in September 1932. In the following year his results were confirmed by Patrick Blackett and Giuseppe Occhialini. Anderson won the 1936 NOBEL PRIZE for physics. In the same year Anderson noted some further unusual cosmic-ray tracks, which appeared to be made by a particle more massive than an electron but lighter than a proton. The particle was initially named the mesotron or yukon. From 1938 the particle became known as the meson. The confusion was partly dispelled in 1947 when Cecil Powell discovered another and more active meson, which became known as the pi-meson or pion, to distinguish it from Anderson's mu-meson or muon.

Anderson, Jack (Northman) (1922–). American newspaper columnist. Born in Long Beach, California, Anderson was raised in Salt Lake City and began his career in journalism in the 1930s as a reporter for the *Deseret News* and later for the *Salt Lake Tribune*. Much of the moral fervor that has marked his reporting was shaped by his Mormon upbringing and his years (1941–44) as a missionary in the South. After service as a war correspondent in 1945, he became (1947) an assistant to the muckraking columnist Drew PEARSON, inheriting the column after Pearson's death in 1969. Anderson is particularly noted for his expose of the pro-Pakistan U.S. policy during the INDO-PAKISTAN WAR OF 1971 (which won him a 1972 PULITZER PRIZE), of CIA plots to assassinate various foreign leaders, including Fidel CASTRO, of FBI wiretappings and of the WATERGATE Affair. His syndicated column remained influential into the 1990s.

Anderson, John (1922–). U.S. congressman. Born in Rockford, Illinois, Anderson graduated from the University of Illinois in 1943 and obtained his law degree there in 1946. He was an adviser to the U.S. High Commission for Germany (1952–55) before returning home to become State's Attorney (1956–60). A Republican, he entered the House of Representatives in 1961, serving there for 20 years. Gradually moderating his once conservative views, he often opposed party policy, but was nevertheless elected chairman of the House Republican Conference, serving from 1968 to 1979. In 1979 he campaigned for the Republican nomination for president but was defeated by Ronald REAGAN. In the 1980 campaign, Anderson ran as an independent and garnered some 7% of the popular vote. He retired from the House in 1981.

Anderson, Lindsay (1923–). British film director and critic. A controversial figure in British cinema, Anderson is best known for combining cinematic experimentation with a strident social consciousness. Born in India, the son of a Scottish general, Anderson moved to London as a young man and, in the 1950s, became a leading film critic who called for British cinema to tackle the issues of a troubled postwar society. In 1954 his short documentary film, *Thursday's Children*, won an Oscar, and Anderson became a key figure in the emerging British Free Cinema movement that also included Tony Richardson and Karel Reisz. Anderson made his full-length directorial debut in 1963 with the highly acclaimed *This Sporting Life*, starring Richard Harris. Other Anderson films include *If...* (1968), *O Lucky Man!* (1973) and *The Whales of August* (1987). He also had a small acting role in *Chariots of Fire* (1981).

Anderson, Marian (1902–). American concert and opera singer. Born in Philadelphia, Anderson began singing in church choirs and studied voice privately. Possessed of an extraordinarily rich contralto voice, she began her concert career after graduation from high school, winning a New York Philharmonic Orchestra guest appearance in 1925. Her first CARNEGIE HALL recital was held in 1929, and she soon made extremely popular tours of Europe. Primarily a concert singer, she excelled at spirituals as well as at the classical repertoire, but as a black artist she encountered prejudice in her native country. In 1939 she was denied access to Constitution Hall in Washington, D.C. by the Daughters of the American Revolution, and instead gave a triumphal concert to some 75,000 on the steps of the Lincoln Memorial. In 1955 she became the first black permanent member of the Metropolitan Opera Company. Named a delegate to the United Nations in 1958, she retired from her performing career in 1965. One of the most popular classical artists of her day, she is known for a variety of

Marian Anderson.

outstanding recordings. Anderson was named to the National Arts Hall of Fame in 1972 and was one of the Kennedy Center's first honorees in 1978. Her autobiography, *My Lord, What a Morning,* was published in 1956.

Anderson, Maxwell (1888–1959). American playwright known for historical dramas that embody satire and social commentary. Originally a journalist, Anderson gained success with the production of his first play, *What Price Glory?,* an antiwar drama. *Winterset* (1935), written in verse, examines the SACCO AND VANZETTI CASE. *Key Largo* (1939) and *Anne of the Thousand Days* (1948) were later adapted as movies. Anderson collaborated with composer Kurt WEILL on the musicals *Knickerbocker Holiday* (1938) and *Lost in the Stars* (1940) and won a PULITZER PRIZE for *Both Your Houses* (1933), a satire on the U.S. Congress.

Anderson, Philip Warren (1923–). American physicist. Anderson obtained his B.S. (1943), M.S. (1947), and Ph.D. (1949) at Harvard University, doing his doctoral thesis under John Van Vleck. He spent 1943 to 1945 at the Naval Research Laboratory working on antenna engineering. Upon receiving his doctorate, Anderson joined the Bell Telephone Laboratories at Murray Hill, N.J. Anderson's main research has been in the physics of the solid state, incorporating such topics as superconductors and nuclear theory. In 1959 he developed a theory to explain "superexchange"—the coupling of spins of two magnetic atoms in a crystal through their interaction with a nonmagnetic atom located between them. He went on to develop the theoretical treatments of antiferromagnetics, ferroelectrics, and superconductors. In 1961 Anderson conceived a theoretical model to describe what happens where an impurity atom is present in a metal—now widely known and used as the **Anderson model**. Also named for him is the phenomenon of **Anderson localization,** describing the migration of impurities within a crystal. In the 1960s Anderson concentrated particularly on superconductivity and superfluidity. Along with Van Vleck and the British physicist Nevill MOTT, Anderson shared the 1977 NOBEL PRIZE for physics "for their fundamental theoretical investigation of the electronic structure of magnetic and disordered systems."

Anderson, Sherwood (1876–1941). U.S. author. After a childhood of poverty in Camden, Ohio, he moved to Chicago where he joined the National Guard. He served in Cuba during the Spanish-American War (1898–1899). After preparatory studies in Chicago, he became an advertising executive. He went back to Elyria, Ohio, where he opened a paint factory. After five years in the business, he came back to Chicago and associated himself with the Chicago Circle of writers. His first novel was *Windy McPherson's Son* (1916), followed by *Marching Men* (1917). His most famous book was a collection of short stories and sketches with interrelated themes, entitled *Winesburg, Ohio* (1919); it was followed by *Poor White* (1920) and *The Triumph of the Egg* (1921). He dealt with the conflict of the individual against organized industrial society. Many critics contend that his short stories contain the best expression of his talent.

Andorra [Principality of Andorra]. Andorra is a small, neutral European coprincipality (formed by a treaty in 1278) situated in the Eastern Pyrenees roughly midway between Barcelona, Spain, and Toulouse, France. Historically protective of the right to Andorran citizenship, Andorrans reacted to a modest extension of the franchise in 1933 by staging a mild revolution, which was eventually ended by a force of French gendarmes. In the post-war era, as tourism rapidly developed into the main industry, the non-Andorran (mainly Spanish) population increased. Previously confined to male citizens of the third generation, the franchise was progressively extended to all citizens in the 1970s, although with a higher age qualification for first-generation Andorrans. Under a 1981 constitutional agreement providing for a separation of legislative and executive functions, Andorra's first executive council (government) was formed in January 1982 under the leadership of a prime minister. This office was initially held by Oscar Ribas Reig and after May 1984 by Josep Pintat Solens. The December 1985 elections to the General Council of the Valleys produced, in the absence of formal parties, a mainly conservative new legislature, which confirmed Pintat in his post. In a general election in December 1989, however, Ribas Reig was returned to office.

Andrea Doria. Shortly before midnight on July 25, 1956, the 29,083-ton Italian luxury liner *Anrea Doria,* en route from Genoa to New York, was rammed by the 12,644-ton Swedish liner *Stockholm,* en route from New York to Europe. The *Andrea Doria* began taking on water and sank at 10:15 A.M. on July 26. More than 500 survivors were picked up off Nantucket Island by the *Stockholm,* which remained afloat and returned to New York. The liner *Ile de France* also helped in the rescue, arriving three hours after the collision and taking aboard 753 of the *Doria*'s 1,709 passengers and crew. More than 50 passengers died. Both liners in the collision were equipped with RADAR. An investigation later determined that crew members on both ships had made errors that resulted in the collision.

For further reading:

Gentile, Gary, *Andrea Doria: Dive to an Era.* Gary Gentile, 1988.

Andretti, Mario (1940–). Italian-born race car driver. Born in Trieste, Italy, Andretti began driving in the Formula, Jr. class at the age of 13 in Italy. In 1955 his family immigrated to the U.S. In 1965 he captured his first national championship with 3,110 points. In 1966 he repeated as national champion, posting eight wins. In 1969 he won the Indy 500 with a record speed of 156.867 mph and was again national champion. He has competed in every Indy 500 from 1965 to 1990 except one and has the record for number of laps driven—7,236. He is second to A.J. FOYT in career victories, with 67.

Andrew, Bishop Agnelius (1908–1987). Pioneer of religious broadcasting on radio and television for the BRITISH BROADCASTING CORPORATION (BBC). He was the first Roman Catholic priest to appear on British television and the first in Europe to become a television producer.

Andrews, Julie [Julia Elizabeth Welles] (1935–). Gifted English singer and actress of stage, screen and television, Andrews was born in Walton-on-Thames, a small town west of London. Boasting a full-grown larynx as a child, Andrews quickly became a professional singer and performer. She made her stage debut at 12 in a musical review, and at 19 she became a star in the U.S. in the British musical *The Boy Friend.* Her next stage appearance, in 1956 as Eliza Doolittle in *My Fair Lady,* received glowing reviews in England and the U.S.; but it was 1964 before a movie version was made, with a mistakenly cast Audrey Hepburn. Meanwhile, Andrews had triumphed in Lerner and Loewe's *Camelot* and become a popular figure on American TV variety shows. Turned down for the movie of *My Fair Lady,* Andrews in-

The Andrea Doria *sinks to the bottom of the Atlantic after colliding with the Swedish liner* Stockholm.

stead made her movie debut in the Walt Disney adaptation of the P.L. Travers fantasy, *Mary Poppins* (1964)—and won a best actress ACADEMY AWARD. This was followed by a straight role in the antiwar comedy *The Americanization of Emily* (1964).

But her most successful film was undeniably *The Sound of Music* (1965), which earned her a second Oscar nomination and brought her "Star of the Year" awards in 1966 and 1967 (voted by the Theater Owners of America). In the late 1960s, film projects like *Star* and *Darling Lili* were expensive failures; but her marriage to director Blake Edwards in 1969 led to several pleasing collaborative film efforts: *The Tamarind Seed* (1974), *10* (1979), *S.O.B.* (1981) and *Victor/Victoria* (1982), which earned her another Oscar nomination. Andrews continues to appear in films and on television specials, and she has even written several children's books (as "Julie Andrews Edwards").

Andrews, Roy Chapman (1884–1960). U.S. explorer and scientist. A graduate of Beloit College in Wisconsin (1906), he joined the staff of the American Museum of Natural History in New York, where he specialized in the study of whales and became recognized as the world's top cetologist. In 1914 he became head of the museum's division of Asian exploration, and from 1914 to 1932 Andrews led scientific expeditions to ALASKA, northern Korea, Tibet, southwestern CHINA, BURMA, northern China and Outer Mongolia. On his 1919 expedition to Central Asia, he was the discoverer of the first known dinosaur eggs, perfectly preserved. He was the first to find evidence of the Baluchitherium, the largest known land animal, and made other important discoveries of prehistoric life, including some of the world's largest fossil fields. Andrews was the director of the American Museum of Natural History from 1935 to 1942.

Andreyev, Andrei (1895–1971). Soviet political leader. Andreyev joined the COMMUNIST PARTY in 1914, and was one of the organizers of the Union of Metalworkers in Petrograd from 1915 to 1917. He took part in the OCTOBER REVOLUTION and in the second ALL-RUSSIAN CONGRESS OF SOVIETS. He was president of the central committee of the Union of Railway Workers (1922–27) and was secretary of the central committee of the All-Union Communist Party (1924–25). Andreyev was a member of the politburo (1932–52) and was again secretary of the central committee of the All-Union Communist Party (1935–46). He was a people's commissar of the workers' and peasants' Red Army and of agriculture, and held several other important positions within the party. In 1953 he became a member of the Presidium.

Andreyev, Leonid (Nikolayevich) (1871–1919). Russian author and playwright. He began his career as a lawyer and then turned to journalism. He was a friend of Maxim GORKY, whose influence is evident in his early short stories; his later works show the influence of Dostoevsky and Tolstoy. In his prime he was regarded as highly as Gorky, but his popularity did not endure. His best known works include the short stories *The Red Laugh* (1904) and *The Seven Who Were Hanged* (1908) and the plays *To The Stars* (1906) and *Anathema* (1909). While he supported the moderates in the early phases of the RUSSIAN REVOLUTION, he became fiercely anti-BOLSHEVIK, and in 1917 fled to Finland, where he died in poverty two years later.

Andric, Ivo (1892–1975). Yugoslavian author and diplomat. Born in the village of Dolac in Bosnia (now part of Yugoslavia), he joined the revolutionary organization Young Bosnia (*Mlada Bosna*) while a student in Zagreb. When Gavrilo Princip, another member of the organization, assassinated Archduke Francis Ferdinand in 1914, precipitating WORLD WAR I, Andric was among those arrested. He spent three years in jail, where he immersed himself in the works of Dostoevsky and Kierkegaard, which greatly influenced his outlook. After the war he studied languages, history and philosophy at the universities of Zagreb, Vienna, Krakow and Graz. Shortly thereafter he joined the diplomatic corps, serving in various European capitals during the 1920s and 1930s. On the eve of World War II he was in Berlin as Yugoslavia's minister to Germany. He spent the war in Belgrade under German house arrest, and during this time (1941–45) wrote the three novels (known as the Bosnian Trilogy) that made his reputation: *NaDrini cuprija* (*The Bridge on the Drina*, 1945), *Travnicka chronika* (*Bosnian Chronicle*, 1945), and *Gospodjica* (*The Woman from Sarajevo*, 1945). These works draw on the complex history, cultural diversity and ethnic folklore of his native Bosnia and reflect his fundamentally pessimistic outlook. After the war Andric, a supporter of Yugoslav Premier Josip TITO, was president of the Union of Yugoslav Writers; in the late 1950s he was elected to Yugoslavia's federal assembly. Andric received the NOBEL PRIZE for literature in 1961. His other works include *Prokletaavlija* (*The Devil's Yard,* 1954) and *Nove pripovetke* (*New Stories,* 1948).

Andropov, Yuri (1914–1984). Soviet official and general secretary of the Communist Party (1982–84). Andropov served as ambassador to Hungary (1954–57), where he played a major role in suppressing the HUNGARIAN UPRISING OF 1956. Secretary to the Central Committee of the Communist Party (1957–67), he was subsequently chairman of the KGB (1967–82). In this latter post he became identified with the 1968 invasion of CZECHOSLOVAKIA, the 1979 invasion of AFGHANISTAN and the 1980 military crackdown in POLAND. He became general secretary on BREZHNEV's death in 1982. Although ill-health dimmed his brief tenure as party head (and, thus, as top political leader in the U.S.S.R.), he did initiate a drive for economic reform. His proposal for arms reduction was greeted with skepticism in the West.

Andrzjewski, Jerzy (1909–1983). Polish author and political dissident. His best known novel is *Ashes and Diamonds,* which depicts political struggles in Poland after World War II; in 1961 the book was made into a widely acclaimed film by Andrzej Wajda. Andrzjewski helped found the Workers' Defense Committee (KOR) in 1976 to aid families of striking workers who were jailed or dismissed from their jobs.

"Andy Griffith Show, The". Popular American television series noted for its gentle, homespun comedy. Monday nights on CBS, from October 3, 1960, to September 16, 1968, millions of viewers were willingly whisked away to bucolic Mayberry, tucked away in the North Carolina hills. This was a world you could count on. Folks were dependable. You knew Sheriff Andy Taylor (Andy Griffith) was on the trail of a moonshiner; that Aunt Bea (Frances Bavier) would bring supper down to the jailhouse; that little Opie (Ron Howard) would lose another tooth; and that Deputy Barney Fife (Don Knotts) would accidentally discharge the single bullet in his revolver. It was the most likable formula on television. A spinoff of "The Danny Thomas Show," it portrayed Andy at first as a loutish country sheriff. With the growing popularity of his bumbling sidekick Barney, Andy mellowed and yielded the floor to a growing cast of outrageous but likable characters: the town drunk, Otis (Hal Smith); the loony vagabond, Ernest T. (Howard Morris); the loquacious barber Floyd (Howard McNear); and the drawling gas station attendant, Gomer Pyle (Jim Nabors, who got his own show, "Gomer Pyle, U.S.M.C.," in 1965). Don Knotts left the show in 1965, Griffith and Ron Howard in 1969. A new series, "Mayberry, R.F.D.," retained the setting and some of the characters. During the 1980s, former child star Howard emerged as a successful HOLLYWOOD director.

For further reading:

Brooks, Tim, *The Complete Directory to Prime Time Network TV Shows,* New York: Ballantine, 1968.

Anfinsen, Christian Boehmer (1916–). American biochemist. Anfinsen was educated at Swarthmore College, the University of Pennsylvania and Harvard University, where he obtained his Ph.D. in 1943. He taught at Harvard Medical School from 1943 to 1950, when he moved to the National Heart Institute at Bethesda, Md., where from 1952 to 1962 he served as head of the laboratory of cellular physiology. In 1963 Anfinsen joined the National Institute of Arthritis and Metabolic Diseases at Bethesda, where he was appointed head of the laboratory of chemical biology. Anfinsen was concerned with the shape and structure of the enzyme ribonuclease and the forces that permit it always to adopt the same unique configuration. He found that the minimum of chemical intervention—merely putting the enzyme into a favorable environment—was sufficient to induce the ribonuclease to adopt the one configuration that restores enzymatic activity. From this observation Anfinsen drew the important conclusion that the protein's sequence of amino acids—its primary structure—must contain all the information for the assembly of the three-dimensional protein. He went on to show similar behavior in other proteins. For this work Anfinsen shared the 1972 NOBEL PRIZE for physiology or medicine with Moore and Stein.

Angel Island. Island in California's San Francisco Bay. During WORLD WAR II, it was the site of both a U.S. military base and an immigration intake station, as well as a camp for PRISONERS OF WAR.

Angell, Sir Norman [Ralph Norman Angell Lane] (1873–1967). British writer and peace activist. Born in Lincolnshire, Angell was educated in England, France and Switzerland. In 1891 he traveled to the U.S., where he took odd jobs and worked as a journalist in various cities. Settling in Paris in 1898, he became the editor of the Paris edition of London's *Daily Mail* and wrote *The Grand Illusion* (1910, rev. ed. 1933), a widely celebrated book that pointed out, in economic terms, the interdependence of nations and the stupidity of war. In 1913 the periodical *War and Peace* was established to disseminate his views. Angell's concepts of an international asociation were instrumental in the formation of the LEAGUE OF NATIONS. In 1934, he was awarded the NOBEL PRIZE for peace. Angell was opposed to the British policies of APPEASEMENT toward Nazi Germany, Japan and Italy, views he articulated in *Peace with the Dictators?* (1938). During World War II he worked in the U.S. to seek support for the British war effort, remaining in New York City until 1951. Returning to England, he continued to write and to work for the cause of international peace.

Angelou, Maya [Marguerite Ann Johnson] (1928–). American memoirist and poet. Born in St. Louis, Maya Angelou is best known for four volumes of autobiography: *I Know Why the Caged Bird Sings* (1970), *Gather Together in My Name* (1974), *Singin' and Swingin' and Gettin' Merry Like Christmas* (1976) and *The Heart of a Woman* (1981). Her memoirs describe the small, rural, black community of her childhood, her struggles to support herself as a young unwed mother in San Francisco, her burgeoning theatrical career, and her experiences with the black liberation movement in the 1960s and as a writer and administrator in Africa. Her poetry, which has been less successful than her powerful and engaging prose, ranges from love lyrics to harsh public condemnation of racism in America. She has also produced and acted in a number of plays.

Maya Angelou (1971).

For further reading:

Elliott, Jeffrey M., ed., *Conversations with Maya Angelou.* Jackson: University Press of Mississippi, 1989.

Anghelis, Odysseus (1912–1987). Greek military leader. He was a leading member of the military junta that ruled GREECE from 1967 to 1974 (see GREEK COLONELS). After the junta was overthrown, he was sentenced to 20 years in Korydallos Prison, where he later committed suicide.

Angleton, James J(esus) (1917–1987). U.S. intelligence officer. He joined the CENTRAL INTELLIGENCE AGENCY (CIA) at its inception in 1947 and served for more than 20 years as the head of its counterintelligence office, whose purpose was to protect the agency from infiltration by foreign agents. Over the years his efforts to unmask Soviet agents came to be regarded as overzealous, and at the end of 1974 he was forced to resign his post. With his departure from the CIA, the agency cut its counterintelligence staff from 300 to 80 and moved away from some of the techniques he had introduced.

Anglo-Egyptian Sudan. Former British colony, now the country of SUDAN in northeastern Africa. Jointly ruled by Egypt and Great Britain from 1899, in practice real control was exercised by the British. Sudanese resistance persisted, even after Britain established North and South Sudan as separate colonial entities. In 1952, an agreement in principle was reached to establish Sudan independence, which was accomplished in 1956.

Anglo-French Entente. See ENTENTE CORDIALE.

Anglo-Irish Civil War of 1916–23. Irish nationalism generated by the Anglo-Irish Union of 1800 led to the British granting home rule in 1914 but postponing it until 1920 because of WORLD WAR I. Frustrated, the Irish began the final phase of their struggle against the British in the unsuccessful 1916 EASTER RISING. After executing the rebel leaders, the British tried to achieve an all-Ireland consensus through an Irish National Convention (1917). However, announcement of Irish conscription (1918)—a never-fulfilled plan—resulted in Irish terrorism and political resistance. SINN FEIN, an Irish political society, won 73 parliamentary seats assigned to the Irish; they refused to go to London and instead set up the DAIL EIREANN (Irish Assembly). The British promptly arrested 36 members of the society, but the remaining 37 ratified the Irish republic proclaimed during the EASTER RISING. A provisional Irish government was established, and the IRISH REPUBLICAN ARMY (IRA) and the Irish Volunteers engaged in two and a half years of guerrilla warfare (called "the Troubles" by the Irish) against the Royal Irish Constabulary (Black and Tans). The republicans were supported by the public, Irish-Americans and isolated heroic acts like the Lord Mayor of Cork's successful 1920 hunger strike. The British government was slowly conciliated; after granting a separate Irish parliament in 1920, Sinn Fein took almost all seats. A truce led to an Anglo-Irish Treaty, opposed by both Ulster (NORTHERN IRELAND) and Dublin (EIRE) because it split the country. Fighting broke out between pro-truce and antitruce factions within the IRA. Granted both free state and dominion status (1921), Dublin finally accepted the partition and became the capital of the IRISH FREE STATE in 1922. However, fighting continued into the following year.

For further reading:

Hopkinson, Michael, *Green Against Green: A History of the Irish Civil War*. New York: St. Martin's, 1988.

Anglo-Russian Entente. An agreement signed in St. Petersburg on August 31, 1907, that laid down English and Russian spheres of interest in Persia, England taking the Persian Gulf and Russia the north of Persia. The aim was to keep a check on German expansion in the Near East. The entente formed a link in the ENTENTE CORDIALE among England, France and Russia and was a basis for the Allied coalition in WORLD WAR I.

Angola [People's Republic of Angola]. Angola is situated on the west coast of Africa, south of the Equator, and has an area of 481,226 square miles. The frontiers of Angola were fixed by the conventions of 1891, following the 1884–85 Congress of Berlin, which had divided the map of Africa among the colonial powers. PORTUGAL, which had established a lucrative slave-trading presence on the coast in the 16th century, was granted rights of occupation over Angola, but Portuguese rule did not effectively begin until 1910–20. Following the overthrow of the Portuguese Republic in 1926 and the establishment of Dr. Antonio SALAZAR's Estado Novo four years later, the decentralization policy of the early colonial period ended and was replaced by a system whereby the interests of the colonies were more directly subjugated to the immediate interest of Portugal, eventually leading to a rebellion in Luanda in February 1961. Severe repression followed, but armed resistance to Portuguese rule in Angola was under way. In the 13 years until April 1974, when a military coup in Lisbon led directly to the ending of the Portuguese colonial wars, the nationalist guerrilla armies were able to establish military and political control over large parts of eastern Angola and to press westwards towards the country's central and western districts.

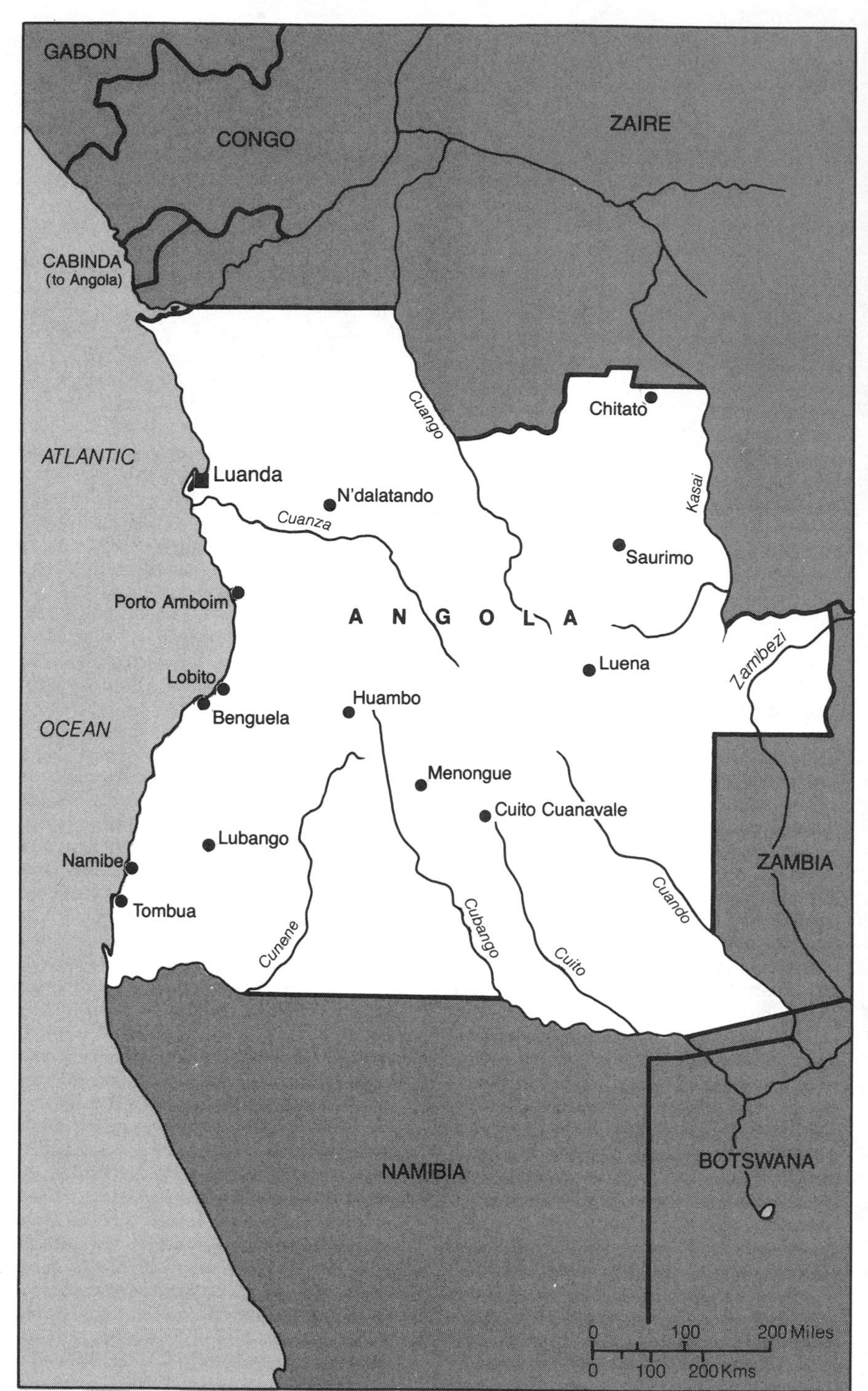

ANGOLA

ANGOLA

1954-74	Rival rebel groups MPLA, FNLA and UNITA fight Portuguese rule.
1975	Portugal grants Angolan independence; MPLA takes power, forms Marxist-Leninist government and establishes ties to SWAPO movement in Namibia.
1976	UNITA calls on U.S. blacks to come and fight for "liberty"; one American and three British mercenaries executed despite U.S. and U.K. appeals for clemency.
1988	Namibian independence linked to Cuban troop withdrawal in Brazzaville Accord.
1990	Angolan government and UNITA rebels agree to ceasefire; ruling party adopts "democratic socialism."
1991	Rivals expected to sign peace agreement in Portugal; talks fail over disagreement on date to begin ceasefire.

Three nationalist movements were involved in the struggle for independence. The Popular Movement for the Liberation of Angola (Movimento Popular de Libertacao de Angola—MPLA) was formed in December 1956 with the aim of ending colonial rule and building a new and unified society. It was led by Agostinho NETO. The National Front of Angolan Liberation (Frente Nacional de Libertacao de Angola—FNLA), essentially a tribalist movement, was formed in 1962, operating in the north of the country and led by Holden Roberto. The National Union for the Total Independence of Angola (Uniao Nacional para a Independencia Total de Angola—UNITA) was formed in 1966 under Dr. Jonas SAVIMBI, operating mainly in eastern Angola.

Following the military coup in Portugal a tripartite transitional government was formed by the three nationalist movements, but armed conflict soon broke out between the MPLA and the others (see ANGOLAN CIVIL WAR). A socialist regime was established; in December 1977 the MPLA was restructured as a Marxist-Leninist party, with the state becoming an instrument of the party. President Neto died on September 10, 1979, and was succeeded by MPLA veteran Jose Eduardo DOS SANTOS. Elections to the assembly were held in 1980 and 1986, but political power remained firmly in the control of the 90-member central committee and the 15-member political bureau of the MPLA.

South African incursions into Angola continued sporadically until August 1988, despite a formal withdrawal in April 1985 following the signing of the Lusaka Accord in February 1984. South Africa also continued to provide logistical backing to UNITA as the latter waged a guerrilla campaign against the Angolan government. The U.S. Congress in June 1985 voted to repeal the Clark Amendment (enacted in 1976), which prohibited U.S. military and financial support for UNITA.

As part of the peace process designed to bring independence to Namibia, South African forces were finally withdrawn from Angola on August 30, 1988, and, under a

Angolan president Agostinho Neto meets with guerrilla leaders Holden Roberto and Jonas Savimbi during talks on Angolan unity.

U.S.-mediated agreement signed in New York on December 22, 1988, Cuba and Angola agreed on a gradual and total withdrawal of the estimated 50,000 Cuban troops from Angola, while South Africa agreed to withdraw from Namibia to allow free elections to be held there prior to independence. In December 1988 the Angolan government offered a one-year amnesty to UNITA supporters, but this was rejected by the UNITA leadership. Pres. dos Santos had declared in mid-1987 that the war against UNITA and its South African backers had cost Angola $12 billion in terms of economic sabotage, 60,000 citizens killed and 600,000 displaced.

Angolan Civil War of 1975. When the Popular Movement for the Liberation of Angola (see MPLA) gained control of the government of Angola in 1976 (see ANGOLAN WAR OF INDEPENDENCE), UNITA and the FNLA refused to recognize the new Marxist-oriented government. In 1977 the MPLA captured UNITA's major stronghold and drove its leaders into ZAIRE and ZAMBIA. UNITA regrouped and revived its guerrilla activities. It was aided by South African and Portuguese white mercenaries and by covert American arms. In the early 1980s UNITA had extended its control over central and southeastern Angola. UNITA also won support from Great Britain, France, the U.S., Saudi Arabia and several African nations. The MPLA was backed by the U.S.S.R. and Cuba. Continual warfare disrupted the Angolan economy and displaced one-sixth of its people, many of whom became refugees in Zaire, Zambia and the Congo. In 1988 Cuba, Angola and South Africa signed accords that promised the departure of all Cuban troops by July 1991. Cuban withdrawal began in 1989.

Angolan War of Independence (1961–76). The Marxist Popular Movement for the Liberation of Angola (see MPLA) revolted against Portuguese rule in the capital of Portuguese West Africa (ANGOLA) in February 1961. About a month later the moderate Union of Peoples of Angola (UPA) joined the rebellion in the north. The rebels were suppressed, and an estimated 20,000 black Africans were killed in the fighting. The MPLA shifted its activities to the country's eastern section, where it waged guerrilla campaigns from bases in neighboring ZAMBIA. In 1966 the UPA split into two pro-western groups, the socialist Front for the Liberation of Angola (FNLA) and the National Union for the Total Independence of Angola (UNITA), which moved its guerrilla operations into the south-central region. The antigovernment forces confined their actions to ambushes and hit-and-run attacks, but they tied down a sizable Portuguese force. By the late 1960s half of Portugal's national budget was being spent on its armed forces in Africa (see GUINEA-BISSAUAN WAR OF INDEPENDENCE; MOZAMBIQUE; PORTUGAL). Many young Portuguese officers came to resent the unrelieved bush fighting and the inefficiency of the bureaucracy running the war in Lisbon. In April 1974 they toppled the national government and installed a leftist regime that was willing to relinquish Portuguese West Africa once an orderly succession could be ensured. Twice the three main liberation movements formed a coalition government, and twice the coalitions collapsed. When the Portuguese finally withdrew in November 1975, they left a country divided by civil war, with UNITA and the FNLA pitted against the MPLA. The MPLA held the capital and received Soviet aid and Cuban soldiers, which turned the tide in its favor. Although South African forces and American supplies came to the aid of FNLA and UNITA, the MPLA seized control of the government (February 1976) and was recognized by the ORGANIZATION OF AFRICAN UNITY (OAU) as the legitimate authority in newly independent Angola. Portuguese colonialism in Africa had ended. (See also ANGOLAN CIVIL WAR OF 1975.)

Angry Young Men. A term coined in the mid-1950s to describe several young British writers including Kingsley AMIS, John BRAINE, and John OSBORNE, among others, whose works are characterized by their protagonists' anarchistic, antiestablishment views, lower middle-class origins, restlessness and sense of social ostracism. Among the most notable and representative works fitting this description are Amis's LUCKY JIM, Braine's *Room at the Top,* Osborne's *Look Back in Anger,* and John WAIN's *Hurry on Down.* Ironically, most of the angry young men resisted the label, and several of them later became figures of the establishment. The name is believed to have been taken from the book *Angry Young Men* (1951) by Irish writer Leslie Paul.

Anheuser, Eberhard (1880–1963). U.S. businessman. He formed a partnership with Adolphus Busch in 1896 and purchased a bankrupt St. Louis brewery. Together they developed a method of brewing beer without pasteurization and pioneered in bottling beer. Anheuser began serving as chairman of the board in 1950.

Animal Farm. An allegorical satire of the aftermath of the RUSSIAN REVOLUTION, the novel by George ORWELL describes the revolt of the animals on a farm and their overthrow of their human keepers. The clever pigs seize power and are soon corrupted by it; their slogan is "All animals are equal, but some animals are more equal than others." The calculating, tyrannical pig Napoleon, who represents Josef STALIN, ousts the more idealistic Snowball, who represents Leon TROTSKY. The kind-hearted horse Boxer symbolizes the strength, goodness and innocence of the common man, and is eventually crushed by the despotic government imposed by the pigs.

animal rights movement. The modern animal rights movement dates from the publication of *Animal Liberation* (1975) by Peter Singer, a philosophy lecturer at University College, Oxford. Singer documented inhumane conditions under which animals were used as subjects for medical experiments and in which they were kept on so-called factory farms. According to Singer, research animals were subjected to extreme pain and distress in the course of cruel "experiments," while farm animals were confined for their entire lives in small, crowded pens. Subsequent investigations, reported in newspapers and magazines and on television, have periodically uncovered similar stories. The animal rights movement seeks to stop these practices and to ensure that all animals can live natural, healthy lives. However, animal rights activists have sometimes crossed the line into activity that the law may deem criminal. This often involves releasing animals from cages where they are confined; it has occasionally extended to bombing or otherwise damaging facilities where animals are allegedly mistreated. Most medical researchers defend experiments on animals, claiming that important medical advances that save human lives would not be possible without such experiments, and charging that animal rights activists are naive in their assumptions about the use of animals for such testing. While the animal rights movement has not developed the sort of political influence that other contemporary rights movements (for the blacks, women, homosexuals, the handicapped and other minorities, for example) have come to enjoy, it has received public attention and has helped to change many people's attitudes toward the treatment of animals, particularly in the U.S., Britain and Western Europe. For example, many people now find the purchase and wearing of fur coats unacceptable; many boycott specific products, such as brands of shampoo or cologne whose development involved animal testing; still others have become vegetarians.

animated film. Animated film creates the illusion of life in static drawings and inanimate objects by adapting graphic arts techniques to the film process. Animation is produced by a progressive build-up of images, frame by frame, using one of several methods, such as "cel animation" or "silhouette animation," to make each frame and link them together. The introduction of a computerized animation process by Bell Telephone Company in the mid-1960s revolutionized animation. Walt DISNEY Studio has produced the best known animated films, from short cartoons featuring such characters as MICKEY MOUSE to the full-length *Snow White and the Seven Dwarfs.* The memorable animated images of Disney's FANTASIA (1941) reflect the mood of particular works of classical music. Animated films are also used in television commercials, industrial presentations and in education. In recent years several Eastern European countries have taken animation in another direction by using fable and myth to deal with serious subjects.

Ankara [Angora]. Capital of Turkey, at

the juncture of the Ankara and Cubuk rivers. In 1920, it was established as the nationalist capital by Kemal ATATURK, and in 1923 it became the official capital of the Republic of TURKEY.

Anouilh, Jean (-Marie-Lucien-Pierre) (1910–1987). French playwright. Anouilh first achieved international popularity with theater audiences through the success of his modern adaptation of *Antigone* (1944), from the classic Greek tragedy by Sophocles. Born in the Bordeaux region, Anouilh began his career as a playwright in the 1930s and continued to produce plays at a prolific rate for over five decades. Anouilh cannot easily be linked with any particular school or trend in the modern theater. Rather, he maintained an intellectual independence that showed itself in the sheer diversity of his works, which ranged in tone from high drama to absurdist farce. His plays frequently dealt with the themes of loss of idealistic innocence and the societal pressures that dictate compromise of one's most cherished values. Other major plays by Anouilh include *The Traveller Without Baggage* (1937), *Point of Departure* (1942), *Ring Round the Moon* (1947), *The Rehearsal* (1950), *The Waltz of the Toreadors* (1952), *Medea* (1953) and *Becket, or the Honour of God* (1959).

Anschluss. German term for the 1938 union of Austria with Germany. Favored by German-speaking subjects of the failed Hapsburg monarchy, by German nationalists and by Austrians who wished to expand their country's status after World War I, it was forbidden by the terms of the Treaties of VERSAILLES and St. Germain (both 1919). Demands for Anschluss became insistent with the ascendancy of Adolf HITLER as German chancellor in 1933. It was accomplished in March 1938, when Hitler occupied Austria and incorporated it into Germany as a province. The Anschluss was annulled by the Allied powers in 1943 when they also agreed on the establishment of an independent Austria after World War II; Austria was formally recognized in 1946.

Ansermet, Ernest (1883–1969). Swiss conductor and founder of the L'Orchestre de la Suisse Romande, renowned for his interpretations of Russian and French ballet music. Ansermet was born into a musical family in Vevey in the French-speaking region of Switzerland. After several years spent teaching mathematics in Geneva and Lausanne, he turned to music and from 1919 to 1923 conducted the BALLETS RUSSES of Serge DIAGHILEV. He led world premieres of many important works, including Maurice RAVEL's *La Valse* and Manuel DE FALLA's *The Three-Cornered Hat*. In 1922 he gave the first performance in Germany of Igor STRAVINSKY's *Le Sacre du printemps*. In 1918 he founded the L'Orchestre de la Suisse Romande with which he would be linked for the next 50 years. His extensive recording career began in 1929. His most notable records were made with Decca, beginning in 1946. Never wholly comfortable with the German repertoire, Ansermet specialized in the ballet music of Stravinsky, Ravel, BARTOK, PROKOFIEV and DEBUSSY. His cool temperament and precise, elegant sensitivity to textures made him the ideal interpreter of these scores. He regarded the atonal ambitions of Arnold SCHOENBERG with hostility and expressed his distrust of these contemporary directions in his book, *The Foundations of Music in the Human Consciousness* (1916). His lifelong conviction was that the spirit of the composer, not the temperament of the conductor, should be observed.

For further reading:

Schonberg, Harold C., *The Great Conductors*. New York: Simon & Schuster, 1967.

An-Shan. City in China's Liaoning province. Its growth was bolstered by the establishment of steelworks in 1918. Expansion continued during the lengthy occupation by Japanese forces, from 1931 to 1944. An-Shan is one of the major metal-processing centers of the world.

Antarctica. Southernmost continent, encompassing the South Pole and composed of two major landmasses joined and overlayed by an ice cap thousands of feet thick. Within the Antarctic Circle, it has the coldest climate on Earth. The first permanent base was established by Norwegian naturalist Carsten E. Borchgrevink in 1899. A major expedition from 1907 to 1909, led by British explorer Sir Ernest Shackleton, resulted in the discovery of the magnetic South Pole and the first ascent of Mount Erebus, one of the tallest volcanoes on Earth. On December 14, 1911, Norwegian explorer Roald AMUNDSEN became the first person to reach the South Pole. He was followed, a month later, by British naval officer Robert F. SCOTT. Airplanes were first used for exploration in the 1920s. Sir Hubert Wilkins of Britain became the first person to fly over the continent in 1928, while Americans Richard E. BYRD and Bernt Balchen became the first to fly over the South Pole itself in 1929, and American Lincoln Ellsworth the first pilot to traverse the entire continent in 1936. In 1958–59, Sir Vivian FUCHS of Britain made the first complete overland crossing. In 1989–90, an international team led by Will Steger made the first crossing by dog sled. Since the 1930s, numerous claims have been made by various nations as to control of Antarctic territory. The United States has refrained from such claims and recognizes none made by other countries. Antarctica has become the site of several major scientific research stations. The Antarctic Treaty of 1959 was signed by 12 nations that participated in the 1957–58 INTERNATIONAL GEOPHYSICAL YEAR. In the late 1980s, Antarctica again became a subject of international debate between those who wished to exploit its natural resources and those who favored leaving the continent in its natural state.

Antheil, George (1900–1959). American composer, pianist and writer whose music in the 1920s was an important force in the avant-garde. He was born in Trenton, N.J., of German-Polish ancestry. His early musical studies were with Ernest BLOCH and at the Settlement School in Philadelphia (renamed the Curtis Institute). He toured London, Berlin and Paris in the early 1920s as a pianist/composer. He earned the nickname "the Bad Boy of Music" because of his iconoclastic music, feisty manner, and the loaded .32 automatic revolver he reputedly kept in his coat pocket to master unruly audiences. His *Mechanisms* (later renamed *Ballet Mecanique*) caused a riot in 1923. This "Message to Mars," as he called it, utilized 10 pianos, bells, sirens and an airplane propeller to create a cold, hard, precise sound—a prophecy and a warning about the impending mechanization of society. He injected jazz idioms into his opera, *Transatlantic* (1930), and contemporary "pop" music into his six symphonies. After 1933 Antheil spent much of his time in HOLLYWOOD, writing a column on music and the movies and scoring many motion pictures, including *The Plainsman* (1937), *In a Lonely Place* (1952) and *The Pride and the Passion* (1955). A man of diverse interests, he also wrote mystery stories under the pen name Stacey Bishop and studied electronics and criminology. His importance as a composer stems largely from the pre-Hollywood period; and he was an innovator in the use of sounds produced by nonmusical instruments. "I have only used these sounds because they are part of the musical sound of our modern life," he wrote, ". . . as steel and aluminum are now part of the material of modern buildings." Before his death he wrote an opera and a ballet for the new medium of television—*Volpone* and *Capital of the World* (both 1953).

For further reading:

Antheil, George, *The Bad Boy of Music: An Autobiography*. Garden City, N.Y.: Doubleday, Doran and Co., 1945.

Anti-Comintern Pact. A five-year agreement for mutual defense against communist subversive activities; signed by Germany and Japan on November 24, 1936, and later joined by Italy (1937). The Western democracies held that the pact was designed to dominate Europe rather than to combat COMMUNISM. From 1939 to 1941 other countries, including Bulgaria, Finland, Hungary, Romania, Slovakia and Spain, signed the pact.

anticommunist bloc. Following WORLD WAR II the U.S.S.R.'s hold over countries in Eastern Europe grew stronger. In April 1949 a Western military alliance, the NORTH ATLANTIC TREATY ORGANIZATION (NATO), was established. Fear of COMMUNISM in the anticommunist countries intensified, especially during the McCarthy era (see Joseph MCCARTHY; MCCARTHYISM) and especially after the U.S.S.R. announced that it possessed the HYDROGEN BOMB. In 1955 West Germany joined NATO, and plans were made for the rearming of West Germany. The U.S.S.R., alarmed, retaliated by creating the Warsaw Treaty Organization (see WARSAW PACT), which bound the Eastern European countries in a close military alliance. Thus the world was divided roughly into the communist bloc, the anticommunist bloc, headed by the United States, and the nonaligned countries.

Antigua and Barbuda. The nation of Antigua and Barbuda consists of three islands in the eastern Caribbean, along the outer rim of the West Indies' Leeward Islands chain. Antigua, formerly a British colony, saw universal adult suffrage introduced in 1951, when the Antigua Labour Party (ALP), the political arm of the Antigua Trade and Labour Union, led by Vere Bird, won all eight elective seats on the Legislative Council. A system of ministerial government was introduced in 1956, and in 1960 Bird became chief minister. The territory became an "associate state" in 1967, with full internal government. The ALP lost the 1971 general election to the opposition Progressive Labour Movement, and George Walter became premier. The ALP regained power at elections in 1976 and, after elections in 1980, opened negotiations with Britain for full independence. Opposition to independence came from the island of Barbuda, which wanted greater autonomy for itself. The territory became an independent state within the COMMONWEALTH on November 1, 1981. Vere Bird became the first prime minister.

Anti-Party Group Crisis. The Anti-Party was the name given by Soviet Premier Nikita KHRUSHCHEV to large and inefficient central ministries that, he felt, were usurping the COMMUNIST PARTY's role in industry. Members of the group included MALENKOV, MOLOTOV and KAGANOVICH. In meetings of the central committee and the Supreme Soviet, seven members of the Presidium had remained silent, forming a majority against Khrushchev and calling on him to resign as first secretary. Khrushchev refused, and rallied his supporters. On June 22, 1957, the vast majority of central committee members supported Khrushchev, the Anti-Party group was defeated and a new Presidium of the U.S.S.R. elected.

anti-Semitism. Prejudice against JEWS. Anti-Semitism had a religious basis until the 19th century. The liberalization of Western Europe in the 18th century, brought on by the Enlightenment and the French Revolution, resulted in the emancipation of Europe's Jews and the granting of legal and religious freedoms. Subsequent 19th-century prejudices were based on theories that saw Jews as a distinct and inferior race and nationalist concerns, especially where Jews formed a large minority. In Czarist RUSSIA, ROMANIA, POLAND and HUNGARY, attacks on Jews, known as POGROMS, were organized and deadly. Pseudoscientific theories of Aryan racial superiority and Jewish inferiority, espoused by the French ethnologist J.A. Gobineau (1816–82) and the Anglo-German Houston Stewart CHAMBERLAIN, were important in the formation of racist policies.

In GERMANY, Adolf HITLER and his NAZI Party advocated the idea of an ARYAN "master race" and targeted Jews as scapegoats for Germany's misfortunes after World War I. German anti-Semitism was codified in the Nuremberg Laws of 1935, and Jewish property was confiscated in 1938. Ultimately, Germany's official FINAL SOLUTION resulted in the extermination of some six million Jews in the HOLOCAUST. After WORLD WAR II anti-Semitism was particularly prevalent in Russia, where continued persecution in the 1950s, '60s and '70s led to large-scale immigration of Jews to ISRAEL and the U.S. Anti-Semitism remains a factor in the Middle East, where it is related to the ongoing Arab-Israeli conflict. With the waning of the Soviet empire in Russia and Eastern Europe in the late 1980s and early 1990s and the concurrent rise of religious orthodoxy and political nationalism, anti-Semitism again became a serious problem in Europe.

antiwar movement. Term generally used for the movement that developed in the U.S. in opposition to American involvement in the VIETNAM WAR. The earliest dissent originated with foreign policy experts who saw little of vital interest for the U.S. in Southeast Asia. Opposition among private citizens was first manifested by pacifists and social activists. Many of these early opponents spoke at college campuses, where a core of student activists against the war was formed. Gaining momentum after President JOHNSON's escalation of the war in 1965, the movement came to encompass a large and vocal segment of the American population. The first college "teach-in" was held at the University of Michigan, Ann Arbor, in March 1965, with such events occurring regularly at colleges and universities thereafter. That same year a number of organizations and peace coalitions were formed to try to put an end to the war: the Women's Strike for Peace, Committee for a Sane Nuclear Policy (SANE) and the Vietnam Day Committee. Their tactics varied from peaceful marches to draft-card burnings.

By 1967 a radical and confrontational segment had formed, helping to create the mass march on the Pentagon in October 1967, student takeovers of university buildings at various campuses and the bloody riots outside the Democratic Convention in Chicago in August 1968. As war casualties rose and the cost increased, a credibility gap arose between the Johnson administration and the American public. The TET OFFENSIVE of 1968 lent momentum to the antiwar movement, and vocal elements within the public, the Congress and the media all

Protest march against the Vietnam war in Dallas, Texas (Feb. 27 1968).

pressed for an end to the war. Within the DEMOCRATIC PARTY, Senators Eugene MCCARTHY and Robert KENNEDY entered the 1968 presidential primaries as antiwar candidates. This opposition forced Johnson from the White House and helped to defeat his heir, Hubert HUMPHREY, and to elect Richard NIXON, who claimed to have a secret plan to finish the war.

In January 1969, the first Moratorium Against the War was held in a number of U.S. cities, and public opposition grew after the KENT STATE killings in 1970. The Nixon administration felt besieged as the antiwar movement grew, and pressure increased with the publication of the PENTAGON PAPERS in 1971. Two mass bombings of Hanoi in 1972 brought further criticism from press and public alike. Vice President Spiro AGNEW vociferously denounced the antiwar protesters as left-wing radicals, and Nixon himself appealed to what he called the "silent majority," those who did not protest but who patriotically supported the government. The movement quieted as Nixon deescalated the war, and it was finally silenced when South Vietnam fell in 1975.

Arguments continue as to the antiwar movement's effectiveness and its motives; some critics of the movement have charged that it undermined the U.S. war effort, giving aid and comfort to the Vietnamese communists and thus contributing directly to the perceived U.S. defeat and the eventual communist takeover of all of Vietnam.

For further reading:

DeBenedetti, Charles, and Charles Chatfield, *An American Ordeal: The Antiwar Movement of the Vietnam Era*. Syracuse, N.Y.: Syracuse University Press, 1990.

Antonescu, Ion (1882–1946). Romanian dictator during WORLD WAR II. A military officer, he served in World War I and was briefly chief of the general staff (1937). Pro-NAZI and supported by the fascist Iron Guard and the German government, he was appointed premier by King CAROL II in 1940. He quickly forced the king's abdication, and Antonescu ruled Romania in the name of Carol's young son King Michael. During his four years in power, Antonescu allied Romania with the AXIS powers, giving HITLER virtual control over the country. On August 23, 1944, with Soviet troops at Romania's borders, King Michael seized control of the government and arrested Antonescu. Tried for war crimes, he was condemned and executed on June 1, 1946.

Antoniadi, Eugene Michael (1870–1944). Greek-French astronomer. Antoniadi established quite early a reputation as a brilliant observer and in 1893 was invited by Camille Flammarion to work at his observatory at Juvisy near Paris. From 1909 Antoniadi worked mainly with the 33-inch refracting telescope at the observatory at Meudon. He became a French citizen in 1928. In his two works *La Planete Mars* (1930) and *La Planete Mercure* (1934) Antoniadi published the results of many years' observations and presented the best maps of Mars and Mercury to appear until the space probes of recent times. He took a strong line regarding Mars: "Nobody has ever seen a genuine canal on Mars," attributing the "completely illusory canals" "seen" by astronomers such as Percival LOWELL and Flammarion to irregular natural features of the Martian surface. Antoniadi also observed the great Martian storms of 1909, 1911 and 1924, noting after the last one that the planet had become covered with yellow clouds and had a color similar to Jupiter. On Mercury his observations made between 1914 and 1929 seemed to confirm Giovanni Schiaparelli's rotation period of 88 days, identical with the planet's period of revolution around the sun. The effect of this would be for Mercury always to turn the same face to the sun, in the same way as the moon always turns the same face to the Earth. Antoniadi cited nearly 300 observations of identifiable features always in the same position, as required by the 88-day rotation period. However, radar studies of Mercury in 1965 revealed the planet has a 59-day rotation period. When the planet returns to the same favorable viewing position in the sky, at intervals of 116 days, it does present the same face to observers.

Antonioni, Michelangelo (1912–). Italian film director. A graduate of the University of Bologna, Antonioni won worldwide praise for his film *L'Avventura* in 1959. In this film and in his other works, including *La Notte* (1961), *The Eclipse* (1962), *Red Desert* (1964), *Blow-Up* (1966), *Zabriskie Point* (1970) and *The Passenger* (1975), Antonioni explores the alienation of modern life.

Antonov-Ovseyenko, Vladimir Aleksandrovich (1884–1939?). Russian revolutionary with MENSHEVIK leanings who joined the Social-Democratic Labor Party in 1903. He was an organizer of the OCTOBER REVOLUTION and conducted the capture of the Winter Palace. He commanded various army groups during the Russian Civil War, but as a supporter of TROTSKY he was dismissed from the army in 1925. He then held diplomatic posts abroad and disappeared in the GREAT PURGE of 1936–38.

Antonov Uprising (1919–1921). An uprising in the Tambov province of Russia, led by A.S. Antonov, a socialist revolutionary. It was anticommunist, and as many as 50,000 peasants and deserters from the Red Army took part. Soviet troops defeated the movement on several occasions, but it collapsed only with the onset of the NEW ECONOMIC POLICY.

Anzac. Acronym for the Australian and New Zealand Army Corps. Anzacs became famous for their eight-month stand against the Turks during the disastrous GALLIPOLI campaign of 1915. They later fought at Arras and Messines, served under General ALLENBY in Palestine (1917) and resisted German advances on the Western Front (1918).

Aparicio, Luis (1934–). Venezuelan-born baseball player. Considered by many to be the finest shortstop ever, Aparicio won the Gold Glove for that position nine times. He was named Rookie of the Year in 1956, and while with the Chicago White Sox (1956–63), he and Nellie Fox formed one of the most efficient infield combinations in baseball history. Traded to the Orioles in 1963, he returned to Chicago five years later, and finished his career in Boston in 1973. Aparicio led American League shortstops in fielding eight consecutive years and was a 10-time All-Star. A workmanlike hitter, he reached the .300 mark only once, in 1970. His basepath speed gave him seventh position on the all-time stolen bases roster, with 506. Aparicio was named to the Hall of Fame in 1984.

Apartheid. An Afrikaner term (literally, "apartness") referring to the South African policy of racial segregation and economic and political discrimination against nonwhites. Practiced unofficially since colonial times, the policy became politically entrenched with the 1948 victory of the white supremist Afrikaner National Party. As part of apartheid the Bantu Self-Government Act (1959) provided for the establishment of seven native African areas to be run by non-white chief ministers. International opposition to the policy began in 1952 and intensified during the 1970s and 1980s, resulting in an economic boycott of SOUTH AFRICA by many countries. The controversy led to South Africa leaving the British COMMONWEALTH and becoming an independent republic in 1961. Major anti-apartheid riots occurred at Sharpeville (1960; see SHARPEVILLE MASSACRE) and SOWETO (1976). Black leader Steve BIKO died in detention in 1977, causing increased anger over the policy. Since 1989 the government of South Africa under F.W. DE KLERK has slowly moved toward discussions on ending apartheid, and has released AFRICAN NATIONAL CONGRESS leader Nelson MANDELA from prison.

For further reading:

Lelyveld, Joseph, *Move Your Shadow: South African Black and White*. New York: Time Books, 1985.

Apollinaire, Guillaume [born Wilhelm-Apollinairis de Kostrowitski] (1880–1918). French poet and art critic. Apollinaire is perhaps the most widely read and influential French poet of this century. Born of a Polish mother and an Italian-Swiss father, young Apollinaire adopted the French language when he was sent to school in Monaco. His first lyric poems, written in his early twenties in Paris, showed the marked influence of 19th-century French Symbolist poets, such as Baudelaire, Rimbaud and Verlaine. But in 1905, Apollinaire established friendships with a group of young painters, including Pablo PICASSO, who were creating the new aesthetics of CUBISM. Apollinaire championed their work and was also the first critic to praise the visionary canvases of Henri Rousseau. In his poems, Apollinaire combined Cubist experimentation with his own natural lyrical bent. *Alcools* (1913) and *Calligrammes* (1918) are his two major volumes of poems. He served in the French Army during WORLD

Edwin E. "Buzz" Aldrin Jr. descends the lunar module to take his first steps on the moon (June 20, 1969).

WAR I and died on November 9, 1918, two days before the Armistice, of complications from a head wound.

Apollo 11. Manned space flight launched on July 16, 1969, as a part of the APOLLO PROJECT; on July 20 it landed the first men on the moon. The mission's crew consisted of its commander, Neil ARMSTRONG, Edwin "Buzz" ALDRIN and Michael Collins. With Collins orbiting the moon in the command module *Columbia,* Armstrong and Aldrin piloted the lunar module *Eagle* to a landing on the moon's Sea of Tranquility. Upon landing, they broadcast to Earth: "Houston, Tranquility Base here. The *Eagle* has landed." Armstrong was the first man to stand upon the lunar surface. Stepping onto Earth's satellite at 10:56 P.M., EST, he made the now-famous statement: "That's one small step for [a] man, one giant leap for mankind." Aldrin then joined Armstrong, and the two spacesuit-clad men set up a battery of scientific instruments, including a seismometer, an aluminum foil apparatus to catch solar wind particles, and a laser beam reflector. They also erected an American flag. The two astronauts photographed the moon's surface and collected over 50 pounds of lunar rock and soil. Altogether, the two Earthmen spent two hours and 13 minutes on the moon. Returning to *Columbia* in the ascent stage of the lunar module, Armstrong and Aldrin rejoined the command module, jettisoned *Eagle* into lunar orbit and returned to a splashdown in the Pacific Ocean on July 24, 1969.

For further reading:

Aldrin, Edwin E., Jr., Armstrong, Neil, and Collins, Michael, et al., *First on the Moon.* Boston: Little, Brown, 1970.

Apollo Project. American space program initiated in 1961 by President John F. KENNEDY, who pledged the nation to land men on the moon and return them safely to Earth by 1970. The undertaking that realized that goal became the biggest technological program to date, encompassing 17 missions, and the most expensive, costing some $25 billion. Overseen by the NATIONAL AERONAUTICS AND SPACE ADMINISTRATION (NASA), the Apollo spacecraft was developed from research conducted in the earlier MERCURY and GEMINI programs. The Apollo spacecraft were launched from the Kennedy Space Center in Florida by a three-stage Saturn V rocket, 363 feet in length, weighing over 3,000 tons and developing a liftoff thrust of 7.5 million pounds. The spacecraft itself consisted of a three-man command module, a service module and a Lunar Excursion Module (LEM). When in moon orbit, the LEM, with a crew of two, detached from the command and service modules and landed on the moon. After exploration, one part of the LEM remained on the lunar surface, while the other rejoined the spacecraft and was discarded after the astronauts reentered the command module. On returning to Earth, the service module was jettisoned, and only the command module and its crew splashed down to complete the journey.

The first six Apollo flights were unmanned tests. The only fatalities of the project occurred during this testing phase when three astronauts were killed in a launchpad fire early in 1967. The first manned flight, Apollo 7, took place in October 1968 and demonstrated the spaceworthiness of the craft. Apollo 8, in December 1968, was successful in orbiting both the Earth and the moon. Apollo 9 (March 1969) tested a lunar module in Earth orbit, and Apollo 10 (May 1969) saw the piloting of the LEM within 50,000 feet of the moon. The goal of the Apollo program was finally reached with APOLLO 11, which successfully landed men on the moon. Scientific exploration began in earnest in November 1969 with Apollo 12, which employed the first Apollo Lunar Scientific Package (ALSEP) and brought back almost 75 pounds of lunar material. Apollo 13 (April 1970) was aborted after an explosion in the service module but returned safely to Earth. Apollo 14 (January-February 1971) did additional scientific exploration, and Apollo 15 (July-August 1971) was the first mission to use an exploration vehicle, the Lunar Rover, on the surface of the moon. The last two Apollo missions, Apollo 16 (April 1972) and Apollo 17 (December 1972), explored the lunar highlands with the aid of the Lunar Rover and collected a total of over 450 pounds of lunar rocks.

Altogether, Apollo astronauts collected and brought back to Earth for investigation some 900 pounds of lunar material. The Apollo Project also involved a Soviet-American cooperative effort in space. Initiated in an agreement of 1972, a link-up of Soviet and U.S. spacecraft was achieved on July 17, 1975, when Apollo 18 docked in space with the Soviet Soyuz 19 spacecraft. The two ships were linked for almost two days. Mounting costs finally terminated the Apollo Project, and work on manned space exploration was continued with the SKYLAB program.

For further reading:

Hurt, Harry, *For All Mankind.* Boston: Atlantic Monthly Press/Little, Brown, 1988.

Apollo-Soyuz Test Project [ASTP]. Historic cooperative program between the U.S. and the U.S.S.R. resulting in a joint space mission in July 1975. Two Soviets and three Americans met in space when the orbiting SOYUZ and APOLLO spacecraft linked up. The term "test project" was used because only one mission was planned.

Apostles, the. A secret society at Cambridge University whose members idealized the Soviet Union. During the 1930s, Cambridge don Anthony BLUNT worked with undergraduate Guy Burgess to turn the Apostles into a Marxist cell and to recruit potential spies from among its ranks. In addition to Blunt and Burgess, the group's most notable members included Donald Maclean and Kim PHILBY, all of whom actively worked as double agents for the Soviet Union during WORLD WAR II and in the early stages of the COLD WAR. (See also BURGESS-MACLEAN SPY CASE.)

appeasement. Foreign policy that causes a nation or nations to concede certain matters to an aggressor country rather than risk war. In the 20th century the term is usually applied to attempts by Great Britain and France to appease Adolf HITLER by making agreements with Germany and Italy in the years from 1936 to 1939. It is particularly associated with the efforts of British Prime Minister Neville CHAMBERLAIN. Appeasement permitted German reoccupation of the RHINELAND, the ANSCHLUSS with Austria and Czechoslovakia's surrender of the Sudetenland in the MUNICH PACT. The policy came to an end as a result of Germany's occupation of the rest of Czechoslovakia in 1939.

Appiah, Joseph "Joe" Emmanuel (1918–1990). Ghanaian political leader and diplomat. Appiah was a close associate of Ghanaian leader Kwame NKRUMAH before GHANA achieved independence from Britain in 1957. However, he eventually split with Nkrumah over Nkrumah's increasingly authoritarian policies and became a prominent opposition leader. Appiah served as Ghana's representative to the UNITED NATIONS (1977–78). Appiah attracted widespread publicity in 1953 when he married an English woman, Peggy Cripps, the daughter of former Chancellor of the Exchequer Sir Stafford CRIPPS.

Apple Computer. Computer manufacturing firm based in Cupertino, California, founded by Steven Jobs, a computer expert who successfully challenged such major manufacturers as IBM with a product line not compatible with other manufacturers' systems. Apple computers have been of distinguished design, developed by the German-American industrial design firm Frogdesign. The very successful Apple IIC, the Macintosh, and Apple IIGS units are examples of the compactness and neat detailing typical of Apple products. Apple introduced a new line of Macintosh computers in 1990.

Appleton, Sir Edward Victor (1892–1965). British physicist. Appleton studied physics at Cambridge University from 1910 to 1913. During World War I, while he was serving in the Royal Engineers, he developed his interest in radio that was to influence his later research. After the war he returned to Cambridge and worked in the Cavendish Laboratory from 1920. In 1924 he was appointed Wheatstone Professor of Experimental Physics at King's College, London. There, in his first year, he used a BBC transmitter to conduct a famous experiment that established beyond doubt the presence of a layer of ionized gas in the upper atmosphere capable of reflecting radio waves. The existence of such a layer had been postulated by Oliver Heaviside and Arthur Kennelly to explain MARCONI's transatlantic radio transmissions. Furthermore, the experiment measured the height of the layer, which Appleton estimated at 60 miles. He proceeded to do theoretical work on the reflection or transmission of radio waves by the ionized layer and found, using further measurements, a second layer above the **Heaviside-Kennelly** layer. The **Appleton layer** undergoes daily fluctuations in ionization, and he established a link between these variations and the occurrence of sunspots. In 1936 he became the Jacksonian Professor of Natural Philosophy at Cambridge, and during the war years until 1949 he was secretary of the department of scientific and industrial research, while he led research into RADAR and the ATOMIC BOMB. For his great achievements in ionospheric physics he was knighted in 1941 and in 1947 won the NOBEL PRIZE for physics.

April Theses (April 1917). On his return to Petrograd, April 16, 1917, LENIN published the so-called April Theses, a policy statement that defined his own position and was intended to direct the BOLSHEVIKS toward the seizure of power. The theses contributed to the OCTOBER REVOLUTION because in effect they were asking the Bolsheviks to withdraw support from the provisional government. In the theses Lenin opposed continuation of WORLD WAR I; proposed that power be handed over to the Soviets, including control of banks, production and distribution of goods; advocated abolition of the existing police force, army and bureaucracy and the confiscation of all private land; and suggested that the Social-Democratic Party be called the COMMUNIST PARTY, and that the Socialist International be reconstructed.

The theses met with considerable opposition even from within the Bolshevik Party; and the Petrograd and Moscow Bolshevik committees voted against them, but within a few weeks they were adopted by the Bolsheviks.

Aquino, (Maria) Corazon [Cori Aquino] (1933–). President of the Philippines since February 1986. From 1980 to 1983 Aquino lived in exile with her husband, **Benigno Aquino,** who led the opposition to President Ferdinand MARCOS. Following Benigno Aquino's assassination on his return to MANILA in 1983, she became increasingly active politically and was chosen as a compromise candidate to contest the presidential election against Marcos in 1986. Although Marcos claimed victory, international pressure in the face of widespread corruption led to his resignation and Aquino's accession to the presidency. As president, Aquino pledged economic and political reforms but faced opposition from both the right and the left, including several attempted coups.

For further reading:
Burton, Sandra, *Impossible Dream: The Marcoses, the Aquinos, and the Unfinished Revolution.* New York: Warner Books 1989.

Corazon Aquino during a press conference in 1987.

Arab-Israeli War of 1948–49. Arab forces from Egypt, Syria, Transjordan (Jordan), Lebanon and Iraq invaded ISRAEL on May 14, 1948, the day the state of Israel was proclaimed. The Arabs pushed into southern and eastern PALESTINE and Jerusalem's Old City before the Israelis halted them. In June the UNITED NATIONS succeeded in a securing a four-week truce. After fighting resumed in July, the Israeli forces gained territory until another truce went into effect for about three months. The Israelis then pushed the Arab forces back on all fronts, gaining the Negev desert region (except for the GAZA STRIP). Between February and July 1949 Israel signed armistice agreements with the Arab states (except Iraq, which refused to sign but did withdraw its troops). At the end of the war, Israel occupied most of the disputed areas of Palestine, increasing its territory by one-half. It also developed a formidable standing army. About 400,000 Palestinian Arabs fled, settling in refugee camps in neighboring Arab countries. (See also ARAB-ISRAELI WAR OF 1956.)

For further reading:
Collins, Larry, and Dominique Lapierre, *O Jerusalem.* New York: Simon & Schuster, 1972.
O'Ballance, Edgar, *The Arab-Israeli War, 1948.* Westport, Conn.: Hyperion Press, 1981.

Arab-Israeli War of 1956 (October 29–November 6, 1956). Brief war between ISRAEL and EGYPT, prompted by the Egyptian nationalization of the SUEZ CANAL. The Israeli attack on Egypt (October 29) was secretly instigated by Britain and France, which sought to topple Egyptian President NASSER and protect their own interests in the Canal Zone. Actively supported by Britain and France, Israel achieved its military goals in less than a week. However, the French and British role in the affair resulted in severe domestic and international political crises for these nations. (See also SUEZ CRISIS.)

Arab-Israeli War of 1973 [Yom Kippur War]. Fighting continued off and on between the Arabs and Israelis after the SIX-DAY WAR of 1967. Frustrated over Israeli refusal to negotiate return of the Occupied Territories, Arab states launched a surprise attack on Israel on October 6, 1973, the Jewish holy day of Yom Kippur. Egyptian forces attacked from the east across the SUEZ CANAL, while Syrian troops moved from the north into Israel. The Egyptian and Syrian armies, joined by Iraqi, Jordanian and Libyan units, inflicted heavy losses on the Israelis, who were caught off guard. The Israeli armies eventually counterattacked and drove into Syria to within 20 miles of Damascus. They also encircled the Egyptian army by crossing the Suez and establishing troops on the canal's west bank. Israel agreed to a cease-fire called for by the U.S. and the U.S.S.R., but fighting continued until a United Nations peacekeeping force was moved into the war zone and a cease-fire agreement was signed on November 11, 1973. By a 1974 agreement Israel withdrew into SINAI west of the Mitla and Gidi passes, and Egypt reduced forces on the Suez's east bank. A UNITED NATIONS buffer zone was established between Israel and Syria.

Arab League [League of Arab States]. Organization formed in 1945 by EGYPT, IRAQ, LEBANON, SAUDI ARABIA, SYRIA, Transjordan (now JORDAN) and YEMEN (later North Yemen, or the Yemen Arab Republic). Its purpose was to provide a political voice for the Arab states, to strengthen ties among Arab nations and to preserve the sovereignty of member states. The league has remained a loose confederation without a strong central

Yasir Arafat (Jan. 11, 1989).

authority. At first involved in anti-Israeli activities and in efforts to curb French influence, its militancy was tempered by the founding of the PALESTINE LIBERATION ORGANIZATION (PLO). In the early 1990s the League had a membership of 22 (including the PLO) and acted largely as a spokesman for moderate Arab thought and as a coordinator of Arab economic affairs.

Arafat, Yasir (1929–). Palestinian leader, chairman of the PALESTINE LIBERATION ORGANIZATION (PLO) since 1968. Active in the **League of Palestinian Students** in the 1940s and 1950s, he formed the Al Fatah movement in 1956. Although the PLO has been associated with many terrorist incidents, Arafat has been regarded as a moderate Palestinian leader and, as such, has been recognized by much of the international community as someone with whom negotiations should take place.

For further reading:

Wallach, Janet, and John Wallach, *Arafat: In the Eye of the Beholder*. New York: Carol Publishing Group, 1990.

Aragon, Louis (1897–1982). French poet, novelist, essayist and journalist. Aragon first came to prominence as a Surrealist poet in the 1920s, most notably in his book *Perpetual Movement* (1926). That same year he published a novel, *Le Paysan de Paris,* which evokes the everyday life of Paris in a fantastical style. Aragon joined the Communist Party in 1927 and visited the Soviet Union in 1930. In the 1930s and after, he abandoned his Surrealistic style in favor of a committed political realism. During World War II, Aragon became a hero of the French RESISTANCE both by publishing clandestine newspapers and by expressing the yearning for liberty in his traditional lyric poems of the war years. Aragon continued to write novels in the postwar years, such as the six-volume series *The Communists* (1949–51), as well as volumes of love poems, such as *Elsa* (1959).

Arbenz Guzman, Jacobo (1913–1971). Guatemalan political leader. Arbenz served as Guatemala's defense minister (1945–50) before being elected president in 1950. An independent radical with the support of both the army and left-wing political groups, Arbenz in 1952 launched a controversial land reform program that resulted in the confiscation of holdings of the United Fruit Company, an American firm. As a result, the U.S. government denounced the Arbenz government as communist, and in 1954 a U.S.-backed coup replaced Arbenz with the right-wing Castillo Armas.

Arber, Werner (1929–). Swiss microbiologist. Arber graduated from the Swiss Federal Institute of Technology in 1953 and gained his Ph.D. from the University of Geneva in 1958. He spent a year at the University of Southern California before returning to Geneva where he became professor of molecular genetics in 1965. In 1970 Arber moved to Basel to take the chair of molecular biology. In the early 1950s Giuseppe Bertani reported a phenomenon he described as "host-controlled variation" in which phage (the viruses that infect bacteria) successfully growing on one host found it difficult to establish themselves on a different bacterium. In 1962 Arber proposed that bacteria possess highly specific enzymes capable of destroying invading phage by cutting up their DNA. The existence of such "restriction enzymes," as they came to be called, was later established by Hamilton Smith. As restriction enzymes were found to leave DNA strands "sticky" and ready to combine with certain other "sticky" strands, it was soon apparent to molecular biologists that genetic engineering was at last a practical proposition. For his work on restriction enzymes Arber shared the 1978 NOBEL PRIZE for physiology or medicine with Smith and Daniel Nathans.

Arbuckle, (Roscoe) "Fatty" (1887–1933). American comedy film actor. Originally a member of the silent screen's bumbling Keystone Kops, the chubby clown became a star in his own right at the Mack SENNETT studio from 1912 to 1915. In 1920 he began to make his own feature-length comedies. His career ended after a 1921 scandal involving the death of a young actress. Although cleared of rape and manslaughter charges, a discredited Arbuckle was unable to work in the film industry again, although he had a brief stint as a writer and director under the pseudonym William B. Goodrich from 1931 to 1932.

Arbus, Diane [born Diane Nemerov] (1923–1971). American photographer. The sister of American poet Howard Nemerov, she married fellow fashion photographer Allan Arbus in 1941, and the two operated a successful commercial studio until 1958. In 1959 she studied with the photographer Lisette Model. She is best known for her unblinkingly direct studies of unconventional, strange or freakish people. Among her best known photographs are images of twins (1966), a photograph of a Jewish "giant" (1970) and studies of prostitutes, transvestites and

Fatty Arbuckle.

dwarfs. Not all of her subjects are unusual, but she brings a jarringly powerful vision and a pervasive sense of unease to portrayals of even the most ordinary people. Arbus committed suicide in 1971.

Arbuzov, Alexei Nikolayevich (1908–). Russian playwright. Arbuzov is one of the best known of contemporary Soviet dramatists, both at home and abroad. His plays were first published in 1930. *Tanya* is generally considered to be one of the foremost plays of the 1930s. In later years, music hall and vaudeville features have colored his work.

Arcaro, Eddie [George Edward Arcaro] (1916–). American jockey. Over a 30-year career, Arcaro rode in 24,092 races. A stable boy at the age of 13, he rode the first of his 4,779 winners at a Mexican track in 1932. A four-time Kentucky Derby winner, he was the only jockey ever to ride two Triple Crown winners, WHIRLAWAY in 1941 and CITATION in 1948. He was known early in his career as a down-and-dirty rider, and was suspended during the 1942–43 racing season for his tactics. He later reformed and became known for his skill and tactical ability. Among his best-known mounts were NATIVE DANCER, NASHUA and the incomparable KELSO.

Archipenko, Alexander (1887–1965). Russian sculptor. His development paralleled that of the Cubist painters (see CUBISM). A gradual simplification of human contours brought him to the point of expressing the nude figure entirely in geometrical shapes.

Arcos Raid. Diplomatic incident of May 1927 in the UNITED KINGDOM. Under orders from Stanley BALDWIN's government, which suspected that the U.S.S.R. was meddling in British affairs, Scotland Yard agents raided and searched the London offices of the Soviet trading company known as Arcos. Although no evidence was found, the British nevertheless maintained that the Soviets were plotting against British imperial interests. Diplomatic relations were subsequently broken off, but were resumed in 1929 when anti-Soviet sentiments had somewhat subsided.

Arden, Eve [Eunice Quedens] (1908–1990). U.S. film and television actress. She appeared in such films as *Stage Door* (1937), *Mildred Pierce* (1945), for which she was nominated for an ACADEMY AWARD, and *Anatomy of a Murder* (1959). She was best known for her role as the sharp-tongued but lovable schoolteacher in the long-running television series "Our Miss Brooks" (1948–57). She went on to star in "The Eve Arden Show" and costarred with Kaye Ballard in the series "The Mothers-in-Law."

Arendt, Hannah (1906–1975). German-born American philosopher and social critic. Arendt was one of the most influential political writers in the U.S. in the decade following World War II. She earned her Ph.D. in philosophy in 1928 at the University of Heidelberg, where she studied under the renowned philosopher Karl JASPERS. Due to her Jewish ancestry, Arendt was forced to flee the German Nazi regime in 1933, moving first to Paris and then, in 1941, to the U.S., where she was actively involved in Jewish refugee relief efforts. Her first major work, *The Origins of Totalitarianism* (1951), argued that totalitarian regimes were growing in strength throughout the Western world due to an increasing sense of political and personal alienation among the ruled populaces. Considerable controversy developed over *Eichmann in Jerusalem* (1963), in which Arendt stated that the trial of Nazi death camp officer Adolf EICHMANN illustrated the "banality of evil." Her other major works include *The Human Condition* (1958) and *On Violence* (1970).

For further reading:
May, Derwent, *Hannah Arendt*. New York: Penguin, 1986.

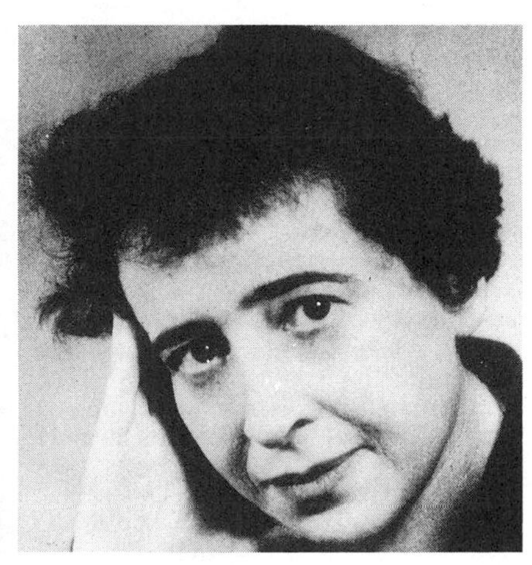

Hannah Arendt (1954).

Arens, Egmont (1888–1966). American industrial and packaging designer whose work of the 1930s followed the streamlined direction typical of the most advanced work of the time. His book, *Consumer Engineering*, of 1932 (written with Roy Sheldon) was influential during the Depression in promoting the idea that improved design could be a tool to increase product sales. Many of his package designs, such as the coffee bags for A&P food stores, were once universally familiar. His Kitchen Aid mixer (c. 1946) is a typical example of his approach to product design.

Arevalo, Juan Jose (1904–1990). President of GUATEMALA (1945–51). Arevalo began his career in Guatemala's Education Ministry but soon exiled himself in political protest to Argentina, where he was a professor of literature and ethics and wrote textbooks. After a 1944 coup ended 14 years of military dictatorship in Guatemala, Arevalo returned and was elected president, his tenure beginning in 1945. He overturned repressive laws banning free press and labor unions and encouraged the formation of political parties. He also initiated social security and public health reforms and attempted to bring Guatemala's Indian population into government. Arevalo described himself as a socialist, but many accused him of being a communist. As a more radical left gained increasing control of his party, he faced many attempts to oust him by the right. He was succeeded in 1951 by Jacobo ARBENZ GUZMAN, who was overthrown in 1954 by a military coup backed by the U.S. CENTRAL INTELLIGENCE AGENCY. A military dictatorship was reestablished that eliminated many of Arevalo's reforms and maintained a brutal repression almost continuously until 1985. Arevalo went into exile and did not return permanently to Guatemala until the mid-1970s. He is the author of *The Shark and the Sardines* (1961), which criticizes U.S. involvement in Latin America.

Argentina. Argentina occupies almost the whole of the southern part of the South American continent and extends from Bolivia to Cape Horn, a distance of nearly 2,149 miles. From 1880 to the 1920s, the attraction of foreign investment and labor became the primary concern of governments. Argentina's population was

ARGENTINA

1902	Long dispute with Chile over Patagonian border settled.
1910	International exhibition in Buenos Aires marks centennial of first independence struggle; peak of economic and population boom based on export of beef to Europe.
1916	After electoral reforms, Radical Party takes over government; fails to challenge entrenched agricultural and business interests.
1919	Argentina joins League of Nations; withdraws following year to protest Allied treatment of defeated Germany.
1930	First military coup ends period of reform.
1943	Labor unrest leads to second coup, by army colonels including Juan Peron.
1944	Publication of *Ficciones* by Jorge Luis Borges.
1946	Peron elected president; attempts to pacify labor movement and industrialize the country.
1952	Death of Peron's wife Eva, whose advocacy of social programs made her a hero to many Argentines.
1966	Military suspends congress and dissolves political parties.
1973	Elections resume and Peron returns from exile; he is re-elected.
1976	Inflation cripples economy; Peron forced out in coup.
1977	"Dirty War"; army kills thousands of perceived subversives.
1982	Military discredited after defeat by Britain in war over Malvinas (Falkland) Islands; junta leaves power and elections are scheduled.
1986	Argentina wins the World Cup in soccer.
1989	Peronists return to power with election of Carlos Saul Menem; hyper-inflation again batters the economy.

ARGENTINA

boosted by European immigration. The honest administration of the 1912 Electoral Law, which insisted on universal and compulsory male suffrage, secret ballots and permanent voter registration, brought the radicals to power in 1916 under Hipolito Yrigoyen. The radicals held the presidency for the next 14 years but never seriously threatened the power base of the ruling class. In September 1930, amid economic crisis, government corruption and popular disillusionment, a coup brought Argentina's first military government to power. Far from providing stability, the coup brought harsh repression and corruption, the period from 1930 to 1943 being known as the "Era of Patriotic Fraud," when the Conservatives, together with civilian and military political opportunists, rigged successive elections. Such abuses in turn antagonized the growing industrial middle class and an increasingly militant working class. The heightened tension developing between these two forces persuaded the military to take the helm again in 1943.

The 1943 coup brought Col. Juan Domingo PERON on to the political stage. As the military's minister of labor, Peron believed that the state could play the key role in industrializing and diversifying the economy and that it could be assisted by the urban working class. Peron sanctioned progressive labor legislation, encouraged trade union growth and organization, and substantially raised wages. In the presidential elections of 1946 Peron, now the candidate of the Argentine Labor Party, defeated the single candidate of the traditional parties. He, along with his second wife Eva ("Evita," a legend for her social welfare programs), mobilized the labor movement into a single General Labor Confederation (CGT) fiercely loyal to him. Such loyalty persisted even when Peron (re-elected in 1951 as the automatic candidate of the new Peronist Party) became increasingly authoritarian as economic growth slowed. Strikes were repressed, wages driven down and opposition leaders were harassed or exiled. By 1955, Peronism had strained its appeal among the rank-and-file of the labor movement, and the Catholic Church had withdrawn its support. In September, the military overthrew Peron and forced him into an 18-year exile.

The succeeding 20 years were characterized by accelerating inflation, strikes, high unemployment and political instability. The military, which had closed the Congress and dissolved all political parties in 1966, was unable to deal with the high level of political violence, which their own repression had stoked up. Gen. Alejandro Lanusse allowed the Peronists to contest the elections of March 1973, and their successful candidate, Hector Campora, then resigned within 50 days, forcing fresh elections to clinch the presidency for Peron, who had returned from exile. Both Peron and his third wife "Isabelita" (who succeeded him as president after his death) failed to deliver any significant social and economic changes, with record inflation in 1975 and 1976. In 1975 there was the threat of the first general strike against a Peronist government. The radical youth wing of the Peronist movement initiated a campaign of urban guerrilla warfare to destabilize the government. The military returned to power in a coup on March 24, 1976, arresting Isabel Peron and proceeding to torture, murder and abduct thousands of perceived opponents in a campaign later known as the "dirty war."

At the end of 1981 military hardliners installed a junta led by the commander-in-chief of the army, Gen. Leopoldo GALTIERI. By 1982 the military had so discredited itself that it gambled on invasion of the Falkland (Malvinas) Islands on April 2 to restore its national credibility (see FALKLAND ISLANDS WAR). Defeat by British forces made the resignation of Galtieri's military junta inevitable. In the presidential elections of October 1983 Raul ALFONSIN was the surprise victor. The Alfonsin administration promised peace, freedom and progress, but faced military unrest and a multitude of economic problems that deepened throughout its term, notably the spiraling inflation and foreign debt that topped U.S. $60 billion at the close of 1988. Groups of army officers led a series of rebellions in 1987 and 1988, protesting against government efforts to bring to trial the military personnel responsible for human rights violations. The Peronists returned to power with the victory of Carlos Saul Menem over the UCR candidate Eduardo Angeloz in May 1989. They also won control of the Congress.

Argentine "Dirty War" (1976–83). On March 24, 1976, the Argentine armed forces overthrew the government of President Isabel Peron (see Juan PERON). A three-man junta led by General Jorge Videla began a ruthless campaign against leftists, liberals and terrorists. An estimated 6,000 to 15,000 Argentines disappeared between 1976 and 1981. The flagrant violations of human rights caused the U.S. government under President CARTER to stop sending Argentina military aid. Several prominent prisoners were freed and allowed to leave the country, and gradually the security forces reduced their "dirty war" activities in response to worldwide public opinion. Argentina's return to civilian rule under President Raul ALFONSIN (December 10, 1983) resulted in the prosecution of former military presidents Videla, General Roberto Viola and General Leopoldo GALTIERI and six other members of the former junta.

Argentine Revolt of 1951. Argentina became a virtual dictatorship under President Juan Domingo PERON, who was assisted by his wife Eva (Evita) PERON. In 1951 the country's economy was in bad shape, with decreasing exports, climbing inflation and several strikes. Declaring martial law, Peron broke the strikes with force and claimed they were instigated by "foreign agitators." Riots erupted when he suspended the newspaper *La Prensa,* Argentina's largest independent newspaper, which had criticized the government. Peron attempted to have his wife nominated for vice president, but the prospect of a woman succeeding to the presidency and as commander of armed forces outraged some generals, who led an unsuccessful revolt in September 1951. Eva withdrew her bid for the vice presidency. In the national election on November 11, 1951, Peron was reelected by a two-to-one majority.

Argentine Revolt of 1955. Juan Domingo PERON, president and dictator of ARGENTINA, began to lose power after the death of his wife Eva (Evita) PERON (1952), who had a strong political following among women, labor and the poor. Many Argentines were also upset by the deteriorating economy and increasing totalitarianism. Fearing a growing Christian socialist movement, Peron turned against the Catholic Church, a former ally. He arrested priests, fired clerical teachers and stopped all financial support of church educational facilities. Opposition to these measures increased, and many government officials resigned in protest. Peron introduced bills to end religious instruction in the schools and to tax church property. Catholics held religious processions that turned into antigovernment demonstrations, which the police suppressed. After a Corpus Christi celebration in June 1955, two high-ranking bishops were deported. The Vatican retaliated by excommunicating Peron (June 16, 1955). That same day part of the navy and air force staged an unsuccessful revolt in Buenos Aires. Peron later offered to resign (August 31, 1955), but the workers, who still supported him, called a general strike until he promised to remain in office. On September 16, 1955, army revolts broke out against Peron. The navy and air force soon joined and threatened to bomb Buenos Aires unless Peron resigned. Peron fled to Paraguay and went on to exile in Spain. Five days after Peron was ousted, General Eduardo Lonardi became provisional president (September 23, 1955).

Argentine Revolts of 1962–63. Peronist candidates were permitted to run for the first time since President Juan Domingo PERON's ouster (1955). The Peronistas won a slight majority in the Chamber of Deputies and nine of 14 governorships. The anti-Peronist military leadership refused to allow the Peronists to take office, deposed President Arturo Frondizi and seized control of the government. Fighting erupted within the military over whether to allow elections or to establish a dictatorship. In the elections of 1963 Peronistas were forbidden to run candidates, and so cast blank ballots in protest as they had in 1957, when they tried to disrupt the voting. Intrigue, secret alliances, street fighting, intimidation by the military, hardening hatreds and an economy in shambles characterized Argentina when Umberto ILLIA (1900–1983) was elected president in 1963.

Arghezi, Tudor (1880–1967). Romanian poet. A controversial figure, Arghezi began publishing his work in 1896 while eking out a modest existence in Bucharest. He entered a monastery in 1899 and stayed for four years before returning to Bucharest to write and edit a literary journal of his own devising, *The Straight Line* (it was the first in a succession of such magazines). Frequently in trouble for his tendency to issue alienating, radically inconsistent political tirades, he was imprisoned after World War I for contributing to a pro-German newspaper. His first book of poems was not published until 1927. Five novels appeared in the 1930s, as well as further collections of poetry. Called a "Faustian" by some, Arghezi was nonetheless seen as a poet of the first rank, writing with ferocity of the world's evils and compensatory pleasures.

Ariane. Three-stage rocket developed by the European Space Agency (ESA). The Ariane project, designed to create an independent European capability in launching a variety of satellites, ran into a number of difficulties in its early days, at the beginning of the 1980s. Declared operational in January 1982, Ariane 1 failed in its first launch in September 1982. Subsequent launches met with some successes and some failures, including rockets that had to be destroyed after launching in September 1985 and May 1986. Ariane 4 was developed during 1987–88 and successfully launched for the first time in June 1988. Ariane 5, scheduled for development in the 1990s, is planned to bring Europe into satellite-launching parity with the U.S. and the U.S.S.R. and is slated to place the ESA's planned Hermes space shuttle in orbit. Launched from Kourou, French Guiana, Ariane is 155.45 ft. tall, has a lift-off weight of 463,643 lbs. and can carry a payload of up to 4.6 tons.

Arias, Roberto Emilio (1918–1989). Panamanian lawyer, journalist and diplomat. In 1955 he married the British ballerina Dame Margot FONTEYN, whom he had known for many years. In 1959 he and Fonteyn were charged with attempting to smuggle guns into PANAMA aboard their yacht as part of a plot to overthrow President Ernesto de la Guardia Jr. Fonteyn was deported and Arias took refuge in the Brazilian embassy until the charges were dropped. In 1964 Arias was shot and partially paralyzed by a former political associate in a dispute over his election to the national assembly.

Arias Madrid, Arnulfo (1901–1988). Panamanian politician; three times elected president of Panama, he was three times overthrown by the Panamanian military or police. An old-style nationalist, Arias Madrid first popularized the slogan "Panama for the Panamanians" in an unsuccessful attempt to gain the PANAMA CANAL Zone from the U.S. His fascist sympathies and his refusal to allow the U.S. to arm Panamanian ships bringing Lend-Lease weapons to Great Britain led to his first U.S.-backed removal in a bloodless coup in 1940.

Arias Navarro, Carlos (1908–1989). Spanish politician. He was the last prime minister of SPAIN under the regime of General Francisco FRANCO. Appointed to the post by Franco in 1973, he was reappointed by King JUAN CARLOS, following Franco's death in November 1975 but was dismissed a year later. Thereafter his influence waned.

Arledge, Roone (Pinckney, Jr.) (1931–). American TELEVISION producer. As president of ABC Sports (1968–77), Arledge transformed the very "look" and pacing of live and taped sports television. He insisted on using the latest technical advances in his programs, and his innovations were copied by other networks and quickly became standard practice in television sports broadcasting. Most notably, Arledge introduced the instant replay and its variations: stop-action replay, slow-motion replay and replays shot from different cameras and camera angles. He also pioneered the use of computer-generated graphics on the screen. The two showcases for Arledge's style were "Monday Night Football" and "Wide World of Sports"; he also brought a new level of coverage to the OLYMPIC GAMES in 1968 and subsequent years. In 1977, Arledge became head of ABC News.

Arlen, Harold [Hyman Arluck] (1905–1986). U.S. composer. During his Broadway and HOLLYWOOD career, Arlen created some of the most enduring and popular tunes in the history of American popular music. He started out hoping to succeed as a singer but switched full time to composition in the late 1920s. His first hit was "Get Happy," written in collaboration with lyricist Ted Koehler. Among their other hits were "I Love A Parade" and "Stormy Weather." During the Great Depression, Arlen left Broadway for Hollywood, where he collaborated with E.Y. Harburg on the songs for *The Wizard of Oz*. Arlen won an Oscar in 1939 for that film's "Over the Rainbow." He was nominated for five other songs, including "Blues in the Night" and "That Old Black Magic."

Armani, Giorgio (1935–). Italian fashion designer, known for work that is characterized by a quality of casual elegance, a quality that has even been described as "over-serious." Armani's educational background included two years of medical school followed by military service. In the 1950s he took a job designing windows for La Rinascente, moving into buying and then to fashion design. He was associated with La Rinascente until he established his own design studio in 1970, producing designs for various manufacturers. In 1975 he founded his own label. He now operates a chain of shops, designs leatherware for Mario Valentino and has even designed uniforms for the Italian Air Force. His style depends heavily on the traditional detailing of men's clothing, adapting that vocabulary to jackets and skirts for women with a reserved, tailored dignity. He was the winner of a 1979 Neiman-Marcus Award.

Armenian Massacres of 1909. In April 1909 thousands of Armenians were killed by Turks in Cilicia, present-day southern Turkey, on the order of Sultan ABDUL HAMID II. The massacres were reprisals for Armenian revolutionary activity. The U.S. and other major powers intervened to stop the slaughter. (See also YOUNG TURKS.)

Armenian Massacres of 1915–23. Armenian revolutionaries, hoping to achieve independence, captured the Ottoman fortress of Van, in the east of the empire, on April 20, 1915. Aided by the Russians, they held the fortress until August, when Turks regained control. The YOUNG TURK government declared the Armenian people dangerous, accused them of helping Russian invaders in WORLD WAR I, and ordered them killed or deported. About 1 million Armenians fled or were killed, and 600,000 died of starvation, disease and exhaustion during forced marches through swamps and deserts of Syria and Mesopotamia. Many were massacred when they could go no farther.

Armory Show [International Exposition of Modern Art]. Popularly known as the Armory Show, the International Exposition of Modern Art was held February 15 to March 15, 1913, in the 69th Regiment Armory in New York City. It introduced modern art in America. Organized by the Association of American Painters and Sculptors (founded in 1911), the show provided an outlet for artists ignored by the academically dominated shows usually presented, and introduced Americans to the European art movements of FAUVISM and CUBISM. Approximately 1,000 American artists, including John SLOAN and Maurice PRENDERGAST, and 500 Europeans, such as Pablo PICASSO and Paul Cezanne, were represented. Although the public and the press ridiculed and condemned many of the paintings and sculptures, the show became a watershed in the development of American art.

Armstrong, Edwin (1890–1954). American inventor, radio pioneer. Armstrong received his bachelor of electrical engineering from Columbia University, New York City, in 1913 and taught there from 1934 to 1954. He is best known for developing the regenerative or feedback circuit (1912) and superheterodyne circuit (1918) that formed the basic design for AM radios. In 1933 Armstrong invented the frequency modulation (FM) technique, which reduced static and improved radio reception. Patent disputes over his inventions marred his later years, and in 1954 he committed suicide.

Armstrong, Henry [born Henry Jackson] (1912–1988). American boxer, the only man to have held three world titles simultaneously. In 1938, Armstrong reigned as the featherweight, lightweight and welterweight champion. He was inducted into boxing's Hall of Fame in 1954. He suffered a series of illnesses in his later years, some of which doctors suspected were caused by the many punches he had taken.

Armstrong, (Daniel) Louis (1900–1970). American jazz musician. Born in New Orleans, Armstrong began playing the cornet at the age of 13 in the Waifs' Home band in his native city. He subsequently (1918–21) became a soloist with various New Orleans and Mississippi riverboat bands. He moved to Chicago in 1922 and gained recognition as a trumpet player with King OLIVER, later soloing with Fletcher HENDERSON in New York. Armstrong returned to Chicago in 1925 and organized his own band, the Hot Five. He made the first of many successful European tours in 1932 and gained the nickname of "Satchmo," a London critic's mispelling of the earlier appellation "Satchelmouth." Armstrong made a number of memorable recordings and became a familiar figure at jazz festivals and on television. An enormously popular musician, he was known for his brilliant improvisational style with the cornet and trumpet and for his gravelly-voiced "scat" singing. His autobiography, *Satchmo*, was published in 1954.

Armstrong, Neil Alden (1930–). U.S. astronaut and the first man on the moon. He received his pilot's license at the age of 16. A naval air cadet at Purdue University, he was called to active duty in the Korean War. He received the Air Medal three times for his 78 combat missions. He returned to Purdue where he graduated in 1955. In 1962 he was accepted as a NASA pilot. On his first space flight in 1966, he commanded Gemini 8 and performed the first manual docking maneuver in space. He commanded the APOLLO 11 flight, and on July 10, 1969, he landed the lunar landing module on the moon's surface. As the first man to set foot on a non-terrestrial surface, he made one of the notable comments of all time when he declared: "That's one small step for (a) man, one giant leap for mankind." With his companion Edwin E. ALDRIN, he set up experiments on the moon and gathered a quantity of moon material. In 1970 Armstrong resigned from the astronaut program and became a NASA administrator. In 1971 he joined the faculty of the University of Cincinnati.

Army-McCarthy Hearings. Soon after the end of World War II, the U.S. found itself in the grip of an anticommunist hysteria that became known as MCCARTHYISM, in tribute to the senator from Wisconsin. Like the PALMER RAIDS that followed World War I, many individuals were unfairly labeled as communists or FELLOW TRAVELERS and careers and lives were ruined as a result. Although Joseph R. MCCARTHY's tactics were brutal he initially enjoyed broad popular support because of his seemingly patriotic opposition to COMMUNISM. McCarthy met his own downfall in 1953 at televised hearings in which the senator attempted to implicate the U.S. Army as harboring subversives. McCarthy was aided by his chief counsel, attorney Roy COHN, who held a personal grudge against the Army because of its perceived abuse of his friend G. David Schine. McCarthy and Cohn, relishing the spotlight, turned the proceeding into a televised witchhunt. But McCarthy's antics and bullying of witnesses soured the public who came to admire Army counsel Joseph Welch. The most memorable moment occurred when McCarthy accused Welch himself of employing subversives, and Welch shot back asking McCarthy "have you no sense of decency at long last?" After the hearings McCarthy's power and prestige waned and in late 1954 he was censured by the full Senate.

Arnaz, Desi [Desiderio Alberto Arnaz y de Acha 3rd] (1917–1986). Cuban-born entertainer and producer. He and his first wife, Lucille BALL, designed, starred in and produced the pioneering TELEVISION comedy series "I LOVE LUCY." The show dominated the U.S. airwaves from 1951 to 1957 and continues to entertain in syndication throughout the world. In the show Arnaz played Ricky Ricardo, a bandleader bedeviled by his wife's attempts to break into show business. The couple, married for 20 years, built a show business empire called Desilu Productions. They were divorced in 1960. After selling his interest in Desilu to Ball, Arnaz devoted himself to raising thoroughbred horses.

Arness, James (1923–). American television and movie actor. Arness (originally spelled Aurness) began his movie career after working in advertising. He played minor roles in such movies as *The Thing* in 1951 before creating the role of Marshal

Louis Armstrong, "Satchmo," hitting a high note.

Matt Dillon on television's long-running dramatic series, "Gunsmoke" (1955–1975). Arness, six feet seven inches in height, was suggested for the role by John WAYNE. From February 12, 1978, to April 23, 1979, Arness played the role of Zeb Macahan in the television series *How the West Was Won.*

Arnheim, Rudolf (1904–). Theorist, teacher, and writer in the field of Gestalt perception often called "experimental aesthetics." His 1954 book, *Art and Visual Perception,* deals with such concepts as balance, form, light, color, tension, and expression and their significance in architecture and design as well as in the fine arts of painting and sculpture.

Arnhem. Netherlands port on the lower Rhine River. In September 1944, during WORLD WAR II, it was the target of a major Allied airborne and armored offensive, led by British General Bernard MONTGOMERY, that was designed to capture the Rhine River bridges and drastically shorten the war—a tragically bungled operation. Arnhem was not taken by the Allies until April 1945.

Arno, Peter (1904–1968). American cartoonist. Born Curtis Arnoux Peters in Rye, N.Y., he attended Yale University. He became famous for his cartoons, principally published in THE NEW YORKER. Heavily outlined with spikey expressive lines, the charcoal and watercolor drawings cleverly portray New York society, from high to low life, from the flapper-era '20s to the hippie-filled '60s. Recurrent in his delightful cast of characters were pompous businessmen, endearing drunks, overstuffed socialites and bosomy young things. Among his cartoon collections are *Peter Arno's Parade* (1929), *Man in the Shower* (1944), *Sizzling Platter* (1949) and *Lady in the Shower* (1967).

Arnold, Henry Harley "Hap" (1886–1950). American Army and Air Force general. Born in Gladwyn, Pennsylvania, Arnold attended West Point, graduating in 1907. He took flying lessons from Orville Wright (see WRIGHT BROTHERS), and for the next three decades he advanced in the Army Air Corps, finally becoming chief of the corps in 1938. Arnold was long a believer in the strategic importance of air power, and in the years preceding WORLD WAR II he aggressively maximized the Air Corps' combat readiness despite a sharply limited budget. At his urging, American airplane manufacturers increased their production capacity six-fold during this period, and the Air Corps' pilot-training program greatly expanded its capacity through Arnold's scheme of sending pilots to civilian training programs. In World War II, Arnold was commander of the U.S. Army Air Force and played an instrumental role in planning the Allied war effort. In 1944, he was promoted to general of the army. In 1947, due largely to Arnold's lobbying, the Air Force was made an independent branch of the armed forces, and in 1949, Arnold was named the first general of the Air Force.

Arnoldson, Klas (Pontus) (1844–1916). Swedish journalist and peace activist. Born in Goteborg, he was a railway stationmaster who was self-taught in many disciplines. During the 1870s he began to write articles that stressed individual conscience and freedom of thought. In 1881 he decided to devote all his time to journalism and the promotion of world peace. The following year he was elected to parliament, where he advocated neutrality and served until 1887. He edited a number of progressive journals and wrote several novels and many widely read books on peace and religion. One of the most influential figures in the European peace movement, he was important in preventing war with Norway after the Norwegian parliament voted for independence in 1905. In 1908 Arnoldson shared the NOBEL PRIZE for peace with the Danish pacifist Fredrik BAJER.

Arno River. River that rises in Italy's northern Apennines and flows westward into the Ligurian Sea. From June to August 1944, during WORLD WAR II, it saw heavy fighting in the course of the Allied push toward Rome.

Aron, Jean-Paul (1925–1988). French writer and philosopher. Aron was the nephew of philosopher Raymond ARON and member of a distinguished Alsace family. Aron taught philosophy at the universities of Tourcoing and Lille and wrote books on the social manners and mores of 19th-century France. He also wrote novels and plays, and contributed to the newspapers *Le Matin* and *Le Monde.* One of the first public figures in France to admit that he was suffering from AIDS, he said on French television that he would never have admitted he was homosexual had he not suffered from AIDS.

Aron, Raymond (Claude) (1905–1983). French political theorist, sociologist, historical philosopher, writer and teacher.

During WORLD WAR II, after the Germans occupied FRANCE, he escaped to England and became editor of *La France Libre,* the official newspaper of Charles DE GAULLE's FREE FRENCH government-in-exile. After the war he was a political columnist for *Le Figaro* for 30 years (1947–77), then served on the editorial board of the weekly *L'Express* (1977–83), for which he also wrote a regular column. Politically right of center, Aron championed individual freedom above all else and vigorously opposed COMMUNISM and TOTALITARIANISM. He carried on a well-known, long-standing antagonistic relationship with the French philosopher and writer Jean-Paul SARTRE. He wrote more than 30 books including *Main Currents in Sociological Thought* (1965).

Arp, Jean (Hans) (1887–1966). French painter, sculptor and poet. A student at the Weimar Academy (1905–07) and the Academie Julien, Paris (1908), he was associated with the BLAUE REITER group in Germany, exhibiting with them in 1913. In 1916 he was a cofounder of the DADA movement, contributing art and poetry to Dada publications. From 1919 to 1920, he worked on Dadaist projects with Max ERNST and in 1925 he collaborated with El LISSITZKY on *The Isms of Art,* a survey of contemporary art. The following year he moved to Meudon near Paris and became a member of the Surrealist group (1926–30). Arp is known for his inventive abstract work in many media—painted reliefs, collages, cut-outs, basreliefs and sculptures in the round. He is best remembered for the sculptures he began about 1930, works called "Concretions" that are richly organic in form. Represented in many museum collections, he is also noted for large commissioned works such as the wood relief executed for Harvard University in 1950 and the bronze created for the University of Caracas in 1953.

Arpino, Gerald (1928–). American dancer and choreographer. Born in New York City, Arpino studied with Mary Ann Wells and May O'Donnell. He was one of six dancers who, with Robert JOFFREY, formed the Joffrey Ballet in 1956. Now best known as a choreographer and, after Joffrey's death in 1989, as artistic director of the company, Arpino has set a distinctly contemporary stamp on ballet with such works as his rock ballet *Trinity* (1970), *Viva Vivaldi!* (1965) and *Italian Suite* (1983). He has also danced in and choreographed Broadway musicals, opera and worked for televison. In 1974 he received a Dance Magazine Award. Arpino is noted for his use of avant-garde music and the contemporary themes of his works.

Arras. Capital of France's Pas-de-Calais department, located on the Scarpe River. During WORLD WAR I, it was occupied by German forces and saw heavy fighting during the Allied offensive of April-May 1917.

Arrhenius, Svante August (1859–1929). Swedish physical chemist. Arrhenius originally went to Uppsala University to study chemistry, changing later to physics. He transferred to Stockholm in 1881 to do research under the physicist Erik Edlund, working initially on electrical polarization and then on the conductivity of solutions (electrolytes). This work won Arrhenius a high international reputation but only limited acclaim in Sweden. Despite this he returned to Stockholm in 1891 as lecturer at the Technical Institute and in 1895 became professor there. In 1903 he was awarded the NOBEL PRIZE for chemistry, and in 1905 he became the director of the Nobel Institute, a post he held until shortly before his death.

Arrhenius was a man of wide-ranging intellect. Besides developing his work on solutions, in later life he worked on cosmogony and serum therapy, being especially interested in the relation between toxins and antitoxins. He also investigated the GREENHOUSE EFFECT by which carbon dioxide regulates atmospheric temperature and calculated the changes that would have been necessary to have produced the Ice Ages.

Arromanches-les-Bains. Village on the English Channel, in France's Calvados department. During WORLD WAR II, as part of the June 6, 1944, D-day offensive, it was taken by landing Allied forces and transformed into an artificial harbor that served as a key supply conduit.

Artaud, Antonin (1896–1948). French playwright, poet, actor and theoretician of the theater. Artaud, who has attained a legendary status as a personification of the mad, tortured artist, ended his life in an insane asylum after a long, creative career that spanned many genres. In the 1920s Artaud won renown both as a Surrealist poet, whose best work was collected in *Art and Death* (1929), and as a powerful film actor, notably in his role as a monk in *The Passion of Joan of Arc* (1928) by Danish director Carl DREYER. But Artaud was drawn first and foremost to the theater, writing several plays, including *The Cenci* (1935), as well as a theoretical work, *The Theater and Its Double* (1938), which advocated what has become known as "The Theater of Cruelty"—an impassioned, emotive style of dramatic presentation that rejects all moralizing and censorship and aims for truthful depiction of all dimensions of the human spirit.

Art Brut. A name originated by the French painter Jean DUBUFFET to designate art produced by persons with no connection to the societally established worlds of art and culture. Dubuffet amassed a collection of over 5,000 works of Art Brut, which he donated in 1972 for permanent showing in the Chateau de Beaulieu in Lausanne, France. The creators of these Art Brut works were predominantly prisoners, hermits, psychiatric hospital residents—in short, societal outsiders. Dubuffet claimed that their works represented "pure invention" as opposed to the influence-laden techniques of officially recognized art. Dubuffet denied that Art Brut represented a form of "psychiatric art," insisting that "there is no art of the insane any more than there is an art of dyspeptics." The common threads of Art Brut, according to Dubuffet, were a disinterest in prevailing aesthetic standards and a focus on expression of vital personal crises.

Art Deco. Name given to an ornately fashionable mode of interior decoration and product design that was highly popular in both America and Europe in the 1920s and 1930s. The name Art Deco arose from the Exposition Internationale des Arts Decoratifs et Industriels Modernes, held in Paris in 1925, which marked the debut of the Art Deco style. Art Deco emphasizes geometric patterns that are lavishly stylized by means of intricate tracery and ornamental details. Originally, Art Deco designs were noted for their use of rare and expensive materials such as marble, ivory, jade and lacquer. But in the 1930s Depression era, its focus shifted from fine material workmanship to dramatic design impact achieved with ordinary materials. Art Deco designs were most prominently used in public lobbies and railway stations of the era. The French ocean liner NORMANDIE was also a crowning achievement of the Art Deco style.

Art Nouveau. A decorative style that was highly popular in Europe and America from the Gay Nineties era to the outbreak of World War I. Art Nouveau, which was utilized both in architecture and in product design, was distinguished by its delicate craftsmanship and its use of organic design forms such as fruits, flowers and twining leaves. It first emerged in England as an offshoot of the Arts and Crafts movement led by William Morris, although it derives its name from an 1895 exhibition held at the L'Art Nouveau gallery in Paris. The famous Tiffany lamps and stained glass windows produced in America are the most well-known examples of the Art Nouveau style. The Spaniard Antonio Gaudi is the most famous Art Nouveau architect. Art Nouveau, while predominantly influential in the applied arts, also showed itself in the fields of painting and book illustration, most notably in the works of Aubrey Beardsley.

Artois. Area in northeastern France that during WORLD WAR I was a scene of heavy trench warfare. Between 1914 and 1916 three bloody, inconclusive battles were fought around the town of Arras. A ridge near Vimy was captured and recaptured three times. During the second battle French forces incurred over 3,000 casualties in 10 minutes. Between May 9 and June 18, 1915, the French lost 102,000 men. Both sides incurred heavy shelling and gas attacks.

Arts Council of Great Britain. Established in 1946 by Royal Charter, the Arts Council was developed to promote high standards in the arts and to foster public appreciation and accessibility throughout Britain. The Arts Council evolved from the wartime Council of the Encouragement of Music and the Arts (CEMA). It receives its grant directly from the goverment and has contributed to the abolition of weekly repertory, the maintenance of relatively low-priced seats and the development of new works of writing, music and architecture. In the 1970s regional and local arts councils took more responsibility for supporting small-scale, community and young people's productions. Under the government of Prime Minister Margaret THATCHER, the Arts Council budget was severely cut, and the government suggested that the council look to corporate donations. In 1987, due largely to a noisy arts lobby and a government response to charges of philistinism, a modest increase was announced. Some critics suggested that the Arts Council should be abolished and the subsidy handed out by the Office of Arts and Libraries; arts organizations strongly oppose this idea.

Artsybashev, Mikhail Petrovich (1878–1927). Russian novelist, essayist and playwright. His novel *Sanin* (1907) was one of the first in Russia to include a frank discussion of sex. Other works include *Breaking Point* (1915) and *War* (1918). He left Russia following the Russian Revolution.

Aruba. Island in the Netherlands Antilles, off the northwest coast of Venezuela; a key refining and shipping center for Venezuelan oil since 1925. In February and April 1942, during WORLD WAR II, its refineries were shelled by German submarines.

Arup, Sir Ove (1895–). English engineer, educated in Germany and Denmark. Arup was a consultant to Berthold Lubetkin and the Tecton group, architects, when they were designing the Highgate flats and the penguin pool at the London Zoo. Arup helped design the Sydney Opera House by Jorn Utzon. His bridge in Durham, England, is a fine example of the elegance of his work.

Arusha Declaration. A 1967 call by Tanzanian President Julius NYERERE to develop TANZANIA's national economy through state ownership but locally administered village planning and for the Tanzanian people to emulate his own simple life-style.

ASCAP [American Society of Composers, Authors & Publishers]. Founded in 1914, this New York City-based professional association licenses nondramatic rights of members' musical compositions and apportions royalties to its members from public performances. The organization currently maintains 20 branch offices in the United States and serves 35,000 composers, lyricists and music publishers.

Asch, Moses (1905–1986). U.S. record producer. He founded Folkways Records in 1947 and ran the company until his death. Folkways recordings of such artists as LEADBELLY, Woody GUTHRIE, and Brownie McGhee helped spark the U.S. folk music revival of the 1950s and 60s. The company's catalog consisted of more than 2,000 albums that Asch kept in print. Beyond international folk music, notable titles included *Agitprop Music* and *Sounds of North American Frogs.*

Aschoff, Karl Albert Ludwig (1866–1942). German pathologist. Educated at Bonn, Berlin, and Strasbourg, Aschoff was later professor of pathological anatomy first at Marburg (1903–06) and then at Freiburg, where he remained for the rest of his career. He carried out investigations of a number of human pathological conditions, including jaundice, appendicitis, cholecystitis, tuberculosis and thrombosis. In 1904 he described the inflammatory nodules located in the muscle of the heart and associated with rheumatism (*Aschoff's bodies*). He recognized the bacteria-engulfing activity of the phagocytes in various tissues and named them the reticuloendothelial system. Students from all over the world attended the pathological institute that Aschoff built up at Freiburg.

Aseyev, Nikolai Nikolayevich (1889–1963). Russian poet. His early works include *Night Flute* (1914), *Letorey* (1915) and *Queen of the Cinema* (early 1920s). In 1923 he joined the literary LEF (Left Front); although later works, such as *The Steel Nightingale* (1922), *Twenty-Six* (1923), *The Sverdlov Storm* (1924) and *Semyon Proskakov* (1926), contained a political element, they still expressed much romanticism.

Asgeirsson, Asgeir (1894–1972). President of ICELAND (1952–68). Asgeirsson was a member of the Icelandic parliament from 1923 to 1952. While in parliament he served as minister of finance (1931–34), prime minister (1932–34) and governor of the International Monetary Fund (IMF, or WORLD BANK, 1946–52).

Ashbery, John (1927–). American poet and art critic. Raised on a farm in upstate New York, Ashbery attended Harvard, Columbia and New York University. In 1955 he went to Paris on a Fulbright scholarship to translate French poetry. A contributor (1955–65) to *Art News* and the Paris *Herald Tribune,* he later became art critic for *Newsweek.* He was associated with the avant-garde New York School of poets. His first book, *Some Trees* (1956), won the Yale Younger Poets prize. His reputation was enhanced when *Self-Portrait in a Convex Mirror* (1975) won the PULITZER PRIZE, the National Book Award and the National Book Critics Circle Award. Later collections include *Houseboat Days, As We Know* and *A Wave* (1984). He was cowinner of the 1985 BOLLINGEN PRIZE. His playful, dreamlike and often obscure poems have often baffled readers and critics alike. Ashbery is sometimes compared to Wallace STEVENS.

For further reading:
Kalstone, David, *Five Temperaments: Elizabeth Bishop, Robert Lowell, James Merrill, Adrienne Rich, John Ashbery.* New York: Norton, n.d.

Ashcan School. See the EIGHT.

Ashcroft, Peggy (Edith Margaret Emily) (1907–1991). British actress. One of the greatest actresses of the British theater, Ashcroft made her acting debut in James Barrie's *Dear Brutus* at the Birmingham Repertory Theatre in 1926. Many of her theatrical triumphs were in Shakespearean roles opposite Sir John Gielgud: Juliet in *Romeo and Juliet* (1935) and Beatrice in *Much Ado About Nothing* (1950), among others. Other acclaimed performances were in Chekhov's *Three Sisters* (1936–37), Goetz's *The Heiress* (1949) and Hellman's *Watch on the Rhine* (1980). A founder member and a director of the ROYAL SHAKESPEARE COMPANY, she played Margaret of Anjou in their monumental production of *The Wars of the Roses* (1963–64).

For further reading:
Billington, Michael, *Peggy Ashcroft.* London: David & Charles, 1990.

Ashe, Arthur Robert (1943–). U.S. tennis player. In 1968, while still an amateur, Ashe became the first black man to win the U.S. Open title. He turned professional the following year and became a consistent winner, leading an overpowering U.S. Davis Cup team from 1968 to 1972. In 1975, he became the first black man ever to take the Wimbledon singles title, defeating the much-favored Jimmy CONNORS. Ashe retired after a heart attack in 1979 and was named captain of the Davis Cup team in 1980. He went on to a career in tennis broadcasting.

Ashkenazy, Vladimir (1937–). Russian pianist and conductor. Born to pianist parents in Gorki, Ashkenazy began piano lessons at six, made his debut at seven and studied at the Central Music School, Moscow, and the Moscow State Conservatory. He achieved international prominence when he won the second prize in the Chopin Competition, Warsaw, in 1956 and first prize in the Queen Elisabeth Competition, Brussels, in 1957. His busy touring schedule included an American debut in 1958. In 1963 he and his wife left the U.S.S.R. They settled in Reykjavik, Iceland, in 1968. He became a citizen of Iceland in 1972. As a pianist, Ashkenazy is noted for his sensitive, poetic yet energetic style and for a repertoire that includes Beethoven, Brahms, Mozart, RACHMANINOFF, SIBELIUS and PROKOFIEV. He made his conducting debut in Iceland in 1973 and has since turned his attention to conducting while remaining an active pianist. Ashkenazy's autobiography is titled *Beyond Frontiers.*

Ashley, Laura (1926–1985). Welsh-born British designer. Ashley's romantic, Victorian-inspired clothes and home furnishings have found favor with "Sloane Rangers" and romantics the world over. In 1953 she and her husband, Bernard, set up the company that bore her name by printing fabric on the kitchen table of their London home. The business grew into a global enterprise headquartered in Carno, Wales, with 4,000 employees, some 200 stores and annual sales of $130 million. Since its inception, chairman Bernard Ashley has been in charge of the business aspects of the company while Laura Ashley has created its designs.

Ashton, Frederick (1906–1988). English dancer and choreographer. Considered

Vladimir Ashkenazy directing the Royal Philharmonic in the prestigious Grand Hall of the Moscow Conservatory.

Britain's greatest choreographer, Ashton was born in Ecuador of English extraction and was inspired to become a dancer after seeing ballerina Anna PAVLOVA in 1917. He began to study dance in 1924 with Leonide MASSINE and Marie RAMBERT in London, and took up choreography shortly thereafter. In 1935 he joined the Vic-Wells Ballet (now the ROYAL BALLET) and began his successful association with ballerina Margot FONTEYN for whom he created leading roles in many of his ballets during the next 25 years (*Ondine* in 1958, *Marguerite and Armand* in 1963). Some of Ashton's well-known ballets are *Illuminations* (1950), *Romeo and Juliet* (1955), *La Fille Mal Gardee* (1960) and *Monotones I* (1965). Known for his sure poetic touch in delicately evoking scenes and moods, he helped develop a distinctly British balletic style marked by elegance, lyricism and graciousness. As a dancer he achieved his greatest acclaim in character roles, such as Carabosse in *Sleeping Beauty*. He also served as director of the Royal Ballet from 1963 to 1970. In 1950 Ashton was made a Commander of the Order of the British Empire and, in 1962, was knighted; he was also a recipient of the Legion d'Honneur.

Ashton-Warner, Sylvia (Constance) (1908–1984). New Zealand author and educator. Born in Stratford, New Zealand, she was educated at Wairapa College and the Teacher's College, Auckland. Her novels describe her experiences teaching Maori children. Her first and best known book, *Spinsters* (1959), was the basis of a British film, *Two Loves* (1961). Other work includes the novels *Bell Call* (1964), *Three* (1970) and an autobiography, *Myself* (1967). Ashton-Warner also published poetry and short stories under the name Sylvia Henderson, her husband's surname.

Asia, Soviet Central. Region of the U.S.S.R. Soviet Central Asia embraces the Kazakh SSR (Soviet Socialist Republic), the Uzbek SSR, the Turkmen SSR, the Tadzhik SSR and the Kirghiz SSR. Until 1917 Russian Central Asia was divided politically into the khanate of Khiva, the emirate of Bokhara and the governor-generalship of Turkestan. In the summer of 1919 the authority of the Soviet government became definitely established in these regions. The khan of Khiva was deposed in February 1920, and a People's Soviet Republic was set up. In August 1920 the emir of Bokhara suffered the same fate, and a similar regime was set up in Bokhara. The former governor-generalship of Turkestan was constituted an autonomous Soviet socialist republic within the Russian Soviet Federated Socialist Republic on April 11, 1921.

In the autumn of 1924 the Soviets of the Turkestan, Bokhara and Khiva republics decided to redistribute the territories of these republics on a nationality basis; at the same time Bokhara and Khiva became socialist republics. The redistribution was completed in May 1925, when the new states of Uzbekistan, Turkmenistan and Tadzhikistan and several autonomous regions were established. The remaining districts of Turkestan populated by Kazakhs were united with Kazakhstan. Kirghizia, until then a part of the Russian Soviet Federal Socialist Republic, was established as a union republic in 1936.

Asimov, Isaac (1920–). Popular American writer whose more than 300 books embrace popular science, history, literary criticism, crime fiction and science fiction. His family emigrated from Russia to the U.S. when he was three years old. He grew up near New York City, where he still lives. Throughout most of his life he has been torn between careers in science education—he was an associate professor of biochemistry at Boston University—and professional writing—his early enthusiasm for pulp magazines led to his first story sale in 1938. He has been able to combine both interests in his numerous science fiction stories. Whether his subject is fact or fancy—the action of enzymes, the plays of Shakespeare or the flight of rocketships—he insists on accuracy. "I am a working scientist," he says, "I don't want to write poetically; I want to write clearly." It is enough if his stories "stimulate curiosity and the desire to know." Two ongoing series dominate his fiction. His "ROBOT" stories and novels, including *I, Robot* (1950) and *Caves of Steel* (1954), brought dignity to a cliched genre. "Metal men" stereotypes were replaced with the more thoughtful, mature images of the "positronic robots," machines that could be "the servants, friends, and allies of humanity." His Foundation novels, for which he won a Hugo Award in 1966, are a "psychohistory" of the rise and fall of future Galactic Empires.

For further reading:

Asimov, Isaac, *Asimov on Science Fiction.* New York: Doubleday, 1979.

Aslan, Ana (1897–1988). Romanian gerontologist who developed a controversial drug called Gerovital H3 that she claimed could restore youth. Among those rumored to have taken her treatments were such heads of state as Charles DE GAULLE, Nikita KHRUSHCHEV and Indira GANDHI, and such show business luminaries as Lillian GISH and Marlene DIETRICH. Most scientists outside Romania remained unconvinced that Gerovital had any rejuvenating effect. Detractors pointed out that the drug was simply a form of procaine, which under the brand name Nov-

Isaac Asimov.

ocain had been in use for decades as a local anesthetic.

Asmara [Asmera]. Capital of ETHIOPIA's province of ERITREA, located on the Hamasen Plateau near the Red Sea. In 1900, it was annexed by Italy as part of its colony of Eritrea. During WORLD WAR II, it was captured by the British (in 1941) and was held by them until it was annexed by Ethiopia in 1952. For a time, it served as the site of a U.S. military communications base. In February 1972, it was the scene of a mutiny by officers of the Ethiopian army, which sparked the overturn of the monarchy of Emperor HAILE SELASSIE and the implementation of a socialist regime.

Asplund, Erik Gunnar (1885–1940). Swedish architect. Born in Stockholm, he studied architecture at the city's Academy of Art. From 1917 to 1920 he edited the influential magazine *Arkitektur*. His early neoclassical style is evident in his design of the Stockholm City Library (1924–28). Asplund's most celebrated contributions to architecture were the pavilions he designed for the Stockholm Exhibition of 1930, Sweden's first foray into the INTERNATIONAL STYLE. He is known for his spare and elegant buildings and accessories, designs that contributed greatly to the development of Swedish Modern architecture.

Asquith, Herbert Henry [Earl of Oxford and Asquith (1925)] (1852–1928). British statesman, prime minister (1908–16). He was educated at Oxford and became a London barrister in 1876. Entering politics, he was elected to Parliament as a Liberal in 1886. Recognized as a persuasive and powerful speaker, he gained fame as a counsel to Irish nationalist Charles Stewart Parnell (1846–91) and a supporter of the South African War. Asquith served as home secretary (1892–95) and chancellor of the exchequer (1905–08). Succeeding Sir Henry CAMPBELL-BANNERMAN as prime minister in 1908, Asquith presided over a number of important social reforms. These included health and unemployment insurance, old-age pensions and trade union protection. He also set the nation on a program of naval expansion. In order to finance his programs, his government levied heavy taxes on wealthy Britons. When the House of Lords rejected his budget, Asquith ultimately fought back with the Parliament Act of 1911, which ended the Lords' veto power.

During his ministry, Asquith also faced problems with militant woman suffragists and socialists and with the Irish HOME RULE question. Asquith brought Britain into WORLD WAR I in 1914, but he did not prove a vigorous wartime leader and he resigned in 1916. Succeeded by David LLOYD GEORGE, Asquith headed the waning LIBERAL PARTY until 1926, entering the House of Lords in 1925.

Assad, Hafez al- (1930–). Syrian general and president. Born at Quaradah in a minority Alawite (Shiite) sect, Hafez al-Assad was trained as an air force pilot in the U.S.S.R. He rose to the rank of air force commander in 1964 and became defense minister in 1966. As a member of the nationalist faction of the Ba'ath Party (pro-PLO, anti-ISRAEL and opposed to close Soviet ties), he instigated the November 1970 coup, became prime minister in 1970 and president in 1971. His attempts to merge SYRIA with IRAQ failed, and hostility developed between these two nations, especially after Saddam HUSSEIN became Iraqi president. Assad was reelected in 1978 and 1985. He also heads the Ba'ath Party and the Syrian armed forces. The 1986 Syrian involvement in terrorism led to Great Britain's breaking off diplomatic relations and limited EUROPEAN COMMUNITY sanctions against Syria. Assad's relations with the West improved when he supported UNITED NATIONS action against Sadam Hussein and Iraq after Iraq's 1990 invasion of KUWAIT.

Hafez al-Assad.

Assam. Indian state bordered to the north by Bangladesh and to the south by Burma. The British East India Company took control of Assam in 1826, but it was not established as a separate province until 1919. It was the site of intense fighting between Japanese and Allied forces during WORLD WAR II. In 1950, it became a constituent state of India. It was invaded by Chinese troops in 1962. Rebellions on the part of various indigenous tribes led to the establishment of two separate and smaller states within Assam: Nagaland (in 1963) and Meghalaya (in 1971).

Assault (1943–1971). Thoroughbred racehorse. A son of Bold Venture, in 1946 Assault became the seventh Triple Crown winner in history, and was named three-year-old of the year. The following year saw three of the greatest racehorses ever—Assault, Armed and Stymie—battle for top money-winning honors, a title eventually taken by the six-year-old Stymie. Never entirely sound due to injuries suffered as a yearling, he retired in 1950 with a record of 42 starts, with 18 wins and finishing out of the money only 11 times. Retired to stud at the King Ranch, he was found to be sterile, but still enjoyed a lengthy retirement until his death in 1971.

Asser, Tobias (1838–1913). Dutch statesman, jurist and legal scholar. Asser served in a series of governmental posts in the latter half of the 19th century as a legal advisor and treaty negotiator. As a member of the Dutch Council of State, he presided over international law conferences at THE HAGUE in 1893, 1894, 1900 and 1904. He was instrumental in the formation of The Hague Permanent Court of Arbitration to which he was appointed in 1900. In 1911, Asser shared the NOBEL PRIZE for peace with Alfred FRIED.

As-Suwayda. Town in As-Suwayda province of Syria. First settled by the Romans, it has stood since the 10th century as the leading center of the DRUSE religious sect. During French Mandate rule (1921–42), it was the capital of the state of Jebel Druse. When the Druse revolted against French rule, they conducted a successful siege against As-Suwayda's French garrison, from July to September 1925, but were forced to relinquish their prize in 1926.

Astaire, Fred [Frederick Austerlitz] (1899–1987). American dancer and choreographer. Immortalized in films from *Top Hat* to *Carefree*, Nebraska-born Astaire began his career in a brother-sister vaudeville act at the age of eight. With his sister Adele he appeared on the Broadway and

Fred Astaire with dance partner and costar Ginger Rogers.

London stage in various musicals and revues, starting with *Over the Top* in 1917 and including the GERSHWIN *Funny Face* (1927). After his sister retired in 1932, he appeared in Cole PORTER's *Gay Divorce* (1932). In 1933 Astaire made his first film, *Dancing Lady,* and then was teamed with Ginger ROGERS in RKO's film, *Flying Down to Rio*—thus beginning a legendary partnership that was showcased in nine more films. In over 30 musical films Astaire sang and danced with other leading ladies, among them: Judy GARLAND (*Easter Parade,* 1948), Rita Hayworth (*You Were Never Lovelier,* 1942), Cyd Charisse (*The Band Wagon,* 1953) and Audrey Hepburn (*Funny Face,* 1957).

He starred in several award-winning television specials, and won acclaim as a dramatic actor in his later years, most notably in such films as *On the Beach* (1959) and *The Towering Inferno* (1974). As a singer, Astaire introduced many of the great songs of Irving BERLIN, Jerome KERN and George and Ira Gershwin, both on the stage and in movies. Considered one of the greatest dancers of the 20th century, Astaire was a perfectionist noted for his elegance and originality in choreography, and his canny grasp of the movie camera's possibilities. In 1949 Astaire received a special Academy Award "for his unique artistry and his contributions to the technique of musical pictures."

For further reading:

Astaire, Fred, *Steps in Time: An Autobiography.* New York: Harper & Row, 1988; first published, 1959.

Croce, Arlene, *The Fred Astaire and Ginger Rogers Book.* New York: Outerbridge, 1972.

Thomas, Bob, *Astaire: The Man, the Dancer.* New York: St. Martin, 1985.

Astbury, William Thomas (1889–1961). British X-RAY crystallographer and molecular biologist. In 1916 he won a scholarship to Cambridge University, to study chemistry, physics and mathematics, and graduated in 1921 after spending two years of the war doing X-ray work for the army. He then joined William Henry BRAGG's brilliant group of crystallographers, first at University College, London, and from 1923 at the Royal Institution. In 1928 he moved to the University of Leeds as lecturer in textile physics and by 1930 had produced an explanation of the extensibility of wool in terms of two keratin structures. A popular account of this work was given in *Fundamentals of Fibre Structure* (1933). The keratin structure established his reputation, and he quickly extended his studies to other fibers and proteins. This work laid the foundation for the X-ray structural investigations of hemoglobin and myoglobin. In 1935 Astbury began to study nucleic acids by X-ray crystallography, and in 1938 he and his research student Florence Bell produced the first hypothetical structure of DNA. In 1945 Astbury was appointed to the new chair of biomolecular structure at Leeds.

Aston, Francis William (1877–1945). British chemist and physicist. He was educated at Mason College, the forerunner of Birmingham University, where he studied chemistry. From 1898 until 1900 he did research on optical rotation under P.F. Frankland. He left Birmingham in 1900 to work in a Wolverhampton brewery for three years. During this time he continued with scientific research in a home laboratory, where he worked on the production of vacua for X-ray discharge tubes. This work came to the notice of J.H. Poynting of the University of Birmingham, who invited Aston to work with him. He remained at Birmingham until 1910 when he moved to Cambridge as research assistant to J.J. Thomson. He became a research fellow at Cambridge in 1920 and stayed there for the rest of his life, apart from the war years spent at the Royal Aircraft Establishment, Farnborough. Aston's main work, for which he received the NOBEL PRIZE for chemistry in 1922, was on the design and use of the mass spectrograph, which was used to clear up several outstanding problems and became one of the basic tools of the new atomic physics. Contained in Aston's work were the implications of atomic energy and destruction. He believed in the possibility of using nuclear energy and warned of the dangers. He lived just long enough to see the first ATOMIC BOMB dropped in August 1945.

Asturian Uprising of 1934. In Spain in the early 1930s political parties were polarized over powers to be granted the Roman Catholic Church. In 1934 the Socialist Party planned a nationwide general strike and various uprisings to prevent the pro-church CEDA from joining the government. On October 5, 1934, communist-oriented miners revolted in Asturias (northwestern Spain), occupying the city of Oviedo and the surrounding region, subsequently burning churches and killing about 40 people. Francisco FRANCO and another general brutally put down the uprising, killing 3,000 and capturing 35,000, who were tortured and tried in 1935. The ferocious suppression divided Spain, helping to precipitate the SPANISH CIVIL WAR (1936–39).

Asturias, Miguel Angel (1899–1974). Guatemalan novelist, poet, diplomat and journalist. As a student, Asturias was active in the overthrow of the dictator Manuel Estrada Cabrera; but in 1923 he was forced into exile. For five years he studied Mayan ethnology at the Sorbonne, meanwhile associating with SURREALISTS Andre BRETON and Paul ELUARD. *El senor presidente,* completed in 1930, was not published until 1946. Returning to Guatemala, he joined the diplomatic service and published *Hombres de maiz* (1949, *Men of Corn*). His Banana Trilogy—*Viento fuerte* (1950, *Strong Wind*), *El papa verde* (1954, *The Green Pope*) and *Los ojos de los enterrados* (1960, *The Eyes of the Interred*)—examined U.S. economic and political influence in Central America. In 1954 he again went into exile, first in Chile and Argentina, later in Italy. *Mulata de tal* (1963, *Mulata*) and *Maladron* (1969, *Bad Thief*) described the clash between Indian and European culture. His poetry includes *Alcazan* (1940), *Bolivar* (1955) and *Clarivigilia primaveral* (1965). In 1966 he received the Lenin Peace Prize and was named ambassador to France. He was awarded the NOBEL PRIZE for literature in 1967. His work marks the beginning of EL BOOM in Latin American literature.

Aswan Dam. On the Nile River, about 450 miles south of Cairo. Construction of this dam was central to NASSER's industrial and agricultural development program for EGYPT. Its construction appeared thwarted when the U.S. and Britain withdrew a promise of aid on July 20, 1956. Nasser retaliated by nationalizing the SUEZ CANAL on July 26, leading to the SUEZ CRISIS and Nasser's appeal to the U.S.S.R. for funds, which Egypt received until 1970. The huge lake created by the dam threatened the ancient archaeological site of Abu Simbel, whose massive temple and statues were moved to higher ground with U.S. aid.

Ataturk, Mustapha Kemal [born Mustapha Kemal] (1880–1938). Turkish statesman, reformer, founder and first president of the Republic of TURKEY. After attending the Military Academy at Constantinople, he advanced in the military and served as a leader in the Balkan Wars (1912–13) and World War I. He resigned from the army in 1919, and in 1920, after Britain formally occupied Turkey, he set up a provisional government. After the CHANAK CRISIS and the victory over the Greeks, he secured the revision of the Turkish peace settlement by the Treaty of LAUSANNE. He was elected the Turkish republic's first president in 1922. He abolished the caliphate in 1924 and started sweeping reforms of Turkish politics. His dictatorial regime secularized Turkey. In 1933 he was given the name "Ataturk" ("father of the Turks") by the National Assembly. His ideas inspired nationalism elsewhere in the MIDDLE EAST, notably in EGYPT under NASSER.

Kemal Ataturk.

The ancient and the modern worlds meet at the giant Aswan Dam.

Atget, Eugene (1856–1927). French photographer. Atget was a latecomer to photography, pursuing long stints as a stage actor and as a sailor before turning to photography at age 42. Atget is today regarded by critics as one of the pioneers of artistic photographic technique. Atget was not a self-conscious artist, but devoted himself primarily to commercial work. He is best remembered for his delicate, detailed renditions of the streets, parks and buildings of Paris, photographs noteworthy for their masterful use of light and their classical sense of order and proportion. A representative sampling from Atget's more than 10,000 photographs is included in *The Work of Atget,* published in three volumes (1981–1983). Berenice ABBOTT wrote a biography, *The World of Atget* (1964).

Atkinson, Brooks (1894–1984). American journalist, editor and theater critic. He graduated from Harvard in 1917, then served as assistant to the legendary H.T. Parker, music and drama critic for the *Boston Evening Transcript,* before moving to the *New York Times* in 1925. During his tenure at the *Times* (1925–60) he was considered "the conscience of the theater." He was also acclaimed as a foreign correspondent, receiving a Pulitzer Prize in 1947 for his articles on conditions in Moscow. Known for his wit, urbanity and candor, Atkinson declared that "to believe in the original principles of America is to be a dissenter." He was author of nearly a dozen books and an editor of the writings of Ralph Waldo Emerson and Henry David Thoreau.

Atlanta serial murders (1979–81). Killings of 29 young people in Atlanta, Ga. All those murdered were black and most were under the age of 20. An intensive manhunt included investigations by local and federal authorities as well as by the FBI. A 23-year-old Atlantan, Wayne B. Williams, was arrested in June 1981 and was convicted of two of the murders in February 1982. Although Williams continued to protest his innocence, the slayings stopped with his arrest.

Atlantic, Battle of the (1940–43). After the start of WORLD WAR II, Great Britain blockaded German-controlled Europe, but German U-boats (SUBMARINES) disrupted the sea lanes. U-boats in the North Atlantic torpedoed and sunk many merchant ships carrying food and materiel to Britain, thus forcing the need for food rationing in the British Isles in 1940. When the U.S. began LEND-LEASE shipments, U.S. naval vessels began patrolling the western Atlantic, while British Royal Air Force planes patrolled the east. Large convoys of American merchant ships assembled west of Iceland to be escorted across the Atlantic by British warships. After the U.S. destroyer *Reuben James* was sunk by a U-boat off Iceland (October 31, 1941), the U.S. Congress repealed the Neutrality Act, and U.S. ships armed themselves and entered war zones. In 1942 and early 1943 sinkings by U-boats increased when the Germans began hunting their targets in "wolf-packs" of 15 to 20 submarines. The British, however, had invented two devices that eventually turned the tables—high frequency direction finding and RADAR, both of which enabled the Allies to pinpoint the U-boats and sink them. So many submarines were sunk that the Germans could not disrupt shipping much after mid-1943, and the Allies soon controlled the sea lanes of the Atlantic and elsewhere. The name "Battle of the Atlantic" was coined by Winston CHURCHILL.

Atlantic Charter. A declaration of principles for a postwar world and shared democratic ideals that emerged from a meeting off Newfoundland between U.S. President Franklin D. ROOSEVELT and British Prime Minister Winston S. CHURCHILL on August 9–12, 1941. Among the principles agreed to by the U.S.S.R. and 14 other states at war with AXIS powers in September 1941 were: open seas, equal access to trade and raw materials, lives without fear and want, renunciation of force as a way of settling disputes and the creation of a means for securing world security, democratic government, the disarming of aggressors and the easing of the international arms burden.

Atlantic City. A city of 37,986 residents (1990) on the New Jersey shore, Atlantic City was a fashionable resort in the latter half of the 19th century. Tourism waned and the city's fortunes declined through-

Franklin Roosevelt and Winston Churchill during the signing of the Atlantic Charter.

out the 20th century. In 1976, the state legislature legalized gambling in Atlantic City in an attempt to revive the area's economy. Although more than a dozen casinos were built and thousands of new jobs were created, the hoped-for economic benefits were not felt by many of the city's residents.

atomic bomb development (1942–1945). The American project to develop an atomic bomb—which would derive its force from the release of energy through the process of the splitting (or fission) of the nuclei of a heavy chemical element—started on August 13, 1942, and changed the world completely. Shrouded in the utmost secrecy, the project involved some of the world's top scientists laboring in a few laboratories. The great Italian scientist Enrico FERMI was in charge of a program to unleash the power of the atom at the University of Chicago. Working with Nobel scientist Arthur COMPTON and others, Fermi built a "pile" consisting of aluminum and graphite in layers. At the final experiment, scientist George Weil withdrew the cadmium-plated control rod and by this action released and controlled the energy of the atom. The first chain reaction in nuclear fission was accomplished at 3.25 P.M. on December 2, 1942. The first atomic bomb was completed in 1945 after three additional years of research and an additional cost of $2 billion. The first experimental explosion of an atomic bomb occurred on July 16, 1945, near ALAMOGORDO, New Mexico. The first military use of the bomb came on August 6, 1945, when it was dropped on HIROSHIMA, Japan, and again on August 9, 1945, at NAGASAKI, Japan. The vast network laboring on the development of atomic energy later became known to the public by its codename, the MANHATTAN PROJECT.

Atsugi. Town in Japan's Kanagawa prefecture; site of the airbase where U.S. troops first landed on the Japanese homeland, on August 28, 1945, after the end of hostilities in WORLD WAR II.

AT&T [American Telephone & Telegraph Company]. American telecommunications corporation, headquartered in New York City. Incorporated in 1885, AT&T grew into the largest telecommunications company in the world and one of the largest corporations in the U.S.; the firm developed a virtual monopoly on telephone service in the U.S. A government lawsuit (1974) eventually forced AT&T to divest itself of its local companies. Since then, it has had to compete against other long-distance telephone companies. AT&T is the parent company to other corporations, including Bell Laboratories, a research and development arm of the firm.

At-Ta'if [Taif, Tayif]. Town in Hejaz, southeast of Mecca. A part of the OTTOMAN EMPIRE until 1916, it was captured in 1924 by King IBN SAUD of Saudi Arabia during his war against King Hussein of Hejaz. In 1934, it was the site of a treaty signing between King Ibn Saud and Yemeni peoples whom he had conquered in a six-week war.

Attica prison riot. A 1971 riot at Attica State Prison, east of Buffalo, New York, in which 28 prisoners and nine prison guards were killed. Over 1,000 prisoners rioted and took control of one-half of the facility. They also seized over 30 guards and other employees. The head of the state prison system negotiated with the riot's leaders who demanded reforms plus total amnesty for the prisoners. Governor Nelson ROCKEFELLER refused the prisoner demands that he personally join the negotiations and he rejected the call for total amnesty. After negotiations collapsed the prisoners displayed a number of hostages with knives held to their throats. State police stormed the prison and 28 prisoners and nine guards were killed. Although state officials initially claimed the guards had their throats slit by prisoners, a subsequent investigation revealed this to be false. In fact, all nine guards died from gunshots fired by the state police. Later investigations criticized prison officials and the governor for the entire affair, including the brutality and inadequate medical care afforded the prisoners after the riot.

Attlee, Clement (Richard) [1st Earl Attlee] (1883–1967). British statesman, prime minister (1945–51). Born into a middle-class family in Putney, Attlee attended Oxford University. He was admitted to the bar in 1906 and soon involved himself in social problems, lecturing at the London School of Economics and becoming a socialist in 1907. After service in WORLD WAR I, he was elected mayor of Stepney (1919–20) and became a Labour M.P. in 1922. He was a member of the Simon Commission on Indian government, visiting India in 1927 and becoming convinced of the justice of Indian independence. Attlee was a junior minister in the Labour government from 1930 to 1931 but refused to join the national government in 1931. He was elected LABOUR PARTY leader in 1935, strongly criticizing the foreign policies of the Conservative government. During WORLD WAR II he was a part of Winston CHURCHILL's coalition cabinet (1940–45). When Labour was victorious in the elections of 1945, Attlee became prime minister. Committed to radically changing the structure of British society in order to create a modicum of social equality, he instituted numerous WELFARE STATE reforms. These included the nationalization of the Bank of England, the railways, the bulk of public utilities and large industry, as well as the establishment of the NATIONAL HEALTH SERVICE. In addition, he was a leading force in granting independence to India, Pakistan, Ceylon and Burma. Maintaining Britain's alliance with the U.S, he also encouraged his nation's charter membership in NATO. After instituting an economic austerity program to deal with Great Britain's growing economic ills, he narrowly won the elections of 1950 but lost the elections of 1951. Attlee was leader of the opposition to the Conservative government until his retirement in 1955, when he was created an earl.

Clement Attlee

For further reading:

Haney, John, *Clement Attlee.* New York: Chelsea House, 1988.

Williams, Francis E., ed., *Twilight of Empire: Memoirs of Prime Minister Clement Attlee.* Westport, Conn.: Greenwood, 1978.

Atwood, Margaret (1939–). Canadian novelist, poet and feminist. Born in Ottawa, she published her first book of poetry, *Double Persephone,* in 1962; her first novel, *The Edible Woman,* appeared in 1969. Atwood's acute and often wry fiction reflects her concern with individual autonomy and the relations between men and women. *The Handmaid's Tale* (1986) describes a futuristic, totalitarian society in which women, ostensibly for their own protection, are relegated to specific, subservient roles; it was a highly acclaimed best seller. It was followed by *Cat's Eye.* Atwood also edited *The New Oxford Book of Canadian Verse in English* (1983).

Aubock, Carl (1924–). Austrian Modern architect and designer trained in Vienna and at the Massachusetts Institute of Technology. Aubock's work includes designs for furniture, metalware, ceramics, and glass as well as industrial products and sports equipment. A metal cocktail shaker of Aubock's design is in the design collection of the MUSEUM OF MODERN ART in New York. A number of his designs are produced and distributed by the Vienna firm operated by his family.

Auchinleck, Sir Claude John Eyre (1884–1981). British general. He began his long army career in 1904, joining the Indian army and serving in the Middle East during World War I. In WORLD WAR II he was briefly (1940) commander of British forces at Narvik, Norway, but was soon posted as British commander-in-chief, first in India (1941), then in the Middle East (1941–42). While he gained ground in

Libya in a 1941 offensive, he was pushed back to Egypt in ROMMEL's 1942 counter-offensive. As head of the Eighth Army, Auchinleck was victorious at the battle of EL ALAMEIN (July 1–3, 1942). He resumed the post of commander-in-chief in India (1943–47), where he aided in the transition to independence.

Auden, W(ystan) H(ugh) (1907–1973). Anglo-American poet, playwright, critic, translator and editor. The son of a physician, Auden was born in York, England. Despite an early interest in practical science, as a student at Oxford in the 1920s he declared his intention to become a great poet, and became the leading member of an influential left-wing literary circle that included Christopher ISHERWOOD, Cecil DAY LEWIS, Stephen SPENDER and Louis MACNEICE. After graduating, he briefly taught school; thereafter, he spent most of his time traveling, writing and solidifying his reputation as the most brilliant poet of his generation. He collaborated with Isherwood on *The Dog Beneath the Skin* (1935) and *The Ascent of F6* (1936) and with MacNeice on *Letters from Iceland* (1937). In 1935 he married Erika Mann, daughter of Thomas MANN, to provide her with a British passport. His travels to Spain and China in 1937–38 yielded *Spain* (1937) and *Journey to a War* (1939). In 1939 he moved to the U.S., where he spent the years of WORLD WAR II; he was naturalized as a U.S. citizen in 1946.

During the 1930s, Auden's work celebrated elements of the modern world previously considered "unpoetic," such as machinery, railways and other implements of mass living; his outlook was influenced by Marx and FREUD. In the 1940s, his poems began to express a Christian existential view influenced by Kierkegaard and NIEBUHR. *The Age of Anxiety* won a PULITZER PRIZE in 1948. From 1947 to 1962 he was editor of the Yale Younger Poets series. In New York City, as at Oxford, Auden held court and was effectively the arbiter of poetic taste in the United States. He was professor of poetry at Oxford (1956–61). The last works of the poet known in the 1930s as the conscience of his generation astonished critics with their modesty, domesticity and light comic tone. He died at Kirchstetten, Austria. A brilliant, fluent and versatile poet whose work was distinguished by a playful and mordant wit, Auden is widely considered to rank among the greatest literary figures of the 20th century.

W.H. Auden, English poet.

For further reading:

Mendelson, Edward, *Early Auden*. Cambridge: Harvard University Press, 1983.
Carpenter, Humphrey, *W.H. Auden: A Biography*. Boston: Houghton-Mifflin, 1982.
McDiarmid, Lucy, *Saving Civilization: Yeats, Eliot and Auden Between the Wars*. New York: Cambridge University Press, 1984.

Auerbach, Arnold Jacob "Red" (1917–). American basketball coach. The Brooklyn-born Auerbach was perhaps more closely associated with Boston sports over a longer period of time than any other man. After an undistinguished college athletic career, he coached at that level before assuming the helm of the Washington Capitols for three seasons (1946–49). In 1951, he joined the Boston Celtics, leading them to 938 victories and nine championships over 16 seasons (1950–1966). He was named to the Basketball Hall of Fame in 1968; in 1980, the Professional Basketball Writers' Association, named Auerbach the greatest coach in NBA history. Auerbach continues his involvement with the Celtics as president and general manager of the team.

Auger, Pierre Victor (1899–). French physicist. Auger was educated at the Ecole Normale Superieure, where he obtained his Ph.D. in 1926. He was later appointed to the staff of the University of Paris. After serving there as professor of physics from 1937, he became director of higher education for France in 1945. From 1948 until 1960 he was director of the science department of UNESCO; he left UNESCO to become president of the French Space Commission, but in 1964 he took the post of director-general of the European Space and Research Organization, a post he retained until his retirement in 1967.

Auger's work has mainly been on nuclear physics and cosmic rays. In 1925 he discovered the **Auger effect** in which an excited atom emits an electron (rather than a photon) when it reverts to a lower energy state. In 1938 Auger made a careful study of "air showers," a cascade of particles produced by a cosmic ray entering the atmosphere and later known as an **Auger shower**.

Auric, Georges (1899–1963). French composer of symphonic music, film scores and ballets. Auric first came to musical prominence in the 1920s, during which he was a key member of a group of young avant-garde classical composers known as LES SIX—other members were Arthur HONEGGER, Darius MILHAUD and Francis POULENC. As a youth, Auric studied in Paris under the composers Vincent D'INDY and Albert ROUSSEL, living embodiments of the rich romanticism that had dominated late-19th-century French music. But Auric rebelled against this tradition and distinguished himself with compositions in a spare, playful manner that mocked the romantic conventions of melancholy and lush melody. In the 1920s, Auric wrote a number of ballets for the Paris dance company of renowned impressario Serge DIAGHILEV. He also composed music for several films, including Jean COCTEAU's *The Blood of a Poet* (1930), *Orpheus* (1950) and *Beauty and the Beast* (1946).

Auriol, Vincent (1884–1966). French politician, president of FRANCE (1947–54). A member of the Socialist Party, Auriol was elected to the Chamber of Deputies in 1914. He became a leading figure in the party in the 1930s and served as finance minister in the cabinet of Leon BLUM (1936–37). An early opponent of the VICHY government established after the German defeat of France in WORLD WAR II, he was a leader of the RESISTANCE and in 1943 joined Charles DE GAULLE'S FREE FRENCH government-in-exile. Auriol served in the provisional government established at the end of the war and in 1946 was elected president of the national assembly. He was the first president of the Fourth Republic. He initially supported De Gaulle's presidency in 1958 but split with De Gaulle in 1960.

Auschwitz. The most notorious of the Nazi CONCENTRATION CAMPS during WORLD WAR II; located near Oswiecim, Poland. Auschwitz was opened in June 1940 and was run by Heinrich HIMMLER's SS. Originally a detention and forced labor camp, in January 1942 it was designated as an extermination camp—the primary center in which the Nazis would carry out Adolf HITLER'S so-called FINAL SOLUTION, the destruction of Europe's JEWS. Special gas chambers, disguised as showers, were built for the mass execution of prisoners, and crematoria (ovens) were installed to cremate the bodies of the dead. At least half of the prisoners sent to Auschwitz from various parts of German-occupied Europe—many of them women, children and elderly people—were sent immediately to the gas chambers. The remaining able-bodied were assigned to forced labor, usually at the adjacent camp of Birkenau or at another nearby camp (operated by the German industrial firm I.G. Farben), until they too were ordered to the gas chambers. The camp operated until the spring of 1945, when in the waning days of the war it was overrun and liberated by the advancing Soviet armies. Because the SS destroyed the camp records, the exact number of people killed at Auschwitz is unknown; many authorities estimate that as many as four million died. After the war, Auschwitz's commandant, Rudolf Hoess, was tried and convicted of war crimes at the NUREMBERG TRIALS and executed. The sheer magnitude and inhumanity of the crimes committed at Auschwitz have been the subject of much analysis, and the name of the camp has become synonymous with

Auschwitz concentration camp surrounded by a double fence of electrified barbed wire.

the darkest deeds of the 20th century. (See also HOLOCAUST; NAZISM.)

Austin, John Langshaw (1911–1960). British philosopher. Austin, who was educated at Oxford and taught there for over two decades, became the most important postwar proponent of the "ordinary language" approach to philosophical analysis. According to Austin, the first task of any philosopher was to consider the linguistic terminology at his disposal. This was valuable not only in order to avoid confusion and ambiguity insofar as was possible, but also because the nature of language was a worthy philosophical problem in its own right. Austin believed that the subtle ethical and perceptual distinctions embedded in daily language usage could provide a valuable impetus to philosophical thought, which was too often based strictly on isolated intellectual analysis. Austin's methodology was one of rigorous analysis unencumbered by a priori conceptions. His major works, which are suggestive rather than conclusive, are *Philosophical Papers* (1961), *Sense and Sensibilia* (1962) and *How to Do Things With Words* (1962).

Australia [Commonwealth of Australia]. Australia, the sixth-largest country on Earth, is located between the Indian and Pacific Oceans. On January 1, 1901, the British colonies of New South Wales, Victoria, Queensland, South Australia, Western Australia and Tasmania federated to form the Commonwealth of Australia. (The Northern Territory was transferred from South Australia to the Commonwealth in 1911.) The federal government was to have control of foreign affairs, defense, trade. The head of state was the governor general, appointed by the Crown, and a parliament was set up, consisting of a senate and a house of representatives. The first Commonwealth parliament passed an Immigration Restrictions Act in 1901, which put the "White Australia" policy into effect. It was aimed in particular at keeping out Chinese immigrants, who had arrived in large numbers to work in the gold fields. The policy also caused the repatriation of Pacific Islanders. A great deal of social legislation was enacted in the years leading up to World War I. In 1902 woman suffrage was adopted by the federal government. An industrial arbitration court was established in 1906 that laid down the principle of a basic wage. Old-age and invalid pensions were brought in, along with free and compulsory education. In 1909 the first ship of the Australian navy was ordered. In 1911, territory was ac-

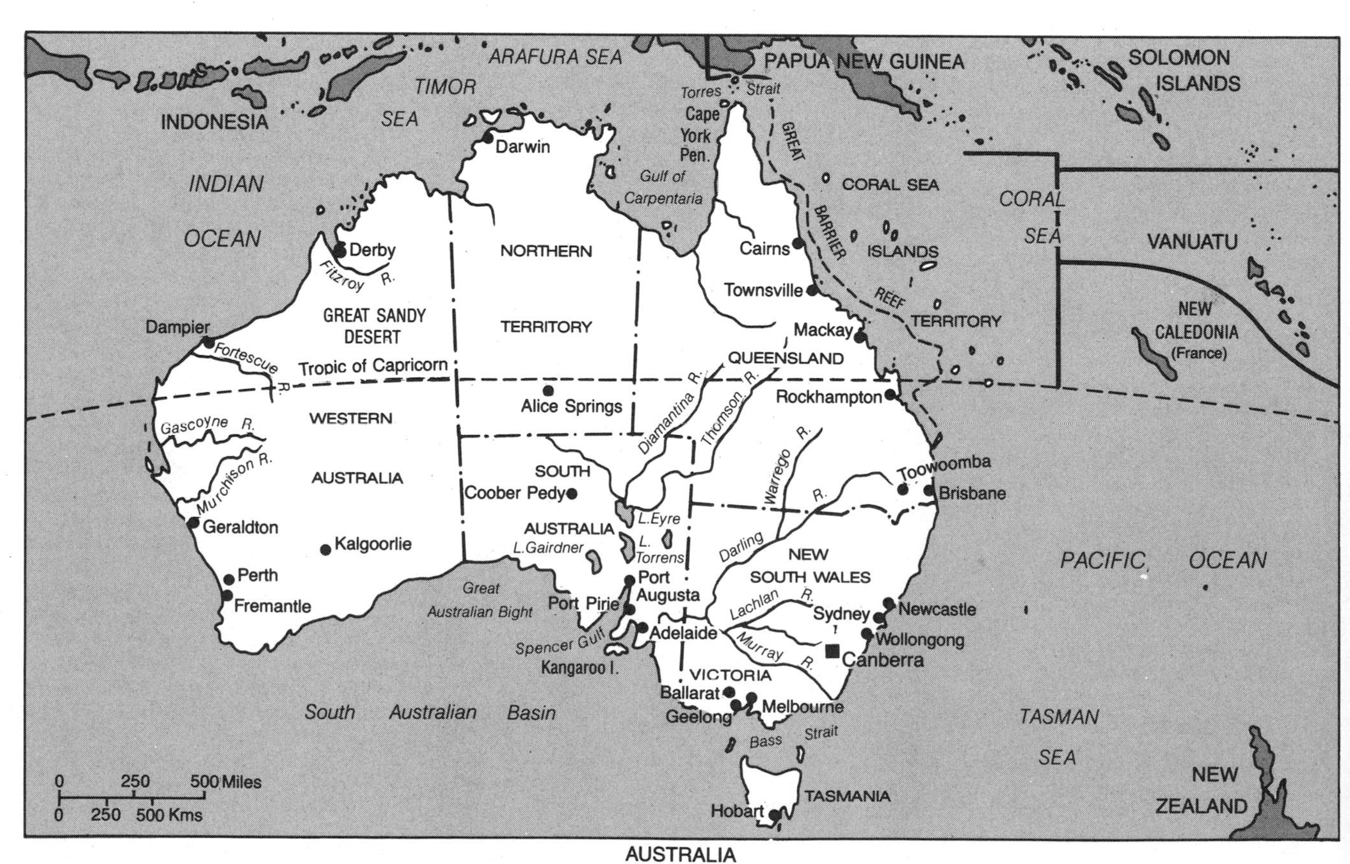

AUSTRALIA

AUSTRALIA

1901	(Jan. 1) Colonies of New South Wales, Victoria, Queensland, South Australia, Western Australia and Tasmania federate to form Commonwealth of Australia.
1902	Woman suffrage adopted.
1914-18	300,000 Australians fight alongside Britain in World War I.
1941	Australian Labor Party takes office.
1942	Australia becomes main Allied base in the Pacific during World War II.
1949	ALP voted out of office after Prime Minister Chiffley attempts to nationalize banks. Liberal and Country Parties form coalition government, remain in power for 23 years.
1950	Australia-New Zealand-United States (ANZUS) defense treaty signed.
1954	Australia joins South East Asia Treaty Organization (SEATO).
1965	Australian troops support the U.S. in Vietnam War.
1965	Aborigines given the vote.
1983	Australia wins America's Cup yachting trophy; ALP returns to power under Robert Hawke.
1984	Law passed giving greater protection to sacred Aboriginal sites.
1986	Australia Act gives full legal independence from Britain, keeping the queen as sovereign.
1987	Royal commission established to investigate high death rate of Aborigines in police custody.
1988	Bicentennial of European settlement celebrated—protested by Aborigines.
1990	(April) Hawke returned to power for fourth time, with reduced parliamentary majority reflecting gains by Liberal-National coalition.

quired from New South Wales to form the federal capital of Canberra, and parliament began meeting there in 1927. In 1911 the Commonwealth Bank was established.

During WORLD WAR I Australia sent about 330,000 men to Europe to fight alongside Britain. In 1920 Australia was a founder member of the LEAGUE OF NATIONS. With the passage of the STATUTE OF WESTMINSTER in 1931 Australia became a dominion within the British COMMONWEALTH. During the 1920s the Australian economy expanded, benefiting from high prices for wool and meat. Tariffs were introduced to protect new manufacturing industries, and primary producers were given subsidies. The worldwide GREAT DEPRESSION in the early 1930s caused widespread unemployment and hardship in Australia, which had an economy largely dependent on that of Britain. But it recovered more quickly than many countries, due to the rising price of wool and gold.

In WORLD WAR II Australia once again supported Britain. Australian troops fought in the Middle East between 1940 and 1942. When Japan entered the war, Australian forces returned to the Pacific theater, and the United States made Australia the Allied base in the Pacific. The AUSTRALIAN LABOUR PARTY (ALP) took office in 1941, after the United Australia Party lost ground in federal elections. At the end of the war there was an influx of displaced persons from Europe. In 1947 the Labor Prime Minister John Chiffley made a controversial attempt to nationalize the banks, which failed in the courts. A bitter coal strike was put down with the use of troops and emergency legislation.

The ALP was voted out of office in 1949. The Liberal and the Country Parties formed a coalition government that stayed in power for the next 23 years. The new prime minister was Robert MENZIES. In 1950 the High Court prevented his government from outlawing the Communist Party. The 1950s saw the trade deficit rise, along with wages, and inflation spiralled. A secret ballot for trade union elections was introduced. Australia's foreign policy now concentrated on non-communist Asian nations, and on strengthening ties with the United States. Australia took a prominent part in the COLOMBO PLAN (1950), giving economic aid to underdeveloped countries of South and Southeast Asia. Australia, New Zealand and the United States signed the ANZUS defense treaty the following year. In 1954 it was a signatory to the South East Asia Treaty Organization, whose members pledged to help each other in the event of outside aggression. In 1952 Britain began testing atomic bombs on Australian territory, and continued to do so for more than a decade. The government agreed to the establishment of an American naval communications base in Western Australia, in 1963. In 1965 Australia sent troops to support the U.S. in South Vietnam.

At home, Aborigines were given the vote and access to social benefits, which had previously been denied them. Menzies retired as prime minister in 1966. Harold Holt took over, but died in a swimming accident the following year. John Gorton became prime minister and then in 1971, the Liberal leader William McMahon took over the premiership. The government was beset by problems of inflation and industrial unrest. It lost a general election for the House of Representatives, to the ALP, led by the charismatic socialist, Gough WHITLAM. The Whitlam government ended Australia's military involvement in the VIETNAM WAR in 1972. Among the administration's domestic achievements was the introduction of a national health scheme to provide free health care for all. In 1974, Whitlam dissolved both houses of Parliament, following a conflict between the government and the Senate. On Nov. 11, 1975, the governor general, in an unprecedented move, dismissed Whitlam and dissolved Parliament. The Liberal Party leader, Malcolm FRASER, was declared caretaker prime minister, pending new elections in December.

A coalition of Fraser's Liberals and the National Country Party subsequently won majorities in both houses. The coalition government was beaten in the March 1983 general elections, by the ALP under Bob HAWKE. The new prime minister immediately called an economic summit, and an accord on pay and prices was reached between the government, trade unions and employers. In 1984 a law was enacted giving greater protection to sacred Aboriginal sites. The Medicare system, providing universal health insurance, was introduced. The Australia Act (1986) gave the nation full legal independence from Britain, but left the queen's status as sovereign unaltered. In 1988 Australians celebrated the bicentenary of European settlement.

Australian Labour Party (ALP). Australian political party established in 1890. The ALP arose when trade unions sought political representation in the recessionary period at the end of the 19th century. The ALP held the balance of power in the first Commonwealth Parliament, formed minority national governments briefly in 1904 and 1908, and then won clear control of both houses in 1910. Under the leadership of William HUGHES, the party split in 1916 over the issue of conscription. Hughes left the ALP, which was out of power until 1929. From 1929 to 1931 party leader James Scullin was prime minister, but the party ruptured again over its response to the GREAT DEPRESSION. The party rose to power between 1941 and 1949 under the leadership of Prime Ministers John CURTIN and Ben CHIFLEY when many social reforms were initiated. In the-mid 1950s another split occurred when an anticommunist faction broke away and formed the Democratic Labour Party. From 1972 to 1975 ALP leader Gough WHITLAM

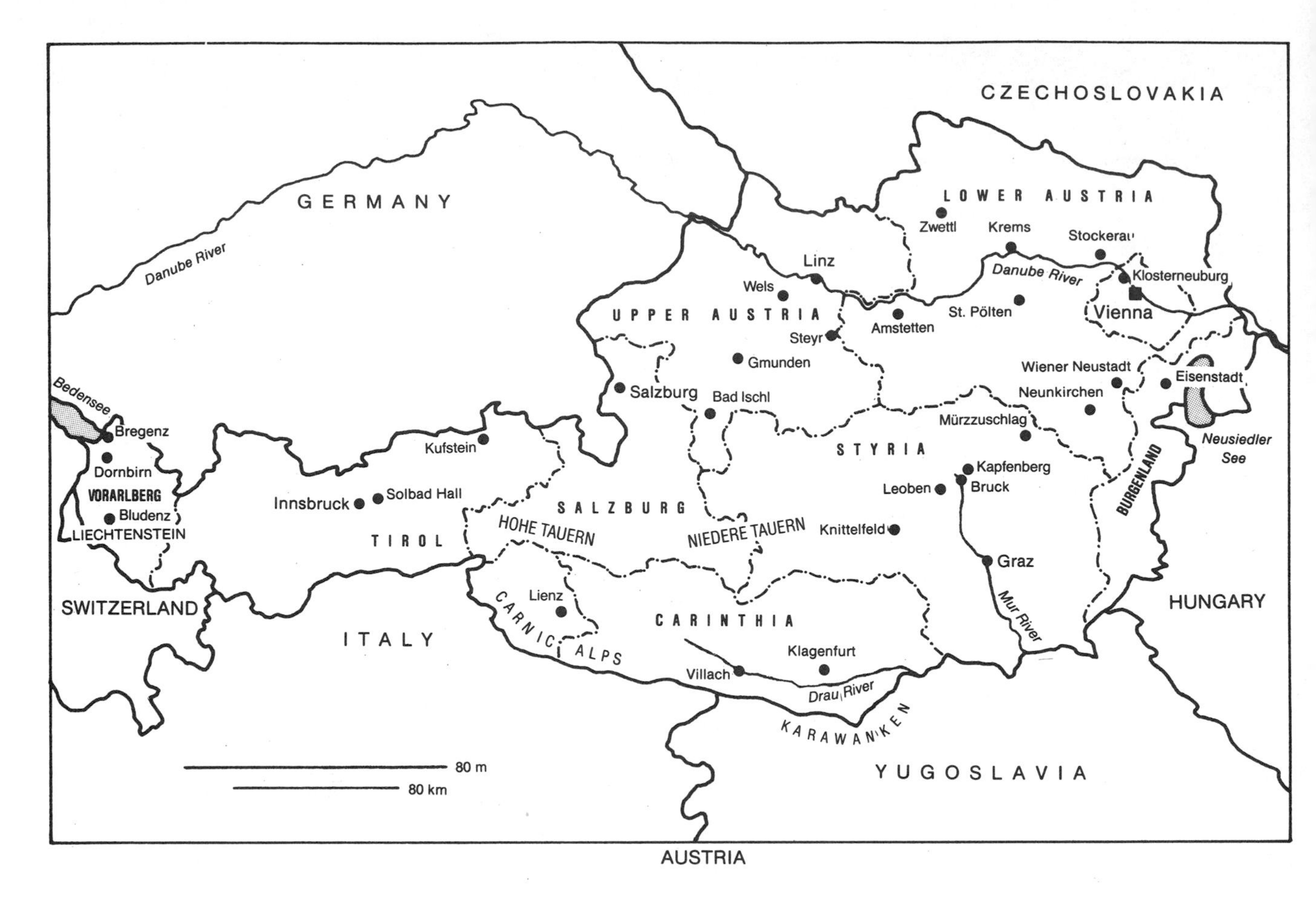

AUSTRIA

was prime minister. Although his tenure ended in a constitution crisis, Labour came to power again in 1983.

Austria. Austria is a landlocked country in central Europe, divided into nine federal states with an area of 32,368 square miles. Austria entered the 20th century as the dual monarchy of Austria-Hungary (see AUSTRO-HUNGARIAN EMPIRE). The final decades of Habsburg rule were a glorious twilight of economic, social and cultural achievement, and political corruption. Despite the introduction of universal suffrage in the Austrian half in 1907, the empire remained essentially an autocracy, inimical to its subject Slav peoples and the growing working-class movement, represented by the Social Democratic Party. Austria's annexation of BOSNIA AND HERZEGOVINA (1908) was to lead indirectly to the empire's downfall.

WORLD WAR I not only ended in defeat for Germany and Austria-Hungary but also unleashed a tide of revolutionary and national aspirations that swept away the old order in central Europe. In November 1918 the first Austrian republic was proclaimed, with Karl Renner (Social Democrat) becoming chancellor. A "Habsburg Law" (1919) barred members of the former imperial family from Austria unless they declared allegiance to the republic. Various postwar peace treaties dismembered the empire on the basis of national self-determination, and Austria was reduced to its present-day borders, being roughly the German-speaking area except South Tirol, which was ceded to ITALY. Beset by economic problems, the new republic experienced chronic strife between left and right, leading to the suspension of parliamentary government by Chancellor Englebert DOLLFUSS in 1933, Dollfuss's murder by Austrian Nazis, and the suppression of the Social Democrats in 1934. Growing internal pro-fascist agitation and pressure from Nazi GERMANY culminated in the unopposed entry of German forces in March 1938 and the ANSCHLUSS (annexation), under which Austria was fully incorporated into HITLER's Reich.

After WORLD WAR II the victorious Allies established a four-power (Soviet, U.S., British and French) occupation regime in Austria and recognized the newly declared second republic in December 1945. Economic recovery was assisted by the MARSHALL PLAN. After lengthy negotiations, the 1955 Austrian State Treaty achieved the withdrawal of all occupation forces and accorded international recognition of Austria as a sovereign, independent and democratic state within its frontiers of January 1938. The treaty specifically banned any future political or economic union with Germany and reaffirmed the

AUSTRIA

1907	Universal suffrage introduced.
1908	Austria annexes Bosnia-Herzegovina.
1914	Gavrilo Princip assassinates Archduke Franz Ferdinand; World War I begins.
1918	Emperor Charles abdicates; Austria proclaimed a republic.
1934	Chancellor Dollfuss murdered by Austrian Nazis.
1938	"Anschluss" (annexation) of Austria by Germany.
1945-55	Austria occupied by U.S.S.R., U.S., France and Britain after World War II.
1970-83	Socialist government under Bruno Kreisky.
1986	Election of Kurt Waldheim as president stirs controversy.
1989	Austria applies for EEC membership.

1919 Habsburg Law, while an associated constitutional law provided for Austria's permanent neutrality. The resumption of full sovereignty was followed by rapid industrialization and economic advance. A founder member of EFTA from 1959, Austria signed an industrial free-trade agreement with the EUROPEAN ECONOMIC COMMUNITY (EEC) in 1972 and applied for membership in the latter in July 1989.

Austria-Hungary. See AUSTRO-HUNGARIAN EMPIRE.

Austrian state treaty. Treaty signed on May 15, 1955, by the U.S., U.S.S.R., Britain and France to end their joint post-World War II occupation of Austria and withdraw all troops by October 25, 1955. Austria was restored to its frontiers of 1937, and union with Germany was forbidden. The treaty raised hopes of Soviet agreement to withdraw troops from Eastern Europe.

Austro-Hungarian Empire. The Compromise (*Ausgleich*) of 1867 united Austria and Hungary under the banner of the dual monarchy of Austria-Hungary. The Austro-Hungarian empire covered much of central Europe; it included not only the Austrians and Hungarians, but a whole host of mostly Slavic peoples—Czechs, Slovaks, Serbs and Croats as well as Romanians. In the early 20th century, increasingly resentful of the predominance of the Austrians and Hungarians, these subject peoples agitated for independence. Tensions within the empire contributed to the general European unease that led up to WORLD WAR I; the assassination of the Austrian Archduke FRANZ FERDINAND by a Serbian nationalist, Gavrilo Princip (June 28, 1914, at Sarajevo), was the event that sparked the great conflagration. Austria-Hungary fought alongside GERMANY; her troops were engaged mainly against the Russians in the east and the Italians in the south. Defeated in the war, the Austro-Hungarian empire disintegrated as new countries were created from its outlying areas. The Corfu Pact of 1917 provided for a kingdom of Serbs, Croats and Slovenes; that kingdom came into being at the end of 1918; in 1929 the new country adopted the name YUGOSLAVIA. Independent CZECHOSLOVAKIA was created in 1918, and the treaties of St. Germain and Trianon in 1919–20 formalized the breakup of the old empire; AUSTRIA and HUNGARY went their separate ways as distinct nations.

Autobiography of Alice B. Toklas, The. Book by Gertrude STEIN, published in 1933. It is not an autobiography at all, but rather Stein's own memoir written as if by her longtime companion and secretary, Alice B. Toklas. The book was Stein's first popular work, and describes Stein and Toklas's life together in Paris where they maintained a literary and artistic salon where Pablo PICASSO, Henri MATISSE, Ernest HEMINGWAY and many other luminaries of the time gathered. The book expresses Stein's opinions of their talent and her views on art and literature and her own "genius."

automobile. Although a 19th-century invention, the automobile is a 20th-century phenomenon that transformed the way of living in much of the Western world. The automobile revolution is due in large measure to Henry FORD, who believed that every person ought to be able to own a car. Ford perfected the system of MASS PRODUCTION and in 1908 introduced his Model T, the first car available to a mass market. By the 1920s, the automobile was a common means of transportation in the U.S. and much of Europe. The automobile age was encouraged as much by new roads designed for auto traffic as by the cars themselves. The German autobahn—an innovation of HITLER's Third Reich—was the first long-distance, high-speed, controlled-access highway. In 1956, U.S. President EISENHOWER signed a bill providing for the construction of an extensive interstate highway system linking virtually every region of the U.S.; in Britain, the first motorway opened in 1958.

However, nowhere more than in the U.S. did the automobile become a way of life. With more than 42,000 miles of controlled-access roads linking major cities, the interstate highway system made it possible to drive thousands of miles across country—from Portland, Maine, to Key West, Florida, or from New York City to Los Angeles, California—at high speeds, without having to use local roads. The economic boom of the 1950s and 1960s made the automobile affordable for most middle-class American families; moreover, the car was transformed from merely a means of transportation into a symbol of economic status and personal freedom, and an entire subculture was built around the automobile. The availability of plentiful and cheap gasoline had further spurred auto sales, increased the mobility of the American public and fueled a boom in the interstate trucking business. On the other hand, the proliferation of private automobiles and of highways (along with passenger airliners) spelled doom for the American railways and led to severe air pollution in many U.S. cities, most notably LOS ANGELES. The oil crises of the 1970s affected Americans' driving habits as the cost of gasoline soared. Many American drivers switched to more fuel-efficient cars; from this point into the 1990s, Japanese and other foreign imports made a significant impact on the U.S. market. By the last decade of the century, the automobile had become a universal phenomenon, traveling the roads of virtually every country in the world.

Autry, Gene (1907–). American singing cowboy and businessman. A familiar figure on the airwaves and the silver screen during the 1930s and 1940s, Autry recorded numerous "cowboy" songs and starred in over 100 B-movies with his horse Champion. After WORLD WAR II service, Autry returned to show business with such perennial song hits as "Rudolph the Red-nosed Reindeer" and "Here Comes Peter Cottontail." Autry's holdings include hotels, radio stations and the California Angels baseball club.

Avedon, Richard (1923–). American photographer known for his creative approach to fashion and portrait photography. Avedon studied with Alexey BRODOVITCH at the New School in New York, establishing his own studio in 1946. He was a regular contributor to *Harper's Bazaar* from 1945 to 1965, where Brodovitch was art director, and also was frequently published in LIFE and *Theater Arts* magazines. Although at first primarily a fashion photographer, his portraits, often of famous people, became equally well known, while his work became constantly more varied and more creative. His work is often exhibited, and he has published a number of books, including *Observations* of 1959 (with a text by Truman CAPOTE), a collection of his celebrity portraits up to that time.

Averoff-Tositsas, Evangelos (1910–1990). Greek politician. Averoff served as Greek foreign minster from 1956 to 1963 and was instrumental in negotiating the 1959 settlement that led to independence for CYPRUS. While holding the post of defense minister (1974–80), he helped oversee the restoration of democracy in GREECE in 1974, by successfully advocating the recall of President Constantine CARAMANLIS. Averoff served as the leader of New Democracy, the country's main conservative party, from 1981 until his retirement in 1984.

Avery, Fred "Tex" (1907–1980). American cartoon animator, producer and director. Working for WARNER BROS. in the late 1930s he created and/or developed such classic cartoon characters as Daffy Duck (in *Porky's Duck Hunt*, 1937) and BUGS BUNNY (in *A Wild Hare*, 1940). In the latter film Avery came up with Bugs's famous greeting, "What's up, doc?" From 1941 to 1954 Avery ran his own animation unit at METRO-GOLDWYN-MAYER, where he developed the character of Droopy the Dog. During his later years he produced a number of cartoons for the Walter Lantz company. A self-styled anarchist, Avery was known for creating irreverent caricatures, outrageous spoofs and absurd situations. Avery's influence upon younger generations of animation directors, like Chuck Jones and Friz Freleng, has been enormous. Always the exponent of slapstick humor, Avery said: "Dialogue gags are a dime a dozen, but a good sight gag is hard to come by."

For further reading:

Adamson, Joe, *Tex Avery: King of Cartoons*. New York: Popular Library, 1975.

Avery, Milton (1893–1965). American painter. Born in Altmar, N.Y., he studied briefly at the Art Students League, New York City, traveled in Europe and settled in New York in 1925. His first one-man show was held in the city in 1928. Working within the MATISSE tradition, he is noted for flat, figurative canvases of great boldness and originality. His mature landscapes, such as *Green Sea* (1954, Metropolitan Museum of Art, N.Y.C.), border on pure abstract art.

Avery, Oswald Theodore (1877–1955). American bacteriologist. Educated at Colgate University, Avery received his A.B. in 1900 and his M.D. in 1904. After a time at the Hoagland Laboratory, N.Y., as a lecturer and researcher in bacteriology, he joined the Rockefeller Institute Hospital (1913–48). While investigating the pneumococcus bacteria responsible for causing lobar pneumonia, Avery found that the bacteria produced soluble substances, derived from the cell wall and identified as polysaccharides, that were specific in their chemical composition for each different type of pneumococcus. This work provided a basis for establishing the immunologic identity of a cell in biochemical terms. In 1932 Avery started work on the phenomenon of transformation in bacteria. It had already been shown that heat-killed cells of a virulent pneumococcus strain could transform a living avirulent strain into the virulent form. In 1944 Avery and his colleagues Maclyn McCarthy and Colin MacLeod extracted and purified the transforming substance and showed it to be deoxyribonucleic acid (DNA). Previously it had been thought that protein was the hereditary material. Thus Avery's work was an important step toward the eventual discovery, made nine years later by James WATSON and Francis CRICK, of the chemical basis of heredity.

aviation. The 20th-century development of practical aviation has had an incalculable effect on human history. The WRIGHT BROTHERS made the first successful powered flight in December 1903, just a week after LANGLEY's failed attempt. In 1909, Louis BLERIOT was the first to fly across the watery perils of the English Channel. The airplane's military potential was seen in WORLD WAR I, while air-mail service began in the 1920s in the U.S. Charles LINDBERGH's solo transatlantic flight in 1927 made long-distance flight acceptable. Commercial passenger service was established in the 1930s. WORLD WAR II saw warplanes that were faster, could fly farther and carry heavier payloads. The Germans introduced jet planes—but too late to do more than startle Allied pilots. RADAR, a wartime development, had a tremendous impact on postwar commercial aviation. Well into the 1950s, the piston-engine propeller airplane and the turboprop aircraft remained the mainstay of long-distance commercial aviation. However, the JET ENGINE (developed by British aviation engineer Frank Whittle in the 1930s) was perfected in the 1950s, and the first jet-powered commercial aircraft entered service. Aircraft such as the BOEING 707 were able to cross the Atlantic Ocean in half the previous time. Long-distance passenger aviation boomed—with dire consequences for the passenger OCEAN LINERS and the railroads. By the last decade of the century, there were few inhabited places on Earth that could not be reached by airplane.

AVIATION

1900	First Zeppelin airship flight.
1903	Orville and Wilbur Wright make first flight in motor-powered heavier-than-air machine.
1909	Bleriot makes first flight across English Channel.
1911	Anthony Fokker builds first fighter plane.
1915	Hugo Junkers produces all-metal plane.
1918	First regular air service between Kiev and Vienna, also New York and Washington.
1919	Alcock and Brown first to fly across Atlantic, also London to Australia.
1927	Charles A. Lindbergh makes first nonstop solo flight across Atlantic (New York-Paris).
1928	First flight across the Pacific.
1928-29	Dirigible *Graf Zeppelin* makes transatlantic and world flights.
1930	Amy Johnson flies solo from U.K. to Australia.
1931	Auguste Piccard ascends to stratosphere in balloon.
1932	Amelia Earhart flies solo from Newfoundland to Ireland.
1934	DC-3 enters service.
1936	Louis Breguet flies first successful helicopter; Beryl Markham makes first solo east-to-west transatlantic flight; first flight of Mitchell's Spitfire fighter plane.
1937	Frank Whittle (RAF) runs first jet engine on test bed; *Hindenburg* disaster.
1939	Pan American begins New York-Southampton flying-boat service.
1939	First turbojet test flight by Heinkel 178, Germany.
1947	Chuck Yeager breaks sound barrier in X-1 rocket plane.
1949	First passenger jet flight by British Comet.
1952	Comet jetliner enters service.
1954	First test flight of Boeing 707 jetliner.
1955	British designer Cockerell patents Hovercraft.
1958	Boeing 707 jetliner enters service.
1959	Hovercraft crosses English Channel.
1969	First flight by Concorde supersonic airliner.
1970	Boeing 747 "Jumbo Jet" enters service.
1976	Concorde enters service.
1977	Laker Airways inaugurates cheap transatlantic "Skytrain" flights.
1978	Airline deregulation in U.S.
1981	First flight of space shuttle
1990	Eastern Airlines goes out of business after prolonged strike, bankruptcy.

Axelrod, Julius (1912–). American neuropharmacologist. Axelrod was educated at the City College of New York. Denied a medical career by poverty during the great depression, Axelrod instead worked as a technician in a food-testing laboratory for 12 years. But still with an ambition for a career in scientific research, and after some years at the Goldwater Memorial Hospital and the National Heart Institute, he took a year off in 1955, obtained a Ph.D. from George Washington University, and moved to the National Institute of Mental Health as chief of the pharmacology section.

Axelrod has thrown much light on the action of the catecholamines, the neurotransmitters of the sympathetic nervous system. For work on the catecholamines, Axelrod shared the 1970 NOBEL PRIZE for physiology or medicine with Ulf VON EULER and Bernard Katz.

Axelrod has also worked on the role of the pineal gland in the control of circadian rhythms, and the neuropharmacology of schizophrenia.

Axis. Term used to describe the alliance among GERMANY, ITALY and JAPAN immediately before and during WORLD WAR II. The term was coined by Italian dictator Benito MUSSOLINI. On October 25, 1936, Mussolini and Adolf HITLER signed a treaty that recognized the two nations' common foreign policy goals; this alliance was reinforced when the two leaders concluded a formal military alliance, known as the "Pact of Steel," on May 22, 1939. This so-called "Rome-Berlin Axis" expanded to become the "Rome-Berlin-Tokyo Axis" on September 27, 1940, when Japan joined the two nations in the Tripartite Pact of September 27, 1940.

Axis Sally [Mildred Elizbeth Siek] (1900–1988). U.S.-born radio propagandist for the NAZIS. She was convicted of treason in 1949 for broadcasting English-language programs from Berlin to Allied troops during WORLD WAR II. She served 12 years in prison. After her release at the age of 60, she taught music at a Roman Catholic convent school in Columbus, Ohio.

Ayckbourn, Alan (1939–). British playwright and theatrical director. Born in London, he is known for his numerous successful farces portraying a dark view of British middle-class life in the late 20th century. He began his career at 17 working as assistant stage manager to Donald Wolfit and supported his early writing by producing plays for the BBC. His first major success, *Relatively Speaking* (1967), is characteristic of his work with its suburban setting and bitter undertones—although the bitterness increases in his later work. Author of some 39 plays through 1989, in 1975 Acykbourn had five plays running simultaneously in London. His work has been performed worldwide, but he did not gain the popularity in the U.S. he enjoyed in England. His works include *The Norman Conquests* (1974), *It Could be Any One of Us* (1983), *Man of the Moment* (1989) and *The Revenger's Comedies* (1990), which depicts two suicidal people deciding instead to seek revenge on one another's enemies. Ayckbourn is artistic director of the Stephen Joseph Theatre-in-the-Round in the seaside resort town of Scarborough, where much of his work is first performed. He is admired by his contemporary Harold PINTER, who describes him as "a very serious playwright."

Ayer, A(lfred) J(ules) (1910–). British philosopher. Ayer has been one of the most influential philosophers of the century due to his controversial definition of "truth" as applying only to logical or empirical statements. Ayer, who studied LOGICAL POSITIVISM in Vienna following his graduation from Oxford in 1932, was the first English-speaking philosopher to apply the teachings of that Continental school of philosophy to problems of language and meaning. In his first major work, *Language, Truth and Logic* (1936), Ayer argued that logical statements were empty of factual content but were true as defined by the conventional rules of mathematics and logic. As for empirical statements, they were only meaningful in so far as they could be verified by observation. This left all metaphysical and ethical statements as emotive assertions without essential meaning. Ayer developed these ideas in *The Foundations of Empirical Knowledge* (1940) and *Philosophical Essays* (1954). In *The Problem of Knowledge* (1956), however, Ayer showed that analytical skepticism had its limits—it could not disprove the possibility that certain statements could be true even if they could not be logically or empirically justified.

Ayres, Lew (1908–). American screen actor. A leading man in films of the 1930s, Ayres hurt his career by declaring himself a conscientious objector in WORLD WAR II. His best known film is *All Quiet on the Western Front* (1930). Among his other films are *Holiday* (1938), *Advise and Consent* (1961) and *The Carpetbaggers* (1964).

Ayub Khan, Mohammed (1908–1974). Military leader and president of PAKISTAN (1958–69). Educated at the Royal Military College at Sandhurst, he was commissioned in the British Indian army in 1928 and served as a battalion commander in World War II. After the creation of the Muslim state of Pakistan in 1947, he headed the military forces in East Pakistan (now the state of BANGLADESH) and later became Pakistani commander in chief (1951–58). He also served as defense minister from 1954 to 1956. In 1958, a military coup toppled the government, martial law was declared and Ayub Khan proclaimed himself president. He became a field marshal in 1959, and his presidency was confirmed in a 1960 referendum. Ayub Khan began ambitious social, political and economic programs, including land reform, economic development and a system of local government councils he dubbed "basic democracies." He was reelected in 1965, the same year he led Pakistan in a one-year war with India. Despite his attempts at reform, dissatisfaction with the repressiveness of his government, continued social inequalities and his lack of success in conflicts with India led to criticism, unrest and finally to riots in 1968. Ayub Khan resigned on March 26, 1969, turning the presidency over to General YAHYA KHAN.

Azana, Manuel (1880–1940). President of SPAIN (1936–39). A distinguished liberal journalist and critic, Azana became politically active in the early 1930s. After the flight of ALFONSO XIII in 1931, he served first as minister of war in the Republican cabinet, then as prime minister (1931–33). During his ministry, Azana inaugurated various social, military and educational reforms. Becoming prime minister again with the victory of the Popular Front in 1936, he was soon elected president. Azana acted as a virtual figurehead during the SPANISH CIVIL WAR, fleeing to France in 1939 just before the collapse of the Republic.

Azikiwe, Benjamin (1904–). President of NIGERIA (1963–66). An Ibo active in nationalist politics as editor of various newspapers and executive member of the **Nigerian Youth Movement** (1934–41), he was elected member of the Eastern Region House of Assembly (1954–59), and premier, Eastern Region (1954–59). He served as governor-general of Nigeria (1960–63) and first president of the republic (1963–66).

AZT. See AIDS.

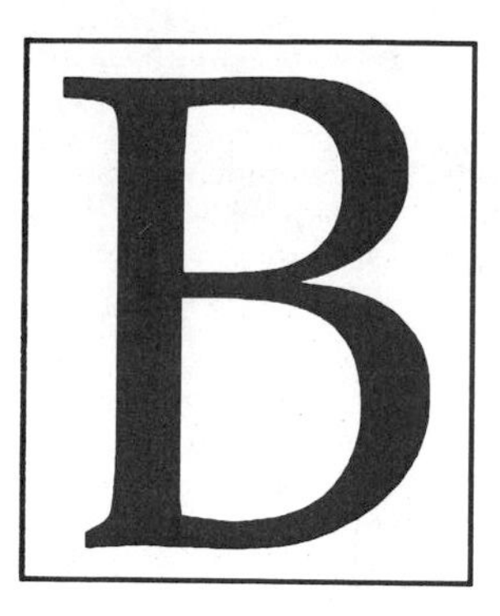

Baade, Wilhelm Heinrich Walter (1893–1960). German-American astronomer. Baade was educated at the universities of Munster and Gottingen where he obtained his Ph.D. in 1919. He worked at the University of Hamburg's Bergedorf Observatory from 1919 to 1931, when he moved to the U.S. He spent the rest of his career at the Mount Wilson and Palomar Observatories, retiring in 1958. In 1920 Baade discovered the minor planet Hidalgo, whose immense orbit extends to that of Saturn, and in 1949 he detected the minor planet Icarus, whose lopsided orbit lies within that of Mercury but can bring Icarus very close to Earth. In the 1930s he did important work with Fritz Zwicky on supernovae, with Edwin HUBBLE on galactic distances and with his old Hamburg colleague Rudolph Minkowski on the optical identification of radio sources.

Baade's most significant work began in 1942. Of German origin, he was precluded from the general induction of scientists into military research. In early 1943 Baade took some famous photographs with the 100-inch reflecting telescope of the central region of the Andromeda galaxy. He was able to distinguish stars in the inner region where Hubble had found only a blur of light. These observations allowed Baade to introduce a fundamental distinction between types of stars. The first type, Population I, he found in the spiral arms of the Andromeda galaxy. They were hot young blue stars as opposed to the Population II stars of the central part of the galaxy, which were older and redder, with a lower metal content. This distinction, now much expanded, has played a crucial role in theories of galactic evolution. Baade found that the Andromeda galaxy was two million light-years distant. The distance to the Andromeda galaxy had been used by Hubble to estimate the age of the universe as two billion years. Baade's revised figure gave the age as five billion years. With Baade's revision of the distance of the Andromeda galaxy—without any change in its luminosity—it became clear that its size must also be increased together with the size of all the other galaxies for which it had been a yardstick. Baade was thus able to establish that, while our galaxy was somewhat bigger than normal, it was not the largest, as Hubble's work had implied.

Baader-Meinhof Group [also known as Red Army Faction]. Post-1968 West German urban guerrillas, emerging from the radical student movement, led by **Andreas Baader** and **Ulrike Meinhof**. The group was responsible for six killings, 50 attempted killings, bombings of U.S. military installations, and bank raids. Captured in June 1972, Baader and Meinhof later committed suicide while in custody.

Ba'ath. "Revival" or "renaissance"—an Arabic party founded in 1910 by a Syrian Christian, Michel AFLAQ. The Ba'ath Party propounds a policy of pan-Arabism and principles of freedom, unity and socialism. It became the Ba'ath Socialist Party in 1952 after merging with the Syrian Socialist Party. However, Ba'athists are not confined to SYRIA, and their pan-Arab philosophy has been influential in IRAQ, JORDAN, LEBANON and the PERSIAN GULF states. Ba'athists were most influential during the UNITED ARAB REPUBLIC (EGYPT and Syria) of the late 1950s, but supporters became disillusioned by the authoritarianism of Egyptian President NASSER. A military coup in 1961 was followed by Syria's withdrawal from the union the same year. The Ba'athist cause suffered from the failure of this experiment and from antidemocratic tendencies of Ba'athist governments in Iraq and Syria since 1963—tendencies displayed in the 1980s by Hafez al-ASSAD (Syria) and Saddam HUSSEIN (Iraq), both professed Ba'athists.

Babbitt, Irving (1865–1933). American educator and author. After attending Harvard University and the Sorbonne in Paris, Babbitt taught French and comparative literature at Harvard from 1894 until his death. He opposed the romantic movement and established a new literary movement, neo-humanism, that emphasized human concerns based on studies of art and literature and the civilizations of ancient Greece and China. H.L. MENCKEN was a critic of Babbitt; early followers included T.S. ELIOT and George SANTAYANA, who later disagreed with his philosophy. His books include *Literature and the American College* (1908).

For further reading:

Brennan, Stephen, *Irving Babbitt*. Boston: G.K. Hall, 1987.

Babbitt, Milton (1916–). American composer. Babbitt is one of the pioneers of modern musical composition for electronic instruments. He earned his M.A. in fine arts in 1942 from Princeton University, where he studied with Roger SESSIONS. Babbitt subsequently taught at Princeton while pursuing an active and influential career as a composer. Among his most noted works are *Three Compositions for Piano* (1946–1947), *Composition for Four Instruments* (1947), *Composition for Synthesizer* (1961) and *Vision and Prayer* (1961). In many of his works, Babbitt employed a 12–tone, serialized method of composition that featured marked variations in timbre, pitch and dynamics.

Babcock, Harold Delos (1882–1968). American astronomer. Babcock was educated at the University of California, Berkeley, where he graduated in 1907. In 1908 he joined the staff of the Mount Wilson Observatory where he remained until his retirement in 1948, after which he continued to work for many years with his son Horace BABCOCK. When he joined the observatory Babcock's first task was to supply the basic laboratory data on the effects of strong magnetic fields on various chemical elements. Many years later, in collaboration with his son, he used their joint invention, the magnetograph, to detect the presence of weak and more generalized magnetic fields on the sun. In 1948, they also revealed the existence of strong magnetic fields in certain stars.

Babcock, Horace Welcome (1912–). American astronomer. Babcock was the son of Harold Delos BABCOCK. Horace Babcock graduated in 1934 from the California Institute of Technology and obtained his Ph.D. in 1938 from the University of California. He worked at Lick Observatory from 1938 to 1939 and at the Yerkes and McDonald observatories from 1939 to 1941. He was engaged in war work at the radiation laboratory at the Massachusetts Institute of Technology (1941–42) and at Cal Tech (1942–45). In 1946 Babcock returned to astronomy and joined his father at Mount Wilson where they began an enormously profitable collaboration. Babcock later served from 1964 until his retirement in 1978 as director of the Mount Wilson and Palomar Observatories, which became known in 1969 as the Hale Observatories.

Babcock, Stephen Moulton (1843–1931). American agricultural chemist. After graduating from Tufts College in 1866, Babcock studied at Cornell, and in 1879 took a Ph.D. at the University of Gottingen. He taught at Cornell in 1881 and 1882, and later worked for five years as a chemist at Cornell's agricultural experiment station. He joined the University of Wisconsin faculty in 1887 as professor of agricultural chemistry and served until he retired in 1913. During this time he made possible some of the most notable advances in his field. In 1890 he invented the still-used method of testing the amount of butterfat in milk. The test helped both milk producers and sellers in quality control, and thus paved the path for the modern dairy industry, especially in Wisconsin. Babcock made extensive studies in the nutritional requirements of animals. This formed the basis for the discovery of vitamin A by E.V. McCollum in 1912. Babcock never patented his discoveries, making them available to benefit all.

Babel, Isaac Emmanuelovich (1894–1941). Russian novelist, playwright and short story writer. Babel wrote mainly about violence and brutality, from the viewpoint of an intellectual both fascinated and repelled by his material, yet striving to be objective. He gained fame with *Odessa Tales* (1923–24), which was published by Maxim GORKY. *Red Cavalry* (1924) was written as a result of his service as a soldier in the war against POLAND. He also wrote two plays, *Sunset* (1928) and *Maria* (1935). He was arrested in 1937 or 1938 and died in a Soviet CONCENTRATION CAMP, a victim of STALIN's GREAT PURGE.

Babi Yar Massacre. In September 1941 large numbers of Ukrainian JEWS and communists in Nazi-occupied KIEV were summoned to be registered. Many were then transported to a deep gully called Babi Yar ("Old Woman's Gully") outside the city, where they were machine-gunned in front of pre-dug graves by Nazi SS troops commanded by General Otto Rasch. The mass graves were covered over by bulldozers. Perhaps 100,000 inhabitants of Kiev, including 34,000 Jews, were massacred by the Nazis in two days.

Baby M Case. American court case in 1987 that considered a surrogate mother's plea for the return of the child she bore, pitting the child's natural mother against the child's adoptive parents. Mary Beth Whitehead, a married mother of two, agreed to bear a child for Mr. and Mrs. William Stern, who wanted a child but knew a pregnancy and childbirth would be dangerous because of Mrs. Stern's medical condition. Mrs. Whitehead agreed in a written contract to be artificially inseminated with Mr. Stern's semen and to bear a child, which would be turned over to the Sterns. In return she received $10,000 and the Sterns paid all costs. After the delivery Whitehead refused to turn over the baby and vanished with the child. After Mrs. Whitehead and the child were found the Sterns sued for breach of contract. The ensuing court battle caught the attention of the public at large and precipitated a vigorous national debate over the issue of surrogacy. The Sterns ultimately gained custody of the child, but a number of state legislatures passed laws outlawing surrogacy contracts in the future.

Bacall, Lauren [Betty Joan Persky] (1924–). American actress; one of Hollywood's most engaging film stars of the 1940s and '50s. After graduating from the American Academy of Dramatic Arts, Bacall was cast—at only 19 years of age—opposite Humphrey BOGART in the film *To Have and Have Not* (1944). She married the great actor a year later and costarred with him in three more film noir classics: *The Big Sleep* (1946), *Dark Passage* (1947) and *Key Largo* (1948). Bacall's model-like figure (she was nicknamed "slim"), husky voice and cool sex appeal formed a perfect chemistry with Bogart's famed "tough" exterior. After Bogart died in 1957, Bacall's career slipped somewhat, although she continued to appear in films such as *Harper* (1966) and *The Shootist* (1976). In the 1970s and '80s she turned more to stage work, with acclaimed performances in *Cactus Flower* and *Woman of the Year.* In the 1990s Bacall continues to make intermittent television, stage and film appearances.

Bachauer, Gina (1913–1976). Greek pianist. Born in Athens, Bachauer studied at the Athens Conservatory, the Ecole Normale de Musique in Paris with Alfred Cortot, and privately with Sergei RACHMANINOFF from 1932 to 1935. She made her debut as a soloist with the Athens Symphony Orchestra in 1935 and debuted with the Paris Symphony Orchestra two years later. When the Nazis invaded Greece, her immediate family was killed and she fled to Egypt, where she performed in hundreds of concerts for the Allied troops. After the war she settled in London, making her English debut with the New London Symphony in 1946. From then on she toured the world as a high-ranking international soloist, making her first American appearance at New York City's Town Hall in 1950. Bachauer was known for her accomplished and sometimes bravura technique, her penetrating tone and liquid playing style.

Bache, David (1926–). British automobile designer whose best-known works include the Land Rover of 1959, the Rover 2000 of 1963, and the Range Rover of 1970. His influence was present in many products of the automotive firm British Leyland until his departure from that firm in 1981.

Bachmann, Ingeborg (1926–1973). Austrian poet, short story writer, novelist, critic and dramatist. Bachmann studied law and philosophy at Graz, Innsbruck and the University of Vienna. *Die gestundete Zeit* won the Gruppe 47 prize in 1953; these pessimistic poems showed an awareness of German guilt and ambivalence. *Anrufung des grossen Baren* appeared in 1956. In 1959–60 she gave a series of lectures on the existential situation of the writer and published an essay on the philosopher Ludwig WITTGENSTEIN that addressed the "language problem." She also collaborated on libretti with composer Hans Werner HENZE. In 1964 she won the Georg Buchner prize. She ceased to write poetry in the 1960s, but went on to write a novel, *Malina*, part of a trilogy left unfinished at her death, and *Simultan* (1972), a cycle of short stories. FEMINISM is a major theme of her later work.

Bach-Zelewsky, Erich von dem (1899–1972). German Nazi general who crushed the 1944 WARSAW UPRISING during WORLD WAR II. In putting down the uprising, his troops killed 100,000 Poles and leveled 90% of the city. Bach-Zelewsky later testified against Nazi leaders at the NUREMBERG TRIALS. He was sentenced to life imprisonment for the murder of six communists.

Backhaus, Wilhelm (1884–1969). German pianist. Born in Leipzig, he studied at that city's conservatory and made his concert debut there at the age of eight. He pursued further studies with Eugene d'Albert in Frankfort am Main. A 1900 concert tour marked the beginning of his solo career. Backhaus settled in London in 1905, becoming a professor of piano at the Royal College of Music, Manchester. He continued to tour Europe, establishing a distinguished reputation for his interpretations of Beethoven and Brahms. He debuted in the U.S. in a concert with the New York Symphony Society in 1912. Beginning in 1909, Backhaus made a great many recordings, and he is particularly noted for his two series of Beethoven piano sonatas, the last of which he recorded at the age of 80. He was especially known for his boldness, clarity, breadth and devotion to accuracy. He and his wife moved to Lugano in 1930 and became Swiss citizens. Backhaus remained an active and admired soloist up until the time of his death.

Backus, Jim (1913–1989). Television, radio, film and theater actor. He provided the voice for the bumbling, nearsighted cartoon character Mr. Magoo beginning in 1949 and into the 1970s. His film roles included James DEAN's father in *Rebel Without a Cause* (1955).

Bacon, Francis (1909–). British painter. Bacon emerged in the postwar generation of British "pessimistic" painters that also included Graham SUTHERLAND. He earned worldwide recognition in the 1960s for his strikingly bizarre canvases that probed highly charged emotional themes through the use of incongruent and violent images. One of Bacon's best-known paintings is *Three Studies for a Crucifixion* (1962), a triptych in which the Christian symbolism of death and resurrection is transformed into a series of brutal scenes of dismembered torsos locked in seemingly erotic postures. Because Bacon frequently employed nonpainted images—such as photographs—for his canvasses, he was linked by critics to the American POP ART movement, although the emotional tenor of Bacon's work was far removed from the light satire of most Pop Art productions.

Baddeck. Village and resort on Cape Breton Island, Nova Scotia, Canada; onetime summer home of inventor Alexander Graham Bell. In 1909, it was the site of early airplane flights by the Aerial Experiment Association, formed by Bell in 1907 in conjunction with Glenn CURTISS and others. The association achieved record flights through the aileron principle of flight control.

Baden [Baden bei Wien]. Town in Austria's Miederosterreich province, southwest of Vienna; Aquae Panoniae, in the ancient world. It was the headquarters of the Soviet occupation zone from 1945 to 1955 and is one of the most famous health and tourist spas in the world.

Baden-Powell, Robert (Stephenson Smyth) [1st Baron Baden-Powell of Gilwell] (1857–1941). British soldier and founder of the Boy Scouts and Girl Scouts. An officer in the 13th Hussars cavalry regiment, Baden-Powell first gained fame as the defender of Mafeking during the South African BOER WAR (1899–1900). Back home, he initiated a program for boys that stressed self-reliance, resourcefulness and courage; this developed into the Boy Scouts organization in 1908. In 1909, with the help of his sister Agnes Baden-Powell, he founded the Girl Guides (became the Girl Scouts in the U.S.A.). His wife, Lady Olave Baden-Powell, was the first and only World Chief Guide (1918–77). He was created a peer with the title of Baron in 1929. His many books include *Scouting for Boys* (1908) and *Scouting and Youth Movements* (1929).

For further reading:

Jeal, Tim, *The Boy-Man: The Life of Lord Baden-Powell*. New York: Morrow, 1990.

Badoglio, Pietro (1871–1956). Italian soldier and premier (1943–44). A career officer, he served in WORLD WAR I and later became ITALY's governor of LIBYA (1929–33). He was commander-in-chief during the Italian conquest of ETHIOPIA (1935–36) and the failed invasion of GREECE (1940). An opponent of Italy's entry into WORLD WAR II, he became premier after the fall of MUSSOLINI and negotiated a 1943 alliance with the Allies. Badoglio resigned in 1944.

Baez, Joan (1941–). American folk and rock vocalist. Baez, who was one of the major figures in the widespread folk music revival of the early 1960s, was a musical star before the age of twenty by virtue of her haunting and powerful soprano voice. Her father was a Mexican-American scientist and her mother an American professor of English. Baez attended Boston University for a time but gave up her academic career to become involved in the active folk scene then based in Cambridge, Massachusetts. Baez enjoyed phenomenal success with albums including *Joan Baez in Concert* volumes I, 1962, and II, 1964, and *Daybreak* (1968). Her rendition of "We Shall Overcome" was an anthem of the 1960s CIVIL RIGHTS MOVEMENT. In the 1960s and 1970s, she toured with Bob DYLAN, with whom she was also romantically linked. Baez enjoyed hits in the 1970s with two different singles—"The Night They Drove Old Dixie Down" and "Diamonds and Rust." She remains active both in music and in libertarian politics.

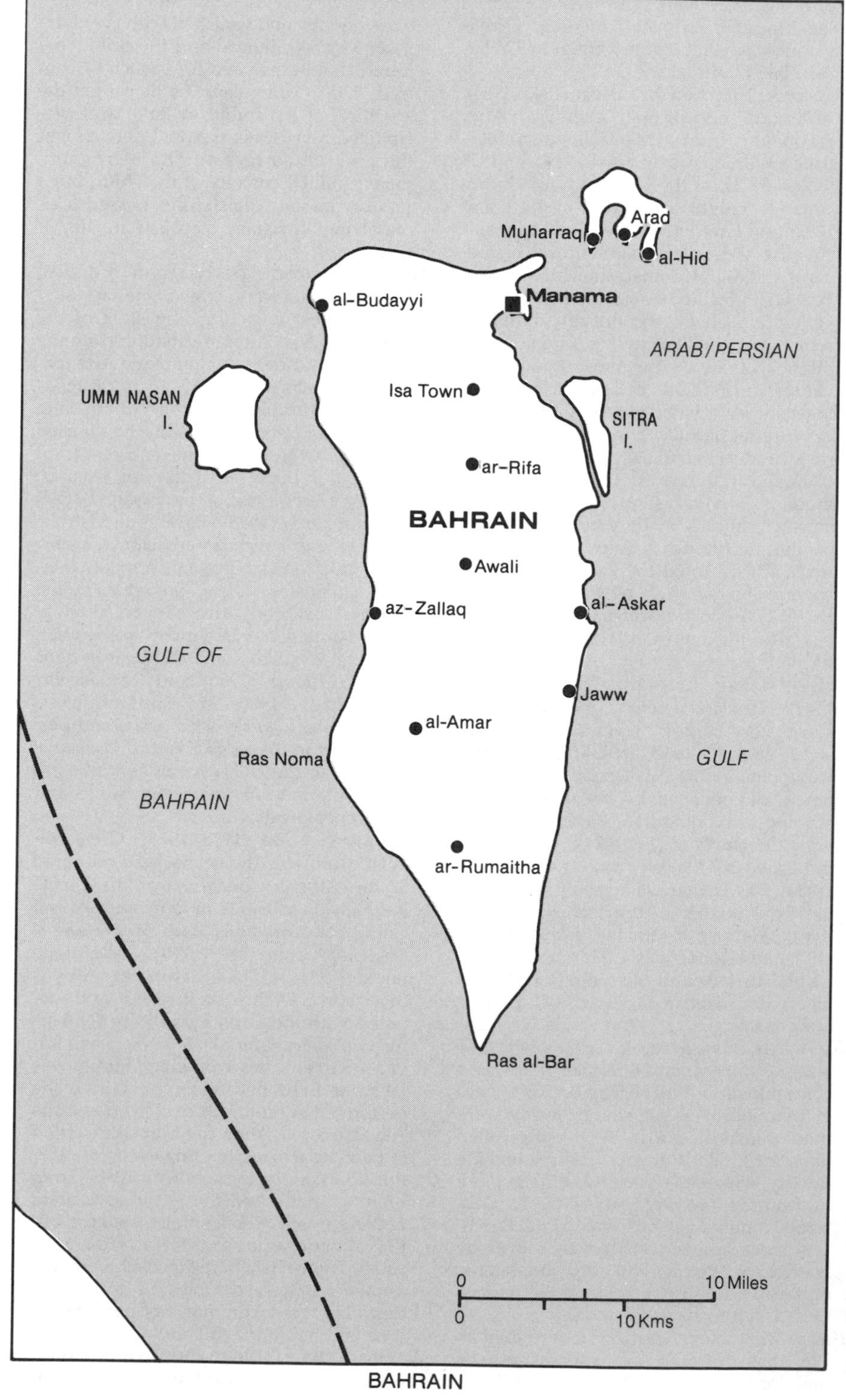

BAHRAIN

Baffi, Paolo (1911–1989). Italian financier and politician. He was one of the major economic figures in post-World War II Italy and served as governor of the Bank of Italy from 1975 to 1979, during one of the most turbulent periods in the country's recent economic history. He resigned in 1979 after he was arrested on charges of misconduct, but was later cleared and remained honorary governor of the bank until shortly before his death. It was afterwards reported that his arrest had been prompted by angry members of the ruling Christian Democratic Party who had been upset by an investigation he had conducted into the misuse of government credit for political purposes.

Baghdad. Capital city of Iraq located on both banks of the Tigris River. This ancient city was captured by British forces in 1917, during WORLD WAR I. In 1921 the British made Baghdad the capital of Iraq and saw an Arab monarchy installed. A violent revolution in 1958 toppled the monarchy after major fighting in Baghdad. The capital was a main target of U.S. bombing raids during **Operation Desert Storm** in the PERSIAN GULF WAR (Jan.-Feb. 1991).

Bahama Islands [Bahamas]. Nation of over 700 islands extending in a chain north of the West Indies, on a rough line from Florida to Haiti. Once a member of the British COMMONWEALTH, the Bahamas was granted independence in 1973. Its main industries are tourism and international banking; Nassau is the capital.

Bahrain. Emirate state consisting of a group of islands in the Persian Gulf, off the east coast of Saudi Arabia. Key islands are Bahrain, on which the capital of Manama is located, and Muharraq. In topography they are flat and sandy, with a humid climate. Bahrain became a British protectorate in 1861; after resistance to colonial rule in the 1950s and 1960s, Britain granted independence in 1971. Bahrain is ruled by an emir of the al-Khalifah family. Its key source of income is oil, first discovered in 1931, but it is also an international banking center.

Baikonur. See TYURATAM.

Bailey, Sir Donald Coleman (1901–1985). British civil engineer. Bailey was the inventor of the portable **Bailey bridge,** a device that played a key role in the Allied victory in WORLD WAR II. The bridge, assembled from welded panels of light steel connected by pinned joints, was extremely portable and could hold loads weighing tons. It was particularly useful during the June 1944 Allied invasion of NORMANDY.

Bailey, F. Lee (1933–). American criminal attorney and author. A graduate of Harvard University and Boston University Law School, Bailey handled many high-profile cases during the years after World War II. He gained national notice for his defense of Sam SHEPPARD, a Cleveland doctor who had been convicted of murdering his wife. After the U.S. Supreme Court granted Sheppard a new trial on the charge, Bailey won an acquittal. A decade later Bailey was hired to defend Patty HEARST, the daughter of newspaper magnate William Randolph Hearst Jr., who after her kidnapping by an extremist group voluntarily joined the group and robbed a California bank. Because of the overwhelming evidence against her even Bailey was unable to convince a jury of her innocence. Bailey, a celebrity in his own right, is the author of several books including *The Defense Never Rests.*

Pearl Bailey moments before she collapsed during a performance at the Americana Hotel after suffering a mild heart attack a few days earlier (April 26, 1965).

Bailey, Pearl Mae (1918–1990). U.S. singer. A Broadway musical star and cabaret singer, she was known for her campy, bawdy singing style and her dedication to performing. Her career began in VAUDEVILLE in the 1930s. She appeared in several films, including *Carmen Jones* (1954) and *Porgy and Bess* (1959). She played the title role in the acclaimed all-black production of the stage musical *Hello, Dolly!* (1967–69). Among her best known songs were "Tired," "Birth of the Blues," "That's Good Enough for Me" and "Takes Two to Tango." She won a special Tony Award in 1968 and the Presidential Medal of Freedom in 1988.

Bailey Bridge. See Donald Coleman BAILEY.

Bailey v. Drexel Furniture Co. (1922). U.S. Supreme Court decision overturning a federal law that attempted to outlaw child labor. The exploitation of children in factories was widespread in the early years of the 20th century. In response to an outcry from the public, Congress passed the Child Labor Tax Act to discourage employers from exploiting children. The law placed a 10% tax on the net profits of businesses who employed child labor. The Supreme Court declared the law unconstitutional on the grounds that, since the purpose of the tax was to regulate rather than raise revenue, the tax was an impermissible intrusion on business. The case was a major blow to reformers and child labor remained common until World War II, when the practice was finally outlawed.

Baillie-Scott, Mackay Hugh (1865–1945). English architect and designer involved with the Arts and Crafts movement. Baillie-Scott received his training while working in the office of the Bath city architect from 1886 to 1889. His commission to decorate rooms in a palace at the art colony at Darmstadt in 1898 led to his developing a reputation in Germany. He continued architectural practice and produced furniture designs for production and publication in Germany and Switzerland until his retirement from active practice in 1939.

Baird, Bill (William Britton) (1904–1987). U.S. puppeteer. Baird's impish creations, including Charlemane the Lion and Slugger Ryan, delighted millions of U.S. television viewers during the 1950s. With his third wife, Cora, he staged puppet shows around the world, including some in the Soviet Union. He trained a generation of other gifted puppeteers, most notably Muppets' creator Jim HENSON.

Baird, John Logie (1888–1946). British inventor. Baird studied electrical engineering at the Royal Technical College in Glasgow and then went to Glasgow University. His poor health prevented him from active service during World War I and from completing various business enterprises in the years following the war. After a breakdown in 1922 he retired to Hastings and engaged in amateur experiments on the transmission of pictures. Using primitive equipment he succeeded in transmitting an image over a distance of a couple of feet, and in 1926 he demonstrated his apparatus before a group of scientists. Recognition followed, and the next year he transmitted pictures by telephone wire between London and Glasgow. In the same year he set up the Baird Television Development Company. He continued to work on improvements and on September 30, 1929, gave the first experimental BBC broadcast. Synchronization of sound and vision was achieved a few months later. In 1937, however, the Baird system of mechanical scanning was ousted by the all-electronic system put forward by Marconi-EMI. Baird was at the forefront of virtually all developments in television; he continued research into color, stereoscopic and big-screen television until his death.

Baj, Enrico (1924–). Italian artist. An influential figure in the Milan art world, Baj was the cofounder of the journal *Il gesto* in 1955. Working in oils, collages and graphics, he underwent a number of stylistic changes during his career. Beginning as an abstract painter, he turned to a kind of surrealist imagery in semi-figurative paintings inhabited by otherworldly human-like creatures. He is also known for his POP ART parodies of paintings by modern masters.

Bajer, Frederik (1837–1922). Danish author and pacifist. In the Danish army from 1856 to 1864, he became interested in social problems. He started to write newspaper articles, and in 1867 he attempted to found a peace society. In 1870 he established the Association of Scandinavian Free States, which advocated the union of Scandinavian nations. As a member of parliament (1872–95), he worked for various progressive reforms including neutrality and women's rights. From 1891 to 1907, he served as chairman of the International Peace Bureau, headquartered in Bern, Switzerland. In 1908, he was instrumental in the establishment of a Scandinavian Interparliamentary Union, and that same year he was awarded the NOBEL PRIZE for peace along with the Swedish peace advocate Klas ARNOLDSON.

Bakelite. Trade name of one of the first PLASTICS to come into wide use. A phenolic invented in 1907 by chemist Leo Baekeland, the material is a good insulator against heat and electric current, can easily be molded in varied shapes, and is relatively inexpensive. It has a wide application in electrical hardware, for example, for handles and enclosure elements on kitchen wares, irons, and similar products. The material is brittle, making it easily damaged by impact; its color is normally limited to browns and black. The term has become a generic name for any phenolic plastic, regardless of manufacturer.

Baker, Chet (Chesney) (1929–1988). American JAZZ trumpeter and vocalist. Baker helped set the standard for West Coast "cool jazz" in the early 1950s, when he appeared with the Gerry Mulligan Quartet, a revolutionary, pianoless ensemble. Baker's career was blighted by heroin addiction. He was arrested repeatedly during the 1950s and 1960s on drug-related charges, both in the U.S. and in Europe. After a 1968 beating in which he lost most of his teeth, he did not play again for several years.

Baker, Ella (1903–1986). American CIVIL RIGHTS activist. Baker's talents as an organizer led to her becoming director of the New York branch of the NATIONAL ASSOCIATION FOR THE ADVANCEMENT OF COLORED PEOPLE during World War II. After the SOUTHERN CHRISTIAN LEADERSHIP CONFERENCE was established in 1957, she was asked to set up its national office and serve as its executive director. In 1960, she organized the conference that created the Student Nonviolent Coordinating Committee and later played a key behind-the-scenes role in that group's efforts to register black voters in Mississippi.

Baker, George Pierce (1866–1935). American educator. After graduating from Harvard University in 1887, Baker remained there for 36 years, beginning a career that influenced a whole generation of playwrights and actors. At Harvard he instituted a playwriting laboratory known as the 47 WORKSHOP, in which he taught talented students such as Eugene O'NEILL and Thomas WOLFE. From 1925 to 1933 Baker taught drama history and technique at Yale, and he headed the Yale department of drama. He was the first president of the National Theatre Conference (1932). His works include: *The Principles of Argumentation* (1895), *The Development of Shakespeare as a Dramatist* (1907) and *Dramatic Technique* (1919). Works that he edited include: *The Forms of Public Address, Plays of the 47 Workshop* and *Yale Long Plays.*

Baker, Dame Janet (1933–). English mezzo-soprano. Born in York, she studied with Helene Isepp and Meriel St. Clair in London and with Lotte LEHMANN in Salzburg. She made her English debut with the Glyndebourne Festival Chorus in 1956 and her American debut with the San Francisco Symphony in MAHLER's *Das Lied von der Erde* 10 years later. Her first American recital, also in 1966, was given at New York's Town Hall. Singing in a wide range of recitals, oratorios and operas, and as a soloist with major orchestras, Baker became an international star. She is known for her vocal warmth and richness, her exquisite phrasing, her sensitive musicianship and her breadth of repertoire. A superb interpreter of lieder, she also has a broad operatic range. Baker was named a Dame of the British Empire in 1970.

Baker, Josephine (1906–1975). American dancer, singer, entertainer and CIVIL RIGHTS activist. Baker, an African-American whose mother was a St. Louis washerwoman, first achieved international fame as an entertainer in the 1920s. Unable to find acceptance in her native land due to racial prejudice, Baker immigrated to Paris where in 1925, at age eighteen, she became a star while appearing in *La Revue Negre.* A beautiful woman with exceptional dancing and singing ability, Baker was also adept at presenting herself in a unique manner—such as walking on with her pet cheetah or having herself lowered upside down onto center stage. In the United States, her career fared less well. While Baker appeared with the ZIEGFELD FOLLIES in the 1930s, she was barred from many segregated clubs in the 1950s. In 1963, she marched for civil rights in Washington, D.C., with Rev. Martin Luther KING Jr. In 1937, Baker became a French citizen; her autobiography, *Josephine,* was published in 1977.

Josephine Baker models one of her spectacular Parisian gowns created for her American tour in 1951.

Baker, Newton Diehl (1871–1937). U.S. secretary of war (1916–21). After graduating from Johns Hopkins University in 1892, Baker earned his law degree from Washington and Lee University, and returned to Martinsburg, West Virginia, to practice law. Moving to Cleveland, Ohio, he was city solicitor (1902–12) and mayor (1912–16). Appointed secretary of war by Woodrow WILSON in March 1916 he began his service as WORLD WAR I was grinding on in Europe. During his first year in office, he was investigated by Congress for not doing much to strengthen the U.S. armed forces, but he was not removed from office. Baker overcame the early judgments of his administration and ended his service to the War Department with almost universal praise for his mobilization effort. Nevertheless, he remained one of the most ardent advocates of peace and continued to urge U.S. entry into the LEAGUE OF NATIONS. In 1928 President Calvin COOLIDGE appointed him to the Permanent Court of Arbitration at THE HAGUE.

Baker scandal. Political scandal involving President Lyndon JOHNSON's close political aide, Bobby Baker, a former Senate page. While Johnson was Senate majority leader, his aide Baker improperly used his political contacts to get contracts for his vending machine business and to amass a sizable personal fortune. When Johnson became vice president in 1961, additional accusations were raised that Baker received illegal payments and also bribed public officials. The outcry against Baker continued after Johnson became president following the assassination of President John KENNEDY. A Senate investigation raised additional accusations of wrongdoing against Baker, including financial improprieties involving Baker, President Johnson and Mrs. Johnson's Texas radio station. Although Baker himself testified, he added little damning nor exculpatory evidence. The committee found Baker had committed gross improprieties. Although Barry GOLDWATER, the Republican presidential nominee in 1964, raised the Baker scandal in his campaign, President Johnson won reelection handily. Baker was eventually convicted of tax evasion, theft and conspiracy to defraud the government. He served time in a federal penitentiary before being paroled in 1972.

***Baker v. Carr* ["One Man, One Vote"]** (1962). Landmark Supreme Court case holding that citizens could challenge the makeup of state legislatures in federal courts. From the earliest days of the Republic state legislatures employed considerable ingenuity in drawing legislative district boundaries, a process referred to as "gerrymandering." Legislative district lines were also often drawn to favor rural areas: A rural district with only a few thousand voters would enjoy the same voting power as an urban area with hundreds of thousands of voters. Despite suits protesting such disenfranchisement, federal courts traditionally declined to hear such cases on the grounds that they were "political" matters. In *Baker v. Carr* the Supreme Court reversed its previous position and held that state apportionment could be challenged in the federal courts. The decision, also known as the "one man, one vote" decision, started the process of reapportionment of state legislatures in favor of urban areas, which were often populated by minority groups.

Bakhtin, Mikhail (1895–1975). Russian theorist and critic. Descended from the nobility, Bakhtin was born in Orel, a small town outside Moscow, and was educated at Odessa and Petersburg Universities. His complex intellectual nature led him to write literary criticism and to work in the disparate fields of theology, anthropology, philosophy, political science, linguistics and psychology. Bakhtin worked in obscurity until the last 12 years of his life, and some of his books languished unpublished for 25 years or more. He made important contributions to the development of Marxism, Formalism and Freudianism. Bakhtin's books include *Problems of Dostoevsky's Poetics, The Dialogic Imagination* and *Rabelais and His World.*

Bakke case. Legal case, formally known as *University of California v. Bakke,* decided by the U.S. Supreme Court in 1978. It was brought by Allan Bakke, a white applicant for admission to the medical school at the University of California at Davis. Twice-rejected, Bakke claimed that he was the victim of reverse discrimination, in that he was denied admission while various minority group members with lower scores than his had been admitted to the school. The decision was close (5–4) and complex. It upheld the principle of race-based AFFIRMATIVE ACTION PROGRAMS, while denying institutions the right to establish race-based quotas. In this case, the University of California was found to have discriminated against Bakke by maintaining a 16% minority quota, and the Court ordered that Bakke be admitted. The decision was viewed by many civil rights advocates as a setback to affirmative action programs.

Bakr, Ahmed Hassan (1914–1982). President of IRAQ (1968–79). An army officer and a member of the Ba'ath Party (see BA'ATH), Bakr participated in the 1958 coup that overthrew the monarchy in Iraq. He became president after a bloodless coup in 1968. Bakr was ousted in 1979 by Saddam HUSSEIN.

Bakst, Leon Samoylovich (1866–1924). Russian painter and stage designer. Bakst designed settings for the Imperial Theater at St. Petersburg and later for many of Serge DIAGHILEV's ballets, including *The Sleeping Beauty, Carnaval, Scheherazade* and *L'Apres-Midi d'un Faune.*

Baku. City on the western shore of the Caspian Sea. During the RUSSIAN CIVIL WAR Baku was held by the WHITES. It became the capital of the U.S.S.R.'s Azerbaijan SSR in 1920. During WORLD WAR II, the city and its surrounding oilfields were almost within the grasp of the Germans before the invading fascists were stopped—and then rolled back all the way to Berlin.

Balaguer, Joaquin (1907–). President of the DOMINICAN REPUBLIC. Balaguer served in the government of dictator Rafael TRUJILLO MOLINA before becoming vice president (1957–60). He assumed the presidency in 1961, although Trujillo held effective power until his assassination in May 1961. Unable to govern in the chaos that followed Trujillo's death, Balaguer was overthrown in a military coup in January 1962. He was elected president in 1966 and reelected in 1970 and 1974 with overwhelming majorities. Balaguer's administration restored order and promoted economic development but was subject to attempted coups from both the right and the left. Balaguer lost the election of 1978 but was returned to office in 1986.

Balanchine, George [born Georgi Balanchivadze] (1904–1983). Russian dancer, choreographer and ballet director. One of the greatest and most influential choreographers of the 20th century, Balanchine was born in St. Petersburg. After studying dance at the Imperial School of Ballet (1914–21) and music at the Petrograd Conservatory of Music, he organized a short-lived touring company with fellow dancers in 1923. Denounced for his experimentation in dance, Balanchine left Russia in 1924 and joined Serge DIAGHILEV'S BALLETS RUSSES, for which he choreographed 10 ballets, including the seminal works *Prodigal Son* and *Apollo.* During this time he began to work with composer Igor STRAVINSKY, a collaboration that lasted over 50 years and resulted in 26 ballets, such as *Firebird* and *Orpheus.* After the company disbanded in 1929 upon Diaghilev's death, Balanchine formed associations with several other companies before Lincoln KIRSTEIN and Edward Warburg invited him to establish a ballet school (the School of American Ballet) and company (later named the NEW YORK CITY BALLET) in the United States. As artistic director of NYCB from 1948, Balanchine choreographed dozens of ballets, including *Midsummer Night's Dream, Leibeslieder Walzer* and *Sonnambula.* His oft-repeated maxim, "Ballet is woman," led to his association with many prominent ballerinas (such as Vera Zorina, Maria TALLCHIEF, Suzanne FARRELL and Patricia McBride), who were the inspiration for many of his ballets. The hallmarks of Balanchine's choreography are his musicality, his development of the plotless ballet that emphasized the dance element, his full use of a large dance ensemble and his emphasis on the ballerina. An innovative teacher, he also set a standard for ballet pedagogy and technique rarely equaled. Balanchine also created dances for Broadway musicals (*On Your Toes,* 1936) and films (*Goldwyn Follies,* 1938).

For further reading:

Ashley, Merrill, *Dancing for Balanchine.* New York: Dutton, 1984.

Buckle, Richard, *George Balanchine: Ballet Master.* New York: Random House, 1988.

Kirstein, Lincoln, ed., *Union Jack—the New York City Ballet.* New York: Eakins Press Foundation, 1977.

McDonagh, Don, *George Balanchine.* Boston: G.K. Hall, 1983.

Taper, Bernard, *Balanchine,* rev. New York: Random House, 1984.

Balch, Emily Greene (1867–1961). American economist and sociologist. Born in Jamaica Plains, Mass., she was educated at Bryn Mawr College, Harvard Annex (later Radcliffe), the University of Chicago and the University of Berlin. In

George Balanchine assisting prima ballerina Patricia McBride in an arabesque.

1896, she began teaching at Wellesley College. Also interested in social reform, she was cofounder of the Boston branch of the Women's Trade Union League and worked to promote the minimum wage. Her researches in Slavic immigration resulted in her book *Our Slavic Fellow Citizens* (1910). Balch's advocacy of liberal causes and world peace brought about her dismissal from Wellesley in 1918. Secretary-treasurer of the Women's International League for peace, she spent the next 40 years promoting international peace. In 1946 she shared the NOBEL PRIZE for peace with John MOTT.

For further reading:

Randall, Mercedes M., *Improper Bostonian: Emily Greene Balch.* New York: Irvington Publishers, 1964.

Baldwin, Faith (1893–1978). American popular author. During her career Baldwin wrote some 85 books of light fiction, as well as light verse. She reached the peak of her success during the GREAT DEPRESSION of the 1930s with magazine serializations and popular novels such as *Office Wife, District Nurse, Honor Bound* and *Rich Girl, Poor Girl.* Four movies were made from her books, with such stars as Henry FONDA, Jean HARLOW and Clark GABLE.

Baldwin, James (1924–1989). American author. Born in New York City, the son of a preacher, Baldwin felt the "rhetoric of the storefront church" to be an influence on his work, which examines racial, national, sexual and personal identity. He left home at 17 and eventually settled in Paris (1948). His first novel, *Go Tell It on the Mountain* (1953), the story of one day in the lives of the members of a HARLEM church, established him as a leading novelist of Black American life and drew inevitable comparisons to his mentor Richard WRIGHT, whose work Baldwin later rejected. His second novel, *Giovanni's Room* (1956), explored a man's struggle with his homosexuality. During the American CIVIL RIGHTS MOVEMENT, he wrote *Nobody Knows My Name* (1961), essays on race relations, and *The Fire Next Time* (1963), a powerful nonfiction book. Other works include *Another Country* (1962), *The Evidence of Things Not Seen* (1985), *The Price of a Ticket: Collected Non-Fiction* (1985) and *Perspectives: Angles on African Art* (1987).

Author James Baldwin.

For further reading:

Porter, Horace A., *Stealing the Fire: The Art and Protest of James Baldwin.* University Press of New England, 1988.

Standley, Fred L., ed., *Conversations with James Baldwin.* Jackson: University Press of Mississippi, 1989.

Weatherby, W.J., *James Baldwin: Artist on Fire.* New York: Dell, 1990.

Baldwin, Roger (1884–1981). Founder of the AMERICAN CIVIL LIBERTIES UNION (ACLU) and self-styled political reformer. As executive director of the ACLU from its formation in 1920 until 1950, he defended such disparate clients as communists, Nazis, members of the KU KLUX KLAN, Henry FORD and SACCO AND VANZETTI, all with equal vigor and dispassion. He was widely regarded as a leftist because of his defense of radical labor unions and other left-wing groups in the 1920s and 1930s. However, he also coordinated the defense of such underdogs as John Scopes in the SCOPES TRIAL (1925), and the Jehovah's Witnesses in 1938, achieving free-press rights for that religious group. After retiring as director, he remained the ACLU's international affairs adviser until his death. In January 1981 he received the White House Medal of Freedom.

Baldwin, Stanley [Earl Baldwin of Bewdley (1937)] (1867–1947). British statesman, three-time prime minister (1923, 1924–29, 1935–37). Educated at Cambridge he entered the political arena as a Conservative member of Parliament, where he served from 1908 to 1937. He became parliamentary private secretary to Andrew Bonar LAW in 1916, financial secretary of the treasury in 1917 and entered the cabinet as the president of the Board of Trade in 1921. After serving as chancellor of the exchequer (1922–23), he succeeded Law as prime minister in 1923. He left office briefly in 1923, returning as prime minister from 1924 to 1929. During this tenure in office, economic distress and rising unemployment led to the GENERAL STRIKE OF 1926, a crisis that Baldwin handled with considerable firmness and skill. After losing the election of 1929, he joined the coalition government of Ramsay MACDONALD in 1931 and again assumed the prime minister's office in 1935. Opposing the marriage of King EDWARD VIII, he deftly handled the ABDICATION CRISIS of 1936. Baldwin has been widely criticized for his underestimation of the NAZI threat during his last years in office. He resigned in 1937 and was made a peer later that year.

Balearic Islands [Islas Baleares]. Archipelago of 16 islands in the Mediterranean Sea, east of Spain (of which they are a province). Ibiza, Minorca and Majorca are the major islands. During the SPANISH CIVIL WAR (1936–39), Ibiza and Majorca were held by insurgents from the outset, but Minorca was held until 1939 by the losing Loyalists.

Balenciaga, Cristobal (1895–1972). Fashion designer whose work suggested the influence of his Spanish Basque origins. Balenciaga is viewed as a "dean" of fashion design, sometimes called "the greatest of the century." At the age of eighteen he established Elsa, a retail shop in San Sebastian, and shortly thereafter in Madrid and Barcelona. He made regular buying trips to Paris to augment his own design productions. In 1937, in response to the SPANISH CIVIL WAR, he relocated to Paris, opening a shop there that remained in business for thirty years. His first offerings were quiet and simple, but he soon developed design directions generally independent of the trends of any particular moment. His work was characterized by a bold sense of color, use of much black, strong and stiff fabrics, and rich ornament suggestive of traditional Spanish origins. Hats, scarfs, and rich jewelry were frequent additions to his productions. His work had a quality of timeless elegance.

Balewa, Alhaji [Sir Abubakar Tafawa] (1912–1966). Nigerian political leader. A member of the northern Hausa tribe, he was a founder of the Northern People's Congress political party, entering the regional house of assembly in 1947 and the federal house of representatives in 1951. Serving in various ministerial positions, he became the first prime minister of the Federation of NIGERIA in 1957, retaining the office when Nigeria became independent in 1960. A respected statesman, knighted by the British in 1960, he was nevertheless criticized by members of western and eastern tribes for favoritism toward the north. Balewa was assassinated in a 1966 military coup.

Balfour, Arthur James [1st Earl of Balfour (1922)] (1848–1930). British statesman, prime minister (1902–05). He entered Parliament as a Conservative in 1874. Balfour gained his first international experience serving as secretary to his uncle, the 3rd marquess of Salisbury (1830–1903) at the Congress of Berlin (1878). He first achieved prominence as chief secretary for Ireland (1887), opposing HOME RULE and championing land reform. He served as first lord of the treasury in 1891–92 and 1895–1902, and in 1902 he succeeded Salisbury as prime minister. During his term in office, Balfour introduced educational reforms (1902) and negotiated the ANGLO-FRENCH ENTENTE (1904). When the government split in 1905 over Joseph CHAMBERLAIN's tariff proposals, Balfour resigned. He was the leader of the opposition from 1906 to 1911.

During WORLD WAR I, Balfour served as first lord of the admiralty (1915–16) and foreign secretary (1916–19). In this capacity, he issued the BALFOUR DECLARATION in 1917, a document he considered the most important achievement of his political career. Balfour was prominent in the reshaping of Europe and the promotion of international peace, serving at the VERSAILLES Peace Conference (1919), the LEAGUE OF NATIONS (1920) and the WASHINGTON CONFERENCE (1921–22). He was lord president of the council in Stanley BALDWIN's cabinet from 1925 to 1929. An outstanding actor on the world stage, Balfour was also a profound thinker and the author of a number of books on philosophy and theology.

Balfour Declaration. Statement of British policy regarding ZIONISM. It was formulated in a letter of November 2, 1917, from British Foreign Secretary Arthur BALFOUR to Lord Rothschild, head of the British Zionist Federation. It endorsed the creation of a Jewish national home in PALESTINE, providing that the rights of non-Jewish communities in Palestine and the rights of Jews in other countries were not abridged thereby. Confirmed by the Allied governments, the declaration was written into the LEAGUE OF NATIONS mandate for Palestine (1922).

Bali. Island province of Indonesia, between the Bali Sea and the Indian Ocean. Unlike the remainder of Indonesia, which is Muslim, Bali has been a Hindu island since the seventh century. Conquered by Japanese forces during WORLD WAR II, it became a part of Indonesia upon the founding of that independent nation in 1949. In 1965, it saw fierce fighting when the Indonesian government murdered members of the nation's Communist Party.

Balikpapan. Indonesian port city on the northeast coast of the island of Borneo. Throughout the century, it has been a major oil producing and refining center. In January 1942, during WORLD WAR II, the Japanese navy met U.S. naval forces in the adjacent Makassar Strait and thereafter maintained control of it until 1945.

Balkans. The Balkan Peninsula, a large, ethnically diverse region of southeastern Europe, is crossed by the borders of six European and Asian nations: ALBANIA, BULGARIA, GREECE, ROMANIA, YUGOSLAVIA and TURKEY. The border between the Balkans and central Europe is generally considered to be the course of the Danube and Sava rivers. Since ancient times, the Balkans have been a violent blending-pot of peoples and cultures, of migrating horsemen and invading armies, the arena for numerous battles, conquests and revolutions. From the late 14th century until WORLD WAR I, the Balkans were largely dominated by the OTTOMAN EMPIRE. In 1815, Istria and Dalmatia were ceded to the Austrian Empire. In 1867, the Austro-Hungarian Empire included Croatia, Slovenia and Transylvania; in 1908, Bosnia and Herzegovina as well. Serbian nationalism was the spark that lit the conflagration of WORLD WAR I. Border conflicts and ethnic readjustments have continued into the last decade of the 20th century.

Balkan War, First (1912–1913). SERBIA, BULGARIA, GREECE and Montenegro attacked the OTTOMAN EMPIRE soon after its defeat in the Italo-Turkish War (1911–12), with the intent of seizing its remaining Balkan possessions. The Turks were unprepared, and the Balkan allies were prevented only by Bulgarian supply problems from advancing all the way to Constantinople (now ISTANBUL). Despite an armistice and an attempted peace conference, fighting resumed. Additional Turkish losses caused the new YOUNG TURK government to accept peace terms temporarily, but fighting began again, when it rejected them. The **Second Balkan War** (1913) was largely between Bulgaria and its former allies, joined by ROMANIA, over dismemberment of Macedonia, with Turkey attempting to regain its territories. In the **Treaty of Bucharest** (August 10, 1913), Bulgaria ceded its gains to its former allies, and the Ottoman Empire retained Adrianople, but lost 80% of its Balkan territories.

Ball, Lucille (Desiree) (1911–1989). American actress. Lucille Ball was one of television's most popular commediennes. In the 1930s and 1940s she was a contract player at the RKO movie studio, and she also performed on radio. Her greatest success came with the debut of the television series "I LOVE LUCY" in 1951. The slapstick situation comedy featured Ball as the zany, redheaded wife of a Cuban bandleader (played by her coproducer and real-life husband, Desi ARNAZ); it soon became the most popular television program in the U.S. The show was the first to be filmed in front of a live audience, thus ensuring its preservation on high-quality film (rather than by a film, or kinescope, shot off a live TV transmission). Years later, reruns continued to be shown in syndication in more than 70 countries around the world. In 1957, after the series ended, Ball and Arnaz bought out RKO and began producing other shows. After they divorced in 1960, she bought out his share of their Desilu Productions company for $3 million and eventually sold Desilu to Gulf and Western for $17 million in 1967. She also starred in two other series of her own, "The Lucy Show" (1962–68) and "Here's Lucy" (1968–74), as well as in films, television movies and specials.

Lucille Ball with her television and real-life husband Desi Arnaz at the height of their popularity.

Balla, Giacomo (1871–1958). Italian Futurist painter. Early in his career, Balla created academic paintings. While on a trip to Paris, he discovered Impressionism and Divisionism, and became fascinated by the interaction of light and color. He began to paint in the Futurist style in 1901 and was one of the signers of the Futurist manifesto in 1910 (see FUTURISM). Influenced by Cubist dissections of form and by the flickering images of the cinematograph, he developed a visual language that expressed dynamic motion. He is known for his whimsical Futurist work *Dog on a Leash* (1904), as well as for such later paintings as *Speeding Automobile* (1912, both Museum of Modern Art, N.Y.C.). (See also CUBISM.)

Ballard, (Edwin) Harold (1903–1990). Canadian sports executive. As owner of the National Hockey League's Toronto Maple Leafs, Ballard became one of sport's most controversial figures. He acquired control of the team after being released from prison after serving a sentence for income tax evasion. The team rapidly deteriorated into one of the worst in the NHL, as Ballard would not sign free agents and had a poor opinion of most non-Canadian players. Shortly before his death he dismantled the once awesome junior A franchise, the Toronto Marlboros, for financial reasons.

Ballard, J(ames) G(raham) (1930–). British novelist. Ballard began writing short stories for *New Worlds* in 1956 and established himself as one of the "New Wave" science fiction writers of the 1960s. His novels include *The Drowned World* (1962), *High Rise* (1975) and *Hello America* (1988). His short story collections, which are more admired, include *The Terminal Beach* (1964), *The Disaster Area* (1967) and *Vermilion Sands* (1971). Ballard was born and raised in Shanghai before returning to England to attend Cambridge; turning away from science fiction, he drew on his experiences in Japanese-occupied China in *Empire of the Sun* (1984, filmed 1988).

Ballets Russes (de Serge Diaghilev). The Ballets Russes, composed of some of the best Russian dancers of the day (such as Anna PAVLOVA and Vaslav NIJINSKY), was founded by Serge DIAGHILEV in 1909. The company's sensational debut at the Theatre du Chatelet in Paris (1909) is regarded as the birth date of modern ballet. For the next 20 years the company dominated the international ballet scene and became known for Diaghilev's ability to integrate all aspects of dance through his collaborations with such composers as Igor STRAVINSKY, Claude DEBUSSY and Serge PROKOFIEV, painters such as Leon BAKST, Alexander BENOIS and Pablo PICASSO, and choreographers such as Mikhail FOKINE, Leonid MASSINE and George BALANCHINE. In addition, the talents of dancers like Anton DOLIN and Tamara KARSAVINA were showcased. Notable ballets of the company include *Les Sylphides* (1909), *Le Sacre du Printemps* (1913), *Tricorne* (1919) and *Prodigal Son* (1929). The company disbanded in 1929 upon Diaghilev's death.

For further reading:

Kochno, Boris, *Diaghilev and the Ballets Russes.* New York, 1970.

Ballinger-Pinchot controversy. Conflict between U.S. Secretary of the Interior Richard Ballinger and Gifford Pinchot, head of the U.S. Forest Service, that badly split the REPUBLICAN PARTY in 1910, allowing the election of Democrat Woodrow WILSON as president in 1912. Ballinger, appointed as interior secretary by President William Howard TAFT, approved the sale of an Alaskan coal field to one of his former law clients. The same sale had been declared illegal by President Roosevelt's secretary of the interior, James Garfield. Pinchot, an ardent conservationist and the head of the Forest Service, opposed the sale. President Taft himself became involved, ultimately supporting the sale and his appointee Ballinger. The president fired both Pinchot and Louis Glavis, an employee of the Interior Department's land office who had opposed the sale and urged the Justice Department to intervene. Taft's strategy backfired when Pinchot and Glavis brought the matter to the public's attention. Glavis wrote an article for *Collier's* magazine that led to a congressional investigation in which Louis BRANDEIS—later to become a Supreme Court associate justice—demonstrated improprieties by both Ballinger and Taft himself. Taft's lame excuse that he "misremembered" events only worsened the situation; Teddy ROOSEVELT split from the Republicans and formed the Bull Moose Party, allowing Democrat Wilson to win the White House in 1912.

Baltimore, David (1938–). American molecular biologist. Baltimore studied chemistry at Swarthmore College and continued with postgraduate work at the Massachusetts Institute of Technology and Rockefeller University, where he obtained his Ph.D. in 1964. After three years at the Salk Institute in California, he returned to MIT in 1968 and in 1972 became professor of biology. In June 1970 Baltimore and, quite independently, Howard TEMIN announced the discovery of an enzyme, later to be known as reverse transcriptase, which is capable of transcribing RNA into DNA. For this work Baltimore shared the 1975 NOBEL PRIZE for physiology or medicine with Temin and Renato DULBECCO. Earlier (1968) Baltimore had done important work on the replication of the polio virus. In 1989, Baltimore became president of Rockefeller University. In 1991, he became the center of controversy when it was revealed that he had fabricated research data in a scientific paper earlier in his career.

Bamboo Curtain. Term given to the physical and ideological barrier to movement across the borders of the People's Republic of CHINA. The bamboo curtain was apparently lifted with the end of U.S. embargoes on exports to China in 1971, admission of China to the United Nations, President NIXON's visit to China (February 1972), and establishment of official relations with the European Communities in 1975. (See also IRON CURTAIN.)

Band, The. Canadian rock band. Comprised of Robbie Robertson, guitar; Garth Hudson, organ; Richard Manuel, piano and vocals; Rick Danko, bass and vocals; and the group's only American, Levon Helm on drums and vocals. Initially touring as a backup group for Ronnie Hawkins, they toured much of North America before hooking up with Bob DYLAN. Dylan, who was in the midst of his controversial transition from acoustic to electric, hired them for a world tour. Their debut album *Music from Big Pink* (1968) catapulted them to the top of the American rock scene. Other notable albums include *Stage Fright* (1970), *Moondog Matinee* (1970) And *Before the Flood* (1974). The Band's last performance is chronicled in Martin SCORSESE's *The Last Waltz* (1976).

Banda, Hastings Kamuzu (1906–). President of MALAWI (1966–). After practicing medicine in the United Kingdom and Ghana, he returned to Nyasaland as

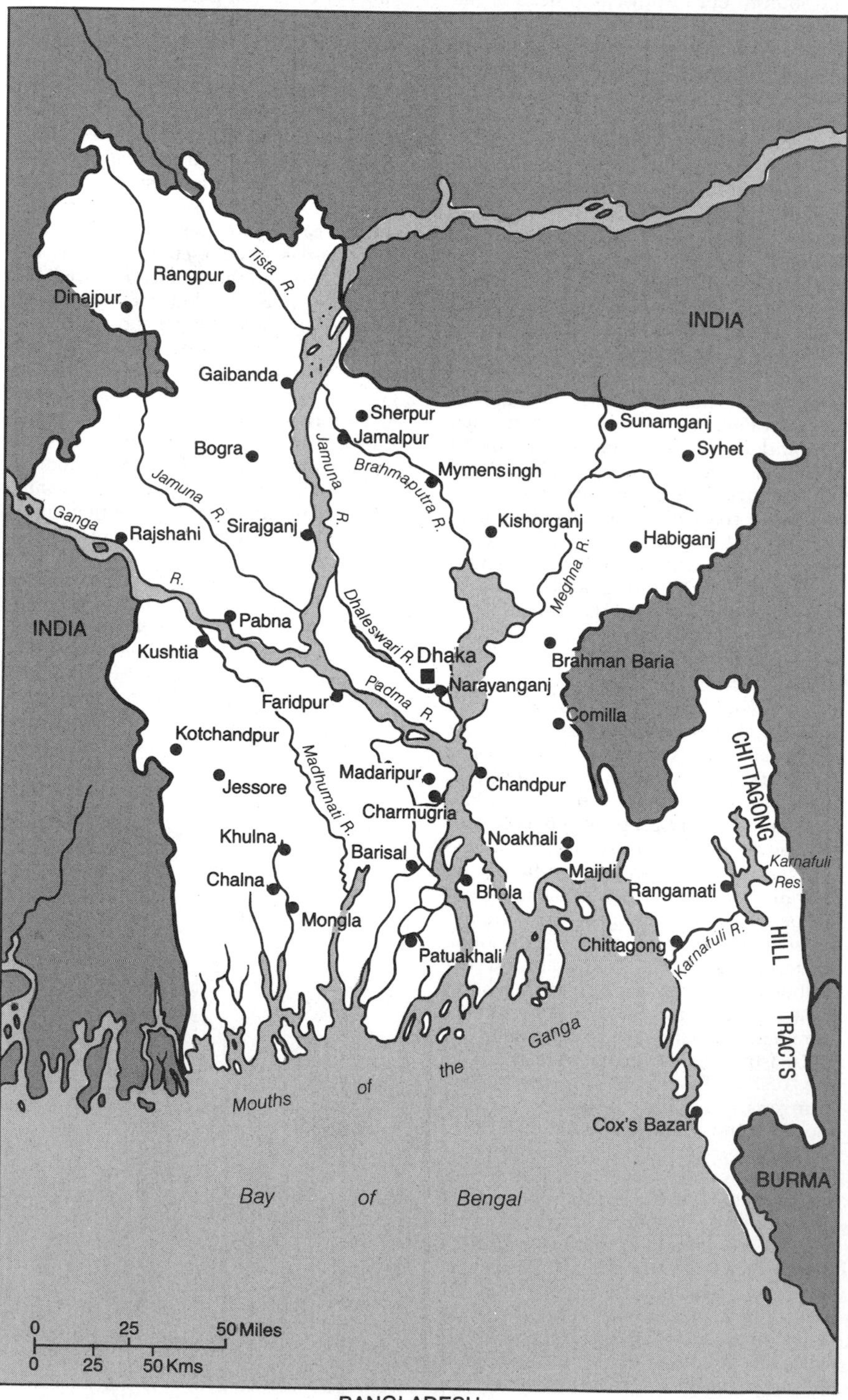

BANGLADESH

president-general of the AFRICAN NATIONAL CONGRESS (ANC) in 1958. He was imprisoned in 1959–60. He became leader of the Malawi Congress Party in 1961, minister of natural resources and local government (1961–63), prime minister of Nyasaland (1963–64) and of independent Malawi (1964–66).

Bandaranaike, Sirimavo (1916–). Sri Lankan political leader. Bandaranaike became the world's first female prime minister in 1960. She was the wife of the founder of the Sri Lanka Freedom Party, S.W.R.D. BANDARANAIKE, who was prime minister from 1956 until his assassination in 1959. His widow took over leadership of the party, then as prime minister she vigorously pursued a policy of socialist economics and Sinhalese domination of culture and politics. Defeated in 1965, she returned to office in 1970 and in 1972 was instrumental in the adoption of a new constitution. She was decisively beaten in the 1977 elections and, accused of abuses while in office, was stripped of her civil rights in 1980. She ran against Premadasa in the 1988 presidential elections and lost.

Bandaranaike, Solomon West Ridgeway Dias (1899–1959). Sri Lankan political leader and prime minister (1956–59). An Oxford-educated barrister, he returned to Ceylon (later renamed SRI LANKA) where he entered politics and was elected to the legislative assembly in 1931. From 1948 to 1951, he was minister of health and led the fight against malaria. In 1951 he resigned from the government and from the ruling United National Party, forming the socialist Sri Lanka Freedom Party. In 1956 he organized a leftist alliance, which was victorious in the elections of 1956. Becoming prime minister that year, he promoted neutralism in Ceylon's international policy and Sinhalese nationalism and language at home, while dealing with severe economic problems. He was assasinated by a Buddhist monk in 1959.

Bandung Conference. Conference of 29 African and Asian states, held April 17–24, 1955. Agreement was reached on economic and cultural cooperation, opposition to Dutch and French colonialism, and the development of a specifically THIRD WORLD non-aligned and neutral political stance in the COLD WAR.

Bane, Frank B. (1893–1983). U.S. government official. A strong proponent of federal welfare policies, Bane played a prominent role in shaping the programs of Franklin D. ROOSEVELT'S NEW DEAL. He was an author of the legislation that created the nation's SOCIAL SECURITY system and served as the system's first administrator from 1935 to 1938. During WORLD WAR II he played an important role in directing the rationing of goods and food. In addition to other government offices, he headed the Council of State Governments for 20 years.

Bang & Olufsen. Danish manufacturer of high-quality audio and video equipment. Peter Bang and Svend Olufsen began building wireless sets in the attic of the Olufsen family home in Struer, Denmark, in 1925. By 1929 they were operating a small factory that produced such innovative equipment as an early push-button tuning radio. A pick-up arm of 1965 designed by B&O staff designer E. Rorbaek Madsen was one of the first products to attract design attention to the firm. B&O products are of consistently high quality (and high price); their external designs are unique in emphasizing simplicity, unobtrusive controls, genuine wood panels, and black-finished metal, in contrast to the complex display of controls and high-tech look of most comparable equipment.

Bangkok [Krung Thep]. Capital and commercial center of THAILAND. In December 1941, during WORLD WAR II, it was conquered by the Japanese; later in the war, it was heavily bombed by the Allies. Severed into two municipalities in 1937—Krung Thep and Thon Buri—it was reunited into one city, Bangkok, in 1971. Bangkok has undergone much developement since the 1960s, and consequently combines the features of both first-world and third-world cities—modern opulence, pollution and poverty.

Bangladesh. Nation in South Asia, bound on the east, north and west by India and to the southeast by Burma. Formerly known as East Pakistan, it is the most densely populated country on Earth. Located in the Bengal region, its topography is dominated by the delta created by the confluence of the Brahmaputra, Ganges and Meghna rivers, and the land is prone to recurrent flooding. The population is 80% Muslim. From 1857 to 1947, the region was ruled as a part of British India. In 1947, it was granted independence as **East Pakistan,** separated (by 1,000 miles of India) from **West Pakistan**. The government of the new nation was located in West Pakistan, despite the East's larger population. Matters came to a head in 1970, when the Awami League of East Pakistan, led by Mujibur RAHMAN (known as Sheikh Mujib), won a majority of the parliamentary seats but was not allowed to convene. On March 15, 1971, civil war began; on the next day Bangladesh declared its independence. Shocking, large-scale massacres of Bangladesh civilians by the Pakistani military ensued. In December 1971, India entered the war on the side of Bangladesh, which it formally recognized as a new nation. In two weeks, the Pakistani military was defeated, but PAKISTAN did not recognize the nation of Bangladesh until 1974.

Sheikh Mujib became president of the new nation, its capital in Dacca. He nationalized several banks and businesses and assumed full dictatorial control in 1975, the same year he was assassinated by army officers. Subsequent President ZIAUR RAHMAN, who took office in 1977, was assassinated in 1981, after numerous coup attempts. The following year General Hossain Mohammad ERSHAD seized power and declared martial law. Disastrous floods in 1988 put three-quarters of Bangladesh under water and left 25 million people homeless. A cyclone in 1991 caused a reported 125,000 deaths, destroyed crops and contaminated drinking water. Apart from these natural disasters, Bangladesh remains plagued by the problems of famine, overpopulation and poverty.

BANGLADESH

1947	Eastern region of Bengal becomes East Pakistan.
1971	East Pakistan becomes independent state of Bangladesh.
1982	Hussein Mohammed Ershad takes power in military coup; martial law imposed.
1988	Record floods leave three-quarters of Bangladesh under water and 25,000,000 homeless.
1989	Rioting against Salman Rushdie's *Satanic Verses* kills 100 in Dacca.
1990	Ershad resigns; Awami League (AL) and Bangladesh National Party (BNP) unite to choose president.
1991	BNP wins first free elections in 20 years.

Bankhead, Tallulah (1903–1968). American stage and screen actress known for her sultry voice and sophisticated manner. The daughter of politician William Brockman Bankhead, speaker of the U.S. House of Representatives in the late 1930s, Bankhead made her stage debut in New York in 1918 and spent the 1920s in London. Returning to the U.S. in 1930, she became a familiar personality and was admired for her leading performances in such plays as *Dark Victory* (1934), *Rain* (1935), *Anthony and Cleopatra* (1937) and *The Little Foxes* (1939). Her most memorable film performance was in Alfred HITCHCOCK'S *Lifeboat* (1944).

Banks, Ernest "Ernie" (1931–). American baseball player. Known as much for his effusive personality as for his playing skills, Banks was the first black player on the Chicago Cubs. By the end of his career, which spanned 17 seasons (1954–71), he was known as "Mr. Cub." He was named Most Valuable Player in 1958 and 1959, both years in which he hit over .300. Dividing his career between shortstop and first base, his fielding skills were mediocre at the beginning of his career, but he

Mukti Bahini soldiers bayoneting execution victims in Dacca, Bangladesh.

improved enough to win a Gold Glove in 1960. He hit his 500th home run in 1970, and retired the following year. An 11-time All-Star, he was named to the Hall of Fame in 1977.

Banks, Harold Chamberlain "Hal" (1909–1985). American-born union leader. Banks led the Seafarers International Union of Canada in the 1950s and early 1960s. A militant anti-communist, he was at first welcomed by Canadian authorities but later accused of trying to destroy Canada's shipping industry. He returned to the U.S. as a fugitive in 1964 after conviction by a Canadian court on charges of conspiracy in an attack on a rival union leader. Canadian authorities tried unsuccessfully to have him extradited.

Bannister, Sir Roger (Gilbert) (1929–). English runner, physician and amateur athlete. While still a medical student Bannister became the first person to run a mile in less than four minutes. His record-setting run occurred on May 6, 1954, at Oxford; his time was 3 minutes 59.4 seconds. His record was soon broken by the Australian runner John Landy, who ran a 3:58 mile a month and a half later. Bannister came back to beat Landy at the Commonwealth Games, clocking 3:58.8 on August 7, 1954. He retired from competition shortly thereafter. Becoming a neurologist, he was knighted in 1975.

Banting, Sir Frederick Grant (1891–1941). Canadian physiologist. Banting, a farmer's son, began studying to be a medical missionary at Victoria College, Toronto, in 1910. During his studies he concentrated increasingly on medicine and graduated an M.D. in 1916, whereupon he immediately joined the Canadian Army Medical Corps and served in France in WORLD WAR I. In 1918 he was awarded the Military Cross for gallantry in action. Banting returned to Toronto and for a time studied children's diseases before setting up practice in London, Ontario, in 1920. He also began work at the London Medical School, specializing in studies on the pancreas, particularly the small patches of pancreatic cells known as the islets of Langerhans. Earlier work had shown a connection between the pancreas and diabetes, and Banting wondered if a hormone was produced in the islets of Langerhans that regulated glucose metabolism. In 1921 he approached John Macleod, professor of physiology at Toronto University, who was initially skeptical. Feeling that Banting needed help in physiological and biochemical methods, Macleod suggested the assistance of a young research student, Charles Best. Over the next six months Banting and Best devised a series of experiments. They tied off the pancreatic ducts of dogs and made extracts of the islets of Langerhans free from other pancreatic substances. These extracts, called "isletin," were found to have some effect against diabetes in dogs. Prior to trials on humans, Macleod asked a biochemist, James Collip, to purify the extracts, and the purification method for what is now known as INSULIN was patented by Banting, Best and Collip in 1923. They allowed manufacturers freedom to produce the hormone but required a small royalty to be paid to finance future medical research.

The pharmaceutical firm Eli Lilley began industrial production of insulin in 1923, and in the same year Banting was awarded the chair of medical research at Toronto University and a government annuity of $7,000. The NOBEL PRIZE for physiology or medicine was awarded jointly to Banting and Macleod in 1923; Banting was furious that Best had not been included in the award and shared his part of the prize money with him. In 1930 the Banting Institute opened in Toronto and under Banting's guidance this was to become the home of Canadian medical research, with work on cancer, coronary thrombosis and silicosis as well as diabetes. Banting was knighted in 1934. When war broke out in 1939 he joined an army medical unit and worked on many committees linking Canadian and British wartime medical research. His bravery was much in evidence at this time, particu-

Roger Bannister cracks the four-minute mile barrier by running the distance in three minutes 59.4 seconds.

larly his personal involvement in research into mustard gas and blackout problems experienced by airmen. In 1941 on a flight from Gander, Newfoundland, to Britain his plane crashed and he died in the snow.

Bao Dai (1913–). Last emperor of VIETNAM. Enthroned in 1932 (though he succeeded as emperor in 1926), Bao Dai abdicated in 1945 under communist pressure and retired to Hong Kong, leading a playboy existence. He returned as head of state in 1949 at the request of FRANCE. When a separate **South Vietnam** came into existence in 1954, he was only a figurehead ruler, with Ngo Dinh DIEM as prime minister. In 1955 he was deposed by Diem in a referendum held while he was out of the country.

Bara, Theda [Theodosia Goodman] (1890–1955). A HOLLYWOOD star of the SILENT FILM era, Bara had a short, but sensational career as the original vamp—her name, an anagram for "Arab death," was coined to describe the evil temptress characters she played. A publicity campaign describing her as a seductress who was poison to men made her a star. Bara made over 40 films between 1916 and 1919.

Baraka, Amiri [born LeRoi Jones] (1934–). American poet, playwright, social activist. Baraka had a middle-class childhood in Newark, N.J., and attended Rutgers and Howard University. In the late 1950s and early 1960s he lived in New York's Greenwich Village and associated with the BEAT GENERATION poets. After the publication of *Preface to a Twenty-Volume Suicide Note,* he became a well-known avant-garde artist. In 1964 *Dutchman* received an Obie Award for best off-Broadway play. In the mid-1960s he became a militant black spokesman and moved to Harlem. Later he returned to Newark, where he became involved with local politics. His later writing is highly revolutionary, directed primarily to blacks. As the tone of his work grew more violent, his stature in the white literary establishment dwindled, but he is still regarded as an important African-American poet.

Barany, Robert (1876–1936). Austro-Hungarian physician. Barany was educated at the University of Vienna, graduating in medicine in 1900. After studying at various German clinics, he returned to Vienna to become an assistant at the university's ear clinic. In 1909 he was appointed lecturer in otology. Through his work at the clinic he devised a test, now called the **Barany test,** for diagnosing disease of the semicircular canals of the inner ear by syringing the ear with either hot or cold water. For this he was awarded the 1914 NOBEL PRIZE in physiology or medicine. At this time he was being held as a prisoner of war in Siberia, but through the offices of the Swedish Red Cross he was released and the award presented to him. In 1917 Barany was appointed professor at Uppsala University where he continued his investigations on the inner ear and the role of the cerebellum in the brain in controlling body movement. *Barany's pointing test* is used to test for brain lesions.

Barbados. Island nation in the Windward Islands of the West Indies; formally became a British colony in 1885. The first elections with local participation were held in 1944 and were won by Grantly Adams' Barbados Labour Party (BLP). Barbados was a part of the now-defunct Federation of the West Indies from 1958 to 1962, with Adams as federation prime minister. Britain granted Barbados independence on November 30, 1966, and Earl Barrow, leader of the Democratic Labour Party, was the country's first prime minister. In 1976 Grantly's son, J.M.G. Tom ADAMS, was elected and pursued a conservative, pro-American policy. Barbados has remained a parliamentary democracy and is one of the more stable and prosperous West Indian nations. Its population is roughly 90% of black African ancestry. Barbados contains no rivers, and its water supply is pumped from underground caves. Sugar, rum and molasses are its primary exports, but tourism is also a major source of revenue. The capital is Bridgetown.

Barbarossa. German code name for the invasion of the U.S.S.R. in 1941. "Operation Barbarossa" was approved by Adolf HITLER late in 1940 and called for an invasion by the following May. The invasion aimed at creating LEBENSRAUM ("living space") for GERMANY and at the establishment of German colonies within Russia. German intervention in the Balkans postponed her plans slightly, but on June 22, 1941, 121 massed divisions crossed the Russian frontier, attacking on a front from the Baltic to the Black Sea. Hitler was completely confident of success in this undertaking, so convinced of early victory that he failed to outfit his troops for possible winter fighting. Catching the Soviets by surprise, German troops met with overwhelming initial success. By the fall of 1941, Russian resistance to the invasion began to solidify while German resolve began to falter and their supply lines to break down. A counteroffensive by Soviet General Georgi ZHUKOV forced back German troops in central Russia. The largest military undertaking in history, Barbarossa failed largely because of Germany's underestimation of Russian resistance and her inability to subdue Moscow before the coming of winter. (See also WORLD WAR II ON THE RUSSIAN FRONT.)

Barber, Samuel (1910–1981). American composer. Barber is one of the outstanding composers of the century, especially noted for his lyrical, melodic style and mastery of modern counterpoint. In 1937 his Symphony No. 1, in one movement, became the first American work to be performed at the Salzburg Festival of Contemporary Music. He collaborated with his lifelong friend Gian Carlo MENOTTI on his first opera, *Vanessa,* which won the PULITZER PRIZE for music (1958). A second Pulitzer was awarded for his 1962 Piano Concerto. Other major works include his most popular piece, *Adagio for Strings* (1938); the Violin Concerto (1941); and the ballet score for Martha GRAHAM'S *The Cave of the Heart* (1946).

Barbie Trial. Klaus Barbie, a former officer in the Nazi SS, was tried and convicted of crimes against humanity in a widely-publicized trial held in Lyons, France, in 1987. During WORLD WAR II, Barbie had been an SS lieutenant in charge of the German GESTAPO in Lyons, France, where he became known as the Butcher of Lyons for his sadistic treatment of Jewish and French RESISTANCE prisoners. After World War II the U.S. Army employed Barbie and later assisted his secret escape to Bolivia, where he lived until his discovery in 1983.

Although Barbie had been tried in absentia years before, the statute of limitations had run out on his specific crimes, so he was tried for the more general charge of crimes against humanity. Although he appeared only briefly during the trial, he protested his innocence and any responsibility. The judges and jury, however, convicted him of deporting 842 people, resulting in the known deaths of 373 individuals. Barbie was sentenced to life imprisonment, although he was eligible to be released on parole in 1993 at age 88.

For further reading:

Morgan, Ted, *An Uncertain Hour: The French, the Germans, the Jews, the Barbie Trial, and the City of Lyon, 1940–1945.* New York: Arbor House, 1990.

Wilson, Robert, *Confession of Klaus Barbie, Gestapo Commandant.* Seattle: Left Bank Books, 1984.

Barbirolli, Sir John (Giovanni Battista) (1899–1970). British conductor noted for his rich interpretations of 20th-century British and late-romantic composers. Born in London to a French mother and Italian father, Barbirolli studied at the Royal Academy of Music. After service in World War I, he played the cello in a London orchestra and in several string quartets. He made his conducting debut in 1925 directing his own chamber orchestra. Over the next decade he conducted various British orchestras. He succeeded Arturo TOSCANINI as director of the New York Philharmonic (1937–43); despite his generally fine performances, he inevitably suffered from comparisons to his legendary predecessor. Returning to England in 1943, he became director (1943–58) of the Halle Orchestra in Manchester and built it into an orchestra of international caliber. He later directed the Houston Symphony Orchestra (1961–67). During his last decade, Barbirolli made many outstanding recordings with the Philharmonia and the London Symphony Orchestra, among others. His performances of the works of Sir Edward ELGAR, Ralph VAUGHAN WILLIAMS, Jean SIBELIUS and Gustav MAHLER were particularly acclaimed.

For further reading:

Kennedy, Michael, *Barbirolli.* New York: Da Capo Press, 1982.

Barbusse, Henri (1873–1935). French novelist, biographer and journalist. Barbusse played an influential role in the French society of his era due to the political forcefulness of his writings. He worked as a journalist prior to WORLD WAR I, in which he served in the French army and was wounded. *Under Fire* (1916), his best-known work, is one of the major works of literature on the sober realities of warfare. In it, Barbusse advocated a committed pacifism. In the 1920s, Barbusse joined the Communist Party; in the 1930s, he was active in various antifascist movements. Barbusse wrote biograpies of Jesus (1927) and the French writer Emile Zola (1932). *I Saw It Myself* (1928) is his autobiography.

Barcelona [Barcino, Barcinona]. City on the Mediterranean coast of northeastern SPAIN. In 1938–39, Barcelona was the capital of the Loyalist Republicans during the SPANISH CIVIL WAR. It was also a key center of the Catalan separatist movement.

Barcelona Chair. Chair, together with an ottoman, designed by Ludwig MIES VAN DER ROHE in 1929 for the BARCELONA PAVILION. Its design consists of a simple X frame of steel bars supporting leather straps that carry seat and back cushions covered in leather. The Barcelona chair has become known as a modern design classic.

Barcelona Pavilion. German Pavilion at the Barcelona Exhibition of 1929 that became one of the best-known and most admired works of INTERNATIONAL STYLE modern architecture by Ludwig MIES VAN DER ROHE. The building, demolished after the close of the exhibition, was reconstructed in 1986 in its original location.

Barcroft, Sir Joseph (1872–1947). Irish physiologist. Professor of physiology at Cambridge University (1926–37) and director of animal physiology for the Agricultural Research Council (1941–47), Barcroft carried out extensive research into human embryology, physiology and histology. He investigated the oxygen-carrying role of hemoglobin and devised (1908) an apparatus for the analysis of blood gases. Barcroft led three high-altitude expeditions—to Tenerife (1910); Monte Rosa, Italy (1911); and the Peruvian Andes (1922)—in order to study acclimatization and the effects of rarefied atmospheres on respiration. During WORLD WAR I, Barcroft was chief physiologist at the Experimental Station at Porton, Wiltshire, where he studied the effects of poisonous gases. Elected a fellow of the Royal Society in 1910 and knighted in 1935, Barcroft wrote the famous text *Respiratory Function of the Blood* (1914), as well as publications on the brain and its environment and on prenatal conditions.

Bardeen, John (1908–1991). American physicist. Bardeen, the son of a professor of anatomy, studied electrical engineering at the University of Wisconsin and obtained his Ph.D. in mathematical physics at Princeton in 1936. He began work as a geophysicist with Gulf Research and Development Corporation, Pittsburgh, in 1931 but in 1935 entered academic life as a junior fellow at Harvard, moving to the University of Minnesota in 1938. Bardeen spent the war years at the Naval Ordnance Laboratory, followed by six creative years from 1945 until 1951 at the Bell Telephone Laboratory, after which he was appointed professor of physics and electrical engineering at the University of Illinois. Bardeen was a unique figure in science—the only recipient of two NOBEL PRIZES in physics. The first, awarded in 1956, he shared with Walter BRATTAIN and William SHOCKLEY for their development of the point-contact TRANSISTOR (1947), thus preparing the way for the development of the more efficient junction transistor by Shockley. Bardeen's second prize was awarded in 1972 for his formulation, in collaboration with Leon Cooper and John Schrieffer, of the first satisfactory theory of superconductivity—the so-called BCS theory. (See also SUPERCONDUCTORS.)

Bardot, Brigitte (1934–). French film actress. Bardot began her career as a model but soared to immediate international fame as a sex symbol with the release of her first film, *And God Created Woman* (1956). The Bardot look—blonde hair, cat-like eyes and full, pouting lips—became the rage on both sides of the Atlantic Ocean. She went on to star in numerous sex farces, not all of which were box office successes. Nonetheless, and in spite of long inactivity on the screen, Bardot has retained a high celebrity status. Her more notable films include *Contempt* (1963) and *Viva Maria* (1965).

Barenboim, Daniel (1942–). Israeli pianist and conductor, considered one of the most talented and glamorous classical musicians of his generation. Born in Buenos Aires, Barenboim was a child prodigy and gave his first public piano recital at age seven. His family subsequently moved to Europe, where the young Barenboim gave frequent concerts and recitals and also studied conducting and composition (with Nadia BOULANGER, among others). During the 1960s he established his reputation as a brilliant pianist and made extensive recordings of Mozart and Beethoven. He married the celebrated British cellist Jacqueline DU PRE in 1967. By the late 1960s he had also become well known as a conductor in Britain, Europe and the U.S. He was named director of the Orchestre de Paris in 1975. In the late 1980s Barenboim was appointed artistic and music director of the new Bastille Opera in Paris; his abrupt firing by the board's director before the company's first season in 1989, over the issue of artistic control, caused a major artistic and political controversy in France. Barenboim succeeded Sir George SOLTI as director of the Chicago Symphony Orchestra in 1991. Barenboim's repertoire includes relatively little 20th-century music, although he has championed the works of Sir Edward ELGAR.

Brigitte Bardot in a scene from the film Voulez-vous Danser Avec Moi (Do You Want to Dance with Me).

Barger, George (1878–1939). British organic chemist. Barger, of Anglo-Dutch parentage, went to school in Holland and read natural sciences at Cambridge University, where he graduated with equal distinction in chemistry and botany. While a demonstrator in botany at the University of Brussels (1901–03) Barger discovered a method of determining the molecular weight of small samples by vapor-pressure measurements. From 1903 to 1909 he was a researcher at the Wellcome Physiological Research Laboratories, where he worked mainly on ergot, isolating ergotoxine in collaboration with Francis Carr (1906). Work on ergot by Barger and Henry Dale led to a better understanding of the nervous system and to the development of new drugs. From 1909 to 1919 Barger worked in London, as head of chemistry at Goldsmiths' College, professor of chemistry at Royal Holloway College and from 1914 as chemist with the National Institute of Medical Research. In 1919 he was elected a fellow of the Royal Society and appointed to the new chair of chemistry in relation to medicine at Edinburgh. In 1938 Barger became professor of chemistry at the University of Glasgow. He was a pioneer of medicinal chemistry, an excellent linguist and a tireless ambassador for science.

Barkan, Alexander Elias (1909–1990). U.S. labor leader. He served as political director of the AMERICAN FEDERATION OF LABOR AND CONGRESS OF INDUSTRIAL ORGANIZATIONS (1963–81). As director of the AFL-CIO's Committee on Political Education, he was the chief political fund raiser and campaign operator for much of the organized labor movement and was instrumental in winning the election of sympathetic U.S. House and Senate candidates. He became disenchanted with the DEMOCRATIC PARTY in the late 1970s and retired in 1981.

Barkhausen, Heinrich Georg (1881–1956). German physicist. After attending the gymnasium and engineering college in Bremen, Barkhausen gained his Ph.D. in Gottingen and in 1911 became professor of electrical engineering in Dresden. Here he formulated the basic equations governing the coefficients of the amplifier valve. In 1919 he discovered the **Barkhau-**

sen effect, observing that a slow, continuous increase in the magnetic field applied to ferromagnetic material gave rise to discontinuous leaps in magnetization, which could be heard as distinct clicking sounds through a loudspeaker. This effect is caused by domains of elementary magnets changing direction or size as the field increases. In 1920, with K. Kurz he developed an ultrahighfrequency oscillator, which became the forerunner of microwave technology developments. After World War II he returned to Dresden to aid the reconstruction of his Institute of High-Frequency Electron-Tube Technology, which had been destroyed by bombing, and remained there until his death.

Barkla, Charles Glover (1877–1944). British X-ray physicist. After taking his master's degree in 1899 at Liverpool, Barkla went to Trinity College, Cambridge, but transferred to King's College to sing in the choir. At King's College he started his important research on X RAYS. In 1902 he returned to Liverpool as Oliver Lodge Fellow and in 1909 became Wheatstone Professor at King's College, London. From 1913 onward he was professor of natural philosophy at Edinburgh University. His scientific work, for which he received the 1917 NOBEL PRIZE for physics, concerned the properties of X rays—in particular, the way in which they are scattered by various materials. Barkla also demonstrated X-ray fluorescence. From about 1916, Barkla became isolated from modern physics, with an increasingly dogmatic attitude, a tendency to cite only his own papers and a concentration on untenable theories.

Barkley, Alben (1877–1956). U.S. political leader. Barkley served as a Democrat in the House of Representatives (1912–23) and in the Senate (1926–48, 1954–56), where he acquired a reputation as an ardent internationalist and supporter of progressive and NEW DEAL legislation. He was Harry S TRUMAN's vice president from 1948 to 1953. The following year he was reelected to the Senate.

Barlach, Ernst (1870–1938). German playwright and sculptor. Barlach was one of the leading figures in the Expressionist dramatic movement that dominated German theater in the decade following World War I. He frequently dealt with theological themes, such as the nature of the relationship between God and a troubled world, as well as with the tangled dynamics of family relationships. His major works include *The Dead Day* (1919), *The Poor Cousin* (1919), and *The Foundling* (1922).

Barmen. Suburb of East Wuppertal, in the German state of North Rhine-Westphalia; located on the RUHR River. In May 1934, German Protestant leaders met here at the **Synod of Barmen** to confer over possible resistance to NAZI control of GERMANY.

Barmine, Alexander G. (1899–1987). Soviet-born U.S. diplomat. A brigadier general in the Soviet army, in 1937 he became one of the earliest high-level Soviet defectors. Three years later he arrived in the U.S., where he became a journalist and government official. He served for 16 years (1948–64) as chief of the Russian branch of the VOICE OF AMERICA and for eight years (1964–72) as senior adviser on Soviet affairs at the U.S. Information Agency.

Barnack, Oscar (1879–1936). Inventor-designer of the LEICA, the first successful 35mm camera. Barnack grasped the possibility of using 35mm motion picture film for still photographs and developed a light, portable instrument and the optics to make this practical. The Leica camera has become a greatly admired icon of modern technological design, sternly functional in the tradition of Leitz optical instruments, but beautiful in a way that has made it a key example of industrial design in the 20th century.

Barnard, Christiaan Neethling (1922–). South African surgeon who performed the first human heart transplant. Barnard was awarded his M.D. from the University of Cape Town in 1953 and joined the Medical Faculty as a research fellow in surgery. After three years at the University of Minnesota (1955–58), where he studied heart surgery, he returned to Cape Town as director of surgical research. He concentrated on improving techniques for artificially sustaining bodily functions during surgery and for keeping organs alive outside the body. On December 2, 1967, Barnard performed the first heart-transplant operation on a human patient, a 54-year-old grocer named **Louis Washkansky.** He received the heart of Denise Duvall, a traffic accident victim. The heart functioned but the recipient died of pneumonia 18 days after the operation. The body's immune system had broken down following the administration of drugs to suppress rejection of the new heart as a foreign protein. Barnard subsequently performed further similar operations with improved postoperative treatment giving much greater success. His pioneering work generated worldwide publicity for heart-transplant surgery, and it is now fairly widely practiced.

Dr. Christiaan Barnard, South African surgeon who performed the first human heart transplant.

Barnard, Joseph Edwin (1870–1949). British physicist. While working in his father's business, Barnard used his spare time to study at the Lister Institute, King's College, London, where he developed an interest in microscopy, especially photomicrography, which led to his receiving a chair at the Charing Cross Medical School. He was a fellow and three-time president of the Royal Microscopical Society and in 1920 became honorary director of the applied optics department at the National Institute for Medical Research. His research and experience in photomicrography led him to write *Practical Photomicrography* (1911), which became a standard work. Later he developed a technique for using ultraviolet radiation, which is of shorter wavelength than visible light, and therefore gives greater resolution. With W.E. Gye he used this method to identify several ultramicroscopic organisms connected with malignant growths that were too small to see using standard microscopy.

Barnes, Djuna (1892–1982). American author. Born in Cornwall-on-Hudson, New York, Barnes later studied art in New York City and eventually settled in Paris. Her first works, *A Book of Repulsive Women* (1911) and *A Book* (1923), were collections of poems and plays. Her most enduring work of fiction, *Nightwood* (1936), a STREAM OF CONSCIOUSNESS narrative about five malevolent characters, was praised by T.S. ELIOT. Other works include *Ryder* (1928), a novel exploring the relationships of a man, his wife, mother, and mistress; *Ladies Almanack* (1928), which dealt with lesbianism; and *Selected Works* (1962). Her work is characterized by a dark decadence.

Barnett, Ross (Robert) (1898–1987). American politician. A white supremacist and segregationist, Barnett was governor of Mississippi from 1960 to 1964. Elected as a Democrat, he left that party during the 1960 presidential election. In 1962, in defiance of a court order, he refused to allow a black student, James MEREDITH, to be admitted to the University of Mississippi. This incident touched off one of the great confrontations of the CIVIL RIGHTS era.

Baron, Salo Wittmayer (1895–1989). Professor of Jewish history at Columbia University, widely regarded as one of the greatest Jewish historians of the 20th century. In 1961, Baron testified in Jerusalem at the trial of former Nazi official Adolf EICHMANN, setting the historical framework for the Israeli government's case against Eichmann. Baron wrote 13 works on Jewish history, including the 18-volume *A Social and Religious History of the Jews*.

Barr, Alfred Hamilton, Jr. (1902–1981). American art scholar. He was director of New York City's MUSEUM OF MODERN ART (MOMA) from its opening in 1929 until 1943 and was its director of collections from 1947 until 1967. An innovative exhibition designer, he expanded the museum's collection of 20th-century art to include industrial design as well as PI-

CASSO, avant-garde impressionists, architecture and motion pictures. Dubbed the "soul" of MOMA, he was considered by many the premier museum curator and tastemaker of the century.

Barragan, Luis (1902–1988). Mexican engineer and architect whose work combines the austerity of the INTERNATIONAL STYLE, or minimalist modernism, with a strong use of chromatic color (see MINIMALISM). Barragan was a self-taught architect, although he had some training in engineering and experience in his family's building business in Guadalajara. He traveled in Spain and was influenced by the Vernacular architecture of that country as well as that of his native Mexico. His work also shows influences of LE CORBUSIER and of many artists, historic and contemporary. His own house in Mexico City (1947) and the 1954 chapel at Tlalpan, Mexico, are well-known examples of his work. His work was exhibited at the MUSEUM OF MODERN ART in New York in a 1976 retrospective, and he was the recipient of the Pritzker Prize in 1980 in recognition of his work's international reputation.

Barrault, Jean-Louis (1910–). French actor, director and theater manager. Barrault is one of the leading figures of French theater in this century, having served at various times as the guiding force behind such renowned theatrical companies as the Comedie Francaise, the Theatre Marigny of Paris and the Odeon-Theatre de France. Barrault first came into prominence as a film actor in the 1940s, most notably for his romantic lead role in *Les Enfants du Paradis* (1944). Also during that decade, Barrault staged numerous premieres of works by the prominent French playwright Paul CLAUDEL. In the 1950s and 1960s, Barrault became a proponent of the THEATER OF THE ABSURD and directed plays by Samuel BECKETT, Jean GENET and Eugene IONESCO, among others. In 1968, having been dismissed by the Odeon-Theatre for his support of the French student uprising in May of that year, Barrault staged his play adaptation *Rabelais* in a Montmartre wrestling arena to great critical acclaim. With his wife, the actress Madeleine Renaud, Barrault founded the renowned Compagnie Renaud-Barrault.

Barrie, Sir James Matthew (1860–1937). Scottish-born novelist and playwright, the creator of PETER PAN. Barrie was born at Kirriemuir in Forfarshire, Scotland. After education at the Dumfries Academy and Edinburgh University he worked as a journalist for the *Nottingham Journal* and the *St. James Gazette.* Publication of his vivid recollections of his boyhood—*Auld Licht Idylls* (1887) and *A Window on Thrums* (1889)—brought him his first public notice. Many popular books and plays quickly followed. The plays, *Quality Street* (1901), *The Admirable Crichton* (1902), *Peter Pan* (1904), and *What Every Woman Knows* (1908) established him as the most popular playwright of his time. The devoted efforts of his longtime friend, theater producer Charles Frohman, brought them to equally enthusiastic audiences in America. Today, Barrie's works find a mixed reception. As a member of the so-called "Kailyear School"—a term applied to writers of romantic fiction utilizing the vernacular and common life of Scotland—he is without equal. However, other aspects of his work are more problematic. Barrie continued to write until the end of his life, finishing his last play, *The Boy David,* just before his death from a long illness in 1937.

For further reading:

Dunbar, Janet, *J.M. Barrie; The Man Behind the Image.* Boston: Houghton Mifflin Co., 1970.

Barringer, Daniel Moreau (1860–1929). American mining engineer and geologist. Barringer graduated from Princeton in 1879 and then studied law at Pennsylvania, geology at Harvard and chemistry and mineralogy at the University of Virginia. In 1890 he established himself as a consulting mining engineer and geologist; he was the author of the standard work *Law of Mines and Mining in the U.S.* (1907). Barringer is remembered for his investigation of the massive Diabolo Crater in Arizona, which is nearly 600 feet deep and over 4,000 feet in diameter. Barringer, finding numerous nickel-iron rocks in the area, became convinced that the remains of an enormous meteorite lay buried at the center of the crater. He began drilling in 1902 but failed to find anything of significance. After his death the crater became known as the **Barringer Meteor Crater.**

Barron, Clarence (1855–1928). American newspaper editor and author. Born in Boston, Barron joined the staff of the *Boston Evening Transcript* as a young man in 1875, and remained until 1884. Three years later, he established the Boston News Bureau and, in 1897, its counterpart in Philadelphia. Later in his career, he edited *Barron's Financial Weekly* and served as manager of Dow Jones & Company, publisher of the WALL STREET JOURNAL. Among Barron's books are *The Audacious War* (1915) and *A World Remaking* (1920).

Barrow, Clyde. See BONNIE AND CLYDE.

Barrow, Errol W(elton) (1920–1987). Barbadian statesman. Barrow helped lead BARBADOS to independence from Great Britain in 1966 and in the process became the Caribbean island's first prime minister after 350 years of constitutional rule. He governed Barbados for three consecutive terms before being voted out of office in 1976. In 1986 he was voted back into office.

Barrow Canyon. Submarine canyon in the Arctic Ocean of Canada and the U.S., running northwest into the Beaufort Sea. It was utilized in 1957 by the USS NAUTILUS, the first nuclear-powered SUBMARINE, in the course of its historic voyage beneath the polar ice cap.

Barry, Philip (1896–1949). American playwright. With wry comedies such as *Holiday* in 1928 and *The Animal Kingdom* in 1932, Barry became a prominent playwright of his time. His 1939 play *Philadelphia Story* was a hit and was adapted into a classic film. He also wrote serious dramas. His other plays include *Cock Robin* (1928), *Hotel Universe* (1930), *Here Come the Clowns* (1938), *Liberty Jones* (1941), *Without Love* (1942) and *The Foolish Notion* (1945).

Barry, Tom (1898–1980). Irish revolutionary, IRISH REPUBLICAN ARMY (IRA) leader and expert on guerrilla warfare. Barry trained and led the **West Cork Flying Columns,** an IRA guerrilla group, in the struggle against British rule during the ANGLO-IRISH CIVIL WAR OF 1916–23. He authored *Guerrilla Days in Ireland,* a book on tactical warfare that influenced guerrilla movements worldwide. (See also IRELAND.)

Barrymore. America's "first family" of stage and motion picture performers. The Barrymore saga begins in the middle of the 19th century with the distinguished actors, Mr. and Mrs. John Drew. Their daughter Georgiana married Herbert Blythe, who adopted the name "Maurice Barrymore." The three children of that union were born as "Barrymores": **Lionel** (1878–1954), **Ethel** (1879–1959) and **John** (1882–1944). Each at an early age followed in the family acting tradition. Lionel was a Broadway star at age 22 and a movie actor eight years later in 1909, when he began appearing in many BIOGRAPH films directed by D.W. GRIFFITH. Ethel was a smash hit on broadway in *Captain Jinks of the Horse Marines* (1900) and began movie acting after 1914. Handsome, rambunctious John, who was a sensation on Broadway and in London with the record-breaking *Hamlet* (1922–25), had the brightest success of the three in SILENT FILM, where he was a top star for WARNER BROS. in the 1920s, his appearance eliciting the memorable remark from Heywood Broun: "He now edges into pictures like a beautiful paper knife."

All three siblings made successful TALKING PICTURES. Lionel won an Oscar in *A Free Soul* (1931) and, after an accident that confined him to a wheel chair, played the crusty "Dr. Gillespie" in the Dr. Kildare series. Ethel won an Oscar for *None but the Lonely Heart* (1944) and appeared as a character actress in many subsequent films and television shows. John never got an Oscar but left a proud gallery of characters: the evil hypnotist in *Svengali* (1931), the disturbed father in *Bill of Divorcement,* the gentle teacher in *Topaze* (1933). Surprisingly, the three never appeared together on stage. Lionel and John costarred in the plays *Peter Ibbetson* (1917) and *The Jest* (1919) and on film in *Night Flight* (1933). John and Ethel occasionally appeared together on stage, most notably in *Clair de Lune* (1920). But the three were destined to appear together only once, on film, in MGM's *Rasputin and the Empress* (1932). It was a brilliant, if unstable, family, full of eccentricities and temperament. For all their glitter, the Barrymores lived under a shadow. As Ethel put it, "I think that both my brothers and I were born under a dark star so that there was no such thing for us as enduring happiness." Later generations of Barrymores

Three profiles of the Barrymore family—Lionel, Ethel and John—as they appeared together for the only time on screen in Rasputin and the Empress.

fared little better. John's children, John Jr. and Diana, pursued unsuccessful film careers. Drew Barrymore, daughter of John Jr., a successful child prodigy in films like *E.T.* (1982) and *Irreconcilable Differences* (1985), publicly revealed her problems with drug abuse.

For further reading:

Peters, Margot, *The House of Barrymore*. New York: Alfred A. Knopf, 1990.

Barth, John (1930–1990). American novelist and story writer. Barth, a native of Maryland who attended Johns Hopkins University in Baltimore and taught there for many years, first rose to prominence in the 1950s when his novels *The Floating Opera* (1956) and *The End of the Road* (1958) earned him a reputation as a gifted comic writer with a keen eye for the absurdities of American pop culture. Barth then proceeded to write two epic-length novels, *The Sot-Weed Factor* (1960) and *Giles Goat Boy* (1966), that both consolidated his reputation as a satiric explorer of existential themes and won him a broad popular readership. A book of novellas, *Chimera* (1972), earned Barth the National Book Award. Subsequent works by Barth include *Letters* (1979) and *Tidewater Tales* (1987). Barth also appeared frequently as a book reviewer in prominent national publications.

Barth, Karl (1886–1968). Swiss theologian. Barth was one of the leading Protestant theologians of this century, proclaiming as his central credo that "Faith, not reason, is the basis of Christian knowledge." Barth's father was a theologian of the Swiss Reformed Church, and Barth himself, after university study in Germany, became a Reformed Church minister in the small Swiss village of Safenwil, where he remained for 10 years. In 1918 Barth published his first book, *Epistle to the Romans*, which attacked liberal Protestant theology as having produced a "God-forgetting humanism." Over the next four decades, works such as *The Word of God and the Word of Man* (1928) and *Dogmatics in Outline* (1949) established Barth as a leading existential theologian whose defense of absolute faith echoed that of the 19th-century Danish philosopher Soren Kierkegaard. Although he felt that the church should stay out of politics, Barth personally was an active opponent of the HITLER government, joining the Swiss Army at age 54 in order to serve sentry duty on the Swiss-German frontier.

Barthelme, Donald (1931–1990). American novelist and story writer. Barthelme, who is best known for his short stories that appeared frequently in THE NEW YORKER, is often termed a POSTMODERN writer by virtue of his use of nontraditional, episodic narratives filled with black humor and absurdist irony. Barthelme, who was raised in Texas, was a gifted stylist fond of puns, neologisms and tangled literary allusions. His short story collections include *Come Back, Dr. Caligari* (1964), *Unspeakable Practices, Unnatural Acts* (1968), *City Life* (1970), *Sadness* (1972), *Guilty Pleasures* (1974), *Amateurs* (1976) and *Great Days* (1979). Barthelme also produced acclaimed novels such as *Snow White* (1967), a deadpan, disturbing retelling of the traditional fairy tale, and *The Dead Father* (1975), a fable-like account of a father who is at one and the same time alive and a gigantic dead carcass.

Barthes, Roland (1915–1980). French literary critic and philosopher. Barthes was one of the most influential literary critics of his era, a proponent of the "nouvelle critique" method that brought stringent philosophical analysis into the domain of textual criticism, where traditional stylistic analysis had long prevailed. Barthes drew heavily from Marxism, Freudian psychoanalysis, EXISTENTIALISM and STRUCTURALISM in his works, as well as from the study of SEMIOTICS, a linguistics-based school of thought proposing that a structure of basic signs underlies all forms of human communication, including literary expression. A suave stylist and versatile observer of cultures as well as of literature, Barthes' major works include *Writing Degree Zero* (1953), *Mythologies* (1957), *On Racine* (1963), *Critical Essays* (1964), *The Empire of Signs* (1970), *Sade, Fourier, Loyola* (1971), *S/Z* (1971) and *The Pleasures of the Text* (1972).

Bartlett, Sir Frederick Charles (1886–1969). British psychologist. Bartlett earned distinction both in theoretical and applied psychology over a long academic career that saw him become the first-ever professor of experimental psychology at Cambridge University in 1931. As a theoretician, Bartlett is best known for his book *Remembering* (1932), in which he argued—contrary to the schools of behaviorism and gestalt theory, both of which argued for a passive model of memory processes—that the human mind is highly selective, reconstructive and goal-oriented in its use of memory. During WORLD WAR II, Bartlett conducted practical psychological testing to improve British Army performance on gunnery and radar control systems. After the war, he became active in research on issues of industrial psychology. From 1924 to 1948, Bartlett was editor of the prestigious *British Journal of Psychology*. Bartlett was knighted in 1948.

Bartlett, Neil (1932–). British-American chemist. Bartlett was educated at the University of Durham, England, where he obtained his Ph.D. in 1957. He taught at the University of British Columbia, Canada, and at Princeton before being appointed to a chemistry professorship in 1969 at the University of California, Berkeley. Bartlett was studying metal fluorides and found that the compound platinum hexafluoride is extremely active. At the time it was an unquestioned assumption of chemistry that the noble gases—helium, neon, argon, krypton and xenon—were completely inert, incapable of forming any compounds whatsoever. Further, there was a solid theory that provided good reasons why this should be so. So struck was Bartlett with the ability of platinum hexafluoride to react with other substances that he tried, in 1962, to form a compound between it and xenon. To his and other chemists' surprise xenon fluoroplatinate was produced—the first compound of a noble gas. Once the first compound had been detected xenon was soon shown to form other compounds. Krypton and radon were also found to form compounds.

Bartlett, Paul Doughty (1907–). American chemist. Bartlett was educated at Amherst College and Harvard, where he obtained his Ph.D. in 1931. After teaching briefly at the Rockefeller Institute and the University of Minnesota he returned to Harvard in 1934 and served there as professor of chemistry from 1948 until his retirement in 1975. Bartlett worked mainly on the mechanisms involved in organic reactions. He also investigated the chemistry of elemental sulfur and the terpenes (a family of hydrocarbons found in the essential oil of plants).

Bartok, Bela (1881–1945). Hungarian composer and pianist, one of the foremost figures in 20th-century music. Born in Nagyszentmiklos, Hungary, Bartok was a sickly child with precocious music talents. With the encouragement of friend and mentor, Ernst von DOHNANYI, he went to Budapest's Royal Academy of Music in 1899. Although trained in the Germanic tradition exemplified by Franz Liszt and Richard STRAUSS, Bartok displayed a growing interest in the Magyar music and poetry of his native Hungary. Beginning in 1905 he made a series of trips across Hungary with his friend, composer Zoltan KODALY, to collect and record thousands of peasant folk songs. Far different from the "gypsy" music of Liszt, these colorful melodies and strange rhythms became the basis of Bartok's mature musical expression. They freed him from classical major-minor systems and instead utilized many modes, like the pentatonic scale and so-called "acoustic octaves" (with their augmented fourth intervals) with which he established a system of 12 semitones that functioned tonally, as opposed to the atonality of Arnold SCHOENBERG. Examples of this new musical vocabulary abound in Bartok's many sets of piano pieces, particularly the two books of *For Children* (1908–1909) and the collection of 137 tiny pieces called *Mikrokosmos* (1932–1937). During Bartok's tenure as professor of piano at the Royal Academy (1907–1936) and later residence at Columbia University in New York (1940–1942), he composed *Bluebeard's Castle* (1911), the *Dance Suite* (1923), *Music for Strings, Percussion, and Celesta* (1936), six string quartets and two piano concertos. However, living in virtual poverty in his last years, he was commissioned by Serge KOUSSEVITZKY to write what would be one of his most beloved works, the *Concerto for Orchestra* (1944), in which he quoted a theme from SHOSTAKOVICH's *Leningrad* Symphony. Bartok died of leukemia in 1945 before he could return to Hungary. "Bartok was not a robust man," recalled pianist and student of Bartok, Gyorgy Sandor, who premiered many of Bartok's works, including the unfinished Third Piano Concerto. "But his emotional and intellectual qualities were superb. He spoke fourteen languages and dialects. He was honest and extremely civilized. Everywhere in his music you find the most complete range and expression of human emotion."

Bela Bartok, composer.

For further reading:

Bonis, Ferenc, *Bela Bartok*. Budapest: Kossuth Printing House, 1980.

Milne, Hammish, *Bartok: His Life and Times*, Midas Books, 1981.

Barton, Sir Derek Harold Richard (1918–). British chemist. Barton was educated at Imperial College, London, where he obtained his Ph.D. in 1942. After some industrial research he spent a year as visiting lecturer at Harvard before being appointed reader (1950) and then professor (1953) in organic chemistry at Birkbeck College, London. Barton moved to a similar chair at Glasgow University in 1955 but returned to Imperial College in 1957 and held the chair of chemistry until 1978, when he became director of the Institute for the Chemistry of Natural Substances at Gif-sur-Yvette in France. In 1950 Barton published a fundamental paper on conformational analysis in which he proposed that the orientations in space of functional groups affect the rates of reaction in isomers. He confirmed these notions with further work on the stability and reactivity of steroids and terpenes. It was for this work that he shared the 1969 NOBEL PRIZE for chemistry with Odd Hassell. Barton's later work on oxyradicals and his predictions about their behavior in reactions helped in the development of a simple method for synthesizing the hormone aldosterone.

Baruch, Bernard M(annes) (1870–1965). American financier who acted as an adviser to every president from Woodrow WILSON to John F. KENNEDY. Born in Camden, S.C., he studied at City College in New York City. Starting as a Wall Street office boy, he quickly rose in the world of high finance, becoming a millionaire before he was 30. During WORLD WAR I he headed (1918–19) the War Industries Board and after the war (1919) served as a U.S. delegate to the PARIS PEACE CONFERENCE. After the election of President Franklin D. ROOSEVELT, he was offered the post of secretary of the treasury but declined the office in order to be an unofficial presidential adviser on economics and politics, a role he played until Roosevelt's death in 1945. During WORLD WAR II, Baruch was special adviser to James F. BYRNES (1942). Appointed U.S. representative to the United Nations Atomic Energy Commission in 1946, he was an important force in the attempt to control the forces of the atom. He described his life in two volumes of autobiography, *Baruch: My Own Story* (1957) and *Baruch: The Public Years* (1960).

Bernard Baruch.

Baryshnikov, Mikhail (1948–). Russian-born author and ballet director. Considered one of the greatest male dancers of the 20th century, Baryshnikov was born in Riga, Latvia. After training in Riga and Leningrad, Baryshnikov joined the Kirov Ballet as a soloist in 1966. That same year he won international acclaim and a gold medal at the Varna ballet competition. Then in 1969 he won the gold medal at the prestigious International Ballet Competition in Moscow. But limited repertory at the Kirov proved frustrating, and in 1974 Baryshnikov defected to the West. His search for artistic freedom led to a memorable partnership with Gelsey Kirkland at AMERICAN BALLET THEATRE, which he joined in 1974. As an ABT principal and guest artist with other companies, he achieved brilliant success in a variety of roles, ranging from Albrecht in *Giselle* to the lead in the modern dance *Push Comes to Shove* created for him by Twyla THARP (1976). In 1978 he left ABT for the NEW YORK CITY BALLET and the opportunity to work with George BALANCHINE.

He returned to ABT in 1980 as artistic director. During his nine-year tenure as director, he restaged classic works, commissioned pieces in the postmodern idiom and launched many dancers' careers, while also pursuing a career as an actor in movies (*The Turning Point, White Nights*) and on Broadway (*Metamorphosis*). In ad-

Mikhail Baryshnikov as the Nutcracker Prince in the 1980 American Ballet Theatre production of The Nutcracker.

dition, he has choreographed some works, most notably new versions of the *Nutcracker* and *Don Quixote*. As a dancer, Baryshnikov is best known for his spectacular jumps and turns.

For further reading:
Aria, Barbara, *Misha: the Mikhail Baryshnikov Story*. New York: St. Martin, 1989.
Baryshnikov, Mikhail, *Baryshnikov*. New York: Abrams, 1980.

Barzani, Mustafa (1904–1979). General Barzani was leader of an estimated 12 million Muslim KURDS. Under his leadership, the Kurds waged guerrilla war on and off against IRAQ for more than 40 years, beginning in the 1940s. Barzani hoped to establish an autonomous Kurdistan in northern Iraq. His secessionist movement collapsed in 1975.

Barzini, Luigi (1908–1984). Italian author, journalist and politician. Barzini began his career as a proponent of Benito MUSSOLINI and FASCISM. However, he became disillusioned and was later jailed for his opposition. As a journalist, he covered wars in GERMANY and ETHIOPIA and wrote for such U.S. magazines as *Harper's*, THE NATION and LIFE. Barzini also served as a member of the Italian parliament. His books on European culture include *The Italians*, a bestseller that offended many of his countrymen with its biting criticism, and *The Europeans*.

Barzun, Jacques Martin (1907–). American cultural historian and literary critic. Barzun was born in France but immigrated to the U.S. just after World War I. He graduated at the head of his Columbia College class in 1927 and commenced a lifelong career as a writer and teacher, ultimately becoming a professor of history at Columbia. Barzun's approach to historical and literary criticism was humanistic and eclectic, without recourse to absolute ideologies. He wrote a highly influential work on educational method, *The Teacher in America* (1945); in an essay for LIFE magazine (1950) he asserted that the true test of education was that the student "finds pleasure in the exercise of his mind." Other works by Barzun include *Darwin, Marx, Wagner: Critique of a Heritage* (1941), *Romanticism and the Modern Ego* (1943) and *God's Country and Mine* (1954), a book of reflections on American life.

Basic Treaty. A December 21, 1972, treaty of friendship and mutual recognition between the Federal German Republic (WEST GERMANY) and the German Democratic Republic (EAST GERMANY). The Basic Treaty was the culmination of West German Chancellor Willy BRANDT'S OSTPOLITIK and was followed by the entry of both nations into the UN in 1973.

Basie, William "Count" (1904–1984). American jazz legend, born in Red Bank, New Jersey. Count Basie, the seminal big band leader-pianist, forged a uniquely swinging style and subsequently achieved his initial fame and influence in the mid-1930s through national radio broadcasts from Kansas City, Missouri. His band's great appeal was based on an insistent yet subtly syncopated rhythmic pulse, a penchant for loosely sketched blues-based arrangements, and a "riff" style where the brass and saxophone sections alternated repeated background motifs, punctuating the impassioned improvisations of the band's always great stable of soloists. The Count Basie Orchestra, with only a few brief hiatuses, succeeded with its big band format (generally including five saxophones, three trombones, four trumpets, piano, rhythm guitar, bass and drums) in impressing critics and jazz fans, as well as dancers. Basie's Orchestra, one of the most potent incubators of jazz talent, brought to fame such fabled jazz soloists as trumpeters Harry "Sweets" Edison and Thad Jones, plus saxophonists Lester YOUNG, Eddie "Lockjaw" Davis and Frank Wess; Basie also featured arrangements by such noted composer-arrangers as Neal Hefti, Benny Carter and Quincy Jones. The Basie Orchestra continues to tour and record under the direction of one of its most outstanding alumni, saxophonist Frank Foster.

Count Basie (1950).

For further reading:
Basie, Count, and Albert Murray, *Good Morning Blues: The Autobiography of Count Basie*. New York: Random House, 1985.

Baskin, Leonard (1922–). American artist and illustrator. Born in New Brunswick, N.J., Baskin studied at New York University and the New School and at art schools in Paris and Florence. A figurative sculptor and printmaker, he is noted for expressive figures, often of bloated, corrupt humans and powerful animals. Noted also for his dramatic, spikey line, Baskin is particularly acclaimed for his dramatic woodcuts. He has illustrated several books by the British poet Ted HUGHES as well as numerous books on Jewish traditions. An articulate advocate of humanistic values in the visual arts, he is a noted teacher who has been a member of the faculty at Smith College since 1953. One of his best-known sculptures, *Man with a Dead Bird*, is in the collection of the Museum of Modern Art, New York City.

Basque separatist movement. The Basques are a people whose homeland, in the western Pyrenees Mountains, is spread across four Spanish and three French provinces; they are a group with their own culture and language and have long sought political autonomy. Under the leadership of Jose Antonio Aguirre y Lecube (1904–60), the Basques supported the Republicans in the SPANISH CIVIL WAR and briefly (1936) were granted autonomy in Spain. The Basque Republic, called "Euzkadi," with Aguirre as president, was destroyed with the victory of FRANCO, although a government-in-exile was maintained, first in Spain and later in France. Largely ignored by Franco, the Basques reemerged as a political force in 1959 with the formation of a militant separatist group known as the ETA. This organization became particularly active in the 1970s, causing a good deal of violence and embarking on a campaign of terrorism. In 1980 the Basques gained home rule as an entity within the Spanish state, but Basque violence and the quest for complete political autonomy continued.

Basra [Al-Basrah]. Sole port and second largest city of Iraq, located on the Shatt-al-Arab in the southeastern part of the country, near the Persian Gulf. Basra was occupied by British forces in 1941, during WORLD WAR II. A vital port for oil shipping, it was the site of intense fighting during the IRAN-IRAQ WAR (1980–88). During the PERSIAN GULF WAR it was bombed by the UN allies in **Operation Desert Storm** (1991). After the war there was fighting between forces loyal to Saddam HUSSEIN and Iraqis who opposed Hussein.

Bastin, Jules (1889–1944). Belgian army officer. A PRISONER OF WAR during WORLD WAR I, Bastin achieved public notice for his repeated and finally successful attempts to escape captivity. He commanded the Belgian cavalry in 1939–40, at the outset of WORLD WAR II. Following the German invasion of BELGIUM in May 1940 he joined the Belgian forces in

FRANCE. Commander of the Belgian Legion, he was appointed commander-in-chief of Belgium's underground military forces in 1942. Bastin was imprisoned in 1943 and died the following year while still in prison. He was posthumously (1946) awarded the title of general.

Bastogne. Town in southern Belgium. During WORLD WAR II, Bastogne was the keystone of U.S. resistance to the December 1944 German counteroffensive known as the BATTLE OF THE BULGE. The forces in Bastogne commanded by Gen. MCAULIFFE resisted repeated German attacks.

Bataan Peninsula. On Luzon Island in the Philippines. During WORLD WAR II, U.S. forces under Gen. Douglas MACARTHUR retreated here after Manila fell to Japanese forces. In April 1942, some 12,000 American and 64,000 Philippine soldiers surrendered to Japanese forces in Mariveles, a town on the Bataan Peninsula. It was the largest surrender of U.S. forces in history. Some Americans retreated farther to CORREGIDOR, an island off the south end of the peninsula, but these too surrendered in May 1942 after fierce resistance. The Japanese forced their U.S. and Philippine prisoners to march to northern Luzon under extremely desperate conditions; some 10,000 died and the march earned notoriety as the **Bataan Death March**. In February 1945, U.S. forces reconquered Bataan. The area of the peninsula overlooking Manila Bay to the east is today a Philippine national shrine.

Bates, H(erbert) E(rnest) (1905–1974). British author. Born in Northampton and educated at Kettering Grammar School, Bates later worked at a local newspaper. On the advice of publisher Edward Garnett, Bates' first novel, *The Two Sisters,* was published in 1926, followed by many short stories. He achieved great success during WORLD WAR II with his stories of wartime flying and maintained his reputation with such postwar books as *Love for Lydia* (1952), which was later adapted and televised by the BBC, and *The Darling Buds of May* (1958). Bates' work is marked by lyricism, simplicity, nostalgia for the countryside and rural traditions, and insight into the lives of ordinary people. He also published an autobiography in three volumes: *The Vanished World* (1969), *The Blossoming World* (1971) and *The World in Ripeness* (1972).

Bates, Leslie Fleetwood (1897–1978). British physicist. Bates was educated at Bristol University and at Cambridge University, where he obtained his Ph.D. in 1922. After teaching first at University College, London, he moved to Nottingham where he served as professor of physics from 1936, apart from wartime duties on the degaussing of ships, until his retirement in 1964. Most of Bates' work was on the magnetic properties of materials. He was the author of a widely used textbook, *Modern Magnetism* (1938), which went through many editions.

Bateson, William (1861–1926). British geneticist. Bateson graduated in natural sciences from Cambridge University in 1883, having specialized in zoology. At Cambridge Bateson began studying variation within populations and soon found instances of discontinuous variation that could not simply be related to environmental conditions. He believed this to be of evolutionary importance and began breeding experiments to investigate the phenomenon more fully. These prepared him to accept Mendel's work when it was rediscovered in 1900, although other British scientists were largely skeptical of the work. Bateson translated Mendel's paper into English and set up a research group to investigate heredity in plants and animals. He found that certain traits are governed by two or more genes, and in his sweet pea crosses showed that some characteristics are not inherited independently. This was the first hint that genes are linked on chromosomes, but Bateson never accepted the chromosome theory of inheritance. In 1908 Bateson became the first professor of the subject he himself named—genetics. However, he left Cambridge only a year later and in 1910 became director of the newly formed John Innes Horticultural Institution at Merton, Surrey, where he remained until his death. He was the leading proponent of Mendelian genetics in Britain.

Batista y Zaldivar, Fulgencio (1901–1973). President (1939–44) and dictator (1952–58) of CUBA. Batista joined the army, rising to the rank of sergeant before participating in a military coup against President Gerardo Machado. He promoted himself to colonel and established a fascist-inspired corporate state (see FASCISM). Elected president after permitting the formation of rival political parties in 1939, he went into voluntary exile in 1944 when he lost to Ramon Grau San Martin in the presidential elections. Batista returned to power in 1952 after a coup d'etat, but from 1956, faced by Fidel CASTRO's left-wing guerrilla movement, he lost support in the army and in January 1959 was forced to flee the country.

Batman. Celebrated American comic book hero, second only to SUPERMAN in international popularity. Batman first appeared in a six-page story in *Detective Comics* (1939). Identified at first as simply "The Bat-Man," he was the creation of 18-year-old artist Bob Kane. Like Superman, Batman wore a uniform and cape, possessed a dual identity and fought against the underworld. However, he possessed no super powers beyond his native intelligence and training in science and criminology. Batman's nemesis the Joker (one of a gallery of colorful super villains) appeared in late 1939; Batman's young assistant Robin ("the Boy Wonder") followed the next year. COLUMBIA PICTURES produced two film serials in 1943 and 1949, respectively. In 1964 the character was revived by the popular tongue-in-cheek "Batman" television series, which featured well-known actors in the roles of various villains. The hit film *Batman* (1989), starring Michael Keaton as Batman and Jack NICHOLSON as the Joker, brought the character back to its original conception.

Battle of Britain (1940). After France fell to the invading Germans in WORLD WAR II, the Nazis planned to bomb Great Britain into submission before invading across the English Channel. On August 15, 1940, the Luftwaffe (German air force) sent its first wave of bombers to southern England, encountering stiff resistance from British fighter planes. At first focusing on airfields, then intensively bombing London and other cities (the blitz), great damage was caused, but British morale was unbroken. The Royal Air Force (RAF) fought tenaciously, shooting down many German aircraft, and the Luftwaffe failed to establish air superiority. Germany called off the operation, and Prime Minister Winston CHURCHILL (1874–1965) said of the RAF pilots, "never . . . was so much owed by so many to so few."

battleship. See DREADNOUGHT.

Bauer, Riccardo (1896–1982). Italian socialist leader. He was a founder of the Action Party during the 1920s and of the underground "Justice and Liberty" organization that opposed MUSSOLINI during the 1930s and 1940s. During WORLD WAR II, he led guerrilla strikes against German troops occupying northern ITALY.

Bauhaus. German college of architecture and applied design that became a highly influential center of the arts in the 1920s. The Bauhaus was founded in Weimar by Walter GROPIUS in 1919. Gropius, inspired in part by the aesthetic craft movement of the British writer and artist William Morris, created the Bauhaus to further the role of the artist in industrial mass production. The Bauhaus became known for an architechtonic approach to design in which purely ornamental touches were eliminated in favor of a spare, geometric approach that utilized component materials with strict economy. The Bauhaus worked closely with industrial firms, and its furniture, textile and light-fixture designs were mass produced successfully. Bauhaus faculty members included painters Wassily KANDINSKY and Paul KLEE and the architect Ludwig MIES VAN DER ROHE. The Bauhaus moved from Weimar to Dessau in 1925 and again to Berlin in 1931. In 1933 it was closed down by the Nazis. The subsequent emigration of Bauhaus faculty and students has contributed to its enduring worldwide influence.

Baum, L(yman) Frank (1856–1919). American author. Born in Chittenango, N.Y., he worked as a journalist in South Dakota and Chicago. In 1899 he published his first book, *Father Goose: His Book,* which quickly became a best-seller. His next book, *The Wonderful Wizard of Oz* (1900), was to be his most famous. This story of little Dorothy from Kansas who is transported by a "twister" to a magical realm was made into a musical comedy in 1901 and into one of America's most popular motion pictures in 1939. The tale was the first of 14 Oz books by Baum, such as *Ozma of Oz* (1907) and *The Scarecrow of Oz* (1915), and many more written by others after his death. During his career, Baum wrote more than 60 books, many of them for children.

Baumeister, Willi (1889–1955). German painter. Born in Stuttgart, Baumeister was a student of Adolf Hoelzel. At first influenced by the Postimpressionists, he turned to a CONSTRUCTIVISM strongly associated with Fernand LEGER, creating abstract paintings filled with mechanical shapes. Dismissed from his teaching post in Frankfurt am Main in 1933 for tendencies deemed "degenerate" by the Nazis, he remained in Germany during World War II, researching color theory and archaeology. Influenced in his later works by these studies as well as by the work of Paul KLEE and Joan MIRO, his later work swarms with organic forms and ideographic signs.

Bavaria. State in southern GERMANY; formerly an independent duchy, kingdom and republic. Its major cities are Munich, the capital, and Nuremberg. After Germany was unified by Prussian Chancellor Otto von Bismarck in 1871, Bavaria joined the German Empire. After WORLD WAR I, King Louis III, the last of the Wittelsbach royal lineage, was deposed and a socialist republic was established under the leadership of Kurt Eisner. But Eisner was assassinated a few months later, and a subsequent communist revolt was crushed by the German military. Bavaria joined the WEIMAR REPUBLIC. Munich saw the rise of HITLER and his failed Munich BEER HALL PUTSCH of 1923. When Hitler finally came to power in 1933, Bavaria became a part of the Nazi Reich. After WORLD WAR II, it was in the U.S. occupation zone and was merged into West Germany in 1949.

Bawden, Sir Frederick Charles (1908–). British plant pathologist. Bawden was educated at Cambridge University, receiving his MA in 1933. From 1936 to 1940 he worked in the virus physiology department at Rothamsted Experimental Station, becoming the head of the plant pathology department in 1940 and director of the station in 1958. In 1937 Bawden discovered that the tobacco mosaic virus (TMV) contains ribonucleic acid, this being the first demonstration that nucleic acids occur in viruses. With Norman Pirie, Bawden isolated TMV in crystalline form and made important contributions to elucidating virus structure and means of multiplication. Bawden's work also helped in revealing the mechanisms of protein formation.

Bax, Arnold (1883–1953). British composer known for his romantic symphonic works. Bax was acquainted with the Irish poet W.B. YEATS, and his first work to gain recognition, *In the Faery Hills* (1909), was inspired by Yeats' narrative poem *The Wanderings of Oisin*. Bax's output includes seven symphonies and the tone poem *Tintagel* (1917), among numerous other works. His music is marked by rich orchestration and soaring melodies; quiet, poetic passages are frequently interrupted by rhapsodic outbursts. Bax never achieved the critical acclaim or popularity of ELGAR, VAUGHAN WILLIAMS or DELIUS, but his music has been widely performed and recorded in Britain and has undergone something of a revival in the latter part of the 20th century.

Bayar, Celal (1882–1986). Turkish statesman. Bayar was one of the founding fathers of the modern Turkish republic (see YOUNG TURKS). In the 1920s and 1930s he held a number of key cabinet posts under ATATURK; he was prime minister from 1937 to 1939. In 1945 he founded the opposition Democratic Party, and five years later he was overwhelmingly elected president of TURKEY. Ousted in a military coup in 1960, he was condemned to death; the sentence was commuted to life in prison. He was freed during a general political amnesty in 1964 but thereafter refused to sit in the Turkish senate, although this was his right as a former president.

Bayer, Herbert (1900–1985). Austrian artist; one of the last major figures associated with the BAUHAUS design school. Bayer arrived in the United States as a refugee from NAZISM in 1938 and soon became a major contributor to the advancement of graphic and industrial design, as well as advertising and urban planning. During the 1940s, he helped develop the town of Aspen, Colorado, as a cultural and resort center. From the 1960s until his death he served as art and design consultant to the Atlantic Richfield Company.

Bayliss, Sir William Maddock (1860–1924). British physiologist. Bayliss was the son of a wealthy iron manufacturer. In 1881 he entered University College, London, as a medical student but when he failed his second MB exam in anatomy he gave up medicine to concentrate on physiology. He graduated from Oxford University in 1888, then returned to University College, London, where he worked for the rest of his life, holding the chair of general physiology from 1912. Bayliss was elected a fellow of the Royal Society in 1903 and was knighted in 1922. He was chiefly interested in the physiology of the nervous, digestive and vascular systems, on which he worked in association with his brother-in-law, Ernest Starling. Their most important work, published in 1902, was the discovery of the action of a hormone (secretin) in controlling digestion. In 1915 Bayliss produced a standard textbook on physiology, *Principles of General Physiology*, which treated the subject from a physiochemical point of view.

Baylor, Elgin Gay (1934–). American basketball player. In 1958, Baylor was a first-round draft pick of the then-Minneapolis Lakers and was named rookie of the year in his first professional season. He remained with the Lakers for 14 years, a tenure that might have lasted even longer had it not been for his troublesome knees. He finished his career 11th on the all-time scoring list, with 23,149 points and, in 1960, set a record for most points in a game with 71. A 10-time all-star, Baylor went on to a less-successful career as a coach in the late 1970s. He was named to the Basketball Hall of Fame in 1976.

Bay of Pigs Invasion (1961). Abortive attempt by anticommunist Cuban exiles to invade CUBA and overthrow the government of Fidel CASTRO. The 1959 takeover of Cuba by Castro and his revolutionary followers prompted the exodus of many Cubans, especially to the United States. When Castro's regime began confiscating private property and established close ties to the Soviet Union, the United States imposed an embargo on all exports to Cuba (except food and medicine) and broke diplomatic relations (1960–61). Anti-Castro Cuban exiles demanded that the United States back an invasion of their homeland to topple the government; as early as 1960 the American CENTRAL INTELLIGENCE AGENCY (CIA) began to train an exile army in Guatemala. On April 17, 1961, about 1,400 exiles invaded southern Cuba at the Bahia de los Cochinos (Bay of Pigs), but by April 20 they were totally defeated by the Cuban army. Most of the invaders were killed or taken prisoner. Critics of this failure blamed the last-minute withdrawal of naval air support by U.S. President John F. KENNEDY, but closer investigation disclosed that the CIA scheme, meant to be secret but long a matter of public knowledge, had been based on faulty intelligence information and was poorly planned and executed. The failed invasion aggravated already hostile U.S.-Cuban relations and eventually required the expenditure of $53 million in food and medicine (raised by private donors) to secure the release of 1,113 surviving captive invaders (1962–63).

Bayreuth Festival. Located in the town of Bayreuth in Bavaria, Germany, where Richard Wagner built his home, the festival has given regular performances of Wagner's operas since 1892 (interrupted only by the world wars). The first festival was given in 1876 after Wagner had a theater built to house performances of his *Der Ring des Nibelungen*. Directors of the festival have all been members of the Wagner family, and no opera by any other composer has been given there.

Bazelon, David (1909–). American judge. A graduate of Northwestern University Law School, Bazelon was appointed to the powerful U.S. Court of Appeals for the District of Columbia where he helped shape criminal and administrative law for the nation. Among other notable achievements, Bazelon formulated the famous Durham rule, an insanity defense under which an accused would not be criminally responsible if a criminal act was the product of mental disease or mental defect. Although the rule was hailed as an advance, it was abandoned because it proved unworkable in practice.

Baziotes, William (1912–1963). American painter. Born in Pittsburgh, Pa., he studied at the National Academy of Design, New York City (1933–36) and held a number of teaching posts in the city. Influenced by CUBISM and SURREALISM, he developed a highly personal form of

ABSTRACT EXPRESSIONISM in the 1940s, which he refined in the 1950s. His brooding abstract canvases, usually painted in subdued colors, are inhabited by mysterious, otherworldly and faintly organic shapes. Characteristic works are *Dragon* (Metropolitan Museum, N.Y.C.) and *The Dwarf* (Museum of Modern Art, N.Y.C.).

BBC. See BRITISH BROADCASTING CORPORATION.

Beach, Amy Marcy Cheney (1867–1944). American composer and concert pianist. A child prodigy, in 1883 in Boston she premiered as a concert pianist to critical praise. In 1892 her *Mass* in E flat major became the first woman's composition performed by the prestigious Handel and Haydn Society of Boston, as was her *Eilende Wolken* (Opus 18) for the New York Symphony. Her reputation was solidified with a commission to write the *Festival Jubilate* for the 1892 World Columbian Exposition in Chicago. Beach toured Europe to critical and popular acclaim (1911–14). Her 150 works have generally been discussed with those of the Boston classicists, well constructed, late romantic, with broad melodies and beautiful harmonies. Her *Gaelic Symphony* (Opus 32) and Browning songs are still popular.

Beach, Sylvia (Woodbridge) (1887–1962). American literary publisher, bookseller and author. Born in Baltimore, Md., she immigrated to PARIS, where for many years she ran the renowned book shop and lending library, Shakespeare and Company. During the 1920s and 1930s it was a gathering place for such writers as Ernest HEMINGWAY, Andre GIDE, T.S. ELIOT, James JOYCE, Gertrude STEIN and many other lions of the Paris literati. Beach gained additional fame when she published Joyce's ULYSSES (1922) and, with the help of Hemingway, arranged for copies of the book to be smuggled to the United States, where it was banned until 1933. Shakespeare and Company was forced to close during the NAZI occupation of Paris in WORLD WAR II, but Beach and friends saved her vast collection of correspondence, books and memoirs from Nazi confiscation. She was detained in a CONCENTRATION CAMP for several months. In 1959 Beach presented the collection in an exposition at the United States Embassy in Paris. Much of it was later housed at the Sylvia Beach collection at Princeton; her Joyce collection was donated to the University of Buffalo. Her memoir is *Shakespeare and Company* (1959).

For further reading:

Fitch, Noel R., *Sylvia Beach and the Lost Generation: A History of Literary Paris in the Twenties and Thirties,* New York: W.W. Norton, 1985.

Beach Boys, The. American rock and roll band. The Beach Boys are one of the best known rock groups in history. Their hit songs of the 1960s, such as "I Get Around" (1964), "Help Me Rhonda" (1965) and the classic "Good Vibrations" (1966), have never left the radio airwaves since the time of their first airings. The five white male members of the Beach Boys included three brothers, Brian, Carl and Dennis Wilson, along with Al Jardine and Mike Love. Brian Wilson, who produces, composes and plays keyboard, has been the guiding musical force behind the group since its founding in 1961. In the mid-1960s, the Beach Boys linked themselves indelibly to the California beach scene with hits such as "Surfin' U.S.A.," "Fun, Fun, Fun" and "California Girls." While the group has continued to perform and record to the present day, it is these early hits—featuring the Beach Boys' trademark lilting vocal harmonies—that have won them a worldwide following of loyal fans.

Beadle, George Wells (1903–). American geneticist. Beadle graduated from the University of Nebraska in 1926 and gained his Ph.D. from Cornell University in 1931. He then spent two years doing research in genetics at the California Institute of Technology. In 1937 Beadle went to Stanford University, where in 1940 he began working with Edward Tatum on the mold *Neurospora.* From this and similar work Beadle and Tatum concluded that the function of a gene was to control the production of a particular enzyme and that a mutation in any one gene would cause the formation of an abnormal enzyme that would be unable to catalyze a certain step in a chain of reactions. This reasoning led to the formulation of the one gene-one enzyme hypothesis, for which Beadle and Tatum received the 1958 NOBEL PRIZE for physiology or medicine, sharing the prize with Joshua Lederberg, who had worked with Tatum on bacterial genetics.

Beamon, Bob (1946–). American athlete who set the world record for the long jump at the 1968 OLYMPIC GAMES in Mexico City. His spectacular jump of 29 feet, 2.5 inches shattered the previous record by 1 foot, 9 inches, and has never been equaled since by Beamon or any other athlete. Some critics point out that Beamon achieved his record at high altitude and that he was helped by a tail wind; Beamon's supporters feel that he has never gotten the recognition he deserves. Beamon retired from competition before the 1972 Olympics.

Bean, Alan (1932–). U.S. astronaut. Presently a professional artist, his paintings, like those of Russian cosmonaut-artist Alexei LEONOV, are enhanced not only by his creative imagination but also by his actual experiences; he was the fourth human to walk on the moon. Bean's moonwalk (November 18, 1969) came after he and Commander Charles CONRAD landed the lunar module of Apollo 12 on the surface of our nearest space neighbor. It was a near pinpoint landing, about 600 feet away from a U.S. Surveyor that had landed 31 months before. Curiously, among the parts of SURVEYOR returned to Earth, scientists found a colony of bacteria in the foam insulation of its TV camera—alive after two-and-a-half years. It can thus be said that Bean and Conrad "encountered" life on the moon. In one of the most successful of the APOLLO missions, Bean and Conrad spent over 30 hours walking the moon's dusty surface before returning to Earth on November 24, 1969. Bean commanded his second and last flight aboard Skylab 3, the second of three manned missions on America's first space station. With fellow astronauts Owen Garriott and Jack Lousma, Bean spent over 59 days (July 28–September 25, 1973) conducting experiments and making observations of the Earth and sun. Although he was in line to command the first Shuttle/Spacelab mission, Bean decided to work full time as an artist and resigned from NASA on June 26, 1981.

Beard, Charles Austin (1874–1948). U.S. historian and political scientist. After graduating from De Pauw University in 1898, he studied abroad for four years. From 1907 to 1917 he taught political science and history at Columbia University. During this time he became more interested in American history and economics, and became an intellectual leader of the Progressive movement. Beard was named director of the Training School for Public Service in 1917, and in 1919 he founded the New School for Social Research. He continued to write on political and historical matters and is considered one of America's most influential historians. With his wife Mary, Beard began work in 1927 on a four-part series called *The Rise of American Civilization.* His book *A Basic History of the United States* (1944) has continued to be a standard text. Beard's writings include *The Development of Modern Europe* (1907), *The Supreme Court and the Constitution* (1912), *President Roosevelt and the Coming of War* (1948) and *An Economic Interpretation of the Constitution of the United States* (1913).

Beard, James (Andrews) (1903–1985). American food authority. In 1945, Beard became the first chef to give cooking demonstrations on network television. A chef, lecturer and syndicated columnist, he wrote or coauthored 24 books, most of which celebrated American food. His best known work, *James Beard's American Cookery,* published in 1972, is considered a classic. For many years he also ran a New York-based cooking school.

For further reading:

Jones, Evan, *Epicurean Delight.* New York: Knopf, 1990.

Beat Generation, The. A group of American writers and poets whose work came into international prominence in the 1950s and continues to exercise a worldwide influence. The three key figures of the Beat Generation are novelist and poet Jack KEROUAC (*On The Road,* 1957), poet Allen GINSBERG (*Howl,* 1956) and novelist William BURROUGHS (*The Naked Lunch,* 1962). The term "Beat" was originally devised by writer John Clellon Holmes, a friend of Kerouac's, to connote a person who had abandoned the materialism of postwar American life in favor of a bohemian quest for worldly experience and spiritual meaning. Kerouac and Ginsberg first met in 1944 while both were still students at Columbia University; Burroughs, an older Harvard graduate who was holding various odd jobs, joined their circle and ex-

The "Fab Four" in 1963: John Lennon, Ringo Starr, Paul McCartney and George Harrison.

ercised a mentor's influence. In the late 1940s, Neal Cassady, a brilliant and charismatic blue-collar worker from Denver, befriended Kerouac and became Ginsberg's lover. Cassady's exuberant love of life became a vital source of inspiration for both authors; the central character of *On The Road,* Dean Moriarty, is based upon Cassady.

The Beat Generation literary movement, which also included poets such as Gregory Corso, Lawrence FERLINGHETTI, Gary Snyder and Philip Whalen, celebrated intuition over intellect, impulsive passion over puritanism, and the joys of bohemian simplicity and the open road. It exercised a tremendous influence on the youth of America and helped to spur the social and political protest movements of the 1960s.

Beatles, The. British rock and roll group of the 1960s. The Beatles were and remain the most popular band in the history of ROCK and roll. They were more than just a music group—they were a phenomenon, and they influenced and reflected the social history of the 1960s. The group had its origins in Liverpool, England, in the late 1950s when several teenagers got together to play "skiffle" music, a form blending JAZZ and folk music, in local nightclubs. The group performed for several years (under a number of names and with various members) in Liverpool and in Hamburg, Germany, before finally emerging as a hit group in England in 1963. By this time, the Beatles had coalesced and had developed a distinctive style that placed them far above run-of-the-mill pop groups. By 1964, "Beatlemania" spread to America and then around the world. The four musicians known to the world formally as the Beatles and informally as the "Fab Four" were guitarists George Harrison (1943–) and John LENNON (1940–1980), guitarist and pianist Paul MCCARTNEY (1942–) and drummer Ringo Starr (born Richard Starkey, 1940–). Manager Brian Epstein (1934–67) and producer-arranger George Martin (1926–) also contributed substantially to the group's success. The Lennon-McCartney songwriting team is now regarded as one of the finest in the history of popular music. The Beatles still hold the record for the most Number One hits (20), including "I Want To Hold Your Hand" (1964), "A Hard Day's Night" (1964), "Penny Lane" (1967), "Hey Jude" (1968) and "Let It Be" (1970). Their 1967 album, *Sgt. Pepper's Lonely Hearts Club Band,* is considered a classic. The Beatles stopped giving live performances in 1966, and thereafter devoted themselves to songwriting and recording. The Beatles disbanded in 1970, after several years of increasing tensions among Lennon, McCartney and Harrison. The four musicians went on to new solo careers, but none was as successful alone as they had been together as the Beatles. Lennon was murdered in New York City in 1980.

For further reading:

Brown, Peter, and Steven Gaines, *The Love You Make: An Insider's Story of The Beatles.* New York: McGraw-Hill, 1983.

Davies, Hunter, *The Beatles: An Authorized Biography.* New York: McGraw-Hill, 1968.

Martin, George, *All You Need Is Ears.* New York: St. Martin's, 1982.

Philip, Norman, *Shout!: The Beatles in Their Generation.* New York: Simon & Schuster, 1981.

Stokes, Geoffrey, *The Beatles.* New York: Times Books, 1980.

Beaton, Cecil (1904–1980). English designer and photographer. Educated at Cambridge University, Beaton worked from 1939 to 1945 as a war photographer in the British Ministry of Information. After the war he won acclaim as a photographer in England and the United States. He was known for his sartorial style and became the favorite photographer of the British royal family, and of the rich and famous in theater, film, ballet and opera. Beaton's photographs have been published widely in magazines and books. Among the milestones of his career were set and costume designs for the Academy Award-winning films *Gigi* (1959) and *My Fair Lady* (1965). In 1957 he was made Commander of the Most Honourable Order of the British Empire, and in 1960 he received the Legion d' Honneur.

For further reading:

Vickers, Hugo, *Cecil Beaton: a Biography.* New York: Donald I. Fine, 1987.

Beattie, Ann (1947–). American novelist and short story writer. Her first collection, *Distortions* (1976), established her as an acute observer of self-absorbed contemporary Americans. Her first novel, *Chilly Scenes of Winter* (1976), describes a man with 1960s sensibilities coming to terms with the 1970s. Other works include *Secrets and Surprises* (1979), a collection of short stories, and *Picturing Will* (1989), a novel. Beattie is a frequent contributor to THE NEW YORKER, where many of her short stories first appeared.

Beaubourg. See POMPIDOU CENTER.

Beauclerk, Charles Frederic Aubrey de Vere (1915–1988). English duke. A direct descendant of King Charles II and his mistress Nell Gwyn, Beauclerk was the 13th Duke of St. Albans and Hereditary Grand Falconer of England. Reputedly one of the first English dukes to hold a job, he gained notoriety through his involvement in financial scandals during the 1970s, when he was chairman of the Grendon Trust. Sued by the Inland Revenue for tax dodging, he settled in the south of France. Beauclerk reportedly returned to the U.K. only for his regular haircut at the Ritz hotel.

Beauvoir, Simone de. See Simone DE BEAUVOIR.

Beaux-Arts style. Style characteristic of architecture, interior design, and related objects (such as textiles and furniture) designed under the influence of the French Ecole des Beaux-Arts during the second half of the 19th century. Beaux-Arts design combines a concern for rational, functional planning with a florid decorative style based generally on the classic architecture of ancient Rome and the Renaissance. Many prominent American architects, including Raymond HOOD, George HOWE, Charles Follen McKim, and John Russell Pope, studied at the Beaux-Arts in Paris in the late 19th and early 20th century. They introduced Beaux-Arts thinking into American architectural education and into their own and their students' work. Outstanding examples of Beaux-Arts design in the U.S. include the New York Public Library by Carrere and Hastings (1897–1911) and Grand Central Station in New York by Warren and Wetmore (1907–1913).

Beaverbrook, William Maxwell Aitken [1st Baron (1917)] (1879–1964).

Lord Beaverbrook at a dinner in honor of his work in furthering American-Canadian Commonwealth relations.

British newspaper owner and political figure. Born in Canada, he was already an extremely wealthy businessman by the time he immigrated to England in 1910. There he established close ties with the Conservative leader Andrew Bonar LAW and soon was elected a Conservative member of Parliament (1910). He was minister of information in 1918, and left Parliament after World War I. He had purchased the *Daily Express* in 1916, and he founded the *Sunday Express* in 1918 and acquired the *Evening Standard* in 1923. An influential man of strong prejudices and opinions, he used his newspapers to advocate free trade within the BRITISH EMPIRE and favor imperial isolationism. During the ABDICATION CRISIS, Lord Beaverbrook sided with EDWARD VIII against Stanley BALDWIN, favoring the option of morganatic marriage. He returned to public office during WORLD WAR II in the cabinet of his friend Sir Winston CHURCHILL, assuming a number of important wartime posts. He was minister of air force production (1940–41), minister of supply (1941–42), minister of production (1942) and lord privy seal (1943–45). He continued to be active in his newspapers after Churchill's defeat in 1945.

bebop. Bebop, the predominant postwar jazz style, appeared in the mid-1940s largely in reaction to the limitations of big band swing. Bebop, generally a small group affair, emphasized the individual soloist and a highly interactive and dynamic rhythm section. Whereas big bands had relied largely on the contributions of the arranger, bebop, in contrast, put the spotlight on the spontaneously improvising musician. The big bands of the SWING ERA had attracted a mass following because of their danceable beats, attractive singers and entertaining novelty numbers. As the audience for jazz changed, bebop grew in popularity. It was pioneered by alto saxophonist Charlie PARKER, trumpeter Dizzy GILLESPIE, pianists Bud Powell and Thelonious MONK and the drummers Max Roach and Kenny CLARKE, who introduced new levels of virtuosity, harmonic daring and rhythmic audacity. Though bebop has been periodically eclipsed by such alternate jazz styles as the modal and fusion approaches, it has remained jazzdom's most sophisticated and demanding form. For musicians, a good part of bebop's challenge comes from its reliance on a repertoire of "standards" from 1930s-1940s Broadway and Hollywood shows, whose complex harmonic changes and intriguing melodies continue to constitute a litmus test for a musician's improvisatory mettle. In the 1990s, bebop is once again in vogue due to the tremendous popularity of trumpeter Wynton MARSALIS and his young followers.

For further reading:

Gitler, Ira, *Swing to Bop: An Oral History of the Transition in Jazz in the 1940s*. New York: Oxford University Press, 1985.

Bechtel, Stephen Davison (1900–1989). American businessman, president of the Bechtel Corporation. In 1935 Bechtel assumed control of his family's San Francisco-based business and helped mold it into one of the world's most prominent international construction and engineering firms. Among the projects completed under his guidance were the HOOVER DAM and the San Francisco Bay Area Rapid Transit System. In the 1980s, several of his top executives—notably George P. Schultz and Caspar Weinberger—served in key positions in the REAGAN administration.

Beck, Julian (1925–1985). American actor and director. In 1947, with his wife Judith Malina, he founded the LIVING THEATRE, which became one of the most influential of all American avant-garde theater companies. The company came to the fore in the 1960s with such landmark productions as *The Connection*, *The Brig* and *Antigone*. In these and other productions the company aimed for maximum audience involvement and sought to promote revolutionary political ideals. In the mid-1980s, the Becks brought the Living Theatre back to New York City after a long self-imposed exile in Europe.

Beck case. Investigation and conviction of the president of the International Brotherhood of Teamsters in 1957. Dave Beck was a aggressive union leader from Seattle who rose to become president of the 1.4–million-member Teamsters' Union. In 1957 he was called before the Senate Select Committee on Improper Activities in Labor or Management, headed by Senator John McClellan of Arkansas. The committee presented evidence that Beck had become a millionaire by siphoning off union funds. Beck was expelled from the AFL-CIO after he asserted his Fifth Amendment right against self-incrimination 7,200 times during the hearings. He was convicted of filing false tax returns and served a prison sentence. After his parole in 1964 he still owed the government $1.3 million in back taxes. This debt was eventually forgiven by the NIXON administration: the Teamsters were among President Nixon's more ardent supporters.

Beckenbauer, Franz (1945–). German soccer player and manager—and the only man to have captained and managed a World Cup winning team, in 1974 and 1990, respectively. Beckenbauer first gained recognition as a stylish midfield player for Bayern Munich and West Germany in the 1960s, but his greatest contribution to the game came with his conversion from midfield player to "libero" in the early 1970s. His unsurpassed ability to read the game, combined with his speed and outstanding passing skills, allowed him to orchestrate offensive plays from defensive zones, a novel tactic that produced enormous success for his club and national teams. Bayern captured three European Cups (1974–76), and West Germany won the European Championship in 1972 and the World Cup in 1974, all under Beckenbauer's captaincy. Beckenbauer retired in 1983, after stints with the New York Cosmos and SV Hamburg. In 1984 he was appointed West Germany team manager. Under his guidance West Germany was runner-up in the 1986 World Cup and was the winner of the tournament in 1990.

Becker, Boris (1967–). German tennis player. Becker achieved instant tennis stardom when at age 17 he became the youngest competitor to win the Wimbledon men's singles title (1985). His aggressive, rough and tumble style and skinned knees made him an audience favorite. He won Wimbledon again in 1986 and 1989. Although Becker has also won the U.S. Open (1989) and Australian Open (1991), his level of play is sometimes erratic and he has yet to reach his full potential.

Beckett, Samuel (1905–1989). Irish writer who spent most of his creative life in France. Beckett, who won the NOBEL PRIZE for literature in 1969, is closely linked to EXISTENTIALISM by virtue of his absurdist novels and plays that capture the emptiness and desperate humor of modern life, in which abiding values are lacking. Beckett studied at Trinity College, Dublin, before moving to France and establishing a friendship with James JOYCE, who served as Beckett's literary mentor. Beckett's first major work was the comic novel *Murphy* (1937), which showed the influence of Joycean punning and wordplay. In the postwar years came an important novelistic trilogy—*Molloy* (1951), *Malone Dies* (1951) and *The Unnameable* (1953)—written in French, which Beckett had adopted as his new literary language. Beckett also emerged as a master of the THEATER OF THE ABSURD with his 1953 play WAITING FOR GODOT, his most famous work and still widely performed. Two other important Beckett plays are *End Game* and *Krapp's Last Tape*, both written in 1958.

Beckmann, Max (1884–1950). German painter. The expressionist artist was born in Leipzig, studying at the Weimar Acad-

Samuel Beckett, playwright, poet and author, as he appeared in 1987.

emy. In 1906 he moved to Berlin, where he was a member of the Berlin secession from 1908 to 1911. After terrible experiences as a medical corpsman in WORLD WAR I, his style changed from a gently realistic Impressionism to a savage and symbolic depiction of the human form that grew more personal and allegorical through the years. Beckmann taught at the Frankfort Art Institute from 1925 to 1933, when he was dismissed by the Nazis, who branded his art "decadent." He moved to Amsterdam in 1936 and spent the war years there. In 1947, he immigrated to the U.S., teaching at Washington University (1947–49) and the Brooklyn Museum School (1949–50). One of his best-known paintings is the triptych *Departure* (1932–35; Museum of Modern Art, N.Y.C.).

Becquerel, Antoine Henri (1852–1908). French physicist. Becquerel's early scientific and engineering training was at the Ecole Polytechnique and the School of Bridges and Highways, and in 1876 he started teaching at the Polytechnique. In 1899 he was elected to the French Academy of Sciences. He held chairs at several institutions and became chief engineer in the department of bridges and highways. Becquerel is remembered as the discoverer of radioactivity in 1896. Following Wilhelm RONTGEN's discovery of X RAYS the previous year, Becquerel began to look for X rays in the fluorescence observed when certain salts absorb ultraviolet radiation. His method was to take crystals of potassium uranyl sulfate and place them in sunlight next to a piece of photographic film wrapped in black paper. The reasoning was that the sunlight induced fluorescence in the crystals and any X rays present would penetrate the black paper and darken the film. The experiments appeared to work and his first conclusion was that X rays were present in the fluorescence. The true explanation of the darkened plate was discovered by chance. He left a plate in black paper next to some crystals in a drawer and some time later developed the plate. He found that this too was fogged, even though the crystals were not fluorescing. Becquerel investigated further and discovered that the salt gave off a penetrating radiation independently, without ultraviolet radiation. He deduced that the radiation came from uranium in the salt. Becquerel went on to study the properties of this radiation; in 1899 he showed that part of it could be deflected by a magnetic field and thus consisted of charged particles. In 1903 he shared the NOBEL PRIZE for physics with Pierre and Marie CURIE.

Bedny, Demyan (1883–1945). Soviet poet and propagandist. In the 1920s he was considered to be the chief proletarian poet of the U.S.S.R. Official approval was such that LENIN advised GORKY to read Bedny's fables. His RUSSIAN CIVIL WAR poems did much to spur on the fighters, but his poems of the NEP (NEW ECONOMIC POLICY) period were considered lewd. The obedient puppet of STALIN, he glorified Stalin's policies. Bedny also produced pornographic and antireligious verse. The production of his play *Ancient Warriors,* in which the Orthodox Church is ridiculed, occurred just as the Communist Party proclaimed that the church had had a positive effect on the development of early Russia, and brought Bedny's career to a halt. He was later allowed to continue publishing.

Beebe, Charles William (1887–1962). American naturalist. Beebe graduated from Columbia University in 1898 and the following year began organizing and building up the bird collection of the New York Zoological Park. After serving as a fighter pilot in WORLD WAR I he became, in 1919, director of the Department of Tropical Research of the New York Zoological Society. Beebe is noted as one of the pioneers of deep-sea exploration. His first observation capsule was a cylinder; later collaboration with the geologist and engineer Otis Barton resulted in the design of a spherical capsule (the *bathysphere*). Various dives were made and in August 1934 Beebe and Barton were lowered to a (then) record depth of 3,028 feet near Bermuda. Beebe made many interesting observations, such as the absence of light at 2,000 feet, phosphorescent organisms and an apparently unknown animal estimated to be some 20 feet long. He abandoned deep-sea exploration after making 30 dives. Descents to even greater depths were subsequently made by Auguste PICCARD and others.

Beecham, Sir Thomas (1879–1961). English orchestral and operatic conductor. The wealthy grandson of a prominent pharmaceutical manufacturer, he attended Oxford University. Instead of going into the family business, he chose a musical career and formed his own orchestra. Musically self-educated, and at first regarded as a dilettante, he gained public attention and critical respect in 1910 when he conducted at the Royal Opera House,

Sir Thomas Beecham (1956).

Covent Garden; he was later the company's artistic director (1933–40). Beecham also founded two of Britain's leading orchestras, the London Philharmonic (1932) and the Royal Philharmonic (1947). A musician of strong and often idiosyncratic tastes, he championed the music of Mozart, Berlioz, DELIUS and SIBELIUS. He gave many concerts throughout Britain, Europe and the United States; his performances were noted for their elegance and spontaneity, and his recordings are prized by collectors. Beecham was also acknowledged as one of the great wits of the 20th century.

For further reading:

Beecham, Thomas, *A Mingled Chime: An Autobiography*. New York: G.P. Putnam's Sons, 1943.

Beeching, Lord Richard (1913–1985). British scientist, businessman and railway director. In 1961, while serving as a director of Imperial Chemical Industries (ICI), one of the largest corporations in Britain, he was asked to join British Transport Commission as chairman-designate of the newly created British Railways Board. In this role, he took radical measures to increase the efficiency and profitability of British Rail. In 1963, he produced the historic and controversial **Beeching Report,** which called for a much smaller British railway system with far fewer employees. His plan met with much opposition from railway workers and the railway riding public. However, it was adopted and many rural lines and stations were closed. Beeching also succeeded in restructuring the railway's management before departing in 1965, after the LABOUR PARTY regained power. That same year he was made a life peer.

Beel, Louis J.M. (1902–1977). Prime minister of the NETHERLANDS (1946–48, 1958–59). Beel was one of the postwar leaders who steered the Netherlands' recovery from the Nazi occupation of WORLD WAR II.

Beene, Geoffrey (1927–). American fashion designer known for his youthful, almost playful approach, combined with respect for traditional craftsmanship and detail. Beene was a medical student at Tulane University in New Orleans before dropping out to relocate in Los Angeles. His fashion sketches led to his enrolling at the Traphagen School in New York and then to study in Paris. In 1962 Beene opened his own firm. His work often crosses the lines between sportswear and more formal costume, using the best of materials and fine details along with generally bright and lively color. An element of humor appears in his designs, which sometimes verge on the shocking. Beene has won many awards, including a 1964 Neiman-Marcus Award and a series of Coty Awards, his fifth in 1982.

Beerbohm, (Sir Henry) Max(imilian) (1872–1956). British playwright, critic, essayist and caricaturist. Born in London, Beerbohm was educated at Charterhouse School and at Merton College, Oxford. Beerbohm entered the world of the arts and society through his elder half-brother, Sir Herbert Beerbohm-Tree. Turning a gimlet eye on the social, artistic and literary personalities of the day, he produced witty caricatures, essays and also drama criticism for the *Saturday Review,* where he succeeded George Bernard SHAW. He was also author of several plays, most notably *The Happy Hypocrite* (1900). His first collection of essays was called *The Works of Max Beerbohm* (1896), followed by *More* (1899), *Yet Again* (1909) and *And Even Now* (1920). In *A Christmas Garland* (1912) he parodied the works of Henry JAMES, H.G. WELLS and Rudyard KIPLING, among others. He lived primarily in Italy after 1911, but during WORLD WAR II he broadcast commentaries for the BBC in London; these were collected in *Mainly on the Air* (1957).

Beer Hall Putsch. Name given to Adolf HITLER's abortive attempt to overthrow the German WEIMAR REPUBLIC. On November 8, 1923, his NAZI Party storm troopers invaded a large political meeting in a MUNICH beer hall, coercing Bavarian leaders to proclaim loyalty to the Nazis. But the leaders escaped, mobilized the army against the Nazis and soon arrested Hitler. The fiasco brought him to national prominence, however. During his nine-month imprisonment Hitler dictated MEIN KAMPF, the bible of National Socialism, to his aide Rudolf HESS.

Begin, Menachem (1913–). Prime minister of ISRAEL (1977–83). Having emigrated from Siberia to PALESTINE in 1941, he led IRGUN ZVAI LEUMI extremists. A member of the Knesset (parliament) from 1948, he was a junior minister (1967–70), leader of the right-wing LIKUD (Unity) Party from 1970 and prime minister on winning the 1977 elections. His premiership was marked by his tough line against the PALESTINE LIBERATION ORGANIZATION (PLO) and on Israeli control of the WEST BANK of the Jordan, but also by relaxation of tension with EGYPT, following talks with President SADAT in 1977. He was joint recipient of the NOBEL PRIZE for peace (with Sadat) in 1978. He retired due to ill health in 1983. (See also CAMP DAVID TALKS; KING DAVID HOTEL ATTACK.)

For further reading:

Silver, Eric, *Begin: The Haunted Prophet.* New York: Random House, 1984.

Behan, Brendan (1923–1964). Irish playwright. Behan was born in Dublin to a lower-middleclass family. Active in the IRISH REPUBLICAN ARMY (IRA) as a teenager, he was arrested in 1939 and spent several years in British borstals (reform schools) and in jail; he later recounted his experiences in the autobiography *Borstal Boy* (1958). His most popular works are *The Hostage* (1958), which showed the influence of Bertolt BRECHT, and *The Quare Fellow* (1959). Both were produced in Britain by Joan Littlewood; *The Hostage* was staged in New York and Dublin as well. He also wrote a television play, *The Big House* (1957). Celebrated for his radical views, irreverent wit, and public rowdiness, Behan died an alcoholic. An unfinished play, *Richard's Cork Leg,* was posthumously presented at the ABBEY THEATRE in 1972.

Behrens, Peter (1868–1940). German architect. An influential figure in the development of modern architecture, Behrens was born in Hamburg and at first studied painting. He worked as an architect and designer from 1890 to 1898. Moving to Darmstadt in 1899, he joined a leading artists' colony, designing his house and all its furnishings, which were exhibited in the 1901 Darmstadt Exhibition. Behrens made a lasting contribution to modern industrial design with the works he created as architect for the huge Berlin electrical company A.E.G. from 1907 to 1914. His factory buildings, notably the turbine plant of 1909, are celebrated for their monumental and utilitarian clarity. His other A.E.G. designs, including furnishings, equipment, stationery and catalogs, are early examples of functional modernism. His other works include apartment blocks and workers' housing as well as the Abbey of St. Peter, Salzburg, and the German Embassy, Leningrad. An influential teacher, he was a professor of architecture at the Dusseldorf Academy (1921) and director of the architecture school at the Vienna Academy (1922–36) before heading up the architecture department of Berlin's Prussian Academy in 1936. His students included LE CORBUSIER and Ludwig MIES VAN DER ROHE.

Behring, Emil Adolf von (1854–1917). German immunologist. Behring graduated in medicine at Berlin University and entered the Army Medical Corps before becoming (in 1888) a lecturer in the Army Medical College, Berlin. In 1889 he moved to Robert Koch's Institute of Hygiene and transferred to the Institute of Infectious Diseases in 1891, when Koch was appointed its chief. In 1890, working with Shibasaburo Kitasato, Behring showed that injections of blood serum from an animal suffering from tetanus could confer immunity to the disease in other animals. Behring found that the same was true for diphtheria, and this led to the development of a diphtheria antitoxin for human patients, in collaboration with Paul EHRLICH. This treatment was first used in 1891 and subsequently caused a dramatic fall in mortality due to diphtheria. Behring's success brought him many prizes, including the first NOBEL PRIZE for physiology or medicine, awarded in 1901. In 1913 he introduced toxin-antitoxin mixtures to immunize against diphtheria, a refinement of the immunization technique already in use. He also devised a vaccine for the immunization of calves against tuberculosis.

Beiderbecke, (Leon) Bix (1903–1931). American jazz cornetist, pianist and composer—one of the legends of jazz history. Beiderbecke was an astonishingly gifted cornet player who was devoted to his music but died at the young age of 28 from a combination of excessive drinking and ill health. He never achieved great public fame in his own lifetime, but he was highly esteemed among his fellow musicians. In the late 1920s, he was the featured cornetist with the Paul WHITEMAN band, with which he made numerous recordings. A gifted piano player, Beiderbecke composed several pieces principally for that instrument, including "In a Mist" and "Candlelights."

Beilby, Sir George Thomas (1850–1924). British industrial chemist. The son of a clergyman, he was educated at Edinburgh University. He began work with an oil-shale company as a chemist in 1868 and increased the yield of paraffin and ammonia from oil shales by improving the process of their distillation. He also worked on cyanides, patenting in 1890 a process for the synthesis of potassium cyanide in which ammonia was passed over a heated mixture of charcoal and potassium carbonate. This had wide use in the gold-extracting industry. From 1907 to 1923 Beilby was chairman of the Royal Technical College, Glasgow, later the University of Strathclyde. He became interested in the economic use of fuel and smoke prevention, submitting evidence to the Royal Commission on Coal Supplies in 1902. In 1917 he was appointed as the first chairman of the Fuel Research Board. He was knighted in 1916.

be-in. Be-in is a term that originated in the 1960s to describe a large-scale gathering of people that generally emphasized freedom, spontaneity and a lack of social and sexual inhibitions. The genesis of the be-in concept owed a great deal both to the art world conception of a HAPPENING, and to the libertarian outlook that pervaded many of the prominent political and psychological theories of the era. Be-ins were usually organized in open public spaces, such as parks, and invited all comers to participate in a spirit of peace and joy. Activities were unstructured and ranged from political protest to free-form theatrical and musical events to frank sexuality to friendly, innocuous conversation.

Being and Nothingness. Influential philosophical work by the French writer Jean-Paul SARTRE. *Being and Nothingness* (1943) was written prior to the onset, in the late 1940s, of Sartre's political commitment to Marxism, a commitment that showed itself strongly in his philosophical writings thereafter. Nonetheless, *Being and Nothingness* stands as Sartre's most famous work, a seminal text of EXISTENTIALISM. In it, Sartre argued that there was no a priori value structure to human existence. Existence and activity alone could define the essence and meaning of one's life. Absolute freedom was thus the natural human condition—in Sartre's famous phrase, man is "condemned to liberty." Genuine "being" consists in seizing and making use of this freedom and thereby emerging from the "nothingness" that submerges the passive man who seeks to justify his life in terms of accepted bourgeois values, externally imposed philosophical systems, or religious dogma.

Beirut. Capital of Lebanon, located on its Mediterranean Sea coast. Conquered by French troops during WORLD WAR I, Beirut was made capital of LEBANON in 1921, pursuant to a French mandate awarded by the LEAGUE OF NATIONS. It was held by French and British forces during WORLD WAR II and was declared the national capital in 1945 when Lebanon earned its independence. In recent decades it has been the site of Palestinian refugee camps and of violent fighting between various Christian and Muslim paramilitary factions. Numerous Westerners have also been taken hostage by terrorists in Beirut. In June 1982, the city was invaded by Israeli military forces seeking to oust PALESTINE LIBERATION ORGANIZATION guerrillas who had used it as a key base of operations against Israel. In September 1982, in spite of the presence of Israeli troops, Lebanese Christian Phalangists massacred Palestinians in the SABRA AND SHATILA refugee camps. By October, an international peacekeeping force had helped to restore order, but the massacre spurred major political debate in Israel. U.S. forces withdrew after several terrorist attacks on their base caused high American casualties. Devastation continued in the late 1980s in fierce fighting between rebel Christian leader General Michael Aoun and Syrian and other Muslim forces. Aoun was finally forced to surrender in October 1990, and the city assumed a semblance of calm for the first time in many years. (See also LEBANESE CIVIL WAR OF 1975–90.)

Bejart, Maurice [born Maurice Berger] (1928–). French dancer and choreographer. The son of philosopher Gaston Berger, Bejart studied at the Marseille Opera Ballet School and danced with the Marseille Opera Ballet until 1945, then joined the Ballets de Roland Petit (1947–49) and the International Ballet. He first became known and celebrated as a choreographer in the 1950s for work that synthesized elements of ballet, modern, jazz and acrobatics. He formed a company of his own (Ballet Romantiques, then Ballet de l'Etoile) in 1953. In 1960 he formed the Belgium-based Ballet of the Twentieth Century, which showcased his eclectic explorations of dance in such works as *Contes d'Hoffman* (1961), *Damnation de Faust* (1966) and *Symphonie Pour Un Homme Seul* (1971). Controversially, Bejart has staged unambiguously sexual scenes, including nudity, and characteristically works in a heroic mold. He has also worked as a director of operas, and is currently director of the Bejart Ballet Lausanne.

Bejerot, Nils (1921–1988). Swedish physician and psychiatrist. Bejerot won worldwide recognition for his investigation into the spread of drug addiction and his search to find ways of preventing that addiction. He remained a controversial figure in Sweden because of his emphasis on the prevention rather than the treatment of drug abuse. Until his retirement in 1987, he was a professor in the Department of Social Medicine at the Karolinska Institute.

A U.S. Marine with his leg torn open is carried by comrades away from barracks devastated by a terrorist car bomb attack in Beirut (Oct. 23, 1983).

Belafonte, Harry [Harold George] (1927–). American folksinger. Although he was born in New York, Belafonte spent many years in his parents' native Jamaica. There he developed a love for the calypso music of the West Indies that became his trademark. During the 1950s his Calypso hits included "Jamaica Farewell" (also known as the "banana boat song"), "Matilda" and "Mary's Boy Child." Belafonte also appeared in a number of films, including *Carmen Jones* (1953) and *Island in the Sun* (1957).

Belasco, David (1853–1931). Important American playwright, producer, stage manager and theater owner whose innovations in popular melodrama and realism at the turn of the century marked an important phase of American stagecraft. Belasco was born in San Francisco to Portuguese Jews recently emigrated from England. He filled his early years with touring as an actor and collaborating as a playwright, with important writers of the time like James A. Herne and Dion Boucicault. After his arrival in New York City in 1882 as stage manager for the Madison Square Theater he began writing and producing plays noted for their flair for, by turns, thrilling melodrama and intimate realism. By the turn of the century Belasco was one of the most powerful and influential men of the theater. He opened two theaters of his own, the Belasco and the Stuyvesant, in an ongoing conflict with the controlling interests of the notorious New York-based Syndicate. In 1913 he turned to the new medium of the motion picture to ensure his plays could reach wider audiences. The Protective Amusement Company in association with the BIOGRAPH company released movies of his De Mille collaborations. The Jesse L. Lasky Feature Play Company, in association with director Cecil B. DE MILLE, released *The Girl of the Golden West* and *The Warrens of Virginia*, among others, in 1914. The decline of Belasco in later years was in part due to his resistance to the growing "Little Theater" movement and to emerging playwrights like Eugene O'NEILL. He is regarded today not as a great playwright but as an innovator of scenic, electrical, and aural stage effects.

For further reading:

Marker, Lise-Lone, *David Belasco; Naturalism in the American Theatre*. Princeton: Princeton University Press, 1975.

Belau. Belau is composed of over 200 islands at the western end of the Caroline Islands chain in the Pacific Ocean; total land area is 177 square miles. From 1921 the territory of Micronesia, of which Belau is part, was administered by Japan under a LEAGUE OF NATIONS mandate. After withdrawal from the league in 1935, Japan constructed military installations on the islands, which became strategically important during WORLD WAR II. All of Micronesia became a UNITED NATIONS trusteeship under U.S. administration in 1947. After Belau rejected a teritorial constitution in 1978, the trust territory was dissolved. With its own constitution approved in 1981, Belau signed a Compact of Free Association (1982) with the United States, giving America the right to install military installations. However, the compact has yet to be ratified because of conflict between a ban on nuclear weapons in Belau's constitution and a clause permitting them in the compact.

Belem [Santa Maria de Belem do Grao Para]. Capital of Para state in northern Brazil and key port for the vast Amazon basin. During the rubber production boom of the late 19th and early 20th centuries, Belem expanded as a commercial center. The GREAT DEPRESSION of the 1930s brought hard times. After WORLD WAR II, Belem grew again due to increased development in the basin.

Bel Geddes, Norman (1893–1958). American industrial and stage designer with a prominent role in the use of STREAMLINING in the design style of the 1930s. Bel Geddes was born in Michigan and studied briefly at the Art Institute of Chicago before establishing his own office as an industrial designer. His work included Toledo scales, Philco radio cabinets, and a Graham Page automobile, but his influence was greatest through the publication of unrealized, generally futuristic projects. His 1932 book, *Horizons,* described and illustrated such projects as a fully streamlined ocean liner and a huge passenger airplane with public lounges, promenade decks (in the wings), and a gymnasium. His best known and most influential work was the FUTURAMA exhibit for GENERAL MOTORS at the 1939 NEW YORK WORLD'S FAIR in which visitors traveled above a model landscape complete with cities and highways as Bel Geddes anticipated they might be in the future. The exhibit is often credited as a major force in the development of modern superhighways.

Belgian Congo. Former Belgian colony in south-central Africa, now the independent nation of ZAIRE. In the 1870s, British explorer Henry M. Stanley was hired by Belgian King Leopold II to help expand Belgian power in Africa. As a result, the Congo Free State was established as a personal possession of Leopold II in 1885, with borders roughly corresponding to those of present-day Zaire. The European population remained low, while native laborers were grossly exploited. This led to an international scandal in 1904, when Britain brought the extent of Congo exploitation to the world's attention. The Belgian government responded by annexing the Congo Free State in 1908 and reopening it to free trade. During WORLD WAR I, it was a base of operations against German colonial forces in Africa. Free trade led to development of natural resources; the diamond and copper deposits of the Katanga (now Shaba) region led to the Congo becoming the world's leading supplier of these commodities by 1928. During WORLD WAR II, it was a major raw material supplier for the Allied war effort. After the war, the colonial economy boomed, but resistance to Belgian colonial rule culminated in riots in the capital city of Leopoldville in 1959. In 1960, Belgium granted independence to the new country of Zaire.

BELGIUM

1908	Belgium annexes the Congo.
1909	Death of King Leopold II, succeeded by Albert I.
1914	Germany invades Belgium in opening days of World War I.
1925	Locarno Pact sets aside neutrality forced on Belgium since the 19th century.
1932	Flemish language accorded equal status with French.
1934	Albert I dies in accident; Leopold III crowned.
1940	Belgium invaded after attempting to remain neutral in World War II.
1946	Belgium, Netherlands, Luxembourg sign Benelux economic pact.
1951	Unpopular Leopold III abdicates, succeeded by his son as Baudoin I.
1958	Women gain right to vote.
1962	Congo and other colonies gain independence.
1971	New constitution recognizes separate Flemish, Walloon and French cultural communities.
1986	Former Prime Minister Boeyants convicted of tax evasion and fraud.
1991	Belgium sends fighter planes to Turkey as part of Allied coalition against Iraq in Persian Gulf War.

Belgium. Country in northeastern Europe; a highly industrialized, densely populated lowlands nation. First established as an independent state by the London Conference of 1830–31, it expanded economically under the rule of King Leopold II (1865–1909) and forged a valuable colonial empire in Africa (see BELGIAN CONGO). Its two major ethnic regions are Flemish-speaking FLANDERS in the north and French-speaking Wallonia in the south. In the 1960s, political conflict between these two groups threatened the unity of the nation. The capital, BRUSSELS, is home to both languages and also serves as headquarters of the EUROPEAN ECONOMIC COMMUNITY and of NATO (North Atlantic Treaty Organization). The German invasion of Belgium in WORLD WAR I was met by the British Expeditionary Force, but—except for the vicinity of YPRES—Belgium was held by Germany throughout the war; some of the most bloody battles of that bloody war were fought on Belgian soil. The nation was again occupied by Germany in WORLD WAR II. In 1948, Belgium joined the BENELUX economic union, with the Netherlands and Luxembourg, and was a founding member (1951) of the EUROPEAN COAL AND STEEL COMMUNITY. The 1985 decision to base U.S. CRUISE MISSILES in Belgium caused political controversy.

Belgrade. Capital of both YUGOSLAVIA and its constituent republic of SERBIA. Located at the juncture of the Danube and Sava rivers, it occupies a key position in trade routes between the Balkans and central Europe and has also been the site of numerous battles. By 1867, the newly-independent Serbs had thrown off the centuries-long shackles of Ottoman rule, declaring Belgrade their new capital. In 1915, during WORLD WAR I, the country was conquered by the CENTRAL POWERS, which occupied Belgrade. In 1918, a new Kingdom of the Serbs, Croats and Slovenes was declared and subsequently named Yugoslavia. During WORLD WAR II, Belgrade was held by German forces from 1941 to 1944. It remains the center of Yugoslavian commerce and is well known for its elegant parks and palaces.

Beliveau, Jean Arthur (1931–). Canadian athlete. The captain of the Montreal Canadiens during their dynastic run of the 1960s, Beliveau was known as a gentlemanly and unselfish player. A two-time Hart Trophy winner as most valuable player, he also won the Conn Smythe Trophy in 1965 as the Stanley Cup playoff's most valuable player. A gifted passer and playmaker, he finished his career with 507 goals and 712 assists. He was named to the Hockey Hall of Fame in 1972.

Belize [Belize City]. Port city on the Caribbean Sea coast of BELIZE, at the mouth of the Belize River; the former capital of the colony of British Honduras. After it was severely damaged by Hurricane Hattie in 1961, BELMOPAN was designated as the new colonial capital.

Belize. Nation in Central America bordered on the north by Mexico and on the south and west by Guatemala; formerly known as British Honduras. The capital is BELMOPAN and the largest city is BELIZE. From 1862 to 1884, it was subject to the rule of British colonial authorities in Jamaica but thereafter designated as an individual colony under the name of British Honduras. In 1964, it was granted internal autonomy by Britain. In 1973, it was designated as the Colony of Belize. In 1981, it was accorded independence within the British Commonwealth. During this period, Britain and Guatemala entered into a dispute over the latter's claims, stemming from an 1859 treaty, to certain of the territory of Belize. The population of Belize, unlike that of the rest of Central America, is English-speaking and largely of black African ancestry.

Bell, Alexander Graham (1847–1922). Inventor of the telephone, who also designed early telephone instruments and made a contribution to the development of aircraft. Born in Scotland, Bell moved to Canada in 1870 and then to the U.S. in 1872. The first telephone was demonstrated in 1876, and the first commercial model, a simple wood box of Bell's own design, was introduced in 1877. In 1907 Bell organized the Aerial Experiment Association (AEA) to promote work on aircraft design and was the designer of a spectacular man-lifting kite. In spite of their striking appearance, Bell's aircraft designs were not particularly successful and never equaled the earlier (1903) efforts of the WRIGHT BROTHERS.

Bell, (Arthur) Clive (Heward) (1881–1962). British critic and author. Born into a wealthy country family, Bell was educated at Marlborough College and Trinity College, Cambridge, where he met many of the people with whom he would later form the BLOOMSBURY GROUP. In 1907 he married Vanessa Stephen (see Vanessa BELL), the elder sister of Virginia WOOLF. Noted for his ability to write evocatively about the visual arts, he contributed regularly to the *New Statesman* and *Nation*. He was a friend of Roger FRY, who coined the term POSTIMPRESSIONISM, of which Bell was a great admirer. In *Art* (1914), he attempted to develop a cohesive theory of visual art, and put forth the notion of "significant form," which held that form is the most important component of visual art. In *Civilization* (1928), he reasoned somewhat ironically that civilization depends upon the leisured elite. Other works include *Poems* (1921), *An Account of French Painting* (1931), and a memoir, *Old Friends: Personal Recollections* (1956).

Bell, James "Cool Papa" (1903–1991). American baseball player. The greatest star of the NEGRO LEAGUES, Bell was known for his outstanding speed. He played from 1922 to 1950, including 21 seasons of winter ball, which totaled 50 seasons of pro baseball. While statistics are sketchy, he was renowned for both his fielding and his batting ability, hitting over .400 several times. He himself estimated that he once stole 175 bases in a 200–game season. He was named to the Baseball Hall of Fame in 1972.

Bell, Vanessa [nee Stephen] (1879–1961). The elder sister of Virginia WOOLF, she married the critic Clive BELL in 1907. She is known chiefly for these associations and as a member of the BLOOMSBURY GROUP. After 1914, she lived with the painter Duncan GRANT.

For further reading:
Garnett, Angelica, *Deceived with Kindness: A Bloomsbury Childhood*. New York: Harcourt Brace, 1985.

Belleau Wood [Bois de Belleau, Bois de la Brigade Marine]. French village northeast of Paris and northwest of CHATEAU-THIERRY. It was the site of a major and bloody battle between Allied and German forces from June 6 to 25, 1918, during WORLD WAR I. U.S. troops, primarily the Fourth Marine Brigade, combined with French forces to halt a German offensive directed at Paris as a part of the Second Battle of the MARNE. Losses were heavy. In 1923, the battlefield was dedicated as a permanent memorial to U.S. servicemen slain during the war.

Belli, Melvin (1907–). American attorney and author who revolutionized trial practice by the introduction of physical evidence in tort claim cases. Highly visible and well-known to the public, Belli was dubbed the "King of Torts" for his success on behalf of injured clients. Through his efforts, and those of ATLA—the American Trial Lawyers Association, an organization he helped to found—injured plaintiffs were able to battle large corporations and insurers on an equal basis. Indeed, the success of trial lawyers before juries in the later years of the century led some states to limit the amounts that victims could recover. Belli, a graduate of Boalt Hall, is also the editor of the multivolume treatise, *Proof of Facts*, and the author of *My Life On Trial*. A flamboyant character both inside and outside the courtroom, he gained notoriety as the attorney for Jack RUBY, the killer of Lee Harvey OSWALD, who assassinated President John F. KENNEDY. Belli's law office, located at street level on Montgomery Street in downtown San Francisco, and filled with an eclectic collection of objects, became a well-known stop for tourists visiting the city.

Belloc, (Joseph) Hilaire (Pierre) (1870–1953). British poet and prose writer. With G.K. CHESTERTON, George Bernard SHAW and H.G. WELLS, Belloc was one of the "big four" literary figures in Edwardian England. Born in France of a French father and English mother, he graduated from Balliol College, Oxford, where he was a brilliant student. A prolific and versatile writer, he published some 150 books, including novels, histories, biographies, travel books and poetry collections. He published several collections of essays on literary, social, religious and political topics. He also edited or contributed to some of the most influential journals of the Edwardian period, and served as a Liberal member of Parliament (1906–10). His staunch Roman Catholicism (which he shared with Chesterton) was evident in his many essays. He was renowned in his lifetime, particularly through the period of World War I, but his reputation later declined. Today he is best remembered for such books of light verse as *The Bad Child's Book of Beasts* (1896).

For further reading:
Speaight, Robert, *Life of Hilaire Belloc*. Salem, New Hampshire: Ayer, 1957.

Bellow, Saul (1915–). American writer. Born in Quebec to an Orthodox Jewish, Russian emigre family, Bellow moved as a child to Chicago, which was later to be the inspiration and setting for much of his work. He was educated at the University of Chicago, Northwestern University and the University of Wisconsin at Madison. He worked in the editorial department of the *Encyclopaedia Britannica* and has taught at various universities intermittently since 1946. In 1962 he was appointed a professor at the University of Chicago. His first book, *Dangling Man*, was published in 1947; others include *The Adventures of Augie March* (1953) and *Herzog* (1964), each of which won a National Book Award, *Mr. Sammler's Planet* (1970), *Humboldt's Gift* (1975), *The Dean's December* (1982) and *Him with His Foot in His Mouth* (1984). Bellow avows that "art has something to do with the achievement of stillness in the midst of chaos."

In his novels he focuses on the conflicts that vex the individual in a modern, indifferent industrial society, and often deals with Jewish life in contemporary America. He is especially noted for his skill at characterization and his sense of humor. Bellow has exerted an enormous influence on contemporary American letters, and was awarded the PULITZER PRIZE and the NOBEL PRIZE for literature in 1976.

For further reading:
Bloom, Harold, ed., *Saul Bellow*. New York: Chelsea House, 1986.
Glenday, Michael K., *Saul Bellow and the Decline of Humanism*. New York: St. Martin, 1990.

Saul Bellow after winning the 1976 Nobel Prize for literature.

Goldman, L.H., ed., *Saul Bellow in the 1980s: a Collection of Critical Essays*. East Lansing: Michigan State University Press, 1989.
Kiernan, Robert, *Saul Bellow*. New York: Continuum, 1988.
Miller, Ruth, *Saul Bellow: a Biography of the Imagination*. New York: St. Martin, 1990.
Pifer, Ellen, *Saul Bellow Against the Grain*. Philadelphia: University of Pennsylvania Press, 1990.

Bellows, George (Wesley) (1882–1925). American painter. Born in Columbus, Ohio, he studied painting under Robert HENRI in New York City. Inspired by his teacher's vigorous style and everyday subject matter, he developed a direct and unsentimental realism. Deeply humane in approach, his work is among the best produced by the so-called Ashcan School. Bellows was also central in the promotion of lithography as an American art form, and he produced a number of important prints. An influential teacher, he taught for many years at New York's Art Students League, and was one of the organizers of the ARMORY SHOW. Among his most famous works are his dramatic boxing paintings, such as *Both Members of This Club* (1909; National Gallery of Art, Washington, D.C.) and *Stag at Sharkey's* (1909; Cleveland Museum of Art). He is also known for his landscapes and portraits.

Belmondo, Jean-Paul (1933–). French actor. An international film star with great personal magnetism, Belmondo is especially known for his portrayals of appealing outlaws in the vein of Humphrey BOGART. His acting style evokes the techniques of the NOUVELLE VAGUE. International acclaim came with his performances in Jean-Luc GODARD's *A Bout de Souffle* (1960), *Une femme est une femme* (1961) and *Pierrot-le-fou* (1965). Other important films include *That Man from Rio* (1964) and *Le Guignolo* (1980).

Belmopan. Town on the Belize River of Central America's BELIZE. It was constructed in 1966, after the 1961 devastation of Belize City by a hurricane had necessitated the founding of a new capital for the then-colony. It became the official capital in 1970.

Belorussia [Byelorussia; White Russia]. Soviet republic and region in the western U.S.S.R., bordered on the north by Latvia and Lithuania, to the east by the Russian SFSR, to the south by the Ukraine and to the west by Poland. Its capital is Minsk. Belorussia has been repeatedly devastated by wars—by the 16th- through 18th-century conflicts between Poland and Russia, by the invasion of Napoleon in 1812, during WORLD WAR I, by the Polish-Soviet War of 1919–20, and finally during WORLD WAR II. It briefly declared independence in 1918 but was annexed by the U.S.S.R. the following year. After another Polish-Russian conflict in 1921, it was ceded to Poland but was retaken by the U.S.S.R. during WORLD WAR II. Afterwards, its western border was slightly altered in favor of Poland.

Beltran Espantoso, Pedro Gerardo (1897–1979). Prime minister and finance minister of PERU (1959–61). Beltran published the Lima newspaper *La Prensa* from 1934 until it was taken over by the military government in 1974.

Bely, Andrei (1880–1934). Russian novelist, poet and literary critic. Bely was the son of an eminent Moscow University mathematician and "became a writer by accident." He became a guiding figure in the Russian Symbolist movement, and was an intrepid literary experimentalist in the Joycean mold who, in the eyes of one Soviet critic, was "the most audacious reformer of Russian prose." He wrote many influential works of poetry, literary criticism, memoirs and, most notably, novels such as *St. Petersburg, The Dramatic Symphony, Kotik Letaer* and *The Silver Dove*.

Belyayev, Pavel (1925–1970). Soviet military pilot and cosmonaut. Belyayev was commander aboard Voskhod 2 when fellow cosmonaut Alexei LEONOV made the world's first space walk (March 18, 1965). Upon its return the spacecraft ran into trouble, and Belyayev was forced to take over the controls and make a manual reentry. Although the crew landed safely, they were far off course and after the rigors of their space flight were forced to endure two cold days in the wilderness until a rescue team arrived to help them.

Benavente y Martinez, Jacinto (1866–1954). Spanish playwright and critic. Recipient of the NOBEL PRIZE in 1922, he wrote over 150 plays. He is noted for his use of satire, irony, psychological probing and social commentary. *Los intereses creados* (1907; produced in New York as *The Bonds of Interest*, 1919) and *La Malquerida* (1913; produced in New York as *The Passion Flower*, 1920) are his best known plays. In addition, he was a columnist for a Madrid newspaper from 1908 to 1912, and became Spain's foremost literary critic.

Ben Bella, Mohammed Ahmed (1916–). Prime minister of ALGERIA (1962–66). Leader of the extremist **Algerian National Movement** in 1947, he was imprisoned by the French in 1950. He escaped in 1952 and founded the Front de Liberation Nationale in 1954. He led the armed revolt against French rule and was captured and imprisoned by the French from 1956 to 1962. First prime minister of newly independent Algeria from 1962 to 1965, he was deposed by BOUMEDIENNE's military coup and kept under house arrest until 1979.

Bench, Johnny (1947–). American baseball player. There is little doubt that Bench was one of the greatest catchers ever. The first catcher ever to take National League rookie of the year honors, he spent his entire 16–year major league career (1967–83) with the Cincinnati Reds. The team that became known as the "Big Red Machine" dominated its league competition throughout the 1970s, winning four pennants and two World Series. Twice named the league's most valuable player, he was first-team all-star catcher 13 times, and won 10 consecutive Gold Glove awards. He retired in 1983 and was named to the Hall of Fame in 1989.

Benchley, Robert Charles (1889–1945). American humorist, editor and writer. Educated at Harvard University, Benchley served as writer and editor for the Curtis Publishing Company and the *New York Tribune*. He later became a regular contributor to a variety of magazines, including *Life* and the NEW YORKER, and acted in a number of feature films and short comedies. His books include *The Early Worm* (1927).

For further reading:

Altman, Bill, *Robert Benchley: A Biography*. New York: W.W. Norton, n.d.
Rosmond, Babette, *Robert Benchley: His Life and Good Times*. New York: Paragon House, 1989.

Benda, Julien (1867–1956). French essayist, philosopher and novelist. Benda, born of Jewish parents, was one of the most influential French thinkers of the first half of this century. In the years just prior to World War I, Benda earned a reputation as a fierce polemicist for his essays in opposition to the philosophy of Henri BERGSON. Bergson emphasized creative intuition; Benda, by contrast, was a classicist who held that detached reason was the key to the development of the human spirit. Benda deplored the use of emotional appeals and political polemics. In his most famous work, *The Treason of the Intellectuals* (1927), Benda argued that the supremacy of reason was threatened by a decline in rigor and courage among philosophers. He wrote: "Once the moralist gave lessons to actuality. Now he takes his hat off to it." In the 1930s, Benda lectured at Harvard and became active in anti-fascist organizations. Other works by Benda include *The Ordination* (1910), a novel, and *Belphegor* (1929), an analysis of French aesthetics.

Bender, Lauretta (1897–1987). Child neuropsychiatrist known for the development in 1923 of the **Bender Gestalt Visual Motor Test,** a neurophysiological examination that became a worldwide standard. She spent many years investigating the causes of childhood schizophrenia, and published studies on child suicides and violence.

Bendery [Romanian: Tighina]. City on the Dniester River in the southwestern U.S.S.R.; historically, the primary entranceway to Bessarabia. Formerly known as Tigin, it was conquered by Russia in 1812 and thereafter became a rail and river transport center. In 1918, after WORLD WAR I, it was ceded to Romania, with a subsequent adverse impact on its economy. It was taken by the U.S.S.R. in 1940, retaken by Romania during WORLD WAR II and returned to the Soviet Union after the war.

Benedict XV (1854–1922). Roman Catholic Pope. Born Giacomo della Chiesa in Pegli, Italy, Pope Benedict XV reigned from September 3, 1914, to January 22, 1922. On August 1, 1917, Benedict offered a seven-point peace plan for ending WORLD WAR I, but it was rejected by the combat-ant nations. He personally directed Vatican relief efforts during the war.

Benedict, Ruth (1887–1948). American anthropologist. Benedict studied with Franz BOAS at Columbia University, receiving her Ph.D. there in 1923. She subsequently taught at Columbia until her death. Considered one of the most influential anthropologists of the 20th century, Benedict formulated a number of important theories in cultural anthropology and human behavior. She was particularly active in popularizing the notion of cultural relativism. Among her books are *Patterns of Culture* (1934), *Zuni Mythology* (1935) and *Race: Science and Politics* (1940).

Benelux. Acronym for *Be*lgium, *Ne*therlands and *Lux*embourg, used as the name of a customs union created in 1948 among the three Low Countries. A treaty establishing an economic union was concluded at The Hague in the Netherlands in 1958 and came into force on November 1, 1960. This provided for free movement of goods, traffic, services and population among the three member states; a common trade policy and coordination of investment; and agricultural and social policies.

Benes, Eduard (1884–1948). Czechoslovakian nationalist and diplomat; president of CZECHOSLOVAKIA (1935–38, 1945–48) and of the Czechoslovak government-in-exile (1941–45). Benes was born into a peasant family in Bohemia, then part of the AUSTRO-HUNGARIAN EMPIRE (now in western Czechoslovakia). He studied at the Universities of Prague, Dijon and Paris, earning a doctorate in sociology. Benes spent World War I in exile in Paris, where he joined Tomas MASARYK in working for Czechoslovak independence. As the landlocked country's first foreign minister (1918–35) he gave it a strong presence in international affairs. Benes supported the LEAGUE OF NATIONS and established good relations with France and the U.S.S.R. He succeeded Masaryk as president in 1935. In 1938 Benes was forced to accept the MUNICH PACT that HITLER dictated to British Prime Minister CHAMBERLAIN, giving Germany the SUDETENLAND of northwestern Czechoslovakia. He thereupon resigned and went into exile. After the German occupation he was joined in exile by other Czechoslovakian leaders, and in 1941 he formed the Czechoslovak government-in-exile, which the Allies recognized as the legitimate government of the country. At the end of the war he accompanied Ludwik SVOBODA's forces into Prague. Benes sought to maintain democracy in Czechoslovakia despite increasing pressure from the communists. He resigned in despair after the de facto communist coup by Klement GOTTWALD, and died three months later.

BELGIUM, THE NETHERLANDS AND LUXEMBOURG (BENELUX)

Benet, Stephen Vincent (1898–1943). American poet. Born in Pennsylvania, Benet was educated at Yale and at the Sorbonne. He began publishing poetry while still a student. He is best remembered for his epic poem about the Civil War, *John Brown's Body* (1928), and his later folk opera, *The Devil and Daniel Webster* (1939; filmed 1941), based on his 1937 short story. Benet also wrote five unmemorable novels and worked in HOLLYWOOD as a screenwriter. Other poetry includes *Ballads and Poems* (1931) and *Western Star* (1943), an epic poem published posthumously. His elder brother, **William Rose Benet** (1886–1950), was a journalist who helped found the *Saturday Review of Literature* in 1924 and a poet whose verse autobiography, *The Dust Which Is God* (1941), won a PULITZER PRIZE.

For further reading:

Fenton, Charles A., *Stephen Vincent Benet: The Life and Times of an American Man of Letters*. Westport, Conn.: Greenwood, 1978.

Stephen Vincent Benet, poet.

Benetton, Giuliana (1938–). Founder of an Italian company in 1965, a manufacturer and retailer of knitwear. With her three brothers, Benetton has built up a firm with over 2,500 shops all over the world offering clothing of simple design in attractive colors. The design of the shops and the merchandise offered are of high quality and support each other in conveying an image of bright modernity. The firm has adopted advanced computer and automation techniques in manufacturing and business management.

Bengal. Ancient region in northeastern INDIA, now divided among BANGLADESH and India; a former province of British India. The British took it from the Muslims in 1757, when General Robert Clive defeated Siraj-ud-Daula in the battle of Plassey. When India was granted independence some two centuries later, Bengal was divided along religious lines, with its eastern, Muslim population becoming East Pakistan (Bangladesh). West Bengal is now an Indian state. The region has been marked by political turmoil in recent decades, due to Hindu-Muslim tensions, a large influx of Bangladesh refugees and the efforts of a Maoist group named the Naxalites.

Benghazi. Coastal city in northeastern LIBYA. Held by the OTTOMAN EMPIRE through 1911, it was occupied by Italy until 1941, when it was captured by the British on February 7, during WORLD WAR II. It was taken by the Germans on April 4, retaken by the British on Dec. 25, surrendered by the British on Jan. 28, 1942, and recaptured by the British on Nov. 20. It is a key port and center of commerce for Libya.

Bengsch, Alfred Cardinal (1921–1979). Roman Catholic archbishop of BERLIN and spiritual leader of 1.4 million Catholics in EAST GERMANY, East Berlin and West Berlin from 1967 until his death. Bengsch was considered a conservative theologian with impressive oratorical skill and was known for his struggle for religious freedom in East Germany.

Ben Gurion, David [born David Green] (1886–1973). Israeli statesman, considered the "father of ISRAEL." Born in Russia, he immigrated to PALESTINE in 1906. During the 1920s and 1930s he emerged as leader of the Labour Zionists and became leader of the Labour Party. In 1948 he proclaimed the restoration of the state of Israel, becoming its first prime minister. In his two terms (1948–53, 1955–63) he forged the image of Israel as a modern democratic state and consolidated its international position. During his premiership, over one million JEWS immigrated to Israel. (See also ZIONISM.)

Ben Haim, Paul [born Paul Frankenburger] (1897–1984). German-born composer. After the rise of Adolf HITLER, he fled to Palestine from Germany. By the time of his death, he was Israel's leading composer. His music was late romantic in style. Ben Haim was also known for his attempts to unite oriental and occidental musical traditions. His orchestral piece *The Sweet Psalmist of Israel* won the 1957 Israel State Prize.

Benin. Nation in West Africa, on the "Gold Coast"; bordered on the west by Togo and on the east by Nigeria. France established its colony of FRENCH WEST AFRICA in the 19th century and actively suppressed the Abomey people, exploiting the country's agricultural production—predominantly cocoa, cotton and palm tree products—until 1960, when it granted independence to "Dahomey," a name of long usage for the region. Extreme political instability followed, with 11 different regimes holding power from 1960 to 1972. A 1972 coup by Major Mathieu Kerekou had as its goal the imposition of a Marxist-Leninist socialist economy. The Kerekou regime has withstood several coup attempts, including a 1977 airborne assault that Kerekou accused France of backing.

David Ben Gurion with Richard Nixon (1960).

Benn, Gottfried (1886–1956). German poet. Trained as an army medical officer at the Kaiser Wilhelm Academy in Berlin, Benn practiced medicine all his life. His first volumes of expressionist verse appeared in 1912–13 (see EXPRESSIONISM) His best works were written in the 1920s. Like the French Surrealists (see SURREALISM), Benn attempted to write "absolute" poetry that used language for incantatory effect, dispensing with conventional structure and meaning; as a result, little of his work has been translated. Despite his initial sympathy with NAZISM, the Reich eventually banned his writing as "degenerate." However, he remained in Germany during WORLD WAR II. After 1948 he enjoyed a comeback. His reflections on his political career, *Doppelleben* (*Double Life*), were published in 1950.

Benn, Tony [Anthony Neil Wedgwood Benn] (1925–). British politician. An aristocrat by birth but socialist by inclination, Benn was a Labour M.P. from 1950 to 1960, when he had to leave the House of Commons because he succeeded his father as the second Viscount Stansgate. Benn never used his title and campaigned for the right to disclaim it. This led to passage of the Peerage Act (1963), under which Benn became the first person to disclaim an inherited title. Becoming a member of Labour's National Executive Committee in 1962, Benn served in the Harold WILSON government as postmaster general (1964–66), minister of technology (1966–70) and industry secretary (1974–75). Opposed to Britain's entry into the EUROPEAN ECONOMIC COMMUNITY, he was shifted to the Department of Energy, where he served in the James CALLAGHAN government until Labour's defeat in 1979. In 1981, Benn ran against Denis HEALEY for the deputy leadership of the LABOUR PARTY. Defeated by a narrow margin, the charismatic Benn established himself as a leader of the party's left wing. He lost his seat in 1987 but reentered Parliament in a later by-election. Benn is the author of *Arguments for Socialism* (1979).

Bennett, Alan (1934–). British actor and playwright. Bennett initially gained recognition as coauthor of and actor in the 1960 BEYOND THE FRINGE revue. His reputation as a playwright was established with his first play, *Forty Years On*, in 1968. As a playwright he is known for his use of satire, irony, farce and everyday language. His many successful plays include *Getting On* (1971), *Habeas Corpus* (1973) and *Kafka's Dick* (1986). In addition, he has written several one-act plays and monologues for television.

Bennett, (Enoch) Arnold (1867–1931). British author. Born in the Potteries district of Staffordshire and educated at the Burslem Endowed School and the Middle School of Newcastle-under-Lyme, he went to London in 1888 and began writing. He edited the periodical *Woman* from 1893

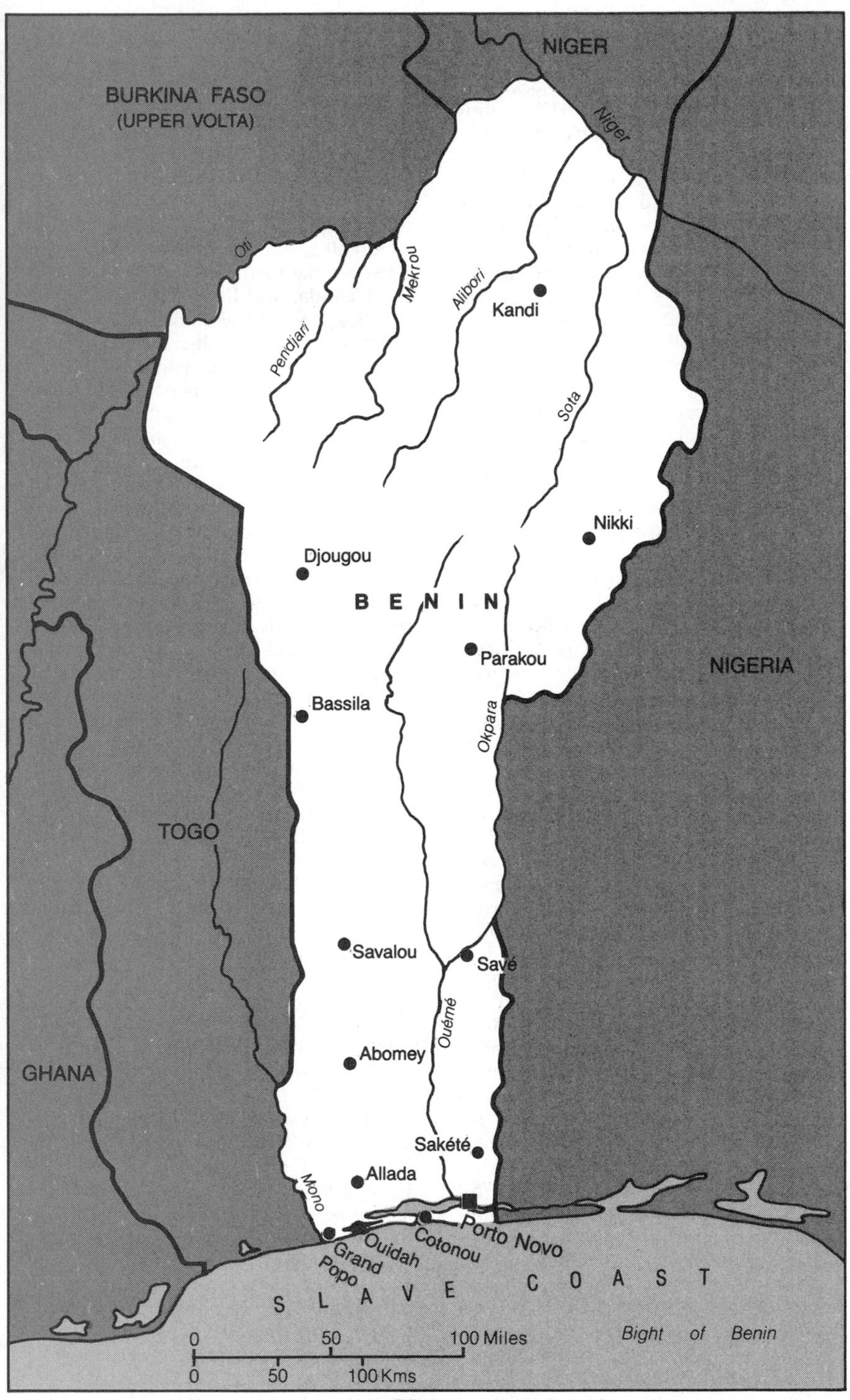

BENIN

until 1902, when he moved to Paris. His first short stories appeared in periodicals in the 1890s; his first novel, *The Man from the North,* was published in 1898. Although he was also a successful playwright, he is best remembered for the series of novels that take place in his provincial birthplace, renamed in the books the "Five Towns." These novels include *Anna of the Five Towns* (1902), *The Old Wives Tale* (1908) and *Clayhanger* (1910). Influenced by the techniques of Naturalism practiced by Emile Zola and other French writers, they are wry and yet affectionate, clear-eyed portraits of provincial personalities and their ordinary lives. Bennett returned permanently to England in 1912, continuing his prolific literary output and also contributing a weekly column on books to the *Evening Standard* until his death from typhoid. An important writer, though not a great one, he was one of the last English realists. Much admired in his time, he was later derided by the modernists, but he is still read.

Bennett, D(onald) C(lifford) T(yndall) (1910–1986). Australian-born British aviator. During WORLD WAR II, at the age of 33, Bennett became the youngest air vice marshal in the history of the ROYAL AIR FORCE. He formed and commanded the Pathfinder Force, which became the spearhead of Bomber Command's mass attacks on German cities. After the war, he became the first chief executive of British Overseas Airways Corp. He was also involved in politics, moving from a LIBERAL PARTY affiliation further to the right as he grew older.

Bennett, Floyd (1890–1928). American aviator. After becoming a pilot in the Navy, Bennett was chosen by Richard BYRD to accompany the MacMillan Expedition to Greenland. On May 9, 1926, Bennett piloted Byrd over the NORTH POLE, in the first successful flight over either Pole. Bennett was awarded the Congressional Medal of Honor as well as a medal by the NATIONAL GEOGRAPHIC SOCIETY. Also in 1926, Bennett made an 8,000–mile test flight around the United States to prove the viability of scheduled commercial flights. While planning a trip with Byrd to the SOUTH POLE, Bennett volunteered to rescue two downed German aviators in the Gulf of St. Lawrence. Bennett became ill during the flight and died of pneumonia in Quebec in 1928. Brooklyn, New York's first airport was named for him in 1931.

Bennett, Jill (1931–1990). British actress. She specialized in stylish comedy, appearing in such films as *Moulin Rouge* (1952) and *Lust for Life* (1956). She is perhaps best remembered for her role as a heavy-drinking actress in the play *Time Present,* written for her by her second husband, John OSBORNE.

Bennett, Joan (1910–1990). American actress; she and her sisters Constance and Barbara, all actresses, were the daughters of stage star Richard Bennett. Bennett began her film career playing ingenue roles and went on to become one of the most glamorous leading ladies of the 1930s and 1940s. Her 75 films ranged from melodramas and thrillers to comedies, and included *Bulldog Drummond* (1929), *The Woman in the Window* (1944), *Scarlet Street* (1946) and *Father of the Bride* (1950). In the 1950s, after her film career began to fade, she turned to stage and television. She starred in the gothic daytime soap opera "Dark Shadows" (1966–71), which became a television cult classic.

Bennett, Michael (1943–1987). American dancer, choreographer and director. Bennett is best known for the landmark musical *A Chorus Line* (1975), which he conceived, choreographed and directed, with Marvin Hamlisch as composer. The musical won nine Tony Awards, a PULITZER PRIZE and the New York Drama Critics Award. Bennett began his career as a dancer in the musical *West Side Story,* then choreographed the musicals *Promises, Promises* (1968) and *Company* (1971), among other shows. He directed and choreographed the shows *Seesaw, Ballroom* and *Dreamgirls* before his untimely death.

For further reading:

Kelly, Kevin, *One Singular Sensation: the Michael Bennett Story*. New York: Doubleday, 1990.

Bennett, Richard Bedford [Viscount Bennett (1941)] (1870–1947). Canadian statesman, prime minister (1930–35). A successful businessman and lawyer, he became a member of the Parliament for Calgary in 1911 and leader of the Conservative Party in 1927. After the Conservative electoral victory in 1930, he became prime minister. During his tenure, Bennett advocated free trade within the empire and attempted to deal with the GREAT DEPRESSION through a broad program of social legislation. His government was defeated in 1935, and he retired to England in 1941, where he was made a viscount.

Bennett, Ward (1917–). Distinguished American furniture and interior designer. Bennett studied art with Hans Hofmann in New York and with the sculptor Constantin BRANCUSI in Paris before working briefly for LE CORBUSIER beginning in 1938. As an interior designer, he has been a consultant to SKIDMORE, OWINGS & MERRILL, for example, designing the interiors of the executive offices of the Chase Manhattan Bank in New York. He has also designed office and residential projects for a number of private clients. His style is generally quiet, reserved, and elegant, with an implication of luxury conveyed through simplicity. Bennett has also been active as a sculptor, jewelry designer, and designer of china and silver tableware.

Bennett, W(illiam) A.C. (1911–1979). Canadian politician. Leader of the SOCIAL CREDIT PARTY for 20 years, Bennett served as premier of British Columbia. He left politics in 1972 after an upset defeat. His son **William Bennett** (1932–) became premier of British Columbia in 1975 and was also a party leader.

Bennite. Supporter of British LABOUR PARTY politician Tony BENN, M.P., former minister and member of the Labour Party National Executive Committee. The term has been misused to refer to all sections of the British left indiscriminately, including the Trotskyist **Militant Tendency,** of which Benn was not a member.

Benny, Jack [Benjamin Kubelsky] (1894–1974). Born in Chicago, Illinois, Benny went on to become one of America's most beloved comedians. Beginning as a violinist and singer, he was known onstage as "the Aristocrat of Humor." In 1932 he took his act to radio and gradually formed his own stock company of performers: Mary Livingston (who became his wife in 1927), sidekick Eddie "Rochester" Anderson, Dennis Day and Mel BLANC. By the mid-1930s his show had caught on, and Benny developed his trademark "stingy" character, which included the catchphrase "Now cut that out!" and his brilliantly timed pauses. Benny continued his radio program until 1955, but was also the star of various television shows and specials from 1950 to 1965. His humor also found its way into the movies, few of them successful; his one unanimously hailed screen role was in the ahead-of-its-time black comedy *To Be or Not To Be* (1942). Benny continued to make television appearances until his death in 1974.

Benois, Alexandre (1870–1960). Russian designer, painter and art historian. Born the son of an architect in St. Petersburg, Benois was descended on his mother's side from the builder of the Maryinsky and Bolshoi Theaters. Benois came to view his calling as "the propagation of art." He served as artistic director and designer of Konstantin STANISLAVSKY'S MOSCOW ART THEATRE, but his metier was ballet. He played an important role in the BALLETS RUSSES company led by Serge DIAGHILEV. Ballet productions for which his costumes or decor are well-known include *Les Sylphides* (1909), *Giselle* (1910), *Petrouchka* (1911), for which he also cowrote the libretto with Igor STRAVINSKY, *Graduation Ball* (1940) and *The Nutcracker* (1957). Benois was also the author of several books, including *Reminiscences of the Ballets Russes* and *Memoirs*. The hallmark of his ballet design was historical accuracy combined with delicate stage settings.

Benson, E(dward) F(rederic) (1867–1940). British novelist. Benson's witty series of novels, such as *Dodo: a Detail of the Day* (1893), followed by other "dodo" novels (*Dodo the Second* [1914], *Dodo's Daughter* [1914] and *Dodo Wonders* [1921]), and *Queen Lucia* (1920), followed by several other "Lucia" novels, were—and are—enormously popular. The "Lucia" novels were collected in *Make Way for Lucia* (1977). An extremely prolific writer, Benson was also renowned as one of the century's most anthologized ghost story writers. His two brothers were also men of letters. The elder, **A(rthur) C(hristopher) Benson** (1862–25), was a biographer and critic; **R(obert) H(ugh) Benson** (1871–14) was a religious writer. E.F. Benson spent his later years at Lamb House in Rye, Sussex, the former home of Henry JAMES.

Benton, Thomas Hart (1889–1975). American painter, illustrator and folk music collector. With other midwestern artists Iowan Grant WOOD and Kansan John Steuart Curry, Benton was a leading example of the movement in the 1930s dubbed REGIONALISM. He was born in Missouri; his great uncle was the legendary "Thunderer," Senator Thomas Hart Benton; and his father was a member of the U.S. House of Representatives. However, young Benton preferred painting to politics and from 1908 to 1911 studied in Paris, dabbling in experimental movements like CONSTRUCTIVISM, CUBISM and, later, Synchronism. After World War I, Benton became convinced that the avant-garde did not mirror the real life and history around him. Soon, he was embroiled in controversy for attacking what he called the "aesthetic drivelings" and "morbid self-concerns" of modernist styles. The 1920s and 1930s were spent painting the murals that would establish his reputation as an observer of southern, midwestern and urban American life: the "America Today" cycle for the New School in New York; the cycle of murals for the Whitney Museum; the great "Social History of Indiana" cycle; and the "Social History of Missouri" cycle for the Jefferson City statehouse. At the same time he began his annual rambles through the countryside. He sketched field hands, attended church services in the Smoky Mountains, sat in with Virginia politicians, worked with cotton pickers in central Georgia, and lived with the farming families of the Texas flatlands.

By the time his self-portrait appeared on the cover of TIME magazine in 1934, he was the most famous painter in America. He left New York City in 1935 after bickering with the art establishment to take on a teaching position at the Kansas City Art Institute. Six years later his increasingly strident attacks against art museums ("graveyards" run by "pretty boys") ran him afoul of both Kansas City's Nelson-Atkins Museum and the Art Institute. He was fired. It was at this time that his most notorious comment was voiced, that he would prefer his paintings be hung in a saloon than in a museum. (His controversial nude, "Persephone," was subsequently hung in Billy ROSE'S Diamond Horseshoe Saloon in New York.) Benton's last years were spent in what his biographer Henry Adams has called "an artistic retreat" into landscapes and nostalgia. Benton's autobiography, *An Artist in America*, written in three installments in 1937, 1951 and 1968, remains an important document of Benton's times.

For further reading:

Adams, Henry, *Thomas Hart Benton: An American Original*. New York: Alfred Knopf, 1990.

Bentsen, Lloyd (Millard, Jr.) (1921–). American politician. Born in Mission, Tx., he received a law degree from the University of Texas in 1942. Becoming a judge after World War II, he was elected to the House of Representatives in 1948. Returning to business in Texas in 1954, he reentered politics when he was elected to the Senate in 1970, defeating Republican candidate George BUSH. One of the most conservative Democratic senators, he was a financial expert, a powerful advocate of the oil, banking and real estate industries of his native state, and an extremely effective fund raiser. Chosen as the vice presidential running mate of Michael DUKAKIS, Bentsen was defeated in the 1988 election. However, he remained an influential figure in the Senate.

Beny, Roloff (Wilfred Roy) (1924–1984). Canadian photographer and artist. Beny's sumptuous books exploring the beauties of Canada, Japan, Iran and the ruins of Greece were internationally acclaimed. His *To Every Thing There Is a Season* was the official Canadian gift to visiting heads of state during the country's 1967 centennial year. His *India* was chosen by the Indian government to celebrate the 100th anniversary (1968) of Mohandas K. GANDHI'S birth. Beny's paintings and engravings were featured in more than 25 one-man exhibitions.

For further reading:

Matheson, Sylvia, *Rajasthan: Land of Kings*. New York: Vendome, 1984.

Berchtesgaden. Town in the southeast of the German state of Bavaria. A popular resort, in the 1930s and 1940s its mountaintop Berghof was the favorite retreat of Adolf HITLER. Consequently, it was a target of heavy Allied bombing during WORLD WAR II. Most of the Berghof was destroyed following its capture in May 1945 by the Allies.

Berdyaev, Nikolai Aleksandrovich (1874–1948). Russian theologian and philosopher. Berdyaev, who was born in Kiev, published his first philosophical work when he was 26 and went on to become one of the most prolific and influential Russian writers of his epoch. In his youth, Berdyaev was briefly drawn to Marxism, but he soon rejected its materialist viewpoint in favor of a spiritual existentialism that emphasized the power of faith to transform human lives. After the Russian Revolution, Berdyaev was appointed to the chair of philosophy at the University of Moscow, but in 1922 he was expelled from his native land (on the charge of being an anti-communist upholder of religion) and died in exile in Paris. Berdyaev insisted that faith could not be achieved by rational argument but was instead a matter of intuition and of the natural impulse of the soul to seek for spiritual freedom. Berdyaev's major works in English translation include *Spirit and Reality* (1939) and *Slavery and Freedom* (1948).

Beregovoy, Georgy (1921–). Soviet cosmonaut and veteran of over 100 combat missions against the Nazis in WORLD WAR II. The first Soviet test pilot to fly in space, Beregovoy was 47 (the oldest cosmonaut at the time) when he flew aboard Soyuz 3 in October 1968. After his flight, he was appointed director of the Gagarin Cosmonaut Training Center.

Berenson, Bernard (1865–1959). American art critic. In his lifetime, Berenson established himself as a leading writer on the Italian Renaissance and as an unquestioned expert on the authenticity of Renaissance paintings. Born in Lithuania of a poor Jewish family, Berenson immigrated to Boston as a young boy. Educated at Harvard and Oxford, he published his first essays on Renaissance art in the 1890s. Berenson championed the view that form—not subject matter—is the preeminent criterion for excellence in painting. His major critical work is *Italian Pictures of the Renaissance* (1932). As an authenticator of Renaissance paintings offered for sale, Berenson acquired an legendary status among art dealers and museum curators and managed to amass a sizable personal fortune, which he used to acquire a villa on the outskirts of Florence in which he lived for most of the last six decades of his life. In *Sketch for a Self-Portrait* (1949), Berenson recounted his difficult years of hiding from the Nazis during World War II.

Berg, Aksel Ivanovich (1893–1979). Soviet radio engineer and pioneer of cybernetics. Berg started his career as a submarine navigator and from 1918 to 1921 commanded a submarine in the Soviet navy's Baltic fleet. He later taught advanced training courses for naval radio operators at Leningrad Naval Academy. His main work concerns theories and methods of design and calculation of tube generators. He was awarded many orders and medals, and in 1946 became a member of the U.S.S.R. ACADEMY OF SCIENCES.

Berg, Alban (Maria Johannes) (1885–1935). Viennese composer, influential disciple of the modern 12–tone techniques of Arnold SCHOENBERG, and composer of the opera *Wozzeck*. He was born in Vienna where his association with Schoenberg overturned his enthusiasm for Wagner and led him in the direction of atonality in early works like the *Five Songs with Orchestra* (1912) and the landmark opera *Wozzeck* (begun in 1913 and completed in 1920). Unlike his colleagues Anton von WEBERN and Schoenberg, Berg achieved at least a degree of popularity in his lifetime. Major works like the *Lyric Suite* (1926), the *Chamber Concerto* (1923–25) and the Violin Concerto (1935) held an elusive appeal because of their ambiguous tonal commitments. Such traditional forms as waltzes, major-minor triads and baroque quotations (like the Bach chorale at the end of the Violin Concerto) were nostalgic reminders of a rapidly vanishing past. The emotional impact of these works was overwhelming. "Musical theories and systems never supplanted an essential humanism in Berg," writes biographer Karen Monson. On the one hand, wit and humor are everywhere. Note-ciphers, musical descriptions of himself, Schoenberg and Webern, pervade the *Chamber Concerto*. On the other hand, deeply felt love and sorrow illuminate the Violin Concerto (inspired by the death of a beloved friend) and the *Lyric Suite* (expressive of Berg's clandestine love affair with Hanna Werfel-Robettin, his "one eternal love"). "I can tell you, dear friend," he wrote Schoenberg, "that if it became known how much friendship, love, and how many spiritual references I have smuggled into [my music] . . . the adherents of program music. . . would go mad with joy." He died of blood poisoning on Christmas Eve, 1935, before he completed his opera *Lulu* (the entire work was finally staged in 1979). (See also SERIAL MUSIC.)

For further reading:

Monson, Karen, *Alban Berg*. Boston: Houghton Mifflin Co., 1979.

Berg, Patty (1918–). American professional golfer. In 1946, Berg won the first U.S. Women's Open ever held. Between 1935 and 1964 she won 83 tournaments and served as the first president of the Ladies Professional Golf Association. Chosen by the Associated Press as Athlete-of-the Year three times, Berg was elected to the American Golf Hall of Fame in 1972.

Bergen, Edgar [Edgar Bergren] (1903–1978). American comedian. One of the top radio personalities for over 10 years (1937–late 1940s), Bergen initially gained fame on the VAUDEVILLE circuit as a ventriloquist. His two wooden dummies, Charlie McCarthy and Mortimer Snerd, became household names. He also toured Europe and appeared on television and in several films, including *The Goldwyn Follies* (1938).

Bergen-Belsen. Nazi CONCENTRATION CAMP in northwestern GERMANY. Bergen-Belsen was opened in 1941 to house Russian PRISONERS OF WAR. In 1943 HIMMLER turned it into a concentration camp for JEWS and incapacitated victims from other camps. The lack of medical care and hygiene caused many deaths—including that of diarist Anne FRANK in March 1945. When the camp was liberated by the U.S. Army on April 14, 1945, 10,000 corpses were found. Of the 38,000 living prisoners, barely one-third survived.

Berger, Erna (1900–1990). German opera singer. Berger was one of the best known and most popular lyric and coloratura sopranos of the pre- and post-World War II era. She was especially noted for her performances as the Queen of the Night in Mozart's *Die Zauberfloete* and her singing of the German lieder.

Berger, John Peter (1926–). British art critic, novelist, social critic and screenplay writer. Berger, one of the most influential art critics of the postwar era, is noted for his Marxist-influenced insistence on placing art in the social context of its times. He was for a long period the art critic of the *New Statesman* and has appeared frequently on British television. His book *Art and Revolution* (1968) underscores the revolutionary content in much of modernist European painting. *The Moment of Cubism* (1969) reevaluates the origins of the Cubist movement in terms of the social implications of its new vision. A representative sampling of his work is included in *The Look of Things: Essays* (1972). Berger has also published several novels, notably *G* (1972), and has written screenplays for several films by the French director Alain Tanner, including *Jonah Who Will Be 25 in the Year 2000* (1976).

Berghof, Herbert (1909–1990). Austrian-born actor, director and teacher. Among the plays he directed was the U.S. debut of Samuel BECKETT'S WAITING FOR GODOT in 1956. His students included Robert DE NIRO, Al Pacino, Anne Bancroft, Matthew Broderick and Geraldine Page.

Bergman, Ingmar (1918–). Celebrated Swedish stage and film director. Bergman was born in Uppsala, Sweden, the son of a stern Lutheran pastor, and brought up in a household full of what he has called "misery and exhausting conflicts." He sought refuge in two interests that became lifelong passions: the theater, especially the plays of August STRINDBERG, and the movies, which he described as "a fever which has never left me." After completing his education at the University of Stockholm, he went to work as a script writer for the Svenskfilmindustri studio. From 1946 to 1982 he divided his time between the theater (mostly at the

Ingmar Bergman with fellow director Billie August (Stockholm, 1989).

Royal Dramatic Theater) and the direction of 40 films, a body of distinguished work unparalleled in modern cinema. With favorite cameraman Sven Nykvist and a stock company that included Liv Ullmann (his wife), Gunnar Bjornstrand, Bibi Andersson and Max von Sydow, he worked with the precision and nuance of a master sculptor. Themes frequently overlap from film to film: the carnal comedy (*Sommarnattens Leende/Smiles of a Summer Night*, 1955); studies of women (*Autumn Sonata*, 1978); historical allegories (*Det Sjunde Inseglet/The Seventh Seal*, 1957); and his most personally-felt theme, the isolation and alienation of modern man (the 1961–63 trilogy of *Sasom i en Spegel/Through a Glass Darkly*; *Nattsvardsgasterna/Winter Light*; and *T Lysnaden/The Silence*). Autobiography is everywhere, especially in his final film, *Fanny and Alexander* (1982). The images scattered through his *oeuvre* are unforgettable: the peasant by the windmill lustily saluting the dawn in *Smiles of a Summer Night*; the minister's altar rituals in an empty church in *Winter Light*; the appearance of the "spider god" in *Through a Glass Darkly*; the violent rape in *The Virgin Spring*; and the sweeping "dance of death" at the conclusion of *The Seventh Seal*. As biographer Birgitta Steene has written, "Bergman has focused his lens on an interior landscape...on the progress of the soul." Bergman retired from filmmaking after *Fannie and Alexander* (1982).

For further reading:

Bergman, Ingmar, *The Magic Lantern: An Autobiography*. New York: Viking Press, 1985.

Cowie, Peter, *Ingmar Bergman: A Critical Biography*. New York: Scribner, 1982.

Bergman, Ingrid (1915–1982). Swedish-born actress, one of the most acclaimed—and controversial—film stars of her time. Trained at the Royal Dramatic Theater in Stockholm, she was brought to HOLLYWOOD to star in a 1939 remake of her earlier Swedish film *Intermezzo*. She starred in several successful films but was catapulted to stardom as Ilsa Lund in the classic *Casablanca* (1943), opposite Humphrey BOGART. She continued to be one of the most popular Hollywood stars through the 1940s, giving acclaimed performances in *For Whom the Bell Tolls* (1943), *Gaslight* (1944; ACADEMY AWARD) and Alfred HITCHCOCK's *Notorious* (1946), among others. However, she became the center of a major scandal in 1948 when she left her husband and child to marry the Italian director Roberto ROSSELLINI, and her career floundered. She returned to the U.S. in 1957 and worked intermittently; her notable later films were *Anastasia* (1957), *Indiscreet* (1957), *Murder on the Orient Express* (1974) and *Autumn Sonata* (1978), her last film. She also played Israeli Prime Minister Golda MEIR in a made-for-television drama.

Bergonzi, Carlo (1924–). Italian tenor. Born in the village of Vidalenzo, Bergonzi studied at the Arrigo Boito Conservatory in Parma. He debuted in the role of Figaro in *The Barber of Seville* in 1948. In 1951 he began singing as a tenor, performing in the title role of *Andrea Chenier*. Bergonzi made his first U.S. appearance with the Chicago Opera in 1955 and debuted with the Metropolitan Opera the following year as Radames in Verdi's *Aida*. Not a particularly robust singer, he made up for a certain lack of strength with his beautiful tone, subtle phrasing and elegant style. The nearly 70 roles in his operatic repertoire included Cavaradossi in *Tosca*, Rodolfo in *La Boheme*, Pinkerton in *Madama Butterfly*, Des Grieux in *Manon Lescaut* and Riccardo in *Un Ballo in Maschera*.

Bergson, Henri (1859–1941). French philosopher. Bergson was a rarity—a philosopher with a style so rich and evocative that he was awarded the NOBEL PRIZE for literature in 1927. Bergson is best known for his speculative concept—best articulated in *Creative Evolution* (1907)—of the "elan vital" (vital impetus), which he posited as "a current of consciousness" that penetrates matter, gives rise to all forms of life and determines the nature of their evolution. The "elan vital" is conveyed from one generation to the next through physical means of reproduction, though it remains something apart from matter in order to assure the maximum intedeterminacy in physical evolutionary development. Bergson asserted that humankind was the highest creation of the "elan vital" and hence the focus of all evolution. Bergson's other major works include *Matter and Memory* (1896), *Laughter* (1900) and *The Two Sources of Morality and Religion* (1932). A Jew, Bergson died an invalid as a result of harassment from the Vichy French government.

Beria, Lavrenti (1899–1953). Head of the Soviet SECRET POLICE (NKVD) (1935–53). Beria organized a BOLSHEVIK group during the RUSSIAN REVOLUTION and directed the secret police in Soviet Georgia from 1921 to 1931. He was first secretary of the Georgian Communist Party and was appointed commissar for international affairs by Joseph STALIN in 1938 and head of the NKVD (Soviet Security Service). After Stalin's death Beria was dismissed and executed by other leading communists, who believed he had been planning to succeed Stalin. Along with YEZHOV and Stalin himself, Beria was one of the most feared figures in the U.S.S.R. during the Stalinist era.

Berkeley. U.S. city on the east side of California's San Francisco Bay; since 1873, the site of the largest campus of the University of California. In the 1960s, Berkeley was the tinderbox for the FREE SPEECH MOVEMENT that influenced campus political activism nationwide.

Berkeley, Busby [William Berkeley Enos] (1895–1976). American choreographer and dance director and one of the few authentic geniuses of the motion picture; famous for the lavish musical extravaganzas he created for such HOLLYWOOD films as *42nd Steet* (1933), *Gold Diggers of 1933* (1933) and *Easy to Love* (1953) (directed by Lloyd Bacon, Mervyn Leroy and Charles Walters), and *Strike Up the Band* (1940) and *The Gang's All Here* (1943) (directed by Berkeley himself). Berkeley, a Broadway veteran, almost immediately grasped the possibilities of the motion picture camera to liberate him from the proscenium-bound stage. Berkeley numbers were hallucinogenic extravaganzas that wandered in space and time and invited the viewer to wink at the conceit that they were being performed on a normal stage. He filled the screen with an energetic movement that was created as much by his trick photography as by the dancing, swimming or flying around of hordes of blonde, brunette and redhead chorines ("350 of the most gorgeous creatures on Earth"—according to the *Dames* publicity). Berkeley had a great deal of success from the 1930s into the 1950s but began to struggle with personal problems and a declining public interest in extravagant musicals. He returned to the spotlight in 1970 as director of a successful Broadway revival of Vincent YOUMANS' *No, No, Nanette*.

Berkeley, Sir Lennox (Randal Francis) (1903–1989). British composer. He studied French, Old French and philology at Oxford University before deciding upon a career in music. Beginning in 1930 he studied with Nadia BOULANGER in Paris for five years. He completed his first major work, the oratorio *Jonah*, in 1935. During his career he composed choral, solo, chamber and orchestral music, including four symphonies as well as several operas. He was knighted in 1974.

Berkshire Festival. Summer music festival held in Lenox, in western Massachusetts, one of the popular Berkshire summer resorts and summer home of the Boston Symphony Orchestra. In 1936, Tanglewood—a private estate consisting of some 200 acres—was donated to the orchestra, then under the direction of Serge KOUSSEVITZKY. Thus was born the Berkshire Festival. Each year, the orchestra presents 24 weekend performances, as well as concerts by the orchestra's chamber players and guest performers. Facilities include a 6,000-seat music shed, several smaller theaters, chamber music halls and studios.

Berle, Adolf Augustus, Jr. (1895–1971). U.S. lawyer and public official. Berle was a member of the PARIS PEACE CONFERENCE after WORLD WAR I, but resigned in protest over the terms of the VERSAILLES TREATY. He later became professor of law at Columbia University and an influential figure in President Franklin ROOSEVELT'S NEW DEAL and Good Neighbor Policy. In 1945, Berle became ambassador to Brazil. He was a founder and chairman of the New York State Liberal Party and author of *Power* (1969).

Berle, Milton (1908–). Prominent American stage and screen entertainer; known as "Uncle Miltie" in the early days of television. After only middling success in VAUDEVILLE, the movies (from *The Perils of Pauline* in 1914 to *Sun Valley Serenade* in 1937), radio and nightclubs, he found his metier in television. Tuesday evenings became known as "Milton Berle Night," beginning on June 8, 1948, on NBC and extending through 1951. At a time when only 9% of homes had television sets, millions watched The TEXACO STAR THEATER inside taverns and in front of appliance store windows. Berle's program led a wave of variety programming at the time. But by 1952 Berle's popularity was beginning to fade, and new sponsors started "tinkering" with his on-air persona, a process that Berle described as softening the "aggressive, pushy 'Milton Berle' into a passive straight man." Also, the technical achievement of coast-to-coast network transmissions had unleashed Berle's essentially "urban" comedy on rural audiences. After a few more seasons with different sponsors in different timeslots, Berle left television, and he has not had his own series again. Although he has not had the enduring popularity of rivals like Jack BENNY and Jackie GLEASON, he was an essential factor in the postwar success of television.

For further reading:

Berle, Milton, *Milton Berle: An Autobiography*. New York: Delacorte Press, 1979.

Berlin, Irving [born Israel Baline] (1888–1989). Russian-born American popular songwriter. His Russian-Jewish family immigrated to the U.S. when he was a few years old, and he grew up in a poor neighborhood on the Lower East Side of New York City. He began working at age eight, first as a newspaper seller then as a street singer and as a singing waiter. He began writing songs in 1907, and in 1911 had his first hit, "Alexander's Ragtime Band." He went on to write such well-known songs as "Puttin on the Ritz," "Always," "Mammy" (for the first TALKING PICTURE, *The Jazz Singer*, 1927), "Cheek to Cheek" (for the Fred ASTAIRE-Ginger ROGERS film *Top Hat*), "Oh How I Hate to Get Up in the Morning" (featured in both a 1917 revue and in the 1943 film *This Is the Army*), "Easter Parade" and "There's No Business Like Show Business" (for the musical *Annie Get Your Gun*). Perhaps his two greatest classics were "God Bless America" and "White Christmas," which is believed to have sold more copies than any other song in history. He received a congressional gold medal and a proclamation of appreciation from President Dwight D. Eisenhower in 1954. Altogether, Berlin composed some 1,500 songs, 19 Broadway musicals and 18 movie scores, despite the fact he never learned to read or write music. His songs captured the mood of 20th-century American experience, whether it was WORLD WAR I, the GREAT DEPRESSION of the 1930s, WORLD WAR II or the post-war prosperity of the 1950s and 1960s. He died at the age of 101, still young in spirit.

Irving Berlin, one of America's most popular and prolific composers.

For further reading:

Bergreen, Laurence, *As Thousands Cheer: The Life of Irving Berlin*. New York: Viking Penguin, 1990.

Berlin. Past and future capital of GERMANY; lying along the Spree River, it is the largest city in Germany, with a population of over three million and was once the capital of Prussia. By 1900, the city had a population of 2,712,000. It entered a period of social unrest after the German defeat in World War I and was the scene of the leftist SPARTACIST UPRISING in 1919 and the rightest KAPP PUTSCH in 1920. While under great economic strain, it was nonetheless a noted cultural center as capital of the postwar WEIMAR REPUBLIC. The city prospered materially but declined spiritually after it became HITLER'S capital in 1933. During WORLD WAR II, Berlin was severely damaged by Allied bombs and by the Soviet artillery fire that preceded the capture of the capital in May 1945. Agreements reached at the YALTA and POTSDAM CONFERENCES divided the conquered city into four occupied sectors, individually administered by the U.S., U.S.S.R., Great Britain and France.

Berlin soon became a major issue in the COLD WAR, with the U.S.S.R. demanding Western withdrawal from a city that was totally within the boundaries of the Soviet occupation zone (which became EAST GERMANY). In 1948 the Soviets established a blockade between West Berlin and WEST GERMANY, which was successfully broken by an Anglo-American airlift (see BERLIN AIRLIFT). In 1949 East Berlin was made the capital of East Germany, and the three Western zones were formally unified to create West Berlin, which became a West German state in 1950. In the years that followed, West Berlin was totally rebuilt, and it quickly developed into one of the most thriving cities in Europe. East Berlin, on the other hand, was much slower to rebuild and never experienced the economic rebirth of its sister city. A stream of refugees fled to West Germany from East Germany, via East Berlin, throughout the 1950s. This exodus was abruptly ended in 1961, when the East German authorities erected the BERLIN WALL, a barrier that prevented traffic between the divided cities. Allied disapproval of the wall was perhaps best crystallized in President John F. KENNEDY'S 1963 visit to the divided city. Tensions were eased somewhat in 1972, when

East German soldier leaps to freedom over barbed wire barricade before the Berlin Wall is completed.

visits across the wall and access to West Berlin from West Germany were formalized in the so-called Berlin accords.

The wall remained a hated symbol of communist repression and of a divided Germany until November 1989, when, in the wake of revolutions sweeping Eastern Europe, East Germany lifted restrictions on travel between East and West Berlin. The impromptu celebration at the wall turned into a joyous occasion, with jubilant, dancing crowds picking at and hurling away chunks from the wall. A September 1990 agreement ended four-power responsibility over Berlin and pledged to unite the city. On October 3, 1990, Germany and Berlin were formally reunited.

Berlin Airlift (June 1948–May 1949). With BERLIN under the four-power administration of the victorious Allies after WORLD WAR II, the U.S.S.R. hoped to force the U.S., Britain and France out of the city. Alleging that the West had broken postwar agreements on German status, the Soviets imposed obstacles to road and river traffic crossing into the western (U.S., British, French) sector of Berlin. The West responded with a round-the-clock airlift of fuel, food, mail and personnel to relieve the beleaguered city.

Berlin-Baghdad Railway. Railway from the Bosporus to the PERSIAN GULF that was proposed by a German company in 1899. The idea of this project was greeted with anger by the Russians, who had their own plans for such a railway. In Britain, some who wished to encourage German-Russian conflict favored the project, but many who feared a Gulf port dominated by Germany spoke out against it. By 1914, most European objections to the plan had been settled. However, the argument proved academic as only a small part of the railway line had been completed by the outbreak of WORLD WAR I, and the war caused the cessation of construction.

Berlinguer, Enrico (1922–1984). Italian communist politician and popular founder of eurocommunism. Berlinguer led ITALY'S 1.7-million-member Communist Party—Europe's largest—from 1972 until his death. In 1973 he called for a "historic compromise" between communist and democratic parties in Western Europe. He urged Western communists to act independently of the Soviet Union, renounce the idea of violent revolution and embrace democratic coalition politics. He nearly brought his party to power in the 1976 Italian parliamentary elections, with 34.5% of the vote. Although the party's strength later declined from that high point, Berlinguer remained a dominant and respected force in Italy's political and intellectual life. His funeral in Rome was attended by more than 1 million people, the city's biggest crowd since the end of World War II.

Berlin Wall. Fortified barrier between East and West BERLIN that existed from 1961 to 1989–90. After the East Berlin riots of 1953, many East Berliners fled into West Berlin to find freedom and better living conditions. This stream of refugees continued throughout the 1950s, until August 13, 1961, when communist authorities closed 68 border crossing points and began to erect a wall between the eastern and western zones of the city. Barbed wire, ditches and guard towers were added and became a part of the landscape. Escape attempts continued but became deadly affairs, many fewer in number and in success. On June 26, 1963, U.S. President John F. KENNEDY traveled to Berlin where he made his famous "Ich bin ein Berliner" speech denouncing the wall and communism and expressing his solidarity with the people of Berlin. Nonetheless, the wall remained for nearly three decades as a physical manifestation of the IRON CURTAIN. After a mass exodus of East Germans to the West in the summer of 1989, political demonstrations against the communist government led to the downfall of hardline East German leader Erich HONECKER (October 1989); reform Premier Egon KRENZ announced the lifting of travel restrictions between East and West Berlin. East and West Berliners responded by mounting the wall and holding an impromptu celebration. By the end of 1990 the last remnants of the wall had been dismantled and East and West Berlin were one—a part of a reunited GERMANY. (See also COLD WAR.)

Berman, Jakub (1901–1984). Polish Communist Party and government official. Trained in the U.S.S.R. during World War II, Berman came to power in postwar POLAND under Nationalist Party leader Wladyslaw GOMULKA. Berman is believed to have helped engineer Gomulka's ouster in 1948. As a member of the ruling Politburo in the early 1950s, Berman's responsibilities included national security, ideological purity and propaganda. He probably played a crucial behind-the-scenes role as the chief exponent of Soviet policy under Joseph STALIN. Berman served as vice premier from 1954 to 1956. Because of his close identification with the Soviets, he was ousted from the party and the government in 1957, after Gomulka's comeback. Thereafter he lived quietly in Warsaw until his death.

Bermuda. A group of islands in the North Atlantic Ocean, approximately 700 miles southeast of New York City, Bermuda covers an area of 19.3 square miles. The population of some 58,000 is approxi-

East German border guards look on as demonstrators pull down a segment of the Berlin wall near the Brandenburg gate (November 1989).

mately two-thirds black and one-third white of mainly British descent. Bermuda is a dependent territory of the UNITED KINGDOM with a constitution dating from June 1968. In the 1970s clashes between those favoring dependent status and those wanting independence, exacerbated by racial tension, resulted in the murder of the governor (1973) and riots (1977). Since 1980 the political party that endorses continued ties with Britain has been in power. Tourism is the main industry; since the 1930s, Bermuda has been a popular tourist and honeymoon destination for Americans. It has managed to retain much of its old world charm and scenic beauty.

Bernadotte, Count Folke (1895–1948). President of the Swedish RED CROSS and UNITED NATIONS mediator. A Swedish soldier involved with the Red Cross in WORLD WAR I, in WORLD WAR II he arranged exchanges of sick and disabled PRISONERS OF WAR at Goteborg in 1943 and 1944. He was used by Heinrich HIMMLER in 1945 as intermediary to seek a surrender of German forces to the British and Americans, but the proposal was rejected in London and Washington. He was invited by United Nations Secretary General Trygve LIE to serve as United Nations mediator in PALESTINE, where he was assassinated by Jewish terrorists in 1948.

Bernadotte, Sigvard (1907–). Leading Swedish craft and industrial designer. Bernadotte, son of the Swedish king Gustave V, began his design career in the firm of Georg Jensen, working in silver, furniture, textiles and helping to build that firm's international reputation. In 1949 he opened an industrial design office in Copenhagen, with the Danish designer Acton Bjorn, where he made a wide variety of industrially produced products. The dignified audio equipment of Bang & Olufsen is an example of distinguished work of the firm. Since 1964 he has been the head of his own design firm in Stockholm, serving a number of major clients.

Bernhard, Thomas (1931–1989). Austrian playwright and novelist. Several of his works were highly controversial. His last play, *Heldenplatz* ("Heroes' Square"), provoked protests in 1988 for its implicit denunciation of Austrian President Kurt WALDHEIM and Austrian ANTI-SEMITISM.

Bernhardt, Sarah (1844–1923). French actress. Considered one of the finest actresses of the French theater, Bernhardt was acclaimed for her distinctive voice and her tragic characterizations. Her career began at the Comedie-Francaise in 1862; 10 years later she had achieved an international reputation. Her most famous parts included title roles in *Phedre* and *Hamlet* (played *en travesti*), Dona Sol in *Hernani*, Marguerite Gautier in *La Dame aux Camelias*, and leading roles in the melodramas of Victorien Sardou. She continued to act even after the amputation of her right leg in 1915.

For further reading:

Skinner, Cornelia Otis, *Madame Sarah*. New York: Paragon, 1988.

Bernstein, Carl. See WOODWARD AND BERNSTEIN.

Sarah Bernhardt (ca. 1917).

Bernstein, Leonard (1918–1990). American composer, orchestra conductor, and educator. An exuberant larger-than-life figure, Bernstein was perhaps the best-known if not the most talented American musician of the 20th century. He was the first native-born American to lead a major American orchestra (the New York Philharmonic), and much of his concert and popular stage music has become standard in the modern repertoire. Born in Lawrence, Massachusetts of a family of Russian Jewish immigrants, he did not hear an orchestral concert until he was 16. He studied at Harvard after 1935 with composer Walter PISTON and at the Curtis Music Institute after 1939 with conductor Fritz REINER. He subsequently worked with Serge KOUSSEVITZKY at Tanglewood, Mass. Bernstein's big break has become the stuff of legend: He created a sensation when in November 1943 he appeared before the New York Philharmonic-Symphony Orchestra as a substitute for the ailing Bruno WALTER. Thereafter, his activities were numerous and diverse. He composed three symphonies, ballets (*Fancy Free*, 1944), musicals (*On the Town*, 1944; *Wonderful Town*, 1953; *West Side Story*, 1957), operas (*Candide*, 1956; *Trouble in Tahiti*, 1952) and the *Mass* (1971). He appeared on the "Omnibus" television program in 1955 for the first of his more than 100 discussion/demonstrations of music. A concert pianist, he conducted and performed many major works. As music director, he led the New York Philharmonic with a flamboyant, emotionally self-indulgent style from 1959 to 1969; he later appeared often with the Vienna Philharmonic. Bernstein made several hundred recordings, including a landmark cycle of the MAHLER symphonies as well as important readings of COPLAND, STRAVINSKY, and IVES. An effective educator, in 1973 he presented six Charles Eliot Norton lectures at Harvard, collectively entitled "The Unanswered Question." Many of his lectures, articles, television scripts and discussions were published in *The Joy of Music* (1959) and *The Infinite Variety of Music* (1966).

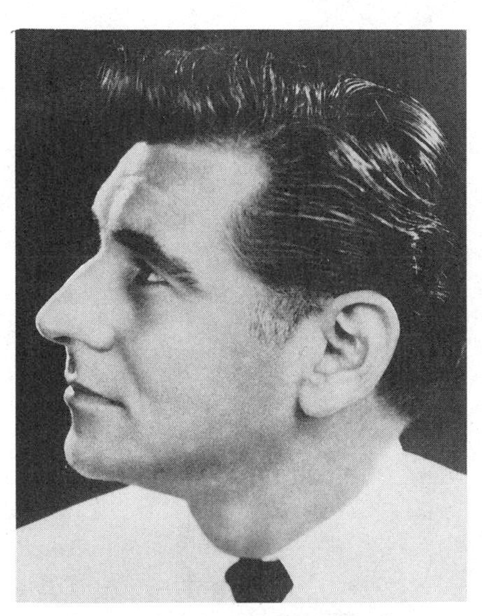

Leonard Bernstein, American conductor and composer.

A political activist, he was well-known for his left-wing views. In the 1960s he vigorously opposed the VIETNAM WAR; his public support of the BLACK PANTHERS led author Tom WOLFE to coin the term "radical chic." Bernstein's occasionally brash conducting style, eclectic approach to composition and love of popular musical idioms might make his description of Charles Ives apply equally well to himself: "He is a native American wandering in the grand palaces of Europe . . . Tossing odd bits of Americana into this European soup pot, thus making a new brew out of it, very American in flavor." Bernstein unashamedly embraced the credo of tonality in music, insisting that there was a "worldwide, inborn musical grammar," a tonality that "persists beyond the changes, imperturbable and immortal."

For further reading:

Bernstein, Leonard, *The Joy of Music*. New York: Simon and Schuster, 1959.

Gradenwitz, Peter, *Leonard Bernstein*. New York: Berg/St. Martin's Press, 1987.

Peyser, Joan, *Bernstein: A Biography*. New York: Beech Tree Books, 1987.

Berra, Yogi [Lawrence Peter Berra] (1925–). American baseball figure. Berra spent his entire playing career (1946–65) with the New York Yankees. He is primarily remembered as one of the all-time great catchers, but he also played in the outfield. Berra had a lifetime batting average of .285, with 358 home runs. He appeared in 14 all-star games and in 14 World Series (more than either Joe DIMAGGIO or Mickey MANTLE, teammates whose careers overlapped his). Berra later coached and managed various teams, including the Yankees (1964 and 1984–85) and the New York Mets (1972–75). He was elected to the Baseball Hall of Fame in 1972. Regarded as one of the sages of the game, he is also known for his humorous aphorisms, such as "It ain't over till it's over" and "50 percent of the game is half mental."

For further reading:
Berra, Yogi, *Yogi: It Ain't Over*. New York: McGraw-Hill, 1989.
Pepe, Phil, *The Wit and Wisdom of Yogi Berra*. Westport, Conn.: Meckler, 1988 (2nd. rev. ed).

Berrigan brothers. Daniel (1921–) and Philip (1923–) Berrigan, both Roman Catholic priests and political activists, became famous in the late 1960s as leaders of the American-based Catholic resistance to the VIETNAM WAR. Both brothers were raised in a working-class family in Syracuse, New York. Their father, a political activist, encouraged his sons in both their Catholic vocation and their concern for social issues. Daniel became a Jesuit priest while Philip joined the Josephite order. In 1965, the brothers became the only priests to support a "declaration of conscience"—its signatories including Dr. Martin Luther KING Jr. and Dr. Benjamin SPOCK—calling for total noncooperation with the Vietnam War effort. The most famous of the brothers' draft resistance efforts was the May 1968 break-in (with seven others) into draft board offices in Catonsville, Maryland. As members of the "Catonsville Nine," both brothers served prison terms. They remained politically active in antinuclear weapons protests throughout the 1980s. (See also ANTIWAR MOVEMENT.)

Berry, Chuck [Charles Edward Berry] (1926–). Black American rock and roll songwriter, guitarist, and vocalist. Berry is one of the seminal figures in the history of ROCK and roll. From the release of his hit single "Maybelline" (1955), Berry set a standard for songwriting that has deeply influenced every subsequent generation of rock musicians. The standard Berry song begins with a rhythmically compelling guitar solo and features witty and knowing lyrics on teenage dreams and frustrations. Berry's pure vocal range is limited, but his slyly articulate phrasing lends spirit and conviction to his songs. Berry's signature stage movement—walking quickly in a low squat while playing his guitar—is known as the "duckwalk." Born in San Diego and raised in St. Louis, Berry began his career as a blues performer in the late 1940s before creating the guitar style that made him a rock and roll star. In 1988 there appeared both his *Autobiography* and a tribute film, *Hail! Hail! Rock and Roll*. Major hits by Berry include "School Days" (1957), "Rock 'n' Roll Music" (1957), "Sweet Little Sixteen" (1958), "Johnny B. Goode" (1958), "No Particular Place to Go" (1964), "My Ding-A-Ling" (1972), and "Reelin' and Rockin" (1972).

Berry, Wendell (Erdman) (1934–). American poet, essayist, novelist, farmer. Born in a rural county northeast of Louisville, Berry earned two degrees from the University of Kentucky at Lexington, where he also taught (1964–77). After a brief sojourn in New York, he settled down on a small farm once owned by his family. He is best known as a philosophical proponent of the environmental movement. The essays of *A Continuous Harmony* (1972), *The Unsettling of America* (1977), *The Gift of Good Land* (1981) and *What Are People For?* (1990) argue for ecological responsibility and the maintenance of the integrity of the land. Berry's lyrical, psalmic poems are similarly earnest pleas for the traditional values of the farmer. His novels are forthright studies of honest country people.

Berryman, John (1914–1972). Major American poet and critic noted for his tragic view of life, intermingled with a razorsharp sense of humor in his works. Berryman taught at various American universities from 1939 to 1953 before becoming professor of humanities at the University of Minnesota in 1954, where he remained until his death by suicide. His intensely autobiographical poems show a marked shift in style from the earlier works, such as *The Dispossessed* (1948), to the later volumes, which include *Homage to Mistress Bradstreet* (1956) and *77 Dream Songs* (1964), for which he received the 1965 PULITZER PRIZE for poetry. He also wrote a critical biography of Stephen Crane (1950) and several critical reviews, which appeared in such publications as PARTISAN REVIEW.

For further reading:
Mariani, Paul L., *Dream Song: The Life of John Berryman*. New York: Morrow, 1990.

Bertoia, Harry (1915–1978). Italian-born sculptor and designer. Bertoia was best known for his design of a chair with a padded, diamond-shaped wire web suspended in a steel cradle. He also crafted massive architectural sculptures in metal featuring honeycomb shapes, and sculptures of rods in dandelion-like bursts. Bertoia worked with Charles EAMES from 1949 to 1952 and probably had some influence on Eames's designs.

Bertolucci, Bernardo (1940–). Italian-born motion picture director, leader of that post-war generation of filmmakers who came after Vittorio DE SICA, Federico FELLINI, and Luchino VISCONTI. Born in Parma, his enthusiasm for the movies was influenced by the politics and innovative styles of Alain RESNAIS and Jean-Luc GODARD. "I am Italian but, in fact, I always felt closer to the French filmmakers than to the Italian cinema," Bertolucci has declared. "The Nouvelle Vague was, for me, the real explosion in my youth of new cinema." Bertolucci's early films were a heady mixture of leftist politics and striking imagery. *Partner* (1968) was a melodramatically charged adaptation of Dostoevski's *The Double; Prima della rivoluzione* (*Before the Revolution*, 1965), *La Strategia del ragno* (*The Spider's Stratagem*, 1970), and *Il Conformista* (*The Conformist*, 1970) all dealt to a degree with radical politics and revolution in modern-day Italy. With *Last Tango in Paris* (1972), which was filmed in English, his films more openly confronted the international audience. Its candid, frequently brutal dissection of a sexual obsession challenged censorship codes and provoked critic Pauline Kael's remark that it was "the most powerfully erotic movie ever made." Since then, his epic vision has enlarged

Chuck Berry performing (April 4, 1980).

with the five-hour *1900* (1976); the extraordinary history of China during WORLD WAR II, *The Last Emperor;* and the spacious silences of *The Sheltering Sky* (1990). Elements of fantasy, an almost neurotic inner vision and intensity, a sprawling operatic opulence, and a complete command of camera technique distinguish his finest films. Nowhere is this better demonstrated than in his masterpiece, *The Spider's Stratagem,* where a young man must confront the truth of his father's traitorous activities during the anti-fascist RESISTANCE—all of this to the strains of opera music by Verdi. "Everything is possible when you use this kind of music," Bertolucci has remarked. "It is the music which helps everything to levitate—to lose the weight of realism."

Bertone, Flaminio (1903–). Italian automobile body designer. His most visible work was for CITROEN and included the design of the Traction Avant, the 2CV, and, most striking of all postwar Citroen cars, the DS models.

Bertone, Nuccio (Giuseppe) (1914–). Italian automobile body designer. Bertone has been responsible for a number of distinguished automobile designs, including the Alfa Romeo Giulietta Sprint of 1954, the Lamborghini of 1966, and the CITROEN BX of 1982. His work has been central in the development of typically Italian automotive design.

Bessarabia. Region of the southwestern U.S.S.R., on the western shores of the Black Sea. Annexed by Russia in 1812, Bessarabia declared itself independent in 1917, during WORLD WAR I, and was united with Romania in 1918. Romania surrendered it to the U.S.S.R. in 1939 but again took control of the region during WORLD WAR II. In 1947, the U.S.S.R. regained control.

Bessell, Peter (Joseph) (1921–1985). British politician. Bessell was a LIBERAL PARTY member of Parliament (1964–1970) and a key witness for the prosecution in the 1979 trial of former Liberal Party leader Jeremy THORPE. Thorpe was accused of having planned to murder Norman Scott, a male model with whom Thorpe was alleged to have had a homosexual affair. Bessell's credibility as a witness came under severe attack, and Thorpe was acquitted. Bessell returned to the U.S. where he had been working as an investment banker. He wrote his own account of the matter, *Cover-Up: The Jeremy Thorpe Affair,* which was published in the U.S. in a limited edition in 1981.

Betancourt, Romulo (1908–1981). Venezuelan politician, president of VENEZUELA (1945–48, 1959–64). He first took power as the head of a revolutionary leftist junta that in 1945 toppled the dictatorship of General Isaias Medina Angarita. Three years later, after the first democratic elections ever held in Venezuela, an army coup forced Betancourt into exile for a decade. In 1959, when the leadership again changed, he returned to Venezuela and won a free presidential election by an overwhelming margin. As president, he worked for social and political reforms.

Bethe, Hans A(lbrecht) (1906–). German-American physicist. The son of a distinguished physiologist, Bethe was educated in Germany, where he received his doctorate in physics in 1928. He taught at various German universities but, because of his part-Jewish ancestry, fled the country in 1933. After a year in England he settled in the U.S. and joined the faculty of Cornell University, where his research into celestial energy aided scientists in developing the HYDROGEN BOMB. From 1943 to 1946 Bethe worked on the MANHATTAN PROJECT under the direction of J. Robert OPPENHEIMER. Bethe and Oppenheimer became leading spokesmen for "finite containment" in the postwar debate over research on the HYDROGEN BOMB. These scientists believed that a large stockpile of American nuclear arms was necessary to contain Soviet aggression. However, they maintained that further technological advances would bring the supply of weapons to dangerous levels unwarranted by strategic considerations. Declaring that the Soviet Union was "largely imitative" in its atomic energy programs, they maintained that the U.S. could forego the hydrogen weapon without incurring a serious security risk. Instead, they suggested that work on the bomb be conducted only at a theoretical level. President Harry TRUMAN rejected their advice; reacting to recommendations of Edward TELLER, he authorized production of the weapon in 1950.

During the early years of the EISENHOWER administration, Bethe became a leading defender of Oppenheimer, who had been suspended from his post as an Atomic Energy Commission (AEC) consultant in 1953 as an alleged security risk. Bethe was among the many outstanding scientists who declared their confidence in Oppenheimer and testified on his behalf. Following the AEC's decision not to reinstate Oppenheimer, despite its finding that he was loyal, Bethe released a statement by the American Physical Society denouncing the ruling as based on differences over nuclear weapons policy rather than on actual security risk.

In 1956 Bethe was appointed to the President's Science Advisory Committee. Two years later he became chairman of a special panel formed to study the possible effects of a NUCLEAR TEST BAN agreement between the U.S. and the Soviet Union and to research the efficiency of various methods of detecting atomic blasts. Bethe attended the 1958 U.S.-Soviet disarmament talks in Geneva, where the two delegations agreed that any test ban accord would include acoustical, radiological, seismic and electromagnetic detection systems. Bethe continued to serve as a presidential adviser in the KENNEDY administration. During his career he won many scientific honors, including the Max Planck Medal, West Germany's highest scientific honor, for his research on celestial energy. He received the AEC's Enrico Fermi Award in 1961 and the NOBEL PRIZE in physics in 1967. Bethe continued to teach at Cornell through the 1970s.

Bethmann-Hollweg, Theobald von (1856–1921). German chancellor (1909–17). A career civil servant, he was Prussian minister of the interior (1905–07) and German secretary of state (1905–07). He succeeded von Bulow as chancellor of the Reich in 1909. At home, he was a moderate reformer who extended the franchise and insurance laws while granting considerable autonomy to ALSACE-LORRAINE and attempting to modernize the constitution. A bureaucrat who was largely inexperienced in international affairs, he was opposed to WORLD WAR I, but was unable to effectively challenge the army, Kaiser WILHELM II and Admiral Alfred von TIRPITZ. When the war began, he justified the German invasion of Belgium, portraying Russia as the aggressor. He attempted to restrict submarine warfare, but was forced out of office in 1917 after conflicts with Generals HINDENBURG and LUDENDORFF.

Bethune, Mary McLeod (1875–1955). American educator. Bethune was special adviser to President Franklin ROOSEVELT on the problems of minorities in the U.S. A teacher in Southern schools (1895–1904), she later founded the Institute for Girls in Daytona (1904), which became the Bethune-Cookman College in 1923. During WORLD WAR II she assisted the secretary of war in selecting officer candidates for the Women's Army Corps and was an observer for the state department at the 1945 UN conference. From 1936 to 1944, she directed the Negro affairs division of the National Youth Administration.

For further reading:

Hurd, Carol and Sicherman, Barbara, eds., *Notable American Women: The Modern Period.* Cambridge, Mass.: Belknap Press of Harvard University Press, 1980.

Betjeman, Sir John (1906–1984). British poet. Born in Highgate, London, Betjeman was educated at Marlborough and Magdalen College, Oxford, though he did not complete a degree. He taught for a time, then in 1931 began writing for *Architectural Review.* His first volumes of poems, *Mount Zion* (1933), *Continual Dew: A Little Book of Bourgeois Verse* (1937) and *New Bats in Old Belfries* (1945), had a limited readership, but his *Collected Poems* (1958, expanded 1962) was enormously popular. His work, on the surface light and witty, has been dismissed by some as facile, but his champions, including W.H. AUDEN and Philip LARKIN, found undertones of wistfulness. Betjeman also wrote on architecture: *Ghastly Good Taste* (1933) and *First and Last Loves* (1952). He was named poet laureate in 1971.

Bettelheim, Bruno (1903–1990). Austrian psychologist. Bettelheim, who immigrated to the United States in 1939 after having been interned in two Nazi CONCENTRATION CAMPS, AUSCHWITZ and BUCHENWALD, first became renowned for his psychological writings on the meaning of the concentration camp experience. He continued to write prolifically for five decades, winning the National Book Award in 1977 for *The Uses of Enchantment* (1976), which argued that the "dark side" of children's fairy-tales—occult spells, terrible bodily transformations, willful violence—was part and parcel of their value in helping children to come to recognize and to assimilate all parts of their psychological make-up. *Surviving and Other Essays* (1980) is a representative sampling of Bettelheim's writing on a variety of therapeutic themes. In *Freud and Man's Soul* (1982), Bettelheim drew upon his own psychiatric training in Vienna to argue for a flexible, non-mechanistic view of the psychoanalytic theories of Sigmund FREUD.

Beuve-Mery, Hubert (1902–1989). French journalist and newspaper publisher. In 1944, following the liberation of France, General Charles DE GAULLE selected Beuve-Mery to establish a new newspaper of record; the existing French newspapers were not permitted to resume publishing because of their association with the German occupation. Beuve-Mery created *Le Monde,* an austere paper that carried very few photographs but became widely respected for its independent viewpoint and its authoritative coverage of foreign and domestic news. Beuve-Mery retired in 1969 and later directed a journalism school and wrote several books.

Beuys, Joseph (1921–1986). West German sculptor and teacher. Soon after being appointed professor of sculpture at the Academy of Arts in Dusseldorf in 1961, he began to acquire an international reputation as a highly politicized artist, who drew freely on GERMANY's NAZI past for artistic images. Much of his work drew on a strange incident that befell him during WORLD WAR II. Downed in a plane crash on the Russian front, he was rescued by Tartar tribesmen who kept him from freezing to death by wrapping him in felt and fat. These two materials became central to his work as an artist. Among his best-known creations were a grand piano constructed of felt and a 20–ton bank of mutton fat.

Bevan, Aneurin (1897–1960). British political leader. A coal miner, he was active in the trade union movement and was elected to Parliament as a LABOUR PARTY member in 1929. He served there until his death. Minister of health (1945–52) in Clement ATTLEE's Labour government, he was instrumental in developing and administering Britain's NATIONAL HEALTH SERVICE. He resigned from the cabinet in 1951 in a dispute over health and defense costs and thereafter led the Labour Party's left wing. A fiery speaker, Bevan was Labour's foreign policy spokesman from 1956 on, strongly advocating nuclear disarmament.

Beveridge, Albert J. (1862–1927). U.S. historian and politician. He was a successful Republican compromise candidate for the United States Senate in 1899, and served in the Senate until 1911. As an Indiana senator, he was the chief spokesman for United States imperialism. Renominated in 1905, he was a firm supporter of President Theodore ROOSEVELT's policies. Beveridge assisted the passage of the Pure Food and the Meat Inspection acts of 1906 and championed child labor legislation. Defeated in 1910, he joined Roosevelt's Progressive Party and gave the keynote speech in 1912. He rejoined the REPUBLICAN PARTY in 1916, but was defeated in 1922 in his attempt to return to the Senate from Indiana. After 1917 he supported the war effort but opposed United States participation in the LEAGUE OF NATIONS. His well known work is a four-volume biography of Chief Justice John Marshall.

Beveridge, William Henry (1879–1963). British economist, 1st Baron Beveridge. A civil servant, Beveridge had served as lieutenant to LLOYD GEORGE in the Liberal government prior to WORLD WAR I, had been director of the London School of Economics from 1919 to 1937 and master of University College, Oxford, from 1937 to 1945. Beveridge created a plan for social security in 1941 that was published as *A Report on Social Insurance and Allied Services* in 1942 and came to be known as the BEVERIDGE REPORT. It served as the basis for the British postwar WELFARE STATE. Beveridge is also the author of *Full Employment in a Free Society* (1944).

Beveridge Report. Popular name of *A Report on Social Insurance and Allied Services,* written by British economist Sir William Henry BEVERIDGE and published in 1942. It recommended an extensive plan for social insurance to stamp out poverty and unemployment. Although Beveridge himself was a Liberal, the report was embraced by the LABOUR PARTY. Against party leader Clement ATTLEE's wishes, some Labour members of Parliament criticized CHURCHILL's wartime coalition government for neglecting the report, causing some friction in the coalition. After the Labour Party came to power in 1945, the Beveridge Report became the basis for Britain's postwar social legislation, including the NATIONAL HEALTH SERVICE.

Beverly Hills. U.S. city, a part of LOS ANGELES County, California; a wealthy municipality best known for the HOLLYWOOD movie personalities who live within it.

Bevin, Ernest (1879–1951). British labor organizer and politician. The uneducated son of a laborer, Bevin became an official in the Docker's Union in 1911 and was an eloquent spokesman for it. Bevin organized disparate unions into the Transport and General Workers' Union in 1922 and served as its general secretary until 1940, when he entered into the war cabinet as minister of labour. He was highly successful at maintaining industry during the war and created the "Bevin Boys," men who worked in the coal mines as war service. From 1945 to 1951, Bevin served as foreign secretary in Clement ATTLEE's Labour government and was instrumental in the acceptance of the MARSHALL PLAN and in the creation of the BRUSSELS TREATY (1948), NATO and the COLUMBO PLAN (1950).

Beyond the Fringe. Popular British satirical revue of the early 1960s. *Beyond the Fringe* was conceived by and featured four Cambridge University undergraduates: Alan BENNETT, Peter COOK, Dudley MOORE and Jonathan MILLER. The revue was first presented as part of the "fringe" entertainment at the 1960 EDINBURGH FESTIVAL; the following year it moved to London's West End, where it ran for over 1,100 performances. In 1962 *Beyond the Fringe* was brought to New York City, with more than 600 Off-Broadway performances; another West End run in 1964, featuring new material, saw more than 1,000 performances. At the cutting edge of comic satire, *Beyond the Fringe* had its roots in the GOON SHOW of the 1950s; it influenced the British comedy troupe MONTY PYTHON'S FLYING CIRCUS, the American television show SATURDAY NIGHT LIVE and the Canadian "SCTV" television program. The four members of the troupe each went on to successful individual careers in theater and film.

Bezobrazov, Alexander Mikhailovich (1866–1933). Russian statesman who served under Czar NICHOLAS II. In 1903 Bezobrazov was promoted to state secretary and a member of the Special Committee for the Affairs of the Far East. It has been suggested that Russia was forced into the RUSSO-JAPANESE WAR of 1904–5 by the Bezobrazov group of adventurers, who made the czar ignore the advice of Count WITTE. Certainly Bezobrazov's comments on Far Eastern affairs aggravated international relations.

Bhopal disaster. Leak of a highly toxic gas (methyl isocyanate) at the Union Carbide pesticide plant in the central Indian city of Bhopal on December 3, 1984. The leak killed over 2,000 and injured some 50,000 others out of a total population of about 800,000. The gas severely affected the functioning of the lungs, causing severe asthma, and many suffered permanent lung, kidney, liver and eye damage. The Indian government sued Union Carbide for the disaster and, in a settlement reached by the Indian Supreme Court in 1989, Union Carbide paid the country $465 million.

Bhutan [Drukyul]. Nation in central Asia, wedged between northeastern India and Tibet; the capital is Thimbu, but the traditional capital is Punaka. The Himalaya Mountains criss-cross the country from north to south, with the resultant valleys serving as agricultural land for the kingdom. The population shares its ethnic heritage with Tibet, and the dominant religion is a Lamaist form of Buddhism. In 1907, the British installed Sir Ugyen Wangchuk as the first of a hereditary line of kings. In 1949, India assumed responsibility for the defense and foreign policy of Bhutan. In 1950, China took control over Tibet and made claim to Bhutan as well—a claim that India rejected. From 1953 to 1972, King Jigme Dorji Wangchuk made improvements, including the abolition of the caste system and slavery, the emancipation of women and the partition of large land holdings. A democratization of the monarchical government took place in 1969. In 1972, JIGME SINGYE WANGCHUK was crowned as king.

Bhutto, Benazir (1953–). Politician and prime minister (1988–90) of PAKISTAN.

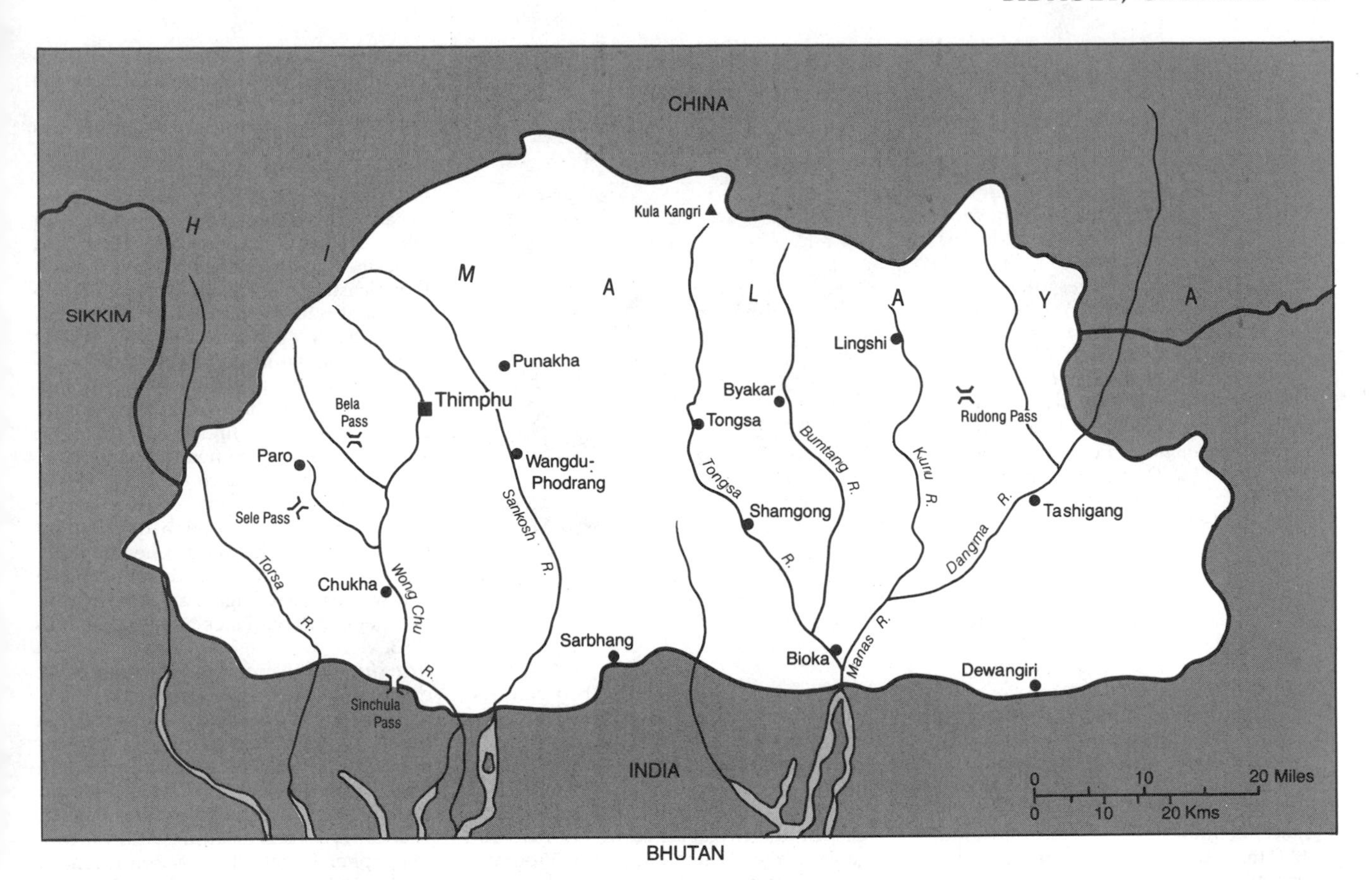

BHUTAN

Benazir Bhutto graduated from Radcliffe College in 1969 and obtained a master's degree from Oxford University in 1976. She is the daughter of former Pakistan Prime Minister Zulfikar Ali BHUTTO, who was executed in 1979. With her mother, Begum Nusrat, she assumed the leadership of the Pakistan People's Party (PPP). She returned to Pakistan from exile in 1986 and became prime minister in December 1988. In August 1989 Pakistan President Ghulam Ishag Khan dismissed Bhutto's government amid charges of nepotism and corruption. Bhutto called the charges politically motivated and asserted she would be returned to office by the voters. She was, however, decisively defeated by the opposition Islamic Democratic Alliance in October 1990.

Benazir Bhutto, Pakistan's premier (December 1988).

Bhutto, Zulfikar Ali (1928–1977). President (1971–73) and prime minister (1973–77) of PAKISTAN. A barrister (lawyer), Bhutto served under President AYUB KHAN from 1958 to 1966. Foreign minister from 1963 to 1966, he resigned over the Indo-Pakistan truce (see INDO-PAKISTANI WAR OF 1965). Founder of the People's Party, which won a majority of seats in the assembly in 1970, he was elected president in 1971 when Pakistan was defeated in the war with INDIA over BANGLADESH (see INDO-PAKISTANI WAR OF 1971). He led Pakistan out of the COMMONWEALTH OF NATIONS in 1972 (when Britain, Australia and New Zealand recognized Bangladesh independence). Under a new constitution introduced in 1973, he became prime minister. Accusations of ballot rigging led to riots in 1977, his overthrow by a military coup led by General ZIA UL-HAQ and his execution in 1979.

Biafra. Region in eastern NIGERIA. Formerly a republic, it is populated by the Ibo tribe, as opposed to western Nigeria, which is populated by the Hausa tribe. In 1967, ethnic tensions spurred a declaration of independence by Biafra's General O. OJUKWU. Civil war resulted, and the population of Biafra was forced into starvation by the tactics of the Nigerian governmental forces. In 1970, Biafra surrendered. Since then, the Nigerian government has adopted a policy of leniency.

Zulfikar Ali Bhutto, Pakistan's premier in 1971. He was convicted of ordering the death of a political opponent and was hanged in 1979.

Bidault, Georges (1899–1983). French government official. During WORLD WAR II, Bidault was active in the French RESISTANCE, and in 1943 he became president of the National Council of the Resistance. In 1944, he was named foreign minister in Charles DE GAULLE's provisional government. As founder of the Popular Republican Movement, Bidault played a pivotal role in the coalition governments of the Fourth Republic, and he served in the French cabinet almost constantly from 1944 to 1954, playing a dominant role in French foreign policy during these years. A strident opponent of independence for

ALGERIA, Bidault quit France to lead the underground opposition. He accepted political asylum in Brazil in 1963, eventually returning to France after the political amnesty in 1968.

Bierce, Ambrose (1842–1914?). American author. Born in Ohio, he fought in the U.S. Civil War. He subsequently worked as a journalist in California and later in London (1872–76), where he published some volumes of sketches and epigrams. He eventually settled in Washington. He is best known for his numerous short stories collected in *Tales of Soldiers and Civilians* (1891; renamed *In the Midst of Life,* 1892, revised 1898), which show the influence of Edgar Allen Poe. His fiction is darkly realistic and bitterly ironical. He also wrote *The Devil's Dictionary* (1906), a peevish and droll collection of definitions. In 1913 he traveled to Mexico and vanished mysteriously, perhaps perishing in the MEXICAN CIVIL WAR, although the actual date and cause of his death are unknown. A fictional account of his last days is given in the novel *The Old Gringo* by Carlos FUENTES.

big bands. See SWING ERA.

big bang theory. Theory that at one time all the matter in the universe was condensed into an area infinitesimally small and infinitesimally dense, and that a massive explosion threw this matter out into space, creating the universe as we know it. After Albert EINSTEIN published his general theory of relativity (1916), scientists began to consider various non-traditional views of the universe and its origin. Russian mathematician and physicist Alexander FRIEDMANN (1922) and Belgian astronomer Georges LEMAITRE (1927) independently proposed that the universe is not static but constantly expanding. In 1929, astronomer Edwin HUBBLE made observations that confirmed these views. Friedmann, Lemaitre and Hubble's findings pointed to the big bang theory, although not all scientists were ready to accept this theory. British astronomer Fred HOYLE and others proposed the **steady-state theory,** which posited that new matter was being created continuously. In 1970, British physicists Roger Penrose and Stephen HAWKING published a paper offering mathematical proof of the big bang theory, again on the basis of Einstein's general theory of relativity. The big bang theory has been widely accepted in the scientific community, although some scientists and mathematicians have questioned various assumptions or conclusions.

For further reading:

Hawking, Stephen W., *A Brief History of Time: From the Big Bang to Black Holes*. New York: Bantam Books, 1988.

Bikini. U.S.-owned atoll, a part of the Marshall Islands chain in the central Pacific Ocean. First discovered by Europeans in 1825, it was formerly known as Escholtz Atoll. From 1946 to 1958, when it was used by the United States as an atomic testing site, the indigenous population was forced to leave and not allowed to return until 1969 (under medical supervision). In the late 1940s, it lent its name to a woman's swimsuit style.

Steve Biko

Biko, Steve (1947–1977). South African nationalist leader. One of the founders of the **Black Consciousness** movement and president of the South African Students Organisation established in 1969, he organized the Black Community Program banned by the South African government following the Durban strikes in 1973. He was arrested and died in police custody, his death sparking major international concern. (See also APARTHEID; SOUTH AFRICA.)

Bill, Max (1908–). Swiss architect and designer whose work is identified with the austere MODERNISM thought of as characteristically Swiss. Bill studied at the BAUHAUS and was director of the Hochschule Fur Gestaltung at Ulm from 1951 to 1956. His influence, through his teaching, writing, and the Gute Form exhibitions that he organized, has been a continuing force in favor of the functionalist ideas that stem from Bauhaus origins. His work as a painter and sculptor equals his design production in importance and quality.

Billings-Mooney Affair. In 1916, during WORLD WAR I, a patriotic parade in San Francisco was bombed. Warren K. Billings and Tom Mooney, two controversial labor organizers and agitators, were charged with the bombing. The two were convicted and imprisoned, but the case became an international cause celebre after witnesses changed their testimony and fraudulent evidence was revealed. Both men were released from prison in 1939.

For further reading:

Frost, Richard H., *The Mooney Case*. Palo Alto: Stanford University Press, 1968.

Hopkins, Ernest J., *What Happened in the Mooney Case*. New York: Da Capo Press, 1970.

Hunt, Henry T., *The Case of Thomas J. Mooney & Warren K. Billings*. New York: Da Capo Press, 1971.

Billy Sol Estes scandal. A scandal involving prominent Democrats during the administration of President John KENNEDY. Billy Sol Estes, a self-made Texas millionaire, swindled millions of dollars from commercial finance companies by mortgaging non-existent fertilizer tanks. He also circumvented government cotton allotment price supports by selling land to farmers with unused allotments and then leasing it back to get around the allotment limit. A newspaper expose revealed Estes' operations and precipitated a congressional investigation of his connections in the Department of Agriculture. Although the investigation found no collusion, it did find lax controls that allowed Estes to circumvent several rules. Estes was tried and convicted for mail fraud and conspiracy and served a lengthy prison sentence in addition to paying a large fine. After his release he again became involved in a fraudulent scheme and was convicted again and returned to the penitentiary. Estes was paroled in 1983.

Billy the Kid. Landmark American ballet choreographed by Agnes DE MILLE which, with FILLING STATION, was one of the first ballets of specifically American inspiration. First performed by Ballet Caravan in Chicago on October 16, 1938, it brought together the talents of impresario Lincoln KIRSTEIN, composer Aaron COPLAND, choreographer Eugene Loring (who danced the title role), and dancers Lew Christensen, Todd Bolender, and Marie-Jeanne. Its 11 episodes depict the lawless career of William Bonney. Choreographically the dancers' movements are derived from natural gesture rather than from the ballet vocabulary. Aaron Copland's music teases the ear with its elusive references to cowboy songs such as "Old Paint" and "The Old Chisholm Trail." The ballet is best known today through a suite of music for which Copland used approximately two-thirds of the ballet score.

For further reading:

Dictionary of Modern Ballet. New York: Tudor Publishing, 1959.

Binet, Alfred (1857–1911). French psychologist. Binet was a pioneering figure in modern psychological research who played a major role in the development of biometrics and psychometrics. Binet invented, in 1905, a series of intelligence tests for children that formed the basis for much of the scholastic intelligence testing done in Europe and America for decades to come. Throughout his career, Binet argued that psychological research should closely follow the models offered by the natural sciences and physiology and include within its focus animal behavior and genetic development. In his own researches, Binet established new techniques for statistical measurement, evaluation of higher mental faculties, and control group comparisons. His writings include *The Psychology of Reasoning* (1886) and *Alterations of Personality* (1892).

Bing, Sir Rudolph (1902–). Viennese-born opera director and impresario. Bing studied at the University of Vienna but chose to work in music as an administrator rather than a performer, associating himself first with a musical agency in Vienna, from 1923 to 1927, then with the Darmstadt State Theater and the Municipal Opera at Charlottenburg-Berlin. He helped to found the Glyndebourne Opera Festival in England in 1933 and became its manager from 1935 to 1939 and again from 1946 to 1949. In 1947 he helped to found the Edinburgh International Festival of Music and Drama, and served as its first director. In 1950 Bing was made general manager of the Metropolitan Opera in New York City, and guided the development of the Metropolitan Opera House at Lincoln Center, which opened in 1966. His memoir, *Five Thousand Nights at the Opera* (1972), tells of his time at the Met, from which he resigned in 1972. A British subject since 1946, he was knighted in 1971. Among the many opera singers that Bing presented at the Met were Maria CALLAS, Joan SUTHERLAND, Franco CORELLI and Tito GOBBI. He also presented the first black in a leading role at the Met when Marion ANDERSON sang Ulrica in Verdi's *Un Ballo in Maschera* (1955).

For further reading:

Bing, Rudolph, *Five Thousand Nights at the Opera*. Garden City, N.Y.: Doubleday, 1972.

Bingham, Hiram (1875–1956). American explorer, statesman, educator. An expert on South American history, Bingham taught at Yale University from 1907 to 1923, served as a U.S. delegate to the Pan-American Scientific Congress in 1908 and made several important scientific/historical expeditions to South America between 1906 and 1915. On his most famous expedition in 1911, he discovered the great Inca ruins of Machu Picchu and Vitcos, the last Inca capital, in Peru. He also served briefly as governor of Connecticut, in 1924, then as that state's U.S. senator from 1924 to 1933.

For further reading:

Bingham, Alfred M., *Portrait of an Explorer: Hiram Bingham, Discoverer of Machu Picchu*. Ames: Iowa State University Press, 1989.

Biograph Company. One of the first important American motion picture studios. As a chief competitor to the EDISON COMPANY, founding member of the Motion Picture Patents Company and home studio to such developing talents as Edwin S. Porter and D.W. GRIFFITH, it would have enormous impact upon the course of the American movie industry. Originally named the American Mutoscope Company, it was founded in 1895 by Henry Norton Marvin to manufacture a peep-show machine called the Mutoscope. With the help of former Edison associate, W.K.L. Dickson, the company made a camera that did not infringe on the Edison patents and presented its first program of short films at Hammerstein's Olympia Music Hall in New York City on October 12, 1896 (just six months after a program of Edison films was premiered). Now called the American Mutoscope and Biograph Company (later shortened to simply "Biograph"), in 1908–09 the company engaged in a series of court battles with Edison for control over patents of motion picture equipment. In 1909 the two rival companies formed the nucleus of the notorious Motion Picture Patents Company, which sought to monopolize the patents governing film production, distribution and exhibition in the U.S. Most Biograph films were made at a studio located at 11 East 14th Street in New York. Former actor and playwright, D.W. Griffith directed his first film for Biograph, *The Adventures of Dollie* (1908); thereafter until 1913 Griffith supervised virtually all Biograph product, personally directing some of his greatest and most influential one- and two-reel movies, including *The Lonely Villa* (1909), *Enoch Arden* (1911), *The Lonedale Operator* (1911) and *The Musketeers of Pig Alley* (1912). He also built up a stock company of players, including Mary PICKFORD, Lillian and Dorothy GISH, Mae Marsh and Robert Harron. In 1913 Biograph signed with the Broadway firm of Klaw and Erlanger to produce feature-length adaptations of popular stage plays. However, after Griffith's departure late in 1913, Biograph began to decline. Its policy of limiting publicity for its stars and the dissolution of the Patents Company hastened its demise in 1915.

For further reading:

Everson, William K., *The American Silent Film*. New York: Oxford University Press, 1978.

Birdseye, Clarence (1886–1956). American inventor and the father of the frozen foods industry. Although attempts to commercially freeze foods had begun as early as the 1840s, the technology was not perfected until 1917, when New York inventor and businessman Clarence Birdseye began to quick-freeze food in individual packages. Birdseye's technique, which he had seen used by the native peoples of Labrador, was the first to retain the original flavor and texture of the food; after his breakthrough, the frozen foods industry expanded rapidly. In 1929, he sold his General Seafoods Corp. for $22 million. The new owners, the Postum Co. and the investment firm Goldman-Sachs, renamed it General Foods.

Birendra Bir Bikram Shah Dev (1945–). King of NEPAL (1972–); received his schooling in St. Joseph's Public School in India and Eton in England, and his higher education at the University of Tokyo and Harvard. As crown prince he established a group of technocratic advisers called the *Janch-Bujh Kendra*. After ascension to the throne he moved toward a more technocratic and administrative style than his father had followed. In 1979, there were student riots protesting the panchayat system—a complex, multi-leveled form of partyless government. In response, King Birendra called a referendum, and a reformed version of the panchayat system received majority support. However, opposition to the monarchy has continued, and King Birendra finds himself increasingly isolated in South Asia as an advocate of nondemocratic government.

Birmingham. Largest city in Alabama (1990 population: 265,968) and the industrial and cultural capital of the state; site of major CIVIL RIGHTS protests from April 3 to May 10, 1963. On April 3, 1963, the SOUTHERN CHRISTIAN LEADERSHIP CONFERENCE, directed by Martin Luther KING Jr., began a boycott of Birmingham businesses to draw attention to the grievances of the city's blacks. Daily protest marches began on April 6, until halted by an injunction four days later. On April 12, King led another march, in defiance of the injunction, and was arrested and later convicted of criminal contempt. More than 900 youngsters between the ages of 6 and 16 were arrested for taking part in a children's march on May 2. On May 3, nearly 1,000 marching protesters were attacked by police with nightsticks, dogs and fire hoses.

As print and broadcast journalists documented the violent reaction of the police over the next four days, American public opinion tilted in favor of the SCLC. On May 7, two demonstrations degenerated into rioting in reaction to the actions of the police. Eager to end the escalating violence, on May 10, white leaders announced an agreement with the civil rights organizers, the key points of which included gradual integration of the city's businesses. That night, however, bombs exploded at the house of Rev. A.D. King, brother of Martin Luther King Jr., and at the SCLC's headquarters, sparking a night of rioting in the city. On September 15, 1963, a church in Birmingham was bombed, killing four black girls. Although white city leaders honored their promises only incompletely, the SCLC campaign in Birmingham had the effect of enhancing King's prestige within his movement and around the nation, and it moved the Kennedy administration toward direct action on the issue of civil rights.

Birmingham Six. Popular name given to six Northern Ireland men found guilty of the November 1974 bombings of two pubs in Birmingham, England, which resulted in 21 deaths. The attacks had been claimed by the outlawed Provisional Wing of the IRISH REPUBLICAN ARMY. Although they steadfastly claimed innocence of the bombings, the six were convicted in 1975 and each given 21 life sentences. Amidst charges of misconduct by the police and prosecutors, they were freed from prison in March 1991 by a Court of Appeal panel that found a number of irregularities in the evidence used in their trial.

Birnbaum, Solomon (1891–1989). German-born Jewish scholar. He fled Germany when Adolf HITLER came to power in 1933. Later he was widely credited with establishing the authenticity of the Dead Sea Scrolls (which contained the earliest known manuscripts of the Bible) following their discovery in 1947.

Biro, Ladislao Jose (1899–1985). Hungarian-born inventor. At the outset of WORLD WAR II, Biro fled to Argentina where he patented the first practical ball-point pen. With the development of lighter inks, his invention became the world's

Police dog is used against a civil rights demonstrator in Birmingham, Alabama (May 3, 1963).

best-selling writing tool, outstripping even the pencil. In 1954 Biro's patents were acquired by the U.S.-based Parker Pen Company. Ballpoint pens are commonly known as "biros" in Britain.

Birth of a Nation, The. Classic American silent film and among the top box-office blockbusters in history. No other motion picture has ever received more praise—and blame. It was directed by D.W. GRIFFITH and premiered at the Clunes Auditorium in Los Angeles, February 8, 1915, as *The Clansman* (the title was changed after the premiere). The story of two families separated by the Civil War and the subsequent Reconstruction was adapted from Thomas Dixon's controversial, racist novel *The Clansman* (1906). The film validated the feature-length format, vaulted the American film industry into the front rank of international cinema, influenced narrative techniques for the next decade, and brought an expanded critical awareness to the new medium. Its use of pioneering techniques—flashbacks, parallel editing, moving camera, masked frames, close-ups and panoramas—was dazzling, prompting the remark attributed to President Woodrow WILSON, "It is like history written in lightning." However, the depiction of blacks—especially mulattos—in the Reconstruction sequences triggered black protests from the NAACP and other groups. Charges of racism dogged the film wherever it opened, precipitating riots. Attempts to censor and ban the film led to an important Supreme Court decision in 1915 (*Mutual Film Corporation v. Industrial Commission of Ohio*) denying motion pictures protection under the First Amendment—a decision not reversed until 1952. Distribution was on a states-rights basis, and *Birth of a Nation* was in almost continual release throughout the silent film period and, with synchronized music, well into the sound period—generating repeated waves of protest. And so it has been ever since. Griffith himself vigorously refuted charges of racism and, in a pamphlet he wrote in 1916 called "The Rise and Fall of Free Speech in America," argued for the movies' right to protection as a form of the press right. (Griffith had some justice on his side, since he had cleaned up considerably Dixon's racist rag of a novel.) In the final analysis, film historian Kevin Brownlow has said its reputation must reside in its importance as a cornerstone in the development of the medium. "It established the classic format of the American motion picture and separated it for all time from the stage."

Bishop, Elizabeth (1911–1979). American poet. Bishop's first book, *North and South* (1945), established her reputation as a gifted poet. Her second book, *A Cold Spring* (1956), won a PULITZER PRIZE. For many years she lived abroad, mainly in Brazil. Her poems deal with exile, travel, and the longing for identity in an impersonal and threatening world, and her best work is characterized by a sense of the strangeness that underlies ordinary events. Although she was a member of the generation of CONFESSIONAL POETS, her treatment of personal themes is calm and understated. Her other books include *Questions of Travel* (1965) and *Georgraphy III* (1976). She served as a consultant in poetry at the Library of Congress (1949–50).

Bishop, Ronald Eric (1903–1989). British aircraft designer. Bishop was the creator of the Comet, the world's first production jet airliner, as well as the wooden DH-98 Mosquito bomber, which proved to be one of Britain's most versatile military planes in WORLD WAR II. Although the Comet won the postwar race to become the first jet-powered commercial airliner, it fell into disfavor following a series of crashes caused by structural failure induced by metal fatigue. However, Bishop continued to design civil and military aircraft until he retired from the De Haviland Aircraft Company in 1964.

Bishop, William Avery ["Billy"] (1894–1956). Canadian WORLD WAR I flying ace. The top-ranking Imperial or Canadian ace of the war, the flamboyant "Billy" Bishop was credited with shooting down 72 enemy aircraft. He was the first Canadian airman to win the Victoria Cross, for a single-handed attack on a German airfield.

Bismarck. The most famous German battleship of WORLD WAR II, the *Bismarck* was completed at Hamburg toward the end of 1940. After a shakedown cruise in the Baltic Sea, the ship, one of the largest and fastest vessels of the war, sailed from Gdynia on May 18, 1941, with the cruiser *Prinz Eugen*, their mission to harass Atlantic shipping. On May 24, the *Bismarck* was intercepted at the Denmark Strait by the British battle cruiser *Hood* and the battleship *Prince of Wales*. In the fighting the *Hood* was sunk, with nearly 1,400 men killed, and the *Prince of Wales* was damaged. The *Bismarck*, also damaged, sailed toward German-occupied France, with other ships of the royal navy in pursuit. On the night of May 24, the German battleship was attacked by torpedo-bombers from the *Victorious*. After temporarily slipping away from the British, the *Bismarck* was assaulted again on the morning of May 26 by planes from the *Ark Royal* and on the next day by the *King George V*, the *Rodney* and the *Dorsetshire*. The *Bismarck* sank at 10:30 A.M. on May 27, with the loss of more than 2,000 crewmembers. By destroying the *Bismarck,* following the 1939 sinking of Germany's GRAF SPEE, Britain had struck an important blow in the BATTLE OF THE ATLANTIC.

Bismarck Archipelago. Archipelago northeast of the island of New Guinea. Now a part of Papua New Guinea, the archipelago includes the ADMIRALTY ISLANDS, New Britain and New Ireland. Topographically, the islands were formed by volcanic activity and support heavy forest growth. They were seized by Germany in 1884 and subsequently named after Otto von Bismarck, the German chancellor. During WORLD WAR I they were occupied by Australian forces. During WORLD WAR II, they were conquered by the Japanese but regained by Allied forces in 1944.

Bizerte. Capital and port city of TUNISIA, on North Africa's Mediterranean Sea coast. Its strategic importance lies in its position at the narrowing point between the western and eastern waters of the Mediterranean. After Tunisia won its independence in 1955, a French naval base remained here and sparked a violent conflict in 1961 that resulted in UNITED NATIONS intervention. The naval base was abandoned in 1963.

Bjorling, Jussi (John Jonaton) (1911–1960). Swedish operatic tenor known for the beauty and purity of his voice and for his stylish singing in the great tenor roles of Italian opera. Bjorling made his operatic debut in 1930 in Stockholm, singing Don Ottavio in Mozart's *Don Giovanni.* In the next half-dozen years he sang major roles with opera companies throughout Europe. In 1937 he went to the U.S., where he quickly received public and critical acclaim. In 1938 he gave his first recital at CARNEGIE HALL and shortly thereafter was signed to a contract at the Metropolitan Opera in New York. Bjorling spent WORLD WAR II in Scandinavia. After the war he returned to the Metropolitan, where he remained (except for three seasons) one of the company's principal tenors until his untimely death from a heart attack. During this time he was virtually unparalleled in such leading roles as Rodolfo in *La Boheme* and Cavaradossi in *Tosca* (both by PUCCINI) and the Duke in Verdi's *Rigoletto.* Many critics consider Bjorling's voice comparable to that of the great CARUSO. Bjorling's golden tones have been captured in many distinguished recordings, including a classic record of *La Boheme* conducted by Sir Thomas BEECHAM.

Blachownia [Blachownia Slaska; German: Blechhammer]. Town in Poland's Opole province, on the Klodnica River. It was the site, during WORLD WAR II, of a Nazi CONCENTRATION CAMP designed exclusively for the systematic murder of Jews and other civilians.

Black, Davidson (1884–1934). Canadian anthropologist whose work expanded the knowledge of human evolution. Trained in medicine at the University of Toronto, Black went to China in 1918 to teach at a medical college in Peking. In 1927, after the discovery of some fossilized remains at a cave near Peking, Black classified a hitherto unknown genus and species of prehuman hominid. This he called *Sinanthropus pekinensis,* or Peking man. Peking man was dated at nearly half a million years old.

Black, Hugo L(afayette) (1886–1971). Associate justice, U.S. Supreme Court (1937–1971). A graduate of Birmingham Medical College and the University of Alabama Law School, Hugo Black grew up in rural Alabama. After abandoning medicine he studied law and became a lawyer in private practice and later a local judge. Black won an upset election as U.S. senator from Alabama in 1926. In the Senate he was a loyal and vocal supporter of President Franklin D. ROOSEVELT'S NEW DEAL. Roosevelt appointed Black to the Supreme Court in 1937. The nomination was controversial because Black was a former member of the KU KLUX KLAN. However, on the Court he proved an effective champion of CIVIL RIGHTS and continued as a strong supporter of New Deal legislation. He was later an important member of the WARREN Court. Black wrote many of the era's important decisions, including ENGEL V. VITALE, which banned public school prayer, and GIDEON V. WAINWRIGHT, which required counsel in criminal cases.

For further reading:

Simon, James F., *The Antagonists: Hugo Black, Felix Frankfurter & Civil Liberties in Modern America.* New York: Simon & Schuster, 1989.

Yarbrough, Tinsley E., *Mr. Justice Black and His Critics.* Durham, N.C.: Duke University Press, 1988.

Black, Misha (1910–1977). British designer and design teacher. Born in Russia, Black was trained as an architect and became a prominent figure in English design when he founded the Design Research Unit with Milner Gray in 1944. His best-known work was in exhibition design, as in the *Britain Can Make It* exhibit of 1946 and in portions of the 1951 Festival of Britain. He was an influential teacher of industrial design at the Royal College of Art.

Black Consciousness. See Steve BIKO.

Black Hand, The. Popular name of a Serbian secret society known as "Unity or Death," which was founded in 1911 in an attempt to unite Serbs from Austria-Hungary and Turkey with those living in independent Serbia. Led by Colonel Dragutin Dimitrievic, the group has been blamed for the assassination of Archduke FRANCIS FERDINAND, heir apparent to the Austro-Hungarian throne, on June 28, 1914. In 1916 Black Hand leaders were arrested by Serbian government authorities and accused of plotting to murder the Serbian prince regent. Dimitrievic and two others were tried, found guilty and executed, and the Black Hand society was disbanded. The name has also been used to designate an alleged organization held responsible for crime in the U.S. Italian community during the early 20th century. Many immigrants received extortion letters signed with a black hand, and the senders were thought to belong to an organization with links to the MAFIA. However, modern researchers doubt a criminal band was actually responsible for most of the threats and have seen the black hand as a symbol of terror, not as the signature of an organized group.

black hole. Term coined by American physicist John Wheeler in 1969 to describe a star that has collapsed and become so dense that no light can escape from it. The concept of the black hole was actually originated in 1783 by a Cambridge don. In the 20th century, the black hole phenomenon has been studied and verified by a number of scientists. Black holes hold fascination for scientists because matter and energy behave very differently in black holes than they do in the rest of the universe.

For further reading:

Hawking, Stephen W., *A Brief History of Time: From the Big Bang to Black Holes.* New York: Bantam Books, 1988.

Black Hundreds, Raids of the (1906–1911). As a reaction against the RUSSIAN REVOLUTION OF 1905, the czarist government secretly sanctioned a reactionary, anti-Semitic group, **League of the Russian People,** also known as the Black Hundreds. Made up of landowners, wealthy peasants, officials and police, it attacked revolutionaries in the provinces and organized frequent, violent pogroms in more than 100 cities. In Odessa, Jews and others were slaughtered for four days before order was restored. These repressions encouraged Russia's autocratic leadership to delay enactment of the constitution of 1905. (See also ANTI-SEMITISM.)

blacklist. A list of persons who would be denied employment. Early in the century employers maintained "blacklists" of workers who were union members or sympathetic to unions; but blacklists gained their greatest notoriety in HOLLYWOOD after World War II, at the height of the anticommunist McCarthy era. In 1946 President Truman required federal employees to sign loyalty oaths. After a private consulting firm founded by former FBI agents wrote that many broadcasters had alleged leftist leanings, hundreds of writers, directors, producers and performers were fired and blacklisted from the industry. Some of the most talented were able to work under pseudonyms but many others lost their livelihoods. The blacklisting episode eventually widened into the MCCARTHYISM hysteria that gripped the nation for a number of years.

"Black Mask School," The. The name of the so-called "hard-boiled" school of American detective fiction—and the magazine that spawned it in the 1920s and 1930s. When H.L. MENCKEN and George Jean Nathan began publishing *Black Mask* magazine in the spring of 1920, most detective stories followed the formulas laid down by 19th-century masters like Emile Gaboriau and A. Cohan DOYLE. Dapper detectives and shrewd policemen matched their feats of ratiocination against the enigmatic clues and ingenious puzzles of the criminal mind. However, a succession of editors at *Black Mask* including Phil Cody, Harry North and especially Captain ("Cap") Joseph T. Shaw, encouraged a new generation of writers in rather different directions. Beginning with the appearance of the "Race Williams" stories of Carroll John Daly, the "Continental Op" tales of Dashiell HAMMETT and, later in the decade, the "Sam Spade" adventures (also by Hammett), detective fiction developed a new "American language," as Mencken put it. The stories were told in terse, clipped diction at a racehorse gallop. Race, the Op and Spade were violent, even brutal characters who nonetheless adhered fiercely to their own highly individualistic codes of honor. "I trusted myself," said Race; "that was what counted." In a murky world bereft of values, these men knew violence was the only act of human courage and decision. Women and relationships were, as the Op put it, "nuisances during business hours." With the publication in *Black Mask* between 1927–30 of Hammett's four novels, *Red Harvest, The Dain Curse, The Maltese Falcon* and *The Glass Key,* and the appearance late in the 1930s of Raymond CHANDLER's Philip Marlowe in *The Big Sleep* (1939), the hard-boiled school reached its peak. Chandler, particularly, brought to the form a richly poetic style full of colorful similes and evocative images. Motion pictures in the 1930s and 1940s like *The Thin Man* (1934), *The Maltese Falcon* (1940), *Murder, My Sweet* (1943) and *The Big Sleep* (1946) further honed the tradition for screen tough guys like William Powell, Humphrey BOGART, and Dick Powell.

Tommie Smith, center, and John Carlos, right, give the Black Power salute during the playing of the Star Spangled Bannner *after coming in first and third in the 200-meter run at the 1968 Olympics in Mexico City.*

Blackmun, Harry A. (1908–). Associate justice, U.S. Supreme Court (1970–). A graduate of Harvard University and Harvard Law School, Blackmun clerked for a federal judge in Minneapolis before entering private law practice. In 1950 he became counsel to the MAYO CLINIC in Rochester, Minnesota. In 1958 he was appointed to the Eighth Circuit Federal Court of Appeals. In 1970 President Richard M. NIXON appointed Blackmun to the Supreme Court to fill the vacancy left by the resignation of Abe FORTAS. Blackmun was Nixon's third choice; the president's two previous nominees—Clement Haynsworth and Harold Carswell—had been rejected by the Senate. Blackmun was confirmed without any protest.

Harry Blackmun, associate justice of the U.S. Supreme Court.

Blackmun, a boyhood friend of then-Chief Justice Warren BURGER, was originally considered a "conservative" on the bench because of his adherence to strict constructionism. The two justices were sometimes referred to as the "Minnesota twins" because of the similarity of their voting records. Over the years, however, Blackmun moved to the center and finally the liberal wing of the Court. Blackmun's best-known and most controversial opinion was the majority opinion he wrote in ROE V. WADE legalizing ABORTION. The decision upheld the right to an abortion as a basic medical procedure protected by the right to individual privacy implied in the Constitution.

Black Patch War (1904–1909). Battles erupting after growers of dark tobacco in western and southwestern Kentucky, known as the Black Patch, opposed monopolistic practices of the tobacco-buying companies and formed a growers association to boycott the buyers. Night riders terrorized buyers and growers not complying until 1907, when Kentucky Governor A.E. Willson declared martial law in 23 counties. The state militia fought the rebels and took control of whole towns. In 1908 an agreement between growers and buyers partially broke the buyer monopoly, but night riders continued into 1909, until the resistance of armed citizens and dissension in the growers' association put an end to the violence.

Black Power. Movement that emerged in the U.S. in the 1960s to express the dissatisfaction of black people with their position in American society. It rejected integration and asserted the intellectual and cultural equality of blacks with whites. The movement was most aggressive in the late 1960s, but improvements in the position of black people in the 1970s and the death of leaders such as George Jackson and MALCOLM X seem to have muted it.

Black September. Palestinian terrorist organization founded in 1970. In February 1970 King HUSSEIN of JORDAN sought to curtail activities of the PALESTINE LIBERATION ORGANIZATION (PLO). The organization responded with violence, leading to civil war (September 17–25). Jordanian government forces eventually imposed authority. Black September, founded following these events, was responsible for the kidnap attempt that resulted in the deaths of 12 Israeli athletes at the MUNICH OLYMPICS in 1972 and for other atrocities. (See also FATAH REVOLUTIONARY COUNCIL, JORDANIAN CIVIL WAR OF 1970–71.)

Black Shirts. Popular name for the Italian fascist paramilitary group formally known

A member of the Arab terrorist group Black September after seizing the Israeli Olympic team quarters at the Munich Olympic village (Sept. 5, 1972).

as the *Fasci di combattimento*. These units, founded by Benito MUSSOLINI in 1919, wore distinctive black shirts as a part of their uniforms. Ultra-rightists and nationalist extremists who opposed communists, socialists and moderate liberals alike, they broke up strikes, attacked trade unions and made other violent assaults on their opponents. In 1922 the Black Shirts marched on Rome and initiated Mussolini's rule. (See also MARCH ON ROME.)

Black Sox Scandal. The unsavory events of the 1919 World Series have passed into literary and celluloid legend as other, unsullied fall classics have not. When the heavily favored Chicago White Sox lost to the National League champion Cincinnati Reds in eight error-riddled games (in a best-of-nine series), persistent rumors of a "fix" led to an investigation by the baseball commissioner, Kenesaw Mountain LANDIS. While the details of the scheme have never come to light, one theory has gangster Arnold Rothstein as a major backer. A grand jury cleared all eight indicted players, but Landis banned them from the game for life. Although the White Sox's legendary "Shoeless Joe" Jackson admitted taking the bribe, he batted .375 in the Series. Jackson was allegedly confronted by a child outside the courtroom who cried, "Say it ain't so, Joe!"

Blagonravov, Anatoli Arkad'evich (1894–1975). Soviet space scientist. Blagonravov played a major role in equipping the armed forces of the U.S.S.R. with modern weapons beginning in WORLD WAR II. He was also an important scientist in the SPUTNIK satellite program in the late 1950s.

Blaize, Herbert Augustus (1918–1989). Grenadan statesman. Blaize served as chief minister in 1960 and 1961 and again from 1962 to 1967, when GRENADA was still a British colony. He then became a member of the opposition in Parliament, remaining in that role once full independence was granted in 1974. He came out of retirement and was elected prime minister in 1984, following the U.S. invasion of Grenada that ousted the Marxist government that had seized power and killed Prime Minister Maurice Bishop (1983). Blaize served as prime minister until his death.

Blake, Eubie (1883–1983). American RAGTIME composer and pianist. Blake reached his centenary year as an acclaimed legend in the field of American popular music. The son of former slaves, he was born in Baltimore. His fundamentalist mother opposed Blake's interest in ragtime music, but by age 12 he had joined a vocal quartet that performed the popular music outside of saloons. In 1921, along with lyricist Noble Sissle, Blake wrote music for, and starred in, *Shuffle Along*, the first all-black Broadway production to successfully draw white audiences. One of the biggest hits from this show was "I'm Just Wild About Harry," which Harry S TRUMAN used as a theme song in his 1948 presidential campaign. In 1954, after years of neglect, a reissued recording of Blake's ragtime tunes won him a new generation of fans. In 1978, the Broadway show *Eubie*—featuring 23 of Blake's songs—began a long and critically triumphant run. In 1981, Blake was awarded the Presidential Medal of Honor.

Blake, Nicholas. See Cecil DAY LEWIS.

Blakely, Colin (George Edward) (1930–1987). British actor. Blakely became one of the most familiar figures in British theater, films and television by giving acclaimed performances in a wide variety of mostly supporting roles. A native of Northern Ireland, he made his London debut at the Royal Court Theater in 1959. In 1963 he joined the newly established National Theatre and achieved critical and popular acclaim as a member of that company for five years. Perhaps his outstanding role was as Dr. Watson in Billy WILDER's *The Private Life of Sherlock Holmes* (1970).

Blakey, Art [also known as Abdullah Ibn Buhaina] (1919–1990). American jazz drummer, band leader and composer. Blakey is one of the preeminent drummers in the history of JAZZ, renowned by fans and fellow musicians alike for the subtlety and force of his rhythms. He was also the founder and leader of a band, the Jazz Messengers, which endured (with numerous changes in personnel) as a musical force from the the late 1940s to the late 1980s. The Jazz Messengers became known as a vital training ground for young jazz musicians who learned their craft under Blakey's expert tutelage. Trumpeters Freddie Hubbard and Wynton MARSALIS, saxophonists Jackie McLean and Branford Marsalis, and pianist Horace Silver are just a few renowned Jazz Messenger alumni. Blakey, who was born in Pittsburgh, first emerged in the BEBOP era of the 1940s, when he played in bands led by Fletcher HENDERSON and Billy ECKSTINE.

Blalock, Alfred (1899–1964). American surgeon. A professor of surgery for many years at Johns Hopkins University, Blalock is known for his work on the vascular system. On the eve of America's entry into WORLD WAR II, Blalock demonstrated that surgical shock is caused by blood loss and accordingly introduced the practice of transfusions during surgery. In 1944, he performed the first "blue baby operation," in which surgery is performed on a fetus in utero to correct the congenital heart condition called pulmonary stenosis.

Blanc, Mel(vin Jerome) (1908–1989). American actor, famous as the voices of such notable cartoon characters as BUGS BUNNY, Daffy Duck, Porky Pig, Elmer Fudd and Woody Woodpecker. In a career that spanned more than 60 years, Blanc provided voices for 800 WARNER BROS. cartoons as well as the animated television series "The Bugs Bunny Show" and "The Flintstones."

Blasket Islands. A group of islands off the coast of the Dingle Peninsula, County Kerry, IRELAND. The largest of the islands, Great Blasket, was home to a small Irish-speaking population until just after the middle of the 20th century. By 1953 it had become impossible for the dwindling community to continue to support itself, and the inhabitants were evacuated to the Irish mainland. Much has been written about these forlorn islands, known as "the last parish before America" because of their position at the western edge of Europe.

For further reading:

O'Sullivan, Maurice, *Twenty Years A-Growing*. New York: Viking Press, 1933.

Sayers, Peig, *Peig: The Autobiography of Peig Sayers of the Great Blasket Island*. Syracuse: Syracuse University Press 1974.

Stagles, Joan, *Blasket Islands: Next Parish America*. Chester Springs, Pa.: Dufour Editions, 1980.

Blass, Bill (1922–). Leading American fashion designer. Blass was self-taught as a fashion artist, drawing inspiration from the films he watched as a boy in his hometown in the American Midwest. He studied for a time at the Parsons School of Design and then began his professional career as a sketch artist in New York in 1940. Blass established his own design house in 1970. Since then his name and work have become well-known, placing him among the leaders of current apparel designers. He is known for women's suits. He has licensed the use of his name to some thirty-five other firms. He has even designed interiors for the LINCOLN CONTINENTAL automobile. Blass won Coty Awards in 1961, 1963, 1968, and 1970.

Blaue Reiter, Der [The Blue Rider]. The name for a group of German expressionist painters who organized themselves in 1911 in order to promote—in their paintings and critical writings—the depiction in abstract form of spiritual realities. The name of the group was derived from a painting by Wassily KANDINSKY, one of its members. Other prominent painters associated with Der Blaue Reiter were Paul KLEE, Auguste MACKE and Franz MARC. While these artists were far from uniform in their styles, they were united in emphasizing spiritual concerns that they felt had been ignored by the Impressionists. Blaue Reiter exhibitions were held throughout Germany to publicize the aims of the group. Artists outside of Germany who exhibited with the group included Georges BRAQUE and Pablo PICASSO. With the outbreak of WORLD WAR I, Der Blaue Reiter ceased its organized activities.

Bleriot, Louis (1872–1936). French pioneer aviator and airplane designer. Bleriot began his career as a manufacturer of automobile accessories, but became interested in flying in 1901. His early efforts at airplane building had very limited success, but by 1907 he arrived at the general plan of a tractor (engine-in-front) monoplane, the Bleriot VI, which managed a number of successful (although brief) flights. In several further steps, he progressed to the Bleriot XI, the design that turned out to be his masterpiece. (The design must be credited, in part, to collaboration with Raymond Saulnier.) In 1909 Bleriot made the first successful flight across the English Channel in this airplane, earning fame for himself and his airplane as well. The structure was made of steel tubing, ash, and bamboo with fabric covering. Power was supplied by a 25-horsepower, three-cylinder engine. The wings were without ailerons, and banking was controlled by warping the entire wing. Bicycle-type wire landing wheels and the open frame of the rear fuselage construction gave the Bleriot XI a fragile, insectlike appearance of great elegance. Its form was a first step toward the development of modern aircraft types. Shortly after his triumphant Channel flight, Bleriot quit flying to devote himself to commercial production of his design. By 1914 over 800 Bleriot aircraft had been produced. A surviving example was restored in 1979 and is displayed in the Smithsonian National Air and Space Museum in Washington, D.C.

Blitzkrieg [*German:* "lightning war"]. Term first used in 1939 to describe the German invasion of Poland in WORLD WAR II and, subsequently, any sudden and overwhelming strike by one country against another. Despite frantic British and French negotiations to prevent it, Adolf HITLER was determined to absorb POLAND. On September 1, 1939, a well-equipped mechanized German army swept into Poland, while the German Luftwaffe (air force) destroyed Polish air defense and transportation systems and blasted industrial centers. A second German army invaded from East Prussia, while the Soviets invaded at the eastern border. The Poles fought valiantly but ineffectually, and although Britain and France declared war, they could do nothing. Warsaw was besieged and fell on September 27, and the last Polish resistance collapsed at Lubin eight days later.

Blitzstein, Marc (1905–1964). American composer. Born in Philadelphia, he studied at the Curtis Institute and traveled to Berlin on a Guggenheim Fellowship in 1940. Composing for the stage, films and orchestra, he was best known for his left-wing political views, particularly as expressed in his satirical light opera *The Cradle Will Rock* (1937). Blitzstein is also noted for his opera *Regina* (1949). He was murdered while on vacation in Martinique.

Bloch, Ernest (1880–1959). Swiss-American composer. Born in Switzerland, he studied abroad and returned to his native country to conduct and teach, notably at the Geneva Conservatory (1911–15). Settling in the U.S. and naturalized in 1924, Bloch taught at New York's Mannes School (1917–19), later becoming director of the Cleveland Institute of Music (1920–25) and the San Francisco Conservatory (1925–30). He returned to Switzerland to pursue his activities as a composer in 1930, coming back to the U.S. in 1938 and teaching part-time at the University of California at Berkeley, beginning in 1943. Bloch is best known for his expressive classical works composed in a specifically Jewish idiom. These compositions include the rhapsody *Schelomo,* the symphonic work *Israel* (both 1916), *Trois poemes juifs* (1918), the *Sacred Service* (1933) and *Cinq pieces Hebraique* (1951). Bloch's intense work includes many pieces in other musical modes, including five string quartets, the opera *Macbeth* (1909), two symphonic poems and various pieces for chorus and orchestra.

Bloch affair. On July 21, 1989, the U.S. State Department announced that Felix S. Bloch, deputy chief of the U.S. embassy in Vienna, was under investigation for espionage activities. Bloch had allegedly been seen passing a briefcase to a Soviet agent. Bloch claimed that he and the other individual were merely stamp collectors exchanging a sheet of stamps. The case gained wide publicity as reporters and the FBI dogged Bloch's steps through the summer of 1989. More than a year later Bloch was finally forced to resign; by that time although he had not been cleared, no formal charges had yet been brought against him. If the State Department's allegations were true, Bloch could have been engaging in espionage activities for nearly a decade; that and his senior position would make the Bloch case one of the worst American spy scandals in several decades.

Bloemfontein. South African city located on a tributary of the Modder River. Bloemfontein was the site, in 1899, of the Bloemfontein Conference, which failed to prevent the outbreak of the BOER WAR; the British occupied the city in 1900. It was also the site of negotiations leading to the establishment, in 1908, of an independent Union of SOUTH AFRICA.

Blok, Alexander (1880–1921). Russian poet. Born to the family of a university professor in St. Petersburg, Blok began publishing his poetry at the age of 20. He studied law and philosophy at the University of St. Petersburg, and published his first book, *Songs to the Beautiful Lady,* in 1904. An early convert to the Russian Symbolist movement, he altered his views with the advent of Bolshevism, seeking an association with the Communist Party. An unhappy marriage, poverty and disillusionment with life, combined with his love of Russia, influenced the themes of social protest and individual despair that dominate the later works. His best-known book is *The Twelve* (1920), which depicts the rise of the Bolshevik movement in poetic form.

For further reading:

Chukovsky, Kornei, *Alexander Blok as Man and Poet.* Ann Arbor, Michigan: Ardis, 1982.

Mochulsky, Konstantin, *Aleksandr Blok.* Detroit: Wayne State University Press, 1983.

Pyman, Avril, *Aleksandr Blok, a Biography: The Distant Thunder, 1880–1908,* vol. 1. New York: Oxford University Press, 1979.

———, *The Life of Aleksandr Blok, a Biography: the Release of Harmony, 1908–1921,* vol. 2. New York: Oxford University Press, 1980.

Bloody Sunday January 9, 1905, massacre of peaceful demonstrators in St. Petersburg, RUSSIA, by Russian imperial guards. A workers' strike in the city at the end of 1904 had led to a lockout by employers. As a consequence, some 200,000 people, mostly workers and their families, marched to the Winter Palace to petition Czar NICHOLAS II to end the lockout and to improve working and living conditions. The demonstration was organized in part by Georgi Capon, a priest and workers' leader who, it was later believed, acted as an agent provocateur. As the marchers approached the palace they were fired on by soldiers and police, and dispersed. Some 130 were killed and many more wounded. Ironically, the majority of the marchers were not revolutionaries but loyal citizens who looked up to the czar as the father of Russia. The events of Bloody Sunday radicalized public opinion within Russia and helped set in motion the events that led to the RUSSIAN REVOLUTION of 1917.

Bloody Sunday January 30, 1972, day on which 13 Catholic civilians were killed by British troops in Londonderry, NORTHERN IRELAND, while demonstrating in favor of civil rights and a united Ireland. The event aroused international condemnation and led to further escalation of the fighting in the province. (See also IRISH REPUBLICAN ARMY.)

Bloom, Allan (1930–). American philosopher, educator and social critic. Bloom, a professor at the University of Chicago, won national renown with the publication of THE CLOSING OF THE AMERICAN MIND: EDUCATION AND THE CRISIS OF REASON (1987). As a result of that book, Bloom became a leading spokesman for a traditional, conservative approach to American education from grade school through college. He has attacked cultural relativism—the view that each culture has a set of beliefs that hold relative truth only within the context of that culture—as a de facto assault upon the Western intellectual tradition. That tradition, according to Bloom, ought to remain the foundation of American educational efforts. Bloom has also argued in favor of more strict curricula that emphasize basic reading, writing and mathematical skills.

Bloomsbury Group, The. A disparate group of British writers, painters and political thinkers that flourished between the two world wars. The key figures in what was designated the Bloomsbury group (after the district of London in which most of them lived) were novelists Virginia WOOLF and E.M. FORSTER, art critic Roger FRY, painter Duncan GRANT, biographer Lytton STRACHEY, political essayist Leonard Woolf and economist John Maynard KEYNES, although there were a host of additional writers and bohemian figures who figured intermittently in the social doings of the group. The "Bloomsberries," as they called themselves, were linked not by any single express ideology, but rather by a common sense of the ultimate value of aesthetic excellence, and of the superiority of the bonds of friendship and love to those imposed by law and social custom. Homosexuality and bisexuality were common among group members, in defiance of the mores of the upper-class Victorian upbringing from which most of them had emerged. The Bloomsbury group exercised a dominant influence upon British culture between the wars, and the social and sexual doings of the group continue to fascinate biographers to the present day.

bluegrass. A distinctive musical blend of COUNTRY AND WESTERN and folk styles that emphasizes acoustic instrumentation, driving tempos and vocal harmonies. Bluegrass took its name from the Blue Grass Boys, a band formed in the 1930s by Grand Old Opry star Bill Monroe, which featured Monroe on lead vocals and mandolin. Monroe was the first great star of bluegrass, and his influence shows itself strongly in the playing of subsequent stars such as guitarist Lester Flatt, banjo player Earl Scruggs, the harmonizing brother duo of Ralph and Stanley Carter, and current-day bluegrass singer-guitarists Ricky Skaggs and Peter Rowan. The reason often given for the acoustic sound in bluegrass is that the original bluegrass players did not have electricity in their homes. This strong sense of rural folk tradition imbues the lyrical content of bluegrass songs, which celebrate simple country living, true love and family loyalty. Acoustic instruments specially featured in bluegrass playing include the fiddle, the string bass and the dobro (a steel or "Hawaiian" guitar).

blues. An American musical form created primarily by blacks living in the Southern states in the early decades of the 20th century. Blues music, with its emphatic, driving beat, emotion-laden vocals and earthy themes, draws musically from two key sources: the chanting field songs of black workers (often with melodies of African origin) and the impassioned gospel music of black church worship. It was in the 1920s that so-called "blues" music began to make an impact with the broad American public. Its first major stars were guitarist Blind Lemon Jefferson and singer Bessie SMITH. The legendary composer-guitarist Robert JOHNSON emerged in the 1930s, when blues music aptly mirrored the concerns of Depression-era America. Also at this time, blues began to exercise a major influence on JAZZ musicians such as Count BASIE and Billie HOLIDAY. In the 1940s, Chicago became a vital center of blues music: vocalist-guitarist Muddy WATERS, vocalist Howlin' Wolf and composer-bassist Willie Dixon were key figures of this era. In the 1950s, when ROCK and roll first came to prominence, many of the early hits of white singers such as Elvis PRESLEY were rerecordings of old blues songs. Leading lights of the current blues scene are guitarist-vocalists Albert Collins and Robert Cray.

Bluford, Guion (1942–). U.S. astronaut. As a mission specialist aboard the U.S. SPACE SHUTTLE mission STS-8 (August 30–September 5, 1983), Bluford was the first black American to go into space. He made a second flight aboard Mission 61–A/Spacelab D1 (October 30–November 6, 1985) as part of an eight-astronaut team on a mission directed by the Federal German Aerospace Research Establishment. Bluford holds a Ph.D. in aerospace engineering.

Blum, Leon (1872–1950). French writer and political leader, premier (1936–37, 1946). A Jewish socialist, he was a literary critic who became politically active during the Dreyfus Affair. He was elected to the office of deputy in 1919 and headed the French Socialist Party in 1925. In 1936 he became premier, presiding over a Popular Front government that included socialists, communists and other left-wing groups. In the year he held office, Blum introduced such reforms as the 40-hour work week and collective bargaining and nationalized the Bank of France. He was ousted from office in 1937, returning for a few weeks in 1938. During WORLD WAR II he was arrested by the VICHY government (1940) and tried at Riom (1942), where he defended himself brilliantly. He was imprisoned until 1945. Growing more moderate in his views toward the end of his life, Blum returned briefly as interim premier in 1946.

Blumberg, Baruch Samuel (1925–). American physician. Blumberg studied physics and mathematics at Union College, Schenectady, and at Columbia where, after a year, he changed to medical studies. He received his M.D. from Columbia in 1951 and his Ph.D. in biochemistry from Oxford University in 1957. After working at the National Institutes of Health in Bethesda, Md., from 1957 until 1964, Blumberg was appointed professor of medicine at the University of Pennsylvania. In 1963, while examining literally thousands of blood samples in a study of the variation in serum proteins in different populations, Blumberg made the important discovery of what soon became known as the "Australian antigen." For his work on the Australian antigen, Blumberg shared the 1976 NOBEL PRIZE for physiology or medicine with Carleton Gajdusek.

Blunt, Anthony (1907–1983). British double agent. A don at Cambridge University in the 1930s, Blunt worked for British intelligence during WORLD WAR II, was later the official art adviser to Queen ELIZABETH II and was knighted for his services to the Crown. In 1979, British writer and broadcaster Andrew Boyle published *The Climate of Treason,* in which he charged that a respected but unnamed figure in the British establishment had been the "fourth man" in the infamous Philby-Burgess-Maclean spy ring during World War II and after (see BURGESS-MACLEAN SPY CASE; Kim PHILBY). On November 15, 1979, Prime Minister Margaret THATCHER told Parliament that Blunt had been the "fourth man." Blunt had secretly confessed to British authorities in 1964 that he had recruited spies for the U.S.S.R. from among his students while he was a don at Cambridge University in the 1930s, that he had passed intelligence to the Soviets during the 1940s and that he had warned Burgess and Maclean of their impending arrest. Blunt's confession was kept from the public, and Blunt was allowed to continue as the queen's art adviser until he retired in 1972. The revelation about Blunt's earlier involvement in Britain's worst spy scandal shocked the nation; the fact that Blunt's crimes had gone unpunished led to charges that the British establishment was more interested in protecting its members than in national security and justice. The Blunt expose also led to speculation that there may have been a highly placed "fifth man"—possibly MI5's director, Sir Roger Hollis—working for the Soviets in British intelligence. (See also the APOSTLES.)

Bly, Robert (Elwood) (1926–). American poet, editor and translator. Educated at Harvard and the University of Iowa, Bly received a Fulbright to translate contemporary Norwegian poetry. Back in his native Minnesota, he began the *Fifties* magazine (later the *Sixties* and the *Seventies*), which also promoted the work of James Wright, Donald Hall and Louis SIMPSON. *Silence in the Snowy Fields* (1962) and *The Light Around the Body* (1967) made his reputation. The latter collection, which also contained polemical antiwar verse, won the National Book Award. Bly and his friends seek the "deep image" in poems characterized by simplicity, subjectivity and surreal imagery.

For further reading:

Davis, William V., *Understanding Robert Bly*. Columbia: University of South Carolina Press, 1989.

BMW [Bayerische Motoren Werke]. German firm noted for its automobile designs. Founded in 1916 by Karl Rapp and Gustav Otto as a manufacturer of aircraft engines, BMW began manufacturing motorcycles in 1923 and finally automobiles in 1929. Many of its products have been of outstanding design quality. The 2002 sedan of 1968–76, designed by BMW staff under the direction of Andreas Glas, was particularly admired for its logical and consistent design, free of meaningless ornament and with a unity of theme rare in automobile design. The 2002 and more recent BMW designs have become popular imports in the U.S..

Boas, Franz (1858–1942). American anthropologist. Educated at the University of Kiel, Boas taught at Clark University and, in 1899, became Columbia University's first professor of anthropology, a position he held for 37 years. The dominant force in American anthropology during the first half of the century, Boas emphasized the importance of culture on human behavior and development. He was one of the first anthropologists to emphasize field research, and many of his theories are based on his own studies of the Indians of northwest Canada. Among his best known works are: *The Mind of Primitive Man* (1911), *Primitive Art* (1927), *Anthropology and Modern Life* (1928) and *Race, Language, and Culture* (1940).

boat people, Vietnamese. Part of the terrible aftermath of the VIETNAM WAR has been the exodus of more than a million refugees from communist oppression. While some have fled overland into THAI-

Twenty-five-hundred Vietnamese refugees stranded aboard a freighter after being denied permission to land at Port Klang, Malaysia (1978).

LAND, the majority have attempted to escape in small boats across the South China Sea to HONG KONG, INDONESIA or the PHILIPPINES or across the Gulf of Siam to Thailand or MALAYSIA. It is estimated that some 200,000 have died from exposure, drowning or attacks by pirates while making this perilous voyage.

Bob and Ray. American comedy team. Bob Elliott and Ray Goulding performed on radio and television from the late 1940s through the mid-1980s. They specialized in offbeat humor and gentle satire. Among their creations were the bumbling interviewer Wally Ballou and Mary Backstage, Noble Wife (a parody of the popular 1940s soap opera, "Mary Noble, Backstage Wife"). They were perhaps best known for a series of commercials they created for Piels beer, in which they appeared as the fictional Piels brothers, Harry and Bert.

Bodenstein, Max Ernst August (1871–1942). German physical chemist. Bodenstein earned his doctorate at Heidelberg (1893) and worked with Wilhelm Ostwald at Leipzig before becoming a professor at Hannover (1908–23) and at the Institute for Physical Chemistry, Berlin (1923–36). He made a series of classic studies on the equilibria of gaseous reactions, especially that of hydrogen and iodine (1897). Bodenstein also worked in photochemistry and was the first to show how a chain reaction could explain the large yield per quantum for the reaction of hydrogen and chlorine.

Boeing, William Edward (1881–1956). Born in Detroit, Boeing founded the Pacific Nero Products Co. in Seattle in 1916. In 1929, the corporation's name was changed to Boeing Aircraft; today it is the world's largest manufacturer of commercial aircraft. In recognition of his pioneering achievement in the AVIATION industry, Boeing was awarded the Daniel Guggenheim medal in 1934. He died 22 years later, on his yacht in Puget Sound, Seattle.

Boer Uprising of 1914–1915. The Union of SOUTH AFRICA entered WORLD WAR I on the side of the Allies in 1914, but many Boers (South Africans of Dutch descent) balked, favoring Germany. Three army commanders led a Boer uprising in the Orange Free State and Transvaal and by the end of 1914 12,000 rebels were involved. Prime Minister Louis BOTHA and Jan SMUTS, former Boer generals, opposed the rebels, and in three campaigns (October and December 1914, and February 1915) overcame the rebel forces. Botha showed unusual clemency, and all prisoners were set free by 1917. (See also BOER WAR.)

Boer War [Second Boer War; Great Boer War] Conflict of 1899–1902 between Boers (South Africans of Dutch descent) and British forces in SOUTH AFRICA; the first major war of the 20th century. The discovery of large, rich deposits of gold in the southern Transvaal in 1886 had brought a rush mainly of Britons to the region and exacerbated longstanding British-Boer tensions. When troops protecting British mining interests failed to comply with a Boer ultimatum to withdraw, the South African Republic (Transvaal) and its ally, the Orange Free State, declared war on Great Britain (October 1899). Well-equipped Boer forces, led by Piet Joubert, Piet Cronje, Louis BOTHA and others scored initial successes, seizing Kimberly, Mafeking and Ladysmith. However, in 1900 the fortunes of war turned with the arrival of British reinforcements under Field Marshal Lord Frederick Roberts and General Lord Horatio Kitchener. Roberts advanced into the Orange Free State, seizing its capital, Bloemfontein (March 13, 1900), and soon occupying the country. The British then invaded the Transvaal and captured Johannesburg and Pretoria (May-June 1900), effectively crushing Boer resistance on the battlefield. The British formally annexed the Boer states, but it took Kitchener's forces two more years of bitter fighting to subdue guerrilla units led by such Boer generals as Jan SMUTS and Botha. Through a line of blockhouses (to split the country) and the detention of Boer women and children in CONCENTRATION CAMPS, Kitchener wore down Boer morale and systematically destroyed guerrilla units. By the Treaty of Vereeniging (May 31, 1902) the Boers recognized British sovereignty in exchange for a large indemnity and other concessions.

Boesky scandal. Wall Street scandal that rocked the U.S. financial world in 1986. Ivan Boesky was a multi-millionaire who had made his fortune through risk arbitrage—speculating on the stocks of cor-

A prototype of the Boeing 707 jetliner in a test flight over Puget Sound in 1955.

porations that are suspected to be involved in mergers. Boesky traded on behalf of many wealthy individuals and corporations in addition to himself. However, his success was largely founded on illegal insider trading. When the SECURITIES AND EXCHANGE COMMISSION prosecuted Wall Street trader Dennis Levine for insider trading, Levine revealed that Boesky had been receiving illegal tips about mergers and takeovers. Boesky eventually cooperated with the SEC and paid a fine of $50 million and a civil indemnity of an equal amount. He retained at least $200 million of his personal fortune. Boesky's disclosures implicated Michael R. Milken and his Wall Street firm DREXEL BURNHAM LAMBERT, which went bankrupt in the wake of the scandal.

Bogan, Louise (1897–1970). American poet and critic. Bogan's poetic output was small, and she continually revised her work throughout her career. Her collected poems *The Blue Estuaries: Poems 1923–1968* brought together a slender oeuvre of short, highly distilled, rhymed and metered lyrics that show the influence of Emily Dickinson. From 1931 to 1970 she served as poetry editor and critic for the NEW YORKER; her influential critical essays were published as *A Poet's Alphabet* (1970). In *Achievement in American Poetry 1900–1950* (1951) she argued that the woman poets of the 19th century were responsible for the revitalization of American poetry. Bogan won the BOLLINGEN PRIZE in 1955 and held the Library of Congress Chair in Poetry in 1945–46.

Bogart, Humphrey (DeForest) (1899–1957). Popular American motion picture actor known for his tough and cynical screen persona. The son of a prominent New York surgeon, Bogart began in the entertainment business with Broadway stage producer William A. Brady. After rising from office boy to stage manager, he began to play juvenile parts in the 1920s. (For one role he came on stage in white trousers to utter the immortal line, "Tennis anyone?") His big break came playing gangster Duke Mantee in *The Petrified Forest* in 1935, a role he repeated a year later in the film version for WARNER BROS. Despite some fine performances in subsequent movies, he almost became mired in second-rate gangster melodramas. Two superior crime thrillers changed everything: *High Sierra* (1939) and *The Maltese Falcon* (1940), a virtually perfect film debut by director-writer John HUSTON. For the next 15 years Bogart perfected the battle-scarred but vulnerable roles for which he is best known: the lovelorn Rick in *Casablanca* (1942), the crafty Phillip Marlow in *The Big Sleep* (1946), the obsessive prospector in *Treasure of the Sierra Madre* (1948), the "river rat" in *The African Queen* (for which he won an ACADEMY AWARD in 1952) and the twitchy, ball-bearings-rolling Captain Queeg in *The Caine Mutiny* (1956). He died of cancer of the esophagus in 1957.

For further reading:

Benchley, Nathaniel, *Bogart*. Boston: Little, Brown, Co., 1975.

Humphrey Bogart with Ingrid Bergman.

Bogoliubov, Nikolai Nikolaevich (1909–). Soviet mathematician and physicist. Bogoliubov did his graduate work at the Academy of Sciences of the Ukrainian Soviet Socialist Republic and subsequently worked there and at the Soviet Academy of Sciences. His main contribution was in the application of mathematical techniques to theoretical physics. He developed a method of distribution-function for nonequilibrium processes and also worked on superfluidity, quantum field theory and superconductivity. His work was partly paralleled by that of John BARDEEN, Leon COOPER, and John Robert Schrieffer. Bogoliubov was a prolific author, with many of his works translated into English. He was active in founding scientific schools in nonlinear mechanics, statistical physics and quantum-field theory. In 1963 he became academician-secretary of the Soviet Academy of Sciences and was made director of the Joint Institute for Nuclear Research in Dubna in 1965. The next year he was also made a deputy to the Supreme Soviet. He has been honored by scientific societies throughout the world, and in his own country received the State Prize twice (1947, 1953) and the Lenin Prize (1958).

Bohm, Karl (1894–1981). Austrian orchestral and operatic conductor. Bohm divided his early studies between law and music, taking piano lessons at Graz Conservatory and the Vienna Conservatory while studying law at the University of Graz. He served in the Austrian army in WORLD WAR I and was wounded. He received his law degree in 1919 but decided on a conducting career, even though he had no formal training. During the 1920s and '30s he held a series of conducting posts in Germany, where he worked under Bruno WALTER and Hans Knappertsbusch. He was music director at Dresden (1934–43) before moving to the Vienna State Opera, which he also directed (1950–53) after World War II. He also frequently conducted at the Metropolitan Opera, Bayreuth, Salzburg, Berlin and London. Bohm was particularly identified with the Austrian-German repertory and specialized in the works of Mozart, Beethoven, Schubert, Wagner, Richard STRAUSS (who was a personal friend) and Alban BERG. His repertory included 150 different operas, and he made numerous recordings. A precise stylist and a purist in interpretation, his performances were less glamorous and flamboyant than those of many of his more popular colleagues. Nonetheless, he was one of the outstanding conductors of the century, and the only person ever designated as Austria's General Music Director.

Bohr, Aage Niels (1922–). Danish physicist. The son of Niels BOHR, he was educated at the University of Copenhagen. After postgraduate work at the University of London from 1942 to 1945, he returned to Copenhagen to the Institute of Theoretical Physics, where he has served since 1956 as professor of physics. When Bohr began his research career, Maria Goeppert-Mayer and Hans Jensen had just proposed, in 1949, the shell model of the nucleus. Almost immediately Leo James Rainwater produced experimental results at odds with the predictions derived from a spherical shell model, and proposed that some nuclei were distorted rather than perfectly spherical. Bohr, in collaboration with Ben Mottelson, followed Rainwater's work by proposing their collective model of nuclear structure (1952), so called because they argued that the distorted nuclear shape was produced by a participation of many nucleons. For this work Bohr shared the 1975 NOBEL PRIZE in physics with Rainwater and Mottelson.

Bohr, Niels Hendrik David (1885–1962). Niels Bohr came from a distinguished scientific family and was educated at the University of Copenhagen where he obtained his Ph.D. in 1911. After four productive years with Ernest RUTHERFORD in Manchester, Bohr returned to Denmark, becoming in 1918 director of the newly created Institute of Theoretical Physics. Under Bohr (after Albert EINSTEIN probably the most respected theoretical physicist of the century) the institute became one of the most exciting research centers in the world. A generation of physicists from around the world were to pass through it, and eventually the orthodox account of QUANTUM theory was to be

Dr. Niels Bohr, Danish scientist who helped develop the atomic bomb.

described as the "Copenhagen interpretation."

In 1913 Bohr published a classic paper, *On the Constitution of Atoms and Molecules,* in which he used the quantum of energy, *h,* introduced into physics by Max Planck in 1900, to rescue Rutherford's account of atomic structure from a vital objection and also to account for the line spectrum of hydrogen. He was able to calculate energies for possible orbits of the electron, receiving the NOBEL PRIZE for physics for this work in 1922. The Bohr theory was developed further by Arnold Sommerfeld. Bohr made other major contributions to this early development of quantum theory. The "correspondence principle" (1916) is his principle that the quantum-theory description of the atom corresponds to classical physics at large magnitudes. In 1927 Bohr publicly formulated the "complementarity principle," which argued against continuing attempts to eliminate such supposed difficulties as the wave-particle duality of light and many other atomic phenomena. It was a principle Bohr remained faithful to, even representing it on his coat of arms in 1947 (the motto *Contraria sunt complementa* above yin/yang symbols). Together with the indeterminancy principle of Werner HEISENBERG and the probability waves of Max BORN, this principle emerged from the 1930 Solvay conference (the last one Einstein attended) as the most authoritative and widely accepted theory to describe atomic phenomena.

Bohr also made major contributions to the work on radioactivity that led to the discovery and exploitation of nuclear fission. It was Bohr who in 1939 made the crucial suggestion that fission was more likely to occur with the rarer isotope uranium-235 than the more common variety uranium-238. In 1943 Bohr, who had a Jewish mother, felt it necessary to escape from occupied Denmark; he eventually made his way to Los Alamos in America where he served as a consultant on the ATOMIC BOMB project. He was quick to appreciate the consequences of using such weapons and in 1944 made an early approach to ROOSEVELT and CHURCHILL, proposing that such an obvious danger could perhaps be used to bring about a rapprochement between Russia and the West. Scientists were in a unique position, he argued, in having the Soviet contacts and the knowledge to make the first approach. Much of Bohr's time after the war was spent working, among scientists, for adequate controls of nuclear weapons, and in 1955 he organized the first Atoms for Peace conference in Geneva.

Bok, Bart Jan (1906–). Dutch-American astronomer. Bok studied at the Universities of Leiden (1924–27) and Groningen (1927–29) and obtained his Ph.D. from Groningen in 1932. He had moved to the U.S. in 1929, was naturalized in 1938 and served at Harvard from 1929 to 1957, being appointed professor of astronomy in 1947. Bok spent 1957 to 1966 in Australia as director of the Mount Stromlo Observatory, Canberra, and professor of astronomy at the Australian National University. He returned to the U.S. in 1966 to become director of the Steward Observatory, Ariz., until 1970 and professor of astronomy (since 1974 emeritus professor) at the University of Arizona, Tucson. Bok's major interest has been the structure of our galaxy, the Milky Way. With his wife, Priscilla, he published a survey of the subject: *The Milky Way* (1941). In 1947 Bok discovered small dark circular clouds visible against a background of stars or luminous gas, since known as *Bok globules*. Since they are thought to be precursors of stars, as Bok himself conjectured, they have received considerable attention in recent years.

Bokassa, Jean-Bedel (1921–). African dictator. Bokassa joined the French army in 1939 and became chief of staff of the newly formed CENTRAL AFRICAN REPUBLIC (CAR) army in 1962. In December 1965 he overthrew the government of his cousin, David DACKO. Bokassa served as president from 1966 to 1979, proclaiming and crowning himself Emperor Bokassa I in 1977. Bokassa's despotic leadership achieved worldwide infamy when 100 schoolchildren were massacred by government troops at his behest in April 1979 in Bangui, the capital, after the children protested a decree requiring them to wear school uniforms. Bokassa was overthrown in a bloodless coup in September 1979, and Dacko was reinstated as president. Bokassa was exiled to the Ivory Coast, and later lived in France before returning to the CAR in 1986. He stood trial and in 1987 was sentenced to death by firing squad. The sentence was later commuted to life imprisonment by General Kolingba.

Bolet, Jorge (1914–1990). Cuban-born pianist. He began his career as a child prodigy, noted for his mastery of such Romantic-era composers as Franz Liszt. His style of playing was not popular among critics or the public for much of his adult life. A revival of interest in Romantic composers won him accolades in the 1970s.

Bolger, Ray(mond Wallace) (1906–1987). U.S. dancer and comic actor. His most celebrated role was as the Scarecrow in the 1939 film classic *The Wizard of Oz.* Among the many Broadway productions in which he appeared was the late 1940s' *Where's Charley,* in which he created his most memorable song-and-dance number, "Once in Love with Amy." During the 1950s he had his own television show.

Bolivia. Nation in west-central South America; Sucre is the constitutional capital, while La Paz is the political capital and main commercial center. Bolivia was named after the South American leader Simon Bolivar, who fought the Spanish colonial power early in the 19th century. From 1879 to 1884, Bolivia was allied with Peru against Chile in the War of the Pacific, which was triggered by a dispute over control of nitrate deposits in the Atacama (now Antofagasta) coastal province of Bolivia. In 1899, the balance of internal political power switched from conservatives to liberals, whose principal leader, Ismael Montes, served as president from 1904 to 1909 and from 1913 to 1917. In 1903, negotiations with Brazil led to Bolivia ceding the Acre rubber production region in exchange for financial and railroad interests. There was an opposition coup in 1920 and a military coup during the GREAT DEPRESSION of the 1930s. From 1932 to 1935, Bolivia and Paraguay waged war over control of the long-disputed GRAN CHACO lowlands, in which oil had been discovered. A 1938 treaty granted 75% of the region to Paraguay. In 1967, Cuban revolutionary leader Ernesto "Che" GUEVARA was captured while organizing guerrilla resistance in Bolivia and was executed. In 1969, Alfredo Ovando Candia became president and nationalized U.S. oil holdings in Bolivia. Lidia Gueiler Tejada later became the first woman president of Bolivia. Political instability has been a constant throughout the country's history.

Bolivian Guerrilla War of 1966–67. In the mid-1960s Ernesto "Che" GUEVARA, the Argentine-born Cuban revolutionary, believed that conditions in Bolivia made it ripe for a Cuban-type revolution. In autumn 1966 he and 15 followers clandestinely established headquarters at Nancahuazu, a wild, unsettled region of Bolivia. Local communists failed to support them. The Bolivian army began to patrol the area, looking for a large force, and in March 1967 fighter planes strafed the area while counterinsurgency troops began an encirclement. On April 26 two couriers were captured; the army later used them to arouse Bolivians against the foreign "invaders." By the fall of 1967 Guevara was retreating through the jungles with only 16 men. On October 8 his band was discovered; some were killed outright, but Guevara was captured. He was executed the next morning.

Bolivian National Revolution (1952). Although outlawed in 1946, the Movi-

BOLIVIA

BOLIVIA

1946	President Gualberto Villarroel shot and killed by rioters; Tomas Manje Gutierez named provisional president.
1956	After a bloody uprising, tin miners overthrow the government; Victor Paz Estenssoro becomes president, enacts land reform and universal suffrage and nationalizes the mines.
1964	Gen. Rene Barrientos overthrows Victor Paz Estenssoro, represses militant miners and the Nancahuazu guerrilla movement led by Che Guevara.
1967	Che Guevara killed in battle with government forces.
1982	(July) Gen. Luis Garcia Meza seizes power; his government becomes notorious for violent repression and cocaine trafficking.
1985	(July) General elections won by Victor Paz Estenssoro; tin prices plummet and unemployed miners turn to coca production.
1989	(August 11) Jaime Paz Zamora, a self-described social democrat, sworn in as president by his 81-year-old second cousin and predecessor, Victor Paz Estenssoro.
1990	Government launches anti-cocaine program, paying farmers to destroy more than 8,400 acres of coca.

miento Nacionalista Revolucionario (MNR) won a plurality for its presidential candidate and founder, Victor Paz Estenssoro in the 1951 elections in BOLIVIA. To prevent Estenssoro coming to power, the president handed power over to a 10–man military junta. On April 8–11, 1952, armed workers, peasants and the national police revolted in La Paz, the administrative capital, and elsewhere, overthrew the junta and recalled Estenssoro from exile. As president, Estenssoro nationalized the tin mines, raised miners' wages, liquidated large landholdings, distributed land to Indians and established universal suffrage. Bolivians gained civil and political rights, but Estenssoro imprisoned many of his political opponents.

Bolivian Revolt of 1946. A popular revolt (July 17–21, 1946) due to severe inflation and unemployment caused by falling mineral prices after World War II. Bolivian tin was vital to the Allies in World War II. After Bolivia declared war on the Axis powers (April 1943), dissident army officers led by Colonel Gualberto Vilardel, supported by German agents, the Argentine government and the National Revolutionary Movement, staged a coup and named Villardel president. The U.S. refused to recognize the new regime until it agreed to cooperate with the Allies. The army stood by during the revolt. Villardel was seized and killed, and a liberal provisional government was installed.

Bolivian Revolt of 1971. The arrest of rightist demonstrators in Santa Cruz, BOLIVIA, triggered a general revolt (April 19–22, 1971). Peasants, students, miners and the air force supported leftist President Juan Jose Torres against rightists of the army and the middle and upper classes. The rightist rebels gained control of Santa Cruz and Cochabamba and, after the air force joined them, captured La Paz, the administrative capital. Torres fled to Peru, then Chile, while a military-civilian coalition established Colonel Hugo Banzer Suarez as head of government.

Boll, Heinrich (Theodor) (1917–1985). German novelist, short story writer and essayist. Boll, who won the NOBEL PRIZE for literature in 1972, is one of the major figures in postwar German literature. Born in Cologne, Boll attended school there and then was drafted into the German army despite having been one of the few boys in his class to refuse to join the HITLER YOUTH movement. He served throughout WORLD WAR II. After the war he studied at the University of Cologne and turned to writing. His first novel, *The Train Was on Time* (1949), which told of a young German soldier's horrific experiences in combat, was a critical success. Boll produced a steady stream of fictional works over the next three decades, most notably the novels *Billiards at Half Past Nine* (1959), *The Clown* (1963) and *Group Portrait with Lady* (1971), all of which dealt with Nazi decadence and the dehumanizing materialism that fueled the postwar German economic success. *What's to Become of the Boy* (1985) is his autobiography.

Boll was a politically engaged writer and an active proponent of artistic freedom.

Bollingen Prize in Poetry. Awarded biennially, with administrative offices maintained at Yale University, this prize is given to the best book of poetry written by an American during the two years preceding each award. Poets are nominated by jury. The prize is $10,000.

Bolotowsky, Ilya (1907–1981). Russian-born sculptor and painter. He was known for his simple, highly geometric forms. In 1937 he helped found the **American Abstract Artists,** a group that included Piet MONDRIAN and Ad REINHARDT. The group's style, known as **Neo-Plasticism,** was one of pure, formal abstraction not based on natural forms.

Bolshevik Revolution. Military defeats, shortages and widespread distrust of government during WORLD WAR I led first (March 1917) to the overthrow of Czar NICHOLAS II. When he failed to subdue rioters in Moscow and Petrograd (Leningrad), the parliament established a provisional government under Prince LVOV and forced Nicholas' abdication. Revolutionary committees (Soviets) agitated for withdrawal from the war, encouraged by Vladimir I. LENIN, leader of left-wing Russian Marxists (Bolsheviks). They attempted to seize power but failed, and Lenin fled. Alexander F. KERENSKY, a socialist moderate, became premier. He soon lost support, and Lenin returned to lead a bloodless coup in November (the OCTOBER REVOLUTION), masterminded by Leon TROTSKY (1879–1940). The Bolsheviks withdrew Russia from the war and consolidated power. They abolished private property and class privilege, nationalized banks and industries, and suppressed opposition with secret police. A bloody civil war followed.

Bolsheviks. Those of the radical faction of the Russian Social Democratic Workers' Party when it split in 1903. The Bolsheviks, meaning those in the majority (MENSHEVIKS were the minority), were headed by LENIN, who believed that the revolution must be led by a single centralized party of professional revolutionaries. After the RUSSIAN REVOLUTION (1917) the Bolsheviks succeeded in eliminating other political parties, and from 1918 until 1952 the COMMUNIST PARTY OF THE SOVIET UNION was termed Communist Party (Bolsheviks).

Bolshoi Ballet. Acclaimed Russian dance company in existence since 1776. The Bolshoi is particularly noted for its dramatic ballet style. The company staged the first productions of the Petipa-Minkus ballet *Don Quixote* (1869) and the Reisinger-Tchaikovsky *Swan Lake* (1877), and presented the first ballet on a modern theme, *The Red Poppy* (1927). Under the direction of Leonid Lavrovsky, who was also chief choreographer (1944–64), the Bolshoi appeared for the first time in London (1956) and New York (1959), presenting acclaimed productions of Lavrovsky's *Romeo and Juliet* and *Giselle* and starring the legendary ballerina Galina Ulanova. Since 1976 the company has been directed by Yuri Grigorovich. His new version of *Spartacus* (1968) and reworking of *Swan Lake* has been performed on the company's world tours with great success. The affiliated ballet school has produced some outstanding dancers for the company, including Natalia Bessmertnova and Nikolay Fadeyechev.

For further reading:

Grigorovich, Yuri & V. Vanslov, trans. Yuri Sviridov, *Bolshoi Ballet*.

Zapevalova, G.M., *The Bolshoi Ballet*. England: Collets, 1981.

Bolt, Robert (1924–). British playwright and screenplay writer. Bolt is best known for his skill in blending historical narrative and Brechtian political commentary into a satisfying dramatic whole. His most famous work is the play *A Man for All Seasons* (1960), a study of Sir Thomas More that was successfully adapted into a 1966 film starring Paul Scofield that earned Bolt an ACADEMY AWARD for best screenplay. Other plays by Bolt include *The Tiger and the Horse* (1960), *Vivat! Vivat Regina!* (1970) and *State of Revolution* (1977). Bolt also wrote screenplays for a number of films directed by David LEAN, most notably *Lawrence of Arabia* (1962).

Bolton, Guy Reginald (1894–1979). British-born playwright and musical librettist. Bolton coauthored the books of dozens of romantic Broadway musicals in the 1920s and 1930s. These included the shows *Lady Be Good* (1924) and *Girl Crazy* (1930) with music by George GERSHWIN and *Anything Goes* (1934) with music by Cole PORTER. He also worked with Jerome KERN. Probably his most celebrated association was his lifelong collaboration with P.G. WODEHOUSE.

Boltwood, Bertram Borden (1870–1927). American chemist and physicist. Boltwood was educated at Yale and the University of Munich. Apart from the period 1900–06, when he served as a private consultant, and the year 1909–10, which he spent with Ernest RUTHERFORD at the University of Manchester, England, he devoted the whole of his academic career to Yale. He occupied the chair of physics (1906–10), the chair of radioactivity (1910–18), and the chair of chemistry from 1918 until his death by suicide in 1927. Boltwood made a number of contributions to the study of radioactivity. In 1905 he demonstrated that lead was always found in uranium and was probably the final stable product of its decay. He argued that in minerals of the same age the lead-uranium ratio would be constant and that in minerals of different ages the ratio would be different. His estimates of the ages of several rocks based on accepted decay rate estimates were good. This was the beginning of attempts to date rocks and fossils by radiation measurements and other physical techniques, which have revolutionized geology and archaeology.

Bond, Edward (1934–). British playwright. Bond is best known for his commitment to leftist politics in his plays. He has been in the forefront of those seeking to emphasize social consciousness in British theater. His first play, *The Pope's Wedding* (1962), debuted in the Royal Court Theatre. Numerous companies, including the National Theatre and the Royal Shakespeare Company, have produced subsequent of his plays including *Saved* (1965), which featured a controversial scene of a baby being stoned that led to the British government censoring the play; *Narrow Road to the Deep North* (1968); *The Sea* (1973); *Summer* (1982); and *Restoration* (1988).

Bond, George F. (1915–1983). U.S. Navy doctor. An authority on the medical effects of deep-sea diving and undersea pressure, Bond was the pioneer of the **Sealab** program of the 1960s. Teams of Sealab "aquanauts" studied the feasibility of undersea living by spending days in a small capsule anchored to the ocean floor.

Bond, (Horace) Julian (1940–). American CIVIL RIGHTS leader and government official. A native of Nashville, Tennessee, Bond was an organizer of the Committee on Appeal for Human Rights while he was a student at Morehouse College in Atlanta. In 1960, he helped to found the Student Nonviolent Coordinating Committee. In 1965, Bond was elected to the Georgia state legislature, one of eight blacks elected under court-order reapportionment. However, his fellow legislators, by a vote of 184–12, voted to bar Bond, citing his vocal criticism of the Vietnam War and his alleged encouragement of draft evasion. He was finally admitted to the legislature under a December 5, 1966, order of the U.S. Supreme Court. Bond also served in the Georgia state senate, and, in an upset, was defeated in a 1986 Democratic congressional primary by John Lewis, who went on to win the election.

Bondarchuk, Sergei (1920–). Russian actor and film director. Bondarchuk is best known as the director of the acclaimed, seven-hours-plus Soviet film *War and Peace* (1966–67), an adaptation of the classic novel by Leo Tolstoy. He was born in the Ukraine and served in the Theater of the Soviet Army during World War II. In the decade following the war, Bondarchuk distinguished himself as the leading actor in the Soviet cinema. While the range of dramatic portrayals open to him under Soviet censorship was severely limited, Bondarchuk gave life to legendary figures in Russian history, playing the title roles in *Michurin* (1948) and *Taras Shevchenko* (1951). He won international acclaim for his lead performance in a Soviet film adaptation of *Othello* (1955). Bondarchuk's debut as a director of full-length features was *Destiny of a Man* (1959), based on a novel by Nobel Prize winner Mikhail SHOLOKHOV. Subsequent Bondarchuk films have included *Waterloo* (1970) and *Uncle Vanya* (1971).

Bondi, Sir Hermann (1919–). British-Austrian mathematician and cosmologist. Bondi studied at Cambridge University, where he later taught. In 1954 he moved to London to take up the chair in mathematics at King's College. Bondi has always been actively interested in the wider implications of science and the scientific outlook, as his membership of the British Humanist Association and the Science Policy Foundation testify. He served as chief scientific adviser to the Ministry of Defence (1971–77), chief scientist at the Department of Energy (from 1977) and chairman of the Natural Environment Research Council (from 1980). He was knighted in 1973. Bondi's most important work has been in applied mathematics and especially in cosmology. In collaboration with Thomas Gold, in 1948 he propounded a new version of the steady-state theory of the universe. Fred HOYLE had first suggested the idea of a steady-state theory to devise a model of the universe that could accommodate both the fact that the universe is the same throughout and yet is expanding. Bondi and Gold suggested that, in order to maintain the universe despite its expansion, matter is created continuously. Although it enjoyed considerable popularity, Bondi and Gold's steady-state model is now considered to have been decisively refuted by observational evidence, and the BIG-BANG THEORY is favored.

Bonestell, Chesley (1888–1986). U.S. space-astronomical artist. Recipient of a special award from the British Interplanetary Society, Bonestell was the world's best known space artist, inspiring a generation of space enthusiasts, scientists, science fiction writers and other artists with his talent for rendering astronomical scenes that were thoroughly researched and had a photographic verisimilitude. Although trained as an architect, he never completed his studies and spent his early years working in various architectural offices in San Francisco. He later worked as an artist, doing background paintings (mats) for such motion pictures as CITIZEN KANE (1941), *Destination Moon* (1950), *When Worlds Collide* (1951) and *War of the Worlds* (1953). From the early 1940s until the 1970s he specialized in works depicting the facts and wonders of space, producing over 10 books, including his most famous, *The Conquest of Space* (1949), with text by rocket pioneer Willy LEY. A 10-by-40-foot mural he did for the Boston Museum of Science in 1950–51 was transferred to the Smithsonian's National Air and Space Museum in 1976.

Bonhoeffer, Dietrich (1906–1945). German theologian. Bonhoeffer has exercised an enormous influence on 20th-century Western theology by virtue of his impassioned writings on moral and political issues and the example set by his martyrdom at the hands of the Nazis. Bonhoeffer combined in his writings a practical view of human psychology and a reverential standard as to the requirements of a truly religious life. In *The Cost of Discipleship* (1937), written in response to the threat posed by the HITLER Reich, Bonhoeffer insisted that true "grace" required direct involvement in the fight against worldly evil. At the outset of WORLD WAR II Bonhoeffer was in America, but he voluntarily returned to GERMANY to work against the Nazi regime. He was arrested in 1943; *Letters and Papers from Prison* (1953) contains writings smuggled out of his prison cell. He was hanged by the Nazis in 1945 just after leading a Sunday prayer service for his fellow prisoners.

Bonnard, Pierre (1867–1947). French painter. Bonnard, though his name has been linked with the Nabi and fauve artistic movements, stands out as an independent visionary of 20th-century French painting (see FAUVISM). His canvases, which are frequently devoted to simple domestic and pastoral scenes, employ a radiant palette of colors and emphasize pictorial values over dramatic content or aesthetic experiment. Born near Paris, he established a close early friendship with fellow painter Edouard Villard, with whom he was active in the Nabi (Prophet) movement that was strongly influenced by the stylized, decorative qualities of Japanese woodblock prints. By 1905, Bonnard had linked himself with the Fauves (including Henri MATISSE) who called for bold, expressive use of color. From 1910 until his death, Bonnard worked in relative solitude in the southern Midi region of France. In addition to painting, Bonnard made frequent use of color lithography, and illustrated books by French contemporaries such as Andre GIDE.

Bonnefoy, Yves (1923–). French poet, critic and scholar. After graduating from the University of Paris with a degree in philosophy, Bonnefoy traveled in Europe and the United States and studied art history. In 1954 *Du Mouvement et de l'immobilite de Douve* (translated in 1967 by Galway Kinnell as *On the Motion and Immobility of Douve*) immediately established him as a major poet. *Hier regnant desert* (1958) received the Prix de l'Express. *Pierre ecrite* (1965) included essays on poets and poetry. Bonnefoy is also acclaimed as a critic for his books on Rimbaud and Joan MIRO, as well as for his translations of Shakespeare. In 1971 he received the Prix des Critiques. Although Bonnefoy was heavily influenced by SURREALISM and the work of Paul VALERY, an interest in Hegel is also evident in his work.

Bonner, James Frederick (1910–). American biologist. Bonner received a degree in chemistry from the University of Utah in 1931 but turned to biology under the influence of Theodosius Dobzhansky. He received his Ph.D. from the California Institute of Technology in 1934, which was then becoming known as the main center for molecular biology. There he became interested in developmental biology and the question of why any one cell expresses only some genes of the chromosome complement of an organism. He discovered that histone, a protein associated with chromosomes, is responsible for shutting off gene activity, and that if the histone is removed then the repressed genes become functional again. He also discovered that certain hormones act by repressing and derepressing genes. Bonner has also conducted research on the artificial synthesis of ribonucleic acid (RNA) and studied ribosomes and mitochondria. In 1946 he became professor of biology at Cal Tech.

Bonnie and Clyde. Texas-born criminals **Bonnie Parker** (1910–34) and **Clyde Barrow** (1909–34) robbed filling stations, restaurants and banks throughout the Southwest in the early 1930s. Both were born into poverty. The two teamed up in 1930, joined by Clyde's brother Buck, his wife Blanche, gunman Ray Hamilton (who left the gang) and William Daniel Jones, who joined the group in 1932. Tireless publicity-seekers, they played to the press with snapshots and Bonnie's ballads of crime, and they became popular heros to some of the poverty-stricken victims of the GREAT DEPRESSION. Their fame and popularity notwithstanding, Bonnie and Clyde were vicious criminals who murdered 12 people during their rampage. They were killed in a Louisiana police ambush on May 23, 1934. Their story formed the basis for the award-winning 1967 film *Bonnie and Clyde.*

Bonn Pact. An international agreement, also known as the Bonn Convention, that provided for the end of the Allied occupation of WEST GERMANY and also made West Germany a member of the Western Alliance—in effect signalling the denazification of Germany and accepting the Western zone back into the community of nations. Signed on May 26, 1952, the Bonn Pact gave West Germany the right of complete self-determination in its domestic and foreign policies. The French, British and American troops stationed in Germany since the end of World War II

Bonnie Parker and Clyde Barrow—Bonnie and Clyde.

would no longer be there as an occupying force, but rather as a defender of Western Europe against possible Soviet aggression. Three years later, West Germany became a member of NATO.

Bonus Army. Popular name for a group of some 20,000 American veterans of WORLD WAR I who marched on Washington, D.C., in the spring of 1932 to demand payment of a bonus voted to them by Congress in 1921. This bonus was payable in 1945 but the men, mainly unemployed, many destitute and some literally starving as a result of the GREAT DEPRESSION, hoped to pressure Congress into passing an alternative bill. This legislation, submitted by Rep. Wright Patman, would have provided for an immediate lump-sum payment. Dubbed the Bonus Expeditionary Force, they camped at Anacostia Flats, Md., and peacefully demonstrated in favor of the bill. Although passed by the House, the bill was defeated in the Senate on June 17. While much of the army returned home, at least 5,000 men remained in their shantytown, demanding action. On July 28 President Herbert HOOVER, claiming that a communist conspiracy was involved, ordered federal troops under the command of General Douglas MACARTHUR to disperse the veterans. A bloody riot ensued in which the shantytown was burned to the ground and the marchers forcibly evicted from the city. Hoover was widely, although perhaps wrongly, blamed for this brutality. The episode is thought to have contributed to his defeat in the 1932 presidential elections.

Book of Common Prayer. See PRAYER BOOK CONTROVERSY.

Boothby, Lord (Robert John Graham) (1900–1986). British politician. An outspoken member of the CONSERVATIVE PARTY, Boothby spent 34 years in the House of Commons as a member representing East Aberdeenshire in Scotland, from 1924 to 1958, when he was created a life peer. He served as parliamentary private secretary to Winston CHURCHILL from 1926 to 1929, when Churchill was chancellor of the exchequer. Boothby's memoirs, published in 1978, presented a somewhat controversial portrait of Churchill.

Borah, William Edgar (1865–1940). U.S. senator. Born near Fairfield, Illinois, Borah was admitted to the bar in 1887. He was elected to the Senate as a Republican from Idaho in 1887 and served there until his death. Borah gained national attention in 1907 as prosecutor in the trial of William Haywood, accused of conspiracy to murder ex-Governor Frank Steurenberg. A political maverick, Borah's support of progressive reform was limited by his distrust of big government and devotion to states rights. He backed labor legislation, prohibition, the income tax and direct election of senators but opposed woman suffrage. Borah led the irreconcilables opposed to the LEAGUE OF NATIONS. He supported international action as long as military sanctions were not involved and hoped to achieve peace through international law. Borah was responsible for calling the WASHINGTON DISARMAMENT CONFERENCE in 1921 and played a major role in the development of the KELLOGG-BRIAND PACT in 1924. A chairman of the Senate Committee on Foreign Relations after 1924, he exercised enormous influence on foreign policy. An isolationist, he opposed U.S. intervention in WORLD WAR II until the end of his life. Borah supported many NEW DEAL measures but was a severe critic of the NATIONAL RECOVERY ADMINISTRATION and Franklin ROOSEVELT's attempt to pack the Supreme Court.

Borden, Sir Robert Laird (1954–1937). Canadian statesman, prime minister (1911–20). A teacher and lawyer, he was elected to Parliament from Halifax in 1896 and became leader of the Conservative opposition in 1901. When his party was victorious in the elections of 1911, he was made prime minister, a post he held throughout WORLD WAR I, and knighted in 1914. He was successful in preparing his nation for the war, sending about half a million soldiers to fight overseas. Head of a Conservative government for his first six years, he was returned to office in 1917 as the leader of a Union coalition. After the war and mainly through Borden's efforts, CANADA achieved separate representation at the PARIS PEACE CONFERENCE (1919) and in the LEAGUE OF NATIONS. He retired from office in 1920.

Bordet, Jules Jean Baptiste Vincent (1870–1961). Belgian immunologist. Bordet graduated in medicine from Brussels University in 1892 and in 1894 joined the Pasteur Institute, Paris, where he worked under the bacteriologist Elie Metchnikoff. In collaboration with Octave Gengou, Bordet discovered that in an immunized animal the antibodies produced by the immune response work in conjunction with another component of blood (which Bordet termed alexin but which is now called complement) to destroy foreign cells that invade the body. This component, Bordet found, was present in both immunized and nonimmunized animals and was destroyed by heating to over 55 degrees C. This work formed the basis of the **complement-fixation test,** a particularly sensitive means of detecting the presence of any specific type of cell or its specific antibody. A notable application of this was the test to detect syphilis devised by August von WASSERMANN. In 1901 Bordet left Paris to found and direct the Pasteur Institute in Brussels, and in 1907 he was appointed professor of pathology and bacteriology at Brussels University. In 1906 Bordet isolated the bacterium responsible for whooping cough, which is named after him: *Bordetella (Haemophilus) pertussis.* For his discovery of complement and other contributions to medicine, he was awarded the 1919 NOBEL PRIZE in physiology or medicine.

Borg, Bjorn (1956–). Swedish tennis player. Borg turned professional at the age of 14 and began winning major tournaments long before his 20th birthday. In 1975 he led Sweden to its first Davis Cup. Borg's methodical and emotionless style of play belied a competitive drive that led him to five successive Wimbledon singles championships (1976–80). His domination of the French Open was equally impressive, with four consecutive singles titles (1978–81) and six titles overall. In 1981 he won an unprecedented 41 singles matches until being defeated by a representative of tennis' next wave, John MCENROE. Borg retired to Monaco in 1983 but announced an attempted comeback in 1990. He was rumored to be experiencing financial difficulties.

Borges, Jorge Luis (1899–1986). Argentinian essayist, story writer and poet. Borges is one of the major figures of 20th-century literature—a master of maze-like plots and imaginative paradoxes. Born in Buenos Aires, Borges immigrated to Spain for a short time but has lived most of his life in his native city. In the 1920s, Borges focused on poetry. His stories and essays, for which he is best known, first began to appear in the 1930s. Much of the best of Borges' prose work can be found in two story collections, *Ficciones* (1944) and *The Aleph and Other Stories* (1949), and in a volume of selected essays, *Other Inquisitions* (1952). Many of his essays and stories take the form of an intricate commentary on another written text, real or imagined. Borges overcame the onset of blindness as a young man to become a prodigious reader and, at one time, director of the National Library of Argentina. Borges won the Prix International des Editeurs in 1961.

Borglum, John Gutzon de la Mothe (1867–1941). U.S. sculptor. Gutzon Borglum is best known as the creator of the gigantic Mount Rushmore sculpture of Presidents George Washington, Thomas Jefferson, Theodore ROOSEVELT and Abraham Lincoln. Borglum was an inventor, engineer and artist of international acclaim when he visited Custer State Park in 1924 to find a suitable site for a massive sculpture. He chose Mount Rushmore in the Black Hills of South Dakota. Using five-foot models of each figure, he multiplied every measurement by twelve in order to guide his workers in removing unnecessary stones (by using dynamite). He designed a "bosun chair" to lower workmen over the edge of the mountain. He worked tirelessly to raise money for the project. He even held a one-man strike, refusing to continue his part of the work until 1938, when an additional $300,000 in federal aid was authorized. He envisaged Mount Rushmore Hall of Records as the most elaborate national archive in the world. Due to overwork and failing health, he died in Chicago from a heart attack.

For further reading:

Fite, Gilbert C., *Mount Rushmore.* Norman: University of Oklahoma Press, 1984.
Zeitner, June C., *Borglum's Unfinished Dream—Mount Rushmore.* Aberdeen, S.D.: North Plains Press, 1976.

Bori, Lucrezia (1887–1960). Spanish singer. Known for her unique operatic style and clear soprano voice, Bori made her debut in Rome as Michaela in *Carmen* (1908).

She made a successful return to opera in 1919 after nodes were removed from her vocal chords. Appearing primarily with the Metropolitan Opera in New York City from 1921 until her retirement in 1936, Bori received acclaim for her performances as Mimi in *La Boheme* and Manon in *Manon Lescaut,* among other roles.

Boris III (1894–1943). King of BULGARIA (1918–43); as crown prince, he fought in WORLD WAR I, and succeeded to the throne at the abdication of his father, FERDINAND I. He was a constitutional ruler until 1935, when he formed a military dictatorship. He allied Bulgaria with the AXIS in 1940, but was unwilling to declare war on the Soviet Union. An angered Adolf HITLER summoned the king to a meeting in 1943, and Boris died mysteriously a few weeks later. He was succeeded by his six-year-old son, Simeon II, who ruled under the regency of Boris' brother Prince Cyril (1895–1945).

Bork, Robert H(eron) (1927–). American jurist and Supreme Court nominee. A graduate of the University of Chicago Law School, Bork taught law at Yale University during the 1960s and served as solicitor general of the U.S. (1973–77) under Presidents Richard M. NIXON and Gerald FORD. He gained prominence during the WATERGATE scandal, when as acting attorney general, he obeyed Nixon's order to fire special prosecutor Archibald COX (October 20, 1973) after Attorney General Elliot Richardson and his deputy, William Ruckelshaus, had refused to do so and resigned. Bork returned to Yale in 1977. In 1982 President Ronald REAGAN named Bork to the Court of Appeals in the District of Columbia. In this post and in his writings, Bork compiled a substantial record as a conservative thinker who emphasized the doctrine of "original intent" in his decisions. When Justice Lewis F. POWELL resigned from the Supreme Court in 1987, Reagan was determined to appoint a conservative to fill the vacancy. He chose Bork, whom he called a "prominent and intellectually powerful advocate of judicial restraint." The controversial appointment sparked a bitter debate between liberals and conservatives throughout the country. Democratic Senator Edward Kennedy and other Senate liberals led the fight against Bork's nomination, claiming that Bork was an extremist who would reverse the CIVIL RIGHTS decisions reached by the Court under Earl WARREN, as well as the 1973 ROE V. WADE decision on ABORTION. Many special interest groups also testified against Bork during his confirmation hearings. The Senate Judiciary Committee ultimately voted 9–5 to reject the nomination; the full senate voted 58–42 for rejection. One Republican senator who voted for Bork said that he had never seen "such an unjustified and untrammeled assault on a distinguished American citizen as I have witnessed in these last few weeks," and other supporters compared the clamor against Bork to the "witch hunts" of MCCARTHYISM.

For further reading:
Bork, Robert H., *The Tempting of America: The Political Seduction of the Law.* New York: Free Press, 1989.

Borlaug, Norman Ernest (1914–). American agronomist and plant breeder. He graduated in forestry from Minnesota University in 1937 and earned his Ph.D. in plant pathology in 1941. He then spent three years with the Du Pont Chemical Company, testing the effects of chemicals on plants and plant diseases. In 1944 he joined the newly formed International Maize and Wheat Improvement Center in Mexico and began the breeding work that was to produce the highly adaptable dwarf wheats that played so large a part in the Green Revolution of the late 1960s and early 1970s. Borlaug's high-yielding cereals increased agricultural production in the developing countries to the extent that many became self-sufficient for grain. For his major role in temporarily alleviating world famine, Borlaug was awarded the NOBEL PRIZE for peace in 1970.

Borman, Frank (1928–). U.S. astronaut and airline executive. As commander of Apollo 8 (December 21–27, 1968), Borman and fellow astronauts James Lovell and William Anders made 10 orbits of the moon, while Borman earned the dubious distinction of becoming the first U.S. astronaut to vomit in space (but certainly not the first to experience space sickness). He also found himself involved in an unusual controversy upon his return to Earth. At NASA's request, the three Apollo 8 crewmen had read passages from the Bible on a live Christmas Eve broadcast from lunar orbit. The act drew some angry protest and even a threatened legal suit to "stop the astronauts from broadcasting religious propaganda from space." Borman's only previous space flight had been aboard Gemini 7 (December 4–18, 1965), when he and copilot James Lovell joined up with Gemini 6–A and its crew of Wally Schirra and James Stafford for NASA's first space rendezvous; Borman and Lovell also went on to set a new space endurance record of 14 days. Borman retired from NASA in 1970 to join Eastern Airlines, becoming that firm's chairman of the board.

Bormann, Martin (1900–1945). German Nazi leader. An important figure in the inner circle of the National Socialist (Nazi) Party, Bormann was devoted to HITLER and became the Fuhrer's personal secretary in 1942. A master bureaucrat, he was not well known to the general public but wielded great power behind the scenes. Bormann disappeared in the final days of WORLD WAR II and was condemned in absentia by the NUREMBERG TRIALS of war criminals. In 1973, a skeleton unearthed in Berlin was positively identified as Bormann's; he had committed suicide on May 2, 1945. (See also NAZISM.)

Born, Max (1882–1970). German physicist. Born was educated at the universities of Breslau, Heidelberg, Zurich and Gottingen, where he obtained his Ph.D. in 1907. From 1909 until 1933 he taught at Gottingen, being appointed professor of physics in 1921. With the rise of HITLER he moved to Britain and from 1936 served as professor of natural philosophy at the University of Edinburgh, returning to Germany on his retirement in 1953. Born is noted for his role in the development of the new QUANTUM theory. Together with Pascual Jordan, he developed (1925) the matrix mechanics introduced by Werner HEISENBERG. He also showed how to interpret the theoretical results of Louis DE BROGLIE and the experiments of such people as Clinton J. DAVISSON, which showed that particles have wavelike behavior. Born shared the 1954 NOBEL PRIZE for physics with Walter BOTHE.

Borneo. Third largest island in the world, north of Java and south of the Philippines. Populated in the interior by the Dyaks and in its coastal areas by Malays, the topography ranges from swampy coastal chain to mountain to jungle. From the end of 1941 to 1945, during WORLD WAR II, it was occupied by Japanese forces. The region of Brunei (an enclave on the northwest coast of Borneo) is a British protectorate, while Kalimantan (the major part of the island) is now a part of Indonesia (after being held by the Dutch until 1949); the regions of Sabah and Sarawak (the northern and northwestern parts of the island) are now a part of MALAYSIA (after being held by the British until 1963).

Bosch, Carl (1874–1940). German industrial chemist. Bosch was trained as both metallurgist and chemist and earned his doctorate under Johannes Wislicenus at Leipzig (1898). He joined the large German dyestuffs company, *Badische Anilin und Soda Fabrik* (BASF), in 1899. Following Fritz Haber's successful small-scale ammonia synthesis in 1909, Bosch began to develop a high-pressure ammonia plant at Oppau for BASF. The plant was opened in 1912—a successful application on a large scale of the Haber process. Bosch also introduced the use of the water-gas shift reaction as a source of hydrogen for the process. After World War I the large-scale ammonia fertilizer industry was established, and in 1923 BASF extended the high-pressure technique to the synthesis of methanol from carbon monoxide and hydrogen. Bosch was chairman of BASF's successor, I.G. Farben (1935–40), and concurrently director of the Kaiser Wilhelm Institutes. He shared the NOBEL PRIZE for chemistry with Friedrich Bergius in 1931.

Bosch, Juan (1909–). President of the DOMINICAN REPUBLIC. Bosch lived in exile from 1937 to 1961 during the Dominican dictatorship of Rafael TRUJILLO. On Trujillo's assassination, Bosch returned home and was elected president in 1963. After seven months, however, he was removed from office by a right-wing military coup. His leftist supporters staged a countercoup in 1965, which was quelled by U.S. troops. Bosch ran for president again in 1966, but was defeated. On May 16, 1990, he lost another bid for reelection, to longtime rival Joaquin BALAGUER; Bosch claimed fraud, although an international panel proclaimed the elections honest.

Bose, Sir Jagadis Chandra (1858–1937). Indian plant physiologist and physicist. He began his studies in London as a medical student. He then won a scholarship to Cambridge University, from where he graduated in natural sciences in 1884. He was appointed professor of physical science at Presidency College, Calcutta, in 1885 and retained this post until 1915. In 1917 he founded and became director of the Bose Research Institute, Calcutta. He was knighted in 1917 and in 1920 became the first Indian to be elected a fellow of the Royal Society. Bose's early research was on the properties of very short radio waves. His most famous work concerned his investigations into plant physiology and the similarities between the behavioral response of plant and animal tissue. While his experimental skill was widely admired, at the time his work did not gain universal acceptance.

Bose, Satyendra Nath (1894–1974). Indian physicist. Bose was educated at Presidency College, Calcutta. Among his teachers was the eminent Indian physicist Jagadis Chandra BOSE. Bose held the post of lecturer at the Calcutta University College of Science from 1917 until he left in 1921 to become a reader in physics at the new University of Dacca in East Bengal. His work ranged over many aspects of physics, including statistical mechanics, the electromagnetic properties of the ionosphere, theories of X-ray crystallography and unified field theory. He is best know for his work in quantum statistics. Bose attracted the attention of Albert EINSTEIN and other European physicists by publishing an important scientific paper in 1924. Because of this work Bose was able to get two years' study leave in Europe. During his visit he came into contact with many of the great physicists of the day, such as Louis DE BROGLIE, Max BORN, and Einstein. Einstein's generalization of Bose's work led to the system of statistical QUANTUM mechanics now known as **Bose-Einstein statistics**.

Bosnia and Herzegovina. Province of Yugoslavia. A part of the AUSTRO-HUNGARIAN EMPIRE from 1878, the streets of the capital, SARAJEVO, witnessed perhaps the most fateful event of the 20th century. On June 28, 1914, Serbian nationalist Gavrilo Princip assassinated the heir to the imperial throne, Austria's Archduke FRANZ FERDINAND, triggering WORLD WAR I. In 1918, the region was united by Serbia with Slovenia, Croatia and Montenegro to form the Kingdom of Serbs, Croats and Slovenes, renamed YUGOSLAVIA in 1929. In 1946, Bosnia and Herzegovina were included within Yugoslavia as one of its six republics. Turmoil in Yugoslavia in the early 1990s made the province's future uncertain.

Boss, Lewis (1846–1912). American astronomer. Boss studied at Dartmouth College where he graduated in 1870. In 1872 he was appointed assistant astronomer to the 49th parallel survey for the American-Canadian boundary, accurately locating stations from which the surveyors could work with confidence. In 1876 Boss was appointed director of the Dudley Observatory, Albany, a post he held until his death in 1912. While working on the parallel survey Boss became aware of the many errors made in the measurement of stellar positions, which caused the current star catalogs to be inaccurate. He consequently made his own observations, publishing the positions of 500 stars in 1878. In 1910 he published the *Preliminary General Catalogue* containing the position and proper motion of 6,188 of the brighter stars, His work was extended by his son, **Benjamin Boss,** who published in 1937 the *General Catalogue* containing comparable details of 33,342 stars.

Boston police strike. Strike (1919) of uniformed Boston police officers in which then-Governor Calvin COOLIDGE called out the Massachusetts State Militia to keep order. In 1919 the vast majority of Boston police officers went out on strike after the police commissioner refused to recognize their right to join the American Federation of Labor (AFL). The result was a rash of crime, including near riots throughout the city. At the time, the police commissioner was appointed by the state governor, not the city's mayor. Before the walkout, the commissioner had ignored the pleas of the mayor to reach a compromise with the strikers. Governor Coolidge broke the strike by sending in the militia to restore order. All striking policemen were fired and replaced. Coolidge's forceful and well publicized action paved the way for his selection as Republican Warren HARDING's running mate in the 1920 presidential election—and his rise to the presidency on Harding's sudden death in 1923.

Botero, Fernando (1932–). Colombian painter. Botero is one of the most acclaimed Latin American painters of modern times. He has taken the bold social realism of precursor Latin American painters such as Diego RIVERA and transformed it into a wry and individualistic commentary on modern life. Botero's distinctive style features bizarre human figures who resemble overinflated dolls; these figures, often set in absurd and jangling urban situations, have a satirical, clownish impact. Botero is also renowned for his parodistic treatments of the themes of the Old Masters of the European painting tradition. Botero has lived and worked in New York and Paris and his works are featured in private collections and museums worldwide.

Botha, Louis (1862–1919). South African soldier and statesman, prime minister (1910–19). An Afrikaner and originally a farmer, he fought the British in the BOER WAR, rising to become a commanding general in the Transvaal (1900) and later leading guerrilla forces. Assuming a more moderate stance after the war, he strived for reconciliation, becoming prime minister of the Transvaal from 1907 to 1910. He worked toward the creation of the Union of SOUTH AFRICA, and became its first prime minister in 1910. In WORLD WAR I, Botha joined the Allies, suppressing a pro-German Boer revolt and, in 1915, sending South African troops into Germany's South West Africa colony. Just prior to his death, Botha participated in the Paris Peace Conference (1919) and signed the Treaty of Versailles.

Botha, P(ieter) W. (1916–). President of SOUTH AFRICA (1984–89). Botha held various federal government offices from 1958 to 1978. He led the ruling **National Party** from 1978 to 1989. Prime minister from 1978 to 1984, he became state president when a constitutional change was introduced in 1984. Although a conservative, he introduced cautious reforms in the APARTHEID system. Caught between increasing international opposition toward South Africa and the diehard reactionaries in his party, he resigned in 1989 following a stroke, and was succeeded by the more moderate F.W. DE KLERK.

Bothe, Walther Wilhelm Georg Franz (1891–1957). German atomic physicist. Bothe studied at the University of Berlin under Max Planck and received his Ph.D. in 1914. For the next few years he was a PRISONER OF WAR in Russia. On his return to Germany in 1920, he taught at Berlin and worked in Hans GEIGER's radioactivity laboratory. He devised the "coincidence method" of detecting the emission of electrons by X rays in which electrons passing through two adjacent Geiger tubes at almost the same time are registered as a coincidental event. He used it to show that momentum and energy are conserved at the atomic level. In 1929 he applied the method to the study of cosmic rays and was able to show that they consisted of massive particles rather than photons. For this research he shared the 1954 NOBEL PRIZE for physics with Max BORN. By 1930 his reputation was established and he was appointed professor of physics at Giessen. While director of the Max Planck Institute in Heidelberg, Bothe supervised the construction of Germany's first cyclotron. This work was finished in 1943. During WORLD WAR II he led German scientists in their search for atomic energy. When the war ended he was given the chair of physics at Heidelberg, which he retained until his death.

Botswana. Nation in central part of southern Africa. Formerly known as Bechuanaland, it is without a seacoast and is populated primarily by the Botswana, a Bantu people who migrated here centuries ago. In 1885, to counter German power in Africa, the British claimed northern Bechuanaland as a protectorate and made southern Bechuanaland a crown colony (which was annexed to Britain's Cape Colony in 1895). According to the constitution of independent South Africa, drafted in 1909, all of Bechuanaland was to become a part of that nation. But the British maintained their rule over Bechuanaland until 1965, when general elections were conducted and a constitution enacted. Gabarone replaced Mafeking as capital, and full independence was granted to the newly named Botswana in 1966. Its first leader was Sir Seretse Khama. Large deposits of copper, diamonds and nickel spurred the

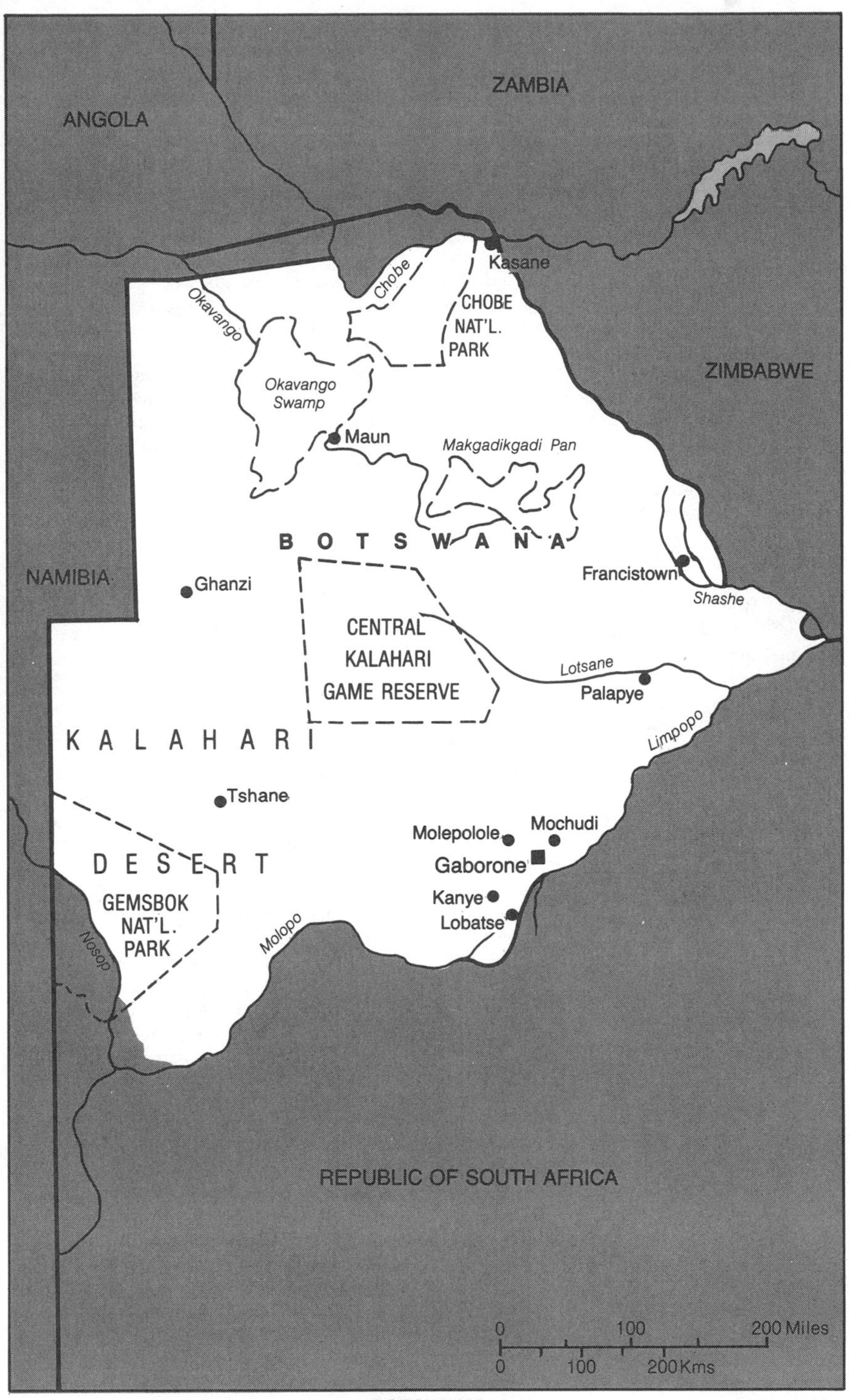

BOTSWANA

new nation's economy. While maintaining relations with white-ruled South Africa, Botswana sought to forge strong ties with its black African neighbors. On Botswana's northwest border, Rhodesia (now ZIMBABWE) became a source of tension during its own struggle for independence; Rhodesian forces invaded Botswana repeatedly during the 1970s in search of Zimbabwe nationalist guerrillas.

Botvinnik, Mikhail Moiseyevich (1911–). Soviet chess player. Born near St. Petersburg, Botvinnik studied electrical engineering at Leningrad Polytechnic. He began playing chess at the age of 12 and won his first Soviet championship in 1931. Beginning to play in international chess tournaments in the 1930s, he became the first preeminent Soviet chess master. A wily strategist who relished difficulty, Botvinnik was world chess champion three times, from 1948 to 1957, 1958 to 1960 and 1961 to 1963, and is considered one of the chess world's all-time greats.

Botwood. Canadian town in northwestern Newfoundland; formerly known as Botwoodville. In 1939, it was a fuel stop for the first transatlantic flying boat operation; also an air base during WORLD WAR II.

Boudreau, Louis "Lou" (1917–). American baseball player. Boudreau was named playing manager of the Cleveland Indians at the age of 24, the youngest ever to hold that position. He led that team to the American League pennant and a victory in the World Series in 1948, a year in which he was also the league's Most Valuable Player, with a .355 batting average. He was named All-Star shortstop seven times, and was the American League batting champion in 1944. After his retirement as a manager in 1960, he went into a successful career in broadcasting. He was named to the Hall of Fame in 1970.

Boue, Michel (1936–1971). French automobile designer, Boue's brief career with the French manufacturer Renault centered on the development of the Renault 5, or R5 (known in the U.S. as Le Car) in 1972, an economical front-wheel-drive compact car of simple and logical form. The design is notable for its consistency and unity, a reflection of its development by a single person of exceptional talent.

Bougainville Island. In the southwestern Pacific Ocean. Created by volcanic activity, Bougainville was discovered by Europeans in 1768 and placed under German control in 1898. During WORLD WAR I, it was occupied by Australian forces, and during WORLD WAR II it was conquered by the Japanese. After the war, it was returned to Australia, but after considerable secessionist activity, it became a part of Papua New Guinea when the latter became independent in 1975. Its main export is copper ore.

Boulanger, Nadia (1887–1979). French pianist, composition teacher and conductor. A student of Gabriel FAURE, she abandoned a career as a pianist to ultimately become one of the most influential teachers of musical composition, harmony and counterpoint in the 20th century. In the 1920s and 1930s, as her reputation grew,

Nadia Boulanger.

many young American composers flocked to Paris to study with her; among her most celebrated pupils were Aaron COPLAND, Roy HARRIS and Walter PISTON, as well as the British composer Lennox BERKELEY. Boulanger was the first woman to conduct the New York Philharmonic, the Boston Symphony, the Philadelphia Orchestra and London's Royal Philharmonic. She taught at the Paris Conservatory, and for 30 years directed the American Conservatory of Music at Fontainebleu.

For further reading:
Monsaingeon, Bruno, *Mademoiselle: Conversations with Nadia Boulanger*. Manchester: Carcanet, 1985.

Boulanger, Pierre (1886–1950). French engineer who became chief of the CITROEN automobile firm in 1935. He was the person responsible for the development of the Traction Avant, 2CV, ID, and DS models that made Citroen the leader in innovative automobile design from the 1930s until recent years. It is said that Boulanger's insistence that the driver's seat of the DS accommodate him wearing a hat (and he was tall) led to the exceptionally spacious design of the car's interior.

Boulder Dam. See HOOVER DAM.

Boulez, Pierre (1925–). French composer and conductor. Born near Lyons, he studied at the Paris Conservatoire with Olivier MESSIAEN during 1944–45 and learned the 12-tone system from Rene Liebowitz in 1946. A musical rebel, Boulez went beyond Arnold SCHOENBERG in the techniques of SERIAL MUSIC, which rejects traditional melody, tonality, harmony, pitch and rhythm. Rigorously intellectual, difficult to perform and often unpopular with traditional classical audiences, his avant-garde compositions include *Le Soleil des eaux* (1948), *Symphonie concertante* (1950), *Le Marteau sans maitre* (1953–54), *Eclat* (1965), *Domaines* (1968) and *Memoriales* (1975). Boulez has acted as an advocate for avant-garde music, directing Jean-Louis BARRAULT's company, organizing (1954) the "Domaine musicale" concerts in Paris, stressing avant-garde compositions throughout his career as a conductor and becoming deeply involved with electronic and computer-generated music. He has led major symphony orchestras throughout the world, serving as principal guest conductor of the Cleveland Orchestra (1970–71), as music director of London's BBC Symphony Orchestra (1971–75) and of the New York Philharmonic (1971–76) and, since 1976, as director of the Institut de Recherche et de Coordination Acoustique/Musique in Paris.

Pierre Boulez in his first season as music director of the New York Philharmonic (1971).

For further reading:
Stacey, Peter F., *Boulez and the Modern Concept*. Lincoln: University of Nebraska Press, 1987.

Boulogne [Boulogne-sur-Mer]. Port city on France's English Channel coast, in the Pas-de-Calais department. During WORLD WAR II, it was used as a German submarine base and as part of the West Wall German defensive strategy.

Boult, Sir Adrian (Cedric) (1889–1983). British conductor. Born in Chester, Boult studied at Oxford and in Leipzig. Returning to England in 1913, he made his conducting debut the following year. Boult conducted throughout Europe and the U.S., leading the Birmingham City Symphony (1924–30), the BBC Symphony Orchestra (1930–50) and the London Philharmonic (1950–57). He also had a distinguished teaching career at the Royal College of Music. Knighted in 1937, Boult was a tireless champion of 20th-century English music. Among the world premieres he conducted were Gustav HOLST's *The Planets* (1919), Sir Michael TIPPETT's Symphony No. 2 (1958) and several works by Ralph VAUGHAN WILLIAMS, including the *Pastoral* Symphony (1922) and three other symphonies. A modest and self-effacing conductor, Boult believed in adhering to the letter of the score and refrained from imposing his personal interpretation on any music he performed. His autobiography, *My Own Trumpet*, was published in 1973.

Boulting Brothers. British filmmakers. Twin brothers Roy (1913–85) and John (1913–) were a major force in postwar British filmmaking and wrote, produced and directed more than 30 films, many of them comedies. They lampooned such venerable British institutions as the armed forces (*Private's Progress*, 1955), labor unions (*I'm All Right, Jack*, 1959) and the Church of England (*Heavens Above!*, 1963).

Boumedienne, Houari (1925–1978). President of ALGERIA (1965–78). A soldier, he joined the Front de Liberation Nationale in the war against FRANCE in 1955. Appointed minister of defense in 1962 by President BEN BELLA, he led a coup that overthrew Ben Bella in 1965. President of Algeria from 1965 until his death in 1978, he was responsible for the Four Year Plan (1969–73), which developed industry, reformed agriculture and nationalized French oil interests.

Bourbaki, Nicolas. French group of mathematicians. "Nicolas Bourbaki" is the collective pseudonym of a group of some of the most outstanding of contemporary mathematicians. The precise membership of Bourbaki, which has changed over the years, is a closely guarded secret, but it is known that most of the members are French. Since 1939 Bourbaki has been publishing a monumental work, the *Elements de mathematique* (*Elements of Mathematics*), of which over 30 volumes have so far appeared. In this Bourbaki attempts to expound and display the architecture of the whole mathematical edifice starting from certain carefully chosen logical and set-theoretic concepts. As the members are all working mathematicians rather than pure logicians, the influence of Bourbaki's writings on contemporary mathematicians and their conception of the subject has been immense.

Bourguiba, Habib [Muhammad Boukharouba] (1903–). President of TUNISIA (1957–87). A member of the Destour Party from 1921, he split away to form the Neo-Destour Party in 1934. Imprisoned by the French from 1934 to 1936 and from 1938 to 1943, he lived outside Tunisia from 1946 to 1949. On his return to Tunisia he was again imprisoned (1952–54). Prime minister in 1956 when Tunisia became independent, he was elected president in 1957.

Bourke-White, Margaret (1906–1971). American photographer. Bourke-White is famous for capturing in pictures many of the major events of the first half of this century. Initially an industrial photographer for *Fortune* magazine (1929–33), she gained international recognition as a photographer for LIFE magazine (1936–69). Her photo-essay books include *Eyes on Russia* (1931) and *Halfway to Freedom: A Study of the New India* (1949). Briefly married to novelist Erskine CALDWELL (1939–42), she collaborated with him on several books, including *North of the Danube* (1939).

For further reading:
Goldberg, Vicki, *Margaret Bourke-White: A Biography*. Reading, Massachusetts: Addison-Wesley, 1987.

Boussac, Marcel (1889–1980). French textile magnate. After World War I Boussac built a $150 million financial empire that at its peak included 65 textile mills, the fashion house of Christian DIOR, thoroughbred racing stables and the right-wing Paris newspaper *L'Aurore*. During this time Boussac was known as the "King of Cotton" in France. In the 1960s and '70s, however, faced with increasing foreign competition and a lack of modern management and facilities, his textile empire declined.

Bouton, James "Jim" [Bulldog] (1939–). American baseball player. Although Bouton enjoyed a respectable career as a pitcher, making the All-Star team in 1963 with a 21–7 record and a 2.53 ERA, he is best-known for his controversial book *Ball Four*. The book exposed baseball players as people with human foibles and, occasionally, unhealthy off-the-field habits. While it seems mild by today's standards, its 1969 publication unleashed a furor in the baseball establishment and the baseball press. Bouton's early career with the Yankees (1962–64) gave him a World Series win as well as material about some of baseball's most revered figures, including Mickey MANTLE. He converted to the knuckleball in 1968, and played with a variety of expansion teams before retiring in 1975. He tried a comeback in 1977, and finally retired in 1978.

Bovet, Daniel (1907–). Swiss-Italian pharmacologist who was responsible for developing many of the medical drugs taken for granted in the 20th century. Educated at the University of Geneva, Bovet worked at the Pasteur Institute in Paris in the 1930s and was able to isolate sulfanilamide, which destroys streptococcal bacteria both in the body and in laboratory cultures. This work led to the production of the first "wonder drug" that worked directly against the cause of a disease. Bovet later synthesized many drugs derived from sulfanilamide, creating an entire family of sulfa drugs. He also developed the first antihistimine; his work in this field laid the groundwork for virtually all the antihistimines that are now available. Bovet moved to Rome in 1947 and became an Italian citizen. He next worked on the drug curare, a muscle relaxant derived from plants in the South American jungles. He helped to develop synthetic curare for use in surgery. For this work, Bovet was awarded the 1957 NOBEL PRIZE for physiology or medicine. During the 1960s, Bovet investigated the possible chemical causes and treatments of mental illness. In addition to his Nobel Prize, Bovet has received numerous other awards and honors.

Bow, Clara (1905–1965). HOLLYWOOD film star who personified the independent, 1920s JAZZ AGE woman or "flapper." Known as the "It" girl because of her sexual appeal; Bow's clothes, hairstyle and makeup were copied by women everywhere. In films such as *Mantrap* (1926), *It* (1927) and *Roughhouse Rosie* (1927), she played a madcap emancipated woman in search of money, a handsome man and a good time. A scandal in the early 1930s involving adultery, bribery and drugs brought an early end to her career.

Bowen, Edmund John (1898–). British physical chemist. Bowen spent his entire career at Oxford University, beginning in 1915 as a student at Balliol College and continuing after graduation as a fellow of University College from 1922 until his retirement in 1965. He worked mainly on photochemistry, investigating a large number of photochemical reactions and producing a survey of the subject, *Chemical Aspects of Light* (1942).

Bowen, Elizabeth (Dorothea Cole) (1899–1973). Anglo-Irish author. Born in Dublin, Bowen spent much of her early childhood in County Cork and was educated at Downe House School in Kent, England. Orphaned at 13, she was shuttled between relatives in England and Ireland; her resulting sense of displacement is reflected in her fiction. In 1918 she moved to LONDON, which is a moody, vividly described, additional "character" in much of her later work. A prolific short story writer, her first collection, *Encounters,* was published in 1923. Of her novels, perhaps best known are *The Death of the Heart* (1938), the story of an orphaned young woman sent to live with relatives in London, where she has her first experience with love; and *The Heat of the Day* (1949). Wartime London served as inspiration to some of her best work, and in the introduction to *The Collected Stories of Elizabeth Bowen* (1981) novelist Angus Wilson called her one of "two English writers who convey what life in blitzed London was like."

For further reading:

Bowen, Elizabeth, *Bowen's Court.* New York: Ecco Press, 1979; first printed 1942.
Glendinning, Victoria, *Elizabeth Bowen.* New York: Knopf, 1986.

Bowen, Ira Sprague (1898–1973). American atronomer. Bowen graduated from Oberlin College in 1919 and earned his Ph.D. from the California Institute of Technology in 1926. He taught physics at Cal Tech from 1921 to 1945, serving from 1931 as professor. In 1946 he was made director of the Mount Wilson Observatory and, in 1948, of the newly opened Palomar Observatory, posts he held until his retirement in 1964.

Bowers, Claude (1878–1958). U.S. diplomat, journalist and historian. He performed editorial duties for newspapers in Indianapolis, Terre Haute and Fort Wayne, Indiana. He delivered the keynote address to the 1928 Democratic convention in Houston, Texas. He was appointed ambassador to SPAIN in 1933, but resigned his position in 1939 when the United States recognized Francisco FRANCO's regime. He was appointed as ambassador to CHILE, where he served until his retirement in 1953. His writings include *The Party Battles of the Jackson Period* (1922), *The Tragic Era, A History of Reconstruction* (1929) and *Chile Through Embassy Windows* (1958).

Bowie, David (1947–). British ROCK and roll musician and actor. Bowie has maintained a steady popularity with rock and roll listeners for two decades, largely through his ability to create a range of fascinating styles and stage personae. Bowie was one of the first new rock stars to emerge in the 1970s. A 1972 album, "The Rise and Fall of Ziggy Stardust and the Spiders from Mars," coupled with a promotional concert tour, portrayed Bowie as an orange-haired, beglittered, androgynous, alien rock and roller. Bowie borrowed from disco for his 1975 "Young Americans" album, which included his first number one hit, "Fame." The title track of his 1983 album "Let's Dance" also climbed to number one on the charts. By 1990, Bowie's musical image was that of a gaunt, jaded rock aristocrat. He has appeared in a number of films, notably *The Man Who Fell To Earth* (1976), and also starred in a 1980s Broadway run of *The Elephant Man.*

Bowles, Chester (Bliss) (1901–1986). U.S. public official. Bowles held high posts in four Democratic administrations and personified the liberal wing of the DEMOCRATIC PARTY in the 1950s and 1960s. He came to public service after a successful career in advertising, having been a founding partner of the Benton & Bowles agency. During World War II, after serving as head of the Connecticut Office of Price Administration, Bowles was made director of the national Office of Price Administration (1943). After the war he served briefly as director of the Office of Economic Stabilization. In 1948 he was elected governor of Connecticut but was defeated in 1950. The following year he was appointed ambassador to INDIA, where he served until 1953. From 1959 to 1961 he served in the U.S. House of Representatives. As chairman of the Democratic platform committee during the 1960 presidential race, he led the fight for a strong CIVIL RIGHTS plank and for a vigorous policy of foreign aid. In 1961 President John F. KENNEDY appointed Bowles undersecretary of state. From 1963 to 1969 he was again ambassador to India. Bowles wrote several books, including *Ambassador's Report* (1954).

Bowles, Jane (1917–1973). American novelist, story writer and playwright. Bowles, who was born in New York, lived abroad—primarily in Tangiers, Morocco, with husband Paul BOWLES—for most of her creative career. Bowles first gained a reputation in avant-garde literary circles with her experimental novel *Two Serious Ladies* (1943), which concerned two women, one prosperous and conventional, the other sensuous and defiant, whose lives touch obliquely on two occasions. This novel showed the influence of Gertrude STEIN. Bowles' play *In the Summer House* (1954) received critical acclaim during its New York run. *Plain Pleasures* (1966) is a representative selection of Bowles' stories. A posthumous collection, *Feminine Wiles* (1976), includes stories, sketches and letters.

Bowles, Paul (1910–). American novelist, short story writer and composer. Bowles, an expatriate who has lived in Morocco for the past four decades, is regarded as one of the finest short story writers of the 20th century, a master of an incisive style that depicts psychological horror with absolute precision. Born in Long Island, Bowles studied musical composition as a young man with Aaron COPLAND. Throughout the 1930s, Bowles devoted himself to music (including numerous theater scores) and music criticism. In the 1940s, he turned to fiction and won critical acclaim for his first novel, *The Sheltering Sky* (1949), and a story collection, *The Delicate Prey* (1950). The themes examined in these works—the impersonal cruelty of nature, and the gulf between Western cultural values and the stark realities of North African life—have remained dominant in Bowles' subsequent works, which have included forays into travel writing, autobiography and translation. His *Collected Stories* (1976) contains much of the best of Bowles' work. His wife Jane BOWLES was also a highly regarded fiction writer.

Paul Bowles was cofounder of the literary journal *Antaeus*.

For further reading:

Bowles, Paul, *Without Stopping: An Autobiography*. New York: Putnam, 1972.

Boxer, Mark [Marc] (1931–1988). British editor, cartoonist and satirist. Boxer's witty, savage cartoons, which he drew under the pen name Marc, appeared in nearly all British newspapers, including the *Times*, the *Guardian*, the *Observer* and the *Daily Telegraph*. A cartoonist in the tradition of Max BEERBOHM and Oscar Lancaster, he was famous for his creation of a social-climbing couple, the Stringalongs. The first editor of the *Sunday Times* magazine, he was later editor of *Tatler* and editorial director of Conde Nast Publications Ltd.

Boxer Uprising (1899–1901). A secret organization in the Chinese government, the Society of the Righteous Harmonious Fists (Boxers) led an uprising against foreign missionaries and their converts. Britain, France, Italy, Germany, Russia and the U.S. sent military forces to Tientsin and Peking to protect their legations. China's Empress Dowager Tz'u Hsi, supporting the boxers, ordered death to all foreigners. An international expedition subdued the Boxers and captured Peking and the Imperial City, sending the Empress Dowager fleeing, while the Russians occupied southern Manchuria. The Boxer Protocol, signed by China, the western nations and Japan, compelled Chinese reparations payments and established "extraterritorial" rights for foreign powers in China.

Boycott, Geoffrey (1940–). English cricket player. A controversial cricketer, Boycott scored more runs than any other Englishman in Test cricket, but piled up as many critics as he did runs. Noted for his strict discipline at the wicket, Boycott built his innings slowly. He was often accused of playing for himself and that his slow scoring rate was detrimental to the team. Boycott's career statistics place him in the uppermost echelon of batsmen. His 8,114 runs from 108 Tests lead all Englishmen and place him third all-time. During his first-class career (1962–86), he scored 48,426 runs at an average of 56.83. He was one of the few men to have scored 100 centuries, accomplishing the feat in a Test versus Australia on his home ground at Headingley. Boycott played his entire county career for Yorkshire, captaining the side for eight seasons.

Boyd, William Clouser (1903–). American biochemist. Boyd was educated at Harvard and Boston University where he obtained his Ph.D. in 1930 and later taught in the medical school, serving as professor of immunochemistry from 1948 until his retirement in 1969. Karl Landsteiner's discovery of blood groups in 1902 and subsequent studies of their global distribution permitted a far more accurate estimate of racial types than had previously been possible. To this end Boyd began the systematic collection and analysis of blood samples from all over the world. Eventually in the 1950s in such works as *Genetics and the Races of Man* (1950) he began to present evidence for the existence of 13 races—early European, northern and eastern European, Lapp, Mediterranean, African, Asian, Dravidian, Amerind, Indonesian, Melanesian, Polynesian and Australian aborigine.

Boyd Orr, John (1880–1971). British nutritionist, agricultural scientist and educator. Born in Scotland, he attended the University of Glasgow and was a professor of agriculture at the University of Aberdeen from 1942 to 1945. He was the author of a number of influential books on nutrition including *The National Food Supply* (1934), *Food, Health and Income* (1936) and *Food and the People* (1943). Boyd Orr served as the first director general of the United Nations Food and Agriculture Organization, playing a leading role in dealing with post-World War II famine. His United Nations work was largely responsible for his being awarded the 1949 NOBEL PRIZE for peace. Boyd Orr was knighted in 1935 and made a baron in 1949. Vitally concerned with world food problems, he was also an ardent internationalist who favored world government and served as president of the World Federalist Movement.

The debonair Charles Boyer (1942).

Boyer, Charles (1897–1978). French-born actor and movie star, known as "the Great Lover" because of his romantic appeal. Boyer acted in romantic films opposite most of HOLLYWOOD's leading ladies in

Painting by Sgt. John Clymer, USMC, depicting battle between Boxers and U.S. Marines outside Peking Legation.

the 1930s and 1940s. A graduate of the Sorbonne and the Paris Conservatory, he established his reputation on the French stage in the 1920s. He also appeared in some films at this time. His first films in Hollywood in the early 1930s were unsuccessful. However, his films later in the 1930s won larger audiences. He became a star in America in *Algiers* (1938), the film in which he supposedly uttered the line, "Come with me to the Casbah." (In fact, he never said this.) In 1945 he had the highest salary of any star at WARNER BROS. For many years, American audiences regarded Boyer as the archetypal romantic Frenchman, charming, elegant and sophisticated. Later in his career he turned to character roles, and continued to act in films until 1976. He committed suicide two days after his wife died.

Boyer, Herbert Wayne (1936–). American biochemist. He was educated at St. Vincent College in Latrobe, Penna., and the University of Pittsburgh, where he obtained his Ph.D. in 1963. He joined the faculty of the University of California, San Francisco, in 1966 and has served since 1976 as professor of biochemistry. Much of Boyer's work has been concerned with developing some of the basic techniques of recombinant DNA, known more popularly as GENETIC ENGINEERING. In 1973 he succeeded with Robert Helling, and independently of the work of Stanley Cohen and Annie Chang, in constructing functional DNA from two different sources. By 1976 Boyer and others realized that recombinant DNA could be used to produce such important proteins as INSULIN, INTERFERON and growth hormone in commercial quantities. Consequently in 1976 he joined with financier Robert Swanson to invest $500 each to form the company Genentech, which went public in 1980.

Boyington, Gregory "Pappy" (1912–1988). U.S. Marine WORLD WAR II flying ace. Boyington began the war with the FLYING TIGERS in China. From September 1943 to January 1944 he commanded Fighter Squadron 214, known as the Black Sheep, in the SOLOMON ISLANDS. During the war he downed 28 Japanese warplanes, a Marine pilot record. He was shot down over New Guinea in January 1944 and spent the rest of the war in Japanese captivity. For his exploits, he was awarded the Medal of Honor and the Navy Cross. His 1958 autobiography, *Baa Baa Black Sheep,* was the basis of a 1970s television series.

Boyle, William Anthony "Tony" (1904–1985). American labor leader. Born in Bald Butte, Mont., "Tony" Boyle was, like his father, a coal miner in the American West. Joining the United Mine Workers Of America (UMW) in 1922, he rose quickly in the ranks. International vice president of the UMW from 1960 to 1963 and a protege of the powerful John L. LEWIS, he became union president in 1963. For the remainder of the decade he maintained dictatorial control over the burgeoning union and was widely charged with corruption and nepotism. In the 1969 election he was challenged by "Jock" YABLONSKI. Two weeks before the election the Labor Department issued a damning report regarding the UMW's finances. When Boyle was reelected, Yablonski charged vote rigging. Shortly thereafter he, his wife and daughter were murdered. After the killings, the Department of Labor and the FBI began extensive investigations. In 1972 the Labor Department invalidated the 1969 election. The following year Boyle was convicted of illegal use of union funds, and in 1975 he was sentenced to life in prison for conspiring to murder the Yablonski family.

Boys Town. Also known as Father FLANAGAN's home for homeless boys. Established in 1917 by Father Edward J. Flanagan, it started in an old house in Omaha, Nebraska, but soon moved to the larger German Civic Center. Fund-raising led to the purchase of the present land, where wooden shelters were built. The home was incorporated as a village in 1936. The name of the institution spread with the popular 1938 motion picture *Boys Town.* Today most of the buildings on the 320-acre facility are of sturdy red brick construction. Over 10,000 boys may be counted as "alumni." The place now gives shelter to both boys and girls.

Brachet, Jean Louis Auguste (1909–). Belgian cell biologist. Brachet was educated at the Free University of Brussels where his father, an embryologist, was rector. After earning his M.D. in 1934 he joined the faculty as an anatomy instructor and in 1943 was appointed professor of general biology. Brachet began his career by studying the then poorly understood nucleic acids. In 1933 he demonstrated that DNA and RNA occur in both plant and animal cells. In 1942 he proposed the important hypothesis that ribonucleoprotein granules could be the agents of protein synthesis. Later experiments, in which Brachet removed the nucleus from the cell, showed that although protein synthesis continued for a while, the amount of RNA in the cytoplasm decreased until there was none left. This indicated that RNA production occurs in the nucleus and that it is then transported from the nucleus to the cytoplasm.

Bracken, Brendan (1901–1958). British politician. Bracken was educated at Sedbergh and was later publisher of the *Financial Times* and other periodicals. He entered Parliament as a Conservative in 1929 and became minister of information in 1941. During WORLD WAR II, Bracken was one of Winston CHURCHILL's closest advisors, and in 1945 he served briefly as first lord of the admiralty.

Bradbury, Ray (Douglas) (1920–). American fantasy and science fiction writer whose work is characterized by poetic impulse and allegory rather than hard technology. Born in Waukegan, Ill., in 1934 Bradbury moved with his family to Los Angeles. His enthusiasm for science fiction led to the creation of his own magazine, *Futuria Fantasia* (1939), and his first story sales in 1941. He soon published stories in such quality magazines as *Colliers* and *The Saturday Evening Post.* His short story collection *Dark Carnival* (1947) and subsequent books—*The Martian Chronicles* (1950), *Fahrenheit 451* (1953) and *Dandelion Wine* (1957)—established his reputation with readers and critics alike. These remain his most important works, although his later output, while uneven, continues unabated. An author of screenplays (notably *Moby Dick* for John HUSTON, 1957), poetry collections and musical plays, he also hosted his own television

Ray Bradbury, surrounded by toys, prepares for the 1986 debut of his cable television series "The Ray Bradbury Theater."

anthology program, "The Ray Bradbury Theater." His work has appeared in over 800 anthologies, and his name has become synonymous with the modern weird tale. His main themes may be grouped around two frequent locations for his works—Green Town, Ill. (a fictional reworking of his hometown) and the planet Mars. The former is the abode of childhood nostalgia and terror; the latter is the arena where the technology and poetry of mankind clash in an ongoing struggle. Bradbury's prose shows a distinctive flair for unusual metaphors and symbolic imagery, although in his later works it tends to become inflated. He himself prefers *Dandelion Wine* to all his works. Its deeply felt emotion and wonder about childhood may be taken as autobiographical.

For further reading:

Nolan, William F., *The Bradbury Companion*. Detroit: Gale Research Co., 1974.

Braddock, James J. (1905–1974). American boxer. Born and raised in New York City, Braddock began his professional career in 1926 and for three years was undefeated until he lost the light-heavyweight title to Tommy Loughran in 1929. He then suffered several years of defeats and retired in 1933 after breaking both hands in a match. After two years as a dockworker, he attempted a comeback and in 1935 defeated the favorite Max Baer for the heavyweight title. This upset earned him the nickname "Cinderella Man." In 1937 he lost the title to a young Joe LOUIS.

Bradlee, Benjamin (1921–). American journalist and editor. Born in Boston, Bradlee graduated from Harvard University in 1942 and served in the Navy during World War II. An appointment as press attache in the American embassy in Paris was followed by a post as European correspondent for *Newsweek* magazine from 1953 to 1957. Bradlee then went to *Newsweek*'s Washington, D.C., bureau where he was named bureau chief in 1961. Four years later he joined the *Washington Post*, where he was appointed executive editor in 1968. He presided over major investigative stories, including the *Post*'s epoch-making coverage of the WATERGATE scandal. Known for his tough, exacting editorial standards, Bradlee is also the author of *That Special Grace* (1964) and *Conversations with Kennedy* (1975).

Bradley, Francis H(erbert) (1846–1924). British philosopher. Bradley was one of the most influential British philosophers of the Idealist school, which allowed an ultimate reality to nonmaterial concepts. As a metaphysician, Bradley was greatly influenced by German Idealist thought, most notably the works of Georg Hegel. A fellow of Merton College, Oxford, Bradley's works include *Ethical Studies* (1876), *Appearance and Reality* (1893) and *Essays on Truth and Reality* (1914). The poet and critic T.S. ELIOT devoted his youthful master's thesis at Harvard University to Bradley. Eliot later acknowledged that Bradley had greatly influenced his own prose style.

Bradley, Jenny (1886–1983). Belgian-born literary agent. During the 1920s and '30s she was an agent for such eminent authors as James JOYCE, Gertrude STEIN, and F. Scott FITZGERALD. She and her husband acted as a liaison between authors and publishers in New York City and Paris, acquiring options on leading French writers including Andre GIDE, Andre MALRAUX, and Antoine de SAINT-EXUPERY for American publishers.

Bradley, Omar Nelson (1893–1981). U.S. Army general. After graduating from West Point, he served in WORLD WAR I. In 1943 he took command of the Second Corps and played an important role in the invasions of North Africa and Sicily. EISENHOWER chose him to lead the Allied invasion of Normandy in 1944 (see D-DAY). Later the same year, he was placed in command of the Twelfth Army, the largest ever to be led by a single American field commander. In 1945 he received the four stars of a full general. He was the principal figure in Allied operations in the battle to take GERMANY. He served as Army chief of staff from 1948 to 1949, and became first chairman of the Joint Chiefs of Staff, from 1949 to 1953. In 1950 he was promoted to the five-star rank of General of the Army. He retired to a business career in 1953. Among the many commendations earned by Bradley were the Distinguished Service Medal, Silver Star, Bronze Star, Presidential Medal of Freedom and Grand Cross Legion of Honor.

Bradman, Sir Donald (1908–). Australian cricketer, widely regarded as the greatest batsman in cricket history. Bradman holds the record for the highest batting average in Test matches, 99.94 (6,996 runs in 70 innings). He played 52 Tests for Australia from 1928 to 1948, captaining the side 24 times (1936–48). Among his many other batting feats, Bradman holds the record for the fastest double century in Test cricket: 214 minutes from 259 balls, scored on July 11, 1930, for Australia v. England. In this innings he went on to score 334 runs, the fifth highest score in Test history. In Australia, Bradman played state cricket for New South Wales and South Australia (1927–49). Following his retirement, he was knighted for his services to cricket.

Bradshaw, Robert (1917–1978). Prime minister of the British-associated West Indies state of St. Kitts-Nevis from its formation in 1967 until his death in 1978.

Bragg, Sir William Henry (1862–1942). British physicist. Bragg graduated in 1884 from Cambridge University and after a year's research under J.J. Thomson took the chair of mathematics and physics at the University of Adelaide, Australia, in 1886. He returned to England as professor of physics at Leeds University in 1909, moving from there to University College, London, in 1915. In Australia Bragg concentrated on lecturing. There he started original research late in life (in 1904), working first on alpha radiation, investigating the range of the particles. Later he turned his attention to X RAYS. He constructed (1915) the first X-ray spectrometer to measure the wavelengths of X rays.

Sir William Henry Bragg, winner of the Nobel Prize for physics, conducting an experiment (Feb. 18, 1936).

Much of his work was on X-ray crystallography, in collaboration with his son, William Lawrence BRAGG. They shared the NOBEL PRIZE for physics in 1915. During WORLD WAR I Bragg worked on the development of hydrophones for the admiralty. In some ways his most significant work was done at the Royal Institution, London, where he was director from 1923.

Bragg, Sir William Lawrence (1890–1971). British physicist. The son of William Henry BRAGG, William Lawrence Bragg was educated at the University of Adelaide, Australia, and Cambridge University, where he became a fellow and lecturer. In 1919 he was appointed professor of physics at Manchester University. After a short period in 1937 as director of the National Physical Laboratory, he succeeded Ernest RUTHERFORD in 1938 as head of the Cavendish Laboratory and Cavendish Professor at Cambridge. In 1953 he became director of the Royal Institution, London, a post his father had held previously and which he held until his retirement in 1961. Success came early to Bragg, who shared the NOBEL PRIZE for physics with his father in 1915. Following Max von Laue's discovery of X-ray diffraction by crystals in 1912, Bragg in the same year formulated what is now known as the *Bragg law*. Bragg collaborated with his father in working out the crystal structures of a number of substances. He later worked on silicates and on metallurgy and set up a program to determine the structure of proteins.

Brain, Dennis (1921–1957). Legendary British French horn player. Brain was not merely a virtuoso performer on a difficult instrument, he was a consummate musician. During his career he was principle horn player with the Royal Philharmonic (under Sir Thomas BEECHAM) and the Philharmonia (under Otto KLEMPERER). Also well known as a soloist and chamber player, he made several outstanding recordings in this capacity; such composers as Benjamin BRITTEN composed new works for him. Brain was killed in a car crash.

Braine, John (Gerald) (1922–1985). British novelist. Born in Bradford, Yorkshire, he served in the navy during WORLD WAR II. After the war he worked as a librarian in the north of England, settling in London in the late 1950s. One of the ANGRY YOUNG MEN of the 1950s, his successful first two novels, *Room at the Top* (1957; filmed 1958) and *Life at the Top* (1962; filmed 1965), tell the story of Joe Lampton, a disillusioned lower-middle-class Yorkshireman who cynically marries for money and social standing although he is in love with a married woman. Braine's later works, among them *The Queen of a Distant Country* (1975), *The Pious Agent* (1976) and *Waiting for Sheila* (1980), show a departure from the radical, anti-establishment views of his youth.

Brainerd, John Grist (1904–1988). American electrical engineer. Brainerd headed a University of Pennsylvania team that built ENIAC (Electronic Numerical Integrator and Computer), one of the world's first electronic computers. The 30-ton device was unveiled in 1946.

brain trust. Nickname given to the group of informal advisers who helped President Franklin D. ROOSEVELT plan his NEW DEAL program. During his successful 1932 presidential campaign, FDR relied heavily on three professors from Columbia University—Adolf A. BERLE Jr., Raymond MOLEY and Rexford Guy TUGWELL, as well as Harry HOPKINS—to help him in conceptualizing his economic reform program. The brain trust designed a program that was radical in conception, based on massive government intervention in the economy. The program was implemented as FDR's New Deal, and it forever changed the role of the federal government in the U.S. Although the names of these advisers have faded, their work lives on.

Brambell, Francis William Rogers (1901–1970). British zoologist. Brambell earned both his B.A. and Ph.D. from Trinity College, Dublin, and then worked successively at University College and King's College, London. In 1930 he became professor of zoology at Bangor University, remaining there until his retirement in 1968. Brambell's work on prenatal mortality in wild rabbits led to his discovery that protein molecules are transferred from mother to fetus not through the placenta as previously supposed but by the uterine cavity and fetal yolk sac. He further found that this process is selective; for example, the gamma globulins are transferred more readily than other serum proteins. Such work is important in studies of resistance to disease in the newborn and of hemolytic diseases of infants. For this work Brambell received the Royal Medal of the Royal Society of London in 1964.

Brancusi, Constantin (1876–1957). Rumanian sculptor who spent most of his creative life in Paris. Brancusi is among the most revered figures of 20th-century art, a sculptor who belonged to no particular school but whose work is universally admired. After studying art in Bucharest, Vienna and Munich, Brancusi settled in Paris in 1904, where he endured years of poverty and obscurity. In 1906, the great sculptor Auguste Rodin offered to take Brancusi on as an assistant; Brancusi declined with this famous explanation: "No other trees can grow in the shadow of an oak tree." Around 1910, Brancusi turned to highly stylized sculptures made of bronze and other metals that captured the essential forms of birds and other natural fauna. These won him international fame. In 1937 he completed, for the public park at Tirgu Jiu near his birthplace, an immense sculpture called "Endless Column" (over 30 meters high). That same year he designed a Temple of Meditation for the maharajah of Indore in India. Jacob EPSTEIN and Henry MOORE are just two of the many major sculptors who have acknowledged the influence of Brancusi. A recreation of Brancusi's studio is now housed in the POMPIDOU CENTER in Paris.

Brandeis, Louis D(embitz) (1856–1941). American jurist, associate justice of the U.S. Supreme Court (1916–39). Born in Louisville, Kentucky, Brandeis graduated from Harvard Law School in 1877. As a private attorney in Boston (1879–1916), he established a brilliant liberal record, initiating (1907) Massachusetts savings-bank insurance and defending the public interest in such areas as labor law, utility and railroad rates, consumerism and conservationism. His "Brandeis brief," introduced in his Supreme Court argument in *Muller v. Oregon* (1908), revolutionized legal practice by introducing sociological and economic data into legal discourse. A critic of big banks, he was the author of the bestselling *Other People's Money, and How the Bankers Use It* (1914). Also a staunch opponent of corporate monopoly, he strongly influenced Woodrow WILSON, and his views were reflected in the Wilson administration's strong antitrust legislation. In 1916 Wilson appointed "the people's attorney" to the Supreme Court, and Brandeis became the first Jewish justice in U.S. history. During his distinguished career on the bench, he maintained his liberal positions, often dissenting from the opinions of the Court's conservative majority. After the election of Franklin D. ROOSEVELT in 1933, Brandeis became a supporter of NEW DEAL policies, again finding himself often in the Court's minority. After retirement in 1939, Brandeis, a committed Zionist (see ZIONISM), spent much of his time working in the cause of a Jewish homeland.

Brando, Marlon (Jr.) (1924–). American stage and screen actor; acclaimed as the most magnetic and influential American actor of the postwar era. Trained in the 1940s, in the method school of acting by teachers Stella Adler and Elia KAZAN, Brando began his Broadway stage career in 1944 with minor roles, but achieved major stardom with his portrayal of Stanley Kowalski in the Tennessee WILLIAMS play *A Streetcar Named Desire* (1947). Brando played the same role in the successful film adaptation of *Streetcar* (1951) and from that point on devoted himself to film work. His early film successes included *Viva Zapata!* (1952) and *The Wild One* (1954), but his most brilliant role—for which he won an ACADEMY AWARD as best actor—came as boxer Terry Malloy in *On the Waterfont* (1954). Other films featuring Brando include *Guys and Dolls* (1955); *One-Eyed Jacks* (1960), a western in which he directed himself; *The Godfather* (1972), for which he won another best actor Oscar for his portrayal of Don Corleone; *The Missouri Breaks* (1976); and *Apocalypse Now* (1979). More recently Brando has starred in *A Dry White Season* (1989), a look at South African apartheid, and *The Freshman* (1990), an offbeat comedy.

Brandt, Bill (1905–1983). One of the leading British photographers of this century. In the late 1920s, Brandt served as an assistant to the American Surrealist photographer Man RAY in Ray's Paris studio, and the influence of SURREALISM persisted in his work. But Brandt went on to more socially conscious work in documenting British poverty during the GREAT DEPRESSION of the 1930s. He also earned renown for his moody photographs of London during the blackouts of WORLD WAR II. His later work included experimental studies of the human body, published in the collection *Perspective of Nudes* (1961). Other major volumes of photographs include *Literary Britain* (1951) and *Shadow of Light* (1977).

Brandt, Willy [born Herbert Ernst Karl Frahm] (1913–). German political leader. Born in Lubeck, as a teenager he became a socialist in the European democratic tradition. He opposed HITLER in the early 1930s and fled to Norway in 1933. There he changed his name to Willy Brandt, a pseudonym he had used in earlier writings, became a Norwegian citizen, attended Oslo University and began a career as a journalist. When the Germans invaded Norway in 1940 he escaped to Sweden, where he acted as a link between the Scandinavian and German RESISTANCE movements. After the war he was appointed Norwegian press attache to Berlin and soon resumed relations with

Willy Brandt in 1965, after losing his bid to become West Germany's chancellor.

the Social Democratic Party (SPD). He regained German citizenship in 1947 and subsequently (1949–57) served as an SPD member of the West German Bundestag. In 1957 Brandt was elected to the highly visible post of mayor of BERLIN. Becoming SPD chairman in 1964, he was appointed foreign minister in 1966. When the SPD was victorious in the 1969 federal elections, Brandt became chancellor and worked tirelessly to promote reconciliation with eastern European countries and EAST GERMANY. This policy, known as OSTPOLITIK, earned him the 1971 NOBEL PRIZE for peace. Brandt was pressured into resigning in 1974 after an East German spy was discovered among his close advisors. Since 1976 he has served as chairman of the Socialist International, a confederation of worldwide Social Democratic parties. He has contiued to speak on national and international issues.

Brandt Report. A report of February 1980 generated by the Brandt Commission, headed by former West German Chancellor Willy BRANDT. The Brandt Report—*North-South: A Program for Survival*—advocated a restructuring of the world economy and financial institutions, and the development of plans to stimulate growth, trade and confidence—in order to divert the divisions between North (the industrialized "First World") and South (the developing THIRD WORLD) that threatened an eventual crisis.

Brans, Carl Henry (1935–). American mathematical physicist. Brans graduated in 1957 from Loyola University and earned his Ph.D. in 1961 from Princeton. He returned to Loyola in 1960 and in 1970 was appointed professor of physics. Brans has worked mainly in the field of general relativity. He is best known for his production with Robert Dicke in 1961 of a variant of EINSTEIN's theory in which the gravitational constant varies with time. A number of very accurate measurements made in the late 1970s have failed to detect this and some of the other predictions made by the **Brans-Dicke theory**.

Branton, Wiley Austin (1923–1988). American lawyer who gained national prominence by fighting for CIVIL RIGHTS. In 1957, Branton represented the nine students who successfully sought to integrate the public school system in LITTLE ROCK, Arkansas (see BROWN V. BOARD OF EDUCATION). He also led voter registration drives among blacks in the South in the 1960s. From 1977 to 1983, he served as dean of the Howard University Law School.

Braque, Georges (1882–1963). French painter and cofounder, with Pablo PICASSO, of CUBISM. After graduation from the Ecole des Beaux-Arts in Paris in 1900, Braque became actively involved in the FAUVE school of painting that called for the use of bright colors and pure pigments. But in 1907 Braque's style changed dramatically as a result of his study of the geometrically structured late landscapes of Paul Cezanne. Also in that year, Braque was introduced to Picasso, and the two began to work together actively to formulate an abstract Cubist style that fractured and reconstructed traditional pictorial forms. While Braque and Picasso soon went their separate ways, Braque continued to show a Cubist influence throughout his career while experimenting with new techniques. Braque's *The Portuguese* (1911) was the first modern painting to employ stenciled lettering. Braque also frequently employed papier colle—molded surfaces made of papier-mache and other materials—in his paintings. In his final decades, Braque devoted himself primarily to stylized still-lifes, in flat hues, of simple objects such as plants, fruits, bowls and vases.

Bras d'Or. Chain of lakes on Canada's Cape Breton Island in northern Nova Scotia. Alexander Graham Bell, inventor of the telephone, established his Aerial Experiment Association, a pioneering flight research facility, here (see also BADDECK). In February 1909, J. McCurdy conducted a half-mile flight here.

Brasilia. Capital of Brazil; in Goias province. The site was selected in 1956 as the new capital of Brazil, in place of Rio de Janeiro. It was built with an eye to contemporary architectural innovation and was formally instituted as the capital in 1960.

Brassai [born Gyula Halasz] (1899–1984). Hungarian photographer. Brassai is renowned for his candid and revealing portraits of urban life, and it is his remarkable series of black and white photos of what he called "the secret Paris" of the 1930s—its bars, bordellos and street life—that constitute his best-remembered legacy. Born in Hungary, Brassai immigrated to PARIS in 1924 to take part in the thriving artistic community then centered in Montparnasse. The photographs of Brassai have a relaxed, snapshot quality, but they also display a studied, dramatic use of light and shadow. *Picasso and Company* (1966) contains photographs of Brassai's numerous artist friends. *The Secret Paris of the 30's* (1976) is a collection of night life photographs accompanied by his autobiographical reminiscences. Brassai's work is featured in the collections of museums around the world.

Brattain, Walter Houser (1902–1987). American physicist. Brattain, brought up on a cattle ranch, was educated at Whitman College, the University of Oregon and at the University of Minnesota, where he earned his Ph.D. in 1929. He immediately joined the Bell Telephone Company where he worked as a research physicist until his retirement in 1967. After leaving Bell, Brattain taught at Whitman College. Brattain's main field of work was the surface properties of SEMICONDUCTORS. He was particularly interested in using them to amplify signals. Working with John BARDEEN, he investigated various arrangements for achieving this—originally studying silicon in contact with electrolytes, but later using germanium in contact with gold. Their first efficient point-contact TRANSISTOR (1947), consisting of a thin wafer of germanium with two close point contacts on one side and a large normal contact on the other, had a power amplification of 18. For their development of the transistor, Bardeen and Brattain shared the 1956 NOBEL PRIZE for physics with William SHOCKLEY.

Braudel, (Paul Achille) Fernand (1902–1985). French historian, widely considered to be have been one of the great historians of the 20th century. For many years he was the foremost representative of the influential Annales school of historiography, which focused on the daily lives of ordinary people rather than the deeds of those in power. Braudel's two major works were *The Mediterranean and the Mediterranean World in the Age of Philip II* (1949), written from memory while he was in a German prison camp, and a trilogy, *Civilization and Capitalism, 15th-18th Century* (1979).

Braun, Karl Ferdinand (1850–1918). German physicist. Braun studied at Marburg and received a doctorate from the University of Berlin (1872). He taught in various university posts. In 1885 he became professor of experimental physics at Tubingen, and in 1895 he became professor of physics at Strasbourg. In 1874 Braun observed that certain semiconducting crystals could be used to convert alternating to direct currents. At the turn of the century, he used this fact to invent crystal diodes, which led to the crystal radio. He also adapted the cathode-ray tube so that the electron beam was deflected by a changing voltage, thus inventing the oscilloscope and providing the basic component of a television receiver. His fame comes mainly from his improvements to MARCONI's wireless communication system and, in 1909 they shared the NOBEL PRIZE for physics. Braun's system, which used magnetically coupled resonant circuits, was the main one used in all receivers and transmitters in the first half of the 20th century. Braun went to the U.S. to testify in litigation about radio patents, but when the U.S. entered World War I in 1917 he was detained as an alien. He died in New York a year later.

Braun, Werner von (1912–1977). Pioneer German-American rocket engineer and controversial genius behind the early days of the U.S. space program. Von Braun was responsible for America's first space success, the satellite EXPLORER 1, launched January 31, 1958, a few months after the Soviet Union's SPUTNIK satellite rocked the Western scientific establishment. Born in Germany and educated in Switzerland and Berlin, he became interested in rocketry and the idea of space travel after reading a book by Hermann OBERTH. Joining the German Rocket Society in 1930, he aided in the firing of over 80 experimental rockets. When the society disbanded in 1932, some members began working on rocketry for the German army while others dropped out of what was clearly becoming a military project. Undeterred by politics, von Braun stayed on to pursue his all-consuming interest in rockets. By the time HITLER assumed power in 1933, the young von Braun had become one of Germany's most influential rocket pioneers.

Working under the command of Walter DORNBERGER on the Baltic Sea island of PEENEMUNDE when WORLD WAR II broke out, von Braun joined the Nazi Party in 1940. Although he had developed a "V-2" prototype in 1938, it was not until 1943 that von Braun and his fellow engineers and scientists began full-scale development of rockets for military purposes—becoming pioneers not only in space flight but also in the more deadly art of the guided missile. The V-2 missile was capable of carrying its own fuel and oxygen and of reaching a height of 60 miles. The V-2 was developed too late to rescue the German army from defeat, but in its short history the V-2 terrorized London, killing more than 2,500 people, and was also used against advancing Allied troops after D-day. U.S. intelligence officers later calculated that more than 3,000 people, used as slaves by the Nazis to build the missiles, may have died of mistreatment or in accidents.

Fleeing from advancing Russian troops near the end of the war, von Braun and his team surrendered to the American Army, deciding that they would get better treatment from the U.S. than the U.S.S.R., whose countryside the Nazis had ravaged. Von Braun and his group were secretly smuggled into the U.S. under a government program known as OPERATION PAPERCLIP and began working openly and with few restrictions on the fledgling American rocket program. As vocal an American advocate for space exploration and colonization as he had been in Germany in his youth, von Braun went on to become a driving force behind the Saturn 5 rocket that took the first humans to the moon, as well as a popular author and speaker in defense of America's space program.

Brautigan, Richard (1935–1984). American novelist, story writer and poet. In the late 1960s, Brautigan, a writer with great lyric and imaginative gifts, became a best-selling hero of the COUNTERCULTURE. His novel *Trout Fishing in America* (1967), a wry, picaresque tale of love and simple bohemian pleasures, was greeted with both popular and critical acclaim and, in its numerous translations, made the California-based Brautigan one of the best-known American writers of his generation. Other important Brautigan works of this epoch include a volume of poems, *The Pill Versus the Springhill Mine Disaster* (1968), a novel, *In Watermelon Sugar* (1968), and a volume of stories, *The Revenge of the Lawn* (1972). While Brautigan continued to write throughout the 1970s and early 1980s, his novels—although retaining Brautigan's unique, stylish whimsy—fell out of critical favor, and some have speculated that this decline was a factor leading to his suicide.

Brave New World. Novel by the British writer Aldous HUXLEY. *Brave New World* (1932) is by far the most famous of the works of Huxley. It stands alongside *1984*, by George ORWELL, as the most influential vision of a future dystopia in 20th-century literature. The setting of *Brave New World* is the 7th Century AF (After Ford), so designated in honor of the man who set civilization on a scientifically-controlled course in which eugenics and imposed social conformity reign supreme. Human beings are assigned caste status according to intelligence—manual workers being lowest on the scale. To maintain the caste populations, genetically planned infants are birthed from incubators and brought up in communal schools. The plot revolves around Bernard Marx, a Britisher with a high Alpha-Plus status, who is dissatisfied with the bland conditioning of his world and so brings a Savage from a New Mexican Reservation to live in London. The Savage soon develops a repugnance for the new society's lack of spontaneity and warmth. The Savage confronts Mustapha Mond, the World Controller, who insists on the ultimate goods of peace and order and deprives the Savage of his last hope for freedom. Huxley wrote a sequel, *Brave New World Revisited* (1958), in which he argued that his 1932 novel remained a plausible scenario, given the dire growth of both totalitarian power and the scientific means of behavior control.

Bray, John R. (1929–1978). American inventor of the animated cartoon process used by almost all early animators, including Walt DISNEY. Bray also pioneered the use of motion picture training films for WORLD WAR I draftees and syndicated many cartoon strips, including *Out of the Inkwell*. (See also ANIMATED FILM.)

Brazil [Federative Republic of Brazil]. South American country, bordered on the east by the Atlantic Ocean and abutting all other South American countries save Chile and Ecuador. Brazil is the fifth largest country in the world and the largest in South America. Ruled by an emperor from 1822 until a republic was established in 1889, Portuguese is Brazil's national language. Due to profitable coffee and rubber industries, Brazil enjoyed a wave of prosperity in the late 19th and early 20th centuries, and many Europeans and others immigrated there. Its population more than tripled between 1850 and 1920. During WORLD WAR I, Brazil joined the Allies and declared war on Germany in 1917. Following the war, demand for rubber and other Brazilian exports sharply dropped as did the price of coffee. The resulting unemployment led to social unrest and political upheaval during the 1920s. In 1930 a military coup ousted the newly elected president Julio Prestes and replaced him with Getulio Vargas, a former governor of Rio Grande do Sul. Vargas wrought many popular reforms in a

BRAZIL

Brazilian Indians protest a proposal to create a nuclear waste dump at an air force base in the Amazon.

new constitution adopted in 1934, including increased power to labor unions and giving women the right to vote but Brazil, like the rest of the world, remained in the grips of economic depression. In 1937 he wrote yet another constitution, which gave him absolute powers as a dictator. Brazil again joined the Allies in WORLD WAR II, declaring war on the Axis and taking part in the invasion of Italy, the first time any South American forces had fought on another continent. The war also brought about an increased demand for rubber. In 1945 the army forced Vargas to resign and General Eurico Dutra assumed the presidency. Dutra introduced a new constitution restoring some civil rights and creating an elected legislature. When Vargas was reelected in 1950, Brazil was again facing economic disaster and extreme inflation, which his corrupt government was unable to mitigate. In 1954, after another military coup, Vargas committed suicide. In 1956 Juscelino Kubutschek was elected president. To encourage economic recovery, Kubutschek promoted development of Brazil's interior and began construction on the planned city of Brasilia, which replaced Rio de Janeiro as capital in 1960. In 1961 Jasnio Quadros became president, but quickly resigned and was succeeded by his vice president, Joao Goulart, who was deposed in a bloodless coup in 1964 when General Castelo Branco established himself as dictator. His right-wing military regime was maintained by a succession of like-minded presidents. In 1985 Tancredo Neves was elected, the first civilian president since 1964. The 75-year-old Neves was in ill health and died shortly after his election. He was succeeded by his vice president, Jose Sarnay. Sarnay amended the constitution to permit direct presidential elections and introduced other reforms. Faced with 600% inflation, Sarnay also declared a wage and price freeze in 1985. In 1989 the conservative governor Fernando Collor de Mello was elected and vowed to reconstruct the economy. Brazil has increasingly become a focus of attention due to the destruction of the Amazon rain forest, much of which lies within its borders, which has contributed to GLOBAL WARMING and the worldwide GREENHOUSE EFFECT.

BRAZIL

1930	Getulio Vargas establishes right-wing dictatorship following major revolt.
1942	Brazil declares war on Germany and Italy, becoming first South American country to send troops to another continent.
1945	Vargas overthrown in military coup.
1960	Brasilia, a new city on an inland jungle plateau, replaces Rio de Janeiro as capital.
1976	Death-squad victims are found.
1977	Divorce is legalized.
1985	Civilian government is restored; Nazi Joseph Mengele's remains are exhumed and examined.
1988	Rubber-tapper, labor leader and environmentalist Chico Mendes is murdered.
1990	President Fernando Collor de Mello supports "debt-for-nature" swap to preserve Amazon.

Brazilian Revolt of 1964. On March 25, 1964, 1,400 sailors and marines, organized by the Sailors and Marines Association supporting President Joao Goulart, seized a trade union building to protest the arrest of their association's president. After refusing to surrender to the minister of the navy, two days later they yielded to army troops and were pardoned. Military leaders accused Goulart of undermining discipline and staged a revolt against him on March 31, 1964. A general strike staged by the General Confederation of Workers failed to prevent military takeover, and Goulart fled to Uruguay. The new government instituted a purge of all leftists, including officials of Goulart's Labor Party.

Brazilian Revolution of 1930. Suffering from the GREAT DEPRESSION and the collapse of the coffee market, Brazilians were discontented even before President Washington Luiz Pereira de Souza broke with expected practice to name fellow native of Sao Paolo, Julio Prestes, his conservative successor in the upcoming election, instead of someone from Minas Gerais. The leaders of Minas Gerais supported Getulio Dornelles Vargas, governor of Rio Grande do Sul. When Prestes was declared winner (March 1930), his opponents made preparations for overturning the results. Vargas called for a revolt, promised economic and political reforms, gathered loyal troops, and in a bloodless revolution (October 1930) seized the presidency, marking the end of the old, or first, republic.

Brazzaville Declaration. Statement of January 1944 that defined the post-World War II relationship between FRANCE and its overseas colonies. It was the result of a 1944 meeting between the FREE FRENCH, headed by Charles DE GAULLE, and representatives of various French colonies, and was held in Brazzaville, capital of FRENCH EQUATORIAL AFRICA and center for Free French forces. The declaration guaranteed French citizenship to colonial peoples, reaffirmed the colonial unity of France and its colonies and recommended a measure of autonomy for those colonies. It did not, however, address the issue of colonial independence. The document was largely rejected as too stringent by nationalists in ALGERIA and elsewhere and as overly moderate by many French settlers.

Brecht, Bertolt [Eugen Bertolt Friedrich Brecht] (1898–1956). German playwright, stage director and theoretician, and poet. Brecht is one of the seminal figures of 20th-century drama. He wrote his first play, *Baal* (1918), while studying medicine in Munich but began his theater career in earnest in the early 1920s as an assistant director to Max REINHARDT in Berlin. *A Man's a Man* (1926) was his first play to incorporate a Brechtian dramatic trademark—an epic view of history that overlays the action of the individual characters. *The Threepenny Opera* (1928), with

Bertolt Brecht, on the left, at a culture union meeting in the Russian sector of Berlin (1948).

Kurt WEILL composing the music (sung by Lotte LENYA) for Brecht's acerbic text, remains one of the most influential musical plays of the century. Brecht became a socialist in 1927. In 1933 he and his wife fled Nazi GERMANY. While in exile in the U.S., Brecht wrote most of his best plays, including *Mother Courage and Her Children* (1941) and *The Caucasian Chalk Circle* (1945). He returned to East Germany in 1949, where he founded the Berliner Ensemble. *Little Parables for the Theater* (1949) is his major theoretical work.

Breit, Gregory (1899–). Russian-American physicist. Born in Russia, Breit moved to the U.S. in 1915 and became a naturalized citizen in 1918. He studied at Johns Hopkins University, earning his Ph.D. in 1921. From 1921 until 1924 he worked at the Universities of Leiden, Harvard and Minnesota, before joining the Carnegie Institution, Washington, D.C. (1924–29). At Carnegie he worked in the department of terrestrial magnetism as a mathematical physicist. There, with Merle A. TUVE, he conducted some of the earliest experiments to measure the height and density of the ionosphere. Their technique was to transmit short bursts of radio waves and analyze the reflected waves received. Their work was a significant step in the historical development of RADAR. Besides his pioneering work on the ionosphere, Breit researched quantum theory, nuclear physics and quantum electrodynamics. Between 1929 and 1973 Breit held professorial posts at the universities of New York, Wisconsin, and Yale, and the State University of New York, Buffalo.

Brel, Jacques (1929–1978). Belgian-born singer and composer. In the United States he was best known for a musical based on his lyrics, *Jacques Brel Is Alive and Well and Living in Paris.* He stopped giving concerts in 1966 and devoted himself to acting and directing. In 1973, when he learned he had cancer, he settled in the South Pacific. He returned to France in 1977 to record *Brel,* which sold a million advance copies.

Brennan, William J., Jr. (1906–). Associate justice, U.S. Supreme Court (1956–1990). Brennan, the son of Irish immigrants, graduated with distinction from the University of Pennsylvania and Harvard Law School. Before and after service in WORLD WAR II, Brennan was a labor lawyer in private practice in Newark, New Jersey. He was appointed as a justice of the New Jersey Superior Court and eventually rose to the state's Supreme Court. Appointed to the U.S. Supreme Court by President EISENHOWER, Brennan was known as a strong advocate of CIVIL RIGHTS on the WARREN court of the 1960s. Brennan remained the leader of the liberal minority after 1970, and his ability to build consensus positions preserved and often extended the liberal decisions of the Court even after the appointment of a number of conservatives. Brennan was accused by critics of legislating from the bench because he normally interpreted the Constitution flexibly rather than literally.

Brenner, Sydney (1927–). South African-British molecular biologist. Brenner, the son of a Lithuanian exile, was educated at the Universities of the Witwatersrand and Oxford, where he earned his D.Phil. in 1954. In 1957 he joined the staff of the Medical Research Council's molecular biology laboratory in Cambridge. Brenner's first major success came in 1957 when he demonstrated that the triplets of nucleotide bases that form the genetic code do not overlap along the genetic material (DNA). A greater triumph followed in 1961 when Brenner, in collaboration with Francis CRICK and others, reported the results of careful experiments with the bacteriophage T4, which clearly showed that the code did consist of base triplets that neither overlapped nor appeared to be separated by "punctuation marks." Also in 1961 Brenner, in collaboration with Francois Jacob and Matthew Meselson, introduced a new form of RNA, messenger RNA (mRNA). With this came one of the central insights of molecular biology—an explanation of the mechanism of information transfer whereby the protein-synthesizing centers (ribosomes) play the role of nonspecific constituents that can synthesize different proteins, according to specific instructions, which they receive from the genes through mRNA. After such early successes in the pioneering days of molecular biology, Brenner became involved in a major investigation into the development of the nervous system of nematodes.

William J. Brennan Jr. at the time of his appointment to the U.S. Supreme Court in 1956.

Brenner Pass. Alpine mountain pass between Innsbruck, Austria, and northeastern Italy; an ancient, major trade route between central Europe and Italy. From 1940 to 1943, during WORLD WAR II, it was a site for recurrent meetings between Axis leaders Adolf HITLER and Benito MUSSOLINI.

Bresson, Robert (1907–). French film director. Bresson is regarded by film critics as the ultimate directorial auteur—one who carefully creates and controls every aspect of the finished film, from script to cinematography to the casting of nonprofessional actors so as to use, in Bresson's words, "not what they do but what they are." While Bresson wrote screenplays in the 1930s, it was his first full-length film, *Angels of the Streets* (1943), that brought him to international prominence. During WORLD WAR II Bresson was a PRISONER OF WAR under the Nazis; he drew from this experience to make *A Man Escaped* (1956). While not a prolific filmmaker, virtually all of Bresson's finished work is highly regarded. His other films include *Diary of a Country Priest* (1951), *The Trial of Joan of Arc* (1962) and *Lancelot of the Lake* (1974). His *Notes on Cinematography* (1977) emphasizes the importance of minute attention to detail and the use not of "beautiful" images but of "necessary" ones.

Brest. Port city at the northern head of the Bay of Biscay on France's Atlantic coast; in the Finistere department. During WORLD WAR I, it was used as a debarkation point for U.S. military forces. During WORLD WAR II, it served as a major Nazi SUBMARINE base and was severely damaged in the course of the fighting.

Brest-Litovsk, Treaty of. Treaty, signed on March 3, 1918, by the CENTRAL POWERS of Germany and Austria and the newly formed Soviet Union, that created a separate World War I peace for Russia. Hard-pressed by advancing German troops, the fledgling government of the U.S.S.R. was forced to accede to extremely harsh provisions, giving up the Ukraine, Finland, the Baltic provinces, the Caucasus, White Russia and Poland, and obliged to pay a large indemnity as well. The treaty was invalidated upon the signing of the general armistice that ended the war on November 11, 1918. (See also UNION OF SOVIET SOCIALIST REPUBLICS.)

Breton, Andre (1896–1966). French poet, essayist and novelist. In his early poems, Breton revealed the marked influence upon him of the lyricism of Guillaume Apollinaire and of Dadaism. But in 1924, with the publication of his first Surrealist Manifesto, Breton became the unquestioned leader of SURREALISM, a literary movement that extolled the value of dreams and of uncensored, automatic writing from the depths of the human psyche. Breton composed two more Surrealist Manifestos (1930, 1942) as well as a book of essays, *What Is Surrealism?* (1934), and remained an active proponent of Surrealist theories unto his death. Breton scored a major critical success with his evocative prose fantasy, *Nadja* (1928), in which Paris is evoked through meetings with a mysterious woman. He collaborated with his fellow surrealist poet Paul ELUARD on *Immaculate Conception* (1930). In *Arcane 17* (1945), Breton explores occult themes. *Poems* (1948) was a major collection of his verse over three decades.

Bretton Woods Conference. International conference held in July 1944 to establish a structure for international monetary and economic cooperation in the postwar world. The Bretton Woods Conference was called by U.S. President Franklin D. ROOSEVELT, who saw a need to prevent a recurrence of the economic crises (notably the GREAT DEPRESSION) that had troubled the world during the 1920s and 1930s. Held in the resort town of Bretton Woods, N.H., the conference was attended by representatives of 28 Allied nations. Treasury Secretary Henry MORGENTHAU Jr. headed the U.S. delegation and greatly influenced the conference. The Bretton Woods Conference laid the groundwork for the establishment of the International Monetary Fund (see WORLD BANK).

Breuer, Marcel (Lajos) (1902–1981). Hungarian-born architect and designer. Breuer introduced architectural MODERNISM to the U.S. and later helped create and establish the INTERNATIONAL STYLE. He was trained under Walter GROPIUS at Germany's famous BAUHAUS in the 1920s. While there he designed the now-ubiquitous Wassily and Cesca chairs, curved-steel-framed, tensile structures that created a revolution in furniture design. In 1937 he fled Nazi Germany and immigrated to the U.S., joining Harvard's Graduate School of Design. There he taught some of this century's preeminent architects. Breuer's later conceptions made extensive use of concrete as a prime building material and were more massive and austere than his earlier designs. Among his creations of the 1950s and 1960s were such buildings as New York's Whitney Museum and Pan Am Building and the Paris headquarters of UNESCO.

Brewer, David J. (1837–1910). Associate justice, U.S. Supreme Court (1889–1910). A graduate of Yale University and Albany Law School, and a nephew of industrialist Cyrus Field, Brewer moved west to Kansas where he was appointed a judge. He later became a judge of the Kansas Supreme Court and was eventually appointed to the Federal Court of Appeals for the Eighth Circuit. Although his nomination to the Supreme Court by President Benjamin Harrison was opposed by prohibitionists, Brewer was confirmed in 1889. Brewer was uncharacteristically outspoken for a justice and while on the Court he spoke out in favor of independence for the PHILIPPINES, and women's suffrage—two controversial issues of the day. Brewer was also appointed as the head of a U.S. commission that arbitrated the Venezuela-British Guiana boundary issue. He died unexpectedly in 1910 while still on the Court.

Breytenbach, Breyten (1939–). South African poet, prose writer and painter. He writes in Afrikaans. Breytenbach left the University of Cape Town to travel to Europe. He settled in Paris in 1961, where he gained a reputation as a painter. His early anti-APARTHEID poetry *Die Ysterkoi Moet Sweet* (*The Iron Cow Must Sweat*) and *Katastrofes* (*Catastrophes*) established him as a writer. In 1975 on an illegal visit to SOUTH AFRICA he was arrested under the Terrorism Act. Charged with being a founder of Okehela, a white wing of the AFRICAN NATIONAL CONGRESS, he was sentenced to nine years in prison. Some of his finest poems and *Mouroir: Mirrornotes of a Novel* (tr. 1984) were written in prison. Under pressure from the French government, South Africa released Breytenbach in 1982, and he returned to Paris.

Brezhnev, Leonid Ilyich (1906–1982). Soviet political leader. Born in Dneprodzerzhinsk in the Ukraine, Brezhnev was educated at the Dneprodzerzhinsk Metallurgical Institute and later became deputy chief of the Urals regional land department. In 1935–36 he served in the Soviet army. From 1937 to 1939 he was chief of a department in the Dnepropetrovsk regional party committee. A political officer in the army from 1941 to 1946, in 1944 he was made major general. The first secretary of the central committee of the COMMUNIST PARTY in Moldavia in 1950–52, Brezhnev was made a member of the central committee of the CPSU in 1952. His political career continued to climb and in 1956 he was made a member of the Politburo, and from 1956 to 1960 he served as secretary of the central committee of the CPSU. Chairman of the Presidium of the Supreme Soviet of the U.S.S.R. from 1960 to 1964, and also from 1977, in 1963 he was appointed as secretary of the central committee of the CPSU and general secretary from 1966. In 1976 he was made marshal of the Soviet Union and in 1977 became president of the Presidium of the Supreme Soviet. He died on November 10, 1982. Yuri ANDROPOV succeeded him.

Leonid Brezhnev, Soviet premier (date unknown).

Aristide Briand.

Brezhnev Doctrine. An assertion by Soviet Communist Party First Secretary BREZHNEV of the legitimacy of the intervention of one socialist state in the affairs of another, when the central role of the COMMUNIST PARTY itself appeared threatened. The doctrine was demonstrated in the WARSAW PACT invasion of CZECHOSLOVAKIA (August 20–21, 1968), which ended the liberal PRAGUE SPRING.

Briand, Aristide (1862–1932). French statesman, 11-time premier. A socialist lawyer, he entered the Chamber of Deputies in 1902 and was known for his work in separating church and state (1905). He became premier in 1909, between that year and 1929 holding the office 11 separate times. Briand is best remembered, however, for his post-WORLD WAR I efforts in promoting international reconciliation and peace through arbitration. As foreign minister, Briand was the driving force behind the LOCARNO PACT of 1925, and the following year he shared the NOBEL PRIZE for peace with Germany's Gustav STRESEMANN. He went on to help formulate the KELLOGG-BRIAND PACT (1928), which attempted to eradicate war altogether, and in 1929–30 advocated a United States of Europe. He retired in 1932 after running unsuccessfully for the presidency.

Brice, Fanny [Fanny Borach] (1891–1951). One of the great legends of burlesque, vaudeville and Broadway, Fanny Brice began her career at age 14 when she won a singing contest at Keeney's Theater in Brooklyn. Working both the VAUDEVILLE circuit and Broadway (in revues such as the ZIEGFELD FOLLIES), she developed a popular routine consisting of physical comedy, jokes in Jewish dialect, and a wide assortment of humorous songs, including "Sadie Salome," "Oh How I Hate That Fellow Nathan" and "Mrs. Cohen at the Beach." After her marriage to producer Billy ROSE ended in divorce in 1938, Brice became popular for her regular radio programs, which included "Good News of 1938" and the "Baby Snooks Show" (named after her famous character) in 1944. Before Brice had a chance to prove herself in the new medium of television, she died in 1951, several days after suffering a stroke. Her life story has been told, sometimes with names disguised, in several films, including the Barbra STREISAND vehicles *Funny Girl* (1968) and *Funny Lady* (1975).

Bricktop [born Ada Beatrice Queen Victoria Louis Virginia Smith] (1894–1984). Black American entertainer, singer and nightclub owner. Like many black artists of her day, Bricktop did not gain wide recognition until she moved abroad. Her nightclub in PARIS, also called Bricktop, was a gathering place during the 1920s for members of cafe society and for such prominent American expatriate writers as Ernest HEMINGWAY and F. Scott FITZGERALD. During the 1940s, she presided over clubs in Rome and Mexico City. Cole PORTER wrote his song "Miss Otis Regrets" in her honor. Her proteges included Josephine BAKER, Mabel MERCER and Duke ELLINGTON.

Brico, Antonia (1902–1989). American orchestra conductor. Brico led her own orchestras in New York in the 1930s and helped lead the fight to overturn prejudice against female conductors around the world. She was the subject of the 1974 documentary film, *Antonia: Portrait of a Conductor*.

Bridge, Frank (1879–1941). English composer, conductor and teacher. A distinguished viola player, Bridge began his career performing with the Joachim String Quartet and the English String Quartet. He also appeared as a conductor with several orchestras in Britain (1910–20) and in the U.S. (1923). As a composer he is known for his careful craftsmanship and versatility. Major works include the 4th String Quartet (1937), a symphonic poem, *Isabella* (1907), sonatas for violin and cello, and about 100 songs and choruses for voice and orchestra. He was a master teacher, inspiring such students as Benjamin BRITTEN, his most famous pupil.

Bridges, Alfred Renton Bryant "Harry" (1901–1990). Australian-born U.S. labor leader. Bridges organized the International Longshoremen's and Warehousemen's Union in 1933 and served as its president from 1934 to 1977. The union staged a strike in May 1934 that led to a general strike that virtually shut down the city of San Francisco for three days. Long accused of being a communist, Bridges denied the charge, although he willingly accepted financial aid from the Communist Party. He was the target of repeated attempts to deport him to his native Australia in the 1940s and 1950s. Upon Bridges' death, San Francisco's mayor ordered all city flags to be flown at half-mast in his honor. (See also BRIDGES V. CALIFORNIA.)

Bridges, Robert (Seymour) (1844–1930). English poet. Educated at Eton and Corpus Christi College, Oxford (1863–67), Bridges worked as a physician in London until 1881. His first book appeared in 1873, but it was the publication of *Shorter Poems* in 1890 that earned him a reputation as a master of the lyric form. A technically accomplished metricist, he was named poet laureate in 1913. Bridges has been blamed for delaying the publication of the more innovative poems of his friend Gerard Manley Hopkins until 1918. Although his diction is now regarded as stilted and cold, he is remembered for *The Testament of Beauty* (five volumes, 1927–29) and some fine, short lyric poems, such as "London Snow."

For further reading:

Young, F.E., *Robert Bridges*. Brooklyn, N.Y.: Haskell, 1970.

Stanford, Donald E., ed., *The Selected Letters of Robert Bridges*. Newark: University of Delaware Press, 1984.

Bridges v. California (1941). U.S. Supreme Court decision involving the First Amendment; brought against union leader Harry BRIDGES. At the start of WORLD WAR II, when the U.S. government was stepping up its war effort, Harry Bridges, the left-wing leader of the West Coast Longshoreman's Union, was held in contempt by a California state court. While his trial was in progress Bridges issued a press release threatening to tie up all shipping from West Coast ports in the event he was convicted. Two California state courts held Bridges in contempt of court, but he appealed to the Supreme Court, arguing that the action violated his First Amendment right to free speech. Despite the wartime setting the Supreme Court threw out the contempt conviction. Applying the clear and present danger test, the Court held that the state court's contempt order had violated Bridges' free speech rights.

Antonia Brico.

Bridgman, Percy Williams (1882–1961). American physicist. The son of a journalist, Bridgman was educated at Harvard, where he earned his Ph.D. in 1908. He immediately joined the faculty, leaving only on his retirement in 1954 after serving as professor of physics (1919–26), professor of mathematics and natural philosophy (1926–50), and a Huggins Professor (1950–54). Most of Bridgman's research was in the field of high-pressure physics. When he began he found it necessary to design and build virtually all his own equipment and instruments. In 1909 he introduced the self-tightening joint. With the appearance of high-tensile steels, he could aim for pressures well beyond the scope of earlier workers. Bridgman used such pressures to explore the properties of numerous liquids and solids. In the course of this work he discovered two new forms of ice, freezing at temperatures above 0 degrees C. In 1955 he transformed graphite into synthetic diamond. Bridgman was awarded the 1946 NOBEL PRIZE for physics for his work on extremely high pressures. He was also widely known as a philosopher of science. While in his 70s Bridgman developed Paget's disease, which caused him considerable pain and little prospect for relief. He committed suicide in 1961.

Brightman, Edgar Sheffield (1884–1953). American philosopher. Brightman was the leading American proponent of personalism—the view that each individual human consciousness creates a unique reality that is not subject to objective verification or dispute. Brightman argued that these individual realities were unified by the conscious will of God, who creates individuals and cooperates with them in the creation of a cosmic Reality. The most controversial position taken by Brightman concerned the nature of evil, which he called "the Given" and held to be a nonrational aspect of reality that was neither created nor approved by God, but that God was capable of holding in check. Brightman taught for several decades at Boston University. His chief works include *Introduction to Philosophy* (1925), *The Problem of God* (1930), *Moral Laws* (1933) and *Nature and Values* (1945).

Brighton Bombing. On October 12, 1984, during the 1984 CONSERVATIVE PARTY conference in Brighton, England, a bomb exploded at the hotel where party leaders, including Prime Minister Margaret THATCHER and cabinet members, were staying. Five people were killed and 32 wounded, including top party official Norman Tebbitt and his wife. The Provisional IRISH REPUBLICAN ARMY claimed responsibility for the blast. Thatcher herself narrowly escaped injury. The blast occurred a few hours before the party's debate on Northern Ireland policy. The bombing was denounced by British and international leaders. In 1986 a London jury found a Belfast man guilty of the bombing, along with four codefendants. Charges against some codefendants were later dropped.

Brinkley, David (McClure) (1920–). American news commentator. He helped develop documentary television techniques for NBC with the *Huntley-Brinkley Report* (1956–71), which won Peabody, Sylvania and Emmy awards. In the 1980s he hosted an influential weekly political discussion program from Washington, D.C., "This Week with David Brinkley," on ABC. Brinkley is noted for his terse, dry sense of humor.

brinksmanship. In foreign affairs, the policy of forcing a rival power to reach agreement by deliberately creating the risk of nuclear war. In 1956 U.S. Secretary of State John Foster DULLES told LIFE magazine that "if you are scared to go to the brink you are lost."

Brinks Robbery. Robbery on January 17, 1950, of the Brinks Security company's North Terminal Garage in Boston. In 15 minutes 11 middle-age Bostonians, who had carefully planned the caper, stole some $2.7 million in cash, checks and securities. The robbers had intended to maintain low profiles until the seven-year statute of limitations ran out. However, one of their number, Joseph "Specs" O'Keefe, felt cheated. Fearing that he might turn informer, the others unsuccessfully tried to have him killed. After the attempt on his life, O'Keefe did talk with the authorities, and eventually eight of the Brinks thieves were tried, convicted and sentenced to life imprisonment. The Brinks Robbery was one of the largest and most highly publicized of all 20th-century crimes. It was the subject of a 1980 film, *The Brinks Job.* (See also GREAT TRAIN ROBBERY.)

British Antarctic Territory. A vast territory that lies south of 60 degrees South Latitude, stretches to the South Pole and is bounded by Longitudes 20 degrees and 80 degrees West. About 659,828 square miles in area, the territory includes the South Orkney Islands, the South Shetland Islands, Palmer Land and Graham Land on the Antarctic Peninsula, the Filcher and Ronne ice shelves and Coats Land. The territory was formed in 1908 when the various areas were grouped together; they are administered by a British high commissioner based in the Falkland Islands. The first permanent settlement was established on the South Shetland Islands in the early 20th century; scientific bases followed in the 1940s. Both CHILE and ARGENTINA have territorial claims to parts of the territory. Clashes between Argentina and Britain occurred in 1952 and again in 1982 when Britain expelled Argentina from its occupation of the South Shetland Islands during the FALKLAND ISLANDS WAR.

British Broadcasting Corporation (BBC). The state-owned broadcasting service of the UNITED KINGDOM. Established as a private company in 1922, the BBC was converted by royal charter to a public corporation in 1927. Its first director-general (1922–38) was the legendary John Reith, who established strict guidelines and a tone of high moral seriousness. Since 1932 the BBC's headquarters have been in Broadcasting House in Portland Place, London. During WORLD WAR II the BBC served as the "voice of Britain" and broadcast war news to Britain and to occupied Europe. It also relayed coded messages to RESISTANCE fighters in FRANCE and other occupied countries. Television broadcasting began in 1936, was suspended at the beginning of the war (1939) and resumed in 1946. The BBC is now responsible for four national radio stations (Radio 1—contemporary pop and ROCK and roll; Radio 2—pop standards, JAZZ and light music; Radio 3—classical music and drama; Radio 4—news, quiz and game shows and information and educational programs). It also operates several regional services, the world service and two national television services (BBC 1 and BBC 2). It is financed by fees from annual television licenses (for domestic services) and the government (for the world service). A board of 12 governors (appointed by the crown) oversees its operations and appoints a governor-general, the corporation's chief executive. While the British government has power over technical and related matters and final review of programming, the BBC theoretically has independent control over the content of programming. In the 1980s and 1990s the establishment of a fourth independent television network (Channel 4), the advent of cable television, and Prime Minister THATCHER's emphasis on "free-market values" as well as government attempts to censor certain news and documentary programs posed a serious challenge to the BBC's traditional role as a public service committed to excellence. The BBC has played a major and controversial role in weakening the hold of regional accents and spreading "standard English" (also known as "BBC English") throughout the United Kingdom. Over the years the BBC has provided a livelihood for many distinguished writers, actors, directors, musicians and other personalities. In the U.S., the BBC is known as a purveyor of quality programs to American public television stations.

British Council. An organization established in 1934 and incorporated by Royal Charter in 1940 dedicated to promoting British culture abroad. It established a specialist drama department in 1939, incorporating dance in 1980, and organizes overseas tours of British companies and writers as well as arranges visits to Britain by foreign theatrical dignitaries. The council also publishes a continually updated series *British Writers* and runs libraries and English-language schools around the world.

British Ecology Party. See GREENS.

British Empire. A collection of colonies, settlements, protectorates and outposts throughout the world that were administered by, or owed their loyalty to, the UNITED KINGDOM. Dating from the Age of Discovery, the British empire grew throughout the Victorian era and reached its zenith early in the 20th century—from which point it almost immediately began a decline that turned into a dismantling after WORLD WAR II. Some of the colonies—notably INDIA, the jewel in the imperial crown—had never been settled by large numbers of Britons but were administered by an efficient British-organized civil service. India, along with various other colonies and/or protectorates in Asia (e.g., BURMA and Malaya [now MALAYSIA]) and Africa (e.g., EGYPT, NIGERIA and Rhodesia [now ZIMBABWE]) were viewed mainly as sources of raw materials and markets for British manufactured goods or as military outposts, buffers against potentially hostile states. On the other hand, CANADA, AUSTRALIA and NEW ZEALAND were populated largely by British emigres and their descendants who outnumbered the native populations (American Indian in Canada, Aborigine in Australia, Maori in New Zealand); these self-governing dominions (notwithstanding a significant number of French Canadians) remained loyal to the British Crown while evolving their own particular national identities and institutions.

Some historians have asserted that the far-flung empire was held together by bluff, bluster, pomp and circumstance, rather than overwhelming military force; there is more than a grain of truth to this. There was also a good deal of racism in British attitudes toward the empire's non-British subjects. In some parts of the empire, local movements for independence (most notably in India) gained momentum in the first four decades of the century. Britain, though a victor in WORLD WAR II, had been pauperized by the long and costly struggle and was in no position to contest an empire. After India was granted independence in 1947, the empire began to unravel; Britain's humiliation in the SUEZ CRISIS (1956) demonstrated that the U.K. was no longer an unchallenged world power. A large number of colonies gained independence in the late 1950s and early 1960s. Despite guerrilla movements in KENYA (see MAU MAU) and Malaya, the dismantling of the British empire was generally a peaceful and orderly affair. Most former colonies continued their association with Britain as members of the COMMONWEALTH OF NATIONS.

British Indian Ocean Territory. Island colony in the southwestern Indian Ocean. In 1965, the territory was created by the unification of Aldabra, Destoches and Farquhar islands (formerly with SEYCHELLES) and the Chagos Archipelago (formerly with MAURITIUS). In 1976, when the Seychelles were granted independence, the above three islands were restored to it, leaving only the Chagos Archipelago within the Indian Ocean Territory. The major island, Diego Garcia, became in 1972 a communications and defense base for British and U.S. forces. At that time, the extant population—primarily copra plantation workers—were moved elsewhere.

British Legion. A British organization to aid war veterans and their dependents. The Legion was created largely by Douglas HAIG in 1921, was recognized by royal charter in 1925 and became the Royal British Legion in 1971. Much of its funding is generated by its disabled members selling Flanders poppies on Remembrance Sunday, when Britain honors the dead of WORLD WAR I.

British Library. Built in 1857 as part of the British Museum, the famous domed reading room was planned by the librarian Sir Antonio Panizzi. In 1963, due to the huge increase in the library's collection, much of which is being stored in various locations around London, plans were first laid to build a new headquarters. After much delay and difficulty with financing, the first phase of construction of the new library designed by Colin St. John Wilson is to be completed in 1993. Throughout the 1980s the project was still beset by financial woes due to construction cost inflation. The anticipated date of the completion of the entire new building is 2010, at a total cost of over 1 billion pounds. The library is home to many treasured first editions and manuscripts, such as the manuscript of Jane Austen's *Juvenilia,* which it acquired in 1988. In 1990 it acquired an important collection of manuscripts by major 20th-century writers from the British publisher Macmillan. It also serves a function similar to that of the Library of Congress in the U.S., holding a copy of every book published in the U.K.

British Telecom. British telecommunications company. Prior to 1980, British Telecom was a nationalized service, part of the Post Office; it was privatized in 1984 as part of Margaret THATCHER's program of PRIVATIZATION. It operates radio and television broadcasting, the telephone system and Britain's viewdate network, Prestel. Formerly a monopoly, British Telecom faces increasing competition from other commercial suppliers.

British Union of Fascists. See Oswald MOSLEY.

British Volunteer Programme. Since 1966, an umbrella organization overseeing associations such as Voluntary Service Overseas (VSO) that send British volunteers to work in developing countries. VSO served as a model in the creation of the U.S. PEACE CORPS.

Brittain, Donald (1928–1989). Canadian documentary filmmaker. His films, many of them done for the National Film Board of Canada or the Canadian Broadcasting Corporation (CBC), included *The King Chronicle,* a documentary on the life of Prime Minister William Lyon Mackenzie KING, and *Memorandum,* a film about the HOLOCAUST. He received three ACADEMY AWARD nominations and was an officer in the Order of Canada.

Brittain, Vera (Mary) (1894–1970). British author, pacifist and feminist. Brittain interrupted her studies at Somerville College, Oxford, to serve as a nurse during WORLD WAR I. *Testament of Youth* (1933) draws on her experiences and reflects her beliefs. She returned to Oxford after the war where she became close friends with the like-minded Winifred HOLTBY, about whom Brittain wrote in *Testament of Friendship* (1940). Brittain also wrote poetry and essays as well as fiction. She was married to the political scientist Sir George Catlin (1896–1979); their daughter, Shirley WILLIAMS, was a prominent LABOUR PARTY politician in the 1970s and cofounded the SOCIAL DEMOCRATIC PARTY (1981).

Britten, Benjamin (1913–1976). One of Britain's most important 20th-century composers, Benjamin Britten was born at Lowestoft, Suffolk. Displaying early musical talent, he was a pupil of the composer Frank BRIDGE and studied at the Royal College of Music, London, with John IRELAND. His early work consists mainly of instrumental music written to accompany films, dramas and plays. Britten achieved early fame with his choral work *A Boy Was Born* (1933) and his Fantasy Quartet for Oboe and Strings (1934). He excelled at vocal works, many of them written for his friend, the English tenor Peter PEARS. His song cycles and choral works include a setting of Rimbaud's *Illuminations* (1940), *Seven Sonnets of Michelangelo* (1942), *A Ceremony of Carols* (1942) and the *War Requiem* (1962). Also a superb operatic composer who often explored themes of innocence and corruption, Britten is particularly noted for *Peter Grimes* (1945). His other operas include *The Turn of the Screw* (1954) and *Death in Venice* (1973). A traditionalist in style with an enormous lyrical gift, Britten was also a noted conductor.

Benjamin Britten, British composer (1968).

For further reading:

Herbert, David, *The Operas of Benjamin Britten.* New York: New Amsterdam Books, 1979; rev. 1989.

Palmer, Christopher, ed., *The Britten Companion.* Cambridge: Cambridge University Press, 1984.

Parsons, Charles H., ed., *A Benjamin Britten Discography.* San Francisco, Calif.: Edwin Mellen Press, 1990.

Broad, Charlie Dunbar (1887–1971). British philosopher and essayist. Broad is one of the best-known and most eclectic of modern British philosophers. In the course of a long academic career as a fellow at Trinity College, Cambridge, Broad wrote on subjects as diverse as epistemology and the philosophy of science, psychical research and ethics, and wrote analyses of the works of thinkers Francis Bacon and Immanuel Kant, both of whom exercised a strong influence on Broad's skeptical but open-minded approach to philosophical issues. Broad is best known for his writings on the scope and limits of scientific knowledge, especially *The Mind and Its Place in Nature* (1925) and *Religion, Philosophy and Scientific Research* (1953). In these works, Broad argued for a skeptical empiricism that distinguished between persistent substances (with consistently perceived shape, mass, position and the like) and sense-qualified occurrents (such as mirages and other light reflections) that are seen because of the unique perceptual capabilities and limitations of human beings.

Broch, Hermann (1886–1951). Austrian novelist, essayist and poet Broch turned to writing at the relatively late age of 41, after having devoted two decades to working in the textile business. But the novels he produced thereafter established him as one of the modern literary masters in the German language. *Die Schlafwandler* (*The Sleepwalkers*), which appeared in three volumes (1930–32), dealt with political apathy and social cynicism in the WORLD WAR I era. This was followed by *Die unbekannte grosse* (1933; *The Unknown Quantity,* 1935). Shortly thereafter Broch immigrated to the U.S. after being detained by the Nazis. *Der Tod des Bergil* (1945; *The Death of Virgil*), Broch's most famous work, drew parallels between the decline of modern Europe and that of the ancient classical era as symbolized by the death of the Roman epic poet Vergil. It, along with *Die Schuldlosen* (1950; *The Guiltless* 1974), was published posthumously. In addition to his novels, Broch wrote poems, dramatic works and literary criticism.

Brock, Louis Clark "Lou" (1939–). American baseball player. Best remembered for his years with the St. Louis

Cardinals, Brock began his career with the Chicago Cubs in 1961. He joined the Cardinals during the 1964 stretch drive, and batted .348 while leading the team to an eventual World Series victory. He led the league in batting in 1967, and batted an astonishing .414 during the World Series, with seven steals, as the "Cards" won another title. Always at or near the top in stolen bases, his 118 thefts in 1974—at the age of 35—broke the old record of 104. Never known as a fielder, he led the National League in errors seven times. His basepath speed and batting prowess, however, won him a place in the Hall of Fame in 1985.

Brockway, Lord (Archibald) Fenner (1888–1988). British socialist and pacifist; a leader of the anticolonial movement and a founder of the nuclear disarmament movement (see CAMPAIGN FOR NUCLEAR DISARMAMENT [CND]). In 1964, after many years as a militant LABOUR PARTY MP in the House of Commons, Brockway reluctantly accepted a life peerage from Queen ELIZABETH II. He thus became a member of the House of Lords, a body he had sought to abolish throughout his career.

Brod, Max (1884–1968). Czech biographer, novelist, poet and dramatist. Brod, best remembered today for his biography of his close friend Franz KAFKA, was born of Jewish parents in Prague, then within the AUSTRO-HUNGARIAN EMPIRE. Brod earned a law degree but soon thereafter devoted his energies exclusively to journalism and literary writing. He first befriended Kafka in 1908. In 1912 Brod became a Zionist. At the outset of World War II, Brod fled to Tel Aviv, Israel, where he became the director of the renowned Habimah Theater. But Brod's greatest contribution to world literature came in 1924, following the death of Kafka, when Brod ignored his friend's express wish that all of his manuscripts be destroyed. Instead, Brod, who was convinced of Kafka's genius, edited and arranged for the publication of many of Kafka's classic novels and stories.

Brodie, Bernard Beryl (1909–1989). American pharmacologist. Brodie was educated at McGill University in Canada and at New York University, where he earned his Ph.D. in 1935. He worked at the Medical School there from 1943 to 1950 when he moved to the National Institutes of Health at Bethesda, Md., where he served as chief of the chemical pharmacology laboratory until 1970. Brodie has worked in a wide variety of fields including chemotherapy, anesthesia, drug metabolism and neuropharmacology. In 1955 Brodie and his colleagues produced some results that once more raised the possibility of a chemical basis of mental disease. The speculations arising from Brodie's work have turned out to be surprisingly difficult to confirm or reject.

Brodkin, Herbert (1912–1990). U.S. television producer. He helped create such innovative programs as "The Defenders" (1961–65) and "Playhouse 90." After forming an independent production company in the 1960s, he went on to create a series of highly acclaimed, often controversial made-for-television movies and mini-series. Among the most notable were *Holocaust* (1978), *Skokie* (1981) and *The Missiles of October* (1981).

Brodovitch, Alexey (1898–1971). Russian-born art director, graphic designer, and teacher with major influence in the U.S. Born in Ogolitchi, Russia, Brodovitch came to the U.S. in 1930 to take up a design career. From 1934 to 1956 he was art director of *Harper's Bazaar* magazine, a post in which his own design and his influence on other designers and photographers was extensive. His use of strong photographic images, emphatic typography, simple layout with generous white space characterized his innovative style. He continued in practice as a consultant after leaving *Harper's Bazaar* until his retirement in 1967. Classes he conducted in design and photography were attended by many younger designers and photographers, who looked toward him as their mentor. The character of the American fashion magazine and of modern fashion photography was largely molded by Brodovitch.

Brodsky, Joseph (1940–). Russian-born poet and critic. Brodsky quit school after the eighth grade. As a young man, he befriended the elderly Anna AKHMATOVA and began writing poetry of lyric intensity and metaphysical inwardness. He was arrested and tried by Soviet authorities for "social parasitism" in 1964, and as a result served 20 months of hard labor, during which time he began studying English seriously. In 1972 he was asked to leave the U.S.S.R. permanently; he settled in the United States where he took up a series of academic appointments at the University of Michigan, Mt. Holyoke College and elsewhere. He received a National Book Critics Circle award for criticism in 1986 and the NOBEL PRIZE for literature in 1987. Brodsky's books include *Selected Poems* (1973), *Less Than One: Selected Essays* (1986) and *To Urania* (1988). He was characterized by poet W.H. AUDEN as "a traditionalist" who "shows a deep respect and love for the past of his native land," but appears to be irrevocably estranged from it.

Poet Joseph Brodsky in his Greenwich Village apartment (1981).

For further reading:

Polukhina, Valentina, *Joseph Brodsky: a Poet for Our Time.* New York: Cambridge University Press, 1989.

Bronk, Detlev Wulf (1897–1975). American physiologist. The son of a Baptist minister, Bronk came from Dutch stock; the family name survives in the Bronx district of New York. He was educated at Swarthmore College and the University of Michigan, where he earned his Ph.D. in 1922. Bronk spent some time in England working with Edgar ADRIAN in Cambridge before accepting, in 1929, the post of director of the Johnson Institute, attached to the University of Pennsylvania, where he was already serving as professor of biophysics and director of the Institute of Neurology. In 1949 Bronk became president of Johns Hopkins University but left there in 1953 to take the presidency of the Rockefeller Institute (later Rockefeller University) in New York, where he remained until his retirement in 1968. Bronk established an early reputation with his fundamental work with Adrian on nerve impulses (1928–29). They demonstrated that both motor and sensory nerves transmit their messages by varying the number of impulses sent rather than by using impulses of different intensities. By careful experiments they established that the range of the impulses is between 5 and 150 per second, with greater stimuli producing higher frequencies. In the 1930s Bronk worked mainly on the autonomic nervous system. He is, however, mainly remembered for his crucial role in organizing the institutional structure of American science.

Bronowski, Jacob (1908–1974). Polish-born philosopher of science. Bronowski immigrated to Britain and earned a Ph.D. in mathematics at Cambridge University. He subsequently pursued the career of a 20th-century Renaissance man; as well as a mathematician, he was a poet, playwright, inventor and held various government, administrative and academic posts. Shortly before his death, Bronowski gained wide public recognition when he hosted "The Ascent of Man." This series, produced by the BRITISH BROADCASTING CORPORATION (BBC), surveyed the history of Western civilization.

Bronsted, Johannes Nicolaus (1879–1947). Danish physical chemist. He studied at the Polytechnic Institute, Copenhagen, from 1897, earning degrees in engineering (1899) and chemistry (1902) and a doctorate (1908). The same year he became professor of chemistry there. Bronsted worked mainly in thermodynamics, especially in the fields of electrochemistry and reaction kinetics. In 1923 he proposed, concurrently with Thomas Lowry, a new definition of acids and bases. This, the **Lowry-Bronsted theory,** states that an acid is a substance that tends to lose a proton and a base is a substance that tends to gain a proton.

Bronx. Borough of the U.S.'s NEW YORK CITY. In the first half of this century, the Bronx was known as a light-industrial center; in recent decades, it decayed considerably (although many believe that its downward slide has bottomed out). The South Bronx became a classic example of urban blight. Yankee Stadium is located in the Bronx.

Brook, Peter (Stephen Paul) (1925–). British theatrical director. Brook has been one of the most influential British theatrical directors of the post-World War II era. He made his mark as a prodigy with his successful direction, at age 18, of *Doctor Faustus* by Christopher Marlowe at the Torch Theatre in London. Brook went on to direct an acclaimed production of Shakespeare's *Love's Labour's Lost* (1946) at Stratford-upon-Avon. In 1950 he directed the renowned British actor Paul Scofield in *Ring Around the Moon* by Jean ANOUILH. In 1962 Brook was named codirector of the new Royal Shakespeare Company. He achieved great success with that company in productions of Shakespeare's *King Lear* (1962) and *Marat/Sade* (1964) by Peter WEISS. Brook's production of Shakespeare's *A Midsummer Night's Dream* (1970) featured intricate stage acrobatics and a white stage setting. He founded the International Centre of Theatre Research in 1970 and there directed a 10-hour stage adaptation of the Indian epic *Mahabharata*. In 1988 Brook staged a revival of Anton CHEKHOV's *The Cherry Orchard* in New York City.

Brooke, Edward W(illiam) (1919–). U.S. senator. Born in Washington, D.C., Brooke attended Howard University and the Boston University Law School. After practicing law during the 1950s, Brooke, a liberal Republican, began his political career as attorney general of Massachusetts (1963–66). In 1966 he became the first black since Reconstruction to be elected to the Senate, and the first black in history to be elected to that office by popular vote. He was a senator from 1967 to 1979, serving (1967) on the President's Commission on Civil Disorders, which looked into urban race riots; advocating a strong CIVIL RIGHTS policy; initiating housing legislation that resulted in the 1970 Housing and Urban Development Act; and breaking (1973) with the NIXON administration over WATERGATE. Brooke was defeated by Democrat Paul Tsongas in the 1978 election.

Brooke, Rupert (Chawner) (1887–1915). British poet. Brooke was born at Rugby, where his father was a master, and was educated at Cambridge. He published his first collection of poetry, *Poems*, in 1911, and his work was featured in *Georgian Poetry*, the periodical he was instrumental in founding along with his friend, editor Sir Edward Marsh (see the GEORGIANS). Brooke served in WORLD WAR I in the Royal Naval Division and was acclaimed for his War Sonnets, which appeared in *New Numbers* in 1915. He died of blood poisoning en route to the Dardanelles and was buried in Scyros. His War Sonnets presented a dreamy, patriotic and heroic view of the war that went out of fashion as the war dragged on and the appalling carnage of the trenches became apparent. Nonetheless, his tragic early death made Brooke seem the romantic embodiment of an age that was about to end. He is now chiefly remembered for his lighter verse and for his Elizabethan scholarship.

Brooklyn. Borough of the U.S.'s NEW YORK CITY. After existing as a wealthy, independent suburb, Brooklyn became a New York City borough in 1898. Its most noteworthy landmark is the Brooklyn Bridge, spanning the East River to Manhattan, which was built from 1869 to 1883. Another bridge, the Verrazano, crosses New York harbor's Narrows and is the longest suspension bridge in the world. As late as the 1930s, some of its land was still under agricultural use. At present, with a population in excess of four million, it would stand as the fourth largest American city—if it were an independent municipality. It is a shipping and small industry center, with neighborhoods such as Bedford-Stuyvesant, Brooklyn Heights, Coney Island and Flatbush. Brooklyn residents have included composer Aaron COPLAND, poet Hart CRANE and novelist Thomas WOLFE.

Brookner, Anita (1928–). British novelist and art historian. Born in London and educated at King's College, London, and the Courtauld Institute of Art in London, where she later taught, Brookner became the first female Slade Professor at Cambridge in 1968. An authority on 18th- and 19th-century art, she has written books on Watteau and Greuze, among others. Her fiction includes *Hotel du Lac* (1984, Booker Prize), *Family and Friends* (1985), *A Friend from England* (1987) and *Lewis Percy* (1990). Her delicate, inward novels explore the themes of family and loneliness; they are peopled with neurotic characters and written with an ironic wit.

For further reading:

Sadler, Lynn Veach, *Anita Brookner*. Boston: Twayne, 1990.

Brooks, Cleanth (1906–). American critic. Brooks first met the Southern FUGITIVES AND AGRARIANS, who laid the groundwork for NEW CRITICISM, at Vanderbilt University (1924–28). After receiving an M.A. from Tulane (1929), he studied at Exeter College, Oxford, on a Rhodes scholarship. With Robert Penn WARREN, he taught at Louisiana State, where he was an editor of the influential *Southern Review*. Together they wrote *Understanding Poetry* (1938), which emphasized close reading rather than subjective response to poetry. In 1946 he moved to Yale where he was associated with the critics Rene Wellek, William K. Wimsatt and Maynard Mack. His major theoretical work, *The Well-Wrought Urn*, appeared in 1947. He collaborated with Wimsatt on *Literary Criticism: A Short History* (1957). He is also known for two key works on FAULKNER and as the critic whose classic essay made T.S. ELIOT'S WASTE LAND accessible.

Brooks, Gwendolyn (1917–). American poet and playwright. Born in Topeka, Kansas, Brooks graduated from Wilson Junior College (1936) and worked for the NAACP Youth Council in Chicago during the 1930s. *A Street in Bronzeville* (1945) won her wide acclaim and several grants and fellowships. Her second book, *Annie Allen*, was awarded a PULITZER PRIZE in 1950. In 1968, she ended a 28-year relationship with her New York publisher in favor of a black-owned firm in Detroit. In 1969, she was made poet laureate of Illinois. She also had a varied teaching career and received numerous honorary degrees. Whereas her early work was largely a realistic portrayal of urban ghetto life, her later work became more overtly polemical and sociopolitical. Her work has set the highest standards for African-American literature.

Gwendolyn Brooks, winner of the 1950 Pulitzer Prize for poetry (Feb. 8, 1968).

For further reading:

Kent, George E., *A Life of Gwendolyn Brooks*. Lexington: University Press of Kentucky, 1990.

Melham, D.H., *Gwendolyn Brooks: Poetry and the Heroic Voice*. Lexington: University Press of Kentucky, 1987.

Brooks, Louise (1906–1985). American actress. Brooks' most memorable performances were in the German SILENT FILM classics, *Pandora's Box* and *Diary of a Lost Girl*, directed by Austrian G.W. Pabst. Spurned by HOLLYWOOD, Brooks made her last film in 1938, and began contributing articles to various film journals. Her memoir, *Lulu in Hollywood*, was published in 1982 to wide critical acclaim.

Brooks, Mel [Melvin Kaminsky] (1926–). American comedic film director, writer, actor and producer. Brooks is one of the best-known figures in American comedy of the second half of the 20th century. He first emerged as a major talent in the 1950s when, as a young man, he became one of the leading writers for the hit Sid CAESAR television program "Your Show of Shows." Brooks enjoyed further success with the comedy album *2,000 Years with Carl Reiner and Mel Brooks* (1960), in which Brooks played a 2,000-

year-old man with cranky attitudes and a poor memory. Brooks was also a key creator of the "Get Smart" television comedy series in the 1960s. But he has made his greatest mark as a film director. He won an ACADEMY AWARD for best animated short subject with *The Critic* (1964), then achieved both popular and critical success with *The Producers* (1967), a classic black comedy with a plot that includes the ultimate bad taste musical, "Springtime for Hitler." Other hit films by Brooks include the Western parody *Blazing Saddles* (1974), the horror film spoof *Young Frankenstein* (1974), the Alfred HITCHCOCK send-up *High Anxiety* (1977) and *Spaceballs* (1987), a satirical rewrite of *Star Wars*. Brooks has also produced films including the acclaimed drama *The Elephant Man* (1980). He is married to the actress Anne Bancroft.

Brooks, Van Wyck (1886–1963). American critic. After a brief flirtation with poetry at Harvard, Brooks worked as a literary journalist to support his critical writing. *The Wine of the Puritans* (1908) introduced his theme of the schism in American culture between idealism, or transcendentalism, and commercialism; *America's Coming of Age* (1915) employed the terms "highbrow" and "lowbrow" to describe the same dialectic. His critical trilogy (1920–32) examined the careers of Mark Twain, Henry JAMES and Emerson; and his five-volume *Makers and Finders: A History of the Writer in America, 1800–1915* (1936–52) presented an anecdotal, impressionistic view of the American literary scene. *The Flowering of New England* won a 1936 PULITZER PRIZE and was a best-seller. In the 1940s, his vision came under fire from adherents of the NEW CRITICISM, the PARTISAN REVIEW group and other academics.

Broom, Robert (1866–1951). British-South African morphologist and paleontologist. Broom graduated in medicine from Glasgow University in 1889. He traveled to Australia in 1892 and in 1897 settled in South Africa where he practiced medicine, often in remote rural communities, until 1928. He also held posts as professor of geology and zoology (1903–10) at Victoria College, now Stellenbosch University, South Africa, and curator of paleontology at the Transvaal Museum, Pretoria, from 1934 until his death. Apart from studies of the embryology of Australian marsupials and monotremes, Broom's major contributions to science have been concerned with the evolutionary origins of mammals, including man. He excavated and studied the fossils of the Karroo beds of the Cape and in the 1940s discovered numbers of Australopithecine skeletons in Pleistocene age quarries at Sterkfontein, Transvaal. These latter have proved of considerable importance in investigations of man's ancestry. Broom's account of their discovery is given in *Finding the Missing Link* (1950).

Brophy, Brigid (Antonia) (1929–). British author. An eccentric, prolific writer of catholic tastes, Brophy is a novelist, critic, biographer and dramatist as well as an advocate of animal rights and a successful campaigner for the Public Lending Right, which provides that authors are paid when their works are borrowed from libraries. Her first collection of short stories was *The Crown Princess and Other Stories* (1953). *Hackenfeller's Ape* (1959), which she considers her best work, won the Cheltenham Literary Festival First Prize for a first novel. Other works include *Mozart the Dramatist: A New View of Mozart, His Operas and His Age* (1964) and *The Adventures of God in His Search for the Black Girl: A Novel and Some Fables* (1973). In the early 1980s Brophy was stricken with multiple sclerosis, which she eloquently describes in *Baroque and Roll and Other Essays* (1987).

Brouwer, Dirk (1902–1966). Dutch-American astronomer. Brouwer studied at the University of Leiden where he earned his Ph.D. under Willem de Sitter in 1927. He then moved to the U.S. to do postdoctoral research at the University of California, Berkeley. He joined the Yale faculty in 1928, serving from 1941 until his death as professor of astronomy and director of the Yale Observatory. Brouwer worked mainly in celestial mechanics, particularly in the analysis of observations concerning orbiting bodies, and on planetary theory, providing new methods by which the motion of a planet could be determined and by which the very long term changes in orbits could be calculated. He collaborated with Gerald CLEMENCE and W.J. Eckert to write in 1951 the basic paper to give the accurate orbits of the outer planets. He introduced new techniques and initiated programs for the measurement of stellar positions, especially in the southern sky. He was also involved in the decision to adopt a new time scale, known at Brouwer's suggestion as **Ephemeris Time** (ET). This became necessary when the rotation rate of the Earth, on which time measurements had been based, was found to vary very slightly. Ephemeris Time is derived from the orbital motions of the moon and the Earth and is perfectly uniform. It is only used by astronomers, however; more general timekeeping now involves atomic clocks.

Brouwer, Luitzen Egbertus Jan (1881–1966). Dutch mathematician and philosopher of mathematics. Brouwer studied at the University of Amsterdam, where he became professor in the mathematics department. From 1903 to 1909 he did important work in topology, presenting several fundamental results, including the fixed-point theorem. Brouwer's best-known achievement was the creation of the philosophy of mathematics known as **intuitionism**. The central ideas of intuitionism are a rejection of the concept of the completed infinite and an insistence that acceptable mathematical proofs be constructive. That is, they must not merely show that a certain mathematical entity (e.g., a number or a function) *exists* but must actually be able to construct it. This view leads to the rejection of large amounts of widely accepted classical mathematics and one of the three fundamental laws of logic, the law of excluded middle (a proposition is either true or not true). Brouwer was able to reprove many classical results in an intuitionistically acceptable way, including his own fixed-point theorem.

Browder, Earl (1891–1973). Longtime American communist leader. Browder, a native of Kansas, became active in the tiny American Communist Party in 1920 and journeyed to Moscow where he met LENIN. At the start of WORLD WAR II, Browder and the party were opposed to U.S. involvement. After Germany invaded the Soviet Union, Browder and the party were ardent supporters of the U.S. war effort. After the war Browder had a philosophical dispute with the leaders of the U.S. party and was ousted from membership. During the anticommunist McCarthy period he was called to testify before a Senate Foreign Relations subcommittee investigating communist infiltration of the State Department. Although he was jailed when he refused to answer certain questions, his conviction was overturned because he had the right to refuse to answer irrelevant questions. Although many considered him the elder statesman of the American Left, he never resumed any formal affiliation with the Communist Party.

Brown, Archie (1911–1990). U.S. labor leader. West Coast leader of the International Longshoremen's Union, he had been convicted in 1962 under a provision of the 1959 Landrum-Griffin Act that barred communists from serving in official union positions. He won a landmark Supreme Court decision in 1965, which found the previous ruling unconstitutional and upheld the right of communists to so serve.

Brown, Sir Arthur Whitten. See ALCOCK AND BROWN.

Brown, Christy (1932–1981). Irish author and painter. Born in Dublin, the 10th of 22 children, Brown was afflicted from birth with cerebral palsy. Almost completely disabled, Brown had the use of his left foot and trained himself to paint and to type with it. His first book, an autobiography, *My Left Foot* (1954; reissued as *The Childhood Story of Christy Brown*, 1972; filmed 1989), describes his efforts to cope with his disability. His next book, *Down All the Days* (1970), is a fictionalized autobiography with a bawdy depiction of life in Dublin slums. Other work includes *Come Softly to My Wake: The Poems of Christy Brown* (1971); *Of Snails and Skylarks* (1977) and the novel *Wild Grow the Lilies* (1976).

Brown, Clarence (1890–1987). American film director. Brown spent his formative years as an assistant director to filmmaker Maurice Tourneur, from whom he inherited a crisp, pictorial eye, a solid craftsmanship and an intelligent sensibility for story and character. Establishing himself with the Rudolph VALENTINO vehicle, *The Eagle* (1925), Brown then became a leading director for METRO-GOLDWYN-MAYER with a series of films starring Greta GARBO, including *Flesh and the Devil* (1927), *Anna Christie* (1930) and *Anna Karenina* (1935) as well as three others. A six-time ACADEMY AWARD-nominee, he directed many splendid character studies that are now regarded as classics, including *Of Human Hearts* (1938), *Edison the Man* (1940), *National Velvet* (1944) and *The Yearling* (1946). His *Intruder in the Dust* (1949), adapted from William FAULKNER's book, was a pioneering indictment of racial prejudice in the American South. In 1971 he established the Clarence Brown Theatre for the Performing Arts at his alma mater in Knoxville, Tenn.

For further reading:

Coursodon, Jean-Pierre, ed., *American Directors*. New York: McGraw-Hill, 1983.

Brown, Clifford (1930–1956). American jazz trumpeter, a pivotal figure of 1950s jazz. While consolidating the BEBOP virtuosity of Dizzy GILLESPIE and Fats Navarro with the moody lyricism of Miles DAVIS, Brown pointed the way for such modern trumpet stylists as Lee Morgan and Freddie Hubbard. As he studied mathematics and music in college in the late 1940s, Brown began sitting in at Philadelphia jazz clubs with such major improvisers as Charlie PARKER and Gillespie and Navarro, who encouraged his musical ambitions. Key engagements with pianist Tadd Dameron, vibraphonist Lionel HAMPTON and drummer Art BLAKEY brought international recognition and further refinements in an extraordinary approach that combined a big brash sound, a crisp percussive attack and consistently inspired improvisatory flights based on the bebop lexicon coined by Parker and Gillespie. Brown's zenith came in 1954–56 when he co-led the Clifford Brown-Max Roach Quintet, a justly celebrated 1950s jazz group noted for its "hard bop" edge, featuring Roach's aggressive drumming and Brown's dazzling yet lyrical and finely structured solos. Brown's genius was cut short at the age of 25 when an automobile accident claimed his life.

For further reading:

Gridley, Mark C., *Jazz Styles*. Englewood Cliffs, New Jersey: Prentice-Hall, 1978.

Brown, Edmund G(erald), Jr. (1938–). American politician; governor of California (1975–82). Jerry Brown, son of California Governor Pat Brown, received his B.A. from the University of California at Berkeley (1961) and his law degree from Yale (1964). In the late Sixties, Brown became active in the ANTIWAR MOVEMENT and in the campaign to unionize migrant workers. In 1970 he was elected secretary of state of California, in which office he conducted some highly publicized reform campaigns that won him wide popularity. In 1974, he was elected governor of the state by a narrow margin. As governor, Brown quickly gained national attention with his quirky style, his commitment to limited government, and the austerity measures he implemented. In 1976, he made a run for the Democratic presidential nomination, losing to Jimmy CARTER. He was reelected governor in 1978, and in 1980 he made another unsuccessful attempt at the Democratic presidential nomination. In 1982, by which time he had acquired a reputation for being mercurial and was widely known as "Governor Moonbeam," Brown ran for the U.S. Senate but was defeated by Pete Wilson. That year, he was succeeded as governor by George Deukmejian, who defeated Democrat Tom Bradley. In 1989, Brown returned to politics as chairman of the California Democratic Party.

Brown, George S(cratchley) (1918–1978). American military officer. A graduate of West Point (1941), Brown served in the U.S. Eighth Air Force in Europe in WORLD WAR II. He won the Distinguished Service Cross for his role in the Allied bombing of the oil refineries at PLOESTI, Romania (August 1943). During the KOREAN WAR he was director of operations for the Fifth Air Force. In 1968 he became head of U.S. Air Force operations in VIETNAM (see VIETNAM WAR). In 1973 President Richard M. NIXON named him Air Force chief of staff. He was later chairman of the Joint Chiefs of Staff (1974–78). His years as America's top-ranking military officer were marked by controversy over his often blunt public statements. Brown blamed South Vietnam's defeat (1975) on congressional cutbacks in military aid to the South.

Brown, Harrison (Scott) (1917–1986). American chemist. Brown played a key role in producing plutonium for the first ATOMIC BOMB. He later emerged as a leading opponent of nuclear weapons development. His varied career included long service as foreign secretary of the National Academy of Sciences. He was also involved in analyses of meteorites for clues to their origin and promotion of birth control and editor of the *Bulletin of Atomic Scientists*. From 1951 to 1977 he was professor of geochemistry at the California Institute of Technology.

Brown, Helen Gurley (1922–). American author and editor. Brown worked as a secretary and award-winning advertising copywriter before becoming editor-in-chief of *Cosmopolitan* magazine in 1965. In that role she has parlayed a bold and brassy view of American women to readers, glamorizing power (often sexual power) and freedom as prime goals for young, professional and primarily unmarried women. Brown has also written two books: *Sex and the Single Girl* (1962) and *Having It All* (1982). She received the Distinguished Achievement Award in journalism from Stanford University in 1981.

Brown, Henry B. (1836–1913). Associate justice, U.S. Supreme Court (1890–1906). A graduate of Yale University, Brown also studied at Yale and Harvard law schools but passed the bar in Detroit after studying law at a law firm in the city. Married into a wealthy Detroit family, he held a number of public posts and was also in private law practice before being appointed a federal district court judge. Brown had considerable experience in admiralty law and once on the bench was considered a national authority on the subject. He was appointed to the Supreme Court by President Benjamin Harrison and served until 1906 when his vision failed him. He died in Bronxville, New York, in 1913.

Brown, Herbert Charles (1912–). American chemist. Brown moved from England to Chicago with his family when he was two years old. Brown left school to help support his mother and three sisters. When he finally did enter Crane Junior College, it was forced to close in 1933 for lack of funds. He eventually went to the University of Chicago where he earned his doctorate in 1938. Brown then worked at Wayne University, from 1943 until 1947, when he moved to Purdue University, where he served as professor of inorganic chemistry until his retirement in 1978. Brown was noted for his work on compounds of boron. He discovered a method of making sodium borohydride, used extensively in organic chemistry for reduction. He also found a simple way of preparing diborane by reacting diborane with alkenes (unsaturated hydrocarbons containing a double bond). He produced a new class of compounds, organoboranes, which are also useful in organic chemistry. Brown also used addition compounds of amines with boron compounds to investigate the role of steric effects in organic chemistry. He received the 1979 NOBEL PRIZE for chemistry.

Brown, H(ubert) "Rap" (1943–). Militant American CIVIL RIGHTS leader. Brown was born in Baton Rouge, Louisiana. In the 1960s he attracted wide attention for his militant views, and in 1967 he assumed the chairmanship of the Student Nonviolent Coordinating Committee. Brown had frequent brushes with the law during these years and was charged with inciting riot, transporting weapons across state lines and arson. In 1971, after living as a fugitive for 17 months, he was wounded in a shootout with New York City police during the holdup of a tavern. He was convicted of the crime and on May 10, 1973, was sentenced to 5–15 years in prison. He was paroled on October 21, 1976.

Brown, J. Douglas (1898–1986). U.S. economist. In 1934 he was one of the three experts who served on President Franklin D. ROOSEVELT's Committee on Economic Security. They were the architects of the U.S. Social Security system. From 1946 to 1966 he was dean of the faculty at Princeton University.

Brown, James (1928–). American singer-songwriter. The flamboyant Brown combined gospel, soul, funk and flat-out showmanship to become a music legend. Early hits included "Papa's Got A Brand New Bag" (1965) and "I Got You (I Feel Good)" (1965). His popularity surged with the emergence of the 1960s BLACK POWER movement and with such hits as "Say It Loud, I'm Black and Proud" (1968), "Super Bad" (1970) and "Soul Power" (1971). He continues to record such hits as "Living in America" (1986) and is a charismatic live performer. Jailed for tax evasion in 1990, Brown resumed recording upon his release.

Brown, James Nathaniel "Jim" (1936–). American football player. A combination of athletic ability and grace under pressure made Jim Brown the most exciting ball carrier in the history of professional football. A star at Syracuse University, he won three letters in addition to football. He was the NFL's 1957 rookie of the year, with a total of 942 yards rushing, and in 1960 was named the best back of the previous decade. The first back ever to surpass 10,000 yards rushing, over a nine-year career he gained a total of 12,312 yards and scored a record 126 touchdowns. In 1965, Brown retired to pursue a career in acting. He was named to the Pro Football Hall of Fame in 1971.

Brown, Robert Hanbury (1916–). British radio astronomer. Brown was educated at the City and Guilds College, London. From 1936 to 1942 he worked on the development of RADAR at the Air Ministry Research Station, Bawdsey. This was followed by three years in Washington with the British Air Commission and two years with the Ministry of Supply. By the late 1940s Brown was keen to enter academic research and persuaded Bernard LOVELL to admit him as a research student at the Jodrell Bank radio observatory. Brown later served there as professor of radio astronomy from 1960 to 1963 when he was appointed to a professorship in physics at the University of Sydney. In 1950 Brown plotted the first radio map of an external galaxy, the spiral nebula in Andromeda. He later identified emissions from four other extragalactic nebulae.

Brown, Sterling Allen (1901–1989). American poet and teacher of black American literature. As a professor at Howard University (as was his father), he introduced the school's first course in Afro-American literature. Among his students were the writers Amiri BARAKA and Toni MORRISON, psychologist Kenneth B. CLARK, and actor Ossie Davis. Brown's own work helped to lay the foundation for studies in black American literature. His collected poems were published in 1983. Brown also wrote the study *A Negro in American Fiction*.

Browning, John Moses (1855–1926). U.S. inventor of the Browning automatic rifle. Browning was born in Ogden, Utah, the son of a Mormon gunsmith. Beginning in 1879, he designed a number of firearms, including some automatic and repeating models, for different firms; he manufactured guns at his own company as well. Many of his designs were purchased by the U.S. military, including his "Peacemaker" machine gun. In 1918, he introduced the Browning automatic rifle (BAR), which became a standard shoulder weapon of the U.S. Army for the next four decades.

Browning, Tod (1882–1962). American film director; one of the great masters of horror film direction. At age 16 he ran away from home to join a circus, and his experiences at that time with carnival life and, in particular, the physical freaks who appeared in the carny sideshows, would leave a lasting mark on his films. In the 1910s, Browning worked as an assistant to famous director D.W. GRIFFITH. He made his own directorial debut with *Jim Bludso* (1917) but found his metier in the 1920s when he teamed with actor Lon CHANEY on a number of successful horror films, including *The Unholy Three* (1925), *The Black Bird* (1926), *The Road to Mandalay* (1926), *The Unknown* (1927), *London After Midnight* (1927) and *Where East Is East* (1929). After Chaney's untimely death, Browning directed Bela LUGOSI in *Dracula* (1931). *Freaks* (1932) was Browning's most controversial film, as it featured an international cast of sideshow performers. Browning depicted them sympathetically, and the film is today regarded as a classic. Browning went into retirement at the end of the 1930s.

Brown Shirts. See Ernst ROEHM.

Brown v. Board of Education (1954). Landmark U.S. Supreme Court case that set the groundwork for the racial desegregation of schools throughout the U.S. Despite the Civil War amendments to the U.S. Constitution guaranteeing legal rights to black citizens, segregated school systems and accommodation persisted for a century after the end of the war. The 1896 Supreme Court case *Plessy v. Ferguson* had legalized SEGREGATION under the "separate but equal" doctrine. Under this doctrine, a state could legally maintain one set of schools for whites and one set of schools for blacks under the guise of their being separate but equal. In fact, the black school systems were nearly always radically inferior to the white school systems.

In the *Brown* decision, written by Chief Justice Earl WARREN, the Supreme Court held that the maintenance of two separate school systems was inherently unequal and a violation of the 14th Amendment's Equal Protection clause. Despite the ruling, many states refused to comply, which led to forced desegregation of public schools by the federal government—accompanied by violence and bloodshed. The tide turned in favor of public school desegregation only after President Dwight D. EISENHOWER threatened to desegregate the LITTLE ROCK, Arkansas, public schools using federal troops. The desegregation of public universities, which came later, was also marked by violence and enforcement by federal troops. The ruling in the case outlawing "separate but equal" schools was later extended to other state-supported facilities. Private facilities were later desegregated by the CIVIL RIGHTS ACT OF 1964. Because of its importance, the Brown case is sometimes simply referred to as "the school desegregation case."

Brubeck, Dave (1920–). In the 1950s, pianist-composer Dave Brubeck rose to the top of the jazz world with the "classic" David Brubeck Quartet, featuring the significant contributions of alto saxophonist Paul Desmond, bassist Eugene Wright and drummer Joe Morello. Brubeck's success, especially with college audiences, was signaled in 1954 when he appeared on the cover of TIME magazine and was signed by Columbia Records; in 1959 Brubeck enjoyed the distinction of having the first million-selling jazz instrumental recording (Desmond's "Take Five" on one side, Brubeck's "Blue Rondo a la Turk" on the reverse). Though an effective jazz popularizer, some critics found his keyboard style dense and overly prolix. Still, his experiments with polyphony, polytonality and polyrhythms, as well as with unorthodox time signatures such as 5/4 ("Take Five") and 9/8 ("Blue Rondo a la Turk"), proved greatly influential. In 1967, Brubeck dissolved his highly visible and very successful Quartet to focus on composition, a decision influenced by early studies with prominent 20th-century composers Darius MILHAUD and Arnold SCHOENBERG. Though he has continued to assemble engaging foursomes through the years, Brubeck's transcendent period was in the 1950s in company with the exceptional Desmond, Wright and Morello.

For further reading:

Lyons, Len, *The Great Jazz Pianists: Speaking of Their Lives and Music*. New York: William Morrow, 1983.

Bruce, Sir David (1855–1931). British bacteriologist. A one-time colleague of Robert Koch in Berlin, Bruce spent the greater part of his career as a military physician. Educated at Edinburgh University, he was assistant professor of pathology at the Army Medical School, Netley (1889–94), and then commandant of the Royal Army Medical College, Millbank, where he was also director of research on tetanus and trench fever (1914–18). He undertook royal commissions of enquiry into various diseases of man and domestic animals in Malta and central Africa. In Malta he was able to trace the cause of Malta fever (brucellosis or undulant fever found in the milk of goats) to a bacterium later named after him as *Brucella melitensis*. Bruce also investigated the cause of nagana, a disease of horses and cattle in central and southern Africa, and found it to be transmitted by a trypanosome parasite carried by the tsetse fly. This work was of great help in his later research on sleeping sickness (trypanosomiasis), which he also proved to be transmitted by the tsetse fly. The recipient of many honors for his humanitarian work, Bruce was chairman of the War Office's Pathological Committee during WORLD WAR I. He was knighted in 1908.

Bruce, Lenny [Leonard Alfred Schneider] (1925–1966). American stand-up comedian. Bruce, who drew considerable hostility and attention from government authorities due to his use of so-called "dirty words" in his nightclub comedy act, was a brilliant satirist who dramatically expanded the style and subject matter of stand-up comedy. Bruce served in the Navy during World War II. He first drew national attention in the mid-1950s when his daring style of satire, in which Bruce probed taboo subjects such as racial fears, sexual fantasies and Jewish-Christian tensions, won him an admiring audience and made his act a cause celebre in liberal literary circles. In 1961, Bruce was imprisoned on obscenity charges. In 1963, his show was banned both in England and in Australia. Bruce published an autobiography, *How to Talk Dirty and Influence People* (1965). In his later years, he became addicted to heroin. He died of an overdose in 1966.

Bruhn, Erik (1928–1986). Danish-born ballet star regarded as one of the greatest classical dancers of the 20th century. For nearly two decades (1953–72), Bruhn was principal dancer with the AMERICAN BALLET THEATER. He also appeared in major roles with most of the world's other major companies, partnering a notable succession of great ballerinas, including the Italian dancer Carla FRACCI. Bruhn was also distinguished as a choreographer, directing the Royal Swedish Ballet from 1967 to 1972. In 1983 he assumed the position of artistic director of the National Ballet of Canada.

Brunei [Islamic Sultanate of Brunei]. The sultanate is located on the northwestern coast of the island of Borneo and covers an area of 2,225 square miles. A British residency from 1906 to 1971, Brunei was ruled by a sultan who was advised by a British resident on all matters except religion and culture. This residency was interrupted from 1941 to 1945 when Japan occupied the country. In 1971 a new United Kingdom-Brunei treaty was signed under which Britain retained control of Brunei's external affairs only. In 1984 Brunei achieved full independence from Britain; it is currently ruled by Sultan Hassanal Bolkiah.

Brunhes, Jean (1869–1930). French geographer. Brunhes came from an academic background—both his father and brother were professors of physics. He was educated at the Ecole Normal Superieure, Paris (1889–92), and taught at the University of Fribourg from 1896 until 1912, when he moved to the College de France, Paris, as professor of human geography. His most important work was his three-volume *Geographie humaine* (1910), which was translated into English in 1920. Following his teacher, Vidal de la Blache, he argued against the geographical determinism implicit in the work of Friedrich Ratzel. Instead he was more interested in revealing the complicated interplay among man, society and the environment.

Bruning, Heinrich (1885–1970). German chancellor (1930–32). A member of the Catholic Center Party and an expert in economics, he was appointed chancellor (1930) by President HINDENBURG in hopes that he would stabilize finances and lessen the appeal of the rising NAZI movement. His program of taxation and budget-cutting was defeated in the Reichstag, but Bruning continued to govern under emergency decrees from Hindenburg, thus helping to undermine parliamentary powers. As GERMANY's economic crisis deepened, he was forced to resign in 1932 and was replaced by Franz von PAPEN. A strong opponent of Adolf HITLER, Bruning fled Germany in 1934 and settled in the U.S. where he taught at Harvard University from 1939 to 1951. He returned to Germany in 1951, assuming a teaching post at the University of Cologne.

Brunner, Emil (1889–1966). Swiss theologian. The writings of Brunner are often closely linked to those of his Swiss contemporary, Karl BARTH. Both men began their careers as ministers in the Swiss Reformed Church and both emphasized, in their writings, the dependence of the human soul on a divine grace that could be achieved only by faith. Brunner, who spent most of his productive years as a professor of practical theology at the University of Zurich, emphasized in works such as *The Word and The World* (1931), *Justice and the Social Order* (1945), *Christianity and Civilization* (1948) and *The Christian Doctrine of Creation and Redemption* (1952), that Christianity is founded not on human reason or observation but rather in a divine revelation that supersedes all questioning. Brunner further held that the church ought to play a definite but limited role in social and political issues; this was necessary in order to fend off totalitarian policies that would constrict the dignity of the human soul.

Brussels, Treaty of. A 50-year mutual guarantee (March 17, 1948) among Belgium, Britain, France, Luxembourg and the Netherlands of military and other assistance in the event of an attack. With the adherence of West Germany and Italy in May 1955, the **Western European Union** was formed, intended to further West European unity.

Brutalism [also called New Brutalism]. Term first used in the 1950s by British architectural critics to describe an aspect of modern architectural design that emphasizes massive forms, usually constructed of reinforced concrete with its rough surfaces left exposed. Much of the later work of LE CORBUSIER is often re-

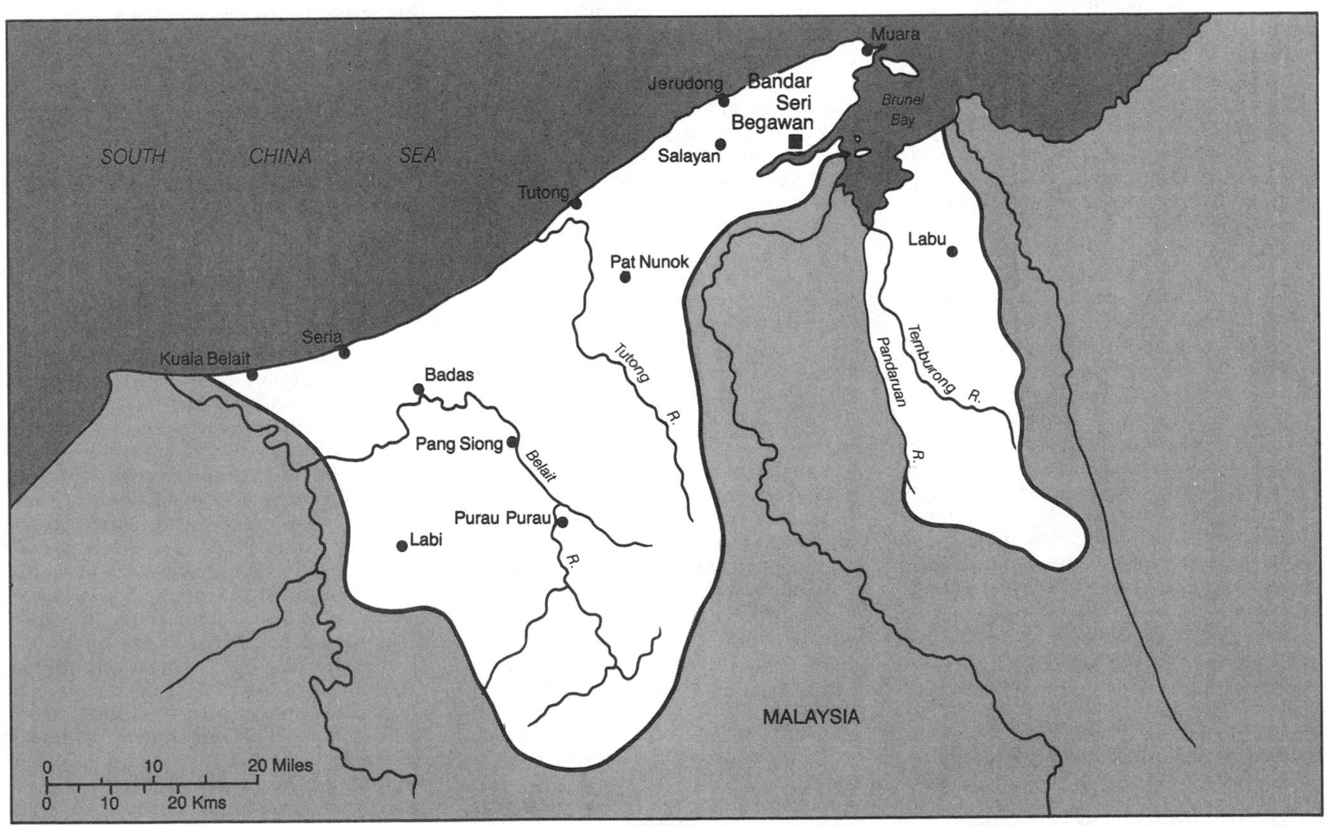

BRUNEI

ferred to as brutalist. The term is applied to the work of such architects as Paul Rudolph in the U.S. or Kenzo Tange in Japan that display similar characteristics.

Bryan, William Jennings (1860–1925). U.S. politician, often called "The Great Commoner" because of his advocacy of the common man. He studied law at Chicago and practiced in Jacksonville, Illinois (1883–87). He moved to Lincoln, Nebraska in 1887 to practice law, but left it for politics. Democrat Bryan was elected to Congress in 1890 and reelected in 1892. He was particularly known in the Congress as an advocate for farm interests. Later he started a career as a newspaper editor in Omaha, Nebraska and soon became a sought-after public speaker. After his speech at the Democratic convention in 1896, he was the Democratic presidential candidate. Although unsuccessful, he stressed the "sectional struggle between Wall Street and the 'toiling masses.'" He became known for his constant support of silver as the basis for U.S. currency. Nominated again for president in 1900, he lost to incumbent President MCKINLEY. Nominated by the Democrats again in 1908, he was defeated again. Later Bryan worked to elect Woodrow WILSON, and served as Wilson's secretary of state from 1912 to 1915. He made his last political appearance at the Democratic convention of 1924. His greatest publicity came when he acted for the prosecution at the trial of J.T. Scopes in 1925 (for teaching of evolutionary theory, see SCOPES TRIAL). Five days after the trial ended, Bryan died in his sleep. His memoirs were unfinished, but they were completed by his wife and published in 1925.

Brynner, Yul (1915–1985). American actor of Swiss-Mongolian descent, best known for his portrayal of the king in the musical play *The King and I* by Richard RODGERS and Oscar HAMMERSTEIN II. Brynner shaved his head for his Broadway debut as the king in 1951, and continued to do so for the rest of his career. He received an ACADEMY AWARD as best actor in 1956 for his appearance in the film version of *The King and I*. Other notable performances were in such films as *Anastasia* and *The Ten Commandments*. Toward the end of his life, when he was terminally ill with lung cancer, he made a series of television commercials warning of the dangers of cigarette smoking.

Bryusov, Valery Yakovlevich (1873–1924). Russian symbolist poet and writer. Bryusov's early work was largely misunderstood and ridiculed. By 1906, however, symbolism was recognized, and Bryusov was hailed as the foremost Russian poet. His *Stephanos* (1906) was warmly received, although his poetic talents were on the wane. Bryusov also wrote stories and plays, translated poetry, reviewed books and became an expert on Armenian poetry. After the Russian Revolution (1917) he became a communist and worked as the head of censorship, but he was not felt to be sufficiently reliable and was replaced.

Buber, Martin (1878–1965). Austrian-born

Martin Buber lecturing at the Washington, D.C. School of Psychiatry (April 18, 1957).

Jewish theologian, philosopher and social critic. Buber is one of the best-known theologians of this century, primarily due to the pervasive influence—in fields as diverse as clinical psychology, social work and existential philosophy—of his classic book *I and Thou* (1923). In this work Buber argued for the primacy of an immediate, unstructured and personal relationship between man and God that must, at times of crisis, supersede the dogma of organized religious faith. Buber, born in Vienna, studied philosophy at the Universities of Vienna, Zurich, and Berlin. As a young man he was politically active as a Zionist and worked with both Theodore HERZL and Chaim WEIZMANN. In the 1930s he immigrated to Israel and taught at the Hebrew University in Jerusalem. Buber's translations of the folktales of the Hasidic Jews of Eastern Europe served as the first popular introduction of Hasidism to the West. His major works include *Moses* (1946), *Eclipse of God* (1952), *Kingship of God* (1956) and *The Origin and Meaning of Hasidism* (1960).

For further reading:

Friedman, Maurice, *Martin Buber's Life and Work*. Detroit: Wayne State University Press, 1988.

Bubnov, Andrei Sergeyevich (1883–1940?). Russian Bolshevik revolutionary. Joining LENIN's Social-Democratic Party in 1903, Bubnov participated in the RUSSIAN REVOLUTION OF 1905, after which he worked in local party committees. Following the OCTOBER REVOLUTION (1917), he was elected to the first Politburo, and during the RUSSIAN CIVIL WAR he was a prominent commissar. A Left Communist in 1918, a Democratic Centralist and a Trotskyite in 1923, he supported STALIN after Lenin's death. In 1929 he was appointed commissar of education in the Russian Soviet Federated Socialist Republic. He disappeared in the GREAT PURGE, but his name was subsequently rehabilitated.

Buchan, John [1st Baron Tweedsmuir] (1875–1940). Scottish author and politician. Buchan published his first novel, *Sir Quixote of the Moors* (1895), while still a student at Brasenose College, Oxford. Although he wrote many biographies, including that of Sir Walter Scott (1932), he is best known for his adventure novels, including *The Thirty-nine Steps* (1915), which was filmed by Alfred HITCHCOCK in 1935; *Mr. Standfast* (1918); and *John Macnab* (1925). Buchan worked in reconstruction in SOUTH AFRICA following the BOER WAR, was a conservative member of Parliament from 1927 to 1935, and from 1935 until his death served as governor-general of Canada, where his last novel, *Sick Heart River* (1941), takes place.

For further reading:

Smith, Janet, *John Buchan: A Biography*. New York: St. Martin's, 1985.

Bucharest [Bucuresti]. Capital of Romania, on the Dimbovita River. Bucharest has been the site of numerous treaty negotiations, including those leading to the 1913 Treaty of Bucharest, which nullified Bulgaria's gains in the Second Balkan War (see the BALKANS). From 1916 to 1918, during WORLD WAR I, it was occupied by Germany and its allied forces. Long known as the "Paris of the East" for its cultural richness, from 1940 to 1944, during WORLD WAR II, it was occupied by the Nazis and damaged by German bombers during 1944 battles for control of the city. Occupied that year by Soviet troops, it became a part of the communist Eastern Europe bloc; it was COMINFORM headquarters from 1948 to 1956. In December 1989, Bucharest was the site of violent civil rebellion leading to the overthrow and execution of Romanian leader CEAUSESCU.

Buchenwald. Nazi CONCENTRATION CAMP located in the Buchenwald forest near Weimar, Germany. Buchenwald was established in 1937 ostensibly as a camp for "rehabilitation and labor." Initially it housed Germans—JEWS and gypsies who were persecuted by the Nazis, as well as socialists and others who opposed Hitler's program of ANTI-SEMITISM. After the outbreak of WORLD WAR II, Buchenwald became a death camp as Hitler tried to implement his FINAL SOLUTION.

Buchman, Frank (1878–1961). American evangelist. Buchman, who was ordained as a Lutheran minister in 1902, first earned public attention for his work in establishing an orphan home for boys. During a visit to Britain, Buchman claimed to have had a vision while sitting on a porch. This led to his founding a religious movement that was known as the OXFORD GROUP and, later, as MORAL RE-ARMAMENT, which also served as the title of a book by Buchman (1938). As leader of the movement, Buchman called for the establishment of a political and social dictatorship of God—God's will being manifested through the Christian values Buchman espoused. Buchman also praised Adolf HITLER as a front-line opponent of COMMUNISM. After WORLD WAR II, Buchman lost his public influence.

Buchner, Eduard (1860–1917). German organic chemist and biochemist. Buchner studied chemistry under Adolf von Bae-

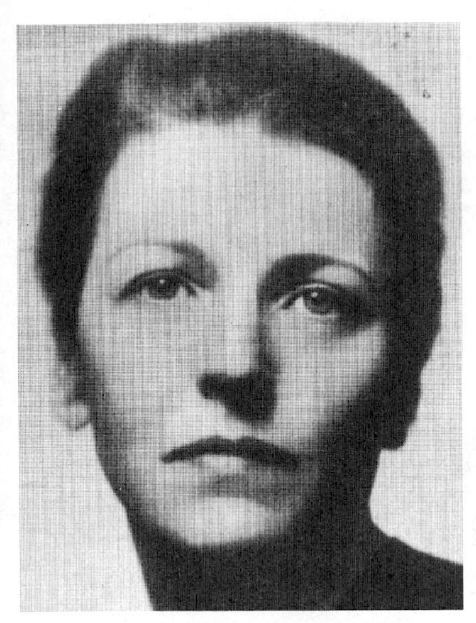

Pearl S. Buck, winner of the Nobel Prize for literature.

yer and botany at Munich, earning his doctorate in 1888. He was Baeyer's assistant until 1893. In 1897, while associate professor of analytical and pharmaceutical chemistry at Tubingen, he observed fermentation of sugar by cell-free extracts of yeast. Following Pasteur's work (1860), fermentation had been thought to require intact cells. Buchner's discovery of zymase was the first proof that fermentation was caused by enzymes and did not require the presence of living cells. Buchner also synthesized pyrazole (1889). He was professor of chemistry at the University of Berlin from 1898 and won the NOBEL PRIZE for chemistry in 1907 for his work on fermentation. He was killed in Romania while serving as a major in World War I.

Buck, Pearl (Comfort Sydenstricker) (1892–1973). American novelist. The daughter of American missionaries, Buck was born in West Virginia but spent most of her early life in China, learning to speak Chinese before she spoke English. Buck returned to the U.S. to attend Randolph Macon Women's College in West Virginia, but returned to China to teach in 1921. There she later met and married the missionary John Lossing Buck. Her most important novels are set in China and address the broader themes of the cyclical quality of life and the need for tolerance. These include *East Wind; West Wind* (1930); *A House Divided* (1935); *The Good Earth* (1931), which won the PULITZER PRIZE; and the biographies of her father and mother, *Fighting Angel* (1936) and *The Exile* (1936). Buck also translated Chinese literature into English. She was awarded the NOBEL PRIZE for literature in 1938.

For further reading:

La Farge, Ann, *Pearl Buck.* New York: Chelsea House, 1988.

Buckler, Ernest (1908–1984). Canadian novelist, essayist and short story writer. Buckler was once described as Canada's least-known best writer. His lyrical works centered around the rural Nova Scotia community where he lived most of his life. His themes included death, solitude, pain and the collapse of ideals. Some critics considered Buckler's best-known novel, *The Mountain and the Valley*, to be one of the great English-language novels of the 20th century.

Buckley, William F(rank), Jr. (1925–). American political writer, essayist, television interviewer and novelist. Buckley is perhaps the best-known conservative political analyst in the post-World War II U.S., due largely to the ongoing success of his television interview program "Firing Line," which has been syndicated since 1966 and earned an Emmy Award in 1969. Raised in a wealthy Roman Catholic family, Buckley was educated in private schools in England, France and the U.S. In 1944 he studied for a year at the University of Mexico and also gathered information for the CENTRAL INTELLIGENCE AGENCY, an experience Buckley would later draw on in writing a series of spy novels—beginning with *Saving the Queen* (1976)—that featured CIA operative Blackford Oakes as their protagonist. During WORLD WAR II, Buckley served in the U.S. Army and earned the rank of second lieutenant. He graduated from Yale University in 1950 and shortly thereafter won acclaim for *God and Man at Yale* (1951), a vituperative lambasting of the liberal policies of his alma mater. *McCarthy and His Enemies* (1954) was a vigorous defense of MCCARTHYISM. Buckley has edited the NATIONAL REVIEW since 1955. A candidate for mayor of New York City in 1965, he served as a member of the American delegation to the United Nations in 1973, an experience he chronicled in *United Nations Journal* (1973). His older brother, **James Buckley** (1923–), was a U.S. senator from New York (1971–77). (See also CONSERVATISM.)

For further reading:

Judis, John B., *William F. Buckley Jr.* New York: Simon & Schuster, 1990.

Budantseyev, Sergei Fedorovich (1896–1938?). Russian writer. His early work, such as *The Revolt* (1922), was conventional in content, but his later *Tale of the Sufferings of the Mind* was denounced as reactionary and extremely anti-Soviet, despite its apparently neutral theme. He died in a Soviet concentration camp in the late 1930s.

Budapest. Capital of HUNGARY, lying on both banks of the Danube River; the Aquincum of the ancient world. Budapest was established in 1873 by the unification of east bank cities Buda and Obuda and left bank Pest; it then served, along with VIENNA, as one of the two capitals of the AUSTRO-HUNGARIAN EMPIRE. It became a major commercial and cultural center but suffered from the defeat and dismemberment of the empire in WORLD WAR I. After the war, Hungary became independent and Budapest became its capital. In March 1919, communists led by Bela Kun took political control for a short while (see KUN'S RED TERROR). At the outset of WORLD WAR II, Hungary was allied with Germany; when it attempted to retract its stance, Budapest was occupied by the Nazis, in October 1944. In February 1945, the Russian conquest of the city brought major destruction to much of Buda's architectural landmarks. A violent revolt against Hungary's Soviet-supported regime occurred in October-November 1956; it was brutally quashed by Soviet troops. Budapest is today a restored and vibrant city. (See also HUNGARIAN UPRISING.)

Budenny, Semyon Mikhailovich (1883–1973). Russian military leader and marshal of the U.S.S.R. Having served in the 48th Cossack Regiment in the Far East, Budenny was involved in revolutionary activity early in 1917. In 1918 he organized a cavalry unit to combat White forces. A member of the COMMUNIST PARTY from 1919, he took an active role in the RUSSIAN CIVIL WAR. He pursued a highly successful military and political career; in 1939 he was deputy commissar for defense and in 1940 was first deputy. Despite a setback to his career in WORLD WAR II, in 1953 he was made inspector of cavalry. From 1939 to 1961 he was a full member of the Communist Party central committee.

Budge, (John) Don(ald) (1915–). American tennis player. Budge had a major impact on the game of tennis as he transformed the backhand from a defensive stroke into a formidable offensive weapon. He played on four U.S. Davis Cup teams, leading the team to its first victory in a decade. In the late 1930s his domination of the game was absolute, as he twice won both the Wimbledon singles title (1937–38) and the men's and mixed doubles. He duplicated the feat at Forest Hills, winning the U.S. Open singles and doubles titles four times from 1936 to 1938. In 1938 he became the first amateur to

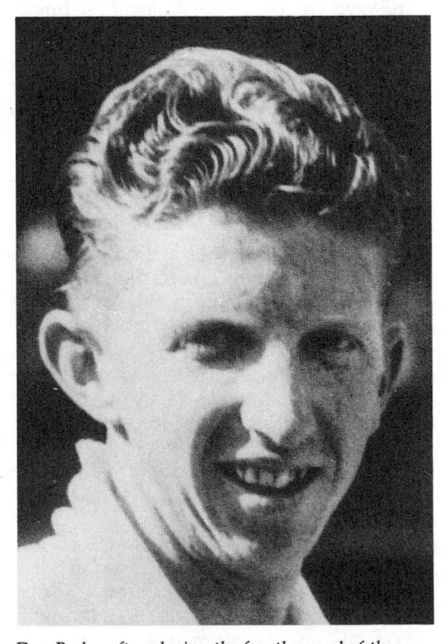

Don Budge after playing the fourth round of the Davis Cup (Aug. 6, 1935).

win the Grand Slam, encompassing the championships of the U.S., Great Britain, Australia and France. He turned professional in 1939 and also published his book *Budge on Tennis.* Budge was named to the National Lawn Tennis Association Hall of Fame in 1964.

Buea [Bouea]. Town in western Cameroon. It was the capital of Germany's Kamerun colony from 1884 to 1919. In 1922, Buea was designated as headquarters of the British commissioner for the Southern Cameroons.

Buffet, Bernard (1928–). French painter. An extremely precocious artist, Buffet was well-known in Parisian art circles by the mid-1940s and was awarded a major French critical prize in 1948. Much influenced by the *Miserabisme* movement, his early work is somber in nature, boldly outlined in black, with drab colors and a distinctive angular signature. He is known for his earlier religious paintings and for later views of London, Paris and New York. Buffet's work became increasingly popular in the 1960s but was dismissed by many critics as mawkish and sentimental.

Buganda. Former kingdom of southern Uganda, located on the north shore of Lake Victoria. Its capital was Kampala, and as an independent kingdom it exercised considerable power in the 19th century. In 1900, pursuant to the Buganda Agreement, it was made a British protectorate. Following the independence of UGANDA, tensions between the former kingdom and the new nation rose to such a point that the political entity of Buganda was formally abolished.

Bugatti, Ettore (1881–1947). Italian designer primarily known as a designer of automobiles. Ettore Bugatti, at one time or another, built cars in Italy, Germany, and France. His product included both racing and sports cars and luxury sedans, such as the legendary Type 41 Royale, a massive vehicle of great elegance. Bugatti's greatest contribution was in the technical and engineering design of engines, but the appearance of many of his cars—even the appearance of their mechanical components—was remarkably sophisticated. A picture of a Bugatti motor appears in LE CORBUSIER's *Vers une architecture* of 1923.

Bugatti, Jean (1909–1939). Italian-born designer and son of Ettore BUGATTI, who joined his father's career as a designer of sport and luxury automobiles. The Type 57 Bugatti of 1934, built in both sedan and open touring versions, is largely his work. His streamlined railcars for the French state railways (also of 1934) are among the earliest examples of modern railroad equipment produced in Europe. Bugatti died in an accident while testing a streamlined version of the Type 57.

Bugs Bunny. Celebrated American animated cartoon character and star of many WARNER BROS.' "Looney Tunes." Bugs, who turned 50 in 1990, is second only to Walt DISNEY'S MICKEY MOUSE in name recognition and popularity among cartoon stars. The "wabbit" (as arch-foe Elmer Fudd called him) was the joint creation of a team of young animators—Ben Hardaway, Chuck Jones, Fritz Freleng and Tex AVERY—working at the Warners animation unit in Burbank in the late 1930s. He first appeared in 1938 as an unidentified white rabbit in Hardaway's *Porky's Hare Hunt.* He was soon refined in Jones' *Elmer's Candid Camera* and Avery's *A Wild Hare* (both 1940), acquiring a name ("Bugs" was Hardaway's nickname), a voice (courtesy of Mel BLANC), and a trademark salutation, "What's up, doc?" (courtesy of Avery). Since then the brash rabbit from Brooklyn has been all over the map. He's played every position on a baseball team, gone to other planets, fought in the bullring, sung grand opera and won an ACADEMY AWARD (in Freleng's *Knighty Knight, Bugs,* 1958). His star was installed on HOLLYWOOD's "Walk of Fame" in 1985 and his television series in television history. In contrast to the Disney characters, the humor of Bugs and friends Daffy Duck, Yosemite Sam and the others was really for adults, quite sophisticated and full of double entendres.

Bugs Bunny with his nemesis Elmer Fudd.

For further reading:

Joe Adamson, *Bugs Bunny: Fifty Years and Only One Grey Hare.* New York: Henry Holt and Co., 1990.

Buhler, Karl L(udwig) (1879–1963). German psychologist. Buhler remains best known for his early writings on the psychology of perception, which contributed to the development of GESTALT theory. In contrast to the contemporary Gestalt school of psychologists, he held that gestalts were merely hypothetical possibilities, not proven realities. Buhler earned a medical degree from the University of Freiburg and a doctorate in psychology from the University of Strassburg. In the 1920s, he operated a psychological institute in Vienna and wrote *The Mental Development of the Child* (1927). In 1938, Buhler was briefly arrested by the Nazis. Upon his release, he immigrated first to Norway and then to America, where he taught at several institutions, including the University of Southern California medical school.

Buick, David Dunbar (1854–1929). Scots-born American auto manufacturer. After starting out in the plumbing supply business, Buick founded the Buick Motor Company in 1903 to build automobiles. In August 1904, the company produced its first model in its plant in Flint, Michigan. Later that same year, Buick's investors invited William C. Durant to assume management of the company, and in 1908 Buick resigned from the firm, which continued to bear his name. Although Buick was paid at least $100,000 to step down, he lost the money in a series of bad business ventures, and he died virtually penniless on March 6, 1929.

Bukharin, Nikolai Ivanovich (1888–1938). Russian communist leader and Marxist theoretician. In 1908 Bukharin was made a member of the Moscow Bolshevik committee. He was imprisoned and deported by the czarist government. After the 1917 RUSSIAN REVOLUTION he returned to Russia, edited PRAVDA (1917–29) and in 1919 was elected to the executive committee of the COMINTERN. The following year he published *The Economy of the Transitional Period.* A member of the Politburo from 1924, Bukharin supported STALIN but distrusted him. In 1928 he disagreed with Stalin over the latter's collectivization and industrialization policy and was expelled from the Politburo in 1929, although he remained on the Central Committee. A victim of the GREAT PURGE, in 1938 he was charged with treason, tried (along with YAGODA and Krestinsky) and shot. His reputation was officially rehabilitated during the GLASNOST period of the late 1980s. (See also KULAKS.)

Bukowski, Charles (1920–). American poet. Born in Germany, Bukowski immigrated to the United States in 1922. As a young man, he worked as an unskilled laborer, emerging on the literary scene in Los Angeles in the early 1960s. Although prolific, he remained a literary outsider who published his work with small presses, primarily on the West Coast. His work is marked by a sordid and brutal realism sometimes tempered with a vein

BULGARIA

of sentimentality. His confessional persona is that of a tough, skid-row, hard-drinking womanizer; his rough, gritty work portrays the underbelly of urban life, populated with bums and criminals; his tone is by turns matter-of-fact, despondent and bored. Frequent subjects include suicide, depression and the loneliness of one-night stands.

Bulgakov, Mikhail Afanasyevich (1891–1940). Russian author. Having graduated as a doctor in 1916, in 1920 Bulgakov turned to literature, earning his living as assistant producer and literary advisor at the MOSCOW ART THEATER. In 1924 he wrote *The Day of the Turbine* (also translated as *The White Guard*). Although he wrote historical plays, Bulgakov achieved fame with his novel *The Master and Margarita* (1938, not published until 1966). Persecuted from 1929, he appealed to STALIN for permission to emigrate, but was denied. He went blind in 1939 and died the following year.

Bulgakov, Sergei Nikolayevich (1871–1944). Russian philosopher, economist and theologian. Bulgakov first emerged as an important Marxist economic thinker in 1897, with the publication of *Markets in Capitalist Production*. His work *Capitalism and Agriculture* (1900) revised accepted notions of the role of agrarian production in a Marxist society. Bulgakov shifted his focus from economic to philosophical questions in *Problems of Idealism* (1902) and *From Marxism to Idealism* (1903). After the 1905 Revolution, Bulgakov joined the Constitutional Democrats reform party. As a result of a religious conversion, Bulgakov became a priest of the Russian Orthodox Church in 1918 and was ultimately expelled from his native land in 1922 for alleged anti-Soviet activities. *Quiet Thoughts* (1918) is representative of his theological writings. Bulgakov died in exile in Paris.

Bulganin, Nikolai (1895–1975). Prime minister of the U.S.S.R. (1955–58). Bulganin joined the COMMUNIST PARTY at the time of the RUSSIAN REVOLUTION (1917). He was chairman of the Moscow soviet (in effect, mayor of Moscow) from 1931 to 1937. He succeeded STALIN as minister of defense in 1946, after World War II. On Stalin's death in 1953 Bulganin initially appeared to share power with KHRUSHCHEV, but Khrushchev rapidly took the ascendancy, ousted Bulganin in 1958 and became prime minister himself.

Bulgaria [People's Republic of Bulgaria (Narondna Republika Bulgariya)]. Nation in southeastern Europe, its boundaries corresponding roughly to those of the ancient countries of Moesia and Thrace. In 1908, following a revolt within the neighboring OTTOMAN EMPIRE (longtime and former master of Bulgaria), Prince Ferdinand declared himself czar over all Bulgaria. The country engaged in two brief wars with other Balkan nations in 1912 and 1913 (see the BALKANS), prevailing in the first but losing in the second—and thus was forced to cede land under the 1913 Treaty of Bucharest. During WORLD WAR I, it sided with the CENTRAL POWERS, including GERMANY. Defeat led to the 1919 Treaty of Neuilly, pursuant to which Bulgaria ceded land to both GREECE and YUGOSLAVIA and also paid reparations. In 1934, BORIS III created a military dictatorship; during WORLD WAR II, he allied Bulgaria with the Nazis. Following that defeat, Bulgaria came under Soviet control as part of the Eastern bloc. Communist Georgi DIMITROV served as leader from 1946 to 1949. In 1954, To-

BULGARIA

1908	Bulgaria declares independence from Turkey; Ferdinand crowned czar.
1912	Allied with Greece against Turkey in First Balkan War.
1913	Loses Macedonia as Greece allies with Turkey in Second Balkan War.
1914	Allied with Turkey and other Axis powers in World War I.
1918	Loses Thrace after defeat of Central Powers; Ferdinand forced to resign; Boris II crowned.
1920	Agrarians under Prime Minister Stambolisky begin sweeping land reforms.
1922	Death of Ivan Vasov, national poet who recorded struggles for freedom.
1923	Stambolisky assassinated; centrist coalition forms government.
1934	Putsch by fascist Zuevno movement briefly drives out the king; he returns to rule as a royal dictator until 1943.
1941	Bulgaria joins Axis powers in World War II.
1944	Soviet troops enter Sofia; communist Fatherland Front forms government.
1948	Industries nationalized, farms collectivized under new constitution.
1954	Todor Zhivkov named Communist Party chief.
1962	Zhivkov consolidates power, adds prime minister's title.
1985	"Bulgarianization" drive launched against ethnic Turks.
1989	Zhivkov ousted by massive protests; Maldsnov assumes presidency.
1990	Communist Party allows sweeping reforms; changes name to Socialist Party but retains power (only party in Eastern Europe to do so).

dor ZHIVKOV became party secretary, and in 1962 prime minister. He was finally ousted in 1989 due to worsening domestic conditions and a general wave of anti-communist feeling throughout eastern Europe. By the beginning of 1991, reforms in Bulgaria were less advanced than those in CZECHOSLOVAKIA, POLAND and HUNGARY, and the communists (their party renamed) remained in power.

Bulge, Battle of the. As a last desperate gamble to win WORLD WAR II, Adolf HITLER, GERMANY's leader, ordered an offensive in the Ardennes Forest in Luxembourg and southern Belgium. On December 16, 1944, three German armies attacked the line held by four inexperienced U.S. divisions. The Germans, aided by bad weather, advanced 50 miles along a 50-mile front in a week (the bulge). When the skies cleared Allied air forces attacked, stiffening American resistance. U.S. General George S. PATTON rushed in the Third Army, and on December 26, 1944, the Germans began a slow retreat, pushed back to their starting line by January 28, 1945. Both sides suffered heavy losses in personnel and materiel, the Germans losing over one and a half times as much as the Allies.

Bullard, Sir Edward Crisp (1907–1980). British geophysicist. Bullard was educated at Cambridge University. After war service in naval research he returned to Cambridge as a reader in geophysics before accepting a post as head of the physics department of the University of Toronto (1948) and visiting the Scripps Institute of Oceanography in California (1949). After a five-year spell as director of the National Physical Laboratory, he returned to Cambridge as a reader and, in 1964, professor of geophysics and director of the department of geodesy and geophysics. There he remained until his retirement in 1974. Bullard made a number of contributions to the revolution in the Earth sciences that took place in the 1950s and '60s. He carried out major work on the measurement of the heat flow from the Earth. In 1965 Bullard studied continental drift using a computer to analyze the fit between the Atlantic continents. He found an excellent fit for the South Atlantic at the 500-fathom contour line. However, a reasonable fit could be made for the North Atlantic only if a number of assumptions, such as deformation and sedimentation since the continents drifted apart, were taken into account. Later, independent evidence for these assumptions gave powerful support for the theory of continental drift. Bullard was knighted in 1953.

Bullen, Keith Edward (1906–1976). Australian applied mathematician and geophysicist. The son of Anglo-Irish parents, Bullen was educated at the universities of Auckland, Melbourne and Cambridge, England. He began his career as a teacher in Auckland and then lectured in mathematics at Melbourne and Hull, England. In 1946 he became professor of applied mathematics at the University of Sydney. Bullen's chief contributions to science were his mathematical studies of earthquake waves and the ellipticity of the Earth. In 1936 he gave values of the density inside the Earth down to a depth of 3,100 miles. He also determined values for the pressure, gravitation intensity, compressibility and rigidity throughout the interior of the Earth. From the results on the Earth's density he inferred that the core was solid. He applied his results to the internal structure of the planets Mars, Venus and Mercury and to the origin of the moon. Bullen conducted some of his early work on earthquake travel times in collaboration with Harold Jeffreys. This resulted in the publication of the Jeffreys-Bullen (JB) tables in 1940.

Bultmann, Rudolf (1884–1976). German theologian and Biblical historian. Bultmann became a center of controversy in Christian theological circles by virtue of his advocacy of a "demythologizing" approach to Biblical interpretation. Bultmann adopted as a starting point the disparity in consciousness between the scientific 20th century and the New Testament period, in which the possibility of miracles was readily embraced. Bultmann argued that Christian faith could best survive by embracing the "mythic" teaching aspects of the Gospels and refusing to be caught up in debates over the historical reality of such events as the Resurrection. For Bultmann, the Bible retains its human value as a source of inspiration and wisdom capable of pointing one to an existentially authentic personal existence. Bultmann's major works include *History and Eschatology* (1957), *Jesus Christ and Mythology* (1958) and a volume of selected essays, *Existence and Faith* (1961).

Bunche, Ralph (1904–1971). American statesman. A graduate of UCLA, Bunche earned a master's and a Ph.D. in government from Harvard in 1934. He did postdoctoral study in anthropology and colonial policy at Northwestern University, the London School of Economics and the University of Capetown, South Africa. Under Rosenwald and Social Science Research Council fellowships, he studied in Africa, Europe, Malaya and the Netherlands Indies (now Indonesia). Bunche was a member of the political science department at Howard University from 1928 to 1950. His diplomatic career began in 1944 when he joined the Department of State. He helped found the UNITED NATIONS, and served as a UN undersecretary from 1955 to 1971. Bunche received the Spingarn Medal of the NAACP in 1949 and the Presidential Medal of Freedom in 1963. He was awarded the NOBEL PRIZE for peace in 1950, the first black to receive a Nobel prize.

Bund [General Union of Jewish Workers]. Active in Russia and Poland, the Bund was a socialist political movement founded in Vilna in 1897. Its aims were an end to anti-Jewish discrimination (see POGROMS) and a reorganized, federal Russian empire. By 1900, it was the most powerful socialist body in Russia. In conflict with LENIN over its emphasis on Jewish interests, it seceded from the Russian Social Democrat Party (1906) and supported the MENSHEVIKS. In 1920 it was divided. The majority of members joined the COMMUNIST PARTY of the Soviet Union, the minority continued as a separate group until suppressed by the government.

Bunde. City in northwestern Germany, in state of North Rhine-Westphalia. From 1945 to 1948, it was the headquarters of the Allied Control Commission for Germany, which was dissolved just prior to the Soviet blockade of BERLIN (1948–49).

Bundy, McGeorge (1919–). U.S. government official. Bundy graduated from Yale in 1940 and served in the Army during World War II. He joined the Harvard faculty in 1949. From 1953 to 1961 he was the dean of the faculty of arts and sciences. Bundy served as special assistant to the president for national security affairs in both the KENNEDY and JOHNSON administrations (1961–66). As special assistant, he played a major role in formulating and directing foreign policy. One of Kennedy's inner circle, he helped determine administration action in the CUBAN MISSILE CRISIS. Under Johnson he strongly advocated escalating the VIETNAM WAR. Bundy resigned in 1966 to accept the presidency of the Ford Foundation (1966–79). In 1968 he came out in support of deescalation of the war.

Bunin, Ivan (Alexeyevich) (1870–1953). Russian poet, short story writer, novelist. After his early publication of nature poetry in the classical style of Pushkin, Bunin turned to prose. *The Village* (1910) was a pessimistic prose poem that recounted the decline of the rural peasantry after the RUSSIAN REVOLUTION OF 1905. A volume of stories published in 1917 included his best-known work, "The Gentleman from San Francisco," a fantasy-satire of bourgeois Western society. After the BOLSHEVIK REVOLUTION (1917), Bunin left Russia and lived as an expatriate, mainly in France. His semi-autobiographical novel, *The Life of Arsenyev: The Well of Days* (1933), earned him the NOBEL PRIZE for literature. He was also a translator of such writers as Byron, Longfellow, Tennyson and Alfred de Musset. During his lifetime he was regarded as a leading Russian writer, but his reputation later declined.

Bunshaft, Gordon (1909–1990). American architect who was the partner in the large firm of SKIDMORE, OWINGS & MERRILL credited with the design of a number of that firm's most distinguished glass wall and steel buildings. Trained at MIT, Bunshaft worked briefly for Edward Durrell STONE before joining Skidmore, Owings & Merrill, where he became a partner in 1949. He was the partner in charge of design for such major SOM projects as Lever House (1951–52), the Pepsi-Cola Building (1959) and the Chase Manhattan Bank headquarters (1961), all in New York; the U.S. Air Force Academy (1956–62) at Colorado Springs; and the Beinecke Rare Book Library (1964) on the Yale campus in New Haven, Connecticut. The Bunshaft aesthetic has generally been austere and mechanistic; seemingly he drew on Ludwig MIES VAN DER ROHE as a major inspiration. His role in raising SOM's work to a high level of design quality was much praised in the 1950s and 1960s, although more recently in the 1980s, this work has also been criticized for a certain coldness and monotony.

Bunting, Basil (1900–1985). British poet. Bunting's poetry first appeared in book form in 1965. Among them was the lengthy autobiographical poem *Briggflatts,* generally considered his masterpiece. The poem was largely an evocation of his youth in Northumbria, drawing on that region's legends and speech patterns. Bunting was also influenced by Persian poetry, as he spoke the language fluently and served as Iranian correspondent for the *Times* of London for a few years after World War II.

Bunuel, Luis (1900–1983). Spanish-born filmmaker. An iconoclastic and scathing critic of bourgeois society, Bunuel was internationally acclaimed for his pioneering surrealistic work. He achieved notoriety with his first short film, *Un Chien Andalou* (1928), made with the surrealist artist Salvador DALI, and *The Age of Gold* (1930). Bunuel went into exile in the 1930s and ultimately settled in Mexico City in 1947. His career did not revive until *Los Olvidados* (1950), for which he received the best director prize at the 1951 Cannes Film Festival. Other well-known Bunuel films included *Viridiana* (1961), *Diary of a Chambermaid* (1964), *Tristana* (1970), *The Discreet Charm of the Bourgeoisie* (1972) and *That Obscure Object of Desire* (1977). His memoirs were published as *My Last Sigh* (1983).

For further reading:

Durgnat, Raymond, *Luis Bunuel,* expanded rev. ed. Berkeley: University of California Press, 1978.

Edwards, Gwynne, *The Discreet Art of Luis Bunuel: A Reading of His Films.* New York: Marion Boyars, 1983.

Mellen, Joan, ed., *The World of Luis Bunuel: Essays in Criticism.* New York: Oxford University Press, 1978.

Burbank, Luther (1849–1926). American plant breeder. Burbank was brought up on a farm and received only an elementary education. He began breeding plants in 1870, when he bought a seven-hectare plot of land. After about a year he had developed the Burbank potato, which was introduced to Ireland to help combat the blight epidemics. By selling the rights to this potato he made $150, which he used to travel to California, where three of his brothers had already settled. He established a nursery and experimental farm in Santa Rosa, where the climate was especially conducive to fruit and flower breeding—his occupation for the next 50 years. He worked by making multiple crosses between native and introduced strains, using his remarkable skill to select commercially promising types. These were then grafted onto mature plants to hasten development, so that their value could be assessed rapidly. In this way he produced numerous new cultivated varieties of plums, lilies and many other ornamentals and fruits.

Luther Burbank.

Burbidge, Eleanor Margaret [born Margaret Peachey] (1922–). British astronomer. Burbidge studied physics at the University of London. After graduation in 1948 she joined the University of London Observatory where she earned her Ph.D. and served as acting director (1950–51). She then went to to the U.S. as a research fellow, first at the Yerkes Observatory of the University of Chicago (1951–53) and then at the California Institute of Technology (1955–57). She spent 1953–1955 in highly productive work at the Cavendish Laboratory in Cambridge, England. She returned to Yerkes in 1957, serving as associate professor of astronomy from 1959 to 1962, and then transferred to the University of California, San Diego, where she has been professor of astronomy since 1964 and has also served since 1979 as director of the Center for Astrophysics and Space Sciences. In 1948 she married Geoffrey BURBIDGE a theoretical physicist, and began a highly productive partnership. They collaborated with Fred HOYLE and William Fowler in 1957 in publishing a key paper on the synthesis of the chemical elements in stars. Their *Quasi-Stellar Objects* (1967) was one of the first comprehensive works on quasars. She had earlier recorded the spectra of a number of quasars with the 120-inch Lick reflector and discovered that their spectral lines displayed different red shifts, probably indicating the ejection of matter at very high speeds. The first accurate estimates of the masses of galaxies were based on Margaret Burbidge's careful observation of their rotation.

Burbidge, Geoffrey (1925–). British astrophysicist. Burbidge graduated in 1946 from the University of Bristol and earned his Ph.D. in 1951 from the University of London. From 1950 to 1958 he held junior university positions at London, Harvard, Chicago, Cambridge (England) and the Mount Wilson and Palomar Observatories in California. He became associate professor at Chicago (1958–62) before being appointed associate professor (1962), then professor of physics (1963) at the University of California, San Diego. In 1978 Burbidge accepted the post of director of the Kitt Peak National Observatory, Arizona. Burbidge began his research career studying particle physics; after his 1948 marriage to Margaret Peachey (see Eleanor Margaret BURBIDGE), who was to become one of the world's leading optical astronomers, he turned to astrophysics and began a productive research partnership with his wife. The Burbidges worked on the mysterious quasars, first described by Allan Sandage in 1960, and produced in their *Quasi-Stellar Objects* (1967) one of the earliest surveys of the subject. Burbidge was reluctant to accept without reservation the BIG BANG THEORY on the origin of the universe. In 1971 he published a paper in which he maintained that we still do not know whether the big bang occurred and that much more effort must be devoted to cosmological tests. Although such views found little favor, Burbidge continued to be highly productive, rich in new ideas, and yet outside and somewhat skeptical of prevailing cosmological and astrophysical orthodoxy.

Burchfield, Charles (1893–1967). American painter. Born in Ashtabula, Ohio, Burchfield studied at the Cleveland School of Art and was a wallpaper designer from 1921 to 1929. Painting mainly in watercolors, he is best known for his evocative portrayals of ghostly midwestern towns, replete with Victorian houses and crumbling wooden shacks in wintry snows, blustery storms or bright sunshine. In the early and late phases of his career, Burchfield also painted lyrical nature studies. Typical of his work are *Night Wind* (1918, Museum of Modern Art, New York City), *Ice Glare* (1933, Whitney Museum of American Art, New York City) and *Freight Cars Under a Bridge* (Detroit Institute of Arts).

Burden, William Douglas (1898–1978). American naturalist and explorer. Burden established the Department of Animal Behavior at the American Museum of Natural History in New York. In 1926 he led an expedition to the Dutch East Indies. On this expedition he captured the Komodo dragon, the world's oldest and largest lizard. This exploit inspired the film *King Kong* (1933).

Burgee, John (1933–). American architect known for his partnership with Philip JOHNSON. Burgee received his architectural education at Notre Dame University in Indiana and worked for the Chicago firms of Holabird and Root and Naess-Murphy before collaborating with Johnson on a 1965 project. The relationship led to a Johnson/Burgee partnership in 1967. Many major projects often viewed as Johnson designs are in fact the work of this partnership—for example, Pennzoil Plaza in Houston, Texas (1972–76), the AT&T Building in New York (1985), and the elliptical office tower at 53rd Street and Third Avenue in New York (often called the Lipstick building, in reaction to its shape). Since 1987, the firm has been called John Burgee Architects to reflect Johnson's current role as design consultant while Burgee, with two partners, has

Warren Burger, chief justice of the United States (1982).

primary responsibility for the firm's operation.

Burger, Warren (1907–). Chief justice, U.S. Supreme Court (1969–86). The son of immigrant parents, Burger worked his way through two years of the University of Minnesota and the St. Paul College of Law (later Mitchell College of Law). He then spent about 20 years in private practice. An active Republican, Burger was appointed assistant attorney general in charge of the civil division of the Justice Department. He first gained national attention when he supported the federal government's prosecution of John Peters for disloyalty after the U.S. solicitor general had refused to prosecute. Burger was appointed as a judge of the important U.S. Court of Appeals for the District of Columbia. Appointed by President Richard M. NIXON to succeed Earl WARREN as chief justice of the Supreme Court, Burger was known as a strict constructionist. Although the Burger court proved more conservative than the Warren court, the Court was judicially active. During Burger's term the Court delivered several controversial opinions that led to liberalized ABORTION laws. After resigning from the Court, Burger served as head of the U.S. Bicentennial Commission.

For further reading:

Blasi, Vincent, *The Burger Court: The Counter-Revolution That Wasn't.* New Haven, Conn.: Yale University Press, 1986.

Burgess, Anthony (1917–). British novelist, critic and dramatist. Burgess is one of the most prolific and versatile British writers of his generation, having worked in genres as diverse as journalism, screenplay and television writing, theatrical adaptations and a 1970 biography of Shakespeare. But he is best known as a novelist. His most famous work is *A Clockwork Orange* (1962), a dire futuristic vision of street violence, repressive government and high-technology mind control, which was adapted into an evocative 1971 film by Stanley KUBRICK. Other notable Burgess novels include his "Malayan Trilogy" on British colonial life—*Time for a Tiger* (1956), *The Enemy in the Blanket* (1958), and *Beds in the East* (1959)—and *Earthly Powers* (1980), which mingles real and imagined characters to chronicle the events of the 20th century. Burgess is a prolific book reviewer and has written a full-length study of James JOYCE.

Burgess, W. Starling (1878–1947). American naval architect and designer of sailing yachts known for his successful designs for racing craft, including several winners of America's Cup races. He was, in 1910, the designer of the first successful airplane built in New England and, shortly after, of the first successful flying boat. His design for the 59-foot schooner Nina of 1928 was a great success in racing in both American and British waters and established his reputation as a master designer of fast sailing craft. His most famous designs were *Enterprise* (1930), *Rainbow* (1934), and *Ranger* (1937); the last designed in collaboration with Olin STEPHENS. All three were America's Cup winners. Burgess was largely responsible for establishing the characteristic design of the modern racing sailboat.

Burgess-MacLean spy case. On May 26, 1951, two officials of the British foreign office slipped out of England on a ferry bound for France and vanished; it was later learned that they had defected to the U.S.S.R. **Guy Burgess** had been an attache at the British embassy in Washington, D.C.; **Donald MacLean** had been chief of the Foreign Office's American section. MacLean had had access to high-level Anglo-American diplomatic, military and intelligence secrets. The two finally surfaced in Moscow in 1956 and admitted that they had become communists while they were students at Cambridge in the 1930s. They had disagreed with British and American foreign policy and believed that the U.S.S.R. offered the most reasonable hope for world peace; while serving in the foreign office, they had passed British and American secrets to Soviet agents. In 1950 or '51, British and U.S. counterintelligence had become suspicious of the two and placed them under surveillance. However, Burgess and MacLean were tipped off by a "third man" in the spy ring who knew that they were about to be arrested. The "third man" turned out to be the high-ranking British diplomat and intelligence agent Kim PHILBY, who had been MacLean's superior in Washington. Philby himself defected to the U.S.S.R. in 1963.

For further reading:

Cecil, Robert, *A Divided Life.* New York: Morrow, 1989.

Burkina Faso [People's Republic of Burkina]. Landlocked republic in west Africa, lying south of the Sahara; its total area of 105,811 square miles is divided into 30 provinces. Over 90% of the population is rural-based, yet only 8%-10% of the republic's land is arable; soil conditions are poor. The area came under French rule at the end of the 19th century, when it was incorporated into the colony of the French Sudan, which itself formed part of the Federation of FRENCH WEST AFRICA. In 1920 the area became a separate colony known as Upper Volta, but in 1932 it was divided among the neighboring colonies of French Sudan, Niger and the Ivory Coast; in 1947 it reemerged as a separate administrative unit in its current boundaries. Throughout the colonial period Upper Volta was a backwater of France's West African empire. There was little investment, and many inhabitants worked in the coffee plantations of neighboring Ivory Coast (to which it was linked by a railway started before World War I but not completed until 1954). After World War II the Mossi king was a pro-French conservative influence in opposition to the more radical Rassemblement Democratique Africain Party (RDA), which campaigned for independence for the whole of French West Africa as a single state. The country became independent as Upper Volta on August 5, 1960, with Maurice Yameogo, leader of the Union Democratique Voltaique Party (UDV), as president. Yameogo soon moved to a one-

BURKINA FASO

1960	(Aug. 5) Country becomes independent from France as Upper Volta with Maurice Yameogo, leader of Union Democratique Voltaique (UDV), as president.
1966	Following a general strike, mobs attack the national assembly; army chief of staff Sangoule Lamizana removes Yameogo and assumes power.
1973	Drought of unprecedented severity hits the Sahel.
1981	Lamizana, elected president in 1978, is overthrown in a military coup led by Col. Saye Zerbo.
1982	Zerbo ousted in army coup led by Jean Baptiste Ouedraogo.
1983	Thomas Sankara ousts Ouedraogo and sets up left-leaning regime, "National Council of the Revolution".
1984	(Aug. 3) Upper Volta renamed Burkina Faso, meaning "country of honest men."
1987	(Oct. 15) Sankara assassinated, replaced by Blaise Compaore.

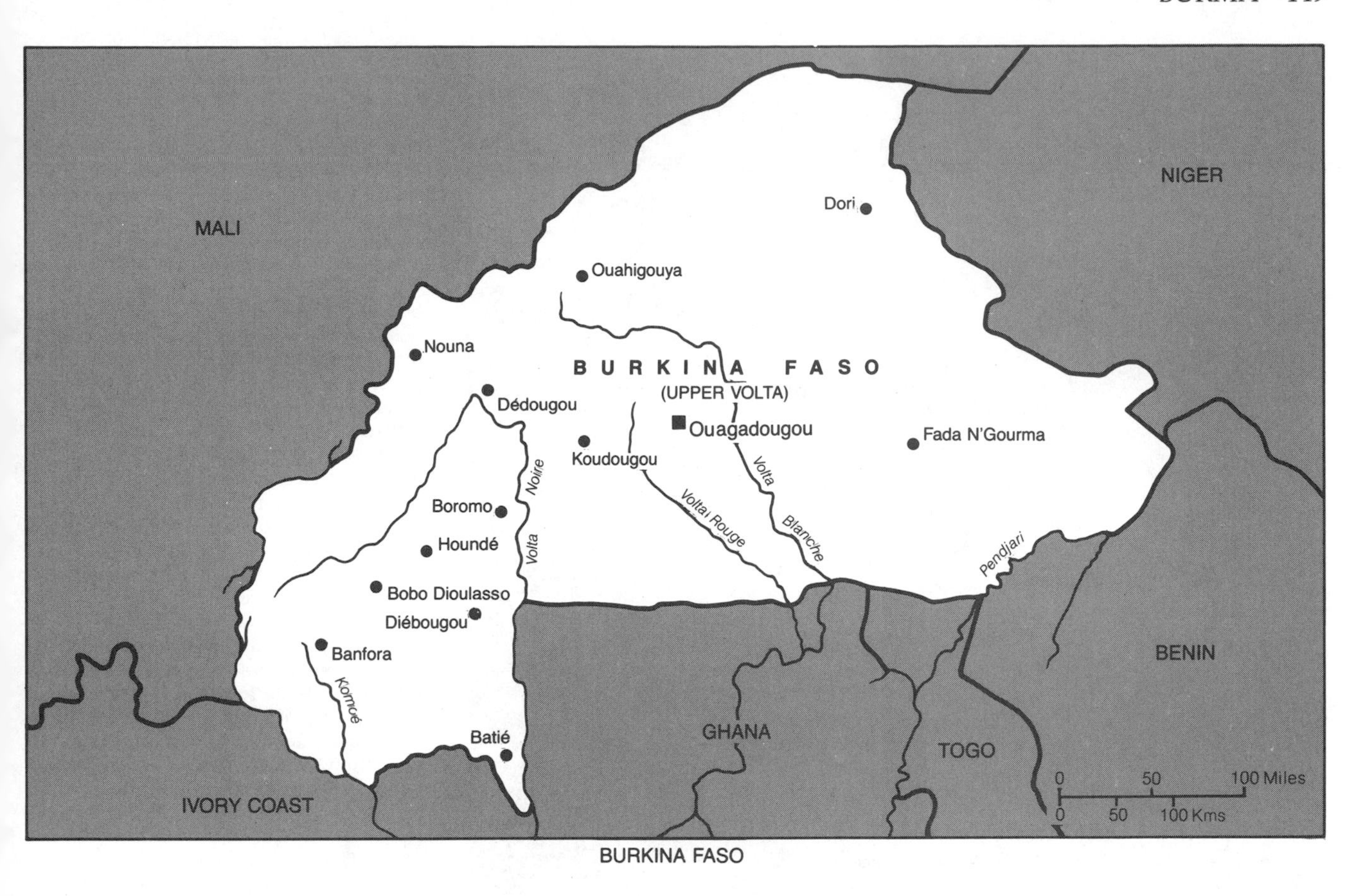

BURKINA FASO

party state but was deposed in a 1966 coup led by Lt. Col. Sangoule Lamizana. A new constitution, providing for a return to civilian rule, was approved in a June 1970 referendum. Severe hardship caused by the Sahelian drought combined with political ineptitude led to another military intervention, with Lamizana resuming power on February 8, 1974. During the 1970s the trade unions became the principal mouthpiece for opposition politics. Full party politics were restored in assembly and presidential elections in April and May 1978 in which the UDV again won a majority of the votes and Lamizana was confirmed as president. His regime was overthrown in a 1980 military coup that installed Col. Saye Zerbo as president; he was overthrown in November 1982 in a coup of junior officers led by Capt. Thomas Sankara. Sankara's new government, the Peoples' Salvation Council, had a radical reform program closely modeled on policies pursued in GHANA by Flt. Lt. Jerry Rawlings. On August 3, 1984, Upper Volta was renamed Burkina Faso—country of honest men. War broke out with neighboring Mali in December 1985, when Burkinabe troops crossed the disputed border and were driven back by superior Malian air power; relations were normalized the following year. Sankara's drive against corruption and his authoritarian policy of forcing city-dwellers to return to the countryside caused resentment against the urban elite; on October 15, 1987, he was assassinated. Blaise Compaore, his replacement, had been one of his closest friends but was not thought to have been directly involved in the assassination. With one of the lowest GNPs in the world, Burkina Faso is increasingly dependent upon foreign aid for its survival.

Burleigh, Harry Thacker (1866–1949). African-American art song composer, best known for his many arrangements of Negro spirituals. During his boyhood in Erie, Pennsylvania, Burleigh heard the Negro folk songs as well as the songs of Stephen Foster from his blind grandfather, Hamilton E. Waters, a former slave. In 1892 he enrolled in the National Conservatory in New York, where he worked as a copyist for its director, Antonin Dvorak. His singing of spirituals for Dvorak—especially "Swing Low, Sweet Chariot"— resulted in the composer's incorporation of them into his famous "New World" Symphony. In 1894 Burleigh gained the important post of baritone soloist at St. George's Church, the only black man in an otherwise white congregation. He held the post for the next 50 years. His arrangements of spirituals and folk songs included the *Six Plantation Melodies for Violins and Piano* (1901), *From the Southland* (1914), *Jubilee Songs of the United States of America* (1916), and *Old Songs Hymnal* (1929). The popularity of "Deep River" and "Go Down, Moses," for example, may be attributed to his efforts. He also had a profound impact upon the next generation of black composers, including Duke ELLINGTON. "He was America's first great black composer of art songs," says biographer Jean Snyder. "This helped create the audience and the acceptance among white singers of the artistic value of the arrangements of the spirituals as well." Today his life and work are enjoying a great revival in interest and popularity.

Burma [Myanmar Naingngan (Union of Myanmar)]. Nation of Southeast Asia, located on the western side of the Indochina Peninsula, with a lengthy coastline on the Bay of Bengal and the Andaman Sea. Its landward borders dominated by mountains, Burma developed as an isolated nation with a unique culture, lying athwart the ancient, overland trade route between India and China. In 1885, following its defeat in the third Anglo-Burmese war, Burma was annexed as a province of British India. Under British exploitation, it became a major rice exporter but suffered from a degeneration of its own culture. Nationalist movements became recurrent; a serious rebellion against British rule broke out in 1931 and was quashed after two years of violent struggle. During WORLD WAR II, it was occupied by Japanese forces and was forced to support Japan through 1943, but Burmese troops fought for the Allies in 1945. In 1947, Burma was granted independence by Britain, on January 4, 1948. It has since maintained a neutral stance in international affairs. In 1962, a military coup established General NE WIN as a socialist dictator, through 1973, when a new constitution was enacted and civilian rule restored, although Ne Win has remained

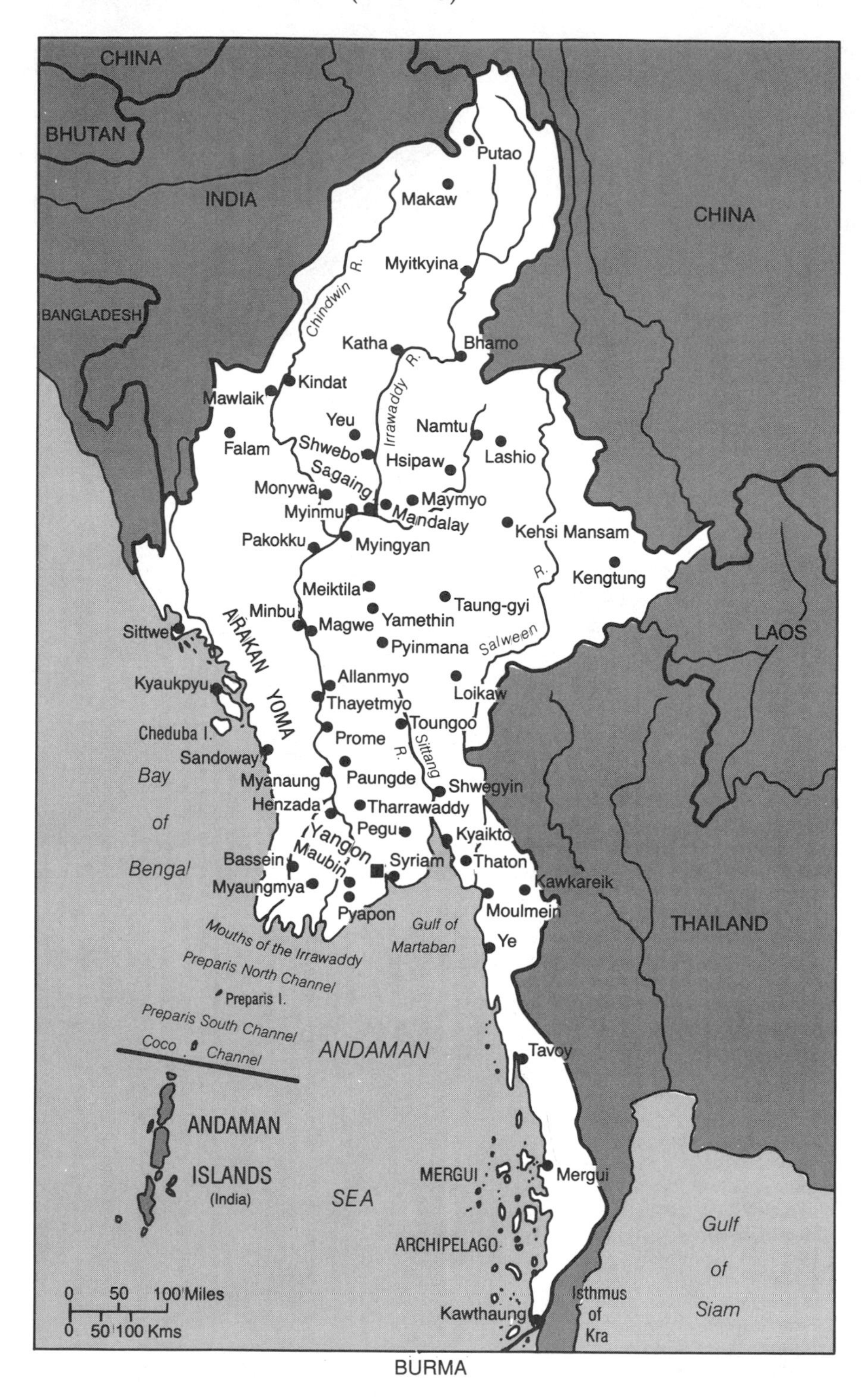

BURMA

a powerful figure behind the scenes. After another period of intense turmoil (1987–88), the military again assumed power and used terror to crush any opposition.

Burma Campaign (1943–45). The Japanese occupied BURMA in 1942, closing the BURMA ROAD, the only supply route from northern Burma to China. British, Gurkha and Burmese guerrillas maintained resistance, while a joint American-Chinese army trained and led by General Joseph "Vinegar Joe" STILWELL attacked from the north, traversing extremely rugged terrain and fighting experienced Japanese troops. Joined by 3,000 volunteers ("Merrill's Marauders") recruited by Stilwell aide Frank Dow Merrill, the combined forces seized Myitkyina airfield in northern Burma (May 17–18, 1944) after much hardship, permitting reinforcements and supplies to be flown in. After fierce fighting the Japanese surrendered the city of Myitkyina on August 3, while the Chinese moved against them at Lun-ling on the Burma Road. Much bloody fighting continued into 1945 before the road was opened, marking the only Chinese victory against the Japanese in eight years of war.

For further reading:

Time-Life, *China-Burma-India* (World War II Series). Alexandria, Va.: Time-Life, 1978.

Burma Road. Road running north-south between central Burma (Myanmar) and southern China; it was built from 1937 to 1939. During the SINO-JAPANESE WAR, it was utilized as a supply route into China but was closed in 1942, during WORLD WAR II, when Japanese forces took control of its southern terminus at Lashio. At present, it serves as a trade route between Chungking in China and Rangoon in Burma. (See also BURMA CAMPAIGN.)

Burmese Guerrilla War of 1948–. The establishment of the Union of BURMA in 1948 provoked minorities to rebel, demanding autonomous states. Aided by communists in south-central Burma, separatists seized Mandalay and besieged the government in Rangoon. A separate independent state was proclaimed at Toungoo (1949); the city was retaken by the government (1950), and the main communist center, Prome, was also seized, but fighting continued. Chinese Nationalist forces fleeing the Chinese communist takeover moved into eastern Burma, resisting Burmese control until evacuated to Taiwan under United Nations auspices (1953–54). About that time Burmese troops under General U NE WIN gained control of most of the country. U Ne Win established a military dictatorship in 1962 to prevent communist takeover, but separatist and communist resistance continued. General U San Yu succeeded U Ne Win as president in 1981, holding Burma together despite continued strong rebel opposition.

Burnet, Sir (Frank) Macfarlane (1899–1985). Australian microbiologist and virologist. Burnet shared the 1960 NOBEL PRIZE for medicine with British scientist Peter MEDAWAR. The two were honored for their independent work in the discovery of acquired immune tolerance, a discovery that led to major advances in organ transplantation. Burnet also did pioneering work in the field of viral genetics that formed the basis for current theories about viruses as cancer-causing agents. After his retirement in 1965 as professor of experimental medicine at the University of Melbourne, a post he held for more than 20 years, he wrote 16 books dealing mainly with science and medicine in a nontechnical manner.

Burnett, Frances Eliza Hodgson (1849–1924). Anglo-American author. Born in Manchester, England, Burnett moved to Tennessee with her family in 1865. She began writing for periodicals and published her early short stories in *Scribner's* beginning in 1872. Although she also wrote fiction for adults, Burnett is chiefly remembered for her popular and successful children's books, which include *Little Lord Fauntleroy* (1886) and *The Secret Garden* (1911).

For further reading:

Thwaite, Ann, *Waiting for the Party: The*

BURMA

1937	Burma separates from India to become British dependency.
1942	Japan invades Burma.
1948	Union of Burma becomes independent.
1949	Karen nationalists capture Mandalay with the help of communist guerrillas.
1962	Gen. Ne Win seizes power, publishes *The Burmese Way to Socialism,* combining Buddhist thought with Marxist theory, as the nation's official policy.
1964	All political parties banned.
1981	Ne Win steps down as president but maintains influence.
1989	Official name of Burma changed to Myanmar; Rangoon becomes Yangon.
1990	World Resources Institute study finds that 1.7 million acres in Burma have been lost to deforestation.

Life of Frances Hodgson Burnett. Boston: David R. Godine, 1989.

Burnett, W(illiam) R(iley) (1899–1982). American novelist and screenwriter. Along with James N. CAIN, Raymond CHANDLER and Dashiell HAMMETT, he was a master of the "hardboiled" school of gangster and detective fiction, known for its crisp, cynical dialogue. Burnett wrote 39 books, beginning with *Little Caesar* (1929, filmed 1930) and ending with *Goodbye, Chicago* (1981). As a HOLLYWOOD screenwriter he authored 40 screenplays, creating memorable tough-guy roles for such leading actors as Edward G. ROBINSON, Humphrey BOGART, Paul Muni and Alan Ladd. His credits included *The Iron Man, High Sierra* and *The Great Escape*.

Burnham, James (1905–1987). American conservative activist. Burnham was founding editor of NATIONAL REVIEW magazine (1955), and his warnings about the dangers of COMMUNISM had a profound impact on U.S. political debate. In his 20s he was a follower of Leon TROTSKY, but switched to CONSERVATISM after concluding that Marxism would lead to totalitarian despotism. He wrote a number of books, among them two that sparked great debate because of their prediction of an inevitable clash between the U.S. and the U.S.S.R.—*The Struggle for the World* (1947) and *The Coming Defeat of Communism* (1950). He worked briefly for the CENTRAL INTELLIGENCE AGENCY in the 1950s, organizing anticommunist intellectual movements abroad. In 1983 he was awarded the Presidential Medal of Freedom for his contributions to conservative thought in the U.S.

Burns, Arthur F. [born Arthur Frank Burnzelg] (1904–1987). American economist. Burns taught at Columbia University for two decades, until in 1953 he was chosen by President Dwight D. EISENHOWER to head the Council of Economic Advisers. Burns held the post for three years before returning to academia and a 10–year stint as president of the National Bureau of Economic Research. He returned to government service in 1969 as economic counselor to President Richard M. NIXON. One year later, Nixon named him to the first of two four-year terms as chairman of the Federal Reserve Board. From 1981 to 1985 he was U.S. ambassador to West Germany.

Burns, John (1858–1943). British trade unionist and political leader. Working in a factory as a child and self-taught, he became a radical socialist and a powerful orator. He was a leader in the London dock strike of 1889, and in 1892 was elected a member of Parliament. After a quarrel with James Keir HARDIE, Burns joined the Liberal ranks. The first working-class member of a cabinet, he was president of the Local Government Board (1905–14) and the Board of Trade (1914). He resigned from the cabinet in 1914 in protest over Britain's involvement in WORLD WAR I, and retired from Parliament and the public arena in 1918.

Burns and Allen. From the early days of VAUDEVILLE and RADIO to movies and TELEVISION, Burns and Allen were America's most popular husband and wife comedy team. **George Burns** (born Nathan Birnbaum in 1896) and **Gracie (Ethel Cecile Rosalie) Allen** (1902–1964) first teamed in 1923. George—already a veteran vaudeville performer in various acts—elected to be the "comedian," while his partner Gracie (then in secretarial school) was the "straight man." The act didn't quite work, as Gracie began to get more laughs than her partner. The duo switched roles and found success: Burns became the wisecracking straight man and Gracie the silly, often air-headed comic focus. The Jewish George and Irish-Catholic Gracie were happily married in 1926. Burns and Allen subsequently worked the Palace in the early 1930s and starred in a series of short films. In 1932 they became national stars over the radio waves, continuing for 18 years until they brought their tremendous appeal to the new medium of television. They also appeared in a number of feature films, including *International House* (1933), *College Holiday* (1936), *The Big Broadcast of 1937* (1937), *College Swing* (1938) and *The Gracie Allen Murder Case* (1939). Gracie's retirement from the entertainment world in 1958—and her death six years later—were tragic blows to her adoring fans. George pressed on, with limited success; HOLLYWOOD considered him worthless without Gracie, in spite of the fact that for years he had supplied most of the team's jokes. But in 1975—at the age of 79—he made a comeback with his ACADEMY AWARD-winning performance in *The Sunshine Boys*. This was followed by another movie hit, *Oh God* (1977), and other films. Going into his 90s, the "grand old master of comedy" continues to make television and film appearances and write books.

Burpee, David (1893–1980). American horticulturist and seed merchant. Burpee headed the world's largest mail-order seed company, W. Atlee Burpee Co., for 55 years. He developed hundreds of new varieties of flowers and vegetables, created many successful merchandising methods and sent out as many as four million seed catalogues annually.

Burroughs, Edgar Rice (1875–1950). American writer of fantastic novels and stories, creator of the character TARZAN OF THE APES. Born in Chicago, Burroughs led a life full of failures. He flunked entrance exams for West Point. He tried to be a clerk, cowboy, railroad policeman, gold miner and shop owner. Finally, in 1911 at the age of 35, surrounded by a growing family and debts, he began his first successful story, "Dejah Thoris, Princess of Mars" (first published in *All-Story* magazine in 1912 as "Under the Moons of Mars"; later published in book form in 1917 as *A Princess of Mars*). The 11 Mars books (the planet is called "Barsoom" in the series) chronicled the adventures of an earthling, Captain John Carter, on a hostile but savagely beautiful planet. A few months later in 1912 appeared Burroughs' biggest success, *Tarzan of the Apes*. In a total of 24 books the ape-man roamed an unlikely but exotic and dangerous jungle, discovered lost races, penetrated to the Earth's core and fought in two world wars. Other series flowed from Burroughs' incredibly prolific pen—the Carson of Venus books, the Pellucidar tales (located at the center of the Earth), the Land That Time Forgot trilogy (located on an unknown continent in the South Seas); a trilogy of books located on the moon; and many other titles. Most of Burroughs' works could not be called science fiction, because their science is inconsistent and implausible. Rather, they blend the color and sheer storytelling exuberance of such 19th-century masters as H. Rider Haggard with the more modern zest for science and space travel of H.G. WELLS. While criticized as repetitious and frequently clumsily written, Burroughs' works display superb pacing and an unflagging imagination. They have never been out of print and continue to be adapted to radio, comic strips and movies. *The Gods of Mars* (1913), *Tarzan of the Apes* (1912) and *The Moon Maid* (1926) will likely endure as narrative masterpieces. Burroughs died of a heart ailment after serving as a war correspondent in WORLD WAR II.

For further reading:

Porges, Irwin, *Edgar Rice Burroughs.* Provo, Utah: Brigham Young University Press, 1975.

Holtsmark, Erling B., *Edgar Rice Burroughs.* Boston: G.K. Hall, 1986.

Burroughs, William S(eward) (1914–). American novelist and essayist. Burroughs is a highly controversial yet critically acclaimed author whose best-known work, *The Naked Lunch* (1959), sparked a well-publicized obscenity trial in the U.S. upon its first publication. Burroughs, the scion of a wealthy St. Louis family, was educated at Harvard. But he rejected his background and instead plunged into an alternative life-style that included travel, odd jobs, bisexualty and drug addiction; he also accidentally shot his wife. In the mid-1940s in New York, he befriended younger writers Allen GINSBERG and Jack KEROUAC, with whom he would be linked—in the 1950s—as key figures in the BEAT GENERATION. With painter Brion Gysin, Burroughs developed a "cut-up" system of prose composition that employed cutting and blending of several random texts into one hybrid narrative. Burroughs' works include *Junky* (1953), *The Soft Machine* (1961), *Nova Express* (1964) and *The Western Lands* (1987).

Burstyn, Ellen (1932–). U.S. film and television actress who won an ACADEMY AWARD for best actress for the film *Alice Doesn't Live Here Anymore* (1974). She also won a Tony Award for *Same Time Next Year* in 1978. Burstyn was also nominated for an Academy Award for *The Exorcist* (1973) and *The Last Picture Show* (1971).

Burt, (Sir) Cyril L(odowic) (1883–1971). British psychologist. Burt was one of the most influential psychologists of his era, particularly in his native land. Burt designed widely used tests to measure the intelligence of British schoolchildren. In books such as *Measurement of Mental Capacities* (1927) and *Factors of the Mind* (1940), he stressed the importance of intelligence differences between individuals and argued that these were largely determined by heredity. Burt taught education and psychology at the University of London from 1924 to 1950. After his death, in 1976, it was proven that Burt had published falsified data in support of his theories. As a result, Burt's scientific credibility has suffered.

Burton, Harold H(itz) (1888–1964). Associate justice, U.S. Supreme Court (1945–58). A graduate of Bowdoin College and Harvard University Law School, Burton first entered private practice in Ohio before working in Utah and Idaho. After service in World War I, he resumed private law practice in Cleveland. An active Republican, Burton was elected mayor of Cleveland, vowing to rid the city of racketeers and gangsters. An extremely popular mayor, he was next elected to the U.S. Senate (1941), where he took a leadership role. In 1945 Burton was nominated to the Court by President Harry S TRUMAN, who had been under pressure to name a Republican to the overwhelmingly Democratic Court. Burton generally took a conservative approach to civil liberties cases but was impartial and open-minded, judging each case on its own merits and often basing his decisions on technical rather than philosophical grounds. He gained a reputation as a conciliator between the more contentious justices. He served on the Court for 13 years before retiring for health reasons.

Burton, Phillip (1926–1983). American politician. A Democrat from California, Burton served in the U.S. House of Representatives from 1964 until his death. In 1976 he came within one vote of being elected House Democratic majority leader. A champion of liberal causes, he helped pass legislation that established a cost-of-living adjustment for social security recipients, raised the minimum wage, and improved benefits for the disabled and elderly and miners with black lung disease. He also introduced the largest national parks bill in history, which established more than 100 parks around the U.S.

Burton, Richard (Walter) [Richard (Walter) Jenkins] (1925–1984). Welsh-born actor, noted for his intense performances and his stormy life. Widely regarded as one of the most talented actors of the 20th century, Burton is remembered for his spectacular failures as well as his considerable successes. One of 13 children of a Welsh coal miner, he spoke only Welsh before the age of 10. His schoolteacher-mentor, Philip Burton, recognizing the boy's talent, adoped him and gave the boy his own name. He made his stage debut in *The Devil's Rest* (1943) by playwright-actor Emlyn Williams, who further encouraged Burton's career. By the early 1950s, Burton had emerged as one of Britain's finest Shakespearean actors, appearing at Stratford and the Old Vic. He soon moved on to films, making his breakthrough as Jimmy Porter in John OSBORNE's *Look Back in Anger* (1959). He became an international star in the HOLLYWOOD spectacle *Cleopatra* (1963), playing opposite Elizabeth TAYLOR, whom he subsequently married. Burton's stormy relationship with Taylor, whom he later divorced and then remarried, was well publicized and earned the couple considerable notoriety. Of his more than 40 films, *Becket* (1964), *The Spy Who Came in From the Cold* (1965) and *Who's Afraid of Virginia Woolf* (1966) are the most notable. Burton was the most-nominated actor never to win an ACADEMY AWARD. His Broadway performances in *Hamlet, Camelot* and *Equus* were also acclaimed. However, he also appeared in many inferior films. Critics have explained Burton's inability to sustain his early promise in terms of his womanizing, his heavy drinking and the debilitating demands of fame. His last appearance was in a movie adaptation of George ORWELL's *1984* (1984).

Richard Burton as Mark Antony in the 1963 film Cleopatra.

For further reading:

Bragg, Melvin, *Richard Burton: A Life.* Boston: Little, Brown, 1989.

Jenkins, Graham, *Richard Burton, My Brother.* New York: Harper & Row, 1988.

Burundi. In east-central Africa, just south of the equator and across the Nile-Congo watershed, Burundi is a land-locked country with an area of 10,744 square miles. Twa (Batwa) pygmies were the earliest peoples of the Burundi forests. Hutu (Bahutu) cultivators settled in the 14th century but over the next two centuries were swept aside by Tutsi (Batutsi) herders, who made virtual serfs of the majority Hutu. Germany took control as a colonial power after 1884, merging Burundi with Rwanda (1899) and making Ruanda-Urundi part of German East Africa. Troops from the adjoining Belgian Congo occupied Ruanda-Urundi during WORLD WAR I, after which Belgium administered it under a LEAGUE OF NATIONS mandate and, from 1946, a UNITED NATIONS trusteeship. In 1959 Rwanda and Burundi were separated. The Parti de l'Unite et Progres National (UPRONA) won UN-supervised elections in September 1961, and Prince Louis Rwagasore became prime minister; he was assassinated less than a month later.

Burundi became an independent kingdom on July 1, 1962. By October 1965, when an attempted coup was crushed and thousands were killed, two more prime ministers had been assassinated. An army coup in November 1966 overthrew the monarchy, and Burundi became a republic under President Michel Micombero. The exiled former king, Mwami Ntare V, was killed in 1972 during an abortive coup attempt, which was blamed on the Hutu. About 100,000 Hutu died in the subsequent Tutsi crackdown, and thousands more fled (see BURUNDIAN CIVIL WAR OF 1972). Another military coup ousted Micombero in 1976, and Jean-Baptiste Bagaza became president, introducing some pro-Hutu reforms, although Tutsi dominance continued. Fellow Tutsi Pierre

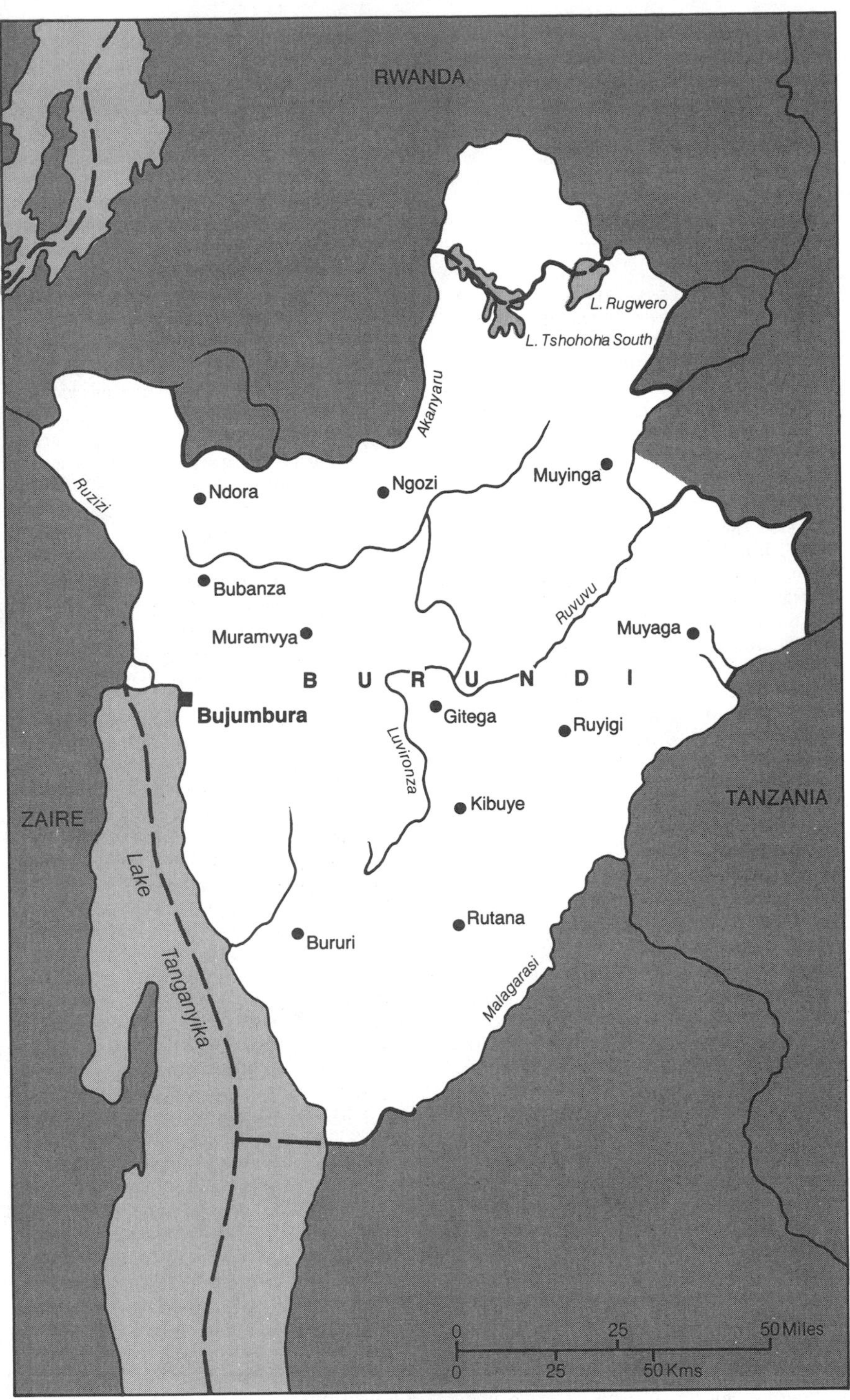

BURUNDI

Buyoya deposed Bagaza in a September 3, 1987, coup; up to 20,000 Hutu were massacred by the Tutsi in August 1988, when ethnic fighting again flared up, resulting in many deaths and a (temporary) mass exodus of refugees, mostly Hutu, to Rwanda.

Burundian Civil War of 1972. War between the Tutsi and Hutu ethnic groups in BURUNDI. The very tall Tutsi had long ago conquered the medium-height Hutu peasant farmers in east-central Africa. The Tutsi became the aristocratic ruling minority and held the Hutus in serfdom. When Burundi (which had been governed under a United Nations mandate since 1946) gained independence in 1962, a Tutsi monarchy was established. A struggle for power resulted in a military coup (1966), deposing the monarch and creating a republic, but with the Tutsi still in control. In 1970 the Hutu rebelled, massacring many Tutsi; most Hutu leaders were eventually executed. After a failed coup by the deposed monarch (1972), the Hutu attacked the Tutsi throughout Burundi. The government slaughtered over 100,000 Hutu to suppress the rebellion. About 10,000 Tutsi died, but they regained firm control of the country and put down another Hutu rebellion in 1973.

Busch, August Anheuser, Jr. (1899–1989). American brewery and baseball executive. In 1946 Busch took control of his family's small, financially ailing St. Louis brewing firm, Anheuser-Busch, and built it into the largest brewing operation in the world. The company's several brands included the world's top-selling beer, Budweiser. In Busch's 29 years as head of the company, Anheuser-Busch increased its production more than 12–fold and eventually became a major sponsor of sporting events worldwide. After his retirement in 1975, Busch remained active as president of the St. Louis Cardinals baseball team, which Anheuser-Busch had purchased in 1953. He was also a breeder of Clydesdale horses.

Busemann, Adolf (1901–1986). German-born aerospace engineer. Busemann's design of the swept wing for aircraft helped make supersonic flight possible. After settling in the U.S. in 1947, he worked for the forerunner of the NATIONAL AERONAUTICS AND SPACE ADMINISTRATION and later for NASA itself. He designed a rotating space station for NASA and recommended the use of ceramic tiles as heat shields on the SPACE SHUTTLE.

Bush, George (Herbert Walker) (1924–). Forty-first president of the United States (1989–). Bush was born into a prominent Connecticut family; his father, Prescott Bush, served as a U.S. senator (1952–63). Bush attended Phillips Acad-

George Herbert Walker Bush, 41st president of the United States.

emy in Andover, Mass., before joining the Navy in 1942. The youngest American pilot during WORLD WAR II, he was based on a carrier in the Pacific, saw combat and was shot down once. Bush won three Air Medals and the Distinguished Flying Cross. Discharged in 1945, he entered Yale University, where he completed his bachelor's degree in economics in two-and-a-half years and won Phi Beta Kappa honors. In 1948 Bush and his wife, Barbara Pierce Bush, moved to Texas, where he worked in the oil industry and eventually founded a number of successful businesses that made him wealthy. Bush entered politics in 1964, running unsuccessfully for a U.S. Senate seat, but in 1966 he won election to the U.S. House of Representatives. In his two consecutive terms in the House he compiled a generally conservative record and favored stringent environmental protection measures. In 1968 Bush was reportedly considered as a vice presidential running mate by Richard M. NIXON; he was apparently considered again in 1973, after the resignation of Vice President Spiro AGNEW; and again in 1974, when Gerald FORD had to name his own successor after Nixon resigned the presidency.

Following his defeat (by Lloyd BENTSEN) in a second bid for the Senate (1970), Bush was appointed U.S. ambassador to the UNITED NATIONS. After the 1972 elections he was named chairman of the Republican National Committee. In September 1974, President Ford named Bush to head the U.S. Liaison Office in Beijing; although the U.S. and China did not have full diplomatic relations at the time, Bush was in effect ambassador. From late 1975 to January 1977, Bush headed the CIA and was credited with improving the agency's professionalism. Out of government during the CARTER administration, Bush was chairman of a Houston, Texas, bank. He announced his candidacy for the Republican presidential nomination in May 1979 and remained in the race longer than any of front-runner Ronald REAGAN's rivals. Bush caused a stir during one televised debate when he criticized Reagan's economic proposals as "voodoo economics." Nonetheless, Reagan chose Bush as his vice presidential running mate at the convention, and Bush served as vice president throughout Reagan's two presidential terms (1981–89).

Bush won the Republican presidential nomination in 1988 and defeated Democrat Michael DUKAKIS for the presidency after a bitter campaign. Bush promised to work for "a kinder, gentler nation" and urged a new spirit of public service and volunteerism. In office he largely continued Reagan's conservative policies but proved more willing to compromise with Congress. Domestically, much of his attention was devoted to dealing with the effects of the SAVINGS AND LOAN SCANDAL, which had caused many banks to collapse. Drugs, crime and education were also priorities on Bush's domestic agenda. However, the huge budget deficit and a new recession made his task difficult.

When IRAQ invaded and occupied KUWAIT in August 1990, Bush condemned Iraqi President Saddam HUSSEIN and acted decisively to counter this aggression. He announced **Operation Desert Shield,** sending more than 200,000 U.S. troops to Saudi Arabia to deter an Iraqi invasion of that country, but promised that the U.S. would not repeat the mistakes of the VIETNAM WAR. In Nov. 1990 Bush doubled the number of U.S. personnel in the region, achieving a U.S. offensive capability. He rallied the United Nations to impose tough sanctions on Iraq and to declare a deadline (January 15, 1991) for Iraq's withdrawal from Kuwait. A UN resolution gave him a supranational authority to use force against Iraq after the deadline. When Iraq refused to comply, Bush ordered **Operation Desert Storm** to dislodge the Iraqis (see PERSIAN GULF WAR). On March 6, 1991, Bush addressed Congress and nation and proclaimed victory in the Gulf. He also announced a four-point plan for restoring peace and stability to the region, including a proposal that ISRAEL give up land in return for peace. At the end of the Gulf War, national polls put Bush's approval rating at over 90%—the highest ever recorded for any U.S. president.

For further reading:

Hyams, Joe, *Flight of the Avenger: George Bush at War*. San Diego: Harcourt Brace Jovanovich, 1991.

Bush, Vannevar (1890–1974). American engineer and public official. Bush earned his B.S. and M.S. degrees from Tufts College in 1913 and received his Ph.D. in engineering jointly from Harvard and the Massachusetts Institute of Technology in 1916. The following year he worked in a special Navy anti-submarine laboratory. Bush joined MIT's faculty in 1919, becoming the institute's vice president and dean of the school of engineering in 1932. A prolific inventor, he designed a number of advanced mathematical analyzing instruments, including the differential analyzer, a forerunner of the computer. In 1939 he became president of the Carnegie Institution of Washington. In 1940 Bush served as chairman of the National Defense Research Committee (NDRC), formed at his suggestion to direct war-related scientific research. The following year he became chairman of the Office of Scientific Research and Development (OSRD), which included the NDRC.

Bush made no technical contribution to the war effort, but as an administrator he was responsible for the development of an array of new weapons, including RADAR, amphibious vehicles and the ATOMIC BOMB. In June 1945 he advised President Harry S TRUMAN to use the atomic bomb against Japan without prior warning. After the war Bush continued to serve on government policy committees. He prepared recommendations on ways in which wartime research could be applied to peace; "Science, the Endless Frontier," urged massive government support for basic research. His recommendations resulted in the establishment of the National Science Foundation in 1950. Bush opposed the development of the HYDROGEN BOMB and urged negotiations to end the arms race.

In the 1950s Bush was a vocal critic of abuses in security investigations, which he thought had retarded weapons research by undermining scientists' morale. He was particularly alarmed by the 1954 OPPENHEIMER security hearings. Because of Oppenheimer's prewar involvement with leftist groups and his postwar reservations about the development of the hydrogen bomb, President Dwight D. EISENHOWER ordered his security clearance suspended in late 1953 pending a hearing. Bush objected to the charges, urging that they be "redrafted in such a way as to remove all implication that Oppenheimer was being tried for his opinions." Bush declared that "useful men" were "denied the opportunity to contribute to our scientific efforts because of their youthful indiscretions." In an apparent reference to Sen. Joseph R. MCCARTHY, he accused "ruthless, ambitious men" of using "our loyalty procedures for political purposes."

In 1957 Bush became chairman of the MIT Corporation and in 1959 its honorary chairman. He continued to write and lecture on national defense through the 1960s. In 1970 he and James CONANT received the Atomic Pioneers Award from the AEC.

Bushuyev, Konstantin D. (1914–1978). Soviet space scientist. Bushuyev was the director of the historic 1975 U.S.-Soviet APOLLO-SOYUZ TEST PROJECT, in which American astronauts and Soviet cosmonauts linked their spacecraft in orbit above the earth.

Busia, Kofi (1913–1978). Prime minister of GHANA (1969–72). Following Ghana's independence (1957), Busia was a leader of conservatives and a strong critic of the socialist Prime Minister Kwame NKRUMAH. He went into exile in the early 1960s. In September 1969, the military government that had deposed Nkrumah turned power over to Busia and his Progress Party. However, he was unable to solve Ghana's social and economic problems, and was himself overthrown by the army while he was out of the country in January 1972. Busia went into exile in Great Britain.

Busignies, Henri Gaston (1905–1981). French-born electronics engineer and inventor. Busignies' 140 patented inventions included the first automatic direction finder for aircraft. His many innovations in aerial navigation, RADAR and other areas contributed significantly to the Allied military capability during WORLD WAR II. After the war he became chief scientist with the International Telephone and Telegraph Corporation (ITT).

Busoni, Ferruccio B(envenuto) (1866–1924). Italian composer, pianist and music critic. Born of an Italian father and a German mother who were both musically gifted, Busoni was a piano prodigy who made his debut in Vienna at age eight. In addition to his acclaimed status as a concert performer throughout Europe and America, Busoni earned a reputation as a gifted composer who combined both classicism and romanticism in his works. His major compositions include *Piano Concerto* (1904) and *Indian Fantasy* (1913). Busoni also wrote *Sketch of a New Esthetic of Music* (1907), one of the earliest critical pieces to point toward the new compositional techniques that would emerge with Igor STRAVINSKY and his fellow modernists.

busing. Local government policy in the U.S. to promote racial integration by transporting schoolchildren by bus from predominantly white or black neighborhoods to racially mixed schools. Ordered by court decisions in the 1960s and 1970s, the policy has proven controversial and has attracted much hostility from members of both races.

Bustamante, Sir (William) Alexander (1884–1977). Jamaican political leader, prime minister (1962–67). Taken to Spain as a child, he traveled extensively before returning to JAMAICA in 1932. There he became active in the trade union movement, making a name for himself with his fiery oratory. Jailed in 1941–42 for his union activities, he founded the Jamaican Labour Party, a relatively moderate political group, in 1943. Chief minister from 1953 to 1955, he was knighted in 1955, became prime minister in 1962 and welcomed Jamaican independence later that year. The voluble and flamboyant leader instituted ambitious public works and agrarian reform programs before his retirement in 1965.

Bustamante y Rivero, Jose Luis (1894–1989). Peruvian political leader. Bustamante was elected president of PERU in 1945 but was ousted three years later in a military coup. Following the coup, he taught law and served as a judge at the International Court of Justice in The HAGUE; he served as president of the court from 1967 to 1970.

Alexander Bustamente shortly before becoming prime minister of Jamaica on August 6, 1962.

Butenandt, Adolf Friedrich Johann (1903–). German organic chemist and biochemist. Butenandt took his first degree in chemistry at the University of Marburg and earned his doctorate in 1927 under Adolf Windaus at Gottingen, where he remained until 1933. Following the work of Windaus on cholesterol, Butenandt investigated the sex hormones and in 1929 isolated the first pure sex hormone, estrone. (The compound was also discovered independently by Edward Doisy.) A search for the male sex hormone resulted in the isolation in 1931 of androsterone. In 1933 he became professor of organic chemistry at the Danzig Institute of Technology. There he demonstrated the similarities between the molecular structure of androsterone and cholesterol. His proposed structure for androsterone was confirmed by Leopold Ruzicka in 1934. Butenandt and Ruzicka synthesized the male hormone testosterone only months after its isolation in 1935. They were jointly awarded the NOBEL PRIZE for chemistry in 1939 but Butenandt was forbidden to accept it by the Nazi government. Butenandt was also the first to crystallize an insect hormone, ecdysone, and found that this too was a derivative of cholesterol. Later he led research on the isolation and synthesis of the pheromones. From 1936 to 1945 Butenandt was director of the Max Planck Institute for Biochemistry at Tubingen and from 1945 to 1956 professor of physiological chemistry there. He retained these posts when the institute moved to Munich in 1956, and in 1960 he succeeded Otto HAHN as president of the Max Planck Society.

Buthelezi, Mangosuthu Gatsha (1928–). Black South African political figure and hereditary Zulu chief. Buthelezi was installed as leader of the Buthelezi tribe in 1953 and appointed chief minister of Zululand, one of SOUTH AFRICA's black homelands, in 1972. In 1975 he revived the Zulu cultural organization INKATHA and became its president. As leader of South Africa's Zulus, Buthelezi has been a controversial figure. Some observers regard him as a puppet of the white-dominated South African government and claim that he has received government backing to counteract the more radical AFRICAN NATIONAL CONGRESS. In 1990 and into 1991, while President F.W. DE KLERK initiated reforms, hundreds of blacks were killed in violent clashes between Buthelezi's supporters and rival blacks. Nelson MANDELA has met with Buthelezi and attempted to mediate the ideological dispute between Inkatha and his own ANC.

Butler, Nicholas M(urray) (1862–1947). American educator who was awarded, jointly with Jane ADDAMS, the NOBEL PRIZE for peace in 1931. Butler, who was born in New Jersey and received a doctoral degree in philosophy from Columbia University in 1884, became one of the guiding voices of American education in the first half of this century. He became president of Columbia University in 1901 and was the first to introduce education as a distinct field of study there. Butler became a major lobbying force behind the unified administration of public education in New York state. In 1910 he was instrumental in convincing steel magnate Andrew Carnegie to establish the Carnegie Endowment for International Peace. A conservative Republican, Butler became a controversial figure during World War I when he fired two Columbia faculty members in 1917 for their opposition to the Conscription Act. In the 1930s Butler was critical of American neutrality and urged economic unity for Europe.

Butler, Pierce (1866–1939). Associate justice, U.S. Supreme Court (1923–39). A graduate of Carleton College, Butler was admitted to the bar after reading law at a law firm. He was in private practice in St. Paul, Minnesota, when the federal government enlisted him to prosecute several antitrust cases. Butler's success enhanced his reputation and in 1922 President Warren G. HARDING followed the advice of Chief Justice William Howard TAFT and nominated Butler to the Supreme Court. Nominated, at least in part, because he was a Roman Catholic, Butler's nomination had been challenged because of his close association with large railroads while he was in law practice. On the court Butler did prove to be a supporter of big business and a foe of government regulation.

Butler, Richard Austen "Rab" [Baron Butler of Saffron Walden] (1902–1982). British statesman. He was a leading politician in Britain for half a century and the most influential figure in the reconstruction of the CONSERVATIVE PARTY after WORLD WAR II. During his career he served in top ministerial posts in seven Conservative governments. He was chancellor of the exchequer (1951–55), leader of the House of Commons (1955–61), home secretary (1957–62), foreign secretary (1963–64) and deputy prime minister (1962–63). He was first elected to Parliament in 1929. He was largely responsible for the India Act of 1935, which established greater constitutional freedom for INDIA by creating provincial legislatures. He supported Neville CHAMBERLAIN'S MUNICH PACT with Adolf HITLER (1938). As minister of education (1941–45) he was responsible for the Education Act of 1944, which restructured secondary education in Britain and secured the right of free education for British children. A leading contender for prime minister in 1957 and 1963, he was defeated by Harold MACMILLAN and Alec DOUGLAS-HOME, respectively. He was made a life peer in 1965 and served as master of Trinity College, Cambridge (1965–78).

Butor, Michel (1926–). French novelist, literary critic and philosophical essayist. Butor came to prominence in the 1950s as one of the NOUVEAU ROMAN (New Novel) school of postwar French novelists—also including Marguerite DURAS and Alain ROBBE-GRILLET—who had abandoned the traditional space-time plot conventions of the novel in favor of episodic disjunctions and philosophical explorations of the consciousness of the fictional characters. Butor's first novel was *Passage to Milan* (1954); other notable novels include *The Modification* (1957), *Degrees* (1960) and *Intervalle* (1973). He has also been active as a literary critic, producing a psychological study of 19th-century French poet Charles Baudelaire, *Histoire Extraordinaire* (1961), as well as analyses of Proust and of the nature of artistic creation. Beginning in 1963, Butor published several volumes of *Illustrations*, an ongoing "journal intime."

Butterworth, George (Santon) (1885–1916). British composer. Butterworth was educated at Eton School and at Oxford and then went on to study composition under Charles Wood at the Royal College of Music. Subsequently he devoted himself to the collecting of authentic British Isles folksongs, which were the primary inspiration for Butterworth's compositions. In the course of this endeavor Butterworth became an assistant to the renowned British composer Ralph VAUGHN WILLIAMS, who was also deeply influenced by folksongs. Butterworth's most famous composition was an orchestral setting (1912) of the poem *A Shropshire Lad* by British poet A.E. HOUSMAN. Butterworth was killed during WORLD WAR I at the battle of the SOMME.

Button, Richard Totten "Dick" (1929–). American figure skater. Button brought the first breath of athleticism to figure skating and was the first to perform a triple loop jump. He dominated the sport as no other had before him, holding the U.S. title from 1946 to 1952 and winning the world title five times from 1948 to 1952. He turned professional in 1953 and skated for some years with the Ice Capades. Today he is known throughout the world as an insightful figure skating commentator.

buzz bomb. See V-1 AND V-2 ROCKETS.

Byalik, Chaim Nachman (1873–1934). Russian-born Hebrew poet, essayist and story writer. Byalik's poem "Into the City of Slaughter" (1905) was written in reaction to the Kishinev POGROM; it is a moving account of human suffering and an admonition to the JEWS for their passivity under oppression. In 1924 Byalik settled in Palestine, where he was the leader of a cultural revival. He translated Shakespeare's *Julius Caesar* and Cervantes' *Don Quixote* into Hebrew and is regarded as the greatest modern Hebrew poet.

Byatt, A.S. See Margaret DRABBLE.

Bykova, Yelizaveta Ivanovna (1913–). Soviet chess player and economic planner. The women's world chess champion (1953–56 and 1958–62), she became an international chess master in 1953 and an honorary master of sport of the U.S.S.R.

Bykovsky, Valery (1934–). Soviet cosmonaut who made space history in June of 1963, when he spent nearly five days alone in the Vostok 5 spacecraft, the longest solo space flight up to that date. Bykovsky later commanded Soyuz 22 (1976) and Soyuz 31 (1978), both scientific missions.

Byrd, Harry F(lood) (1887–1966). Harry Byrd was the scion of a Virginia line dating back to 1674. He left school at the age of 15 to restore his father's newspaper, the *Winchester Star*, to solvency, and at age 20 established his own newspaper in Martinsburg, W.Va. In 1915 Byrd entered the Virginia State Senate and within a decade was the dominant figure in Virginia politics. He remained so for the next 40 years. A master political technician, he served as Virginia's governor from 1926 to 1930, and his frugal regime was considered innovative and successful. Appointed to the Senate in 1933 at the urging of President Franklin D. ROOSEVELT, Byrd ironically became one of the most bitter opponents of the NEW DEAL. As chairman of the newly created Joint Committee on Reduction of Nonessential Federal Expenditures in 1941, he attained a forum for his sallies against unbalanced budgets and social welfare programs.

In the 1950s Byrd was one of the Senate's most influential members. He sat on the powerful Armed Services Committee and became chairman of the Finance Committee in 1955. In the presidential election of 1952, he refused to endorse the Democratic ticket headed by Adlai STEVENSON. Byrd often voted against public works bills, including the ST. LAWRENCE SEAWAY and the national highway program. He consistently fought to eliminate all economic assistance from foreign aid packages. Byrd also worked to block enactment of his Democratic colleagues' social measures. In 1960 he opposed federal aid to education, federal aid for areas beset by chronic unemployment, an increase in the minimum wage and medicare.

In the wake of the Supreme Court's 1954 ruling banning school SEGREGATION, Byrd moved to the forefront of the Southern crusade to maintain segregation and STATES' RIGHTS. His February 1956 call for "massive resistance" became a rallying cry for those determined to oppose even token desegregation. In March he helped mobilize the signing of the "Southern Manifesto," a rhetorical defiance of the Court signed by 101 Southern members of Congress. A national symbol of unbudging resistance to integration, deficit-spending and the WELFARE STATE, Byrd received support in the presidential elections of 1956 and 1960. Although not a declared candidate, he won 134,157 votes for president in 1956. In the election of 1960 he received the electoral votes of Mississippi, Alabama and one Oklahoma Republican elector, for a total of 15. Byrd resigned from the Senate in November 1965; his son, Harry F. Byrd Jr., was appointed his successor.

Byrd, Richard Evelyn (1888–1957). American pilot, military officer and explorer. A member of Virginia's famous Byrd family, and brother of Harry Flood BYRD, Richard Byrd graduated from the U.S. Naval Academy in 1912 and served in WORLD WAR I. Forced in 1916 to resign from the Navy with an injured leg, he joined its fledgling air arm. After the end of World War I he became interested in polar aviaton. He joined the MacMillan expedition to the Arctic in 1924 and, with Floyd BENNETT, made the first flight over the NORTH POLE on May 9, 1926. Byrd then became interested in Antarctic exploration, leading his first expedition there in 1928. He established a base camp, Little America, on the Ross Ice Shelf and, in 1929, flew over the SOUTH POLE. The Antarctic was the largest unmapped and unexplored area of the world, and Byrd contributed greatly to opening up and mapping the continent. A more extensive expedition was undertaken in 1933–35, during which Byrd spent five months alone at an Antarctic weather station; there were three more expeditions, the last in 1955–56. A large section of the Antarctic was named Marie Byrd Land, after his wife.

For further reading:

Byrd, Richard Evelyn, *Alone*. Covelo, California: Island Press, 1984.

Rogers, Eugene, *Beyond the Barrier: The Story of Byrd's First Expedition to Antarctica*. Annapolis, Md.: Naval Institute Press, 1990.

Byrds, The. American folk-country-rock band. The original band lineup was Roger McGuinn, vocals, guitar; Gene Clark, vocals, percussion, guitar; Chris Hillman, bass, mandolin, vocals; Michael Clarke, drums; and David Crosby, guitar, vocals. The band's pedigree, via various members, included the Limelighters, the Scottsville Squirrel Barkers, the Hillmen and the New Christy Minstrels. In 1965 they hit number-one on both sides of the Atlantic with a cover of Bob DYLAN's "Mr. Tambourine Man." The group charted with two other covers, "All I Really Want to Do" and "Turn, Turn, Turn." By 1966, the group's personnel began to shift, with Gene Clark departing. David Crosby left the following year, which also saw the release of *Younger than Yesterday*. Gram Parsons was part of the Byrds for the 1968 albums *Notorious Byrd Brothers* and *Sweetheart of the Rodeo*. The group dissolved for good in 1973, having introduced a shot of country music into mainstream rock. McGuinn, Clark and Hillman would resurface in 1979 as the group McGuinn, Clark and Hillman.

Byrnes, James F(rancis) (1879–1972). American lawyer, politician and government official. A leading Democrat, Byrnes had a long and distinguished career at the highest levels of government. He served as U.S. representative from South Carolina (1911–25), U.S. senator (1931–40), South Carolina state supreme court justice (1941–42), director of war mobilization (1942–45), U.S. secretary of state (1945–47) and governor of South Carolina (1951–55). President Franklin D. ROOSEVELT described the powerful Byrnes as "assistant president" during WORLD WAR

II. He attended the YALTA CONFERENCE (1944) and the POTSDAM CONFERENCE (1945). However, his tenure as secretary of state was stormy. Byrnes was often at odds with the TRUMAN administration and Congress on foreign and domestic policy and on the way he handled his job. As governor of South Carolina, he championed STATES' RIGHTS, favored school segregation and opposed the Supreme Court's decision in BROWN V. BOARD OF EDUCATION (1954).

For further reading:

Byrnes, James F., *Speaking Frankly*. Westport, Conn.: Greenwood 1974.
Clements, Kendrick A., ed., *James F. Byrnes and the Origins of the Cold War*. Durham, N.C.: Carolina Academic Press, 1982.

Cabaret. Long-running Broadway musical show and ACADEMY AWARD-winning motion picture. The songs, by John Kander and Fred Ebb, and the book, by Joe Masteroff, signaled a shift from the conventional musicals of the 1950s to the edgy and raffish style of the 1960s. "It mocked emotion and emphasized decadence and immorality in its depiction of the mood of pre-Nazi Germany," writes historian Abe Laufe; but it intrigued theater-goers and had "a morbid fascination for others." The source was John VAN DRUTEN's adaptation of a number of stories by Christopher ISHERWOOD about a young writer, Clifford, living in Berlin during the pre-Hitler era. Van Druten's I AM A CAMERA opened on Broadway in 1951 with Julie Harris in the leading role of Clifford's pregnant girl friend, Sally Bowles (a nightclub entertainer). Kander and Ebb's musical version, *Cabaret,* opened on November 12, 1966, at Broadway's Broadhurst Theater. It ran for a total of 1,166 performance and garnered 10 Tony Awards as well as the Critics' Circle Award as best musical for 1966–67. The cast included Joel Grey as the Master of Ceremonies, Jill Haworth as Sally, Bert Convy as Cliff, Jack GILFORD as Schulz and Lotte LENYA as Fraulein Schneider. Joel Grey repeated his role in the Bob FOSSE film adaptation (1972), which starred Liza Minnelli as Sally and received eight Oscars.

For further reading:
Laufe, Abe, *Broadway's Greatest Musicals* New York: Funk & Wagnall's, 1970.

Cabell, James Branch (1879–1958). American novelist and essayist. Cabell attended the College of William and Mary, and taught Greek and French there for one year (1896–97). This was followed by newspaper work in Virginia, New York and West Virginia. His principal work was a 20–volume series of novels, short stories, essays, sketches and genealogies set in the mythical French province of Poictesme and concerning the history of the descendants of one Dom Manuel, from 1234 to 1750. Cabell's greatest success was *Jurgen* (1919), which was prosecuted in the U.S. in 1920 by the Society for the Suppression of Vice. Considered important and sexually controversial in his day, Cabell's reputation has declined since his death, and his works today are read strictly by fantasy aficionados. His nonfictional works include *Beyond Life* and *Some of Us.*

Cabinda [Kabinda]. District and town on the Atlantic Ocean, in an enclave north of the Congo River; sequestered from the rest of Angola by a span of Zaire's coastline. Cabinda actively supported the Angolan effort for independence from Portugal (see ANGOLAN WAR OF INDEPENDENCE). After liberation in 1975, some local residents wanted Cabinda to become a separate nation so that it could retain its copious oil reserves.

CAD. Popular acronym for "computer-aided drawing" and "computer-aided design." The development of compact and inexpensive COMPUTER equipment in the 1960s and the availability of programs for computer design and drafting have made CAD techniques increasingly popular. Designs and drawings are developed on a computer CRT screen, where revision is easy and the creation of various perspective views virtually automatic and instantaneous. Hard copy is printed on paper by a printer or plotter as needed. CAD techniques are now in general use in engineering and architectural offices, and their use is increasing in interior and industrial design firms. While CAD has demonstrated its ability to augment and even replace conventional drafting in many applications, skill in drawing will remain an important element in architects' and designers' professional practice for the foreseeable future.

Caesar, Sid (1922–). One of the great pioneers of television during its "Golden Age of Comedy" in the 1950s, Sid Caesar was known for his brilliant pantomime, hilarious foreign accents (e.g., "the Professor") and portrayals of "everyman" characters frustrated by day-to-day problems. Born and raised in New York, Caesar began his career as a saxophonist, forming a band with composer Vernon Duke in the 1940s. Slipping imitations, jokes, double-talk and funny faces in between songs, Caesar was selected to perform comedy in various Coast Guard shows, until he landed a role in the Broadway hit *Make Mine Manhattan* (1948). In 1949 Caesar moved to television, where he became the star of the program "American Broadway Review," which was

Liza Minnelli as "Sally Bowles" and Joel Grey as the "Master of Ceremonies" in the movie version of Cabaret.

retitled "Your Show of Shows" a year later. The live, weekly comedy program featured dozens of hilarious comic sketches with Caesar and costars Imogene Coca, Carl Reiner and Howard Morris; the shows were written by Caesar, Reiner and future comedy greats Mel BROOKS, Neil SIMON, Woody ALLEN, Larry Gelbart and Reiner, among others. Caesar won two Emmys for the show (in 1951 and 1956), but the strain of performing live each week proved too much for him. He suffered serious bouts with drugs and alcohol (recounted in his autobiography *Where Have I Been?*) and had only intermittent success after the 1950s, with featured parts in films such as *It's a Mad, Mad, Mad, Mad World* (1963) and *Silent Movie* (1975). In 1989 he returned to the Broadway stage for the acclaimed nostalgic comedy revue, *Sid Caesar and Company*.

Caetano, Marcello (1906–1980). Prime minister of PORTUGAL (1968–74). A minister under Antonio de Oliveira SALAZAR in the 1940s and 1950s, Caetano retired from politics in 1959 to become rector of the University of Lisbon. He was recalled as prime minister on Salazar's retirement in 1968. He was more inclined than his predecessor to favor social change; however, his conservative pace for implementing reforms led to a left-wing military coup in 1974 that sent him into exile in Brazil and brought an end to Portugal's colonial empire in Africa. (See also ANGOLAN WAR OF INDEPENDENCE.)

Cage, John Milton (1912–). American composer, self-styled Zen philosopher, social anarchist and tinkerer in sounds. The son of an inventor, Cage was born in Los Angeles. In 1934 at age 22 he went to the University of California, Los Angeles, to study with composer Arnold SCHOENBERG. Experiments in the twelve-tone (see SERIAL MUSIC) techniques led to such early works as the "Six Short Inventions" (1933). Other influences included the concepts of "organized sound" of Edgard VARESE and the tone clusters of Henry Cowell. After teaching at the Cornish School in Seattle, Cage began presenting concerts of his works in the 1940s. Renown and notoriety followed him everywhere. He developed the "prepared piano," attaching metal and fiber objects to the strings in order to produce new and unusual sounds ("Sonatas and Interludes," 1946–48). He scored music for unlikely sound-producing artifacts. "Imaginary Landscape, No. 4" (1951) was scored for 12 radios and 24 "players." "Water Music" (1952) instructed the pianist to use a radio, whistle, water containers and a deck of cards during the performance. Cage attached microphones to house furniture. He even experimented with producing no sounds at all. His famous "Four Minutes 33 Seconds" (1952) presented a pianist sitting motionless before a closed piano for the prescribed period of time. Throughout the 1960s he presented multi-media HAPPENINGS, interfacing audience and performers. After numerous appointments and honors, including membership in the National Institute of Arts and Letters (1968) and the chair of Charles Eliot Norton Professor of Poetry at Harvard (1988–89), Cage continues his radical reorganization of traditional concepts of creativity and expression. His "change" music short-circuits the composer's intent and substitutes spontaneous operations as determinates of the sequencing of sounds. This he derives from studying the *I Ching* (the Chinese *Book of Changes*).

For further reading:
Ewen, David, *Composers Since 1900*. New York: The H.W. Wilson Co., 1969.

Cagney, James (1899–1986). American actor of Irish decent, Cagney rose from the streets of New York City to become one of the greatest stars of HOLLYWOOD'S Golden Age. He became an overnight sensation with the 1931 release of *The Public Enemy*, in which he portrayed a gangster. He followed that film with a series of gangster films interspersed with musicals. He won his only ACADEMY AWARD for the 1942 musical *Yankee Doodle Dandy*, in which he portrayed songwriter George M. COHAN. Other memorable roles were in *Angels with Dirty Faces* (1938), *White Heat* (1949) and *Mister Roberts* (1955). After appearing in more than 60 films, he retired from the screen in 1961. He came out of retirement in 1981 to appear in Milos FORMAN'S *Ragtime*. His last appearance was in the television movie *Terrible Joe Moran* (1984).

Cahiers du Cinema. The most influential journal of film criticism in the 20th century, founded in 1951 by the French film critics Andre Bazin, Jacques Doniol-Valcroze and Lo Duca. Edited primarily by Bazin until his death in 1958, *Cahiers* broke with the traditional approach of film criticism that habitually valued "art" films over "commercial" HOLLYWOOD productions. Instead, *Cahiers* proclaimed the directorial genius of certain commercial filmmakers, especially Alfred HITCHCOCK. Another critical approach championed by *Cahiers* was the "auteur" theory that directors—not actors, scriptwriters or producers—are the governing force in the making of a film. *Cahiers* also featured the critical writings of a number of young French film enthusiasts—such as Claude CHABROL, Jean-Luc GODARD, Eric ROHMER, and Francois TRUFFAUT—who would shortly thereafter emerge as leading directors in the French NOUVELLE VAGUE (New Wave) cinema of the 1960s.

Cahn, Sammy [Samuel Cohen] (1913–). American lyricist and librettist. Cahn first gained success in the 1940s writing for films and Broadway (e.g., *High Button Shoes*, 1947) with composer Jule STYNE. He has also collaborated with Johnny Burke and Jimmy VAN HEUSEN. Cahn won ACADEMY AWARDS for his lyrics to "Three Coins in the Fountain," "All the Way" and "High Hopes"—the latter was used as John F. KENNEDY'S campaign theme in 1960. Frank SINATRA has recorded many Cahn songs, such as "Saturday Night Is the Loneliest Night of the Week." The Broadway show *Words and Music* (1974) was a retrospective devoted entirely to Cahn's lyrics.

Caillaux, Joseph (Marie Auguste) (1863–1944). French statesman. A tax inspector and son of a former cabinet minister, he was elected to the Chamber of

James Cagney (seen here with Jean Harlow) plays a hardbitten gangster in the film classic Public Enemy.

Deputies in 1898. He was soon made minister of finance (1899), and served in that post at various times over the next 36 years. Among his financial reforms was an extremely unpopular income tax. During his brief tenure as premier (1911–12), Caillaux reached a settlement with GERMANY over MOROCCO that was as unpopular as his tax proposals and led to his resignation. While again serving as finance minister, he was involved in a scandal when his wife assassinated a Parisian newspaper editor in 1914. A pacifist, he was imprisoned by the CLEMENCEAU government after the outbreak of WORLD WAR I, and was deprived of his civil rights. After a 1924 amnesty, he served as minister of finance under Paul Painleve (1925) and Aristide BRIAND (1925), serving in that post for the last time in 1935. Losing his seat in the Chamber of Deputies in 1919, he was elected to the Sen- in 1925, remaining there until his death.

Cain, James M(allahan) (1892–1977). American novelist. Cain stands alongside Raymond CHANDLER and Dashiell HAMMETT as one of the great American writers of mystery and thriller fiction. Cain's novels were both widely read and critically acclaimed and were frequently adapted into Hollywood films. Cain was particularly noted for his extremely spare and hard-boiled style. His best known novel is *The Postman Always Rings Twice* (1934), which was adapted into a 1946 film starring John Garfield and Lana Turner. A 1981 remake starred Jessica Lange and Jack NICHOLSON. Other novels by Cain include *Double Indemnity* (1936), *Serenade* (1937), *Mildred Pierce* (1941), *The Butterfly* (1947), *The Moth* (1948), *Root of His Evil* (1954), *Magician's Wife* (1965) and *Rainbow's End* (1977).

Caine, Michael [Maurice Joseph Micklewhite] (1933–). British film actor. Born into a poor Cockney family, Caine played small roles in over 30 films from 1956 to 1963. Although he received attention from a supporting role in *Zulu* (1963) and the starring role of Harry Palmer in *The Ipcress File* (1965), it was his portrayal of the charming, self-centered *Alfie* (1966) that made him a star. Despite the box-office failure of many of his films, Caine is praised by critics for his versatility and craft. He received ACADEMY AWARD nominations for *Alfie* and *Sleuth* (1972) and won best-supporting actor for *Hannah and Her Sisters* (1986). Other memorable films include *The Man Who Would Be King* (1976), *Dressed To Kill* (1980), *Death Trap* (1982) and *Educating Rita* (1983).

Cairo Conference. Conference of Allied leaders in Cairo, Egypt November 22–26, 1943, during WORLD WAR II to discuss the war in Asia. After the conference U.S. President Franklin D. ROOSEVELT, British Prime Minister Winston CHURCHILL, and Chinese leader CHIANG KAI-SHEK issued a declaraton on December 1st demanding JAPAN's unconditional surrender to end the war in Asia. Japan was to be forced back to its 1894 boundaries; Formosa was to be restored to CHINA; and the Japanese presence in KOREA and MANCHURIA was to be ended.

Calais. Ancient city and port on the Strait of Dover in Pas-de-Calais department, France. A target of Germany's thrust to the sea in both world wars, it was held by them from 1940 to 1944 and used as a launching pad for V-1 buzz bombs targeted against England. Much of Calais' ancient architecture was demolished during the war.

Calcutta. Primary manufacturing center and port, on the Hooghly River about 85 miles from the Bay of Bengal. Currently the capital of West Bengal State, INDIA, it was the capital of British India from 1773 to 1912. By 1900 it was the second most populous city in the British Empire; now it is India's third largest city. Tension between Muslims and Hindus led to heavy riots during the late 1940s when India gained independence. In the 1960s and 1970s displeasure with the government spurred more unrest. The city's slums and large homeless population remain persistent problems.

Calder, Alexander (1898–1976). American sculptor. Calder received a degree in mechanical engineering at Hoboken, New Jersey's Stevens Institute of Technology (1919) and later studied at the Art Students League, New York (1923–26). Traveling widely in the U.S., Latin America, India and Europe, he arrived in Paris in 1928 and was influenced by the constructivism of Naum GABO, the severe structure and primary colors of Piet MONDRIAN, the organic forms of Jean ARP and the playfulness and coloristic bravura of Joan MIRO. Forsaking the fanciful representational wire sculpture typical of his early work (such as the small 1925 *Zoo* now at New York's Museum of Modern Art), he created a new form of sculpture—christened "mobiles" by Marcel DUCHAMP. First shown in 1932, these sheet-metal and wire constructions mingled the principles of mechanics with the images of abstract art. Calder's mobiles are brightly-colored or black sheet-metal cutouts in organic shapes, attached by wires, finely balanced and set in motion by currents of air. From the 1950s on, he also produced a series of monumental "stabiles," constructed of sheet metal, in soaring but firmly ground-based sculptures. Calder was also a gifted printmaker and book illustrator and created a number of notable stage sets.

Caldwell, Erskine (1903–). American author and journalist. Although he had gained a modest reputation from his early short stories, Caldwell achieved notoriety with the successful staging in 1935 of his first novel, *Tobacco Road* (1932). He continued writing stories and novels about the lives of poor black and white farmers in the deep South, which include *God's Little Acre* (1933; filmed 1958), *The Sure Hand of God* (1947) and the memoir *Deep South: memory and observation* (1980).

For further reading:
Arnold, Edwin T., ed., *Conversations with Erskine Caldwell.* Jackson, Miss.: University Press of Mississippi, 1988.

Author Erskine Caldwell in his New York hotel room (1958).

Caldwell, (Janet Mirriam) Taylor (Holland) (1900–1985). Anglo-American novelist who also wrote under the pseudonyms Marcus Holland and Max Reiner. A prolific author of popular fiction, Caldwell's first novel, *Dynasty of Death* (1938), a family saga rife with intrigue and romance, is typical of her work. Though some praise her narrative ability, she has never received critical acclaim for her literary style. Other titles include *Captains and the Kings* (1972), *Bright Flows the River* (1978) and *Answer as a Man* (1981).

California. U.S. state on the Pacific Coast, bordered on the north by the state of Oregon and on the south by Mexico. During the 20th century, California became one of the largest, wealthiest and most politically influential U.S. states. Early in the century the SAN FRANCISCO EARTHQUAKE and fire levelled the northern California city, in April 1906, but the city and California itself were growing so rapidly that San Francisco was quickly rebuilt. Prejudice against Japanese immigrants who were purchasing truck gardening land was also evident early in the century; in 1913 a law prohibited them from owning agricultural land. During the 1920s real estate speculation flourished, bringing more people to California, but the GREAT DEPRESSION of the 1930s caused widespread hardship as the state became a magnet for the nation's homeless and hopeful.

Affluence rebounded with WORLD WAR II as ports and aircraft assembly plants fueled the demands of the Pacific phase of the war. Racist paranoia, another product of the war, saw the native Japanese of California sent to "relocation centers." After the war California emerged as one of the fastest growing states, the driving force of the American dream, and its population doubled between 1950 and 1970.

The 1960s revealed the disparities of affluence and opportunity spawned by this growth. In August 1965 increasing racial pressures exploded in WATTS, a black area of LOS ANGELES, and within six days 34 people were killed and millions of dollars of property damaged. Later in the 1960s, a succession of agricultural strikes were joined by riots as migrant farm workers fought for union recognition and a share in the state's affluence. Student dissension also erupted during the 1960s and 1970s, mainly at the University of California campus at BERKELEY. Ronald REAGAN became a national political figure as an adversary of many of these social changes. In 1966 he was elected governor, serving two terms and paving the way for the state's growing conservatism in the 1970s.

California's economic strength comes from the manufacturing of aircraft, the growing of fruits and vegetables; it is the country's major wine producer. HOLLYWOOD has been the movie production capital of the world for nearly 75 years. Sacramento is the state capital, Los Angeles is the largest city; Oakland, San Diego, San Francisco and San Jose are also important cities.

Calkins, Mary Whiton (1863–1930). American philosopher and psychologist. A graduate of Smith College (1885), Calkins taught Greek at Wellesley College. Later she studied at Clark University and Harvard, and returned to Wellesley to teach philosophy and psychology (1890–1926). Her experimental research and publications in both fields revolved around her interpretations of the psyche and reality. She published over a hundred articles and several books, the most influential of which were *The Persistent Problems of Philosophy* (1907) and *The Good Man and the Good* (1918).

Callaghan, (Leonard) James (1912–). British prime minister (1976–79). The son of a naval chief petty officer, Callaghan was educated at Portsmouth and joined the Inland Revenue in 1929. He served in the navy throughout World War II and was elected as a Labour member of Parliament in 1945. He served as parliamentary secretary in the Ministry of Transport (1947–50) and as financial secretary to the Admiralty (1950–51). In 1963 he was defeated by Harold WILSON for leadership of the LABOUR PARTY. Callaghan went on to become chancellor of the exchequer (1964–67) and home secretary (1967–70). As foreign secretary (1974–76) he renegotiated Britain's membership in the EUROPEAN ECONOMIC COMMUNITY. When Wilson retired, Callaghan narrowly defeated Michael FOOT as head of the Labour Party, and served as prime minister from 1976 to 1979. Economic instability and widespread strikes in 1978 and early 1979 (the so-called Winter of Discontent) caused the House of Commons to force an election in May 1979, when Callaghan was defeated by Margaret THATCHER. Callaghan resigned the Labour Party leadership in 1980 and in 1985 declared he would not run again for Parliament.

Callaghan, Morley Edward (1903–1990). Canadian writer. A novelist and short story writer, he was noted for his hard-boiled style and use of Roman Catholic themes. He wrote 13 novels, including *Strange Fugitive* (1928) and *A Many-Colored Coat* (1960). While living in Paris in 1929, he got into a famous boxing match with Ernest HEMINGWAY. Timekeeper F. Scott FITZGERALD forgot to signal the end of the first round, and Callaghan knocked Hemingway to the ground. The match ended in friendship among the three, and the fight appeared in lightly fictionalized accounts by all three men.

Maria Callas before a performance of La Traviata *at the Royal Opera House in London (1958).*

Callas, Maria (1924–1977). American opera singer. Considered one of the great sopranos of the post-World War II era, Callas was especially noted for her precise diction, musical phrasing and dramatic intensity in the *bel canto* operas of Donizetti, Bellini, and Rossini. Of Greek heritage, she studied at the Royal Conservatory in Athens and joined the Royal Opera in 1942, making her debut in *Tosca*. Her first great success was in *Tristan and Isolde* in Venice (1947). She married businessman Giovanni Battista Meneghini in 1949 and joined La Scala Opera in Milan in 1950. She made her Metropolitan Opera debut in 1956 in *Norma*, one of her most famous roles. She also gained renown for her heroines *Lucia di Lammermoor* and PUCCINI's *Tosca*. A celebrity even among the non-opera-going public, Callas was known for her fiery temper and her stormy personal relationships.

For further reading:

Stanicoff, Nadia, *Maria Callas Remembered*. New York: Dutton, 1987.

Stassinopoulis, Arianna, *Maria Callas: The Woman Behind the Legend*. New York: Ballantine, 1982.

Calles, Plutarco Elias (1877–1945). Mexican politician, president of MEXICO (1924–28). An active figure in the complex Mexican politics of the 1910s, '20s and '30s, Calles began as a revolutionary. He was governor of the state of Sonora (1915–19) and secretary of the interior (1920–24). He played an important role in the MEXICAN CIVIL WAR OF 1920 and was subsequently secretary of the interior in the revolutionary government of Alvaro Obregon. As president, Calles' actions against the Roman Catholic Church led to the MEXICAN INSURRECTIONS OF 1926–29. He became increasingly conservative and remained a powerful figure even out of office. He was exiled in 1936 but allowed to return to Mexico in 1941.

Calley, Lt. William L. See MY LAI MASSACRE.

Calloway, Cab(ell) (1907–). American bandleader, singer and composer. Born in Rochester, New York, Calloway worked as a singer, musician and bandleader in Baltimore, Chicago, New York and elsewhere, before becoming leader of the band the Missourians in 1930. In New York, Calloway's band played at the Savoy and the Cotton Club, scoring a hit in 1931 with "Minnie the Moocher." The band began to tour, and their hits during this period included the 1939 million-seller "Jumpin' Jive." Calloway quit the big band in 1948. In 1952, he sang the role of Sportin' Life in a revival of PORGY AND BESS, then toured with the production for many years. He appeared in Broadway shows and in films and entertained in other capacities through the 1980s.

Calvin, Melvin (1911–). American biochemist. Calvin studied chemistry at the Michigan College of Mining and Technology and earned his B.S. degree in 1931. After obtaining his Ph.D. from the University of Minnesota in 1935, he spent two years at the Victoria University of Manchester, England, working with Michael Polanyi. There he became interested in chlorophyll and its role in the photosynthetic process in plants. In 1937 Calvin began a long association with the University of California, Berkeley. From 1941 to 1945 he worked on scientific problems connected with the war, including two years on the MANHATTAN PROJECT (the ATOMIC BOMB). In 1946 Calvin became director of the Bio-organic Division of the Lawrence Radiation Laboratory at Berkeley, where he used the new analytical techniques developed during the war to investigate the "dark reactions" of photosynthesis—those reactions that do not need the presence of light. This work earned Calvin the NOBEL PRIZE for chemistry in 1961. Calvin remained at Berkeley as director of the Laboratory of Chemical Biodynamics (1960–63), professor of molecular biology (1963–71) and professor of chemistry (1971).

Calvino, Italo (1923–1985). Italian novelist and short story writer. Calvino was widely considered one of the major figures in contemporary world literature. His earliest published stories, which were in a realistic mode, appeared shortly after World War II. He later made increasing use of allegory and fantasy, his reputation largely accruing from his work as an experimental writer. His best known works were *Cosmicomics, Invisible Cities* (1972) and his most familiar work, Italian Folktales (1956), a retelling of traditional stories.

Cambodia [Kampuchea]. Located in the southwest of INDOCHINA, in Southeast Asia, Cambodia covers 69,880 square miles. A French colony, Cambodia was occupied by Japanese forces in late 1940, who left the pro-VICHY colonial administration intact. In April 1941, the French

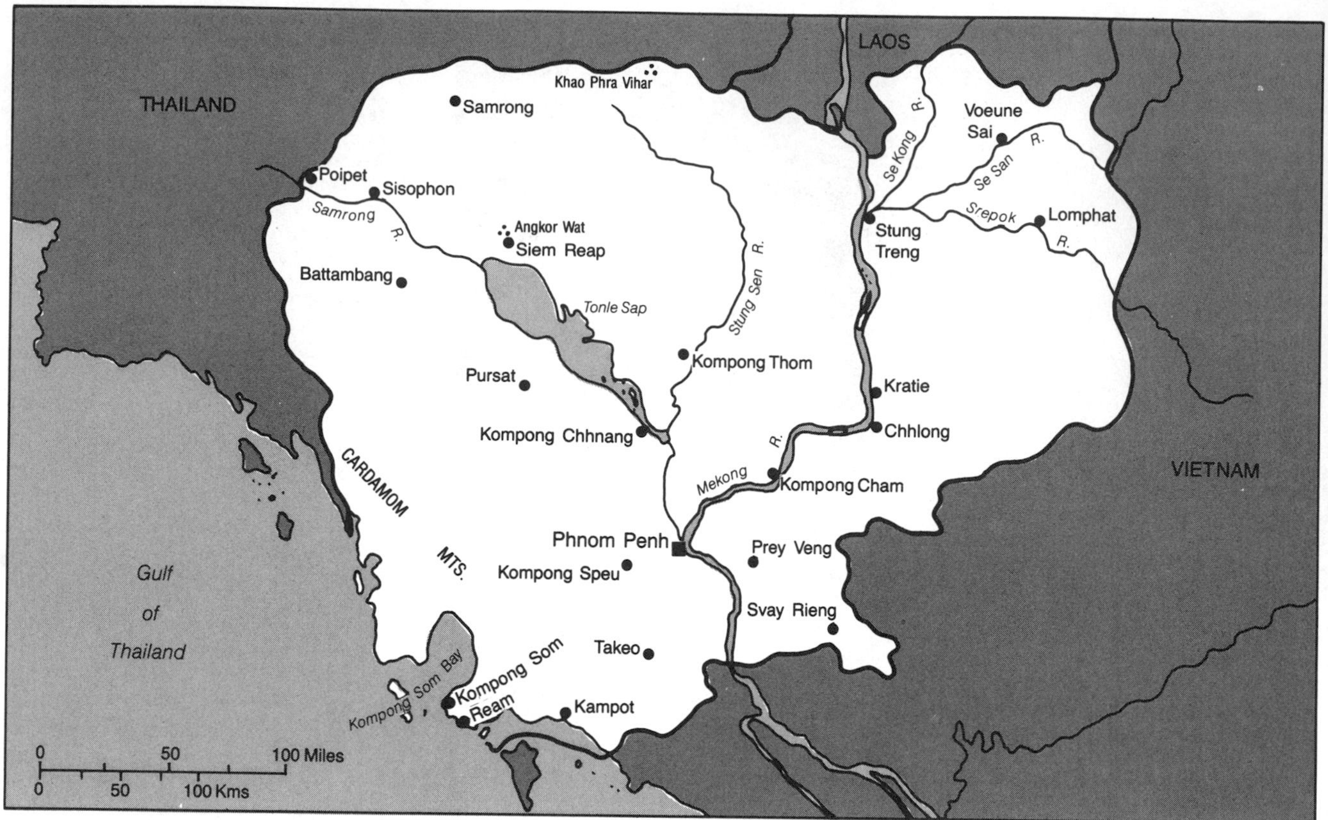

CAMBODIA

authorities placed 18-year-old Prince Norodom SIHANOUK on the Cambodian throne. In early 1945, the Japanese attempted to foster local support by offering limited independence to Cambodia, VIETNAM and LAOS. A few weeks later Sihanouk was pressured into proclaiming his country's independence. After Japan's surrender in 1945, the French returned to Cambodia and in 1946 the absolute monarchy was abolished. A constitution was introduced in 1947 that permitted popular political activity. However, by 1950 anti-French rebels controlled large areas of the countryside. Sihanouk abolished the National Assembly and declared martial law in early 1953 before embarking on a "Royal Crusade for Independence." The French, facing an increasingly stiff military test in Vietnam and Laos conceded Cambodia's independence (November 9, 1953). Sihanouk's royal government was accorded international recognition at the 1954 Geneva Conference. To avoid constitutional constraints on his rule, Sihanouk abdicated in 1955. His newly created political party won an overwhelming victory in national elections that year.

As head of state Sihanouk attempted to preserve Cambodia's neutrality during the VIETNAM WAR. He approved both the establishment of Vietnamese communist sanctuaries in eastern Cambodia and America's clandestine bombing of these bases. Eventually, external pressures destabilized Sihanouk's government. In March 1970 LON NOL and Sirik Matik led a right-wing coup and renamed the country the Khmer Republic. In response, Sihanouk forged an alliance with his former communist enemies, the radical KHMER ROUGE, and formed a government-in-exile in Beijing. In April 1975, PHNOM PENH fell to the Khmer Rouge.

Severing the country's links with the outside world (except China and North Korea), the new government embarked on an economic and social experiment modeled on China's GREAT LEAP FORWARD of the late 1950s. The experiment failed and hundreds of thousands of people died from brutal treatment, starvation and disease. In 1978 an ultra-nationalist faction led by POL POT and Ieng Sary gained full control of the revolution. Villages and communes previously under Pol Pot opponents were subjected to ferocious purges; the population of Phnom Penh was forcibly removed to the countryside in order to work on the land.

Border clashes between Cambodia and VIETNAM broke out in May 1975. After organizing anti-Pol Pot refugees into a United Front, Vietnamese troops swept into Cambodia in late December 1978; Pol Pot's forces were driven toward the Thai border. On January 10 the People's Republic of Kampuchea (PRK) was proclaimed by members of the United Front and other (Hanoi-based) Khmer exiles. Western pressure ensured that Pol Pot's regime retained its UN seat, but unease over his genocidal record led to the formation of the Coalition Government of Democratic Kampuchea (CGDK) in 1982, once again bringing together the Khmer Rouge and Sihanouk. The CGDK guerrilla forces on the Thai border were routed

CAMBODIA

1940	Japanese occupy Cambodia.
1941	Prince Norodom Sihanouk assumes throne.
1945	Sihanouk proclaims Cambodian independence.
1953	France recognizes Cambodian independence.
1970	Right-wing coup by Marshal Lon Nol.
1975	Khmer Rouge forces capture Phnom Penh.
1975-78	Pol Pot's reign of terror kills millions of Cambodians.
1978	Vietnam invades Cambodia; pro-Vietnamese government installed.
1989	Vietnamese withdraw from Cambodia.

Remains of victims unearthed from the killing fields of the Pol Pot regime in Cambodia (1983).

by Vietnam in 1984–85. In late 1987 Sihanouk and PRK Premier Hun Sen held talks in France. In late 1989 Vietnam withdrew the last of its armed forces from the country. The withdrawal heralded a period of increased fighting between the various Khmer protagonists.

Cambodian Civil War of 1970–75. Cambodia became involved in the VIETNAM WAR when its ruler, Prince Norodom SIHANOUK, tolerated communist infiltration and permitted North Vietnam to supply its forces in South Vietnam through the port of Sihanoukville and the HO CHI MINH TRAIL. When Sihanouk closed the port in 1970, North Vietnamese troops began to aid the KHMER ROUGE in their fight against him. A pro-Western coup led by General LON NOL overthrew Sihanouk when he was abroad in March, 1970. Lon Nol demanded North Vietnamese withdrawal. In support, American and South Vietnamese forces attacked enemy sanctuaries in Cambodia and U.S. bombing raids increased. Nevertheless, North Vietnamese and Khmer Rouge control advanced steadily; PHNOM PENH, the capital, was frequently shelled and besieged between 1972 and 1975, and fell to the Khmer Rouge on April 16, 1975. Cambodia was renamed Democratic Kampuchea. The new government evacuated inhabitants from Phnom Penh in a terror campaign that left about 1 million dead from executions, starvation and forced marches. (See also POL POT.)

Cambon brothers. Jules (Martin) Cambon (1845–1935) and (Pierre) Paul Cambon (1843–1924) were French diplomats. Brilliant practitioners of statecraft, the Cambon brothers played major parts in the international politics of their day. Both were born in Paris. Jules was governor general of Algeria (1891–96), where he helped to promote Algerian autonomy. He then served as ambassador to the U.S. (1897–1902), where he was important in beginning the peace process that ended the Spanish-American War. He subsequently assumed ambassadorial posts to Madrid (1902–07) and Berlin (1907–14). A delegate to the PARIS PEACE CONFERENCE in 1919, from 1920 to 1922 he was chairman of the group that enforced the provisions of the TREATY OF VERSAILLES. Paul Cambon began his career as resident minister to Tunis in 1882. He was ambassador to Madrid (1886–91), Constantinople (1891–98) and London (1898–1920), where he encouraged English cooperation with France and Russia and helped to engineer the ANGLO-FRENCH ENTENTE of 1904 and the Anglo-Russian agreement of 1907. Both Cambon brothers were known as diplomats of the utmost subtlety and skill.

"Camel News Caravan". One of the first nightly news programs in American television, the 10-minute show began on NBC in 1948 as *Camel Newsreel Theatre* (the name was changed within a year), with a boutonniered John Cameron Swayze as news anchor. Adapting the formula of the standard theatrical newsreel, it contained several filmed items from FOX Movietone crews stationed in principal news centers. Swayze kept the pace brisk with his famous: "Now, let's go hopscotching the world for headlines!" Within the next four years the standard formula of the nightly newscast had taken shape. Correspondents reporting from other cities were added (a device borrowed from radio news formats), and NBC organized its own film crews. As influential as the program was, writes historian Erik Barnouw, it also represented a diminution of the coverage that had been standard in radio: "The camera, as arbiter of news value, had introduced a drastic curtailment of the scope of news...Analysis, a staple of radio news in its finest days, was being shunted aside as non-visual." Further, the sponsor, Camel Cigarettes, influenced the show; for example, it forbade the depiction of "No Smoking" signs and personages who smoked cigars. Swayze and the program were dropped when the "Huntley-Brinkley Report" took over on NBC in October 1956.

Cameron, Sir Gordon Roy (1899–1966). Australian pathologist. The son of a Methodist minister, Cameron studied medicine at Melbourne University, graduating in 1922. He worked first at the university and then at the Walter and Eliza Hall Institute before leaving for Europe in 1927 to do postgraduate work at Freiburg. Shortly afterward he was appointed to the staff of University College Hospital, London, where he served as professor of morbid anatomy from 1937 until his retirement in 1964. Cameron worked on a wide range of problems including pulmonary edema, inflammation and the pathology of the spleen and liver. His *Pathology of the Cell* (1952) was a major survey of all aspects of the field.

Cameron, James (1911–1985). British journalist and television commentator. Cameron was perhaps the best known British foreign correspondent of his era. One of his first major assignments was to cover the first postwar ATOMIC BOMB test at BIKINI atoll in the Pacific Ocean. The experience prompted him to become a founding member of the CAMPAIGN FOR NUCLEAR DISARMAMENT (CND). An avowed socialist, he was the first Western correspondent to tour North Vietnam after the U.S. began bombing the country in 1965. (See VIETNAM WAR.) His reports from Hanoi, published simultaneously in the London *Evening Standard* and the New York *Times*, helped fuel the ANTIWAR MOVEMENT of the 1960s.

Cameroon [French: Cameroun; German: Kamerun]. Republic on the Bight of Biafra, southeast of Nigeria. During the 19th century Britain exercised commercial control over the coastal area but was later deposed by Germany. Germany's colony was occupied during WORLD WAR I by France and Britain; in 1919 the territory was split into French and British districts. The French district became independent on January 1, 1960. In 1961 the northern division of the British district joined with NIGERIA, while the southern division fused with the self-governing Cameroon. Ahmadou AHIDJO served as president from 1961 to 1982. There was much political unrest during the 1980s. In a bizarre natural disaster, as many as 2,000 people were killed when toxic gas spewed from a volcanic lake on August 21, 1986.

Campaign for Nuclear Disarmament [CND]. Movement to promote the abandonment of nuclear weapons and a reduction in British defense spending. The CND was founded in Great Britain in 1958 by philosopher Bertrand RUSSELL and Canon L. John Collins. The movement reached its peak in 1960–61, when it attracted many thousands of adherents, and it sponsored a number of mass demonstrations against nuclear weaponry, notably those in Trafalgar Square. The CND helped to spawn similar movements in the U.S., France and Australia. CND groups were again active in the early-to mid-1980s, when they protested the U.S. decision to base CRUISE MISSILES with nuclear warheads in Britain and other NATO countries.

Campana, Dino (1885–1932). Italian poet. Campana abandoned the study of chemistry at the University of Bologna to travel in Europe and the U.S., where his jobs included doorman and triangle player. The onset of schizophrenia led to his imprisonment (1903) and institutionalization (1906, 1909), and he was rejected for service in WORLD WAR I. His reputation is based on *Canti Orfici* (1914; reissued with additions, 1928), translated as *Orphic Songs*. In 1918 he entered a mental asylum where he remained until his death. His fragmentary, nihilistic and intensely personal poetry was largely ignored at first, but several of his lyrics—including "The Chimera," "Autumnal Garden," "The Glass Window" and "Journey to Montevideo"—are counted among the most beautiful of this century. As a poetic innovator, Campana's work marks a transition from the traditionalism of CARDUCCI to the MODERNISM and hermeticism of MONTALE, QUASIMODO and UNGARETTI.

Campanella, Roy "Campy" (1921–). American baseball player. After nine years in the NEGRO LEAGUES, Campanella became the first black catcher in major league baseball upon signing with the Brooklyn Dodgers. During the Dodgers' glory years in the late 1950s, he was named Most Valuable Player three times. His most outstanding year was 1953, when he hit .312 with a league-leading 142 runs batted in. His career, always plagued by inju-

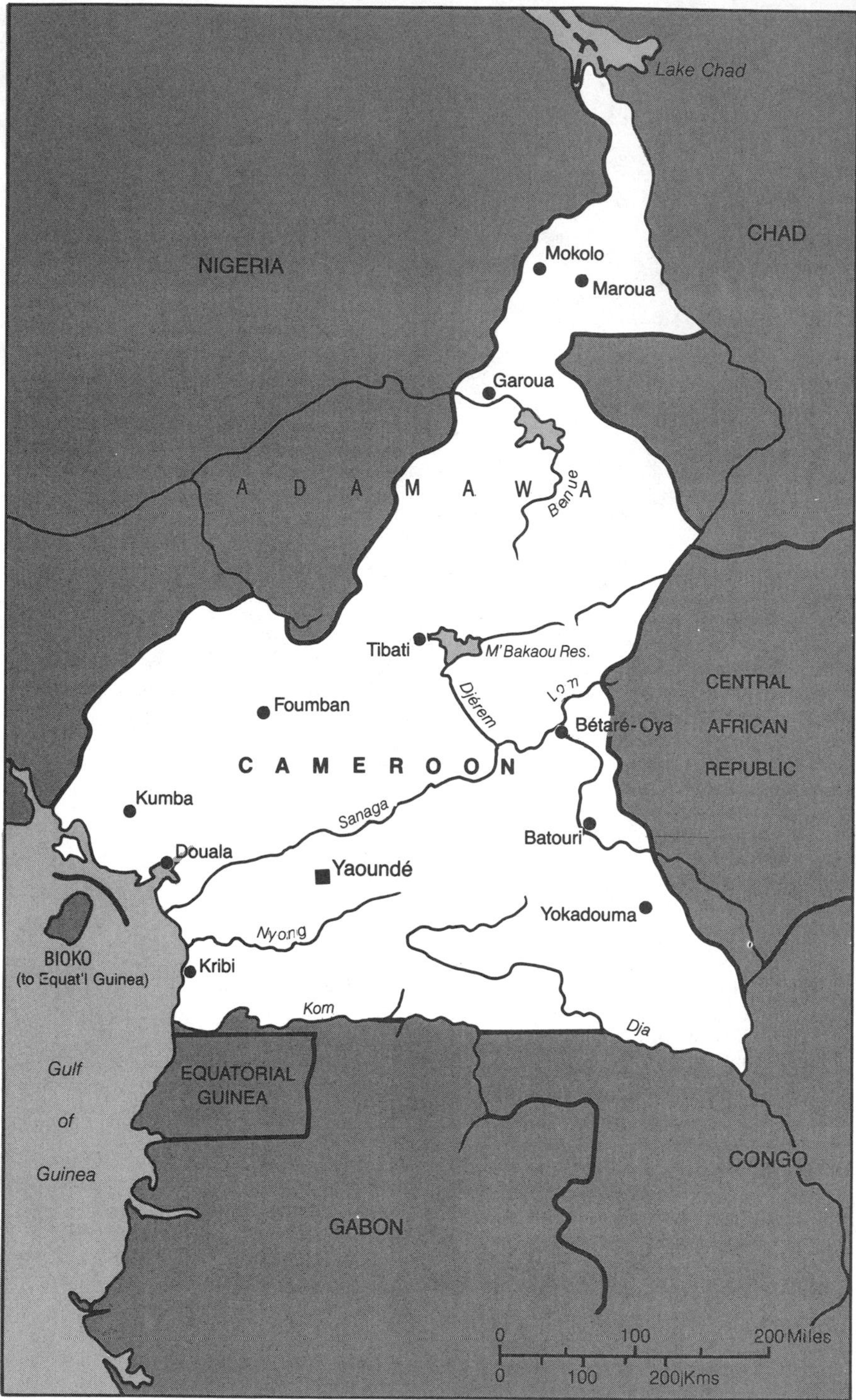

CAMEROON

CAMEROON

1900	Following the invasion of the Fulani tribe from the north during the 19th century, adjustments and migrations among the area's 200 ethnic groups continue.
1904	Sporadic revolts against German colonial authorities.
1916	British and French forces end German rule.
1919	Divided into British and French protectorates under League of Nations (and, later, United Nations).
1930	European plantation companies continue to dominate local economy.
1948	Union des Populations en Cameron founded to seek reunification and independence.
1955	Unsuccessful revolt by U.P.C.
1957	Disturbances continue despite grant of limited self-government by French.
1960	French Cameroon gains independence; Ahmadou Ahidjo is first president.
1961	Part of British Cameroon absorbed into Nigeria; remainder joins former French territory to create Federal Republic of Cameroon.
1962	University of Yaounde founded.
1972	Ahidjo consolidates power of presidency under new constitution; pursues repressive policies to stifle tribal forces and still-active U.P.C.
1983	Struggles between Ahidjo and his protege, Paul Biya. Ahidjo flees.
1984	Biya elected president, begins reported "liberalization programs"; popular unrest continues.
1986	1,200 people killed by release of natural toxic gas from Lake Nyos.
1988	Biya reelected.

ries, came to an end when he was paralyzed by an automobile accident in January 1958.

Campbell, Clarence Southerland (1905–1977). Canadian soldier, attorney and seminal figure in professional ice hockey. A Rhodes scholar, during WORLD WAR II Campbell rose from the rank of private to lieutenant colonel in the Canadian Army. After the war he was a prosecutor at the NUREMBERG TRIALS. A onetime referee, Campbell served as president of the National Hockey League from 1946 to 1977. He established the Players' Pension Plan, which became a model for other professional sports. Campbell's most difficult moment came when he was forced to suspend the popular and valuable Maurice RICHARD for a brawl just prior to the 1955 NHL playoffs. Campbell's life was threatened, but he stood firm and established his managerial style once and for all. He presided over the league's most significant expansion, from six to 12 teams, in 1967, and several other expansions thereafter. He was named to the Hockey Hall of Fame in 1966.

Brooklyn Dodger catcher Roy Campanella.

Campbell, Douglas (1896–1990). American aviator. A graduate of Harvard University, Campbell joined the Army Air Service at the outbreak of WORLD WAR I. Schooled as a pilot in the U.S., he was sent to France and became the first American-trained air ace in the war. Campbell achieved six confirmed kills of German planes and was awarded the French Croix de Guerre. After the war he returned to the U.S. and became a successful aircraft industry executive.

Campbell, Joseph (1904–1987). American writer on mythology and comparative religion. Campbell, who gained considerable posthumous fame by virtue of a 1988 Public Broadcasting System series of television interviews with Bill Moyers, was both an erudite scholar and a gifted writer capable of popularizing the key discoveries of comparative religion and the psychology of Carl Gustav JUNG. Campbell began his writing career as a literary critic, coauthoring *A Skeleton Key to Finnegans Wake* (1944), a study of the final novel of James JOYCE. He then turned his attention to explicating the great myths of the world's religions in terms of the Jungian concept of the collective unconscious—an innate mental stratum to be found in all peoples that shows itself in their common mythic symbols. *The Hero With a Thousand Faces* (1948), *The Mythic Image* (1983) and the multi-volume *Historical Atlas of World Mythology* (1989) are his major works. Campbell was a longtime member of the faculty of Sarah Lawrence College.

Campbell, Sir Malcolm (1885–1949). British auto and speedboat racer. Campbell set world speed records on both land and water. In 1935 at Bonneville Flats, Utah, he became the first person to go over 300 mph on land (301.1 mph). During World War II, the Royal Air Force developed the SPITFIRE engine from Campbell's engine design. His son **Donald Malcolm Campbell** (1921–1967) was also an auto and speedboat racer. In 1955 Donald Campbell became the first person to break the 200 mph barrier on water (202.3 mph). In 1964 he held both water (276.3 mph) and land (403.1 mph) speed records. In 1967, while trying to break his own record, Donald Campbell was killed when his hydroplane crashed at a speed in excess of 300 mph.

Campbell, Roy (1901–1957). South African poet and translator. Campbell was a paradoxical poet, combining a flamboyant romanticism with a highly conservative approach to aesthetics and politics. Raised in South Africa, Campbell briefly attended Oxford but failed to pass the required examinations. His peripatetic life during the 1920s and 1930s included stints of running a fishing boat on the Mediterranean and working as a professional steer-thrower in the Provence region of France. Campbell's first volume of poems, *The Flaming Terrapin* (1924), was hailed by influential critics. Subsequent volumes won less praise, though Campbell did establish himself as a masterful translator of St. John of the Cross and Federico GARCIA LORCA. In 1935, while living in Spain, Campbell declared himself a fascist and later fought on the side of FRANCO's troops in the SPANISH CIVIL WAR. During WORLD WAR II, Campbell served as a private in the British Army and saw action in North Africa. His *Collected Poems* appeared in 1949.

Campbell-Bannerman, Sir Henry (1836–1908). British statesman, prime minister (1905–08). A Liberal, he was elected to Parliament in 1871 and served there for 40 years. He was secretary of the admiralty (1882–84), secretary of state for Ireland (1884) and secretary of war (1886 and 1892–95); knighted in 1895, he was elected leader of his party in 1899. "C-B" was opposed to the BOER WAR, and after his appointment as prime minister in 1905 he granted self-government to the Transvaal (1906) and the Orange Free State (1907). In England, he favored a number of liberal reforms, most of which were vetoed by the House of Lords. Ill health forced him to resign in 1908 just weeks prior to his death.

Camp David. Official retreat of the U.S. president and his family, located in the Catoctin Mountains about 70 miles from Washington, D.C. This 200-acre complex was acquired by President Franklin ROOSEVELT in 1942 and was originally named "Shangri-La." In 1953 President Dwight D. Eisenhower renamed the retreat Camp David after his grandson. The complex, featuring both entertainment and meet-

Egyptian President Anwar Sadat, U.S. President Jimmy Carter and Israeli Prime Minister Menachem Begin celebrate the signing of the peace treaty between Israel and Egypt.

ing areas, is under the jurisdiction of the office of the military assistant to the president, and is patrolled by the U.S. Marine Corps. Notable among the important international meetings held here is the Camp David Peace Accords between Israel and Egypt, in 1979.

Camp David Talks. Peace talks of September 5–17, 1978, among Egyptian President Anwar el-SADAT, Israeli Premier Menachem BEGIN, and U.S. President Jimmy CARTER. The talks resulted in a treaty (known as the **Camp David Accords**) signed in Washington on March 25, 1979, opening Egyptian-Israeli economic and diplomatic relations and returning the occupied SINAI PENINSULA to EGYPT. Hopes of developing an autonomous Palestinian state on the WEST BANK foundered in the face of Israeli internal opposition and PALESTINE LIBERATION ORGANIZATION (PLO) antagonism to the treaty. Arab nations publicly denounced EGYPT for its role in the talks, but privately many moderate Arabs approved. Carter's role in sponsoring the talks and mediating differences between Begin and Sadat is widely regarded as the most significant foreign policy achievement of his administration. For their part, Begin and Sadat shared the NOBEL PRIZE for peace (1978). (See also ARAB-ISRAELI WAR OF 1973, ISRAEL.)

Campora, Hector J. (1909–1980). Argentinian politician. In 1973 Campora served as president of ARGENTINA for 49 days before resigning to allow the election of Juan PERON. During his presidency he released more than 500 jailed leftist guerrillas, thereby angering the country's military. After living in the Mexican embassy in Buenos Aires for three and a half years, in 1979 he was granted safe conduct to Mexico, where he lived in exile.

Camranh Bay [Kamranh Bay, Vinh Cam Ranh]. Harbor and port on the South China Sea north of Phan Rang, VIETNAM. Captured by the Japanese in 1941, during WORLD WAR II it served as a major Japanese naval base. Located in South Vietnam when the country was partitioned, Camranh Bay was a major U.S. base during the VIETNAM WAR.

Camus, Albert (1913–1960). French novelist, essayist and story writer. Camus, who won the NOBEL PRIZE for literature in 1957, is one of the most influential writers of this century, a champion of individual freedom and of an existential philosophy that extols the courage of socially committed political action. Born in Algiers, Camus published his first philosophical essays in the late 1930s. But it was with the appearance of his novel *The Stranger* (1942), the story of an inadvertent murderer who arrives at a kind of happiness by embracing the absurdity of both his crime and his punishment, that Camus first came to international attention. During WORLD WAR II Camus, who had immigrated to France, was active in

Albert Camus (1957).

CANADA

the RESISTANCE. Camus' other novels include *The Plague* (1948) and *The Fall* (1956); *Exile and the Kingdom* (1957) contains a selection of his stories. His major philosophical works are *The Myth of Sisyphus* (1942) and *The Rebel* (1954). For a time, Camus was a close friend of Jean-Paul SARTRE, but Camus broke with Sartre over the latter's support of Stalinist policies in the early 1950s. Camus died in an auto accident.

Canada. Covering 40% of the North American continent, Canada occupies a total area of some 3,850,790 square miles and is geographically the second largest country in the world. An influential member of Britain's COMMONWEALTH OF NATIONS, especially after World War I, Canada also has close economic ties to the neighboring United States. Liberal Prime Minister William Lyon Mackenzie KING, the country's longest-serving leader in this century, gave Canada strong leadership in the 1920s, 1930s and 1940s. After World War II, Canada helped establish the NORTH ATLANTIC TREATY ORGANIZATION (NATO). During Pierre TRUDEAU'S first terms as prime minister (1967–79) the separatist cause of French-speaking Quebec mushroomed, as the PARTI QUEBECOIS, led by Rene LEVESQUE, pushed for secession from Canada. During the 1970s terrorist bombings and murders were associated with the movement, but a 1980 referendum in Quebec defeated the separatist plan. The Canada Act of 1982 officially recognized Canada's multicultural heritage, but the defeat of the Meech Lac Accord (1990), which would have given Quebec special status within Canada, led to further talk of secession. Prime Minister Brian MULRONEY succeeded in negotiating a free-trade agreement with the United States in 1988.

For further reading:

Bothwell, Robert, *Canada Since 1945*, 2nd ed. Toronto: University of Toronto Press, 1989.

McNaught, Kenneth, *The Penguin History of Canada*. New York: Viking Penguin, 1988.

Canaris, Wilhelm (1887–1945). German admiral. A career officer, Canaris served in the German navy during WORLD WAR I and in the postwar era. The conservative officer was appointed chief of German's military intelligence agency, the ABWEHR, in 1935. At first a supporter of HITLER, Canaris came to oppose the fuhrer's brutality and to fear the war that seemed inevitable with Hitler as Germany's leader. Under Canaris'direction, the *Abwehr* became an important part of an anti-Hitlerite movement. After the failed attempt to assassinate Hitler in July 1944, Canaris was arrested and, although he was never directly implicated in the plot, was hanged by the GESTAPO in April 1945.

Canaveral, Cape. Cape, located in Brevard County on the east central coast of Florida; part of a system of barrier islands paralleling the coast of the U.S. and projecting into the Atlantic Ocean. Longtime site of a lighthouse, part of the cape also became a U.S. Air Force installation for launching missiles, the first missile being launched in 1950. The base was called the Kennedy Space Center, after President KENNEDY'S assassination, and in 1969 was the launching site of the first spacecraft to send men to the moon, land them and bring them back. For a short time after the president's death the entire cape was known as Cape Kennedy.

Canberra [originally Canberry, Canbury]. Capital of AUSTRALIA, on the Molonglo River 150 miles southwest of Sydney. First colonized in the 1820s, it was formally named the capital of Australia on May 9, 1927, when King GEORGE V opened the parliament. The Australian National University was established here in 1936.

CANADA

1926	Commonwealth Conference of 1926 accepts principle of equality of status; curtailment of the powers of the governor general follow.
1936	Reciprocity Treaty increases economic links with U.S.
1957	Long Liberal rule ends as John Diefenbaker of the Progressive Conservative Party is chosen prime minister.
1963	Lester B. Pearson leads Liberals back into office.
1967	Charles de Gaulle visits Canada, fueling French nationalism.
1967	The Parti Quebecois led by Rene Levesque is formed and demands complete separation from the government.
1968	Pearson is succeeded by Pierre Trudeau.
1970	(Oct.) Members of the separatist movement kidnap British diplomat James Cross.
1970	War Measures Act is passed to deal with Francophone terrorist activity in Quebec.
1974	Quebec declares French to be its official language.
1979	(May 22) Conservatives form minority government under Joe Clark.
1980	(Feb.) Liberals, led by Trudeau, resume power.
1982	Constitution Act of 1982 and Charter of Rights and Freedoms are passed.
1984	(June) Trudeau resigns and is replaced by Liberal leader John Turner.
1984	(Sept. 4) Brian Mulroney of the Conservatives is elected prime minister.
1986	Canada proclaims sovereignty over the Arctic region, including inter-island channels, despite objections from the U.S.
1989	(Jan.1) The Canada-United States free-trade agreement comes into force.
1990	(June 22) Meech-Lake Accord (a series of constitutional amendments meant to persuade Quebec to ratify the 1982 constitution) fails when it is rejected by the provinces of Newfoundland and Manitoba.

CANADA: PRIME MINISTERS

1896-1911	Wilfred Laurier (Liberal)
1911-20	Robert Borden (Conservative)
1920-21	Arthur Meighen (Conservative)
1921-26	William Lyon Mackenzie King (Liberal)
1926	Arthur Meighen (Conservative)
1926-30	William Lyon Mackenzie King (Liberal)
1930-35	Richard Bedford Bennett (Conservative)
1935-48	William Lyon Mackenzie King (Liberal)
1948-57	Louis Stephen St. Laurent (Liberal)
1957-63	John G. Diefenbaker (Conservative)
1963-67	Lester Pearson (Liberal)
1967-79	Pierre Trudeau (Liberal)
1979-80	Joe Clark (Progressive Conservative)
1980-84	Pierre Trudeau (Liberal)
1984	John Turner (Liberal)
1984-	Brian Mulroney (Progressive Conservative)

Candler, Asa Griggs (1851–1929). U.S. pharmacist and soft-drink manufacturer. A student of medicine and a successful wholesale drug manufacturer, he bought the formula for Coca-Cola in 1887, developed a method of manufacture and engineered its worldwide success. In 1919 he received $25 million for the rights to the industry he had created. Much of his fortune was given to develop the medical school of Emory University, Atlanta, Georgia.

Canetti, Elias (1905–). German novelist, essayist and sociologist. Canetti, who received the NOBEL PRIZE for literature in 1981, came to great prominence as a writer only after decades of obscurity. A Jew raised and educated in Vienna, Canetti immigrated to London in 1938 to escape the Nazi regime. The novel for which he is best known, *Auto da Fe* (1936), did not receive widespread critical attention until it was reprinted in the 1960s, by which time its existential tale of an isolated, bookish intellectual who is frightened of the mass manipulations of society was seen to have universal relevance. Canetti explicitly analyzed the nature of FASCISM and of mass action in a sociological work, *Crowds and Power* (1960). Canetti is also a prominent literary critic as evidenced by his full-length study, *Kafka's Other Trial* (1969). He has also written travel books and a multi-volume autobiography.

Cannes Film Festival. An annual international celebration of films that takes place in the spring in Cannes, France; first held in 1946. Each country enters feature-length and short films in the competition. Awards are presented for best director, actor, actress and best film (the Palme d'Or or Golden Palm Award). Awards are sometimes given for such aspects as set design, and the judges may award a Special Jury Prize to deserving films. Much of the festival revolves around publicity for the films and their stars. Recent winners for best film include Steven Soderbergh's *sex, lies, and videotape* (1989) and David Lynch's *Wild at Heart* (1990).

Cannon, Annie Jump (1863–1941). American astronomer. The daughter of a Delaware state senator, Cannon was one of the first women from Delaware to attend university, studying at Wellesley College from 1880 to 1884. After spending a decade at home, where she became deaf due to scarlet fever, she entered Radcliffe College in 1895 to study astronomy. In 1896 she was appointed to the staff of the Harvard College Observatory, as it was the practice of the observatory, under the direction of Edward Pickering, to employ young well-educated women as computers. She worked there for the rest of her career, serving from 1911 to 1932 as curator of astronomical photographs. In 1938, after nearly half a century of distinguished service, she was appointed William Cranch Bond Astronomer. One of the main programs of the observatory was the preparation of the *Henry Draper Catalogue* of a quarter-million stellar spectra. Stars were originally to be classified into one of the 17 spectral types, A to Q, which were ordered alphabetically in terms of the intensity of the hydrogen absorption lines. Cannon saw that a more natural order could be achieved if some classes were omitted, others added, and the total reordered in terms of decreasing surface temperature. Her classification scheme has since been altered only slightly.

Cannon developed a phenomenal skill in cataloging stars, and at the height of her power it was claimed that she could classify three stars a minute. Her classification of over 225,000 stars brighter than 9th or 10th magnitude and the compilation of the *Catalogue* took many years. It was finally published, between 1918 and 1924, as volumes 91 to 99 of the *Annals of Harvard College Observatory*. She continued the work unabated, later publications including an additional 47,000 classifications in the *Henry Draper Extension* (*Annals*, vol. 100, 1925–36). Even as late as 1936, when she was over 70, she undertook the classification of 10,000 faint stars submitted to her by the Cape of Good Hope Observatory.

Cannon, James, Jr. (1864–1944). American clergyman and prohibitionist. Cannon entered the ministry as a Methodist Episcopalian in 1888, was elected a bishop in 1918 and retired in 1938. A leading Anti-Saloon Leaguer and head of the World League Against Alcoholism, his influence was extensive until the repeal of Prohibition in 1933. Called before a Senate lobby committee to answer charges concerning his use of funds in Virginia during the campaign of presidential candidate Alfred E. SMITH (1928), he defied the committee and was later acquitted in federal court.

Cannon, Joseph Gurney (1836–1926). U.S. congressman, considered the most domineering speaker of the United States House of Representatives. He was elected to the House as a Republican in 1872, and again in 1892, but was defeated for re-election in 1912. He returned in 1914 and remained until 1923. He served as speaker from 1903 to 1911. As a speaker he began an arbitrary and partisan control of House procedures that became known as "Cannonism." As chairman of the House Rules Committee, he and his committee members could block almost any measure they opposed and carry any measure they approved. He could block important legislation, such as civil rights. A combination of insurgent Republicans and Democrats managed to pass a resolution that stripped House Speaker Cannon of much of his power—an action that became known as the "Revolution of 1910."

Cannon, Walter Bradford (1871–1945). American physiologist. Cannon graduated from Harvard in 1896 and was professor of physiology there from 1906 to 1942. His early work included studies of the digestive system, in particular the use of X RAYS to study stomach disorders. Most of his working life, however, was spent studying the nervous system, particularly the way in which hormones regulate various body functions. As early as 1915 he showed the connection between secretions of the endocrine glands and the emotions. In the 1930s he worked on the role of epinephrine in helping the body to meet fight-or-flight situations. He also studied the way hormonelike substances are involved in transmitting messages along nerves.

Cantelli, Guido (1920–1956). Italian conductor. Born in Novara, Cantelli studied at the Milan Conservatory, returning to his native city in 1941 to conduct the Teatro Coccia, a theater founded by Arturo TOSCANINI. An opponent of MUSSOLINI's fascist regime during WORLD WAR II, he was imprisoned in a CONCENTRATION CAMP from 1943 to 1945. Hospitalized, he escaped, but was captured by the Nazis and sentenced to death—a fate he eluded when Italy was liberated by the Allies. After the war he became the conductor of the La Scala Orchestra and made a number of appearances conducting major European orchestras. He soon won the attention and admiration of Toscanini, who invited the younger musician to make his American debut with the NBC Symphony Orchestra (1949). Thereafter, Cantelli returned annually to the U.S. as guest conductor of various orchestras. Cantelli's performances were particularly noted for their precision, clarity and intensity. His career was cut short when he was killed in a plane crash.

Canton [Kuang-chou, Kwangchow]. City and port of Kwangtung province, China, on the Pearl River 80 miles from the sea. In 1911 it was the site of the revolutionary operations of SUN YAT-SEN and of the declaration of the Republic of CHINA; briefly the seat of one of the first communist communes in China, in 1927. Held by the Japanese from 1938 and throughout WORLD WAR II, it surrendered to the communists in October 1949, marking the communist domination of the country. Today it is the most prominent city of southern China.

Canton Atoll [formerly Mary Island]. Coral group in the west-central Pacific, southwest of Hawaii; part of the Phoenix Islands group. In the 1930s the islands served as an important stopover place for transpacific flights. After a quarrel concerning ownership they were placed under mutual U.S.-British supervision. During WORLD WAR II the islands served as a key Allied air base.

Cantor, Eddie [Isidore Itzkowitz; Edward Israel Iskowitz] (1892–1964). Cantor was a successful VAUDEVILLE, revue, musical comedy and Broadway and film comedian who was known not for great comic skills, but for an overpowering, enthusiastic stage persona that was every bit as formidable as Al JOLSON's. Cantor's parents died before he was two years old. Raised by his grandmother, Cantor quit school to perform in contests, on the street and ultimately on the vaudeville circuit. He worked with other performers with limited success, until he was signed for *The Ziegfeld Follies* in 1917. The show led to superstar status in the 1920s, climaxing with the ZIEGFELD smash hit, *Whoopee*, in 1928. Moving into films such as *Whoopee* (1930), *Roman Scandals* (1933) and *Kid Millions* (1934), Cantor's bulging eyes and cheerful demeanor became a trademark, and his high tenor voice made instant hits out of songs such as "Potatoes are Cheaper, Tomatoes are Cheaper, Now It's Time to Fall in Love" and "Makin' Whoopee." In the 1950s Cantor spoke openly against ANTI-SEMITISM, and lost some of his popular appeal. In 1956 he was given an honorary ACADEMY AWARD, but health problems caused him to limit his public appearances. After his death in 1964, Cantor's reputation plummeted, as comedians and writers such as Milton BERLE, Steve ALLEN and George S. KAUFMAN remarked that he lacked natural comic ability and had to "struggle for his laughs."

Cantos, The. The major work of Ezra POUND's poetic career, this epic cycle of poems, begun in 1925, was originally planned to include 100 cantos, or chapters, but that number was surpassed before 1960. Hugely ambitious in compass, the cycle's complex structure borrows from Dante's *Divine Comedy,* Ovid's *Metamorphoses* and Homer's *Odyssey;* the cantos also weave together myth and legend, Oriental poetry and philosophy, troubador ballads, and political and economic theory to reconstruct the history of human civilization. Most famous are Canto XLV, on "usura," or usury, and the "Pisan Cantos," which describe Pound's imprisonment by the U.S. Army in Italy at the end of WORLD WAR II. Despite their influence on modern poetry, in his embittered old age Pound declared them "a failure." They remained unfinished at his death.

Capa, Cornell (1918–). American photographer. The brother of photographer Robert CAPA, he was born in Hungary and began his photography career in Paris during the 1930s. He fled to the U.S. in 1937, worked for the photo intelligence section of the air force during WORLD WAR II and joined the staff of LIFE magazine in 1946. Becoming a well-known photojournalist, he contributed many photo essays to the magazine, even after leaving it to join his brother's photo agency, Magnum, in 1954. In 1974 he became the founder and director of the International Center of Photography in New York City. His deep political and social concerns are evident in his study of Latin America, *Margin of Life* (1974).

Capa, Robert (1913–1954). American photographer. Born in Hungary, Robert Capa was active in Paris in the 1930s along with such other photographers as CARTIER-BRESSON and David Seymour. Renowned for his portrayals of humanity at war, he became well-known for his superb photographs of the 1936 SPANISH CIVIL WAR and is particularly famous for his classic photo of a Loyalist soldier's "Moment of Death." He traveled throughout Africa, Italy and Sicily for LIFE magazine during WORLD WAR II, contributing powerful battlefield photos, and participated in the landing at NORMANDY. In all, Capa covered five wars, producing a profoundly moving body of work. In 1946 he cofounded the photojournalist agency Magnum. He was killed by a landmine while covering the FRENCH INDOCHINA WAR. His books include *Death in the Making* (1938) and *Images of War* (1964).

Cape Esperance, Battle of. On October 1–12, 1942, one of six WORLD WAR II naval engagements that occurred during the fighting at GUADALCANAL. It involved a Japanese naval bombardment force and convoy under the command of Rear Admiral Aritomo Goto and a U.S. task force under Rear Admiral Norman Scott. Mainly a nighttime battle, it pitted a Japanese force of four cruisers and two destroyers against a U.S. force of four cruisers and five destroyers that had been escorting an American regiment. During the encounter, in which Goto was killed, a Japanese heavy cruiser and a destroyer were sunk, while the Americans lost one destroyer, USS *Duncan,* and sustained damage to two other ships. In daytime fighting, the Japanese lost another two destroyers to U.S. air forces. While considered an American victory, the battle did not utterly destroy the Japanese bombardment force nor prevent the convoy from getting through and the furious battle at Guadalcanal continued. (See also WORLD WAR II IN THE PACIFIC.)

Capek, Karel (1890–1938). Czechoslovakian novelist and playwright. Capek is one of the leading Czech writers of the 20th century. He achieved international prominence between the two world wars by virtue of his distinctive satiric plays set in imagined future worlds that incorporated elements of pulp science fiction. Notable among his plays are *R.U.R.* (1920), which featured a robot as a central character, and *The Insect Play* (1921). In the 1930s Capek devoted his primary energies to fiction writing in a philosophical vein. His novel *War with the Newts* (1936),

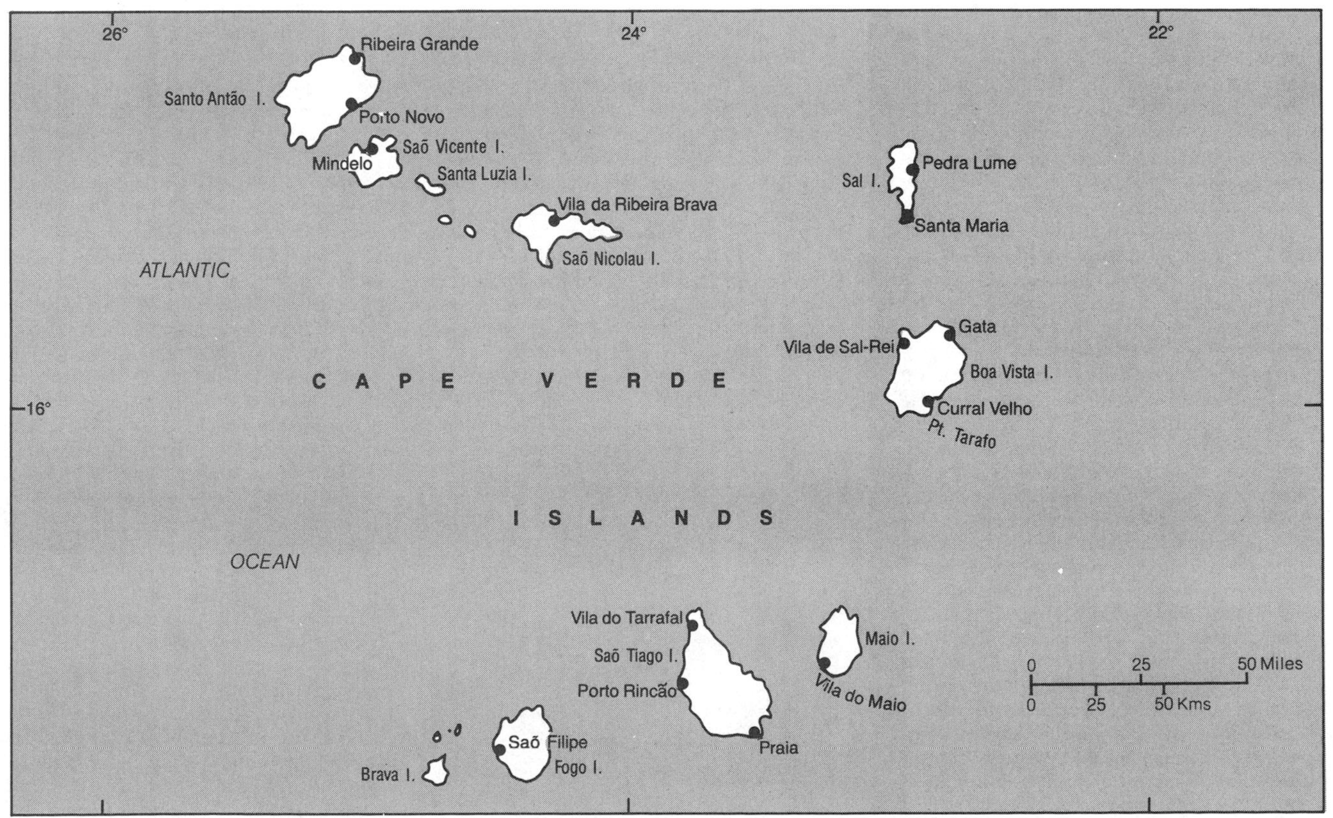

CAPE VERDE

which satirically depicted the rise of a totalitarian regime in a disintegrating society, achieved a wide readership. Politically Capek was a liberal democrat who wrote an admiring biography of Czech president Thomas MASARYK.

Cape Kennedy. U.S. government space center, in Brevard County, Florida. The term is used to refer to the Kennedy Space Center located on the part of Cape CANAVERAL that has been used for launching U.S. research missiles. For a time the entire cape was named for the late President John F. KENNEDY but the local name, Cape Canaveral, has prevailed for the geographical area.

Cape Verde, Republic of [Portugese: Republica de Cabo Verde]. Island nation in the Atlantic Ocean, off the west coast of Africa. Located approximately 385 miles west northwest of Dakar, SENEGAL, the republic consists of 10 main islands with a population of some 358,000 people. The islands began the 20th century as a colony of PORTUGAL and were granted overseas province status in 1951. An independence movement led by Amilcar Cabral began an armed rebellion in Cape Verde and Portugese Guinea in 1961. Cape Verde was granted independence on July 5, 1975. Aristides Pereira became the first president and remained in power as of late 1990. Sao Tiago is the capital.

capitalism. Economic system in which the means of production and distribution of goods and services are privately owned and operated; also known as "private enterprise" or "free enterprise." In the 20th century, capitalism has been diametrically opposed to COMMUNISM. The UNITED STATES has long been seen as the showcase of capitalism (although GERMANY and JAPAN have developed highly successful capitalist economies); the UNION OF SOVIET SOCIALIST REPUBLICS and, after 1949, CHINA, have been strongholds of communism. Advocates of capitalism argue that it is the only economic system that can guarantee personal and political freedom, because only in a capitalist system are individuals free to choose their jobs and to spend their money as they wish. Capitalists believe that prices and levels of production should be determined by "market forces," not by government planning. Competition (in order to achieve higher profits and, sometimes, to remain in business) is considered a cornerstone of traditional capitalism, encouraging efficiency and progress. Critics of capitalism point to unemployment, homelessness, unfair business practices and inequitable salaries and wages as its inevitable by-products. In many parts of the world, private enterprise mixed with some government ownership and regulation is seen as an alternative to both capitalism and communism. The movement toward market economies in Eastern Europe in the late 1980s was seen by many as the victory of capitalism over communism. In 1991, Pope JOHN PAUL II cautiously endorsed capitalism while calling for greater attention to spiritual and humanitarian values in capitalist societies.

capital punishment. The use of the death penalty in U.S. criminal cases was one of the most controversial legal issues of the 20th century. Although implementation of the death penalty had waned, by 1971 the penalty still existed in a great majority of the states. In 1972 the U.S. Supreme Court cast doubt on the constitutionality of the death penalty. The Court ruled that when the penalty was imposed in an arbitrary manner it amounted to unconstitutional cruel and unusual punishment. However, supporters of the death penalty made capital punishment a national issue, and a majority of Americans seemed to favor it. Because of these concerns, no convicts were executed in the U.S. for over 10 years. In 1976 the Supreme Court made clear that capital punishment was not inherently cruel and unusual, so long as it was imposed consistently with ample procedural protections for the accused. By 1980, executions had resumed in a number of states, although capital punishment is still outlawed in many other states. Overseas, 41 nations—mostly in the Western world—have banned capital punishment.

Capone, Al(phonse) (1899–1947). American gangster. Born and raised in Brooklyn, N.Y., Capone became a small-time criminal early in life, earning the nickname "Scarface" for the razor slash across his face. Settling in CHICAGO in 1920, he quickly moved up in the crime syndicates, ruthlessly eliminating his competition and gaining control of bootleg liquor traffic during PROHIBITION. Terrorizing Chicago during the 1920s, he extorted money from businessmen and politicians and gained control of such lucrative illicit activities as prostitution and gambling. By the end of the 1920 Capone was estimated to have an annual income of over $20 million. His ruthless slaughter culminated in the ST. VALENTINE'S DAY MASSACRE of 1929, in which his henchmen machine-gunned seven members of the "Bugs" Moran gang. After a decade of corrupting the Chicago police and eluding prosecution, Capone was finally indicted (1931) by a federal grand jury for tax evasion. He was released from prison late in 1939. Racked by terminal syphilis, he retired to his Florida estate, where he died.

Chicago mob giant Al Capone.

For further reading:

Pasley, Fred, *Al Capone: The Biography of a Self-Made Man.* New York: Ayer Company, n.d. (repr).

Enright, R. T., *Capone's Chicago.* Northstar Books, 1987 (rev).

Capote, Truman (1924–1984). American author. As famous for his witty conversation on the television talk show circuit as for his evocative, disciplined prose style, Capote provoked controversy from the debut of his first novel, *Other Voices, Other Rooms* (1948), with its homosexual theme. He had already received attention with his "Southern Gothic" stories, such as *Miriam* (1945; winner of the O. Henry Memorial Award, 1946). In his novels *The Grass Harp* (1951; dramatized, 1952) and *Breakfast at Tiffany's* (1958; filmed, 1961) he shed the gothicism for a lighter, wittier approach. His most famous work is the 1966 nonfiction work *In Cold Blood* about multiple murders. His 1956 short story *A Christmas Memory* became an acclaimed television show (1967). His last novel was *Music for Chameleons* (1980).

For further reading:

Clarke, Gerald, *Truman Capote.* New York: Ballantine, 1989.

Capp, Al [born Alfred Gerald Caplin] (1909–1979). American cartoonist, creator of the satirical comic strip *L'il Abner.* Al Capp created the fictional community of Dogpatch and filled it with frolicsome hillbilly characters who lampooned the foibles of the high and the mighty in newspapers for 43 years. The comic strip gained a following of tens of millions of readers, inspired a Broadway musical, two movies and a television show, and earned Capp $500,000 a year at its peak.

Capra, Frank (1897–1985). American motion picture director whose films include several HOLLYWOOD classics. Born in Sicily, Capra immigrated to the U.S. with his family in 1903. He worked as a chemical engineer, army ballistics instructor, laborer and salesman before becoming a gag writer for Mack SENNETT in Hollywood (1925), then teamed up with slapstick comedian Harry LANGDON (1926) to make his first important films. His association with producer Harry COHN and COLUMBIA PICTURES (1928–39) resulted in some of his best known films, including *It Happened One Night* (1934), for which he won the first of his three ACADEMY AWARDS for best director; *Mr. Deeds Goes to Town* (1936); *Lost Horizon* (1937); and *Mr. Smith Goes to Washington* (1939). These pictures contain Capra's hallmarks—the topsy-turvey class mixtures of the screwball comedy; optimistic faith in democracy and the values of simplicity and honesty (called "Capra-corn" by critics); rapid pacing and snappy dialogue; and Capra's own insistence that his vision shape the entire picture. In 1940 he resigned as president of the Academy of Motion Picture Arts and Sciences and was commissioned as a major in the Army Signal Corps, where he made an important series of documentaries and training films, *Why We Fight;* these contributed to U.S. morale in WORLD WAR II. His postwar years were marked by numerous independent projects, most notably *It's a Wonderful Life* (1946), which eventually became perhaps his most popular film. He also produced a series of science films for Bell Telephone (1952–56). His last features were *A Hole in the Head* (1959) and *A Pocketful of Miracles* (1961).

For further reading:

Capra, Frank, *The Name Above the Title.* 1971.

Capucine [born Germaine Lefebvre] (1933–1990). French actress. A glamorous movie star of the 1960s, Capucine starred in such films as *Walk on the Wild Side* (1962), *The Pink Panther* (1964), *What's New Pussycat* (1965) and *Fellini Satyricon* (1969). She took her name from the French name for the nasturtium flower.

Caradon, Lord [Hugh Mackintosh Foot] (1907–1990). British diplomat. He served as governor of CYPRUS from 1957 to 1960, and was credited with bringing together the governments of GREECE and TURKEY to forge a compromise that established Cyprus as a nation. He joined the UNITED NATIONS in 1961 as Britain's representative to the Trusteeship Council, but resigned 15 months later in protest against the white government of RHODESIA's repression of black nationalists. Appointed a life peer in 1964, he was appointed by Britain's Labour government as its chief UN representative. He held the post until the Conservatives' return to power in 1970.

Caramanlis, Constantine (1907–). Greek political leader, premier (1955–63, 1974–80), president (1980–85). Born in Macedonia, he attended the University of Athens and was first elected to parliament in 1936. After entering the cabinet as minister of labor in 1946, Karamanlis served in a succession of posts until he was named premier in 1955. The following year he was a founder of a right-wing political party, the National Radical Union. During his first term in office, he supported the NORTH ATLANTIC TREATY ORGANIZATION, came to an accord with TURKEY and Great Britain regarding CYPRUS (1959) and in the early 1960s conceived and implemented a five-year agricultural and industrial reform plan. He resigned in 1963 and went into exile in France. Opposing the military junta that ruled GREECE in the interim, he returned to the premiership when the military government fell in 1974. Founding another new party, New Democracy, he remained in office until 1980, when he was elected president.

carbon-14 dating. See Willard LIBBY.

Cardiff [Welsh: Caerdydd]. Situated on the Bristol Channel, 130 miles west of London, Cardiff has been the official capital of Wales since 1955. Cardiff began the 20th century as the world's largest coal exporting port, but its coal business suffered a severe setback during as the century progressed. During WORLD WAR II, the Luftwaffe bombed the city, causing extensive destruction.

Cardin, Pierre (1922–). French fashion designer (born in Venice) who has expanded his activities into a wide variety of design fields with licensing to some 500 firms in 93 countries. He was apprenticed to a tailor before World War II and after the war worked for several Paris fashion houses before spending three years with the House of DIOR. He opened his own firm in 1953. His early work focused on traditional suits and coats, but by the 1960s he had become an innovator, using big patterns with references to the OP ART of the day. He has been a key figure in turning the concept of haute couture into a commodity for the mass market, applying a name and monogram to a range of goods. Perfumes, luggage, men's fashions, and wigs, among other items, all bear his label. His work has included interior design for restaurants and aircraft along with a continuing flow of fashion apparel products.

Cardozo, Benjamin N. (1870–1938). Associate justice, U.S. Supreme Court (1932–1938). Cardozo is recognized as one of the giants of modern jurisprudence. A graduate of Columbia University, he served as a judge in New York. His father, also a judge, resigned after being implicated in Tammany Hall corruption in New York City. The younger Cardozo never married. While he was chief judge of New York's highest court, Cardozo's judicial opinions set new standards for legal analysis. He wrote a number of landmark business opinions that are still carefully studied by law students and that still carry great weight with jurists, perhaps the most famous being *Palsgraf v. Long Island R.R.* His books, including *The Nature of the Judicial Process* (1921), established him as one of the great legal theorists of the century.

After Oliver Wendell HOLMES resigned from the Supreme Court, Cardozo was the favored nominee, although President Herbert HOOVER at first resisted the nomination because three New Yorkers already sat on the Court. However, Hoover nominated Cardozo after Chief Justice Harlan Fiske STONE threatened to resign unless Cardozo was appointed. A supporter of Franklin D. ROOSEVELT'S NEW DEAL legislation, Cardozo was known as a champion of liberal causes. He served only six years before his death. His legal writings and lectures established him as a leading legal intellectual.

For further reading:

Cardozo, Benjamin N., *Selected Writings of Benjamin N. Cardozo.* New York: Bender, Matthew, 1947.

Pollard, Joseph P., *Mister Justice Cardozo: A Liberal Mind in Action.* Westport, Conn.: Greenwood, 1970.

Carducci, Giosue (1835–1907). Italian poet and critic. The son of a member of the Carbonari who later embraced Roman Catholicism, Carducci was known for his own mercurial politics. He was alternately pro- and anti-republican. A professor of literature at the University of Bologna from 1860 to 1904, he was a scholar, an editor, an orator and a patriot. He was generally regarded as Italy's unofficial poet laureate. His historical verse, *Odi barbari* (1878–89), attempted to capture the spirit of the classical world by emulating ancient Greek and Latin poetry. His personal poetry includes *Rime nuove* (New Lyrics, 1861–87). He received the NOBEL PRIZE for literature in 1906. Carducci's work reflects the spirit that infused the *Risorgimento;* it avoids the excesses of romanticism in favor of a restrained and classical style.

CARE. Acronym for Cooperative for American Relief Everywhere, a nonprofit volunteer agency in the U.S. that provides assistance to people in developing nations. To the general public, the agency is best known for its "CARE packages" sent to needy people around the world during natural emergencies. CARE was founded in 1945 at the end of WORLD WAR II to provide donations of food and clothing to the people of war-torn Europe. It subsequently developed into a full-time service agency that coordinates relief efforts in Africa, Asia and Latin America. CARE's activities are funded by private donations.

Caretan. Town in Manche department, France, a targeted area of the INVASION OF NORMANDY in WORLD WAR II. Its seizure by U.S. troops after brutal combat from June 8 to 12, 1944, connected the Utah and Omaha invasion beaches.

Carey, George (Leonard) (1935–). Archbishop of Canterbury and spiritual leader of the Anglican Church (1990–). Carey, who was named archbishop of Canterbury in 1990, had previously served for three years as bishop of Bath and Wells. An evangelical Anglican, Carey stresses traditional church dogma while arguing for certain controversial innovations, including an active church role in environmental issues and the ordination of women as priests. Carey was raised in the lower-class East End of London. He took a degree in divinity from King's College, University of London, in 1962. Prior to becoming a bishop, Carey had been a vicar in Durham and served for five years as principal of Trinity Theological College in Bristol.

Carmichael, (Hoagland) Hoagy (1899–1981). U.S. composer and actor. He first encountered jazz music as a student at Indiana University, when his song "Riverboat Shuffle" was given to Bix BEIDERBECKE for recording. Carmichael formed a band of his own, but continued with his studies and earned a law degree in 1926. He practiced law for a while, but finally moved to New York City in 1929. His most popular song, "Stardust," established him as a composer. "Rockin' Chair" and "Georgia on My Mind" were published in 1930. In 1931 he assembled a band that included Jimmy DORSEY, Benny GOODMAN, Bix Beiderbecke and Gene KRUPA. The group was called the most impressive jazz ensemble ever gathered together. Carmichael's "Lamplighter's Serenade" was the first song recorded by Frank SINATRA. He also appeared in feature films and had popular radio and television programs. He won an ACADEMY AWARD in 1951 for his song "In the Cool, Cool, Cool of the Evening." In 1971 he was one of the first 10 popular composers elected to the Songwriters' Hall of Fame.

Carmichael, Stokely (1941–). U.S. CIVIL RIGHTS leader. Carmichael was born in Port-of-Spain, Trinidad. He attended Howard University, graduating in 1964. Both during his college years and later, Carmichael worked with the CONGRESS OF RACIAL EQUALITY (CORE) and the Student Nonviolent Coordinating Committee, participating in protest and voter registration drives in Southern states. In 1966, he was named head of the SNCC, and shortly afterward he took part in James MEREDITH's Freedom March in Mississippi. Carmichael was active in the BLACK PANTHERS beginning in 1967; he was prime minister of the group before his resignation in 1969.

Carnap, Rudolf (1891–1970). German-American philosopher and logician. Carnap had a rigorous scientific and philosophical education, which was reflected in the style and content of all his later work. He studied mathematics, physics and philosophy at the universities of Jena and Freiburg (1910–14) and obtained a doctorate from Jena with a thesis on the concept of space in 1921. In 1926 Carnap was invited to take up a post at the University of Vienna, where he became a major figure in the Vienna Circle—a group of philosophers and mathematicians founded by Moritz Schlick. This group had an empiricist outlook (all our ideas, concepts and beliefs about the external world derive from our immediate sensory experience). Out of this evolved the logical empiricist or LOGICAL POSITIVISM school of thought, which states that the meaningful statements we can make are just those that have logical consequences that are observably verifiable. That is, meaningful statements must be testable by experience; those that are not, such as the propositions of metaphysics and religion, are, strictly, meaningless.

Throughout his life Carnap used the tools of symbolic logic to bring a greater precision to philosophical inquiry, including investigations into the philosophy of language and into probability and inductive reasoning. He produced his first major work in 1928, *Der Logische Aufban der Welt,* translated into English in 1967 as *The Logical Structure of the World.* In this he developed a version of the empiricist reducibility thesis, holding that scientific theories and theoretical sentences must be reducible to sentences that describe immediate experiences, which are observably verifiable. His other works included *Logishe Syntax der Sprache* (1934) and *Logical Foundations of Probability* (1950). He immigrated to the U.S. in 1936, becoming professor of philosophy at Chicago until 1952 and at UCLA until 1961. (See also A.J. AYER, Ludwig WITTGENSTEIN.)

Carne, James Power (1906–1986). British military officer. In 1951, during the KOREAN WAR, he led the 1st Battalion of the Gloucestershire Regiment in a heroic three-day stand against vastly superior Chinese forces in the Battle of the Imjin River. Carne and those of his men who survived were captured and endured 19 brutally taxing months as prisoners of the North Koreans.

Carne, Marcel (1909?-). French film director; came to prominence in French films in the 1930s and 1940s for a series of films on which he collaborated with French poet and performance artist Jacques PREVERT, who wrote the screenplays. These films include *Port of Shadows* (1938), *Daybreak* (1939) and the internationally acclaimed *Children of Paradise* (1943), which featured French actor Jean-Louis BARRAULT. *Children of Paradise,* set in the 19th century and concerning a romance between an actor and an actress, was shot during the German occupation of France in WORLD WAR II. Carne is highly regarded by film critics for his moody, evocative style and lush romantic sensibility.

Carnegie, Dale (1888–1955). American salesman, lecturer and author who developed and taught the arts of self-confidence and public speaking. Carnegie was the first of the "how-to" authors. His 1936 book *How to Win Friends and Influence People* became a publishing phenomenon and instant bestseller; by the time of his death some five million copies had been sold worldwide, a number that has now doubled. Carnegie founded the Carnegie Institute for Effective Speaking and Human Relations. He also wrote the popular book *How to Stop Worrying and Start Living* (1948).

Carnegie Hall. Legendary concert hall in NEW YORK CITY. Opened in 1891, Carnegie Hall has been a venue for cultural events of the highest order. The long list of personalities who have appeared there is a who's who of the modern era. Early in the century, lectures were given by Winston CHURCHILL, Theodore ROOSEVELT, Woodrow WILSON, Sigmund FREUD and W.B. YEATS. Classical musicians who have graced the hall's stage include conductors Gustav MAHLER, Wilhelm FURTWANGLER, Arturo TOSCANINI, Leopold STOKOWSKI, Bruno WALTER, Thomas BEECHAM, Leonard BERNSTEIN, Carlo Maria GIULINI, George SOLTI and Herbert von KARAJAN; pianists Sergei RACHMANINOFF, Josef and Rosina LHEVINNE, Vladimir HOROWITZ, Arthur RUBINSTEIN, Emil GILELS, Rudolf SERKIN, Van CLIBURN and Vladimir FELTSMAN; violinists Jascha HEIFETZ, David OISTRAKH, Yehudi MENUHIN and Itzhak PERLMAN; cellists Pablo CASALS, Gregor Piatagorsky, Mstislav ROSTROPOVICH and Jacqueline DU PRE; operatic and concert singers Marian ANDERSON, Maria CALLAS, Leontine PRICE, Janet BAKER, Joan SUTHERLAND, Luciano PAVAROTTI, Placido DOMINGO, Dietrich FISCHER-DIESKAU; JAZZ, big band and popular music performers Benny GOODMAN, Fats WALLER, Ella FITZGERALD, Sarah VAUGHAN, Duke ELLINGTON, Count BASIE, Paul WHITEMAN and Frank SINATRA; folk singers Woody GUTHRIE, Burl IVES, the WEAVERS, Pete SEEGER and Bob DYLAN; ROCK and roll groups such as the BEATLES and the ROLLING STONES.

In the late 1950s, Carnegie Hall was threatened with demolition in order to make room for a new office building; a group of music lovers, led by violinist Isaac STERN, intervened to save it. In 1986, Carnegie Hall was renovated; despite new amenities, many musicians and critics claim that its accoustics, hitherto near-perfect, were adversely affected. The hall celebrated its centennial in 1991–92 with a series of gala events.

For further reading:

Schickel, Richard, and Michael Walsh, *Carnegie Hall: The First One Hundred Years.* New York: Harry N. Abrams, 1987.

Carney, Robert Bostwick (1895–1990). American admiral. While chief of staff to Admiral William F. HALSEY, Jr., in the Pacific during WORLD WAR II, he helped plan several key naval battles. He served as commander in chief of the NORTH ATLANTIC TREATY ORGANIZATION (NATO) forces from 1951 to 1953. Under President Dwight D. EISENHOWER, he served as U.S. chief of naval operations from 1953 to 1955. His failure to be reappointed in 1955 was attributed to his clashes with Defense Secretary Charles E. Wilson, particularly his outspoken advocacy of a stronger navy to counter the Soviet naval buildup.

Carnovsky, Morris (1897–). American actor. Carnovsky was an acclaimed stage actor who enjoyed a lengthy career. He first came to the attention of critics and the public with his performance in the New York production of *The God of Vengeance* (1922) by Sholom Asch. Over the next two decades Carnovsky worked with both the Theater Guild and the GROUP THEATRE in New York City. With the latter company, he starred in two plays by Clifford ODETS, *Awake and Sing!* (1935) and *Golden Boy* (1937). In the 1950s and after, Carnovsky appeared frequently at the American Shakespeare Festival in Stratford, Conn., where his roles included that of King Lear.

Carol II (1893–1953). King of ROMANIA (reigned 1930–40); the son of King FERDINAND I and Queen Marie (1875–1938), as crown prince his first marriage, a morganatic union, was dissolved and he married Princess Helen of Greece in 1921. Carol became infamous for his liaison with Magda Lupescu, and when his father forced him to renounce his rights to the throne (1925), he settled in France with his mistress. On Ferdinand's death, the throne was assumed by Carol's six-year-old son Michael under a regency. Divorcing Queen Helen in 1928, Carol returned from exile and was proclaimed king in 1930. Ruling at first under a parliamentary system, Carol assumed dictatorial powers in 1938. After the outbreak of WORLD WAR II, he was obliged to cede territory to Hungary, Bulgaria and the U.S.S.R. and came into violent conflict with Romania's fascist Iron Guard. When Ion ANTONESCU formed a government in 1940, Carol was forced to flee and Michael again became king. Carol married Lupescu in Brazil in 1947 and died in exile in Portugal six years later.

Caroline Islands. A group of several hundred small islands in the western Pacific Ocean, north of the equator. Although uninhabited in modern times, ruins show that there was life here several centuries ago. Germany bought the islands in 1899 following the Spanish-American War; JAPAN seized them in 1914 and reinforced them during WORLD WAR II. The islands became U.S. trust territories in 1947.

Carothers, Wallace Hume (1896–1937). American industrial chemist. Carothers earned a B.S. degree from Tarkio College, Mo. (1920), after working his way through college. He gained his Ph.D. in 1924 from the University of Illinois and was an instructor in chemistry at Illinois and Harvard before joining the Du Pont company at Wilmington, Del., as head of organic chemistry research in 1928. Carothers's early work was in the application of electronic theory to organic chemistry, but at Du Pont he worked on polymerization. His first great success was the production of the synthetic rubber neoprene (1931). In a systematic search for synthetic analogs of silk and cellulose he prepared many condensation polymers, especially polyesters and polyethers. In 1935 one polyamide proved outstanding in its properties and came into full-scale production in 1940 as Nylon 66. But Carothers did not live to see the results of his achievements; despite his brilliant successes, he suffered from fits of depression and took his own life at the age of 41.

Carpenter, John Alden (1876–1951). American composer whose work marks a transition between 19th-century Impressionism and 20th-century JAZZ. Carpenter was born in Park Ridge, Ill., the son of a wealthy industrialist. After studies at Harvard and musical training in England with Edward ELGAR, Carpenter divided his time between the family shipping business and composing. His works revealed a wide range of eclectic interests. The song cycle *Gitanjali* (1914) derived from the poetry of Rabindranath TAGORE. The *Krazy-Kat* orchestral suite brought jazz idioms to the slapstick comedy of the popular George Herriman comic strip. His most complex and innovative score was the ballet *Skyscrapers* (1926), first performed at the Metropolitan Opera House. Rather than merely quoting jazz tunes, Carpenter thoroughly assimilated jazz idioms into his own unique expression, portraying in music the rhythmic movements and sounds of modern urban American life. Carpenter's most famous work, however, is the whimsical *Adventures in a Perambulator* (1914), which evokes the sights and sounds recorded by a wide-eyed infant in a baby buggy.

For further reading:

Ewen, David, *Composers Since 1900*. New York: The H.W. Wilson Co., 1969

Carpenter, Scott (1925–). U.S. astronaut. "Spectacular, like a very brilliant rainbow" was how Carpenter described his first sunset viewed from Earth orbit aboard Mercury 7 (May 24, 1962), his only space flight. The second American astronaut to orbit the Earth, Carpenter circled three times but used up too much fuel and fell behind schedule. He was forced to reenter Earth's atmosphere under manual control and splashed down 250 miles from his recovery ship. He was safely retrieved 40 minutes after splashdown, but not before some television newscasters announced to their nervous viewers that America might have "lost an astronaut." Critical of Carpenter's performance during the flight, some NASA officials held him responsible for the anxious moments surrounding his recovery. In 1965, taking a leave of absence from NASA, he participated in the Navy's Sealab 2 experiment, spending 30 days living and working in another alien environment, the challenging depths of the ocean floor. After retiring from NASA he continued with the Sealab experiments and served as assistant for aquanaut operations for Sealab 3. In 1969 he retired from the Navy with the rank of commander and became an engineering consultant and wasp breeder. (See also MERCURY PROGRAM.)

Carr, Edward (1892–1982). British historian known for his 14-volume *History of Soviet Russia*. Written over a period of 30 years, this work was considered one of the most comprehensive studies of the development of the U.S.S.R. and Soviet COMMUNISM.

Carr, John Dickson (1906–1977). American crime and detective story writer best known for his mastery of the "locked room" school of fiction. Born in Uniontown, Penn., Carr began writing his first detective short stories while a student at Haverford College. After the success of his first novel, *It Walks by Night* (1930), which introduced French police magistrate Henri Bencolin, Carr moved to England. For the next 15 years he introduced a series of fictional detectives. Dr. Gideon Fell, a Scotland Yard consultant, first appeared in *Hag's Nook* (1933); Sir Henry Merrivale, a barrister, debuted in *The Plague Court Murders* (1934); and Colonel March, chief of the "Department of Queer Complaints," came along in a volume of short stories under that name in 1940. Writing under his own name or the pseudonym Carter Dickson, Carr emerged the pre-eminent master of the "locked room" form. In a number of classics, like *The Crooked Hinge* (1938) and *The Problem of the Wire Cage* (1939), the operative question was not *who*-dunnit, but *how*-dunnit. Not locked doors, sealed rooms or trackless sands seemed to daunt the incredible ingenuity of his criminals. It was to Carr's credit, however, that the triumph of reason over superstition rarely disappointed the reader. Carr's later years after World War II were increasingly devoted to historical novels with crime/detection themes, such as *The Bridge of Newgate* (1950) and *The Devil in Velvet* (1951).

For further reading:

Nevins, Francis M., *The Mystery Writers' Art*. Bowling Green, Ohio: Bowling Green University Press, 1970.

Carra, Carlo (1881–1966). Italian painter. Carra was one of the leading Italian painters to be influenced by FUTURISM as articulated by Italian poet F.M. MARINETTI. A major painting from Carra's Futurist period is *The Funeral of the Antichrist Galli* (1911). In 1917 Carra met fellow Italian painter Giorgio de CHIRICO. Together they became the key proponents of the *Scuola Metafisica* (Metaphysical School) movement in painting. This new movement called for the pictorial evocation—through clearly defined geometrical constructions—of disquieting states of mind that pierced through the illusion of objective, impersonal existence. Carra and de Chirico soon quarreled over who had originated the movement. In his later years Carra turned to a neo-Classical painting style.

Carrel, Alexis (1873–1944). French surgeon. Carrel received his medical degree from the University of Lyons in 1900. In 1902 he started to investigate techniques for joining (suturing) blood vessels end to end. He continued his work at the University of Chicago (1904) and later at the Rockefeller Institute for Medical Research, N.Y. (1906). Carrel's techniques, which minimized tissue damage and infection and reduced the risk of blood clots, were a major advance in vascular surgery and paved the way for the replacement and transplantation of organs. In recognition of this work, Carrel was awarded the 1912 NOBEL PRIZE for physiology or medicine. During WORLD WAR I Carrel served in the French army. With the chemist Henry Dakin he formulated the Carrel-Dakin antiseptic for deep wounds. Returning to the Rockefeller Institute after the war, Carrel turned his attention to methods of keeping tissues and organs alive outside the body. With the aviator Charles LINDBERGH he devised a so-called artificial heart that could pump physiological fluids through large organs, such as the heart or kidneys. In *Man, the Unknown* (1935) Carrel published his controversial views about the possible role of science in organizing and improving society along authoritarian lines. During WORLD WAR II he founded and directed the Carrel Foundation for the Study of Human Problems under the VICHY government, in Paris. Following the Allied liberation, Carrel faced charges of collaboration but died before a trial was arranged.

Carreras, Jose (1946–). Spanish opera singer. Carreras was born in Barcelona, where he received his musical training. His rise as an operatic superstar was meteoric. A tenor, he made his professional debut in Spain in 1970, won first prize at the International Verdi Competition in Italy in 1971 and appeared in the U.S. in 1972 to wide acclaim. He first sang at New York's Metropolitan Opera in 1974, at La Scala in 1975 and at the SALZBURG FESTIVAL in 1976 (at the invitation of Herbert von KARAJAN). He made numerous recordings, telecasts and live appearances throughout the world. However, his large number of engagements and choice of some unsuitable roles seemed to affect the quality of his voice and his interpretations. In 1987 Carerras became seriously ill with leukemia. After intensive treatment he went into remission and returned to the stage in 1988. Critics noted a new vocal refinement and musical depth in his performances.

Carrizal. Village and battlefield in Chihuahua State, 85 miles south of Ciudad Juarez, Mexico. On June 21, 1916, Mexican troops routed an American expeditionary force under command of General John J. PERSHING, who was in pursuit of Pancho VILLA after the revolutionary's raid on an American border town.

Carruthers, Jimmy (1929–1990). Australian boxer. The world bantamweight champ from 1952 to 1954, he was the first Australian to win a world title. After his retirement, he became a boxing referee and hotel owner.

Carry Back (1958–1983). Thoroughbred racehorse. Carry Back's remarkable career was all the more astonishing because of his undistinguished ancestry. He was sired by Saggy out of a mare named Joppy, who was once used to pay off a $300 debt. Carry Back went on to become only the fifth racehorse to win over one million dollars. Most famous for his rivalry with KELSO, he bested the older horse in the 1961 Metropolitan Handicap. He won the Kentucky Derby and Preakness that year, but suffered an injury in the Belmont that destroyed his chances for the Triple Crown. Named three-year-old of the year for that campaign, he faced Kelso again as a four-year-old but was unable to best the old champion. He retired to stud in 1962.

Carson, Sir Edward Henry (1854–1935). Irish political leader. A Dublin lawyer, he was elected to the British Parliament in 1892; a superb trial lawyer, he was solicitor general from 1900–05. Carson led Irish Protestant opposition to HOME RULE, and in 1912 he raised an army of some 80,000 men in an attempt to defeat it. The threat of civil war led Parliament to concede NORTHERN IRELAND to the Protestants in 1914. Carson was attorney general (1915), first lord of the admiralty (1916–17) and a member of the cabinet during WORLD WAR I (1917–18). Knighted in 1900 and made a baron in 1921, he served as lord of appeal from 1921 to 1929.

Carson, Johnny (1925–). U.S. radio and television talk show host and comedian. After spending his early years in Iowa, he moved to Nebraska with his family. Initially Carson entertained with magic, card tricks and ventriloquism. His WORLD WAR II service took him to duty in the Pacific on the U.S.S. *Pennsylvania*, where he often entertained his shipmates with tricks and humor. He graduated from the University of Nebraska in radio and drama (1949) and finally moved to Los Angeles, where in 1951 he had a comedy show called *Carson's Cellar*. He also started writing for the comedy stars. He was offered "The Johnny Carson Show" by CBS in 1955. After the show closed, he moved to New York in 1957 to host ABC's "Who Do You Trust?" for five years. A hit as a substitute on NBC's TONIGHT SHOW in 1958, he later became host of the show and one of the best-known personalities in American television. He announced his retirement in 1991.

For further reading:

De Cordova, Fred, *Johnny Came Lately*. New York: Pocket Books, 1989.

Carson, Rachel (1907–1964). American biologist, environmentalist and writer. Following postgraduate research in zoology at Johns Hopkins University (1932), Carson joined the U.S. Fish and Wildlife Service as an aquatic biologist; she was later the service's editor-in-chief of publications. In 1952 she received the National Book Award for *The Sea Around Us*. Her most important book was *Silent Spring* (1962), which warned of the dangers of pesticides, particularly DDT; the book virtually launched the environmental movement and prompted regulatory legislation. Although the chemical industry attacked Carson's findings, President KENNEDY's Science Advisory Committee confirmed them in 1963. In addition to receiving numerous awards from CONSERVATION and animal welfare societies, Carson was elected to the American Academy of Arts and Letters. In 1980 she was posthumously awarded the presidential Medal of Freedom.

For further reading:

Brooks, Paul, *The House of Life: Rachel Carson at Work*. Boston: Houghton Mifflin, 1989.

Jezer, Marty, *Rachel Carson*. New York: Chelsea House, 1988.

Cartan, Elie Joseph (1869–1951). French mathematician. Cartan is now recognized as one of the most powerful and original mathematicians of the 20th century, but his work became widely known only toward the end of his life. He studied at the Ecole Normale Superieure in Paris and held teaching posts at the universities of Montpellier, Lyons, Nancy and, from 1912 to 1940, Paris. Cartan's most significant work was in developing the concept of analysis on differentiable manifolds, which now occupies a central place in mathematics. He began his research career with a dissertation on Lie groups, a topic that led him on to his pioneering work on differential systems. The most important innovation in his work on Lie groups was his creation of methods for studying their global properties. The global approach also distinguished his work on differential systems. One of his most useful inventions was the "calculus of exterior differential forms," which he applied to problems in many fields, including differential geometry, Lie groups, analytical dynamics and general relativity. Cartan's son Henri was also an eminent mathematician.

Carter, Angela (1940–). British author. Carter was born in London and educated at the University of Bristol. The daughter of a journalist, Carter began her career in journalism before turning to writing fiction. With her first novel, *Shadow Dance* (1966; published in the U.S. as *Honeybuzzard*, 1967), she established her style, a surreal treatment of Gothic themes laced with violence and eroticism, akin to MAGIC REALISM. Other fiction includes *The Passion of New Eve* (1977), *Nights at the Circus* (1984) and *Saints and Strangers* (1986). Carter, a feminist, also wrote *The Sadeian Women: An Exercise in Cultural History*, (1979), which, surprisingly, defends the Marquis de Sade's portrayals of women. Carter has served as Arts Council fellow at Sheffield University, England, and as a visiting professor of creative writing at Brown University and has also written short stories and articles.

Carter, Elliot (Cook), Jr. (1908–). American composer. Carter was one of the most highly regarded of modern American composers. He earned his master's degree at Harvard University in 1932 and subsequently studied in Paris under Nadia BOULANGER. Carter's major compositional works were completed in the postwar era. He twice won the Pulitzer Prize for music—in 1960 for String Quartet No. 2 and in 1973 for String Quartet No. 3. Carter's style is marked by the use of highly intricate tempos and rhythms. *The Writings of Elliot Carter* (1977) is a major collection of his critical essays on music.

Carter, Howard (1873–1939). English archaeologist and Egyptologist. A draftsman with the Egyptian Exploration Fund from 1891–1899, Carter was trained in the then-current techniques of archaelogical excavation. He became inspector general of the Egyptian government's antiquities department in 1899 and supervised various excavations in Luxor's Valley of the Kings in 1902–03. Associated with Lord Carnarvon from 1906 on, he excavated many tombs, including those of Amenophis I and Queen Hatshepsut. He is famous for his discovery of the tomb of Tutankhamen in November 1922. Carter described the excavation of this world-renowned site in a three-volume work written with A.C. Mace, *The Tomb of Tutankh-Amen* (1923–33).

Carter, Jimmy (1924–). Thirty-ninth president of the UNITED STATES (1977–81). Born in Plains, Georgia, Carter attended the U.S. Naval Academy, graduating in 1946. He served in the Navy as a nuclear engineer until 1953, when he returned to Georgia to head his family's successful peanut business. Carter entered political life as a state senator (1962–66), ran un-

Jimmy Carter.

successfully for governor of Georgia in 1966 and attained the governor's office in 1970. He ran a vigorous campaign for the presidential nomination in 1975 and narrowly defeated President Gerald FORD in the election of 1976. Carter was something of a phenomenon as president: an amiable but tough outsider, a Southerner, a moralist and a fundamentalist Christian. On the domestic front, Carter attempted to implement new national energy policies and to reform the income tax system.

However, his status as a Washington outsider circumscribed his power with Congress, and his attempts to pass legislation met largely with failure. Moreover, the economy suffered during his presidency, experiencing high interest rates, inflation and, later, recession. In foreign affairs, he was both praised and censured for the two PANAMA CANAL treaties of 1977 that gave control of the canal to PANAMA. Carter's lack of power with the Congress was mirrored in his 1979 failure to gain ratification of a U.S.-Soviet arms control treaty. He scored his main foreign policy success in 1979 when he engineered and presided over the Camp David peace treaty between Israel and Egypt. His popularity tumbled after Muslim militants took over the U.S. embassy in Teheran in November 1979, holding a group of U.S. citizens hostage (see IRAN HOSTAGE CRISIS). The failure of a rescue mission in April 1980 added to his unpopularity, and Carter was easily defeated by Ronald REAGAN in the 1980 elections. Carter managed to secure the release of the hostages in the last month of his presidency, and he retired to private life in 1981—a private life of selfless volunteerism that has set him apart from the post-presidential activities of other former chief executives.

Carter, "Mother" Maybelle (1909–1978). American country music singer. Carter was the matriarch of the Original Carter Family, the first group named to the Country Music Hall of Fame. Her guitar style changed that instrument's role in country music. She was identified with such songs as "Wabash Cannonball," "Will the Circle Be Unbroken" and "Wildwood Flower." (See also BLUEGRASS; COUNTRY AND WESTERN MUSIC.)

Carter, William Hodding, Jr. (1907–1972). American journalist. In 1938 he became editor and publisher of the *Delta Democratic-Times* in Greenville, Mississippi. He won the 1945 Pulitzer Prize for his editorials against racial segregation in the South and was called "the spokesman for the New South." His son **Hodding Carter 3d** was a prominent adviser to President Jimmy CARTER.

Carter v. Carter Coal Co. (1936). U.S. Supreme Court decision that declared one of President Franklin D. ROOSEVELT'S NEW DEAL programs illegal. An important part of the New Deal program to revive the U.S. economy, the Bituminous Coal Conservation Act allowed mine operators to set work and hour standards for workers. The Supreme Court declared that the federal government could not regulate mining because mining was not interstate commerce. The Supreme Court also declared illegal the act's requirement that mine operators collectively bargain with the mineworkers' unions. This case followed the Supreme Court's rejection of FDR'S AGRICULTURAL ADJUSTMENT ACT and amounted to a serious roadblock to FDR's economic reform program and also led to FDR'S COURT-PACKING ATTEMPT, when he sought to add additional justices to the Court who were more sympathetic to his New Deal programs.

Cartier-Bresson, Henri (1908–). French photojournalist. He began his career as a photographer in 1930 and became a cinematographic assistant to Jean RENOIR in 1936. Widely exhibited throughout the world, he was one of the founders of the photographic agency Magnum in 1947. Cartier-Bresson has photographed around the globe, employing black and white and refusing to crop his images. His expressive compositions are considered among the most effective of all documentary photographs. His numerous books of photographs include *The Decisive Moment* (1952), *China in Transition* (1956), *The World of Henri Cartier-Bresson* (1968), *About Russia* (1974) and *Henri Cartier-Bresson: Photographer* (1979).

Cartland, Barbara Hamilton (1901–). British novelist. A writer of popular romantic fiction, Cartland is notable for her extraordinary output. Between the mid-1920s and the late 1980s she wrote literally hundreds of books, all following a basic plot formula; she is listed in the GUINNESS BOOK OF RECORDS as the best-selling author in the world. Cartland, who claims to write a novel in seven days, has also published under her married name, Barbara McCorquedale.

Carty, John Joseph (1861–1932). American telephone engineer. Carty went to high school in Cambridge, Mass., but because of eye trouble his entrance to college was put off. During this period his imagination was captured by the invention of the telephone (1875) by Alexander Graham Bell. He joined the Bell System in 1879, eventually becoming chief engineer of the New York Telephone Company (1889–1907) and of the American Telephone and Telegraph Company (1907–19) and finally becoming vice president of the latter company until his retirement in 1930. Carty was responsible for a number of technical innovations in the development of commercial telephone use. These included the introduction of the "common" battery that, by providing current from a central source to a number of interconnected telephones, allowed the development of a complex urban network. He also directed the project to provide the first transcontinental telephone line, completing in 1915 the 3,400-mile link between New York and San Francisco.

Caruso, Enrico (1873–1921). The legendary Caruso is commonly regarded as the greatest operatic tenor—if not the greatest singer—of the 20th century. He was certainly the most famous singer of his lifetime, and 70 years after his death his name remains a household word, even in households where opera is never heard. Caruso was born in the slums of Naples, the 18th of 21 children. His father intended him to become a mechanic; however, Caruso discovered his musical gifts at an early age and ran away from home at 16 to pursue his vocation. His professional operatic debut was in 1894 in Naples; over the next few years he sang at provincial opera houses throughout Italy, building his repertoire and his reputation. He debuted at Milan's La Scala in 1900 (as Rodolfo in PUCCINI'S *La Boheme*) and made his first appearance at the Metropolitan Opera in New York in 1903 as the Duke in *Rigoletto.* For the next 17 seasons he was the leading Italian tenor at the Met, singing over 600 performances at that house. He also sang frequently in Europe and toured Latin America. Among his many famous roles were Alfredo in *La Traviata,* Manrico in *Il Trovatore,* Canio in *Pagliacci,* Des Grieux in *Manon Lescaut.* Before the end of the century's first decade, Caruso had become an international celebrity, known as much for his zest for life and his sense of humor as for his singing.

Legendary opera singer Enrico Caruso as Canio.

Part of Caruso's fame during his lifetime stems from the fact that he took full advantage of the new recording technology. If recordings helped to secure Caruso's fame, his voice helped to establish the record industry. His rendition of "Vesti la giubba" was the first recording ever to sell one million copies. Caruso's contemporaries, including many other celebrated singers, acknowledged the greatness of his voice. Much has been written about that voice: it has been called warm, powerful, beautiful and golden; it was (and is, even in the primitive acoustic recordings of his time) instantly recognizable. Caruso died at the peak of his career from bronchial pneumonia.

For further reading:

Scott, Michael, *The Great Caruso.* New York: Alfred A. Knopf, 1988.

Carvel, Tom [born Thomas Andreas Carvelas] (1906–1990). Greek-born inventor and entrepreneur. He invented a machine to make soft ice cream, later known as frozen custard. With a $15 loan from his future wife, he started a business that grew into the Carvel Corp., the nation's third-largest chain of ice cream stores. He sold the chain to Investcorp in 1989 for more than $80 million. He became known to millions of people with his gravel-voiced radio and television advertisements, asking listeners to "please visit your local Carvel store."

Former slave and renowned American scientist George Washington Carver (1939).

Carver, George Washington (1864–1943). U.S. agricultural scientist. Born to a black farm family in Missouri, he and his mother were stolen and taken to Arkansas, where his mother was sold and he was traded for a race horse. After he returned to his former home in Missouri, he worked his way through high school and college, and graduated in 1894. He was elected to the faculty of Iowa State University, where he devoted himself to bacterial laboratory work in botany. After gaining his master's degree in 1896, he was named chairman of the department of agriculture at Tuskegee Institute in Alabama, where he devoted the rest of his life to agricultural research. He won international recognition for discovering industrial uses for such agricultural products as peanuts, sweet potatoes and soybeans, as well as cotton wastes. His discovery of 300 by-products of the peanut gave hope for a crop to replace the sagging cotton economy of the South.

Carver is noted for his work to elevate the position of fellow blacks. He was chosen a member of the Royal Society of Arts in London in 1916. In 1939 he received the Roosevelt medal for his valuable contribution to agricultural science. During World War II, he developed many dyes to replace those that could no longer be imported from Europe. January 5 has been designated George Washington Carver Day by the United States Congress. The George Washington Carver National Monument was established on the Missouri farm where he was born.

For further reading:

Adair, Gene, *George Washington Carver.* New York: Chelsea House, 1989.
McMurry, Linda O., *George Washington Carver: Scientist and Symbol.* New York: Oxford University Press, 1981.

Carver, Raymond (1938–1988). American short-story writer. Carver was widely regarded as the laureate of America's working poor. Writing in short, declarative sentences, he portrayed the hard underside of blue-collar life in the Pacific Northwest, where he spent his childhood. Among his most highly regarded works were *Will You Please Be Quiet, Please?* (1976), *What We Talk About When We Talk About Love* (1981), *Cathedral* (1984) and *Fires* (1983). Married twice, he spent much of his life struggling with alcohol and poverty.

Cary, (Arthur) Joyce (Lunel) (1888–1957). Anglo-Irish novelist. Born in Londonderry, Northern Ireland, of an old Anglo-Irish family, Cary studied art at Edinburgh Art School and law at Trinity College, Cambridge. He served in the BALKAN WAR OF 1912–13 and in WORLD WAR I in Nigeria, returning to England in 1920. His first novel *Aissa Saved,* appeared in 1932 when he was 44. His first seven novels feature Nigerians and Irish peasants and children. *A House of Children* (1941) was based on his own youth. His greatest achievements were two trilogies (1941–44 and 1952–55) on the subjects of art and politics in 20th-century England; a third trilogy, on religion, remained unfinished at his death. Each volume is narrated by a different protagonist, thus allowing three points of view for each story. Most famous is *The Horse's Mouth* (1944), narrated by the scoundrel Gully Jimson.

For further reading:

Fisher, Barbara, ed., *Joyce Cary Remembered.* New York: Barnes & Noble, 1988.
Closter, Susan V., *Joyce Cary & Lawrence Durrell: A Reference Guide.* Boston: G.K. Hall, 1985.
Robey, Kinley E., *Joyce Cary.* Boston: G.K. Hall, 1984.

Casablanca [Arabic: Dar el Beida]. Port city 180 miles southwest of Tangier, Morocco, on the Atlantic Ocean. Early in the 20th century the town went through massive improvements under French control. It was the November 1942 site of one of the major Allied landings in North Africa and also hosted the CASABLANCA CONFERENCE between President Franklin D. ROOSEVELT and Prime Minister Winston CHURCHILL (January 14–26, 1943). The two Allied leaders agreed that peace could be achieved only when Germany capitulated unconditionally. Casablanca's image as a city rife with romantic intrigue stems from the 1942 movie of the same name starring Humphrey BOGART and Ingrid BERGMAN—but the movie was filmed in a HOLLYWOOD sound stage.

Casablanca Conference. Meeting on January 14, 1943, between U.S. President Franklin D. ROOSEVELT and British Prime Minister Winston CHURCHILL in CASABLANCA, MOROCCO, during WORLD WAR II. The Allied leaders reiterated their insistence on the unconditional surrender of the AXIS powers, decided to invade ITALY through Sicily and to intensify the bombing of GERMANY before mounting an invasion of occupied FRANCE, and agreed that more British forces should be sent to the Asian theater following victory in Europe.

Casadesus, Robert (1899–1973). French pianist and composer. Born in Paris, he was a member of a family of eminent 20th-century musicians. He studied at the Paris Conservatory, began his distinguished concert career in 1922 and continued to travel and concertize for the rest of his life. Casadesus moved to the U.S. in 1940, returning to France to become

Joseph Stalin, Franklin Roosevelt and Winston Churchill at the Teheran Conference.

The great cellist Pablo Casals (1957).

director of the American Conservatory at Fontainebleau (1945–49). A pianist with a limpid and lyric style, he was particularly noted for his performance of French music and often appeared with his wife, pianist **Gaby Casadesus**. A gifted teacher and composer, he wrote seven symphonies, numerous piano and violin concertos, songs and other orchestral and piano works.

Casals, Pablo (1876–1973). Spanish cellist and conductor. A prodigy, Casals first studied violin, then adopted the cello as his primary instrument at the age of 12. He began giving concerts in 1891, touring Europe and the U.S. to great acclaim. He, the violinist Jacques THIBAUD and the pianist Alfred CORTOT formed a chamber trio in 1905. He began conducting in 1908 and founded the Orquestra Pau Casals in Barcelona in 1919. In 1939, Casals went into self-imposed exile in the south of France in protest against Spain's FRANCO regime. After organizing many music festivals in France, in 1956 he settled in Puerto Rico, where he again put together many successful musical events. Famed for his interpretations of the Bach suites for unaccompanied cello, he was an adored public figure and one of the greatest musicians of the 20th century as cellist, conductor, composer, pianist and teacher.

Casement, Sir Roger (David) (1864–1916). Irish revolutionary leader. In the British consular service early in his career, he exposed atrocities in the rubber plantations of the Congo in 1903–04 and in South America in 1910–12, and was knighted in 1911 for these achievements. A committed Irish nationalist, he retired from the consular service to further the nationalist movement. After the outbreak of World War I, Casement traveled to the U.S. and then to Germany (1914) in search of aid for an Irish uprising. Securing only promises, he was landed in IRELAND by a German U-boat in 1916 on the eve of the EASTER REBELLION. Arrested by the British, he was tried for treason, convicted and hanged. In order to lessen his credibility, British agents circulated his diaries, which contained homosexual passages. Nonetheless, Casement was considered an Irish martyr and continues to be revered by Irish nationalists.

Casimir, Hendrik Brugt Gerhard (1909–). Dutch physicist. Casimir studied at the universities of Leiden, Copenhagen and Zurich, and held various research positions between 1933 and 1942. He published many papers in the fields of theoretical physics, applied mathematics and low-temperature physics. His most notable work has been in the theory of the superconducting state. Following the work of W. Meissner, Casimir and his colleague Cornelis Gorter advanced a "two-fluid" model of superconductivity in 1934. They were successful in explaining the high degree of interrelationship between the magnetic and thermal properties of superconductors. After 1942 Casimir pursued a highly successful career with the Philips company, becoming director of the Philips' Research Laboratories in 1946 and a member of the board of management (1957–72). He supervised Philip's research activities in several countries.

Caspersson, Torbjorn Oskar (1910–). Swedish cytochemist. Caspersson earned his M.D. from Stockholm University in 1936. He then joined the staff of the Nobel Institute, where he was appointed professor of medical cellular research and genetics in 1944. In the late 1930s Caspersson spent a few years working on DNA. In 1936 with the Swiss chemist Rudolf Signer he made fundamental measurements of the molecule. These measurements showed nucleic acids to be larger than protein molecules. Further important data were collected by a photoelectric spectrophotometer developed by Caspersson. This work showed that protein synthesis in the cell was associated with an abundance of RNA. Despite this Caspersson remained committed to the orthodox view that genes were proteins and believed nucleic acids to be a structure-determining supporting substance.

Cassatt, Mary (1845–1926). American painter. Born in Pittsburgh, she studied at the Pennsylvania Academy of the Fine Arts (1861–65) and at the Academy of Parma, Italy (1872), before settling in Paris. Spending most of her life in France, she was a friend of such artists as Manet and Degas, who became important influences on her work. Associated with the French Impressionists and the only American to exhibit with them, she was also influenced by the color and pattern of Japanese prints. Taking motherhood as her most frequent subject, Cassatt was an accomplished painter, pastel artist and etcher. Her images are intimate and colorful, very personal interpretations of the Impressionist esthetic. Included in many of the world's most important public collections, her best-known paintings in American museums include versions of *Mother and Child* in the Metropolitan Museum of Art, N.Y.C., and the Museum of Fine Arts, Boston, as well as *Morning Toilette* (1886) and *The Boating Party* (1893), both at the National Gallery of Art, Washington, D.C.

Cassavetes, John (1929–1989). American actor, screenwriter and film director. Cassavetes starred in such films as *Rosemary's Baby* and *Edge of the City;* in 1967 he was nominated for an ACADEMY AWARD for his performance as a psycopathic soldier in *The Dirty Dozen*. His own films, which he financed through his acting, were distinguished by a quirky, improvisational quality; several of them starred his wife, actress Gena Rowlands, and his friends actors Ben Gazzara and Peter Falk. Although his work was never popular with mass audiences, Cassavetes garnered Academy Award nominations in 1968 for his screenplay *Faces* and in 1974 for directing *A Woman Under the Influence*.

Cassin, Rene (1887–1976). French jurist. Cassin served in WORLD WAR I before becoming a professor of international law. Deeply interested in veterans' affairs, he founded and ran the Federal Union of Associations of Disabled and Aged War Veterans. Secretary of defense for the French government-in-exile during WORLD WAR II, he directed the military activities of the FREE FRENCH. After the war he became one of France's most prominent jurists, serving on numerous boards and commissions. Cassin became an important figure in the human rights movement as a delegate to the United Nations Commission on Human Rights, the author of its Universal Declaration of Human Rights and later as its chairman. He was a founder of the UNITED NATIONS EDUCATIONAL, SCIENTIFIC AND CULTURAL ORGANIZATION (UNESCO) and president of the International Institute of Human Rights. In 1968 Cassin was awarded the NOBEL PRIZE for peace.

Cassino. Town, monastery and battleground in Frosinone province, Italy. During WORLD WAR II the monastery, in a key location on a hill (HILL 516), was a part of the German Gustav Line that blocked the Allied road to Rome. Some of the fiercest fighting of the war occurred here from February to May 1944, when the town and monastery were destroyed. Both were subsequently reconstructed. (See also WORLD WAR II ON THE ITALIAN FRONT.)

Cassirer, Ernst (1874–1945). German philosopher. Cassirer became renowned as one of the leading exponents of neo-Kantian philosophy in this century. As a professor at the University of Hamburg, he was an influential philosopher in his native land. Due to his Jewish heritage, he was forced to leave Nazi Germany in 1933 and subsequently taught at Oxford University in England and at Yale University in the U.S., where he died in 1945. The key philosophical issues to which Cassirer devoted himself were the history of scientific theory, the epistemological problem of the nature of human knowledge and the structure of mythic thought. As a neo-Kantian, Cassirer stressed the need for symbolic representations to interpret reality. His major works include the three-volume *Philosophy of Symbolic Forms* (1923–29), *Language and Myth* (1925), *An Essay on Man* (1944) and *The Myth of the State* (1946).

Castaneda, Carlos (1925?–). American anthropologist and spiritual philosopher. Castaneda created a sensation both in America and in Europe with his first book, *The Teachings of Don Juan: A Yaqui Way of Knowledge* (1968), which was originally submitted as an academic thesis by Castaneda while he was a graduate student in anthropology at the University of California at Santa Cruz. The book detailed the life of a Yaqui Indian shaman living in Mexico who taught Castaneda, in part through the use of peyote and other hallucinogenic plants, of the existence of an alternative mode of reality in which man and nature merged and communication with nonhuman life forms and energies was possible. Since its publication, a scholarly controversy has arisen as to whether or not Castaneda fictionalized the character of Don Juan in part or in whole; no definitive answer has been reached. Whether regarded as anthropology or literature, the works of Castaneda have exercised a major influence on the NEW AGE MOVEMENT. His other books include *Tales of Power* (1974), *The Fire from Within* (1984) and *The Power of Silence* (1987).

Castelnuovo-Tedesco, Mario (1895–1968). Italian-American composer. Born in Florence, Castelnuovo-Tedesco was educated there under Ildebrando Pizzetti. He undertook commissions for such performers as Andres SEGOVIA, Jascha HEIFETZ and Gregor Piatigorsky beginning in the mid-1920s. By the 1930s he was one of the most frequently performed contemporary Italian composers. When anti-Semitic laws were promulgated in Italy in 1938, Castelnuovo-Tedesco, who was Jewish, emigrated to the U.S. (1939), where he became an American citizen and an influential music teacher. Known for their delicacy and refinement, his numerous compositions include film scores, songs, operas, orchestral music, chamber pieces, oratorios, concertos and piano music.

Castle, Barbara Anne (1911–). British politician. Castle was elected to Parliament in 1945 and became a member of the LABOUR PARTY national executive committee in 1950. She served as minister of overseas development from 1964 to 1965, minister of transport from 1965 to 1968, secretary of state for employment and productivity from 1968 to 1970 and secretary of state for social services from 1974 to 1976. In 1979 Castle was elected a member of the European Parliament.

Castle, Irene and Vernon. Irene Castle (1893–1969, born Irene Foote) and Vernon Castle (1887– 1918, born Vernon Castle Blythe) were noted exhibition ballroom dancers and teachers. British-born Vernon married New Yorker Irene in 1911, and they became one of the most successful and influential ballroom dance teams of their day. Noted for their elegant style, the Castles introduced such dances as the Castle Walk and the Castle Polka, and created a new style for ballroom dancing by popularizing such dances as the tango and the hesitation waltz. Together they wrote *The Modern Dance* in 1914. When Vernon was killed in an air crash in 1918, Irene retired from dancing and wrote *Castles in the Air* in 1958. Fred ASTAIRE and Ginger ROGERS starred in the 1939 film of their lives, *The Story of Vernon and Irene Castle*.

Castle, The. Classic 1926 novel by Czech writer Franz KAFKA. *The Castle* has been broadly acclaimed as one of the most piercing literary depictions of the spiritual crisis of the 20th century. Its basic plot concerns the arrival of K., a land surveyor, to a village to which he has been summoned by officials of the Castle that overshadows, both physically and psychologically, the life of the village. K. had understood that he had been appointed the official surveyor for the village, but the villagers deny his authority and even the need for such services. All of K.'s attempts to confirm his mission from the Castle officials end in confusion and doubt. In the course of K.'s dealings with the Castle and with the persons of the village, a symbolic tale emerges of the quest for life's meaning and the yearning for divine revelation.

Castro, Fidel [Fidel Castro Ruz] (1926–). Cuban revolutionary and premier of CUBA (1959–). As a young lawyer, Castro was an outspoken critic of the regime of Fulgencio BATISTA, which he toppled on January 1, 1959, after two previous, unsuccessful attempts. Initial American support for Castro eroded as he broadened his ties with the Soviet Union. In December 1961, shortly after the disastrous American-backed BAY OF PIGS INVASION, Castro declared himself to be a Marxist-Leninist. The CUBAN MISSILE CRISIS (1962) added to international tensions, as U.S. President John F. KENNEDY demanded that the Russians withdraw their offensive missiles from Cuban soil. The Russians complied, but the world lay on the brink of war throughout the crisis. Castro's domestic policies—especially his nationalization of the economy—have been brought into question by such crises as the failed sugar harvest of 1970, while Cuban military involvement in Africa and elsewhere has drawn strong condemnation. With the end of the COLD WAR, as Eastern European nations turned from communism in 1989–90, and the defeat of the Marxist Sandinista regime in Nicaragua, Castro became increasingly isolated. However, he continued to espouse his belief in revolutionary Marxism.

For further reading:

Geyer, Georgie Anne, *Guerrilla Prince: The Untold Story of Fidel Castro*. Boston: Little, Brown, 1991.

Cuban President Fidel Castro addresses the nation on the 35th anniversary of the revolution.

Castroviejo, Ramon (1904–1987). Spanish-born eye surgeon. Castroviejo was one of the first surgeons to perform successful cornea transplants. In 1938 he made a public appeal to Americans to will their eyes to science to help restore the eyesight of others. His appeal helped lead to the creation of present-day eye banks. He was based in New York for most of his career.

Catastrophists. Literary group founded in Wilno, Poland, in 1929. Among the writers associated with the group were the Lithuanian poet Oscar Venceslas Lubicz-Milosz and his nephew, the Polish poet and essayist Czeslaw MILOSZ. The group's name referred to two key convictions held by its members. The first was that a socialist upheaval would be forthcoming in Europe. The second was that such an upheaval would serve as a necessary purification of the corrupted capitalistic social structure. Thus the Catastrophists focused on politics as an eschatological movement leading to a redeemed humanity, without reference to religion. Their predictions were only partly correct: immense upheavals came in the form of the rise of NAZISM, WORLD WAR II, and the subsequent communist domination of Eastern Europe.

Catcher in the Rye. The most famous novel of American writer J.D. SALINGER. *Catcher in the Rye* (1951) was a sensation upon its first appearance, earning both critical acclaim and best-seller status. It went on to become a cult classic avidly read by the youth of the 1950s and 60s and continues to be popular to this day. Its protagonist, Holden Caulfield, is a sarcastic but inwardly warm teenager who has dropped out or been expelled from a series of private schools. After the latest such disaster, Caulfield returns home to New York City, where during the weekend in which the bulk of the action occurs both his cynicism and his idealism are put to the test by the harsh realities of the city. Caulfield's contempt for human phoniness inspired the same in many readers.

Catch-22. Novel by American writer Joseph HELLER. *Catch-22* (1961) stands as one of the classic black comedies of modern literature. Its hilarious, absurdist indictment of the horrors of war remains unsurpassed among satires on the relentless inhumanity of man to man. The plot concerns the efforts of Yossarian, an American pilot stationed with a bomber squadron in Italy during WORLD WAR II, to have himself certified as insane by the

American author Willa Cather.

military doctors so that he can stop flying the missions that put his own life at risk and bring death to untold others. But the stumbling block is that, if Yossarian is aware enough to want to stop flying the missions, he cannot possibly be insane. The term "catch-22" has earned a place in common American parlance as signifying bureaucracy operating at its most inane, paradoxical level. A film version of the novel, directed by Mike NICHOLS, was produced in 1970.

Cather, Willa (Sibert) (1876–1947). American novelist. Born in Virginia, she was raised in Nebraska and later attended the University of Nebraska. She taught, worked as a journalist and published her first volume of poetry, *April Twilight*, in 1903, followed by a collection of short stories, *The Troll Garden* (1905). In 1906 she moved to New York, working on the staff of *McClure's Magazine* until 1912, when she published her first novel, *Alexander's Bridge*. With *O, Pioneers* (1913), the story of Swedish immigrants in Nebraska, she found her characteristic voice and themes. *My Antonia* (1918) tells the story of an immigrant girl from Bohemia in Nabraska; the convincing first-person narrative is written from a male character's viewpoint. Other works include *The Song of the Lark* (1915); her best known book, *Death Comes for the Archbishop* (1927), a historical novel set in a New Mexico mission; *Lucy Greyheart* (1935), in which a music student is torn between traditional values and those of the artistic world; and *Not Under Forty* (1936).

CAT scan. Popular name for computerized axial tomography, a merger of computer and X-RAY technology that can be used to diagnose problems in any internal organ of the body, including the brain. Invented in 1961, introduced in 1972 and widely available since the mid-1970s, the tomograph focuses X rays 100 times more sensitive than ordinary X rays on specific planes of the body by rotating a scanner around the body. The X-ray beams are picked up by a detector and fed into a computer, which then creates an analysis of the information provided on tissue density. This analysis is converted into cathode-ray-tube pictures of detailed cross-sections of these complicated structures. By allowing doctors to examine the body and brain without invasive procedures, this painless procedure has created a revolution in the diagnosis of tumors, blood clots, cysts, abscesses and other disorders.

Catton, Bruce (1899–1978). American journalist and historian. Catton wrote 13 volumes on the American Civil War, and won the PULITZER PRIZE (1954) for his book *A Stillness at Appomattox*. He was also senior editor of *American Heritage* magazine.

Caucasia [Caucasus]. Area of the U.S.S.R. between the Black Sea and the Caspian Sea, on the west and east, and southwestern Russia and the Caucasus Mountains, on the north and south. A blend of various peoples, it was under Russian domination in the 19th century following wars with Turkey and Persia; but Russian control was rigorously challenged by the Muslims of Azerbaijan. Oil-rich Caucasia was critically important to the U.S.S.R. in WORLD WAR II, and a German attack was aimed at the area in July 1942. The initial assault was triumphant, but the Germans were driven back by a counteroffensive in January 1943.

Cauthen, Steve (1960–). American jockey. Born in Texas, Cauthen was licensed to ride professionally at age 16. The 1977 jockey of the year, Cauthen set the American racing world on fire, riding AFFIRMED to the TRIPLE CROWN one year later. The crush of publicity that attended his every move contributed to his decision in 1979 to move his career to England. The first American in nearly 80 years to win the Epsom Derby, he is the only jockey to have ridden winners in both the Epsom and Kentucky derbies. The first jockey to win over $6 million, he had already ridden more than 1,000 winners before the end of 1990.

Cavafy, Constantine (Peter) (1863–1933). Greek poet. Except for a few years in Liverpool and Constantinople, Cavafy spent most of his life in the cosmopolitan, half-oriental city of Alexandria. Scion of a wealthy merchant family, he worked intermittently as a journalist, broker and civil servant but generally lived a sybaritic existence. Though only a few of his poems were privately printed in his lifetime, he was nonetheless celebrated as the greatest Mediterranean poet of modern times. His main themes were homosexual love, art and politics. His political poems are set in the Levantine provinces and the East Roman and Byzantine empires. His poetry is devoid of imagery, written in a mixture of demotic and pure Greek that is remarkable for its simultaneous ordinariness and lyrical beauty. *Complete Poems of C.P. Cavafy* (1961) and *Passions and Ancient Days* (1971) were published posthumously. Cavafy is also known as the "poet of the city" in Lawrence DURRELL'S ALEXANDRIA QUARTET.

For further reading:
Robinson, Christopher, *C.P. Cavafy*. New Rochelle, N.Y.: Aristide D. Caratzas, 1990.

Cavallero, Ugo (1880–1943). Italian general. A successful industrialist and an undersecretary of war during the 1920s, Cavallero served as head of Italian forces in West Africa from 1936 to 1937. He headed the Italian campaign in Greece and was appointed chief of the general staff late in 1940. Displeased with a number of defeats Cavallero had suffered in Africa and with his increasing closeness with the Germans, MUSSOLINI replaced him with General Ambrosio in 1943. After Mussolini's fall later that year, Cavallero was arrested on orders from premier Pietro BADOGLIO. He committed suicide on September 12, 1943.

Cavalli-Sforza, Luigi Luca (1922–). Italian geneticist. He was educated at the University of Pavia, where he earned his M.D. in 1944. After working on bacterial genetics at Cambridge (1948–50) and Milan (1950–57), he held chairs in genetics at Parma (1958–62) and Pavia (1962–70). In 1970 he was appointed professor of genetics at Stanford University in California. Cavalli-Sforza specialized mainly in the genetics of human populations. He also did much to show how genetic data from current human racial groups could be used to reconstruct their past separations. This reconstruction, based on the analysis of 58 genes, yields an evolutionary tree with Caucasian and African races in one branch and Orientals, Oceanians and Amerinds in the other. The main division appeared, according to Cavalli-Sforza, some 35,000 to 40,000 years ago.

Cavell, Edith (1865–1915). English nurse. Appointed head of a Brussels hospital in 1907, she remained there after the German occupation in 1914. She was arrested by the Germans in 1915, admitted to aiding Allied soldiers to escape to Holland

Undated photograph of Edith Cavell, a World War I Allied nurse and martyr.

and was executed by firing squad. Her death caused a furor in Great Britain, and was used for anti-German propaganda throughout WORLD WAR I.

Cavite [City of Cavite]. City of the Cavite region on the island of Luzon, the Philippines; site of a U.S. naval base, eight miles across Manila Bay from the capital city. From 1898 to 1941 the city was the main Asiatic naval base of the U.S. Japan controlled it from January 2, 1942, to February 13, 1945. (See also BATAAN PENINSULA; CORREGIDOR.)

Cayman Islands. The Cayman Islands (Grand Cayman, Little Cayman and Cayman Brac) cover a total area of 100 square miles in the Caribbean. Currently a dependent territory of the United Kingdom and a member of the COMMONWEALTH, the islands were a dependency of JAMAICA until 1962. Administered by a governor (currently, A.J. Scott) and a partially elected executive council, the islands are noted for their offshore banking and financial services, which developed in the 1960s and 1970s.

CBS. American TELEVISION and RADIO network, one of the three major broadcasting networks in the U.S. The company was founded in New York in 1927 by impresario Arthur JUDSON as United Independent Broadcasters, Inc. In 1929 William S. PALEY bought a controlling interest in the company. During the GREAT DEPRESSION, the CBS radio network broadcast a wide variety of programs, including radio dramas, serials, comedy and variety shows and news. During WORLD WAR II the network broadcast regular reports from Britain by Edward R. MURROW, perhaps the most famous of all broadcast journalists. Murrow brought other distinguished journalists into the broadcast medium via CBS; after the war he originated such documentary programs as "Hear It Now" and SEE IT NOW on the network.

CBS made a successful transition into television broadcasting in the postwar era. Comedy and variety shows of this period established entertainers like Lucille BALL, Milton BERLE, Jackie GLEASON and Ed SULLIVAN as masters of the new medium. In the 1960s, CBS news was renowned for its coverage of political conventions, the space program and the VIETNAM WAR; anchorman Walter CRONKITE achieved a reputation as perhaps the most trusted man in the U.S. In the 1970s, CBS presented situation comedies with a social message; foremost among these programs were ALL IN THE FAMILY and MASH. Like the other networks, CBS was challenged in the 1980s by the advent of cable television and alternate forms of home entertainment.

Ceausescu, Nicolae (1918–1989). Communist dictator of ROMANIA. Born into a large peasant family, Ceausescu joined the illegal Communist Party youth organization in 1933 and was jailed by King CAROL II's government for his political agitation prior to World War II. After the war he rose rapidly in the now-ruling Communist Party. He became a full member of the Central Committee in 1952 and by 1957 was second only to his mentor, party leader Gheorghe GHEORGHIU-DEJ. Upon the death of Gheorghiu-Dej (1965), Ceausescu became the party's first secretary. In 1968 he assumed the title of president, moved his relatives into important government and party positions and made himself the center of a cult of personality rivaled in Eastern Europe only by the late Soviet leader Joseph STALIN. However, Ceausescu followed a foreign policy independent of the U.S.S.R.; he maintained good relations with ISRAEL, condemned the SOVIET INVASION OF CZECHOSLOVAKIA and did not join the East-bloc boycott of the 1984 summer OLYMPIC GAMES. Ceausescu's maverick stance irritated the Kremlin but gained him favor among both Western and developing nations.

Romanian dictator Nicolae Ceausescu before his overthrow (1985).

While he was feted abroad, many Romanians regarded him as a ruthless tyrant. As Romania's economy faltered in the late 1980s, Ceausescu pressed ahead with grandiose, disastrous schemes. He created severe shortages at home with the wholesale export of food and fuel to pay off Romania's foreign debt. He destroyed many rural villages and forcibly displaced their populations to make way for agricultural-industrial complexes that were never built. He steadily opposed any reforms in Romania, as communist governments began to topple elsewhere in Eastern Europe. After a massacre of unarmed protesters in Timisoara (Dec. 17, 1989), armed rebellion broke out, with much of the army joining the people against the dreaded Securitate, Ceausescu's elite paramilitary secret police. Ceausescu and his wife fled the presidential palace on December 22 but were apprehended the following day. A tribunal of the provisional government tried and convicted the couple of genocide, abuse of power, undermining the economy and theft of government funds; they were executed on Dec. 25.

Cecil, (Lord Edward Christian) David (Gascoyne) (1902–1986). British biographer and literary critic. Cecil was educated at Eton and Christ Church, Oxford, where from 1948 until 1969 he was Goldsmith's Professor of English Literature. An eminent man of letters, Cecil is known for his balanced, thoughtful biographies that are at once scholarly and accessible to the average reader. His first, *Stricken Deer* (1929), was a life of the poet William Cowper, who suffered bouts of severe depression. Other of Cecil's many works include *The Young Melbourn* (1939); its sequel, *Lord M* (1950); *A Portrait of Jane Austen* (1978); and *A Portrait of Charles Lamb* (1983).

Cecil, (Edgar Algernon) Robert (Gascoyne) [Viscount Cecil of Chelwood] (1864–1958). British statesman. A son of the Marquess of Salisbury, Cecil was educated at Eton and Oxford and became a London barrister. A Conservative, he was elected to Parliament in 1906 and became known for his progressive views on free trade, women's suffrage and internationalism. During WORLD WAR I he was active with the International Committee of the RED CROSS. In 1919 he and U.S. President Woodrow WILSON drafted the Covenant of the LEAGUE OF NATIONS. In 1923 he was created a viscount. Cecil remained a leading figure in the League until it dissolved in 1946. For his League work, Cecil was awarded the 1937 NOBEL PRIZE for peace. His autobiography, *All the Way*, was published in 1949.

Celan, Paul [Paul Antschel] (1920–1970). German poet. Celan was born in a German-speaking area of ROMANIA and largely educated there. In 1942, his Jewish parents were deported to a CONCENTRATION CAMP, but he managed to escape. In 1948, he immigrated to Paris, eventually becoming a French citizen. His poems began to appear in periodicals in the late 1940s. His second book, *Mohn und Gedachtnis* (*Poppy and Memories*, 1952), established his reputation as an important poet of the HOLOCAUST. His most famous poem, "Todesfugue" ("Death Fugue"), describes the Jewish experience under NAZISM. Its dark images and tragic themes recur throughout his subsequent collections. Readers occasionally find Celan's innovative diction difficult; he described his poetry as "a message in a bottle." In 1960 he received the Georg Buchner Prize. He committed suicide in 1970 at the age of 49.

Celibidache, Sergiu (1912–). Romanian composer and conductor. Celibidache studied in Paris and Berlin, and acted as the permanent conductor of the Berlin Philharmonic Orchestra from 1945 to 1952, introducing many avant-garde works to its repertoire. He later directed the Munich Philharmonic, but rarely appeared with other major orchestras because he insisted on extensive rehearsal time. Because of this and his refusal to make recordings, Celibidache reached a limited audience but became something of a cult figure. He was noted for his discipline, accuracy and finesse, as well as for his eccentric musical theories and his personal elusiveness. His own compositions include four symphonies, a piano concerto and an orchestral suite, *Der Taschengarten*.

Celine, Louis-Ferdinand [pen name of Louis Ferdinand Destouches] (1894–1961). French novelist. Educated at Rennes Medical School, Celine practiced medicine throughout his life in addition to writing, working from 1925 to 1928 at the Rockefeller Foundation in New York. Celine's first novel, *Voyage au bout de la nuit* (1932; translated as *Journey to the End of Night*, 1934), is a sordid story of a ruthless doctor working in the slums following WORLD WAR I. The relentless misanthropy of Celine's work, combined with his later expressions of ANTI-SEMITISM and FASCISM, thwarted much critical or popular praise for it. However, his writing is nightmarishly evocative, and his powerful use of language has been praised. His writing has been likened to that of James JOYCE and Marcel PROUST and compared to the paintings of Goya and Dürer. Others of his many novels include *Mort a credit* (1936; translated as *Death on the Installment Plan*, 1938); *Ballet sans personne, sans musique, sans rien*, ("A Ballet Without Anyone, Without Music, Without Anything," 1959), and *Nord* ("North," 1960).

Celler, Emanuel (1888–1981). American politician. A Democrat from New York, Celler served in the U.S. House of Representatives for half a century (1922–72). Known for his liberal views, he chaired the influential House Judiciary Committee for a record 22 years (1949–53, 1955–72). He supported key programs of the NEW DEAL and the FAIR DEAL and opposed the HOUSE UN-AMERICAN ACTIVITIES COMMITTEE. He was credited with authoring and handling the passage of the landmark CIVIL RIGHTS ACTS of 1957, 1960 and 1964. He also left his mark on major antitrust, labor and immigration legislation. He gained a reputation as a combative, colorful debater.

Celles. Village and battlefield in southwest BELGIUM. During WORLD WAR II, it was the deepest penetration achieved by the German counteroffensive of December 1944, which was known as the BATTLE OF THE BULGE.

Cendrars, Blaise [pen name of Frederic Sauser-Hall] (1887–1961). French novelist and poet. Cendrars was born, educated and died in Paris; he first ran away from home at the age of 15. He traveled to Siberia, Panama, China, Persia, Mongolia and America and visited most of Europe, working variously as a film maker, journalist, art critic, horticulturist and businessman. His semi-autobiographical works feature resilient heroes, rich images and striking effects. During WORLD WAR I he served with the French Foreign Legion. His best-known works include *L'Or* (1925; tr. *Sutter's Gold*, 1926), *L'Homme foudroye* (1945; tr. *The Astonished Man*, 1970) and *Le Panama; ou Les Aventures de mon sept oncles* (1918; tr. *Panama; or The Adventures of My Seven Uncles*, 1931). His poetry, which influenced APOLLINAIRE, includes *Dix-neuf poemes elastiques* (1919) and *Du monde entier* (1919).

Central African Empire. Formal name of the CENTRAL AFRICAN REPUBLIC during the period from December 1976 to September 1979. This name was proclaimed by the country's self-styled emperor, Jean-Bedel BOKASSA, who was overthrown in 1979.

Central African Federation. A British attempt to protect the interests of the white minority population and to encourage economic development by uniting the African territories of Nyasaland, Northern Rhodesia and Southern Rhodesia. The federation was established on September 3, 1953. Unpopular with the predominantly black population, it collapsed in 1963.

Central African Republic. Landlocked country in Africa, bordered by Chad to the north, Sudan to the east, Zaire and the Congo Republic to the south and Cameroon to the west. At the end of the 19th century, the French occupied the CAR and organized it as the colony of Ubangi-Shari. In 1906 Chad was linked with the colony, and in 1910 the two were joined with Congo and Gabon to form FRENCH EQUATORIAL AFRICA. Despite occasional rebellions, the CAR supported the French RESISTANCE forces in WORLD WAR II. Following the war, a rebellion forced the French to allow the establishment of a territorial government and parliament. In 1958 the CAR took its current name and voted to become an indepen-

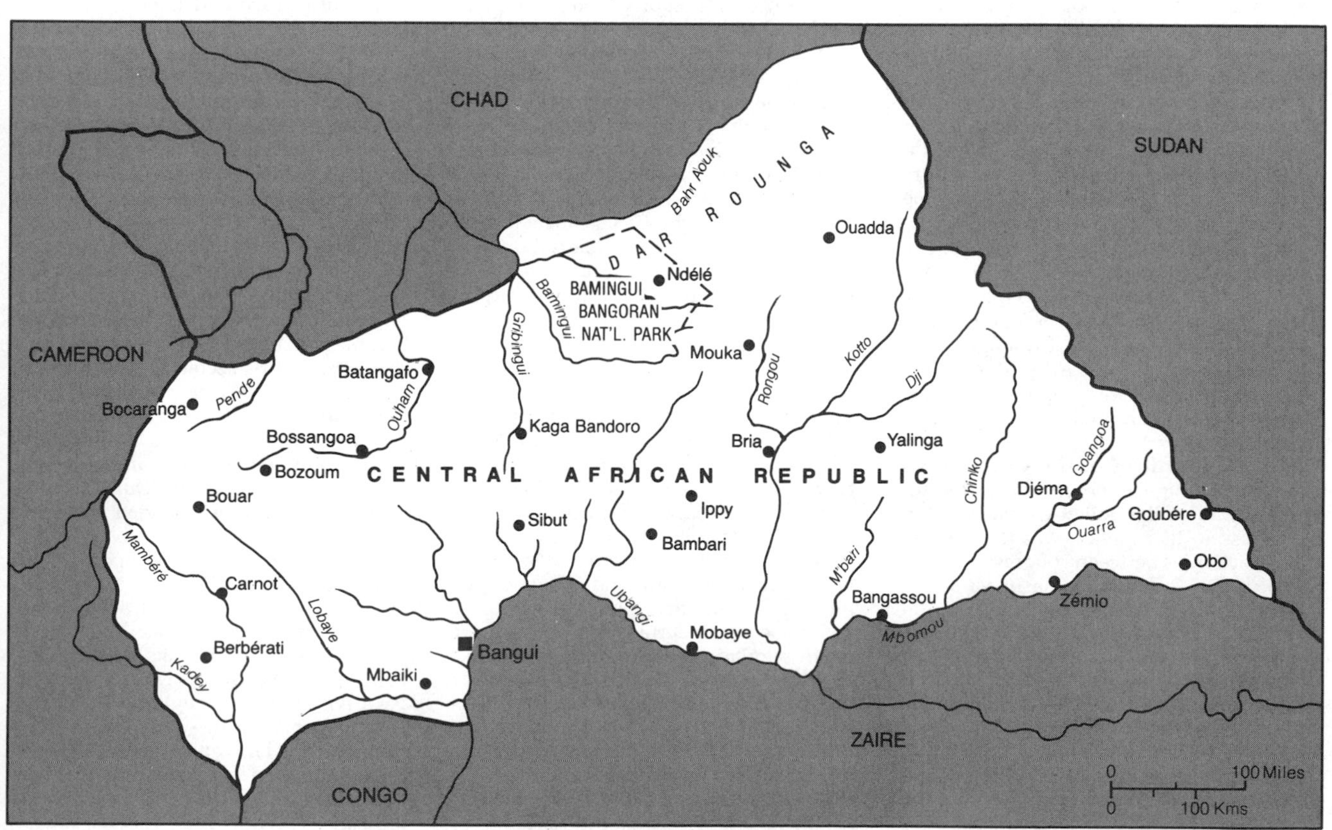

CENTRAL AFRICAN REPUBLIC

CENTRAL AFRICAN REPUBLIC (CAR)

1911	France secures complete control.
1960	(Aug. 13) CAR achieves full independence with David Dacko as president.
1966	Dacko overthrown by his cousin Col. Jean-Bedel Bokassa.
1977	(Dec. 4) Bokassa spends $20-30 million to have himself crowned emperor in imitation of Napoleon.
1979	Amnesty International charges Bokassa in the massacre of 80 school children.
1979	(Sept.) With the aid of French paratroopers, Bokassa is exiled and Dacko is restored to the presidency.
1986	(Oct.) Bokassa escapes from France and returns to CAR expecting an enthusiastic reception; captured and sentenced to life imprisonment.

dent republic of France. Barthelemy Boganda, a founder of the Movement for the Social Evolution of Black Africa (MESAN), became its first prime minister. Upon his death in an airplane accident in 1969, his nephew, David DACKO, assumed power, becoming president in 1960 when the CAR achieved complete independence. In December 1965 Dacko was ousted by a military coup, and Colonel Jean-Bedel BOKASSA took power. Bokassa established himself as president-for-life in 1972, Marshal of the Republic in 1974 and, in an ostentatious and expensive ceremony in 1976, Emperor of the Central African Empire. Bokassa's increasingly brutal and repressive regime achieved worldwide notoriety in 1979 when government troops murdered approximately 100 schoolchildren who had protested mandatory school uniforms made by a Bokassa family company. Dacko reassumed power in a bloodless coup later that year and restored the republic. In 1981 yet another coup deposed Dacko, and army chief of staff General Andre Kolingba took power. Kolingba's regime voided the constitution and banned political parties. Opposition to the regime received some French support, and French president MITTERRAND visited the country to influence Kolingba. There was some evidence of a loosening of Kolingba's autocratic control of the CAR in 1985, when a new constitution was proposed and some civilians were admitted into the government.

Central Committee of the Communist Party. The highest organ of the COMMUNIST PARTY of the Soviet Union between congresses. Its function was to direct all party activities between congresses. From 1917 to 1934, it acted as a quasi-parliament. In order to free himself from dependency on majority support in the central committee, STALIN liquidated 70% of the members between the 17th and 18th party congresses (1934–39). During the period of "collective leadership" after Stalin's death, leaders again had to win the support of the various factions of the central committee. Wider in scope than the Supreme Soviet, the central committee was the main tool of the government until the late 1980s, when GORBACHEV began to alter the Soviet system of government.

Central Executive Committee. From 1917 to 1936, the executive organ of the congresses of Soviets of workers' and soldiers' deputies. It was elected at the first congress of Soviets in July 1917. In 1922, following the formation of the U.S.S.R., there were all-union and also republic central executive committees. The chairmen of the committees acted as the heads of state. As a result of the STALIN constitution of 1936, the role of the central executive committee was bestowed on the Supreme Soviet and its Presidium.

Central Intelligence Agency [CIA]. U.S. government agency established in 1947 to coordinate and analyze foreign intelligence. The CIA reports to the U.S. president, to whom alone it is responsible. Under the directorship of Allen DULLES in the 1950s, the CIA moved into more active involvement in foreign affairs, initiating a series of "covert operations" designed to eliminate anti-American interests in such countries as GUATEMALA and IRAN. The 1961 BAY OF PIGS debacle forced a reassessment of the CIA's function, and subsequent scandals and alleged domestic civil rights abuses led to further calls for accountability and reform. Despite criticism, the agency maintained its controversial dual role of overseas intelligence source and coercive arm for American interests.

Central Powers. The nations that fought against the Allies in WORLD WAR I. They included Germany, Austria-Hungary, the Ottoman Empire (Turkey) and Bulgaria.

Century of Progress Exhibition. Chicago World's Fair of 1933–34; a major showcase of both ART DECO and MODERNISM in architecture and industrial design. Its role as the first publicly accessible showcase for modernist directions was of major significance. Although it occurred at a low point in the GREAT DEPRESSION, the Century of Progress Exhibition included many elements pointing toward future optimism. Architecturally, the fair leaned on established figures. Also present were many more adventurous, smaller projects such as the *House of Tomorrow,* a steel-and-glass octagon complete with airplane hangar for the predicted family plane. Buckminster FULLER's DYMAXION automobile and the Burlington Zephyr railroad train were first seen at this fair. Critics from the historicist Ralph Adams CRAM to the still-controversial modernist Frank Lloyd WRIGHT tended to offer negative comments, finding the fair either too advanced or not advanced enough.

Cerf, Bennett (1898–1971). American publisher. Born in New York City, he was a lifelong resident; he founded the publishing companies Modern Library (1925) and Random House (1927), where he served as president until 1966. Involved in censorship issues, he fought in the courts to publish James JOYCE's *Ulysses* in the U.S., succeeding in 1933. A witty and punning commentator, he wrote a variety of newspaper columns and several books, but became a recognized public figure in the U.S. through his regular appearances on the television show "What's My Line?" (1952–66).

Cernan, Eugene (1934–). U.S. astronaut. Neil ARMSTRONG had been the first astronaut to walk on the moon. Eugene Cernan is the last—to date. Along with fellow crewman geologist Harrison SCHMITT, Cernan spent more than 22 hours on the moon, while the third member of the Apollo 17 (December 7–19, 1972) crew, Ronald Evans, orbited overhead. Humankind's last official words from the moon lacked much poetry but were simple and heartfelt. Cernan said, "As we leave the Moon at Taurus-Littrow, we leave as we came and, God willing, as we shall return, with peace and hope for all mankind. God bless the crew of Apollo 17." In his two previous space flights, Cernan had been pilot of Gemini 9–A (June 3–6, 1966) and lunar module pilot of Apollo 10 (May 18–26, 1969), which had flown to within 10 miles of the moon in a test flight. A former Navy pilot, Cernan resigned from NASA to enter private industry.

Cernik, Oldrich (1921–). Prime minister of CZECHOSLOVAKIA (1968–70). Cernik held various posts in the Communist Party and government from 1948 to 1968. He became associated with Alexander DUBCEK, who as first secretary introduced reform programs. (See PRAGUE SPRING.) After the SOVIET INVASION OF CZECHOSLOVAKIA in 1968, Cernik continued in office until 1970, when, along with many other progressives associated with Dubcek, he resigned and was suspended from the Communist party.

Cernuda, Luis (1904–1963). Spanish poet. Cernuda was born in Seville and studied at its university with Pedro Salinas. A member of the GENERATION OF 1927, he was associated with GARCIA LORCA, ALBERTI and ALEIXANDRE. During the SPANISH CIVIL WAR, he fought with the Loyalists; after 1938 he went into exile in England, the U.S. and Mexico, where he took up permanent residence in 1952. *Perfil del aire* (1927, *The Air in Profile*), *Un rio, un amor* (1929, *A River, a Love*) and *Los placeres prohibidos* (1931, *Forbidden Plea-*

sures) show the influence of Symbolism and SURREALISM; *Donde habite el olvido* (1934, *Where Forgetfulness Dwells*) was inspired by his reading of Holderlin. His collected poems, *La realidad y el deseo* (1936, 1940, 1958, 1964, *Reality and Desire*), run a gamut of styles from traditionalism to free verse. His poetry is also notable for its frank homosexual themes.

Cesaire, Aime Ferdinand (1913–). West Indian poet, dramatist and essayist. Though born in poverty in Martinique, in 1931 Cesaire went to Paris to study. At the Sorbonne he specialized in Latin, Greek and French literature. There he met the poet Leopold Sedar SENGHOR, later president of Senegal; together they formed the group known as the NEGRITUDE poets. The negritude movement was based on a revitalization of black and African culture and a rejection of the rationalism of Western white society. After his return to Martinique in the late 1930s, Cesaire met Andre BRETON, then a refugee from occupied France, and was influenced to write Surrealist poetry to free himself from conventional "white" language (see SURREALISM). In the 1950s and 1960s he wrote plays on the theme of black liberation, including *Une Saison au Congo* (*A Season in the Congo*, 1967), based on the struggle of Patrice LUMUMBA.

Cesca chair. Design classic of the BAUHAUS era by Marcel BREUER. This metal tube cantilever design was derived from various prototypes of a year or two before. Mart Stam developed a similar design as early as 1926, which resulted in bitter debate over credit for origination of the design concept. As it is now produced, the Cesca chair, with or without arms, is clearly Breuer's design. Its popularity and broad acceptance in modern contexts are a tribute to the long life of a design that was originally ahead of its time.

Cessna, Clyde Vernon (1879–1954). U.S. aircraft manufacturer. He built the first cantilever airplane and in 1927 founded the Cessna Airplane Company in Wichita, Kansas. The company supplied some of the first commercial passenger planes to an early airline, the **Curtiss Flying Service** (see Glenn CURTISS). The company was famous for its small single-engine aircraft sold to recreational flyers and businesses.

Ceylonese Rebellion of 1971. Sirimavo BANDARANAIKE, widow of independent Ceylon's first prime minister, became leader of the Sri Lanka Freedom Party (SLFP) upon his assassination in 1958. In 1960 she became prime minister, heading a strongly leftist, pro-Sinhalese government. After being out of power from 1965, she again became prime minister in 1970, heading a coalition of the SLFP and Marxist parties. The extreme left, impatient for reform, attempted a takeover of Columbo, the capital, and other cities (April–May, 1971). Ceylon received military aid from the U.S.S.R., India, Pakistan and Britain, suppressing the rebels in the cities and then by mid-June in the rural areas. In 1972 Mrs. Bandaranaike proclaimed a republic, a new constitution and a new name for the country: SRI LANKA, meaning "resplendent land" in Sinhalese, language of the majority.

Chabrol, Claude (1930–). French film director. Chabrol first earned recognition as a film critic who contributed to the renowned journal CAHIERS DU CINEMA in the 1950s. With Eric ROHMER, a fellow critic who would also go on to achieve fame as a director, Chabrol wrote *Hitchcock* (1957), which examined the work of American director Alfred HITCHCOCK from a moral perspective. Chabrol's directorial debut, *Le Beau Serge* (1959), is considered to be the first film of the French cinematic New Wave that also included Alain RESNAIS and Francois TRUFFAUT. Chabrol's wife, the French actress Stephane Audran, frequently stars in his films. Chabrol is a versatile director whose work ranges from light comedies to intensive examinations of bourgeois morality. Other films by Chabrol include *Killer!* (1969), *Ten Day's Wonder* (1971) and *Nada* (1974).

Chaco Boreal. Region of South America, in the fork of the Paraguay and Pilcomayo rivers. Located primarily in northwest Paraguay, this 100,000-square-mile area was long disputed by BOLIVIA and PARAGUAY. In December 1928 Paraguay attacked Bolivia, and the fighting lasted until 1935. In 1938 a peace treaty was signed that gave the larger section to Paraguay and a small, western section to Bolivia.

Chaco War (1932–35). Paraguayan ownership of the GRAN CHACO region was long disputed by Bolivia, which sought an outlet to the Atlantic. In 1928 there was sporadic fighting between the countries. After launching a major offensive, Paraguay declared war on May 10, 1933. The larger Bolivian army seized northern and central parts of the Chaco, precipitating Paraguayan mobilization in defense of its homeland. In a major offensive led by Colonel Jose Felix Estagarribia (1888–1940), Paraguayan forces recaptured most of the Chaco in 1934 and advanced into eastern Bolivia in early 1935 before being pushed back. The U.S. and five South American nations arranged a truce on June 12, 1935. The two nations signed the **Treaty of Buenos Aires** (July 21, 1938) giving Paraguay most of the Chaco but granting Bolivian access to the Atlantic.

Chad. Central North African country, bounded to the north by Libya, to the east by Sudan, to the south by the Central African Republic and to the west by Cameroon, Nigeria and Niger; capital is Ndjamena, formerly called Fort-Lamy. The French began exploring the region late in the 19th century. In 1913, Chad became a part of FRENCH EQUATORIAL AFRICA; in 1958 it became an autonomous state, with Francois Tombalbaye as its prime minister. In 1960, Chad gained full independence, and Tombalbaye became the first president. Since independence, Chad has been torn by disputes between the Muslim north, which aligns itself with the Arab nations, and the Christian south. As early as 1963, the northern, Libya-backed Chadian National Liberation Front (Frolinat) began a violent revolt, quelled in 1968 with military assistance from the French. In 1975 Tombalbaye was killed during a coup led by Felix Malloum, a former army chief of staff. Malloum became president, but his government was still threatened by Frolinat. In an effort to achieve unity, Malloum named Hisseme Habre, a former leader of Frolinat, as prime minister in 1978, but the two could not reconcile their differences.

Meanwhile, LIBYA had occupied a Chadian border area known as the Aouzou Strip—thought to contain uranium—and continued its backing of Frolinat, which had increased the territory under its influence through the leadership of General Goukouni Oueddei. In 1979, intense fighting forced Malloum to leave the country. A provisional government (GUNT) established Oueddei as president, with the approval of Libya. Meanwhile, Habre and the Army of the North (FAN) continued to oppose the Libya-backed government, and in 1980 civil war broke out. The Organization for African Unity (OAU) intervened and set up a peacekeeping force. Libyan troops withdrew, Habre and FAN gained control and Oueddei fled to the north. In 1983, the OAU recognized Habre's regime, but Libyan-backed Oueddei still fought. Habre received 3,000 French "instructor" troops and American financial aid and arms. A 1983 ceasefire divided the country in half between north and south.

In 1984, Libya's Colonel QADDAFI proposed that all foreign troops withdraw from Chad. France did so, but some Libyan forces remained in the north. By 1985 fighting had again intensified between the two factions. In 1986, there was a rift between Qaddafi and Oueddei, whose forces defected. Habre, with French assistance, retaliated against the Libyans; in 1987, France, Chad and Libya agreed to another ceasefire called for by the OAU.

Chadwick, Bill (1915–). American hockey figure. A native New Yorker, Chadwick (affectionately known as The Big Whistle) had an enormous impact on the Canadian game as a referee. Chadwick refereed for 16 years and, throughout that time, was blind in his right eye. He instituted hand signals on the part of officials, so that spectators were aware of calls as they were being made, and was responsible for many other innovations. The only man to be inducted into both the American and Canadian Hockey halls of fame, he is also the only official to ever be honored with a "night." He went on to a successful career as a hockey commentator with the New York Rangers.

Chadwick, Sir James (1891–1974). British physicist. Chadwick was educated at the University of Manchester, where he graduated in 1911 and remained as a graduate student under Ernest RUTHERFORD. In 1913 he went to Leipzig to work under Hans GEIGER. In 1914 he was interned near Spandau as an enemy alien. There he remained for the duration of the war, cold and hungry but permitted, with

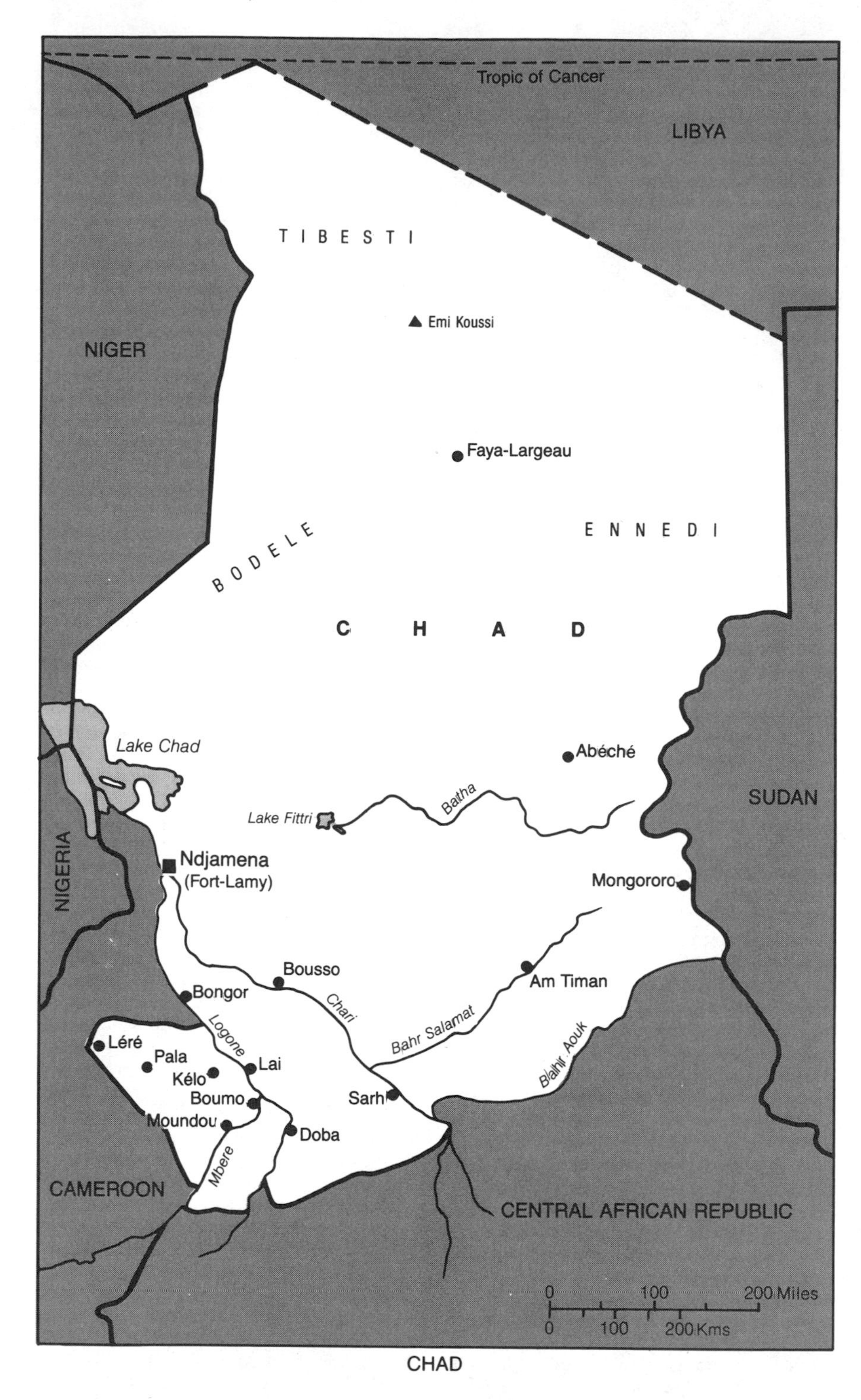

CHAD

the help of Walther Nernst, to carry out rudimentary research. On his return to England in 1919 he was invited by Rutherford to Cambridge University, where he served as assistant director of research at the Cavendish Laboratory (1922–35). In 1932 Chadwick made his greatest discovery—the neutron. Before this, physicists had accepted the existence of only two elementary particles: the proton (p) with a positive charge and the electron (e) with a negative charge. All physicists recognized that these two particles could not account for the atomic phenomena observed. In 1920 Rutherford had introduced the possibility of "an atom of mass 1 which has zero nuclear charge." Chadwick attempted unsuccessfully to discover such a particle in the 1920s by bombarding aluminum with alpha particles (helium nuclei). More promising, however, was the report in 1930 that the bombardment of beryllium with alpha particles yielded a very penetrating radiation. In 1932 Irene and Frederic JOLIOT-CURIE found that this radiation could eject protons with considerable velocities from matter containing hydrogen. They thought such radiation consisted of gamma rays—electromagnetic radiation of very short wavelength. Chadwick showed that the gamma rays would not eject protons but that the result was explained if the particles had nearly the same mass as protons but no charge—neutrons. It was for this work that Chadwick was awarded the 1935 NOBEL PRIZE for physics. In 1935 Chadwick accepted the offer of the chair of physics at Liverpool University. There he built Britain's first cyclotron and was on hand at the outbreak of World War II to support the claims made by Otto Frisch and Rudolph Peierls on the feasibility of the ATOMIC BOMB. Chadwick consequently spent most of the war in the U.S. as head of the British mission to the MANHATTAN PROJECT. For this service he was knighted in 1945. He returned to Cambridge in 1958 as master of Gonville and Caius College, an office he held until his retirement in 1958.

Chadwick, Lynn (1914–). English sculptor. Trained as an architect, Chadwick worked in architecture until the outbreak of WORLD WAR II, when he became a pilot in the Royal Air Force. After the war he turned to sculpture, at first producing mobiles influenced by Alexander CALDER. He had his first one-man show in 1950. Around 1955 he began to create stationary figures whose roughly textured surfaces are welded of iron, steel, copper or bronze. These brooding abstract pieces are built on geometric forms and suggest totemic personages. His later work maintains an angular menace while making more direct references to human and animal forms.

Chafee, Zechariah, Jr. (1885–1957). U.S. legal scholar. A graduate of Harvard, Chafee taught at the Harvard Law School as a professor for 40 years, beginning in 1916. Noted for his advocacy of civil liberties, he wrote *Freedom of Speech* (1920), an extended version of which became a leading text of U.S. libertarian philosophy. He was considered a leading authority on equity and unfair business competition.

Chaffee, Roger (1935–1967). U.S. astronaut. America's first space tragedy took place on January 27, 1967, when Chaffee, Edward WHITE and Gus GRISSOM were killed in a flash-fire aboard the APOLLO 1 spacecraft while training for the first manned Apollo flight. The mission would have been Chaffee's first space flight. He had received a B.S. in aeronautical engineering from Purdue University and was an experienced pilot who had logged nearly 2,300 hours of flying time. As a member of Heavy Photographic Squadron 62, he had flown photo-reconnaissance missions over Cuba during the CUBAN MISSILE CRISIS of 1962.

Chagall, Marc [born Moyshe Shagall] (1887–1985). Russian-born artist. Born into a poor orthodox Jewish family in czarist RUSSIA, Chagall became one of the most famous artists of the 20th century. He moved to Paris in 1910 thanks to a rich patron and, during his four years there, produced a series of paintings that marked him as a forerunner of SURREALISM. He returned to Russia in 1922, and briefly held the post-revolutionary position of cultural commissioner before returning to France (1922), where he lived for most of his life. His subject matter was drawn largely from Jewish life and folklore, with flowers, birds and animals among his favorite motifs. In addition to producing numerous easel paintings and a great many theatrical designs and book illustrations, he created some of the best known public art of the century.

Chain, Ernst Boris (1906–1979). German-British biochemist. Chain graduated in 1930 from the Friedrich-Wilhelm University with a degree in chemistry. He left Germany for England in 1933 and, after two years' research at Cambridge University, joined Howard Florey at Oxford. There his brilliance as a biochemist was put to good use in the difficult isolation and purification of PENICILLIN—work Alexander FLEMING had been unable to carry out. He shared the 1945 NOBEL PRIZE for physiology or medicine with Florey and Fleming for this work. After 1945 he was professor of biochemistry at the Superior Institute of Health in Rome, returning to England in 1961 for the chair of biochemistry at Imperial College, London. During this time he discovered penicillinase, an enzyme that some bacteria can synthesize and so destroy the drug.

Chakravarti Rajagopalachari, Rajaji (1878–1972). Indian political leader. He joined Mohandas K. GANDHI's nonviolent movement against British rule in 1919. After INDIA gained independence (1947), he served as the country's first governor-general (1948–50). He split with the CONGRESS PARTY and formed his own Swatantra Party in 1959. In 1971, at the age of 92, he organized a right-wing coalition to oppose Indira K. GANDHI but was defeated. Upon his death, the government declared a seven-day period of mourning.

Chaliapin, Feodor (1873–1938). Russian singer. Acclaimed for his beautiful basso voice and electrifying acting, Chaliapin became the first Russian singer to gain international stature. While with Mamontov's Opera in Moscow (1896–98), he was the premier interpreter of such roles in the Russian repertory as Ivan the Terrible in Rimsky-Korsakov's opera of the same name. Chaliapin first achieved fame outside Russia as Boris in Serge DIAGHILEV's production of *Boris Godunov* (1908). This became his most famous role; as a result of his exciting performances as Boris the opera was included in the standard repertory of many companies. He triumphed as Boris at the Metropolitan Opera in New York City (1921) and appeared with the company until 1929. He also made several classic recordings, toured the U.S. in recital and made a world tour in 1926. Other outstanding roles included Mephistofeles in both Gounod's *Faust* and Boito's *Mephistofele,* and the title role in Massenet's *Don Quichotte,* which he first created in 1910.

Opera singer Feodor Chaliapin (1924).

For further reading:

Borovsky, Victor, *Chaliapin: A Critical Biography.* New York: Knopf, 1988.

Challe, Maurice (1905–1979). A career army officer, Challe served as chief of staff of the French armed forces (1955), commander in chief of French forces in ALGERIA (1958–60) and commander of the European Sector of NATO (1960–61). He led the unsuccessful coup attempt against French President Charles DE GAULLE in 1961, for which he was sentenced to 15 years in prison. He was subsequently pardoned. (See also ALGERIAN WAR OF 1954–62; ORGANIZATION DE L'ARMEE SECRETE.)

***Challenger* disaster.** January 28, 1986, explosion of the U.S. space shuttle *Challenger,* with the loss of all seven astronauts aboard. The *Challenger* exploded 74 seconds after it was launched from Cape Canaveral, Florida, on its 10th mission. The disaster was witnessed by a crowd of ground observers and by millions of people watching on television. The launch had been highly publicized because one of the crew, Christa MCAULIFFE, was a high school teacher who had been selected as the first citizen-in-space. The disaster—the first time U.S. astronauts had been killed on a space mission—stunned the nation and resulted in the grounding of all manned missions for two years. A presidential commission comprised of current and former astronauts as well as distinguished scientists and public figures was appointed to investigate the tragedy. The investigation revealed that NASA had disregarded many safety considerations because of pressure to maintain the launching schedule. It also concluded that the explosion had been caused when hydrogen leaked through a faulty seal in one of the booster rocket joints.

Chamberlain, Sir (Joseph) Austen (1863–1937). British political leader. Son of Joseph CHAMBERLAIN and half-brother of Neville CHAMBERLAIN. A Conservative, he was elected to Parliament for the first time in 1892. Chamberlain served in a number of important posts, including chancellor of the exchequer (1903–05 and 1919–21), secretary of state for India (1915–17), member of the war cabinet under LLOYD GEORGE (1918–19) and lord privy seal (1921–22). He became leader of the CONSERVATIVE PARTY in 1921. As foreign secretary under Stanley BALDWIN from 1924 to 1929, he was instrumental in the creation of the LOCARNO PACT in 1925, a year in which he was knighted and awarded the NOBEL PRIZE for peace (along with U.S. Vice President Charles G. DAWES). Chamberlain remained an important member of Parliament until his death.

Chamberlain, Houston Stewart (1855–1927). Anglo-German writer. Son of a British admiral, he settled in Germany, marrying the daughter of composer Richard Wagner (1908) and becoming a naturalized German citizen (1916). His best-known work, *The Foundations of the Nineteenth Century* (1899), became one of the 20th century's most influential racist polemics. In it, Chamberlain celebrated the so-called Aryan race and vilified the JEWS. The book was important in shaping the thought of Adolf HITLER and other Nazi leaders.

Chamberlain, (Arthur) Neville (1869–1940). British statesman, prime minister (1937–40). Son of Joseph CHAMBERLAIN and half-brother of Sir Austen CHAMBERLAIN. A successful Birmingham businessman, he became the city's mayor from 1915 to 1916. Elected a Conservative member of Parliament in 1918, he was chancellor of the exchequer (1923 and 1931–37) and minister of health (1923 and

British Prime Minister Neville Chamberlain returns from a meeting with Hitler at Berchtesgaden, hopeful that England may be safe from German aggression (1938).

1924–29). An able administrator, he initiated a number of reforms in social services, helped to systemize local government and aided in the rebuilding of Britain's economy in the late 1930s. His domestic successes led to his appointment as prime minister in 1937, but he was ill-prepared to cope with the foreign crises that soon engulfed him. Faced with the aggression of Adolf HITLER, Chamberlain opted for negotiation and followed a policy of APPEASEMENT, signing the MUNICH PACT in 1938 and proclaiming "peace in our time." With the continuation of German advances in 1939, Chamberlain altered his views and led his nation into WORLD WAR II. After the German occupation of Norway in 1940, he was forced to resign and Sir Winston CHURCHILL succeeded him as prime minister. He served as lord president of the council in Churchill's coalition cabinet until shortly before his death.

Chamberlain, Owen (1920–). American physicist. The son of a prominent radiologist, Chamberlain followed his father's interest in physics. He graduated from Dartmouth College in 1941 and earned his doctorate in physics from the University of Chicago in 1949. From 1948 until 1950 he was an instructor in physics at the University of California at Berkeley becoming associate professor in 1954 and professor in 1958. WORLD WAR II interrupted his university studies, and he spent the years 1942–46 under the leadership of Emilio Segre working on the MANHATTAN PROJECT at LOS ALAMOS. There he investigated spontaneous fission of the heavy elements and nuclear cross sections. Later he worked with Enrico FERMI on neutron diffraction by liquids. At Berkeley, Chamberlain experimented with the bevatron particle accelerator of the Lawrence Radiation Laboratory, and in 1955 (with Segre, C. Weigand and T. Ypsilantis) discovered the antiproton. For their discovery Chamberlain and Segre received the 1959 NOBEL PRIZE for physics. Chamberlain's later work was on the interaction of antiprotons with hydrogen and deuterium, the production of antineutrons from antiprotons and the scattering of pions.

Chamberlain, Wilt(on Norman) (1936–). American basketball player. An outstanding offensive center even in high school, Chamberlain was recruited by scores of colleges before deciding on the University of Kansas in 1956. He left the school after only two years, and signed on with the Harlem Globetrotters. He played 16 years in the pros: with the Warriors in both Philadelphia and San Francisco (1959–65), the Philadelphia 76ers (1965–68) and the Los Angeles Lakers (1968–73). In 1962, while with the Warriors, he became the only NBA player to score 100 points in a single game. In later years his defensive and playmaking skills caught up with his offense, and he came to be regarded as one of the game's greatest players, He retired in 1973 with career totals of 31,419 points scored and a game point average of 30.1. He published his

Basketball great Wilt Chamberlain.

biography *Just Like Any Other 7–Foot Black Millionaire Who Lives Next Door* in 1973 and was named to the Basketball Hall of Fame in 1978.

Chamberlin, Thomas Chrowder (1843–1928). American geologist. Chamberlin came from a farming background. His discovery of fossils in a local limestone quarry aroused his interest in geology, which he pursued at the University of Michigan. From 1881 until 1904 he was in charge of the glacial division of the U.S. Geological Survey. After a period as president of the University of Wisconsin (1887–92), he became professor of geology at the University of Chicago (1892–1918). Apart from his work on geological surveys, Chamberlin's most significant work was in the field of glaciation. Early work on glaciation had assumed that there had been one great ice age, but James Geikie collected evidence that there had been several ice ages separated by nonglacial epochs. Chamberlin went on to establish four major ice ages, named the Nebraskan, Kansan, Illinoian, and Wisconsin after the states in which they were most easily studied. Together with the astronomer Forest Moulton, in 1906, Chamberlin formulated the planetismal hypothesis on the origin of the planets in the solar system. Chamberlin and Moultin supposed that a star had passed close to the sun causing matter to be pulled out of both. Within the gravitational field of the Sun, this gaseous matter would condense into small planetismals and eventually into planets. The theory was published in *The Two Solar Families* (1928), but it has little support today as it cannot account for the distribution of angular momentum in the solar system.

Chambers, Whittaker. See HISS-CHAMBERS CASE.

Chaminade, Cecile (Louise Stephanie) (1857–1944). French composer and pianist. Chaminade was one of the most esteemed pianists of her era and was especially popular for her moving performances of salon pieces. As a youth, she studied piano in Paris under Benjamin Godard. Her compositions include *Les Amazones,* a lyric symphony for orchestra and chorus, as well as other orchestral works and solo pieces for the piano. In her later years, Chaminade performed frequently in Britain, where she became a special favorite of concert audiences.

Chamonix [Chamonix-Mont-Blanc]. Town in the Haute-Savoie department of eastern France, in the French Alps, at the foot of Mont Blanc. A favored year-round resort and winter skiing center, it is a base for the ascent of Mont Blanc and is close to Mer de Glace, a glacier on the northern bank of the mountain. It is here that the world's highest cable car scales 12,605 feet; beneath Mont Blanc an automobile tunnel joins France with the village of Courmayeur, Italy. The winter OLYMPICS were held in the Chamonix Valley in 1924.

Chamorro, Violeta Barrios de (1930–). President of NICARAGUA (1990–). Born into an upper-class Nicaraguan family, Chamorro married Pedro Joaquin Chamorro Cardenal in 1950, who became a newspaper publisher and a guerilla fighter during the rule of the SOMOZA family. He was assassinated in 1978. Chamorro was later a publisher of *La Prensa* and a member of the junta that took power in Nicaragua after the Sandinista revolution in 1979, but she resigned in 1980 in disagreement with the Sandinistas' increasingly dictatorial policies. Although Chamorro was not a member of any political party, she was chosen by the 14 parties in the National Opposition Union (UNO) as their presidential candidate in 1989, after the Sandanistas agreed to hold free elections. In February 1990 she was elected president with Virgilio Godoy Reyes, a member of the Independent Liberal Party and a former labor minister, as her running mate. Chamorro's surprise upset of the Sandinista regime was widely hailed as a victory for democracy in Nicaragua. However, as president, Chamorro faced considerable political and economic problems. (See also Daniel ORTEGA SAAVEDRA.)

Chamoun, Camille Nimer (1900–1987). Lebanese political leader. A powerful Maronite Christian leader, he was a wealthy businessman, lawyer, parliamentarian and holder of many cabinet posts since 1938. He served as president of LEBANON from 1952 to 1958. At the time of his death, he was finance minister in Lebanon's caretaker cabinet. He was an outspoken critic of SYRIA, the PALESTINE LIBERATION ORGANIZATION and the pro-Iranian Shiite Moslem militia factions. He survived at least three major assassination attempts.

Champassak. Former empire of southern LAOS along the Mekong River. Founded in 1713, it was one of the three Laotian kingdoms. Its western lands were assimilated by Siam (modern THAILAND) in the 19th century. Franco-Siamese treaties re-established the empire in 1904 and 1905. During WORLD WAR II, Thailand repeated its occupation of the western portion, and in 1946 Prince Boun Oum of Champassak abdicated his reigning territorial rights for a united Laos.

Champion, Gower (1919–1980). Broadway stage choreographer, musical director and dancer. Champion began his career in VAUDEVILLE and achieved national prominence in the 1950s for his work with his wife, **Marge Champion,** in television variety shows and HOLLYWOOD film musicals. On Broadway he directed such hits as *Hello, Dolly, Carnival, Bye Bye, Birdie* and *42nd Street*.

Chanak Crisis. Crisis in Anglo-Turkish relations (Sep.-Oct. 1922) arising from Turkey's victory over Greece at Smyrna. Great Britain feared that Turkey, under the leadership of Kemal ATATURK, would attack Allied troops near Constantinople. British Prime Minister LLOYD GEORGE was in favor of reinforcing the British garrison at Chanak (now Canakkale). A convention held on October 12, 1922, between British and Turkish representatives eased the crisis by pledging the return of some European territory to Turkey provided Turkey accepted the neutrality of the Dardanelles and Bosporus; this was the basis of the Treaty of LAUSANNE (1923). The crisis precipitated the fall of Lloyd George's government, when conservative leaders, fearing war as the outcome of his actions, pulled out of Britain's coalition government.

Chance, Britton (1913–). American biophysicist. Chance, an engineer's son, was educated at the University of Pennsylvania where he earned his Ph.D. in 1940 and where, in 1949, he was appointed to the E.R. Johnson Professorship of Biophysics. In 1943 he carried out a spectroscopic analysis that provided firm evidence for the enzyme-substrate complex whose existence biochemists had confidently assumed since the beginning of the century. Chance also contributed to one of the great achievements of modern bio-chemistry, namely the unraveling of the complicated maze through which energy is released at the cellular level. His studies led to a better understanding of how glucose is used in the body.

Chancellor, Sir Christopher John (1904–1989). British journalist and publisher. Chancellor joined Britain's **Reuters** news agency in 1930 and served as a correspondent in China. Returning to London during WORLD WAR II, he was named general manager of Reuters (1944–59) and helped build it into a major international news agency. He later served as chairman of the *Daily Herald* and of Bowater Paper Co. He was knighted in 1951.

Chandigarh. City in northwestern INDIA, 150 miles north of Delhi; capital of Punjab and Haryana. When India was granted independence and divided in 1947, Lahore, formerly the capital of the Punjab, joined with PAKISTAN. The Indians wanted to erect a brand new capital city and commissioned the renowned French architect LE CORBUSIER for the project. In 1951 he undertook his challenging work on a site that was noted for its beneficial climate and bountiful water supply. Le Corbusier designed Chandigarh in 36 rectangular sections, 30 of which were residential. The government buildings are in one area, the industrial in another; he also designed an artificial lake. Jullundur was the provisional capital of the Punjab during the construction of the new capital.

Chandler, Albert Benjamin "Happy" (1898–). American politician and baseball commissioner. He was governor of Kentucky (1935–39, 1955–59), as well as U.S. senator from the state (1939–45). He resigned as senator to become commissioner of organized baseball and served until 1951.

Chandler, Raymond (1888–1959). American motion picture screenwriter and author of detective fiction. Born in Chicago, Chandler grew up in England, where he attended Dulwich College. Back in America he worked in the oil business. When he lost his job during the GREAT DEPRESSION he began writing stories for *Black Mask* magazine, a publication noted for its "hard-boiled" crime fiction that also spawned Dashiel HAMMETT. Chandler's first story, "Blackmailers Don't Shoot" (1933), established the tough but honest protagonist who eventually would evolve into the archetypal Chandler detective, Philip Marlowe. In seven novels, including *The Big Sleep* (1939), *The Little Sister* (1949) and *The Long Goodbye* (1953), Marlow prowled the "mean streets" of Los Angeles, "looking for," in the words of historian Philip Durham, "ladies to rescue, for the little fellow who needed help, for the big man who deserved a shot of old-fashioned justice." Chandler's prose was full of colorful similes: "As a bluff, mine was thinner than the gold on a week-end wedding ring." There was "the hard-boiled redhead" who sings "in a voice that could have been used to split firewood." And there was the beer that's as "tasteless as a roadhouse blonde." Chandler wrote a number of screenplays, most notably the FILM NOIR thrillers *Double Indemnity* (1944) and *The Blue Dahlia* (1946). Marlowe has been portrayed on screen by an assortment of actors, including Humphrey BOGART (*The Big Sleep*, 1946) and Elliott Gould (*The Long Goodbye*, 1973), but perhaps the definitive interpretation was Dick Powell's in the Edward Dmytryk classic *Murder, My Sweet* (1943).

Chandrasekhar, Subrahmanyan (1910–). Indian-American astrophysicist. Chandrasekhar studied at the Presidency College, Madras, earning his M.A. in 1930. He then went to Cambridge University, England, where in 1933 he earned his Ph.D. and was elected to a fellowship. In 1936 he moved to the U.S. and has worked since 1937 at the University of Chicago and the Yerkes Observatory. He became a U.S. citizen in 1953. Chandrasekhar's major fields of study have been stellar evolution and structure and the processes of energy transfer within stars.

French fashion designer Coco Chanel (1958).

He showed that when a star has exhausted its nuclear fuel, an inward gravitational collapse will begin. The star will shrink into an object so dense that a matchbox of it would weigh many tons. Chandrasekhar showed that such a star would have the unusual property that the larger its mass, the smaller its radius. There will therefore be a point at which the mass of a star is too great for it to evolve into a white dwarf. He calculated this mass to be 1.4 times the mass of the Sun. This has since become known as the **Chandrasekhar limit**. A star lying about this limit must either lose mass before it can become a white dwarf or take a different evolutionary path. In support of Chandrasekhar's theoretical work, it has been established that all known white dwarfs fall within the predicted limit.

Chanel, Gabrielle "Coco" (1883–1971). Leading French fashion designer. A British admirer encouraged Chanel to set up a Paris shop in 1910. Chanel's social reputation as a favorite of the Paris avant-garde added to her fame as she designed costumes for COCTEAU's *Antigone* (which also had sets by PICASSO) and for STRAVINSKY's ballet *Le Train Bleu*. Chanel's characteristic style was established during the 1920s, a style based on simplicity and neatness of a timeless sort. She was a designer of jewelry, both real and costume, often of massive and flamboyant form. Her Paris shop was closed during World War II, but reopened in 1954 and has continued to emphasize the same themes of style without undue pretension. Chanel was the winner of a Neiman Marcus Award in 1957. The famous perfume *Chanel No. 5*, with its simple and elegant packaging (and high price), remains one of the best-known products bearing her name.

Chaney, Lon [Alonzo Chaney] (1883–1930). American film actor. Chaney, dubbed the "Man of a Thousand Faces" due to his penchant for appearing in elaborate physical disguises in his films, stands as one of the premier actors of the horror film genre. He began his career as a comic and dancer on the VAUDEVILLE circuit and came to HOLLYWOOD in 1914, where he

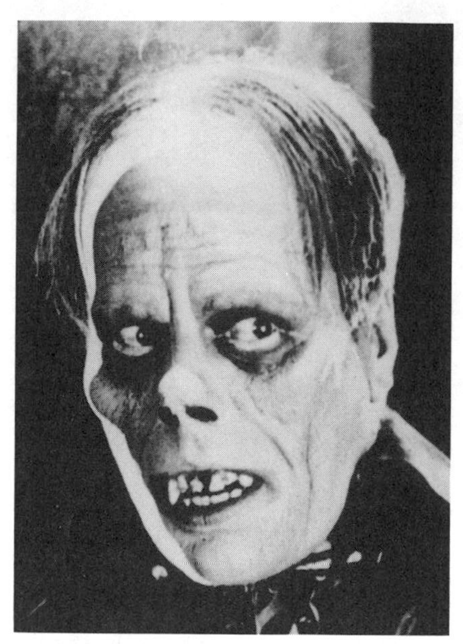

Lon Chaney in character as the Phantom of the Opera.

played bit parts in a number of films until 1919, when his portrayal of a man who feigns to be a cripple in *The Miracle Man* won him acclaim and larger roles. Chaney achieved international fame in the 1920s when he teamed with director Tod BROWNING on a number of successful horror films including *The Unholy Three* (1925), *The Black Bird* (1926), *The Road to Mandalay* (1926), *The Unknown* (1927), *London After Midnight* (1927) and *Where East Is East* (1929). Chaney was slated to play the lead role in Browning's *Dracula* (1931) but died of throat cancer. His son Lon Chaney Jr. appeared in a number of horror films in the 1930s and 1940s.

Chang, Min Chueh (1908–). Chinese-American biologist. Chang was educated at the Tsinghua University in Beijing and at Cambridge University, England, where he earned his Ph.D. in 1941. He emigrated to the U.S. in 1945 and joined the Worcester Foundation in Shrewsbury, Mass. In 1961 he became professor of reproductive biology at Boston University. Chang carried out a number of major research projects from which emerged not only greater understanding of the mechanisms of mammalian fertilization but also such practical consequences as oral contraceptives and the transplantation of human ova fertilized *in vitro* (by Robert Edwards and Patrick STEPTOE in 1978).

Ch'ang-Ch'un [formerly Hsinking, Shinkyo]. City in Kirin province, China. Ch'ang-Ch'un became the capital of the Japanese puppet state of MANCHUKUO in 1932. On August 22, 1945, at the end of WORLD WAR II, it was seized by Soviet paratroopers.

Chang-Ku Feng [Russian: Gora Zaozernaya]. Hill and battlefield, 100 miles southwest of Vladivostok on the left bank of the Tumen River where the perimeters of the U.S.S.R., NORTH KOREA and CHINA converge. JAPAN claimed it in 1938; fighting broke out there in July and August 1938 between Japan and the U.S.S.R.

Ch'ang-sha [formerly Tanchow]. City in Hunan province, China, known for its educational institutions. MAO TSE-TUNG [Mao ze-Dong] received his schooling here; he directed revolutionary activity in the city during the early part of his career.

Channel Islands [French: Iles Normandes]. A cluster of islands that includes Aldernay, Guernsey, Jersey and Sark, situated 80 miles south of the British Coast at the opening to the Gulf of St. Malo in the English Channel; part of the UNITED KINGDOM. The islands were the only section of Britain occupied by Germany during WORLD WAR II (from June 30, 1940, to May 9, 1945).

Channing, Edward (1856–1931). American historian. In 1925 Channing won the PULITZER PRIZE for the sixth volume of his *History of the United States* series. The series ranks high in American historical writing for its inclusive chronological coverage, original research and range of interpretation. A teacher at Harvard (1883–1929), his unique insight brought clarity to obscure historical situations. Channing's emphasis on national union as opposed to localism, and the effects of urbanization and transportation, provided a contrast to the emphasis on frontier exploration.

Chapayev, Vasily Ivanovich (1887–1919). Soviet hero of the RUSSIAN CIVIL WAR. Originally a laborer, he commanded a division in the Urals during the Civil War. He has remained popular in Soviet lore as a result of Dmitry FURMANOV's book about him (1923) and the film *Chapayev* (1934) about his Civil War exploits.

Chapaygin, Alexei Pavlovich (1870–1937). Soviet writer. He worked first as a shepherd and then as a decorator in St. Petersburg. His first work was published in 1903. His novel *The White Monastery* (1913) depicts life on the eve of the RUSSIAN REVOLUTION OF 1905. He also wrote short stories and sketches, including the autobiographic tale *My Life* (1929). His historical novel *Stepan Razin* was warmly received in Soviet Russia, particularly by Maxim GORKY.

Chaplin, Charlie [Sir Charles Spencer Chaplin] (1889–1977). British-born film actor and director; one of the most revered figures in the history of the cinema. Chaplin's screen alter ego of the "Little Tramp," with a black mustache, bowler hat and baggy pants, remains one of the archetypal figures of comedy and an icon of popular culture. Chaplin began his career working as a British music hall performer in the years prior to World War I. He made his HOLLYWOOD film debut in *The Little Tramp* (1915) and at once became an international star. Chaplin wrote and directed as well as starred in his classic films, which successfully spanned both the silent and sound eras and include *Easy Street* (1917), *The Kid* (1920), *The Gold Rush* (1925), *City Lights* (1931), *Modern Times* (1936), *The Great Dictator* (1940) and *Limelight* (1952). In 1952, adverse public reaction to Chaplin's leftist politics and sexual scandals led to a self-imposed exile from America for 20 years. Chaplin wrote an *Autobiography* (1964) and returned to

Charlie Chaplin and Jackie Coogan.

America for a gala Hollywood tribute in 1972.

Chapman, Richard D. "Dick" (1911–1978). American golfer. Chapman retained his amateur status during three decades of competitive play. He won the U.S. Amateur championship (1940), the British Amateur (1951) and other international titles. He qualified to play in 19 Masters tournaments and was a member of five Walker Cup teams.

Chapman, Sydney (1888–1970). British mathematician and geophysicist. Chapman entered Manchester University in 1904 to study engineering. After graduating in 1907, his interest was diverted into more strictly mathematical areas, and he went to Cambridge to study mathematics, graduating in 1910. His first post was as chief assistant at the Royal Observatory, Greenwich. His work there sparked his lasting interest in a number of fields of applied mathematics, notably geomagnetism. In 1914 Chapman returned to Cambridge as a lecturer in mathematics, and in 1919 he moved back to Manchester as professor of mathematics. From 1924 to 1946 he was professor of mathematics at Imperial College, London. After working at the War Office during WORLD WAR II he moved to Oxford to take up the Sedleian Chair in natural philosophy, from which he retired in 1953. He continuted teaching and research for many years at the Geophysical Institute in Alaska, and at the High Altitude Observatory at Boulder, Colo. The two main topics of Chapman's mathematical work were the kinetic theory of gases and geomagnetism. Highlights of Chapman's work on geomagnetism include his work on the variations in the Earth's magnetic field. In collaboration with one of his students, in 1930, he also developed what has bcome known as the **Chapman-Ferraro theory** of magnetic storms.

Chappaquiddick Incident. Accident in 1969, and its aftermath, involving Senator **Edward M. Kennedy,** a leading Democratic politician and brother of the late President John F. KENNEDY and the late Senator Robert F. KENNEDY. On the night of July 18, 1969, Kennedy left a party on Chappaquiddick Island, Mass., presumably to drive secretary Mary Jo Kopechne home. The senator mistook turns on a country road and accidently drove his car off the Dike Bridge into Poucha Pond. Kennedy escaped, but his passenger was drowned. Kennedy's actions were widely questioned, and he later pled guilty to leaving the scene of an accident. The incident followed Kennedy for the rest of his career and proved a serious impediment to his seeking higher political office.

Chapultepec. Fortress and hill, three miles southwest of Mexico City, inside Mexico's Federal District. From the 1860s to the 1940s the presidents of MEXICO officially resided here. The nations of the Western Hemisphere signed the **Act of Chapultepec** in March 1945, acknowledging the perimeters of American states. Modern Chapultepec is noted as a cultural and recreational center of Mexico City.

Char, Rene (1907–1988). French poet. A native of the Vaucluse region, Char first visited Paris after the publication of his first book, *Le Marteau sans maitre* (1934, *Hammer Without a Master*). There he met Paul ELUARD and Andre BRETON, and was closely associated with the Surrealist movement (see SURREALISM). Thereafter he divided his time between his country home and the capital. He broke with the Surrealists in 1937. *Placard pour un chemin des ecoliers* (1937) focused on social issues, specifically the victims of the SPANISH CIVIL WAR. *Seuls demeurent* (1945) and *Feuillets d'Hypnos* reflected his experiences in the French RESISTANCE during WORLD WAR II. His postwar poetry again moved away from social issues. Later works included *Poemes des deux annees* (1955), *Fureur et mystere* (1967) and *Dans la pluie giboyeuse* (1968).

For further reading:

Caws, Mary Ann, *The Presence of Rene Char*. Princeton: Princeton University Press, 1976.

Charbonneau, Robert (1911–1966). French-Canadian fiction writer, essayist and poet. Charbonneau, who was born in Montreal, Canada, and educated at the University of Montreal, spent many years as a script supervisor for the Canadian Broadcasting Corporation. But he is best remembered for his literary works, which include *Ils possederont la terre* (1941), *Petits poemes retrouves* (1944), *Connaissance du personnage* (1945), *La France et nous* (1947) and *Les desirs et les jours* (1948).

Chareau, Pierre (1883–1950). French designer and architect whose work of the 1920s and 1930s forms a link between ART DECO and the more purist architectural MODERNISM of the INTERNATIONAL STYLE. Chareau's best-known work is a Paris house of 1929–31 called *Maison de Verre* (House of Glass) designed in collaboration with Dutch architect Bernard Bijvoet. It uses steel framing and glass block in a way that seems to anticipate high-tech of recent years. Furniture Chareau designed is used along with tapestries by Jean LURCAT.

As editor of the 1929 publication *Meules,* he played a significant role in publicizing the work of many of the leading modernists of the time. Chareau came to the U.S. in 1939 and continued work in a generally Art Deco style that never received wide recognition.

Chargaff, Erwin (1905–). Austrian-American biochemist. Chargaff earned his Ph.D. from the University of Vienna in 1928 and then spent two years at Yale University. He returned to Europe, working first in Berlin and then at the Pasteur Institute, Paris, before returning permanently to the U.S. in 1935. He then joined the staff of Columbia University. Initially Chargaff's work covered a range of biochemical fields, including lipid metabolism and the process of blood coagulation. Later his attention became concentrated on the DNA molecule, following the 1944 announcement by Oswald AVERY that pure DNA is the factor causing the heritable transformation of bacteria. Chargaff reasoned that, if this were so, there must be many more different types of DNA molecules than had been believed. He examined DNA using the recently developed techniques of paper chromatography and ultraviolet spectroscopy and found its composition to be constant within a species but to differ widely between species. This led him to conclude that there must be as many different types of DNA as there are different species. However, some interesting and very important consistencies emerged. First, the number of purine bases (adenine and guanine) is always equal to the number of pyrimidine bases (cytosine and thiamine); second, the number of adenine bases is equal to the number of thiamine bases and the number of guanine bases equals the number of cytosine bases. This information, announced by Chargaff in 1950, was of crucial importance in constructing the Watson-Crick model of DNA.

Charleroi. Town on the Sambre River, 31 miles south of BRUSSELS, BELGIUM, where the first battle of WORLD WAR I was fought (August 22, 1914.)

Charles [Prince of Wales] (1948–). Charles Philip Arthur George Windsor-Mountbatten, eldest son of Queen ELIZABETH II and Prince Philip; heir to the British throne. Educated at Gordonstoun school in Scotland, he became the first

Britain's Prince Charles and Princess Diana.

member of the royal family to receive a university education when he attended Trinity College, Cambridge (1967–70). During the 1970s he served in both the Royal Navy and the RAF, commanding a ship and also qualifying as a pilot. His investiture as Prince of Wales at Carnarvon Castle (July 1, 1969) was a ceremony of great pomp, as was his wedding to his distant cousin Lady Diana Spencer (b. 1961) at St. Paul's Cathedral, London, in 1981. Although his royal responsibilities and authority were strictly defined by the constitution, he took an active and sometimes controversial role in many areas of public life. Outspoken in his criticism of modern architecture, he publicly urged a return to more humane styles; his views prompted much debate in the late 1980s and into the 1990s. He also spoke out in favor of rehabilitating Britain's inner cities, and sponsored several programs that provided educational and economic opportunities for young people.

Charles [Prince Karel van Vlaanderen] (1903–1983). Prince of BELGIUM. He served as regent from 1944 through 1950 while his brother, King LEOPOLD III, was in exile. Prince Charles helped restore Belgium after the German occupation of the country in WORLD WAR II. He was credited with having saved the Belgian monarchy.

Charles I (1887–1922). Last emperor of Austria (reigned 1916–18) and king of Hungary (as Charles IV); son of Archduke Otto, grandnephew and successor of Emperor FRANZ JOSEPH II. After his accession to the throne, he vainly attempted to secure peace negotiations, secretly contacting Great Britain and France through Prince Sixtus of Bourbon-Parma, brother of his wife Empress ZITA. After World War I, he was forced to abdicate and in 1921 twice failed to regain the throne.

Charles, Ray [Ray Charles Robinson] (1930–). American pianist and popular singer. Blind from age six, Charles developed into one of America's most versatile performers. His first hits—rhythm-and-blues numbers—appeared in the mid-1950s. Charles's career subsequently took him into such genres as jazz, soul and country. He has made numerous recordings and appears frequently in television specials and in commercials.

Charleville-Mezieres. Capital city of Ardennes department, on the Meuse River in northeastern France; the two towns were joined in 1966. Both had succumbed to the Germans, in 1914 and 1940, and during WORLD WAR II they were the site of the German high command headquarters for Western Europe. Mezieres, which was rescued by the Allies in 1918, was the last major campaign of WORLD WAR I.

Charlottenburg. A district of (West) BERLIN, Germany. A portion of the 1936 summer OLYMPIC GAMES was held at the Charlottenburg stadium.

Charlotte's Web. Children's book by E.B. WHITE published in 1952. *Charlotte's Web* takes place on a farm where the pig, Wilbur, the runt of the litter, is saved by the daughter of the family, Fern, who, as she grows up grows less interested in Wilbur. Wilbur has made friends with the spider Charlotte, who contrives a way to save Wilbur from the inevitable lot of pigs. Charlotte weaves "some pig" into her web, and Wilbur is soon a local hero, displayed at the local fair. Charlotte eventually dies, yet her children and the offspring of the other animals on the farm carry on. The book ends with Wilbur reflecting "It is not often that someone comes along who is a true friend and a good writer. Charlotte was both." The book is an American classic in children's literature, notable for its handling of the sadness of death and life's renewal, and the transitory nature of childhood.

Charlotte von Nassau-Weilburg, Grand Duchess (1896–1985). Charlotte was constitutional ruler of LUXEMBOURG from 1919 until 1964, when she abdicated in favor of her eldest son, Jean. After GERMANY invaded her country in May 1940, she went into exile in London but continued to address her subjects by radio. When she returned home in April 1945, she received a tumultuous welcome. She was later praised for her efforts in rebuilding the country.

Charlton, Robert "Bobby" (1937–). One of England's greatest soccer players, Charlton played 106 times for England (1958–70) and was the star of the 1966 World Cup winning side. Charlton joined Manchester United in 1954 and played on two League Championship teams (1964–65, 1966–67) and one F.A. Cup winning side (1963). In 1969 he scored two goals in Manchester United's emotional 4–1 defeat of Benfica in the European Cup. In 1956 Charlton had survived the Munich air crash that had taken the lives of the majority of the United team, returning from a European Cup game; the 1969 victory reenforced United, and Charlton's, position in the folklore of the English game. Noted for his "thunderbolt" shot, Charlton scored a record 49 goals for England. In 1966 he was awarded both the English and European Player of the Year awards. He was awarded the CBE for services to soccer.

Charpentier, Gustav (1860–1956). French composer. Charpentier was deeply influenced by the musical tradition of Romanticism that dominated French composition in the latter half of the 19th century. His major works were in the genres of opera and the orchestral suite. Charpentier remains best known for his opera *Louise* (1900), which continues to be frequently performed. Other of his compositions include *Didon* (1887), *The Life of a Poet* (1888–89) and *Coronation of the Muse* (1897). Charpentier devoted much of the final decades of his life to teaching.

Charteris, Leslie C(harles Bowyer Yin). British mystery writer. Charteris created one of the most popular fictional characters of this century—Simon Templar, "The Saint," who was the subject of dozens of novels by Charteris as well as of numerous successful adaptations to radio, television and film. Charteris was born of a British mother and a Chinese father. He attended Cambridge University in 1926 but dropped his academic studies after the sale of his first mystery novel. *Meet the Tiger* (1928) was the first novel to feature the wealthy and dapper Simon Templar, whom Charteris regarded as a kind of fictional brother. Charteris moved to the U.S. in 1932 and worked for many years as a HOLLYWOOD scriptwriter.

Charter 77. Organization formed in PRAGUE, CZECHOSLOVAKIA, in 1977 by the country's leading dissident intellectuals to monitor the Czechoslovak government's adherence to the UN Declaration of Human Rights, the HELSINKI ACCORD and UN covenants on civil, political, economic, social and cultural rights. The group's initial manifesto was signed by 242 members; the total membership was reportedly over 1,000. Playwright Vaclav HAVEL was a cofounder and leading spokesman for the group. Many members were imprisoned for their activities.

Chase, Lucia (1897–1986). American dancer and ballet director. Although Chase began her career as a dancer with the Mordkin Ballet (1938–39), she is best known as a founder of AMERICAN BALLET THEATRE (1940, originally known as "Ballet Theatre") and as a company director for 40 years. She was the primary force in making ABT a major U.S. ballet company with an international reputation. As a dancer she created the roles of the Nurse in Antony TUDOR's *Romeo and Juliet* and the Eldest Sister in Tudor's *Pillar of Fire.*

Chase, Stuart (1888–1985). American economist. Chase was a member of Franklin D. ROOSEVELT'S BRAIN TRUST, the group of advisers who helped shape the NEW DEAL economic programs during the GREAT DEPRESSION of the 1930s. It was believed that the source of "new deal" was Chase's book *A New Deal*, published in 1932. He was the author of many other books on topics ranging from ecology to semantics.

Chase, William C(urtis) (1895–1986). U.S. Army general. During WORLD WAR II, Chase served as leader of the American forces reentering Manila and those entering Tokyo. He became chief of staff of the 3rd Army in 1949 and from 1951 until his retirement in 1955 served as a military adviser to Chinese Nationalist leader CHIANG KAI-SHEK.

Chateau-Thierry. Town on the Marne River, in the Aisne department of northeastern France. In 1918, Chateau-Thierry was the deepest location reached by the last German offensive of WORLD WAR I.

Chatichai, Choonhavan (1922–). Chatichai became prime minister of THAILAND in late July 1988 when former Prime Minister Prem Tinsulanonda declined a fourth term. Chatichai's colorful lifestyle, which has earned him the title "playboy minister," contrasts sharply to that of the mild-mannered Prem. Chatichai was a former army major general, serving in Indochina in 1940–41 and as part of the first Thai expeditionary force to Korea in 1950–52. His army service abruptly ended in 1958 when the regime, of which his father was deputy prime minister, was toppled in a military coup. For the next 15 years Chatichai served in various ambassadorial postings in Latin America and Europe. In 1973 he returned to Bangkok to serve as deputy foreign minister and has held senior government posts since. He became deputy premier under Prem but was not expected to be able to exert the same degree of influence over the military as his predecessor.

Chatwin, (Charles) Bruce (1940–1989). British author. Chatwin, who began his career working as a picture expert for Sotheby and Company in England, later studied anthropology and became a journalist, traveling to remote locations and writing for the *Sunday Times Magazine*. He achieved recognition for his writing with *In Patagonia,* (1977), a travel adventure that describes a desolate area in southern South America. His travel fiction is rich in detail and broad in scope. Other works include *On the Black Hill* (1983), *Utz* (1989) and *What am I Doing Here* (1989).

Chavez, Carlos (1899–1978). Mexican composer and conductor. Widely considered the foremost Mexican composer of the 20th century, he began writing music in his youth and composed his first symphony at the age of 20. In 1928, he founded the Mexican Symphony Orchestra, conducting it until 1949. He also became director of the National Conservatory of Music, guiding its development from 1928 to 1934. As a composer, Chavez often employed Mexican Indian elements. Two of his best known works in this idiom are the *Sinfonia India* (1936) and *Xochipilli Macuilxochitl* (1940), both of which incorporate native Indian instruments. Often influenced by Mexican folk music, Chavez's music is usually powerfully rhythmic. His many other compositions include the ballet *HP* (Horsepower, 1927), *Sinfonia Antigona* (1933), the choral work *La Paloma Azul* (1940), the string trio *Invention* (1965), as well as several symphonies, concertos and pieces for chamber ensemble and piano.

Chavez, Cesar (Estrada) (1927–). American labor leader. The son of migrant farm workers, Chavez was born near Yuma, Ariz. Attending over 30 elementary schools through the seventh grade, he is mainly self-taught. After service in the navy (1944–45), in 1952 he joined a Mexican-American self-help group, the Community Service Organization, becoming its general director in 1958. Four years later he left the group to found the National Farm Workers Association (NFWA) and, against strong opposition from growers, attempted to organize migrant workers in California. In 1966 the NFWA merged with an AFL-CIO agricultural affiliate to form the United Farm Workers (UFW). Through a series of long and bitter strikes, marches and national boycotts of grapes, wine and lettuce, Chavez brought pressure on the growers and was able to obtain a number of contracts between growers and the UFW. The union became a part of the AFL-CIO, with Chavez as president, in 1972. Jurisdictional disputes with the International Brotherhood of Teamsters plagued Chavez and his union during the 1970s. Nonetheless, he continued to head the UFW, which, by 1990, claimed a membership of 100,000.

Cesar Chavez, leader of the migrant farm labor movement in the U.S. in the 1960s, '70s and '80s.

Chayevsky, (Sidney) "Paddy" (1923–1981). American playwright and screenwriter. Beginning as a writer of domestic dramas during television's "golden age" in the 1950s, he later wrote naturalistic plays and films whose satiric slant bordered on SURREALISM. He characterized his own specialty as the portrayal of "characters caught in the decline of their society." His three ACADEMY AWARDS as best screenwriter were for *Marty* (1955), the story of a lonely butcher; *Hospital* (1971), a satirical and frightening account of daily life in a city hospital; and *Network* (1976), a satirical look at network TV through the eyes of a disillusioned news anchorman. Chayevsky had three Broadway successes (including *The Tenth Man,* 1959) before suffering a failure with *The Passion of Josef D.,* a play about STALIN. After this he refused to return to the theater but wrote exclusively for television and film.

Chechaouen [Xauen; Shaf Shawan]. Holy city in northern Morocco, established by Moors ousted from Spain in the 15th century as a shelter from Christian Ceuta. Non-Muslims were not allowed entrance until 1920, when it came under the control of SPAIN. The Spanish evacuated the city during the Rif revolt, from 1924 to 1926.

Chechen-Ingush Autonomous Soviet Socialist Republic. Caucasus-area subdivision of the Russian Soviet Federated Socialist Republic (RSFSR). Its name is derived from the Chechen and Ingush people, who largely populate the area and who vigorously opposed the efforts of czarist Russia to control them. Following the RUSSIAN REVOLUTION, the BOLSHEVIKS asserted control of the area in 1918. Counterrevolutionary forces under Anton I. DENIKIN chased them out in 1919, but they regained control in 1921. The Chechen and Ingush oblasts were united in 1924, and they became a self-sufficient republic in 1936. In WORLD WAR II, when the Germans tried unsuccessfully to capture the area's oil fields, the Chechen and Ingush collaborated with the Nazis. The victorious Soviets terminated the republic and expatriated the people to central Asia. In 1956 they were permitted to come back, and the following year the republic was restored.

Chechens. Caucasian-speaking people in the Chechen-Ingush Autonomous Republic, U.S.S.R. They fought both the Cossacks and the Bolsheviks during the RUSSIAN CIVIL WAR, and continued to oppose the communists by means of guerrilla warfare in the mountains. In 1943, as a result of their anti-communist uprising, they were all deported to Kazakhstan and W. Siberia, but they were rehabilitated in 1957. They are Sunni Moslems.

Checkers Speech. See Richard M. NIXON.

Cheever, John (1912–1982). American novelist and short story writer. While a student at Thayer Academy, the 16–year-old Cheever was expelled. This experience was the nucleus of his first published story, "Expelled" (1930). Many of his short stories, most of which appeared in the NEW YORKER, dealt with the constricting pressures of suburbia. Among his novels are *The Wapshot Scandal* (1964), which earned the Howells Award from the American Academy of Arts and Letters. *The Stories of John Cheever* (1978) won the PULITZER PRIZE for fiction, the National Books Critics Circle Award and an American Book Award. Other short story collections include *The Enormous Radio, and Other Stories* (1953) and *The World of Apples* (1973).

For further reading:

Donaldson, Scott, *John Cheever: A Biography*. New York: Random House, 1988.

Cheka [acronym for *Chrezvychaynaya Kommissiya*]. All-Russia extraordinary commission for fighting counterrevolution and sabotage, established on December 7, 1917. It was in operation until 1922, when it became the GPU. It was headed by Felix DZERZHINSKY. Although its sphere of work was wider than mere political repression (it also dealt with speculation and abuse of authority, for example), it did not hesitate to use terror as a means of eliminating inefficiency and opposition. It established CONCENTRATION CAMPS and internal security camps, as well as censorship of the press. The KGB took over many of the functions of the Cheka, and KGB agents were often referred to as *chekisty*.

Chekhov, Anton (1860–1904). Russian playwright and short story writer. While Chekhov produced the bulk of his writings in the 19th century, his enormous influence on 20th century literature sets him within the modern era. Chekhov spent his childhood in Taganrog, a country village in southern Russia, and first went to Moscow in 1879 to study medicine. While attending the university, Chekhov began producing humorous sketches and short stories to sell to supplement his meager income. His stories were an immediate success, and Chekhov went on to pursue dual careers as a physician and a writer. In 1887 Chekhov's first full-length play, *Ivanov,* was produced in Moscow. In 1900, with his health failing, Chekhov moved to Yalta in the Crimea, where he befriended Leo Tolstoy and Maxim GORKY. In the final years of

A formal portrait of Russian author Anton Chekhov (1904).

his life Chekhov wrote four classic plays—*The Seagull* (1898), *Uncle Vanya* (1900), *Three Sisters* (1901) and *The Cherry Orchard* (1903)—that continue to be performed frequently.

Chelm [Russian: Kholm]. Town and battlefield in the Lublin province of eastern Poland. The Germans won a skirmish here during WORLD WAR I, August 1–3, 1915. During WORLD WAR II a German CONCENTRATION CAMP was erected in Chelm. Following emancipation the Polish Republic was declared at Chelm on July 22, 1944.

Chemin Des Dames. Highway and battlefield north of the Aisne River between Craonne and Fort Malmaison in northeastern France. The area was repeatedly and savagely contested during WORLD WAR I.

Chen Boda [Ch'en Po-ta] (1905–1989). Chinese communist political figure. He joined the communists in 1937 and soon became a leading ideologist and secretary to Mao Zedong (MAO TSE-TUNG), whom he served in this capacity for more than 30 years. He was believed to have ghost-written many of Mao's speeches and articles. He rose to public prominence in 1968, when Mao appointed him leader of the Central CULTURAL REVOLUTION Group, which ran the day-to-day operation of the PURGES that swept China at this time. He fell into disgrace in the early 1970s and eventually stood trial in 1980 with the GANG OF FOUR who had led the Cultural Revolution. He was sentenced to an 18-year prison term but was released a year later for medical reasons.

Cheng-Chou [Chengchow, Chenghsien]. Capital city of Honan province, on the Yellow River (Hwang Ho) in central China. In 1938, during the war with Japan, the Nationalists flooded the Yellow River near Cheng-Chou. The city became capital of Honan in 1954.

Chennault, Clair. See FLYING TIGERS.

Chen Yonggui (1913–1986). Chinese politician. Chen originally became known throughout CHINA as the leader of a model agricultural commune in his home village of Dazhai. He was brought to Beijing by Chairman MAO TSE-TUNG in 1973 and installed as a member of the ruling Politburo. From to 1975 to 1980 he served as deputy premier, although many of his accomplishments came to be questioned after Mao's death in 1976. He was dropped from the Politburo in 1982.

Cherbourg. English Channel port town at the tip of the Cotentin Peninsula in Normandy, 190 miles west-northwest of Paris. During WORLD WAR II it was controlled by the Germans, who used it as a naval base. The Allies recaptured Cherbourg on June 27, 1944, three weeks after the INVASION OF NORMANDY, but the harbor was severely damaged in the fighting.

Cherenkov, Pavel Alekseyevich (1904–). Soviet physicist. Cherenkov came from a peasant family. He was educated at the University of Voronezh, where he graduated in 1928. In 1930 he became a member of the Lebedev Institute of Physics in Moscow and later (1953) became professor of experimental physics. In 1934 Cherenkov was investigating the absorption of radioactive radiation by water when he noticed that the water was emitting an unusual blue light. At first he thought it was due simply to fluorescence. He was forced to reject this idea when it became apparent that the blue radiation was independent of the composition of the liquid and depended only on the presence of fast-moving electrons passing through the medium. In 1937 Ilya FRANK and Igor Tamm showed that the radiation was caused by electrons traveling through the water at a speed greater than that of light in water (though not greater than that of light in a vacuum). This **Cherenkov radiation** can be produced by other charged particles and can be used as a method of detecting elementary particles. Cherenkov, Frank and Tamm shared the NOBEL PRIZE for physics in 1958.

Chernenko, Konstantin (1911–1985). General secretary of the Soviet Communist Party (1984–85). Chernenko was a protege of BREZHNEV, under whose regime he became a member of the Central Committee and the Politburo. His rise to general secretary after having been passed over for Yuri ANDROPOV was seen as the last stand of the old guard in Soviet politics. Chernenko died after less than a year in office and was succeeded by Mikhail GORBACHEV.

Chernobyl disaster. Catastrophic explosion and fire in April 1986 at a Soviet light-water nuclear reactor in the Ukrainian city of Chernobyl. The accident spewed clouds of radiation that spread into the atmosphere over parts of the U.S.S.R. and other European nations. According to Soviet authorities, who at first downplayed the disaster, 26 people were killed, as many as 1,000 suffered from radiation poisoning and over 90,000 were evacuated from the area as immediate results of the accident. About 100,000 Ukranians were considered at risk of developing cancer from the Chernobyl fallout, and other Europeans in the path of the radioactive cloud were also deemed to be at risk. Farm animals as far away as Scandinavia and Britain were exposed to the radiation and were subsequently destroyed. The disaster caused a reevaluation of nuclear power plants throughout the U.S.S.R. and in other nations, as well as a rethinking of the whole issue of nuclear power.

For further reading:

Medvedev, Zhores A., *The Legacy of Chernobyl.* New York: W.W. Norton, 1990.
Scherbak, Yuri, *Chernobyl: A Documentary Story.* New York: St. Martin's, 1989.

Chernovtsy [German: Czernowitz; Romanian: Cernauti]. Town and battlefield in the Ukraine, 140 miles southeast of Lvov on the Prut River. A battle-

The burned-out ruins of the Chernobyl nuclear powerplant, site of the worst recorded nuclear power accident in history.

field from 1915 to 1917, it was transferred to ROMANIA at the end of WORLD WAR I and to the U.S.S.R. in 1940.

Chervenkov, Vulko (1900–1980). Premier of BULGARIA (1950–56). Nicknamed "Little STALIN" by Russian admirers before World War II, Chervenkov rose rapidly within the Communist Party ranks in the late 1940s to become head of the Bulgarian Communist Party. As party chief and premier, he followed a Stalinist policy (see STALINISM). However, following Nikita KHRUSHCHEV's denunciation of Stalin at the TWENTIETH PARTY CONGRESS in the U.S.S.R. (1956), Chervenkov was ousted from his post and from the party.

Chesapeake Bay Bridge-Tunnel. Often referred to as one of the Seven Wonders of the Modern World, the complex system consists of two tunnels (totaling two miles in length), two bridges (totaling 3.6 miles) and trestles (12 miles)—for a total length of 17.6 miles. Opened in 1964 after three-and-a-half years of construction time, it connects Virginia Beach/Norfolk, Virginia, with the Eastern Shore (peninsula) of Virginia.

Chessie. Cat who was the emblem of the Chesapeake & Ohio Railroad and, later, Chessie System Inc. Chessie was first drawn by the Viennese artist artist G. Gruenwald in 1933 and was a familiar sight in numerous posters advertising the Chesapeake & Ohio R.R. in the 1930s through the 1950s, including classic World War II posters. Chessie symbolized the comfort and safety that passengers could expect riding the Pullman coaches of the C&O. The figure of the sleeping Chessie cat tucked under a blanket and with her head on a pillow continues to appear on thousands of railroad boxcars and on railroad memorabilia.

Chessman case. Caryl Chessman, a convicted rapist, was executed in California's San Quentin Penitentiary after 12 years of appeals. Chessman had confessed to being the notorious "Red Light Bandit," a robber who approached victims in lonely spots, flashing a red light that resembled the one used on a police car; sometimes the robber drove off with women, forcing them to perform sexual acts. Chessman later claimed innocence and that his confession was coerced through police torture. However, he was convicted under California's "little Lindburgh Law," received a mandatory death penalty and was moved to Cell 245, Death Row. Chessman's new prison address became internationally famous after he used it as the title for a best-seller penned in his prison cell. He followed up with three more books, whose manuscripts were smuggled out of the prison. Chessman escaped death for 12 years by appealing his sentence, but he was finally executed in 1960 despite worldwide pleas for mercy. Ironically, Chessman would have received one last hearing and stay of his execution, but the call to stop the execution came just moments too late.

Chesterton, G(ilbert) K(eith) (1874–1936). British writer, artist, lecturer and broadcaster. With George Bernard SHAW, Hilaire BELLOC, and H.G. WELLS, Chesterton was one of the big four Edwardian men of letters. Born in London, he attended University College and the Slade School of Art. In 1899 he embarked on a career in journalism; and for the rest of his life he worked steadily as an essayist, editor and pamphleteer for such publications as *The Speaker, The Daily News, The New Witness* and *G.K.'s Weekly*. His enthusiasms and causes were numerous, as were his books. The novel *The Napoleon of Notting Hill* (1904) and the biography of Chaucer (1932) celebrated the Middle Ages. *The Thing*, a collection of essays (1929), examined his own conversion to Roman Catholicism. Other essay collections such as *What's Wrong with the World* (1910), and short story volumes, including *Takes of the Long Bow* (1925), propounded social and political theories of the movement known as Distributism. His love of detective stories produced probably his best known creation, the mild-mannered priest FATHER BROWN, who cared more about saving souls than solving crimes. He appeared in five collections of short stories from 1911 to 1935. Chesterton's love of paradox was constant—and notorious; although he preferred to think his juxtaposition of contradictions produced revelation rather than confusion. His colorful bearing and appearance—boxcape, swordstick, and slouch hat surmounting his enormous bulk—was lovingly satirized by detective novelist John Dickson CARR in his Gideon Fell mysteries. Today his reputation is growing again after the post-World War II decline, largely thanks to the efforts of the Chesterton Society in Canada.

For further reading:
Michael F. Finch, *G.K. Chesterton*. New York: Harper and Row, 1986.

Chetniks. Serbian guerrilla force. The original Chetniks operated from 1907 into the BALKAN WARS and WORLD WAR I and attempted to liberate their homeland from the Turks. Relatively inactive between the wars, the group was revived in 1941 and placed under the leadership of Yugoslav General Draza MIHAJLOVIC, who had fought with them earlier. They resisted the German occupation, engaged in acts of sabotage and helped downed Allied airmen. However, with a Serbian rather than a Yugoslav allegiance and a strongly anticommunist ideology, they also collaborated with AXIS forces against TITO and his followers. Greatly reduced in number by the end of WORLD WAR II, they were largely eliminated by Tito's government and by the Soviet troops that occupied Yugoslavia after the war.

Chevalier, Maurice (1888–1972). A charming French singer and comic actor, Chevalier was the son of an alcoholic house painter. Struggling at first as an acrobat and street performer, he became mildly successful in French music halls. After confinement in a PRISONER OF WAR camp during WORLD WAR I, Chevalier became a film star in light bedroom comedies directed in the U.S. by Ernst LUBITSCH, such as *The Love Parade* (1929), *One Hour With You* (1932) and *The Merry Widow* (1934). Chevalier's activities during WORLD WAR II caused much controversy; his performances in Germany brought charges that he was a collaborator. After several years of lost popularity in the 1940s, Chevalier returned with even greater success in the late 1950s in Billy WILDER'S *Love in the Afternoon* (1957) and Vincente MINNELLI'S *Gigi* (1958), which featured his famous rendition of Alan J. LERNER and Frederick LOEWE'S "Thank Heaven for Little Girls."

Chevrier, Lionel (1903–1987). Canadian politician. Prominent in Canadian Liberal politics in the 1940s and 1950s, Chevrier was known as the father of the ST. LAWRENCE SEAWAY. He served as minister of transport from 1945 until 1954, when he was named first president of the seaway authority, a post he held until 1957. From 1957 to 1963, when the Liberals were out of power, he was one of a group of ex-Liberal ministers known as the Four Horsemen for their attacks on the Conservative administration of John DIEFENBAKER. Chevrier was Canadian high commissioner to Britain from 1964 to 1967.

Chiang Ch'ing (1914–1991). Chinese political leader and wife of MAO ZEDONG. Born in Shantung province, Chiang Ch'ing became an actress, touring China and settling in Shanghai. In 1933 she joined the Communist Party, meeting Mao in Yenan and marrying him. She stayed removed from politics until the 1960s, when she became an enormous force in the CULTURAL REVOLUTION, wielding great power over all aspects of Chinese culture and propaganda. In 1969 she was appointed to the Politburo. After Mao's death in 1976, Chiang and three colleagues, known as the GANG OF FOUR, were arrested and tried for crimes against the state. Convicted in 1981, she was sentenced to death, but she remained imprisoned after several reprieves.

Chiang Kai-shek (1887–1975). Chinese president and nationalist general. After serving in the Japanese army for several years, Chiang returned to CHINA in 1911 to help SUN YAT-SEN establish a republican army. Chiang consolidated his power after Sun's death and became president of the Chinese Republic in 1928. Conflicts with communists, autocratic warlords and periodic army rebellions culminated in Chiang's kidnapping in 1936 (see XIAN INCIDENT). He was released contingent upon ending his campaign against the communists and stopping Japanese encroachments. After WORLD WAR II Chiang's party, the KUOMINTANG, resumed its Japan-interrupted civil war with the communists (see CHINESE CIVIL WAR OF 1945–49). In 1949 he resigned as president of China, after the communists captured Peking, and moved his followers to the island of TAIWAN. There he established the Republic of China, serving as president until his death.

For further reading:
Dolan, Sean, *Chiang Kai-shek*. New York: Chelsea House, 1988.

Chiang Kai-shek, Madame Chiang Kai-shek and Gen. Joseph W. Stilwell share a light moment in Maymyo, Burma (April 19, 1942).

spiracy to incite a riot. The trial, which got international attention, was presided over by a crusty 74–year-old federal judge, Julius Hoffman, who was openly hostile to the defendants and their attorneys and made a number of unusual rulings, including trying to jail four defense attorneys who had participated in the early stages of the trial. Bobby SEALE, a leader of the radical BLACK PANTHER Party who was later dropped from the trial, was initially tied up in the courtroom. The defendants and their attorneys, including William KUNSTLER, used the trial to publicize their radical views and opposition to the Vietnam War. A divided jury eventually reached a compromise verdict that acquitted the defendants on the more serious charges.

Chicago. One of the major cities in the United States, it is situated at the lower end of Lake Michigan, in Illinois. Notable events of the 20th century include the IROQUOIS THEATER FIRE in 1903, costing more than 550 lives, and the 1915 Eastland steamer disaster, which took 812 lives. In the 1930s Chicago triumphed over the GREAT DEPRESSION with a world's fair, the 1933–34 CENTURY OF PROGRESS, in which a number of future trends were correctly anticipated. Chicago today has done much to overcome its image as a gangster city, the home of Al CAPONE and the site of the ST. VALENTINE'S DAY MASSACRE, but some of the old stigma remains, especially abroad.

During the 1980s, new construction placed Chicago in the first or second rank among major U.S. cities. In the 1970s and 1980s, three of the nation's five tallest buildings were constructed here, including the Sears Tower, the world's tallest. The city has also been ranked among the world's top 10 cities for outdoor sculpture. Chicago's National Football League Bears were Super Bowl champions in 1986.

Chicago, University of. The University of Chicago opened for classes on October 1, 1892, with facilities for both graduate and undergraduate study. It was the first to establish a department of sociology. Many internationally recognized experts have served on its faculty. Enrico FERMI (1901–54) with his fellow scientists conducted the first nuclear chain-reaction at the university, which later established the Enrico Fermi Institute for research in higher energy physics. Leading economists such as Thorstein VEBLEN, Milton FRIEDMAN and George Shultz, have taught here. The university laboratory schools in education were established by John DEWEY (1859–1952) in 1896. The university operates the Argonne National Laboratory for the U.S. Department of Energy and the Yerkes Observatory, the latter in Wisconsin. Chicago was designed by its first president W.R. Harper to be a model university. In 1892 he established the first correspondence course in the nation and also the University of Chicago Press—now one of the largest academic publishers. The university's school of law has been rated number five of the top 10 and its medical school number six of the top 11.

Chicago jazz. Chicago jazz flourished in the 1920s during the Windy City era of speakeasies and mob-influenced political corruption. Stylistically, the Chicago style can be regarded as a subspecies of New Orleans jazz, booted out of the Crescent City by progressive reform forces cleaning up the red light districts, and brought north by Chicago gangsters (and their "hired" friends in government), who were establishing a thriving nightlife based on speakeasies, bootleg liquor and jazz in order to meet the needs of a "thirsty" public deprived of alcohol during PROHIBITION. This dislocation caused a number of New Orleans musicians to move to Chicago, including Jelly Roll MORTON and Louis ARMSTRONG. With access to such accomplished and revered musicians, an avid group of young white players adapted the basic elements of the New Orleans style. There was the so-called Austin High School Gang (Jimmy McPartland, Dave Tough and Bud Freeman) and then other Chicagoans, like Benny GOODMAN, Gene KRUPA and Muggsy Spanier. This group is generally credited with adding a greater level of virtuosity, a more exuberant rhythmic interplay and an expanded emphasis on the role of the soloist. In the late 1920s, when Chicago's own reform politicos successfully dampened the speakeasy culture that supported jazz, most of the city's prominent young players relocated to New York, many to become important figures of the SWING ERA.

For further reading:
Steiner, John, "Chicago," in *Jazz: New Perspectives on the History of Jazz by Twelve of the Foremost Jazz Critics and Scholars*, ed. by Nat Hentoff and Albert J. McCarthy. New York: Rinehart, 1959.

Chicago 7 trial. Highly-publicized 1968 trial of political protesters. In 1968 the Democrats held their national party convention in Chicago. Protesters opposed to the VIETNAM WAR staged a violent demonstration that erupted into a riot, and many protesters were injured when the Chicago police moved to subdue them. Eight protesters were charged with con-

Chicago Symphony Orchestra. Founded in 1891 by Theodore Thomas, it began playing concerts in the Auditorium Theater in Chicago. Thomas considered the Auditorium too large for the symphony, and solicited contributions from 8,500 wealthy Chicagoans to build a new home for the symphony. He moved the orchestra to Orchestra Hall in 1905, but lived long enough to conduct only three concerts there. He was succeeded by Fredrick STOCK (1872–1942), who directed the symphony for the next 37 seasons. He brought the orchestra to international stature through his introduction of the classical music of many of the great composers of the first half of the 19th century. Sir George SOLTI, who became the musical director and conductor in 1969, was the first to take the orchestra abroad, greatly enhancing its international reputation. Ranked regularly as the finest in the country by TIME magazine, many critics have called it the finest in the world. Solti was succeeded as music director by Daniel BARENBOIM in 1991.

Chichester, Sir Francis (1901–1972). English sailor and adventurer. Chichester won international fame in 1966 when he became the first person to make a solo nonstop voyage around the world. He accomplished the feat in 226 days in his 54-foot ketch, the *Gipsy Moth IV*.

Chieftains, The. Band of Irish musicians who helped revive and popularize the traditional music of IRELAND in the 1960s, '70s, '80s and '90s. The Chieftains' membership has varied slightly over the years; Matt Molloy and Paddy Moloney are generally regarded as the group's guiding spirits. They began performing traditional music with the Irish composer Sean O'Riada and have since performed all over the world; they tour the U.S. annually and have even performed in the People's Republic of China. They have made over a dozen albums and have recorded the scores for several films and television programs. The Chieftains played before a crowd of more than one million people—the largest audience ever—when they performed for Pope JOHN PAUL II in Phoenix Park, Dublin, on the Pope's visit to Ireland in September 1979.

Chifley, (Joseph) Benedict (1885–1951). Australian statesman, prime minister

(1945–49). A prominent New South Wales trade unionist, he entered Parliament in 1928 as a Labour member. He was minister of defense (1929–31), later serving as John CURTIN's treasurer (1941) and minister in charge of planning postwar reconstruction (1942). As prime minister, he proposed banking reforms, expanded social services and led postwar economic growth. Chifley was defeated by a Liberal-Country Party coalition under Sir Robert MENZIES in the election of 1949.

Chile. The Spanish-speaking nation stretches for some 2,700 miles along the Pacific coast of South America. In 1904 ARGENTINA and Chile celebrated an end to old boundary feuds by erecting a statue, the Christ of the Andes, on a mountaintop on their mutual border. In 1914, Chile temporarily merged with Brazil and Argentina (as the ABC Powers) to settle an argument between the UNITED STATES and MEXICO. The worldwide GREAT DEPRESSION caused much suffering during the 1930s, and anti-government sentiments increased. In 1938 a league of democrats and leftists achieved control. Nazi sympathizers pushed for ties with Germany during WORLD WAR II, but in 1943 Chile severed diplomatic ties with the Axis powers and in 1945 went to war with Japan.

During the 1950s and 1960s inflation soared, and Chile's economy wavered. In 1964 Eduardo FREI MONTALVA of the Christian Democratic Party was elected president, and his government took control of foreign-owned corporations and allocated land to small farmers. Salvador ALLENDE GOSSENS won by a narrow margin in the election of 1970, becoming the first democratically elected Marxist leader in the Western Hemisphere. Allende's policies were not universally admired, and he was killed during a bloody military revolt on September 11, 1973. He was succeeded by General Augusto PINOCHET Ugarte, who headed a repressive right-wing regime. In 1988 Pinochet permitted a referendum on his continued leadership; he lost. In December 1989 Patricio Aylwin, the candidate of the opposition Coalition for Democracy, was elected president, ending 17 years of military rule.

For further reading:

Falcoff, Mark, *Modern Chile, 1970–1989: A Critical History*. New York: Transaction Publishers, 1989.

CHILE

1906	Massive earthquakes rock Chile.
1910	Opening of trans-Andes railway to Buenos Aires; nitrate boom peaks as Chile exports 64% of world's nitrogen fertilizer.
1920	Nitrate boom subsides; labor unrest and political confusion follow; foreign-owned copper mines assume new importance.
1924	Parliamentary republic ends in military coup.
1932	Rebellious colonels group founds socialist republic lasting 13 days.
1938	Despite violent opposition of Nacisti (Chilean Nazis), Popular Front composed of radicals, socialists and communists forms government.
1939	Earthquakes kill 8,000 to 15,000.
1948	Radical President Videla, in line with U.S. cold war policies, breaks with communists, then bans party.
1960	Earthquakes kill 2,500.
1964	President Fesi attempts limited reforms with U.S. backing, satisfying neither right nor left.
1970	Marxist Salvador Allende elected president.
1971	While serving as ambassador to France, poet Pablo Neruda wins Nobel Prize for literature; Allende nationalizes American copper holdings.
1973	With U.S. backing, Gen. Augusto Pinochet overthrows Allende, suspends political parties and civil liberties; Allende and Neruda die during coup.
1974	Mass arrests and torture of Pinochet opponents continue.
1976	Former Defense Minister Orlando Letelier killed by a bomb in Washington, D.C.
1981	Pinochet's experiment with free-market economy fails, producing record 14% drop in GNP the following year. Popular and labor movements resurface with support of the Catholic Church.
1989	Patricio Aylwin elected president, but Pinochet remains as commander-in-chief of military.
1991	Commission on Truth and National Reconciliation documents torture and murder under Pinochet.

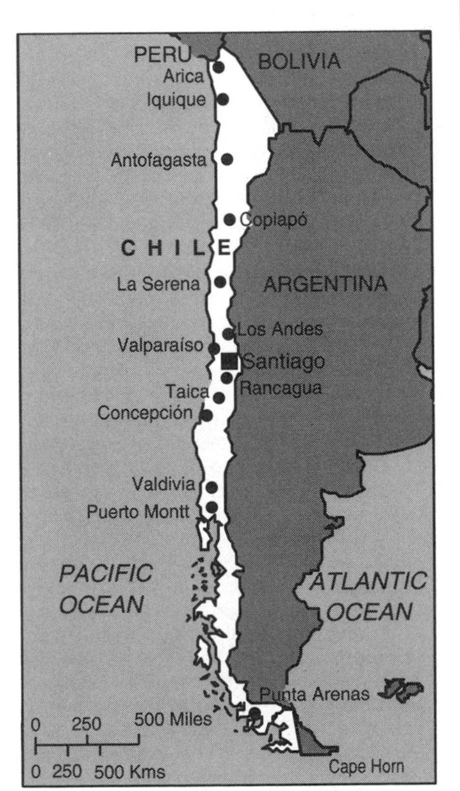

CHILE

Chilean Revolution of 1973. In 1970 Salvador ALLENDE GOSSENS (1908–73), an avowed Marxist, was elected president of CHILE. He began to establish democratic socialism by freezing prices and raising wages, nationalizing U.S.-owned copper mines, heavy industries and breaking up large plantations to distribute land to peasants. These actions antagonized foreign countries, the middle and upper classes and right-wing parties. The economy worsened as food shortages developed, strikes cut production, foreign loans were refused and inflation rose. A two-month strike of trucking industry owners resisting nationalization crippled the nation, and on September 11, 1973, the armed forces staged a successful coup d'etat. Allende apparently committed suicide. Reportedly, the U.S. CIA helped plan and finance the takeover. A four-man military junta headed by Augusto PINOCHET Ugarte took power.

China [People's Republic of China]. China encompasses 3,704,427 square miles of central and east Asia and is the most populous nation on Earth. The BOXER UPRISING of 1900 attempted to oust foreigners but was suppressed by a British-led, six-nation foreign army. Manchu Dynasty rule was overthrown during the CHINESE REVOLUTION OF 1911–12, and China became a republic in 1912. SUN YAT-SEN is regarded as the father of modern China. In 1916 civil war erupted between rival warlords, leading to conflict between two major political factions: the KUOMINTANG (KMT), led by CHIANG KAI-SHEK, and the Chinese Communist Party (CCP), led by MAO TSE-TUNG (see CHINESE CIVIL WAR OF

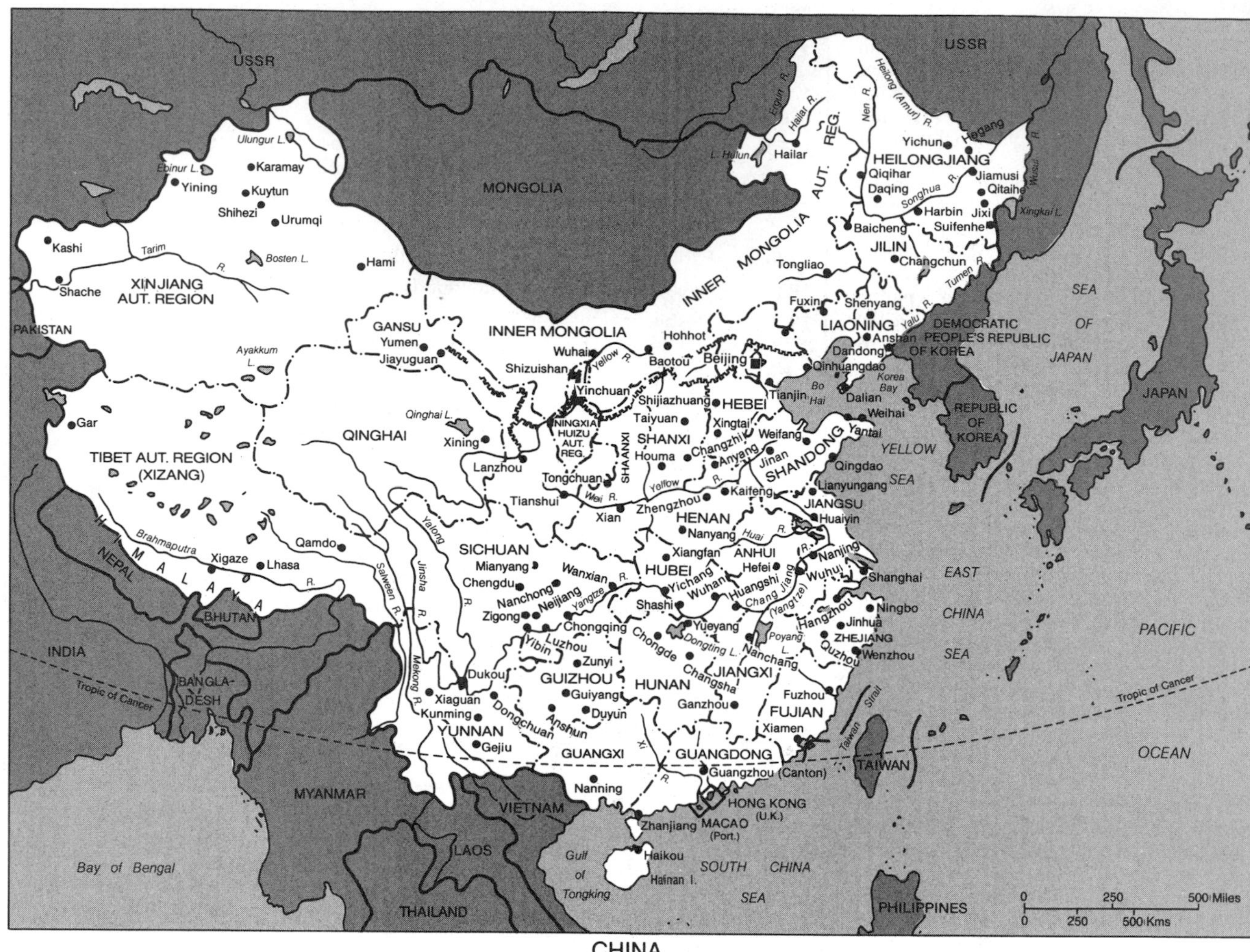

CHINA

1930–34; LONG MARCH). After the Japanese occupation (1937–45), the communists gained control, and the People's Republic of China was established on October 1, 1949 (see CHINESE CIVIL WAR OF 1945–49). The KMT was left in control of TAIWAN and several offshore islands. In 1951 Tibet became an autonomous region of China. From 1950 to 1976 a central council under the chairmanship of Mao Tse-tung held absolute power. China supported NORTH KOREA during the KOREAN WAR (1950–53), and Chinese troops fought against U.S. and UN forces during the conflict. The CULTURAL REVOLUTION (1966–76) brought violence and chaos as the RED GUARDS tried to eliminate old customs, revive the Maoist revolutionary spirit and suppress "revisionism." U.S. envoy Henry KISSINGER's secret visit to Beijing in 1971, followed by President NIXON's visit in 1972, began an era of dialogue between China and the U.S.—after more than 20 years of mutual antipathy. Upon Mao's death in 1976, the GANG OF FOUR led by Mao's widow, CHIANG CH'ING, tried to seize power but failed; they were tried and jailed.

New leader DENG XIAOPING initiated a decade of reform in 1978, attempting to modernize the economy and forging new trade ties with the West. A new constitution was established in 1982. China seemed poised to turn away from its isolationist, communist past. Student-led prodemocracy demonstrations occurred in April 1989, but were quelled when the army killed hundreds in Beijing's TIANANMEN SQUARE in June. The communist government has since tightened its control in China, cracking down on dissidents and making it clear that economic reforms would not mean the introduction of democratic government.

For further reading:

Associate Press Staff, *China: From the Long March to Tiananmen Square.* New York: Holt, 1990.

Hsu, Immanuel C., *The Rise of Modern China,* 4th ed. Oxford: Oxford University Press, 1990.

Mackerras, Colin, *The Cambridge Handbook of Contemporary China.* Cambridge: Cambridge University Press, n.d.

Salisbury, Harrison E., *The Long March.* New York: McGraw-Hill, 1987.

Woodruff, John, *China in Search of Its Future: Reform vs. Repression, 1982–1989.* New York: Carol Publishing Group, 1990.

Chindwin River. River coursing from northern BURMA southward to the Irrawaddy River at Myingyan. During WORLD WAR II many battles were fought on this site in the BURMA CAMPAIGN. The British crossed the river in November 1944 as they progressed into Burma from India.

Chinese Civil War of 1930–34. Although the KUOMINTANG (Nationalist) armies had reunited CHINA in 1928 (see NORTHERN EXPEDITION), the problems of turning CHINA into a modern state were enormous and complex. It could not be done in a few years, and discontent smoldered all over the country as former warlords tried to regain power and the peasants suffered the ravages of floods and famines. Revolts were put down in one province, and a fresh one broke out in another. However, the Kuomintang's Generalissimo CHIANG KAI-SHEK considered his chief enemies to be the communists, who had been driven from the large cities and found refuge in the Jing Gang Mountains in the south. Five times between 1930 and 1934 Chiang's troops tried to encircle their strongholds. The first two efforts and the fourth failed. In the third campaign of 1931 a furious battle was fought at Goaxing with heavy losses on both sides. Chiang claimed a victory, but the Red (communist) Army was not annihilated and moved its bases farther south. By 1933 Chinese communist communes had been set up in four other

CHINA

1900	Boxer rebellion—failed atttempt to expel foreigners.
1911	British Parliament bans opium trade.
1912	(Feb. 12) China becomes a republic, which lasts until the death of its leader Yuan Shikai in 1916.
1916	(approx.) Shikai's followers set up government in Beijing. Rival government established in Canton by Sun Yat-sen's Kuomintang, sending the country into civil war.
1921	Chinese Communist Party established.
1927	Chaing Kai-shek attacks communists at their base in Shanghai.
1931	Japan occupies Manchuria.
1934-35	Mao Tse-tung leads communists in "Long March" to Yenan.
1936	Chiang is kidnapped and agrees to halt his campaign against the communists.
1937	Japan launches full-scale invasion.
1945	Japan surrenders; the Nationalists take over areas formerly held by the Japanese; U.S. attempts to mediate between Nationalists and CCP.
1949	(Jan.) Peoples' Liberation Army captures Beijing.
1949	(Oct.1) The People's Republic of China formally established; Nationalists under Chiang flee to Taiwan.
1950	Chinese troops intervene in Korean War, push UN troops back into South Korea.
1950	(Oct.) China invades Tibet.
1954	Soviet-style collective farms established.
1958	Chinese crush Tibetan revolt.
1960	China breaks relations with the U.S.S.R.
1962	Sino-Indian war erupts over Chinese occupation of areas in Northern Kashmir.
1964	China successfully tests atomic bomb.
1966	Cultural Revolution begins.
1971	People's Republic of China is seated at the UN, Republic of China (Taiwan) is expelled.
1972	U.S. President Richard Nixon visits Beijing.
1976	Death of Mao.
1981	Gang of Four is convicted.
1982	Deng Xiaoping emerges as paramount ruler, begins economic reforms.
1984	Sino-British agreement is signed on reversion of Hong Kong to China in 1997.
1989	(June 4) Pro-democracy demonstrators in Tiananmen Square in Beijing are violently crushed by the army.
1990	(Nov. 29) China abstains from UN vote to use force against Iraq.

remote provinces. The fifth campaign started in October 1933 with a 700,000–man Nationalist army. This time, with the coaching of a German general and the aid of modern planes and artillery, the Nationalist troops adopted a scorched-earth policy to starve the enemy into submission. Pillboxes, forts and checkpoints on all roads discouraged the communists' usual aggressive guerrilla methods, and the peasants were exterminated. The ruthless campaign continued for a year until the communists in the southern mountains of China were finally dislodged and began their long trek to a new base. (See also LONG MARCH.)

Chinese Civil War of 1945–49. After Japan's defeat in WORLD WAR II (see also WORLD WAR II IN CHINA; WORLD WAR II IN THE PACIFIC) and the expulsion of its troops from mainland China, both the communists in the north and the KUOMINTANG (Nationalist) armies in the south rushed to seize the Chinese areas formerly occupied by the Japanese. American planes airlifted thousands of Kuomintang troops to Shanghai, Nankin and other major Chinese cities; U.S. General George C. MARSHALL was sent to negotiate a peace between the opposing Chinese sides. MAO TSE-TUNG, the communist leader, seemed willing to bargain, but CHIANG KAI-SHEK, the Nationalist leader, refused to talk with the communists. Marshall warned Chiang that China's faltering economy would collapse if negotiations were not conducted, but Chiang would not listen. Marshall reported that his mission had failed and returned home in early 1947. U.S. troops were also withdrawn, but U.S military and economic aid continued. Meanwhile, whole divisions defected to the communists; Kuomintang commanders quarreled among themselves and refused to take the offensive; and rampant inflation and government corruption discredited the once popular Kuomintang. In October 1948 300,000 Nationalist troops surrendered to the communists in Manchuria, and two months later 66 Nationalist divisions were surrounded and captured—or they deserted—in north-central China. The following April the communists crossed the Yangtze River and spread throughout the south. Shanghai fell to them in May, Canton in October and the former capital of Chungking in November. In December 1949 Chiang, his Nationalist government and their followers fled to the island of Formosa (Taiwan), where Chiang set up the Republic of China (1950). Millions of Chinese died in this civil war and millions more were impoverished by the runaway inflation. U.S.aid to the Kuomintang created anti-American sentiments among much of China's population. The communists had triumphed and proclaimed the People's Republic of China (1949), with their capital at Beijing and Mao as chairman; soon they would chart a completely new social, economic and political course for China. (See also SINO-JAPANESE WAR OF 1937–45.)

Chinese Revolution of 1911–12. Although the Manchu (Ch'ing) dynasty (1644–1911) had ruled CHINA for more than 260 years, many Chinese still considered the Manchus (who originated in Manchuria) foreigners and hated them as much as they hated and feared the Western foreigners who had gained control of the coastal ports and had been granted concessions to build railroads, roads and mines. Throughout the first decade of the 20th century, China seethed with unrest and turmoil, revolutionary societies sprang up everywhere, new public and private schools graduated students who wanted a better life for themselves and their countrymen, and overseas Chinese sent money home to finance reform and resistance movements. The weak Manchu emperor made some attempts at reform, but these were abruptly canceled by the dowager empress, who was out of touch with the realities in the country. On October 8, 1911, an explosion in the city of Hankow revealed the presence of a revolutionary group, whose leaders were promptly arrested and executed. Soldiers in Wuchang (part of Wuhan) across the Yangtze River from Hankow knew of the

Exhaustion etching their faces, Chinese Nationalist troops wait to be evacuated after defeat by communist forces.

group's plot and, fearing to be implicated, mutinied on October 10, sacked the governor's residence, took control of the city and declared a rebellion against the Manchus. This date, celebrated as the "Double Ten," sparked similar uprisings all over the country. Soon all the provinces in the Yangtze valley and southern and northwestern China were in rebel hands. They proclaimed their territory a republic. There was comparatively little bloodshed because most Chinese officials and military leaders realized the days of the Manchus were numbered. In desperation, the prince regent recalled the Assembly, an advisory body of appointed and elected members, which elected YUAN SHIH-K'AI (1859–1916) prime minister, a post he reluctantly accepted. Yuan had organized China's modern army. A capable leader not strongly devoted to the Manchus, Yuan wanted mainly to direct China's development as a strong modern nation. His army retook several cities from the revolutionaries, and then Yuan ordered the revolution to halt. Meanwhile SUN YAT-SEN hurried home from the U.S. where he had been lecturing and raising funds for the revolution. On his return to China, he was offered the position of provisional president and was inaugurated on January 1, 1912, at the provisional capital in Nanking. Sun knew he had no military support and no government experience; he was chiefly a theorist and democratic idealist. Thus, when the young emperor, Hsuan T'ung, abdicated on February 12, bringing the Ch'ing dynasty to an end, Sun resigned. The newly formed National Assembly then elected Yuan provisional president, and the north and south of China were reunited as a republic.

Chinh, Trong (1908–1988). Vietnamese politician; one of the last of the original group of Vietnamese communist revolutionaries who governed VIETNAM from the 1940s through the 1980s. He served as general secretary of the Communist Party from 1941 to 1956 and again for six months in 1986 before being replaced. His attempt at radical agrarian reform in the mid-1950s caused the widespread dispossession of families and the killing of as many as 50,000 people. In the fight against the U.S., he advocated guerrilla and political warfare rather than the throwing of North Vietnamese troops into battle.

Chinhae. City and naval base in South Kyongsang province, 20 miles west of Pusan, South Korea. Chinhae was the headquarters for the Japanese navy during the RUSSO-JAPANESE WAR of 1904–5. It is now a major South Korean naval base.

Chin Hills Special Division. In Burma, northwest of Magwe division and southeast of the Indian border. This region was established in 1948 to acknowledge the Tibetan descent of the Chins. Massive fighting occurred here from 1942 to 1944 during the WORLD WAR II Japanese operation against Manipur.

Chirac, Jacques (1932–). Prime minister of FRANCE (1974–76, 1986–88). Elected to the National Assembly in 1967, Chirac held various government posts under presidents Charles DE GAULLE and Georges POMPIDOU from 1967 to 1974. He became prime minister under President Valery GISCARD D'ESTANG from 1974 to 1976. Increasing tension between Chirac, as leader of the **Gaullist** Party, and Giscard led to his emergence as a political rival to Giscard. Elected mayor of PARIS in 1977, he ran unsuccesfully in the 1981 presidential election against Giscard and Francois MITTERRAND. Following a Gaullist victory in the 1986 parliamentary elections, he was appointed prime minister by President Mitterrand.

Chirau, Chief Jeremiah (1923–1985). Zimbabwean politician. As head of the ZIMBABWE United People's Organization in what was then RHODESIA, in 1978 he helped negotiate a settlement with Prime Minister Ian SMITH for the transfer of power to the country's black majority. He was part of the joint leadership (with Bishop Abel MUZOREWA and Ndabaningi Sithole) that governed the country briefly and was widely seen as a puppet government controlled by the white minority. In any event, Chirau lacked the broader political base enjoyed by his colleagues and by their more radical rivals, Joshua NKOMO and Robert MUGABE, and his influence quickly waned.

Chirico, Giorgio de (1888–1978). Italian painter. Born in Volos, Greece, he studied at Athens and Munich. Moving to Italy in 1909, he began to create his *Enigma* paintings, dreamlike canvases in which anonymous figures stand in starkly lit piazzas often marked by classical statues or great towers. Working in Paris from 1911–15, he became acquainted with CUBISM, struck up a friendship with the poet Guillaume APOLLINAIRE and further developed his enigmatic imagery. Returning to Italy in 1915, he settled in Ferrara. Inspired by the city's architecture and continuing to explore strangely juxtaposed figurative images, he developed the movement he termed METAPHYSICAL PAINTING, and in 1920, along with the artist Carlo CARRA, he founded the magazine *Pittura metafisica*. Chirico's works characteristically include architecturally-constructed mannequins, statues or still-life elements placed in shadowed and mysteriously empty spaces influenced by classical perspective. These lonely and symbolic images were important precursors of SURREALISM. Chirico moved to Paris in 1924. In 1930 he abandoned his earlier style, and his later works are widely considered academic and imitative.

Chisholm, Shirley (1924–). U.S. congresswoman. Born in Brooklyn, New York, Chisholm attended Brooklyn College and Columbia University, obtaining a degree in childhood education in 1952. From 1953 to 1964, she was a child care specialist and educational consultant in New York and was active in various CIVIL RIGHTS organizations. In 1968 Chisholm, a Democrat, became the first black woman to be elected to the U.S. House of Representatives. In the House, she proved herself a skilled politician and an effective advocate of the rights of minorities, the urban poor and women. She was also an outspoken opponent of the VIETNAM WAR (see ANTIWAR MOVEMENT). She briefly sought the Democratic nomination for president in 1971. An extremely popular legislator, Chisholm served seven terms and retired in 1982.

Chissano, Joaquim (1939–). President of MOZAMBIQUE (1986–). Active in the **Frente de Liberticao de Mozambique (Frelimo)** in the struggle against Portuguese rule, on independence in 1975 he was appointed minister of foreign affairs. He succeeded President Samora Machel following Machel's death in an air crash in 1986.

Chomsky, Noam (1928–). American linguistics theorist and political and social critic. Chomsky is one the leading thinkers of this century in the field of linguistics. Son of a Hebrew language scholar, Chomsky earned his doctorate in linguistics at the University of Pennsylvania and has taught at the Massachusetts Institute of Technology since 1955. Chomsky single-handedly created a theoretical revolution in linguistics with the publication of his first major work, *Syntactic Studies* (1957), which asserted that language and grammatical structures were learned primarily through innate structures within the human brain as opposed to cultural conditioning. Chomsky elaborated this theory in *Aspects of a Theory of Syntax* (1965). In the 1960s he emerged as a prominent left-wing libertarian critic of U.S. foreign and domestic policies, most notably the VIETNAM WAR. He was also critical of U.S. military involvement in the Middle East after IRAQ's invasion of KUWAIT (1990). His writings on politics include *American Power and the New Mandarins* (1969), *At War with Asia* (1970), *Towards a New Cold War* (1982) and *The Fateful Triangle* (1983).

Chou En-lai (1898–1976). Chinese political leader; premier of the People's Republic of CHINA (1949–76). Born in Chekiang province of an upperclass family, he attended a Japanese university from 1917 to 1919. Imprisoned briefly in 1920 for his participation in the MAY FOURTH MOVEMENT, Chou went to France later that year to study. There he was impressed with European radicalism and cofounded the Chinese Communist Party and the Chinese Communist Youth Group. Returning to China in 1924, he joined the KUOMINTANG (KMT), which was then cooperating with the communists, and organized labor groups in SHANGHAI, opening the city to CHIANG KAI-CHEK's forces. When Chiang broke with the communists, Chou was imprisoned and released. He then journeyed to Nanchang, where he took part in an abortive 1927 uprising. He made several trips to Moscow, participating in Communist Party congresses. Important in the political and military policy of the Chinese Communist Party, Chou became a leading adviser to MAO TSE-TUNG and participated in the LONG MARCH of 1934–35. An able negotiator with a broad knowledge of the Eastern and Western worlds, he negotiated Chiang's release from the Xian Kidnapping (1936), served as a liaison officer for the communists in Chunking during the SINO-JAPANESE WAR (1937–45) and represented the communists in civil war mediation talks with the U.S. (1945–47).

Upon the establishment of the People's Republic of China in 1949, Chou became premier, holding this position until his death. He also served as foreign minister from 1949 to 1958. He was instrumental in procuring the Sino-Soviet friendship treaty of 1950 and was China's chief representative at the Geneva Conference of 1954 and the Bandung Conference of 1955. Chou used his skills to stay in power through the upheavals of the GREAT LEAP FORWARD (1958) and the CULTURAL REVOLUTION (1966–70). Emerging from these troubled times, he spent much of the early 1970s securing a rapprochement with the U.S. and remained China's major international spokesman until his death.

China's Premier Chou En-lai (1958).

Chou Yang. See ZHOU YANG.

Chretien, Jean-Loup (1938–). French "spationaut." Serving as a researcher aboard the Soviet Soyuz T-6 (June-July 1982), Chretien was the first Western participant in the Soviet space program. Spending eight days in space, including seven aboard the space station Salyut 7, Chretien supervised the operation of a specially built heart monitoring system for use in space health studies. He made his second space flight aboard Soyuz TM-7, visiting the Mir space station from November 26 to December 21, 1988. Chretien was accompanied by Soviet cosmonauts Alexander Volkov and Sergei Krikalov. During his stay aboard Mir, he became the first West European to perform a space walk. Chretien was also backup for French spationaut Patrick Baudry aboard U.S. Shuttle mission 51–G, flown in May 1985, and trained with him in Houston.

Christian X (1870–1947). King of DENMARK. Christian ascended the Danish throne in 1912. During his reign the Danish government passed a wide variety of reform legislation, including social security laws. In 1915 Christian signed a new constitution granting women the franchise and ending the special rights of the upper classes. A symbol of national resistance to Nazi occupation during WORLD WAR II, he defied German authority and was placed under house arrest after open opposition to the occupation broke out in 1943.

Christian Democratic Union (CDU). Founded in 1945 as the postwar successor of the Catholic Center Party, the CDU (led in the 1980s by Helmut KOHL) was WEST GERMANY's major conservative party. A coalition headed by the CDU and including two smaller parties, the Christian Social Union and the Free Democratic Party, held office under Kohl's chancellorship from 1982 into the 1990s. The CDU was victorious in the national elections held shortly after the reunification of GERMANY (October 3, 1990).

Christie, Dame Agatha (1890–1976). English detective fiction writer. The most acclaimed of all British mystery writers, she is best known for two characters: the sly and egotistical Belgian detective, Hercule Poirot, who first appeared in *The Mysterious Affair at Styles* (1920), and the implacable village spinster and snoop, Jane Marple, who was introduced in *Murder at the Vicarage* (1930). Married to archaeologist Sir Max Mallowan, Christie assisted him in a number of Middle Eastern digs and used the locale for some of her most famous mysteries: *Death on the Nile* (1937), which became the play *Murder on the Nile* (1946) and a film (1978); *Murder in Mesopotamia* (1936); and *Appointment with Death* (1938). Among the best known of her almost 100 other novels are *The Murder of Roger Ackroyd* (1926), *Murder on the Orient Express* (1934; U.S. title *Murder in the Calais Coach;* film, 1975), *Ten Little Niggers* (1939; retitled *Ten Little Indians;* U.S. title *And Then There Were None;* films, 1945, 1965, 1975) and *The Pale Horse* (1962). Also an extremely successful playwright, she was the author of such works as *Witness for the Prosecution* (1954; film, 1958) and *The Mousetrap* (1952). She was made a Dame Commander, Order of the British Empire, in 1971. Her autobiography was published in 1977.

Christie, John Reginald Halliday. British mass murderer. On March 24, 1953, a tenant at 10 Rillington Place, London, discovered the bodies of three women hidden inside a cupboard. He called the police, who found the bodies of three other women—two buried in the garden and one hidden underneath the floorboards. The investigation led to the arrest of John Christie, a former tenant. Christie confessed to the murders and was also found to have murdered two other female tenants in 1949—a crime for which an innocent man had been hanged. Christie had strangled the women while having sexual intercourse with them. He was hanged at Pentonville Prison on July 15, 1953.

Christie, Julie (1940–). With her striking beauty and cool sexuality, Christie was Britain's leading actress in American films in the 1960s and early '70s. Born in Chukua, Assam, India, she made her film debut in 1962 as a stripper in the British film *Crooks Anonymous.* Thereafter she starred predominantly in dramas and big-screen epics, such as *Billy Liar* (1963), *Doctor Zhivago* (1965), *Far From the Madding Crowd* (1967), *Petulia* (1968), *The Go-Between* (1971), *Shampoo* (1975), although was equally appealing in science fiction and suspense, such as *Fahrenheit 451* (1967), *Don't Look Now* (1973) and *Demon Seed* (1977). In 1965 Christie won the ACADEMY AWARD for best actress for her performance in the satire *Darling.* After an absence, she returned to the screen in the mid-1980s in *Heat and Dust.*

Christmas Island. Island in the Indian Ocean, about 186 miles south of Java; 52 square miles in area. The island was apparently uninhabited until 1888, when it was claimed by Britain. In 1891 it was leased to John Clunies-Ross (who also held the COCOS ISLANDS) and Sir John Murray, who ran the island as a private concession and brought in Malay and Chinese workers to mine the local phosphate. Australia and New Zealand acquired the mining interests in 1948. Christmas Island is now a self-governing dependency of Australia. The population in 1989 was slightly over 2,000. Another island of the same name, in the Pacific, is part of Kiribati.

Christo [Christo Javacheff] (1935–). Bulgarian artist. Known for wrapping objects, a technique that at once mocks modern packaging and gives objects new and mysterious presence, he began in Paris during the 1950s, wrapping small objects such as bottles or chairs in plastic. By the 1960s he was wrapping whole buildings in temporary projects that turned commonplace structures into ambiguous entities. He turned to environmental pieces in 1969, wrapping a mile of Australian coastline in polypropylene sheeting. His best known environmental pieces are *Valley Curtain* (1972), a drape across a Colorado mountain valley, and *Running Fence* (1976), a 5.5-mile-long curtain constructed in northern California. Both these projects were subjects of documentaries by the MAYSLES brothers. While Christo's "spectacles" are ephemeral by nature, they are carefully planned in drawings and meticulously recorded.

chromium. Metallic element used in making various alloys and a material for electroplating. Chromium (or "chrome") plating is a favorite way of surfacing steel since it protects against rust and creates a coating that can be polished to a mirrorlike reflective shine. Chromium is a very hard metal, making chromium plate a more durable alternative to paint as a surface treatment for steel and other metals such as the alloys used for die casting. Although the practical value of chrome plating is often quite important, its gleaming appearance is an equally important factor in its use on metal trim elements where the bright glitter of chrome provides bright, silvery accents. The excessive use of chrome-plated trim is an aspect of the styling of American automobiles that has been subject to much criticism, though it retains strong popular appeal.

Chrysler, Walter P. (1875–1940). U.S. auto manufacturer and founder of the Chrysler Company. Chrysler initially worked as a machinist's apprentice, but by 1912 he was manager of the BUICK Motor Company. By 1916 he was appointed president and general manager. He was put in charge of operations for GENERAL MOTORS in 1919. In 1920 he became vice president of the Willys-Overland Company and president of the Maxwell Motor Corporation. In 1925 he launched his own company, the Chrysler Corporation, and in 1928 took control of the DODGE Company and merged it into Chrysler. The Chrysler Corporation introduced the high compression engine and torsion bar suspension to the automobile industry. Chrysler ranks among the top three American automobile manufacturers.

Chrysler Building. New York skyscraper, a key monument of the ART DECO phase of American architecture. A 1930 design of architect William Van Alen, the Chrysler Building was, until the EMPIRE STATE BUILDING was constructed in 1931, the tallest building in the world, with a height of 1,048 feet. Its ornamentation with "gargoyles" fashioned after automobile radiator caps, its spectacular Deco lobby spaces with rich materials, geometric ornamentation, and decorative lighting, its setback forms, and stainless steel spike top makes it a striking example of the Art Deco architectural design of its time as well as one of New York's most famous landmarks.

Chuikov, Marshal Vasily Ivanovich (1900–1982). Soviet general and hero of WORLD WAR II who led the defense of STALINGRAD. Chuikov joined the Red Army in 1919 and was later military attache to CHIANG KAI-SHEK. He commanded the Soviet forces at Stalingrad (consisting of the 62nd Army) and held off German forces for five months; the result of the bloody battle was a decisive German defeat (see STALINGRAD, SIEGE OF). Under General ZHUKOV, he led a Soviet army into Poland and Berlin, where he accepted the German surrender (May 1, 1945). After the war he became a member of the Central Committee of the Communist Party. He was commander in chief of the Soviet occupation force in Germany until 1953 and rose to commander of all Soviet land forces and deputy minister of defense.

Chungking [Ch'ung-ch'ing, Tchongking]. City on the Yangtze River in Szechwan province, central CHINA. The city, remote from the invading Japanese, was headquarters of the KUOMINTANG and capital of Nationalist China from 1938 to 1946 and again in 1949, until it was seized by the communists. During WORLD WAR II it was also a U.S. air base, from 1944 to 1945.

Church, Frank (Forrester) (1924–1984). U.S. senator (1957–81). An Idaho Democrat known as the "boy orator" of the Senate, Church came to national prominence when he delivered the keynote address at the 1960 Democratic National Convention. A spokesman for liberal and conservationist causes, he broke with the JOHNSON administration and called for a halt in the U.S. bombing of VIETNAM in 1966. As a leading member of the ANTI-WAR MOVEMENT, Church later sought to end all American military involvement in Southeast Asia. As chairman of the Senate Select Committee on Intelligence, he led an investigation of U.S. intelligence agencies in 1975–76 that uncovered an array of civil rights abuses. His investigation resulted in closer monitoring of the agencies.

Churchill, Winston (1871–1947). American novelist. Churchill (no relation to the British prime minister) graduated from the naval academy at Annapolis in 1894 but pursued a career in writing and went on to become one of the most widely read authors of his day. His best-selling novels include *Richard Carvel* (1899), *The Crisis* (1901) and *The Crossing* (1904). His later works reflect his interests in political, religious and social problems.

Churchill, Sir Winston Leonard Spencer (1874–1965). British statesman, widely considered the greatest political figure in 20th-century Britain. Born at Blenheim Palace, in Oxfordshire, Winston Chur-

Winston Churchill surveys damage from German bombing in Manchester, England (1941).

chill was the third son of conservative politician Lord Randolph Churchill and his American wife, Jennie Jerome, and was descended from the first Duke of Marlborough. He attended Harrow and Sandhurst and in 1894 was commissioned in the Fourth Hussars. He served in Cuba, where he was also a reporter for a London daily, and in India and the Sudan, where he fought at the battle of Omdurman (1898). The following year he resigned his commission and was assigned to cover the BOER WAR by a London newspaper. Captured and imprisoned by the Boers, he engineered a daring escape, which made him an overnight celebrity and hero. Churchill was first elected to Parliament in 1900 as a Conservative, switching to the LIBERAL PARTY in 1904 after disputes over the Conservatives' high-tariff policy. He served as undersecretary for the colonies (1906–08), president of the Board of Trade (1908–10) and home secretary (1910–11). Appointed lord of the admiralty in 1911, he helped to prepare Britain's naval forces for war. After the outbreak of WORLD WAR I, he supported the DARDANELLES CAMPAIGN; he was widely blamed when the campaign failed and was forced to resign from the government. In 1917, after active service in France, he was appointed LLOYD GEORGE's minister of munitions, subsequently becoming the state secretary for war and air (1918–21). As colonial secretary (1921–22), he helped to support the Irish Free State (see IRELAND) and affirmed PALESTINE as a Jewish homeland while recognizing Arab rights (see BALFOUR DECLARATION). He left Parliament in 1922, returning to the House as a Conservative two years later and subsequently serving as chancellor of the exchequer (1924–29) under Prime Minister Stanley BALDWIN. Out of office after the Conservative defeat in 1929, he wrote a four-volume biography of his ancestor, Lord Marlborough, and spent much of his time warning the nation about the looming Nazi threat in GERMANY and roundly condemning British APPEASEMENT of HITLER.

He returned to the government as first lord of the admiralty under Neville CHAMBERLAIN upon the outbreak of WORLD WAR II (September 3, 1939). He immediately took action against German SUBMARINE warfare. When the GERMAN INVASION OF NORWAY toppled Chamberlain's government, Churchill became prime minister on May 10, 1940. His first report to Commons promised Britain's total devotion to the defeat of Germany and contained the famous phrase "I have nothing to offer but blood, toil, tears and sweat." Churchill's superb oratory, his courageous spirit and his absolute refusal to consider British defeat helped to rally Great Britain in the dark years of 1940 to 1942 and to unite the nation throughout WORLD WAR II (see BATTLE OF BRITAIN). Establishing close ties with U.S. President Franklin D. ROOSEVELT, he secured badly-needed LEND LEASE aid and urged U.S. entry into the war. He also met several times with Joseph STALIN and supported the U.S.S.R. after the German invasion in 1941. Attending a series of conferences in CASABLANCA, QUEBEC, Cairo, Teheran, YALTA and POTSDAM, he helped to plan wartime strategy and to unite the Allied countries.

Emerging from the war as a national hero, he was nonetheless replaced as prime minister in the 1945 elections, as a nation yearning for social and economic change voted in the LABOUR PARTY of Clement ATTLEE. Out of office for several years, he led the Conservative opposition, wrote the magisterial six-volume work *The Second World War* (1948–54) and continued to be politically active, warning a 1946 audience of the dangers of the new communist IRON CURTAIN. He again became prime minister in 1951, and was knighted in 1953. The author of dozens of works of history, political analysis, biography and autobiography, Churchill was awarded the 1953 NOBEL PRIZE for literature. In ill health, he reluctantly resigned from the prime minister's office in 1955. After his retirement he published the monumental *A History of the English-Speaking Peoples* (4 vols., 1956–58). His death marked the end of an era in the history of the UNITED KINGDOM and the Western World.

For further reading:

Manchester, William, *The Last Lion: Winston Spencer Churchill,* 3 vols. Boston: Little, Brown, 1983–84.

Gilbert, Martin, *Winston S. Churchill,* 8 vols. Boston: Houghton Mifflin, 1973–88.

Gilbert, Martin, *Churchill: A Photographic Portrait*. Boston: Houghton Mifflin, 1988.

Chu Teh (1886–1976). Chinese military leader. Born in Szechwan, he attended the Yunnan Military Academy, where he joined SUN YAT-SEN's Revolutionary Party in 1909. Graduating in 1911, he entered the army and soon participated in the overthrow of the Ch'ing Dynasty. A warlord from 1916 to 1920, he traveled to Europe in 1922, meeting CHOU EN-LAI and joining the newly formed Chinese Communist Party. Expelled from Germany in 1925 for his radical activities, Chu journeyed to the U.S.S.R. and then returned to CHINA. After CHIANG KAI-SHEK purged the communists from the KUOMINTANG in 1927, Chu led the NANCHANG UPRISING and thus played a key role in forming the Red Army. The following year he and his followers combined with the forces of MAO TSE-TUNG in Kiangsi. Chu then led his troops in the LONG MARCH (1934–35). He commanded the communist forces in the SINO-JAPANESE WAR (1937–45) and the CHINESE CIVIL WAR (1946–49). After the establishment of the People's Republic of China in 1949, Chu continued to hold the post of commander-in-chief until he left the military in 1954 to serve in various high political offices.

CIA. See CENTRAL INTELLIGENCE AGENCY.

CIAM [The International Congress of Modern Architects]. Organization founded in 1928 at Chateau de la Sarraz by a group of first-generation modernists to advance the cause of MODERNISM within the architectural profession. Twenty-four leading architects, including LE CORBUSIER and Walter GROPIUS, were CIAM's founders, while Swiss historian Sigfried GIEDION acted as a spokesman for the organization in building up the now widely accepted history of the modern movement. From time to time organizational conferences served to maintain some degree of unity among the members from different countries despite many debates and conflicts. Urban planning was a subject of particular interest, but one that produced theoretical differences that were impossible to resolve. The organization dissolved after the 1956 meeting in Dubrovnik, Yugoslavia. Attempts by a group designated Team X to take over and carry on the work of CIAM have had only limited success.

Ciano, Count Galeazzo (1903–1944). Italian political leader. A fascist diplomat, he married the daughter of Benito MUSSOLINI in 1930. Foreign minister from 1936 to 1943, he negotiated the AXIS pact with Germany in 1936. He was appointed ambassador to the VATICAN in 1940. Dissatisfied with the progress of WORLD WAR II, he voted for Il Duce's dismissal in 1943. Blamed by HITLER for Mussolini's downfall, Ciano was arrested by the Germans, tried for treason by Italian fascists and executed. (See also ITALY; FASCISM.)

Ciardi, John Anthony (1916–1986). American writer. A poet, critic and essayist, Ciardi was the author of some 40 books, including many volumes of children's verse and an internationally acclaimed translation of Dante's *Divine Comedy* (1954). He was poetry editor of the *Saturday Review* magazine from 1956 to 1972, and from 1980 until his death produced a weekly feature on word origins for NATIONAL PUBLIC RADIO.

Cines. Important early Italian motion picture studio that helped vault Italy's films to world prominence in the years before WORLD WAR I. An outgrowth of Italy's very first studio, the Alberini-Santoni Studio in Rome, it produced numerous short comedies and action pictures before leading the way toward the feature-length format with the landmark *Quo Vadis* (1913). This historical épic set the standard not only for subsequent Italian epics, such as *Cabiria* (1914), but for the feature-length aspirations of American director, D.W. GRIFFITH. During a time of recession in the European film industry after 1907, Cines assumed leadership in the Congres des Dupes, a collective of the principal manufacturers and producers of Europe. Although Cines ceased operation in 1921, the name was resurrected in 1929 and again in 1949. Today it designates a studiocombine under part ownership of the state.

For further reading:
Fifty Years of Italian Cinema. Rome: Carlo Bestetti, 1954.

CIO. See AMERICAN FEDERATION OF LABOR AND CONGRESS OF INDUSTRIAL ORGANIZATIONS.

Citation (1945–1970). Thoroughbred racehorse. Two-year-old of the year in 1947, this versatile Calumet Farms bay colt could win at any length and under any conditions. The 1948 Triple Crown winner, he went on that year to win 19 of 20 starts, including the Jockey Club Gold Cup. He scored a rare walkover in the Pimlico Special, as no other stable sent a horse to challenge him. Injuries forced him to skip his campaign as a four-year-old, and he ran unevenly the following year, some saying he was still unsound. His owner, Warren Wright, obsessed with making Citation the first million-dollar winner, continued to race him at the age of six. He achieved that mark as he won the Hollywood Gold Cup, and was immediately retired to stud. His career saw him start 45 times, winning 32 and finishing out of the money only once.

Citizen Kane. Motion picture directed in 1940 by Orson WELLES; regarded by many critics and viewers as the greatest film ever made. "Everything that matters in cinema since 1941," said Francois TRUFFAUT, "has been influenced by *Citizen Kane.*" Fresh from his triumphs on radio in the late 1930s, Welles and his Mercury Theater staff—including composer Bernard HERRMANN, producer John HOUSEMAN and 15 actors (Agnes Moorehead, Joseph Cotten, Everett Sloane)—came to the RKO studios. There Welles forged an alliance with noted cinematographer Gregg Toland, hammered out a screenplay with Herman MANKIEWICZ and for $686,033 created a masterpiece. It was filmed at RKO between July 30 and October 23, 1940.

The story concerns the efforts of a newsreel reporter named Thompson (William Allan) to ferret out the private life of dead newspaper tycoon Charles Foster Kane, and the narrative is comprised of this "framing" story and a series of interviews with figures in Kane's life, an interplay between gothic melodrama and tabloid journalism. As the stories intertwine and sometimes contradict each other, the reporter feels that he has failed to penetrate to the truth behind Kane—although the audience may have arrived at its own conclusions. The story's similarity to the saga of newpaper tycoon William Randolph HEARST and Hearst's relationship with his mistress Marion Davies, were enough to bring pressure against the film's distribution and exhibition. The scheduled premiere at Radio City in New York was canceled, and subsequent showings that year were limited to RKO-owned theaters. Nominated for nine ACADEMY AWARDS, *Kane* received only one, for best screenplay.

Proper "authorship" of *Citizen Kane* is still disputed, with the honors divided among Mankiewicz, cameraman Toland and director Welles. Critic Pauline Kael suggests that Mankiewicz was slyly making Welles the real target of the screenplay. Even the dying Kane's reference to the mysterious "Rosebud" has been open to interpretations different from the one offered at the end of the picture.

Citroen. French automobile manufacturer noted for its innovative technology and design. The firm was founded before World War I as an arms manufacturer, but after the war it turned to production of cars, introducing the Type A in 1919, the first popular mass-produced automobile in Europe, designed by Jules Saloman. In 1934, Citroen introduced the first front-wheel-drive car, the Traction Avant model 7A, ahead of its competition in both engineering and design by many years. Pierre BOULANGER is credited with the design of the 2CV of 1939, a highly economical and practical four-seat car. This design, with various improvements, remained in production until 1990 and enjoyed enormous popularity in Europe where it was the only major competition for the popular VOLKSWAGEN. In 1957 the extraordinary DS19 appeared, combining front wheel drive with a hydropneumatic suspension that eliminated springs and shock absorbers while offering superior comfort and handling characteristics. More recent models retained many innovative features, but never attained the remarkable advanced status of earlier Citroen products.

Ciudad Juarez [formerly El Paso del Norte]. City in Mexico's Chihuahua state, on the Rio Grande River opposite El Paso, Texas. Pascual Orozco and Francisco VILLA seized it in 1910, leading to the MEXICAN CIVIL WAR OF 1911.

Civilian Conservation Corps [CCC]. U.S. government program, part of President Franklin D. ROOSEVELT'S NEW DEAL during the GREAT DEPRESSION of the 1930s. The CCC was designed to provide work for unemployed young men. CCC work crews, organized along military lines, were assigned to conservation projects throughout the country. They planted trees and did other work to prevent erosion and protect the environment.

Civil Rights Act of 1964. Landmark legislation granting equal public accommodations to all, regardless of race, religion or national origin. For almost 90 years after the Civil War the southern U.S. was a largely segregated society. Private businesses often excluded African-Americans, and the states ran two, so-called separate but equal school systems. Although the 1954 Supreme Court case BROWN V. BOARD OF EDUCATION ruled segregated school systems illegal, the decision did not affect private businesses. The CIVIL RIGHTS MOVEMENT of the 1960s, characterized by both peaceful protest and armed conflict and the use of troops, culminated in federal legislation outlawing both public and private discrimination. The Civil Rights Acts of 1964 and 1968, and the VOTING RIGHTS ACT OF 1965, made illegal any discrimination in providing public accommodations, admission to schools, employment or voting.

Civil Rights Movement. Name given to an American movement that struggled for the civil rights of black citizens in the 1950s and 1960s. It was led by such groups as the CONGRESS OF RACIAL EQUALITY (CORE), NATIONAL ASSOCIATION FOR THE ADVANCEMENT OF COLORED PEOPLE (NAACP), URBAN LEAGUE, Student Nonviolent Coordinating Committee and the SOUTHERN CHRISTIAN LEADERSHIP CONFERENCE, headed by the movement's most charismatic leader, Dr. Martin Luther KING, Jr. Highlights of judicial and legislative attempts to provide for civil rights in the 1950s include the 1954 Supreme Court decision in BROWN V. BOARD OF EDUCATION of Topeka, which prohibited SEGREGATION in public education, and the Civil Rights Acts of 1957 and 1960, which provided a federal agency to deal with the denial of equal rights. When these measures provoked riots over desegregation in LITTLE ROCK, Ark., in 1957 and a general lack of compliance in the South, civil rights forces mobilized. The many demonstrations by blacks and their supporters included sit-ins at segregated lunch counters, Freedom Rides on interstate buses and other forms of direct action. These culminated in the massive MARCH ON WASHINGTON of August 1963 and the dramatic march from SELMA to MONTGOMERY, Ala., in 1965, both led by King. The demonstrations helped to prod Congress into passaging the CIVIL RIGHTS ACT OF 1964 and 1968 and the VOTING RIGHTS ACT OF 1965. Together they prohibited discrimination in employment, public accommodations, housing, education and

Organized picketing and boycotts helped gain attention and support for the civil rights movement in the U.S. in the 1950s and '60s.

voting. Toward the end of the 1960s, the movement became increasingly fractured, with some factions supporting a more militant and sometimes violent approach. While the movement was weakened, it had created revolutionary legislation and contributed to enormous gains by some U.S. black Americans. However, by the end of the 20th century, blacks remained among the nation's poorest citizens and racial prejudice was still a fact of life in the U.S.

For further reading:

Powledge, Fred, *The Civil Rights Movement and the People Who Made It*. Boston: Little, Brown, 1991.

Moore, Charles, *Powerful Days: The Civil Rights Photography of Charles Moore*. New York: Stewart, Tabori & Chang, 1991.

Claiborne Case. Conviction and impeachment of Federal Judge Harry Claiborne for tax evasion. Claiborne was the first sitting federal judge ever to be sent to prison. An active Democrat from Nevada, appointed to the bench by President CARTER, he was under financial pressure due to a recent divorce and failed to report on his tax return over $100,000 in legal fees received from his old law firm. Claiborne was initially tried for both tax evasion and taking bribes, but the trial resulted in a hung jury. A retrial on only the tax evasion charge resulted in a conviction for which Claiborne served a prison term. Claiborne declined to resign his judicial post however, and the House of Representatives voted unanimously for articles of impeachment. The Senate found him guilty of betraying the trust of the people of the United States and of bringing disrepute on the federal courts and the administration of justice. Claiborne was permanently removed from office in October 1986.

Clair, Rene [born Rene-Lucien Chomette] (1898–1981). French screen writer and film director who was one of the acknowledged masters of the French cinema in the first half of the 20th century. Born in Paris, he began acting in movies after suffering a back injury during service in WORLD WAR I. Dissatisfied with contemporary cinema, he experimented with techniques of DADAISM and SURREALISM in his first two films, *Paris qui dort* (1923) and *Entracte* (1924). Their freewheeling camera effects, absurd juxtapositions of images and bizarre humor would all be incorporated into his later mature work. Another important influence, evident particularly in his first masterpiece, *Un Chapeau de Paille d'Italie* (*The Italian Straw Hat*) in 1928, were the slapstick chases of the American comedy master, Mack SENNETT. Clair described these chases as "a world of light in which the law of gravity seems to be replaced by the joy of movement." In 1929–31 he secured his world fame and reputation with three successful pioneering efforts in the creative use of synchronized sound—*Under the Roofs of Paris*, *Le Million* (1931) and *A Nous la Liberte* (1931). For the next 15 years he made films in England and in HOLLYWOOD. Back in France after World War II, he made one of his last authentic masterpieces, the fantasy *Les Belles-de-Nuit* (*The Beauties of the Night*) in 1952. Clair's films are striking blends of comic slapstick and subtle beauty and romance.

For further reading:

R.C. Dale, *The Films of Rene Clair*. Metuchen, N.J.: Scarecrow Press, 1986.

Clancy, Tom (1923-1990). Irish folk singer and actor. Although Tom Clancy and his brother Liam began their careers as actors, they achieved fame through the **Clancy Brothers** folk group, which they formed with **Tommy Makem**. They started singing and recording traditional Irish folk songs in America in the late 1950s and had a major influence on the folk music revival of the 1960s. Clancy went on to act in several American television shows.

Clapton, Eric (1945–). English rock guitarist and vocalist; considered the most important rock guitarist of his generation, if not all time. Clapton's style is utterly unmistakable and sensual. He began his career in rhythm and blues. His first breakthrough came with the Yardbirds, who achieved a degree of chart success that was to be eclipsed by a later group, Cream. Clapton achieved unwanted superstar status with the "power blues" trio, and went on to form and dissolve a number of groups in a search for relative anonymity. He recorded *Derek and the Dominos* (1970) with Duane Allman, which included the instant classic "Layla," written for BEATLE George Harrison's wife, whom Clapton later married. Clapton became addicted to heroin and did not record for some years. In 1974, he returned to prominence with the number-one hit "I Shot the Sheriff." His albums include *Ocean Boulevard* (1974), *Slowhand* (1977) and *Behind the Sun* (1985), as well as numerous compilations.

Clark, Dick (Richard Augustus) (1929–). American TV host and entrepreneur. The ageless Clark, America's "oldest teenager," began his career in radio with a pop music show called "Bandstand." The show became a Philadelphia hit after its move to television, and became "American Bandstand" when national network ABC began carrying it. The program became a showcase for new musical talent, particularly of the teen idol variety, including Frankie Avalon, Fabian and Bobby Rydell. The format included dance regulars and took on the air of a soap opera as viewers watched real-life teenage romances blossom and fade in a matter of weeks. Clark ran into difficulty in payola investigations, losing $8 million but managing to emerge with his squeaky-clean image intact. "Bandstand" survived in a variety of forms into the 1980s and was a forerunner of such shows as "Soul Train" and "Hullaballoo." Clark has diversified into game shows and is a millionaire many times over.

Clark, James Beauchamp (1850–1921). U.S. politician. Settled in Missouri in 1876, he began a career as a newspaper editor, city and county prosecuting attorney, state legislator and member of the U.S. House of Representatives (1893–95, 1897–1921). His philosophy was progressive. As Democratic leader in the House, Clark led a successful fight against the dictatorial control of speaker Joseph G. CANNON. He served as speaker of the House from 1911 to 1919. Clark was a candidate for the Democratic presidential nomination in 1912.

Clark, Joe (1939–). Prime minister of CANADA (1979–80) and secretary of state for external affairs (1984–). Clark, from the province of Alberta in western Canada, was first elected to the Canadian Parliament in 1972. He was elected leader of the opposition PROGRESSIVE CONSERVATIVE PARTY in 1976. His party unseated the government of Liberal Prime Minister Pierre Elliott TRUDEAU in 1979, only to lose control of the government to Trudeau and the Liberals the following year. He was subsequently replaced as Progressive Conservative Party leader by Brian MULRONEY (1984) but reentered the government as foreign minister in the Mulroney administration, after the Progressive Conservatives' election victory in 1984.

Clark, Kenneth (Mackenzie) (1903–). British art historian and author. Born to a wealthy London family, Clark was educated at Winchester and at Trinity College, Oxford. He later worked with the art historian and philosopher Bernard BERENSON. Clark published his first book, *The Gothic Revival* (1928), at age 26. By the time he was 30 he was appointed director of London's National Gallery. He later served as chairman of ARTS COUNCIL OF GREAT BRITAIN, (1963–1960). Clark's numerous works on the arts include *Leonardo Da Vinci: An Account of His Development as an Artist* (1939); the notable *The Nude: A Study of Ideal Art* (1953); *Introduction to Rembrandt* (1978); and *The Art of Humanism* (1983). To non-academics, he is perhaps best known for creating the BBC television series "Civilization" which was published as a book, *Civilization: A Personal View*, in 1969. Clark has also written two volumes of autobiography, *Another Part of the Wood: A Self Portrait* (1974) and *The Other Half: A Self Portrait* (1977).

Clark, Mamie and Kenneth B. American psychologists. Mamie (1917–83) and Kenneth (1914–) did important research on the effects of school desegregation on black children. Their joint writings were used extensively in the U.S. Supreme Court's landmark decision in BROWN V. BOARD OF EDUCATION (1954). Mamie Clark founded the Northside Child Development Center in New York in 1946, remaining as director until 1980.

Clark, Mark (Wayne) (1896–1984). A graduate of the U.S. Military Academy at West Point (1917), Clark commanded an infantry battalion in FRANCE during WORLD WAR I. At age 46 he became the youngest three-star general in the U.S. Army and was General Dwight D. EISENHOWER'S deputy in the World War II European theater of operations (see WORLD WAR II IN EUROPE). He helped plan the Allied invasion of North Africa (1942). Promoted to full (four-star) general, he led the U.S. Fifth Army throughout the Italian campaign and the capture of Rome in 1944. After the war, he served as the Allied high commander in occupied Austria. During the KOREAN WAR, Clark succeeded General Matthew B. RIDGWAY as supreme commander of the UNITED NATIONS forces in KOREA (1952). He signed the Korean armistice in 1953. After retiring from the Army, he was president of the Citadel military college in Charleston, South Carolina (1954–65).

Clark, (William) Ramsey (1927–). American lawyer and political figure. A graduate of the University of Texas and the University of Chicago Law School, Ramsey Clark was the son of Supreme Court Justice Tom CLARK. After graduating from law school, the younger Clark practiced law in Dallas before before becoming an assistant attorney general in the U.S. Justice Department. He became deputy attorney general in 1965 and was appointed U.S. attorney general in 1967, serving in that post until 1969. A prominent liberal, Clark, was an active opponent of the VIETNAM WAR when that stance was considered radical. He was also involved in controversial left-wing causes and was a leading U.S. opponent of the U.S. bombing of Iraq in 1991. After government service he returned to law practice in New York and also taught at Brooklyn Law School. He is the author of *Crime in America*.

Clark, Septima Poinsette (1898–1987). American civil rights activist. The daughter of a slave, she became a teacher and a U.S. CIVIL RIGHTS pioneer. As early as 1918, she campaigned for the hiring of black teachers in South Carolina. In the 1950s she organized citizenship schools through the Deep South to train blacks to pass voter literacy tests. The schools were later incorporated into Martin Luther KING Jr.'s SOUTHERN CHRISTIAN LEADERSHIP CONFERENCE. She accompanied King to Norway in 1964 when he was awarded the NOBEL PRIZE for peace.

Clark, Tom C(ampbell) (1899–1977). Associate justice, U.S. Supreme Court (1949–67). A native of Dallas, Clark was a graduate of the University of Texas and its law school. After law school he joined his politically-influential father in law practice. He held a number of state and federal posts. Clark actively championed Harry S TRUMAN'S vice presidential ambitions, and when Truman became president he appointed Clark as attorney general. As attorney general, Clark prosecuted a number of antitrust cases but is best-remembered for his vigorous pursuit of alleged communists and other so-called subversives during the early postwar era. In 1949 Truman appointed Clark to the Supreme Court, where he was generally a centrist. He resigned in 1967 when his son, Ramsey CLARK, became attorney general in Lyndon B. JOHNSON'S administration. Tom Clark remained active in public affairs until his death in 1977.

Clarke, Arthur C. (1917–). British author. A graduate of King's College, London, with honors in physics and mathematics, Clarke is a past chairman of the British Interplanetary Society and a member of the Academy of Astronautics and the Royal Astronomical Society. The author of over 50 books, his work has been translated in more than 30 languages and he has been the recipient of prizes in both the science and science fiction fields. One of the most influential of modern science fiction writers and author of the seminal *Childhood's End* (1953), Clarke is best known to the general public for his science fiction writing, including the popular novel and later hit motion picture *2001, A Space Odyssey*. His now-famous 1945 technical paper describing geostationary orbits helped form the basis of today's communications satellite system. Clarke joined newscaster Walter CRONKITE as part of the televised coverage of many of the U.S. APOLLO missions, sharing his insights with television viewers of the historic moon flights.

Clarke, Austin (1896–1974). Irish poet, playwright, prose writer. Clarke was educated at Belvedere College and University College, Dublin. His early work, influenced by YEATS and the other IRISH LITERARY REVIVAL poets, was largely drawn from Irish folklore and legends. Later he focused on the stultifying influence of religious parochialism in IRELAND. His prose-romances and many of his verse plays and poems are set in the Celtic-Romanesque period from the 5th to the end of the 12th centuries. His later works, after 1955, are more personal and contemporary, focusing on the realities of modern Ireland. In his poems Clarke skillfully and subtly adapted Celtic rhythms and speech patterns to the English line. He also worked as a book reviewer in London from 1923 to 1937 and was a founding member (1932) and president (1952–54) of the Irish Academy of Letters.

For further reading:

Harmon, Maurice, *Austin Clarke, 1886–1974: A Critical Introduction*. New York: Barnes & Noble, 1989.

Clarke, Sir Cyril Astley (1907–). British physician. Clarke was educated at the University of Cambridge and Guy's Hospital, London, where he qualified in 1932. He remained at Guy's until 1936 when he engaged in life insurance work before spending the war years in the Royal Navy. Clarke worked as a consultant physician in Liverpool from 1946 until 1958, when he joined the staff of the university. There he later served as professor of medicine from 1965 to 1972 and also, from 1963 to 1972, as director of the Nuffield unit of medical genetics. Clarke was also a skilled amateur lepidopterist. In 1952 he became interested in the genetics of the wing colors of swallowtail butterflies and began a collaboration with Philip Sheppard, a professional geneticist who later became a colleague at Liverpool University. In particular, they worked on the inheritance of mimicry in the wing patterns of certain swallowtails. They noted that the gene controlling the wing pattern is actually a group of closely linked genes behaving as a single unit—a supergene. They also found that even though the males also carry such supergenes, the patterns show only in the females. Clarke was struck by certain striking parallels between the inheritance of swallowtail wing patterns and human blood types, which aroused his interest in Rhesus babies. This condition arises when an Rh-negative mother (a woman whose blood lacks the Rh factor or antigen) and an Rh-positive father produce a Rh-positive child. Occasionally the fetus' blood leaks from the placenta into the mother's blood and stimulates the production of Rh antibodies. This will cause her body to destroy the red cells of any subsequent Rh-positive babies she may carry. Clarke and Sheppard puzzled over how to prevent the mother producing the destructive Rh antibodies. The answer eventually came from Clarke's wife, who in an inspired moment told him to inject the Rh-negative mothers with Rh-antibodies. As this is what destroys the blood of the fetus in the first place, the answer initially sounds absurd. However, the Rh-antibodies should destroy incompatible Rh-positive cells before the woman's own antibody machinery can act, that is, before the woman could become sensitized to Rh-positive blood. In 1964 Clarke and his colleagues were able to announce a major breakthrough in preventive medicine. Since then thousands of women have received injections of Rh-antibodies with only a few failures.

Clarke, Edith (1883–1959). U.S. electrical engineer. A graduate of Vassar and MIT (M.S., 1919), Clarke worked for American Telephone & Telegraph in New York City (1912–18), taught at Constantinople Woman's College in Turkey (1921), and was employed as an engineer by General Electric (1922–45). At GE she pioneered systems analysis for large power networks. She also taught at the University of Texas, Austin (1947–56). Her *Circuit Analysis of A-C Power Systems* (2 vols., 1943–50) is a standard. She was the first woman elected to membership in the American Institute of Electrical Engineers (1948).

Clarke, John H. (1857–1945). Associate justice, U.S. Supreme Court (1916–22). A native of Ohio, Clarke was a graduate of Western Reserve College (now Case Western Reserve University). He read law in his father's law office and became a lawyer in 1878. He was also active in progressive politics, and at one time published a newspaper. He later moved to a large law firm in Cleveland and worked as general counsel for the Nickel Plate Railroad, but continued to participate in progressive reform politics. After a few unsuccessful runs for elective office he was appointed a federal judge by President Woodrow WILSON. When Charles Evans HUGHES resigned from the Supreme Court to run for president against Wilson in 1916, Wilson appointed Clarke to the Court. (Wilson had also considered appointing Warren G. Harding, at the time a senator from Ohio.) On the Court Clarke proved a progressive despite his background as a corporate lawyer. He unexpectedly resigned from the Court in 1922 to champion American membership in the LEAGUE OF NATIONS. He later spoke out in favor of President Franklin D. ROOSEVELT'S COURT-PACKING plan.

Clarke, Kenny "Klook" (1914–1985). American jazz drummer. In the 1940s Clarke made a major contribution to the development of the complex rhythmic patterns of what came to be known as BEBOP. During this time he performed with such JAZZ greats as Charlie PARKER and Dizzy GILLESPIE. In 1952 he became a founding member of the Modern Jazz Quartet, in which he played until 1955. Thereafter he settled in France and pursued his career in Europe.

Clarke, T(homas) E(rnest) B(ennett) (1907–1989). English screenwriter. T.E.B. Clarke wrote many of the classic comedies produced by Britain's EALING STUDIOS in the 1950s. In 1952 he received an ACADEMY AWARD for his script for the film *The Lavender Hill Mob,* which starred Alec GUINNESS as a clerk who steals a bullion shipment. In the movie *The Blue Lamp* he created the popular fictional policeman PC Dixon, who was later featured in the long-running British television series "Dixon of Dock Green."

Claude, Albert (1898–). Belgian-American cell biologist. Claude was educated at the University of Liege where he obtained his doctorate in 1928. In 1929 he joined the staff of the Rockefeller Institute in New York, and in 1941 became a U.S. citizen. Claude returned to Belgium in 1948 to serve as director of the Jules Bordet Research Institute, a post he retained until his retirement in 1972. For 20 years (beginning in the 1930s), using electron microscopes as well as improved centrifuges, Claude began to chart the constitution of the cell protoplasm. For his work in opening up the study of cell structures, Claude shared the 1974 NOBEL PRIZE for physiology or medicine with George PALADE and Christian de Duve.

Claude, Georges (1870–1960). French chemist. Claude was educated at the Ecole de Physique et Chimie, after which he worked as an engineer in various industries. He made a number of important contributions to technology, including a method of liquefying air (1902), which he used for the large-scale production of nitrogen and oxygen. In 1910 he introduced neon lighting, using neon gas at low pressure excited by an electric discharge to emit a bright red light. The latter part of his life was, however, less successful. From 1926 onward he worked on new sources of energy. In particular, he tried to show how energy could be extracted from the temperature difference between the surface and the bottom of the sea. His argument was sound but he never overcame the formidable engineering difficulties. Although 75 when WORLD WAR II ended, Claude was imprisoned as a VICHY sympathizer.

Claudel, Paul (Louis Charles Marie) (1888–1955). French poet and dramatist. Claudel underwent a spiritual epiphany in 1886 that led to his conversion to Roman Catholicism, which he eloquently championed in his later writing. A career diplomat beginning in 1890, Claudel lived in the U.S., South America and the Orient. His poetic dramas, such as *L'Annonce faite a Marie* (*The Tidings of Mary,* 1912) and *Le Soulier de Satin* (*The Satin Slipper,* 1925), so effectively proselytized for the Roman Catholic Church that Claudel was publicly honored by Pope PIUS XII in 1950. His plays were collected into *Oeuvres complete* (13 volumes, 1950–59). His poetry, which includes *Cinq grandes Odes* (1910) and *La Cantate a troix voix* (1913), evidences the influence of the Symbolist poets. Claudel also wrote essays on metaphysics, poetry and religion, and later in life concentrated on studying and interpreting the Bible, writing commentary endorsing its symbolic interpretation.

Clay, Lucius D(uBignon) (1897–1978). American army officer and diplomat who played a prominent role in the reconstruction of Germany after WORLD WAR II and in two major crises of the COLD WAR. Clay came from a distinguished Southern family: his father was a U.S. senator, and he was descended from the 19th-century American statesman Henry Clay. Graduating from West Point in 1918, Clay served in the Army Engineering Corps until 1942. Known for his organizational ability and leadership qualities, for much of World War II he was head of the Army's procurement program (1942–44). He saw action in France briefly after the INVASION OF NORMANDY (1944). At the end of the war he was appointed commander of U.S. forces in Europe and military governor of Germany. In these roles he was directly involved in the denazification of Germany, in German reconstruction, and in implementing the MARSHALL PLAN. In response to the Soviet blockade of West Berlin (1948–49), he ordered and supervised the successful massive airlift of supplies (see BERLIN AIRLIFT).

After retiring from the Army he entered business as chairman of the Continental Can Co. He campaigned for Dwight D. EISENHOWER in the presidential election of 1952. When communist authorities erected the BERLIN WALL (1961), Clay returned to Berlin as the personal representative of President John F. KENNEDY, with the rank of ambassador (1961–62). He was later a senior partner of the investment banking firm Lehman Brothers (1963–73) and served on the boards of numerous other corporations.

For further reading:

Clay, Lucius D., *Decision in Germany.* Westport, Conn.: Greenwood, 1970.

Gelb, Norman, *The Berlin Wall: Kennedy, Khrushchev & a Showdown in the Heart of Europe*. New York: Simon & Schuster, 1988.

Smith, Jean E. (ed.), *The Papers of General Lucius D. Clay: Germany 1945–1949*. Bloomington: Indiana University Press, 1975.

Tusa, Ann and Tusa, John, *The Berlin Airlift*. New York: Atheneum, 1989.

Cleaver, A.V. (?–1977). British engineer. A leading space activist, Cleaver was a member of the British Interplanetary Society and served as its chairman in the 1950s. Author of many papers on space technology, exploration and development, Cleaver also worked as chief engineer and manager of the Rocket Department of Rolls-Royce, Ltd., England.

Cleaver, (Leroy) Eldridge (1935–). American black activist leader. Born in Wabbaseka, Ark., Cleaver was raised in Los Angeles' Watts section. Involved in various crimes, including rape, he was sentenced to a number of reformatories and jails. While in Folsom Prison, he became a Black Muslim and began writing. On his release in 1966, he joined the BLACK PANTHERS. *Soul on Ice* (1968), a collection of his powerful and immensely personal prison writings, became one of the best known radical works on the black experience in the U.S. In 1968 Cleaver's parole was revoked and he fled to Algeria, remaining in exile there until 1975. Returning to the U.S., he was converted to Christianity and CONSERVATISM, subjects he discussed in lectures and the book *Soul on Fire* (1978).

Clemence, Gerald Maurice (1908–1974). American astronomer. Clemence studied mathematics at Brown University. After graduating, in 1930 he joined the staff of the U.S. Naval Observatory where he remained until 1963, serving as head astronomer and director of the Nautical Almanac from 1945 to 1958 and science director of the observatory from 1958. In 1963 he was appointed senior research associate and lecturer at Yale, becoming professor of astronomy in 1966, a post he held until his death. Clemence's work was primarily concerned with the orbital motions of the Earth, moon, and planets. In 1951, in collaboration with Dirk BROUWER and W.J. Eckert, Clemence published the basic paper *Coordinates of the Five Outer Planets 1653–2060*. This was a considerable advance on the tables for the outer planets calculated by Simon Newcomb and George W. Hill 50 years earlier. Clemence and his colleagues calculated the precise positions of the outer planets at 40–day intervals over a period of 400 years. It was the first time that the influence of the planets on each other was calculated at each step; the prevailing custom was to assume that the paths of all except one were known in advance. Such an ambitious scheme was made possible only by the emergence of high-speed computers, one of which was made available to them by IBM from 1948. For each step some 800 multiplications and several hundred other arithmetical operations were required. Clemence said they would have taken a human computer 80 years if he could have completed the work without committing any errors en route. Clemence also conceived the idea that Brouwer named **Ephemeris Time,** by which time could be determined very accurately from the orbital positions of the moon and the Earth. Ephemeris Time came into use in 1958, although it has been superseded for most purposes by the more accurate atomic time scale.

French Premier Georges Clemenceau (1929).

Clemenceau, Georges (1841–1929). French statesman, an ardent republican and two-time premier (1906–09, 1917–20), nicknamed "the Tiger." Trained as a doctor, he was a journalist and teacher. He began his stormy political career as mayor of Montmartre (1870), after the fall of Napoleon III. Elected as a Radical member of the chamber of deputies in 1876, he served until 1893 when he was unjustly implicated in the Panama Canal scandal. Clemenceau devoted the next nine years to journalism, returning to the political arena when he passionately defended Alfred Dreyfus. He became a senator in 1902, and served as premier for the first time from 1906 to 1909. During that period, he strengthened the alliance with Great Britain and approved the ANGLO-RUSSIAN ENTENTE of 1907 that led to the TRIPLE ENTENTE. At home, he battled labor unrest; his harsh treatment of strikers caused a rift with the Radicals and his fall from office. Resuming his journalistic activities, Clemenceau lashed out at Germany and called for French military strength.

In November 1917, he again became premier, forming a coalition government. An indomitable leader, he almost singlehandedly rallied national morale, helping his nation weather the German onslaughts of 1918 and ultimately leading it to victory. As leader of the French delegation at the PARIS PEACE CONFERENCE of 1919, he came into conflict with the idealistic American President Woodrow WILSON. He fought for buffer states on the Rhine and demanded German reparations, ultimately feeling that the Treaty of VERSAILLES did not adequately protect France. Although his attitude was the harshest of any of the Allies, many of his countrymen accused him of leniency, and he was defeated in the elections of 1920. In retirement, the fallen "Tiger" continued to warn of future German threats to Europe.

Clemente, Roberto (1934–1972). Puerto Rican-American baseball player. One of the greatest outfielders ever to play the game, Clemente won 12 Gold Gloves during his Pittsburgh Pirate career. From 1960 through 1968, his batting average never fell below .300, and he was named to 12 All-Star teams during the late 1960s and early 1970s. During that time, he also led the National League in batting four times. In 1971, he was named World Series MVP, as his .414 batting average and brilliant fielding led Pittsburgh to the championship. He hit his 3,000th base hit in 1972. Clemente died later that year in the crash of a plane bringing relief supplies to Nicaraguan earthquake victims. He was named to the Hall of Fame in 1973, when the five-year waiting period was waived in his honor.

Cliburn, Van [born Harvey Lavan Cliburn Jr.] (1934–). American pianist. One of the great piano virtuosos of his time, Van Cliburn was catapulted to international fame in 1958 when, at the height of the COLD WAR, he became the first American (and first non-Soviet) to win the prestigious Tchaikovsky Piano Competition in Moscow. Born in Shreveport, La., Cliburn gave his first public performance at the age of four. Shortly thereafter the Cliburn family settled in Kilgore, Tex., where Cliburn studied with his mother, a concert pianist and piano teacher. He later attended the Juilliard School of Music in New York, where he studied with Rosina LHEVINNE and Olga SAMAROFF. He made his solo concert debut with the Houston Symphony Orchestra (1947) and first performed at CARNEGIE

Van Cliburn.

HALL in 1948 as a winner of the National Music Festival Award. Graduating from Juilliard in 1954, he won the Leventritt Competition in New York that same year. For the next few years he gave concerts throughout the U.S. When his career began to falter, Lhevinne and Cliburn's manager, Arthur JUDSON, decided to enter him in the 1958 Tchaikovsky Competition. Cliburn's victory has become legendary; he made world headlines and became an instant celebrity. Gala receptions, parades, concert tours, television appearances, a recording contract and a Grammy Award (1959) followed. In 1962 a piano competition, named in his honor, was organized in Fort Worth, Tex. At the height of his powers, Cliburn was particularly known for his interpretation of Tchaikovsky's Piano Concerto No. 1 and RACHMANINOFF's Piano Concerto No. 3. In 1976 Cliburn retired from the concert stage and the recording studio. He began a "comeback" in 1989, although his repertoire was limited to the few works that had made his initial reputation.

For further reading:

Chasins, A., *The Van Cliburn Legend*. New York, 1959.

Clift, Montgomery [(Edward)] (1920–1966). American theater and film actor. Although Clift made only 17 films, he received four ACADEMY AWARD nominations in recognition of his intense and brilliant acting style. Clift began his career as an acclaimed stage actor in the 1940s, appearing in a number of Broadway productions, most notably *The Skin of Our Teeth* (1942) by Thornton WILDER and *You Touched Me* (1945) by Tennessee WILLIAMS. He made his Hollywood debut in *The Search* (1948) and followed up with a role in the classic western *Red River* (1948), in which he was directed by Howard HAWKS and starred alongside John WAYNE. Other notable films featuring Clift include *The Heiress* (1949), *A Place in the Sun* (1951), *From Here to Eternity* (1953), *The Young Lions* (1958), *Suddenly Last Summer* (1959), *The Misfits* (1961) and *Judgment at Nuremberg* (1961). Clift suffered a severe auto accident in 1957, which left him with lingering pain and led him to alcohol and drug abuse, which is thought to have contributed to his early death by a heart attack.

Closing of the American Mind: Education and the Crisis of Reason, The. Book by American philosopher and educator Allan BLOOM. *The Closing of the American Mind* (1987) has been one of the most discussed works of social criticism to be published in the U.S. in recent years. In it, Bloom raises the highly controversial argument that the trends toward cultural relativism and curricula innovation, which began in the 1960s and continued through the 1980s, have sapped the strength of the Western intellectual tradition, which ought to remain the primary foundation of American educational efforts. Bloom identifies the Western intellectual tradition as commencing with Socrates and Plato and extending through the great philosophical tradition of Machiavelli, Hobbes, Rousseau and Nietzsche, all of whom utilized reason to critique and enlarge upon societal values. Because students are no longer trained in this tradition, they cannot appreciate the value of liberal education as offered by American colleges—which seeks to instill techniques of rational analysis as a means of guiding public and private decision-making. *The Closing of the American Mind* has become a seminal text for those advocating a more conservative approach to education in America.

Clubb, O(liver) Edmund (1901–1989). U.S. diplomat. Clubb was the last U.S. diplomat stationed in CHINA after the communists took control in 1949. He returned to the U.S. in 1950, but the following year he became one of several State Department officials to have his career wrecked by Senator Joseph MCCARTHY's anticommunist "witch hunts." McCarthy accused him of being a communist sympathizer, and Clubb was suspended as head of the State Department's China section. He fought the suspension and was cleared, but quit after being reassigned because he felt the government had been disloyal to him.

Club Mediterranee. An empire of vacation villages, founded by Belgian Gerard Blitz in 1950. "Club Med" began as a nonprofit association in which travelers would pay a set fee in exchange for a tropical, get-away-from-it-all vacation in which no money was required. Billed as an "antidote to civilization," Club Med grew into one of the world's largest tourism groups, with more than 87,000 beds around the world.

Club of Rome. An international organization of scientists, industrialists and economists founded in Rome, Italy, in 1968 by Italian business executive Aurelio Peccei. The club studied problems of industrialization, population growth and depletion of natural resources. In 1972 it published *The Limits to Growth,* which predicted the collapse of society wihin 100 years if current trends continued. The book's conclusions were based on a computer model.

For further reading:

Meadows, Donella H., *The Limits to Growth: A Report for the Club of Rome's Project on the Predicament of Mankind*, 2nd ed. New York: Universe Books, 1974.

Clurman, Harold (Edgar) (1901–1980). American theater director, drama critic, author and teacher. Clurman's stage productions and scholarship influenced the American theater for nearly 50 years. He founded the GROUP THEATER in 1931, which became known for landmark stage productions in the 1930s. He directed numerous plays there. He also served as drama critic for *The Nation* and wrote several books, including *All People Are Famous* (1974).

Clyde River and Firth of Clyde. River and its estuary, the most prominent in Scotland. Shipbuilding leads all other industry in this heavily populated area. Glasgow, on the river's bank, is Scotland's largest city, seaport and industrial and shipbuilding hub, but was faltering late in the century. The famous OCEAN LINERS QUEEN MARY and *Queen Elizabeth* were constructed here in the 1930s. Another city on the Clyde is Hamilton, close to where Rudolf HESS, the Nazi leader, landed after he fled Germany in a small airplane in May 1941.

Coates, Wells (1895–1958). English architect and industrial designer, one of the first practitioners of MODERNISM in Great Britain. Coates was born in Japan and studied engineering at McGill University in Montreal, Canada. In 1929 he moved to London where he took up architectural practice. His Lawn Road Flats of 1934 in London is his best-known building in the INTERNATIONAL STYLE. In 1931 he founded Isokon with Jack Pritchard to manufacture furniture and other products of modern design in plywood. In 1933 he was among the founders of the Mars group, the English chapter of CIAM. As an industrial designer, he became known for furniture design using tubular steel and plywood in a BAUHAUS-related style. His best-known work is an Ekco radio (Model ADD65) of 1934, a cylindrical table model of ART DECO character with a case of BAKELITE plastic. He was also the designer of a variety of other Ekco electrical products, of BBC radio studio interiors, and of aircraft interiors for British Overseas Airways Corporation.

Cobb, Arnett Cleophus (1918–1989). American jazz saxophonist. Cobb first came to prominence after he joined the Lionel HAMPTON Orchestra in 1942. An automobile accident in 1956 temporarily halted his performing career; after he returned, he performed on crutches for the remainder of his life. His frail appearance contrasted with the robust sound of his tenor sax playing.

Cobb, Ty(rus Raymond) (1886–1961). Legendary American baseball outfielder. In 22 seasons with the Detroit Tigers, Cobb had the highest lifetime batting average (.367) and, until recent years, the

Baseball star Ty Cobb.

most hits (4,191) and the most stolen bases (892). Manager of the Tigers from 1921 to 1926, he was inducted into the Baseball Hall of Fame in 1936. While venerated as an icon of the game, Cobb has also been criticized for his racism and his violent temper.

For further reading:

Alexander, Charles C., *Ty Cobb*. New York: Oxford University Press, 1984.

Coblentz, William Weber (1873–1962). American physicist. Coblentz was educated at the Case Institute of Technology and at Cornell, where he earned his Ph.D. in 1903. In 1904 he joined the National Bureau of Standards in Washington and in the following year founded the radiometry section of the Bureau, where he remained until his retirement in 1945. Coblentz worked mainly on studies of infrared radiation. At the Lick Observatory he began, in 1914, a series of measurements aimed at determining the heat radiated by stars. He was also one of the pioneers of absorption spectroscopy in the infrared region as a technique for identifying compounds.

CoBrA. International arts movement (1948–51), an acronym of its founders' home cities: "Co"penhagen (painter Asger Jorn), "Br"ussels (Belgian writer Christian Dotremont) and "A"msterdam (Dutch artists Karel Appel, Constant [A. Nieuwenhys] and Corneille [Guillaume van Beverloo]). Among the other artists associated with CoBrA was the Belgian painter Pierre Alechinsky. Formed in reaction against the formalism of the School of Paris, the movement stressed a spontaneous expressionism, a bold use of color and a dramatic visual vocabulary of figures and symbols.

Coburn, Alvin Langdon (1882–1966). American photographer. Born in Boston, Coburn started experimenting with photographs at the age of eight. He joined the American PHOTO-SECESSION Group in 1902 and the British Salon of the Linked Ring the following year. Moving to London, Coburn became widely known for his probing portraits of literary and artistic figures, photographs that were collected in the two volumes of *Men of Mark* (1913, 1922). He also created notable landscapes, city scenes and seascapes, as well as the so-called vortographs, the first completely abstract photographs. His autobiography *Photographer* was published in 1966.

Coca-Cola. Brand name of an American soft drink that in the 20th century has become one of the most widely-consumed beverages worldwide. Although closely identified with the 20th century, Coca-Cola was invented in the 19th century (1866). The formula was later purchased by Asa Griggs CANDLER. Coca-Cola is made almost exclusively of sugar and water; early in the century, COCAINE was reputedly an ingredient. The drink's popularity spread after World War II, helped by a massive advertising campaign and by the emergence of the U.S. as the leading free-world power. In the 1980s, the company changed the formula and introduced "the new coke," but there was such an outcry that the company was forced to bring back the old formula, under the name "Coke Classic." In many places, Coke is now made with fructose. The drink's main rival is Pepsi-Cola.

cocaine. Powerfully stimulative alkaloid-based drug derived from the leaves of coca plants (grown mainly in Colombia, Peru and Bolivia). For many years coca leaves were chewed by Peruvian Indians in the Andes Mountains to counteract the effects of altitude. Cocaine became known in the West in the late 19th century, and (in a refined and more potent powder form) was used for a number of medical purposes. Realization of its dangerous physical and psychological effects ended most medicinal use. Cocaine resurfaced in the 1970s as the so-called "recreational" use of illicit drugs expanded; cocaine acquired the reputation of a "glamour" drug and use soared. In the mid-1980s, a new, cheap, smokable form of cocaine known as **crack** became available. Crack produces an even more intense (but shorter-lived) "high" in the user, followed by a period of deep depression. Crack also causes erratic, often violent behavior and is instantly addictive. By the late 1980s, the widespread use of cocaine and crack had become a major social problem in the U.S.

Cochran, Jackie (1906 or 1910–1980). Pioneer American flier. Cochran learned to fly in her early 20s and went on to set more than 200 aviation records. She held more speed, distance and altitude records than any other flyer of her era. During WORLD WAR II she was director of the Woman's Air Force Service Pilots, a program that trained over 1,200 female pilots. In 1953 she became the first woman to break the sound barrier, and in 1964 she set another speed record of some 1,425 miles per hour.

Cockcroft, Sir John Douglas (1897–1967). British physicist. Cockcroft entered Manchester University in 1914 to study mathematics, but left the following year to join the army. After WORLD WAR I he was apprenticed to the engineering firm Metropolitan Vickers, which sent him to study electrical engineering at the Manchester College of Technology. He later went to Cambridge University, graduated in mathematics, and joined Ernest RUTHERFORD's team at the Cavendish Laboratory. Cockcroft soon became interested in designing a device for accelerating protons and, with E.T.S. Walton, constructed a voltage multiplier. Using this the two bombarded nuclei of lithium with protons and, in 1932, brought about the first nuclear transformation by artificial means. For this work Cockcroft and Walton received the 1951 NOBEL PRIZE for physics. During WORLD WAR II Cockcroft played a leading part in the development of RADAR. In 1940 he visited the U.S. as a member of the Tizard mission to negotiate exchanges of military, scientific and technological information. In 1944 he became director of the Anglo-Canadian Atomic Energy Commission. He returned to Britain in 1946 to direct the new Atomic Energy Research Establishment at Harwell and remained there until 1959, when he was appointed master of Churchill College, Cambridge, a new college devoted especially to science and technology. Cockcroft was knighted in 1948.

Cocos Islands [Keeling Islands]. Australian territory comprising a chain of islands in the Indian Ocean, about 580 miles southwest of Java. During WORLD WAR I, on November 9, 1914, the German cruiser *Emden* was demolished by the Australian cruiser *Sydney* off the Cocos Islands. In 1886 Britain granted the islands to the Clunies-Ross family. Australia took possession of the islands in 1955 and purchased most of the Clunies-Ross' interest in 1978. The islanders have the rights of Australian citizens and are represented in the Australian parliament. Only two of the islands are inhabited; the population—Cocos Malays and inhabitants of European descent—numbers only 600.

Cocteau, Jean (1891–1963). French poet, dramatist, novelist, playwright, literary critic and film director. Cocteau was perhaps the most versatile writer of the 20th century, scoring critical successes in virtually every literary genre and earning the friendship of great contemporaries such as painter Pablo PICASSO and composer Igor STRAVINSKY. While he was loosely associated with CUBISM and SURREALISM, Cocteau ultimately remained free of all artistic schools, pursuing his own unique blend of imaginative myth and elegant wit. Cocteau published his first volume of poems when he was 17 but dated his real emergence as a writer with *Le Potomak* (1919), a prose fantasy. In 1917, he wrote the ballet *Parade* for a score by Erik SATIE. In the 1920s he turned to the psychological novel with *Thomas the Impostor* (1923) and *Les Enfants Terribles* (1929). His successful plays of the 1920s and 1930s include adaptations of *Antigone* (1928) and *The Infernal Machine* (1934). His pathbreaking films include *The Blood of a Poet* (1931) and *Beauty and the Beast* (1945).

Coetzee, J(ohn) M. (1940–). South African author. Coetzee was educated at the University of Cape Town and the University of Texas, and after working in Britain, he returned to the University of Cape Town, where he eventually became professor of general literature. His work, which examines the themes of the abuse of power and moral conscience in contemporary SOUTH AFRICA, includes *Dusklands* (1974), *The Life and Times of Michael K.* (1983, Booker Prize), *Foe* (1986) and *White Writing: On the Culture of Letters in South Africa* (1988). He received the Booker Prize in 1983 and the Prix Femina Etrange in 1985.

Coffin, Henry S(loan) (1877–1954). American religious leader. Coffin, who was ordained as a Presbyterian minister in 1900, became the pastor of the Madison Avenue Church in New York City in 1905 and served there for over 20 years. His sermons drew considerable public attention due to their emphasis on social issues and contemporary Christian ethical dilemmas. Coffin went on to become the president of the Union Theological Seminary in New York City from 1926 to 1945. *Memory of the Cross* (1931) is noteworthy among his many works.

Coffin, William Sloane, Jr. (1924–). American Presbyterian minister; well-known in the 1960s for his fervent involvement in the ANTIWAR MOVEMENT during the VIETNAM WAR. Coffin's background made this involvement particularly ironic—he had served as an intelligence officer during WORLD WAR II and worked for the CENTRAL INTELLIGENCE AGENCY (CIA) in the early 1950s before graduating from the Yale Divinity School in 1956. Subsequently, he served as chaplain for Yale University, and it was while holding this position that he was charged, in 1968, with criminal conspiracy to violate federal draft laws. The charges were overturned in 1970. Coffin became a minister at the interdenominational Riverside Church in New York City in 1977. *Once to Every Man* (1977) is his autobiography.

Coggan, Donald (1909–). Archbishop of Canterbury and spiritual leader of the Anglican Church. Coggan, who served as archbishop of Canterbury from 1974 to 1979, was best known for his break with longstanding Anglican tradition by advocating the right of women to become ordained as priests. He also suggested a reconciliation with the Roman Catholic Church through intercommunion—the receiving of the sacrament of communion by and between priests of both the Anglican and Catholic churches. Prior to his election as archbishop, Coggan had taught theology at Wycliffe College in Toronto and at the London School of Divinity and had served as bishop of Bradford.

Cohan, George M(ichael) (1878–1942). U.S. actor, composer, playwright and producer. He started performing with his family and later played comedy roles in vaudeville and on the stage. In 1893, he began writing skits and songs for vaudeville shows, and in 1901 his first full-length play opened in New York. His musicals include *Little Johnny Jones* (1904), *The Talk of New York* (1907) and *The Song and Dance Man* (1923). He wrote numerous songs, including "Give My Regards to Broadway" and "Over There," for which Congress awarded him a special medal in 1940. His career was the subject of an enduring movie classic, *Yankee Doodle Dandy* (1943).

"Yankee Doodle Dandy"—George M. Cohan (1923).

Cohen, Benjamin Victor (1894–1983). American attorney. A member of President Franklin D. ROOSEVELT'S BRAIN TRUST, Cohen was one of the principal architects of the NEW DEAL legislation enacted during the GREAT DEPRESSION of the 1930s. Along with his close associate Thomas G. CORCORAN, Cohen was credited with writing such key measures as the **Securities and Exchange Act,** the first Wage and Hours bill, and the Public Utilities Holding Company act. He later held a number of political posts, most notably delegate to the UNITED NATIONS (1948–52).

Cohen, Seymour Stanley (1917–). American biochemist. Cohen was educated in New York, at the City College and at Columbia, where he earned his Ph.D. in 1941. He joined the University of Pennsylvania in 1943, serving as professor of biochemistry from 1954 until 1971, when he moved to the University of Denver as professor of microbiology. Cohen returned to New York in 1976 to take the chair of pharmaceutical sciences at the State University, Stony Brook. In 1946 Cohen began a series of studies in molecular biology using radioactive labeling. Cohen used this technique in a number of experiments in the late 1940s that suggested rather than demonstrated the vital role of DNA in heredity. It was not until 1952, when Alfred Hershey and Martha Chase used Cohen's labeling technique, that more substantial results were available.

Cohn, Harry (1891–1958). Cofounder, president and head of production at COLUMBIA PICTURES in HOLLYWOOD. Said to have been the most tyrannical of the old-guard studio barons, Cohn came from an immigrant family on New York's Upper East Side. He worked in vaudeville and as a songwriter before forming the C.B.C. Film Sales Company with his brother Jack in 1920. Cohn relocated to Hollywood as production chief, and four years later the studio was renamed Columbia Pictures. From humble beginnings, Columbia became one of Hollywood's most successful studios in the 1930s and 1940s. After a long power struggle with his brother, Cohn became president of the studio in 1932—and the only production chief in Hollywood to double as president of his company. To director Frank CAPRA, an important Cohn discovery, he was one of a breed of "tough, brassy, untutored buccaneers. . .indigent, hot-eyed entrepreneurs, gamblers who played longshots." Cohn was obsessed with movies, maintaining absolute control of studio operations down to the last detail. Some hunches, such as the discovery of Rita HAYWORTH in the mid-1930s, paid off; others, such as the dismissal of Marilyn MONROE in 1949, didn't. After a "last hurrah" of several successful pictures, including *On the Waterfront* (1954), Cohn died following hernia surgery.

Cohn, Roy (1927–1986). Controversial American attorney who first gained notoriety for his role in the ARMY-MCCARTHY HEARINGS. Cohn served as council for Senator Joseph MCCARTHY'S committee investigating alleged communists in the U.S. government in the late 1940s and early 1950s. He gained national prominence during the committee's televised hearings in which McCarthy denounced numerous people as communists or dangerous "fellow travelers." Cohn was also a prosecutor in the famous ROSENBERG TRIAL. In later years Cohn turned to private practice where he earned a reputation as a combative lawyer and was often accused of being abrasive and relying on intimidation. Cohn, a friend of many in New York's society, became a minor celebrity. He also had a running battle with the Internal Revenue Service and was audited annually. He was tried and acquitted three times on bribery, extortion, blackmail and obstruction of justice charges. Even the true cause of his death proved controversial. He claimed to be suffering from liver cancer, but the White House was said to have moved him ahead of other patients waiting to receive experimental treatments for AIDS.

Colani, Luigi (1928–). German industrial designer known for his aggressively futuristic approach to design. Colani was educated in Berlin and Paris in painting, sculpture, and, later, aerodynamics. His drawings of futuristically streamlined cars led to his development of a variety of racing and sports cars built as prototypes but never actually produced. Only the Colani T Spider, a two-seat sports body for a VOLKSWAGEN chassis, was produced as a do-it-yourself FIBERGLASS kit. About 500 were sold from 1950 to 1960. More recent projects have included furniture designs, a design for a small TV set, and various designs for cars, trucks, and boats.

Cold War. Protracted state of tension between countries falling short of actual warfare. The term was first used in the U.S. Congress to describe deteriorating post-World War II relations between the U.S. and the U.S.S.R. It especially describes the period of tension between 1946 and the early 1970s, marked by such international crises as the GREEK CIVIL WAR, the construction of the BERLIN WALL and the CUBAN MISSILE CRISIS. The division between the West and the communist world was formalized by the creation of NATO (1949–50) and the WARSAW PACT (1955). The momentous events of 1989–90 in Eastern Europe, marking the transition from communist to non-communist governments, are widely seen as marking the end of the Cold War.

Cole, Nat "King" [Nathaniel Adams Coles] (1919–1965). Black American JAZZ and popular music vocalist and pianist.

A view of the Berlin Wall; the swath of steel-spiked matting underlines the Cold War division of communist from non-communist (1978).

Cole began his career as a jazz pianist. He founded his own jazz group, the King Cole Trio, in the late 1930s. But within a decade, his playing had been overshadowed by his distinctive vocal talent—soft and smooth, yet emotionally compelling—which made him a star. Major hits by Cole in the 1940s and 1950s include "Mona Lisa," "Nature Boy" and "Too Young." He also hosted his own radio and television shows. Cole was a major breakthrough figure as a black performing for mainstream white audiences. As such, he was a major influence on the next generation of black vocalists, especially Sam Cooke and Marvin GAYE.

Velvety-voiced Nat "King" Cole (1964)

Coleman, Ornette (1930–). American alto saxophonist-composer. Coleman is one of modern jazz's most enigmatic figures. Though reflecting influences from the 1940s' BEBOP revolution spawned by Charlie PARKER and Dizzy GILLESPIE, Coleman also has drawn from the collective improvisational approach of the New Orleans tradition and the raw emotion of Mississippi BLUES. For some, Coleman has "liberated" jazz from its dependence on predetermined harmonic patterns and the convention of melodic variation; for others, including modern jazz giants Miles DAVIS and Charles MINGUS, Coleman's collective "music" is primitive, a cacophonous collage lacking either form or substance. Depending on one's point-of-view, the controversy stirred by Coleman's radical style can be seen as pitting "freedom" against "anarchy." In the U.S., the impact of Coleman's approach—with its emphasis on group rather than virtuosic solo improvisation—has waned since its heyday in the 1960s; however, it continues to be a force in European FREE JAZZ circles. Coleman's most inspired playing and writing came in the late 1950s and 1960s; "Blues Connotation" and "Lonely Woman" are among the tunes Coleman has contributed to the repertory of "jazz standards." Overall, Coleman's greatest influence may have been in provoking—like John CAGE in conservatory music—broadly based questions on the very nature of jazz, its basic assumptions, materials and improvisational procedures.

For further reading:

Litweiler, John, "Ornette Coleman: the Birth of Freedom," in *The Freedom Principle: Jazz After 1958.* New York: William Morrow, 1984.

Colette [Sidonie Gabrielle Colette] (1873–1954). French novelist. Colette spent her childhood in the countryside of Burgundy, which inspired a responsiveness to nature apparent in her later work. In 1893 she married the writer Willy (Henry Gauthier-Villars), who encouraged her to write about her childhood and to make the stories as risque as possible. This resulted in the Claudine series: *Claudine a l'Ecole* (1900; tr. *Claudine at School,* 1930) *Claudine a Paris* (1901; tr *Claudine in Paris,* 1958) *Claudine en Menage* (1902; tr. Claudine Married 1960) and *Claudine s'en va* (published in English as *Claudine and Annie,* which Willy usurped and first had published under his name between 1900 and 1903). The marriage was an unhappy one, and Colette left Willy in 1906, working as a dancer and a mime in music halls while continuing to write novels, including *La Vagabond* (1911). Her writing is rich, sensuous and sensitive to the influence of nature. Her later works evocatively depict the phases in a woman's life. Colette married twice more and was the first woman to be elected to the Goncourt Academy as well as the first to be honored by a state funeral. Other important novels include *Mitsou; ou, Comment l'esprit vient aux filles* (1919, translated as *Mitsou, or How Girls Grow Wise*), *Cheri* (1920) and *Gigi* (1944), which inspired a musical film of the same name in 1958.

collage. Technique of creating art or graphic works by assembling various material fragments and pasting them on a flat surface. Collage became a widely used technique for the production of abstract works of modern art during the 1920s and has continued as a significant alternative to painting used by many artists. Typical

COLD WAR

1945	Roosevelt, Churchill and Stalin meet at Yalta Conference to plan postwar division of Europe; end of World War II.
1947	U.S. Secretary of State George C. Marshall proposes European Recovery Program (Marshall Plan).
1948	Communist takeover of Czechoslovakia.
1948-49	Soviets blockade West Berlin; U.S. and Allies respond with Berlin Airlift.
1949	Communists defeat Nationalists in Chinese Civil War, proclaim People's Republic of China; pro-Western forces defeat communists, ending Greek Civil War; U.S. and its Western allies form NATO alliance; U.S.S.R. successfully tests atomic bomb.
1950-53	Korean War.
1951	U.S. successfully tests first hydrogen bomb.
1953	Julius and Ethel Rosenberg executed for passing U.S. atomic secrets to the U.S.S.R.
1955	Warsaw Pact formed by U.S.S.R. and its Eastern bloc satellites.
1956	Hungarian uprising—rebellion against communist rule crushed by Soviet invasion.
1957	U.S.S.R. launches first artificial satellite, Sputnik 1.
1960	U2 incident—Soviets shoot down U.S. spy plane over U.S.S.R., convict pilot Gary Powers of spying.
1961	Berlin Wall erected; anti-Castro Cubans land in Cuba in abortive Bay of Pigs invasion.
1962	Cuban Missile Crisis.
1968	Soviet invasion of Czechoslovakia ends Prague Spring reforms.
1972	U.S., U.S.S.R. sign SALT-1 strategic arms limitation treaty.
1975	Vietnamese communists capture Saigon (Ho Chi Minh City), Vietnam unified under communists; Andrei Sakharov wins Nobel Prize for peace.
1983	U.S. invasion of Grenada deposes communist government; U.S. President Reagan denounces U.S.S.R. as "evil empire," proposes Strategic Defense Initiative.
1985	Mikhail Gorbachev becomes leader of U.S.S.R., ushering in period of *glasnost* and *perestroika.*
1986	Reykjavik summit between Gorbachev and Reagan; Reagan rejects Gorbachev plan to eliminate all nuclear weapons by 2000.
1988	U.S. President Reagan and Soviet leader Gorbachev hold summit meeting in Moscow.
1989	Tiananmen Square massacre—Chinese troops crush reform movement in China.
1989-90	Downfall of communist governments in Czechoslovakia, East Germany, Hungary, Poland, Romania; opening and dismantling of Berlin Wall.
1990	Reunification of Germany under democratic government; Lech Walesa elected president of Poland.
1991	Soviet troops use force to quell independence movements in Lithuania and Estonia; Soviet republic of Georgia declares independence from U.S.S.R.

collage materials are colored papers, fragments of cloth, wood, or other materials, and bits of printed material or actual objects, often cut or torn before being combined in a finished work. Collage was developed, to an exceptional degree, by the German artist Kurt Schwitters, an important figure in the DADA movement. The technique was taken up and used by many leading modern artists including Henri MATISSE, Georges BRAQUE, and Pablo PICASSO.

collective unconscious. See Carl Gustav JUNG.

collectivization. Policy first carried out in the UNION OF SOVIET SOCIALIST REPUBLICS under Joseph STALIN. The collectivization of agriculture was part of Stalin's plan to give the communist state complete control of the economy. In his first FIVE-YEAR PLAN (1928–33), Stalin attempted to consolidate small peasant farms into large **collective farms**. By abolishing privately owned farms, the government, not the farmers, could set food prices. In theory, collective farms were to be a source of cheap and plentiful grain with which to feed the nation and sustain the revolution. The KULAKS (prosperous peasant farmers) opposed collectivization; many were executed or deported to Siberian labor camps, and their property was seized by the government. By the early 1930s, the Soviet collectivization policy was well underway. However, contrary to Stalin's wishes, production did not increase; rather, it plummeted. The ensuing famine in the UKRAINE—traditionally the breadbasket of Russia—resulted in several million deaths during the early 1930s.

Collier, John (1901–1980). British novelist, screenwriter, poet and modern master of the wickedly macabre short story. Perhaps only SAKI at the turn of the century and Roald DAHL more recently have rivalled his gleefully diabolical touch. Although he worked as a literary critic for the *London Telegraph,* poetry editor for *Time and Tide,* novelist (*His Monkey Wife,* 1930), and screenplay writer in HOLLYWOOD (sharing scenario credit with James AGEE for *The African Queen,* 1951), it is upon his remarkable short stories that his fame must ultimately reside. Originally appearing in magazines like THE NEW YORKER, they have been collected in *Presenting Moonshine* (1941), *Fancies and Goodnights* (1951) and *Pictures in the Fire* (1958). The tales range from the gruesome (a man-eating orchid in "Green Thoughts") to the whimsical (the night-life among department store mannequins in "Evening Primrose") to the naughty (the erotic fables "Bottle Party" and "The Chaser") to the most outrageous degree of grand guignol (the cheerfully grisly "Another American Tragedy"). They are, in the words of Anthony Burgess, "quaint, precise, bookish, fantastic." All the same, they *bite,* frequently snatching up hapless readers in the jaws of a double-take.

Collins, J(oseph) Lawton (1896–1987). U.S. general. Collins was a U.S. combat leader in WORLD WAR II and subsequently Army chief of staff. He earned the nickname "Lightning Joe" when he commanded a division early in the war on the Pacific island of GUADALCANAL. Later, on the European front, he led the Army 7th Corps to the capture of Cherbourg. He led one of the two Army corps that landed at NORMANDY on D-day, on to the capture of Aachen and Cologne, and thence to a meeting with the Soviets at Dessau. As army chief of staff from 1949 to 1953, he was at the head of that service throughout the KOREAN WAR.

Collins, Judy (1939–). American folk and popular music vocalist and songwriter. Collins emerged as a major folk music star with her very first album, *Maid of Constant Sorrow* (1961), which featured her trademark, bell-clear vocals and affecting lyrical delivery. Two other successful albums followed during this period of peak popularity for Collins—*In My Life* (1966) and *Wildflowers* (1967), the first album to feature songs written by Collins herself. During the 1960s, Collins was politically active in support of civil rights and in opposition to the VIETNAM WAR. She was also the inspiration for the Crosby, Stills & Nash hit song "Judy Blue Eyes" (1970). Subsequent albums by Collins, which have been less commercially successful, include *Judith* (1975) and *Hard Times for Lovers* (1979).

Collins, Michael (1890–1922). Irish revolutionary leader. After working in England (1907–16), he returned to Ireland and participated in the EASTER REBELLION of 1916. A member of SINN FEIN and a leader of the IRISH REPUBLICAN ARMY, he was one of the organizers of the Dail Eireann in 1919 and became a member of that assembly. Three years later he helped formulate the treaty that created the IRISH FREE STATE. Serving briefly as finance minister in the government of Arthur GRIFFITH, he was assassinated by extremists in 1922.

Collins, Michael (1930–). U.S. astronaut. "O.K., Eagle...You guys take care." With those words, Collins watched Neil ARMSTRONG and Edwin "Buzz" ALDRIN maneuver the APOLLO 11 (July 16–24, 1969) lunar module away from the command module and begin their historic descent to the moon. During the next 24 hours Collins continued to circle the moon while his crewmates made history on its surface. This was Collins' second space flight; as pilot of Gemini 10 (July 18–21, 1966) he had made two space walks during the three-day rendezvous and docking mission. Son of a Army major general, Collins was born in Rome and is the author of *Carrying the Fire,* a book of memoirs, *Flying to the Moon and Other Strange Places,* a children's book, and *Liftoff: The Story of America's Adventure in Space.*

Cologne [German: Koln]. German city in North Rhine-Westphalia, on the Rhine River 20 miles south-southeast of Dusseldorf. It was demolished by Allied air raids in WORLD WAR II but has been reconstructed as a key industrial and commercial area.

Colombia. Nation at the northwestern edge of South America, bordering on both the Caribbean Sea and the Pacific Ocean. Liberated from Spanish control, the 19th century saw political friction between right and left blocs and intermittent civil war. In 1878 Colombia granted a French firm a concession to construct a canal across the Isthmus of Panama, but the venture floundered. The **Hay-Herran Treaty** of 1903 consigned this right to the U.S.; in exchange, Colombia was to collect $10 million and an annuity of $250,000. The Colombian senate denied the ratification of the treaty, but a Panamanian uprising on November 3, assisted by the U.S., made PANAMA a separate country. In 1921 Colombia acknowledged Panamanian autonomy after a U.S. payment of $25 million.

In 1932 a rift with PERU occurred over ownership of Leticia and its region; the LEAGUE OF NATIONS granted it to Colombia in 1934. From the late 1940s to the late 1950s bloody civil turmoil ran rampant—*la Violencia* (see COLOMBIAN REVOLT OF 1948). In 1957 fatigued liberals and conservatives joined forces to reduce disorder. In 1978 liberal Julio Cesar Turbay Ayala was elected president; his government took credit for destroying the main guerrilla circle, but disorder extended into the 1980s. Conservative Party candidate Belisario Betancor was elected president in 1982. In the late 1980s Colombia was besieged by the brutality of criminal cocaine traffickers (see MEDELLIN CARTEL); many police officers, judges and govern-

COLOMBIA

COLOMBIA

1903	Panama secedes from Colombia with U.S. backing.
1940	Colombia's oil pipelines are destroyed, allegedly by German fifth columnists.
1948	Bogota Mayor Jorge Eliecer's assassination begins "La Violencia," 10 years of lawlessness.
1957	First vote on basis of universal suffrage.
1985	22,000 people are killed in volcanic disaster at Armero
1989	Medellin cocaine traffickers kill presidential candidate Luis Carlos Galan (August).
1990	Medellin drug cartel issues declaration of surrender.

ment officials were bribed, intimidated or assassinated. When a prominent politician, Carlos Galan was murdered during a campaign rally (August 1989), President Virgilio Barco Vargas declared war on the drug cartels. The government subsequently made progress against the cartels, arresting many top figures. Colombia's capital and largest city is Bogota; other cities include Medellin, Cali and Barranquilla.

Colombian Guerrilla War of 1976. In 1976 the Colombian government instituted a state of siege against left-wing guerrillas, but leftist violence continued leading to a "security statute" (1978) that curtailed individual liberties. On January 1, 1979, guerrillas of the Movement of April 19 (M-19) captured more than 5,000 weapons from the Bogota arsenal, inducing violent government reprisals. Another left-wing group, the Colombian Revolutionary Armed Forces (FARC), simultaneously increased its attacks, while M-19 seized 15 diplomats in 1980, demanding a ransom and release of political prisoners. A settlement was reached after 61 days. Many M-19 leaders were killed or captured in a shootout with the army (March 18, 1981), but M-19 and FARC activities continued, while right-wing paramilitary groups engaged in reprisals. An amnesty (1982–83) had little success. Successive governments have attempted to improve living conditions and induce guerrillas to join the peaceful political process, but guerrillas and right-wing death squads continue to terrorize Colombia.

Colombian Revolt of 1948. Colombia, plagued by economic and social problems, was also embroiled in a political feud between Liberals and Conservatives. When popular left-wing Liberal Jorge Eliecer Gaitan (1902–1948) was assassinated on April 9, 1948, long repressed tensions overflowed in violence. This initiated a period called "La Violencia" (1948–1958), a state of constant insurrection and criminality. Over 200,000 people were killed and billions of dollars of damage was done. Arch-conservative Laureano Eleuterio Gomez (1889–1965) served as president from 1950 until ousted in 1953 by army chief of staff General Gustavo Rojas Pinilla. Rojas ruled as dictator until his corrupt rule was ended by a military junta (1957). In 1958 democracy returned with a National Front government, a Liberal-Conservative coalition, under newly elected President Alberto LLERAS CAMARGO, who slowly stabilized the country.

Colombo. Capital city and harbor on the west coast of SRI LANKA (formerly Ceylon), on the Indian Ocean. It served as an Allied naval base in WORLD WAR II and was named the capital in 1948. In June 1951 an economic improvement group, the COLOMBO PLAN, was created at an international conference here. The Portuguese fort and a large area of old streets are historic sites.

Colombo Plan. An international plan for economic development aid to countries of south and southeast Asia. First proposed in 1950, at a meeting of British COMMONWEALTH OF NATIONS foreign ministers in Colombo, Ceylon (now Sri Lanka), the Colombo Plan was intended for regional Commonwealth nations only. Australia's Prime Minister Robert Gordon MENZIES foresaw its potential to counter communism in the region and U.S. backing was sought. The program is now administered through headquarters in Colombo. Regional members include most most nations from IRAN east to FIJI, excepting Vietnam, China, North Korea and Brunei. Nonregional members are AUSTRALIA, CANADA, the UNITED KINGDOM, JAPAN, NEW ZEALAND and the U.S. Regional members plan their own development programs. Nonregional members contribute financially and provide training, research and consultative services. The U.S. has provided a large share of the funding.

Colonels, Greek. Military junta that seized power in GREECE on April 21, 1967. The coup was led by two colonels, George PAPADOPOULOS and Stylianos Pattakos, who suspended the democratic constitution. The regime collapsed in July 1974, following its intervention in CYPRUS. (See also Greek-Turkish CYPRIOT WAR OF 1974.)

color-field painting. Style of painting that originated with one wing of ABSTRACT EXPRESSIONISM. Using pure color in two-dimensional space on enormous canvases, such painters as Mark ROTHKO and Barnett Newman created a unified color field of closely valued color. The technique was used in new ways by painters of the next generation, such as Friedel DZUBAS, Morris Louis, Kenneth NOLAND and Jules Olitsky, who also used monumentally scaled canvases (sometimes shaped), two-dimensional space and their own configurations of pure color. The work of this second group of painters was dubbed "post-painterly abstraction" by the critic Clement Greenberg.

Coltrane, John (1926–1967). Tenor and soprano saxophonist; arguably the most influential jazz innovator of the 1960s. Coleman's earliest professional experiences were in rhythm-and-blues, then with jazz stalwarts Dizzy GILLESPIE and Johnny Hodges. Initially obsessed with pushing the boundaries of BEBOP chord progressions to the limit, Coltrane developed an unparalleled virtuosity in articulating scalular and arpeggiated patterns with a steely sound aptly described by critic Ira Gitler as "sheets of sound." These successful, if then controversial, experiments were explored by Coltrane in the late 1950s as a key member of the highly visible Miles DAVIS Quintet. In 1960, the tenorman formed the pivotal John Coltrane Quartet, whose seminal edition included pianist McCoy Tyner, bassist Jimmy Garrison and drummer Elvin Jones. He also added soprano saxophone to his arsenal; though the soprano was considered a relic from the 1920s, Coltrane developed a singularly muscular approach that proved the instrument a potent jazz voice, and by 1970 a virtually mandatory "double" for all tenorists. While best known for his unprecedented up-tempo harmonic explorations, Coltrane was also a consummate interpreter of ballads. In the mid-1960s, Coltrane's relentless quest led him to controversial explorations of the avant-garde, but with the deep spirituality that marked each phase of his career. In addition to his enormous influence as a stylistically innovative player, Coltrane left a number of now-standard jazz compositions, including "Giant Steps," "Impressions" and "Naima."

Jazz saxophonist John Coltrane (1967).

For further reading:
Thomas, J.C., *Chasin' the Trane: The Music and Mystique of John Coltrane.* Garden City, New York: Doubleday, 1975.

Colum, Padraic (1881–1972). Irish-American poet. Born in Ireland, he was an important figure in the IRISH LITERARY REVIVAL, and helped to found the Abbey Theater (1902) and the *Irish Review* (1911). In 1912 he married the Irish literary critic and short story writer Mary Maguire (1880?-1957), and they settled in the U.S. in 1914. His volumes of poetry include *Wild Earth* (1907), *Creatures* (1927) and *Collected Poems* (1953). Colum also wrote a number of plays and stories for children based on Irish folktales.

Columbia Basin Project. Launched on the Columbia River in the northwestern U.S. in 1948—a U.S. government irrigation, hydroelectric power and flood-control plan, with Grand Coulee Dam as its major facility.

Columbia Broadcasting System. See CBS.

Columbia Pictures. One of HOLLYWOOD's "Little Three" production companies (along with UNITED ARTISTS and UNIVERSAL PICTURES) and the only studio to transcend its "Poverty Row" origins to become a major corporation. The driving force behind Columbia was the colorful, indomitable Harry COHN, who personally supervised all studio production until his death in 1958. Cohn and his brother Jack had been producing cheap westerns and comedies since the early 1920s for their C.B.C. Film Sales Corporation in Hollywood. In 1924 they changed the company name to Columbia and in 1926 released their first feature-length film, *Blood Ship.* The arrival of director Frank CAPRA a year later had an enormous impact on the studio's rising fortunes. For the next 10 years his remarkable comedies and dramas, including *It Happened One Night,* which walked off with every major ACADEMY AWARD for 1934, vaulted the studio into the front rank. However, the 1940s saw primarily the production of formula programmers, except a handful of big-budget pictures such as *Gilda* (1946), *The Jolson Story* (1947) and *Born Yesterday* (1950). Unlike the other studios Columbia was not adversely affected by government antitrust actions after 1948 and the advent of television. Columbia owned no theaters, so the government-enforced divorcement of theaters had no impact. At the same time, the formation of Screen Gems in 1952 allowed Columbia to become the first studio to produce programs for TV. Profits from sales of Columbia films to TV were channeled into new film production. In 1968 the studio was reorganized as Columbia Pictures Industries. In 1972 it left its original studios at Sunset Boulevard and Gower in Hollywood to share the WARNER BROS.'s new Burbank Studios. Several corporate takeovers have ensued. Coca-Cola Corp. acquired the studio in 1981 and Sony Corporation purchased it in 1989. Some of the more recent successes have included *Easy Rider* (1969), *Five Easy Pieces* (1970) and *Tootsie* (1985).

For further reading:

Larkin, Rochelle, *Hail Columbia.* New York: Arlington House, 1975.

Columbus. New Mexico village on the U.S.-Mexico border, 70 miles west of El Paso, Texas. On March 9, 1916, followers of Francisco "Pancho" VILLA, Mexican revolutionary, crossed the border at Columbus and slaughtered 19 Americans. Although it was never determined whether Villa himself was a part of the mob, the U.S.'s President WILSON struck back and ordered American troops into MEXICO to apprehend and punish Villa—a fruitless, 11-month expedition.

Colville, Sir John (Rupert) (1915–1987). British political secretary and principal private secretary to Winston CHURCHILL during most of Churchill's tenure as British prime minister. Colville also served briefly as secretary to two other prime ministers, Neville CHAMBERLAIN and Clement ATTLEE. From 1947 to 1949, he was secretary to Princess ELIZABETH before she became queen. After leaving government service in 1955, he became a merchant banker. Colville was knighted in 1974.

Comaneci, Nadia (1961–). Romanian gymnast. Her career began at the age of six, when Comaneci was discovered by the sports' most influential coach, Bela Karolyi. She began winning multiple gold medals as a junior competitor during the 1970s, and, in her first senior event, dethroned five-time European champion Lyudmila Turishcheva. At the 1976 Montreal OLYMPIC GAMES, she became the first gymnast to be awarded a perfect 10 in international competition, receiving seven perfect scores as she won gold medals for the uneven bars and the balance beam. Dark and petite, her gravity and intensity contrasted sharply with the winning ways of the previous Olympic star, Olga KORBUT. Comaneci retired from competition in 1984 and defected to the U.S. in 1990.

Comden and Green. American librettists and lyricists. **Betty Comden** (1919–) and **Adolphe Green** (1915–), a celebrated team, have written with equal success for the Broadway stage and the Hollywood musical. Among their most celebrated theatrical works are *On the Town* (with Leonard BERNSTEIN, 1944), *Two on the Aisle* (1951), *Peter Pan* (with Jules Styne, 1954), *Bells Are Ringing* (1956), *Subways Are for Sleeping* (1961) and *Applause* (1970). Their film successes include *Singin' In the Rain* (1952) and *The Band Wagon* (1953). Beginning in 1958, they toured in a musical autobiography entitled *A Party,* a dual performance of their songs and lyrics that they continued into the 1990s.

Cominform. Communist information agency formed in 1947 and dissolved in 1956. Its members were the communist parties of Bulgaria, Czechoslovakia, France, Hungary, Italy, Poland, Romania, the U.S.S.R. and Yugoslavia (expelled in 1948), though membership was not obligatory for communist parties. It sought to promote party unity through dissemination of information.

Comintern [Communist International]. Also known as the Third International, the Comintern was founded by LENIN and the Russian COMMUNIST PARTY in 1919. The organization was intended to give the Russian communists control of the communist movement throughout the world; under the Comintern's "Twenty-one Conditions" (1920), the U.S.S.R. prohibited communist cooperation with non-communist socialist parties. ZINOVIEV was the Comintern's first president. The Comintern was viewed with alarm in many Western countries, but it had little practical influence. The German-Japanese ANTI-COMINTERN PACT (1936) was designed to counter the world influence of the Comintern. The Comintern was dissolved in 1943.

Commentary. American periodical. Founded as a liberal Jewish journal in 1945, *Commentary* lapsed into what was considered boring stagnancy in the late 1950s. When editor Eliot Cohen died in 1960, he was replaced by Norman Podhoretz, who revolutionized the magazine. Expanding its coverage to include a wide spectrum of ideas as well as political and social concerns, Podhoretz published material from a variety of well-known authors and critics. During the mid and late 1960s, *Commentary* increasingly became a journal of right-wing opinion. Among its editorial positions are opposition to government spending programs, affirmative action plans and university quotas as well as strong support of Israel. Widely respected for the intellectual rigor of its content and often criticized for the CONSERVATISM of its outlook, *Commentary* continues, under Podhoretz's direction, to be an important journal of American thought.

Committee of One Million. See Gerald L.K. SMITH.

Common Market. See EUROPEAN ECONOMIC COMMUNITY.

Commonwealth of Nations. Voluntary group of self-governing nations and dependencies of the UNITED KINGDOM, embracing certain affiliated states whose foreign activities are managed by the United Kingdom; formerly known as the British Commonwealth. The commonwealth is an offshoot of the BRITISH EMPIRE and includes members from all hemispheres. It developed out of the Statute of Westminster, an act of the British Parliament, passed in 1931, that acknowledged the right of self-rule for those states with dominion status within the British Empire. A free association, the commonwealth is constrained only by loyalty to the British Crown. The legislatures of the jurisdictions are equal to that of the British Parliament. The statute was considered an extension to the group of Imperial Conferences, begun in 1887, which were originally known as the Colonial Conferences. WORLD WAR I pushed the advancement of autonomy within the empire, and WORLD WAR II completed the procedure. Meetings are held on a regular basis for consultation, but no binding motions are made; the U.K., however, still plays an active role. Economic ties and trade agreements are emphasized. The 46 members of the commonwealth are: Antigua, Australia, Bahamas, Bangladesh, Barbados, Belize, Botswana, Canada, Cyprus, Dominica, Fiji, Gambia, Ghana, Grenada, Guyana, India, Jamaica, Kenya, Kiribati, Lesotho, Malawi, Malaysia, Malta, Mauritius, Nauru, New Zealand, Nigeria, Papua New Guinea, Saint Lucia, Saint Vincent and the Grenadines, Samoa, Seychelles, Sierra Leone, Singapore, Solomon Islands, Sri Lanka, Swaziland, Tanzania, Tonga, Trinidad and Tobago, Tuvalu, Uganda, United Kingdom, Vanuatu, Zambia and Zimbabwe. The Republic of South Africa withdrew from the Commonwealth in 1961 and Pakistan in 1972.

communism [also known as Marxism or Marxism-Leninism]. Political, economic and social ideology formulated in the 19th century by Karl Marx and Friedrich Engels; it was embraced and "refined" in the 20th century by V.I. LENIN, MAO TSE-TUNG and numerous other theorist-practitioners. Communism has been one of the most powerful and pervasive ideologies of the 20th century, and also the most controversial. Its proponents insist that it presents the only rational and comprehensive program for correcting social ills and achieving an equitable society. Opponents point to the vast human suffering that has been inflicted in the name of communism.

In practical terms, 20th-century communism has emphasized the state ownership of all means of production; central planning of the economy; and the guiding role of the COMMUNIST PARTY in all facets of society. Communism has also flourished in many places as a revolutionary movement dedicated to the overthrow of colonial, right-wing, authoritarian or democratic governments. Communism regards the party and the state as more important than the individual. The main features of 20th-century communism have been a totalitarian form of government, the use of terror and coercion to stifle political opposition or deviation, and the support of revolutionary movements throughtout the world.

Communism gained hold first and foremost in Russia, where Lenin's BOLSHEVIK REVOLUTION (or October Revolution, 1917) eventually led to the Communist Party's domination of virtually every aspect of life in the country (see UNION OF SOVIET SOCIALIST REPUBLICS). According to Lenin, the "dictatorship of the proletariat" was to be simply one phase in the revolutionary transition to a purely communist society; however, this dictatorship proved to be a prevalent feature of communism. Lenin favored the spread of revolutionary communism to other nations. His successor, Joseph STALIN, adhered to a policy of communism "in one nation," consolidating his power and that of the party in the U.S.S.R.

After WORLD WAR II, however, communist regimes seized power in most countries of Eastern Europe. Many of these regimes were installed by the Soviets, whose army had occupied the region at the end of the war. A few (YUGOSLAVIA and, later, ALBANIA and ROMANIA) followed a policy independent from the U.S.S.R. but generally employed similar methods in maintaining power (see STALINISM). Communism was also adopted in CHINA under Mao (see CHINESE CIVIL WAR OF 1945–49), and communist revolutionary movements spread to many of the European colonies in Asia and Africa. The COLD WAR between (primarily) the U.S.S.R. and the UNITED STATES was seen as a worldwide competition between communism and democracy.

Forty years of communism in Eastern Europe (and 70 years in the U.S.S.R.) failed to bring about the transformation of society. By the late 1980s, communism was being openly challenged in a number of Eastern European nations that had been under communist governments since the end of World War II. In 1989–90, communist governments were deposed or reformed in POLAND, CZECHOSLOVAKIA, HUNGARY, EAST GERMANY and ROMANIA. Elections in NICARAGUA also resulted in the ouster of the communist-oriented government of Daniel ORTEGA and the Sandinistas. In the U.S.S.R., Mikhail GORBACHEV's economic reforms (PERESTROIKA) and policy of openness (GLASNOST) signalled a departure from orthodox Soviet communism.

Communist Party of the U.S.S.R. Following the RUSSIAN REVOLUTION (1917) the BOLSHEVIKS under LENIN emerged as the single, dominant party and adopted the name "Communist Party (Bolsheviks)." Under STALIN the party grew from a relatively small, elite group to a ruling bureaucracy with a much larger membership. In 1952 "Bolsheviks" was dropped from the party's official name. According to the rules adopted by the 22nd Congress of the party on October 31, 1961, the Communist Party of the Soviet Union "unites, on a voluntary basis, the more advanced, politically more conscious section of the working class, collective-farm peasantry and intelligentsia of the U.S.S.R.," whose principal objects are to build a communist society by means of gradual transition from socialism to communism, to raise the material and cultural level of the people, to organize the defense of the country, and to strengthen ties with the workers of other countries.

The party remained the sole and overwhelmingly dominant political force throughout the regimes of BREZHNEV and his short-lived successors, ANDROPOV and CHERNENKO. However, under GORBACHEV in the late 1980s, the party's structure and its role in Soviet society underwent profound changes. The constitution of the U.S.S.R. was revised, the government structure reformed and non-communist politicians were elected to the new Congress of People's Deputies. Although the Communist Party remained a strong force, at the beginning of 1991 its future direction seemed unclear.

Up to the Gorbachev era, the party was built on the territorial-industrial principle. The supreme organ was the party congress; ordinary congresses were convened not less than once in four years. The congress elected a central committee, which met at least every six months, carried on the work of the party between congresses and guided the work of central Soviet and public organizations through party groups within them. The central committee formed a political bureau to direct the work of the central committee between plenary meetings, a secretariat to direct current work, and a commission of party control to consider appeals against decisions about expulsion. Similar rules hold for the regional and territorial party organizations.

By the late 1970s, over 398,340 primary party organizations existed in mills, factories, state machine and tractor stations, and other economic establishments; in collective farms and units of the Soviet army and navy; in villages, offices, educational establishments and so forth, where there were at least three party members. On January 1, 1978, nearly 42% of the members were industrial workers; 13% were collective farmers; and 44% were office and professional workers. Women accounted for 25.1% of all members. In 1981 the Communist Party had 17,500,000 members; membership of the Young Communist League was 37,800,000 in 1978.

Comoros [Federal Islamic Republic of the Comoros]. Four major, and several smaller, islands located in the Mozambique Channel of the Indian Ocean, 300 miles northeast of MADAGASCAR. In the 19th century, FRANCE saw the strategic worth of the island of Mayotte and assumed control after negotiating a treaty with the ruling sultan. France claimed the remaining islands of Grand Comoro, Anjouan and Moheli to squelch imperial German development. By 1961 the Comoros had acquired internal self-control, and Independence was claimed in 1975. Mayotte chose to remain French, but the new government opposed this and was supported by the U.N. General Assembly in 1979. Ahmed Abdallah was president from 1975 to 1989, except for a period (1975–78) when he was temporarily deposed by a left-wing coup. Abdallah was assassinated in 1989, and the country was run briefly by his top advisor, the French mercenary Bob Denard. After Denard's departure, Said Mohammed Djohar became acting president, but the political situation remained uncertain.

Compton, Arthur Holly (1892–1962). American physicist. Compton came from a distinguished intellectual family. His father, Elias, was a professor of philosophy at Wooster College while his brother, Karl, also a physicist, became president of the Massachusetts Institute of Technology. He was educated at Wooster College and at Princeton, where he earned his Ph.D. in 1916. He began his career by teaching at the University of Minnesota. After two years with the Westinghouse Corp. in Pittsburgh, he returned to academic life. In 1920 he was appointed professor of physics at Washington University, St. Louis. He spent most of his career at the University of Chicago, where he served as professor of physics from 1923 to 1945. Compton then returned to Washington University first as chancellor and then as professor of natural philosophy (1953–61). Compton is best remembered for the discovery and explanation in 1923 of the effect named for him for which, in 1927, he shared the NOBEL PRIZE for physics with Charles T.R. Wilson. His work on X RAYS provided the first hard experimental evidence for the dual nature of electromagnetic radiation; that is, that it could behave both as a wave and a particle. This would be developed much further in the 1920s as one of the cornerstones of the new quantum physics. In the 1930s Compton concentrated on a major investigation into the nature of cosmic rays. During World War II he was an important figure in the manufacture of the ATOMIC BOMB and a member of the committee directing research on the MANHATTAN PROJECT. He also set up the Metallurgical Laboratory, at Chicago, which acted as a cover for the construction of

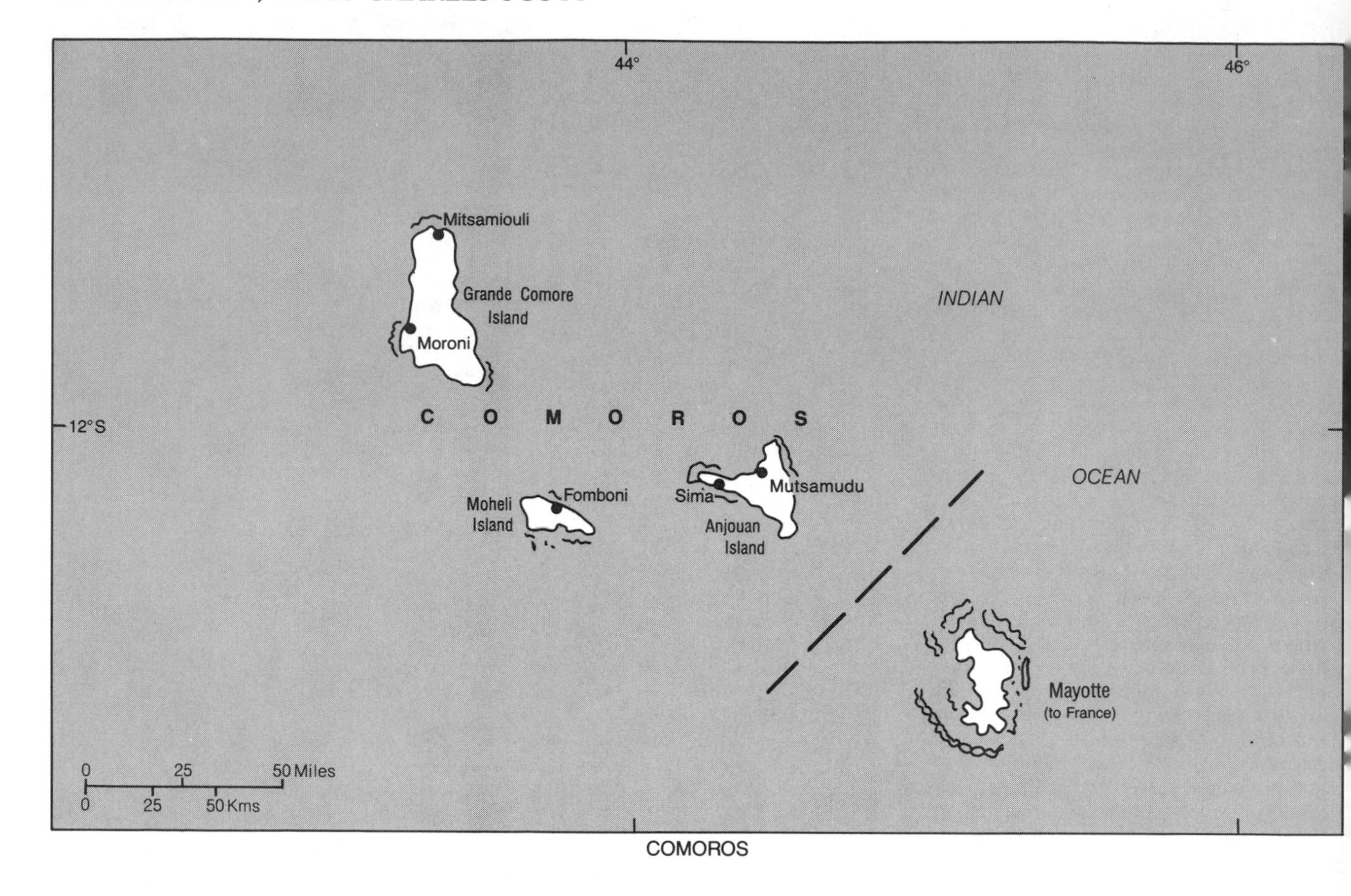

COMOROS

the first atomic pile under the direction of Enrico FERMI and took responsibility for the production of plutonium. The book *Atomic Quest* (1956), is Compton's full account of this work.

Compton, Denis Charles Scott (1918–). English cricket player. Noted for his batting technique, entertaining style and courage, Compton established himself as one of English cricket's all-time greats. Despite losing six years of his career to World War II and being hampered by a series of knee injuries, Compton was the dominant batsman of his day. He made his county debut with Middlesex in 1936 and played for England the following year at age 19. In 1947 Compton scored 3,816 runs, 18 of them centuries. Overall Compton played 78 Test matches, scoring 5,807 runs and 17 centuries. He retired from first-class cricket in 1964 having scored 38,942 runs. Although best known as a cricketer, Compton also played soccer at the professional level. His soccer career was curtailed by his knee ailments, but he did gain an FA Cup winners medal with Arsenal in 1950.

Compton-Burnett, Ivy (Dame) (1884–1969). British novelist. Educated at Holloway College, Compton-Burnett received a degree in classics, which influenced her later work. Her first novel, *Delores* (1911), was an unsuccessful imitation of the work of George Eliot. Deeply affected by the tragedy of WORLD WAR I, she suffered a physical and emotional collapse and did not produce her first serious novel, *Pastors and Masters,* until 1925. It began an extraordinary series of 18 chilling—but not humorless—novels depicting late Victorian upper-class families and their dependents. Written almost entirely in dense, sometimes cryptic dialogue, her work explores the corrupting influence of power within families and the dark themes of incest, child abuse, murder and fraud. Later works inlcude *A House and Its Head* (1935), *Manservant and Maidservant* (1947) and *A God and His Gifts* (1963). Defying conventional literary classification, her individualistic fiction has been described as the literary counterpart of POSTIMPRESSIONISM.

For further reading:
Spurling, Hilary. *Ivy: The Life of Ivy Compton Burnett.* New York: Knopf, 1984.

computers. In the second half of the 20th century, the computer has not only revolutionized business but also had a profound impact on personal life. The early stages of computer development were slow and painstaking. Vannevar BUSH designed a mechanical computer in 1930, and several other models were introduced during the '30s. The first truly digital electronic computer, ENIAC, was invented in 1946; it was followed in 1951 by UNIVAC. The invention of the TRANSISTOR did away with the need for vacuum tubes and allowed for the miniaturization of computers. In 1959, IBM (International Business Machines) introduced its first fully transistorized computer. Many businesses began utilizing computers for accounting and recordkeeping, but it was not until the 1970s that the most significant computer revolution occurred. The perfection of the silicon microchip, which could hold thousands of miniaturized computer circuits, led to the invention of the **personal computer**. The APPLE II, designed by Steven Jobs and Stephen Wozniak, two young American entrepreneurs and computer wizards, was the first widely accepted personal computer. Entering the market in 1977, it revolutionized not only the entire computer industry but also the way in which individuals used computers. In less than a decade, the personal computer became a common tool in homes, schools and offices.

Conant, James Bryant (1893–1978). American chemist. Conant studied at Harvard, earning his Ph.D. in 1916. He was professor of chemistry there (1919–33) and then president (1933–53). He had a multifaceted career as a research chemist, administrator, diplomat and educationalist. In the research phase he worked on organic reaction mechanisms and also showed that oxyhemoglobin contains ferrous iron (1923). During WORLD WAR II he was head of the National Defense Research Committee and deputy head of the Office of Scientific Research and Development; he played an important role in the development of the ATOMIC BOMB. On retiring from Harvard he became commissioner and then ambassador to Germany (1953–57) and wrote many controversial books on education.

concentration camps. Places for confining political prisoners and prisoners of war. While the term "concentration camp"

Survivors of a Nazi concentration camp (1945).

is most associated with the notorious prisons in NAZI GERMANY, the first concentration camps were established by Lord Kitchener and the British army during the BOER WAR in SOUTH AFRICA around 1900. After 1928, during the rule of Joseph STALIN in the U.S.S.R., millions of people were confined in labor camps for "reeducation" but many perished, particularly in camps in the brutal Arctic region. The Japanese also confined prisoners in harsh prison camps in wartime. The Nazis began establishing camps in 1933, DACHAU being among the first. The camps initially were used to confine communists and other political opponents; later homosexuals, Gypsies, JEWS and anyone deemed unsuitable by the Nazis were arrested. By the time WORLD WAR II began there were 22 camps where inmates were brutalized and used as slave labor. In 1941, Adolf HITLER conceived of the FINAL SOLUTION, a plan to exterminate all European Jews, and many camps were outfitted with gas chambers for mass murder. Victims' hair and bodies were collected for use in manufacturing. At some camps doctors performed medical experiments, usually on women and children, who were often killed. Many others were shot or starved. Between 7 and 11 million people were killed in the Nazi concentration camps. Some of the infamous camps include AUSCHWITZ, BERGEN-BELSEN, BUCHENWALD and TREBLINKA.

Conference on Security and Cooperation in Europe. See HELSINKI ACCORDS.

Confessional Poets. Although none of the major poets yoked together under the confessional heading would call themselves a formal group with a shared agenda, this term is used particularly to decribe John BERRYMAN, Robert LOWELL and Lowell's proteges, notably Sylvia PLATH and Anne SEXTON. This piercingly subjective poetry is tinged with suffering and self-revelation. Its seminal work was Lowell's *Life Studies* (1959). In the 1970s the popularity of the confessional poets led to a spate of self-indulgent imitators, who saw such deeply personal statements as a means of approaching the human condition. At their best, the confessional poets established a new mode of discourse by making art from subject matter that had previously been taboo.

For further reading:

Phillips, Robert, *The Confessional Poets.* Carbondale: Southern Illinois University Press, 1973.

Congo, People's Republic of. A nation of west-central Africa, densely covered by equatorial forest and marshland; formerly, the Middle Congo. In the late 19th century French colonial ambition was turned toward the interior of central Africa. The area covered by present-day Congo eventually became part of French Equatorial Africa and was governed by business interests as a private concession. By 1907 international anger compelled France to exercise some authority over rapacious private enterprises, but the indigenous population and local economy (in the form of the ivory and rubber trade) had already suffered immensely. The Africans of the Congo were also exploited as workers to build the Congo-Ocean railway after WORLD WAR I; approximately 17,000 people died during its construction.

During WORLD WAR II, the capital city of Brazzaville was a headquarters of the FREE FRENCH. In 1958 the Congo became an autonomous republic within the French Community; it gained full independence on Aug. 15, 1960. Fulbert YOULOU, a former Catholic priest, was the first president. Marien Ngouabi grabbed power after a military coup in 1968 and allied the Congo with the U.S.S.R. He was assassinated in 1977, and the new military regime quickly renewed diplomatic ties with the U.S. and the West, although continuing a Marxist-Leninist state with close Soviet and Chinese affiliations. Political tensions between northern and southern tribes continued.

Congress of Industrial Organizations. See AMERICAN FEDERATION OF LABOR AND CONGRESS OF INDUSTRIAL ORGANIZATIONS.

Congress Party. Indian political party established in 1885. The National Congress, initially an association to inculcate Indians into government service, was supported by the British viceroys prior to George CURZON whose 1905 splitting of Bengal brought about violent opposition by Congress and a rift between its more radical leader, Bal Gangadhar Tilak, and the more moderate, Western-influenced G.K. Kokhale. Mohandas K. GANDHI became its primary leader in 1920 and retained an enormous influence until his assassination in 1948. He established the doctrine of nonviolent civil disobedience to effect political change. The Congress Party took office in six provinces in 1937, but its leaders refused to support entry into WORLD WAR II, because the British neglected to check Indian opinion on the issue. Congress leaders were subsequently interned from 1942 to 1945. Following independence in 1947, the Congress Party came to power under Prime Minister Jawaharial NEHRU with sustaining, broad-based support. He was succeeded by Lal Bahadur SHASTRI in 1964, but Shastri died suddenly in 1966. At that time a group of party bosses known as the Syndicate were vying for control of the party, but Indira GANDHI became the dominant figure of the party following the 1971 elections, and she remained so until her assassination in 1984. Although she and the Congress Party were out of power between 1977 and 1980, her role was so strong the party is now labeled Congress (I) for Indira Congress, to distinguish it from other offshoots of the party. Congress (I) remained India's dominant party under the leadership of Rajiv GANDHI until his defeat in 1990.

Connally, John B(owden) (1917–). U.S. politician. Connally was twice elected governor of Texas (1963–69) and was secretary of the Navy under President John F. KENNEDY. He was seriously wounded in Dallas during the shooting that claimed President Kennedy's life in 1963. Originally a conservative Democrat, he joined the REPUBLICAN PARTY in 1975, having served as President Richard M. NIXON's secretary of the treasury in 1971–72. Connally retired to private life in 1976. His investments in real estate toppled during the decline of Texas oil fortunes in the 1980s, and he entered bankruptcy in 1988.

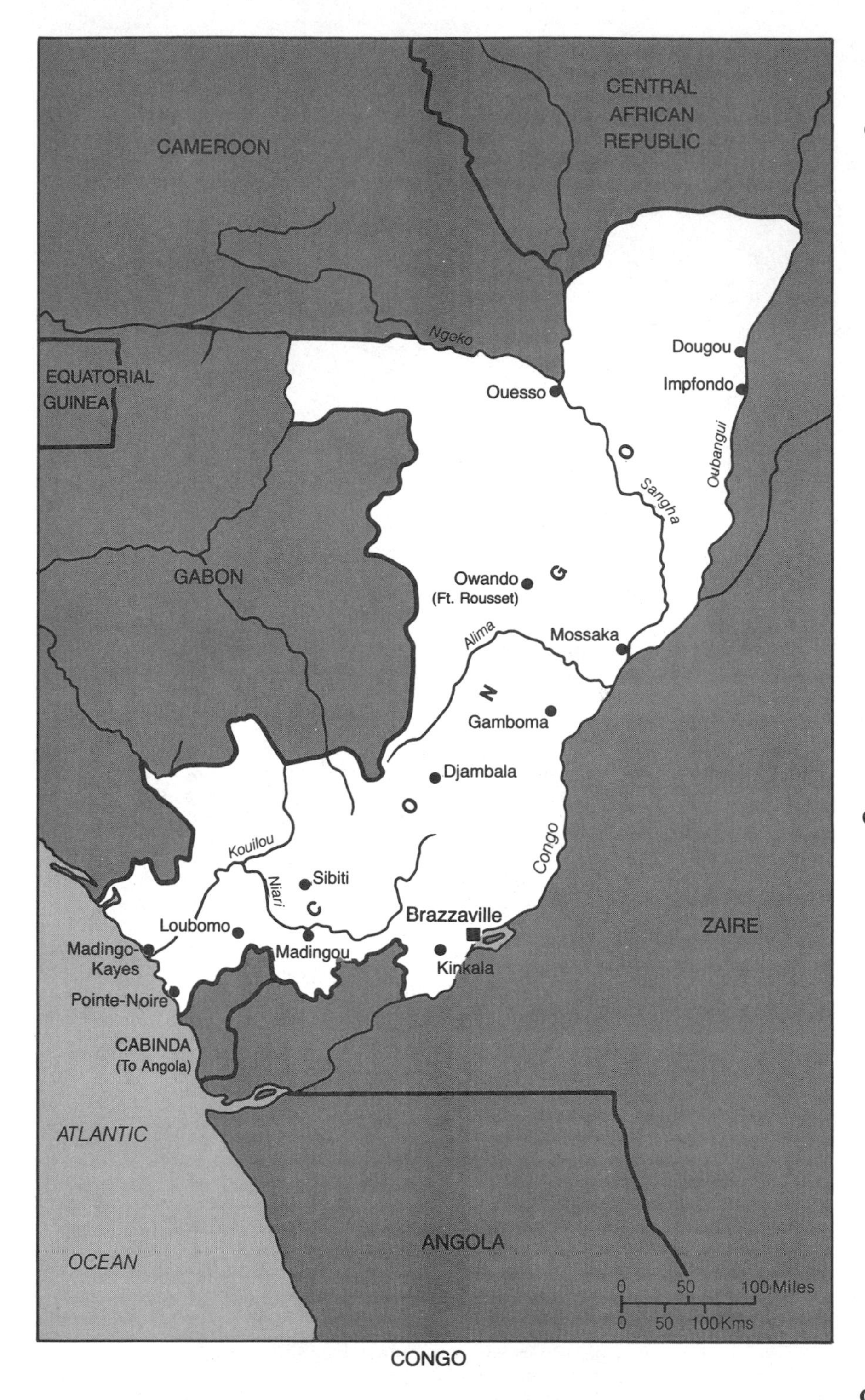

CONGO

For further reading:
Reston, James R., *The Lone Star: The Life of John Connally*. New York: HarperCollins, 1989.

Connally, Thomas "Tom" (1877–1963). American politician. A Texas Democrat, Connally entered the House of Representatives in 1917 but resigned to serve WORLD WAR I. After the war he returned to the House, gained a seat on the Foreign Affairs Committee and began a lifelong interest in diplomacy. Supporting Woodrow WILSON, he campaigned for U.S. involvement in the LEAGUE OF NATIONS. During the 1920s he represented the U.S. at several international conferences. Elected to the Senate in 1928, he later opposed Franklin D. ROOSEVELT's NEW DEAL but supported the president's foreign policy. After Harry S. TRUMAN became president, Connally was a frequent adviser on foreign affairs and led the fight for ratification of the UNITED NATIONS charter. With Republican senator Arthur VANDENBURG, he championed the TRUMAN DOCTRINE and the MARSHALL PLAN, but he expressed reservations about NATO. He supported the TAFT-HARTLEY ACT and opposed CIVIL RIGHTS legislation. He retired from the Senate in 1952.

Connery, Sean (Thomas) (1929–). Popular Scottish actor known for his suave and manly roles in adventure and suspense films. Born in Edinburgh, Scotland, Connery at age 15 enlisted in the Royal Navy in World War II, and on his return to England he became a physical fitness addict. In the 1950s his muscular build and dashing goods looks led to a career in modeling and then to theater and television work. He played bit parts and featured roles in several poorly received films (both British and American), until he landed the title role in a low-budget spy thriller, *Dr. No* (1962). Based on Ian FLEMING's internationally famous secret agent, JAMES BOND ("007"), it became a mega-hit and boosted Connery to stardom. He continued his debonair but gritty portrayal of Bond in *From Russia With Love* (1963), *Goldfinger* (1964), *Thunderball* (1965), *You Only Live Twice* (1967), *Diamonds Are Forever* (1971) and, 12 years later, *Never Say Never Again*. Connery was equally larger than life in *The Hill* (1965), *The Molly Maguires* (1970), *The Man Who Would Be King* (1975) and *Indiana Jones and the Last Crusade* (1989). In 1987 Connery received the best supporting actor ACADEMY AWARD for his performance in *The Untouchables*.

Connolly, Cyril (Vernon) (1903–1974). British critic, editor and author. Born in Coventry, Connolly was educated at Eton and at Balliol College, Oxford, where he was acquainted with Graham GREENE. He began working as a journalist and critic and was soon contributing regularly to *The New Statesman*. In 1939 he and Stephen SPENDER founded the literary magazine *Horizon*, which Connolly edited until its demise in 1950. He also served as literary editor of the *Observer* from 1942 to 1943, and from 1951 until his death was a book reviewer for *The Sunday Times*. His sole novel, *The Rock Pool* (1936), is a clever satire about a smug British stockbroker attempting to gain entree into an artistic colony on the French Riviera. Other important works include *Enemies of Promise* (1938), a partly autobiographical collection of essays; *The Unquiet Grave* (1944), a collection of thoughts and aphorisms published under the pseudonym Palimurus (the drowned Trojan pilot in the *Aenied*); and *The Evening Colonnade* (1973), essays.

Connolly, James (1870–1916). Irish labor leader and revolutionary. A socialist, Connolly spent some time in the U.S. at the beginning of the 20th century and was an organizer for the radical INTERNATIONAL WORKERS of the World (IWW). He returned to IRELAND to lead the dockworkers in Belfast. In Dublin he and union leader James Larkin organized the powerful Irish Transport and General Workers Union. During a 1913 lockout of the workers, he organized a citizen army. Connolly did not share the romantic nationalist fervor of Patrick PEARSE and other anti-British rebels, but he joined them as a leader of the EASTER RISING in 1916. He was wounded during the fighting; after the rebellion was suppressed, he was one of 16 rebels executed by the British.

Connolly, Maureen Catherine (1934–1969). American tennis player. At 16, "Little Mo" Connolly was the youngest woman in nearly half a century to win the U.S. title; she was also the first woman ever to win the U.S., British, French and Australian championships in a single year (1953). Her string of victories continued with U.S., French and Wimbledon titles in 1954. After suffering a serious injury in a horseback riding accident, she was forced to retire from tennis at the age of 20. She embarked upon a successful coaching career, cut short when she died of cancer at the age of 35.

Connors, James Scott "Jimmy" (1952–). American tennis player. Connors' heart and spirit revolutionized how the world viewed the genteel sport. Connors cursed on court, challenged umpires and drove himself mercilessly. One of the dominant players of the 1970s, he had his best year in 1974, when he won three of the Big Four tournaments—the U.S. and Australian Opens and Wimbledon. That year he entered into a much-publicized engagement with the women's champion, Chris EVERT, but both went on to marry others. A perennial favorite at the U.S. Open, he won that title five times, the last in 1983. He played in occasional tournaments into the 1990s, vowing to compete as long as he continued to enjoy the sport.

Conrad, Charles "Pete" (1930–). U.S. astronaut. In his four NASA missions—from his first flight on Gemini 5 in August 1965 until his last flight on Skylab 2 in May-June 1973—Conrad logged approximately 1,180 hours in space, including 14 hours of EVA (extravehicular activity). In between he commanded Gemini 11 (September 1966), which established a world altitude record at that time of 850 miles, and, as commander of Apollo 12 (November 1969), landed on the moon and spent over 30 hours romping over its surface.

Conrad, Joseph [born Teodor Jozef Konrad Nalecz Kozeniowski] (1857–1924). Polish-British novelist. Conrad was born in the Ukraine to Polish parents. His father's anti-Russian political views caused the family to be exiled to northern Russia. Conrad's mother died there when he was seven. Following their return to Poland, Conrad's father died when he was 11 and his uncle, Thaddeus Bobrowski, became his guardian and mentor. In 1874 he went to Marseille and became a sailor; he was essentially educated at sea. His experiences and travels provided him with the raw material for the best of his later work. Conrad became a British subject in 1886, continuing his seafaring career until 1894, when he settled in England, married and turned to writing. Although Conrad did not learn to speak English until he was 20, he eventually became one of the most renowned 20th-century English-language novelists. His first two novels, *Almayer's Folly* (1895) and *An Outcast of the Islands* (1896), demonstrate his unfamiliarity with both the English language and the craft of writing, but by *The Nigger of the Narcissus* (1897), *Lord Jim* (1900) and THE HEART OF DARKNESS (1902), he had found his characteristic voice. These three works are now among his best known, but Conrad did not realize much popular success until the publication of *Chance* in 1913. Many consider his finest novel to be *Nostromo* (1904), a profound study of the corrupting effects of colonialism and greed in a small South American town; *The Secret Agent* (1907), about anarchist revolutionaries in turn-of-the-century London, and *Under Western Eyes* (1911) about the political and spiritual state of contemporary Russia, have also been highly praised. Conrad's work has been described as impressionistic, and while it takes place in varied (often exotic) locations, it all reflects his fundamental concern with man's physical and moral weakness. Early in his career Conrad collaborated with Ford Maddox FORD on *The Inheritors* (1900) and *Romance* (1903), but personal disagreements ended their association. Conrad's writing was admired by Arnold BENNETT, Henry JAMES and John GALSWORTHY, but during his lifetime his serious work never found a large audience. He is now considered, along with James, as the most important transitional figure between 19th-century realism and 20th-century MODERNISM. His work has had a significant influence on such later writers as Graham GREENE, John LE CARRE, V.S. NAIPAUL and Paul Theroux.

Novelist Joseph Conrad (1923).

For further reading:

Karl, Frederick R., *Joseph Conrad: The Three Lives*. New York: Farrar Straus & Giroux, 1979.

Knowles, Owen, *A Conrad Chronology*. Boston: G.K. Hall, 1990.

Conran, Terence (1931–). British designer best known as a popular merchandiser of home furnishings. Trained as a textile designer, Conran founded his own firm, the Conran Design Group, in 1955. In 1957 he opened a London shop with Mary QUANT and, thereafter, his own London shop called HABITAT. Its success led to the opening of more stores, eventually leading to an international chain including shops in the U.S. that carry the name Conran's. Conran has also produced a number of consumer-oriented books with rich illustration and texts by a number of writers that give design and technical advice to householders.

Conroy, Jack [John Wesley Conroy] (1899–). American novelist and poet. The son of a union organizer, Conroy was born in a coal mining camp in Missouri, and spent much of his early life traveling the country as a migrant worker. Conroy edited the verse collection *Unrest* (1929) and served as editor of *Rebel Poet* from 1931 to 1932, *Anvil* from 1933 to 1937 and *New Anvil* from 1939 to 1941. In these journals he published the early works of Nelson ALGREN and Richard WRIGHT, among others. Conroy is best known for his novel *The Disinherited* (1933), which received little attention when it was first published but was critically acclaimed when it was rereleased in 1963. Conroy's writing reflects his left-leaning, proletarian politics, which, unlike many other young rebels, he maintained throughout his life. Conroy's work has been collected in *The Jack Conroy Reader* (1980); he has also written children's books and written under the pseudonyms Tim Brennan, Hoder Morine and John Norcross.

conservatism. Political and social philosophy, or set of attitudes, contrasted to LIBERALISM. Like liberalism, 20th-century conservatism has its roots in 18th-century thought. Irish statesman Edmund Burke, economist Adam Smith and several founding fathers of the U.S. (notably Alexander Hamilton) were forerunners of modern conservatism. Broadly speaking, conservatism is marked by respect for tradition, suspicion of social change and of movements that advocate radical change, and a cautious if not pessimistic view of human nature. Many conservatives also believe that political power should be held by an educated elite. In the course of the 20th century these tenets have often been simplified, distorted or misused both by proponents and critics. Conservatism has sometimes been obscured by particular issues of the moment and confused with authoritarianism, racism and even FASCISM. In the U.S., political conservatism is generally associated with the REPUBLICAN PARTY, although there have been liberal Republicans and conservative Democrats and many who did not follow strict conservative or liberal views on all issues. Prominent conservative U.S. presidents include William Howard TAFT and Herbert HOOVER. Calvin COOLIDGE was also conservative in that he took a laissez-faire stance on most issues. Richard M. NIXON took some conservative positions, but his reliance on public expenditure in domestic welfare programs and, more significantly, his blatant disregard of constitutional principles in the WATERGATE scandal were uncharacteristic of classical conservatism. Like Nixon, Ronald REAGAN shared an active opposition to COMMUNISM—a fundamental feature of 20th-century conservatism—but both were pragmatic in their dealings with Soviet and Chinese communist leaders. Reagan's conservatism introduced a new radical emphasis on "free-market" economics, called "Reaganomics" by its detractors. Other notable American conservatives include Russell KIRK, William F. BUCKLEY, Jr., George WILL and 1964 Republican presidential candidate Barry GOLDWATER. A more radical and activist form of conservatisim, often embraced by former liberals and socialists who have rejected their earlier beliefs, is known as **neoconservatism**. In the United Kingdom, conservative principles found a natural home in the CONSERVATIVE PARTY. Stanley BALDWIN and Harold MACMILLAN were mainstream conservatives, but no one more embodied the central values of conservatism than Winston S. CHURCHILL, who rallied the British people against Adolf HITLER and NAZISM in the darkest days of WORLD WAR II. Churchill's conservatism was manifested in his faith in British political and social institutions as they had evolved over the centuries, and in his uncompromising opposition to TOTALITARIANISM, whether in the form of German Nazism or Soviet communism. Churchill's conservatism was also colored by his imperialism and by his belief in the natural superiority of Western civilization and especially of the English-speaking peoples. Margaret THATCHER, who governed Britain throughout the 1980s, revived many of the features of Churchill's conservatism but, like Reagan, added an emphasis on market economics and a determination to uproot all traces of the WELFARE STATE. Some traditional conservatives (see WETS) felt that Thatcher's determined assault on established British institutions was contrary to the main tenets of conservatism, which stress the preservation of existing institutions.

Conservative Party. British political party, established in 1832. The well-organized Conservative Party has constituency committees in all districts in Great Britain and Northern Ireland joined at the national level by the National Union of Conservative and Unionist Associations, which holds an annual rallying conference. The party maintains a well-financed Central Office as well as 11 area offices in England and Wales. Current Conservative policy is distinguished by the party's commitment to monetarist economics (see MONETARISM). Its domestic policies generally coincide with those of conservative Republicans in the U.S. Additionally, the Conservative Party favors British rule in Northern Ireland, a strong military defense, firm allegiance to NATO, and membership in the EUROPEAN ECONOMIC COMMUNITY. Conservatives were in power at the turn of the century and until 1905, when Prime Minister BALFOUR left office and the party went into eclipse. In 1912 a faction of the LIBERAL PARTY opposed to Irish HOME RULE allied itself to the Conservatives, and the word "Unionist" replaced "Constitutional" in the National Union of Conservative and Constitutional Associations, the party's formal name. The party came to power again in 1922 under the leadership of Bonar LAW, who was succeeded by BALDWIN, Neville CHAMBERLAIN and Winston CHURCHILL. The LABOUR PARTY came to power after WORLD WAR II and instituted many social welfare policies. (See WELFARE STATE.) Conservatives returned to power in 1951 with Churchill as prime minister until 1955, when EDEN took office. Following the SUEZ CANAL crisis, Eden's government was disgraced and he left office in 1957. Under the leadership of Harold MACMILLAN, the Conservatives won the 1959 elections. A dispute over his successor and the appointment of Lord Home (see Alec DOUGLAS-HOME) led to the adoption in 1965 of the party's current balloting system of choosing its leader. The Conservative Party remained in power until 1974, when labor conflicts brought about its defeat. In 1975 Margaret THATCHER became leader of the party and became Britain's first female prime minister when the Conservatives returned to power in 1979. She oversaw a sweeping Conservative victory in 1983. While Thatcher was criticized for her dogmatic policies and inability to lower unemployment, she remained in office longer than any prime minister in the preceding 150 years. She stepped down in 1990 and was succeeded by her protege, John MAJOR.

Constantine I [King of the Hellenes] (1868–1923). Married to Sophia, sister of Germany's Kaiser WILHELM II, he came to the throne after the assassination of his father, George I, and reigned from 1913 to 1917 and 1920 to 1922. He was opposed to the pro-Allied policies of Greek Premier Eleutherios VENIZELOS, and in 1917 was forced to abdicate in favor of his son, Alexander. After Alexander's death in 1920, a plebiscite restored him as monarch. When Greece was defeated by the Turks in 1922, the king was widely held accountable, and was again forced to abdicate. He was succeeded by his son, George II.

Constantine II [King of the Hellenes] (1940–). King of GREECE (1964–1973). He succeeded to the throne upon the death of his father, King Paul. After a military junta staged a coup in 1967, Constantine unsuccessfully sought to overthrow the new government. He fled to Italy, and in 1973 a republic was declared and he was formally deposed. A 1974 national referendum opposed his return to the throne.

Constantinople Agreements. Secret accords provided to RUSSIA by Great Britain and France in the spring of 1915. The Constantinople Agreements promised that the city of Constantinople (Istanbul), parts of the Bosphorus strait and the Dardanelles would be ceded to the Russian Empire upon an Allied victory in WORLD WAR I. The agreements provided long sought-after territory to Russia as an inducement to Czar NICHOLAS II not to conclude a separate peace with Germany. After the RUSSIAN REVOLUTION, the Bolsheviks repudiated czarist agreements and in 1918 they angered Turkey, Britain and the U.S. by publishing the secret Constantinople treaties.

Constructivism. Abstract art movement that was originated in Russia in 1913 by the artist Vladmir TATLIN. Major figures in the movement included Naum GABO, Antoine PEVSNER, and Alexander RODCHENKO. The works of the Constructivists emphasized abstract geometric shapes that were inspired by modern machine technology. The Constructivists denied that art required a socially useful purpose, but they did advocate the use in works of art of modern, nonclassical materials such as glass and plastic. Constructivism was condemned by the Soviet government in 1922. Most of the artists in the movement immigrated to other parts of Europe. As a result, Constructivism exercised a substantial influence upon the DE STIJL movement in Holland and the teachings of the BAUHAUS in Germany.

Consumer Price Index. The Consumer Price Index (CPI), also known as the cost of living index, is a monthly U.S. government index that measures consumer prices; it is widely-used to set wage increases and other price-level changes. The index, maintained by the Bureau of Labor Statistics, attempts to present a picture of the average household's costs of living and has been compiled for a number of years, which allows yearly comparisons of price changes. Currently, prices are represented as a percentage of the prices in the base year of 1967. In other words, the index for 1967 is 100 and later years are all in excess of 100.

The bureau carefully selects and weights purchases of goods and services, like food, clothing, and transportation, to typify average household expenditures. The CPI is also tabulated for major metropolitan areas, for commodity and service groups, and for individual items.

Contras. Rebel force in NICARAGUA opposed to the left-wing Sandinista regime of Daniel ORTEGA SAAVEDRA. Many of the Contras had been members of the Nicaraguan National Guard during the Somoza regime; others had fought in the revolution against Somoza but were disillusioned with Ortega's Marxist methods. Operating from bases in HONDURAS and sometimes inside Nicaragua itself, the Contras received U.S. military aid until June 1984, when the U.S. Congress voted to cut their funding. U.S. President Ronald REAGAN was a strong supporter of the Contras, hailing them as freedom fighters. The Reagan administration's zeal to aid the Contras helped lead to the 1986 IRAN-CONTRA SCANDAL. Later in the decade the Contras entered into negotiations with the Sandinista regime; they laid down their arms in return for a promise of amnesty and free elections. The upset election of Violetta CHAMORRO and the defeat of Ortega in 1989 was widely viewed as a political vindication of the Contras' cause.

Coogan, Jackie (1914–1984). Coogan was the first child star in movie history. In 1919, at age four, he starred in Charlie CHAPLIN's *The Kid* and became an overnight success. In 1923 he led Rudolph VALENTINO and Douglas FAIRBANKS Sr., in box-office popularity. At age 21 he discovered that his mother and stepfather had squandered the more than $2 million he had earned. This incident prompted the passage of a California law requiring that the earnings of juvenile actors be deposited in court-administered trust funds. In all, Coogan appeared in more than 100 movies and 800 television programs.

Cook, Bill (1896–1986). Canadian hockey player. Before the advent of Gordie HOWE, he was regarded as the premier right winger in the National Hockey League. He was with the New York Rangers for 12 years, captaining the team from its inception in 1926 until his retirement after the 1936–37 season. He led the Rangers to two Stanley Cup championships. He was elected to the Hockey Hall of Fame in 1952.

Cook, Frederick (1865–1940). American physician and discredited explorer. Cook served as a surgeon on Robert PEARY'S exploratory arctic expedition of 1891–92 and took part in a Belgian expedition in ANTARCTICA in 1897–99. In 1909 he announced that he had reached the NORTH POLE in 1908, a year before Peary's successful expedition. Cook described his feat in *My Attainment of the Pole* (1909) and for a short time enjoyed worldwide fame. However, he was unable to prove that he had reached the Pole, and after his own journey Peary challenged Cook's claims. Cook's claim that he had scaled Alaska's Mt. McKinley in 1906 was also questioned, and he was eventually declared a fraud. However, he continued to insist that he had told the truth about his expeditions. In 1923 Cook was convicted of mail fraud in a crooked investment scheme and spent 10 years in prison before he was pardoned by President Franklin D. ROOSEVELT in 1933. He died in poverty. In 1988, when the NATIONAL GEOGRAPHIC SOCIETY found that Peary may have missed the North Pole by as much as 60 miles, some support for Cook's claims resurfaced, although many scholars believe that neither man reached the North Pole at all.

Cook, Peter (1937–). British comedic actor and writer. Cook, one of the best-known British comedic actors of his generation, began his career at Cambridge University by writing two highly regarded comic revues—*Pieces of Eight* (1959) and *One Over the Eight* (1960)—for the University Footlights Club. He then co-authored a satiric revue, BEYOND THE FRINGE (1960), which was critically acclaimed at the Edinburgh Festival. During this period Cook met Dudley MOORE, with whom he collaborated on a subsequent revue, *Behind the Fridge*. Cook and Moore were featured together in *Bedazzled* (1967), a film comedy directed by Stanley Donen that was based on the Faust legend. Cook later appeared in comedic character roles in a wide range of film and television projects.

Cooke, (Alfred) Alistair (1908–). Anglo-American journalist, commentator and author. Born in Manchester, Cooke was educated at Jesus College, Cambridge, and at Yale and Harvard. He went to the United States in 1932 to study drama at Yale with the intention of becoming a theater director but became interested in the larger theater of America itself. Cooke became an American citizen in 1941. He had been a film critic for the BBC, but in 1936 he began a radio commentary about the U.S. that became "Letters from America" in 1946, and thus started his career as an interpreter of the U.S. for the British. His broadcasts, conversational and keenly observed, became enormously popular, and the program is listed in THE GUINNESS BOOK OF RECORDS as the longest-running radio talk show in the world. Cooke's early writing, such as *Garbo and the Night Watchman* (1937), reflect his interest in acting. His numerous articles and commentaries have been collected in such works as *One Man's America* (1952) and *The Americans: Fifty Talks on Our Life and Times* (1979). Cooke is well-known to Americans as the host for the television programs "Omnibus" (1952–1961), "International Zone" (1961–1967) and "Masterpiece Theatre" (1971–). His varied other work includes *Return to Albion: American in England 1760–1940* (1979), *The Patient Has the Floor* (1986) and *America Observed: The Newspaper Years of Alistair Cooke* (1988), a collection of his journalism.

Cook Islands [aka Hervey Islands]. Nation comprised of 15 scattered islands in the Pacific Ocean, 2,000 miles northeast of NEW ZEALAND. The islands were acquired by New Zealand in 1901 and became autonomous in 1965. In 1986 the prime minister declared the Cook Islands a neutral country; the nation is also part of the South Pacific Nuclear Free Zone. The population, mostly of Polynesia descent, numbers approximately 18,000.

Coolidge, Calvin (1872–1933). Thirtieth president of the United States (1923–29). After studying law and graduating from Amherst College in 1895, Coolidge settled in Northampton, Massachusetts. Elected to the state legislature in 1912, he quickly rose through political ranks. Elected governor of Massachusetts in 1919, he gained national fame for his stern handling of a Boston police strike in that year. He was nominated for the vice presidency by the Republicans on the Warren HARDING ticket of 1920. Harding died in office, and Coolidge was sworn in as president on August 2, 1923. Coolidge's administration coincided with an era of great prosperity that preceded the GREAT DEPRESSION of the 1930s. His administration succeeded in reducing the national debt, and he was elected by a landslide in 1924. Although eligible for a second, full term, Coolidge declined the opportunity in 1928.

For further reading:

McCoy, Donald R., *Calvin Coolidge: The Quiet President*. Lawrence, Kan.: University Press of Kansas, 1988.

Coolidge, William D. (1873–1975). American inventor. Coolidge was a researcher for General Electric for some 40

U.S. President Calvin Coolidge.

years (1905–44). While at GE he developed a ductile tungsten filament (1908), which is still used in electric light bulbs. In 1913 he invented the X-RAY tube that became the prototype for modern X-ray tubes.

Cooper, David (1931–1986). South African-born psychiatrist. After his move to London, Cooper worked with R.D. LAING on the radical movement that came to be known as "antipsychiatry." Cooper rejected the notion that "madness" was a sickness but maintained that the "madman" was merely asserting his autonomy against social and familial restrictions. The movement sought to set up therapeutic communities in which those restrictions would be overcome. He published a number of books, including *The Death of the Family* and *The Language of Madness*.

Cooper, Lady Diana [the Dowager Viscountess Norwich, born Diana Olivia Winifred Maud Manners] (1892–1986). British actress and socialite. Lady Diana Cooper was a legendary beauty and glittering social personality of British high society in the 1920s and 1930s. After a brief career in silent films, she was offered the part of the Madonna in Max REINHARDT's theatrical pageant *The Miracle*. From 1923 to 1935 she toured with the production on and off on both sides of the Atlantic. She became one of the world's most photographed women, and her income enabled her to further the political ambitions of her husband, Alfred Duff Cooper. After his death in 1954, she published three witty volumes of memoirs. She was the model for Mrs. Stitch in Evelyn WAUGH's comic novel *Scoop*.

Cooper, Douglas (1911–1984). British art collector, critic, historian and organizer of major exhibitions in Britain and the U.S. Cooper was closely associated with the cubist painters Pablo PICASSO, Georges BRAQUE, Juan GRIS and Ferdinand LEGER. He collected, wrote about and arranged their work for exhibition. (See also CUBISM.)

Cooper, Gary (Frank J). (1901–1961). American movie actor, born in Montana to English parents; from the late 1920s through the 1950s Cooper may have had more successes and fewer failures than any other Hollywod actor. After working as an extra in such silent Westerns as *The Thundering Herd* (1925), Cooper became an established star only a year later, with his featured role in *The Winning of Barbara Worth.* Equally adept at Westerns, comedies and dramatic films, his magnetic appeal as "the strong, silent type"—and a genuine acting ability—made box-office hits of *The Virginian* (1929), *Morocco* (1930), *City Streets* (1931), *Design for Living* (1934), *For Whom the Bell Tolls* (1943) and many others. His legendary status and continuing reputation rest on such classics as *Mr. Deeds Goes to Town* (1936), *Beau Geste* (1939), *Meet John Joe* (1941), *Ball of Fire* (1941), *The Pride of the Yankees* (1942), *Love in the Afternoon* (1957) and his ACADEMY AWARD-winning roles in *Sergeant York* (1941) and *High Noon* (1952). Cooper died of cancer at only 60 years of age; but in his brief lifetime he produced an impressive body of work that earned him a special Academy Award in 1960.

Cooper, Gordon (1927–). U.S. astronaut. Youngest of the original "Mercury Seven" astronauts selected by NASA in 1959, Cooper made the sixth and last flight in the MERCURY series (May 15–16, 1963). He orbited the Earth 22 times, at that time a record exceeding the combined total of all previous Mercury missions. The self-assured and thrill-seeking Cooper, who had made NASA officials nervous by his love for fast cars and boats, took his first mission so much in stride that he fell asleep inside the spacecraft during one of the mission's almost inevitable "holds." Cooper's second and final mission was Gemini 5 (August 21–29, 1965), with fellow astronaut Pete CONRAD. The two spent eight days in space and set a record at that time of 120 revolutions around the Earth. Cooper, who once said "I'm *planning* on getting to the Moon, I *think* I'll get to Mars," didn't get a chance to visit either; he retired from NASA in July 1970 to enter private industry.

Cooper, Irving S. (1922–1985). American brain surgeon. Cooper pioneered in the development of surgical techniques, including cryogenic surgery, for treating Parkinson's disease and other neurological disorders. He also developed a "pacemaker" brain implant of benefit to epileptics, stroke victims and victims of cerebral palsy.

Cooper, John Montgomery (1881–1949). American anthropologist, priest and author. In 1935, Cooper became head of the department of anthropology at Catholic University, Washington, D.C. His work dealt with the "marginal peoples" of the Americas, the Algonquian tribes of northern Canada, and the natives of Tierra del Fuego, South America, whom he believed had been driven to less desirable habitats by later migrations. He was president of the American Anthropological Association (1940) and founded the quarterly *Primitive Man.*

Cooper, Kent (1880–1965). U.S. newspaperman. While working as a reporter in Indianapolis from 1901 to 1909, Cooper started working for the Associated Press. He established the Associated Press in South America, Great Britain and Germany, as well as the AP Wirephoto system, the wire method of news photo delivery, the first of its kind. Cooper served as president of the Press Association (1940–1951), Wide World (1941–1951) and New York City News Association (1942–1951). He established four journalism scholarships, two each for men and women, at Indiana University.

Cooper, Leon Neil (1930–). American physicist. Cooper was educated at Columbia where he earned his Ph.D. in 1954. After brief spells at the Institute for Advanced Study at Princeton, the University of Illinois and Ohio State University, he moved in 1958 to Brown University and was later (1962) appointed to a professorship of physics. Cooper's early work was in nuclear physics. In 1955 he began work with John BARDEEN and John Robert Schrieffer on the theory of superconductivity. In 1956 he showed theoretically that at low temperatures electrons in a conductor could act in bound pairs (now called **Cooper pairs**). Bardeen, Cooper and Schrieffer showed that such pairs act together with the result that there is no electrical resistance to flow of electrons through the solid. The resulting BCS theory stimulated further theoretical and experimental work on superconductivity and won its three authors the 1972 NOBEL PRIZE for physics. Cooper has also worked on the superfluid state at low temperatures and, in a different field, on the theory of the central nervous system.

Cooper, William [pen name of Harry Summerfield Hoff] (1910–). British novelist. Cooper was born in Crewe and educated at Cambridge University. He taught physics, joined the civil service in 1945 and in 1958 became Personnel Consultant to the U.K. Atomic Energy Authority. He published four early novels under his own name, but it is for his later work, beginning with *Scenes from Provincial Life* (1950), that he is known. With its provincial setting and lower-middle class antihero, his work led the way for the ANGRY YOUNG MEN who followed him. Other works include *Scenes from Married Life* (1961), *Scenes from Metropolitan Life* (1982) and *Scenes from Later Life* (1983); all of which continue the story of Joe Lunn. Cooper also wrote a critical study *C.P. Snow* (1959).

Copeau, Jacques (1879–1949). French theatrical director, actor and critic. Copeau was a leading force in French theater in the first decades of the century. He was best known for his insistence that the tenets of Realism were unnecessarily constricting for theatrical productions. Copeau, whose troupe of actors at the Theatre du Vieux-Colombier in the 1910s included Charles DULLIN and Louis Jouvet, emphasized a focus on the play itself as opposed to elaborate set design. His productions of Moliere, Shakespeare and others featured strong acting, dramatic lighting and a simplified-Elizabethan style stage. In 1924, Copeau formed a highly regarded troupe of actors—called *les Copiaus*—whom he trained in mime and other techniques. In 1936 he became a director of the prestigious Comedie-Francaise.

Copland, Aaron (1900–1990). Dean of modern American composers, whose popular works include the ballet *Rodeo* and *The Fanfare for the Common Man.* Copland was born of Russian immigrant parents (originally named Kaplan) and grew up in Brooklyn where he studied piano with his sister. Later in Paris at the Fontainebleau School of Music he became Nadia BOULANGER's first student and met conductor Serge KOUSSEVITZKY who subsequently commissioned three of Copland's most important works, *Music for the Theatre* (1925), the *Piano Concerto* (1927) and the *Third Symphony* (1946). Copland's best known music is full of characteristic "Americanisms," most notably the quotations from cowboy songs and folk tunes in the ballets BILLY THE KID (1938), RODEO (1942) and *Appalachian Spring* (1945), for which he won a PULITZER PRIZE. He also wrote music for movies, including *The Red Pony* (1948), which brought Bronx inflections to cowboy music, and *The Heiress* (1949), for which he won an ACADEMY AWARD—and for the theater, including the Orson WELLES production in New York of *Five Kings* (1939). More sophisticated purely abstract works include the *Symphonic Ode* (1929), the dodecaphonic *Inscape* (1967) and several piano works that rank among the keyboard masterpieces of the century—the complex *Piano Variations* (1930) and the extraordinary *Piano Sonata* (1939–41). An important critic (*Copland on Music,* 1963) and force in modern music (the "Copland-Sessions Concerts" and organizer of the American Composers Alliance), Copland left an indelible stamp on every phase of American music.

For further reading:

Ewen, David, *Composers Since 1900.* New York: H.W. Wilson, 1969

Composer Aaron Copland, "the Dean of American Music" (1981).

Coppola, Francis Ford (1939–). American motion picture director, producer and screenwriter, most celebrated for his GODFATHER trilogy. After attending the UCLA Film School in the early 1960s, he began a valuable association with low-budget film master Roger CORMAN. This experience produced two successful pictures, *Dementia 13* (1963), a horror film set in Ireland, and *You're a Big Boy Now* (1967). Despite the lackluster box office of his next pictures, the lavish musical, *Finian's Rainbow* (1968), and the deeply felt *The Rain People* (1969), Coppola established his own company, the San Francisco-based Zoetrope Studio, whose vicissitudes took him in and out of bankruptcy. Although Coppola has profited little from his films, his achievements have been impressive. The *Godfather* trilogy to date has won 10 ACADEMY AWARDS. *Apocalypse Now* (1979) and *Tucker* (1988) were exhilarating blends of razzle-dazzle technique and sumptuous period detail (the VIETNAM WAR and the 1940s). But it is *The Conversation* (1974) that best demonstrates what biographer Diane Jacobs suggests is his main theme: "freedom versus privacy." Its depiction of a professional eavesdropper—a man as obsessed with invading the privacy of others as he is of guarding his own—concludes with the chilling (and perhaps autobiographical) realization that he himself cannot escape the prying eyes of others.

For further reading:

Jacobs, Diane, *Hollywood Renaissance*. Cranbury, N.J.: A.S. Barnes, 1977.

Coral Sea. Southwest arm of the Pacific Ocean; site of WORLD WAR II naval battle between the American and Japanese navies. The battle of the Coral Sea, May 7–8, 1942, marked the beginning of the United States' Pacific counteroffensive after the bombing of PEARL HARBOR. It is also noteworthy as the world's first large-scale aircraft carrier conflict; the battle was fought entirely by carrier-based planes, and during its progress no surface ships came within sight of the enemy. On the American side, the carrier *Lexington* was sunk and the carrier *Yorktown* damaged; on the Japanese side, the light carrier *Shoho* was sunk and the carrier *Shokaku* badly damaged; the Japanese lost 43 planes, the Americans 33. The battle of the Coral Sea checked the southward progress of Japanese forces in the Pacific. In addition, by reducing the number of ships available to the Japanese for the impending battle of MIDWAY, the conflict in the Coral Sea may have played a crucial role in the other, critical battle. (See also WORLD WAR II IN THE PACIFIC.)

Corcoran, Thomas G. (1900–1981). American lawyer and lobbyist. Corcoran was instrumental in pushing President Franklin D. ROOSEVELT'S NEW DEAL legislation through Congress during the GREAT DEPRESSION. A deft backstage strategist with countless influential allies, he helped write the Securities and Exchange Act of 1934 and the Fair Labor Standards Act of 1938. After his efforts to aid Roosevelt in enlarging the Supreme Court and dislodging certain congressmen failed, he went into private practice. He represented many powerful corporate clients, provoking four congressional inquiries on charges of influence-peddling. The charges were never proved. (See also BRAIN TRUST.)

Cord Automobile. The Cord 810 model of 1936 is widely recognized as a classic of American automobile design. The car was named for E.L. Cord, the Auburn Company president who supported its development. The introduction of front-wheel drive made the car strikingly advanced in engineering terms, while the body and interior design made it equally striking in visual terms. Only about 3,000 Cords were built, but surviving examples continue to be admired, collected, and valued.

Corea, Chick (1941–). Pianist-composer; one of modern jazz's most influential and versatile personalities. As a child, Corea learned the basics of jazz from his father, and by listening to the recordings of Charlie PARKER and Dizzy GILLESPIE. Following important engagements with the Latin bands of Mongo Santamaria and Willie Bobo, Corea worked with trumpeter Blue Mitchell; at the same time, he was absorbing the latest developments of pianists Bill Evans and McCoy Tyner. Corea joined Miles DAVIS' electronic jazz-rock unit of 1968–70 but departed to pursue freer forms of improvisation, largely within acoustic contexts. In the 1970s, Corea successfully "crossed over" to the various jazz-Latin-rock combinations in three editions of his group Return to Forever. Unlike many who have scored big with commercial jazz, Corea has regularly returned to pure, BEBOP-based formats, most prominently in duo associations with fellow pianist Herbie HANCOCK and vibraphonist Gary Burton. In 1985, he formed the popular Elektric Band with electric bassist John Patitucci and drummer Dave Weckl; with the same personnel, but playing acoustic versions of their electric instruments, Corea also established the highly regarded Akoustic Bank. Among his many attractive and romantic compositions are "Spain," "Windows" and "Crystal Silence."

For further reading:

Lyons, Len, *The Great Pianists: Speaking of Their Lives and Music*. New York: William Morrow, 1983.

Corelli, Franco (1923–). Italian tenor. Born in Ancona, he was relatively untrained but possessed a strong, natural voice. Corelli made his operatic debut at the SPOLETO FESTIVAL in 1952, singing Don Jose in Bizet's *Carmen*. Two years later, he appeared at La Scala for the first time opposite Maria CALLAS in Spontini's *La Vestale*. With a growing reputation, Corelli first appeared outside Italy at Covent Garden, London, in 1957, and he made his Metropolitan Opera debut in 1961 as Manrico in Verdi's *Il Trovatore*, one of his finest roles. Corelli continued to be a featured singer at La Scala and the Metropolitan, as well as at other important opera houses around the world. A handsome man with fine stage presence, he is noted for his passionate style and for the golden brilliance of his voice. Among his other important roles are Calaf in PUCCINI'S *Turandot*, Cavaradossi in *Tosca* and the title part in *Don Carlo*.

Corey, Elias James (1928–). American chemist. Corey was educated at the Massachusetts Institute of Technology where he earned his Ph.D. in 1951. He immediately joined the staff of the University of Illinois and was appointed professor of chemistry there in 1955. In 1959 he moved to a similar chair at Harvard. Corey made a number of organic syntheses and was particularly successful in synthesizing a variety of terpenes, a family of hydrocarbons found in natural plant oils and im-

Jazz musicians Herbie Hancock and Chick Corea (1989).

portant precursors of several biologically active compounds. In 1968 Corey and his colleagues announced they had synthesized five of the prostaglandin hormones.

Corfu. Greek island in the Ionian Sea, off the coasts of Greece and Albania. The **Pact of Corfu,** signed here on July 20, 1917, created the new Serb, Croat and Slovene state that later became YUGOSLAVIA. ITALY controlled Corfu for one month in 1923; this so-called **Corfu Incident** was settled through the new LEAGUE OF NATIONS—the League's first practical test. During WORLD WAR II Corfu was controlled by the Italians and Germans (1941–44).

Cori, Carl Ferdinand (1896–1984). Czechoslovakian-American biochemist. Cori was educated at the gymnasium in Trieste, where his father was director of the Marine Biological Station, and the University of Prague Medical School. He graduated in 1920, the year he married Gerty Radnitz, a fellow student who was to become his lifelong collaborator (see Gerty Theresa Radnitz CORI). The Coris moved to the U.S. in 1922, taking up an appointment at the New York State Institute for the Study of Malignant Diseases in Buffalo. In 1931 they both transferred to the Washington University Medical School, where Cori was successively professor of pharmacology and then of biochemistry until his retirement in 1966. In the mid-1930s the Coris began work to find out how the complex carbohydrate glycogen is converted to glucose in the body. (Glucose provides energy for the body.) Through their researches they discovered that an enzyme called phosphatase is responsible. The value of the Coris' work is undeniable. Above all they pointed the way to the crucial role of phosphates in the provision of cellular energy, the details of which were soon to be worked out by Fritz Lipmann. For their work the Coris shared the 1947 NOBEL PRIZE for physiology or medicine with Bernardo Houssay.

Cori, Gerty Theresa Radnitz [born Gertrude Radnitz] (1896–1957). Czech-American biochemist. She graduated from the Medical School of Prague University in 1920, the year in which she married her lifelong collaborator, Carl CORI. She moved with him to the U.S., taking a post in 1922 at the New York State Institute for the Study of Malignant Diseases in Buffalo. In 1931 she went with her husband to the Washington University Medical School, where she became professor of biochemistry in 1947. That year the Coris and Bernardo Houssay shared the NOBEL PRIZE for physiology or medicine for their discovery of how glycogen is broken down and resynthesized in the body.

Cormack, Allan Macleod (1924–). South African-born physicist. Cormack was educated at the University of Cape Town. He became interested in X-ray imaging at the Groote Schuur Hospital in Johannesburg, where he worked as a physicist in the radioisotopes department. In 1956 he moved to the U.S. where he became a professor at Tufts University. Cormack was the first to analyze theoretically the possibilities of developing a radiological cross-section of a biological system. Independently of the British engineer Godfrey HOUNSFIELD, he developed the mathematical basis for the technique of computer-assisted X-ray tomography (CAT), describing this in two papers in 1963 and 1964, and provided the first practical demonstration. X-ray tomography is a process by which a picture of an imaginary slide through an object (or the human body) is built up from information from detectors rotating around the body. The application of this technique to medical X-ray imaging was to lead to diagnostic machines that could provide very accurate pictures of tissue distribution in the human brain and body. Hounsfield was unaware of Cormack's work when he developed the first commercially successful CAT SCANS for EMI in England. Cormack also pointed out that the reconstruction technique might equally be applied to proton tomography or to gamma radiation from positron annihilations within a patient, and he is investigating these as possible imaging techniques. Cormack shared the 1979 NOBEL PRIZE for physiology or medicine with Hounsfield for the development of CAT.

Corman, Roger (1926–). American motion picture producer and director; his ability to churn out low-budget productions earned him the title "King of the Bs." Corman divided his time in the 1940s as messenger boy and story analyst for 20TH CENTURY-FOX and student in English literature at Oxford. He hit his stride at American-International in the 1950s, directing and/or producing many such forgettable cheapies as *The Monster from the Ocean Floor* (1954) and *Viking Women and the Sea Serpent* (1957), as well as a few minor masterpieces, notably *Little Shop of Horrors* (1960). Corman's quickness is legendary: *War of the Satellites* (1958) appeared only two months after the Russians launched their first Sputnik satellite. After setting his sights and budgets higher with a series of successful Edgar Allan Poe adaptations (e.g., *The Masque of the Red Death* [1964]), Corman formed New World Pictures in 1970 as a kind of training school for soon-to-be prominent directors. Among his discoveries were the young Francis Ford COPPOLA and Martin SCORSESE. In the early 1970s Corman branched out into distribution and handled the American release of several BERGMAN and FELLINI films.

Cornell, Joseph (1903–1972). American artist. Born in Nyack, N.Y., Cornell was self-taught and had his first exhibition in 1932. During World War II he came to know Max ERNST and other expatriate Surrealists. The influence of SURREALISM is strong in his best known works, shallow glass-fronted wooden shadow boxes that contain three-dimensional collages. In these works, everyday objects, photographs, old engravings and other elements are arranged and juxtaposed to create delicate, evocative, mysteriously symbolic and strangely haunting images. Reclusive and bookish, Cornell often made visual references to other works of art or artists, as in *Medici Slot Machine* and *A Pantry Ballet for Jacques Offenbach* (both 1942). Never a part of the New York art scene, Cornell lived in an unfashionable suburb of the city and joined no movements. His intensely personal style made him an important figure in contemporary American art and his work is in the collections of many prominant museums, e.g., *Hotel du Nord* (1953) at the Whitney Museum, N.Y.C.

Cornell, Katherine (1893–1974). American actress. The leading stage actress of her day, Cornell was often directed by her husband, Guthrie McClintic. She made her London debut in Clarence Dane's *A Bill of Divorcement* (1921). Her most famous roles included the title role in *Candida,* Juliet in *Romeo and Juliet,* Elizabeth in *The Barretts of Wimpole Street* and the Countess in *The Light Is Dark Enough.*

Corner, Edred John Henry (1906–). British botanist. Corner graduated from Cambridge University in 1929. He then spent 20 years overseas, first as assistant director of the Gardens Department of the Straits Settlements (Singapore) and from 1947 to 1948 as a field officer for UNESCO in Latin America. Corner returned to Cambridge in 1949 and later, from 1966 until his retirement in 1973, served as professor of tropical botany. Although he originally began as a mycologist, so little was known about tropical plants that he specialized there. He produced a large number of books on the subject; his *Life of Plants* (1964) and *Natural History of Palms* (1966) are widely known.

Cornforth, Sir John Warcup (1917–). Australian chemist. Cornforth was educated at the universities of Sydney and Oxford, England, where he earned his D.Phil. in 1941. He spent the war in Oxford working on the structure of PENICILLIN before joining the staff of the Medical Research Council in 1946. In 1962 Cornforth moved to the Shell research center at Sittingbourne in Kent to serve as director of the Milstead Laboratory of Chemical Enzymology. In 1975 he accepted the post of Royal Society Research Professor at Sussex University. In 1951 the American chemist Robert Woodward had succeeded in synthesizing the important steroid, cholesterol; Cornforth was interested in how the molecule is actually synthesized in the living cell. Using labeled isotopes of hydrogen, he traced out in considerable detail the chemical steps adopted by the cell to form cholesterol from the initial acetic acid. It was for this work that he shared the 1975 NOBEL PRIZE for chemistry with Vladimir Prelog.

Corregidor. Island fortress in Manila Bay, the Philippines, at the southern end of Luzon Island's Bataan Peninsula. Originally an 18th-century Spanish fortress, it became a U.S. military base in 1900. In 20th-century history, the name Corregidor is synonymous with the island's heroic defense against the numerically superior Japanese invaders after the fall of BATAAN, at the beginning of WORLD WAR II. It succumbed on May 6, 1942, after five months of battle; it stood alone for those last 27 days, when the rest of the Philippines had been captured. The surviving U.S. defenders of Corregidor became PRISONERS OF WAR. The American commander, Lt. Gen. Jonathan WAINWRIGHT, survived his captivity and was present when the Japanese signed their surrender aboard the battleship U.S.S. MISSOURI in 1945.

Correns, Karl Erich (1864–1933). German botanist and geneticist. Correns was the only child of the painter Erich Correns. He studied at Tubingen University, where he began his research on the effect of foreign pollen in changing the visible characters of the endosperm (nutritive tissue surrounding the plant embryo). His later research concentrated on establishing how widely Mendel's laws could be applied. In 1909 he obtained the first conclusive evidence for cytoplasmic, or non-Mendelian, inheritance, in which certain features of the offspring are determined by the cytoplasm of the egg cell. Other contributions to plant genetics include his proposal that genes must be physically linked to explain why some characters are always inherited together. Correns was also the first to relate Mendelian segregation (the separation of paired genes, or alleles) to meiosis and the first to obtain evidence for differential fertilization between gametes. From 1914 until his death he was director of the Kaiser Wilhelm Institute for Biology in Berlin.

Corrigan, Mairead (1944–). Irish peace activist. Raised as a Catholic in Belfast, Corrigan witnessed the violence and brutality of the conflict between Catholics and Protestants in NORTHERN IRELAND through her voluntary work for the Catholic welfare organization the Legion of Mary. In 1976, an IRA member was killed at the wheel of his van by British soldiers. The uncontrolled van struck Corrigan's sister and killed three of her children. The event, witnessed by **Betty Williams**, a Protestant, galvanized the two women to action against the internecine terrorism in Belfast. Williams began collecting signatures for a peace petition, and Corrigan appeared on television denouncing the IRA and announcing a peace march. At the march, 10,000 Protestant and Catholic women appeared and Corrigan and Williams were motivated to form the Community of Peace People, which grew into a worldwide organization demonstrating and acting for peace. In 1975, groups in Norway raised money and presented it to Corrigan and Williams as a Peoples Peace Prize. The following year Corrigan and Williams received the NOBEL PRIZE for Peace. Corrigan continues to live in Belfast, promoting the integration of Catholics and Protestants.

Founders of Northern Ireland's Women's Peace Movement, Mairead Corrigan and Betty Williams, with Queen Elizabeth II (1977).

Cortazar, Julio (1914–1984). Argentinian novelist and short story writer. Born in Brussels, Cortazar attended Buenos Aires University and held dual citizenship in Argentina and (after 1981) France. A popular as well as a critical success, his avant-garde, circular *Rayela* (1963; tr. 1966 as *Hopscotch*) was the first great novel of EL BOOM in Latin American literature. Other experimental works include *62: Modelo para armar* (1968; tr. 1972 as *62: A Model Kit*), *Libro de Manuel* (1973; tr. 1978 as *A Manual for Manuel*) and *Queremos tanto a Glenda* (1980; tr. 1983 as *We All Love Glenda So Much*). His short story "Las babas del diablo," from the 1959 *Las armas secretas*, was the basis for Michelangelo ANTONIONI's 1966 film *Blow Up*. His work tends to be playful, fantastic and socially committed; it attempts to jolt the reader out of traditional ways of viewing reality. His final years were devoted to political activism. Cortazar was a supporter of the Cuban and Nicaraguan revolutions.

For further reading:

De Mundo Lo, Sara, *Julio Cortazar: His Works and his Critics*. Albatross, 1985.

Peavler, Terry J., *Julio Cortazar*. Boston: G.K. Hall, 1990.

Cortot, Alfred (Denis) (1877–1962). French pianist and conductor. Born in Switzerland, Cortot studied piano at the Paris Conservatory and made his concert debut in Paris in 1896. He taught piano at the Paris Conservatory from 1907 and was a cofounder (1919) and director of the Ecole Normale de Musique, Paris. Also active in chamber music, he was particularly noted for his trio work with cellist Pablo CASALS and violinist Jacques THIBAUD. Touring Europe and the U.S. as a performer and a conductor, he became a popular fixture of the classical music scene between the two world wars and was especially known for his performances of Chopin, Schumann and Liszt. Accused of collaboration with the Nazis because of his ties with the VICHY government's musical establishment, Cortot was arrested and released in 1944. He then settled in Lausanne, Switzerland, and made far fewer concert appearances.

Corvette. GENERAL MOTORS (Chevrolet) automobile designed as an American rival to European sport cars. General Motors Vice President Harley J. EARL is viewed as the motive power behind the decision to produce a two-seater car with advanced body design, which first appeared in 1953. The FIBERGLASS body was a blend of functional STREAMLINING and somewhat gross styling elements. In 1956 the design was changed and a V-8 engine substituted for the original 6. Debate about the merit of the Corvette centered on whether it was a "true" sport car or merely a typically American consumer product disguised to appeal to a special audience. The redesigned Stingray model of 1963 was a striking visual form that brought new popularity to the Corvette. Since that time, the Corvette has become something of a cult object, valued, collected, and displayed by ardent devotees.

Cosby, Bill (1937–). Specializing in warm, wholesome family humor, Bill Cosby is the most successful comic television performer of the last 25 years. Although the Philadelphia-born comedian began his career as a phenomenally popular stand-up comedian—garnering a record six straight Grammy awards (1964–69) for his albums, more than a dozen of which became certified Gold bestsellers—as early as 1965 he was making history of another kind, as the black costar (not chauffeur) of Robert Culp on the successful TV drama "I Spy" (1965–68), for which he won three Emmy awards. In the 1970s Cosby appeared in several films, including *Hickey and Boggs* (1972), *Uptown Saturday Night* (1974) and *Mother, Jugs and Speed* (1976). It was on television, however, that his brand of down-to-earth observational comedy struck home. In the 1970s he had success with several different formats, on shows such as "The Bill Cosby Show" (1969–71), "The New Bill Cosby Show" (1972–73), "Cos" (1976) and an animated kiddie-show "Fat Albert and the Cosby Kids." But his greatest achievement is his television sitcom "The Cosby Show" (1984–), rated as the number one show in America through most of its first six years. Cosby's fame and wealth continue; he earned an honorary Ph.D. in 1977, has written several bestselling books (including *Fatherhood*, which sold nearly five million copies in hardcover and paperback in 1986) and has become perhaps the most recognizable face in the country as a result of his commercial testimonials for Coca-Cola softdrinks and Jello pudding products.

Costa-Gavras [Kostantinos Gavras] (1933–). Greek film director. Costa-Gavras, who was educated at the Sorbonne, began his film career in the 1950s as an assistant to the French film director Rene Clement. His first solo directorial effort was *The Sleeping Car Murder* (1965), a mystery thriller. But Costa-Gavras, with the patronage of French actor and singer Yves MONTAND, soon turned his attention to more politically involved filmmaking. *Z* (1969), which starred Montand, Irene Papas and Jean-Louis Trintignant, grippingly portrayed the murder of a Greek peace movement leader at the orders of a right-wing terrorist group tied to the ruling Greek junta (see GREEK COLONELS). *The Confession* (1970), with Montand and Simone SIGNORET, was set in 1952 and explored the psychological breakdown of a Communist Party bureaucrat who is forced by his Stalinist superiors into giving a false confession. Other films by Costa-Gavras include *State of Siege* (1972) and *Missing* (1982).

Costa Rica [Republic of Costa Rica]. Central American country bordered on the north by Nicaragua, on the south by Panama, on the east by the Caribbean Sea and on the west by the Pacific Ocean; capital is San Jose. Since 1838 and with few exceptions, Costa Rica has remained one of the most stable and prosperous of Central American countries. In a bloodless coup d'etat in 1917, Federico Tinoco established a junta government but was deposed in 1919. In 1948, a six-week civil war followed an election dispute. In 1949, a new constitution was adopted, abolishing the army in favor of a Civil and a Rural Guard. Jose FIGUERES, who had led the anti-government forces in the brief war, became president and was reelected in 1953. He was a cofounder of the National Liberation Party (PLN) and instituted social reforms such as nationalized banks and a social security system. Subsequent leaders drifted toward conservatism and overrode some of the PLN reforms. In 1974, PLN candidate Daniel Oduber was elected president, reinstituting social programs. In 1978, Rodrigo Carazo Odio, a conservative of the Unity Coalition (CU), was elected. During his presidency, Costa Rica was brought to the verge of economic collapse, and he was accused of illegal arms trafficking. In 1982, Louis Alberto Monge Alvarez, another cofounder of the PLN, won a landslide victory and managed to salvage the economy. At issue in the 1986 elections was Costa Rica's neutrality. The U.S. had been pressuring Monge to condemn the Nicaraguan Sandinistas and to reestablish an army. However, Oscar Arias Sanchez won the election with a neutral platform and implemented a policy to prevent the U.S.-backed Contras' presence in Costa Rica.

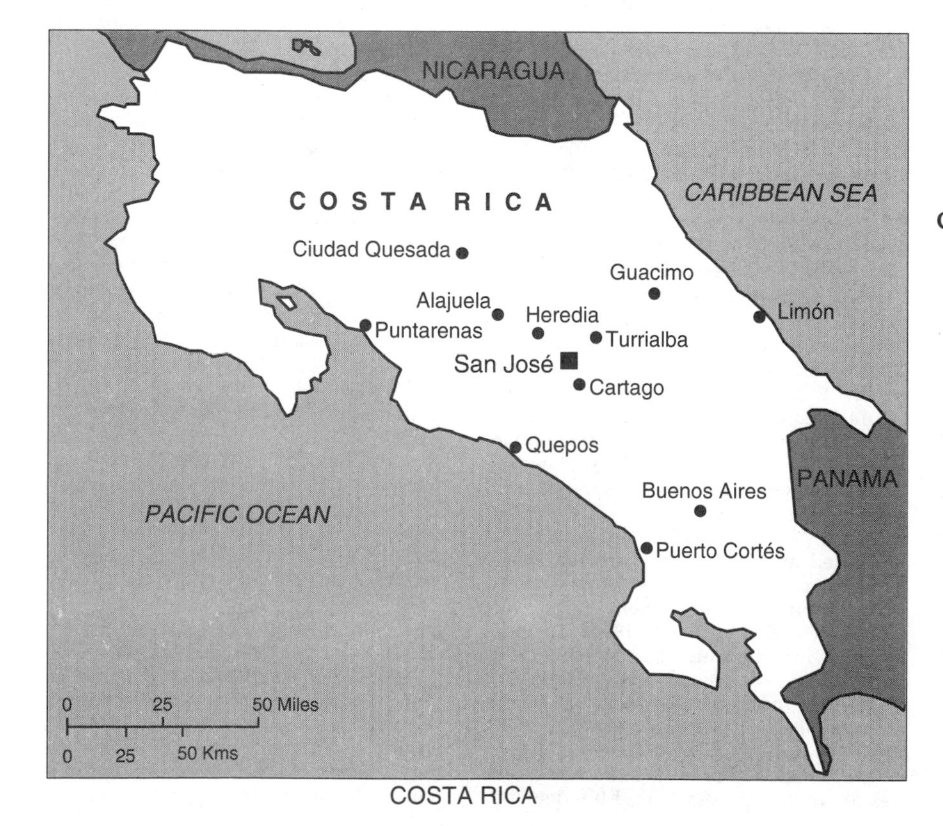

COSTA RICA

Costa Rican Civil War of 1948. COSTA RICA's election of 1948, won by Ottilio Ulate was invalidated by the Congress on March 1, 1948. Civil war broke out between Ulate's followers, led by Colonel Jose "Pepe" FIGUERES FERRER, and the government and supporters of the defeated candidate, Rafael Calderon Guardia. In six weeks of fighting Figueres' forces ousted the government, despite Calderon receiving outside aid from Nicaragua and Honduras. On May 8, 1948, Figueres established a military junta, which dissolved the army, outlawed the communists, nationalized banks and began civil service reform. Resistance by armed Calderonista rebels invading from Nicaragua was repulsed, and in early 1949 a Costa Rican constitutional assembly met, confirmed Ulate's election and drafted a new constitution. On November 8, 1949, Figueres turned over the government to Ulate.

Costa Rican Rebellion of 1955. Jose "Pepe" FIGURES FERRER (b. 1908), a moderate socialist was elected president of Costa Rica in 1953. Dictatorial President Anastasio Somoza (1896–1956) claimed that Figueres'election supporters had plotted against him. To retaliate, Somoza backed disgruntled former Costa Rican President Rafael Calderon Guardia (1900–1970) to lead a rebel force into northern Costa Rica. Figueres appealed to the Organization of American States, whose investigation revealed the rebels' Nicaraguan backing, resulting in Somoza's withdrawal of support. The rebels, no match for the popular government forces, were driven out, and in early 1956 Costa Rica and Nicaragua agreed to cooperative border surveillance.

Costa Rican Revolution of 1917. The proposed reforms of Alfredo Gonzalez Flores elected president of Costa Rica in 1913, were opposed by General Federico Tinoco Granados, who overthrew Gonzalez and set up a military dictatorship. Insurrections broke out, and the U.S. which had refused to recognized Tinoco, threatened intervention. Tinoco resigned in May 1919, and a month later U.S. Marines landed to protect U.S. interests. In 1920 a democratic government was restored under newly elected president Julio Acosta Garcia.

Costello, Elvis [Declan Patrick McManus] (1955–). English singer-songwriter. Costello emerged on the British punk scene as it was evolving into NEW WAVE, and he remains the genre's most enduring figure. He signed with the legendary Stiff label in 1977, joining a stable of talent that included Ian Dury, Wreckless Eric and Nick Lowe. His first hit "Watching the Detectives" showcases the influence of reggae on his work, as well as his unusually cerebral and literate lyrics. His 1979 *Armed Forces* was his best-selling album and included the singles "Oliver's Army" and "Accidents Will Happen." *Almost Blue,* a dense and lovely homage to the country genre, included the 1981 hit "A Good Year For the Roses." His albums and singles continued to sell well through the 1980s and included his first top-40 hit "Everyday I Write the Book." Despite his success, Costello portrays himself as a bitter and angry man. He is married to Pogues' bassist Cait O'Riordan.

COSTA RICA

1900	Boundary dispute with Panama (then part of Colombia); arbitrated by president of France, but dispute continues.
1913	United Fruit Company develops plantations along the Atlantic coast; bananas for a time surpass coffee as leading export.
1916	Costa Rica claims that Betan-Chamorro Treaty (U.S.-Nicaragua) ignores its rights to San Juan River.
1917	Federico Tinoco installs revolutionary government that lasts for two years.
1921	With U.S. backing, Costa Rica occupies area disputed with Panama.
1936	National Republican Party (PRN) comes to power; begins moderate reforms.
1945	United Fruit Company builds plantations on Pacific coast, imports workers from Jamaica.
1948	PRN defeated at polls; refuses to abide by election and vacate presidency. Civil war ensues; PRN strongman Calderon driven from country.
1949	As a result of civil war, new constitution adopted banning national army in perpetuity; Catholicism made official religion.
1955	Calderon and supporters reinvade but are defeated despite help from regional strongmen Somoza, Trujillo and Batista.
1963	Costa Rica joins Central American common market.
1968	Arenal volcano's first eruption in centuries kills many.
1979	Costa Rica supports Sandinista rebellion against Nicaraguan dictator Somoza.
1983	Basing of anti-Sandinista Contra rebels in Costa Rican territory causes friction with Nicaragua.
1985	United Fruit (now United Brands) sells Costa Rican plantations.
1987	President Oscar Arias' Nicaraguan peace plan adopted by other nations of the region; Arias wins Nobel Prize for peace.
1989	Arias plan is basis of regional agreement leading to free elections in Nicaragua in 1990, disbanding of Contras.
1990	Angel Calderon, son of former strongman and opponent of Arias' peace plan, elected president with help of U.S. media consultant Roger Ailes; Costa Rican judge seeks extradtion from U.S. of John Hull, CIA operative in Iran/Contra affair.

Costello, Lou. See ABBOTT AND COSTELLO.

Coster, Dirk (1889–1950). Dutch physicist. Coster was educated at the University of Leiden where he earned his doctorate in 1922. From 1924 to 1949 he was professor of physics at the University of Groningen. In 1923, in collaboration with Georg van Heyesy, he discovered the element hafnium (named for Hafnia, an old Roman name for Copenhagen the home of Niels BOHR, who had suggested that the new element would most likely be found in zirconium ores).

Cote D'Ivoire [formerly, Ivory Coast]. Situated on the west coast of Africa, Ivory Coast covers a total area of 124,471 square miles. In 1904 the Ivory Coast became a member of the federation of FRENCH WEST AFRICA; it gained representation in the French National Assembly after World War II. Opposition to colonial representation led to the formation of the Parti democratique de la Cote d'Ivoire in 1945. The party leader, Felix HOUPHOUET-BOIGNY, became Ivory Coast president when the country declared its independence in 1960. The country has remained quite stable politically, except for brief periods of unrest in the early 1970s. The nation's name was officially changed to Cote d'Ivoire in 1990.

Cottrell, Sir Alan Howard (1919–). British physicist and metallurgist. Cottrell studied at the University of Birmingham, earning his B.Sc. in 1939 and Ph.D. in 1949. After leaving Birmingham in 1955, he took the post of deputy head of the metallurgy division of the Atomic Energy Research Establishment at Harwell until 1958, when he became Goldsmiths Professor of Metallurgy at Cambridge University. From 1965 he held a number of posts as a scientific adviser to the British government. In 1974 he became master of Jesus College, Cambridge, and subsequently vice-chancellor of the University of Cambridge (1977–79). Cottrell's most notable research has been in the study of dislocations in crystals. He also worked on the effect of radiation on crystal structure—work that was important in design changes to the fuel rods in early nuclear reactors.

Coughlin, Charles E(dward) (1891–1979). Canadian-born American Catholic "radio priest" ("the fighting priest") of the 1930s. He started his own radio show in Detroit to crusade against injustice, but his views became increasingly extreme. During the GREAT DEPRESSION he was a leading critic of President Franklin ROOSEVELT. On radio and at mass rallies he preached against the banks, COMMUNISM, the NEW DEAL, the JEWS and Wall Street. In the late 1930s his National Union for Social Justice, renamed the Christian Front, took on fascist overtones. The Catholic Church ended his broadcasts in 1942. A forerunner of the televangelists, Coughlin was among the first to use radio to reach a mass audience; at the height of his popularity, he was heard by 40 million Americans each week. (See also DEMAGOGUES; FASCISM; Huey LONG; Gerald SMITH.)

Coulson, Charles Alfred (1910–1974). British theoretical chemist, physicist and mathematician. Coulson was educated at Cambridge University, where he earned his Ph.D. in 1935, and afterward taught mathematics at the universities of Dundee and Oxford. Coulson then held appointments as professor of theoretical physics at King's College, London (1947–52), Rouse Ball Professor of Mathematics at Oxford (1952–72) and, still at Oxford, professor of theoretical chemistry from 1972 until his death in 1974. As a physicist Coulson wrote the widely read *Waves* (1941) and *Electricity* (1948). His most creative work, however, was as a theoretical chemist. Later he turned to theoretical studies of carcinogens, drugs and other topics of biological interest. Coulson was also one of the leading Methodists of his generation and, from 1965 to 1971, chairman of Oxfam, the third-world charity. He produced a number of works on the relationship between Christianity and science of which *Science and Christian Belief* (1955) is a typical example.

counterculture. Term that first emerged in the U.S. in the 1960s. At that time, the word referred specifically to the HIPPIES, who rejected middle-class American values and advocated drug use, "free love" and an "alternative lifestyle" in general. It is now widely used to refer to the cumulative societal impact exercised by disaffected political and social groups and the artistic avant-garde. The counterculture is the collective embodiment of ideals and values that are not highly valued by mainstream culture. Members of the counterculture act as political, social and artistic gadflies, calling attention to issues that might otherwise be overlooked in the mainstream consensus. Over time, certain countercultural ideals may become accepted by the mainstream, and the counterculture moves on to emphasize different issues. There is, therefore, an ongoing dialectical interaction between the mainstream and the counterculture; both can be viewed as necessary to overall societal functioning and development.

country and western music. Popular American musical form that originated in the South among rural whites. In the 19th

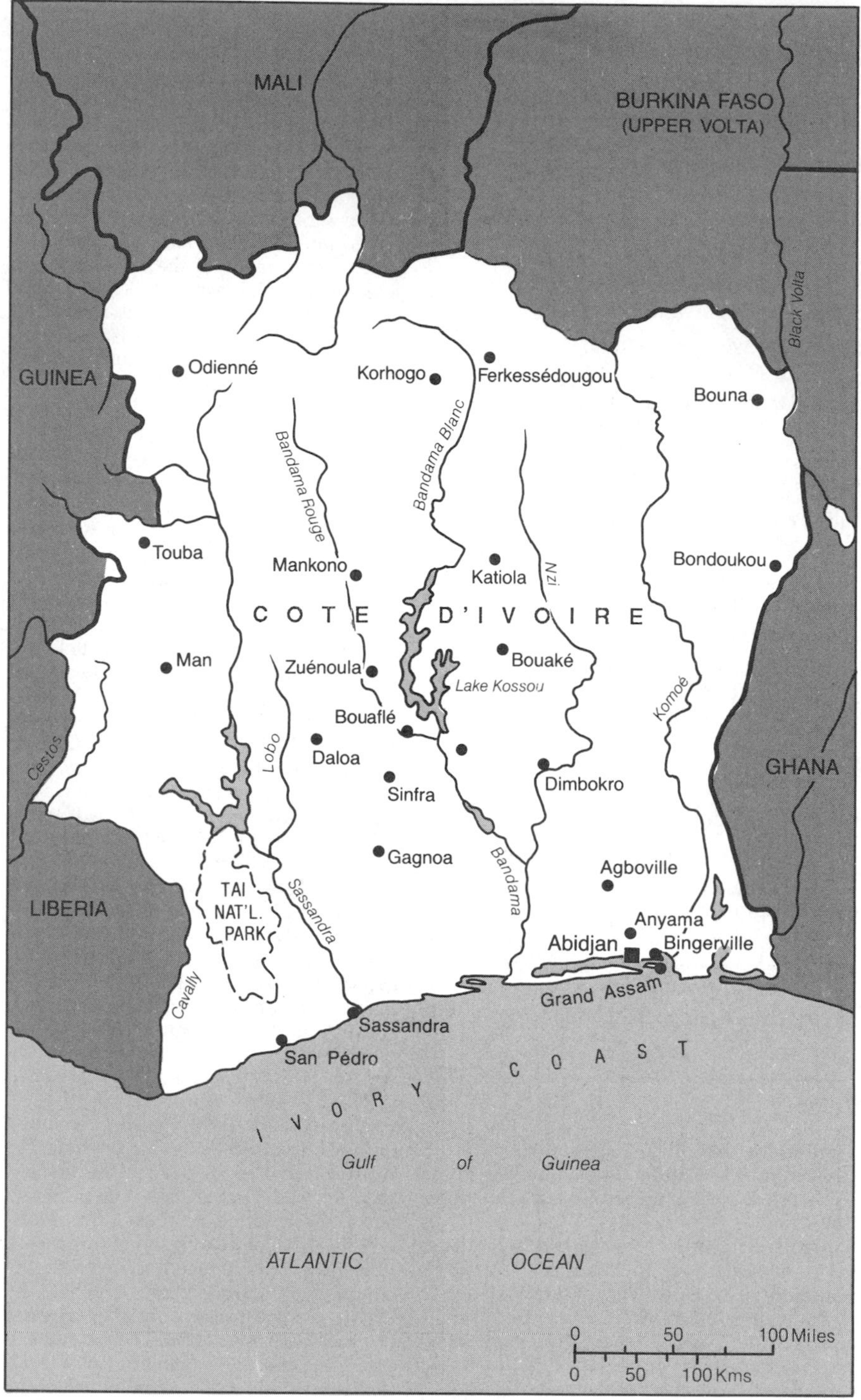

COTE D'IVOIRE

century, a folk music tradition derived from British roots combined with Afro-American and other ethnic sources and took a new twist in the form of what came to be called "hillbilly" music, in the mountainous Appalachian region of the South. At first the music was performed at county fairs, churches and other local occasions. The music was given a great boost during the 1920s by the arrival of radio and the popularity of groups such as the Carter Family, and Jimmie Rodgers (1897–1933), often dubbed "the father of country music."

The mainstream of country music received a major boost in 1927 with the establishment of the Grand Ole Opry, a music show that made Nashville, Tennessee, the Mecca for country music. A variation on the country theme appeared in the 1930s with the rise of western music, popularized by Gene AUTRY, Tex Ritter and Roy ROGERS. Western was but one of a variety of allied forms ranging from the folk traditions of Woody GUTHRIE to the banjo instrumentals of bluegrass music. The postwar era has seen a widespread growth in the popularity of country and western music, although it is strongest in the South and Southwest, which still supply most of the performers. While it has been influenced by other forms, notably rock music, the tradition has been maintained by such artists as Johnny Cash, Willie Nelson, Loretta Lynn, Merle Haggard, Kenny Rogers, Dolly Parton and Barbara Mandrell.

For further reading:

Carr, Patrick, ed., *The Illustrated History of Country Music.* New York, 1980.

Country Party. Australian political party established in 1920. The Country Party arose from an group of farmers from New South Wales who, in 1913, began supporting Conservative politicians who would represent agricultural interests. In 1920 these politicians within the Federal Parliament were organized by W.J. Williams into the Country Party. Under the leadership of Sir Earle Page, the Country Party won 14 seats by 1922 and could influence the LABOUR and Nationalist parties. Under the leadership of Stanley Bruce, the Nationalist Party formed a coalition with the Country Party and shared power from 1922 to 1929, 1934 to 1941 and 1949 to 1971. Sir Arthur Fadden, Country Party leader, was prime minister for the coalition government briefly in 1949.

Cournand, Andre Frederic (1895–1988). French-born physician and physiologist; a professor of medicine at Columbia University for many years. While there, Cournand teamed with Dickinson Richards in researching the practical uses of the heart catheter, invented by Werner FORSSMANN of Germany in 1929. In 1956, the three men shared the NOBEL PRIZE for medicine or physiology.

Courtauld Institute of Art. Museum and art school in London. The Courtauld was established in 1931 under the auspices of the University of London when **Samuel Courtauld** (1876–1947) donated his collection of Impressionist and Post-Impressionist paintings and Home House to quarter it. Subsequent additions to the collection include the Lee and Gambier-Perry collection of Old Masters, the Roger FRY collection of early 20th-century French and English painting and the Spooner collection of English landscape watercolors and drawing. The institute encourages the study and research of art history, and many prominent art historians, including Anita BROOKNER, have taught on its staff. In 1990 the Courtauld was relocated to Somerset House in London.

Court-packing attempt by FDR. An unsuccessful attempt by President Franklin D. ROOSEVELT to add six extra members to the U.S. Supreme Court, which had struck down a number of key NEW DEAL acts as unconstitutional. During his first term Roosevelt did not have the opportunity to fill a single vacancy on the Court. Some of the justices were openly hostile to FDR's program, which seemed radical at the time. On Feb. 5, 1937, frus-

COTE D'IVOIRE (IVORY COAST)

1904	Ivory Coast becomes member of the Federation of French West Africa.
1960	(Aug. 7) The Republic of the Ivory Coast declares independence from France, with Houphouet-Boigny of the Parti democratique de la Cote d'Ivoire (PDCI) as president.
1964	Polygamy, bride price and matrilineal inheritance are abolished.
1969	Relations with the U.S.S.R. are broken.
1971	President Houphouet-Boigny calls for dialogue with South Africa as an alternative to confrontation.
1973	(June) Military coup plot uncovered, seven officers sentenced to death.
1975	5,000 political prisoners granted amnesty; Houphouet-Boigny reelected to a fourth five-year term.
1986	The nation is given its French appellation—Cote d'Ivoire.
1990	Austerity measures imposed in Feb. provoke nationwide unrest, are rescinded.
1990	(May 3) Implementation of multiparty system is begun; (Oct. 28) Houphouet-Boigny reelected for a seventh five-year term, making him Africa's longest-serving leader.

trated at the aged justices' opposition to his New Deal legislation, FDR proposed a plan to allow him to appoint one additional justice to the Court for every sitting justice over the age of 70. The plan was harshly criticized as a blatant attempt to influence the Court, and the proposal was never voted upon by the full Congress. However, for whatever reason, after the unsuccessful plan to pack the Court, the justices were less hostile to FDR's New Deal legislation. Because of advancing age and a more generous pension plan, eight of the nine justices retired during the next six years, and FDR was able to fill the vacancies with appointees more sympathetic to his New Deal program.

Cousins, Frank (1904–1986). British LABOUR PARTY politician and trades union leader. From 1956 to 1964 and again from 1966 to 1968, Cousins headed one of Britain's most powerful trades unions, the Transport and General Workers' Union. Between those two periods, he was in Prime Minister Harold WILSON's Labour government as Britain's first minister of technology.

Cousins, Norman (1915–1990). American magazine editor, author and educator. Cousins was best known for his highly successful tenure as editor of *The Saturday Review,* a general interest magazine on the arts, education, science and other topics. Educated at Columbia University, Cousins became editor of *The Saturday Review* in 1940 and gradually increased its circulation from 20,000 to a high of 600,000. Under Cousins, the magazine became a major liberal voice in American culture, calling for restrictions on nuclear armaments and increased power for the United Nations. Forced to resign his editorship in 1971 due to a change of ownership, he returned in triumph two years later and edited *The Saturday Review* until 1977, when he resigned to devote himself to teaching and writing. In his book *Anatomy of an Illness: As Perceived by the Patient* (1979), Cousins argued—based on his own experience with a life-threatening form of arthritis—that emotional attitudes of the patient can play a vital role in healing. This theme was taken up again in Cousins' last book, *Head First: The Biology of Hope* (1989).

Cousteau, Jacques Yves (1910–). French oceanographer, explorer, inventor, filmmaker and author. Cousteau studied at the Ecole Navale in Brest and on graduation entered the French navy. During WORLD WAR II he served in the French RESISTANCE and was awarded the Legion d'Honneur and the Croix de Guerre. During the war he also made his first two underwater films and, despite German occupation of France, designed and tested an aqualung. For this he adapted a valve (hitherto used by Emile Gagnan to enable car engines to work with cooking gas) to make an underwater breathing apparatus. Using compressed air, the **Cousteau-Gagnon aqualung** allows long periods of underwater investigation at depths of more than 200 feet and frees the diver of the need for a heavy suit and lifeline. In 1946 Cousteau became head of the French navy's Underwater Research Group and the following year set a world record of 300 feet for free-diving. In 1951–52 he traveled to the Red Sea in a converted British minesweeper, the *Calypso,* and made the first underwater color film to be taken at a depth of 150 feet. Later he helped Auguste PICCARD in the development of the first bathyscaphes. Cousteau also designed and worked on a floating island off the French coast that enabled long-term study of marine life. He is the designer of an underwater diving saucer capable of descents to more than 600 feet and able to stay submerged for 20 hours. More significantly, he has worked on the future exploitation of the seabed as a living environment for humans, conducting various experiments on short-term undersea living. Cousteau has made more significant contributions to undersea exploration and study than any other individual. His work has been brought to a wide audience by means of cinephotography and television, and a number of his films, for example, *The Silent World,* have won ACADEMY AWARDS. His many books and his television documentaries in the series "The Undersea World of Jacques Cousteau" have captured the imagination of millions.

Cousy, Bob (1928–). American basketball player, considered one of the all-time greats of the game. A guard for the Boston Celtics of the NBA, Cousy played from 1950 to 1963. He led the NBA in assists for eight straight seasons and helped the Celtics win six NBA championships. After his retirement he coached basketball at Boston College (1963–69) and subsequently returned to the NBA as head coach of the Cincinnati Royals.

Coveleski, Stan (1890–1984). American baseball player. A pitcher, Coveleski played from 1912 to 1928. He spent the prime of his career with the Cleveland Indians but also pitched for the Philadelphia Athletics, Washington Senators and New York Yankees. In 1920 he led the American League in strikeouts and was credited with three of the Indians' four victories over the Brooklyn Dodgers in that year's World Series. His lifetime record was 217 wins and 141 losses. He was inducted into the Baseball Hall of Fame in 1969.

Coventry. City in the West Midlands of England, 18 miles from Birmingham. A major manufacturing center, it was bombed by the Luftwaffe on the night of November 14–15, 1940 during WORLD WAR II. The surviving tower of St. Michael's Cathedral has been incorporated into the structure of a spectacular (though controversial) contemporary cathedral.

Coward, Sir Noel (Pierce) (1899–1973). British playwright, director, actor and

French SCUBA pioneer and ocean explorer Jacques Cousteau.

Moss Hart, Gertrude Lawrence and Noel Coward backstage at the Alvin Theater (1941).

songwriter. Known for his sophisticated wit, he was perhaps the foremost writer of the English comedy of manners in the 20th century. He made his stage debut at age 10, and by 1920 was appearing regularly in West End comedies and writing songs, sketches and plays. His most successful plays, frequently revived, included *Hay Fever* (1925), *Private Lives* (1930), *Design for Living* (1933) and *Blithe Spirit* (1941). He wrote the book and score for the 1929 operetta *Bitter Sweet* and also wrote the screenplays for the World War II film *In Which We Serve* (1942), which he directed and starred in, and for *Brief Encounter* (1946), directed by David LEAN; both are considered classics. His work appealed less to postwar tastes, but he continued to enjoy success in films and on the stage in Britain and the U.S. until his retirement shortly before his death.

Cowl, Jane (1884–1950). U.S. actress and playwright. She made her New York City debut on the stage of the Belasco Theater in *Sweet Kitty Bellairs* (1903). Acting primarily in light comedy, her best known roles were in *A Grand Army Man, The Easiest Way* and *Within the Law*. She coauthored and performed in *Lilac Time, Information Please* and *Smilin' Through*.

Cowles, Henry Chandler (1869–1939). American botanist. Cowles did pioneer ecological studies of dune vegetation, the floral balance in the Chicago area, and the use of trees as indicators of earlier environmental conditions. He taught at the UNIVERSITY OF CHICAGO from 1902 to 1934. Author of several publications on the subject of botany, Cowles edited the *Botanical Gazette* (1925–34).

Cowley, Malcolm (1898–1989). American literary critic, author and editor. Cowley was a member of the so-called LOST GENERATION of American writers who settled in Paris in the 1920s, and which he later chronicled in *Exile's Return*. As editor at the *New Republic* magazine in the 1930s and at Viking Press from 1944 to 1985, Cowley championed the cause of such post-World War I writers as John DOS PASSOS and William FAULKNER. Cowley's edition of *The Portable William Faulkner* (1946) brought about renewed interest in Faulkner's work and led to his receiving the NOBEL PRIZE. Cowley's other work includes *Thinking Back on Us: A Contemporary Chronicle of the 1930's* (1964) and the memoirs *And I Worked at the Writer's Trade* (1963) and *The Dream of the Golden Mountain: Remembering the 1930's* (1980). *The Selected Correspondence of Kenneth Burke and Malcolm Cowley, 1915–1981* was published in 1988.

Cox, Archibald (1912–). American lawyer, law school professor and author. Cox, a graduate of Harvard University, left a private law practice in Boston to work first with the U.S. Justice Department and then the Labor Department during World War II. After the war he returned to Boston as a professor of law at Harvard, although he interrupted his teaching to act as U.S. solicitor general during the early 1960s. Cox is best remembered as the special prosecutor appointed to investigate the WATERGATE scandal that rocked the administration of President Richard M. NIXON. After the Supreme Court upheld Cox's demand for tapes of Nixon's White House conversations, Nixon ordered his attorney general, Elliot Richardson, to fire Cox. Instead, Richardson and his deputy, William Ruckelshaus, resigned. Subsequently, Solicitor General Robert BORK, then acting attorney general, fired Cox in what became known as the Saturday Night Massacre. Cox's dismissal intensified calls for Nixon's impeachment and helped lead to the president's eventual resignation.

For further reading:

Knappman, Edward, ed., *Watergate and the White House*. Volume I: June 1972–July 1973. New York: Facts On File, 1973.

Drossman, Evan and Knappman, Edward, eds., *Watergate and the White House*. Volume II: July-December 1973. New York: Facts On File, 1975.

Kutler, Stanley I., *The Wars of Watergate: The Last Crisis of Richard Nixon*. New York: Knopf, 1990.

Cox, Harvey G(allagher) (1929–). American Protestant theologian and sociologist. Cox rose to national prominence in the 1960s due to widespread acclaim for his first book, *The Secular City* (1965), which examined the difficulties of maintaining religious faith in a secularized American society. Cox, who was educated at Yale and Harvard, taught church history and sociology for nearly three decades at Harvard. His other works include *God's Revolution and Man's Responsibility* (1965), *The Feast of Fools* (1969), *The Seduction of the Spirit: The Use and Misuse of People's Religion* (1973) and *Turning East: The Promise and Peril of the New Orientalism* (1977).

Cox, James Middleton (1870–1957). U.S. newspaper journalist and politician. Cox started his newspaper career at the *Cincinnati Enquirer* and later bought the *Dayton Daily News* (1898). He subsequently bought several other newspapers in various states. Beginning in 1909, he served two terms in the U.S. House of Representatives. He supported the political philosophy of President Woodrow WILSON. Cox was strongly in favor of Wilson's international policies, such as freedom of the seas, arms reduction, freedom of trade and, particularly, some kind of union of nations. In 1920 he was nominated for the presidency by the DEMOCRATIC PARTY, with F.D. ROOSEVELT as his running mate, but was defeated by Warren G. HARDING.

Cozzens, James Gould (1903–1978). American novelist and short story writer. Cozzens was educated at Kent School in Connecticut, which he would later portray in short stories and the novel *The Last Adam* (1933, published in England as *A Cure of Flesh;* filmed as *Doctor Bull* in 1933), and at Harvard University, although he did not complete a degree there. Cozzens published his first novel, *Confusion* (1924) at the age of 19. Although not well received, it expressed one of Cozzens' recurrent concerns, that of a gifted youth finding her destiny. Cozzens moved to Canada and then to Cuba, where he taught children of American mill employees and gleaned the material for his next two novels, *Cock Pit* (1928) and *The Son of Perdition* (1929). After returning to New York in 1927, Cozzens met and married Bernice Baumgarten, a literary agent who subsequently managed his career. Although he produced many novels and short stories between 1927 and 1948, Cozzens' best known work is *Guard of Honor* (1948), which is based on his experiences while stationed in Washington, D.C., during WORLD WAR II and on the detailed diaries he kept. The novel won a PULITZER PRIZE in 1949. Cozzens was often criticized for his cranky iconoclasm and controversial elitism. Many critics feel that his work has not received the attention that its complexity merits. Other of his many works include *By Love Possessed* (1957; filmed 1961), *Morning, Noon and Night* (1968), and the short stories *Children and Others* (1964).

Crabbe, Buster [Clarence Linden Crabbe] (1907–1983). American athlete and actor. During an impressive swimming career in the 1920s and early 30s, Crabbe broke five world records. He placed third in a race in the 1928 OLYMPICS and captured the gold medal in the 400-meter freestyle event in the 1932 Olympics. He then parlayed his impressive physique and rugged looks into a career in HOLLYWOOD "B" movies in the 1930s and '40s. He first played TARZAN in *King of the Jungle* (1932), but he was most familiar to audiences for his starring roles in the serials *Flash Gordon* and *Buck Rogers*.

Craig, Edith G(eraldine Ailsa) (1869–1947). British theatrical actress and director. Craig, daughter of the legendary British actress Ellen Terry, did not equal her mother's achievements as an actress, but she did win renown as a director. Early in her career Craig appeared in plays with both her mother and the famous actor Sir Henry Irving. After managing an American tour by her mother in 1907, Craig turned to the study of music in Berlin and London. She then returned to the theater, directing over 100 plays for the Pioneer Players in London from 1911 to 1921. Her brother, Gordon CRAIG, was a well-known theatrical set designer and dramatic theorist.

Craig, (Edward Henry) Gordon (1872–1966). British stage designer, dramatic theorist, actor and director. Craig, the son of the legendary British actress Ellen Terry, achieved great renown both as a set designer and as a theorist on dramatic presentation. After beginning his career as an actor, Craig turned to directing in the early 1900s, including a production of Shakespeare's *Much Ado About Nothing* that featured his mother. Craig then focused on stage design for numerous plays including *Venice Preserv'd* (1904), *Hamlet* (1911) and *The Pretenders* (1926). Craig, who articulated his stage design theories in his book *On the Art of the Theatre* (1911), was best known as an advocate of nonrepresentational design. His sister, Edith CRAIG, was a prominent actress and director.

Craig, Lyman Creighton (1906–1974). American biochemist. Craig was educated at Iowa State University where he earned his Ph.D. in 1931. After two years at Johns Hopkins University he moved to Rockefeller University, New York, where he was appointed professor of chemistry in 1949. Craig concentrated on devising and improving techniques for separating the constituents of mixtures. His development of a fractional extraction method named countercurrent distribution (CCD) proved to be particularly good for preparing pure forms of several antibiotics and hormones. The method also established that the molecular weight of insulin is half the weight previously suggested. Craig also used CCD to separate the two protein chains of hemoglobin. During work on ergot alkaloids Craig, with W.A. Jacobs, isolated an unknown amino acid, which they named lysergic acid. Other workers managed to prepare the dimethyl amide of this acid and found the compound, LSD, to have considerable physiological effects.

Cram, Donald James (1919–). American chemist. Cram, a lawyer's son, was educated at Rollins College and the University of Nebraska. After working for Merck and Company on streptomycin and PENICILLIN, he entered Harvard, where he earned his Ph.D. in 1947. He then joined the University of California at Los Angeles, becoming professor of chemistry there in 1956. Cram has coauthored with George Hammond a standard textbook, *Organic Chemistry* (1959). He also produced *Fundamentals of Carbanion Chemistry* (1965), the first general work on the subject.

Cram, Ralph Adams (1863–1942). American architect known for his achievements in eclectic Gothic Revival work, primarily in religious and academic buildings. Cram studied art in Boston and was an art critic for a time before forming an architectural partnership with Charles Wentworth in 1889. In 1892 Bertram G. Goodhue joined the firm, which became, in 1913, Cram, Goodhue, & Ferguson. Among the many Gothic buildings designed by the firm are the East Liberty Presbyterian Church in Pittsburgh, the Swedenborgian Cathedral at Bryn Athyn, Pennsylvania, and St. Thomas Church (1914) in New York. In 1911, Cram took over design of the then-partly-built Cathedral of St. John the Divine in New York, revising the design from Byzantine to Gothic style. The Gothic buildings of Princeton University are the result of his role as supervising architect for that institution. Cram was an energetic propagandist for the Gothic style and was the author of a number of books, such as his *Church Building* of 1901, which offers "good" and "bad" examples, including a number of Cram's early works in the former category. Other books include *The Ruined Abbeys of Great Britain* (1906), *The End of Democracy* (1937) and *Black Spirits and White*, a renowned collection of ghost stories.

Crane, Barry [born Barry Cohen] (?-1985). U.S. television director and bridge player. Crane was one of the world's foremost tournament bridge players. The winner of more titles than anyone else in history, he had accumulated nearly 35,000 master points in tournament play, some 11,000 points more than his nearest rival.

Crane, Hart (1899–1932). American poet. The son of a Midwestern candy manufacturer, Crane was largely self-educated. At 16 he left home to make a career in New York as a writer. There his literary friends included Vachel LINDSAY, Sherwood ANDERSON and Malcolm COWLEY, and he contributed to *The Little Review* and *Poetry*. However, he was dogged by the necessity of earning a living and by frequent bouts of depression. His first volume, *White Buildings*, appeared in 1926. The banker Otto Kahn then provided him with funds to work on *The Bridge* (1930). In 1931 he received a Guggenheim grant to go to Mexico and write a long poem, but a year later he committed suicide by jumping overboard from the ship on which he was returning to New York. A poetic innovator who was greatly underestimated and misunderstood in his lifetime, Crane is now regarded as one of the giants of 20th-century American poetry.

For further reading:
Unterecker, John, *Voyager: A Life of Hart Crane*. New York: Farrar, Straus & Giroux, 1969.

Cranko, John [born John Rustenburg] (1927–1973). South African-born dancer, choreographer and ballet director. After studying at the Cape Town University Ballet School in South Africa and the Sadler's Wells School in London, Cranko joined the Sadler's Wells Ballet in 1947, quickly moving from dancer to choreographer. He created several ballets for the company, including *Pineapple Poll* (1951), and works for other companies as well, before becoming director of the Stuttgart Ballet in 1961. He built the Stuttgart into one of the leading ballet companies in the world, particularly noted for its large, diversified repertory and the strong commitment of such dancers as Marcia HAYDEE and Richard Cragun to his artistic vision. Full-length dramatic works such as the popular *Romeo and Juliet* (1962), *Onegin* (1965) and *Taming of the Shrew* (1969) were his forte. He also served as principle choreographer for the Bavarian State Opera in Munich (1968–71). After Cranko's untimely death in 1973, Glen TETLEY became director of the Stuttgart until Haydee succeeded him in 1976.

Crater, disappearance of Judge. In 1930, a New York judge abruptly vanished. Joseph Crater had maintained a very successful commercial law practice in New York City. Despite being married, he was also a man-about-town who had numerous affairs with a succession of models and show girls. Crater had been appointed a New York Supreme Court justice for only a short time when he mysteriously disappeared without a trace. After vacationing with his wife at their summer home in Maine, he planned a short trip to his Manhattan office and promised to return in a few days to celebrate her birthday. Crater gathered various papers and $5,000 from his office, had dinner with friends, then took a taxi and was never to be seen again. News of Crater's disappearance made headlines nationwide, with many reported sightings of the missing judge. Although never firmly established, Crater's disappearance may have been linked to an investigation of graft and corruption in Tammany Hall.

Crawford, Joan [Lucille le Sueur] (1906–1977). An enormously popular American film actress, Crawford became famous for her brilliant portrayals of the "ruthless working woman." Starting out in local talent shows and contests, Crawford appeared as a chorus girl on Broadway, then as a contract player at MGM in the final days of silent movies (*Our Dancing Daughters*, 1928) and finally as a star in such early talkies as *Grand Hotel* (1932). In the 1930s and early 1940s she starred in several sensationally successful melodramas of the "modern woman" (with Clark GABLE, among others) that won her a huge and adoring female audience; of these roles, perhaps only *The Women* (1939) stands out as more than a star turn. It wasn't until she left MGM and made the film noire classic *Mildred Pierce* (1945) that she became recognized as one of Hollywood's most talented actresses. Subsequent hits included *Humoresque* (1946), *Possessed* (1947), *Daisy Kenyon* (1947) and *Flamingo Road* (1949). In the 1950s and '60s her career slipped, and *Whatever Happened to Baby Jane?* (1962) was one of her few successes. Although the Crawford mystique has continued and she is almost always ranked among the top actresses of her time, revelations about her character and personal life have cast a shadow on her career.

Craxi, Benedetto (1934–). Italian politician, prime minister of ITALY (1983–87). A native of Milan, Craxi joined the Socialist Party at an early age. He was elected to the Italian Chamber of Deputies in 1968 and became party leader in 1976. In 1983, Craxi became the country's first Socialist premier, presiding over a five-party coalition government. A moderate in both his foreign and domestic policies, Craxi broadened the base of the Socialist Party, advocated cooperation with the United States, introduced austerity measures to control inflation, fought organized crime and abolished Catholicism as Italy's official religion. He resigned in March 1987, after three years and seven months in office—the longest tenure of any Italian premier since World War II.

Creedence Clearwater Revival. American band cofounded by brothers Tom and John Fogerty. The band blended basic rock, country and rhythm and blues. The band had six gold records and eight Top 10 singles between 1968 and 1972, including "Suzie Q," "Proud Mary," "Bad Moon Rising" and "Traveling Band." Tom Fogerty left the group in 1971.

Creel, George Edward (1876–1953). U.S. journalist. He began his career as a news reporter for the *Kansas City World* (1894). Later, when he established his own newspaper, the *Kansas City Independence* (1899), his reputation as a dedicated investigative reporter was firmly established. In 1917 President Woodrow WILSON appointed him head of the U.S. Committee on Public Information. Creel ran unsuccessfully against novelist Upton SINCLAIR for the Democratic nomination for governor of California in 1934. He published more than a dozen books, including *War Criminals and Punishment* (1944).

Creeley, Robert (White) (1926–). American poet and fiction writer. Educated at Harvard (1943–46), Black Mountain College (B.A., 1955) and the University of New Mexico (M.A., 1960), Creeley was influenced by the colloquial language of William Carlos WILLIAMS, the Projectivism of Charles OLSON and the freewheeling and far-ranging compositions of Robert Duncan. His central theme is love, marriage and the relationship between men and women. His verse tends to be terse and typographically slender. His output has been prolific; starting with his first book in 1952, he has published more than a book a year.

Cret, Paul Philippe (1876–1945). French-born architect who was active and influential in American architecture in the first half of the 20th century. Cret was a graduate of the Paris Ecole des BEAUX-ARTS and was invited to America in 1903 to become the principal teacher and critic at the architectural school (School of Fine Arts) of the University of Pennsylvania in Philadelphia. Under his leadership, the school became preeminent in American architectural education. Particularly well known as a teacher, Cret numbered Louis KAHN among his many distinguished students. Cret also had an active practice. He designed the Pan American Union Building of 1903, the Folger Shakespearean Library of 1930–32, and the Federal Reserve Office Building of 1935–37, all in Washington, D.C. Cret accepted such commissions as the design of the Hall of Science at the Chicago CENTURY OF PROGRESS EXPOSITION of 1933 and the interiors of the Burlington Zephyr railroad train of 1934.

Cretan Uprising of 1935. In early March 1935 the antiroyalist followers of Cretan-born Eleutherios VENIZELOS, Greek premier six times between 1910 and 1933, leader of the Liberal Party and a founder of the republic, rebelled against the government of royalist Panayoti Tsaldaris in protest of the imminent restoration of the monarchy. Government forces under General George Kondylis defeated the rebels, who held out longest in Crete; Venizelos fled to France. In 1935 Kondylis engineered a coup against Tsaldaris, became premier, and prompted parliament to recall Greece's exiled King George II. George was enthroned by nearly unanimous plebiscite on November 25, 1935.

Crichton, (John) Michael (1942–). American author and screenwriter. Educated as a doctor and scientist at Harvard University, Crichton has brought his training to bear in such critically acclaimed best selling suspense novels as *The Andromeda Strain* (1969; filmed 1971), *The Terminal Man* (1972) and *Westworld*, (1974), for which he wrote the screenplay. Other screenplays include *Coma* (1977) and *The Great Train Robbery* (1978), which he adapted from his novel of the same name. Crichton has also written popular thrillers under the pseudonyms John Lange and Jeffrey Hudson; and nonfiction, including *Five Patients: The Hospital Explained* (1970) and *Electronic Life: How to Think About Computers* (1983). Other works include *Sphere* (1987) and *Travels* (1988).

Crick, Francis Harry Compton (1916–). British molecular biologist. Crick graduated from University College, London, and during WORLD WAR II worked on the development of RADAR and magnetic mines. Later he changed from physics to biology and in 1947 began work at the Strangeways Research Laboratory, Cambridge, transferring to the Medical Research Council unit at the Cavendish Laboratory in 1949. Crick received his Ph.D. in 1953. In 1951 a young American student, James WATSON, arrived at the unit. Watson suggested to Crick that it was necessary to find the molecular structure of the hereditary material, DNA, before its function could be properly understood. Much was already known about the chemical and physical nature of DNA from the studies of such scientists as Phoebus Levene, Erwin CHARGAFF, Alexander Todd and Linus PAULING. Using this knowledge and the X-ray diffraction data of Maurice Wilkins and Rosalind FRANKLIN, Crick and Watson had built, by 1953, a molecular model incorporating all the known features of DNA. Fundamental to the model was their conception of DNA as a double helix. The model served to explain how DNA replicates—by the two spirals uncoiling and each acting as a template—and how the hereditary information might be coded—in the sequence of bases along the chains. Ten years' intensive research in many laboratories around the world all tended to confirm Crick and Watson's model. For their work, which has been called the most significant discovery of this century, they were awarded, with Wilkins, the 1962 NOBEL PRIZE for physiology or medicine. Crick, in collaboration with Sydney Brenner, made important contributions to the understanding of the genetic code. He also suggested that in protein synthesis, small adaptor molecules act as intermediaries between the messenger RNA template and the amino acids. Such adaptors, or transfer RNAs, were identified independently by Robert Holley and Paul Berg in 1956. Crick is also known for his formulation of the Central Dogma of molecular genetics, which assumes that the passage of genetic information is from DNA to RNA to protein. David BALTIMORE was later to show that in certain cases, information can actually go from RNA to DNA. In 1966 Crick published the book *Of Molecules and Men*, reviewing the recent progress in molecular biology. He remained in Cambridge until 1977, when he took up a professorship at the Salk Institute in San Diego.

Crimmitschau [Krimmitschau]. German city 36 miles south of Leipzig, in Saxony. A manufacturing area since the 18th century, it became a hub of the working-class movement in the 19th century. An August 1903 to January 1904 strike by textile workers inspired support by textile industry workers all over Germany. The women were led by Clara Zetkin, an early leader of the WOMEN'S MOVEMENT.

Crippen, Harley. (1861–1910). British murderer. A London physician, Crippen was unhappily married and sought a new life with his mistress, Ethel Le Neve. In January 1910 he poisoned his wife with hyoscine, then chopped up her body and hid the pieces in his cellar. In March, Ethel Le Neve moved into Crippen's home, presumably as his housekeeper. Scotland Yard detectives suspected Crippen of having done away with his wife; in July, when Crippen and Le Neve left London (ostensibly for a vacation), Chief Inspector Walter Dew searched Crippen's home and discovered pieces of Cora Crippen's body. Crippen and his mistress were traced to Canada, arrested and returned to England to stand trial. Crippen was found guilty and was hanged on November 23, 1910; Ethel Le Neve was acquitted of having been an accessory to the crime and was released.

Crippen, Robert (1937–). U.S. astronaut. The first person to pilot a manned U.S. SPACE SHUTTLE launch (STS-1, April 12–14, 1981), Crippen, with Commander John Young, began the historic two-day journey aboard Columbia on the 20th anniversary of mankind's first space flight, by Soviet cosmonaut Yuri GAGARIN (April 12, 1961). An experienced pilot, Crippen had served aboard carriers in the Pacific and worked as an instructor for the Aerospace Research Pilot School commanded by Chuck YEAGER. Trained for military space flight in the U.S.A.F. Manned Orbiting Laboratory (MOL) Program, which was canceled in 1969, Crippen joined NASA and worked as a team leader and member of the astronaut support crew for all three SKYLAB missions and the APOLLO/SOYUZ TEST PROJECT before being transferred to the Shuttle development program. Crippen also commanded Shuttle mission STS-7 (June 18–24, 1983), which included Sally RIDE, America's first woman in space, as well as missions 41–C (April 6–13, 1984) and 41–G (October 5–13, 1984). Logging over 23 days and 14 hours in his four space voyages, Crippen is NASA's "old pro" of the post-Apollo, post-Skylab era. He is currently director of the space shuttle program at NASA headquarters in Washington, D.C.

Cripps, Sir (Richard) Stafford (1889–1952). British statesman. A brilliant lawyer, he was knighted in 1930 and was made solicitor general (1930–31). A radical socialist in the 1930s, he was a Labour MP, but was expelled from the party in 1939 for advocating an alliance with the communists in a united front. He was CHURCHILL'S ambassador to the U.S.S.R. from 1940 to 1942 and later served as lord privy seal, leader of the House of Commons and minister of aircraft production. In 1945, Cripps was readmitted to his party and became president of the board of trade (1945–47) and chancellor of the exchequer (1947–50) in Clement ATTLEE'S postwar Labour government. He is remembered best for the tight controls of the austerity program that he instituted while guiding Britain's economic life. Cripps retired in 1950.

Crittenberger, Willis D. (1890–1980). U.S. Army officer. Crittenberger began his military career as a cavalry officer. In the late 1930s and early '40s he set up the U.S. Army's first armored forces. Attaining the rank of lieutenant general, he commanded the IV Corps in ITALY during WORLD WAR II. In this capacity he directed infantry and armored divisions in 326 days of continuous combat. During this period his forces freed more than 600 cities and towns and accepted the unconditional surrender of the German Ligurian Army. This marked the imminent collapse of German resistance to the Allies in Italy. (See also WORLD WAR II ON THE WESTERN FRONT.)

Croatia [*Serbian:* Hrvatska]. Constituent republic of YUGOSLAVIA, bordering on the northeastern shore of the Adriatic Sea; encompasses Slavonia, Dalmatia and most of Istria, as well as Croatia itself. In 1867, with the establishment of the Austro-Hungarian dual monarchy, Croatia proper was incorporated into Hungary with Zagreb as its capital. When the AUSTRO-HUNGARIAN EMPIRE collapsed after WORLD WAR I, Croatia affiliated itself with the realm of the Serbs, Croats and Slovenes, named Yugoslavia in 1929; but until WORLD WAR II some Croat loyalists still fought for independence. In 1941 the Nazi conquest of Yugoslavia put the area under German and Italian rule until 1945, when Yugoslavian sovereignty was reinstated. During WORLD WAR II many Croatians joined the anti-communist CHETNIKS. The Croatians have never fully accepted their status as part of Serbian-dominated Yugoslavia; with the fall of communist governments throughout Eastern Europe at the end of the 1980s, Croatian demands for independence increased.

Croce, Benedetto (1866–1952). Italian philosopher, historian and statesman. After studying in Rome and Naples, Croce founded a critical review, *La Critica,* in 1903. His philosophy emphasized reconciliation between human activities and an aesthetic theory. Croce was minister of education from 1920 to 1921. He resigned from his professorship at Naples when MUSSOLINI came to power in 1923. Croce strongly attacked TOTALITARIANISM in his work *History as the Story of Liberty* (1941), and with the fascist regime's downfall (see FASCISM) promoted LIBERALISM through his writings. He also wrote critical studies of Dante, Ariosto and Corneille as well as an autobiography.

Cronin, A(rchibald) J(oseph) (1896–1981). British novelist. Educated at Glasgow University Medical School, Cronin worked as a medical inspector of mines and as a general practictioner in Wales and in London, which experiences figure in his work. His extremely popular, though not particularly literary, novels include *Hatter's Castle* (1931), the success of which allowed him to give up practicing medicine in favor of writing; *The Citadel* (1937; filmed 1938); *The Judas Tree* (1961); and *A Question of Modernity* (1966). Much of his work has been adapted for films or television programs.

Cronin, James Watson (1931–). American physicist. Cronin was educated at the Southern Methodist University and at Chicago, where he earned his Ph.D. in 1955. After a period at the Brookhaven National Laboratory he moved to Princeton in 1958 and later served as professor of physics from 1965 until 1971, when he was appointed to a comparable chair at the University of Chicago. Cronin and Val FITCH shared the 1980 NOBEL PRIZE in physics for their work.

Cronin, Joseph Edward (1906–1984). American baseball player and executive. A shortstop, Cronin played principally with the Boston Red Sox. He was manager (1934–45) and general manager (1945–58) of the Red Sox, and president of the American League (1959–73). He was inducted into the Baseball Hall of Fame in 1956.

Cronkite, Walter (1916–). American radio and television journalist. Cronkite became a trusted and ubiquitous figure in postwar America through his preeminent role with CBS television news. From 1962 to 1981, he was the anchorman of the CBS Evening News. His trademark sign-off line, "And that's the way it is," was familiar to millions of devoted viewers. In a 1973 public opinion poll, Cronkite was voted the most trusted man in America. Among the major stories he covered were the 1963 assassination of President John F. KENNEDY (during which Cronkite openly wept on camera), the 1969 United States moon landing, WATERGATE and the VIETNAM WAR. Cronkite was born in Missouri and educated at the University of Texas, which he left in his junior year to become a reporter for the *Houston Post.* He covered WORLD WAR II for United Press and joined CBS in 1950.

Walter Cronkite (1987).

Bing Crosby (left) on the set of The Road to Bali, *with perennial costars Dorothy Lamour and Bob Hope (1952).*

Crosby, Bing [Harry Lillis Crosby] (1901–1977). American JAZZ and popular music singer and film actor. Crosby enjoyed outstanding success both as a vocalist and as a HOLLYWOOD star. Born in Tacoma, Washington, he began his career as a singer with various jazz bands in the 1920s, most notably the big band led by Paul WHITEMAN. In the early 1930s, Crosby hosted his own radio program and gained national popularity both as an entertainment personality and as a singer. His mellifluous baritone led to ultimate record sales of over 30 million, with "White Christmas" (1942) heading the list as the most enduringly popular single in the history of the recording industry. He was a success in Hollywood as well, making numerous films from the early 1930s through the 1960s, including *The Road to Singapore* (1940) and six other "Road" comedies in which he was memorably teamed with Bob HOPE. Crosby could also play dramatic parts, as an ACADEMY AWARD for best actor for his role as a priest in *Going My Way* (1944) testifies.

Crosby, Harry (1897–1929). American poet, essayist and small press publisher. Crosby was raised in a wealthy Boston family and attended Harvard University but rejected a banking career for the life of a poet and bohemian. He married Caresse Crosby, who also wrote poetry and held a patent for having invented the strapless brassiere. Together, the two financed their own small literary enterprise, the Black Sun Press, an avant-garde fixture in Paris during the 1920s. Crosby books published by the press include *Shadows of the Sun* (1922) and *Chariot of the Sun* (1927). Solar imagery reoccurs obsessively in Crosby's verse. With his illicit lover of the time, Crosby committed suicide in 1929.

Crosby, Stills, Nash and Young. American ROCK AND ROLL band originally formed in 1968. The original members of the group—three singer-guitarists—were David Crosby, Graham Nash and Steven Stills. All had enjoyed success with prior bands—Crosby with the BYRDS, Nash with the Hollies and Stills with Buffalo Springfield. Their first album, *Crosby, Stills & Nash* (1969), combined sensitive songwriting with pleasing vocal harmonies and featured a hit single, "Marrakesh Express." Shortly thereafter another Buffalo Springfield alumnus, Neil Young, joined the band to contribute to its second album, *Deja Vu* (1970), which spawned three hit singles, "Woodstock," "Teach Your Children" and "Ohio." The band broke up in 1971 but has since enjoyed several reunions in its original trio grouping, without Young.

Crosland, Anthony (1918–1977). British politician. A member of the LABOUR PARTY, Crosland was a leading theorist of democratic socialism. He held six ministerial posts in Labour governments between 1964 and his death. From 1976 until his death he was foreign secretary.

Cross, Charles Frederick (1855–1935). British industrial chemist. Cross studied chemistry at King's College, London, in Zurich and at Owens College, Manchester, where he met Edward Bevan, whose partner he became and with whom he developed the viscose process of rayon manufacture. Cross was subsequently involved in the industrial development of this process. He wrote several books on cellulose and papermaking.

Cross, Hardy (1885–1959). U.S. engineer. He made outstanding contributions to the field of structural engineering. Cross discovered a new method of calculating "moments" in the framework of a structure that eliminated previously needed, lengthy calculations. His discovery became known as the Moment Distribution Method or the Hardy Cross Method. He was named professor of structural engineering at the University of Illinois, and in 1937 he became a professor at Yale. He retired from Yale in 1951, and was awarded a gold medal by the British Institute of Structural Engineers in 1958.

Cross, Wilbur Lucius (1862–1948). American scholar and public official. Cross taught at Yale University from 1894 to 1930. Noted as an outstanding literary critic, he edited the *Yale Review* for 30 years. As Democratic governor of Connecticut (1931–39), he worked for labor reform.

Crossfield, Scott (1921–). U.S. test pilot, the first person to fly at twice the speed of sound. After earning his Navy pilot wings at the Naval Aviation Cadet School in 1942, Crossfield spent World War II as a flight instructor in Texas and after the war attended the University of Washington, receiving a master's degree in aeronautical engineering. In 1950 he joined NACA, the National Advisory Committee for Aeronautics, which would later become NASA, the NATIONAL AERONAUTICS AND SPACE ADMINISTRATION. NACA was doing work in experimental aircraft, and Crossfield signed on as a test pilot. Working out of Edwards Air Force Base deep in the Mojave Desert of California, Crossfield quickly established a reputation as one of America's top test pilots.

Flying such advanced aircraft as the X-1, America's first rocket plane, Crossfield developed a friendly rivalry with Charles "Chuck" YEAGER, the first human being to fly at the speed of sound. The rivalry led to an undeclared race between Crossfield and Yeager to see who would be the first to break Mach 2 (twice the speed of sound). In November 1953, Crossfield reached that speed, not in the specially developed X-1 but in a Douglas D-558-1 Skyrocket test plane hastily upgraded for the purpose. Leaving NACA for North American Aviation in 1955, Crossfield became instrumental in the development of America's most advanced rocket plane, the X-15. As engineer and test pilot he was inseparable from the plane, the pride of North American until it was turned over to NASA in 1960. During that time Crossfield had flown the X-15 in 14 of its 30 test flights for North American, including its first "captive flight" attached to the wing of a B-52 "mother ship," its first glide flight and its first powered flight.

Crossley, Archibald M. (1896–1985). U.S. pollster. Along with Elmo Roper and George GALLUP, he was considered one of the founders of modern public opinion polling. In the mid-1930s the three men introduced the use of scientifically selected random samples to proportionately reflect the views of the entire population. Crossley was the first to use questions designed to measure the reliability of those polled.

Crothers, Rachel (1878–1958). The most important female playwright in American theater during the early decades of the 20th century. She was born in Bloomington, Ill. Her mother was a physician, rather unusual in those days, and perhaps that kind of family background inspired her to concentrate upon women's issues in her subsequent work. After several years writing and staging one-act plays for the Stanhope-Wheatcroft School of Acting in New York, she turned to full-length works. *The Three of Us* (1906) was her first successful Broadway production. Her most important plays examined "women's themes"—subjects such as prostitution, the double standard, birth control, new professions. *A Man's World* (1910) and *He and She* (1912) were her first fully developed examples. In the first, heroine "Frank" Ware stubbornly refuses to sacrifice her independence for a man. In the second, Ann Herford, a sculptress, tragically relinquishes a career in art for the sake of harmony in a marriage. Later plays such as *Young Wisdom* (1914), *Nice People* (1921), *Mary the Third* (1923), *When Ladies Meet* (1932) and *Susan and God* (1937), her most acclaimed play, all deal with aspects of women's search for freedom in a male-dominated society. "Most of the great modern plays are studies of women," she said in 1912. "If you want to see the signs of the times, watch women. Their evolution is the most important thing in modern life." She was more than a mere polemicist, however, and her chosen subject of the tensions between men and women (not to mention an astute sense of stagecraft) make much of her work relevant today.

For further reading:
Twentieth Century American Dramatists. Detroit: Gale Research Co., 1981.

Crowder, Enoch Herbert (1859–1932). U.S. Army officer. An 1881 graduate of the U.S. Military Academy at West Point, Crowder fought with the cavalry against the Indians in the West and served as judge advocate to U.S. troops in the Philippines in the Spanish-American War (1898). He also served as secretary of state and justice (1906–08) in occupied CUBA. In 1911, he was appointed judge advocate general of the U.S. Army and became the provost marshal to administer the Selective Service Act when the law was enacted in May 1917. He also served four years as the first U.S. ambassador to Cuba, beginning in 1923.

Crowley, Aleister (Edward Alexander) (1875–1947). English writer and occult figure, popularly known as "the Great Beast" and "the wickedest man in the world." He was educated at Cambridge Unversity. Rejecting his strict Christian upbringing, he became notorious as a "black magician" because of his anti-Christian writings, his drug-taking, his hedonism and his public pagan celebrations. During his lifetime he published numerous volumes of poetry, fiction and essays. *Magick in Theory and Practice* (1929), a brilliant and stylish guide to occult self-development, is his masterwork. His writings influenced the NEW AGE MOVEMENT of the 1980s and 1990s.

For further reading:
Sutin, Lawrence, *Do What Thou Wilt.* New York: Simon & Schuster, 1992.

Crown Film Unit. The most important documentary film production company in the history of the British cinema. It grew out of the Film Unit formed by John GRIERSON for the Empire Marketing Board in 1930. For the next three years, from its location in Oxford Street in London, the unit was staffed by rising young filmmakers who, shielded by Grierson and sponsor Sir Stephen Tallents from bureaucratic interference, produced a group of minor masterpieces lumped under the catchphrase, "Bring the Empire alive!" In 1933 the unit was taken over by the General Post Office and in 1939 it was transferred to the Ministry of Information, where it was renamed the Crown Film Unit. When the Conservatives returned to power in 1951, the unit was dismantled. Brash young Harry Watt made *Night Mail* (1936), a glorious tribute to the mail trains running between London and Edinburgh, with verse narrative by W.H. AUDEN and music by Benjamin BRITTEN. (Britten's *Young Person's Guide to the Orchestra* was written for the unit's *Instruments of the Orchestra,* 1946.) Basil Wright and Alberto Cavalcanti's *Song of Ceylon* (1934) transmuted into visual poetry the incursion of the British tea trade into that country. During WORLD WAR II, Humphrey Jennings produced *Listen to Britain* (1943), a sensitive masterpiece about the British homefront. Other major figures in the unit included Paul Rotha (the group's historian), Edgar Anstey, Stuart Legg and John Taylor. Through theatrical and 16mm distribution these films celebrated the British working person.

For further reading:
Barnouw, Erik, *Documentary: A History of the Non-Fiction Film.* New York: Oxford University Press, 1974.

Crucible, The. Play by American playwright Arthur MILLER. *The Crucible* (1953), which deals with the impact of panic and persecution when society allows them free rein, was written at the height of the anticommunist blacklistings being conducted by Senator Joseph MCCARTHY in the early 1950s. These blacklistings were often termed "witch hunts" by critics who opposed McCarthy's slanders and excesses. Miller borrowed the metaphor quite literally, setting *The Crucible* in Salem, Massachusetts, during the late 17th century in an attempt to cast a comparative historical light on the McCarthy era. The plot concerns two adolescent girls who are obsessed with dark, erotic fantasies that they repress and project by means of accusing other, innocent persons in Salem of heresy and witchcraft. Jean-Paul SARTRE adapted *The Crucible* into a screenplay for a 1956 French-German film version. *The Crucible* continues to be widely performed and is regarded as a classic of the post-World War II American theater.

cruise missile. An accurate, low-flying and virtually undetectable missile with first-strike capability. The U.S. deployment in 1983 of cruise missiles with nuclear warheads in Western Europe encouraged a growth in antinuclear agitation, particularly in Britain, West Germany and the Netherlands. Medium-range cruise missiles, carrying conventional warheads, were used for the first time in the PERSIAN GULF WAR (1991). They were launched by the U.S. against strategic targets in IRAQ with great effectiveness.

Crumb, George (1929–). American composer. Crumb, who won the PULITZER PRIZE in 1968 for his composition *Echoes of Time and the River,* is one of the major American composers of the postwar era. Educated at the universities of Illinois and Michigan, as well as at the Berlin Hochschule fur Musik, Crumb has held a series of academic teaching posts since the 1950s while producing a broad range of compositions. Crumb's musical style is distinctly unpretentious and idiosyncratic, falling into none of the prevailing schools of composition of his era. At the same time, Crumb is not at all simplistic in his approach, drawing from the tonal techniques of Anton von WEBERN as well as from the romanticism of 19th-century masters such as Claude DEBUSSY. Other works by Crumb include *String Quartet* (1954), *Night Music I* (1963) and *II* (1964), and *Songs, Drones, and Refrains of Death* (1968).

Cruyff, Johan (1947–). Dutch soccer player and manager. Cruyff was the symbol of "total football," which revolutionized soccer in the 1970s. He was spotted as a 10-year-old by the scouts of Amsterdam's premier team, Ajax, and at 17 made his professional debut with them. Cruyff came to world prominence as the leader of Ajax's three European Cup winning sides, from 1971 to 1973. At the 1974 World Cup in West Germany, Cruyff led the Netherlands to a second-place finish. However, the Dutch style of play in the tournament had introduced a new concept, "total football." The free-flowing style of play allowed defenders to move into attack at will, and forwards to play one-touch soccer in defensive zones. Cruyff with his razor-sharp reactions, deft ball control, acceleration and ability to change direction with a subtle swerve became the symbol of the Dutch style. In 1973 he was traded to Barcelona of Spain, which he led to the Spanish championship. He retired from international soccer prior to the 1978 World Cup and ended his playing career with a stint in North America, and a final return to Ajax, 1982–83. Since his retirement, Cruyff has emerged as one of Europe's leading managers, guiding Ajax to the Cup Winners Cup in 1987, and his current team, Barcelona, to the same title in 1989.

Cry, The Beloved Country. Novel by South African writer Alan PATON. The 1948 book tells the story of Rev. Stephen Kumalo who searches for and finds his sister, Gertrude, and son Absolom in Johannesburg, SOUTH AFRICA. Circumstances have forced her into prostitution, and Absolom has murdered the son of a white farmer, James Jarvis. Absolom is sentenced to death for the crime, but the novel ends on a hopeful note as Jarvis and Kumalo are reconciled, and Jarvis commits himself to the struggle of the impoverished blacks of Johannesburg. The novel is not only an eloquent plea for racial equality but also examines how a squalid and deprived environment can thwart and pervert the human spirit. An American film, for which Paton wrote the screenplay, appeared in 1951. (See also APARTHEID.)

Cuala Press. Private press in Dublin founded in 1902, originally as part of the Dun Emer Craft Center. Its first publication was *In the Seven Woods* (1903) by W.B. YEATS. The press also printed prints and Christmas cards and books selected by Yeats, its editor. Elizabeth Corbet Yeats and Susan Mary Yeats, his sisters, changed the name to Cuala Press when they expanded the business to Churchtown, where their first publication was *A Broadside* (1908) by Jack B. YEATS, which eventually became *Broadsheets,* publishing poetry and contemporary Irish art. The press continued publishing the works of Yeats, John SYNGE, and Lady GREGORY, among others, until the 1940s.

Cuba. The largest island and nation of the West Indies, flanked by the Caribbean Sea on the south, the Atlantic Ocean on the northeast and the Gulf of Mexico on

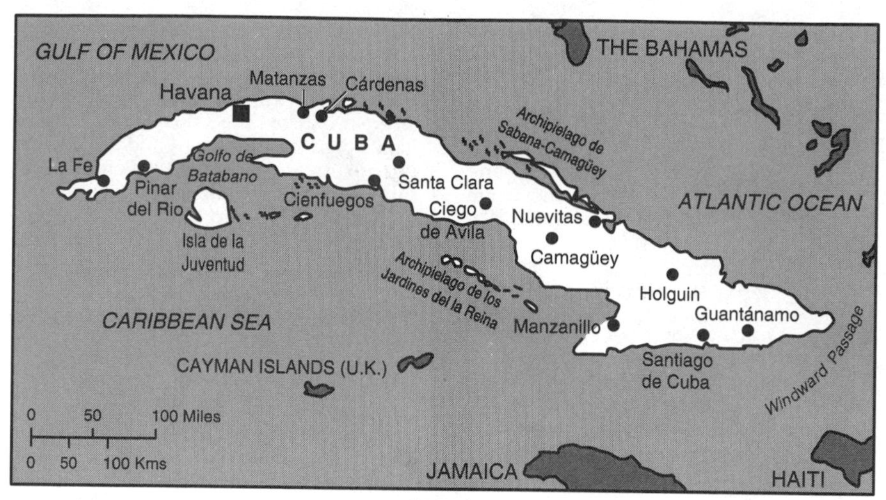

CUBA

the northwest; the nation includes a few other islands of which the Isle of Youth (Isle of Pines until 1978) is the largest. Connections with the UNITED STATES have played a significant role in Cuban affairs for over a century. Active American attention dates to the Spanish-American War of 1898, provoked by the explosion of the U.S. battleship *Maine* in Havana harbor. On May 20, 1901, a Cuban government independent of Spain assumed control, although an act of the U.S. Congress, the Platt Amendment, granted the U.S. the power to intercede in Cuban matters—a right exercised in 1906 and not relinquished until 1934. Fulgencio BATISTA Y ZALDIVAR, an unscrupulous dictator who had seized power in 1933, was ousted in 1959 by rebels led by Fidel CASTRO.

Castro instituted extensive social and economic changes. He quickly aligned Cuba with the U.S.S.R. and got in return monetary and military aid. In 1961 Castro proclaimed himself a Marxist-Leninist. On April 14, 1961, a force of anti-Castro Cubans, trained by the U.S., landed at the island's BAY OF PIGS and was utterly crushed. In the summer of 1962 a U.S. air survey discovered that the U.S.S.R. was erecting missile sites in Cuba. In a tense COLD WAR face-off, the U.S. imposed a naval blockade of Cuba; the Russians capitulated and removed their missiles (see CUBAN MISSILE CRISIS).

In 1976 Castro deployed large numbers of Cuban troops abroad, chiefly to ANGOLA, to bolster Soviet-backed governments or rebels; by 1978 approximately 50,000 Cubans were in Africa. In 1980 Castro temporarily withdrew an embargo on emigration, and by September nearly 125,000 Cubans had sought sanctuary in the U.S. (see MARIEL BOATLIFT). The U.S. has leased a naval base at GUANTANAMO Bay, on Cuba's southeastern coast, since 1903. Relations have yet to fully normalize between Cuba and the U.S. Following the fall of communist governments in Eastern Europe in 1989–90 and political and economic reforms in the U.S.S.R., Castro repeatedly insisted that Cuba would continue to develop as a Marxist-Leninist state.

CUBA

1902	Independence from U.S.; U.S. retains right to intervene and retains naval bases.
1933	Military revolt brings army Sergeant Fulgencio Batista to power.
1944	Batista retires after official four-year term as president.
1952	Batista returns to power in bloodless coup.
1953	Radical group led by Fidel Castro attacks army barracks; Castro is captured but later released and exiled.
1956	(December) Castro lands in Cuba at head of small revolutionary group, begins guerrilla campaign against Batista government.
1959	(January) Castro's guerrillas force Batista to flee Cuba; Castro assumes power.
1960	(October) Castro nationalizes U.S. business interests in Cuba.
1961	(April) U.S.-sponsored anti-Castro Cuban emigres land at Bay of Pigs; invasion fails.
1962	Soviet missiles are withdrawn following U.S. naval blockade.
1980	125,000 Cuban "marielitos" land in Florida.
1990	38,000 of 50,000 troops pulled out of Angola; Castro denounces anti-communist reforms in Eastern Europe, pledges to maintain socialism in Cuba.

A multitude of supporters presses toward Fidel Castro, leader of the revolution (1959).

Cuban missile crisis. Confrontation of October 1962 between the U.S. and the U.S.S.R., resulting from a Soviet attempt to base nuclear missiles in CUBA and U.S. insistence that the missiles be removed. When American reconnaissance flights over Cuba confirmed allegations that the U.S.S.R. was constructing ballistic missile-launching sites, President John F. KENNEDY issued (October 22) a public denunciation of the Soviet action. He announced a U.S. naval blockade of Cuba to prevent any further shipments and demanded withdrawal of all Soviet missiles from the island. On October 26 the Russians countered with an offer to remove their missiles from Cuba if all NATO missiles were withdrawn from Turkey. The U.S. refused, tension mounted and war seemed imminent until October 28 when Soviet Premier Nikita KHRUSHCHEV agreed to withdraw the missiles and dismantle the launching sites providing the U.S. lifted the naval blockade and promised not to invade Cuba. With these assurances from the U.S., the naval blockade ended on November 20 and Soviet missiles were withdrawn. Kennedy's stand during this crisis is widely regarded as a significant U.S. victory in the COLD WAR.

For further reading:

Blight, James G., *On the Brink*. New York: Farrar, Straus & Giroux, 1990.

Kennedy, Robert F., *Thirteen Days: A Memoir of the Cuban Missile Crisis*. New York: NAL/Dutton, 1969.

Cuban Revolt of 1917. Mario Garcia Menocal, CUBA's incumbent conservative president, was reelected in 1916, but the opposition liberals claimed fraud, a protest upheld by Cuba's supreme court, and new elections were scheduled for February 1917 in several provinces. However,

President John F. Kennedy and his brother Attorney General Robert F. Kennedy confer at the White House as tension increases over missiles in Cuba (1962).

liberals rose in revolt, Menocal assembled an army and blocked them, while U.S. Marines landed in Santiago to restore order. Within weeks Menocal's forces, supported by the U.S., had crushed the rebels, and Menocal was inaugurated president on May 20, 1917. To maintain order, Menocal asked for and received U.S. troops; they remained until 1923.

Cuban Revolts of 1930–33. After securing a constitutional amendment providing for a six-year term, President Gerardo Machado y Morales was reelected president of Cuba in 1928. Students at the University of Havana opposed his dictatorial policies and the university was closed in 1930. While the army easily defeated a band of revolutionaries landing at Gibara in August 1931, Cubans continued to resist with terror and sabotage, organizing secret societies such as ABC, estimated to have 30,000 to 40,000 members. Government reprisals were murderous, but mediation by U.S. Ambassador Sumner Wells in June 1933 did not prevent a general strike and a clash between police and citizens. The army rebelled, forcing Machado from office on August 12, 1933; Carlos Manuel de Cespedes y Quesada became provisional president but was ousted on September 5 in an army coup staged by Sergeant Fulgencio BATISTA Y ZALDIVAR, who installed professor Ramon Grau San Martin as president and himself as commander in chief of the army and virtual dictator.

Cubism. Important movement in painting and other arts during the first two decades of the 20th century. Cubism was largely based in France. The painters Georges BRAQUE and Pablo PICASSO are commonly accorded joint status as the creators of Cubism by way of their 1907–08 collaborative efforts in Paris. Cubism sought to project standard visual realities onto randomly intersecting planes, producing an effect resembling that of a broken mirror. Cubist theory held that a new and intense aesthetic significance could be achieved by recombining ordinary aspects of daily life in this manner. *Les Demoiselles d'Avignon* (1907) by Picasso, which portrays five nude women in highly varied styles, is regarded as the first Cubist painting. Subsequent painters influenced by Cubism include Marcel DUCHAMP, Juan GRIS, Fernand LEGER and Francis Picabia. The poet Guillaume APOLLINAIRE championed Cubism in his critical writings and adopted its tenets to verse. Other Cubist-influenced poets included Jean COCTEAU and Pierre REVERDY.

Cugat, Xavier [born Francisco de Asis Javier Cugat Mingall de Brue y Deulofeo] (1900–1990). Spanish-born band leader. He began his musical career in Cuba and helped popularize Latin American dance music in the U.S. in the 1930s and 1940s. He and his band, the Gigolos, appeared in many of the U.S.'s top nightclubs, as well as in such films as *A Date with Judy* (1948) and *Neptune's Daughter* (1949). He was married five times, and his wives included singers Abbe Lane and Charo.

Cukor, George (1899–1983). American motion picture director, best known for his sensitive direction of actors and of "women's theme" pictures. His career spanned more than 50 years, in which he directed some 50 films. After some success as a Broadway director, he moved to HOLLYWOOD where, working with David O. SELZNICK at RKO and METRO-GOLDWYN-MAYER, he directed several 1930s classics, including an adaptation of Dickens' *David Copperfield* (1935). During this time he made a notable series of pictures with Katharine HEPBURN and guided Greta GARBO through one of her best films, *Camille* (1937). He was chosen to direct GONE WITH THE WIND (1939) but was fired by Selznick. His subsequent movies included *The Philadelphia Story* (1940) and *Adam's Rib* (1949, both with Hepburn), *Gaslight* (1944, with Ingrid BERGMAN), *A Star Is Born* (1954, with Judy GARLAND), *Born Yesterday* (1950), and *My Fair Lady* (1964), for which he won his only ACADEMY AWARD.

For further reading:

Phillips. Rev. Gene, *George Cukor*. Boston: G.K. Hall, 1982.

Cullen, Countee (1903–1946). American poet. Educated at New York University (B.A., 1925) and Harvard (M.A., 1926), Cullen was a major figure of the HARLEM RENAISSANCE. His early works—*Color* (1925), *Copper Sun* (1927), *The Ballad of the Brown Girl* (1927) and *The Black Christ* (1929)—explored racial themes but were criticized for their romanticism and absence of black rhythms and idiom. *The Medea and Some Poems* (1935) included a translation of Euripides. Cullen also published a novel about HARLEM life (*One Way to Heaven*, 1932), an anthology of black verse (*Caroling Dusk*, 1932) and books for children.

For further reading:

Shucard, Alan R., *Countee Cullen*. Boston: G.K. Hall, 1984.

Cultural Revolution. Directed at young people, a new political campaign (1966–69) known as the Great Proletarian Cultural Revolution was launched by MAO TSE-TUNG, China's communist leader. Mao, whose power base was in the Chinese army, wanted to regain control from the bureaucracies that had grown up in education, industrial management and agricultural and economic development and to encourage the continuation of the revolution in Chinese cultural life. Free rail passes were issued and hundreds of thousands of militant young men and women flocked to Beijing, China's capital, to march in massive parades reviewed by Mao in Tiananmen Square. These communists or RED GUARDS vied with each other to express their patriotism and devotion to Mao. They covered walls with posters denouncing Mao's enemies and traveled around China spreading the doctrines contained in Mao's "little red book." This endeavor to re-create and experience the fervor of the Red Army's LONG MARCH of 1934–35 soon got out of hand, however. Bands of Red Guards destroyed works of art and historical relics, denounced intellectuals, burned books and attacked those they considered elitists or anti-Mao. Schools and universities were closed and the economy almost came to a standstill. Red Guards fought each other over ideological differences, and armed Chinese factions clashed in most provinces, especially in the south. Gradually the violence and chaos waned as new Revolutionary Committees, made up of representatives of the army, the more responsible Red Guards, and peasants and workers, were organized to restore order and stamp out factionalism. In the spring of 1969 schools were reopened, but the universities did not reopen until September 1970. According to some accounts, the Cultural Revolution did succeed in eliminating many of the age-old differences between rich and poor and city and country, but it did so at enormous cost and loss.

Cummings, E(dward) E(stlin) (1894–1962). American poet, prose writer and painter. After graduating from Harvard, Cummings served as a volunteer ambulance driver in France during WORLD WAR I. *The Enormous Room* (1922) is a novelistic account of his brief internment there. His first collection, *Tulips and Chimneys* (1923), contrasted the evils of war to the "sweet spontaneous earth." In 1925, he won the Dial prize. His series of Norton Lectures at Harvard were published as *i: six nonlectures* (1953). In 1955 Cummings received a special citation from the National Book Award committee for *Poems, 1923–1954*, and in 1957 he won the BOLLINGEN PRIZE. Despite its typographical eccentricities, Cummings's work is in many respects quite traditional. It has always been popular with readers, and his innovations have influenced numerous American poets although many critics have found his romantic lyrics somewhat cloying.

For further reading:

Marks, Barry A., *E.E. Cummings*. Boston: G.K. Hall, 1965.

Waving their "little red books," militant Red Guards of the Cultural Revolution swarm across China to enforce strict adherence to Maoist principles (1966).

Firmage, George J., *E.E. Cummings*. New York: Liveright, 1990.

Cummings, (Charles Clarence) Robert (Orville) (1908–1990). American actor. Cummings starred in dozens of films and four television series. He won an Emmy Award for his 1954 portrayal of a conscientious juror in the original television drama, *Twelve Angry Men*. He starred in the series "My Hero" (1952–53), "The Bob Cummings Show" (1955–59), The New Bob Cummings Show" (1961–62) and "My Living Doll" (1964–65). His film work included Alfred HITCHCOCK's *Saboteur* (1942), *King's Row* (1942) and *Dial M for Murder* (1954).

Cunningham, Glenn (1909–1988). American athlete. As the top U.S. miler of the 1930s, Cunningham set six world records for the mile and the 1,500 meters, and another record at 1,000 yards. In 1979, he was named the greatest track athlete in the history of New York City's Madison Square Garden.

Cunningham, Imogen (1883–1976). American photographer. Born in Portland, Ore., she began her career in photography at the age of 18. She studied abroad and opened her own photographic studio in Seattle in 1910. A leading member of the West Coast photographers' Group f/64, she is probably best remembered for her powerful portraits. Cunningham is also known for the sensuous studies of flowers she began in the late 1920s, such as *Magnolia Blossom* (*Tower of Jewels* (1925), and for her innovative multiple and negative images.

Cunningham, Merce (1919–). American dancer and choreographer. The much-honored Cunningham, whose iconoclastic work in the modern dance idiom was at one time considered "a unique audio-visual torture technique," studied tap, folk and ballroom dancing in his native Washington state before performing with modern dancer Lester Horton. He joined the Martha GRAHAM company in 1939, where he remained as a soloist until 1945, inspiring Graham to create many leading roles for him in such works as *Appalachian Spring*. Since 1944 he has choreographed over 100 dances, including such well-known works as *Summerspace* (1958), *Winterbranch* (1964) and *Rainforest* (1968). Also in 1944 Cunningham began his lifelong collaboration with American composer John CAGE, a fellow experimentalist. Other collaborations with noted painters, sculptors and designers such as Andy WARHOL, Robert RAUSCHENBERG and Jasper JOHNS, are a hallmark of Cunningham's approach to dance. He employs "chance" methods as his favored compositional device, virtually eliminating narrative from dance; combines everyday actions and gestures with more formal movements; and casts performers of independent mind with a strong foundation in ballet and modern. His dance company was founded in 1952.

For further reading:

Cunningham, Merce, *The Dancer and the Dance: Merce Cunningham in Conversation with Jacqueline Lesschaeve*. New York: Marion Boyars, 1985.

Klosty, James, *Merce Cunningham*. New York: Limelight Editions, 1987.

Cunningham-Bendix controversy. Widely-publicized 1980 controversy involving charges that Mary Cunningham was promoted in Bendix Corporation because of her liaison with Bendix chairman and president, William Agee. During the 1970s it had become more common for women to become senior managers in large corporations. Mary Cunningham, an attractive woman of 29 with a Harvard MBA, rose to assistant to the vice president for strategic planning at Bendix Corporation in a mere 15 months. However, rumors of favoritism accompanied her rapid rise because she was linked romantically with Agee. The controversy gained national attention, including a nationally syndicated series of newspaper stories. The merit of Mary Cunningham's promotions became widely debated across America. Eventually Cunningham resigned at the urging of the corporation's board of directors. She became a successful executive elsewhere and married Agee, who also left Bendix.

Curie, Marie [born Marie Sklodowska] (1867–1934). Polish-born chemist whose work on the sources and uses of radioactivity helped set the foundation for 20th-century atomic science. She was the first woman to receive a NOBEL PRIZE, and the first person to be awarded the prize twice. Raised in Warsaw, Marie Sklodowska developed an early interest in science (particularly chemistry) and in Polish nationalism. Prohibited from attending the University of Warsaw because she was a woman, she moved to Paris and entered the Sorbonne; she spent most of the remainder of her life in France. She graduated in 1893 at the top of her class with the equivalent of a master's degree in physics. The following year she also obtained a degree in mathematics, placing second in her class. That same

Undated photograph of Polish-born chemist and physicist Marie Curie.

year (1894) she met the French physicist Pierre CURIE, whom she married in 1895. Inspired by Henri BECQUEREL's discovery that uranium emits radiation, she began her experiments on radioactivity. For several years she and her husband worked painstakingly to discover and isolate the source of radioactivity in pitchblende, a radioactive ore. They finally isolated and analyzed the element in 1902, naming it radium. In 1903 Marie Curie presented her findings in her doctoral dissertation; that year, she and her husband gained international recognition when, with Becquerel, they were awarded the Nobel Prize for physics. Curie continued her research into radium and radioactivity and suggested that radiation might be used to treat tumors. She received a second Nobel Prize in 1911, this time "for her services to the advancement of chemistry." During WORLD WAR I she directed the basic research division of the Radium Institute (established by the University of Paris and the Pasteur Institute). She taught army medical staff how to use X-RAYS to find bullets and shrapnel in wounded soldiers, and also worked to ensure that wartime ambulances carried portable X-ray equipment. Throughout the 1920s she worked to promote the medical use of radiation, advising many students and researchers on the new technology she had helped to create. She died at the age of 66 from leukemia caused by her long exposure to radiation. Her daughter, Irene JOLIET-CURIE (1897–1956), won the Nobel Prize for chemistry the year after Marie Curie's death.

For further reading:

Pflaym, Rosalynd, *Grand Obsession: Madame Curie and Her World.* New York: Doubleday, 1989.

Curie, Pierre (1859–1906). French physicist. The son of a physician, Curie was educated at the Sorbonne, where he became an assistant in 1878. In 1882 he was made laboratory chief at the School of Industrial Physics and Chemistry, where he remained until he was appointed professor of physics at the Sorbonne in 1904. In 1895 he married Marie Sklodowska, with whom he conducted research into the radioactivity of radium and with whom he shared the NOBEL PRIZE for physics in 1903. Curie's scientific career falls into two periods, the time before the discovery of radioactivity by Henri BECQUEREL, when he worked on magnetism and crystallography, and the time after, when he collaborated with his wife Marie CURIE on this new phenomenon. In 1880 with his brother Jacques he had discovered piezoelectricity. The brothers used the effect to construct an electrometer to measure small electric currents. Marie Curie later used the instrument to investigate whether radiation from substances other than uranium would cause conductivity in air. Pierre Curie's second major discovery was in the effect of temperature on the magnetic properties of substances, which he was studying for his doctorate. In 1895 he showed that a substance at a certain temperature specific to it will lose its ferromagnetic properties; this critical temperature is now known as the Curie point. Shortly after this discovery he began to work intensively with his wife on the new phenomenon of radioactivity. Two new elements, radium and polonium, were discovered in 1898. The rays these elements produced were investigated and enormous efforts were made to produce a sample of pure radium. Pierre Curie received little recognition in his own country. He was initially passed over for the chairs of physical chemistry and mineralogy in the Sorbonne and was defeated when he applied for membership of the Academie in 1902. (He was, however, admitted in 1905.) The only reason he seems eventually to have been given a chair at the Sorbonne (in 1904) was that he had been offered a post in Geneva and was seriously thinking of leaving France. Partly this may have been because his political sympathies were very much to the left and because he was unwilling to participate in the science policies of the Third Republic. Pierre Curie may have been one of the first people to suffer from radiation sickness. No attempts were made in the early days to restrict the levels of radiation received. He died accidentally in 1906 in rather strange circumstances—he slipped while crossing a Paris street, fell under a passing horse cab and was kicked to death. The Curies' daughter Irene JOLIOT-CURIE carried on research in radioactivity and also received the NOBEL PRIZE for work done with her husband, Frederic.

Curley, James Michael (1874–1958). American politician. A Democrat, Curley began his public career in 1902 in the Massachusetts legislature and subsequently served as congressman (1911–14, 1943–45), Boston mayor (1914–18, 1922–26, 1930–34, 1946–50) and governor (1935–37). In 1946 he was convicted of mail fraud and served five months in prison before President Harry TRUMAN pardoned him—and he returned to complete his last term as mayor.

Curragh, the. Plain in County Kildare, Ireland, where the yearly Irish Derby is held. The Curragh is at the center of the Irish racing industry; horse races have been run at this ancient site since the first century A.D. In 1913, the CURRAGH INCIDENT involved British officers who rebelled against the HOME RULE Act.

Curragh Incident. As Ulster opposition to Irish HOME RULE mounted in early 1914, the British government considered sending troops to Northern Ireland. However, in March 1914 the government informed officers stationed at the Curragh, near Dublin, that they might resign their commissions and be dismissed from the army if they were unwilling to fight the Ulstermen. Of the 71 officers in the Third Cavalry Brigade, 58 of them, including the commander, said they would resign if ordered north. British military officials responded by assuring the officers that they would not be ordered to force Home Rule on Ulster, and the officers withdrew their resignations. The incident was an unusual case of military officers influencing the government away from an unpopular policy.

Curtin, John (Joseph Ambrose) (1885–1945). Prime minister of AUSTRALIA (1941–45). Curtin, who had become a socialist in 1906, began his career as a secretary to the Victorian timber-worker's union in 1911. From 1917 to 1928 he was editor of the *Westralian Worker,* meanwhile working to promote the LABOUR PARTY, and was a Labour member of Parliament from 1928 to 1931 and from 1934 to 1945. He became leader of the party in 1935 and in 1941 became prime minister. Curtin was an asset to the Allies during WORLD WAR II, offering full support to Britain in the war against HITLER and joining with the U.S. in the Pacific war against JAPAN. (See WORLD WAR II IN THE PACIFIC.) However, when a joint defense with the U.S. was set up under General Douglas MACARTHUR, Curtin sought an increased British naval presence to counteract MacArthur's growing authority. Curtin was reelected in a landslide victory in 1943 and died in office five weeks before the end of the war in Asia.

Curtis, Cyrus H.K. (1850–1933). American publisher. A self-made man, Curtis began his publishing career as a newspaper delivery boy in his hometown of Portland, Maine. At 15 he launched *Young America,* a weekly paper, and four years later moved to Boston to work as an ad salesman for the *Boston Times.* Along with a partner he established a newspaper, *The People's Ledger,* which he moved to Philadelphia in 1875. With the editorial aid of his wife, Curtis founded in 1883 the instantly popular *Ladies' Home Journal* as a monthly supplement to another Philadelphia paper, *The Tribune and Farmer.* This success and others led him to expand his business, forming the Curtis Publishing

Company a decade later. In 1897 he bought the *Saturday Evening Post*, which had been started by Benjamin Franklin in 1728 as *The Pennsylvania Gazette*, and in 1911 Curtis acquired *The Country Gentleman*. Curtis said of his chosen profession, "I edit the editors."

Curtis, Heber Doust (1872–1942). American astronomer. Curtis earned his A.B. (1892) and A.M. (1893) from the University of Michigan, where he studied classics. He moved to California in 1894, where he became professor of Latin and Greek at Napa College. There his interest in astronomy was aroused. After earning his Ph.D. from the University of Virginia, in 1902 he joined the staff of the Lick Observatory, where he remained until 1920 when he became director of the Allegheny Observatory of the University of Pittsburg. In 1930 he was appointed director of the University of Michigan's observatory. Curtis' early work was concerned with the measurement of the radial velocities of the brighter stars. From 1910 on, however, he was involved in research on the nature of "spiral nebulae" and became convinced that these were isolated independent star systems. In 1917 he argued that the observed brightness of novas he and George Ritchey had found on photographs of the nebulae indicated that the nebulae lay well beyond our galaxy. He also maintained that extremely bright novas (later identified as supernovas) could not be included with the novae as distance indicators. He estimated the Andromeda nebula to be 500,000 light-years away. Curtis' view was opposed by many, including Harlow SHAPLEY, who proposed that our galaxy was 300,000 light-years in diameter, far larger than previously assumed, and that the spiral nebulae were associated with our galaxy. In 1920, at a meeting of the National Academy of Sciences, Curtis engaged in a famous debate with Shapley over the size of the Galaxy and the distance of the spiral nebulae. The matter was not settled until 1924, when Edwin HUBBLE redetermined the distance of the Andromeda nebula and demonstrated that it lay well beyond our galaxy.

Curtiss, Glenn Hammond (1878–1930). American aviator and inventor. Curtiss, who began his career as a bicycle mechanic, designed the motor for the first American dirigible balloon in 1904. In 1908 he gained renown for the first one-kilometer public flight in the U.S., flying at an average speed of 40 miles an hour in his plane, the *June Bug*. Curtiss invented the aileron in 1911, the same year he developed the first practical seaplane. During WORLD WAR I Curtiss' factories produced military planes, including the NC-4 flying boat that made the first transatlantic flight in 1919.

Curzon, Sir Clifford (1907–1982). British concert pianist. A child prodigy, at the age of 12 Curzon became the youngest student ever admitted to the Royal Academy of Music. He became the academy's youngest professor at the age of 19. Unlike many prodigies, however, he continued to mature as an artist, and at the height of his powers was considered one of the finest pianists in the world. His repertoire included more than 50 concertos. He was best known for his performances of works by Mozart, Beethoven and Schubert. He was knighted in 1977.

Curzon, George Nathaniel [Baron Curzon of Kedleston] (1859–1925). British statesman. Curzon distinguished himself at Balliol College, Oxford, and became a conservative member of Parliament in 1886, serving as under-secretary of state of India from 1891 to 1892 and under-secretary for foreign affairs from 1895 to 1898. He was appointed viceroy to India in 1899. His viceroyalty was marked by substantial administrative reforms, but his imperious manner grated on Indian sensibilities. In 1904 his tenure was extended, but in 1905, after a clash with Lord Kitchener, the commander in chief in India, over their spheres of authority, Curzon resigned. From 1907 on he was chancellor of Oxford University, and in WORLD WAR I he was a member of LLOYD GEORGE'S war cabinet and foreign secretary from 1919. When Bonar LAW resigned in 1923, Curzon was disappointed not to be chosen prime minister. However, he served BALDWIN well as foreign secretary and, from 1924, as lord president of the Council. Again, his hauteur may have cost him the prime ministry, as Law considered him out of touch with public opinion. Curzon was among

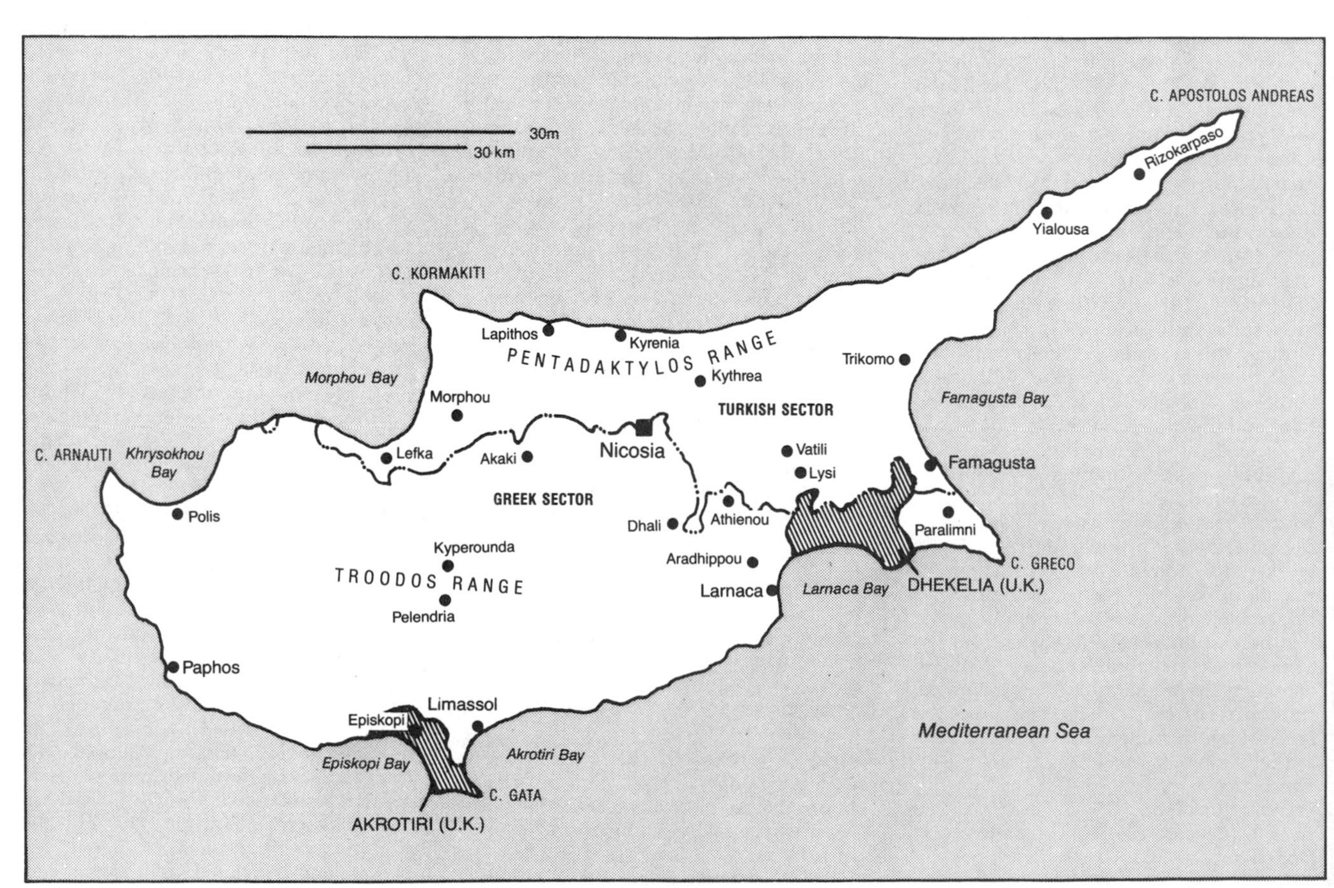

CYPRUS

the last of the British imperialists. He was created baron in 1898, earl in 1911, and marquis in 1921. (See also CURZON LINE.)

Curzon Line. Line proposed as a possible boundary between Poland and the U.S.S.R.; suggested by England's Lord Curzon (see George Nathaniel CURZON) during the Polish-Russian War of 1919–20, it would run south from Grodno through Brest-Litovsk, along the Bug River to Sokal, then west and south past Przemysl to the Carpathian Mountains. It was the basis for the post-World War II boundaries put in place after the YALTA CONFERENCE of 1945.

Cushing, Harvey Williams (1869–1939). U.S surgeon. Cushing received his M.D. from Harvard Medical School in 1895 and joined Massachusetts General Hospital, Boston, before moving to Johns Hopkins Hospital, Baltimore, where he progressed to associate professor of surgery. In 1912 he was appointed professor of surgery at Harvard. Cushing's specialty was brain surgery, and he pioneered several important techniques in this field, especially in the control of blood pressure and bleeding during surgery. From his many case histories, he distinguished several classes of brain tumors and made great improvements in their treatment. Cushing also demonstrated the vital role of the pituitary gland in regulating many bodily functions. He was the first to associate adenoma (tumor) of the basophilic cells of the anterior pituitary with the chronic wasting disease now known as **Cushing's syndrome**. This syndrome is now known to be caused by any of several disorders that result in the increased secretion of corticosteroid hormones by the adrenal glands. Cushing had a lifelong interest in the history of medicine and wrote the *Life of Sir William Ogler*, (1925), which won him a PULITZER PRIZE. He donated his large collection of books and papers to the Yale Medical Library.

Cushman, Robert E., Jr. (1914–1985). U.S. military leader. Cushman was one of the most highly decorated U.S. officers in WORLD WAR II, winning the Navy Cross for Valor in the liberation of GUAM and citations for bravery at BOUGAINVILLE ISLAND and IWO JIMA. In 1957 he was named assistant for U.S. security affairs to Vice President Richard NIXON. In 1967 he became commanding general of the 3d Marine Amphibious Force in VIETNAM, the largest combined combat unit ever led by a marine. He was responsible for the defense of KHE SAHN and the recapture of HUE following the TET OFFENSIVE (see VIETNAM WAR). President Nixon appointed Cushman deputy director of the CENTRAL INTELLIGENCE AGENCY (CIA) (1969–72) and Marine Corps commandant (1972–75).

Cutting, C. Suydam (1889–1972). Explorer and naturalist, reported to be the first white Christian to visit the forbidden city of Lhasa in TIBET (1935).

Cypriot War of 1963–64, Greek-Turkish. The Republic of CYPRUS was established on August 16, 1960, to avoid annexation by either Greece or Turkey. Its population was three-fourths Greek and one-fourth Turkish. Its president, Greek Archbishop MAKARIOS III foreswore union with Greece. However, both Greeks and Turks influenced their Cypriot compatriots to acts of violence. Turkish Cypriots, thinking their rights threatened by Greek constitutional changes, began fighting in late 1963. The UNITED NATIONS sent a peacekeeping force in March 1964. Despite the UN force and the U.S. preventing a Turkish invasion, fighting continued between Greek and Turkish Cypriots. In August 1964 Turkish warplanes attacked Greek Cypriots, and Makarios sought help from Egypt and the U.S.S.R., but the UN arranged a cease-fire. Later tensions were reduced when the government passed laws abolishing de facto abuse of Turkish rights.

Cypriot War of 1974, Greek-Turkish. The shaky peace established in 1964 between Greek and Turkish Cypriots was broken by violent clashes, and in mid-July 1974 the Greek Cypriot National Guard, led by Greek officers, overthrew President Archbishop MAKARIOS III, seeking union with Greece. Since the UNITED NATIONS and a London conference of involved parties failed to act, Turkish forces invaded. The Turks won about 40% of the island, where the inhabitants voted to form a separate state. The UN sponsored two cease-fires. The second, on July 30, 1974, established a UN buffer area between Greek and Turkish zones. The guarantors of the Cypriot constitution (Britain, Greece and Turkey) arranged another cease-fire on August 16, 1974, with the Turks. Makarios returned in late 1974, recognizing Turkish autonomy but not partition.

Cyprus [*Greek:* Kypros; *Turkish:* Kibris]. Island in the eastern Mediterranean, 40 miles south of Turkey and 60 miles west of Syria. At the beginning of the 20th century the population was about 80% Greek and 20% Turkish, with the Greek faction demanding ENOSIS (union) with GREECE. Violence broke out in 1955; the military-political EOKA, directed by Col. George GRIVAS, backed the Greek cause. The British banished Archbishop MAKARIOS III, symbol of Greek-Cypriot nationalism, in an attempt to keep the peace. The U.K., Greece and TURKEY all eventually consented to an independent Cyprus, with balanced representation for Greeks and Turks. The new nation materialized in 1960 with a returned Maka-

CYPRUS

1900	Mixed population of Greeks and Turks is governed as a protectorate by British following pullout of former Ottoman rulers.
1914	Annexed by Britain when Turkey declares war.
1925	Made British crown colony.
1931	Enosis movement begins; Greek Cypriots riot for union with Greece; British respond with polices that drive Turkish and Greek Cypriots further apart.
1935	Law passed governing treatment and export of antiquities.
1940	Cypriot regiment fights in British army.
1943	Local elections held; British announce possibility of self-government.
1955	EOKA begins pro-Enosis guerrilla war; Archbishop Makarios leads anti-British demonstrations.
1956	Makarios deported.
1959	Britain, Turkey and Greece agree to a Cypriot republic set up within British Commonwealth; all three will have a military presence on the island.
1960	Republic established with Makarios as president and Kutchuk (a Turk) as vice president.
1963	Turks withdraw from government; ethnic violence widespread.
1964	UN peacekeeping force arrives.
1968	Provisional government formed by Kutchuk in Turkish northern Cyprus.
1974	Pro-Enosis coup (backed by Greek military government) against Makarios; in response, Turkey invades the island in strength.
1975	Greek Cypriots flee the northern territory; Turkish Federated State of Cyprus proclaimed there.
1983	Turkish Federated State declares independence, renames itself Republic of North Cyprus, recognized only by Turkey.
1988	Leaders of Greece and Turkey meet in Geneva to discuss Cyprus.
1989	Turks claim jurisdiction of waters around North Cyprus; confrontation between Greek and Turkish fighter planes.

CZECHOSLOVAKIA

rios as its president. In 1964 dissension erupted again, and UN troops were brought in to keep the peace. Violence did not subside, and in 1974 a coup overthrew Makarios. Turkey attacked Cyprus and grabbed nearly 30% of the island. The Turkish faction proclaimed its freedom from the Greek-held region, effecting a divided nation and a standoff that continued through the 1980s. (See also CYPRIOT WAR OF 1963–64; CYPRIOT WAR OF 1974).

Cyrankiewicz, Jozef (1911–1989). Polish communist political leader. He headed the Polish government as premier from 1947 to 1970, with a break between 1952 and 1954. In 1970 he signed an accord with West Germany that established POLAND's western border; a few days later his regime was toppled by violent riots over food price increases.

Czechoslovakia. Much-abused country in central Europe; a conglomeration of Czechs, Slovaks and other nationalities, it was carved from the death throes of the AUSTRO-HUNGARIAN EMPIRE. In 1916, during WORLD WAR I, the Czechs and Slovaks joined in a national council directed by Tomas MASARYK to lobby with the Allies for a Czechoslovak national state following the war. In October 1918 the council announced the independence of their state, whose boundaries eventually included not only Bohemia and Moravia, but also Upper Silesia, part of the duchy

CZECHOSLOVAKIA

1918	Independent Czechoslovakia founded with Tomas Masaryk as president.
1935	Eduard Benes becomes president.
1938	Czechoslovakia cedes Sudetenland to Germany under Munich Pact.
1939	Independent, pro-German Slovak state declared; Germany occupies Prague, declares Protectorate of Bohemia-Moravia.
1941	Benes's Czech government-in-exile in London recognized by Allies.
1942	Czech resistance assassinates Heydrich; Germans destroy Lidice.
1945	Creation of National Front government; Soviet troops liberate Prague.
1946	Communist Klement Gottwald becomes prime minister in coalition government.
1948	Communist takeover of Czechoslovakia under Gottwald; death of Jan Masaryk; death of Benes.
1952	Slansky trial; purge of Communist Party.
1953	Death of Gottwald.
1960	New Soviet-style constitution introduced.
1968	Alexander Dubcek becomes first secretary of Communist Party, initiates "Prague Spring" reforms; Soviet invasion of Czechoslovakia (Aug. 20-21).
1977	Charter 77 group formed calling for human rights.
1988	Anticommunists demonstrate in Prague on anniversary of Soviet invasion.
1989	Mass anticommunist demonstrations (Nov.) lead to fall of communists; non-communist government elected under Vaclav Havel.
1991	Czechoslovakian troops join Allies in Saudi Arabia as part of Operation Desert Shield/Desert Storm.

of Teschen and Carpathian Ruthenia. Czechoslovakia's broad constitution of 1918 assured minority rights, but this disparate collection of peoples soon demonstrated its instability.

President Masaryk and Eduard BENES, who replaced him in 1935, managed to lead the state through the minefield of its early years and into the GREAT DEPRESSION of the 1930s. During that decade German upheaval in the SUDETENLAND of Bohemia, led by Konrad Henlein and backed up by Germany's Adolf HITLER, critically endangered the nation. After his annexation of AUSTRIA in March 1938, Hitler insisted that any part of Czechoslovakia whose population was more than half German be under German authority. Unwilling and unready to go to war, Great Britain and France sanctioned the German land-grab—a practice that became known as APPEASEMENT. In a pact signed at MUNICH on September 29, 1938, the Sudetenland was given to GERMANY. POLAND insisted on and received Teschen; Ruthenia and a section of Slovakia went to HUNGARY. In March 1939 Hitler took the balance and made it a German protectorate. German rule during WORLD WAR II was savage, more so after the assassination of Reich Protector Reinhard Heydrich in May 1942; in revenge all male citizens in the town of LIDICE were killed.

The expelled Czech government came under Soviet influence, and when prewar boundaries were restored, Ruthenia became part of the U.S.S.R. Klement GOTTWALD, a communist, was named prime minister in 1946. By February 1948 communist control was absolute. A Soviet-style state was organized with concentrated and strict control of political and economic affairs, and the party was purged in the early 1950s. By the mid-1950s some efforts were being made to combat a growing dissatisfaction, but unrest persisted and erupted in the PRAGUE SPRING of 1968. The Soviet Union, feeling itself to be threatened, led a WARSAW PACT assault on the country on August 20. The military installed Gustave HUSAK as premier, succeeding the reformist Alexander DUBCEK. Strict party rule was restored, and Czechoslovakia again became one of the enslaved nations in the eastern bloc. But by 1989, the people of eastern Europe had had enough of communist governments, and mass demonstrations were held in Prague and in other Czech cities. The communists were forced out; free elections were held for the first time in over 40 years, and playwright Vaclav HAVEL was elected president; Dubcek was elected speaker of parliament.

For further reading:

Stone, Norman, *Czechoslovakia: Crossroads and Crises, 1918–88*. New York: St. Martin's, 1989.

Czechoslovakia, Soviet Invasion of. Early in 1968, the Slovak leader Alexander DUBCEK became first secretary of the Communist Party of CZECHOSLOVAKIA. A brief period of liberalization—labeled the PRAGUE SPRING—began, during which Dubcek attempted to democratize Czechoslovakia by lifting press censorship, establishing ties to the West, promising increases in consumer goods, seeking autonomy for Slovakia within the larger state, and planning a new constitution that allowed individual liberties. The Soviet Union, used to governing Czechoslovakia and its other satellites rigidly, was alarmed, and a Soviet-Czech conference was held in the Slovak town of Cierna (July 29–August 1, 1968), from which the Soviet officials departed amicably. But their views changed, for on the night of August 20–21, 1968, Soviet forces, aided by WARSAW PACT troops from Bulgaria, Hungary, Poland and East Germany, invaded Czechoslovakia, overcame minor resistance, and occupied the country (the invaders numbered at least 600,000). Dubcek and other Czechoslovak leaders were arrested, taken to Moscow, forced to make concessions, and then returned home; a pro-Soviet communist regime was established firmly in Czechoslovakia. By April 1969, all of Dubcek's reforms (except Slovak autonomy) had been invalidated, and Dubcek was out of office. Justifying their action under the so-called BREZHNEV DOCTRINE, the Soviets ordered arrests, union purges, and religious persecutions in 1970 to rid Czechoslovakia of its liberal tendencies.

Czeschka, Carl Otto (1878–1960). Viennese artist and designer associated with the turn-of-the-century MODERNISM of the Vienna SECESSION. In 1904 he was one of a group including Josef HOFFMANN and Koloman MOSER producing designs for the Wiener Werkstatte. Czeschka was the designer of some stained glass for Hoffmann's Palais Stoclet of 1911 in Brussels. He became a teacher of design at the school of applied arts in Hamburg where he continued as a professor until his retirement in 1943.

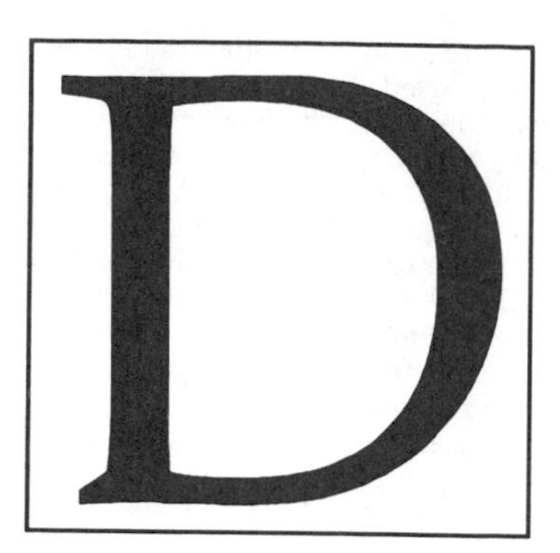

Dacca. City and area of central BANGLADESH, 80 miles northeast of Khulna. From 1905 to 1912 the city of Dacca was the capital of the British jurisdiction of Eastern Bengal and of Assam. It was the capital of East Pakistan from 1956 to 1971. Following INDIA's victory over PAKISTAN in the INDO-PAKISTANI WAR OF 1971, it emerged as the capital of the new nation of Bangladesh.

Dachau. Bavarian town, 11 miles northwest of Munich, Germany. In 1933 Dachau became the site of one of the first CONCENTRATION CAMPS built by the new Nazi regime. Here JEWS and other minorities, along with political inmates and Russian PRISONERS OF WAR, were exploited for slave labor and for so-called medical research. A mass extermination of prisoners also occurred here. It was liberated by the Allies on April 29, 1945, and 32,000 surviving prisoners were set free.

Dacko, David (1930–). President of the CENTRAL AFRICAN REPUBLIC (CAR) (1960–66, 1981). Dacko served as minister of agriculture from 1957 to 1958 in the Central African government council and from 1958 to 1959 as minister of the interior. Following the death of the CAR's first leader, Boganda, in 1959 Dacko, his nephew, became prime minister, and in 1960 he became the first president of the country. In 1966 Dacko's government was overthrown by Jean-Bedel BOKASSA, and Dacko was put under house arrest, later serving as an adviser to Bokassa. In 1979 Bokassa was deposed, and Dacko was reinstated as president. Dacko won a presidential election in 1981 but a faltering economy forced him to retire that same year. He was replaced by General Kolingba.

Dada. International artistic and literary movement that flourished in the 1910s and remains highly influential today. It was formed in 1916 in Zurich by a disparate group of European artists and poets including Jean ARP, Hugo Ball, Richard Huelsenbeck, Marcel Janco, and Tristan TZARA. The word "Dada" literally means "wooden horse" in French. But as it was employed by artists and writers, "Dada" became a cacaphonic nonsense term that was used to shout down all bourgeois artistic pretensions and to embrace the absurdity of modern life. Dada was, in essence, a movement of negation. It posed no positive theories of artistic creation and in part, was a nihilistic response to the horrors of WORLD WAR I. Dadaists composed nonsense poems and cabaret skits and displayed artistic works with satirical themes and an informal, even random, approach to form and composition. For the most part, Dadaists avoided manifestos and ideological commitments of any sort. The Dada movement became a major influence on SURREALISM.

Dahl, Roald (1916–1990). British writer of Welsh and Norwegian parentage, author of popular fantasies, wicked parables and outstanding children's books. After injuries in action with the British Royal Air Force (RAF) in WORLD WAR II, he was assigned as an air attache to Washington, D.C., where he began his first volume of short stories, *Over to You* (1945). Dahl's finest stories appeared in two collections, *Someone Like You* (1953) and *Kiss Kiss* (1960). Their blend of keen-edged satire, dark humor, occasional horror and morbid subjects have been rivaled only, perhaps, by the work of John COLLIER and SAKI. Some, such as "Lamb to the Slaughter" and "Man from the South," were presented on Alfred HITCHCOCK's television series; others were adapted for a television series in the early 1960s hosted by Dahl himself, "Way Out." After the publication of *James and the Giant Peach* (1961), Dahl increasingly turned to children's books—without sacrificing much of the bite of his more adult books. At the same time, his later adult fables, such as the collection *Switch Bitch* (1974) and the novel *My Uncle Oswald* (1979), smack overmuch of scatological jokes and bathroom humor. He also wrote two volumes of an autobiography—*Boy* (1984) and *Solo* (1986). Dahl was married to the American actress Patricia Neal from 1953 to 1983.

For further reading:

Dahl, Roald, *Boy and Solo* (two volumes of autobiography). New York: Farrar, Straus & Giroux, 1984–86.

Dahlberg, Edward (1900–1977). American novelist, essayist and poet. Dahlberg is a highly individualistic figure in American letters. In the course of his long writing career he underwent a decisive transformation from being a proletarian writer concerned exclusively with social issues to the adaptation, in the 1940s and after, of a neoclassical aesthetic. Dahlberg, an illegitimate son, was raised for a time in Kansas City by his mother, a barber. Thereafter he spent some years in an orphanage in Cleveland. These experiences are movingly recounted in Dahlberg's masterful autobiography, *Because I Was Flesh* (1964). In 1929 Dahlberg published his first novel, *Bottom Dogs,* which featured a glowing introduction by D.H. LAWRENCE. Other novels of his proletarian period include *From Flushing to Calvary* (1932) and *Those Who Perish* (1934). In *Can These Bones Live* (1941, revised 1960), Dahlberg explored the course of American literature in a series of stylish, insightful essays. Other of his works include *The Sorrows of Priapus* (1957), on the mind-body split in Hebraic, Hellenic and other cultures, and the autobiograpical *Confessions of Edward Dahlberg* (1971).

Daiches, David (1912–). British literary critic and author. Educated at Balliol College, Oxford, Daiches has served in several academic posts both in Britain and the U.S. A prolific author of nonfiction on a variety of subjects, Daiches is perhaps best known for his definitive biographies, *Virginia Woolf* (1942), *Robert Louis Stevenson* (1947), and *Robert Burns* (1950), and for his literary criticism including *Critical History of English Literature* (four volumes, 1960). Other works include *Scotch*

Whiskey (1969); three volumes of autobiography, *Two Worlds* (1957), *A Third World* (1971) and *Was; a Pastime from Time Past* (1975) and *God and the Poets* (1984).

Dail Eireann [*Irish Gaelic,* "assembly of Ireland"]. House of representatives, lower chamber of the Irish parliament (*Oireachtas*), with 144 members elected for five years by adult suffrage on a system of proportional representation. Often abbreviated to Dail, it is IRELAND's main legislative body, the upper house (**Senaad Eireann,** or senate) being largely consultative and ceremonial.

Daily News. New York City tabloid founded in 1919. The *Daily News* was begun by Capt. Joseph M. Patterson, who coowned the paper with Col. Robert R. McCormick of the *Chicago Tribune.* The *News,* with its sensationalist reporting, comics, snappy headlines and abundant photography, was an immediate success. When Patterson died in 1946, McCormick took over the paper; while continuing to highlight sex and scandal, the *News* maintained a conservative, antiunion, anticommunist, pro-American stance. It began to lose readers in the liberal 1960s and by 1970 was in serious difficulties. It attempted to reshape itself and accommodate changing readership patterns, presenting more straight news and introducing style and business sections, but to little avail. In 1981, the *Tribune* announced that the *Daily News* had lost $11 million that year and was for sale. In 1982, Joe L. Albritton, owner of several other papers, television and radio stations, took an option to buy the *News* but relinquished it a month later. The *Tribune* continued to publish the *News,* but in 1990 the paper's workers began a long strike. The *News* was acquired by British publishing magnate Robert MAXWELL in 1991.

Dainton, Sir Frederick Sydney (1914–). British physical chemist and scientific administrator. Dainton was educated at the universities of Oxford and Cambridge. After World War II he remained in Cambridge until 1950, when he was appointed professor of physical chemistry at the University of Leeds. Apart from a brief period (1970–73) as professor of physical chemistry at Oxford, most of Dainton's time since 1965 has been spent as an administrator. Dainton's early work in physical chemistry was on the kinetics and thermodynamics of polymerization reactions. From about 1945 he turned his attention to studies of radiolysis—chemical changes produced by high-energy radiation (alpha, beta or gamma rays). In particular he has studied the properties and reactions of hydrated electrons in liquids. From 1965 he was a member of the Council for Scientific Policy and was its chairman from 1969. While holding this office he was influential in decisions made about the way British academic research is financed.

Dakar. Harbor and capital of SENEGAL, West Africa, on the south end of the Cape Verde peninsula. It was established by the French in 1857. Dakar became a French naval base and in 1902 was named capital of FRENCH WEST AFRICA; between 1924 and 1946 the city and encompassing areas were self-governing. It was restored to Senegal in 1946 and made capital of the new nation in 1956.

Daladier, Edouard (1884–1970). French politician, three-time premier (1933, 1934, 1938–40). A radical socialist teacher, he entered the chamber of deputies in 1919 and served in successive cabinets beginning in 1924. He was premier for 10 months in 1933 and two months in 1934. He began service as minister of war in 1936, the year that he aided in forming a Popular Front coalition of radicals, socialists and communists. Daladier became premier again in 1938 and, following a policy of APPEASEMENT toward Nazi aggression, was a cosigner of the MUNICH PACT in that same year. A weak and vacillating leader, he was forced to step down as premier in 1940 after FRANCE failed to come to the aid of Finland when that country came under attack from the U.S.S.R. Replaced by Paul REYNAUD, he continued in the post of minister of war, later becoming foreign minister. After the fall of France, he was arrested by the VICHY government (1940), tried at Riom (1942) and imprisoned in Germany (1943–45). Elected to the national assembly in 1946, he served there until 1958.

Dalai Lama (1935–). In 1940, at age five, Tenzin Gyatso was enthroned as the 14th Dalai Lama—the spiritual reincarnation of Buddha and political leader of TIBET. In 1950, communist CHINA invaded Tibet and seized power from the Dalai Lama. He attempted to mediate between the Chinese government and the Tibetan people, but increasing Chinese repression sparked an unsuccessful uprising in 1959. The failure of the revolt led him and 100,000 other Tibetans to seek asylum in India. The Dalai Lama later settled in the town of Dharmsala in the Himalayas, where he continued to call for an end to Chinese control over Tibet and to advocate nonviolent protest. He received the 1989 NOBEL PRIZE for peace; China denounced the award and called it politically motivated.

Dale, Sir Henry Hallett (1875–1968). British physiologist. Educated at Cambridge University and St. Bartholomew's Hospital, Dale became, in 1904, director of the Wellcome Physiological Research Laboratories. His work there over the next 10 years included the isolation (with Arthur Ewins) from ergot fungi of a pharmacologically active extract—acetylcholine—which he found had similar effects on various organs as to the parasympathetic nervous system. Otto Loewi later showed that a substance released by electrical stimulation of the vagus nerve was responsible for effecting changes in heartbeat. Following up this work, Dale showed that the substance is in fact acetylcholine, thus establishing that chemical as well as electrical stimuli are involved in nerve action. For this research, Dale and Loewi shared the 1936 NOBEL PRIZE for physiology or medicine. Dale also worked on the properties of histamine and related substances, including their actions in allergic and anaphylactic conditions. He was the chairman of an international committee responsible for the standardization of biological preparations, and from 1928 to 1942 was director of the National Institute for Medical Research.

Dalen, Nils Gustaf (1869–1937). Swedish engineer. In 1896 Dalen graduated in mechanical engineering from the Chalmers Institute in Goteborg and then spent a year at the Swiss Federal Institute of Technology in Zurich. For several years he researched and improved hot-air turbines, compressors and air pumps, and from 1900 to 1905 he worked with the engineering firm Dalen and Alsing. He then became works manager for the Swedish Carbide and Acetylene Company, which in 1909 became the Swedish Gas Accumulator Company with Dalen as managing director. Dalen is remembered principally for his inventions relating to acetylene lighting for lighthouses and other navigational aids, and in particular an automatic light-controlled valve, for which he received the 1912 NOBEL PRIZE for physics. The valve, known as "Solventil," used the difference in heat-absorbing properties between a dull black surface and a highly polished one to produce differential expansion of gases and thus to regulate the main gas valve of an acetylene-burning lamp. The lamp could thus be automatically dimmed or extinguished in daylight. This allowed buoys and lighthouses to be left unattended and less gas to be used. The system soon came into widespread use and is still in use today. Another of Dalen's inventions was a porous filler for acetylene tanks that prevented explosions. It was ironic that in 1912 he was himself blinded by an explosion during the course of an experiment. This did not, however, deter him from continuing his experimental work up to his death.

Daley, Richard J(oseph) (1902–1976). U.S. politician and mayor of CHICAGO from 1955 to 1976. Working in the stockyards of Chicago, Daley studied law at night and took his degree from Loyola University in 1933. He was elected to the Illinois House of Representatives in 1936, and later also served in the Illinois Senate. Running for sheriff of Cook County, he suffered the only defeat of his career in politics. In 1950 he was appointed clerk of Cook County. His selection as chairman of the Democratic county organization in 1953 brought him major political power. He used harsh measures to quell rioters protesting the VIETNAM WAR during the 1968 DEMOCRATIC PARTY convention. Daley was reelected in 1975 to an unprecedented sixth term as mayor. He was an adviser to Presidents KENNEDY and JOHNSON. His administration reorganized Chicago's scandal-ridden police department, stressed urban renewal and encouraged construction of major downtown buildings. Scandals during his term of office never involved Daley personally.

For further reading:
Sullivan, Frank, *Legend: The Only Inside Story of Mayor Richard J. Daley*. Chicago: Bonus Books, 1989.

Dalglish, Kenneth (1951–). Scottish soccer player and manager. An intelligent forward noted for his goal-scoring skills and ability to create space, Dalglish is Scotland's most capped player with 102 appearances, and shares the all-time goal-scoring record at 30. Unique among British soccer players, Dalglish has won the full array of domestic championships in both Scotland and England, starring for Glasgow Celtic in Scotland and Liverpool in England. Dalglish joined Celtic in 1970 and gained four league championships in seven years, scoring 112 goals in 204 games. In August 1977 he joined Liverpool and embarked on a period of unremitting success with the team. Liverpool won seven championships in nine years and three European Cups, 1978, 1981 and 1984. In May 1985, 39 fans were crushed during a riot by Liverpool fans at the European Cup Final. In the wake of this tragedy Dalglish was appointed player-manager of Liverpool. The team was banned from Europe, but Dalglish led the team in its continued dominance of English soccer. In 1986 and 1988 he was named English Manager of the Year. Although his success in British soccer is unparalleled, Dalglish will always be remembered for his leadership following the HILLSBOROUGH STADIUM DISASTER (April 1989), when 95 Liverpool fans were crushed to death at the English F.A. Cup semifinal. Dalglish led the city in mourning and his influence was credited with restoring the shaken image of the game in England. Dalglish resigned as Liverpool manager in March 1991.

Dali, Salvador [born Salvador Domingo Felipe Jacinto Dali Domenech Cusi y Farres] (1904–1989). Spanish-born surrealist. Dali was one of the best known and most controversial artists of his day; his paintings and other work explored the subconscious mind with images of fantasy, dreams and hallucinations. Dali's lifestyle was as dramatic and well publicized as his art, and he was a well-known figure with his waxed, pointed mustache and silver-handled cane. His career began in 1928, when he visited Paris and was welcomed into the Surrealist group (see SURREALISM). During the next several years he produced some of his best known work, including the painting *The Persistence of Memory* (1931), with its drooping watches and barren landscape. He also collaborated with Luis BUNUEL on the scenario for the surrealist film *Un Chien Andalou*. In 1934, the Surrealists expelled him from their movement for having developed what they considered an unhealthy interest in money. Dali fled Europe at the outbreak of World War II and eventually settled in the U.S., where he worked on films, plays, ballets, paintings and other projects. After returning to Spain in 1949 he became reconciled with the Catholic Church and began a series of large-scale religious paintings. His last years were

Spanish surrealist painter Salvador Dali arrives at the French Academie des Beaux Arts in Paris after his nomination to membership (May 9, 1979).

marred by a forgery scandal, in which Dali was said to have signed thousands of blank sheets of paper to be filled in later by others and sold as Dali originals. After the death (1982) of his wife of nearly 50 years, Dali spent most of his time in seclusion.

Dalkon Shield controversy. Involving the safety of an IUD birth control device. The A.H. Robbins pharmaceutical company developed and in 1971 marketed an intrauterine device (IUD), called the Dalkon Shield, for birth control. Because it was marketed as a safe alternative to birth control pills, nearly five million were sold worldwide. Only three years later the U.S. Food and Drug Administration asked the company to cease marketing the product on the grounds that it was neither safe nor effective. Reportedly, the company had known of potential problems with the IUD and knowingly exposed women to severe medical consequences. Many users experienced serious pelvic inflammatory disease that often led to chronic pain and illness and even death. More than half of the women who did become pregnant lost their babies while other women became infertile. When confronted with thousands of lawsuits Robbins aggressively fought each case, but eventually filed for a bankruptcy reorganization. Ultimately Robbins moved much of its assets to a trust fund for the victims, and itself was acquired by American Home Products Corporation.

Dallapiccola, Luigi (1904–1975). Italian composer and pianist. He was trained at the Conservatory of Florence and later taught there. His difficult personal life—he was interned in an Austrian detention camp in WORLD WAR I and was persecuted by the Italian government during WORLD WAR II because his wife was Jewish—was a profound influence on his music, which often deals with themes of suffering and freedom. The first Italian composer to employ the twelve-tone scale, he is noted for his vocal music, which includes the choral works *Songs of Captivity* (1938–41) and *Songs of Liberation* (1955), the operas *The Prisoner* (1944–48) and *Odysseus* (1968), the oratorio *Job* (1950) and the *Christmas Cantata* (1957). Dallapiccola also composed numerous orchestral and instrumental works as well as several ballets. An influential teacher, he taught in American universities throughout the 1950s and early 1960s.

Dalmatia. Ancient region on the Adriatic coast of the Balkans; now a part of Yugoslavia's constituent republic of CROATIA. In 1915 Dalmatia was pledged to Italy by the Allies, who in return wanted Italy on their side in WORLD WAR I. However, the Allies reneged on their promise, and in 1918 Dalmatia joined with the new kingdom of the Serbs, Croats and Slovenes, named YUGOSLAVIA in 1929. In WORLD WAR II Italy controlled Dalmatia for a brief period, but in 1945 the area was given back to Yugoslavia. Today Dalmatia's coast is brimming with lush scenery and fashionable resorts.

Dalstroy [Far Eastern Construction Trust]. A state corporation in the Magadan oblast and Northeast Yakutia, established in 1930 to exploit mineral resources. Until 1953 it was supervised by the chief of administration of corrective labor camps. The trust was abolished in 1957.

Daly, Edward J. (1922–1984). American airline executive. As chairman and principal stockholder of World Airways, Daly described himself as "the Wyatt Earp of the airlines industry." He bought World Airways in 1950 for $50,000 and turned it into a huge profit-making charter carrier. In the 1970s, he experimented with cheap, no-frills cross-country flights, setting off a nationwide fare war among his competitors. During the VIETNAM WAR, he piloted a World Airways jet on an unauthorized airlift of South Vietnamese orphans.

Damascus. Capital and chief city of SYRIA and its administrative, financial and communications hub; on the Barada River about 57 miles southeast of Beirut, Lebanon. Of indefinite age, some have called it the oldest continually populated city in the Western world. Seized by the OTTOMAN EMPIRE in 1516, it stayed under the domination of the Turks until the end of WORLD WAR I. During WORLD WAR I, Col. T.E. LAWRENCE laid the groundwork for the British capture of the city by General ALLENBY and Emir Faisal, later FAISAL I of Iraq. It was made a French mandate under the LEAGUE OF NATIONS after the war, and the city joined the Druse in a revolt against the French in 1925–26. However, it stayed under nominal French control. During WORLD WAR II British and FREE FRENCH forces infiltrated the city, but it became the capital of a self-governing Syria in 1941. In 1958 Damascus was named the Syrian capital of the short-live UNITED ARAB REPUBLIC, consisting of Syria and Egypt, from which Syria withdrew in 1961.

d'Amboise, Jacques (1934–). American dancer. One of the outstanding interpreters of George BALANCHINE's choreography, d'Amboise joined NEW YORK CITY BALLET in 1950 and created roles in such Balanchine works as *Western Symphony* (1954), *Stars and Stripes* (1958) and *Who Cares?* (1970). He is especially known for his interpretation of Balanchine's *Apollo.* In addition, he has appeared in several movies and television productions, taught at the School of American Ballet and choreographed many works (since 1963). Currently he serves as director of the National Dance Institute and works to involve young people in dance activities.

Dan, Fedor Ilyich (1871–1947). Russian socialist writer and leader. Dan initially collaborated with LENIN, but later joined the MENSHEVIKS. In 1894 he joined the Social Democratic movement and actively supported the St. Petersburg "Union of Struggle for the Liberation of the Working Class." In 1902 the Marxist paper *Iskra* began to publish his articles. Although frequently imprisoned or exiled, he remained active and in 1906 became a permanent member of the Menshevik central committee. Following the FEBRUARY REVOLUTION, Dan was one of the most influential leaders in the executive council of the Soviets and aroused the opposition of the BOLSHEVIKS, who arrested him in 1921. In 1922 he immigrated, first to Berlin, and later to Paris. He became an editor of the *Sotsialisticheskiy Vestnik* (*Socialist Courier*) and was the Menshevik representative to the Second International. In 1940, he settled in the U.S. and wrote *The Origin of Bolshevism* (1946).

Dance Theatre of Harlem. The major, classically oriented, predominantly black American ballet company, Dance Theatre of Harlem made its debut in 1971. Founded by NEW YORK CITY BALLET principal dancer Arthur Mitchell, the dance school was established first in 1968, followed by the formation of the company under the direction of Mitchell and Karel Shook (formerly ballet master of the Dutch National Ballet). Since 1974 the company has had regular seasons in New York City and became the first black ballet company to have a season at Covent Garden in London (1981). Influenced primarily by the neo-classical style of George BALANCHINE, the company performs many of his works, in addition to ballets created by Mitchell and other contemporary choreographers. (See also HARLEM.)

Dance to the Music of Time, A. A 12-volume sequence of novels by the British writer Anthony POWELL. The series began with *A Question of Upbringing* (1951), an examination of class and social values in Britain that immediately earned Powell a preeminent position among the novelists of his generation. Succeeding volumes in the series include *Casanova's Chinese Restaurant* (1960), *The Soldier's Art* (1966), *Temporary Kings* (1973) and *Hearing Secret Harmonies* (1976). Told through the eyes of the self-effacing observer-narrator, Nick Jenkins, these intricately plotted but leisurely paced novels trace the intertwined lives of various characters who reemerge, often transformed, at various points throughout the series. Powell's light, comedy-of-manners touch belies his fiercely satiric evaluation of the transformation of Britain during several decades of the 20th century, from the Roaring Twenties through WORLD WAR II to the tumultuous 1960s.

Daniel, Daniel [Born Daniel Moskowitz] (1890–1981). American journalist who was widely considered the dean of American baseball sportswriters. Daniel changed his name when newspapers refused to carry his byline because he was Jewish. He covered baseball for over half a century, beginning in 1909. He served as chairman of the Baseball Writers Association in 1957.

Daniel, Yuli M. [Nikolai Arzhak] (1925–1988). Soviet dissident satirist and poet; arrested in 1965 and served five years in prison and labor camp for illegally publishing his work abroad. The criminal charge was one of the first ever brought against an intellectual for literary criticism of the Soviet system.

Daniels, Farrington (1889–1972). American chemist. Daniels was educated at the University of Minnesota and at Harvard, where he earned his Ph.D. in 1914. He moved to the University of Wisconsin in 1920, spending his whole career there and serving as professor of chemistry from 1928 until his retirement in 1959. Daniels worked on a wide variety of chemical problems. In addition to a textbook, *Outlines of Physical Chemistry* (1931), he wrote on photochemistry, nitrogen fixation and thermoluminescence. He was also interested in the utilization of **solar energy,** publishing a book on the subject, *Direct Use of the Sun's Energy* (1964), and organizing a symposium on it in 1954, many years before the discussion of solar energy had become fashionable.

Daniels, Josephus (1862–1948). U.S. cabinet member. Born in Washington, D.C., Daniels had a successful career as a newspaper editor, becoming the chief spokesman for Progressive reform in North Carolina and the Upper South. He served on the Democratic National Committee beginning in 1896 and was in charge of publicity for the 1908 and 1912 campaigns. Daniels served as secretary of the Navy through Woodrow WILSON's two terms. Regarded as a great secretary, he was initially criticized for pacifist tendencies and failure to prepare the Navy for possible entry into WORLD WAR I. However, he helped push through Congress the greatest naval building program to that date and improved the conditions and opportunities for enlisted men. Daniels returned to newspaper publishing in 1921. He opposed the KU KLUX KLAN, championed child labor laws and supported U.S. entry into the LEAGUE OF NATIONS and the World Court. As ambassador to MEXICO (1933–41), he was influential in improving relations between the two countries.

Danilova, Alexandra (1906–). Russian ballerina. After training at the Russian Imperial and Soviet State ballet schools in Leningrad, Danilova worked at the Maryinsky Theater. She left the Soviet Union in 1924, joined DIAGHILEV and the BALLETS RUSSES, and worked with them from 1925 to 1929. Her most important roles included *Le Pas d'Acier, Apollon Musagetes* and *The Gods Go a'Begging*. From 1933 to 1937 she was a member of Colonel de Basil's company, and from 1938 to 1958 she was prima ballerina of MASSINE's Ballet Russe de Monte Carlo. For many years she taught and lectured on ballet. In 1975 she choreographed *Coppelia* with George BALANCHINE for the New York City Ballet, and she made her screen debut in *The Turning Point* in 1977.

Danish Modern. Term identifying the MODERNISM developed in post-World War II Denmark by such designers as Kai Bojesen, Finn Juhl, and Hans Wegner. Danish design of the 1930s had developed a cautious modernism based on craft traditions. In the 1950s, Danish design developed in a strongly Functionalist direction, but always with a certain sense of craft tradition that led to qualities of warmth and softness which aided the growth of worldwide popularity for Danish design. At a time when modernism was still somewhat new and frightening to American consumers, Danish modern became a popular compromise, often called "contemporary" or "transitional" to distinguish it from the more mechanistic qualities of BAUHAUS-inspired functionalism. Economic developments in recent years have made Danish products less economical than they were in the 1950s, a tendency that, combined with changing taste, has limited the importance of Danish design in current markets.

D'Annunzio, Gabriele (1863–1938). Italian poet, novelist, patriot and adventurer. Born in Pescara on the Adriatic, he departed for Rome in 1881 and was soon established as a literary figure. His first poems, such as those in *Canto nuovo* (1882), were lyrical, colorful and idyllic. His earliest fiction, exemplified by the short stories in *Terra vergine* (1882), were realistic tales of his native Abruzzi region. D'Annunzio came under the influence of the French symbolists and decadents toward the end of the century and produced a number of rather superficial novels that celebrate the joys of sensuality. These include *Il piacere* (1889; tr. *The Child of Pleasure,* 1898) and *Il trionfo della morte* (1894; tr. *The Triumph of Death,* 1896). During this period D'Annunzio also began the romantic liaisons that made him one of the most controversial figures of his time. He married Duchess Maria Hardouin di Gallese in 1883 and in the mid-1890s began a celebrated affair with the actress Eleonora DUSE, a relationship erotically dissected in his *roman a clef, Il fuoco* (1900; tr. *The Flame of Life*). The affair also prompted him to write 18 plays, including *La citta morta* (1898; tr. *The Dead City,*

1902), *Francesca* (1902; tr. *Francesca da Rimini*) and *La figlia di Iorio* (1904; tr. *The Daughter of Jorio,* 1907). The poetry of the early 20th century, including the patriotic *Laudi* poems (1903–12) and the lushly sensuous *Alcione* (1904), are regarded as his most successful verse.

D'Annunzio lived in Paris from 1910 to 1915, returning home to urge his countrymen to join WORLD WAR I on the Allied side. During the war (1915–18), he fought with distinction as a daring flyer. In 1919, he led 1,000 troops in a raid on the Adriatic port of Fiume, ruling the city until 1921, while wearing the black shirts and using the Roman salute that were later adopted as fascist emblems. The flamboyant D'Annunzio was an admirer of MUSSOLINI and the fascist movement, but he did not take part in their development and retired from politics after the Fiume adventure. His works continue to be admired for their linguistic skill, and he remains a romantic figure in European history.

D'Annunzio's War (1919–20). Italy and Yugoslavia both claimed the city of Fiume (RIJEKA) at World War I's end. Italian soldier-poet Gabriele D'ANNUNZIO (1863–1938), believing it was Italy's, led an expedition of black-shirted troops into Fiume, September 12, 1919, and occupied it. His autocratic rule was opposed by Italy. The Treaty of RAPALLO between Italy and Yugoslavia (November 12, 1920) established Fiume as a free state, causing D'Annunzio to declare war on Italy. He was forced to evacuate by an Italian bombardment, December 27, 1920, and turmoil ensued until a fascist coup overthrew the local government in 1922. Then Italian troops occupied the city. In 1947 Fiume was awarded to Yugoslavia.

Dansgaard, Willi (1922–). Danish meteorologist. Dansgaard was educated at the University of Copenhagen, earning his Ph.D. in 1961. He has studied the applications of environmental isotopes to meteorological, hydrological and glaciological problems and in particular to the climate of the last 100,000 years. In the early 1960s the U.S. Army drilled down into the Greenland icecap, producing an ice core 4,600 feet (1,400 m) long and with a 100,000–year history. Dansgaard realized that by making careful measurement of the core's varying oxygen-18 level he should be able to reconstruct the climatic history of the last 100,000 years. The most recent ice age, ending 10,000 years ago, was clearly marked, as was evidence of a weather cycle during the last 1,000 years.

Dantzig, Rudi van (1933–). Dutch dancer, choreographer and company director. Dantzig made his debut with the Ballet Recital Company in 1952, and was one of the founders of the Netherlands Dance Theatre in 1959. Joining the artistic staff of the Dutch National Ballet in 1965, he became codirector in 1969, then sole artistic director (since 1971). He helped develop a company style, and the company achieved international fame with his work, *Monument for a Dead Boy* (1965). Other major works include *Epitaph* (1969), *Painted Birds* (1971) and *The Ropes of Time* (1970), especially created for Rudolph NUREYEV.

Danzig corridor. See GDANSK.

Dardanelles [Hellespont]. Strait running southwest to northeast between Europe and Asia, uniting the Aegean Sea with the Sea of Marmara and the Bosporus. It is strategically and commercially prominent because, with the Sea of Marmara and the Bosporus, it joins the Black and Mediterranean seas and has been the entrance to Istanbul (Constantinople) for Westerners. Its perennial strategic prominence grew as Russia came to dominate the Black Sea region in the 18th century, while the Ottoman Empire began its ultimately fatal decline. A compact of July 1841, reasserted by the Peace of Paris after the Crimean War in 1856, forbade alien warships from entering the strait without Turkish consent. But in 1914, at the beginning of WORLD WAR I, Admiral Carden led an Anglo-French armada that attempted to occupy the Dardanelles preparatory to attacking the enemy Turks at Constantinople. The postwar Treaty of SEVRES in 1920 demilitarized and internationalized the straits area. In 1923 the TREATY OF LAUSANNE substantiated the demilitarization but restored the strait to Turkish authority; the 1936 Montreux Convention accepted the refortification of the strait, which Turkey had already accomplished covertly. Further adaptations were made during WORLD WAR II to allow the Allies to carry supplies to the U.S.S.R. After the war, the Soviets tried to acquire more advantages but failed. The strait continues under Turkish control.

Australian soldier carries a wounded comrade out of harm's way in the Dardanelles (1915).

Dardanelles Campaign (Gallipoli Campaign). Military campaign waged in 1915, during WORLD WAR I, between the allies and the Turks. Britain and France wanted to control the straits of the Dardanelles and ISTANBUL, so that they could supply their wartime ally, Russia. After naval attacks failed to dislodge the Turks in February 1915, the Allies (mainly Australian and New Zealand forces) launched a land attack, including naval bombardment, on the Gallipoli Peninsula, landing at two points north and south. The Turks, firmly entrenched and aided by German artillery and officers, could not be dislodged. Three bloody battles waged between April and June 1915 gained and lost the Allies a few thousand yards, and another assault in August was also futile. In December 1915 the Allied high command, acknowledging the hopelessness of the campaign, evacuated their disease-ridden troops. First Lord of the (British) Admiralty Winston CHURCHILL was made a scapegoat for the failed campaign that he had urged and was forced to resign from the British government.

Dar-Es-Salaam. Port city and capital of TANZANIA, on the Indian Ocean 45 miles south of ZANZIBAR. It was founded in 1862 by the sultan of Zanzibar, who constructed a palace for himself, and it continued as a fishing hamlet until 1882, when it was came under German control. It was named capital of German East Africa in 1891, but WORLD WAR I saw its occupation by Great Britain in 1916. The city became capital of Tanganyika, which became independent in 1961, and continued as capital after Tanganyika joined with Zanzibar in 1964 to become Tanzania.

Dario, Ruben [Felix Ruben Garcia Sarmiento] (1867–1916). Nicaraguan poet, novelist and journalist. Significant as the architect of Spanish MODERNISM, Dario, whose work is relatively unknown in the U.S., is critically acclaimed as among the foremost writers in the world. Dario worked as a correspondent for various South and Central American newspapers and spent much of his life traveling and living outside of Nicaragua. His most important works are the collections of poetry and short stories *Azul* (1888), *Prosas profanos, y otros* (1896, translated as *Prosas profanos and Other Poems*) and *Cantos de vida y esperanza* (1905; "songs of life and hope"), which evidence a shift away from the romantic tradition.

Darkness at Noon. Novel by Arthur KOESTLER, published in England in 1941. An indictment of communist TOTALITARIANISM, which Koestler had rejected in 1938, the novel depicts the crushing regime of "No. 1" and its arrest and eventual execution of N.S. Rubashov. Rubashov is Koestler's fictional amalgamation of the victims of the show trials that took place during the GREAT PURGE in the U.S.S.R. The book, originally written in German, exposes Joseph STALIN's betrayal of the Russian Revolution.

Darlan, Jean Francois (1881–1942). French admiral and political figure. A career officer, he was a naval commander in WORLD WAR I, executive head of the French navy from 1933 to 1939 and, after that date, commander in chief. His service was the only one in the French military that did not surrender to Germany in 1940. A collaborator, Darlan became foreign minister and vice premier in PETAIN'S VICHY government, and was slated to be the elderly marshal's successor. However, after Pierre LAVAL returned to power in 1942, Darlan was sent to North Africa as French military commander. In Algiers during the Allied landings in November of that year, he again shifted his loyalties, coming to an agreement with U.S. General Mark CLARK and ordering the end of French resistance. He was assassinated by an antifascist Frenchman in 1942.

Darling, J.N. ("Ding") (1876–1962). U.S. political cartoonist and "Father of Conservation." He gained fame drawing political cartoons that depicted national events and human weaknesses. He won the PULITZER PRIZE for editorial cartooning twice, in 1923 and 1943. Darling began his career as a reporter but turned to cartooning in 1901. In 1906 he joined the staff of the *Des Moines Register* where he remained until 1949 (except for 1911–13 when he worked for the *New York Globe*). His cartoons went into syndication in 1917 and appeared in as many as 135 papers. A leader in America's conservation movement, he worked for the establishment of wildlife preservation laws, migratory waterfowl refuges and soil conservation. Among the best collections of his work is the one maintained by the University of Iowa in Iowa City.

Darrow, Clarence (Seward) (1857–1938). American criminal attorney, best remembered for his defense of John Scopes in the famous SCOPES TRIAL, also known as the Monkey Trial (1925). Darrow was perhaps the most celebrated trial attorney of his day, defending both mobsters and businessmen. His most famous client was Eugene DEBS, the socialist labor leader. He also successfully defended the notorious killers LEOPOLD AND LOEB, winning them life sentences instead of the death penalty. Darrow's methods of cross-examination and his appeals to juries were legendary. Darrow volunteered to help the AMERICAN CIVIL LIBERTIES UNION (ACLU) defend John Scopes, a Tennessee teacher who agreed to challenge the state's law prohibiting the teaching of the theory of evolution. The trial gained international attention, pitting Darrow against three-time Democratic presidential candidate William Jennings BRYAN, who railed against Darwin and his theory.

For further reading:

Weinberg, Arthur, *Clarence Darrow: A Sentimental Rebel*. New York: Macmillan, 1987.

Dart, Raymond Arthur (1893–1988). Australian-born anatomist. Dart revolutionized the study of human origins when, in 1924, he discovered the first early human fossil to be found in Africa. Prior to that time, evolutionists had believed that humans developed in Asia. Dart's theory was not widely accepted until Louis LEAKEY confirmed the African origin of humankind with a series of discoveries after World War II. Dart served for many years as professor and dean of the medical school at the University of Witwatersrand in South Africa.

Darwin. Capital city and chief harbor of Australia's Northern Territory, on Beagle Gulf, a waterway of the Timor Sea. Settled in 1869, Darwin was known as Palmerston until 1911. In WORLD WAR II it was Allied headquarters in northern Australia and was heavily bombed by Japan in 1942.

Dash, Jack (1907–1989). British communist. Dash played a leading role in a series of major dock strikes in London from 1945 through 1969. Although he held no official union post, he organized workers as head of his own unofficial liaison committee. Opponents often denounced him as an agitator and a troublemaker.

Dashnaktsutyun. The "Confederacy" party, commonly called Dashnaks, was a national revolutionary grouping founded in Turkish Armenia in 1890. The party started out to recruit Russian Armenians, with the aim of establishing an independent state of Great Armenia. When Czar NICHOLAS II closed many Armenian schools, libraries and newspaper offices in 1903, and took over the property of the Armenian Church, the Dashnaks carried out a policy of civil disobedience in RUSSIA in 1903–05. They supported the provisional government but were opposed to the Bolshevik Revolution Party in the independent Armenian republic of 1918–20, which became the chief party. Even today the party is in existence and aims at achieving an independent Armenia.

Dassault, Marcel [born Marcel Bloch] (1892–1986). French aircraft designer. His career as a designer and builder of both civil and military aircraft spanned most of the century. The best known of all his planes was probably the Mirage, the delta-winged jet fighter that gained world attention when it was used by the Israeli Air Force during the SIX-DAY WAR in 1967. Twice his manufacturing operations were nationalized by French left-wing governments, and, as a Jew, he was stripped of his business interests during WORLD WAR II. Despite this, at the time of his death he was one of the richest men in France. He was also the oldest member of the French parliament, having served almost uninterruptedly since 1951.

Daudet, Leon (1867–1942). French novelist, memoirist and journalist. Daudet, who was the son of the renowned 19th-century story writer Alphonse Daudet, wrote several novels and plays as well as an autobiography (1925), but he never came close to equaling the literary success of his father. Daudet did succeed, however, in making his mark as a political journalist. In 1908 Daudet took over the editorship of the right-wing journal *L'Action Francaise,* in which he called for a restoration of the French monarchy and published vehemently anti-Semitic essays (see ACTION FRANCAISE and ANTI-SEMITISM). Daudet, who served on the Chamber of Deputies from 1919 to 1924, was a severe critic of the democratic French Third Republic in the years between the two world wars.

Daugherty, Carroll R(oop) (1900–1988). U.S. economist and labor arbitrator. During WORLD WAR II, he headed the Wage Stabilization Division of the War Labor Board. After the war, Daugherty led negotiations to settle LEND-LEASE differences between the U.S. and New Zealand. In 1949, as chairman of a U.S. presidential panel seeking to avert a national steel strike, he proposed a noncontributory pension plan for steel workers that set the trend for expanding labor welfare benefits in private industry. A professor emeritus at Northwestern University, where he taught from 1946 to 1968, he was the author of seven college texts on labor matters. He retired from arbitration practice in 1983 after becoming widely known for his *Seven Tests for Just Cause.*

Daugherty, Harry M. (1860–1941). American politician who was reputedly involved in the infamous TEAPOT DOME SCANDAL that rocked the reputation of the administration of President Warren HARDING. Daugherty, a Cleveland lawyer and member of the Ohio legislature with Warren Harding, was a longtime Harding supporter and managed Harding's successful nomination and campaign for the presidency. In gratitude, Harding named Daugherty as his attorney general. Rumors of corruption quickly arose, and Daugherty was accused of benefiting from a less than vigorous enforcement of PROHIBITION regulations; he was already unliked for his vigorous antilabor stance and for packing the Justice Department with questionable men. After Harding's sudden death, Daugherty refused a congressional investigation's efforts to see his department's files. President COOLIDGE dismissed Daugherty from his post in March 1924. Two 1927 trials for conspiring to defraud the government ended in hung juries. He died in 1941.

Dausset, Jean (1916–). French physician and immunologist. Dausset, the son of a doctor, earned his M.D. from the University of Paris in 1945 following wartime service in the blood transfusion unit. He was professor of hematology at the University of Paris from 1958 and professor of immunohematology from 1968. In 1977 he was elected professor of experimental medicine at the College de France.

Dausset's war experience stimulated his interest in transfusion reactions, and in 1951 he showed that the blood of certain universal donors (those of blood group O), which had been assumed safe to use in all transfusions, could nonetheless be dangerous. This was because of the presence of strong immune antibodies in their plasma, which develop following antidiptheria and antitetanus injections. Donor blood is now systematically tested for such antibodies. In the 1950s Dausset noticed a peculiar feature in the histories of patients who had received a number of blood transfusions: They developed a low white blood cell (leukocyte) count. He suspected that the transfused blood might have contained antigens that stimulated the production of antibodies against the leukocytes. With insight and considerable courage Dausset went on to claim that the antigen on the blood cells, soon to be known as the HLA or human lymphocyte antigen, was the equivalent of the mouse H-2 system described by George Snell.

The significance of Dausset's work was enormous. It meant that tissues could be typed quickly and cheaply by simple blood agglutination tests as opposed to the complicated and lengthy procedure of seeing if skin grafts would take. Such work made the technically feasible operation of kidney transplantation a practical medical option, for at last the danger of rejection could be minimized by rapid, simple and accurate tissue typing. Dausset shared the 1980 NOBEL PRIZE for physiology or medicine with Snell and Baruj Benacerraf.

Davao. Port city in Davao del Sur province, on the southeastern end of Mindanao island in the Philippines. Established in 1849, in the 20th century it was cultivated as part of a Japanese settlement. Davao was captured by the Japanese navy on Dec. 20, 1941, and served as a base for naval operations in INDONESIA. It was attacked by U.S. forces in September 1944 and, after much conflict, recaptured by the Allies in May 1945.

Davenport, Charles Benedict (1866–1944). American zoologist and geneticist. Davenport earned a Ph.D. in zoology at Harvard in 1892, where he taught until 1899. From 1901 until 1904 he was curator of the Zoological Museum at the University of Chicago and from 1904 until 1934 was director of the Carnegie Institution's Department of Genetics at Cold Spring Harbor, N.Y. In 1910 Davenport founded the Eugenics Record Office, directing it until 1934. Davenport carried out early studies of animal genetics, using chickens and canaries, at the turn of the century. He was among the first to accept Gregor Mendel's rediscovered theory of heredity. He later turned his attention to man, and in *Heredity in Relation to Eugenics* (1912) offered evidence for the inheritance of particular human traits, suggesting that the application of genetic principles to human breeding might improve the race (eugenics). From 1898 Davenport was assistant editor of the *Journal of Experimental Zoology;* he was also editor of both *Genetics* and the *Journal of Physical Anthropology*.

Davidson, Jo (1883–1952). American sculptor. Born in New York City, Davidson studied at the Art Students League there and at the Ecole des Beaux-Arts, Paris. He was a consummate portraitist who worked in an expressive and naturalistic style, mainly in bronze, to capture the personalities of his sitters. Davidson portrayed many of the most celebrated people of his time, diverse figures that included Woodrow WILSON, George Bernard SHAW, Mohandas K. GANDHI, Franklin D. ROOSEVELT, Albert EINSTEIN, Benito MUSSOLINI, Will ROGERS, Rabindranath TAGORE and Gertrude STEIN. His philosophy of sculpture and his encounters with the celebrated are detailed in his 1951 autobiography, *Between Sittings*.

Davie, Donald (Alfred) (1922–). English poet and critic. Born in Yorkshire, Davie studied at Cambridge (B.A., 1947; M.A., 1949; Ph.D., 1951), where he came under the influence of F.R. LEAVIS. He served in the Royal Navy in World War II and therafter taught at a number of British and American universities. Davie is a literary traditionalist who believes the poet is responsible "for purifying and correcting the spoken language." Among his collections are *Brides of Reason* (1955), *A Winter Talent* (1957), *Essex Poems* (1969) and *In the Stopping Train* (1977). His poems tend to be erudite, abstract, philosophical and highly precise in their use of language. His criticism includes studies of Scott, HARDY, POUND, the Augustans and Boris PASTERNAK.

Davies, Sir Peter Maxwell (1934–). British composer and conductor. Born in Manchester, England, Davies attended the Royal Manchester College of Music and Manchester University. While studying composition in Rome he won the Olivetti Prize (1958). In the early 1960s he studied with Roger SESSIONS at Princeton University. In 1967 in England he formed a chamber ensemble, The Fires of London, to perform his works. In the early 1970s, Davies went to live in the Orkney Islands, off the northernmost tip of Scotland. Much of the music he has written since then reflects the rugged landscape, seascape and local traditions of this isolated region. One of the most gifted and accessible British composers of his generation, Maxwell Davies has written many works in response to commissions. His compositions include *Ave Maris Stella* (1975), two operas, four symphonies and numerous concertos, orchestral works and chamber pieces.

Davies, (William) Robertson (1913–). Canadian author. Davies was born in Ontario and educated at Upper Canada College, Toronto University, Queen's University (Kingston), and Balliol College, Oxford. He began his career as an actor and teacher with the Old Vic Company, London, and subsequently worked in Canada as an editor, publisher and professor of English. Davies' first three novels, *Tempest-Tossed* (1951), *Leaven of Malice* (1959) and *A Mixture of Frailties* (1960), known as the Salterton Trilogy, were well received, but he achieved both critical and popular success with the Deptford Trilogy: *Fifth Business* (1970), *The Manticore* (1972) and *World of Wonders* (1976), which follow the lives of three men connected by an incident in their childhood home of Deptford. Davies' writing, which some say is theatrical, explores the choices between good and evil and evidences his interest in Jungian psychology (see JUNG). While contemporary, his fiction is rich in myth and folklore and is often very funny. Other fiction includes *The Rebel Angels* (1982), *What's Bred in the Bone* (1985) and *The Lyre of Orpheus* (1989). Davies has also written numerous plays, including *Questions Time* (1975) and *Pontiac and the Green Man* (1977), and written newspaper articles under the pseudonym Samuel Marchbanks.

Davis, Angela (Yvonne) (1944–). Black American radical political activist. Davis studied philosophy with Herbert MARCUSE and became involved in radical Marxist politics and the BLACK POWER movement in California in the 1960s. She joined the Communist Party (1968) and was hired by the philosophy department at the University of California in Los Angeles (1969). A furor ensued, and her contract was not renewed at the end of the year. Davis next became involved in a case involving the "Soledad brothers," three black convicts in California. Using guns that Davis owned, a brother of one of the convicts entered a courtroom and seized five hostages. A shootout ensued, in which the gunman, the judge and two inmates were killed. Because she owned the guns, Davis was indicted on charges of murder, kidnapping and conspiracy. She went into hiding and was placed on the FBI's 10–most-wanted list. She was arrested in October 1970, and her trial finally began in March 1972. She was acquitted but remained a focus of controversy. In many ways her case was a microcosm of the political and racial tensions of the late 1960s and early '70s in the U.S.

For further reading:

Davis, Angela, *Angela Davis: An Autobiography*. 1974.

Davis, Benjamin O(liver), Sr. (1877–1970). U.S. military officer. After studying at Howard University (1897), Davis became a lieutenant of volunteers in the Spanish-American War. In 1899 he enlisted in the regular army as a private and rose to the rank of lieutenant in the Philippine service. Davis served as military attache in Liberia (1909–12). He taught at several universities until 1938 when he was given his first independent command, the 369th New York National Guard Infantry Regiment. Despite much criticism based on race and politics, Davis became the first black general in the U.S. Army in 1940, and assistant to the inspector general of the Army in 1941. He served in Europe in WORLD WAR II as an adviser on race relations; he retired in 1948. Davis is the father of retired Air Force General Benjamin Oliver DAVIS Jr.

Davis, Benjamin O(liver), Jr. (1912–). American military officer. The first black graduate of West Point (1936), Davis served as an infantry officer before joining the U.S. Air Force. A distinguished combat pilot during WORLD WAR II, he led the all-black 99th Fighter Squadron (known as the "Tuskegee Airmen") in combat over North Africa and Italy and played a key role in the air war at the battle of Anzio. After leading an integrated fighter force in the KOREAN WAR, Davis became the first black general in the U.S. Air Force in 1954. (In 1940 his father, Benjamin Oliver DAVIS Sr., had become the first black general in the U.S. Army.) In 1961 Davis was appointed director of airpower and organization in the USAF. He com-

Brig. Gen. Benjamin O. Davis Sr., the first black U.S. general, on duty in France during World War II (Aug. 8, 1944).

manded the 13th Air Force during the VIETNAM WAR. He retired in 1970 as a three-star general.

For further reading:

Davis, Benjamin O., Jr., *Benjamin O. Davis, Jr., American: An Autobiography*. Washington, D.C.: Smithsonian, 1991.

Davis, Bette [Ruth Elizabeth Davis] (1908–1989). Legendary American HOLLYWOOD movie star. Born in Massachusetts, Davis worked in small theater companies in New England until she broke into the Broadway theater in the late 1920s. She quickly moved on to Hollywood; although her screen test with Samuel GOLDWYN's studio failed to impress, she played bit roles in pictures at UNIVERSAL, then signed a contract with WARNER BROS., where she remained from 1930 to 1949. There she established a reputation for playing tough, independent women who defied convention. Among her best known films were *Of Human Bondage* (1934), *The Private Lives of Elizabeth and Essex* (1939), *Dark Victory* (1941), *All About Eve* (1950) and *What Ever Happened to Baby Jane?* (1962). She also appeared in several stage roles and, later in her career, in made-for-television movies. Altogether, she made more than 80 films, was nominated for 10 ACADEMY AWARDS, and won the best actress prize twice, for *Dangerous* (1935) and *Jezebel* (1938).

Davis, Edwin Weyerhaeuser (1895–1962). U.S. business executive. As director of the University of Minnesota Bureau of Mines Experiment Station, Davis after years of work developed the inexpensive concentration process that made taconite mining practical. The process, commercially activated in 1955, is known as Beneficiating. This process has been of enormous help to the area and to United States industry.

Davis, Elmer (1890–1958). U.S. broadcast journalist and author. A writer of international note, Davis was a teacher at the Franklin Indiana High School (1909–10), and part of the editorial staff, first at the legendary all-fiction pulp magazine *Adventure* (1913–14) and then at the *New York Times* (1914–24). He was a news analyst for the Columbia Broadcasting System (1939–42) when he became director of the Office of War Information, for which he received the Medal of Merit. He worked at the American Broadcasting Company as a news analyst, from 1945 to 1956. His famous works include *But We Were Born Free* (1953) and *Two Minutes Till Midnight* (1955).

Davis, Francis W. (1887–1978). American inventor. Among his 40 patented inventions was power steering, which he developed in 1926. However, power steering was not adopted as a feature on American cars until 1950.

Davis, John W(illiam) (1873–1955). U.S. lawyer and politician. Davis received both his bachelor (1892) and law (1895) degrees from Washington and Lee University. After election to Congress from West Virginia (1910), he resigned to become solicitor general of the U.S. (1913), simultaneously serving as counselor for the RED CROSS. In 1918, Davis served at a conference in Switzerland concerned with the treatment of World War I PRISONERS OF WAR, and then served as ambassador to Great Britain (1918–21). After election to the presidency of the American Bar Association (1922), he won the Democratic presidential nomination (1924) but was soundly defeated in the election by Calvin COOLIDGE. Davis then returned to private practice. He took 140 cases to the Supreme Court, often without a fee.

For further reading:

Harbaugh, William H., *Lawyer's Lawyer: The Life of John W. Davis*. New York: Oxford University Press, 1973.

Davis, Miles (1926–). Trumpeter-bandleader; perhaps the single most influential figure in postwar jazz due to his introduction and popularization of such significant styles as cool jazz, MODAL JAZZ, jazz-rock and FUSION. Originally inspired by the BEBOP revolutionary and alto saxophonist Charlie PARKER, Davis left his hometown of East St. Louis, Illinois, in 1944 to find his idol in New York City. Parker took the youngster under his wing, and Davis appeared in live and recorded performances with Parker in 1945–48. In 1959, Davis collaborated with arranger Gil Evans in a seminal set of recordings issued as *Birth of the Cool,* thus establishing the "cool" sensibility as one of the dominant styles of the 1950s; Davis turned his back on the movement and instead organized a fiery bop-based quintet. This group, with some modifications, recorded "Kind of Blue" (1959), setting the pace for the modal approach, a dominant force in 1960s' modern jazz. By the early 1970s, Davis had discarded standard tunes such as "Bye Bye Blackbird," a staple of his repertory for nearly two decades, in favor of an evolving style that amalgamated elements from funk, rock and modality; there was an increased reliance on electronic instruments as well. Davis' current work continues in his fusionistic vein. In addition to his status as a stylistic innovator, Davis helped introduce such pivotal contemporary musicians as keyboardists Herbie HANCOCK and Chick COREA, saxophonist Wayne Shorter, guitarist John SCOFIELD and drummer Tony Williams.

For further reading:

Chambers, Jack, *Milestones 1: The Music and Times of Miles Davis to 1960* and *Milestones 2: The Sound and Times of Miles Davis Since 1960*. New York: William Morrow, 1983, 1985.

Carr, Ian, *Miles Davis: A Critical Biography*. New York: Morrow, 1982.

Davis, Sammy, Jr. (1925–1990). American entertainer. Davis' energy and versatility as a singer, dancer, actor and nightclub entertainer made him one of the first black performers to win widespread acclaim from white audiences. He began his career in a family VAUDEVILLE group at age three, and became the group's star performer. A car accident in 1954 led to the loss of his left eye and his widely publicized conversion to Judaism. He appeared in the 1959 film version of PORGY AND BESS, and starred in the Broadway shows *Mr. Wonderful* (1956) and *Golden Boy* (1964). In the 1960s he became a member of, and often performed with, the "Rat Pack," a group of fast-living, hard-drinking, womanizing HOLLYWOOD performers led by Frank SINATRA. He wrote two autobiographies, *Yes I Can* (1965) and *Why Me?* (1989).

Davis, William Morris (1850–1934). American physical geographer. Davis was

Trumpeter Miles Davis has been at the forefront of virtually every major stylistic innovation in postwar jazz.

Entertainer and actor Sammy Davis Jr. was one of the first black performers to gain fame among white audiences.

educated at Harvard, where he returned to teach in 1877 after a period as a meteorologist in Argentina and as an assistant with the North Pacific Survey. He became professor of physical geography in 1890 and of geology in 1898. Davis is acknowledged as the founder of the science of **geomorphology,** the study of landforms. He introduced what later became known as the Davisian system of landscape analysis. His aim was to provide an explanatory description of how landforms change. His most important contribution to this was his introduction of the "cycle of erosion" into geographical thought. He proposed a complete cycle of youth, maturity and old age to describe the evolution of a landscape. Davis also produced an influential work, *Elementary Meteorology* (1894), which was used as a textbook for over 30 years, and in 1928 published *The Coral Reef Problem.*

Davisson, Clinton Joseph (1881–1958). American physicist. Davisson was educated at the University of Chicago and at Princeton, where he earned his Ph.D. in 1911. After working for a short period at the Carnegie Institute of Technology in Pittsburgh, Davisson joined the Bell Telephone Laboratory (then Western Electric) in 1917 and remained there until his retirement in 1946. In 1937 he shared the NOBEL PRIZE for physics with George Thomson for "their experimental discovery of the diffraction of electrons by crystals."

Dawes, Charles Gates (1865–1951). American lawyer and banker; vice president of the UNITED STATES (1925–29). During WORLD WAR I, Dawes served as the head of procurement (purchasing) for the U.S. forces in Europe (1917–18). In the early 1920s he was the chief architect of the DAWES PLAN to reschedule GERMANY'S postwar reparations, thereby helping Germany to survive an economic crisis. For this, Dawes received the 1925 NOBEL PRIZE for peace. A Republican, he was chosen as Calvin COOLIDGE'S vice presidential running mate in 1924 and was elected to that office. During Herbert HOOVER'S administration, Dawes was the U.S. ambassador to Britain.

Dawes Plan. In 1924, American banker Charles Dawes (later vice president of the U.S.) presented a plan to ease GERMANY'S WORLD WAR I reparations payments. The TREATY OF VERSAILLES had set Germany's reparations at $33 billion; however, postwar inflation and other problems confronting the young WEIMAR REPUBLIC resulted in great economic hardship. The Dawes Plan did not reduce Germany's debt but did provide for an international loan, set fixed payments and reorganized the German state bank in order to stabilize the currency. The mark, which had inflated to 4.2 trillion to the dollar, was replaced by the rentenmark (4.2 to the dollar). The plan was superseded by the YOUNG PLAN in 1929, but Germany defaulted on its debts during the GREAT DEPRESSION.

Dawidowicz, Lucy Schildkret (1915–1990). U.S. historian. Her book *The War Against the Jews* was considered a pioneering study of Nazi genocide. The book argued that the extermination of the JEWS had been one of the central aims of the Nazi program, not merely a secondary development. She also clashed with other historians of the HOLOCAUST in refusing to blame Jews for passivity in the face of the Nazi threat.

Dawkins, Richard (1941–). British ethologist. Dawkins was educated at the Oxford University where he worked for his doctorate under Niko TINBERGEN. He initially taught at the University of California, Berkeley, before returning to Oxford in 1970 as lecturer in animal behavior. In *The Selfish Gene* (1976) Dawkins did much to introduce the work of such scholars as William Hamilton, Robert L. Trivers and John Maynard Smith to a wider public. He tried to show that such apparently altruistic behavior as birds risking their lives to warn the flock of an approaching predator can be seen as the "selfish gene" ensuring its own survival (by ensuring the survival of the descendants and relatives of the "heroic" bird).

Day, Clarence "Hap" (1901–1990). Canadian hockey player and coach. Day spent most of his playing career as a defenseman with the Toronto Maple Leafs (1926–37), playing on one Stanley Cup winner in 1932. After finishing his career with the New York Americans, he returned to the Leafs as coach in 1940 and led them to four Stanley Cups in 10 years. Following his retirement from the organization in 1957, he entered private business.

Day, David Talbot (1859–1925). American chemist. Day was educated at Johns Hopkins University, earning his Ph.D. in 1894. He started his career as a demonstrator in chemistry at the University of Maryland but left to become head of the Mineral Resources Division of the U.S. Geological Survey in 1886. Day investigated the reasons for the differences found in the composition of various petroleum deposits. He did much to stimulate the growth of the petroleum industry and in 1922 produced one of its basic texts, *Handbook of the Petroleum Industry.* From 1914 to 1920 he was a consultant chemist with the Bureau of Mines.

Day, Dorothy (1897–1980). American Catholic social activist. A founder of the Catholic Worker Movement in 1933, Day influenced a generation of American priests, intellectuals and laymen. A devout Roman Catholic, she was also a nonviolent social radical who embraced a philosophy of voluntary poverty and care for the destitute through direct involvement. Her philosophy looked to the individual rather than to mass action to transform society. Active in the Church for more than 50 years, she founded many homes for the poor and homeless.

Day, William Rufus (1849–1923). Associate justice, U.S. Supreme Court (1903–22). A graduate of the University of Michigan, Day also attended the University of Michigan Law School before returning to his native Ohio to practice law. After serving as a local judge he was appointed a federal district court judge. He was named first assistant secretary of state by President McKinley, who had known him when both were attorneys in Ohio. After serving as a member of the Paris Peace Commission ending the Spanish-American War, he was appointed as a judge of the U.S. Court of Appeals for the Sixth Circuit. He was appointed to the U.S. Supreme Court by Theodore ROOSEVELT and served until 1922. He was briefly a member of the Mixed Claims Commission, settling World War I claims, until his death in 1923.

For further reading:

McLean, Joseph E., *William Rufus Day, Supreme Court Justice from Ohio.* Baltimore: Johns Hopkins, 1946.

Dayan, Moshe (1915–1981). Israeli military hero and politician. Born in PALESTINE and educated at the Hebrew University in JERUSALEM, he joined the Jewish defense force HAGANAH in the late 1930s. Imprisoned by the British (1939–41), he subsequently fought against Axis forces in Syria during WORLD WAR II, losing his left eye. After ISRAEL became independent (1948), he fought in the ARAB-ISRAELI WAR OF 1948–49, and as chief of staff (1953–58) directed the successful Sinai campaign in the ARAB-ISRAELI WAR OF 1956. He entered politics in 1958 and served in the cabinet of David BEN GURION. Named defense minister several days before the SIX DAY WAR (1976), he launched the attacks that brought speedy victory against EGYPT, JORDAN, and SYRIA. Criticized after Israeli reverses in the YOM KIPPUR WAR (1973), he left the cabinet after a dispute with the Labor prime minister, Golda MEIR (1974). He was named foreign minister by Menachem BEGIN in 1978 but resigned in 1979. A charismatic figure and a bril-

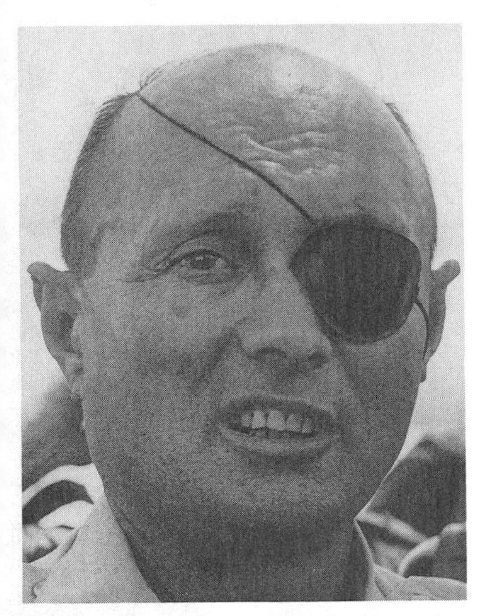

Israeli Defense Minister Moshe Dayan (July 3, 1967).

liant general, Dayan remained a legend even after the setbacks of his later years.

Day Lewis, C(ecil) (1904–1972). British poet, fiction writer, editor, translator. C. Day Lewis's decade of triumph was the proletarian 1930s when, along with AUDEN, SPENDER and (to a lesser degree) MACNEICE, he was a poet-propagandist for socialism in England. However, disillusioned by the events of WORLD WAR II and thereafter, he later returned to writing neo-Georgian verse (see the GEORGIANS). Although he also wrote criticism and children's books, edited anthologies and translated Vergil and VALERY, between 1935 and 1968 he supported himself primarily by producing detective fiction under the pseudonym **Nicholas Blake**. He also lectured at Oxford, Cambridge and Harvard. He was made C.B.E. (Commander, Order of the British Empire) in 1950. In 1968 he succeeded John Masefield as poet laureate of England. His son **Daniel Day Lewis** established a reputation as an accomplished film actor in the late 1980s, winning an ACADEMY AWARD as best actor in 1990.

Dayton. American city, 47 miles northeast of Cincinnati, Ohio. In 1913, after a devastating flood, Dayton was the first major U.S. city to embrace the commission-manager form of government. Aviation pioneers Orville and Wilbur WRIGHT came from Dayton, which became an early and leading center of aviation and aeronautical study. Wright-Patterson Air Force Base and Fairfield Air Depot are in Dayton.

DC-3. Douglas DC-3 airplane of 1934, which proved to be one of the most successful aircraft designs ever developed. Its predecessors, the DC-1, DC-2, and DST, were steps toward the development of the DC-3, all twin-engine, low-wing monoplanes of clean, streamlined form with retractable landing gear and a 21-passenger seating capacity. The success of the DC-3 made passenger air transportation reliable, practical, and widely available. The basic design of the DC-3 established the norm for passenger aircraft and became the basis for many similar designs by other manufacturers and for the gradually larger four-engine transport airplanes that succeeded it. Even modern jet aircraft owe much of their basic form to the DC-3. Including the military version (C-47), some 11,000 DC-3s were built. A surprising number remain in service, particularly in out-of-the-way locations where only short-runway airfields are available.

D-Day. See Invasion of NORMANDY.

DDT. Dichloro-diphenyl-trichloroethane, an insecticide developed by Swiss scientists in 1939–40. DDT was first heralded as a wonder insecticide that would destroy agricultural pests and thus help farmers increase their crop production. During the 1950s and '60s it was routinely sprayed on crops. However, many insects developed a resistance to DDT. Moreover, it was discovered that DDT entered the food cycle and poisoned birds and other animals, as well as contaminating fresh water supplies. The dangerous effects of DDT on the environment were chronicled by Rachel CARSON in her book *Silent Spring* (1962).

Deakin, Alfred (1856–1919). Australian statesman, three-time prime minister (1903–04, 1905–08, 1909–10). A noted lawyer, he served in the Victoria legislature from 1880 to 1899 and pressed for social, labor, tariff and agricultural reform. An advocate of the federation of Australian states, he became the Commonwealth of AUSTRALIA's attorney general in 1901. As prime minister, he initiated important health and old-age pension legislation.

Dean, Arthur H(obson) (1898–1987). American lawyer. While head of the prestigious New York law firm Sullivan & Cromwell, Dean served four U.S. presidents in various diplomatic and advisory capacities. During the ROOSEVELT administration he helped draft landmark securities laws. During the EISENHOWER administration he negotiated for seven weeks in 1953 on behalf of the U.S. and the UNITED NATIONS at talks in Panmunjom that tried to achieve a permanent political settlement to the KOREAN WAR. He conducted important disarmament negotiations during the KENNEDY administration. He later played a key role during the VIETNAM WAR, persuading President JOHNSON to stop the bombing of North VIETNAM in 1968 and to not seek reelection.

Dean, Christopher. See TORVILLE AND DEAN.

Dean, James (1931–1955). American actor; burst into sudden HOLLYWOOD stardom in the 1950s and died at age 24 in an automobile crash. Dean remains an icon of American popular culture in much the same manner as a contemporary Hollywood figure, Marilyn MONROE. He starred in only three films: *East of Eden* (1954) (based on the novel by John STEINBECK), *Rebel Without a Cause* (1955) and *Giant* (1956). In each film Dean portrayed an archetypically rebellious American young man with thick, swept-back hair, piercing eyes and a sneer that could transform suddenly into a vulnerable smile. It is more as an image—one that has graced millions of posters and postcards—than as an imitated actor that Dean has survived in American popular culture to this day.

Dean, Jay Hanna "Dizzy" (1911–1974). American baseball player. Dean joined the world champion "Gas House Gang" St. Louis Cardinals in 1932. An outstanding all-around player, he led the National League in strikeouts his first year, was a stellar fielder, and a solid hitter with a .258 average. He won 102 games over four seasons. His brother Paul ("Daffy") joined the club in 1934 and the two combined for 49 wins. Dizzy led the team to the pennant, and finished the season with two World Series wins. He was traded to the Cubs in 1938 and posted a 7–1 record. He was beloved by fans not only for his skill but also for his colorful personality and cocksure ways. After his retirement, he was a TV commentator for more than 20 years.

Dean, John (Wesley) III (1938–). A minor functionary in the Nixon White House, Dean played a key role in the WATERGATE scandal. As counsel to President Richard M. NIXON from July 1970 to April 1973, he became deeply involved in the coverup. However, fearing prosecution for his own role in the affair, he began to cooperate with federal prosecutors in April 1973. The star witness of

The Douglas DC-3 is the most widely used aircraft in aviation history.

White House aide John Dean testifies in front of the Senate Watergate Committee (June 25, 1973).

Senator Sam ERVIN's Watergate Committee, he was the first administration official to accuse Nixon of direct involvement. Dean testified that, under the direction of Nixon aides H.R. Haldeman and John Ehrlichman, he had managed the day-to-day coverup of the affair and supervised payments of "hush money" to the convicted Watergate burglars. Dean also revealed that the White House kept an "enemies list" of prominent administration critics whom it wished to discredit. Dean received a mild sentence for his part in the affair and served only four months in prison.

For further reading:

Dean, John, *Blind Ambition: The White House Years*. New York: Simon & Schuster, 1976.

De Andrade, Mario Pinto (1928–1990). Angolan writer and historian. He was one of the founders of the Angolan nationalist movement. As the first head of the Popular Movement for the Liberation of ANGOLA, from 1960 to 1974, he helped the country's struggle against Portuguese rule. He became disillusioned with the movement's authoritarian tendencies and split from it a year before Angola gained its independence in 1975.

Dearborn. City in U.S. state of Michigan, 10 miles west of Detroit. Dearborn is the center of research, engineering and manufacturing for the Ford Motor Company. Henry FORD opened his River Rouge plant here in 1917; Dearborn became incorporated as a city in 1927.

Death in Venice. Classic 1911 novella by German author Thomas MANN. The fictional protagonist is Gustave von Aschenbach, a famous but aging author with impeccable work habits who has resolved to take a restful vacation in Venice for the sake of his health. But von Aschenbach is soon distracted by Tadzio, a beautiful boy of 14, with whom he falls chastely in love. The central theme of *Death in Venice* is the painful clash between disciplined artistic creation and wayward passion, which ultimately undermines all values and beckons toward nothingless by virtue of its mindless intensity. While von Aschenbach resists overt advances toward Tadzio, he becomes obsessed by the boy and loses the will to return to the ordered pattern of his previous life. At the end of the novella, the heartsick von Aschenbach dies in a cholera epidemic that sweeps through Venice.

Death of a Salesman. Classic drama by American playwright Arthur MILLER, regarded by many critics as the greatest American play of the 20th century. Miller intended it as a new kind of tragedy: "I believe that the common man is as apt a subject for tragedy in its highest sense as kings were." The basic plot concerns the decline of Willy Loman, a onetime bustling salesman who was inspired by the American Dream of success. Now forsaken by his employer, Loman (note the allegorical last name) is alternately pitied and disrespected by his two sons, Biff and Happy. Only his wife Linda remains loyal, but she cannot save him from his descent into escapist fantasy and ultimate despair. Loman ultimately kills himself in a car accident so his family can have the insurance money. *Death of a Salesman* opened on Broadway on Feb. 10, 1949, directed by Elia KAZAN, with Lee J. Cobb as Loman. The action roams freely through time and space; at Miller's instructions, designer Jo Mielziner created a set—Willy's house—whose rooms could instantly be transformed into other locations—hotel room, office, cemetery. The play is both realistic in its study of a man's professional decline and expressionistic in its projection of a psychological crisis. Frederick March played Willy in the 1951 film version. Perhaps the most memorable of the many stage revivals was one starring Dustin HOFFMAN (1984); it was filmed for television in 1985 by German director Volker Schlondorff. *Death of a Salesman* has become a staple play in the repertoire of theater companies around the world.

de Beauvoir, Simone (1908–1986). French philosopher, novelist and essayist. Born in Paris, Beauvoir was one of France's most esteemed writers and was also well-known for her left-wing political views and iconoclastic personal life. Her writing embraces EXISTENTIALISM and reflects her rejection of her religious up-bringing. Her fiction includes *L'invitee* (1943, translated as *She Came to Stay*, 1949), which depicts a leftist intellectual and his two lovers; *Les Mandarins* (1954), which is based on her love affair with Nelson ALGREN and won the Prix Goncourt; and *Quand Prime Le Spirituel* (1979, translated as *When Things of the Spirit Come First*, 1982), a collection of early short fiction. She is, arguably, best known for the landmark feminist essay *Le Deuxieme Sexe* (1949, *The Second Sex*, 1953), which has enormously influenced subsequent feminist criticism. Beauvoir was an early champion of abortion rights, safety for factory workers and the rights of the elderly. In *La Vieillesse* (1970, translated as *The Coming of Age*, 1972), she assails Western society's treatment of the aged. She was a lifelong companion of Jean-Paul SARTRE, about whom she wrote in *Adieux: A Farewell to Sartre* (1984).

French philosopher Simone de Beauvoir, best known for her influential feminist work The Second Sex *(1964).*

For further reading:

Bair, Deirdre, *Simone de Beauvoir: A Biography*. New York: Summit Books, 1990.

de Beer, Sir Gavin Rylands (1899–1972). British zoologist. De Beer graduated from Oxford University, where he was a fellow from 1923 to 1938. He served in both world wars; during WORLD WAR II he landed in Normandy in 1944, where he was in charge of psychological warfare. He was professor of embryology at University College, London (1945–50), and then director of the Natural History Museum in London (1950–60). In an early publication, *Introduction to Experimental Biology* (1926), de Beer finally disproved the germ-layer theory. He also did work to show that adult animals retain some of the juvenile characters of their evolutionary ancestors (*pedomorphosis*), thus refuting Ernst Haeckel's theory of recapitulation. De Beer also carried out research into the functions of the pituitary gland. In the field of ancient history, de Beer applied scientific methods to various problems, for example, the origin of the Etruscans and Hannibal's journey across the Alps. His other books include *Embryology and Evolution of Chordate Animals* (1962, with Julian HUXLEY), *The Elements of Experimental Embryology* (1962) and a biography of Charles Darwin (1961). He was knighted in 1954.

Debierne, Andre Louis (1874–1949). French chemist. Debierne was educated at the Ecole de Physique et Chemie. After graduation he worked at the Sorbonne and as an assistant to Pierre and Marie CURIE, finally succeeding the latter as director of the Radium Institute. On his retirement in 1949 he in turn was succeeded by Marie Curie's daughter, Irene JOLIOT-CURIE. Debierne was principally a radiochemist; his first triumph came in 1900 with the discovery of a new radioactive element, actinium, which he isolated while working with pitchblende. In 1905 he went on to show that actinium, like radium, formed helium. This was of some significance in helping Ernest RUTHERFORD to appreciate that some radioactive elements decay by emitting an alpha particle (or, as it turned out to be, the nucleus of a helium atom). In 1910, in collaboration with Marie Curie, he isolated pure metallic radium.

Deborin (Ioffe), Abram Moyseevich (1881–1963). Russian historian and philosopher. Deborin became a BOLSHEVIK in 1903, went over to the MENSHEVIKS in 1907, but eventually joined the COMMUNIST PARTY in 1928. He was editor of the chief Marxist philosophical journal, *Under the Banner of Marxism*, and secretary of the department for history and philosophy in the Academy of Sciences (1935–45). His writings argued against mechanical materialism, but he was condemned as a "Menshevik idealist." His works included *Introduction to the Philosophy of Dialectical Materialism* (1916); *Dictatorship of the Proletariat and the Theory of Marxism* (1927); *Dialectical Materialism* (1929); and *Lenin and the Crisis of Modern Physics* (1930).

Deboyne Islands. Volcanic island group in the Louisiade Archipelago, 110 miles southeast of New Guinea in the southwestern Pacific Ocean; a part of Papua New Guinea. A lagoon in the middle of this island chain held a Japanese seaplane base during WORLD WAR II. U.S. forces annihilated it after the Battle of the Coral Sea in May 1942.

de Broglie, Prince Louis Victor Pierre Raymond (1892–1987). French physicist. Educated at the Sorbonne as a historian, de Broglie's interest in science was aroused in World War I when he was posted to the Eiffel Tower as a member of a signals unit. He pursued this interest after the war and obtained a doctorate in physics from the Sorbonne in 1924. He taught there from 1926, serving as professor of theoretical physics at the newly founded Henri Poincare Institute (1928–62). De Broglie is famous for his theory that particles (matter) can have wavelike properties. At the start of the 20th century physicists explained phenomena in terms of particles (such as the electron or proton) and electromagnetic radiation (light, ultraviolet radiation, etc.). Particles were "matter," discrete entities forming atoms and molecules; electromagnetic radiation was a wave motion involving changing electric and magnetic fields. In 1905 two papers by Albert EINSTEIN began a change in this conventional view of the physical world. His work on the special theory of relativity led to the idea that matter is itself a form of energy. More specifically, he explained the photoelectric effect by the concept that electromagnetic radiation (a wave) can also behave as particles (photons).

In 1924 de Broglie, influenced by Einstein's work, put forward the converse idea—that, just as waves can behave as particles, particles can behave as waves. Experimental support was obtained independently by George Thomson and Clinton J. DAVISSON, and the wavelike behavior of particles was used by Erwin SCHRODINGER in his formulation of wave mechanics. Wave-particle duality—the fact that particles can behave as waves, and vice versa—has caused intense debate as to the "real" nature of particles and electromagnetic radiation. De Broglie took the view that there is a true, deterministic physical process underlying quantum mechanics—i.e., that the current indeterminate approach in terms of probability can be replaced by a more fundamental theory. He based his ideas on the concept of particles that are concentrations of energy guided through space by a real wave and exchanging energy with a "subquantum medium." De Broglie received the 1929 NOBEL PRIZE for physics for his "discovery of the wave nature of the electron."

Debs, Eugene V. (1855–1926). U.S. labor leader and Socialist Party presidential candidate. A locomotive fireman, he helped establish the first local lodge of the Brotherhood of Locomotive Firemen. Between 1880 and 1884 he was city clerk of Terre Haute, Ind., and in 1885 he became a member of the lower house of the Indiana legislature. Debs soon came to criticize social conditions, oppose unionization along craft lines, and form the American Railway Union—an organization open to all railroad workers. The union's strike against the Pullman Company resulted in violence in Chicago, and federal intervention. As a result, the union was destroyed and Debs and several associates were sent to jail for six months on contempt of court charges. In 1896 Debs supported William Jennings Bryan for president. He organized the Social Democratic Party of America the next year. Debs was the Socialist Party candidate for president four times successively, between 1900 and 1912, and again in 1920. In 1912 he received 6% of the total vote, the highest total ever gained by a socialist. Indicted under the Espionage Act in 1918 for his opposition to entry of the United States into WORLD WAR I, he was sentenced to 10 years in prison but was pardoned in 1921. Debs had remained a socialist when the communists broke with the Socialist Party in 1919.

U.S. labor leader Eugene V. Debs was presidential candidate for the Socialist Party four times.

For further reading:

Currie, Harold W., *Eugene V. Debs*. New York: Irvington Publishers, 1976.

Salvatore, Nick, *Eugene V. Debs: Citizen and Socialist*. Champaign, Illinois: University of Illinois Press, 1982.

Debus, Kurt Heinrich (1908–1983). German-born electrical engineer and rocket pioneer. During WORLD WAR II he worked with Werner Von BRAUN at PEENEMUNDE, Germany, to develop the V-2 rocket. After the NAZI defeat, he was brought to the U.S. In the 1950s he worked on the Redstone Ballistic program, developing the U.S. Army's first missile equipped with a nuclear warhead. He became a U.S. citizen in 1959. In 1952 he became director of operations at what later became the Kennedy Space Center. He directed the launch of the first American earth satellite and presided over the first American landing on the moon (see APOLLO 11). He also oversaw the three SKYLAB missions in the early 1970s.

Debussy, Claude-Achille (1862–1918). French composer and critic considered the prime architect of modern music in this century. With Bela BARTOK, Igor STRAVINSKY and Charles IVES, Debussy liberated tonality and rhythm from the straitjacket of 19th-century musical practice. He was born in Saint-Germain-en-Laye near Paris. He entered the Paris Conservatory at age 11 and for the next 11 years confounded colleagues and teachers with his unorthodox experiments and improvisations. Contacts with Symbolist poets such as Mallarme and Impressionist painters such as Monet led to an "impressionist" music of his own. Such orchestral works as *Printemps (Spring*, 1887) and *Prelude a l'Apres-Midi d'un Faune* (*Prelude to the Afternoon of a Faun*, 1894), his landmark opera *Pelleas et Melisande* (1902), the piano *Images* (1907) and the ballet *Jeux* (1913) all aroused virulent hostility for their presumed "vagueness" and veiled atmospheres. Reclusive and bitter—one of his few lasting friends was his mentor, Erik SATIE—Debussy lived out his last years suffering from depression, poverty and, ultimately, the cancer that took his life during a German bombardment of Paris in 1918. He was the great tone painter of the ineffable—of silences, foot tracks in the snow, fogs and clouds,

French Impressionist composer Claude Debussy is considered a key architect of modern music.

and drowsy fauns. On the other hand, he reveled in the buoyant RAGTIME rhythms of the music hall, the modal strains of the Far East and sensuous thrummings of Spain. He had the courage to look beyond the standard conceptual and performance trappings of music. "I believe that music has until now rested on false principles," he wrote, anticipating later, oddly similar pronouncements by John CAGE. "We do not listen for the thousands of natural sounds which surround us. This, to my mind, is the new path. But, believe me, I have but caught a glimpse of it."

For further reading:
Dietschy, Marcel, *A Portrait of Claude Debussy*. Oxford: Oxford University Press, 1990.

Decline of the West, The. A two-volume (1918, 1922) analysis of the nature of the growth and decline of world cultures by the German historian Oswald SPENGLER. *The Decline of the West* provoked passionate international debate as to the validity of Spengler's central thesis that all cultures, from classical Greece to the Europe of Spengler's own era, go through an organic evolution from youthful vigor to sterile decay. Spengler insisted that true cultural creativity and religious fervor could only emerge early on in the development of a civilization. In the later period of its decline (as in the case of the modern West), the fitting goal of its members was to consolidate and expand its power rather than to cast about futilely for renewed spiritual meaning, which could only come from a newly emerging culture elsewhere. Spengler thus viewed a commitment to imperialism and warfare as symptoms of a civilization's decline, rather than as evidences of its ongoing vitality. But the Nazis distorted Spengler's views, casting them falsely as a glorification of their own obsession with militarism.

deconstruction. Theory of literary criticism that denies that works of literature have any meaning in and of themselves, and which sees meaning as imposed by the reader, not the writer. Deconstruction is largely the invention of French critic Jacques DERRIDA, who introduced the concept in the late 1960s. The deconstructive analysis is arcane and abstract, but deconstruction has gained a substantial following in the academic community. Nonetheless, many writers, readers and scholars have denounced deconstruction for making the analysis of a text more important than the text itself, and for denying that a literary work—a novel, poem or story—has any reference to the outside world and any inherent moral value.

Decree on the Press (Russia). A set of rules issued by the provisional Russian government in April 1917 to control printing and publishing. A number of copies of the book or journal had to be submitted to various officials for their perusal. Authors and editors were also obliged to print an official denial or correction as directed by the provisional government in the place of passages disapproved of by the government, without altering the text of the alteration provided by the government.

Deferre, Gaston (1910–1986). French politician. A socialist and vigorous anticommunist, Deferre was mayor of Marseilles for 33 consecutive years, where he built a political machine that dominated much of southern FRANCE. He first emerged as a hero of the French RESISTANCE during WORLD WAR II. Under the Fourth Republic, he held a number of ministries and, as minister for France overseas, was the architect of a law that gave autonomy to the African colonies and paved the way for their independence. He played a major role in the regrowth of France's Socialist Party and was a candidate for the presidency of France in 1965 and 1969. As President Francois MITTERRAND's minister of the interior in 1981–82, he set in motion the Socialist master plan for decentralization of some powers from France to the regions.

De Forest, Lee (1873–1961). American inventor whose many creations contributed to the development of radio, motion pictures and television. His most important invention was the Audion Three-Electrode Amplifier Tube (U.S. Patent No. 841,386) in 1907. It was an amplification device for the improved reception of radio broadcasting. In 1912 he used the device to pioneer the development of TALKING PICTURES. Rejecting sound-on-disc processes, he sought a method of transforming sound waves to electrical energy, which in turn could be translated into light waves and recorded on the edge of a film strip. The film projector, correspondingly, contained an incandescent lamp and photoelectric cell, which changed the optical track back into sound. After many experiments, he made his first talking picture in 1921. A year later he founded the De Forest Phonofilm Corporation and afterwards made hundreds of short sound films of stage entertainers like Eddie CANTOR, DeWolf Hopper and Sir Harry LAUDER. But HOLLYWOOD was underwhelmed and would wait several years before taking on the new technology, by which time associates and competitors were poaching on his inventions. De Forest spent many frustrating years in legal disputes. Though the U.S. courts upheld his patents in 1935, proclaiming him the true inventor of the sound-on-film system, he was broke and forgotten. He had made a bold prophecy in 1923 about the sound film: "I think it will add brains to the movies." The jury is still out.

For further reading:
Geduld, Harry M., *The Birth of the Talkies*. Bloomington: Indiana University Press, 1975.

De Gasperi, Alcide (1881–1954). Italian statesman, prime minister (1945–53); born in Pieve Tesino in the Austrian-held Trentino, he attended Vienna University. Involved in Austrian politics from 1911, he became a member of the Italian parliament when his native region became a part of ITALY in 1919, after World War I. That same year he was a cofounder of the Catholic Popular Party. De Gasperi served in parliament and as secretary-general of his party until 1925, when non-fascist parties were banned; the following year he was imprisoned by MUSSOLINI. After 16 months, he was released and took refuge in the Vatican. There he began to organize a new version of the Popular Party, the Christian Democratic Party. After the liberation of all of Italy in 1945, De Gasperi organized a centrist government with himself as premier. He continued in this office through seven more coalition cabinets. A staunch anticommunist and a supporter of the EUROPEAN COMMUNITY, he brought Italy into the EUROPEAN COAL AND STEEL COMMUNITY, the Council of Europe and the NORTH ATLANTIC TREATY ORGANIZATION.

De Gaulle, Charles (1890–1970). French general and statesman, first president of the Fifth Republic (1959–69). The man who was to become the symbol for French RESISTANCE to the Nazis during WORLD WAR II was born in Lille and attended the St. Cyr Military Academy. In WORLD WAR I he served with distinction under PETAIN, was wounded at VERDUN and taken prisoner by the Germans in 1916. After the war, De Gaulle served in the French military mission to Poland, in the forces occupying Germany and in the Middle East. He also taught at the Ecole Superieure de Guerre, becoming expert in the use of tanks and aircraft. As the commander of an armored division, he engaged in one of the few successful sorties against invading German forces in May 1940. He was appointed a member of Paul REYNAUD's government before he was forced to flee to London. There in June 1940 he broadcast to his countrymen, calling for resistance, and there he organized the FREE FRENCH forces. Winning the support of CHURCHILL, ROOSEVELT and STALIN, in 1943 he established a provisional government in Algeria, and a year later he returned to FRANCE. De Gaulle was formally elected president of the Fourth Republic in November 1945 but resigned soon after because of the failure of the constituent assembly to give him sufficient executive power. In 1947 he became head of a new anticommunist party, the Rassemblement du Peuple Francais.

In 1958, the crisis in ALGERIA caused the French government to call the general from retirement and to make him premier. He assumed temporary emergency control, oversaw the drafting of a new constitution that provided for broad presidential power, and in December 1958 was elected president of the Fifth Republic. In this position, he first dealt with the Algerian question, calling for self-determination against the strong opposition of ex-Gaullists who opposed Algerian independence. After an independent Algeria was established in 1962, De Gaulle set out to reestablish France as a great world power. At home, he stabilized the currency by devaluing the franc, established a more favorable balance of trade, asserted his right to the development of a specifically French nuclear deterrent and worked toward full employment and economic well-being. In foreign policy, he called for a dynamic and independent France. Reelected in 1965, he came into conflict with America regarding France's stature in NATO. In 1966 he withdrew French forces from the organization and a year later closed NATO installations in France. A vigorous member of the Common Market, he vetoed Britain's entry into the alliance in 1967. He also strengthened France's ties with West Germany, the U.S.S.R., China and the Third World. In the wake of the 1968 student protest demonstrations in France, he resigned as president. An austere, aloof and even Olympian figure, De Gaulle was undoubtedly France's greatest 20th-century leader.

For further reading:

Cook, Don, *Charles DeGaulle: A Biography*. New York: Putnam Publishing Group, 1984.

Lacouture, Jean, *DeGaulle: The Rebel, 1890–1944*. New York: W.W. Norton, 1990.

de Geer, Derek "Dirk" Jan (1870–1960). Premier of the NETHERLANDS (1939–40). When the Nazis occupied Holland in 1940, de Geer fled to London and formed a government in exile. He resigned in 1941, however, and returned to the Netherlands. Denounced as a traitor, he was convicted of collaboration in 1947, fined 20,000 guilders and given a one-year sentence, which was suspended because of his age.

DeHoffmann, Frederic (1924–1989). American nuclear physicist. While still in his teens, DeHoffman worked on the MANHATTAN PROJECT that developed the ATOMIC BOMB during WORLD WAR II. He later went on to direct the Salk Institute for Biological Studies, building it into one of the world's largest centers of biological research (see Jonas SALK). He died of complications from AIDS acquired through a blood transfusion.

Deighton, Len (Leonard Cyril) (1929–). British author. Born in London, Deighton was educated at the Royal College of Art and held a variety of jobs before publication of his first novel, *Only When I Larf* (1968; filmed 1969). Deighton is known for his many espionage novels, which are unique in the genre because of their irony and wit. These include *London Match* (1985), *Spy Hook* (1988), *Spy Line* (1989) and *Spy Sinker* (1990). His fiction evidences thorough research and historical accuracy also apparent in his nonfiction, which includes *Blitzkrieg: From the Rise of Hitler to the Fall of Dunkirk* (1980) and *The Battle of Britain* (1980). Deighton has also written screenplays, such as *Oh, What a Lovely War* (1969), and has written on food and wine.

De Klerk, F(rederik) W(illem) (1936–). President of SOUTH AFRICA (1989–) and leader of the country's ruling National Party. De Klerk served as education minister in the cabinet of P.W. BOTHA and as leader of the Transvaal branch of the ruling National Party. In these posts he established a reputation as an ultraconservative and party loyalist. However, since becoming president of South Africa, De Klerk has taken steps toward dismantling APARTHEID. After personal talks with black leader Nelson MANDELA, who had been serving a life sentence in prison since 1964, De Klerk released Mandela in 1990. He also legalized the AFRICAN NATIONAL CONGRESS and abolished the pass laws. Early in 1991 De Klerk announced that South Africa would abolish its racial segregation laws. Black nationalists charged that De Klerk was not moving fast enough to end apartheid, while white hardliners denounced De Klerk for betraying them. However, his efforts won considerable praise from U.S. President George BUSH and other Western leaders, as well as from many independent analysts, who view De Klerk as a credible leader undertaking bold and difficult reforms.

de Kooning, Willem (1904–1988). American painter. Born in Rotterdam, Holland, de Kooning studied in Amsterdam (1916–24) and immigrated to the U.S. in 1926, settling in New York City. Like many painters of the period, he worked on the Federal Arts Project and executed murals from 1935 to 1939. His early figural murals enhanced a number of public buildings, including the 1939–40 World's Fair. De Kooning's style became increasingly abstract, especially after his meeting with Arshile Gorky. His mature style evolved from the 1940s to the 1950s, and de Kooning became one of the foremost exponents of ABSTRACT EXPRESSIONISM. Perhaps his best known cycle of paintings is the ferociously-brushstroked *Woman* series of the 1950s-60s. In these monumentally sized works, such as *Woman I* (Museum of Modern Art, N.Y.C.), an elemental figure emerges from slashing strokes and expressive color. De Kooning's other typical paintings are completely abstract. These huge canvases are the quintessence of the highly energetic gestural spontaneity that marks abstract expressionism and are also characterized by a lush color range. De Kooning taught at Black Mountain College (1948) and Yale University (1950–51), and his work influenced and inspired a generation of American artists.

de la Mare, Walter (1873–1956). English poet and novelist. Of Huguenot descent, he worked as an accountant for many years until a government pension allowed him to concentrate on his writing. His poetry and prose often take place in a fantasy world, and much of his verse was written for or about children. De la Mare's poetry includes *Songs of Childhood* (1902), *The Listeners and Other Poems* (1912), *Peacock Pie* (1913), *Poems for Children* (1930) and *Memory and Other Poems* (1938). Among his fictional works are *Henry Brocken* (1904), *Memoirs of a Midget* (1921), *Broomsticks and Other Tales* (1925) and *On the Edge* (1930).

Delaney, Shelagh (1939–). British playwright and screenwriter. Delaney established her reputation at an early age (17) with *A Taste of Honey* (1958), a drama about a rebellious, pregnant teenager named Jo. Its stark realism was in sharp contrast to the sophisticated comedies popular at that time. After her second play, *The Lion in Love* (1960), Delaney concentrated on writing for films and television.

de la Renta, Oscar (1932–). New York–based fashion designer known for ornate and amusing design, often based on exotic themes and cultures. De la Renta was born in the Dominican Republic and studied art in Madrid. He began his professional career in Paris with a job with Cristobal BALENCIAGA before moving to New York to take over couture design for Elizabeth Arden. In 1965 he began work for Jan Derby, taking over the firm in 1967 and giving it his name. De la Renta's reputation as a celebrity of the social world has supported the growing reputation of his work as a designer. He was the winner of a 1968 Coty Award for his Russian- and gypsy-inspired collection of that year, of a Neiman-Marcus Award in 1968, and of a Coty Hall of Fame Award in 1973. In 1977, perfumes were introduced under the de la Renta name, and various other products have been added to his lines, including bathing suits, bed linens, and jewelry.

Delaunay, Robert (1885–1941). French painter. Delaunay was deeply influenced by the emergence of CUBISM in 1907, but he went on to establish himself as a unique artistic visionary who associated with a variety of aesthetic movements but was hidebound by none of them. He first earned critical praise for a series of paintings commenced in 1910, each of which was titled *Window on the City*. The paintings moved from representational cityscapes bathed in light to abstract, gridlike patterns. In 1912 Delaunay painted a new series of canvases, titled *Simultaneous Windows*, that were abstract and dominated by a startling use of brilliant, clashing colors. This series linked Delaunay to "simultaneism," while poet and art critic Guillaume APOLLINAIRE coined the term "Orphism" to describe the Delaunay's new style. Delaunay himself wrote at this time that "Color alone is form and subject." Delaunay, who married the painter Sonia Stern (see Sonia DELAUNAY) in 1910, continued to paint in a style dominated by color in the remaining decades of his life.

Delaunay, Sonia [born Sonia Stern] (1885–1979). Russian-born French artist and designer, considered among the foremost painters of her time. A leading figure in the Paris art world by the time of World War I, she was influenced by folk art, Gauguin, van Gogh and Matisse. She married the artist Robert DELAUNAY in 1910; the couple exerted a stimulating influence on each other and on the modernist movement in art in general (see MODERNISM). In the 1920s, she became increasingly interested in costume design and branched out into other design fields. She was particularly influential in creating new designs for fabrics, ceramics and household goods. Equally capable in virtually all media, she also illustrated books and wove an important series of tapestries at Aubusson.

Delbruck, Max (1906–1981). German-born molecular geneticist. Delbruck began his scientific career as a physicist, receiving his Ph.D. in physics from the University of Gottingen (1930). After Adolf HITLER came to power, Delbruck emigrated to the U.S. (1937) and joined the staff of Vanderbilt University (1940–47). In 1947 he moved to the California Institute of Technology, where he remained until his retirement in 1977. In the U.S., Delbruck turned his attention to biology and genetics. At Vanderbilt he studied a group of viruses called bacteriophages, which were important for understanding the genetic controls that govern the reproduction of living cells. With Dr. Salvador E. LURIA, Delbruck proved that viruses were able to undergo spontaneous mutations and attack cells that were normally resistant to viral invasion. This conclusion was confirmed independently by Alfred Hershey. For this work Delbruck, Luria and Hershey received the 1969 NOBEL PRIZE for physiology or medicine.

Delderfield, R(onald) F(rederich) (1912–1972). British novelist and playwright. Born in London, he later settled in the West Country of England, the setting for such novels as *God Is an Englishman* (1971) its sequel *Theirs Was the Kingdom* (1971) and *To Serve Them All My Days* (1972). Though not critically acclaimed, these books were enormously popular, particularly in the U.S.; several were adapted for television. His plays include *A Worm's Eye* (1945), which ran in the West End of London for more than five years.

Deledda, Grazia (1871–1936). Italian novelist. Deledda wrote in the 19th-century verismo Italian literary tradition, a movement related to naturalism. Her best known novels include *Elias Potolu* (1900; translated as *The Woman and the Priest*, 1928), *Canne al Vento* (1913), *Reeds in the Wind* (1937) and the autobiographical *Cosima* (1939). Deledda was awarded the NOBEL PRIZE for literature in 1926.

Delius, Frederick (1862–1934). English composer. Born in Bradford of German parents, he left England at the age of 20 to become an orange grower in Florida, later teaching piano in Virginia. Returning to Europe, he studied at the Leipzig Conservatory (1886–88), where his romantic impressionism was influenced by his friend Edvard Grieg. His work proved more popular in Germany than in his native country. His suite *Florida* (1886) was first performed there in 1888, followed by performances of such works as the chorale *Sea Drift* (1903) and the opera *A Village Romeo and Juliet* (1907). In England, Delius' reputation began to grow, largely due to the efforts of the conductor Sir Thomas BEECHAM, who performed his choral *A Mass of Life* (1904–05) in 1909. Delius spent the latter part of his life at his home near Fontainebleu. In the 1920s his health failed and he became blind and paralyzed. Nonetheless, he continued to compose with the aid of a secretary, **Eric Fenby**. His finest compositions include the choral works *Mass of Life* and *A Song of the High Hills* (1912) and the orchestral pieces *Brigg Fair* (1907), *On Hearing the First Cuckoo in Spring* (1912) and *North Country Sketches* (1913–14).

Del Monaco, Mario (1915–1982). Italian opera singer. Del Monaco was an impressive dramatic tenor in Italian roles in the 1940s and 1950s—a period that included such outstanding Italian tenors as Carlo BERGONZI, Franco CORELLI and Giuseppi DI STEFANO. He made his debut in a provincial performance of *Cavalleria Rusticana* in 1939. After his appearing at La Scala in Milan in 1941 in PUCCINI's *Madama Butterfly*, his career soared. From 1951 to 1959 he was a leading tenor at the Metropolitan Opera in New York and was acclaimed for the intensity of his performances in such operas as *Otello* and *Tosca*. He also made numerous recordings.

Delon, Alain (1935–). French movie actor. One of France's major actors, Delon has earned an international reputation. He is often cast as the romantic leading man, but has received his greatest acclaim for more offbeat roles in such films as Jean-Pierre Melville's *La Samourai* (1967) and his own production of the comic film *Borsalino* (1970). Among the other films in which he starred are *L'Eclisse* (1961), *Is Paris Burning?* (1966) and *The Investigator* (1974). Delon directed, produced, and starred in his most recent film, *Dance Machine* (1990).

DeLorean, John Z. (1925–). Flamboyant American would-be automobile manufacturer whose venture collapsed in bankruptcy after he was implicated in selling drugs. DeLorean had been a successful executive at General Motors, perhaps in line to head the world's largest manufacturer, when he left GM to head a firm of his own that planned to build an innovative sports car in Northern Ireland with government financing. The venture floundered and DeLorean resorted to smuggling millions of dollars of COCAINE into the U.S., which he planned to resell to save his company. However, the FBI stepped in and he was arrested. Despite videotaped evidence, DeLorean was acquitted of drug charges by a jury that may have felt the FBI was overzealous. DeLorean beat government tax charges and a number of civil lawsuits despite evidence of financial improprieties. Even the bankruptcy of DeLorean Motors was relatively painless to its founder—while creditors received little more than a token repayment of their debts.

de los Angeles, Victoria (1923–). Spanish soprano. Born in Barcelona, de los Angeles studied at the Instituto Balmes and the Conservatorio del Liceo. She made her concert debut at the Barcelona Conservatory in 1946 and her operatic debut at the Teatro Lirico, Barcelona, as the Countess in *The Marriage of Figaro*. After successful European and South American tours, she made her American debut at CARNEGIE HALL in 1950. She performed with the Metropolitan Opera from 1950 to 1961. De los Angeles has performed at Bayreuth, Covent Garden and other leading theaters and festivals throughout the world. She is noted for her exquisitely lyrical voice, her superb musicianship and her extensive command of the operatic repertoire.

De Madariaga, Salvador (1886–1978). Spanish author and diplomat. De Madariaga was Republican SPAIN's ambassador to the U.S. (1931) and its delegate to the LEAGUE OF NATIONS (1932–34). He was a leading critic of Generalissimo Francisco FRANCO and left Spain at the outbreak of the SPANISH CIVIL WAR.

demagogues. Politicians or other public figures who gain power by using oratory that plays on people's fears. During the 20th century, the new mass media of radio, film and television made it possible for demagogues to manipulate the public with great effectiveness. Demagogues flourished in times of crisis and uncertainty, such as the GREAT DEPRESSION of the 1930s, by promising popular but simplistic and fanatical solutions to complex social problems. American demagogues included Charles COUGHLIN, Huey LONG, Joseph MCCARTHY, and Gerald K. SMITH. Benito MUSSOLINI, Adolf HITLER, Joseph GOEBBELS and Juan PERON also used demogogic techniques to attain their ends. (See also PROPAGANDA.)

Demerec, Milislav (1895–1966). Yugoslavian-American geneticist. Demerec graduated from the College of Agriculture in Krizevci, Yugoslavia, in 1916 and after a few year's work at the Krizevci Experimental Station, moved to the U.S. He earned his Ph.D. in genetics from Cornell University in 1923 and then worked at the Carnegie Institution, Cold Spring Harbor, N.Y., where he remained for most of his career, becoming director in 1943. Demerec was concerned with gene structure and function, especially the effect of mutations. He found that certain unstable genes are more likely to mutate than others and that the rate of mutation is affected by various biological factors, such as the stage in the life cycle. He also demonstrated that chromosome segments that break away and rejoin in the wrong place may cause suppression of genes near the new region of attachment. Demerec's work with the bacterium *Salmonella* revealed that genes controlling related functions are grouped together on the chromosome rather than being randomly distributed through the chromosome complement. His radiation treatment of the fungus *Penicillium* yielded a mutant strain producing much larger quantities of PENICILLIN—a discovery of great use in WORLD WAR II. He showed that antibiotics should be administered initially in large doses, so that resistant mutations do not develop, and should be given in combinations, because any bacterium resistant to one is most unlikely to be resistant to both.

Demerec greatly increased the reputation of Cold Spring Harbor while director there and also served on many important committees. He founded the journal *Advances in Genetics* and wrote some 200 scientific articles.

Demichelli, Alberto (1896–1980). President of URUGUAY (1976). A lawyer by profession, Demichelli was a member of the liberal Colorado Party. He was one of a group of political leaders who agreed to cooperate with the Uruguayan armed forces in a 1973 coup that dissolved Congress, banned political and union activities and imposed stiff censorship on all news organizations. In 1976 he was chosen president with the approval of the military; however, he governed for only 80 days.

De Mille, Agnes (1909–). American dancer and choreographer known for her innovative ballets. De Mille used American subjects in her work and transformed American musical theater by integrating dance sequences into the unfolding plot in the landmark show *Oklahoma!* (1943). She first gained fame as a dancer with Ballet Rambert and touring Europe as a solo performer (1929–40). Her first major choreographic works, *Black Ritual* (1940) and *Three Virgins and a Devil* (1941), were for The AMERICAN BALLET THEATRE, and were followed by the popular *Rodeo* (1942) and *Fall River Legend* (1948). Other musicals she choreographed include *Carousel* (1945), *Brigadoon* (1947) and *Paint Your Wagon* (1951). In 1973 she founded the Heritage Dance Theatre at the North Carolina School of the Arts. In addition, she has worked in film and television, served as a dance consultant and written several books on dance, including *Dance to the Piper* (1952), *The Book of the Dance* (1963) and *America Dances* (1981).

For further reading:

De Mille, Agnes, *Portrait Gallery*. Boston: Houghton Mifflin, 1990.

De Mille, Cecil B(lount) (1881–1959). American film director and producer. De Mille enjoyed a long and successful career that spanned both the silent and the talkie film eras. He codirected the very first HOLLYWOOD feature, a western called *The Squaw Man* (1913). In conjunction with Samuel GOLDWYN and Jesse Lasky, De Mille produced numerous silent films in the 1910s, but made his primary mark as a director of action-filled biblical spectacles such as *The Ten Commandments* (1923) and *The King of Kings* (1926). He continued to work in this vein in the sound era, enjoying blockbuster successes with *The Sign of the Cross* (1932), *Samson and Delilah* (1949) and a remake of *The Ten Commandments* (1956), starring Charlton HESTON. Other films by De Mille include *The Greatest Show on Earth* (1952), an extravaganza focusing on circus life. De Mille was one of the few Hollywood directors of his era to enjoy a marquee billing more prominent than that of his actors, a true mark of his popularity with audiences.

Demirel, Suleyman (1924–). Turkish statesman. Demirel was director of water works from 1955 to 1961. One of the founders of the right-wing Justice Party (1961), he was its chairman in 1964. Demirel was prime minister of TURKEY from 1965 to 1971, but was ousted by the military intervention. As leader of a coalition, he was again prime minister from 1975 to 1980 when removed in a military coup. Together with other former opposition leaders, he was forced to renounce political activity in 1983.

Democracy Movement. Political movement in the People's Republic of CHINA, led by students and supported by many Chinese workers in 1989. The Democracy Movement occurred at the same time that Eastern Europeans were pressing for reforms in communist-dominated Eastern Europe, but proved to be less successful in the short run. The Chinese movement was marked by mass demonstrations, especially in the center of Beijing. The students called for an end to government corruption, reform of the Communist Party and public participation in decision making. The Chinese government at first tolerated the movement but repeatedly warned that the demonstrations must stop. While the movement apparently had widespread enthusiastic support, it was poorly organized and its specific goals were unclear. The movement was crushed in the TIANANMEN SQUARE MASSACRE (June 3–4, 1989) in Beijing and subsequent crackdowns on pro-democracy students throughout China as the Communist Party under DENG XIAOPING reasserted its authority. Many students and workers were arrested and imprisoned, while others went into hiding or fled China.

Democratic Party. American political party, founded in 1828. Along with the REPUBLICAN PARTY, the Democratic Party is one of two major American political parties. While each party encompasses a broad range of opinions, generally speaking the Democratic Party is more apt to favor welfare programs, government intervention in the economy, federally funded social programs and a lower military profile abroad. The liberal sector of the party has traditionally embraced the CIVIL RIGHTS MOVEMENT, the WOMEN'S MOVEMENT and labor unions. Southern Democrats tend to be more conservative.

The Democratic National Committee is comprised of a chairperson and representatives from each state and coordinates the party's national conventions and fundraising for Democratic candidates.

Woodrow WILSON was the first Democratic president of the 20th century. His success in the 1912 elections was partly due to opposition to monopolistic trusts that emerged during the prior Republican administration. The modern Democratic Party arose with Franklin D. ROOSEVELT's election in 1932. His NEW DEAL policy of federal programs to offset the GREAT DEPRESSION established the basis for subsequent Democratic administrations. In the following 50 years, Democrats controlled the presidency for 32 years and the House and Senate for 44. While the Republicans won the presidential elections in 1968 and 1972, the Democrats retained control of Congress. In 1976 Democrat Jimmy CARTER of Georgia was elected president, but Republicans returned to office in 1980 when Ronald REAGAN was elected on a platform of reduced government spending and strengthened national defense. Reagan's enormous personal popularity and internal dissention and disorganization within the Democratic Party were widely cited as reasons for the party's apparent decline in the 1980s. Many voters also felt that the national party was controlled by left-wing elements, and the party's presidential candidates in 1980, 1984 and 1988 were perceived as weak and ineffectual. However, the Democratic Party continued to enjoy successes at the local and state levels.

Dempsey, William Harrison "Jack" (1895–1984). World heavyweight boxing champion from 1919 to 1926. Known as the "Manassa Mauler" (after his hometown, Manassa, Col.), he worked as a mucker in Colorado mining camps, where he first fought professionally in 1912. Dempsey knocked out Jess Willard in 1919 to win the title he eventually lost in 1926 to Gene TUNNEY, in the controversial **"long count"** match.

Dempster, Arthur Jeffrey (1886–1950). Canadian-American physicist. Dempster was educated at the University of Toronto. He emigrated to the U.S. in 1914, attended the University of Chicago, earned his Ph.D. in 1916 and began teaching in 1919. In 1927 he was made professor of physics. He is noted for his early developments of and work with the mass spectrograph (invented by Francis W. ASTON). In 1935 he was able to show that uranium did not consist solely of the isotope uranium-238, for seven out of every 1,000 uranium atoms were in fact uranium-235. Niels BOHR later predicted that this isotope was capable of sustaining a chain reaction that could release large amounts of atomic fission energy.

Demy, Jacques (1931–1990). French film director. A director of musical comedies, his best known film was *Les Parapluies de Cherbourg* (*The Umbrellas of Cherbourg*, 1964).

Twice purged for his views, Deng Xiaoping was a major influence in Chinese politics in the latter part of the 20th century.

His other films include *Les Demoiselles de Rochefort* (1966) and *Lola* (1960).

Deneuve, Catherine [Catherine Dorleac] (1943–). French movie actress. The daughter of actor Maurice Dorleac and sister of actress Francoise Dorleac, Deneuve is considered one of the most beautiful women in the world, as well as an accomplished actress. Working with some of the major directors in the world, she has shown her versatility and craftsmanship in such films as Roman POLANSKI's *Repulsion* (1965), Luis BUNUEL's *Belle de Jour* (1966), and Francois TRUFFAUT's *La Sirene de Mississippi* (1969). She won the French Film Academy's best actress award for her performance in *The Umbrellas of Cherbourg* (1964).

Deng Xiaoping (1904–). A member of the Chinese Communist Party since the early 1920s, Deng Xiaoping emerged as the leading political personality in CHINA in the late 1970s. He was twice purged for his views, first during the CULTURAL REVOLUTION, when he was designated the "number-2 capitalist roader" in 1966 and forced to undergo public self-criticism in 1968; and then in 1976, when he was blamed for public demonstrations in April of that year. Eulogizing the recently deceased CHOU EN-LAI after the defeat of the GANG OF FOUR, Deng returned to the political limelight and thereafter largely shaped Chinese politics, even though he held no major, formal position. In 1987 he retired from the politburo of the party but retained his post as chairman of the Central Military Commission until November 1989. Diminutive in stature, he has been praised by foreign leaders for his pragmatism but lost face internationally when in June 1989 he supported the army's massacre of pro-democracy students throughout China, then blatantly lied to the country and the world about what had occurred. (See also TIANANMEN SQUARE MASSACRE; DEMOCRACY MOVEMENT.)

Denikin, Anton Ivanovich (1872–1947). Distinguished Russian general of WORLD WAR I who rose from the ranks. After the RUSSIAN REVOLUTION, Denikin was imprisoned for supporting KORNILOV's attempted revolt against KERENSKY's socialist government but escaped to raise an army in the South. Meanwhile (November 1917) the BOLSHEVIKS under Lenin had seized power and Denikin's "White" army, with Allied support, occupied the Ukraine and North Caucasus. As Bolshevik power grew, the Red Army gradually forced the Whites back to the Crimea, and in 1920 Denikin abandoned the struggle. He died in exile in France.

De Niro, Robert (1943–). American film and theater actor. De Niro is perhaps the most critically acclaimed film actor of his generation. He began his career as a stage actor in New York but soon turned his primary focus to film work. In the 1960s he appeared in student films by the emerging director Brian DE PALMA. But De Niro first attracted the attention of critics—as well as an ACADEMY AWARD for best supporting actor—with his role as a dying catcher in the baseball film *Bang the Drum Slowly* (1973). He won further acclaim for his searing portrayal of a violent youth in *Mean Streets* (1973), directed by Martin SCORSESE. De Niro and Scorsese went on to collaborate on several brilliant films, including *Taxi Driver* (1976); *Raging Bull* (1979), for which De Niro won a best actor ACADEMY AWARD for his portrayal of boxer Jake La Motta; *The King of Comedy* (1983); and *GoodFellas* (1990). De Niro reunited with De Palma in *The Untouchables* (1987), in which he played Al CAPONE. His other films include *The Deer Hunter* (1978), *True Confessions* (1981) and the comedy *Midnight Run* (1988).

Denis, Maurice (1870–1943). French decorator and painter. Denis was, in his youth, influenced by the Symbolist movement and by the theories of the Nabis, who emphasized the technical importance of painting as a two-dimensional depiction of three-dimensional reality. A noted early canvas by Denis was *Hommage a Cezanne* (1900), a still-life tribute to French painter Paul Cezanne. Later in his career Denis became well-known as a theatrical set designer. In 1912, with Georges Desvallieres, Denis founded the Atelier d'Art Sacree, a studio that taught techniques of painting works with religious themes.

Denmark. Denmark occupies the Jutland Peninsula, which runs into the North Sea from north-central Europe; the islands of Sjaelland, Funen, Lolland, Falster and Bornholm in the Baltic Sea; and 480 smaller islands—for a total area of 16,629 square miles. A monarchy since the 14th century, the country has been governed since 1972 by Queen Margrethe II, who shares authority with a parliament. Denmark, which remained neutral during World War I, saw egalitarian reforms and a welfare-state system introduced, after the Social Democratic Party gained power in 1929. Danish attempts to remain neutral during WORLD WAR II were thwarted when Germany occupied the country (1940–45). After the war Denmark became a founding member of the NORTH ATLANTIC TREATY ORGANIZATION (NATO) in 1949 and joined the EUROPEAN COAL AND STEEL COMMUNITY (EEC) in 1973. In 1982 the first conservative-led government since 1901 was elected.

Denmark Strait. Channel between southeastern GREENLAND and ICELAND, 180 miles wide and 300 miles long; links the Arctic Ocean with the North Atlantic Ocean. On May 24, 1941, during WORLD

DENMARK

1915	Universal adult suffrage enacted.
1920	Schleswig votes 3 to 1 in favor of return to Danish rule.
1929	Social Democratic Party comes to power and implements welfare-state legislation.
1940	Germans occupy Denmark during World War II.
1948	Denmark grants home rule to Faroe Islands.
1949	Denmark joins NATO.
1953	Royal succession opened to females.
1966	Odense University is founded.
1969	Pornography legalized.
1972	King Frederick IX dies; his daughter succeeds to the throne as Queen Margrethe II.
1973	Denmark joins EEC.
1976	Government razes "Free City" hangout of drug users and counterculturists.
1979	Greenland granted home rule.
1989	(May 26) Legislation passed allowing civil marriage between homosexuals—the first legislation of its kind among the 12 members of the European Community.

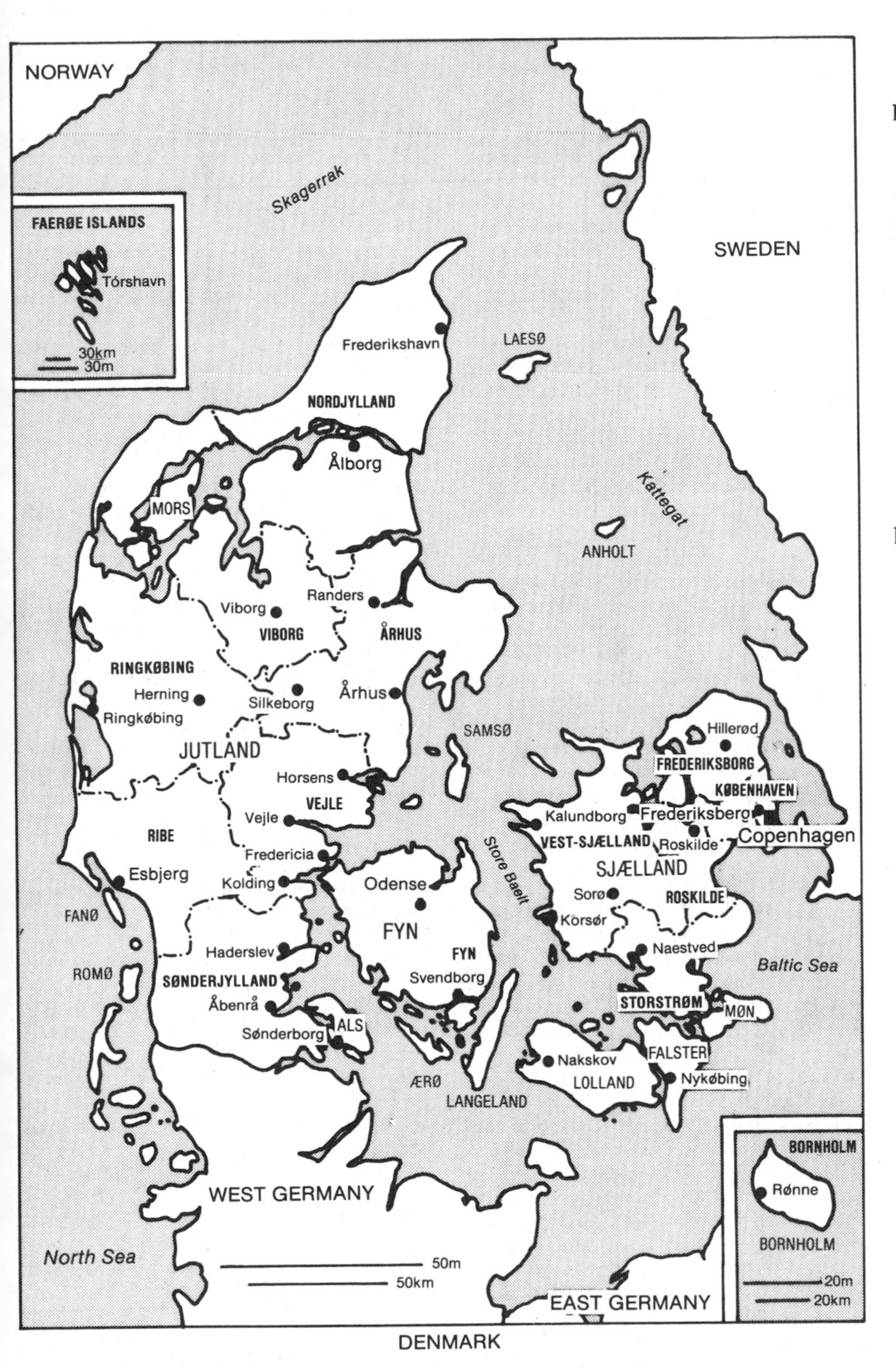

DENMARK

WAR II, the British battleship *Hood* was sent to a watery grave by the German battleship *Bismarck* in this strait.

Dennis, Nigel Forbes (1912–1989). British novelist, playwright and critic. Dennis' best known novel was *Cards of Identity* (1955), a cult hit among young Britons because of its black humor and satire of social pretensions. His other works included the play *The Making of Moo* (1958), the biography *Jonathan Swift* (1964), and the novel *A House in Order* (1966). He also worked as a book and drama reviewer for the *Sunday Telegraph*, THE NEW REPUBLIC, and TIME Magazine.

Dennis v. United States (1951). McCarthy-era U.S. Supreme Court decision upholding a conviction of U.S. Communist Party leaders under the SMITH ACT. The Smith Act, passed in 1940, made it illegal to advocate the violent overthrow of the United States government or to belong to a group that advocated such overthrow. In 1950 Dennis and 10 other U.S. communists were prosecuted under the law. At the trial, the defendants had argued that the provisions of the law were contrary to the Free Speech protections guaranteed by the First Amendment. However, a divided Supreme Court upheld their convictions. Six years later the Warren court largely limited the application of this case by limiting convictions to instances where the speaker incited actual "activity."

Densmore, Frances (1867–1957). U.S. music historian. She made a career of preserving the American Indian heritage. She began studying the music of American Indians in 1893 and, starting in 1907, made special researches into American Indian music for the Bureau of American Ethnology. The Smithsonian-Densmore collection contains sound recordings of American Indian music made between 1941 and 1943. Her writings include *American Indians and their Music* (1926), *Teton Sioux Music* (1918) and many more books on the various Indian tribes and groups. In 1940, Densmore received the National Association of Composers and Conductors award for service to American music.

De Palma, Brian (1940–). American film director. De Palma has inspired both admiration and controversy for his films that so often depict—in a vivid montage style—extreme violence. De Palma has acknowledged the great influence of thriller specialist Alfred HITCHCOCK upon his directorial approach. De Palma began his career with short student films in the 1960s that featured future stars Jill Clayburgh and Robert DE NIRO. He went on to direct a number of features but enjoyed his first great success with *Carrie* (1976), which starred Sissy Spacek and was based on the Steven KING novel. *Dressed to Kill* (1980) was a critically and commercially successful thriller, but numerous other De Palma films of the early 1980s were box office failures. But he has enjoyed two later successes with *The Untouchables* (1987), starring Kevin Costner and De Niro, and *Casualties of War* (1989), a VIETNAM WAR drama.

Depardieu, Gerard (1948–). French movie actor. One of the most popular and acclaimed actors of the French cinema, Depardieu has shown his dramatic range and depth in such internationally-recognized films as Francois TRUFFAUT's *The Last Metro* (1980), *The Return of Martin Guerre* (1982), *Jean de Florette* (1985), *Camille Claudel* (1989) and *Cyrano de Bergerac* (1990). His first American-made film, the comedy *Green Card* (1990), was very successful.

Depression of 1900. Economic depression in Russia following the great industrial expansion of the previous decade. During this period there was considerable political agitation, culminating five years later in the RUSSIAN REVOLUTION OF 1905.

De Priest, Oscar (1871–1951). U.S. congressman. De Priest, from Chicago, Ill., was the first black elected to the United States House of Representatives from the North. As a member of the Republican Party, he voted against Franklin D. ROOSEVELT'S NEW DEAL concepts—a fact that eventually cost him his seat in 1934. His most notable victory was his amendment to the bill creating the CIVILIAN CONSERVATION CORPS; it barred discrimination because of race, color or creed. He called upon the government to live up to its promises to the Indians and introduced a measure to have the government pay a pension to an estimated 100,000 ex-slaves.

De Rochemont, Louis (1899–1978). Documentary film producer. De Rochemont was the originator and producer of the *March of Time* film series (1934–43). Among his numerous films were the documentaries *The Fighting Lady* and *Windjammer* and the documentary-style *House on 92nd Street* and *Martin Luther*.

Derrida, Jacques (1930–). French literary critic and philosopher; gained international attention as the leading spokesperson of the critical school of DECONSTRUCTIONISM, which seeks to evade the metaphysical belief structures of writers and concentrate instead on the inner psychological dynamic mirrored in the creative writing process itself. Derrida was born in Algiers in a Sephardic Jewish family. He immigrated to France and became a contributor to the leading philosophical quarterly *Tel Quel* in the 1960s. His writings show the influence of such disparate thinkers as Hegel, Nietzsche, Sigmund FREUD and Martin HEIDEGGER. Derrida's major works include *Of Grammatology* (1967), *Writing and Difference* (1967), *Dissemination* (1972) and *Margins of Philosopy* (1972).

Dery, Tibor (1894–1977). Hungarian novelist, story writer and playwright. Dery, a politically committed writer, was a radical activist who was involved in the HUNGARIAN REVOLUTION of 1918–19 and joined the Communist Party in 1919. Due to his political beliefs, he spent several years in exile from Hungary. Most of his literary works were not published in his native land until after World War II. These include a three-volume novel, *The Unfinished Sentence* (1947); a two-volume novel, *Response* (1950–52); and the novel *Niki, the Story of a Dog* (1956). *The Portuguese Princess and Other Stories* (1966) is an English translation of his best tales.

Desai, Anita (1937–). Indian novelist. Desai was born in Mussoorie and educated at Delhi University. She writes in English, and her work is known for its realistic portrayal of contemporary India, often focusing on the grittier aspects of urban life. Her novels include *Cry the Peacock* (1963), *Fire on the Mountain* (1977) and *Baumgartner's Bombay* (1990). Desai has also written short stories and books for children.

Desai, Shri Morarji Ranchhodji (1896–). Indian prime minister (1977–79). Active in the civil disobedience movement led by Mohandas K. GANDHI in the 1930s, he emerged as one of the leaders of the CONGRESS PARTY after independence (1947) and held many senior government offices. Increasing conflict with Indira GANDHI led to his imprisonment (1975–77). Leading the **Janata Party** (an electoral alliance of noncommunist parties against Mrs. Gandhi) to victory in 1977, he inflicted the first defeat on the Congress Party since independence. Factionalism within the coalition led to his defeat in an election in January 1980.

Descamisados [*Span.*, "the shirtless ones"]. The urban poor in ARGENTINA, who supported Juan Domingo PERON and whose demonstrations in 1945 helped win his release from prison.

Desch, Cyril Henry (1874–1958). British metallurgist. Desch was educated at King's College, London. He taught in Glasgow from 1909 until 1920, then served as professor of metallurgy at the University of Sheffield from 1920 to 1930. He then moved to the National Physical Laboratory at Teddington, Middlesex, where he was in charge of the metallurgy department until his retirement in 1939. Desch is mainly known for his publication in 1910 of *Textbook of Metallography*, a work that served as the standard account of the subject for the first half of the century.

De Sica, Vittorio (1902–1974). Italian motion picture director, best known for his post-World War II neorealist style. After two decades of success as a leading man on the stage and in films, De Sica turned to filmmaking in the early 1940s. He hit his stride with his fifth film, *I Bambini ci Guardano* (*The Children Are Watching Us*, 1943), a poignant tale of a child's suicide. This was the first of several memorable collaborations with screenwriter Cesare Zavattini, all consistent in their deeply felt observation of contemporary life: the interlocking stories of street children in postwar Italy (*Sciuscia/Shoeshine*, 1946); the Academy-Award-winning tale of a man looking for a stolen bicycle (*Ladri di Biciclette/The Bicycle Thief*, 1948); the fantasy parable (*Miracolo a Milano/Miracle in Milan*, 1950); and the daily activities of an unwanted, elderly man (*Umberto D*, 1952). When his directorial fortunes sagged in the late 1950s, De Sica fell back upon his acting experience; his performance in *General della Rovere* (1959), a wartime story of an Italian traitor, was acclaimed as one of the best character portrayals in the modern cinema. Shortly after directing the Oscar-winning *The Garden of the Finzi-Continis* (1971), De Sica died of complications from lung surgery. He was at his best, notes historian Mario Gromo, when "mirroring some troubled aspect of humanity in travail." In *Umberto D* we share with the old man the agonizing time he must spend waiting to learn if a passing train has killed his faithful dog, and so we understand the intimacy—and the breadth—of De Sica's achievement.

Design Centre. Permanent exhibition center in London devoted to the promotion of design excellence through public educational activities. The Design Centre was opened in 1956 in the Haymarket under the sponsorship of the British Council of Industrial Design. It exhibits selected objects of superior design quality, maintains an index of sources for materials and products of good design quality, and conducts a publishing program of booklets offering advice on design issues of interest to consumers.

De Sitter, Willem (1872–1934). Dutch astronomer and mathematician. De Sitter studied mathematics and physics at the University of Groningen, where his interest in astronomy was aroused by Jacobus Kapteyn. After serving at the Cape Town Observatory in South Africa from 1897 to 1899 and, back at Groningen, as assistant to Kapteyn from 1899 to 1908, he was appointed to the chair of astronomy at the University of Leiden. He also served as director of Leiden Observatory from 1919 to 1934. De Sitter is remembered for his proposal in 1917 of what came to be called the "de Sitter universe" in contrast to the "EINSTEIN universe." The contrast was summarized in the statement that Einstein's universe contained matter but no motion while de Sitter's involved motion without matter. The Russian mathematician Alexander FRIEDMANN in 1922 and the Belgian George Lemaitre independently in 1927 introduced the idea of an **expanding universe** that contained moving matter. It was then shown in 1928 that the de Sitter universe could be transformed mathematically into an expanding universe, the "Einstein-de Sitter universe." De Sitter also worked on celestial mechanics and stellar photometry. He spent much time trying to calculate the mass of Jupiter's satellites.

Deskey, Donald (1894–1989). American industrial designer. Deskey was a renowned and versatile innovator whose projects ranged from building interiors to toothpaste tubes. Among his best known designs was the interior of RADIO CITY MUSIC HALL in New York City (1932), considered a masterpiece of the ART DECO style. He also created memorable packaging for several Proctor & Gamble products, including Crest toothpaste, Aqua-Velva after-shave lotion and Jif peanut butter.

Desmond, Johnny [born Giovanni Alfredo de Simone] (1920–1985). American singer. Desmond became known as the "G.I. SINATRA" when, after joining the U.S. Army, he was assigned to accompany Glenn MILLER's Army Air Force Band in Europe during WORLD WAR II. After returning to civilian life, he became a prominent radio personality and nightclub performer. *The Yellow Rose of Texas* and *Play Me Hearts and Flowers* were among his 1950s hits. He also took up acting and appeared in Broadway shows, films and television.

Desnos, Robert (1900–1945). French poet. Desnos was one of the most gifted poets to be drawn to SURREALISM. He first emerged as a major voice in French letters in the 1920s, when his youthful love lyrics were championed by Andre BRETON. Desnos' poems featured strikingly disjointed and bizarre imagery but nonetheless managed to convey a romantic and melancholy tone. He employed automatic writing techniques by which he sought to evade conscious control over his use of language while evoking the power of dreams and unconscious longings. Desnos' best known volume of poems was *Liberty or Love* (1927). In the 1930s he devoted much of his energies to radio and film scripts. Following the fall of FRANCE in WORLD WAR II, Desnos, a Jew, was arrested by the Nazis and sent to the

Theresienstadt CONCENTRATION CAMP, where he died in 1945.

For further reading:

Desnos, Robert, *The Selected Poems of Robert Desnos*. New York: Ecco Press, 1991.

Dessau. German city in Saxony-Anhalt, 71 miles southwest of BERLIN. Site of the BAUHAUS architectural school from 1925 to 1932. Dessau was heavily attacked during WORLD WAR II, and many historic structures were demolished.

De-Stalinization. Name given to official policy that undermined STALIN's hitherto uncontested infallibility. In February 1956, at the Twentieth Congress of the Communist Party of the U.S.S.R., KHRUSHCHEV attacked the cult of Stalin's personality, and drew attention to the injustices of Stalin's regime. After the Twenty-Second Party Congress, the central committee of the party published a decree condemning the "cult of the individual" and stressing the need for collective leadership. In 1961, Stalin's body was removed from LENIN's side in the mausoleum on Red Square, and numerous busts and pictures of Stalin were destroyed. Places named after Stalin had their names changed, a number of prisoners were released, a freer intellectual atmosphere ensued, and the excesses of forced assimilation were condemned. De-Stalinization also stimulated a process of change in Eastern European countries.

detente. Attempts at relaxing or easing tension, particularly between the countries of Eastern and Western Europe. Intense hostility between the U.S. and the U.S.S.R. ended in 1953 after STALIN's death. After 1963, and the CUBAN MISSILE CRISIS, both superpowers became aware of the need to prevent nuclear warfare. Accordingly, in 1967 the Outer Space Treaty, and in 1968 the Treaty on the Non-Proliferation of Nuclear Weapons, worked toward this goal, as did the normalization of relations between East and West Germany, the Treaty of Non-Aggression between the U.S.S.R. and West Germany in 1970, the Four Power Agreement on Berlin in 1971, and the Seabed Arms Control Treaty, also of 1971. In 1971–72 the U.S.'s decision to end its military intervention in VIETNAM enabled the Kremlin to feel more able to seek detente, although the Sino-American rapprochement made the Soviet leaders apprehensive that the U.S. would curry favor with MAO TSE-TUNG, thus providing Beijing (Peking) with technological aid. In 1972, after his visit to Moscow, President NIXON proclaimed the end of the COLD WAR and the beginning of Soviet-American detente. Such events as the invasion of Afghanistan and the nuclear arms debate did not enhance detente. In the late 1980s, during GORBACHEV's reign, U.S.-Soviet relations improved markedly, beyond the expectations of those who had earlier sought detente.

Detroit. A major city of the midwestern U.S., famous for automobile manufacturing. The early 1900s saw the beginning of the automobile industry. According to historian Raymond C. Miller, Detroit "remade America with the automobile. Henry FORD and the Ford Motor Company, Ransom Olds and his Oldsmobile, the General Motors Corporation, and CHRYSLER Motors of Walter P. Chrysler brought the city its leadership in the field." During World War I, the city was considered a center for German spy activity. After the war, production of the FORD TRIMOTOR airplane gave commercial aviation its early impetus. The Depression of 1929 was particularly difficult for Detroit because of the drop in auto sales. During WORLD WAR II, Detroit surpassed all other cities in war production. The opening in 1959 of the ST. LAWRENCE SEAWAY gave the port of Detroit access to the world's shipping.

The race riots of 1967 caused immense property damage. Much of the downtown area was destroyed, but developments such as the Renaissance Center and Cobb Hall helped to restore the central city. Recessions in the 1970s and the competition of foreign auto makers have brought unemployment, but in the 1980s, the industry was able to rebound substantially. In 1984 Detroit ranked sixth in population among U.S. cities. In sports Detroit teams have won many championships. Professional teams include the football Lions, the hockey Red Wings, basketball Pistons and baseball Tigers. The Tigers won the World Series in 1984. Another principal tourist attraction of the city is its proximity to CANADA, to which it is connected by both a tunnel and the world's longest international suspension bridge, the Ambassador International.

Deutsch, Helene Rosenbach (1884–1982). Austrian-born psychoanalyst. A follower of Sigmund FREUD, Deutsch was the first female psychoanalyst to be analyzed by him. She founded the Vienna Pschoanalytic Institute (1923), remaining its director until 1935, when she emigrated to the U.S. where she helped spread Freudian psychoanalysis. Her important work in personality disorders foreshadowed later research into narcissism. She was also known for her major book, *The Psychology of Women* (1944).

Deutscher Werkbund. German association founded in 1907 to promote excellence in design and design-related craft and manufacturing. In its early years the Werkbund carried forward craft traditions somewhat in the manner of William Morris's Arts and Crafts movement. The orientation turned toward a more clearly modernist direction with the 1914 exhibition in Cologne housed in buildings designed by Walter GROPIUS. Among the personalities associated with the organization were Peter BEHRENS, Ludwig MIES VAN DER ROHE, Hermann Muthesius, Richard Riemerschmidt, and Henry Van de Velde. The organization grew to a membership of over 3,000 and had direct connections with its Austrian counterpart. A 1927 exhibition included the building of a model suburb, Die Weissenhof Siedlung at Stuttgart, that included buildings by many of the major European modernists of the time. The organization was dissolved in 1934 in response to the growing pressure against MODERNISM generated by the rise of the Nazi regime. A revival of the Werkbund began in 1947.

De Valera, Eamon (1882–1975). Irish revolutionary and political leader, prime minister of IRELAND (1932–48, 1951–54, 1957–59) and president (1959–73). De Valera was the dominant force in Irish politics from the 1920s through the 1950s. Born in New York City, the son of a Spanish father and an Irish mother, he moved to Ireland at the age of two after the death of his father. Despite his poor background, he became a mathematician and a teacher. He became involved in the Irish-language movement, then joined the Irish Republican Brotherhood (forerunner of the IRISH REPUBLICAN ARMY) and the paramilitary Irish Volunteers. He participated in the 1916 EASTER RISING, commanding 125 men who seized Westland Row railway station and Boland's Bakery in DUBLIN. Captured by the British, he was sentenced to be executed along with the other 16 leaders of the uprising but was ultimately spared because he held American citizenship. Instead he received a life sentence, but served only one year in prison before being released (1917). He then became president of the revolutionary SINN FEIN nationalist movement. Elected to the British parliament (1919), he refused to take his seat but instead

Eamon De Valera (left), accompanied by Col. Sean Brennen, retires as Ireland's president (June 24, 1973).

joined other nationalists in forming the Irish assembly, the DAIL EIREANN, whose leader he became. He opposed the compromise Anglo-Irish Treaty of 1921, rejecting the partition of Ireland into the 26-county Free State and the 6-county NORTHERN IRELAND. Founder of the FIANNA FAIL Party (1926), De Valera became prime minister in 1932. He followed a nationalist policy, instituting a new constitution (1937) that transformed the country from the Irish Free State to Eire; he later declared Ireland a republic (1947) and formally withdrew the country from the BRITISH COMMONWEALTH (1949). He kept Ireland neutral during WORLD WAR II. He also forged strong ties between the state and the Catholic Church and generally followed conservative domestic and social policies.

For further reading:

Edwards, Owen D., *Eamon De Valera*. Washington, D.C.: Catholic University of America Press, 1988.

MacNamara, Desmond, *Eamon De Valera*. New York: Chelsea House, 1988.

Moynihan, Maurice, ed., *Eamon De Valera: Speeches and Statements 1917–1973*. New York: St. Martin's Press, 1980.

developed socialism. Term used by LENIN, later predominant in Soviet theory. It was used to describe the stage between primative socialism, in which the foundations of socialism were laid down, and full communism, which had not yet been achieved. In 1969, BREZHNEV referred to a "developed socialist party," and after the Twenty-Fourth Party Congress (1971) the term became widespread in theoretical journals. Under GORBACHEV, however, the term became meaningless and was dropped.

Devereux, James P.S. (1903–1988). U.S. military hero. In the Marines, Devereux won fame as the commander of a 522-man detachment that defended WAKE ISLAND, along with 1,200 U.S. construction workers, when the Japanese invaded three days after their attack on PEARL HARBOR. Defending the island against overwhelming odds for 15 days, he reportedly sent out the message "Send us more Japs." Devereux was captured and interned in a Japanese prisoner of war camp for four years. A four-term Republican member of the House of Representatives, he favored public school desegregation.

Devil's Island [Ile du Diable]. One of the Safety Islands off the Atlantic coast of French Guiana. A tiny island, it was organized in 1852 and used as a penal colony, particularly for French political prisoners; the most famous one was Alfred Dreyfus. The French started closing the prison in 1938, but were interrupted by WORLD WAR II. By 1948 all prisoners were returned to their countries of origin. However, the lore of Devil's Island as a place of no escape has continued to hold the imagination.

Devlin, Denis (1908–1959). Irish poet, diplomat and translator. Born in Scotland, Devlin returned with his family to Ireland when he was 10. After a year in a seminary, he turned to the study of languages at University College, Dublin, Munich University and the Sorbonne. His best poetry was marked by religious fervor. He joined the diplomatic corps in 1935, and his first book, *Intercessions*, appeared in 1937. From 1940 to 1947 he was posted to the U.S., where he met Robert Penn WARREN, who championed his work in *The Southern Review*. *Lough Derg*, his masterpiece, was published in 1946. After 1950 he resided in Italy, publishing only sporadically. *Collected Poems* came out in Dublin in 1963; *Selected Poems* (1963) was edited for the U.S. by Warren and Allen TATE. He translated St. John PERSE, APOLLINAIRE, QUASIMODO and Goethe.

Dewar, Michael James Stewart (1918–). British-American chemist. Dewar was educated at Oxford University, where he earned his D.Phil. in 1942. After research at Oxford he worked in industry as a physical chemist until his appointment in 1951 as professor of chemistry at Queen Mary College, London. In 1959 Dewar moved to the U.S. and has served successively as professor of chemistry at the University of Chicago and since 1963 at the University of Texas. Dewar is noted for his contributions to theoretical chemistry. In his *Electronic Theory of Organic Chemistry* (1949) he argued strongly for the molecular-orbital theory introduced by Robert MILLIKEN. He did much to improve molecular-orbital calculations and by the 1960s was able to claim that he and his colleagues could rapidly and accurately calculate a number of chemical and physical properties of molecules.

American philosopher and educator Professor John Dewey.

Dewey, John (1859–1952). U.S. philosopher and educator. After graduating from the University of Vermont and Johns Hopkins University he taught at several universities, and in 1904 was permanently appointed at Columbia University. In philosophy Dewey was the most important heir to the school of American philosophical pragmatism founded by William JAMES. Like James, he challenged all absolute theories of reality and truth. In their place, he espoused a theory of truth that stressed the use of human ideas and hypotheses as limited but necessary instruments for creation of workable truths. To this philosophy he gave the name "instrumentalism." In education Dewey was a prominent proponent of experimentation, or "learning by doing." His most important writings include *Psychology* (1886), *The School and Society* (1900) and *Problems of Man* (1946).

Dewey, Thomas E(dmund) (1902–1971). American attorney, politician, and Republican presidential candidate (1944, 1948). Dewey graduated from the University of Michigan in 1923, took a law degree from Columbia in 1925 and began to practice law in New York City. He gained national fame as special prosecutor between 1935 and 1937, and was elected the district attorney of New York County in 1937. The following year he ran for governor of New York, losing by a narrow margin to Democrat incumbent Herbert Lehman. In 1940 he sought the Republican presidential nomination, losing to Wendell WILLKIE. Dewey was elected governor of New York in 1942 and reelected in 1946 and 1950. He took a moderate stance on most issues, but was renowned for his opposition to the NEW DEAL of President Franklin D. ROOSEVELT. Dewey unsuccessfully challenged Roosevelt for the presidency in 1944. Nominated again in 1948, Dewey choose California governor (later Supreme Court chief justice) Earl WARREN as his running mate. Many polls predicted a Dewey victory over President Harry S TRUMAN, but Truman's aggressive campaigning led to Dewey's surprise defeat. After retiring as governor in 1954, Dewey remained active

Governor Thomas E. Dewey lost the 1948 U.S. presidential election to Democratic candidate Harry S Truman.

in Republican national politics. He was the author of *The Case Against the New Deal* (1940) and *Journey to the Far Pacific* (1952).

For further reading:
Smith, Richard N., *Thomas E. Dewey and His Times*. New York: Simon & Schuster, n.d.

DEW Line. Radar terminals of the Distant Early Warning Network, near 69 degrees North Latitude and extending from northwestern ALASKA to northeastern CANADA—their purpose to give an alert at the approach of unfriendly aircraft. The DEW Line, constructed and run by the UNITED STATES and Canada, began operations in 1957. It was expanded to the ALEUTIAN ISLANDS in 1959 and across GREENLAND in 1961.

de Wolfe, Elsie (1865–1950). American interior decorator and designer, often viewed as the originator of modern professional interior design. After an early career as an actress, de Wolfe took on a total renovation (c. 1910) of her New York townhouse. Notables who visited the house spread word of the de Wolfe style and brought professional commissions. Stanford WHITE, the noted architect, asked her to deal with the interiors of the Colony Club (1905–07), a project that further advanced her vocabulary of light color tones and simple forms. She became a spokesperson for the "good design" direction of its day, giving lectures and writing a popular and influential book of 1913, *The House in Good Taste*. She continued to conduct a successful practice in New York, in Paris (where she became Lady Mendl with her 1926 marriage to Sir Charles Mendl), and finally in Beverly Hills. Although never an advocate of Modernism as that term is now understood, Elsie de Wolfe moved the decorator's profession toward the modern world with her emphasis on professionalism and with her advocacy of simplicity and common sense in design.

Dexter, John (1925–1990). British theater and opera director. Dexter began his career at the Royal Court Theater in London in the late 1950s. Later asked by Sir Laurence OLIVIER to become associate director of the National Theater, he staged such major plays as Peter SHAFFER's *Equus* (1974) and David Henry Hwang's *M. Butterfly* (1988). He won Tony awards in New York for best director for both plays. He also staged operas for the Paris Opera and the Metropolitan Opera in New York.

Deyneka, Alexander Alexandrovich (1899–1969). Russian painter and sculptor. When SOCIALIST REALISM was imposed by the Soviet authorities, he managed to preserve some of his earlier style in his works, which included sports, industrial and military scenes. Many of his murals decorated Moscow Underground stations.

d'Herelle, Felix (1873–1949). French-Canadian bacteriologist. D'Herelle, the son of a Canadian father and Dutch mother, went to school in Paris and later studied medicine at the University of Montreal. He worked as a bacteriologist in Guatemala and Mexico from 1901 until 1909, when he returned to Europe to take up a position at the Pasteur Institute in Paris. D'Herelle moved to the University of Leiden in 1921 but after only a short stay resigned to become director of the Egyptian Bacteriological Service (1923). In 1926 d'Herelle was appointed to the chair of bacteriology at Yale, a position he held until his retirement in 1933. He is best known for his discovery of the **bacteriophage**—a type of virus that destroys bacteria. This work began in 1910. A similar discovery of what d'Herelle termed a "bacteriolytic agent" was announced independently by Frederick Twort in 1915. D'Herelle published his own account first in 1917, followed by his monograph *The Bacteriophage, Its Role in Immunity* (1921). He spent the rest of his career attempting to develop bacteriophages as therapeutic agents. He tried to cure cholera in India in 1927 and bubonic plague in Egypt in 1926 by administering the appropriate phage to patients.

The importance of the bacteriophage as a research tool in molecular biology cannot be disputed. The so-called phage group, centered on Max DELBRUCK, made many of the early advances in this discipline in the 1940s.

Ballet impresario Serge Diaghilev.

Diaghilev, Serge Pavlovich (1872–1929). Russian ballet impresario, born in Novgorod. In pursuit of his goal of introducing Russian art to Western Europe, in 1908 Diaghilev presented the bass Feodor CHALIAPIN in a season of Russian opera in Paris. He followed this up with his famous BALLETS RUSSES, presented in Paris (1909) and London (1911), in the conviction that in ballet he could form a union of all the arts. To this end he secured the services of dancers of outstanding skill—PAVLOVA, NIJINSKY, KARSAVINA and LOPOKOVA—and choreographers such as FOKINE and MASSINE; he commissioned BENOIS, BAKST, MATISSE, PICASSO, BRAQUE and others to design the decor, and DEBUSSY, RAVEL, STRAVINSKY and PROKOFIEV to compose ballet scores. The revolution broke his links with Russia, but with Paris as its headquarters his company continued to enjoy the highest reputation.

Dial, The. American periodical. *The Dial* was founded in Chicago in 1880 and later moved to New York. It began as a conservative literary magazine, but in 1916 evolved into a journal of radical opinion. By 1920, it was an influential champion of modern art and literature. Contributors to the *The Dial* include Sherwood ANDERSON, George SANTAYANA, D.H. LAWRENCE, T.S. ELIOT and Gertrude STEIN. *The Dial* published portions of Oswald SPENGLER's *The Decline of the West* in 1924–25, and Thomas MANN's *Death in Venice* in 1924. Marianne MOORE served as its editor for the last four years of its existence, but it folded in 1929 from lack of finances.

Diamond, I.A.L. (1920–1988). HOLLYWOOD screenwriter. A longtime collaborator of director Billy WILDER, Diamond and Wilder made such films as *Love in the Afternoon* (1957), *Some Like it Hot* (1959), *Irma la Douce* (1963), *Kiss Me, Stupid* (1964) and *The Private Life of Sherlock Holmes*. Diamond won an ACADEMY AWARD for *The Apartment* (1960).

Diamond, Jack "Legs" (1896–1931). American gangster. Diamond's life as a career criminal began in New York City in the early 1900s, when he stole merchandise from the rear of delivery trucks and raced off before he could be caught. His speedy escapes earned him the lifelong nickname "Legs." By the early 1920s, during PROHIBITION, he was working as a bootlegger, bodyguard and sometime killer for the city's top labor racketeer, "Little Augie" Orgen. After Orgen was murdered, with Diamond by his side, in 1927 Diamond made peace with his killers, gangsters Louis Lepke and Jacob "Gurrah" Shapiro, and took over his ex-boss' bootleg and narcotics trade. Thus he graduated to the world of big-time gangsters, and soon he was battling for territory with the infamous "Dutch" SCHULTZ. A dapper ladies' man and ruthless killer, Diamond escaped from many close calls with severe injuries and a reputation as "unkillable." The reputation proved unfounded when he was murdered by unknown mobsters in a hideout in Albany, N.Y.

Diaz, Porfirio (1830–1915). Mexican general and dictator. Diaz's long career straddled the 19th and 20th centuries. Born into a poor mestizo family, he changed his studies from the priesthood to law, but in 1854 joined the revolutionary forces of Benito Juarez. He rose in the military, achieving the rank of general in 1861 and becoming a federal deputy that same year. Diaz fought against France and Maximilian from 1861 to 1867, and was promoted to army commander. In 1871 he unsuccessfully revolted against the Juarez government and lost a presidential bid, and in 1876 he again was defeated in the presidential elections. However, he rebelled again, this time against Juarez's successor, Sebastian Lerdo de Tejada, and succeeded in overthrowing the government. Diaz assumed the presidency in 1877 and, while he was not president from 1880 to 1884, he effectively ruled MEXICO for the next 35 years. He proved a stern dictator, suppressing opposition and almost eliminating the previously prevalent countrywide banditry. He opened Mexico to foreign development, notably by U.S. business interests, bringing enormous revenue into the country and ensuring economic growth. This policy enriched Diaz and his followers but left the peasantry in wretched conditions with diminished landholdings and the workers as poor as ever with a government-opposed labor movement. In 1909 Diaz proclaimed a reinstatement of democracy, but when he again engineered reelection (1910) and showed no evidence of fulfilling his pledge, his regime was overthrown by a 1911 revolution led by Francisco Madero. He fled to Paris, where he died in exile.

Dibelius, Martin (1883–1947). German Protestant theologian. Dibelius became a professor of theology at the University of Heidelberg in 1915 and taught there for most of his adult life. He was known as an interdisciplinary thinker who drew from literature and folkloric oral traditions in his theological works. Dibelius was especially interested in the history of early Christianity. His major books include *Die Formgeschichte des Evangeliums* (1919) and *Geschichte der Unchristlichen Literatur* (1926).

Dick, George Francis (1881–1967). American physician. Dick and his wife, **Gladys Rowena Henry Dick** (1881–1963), also a physician and medical researcher, were renowned for their work on the prevention and treatment of scarlet fever. Until their work, scarlet fever was an endemic and often fatal or crippling childhood disease.

A graduate of Rush Medical College (1905), George Dick studied pathology at the universities of Vienna and Munich. Returning to the U.S. in 1909, he joined the faculty of the University of Chicago, where he eventually became professor of pathology and head of the department of medicine. Gladys Henry obtained her M.D. from Johns Hopkins University School of Medicine (1907) and did postgraduate work in several fields at Johns Hopkins and the University of Berlin. Meeting in 1911 at the University of Chicago, where they were both research pathologists, they were married in 1914.

Collaborating in their research, in the early 1920s the Dicks discovered that hemolytic streptococci bacteria cause scarlet fever. They developed the first test for determining a person's susceptibility to scarlet fever—the Dick test. They also did important work on immunization. However, they became the subject of international controversy because they patented their techniques of toxin and antitoxin development used in the test. In 1935, the LEAGUE OF NATIONS declared that these patents restricted further research into scarlet fever immunization or treatment.

Dick, Philip K(indred) (1928–1982). American novelist and short story writer. Dick has enjoyed a steadily increasing reputation as one of the most original and visionary American fiction writers of the second half of this century. Within the science fiction field, in which he produced most of his best work, he is regarded by peers such as Ursula LE GUIN and Stanislaw LEM as the finest writer in that genre. Dick, who lived in California for nearly all his life, began his career as a prolific short-story writer in the 1950s, contributing to a wide range of science fiction pulp magazines. He first emerged as a major science fiction novelist with *Eye in the Sky* (1956), which was followed by numerous acclaimed works including *The Man in the High Castle* (1962), which won the Hugo Award for best novel, *The Three Stigmata of Palmer Eldritch* (1965) and *Ubik* (1969). *Valis* (1981) is a fictionalized account of Dick's mystical experiences in the final decade of his life. *The Transmigration of Timothy Archer* (1982) is considered Dick's best mainstream fiction novel.

For further reading:

Sutin, Lawrence, *Divine Invasions: A Life of Philip K. Dick.* New York: Harmony Books, 1989.

Dickey, James (Lafayette) (1923–). American poet, novelist, critic. Born in Georgia, Dickey attended Vanderbilt University and began his career as an advertising copy writer. His first volume, *Into the Stone,* appeared in 1960; his fourth, *Buckdancer's Choice,* won the National Book Award in 1965. He is best known for his novel *Deliverance* (1970), an adventure story about four businessmen on a hunting trip in rural Georgia, which became a bestseller and was made into a movie. *The Zodiac* (1976) is a long poem in 12 parts. The title work of *The Strength of Fields* was written for President CARTER's inauguration. *Puella* (1982) describes a girl's coming of age. Dickey is also known for his outspoken criticism of his contemporaries, collected in *The Suspect in Poetry* (1964), *Babel to Byzantium* (1968), *Self-Interviews* (1970) and *Sorties* (1971).

For further reading:

Baughman, Ronald, *Understanding James Dickey.* Columbia: University of South Carolina Press, 1985.

Calhoun, Richard J., *James Dickey.* Boston: G.K. Hall, 1983.

Dick Tracy. The world's most popular detective comic strip, by Chester Gould (1900–85), *Dick Tracy* was first syndicated on October 12, 1931, and is still enjoyed by millions. Over the years, the incorruptible Tracy has used his two-way wrist radio and other high-tech gadgets to do battle with a host of underworld types, including Pruneface, the Mole, Flyface, Itchy and Ugly Christine. Gould retired on Christmas Day 1977, after which the strip was taken over by Max Allan Collins and Rick Fletcher; after Fletcher's death in 1983, Dick Locher was added. The feature-length motion picture *Dick Tracy,* directed by and starring Warren Beatty, was released in 1990.

Didion, Joan (1934–). American author. Born in Sacramento, Cal., which she evokes in much of her work, Didion was educated at the University of California at Berkeley. She went to New York and worked for *Vogue* magazine for eight years, during which time she published her first novel, *Run River* (1963). Returning to California, she wrote a series of essays for the *Saturday Evening Post,* which were collected in the acclaimed *Slouching Towards Bethlehem* (1968). The title essay, a portrait of HIPPIES in the Haight Ashbury district of SAN FRANCISCO, established her as a leading practitioner of the NEW JOURNALISM, with its subjective point of view and detailed impressions. In the best-selling novel *Play It as It Lays* (1970, filmed 1972), she established her unique fictional style, taut, precise and flat. Her writing evidences her fundamentally bleak and hopeless view of life. Other works include *The White Album* (1979), essays; *Salvador* (1983); *Democracy: A Novel* (1984); and *Miami* (1987). Didion is married to the writer **John Gregory Dunne,** with whom she collaborates in the writing of screenplays.

Didrikson, Mildred "Babe" (1913–1956). American athlete. Didrikson became a professional athlete after the 1932 OLYMPIC GAMES in Los Angeles, in which she set two world records. She excelled in a variety of sports, including basketball, baseball, billiards and swimming. In 1947 she began her career as a professional golfer, winning every possible women's title at least once during the next decade and was named outstanding woman athlete of the first half of the 20th century by an Associated Press poll. Her autobiography, *The Life I've Led,* was published in 1955, a year before her death from cancer.

Die Brucke [*German:* The Bridge]. German artistic movement that was heavily influenced by EXPRESSIONISM. The young German painters who initially founded Die Brucke ("The Bridge") were all, at the time, studying architecture at the Dresden Technical School. These artists, who included Ernst-Ludwig KIRCHNER and Fritz Bleyl, were especially drawn to anticlassical forms from non-European cultures, such as African and Oceanic sculpture. Their pictorial style featured intense distortions intended to emphasize spiritual freedom and a shattering of accepted artistic definitions. Die Brucke never formulated a developed and consistent artistic manifesto, but it did create a sense of mission—declaring itself as the bridge to the art of the future. Emil NOLDE was among the painters who associated themselves for a time with the movement, which ultimately disbanded in 1913.

Diederichs, Nicolaas (1903–1978). President of SOUTH AFRICA (1975–78). Diederichs became minister of economic affairs in 1958, and in 1967 was named finance minister.

Diefenbaker, John G(eorge) (1895–1979). Prime minister of CANADA (1957–63). Diefenbaker was first elected to Canada's House of Commons in 1940, and served 13 terms as a representative for Saskatchewan. In 1958, he led his PROGRESSIVE CONSERVATIVE PARTY to the largest electoral victory in Canada's history. His administration was noted for its ambitious efforts to unlock the natural resources of the Canadian north and to increase independence from the U.S. A tireless critic of the opposition LIBERAL PARTY governments that succeeded him, Diefenbaker often demonstrated an acerbic humor and eloquent oratory in debate in the House of Commons.

Diels, Otto Paul Hermann (1876–1954). German organic chemist. The son of Hermann Diels, a famous classical scholar, Diels earned his doctorate under Emil FISCHER in Berlin (1899) and became professor there in 1906. From 1916 until his retirement in 1948 he was professor at Kiel. In 1906 he made an unexpected discovery, that of a new oxide of carbon, carbon suboxide. Diels' second major discovery was a method of removing hydrogen from steroids by means of selenium. He used this method in research on cholesterol and bile acids, obtaining aromatic hydrocarbons that enabled the structure of the steroids to be deduced. In 1928 Diels and his assistant Kurt ALDER discovered a synthetic reaction in which a diene (compound containing two double bonds) is added to a compound containing one double bond flanked by carbonyl or carboxyl groups to give a ring structure. The reaction proceeds in the mildest conditions, is of general application and hence of great utility in synthesis. It has been used in the synthesis of natural products such as sterols, vitamin K, cantharides and synthetic polymers. For this discovery Diels and Alder were jointly awarded the NOBEL PRIZE for chemistry in 1950.

Diem, Ngo Dinh (1901–1963). South Vietnamese leader. Born in Annam, Diem was a member of an important Roman Catholic family, an ardent nationalist and a strong anticommunist. Repeatedly declining offers of political office, he finally became prime minister of South VIETNAM under BAO DAI in 1954 after the partition of his country. Victorious in the presidential elections of 1955, he declared South Vietnam a republic the following year. Strongly supported by the U.S., Diem consolidated his power but became increasingly unpopular due to his nepotism, his dictatorial control and his favoring of Catholics over Buddhists. Under Diem, the South Vietnamese position in the VIETNAM WAR worsened and American support waned. He was assassinated during a 1963 military coup.

Dien Bien Phu. Site of the climactic battle that effectively ended the war between FRANCE and the VIET MINH (1946–54). It was a small village on the border between Laos and North Vietnam. About 180 miles

President Ngo Dinh Diem of South Vietnam during a visit to the United States (May 19, 1957). Diem was later assassinated.

from the nearest French post, it was fortified by some 16,000 French troops, including soldiers of the French Foreign Legion and Vietnamese, Laotians and Cambodians fighting on the French side. The French hoped to draw the Viet Minh into a set-piece battle in which French firepower would destroy them. But the French underestimated their enemy. Viet Minh General VO NGUYEN GIAP entrenched artillery in the surrounding mountains and massed five divisions totaling about 60,000 troops. The battle began with a massive Viet Minh artillery barrage on March 13, 1954 and was followed by an infantry assault. At the height of the battle, the French requested military support from the U.S., but diplomatic and domestic U.S. political considerations caused President EISENHOWER to deny the request. Fighting raged until May 7, 1954, when the French were overrun. The shock of the fall of Dien Bien Phu led France, already plagued by public opposition to the war, to agree to the independence of VIETNAM at the GENEVA CONFERENCE in 1954.

For further reading:
Fall, Bernard, *Hell in a Very Small Place: The Siege of Dien Bien Phu.* Philadelphia: Lippincott, 1966.

Dieppe. Port city on the English Channel north of Rouen, in France's Seine-Maritime department. Dieppe was held by the Germans from 1940 to 1944. On August 19, 1942, during WORLD WAR II, the city was stormed by Allied commandos who were reconnoitering German defenses. The Germans retaliated and inflicted many fatalities on the Allies (who put the experience to good use during the NORMANDY invasion of 1944). Several structures damaged during the war have been reconstructed.

Diesel, Rudolph Christian Carl (1858–1913). German engineer and inventor, designer of the diesel engine. After graduating from the Munich Institute of Technology, Diesel worked as a mechanic for two years in Switzerland and then worked in Paris as a thermal engineer. He was a devout Lutheran and a dedicated pacifist, believing in international religious liberation. In 1893 he demonstrated his first engine, and, although the first few attempts failed, within three years he had developed a pressure-ignited heat engine. The engine named for him is now used universally, for example, in powering boats and in running generators.

By 1898 Diesel was a millionaire but his fortune soon disappeared. He toured the world giving lectures and visited the U.S. in 1912. His health was bad, he suffered from gout and was depressed by the buildup to WORLD WAR I. On the ferry returning to Paris from London in 1913, after dining with a friend, he disappeared and was assumed to have drowned in the English Channel.

Dietrich, Marlene [born Maria Magdalena von Losch] (1901–). German-born film actress. Dietrich, whose primary film triumphs were in the 1930s, has become one of the enduring femme fatale figures of the cinema. Born in Berlin, she studied as a youth for a career as a concert violinist before an injured wrist deflected her into an acting career. After studying at the Max Reinhardt Drama School, she was discovered by film director Josef von STERNBERG, who made Dietrich an international star through her roll as the alluring dance-hall chanteuse Lola-Lola in *The Blue Angel* (1930), a film shot in Germany. Von Sternberg then directed Dietrich in a number of classic HOLLYWOOD films, including *Dishonored* (1931), *Shanghai Express* (1932), *Blonde Venus* (1932) and *The Scarlet Empress* (1934). Dietrich shed von Sternberg's heavy dramatic burden and had a comedy hit alongside James STEWART in *Destry Rides Again* (1939). She made relatively few films in the remaining decades of her life, but her supporting roles in *Witness for the Prosecution* (1958)

One of the great motion picture femme fatales, Marlene Dietrich gained international recognition for her role in The Blue Angel *(1930).*

and *Touch of Evil* (1958) were memorable. Maximilian Schell made a biographical documentary, *Marlene*, in 1986.

Dietrich, Raymond Henry (1894–1980). American automotive designer. Dietrich was credited with designing the flowing, elegant body lines used on the classic luxury cars of the 1920s. He designed cars for such noted celebrities of the period as Al JOLSON, Rudolf VALENTINO, and Gloria SWANSON.

Diffrient, Niels (1928–). American industrial designer best known for his development of chairs based on ERGONOMICS. Diffrient studied at Cranbrook Academy in the 1940s and worked with the SAARINEN office from 1946 to 1951. From 1951 to 1952 he was with the office of Walter B. Ford and thereafter in New York in the office of Henry Dreyfuss, where he became a partner in 1956. His work there included aircraft interiors, road and farm machinery, and studies in ergonomics. After leaving the Dreyfuss office in 1981, Diffrient became an independent designer concentrating on furniture. His chairs and his office systems furniture are his best-known recent projects.

Dillard, Annie (1945–). American essayist. Dillard was educated at Hollins College and was married to the poet and novelist Henry Dillard and later to the novelist Gary Clevidence. Her first book of poetry, *Tickets for a Prayer Wheel,* was published in 1974. That same year her prose reflections, *Pilgrim at Tinker Creek,* was published to great acclaim. Compared to Thoreau's *Walden Pond,* the book won the PULITZER PRIZE in 1974. The book presents Dillard's lyrical reflections on nature, humanity and theology. Dillard has contributed to *Atlantic Monthly, Poetry, Harper's* and many other periodicals and has taught poetry and creative writing. Other works include *Holy the Firm* (1978) and the autobiographical *An American Childhood* (1987).

Dillinger, John (Herbert) (1903–1934). American bank robber. A petty thief during his childhood in Indianapolis, Ind., Dillinger graduated to serious crime in 1924, when he attempted to rob a grocery store. Apprehended, he served nine years in prison where he became a confirmed criminal. After he was released in 1933, his spectacular bank-robbing career lasted a mere 11 months. During that time, he and his two successive gangs held up approximately 20 midwestern banks; he was captured and escaped jail twice; and he was responsible for 16 murders. While the robbery spree was in progress, Dillinger became something of a popular figure to many Depression-era Americans who appreciated his courtesy to individuals and his hatred of banking institutions. Named public enemy number one by the FBI, Dillinger was the object of an intensive manhunt. Apparently betrayed by a female friend, he was killed by FBI agents as he left the Biograph Theater in Chicago on July 22, 1934.

Dillon, Clarence (1882–1979). American financier. In 1925 his firm, Dillon, Read & Co., won a hard-fought battle for control of DODGE BROTHERS Automobile Company. Shortly thereafter, Dillon arranged a merger of Dodge and CHRYSLER, which resulted in Chrysler Corp. becoming the nation's third-largest auto maker. Dillon's son, **C. Douglas Dillon,** held various posts in the EISENHOWER administration and served as secretary of the treasury (1961–65) under presidents KENNEDY and JOHNSON.

DiMaggio, Joe [Joseph Paul DiMaggio] (1914–). American baseball player. Immortalized in song and story, DiMaggio's reputation has reached legendary status. He joined the New York Yankees in 1936 and remained with the team through their "dynasty" years, which included nine world championships. Perhaps the game's all-time best natural hitter, his 1941 56-game hitting streak is one of his more memorable feats. He was an All-Star during each of his major league seasons, and was named Most Valuable Player three times. His career was interrupted by World War II, but he was still a considerable factor in four post-war World Series championships and led the league in home runs in 1948. His legendary status was perhaps fueled by the fact that he was for a time married to another American legend, Marilyn MONROE. His two brothers, Dom and Vince, also played in the majors. DiMaggio retired in 1951, and was named to the Hall of Fame in 1955.

Dimitrov, Georgi (1882–1949). Bulgarian Communist leader. An early trade unionist, Dimitrov was organizing strikes by 1905. Elected to the Bulgarian National Assembly (1913), he was imprisoned in 1915 for his opposition to BULGARIA's entry into WORLD WAR I. From 1917 to 1923 he secretly led the nation's Communist Movement and, in 1923, a Communist uprising against Alexander Tsankov. When it failed, Dimitrov fled the country. In Berlin (1933) he was accused of complicity in the REICHSTAG FIRE, but was acquitted. Settling in the U.S.S.R., Dimitrov served as secretary-general (1935–43) of the COMINTERN. In 1945 he returned to a newly liberated Bulgaria, where he headed the Communist Party and became prime minister in 1946. During his tenure in office, he followed an unswerving Communist line but showed signs of growing independence from the U.S.S.R. He died in Moscow in 1949 while undergoing medical treatment.

d'Indy, Vincent. See INDY, Vincent d'.

Dinesen, Isak [Karen Blixen] (1885–1962). Danish author. Dinesen, who wrote primarily in English, is best known for the acclaimed memoir *Out of Africa* (1937, filmed 1985), which recounts her life on a coffee plantation in Kenya with her philandering husband and her lover. Dinesen was born to an upper-class family and, after studying art in Paris married her cousin, Baron Bror Blixen-Finecke, in 1914. They immediately moved to Africa, but following their divorce and the eventual failure of the plantation, she returned to Denmark and began writing in earnest. Her first important work, *Seven Gothic Tales* (1934), was praised for its use of fantasy and evocative description; it aroused much curiosity about the un-

"Joltin' " Joe DiMaggio, American baseball legend, hits his 17th home run of the year in Philadelphia (June 28, 1941).

known author. Dinesen continued to produce successful and esteemed stories and memoirs, though she suffered ill health as the result of syphilis contracted from her husband. Her works include *Winter's Tales* (1942), *Last Tales* (1957) and the essay collection *Shadows in the Grass* (1961).

For further reading:

Pelensky, Olga Anastasia, *Isak Dinesen: The Life and Imagination of a Seducer*. Athens, Ohio: Ohio University Press, 1991.

Ding Ling [born Jiang Bingzhi] (1904–1986). Chinese writer. She was a feminist whose writings were primarily concerned with the impact of CHINA'S communist revolution on the lives of peasant women. After the communist victory in 1949, she held a number of key literary and cultural posts. A political purge in 1957 led to her banishment from public life and the banning of her works. She was imprisoned for a number of years and was not officially rehabilitated until 1977.

DioGuardi, John [alias Johnny Dio] (1915–1979). American organized-crime leader. DioGuardi was believed to have specialized in labor racketeering, and was alledgedly associated with Teamster official Jimmy HOFFA in the 1950s. He was indicted for arranging the 1956 acid-throwing incident that blinded labor columnist Victor Riesel, but never came to trial for that crime. DioGuardi served several prison terms for tax evasion, extortion and fraud, and died in prison.

Dior, Christian (1905–1957). French fashion designer best known for his 1947 line, with its long skirts and hint of a backward turn toward the austere style of the WORLD WAR I era. Dior studied in PARIS with the intention of becoming a career diplomat, but in 1927 opened a small Paris art gallery showing the works of avant-garde artists such as Salvador DALI and Jean COCTEAU. The GREAT DEPRESSION closed the gallery, leading Dior to turn to fashion design in 1935. In 1947 his firm launched with overwhelming success the style that became known as the New Look. His annual lines thereafter, each with a central theme, were popular and widely copied in the production of ready-to-wear manufacturers. Practicality and a look that was both soft and architectural were typical themes of Dior's designs. His firm was taken over briefly by Yves SAINT LAURENT and then by Marc Bohan after Dior's death. Gianfranco Ferre is currently design director. As the House of Dior, the organization has continued to grow with divisions devoted to hats, furs, shoes, perfumes and jewelry. The New York branch alone employed a staff of about 1,200 by 1948. Dior was the recipient of a 1947 Neiman Marcus Award and a Parsons Medal in 1956.

Diori, Hamani (1916–1989). First president of the independent nation of NIGER. He held several government posts during the years when Niger was an autonomous French territory and was chosen by the French to become president when the nation was granted independence in 1960. His regime was plagued by widespread corruption, and the government's problems were compounded by a severe drought that hit sub-Saharan Africa in the late 1960s and early 1970s. Diori was overthrown by a military coup in 1974. After spending 13 years in prison and under house arrest, he was freed in 1987. He then moved to Morocco.

Dirac, Paul Adrien Maurice (1902–1984). British mathematician and physicist. After graduating in 1921 in electrical engineering at Bristol University, Dirac went on to read mathematics at Cambridge, where he obtained his Ph.D. in 1926. He lectured for several years in America, then was appointed (1932) to the Lucasian Professorship of Mathematics at Cambridge, a post he held until his retirement in 1969. In 1971 he became professor of physics at Florida State University. Dirac is acknowledged as one of the most creative theoreticians of the early 20th century. In 1926, slightly later than Max BORN and Pascual Jordan in Germany, he developed a general formalism for QUANTUM MECHANICS. In 1928 he produced his relativistic theory to describe the properties of the electron. The wave equations developed by SCHRODINGER to describe the behavior of electrons were nonrelativistic; a significant deficiency was their failure to account for the electron spin discovered in 1925 by GOUDSMIT and George Uhlenbeck. Dirac's rewriting of the equations to incorporate relativity had considerable value, for it not only predicted the correct energy levels of the hydrogen atom but also revealed that some of those levels were no longer single but could be split into two. It is just such a splitting of spectral lines that is characteristic of a spinning electron.

Dirac also predicted from these equations that there must be states of negative energy for the electron. In 1930 he proposed a theory to account for this that added a new dimension of matter to the universe—antimatter. It was soon appreciated that Dirac's argument was sufficiently general to apply to all particles. Above all else a quantum theorist, in 1930 Dirac published the first edition of his classic work *The Principles of Quantum Mechanics*. In 1933 he shared the NOBEL PRIZE for physics with Schrodinger for his work on electron theory.

dirigible. See ZEPPELIN.

Dirksen, Everett (McKinley) (1896–1969). American political leader. Born in Pekin, Illinois, Dirksen served in WORLD WAR I, returned to his hometown, practiced law and won election to the House of Representatives as a Republican in 1932. He served as a member of the House until 1948 and was elected to the Senate in 1950, remaining a senator until his death. A popular and colorful conservative, he became party whip in 1957 and minority leader two years later. Dirksen maintained a conservative stance regarding foreign and domestic affairs and supported Senator Joseph MCCARTHY. Moderating his positions in the 1960s, he helped President KENNEDY secure the passage of a NUCLEAR TEST BAN TREATY in 1963. He was an enthusiastic supporter of President Lyndon JOHNSON'S CIVIL RIGHTS program and aided in the passage of landmark civil rights legislation.

Republican Senator Everett Dirksen became Senate minority leader in 1959.

Disney, Walt (Walter Elias) (1901–1966). American motion-picture producer and amusement-park entrepreneur whose work has become synonymous with family entertainment. Born in Chicago, Disney spent his boyhood on a farm in nearby Marceline, Missouri and his later school days in Kansas City, Missouri, where he first experimented with cartooning and ANIMATION. In 1923 he moved to Los Angeles, intending to market his first series of animated films, *Alice in Cartoonland*, which blended live-action characters with animated backgrounds. The appearance of Mickey Mouse in a synchronized-

Walt Disney, creator of Mickey Mouse and Disneyland.

sound cartoon called *Steamboat Willie* in 1928 saved his studio from certain ruin and set the course for future success. With his brother Roy and assistants like the brilliant Ub Iwerks, Disney dominated animation for the next 40 years. *Snow White and the Seven Dwarfs* (1938) demonstrated the viability of a feature-length format. Shorts like *The Old Mill* (1937) and features like *Pinocchio* (1940) pioneered the three-dimensional effects of the multiplane camera technology. For FANTASIA (1941) he developed a stereophonic-sound system; he was also the first filmmaker to contract exclusively with the new Technicolor system. After World War II Disney turned his attention to other interests. *Treasure Island* (1950) inaugurated a successful series of live-action adaptations from children's classics. Several television series, beginning in 1954 with "Disneyland" for ABC, showcased not only the Disney movies, but the new theme parks as well. The DISNEYLAND park opened in Anaheim, California, in 1955. The Disney World project in Orlando, Florida, was well into the planning stages when Disney died in 1966 of an acute circulatory collapse. During his career he amassed 39 ACADEMY AWARDS and hundreds of other awards and honors.

For further reading:

Thomas, Bob, *Walt Disney*. New York: Simon and Schuster, 1976.

Disneyland and Disney World. These two American amusement parks were inspired by animator and film producer Walt DISNEY and are famous throughout the world. Disneyland, located in Anaheim, California, was launched by Disney himself in 1955. The second park, Walt Disney World, was opened outside of Orlando, Florida, in 1971, with a companion park, Epcot Center, opening in 1982. Disney's approach was to create specific themes within each park, such as Fantasyland and Tomorrowland. The first Disney theme park outside the U.S. opened in Tokyo, Japan, in 1983 (Tokyo Disneyland). Another Disney park is located in France (projected opening, 1991). Designed to appeal to adults as well as children, the parks are known for their friendly employees, cleanliness and lavish, innovative attractions that utilize the latest in technology.

Di Stefano, Giuseppe (1921–). Italian tenor. Born near Catania, Sicily, Di Stefano studied privately and made his debut at Reggio Emilia in 1946 as Des Grieux in *Manon Lescaut*. His La Scala debut occurred a year later, and this theater became his European home base. He first performed in the U.S. at the Metropolitan Opera in 1948, singing the Duke in *Rigoletto*. He remained at the Metropolitan for the next five years, singing there again from 1955 to 1956 and 1964 to 1965. Noted for the pure lyricism of his voice, Di Stefano has appeared at most of the world's leading opera houses, singing the major tenor parts in the Italian and French repertoires.

di Stefano Lauthe, Alfredo (1926–). Argentine-born soccer player. Renowned for his achievements with Real Madrid of Spain in the 1950s and 1960s, di Stefano began his career in Argentina with the famous River Plate club. In 1949 he joined the exodus to Colombia, where higher salaries were luring the cream of South America soccer. In 1953, FIFA ruled the Colombian system illegal and forced the release of all non-Colombian players. Di Stefano moved to Spain and embarked upon the golden period of his career and that of Spanish soccer. Real Madrid dominated Spanish domestic competition and helped forge the popularity of the newly created inter-European competitions. Led by di Stefano, Real won the first five European Cups (1956–60) and the first World Club Championship held in 1960. The forward line of Francisco Gento, Ferenc Puskas and di Stefano became the most famed and feared in soccer history. Their mastery reached its peak at the 1960 European Cup Final when Real crushed Eintracht Frankfurt 7–3, Puskas and di Stefano scoring the goals created by Gento's brilliant wing play. Di Stefano played seven times for Argentina and 31 times for Spain.

Dix, Dom Gregory (George Eglington Alston) (1901–1952). Anglican priest and theologian. Dix was one of the leading figures in the Anglican Church in the 20th century. He was noted both for his personal charm and leadership abilities and for his insightful writings on the history and meaning of the Anglican liturgy. Educated at Oxford, he was ordained as an Anglican priest in 1925 and took his final vows in 1940 after a period of monastic life at Nashdom Abbey. In 1946 Dix was named Select Preacher for the University of Cambridge. In 1948 he became the Prior of Nashdom Abbey. His major works include *A Detection of Aumbries* (1942) and *The Shape of the Liturgy* (1945).

Dix, Otto (1891–1969). German painter. Born in Gera, he studied at art schools in Dresden and Dusseldorf. A soldier in WORLD WAR I, he was horrified by the fighting and returned to Dusseldorf to create a series of harrowingly realistic paintings and the cycle of 50 powerful etchings entitled *War* (1925). He lived in Berlin (1925–27), moving to Dresden in 1927 to teach at that city's Academy. Branded a decadent by the Nazis, he was removed from his post in 1933. Although he was arrested in 1939 for plotting against HITLER, he was drafted into the German army in 1945, and was later a French prisoner of war. Dix is known for his bitingly satirical German expressionist works. In these paintings the personalities of the WEIMAR REPUBLIC—often prostitutes, beggars and criminals—are forcefully portrayed in harsh colors and expressively distorted forms. His later paintings were largely religious in subject matter.

Dixieland jazz. Synonymous with "traditional jazz," although the two terms continue to evoke significant polemical resonances. Initially, "dixieland" derived from the ORIGINAL DIXIELAND JAZZ BAND, the white New Orleans group that became an international sensation through its tours and recordings. Since such groups were regarded as essentially imitative of the style developed by black musicians in New Orleans, "dixieland" become associated with white groups like the ODJB and New Orleans Rhythm Kings, with "traditional" and "New Orleans" reserved for the music of the black originators and their followers. But the distinction has lost much of its original specificity, and the terms can now be considered interchangeable. Stylistically, dixieland involves a collective approach to improvisation, with the trumpet generally assigned the melody and with counterpoint provided by a clarinet and trombone; the typical rhythm section consists of drums, banjo (or piano or guitar) and tuba (later, often replaced by the double bass). Today, dixieland is typically rendered with celebratory gusto and, in groups like the Dukes of Dixieland, with great virtuosity and polish.

For further reading:

Schuller, Gunther, *Early Jazz: Its Roots and Musical Development*. New York: Oxford University Press, 1968.

Dixon, Thomas F. (1916–). U.S. rocket design pioneer. Dixon got in on the ground floor of what would later become the Rocketdyne Division of North American Aviation, where he served as vice president of research and engineering from 1955 to 1961. After briefly interrupting his career in the rocket industry to serve as deputy associate administrator of NASA, he returned to the private sector in 1963. Dixon was awarded the Robert H. Goddard Memorial Award by the American Rocket Society in 1957.

Djakarta [Jakarta; formerly Batavia]. Capital city of INDONESIA; on the island of Java's Jakarta Bay, an inlet of the Java Sea. Known to its longtime Dutch occupiers as Batavia, Djakarta is the largest city of Indonesia, as well as its leading commercial and industrial center. During WORLD WAR II, the Japanese captured the city in March 1942 and held it until 1945. In December 1949 Batavia was renamed and made the capital of the newly independent Indonesia.

Djemal, Ahmed (1872–1922). Turkish general and statesman. Djemal, as a staff officer in Salonika (now Thessaloniki, Greece), was the first officer to join the "Society [later Committee] of Union and Progress," also known as YOUNG TURKS. This organization, with military support, overthrew the reactionary government led by Sultan ABDUL HAMID II in 1909, and dominated Ottoman politics until the empire's defeat in WORLD WAR I (1918). Djemal served as military governor of Constantinople, minister of marine and Turkish governor of SYRIA during World War I. After TURKEY's defeat, he became military advisor to AFGHANISTAN.

Djibouti. Republic located on the northeastern coast of the Horn of Africa, fronting the Strait of Bab al Mandeb; the volcanic, mostly infertile country covers a total area of 8,938 square miles. The bulk of the population inhabits the compara-

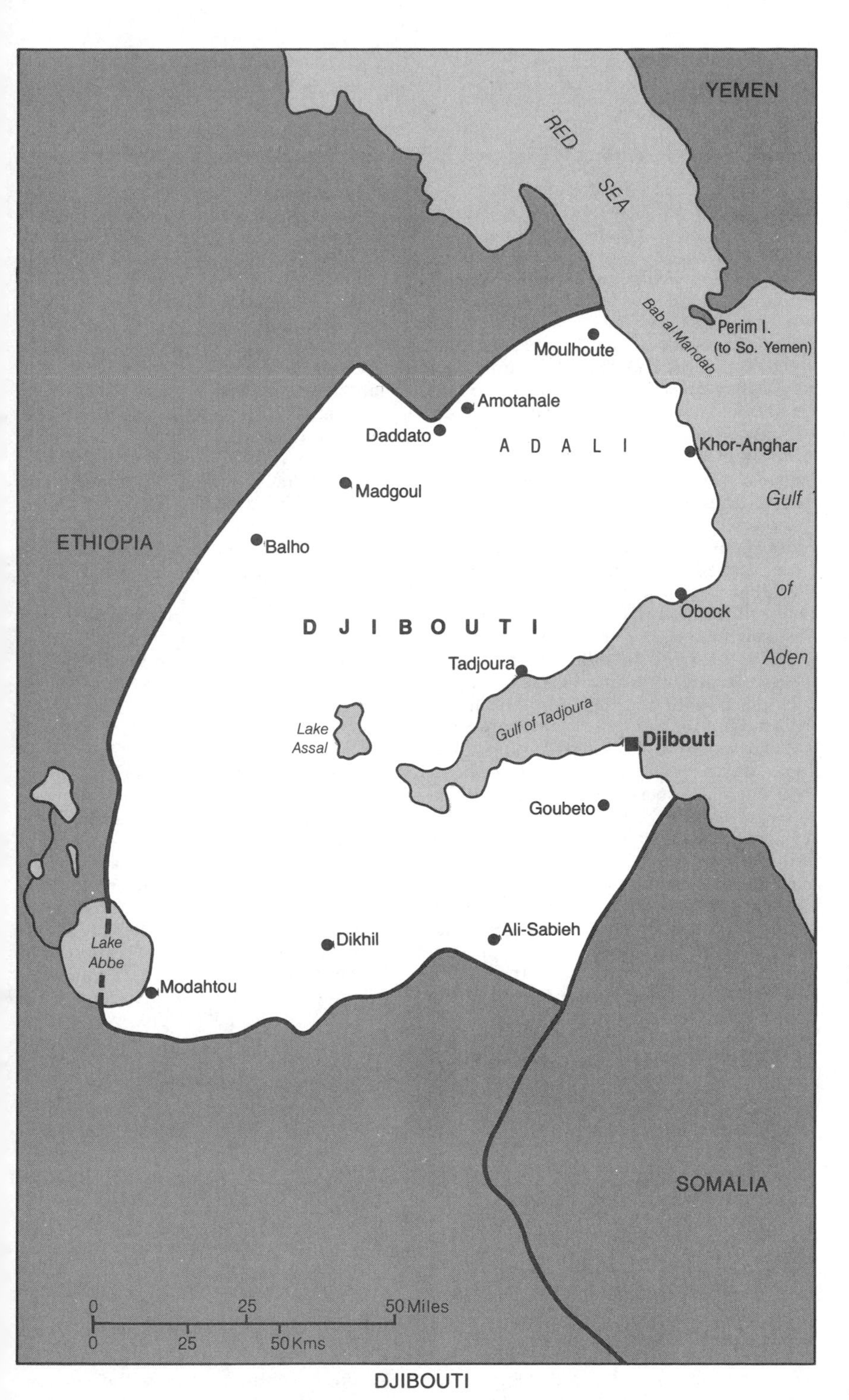

DJIBOUTI

tively fertile coastal strip bordering the Gulf of Tadjoura. The port of Djibouti was an important coal-bunkering station on the SUEZ CANAL route and became the capital of French Somaliland in 1892; a railway to ADDIS ABABA was completed in 1917. In response to the majority Somali community's calls for independence, a referendum was held in March 1967. Although the territory voted to retain its association with France, the Somali community contested the validity of the result. After nearly a decade of Somali agitation and pressure from the ORGANIZATION OF AFRICAN UNITY, the territory acceded to independence in June 1977. A Somali, Hassan Gouled, was elected president, and an Afar, Ahmed Dini, appointed prime minister. In December 1977, Ahmed Dini and four other Afar ministers resigned, alleging discrimination against Afars. As part of a policy of detribalization, the Rassemblement Populaire Pour Le Progres Party (RPP) was formed in 1979; in November 1981 Djibouti became a one-party state. President Gouled was reelected in 1982 and 1987 but stood as sole candidate on both occasions. Ethnic tensions between rival Somali-speaking groups led to serious violence in 1989, when security forces also moved to suppress unrest among the Afar majority.

Djilas, Milovan (1911–). One-time Yugoslav party and government official, Marxist intellectual, chief propagandist and closest friend of TITO. Djilas was born of peasant origins in Montenegro. After studying at Belgrade University he joined the illegal Communist Party of YUGOSLAVIA in 1932, in 1938 was made a member of the central committee by Tito, and in 1940 was made a member of the Politburo. During WORLD WAR II Djilas was a member of Tito's supreme headquarters, and for a while led partisan forces in Montenegro. After Tito had fallen from Moscow's favor in 1948, Djilas was blamed by Moscow for being responsible for "revisionist heresies." Denouncing STALINISM, Djilas assisted Tito in creating Yugoslavia's "self-management socialism." After publishing a series of articles in which he stressed the need for greater freedom, Djilas was brought to trial. He continued to write articles criticizing the regime, and although he was released from prison in 1966, he was forbidden to publish in Yugoslavia. His publications include *The New Class* (1957), *Conversations with Stalin* (1962), *Memoirs of a Revolutionary* (1973) and *Of Prisons and Ideas* (1986).

For further reading:

Sulzberger, C.L., *Paradise Regained: Memoir of a Rebel*. Westport, Conn.: Greenwood, 1988.

Doblin, Alfred (1878–1957). German novelist. Doblin was one of the most important German writers to participate in the modernist movement that dominated European literature in the two decades following World War I. His most famous novel is *Alexanderplatz, Berlin* (1929), which employs multiple viewpoints to create a complex, teeming narrative that mirrors the disjointed style of life in modern urban areas. Three different film versions of this novel have been produced. A Jew, Doblin fled Nazi Germany in 1933 and ultimately established himself in exile in the U.S. His other novels include the four-volume *Men Without Mercy* (1935) as well as *Citizens and Soldiers* (1939), *A People Betrayed* (1948), *Karl and Rosa* (1950) and *Tales of a Long Night* (1956).

Dobrovolsky, Georgi (1928–1971). Soviet cosmonaut. At age 43, Lieutenant Colonel Dobrovolsky was in command of the Soviet SOYUZ 11 mission when he and fellow cosmonauts Viktor Patsayev and Vladislav Volkov became the first travelers to be killed in space. He and his crew had successfully completed more than three weeks aboard the world's first space station, SALYUT 1, and were returning home when tragedy struck. Soyuz 11 had successfully disengaged from the space station and was preparing to separate from its instrument module when a malfunction in the charges used for the separation caused all the charges to fire at once, rather than sequentially. The explosive shock tore open a seal inside one of the craft's pressure-equalization valves, causing the spacecraft's oxygen-nitrogen atmosphere to be sucked out into space. Dobrovolsky and his crew, confident of success, had flown without space suits. The three men gasped for breath and indications were that they attempted to reach the valve and close it manually, but in less than a minute Soyuz 11 was a vacuum chamber, silent and lifeless. Dobrovolsky, buried in the Kremlin wall, is the subject of a 1977 biography, *The Flight Continues*.

Doctorow, E(dgar) L(aurence) (1931–). American novelist. Doctorow was educated at Kenyon College and at Columbia University and began his career reading scripts for Columbia Pictures. Doctorow's first novel, *Welcome to Hard Times* (1960, filmed 1967), is a western that addresses Doctorow's recurrent philosophical concern of the correlation between man and evil. Doctorow frequently places notable figures of recent history in fictional situations, to the chagrin of some critics. *The Book of Daniel* (1971), for example, examines the ROSENBERG TRIAL of the 1950s. *Ragtime* (1971, filmed 1981), arguably Doctorow's most popular novel, includes appearances by J.P. Morgan, Harry HOUDINI, and Henry FORD, among others. Other works include *World's Fair* (1985), *Billy Bathgate* (1989), and the play *Drinks Before Dinner* (1978).

"Doctor's Plot". Alleged plot by some Moscow doctors to kill well-known government officials. The "conspiracy" was fully reported in the press in January 1953. The doctors, many of whom were Jewish, were said to have murdered Andrei ZHDANOV (1896–1948), head of the Leningrad Party Organization. This was probably the pretext for starting another great purge and was part of STALIN's anti-Semitic policy, but the death of Stalin in March 1953 saved the country from this. All but two of the doctors survived their ordeals and were released, and later KHRUSHCHEV stated that there had been no plot whatsoever and that it all had been engineered by Stalin.

For further reading:
Rapoport, Louis, *Stalin's War Against the Jews*. New York: Free Press, 1990.

Author E.L. Doctorow poses with his American Book Award for his novel World's Fair, *at the Waldorf Astoria Hotel, New York (Nov. 17, 1986).*

"Doctor Who". Since 1963, a television series produced by the BRITISH BROADCASTING CORPORATION. "Doctor Who" is a phenomenally popular science fiction program that has been syndicated in over 100 countries. Sets and costumes are resoundingly low budget in look, but outrageous scripts and characters convey an appealing blend of arch comedy and blatant melodrama. The central character, Doctor Who, is a 750–year-old native of the planet Gallifrey who—for convenience's sake—assumes human form for adventures that take him throughout the universe. Doctor Who has been played by over 10 actors during the show's long run. Novelizations of the teleplays have also been big sellers.

***Doctor Zhivago*.** Novel by Boris PASTERNAK, written during the 1940s and 1950s. The novel follows the life of Zhivago, a Moscow physician and poet, as he attempts to come to grips with the tumultuous changes brought by WORLD WAR I, the RUSSIAN REVOLUTION, the RUSSIAN CIVIL WAR and the policies of LENIN and STALIN. Although it does not directly criticize COMMUNISM or the revolution, the book's philosophical and spiritual outlook ran counter to the official doctrine of SOCIALIST REALISM, and Pasternak was refused permission to publish it in the Soviet Union. The manuscript was smuggled out and published in Italy in 1957 and in other Western countries soon thereafter. After Pasternak was awarded the 1958 NOBEL PRIZE for literature, he was denounced by Soviet authorities and forced to refuse the award. The book was not published in the U.S.S.R. until 1987, under GORBACHEV's policy of GLASNOST. It was adapted as a motion picture by David LEAN (1965).

For further reading:
Conquest, Robert, *The Pasternak Affair: Courage of Genius*. New York: Hippocrene Books, 1979.

Dodd, Charles H(arold) (1884–1973). British theologian. Dodd was a highly influential figure in Biblical studies in the 20th century, both as a general director of a major new translation of the New Testament (1966) and as a theological interpreter of the Gospels. Dodd was educated at Oxford and went on to teach there as well as at the universities of Manchester and Cambridge. In three major works—*The Parables of the Kingdom* (1935), *The Apostolic Preaching and Its Developments* (1936) and *History of the Gospel* (1938)—Dodd posed his theory of realized eschatology in which he argued that the coming of the Kingdom of God had already been fulfilled through the Incarnation of Christ and its historical impact upon human civilization. Other works by Dodd include *The Authority of the Bible* (1928), *The Epistle to the Romans* (1932), *The Bible and the Greeks* (1935) and *The Interpretation of the Fourth Gospel* (1953).

Dodd, Thomas (1907–1971). U.S. senator from Connecticut, censured for his misuse of campaign donations. Before entering the Senate Dodd served in the federal government and was a prosecuting attorney at the NUREMBERG WAR CRIMES TRIALS following World War II. A Democrat, Dodd was elected to the House of Representatives in 1952, serving until his election to the U.S. Senate in 1958. Dodd generally supported liberal Democratic domestic programs and was known as a strong anticommunist. As senator, Dodd conducted hearings on the possible relation between crime and violence on television and its possible impact on juvenile delinquency; he charged that the television industry lacked imagination and responsibility. Dodd also favored strong gun-control legislation.

Between 1965 and 1967 columnists Drew PEARSON and Jack ANDERSON revealed that Dodd had used for personal purposes funds earmarked for his election campaign. A Senate investigation followed in 1966–67 and substantiated the allegations against Dodd. The Senate formally censured Dodd in 1967, but he was not expelled. He failed to win reelection to his Senate seat in 1970. His son **Chris Dodd** was later elected senator from Connecticut.

Dodecanese Islands. Island chain in the Aegean Sea, southeast of the Greek mainland, between Crete and Asia Minor. It comprises most of an island area called the Southern Sporades, consisting of about 20 islands. The Turks forfeited the islands to ITALY in the Italo-Turkish War of 1911–12. The Germans gained control from their faltering Italian allies in 1943 during WORLD WAR II, but the Allies took over the islands in 1945; on March 31, 1947, by treaty, they were given to Greece.

Doderer, Heimito von (1896–1966). Austrian novelist. Doderer was educated as a historian in Vienna, and served in the German Air Force in WORLD WAR II. Initially a Nazi sympathizer, he was stripped of his illusions about that ideology during the war, as his diaries of the time, published as *Tangenten* (1964, *Tangents*) indicate. Doderer is best known for his expansive novel *Die Demonen* (1956; *The Demons*, 1961), which he began in 1931 and published on his 60th birthday. The novel, which depicts the nine months leading up to the burning of the Austrian Supreme Court in 1927, was praised as a masterpiece upon its publication in German-speaking countries. It has never received the same acclaim in the U.S., although it was praised by Thornton WILDER. Doderer's other works include *Die Strudlhofstiege* (1951), *Grundlagen und Funktion des Romans* (*Principles and Functions of the Novel*, 1959) and *Die Merowinger* (*The Merovingians*, 1962).

Dodge, Raymond (1871–1942). American educator and experimental psychologist. Best known for his studies of the brain and the motor movements of the eye during the act of reading, Dodge began his academic career at Wesleyan University, where he taught from 1898 to 1924. He was also a member of the Institute of Psychology at Yale. His studies of eye movement were applied directly to gunners during WORLD WAR I. He also studied extensively the psychological effects of alcohol on humans. His written works include *Conditions and Consequences of Human Variability* (1931) and *The Craving for Superiority* (1931).

Dodge brothers. American automobile manufacturers. Horace E. Dodge (1868–1920) and John Dodge (1864–1920) began their careers by making bicycles and stove parts. Soon they were manufacturing engines and auto parts for Ford Motor Company and Olds Motor Works. On November 14, 1914, the first Dodge automobile was produced, and the brothers started their own auto manufacturing business. They built one of the first all-steel American cars, and Horace Dodge invented many improvements for the industry. Both of the Dodge brothers died in 1920, and their company was taken over by the Chrysler Corporation in 1928.

Doenitz, Karl (1891–1980). German admiral. Born in Prussia, Doenitz entered the Imperial German Navy and specialized in SUBMARINE warfare from 1916 onward. The architect and commander of GERMANY's submarine campaign against Allied shipping, he was appointed commander in chief of the navy in 1943. He succeeded Adolf HITLER as leader of Nazi Germany after the Fuhrer's death in May, 1945 and surrendered to the Allies six days later. Doenitz was among those tried and convicted of war crimes at the NUREMBERG TRIALS, and he served 10 years in Berlin's SPANDAU PRISON.

Doesburg, Theo Van [C.E.M. Kupper] (1883–1931). Dutch architect and designer, a major figure in the de Stijl movement of the 1920s. Van Doesburg began his career as a painter, but was drawn toward architecture through collaboration with J.J.P. Oud and Jan Wils beginning in 1916. In 1917 he founded the magazine *De Stijl*. He taught briefly at the BAUHAUS in 1922. His reputation rests on his paintings and in large measure on drawings and models for works never executed. His only completed projects were an entertainment group at the Aubette in Strasbourg, France, of 1928 (since demolished) and a house at Meudon of 1931. A kit for a paper model of the "Maison d'Artiste," reproducing the model van Doesburg and Cornelis van Eesteren designed in 1923 for an exhibition in Paris, is currently available.

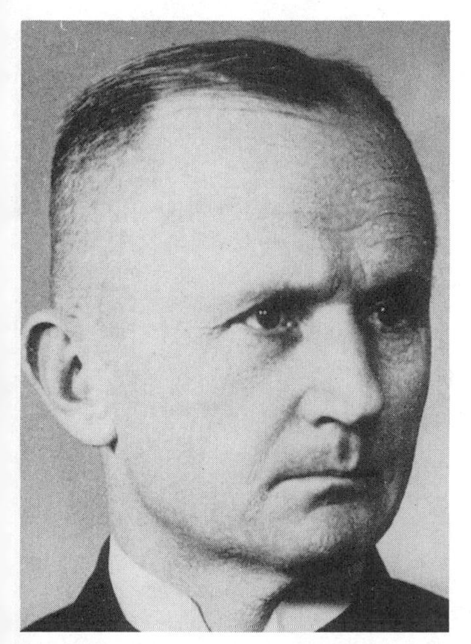

Admiral Karl Doenitz led Nazi Germany for six days after Adolf Hitler's death before surrendering to Allied forces.

Dogger Bank Incident. International incident on October 21, 1904, during the RUSSO-JAPANESE WAR. On its way to the Far East, a Russian fleet under the command of Admiral Zinovy Rozhdestvensky encountered vessels believed to be Japanese torpedo boats on the Dogger Bank, North Sea sandbanks located between Great Britain and Denmark. The Russians fired on the boats, killing two crew members and sinking one vessel. However, the boats were really English fishing trawlers, and fury in Great Britain over the attack was so great the incident almost led to war. Compensation claims for the attack were ultimately paid to Britain by Russia.

Dohnanyi, Ernst von (1877–1960). Hungarian composer, pianist and conductor. Studying at Budapest's Royal Academy (1894–97), he was later its director. He made his piano debut in Berlin in 1897, touring Europe and America to considerable acclaim until 1908, when he began teaching at the Berlin Hochschule. He remained there until 1915 and became associate director of Hungary's Franz Liszt Academy in 1919. Dohnanyi conducted the Budapest Philharmonic Orchestra from 1919 to 1944. He left Hungary after World War II and settled in the U.S. in 1949, teaching first at Ohio State University, then at Florida State University, where he remained until his death. Greatly influenced by Brahms, his compositions include *Variations on a Nursery Song* (1913) and *American Rhapsody* (1954) as well as many other orchestral works, songs, piano pieces, chamber music and three operas. He was the grandfather of conductor Christoph von Dohnanyi.

Dolin, Sir Anton [born Sydney Francis Patrick Chippendall Healey-Kay] (1904–83). The first male British ballet dancer to gain an international reputation. Dolin's work with Serge DIAGHILEV's BALLETS RUSSES in the 1920s helped launch his career. He then formed a highly acclaimed partnership with Alicia MARKOVA, which lasted more than two decades. During the 1940s, Dolin worked as ballet master, choreographer and premier danseur with Ballet Theater, the forerunner of the AMERICAN BALLET THEATER. In 1950 he helped organize the London Festival Ballet.

Dollfuss, Engelbert (1892–1934). Austrian political leader. A WORLD WAR I hero and devout Catholic, Dollfuss became a member of the Christian Social Party and a leader in the Farmers' League. He was an effective minister of agriculture and forestry (1931–32) during the GREAT DEPRESSION, and was appointed chancellor in 1932. Dollfuss suspended parliamentary government in 1933 and subsequently quelled a socialist revolt in 1934. Allied with HORTHY in Hungary and MUSSOLINI in Italy, he promulgated a new fascist constitution in 1934 but opposed ANSCHLUSS with GERMANY in his support of an independent AUSTRIA. He was assassinated by Austrian Nazis during their attempt at a coup d'etat.

Domagk, Gerhard (1895–1964). German biochemist. Domagk graduated in medicine from the University of Kiel in 1921 and began teaching at the University of Greifswald and later at the University of Munster. At this time he carried out important research into phagocytes—special cells that attack bacteria in the body. He became interested in chemotherapy and in 1927 was appointed director of research in experimental pathology and pathological anatomy at the giant chemical factory I.G. Farben at Wuppertal-Elberfeld. Pursuing the ideas of Paul EHRLICH, Domagk tested new dyes—produced by the Elberfeld chemists—for their strength against various infections. In 1935 he reported the effectiveness of an orange-red dye called prontosil in combating streptococcal infections. For the first time a chemical had been found to be active in vivo against a common small bacterium. Earlier dyes used as drugs were active only against infections caused by the much larger protozoa. The work was followed up in research laboratories throughout the world. Alexander FLEMING even neglected his experiments with PENICILLIN to study prontosil in the early 1930s. The most significant ramifications of his work were discovered by Daniel BOVET and his coworkers. Prontosil and the sulfa drugs that followed were effective in saving many people from death, including Franklin D. ROOSEVELT, Winston CHURCHILL and Domagk's own daughter. In 1939 Domagk was offered the NOBEL PRIZE for physiology or medicine. The Nazis forced him to withdraw his acceptance because HITLER was annoyed with the Nobel Committee for awarding the 1935 Peace Prize to Carl von OSSIETZKY, a German whom Hitler had imprisoned. In 1947 Domagk was finally able to accept the prize. In his later years he undertook drug research into cancer and tuberculosis.

Domingo, Placido (1941–). Spanish-born opera singer. Since the 1960s Domingo has been regarded as one of the great dramatic and lyric tenors of his generation. He began his professional career as a baritone in his family's zarzuela (Spanish operetta) company and made his opera debut in 1961 with the Baltimore Civic Opera. That same year he changed his vocal range to tenor and sang the role of

A principal tenor for New York's Metropolitan Opera, Placido Domingo is considered one of the finest tenors of his generation.

Alfredo in *La Traviata.* In 1962 he married soprano Marte Ornelas, and together they appeared with the Hebrew National Opera. He joined the New York City Opera in 1965 and achieved star status after singing the title role in the American premiere of *Don Rodrigo.* He made his Metropolitan Opera debut in 1968, subsequently becoming one of that company's principal tenors. Domingo has performed worldwide and sung a wide range of roles, including Hoffman in *The Tales of Hoffman* and the title roles in *Don Carlo* and *Otello* (also appearing in Franco ZEFFIRELLI's film version of the latter). He has also recorded popular music and has branched out into opera conducting.

Dominica. Small island nation in the Windward Islands of the West Indies, north of MARTINIQUE and south of GUADELOUPE. In 1833 Great Britain incorporated Dominica with the Leeward Islands and in 1940 administration was switched to the Windward Islands. The island was a member of the short-lived WEST INDIES FEDERATION from 1958 to 1962, was given internal self-government in 1967 and achieved independence in 1978.

Dominican Republic. Island nation in the West Indies, inhabiting the eastern two-thirds of the island of Hispaniola, southeast of Cuba. Political upheavals, governmental changes and burgeoning financial difficulties abounded until the early 20th century. It went bankrupt in 1905 when European nations threatened force in collecting money they were owed. U.S. President Theodore ROOSEVELT stepped in, and the U.S. assumed management of customs receipts. The financial picture improved, but the U.S. dominated the country. Unrest persisted, and in 1916 the U.S. Marines began keeping the peace. They stayed until 1924, but customs management continued until 1941. In 1930 Rafael TRUJILLO MOLINA began a 31-year dictatorial reign, one of the most inhumane in history. In 1937 Dominican troops attempting to prevent Haitians from entering the country stormed Haiti and slaughtered thousands.

Trujillo was murdered in 1961, and the first free elections since 1924 were held in December 1962. Leftist Juan BOSCH was elected president but was overthrown by a right-wing military revolt. An effort was made in April 1965 to reinstate Bosch, sparking a civil war that was followed by the arrival of U.S. troops sent by U.S. President JOHNSON. The ORGANIZATION OF AMERICAN STATES organized a peacekeeping force that eventually supplanted the U.S. troops, and in September both groups accepted Hector Garcia Godoy as interim president. OAS forces were removed, but the Dominicans continued to be cursed by political upheaval and economic problems, despite the 1966 election of President Joaquin BALAGUER and his 15-year improvement plan. In May 1978 the army interrupted voting when it appeared that Balaguer would lose a reelection attempt. U.S. President CARTER intervened with a forcefully worded diplomatic note, and the army was obliged to allow the election of leftist President Antonio Guzman, who committed suicide after his term in August 1982. His successor, Dr. Jorge Salvador Blanco, was later convicted of corruption and sentenced to 20 years' imprisonment (1988). For several years sugar has been the leading export, and in recent times its low price has caused hardship. Santo Domingo is the capital.

Domino, (Antoine) "Fats" (1928–). African-American ROCK and roll singer and pianist. Domino is one of the distinctive vocal stylists in rock-and-roll history. He has also enjoyed incredible popularity, selling over 65 million records—all featuring his warm, bluesy singing voice—accompanied by his pounding, boogie-woogie piano. Domino was born in New Orleans into a musical family: His father was a well-known violinist, and his brother-in-law later became lead guitarist in Domino's band. Domino recorded his first successful single, "The Fat Man" (1950), when he was 21. Over the next two decades came classic hits including "Ain't It a Shame" (1955), "Blueberry Hill" (1956), "I'm Walkin' " (1957), "Whole Lotta Loving" (1958), "I'm Ready" (1959), "Walkin' to New Orleans" (1960) and "Let the Four Winds Blow" (1961).

domino theory. Theory used by several U.S. presidents as a rationale for U.S. presence and military intervention in Southeast Asia. The domino theory argued that if the U.S. did not make a stand in South VIETNAM, then the rest of the nations of Southeast Asia and beyond—CAMBODIA, LAOS, THAILAND, MALAYSIA, BURMA, INDONESIA, the PHILIPPINES—would accommodate to communist power and eventually topple one after the other like a stack of dominoes. It is true that with American abandonment of South Vietnam in 1975, the Laotian and Cambodian "dominoes" fell in rapid succession. But the almost quarter century of U.S. involvement in Vietnam gave other nations an opportunity to resist communist expansion and build their own defenses. Indonesia fell toward the West in 1965, and Thailand successfully repelled communist attacks on its eastern borders in the 1980s.

Dong, Pham Van. See PHAM VAN DONG.

Donleavy, J(ames) P(atrick) (1926–). Irish author. Born in New York of Irish parents, Donleavy was educated at Trinity College, Dublin and became an Irish citizen in 1967. His first novel, *The Ginger Man* (1955) is a bawdy and scatological tale of a law student in Dublin. The book was refused by many publishers as ob-

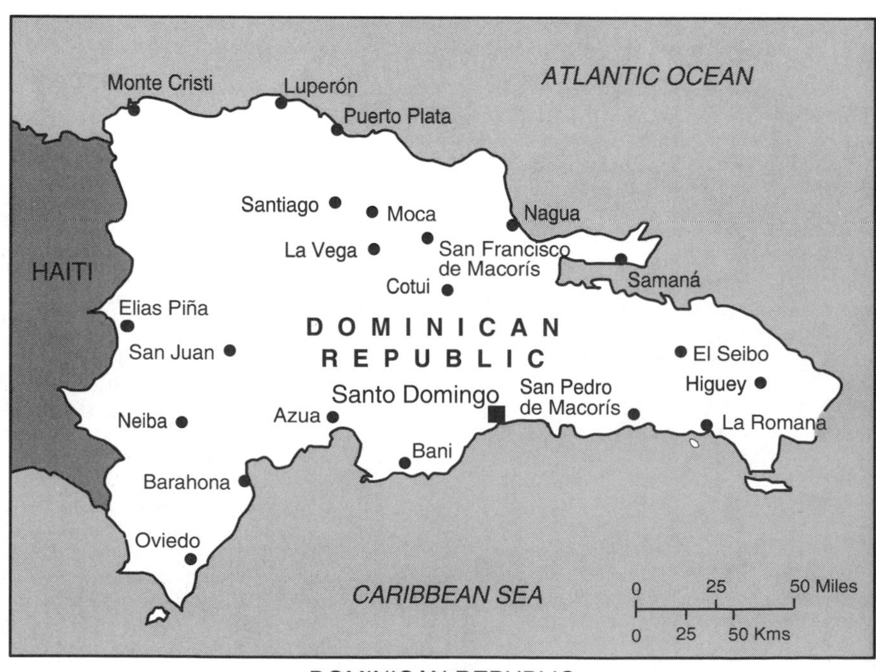

DOMINICAN REPUBLIC

scene; Donleavy was finally able to have it published in Paris. The book, comic in tone, shows the influence of James JOYCE. Critics cited it as his most important work, despite the greater success of his later novels, which include *Schultz* (1979) and *Are You Listening Rabbi Loew* (1987, a sequel to *Schultz*). Donleavy has also written the plays *Fairy Tales of New York* (1961, based on his book of the same title), *A Singular Man* (1964) and others based on his fiction.

Donnan, Frederick George (1879–1956). British chemist. He was educated at Queen's College, Belfast, and the universities of Leipzig and Berlin, where he obtained his Ph.D. in 1896—and acquired some of the German expertise in physical chemistry. On his return to England he worked at University College, London, with William Ramsay from 1898 until 1904, when he accepted the post of professor of physical chemistry at the University of Liverpool. In 1913 Donnan returned to succeed Ramsay at University College and remained there until his retirement in 1937. Donnan is mainly remembered for the *Donnan membrane equilibrium* (1911)—a theory describing the equilibrium that occurs when ions pass through membranes.

Donoso, Jose (1924–). Chilean novelist and short story writer. Born in Santiago, Donoso received a B.A. from Princeton in 1951. His realist works, *Veraneo y otros cuentos* (1955, *Summertime and Other Stories*) and *Coronacion* (1957; tr. 1965 as *Coronation*), were published only after Donoso guaranteed sales of 100 copies by subscription. He also peddled his books on streetcorners. His reputation is based on *El obsceno pajaro de la noche* (1970; tr. 1973 as *The Obscene Bird of Night*), an experimental, hallucinatory novel full of freaks and monsters and narrated by a deaf-mute. His *Historia personal de "boom"* (1972; tr. 1977 as *The Boom in Spanish American Literature*) traces the rise of the Latin novel during the 1960s, focusing on the emergence of such writers as BORGES, FUENTES, VARGAS LLOSA and Donoso himself.

Donovan, William "Wild Bill" (1883–1959). Director of the U.S. OFFICE OF STRATEGIC SERVICES, the WORLD WAR II forerunner of the CENTRAL INTELLIGENCE AGENCY. Born in Buffalo, New York, Donovan attended Columbia University and Columbia Law School. After serving in the Army in WORLD WAR I, Donovan became active in New York state Republican politics and served as U.S. district attorney in the state and as assistant U.S. attorney general; he also ran unsuccessfully for lieutenant governor of New York in 1922 and for governor in 1932. Donovan conducted several sensitive fact-finding missions in Europe for the U.S. government during the early years of WORLD WAR II. In mid-1941, he urged President Franklin D. ROOSEVELT to establish an American intelligence agency comparable to Britain's Secret Intelligence Service; in June 1942, the OFFICE OF STRATEGIC SERVICES (OSS) was formed. During the war, the OSS proved extremely useful to the Allied cause, and in July 1947, the CIA was established as its peacetime successor. After acting as an aide during the NUREMBERG TRIALS, Donovan retired from the military as a major general. From 1953 to 1954, he served as U.S. ambassador to Thailand.

Doodson, Arthur Thomas (1890–1968). British mathematical physicist. Doodson was educated at the University of Liverpool. After working at University College, London, from 1916 to 1918 he joined the Tidal Institute, Liverpool, in 1919 as its secretary. Doodson remained through its reformation as the Liverpool Observatory and Tidal Institute as assistant director (1929–45) and as director until his retirement in 1960. Much of Doodson's early work was on the production of mathematical tables and the calculation of trajectories for artillery. Proving himself an ingenious, powerful and practical mathematician, he found an ideal subject for his talents in the complicated behavior of the tides. He made many innovations to achieve more accurate computations about them and, with H. Warburg in 1942, produced the *Admiralty Manual of Tides.*

Doolittle, Hilda [H.D.] (1886–1961). American poet. Born in Bethlehem, Penna., she moved to England in 1911 and married fellow poet Richard ALDINGTON in 1913. Heavily influenced by Ezra POUND, she became an important member of the imagist group. Her free-form verse is characterized by both vividness and precision. H.D.'s volumes of poetry include *Sea Garden* (1916), *Collected Poems* (1925 and 1940), *The Walls Do Not Fall* (1944) and *Bid Me to Live* (1960).

Doolittle, James (Harold) (1896–). American aviator. Born in Alameda, Calif., he served as a flyer in WORLD WAR I and, after the war, was an aeronautic specialist, civilian test pilot and airborne racer. In 1922 he became the first pilot to cross North America within 24 hours. Recalled to the Army Air Corps in 1940, Doolittle gained worldwide recognition as the commander of the bold bombing RAID ON TOKYO on April 18, 1942. Subsequently, he commanded the 12th Air Force during the landing in North Africa, headed the Anglo-American Strategic Air Force in the Mediterranean (1944) and led the Eighth Air Force in Europe (1944) and the Pacific (1945). Awarded the Medal of Honor, he resigned from the army as a lieutenant general in 1945.

Lieutenant General James Doolittle led the air raid on Tokyo (April 18, 1942).

Doors, The. American rock and roll band. The Doors, featuring lead singer Jim Morrison, remain one of the most popular rock bands to emerge from the psychedelic era of the 1960s. Hits such as "Light My Fire" (1967) and "Hello, I Love You" (1968) are still played regularly on radio stations. Francis Ford COPPOLA featured the group's music prominently in his film *Apocalypse Now* (1979), and Morrison and the Doors have been the subject of numerous biographical works, including a 1991 motion picture. The band first formed in Los Angeles in the mid-1960s. Other band members included keyboard player Ray Manzarek, guitarist Robbie Krieger and drummer John Densmore. Morrison, a charismatic figure who abused both drugs and alcohol, died of a heart attack in 1971, at age 27. Notable albums by the band include *The Doors* (1967), *Strange Days* (1967), *Waiting for the Sun* (1968) and *L.A. Woman* (1971).

Dorati, Antal (1906–1988). Hungarian-born conductor. During a career that spanned more than 60 years, Dorati served as principal conductor for more than a dozen organizations, including the Dallas Symphony, the Minneapolis Symphony, the Stockholm Philharmonic and the Royal Philharmonic. He led the National Symphony in the inaugural concert at the John F. Kennedy Center for the Performing Arts in Washington in 1971. Of the more than 500 recordings Dorati made during his lifetime, his interpretations of the Haydn symphonies were particularly praised.

Dorman-Smith, Eric (1895–1969). British soldier and tactician. A career military man, he supervised the mechanization of the British cavalry in the late 1920s. He served under WAVELL in 1930 and directed military training in India in 1939. After the outbreak of WORLD WAR II, he acted as chief of staff for General AUCHINLECK and planned the strategy for the first battle of EL ALAMEIN in July, 1942. Replaced after British defeats at Tobruk, Libya in 1942, he retired to Ireland.

Dorn, Friedrich Ernst (1848–1916). German physicist. Dorn studied at Konigsberg and in 1873 was made professor of physics at Breslau. In 1886 he transferred to a professorship at Halle and started working with X RAYS. He is noted for his discovery, in 1900, that the radioactive element radium gives off a radioactive gas, which Dorn called radium emanation. The gas was isolated in 1908 by William Ramsay, who named it niton. The name radon was adopted in 1923. Dorn's discovery is the first established demonstration of a transmutation of one element into another.

Dornberger, Walter (1895–1980). German-born rocket engineer. When Germany decided to develop experimental rockets in the 1920s, Dornberger, then an army officer, was named to head the project. His team produced Germany's first rocket engine (1932) and its first launches (1934). During WORLD WAR II, working with Werner von BRAUN, he headed the development of the German V-2 rocket bomb at PEENEMUNDE. A lieutenant general, he directed the firing of more than 1,000 deadly rockets on London and its suburbs in the last years of the war. At the end of the war, he was working on a rocket bomb designed to reach New York from German territory. Along with Kurt DEBUS and von Braun, he surrendered to the U.S. Army rather than to the Russians at the end of the war. Following his de-Nazification, he emigrated to the U.S. and became an American citizen. He served as an adviser to the U.S. Air Force and worked for military industries in the U.S. (See also OPERATION PAPERCLIP.)

Dors, Diana [Diana Fluck] (1931–1984). British actress, once billed as Britain's answer to Marilyn MONROE. Dors was known as the "blond bombshell" of films from the early 1950s to the 1960s. When she was 25 years old she was Britain's highest-paid actress, with a contract valued at more than £500,000. Her films were less than memorable, but she held the public's interest with revelations about her colorful private life and three marriages. Before her death she appeared as a television advice columnist.

Dorsey brothers. Tommy (1905–56) and Jimmy (1904–57) Dorsey were jazz instrumentalists and big band leaders whose Dorsey Brothers Orchestra, one of the premier jazz big bands of the 1930s, lasted only one year, from 1934 to 1935. But both brothers went on to even greater success with their separate big bands from the 1930s and into the 1950s—and became jazz legends. Jimmy, who played alto saxophone and clarinet, and Tommy, who played trombone, had been renowned sidemen in the 1920s and early 1930s, when they were featured with numerous bands and in the Broadway musical *Everybody's Welcome* (1931). With the founding of the Dorsey Brothers Orchestra, they and their theme song *Sandman* became nationally famous. After quarreling in 1935, the brothers went their separate ways for over a decade before working together on the Hollywood biographical film *The Fabulous Dorseys* (1947). From 1953 to 1956, the Dorsey brothers again performed together in a big band led by Tommy.

Dos Passos, John Roderigo (1896–1970). American novelist. After graduating from Harvard University, Dos Passos traveled to Spain intending to study architecture. WORLD WAR I intervened, and he volunteered for the French ambulance corps, later becoming a private in the U.S. Army medical corps. His first two books, *One Man's Initiation—1917* (1920) and *Three Soldiers* (1921), bitterly portray the effects of war on the three main characters. By 1925 in *Manhattan Transfer,* he had arrived at his unique style combining naturalism and STREAM OF CONSCIOUSNESS. Perhaps his best known work is the trilogy *U.S.A.,* which is an expression of his radical approach to life and consists of *The 42nd Parallel* (1930), *1919* (1932) and *The Big Money* (1936). These traced the first three decades of the 20th century, in which he found absurdity, moral deterioration and helplessness—all reflected in the lives of his characters. He incorporated fragments of the era's popular culture into the novels, juxtaposing his characters against prominent Americans of the time. His later work became more conservative, and he eventually expressed disillusion with liberal and radical movements. Later novels included *The Great Days* (1958) and *MidCentury* (1961). He also wrote biographies and works on travel and history.

For further reading:
Ludinton, Townsend, *Twentieth Century Odyssey: The Life of John Dos Passos.* New York: Dutton, 1980.

dos Santos, Jose Eduardo (1942–). Angolan politician. Born in Luanda, Dos Santos joined the Soviet-backed Popular Movement for the Liberation of Angola (MPLA) in 1961 and went into exile that same year. Sent to the U.S.S.R. by the MPLA in 1963, he returned to Africa and graduated from college with an engineering degree in 1969. He fought for Angolan independence from 1970 to 1974, assuming various party offices during the 1970s. He served as planning minister from 1978 to 1979, and became head of the MPLA and president of ANGOLA after the death of Agostinho NETO in 1979.

Dotson case. In 1979, an Illinois man, Gary Dotson, was tried and convicted for the rape of a young woman. Dotson was sentenced to 25 to 50 years in prison, although he insisted that he was innocent. In 1983 the woman admitted that she had made up the story; however, Dotson remained in prison. Prosecutors did not drop the case until 1989, when a Chicago judge granted Dotson's request for a new trial to clear his name. Genetic evidence apparently proved that Dotson could not have committed the rape. The Dotson case was cited as an example of the bureaucracy and confusion of the American criminal justice system.

Douaumont. Village in France's Meuse department. In WORLD WAR I Douaumont was one of the great fortresses of the Western Front and a part of the battlefield of VERDUN, twice lost but retaken by the French in 1916 following a savage battle. Douaumont was demolished in the process; it was never reconstructed, but is now a French national memorial.

***Double Eagle II,* flight of the.** First transatlantic crossing by balloon—August 17, 1978. Three Americans—Max Anderson, Ben Abaruzzo and Larry Newman—successfully completed the trip in the *Double Eagle II* when they landed in a wheat field 60 miles west of Paris. They had departed from Presque Isle, Maine on August 11 and had set an endurance record of 137 hours 18 minutes aloft, during which they had withstood icy conditions and extreme cold over the Atlantic. Abaruzzo and Anderson had attempted the journey in 1977 in the *Double Eagle I* but had been forced down five miles off the coast of Iceland.

Doubrovska, Felia [born Felizata Dluzhnevska] (1896–1981). Russian ballerina. Doubrovska was trained at the Imperial Academy in St. Petersburg. After graduating (1913) she joined the Maryinsky Theater there and with that troupe remained through the RUSSIAN REVOLUTION. In 1920 she fled to Paris and joined Serge DIAGHILEV'S BALLETS RUSSES, dancing in many principal roles choreographed by the legendary George BALANCHINE. After moving to the U.S., she became prima ballerina of the Metropolitan Opera Ballet (1938) but retired from the stage the following year. She subsequently joined the faculty at the School of American Ballet at Balanchine's invitation and in a long second career became one of the most highly regarded ballet teachers in the U.S. Doubrovska was known as the archetypal Balanchine dancer.

Douglas, Aaron (1899–1979). Black American painter. A native of Kansas, Douglas studied in New York and Paris. He was a leading artist during the HARLEM RENAISSANCE of the late 1920s. He was the first black artist recognized for incorporating African iconography into American art. He was known for his murals and his illustrations of books by black American authors.

Douglas, Donald Wills, Sr. (1892–1981). American pioneer aircraft designer, engineer and manufacturer. Founder of the DOUGLAS AIRCRAFT CORP., Douglas built airplanes that helped bring about the era of mass commercial air travel. While in his 20s he learned about aircraft design by working on the development of a heavy bomber for Glenn Martin's company. In 1920 he set up his own company with backing from a wealthy investor. He designed the first aircraft (*Cloudster*) that could carry a load heavier than its own weight. He also designed and developed the airplane that made the first flight around the world in the early 1920s. His company, which dominated the aviation industry during the period when airplanes were driven by propellers, was perhaps best known for the twin-engine DC-3, introduced in 1935. This classic and reliable craft became a familiar sight around the world, hauling passengers, cargo and military loads; DC-3s were still in service 50 years after the first one taxied down a runway. Douglas also produced military aircraft used by the U.S. during WORLD WAR II (including the C-47 military transport and the A-20 attack bomber) and the KOREAN WAR. In 1958 the company introduced the DC-8 passenger jetliner, which (with the Boeing 707) helped revolutionize airline travel. Douglas' fortunes declined in the 1960s. In 1967 the company merged with the MCDONNELL Aircraft Corp. to form McDonnell-Douglas Corp.

Douglas, Helen Gahagan [born Helen Gahagan] (1900–1980). American actress, concert singer and politician. A liberal Democrat from California, she served in the U.S. House of Representatives (1944–50). She won national recognition during a bitter election campaign for the U.S. Senate in 1950, in which she was defeated by Representative Richard M. NIXON. During the campaign, Nixon accused her of being a communist sympathizer. Gahagan was married to the actor Melvyn DOUGLAS.

Douglas, Keith (1920–1944). British poet. Douglas was educated at Christ's Hospital and Merton College, Oxford, where the poet Edmund Blunden was his tutor and fostered Douglas' early work. Although he published in various journals in the 1930s, Douglas is best known for his war poetry, made more poignant by his death during the Allied invasion of NORMANDY (1944). His WORLD WAR II poems describe war-beleaguered North Africa, where he was first posted in 1940, and reflect his contemplation of death while evoking the horrors of war. *Selected Poems* (1943) was the only volume of his verse published in his lifetime. Posthumously published books include *Alemein to Zem Zem* (1946), *Collected Poems* (1951) and *Complete Poems* (1979). (See also Sidney KEYES, Alun LEWIS.)

Douglas, Kirk [Issur Danielovitch] (1916–). American actor; son of an illiterate Russian ragpicker and junkman, Douglas grew up to become one of Hollywood's legendary "tough guy" stars in the 1940s and '50s. After graduating from the American Academy of Dramatic Arts, he starred on Broadway in shows such as *Spring Again* (1941), then enlisted in the Navy. In 1946 he made his film debut in *The Strange Love of Martha Ivers,* but it wasn't until his eighth film—*Champion* (1949)—that he became a recognized star. His dynamic, powerhouse performances can be found in such films as *Ace in the Hole* (1951), *Detective Story* (1951), *The Bad and the Beautiful* (1952), *Lust for Life* (1956), *Paths of Glory* (1957), *Lonely Are the Brave* (1962) and many others. Douglas was also the producer of several films in which he acted, including *The Vikings* (1958) and *Spartacus* (1960), for which he courageously hired the blacklisted writer Dalton Trumbo. In 1988 Douglas earned praise for his autobiography, *The Ragman's Son;* he has also written fiction. Douglas' son Michael (by his first wife, Diana Douglas) is also a respected film actor and has won acclaim for his roles in *Fatal Attraction* (1987) and *Black Rain* (1989).

Douglas, Melvyn [born Melvin Edouard Hesselberg] (1901–1981). Melvyn Douglas began his career as a leading man in HOLLYWOOD romantic films of the 1930s and 1940s, playing opposite some of the leading female stars of the day; he later shifted to character roles on stage and screen. He appeared in 77 films and won two ACADEMY AWARDS for best supporting actor (1963, 1980).

Douglas, (George) Norman (1868–1952). British author. Douglas was brought up in Austria and traveled extensively in Europe, later residing in Italy. He is best known for his vivid travel literature, which includes *Siren Land* (1911), *Fountains in the Sand* (1912) and *Old Calabria* (1915). Of his novels, perhaps best known is *South Wind* (1917). The novel takes place on the fictional island of Nepenthe, which Douglas drolly depicts as a haven of civilized sensualism. Douglas was later acquainted with D.H. LAWRENCE and published *D.H. Lawrence and Maurice Magnus: A Plea for Better Manners* (1924), describing his quarrel with Lawrence.

Douglas, T(homas) C(lement) (1904–1986). Scottish-born Canadian political leader. Douglas set up the first socialist government in North America after being elected premier of the province of Saskatchewan in 1944 on the Cooperative Commonwealth Federation slate. During the 16 years that he served as premier, he introduced a host of social and economic reforms and laid the groundwork for North America's first medicare plan. He resigned in 1961 to become the first national leader of the NEW DEMOCRATIC PARTY, a socialist coalition of farmers, intellectuals and trade unionists. He led the party through four general elections and represented it in Parliament from 1962 to 1968 and again from 1969 to 1979.

Douglas, William O(rville) (1898–1980). Associate justice of the U.S. Supreme Court. With a law degree from Columbia University in 1925, he taught at the university between 1925 and 1928. After serving in various federal posts, he was made chairman of the Securities and Exchange Commission in 1937, and was appointed to the Supreme Court in 1939. Generally considered a liberal, Douglas defended individual liberties throughout his career, and was one of the most controversial figures in the recent history of the Court. He retired from the Court in 1975, but continued an active public life. An aggressive outdoorsman, Douglas wrote several books, including *Men and Mountains* (1950), *A Wilderness Bill of Rights* (1965), *The Bible and the Schools* (1966) and *Points of Rebellion* (1969).

For further reading:
Wasby, Stephen L., ed., *He Shall Not Pass This Way Again: The Legacy of Justice William O. Douglas.* Pittsburgh, Penn.: University of Pittsburgh Press, 1990.

Douglas Aircraft Co. Leading American airplane builder whose 1930s products are credited with having made air transportation practical as a form of mass transport. The firm was founded in 1920 by Donald Wills DOUGLAS and developed the pioneer low-wing, twin-engined monoplanes, the DC-1 and DC-2, predecessors of the famous DC-3, one of the most successful airplanes ever produced. Later Douglas products, beginning with the DC-4, introduced tricycle landing gear and moved to four engines. The DC-8 was a highly successful four-engined jet transport. The successor company, McDonnell Douglas, continues production of the modern DC-9 and DC-10 jet transport aircraft.

Douglas-Home, Sir Alec (Alexander Frederick) [Lord Home; Baron Home] (1903–). British politician, prime minister (1963–64). Born into a titled family, he was educated at Eton and Oxford. A member of the CONSERVATIVE PARTY, he entered the House of Commons in 1931. Parliamentary private secretary to Prime Minister Neville CHAMBERLAIN from 1937 to 1939, he succeeded his father as 14th earl of Home in 1951 and resigned from his seat in the Commons, moving automatically to the House of Lords. He served as minister of state from 1951 to 1955, minister for commonwealth relations (1955–60), leader of the House of Lords (1957–60) and foreign secretary (1960–63). Following Harold MACMILLAN's resignation in October 1963, Douglas-Home disclaimed his peerage to become prime minister as Sir Alec Douglas-Home (winning a by-election to return to the House of Commons). Following his defeat by Harold WILSON in the October 1964 general election, he became leader of the Opposition until 1965, when he stood down, being replaced by Edward HEATH. In 1970 he was appointed foreign secretary by Heath. Following the Conservative defeat in 1974, he was created a life peer as Lord Home. His brother, William Douglas-Home, was a noted playwright.

Douglass, Andrew Ellicott (1867–1962). American astronomer and dendrochronologist. Douglass came from a family of academics, and his father and grandfather were college presidents. He graduated from Trinity College, Hartford, Connecticut in 1889 and in the same year was appointed to an assistantship at Harvard College Observatory. In 1894 he went with Percival Lowell to the new Lowell Observatory in Flagstaff, Arizona and became a professor of astronomy and physics at the University of Arizona in 1906.

Initially Douglass was interested in the 11-year sunspot cycle. While trying to trace its history he was led to the examination of tree rings in the hope that he would find some identifiable correlation between sunspot activity and terrestrial climate and vegetation. Soon tree rings became the center of his studies. Douglass found that he could identify local tree rings with confidence and use them in dating past climatic trends. He thus founded the field of dendrochronology. By the late 1920s he had a sequence of more than a thousand tree rings having six thin rings presumably records of a severe drought that correlated with the end of the 13th century. In 1929 he found some timber that contained the six thin rings and plus a further 500. This took him to the 8th century and over the years he managed to get as far as the 1st century. This was extended still further and by careful analysis scholars have now established a sequence going back almost to 5000 BC. The dated rings of Arizona and New Mexico, however, were found not to correlate with sequences from other parts of the world: The tree-ring clock was a purely local one. The search for a more universal clock continued, and the method of **radiocarbon dating** was developed by Willard LIBBY in 1949.

Dove, Arthur G(arfield) (1880–1946). American painter. Born in Canandaigua, N.Y., he moved to N.Y.C. and became a commercial illustrator. He traveled to Europe in 1907 and began painting in a style influenced by the Impressionists and Cezanne. Returning to the U.S. in 1909, his painting became more abstract and organic in form. He met Alfred STIEGLITZ in 1910 and had his first one-man show at the gallery 291 in 1912. In the 1920s and 1930s, his style became increasingly flowing and abstract, filled with lyrically organic shapes and velvety color. Dove's canvases were among the first abstract works by an American and influenced later generations of abstractionists in the U.S.

Dover. British port on the English Channel, 71 miles southeast of London, in Kent. A key crossing point between Britain and France, it served as a naval base in WORLD WAR I and was heavily shelled by German guns in WORLD WAR II. The British end of the ENGLISH CHANNEL TUNNEL is near Dover.

doves. Term originally used to describe Americans advocating negotiation or reduction of U.S. involvement in VIETNAM in the 1960s and 1970s. The term came to be applied to politicians taking moderate stances on foreign policy issues and opposed to the use of military force in general. (See also HAWKS, VIETNAM WAR.)

Dovzhenko, Alexander Petrovich (1894–1956). Film director, of a Cossack family. Dovzhenko was appointed People's Artist of the Russian Soviet Federated Socialist Republic in 1950. He started in films in 1926, having previously been a teacher and a painter. His *Arsenal* (1929) and *Earth* (1930), in which he used a variety of techniques, all infused with poetic lyricism, brought him fame but were denounced by official critics as counterrevolutionary. *Shchors,* made in 1939, is the story of a Ukranian Red Army hero. Among his other films were *Battle of the Ukraine* (1943), an important war documentary made by giving personal instruction to 24 different cameramen distributed along a battle front; the color film *Michurin* (1949); and *Poem of the Sea,* completed in 1958 after his death.

Dow, Herbert H. (1866–1930). U.S. chemist and industrialist. His college thesis at the Case School of Applied Sciences (1888) was about extracting minerals from the brines underlying much of Ohio. Encouraged by his teachers, he studied the vast underground resources of brines also found in nearby states, and presented his studies at a meeting of the American Association for the Advancement of Science in 1888. In 1889, he discovered and patented an inexpensive method of extracting bromine, chromium and lithium from brine by electrolysis. He founded Dow Chemical Company in 1897 at Midland, Michigan. Dow was the first U.S. company to manufacture indigo and phenol, a compound used in explosives. During WORLD WAR I, the company manufactured mustard gas for troops in Europe. A major industrial enterprise of the day, the company has continued as a producer of a wide variety of chemicals.

Dowell, Anthony (1943–). British dancer. One of the great classical male dancers of his generation, Dowell is famous for his elegance and flawless technique. He joined Britain's ROYAL BALLET in 1961 and quickly received acclaim dancing the leading classical roles. He created roles in Frederick ASHTON's *The Dream* (1964) and *A Month in the Country* (1976), and in Antony TUDOR's *Shadowplay* (1967), among others. From 1978 to 1980 he was a principal dancer with AMERICAN BALLET THEATRE. Since 1986 he has served as the artistic director of the Royal Ballet.

DO-X. Giant flying-boat airplane built by the German firm of Dornier and first flown in 1929. The DO-X had been preceded with some success by the flying boats Dornier WAL and Super-WAL, the latter operating on a regular schedule between Europe and South America. Each carried eight to ten passengers and mail. The huge DO-X, however, carried up to 150 passengers and was intended to provide a regular trans-Atlantic passenger service. It had three decks and provided spacious passenger accommodation somewhat in the manner of a ship. Twelve engines mounted above the single wing, six facing forward and six facing aft, were required to power it. A flight to New York was made, but because the DO-X was underpowered and unable to gain safe altitude, its use was discontinued.

Doyle, Sir Arthur Conan (1859–1930). British writer and physician, best known for his stories about the greatest of all consulting detectives, SHERLOCK HOLMES. Born in Edinburgh and educated at Stonyhurst College and Edinburgh University, Doyle took up his medical practice as an eye specialist near Portsmouth in 1882. He began supplementing his income by writing, and in 1887 the first Sherlock Holmes novel appeared, *A Study in Scarlet,* followed by a spectacularly popular series of Holmes short stories in *The Strand Magazine* (1891–92). Although his fame would ultimately rest on his detective stories, Doyle preferred other literary pursuits. His most cherished projects were historical novels such as *Micah Clarke* (1889) and *The White Company* (1891). His patriotic fervor fueled works like *The War in South Africa: Its Cause and Conduct,* a defense of the British involvement in the BOER WAR (1902); his scientific background led to the creation of Professor George Edward Challenger in *The Lost World* (1912) and *The Poison Belt* (1913)—stories that blended scientific fact with fantastic romance. His growing interest in Spiritualism after World War I led to such books as *The Coming of the Fairies* (1922), in which he supported the existence of what he called the little people. Doyle devoted most of the decade of the 1920s and more than a million dollars to this cause. Holmes remained a skeptic to the last story *The Case-Book of Sherlock Holmes* (1927). While Doyle's output was prodigious and diverse, his contributions to the modern detective story and to the new field of science fiction remain his most important literary legacies.

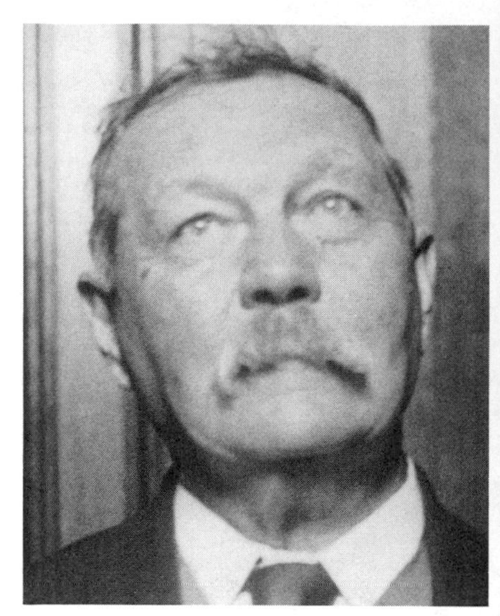

British author and physician Sir Arthur Conan Doyle is best known for his series of detective stories featuring Sherlock Holmes.

For further reading:

Lellenberg, Jon L., ed., *The Quest for Sir Arthur Conan Doyle.* Carbondale: Southern Illinois University Press, 1987.

Drabble, Margaret (1939–). British novelist. Born in Sheffield, Drabble was educated at Victoria University of Manchester. She achieved success with her first novel *A Summer Bird-Cage* (1962), which, like her other early works, depicts intelligent young women facing career and marriage decisions. Leaving behind the almost breathless tone of her early work, Drabble's increasingly complicated novels reflect her earnest concern with contemporary social themes, although some critics have attacked her for her turgid prose and for taking a sociologist's rather than a novelist's view of life. *The Realms of Gold* (1975) depicts archeologist Francis Wingate—a successful, divorced mother, like many of Drabble's women. *The Ice Age* (1977) describes the economic crises of England in the mid-1970s and the social damage wrought by unchecked real estate development. Later works, notably *The Radiant Way* (1987) and its sequel, *A Natural Curiosity* (1989), express her discontent with England under Margaret THATCHER. An outspoken feminist and socialist, Drabble has also written a biography of Arnold BENNETT and edited the *Oxford Companion to English Literature* (1985, fifth edition). She is married to the biographer Michael Holroyd. Her sister **A.S. Byatt** is also a noted novelist.

Drake, Alfred [Alfred Capurro] (1914–). American actor and singer. An outstanding Broadway performer of the 1940s and 1950s, Drake was especially noted for his rich baritone voice and commanding stage presence. He became famous in 1943 playing the lead role in the Broadway musical *Oklahoma!* Several starring roles in such musicals as *Kiss Me, Kate* (1949) and *Kismet* (1953) and in such plays as Shakespeare's *Othello* and *Much Ado About Nothing* followed. He also made many acclaimed recordings and appeared in several television productions during the 1950s and 1960s. His last Broadway appearance was in *Kean* in 1961.

Drake, Frank Donald (1930–). American astronomer. Drake graduated in 1952 from Cornell University and obtained his Ph.D. in 1958 from Harvard. He worked initially at the National Radio Astronomy Observatory (NRAO), West Virginia (1958–63) and at the JET PROPULSION LABORATORY, California (1963–64) before returning to Cornell and being appointed professor of astronomy in 1966. Although Drake has made significant contributions to radio astronomy, including radio studies of the planets, he is perhaps best known for his pioneering search for extraterrestrial intelligence. In April 1959 he managed to gain approval from the director at NRAO, Otto Struve, to proceed with his search, which was called Project Ozma. The name was taken from the Oz stories of L. Frank BAUM. Drake began in 1960, using the NRAO 26–meter radio telescope to listen for possible signals from planets of the sunlike stars Tau Ceti and Epsilon Eridani, both about 11 light-years away. No signals were received. In July 1960 the project was terminated to allow the telescope to be used for other purposes. Drake revived the project in 1975, in collaboration with Carl SAGAN, when they began using the Arecibo 100–ft. radio telescope to listen to several nearby galaxies on frequencies of 1420, 1653 and 2380 megahertz. No contact was made; nor was it likely, for as they declared: "A search of hundreds of thousands of stars in the hope of detecting one message would require remarkable dedication and would probably take several decades."

Draper, Charles Stark (1901–1987). U.S. engineer and physicist. In 1939 Draper helped found the Massachusetts Institute of Technology Instrumentation Laboratory. His work there on gyroscopic systems broke new ground in such developments as gunsights for WORLD WAR II battleships and guidance systems for intercontinental ballistic missiles. Known as the father of inertial navigation, he developed the navigation system that guided the APOLLO astronauts to the moon and back.

Draper, Dorothy (1889–1969). American interior decorator known for her designs for hotels, restaurants, clubs, and other public spaces. She founded her own firm in 1925 and produced early work in a version of the popular ART DECO idiom of the time. In the 1930s, her work took on more eclectic, traditional elements, often in overscaled, exaggerated form. Her book of 1939, *Decorating Is Fun!*, sums up the Draper approach with its energetic, somewhat flamboyant, commercial emphasis. The redecoration of the Pompeiian restaurant of New York's Metropolitan Museum of Art is a highly visible (although now somewhat altered) example of the florid Draper style.

dreadnoughts. Class of "all-big-gun" battleships; derived from H.M.S. *Dreadnought*, a British battleship launched in 1906. The first such ship powered by steam turbines, it carried 10 12–inch guns and five torpedo tubes, giving it about twice the firepower of its predecessors. With heavy armor plate made of Krupp steel and able to reach a cruising speed of 21 knots, the ship outranged and outpaced every other such vessel and immediately became the most powerful ship in the world. Representing a revolution in naval design, the *Dreadnought* provided a model and a name for the battleships that were to render previous capital ships obsolete. Dreadnoughts had a prominent place in WORLD WAR I, but the only engagement in which opposing dreadnoughts faced each other occurred at the battle of JUTLAND in 1916. Limitations were placed on the dreadnoughts by the postwar WASHINGTON CONFERENCE, and their importance was lessened by the growth of air forces and underwater weaponry.

Dream Play, A. An episodic, allegorical drama by the Swedish playwright August STRINDBERG, who described it as "My most beloved drama, the child of my greatest suffering." Strindberg wrote it in 1901, but it was not produced until 1907. In 1961, the Swedish film director Ingmar BERGMAN, who was strongly influenced by Strindberg, produced an adaptation of *A Dream Play* for television. The otherworldly story concerns a daughter of the Indian deity Indra who descends to Earth and observes and experiences—in the course of her wanderings as a human—the anguish of an officer in love with an opera diva, an unsatisfying marriage with a lawyer, social class cruelty on the French Riviera, a conversation with a mythic poet and an acrimonious debate between university specialists. Finally, the daughter reascends to heaven, having seen that human life—as symbolized by the various figures she encountered—entails great suffering. But the play's ending offers the hope that there is meaning in that suffering. *A Dream Play* has influenced both dramatic EXPRESSIONISM and the THEATRE OF THE ABSURD.

Drees, Willem (1886–1988). Dutch politician; premier of the NETHERLANDS from 1948 to 1958 (the longest premiership in Dutch history), he was the architect of the nation's comprehensive welfare system. Under his stewardship, the Netherlands reemerged into prosperity as it recovered from five years of German occupation during WORLD WAR II. Drees, who helped found the Dutch Labor Party after the war, quit the party in the early 1970s, as he felt it was moving too far to the left. His son, Willem Jr., founded the Dutch Democratic Socialist Party.

Dreiser, Theodore (1871–1945). American author who was a major force in the development of modern literary realism. He was born the 11th child to a poor German immigrant family in Terre Haute, Indiana. He came to New York an ambitious journalist in 1894, the same year that critic Hamlin Garland proclaimed that city the "literary center of America." Six years of struggle and privation before the publication of his first novel, SISTER CARRIE (1900), introduced him to many of the greatest young realists of the time—the painter Everett SHINN, photographer Alfred STIEGLITZ, and novelists William Dean Howells, Stephen Crane, and Frank Norris. However, the poor reception accorded *Sister Carrie* caused Dreiser to withdraw into seven years of depression and hospitalization. Back on his feet and encouraged by the successful republication of the novel in 1907, he plunged into a series of 21 books in the next 21 years: *Jennie Gerhardt* (1911), *A Traveller at Forty* (1913), *The "Genius"* (1915), the three Frank Cowperwood novels (*The Financier*, 1912; *The Titan*, 1914; and *The Stoic*, published posthumously in 1946) and his most important novel, AN AMERICAN TRAGEDY (1925).

Despite frequent complaints from his contemporaries that his prose was clumsy, his method ponderous and his subjects sordid, Dreiser managed to secure a lasting reputation as a major novelist. His was a mind, according to colleague H.L. MENCKEN, that was "packed to suffocation with facts directly observed." His greatest characters—Carrie Meeber, Hurstwood, Clyde Griffiths—are superbly realized and, as Dreiser himself put it, "pit their enormous urges" against the limitations "of their pathetic equipment."

For further reading:

Lingeman, Richard, *Theodore Dreiser: An American Journey 1908–1945*. New York: Putnam, 1990.

Moers, Ellen, *The Two Dreisers*. New York: Viking Press, 1969.

Dresden. German city, on the Elbe River in Saxony. Renowned for its music and art collections, its singular architecture and its Dresden china, which has been crafted in nearby Meissen for the past two centuries. Dresden was devastated in WORLD WAR II by Allied fire-bombing in February 1945. In its ferocity and the destruction it caused, the bombing of Dresden, in which thousands of German civilians died, is considered third only to the atomic bombing of HIROSHIMA and NAGASAKI. Dresden was part of EAST GERMANY from 1949 to 1990. Most of the city has been reconstructed and revitalized.

Drew, George A. (1894–1973). Canadian politician. Drew served as premier of Ontario (1943–48) before becoming leader of CANADA'S CONSERVATIVE PARTY (1948–56). He was twice an unsuccessful candidate for prime minister. He was later Canadian high commissioner to London.

Drexel, Mother Katharine (1858–1955). American nun. Katharine Drexel was born into the wealthy and socially prominent Drexel banking family of Philadelphia. She donated her share of the family's fortune to the order she created in 1891, the Sisters of the Blessed Sacrament for Indians and Colored People. At its height, the order (now known as the Sisters of the Blessed Sacrament) maintained 66 schools in 23 states, including the predominantly black Xavier University in New Orleans. In 1988, Mother Drexel was beatified by Pope JOHN PAUL II, leaving her one step from sainthood. The Pope praised Mother Drexel as someone who "would stand up for the rights of the oppressed."

Drexel Burnham Lambert scandal. Financial scandal involving so-called junk bond king Michael R. Milken of Drexel Burnham Lambert, a large Wall Street brokerage firm. During the 1980s American business went through a period of merger mania characterized by "hostile takeovers." At the center of the action was the once obscure investment banking house of Drexel Burnham Lambert, which garnered the limelight when one of its partners, Michael R. Milken, pioneered the use of high-yielding junk bonds to finance corporate takeovers. Both Milken and his firm grew immensely wealthy from these transactions. However, the bubble burst in 1986 when Ivan BOESKY, a multi-millionaire who had made his fortune through risk arbitrage, implicated both Milken and Drexel in illegal insider trading. The federal government prosecuted both Milken and the firm. Drexel, which only a year before had been the most successful firm on Wall Street, went bankrupt in the wake of the scandal.

Dreyer, Carl T(heodor) (1889–1968). Danish film director. Dreyer was one of the most critically acclaimed directors of this century. Many of his films, which span the transition from silent films to the "talkies," are widely regarded as classics. Dreyer, an orphan, was raised by a Lutheran family. He worked as a journalist and as an editor before turning to the cinema in 1919. During his peripatetic career, he made a total of 14 films in Scandinavia, France and Germany. Perhaps his best known work is *The Passion of Joan of Arc* (1928), a highly dramatic black-and-white SILENT FILM that featured the French playwright Antonin ARTAUD as a monk. Other films by Dreyer include *Vampyr* (1932) and *Day of Wrath* (1943), a story of religious persecution, which Dreyer courageously shot in Denmark during the Nazi occupation. *Ordet* (1955) deals with the themes of love and faith, and *Gertrude* (1964) concerns the quest of a woman for absolute love. His writings include *Dreyer in Double Reflection* (1973).

Dreyfuss, Henry (1904–1972). American industrial designer. Born in New York City, Dreyfuss began his career in stage design, working on Broadway productions from 1921 to 1929. In 1929 he opened a his own studio, and from then on he produced a wide variety of industrial designs. Function and ease of use were prime considerations to Dreyfuss in his creation of designs for such products as Bell telephones (1930), Hoover vacuum cleaners (1934), passenger cars for the New York Central Railroad (1941), RCA television sets (1946), refrigerators, hearing aids, typewriters, farm machinery, airplanes, ships, printed materials and myriad other objects. A founder of the American Society of Industrial Design, he expressed his design philosophy in *The Measure of Man* (1959) and an autobiography, *Designing for People* (1955). He and his wife committed suicide in California.

Drickamer, Harry George (1908–). American physicist. Drickamer was educated at the University of Michigan, where he earned his Ph.D. in 1946. He then joined the staff of the University of Illinois, Urbana, serving first as professor of physical chemistry and, after 1953, as professor of chemical engineering. He has specialized in the study of the structure of solids by means of high pressures, producing in the course of his research pressures on the order of some 500,000 atmospheres.

dries. Right-wing members of the British CONSERVATIVE PARTY during Margaret THATCHER's tenure in office. They supported monetarist policies and opposed increases in public expenditure to alleviate social problems. They also supported PRIVATIZATION, curtailment of trade union influence and a vigorous defense policy. (See also WETS.)

Driesch, Hans Adolf Eduard (1867–1941). German biologist. Driesch held professorships at Heidelberg, Cologne and Leipzig and was visiting professor to China and America. A student of zoology at Freiburg, Jena and Munich, he was for some years on the staff of the Naples Zoological Station. Driesch carried out pioneering work in experimental embryology. He separated the two cells formed by the first division of a sea-urchin embryo and observed that each developed into a complete larva, thus demonstrating the capacity of the cell to form identical copies on division. He was also the first to demonstrate the phenomenon of embryonic induction, whereby the position of and interaction between cells within the embryo determine their subsequent differentiation. Driesch is perhaps best known for his concept of entelechy—a vitalistic philosophy that postulates the origin of life to lie in some unknown vital force separate from biochemical and physiological influences. This also led him to investigate psychic research and parapsychology.

Drinkwater, John (1882–1937). British poet, playwright and actor. Drinkwater was a competent Georgian poet and a founding member of the Birmingham Repertory Theatre, where he was a long time actor and manager. His early poetic dramas, the most successful of which was *X = O; a Night of the Trojan War* (1917), were followed by such acclaimed plays as *Abraham Lincoln* (1919) and the comedy *Bird in Hand* (1927) as well as several historical dramas. (See also the GEORGIANS.)

Dr. Seuss [pen name of Theodore Seuss Geisel] (1904–). American children's book author and illustrator. Dr. Theodore Seuss Geisel, known to the world as Dr. Seuss, was born in Springfield, Massachusetts. He has written over 50 delightfully nonsensical tales, including works that have become children's classics, such as *Horton Hears a Who* (1954), *The Cat in the Hat* and *How the Grinch Stole Christmas* (both 1957). His words and rhymes are intended to help preschoolers to recognize and pronounce syllables, and his bold and fanciful cartoon illustrations are designed to enchant. He is also a cartoonist, using the pen name Theo Le Seig for these works.

Drummond, Michael (1960–1990). U.S. heart recipient. He was the first person to be successfully implanted with an artificial heart as a bridge to receiving a human heart. He was given a JARVIK 7 artificial heart, which lasted until he received a human heart transplant nine days later. He later developed an infection that spread throughout his body, weakening the donor heart. A second artificial heart kept him alive for another two months.

Drummond de Andrade, Carlos (1902–1987). Brazilian poet. He was a leader of Brazil's modernist movement in literature. Aside from Fernando PESSOA of Portugal, he was perhaps the foremost Portuguese language poet of the 20th century. According to the *Times* of London, he was also "perhaps the most successful humorous poet of really major stature in this century."

Drury, Allen (Stuart) (1918–). American journalist and novelist. Drury worked as a journalist for 20 years—including a stint at United Press International as a Washington correspondent—before the publication of his first novel, *Advise and Consent* (1959, filmed 1962). The book was an immediate success, largely because it was assumed it was a roman a clef depicting the political and sexual intrigues of prominent Washington figures of the time. It won a PULITZER PRIZE in 1960. Drury wrote several sequels following the careers of the characters of *Advise and Consent*, including *A Shade of Difference* (1962), *That Summer* (1965), *Capable of Honor* (1966) and *Preserve and Protect* (1968). Other works include *A Senate Journal 1942–1945* (1972), *Egypt the Eternal Smile: Reflections on a Journey* (1980) and *Pentagon* (1986).

Druze Rebellion of 1925–27. The Druze, a small Islamic sect in French Mandated Syria, protested their tyrannical treatment by the governor and rebelled under Sultan Al-Atrash in July 1925. They soon controlled much of the countryside. Syrian nationalists joined them forcing the French to withdraw from Damascus. The French unleashed artillery and bombing attacks, but the rebellion, which had spread to southern Lebanon, continued until June, 1927. The Druze then accepted peace. (Lebanon had been declared a republic by the French on May 23, 1927.)

Dryden, Hugh L. (1898–1965). U.S. research scientist and administrator. Although he had never flown an airplane, Dryden was one of the world's great authorities in aeronautics. A graduate of Johns Hopkins University in 1917, he pioneered a series of high-speed flight phenomena projects for the National Bureau of Standards in the mid-1930s and by 1938 had become chief physicist of the agency. After leaving the Bureau of Standards in 1947, that same year he became director of aeronautical research for NACA (the National Advisory Committee on Aeronautics); when that agency became NASA in 1958, Dryden was named deputy administrator. Over a long career he published over 100 papers on aeronautics research and was the recipient of many awards, including the Daniel Guggenheim Medal in 1950 and the Wright Brothers Memorial Trophy in 1955. The Dryden Flight Research Center (formerly known as the High Speed Flight Station) at Edwards Air Force Base in California is named in his honor.

Duarte Fuentes, Jose Napoleon (1926–1990). Salvadoran politician, president of EL SALVADOR (1980–82, 1984–89). A centrist, Duarte helped found El Salvador's Christian Democratic Party in 1961. He ran for the presidency in 1972 and was leading in votes when the military government stopped the count and declared its candidate the winner. Following an unsuccessful coup by military officers who supported him, Duarte was arrested and finally exiled. In 1979, he returned to the country as part of a military-civilian junta. Appointed president in 1980, he was looked on as a force for Central American democracy by the REAGAN administration. He served during most of the 1980s, but large amounts of U.S. aid did not help bring peace. Although himself a man of integrity, his government came to be viewed as inept and riddled with corruption. Ill with cancer, he was forced from office in a 1989 election.

Dubasov, F.V. (1845–1912). Dubasov was the general responsible for the suppression of the RUSSIAN REVOLUTION OF 1905 in Moscow. Initially unsuccessful because the loyalty of his troops was uncertain, he was given reinforcements in the form of the Semenovsky Guards, who ruthlessly quelled the revolt in a few days.

Dubcek, Alexander (1921–). Czechoslovak political leader and reformer. Dubcek joined the Communist Party in 1939, fought with the Slovak RESISTANCE against the Germans (1944–45), and studied political science in Moscow (1955–58). He became principal secretary of the Slovak Communist Party in 1958 and first secretary—in effect, the leader of CZECHOSLOVAKIA—on January 5, 1968. In the following months (see PRAGUE SPRING) he introduced economic and political reforms designed to create what he called "socialism with a human face." Although he assured the U.S.S.R. that he intended to keep Czechoslovakia in the WARSAW PACT, Soviet leader BREZHNEV ordered the SOVIET INVASION OF CZECHOSLOVAKIA (August 20–21, 1968) to crush the reform movement and restore a hard-line communist government; Dubcek was briefly arrested. He remained first secretary until 1969 but was expelled from the party in 1970 and vanished from public life. When the democratic reform movement swept Czechoslovakia in late 1989, he reemerged to popular acclaim and was unanimously elected speaker of the Czechoslovak parliament in December of that year.

Dubinsky, David (1892–1982). American union leader. A major figure in the U.S. labor movement during the middle third of the 20th century, he was president of the International Ladies Garment Workers Union from 1932 to 1966. Under his leadership, the union membership grew tenfold, from 45,000 to 450,000. He took the union from near bankruptcy and built up assets of $500 million. Dubinsky largely eliminated sweatshops in the industry and drove communists out of leadership positions in the union. He pioneered the union role in granting health insurance, housing, severance pay, retirement benefits and a 35–hour work week. He also helped found New York State's Liberal Party and served as its vice chairman. He advised many presidents—from Franklin ROOSEVELT to John F. KENNEDY.

Dublin [Gaelic: Baile Atha Cliath]. Capital city of the Irish Republic, at the mouth of the Liffey River on the island's east coast. The EASTER RISING of April 14–29, 1916, led by Patrick PEARSE, saw a small group of rebels hold public buildings for a week against the British. The formation of the Irish Free State on December 6, 1921, which gave Ireland dominion status within the BRITISH EMPIRE, caused the worst political upheaval in city history as vast numbers of Irish showed their opposition to what they considered a half-measure of freedom. Dublin became capital of a fully autonomous Irish Republic on April 18, 1949. Dublin has long enjoyed its status as a Western cultural haven. The Gaelic League was established here in 1893; the ABBEY THEATRE opened in 1902. Lady Augusta GREGORY, Sean O'CASEY, John Millington SYNGE and William Butler YEATS were familiar Dublin figures in the early part of the century; post-World War II Dublin writers have included Patrick Kavanaugh and Flann O'BRIEN, among numerous others. James JOYCE is Dublin's most prominent literary icon, and the incidents in his novel ULYSSES all occur in Dublin on a single day, June 16, 1904. Dublin is also the location of the Guinness Brewery, Ireland's largest employer.

Du Bois, W(illiam) E(dward) B(urghardt) (1868–1963). Pioneering black American civil rights leader. Born in Great Barrington, Mass., Du Bois attended Fisk University and in 1895 became the first African-American to receive a Harvard Ph.D. He taught history and economics at Atlanta University from 1897 to 1910 and from 1932 to 1944. In the early part of the 20th century, Du Bois was the leading black figure in the fight against racial discrimination. Demanding equal rights, he opposed Booker T. WASHINGTON's credo that hard work alone would improve the status of American blacks. In some 20 books and scores of articles he made great contributions to the historical and sociological understanding of black life in America. His liberationist ideology was eloquently expressed in the classic work *The Souls of Black Folk* (1903). In an attempt to fight racial discrimination he founded (1905) the NIAGARA MOVEMENT, a forerunner of the NATIONAL ASSOCIATION FOR THE ADVANCEMENT OF COLORED PEOPLE (NAACP), which he cofounded four years later. In addition, he edited the organization's influential journal *The Crisis* from 1910 to 1934. Also concerned with colonialism and the international status of blacks, he participated in a number of Pan African Congresses, meeting Kwame NKRUMAH and Jomo KENYATTA at one of these (1945). Impatient with what he felt was the NAACP's timid approach to the civil rights struggle, he resigned from the organization in 1948. Increasingly radical, Du Bois came to view COMMUNISM as the best way to achieve black liberation, and he joined the Communist Party in 1961. That same year he moved to Ghana, becoming a Ghanaian citizen just before his death.

W.E.B. DuBois.

Dubos, Rene Jules (1901–1982). French-born bacteriologist and author. Graduated from France's National Agronomy Institute (1921) with a degree in agricultural science, Dubos worked briefly at the International Institute of Agriculture in Rome and emigrated to the U.S. in 1924. After earning his Ph.D. for research on soil microorganisms (Rutgers University, 1927), he joined the staff of Rockefeller University in New York. There he devoted his career to the study of bacteria and antibacterial substances. He was also a tireless crusader against environmental pollution. The author of more than 20 environmental and scientific works, he received many major scientific awards. He won the 1969 PULITZER PRIZE for nonfiction for his book *So Human an Animal*.

Dubuffet, Jean (1901–1985). French painter and sculptor. Dubuffet was regarded by many as the most important artist to emerge from FRANCE at the end of WORLD WAR II. Supporting himself as a wine merchant, he did not begin his artistic career in earnest until he was in his 40s. Opposed to respectability in art, he reveled in simplicity and created works in a primitive, childlike idiom with a caricatural quality. He was the recipient of a number of large-scale sculptural commissions in the U.S. He also wrote widely on art and other subjects and was considered a master of French prose.

Duchamp, Marcel (1887–1968). French painter and art theorist; in spite of his relatively slim production, one of the most important figures in 20th-century art—an avant-garde icon. The brother of Raymond DUCHAMP-VILLON and half-brother of Jacques Villon, he was born in Blainville and painted his first pictures in an Impressionist style around 1908. Soon thereafter, he produced works influenced by the formal brilliance of Paul Cezanne and the color of FAUVISM. Duchamp quickly developed a style of his own, a merging of CUBISM and FUTURISM that represented form and motion in a series of overlapping planes. This style was manifested in his famous work *Nude Descending a Staircase* (1912), which scandalized a conservative American public when it was shown in the 1913 ARMORY SHOW. Around this time, he began to develop the ideas that crystallized in 1915 in the DADA movement. Duchamp also created the first "readymades," everyday objects—such as bottle rack, bicycle wheel, urinal—exhibited out of context as works of art, which would strongly influence the adherents of POP ART.

He moved to New York City in 1915, became the center of a group of Dada artists and writers and began work on his magnum opus, a symbol-laden composition of painted foil and wire held between two sheets of plate glass and entitled *The Bride Stripped Bare by Her Bachelors, Even* (1915–23). Duchamp is also well known for his moustache-decorated Mona Lisa called *L.H.O.O.Q.* (1919). Although he executed a number of sketches and created his last work, *Etant Donnes* (1949), in the 1940s, Duchamp, who vowed never to repeat himself, officially retired from painting in 1923 and largely devoted himself to the game of chess. Many of his works are in the collection of the Philadelphia Museum of Art.

Duchamp-Villon, Raymond (1876–1918). French sculptor. Duchamp-Villon, who was markedly influenced by CUBISM and was one of the first sculptors to apply its theories to his medium, was also a member of an important artistic family. His brother was the renowned painter and theorist Marcel DUCHAMP, while his half-brother was painter Gaston Duchamp. Duchamp-Villon produced the bulk of his major sculptures in the years just prior to World War I, including *Seated Woman* and *Horse*. He was singled out for praise by French poet and art critic Guillaume APOLLINAIRE as a sculptor who went beyond mere modeling from nature to enlarge and glorify the human spirit.

Ducommun, Elie (1833–1906). Swiss journalist, educator, businessman, administrator and peace advocate. Ducommun was active in Swiss political life during the second half of the 19th century. With Albert GOBAT and Fredrik BAJER, he helped found the International Peace Bureau in 1891 and served as unsalaried director in his spare time. In 1902 he shared the second NOBEL PRIZE for peace with Gobat.

Dudinskaya, Natalya Mikhailovna (1912–). Soviet ballerina. She joined the Leningrad Academic Theater Opera and ballet troupe, and within a year was dancing the main roles. She participated in the creation of new Soviet ballets such as *The Flame of Paris, Laurensya* and *The Bronze Horseman*.

Dudintsev, Vladimir Dmitriyevich (1918–). Soviet author. Trained as a lawyer, during WORLD WAR II he served as defense counsel with a Siberian tribunal (1942–45). He began writing seriously in 1946 as a contributor to *Komsomolskaya Pravda*, the newspaper of the Communist Party's youth organization (see KOMSOMOL; PRAVDA). His most successful work, *Not By Bread Alone* (1957), was a frank description of the Soviet social and political system; it was censored by the authorities.

Dufek, George J. (1903–1977). American naval officer. He commanded the U.S. Navy's **Operation Deep Freeze** Antarctic expeditions (1955–59) and was the first American to set foot on the SOUTH POLE (1956). He retired with the rank of rear admiral.

Dufy, Raoul (1877–1953). French painter. Dufy was strongly influenced by the Impressionists early in his career, but emerged in the 1900s as a practitioner of FAUVISM, a school of painting that emphasized the dynamic use of bright color to create emotional and spiritual impact. Dufy crafted woodcut illustrations for the *Bestiare* (1911) of French poet Guillaume APOLLINAIRE, who was a critical supporter of Dufy's art. Dufy later turned his attention to artistic mass-production of woodblock print, textiles, pottery and tapestries. He also designed theatrical sets and public works displays.

Duggar, Benjamin Minge (1872–1956). American plant pathologist. Duggar devoted his career to studying plant diseases, and while professor of plant physiology at Cornell University wrote *Fungus Diseases of Plants* (1909), the first publication to deal purely with plant pathology. He is known for his work on cotton diseases and mushroom culture, but he made his most important discovery after retiring from academic life. In 1945 he became consultant to the American Cyanamid Co. and soon isolated the fungus *Streptomyces aureofaciens*. Three years' work with this organism resulted in Duggar extracting and purifying the compound chlortetracycline, (marketed as Aureomycin), and first of the tetracycline antibiotics. This drug was on the market by December 1948 and has proved useful in combating many infectious diseases. Duggar was one of the foremost coordinators of plant science research in America and was editor of many important publications.

Dukakis, Michael (Stanley) (1933–). American politician and Democratic presidential candidate (1988). Born in Brookline, Mass., Dukakis attended Swarthmore College and received a law degree from Harvard University. He served in the Massachusetts legislature (1963–70) and was elected governor of the state in 1974. Defeated in 1978, he taught at Harvard (1979–82) before regaining the statehouse in 1982; he was reelected in 1986. During his second term, Dukakis presided over a resurgence in the state economy that was dubbed the Massachusetts Miracle. Due largely to the state's economic successes, Dukakis emerged as the front-runner in the Democratic presidential primaries of 1988, besting such better-known challengers as Senator Al Gore, Representative Richard Gephardt and Jesse JACKSON and capturing the nomination. Dukakis led his Republican rival, George BUSH, in many polls in the summer of 1988. Dukakis, however, was often perceived as a cold and cautious technocrat, and he generated little enthusiasm among the majority of voters. He was resoundingly defeated by Bush. Dukakis com-

Shown campaigning with his wife, Kitty, Massachusetts Governor Michael Dukakis lost the 1988 U.S. presidential election to George Bush.

pleted his term as Massachusetts governor but, burdened by a failing economy, family problems and growing unpopularity in his home state, he declined to run again in 1990.

For further reading:

Kenney, Charles, *Dukakis: An American Odyssey*. Boston: Houghton Mifflin, 1989.

Dukas, Paul (1865–1935). French composer best known for his orchestral scherzo *L'apprenti sorcier* (1897; *The Sorcerer's Apprentice*), which is considered a masterpiece of modern music. Initial recognition as a composer came with his overture to Corneille's drama *Polyeucte* (1892). Among Dukas' most important works are the opera *Ariane et Barbe-Bleue*, with libretto by Maurice Maeterlinck (1907); the ballet score *La Peri* (1912); and the piano Sonata in E Flat Minor (1901). He also was a music critic for several journals, most notably the *Gazette des beaux-arts*, and taught at the Paris Conservatory (from 1918) and the Ecole Normale de Musique.

Duke, Charles (1935–). U.S. astronaut. Apollo 16 was Charles Duke's only space flight, but on that mission he became the 10th human to walk on the moon. As lunar module pilot, Duke, along with Commander John YOUNG, spent almost three days exploring the moon's surface by foot and on the specially built Lunar Rover vehicle.

Duke, James Buchanan (1856–1925). American entrepreneur and philanthropist. Duke was born in North Carolina, the son of a tobacco processor. In 1890, after expanding his father's company into the largest tobacco corporation in America, Duke joined with four competitors to form the American Tobacco Company, which would dominate the industry for two decades, until dissolved by the United States Supreme Court in 1911. Duke University in Durham, North Carolina, is named after Duke, who contributed heavily to the institution.

Dukhonin, Nikolai Nikolayevich (1876–1917). Russian general. He was commander-in-chief of all Russian forces when the OCTOBER REVOLUTION broke out. Having helped several senior officers to escape, he refused to obey an order to open truce negotiations with the Germans. He was shot by mutinous troops in November 1917.

Dulbecco, Renato (1914–). Italian-American physician and molecular biologist. Dulbecco obtained his M.D. from the University of Turin in 1936 and taught there until 1947, when he moved to the U.S. He taught briefly at Indiana before moving to California in 1949. He served as professor of biology (1952–63) at the California Institute of Technology. Dulbecco then joined the staff of the Salk Institute, where—apart from a period (1971–74) at the Imperial Cancer Research Fund in London—he has remained.

Beginning in 1959 Dulbecco introduced the idea of **cell transformation** into biology. In this process special cells are mixed in vitro with such tumor-producing viruses as the polyoma and SV40 virus. With some cells a productive infection results, where the virus multiplies unchecked in the cell and finally kills its host. In other cells, however, this unlimited multiplication does not occur; instead, the virus induces changes similar to those in cancer cells: The virus alters the cell so that it reproduces without restraint and does not respond to the presence of neighboring cells. A normal cell is thus transformed into a cancer cell in vitro. The significance of this work was to provide an experimental set up where the processes by which a normal cell becomes cancerous can be studied in a relatively simplified form. It was for this work that Dulbecco was awarded the NOBEL PRIZE for physiology or medicine in 1975, sharing it with Howard TEMIN and David BALTIMORE.

Dulles, Allen Welsh (1893–1969). U.S. foreign service officer; director of the CIA. Dulles was born in Watertown, New York, and graduated from Princeton University in 1914. In 1916, after earning a master's degree at Princeton, he joined the foreign service, with which he served first in Vienna then in Switzerland during WORLD WAR I; in 1919, he was on the American delegation to the peace conference in Paris. In 1926, Dulles received a law degree from George Washington University and resigned from the State Department to enter private practice. During WORLD WAR II he worked for the OFFICE OF STRATEGIC SERVICES (OSS), first as head of the New York City office and, from November 1942, as director of the office in Bern, Switzerland. Dulles's group made a significant contribution to the war effort, discovering, among other things, that the Nazis were working to develop the V-1 AND V-2 rockets and that Germany had broken the American diplomatic code in use in Europe. In 1946, after the war, Dulles became president of the private Council on Foreign Relations. In 1951 he was appointed deputy director of the CIA, and in 1953 he became the agency's director, about the same time that his brother, John Foster DULLES, was appointed secretary of state. During Dulles's tenure, the CIA was involved in many covert operations, including coups in Iran and Guatemala, U-2 surveillance flights over the Soviet Union (see U-2 INCIDENT) and the BAY OF PIGS INVASION of Cuba. In 1961, after the failure of the latter, Dulles resigned his position at the CIA. In 1964 he was a member of the Warren Commission, which investigated the assassination of President John F. KENNEDY.

Dulles, John Foster (1888–1959). American statesman, secretary of state (1953–59). Born in Washington, D.C., Dulles was the grandson and nephew of previous secretaries of state. He attended Princeton, the University of Paris and George Washington University before becoming a prominent international lawyer. He was a representative to the PARIS PEACE CONFERENCE of 1919, where he was the chief American spokesman on the question of reparations. He subsequently attended a variety of international conferences held between the wars. An adviser

As secretary of state from 1953 to 1959, John Foster Dulles was the main architect of the American Cold War policy.

to the U.S. delegation at the 1945 conference that founded the UNITED NATIONS, he served as a U.S. delegate to the U.N. from 1945 to 1949. In 1951 he negotiated the final peace treaty with Japan. Dulles' long experience in international affairs caused President Dwight D. EISENHOWER to appoint him secretary of state in 1953. Serving in this office until 1959, he became the main architect of America's COLD WAR stance, expanding the anticommunist policies of Dean ACHESON, whom Dulles denounced as too soft on COMMUNISM. He was important in forming a number of anticommunist alliances, such as SEATO and CENTO (Central Treaty Organization), and played a central role in the strengthening of NATO. In his unyielding opposition to communism, which he viewed as an absolute moral evil, Dulles initiated a policy of BRINKSMANSHIP and encouraged the development of nuclear weapons that could be used in a "massive retaliation" against any Soviet aggression. Dulles was a strong backer of the Nationalist Chinese and of the DIEM regime in South Vietnam. However, he strongly opposed the French and British intervention against Egypt in the ARAB-ISRAELI WAR OF 1956 (see SUEZ CRISIS). In ill health, he resigned from his post only five weeks before his death. Dulles' political philosophy was enunciated in his books *War, Peace, and Change* (1939) and *War or Peace* (1950).

For further reading:

Immerman, Richard H., ed., *John Foster Dulles and the Diplomacy of the Cold War*. Princeton, N.J.: Princeton University Press, 1990.

Prussen, Ronald W., *John Foster Dulles: The Road to Power*. New York: Free Press, 1982.

Dullin, Charles (1885–1949). French theatrical actor and producer. Dullin began his career as an actor working under Jacques COPEAU in the Vieux-Colombier theater company. In 1919, Dullin founded an experimental theater company, which he ultimately located at his Theatre de l'Atelier in Paris. It was one of the leading avant-garde troupes of the 1920s, producing plays by notables including Jean COCTEAU and Luigi PIRANDELLO. Dullin was named a director at the prestigious Comedie Francaise in 1936. While there, he provided tutelage to actor Jean-Louis BARRAULT.

duma. The elected legislative assemblies that, with the State Council, comprised the Russian legislature from 1906 to 1917, and which were established in response to the 1905 Revolution. The czar could rule absolutely when the duma was not in session and he could dissolve it at will. The first state duma, elected by universal male suffrage but with limited power over financial and other matters, met for 73 days in 1906 and the second met in 1907 for 102 days. The first and second dumas were unsuccessful in that, although it was expected that the representatives would be conservative, they were mainly liberal and socialist, and their demands for reform were totally unacceptable to the government. The franchise was then restricted, and the third duma ran its full five-year term (1907–12) and gave support to the government's agrarian reforms and military reorganization. The fourth duma sat from 1912 to 1917, but it gradually became opposed to the government's war policy and increasingly critical of the imperial regime. On the abdication of Czar NICHOLAS II the provisional committee established by the duma asked Prince LVOV to form a provisional government.

Du Maurier, Daphne [Dame Daphne] (1907–1989). British novelist. Daughter of the noted actor-manager **Sir Gerald Du Maurier** and granddaughter of novelist George Du Maurier, Dame Daphne was born in London and educated in Paris. A writer of popular romantic fiction, she published her first novel, *The Loving Spirit,* in 1931. Like much of her fiction, her best known work, *Rebecca* (1938, filmed 1940), takes place in Cornwall—where she lived much of her life. Du Maurier has also written lesser-known historical fiction. Other works include *Jamaica Inn* (1938), *Frenchman's Creek* (1941), *My Cousin Rachel* (1951), *The Breaking Point* (1959) and *The Flight of the Falcon* (1965). Du Maurier has written plays as well as nonfiction books about the Brontes, Cornwall and her family's history.

For further reading:
Du Maurier, Daphne, *Enchanted Cornwall: Her Pictorial Memoir.* New York: Viking Penguin, 1990.

British novelist Daphne Du Maurier.

Dumbarton Oaks conferences. From August 21 to October 7, 1944, representatives of China, the U.S.S.R., the U.S. and Great Britain met at Dumbarton Oaks, a mansion in Georgetown, Washington, D.C., to formulate proposals for an organization that eventually became the UNITED NATIONS. Paragraph four of the Moscow Declaration of 1943 had stressed the need for such a postwar organization to succeed the LEAGUE OF NATIONS. The Dumbarton Oaks proposals for the establishment of a general international organization did not establish the voting procedures or qualifications for membership; these were settled at the YALTA CONFERENCE in February 1945, at which a trusteeship system was agreed upon to replace the league mandates. The final proposals formed the basis of negotiations at the San Francisco Conference in 1945, from which the Charter of the United Nations was published.

Dunajec. River in the south of Poland, coursing 128 miles north from the Carpathian Mountains to the Vistula River. Battles were fought here in WORLD WAR I in two phases of General Mackensen's Austro-German attack against czarist Russia from May 1 to 14 and May 24 to June 15, 1915.

Dunand, Jean (1877–1942). Swiss designer. Born near Geneva, he trained as a sculptor and designer in his native city and in Paris, where he settled in 1897. He was particularly well-known for his vases, which he began producing in 1903. His styles ranged from ART NOUVEAU, to ART DECO, CUBISM and naturalism. Beginning to work in hammered metal, he became well-known for his elegant lacquer works, particularly for the panels he executed for the luxury OCEAN LINERS *Ile de France* (1928), *L'Atlantique* (1931) and NORMANDIE (1935). He was also known for his furniture designs.

Dunayevskaya, Raya (1910–1987). Ukrainian-born Marxist philosopher. Raised in the U.S., she is considered the founder of a philosophy called Marxist humanism, on which she wrote four books. From 1937 to 1939, she was secretary to Russian communist revolutionary Leon TROTSKY during his Mexican exile.

Dunayevsky, Isaak (1900–1955). Soviet composer. He worked as a conductor and composer in Moscow, Kharkov and Leningrad. In 1932 he began to compose for films. His works include the operettas *The Golden Valley* (1937), *The Road to Happiness* (1941) and *The Son of the Clown* (1950). He was one of the first composers in the U.S.S.R. to use JAZZ forms.

Dunbar, Paul Laurence (1872–1906). U.S. poet, novelist and one of the country's first black poets to gain international fame. Although from a poor family and the only black in his Dayton, Ohio, class, by the time he reached high school he had been chosen president of the school literary society and editor of the school newspaper. His first poems were published in Dayton newspapers, and his first volume of verses, *Oak and Ivy* (1893), was also published in Dayton. He won wide recognition for his *Lyrics of a Lowly Life* (1896) and took a literary trip to London in 1897. Despite his fame and frail health, Dunbar supported himself and his mother by running a Dayton elevator and by writing in his meager spare time. For the last seven years of his short life, he took no time out to treat the tuberculosis that killed him at the age of 34. His writings include seven volumes of poetry, two volumes of short stories and two novels. The *Ohio State Guide* declared, "Dunbar became the idol of his race and an artist admired by many other Americans, establishing a tradition that undoubtedly encouraged...Countee CULLEN, Claude McKay and Langston HUGHES." A 10-cent U.S. stamp honoring him was issued in the American Poets series, and his house in Dayton has been preserved as a state museum (1938).

For further reading:
Gentry, Tony, *Paul Laurence Dunbar.* New York: Chelsea House, 1988.

Duncan, Isadora (1877–1927). Legendary American dancer. A pioneer of modern dance, Duncan rebelled against the constraints and conventions of classical ballet, adopting a more natural, emotionally inspired dance movement. Her choreography was largely improvisational and based on her ideas of classic Greek drama and her emotional response to the music of such great composers as Beethoven, Chopin and Schubert. Her performances, in which she danced barefoot in a diaphanous tunic, often reflected the passions and tragedies of her unconventional lifestyle. Duncan's dancing shocked American sensibilities, so in 1899 she left for Europe where she remained for most of her life. Her first European performances in Vienna, Paris, Berlin and Budapest (1900–02) were triumphs. She even appeared at the BAYREUTH FESTIVAL in 1904. Her dancing style during her first Russian tour (1904) influenced the balletic reforms of Mikhail FOKINE and Serge DIAGHILEV. She danced in Egypt, Greece and South America and returned to the U.S. for performances in 1908 and 1914, then toured the new Soviet Union (1921, 1923). In addition, she founded several short-lived dance schools in Germany, France and the Soviet Union. Duncan gave her last recital in Paris in 1927, shortly before she was killed when her lengthy scarf caught in the wheelspokes of a car. Her personal magnetism and role as representative of a new dance movement made her the dominant dance influence of her time. Not only did she inspire innumerable later dancers and choreographers (including Frederick ASHTON and Kenneth MACMILLAN), she also influenced other

Dancing barefoot in flowing tunic, Isadora Duncan shocked American audiences as she pioneered modern dance.

arts—the drawings and designs of Gordon CRAIG, the photographs of Edward STEICHEN and the poetry of Sergei ESENIN, to whom she was briefly married (1922–23).

For further reading:

Blair, Fredrika, *Isadora*. New York: McGraw-Hill, 1986.

Duncan, Robert (Edward) (1919–1988). American poet. A prolific lyric poet, Duncan was influenced by Charles OLSON and his work is included in the Black Mountain School of poetry as well as associated with the works of the BEAT GENERATION. His poetry reflects his homosexuality and often deals with the nature of poetry itself. His many works include *The Opening of the Field* (1960), *Roots and Branches* (1964), both poetry; *The Truth & Life of Myth: An Essay in Essential Autobiography* (1968) and *Fictive Certainties: Essays* (1985). Some of his poetry was first published under the pseudonym Robert Edward Symmes. Early in his career, Duncan served as editor of *Experimental Review, Phoenix* and *Berkeley Miscellany*. Duncan was the first recipient of the National Poetry Award and is responsible for San Francisco's role as a center of poetry in the U.S.

Duncan-Sandys, Lord [born Duncan Edwin Sandy] (1908–1987). British politician and a leading figure in British political affairs for nearly four decades. He was elected a Conservative member of Parliament in 1935 and that same year married Winston CHURCHILL's eldest daughter, Diana. He directed key military actions as a junior member of Churchill's cabinet during WORLD WAR II. He lost his seat in Parliament in 1945 but was reelected in 1950 and served uninterruptedly until 1974. During that time, he served successively as minister of supply, minister of housing and local government, minister of defense and minister of aviation. As secretary of state for Commonwealth relations from 1960 to 1964, he helped negotiate the independence of 11 British colonies. After resigning from the House of Commons in 1974, he was elevated to the House of Lords.

Dunedin. City in the southeast of New Zealand's South Island, 190 miles southwest of Christchurch. Admiral Richard E. BYRD used Dunedin as the base for his Antarctic explorations of 1928–30 and 1933–35.

Dunham, Katherine (1912–). American dancer, choreographer, teacher and director. Dunham received an M.A. and a Ph.D. in anthropology from the University of Chicago. After extensive study of Negro dances in the West Indies, she worked with the Federal Theatre Project in Chicago (1938), then became director of the Labor Stage in New York City (1939). The first N.Y. concert featuring her choreography was in 1940, and she danced in the Broadway musical *Cabin in the Sky* that same year. After performing in and/or choreograping several Hollywood films, most notably *Stormy Weather* (1943), she toured the U.S. and Europe with her own dance company. In 1945 she established a dance school, which became the focal point for Afro-American dance until 1955. Her works, such as *Choros* (1943), combine elements of classical ballet, modern and Afro-Cuban dance and are based on her ethnological studies. She became director of the Performing Arts Training Center at Southern Illinois University, East St. Louis Campus.

For further reading:

Beckford, R., *Katherine Dunham*. New York: Dekker, 1979.

Dunkirk, evacuation of. After German armies overran Belgium at the start of WORLD WAR II, they focused on seizing the English Channel ports, bombarding them heavily. Hundreds of thousands of British, French, Belgian and other Allied troops were trapped between the sea and German lines. The British and French navies, merchant fleets and private yachts and trawlers came to rescue the troops off the beaches of Dunkirk. From May 26 to June 4, 1940 more than 1,200 ships sailed back and forth across the channel, despite German bombing and strafing, evacuating about 340,000 troops to the safety of England. Many Allied vessels, including six destroyers, were sunk and all equipment abandoned.

Actress Irene Dunne in The Awful Truth *(1937).*

Dunkirk, Treaty of. An Anglo-French agreement of March 4, 1947, to provide mutual assistance against any future German aggressive threats, together with consultation over economic relations, symbolizing French reemergence as a major European power.

Dunne, Irene Marie (1898–1990). U.S. actress. She was noted for her patrician appearance and an ability to play roles ranging from screwball comedy to sentimental drama. Although she never won an ACADEMY AWARD, she was nominated for her work in *Cimarron* (1931), *Theodora Goes Wild* (1936), *The Awful Truth* (1937), *Love Affair* (1939) and *I Remember Mama* (1948). She also starred in *Roberta* (1935), in which she introduced the song "Smoke Gets in Your Eyes," *Show Boat* (1936) and *Anna and the King of Siam* (1946).

Dunne, John Gregory. See Joan DIDION.

Dunning, John Ray (1907–1975). American physicist. Dunning was educated at Wesleyan University, Neb. and at Columbia University, N.Y., where he earned his Ph.D. in 1934. He took up an appointment at Columbia in 1933 and was made professor of physics in 1950. Dunning was one of the key figures in the MANHATTAN PROJECT to build the first ATOMIC BOMB.

Dunsany, Edward John Moreton Drax Plunkett, Lord (1878–1957). Anglo-Irish author. Born in London of Irish parents, Lord Dunsany was the 18th Baron of Dunsany Castle in County Meath, Ireland. A prolific writer, Dunsany is perhaps best remembered for his mythological tales, such as *The Gods of Pegana* (1905), *The Book of Wonder* (1912) and *The Blessing of Pan* (1927). Although politically aligned with the BRITISH EMPIRE in the question of HOME RULE and other Irish matters, Dunsany is associated with the IRISH LITERARY REVIVAL and was acquainted with Lady GREGORY and W.B. YEATS. Dunsany's first play, *The Glittering Gate,* was performed at the ABBEY THEA-

TRE in 1909. Other plays include *The Gods of the Mountain* (1911) and *A Night at an Inn* (1916). Dunsany also wrote a popular series of story collections beginning with *The Travel Tales of Mr. Joseph Jorkens* (1931) and a series of autobiographies.

DuPont, Clifford W. (1905–1978). First president of RHODESIA (1970–75). A British-born soldier and lawyer, DuPont was appointed head of state following Rhodesia's Unilateral Declaration of Independence (UDI) from Britain in 1965. He held the post until his election as president in 1970. DuPont's roles were largely ceremonial, with Prime Minister Ian SMITH holding the effective decision-making power for the rebellious colony.

Du Pre, Jacqueline (1945–1987). English cellist. Noted for her intense, romantic playing, Du Pre had come to be recognized as one of the world's leading cellists when her career was cut short in the early 1970s by the onset of multiple sclerosis. She and her husband, pianist and conductor Daniel BARENBOIM, had appeared frequently together on concert stages throughout the world and were regarded as the most prominent husband-and-wife musical team of their generation. By the mid-1970s Du Pre was virtually paralyzed, though she continued to teach and work for the cause of the vicitims of multiple sclerosis. Her story became the basis of a play, *Duet for One.* Du Pre left a number of fine recordings.

For further reading:

Easton, Carol, *Jacqueline Du Pre: A Life.* New York: Summit, 1990.

Durand, William Frederick (1859–1958). American engineer. Durand worked mainly on problems connected with the propeller, both marine and, after 1914, aeronautical. He was general editor of an important standard work, *Aerodynamic Theory,* produced in six volumes (1929–36). He also served on the National Advisory Committee for Civil Aeronautics (NACA) from 1915 to 1933 and, in 1941, was recalled to advise the government on the construction of an American jet-propelled airplane.

Durant, Will and Ariel. American historians and writers. William James Durant (1885–1981) was born in North Adams, Massachusetts. After graduating from St. Peter's College in Jersey City in 1907, he taught at Seton Hall and attended the seminary there for two years before moving to New York City and teaching at the Francisco Ferrer Modern School. There he met Ida Kaufman (1898–1981), a Ukrainian immigrant, who was 15 years old when they were married in 1913. "Ariel" was her husband's pet name for her, which she legally adopted after their marriage. Both Durants attended Columbia University, and Will received a doctorate from the school in 1917. In 1926, he published *The Story of Philosophy,* which sold over two million copies in three years. From 1935 to 1975, the Durants labored on their masterwork, *The Story of Civilization,* an 11-volume history of human achievement spanning over 11,000 years; Ariel was credited as coauthor from volume seven on. Criticized by some academic historians but extremely popular among general audiences, the highly readable series has been a perennial bestseller since its publication. Volume 10, *Rousseau and Revolution,* won the PULITZER PRIZE in 1968. While hospitalized, Will Durant died of a heart attack on November 8, 1981, apparently unaware that Ariel had died of natural causes two weeks before, on October 25.

Durante, Jimmy [James Francis Durante] (1893–1980). American vaudeville, nightclub, television and film comedian. Durante gained national popularity in the 1920s in the song-and-dance vaudeville trio of Clayton-Jackson-Durante, performing in PROHIBITION-era speakeasies. In the 1930s he appeared in many Broadway stage shows and in numerous movies for METRO-GOLDWYN-MAYER, where he supplanted Buster KEATON as the studio's top comedian. The Schnozzola, as he was known because of his bulbous nose, extended his fame in the mid-1940s on radio and later on television. He ended his programs with his celebrated sign-off, "Goodnight, Mrs. Calabash, wherever you are." In addition to his nose, his trademarks included a raspy voice, battered hat, butchered diction (with many malapropisms thrown in) and honky-tonk style of piano playing. His last film, *It's a Mad, Mad, Mad, Mad World* (1963), capped a career that spanned half a century.

For further reading:

Fowler, Gene, *Schnozzola.* New York: Viking Press, 1951.

Duras, Marguerite (1914–). French novelist, playwright and screenwriter. Duras was born in Indochina, now Vietnam, and came to Paris in 1932. She published her first of many novels, *Les Impudents,* in 1943. Her experimental fiction, which includes *Blue Eyes, Black Hair* (1977); *The Lover* 1985 and *Emily L.* (1987) is highly esteemed in France. Duras has never enjoyed the same success in the U.S., though her later works have gained more notice. In the States, she is better known for her screenplays, which include *Hiroshima mon amour* (1959). Her plays, which are generally associated with the THEATRE OF THE ABSURD, include *L'Eden Cinema* (1977) and *Savannah Bay* (1984).

Durham. U.S. city in the Piedmont region of north-central North Carolina, northwest of Raleigh. Durham is a component of a large educational and research system called the Research Triangle, which includes the University of North Carolina at Chapel Hill and the high-tech industries and research firms of Research Triangle Park.

Durkheim, Emile (1858–1917). French social theorist; a seminal influence on 20th-century sociology. Through his many writings, he established a scientific framework and methodology for the measurement of societal beliefs, dynamics and change. Durkheim, the son of an Alsatian rabbi, was educated at the Ecole Normale Superieure. In 1887, he taught the first ever university course on sociology in France. As a social theorist, Durkheim emphasized the need for stable political and religious institutions. In *Suicide* (1897), a classic study, Durkheim demonstrated that the per capita suicide rates of various countries were related to the strength of the ongoing social ties in those countries. In *The Elementary Forms of Religious Life* (1915), Durkheim proposed that the major function of religion was to enhance social bonds, and that schismatic movements were symptomatic of societal unrest.

Durnovo, Peter Nikolayevich (1844–1915). Russian politician. Minister of the interior under NICHOLAS II, he replaced General Dimitri Trepov, and was largely responsible for the downfall of Count Sergei WITTE, to whom he owed his post. His measures to quash the 1905 Revolution were ruthless and harsh. His successor as minister of the interior was Peter STOLYPIN.

Durocher, Leo "The Lip" (1905–). American baseball player and manager. An average hitter, Leo Durocher was an outstanding fielder who appeared in three All-Star games over a 17-year playing career. However, he is better known for his long and colorful managerial career, immortalized in his statement, "Nice guys finish last." He managed the Brooklyn Dodgers through most of the 1940s, often feuding with owner Branch RICKEY but winning the pennant in 1941. His temper cost him frequent ejection, and he was indicted for assaulting a fan in 1945. Fired by the Dodgers in 1948, he was quickly signed by the rival Giants and led them to a pennant in 1951 and a World Series victory in 1954. He became a TV commentator in 1955, but returned to manage the Chicago Cubs from 1966 until 1972 and the Houston Astros in 1973. One of the most successful managers in baseball history, he retired with 2,010 wins.

Durrell, Lawrence (George) (1912–1990). British author. Born in India, Durrell was educated at the College of St. Joseph, Darjeeling and St. Edmund's School in Canterbury. He travelled widely, living with his family in Corfu and in Paris in the 1930s. He spent much of his life in the eastern Mediterranean region, which figures in his poetry and fiction as well as his travel writing. Although he had written an earlier collection of poetry and a novel, Durrell first achieved recognition as a poet with collections including *A Private Country* (1943), *On Seeming to Presume* (1948) and *The Tree of Idleness* (1955). His sensuous writing explores the nature of love and knowledge. His first important novel, *The Black Book: On Agon* (1938), was an erotic pastiche that shows the influence of Henry MILLER and James JOYCE. Durrell is best known for The ALEXANDRIA QUARTET, which consists of the novels *Justine* (1957), *Balthazar* (1958), *Mountolive* (1958) and *Clea* (1960). The work shows Durrell's departure from realism; he goes farther in this direction in his later novels, including *Nunquan* (1970), *Monsieur* (1974) and *Constance* (1982). His travel writing includes *Prospero's Cell* (1945), *Reflections on a Marine Venus* (1953) and *Bitter Lemons* (1957). Durrell's brother, Gerald Durrell, is a prominent zoologist and writer.

For further reading:

Friedman, Alan W., ed., *Lawrence Durrell.* Boston: G.K. Hall, 1987.

Pine, Richard, *The Dandy and the Herald.* New York: St. Martin's, 1988.

Durrenmatt, Friedrich (1921–1990). Swiss playwright, screenplay writer, novelist and story writer. Durrenmatt rose to prominence in the 1950s, when his absurdist drama *The Visit* (1956) was performed worldwide to critical and popular acclaim. *The Visit* debuted on Broadway in 1958, starring Alfred LUNT and Lynn FONTANNE, and won the New York Drama Critics Award. Other plays by Durrenmatt, whose pessimistic social vision is thematically linked to the THEATRE OF THE ABSURD, include *The Physicists* (1962) and *The Execution of Justice* (1989). He also wrote prose fiction, notably the novel *Justice* (1985), and coscripted (with actor Maximilian Schell) the film *End of the Game* (1976).

Duse, Eleanora (1859–1924). Italian actress. Duse was considered by many (including George Bernard SHAW) to be the greatest actress of the late 19th and early 20th centuries. Unlike her rival Sarah BERNHARDT, who performed in the florid 19th-century style of acting, Duse was known for the subtlety and naturalness of her performances. This style of acting, developed at the same time in Russia by STANISLAVSKY, replaced the earlier "tragic" style and became the standard for the 20th century. Poet-playwright Gabriele D'ANNUNZIO wrote several plays, including *Francesca da Rimini* (1902), especially for her.

Dust Bowl. The worst droughts in U.S. history. At their peak in the late 1930s, they devastated an overall area of 25,000 square miles in the Central West. As the rain practically ceased the soil dried to dust and unusually high winds created vast dust storms, turning much of the area into a "Dust Bowl." The plight of the people of Oklahoma gained special attention in such works as John STEINBECK's *The Grapes of Wrath* (1939). In South Dakota, from 1933 to 1936, high winds carried choking clouds of dust. In North Dakota one-third of the state's lakes dried up and never refilled.

Great areas of the Central West had been plowed to grow grain for the WORLD WAR I food effort. Much of this land should have been left in its original condition. The dust storms carried off enormous amounts of topsoil—unprotected by roots of the original prairie grasses. The drought added to the hardships of the GREAT DEPRESSION, with banks foreclosing on thousands of farm mortgages.

Gradually the rains returned to the region. The drought taught many conservation lessons. A "shelter belt" of trees was planted from north to south across much of the area to restrain the "dust-busting" winds. Vast reservoirs were created in the Dakotas, Oklahoma and elsewhere to provide more moisture. Subsequent periods of low rainfall have caused substantially less damage, because of the precaution taken. The drought of the summer of 1988 was one of the most severe since the great drought, as many farmers once again faced foreclosure because of the total failure of their crop.

For further reading:

Hurt, R. Douglas, *The Dust Bowl: An Agricultural and Social History.* Chicago: Nelson Hall, 1981.

Worster, Donald, *Dust Bowl: The Southern Plains in the 1930s.* New York: Oxford University Press, 1979.

Du Toit, Alexander Logie (1878–1949). South African geologist. Du Toit studied at the South Africa College, now the University of Cape Town, the Royal Technical College, Glasgow; and the Royal College of Science, London. After a short period of teaching at Glasgow University (1901–03) he returned to South Africa and worked with the Geological Commission of the Cape of Good Hope (1903–20), during which time he explored the geology of South Africa. For the next seven years he worked for the Irrigation Department and produced six detailed monographs on South African geology. He also served as a consulting geologist to De Beers Consolidated Mines (1927–41). Following a visit to South America in 1923, du Toit became one of the earliest supporters of Alfred WEGENER's theory of continental drift, publishing his observations in *A Geological Comparison of South America with South Africa* (1927). He noted the similarity between the continents and developed his ideas in *Our Wandering*

During the Depression, droughts devastated the American Central West, causing dust storms like this one in 1935.

Haitian dictator Dr. Francois "Papa Doc" Duvalier, with his son and successor Jean-Claude (Feb. 25, 1971).

Continents (1937), in which he argued for the separation of Wegener's Pangaea into the two supercontinents, Laurasia and Gondwanaland.

Dutschke, Rudi (1940–1979). German radical student leader and Marxist scholar. Known as "Red Rudi," at the Free University of West Berlin Dutschke was at the forefront of the student revolt in Western Europe in the late 1960s. A fiery orator, he called for the radicalizing of society and the solidarity of workers and students. He moved to Britain in December 1968 for medical treatment of head wounds he suffered from an assailant in Berlin. He attempted to remain for academic studies, but was expelled from the country in 1971 when a British government tribunal ruled that his "meetings and associations have far exceeded normal social activities." Thereafter, he took up a teaching post at Aardhus University in Denmark.

Duvalier, Francois (1907–1971). Haitian dictator (1957–71). Trained as a physician, and a specialist in tropical medicine, Duvalier was popularly known as "Papa Doc." During the 1940s he was an important figure in medicine in the rural parts of HAITI and became involved in various nationalist cultural groups. He served as director of public health (1946–48) and secretary of labor (1949–50) in the regime of President Dumarsais Estime, but was ousted and forced to flee upon Paul Magloire's coup in 1950. After Magloire's resignation, Duvalier was overwhelmingly elected president in 1957. At first enormously popular, he became increasingly dictatorial and in 1964 had himself declared president for life. Duvalier's long reign was marked by poverty, fear and terror, with all signs of opposition suppressed by the dread Tonton Macoutes, his private army of civilian enforcers. On his death in 1971, he was succeeded by his son, Jean-Claude (known as "Baby Doc"), who was overthrown in a popular revolt in 1986.

Dwan, Allan [Joseph Aloysius Dwan] (1885–1981). Canadian-born pioneer motion picture director. Educated at Notre Dame as an electrical engineer, Dwan began providing new lamps for movie lighting to HOLLYWOOD studios in 1909. He was soon writing and editing scripts for silent movies, and in 1911 he directed his first film, a one-reel western. He learned about filmmaking from D.W. GRIFFITH, and created the "dolly shot" by mounting a camera on a moving car—an innovation that revolutionized moviemaking. He discovered Lon CHANEY and Ida Lupino and directed Douglas FAIRBANKS in many films. During the sound era he worked for 20TH CENTURY-FOX in the 1930s, Republic Pictures in the 1940s and RKO in the 1950s. According to his own account, he made about 1,850 films. Among the best known were *The Iron Mask* (1929), *Heidi* (1937), *Rebecca of Sunnybrook Farm* (1938), *Suez* (1938), *The Three Musketeers* (1939) and *The Sands of Iwo Jima* (1949).

Dybenko, Paul Yefimovich (1889–1938). Soviet sailor. Dybenko organized revolutionary sailors in the Baltic fleet in 1917 and was later appointed people's commissar of the Soviet navy. He narrowly escaped execution by the Germans in the Ukraine during the Russian Civil War. He lost his post during STALIN'S PURGE of the armed forces in 1937.

Dylan, Bob [Robert Zimmerman] (1941–). American folk singer and composer. He adopted the given name of Dylan THOMAS, the Welsh poet. He taught himself guitar and other musical instruments at the age of 10, and ran away from home several times. After leaving home for good, he rode freight trains around the country and wrote songs, many inspired by Woody GUTHRIE. In 1961, after occasional coffeehouse appearances, his first record album was released. Dylan is considered the musical symbol of protest by Americans who began to develop their social conscience in the 1960s. His best-known works, like "Blowin' in the Wind" (1962), "The Times They Are A-Changin" (1963) and "Like a Rolling Stone" (1965), are focused on social injustice.

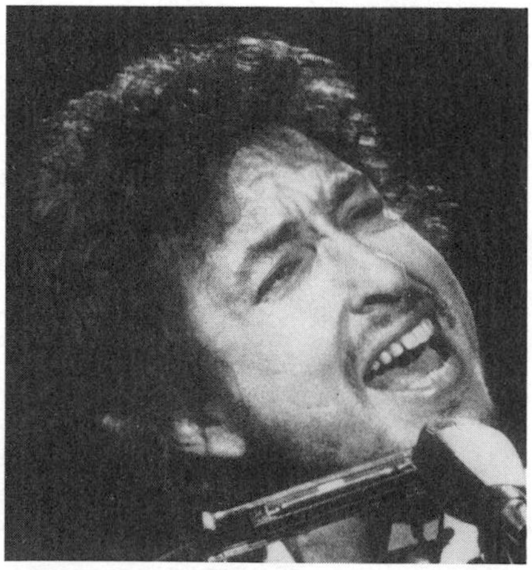

American folk and protest singer-songwriter Bob Dylan.

For further reading:

Krogsgaard, Michael, *Positively Bob Dylan: A Thirty-Year Discography, Concert and Recording Session Guide, 1960–1989*. Ann Arbor, Mich.: Popular Culture Inc., 1990.

Williams, Paul, *Performing Artist: The Music of Bob Dylan. Vol. 1, 1960–1973*. Lancaster, Penn.: Underwood-Miller, 1990.

Dymaxion. Word coined by Buckminster FULLER to describe a number of his projects. The word is made up of dynamic and maximum and is intended to define Fuller's aims toward "maximizing" performance through recognition of "dynamic" forces. The first Dymaxion House of 1927, developed in a model but never constructed, was a hexagonal living space suspended one story above the ground by tension cables radiating from a central vertical mast. His Dymaxion automobile of 1933, a radical, truly streamlined design, was built in three prototype examples, but never accepted for production. The second Dymaxion House of 1946, a domed cylinder, was built as a prototype at Wichita, Kansas, and attracted wide notice, but once again, production was never undertaken because of technical and financial difficulties that made such a radical solution to housing problems seem to be too advanced for its day.

Dyson, Sir Frank Watson (1868–1939). British astronomer. After first working as chief assistant at the Royal Observatory at Greenwich from 1894 to 1905, he was Astronomer Royal for Scotland from 1905 to 1910 and then returned to Greenwich as Astronomer Royal, serving from 1910 to 1933. He was knighted in 1915. Dyson's early observational work was done in collaboration with William G. Thackeray: They measured the positions of more than 4,000 circumpolar stars that had first been observed by Stephen Groombridge at the beginning of the 19th century. They were thus able to determine the proper motions of the stars. Dyson observed the total solar eclipses of 1900, 1901 and 1905, obtaining spectra of the atmospheric layers of the sun. He also organized the detailed observations of the total solar eclipse in 1919, sending expeditions to Principe in the Gulf of Guinea and Sobral in Brazil. The measured positions of stars near the sun's rim during the eclipse provided evidence for the bending of light in a gravitational field, as predicted by EINSTEIN in his theory of general relativity; these measurements were the first experimental support for that theory.

Dyson, Freeman (1923–). English-American physicist. Graduating from Cambridge in 1945, Dyson became an American citizen in 1951 and taught at Cornell University before joining the Institute for Advanced Study at Princeton in 1953. A freewheeling, adventurous thinker, Dyson has done major work in quantum electrodynamics but is best known for his challenging speculations on space science and the possibility of super-intelligent extraterrestrials. Always thought-provoking and often controversial, Dyson's carefully reasoned ideas, although sometimes appearing to be "outlandish," command serious attention and debate.

Dzerzhinsky, Felix Edmundovich (1877–1926). Communist politician, of Polish noble descent. During the reign of Czar NICHOLAS II he was imprisoned for revolutionary activities several times. After the RUSSIAN REVOLUTION he was the first head (1917–24) of the secret police (CHEKA) and of its successors, the OGPU and the GPU.

Dzerzhinsky, Ivan Ivanovich (1909–). Soviet composer. He studied at the Leningrad Conservatory. His works comprise several operas, including *Quiet Flows the Don,* composed 1923–24 but first performed in 1935. This was based on the novel by Mikhail SHOLOKHOV, as was another opera, *Virgin Soil Upturned.* He also composed orchestral and vocal works and music for plays and films.

Dzhanibekov, Vladimir (1942–). Soviet cosmonaut and veteran of five different space missions from 1978 to 1985, Dzhanibekov is unquestionably one of the brightest and most experienced Soviet cosmonauts. His expert piloting of Soyuz spacecraft accounted for five out of five docking successes at a time when the Soviet space program was haunted with a one-in-four failure rate. Dzhanibekov's most spectacular success was docking the SOYUZ T-13 craft with the dead SALYUT 7 space station in 1985. The tricky and exacting mission required unusual expertise, and Dzhanibekov and flight engineer Viktor Savinykh got the job. After a June 6, 1985, launch and two days chasing the dead station, link-up they did, succeeding within a few days in repairing the station's on-board systems. On August 2, in a 6.5–hour space walk, they installed new solar panels, and within a few weeks Salyut 7 was operable again. Praised by French spationaut Jean-Loup CHRETIEN for his calm during a serious docking problem in an earlier flight aboard Soyuz T-6 in 1982, Dzhanibekov also piloted Soyuz 27 in 1978, Soyuz 39 in 1981 and Soyuz T-12 (attempting to repair the Salyut 7 power system in a space walk with Svetlana Savitskaya) in 1984. He is also a deputy in the Uzbek soviet.

Dzubas, Friedel (1915–). German-American painter. Born in Berlin, Dzubas was a student of Paul KLEE (1933–36) in Dusseldorf before immigrating to the U.S. in 1939. His first one-man show was held in New York City in 1952, but his mature style did not develope until the 1960s. Dzubas is a leading figure in COLOR-FIELD PAINTING, using large areas of color in allover patterns on huge canvases.

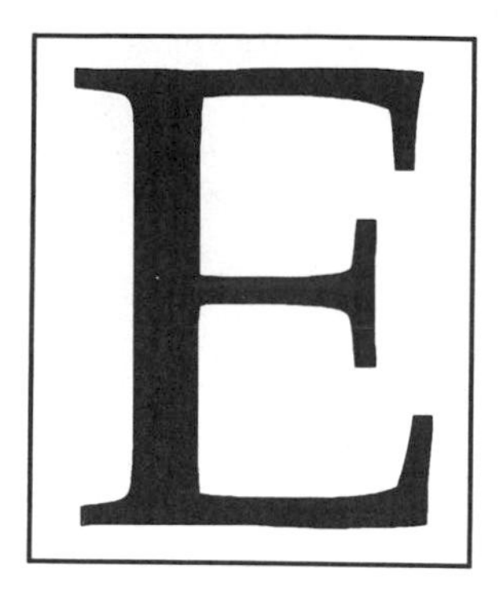

Eagleton, Thomas F(rancis) (1929–). American politician. Born in St. Louis, Missouri, Eagleton attended Amherst College and Harvard Law School; he was admitted to the bar in 1953. After serving as St. Louis' circuit attorney (1957–60), state attorney general (1961–65) and lieutenant governor (1965–68), he was elected to the U.S. Senate as a Democrat in 1968. His liberal views were important to Democratic presidential nominee George MCGOVERN, who chose Eagleton as his 1972 vice-presidential running mate. Shortly afterward, however, rumors surfaced that Eagleton had been hospitalized for depression three times in the 1960s and had undergone electric shock therapy. Eagleton acknowledged this and withdrew from the campaign. The Eagleton affair proved embarrassing to McGovern, whose judgment was called into question. McGovern subsequently selected Sargent SHRIVER as his running mate. Eagleton was reelected to the Senate in 1974 and 1980 but retired from political life in 1986.

Eaker, Ira C(larence) (1896–1987). U.S. Air Force general. An aviation pioneer between the world wars, he made the first blind transcontinental flight (entirely with instruments). He commanded U.S. air forces in Europe during WORLD WAR II and then played a key role in the establishment of the U.S. Air Force as a separate military service. He retired from the Air Force in 1947 and until the late 1970s was a business executive and syndicated newspaper columnist. In 1985 he was promoted to full general on the retired list.

Ealing Studios. British film studio associated with some of the most successful movies in the post-World War II period. The "Ealing comedy" became the standard worldwide for the British style of tasteful yet irreverent entertainment. Established in 1929 under the name Associated Talking Pictures, the studio borrowed the name Ealing in the late 1930s from the London borough where it was located. Under the guidance of Sir Michael Balcon, it functioned during its peak period (1946–58) as a relatively small-scale business enterprise that encouraged the individual creativity of its members—notably actors Alec GUINNESS and Stanley HOLLOWAY, writers T.E.B. White and William Rose, and directors Alberto Cavalcanti, Michael Crichton, Alexander Mackendrick and Robert Hamer. Dry wit, picturesque locations and a sympathy for the "little man" infused the callous black comedy of *Kind Hearts and Coronets* (1949), the grandtheft hijinks of *The Lavender Hill Mob* (1951) and *The Lady Killers* (1955) and the stinging social satire of *Tight Little Island* (1949), to name only a few representative films. Perhaps the masterpiece from this studio was *The Man in the White Suit* (1951), a tragicomedy about a meek little chemist (Guinness) whose invention of an indestructible fabric nearly brings about, ironically, his own destruction. Ealing suffered its own mortal blows when it dissolved in the late 1950s under a burden of debts.

For further reading:

Barr, Charles, *Ealing Studios.* New York: Woodstock, 1980.

Eames, Charles (1907–1978). American industrial designer and filmmaker best known for a molded plywood chair he designed in 1940 with Eero SAARINEN. The chair was later mass-produced in plastic. He and his wife designed a luxurious leather-and-rosewood lounge chair and ottoman in 1952. Charles Eames made over 50 educational movies, many using a multimedia projector approach.

Eames, Ray [nee Ray Kaiser] (1915–1988). U.S. designer. One of the most influential furniture and industrial designers of the post-World War II era, she was founder and partner in the Venice, California, design firm, The Office of Charles and Ray Eames. Eames and her husband Charles designed the Eames chair, two pieces of molded plywood connected by stainless steel tubing. Their work was known for infusing mass production with a high sense of style and comfort.

Earhart, Amelia (1898–1937?). Pioneer American aviator. Earhart was the first woman to fly across the Atlantic Ocean, from Trepassey Bay, Newfoundland, to Burryport, Wales. In 1928 she wrote about that epic journey in her book entitled *20 hrs., 40 min.* In 1931 she married publisher George Putnam. She flew alone across the Atlantic once again in 1932. In 1935 she was the first woman to fly to the mainland of the U.S. from Honolulu, Hawaii, and was the first woman to fly successfully across the U.S. alone in both directions. On a planned around-the-world trip, Earhart vanished near Howland Island in the Pacific Ocean. After her last contact on March 17, 1937, no confirmed report of her fate has ever been made.

For further reading:

Lovell, Mary S., *The Sound of Wings: The Biography of Amelia Earhart.* New York: St. Martin's, 1989.

Rich, Doris L., *Amelia Earhart.* Washington, D.C.: Smithsonian Institution Press, 1989.

Shore, Nancy, *Amelia Earhart.* New York: Chelsea House, 1989.

Amelia Earhart landing in Los Angeles to visit her mother after a flight from Oakland.

Earl, Harley J. (1893–1954). American design executive responsible for the styling of GENERAL MOTORS cars from 1927 until his retirement in 1959. Earl was born in California, the son of a builder of custom auto bodies. After joining General Motors, he exerted a constantly increasing influence in favor of design as a major ingredient in sales success. His 1927 LaSalle, dignified and elegant with its narrow hood and simple radiator grille, is viewed as his first major success. Over the years, particularly after World War II, the styling of General Motors cars became gradually more exaggerated, introducing excess CHROMIUM trim, oversized bodies, wraparound windshields, and, ultimately, tailfins. The concept of forced obsolescence is often associated with the constantly changing body designs developed under Earl's direction and imitated by other American automobile manufacturers.

Easter Rebellion (April 1916). Radical members of SINN FEIN and the older Irish Republican Brotherhood (later known as the IRA) called for rebellion during WORLD WAR I, while vainly sending Sir Roger CASEMENT to Germany for help. Loosely organized, the planned uprising was confined to Dublin and included only 2,000 Irish volunteers and a 200-citizen army. Seizing the General Post Office as headquarters on Easter Monday, April 24, 1916, Patrick PEARSE and James CONNOLLY and their rebels proclaimed a republic. The British, losing about 460 men, put down the uprising in a week. Many Dubliners condemned the rebellion, but when 16 rebel leaders were executed, the rebels became martyrs and the Irish parliamentary party was ruined. The Sinn Fein continued under Eamon DE VALERA, and the IRA became a guerrilla underground. (See also IRELAND; IRISH CIVIL WAR.)

Easter Rising. See EASTER REBELLION.

East Germany [Deutsche Demokratic Republik—DDR, or German Democratic Republic—GDR]. East Germany was located in north-central Europe and covered an area of 41,817 square miles, excluding West Berlin. At the end of WORLD WAR II, Soviet armies occcupied the eastern part of GERMANY. Determined to prevent the reemergence of a large and possibly hostile German nation, the Soviets turned their treaty-ratified zone of occupation (intended, as were the American, British and French zones, to be only temporary), into the German Democratic Republic (GDR) in 1949, with Walter ULBRICHT as leader (until 1971). France, Britain, the U.S. and the new Federal Republic of Germany (WEST GERMANY) refused to recognize the GDR. Ulbricht embraced COMMUNISM and suppressed anti-government uprisings in 1953. The GDR became a founding member of the WARSAW PACT in 1955. Tensions between the GDR and the Western powers, as well as increased escapes by East Germans into West Berlin, led to the construction of the BERLIN WALL (1961). A similar barrier was eventually extended along the entire border between East and West Germany. During

EAST GERMANY

EAST GERMANY (GERMAN DEMOCRATIC REPUBLIC)

1949	(Oct. 7) German Democratic Republic proclaimed in Soviet-occupied zone of Germany.
1951	Walter Ulbricht becomes head of ruling Socialist Unity (Communist) Party.
1953	Anti-government worker riots suppressed with Soviet help.
1955	(May) GDR becomes founding member of the Warsaw Pact.
1961	(August) Construction of Berlin Wall.
1971	Walter Ulbricht resigns; succeeded by Erich Honecker.
1973	(September) GDR admitted to United Nations.
1989	Mass protests and exodus to the West force Honecker's resignation; Berlin Wall opened.
1990	(Oct. 3) Reunification of Germany; GDR absorbed into the Federal Republic of Germany.

Erich HONECKER's leadership (1971–89), the country joined the UNITED NATIONS (1973) and solidified its borders through treaties. However, Honecker's resistance to reform led to mass protests in 1989. Tens of thousands of East Germans fled to the West via Hungary, which had reopened its border with Austria. After Honecker's resignation, interim leader Egon KRENZ opened the Berlin Wall in November 1989, allowing East Germans free passage into the West. The wall was torn down during the next year and East Germans voted for German reunification in March 1990. The GDR ceased to exist as a separate country after the reunification of Germany on October 3, 1990.

For further reading:

Turner, Henry A., Jr., *The Two Germanies Since 1945: East and West*. New Haven, Conn.: Yale University Press, 1987.

Eastland, James O(liver) (1904–1986). U.S. politician. A Mississippi Democrat, Eastland served in the U.S. Senate for more than 36 years. A wealthy plantation owner, he was best known during his years in the Senate as a segregationist and militant anticommunist. He was often at odds with the national DEMOCRATIC PARTY and frequently criticized the U.S. Supreme Court. He left his party during the 1948 presidential election to support the Dixiecrat STATES' RIGHTS ticket. Often sharply critical of President Lyndon B. JOHNSON'S GREAT SOCIETY program, he was nonetheless respected and liked by Senate liberals. When he retired in 1979, Eastland had been chairman of the Senate Judiciary Committee for 22 years and president pro tem of the Senate for six.

Eastman, George (1854–1932). American inventor. Eastman began his career in banking and insurance but turned from this to photography. In 1880 he perfected dryplate photographic film and began manufacturing it. He produced a transparent roll-film in 1884 and in the same year founded the Eastman Dry Plate and Film Co. In 1888 he introduced the simple hand-held box camera that made popular photography possible. The Kodak camera with a roll of transparent film was cheap enough for all pockets and could be used by a child. It was followed by the Brownie camera, which cost just one dollar. Eastman gave away a considerable part of his fortune to educational institutions, including the Massachusetts Institute of Technology. He committed suicide in 1932.

East Pakistan. See BANGLADESH.

East Saint Louis. Illinois city on the Mississippi River, facing St. Louis, scene of an infamous race riot. During WORLD WAR I, on July 2, 1917, whites attacked blacks in retaliation for the employment of blacks by war industries. Forty blacks and eight whites died.

Eastwood, Clint (1930–). American film actor and director; a dominant box-office star since the mid-1960s. Eastwood began his acting career in the 1950s and first achieved success with his cowboy role on the television series "Rawhide" (1959–1966). Real stardom came with his portrayal of the fearsome, gunslinging "man with no name" in a trio of Italian-made "spaghetti" westerns: *A Fistful of Dollars* (1964), *For a Few Dollars More* (1965) and *The Good, the Bad, and the Ugly* (1967). Eastwood's other continuing character (in five films) is ultimate enforcer-cop Harry Callahan, whose "Make my day!" in *Dirty Harry* (1971) became a national catchphrase. Other successful films include *Play Misty For Me* (1971, also his first directing effort), *Tightrope* (1984) and *Heartbreak Ridge* (1986). In recent years, he has concentrated on producing and directing films, most notably *Bird* (1988), based on the life of jazz great Charlie PARKER.

Eaton, Cyrus Stephen (1883–1979). American financier and industrialist. Born in Nova Scotia, Canada, Eaton was a "self-made man." He invested in rubber, steel, coal and utilities. In 1930 he founded the Republic Steel Corporation (1930). Although a champion of U.S. capitalism, he was also an early advocate of trade with communist nations. He was a friend of Soviet Premier Nikita KHRUSHCHEV and other high Soviet officials. In 1955 he established the first of the Pugwash Conferences, annual meetings attended by scientists and scholars from the Eastern and Western blocs designed to lessen international tension. In 1960, the Soviet Union awarded Eaton the Lenin Peace Prize.

Ebashi, Setsuro (1922–). Japanese biochemist. Ebashi received his M.D. (1944) and his Ph.D. (1954) from the University of Tokyo. He became professor of pharmacology in 1959 and, since 1963, has held the chair of biochemistry. Ebashi has for many years been one of the leading workers in the field of muscle contraction. His work has thrown considerable light on the identity and workings of the so-called relaxing factor.

Eboli. Italian town in the Campania, 17 miles from Salerno. It was hit hard during the fighting that followed the Allied landings at Salerno in WORLD WAR II.

Ebro River. River that rises in the Cantabrian Mountains and flows southeastward for 565 miles to a delta on the Mediterranean Sea, between BARCELONA and Valencia, Spain. During the SPANISH CIVIL WAR the Loyalists suffered a major defeat here (August–November 1938). Hydroelectric power plants in the Ebro system now provide nearly 50% of Spain's hydroelectricity.

Eccles, Sir John Carew (1903–). Australian physiologist. Eccles was educated at the University of Melbourne and in England at Oxford University, working at Oxford with Charles Sherrington on muscular reflexes and nervous transmission across the synapses (nerve junctions). For a time he taught in Australia and New Zealand, and in 1966 he began working at the Institute for Biomedical Research in Chicago. While professor of physiology at the Australian National University, Canberra (1951–66), Eccles carried out work on the chemical changes that take place at synapses, pursuing the findings of Alan Hodgkin and Andrew HUXLEY, with whom he subsequently shared the 1963 NOBEL PRIZE for physiology or medicine. Eccles showed that excitation of different nerve cells causes the synapses to release a substance that promotes the passage of sodium and potassium ions and effects an alternation in the polarity of the electric charge. It is in this way that nervous impulses are communicated—or inhibited—by nerve cells.

Ecevit, Bulent (1925–). Turkish statesman and writer. After a career in government and journalism, Ecevit became a member of TURKEY's parliament in 1957. He was minister of labor (1961–65) and chairman of the Republican People's Party (1972). He was briefly prime minister of a coalition government in 1974, again holding that office in 1978–80. After the 1980 military coup, Ecevit was imprisoned and banned from public life in 1983. He voluntarily renounced political activities in 1987, but became chairman of the Democratic Left Party in 1989.

Eckhardt, Tibor (1888–1972). Hungarian statesman and diplomat. Eckhardt was first elected to the Hungarian parliament in 1922. He later organized and led the Smallholders Party (1934). In 1935 he was HUNGARY's chief delegate to the LEAGUE OF NATIONS. He fought for social reforms and against Nazi influence. After WORLD WAR II he organized the anticommunist Hungarian National Council (1948).

Eckstine, Billy (William Clarence) (1914–). American bandleader, singer and trumpeter. Eckstine was born in Pittsburgh, Pennsylvania, and attended Washington University. He began his career as a jazz vocalist, and from 1939 to 1943 was a vocalist and trumpeter with the Earl HINES band. In 1944 he formed his own band and was a pioneer in the development of BEBOP. Jazz greats such as Dizzy GILLESPIE, Charlie PARKER, Miles DAVIS and Sarah VAUGHAN gained valuable experience performing with the band. After the band broke up in 1947, Eckstine continued his career as a solo performer and recording artist. He continued to perform in cabarets until the 1970s.

eclecticism. Term used in design and architecture to refer to the practice of borrowing from various historic styles, sometimes in combination. From about 1900 until World War II, most architecture and interior design was eclectic, using the styles of ancient Greece and Rome, the Middle Ages, and the Renaissance as the taste of architects and clients might suggest. Such buildings as New York's old Pennsylvania Railroad terminal, built in imitation of Roman baths, the Woolworth Building, constructed in the style of a Gothic cathedral tower, and many lesser buildings are typical of the eclectic phase of American architecture. Interiors were similarly designed in imitative styles. Manufacturers of furniture, lighting devices, and similar items produced designs to match the popular periods and styles. Although eclecticism was largely displaced by MODERNISM, it survives in the continuing manufacture of antique reproductions and is currently being revived in a modified form as an aspect of POST-MODERNISM.

Eco, Umberto (1932–). Italian novelist and philosopher. Eco achieved best-seller status in Europe and the U.S. with the publication of his medieval mystery novel, *The Name of the Rose* (1984). A professor of semiotics—the study of human signs and symbols—at the University of Bologna, Eco has written extensively in the fields of philosophy and literary criticism on subjects including Saint Thomas Aquinas and James JOYCE. But he emerged as an important novelist in the 1980s through his ability to combine erudite and esoteric themes, such as Christian scholasticism and Jewish kabbalah, with fast-paced plots set in a historical past that interweave crime and passion with the spiritual quest for meaning in life. *The Name of the Rose,* which is set in a labyrinthine medieval monastery in which a series of murders have taken place, was adapted into a 1986 film starring Sean CONNERY. Eco's second novel was *Foucault's Pendulum* (1988).

ECU [European Currency Unit]. See EUROPEAN MONETARY SYSTEM.

Ecuador. Nation on the Pacific coast of northwestern South America, with Colombia to the north and Peru to the south and east; the Equator, from which the country takes its name, crosses Ecuador near its capital city of Quito. The anticlerical Flavio Eloy Alfaro ruled for nearly 15 years after 1895. From the 1920s to the 1940s there were continual changes of president, a dozen serving between 1931 and 1940. Jose VELASCO IBARRA, a liberal, was elected president five times from 1934 to 1972 but served only one full term. Galo Plaza Lasso served as a liberal president from 1948 to 1952. Camilo Ponce Enriquez was elected in 1956 as the first conservative president in 60 years.

Ecuador's border dispute with PERU dated to 1860 and involved the Oriente, a section east of the Andes Mountains, at the headwaters of the Amazon. The two nations battled in 1941, and the following year Ecuador was compelled to relinquish a large section to Peru, only to have President Velasco Ibarra condemn the treaty in 1960. The 1960s and 1970s brought numerous revolts and different presidents; from 1961 to 1963, however, Carlos Julio Arosemena Monroy's practices enhanced the financial situation. Following several years of government by military junta, Jaime Roldos Aguilera was installed as president in 1979 in a quiet shift of command. When Aguilera died in a plane crash in May 1981, control was transferred quietly to Vice President Osvaldo Hurtado, who carried on Aguilera's reform program. In January 1981 war erupted again over the Peru–Ecuador border; in March, however, both sides started to negotiate. Ecuador's economy surged after the discovery of oil in 1971, but falling oil prices in the 1980s, combined with high inflation, ensure that the standard of living remains low for the average Ecuadoran. Quito is the capital and Guayaquil the largest city.

ECUADOR

ECUADOR

1912	President Eloy Alfaro killed by pro-clerical faction.
1925	"July Revolution" introduces period of reform.
1931-48	Twenty-two governments hold temporary office.
1960	Jose Maria Velasco Ibarra elected president for the sixth time.
1972	General Guillermo Rodriguez Lara overthrows President Velasco; Rodriguez threatens oil contracts and investments of more than 30 foreign companies.
1980	Freedom House lists Ecuador as free country; death of Velasco Ibarra.
1989	Leftist guerrilla group lays down arms after nine-year struggle; two U.S. environmental groups absorb Ecuadoran debt in exchange for rain forest preservation.

Eddington, Sir Arthur Stanley (1882–1944). British astrophysicist and mathematician. Eddington graduated from Owens College (now the University of Manchester) in 1902 and from Cambridge University in 1905. From 1906 to 1913 he was chief assistant to the Astronomer Royal at Greenwich, after which he returned to Cambridge as Plumian Professor of Astronomy. He was knighted in 1930. Eddington was the major British astronomer of the interwar period. His early work on the motions of stars was followed, from 1916 onward, by studies of the interiors of stars—about which he published his first major book, *The Internal Constitution of the Stars* (1926). He showed that for equilibrium to be maintained in a star, the inwardly directed force of gravitation must be balanced by the outwardly directed forces of both gas pressure and radiation pressure. He also proposed that heat energy was transported from the center to the outer regions of a star not by convection, as thought hitherto, but by radiation. It was in this work that Eddington gave a full account of his discovery (1924) of the mass-to-luminosity relationship, which shows that the more massive a star is the more luminous it will be. The value of the relation is that it allows the mass of a star to be determined if its intrinsic brightness is known. Eddington realized that there was a limit to the size of stars. Relatively few would have masses exceeding 10 times the mass of the sun, and any exceeding 50 solar masses would be unstable because of excessive radiation pressure. Eddington wrote a number of books both for scientists and for a lay readership. His more popular books, including *The Expanding Universe* (1933), were widely read, went through many editions and opened new worlds to many inquiring minds of the interwar years. It was through Eddington that EINSTEIN's **theory of general relativity** reached the English-speaking world. Eddington was greatly impressed by Einstein's theory and was able to provide experimental evidence for it. He observed the total solar eclipse of 1919 and submitted a report that captured the intellectual imagination of his generation. It stated that a very precise and unexpected prediction made by Einstein in his general theory had been successfully observed. He had seen the very slight bending of light by the gravitational field of a star—the sun. Further support came in 1924 when Einstein's prediction of the reddening of starlight by the gravitational field of the star was tested. Eddington thus did much to establish Einstein's theory on a sound and rigorous foundation and gave a very fine presentation of the subject in his *Mathematical Theory of Relativity* (1923). Eddington also worked for many years on an obscure but challenging theory, which was only published in his posthumous work, *Fundamental Theory* (1946). Basically, he claimed that the fundamental constants of science, such as the mass of the proton and mass and charge of the electron, were a "natural and complete specification for constructing a universe" and that their values were not accidental. He then set out to develop a theory from which such values would follow as a consequence, but he never completed it.

Eden, Anthony (1897–1977). British Conservative Party statesman, prime minister of the UNITED KINGDOM (1955–57). Eden entered the House of Commons in 1923 and served three times as foreign secretary (1935–38, 1940–45 and 1951–55). He was a leading figure in Winston CHURCHILL's coalition cabinet during WORLD WAR II. Heir-apparent to Churchill for many years, he was deputy prime minister in Churchill's second period in office (1951–55) and succeeded Churchill as prime minister in 1955. Eden's main interests were always in foreign affairs. His ministry was marked by increasing tensions in the Middle East. Eden's hostility toward NASSER's Egypt tempted him to

Sir Anthony Eden.

support Anglo-French military intervention and led to the SUEZ CRISIS (1956). This divided the country, lost Eden the support of most Commonwealth leaders and aroused the ire of U.S. Secretary of State John Foster DULLES. The Suez Crisis contributed to a collapse of Eden's health and his resignation in January 1957. He was created Earl of Avon in 1961.

Ederle, Gertrude "Trudy" (1906–). American swimmer, considered one of the greatest athletes of the 1920s. In the 1924 OLYMPIC GAMES, Ederle won a gold medal as a member of the U.S. women's 400-meter relay team. In 1926 she became the first woman to swim across the English Channel; she made the 35-mile swim in 14.5 hours, two hours faster than the previous record, held by a man. At the peak of her amateur career, Ederle held 29 national or world swimming records.

Edgerton, Harold Eugene "Doc" (1903–1990). American inventor. A professor at the Massachusetts Institute of Technology, Edgerton is credited with inventing the electronic flash for use in photography. His repeating strobe unit, developed in 1931, made high-speed photography possible by "freezing" action. He also devised a flash technique that was used to take night-time reconnaissance photos prior to the Allied Invasion of NORMANDY on D-DAY in 1944. An interest in deep-sea exploration led him to develop an underwater camera for explorer Jacques COUSTEAU. He developed a sonar device that in 1973 helped locate the sunken American Civil War ironclad, *Monitor*. The device was less successful in 1976 in an attempt to find the Loch Ness monster.

Edinburgh Festival. Held annually for a three-week period in August–September in Edinburgh, Scotland, the festival is an international celebration of the arts, with an emphasis on music and, more recently, theater, dance and film. Founded in 1947, the festival was first directed by Rudolph BING. Since 1984 Frank Dunlop has been director. A special feature of the festival is the Fringe, a subfestival composed of hundreds of events, often innovative and experimental, that are outside the official program, but often command much attention. Such distinguished opera companies as La Scala have performed there as well as such famous musicians as opera singer Placido DOMINGO and conductor Zubin Mehta.

Edison, Thomas Alva (1847–1931). One of the most productive of American inventors of the late 19th and early 20th centuries. His invention of the phonograph ("talking machine") in 1877 and of the electric light bulb in 1878 established his reputation as a key figure in the development of modern technology. As with many inventors, Edison combined invention with design through the necessity of giving form to his original prototypes. Although many Edison designs seem crude, others, such as the incandescent bulb, were so well conceived as to become the norm, surviving with little change to the present. Edison was a prolific inventor of many electrical devices and systems and played an important role in the development of modern, near-universally available electrical power distribution systems.

Edison Company. America's first motion picture studio, named after Thomas Alva Edison. A facility called the Black Maria was constructed in West Orange, N.J., in 1891. It was a large structure, covered inside and out with tar paper, with only a removable part of the roof allowing sunlight inside. Utilizing the Edison devices of the **kinetophone** (a device that synchronized film with a sound cylinder), and the **kinetograph** camera, Edison's assistant, W.K.L. Dickson, produced numerous short motion picture strips on the newly developed EASTMAN celluloid film. At first these movies were merely brief actualities of vaudeville acts, strongmen and prize fights; but after April 23, 1896, when the first public performance of Edison's films took place at Koster and Bial's Music Hall in New York's Herald Square, production grew more ambitious. A stock company of players was developed, including Viola Dana, Mary Fuller and Charles Ogle. At a new studio facility in New York, director Edwin S. Porter made many narrative films of one-reel duration (approximately 8 to 12 minutes), including *The Great Train Robbery* (1903). An itinerant actor named D.W. GRIFFITH arrived in 1907 and appeared as a player in *Rescued from an Eagle's Nest*. Later at the rival studio, American Mutoscope and Biograph Company, Griffith would revolutionize filmmaking techniques and effects (see BIOGRAPH COMPANY). After a bitter battle over motion picture equipment patent rights between Edison and Biograph, the two cooperated in the formation (1909) of the notorious Motion Picture Patents Company. The period from 1908 to 1912 saw Edison's peak of success. Several factors, however, caused his

Thomas Edison with his phonograph.

business to decline rapidly. There was a disastrous fire at the new Edison studio in the Bronx. Edison was slow to exploit the popular trend toward feature-length movies after 1914. The Patents Company, moreover, was dissolved by the Supreme Court in 1915 in an antitrust action. The Edison Company disbanded in 1918. Its last film was a feature called *The Unbeliever,* directed by Alan Crosland—who 10 years later would direct the seminal synchronized-sound film *The Jazz Singer* for WARNER BROS.

Edlen, Bengt (1906–). Swedish physicist. Edlen studied at the University of Uppsala, where he gained his Ph.D. in 1934 and also served on the faculty from 1928 until 1944. He was then appointed professor of physics at the University of Lund, a post he retained until his retirement in 1973. Edlen is recognized for his research on atomic spectra and their applications to astrophysics. In the early 1940s he carried out important work on the emission lines in the sun's corona. Edlen succeeded in showing (1941) that the coronal lines were caused mainly by iron, nickel, calcium and argon atoms deprived of 10 to 15 of their electrons; i.e., by highly charged positive ions. The implications of such extreme ionization were not lost on Edlen, who was quick to point out that it must indicate temperatures of more than a quarter of a million degrees in the solar corona.

Edrich, W.J. (Bill) (1916–1986). English cricketer whose career stretched from 1934 to 1958. Edrich's greatest achievement came in 1947 when he scored 3,539 runs and, with Dennis COMPTON, set an English Test record of 370 for the third wicket. The following year he and Compton had an unbroken stand of 424 against Somerset, a Middlesex and Lord's record.

Edsall, John Tileston (1902–). American biochemist. Edsall was educated at Harvard and at Cambridge University, England. He joined the Harvard faculty in 1928 and from 1951 to 1973 served there as professor of biochemistry. Edsall's work focuses mainly on protein chemistry. He spent much time establishing basic data on the constitution and properties of numerous proteins—information that has since been reproduced in innumerable textbooks. With Edwin Cohn he was the author of the authoritative work *Proteins, Amino Acids and Peptides* (1943). In later years Edsall turned his attention to the history of biochemistry; his books in this field included *Blood and Hemoglobin* (1952).

Edsel. Brand name of an automobile introduced by the Ford Motor Company in 1958. The Edsel has become a legend of the failure of a giant company in developing, designing, and marketing a product so badly matched to consumer preferences that it faced almost total public rejection. The Edsel (named for Henry FORD's son) was developed with the aid of consumer preference studies of the time and was designed with heavily exaggerated styling elements of the kind that had become popular in the early 1950s. By the time the Edsel appeared, however, public taste had changed, turning away from such styling toward a slightly more conservative look. The Edsel therefore seemed a caricature of over-design, the subject of derision rather than admiration. The model was discontinued after a very brief production run. Ironically, surviving examples have become collectors' items.

Edward VII (1841–1910). King of Great Britain and Ireland (reigned 1901–10). The eldest surviving son of Queen Victoria and Prince Albert, he did not accede to the throne until he was 59. As Prince of Wales, he traveled widely, was the center of a fashionable social circle and was a noted patron of the arts. He married ALEXANDRA of Denmark in 1863 and the couple had six children. After the death of Albert in 1861, Edward represented the Crown at most official functions. However, he was widely regarded as a playboy, and his libertine ways were roundly disapproved of by his mother, who gave him virtually no political responsibility. He became king after Victoria's death in 1901, and his urbane and genial demeanor made him a popular, if little-experienced, monarch. Edward advanced British foreign policy by his many trips abroad, and he supported the ANGLO-FRENCH ENTENTE of 1904. At home he favored the policies of the LIBERAL PARTY and was a reluctant participant in ASQUITH's attempt to limit the power of the House of Lords. He died in 1910 and was succeeded by his son GEORGE V. In Britain, the first decade of the 20th century is generally known as the **Edwardian** period.

Edward VII (1902).

Edward VIII, Duke of Windsor (1894–1972). King of the United Kingdom of Great Britain and Ireland (1936) who gave up the British throne to, as he said, "marry the woman I love." The eldest son of GEORGE V and Queen Mary, he was proclaimed Prince of Wales in 1911. He served in the Royal Navy in WORLD WAR I. During the 1920s and early 1930s the handsome prince lived the life of a charming playboy and sophisticated trendsetter. He was also a goodwill ambassador for Britain around the world. Much admired by the British people, during the GREAT DEPRESSION he visited working-class areas throughout Britain and expressed genuine concern for the unemployed. Groomed for kingship, he ascended to the throne upon the death of George V (January 20, 1936) but was never formally crowned. By this time, he was involved with Mrs. **Wallis Warfield Simpson,** an American who had been divorced from her first husband and was still married to her second. When Mrs. Simpson obtained her second divorce, the king's decision to marry her provoked the ABDICATION CRISIS (November 1936). Many people felt that as an American and a divorcee, she would be an unsuitable wife for the king. In a moving radio address to the nation (December 11, 1936), Edward announced and explained his decision to abdicate. He was succeeded by his younger brother, GEORGE VI. Taking the title Duke of Windsor, Edward married Mrs. Simpson in France the following year. He was governor (1940–45) of the Bahamas during World War II. The couple then settled in France and rarely visited England.

For further reading:

Ziegler, Philip, *King Edward VIII: The Official Biography*. London: Collins, 1990.

Edwards, Douglas (1917–1990). U.S. broadcaster. He began his broadcast career in radio, and in 1947 became the first major radio announcer to switch to television. The next year, he became the first American news anchorman, as CBS made him the host of its first nightly news program, "Douglas Edwards with the News." He was one of the first television news anchors to do on-the-scene reporting, covering such events as the 1956 sinking of the ANDREA DORIA. He was replaced by Walter CRONKITE in 1962 but continued to work for the network until his retirement in 1988.

Edwards, Hilton (1903–1982). British-born actor and director. Known for his Shakespearean interpretations, he founded the GATE THEATRE in Dublin, Ireland with Micheal MACLIAMMOIR in 1928.

Egk, Werner (1901–1990). German composer. Born in Bavaria, he became a respected conductor, often directing the Berlin State Opera. Egk was also a teacher of music and became director of the Berlin Hochschule in 1950. Strongly influenced by Igor STRAVINSKY in his use of harmony, instrumentation, rhythms and musical irony, he is principally known for his operas, particularly his first, *Die Zaubergeige* (1935), and his second, *Peer Gynt* (1938). Egk's output also included orchestral and chamber works and ballets.

Egypt. Nation on the Mediterranean coast of northeastern Africa, surrounding the fertile valley of the Nile River; officially, the **Arab Republic of Egypt**. Occupied by the British in 1882, it became a British protectorate in 1914 when the OTTOMAN EMPIRE allied itself with England's enemy, GERMANY, in WORLD WAR I. Made an independent kingdom in 1922, it was the site of fierce tank battles between British and German forces in its western deserts during WORLD WAR II. Egypt became a republic in 1953, after Gamal Abdel NASSER led a military coup against King FAROUK; Nasser became president in 1954. Hostility toward the new state of ISRAEL has been a key factor in modern Egypt's history, as it assumed the mantle of major champion of nonaligned Arab solidarity. Although it suffered a military defeat in the ARAB–ISRAELI WAR OF 1956, Egypt won wide respect in the Arab world (see SUEZ CRISIS).

In 1958 SYRIA, YEMEN and Egypt briefly united to create the UNITED ARAB REPUBLIC (UAR)—a venture that ended in 1961. During the SIX-DAY WAR of 1967 Israel solidly defeated Egypt as it outpaced Egyptian, Syrian and Jordanian forces and captured the SINAI PENINSULA and GAZA STRIP; the SUEZ CANAL was closed. Nasser died in 1970 and was succeeded by Anwar al-SADAT. In 1973, war again broke out with Israel, and a section of the Sinai was recaptured by Egypt. Israel withdrew following negotiations, and in 1975 the canal was reopened. U.S. President Jimmy CARTER encouraged Sadat to form cordial relations with Israel, thus distancing Egypt from the rest of the Arab world. Sadat was murdered by a fundamentalist Arab faction in 1981, and Hosni MUBARAK became president. Egypt censured IRAQ'S assault on KUWAIT in 1990 and actively participated in the United Nations' allied coalition against Iraq in the ensuing PERSIAN GULF WAR.

EGYPT

Ehrenburg, Ilya Grigorovich (1891–1967). Writer, of Jewish origin, who spent much of his life in Paris. A Symbolist poet at the start of his career, Ehrenburg was a skillful master of all the genres. His works include *A Street in Moscow* (1932), *Out of Chaos* (1934) and *European Crossroad* (1934). A one-time member of the Supreme Soviet, he was a pioneer of the DESTALINIZATION of literature, and wrote the influential novel *The Thaw* (1954–56). While permitted to strive for the rehabilitation of victims of the Terror, such as Osip MANDELSTAM, at the same time he had to make considerable concessions to the authorities.

Ehricke, Krafft A. (1917–1984). German rocket scientist. Ehricke studied rocket engineering at the Technical University of Berlin, but his studies were interrupted by WORLD WAR II, and he was drafted to work on the V-2 rocket project at PEENEMUNDE. After the war he was brought to the U.S. along with Werner von BRAUN and other German rocket scientists. He subsequently worked on the Redstone, Atlas and Centaur rockets. While heading a committee of the American Rocket Society, Ehricke urged government officials to establish a civilian space agency, which

EGYPT

1900	Nominally autonomous within the Ottoman empire, Egypt is controlled by the British consul-general.
1902	First dam at Aswan to control flooding of the Nile; spread of irrigation to promote cotton as a cash crop.
1914	Declared a British protectorate.
1918	Nationalist movement under Saad Zaghlul.
1922	Britain grants independence but retains military control and possession of Suez Canal; discovery of Tutankhamen's tomb sparks new fashion styles in the West.
1942	British stop Rommel's drive toward the Suez Canal at El Alamein.
1948	Rioting in Cairo after Egypt's defeat in attack on new state of Israel; assassination of pro-Western leaders.
1952	Free Officers' movement forces abdication of King Farouk; proclaims republic.
1954	Col. Gamal Nasser takes power; reorganizes nation, pursues pan-Arab socialism and closer ties with U.S.S.R.
1956	Nasser nationalizes Suez Canal; prevents British and French forces from reclaiming it before UN imposes ceasefire.
1958	Egypt joins Syria to form United Arab Republic.
1961	Syria withdraws from UAR.
1966	Ancient monuments at Abu-Simbel are moved to protect them from waters of immense new flood control dam at Aswan.
1967	Egypt attacks Israel; Egyptian forces crushed in Six-Day War; Egypt loses Gaza Strip.
1970	Death of Nasser; Anwar Sadat begins rapprochement with the West.
1976	Free multiparty elections.
1978	Camp David Accord signed with Israel; Sadat wins Nobel Prize for peace.
1979	Peace treaty with Israel; other Arab states break off relations with Egypt.
1981	Sadat killed by Islamic fundamentalists; succeeded by Hosni Mubarak.
1984	Jordan becomes first Arab state to reestablish ties.
1989	Egypt reaccepted into Arab League at Casablanca summit.
1991	Egypt contributes troops to anti-Iraq coalition in Persian Gulf War.

evolved into NASA. He was also an adviser on the development of the APOLLO spacecraft and the SPACE SHUTTLE.

Ehrlich, Paul (1854–1915). German physician, bacteriologist and chemist. Ehrlich studied medicine at the universities of Breslau, Strasbourg and Freiburg, gaining a physician's degree at Breslau in 1878. For the next nine years he worked at the Charite Hospital, Berlin on many diseases, including typhoid fever, tuberculosis and pernicious anemia. As a result of his laboratory work he contracted tuberculosis and was not restored to health until 1890, when he set up his own small research laboratory at Steglitz on the outskirts of Berlin. When Robert Koch announced the discovery of tuberculin (1890) and suggested its use in preventing and curing tuberculosis, he asked Ehrlich to work on it with him at the Moabit Hospital in Berlin. Ehrlich accepted and for six years studied TB and cholera. In 1896 he accepted the post of director of the new Institute for Serum Research and Serum Investigation at Steglitz and in 1899 moved to the Institute of Experimental

Paul Ehrlich.

Adolf Eichmann grimaces during his war crimes trial in Israel.

Therapy in Frankfurt. Here he investigated African sleeping sickness and syphilis. In 1908 he was awarded the NOBEL PRIZE for physiology or medicine for his work on immunity and serum therapy. Two years later he announced his most famous discovery, **Salvarsan,** a synthetic chemical that was effective against syphilis. Until the end of his life he worked on the problems associated with the use of this compound of arsenic in treating patients. Ehrlich is considered to be the founder of modern chemotherapy because he developed systematic scientific techniques to search for new synthetic chemicals that could specifically attack disease-causing microorganisms.

Eichmann, Adolf (1906–1962). Nazi SS official who oversaw the deaths of millions of JEWS and others during WORLD WAR II. Eichmann rose with GERMANY's Nazi Party to be head of the GESTAPO's Jewish section. After the **Wannsee Conference** (Jan. 1942), he was responsible for the deportation and incarceration of Jews in CONCENTRATION CAMPS throughout Europe. Millions of Jews were ultimately killed in the camps. When the war ended, Eichmann was able to escape to Argentina with the unwitting help of the VATICAN. Although furiously pursued, he eluded detection because he had destroyed all photos of himself. However, Israeli agents traced him to Argentina after his wife rejoined him in Buenos Aires. In 1961, Israeli agents apprehended him and secretly transported him to Israel, where he was tried for crimes against the Jews. He was convicted and hanged.

Eigen, Manfred (1927–). German physical chemist. Eigen was educated at the University of Gottingen, where he obtained his Ph.D. in 1951. He joined the staff of the Max Planck Institute for Physical Chemistry at Gottingen in 1953 and became its director in 1964. Eigen introduced (1954) the so-called relaxation techniques for the study of extremely fast chemical reactions (those taking less than a millisecond). Eigen's general technique was to examine a solution in equilibrium for a given temperature and pressure. If a short disturbance was applied to the solution the equilibrium would be very briefly destroyed and a new equilibrium quickly reached. Eigen studied exactly what happened in this very short time by means of absorption spectroscopy. He applied disturbances to the equilibrium by a variety of methods, such as pulses of electric current, sudden changes in temperature or pressure, or changes in electric field. For this work Eigen shared the 1967 NOBEL PRIZE for chemistry with George Porter and Ronald NORRISH. Eigen later applied his relaxation techniques to complex biochemical reactions. He also became interested in the origin of nucleic acids and proteins.

Eight, the. A popular reference to a group of eight young American painters working and exhibiting in the cause of realism during the first decade of the 20th century. More derisively, they were also branded the Black Gang, the Apostles of Ugliness and the Ash-Can School. In contrast to the prevailing taste of establishments such as the National Academy of Design in New York, these artists—Robert HENRI, Everett SHINN, George Luks, John SLOAN, Arthur B. Davies, William GLACKENS, Ernest Lawson, and Maurice PRENDERGAST—observed and painted the relatively squalid conditions of contemporary American urban sprawl. Since most of them were trained as newspaper illustrators—they had been employed by newspapers like the *Philadelphia Press* and the *New York World* to provide on-the-spot sketches of breaking news stories—they had developed a quick, incisive, unblinking attitude toward the world around them. They knew the police beat, the slums, the rag-pickers. When some of them presumed to present their work for gallery viewing at the National Arts Club in 1904, they were roundly denounced. Three years later several of them were rejected for exhibition at the National Academy. Stung, they decided—under the unofficial leadership of Robert Henri—to exhibit their work collectively in the winter of 1908. The Macbeth Gallery show subsequently became not only the most famous exhibition of the Eight but also the first important event in modern American painting. The titles of some of the works on display tell the story: "Street Scene," "The Shoppers," and "Sixth Avenue and Thirtieth Street." Two years later some of the artists, headed by Sloan and Henri, exhibited in another important modern show: The Independent Artists Exhibition. The way had been prepared for the famous ARMORY SHOW of 1913, when work by the Eight rubbed easels, as it were, with modern works by Cezanne, PICASSO, MATISSE and other famous artists. Apart from their common vision of contemporary American life, there were no philosophical or political bonds among the Eight. They soon disbanded, and some even grew suspicious of the modernist trends they had helped to encourage.

Eijkman, Christiaan (1858–1930). Dutch physician. Eijkman earned a medical degree from the University of Amsterdam in 1883. He served as an army medical officer in the Dutch East Indies from 1883 to 1885, when he was forced to return to Holland to recuperate from a severe attack of malaria. In 1886 he returned to the East Indies as a member of an official government committee to investigate beriberi. After the completion of the committee's work, Eijkman remained in Batavia (now Djakarta) as director of a newly established bacteriological laboratory. In 1896 he took up the post of professor of public health at the University of Utrecht.

Eijkman was responsible for the first real understanding of the nature of and possible cure for beriberi. For this work he shared the 1929 NOBEL PRIZE in physiology or medicine with Frederick Gowland Hopkins. He failed to conclude, however, that beriberi is a deficiency disease. Although Eijkman had clearly demonstrated how to cure and prevent beriberi, it was left to Hopkins to identify its cause as a vitamin deficiency. It was not until the early 1930s that Robert Williams identified the vitamin as B1 (thiamine).

Einstein, Albert (1879–1955). German-born physicist and humanist. Einstein is widely considered one of the greatest and most original thinkers of the 20th century. Although not easily understood by the layman, Einstein's theories of time, space, matter and the nature of the universe radically changed our view of the world. The son of nonreligious German Jewish parents, Einstein taught himself mathematics and physics at an early age. He was far from being an outstanding student, but his intellectual independence and creativity soon brought him into conflict with the strict regimentation of the German Catholic schools to which his parents sent him. While attending the Zurich Federal Institute of Technology from 1896 to 1900, he applied for and received Swiss citizenship. Upon graduation from the Institute, Einstein took a job at the Swiss Patent Office, pursuing scientific studies in his spare time. In 1905 he published four important papers. One of these, *Uber einen die Erzeugung und Verwandlung des Lichtes betreffenden heuristichen Gesichtspunkt* (*On a Heuristic Point of View about the Creation and Conversion of Light*), introduced quantum theory into physics to explain the nature of electromagnetic radiation.

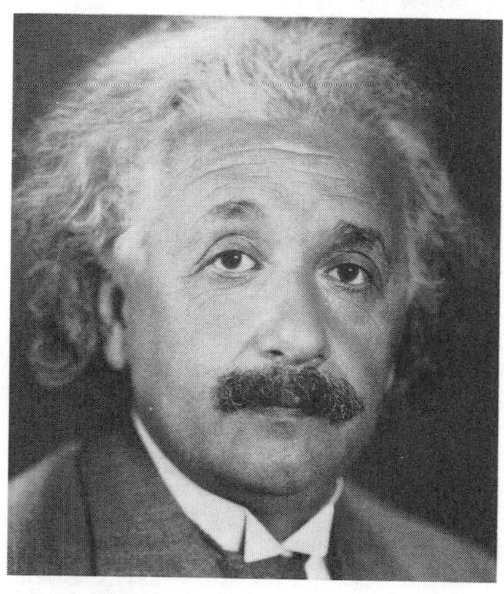

Albert Einstein.

The most famous of the four papers of 1905—*Zur Electrodynamik bewegter Korper* (*On the Electrodynamics of Moving Bodies*)—introduced his revolutionary **special theory of relativity,** showing that space and time, once thought to be absolutes, are actually relative to the observer; the only constant is the speed of light. Einstein's special theory of relativity also states that matter behaves differently as it approaches the speed of light, and that classical Newtonian physics does not apply at these speeds.

In a third paper (only two pages long), *Ist der Tragheit eins Korpers von seinem Energieinhalt abhangig* (*Does the Inertia of a Body Depend on its Energy Content?*), Einstein concluded that matter is really concentrated energy, a most important consequence of relativity. This discovery led directly to the development of the ATOMIC BOMB nearly four decades later.

In 1907, Einstein further developed his ideas about gravity and inertia and predicted that light moving through a gravitational field would be curved. This theory, known as the **general theory of relativity,** was later confirmed when the astronomer Arthur EDDINGTON observed during an eclipse that starlight was indeed curved as it passed near the sun.

As his work gained recognition in scientific circles, Einstein received his doctorate from the University of Zurich in 1909 and then taught in Zurich, Prague and Leyden. He became director of the Kaiser Wilhelm Institute of Sciences in Berlin in 1913. In 1916 he further refined his general theory of relativity in the paper *Die Grundlagen der allgemeinen der Relativitatstheorie* (*The Foundation of the General Theory of Relativity*). This work proposed that space itself is curved. In 1921 Einstein received the NOBEL PRIZE for his work in atomic physics.

The suffering of European Jews after World War I led Einstein to become an active Zionist, traveling extensively during the 1920s to raise money for Jewish settlement in Palestine. (Years later, following the death of Chaim WEIZMANN in 1952, Einstein was asked to become president of Israel, but he declined.) In 1933 he fled Nazi Germany and accepted a professorship at Princeton's Institute for Advanced Study. Appalled by Nazi tyranny and the rearming of Germany, Einstein reversed his lifelong pacifist views in 1933, warning European countries to arm against HITLER's threat.

In 1939 scientists proved the possibility of releasing the atom's energy through a nuclear chain reaction. Acting on the belief that the Germans were close to developing an atomic bomb, Einstein addressed a letter to President Franklin D. ROOSEVELT, describing the destructive potential of the new weapon and urging an accelerated research program so that the U.S. would be the first nation with the bomb. This letter spurred Roosevelt's decision to institute an ultimately successful crash program for the manufacture of the weapon.

With the creation of the first bomb in 1945, Einstein, along with many of the scientists working on the project, began to fear that the U.S. would use the bomb offensively against Japan, thus initiating an atomic arms race. Hoping to preclude the bomb's use, Einstein signed a letter to Roosevelt, warning that any momentary military advantage the bomb might give the U.S. would be offset by grave political and strategic disadvantages. FDR died before receiving the letter. The TRUMAN administration disregarded the warning and dropped atomic bombs on HIROSHIMA and NAGASAKI.

After the war Einstein became a passionate spokesman for the "control" school of thought—those scientists who felt that the only hope for peace was to place all control of nuclear power in a supranational government. In 1945 he organized the Emergency Committee of Atomic Scientists to educate the public about the possibilities and dangers of atomic power. In numerous speeches, broadcasts and letters, he warned against the physical danger and cultural repression that would result from an arms race. He deplored the U.S.' postwar policy of nuclear rearmament, warning, "We must realize that we cannot simultaneously plan for war and peace." In 1948 he joined in a denunciation of universal military training, and in 1950 signed a protest against the penetration of the civilian educational system by the military establishment. He opposed the production of the HYDROGEN BOMB, stating in 1950 that an arms race was the worst method of preventing conflict, and advocated the Gandhian tactic of "nonparticipation in what you believe is evil." He also supported physicist J. Robert OPPENHEIMER against charges that he was a security risk.

In 1953 Einstein completed his last great piece of scientific work, the **unified field theory,** which related his work in quantum mechanics to the theory of relativity. In the year of his death, 1955, he and Bertrand RUSSELL made a world appeal against the dangers of thermonuclear war. This statement, signed by six other Nobel Prize winners, led to the Pugwash Conference, a movement to utilize the internationalism of science as a force for peace.

Although his theories challenged traditional views of the universe, Einstein perceived a rational rather than random force behind creation. "God does not play dice with the universe," he asserted. "He may be subtle, but he is not malicious."

For further reading:

Smith, Kathie B., *Albert Einstein*. New York: Julian Messner, 1989.

Eire. See IRELAND.

Eisenhower, Dwight D(avid) (1890–1969). American general and 34th president of the UNITED STATES (1953–61). Born in Denison, Texas, Eisenhower grew up in Abilene, Kansas, where his family had moved in 1892. He graduated from West Point in 1915, then commanded an Army Tank Corps training camp during World War I, becoming a leading exponent of mobile armored vehicles. He served in the Panama Canal Zone (1922–24), later attending the Command and General Staff School. After a tour on the Battle Monuments Commission, he attended the Army War College and served in the office of the assistant secretary of war (1929–33) and in the Philippines with General Douglas MACARTHUR (1935–40). After the outbreak of WORLD WAR II in Europe, he served in a number of posts before becoming chief of staff of the Third Army in 1941 and leading it successfully in large-scale war games. This performance led directly to his posting as chief of operations under General George C. MARSHALL in Washington, D.C.

Winning Marshall's confidence and friendship, Eisenhower was named U.S. commander in Europe in 1942. He quickly amassed a string of successes, commanding the invasion of North Africa (November 1942), conquering Sicily (July–August 1943) and invading Italy (September 1943). In December 1943, Eisenhower was named supreme commander of the Allied Expeditionary Force. A warm and plainspoken man, he was particularly adept at winning cooperation among the Allies and at achieving a successful integration of the various branches of the armed forces into a fighting machine that could win the struggle for Europe. Under Eisenhower, the NORMANDY INVASION of June 6, 1944, was succesfully planned and mounted, and the Allies pushed into France, driving out German forces. His slow advance allowed the Allied setback at the battle of the Ardennes, but Eisenhower pushed forward, reaching the Elbe in April 1945. Germany's surrender on May 8, 1945 left Eisenhower, a five-star general since December 1944, one of the great heroes of the war.

Afterwards, he served as Army chief of staff, wrote his war memoirs (*Crusade in Europe*, 1948) and was president of Columbia University. In 1951 he returned to Europe as military commander of NATO, further enhancing his international standing. Eisenhower resigned from the Army in 1951 to seek the Republican presidential nomination in 1952; he won the nomination by a close margin over Senator Robert TAFT. That year much of the country adopted the slogan "I Like Ike," and he won a landslide victory over Governor Adlai STEVENSON; he was reelected by an even larger margin four years later.

Early in his first term, Eisenhower fulfilled a campaign promise by securing an armistice ending the KOREAN WAR, in July 1953. Along with his secretary of state, John Foster DULLES, he continued the TRUMAN administration policy of containing COMMUNISM, while also working to ease some COLD WAR tensions. On the homefront, he maintained a business-oriented middle-of-the-road policy, initiating little legislation but overseeing an improved highway and seaway system and taking firm action on CIVIL RIGHTS in the 1957 school desegregation of LITTLE ROCK, Arkansas, and in legislation (1957, 1960).

Eisenhower at Allied headquarters in Europe shortly after his promotion to the newly-created rank of General of the Army (February 1, 1945).

Shortly before leaving office, Eisenhower warned the nation about the growing power of what he termed "the military–industrial complex." He supported the unsuccessful presidential candidacy of his vice president, Richard M. NIXON, in the 1960 election that was won by Democrat John F. KENNEDY. After retiring to his Gettysburg, Pennsylvania, farm in 1961, Eisenhower resumed writing. Among his books were *Mandate for Change* (1963) and *Waging Peace* (1965).

For further reading:

Ambrose, Stephen E., *Eisenhower: Soldier and President*. New York: Simon & Schuster, 1990.

Eisenhower, Milton S(tover) (1899–1985). U.S. educator and public servant, brother of Dwight D. EISENHOWER. Milton Eisenhower was an adviser to every president from Franklin D. ROOSEVELT to Richard M. NIXON. He became perhaps the most important presidential adviser in the nation's history during the administration of his brother. He began his government career in 1926 with the Department of Agriculture. During WORLD WAR II he directed the resettlement of refugees in North Africa after the 1942 Allied invasion. He left government service in 1943 to become president of Kansas State College. In 1950 he was named president of Pennsylvania State University, a post he held for six years. From 1956 to 1967 and again from 1971 to 1972, he was president of Johns Hopkins University. During those years, he held a number of major part-time government posts and served on 12 major government commissions.

Eisenhower Doctrine. Policy promulgated by President Dwight D. EISENHOWER in 1957 during his second term in office. It provided for the use of American military force and economic aid in the protection of Middle Eastern states from internal or external communist aggression. The doctrine was applied twice: In April 1957 the U.S. aided King HUSSEIN of JORDAN in suppressing left-wing threats; and in July 1958 10,000 American Marines were sent to LEBANON to ensure stability after a socialist coup in IRAQ. The doctrine proved unpopular in the Middle East and lapsed after the death of Secretary of State John Foster DULLES in 1959.

Eisenstaedt, Alfred (1898–). American photographer, considered the father of PHOTOJOURNALISM. He introduced the techniques of the photo-essay and news reporting using candid-camera shots. His career began in his native Germany, where he produced candid documentaries (1929–35). Immigrating to the U.S. in 1935, he gained fame for his picture story on the Italian invasion of ETHIOPIA. In 1936 he became one of the original staff photographers for LIFE magazine. He is known for his expressive candid portraits of such people as Albert EINSTEIN (1947) and Marilyn MONROE (1953) and for his evocative photo-essays, such as those from Japan (1945–46). Among his many books is *Witness to Our Time* (1966).

Eisenstein, Sergei Mikhailovich (1898–1948). Russian filmmaker and theoretician. With colleagues Lev KULESHOV, Vsevelod PUDOVKIN, and Dziga VERTOV, Eisenstein stood at the center of the great decade of Soviet filmmaking in the 1920s. He was born in Riga, Latvia and at an early age displayed interests and talents in subjects as diverse as architecture, Japanese culture and theater. As an assistant to the great stage entrepreneur and innovator Vsevelod MEYERHOLD in the early 1920s, he was vitally influenced by the tenets of **Constructivism,** which held that theater and acting were essentially machinelike assemblies of stylized elements in gesture, design, language and light. Eisenstein carried such ideas forward into his great films of the rest of the decade. *Stachka* (*Strike,* 1924), *Bronenosets Potemkin* (*The Battleship Potemkin,* 1925), *Oktiabr* (*October,* 1927) and *Generalnaya Linya* (*The General Line,* 1929) helped vault the Soviet cinema into international prominence. Although nominally about such standard Soviet subjects as revolution and collective agriculture, they were, more importantly, demonstrations of Eisenstein's theories of montage of discrete attractions (his term for the editing together of pieces of film). As opposed to Pudovkin's theory that editing was essentially a linkage process, Eisenstein insisted that it was a dialectic, a collision and contrast of shots. Metaphors could be created with the collision of elements *within* the shot ("potential montage"), in the *juxtaposition* of shots ("metric" and "tonal" montage) and in the *combinations* of image and synchronized sound ("vertical" montage). This "series of explosions," as he cryptically called them, would "drive forward the total film" like an internal combustion engine. Such theories ran him afoul of the STALIN regime in the 1930s and 1940s. Eisenstein completed only two more projects before his death from a heart attack in 1948—*Alexander Nevsky* (1938) and the two parts of *Ivan Groznyi* (*Ivan the Terrible,* 1944). His theoretical writings have been collected into two volumes: *The Film Sense* (1942) and *The Film Form* (1948).

For further reading:

Leyda, Jay, and Zina Voynow, *Eisenstein at Work.* New York: Pantheon, 1982.

Leyda, Jay, *Kino: A History of the Russian and Soviet Film.* London: George Allen and Unwin, 1960.

Ekman, Vagn Walfrid (1874–1954). Swedish oceanographer. Ekman was educated at the University of Uppsala, graduating in 1902. He worked at the International Laboratory for Oceanographic Research in Oslo (1902–08) before he moved to Lund, Sweden as a lecturer in mathematical physics, being made a professor in 1910. Ekman's fundamental paper, *On the Influence of the Earth's Rotation on Ocean Currents* (1905), originated from an observation made by the explorer Fridtjof NANSEN that in the Arctic, drift ice did not follow wind direction but deviated to the right. Ekman showed that the motion, now known as the *Ekman spiral,* is produced as a complex interaction between the force of the wind on the water surface, the deflecting force due to the Earth's rotation (Coriolis force) and the frictional forces within the water layers. Ekman also studied the phenomenon of dead water—a thin layer of fresh water from melting ice spreading over the sea, which could halt slow-moving ships. This, he established, resulted from the waves formed between water layers of different densities. The **Ekman current meter,** which he invented, is still in use.

El Alamein. Town on the Mediterranean Sea, 62 miles west–southwest of Alexandria, Egypt. During WORLD WAR II it was the most advanced point reached by the Axis forces under Gen. Erwin ROMMEL in their attack against Egypt. The Axis advance stalled there on June 30, 1942. Field Marshal MONTGOMERY's Eighth Army counterattacked on October 23; in a battle that lasted until November 3, the Allies won one of their most decisive victories of the war and went on to a total defeat of Axis forces in Africa.

ELAS [*Ellenikos Laikos Apeleutherotikos Stratos,* Hellenic People's Army of Liberation]. Organization founded by the communist resistance in GREECE during WORLD WAR II. ELAS wished to achieve a communist government in postwar Greece along the lines of TITO's PARTISANS. Opposing them, Britain and the U.S. had supported promonarchist groups since 1943, and Britain sent troops to Greece in 1944 to prevent civil war, which eventually broke out following the return of the king in 1946. The **Democratic Army,** successor to ELAS, was defeated in 1949 by the royalists, backed by the U.S. and Britain. (See also GREEK CIVIL WAR.)

Elat. Israeli port city at the head of the Gulf of Aqaba, about 120 miles south of Beersheba. Following its occupation of the area at the conclusion of the ARAB–ISRAELI WAR OF 1948–49, ISRAEL established this modern city to secure its access to the Red Sea, the Far East and Africa. The port was temporarily put out of commission by Egyptian blockades of the Gulf of Aqaba in the 1956 and 1967 Arab–Israeli wars but was expanded after hostilities ceased. The population rose from 529 in 1959 to over 14,000 by the 1970s.

Elath, Eliahu [born Eliahu Epstein] (1903–1990). Ukrainian-born journalist and diplomat. In 1934, he was named head of the political department of the Jewish Agency for PALESTINE, a precursor of the Israeli government. A force in the founding of ISRAEL, he was named that country's ambassador to the United States in 1948, and later its ambassador to Great Britain. He played a major role in negotiations surrounding the 1956 invasion of SUEZ by Britain, France and Israel.

Elbe River. River that rises in northwestern Czechoslovakia and courses through Germany past DRESDEN, then northwest through Hamburg and into the North Sea at Cuxhaven. A prominent river of central Europe, it is about 725 miles long and is linked by canal with BERLIN, with the RUHR area, with the Oder and RHINE rivers and with the Baltic Sea. Toward the end of WORLD WAR II, on April 25, 1945, U.S. and Soviet army units met at Torgau on the Elbe. From 1949 to 1990, a section of the river formed part of the border between East and West Germany.

El Boom. Term applied to a creative flowering of Latin American fiction from the mid-1950s through the 1960s. El Boom, or the Boom, is a highly general label that expresses the breadth and magnitude of the fictional talent that seemed to emerge in unison from numerous Latin American countries in the mid-1950s. There were no distinct themes that unified the writers linked under the El Boom rubric, but what they did have in common was a willingness to explore both political and personal subject matter with a maximum of linguistic and narrative experimentation. The major figures in the El Boom movement included Julio CORTAZAR, Carlos FUENTES, Mario VARGAS LLOSA and Gabriel GARCIA MARQUEZ.

Eldjarn, Kristjan (1916–1982). President of ICELAND (1968–80). An archaeologist by profession, Eldjarn served as curator of the National Museum of Iceland (1947–68) before his election to the country's presidency.

Eldridge, (David) Roy (1911–1989). U.S. jazz trumpeter. A flamboyant and innovative performer, Eldridge was often regarded as the link between Louis ARMSTRONG's pioneering trumpet solos of the 1920s and the instrumental virtuosity of Dizzy GILLESPIE'S BEBOP style of the 1950s.

Although he performed with his own band in the 1930s, Eldridge did not gain national attention until he performed with white bandleader Gene KRUPA in 1941. He also played with Artie SHAW, Benny GOODMAN, and the Jazz at the Philharmonic series. Heart problems forced him to give up trumpet playing in 1980.

electron microscope. The electron microscope is one of the scientific miracles of the 20th century and represents a huge advance over the conventional light microscope. Using beams of electrons to magnify objects that are invisible to the naked eye, the electron microscope can magnify particles up to one million times. Especially valuable in medical research, it allows researchers to study bacteria and viruses; the most powerful electron microscopes can make individual atoms visible.

Elgar, Sir Edward (1857–1934). The first British composer of international stature since Henry Purcell, Elgar is generally regarded as the foremost British composer of the 20th century. He was born into a middle-class Catholic family in Worcestershire, where his father owned a music shop. Largely self-educated, Elgar held various minor posts (including that of bandmaster in the local insane asylum, 1879–84) before becoming organist at St. George's Church, Worcester (1895). During this time he composed steadily but received little recognition until his *Enigma Variations* (1899) and the oratorio *The Dream of Gerontius* (1900) established him as Britain's leading composer. He went on to compose two large-scale symphonies (1908, 1911), the introspective Violin Concerto (1910) and Cello Concerto (1919), several tone poems and the five popular *Pomp and Circumstance* marches, among other works. Although influenced by Brahms and by Richard STRAUSS, his compositions were unmistakably English in character. Distraught over the death of his wife, Alice, the horrors of WORLD WAR I, and the advent of MODERNISM, Elgar composed little during his later years but continued to enjoy both popular and official acclaim as England's greatest living composer.

Sir Edward Elgar.

Eliade, Mircea (1907–1986). Romanian-born historian of religion and fiction writer. Eliade was one of the preeminent interpreters of world religion in this century. A prolific writer, he drew upon the myths and beliefs of virtually all cultures. In his analyses, Eliade synthesized these myths into enduring themes of human spirituality, such as the Golden Age at the beginning of time, the cyclical functioning of nature and the hierarchical structure of being from divine emanation to earthly matter. As a young man, Eliade spent three years in study at the University of Calcutta in preparation for his first book, *Yoga: Essay on the Origins of Indian Mysticism* (1936). In the 1930s and 1940s, he published several works of fiction with a supernatural tone. He joined the faculty of the University of Chicago in 1956 and remained there until his death. His other major works include *Patterns of Comparative Religion* (1949), *Myths, Dreams, and Mysteries* (1957), *Shamanism* (1968) and the three-volume *A History of Religious Ideas* (1976, 1978, 1983).

Elion, Gertrude B(elle) (1918–). American biochemist. Born in New York City, she attended Hunter College and Brooklyn Polytechnic Institute. At first a high-school teacher, she became a researcher during World War II. She joined the laboratory staff of Burroughs Wellcome, Tuckahoe, N.Y., in 1944, beginning her long association with George H. HITCHINGS. Together the two worked on the comparative study of normal and cancer cells, bacteria and viruses. Working with the staff at New York's Sloan Kettering Institute, they developed the first effective chemotherapy to fight leukemia. She and Hitchings investigated the method by which nucleic acids are formed and analyzed their chemical composition, with a focus on purine and pyrimidine. Most importantly, they developed chemotherapies to inhibit nucleic acid formation in diseased cells without damaging normal cells. This discovery led to various advances in drug research, notably the development of AZT, which is used to fight AIDS. In 1988 she, Hitchings and Sir James Black were awarded the NOBEL PRIZE for physiology or medicine.

Eliot, T(homas) S(tearns) (1888–1965). Anglo-American poet, critic and playwright. Born in St. Louis, Missouri, he studied literature and philosophy at Harvard, the Sorbonne and Oxford. In 1914 he settled in London, where he worked briefly as a teacher and then as an officer at Lloyd's Bank; during this time he also wrote and published literary criticism. His first poetry collection, *Prufrock and Other Observations* (1917), attracted some attention, but it was THE WASTE LAND (1922) that established his reputation as a leading modernist poet (see MODERNISM; Ezra POUND). In 1925 he joined the publishing firm of Faber & Gwyer (later FABER & FABER) as an editor, later becoming a director. From 1922 to 1939 he also edited *The Criterion*, an influential literary journal. In 1927 he became a British subject and a member of the Church of England;

T.S. Eliot, English poet and playwright (Jan. 19, 1956).

soon after, he declared himself "an Anglo-Catholic in religion, a classicist in literature, and a royalist in politics." These views are evident in *Ash Wednesday* (1930) and in FOUR QUARTETS (1943), his last and perhaps his greatest poetic work. In his later years, he attempted to revitalize verse drama in such works as *Murder in the Cathedral* (1935), *The Family Reunion* (1939) and *The Cocktail Party* (1949). In 1948 he received the NOBEL PRIZE for literature and the British Order of Merit. Eliot is widely regarded (along with W.B. YEATS) as one of the most significant poets in the English language in the 20th century. His critical theories have also had an enormous influence on other writers.

For further reading:

Ackroyd, Peter, *T.S. Eliot*. London: H. Hamilton, 1984.

Eliot, T.S., *The Letters of T.S. Eliot: Vol. 1, 1890–1922*, ed. by Valerie Eliot. San Diego: Harcourt, Brace, Jovanovich, 1988.

Gordon, Lydall, *Eliot's Early Years*. New York: Oxford University Press, 1977.

Elizabeth II (1926–). Queen of the UNITED KINGDOM of Great Britain and Northern Ireland (1952–). Born in London, Elizabeth became the heir presumptive upon the accession to the throne of her father, GEORGE VI, in 1936 after the abdication of his brother, EDWARD VIII. She married Philip Mountbatten, Duke of Edinburgh, in 1947. The two have four children—Prince CHARLES, Princess Anne, Prince Andrew and Prince Edward. Elizabeth inherited the throne on the death of George VI (February 6, 1952), and her coronation took place in Westminster Abbey on June 2, 1953. An active constitutional monarch, Elizabeth celebrated her Silver Jubilee, the 25th anniversary of her accession to the throne, in 1977. Her eldest son, Prince Charles, the Prince of Wales, is heir apparent.

Queen Elizabeth II and Prince Philip walk in procession during the state opening of Parliament (Nov. 4, 1981).

Elkin, Stanley (1925–1986). U.S. writer. His mystery novels and short stories have been translated into many languages. In some countries, including France, he is regarded as a major literary figure. Such directors as Claude CHABROL and Joseph LOSEY have made films based on his work. In 1981, the Mystery Writers of America honored him with their Grand Master Award for lifetime achievement.

Ellington, Edward Kennedy "Duke" (1899–1974). Composer-bandleader-pianist; one of jazzdom's (and American music's) transcendent figures. In 1923, after developing rudimentary musical skills in his native Washington, D.C., Ellington settled in New York City, where he became a respected bandleader-entertainer at such venues as the Hollywood and Kentucky clubs on Broadway, and then at the fabled Cotton Club in HARLEM (1927–31). Ellington's tremendous productivity as a composer (he is credited with well over 2,000 separate titles) can be attributed to his ability to organize and sustain a relatively stable performing ensemble; indeed, Ellington's orchestra was a veritable workshop in which its leader explored a wide variety of forms, exotic colors and textures, often exploiting the attributes of such individual soloists as baritone saxophonist Harry Carney, alto saxophonist Johnny Hodges and valve trombonist Juan Tizol. Ellington's work of the 1930s to early 1940s is regarded as his most significant. There were popular songs ("I Let a Song Go Out of My Heart," 1938); atmospheric "jungle" pieces ("Jungle Nights in Harlem," 1934); ballads ("In a Sentimental Mood," 1935); swing tunes (including the SWING ERA anthem, "It Don't Mean a Thing If It Ain't Got That Swing," 1932); and the first of Ellington's extended concert pieces ("Black, Brown and Beige," 1943). Ellington achieved international popularity during the postwar period with frequent tours of Europe and the Orient; he also collected an array of honors, including the Presidential Medal of Honor in 1969.

For further reading:

Ellington, Duke, *Music Is My Mistress*. Garden City, New York: Doubleday, 1973.

Elliott, Thomas Renton (1877–1961). British physician. Elliott was educated at Cambridge University and University College Hospital, London, where he later served as professor of clinical medicine from the end of World War I until his retirement in 1939. It was as a research student under John Langley at Cambridge that Elliott made his greatest discovery. In 1901 Langley had injected animals with a crude extract from the adrenal gland and noted that the extract stimulated the action of the sympathetic nerves. **Adrenaline** (epinephrine) had earlier (1898) been isolated by John ABEL at Johns Hopkins University. Elliott decided to inject adrenaline into animals to see if he got the same response as Langley had with the adrenal gland extract. He did indeed achieve increases in heartbeat, blood pressure, etc.—characteristics of stimulation of the sympathetic nervous system. Elliott is remembered for his subsequent suggestion that adrenaline may be released from sympathetic nerve endings—the first hint of neurotransmitters.

Ellis, (Henry) Havelock (1859–1939). British psychologist. Ellis was a true pioneer in establishing a modern, scientific approach to the study of sex. While Ellis did earn a medical degree, he devoted most of his life to writing. His magnum opus was the seven-volume *Studies in the Psychology of Sex* (1897–1928), which explored sexual relations from a multicultural perspective and emphasized the importance of sexuality for mental and physical well-being. The *Studies* were initially declared obscene by a British judge; in the U.S. they were for many years made legally available only to physicians. Ellis was an iconoclast who advocated woman suffrage and birth control at a time when such views were far from respectable (see WOMEN'S MOVEMENTS). *My Life* (1940) is his autobiographical summation of his years of research and political involvement.

Ellis Island. A small, nearly rectangular island of about 27 acres in upper New York Bay, just north of the Statue of Liberty, about a mile southwest of the Battery and some 1,300 ft. east of Jersey City, N.J. Owned by the U.S. government since 1808, it was the site of an early fort and arsenal. It became famous when it served (1892–1943) as the principal immigration port for the U.S. During its peak years (1892–1924) some 16 million prospective Americans passed through Ellis Island,

Duke Ellington (Jan. 8, 1943).

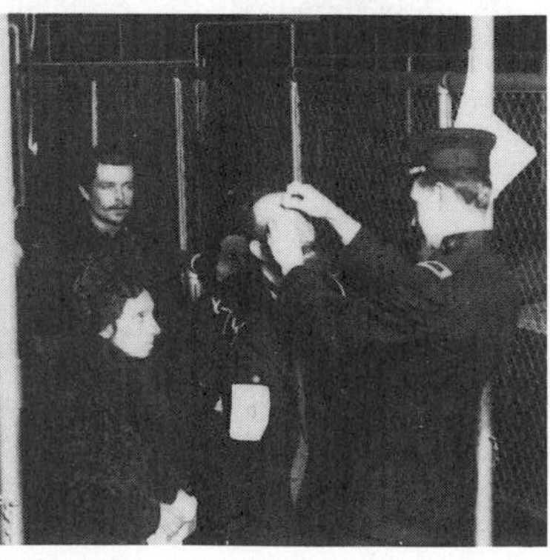

Newly arrived immigrants have their eyes examined at Ellis Island.

where they were given physical examinations and questioned about such matters as political beliefs, job prospects and final destinations in the U.S. Largely a port of entry for poor immigrants (the wealthier arrivals were inspected aboard their ships), Ellis Island was the first taste of the New World for the ancestors of about 100 million present-day Americans. After its buildings were vacated by the Coast Guard in 1955, they fell into disrepair and delapidation. Administered by the National Park Service and a part of the Statue of Liberty National Monument since 1965, the island was restored during the late 1980s to its former imposing appearance. It became the site for a number of permanent exhibitions when it was formally opened as the Ellis Island Immigration Museum in 1990.

For further reading:

Fisher, Leonard E., *Ellis Island: Gateway to the New World.* New York: Holiday House, 1986.

Jacobs, William J., *Ellis Island: New Hope in a New Land.* New York: Macmillan, 1990.

Spencer, Sharon, *Ellis Island: Then and Now.* Franklin Lakes, N.J.: Lincoln Springs Press, 1988.

Ellison, Harlan Jay (1934–). American writer. Although Ellison has published essays as well as short stories about contemporary life, he is known primarily for his gut-wrenching science fiction stories dealing with urban angst, alienation and regimentation. Among his best-known short works are "I Have No Mouth, and I Must Scream," " 'Repent, Harlequin,' Said the Ticktockman" and "A Boy and His Dog." Collections of his stories include *The Beast That Shouted Love at the Heart of the World* and *Deathbird Stories.* His novels include *Doomsman* and *The Man with Nine Lives.*

Ellison, Ralph (1914–). American writer. Born in Oklahoma City, he attended Tuskegee Institute (1933–36). Moving to New York City, he became part of the FEDERAL WRITERS' PROJECT and contributed short stories and nonfiction to various periodicals. His literary reputation rests largely on his first novel, INVISIBLE MAN (1952), a wrenching tale of a nameless black protagonist who loses his sense of identity in a world of prejudice and hostility. The novel won the National Book Award in 1953. Ellison is also known for his collection of essays *Shadow and Act* (1964). He taught at New York University from 1970.

Ellmann, Richard (1918–1987). American literary scholar and biographer. One of the foremost authorities on 20th century Irish literature, Ellmann was the author of a 1959 biography of James JOYCE that is considered the definitive work on the Irish novelist. He also wrote important books on W.B. YEATS and Oscar Wilde. Ellmann had taught at a number of U.S. universities before joining the faculty of Oxford University in 1970. He later became Goldsmiths' professor emeritus of English literature at Oxford.

Ellsworth, Lincoln (1880–1951). American explorer. Born in Chicago, he was left a fortune by his father and became the financial backer and associate of Roald AMUNDSEN. Together, they undertook the Polar Flying Expedition in 1925. Joined by Umberto NOBILE, they accomplished (1926) a transpolar mission in the dirigible *Norge,* flying from Spitzbergen over the NORTH POLE to Alaska. Ellsworth became the first man to fly over ANTARCTICA (1936); three years later he completed an aerial expedition that photographed vast sections of the Antarctic and claimed them for the U.S. His books include *Our Polar Flight* (1925) and *First Crossing of the Polar Sea* (1927), written with Amundsen, as well as *Search* (1932) and *Beyond Horizons* (1938).

Elman, Mischa (1891–1967). Russian-American violinist. Born near Kiev, Elman began studying the violin as a young child and at the age of 11 became a student of Leopold Auer at the St. Petersburg Conservatory. He debuted in that city in 1904 and, on a subsequent tour of Germany and England, became an enormous popular success. He made his U.S. debut in New York in 1908, thereafter touring the world as a soloist with major symphony orchestras and as a chamber player and a recital artist. Elman became an American citizen in 1923. He was known for his sensuous and opulent tone, his expressive playing and his technical mastery of the violin.

El Salvador [Republic of El Salvador]. The smallest and most densely populated of the Central American countries, El Salvador stretches for 208 miles along the Pacific coast and covers an area of 8,259 square miles. Independent since 1821, El Salvador had its political stability shattered in 1932 when the army crushed a popular insurrection led by Agustin Farabundo Marti. The subsequent repressive regime of General Maximiliano Hernandez Martinez lasted until 1944. The army retained power until 1972, when political and social unrest led to the formation of popular organizations and guerrilla groups. Civil war broke out in 1981. The moderate Jose Napoleon DUARTE was elected president in 1984 and, with U.S. support, tried to negotiate a peace with left-wing guerrillas. However, his successor Alfredo Cristiani (elected 1989) opposed negotiation. Increased guerrilla warfare led to declaration of a state of siege in the capital of San Salvador in 1989, and political violence continued. Leftists scored gains in the national election of March 1991.

Elsasser, Walter Maurice (1904–). German-American geophysicist. Elsasser was educated at the University of Gottingen, where he obtained his doctorate in 1927. He worked at the University of Frankfurt before leaving Germany in 1933 following HITLER's rise to power. He taught at the Sorbonne, Paris before emigrating to the U.S. (1936), where he joined the staff of the California Institute of Technology. He became professor of physics at the University of Pennsylvania (1947–50) and at the University of Utah (1950– 58). In 1962 he became professor of geophysics at Princeton; later he was appointed research professor at the University of Maryland from 1968 until his retirement in 1974. Elsasser made fundamental proposals about the origin of the Earth's magnetic field. He proposed that the molten liquid core contains eddies set up by the Earth's rotation. These eddies produce an electric current that causes the familiar terrestrial magnetic field. Elsasser also made predictions of electron diffraction (1925) and neutron diffraction (1936). His works include *The Physical Foundation of Biology* (1958) and *Atom and Organism* (1966).

Elton, Charles Sutherland (1900–). British ecologist. Elton graduated in zo-

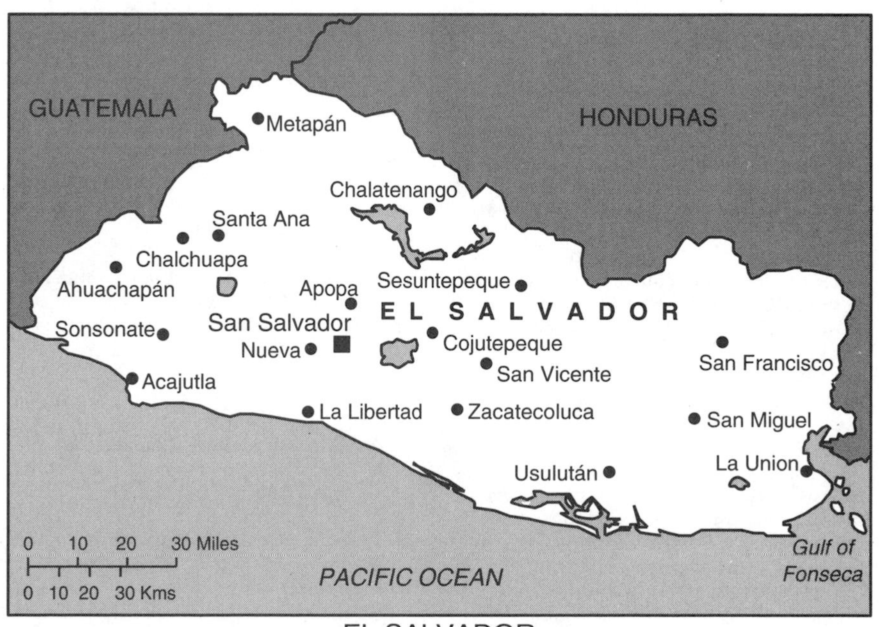

EL SALVADOR

EL SALVADOR

1932	Army crushes popular insurrection led by Agustin Farabundo Marti, killing an estimated 30,000 civilians (mostly Indian peasants).
1969	Riots during a soccer game in San Salvador escalate into armed conflict between Honduras and El Salvador.
1972	Jose Napoleon Duarte, a member of the Nationalist Democratic Union, narrowly loses his presidential bid, accuses the government of massive election fraud and attempts a coup; is arrested and exiled.
1980	Duarte returns from exile and joins the Revolutionary Government Junta.
1981	(January) Civil war breaks out when the Farabundo Marti De Liberation National (FMLN) launches its first major military offensive.
1984	Duarte defeats the extreme right-wing Maj. Roberto d'Aubuisson of the Nationalist Republican Alliance (ARENA).
1989	(March) Alfredo Cristiani of ARENA wins 53.8% of the presidential vote; (November) Peace negotiations break down, the FMLN launches military offensive; government declares the capital, San Salvador, under a state of siege; seven Jesuit priests killed by the military.
1990	Death of Duarte.
1991	Rebels call cease-fire for national election; ruling ARENA Party claims victory amid charges of fraud.

ology from Oxford University in 1922. He was assistant to Julian HUXLEY on the Oxford University expedition to Spitzbergen (1921), where Elton carried out ecological studies of the region's animal life. Further Arctic expeditions were made in 1923, 1924 and 1930. Such experience prompted his appointment as biological consultant to the Hudson's Bay Company. In 1932 Elton helped establish the Bureau of Animal Population at Oxford—an institution that subsequently became an international center for information on and research into animal numbers and their ecology. In the same year he became editor of the new *Journal of Animal Ecology*, launched by the British Ecological Society, and in 1936 was appointed reader in animal ecology as well as a senior research fellow by Oxford University. Elton was one of the first biologists to study animals in relation to their environment and other animals and plants. At the outbreak of World War II Elton conducted intensive research into methods of controlling rats and mice, thus conserving food for the war effort.

Eluard, Paul [Eugene-Emile Paul Grindel] (1895–1952). French poet. Born in Saint-Denis and educated in PARIS, Eluard launched the surrealist movement in the 1920s with Andre BRETON and Louis ARAGON. He collaborated on experimental works with Breton as well as with Max ERNST and Pablo PICASSO. His most famous books are *Les Dessous d'une vie, ou la pyramide humaine* (*The Underside of Life, or the Human Pyramid*, 1926) and *Capitale de la douleur* (*Capital of Sorrow*, 1926). His first wife, Gala, from whom he separated in 1930, became famous as the wife of Salvador DALI. Eluard supported the Republicans in the SPANISH CIVIL WAR, joined the RESISTANCE in 1942, and identified himself with the Communist Party. He is most important as an influence on an international younger generation of writers who were inspired by the avant-garde experiments of the surrealist group to break with traditional forms.

Elvehjem, Conrad Arnold (1901–1962). American biochemist. Elvehjem, the son of a farmer, graduated from and spent his whole career at the University of Wisconsin. He obtained his Ph.D. in 1927 and served as professor of biochemistry from 1936 until 1958, when he became president of the university—a position he held until his retirement in 1962. In 1937, following discoveries by Casimir Funk and Joseph Goldberger, Elvehjem succeeded in producing a new treatment for pellagra. He also worked on the role of trace elements in nutrition, showing the essential role played by such minerals as copper, zinc and cobalt. Elvehjem was a prolific author with more than 800 papers to his credit.

Ely, Paul (1897–1975). French commander in INDOCHINA after the fall of DIEN BIEN PHU. In 1954, General Ely announced in Saigon the partition agreement reached in Geneva ending France's eight-year war in Indochina. He was chief of the French general staff from 1953 to 1961, except for brief periods during that time.

Elytis, Odysseus [born Odysseus Alepoudelis] (1911–). Greek poet. The son of a successful manufacturer in Crete, Elytis studied law at the University of Athens but did not complete a degree there. When he began writing, Elytis changed his name because of its commercial associations. Influenced by the poet Paul ELUARD and the surrealist movement, Elytis published his first poems in *Te Nea Grammata* (*New Letters*) in 1935. He rejected the despair he found in the work of the modernist poets; his early work is characterized by a bright and hopeful tone. After fighting in Albania during World War II, he served as a literary and art critic for the newspaper *Kathimerini* (Daily). In 1948 he went to PARIS, where he studied at the Sorbonne and became acquainted with Pablo PICASSO, Henri MATISSE and others of the Paris art world. Elytis' next major work, *To Axion Esti* (*Worthy It Is*, 1959), was an autobiographical piece alternating between prose and verse in which he explored the use of conversational and literary Greek. Elytis moved to France in 1969 to protest the 1967 coup in GREECE. His works from this time include *O Ilios o iliatores* (*The Sovereign Sun*, 1971), *To fotodendro ke i dekati tetarti omorfia* (*The Light Tree and the Fourteenth Beauty*, 1971) and *Maria Nefeli* (1978), finished after he returned to Greece. Elytis was awarded the NOBEL PRIZE for literature in 1979. (See also MODERNISM, SURREALISM.)

Embden, Gustav George (1874–1933). German physiologist. Embden was educated at the universities of Freiburg, Munich, Berlin and Strasbourg. From 1904 he was director of the chemical laboratory in the medical clinic of the Frankfurt hospital, becoming director (1907) of the Physiological Institute (which evolved from the medical clinic) and director (1914) of the Institute for Vegetative Physiology (which in its turn evolved from the Physiological Institute). In 1918 Otto MEYERHOF threw considerable light on the process of cellular metabolism by showing that it involved the breakdown of glucose to lactic acid. Embden spent much time in working out the precise steps involved in such a breakdown, later known as the **Embden-Meyerhof pathway**. Embden's earlier work concentrated on the metabolic processes carried out by the liver.

Emeleus, Harry Julius (1903–). British inorganic chemist. Emeleus was educated at Imperial College, London and at Karlsruhe and Princeton. He returned to Imperial College in 1931 and taught there until 1945, when he moved to Cambridge University—where he served as professor of inorganic chemistry until his retirement in 1970. In collaboration with John Anderson, he published (1938) the well-known work *Modern Aspects of Inorganic Chemistry*. He also worked on fluorine, publishing a monograph on the subject in 1969: *The Chemistry of Fluorine and its Compounds*.

Emerson, Peter H(enry) (1856–1936). British photographer; one of the world pioneers of nature photography. His works provide an invaluable pictorial record of the British countryside prior to the full-fledged industrial development of the 20th century. Major book collections by Emerson include *Life and Landscape of the Norfolk Broads* (1886) and *Pictures of East Anglia* (1888). Emerson was the first photographer to put forward a written theoretical justification of photography as an independent art.

Emiliani, Cesare (1922–). Italian-American geologist. Emiliani was educated at the University of Bologna. He moved to America in 1948, obtaining his Ph.D. from the University of Chicago in 1950. After teaching at Chicago (1950–56) he moved to the University of Miami, where he was appointed professor of geology in 1963 at the Institute of Marine Science. Emiliani has specialized in using oxygen isotopic analysis of microfossils from ocean sediments. Eduard Bruckner had established (1909) the long-held orthodox view that four ice ages had occurred during the Pleistocene. In his fundamental paper *Pleistocene temperatures* (1955) Emiliani produced evidence that there had been more. Using the principle established by Harold UREY that the climate of past ages can be estimated by the ratio of oxygen-16 to oxygen-18 present in water (i.e., the less oxygen-18 present the colder the climate must have been), he examined the oxygen-18 content of fossils brought up from the mud of the Caribbean. By choosing fossils that he knew had lived near the surface, he could reconstruct the climatic history, and consequently identified seven complete glacial cycles.

Empie, Rev. Dr. Paul C. (1909–1979). International leader of the Lutheran Church, relief official and ecumenical theologian. Empie directed church-sponsored reconstruction aid in Europe during and after WORLD WAR II. He also served as cochairman of official talks between teams of Roman Catholic and Lutheran scholars that led to agreement on critical aspects of papal authority.

Empire State Building. New York City skyscraper of ART DECO design, for many years the tallest building in the world. This structure of 1929–31 was designed by the firm of Shreve, Lamb & Harmon as an 85-floor office tower, but a pylon was added to the top, supposedly as a mooring mast for dirigibles, increasing the height to 102 stories (1,239 feet) and establishing a height record that lasted until 1972. The building has the setback form typical of tall buildings constructed in the 1920-to-1950 era of zoning regulations and regarded as the "skyscraper style." Details are in the Art Deco mode, as are the interiors of the public spaces. The design was generally regarded as banal and commercial, but recent boredom with the INTERNATIONAL STYLE buildings of the post-World War II era has created a cult of reaction that now admires the 1930s skyscrapers, of which this is the largest and most spectacular. Its status as a tourist attraction remains undiminished.

Empson, William (1906–1984). British poet and critic. Empson was educated at Winchester and Magdalene College, Oxford, where he studied physics and English with I.A. RICHARDS, under whose tutelage Empson wrote his dissertation. This work evolved into his first critical book, *Seven Types of Ambiguity* (1930), which made his reputation and became a seminal text in 20th-century literary criticism. Empson taught in China and Japan and then became a professor of English at Sheffeld. His first volume of poems, *Poems* (1935), shows the influence of John Donne. In his second volume, *The Gathering Storm* (1940), which draws on his experiences in the Orient, his voice is more his own. Empson's complex poetry incorporates ideas of modern physics and mathematics and strongly influenced the writers of The MOVEMENT. His critical works, which include *The Structure of Complex Words* (1951) and *Milton's God* (1961), are considered to be a springboard of the NEW CRITICISM, which, ironically, he attacked in a posthumously published collection of essays, *Using Biography* (1984).

END [European Nuclear Disarmament]. British-based movement formed in 1980, originally seeking removal of all nuclear weapons from Europe. It became a pressure group for a reunited Europe free of Soviet or American domination.

Enders, John Franklin (1897–1985). U.S. virologist. In 1954, during his long association with Harvard University, he shared the NOBEL PRIZE for medicine or physiology with two of his former students for their development of a method for culturing the polio virus in large quantities. This procedure made possible the mass production of a safe polio vaccine. Enders conducted other research that led not only to the development of vaccines against measles, German measles and mumps, but also to advances in growing tumor viruses.

Enesco, Georges (1881–1955). Romanian composer. A musical prodigy and violin virtuoso, he began his studies at the Vienna Conservatory at the age of seven. He later studied at the Paris Conservatory under Gabriele FAURE and Jules Massenet. He became an influential teacher, numbering Yehudi MENUHIN among his many students. Enesco toured extensively as a violin soloist and conductor, traveling throughout Europe and the U.S. As a composer, he was influenced by the folk music of his native Romania and evolved a highly personal style. His works include *Romanian Rhapsodies* (1901–02) and other orchestral works, chamber music, three symphonies and the opera *Oedipus* (1932).

Engel v. Vitale (1962). U.S. Supreme Court decision barring state-sponsored school prayer. For many years it was customary for public school children to recite mandatory prayers at the start of the school day. Critics (primarily atheists and Jehovah's Witnesses) charged that requiring the recitation of a state-designated nondenominational school prayer amounted to the establishment of religion. The Supreme Court held that such recitation was not mandatory and that children could either remain silent or be excused during the prayer. Later cases held that daily Bible readings were also unconstitutional.

Engle, Paul (1908–). U.S. educator and poet. Engle attended the University of Iowa, where his thesis, *Worn Earth*, won the prestigious Yale Series of Younger Poets Award in 1932. His further education included work at Columbia University and a Rhodes Scholarship. Increasingly recognized as a poet, he joined the English Department of the University of Iowa in 1936, and was instrumental in founding the famous Iowa Writers' Workshop.

Engler, Heinrich Gustav Adolf (1844–1930). German botanist. Engler studied botany at Breslau University, gaining his Ph.D. in 1866. After teaching natural history he became custodian of the Munich botanical collection and then professor of botany at Kiel University; in 1884 he returned to Breslau to succeed his former teacher in the chair of botany. At Breslau, Engler replanned the botanic garden, ordering the plants according to their geographical distribution. In 1887 he took up the important chair of botany at Berlin and successfully reestablished the garden in Dahlem. Between 1878 and his retirement from Berlin in 1921, Engler contributed greatly to the development of plant taxonomy with his classifications, presented in such books as *The Natural Plant Families* (1887–1911) and *The Plant Kingdom* (1900–1937). Much of his work was drawn from first-hand observation gained during travels through Africa, Europe, India, China, Japan and America.

English Channel Tunnel. A 32.2–mile tunnel running 23.6 miles under the English Channel connecting Folkestone, England and Calais, France. Also called the "Chunnel," the long-debated Eurotunnel was begun in 1986 when Prime Minister Margaret THATCHER and President Francois MITTERRAND signed the Channel Tunnel Treaty. Tunneling was begun from both ends; the two halves of the service tunnel met on December 1, 1990. The Chunnel, scheduled for completion in 1993, actually consists of three tunnels. The outer two are for high-speed trains bearing automobiles and their passengers; in the center is a connected service tunnel, which can also be used for emergency evacuation. The trip will take approximately 35 minutes, and authorities estimate that by 2003, some 44 million people a year will use the tunnel. The trains will carry freight in off-hours. The largest privately financed engineering

A beaming "chunnel" worker gives the "V-for-victory" sign at the English Channel Tunnel breakthrough.

A ghostly, illumined mushroom cloud rises above Eniwetok atoll after a hydrogen bomb test.

project ever undertaken (the estimated cost is $14 billion), the Chunnel will also be the world's longest undersea tunnel when complete. The tunnel has aroused controversy. Many Britons are reluctant to surrender their island status, and many worry about the environmental impact of the tunnel.

ENIAC. Acronym for Electronic Numerical Integrator And Computer. Designed by J. Presper Eckert Jr. and John MAUCHLY and built at the University of Pennsylvania in 1946, the ENIAC was the first true electronic digital COMPUTER. ENIAC occupied an entire large room and used some 18,000 vacuum tubes. It could perform calculations with a rapidity previously unheard of, although by the standards of later computers it was slow and inefficient. Because of its size and complexity, it was never commercially available. In 1951 it was superseded by the more advanced UNIVAC.

Enigma. German cipher machine used to code and decode secret messages during WORLD WAR II. (See also ULTRA.)

Eniwetok. Unpopulated atoll at the northwest end of the Ralik chain in the northwestern MARSHALL ISLANDS of the western Pacific Ocean. Mandated to JAPAN by the LEAGUE OF NATIONS in 1920, it was captured by U.S. forces in February 1944 during WORLD WAR II and became a naval base. In the 1940s and 1950s it was used as a site for atomic weapons testing. (See also BIKINI.)

Enniskillen bombing (November 8, 1987). The explosion of a bomb planted by the outlawed Provisional IRISH REPUBLICAN ARMY killed 11 persons and injured more than 60 others in Enniskillen, County Fermanagh, NORTHERN IRELAND. The explosion came as hundreds of people were gathering for the traditional wreath-laying ceremonies on Britain's Remembrance Day. The death toll was the highest from a single incident in the ongoing strife in Northern Ireland since 17 people were killed in a pub bombing in 1982. All of the 11 killed in the Enniskillen bombing were civilians; seven of them were retired persons over the age of 60. The following day the IRA claimed that the bomb had been intended for soldiers and police who would have been marching in the Remembrance Day parade and said that the bomb had gone off prematurely Both British Prime Minister Margaret THATCHER and Irish TAOISEACH Charles Haughey, among other political leaders, condemned the bombing.

Enosis [*Greek,* "to unite"]. Greek Cypriot movement for the political union of CYPRUS and GREECE. It dates from the 19th century, having been revived in 1954 by Archbishop MAKARIOS III and opposed both by the Turkish minority on the island and by the Turkish government. TURKEY invaded and partitioned the island in 1975. (See also CYPRIOT WAR OF 1963–64, CYPRIOT WAR OF 1974.)

Entebbe, raid on (July 3, 1976). Half-hour battle in which Israeli commandos rescued 106 predominantly Jewish aircraft passengers at Entebbe Airport, UGANDA. The plane had been hijacked by guerrillas of the **Popular Front for the Liberation of Palestine** demanding the release of 53 Arab terrorists. Twenty Ugandan soldiers, seven hijackers, three passengers and one Israeli soldier were killed. (See also Idi AMIN.)

Entente Cordiale [Anglo-French Entente]. A bilateral agreement reached between the UNITED KINGDOM and FRANCE on April 8, 1904, also known as the **Anglo-French Entente**. Overcoming their traditional antagonisms, the two countries ended their colonial rivalry. The pact resolved various international disputes, principally in Egypt, which the British were to develop, and in Morocco, where the French were given free rein. Earlier, an 1890s agreement had sealed the rapprochement between France and Russia. Later, the ANGLO-RUSSIAN ENTENTE of 1907 was to cement relations between England and Russia. These international relationships formed the basis of the TRIPLE ENTENTE that opposed the TRIPLE ALLIANCE in WORLD WAR I.

Enver Bey (1881–1922). Turkish army general. As one of the leaders of the reformist YOUNG TURKS group, Enver Bey led the rebellion in 1908. Later known as Enver Pasha, he served as military attache in Berlin (1909–10) and sought Ger-

Relatives and well-wishers at Ben-Gurion Airport joyously celebrate while awaiting the return of rescued hijack victims from Entebbe (July 4, 1976).

man military support. By 1911 he was de facto ruler of TURKEY. He commanded Turkish forces in the Italo-Turkish War (1911) and the BALKAN WARS (1912). As the war minister in 1913, he commanded Turkish forces against RUSSIA in the Caucasus. After the RUSSIAN REVOLUTION, Enver Bey became involved in a "Pan-Turanian" attempt to unite Turkish people, mostly in Russia. After the Turkish defeat in WORLD WAR I (1918), Enver fled to Turkestan, where he was killed leading an anti-BOLSHEVIK revolt.

Environmental Protection Act. The National Environmental Protection Act (NEPA), signed into law by President NIXON in 1970, declared it a federal policy to consider the environmental impact of government activities. By 1970, Americans had tired of the abuse of the environment and demanded the federal government assume a leadership role. The act established the Council on Environmental Quality, which sets the federal government's environmental policy, and also the better-known Environmental Protection Agency (EPA), which enforces federal environmental laws (its director was later elevated to cabinet rank). Yet even the EPA proved not to be immune from political manipulation and scandals (see EPA–SUPERFUND CONTROVERSY).

NEPA required the federal government to prepare environmental impact statements assessing the environmental effects of any major federal projects. The EPA was given enforcement power over the Clean Air Act and the Clean Water Act and other environmental legislation that also applied to private industry, and the EPA developed national clean air and water standards. Because of this legislation and increased awareness of environmental problems, the degradation of the environment was slowed in the final quarter of the century.

EOKA [*Ethniki Organosis Kypriakou Agonos,* National Organization of Cypriot Struggle]. Anti-British Greek Cypriot guerrilla movement. EOKA members of the National Guard overthrew Archbishop MAKARIOS III, precipitating the Turkish invasion and the partition of CYPRUS. (See also CYPRIOT WAR OF 1974.)

EPA–Superfund controversy. Controversy involving collusion between managers of the Environmental Protection Agency (EPA) and industry during the administration of President Ronald REAGAN. (The Superfund had been established by Congress to clean up the most polluted sites in the country.) When Reagan came into office he had a mandate to reduce government regulation, so lax enforcement of environmental regulations became the order of the day. During the 1980s Congress investigated allegations that Rita Lavelle, the EPA's assistant administrator, had given special favors to her former employer and to others. On orders from the President, EPA head Ann Burford refused to turn over subpoenaed documents to Congress; she was held in contempt of Congress. After months of stalemate Burford resigned, and Reagan fired Lavelle after she refused to resign. Lavelle later served a few months in prison for committing perjury during House hearings. The EPA eventually turned over the requested documents to congressional investigators.

Sir Jacob Epstein.

Ephemeris Time. See Gerald Maurice CLEMENCE.

Epstein, Jacob (Sir) (1880–1959). American-born British sculptor. Epstein, who was born in New York City and studied art as a young man in Paris, lived for most of his life in Britain. There he became renowned as one of the foremost creators of public works of art on the grand scale and was ultimately knighted. But his early career was not without controversy. A massive stone sculptural facade that Epstein produced for the headquarters of the British Medical Association (1907–08) was decried as an aesthetic horror. His memorial sculpture of Oscar Wilde (1911) was similarly received. But Epstein gained ground with the artistic establishment through his famous busts of Joseph CONRAD, Albert EINSTEIN and Jawaharlal NEHRU, among other notables of the day.

Epstein, Julius J. (1909–). Julius J. Epstein and his twin brother **Philip G. Epstein** (1909– 1952) formed one of the most renowned screenplay-writing teams in the history of HOLLYWOOD. They were born on the Lower East Side of New York City, where their Jewish father ran a livery stable. After writing some comedies that were performed on Broadway, they went to work for WARNER BROS. in 1938. It was in Hollywood that the Epstein brothers made their true mark, co-authoring 29 films, including such classics as *Yankee Doodle Dandy* (1942), starring James CAGNEY, *Casablanca* (1943), featuring Ingrid BERGMAN and Humphrey BOGART, and *Arsenic and Old Lace* (1944), with Cary GRANT. After Philip's death in 1952, Julius went on to write numerous screenplays, notably *Pete 'n Tillie* (1972) and *Reuben Reuben* (1983).

Epstein, Philip G. See Julius J. EPSTEIN.

epuration. The purge of suspected Nazi collaborators in France after 1945.

equal employment opportunity. Legally mandated nondiscrimination in employment. During the first half of the century, employers typically discriminated against females and members of minority groups in hiring. In the last half of the century, Congress attempted to enforce the policy of equal employment opportunity by enacting a number of federal laws, including the Equal Pay Act (1963), the CIVIL RIGHTS ACT OF 1964, the Age Discrimination in Employment Act (1967) and the Vocational Rehabilitation Act of 1973. These laws, applying to public and private employers alike, prohibited discrimination in hiring or promotion on the basis of race, religion, national origin, sex, age or physical handicap. The federal government also established the Equal Employment Opportunity Commission (EEOC) to enforce the law by addressing workers' complaints.

Equal Rights Amendment [ERA]. An amendment to the U.S. Constitution, first proposed in 1923, to guarantee the legal equality of men and women. The U.S. Congress passed the ERA in 1972, and it was passed on to the 50 state legislatures for their approval or rejection. However, after an intense lobbying campaign by supporters and opponents of the measure, only 35 states had ratified the measure by the 1982 deadline. This number was three short of the three-quarters majority of 38 required under the Constitution, and the amendment was defeated. The Equal Rights Amendment read: "Equality of rights under the law shall not be denied or abridged by the United States or any state on account of sex."

Equatorial Guinea [Republica de Guinea Ecuatorial]. Equatorial Guinea consists of a mainland area (Rio Muni) of 10,042 square miles on the coast of west–central Africa; and the islands of Bioko (formerly Acias Nguema, formerly Fernando Poo), Annobon (Paualu), Corislo, Elobey Granoe and Elobey Chico in the Gulf of Guinea—for a total offshore area of 10,828 square miles. A Spanish colony since 1778, the area was systematically developed after 1939. Granted partial autonomy in 1963, Equatorial Guinea achieved full independence in 1968. Francisco Macias Nguema ruled the country until 1979, when he was overthrown by his nephew Teodoro Obiang Nguema Mbasogo. Mbasogo currently rules, having survived several attempted coups, most recently in 1988.

Erfurt. Thuringian city on the Gera River, 64 miles west–southwest of Leipzig, Germany. In 1970 it was host to the first meeting between the East and West German heads of state.

ergonomics. Systematic study of relationship between products and human users. The forms and layout of controls and instruments, the design of finger and hand grips, and the arrangement of seating surfaces and other furniture elements to promote efficiency, comfort, and physio-

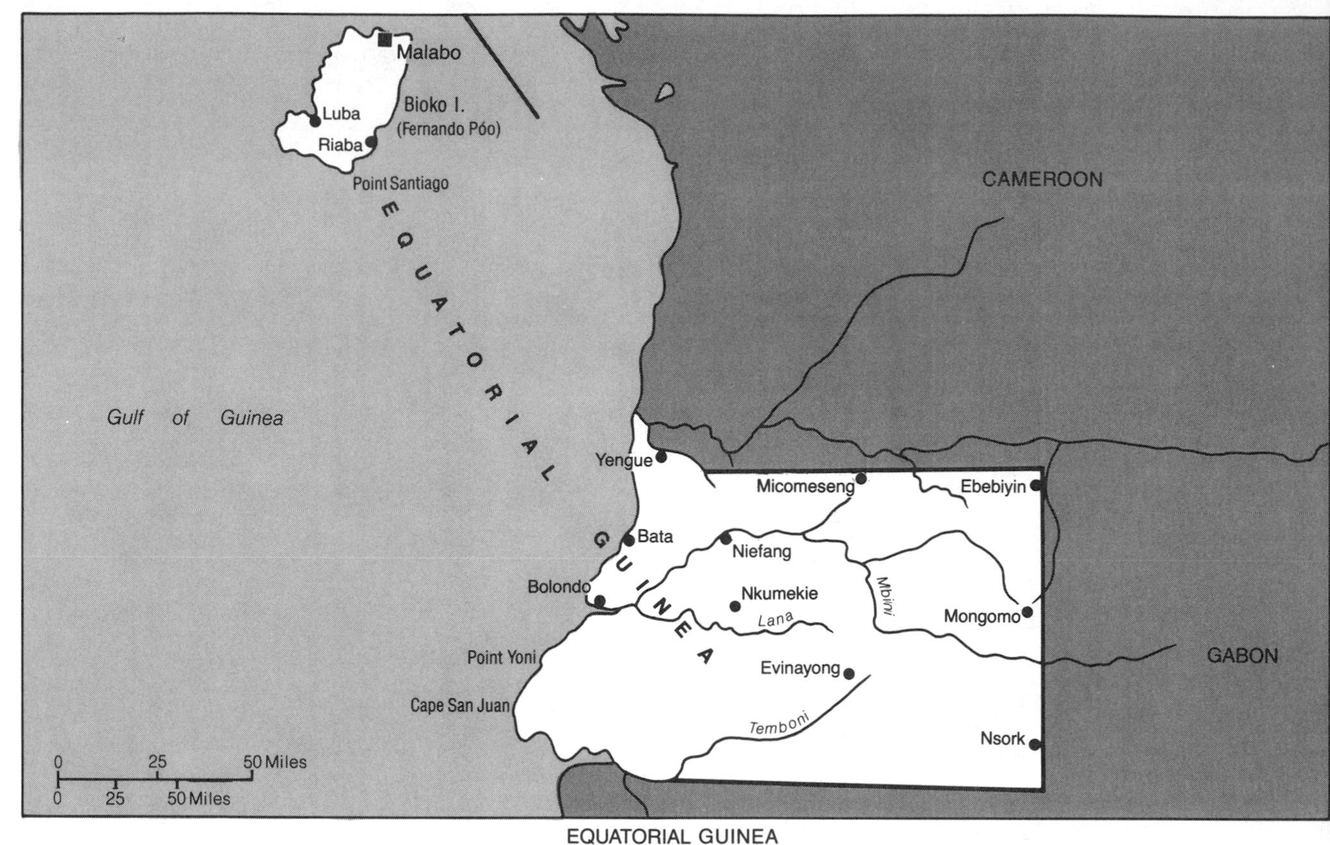

EQUATORIAL GUINEA

logically optimum forms are special concerns of ergonomic study. The term has come into wide use in the promotion of chairs, such as the Herman Miller Ergon chair designed by Bill Stumpf, and other products that are claimed to be designed to maximize human convenience and comfort in use.

Erhard, Ludwig (1897–1977). Chancellor of WEST GERMANY (1963–66). Head of an economics research institute before World War II and professor of economics at Munich University from 1945 to 1949, Erhard was a Christian Democrat member of the Bundestag from 1949 to 1966. He became federal minister of economic affairs (1949–63) and presided over West Germany's "economic miracle," its transition from wartime devastation to prosperity. Deputy chancellor under Konrad ADENAUER (1957–63), he became chancellor on Adenauer's retirement in 1963. Erhard lacked Adenauer's skill in international affairs and, fearing an economic recession, proposed a series of tax increases that were defeated in the Bundestag (1966). He subsequently resigned from office.

Erikson, Erik H(omburger) (1902–). German-born American psychologist. As a young man, Erikson studied art before turning his attention primarily to psychology as a result of undergoing psychoanalytic therapy with Anna FREUD in Vienna in 1927. Erikson then proceeded to train in psychoanalysis, specializing in work with children. Exiling himself from Nazi Germany, he came to the U.S. in 1937. He taught at the the University of California, Berkeley, but was forced to leave in 1950 due to his refusal to sign a MCCARTHY era loyalty oath. For the next three decades, Erikson taught primarily at Harvard University. His first major work, *Childhood and Society* (1950), posited eight major stages of formative personality development. Erikson applied these eight stages to biographical analysis in such renowned works as *Young Man Luther* (1958) and *Gandhi's Truth* (1969). *Insight and Responsibility* (1964) continues Erikson's theoretical researches into developmental issues.

Eritrea. Province on Ethiopia's Red Sea coast; Asmara is the capital. Taken over by Italy in 1882, it was the staging area for Italy's invasion of ETHIOPIA in 1935 and remained under Italian control until captured by the British in 1941 during WORLD WAR II. Eritrea was governed by the British military until 1952, when it became an autonomous unit within the federal structure of Ethiopia, to which it was fully connected in 1962. Since 1962 Eritrean secessionists have been involved in a guerrilla struggle with Ethiopia; active war erupted in 1975, bringing about a critical refugee problem.

Erlander, Tage (1901–1985). Premier of SWEDEN (1946–69). A Social Democrat, Erlander held office longer than any other premier in a modern Western democracy. In a period of industrial growth unprecedented in Sweden, he presided over the vast expansion of the nation's welfare system while maintaining Sweden's neutrality in foreign affairs. (See also WELFARE STATE.)

Erlanger, Joseph (1874–1965). American neurophysiologist. Erlanger was educated at the University of California and Johns Hopkins University in Baltimore, where in 1899 he obtained his M.D. After working on the staff for a few years, Erlanger moved to the University of Wisconsin (1906) to accept the chair of physiology. In 1910 he moved to Washington University, St. Louis, where he held the chair of physiology in the Medical School until his retirement in 1944. Between 1921 and 1931 Erlanger carried out some fundamental research on the functions of nerve fibers with his former pupil and colleague, Herbert GASSER. They investigated the transmission of a nerve impulse along a frog nerve. Their innovation was to study the transmission with the cathode-ray oscillograph, which enabled them to picture the changes the impulse underwent as it traveled along the nerve. They found that when a nerve was stimulated, the resulting electrical activity indicating the passage of an impulse was composed of three waves, as observed on the oscillograph. They explained this by proposing that the one stimulus activated three different groups of nerve fibers, each of which had its own conduction rate. They went on to measure these rates. Erlanger and Gasser produced an account of their collaboration in *Electrical Signs of Nervous Activity* (1937) and they were awarded the 1944 NOBEL PRIZE in physiology or medicine for their work.

Ernst, Max (1891–1976). German painter and writer. Ernst, who began his artistic career as a follower of DADA, emerged in

German-born surrealist painter Max Ernst standing in front of his painting The Temptation of St. Anthony *(1946).*

the 1920s as one of the leading painters of SURREALISM. He was a pioneer figure in the use of collage in Surrealist art, gaining fame and notoriety from his exhibition (1920) of highly unusual collage assemblages such as *Phallustrade* and *The Wet Nurse of the Stars.* Ernst was also a major theoretician of the Surrealist movement, who was influenced by the credo of 19th century French poet Arthur Rimbaud that the true artist should make a conscious effort to disorder all of his senses. Ernst wrote that "I have done everything to render my soul *monstrous.* Blind swimmer, I have made myself see. *I have seen.*" During the Nazi era, Ernst immigrated to the U.S., where he exercised a considerable influence as teacher and exemplar over the postwar generation of American painters.

Ershad, Hussain Mohammed (1930–). President of BANGLADESH (1986–). Ershad was appointed to the 2nd East Bengal Regiment of the Pakistan army after finishing Officers' Training School in 1952. He was promoted to Bangladesh army chief of staff in 1978. General Ershad was instrumental in capturing the assassins of President ZIAUR RAHMAN in 1981. In 1982, he declared martial law and assumed full power. He was elected president in October 1986, in an election boycotted by the major opposition parties.

Erskine, John (1879–1951). American writer, musician, and educator. Erskine was one of the most versatile and influential figures in American academia in the first half of the 20th century. He served as a professor of English at Columbia University from 1909 to 1937, where he taught numerous future writers including Carl Van Doren and Mortimer ADLER. Erskine was also a gifted concert pianist and became the president (1928–37) of the renowned Juilliard School of Music. Remarkably, Erskine also wrote a number of humorous novels, most notably the bestselling *The Private Life of Helen of Troy* (1925), as well as volumes of poetry and literary criticism. His autobiography is in four volumes: *The Names of Certain Persons* (1947), *My Life as a Teacher* (1948), *My Life as a Musician* (1950), and *My Life as a Writer* (1951).

Erte [born Romain de Tirtoff] (1892–1990). Russian-born ART DECO designer. De Tirtoff adopted the name Erte in 1913 and created hundreds of covers for *Harper's Bazaar* magazine between 1915 and 1937. As a theatrical designer, he created costumes for musicals, films, operas and ballets, as well as for the Folies-Bergere and the ZIEGFELD FOLLIES. His lithographs, most of which featured elegant women in Art Deco fashions, became extremely popular in the 1970s and 1980s.

Ertesezek, Olga (?–1989). Polish-born founder of the U.S. manufacturer Olga Co. She designed many of the firm's products and was credited with inventing the seamless brassiere and the nightgown with the built-in bra. She was featured in a widely published series of advertisements for the firm.

Ervin, Sam(uel James, Jr.) (1896–1985). American politician; best known for his role as chairman of the Senate committee that investigated the WATERGATE affair. A North Carolina Democrat, Ervin served briefly in the state legislature in the 1920s and 1930s. Later he became a judge on the North Carolina Supreme Court (1948–54). In 1954 he was appointed to fill a vacant seat in the U.S. Senate, where he served for 20 years, winning election in his own right four times. A conservative known for his integrity and his respect

Erte, renowned for his art deco designs, poses with his sculpture Woman and Satyr *during a Chicago gallery benefit in 1986.*

for the Constitution, he cast his votes according to his strict constructionist principles. Ervin believed that an activist federal government interfered with STATES' RIGHTS and threatened individual liberties, and he opposed many liberal federal domestic programs and most CIVIL RIGHTS legislation. He supported environmental legislation, however, and attempted to strengthen individual liberties. He also supported President Lyndon B. JOHNSON's and Richard M. NIXON's policies on the VIETNAM WAR. In his last three years in the Senate he presided over the Government Operations Committee and chaired three subcommittees of the Judiciary Committee. In early 1973 Ervin was named chairman of the Senate Select Committee on Presidential Campaign Activities, known as the Watergate Committee. The Watergate hearings were broadcast on national television, and Ervin became an American folk hero as he directed the probe that played a key role in the resignation of President Nixon in August 1974. He often quoted from the Bible and the works of Shakespeare, but at one point described himself as simply "an old country lawyer." At one point during the Watergate hearings he sadly remarked, "I think that Watergate is the greatest tragedy this country has ever suffered. I used to think the Civil War was the greatest tragedy, but I do remember some redeeming features in the Civil War in that there was some spirit of sacrifice and heroism displayed on both sides. I see no redeeming features in Watergate."

Ervine, St. John Greer (1883–1971). Irish playwright and author. Born in Belfast, he was acquainted with AE, George Bernard SHAW and others associated with the ABBEY THEATRE, where Ervine's first play, *Mixed Marriage* (1911), was performed, and where he served as manager in 1915. His early plays, which also include *Jane Clegg* (1913) and *John Ferguson* (1915), were realistic social dramas that examined the strife in NORTHERN IRELAND. Ervine later moved to London, where he was drama critic for *The Observer* and the *Morning Post* and continued to write plays, novels and biographies. He achieved success in the London theater with *The First Mrs. Fraser* (1929), which was followed by many other popular comedies. His biographical works include the lives of C.S. Parnell and General Booth, and the notable *Bernard Shaw: His Life, Work and Friends* (1956).

Erving, Julius (Winfield) "Dr. J" (1950–). American basketball player. A standout player in college, Erving signed after his junior year with the Virginia Squires of the fledgling American Basketball Association. He gave the ABA credibility and drew crowds with his dazzling moves and hang time. After leading the New York Nets to three ABA titles, he was again traded, this time to the Philadelphia 76ers of the NBA. With Erving, the team was a four-time championship finalist, taking the title in 1983. A five-time first-team All-Star, at 6 feet 7 inches he was equally adept at both small and power forward. He became only the third player in league history to amass 30,000 points.

Esaki, Leo (1925–). Japanese physicist. Esaki graduated in physics at the University of Tokyo in 1947, where he later gained his doctorate in 1959. His doctoral work was on the physics of SEMICONDUCTORS, and in 1958 he reported an effect known as tunneling. The phenomenon of tunneling is a quantum-mechanical effect in which an electron can penetrate a potential barrier through a narrow region of solid, where classical theory predicted it could not pass. Esaki was quick to see the possibility of applying the tunnel effect, and in 1960 reported the construction of a device with diode-like properties—the tunnel (or *Esaki*) diode. Important characteristics of the tunnel diode are its very fast speed of operation, its small physical size and its low power consumption. It has found applications in many fields of electronics—principally computers, microwave devices and where low electronic noise is required. Esaki shared the NOBEL PRIZE for physics in 1973 with Brian JOSEPHSON and Ivar GAIEVER.

Eschenmoser, Albert (1925–). Swiss chemist. Eschenmoser was educated at the Federal Institute of Technology, Zurich, where he has taught since 1956 and where, in 1960, he was appointed professor of organic chemistry. He is best known for his work in synthesizing a number of complex organic compounds. His first success came with an alkaloid that has important applications in genetic research. He also collaborated with Robert Woodward on the synthesis of vitamin B-12, which had first been isolated and crystallized by Karl Folkers in 1948. Its empirical formula was soon established, and in 1956 Dorothy Hodgkin established its structure. It took many years, with samples passing between Zurich and Harvard, before Eschenmoser and Woodward were finally able to announce its synthesis in 1965.

Escher, Maurits C(ornelis) (1898–1972). Dutch artist. Escher was one of the modern masters of graphic art, specializing in woodcut, wood engraving and lithography. His visually striking and paradoxical works—in which surreal details and trompe l'oeil techniques abound—achieved great popularity in the 1960s and 1970s. Escher was born in Leeuwarden in northern Holland. He began his college studies in Haarlem, Holland, intending to become an architect, but soon switched to the graphic arts, to which he devoted the rest of his life. Escher lived in Italy from 1923 to 1935, and Italian settings predominate in his work of this period. He returned to Holland in 1941. His works of the last three decades of his life—such as *Reptiles* (1943), *Three Spheres I* (1945), and *Relativity* (1953)—tend toward introspective, abstract themes.

Esenin, Sergei Alexandrovich (1895–1925). Poet. Founder of the Imagist school of Russian poets. Esenin presented himself as a "peasant poet" and recited in Moscow salons wearing a peasant smock. He welcomed the revolution, without really understanding it. He married Isadora DUNCAN, the American dancer, in 1922, but they separated after a year and he returned to Russia with an international reputation as a drunken exhibitionist. He never succeeded in adapting either to the new, urban Soviet society or to the changed peasant world; he hanged himself in Leningrad in 1925. His *Confession of a Hooligan* was published in 1918.

Esnault-Pelterie, Robert (1881–1957). French aviation pioneer and aeronautical engineer. Esnault-Pelterie became interested in rocketry in middle age. In 1927, he and banker Andre Louis Hirsch established a 5,000-franc prize to be awarded annually for the best technical book on astronautics (the REP-Hirsch Award). The first award went to German rocket pioneer Hermann OBERTH in 1928. In 1930, Esnault-Pelterie published his own classic, *L'Astronautique,* still regarded as a major work in the history of astronautics. Elected to the French Academy of Sciences in 1936, he was working on the development of a gasoline- and liquid-oxygen-fueled rocket motor when the German occupation cut short his research and forced his retirement in 1940.

Esperance, Cape. In the Solomon Islands, on the northwest coast of GUADALCANAL Island. During WORLD WAR II Japanese forces landed here in 1942–43, and on October 11–12, 1943, Japanese and U.S. naval forces clashed off the cape. It was Japan's last lifeline on Guadalcanal before the invaders were removed from the island in 1943.

Espiritu Santo. Island, also known as Marina, in an autonomous group of islands formerly known as the NEW HEBRIDES but now called VANUATU; in the southwestern Pacific Ocean. A large U.S. airbase was here during WORLD WAR II. Part of an Anglo-French condominium until 1980, independence saw separatist unrest that had to be put down in 1980.

Esposito, Anthony James "Tony" (1943–). Canadian hockey player. Tony Esposito began his career as backup goaltender for the Montreal Canadiens, then came into his own upon joining the Chicago Black Hawks. He won the Calder Trophy as rookie of the year in 1970 and was an All-Star five times. That year, he faced his brother Phil in the Stanley Cup finals, but the Hawks lost in four straight games. Tony was a Vezina Trophy winner three times for lowest goals-against average, and finished his career with 76 shutouts and a 2.92 goals-against average. Active in the Players' Association throughout his career, he went on to a career in hockey administration.

Esposito, Phil(ip Anthony) (1942–). Canadian hockey player. Phil Esposito began his career in Chicago, but the Black Hawks lost patience with the lumbering, slow-developing center and traded him to the Boston Bruins in 1967, thus losing one of the game's greatest players. Although he never became a fluid skater, Esposito's extraordinary balance and puck sense allowed him to score at a virtual goal-a-game rate during the 1971 season.

A five-time scoring champion and perennial All-Star, he was a leader in Team Canada's last-minute triumph over the Soviet Union in 1972. In 1975 he was traded along with Carol Vadnais to the archrival New York Rangers for Jean Ratelle and Brad Park in what is regarded as the biggest trade in hockey history. At first refusing to report, Esposito learned to love New York and went on to become general manager and coach of the team in the late 1980s. He was named to the Hall of Fame in 1984.

Essen [Essen an der Ruhr]. Industrial city on the Ruhr River in North Rhine-Westphalia, GERMANY. The largest manufacturing city of the RUHR Valley, Essen is the heart of the Krupp steel works and the main location for the production of electricity in western Germany. A key center of the German war industry in the 20th century, the city was heavily bombed in WORLD WAR II.

Estonia. Situated on the Gulf of Finland, directly south of Finland itself, Estonia is the northernmost Baltic republic and covers an area of 17,370 square miles. The territory of present-day Estonia was annexed to Russia by Peter the Great in 1709. At the end of WORLD WAR I Estonia became an independent republic, governed by dictator Konstantin Paets (1934–39). The Soviet Union annexed the country in 1940. Since 1988, reforms initiated by Soviet leader Mikhail GORBACHEV have given rise to intense nationalism in Estonia and the establishment of an independence movement. Estonia has declared its sovereignty, but the situation remains tense and unresolved.

Estonian War of Independence (1917–1920). During WORLD WAR I Russian-controlled ESTONIA proclaimed independence on November 28, 1917, following the BOLSHEVIK REVOLUTION. Bolshevik troops advanced to retake the country, but the Germans occupied it. Estonia then declared independence again on February 24, 1918. Although the Treaty of BREST-LITOVSK granted independence to the Baltic states, Soviet forces invaded Estonia after Germany's defeat in renunciation of the treaty. The Estonians, with aid from a British flotilla, expelled the Soviets, and an anti-Bolshevik army from Estonia led by Nikolai Yudenich attempted to seize Petrograd (Leningrad) in October 1919. Leon TROTSKY hastily assembled a force and forced Yudenich's army to retreat to Estonia. Soviet recognition of Estonian independence came about in the Treaty of Dorpat (Tartu) on February 2, 1920. Soviet troops later occupied Estonia in 1940, when it became a Soviet republic.

E.T.: The Extra-Terrestrial (1982). Movie directed by Steven SPIELBERG; commercially the most successful motion picture ever made, it has grossed more than $500 million worldwide. The appearance of an alien creature in a small-town neighborhood creates panic, bewilderment and sympathy (in that order). The film was the result of a superbly coordinated blend of skills: Carlo Rambaldi, who designed the creature; Industrial Light and Magic, which created the special effects; cinematographer Allen Daviau, who captured the wonderfully atmospheric night effects; and director Spielberg. Although attacked by some critics as being emotionally manipulative, *E.T.* is undeniably a cultural phenomenon. Rather than the "monster" threatening normality, the situation is reversed, as in the "trick-or-treat" sequence, when E.T. is surrounded by frights more weird than he is, and terrifyingly reversed in the scenes in which government agents pursue him. The film consistently maintains the viewpoint of a child. It is like a cartoon, says Spielberg, in that adults are usually only *sensed*—only a leg or arm intruding into the frame. Even the lighting contributes to this effect. "We wanted that special kind of 'storytelling' look," cinematographer Daviau later remarked, "the light effects you see in old N.C. WYETH paintings . . . like a fairy tale."

ETA [*Euzakadi Ta Askatasumar*, "Basque Homeland of Liberty"]. A radical group split from the **Basque Nationalist Party** in 1959. It employs terrorist tactics.

Ethiopia. A country on the central plateau of East Africa; bordered by the Red Sea to the north, SUDAN to the west, KENYA to the south and SOMALIA to the east. Formerly known as Abyssinia, it is circled by mountains and has one navigable river, the Blue Nile. In 1882 ITALY, supported by Britain, took the Red Sea harbor of Aseb, but was stopped from moving inland by the Ethiopian army, at Dogali in 1887. In 1889 Menelik II came to power and ended a treaty with Italy, which then claimed Abyssinia as a protectorate. Menelik II denounced the claim, and his army crushed an Italian invasion at Adowa in 1896. Global respect grew, but the new capital at Addis Ababa became a diplomatic hotbed in which Ethiopia kept its autonomy by pitting the colonial powers against each other.

Italy never forgot its 1896 defeat and its interest in Ethiopia. In 1935 Benito MUSSOLINI's fascist fist came down heavily on the medieval country, which nevertheless resisted the weapons of modern warfare for six months before succumbing. Emperor HAILE SELASSIE escaped to Britain but returned in 1941 after Allied forces defeated the Italians. Great Britain labored to upgrade the army and bureaucracy, and full sovereignty was regained after the war; in 1952 Ethiopia took control of the former Italian colony of ERITREA. Eritrea was to have been an autonomous province, but unrest grew as its status was gradually eroded; Eritrean nationalist guerrillas battled the Ethiopian government throughout the 1960s and 1970s. After a cruel famine in September 1974, Haile Selassie was ousted by the military; in December 1974 Ethiopia was proclaimed a socialist state and began a closer relationship with the U.S.S.R. under left-wing radical Col. MENGISTU HAILE MARIAM. All-out war between Eritrean and Ethiopian factions started in 1975, while Somalia challenged Ethiopia's control of the Ogaden region. Intermittent famines persisted throughout the country. Rebel victories forced Mengistu to flee in 1991, ending the Marxist rule of Ethiopia.

Ethiopian–Eritrean Guerrilla War (1961–). Under British control (1941–52), Eritrea became an autonomous province in a federal ETHIOPIA, giving the latter a frontier on the Red Sea. Ethiopian undermining of Eritrean autonomy led to armed

ETHIOPIA

1928	Ras Tafari is crowned as Emperor Haile Selassie (Power of the Trinity) I.
1931-32	Haile Selassie gives Ethiopia its first written constitution and abolishes slavery.
1936	Ethiopia, never before colonized, is conquered and occupied by Italy under Mussolini.
1941	Italians are driven out by British troops during World War II.
1962	Ethiopia annexes Eritrea; secessionists intensify ongoing struggle for independence.
1974	Haile Selassie deposed; military Dergue (coordinating committee) led by Lt. Col. Mengistu Haile Mariam declares Ethiopia a socialist state, institutes large-scale land reform and expands offensive against Eritrean People's Liberation Front (EPLF).
1977	Mengistu government trains peasant militia of 100,000 with Cuban assistance and airlifts them to Eritrea to fight EPLF secessionists and to Ogaden, where rebels seek union with Somalia.
1985	An estimated 1,000,000 die of starvation; in the West Live Aid, an all-star rock telethon broadcast to 152 countries, raises $70 million for famine relief.
1991	Rebels make key advances against Ethiopian government troops; Mengistu flees the country; talks begin on forming new, democratic government.

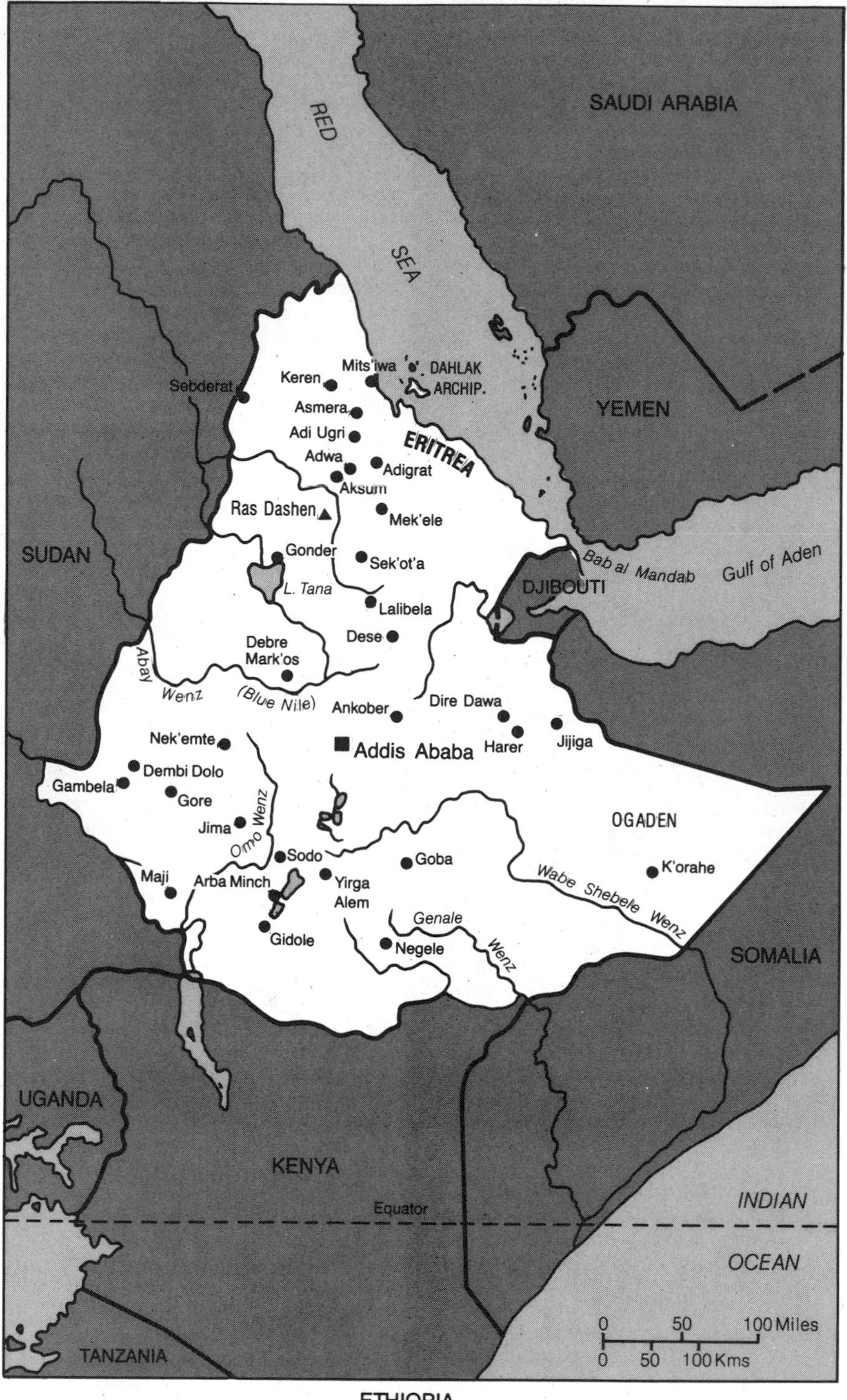

ETHIOPIA

resistance in 1961 by the Eritrean Liberation Front (ELF). Two additional guerrilla parties, the Eritrean Peoples Liberation Front, or EPLF (1970), and the ELF/PLF soon appeared. The rivals often fought among themselves, weakening the anti-Ethiopian effort; the war has been characterized by small skirmishes. A massive military push by Ethiopia (1967) forced out thousands of Eritrean refugees. Martial law, established in 1971, famines in 1973 and 1975, the fall of Ethiopia's imperial government in 1974, reduction of Ethiopian control to Eritrean urban centers by 1977 and rebellions in Ethiopia itself—all complicated the war. Ethiopian-Soviet-Cuban fighters suffered a severe loss at Asmara in 1978.

Ethiopian–Somali Border War (1963–). SOMALIA, the union of Italian and British Somaliland in 1960, demanded additional territories on independence—in DJIBOUTI, KENYA and the Haud, partly in ETHIOPIA'S OGADEN, where Somalis had grazed their herds. As early as 1963 Somalis and Ethiopians fought—Somalis rejecting Ethiopian control of the Ogaden. Discovery of oil (1973), the fall of Ethiopia's imperial government and a major revolt by Somalis in the Ogaden (1977) complicated the issue. In March 1978 Ethiopian troops, with Cuban and Soviet help, drove the Somalis from the Ogaden. The Somalis returned three months later as the Western Somali Liberation Front, and sporadic fighting along the Somali–Ethiopian border ensued.

Euler-Chelpin, Hans Karl August Simon von (1873–1964). German-Swedish biochemist. Euler-Chelpin was educated at the universities of Berlin, Strasbourg and Gottingen as well as at the Pasteur Institute. In 1898 he moved to Sweden, being appointed to the staff of the University of Stockholm, where in 1906 he became professor of general and inorganic chemistry. He also became director of the Institute of Biochemistry (1929), where he remained until his retirement in 1941. Although he became a Swedish citizen in 1902, he served Germany in both world wars. In 1904 important work by Arthur Harden had shown that enzymes contained an easily removable nonprotein part—a coenzyme. In 1923 Euler-Chelpin worked out the structure of the yeast coenzyme, showing that the molecule was made up of a nucleotide similar to that found in nucleic acid. Euler-Chelpin shared the 1929 NOBEL PRIZE for chemistry with Harden for this work. His son, **Ulf von Euler,** won the NOBEL PRIZE for physiology or medicine in 1970 for his work on neurotransmitters and the nervous system. Von Euler had earlier (1935) discovered the substance prostaglandin, which he named. From 1966 to 1975 Von Euler was president of the Nobel Foundation.

Euratom. See EUROPEAN ATOMIC ENERGY COMMUNITY.

European Atomic Energy Community [Euratom]. Community formed in 1958, along with the EUROPEAN ECONOMIC COMMUNITY (EEC), under the terms of the 1957 Treaty of Rome. Its purpose is to achieve the common development and growth of the peaceful nuclear industries of its member states. Euratom is particularly active in the development of nuclear power. It accomplishes its aims by providing technical assistance, permitting the free movement of nuclear materials and equipment, concluding contracts, setting standards for the protection of workers and the public, and establishing common procedures. Euratom became a part of the EUROPEAN COMMUNITY in 1967.

European Coal and Steel Community (ECSC). Proposed by French Foreign Minister Robert Schuman and formulated in the 1951 Treaty of Paris; officially founded in July 1952 by France, West Germany, Italy, Belgium, the Netherlands and Luxembourg, its goal was to unify the coal, iron and steel industries of the member countries. The organization established a single authority to encourage these industries, to eliminate tariffs and other bars to free trade and to favor a free labor market within member states. The community was extremely successful, and its achievements helped to foster other forms of European economic cooperation. The central institutions of the ECSC were merged with the EUROPEAN ECONOMIC COMMUNITY (EEC) and the EUROPEAN ATOMIC ENERGY COMMUNITY (Euratom) in 1967, forming the EUROPEAN COMMUNITY. When Great Britain, Denmark and Ireland became members of the Common Market in 1973, they also became members of the ECSC.

European Community [EC]. Collective term for three post-World War II organizations whose common aim is to create an economically integrated Europe. The European Community emerged from the economic philosophy of Jean MONNET and was implemented by France's Foreign Minister, Robert Schuman. The member communities are the EUROPEAN ECONOMIC COMMUNITY (EEC), the EUROPEAN COAL AND STEEL COMMUNITY (ECSC) and the EUROPEAN ATOMIC ENERGY COMMUNITY (Euratom). Under the provisions of a 1965 treaty, the executive agencies of these organizations were merged in 1967, forming an integrated administrative system. The original member states were Belgium, France, Luxembourg, the Netherlands, Italy and West Germany. In 1973 Denmark, Ireland and Great Britain became members; Greece joined in 1981 and Portugal and Spain in 1986. The European Community achieves its economic aims by creating a common customs tariff, attempting to reduce economic differences between regions, abolishing restrictions on international trade, allowing the free flow of people and services among member states, aiding overseas development, promoting the movement of capital among members, establishing common agricultural goals and, through Euratom, working together to develop the nuclear power industry and other peaceful uses for nuclear energy. Indeed, there is no aspect of the economic life of Europe, including taxes, currency, transportation, antitrust regulations, health, food and much more, that is not governed to some degree by the EC. Implementing the concept of a truly economically unified Europe, the Single European Act, ratified by the community in 1987, sets the close of 1992 as the deadline for the removal of all nontariff barriers among member states.

The community's main policymaking body is the Council of Ministers. With one representative from each member nation, it works closely with the Committee of Permanent Representatives. With a membership of 17 appointed by the council, the committee proposes legislation to the council and carries out the council's decisions in treaties. Both these administrative groups have their headquarters in Brussels; the European Parliament, headquartered in Strasbourg, is the community's advisory body, with a membership of over 500. Supervising its executive agencies, it has power over the budget and can dismiss the commission by the vote of a two-thirds majority. Located in Luxembourg, the European Court of Justice is the community's supreme court. With a judge from each member nation, it decides disputes among member countries that arise from community treaties or legislation. Made up of the heads of state of each member nation and formed in 1974, the European Council meets for general discussions three times a year.

For further reading:

Hackett, Clifford, *Cautious Revolution: The European Community Arrives*. Westport, Conn.: Greenwood, 1990.

European Defense Community [EDC]. Proposed European army, international in character but with common institutions, a kind of military counterpart of the EUROPEAN COMMUNITY. It was originally suggested by French Prime Minister Rene Pleven in 1950. The proposal was formalized in the 1952 Treaty of Paris, signed by the six nations that formed the EUROPEAN COAL AND STEEL COMMUNITY. In spite of the willingness expressed in the treaty, signatory nations, particularly France and Italy, were reluctant to establish this kind of supranational army. The EDC was nipped in the institutional bud when the French National Assembly, largely due to its fears of a reunified Germany, refused to ratify the Paris Treaty in 1954.

European Economic Community [EEC]. Also known as the Common Market, the EEC was formed to integrate the economies of Western Europe through the formation of one economic market for their resources. It is the best known and most important of the three communities in the EUROPEAN COMMUNITY. The EEC and the EUROPEAN ATOMIC ENERGY COMMUNITY (Euratom) were formed through the provisions of the 1957 Treaty of Rome, whose signatories were Belgium, France, Italy, Luxembourg, the Netherlands and West Germany. During the first decade of its operation, the EEC succeeded in abolishing trade restrictions, particularly tariffs, among member nations. It also formulated and put into operation a common tariff in dealing with other world nations. The EEC's success was reflected in the large increase its member states experienced in their production and in their domestic and international sales. The EEC was also responsible for developing a Common Agricultural Policy (CAP), established in 1962 to cover domestic prices paid to farmers and govern the import of all foreign foodstuffs. This community also adopted policies to permit the free flow of goods, people, services and capital among its members and to create uniform taxation. In addition, it worked to create standardized and improved social programs. Largely due to their early achievements, the EEC, Euratom and the EUROPEAN COAL AND STEEL COMMUNITY were formally merged under an umbrella administration in 1967, creating the European Community. In 1973 the EEC admitted Great Britain (whose membership had previously been blocked by French President DE GAULLE), Denmark and the Republic of Ireland as members. Norway, however, rejected a proposed membership by popular referendum in 1972. Greece joined the EEC in 1981, and Spain and Portugal became members in 1986. In addition, associate status has been granted to a number of nations. The Common Market set 1992 as the date for the abolition of trade and legal barriers among all nations of the EEC; there was also movement toward the creation of a common European currency (see ECU).

European Free Trade Association [EFTA]. An organization formed in 1959 to promote economic expansion and free trade; headquarters are in Geneva, Switzerland. EFTA's original seven members were Austria, Denmark, Great Britain, Norway, Portugal, Sweden and Switzerland; Finland joined as an associate member in 1961, and Iceland became a full member in 1970. All members were for a variety of political reasons originally opposed to membership in the EUROPEAN ECONOMIC COMMUNITY (EEC), which was formed two years earlier. EFTA removed all non-agricultural tariffs among member states, in a gradual reduction over a period of seven years. Unlike the EEC, member states maintained preexisting national tariffs on other imports. EFTA was less effective than the EEC in promoting European trade and providing sweeping economic reform. Denmark and Great Britain left EFTA in 1972 to join the EEC in 1973. Thereafter, the remaining six members negotiated a new agreement with the EEC, providing for mutual tariff removal and free industrial trade among all of Western Europe's major nations.

European Monetary System [EMS]. A system of financial exchange-rate controls among nations of the EUROPEAN ECONOMIC COMMUNITY; instituted in 1979. Members include Belgium, Denmark, France, Greece, Ireland, Italy, Luxembourg, the Netherlands and Germany. After initial opposition, Britain joined, but it has been wary of full participation. The EMS sets international currency exchange rates among member states. By the late 1980s, some European leaders had proposed a monetary union of all member states, in which individual national currencies would eventually be replaced by a common European currency, designated the ECU (for European Currency Unit). Supporters of this plan felt that it would improve trade among member nations; it would also be a step toward the political unification of Europe. British Prime Minister Margaret THATCHER strongly opposed this plan, feeling that Britain would lose its national sovereignty. Her open disagreement with leading members of her cabinet over endorsement of the plan led to her resignation in late 1990.

Evans, Bill (1929–1980). Jazz pianist Bill Evans, along with BEBOP practitioner Bud Powell, helped redefine the course of postwar improvisation. After early engagements with guitarist Mundell Lowe, clarinetist Tony Scott and vanguard composer George Russell, Evans catapulted to jazz stardom in 1958 when hired by trumpeter Miles DAVIS; his collaboration with Davis for the seminal recording "Kind of Blue" (1959), which elevated MODAL JAZZ as a viable alternate to bebop, crystallized Evans' place as one of jazzdom's most significant innovators. While assimilating the bebop lexicon of Bud Powell, Evans evolved a highly lyrical and advanced harmonic approach. His greatest accomplishments were achieved in trio contexts with double bass and drums, where highly contrapuntal, interactive dialogues with bassists Scott La Faro, Chuck Israels, Eddie Gomez and Marc Johnson set new standards for the jazz piano format. Evans' rhythmic flair, consistent inventiveness and well-modulated touch also made him a superb accompanist, as his recordings with flutist Jeremy Steig, guitarist Jim Hall and singer Tony Bennett demonstrate. Evans' influence can be discerned in the work of such major contemporary pianists as Chick COREA, Herbie HANCOCK and Richard Beirach. Evans also left a body of provocative compositions, including such standards of the jazz repertory as "Waltz for Debbie," "Peace Piece," "Funkallero" and "Peri's Scope."

For further reading:

Feather, Leonard, "Bill Evans," in *The Encyclopedia of Jazz in the Seventies*. New York: Horizon Press, 1976.

Evans, Charles "Chick" (1890–1979). Dean of amateur golf in the U.S. and the first person to win the U.S. Open and the U.S. Amateur championships in the same year (1916). Evans' career in the sport spanned eight decades. He began as a boy wonder and went on to become, successively, a national star and a golf official. He also founded a college scholarship program that enabled more than 4,000 former golf caddies to attend college. As a player, Evans competed in a record 50 successive U.S. amateur championships. He was voted into every golf hall of fame.

Evans, Gil [Ian Ernest Gilmore Green] (1912–1988). Canadian-born American composer and bandleader. His collaborations with trumpeter Miles DAVIS gave rise to some of the most influential JAZZ albums of the 1950s and 1960s. After Duke ELLINGTON, he was regarded as the most important post-World War II jazz composer and orchestrator. In later years, he embraced rock with as much vigor as he had embraced bebop.

Evans, Robley Dunglison (1907–). American physicist. Evans was educated at the California Institute of Technology, where he obtained his Ph.D. in 1932. He went to the Massachusetts Institute of Technology in 1934 and was appointed professor of physics (1945). In 1940 Evans suggested that radioactive potassium-40 could be of use in geologic dating. It is widespread in the earth's crust and has an exceptionally long halflife of more than a billion years, and allows estimates of the age of potassium-bearing rocks ranging from 100,000 to about 10 million years. This method proved to be particularly valuable as it permitted accurate dating beyond the limits of Willard LIBBY's carbon-14 technique.

Evans, Walker (1903–1975). American photographer. Born in St. Louis, Missouri, Evans began his career as a photographer in 1928. As a documentary photographer for the Farm Security Administation from 1935 to 1937, he created superbly precise photographs of the Depression-era South, sharp-focused images that ranged from beautifully composed, sign-dotted facades of rural buildings to the deeply lined faces of poor sharecroppers. In 1936, he accompanied writer James AGEE on a tour of Alabama, and his strikingly dignified portraits of tenant farmers and other working families are an integral part of their highly acclaimed book *Let Us Now Praise Famous Men* (1941). Walker's other projects included a series of portraits of New York City subway riders (1938–41). Walker was an editor, photographer and writer at *Fortune* magazine (1945–65) and a professor at Yale (1965–75). His books include *American Photographs* (1938), *Many Are Called* (1966), *Walker Evans: Photographs* (1971) and the posthumous *First and Last* (1978).

Evans and Novak. American journalists. Since 1970, Rowland Evans Jr. (1921–) and Robert Novak (1931–) have been coauthors of a successful, conservative political column that is syndicated in over 200 newspapers. The pair also publish a newsletter with a circulation of approximately 2,000, broadcast nightly commentary for Ted TURNER's cable television network and deliver over 50 lectures annually.

Everest, Mount. Mountain in the central Himalayas, on the edge of NEPAL and TIBET—at 29,028 ft., Everest is the tallest mountain in the world. After eight unsuccessful attempts, it was finally scaled on May 28, 1953, by New Zealand explorer and mountain climber Edmund HILLARY and Tenzing Norkay of Nepal. It has since been ascended by numerous expeditions. Everest was named after Sir George Everest, British surveyor of the Himalayas.

Everglades. Swampy area of about 5,000 square miles in southern Florida (U.S.); it spreads from Lake Okeechobee in the north to Florida Bay and is only seven feet above sea level at its highest point. The region is surrounded by water, saw grass, islands of vegetation, coastal mangrove forests and black slime. In the 20th century southern Florida's private and commercial real estate boom has drastically upset the area. Drainage and construction enterprises upset the water flow into the Everglades, and plant and animal life are continually menaced. Hunting, fishing and backwoods life continue to flourish in many sections. At the southwestern end is Everglades National Park (1.4 million acres).

Evergood, Philip (1901–1973). American painter. Born in New York City, Evergood studied at Eton, Cambridge, London's Slade School, New York's Art Students League and Paris' Academie Julian. He is best known for a mixture of figurative realism in his oils and etchings. Evergood gained particular recognition for his 1930s murals, which often explored themes of social deprivation and war. These large works include the narrative Richmond Hill Public Library mural (1936–37), *Cotton from Field to Mill* (1938) for the Post Office in Jackson, Georgia and a commission for Kalamazoo College. His later works included more symbolism and often portrayed specifically American subjects, as in *My Forebears Were Pioneers* (1940, Georgia Museum of Art, Athens), or religious imagery; for instance, *The New Lazarus* (1954, Whitney Museum, N.Y.C.).

Evers, Medgar W. (1926–1963). American CIVIL RIGHTS worker. Medgar Evers was born in Decatur, Mississippi. A graduate of Alcorn A&M University, he served in World War II and received two Bronze Stars. For the nine years preceding his death, Evers was Mississippi field secretary for the NAACP. In 1963, civil rights protests in the state were at their height, and early on the morning of June 12, Evers was ambushed and shot to death in the driveway of his Jackson, Mississippi, home, as he was returning from an integration rally at a nearby church. Blacks in Jackson held mass demonstrations on June 12 to protest the murder, resulting in 158 arrests. Ten days after the killing, Bryon de la Beckwith, of Greenwood, Mississippi, was charged with the crime, but two mistrials were declared and no conviction was ever obtained in the case. Beckwith was rearrested in 1991.

Evert, Chris(tine Marie) (1954–). American tennis player. The daughter of a tennis instructor, she was the dominant woman player of the 1970s. She first reached the finals of the U.S. Open at the age of 16 in 1971 but lost to Billie Jean KING. She turned professional in 1972 and won more than $4 million during the remainder of the decade. She was the U.S. Open singles champion from 1975 to 1978 and came back to win it again in 1980 and 1982. A three-time Wimbledon winner, in 1974 she shared the Wimbledon spotlight with her then-fiance Jimmy CONNORS, winner of the men's singles title that year. While married to tennis player John Lloyd, she was known as **Chris Evert Lloyd**.

Evian Agreements (March 1962). Overwhelmingly ratified by referenda in FRANCE (April, 1962) and ALGERIA (July, 1962), the Evian agreements ended the ALGERIAN WAR OF INDEPENDENCE fought against France since 1954 with an immediate cease-fire and a guarantee of French withdrawal by the end of the year. The talks leading up to the agreements were held in Evian-les-Bains, France; the main participants were French Prime Minister Georges POMPIDOU and the Algerian nationalist leader, Mohammed Ahmed BEN BELLA.

Evren, Kenan (1917–). Turkish statesman and president. Evren rose through an orthodox military career and became chief of the general staff. Under his guidance, the Turkish armed forces' National Security Council (NSC) took over the government in a bloodless coup in 1980. Under the new constitution of 1982, Evren became president of TURKEY for a nine-year term in 1982. His firm and straight-

Chris Evert uses her powerful two-handed backhand stroke to return the ball during the U.S. Open (1984).

forward personality has earned him respect and popularity. Known for his modesty, he has denied a desire for permanent political power.

Ewing, Sir James Alfred (1855–1935). British physicist. Ewing was educated at the University of Edinburgh, where he studied engineering. In 1890 he was appointed professor of applied mechanics at Cambridge but in 1903 moved into higher levels of administration—first as director of naval education, and from 1916 until his retirement in 1929 as principal and vice-chancellor of Edinburgh University. During WORLD WAR I Ewing was in charge of the cryptologists at the admiralty from 1914 to 1916. He described his work there in the posthumously published book *The Man in Room 40* (1939).

Ewing, William Maurice (1906–). American oceanographer. Ewing was educated at the Rice Institute, Houston and earned his Ph.D. in 1931. He taught at Lehigh University, Pennsylvania from 1934 until moving in 1944 to Columbia University, New York, where he organized the newly established Lamont Geological Observatory into one of the most important research institutions in the world. Ewing pioneered seismic techniques to obtain basic data on the ocean floors. He was able to establish that the Earth's crust below the oceans is only about 3–5 miles thick, while the corresponding continental crust averages 25 miles. In 1956 Ewing and his colleagues were able to show that the Mid-Atlantic Ridge constituted a mountain range extending throughout the oceans of the world and was some 40,000 miles long. In 1957, working with Marie Tharp and Bruce Heezen, he revealed that the ridge was divided by a central rift, which was in places twice as deep and wide as the Grand Canyon. Ewing also proposed, with William Donn, a mechanism to explain the periodic ice ages, but no hard evidence has yet been found to support that theory.

Ewins, Arthur James (1882–1957). British pharmaceutical chemist. Ewins went straight from school to join the brilliant team of researchers at the Welcome Physiological Research Laboratories at Beckenham. He worked on alkaloids with George Barger; in 1914, with Henry Dale, he isolated the important neurotransmitter acetylcholine from ergot. Following wartime experience in manufacturing arsenicals with the Medical Research Council, he became head of research with the pharmaceutical manufacturers May and Baker, where he remained until retirement in 1952. Under Ewins in 1939, the company produced sulfapyridine, one of the most important of the new sulfonamide drugs. An important later discovery was the antiprotozoal drug pentamidine (1948). He was elected a fellow of the Royal Society in 1943.

exclusionary rule. A controversial rule of evidence that bars the introduction of evidence gathered in violation of a defendant's constitutional guarantees. Under the U.S. Constitution's Fourth Amendment, citizens are protected against unreasonable searches and seizures. In 1914 the U.S. Supreme Court, in the case *Weeks v. United States*, announced that citizens could bar the introduction of evidence gathered in violation of their Fourth Amendment rights. The rule was later termed the "exclusionary rule."

Although the rule originally applied only to searches by federal officers, it was later applied to searches by state officers as well. The rule was attacked because it only indirectly deters unlawful searches; critics argue that the rule excludes potentially relevant evidence while failing to punish the police officers who unlawfully obtain the evidence. However, despite the criticism, the rule has withstood numerous proposals for its abolition.

executive privilege. The discredited concept that a special legal privilege protects the U.S. president's confidential conversations. In 1973, Congress initiated an investigation of the circumstances surrounding a break-in at DEMOCRATIC PARTY headquarters during the 1972 presidential campaign. The ensuing scandal that rocked the administration of President Richard M. NIXON became known as the WATERGATE scandal, after the hotel in which the break-in occurred. When a special prosecutor subpoenaed taped transcripts of President Nixon's conversations, the president asserted that the tapes were protected by an executive privilege—similar to the attorney–client privilege—that covered the tapes' confidentiality.

In UNITED STATES V. NIXON (1974) the U.S. Supreme Court unanimously rejected the concept of executive privilege, ruling that the prosecutor had a legal right to the tapes. After the tapes were made public the House of Representatives voted to initiate impeachment proceedings, after which President Nixon became the first U.S. president to resign from office.

existentialism. Twentieth-century school of philosophy, perhaps the most influential school of philosophical thought to have emerged in this century. Important 19th-century precursors to existentialism include German philosophers Arthur Schopenhauer and Friedrich Nietzsche and Russian novelist Fyodor Dostoyevsky, all of whom wrote of a world in which ultimate meaning was lacking and humans were called upon to confront the absurdity of existence. Another key precursive influence was PHENOMENOLOGY, a philosophical viewpoint developed largely by German philosopher Edmund HUSSERL, which stressed the epistemological necessity of viewing the world without preconceived value judgments. Existentialism holds that life has no meaning beyond that which each individual accords to it. Atheistic existentialists, such as Martin HEIDEGGER and Jean-Paul SARTRE, denied the existence of the divine. Religious existentialists, such as Martin BUBER and Gabriel MARCEL, asserted that the absurdity of life could be transcended through faith achieved by way of an existential encounter with the divine.

Exner, Virgil (1909–1973). American automobile designer usually credited with having a major role in the design on the 1947 Studebaker. Exner worked on automotive styling in the 1930s under Harley EARL at GENERAL MOTORS. In 1939 he went to work for Raymond LOEWY, eventually developing the Studebaker body that has come to be regarded as a classic of postwar American design. In 1949 he returned to Detroit to work for Chrysler.

Explorer I. The first American satellite, launched from CAPE CANAVERAL on January 31, 1958. After the Soviet Union launched the first artificial satellite (SPUTNIK I, Oct. 4, 1957), the U.S. was eager to send its own satellite into orbit and recoup some of its scientific and national prestige—especially after the launchpad explosion of a VANGUARD rocket in December 1957. Explorer I was a pointed cylinder 80 inches long and some 6 inches in diameter, weighing just over 18 pounds (including 11 pounds of instruments). It achieved an elliptical orbit with an apogee (farthest point from the Earth) of 1,587 miles and a perigee (closest point) of 219 miles. Explorer's instruments included a Geiger counter for measuring cosmic radiation, thermometers for measuring temperatures in space and inside the satellite, gauges to detect the number and effect of micrometeorites striking the satellite, and two radio transmitters to relay all this information to Earth. The instruments and experiments were designed by physicist James VAN ALLEN. Among the findings relayed to Earth by Explorer I was the existence of a belt of radiation above the equator, subsequently named the Van Allen Belt. The information received from Explorer I was made available to the world scientific community as part of the INTERNATIONAL GEOPHYSICAL YEAR of 1957–58. Over the following months, a series of Explorer satellites was sent into orbit. In August 1959, Explorer 6 became the first satellite to send back television pictures of the Earth from space.

Expressionism. Movement in art, literature and theater that developed in GERMANY from about 1910 to 1925. Influenced by the paintings of Vincent Van Gogh and Eduard MUNCH, Expressionist artists aimed at intense depictions of inner reality. Expressionism's distorted forms and often grotesquely unnatural colors led to increasingly abstract works. Wassily KANDINSKY, Paul KLEE and Oskar KOKOSCHKA were among the movement's artists. Inspired by such authors as Dostoyevsky and STRINDBERG, Expressionist writers—among them playwrights Georg KAISER and Ernst TOLLER—stressed a protagonist's psychological state. Expressionism's theme of individual alienation was echoed in the fiction of Franz KAFKA and the plays of both Eugene O'NEILL and Bertolt BRECHT. Brecht's dramatic technique also included such Expressionist devices as highly stylized action, dialogue and setting.

Exxon Valdez. On March 24, 1989, shortly after leaving the Alaskan port of Valdez with a full cargo (1,260,000 barrels) of crude oil, the tanker *Exxon Valdez* ran aground on a reef in Prince William Sound. Over the following days, some 11 million gallons of crude oil leaked into the sound, creating a slick more than 45 miles long—the worst oil spill in U.S. history. Much of the oil washed up on the numerous islands in the sound and on the mainland itself, causing extreme damage to local wildlife and threatening the region's fishing industry. Cleanup crews proved inadequate to cope with the magnitude of the spill, although hundreds of workers scoured the region during the next year. Meanwhile, a routine investigation had revealed that the *Exxon Valdez*'s captain had been drinking shortly before the accident and that the ship was being piloted by the third mate, who was not certified to operate the ship in those waters. The state of Alaska, the federal government and environmental groups claimed that the ship's owner, Exxon, had been criminally negligent. Exxon insisted that the disaster had been a simple accident and that no safety regulations had been violated. However, in 1991, Exxon pleaded guilty to four criminal misdemeanor charges and agreed to pay a $100 million fine—the largest fine ever assessed for an environmental crime. Moreover, the corporation agreed to pay $900 million over the next decade (until 2000) to settle civil suits brought by the state of Alaska and the U.S. government. However, the matter is still unsettled. The *Exxon Valdez* itself was towed to California, repaired and subsequently sailed under a new name.

Eyde, Samuel (1866–1940). Norwegian engineer and industrialist. Eyde was a civil engineer, trained in Berlin. Until 1900 he worked in Germany and on harbor and railroad-station projects in Scandinavia. There he became interested in industrial electrochemical processes—a subject of some potential in Scandinavia because of the availability of cheap hydroelectric power. In 1901 Eyde met Kristian Birkeland, with whom he developed a process (1903) for the fixation of atmospheric nitrogen by reaction of oxygen in an electric arc. Because the **Birkeland-Eyde process** needed plentiful and cheap supplies of electricity, it led to an explosive growth in the production of hydroelectric power. In 1900 Norway had an output of little more than 100,000 kilowatts; by 1905, production had jumped to 850,000 kilowatts. In the same year Eyde started the company Norsk Hydro-Elektrisk Kvaelstof, with the help of French capital, to produce fertilizers by the Birkeland-Eyde process. As a result of this, Norway's export of chemicals was to treble before the start of World War I. Eyde retired from the firm in 1917. He was also a member of the Norwegian Parliament.

Eyring, Henry (1901–1981). Mexican-American physical and theoretical chemist. Eyring was a grandson of American missionaries who had become Mexican citizens. He thus first came to America in 1912 as a Mexican citizen and did not take American citizenship until 1935. He was educated at the University of Arizona and the University of California, where he obtained his Ph.D. in 1927. He then held a number of junior appointments before joining the Princeton faculty in 1931, becoming professor of chemistry there in 1938. Eyring moved to a similar chair at the University of Utah, holding the post until his retirement in 1966. He wrote nine books and over 600 papers and as a chemist was as creative as he was productive. His main work was in the field of chemical kinetics with his transition-state theory. Eyring also worked on the theory of the liquid state and made contributions in molecular biology.

Eyskens, Gaston (1905–1988). Belgian prime minister (1949–50, 1958–61, 1968–72). A professional economist and academic, he served in the Belgian parliament for the Christian Social Party from 1939 to 1973, leading five Belgian governments between 1949 and 1972. Eyskens' first term ended in the controversy surrounding the return to BELGIUM of King LEOPOLD III. During a later tenure in office, he oversaw the independence of the Belgian Congo (now known as ZAIRE), but the onset of the Congolese Civil War (1960–68) forced his resignation. Eyskens also served as finance minister under several administrations.

Faber & Faber. British publishing company. A leading publisher of Modernist poetry and belles lettres in the 1920s and '30s (see MODERNISM), Faber & Faber grew out of the Scientific Press, which had been inherited by Lady Gwyer., With the arrival of Geoffrey Faber in 1924, the company became Faber & Gwyer. In 1929 he bought out Lady Gwyer and established Faber & Faber, although Sir Geoffrey was the only Faber involved. Faber, a poet himself, encouraged his staff to foster innovative writers. T.S. ELIOT served as a director for many years, publishing such writers as W.H. AUDEN, Ezra POUND, and Stephen SPENDER. Sir Geoffrey died in 1961, but the company has maintained its reputation as a leading literary publisher. Other Faber & Faber authors have included James JOYCE, Edith SITWELL, Sylvia PLATH, Philip LARKIN, Samuel BECKETT, Ted HUGHES and Seamus HEANEY, to name but a few.

Fabian Society. British socialist organization formed in 1884. The Fabian Society was begun by a group of middle-class intellectuals, including Beatrice and Sydney WEBB, who were committed to infusing the British system with socialistic principles of public welfare. They took their name from Quintus Fabius Maximus (d. 203 B.C.), a Roman general who avoided battles with the Carthaginians but drained them with a series of harassments instead. The Fabians rejected revolutionary tactics and felt that a long period of political evolution—encouraged by their well-intentioned needling—was necessary for democratic socialism to take hold. The society was instrumental in the formation of the Labour Representation Committee, which evolved into the LABOUR PARTY. The Fabian Society now acts largely as the party's research and support organization. Other prominent members of the society during its history have included George Bernard SHAW (who wrote many of the tracts they distributed), Rupert BROOKE and Shirley WILLIAMS.

"Face the Nation". Long-running CBS television public affairs program; premiered on Sunday, November 7, 1954, with newsman Ted Koop as moderator. Over the years hosts have included Stuart Novins, Howard K. Smith, Paul Niven, Martin Agronsky, George Herman and Leslie Stahl. The format has always been the same: leading politicians and other public figures answer questions from a panel of journalists. One of the most famous guests was Nikita KHRUSHCHEV, soon-to-be Soviet premier, who became something of a television celebrity in 1957 when he consented to be a guest on "Face the Nation." Filmed in Moscow, the program aired on June 2 and was subsequently acclaimed by TIME magazine as "the season's most extraordinary hour of broadcasting." The media experience may have served Premier Khrushchev well in 1959, in his "Kitchen Debate" in Moscow with Vice President Richard NIXON.

For further reading:

O'Connor, John E., ed., *American History, American Television.* New York: Frederick Unger, 1983.

Fadeyev, Alexander Alexandrovich (1901–1956). Novelist. He was influenced by Tolstoy's psychological realism and led campaigns against unorthodox trends in literature. He fought in the revolution and became a member of the Communist Party in 1918. During the 1930s and 1940s he was implicated in the purge of writers. His work includes *The Rout* (1927) and *The Young Guard* (1945), which is probably his best book and which he revised in 1951 following criticism that he had failed to show the party's leading role. He committed suicide after the official denunciation of STALIN.

Faeroe Islands. Island group in the North Atlantic, between the Shetland Islands and ICELAND. Colonized by Norsemen in the eighth century A.D., the Faeroes have belonged to DENMARK since 1380. Mounting patriotism in the 19th century nurtured a longing for independence, which grew during WORLD WAR II when Denmark fell to GERMANY in 1940 and Great Britain was forced to set up a protectorate. After the war, the islands were awarded self-government under the authority of Denmark.

Fagerholm, Karl-August (1901–1984). Three-time prime minister of FINLAND, and one of its best known post-World War II political figures, Fagerholm was premier during a major crisis with the U.S.S.R. in 1958; his coalition government fell within four months because of silent Soviet pressure and internal squabbling. A Social Democrat, Fagerholm was a conciliatory politician who advocated Finnish cooperation with Scandinavian nations. He served as premier three times, as speaker of the chamber five times and as a member of parliament for 36 years. He retired from politics in 1966.

Fahd (1923–). Member of the Saudi royal family; king and prime minister of SAUDI ARABIA (1982–). Fahd ibn Abd al-Aziz Al Saud held the posts of second deputy premier and interior minister in the government of King FAISAL; during this time he was also chairman of the council that formulated Saudi Arabia's oil and investment policies. On Faisal's assassination he became first deputy prime minister in the new government of his half-brother, King Khalid, and was viewed as the power behind the throne. He became king following Khalid's death. A leading Arab moderate, Fahd has pursued a pro-Western policy and used the nation's oil wealth to modernize Saudi Arabia while maintaining the nation's Islamic heritage. Fahd strongly supported the UN allied coalition against IRAQ during the PERSIAN GULF WAR; more than 500,000 coalition soldiers were stationed in Saudi Arabia during the crisis.

Faid Pass. Pass in the Atlas Mountains of northern Tunisia. On February 14 and 20, 1943, during the North African phase of WORLD WAR II, German forces led by ROMMEL targeted the Tunisian mountains to their west via the Faid and KASSERINE passes. After initial setbacks, the invading Americans counterattacked and recaptured the Faid Pass in April, concluding the last Axis offensive in North Africa.

Douglas Fairbanks and Mary Pickford at Pickfair, their palatial California estate.

Fairbank, William Martin (1917–1989). American physicist. Working at Stanford University in California, Fairbank specialized in experiments in low-temperature superconductivity. He also worked on research into the existence of gravity waves and the subatomic particles known as quarks. Some of his work formed the basis for an ongoing multimillion-dollar satellite project intended to test a final unproven prediction from Albert EINSTEIN's general theory of relativity.

Fairbanks, Douglas [born Douglas Elton Ulman] (1883–1939). American motion picture actor and producer whose swashbuckling style and physical agility dominated 43 films from 1915 to 1934. Born in Denver, Colorado, Fairbanks began acting in the Frederic Warde Shakespeare Company. After a succession of juvenile roles on Broadway, he came to HOLLYWOOD in 1914 under contract with the newly established Triangle Film Company. For the next five years he exploited talents for comedy and physical action in dozens of peppy, contemporary comedies breezily satirizing the fads and social pretensions of the day (for example, *His Picture in the Papers, Wild and Wooly, When the Clouds Roll By*). But with the unexpected success of a period drama about old California, *The Mark of Zorro* (1920), Fairbanks settled in to a notable, expensively produced series of costume dramas for which he is best remembered today: *The Three Musketeers* (1921), *Robin Hood* (1922), *The Thief of Bagdad* (1924), *The Black Pirate* (1926), *The Gaucho* (1927), and others. He married Mary PICKFORD in 1920 and the couple established residence in BEVERLY HILLS in a home they named "Pickfair," the prototype of subsequent celebrity homes in the area. He retired in 1934 after his last film, *The Private Life of Don Juan,* and devoted the rest of his life to traveling and planning film projects with his son, **Douglas Fairbanks, Jr.** Apart from his inimitable pantomimic style—a blend of balletic grace and rough-and-tumble acrobatics—Fairbanks was a powerful force in the film industry. With Pickford, Charles CHAPLIN and D.W. GRIFFITH, he formed UNITED ARTISTS in 1919. *The Black Pirate* introduced Technicolor to the commercial arena. He also served as the first president of the Academy of Motion Picture Arts and Sciences. He died of a heart attack in 1939. Fairbanks' son from an earlier marriage, **Douglas Fairbanks, Jr.** was also a noted actor and producer.

For further reading:

Tibbetts, John, and James Welsh, *His Majesty the American: The Films of Douglas Fairbanks, Sr.* Cranbury, New Jersey: A. S. Barnes, 1977.

Fairbanks. U.S. city in central ALASKA, at the intersection of the Tanana and Chena rivers. Fairbanks was established on the site of a 1902 gold strike and was named after a U.S. vice president. The construction of the Alaska Railroad, major highways (most notably the ALASKA HIGHWAY in 1942) and an international airport, the northernmost in North America, greatly helped in making Fairbanks the transportation and distribution center of the Alaskan interior.

Fair Deal. President Harry TRUMAN's domestic program. Following President Franklin ROOSEVELT's death, Vice President Truman assumed the presidency in 1945. After the end of WORLD WAR II, Truman sought to continue and extend the programs initiated by FDR's NEW DEAL reforms. Although Truman put forward his domestic program shortly after assuming office, he first used the term "fair deal" in his 1949 State of the Union address. The Fair Deal proposals centered on a full-employment law, a higher minimum wage, fair employment practices and extension of the social security program. Truman also called for a national housing program to eliminate slums, better price supports for farmers and increased aid to education. Although much of the program was enacted, the results were less dramatic than the New Deal reforms. Shortly after Truman's reelection in 1948 the KOREAN WAR diverted attention from the Fair Deal program.

Fair Labor Standards Act. The Fair Labor Standards Act (1938), more commonly known as the Wage-Hour Law, prohibits oppressive child labor, establishes maximum working hours and fixes a federal minimum wage for many workers. Although Congress had made earlier attempts at regulating wages and hours in private employment, the Supreme Court had struck down all prior laws as beyond congressional power.

The act outlaws oppressive child labor, which includes any labor for a child under 16 years of age and labor that is hazardous to the health of a child under age 18. It establishes 40 hours as the maximum workweek, unless overtime pay is paid at one and one half times the normal wage. The act also sets a minimum wage, which has been gradually increased over the years. The wage and hour rules do not apply to administrative or professional workers, outside sales reps and certain service and retail workers.

Fairport Convention. English folk-rock group; founded in 1966, they created folk-rock virtually out of whole cloth. Their members included Ashley Hutchings, Simon Nicol, Richard Thompson, Martin Lamble, Judy Dyble and Ian Matthews. Their breakthrough album, *Fairport Convention,* included original material and covers, but by their third album they were performing almost entirely their own work. Their membership changed over the years, as performers pursued solo careers, and the band experienced highs and lows of critical and financial success. The group has also split and reformed but continued to release albums into the 1980s.

Faisal (1906–1975). King of SAUDI ARABIA (1964–75). Faisal served as prime minister from 1953 to 1964, before succeeding his brother, King Saud, as king. He used Saudi Arabia's oil wealth to transform the country into a modern nation. In the early 1970s, following the ARAB–ISRAELI WAR OF 1973, he directed the OPEC oil embargo against the U.S. to show his displeasure with America's support for ISRAEL. Faisal was assassinated by his nephew, Prince Faisal ibn Musad Abdel Aziz. He was succeeded by his half-brother, Crown Prince Khalid Abdel Aziz Al Saud.

Falange. Spanish extremist political group that favored nationalism and a fascist-type political and economic structure. It was founded in 1933 by Jose Antonio Primo de Rivera, son of the former Spanish dictator Miguel PRIMO DE RIVERA. After Jose Antonio's execution by Spanish Republicans in 1936 at the start of the SPANISH CIVIL WAR, the party moved closer toward a FASCISM inspired by MUSSOLINI. General Francisco FRANCO organized the party into the only legal political movement in Nationalist SPAIN. The Falange, under Franco's leadership, ruled Spain for many years, but in later years Franco moved away from its ideology. The Falange's influence declined considerably, and it was formally abolished on April 1, 1977.

Falkland Islands [Spanish: Islas Malvinas]. Cluster of 200 islands in the South Atlantic, 300 miles east of the Strait of Magellan, now a dependent territory of the UNITED KINGDOM. Discovered and claimed by John Davis in 1592, it was colonized from 1765 to 1774, and the islands have been continuously occupied since 1833. ARGENTINA also claims the islands, although it failed at colonizing them between 1829 and 1833. The remote islands were the site of a strategic naval battle during WORLD WAR I when on December 8, 1914, a British naval force shattered the German Pacific squadron, which had approached from the Straits of Magellan. In early April 1982, Argentina, asserting its claim to the islands, seized them by force. Great Britain quickly sent a large task force to recover the Falklands and set up a "total exclusion zone" around the islands. In late April the British recovered South Georgia, a chain of islands some 800 miles east of the Falklands, then moved on to attack the main islands. The Argentine cruiser *General Belgrano* and the British destroyer *Sheffield* were sunk, with much loss of life. In May the British established a beachhead on East Falkland. Darwin and then Stanley were secured, and by June 22 the British had triumphed. Although diplomatic relations have since been reestablished between Great Britain and Argentina, there has been no discussion of Britain's continued sovereignty in the islands.

Falkland Islands/Islas Malvinas War (1982). The dispute over control of the Falkland Islands (Sp. *Islas Malvinas*) dates back to the 17th century. In 1833 the British reinforced their claim by deporting Argentine inhabitants, but Latin American nations supported the Argentine claims. Negotiations ended unresolved on February 27, 1982; Argentine forces invaded the Falklands on April 2, 1982, securing all points. Diplomatic efforts to defuse the crisis failing, British Prime Minister Margaret THATCHER dispatched a large naval task force under Rear Admiral John Woodward. The Argentine Air Force inflicted extensive damage on the British fleet. On May 21, 1982 British infantry landed at Port San Carlos led by Major General Jeremy Moore; after establishing a bridgehead they moved inland, forcing the surrender of the Argentines under General Mario Menendez at Stanley on June 14, 1982. The British victory boosted Thatcher's government, while bringing down Argentine president Leopoldo Fortunato GALTIERI.

Fall, Albert (1861–1944). U.S. secretary of the interior involved in the TEAPOT DOME SCANDAL. A rancher, Fall was elected senator from New Mexico. When Warren Harding became president in 1921 he appointed his friend Fall to the Interior cabinet post. In 1922 Fall secretly leased the Navy oil reserve lands at Elk Hills, Calif., and Teapot Dome, Wy., to oil companies controlled by his crony Edward Doheny and Harry Sinclair. About the same time he received $100,000 from Doheny and a $260,000 "loan" from Sinclair. When the leases were revealed, Fall at first explained the $100,000 payment as a loan from an eccentric millionaire named Edward McLean, who promptly denied making any such loan. Fall eventually admitted the source of the funds. The press had a field day when Doheny termed the $100,000 payment "a mere bagatelle." Fall eventually went to prison for one year but emerged an invalid until his death in 1944.

Falla, Manuel de (1876–1946). Spanish composer. Born in Cadiz, he studied at the Royal Conservatory in Madrid and with composer Felipe Pedrell. Living in Paris from 1907 to 1914, he met DEBUSSY, DUKAS and RAVEL and was somewhat influenced by their impressionist style. He settled in Granada in 1921, living there until 1939 when he moved to Argentina, where he died. Falla's music is brilliantly Spanish in character. An expert on flamenco, he succeeded in capturing its driving rhythms while incorporating the brilliance and color of his homeland into the classic structure of his compositions. His most celebrated works include the opera *La Vida Breve* (1913); *Nights in the Gardens of Spain* (1911–15), which symphonically evokes Granada; and his most famous compositions, the ballets *El Amor Brujo* (1914–15) and *The Three-Cornered Hat* (1917). He also created many piano pieces, songs, orchestral works, the guitar solo *Homenajes* (1920–39), and *La Atlantida*, a massive cantata unfinished at his death and completed by his ex-pupil Ernesto Halffter.

Fall Gelb [German for "Yellow Case" or "Yellow Plan"]. "Fall Gelb" was the code name for the German invasion of France, Luxembourg and the Low Countries (Belgium and the Netherlands) in May–June 1940. In broad terms, the plan of attack was similar to the German plan of World War I, the SCHLIEFFEN PLAN. However, it was much better executed. The Germans were well organized and were able to use their superiority in planes and tanks to overrun France in six weeks. However, they failed to destroy the British and French armies at DUNKIRK.

Fallingwater. Famous house by Frank Lloyd WRIGHT at Bear Run, Pa., designed in 1936 for the Kaufmann family of Pittsburgh. Wright placed dramatic concrete cantilevers over a rocky waterfall in a wooded, rural site. The house is generally regarded as one of Wright's most striking masterpieces. Its dramatic form and the charm of its interiors are universally admired. It is now open to the public.

Falwell, Jerry (1933–). American fundamentalist Christian preacher, televangelist and political activist. While a student at Lynchburg College, Virginia, Falwell became a "born-again" Christian; after graduating from a Baptist Bible college, he started his own church in Lynchburg. He took to the television airwaves with a weekly program, "The Old Time Gospel Hour," which was eventually broadcast over some 350 stations throughout the U.S., and gained a large following. In 1979 Falwell founded the **Moral Majority,** a grass-roots conservative lobbying group that was influential throughout the 1980s. The Moral Majority was formed to counter what Falwell and his followers saw as a rising tide of permissiveness, both in politics and in everyday life. Falwell stressed traditional values and scorned contemporary liberal movements; he was a strong supporter of Ronald REAGAN and other conservative candidates in 1980. Falwell disbanded the Moral Majority in 1989, saying that the organization had achieved its goal of getting conservative Christians involved in politics. He subsequently devoted himself to his Lynchburg ministry.

Fangio, Juan Manuel (1911–). Argentine race car driver who dominated Grand Prix auto racing during the 1950s. Five-time world Grand Prix champion, Fangio won 16 Grand Prix races during the decade. After his racing career ended he became president of the Argentine branch of Mercedes-Benz.

Fang Lizhi (1937–). Chinese astrophysicist. Fang's name became internationally known in early 1987 when he was accused by the Communist Party of instigating student demonstrations for general democratic reforms. Fang was expelled from the party for promoting "bourgeois liberalization," but he retained his academic posts and in January 1988 was promoted from fourth- to second-grade academician of the Chinese Academy of Sciences. Dubbed by some the Chinese SAKHAROV, Fang does not want to be considered a dissident and believes that China will eventually become democratic. He and his wife took refuge in the U.S. embassy in Beijing following the army crackdown in June 1989; they later moved to the U.S. (See also TIANANMEN SQUARE MASSACRE.)

Fanon, Frantz Omar (1925–1961). Martinique-born psychiatrist and social critic. Fanon, a black raised under French colonial rule, was seared as a youth by racism and the cultural prejudices of colonialism. He examined the psychological and political significance of these early experiences in his first major work, *Black Skin, White Masks* (1952), which argued that white colonialism imposed an existentially false and degrading existence upon its black victims to the extent that it demanded their conformity to its imperialistic social values. In 1953 Fanon began to practice in a psychiatric ward in Algeria and soon allied himself with the Algerian liberation movement that sought to throw off French rule. In his subsequent writings—*Studies in a Dying Colonialism* (1959), *The Wretched of the Earth* (1961), and *Toward the African Revolution* (1964)—Fanon argued for violent revolution as the only means of ending colonial repression and cultural trauma in the Third World.

Fantasia. Classic Walt DISNEY motion picture. *Fantasia* combined the talents of conductor Leopold STOKOWSKI and Disney, excerpts from classical music and visual interpretations by the Disney animators. Although it lost money after its premiere on November 13, 1940 at the Broadway Theatre in New York (the location of the premiere of Disney's *Steamboat Willie* in 1928), it has since been frequently revived and was accorded cult status by audiences in the 1960s. Stokowski recorded the eight classical selections in the Disney Hyperion Studios and at the Philadelphia Academy of Music. The sequences and their visual interpretations were as follows, in chronological order: 1) "Toccata and Fugue in D minor," by J.S. Bach—abstract shapes shift and change through a universe of freely mixing colors; 2) "The Nutcracker Suite," by Tchaikovsky—flowers and fairies twinkle in the muted twilight; 3) "The Sorcerer's Apprentice," by Paul DUKAS—MICKEY MOUSE brings to life a bunch of sinister brooms; 4) *Le Sacre du Printemps* (THE RITE OF SPRING), by Igor STRAVINSKY—dinosaurs galumph about a primeval landscape; 5) the Sixth Symphony ("Pastoral"), by Beethoven—cupids, nymphs and satyrs cavort about Mount Olympus; 6) "Dance of the Hours," by Ponchielli—hippos and alligators whirl in a mad ballet; 7) "Night on Bald Mountain," by Moussorgsky—an amphibian creature presides over an unholy bacchanale; 8) "Ave Maria," by Schubert—a pilgrim's procession greets the dawning light. Not merely a tour de force of state-of-the-art animation, it was a technical innovation in sound. Stokowski used a nine-track sound system that in some theaters was reproduced by a number of sound horns placed behind the screen and around the walls. This "Fantasound" anticipated stereophonic sound. Disney's attempt to popularize classical music has been both praised and damned by critics. "Gee," Disney allegedly said after viewing the "Pastoral" sequence, "this'll make Beethoven!" Which perhaps accounts for the extra twinkle in Mickey's eye—provided by animators Fred Moore and Les Clark, who placed pupils in his eyes for the first time.

Far Eastern Republic (1920–22). The Far Eastern Republic served as a buffer state between Soviet Russia and Japan. One of the first "people's democracies," it was annexed by the U.S.S.R. after the Japanese left Vladivostok.

Farewell to Arms, A (1929). Novel by Ernest HEMINGWAY. The story takes place during WORLD WAR I ON THE ITALIAN FRONT and depicts a love affair between an American soldier and an English nurse. The novel highlights the transience of human existence and emotions and contains vivid and acclaimed portrayals of the war—particularly the retreat from Caporetto. The publication of *A Farewell to Arms* firmly established Hemingway's reputation as an important literary figure of the time.

Fargue, Leon-Paul (1876–1947). Fargue was an enduring force in the various French poetic movements of the first half of this century. In his earliest verse of the 1890s, he allied himself with the symbolist circle. *Tancrede* (1894) is his major work of this period. In the years prior to World War I, Fargue was influenced by cubist poetics, as is evident in *Poemes* (1912) and *For Music* (1918) (see CUBISM). His later collections include *Espaces* and *Sous la Lampe* (both 1929). A noted raconteur, Fargue was acquainted with most of the major French literary figures of the day. His memoirs, *Le Pieton de Paris* (1939), remain a key source work of the period.

Faris, Muhammed (1951–). Syrian cosmonaut-researcher. The first Syrian in space (July 22–30, 1987), Faris spent six days aboard the Soviet space station *Mir* after being launched and landed there by the SOYUZ TM-3 spacecraft. A pilot in the Syrian air force, Faris, with Munir Habib, was one of two Syrians to be trained for the mission in the Soviet Union's Star City complex.

Farjeon, Herbert (1887–1945). British critic, author and revue librettist. Farjeon began as an actor and was a long-time theater critic in London. He is best known for his highly successful revues, such as *Nine Sheep* (1938) and *The Little Review* (1939). He also collaborated with his sister, **Eleanor Farjeon** (1881–1965)—herself a successful children's author—on such musical plays as *The Glass Slipper* (1944).

Farkas, Bertalan (1949–). Hungarian cosmonaut-researcher. The first Hungarian citizen to make a space flight, Farkas, a skilled air force pilot, was aboard Soyuz 36 (May 1980).

Farley, James A. (1888–1976). American politician. A life-long Democrat, Farley rose through the party ranks in his native New York, becoming state DEMOCRATIC PARTY chairman. In this position he managed Franklin D. ROOSEVELT's electoral races for governor and finally for president in 1932. After managing Roosevelt's landslide reelection in 1936, Farley was able to quip "As goes Maine, so goes Vermont." Roosevelt appointed Farley postmaster general. Farley, who also became chairman of the national Democratic committee, was responsible for building grassroots enthusiasm for Roosevelt's NEW DEAL reform program. In 1940, however, Farley and Roosevelt had a falling out—perhaps over Roosevelt's plan to run for a third term—and Farley quit his twin national posts. He became an executive with the Coca-Cola Corporation but remained active in politics until his death.

Farnsworth House. Famous project of Ludwig MIES VAN DER ROHE, weekend house beside the Fox River near Plano, Illinois, built from 1945 to 1951 for Dr. Edith Farnsworth. The house is an ultimate example of the architect's effort to reduce building to minimal and universal terms. It consists of floor and roof planes supported by eight steel columns placed along their outer edges, with an all-glass rectangular enclosure that extends about two-thirds of the building's length. The interior is totally open except for a small rectangular block enclosing baths, utilities, and storage. Generally regarded as one of Mies' finest works, the house was unfortunately the cause of a bitter and notorious conflict between architect and client. The design seems to have been the inspiration for the equally famous Glass House of Philip JOHNSON at New Canaan, Conn.

Farouk, the 27-year-old king of Egypt, in uniform as commander of the royal armed forces (1947).

Farouk (1920–1965). King of EGYPT (1938–52). Farouk attained his majority in 1938 and ousted the WAFD government of Nahas Pasha, who had ruled following the death of Farouk's father in 1936. He tried to launch schemes of land reform and economic advancement, but corruption was rife, and his popularity rapidly dwindled. Strains in relations with Britain during and after WORLD WAR II and failure of the army in PALESTINE (1948) focused criticism against him, and he was forced to abdicate as a result of a military coup in 1952.

Farr, Tommy (1914–1986). Welsh boxer. After winning the British heavyweight crown, Farr nearly took the world heavyweight title from Joe LOUIS in an August 1937 match at Yankee Stadium. In that title defense by Louis, Farr became the first of only three challengers to go the 15-round distance. Farr fought professionally from 1926 to 1953, winning 80 of 125 fights.

Farrand, Clair Loring (1895–1981). American electronics engineer and inventor. A pioneer in the radio industry, Farrand invented the radio loudspeaker. He worked with WARNER BROS., developing sound, color and cinematography technologies. He also founded and headed several companies, which together eventually held more than 1,000 patents on devices ranging from B-52 bombsights to simulator windows used in the U.S. space program.

Farrar, Geraldine (1882–1967). American opera singer. A great soprano of the early 20th century, Farrar made her debut with the Berlin Royal Opera in 1901 as Marguerite in *Faust*. After successful performances throughout Europe, she made her debut with the Metropolitan Opera in 1906 as Juliet. In 1907 she sang the title role in the American premiere of PUCCINI's *Madama Butterfly,* the role with which she became most identified. Other roles for which she was famous were Carmen and Tosca. She was a star of the Met until her retirement in 1922 and appeared in many world premieres, such as Paul DUKAS' *Ariane et Barbe-Blue* (1911). In addition, she acted in more than a dozen films, including Cecil B. DE MILLE's *Maria Rosa* (1915). She went on several concert tours before finally giving up public life to pursue philanthropic works.

Farrell, James T(homas) (1904–1979). American novelist. Farrell was born in Chicago and worked at a variety of jobs to finance his education at the University of Chicago and later New York University. A naturalistic writer, he is best known for his trilogy consisting of the novels *Young Lonigan* (1932), *The Young Manhood of Studs Lonigan* (1934) and *Judgement Day* (1935). The novels portray Studs Lonigan, a poor Irish Catholic, from his childhood, through his various attempts, some illegal, to get ahead, and ultimately, his death from a heart condition aggravated by poverty. Farrell somberly depicts Chicago during the GREAT DEPRESSION and the deadening effects of poverty, both physical and spiritual. His writing has been compared to that of Theodore DREISER, whose work Farrell edited in *A Dreiser Reader* (1962). Other works include *The Collected Poems of James T. Farrell* (1965), *The Dunne Family* (1976) and *The Death of Nora Ryan* (1978).

Farrell, Suzanne (1945–). American dancer. One of the outstanding ballerinas of the 1960s–1980s, she is most closely identified with the works of George BALANCHINE. Farrell joined the NEW YORK CITY BALLET in 1961 and quickly became Balanchine's muse, creating roles in many of his ballets, such as *Don Quixote* (1965) and *Jewels* (1967). From 1970 to 1974 she was the star ballerina with the Ballet of the 20th Century and created roles in such ballets as *Sonate* (1971) and *Nijinsky, Clown of God* (1971) by Maurice BEJART. Returning to NYCB in 1975, she continued to create roles in Balanchine ballets, such as *Vienna Waltzes* (1977). She retired from dancing in 1989.

For further reading:

Farrell, Suzanne, with Toni Bentley, *Holding On to the Air: An Autobiography*. New York: Summit Books, 1990.

fascism. Political ideology and form of government that emphasizes a strong one-party dictatorship (often embodied in a charismatic leader), extreme militarism and the glorification of the state. Fascist governments seek to instill uniformity and obedience in the populace, which is often manipulated by means of PROPAGANDA and coerced by secret police and informers. Unlike COMMUNISM, which professes to serve the people and to be an international movement, fascism makes little pretense about its dictatorial character or its nationalist and often racist aims. Fascism also allows privately owned industries, although there is some state regulation of the economy. In other respects, however, fascism and communism have generally proved to be merely two sides of the same totalitarian coin. Most 20th-century fascist governments have arisen during severe political and economic crises as people looked for simple, bold solutions to complex social problems. The two main manifestations of fascism in the 20th century occurred in ITALY under Benito MUSSOLINI from 1922 to 1945, and in GERMANY under Adolf HITLER from 1933 to 1945. (However, fascism and NAZISM are not technically equivalent.) Military regimes incorporating some aspects of fascism have also operated in SPAIN (under FRANCO and the FALANGE, 1939–75), HUNGARY (during WORLD WAR II), ROMANIA (again during WORLD WAR II, under ANTONESCU and the Iron Guard), CHILE (under Gen. PINOCHET, 1973–89) and elsewhere. There have also been fascist-style political parties in FRANCE, the U.K. (led by Oswald MOSLEY) and other democratically governed countries, but these have had limited appeal. While fascism has proved popular in certain places at certain times during the 20th century, it has not proved a durable ideology. At most times and in most places, "fascist" and "fascism" have been used as pejorative terms.

Fassbinder, Rainer W(erner) (1946–1982). German film director and actor. Fassbinder was one of the most prolific and controversial directors of the postwar era. He began his career in the theater, working with the avant-garde Anti-Theater in West Germany in the 1960s. Over a 13-year film career that began in 1969, Fassbinder completed an astonishing 41 films, for most of which he wrote the screenplays and appeared as an actor. Left-wing in his politics and a self-proclaimed homosexual, Fassbinder aroused strongly partisan or hostile feelings among cinema audiences. The political and social corruption of postwar Germany was a major theme in his films. Among Fassbinder's best-known films are *The Marriage of Maria Braun* (1979), *Lola* (1981) and *Veronika Voss* (1982). Fassbinder also directed a critically acclaimed 15.5-hour epic, *Berlin, Alexanderplatz* (1979).

Fast, Howard (Melvin) (1914–). American novelist, playwright and screenwriter. Fast is best known for his popular historical novels, which include *Two Valleys* (1933), written when he was eighteen; *Spartacus* (1951), which he first published privately and for which he later co-authored the screenplay with Dalton Trumbo (1960); and the trilogy with more modern themes—*The Immigrants* (1977, televised 1979), *The Second Generation* (1978) and *The Establishment* (1979). Fast was a member of the Joint Anti-Fascist Refugee Committee and as a result he was called before the HOUSE UN-AMERICAN ACTIVITIES COMMITTEE. Following his refusal to cooperate with the committee, he was jailed for a period in 1950. Many of Fast's novels have been adapted for film and television. Other works include the plays *The Hammer* (1950) and *The Crossing* (1962); the screenplays *The Hill* (1965) and *The Hessian* (1971), which were both based on his novels of the same titles; and the novels *The Dinner Party* (1987), *The Pledge* (1988) and *The Confession of Joe Cullen* (1989).

Fatah Revolutionary Council. Palestinian terrorist organization founded in 1974 by ABU NIDAL. It was a radical breakaway group from Yassir ARAFAT's Al-Fatah and the PALESTINE LIBERATION ORGANIZATION (PLO). The council received financial, military and intelligence aid from East Germany, Poland, North Korea, Iraq, Syria and Libya. Its targets included Israel, Westerners, Arab moderates and members of rival Palestinian organizations. At its peak during the late 1970s/early 1980s, the council had some 400 members operating in tightly-knit secret cells in the Mideast, Europe and Asia, plus more than 1,000 Palestinian recruits in training. It claimed more than 900 victims in at least 20 countries, including 56 people killed in the hijacking of an Egyptian airliner in 1985, 21 in the bombing of an Istanbul synagogue in 1986 and several dozen Arab diplomats and PLO officials assassinated in various operations. In 1988 the U.S. State Department characterized the group as "the most dangerous terrorist organization in existence."

Father Brown. Fictional priest-detective created by G.K. CHESTERTON. The most important detective character created in this century, Brown has been ranked by Ellery QUEEN as one of literature's greatest detectives, on a par with Poe's Auguste Dupin and Arthur Conan DOYLE's SHERLOCK HOLMES. Brown first appeared in "The Blue Cross" in *The Storyteller* magazine in 1910. Subsequent collections of stories appeared throughout the rest of Chesterton's life, attesting to his enduring affection for the character—*The Innocence of Father Brown* (1911), *The Wisdom of Father Brown* (1914), *The Incredulity of Father Brown* (1926), *The Secret of Father Brown* (1927) and *The Scandal of Father Brown* (1935). In these 50 stories Brown developed from a mild, nondescript London priest "with a face as round and dull as a Norfolk dumpling" to a formidable world traveler who admonished criminals "with a voice like a rolling drum." Chesterton had been fascinated with priests who, like his friend Father John O'Connor, possessed that paradoxical blend of spiritual authority, worldly innocence and insight into the criminal mind (derived in part from the confessional). "I am a man therefore have all devils in my heart," admits Brown in "The Hammer of God." At the same time Brown's methods refute the relentless logic of some of his more cerebral colleagues. He looks past the deceptive minutiae of facts and surfaces into "the main tendencies of Nature" to the psychological truths and moral depravities behind literature's most bizarre crimes and situations. Neither nightmare nor magical illusion daunt him; and his solutions apply Chesterton's own dictum: "The climax must not be only the bursting of a bubble but rather the breaking of a dawn." Thus if he rarely apprehends a criminal, he almost always saves a soul. Detection of guilt is really just the beginning of redemption.

Faubus, Orval (Eugene) (1910–1980). American politician. As governor of Arkansas (1956–67), Faubus summoned the state National Guard (1957) to block federally directed integration at LITTLE ROCK Central High School. His stand, which forced the use of federal troops to carry out integration, gained Faubus the popularity that won him many terms as governor. (See also BROWN V. BOARD OF EDUCATION.)

For further reading:
Huckaby, Elizabeth, *Crisis at Central High: Little Rock, 1957–58*. Baton Rouge: Louisiana State University Press, 1980.

Faulk, John Henry (1913–1990). American humorist and radio host. In 1956, while serving as host of the popular radio show "Johnny's Front Porch," Faulk was accused by an anticommunist watchdog group, Aware Inc., of having communist ties. The accusations were based, in part, on his having attended a UNITED NATIONS dinner for Soviet foreign minister Andrei GROMYKO. The chief sponsor of his show pulled out and CBS radio fired him later that year. He sued Aware Inc. and two of its founders and was awarded $3.5 million by a jury in 1962. His book about the case, *Fear on Trial*, was made into a television movie in 1975.

Faulkner, William (Harrison) (1897–1962). American novelist, widely considered one of the most original and important American literary figures of the 20th century. Born in Mississippi to a family with well-established roots there, Faulkner was an indifferent student and later held sundry menial positions before and after serving in the Royal Canadian Air Force in WORLD WAR I. Working as a journalist in New Orleans in 1924, he met Sherwood ANDERSON, who encouraged Faulkner to produce his first novel, *Soldier's Pay* (1926). Following a sojourn in Europe, Faulkner returned to Mississippi and began writing the notable series of novels that take place there—in the fictitiously renamed Jefferson in Yoknapatawpha County. *Sartoris* (1929) is the first of these, followed by *The Sound and the Fury* (1929), which depicts the degeneration of the South. *As I Lay Dying* (1930) is a darkly comic story of a poor family's attempt to fulfill a wish of their dying mother; *Sanctuary* (1931) is considered by some to be a sensationalized attempt to increase sales; and *Light in August* (1932) and *Absolom, Absolom* (1936) both firmly established Faulkner as a distinguished modern novelist. The publication of *The Portable William Faulkner* (1946), edited by Malcolm COWLEY, led to Faulkner's receiving the NOBEL PRIZE for literature in 1949. Faulkner also worked as a screenwriter in HOLLYWOOD; among his film

American author William Faulkner at his home in Oxford, Mississippi (1950).

credits is the *The Big Sleep* (1946). Faulkner's later works, less celebrated than his earlier novels, include *The Hamlet* (1940) and *Intruder in the Dust* (1948).

For further reading:
Blotner, Joseph, *Faulkner: A Biography*. New York: Random House, 1991.

Faure, Edgar (1908–1988). French politician. Faure twice served as premier of FRANCE, for 40 days in 1952 and again in 1955–56. Faure held 11 cabinet posts during his 30-year political career and became minister of education after the 1968 Paris student riots.

Faure, Gabriel Urbain (1845–1924). French composer. A student of Camille Saint-Saens, he was an outstanding organist and teacher. Faure became a professor of composition at the Paris Conservatory and was its director from 1905 to 1920. His long list of students included Nadia BOULANGER, Georges ENESCO and Maurice RAVEL. Subtle and intimate, Faure's compositions are remarkable for their melodic lyricism. He was extremely prolific, composing chamber music, orchestral works, nearly 100 songs, piano pieces and two operas. Among his best-known works are the *Pavane* and the *Requiem* (both 1887) and *Pelleas et Melisande* (1898).

Fauvism. Name given to the work of a group of French painters who exhibited at the 1905 Parisian Salon d'Automne and who were called by outraged critics "fauves" (wild beasts), a name they happily embraced. Fauvism, perhaps the first truly modernist movement in 20th-century painting, is most strikingly marked by vivid, spontaneous and often violent color as well as by distorted forms, expressive brushwork and flat patterns—all characteristics that entered the canon of modern art. The movement lasted a brief time (1905–08), but its influence was felt throughout the world and the century. Among the Fauves, not all of whom exhibited in the 1905 show, were such masters as Henri MATISSE, often considered their leader; Maurice de Vlaminck, Georges Rouault, Albert Marquet, Andre Derain, Georges BRAQUE, Raoul DUFY and Kees van Dongen, as well as a number of lesser-known artists.

Fawzi, Mahmoud (1900–1981). Egyptian diplomat and statesman. During his 50-year career the polylingual Fawzi served as EGYPT's ambassador to many nations. During the reign of King FAROUK he was Egypt's first ambassador to the UNITED NATIONS (1946–52). He was a leading figure in the administration of President NASSER, serving as foreign minister (1952–64) during the SUEZ CRISIS and ARAB–ISRAELI WAR OF 1956. He was subsequently Nasser's deputy prime minister (1964–67) and vice president (1967–68) and President SADAT's prime minister (1972–74) and co-vice-president (1972–74).

Fay brothers. Frank J. Fay (1970–1931) and **William George Fay** (1872–1947), Irish theatrical actors and directors. They are best remembered for their active involvement in the Irish National Theater movement and in the creation, in 1904, of the Dublin-based ABBEY THEATRE company. As actors, they appeared in a number of Abbey Theatre productions. William played the lead role of Christy Mahon in the premiere of THE PLAYBOY OF THE WESTERN WORLD (1907), by John Millington SYNGE. In 1908 the brothers traveled to the U.S. to perform in a repertory of Irish plays. In the 1920s, after Frank had retired from the theater to work as a speech teacher, William remained active as an actor and director in England.

Fearing, Kenneth (1902–1961). American novelist and poet. Born in Illinois, Fearing was educated at the University of Wisconsin and worked a variety of jobs before finding his way to New York and taking up writing. His first volume of poems, *Angel Arms*, was published in 1929; much of his work first appeared in journals. Fearing's lyric poetry often portrays ordinary events of urban life in a dark, sometimes frightening manner. Fearing has also written several novels, the best known of which are *The Hospital* (1939), which describes one hour in a large hospital, and *The Big Clock* (1946, filmed 1948), in which a crime reporter investigating a murder discovers that he has been set up as the prime suspect. Other works include the poetry collections *Stranger at Coney Island, and Other Poems* (1948) and *New and Selected Poems* (1956) and the novels *Loneliest Girl in the World* (1951) and *The Crozart Story* (1960).

February Revolution (1917–). Revolution during which the Russian monarchy fell and the provisional government and the Soviets of workers' and soldiers' deputies were established. Over 14 million peasants were engaged in military service, which in turn led to acute food shortages; this proved to be one of the factors that triggered the revolution. Having taken command of the army in 1915, Czar NICHOLAS II was at the front, and the czarina, with the help of RASPUTIN, was responsible for much of the decision-making on domestic matters. In February 1917 there were widespread bread riots, strikes and demonstrations in Petrograd; the troops, summoned to restore order, mutinied. This led to the abdication of the czar, and a provisional government, led by KERENSKY, assumed power. The provisional government and the Soviets vied with one another for power, and the government proved to be incapable of dealing with the rising power of the Bolsheviks.

Fedayeen [*Arabic,* those who risk their lives for a cause]. Palestinian guerrillas who carried out raids in ISRAEL under the leadership of the Grand Mufti. They were eventually absorbed into the PALESTINE LIBERATION ORGANIZATION.

Federal Deposit Insurance Corporation (FDIC). The FDIC is a U.S. government corporation that insures customer deposits in U.S. banks. The 1929 STOCK MARKET CRASH was followed by a number of bank failures in which depositors lost their savings. In 1934 the federal government established the FDIC with the role of providing federal insurance for bank deposits. The current insured limit is $100,000 per account in each bank; however, banks are not required to carry the federal insurance. The depositor insurance is funded by premiums paid by member banks. No depositor has ever lost any money in an FDIC-insured account. After the failure of a number of savings and loan associations in the 1980s, the FDIC absorbed another government corporation, the Federal Savings and Loan Insurance Corporation (FSLIC), which was near insolvency.

Federal Reserve System. The U.S. government's central bank, which controls both the money supply and credit within the economy. Although its board is appointed by the president, the Fed enjoys considerable independence and the chairman of the Fed is influential in setting monetary and exchange policy.

Created in 1913, the Federal Reserve System is comprised of 12 Federal Reserve banks and the Federal Reserve Board, consisting of seven members appointed by the president. The Fed issues U.S. currency—federal reserve notes—and controls monetary policy, lending and interest rates through its reserve requirements and the discount rate for member banks. The Fed also operates in the foreign exchange markets. Each of the 12 federal reserve banks regulates private banks in its geographic area, and provides them with services such as check-clearing and fund transfers.

Federal Writers' Project. Part of the Federal Artists' Project of the WPA, the Federal Writers' Project existed from 1935 to 1939 and was directed by Henry G. Alsberg. The project aimed to hire writers to produce works on American themes, and it was responsible for many groundbreaking studies of black culture, folklore and regional histories. A major accomplishment was the American Guide Series, which profiled each of the 48 states. Many notable writers worked for the project, among them Nelson ALGREN, Conrad AIKEN, Ralph ELLISON, John CHEEVER and Kenneth FEARING.

Fedin, Konstantin Alexandrovich (1892–1977). Russian novelist, fellow-traveler and one of the SERAPION BROTHERS. His *Cities and Years* (1924) is an attempt to analyze the revolution. His work is frequently about revolution, civil war and the intellectual's task of redefining his role in a much-changed world. Head of the Moscow Writers' organization, in 1959 he was appointed secretary-general of the Writers' Union.

Fefer, Itsik [Isaak Solomonovich] (1900–1952). Yiddish poet. Having joined the Communist Party in 1919, Fefer volunteered for the Red Army and took part in the Civil War of 1917–20 and in the war of 1941–45. His first work was published in 1919. In 1943 he toured the United States and Great Britain in the capacity of the first official representative of Soviet Jews. He held a number of important government offices, but was arrested in 1948 during the purge of Jewish writers. He was executed in 1952. The author of lyrical poems, Fefer drew upon his experiences in the Civil War for the subject matter of much of his writing. He also wrote several plays.

Feiffer, Jules (1929–). American cartoonist, playwright and screenwriter. Feiffer studied at the Art Students League in New York City, worked for various cartoon syndicates and served in a cartoon animation unit in the Army Signal Corps before *The Village Voice* began printing his political cartoons with their uniquely neurotic characters in 1956. His first venture as a playwright was the satirical review *The Explainers,* produced in 1961—the same year his animated film *Munro* won an Oscar as the best short-subject cartoon. Feiffer wrote the screenplay for the film *Carnal Knowledge* (1971), which was banned in Georgia and subsequently at issue in the U.S. Supreme Court (1974). His other works include the cartoon collection *Jules Feiffer's America, from Eisenhower to Reagan* (1982) and the play *Eliot Loves* (1990).

The Village Voice *cartoonist Jules Feiffer shortly after he was awarded the Pulitzer Prize (1986).*

Feisal I (1885–1933). King of IRAQ (1921–33). Third son of Husein Ibn Ali of Mecca, he was educated in Constantinople. Serving with the Turkish forces in Syria during WORLD WAR I, he fled to Arabia in 1916, joining T.E. LAWRENCE in the Arab revolt and entering Damascus with Lawrence in 1918. Becoming king of Syria in 1920, within months he was forced to abdicate by the French. Feisal was elected king of Iraq in 1921 under the British mandate, and he maintained a pro-British policy while obtaining Iraq's independence in 1932. He died a year later and was succeeded by his son, Ghazi.

Feisal II (1935–1958). King of IRAQ (1939–58). Grandson of FEISAL I, he assumed the throne upon the death of his father, King Ghazi. Educated at Harrow, he ruled under the regency of his uncle, Emir Abdul Ilah, until his 18th birthday. During his reign, he and his cousin, King HUSSEIN of Jordan, attempted to form a federation of their two nations. Feisal was killed on July 14, 1958, in a revolution led by Abdul Karim KASSEM, who overthrew the monarchy and proclaimed Iraq a republic.

Feld, Eliot (1942–). American dancer, choreographer and dance company director. Feld began his career as a dancer in the Broadway and film productions of *West Side Story.* In 1963 he joined the AMERICAN BALLET THEATRE, receiving acclaim for his roles in many ballets, including *Fancy Free* and *Billy the Kid,* and for his first choreographed works, *Harbinger* and *At Midnight* (1967). He founded and directed the American Ballet Company as the resident company at the Brooklyn Academy of Music (1969–71), then formed the Eliot Feld Ballet in 1974. His choreography is characterized by its athleticism and combination of classical, jazz and modern dance elements. Major works include *Intermezzo* (1970), *Seraphic Songs* (1974) and *Santa Fe Saga* (1978).

Fellini, Federico (1920–). Italian film director and writer. An internationally acclaimed filmmaker, Fellini is noted for his use of personal symbolism and the surrealistic quality of his films, which often deal with the relationship between illusion and reality. He began his career as a cartoonist, journalist and radio scriptwriter (1936–43). Collaboration with actor Aldo Fabrizzi and director Roberto ROSSELLINI on *Open City* (1945) brought him widespread critical acclaim. Among the many subsequent films he directed (and collaborated on as screenwriter) are *Variety Lights* (1950), *La Strada* (1955), *La Dolce Vita* (1959), *8 1/2* (1963), *Juliet of the Spirits* (1965) and *Fellini Satyricon* (1969).

For further reading:

Alpert, Hollis, *Fellini: A Life.* New York: Paragon House, 1987.

Fava, Claudio G., *The Films of Federico Fellini.* New York: Carol Publishing Group, 1985.

fellow traveler. Term coined by Leon TROTSKY in 1925. It described intellectuals, especially writers, who were not communists but had sympathy with COMMUNISM or a modified Soviet regime. During the COLD WAR, and especially during the period of MCCARTHYISM in the 1950s, the term was also used disparagingly by American conservatives to describe U.S. intellectuals with leftist political leanings.

Feltsman, Vladimir (1952–). Russian pianist. Feltsman studied at the Moscow Conservatory and won first prize in the prestigious Marguerite Long Competition in Paris (1971). Hailed by the Soviets as a major pianist, during the 1970s he performed with orchestras throughout the Soviet Union and toured Europe and Japan. In 1979 he and his wife applied to immigrate to Israel. Their application was refused, and thereafter Feltsman was forbidden to perform in the U.S.S.R. During the 1980s the Feltsman case became an international cause celebre. Various foreign governments and individuals pressured the Soviets until the Feltsmans were granted exit visas in 1987 under GORBACHEV's policy of GLASNOST. Feltsman's arrival and initial concerts in the U.S. were greeted with rapturous acclaim. Feltsman has since established a successful concert and teaching career in the West.

feminism. Political, social and personal growth movement dedicated to bettering the lives and raising the status of women. The suffragettes' campaign to gain the vote for women in the U.S. was a vital precursor of modern feminism. As the term is presently used, it refers to a broad movement that came of age internationally in the 1960s and is directed at all aspects of the status of women—sexual, personal, social, economic and political. Key issues include the right to equal pay and to self-determination with regard to reproductive rights. Major theorists and writers in the feminist movement include Simone DE BEAUVOIR, Betty FRIEDAN, Germaine GREER and Gloria STEINEM.

Fender, P(ercy) G(eorge) H(enry) (1892–1985). English cricketer. A legendary captain of Surrey, Fender won 13 England caps as an all-rounder in the 1920s. In 1920, in a match against Northamptonshire, he scored a 35-minute century, the fastest in first-class cricket history. He retired as the world's oldest Test cricketer.

Feodosiya. City in the southeastern Crimea of the U.S.S.R. In October 1914 the bombing of Feodosiya—on TURKEY's behalf by a German naval squadron—compelled the OTTOMAN EMPIRE to enter WORLD WAR I. During WORLD WAR II, Feodosiya was controlled by the Germans in 1941 and again from 1942 to 1944.

Ferber, Edna (1885–1968). American author. Ferber began her career as a reporter in the Midwest. After the publication of her first novel, *Dawn O'Hara* (1911), she took up writing full time. She was a prolific writer of popular magazine stories, which were gathered together in several book collections. With the publication of *So Big* in 1924, she gained a place on the best-seller lists and also won the PULITZER PRIZE. As a keen observer of American life and times, she was noted for her characterizations and choice of settings for her novels. The highly popular SHOW BOAT (1926) formed the basis of musicals and motion pictures. Ferber was the author of many other famous novels, including *Saratoga Trunk* (1941, filmed 1945) and *Giant* (1952, filmed 1956). With George S. KAUFMAN she co-authored several plays, including the perennial *Dinner at Eight* (1932, filmed 1933). Although she was dismissed as a light romantic by many critics, others have praised Ferber's serious approach to her many themes. She wrote two autobiographical works, *A Peculiar Treasure* (1930) and *A Kind of Magic* (1963).

American author and playwright Edna Ferber (1945).

Ferdinand I (1861–1948). King of BULGARIA (reigned 1908–18); a prince of Saxe-Coburg, in 1887 he was elected prince of Bulgaria, then under Turkish sovereignty. The early part of his reign was made difficult by Russian opposition, but in 1896 he was finally recognized by the European powers. In 1908, Ferdinand declared Bulgaria independent and himself king. Forming an alliance with other Balkan countries, he was victorious in the first of the BALKAN WARS (1912–13) against the Turks, but was overwhelmingly defeated in the second of these conflicts (1913). Hoping to win back territory he had lost, Ferdinand brought Bulgaria into WORLD WAR I on the CENTRAL POWERS' side (1915); when his fortunes in war went sour again, he was forced to abdicate (1918). His son, BORIS III, assumed the throne, and Ferdinand went into exile in Germany.

Ferencsik, Janos (1907–1984). Considered Hungary's foremost 20th-century orchestra and opera conductor, Ferencsik helped spread Hungarian music abroad. Educated at the conservatory in Budapest, he conducted at the Budapest State Opera in 1930. He later helped establish the Hungarian State Symphony Orchestra, which he directed from 1952 until his death. He was also music director of the Budapest State Opera (1957–74) and conducted frequently in Europe, the U.S.S.R., the U.S. and South America, as well as in Japan and Australia. Ferencsik was a leading interpreter of Hungary's two greatest 20th-century composers, Bela BARTOK and Zoltan KODALY, whom he knew personally. He twice received Hungary's highest award, the Kossuth Prize (1951, 1961).

Ferguson, James Edward (1871–1944). U.S. politician. A champion of the small farmer, Ferguson became governor of Texas in 1915. Accused of corruption, he was impeached during his second term in 1917 but resurfaced as "the man behind the governor" when his wife, Miriam A. Wallace FERGUSON, served as Texas governor in 1924 and again in 1932.

Ferguson, Maynard (1928–). Canadian-born jazz trumpet virtuoso; a child prodigy whose exceptional technique, range and brassy flair gained him initial prominence in the big bands of Boyd Raeburn and Charlie Barnet during the late 1940s. In 1950, Ferguson was hired by Stan KENTON, who showcased the trumpeter's stratospheric wizardry and helped make Ferguson a star. In the mid-1950s, after achieving acclaim with recordings for Kenton and under his own name, Ferguson formed his first important unit, the Birdland Dream Band, which debuted in New York City to rave reviews and wildly enthusiastic crowds. From that point on, Ferguson has helmed a string of successful bands; in addition to acclaim for his variously sized jazz outfits, Ferguson achieved popularity in the 1970s with the jazz-rock hits "MacArthur Park" (1970) and "Gonna Fly Now" (1978), the theme from the motion picture *Rocky*. Ferguson has secured a place in jazz history by virtue of his exceptional control over the trumpet's high register and BEBOP acrobatics. Like Kenton, Ferguson has been an active jazz educator through his many clinics and school concerts. He has also encouraged a host of players who went on to jazzdom's front ranks; in 1990, when Ferguson returned to a solid, swinging jazz approach with his Bib Bop Nouveau band, he featured the gifted 17-year-old bassist, Nathan Berg. Ferguson can also be regarded as the last of the active big band leaders whose careers were built and sustained by being constantly on the road, playing one-nighters, club engagements and festivals.

For further reading:

Berg, Chuck, "Maynard Ferguson: The Fox Is Big on Bop," *Jazz Educators Journal*, Spring 1990.

Ferguson, Miriam A. (1875–1961). U.S. governor (Texas). Mrs. Ferguson was the wife of state governor James Edward FERGUSON. When he was not allowed to run for reelection in 1924, she ran in his place, winning the vote of small farmers. Although she held the office, it was generally known that James was the one who ran the state. She was reelected governor of Texas in 1932.

Ferlinghetti, Lawrence (1919–). American poet and publisher. Ferlinghetti was one of the key poetic figures to emerge from the BEAT GENERATION. Two volumes of his poems from the 1950s, *Pictures from the Gone World* (1955) and *A Coney Island of the Mind* (1958), sold in the hundreds of thousands—extraordinarily well for poetry—and established Ferlinghetti as a bridge between literary and popular culture. Ferlinghetti, who earned a doctoral degree in literature from the Sorbonne in Paris, has also been highly influential as the founder of City Lights Press in San Francisco, an avant garde publishing house that has published key works by Allen GINSBERG, William S. BURROUGHS and others.

Fermi, Enrico (1901–1954). Italian-American physicist, without doubt the greatest Italian scientist since Galileo and in the period 1925–50 one of the most creative physicists in the world. In an age of ever-growing specialization he excelled as both an experimentalist and a theoretician. Fermi's intelligence and quickness of mind were apparent from an early age, and he gained admission in 1918 to the Scuola Normale in Pisa, a school for the intellectual elite of Italy. He completed his education at the University of Pisa, where he gained his Ph.D. in 1924. After spending time abroad, Fermi returned to Italy, where he was appointed to a professorship of physics at the University of Rome—a considerable achievement for one so young. This advancement was largely due to the reputation he had already established with the publication of some 30 substantial papers, and the support of O.M. Corbino, the most distinguished Italian physicist at the time. Fermi published the first Italian text on modern physics, *Introduzione alla Fisica Atomica* (1928). His reputation attracted the brightest of the younger Italian physicists, but the growth of FASCISM in Italy led to the dispersal of its scientific talent. By 1938 Fermi, with a Jewish wife, was sufficiently alarmed by growing ANTI-SEMITISM to move to America.

However, his period in Rome turned out to be remarkably productive, with major advances in both the theoretical and the experimental field. His experimental work arose out of attempts to advance the efforts of Irene and Frederic Joliot-Curie, who had announced in 1934 the production of artificial radioactive isotopes. Fermi realized that the neutron, discovered by James CHADWICK in 1932, was perhaps an even better tool for creating new isotopes. Fermi stumbled on the phenomenon of slow neutrons, the production of which was later to have a profound impact in the field of nuclear energy. However, Fermi's immediate task was to use them to irradiate as many of the elements as possible and to produce and investigate the properties of a large number of newly created radioactive isotopes. It was for this work, for "the discovery of new radioactive substances . . . and for the discovery of the selective power of slow neutrons" that Fermi was awarded the 1938 NOBEL PRIZE for physics. In the course of their systematic irradiation of the elements, Fermi and his colleagues bombarded uranium with slow neutrons. Fermi thought that transuranic elements were being produced, but in 1938 Otto Frisch and Lise MEITNER first realized that nuclear fission was taking place in such reactions. On the theoretical level Fermi's major achievement while at Rome was his theory of beta decay—the process in unstable nuclei whereby a neutron is converted into a proton with the emission of an electron and an antineutrino. In 1933 Fermi gave a detailed analysis that introduced a new force into science, the so-called "weak" force.

In America Fermi soon became involved in the attempt to create a controlled nuclear chain reaction. In 1942 he built the first atomic pile in the stadium of the University of Chicago at Stagg Field. Using pure graphite as a moderator to slow the neutrons, and enriched uranium as the fissile material, Fermi and his colleagues began the construction of the pile. It consisted of some 40,000 graphite blocks, in which some 22,000 holes were drilled to permit the insertion of several tons of uranium. At 2.20 P.M. on December 2, 1942, the atomic age began as Fermi's pile went critical, supporting a self-supporting chain reaction for 28 minutes. In a historic telephone call afterwards, Arthur COMPTON informed the managing committee that "the Italian navigator has just landed in the new world." Fermi continued to work on the project and was in fact present in July 1945 when the first ATOMIC BOMB was exploded in the New Mexico desert. He is reported to have dropped scraps of paper as the blast reached him and, from their displacement, to have calculated the force as corresponding to 10,000 tons of TNT. After the war Fermi accepted an appointment as professor of physics at the University of Chicago, where he remained until his untimely death from cancer.

Atomic research pioneer Enrico Fermi teaching at the University of Chicago (ca. 1942).

Fermi National Accelerator Laboratory. A U.S. Department of Energy physics research laboratory, near Batavia, Illinois. Commonly known as Fermilab, it is named in honor of Enrico FERMI, the physicist who produced the first nuclear chain reaction. Fermilab contains one of the world's largest particle acclerators, also known as an atom smasher. Within a circular underground tunnel, one-and-one-third miles in diameter, protons are accelerated almost to the speed of light. The protons are directed at a target and the result of the collision is studied. Fermilab is managed by Universities Research Association, Incorporated, a consortium of 53 universities reporting to the U.S. Department of Energy.

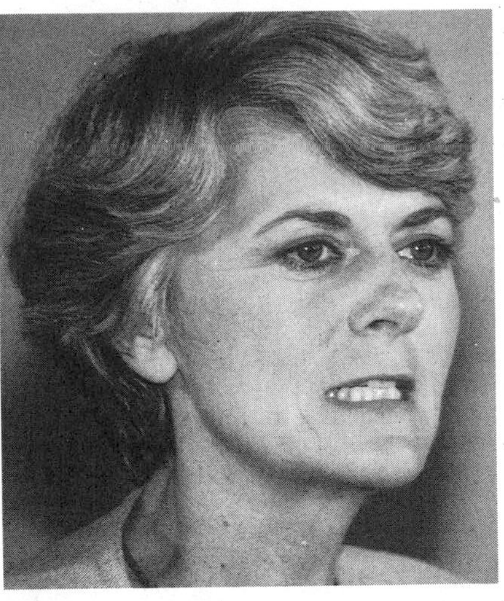
Geraldine Ferraro, the first woman in U.S. history to be chosen as a vice-presidential candidate by a major political party.

Fernandez, Emilio (1904–1986). Mexican actor, screenwriter and director. His socially aware films of the 1940s (*Maria Candelaria, Flor Silvestre, The Pearl*) were the first to draw international attention to the Mexican cinema. Known as "El Indio" for his half-Indian ancestry, Fernandez gained notoriety when he shot and wounded a film critic. He was imprisoned for several years in the 1970s for killing a farm laborer in a brawl. He acted in a number of Hollywood films, including *The Wild Bunch* and *Under the Volcano*.

Ferrari, Enzo (1898–1988). Italian entrepreneur; founder and chairman of the Italian car company that bore his name. Ferrari's factory near Modena produced about 1,000 cars a year, world-renowned for their blood-red color, hair-raising power and acceleration, precise high-speed handling, and exclusivity and expense. The Ferrari Formula 1 racing car, with its distinct prancing black stallion motif, became a symbol of national strength and weaknesses, winning nine world titles since 1952. A race car driver himself, he said that he "built racing cars with the same feverish pleasure with which drug addicts sniff cocaine."

Ferraro, Geraldine (1935–). American politician. Ferraro earned her law degree at Fordham University's evening division while teaching during the day. In 1978 she was elected to the House of Representatives from Queens, N.Y., and served three terms (1979–85). A liberal Democrat, Ferraro became secretary of the Democratic Caucus in the House and a protegee of House Speaker Thomas P. O'Neill. In 1984 she became the first woman vice-presidential candidate of a major party when presidential candidate Walter MONDALE named her as his running mate; they lost the election. Ferraro's career was later troubled by allegations of impropriety against her husband, John Zaccaro, in his real estate business, and by her son's arrest for selling cocaine.

Ferrier, Kathleen (1912–1953). British concert singer noted for her performances of the vocal music of Handel, Bach and Mahler and the lieder of Schubert, Schumann and other masters. Ferrier's career was tragically brief; yet her vocal, musical and personal qualities made her one of the most beloved performers of her time. She possessed one of the purest and most distinctive contralto voices ever recorded. Born in Lancashire, she originally made her living as a piano accompanist and also worked as a telephone operator. After winning first prize in a voice competition she had casually entered in 1938, she devoted herself to the study of singing. She made her professional singing debut as a soloist in Bach's *Passion According to St. Matthew* in 1942 and quickly won the attention of other musicians, critics and the public. During WORLD WAR II she sang for soldiers and civilians throughout England—often in bomb shelters, hospitals or factories. At the GLYNDEBOURNE FESTIVAL in 1946 she sang the title role in the world premiere of Benjamin BRITTEN's opera *The Rape of Lucretia*. The next year at the festival she triumphed as Orfeo in Gluck's *Orfeo ed Euridice*, the only other operatic role she performed during her career. She first appeared at the EDINBURGH FESTIVAL in 1947 under the baton of Bruno WALTER, who became her friend and mentor. In 1948 she made her American debut in MAHLER's *Das Lied von der Erde* with the New York Philharmonic, again conducted by Walter. She toured the U.S. in concert (1948–49; 1950–51) and also appeared throughout Europe. Her career was cut short at its peak when she was stricken with cancer.

Fessenden, Reginald Aubrey (1866–1932). Canadian electrical engineer. After an education in Canada, Fessenden worked for the EDISON COMPANY as an engineer and later as head chemist (1886–90) and as an engineer (1890–91) for the Westinghouse Co., Edison's great rival. In 1900 he was appointed special agent for the U.S. Weather Bureau, adapting the technique of radio telegraphy, newly developed by Guglielmo MARCONI, to weather forecasting and storm warning. In 1902 he became general manager of the National Electric Signaling Co., which was formed by two financiers from Pittsburgh to exploit his ideas. From 1910 he was consultant engineer at the Submarine Signal Co. Fessenden's inventions were prolific and varied: at the time of his death he held over 500 patents. In 1900 he developed an electrolytic detector that was sufficiently sensitive to make radio telephony feasible. His most significant invention was the technique of amplitude modulation. This involved the use of carrier waves to transmit audio signals; he varied the amplitude of a steady high-frequency radio signal so that it corresponded to variations in the sound waves and thus carried the audio information. Using this principle he transmitted on Christmas Eve, 1906, what was probably the first program of music and speech broadcast in America. The program was heard by ships' radio operators at distances of up to several hundred miles.

Festung Europa. See FORTRESS EUROPE.

Fetchit, Stepin [Lincoln Theodore Monroe Andrew Perry] (1902–1985). Black American actor. Stepin Fetchit was the first black actor to be prominently cast in American movies not aimed specifically at black audiences. His career peaked in the early and mid-1930s, when he starred in the all-black *Hearts in Dixie* and was given featured billing with such stars as Will ROGERS and Shirley TEMPLE. He generally portrayed a languorously lazy, simpleminded servant in roles that were later denounced as racist stereotypes. He countered this criticism by stating that he had paved the way for the success of such stars as Bill COSBY and Sidney POITIER. Once a millionaire, in the 1940s he declared bankruptcy and supported himself with nightclub appearances and occasional film roles.

Feuchtwanger, Lion (1884–1958). German novelist and essayist. Born into an Orthodox Jewish family in Munich, Feuchtwanger rose to prominence in German letters with the publication of his novel *The Ugly Duchess* (1923). *Jew Suss* (1925, trans. 1926), his most famous novel, probed the tensions of life as a Jew in German society; in a bitter turnabout, the Nazis adopted this novel into an anti-Semitic propaganda film in 1940. Feuchtwanger fled Germany in 1932, going first to France and then, in 1941, to the U.S. His novels emphasized the molding forces of history and religion over and above the personality traits of the individuals. Major works by Feuchtwanger include a trilogy on Jewish life in Germany—*Success* (1930), *The Oppermanns* (1933) and *Paris Gazette* (1939)—and a second trilogy set in the Biblical era—*Josephus* (1932), *The Jew of Rome* (1935) and *Josephus and the Emperor* (1936). *Jephta and His Daughter*, published in 1957, was Feuchtwanger's final novel.

Feydeau, Georges (1862–1921). French playwright, actor and director; one of the most popular figures in French theater in the 1900s. Feydeau was especially renowned for his farces, such as *Hotel Paradiso* (1894) and *A Flea in Her Ear* (1907), which featured witty and stylized dialogue, quick plot twists, frantic action and imaginative use of stage decor and props. He frequently appeared in his own productions; English translations include *Four Farces* (1970) and *Feydeau, First to Last* (1982).

Feynman, Richard Phillips (1918–1988). American physicist. Feynman received a B.S. in physics from the Massachusetts Institute of Technology (1939) and a Ph.D. from Princeton (1942) after publishing his dissertation on quantum mechanics. During WORLD WAR II, Feynman played a key role in the development of the ATOMIC BOMB at Los Alamos, New Mexico. On the MANHATTAN PROJECT he came into contact with many of the century's greatest physicists, including Hans BETHE, Niels BOHR, Aage BOHR, Enrico FERMI and J. Robert OPPENHEIMER. After the war he taught for several years at Cornell University (and later at the California Institute of Technology), where he carried out the work on quantum electrodynamics that led to the 1965 NOBEL PRIZE for physics, which he shared with Julian S. Schwinger and Sin-itiro Tomonaga. The "Feynman diagrams" he developed gave physicists a way of explaining the behavior of light and matter in terms of fundamental particles. His 1985 autobiography, *Surely You're Joking, Mr. Feynman*, became a surprise best-seller. A turning point in the presidential probe of the space shuttle CHALLENGER DISASTER came when Feynman demonstrated the loss of resiliency in the critical O-ring seals at low temperatures. As well as being an important physicist, Feynman was also a brilliant teacher in the classroom and influenced many younger physicists by his unique approach to problem-solving.

Fianna Fail [*Irish Gaelic*, "soldiers of destiny"]. Political party formed by Eamon DE VALERA in 1926 from moderate members of SINN FEIN, reflecting a reversal of previous opposition to dominion status for IRELAND. One of the two major Irish political parties, it formed the government in 1951–54, 1957–73, 1977–81, 1982–83, and 1987– . Fianna Fail is considered the most nationalist of Ireland's political parties and generally follows conservative domestic policies. It seeks the reunification of Ireland through peaceful means. (See also FINE GAEL.)

Fiat. Largest Italian automobile manufacturer, with original factories near Turin. Founded in 1899 by Giovanni Agnelli, Fiat has often supported design excellence. The 1935 500 Topolino, the 1978 Ritmo, and the 1979 Strada—each small, functional and unpretentious—are good examples of Fiat's dedication to producing basic cars for a mass market. The 124 Spider sports car is an example of quality design, in the tradition of Italian coach building, aimed at a special luxury market.

"Fibber McGee and Molly". American radio network show. This classic NBC RADIO show ran from 1935 to 1957 and starred Jim Jordan and his real-life wife, Marjorie. The McGees' home at Wistful Vista became a familiar place on the U.S. cultural landscape. As one critic commented in 1940, the characters "get their humor from simple things, like fixing the brakes or playing checkers." Molly's rejoinder to her husband, "Tain't funny, McGee," became a national catchphrase.

fiberglass. Generic version of the trade name Fiberglas used by the Owens-Corning Glass Company for the hybrid material made from polyester PLASTIC reinforced with glass fibers. Fiberglass makes it possible to give high strength to glass parts that may be molded, or "hand laid-up," that is, built up on a mold with layers of glass cloth soaked in plastic resin. Fiberglass is increasingly used for automobile body parts and the hulls of small boats. It is also used for various household products and is the material of the first successful plastic chairs designed by Charles EAMES and Eero SAARINEN.

fiber optics. A branch of optics dealing with the passage of light along optical fibers, usually slender strands of glass or plastic. Bundles of fiber optic cables are much thinner and lighter than wire cables, can carry much more information and are immune to electromagnetic interference. Fiber optical cables are widely used in communications equipment, where they can link computers, transmit television signals, carry thousands of telephone conversations or perform a number of other functions. They have also found wide application in medicine, where fiber optic tubes such as the endoscope are often employed to examine the interior of the body without the use of X-ray or exploratory surgery.

Fiedler, Leslie A(aron) (1917–). American literary critic and author. Educated at New York University, the University of Wisconsin and Harvard University, Fiedler has served in a variety of academic posts in the U.S. and abroad. He is perhaps best known for the critical work *Love and Death in the American Novel* (1960), in which he compares American and European novels and contends that Americans are obsessed with death and unable to write about sex, portraying women as either sinners or saints. His many provocative works of criticism include *The Jew in the American Novel* (1959, second edition 1966), *The Inadvertent Epic: From Uncle Tom's Cabin to Roots* (1980) and *Olaf Stapeldon; A Man Divided* (1983). In *Being Busted* (1969) Fiedler describes his own false arrest and incarceration for marijuana use while he was a faculty advisor to a student group fighting for the legalization of marijuana. His fiction includes *The Messengers Will Come No More* (1974) and the short stories *Nude Croquet and Other Stories* (1969).

Field, Marshall, III (1893–1956). American businessman, publisher and philanthropist. The grandson of the wealthy department store owner Marshall Field I (1834–1906), Field was born in Chicago. After his father's apparent suicide in 1906, he was taken to England, where he attended Eton and Cambridge. He returned to the U.S. in 1914, and in 1936 he abandoned his many business activities to devote himself to liberal political and social causes. He was a cofounder (1940) of the liberal N.Y.C. newspaper *PM* and established the Field Foundation to aid in child welfare and race relations. The following year he founded the Chicago *Sun*, which through merger became the *Sun Times* in 1948. Consolidating his ventures into Field Enterprises Inc. in 1944, he also published *The World Book Encyclopedia* and the Sunday supplement *Parade*. He owned four radio stations and other communications enterprises. His social and political philosophy was expressed in his book *Freedom Is More Than a Word* (1945).

Fields, Dorothy (1904–1974). American lyricist and librettist. Fields first gained success with songwriter Jimmy McHugh by writing lyrics for songs in the Cotton Club revues in HARLEM. An early hit was "I Can't Give You Anything But Love, Baby" (1928). Other hits with McHugh included "On the Sunny Side of the Street" and "I'm in the Mood for Love." She also wrote lyrics for Broadway musicals—*Annie Get Your Gun* (1946), *A Tree Grows in Brooklyn* (1951), *Redhead* (1959) and *Sweet Charity* (1964). Fields collaborated on movie musicals with both Harold ARLEN and Jerome KERN. Several songs written with KERN have become standards—"A Fine Romance," "The Way You Look Tonight" and "Lovely to Look At."

Fields, Gracie [born Grace Stansfield] (1898–1979). British music-hall singer and comedienne. Born in Rochdale, Lancashire, she first appeared in the town's Hippodrome in 1910. During the 1920s, 1930s and 1940s she performed frequently in London and toured throughout Great Britain. In her heyday she was believed to be the world's highest-paid star, and is thought to have sold more records than any other British performer in the mid-1920s. Known for her sassy ditties, warm ballads and stouthearted warbling, she was especially popular during WORLD WAR II, entertaining the troops and civilians alike during Britain's darkest hours. Even after her popularity waned she remained a national institution.

Tycoon-philanthropist Marshall Field welcomes British refugee children to safety in America during World War II (1940).

Fields, W(illiam) C(laude) [William Claude Dukenfield] (1879–1946). American comedic stage and film actor. W.C. Fields remains one of the best-loved comic figures in the history of the cinema. He began his career as a teenage juggler on the vaudeville circuit. By his early twenties, he was a top-billed star and in the 1900s and 1910s he was featured with the renowned ZIEGFELD FOLLIES in New York. Fields' first film was a silent short, *Pool Sharks* (1915). In the 1920s, Fields enjoyed success on Broadway with *Poppy* (1923) and also appeared in the D.W. GRIFFITH silent film *Sally of the Sawdust* (1925), which established Fields in HOLLYWOOD at the late age of 46. In the 1930s, with the arrival of the talkies, Fields became a star in his persona as the crafty con artist with a heart of gold. In the 10 years between 1931 and 1941 Fields made his best films; these include *It's a Gift* (1934), *The Man on the Flying Trapeze* (1935), *You Can't Cheat an Honest Man* (1939), *My Little Chickadee* (1940, with Mae WEST) and *The Bank Dick* (1940).

fifth column. Term used just prior to and during WORLD WAR II to denote Nazi sympathizers in Allied and neutral countries who collaborated with the Germans, disseminated pro-German propaganda or committed other treasonous acts. The term was coined during the SPANISH CIVIL WAR by the nationalist general Emilio Mola (1887–1937). Although the attack on Madrid was made by four columns of troops, Mola asserted that he also had a "fifth column," a cadre of pro-FRANCO agents in the city. Fifth-column activities in WORLD WAR II were encouraged and financed by Germany, partially by the creation of German minority organizations under the Nazi Party's foreign relations section. Playing upon the themes of anticommunism and ANTISEMITISM, fifth-column propaganda was somewhat effective among European civilians. Countries in which fifth-column activities were particularly strong included Norway, Belgium, France and Yugoslavia. The term is also more generally used to denote enemy agents or sympathizers who attempt to undermine any nation's structure or institutions from within.

Figueres Ferrer, Jose (1906–1990). Costa Rican politician. Affectionately known as "Don Pepe," he helped establish democracy in COSTA RICA after years of political turmoil. In 1948, he led a brief civil war against a leftist government that had sought to annul the results of an election. He emerged from the struggle as president. In 1949, he dissolved the country's army, leaving only a civil defense force. He also undertook major social and economic reforms, including the adoption of a constitution and the nationalization of the country's banks. Elected to two more terms (1953–58 and 1970–74), Figueres was one of the first Costa Rican leaders to play a major international role in Latin America.

Fiji [Fiji Islands]. Island nation in the southwest Pacific, 1,300 miles north of New Zealand. The archipelago of islands, strategically placed and agriculturally fertile, was seized by Great Britain in 1858. A prime Allied supply site in WORLD WAR II, Fiji was named an independent dominion of the COMMONWEALTH in 1970. Tensions between the Fijian majority (of Melanesian-Polynesian origin) and the Indian minority came to a head in April 1987, when an Indian-dominated coalition won the general election. Two coups were followed by the declaration of a Fijian republic (October 1987) and Fiji's decision to withdraw from the Commonwealth. The country returned to civilian rule at the beginning of 1990 but ethnic tensions lingered. To the outside world, however, Fiji remains an island paradise, and it is a popular stopover for travelers between the U.S. and Australia or New Zealand.

Filene, Edward Albert (1860–1937). U.S. merchant. The president of William Filene's Sons in Boston, he was noted for his innovations in retail distribution, particularly his "bargain basement." He helped organize both the Boston Chamber of Commerce and the Chamber of Commerce of the U.S. and was active in civic reform.

Filling Station, The. Landmark modern American ballet. It was the joint collaboration in 1938 of composer Virgil THOMSON, choreographer Lew Christensen, and impresario Lincoln KIRSTEIN for the newly formed Ballet Caravan of New York. With another Caravan production that same year, BILLY THE KID, it was one of the first ballets to draw primarily upon American national idioms and characters. The filling station itself was the intersection of a diverse group of travelers. Mack, the attendant, is visited by several characters—a golfer and his family, two truck drivers, a tipsy society couple and a gangster. After a holdup, a state trooper arrives to arrest the thief. "Using American music this way was quite avant-garde at the time," recalled Todd Bolender, who danced in the original production in 1938. "Audiences were startled to find anything so intrinsically American could be danced. And they loved the parodies of classical ballet, like the pas de deux danced by the drunken socialites and the use of a more modern jazz style. [Kirstein] wanted Americans to be aware that dance could be an integral part of our own culture and not so dependent upon the Europeans." The ballet is frequently revived, most recently by the State Ballet of Missouri and the San Francisco Ballet.

For further reading:
Dictionary of Modern Ballet. New York: Tudor Publishing, 1959.

film noir. A term applied by French film critics to certain American motion pictures from the WORLD WAR II and postwar era. It was not a specific genre; rather, the term denotes a particular mood and world-view found in a wide range of movies. From roughly the early 1940s to the late 1950s a sense of fatality, despair and nightmare appeared, born out of disillusionment with the recent war. Influential were the psychopathology of themes and characters and the dramatic lighting schemes of the German emigre filmmakers Fritz LANG, Robert Siodmak, and John Alton; the weakening censorship restrictions in HOLLYWOOD; and influences from the Italian neo-realist films of the time. In short, after two decades of bright musicals and fairytale romances, suddenly the American screen was ripe for the ruthless hard-boiled detectives Sam Spade and Philip Marlow in, respectively, John HUSTON's *The Maltese Falcon* (1940) and Edward Dmytryk's *Murder, My Sweet* (1943). There were documentary-like police procedure thrillers, like Jules Dassin's *The Naked City* (1949) and Alfred Werker's "Dragnet" prototype, *He Walks By Night* (1949). *Double Indemnity* (1944) and *The Postman Always Rings Twice* made adultery, murder and sultry passion the cornerstones of romance, and inspired a latter-day *film noir*, *Body Heat* (1981). Alfred HITCHCOCK attacked the smugness of American values in *Shadow of a Doubt* (1943); and Nicholas Ray questioned the future of a new generation of teenagers in *They Live By Night* (1947). Robert Aldrich envisioned in *Kiss Me Deadly* (1957) nothing less than global holocaust. Not even the western and musical genres were left untouched: Raoul WALSH brought psychoanalysis to *Pursued* (1947) and Vincente MINNELLI inserted a Mike Hammer-like character into a sleazy ballet number in *The Band Wagon* (1953). Miraculously, in the face of such unremitting pessimism these movies displayed a dramatic, pictorial flair. Low-key lighting, the violent contrasts of rich chiaroscuro, and crazy camera angles brought a breathtaking look even to conventional thrillers like *T-Men* (1947) and *The Big Combo* (1955).

final solution [German: *Endlosung*]. Nazi euphemism for the secret German plan to systematically exterminate all European JEWS during WORLD WAR II, otherwise known as the HOLOCAUST. Adolf HITLER expressed his extreme ANTI-SEMITISM as early as 1923 in MEIN KAMPF, and anti-Semitism was fundamental in the rise of NAZISM and the Nazi Party during the 1930s. From the mid-1930s until the end of 1941, hundreds of thousands of Jews (at first in GERMANY, and later in the German-occupied countries) were deprived of their property and livelihood and confined to ghettos or sent to CONCENTRATION CAMPS. Hitler did not actually proclaim his deliberate extermination policy, however, until late 1941. The plan to destroy the European Jews—the so-called "final solution to the Jewish problem"—was formalized at the Wannsee Conference chaired by Reinhard HEYDRICH on January 20, 1942. Responsibility for implementing the final solution was given to Heinrich HIMMLER, who was assisted by Adolf EICHMANN and hundreds of lesser Nazi functionaries. The extermination policy was carried out at selected concentration camps, of which AUSCHWITZ was the most notorious.

Finch, George Ingle (1888–1970). Australian physical chemist. Finch was educated at Wolaroi College in Australia and the Ecole de Medecine in Paris. Finding the study of medicine unappealing, he moved to Switzerland and studied physics and chemistry, first at the Federal Institute of Technology in Zurich and later at the University of Geneva. On moving to Britain in 1912 he worked briefly as a research chemist at the Royal Arsenal, Woolwich, joining the staff of Imperial College, London in 1913. Finch remained there until his retirement in 1952, having been appointed professor of applied physical chemistry in 1936. After his retirement Finch traveled to India, where he was the director of the National Chemical Laboratory (1952–57).

Finch worked mainly on the properties of solid surfaces. In the 1930s he developed the technique of low-energy electron diffraction, using the wavelike properties of electrons, demonstrated by George Thomson and Clinton J. DAVISSON in 1927, to investigate the structure of surfaces. Finch was also widely known as a mountaineer. As one of the leading climbers of his generation he was a member of the 1922 Everest expedition, climbing to the then-unequaled height of 27,300 feet.

Fine Gael [*Irish Gaelic:* "Irish tribe"]. Moderate national party and one of two major Irish political parties. It won elections in 1973, 1982 and 1983. It generally avoids the nationalist rhetoric of the rival FIANNA FAIL Party and has shown willingness to compromise on the complex NORTHERN IRELAND issue.

Fini, Leonor (1908–). Italian-Argentine painter. Raised in Buenos Aires, Fini received no formal artistic training as a youth, but after immigrating to Italy, she was influenced by painter Carlo CARRA while living in Milan and became one of his protegees. In 1933 Fini moved to Paris, where she became involved in the surrealist movement (see SURREALISM). Her fantastical paintings of the 1930s remain her best known works. In the 1940s Fini won renown as a portraitist of famous personages of her era. She also did ballet stage designs and set designs for films.

Finland, Republic of [*Finnish:* Suomi]. Nation of northeastern Europe; located between the Gulf of Bothnia and the Gulf of Finland and flanked by NORWAY and SWEDEN on the north and west and the U.S.S.R. on the east and south. The north of Finland stretches above the Arctic Circle, in Lapland, and the south is flecked with lakes and waterways. Independent since 1917, Finland has been connected with either Russia or Sweden for much of its history; in fact, Swedish continues as one of the country's two official languages. The capital, Helsinki, is on the southern coast. After the RUSSIAN REVOLUTION in 1917, the Finns proclaimed their independence from the new Soviet Union. Right-wing factions emerged triumphant after a five-month civil war in 1918; in 1920 the Soviet Union acknowledged the new republic in the Treaty of Tartu (see FINNISH WAR OF INDEPENDENCE). Finnish politics were unstable during the 1920s and 1930s, as reminders of the civil war were slow to fade. At the beginning of WORLD WAR II, in the winter of 1939–40, Finland was attacked by the U.S.S.R., in violation of a nonagression pact. The Finns fought bravely but were defeated; quickly recuperating, they themselves attacked Russia when GERMANY invaded the U.S.S.R. in 1941. The Finns were victorious at first but were routed in 1944, losing the Isthmus of Karelia, Vyborg, the Finnish shores of Lake Ladoga, and the Pechenga region to the Soviet Union. Since 1945 relations with the U.S.S.R. have been friendlier, and Finland's industries have grown considerably. Finland enjoys good trade with the nations of the EUROPEAN ECONOMIC COMMUNITY and has a stable multiparty government.

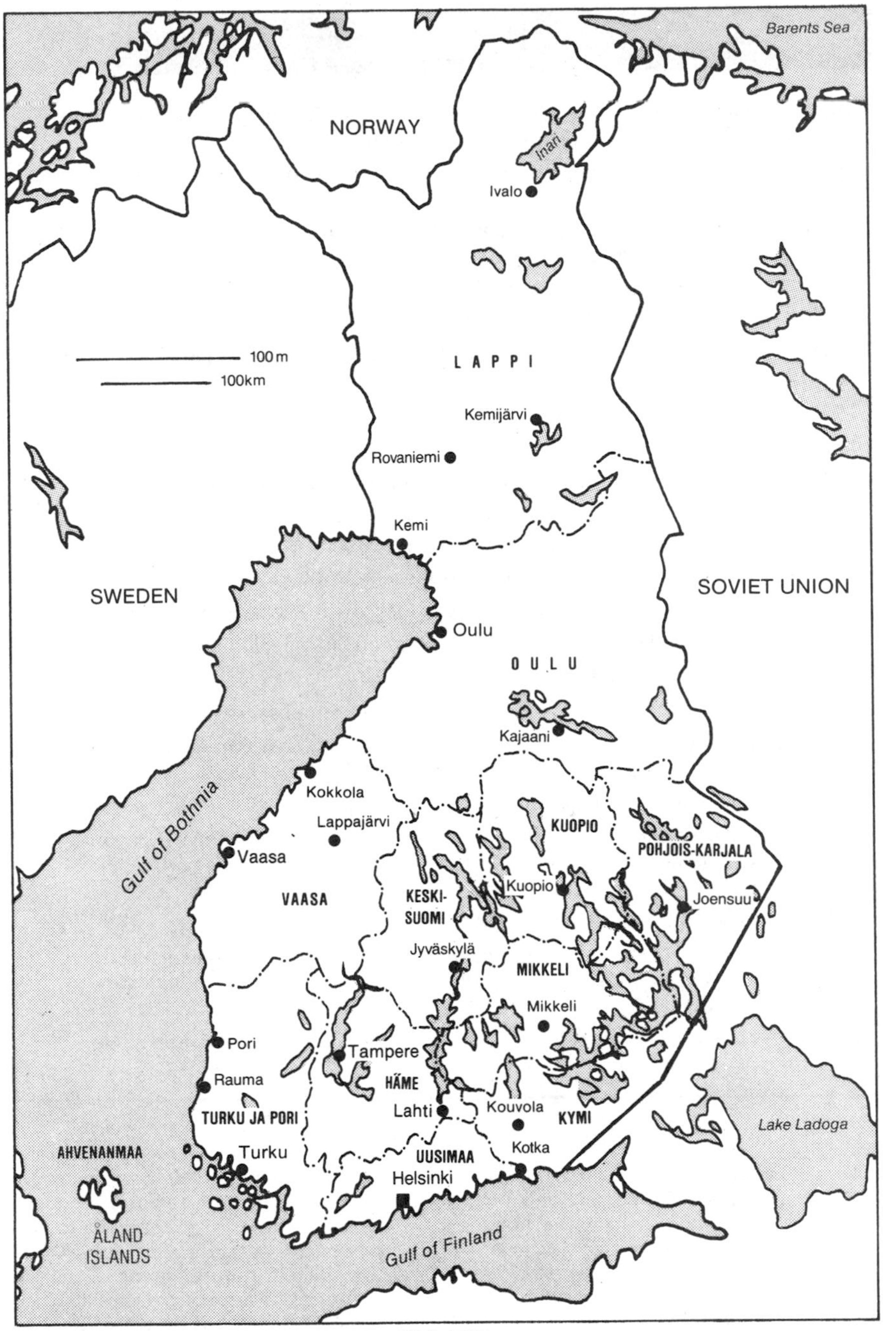

FINLAND

Finley, David (1890–1977). Planner and first director (1938–56) of the National Gallery of Art in Washington, D.C. He was chairman of the U.S. Commission of Fine Arts (1950–63) and headed the National Trust for Historic Preservation during the same period.

Finney, Albert (1936–). British stage and film actor and stage director. Finney remains most familiar to audiences worldwide for his tour de force performance in the title role of the film *Tom Jones* (1963), based on the picaresque 18th-century novel by Henry Fielding. Other films starring

FINLAND

1900	Finland enjoys limited autonomy within the Russian empire, with its own legislature (the Diet) and a tradition of personal freedoms.
1905	Russian campaign to restrict freedoms and the power of the Diet is resisted in the "National Strike."
1906	Its power restored, Diet guarantees freedom of press, assembly, etc. and universal suffrage; first film made.
1910	Russians reassert authority; freedoms erode.
1917	Diet declares independence during Russian Revolution.
1918	Brief civil war; "Whites" backed by Germany defeat and massacre "Reds" backed by Moscow.
1919	Republic declared; Staahlberg is first president.
1920	Treaty of Tartu with Soviet Union.
1925	Cultural renaissance in Helsinki, with composer Sibelius, architect Saarinen and others.
1930	Unsuccessful revolt by "Lapua," right-wing peasant movement.
1939	Soviet invasion meets tough resistance in Winter War.
1940	Finland cedes territory in Treaty of Moscow but retains independence.
1941	Embittered Finland joins Hitler's invasion of Soviet Union.
1944	Finland defeated by Soviet army.
1947	Treaty of Paris grants more territory and enormous reparation to Soviets.
1948	President Paasikivi seeks to placate Soviet neighbor through close cooperation; signs limited defense pact.
1952	Olympics held in Helsinki.
1955	Joins Nordic Council; this and other economic ties to the West, coupled with final stabilization of Soviet question, allows for long period of economic growth under center-left coalition governments.
1969	First Finnish auto factory opens as industry booms.
1975	Helsinki Conference and Accords; attempt by 35 nations to achieve East-West cooperation; accords set out basic human rights standards worldwide.
1987	Harri Holkeri becomes Finland's first post-World War II conservative prime minister.

Finney include *Two for the Road* (1967) and *Shoot the Moon* (1982). But the bulk of his acting work took place on the London stage, where he earned critical acclaim for his lead roles in plays as diverse as *Billy Liar* (1960), *Luther* (1961), *Hamlet* (1975) and *Tamburlaine the Great* (1976). In 1983, he both directed and starred in *Armstrong's Last Goodnight,* by British playwright John Arden, in a production by the Old Vic Company.

Finnish War of Independence (1918–1920). In 1917 the new Russian provisional government granted Finland a democratic government. After the BOLSHEVIK REVOLUTION, the Finns declared independence on December 6, 1917. The new Soviet government recognized it, but Finland's coalition government was ousted by Soviet-backed Finnish radicals (Reds) on January 28, 1918. This started a civil war between WHITES in the north, led by Baron Carl Gustaf MANNERHEIM, and Reds controlling the south. Mannerheim attacked the Reds but was halted until aid arrived from German troops under Count Rudiger von der Goltz, who seized Helsinki and drove the Reds from the country. At the **Battle of Vyborg,** April 29, 1918, the Whites forced the Reds to surrender and then launched a terror campaign, killing thousands of suspected communists. A Republic was established on June 17, 1919, but desultory fighting continued with Russia over conflicting claims to western Karelia until the Treaty of Dorpat (Tartu), October 14, 1920, ended hostilities, reaffirming Finland's independence.

Finsen, Niels Ryberg (1860–1904). Danish physician and medical researcher. He was educated in Reykjavik, Iceland, and at the University of Copenhagen, where he earned his M.D. In the 1890s Finsen began to investigate previous suggestions that light could be used to kill bacteria. He experimented and found that ultraviolet rays had the greatest power to kill bacteria. In 1896 he founded the Institute of Phototherapy, directing it until his death. Here he used ultraviolet light to treat lupus vulgaris, a skin infection caused by the tubercle bacillus. Half of his 800 lupus vulgaris patients were completely cured, and nearly all the rest showed significant improvement. For this work he received the 1903 NOBEL PRIZE in physiology or medicine. Finsen was not only among the first to use light to treat medical conditions, but he was also among the first to note the effects of sunlight, and its absence, on mood.

Finzi, Gerald (1901–). British composer. Finzi, who as a youth studied music under Ernest Farrar and Edward Bairstow, was a prolific composer whose works often reflected the melodic influence of English folk songs. Finzi taught composition at the Royal Academy of Music in London from 1930 to 1933 and in 1939 founded the Newbury String Players, whose performances helped to bring about a revival of interest in 18th century music. Major compositions by Finzi include *A Severn Rhapsody* (1923), *Interludium* (1936), *For St. Cecilia* (1947) and *In Terra Pax* (1954, revised 1956). Finzi's music has enjoyed a revival in the late 20th century.

Firbank, (Arthur Annesley) Ronald (1886–1926). British author. Born to a wealthy family, Firbank was educated privately as a child and later attended Trinity College, Cambridge, though he did not complete a degree there. In 1908 Firbank left Cambridge and converted to Catholicism under the influence of R.H. Benson (brother of E.F. BENSON). He traveled and then settled in London, where he was noted as a personality as well as for his writing. Firbank's fiction, which has been compared to that of Max BEERBOHM, often revolves around the dark themes of the isolation of the individual in a depraved world, but is written in a sophisticated, witty style. His work is considered to have influenced the writing of Evelyn WAUGH and Ivy COMPTON-BURNETT, among others. His novels, the first three of which he originally published privately, include *Vainglory* (1915), *Inclinations* (1919), and *The Flower Beneath the Foot* (1924). *Sorrow in Sunlight* (1924, published in the U.S. as *Prancing Nigger* in 1925) and *Concerning the Eccentricities of Cardinal Pirelli* (published posthumously in 1926) take place in varied picturesque locales. Firbank was also a playwright.

Fire Next Time, The (1963). Book of essays by James BALDWIN. The book consists of two essays, the main one of which caused a sensation when it was first published in THE NEW YORKER in 1962 as "Letter from a Region in My Mind." The essay resulted from Baldwin's meeting with the Honorable Elijah Muhammad, the leader of the BLACK MUSLIMS, a group espousing black separatism, and violence, if necessary, to achieve it. The other essay, "My Dungeon Shook," was an adapted letter originally published in *The Progressive.* Baldwin, though not an advocate of separatism, bitterly and eloquently depicted black rage and frustration in a racist society, and the book was taken by some as a warning to respond to the more moderate efforts of Martin Luther KING, Jr. The book was widely read and enormously influential; it established Baldwin not only as an important writer, but also as an advocate and spokesman for the CIVIL RIGHTS MOVEMENT.

fireside chats. Informal radio talks begun by U.S. President Franklin Delano ROOSEVELT. The first fireside chat was broadcast on March 12, 1933; the format proved popular and was continued by Roosevelt's successors.

first strike. Tactic of nuclear warfare in which the aim is to destroy an enemy's missiles while they are still on the ground, thereby forestalling retaliation. During the COLD WAR the U.S. would not rule out the possibility of launching a first strike in the event of war. The possibility of first strike was meant to deter an aggressor from launching a conventional attack that might escalate into nuclear war. (See also MUTUAL ASSURED DESTRUCTION.)

Firth of Clyde. See CLYDE RIVER AND FIRTH OF CLYDE.

Fischer, Emil Hermann (1852–1919). German organic chemist, widely regarded as the father of biochemistry. During the 1870s he worked closely with Adolf von Bayer. Before the end of the 19th century he did important work in three fields: purines, sugars and peptides. This work helped lay the foundation for 20th-century biochemistry, and Fischer received the 1902 NOBEL PRIZE for chemistry. Later he was the first scientist to produce a polypeptide containing 18 amino acids (1907) and the first to synthesize a nucleotide (1914). He also studied enzymes and recognized the importance of proteins as building blocks of life.

Fischer, Ernst Otto (1918–). German inorganic chemist. Fischer was educated at the Munich Institute of Technology, where he obtained his Ph.D. in 1952. He taught at the University of Munich, serving as professor of inorganic chemistry from 1957 to 1964, when he became the director of the Institute for Inorganic Chemistry at the Institute of Technology. Fischer is noted for his work on inorganic complexes. He shared the NOBEL PRIZE for chemistry with Geoffrey Wilkinson in 1973. Fischer went on to do further work on transition-metal complexes with organic compounds and is one of the leading workers in the field of organometallic chemistry.

Fischer, Hans (1881–1945). German organic chemist. Fischer gained his doctorate in chemistry at the University of Marburg in 1904. He also studied medicine at the University of Munich, earning his M.D. in 1908. He was assistant to Emil FISCHER before occupying chairs of medical chemistry at Innsbruck (1916) and Vienna (1918). In 1921 he succeeded Heinrich Wieland as professor at the Technical Institute in Munich. Fischer's life work was the study of the immensely important biological molecules hemoglobin, chlorophyll and the bile pigments, especially bilirubin. He synthesized hemin in 1929 and extensively investigated similar molecules—the porphyrins. He was awarded the NOBEL PRIZE for chemistry for this work in 1930. He then turned to the chlorophylls. Fischer took his own life at the end of WORLD WAR II, after his laboratories had been destroyed in the bombing of Munich.

Fischer, Robert James "Bobby" (1943–). American chess champion. Considered among the greatest chess players of all time, Fischer was known for his aggressive style of play as well as for his demanding personality. He became a grandmaster in 1958, then went on to win the U.S. championship. In 1972, he beat the Soviet Union's Boris SPASSKY for the world championship, becoming the first American to hold that title; then he abruptly quit all competitive play. During his brilliant career, Fischer helped to popularize chess throughout the world and helped to break the Soviet domination of the sport.

Fischer-Dieskau, Dietrich (1925–). German lieder (art song) and operatic baritone singer. His interpretations of the great German lieder cycles of Schubert, Schumann and Wolf are incomparable. He was born in Berlin in 1925 and studied voice with G.A. Walter and Hermann Weissenborn. While serving in the German army during WORLD WAR II, he was captured by American forces near Pisa, Italy, and spent the remainder of the war singing lieder to his fellow prisoners. His subsequent concert and recording career with accompanists Joerg Demus, Gerald MOORE and Hartmut Hoell has encompassed an incredibly diverse roster of composers, from Purcell and Handel to Meyerbeer and Strauss to Pfitzner, Charles IVES, Hans-Werner HENZE, and Benjamin BRITTEN (for whom he inspired the baritone part in the *War Requiem*, 1962). On the opera stage Fischer-Dieskau has particularly excelled in the roles of Falstaff, Don Giovanni and Macbeth. In recent years he has established a conducting career, written several books (*Wagner and Nietzsche*, 1974; *Robert Schumann*, 1981; and a biographical study of Schubert's songs, 1976); and presented distinguished master classes. Arguably, his finest achievement was a 25-record project in the late 1960s for the Deutsche-Grammophone label of the approximately 600 Schubert songs. Many of these songs had never before been publicly performed and/or recorded. Although there are some detractors who criticize his tendency to "push" what is a rather lightweight vocal instrument, there is no denying his unparalleled dramatic insight and his complete command of any concert stage.

Fisher, Dorothy Canfield (1879–1958). American author and humanitarian. Using the name Dorothy Canfield, she contributed many stories to magazines. After graduating from Ohio State University in 1899, she went to the Sorbonne in Paris, and took a Ph.D. in 1904 from Columbia University. After marrying John R. Fisher, she lived on her ancestral farm near Arlington, Vermont for the rest of her life. During WORLD WAR I she and her husband undertook relief work in France, resulting in her collection of short stories *Home Fires in France* (1918). She was selected as the only woman on the board of the Book-of-the-Month Club, continuing for 24 years. She introduced and popularized the Montessori method of early childhood education in her *A Montessori Manual* (1913). Her work includes *The Bent Twig* (1915); *Understood Betsy* (1916), considered a children's classic; *Day of Glory* (1919); and *American Portraits* (1946).

Fisher, Geoffrey Francis [Lord Fisher of Lambeth] (1887–1972). English clergyman, Archbishop of Canterbury. Fisher, who also served as primate of the Church of England, was one of the leading supporters of ecumenical unity in the modern Anglican church. In 1960 he paid a visit to Pope JOHN XXIII in the Vatican. That occasion marked the first formal meeting between the heads of the Anglican and the Roman Catholic churches since the initial split between the two churches in 1534. In a 1961 speech, Fisher declared that the terms "Catholic" and "Protestant" were out of date and no longer held real meaning. Fisher's ultimate goal was what he termed a "commonwealth of churches"—with all denominations spiritually unified while each maintained organizational independence. Fisher served as Bishop of Chester (1932) and of London (1939) before becoming Archbishop of Canterbury (1945–61).

Fisher, Sir John (1892–1983). British naval officer and government official. Fisher was one of those responsible for the "little ships" evacuation of Allied troops from DUNKIRK early in WORLD WAR II. Fisher was serving as director of the coastal division of Britain's Ministry of War when he planned **Operation Dynamo,** in which an armada of small boats, most of them privately owned and sailed by civilians, ferried 338,226 Allied troops to England in May and June of 1940.

Fisher, John Arbuthnot [1st Baron Fisher of Kilverstone (1909)] (1841–1920). British admiral. He joined the navy in 1854 and, while trained in sailing ships, became an advocate of technical advances and aided in the development of the torpedo. He developed ordnance (1886–90) and served as third sea lord (1892–97), commander in chief in the Mediterranean (1899–1902), second sea lord (1902–03) and first sea lord (1903–10). Largely responsible for revamping Britain's navy to face the emerging threat from Germany, the fiery admiral helped to build the *Dreadnought* and encouraged the construction of an expanded fleet and the development of the SUBMARINE. He retired in 1910, but returned as first sea lord at the outbreak of WORLD WAR I (1914). Opposed to CHURCHILL's Dardanelles expedition, he resigned in 1915.

Fisher, M(ary) F(rances) K(ennedy) (1908–). American author. After attending the University of California, Fisher spent three years in France studying at the University of Dijon. The author of numerous essays and books on food and cookery, Fisher is known for the clarity and elegance of her writing as well as her ability to intersperse personal reflection and reminiscence throughout her culinary books. Her prose has been praised by W.H. AUDEN, among others. Her works include *Serve it Forth* (1937), which she published as **Mary Frances Parrish,** using her second husband's name; *Here Let Us Feast: A Book of Banquets* (1946); *An Alphabet for Gourmets* (1949); *Not Now but Now: a Novel* (1982); and *Dubious Honors* (1988). Fisher also translated into English *The Physiology of Taste,* by Jean Anthelme Brillat-Savarin (1946).

Fisk, James B. (1910–1981). American physicist. Fisk headed a group that pioneered the development of RADAR during WORLD WAR II. He was appointed the first director of the U.S. Atomic Energy Commission (AEC) in 1947. In 1958 President EISENHOWER sent him to Geneva to head a team of scientists preparing the groundwork for negotiations on the NUCLEAR TEST BAN TREATY. From 1959 to 1973 Fisk was president of Bell Laboratories.

Fitch, (William) Clyde (1865–1909). American playwright whose work at the turn of the century marked an important development in the commercial acceptance of stage realism. Fitch was born in Elmira, New York, the son of an army officer. Defying his father's wishes that he become an architect, Fitch wrote, designed and directed plays at Amherst College. From 1880 to the year of his death, 1909, he wrote 33 original plays and 23 adaptations and became the most popular and successful playwright in the U.S. (and one of the few internationally recognized American playwrights). Many plays, according to the accepted formulas of the day, were historical dramas, salon farces and actor-vehicles, such as *Beau Brummel* (1890), *Barbara Frietchie* (1899) and *Captain Jinks of the Horse Marines* (1901). Weary of mere commercial acclaim, however, "Clyde" Fitch, as he now called himself, wrote *The Climbers* (1901), *The Girl with the Green Eyes* (1902) and *The City* (1909), more obviously patterned after European realistic models by Henry Becque and Henrik Ibsen. *The City,* especially, created some notoriety for its stinging attacks on social hypocrisy and political and personal corruption—and in its free use of profanity. "I'm tired of the narrow point of view here!" declares one of the characters, as if speaking Fitch's own discontent. "The 20th century is to be a glorification of selfishness, the Era of Egotism," says another character in *The Truth.* Fitch must be ranked with Edward Sheldon and William Vaughn Moody as the most important modern playwright prior to the appearance of Eugene O'NEILL. Just before his death of acute appendicitis in 1909, he wrote in an essay, "The Play and the Public," that America must encourage a "National Drama" that is capable of "reflecting absolutely and truthfully the life and environment about us."

Fitch, Val Logsdon (1923–). American physicist. Fitch was educated at McGill and Columbia universities and obtained his Ph.D. from Columbia in 1954. He then joined the staff of Princeton University, where he became professor of physics in 1960. Working with Leo James Rainwater, Fitch was the first to observe radiation from muonic atoms, i.e., from species in which a muon is orbiting a nucleus rather than an electron. This work indicated that the sizes of atomic nuclei were smaller than had been supposed. He went on to study kaons and in 1964 collaborated with James CRONIN, James Christenson and Rene Turley in an experiment that disproved CP conservation. In 1980 Fitch and Cronin shared the 1980 NOBEL PRIZE for physics for this fundamental work.

Fitzgerald, Barry [born William Joseph Shields] (1888–1961). Irish actor. Born in Dublin, Fitzgerald acted part-time at the ABBEY THEATRE from 1918 until 1929, after which he became a permanent member of the company. Fitzgerald established his reputation in the role of Captain Boyle, in Sean O'CASEY's *Juno and the Paycock* (1924). He appeared first in London in O'Casey's *The Silver Tassie* (1929). Following 1937, Fitzgerald appeared primarily in films, such as *Going My Way* (1944) and *The Quiet Man* (1952).

Fitzgerald, Ella (1918–). American jazz and popular singer known for her elegant song stylings. Born in Newport News, Virginia, Fitzgerald was raised by her aunt in New York. After winning the Harlem Amateur Hour contest, she became a vocalist with the Chick WEBB band in 1934. She first gained wide attention with her recording (with Webb) of "A-Tisket, A-Tasket"; although the song itself is mediocre, Fitzgerald's vocalization made it an instant hit. She displayed her characteristic traits—swing rhythm, improvisatory spirit, vocal range, control and clarity. After Webb's death (1939) she became the leader of the band. Fitzgerald's career has been remarkable for its longevity and its sustained excellence. She has worked with many of the notable jazz musicians of her time, toured extensively in the U.S. and Europe and made numerous concert, festival, nightclub and television appearances. Her repertoire, well represented in recordings, ranges from the sophisticated lyrics of George and Ira GERSHWIN to BLUES and scat songs.

Ella Fitzgerald, First Lady of Song, in concert at Carnegie Hall (1989).

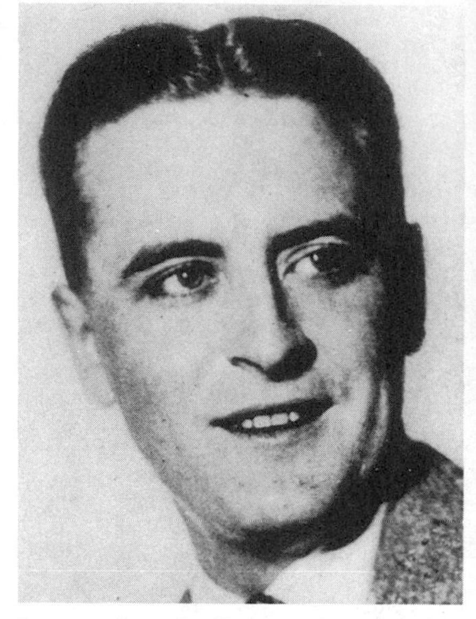

Jazz-age author and sophisticate F. Scott Fitzgerald (ca. 1920s).

For further reading:

Kliment, Bud, *Ella Fitzgerald.* New York: Chelsea House, 1989.

Fitzgerald, F(rancis) Scott (1896–1940). American novelist and short story writer. Fitzgerald captured in his writings the perceived moral emptiness of the wealthy American society of the "Roaring Twenties." Although not a member of the wealthy set, his elite education in private schools provided insight into the life of the privileged. Born in St. Paul, Minnesota, he attended Princeton University but resigned to join the Army (1917) and served in France during WORLD WAR I. While in the Army, he published his first book, *This Side of Paradise,* in 1920. In *Tales of the Jazz Age* (1922) he coined the term "Jazz Age" to describe his era. In 1924 Fitzgerald went to Europe, where he lived for six years. He published his best-known work, THE GREAT GATSBY (1925), while living abroad. *Gatsby* is now widely acclaimed both for its formal perfection and for its insights into the American experience, but its initial reception was disappointing. The mental illness of his wife, Zelda Sayre Fitzgerald, and his bouts with alcohol hampered his literary progress and left Fitzgerald in a difficult financial position. *Tender Is the Night* (1934), perhaps his most ambitious book, was a financial failure. Fitzgerald turned to scriptwriting for HOLLYWOOD in 1936, and died of a heart attack before his *The Last Tycoon* was finished.

For further reading:

Bruccoli, Matthew J., *Some Sort of Epic Grandeur.* Orlando, Florida: Harcourt Brace Jovanovich, 1983.

Fitzgerald, Robert Stuart (1910–1985). American scholar, critic and poet. Fitzgerald was a Harvard professor best known for his translations of the Greek classics. In 1961, his version of Homer's *Odyssey* won the first Bollingen award for translation of poetry. He also translated some major modern French literature.

Fitzmaurice, George (1877–1963). Irish playwright. Fitzmaurice's first play, *The Country Dressmaker* (1907), was performed at the ABBEY THEATRE and was an enormously popular realistic comedy. His later works, which include *The Pie-Dish* (1908), *The Dandy Dolls* (1908) and *The Magic Glasses* (1913), were more difficult, involving elements of the fantastic and grotesque; they were not popular during his lifetime. He remained a civil servant in Dublin. Following his death there was a revival of interest in his work, which has been compared to that of James STEPHENS.

Fitzsimmons, Frank E(dward) (1908–1981). American labor leader and head of the International Brotherhood of Teamsters (1971–81). Beginning as a truck driver, Fitzsimmons rose through the union ranks. He took temporary charge of the largest U.S. union when Jimmy HOFFA, his predecessor, was sent to prison (1967). After his election as head of the Teamsters, he expanded the union as a political force, improved relations with the AFL-CIO and maintained close ties with the White House. Nonetheless, charges of misuse of funds and other abuses continued to plague Fitzsimmons and the Teamsters.

five-year plan. In communist and socialist countries, a plan during which the economic growth of the country is structured for the following five years. The first five-year plan was ordered in the UNION OF SOVIET SOCIALIST REPUBLICS by Joseph STALIN and lasted from 1928 to 1932. In 1958, Nikita KHRUSHCHEV hit on the idea of a seven-year plan. Although the U.S.S.R. made immense industrial strides through its five-year plans during the Stalinist period, the cost in human suffering was also immense. Invariably, five-year plans have failed to meet their ambitious goals; they are often seen more as PROPAGANDA exercises than as realistic programs.

Flagstad, Kirsten (1895–1962). Norwegian opera singer, considered the greatest Wagnerian soprano of the 1930s and 1940s. Flagstad made her debut in *Tiefland* in Oslo (1913) and continued to sing in operettas until she joined the Storm Theater in Gothenburg, Sweden (1930) and devoted herself to opera. Her performance as Sieglinde in *Die Walkure* in Bayreuth (1934) established her international reputation. Her 1935 debut in the same role at the Metropolitan Opera in New York was a triumph, and her subsequent sold-out appearances over the next five years helped save the Met from financial ruin during the GREAT DEPRESSION. Her greatest roles were as Sieglinde, Isolde (*Tristan and Isolde*), Kundry (*Parsifal*) and the three Brunnhildes of Wagner's Ring Cycle. After retiring from live performance in 1954, she founded the Norwegian State Opera in 1959 and became its director.

For further reading:
McArthur, Edwin, *Flagstad: A Personal Memoir*. New York: DaCapo, 1980 (repr. of 1965 edition).

Flaherty, Robert (1884–1951). American documentary filmmaker. Flaherty came to know the Canadian and Alaskan wildernesses as a child when he accompanied his father in travels throughout the Northwest Territory. These experiences came to fruition when Flaherty shot a silent documentary, *Nanook of the North* (1922), that documented Eskimo life and became a box-office success. He followed with *Moana* (1926), a documentary on the South Sea islands. *Man of Aran* (1934) is the work most acclaimed by film critics—a beautifully photographed study in black and white of the harsh conditions of village life on the Aran Islands of Ireland. *Elephant Boy* (1936) was a film on India. Flaherty's final documentary, sponsored by Standard Oil, was *Louisiana Story* (1948).

For further reading:
Calder-Marshall, Arthur, *The Innocent Eye*. London: W.H. Allen, 1963.

Flanagan, (Father) Edward Joseph (1886–1948). American priest and founder of BOYS TOWN. A parish priest in Nebraska, Father Flanagan became interested in the treatment of homeless or lawbreaking boys, and founded Boys Town near Omaha in 1917. The work began with five boys in a rented house. Next year he bought a small tract of land where he and the boys began to build the institution. Boys Town was incorporated as a municipality in 1922. His belief that "there is no such thing as a bad boy" was confirmed by his spectacular success in training young men, many of whom went on to successful careers. Father Flanagan's work was featured in the popular 1938 movie *Boys Town*. Following World War II, he became a special consultant on youth to the U.S. government and traveled to the Orient and Europe to inspect youth work and facilities.

Father Flanagan, Jesuit priest and founder of the home for needy boys that inspired the 1938 film Boys Town *(1945).*

Flanders. Ancient, strategically located area on the English Channel–North Sea coast of Europe, running from what is now the north of France through Belgium and into the Netherlands. Parts of it are in the French departments of Pas-de-Calais and Nord, the Belgian provinces of East and West Flanders and the Zeeland province of the Netherlands. It has had a turbulent history and was a perpetual battlefield during WORLD WAR I and a critical area during WORLD WAR II. The continuous battles in both French and West Flanders during World War I were depicted in John McCrae's poem, *In Flanders' Fields*. During World War II the battle of Flanders commenced with the Nazi attack on Belgium in 1940 and finished with the capitulation of the Belgian army and the British evacuation at DUNKIRK, from May 26 to June 4, 1940.

Flanner, Janet (1892–1978). American writer. Flanner was a correspondent for the NEW YORKER magazine for almost 50 years. Her regular "Letter from Paris" feature in the magazine gave insight into the French mind and way of life. She also wrote profiles of such diverse figures as Adolf HITLER, Henri MATISSE and Queen Mary.

Fleetwood Mac. Anglo-American ROCK AND ROLL band. While the band Fleetwood Mac has experienced numerous changes in musical personnel since its founding in 1967, its most prominent members have been guitarist Lindsay Buckingham, drummer Mick Fleetwood, pianist and vocalist Christine McVie, bass player John McVie and vocalist Stevie Nicks. Fleetwood and John McVie, the two key founders of the band, met in the 1960s while playing together in a British group, John Mayall's Bluesbreakers. In 1969, Fleetwood Mac enjoyed a number-one hit in Britain with an instrumental single, "Albatross." In 1974 Americans Buckingham and Nicks joined the band, and still greater commercial success ensued. A 1977 album, *Rumours*, became the first album by a rock-and-roll band to produce four singles that each reached the *Billboard* Top Ten pop chart—"Go Your Own Way," "Dreams," "Don't Stop" and "You Make Loving Fun." Fleetwood Mac disbanded for a time in the mid-1980s, but the group later reunited and resumed actively performing and recording. Nicks also pursued a successful solo career.

Fleischer, Max (1883–1972). American cartoonist. Fleischer created the "Popeye" and "Out of the Inkwell" cartoon series (1917). He also invented more than 20 devices used in animation and motion picture production.

Fleming, Sir Alexander (1881–1955). British bacteriologist. After his early education at Kilmarnock Academy and the London Polytechnic Institute, Fleming began his career at the age of 16 as a shipping clerk in a London office. With encouragement from his brother, who was a doctor, he became a medical student at

Sir Alexander Fleming, discoverer of the miracle drug penicillin (1952).

St. Mary's Hospital Medical School in 1902 and graduated from the University of London in 1908. He worked at St. Mary's all his life apart from his service in the Royal Army Medical Corps (1914–18). During his time with the Medical Corps he became interested in the control of wound infections and was a vigorous supporter of the physiological treatment of wounds rather than treatment using harsh chemicals, such as carbolic acid.

In 1928 Fleming was appointed professor of bacteriology and in the same year he made his most important discovery. After accidentally leaving a dish of staphylococcus bacteria uncovered, Fleming noticed certain clear areas in the culture. He found these areas were due to contamination by a mold he identified as *Penicillium notatum,* which produced a substance that killed the bacteria. Fleming named this substance PENICILLIN and tested the bactericidal effect of the mold on various bacteria, observing that it killed some but not others. He appreciated the potentialities of his discovery but was unable to isolate and identify the compound. It was not until WORLD WAR II, with the urgent need for new antibacterial drugs, that penicillin—the first antibiotic—was finally isolated by Howard Florey and Ernst CHAIN. Fleming was awarded the 1945 NOBEL PRIZE for physiology or medicine jointly with Florey and Chain for his discovery, which initiated a whole new range of life-saving antibiotics. He received a knighthood in 1944 and many other honors.

Fleming, Lady Amalia [born Amalia Koutsouris] (1909–1986). Greek political activist. She was the wife of Sir Alexander FLEMING, the discoverer of PENICILLIN. She became internationally known for her resistance to the military junta that ruled GREECE from 1967 to 1974. Expelled from Greece in 1971, she returned there after democracy was restored. In 1977 she was elected to Parliament as a Socialist Party member, and later reelected in 1981 and 1985.

Fleming, Ian (Lancaster) (1908–1964). British novelist and journalist. The son of a Conservative M.P., Fleming was educated at Eton, Sandhurst and the universities of Munich and Geneva. He served as Moscow correspondent for Reuters from 1929 to 1933 and later as a reporter for *The Times* of London. Fleming wrote the enormously popular series of espionage novels featuring JAMES BOND, agent 007, the embodiment of many a male adolescent fantasy. The Bond books, nearly all of which have been filmed, include *Casino Royale* (1953, filmed 1967), *Goldfinger* (1959, filmed 1964) and *The Spy Who Loved Me* (1962, filmed 1977). The series was given an additional boost in the U.S. by the praise of President John F. KENNEDY. Fleming also wrote the children's book *Chitty-Chitty-Bang-Bang* (1964, adapted as a musical film, 1968) and contributed to many periodicals under the pseudonym Atticus. The popular James Bond image of the spy as a glamorous superhero has been largely refuted by John LE CARRE.

Fleming, Peggy Gale (1948–). U.S. figure skater. One of the great balletic stylists, she won the first of her five straight U.S. ladies' championships at the age of 15. The ladies' world champion from 1966 through 1968, she was an Olympic gold medal winner in 1968. After the Olympics, she turned professional and performed with a number of ice shows and in professional competitions.

Fleming, Williamina Paton Stevens (1857–1911). U.S. astronomer. She was a housekeeper in Boston when her employer, E.C. Pickering, hired her onto his Harvard College Observatory staff in 1881. Here she helped develop the "Pickering-Fleming" stellar classification system of photographic spectroscopy. She published her *Draper Catalogue of Stellar Spectra* of over 10,000 stars in 1890. She also established the first photographic system of measuring stellar magnitude, discovered half of the then known novae and over 200 variable-magnitude stars. In 1898 Harvard appointed her curator of astronomical photographs, and between 1892 and 1910 she cataloged over 200,000 plates. During her lifetime, Fleming was America's most famous woman astronomer.

Flerov, Georgi (1913–). Soviet nuclear physicist. Educated at the Leningrad Industrial Institute of Science, Flerov started his career at the Leningrad Institute of Physics and Technology in 1938. He later became chief of the laboratory of multicharged ions at the Kurchatov Institute of Atomic Energy, Moscow. Throughout his life, Flerov has been involved in the search for new elements and isotopes through synthesis and discovery. In many ways his work parallels that of Glenn SEABORG in America. In 1960 Flerov became director of the nuclear radiation laboratories of the Joint Institute for Nuclear Research, Dubna, near Moscow.

Fletcher, Harvey (1884–1981). American physicist and expert on electronic acoustics. Fletcher joined Bell Telephone Laboratories in 1916. His acoustical research resulted in the development in 1934 of stereophonic sound. As head of physical research at Bell from 1933 to 1949, he helped develop the first electronic hearing aids and directed pioneering work on sound in motion pictures, television, and transistors.

Fletcher, James (1919–). U.S. space administrator and head of NASA for two separate terms, April 1971–May 1977 and, following the CHALLENGER Shuttle disaster in January 1986, from May 1986 to April 1989, when he resigned. Fletcher began his career in 1940 as a research physicist with the U.S. Navy Bureau of Ordnance. As a research scientist he developed patents in SONAR devices and missile guidance systems and served on many government–industry committees, as well as on the influential President's Science Advisory Committee.

Fletcher, John Gould (1886–1950). American poet and critic. Born in Arkansas, Fletcher later lived for many years in England. His early poetry, such as *Irradiations: Sand and Spray* (1915) and *Goblins and Pagodas* (1916), was experimental and associated with that of the imagist poets. Fletcher later became concerned with issues of philosophy and spirituality, during which period he published *The Black Rock* (1928). This poetry, although mysti-

Creator of the wildly successful James Bond series, author Ian Fleming and Mrs. Fleming (1962).

cal in nature, is more traditional in form. Late in life, Fletcher returned to rural Arkansas, retreating from what he deemed the dehumanization of modern life. For *Selected Poems* (1938) he was awarded the PULITZER PRIZE in poetry. Other works include *The Epic of Arkansas* (1936) and *South Star* (1941). (See also IMAGISM.)

Flexner, Simon (1863–1946). American pathologist and authority on infectious diseases. In 1900, as professor of pathology at Johns Hopkins, Flexner discovered the bacillus that was causing a virulent form of dysentery among American troops in the Philippines; the organism was later named *Shingella flexneri*. In 1907, in response to an outbreak of meningitis in New York City, Flexner, then director of the laboratories at the Rockefeller Institute for Medical Research, developed a serum that remained a standard treatment of the disease for three decades. He headed the Rockefeller Institute from 1920 until 1935.

Floody, C. Wallace (1918–1989). Canadian air force officer. As a PRISONER OF WAR (POW) in a German prison camp during WORLD WAR II, he engineered the tunnel for a 1944 escape attempt. Although 76 Allied officers made their way out of the camp during the escape, only three made their way out of German-occupied Europe to safety. At least 50 were recaptured and executed. The story formed the basis of a 1963 film, *The Great Escape*. Floody himself did not take part in the breakout, having been transferred to another compound shortly before the attempt.

Florensky, Paul Alexandrovich (1892–?). Russian Orthodox priest, philosopher and physicist. One of the founders of the Union of Christian Struggle as a student, he then lectured at the Moscow Theological Academy. Banished to Central Asia before the 1917 Bolshevik seizure of power, he returned afterwards and studied advanced physics at the Academy of Sciences. He was deported to a CONCENTRATION CAMP in the 1920s, and nothing more is known about him. His *The Pillar and Foundation of Truth* (1914) has influenced philosophical and theological thought in the U.S.S.R.

Florida. In the far southeast of the U.S., Florida became the 27th state in 1845. A low peninsula 500 miles long, it is bordered by the Atlantic Ocean on the east and the Gulf of Mexico on the west; the West Indies lie to the south and the states of Alabama and Georgia are to the north. A real estate boom and a bid for tourism were the eventual result of a huge land sale to developers in 1881. In 1898 Florida reaped benefits from the Spanish-American War, when Tampa served as the primary military base. Another real estate boom failed in 1925 when inflated prices toppled the market. WORLD WAR II was a boon to Florida's industry, and the state's industrial and population growth continued long after the war's end. CAPE CANAVERAL achieved fame in the late 1950s as a busy center for spaceflight operations. Schools were desegregated after 1954. In the years following the Cuban Revolution of 1958 a deluge of refugees descended on the state, a mass movement repeated in 1980 when 125,000 Cubans landed in Key West; there have also been many Haitian refugees. Race relations have often been difficult. In May 1980, Miami was the scene of 18 deaths and property damage of $100 million, after the acquittal of white police officers charged with beating a black man to death. Florida was considered a Democratic state, but recent years have seen a surge of Republican fervor and the state frequently votes Republican in national elections. Elderly and retired people comprise a large part of the population. The state suffers from water shortages and conservation problems caused primarily by its rapid expansion. Tallahassee is the capital; Miami is the largest city.

Floyd, (Charles Arthur) ["Pretty Boy"] (1901–1934). American gangster. Raised in Oklahoma's Cherokee Indian Territory, bank-robber Floyd became a folk hero to Depression-era sharecroppers in his home state. Unable to find work, he turned to robbery in the mid-1920s. He served (1925–26) one short term in jail, escaped (1930) a second, longer sentence, and was soon robbing banks throughout the Midwest along with a succession of partners. Along the way, he made a considerable reputation as a Robin Hood, distributing money to the poor and ripping up bank mortgages. At the same time, he became a confirmed killer, murdering an estimated 10 men. Labeled "public enemy number one" in the early 1930s, he was killed in an Ohio cornfield on October 22, 1934, by FBI agents under Melvin PURVIS.

Flushing. A northern section of the NEW YORK CITY borough of QUEENS, at the head of Flushing Bay in southeastern New York state. Assimilated by New York City in 1898, Flushing hosted two world's fairs, in 1939–40 and in 1964–65, and was the headquarters of the UN General Assembly from 1946 to 1949.

Flying Tigers. Popular term for the American Volunteer Group (AVG), an organization formed in 1941 by Colonel Claire Chennault and directed by him. Recruited from the U.S. armed forces, the men of the Flying Tigers fought for CHIANG KAI-SHEK's China against the Japanese from 1941 to 1942. Based in Burma, the three squadrons that comprised the AVG flew American P-40 fighter planes, their wings marked with the Chinese Nationalist sun, their noses emblazoned with menacing red, white and blue shark's teeth. The Flying Tigers proved invaluable in protecting the BURMA ROAD supply line from Japanese incursions and were an important factor in delaying the Japanese capture of Rangoon until March 1942. Four months later, the AVG was transferred to American auspices and ceased to exist as a separate military entity.

Flynn, Errol (1909–1959). Australian-born film actor; achieved enduring success during the 1930s and 1940s as the archetypal HOLLYWOOD swashbuckler. Born on

Hollywood leading man and action hero Errol Flynn exhibits his famous good looks in this still from Santa Fe Trail *(1940).*

the island of Tasmania off the Australian coast, Flynn began his acting career with roles on the British stage before coming to Hollywood in 1934. After playing a few bit parts, he shot to stardom playing the romantic lead in the pirate film *Captain Blood* (1935), directed by Michael Curtiz and featuring Olivia de Havilland as Flynn's leading lady. Flynn then enjoyed a string of hits including *The Charge of the Light Brigade* (1936), *The Adventures of Robin Hood* (1938), *Dodge City* (1939) and *They Died With Their Boots On* (1941). In 1942 he was charged with statutory rape but acquitted, prompting the popular saying "In like Flynn." In his last years, Flynn turned to character roles in films including *The Sun Also Rises* (1957) and *The Roots of Heaven* (1958). *My Wicked, Wicked Ways* (1959) is his revelatory autobiography.

FNLA [National Front for the Liberation of Angola]. An independence movement that fought alongside UNITA against the ultimately victorious MPLA in the ANGOLAN CIVIL WAR begun in 1975. It was funded from CHINA, and initially from the U.S. and ZAIRE.

Fo, Dario (1926–). Italian playwright, actor and theatrical producer. Fo has been a highly political figure in the postwar Italian theater and has avoided the twin extremes of COMMUNISM and FASCISM. He first attained success as a cabaret mime artist in the 1950s, performing satiric reviews with his wife, Franca Rama. Fo subsequently began to write plays that parodied the prevailing COLD WAR politics of the time. His work includes *Archangels Don't Play the Pin-Tables* (1959) and *Seventh: Thou Shalt Steal a Little Less* (1964). Fo achieved success throughout Europe with his play *Accidental Death of an Anarchist* (1970). His more recent plays include *We Won't Pay! We Won't Pay!* (1974) and *Trumpets and Raspberries* (1984).

Foch, Ferdinand (1851–1929). French general. A veteran of the Franco-Prussian War of 1870–71 and commandant of the Ecole de Guerre (1907–11), Foch was an official observer at Germany's army maneuvers in 1913. At the outbreak of WORLD WAR I he led the French Ninth Army at the MARNE. He also served in FLANDERS and commanded a French army group on the SOMME in 1916. After a brief retirement, he became General PETAIN's chief of staff in May 1917. His impressive performance led to his appointment as supreme commander of Allied forces on the Western Front in the spring of 1918 (see WORLD WAR I ON THE WESTERN FRONT). He commanded the successful Marne counteroffensive (July 1918) and the subsequent offensive that led the Germans to sue for an armistice in November 1918. At the PARIS PEACE CONFERENCE (1919) he urged CLEMENCEAU to impose strong conditions on Germany. Foch was created a marshal of France in 1918; he was also made an honorary field marshal in the British army, the only Frenchman so honored.

Focke, Heinrich (1890–1979). German aircraft designer. Focke was an aviation pioneer whose FW-61 helicopter made the first free flight of a rotary-wing aircraft (1936). His VA-61 was the world's first helicopter to receive a certificate of airworthiness. One of his airplanes held the altitude record until 1954.

Fokine, Michael (1880–1942). Russian dancer and choreographer. He was one of the founders of modern ballet. Isadora DUNCAN inspired Fokine to free himself from the rigid classical discipline of the Imperial Ballet to create ballets in which dancing, music and scenery are combined in a related whole. *Le Cygne* (*The Dying Swan,* 1905), created as a solo for Anna PAVLOVA, and *Chopiniana* (later known as *Les Sylphides,* 1906) were early works. His great period was with DIAGHILEV in Paris (from 1909), when he created *Petrushka, Scheherazade, The Firebird* and *Le Spectre de la Rose.* He left Russia for France at the outbreak of the revolution and moved to the U.S. during World War II.

Fokker, Anton Hermann Gerard (1890–1939). German-American aircraft designer and manufacturer. Born in Java of Dutch parents, Fokker moved to Germany, where he established a number of airplane factories. During WORLD WAR I, he manufactured more than 40 kinds of airplanes for the German military, including the famous Fokker biplanes and triplanes. In addition, he developed a system for gear synchronization that allowed pilots to fire machine guns through spinning propellers. In 1922 he settled in the U.S., where he became a citizen and concentrated on the development of commercial aviation. His autobiography, *The Flying Dutchman,* was published in 1931.

Folsom, James E(lisha) "Big Jim" (1908–1987). American politician. Folsom served two terms as governor of Alabama, from 1947 to 1951 and from 1955 to 1959. Known as "the little man's big friend," he stood six feet eight inches tall. In an era when his state was regarded as a bastion of racism, he was regarded as a moderate or liberal on most issues.

Henry Fonda, surrounded by his children, receives the Life Achievement in Motion Pictures and Television Award from the American Film Institute (1978).

Fonda, Henry (1905–1983). American actor. Widely acclaimed as one of America's greatest actors, Fonda starred in 80 films, 15 plays and numerous television dramas during a career that spanned nearly 50 years. Born in Nebraska, he joined the University Players in New England (1928), where he met Joshua LOGAN as well as James STEWART, who became a lifelong friend and later a frequent co-star. In the early 1930s he appeared on Broadway, then moved to HOLLYWOOD to appear in films. In 1939 he began a long and successful collaboration with director John FORD, starring (as Abraham Lincoln) in *Young Mr. Lincoln* and in *Drums Along the Mohawk.* His role in Ford's adaptation of John STEINBECK's *The Grapes of Wrath* (1940) established his quintessential screen persona as a soft-spoken but determined idealist. Among his notable later films are *The Ox-Bow Incident* (1943), *My Darling Clementine* (1946), *Mr. Roberts* (1955), *Twelve Angry Men* (1956), *Fail-Safe* (1964) and *On Golden Pond* (1981), his last movie. Fonda was equally adept in comedies, westerns, and social dramas. He returned to the stage periodically and gave acclaimed performances in such plays as *Mr. Roberts* and *Clarence Darrow.* Many of his roles reflected his commitment to liberal social and political causes. His daughter, Jane FONDA, is also a noted actress and controversial social activist; his son Peter has been somewhat less successful as an actor, director, and producer.

Fonda, Jane (1937–). American film actress; from a renowned HOLLYWOOD family that includes her father Henry FONDA, and her brother, Peter. At age 16, Fonda acted alongside her father in an Omaha stage production of *The Country Girl.* She made her film debut in *Tall Story* (1960). In 1965, Fonda married French film director Roger Vadim and starred in a number of his films, notably the futuristic sex fantasy *Barbarella* (1968), before their divorce. In the late 1960s, she became a leading anti-VIETNAM WAR activist, visiting HANOI and making documentaries such as *Introduction to the Enemy* (1974); her widely publicized and highly controversial visit stirred charges that she was at best naive, at worst a traitor. During this period Fonda married political activist Tom Hayden. She enjoyed a major Hollywood success with the thriller *Klute* (1971), for which she won an ACADEMY AWARD as best actress. She has been a major star ever since, with films including *Julia* (1977), *Coming Home* (1978), for which she won a second best actress Oscar, *Nine to Five* (1981), *On Golden Pond* (1981), in which she co-starred with her father, and *The Old Gringo* (1989). Fonda also became well-known for her physical fitness books and videotapes.

Fontainebleau. Town in France's Seine-et-Marne department, 35 miles south–southeast of PARIS. Now a resort area, Fontainebleau grew around a royal residence that itself evolved from a medieval hunting lodge into a magnificent Renaissance palace. Fontainebleau was a headquarters first for the Germans, then for the Allies, in WORLD WAR II, and for NATO's military branch from 1945 to 1967.

Fontanne, Lynn. See LUNT AND FONTANNE.

Dame Margot Fonteyn at London's Covent Garden, in her 35th year with the British Royal Ballet (1962).

Fonteyn, Dame Margot [born Margaret Hookham] (1919–1991). Legendary British ballerina considered one of the greatest dancers of the 20th century. Born in England to an English father and a Brazilian-Irish mother, Fonteyn spent much of her childhood with her parents in North America and China. She entered the Sadler's Wells Ballet School (now the Royal Ballet School) in 1934, making her dancing debut in a child's role in *The Nutcracker.* She soon come to the attention of Dame Ninette DE VALOIS, who selected her (1935) to follow Alicia MARKOVA as the company's prima ballerina. At 17, Fonteyn danced the title role in *Giselle,* and for more than four decades thereafter she held center stage in British ballet. At the Royal Ballet, she was known for her brilliant characterizations and flawless technique in such classics as *Swan Lake* and *The Sleeping Beauty,* as well as for the dances created for her by the choreographer Sir Frederick ASHTON, including *Ondine* (1958) and *La Fille Mal Gardee* (1960). In 1962 Fonteyn began a legendary partnership with Rudolf NUREYEV. Created a Dame of the British Empire in 1956, she retired from dancing at 60 and was awarded the rarely bestowed title *prima ballerina assoluta.* Her husband was the Panamanian politician Roberto Emilio ARIAS. Their long courtship and, later, Fonteyn's devotion to her husband after he was paralyzed by a would-be assassin, is one of the great romantic stories of the 20th century.

Foot, Michael (1913–). British politician and journalist. After leaving Oxford, Foot became a journalist noted for his disputatious left-wing columns. He entered Parliament in 1945, served as editor of the LABOUR PARTY journal *Tribune* from 1948 to 1952 and from 1955 to 1960, and was secretary of state for employment from 1975 to 1979. In 1976 Foot became deputy prime minister and leader of the House of Commons. Following James CALLAGHAN's resignation in 1980, Foot served as leader of the Labour Party until 1983, attempting to maintain the party's traditional lines against resistance by the more conservative Social Democrats. A gifted orator, Foot is also the author of a two-volume biography of Aneurin BEVAN published in 1962 and 1973. (See also SOCIAL DEMOCRATIC PARTY.)

Forbes, Esther (1891–1967). U.S. novelist and biographer. After studying writing at the University of Wisconsin (1916–18), she worked for publisher Houghton Mifflin in Boston (1919–26). She was awarded the O. Henry Prize for her story "Break-Neck Hill" in 1920. She published a steady stream of successful novels blending sexual passion and social repression in Puritan New England. Among the most famous are: *O, Genteel Lady* (1926), *A Mirror for Witches* (1928) and *Miss Marvel* (1935). She also wrote the PULITZER PRIZE-winning biography *Paul Revere and the World He Lived In* (1942), and the Newberry Prize-winning *Johnny Tremain* (1943).

Forbes, Malcolm Stevenson (1919–1990). American businessman. Forbes was chairman of Forbes Inc. and publisher of *Forbes* business magazine, which had been founded by his father in 1917. He was a flamboyant millionaire who was known for his love of yachting, motorcycling and hot-air ballooning. In his later years a frequent escort of actress Elizabeth TAYLOR, Forbes generated widespread publicity in 1989 with a $2 million 70th-birthday party he threw for himself in Morocco shortly before his death.

Flamboyant publishing magnate Malcolm Forbes (1987).

Forbush, Scott E. (1904–1984). American geophysicist who pioneered research into cosmic rays. Forbush gave his name to the **Forbush effect,** a sharp lessening of the incidence of cosmic rays on Earth as the planet passes through a cloud of gas ejected by a solar flare.

Ford, Edsel Bryant (1893–1943). U.S. automotive executive and son of Henry FORD. In 1919 he succeeded his father as president and treasurer of the Ford Motor Company. However, industry opinion held that Edsel's authority was almost entirely nominal and that he merely carried out his father's wishes. Together the Fords established the FORD FOUNDATION. Henry Ford resumed the presidency when Edsel died in 1943. Edsel's name is perhaps best remembered for the ill-fated Edsel car of the 1950s, which proved to be well ahead of its time and now is in great demand as a classic car.

For further reading:

Lacey, Robert, *Ford: The Men and the Machine.* Boston: Little, Brown, 1986.

Ford, Ford Maddox [born Ford Hermann Hueffer] (1873–1939). British novelist. Ford changed his name in 1917 because of its German connotations. (His maternal grandfather was the noted pre-Raphaelite painter Ford Maddox Brown.) Ford was the son of a music critic, and his childhood environment was an intellectual one. He was educated at University College School in London and converted to Catholicism at the age of 18. Ford published some fairy tales in the early 1890s and became acquainted with Joseph CONRAD, with whom he collaborated on the novels *The Inheritors* (1901) and *Romance* (1903). The two parted due to disagreements, the details of which Ford later obfuscated in his memoirs. On his own, Ford published *The Fifth Queen* (1906), the first of a trilogy about Catherine Howard, wife of Henry VIII; and in 1908 founded and edited the *English Review.* It was with the publication of *The Good Soldier* (1915), still considered Ford's most important novel, that he received some critical attention; however, he was never to realize great success in his lifetime. Also in 1915, he enlisted in the army, later to be invalided home in 1917, after having been gassed. His next major work, *Parade's End,* was published originally in four separate parts: *Some Do Not* (1924), *No More Parades* (1925), *A Man Could Stand Up* (1926) and *The Last Post* (1928). The books characterize the era prior to WORLD WAR I. In 1922 Ford moved to Paris, where he founded the seminal *Transatlantic Review,* which published work by James JOYCE and Ezra POUND, among others. Ford's interesting and idiosyncratic memoirs include *Return to Yesterday* (1931) and *It Was the Nightingale* (1933). His last publication was an original work of literary criticism, *The March of Literature* (1938). Although his work has never garnered popular acclaim, Ford's writing has received important critical recognition. As an editor, Ford had an enormous influence on subsequent 20th-century literature.

Gerald R. Ford, 38th president of the United States.

For further reading:
Judd, Alan, *Ford Maddox Ford*. Cambridge, Mass.: Harvard University Press, 1991.

Ford, Gerald (1913–). American statesman and president of the UNITED STATES (1974–77). Ford served in the Navy during WORLD WAR II, then practiced law until he was elected to the U.S. House of Representatives from Michigan in 1948. A conservative Republican, Ford served as minority leader from 1965 to 1973, when President Richard M. NIXON named him to replace Spiro T. AGNEW as vice president. In 1974, after Nixon resigned, Ford became the 38th president. His pardon of Nixon and his program of limited amnesty for Vietnam-era deserters and draft dodgers stirred controversy. In foreign affairs Ford pursued a policy of DETENTE with the Soviet Union, signing the Vladivostok Arms Limitation Agreement in 1974. On the domestic scene he was plagued by an inflation–recession economy, incurring huge budget deficits. He survived two separate assassination attempts in 1975. Although he lost the 1976 presidential election to Jimmy CARTER, Ford has remained politically active.

For further reading:
Randolph, Sallie G., *Gerald R. Ford, President*. New York: Walker, 1987.

Ford, Henry (1863–1947). American automobile manufacturer. Starting as a mechanic in Detroit, Ford began experimenting with engines about 1890, and completed his first gasoline engine in 1893. The first Ford automobile was completed in 1896. Encouraged by Thomas EDISON, Ford organized the Ford Motor Company in 1903. He started the development of the Model T car in 1908 and managed to reduce the price to within the reach of almost everyone. The car brought fame and fortune to the company, which in turn shared its profits with employees. To avoid stockholders' complaints about profit sharing, Ford bought them all out. From 1919 to 1956 the Ford family had sole control of the company. In 1932 Ford developed the V-8 engine.

Ford paid expenses for 150 people for a "peace trip" to Europe in 1915, but the trip ended in failure. While opposed to the entry of the U.S. into WORLD WAR I and WORLD WAR II, Ford quickly made his plants available for the manufacture of war materials. The Willow Run, Michigan plant was the largest aircraft assembly plant in the world; during World War II, it manufactured B-24 bombers until hostilities ceased.

Ford established Greenfield Village and the Ford Museum in Dearborn, Michigan. With Edsel, his son, he established the FORD FOUNDATION. He passed on the presidency of the company to Edsel in 1919, and then resumed the office when Edsel died in 1943. In 1945, he once again relinquished the company presidency, to Edsel's son Henry Ford II.

For further reading:
Bryan, Ford R., *The Fords of Dearborn: An Illustrated History*. Detroit: Wayne State University Press, 1989.
Collier, Peter, *The Fords: An American Epic*. New York: Summit Books, 1987.
Gelderman, Carol, *Henry Ford: The Wayward Capitalist*. New York: St. Martin's, 1989.

Ford, Henry, II (1917–). Grandson of Henry FORD, the younger Henry Ford was named president of Ford Motor Company

Three Americans who helped shape the 20th century—John Muir, Henry Ford and Thomas Edison—take a drive in the Florida sunshine (1914).

in 1945 at the age of 28. Unlike his grandfather, who was an autocratic manager and foe of unionism, Ford developed a flexible policy toward unions. He also initiated a sweeping reform of the administrative structure of the company to modernize the firm's inefficient managerial system and production techniques. In 1960 he became chairman and chief executive officer of the corporation. He resigned as chairman in 1979.

Ford, John [Sean Aloysius O'Feeney] (1895–1973). American film director best known for his westerns and Americana films. Ford was one of the screen's greatest lyric poets and a master of the offhand gesture and the fugitive moment. He was born in Cape Elizabeth, Maine. In 1913 he joined his older brother in HOLLYWOOD and was soon making films of his own. His first major project was a western, *Straight Shooting* (1917), whose central character and specific imagery anticipate his later, fully mature works, especially *The Searchers* (1956). During WORLD WAR II Ford headed a film unit for the OSS and made such classic documentaries as *The Battle of Midway* (1942). In 1947 he formed his own production company, Argosy Productions, for which he made some of his best-known westerns between 1947 and 1950.

Over the course of 60 years and 112 films, Ford remained remarkably consistent. Whether chronicling America's Manifest Destiny (*The Iron Horse* [1924], *Wagonmaster* [1950]) or his own Irish heritage (*The Informer* [1935] and *The Quiet Man* [1952]), Ford's big subject is the institution of the family. His wagon trains, coal miners, cavalry, "Okies," West Point cadets, air mail pilots and homesteaders are all different kinds of family under threat of dissolution and change. Ford celebrates their tradition and laments their passing. Despite his brusque manner and frequent fights with studio heads and film crews, Ford earned several ACADEMY AWARDS (*The Informer; The Grapes of Wrath* [1939]; *How Green Was My Valley* [1941]; and *The Quiet Man* [1952]) along with the loyalty of friends like John WAYNE and Maureen O'Hara. In 1939–41 alone, he directed seven masterpieces: *Drums Along the Mohawk, Stagecoach, The Grapes of Wrath, Young Mr. Lincoln, The Long Voyage Home, Tobacco Road* and *How Green Was My Valley*—a feat unequaled by any other American filmmaker. Describing Ford's essential genius, Orson WELLES remarked "He knows what the earth is made of."

For further reading:

Ford, Dan, *The Life of John Ford.* Englewood Cliffs, N.J.: Prentice-Hall, 1979.

Ford Foundation. World's wealthiest philanthropic organization, established by Henry FORD and his son Edsel. The organization seeks to promote human welfare through grants for educational purposes. In its early years, the foundation served only the state of Michigan, but in 1950 it became national. The foundation has awarded or pledged nearly $4.8 billion since its establishment in 1936. The money has gone to 95 countries outside the U.S., and to 7,100 organizations within the U.S. Foundation money supports programs in the fields of education and research, the arts, national and international affairs, communications, resources and environment. Foundation money helped establish the Public Broadcasting Service.

Ford Peace Ship. Vessel used by Henry FORD on his peace mission to Europe. On December 4, 1915, Ford and 150 men and women left New York City on a ship privately chartered by the auto pioneer. Ford's object was to organize a conference of peace advocates who would then attempt to influence WORLD WAR I's warring governments to come to terms early. Ford returned home after reaching Christiania (Oslo), Norway, but the rest of the mission continued on through Sweden, Denmark, Germany and the Netherlands. This peace mission was not sponsored by the U.S. government, and despite the best intentions, no peace was achieved.

Ford Trimotor. Airplane developed under the auspices of Henry FORD. Generally remembered for his role in the development of the automobile, Ford also did a great deal to promote the aircraft industry. With W.B. Stout he developed the famous Trimotor plane based on Stout's all-metal airplane, which Ford bought in 1925. He developed the single-engine plane into a plane of three engines, still all-metal. The Trimotor had a great influence on the development of the commercial air travel industry.

Foreman, Carl (1914–1984). American film producer and screenwriter. In 1951 Foreman appeared before the HOUSE COMMITTEE ON UN-AMERICAN ACTIVITIES (HUAC) investigating alleged communist influence in HOLLYWOOD. He was labeled an "uncooperative witness" and later blacklisted. Unable to find work, Foreman moved to London, where he continued to write film scripts under a pseudonym. His script for *High Noon* (1952) was nominated for an ACADEMY AWARD, as were his scripts for *Champion* (1949), *The Men* (1950), *The Guns of Navarone* (1961) and *Young Winston* (1972). Foreman also co-authored the Academy-Award-winning screenplay for David LEAN's *The Bridge on the River Kwai* (1958), but as a blacklisted writer working under a pseudonym he was unable to claim the award.

Foreman, George (1949–). American boxer. Foreman came to world attention as the flag-waving Olympic heavyweight champion during the politically fraught 1968 OLYMPIC GAMES. His professional career included 40 consecutive victories, culminating in an upset victory over Joe FRAZIER for the heavyweight crown in 1973. Foreman lost the title the following year to Muhammad ALI in the "rumble in the jungle" at Kinshasha, Zaire. Foreman retired in 1977 with a 46–2 record and became a preacher but, amazingly, hit the comeback trail in 1990. Initially, he fought unknowns before small crowds, but he earned his way back to the top and fought Evander Holyfield for the heavyweight championship 18 years after he first won the crown. Foreman's late-blooming wit and self-deprecating humor, unusual in the world of boxing, made him a popular favorite, but he was defeated by Holyfield in a unanimous decision. Many considered the 42-year-old Foreman's going the distance with Holyfield a victory in itself.

Foreman, Percy (1902–1988). American trial attorney who compiled a remarkable record in defending accused murderers. Foreman was known for his ability to save convicted murders from the gallows. He is perhaps best-remembered for his unsuccessful defense of James Earl Ray, the man who allegedly shot CIVIL RIGHTS MOVEMENT leader Martin Luther KING, Jr. Following Foreman's advice, Ray pleaded guilty but later appealed, arguing unsuccessfully that he had been misled about the plea.

Forester, C(ecil) S(cott) (1899–1966). American novelist and screenwriter. Forester was born in Cairo, Egypt and studied medicine. He began his literary career writing the biographies *Napoleon and His Court* (1924) and *Josephine, Napoleon's Empress* (1925). He brought his knowledge to bear on his popular series of historical novels about Horatio Hornblower, a fictional British sailor in the Napoleonic Wars. These books include *Beat to Quarters* (1937), *Lieutenant Hornblower* (1952) and *Hornblower and the Atropos* (1953). Forester worked intermittently as a screenwriter, often adapting his own fiction for the screen, notably in *The African Queen* (1935, filmed 1951) and *Captain Horatio Hornblower*, an adaptation of the first three Hornblower novels filmed in 1951.

Formalists. Name given to Soviet literary critics belonging to the Opoyaz group (Society for the Study of Poetic Language). Leading Formalist critics include V. Shklovskiy, B. Eykhenbaum and R. Jakobson. The Formalists issued their manifesto, a collection of essays entitled *Poetika*, in 1919. For the Formalists, art is mainly a collection of devices and techniques; attention is paid to style rather than to ideas expressed or the "message" conveyed; a typical work of Formalist criticism is Shklovskiy's essay "The Plot as a Phenomenon of Style." The extremists amongst the Formalists identified the study of literature with that of linguistics and were interested primarily in the phonetic qualities of poetry; Osip Brik, for instance, produced a study of the phonetic structure of Pushkin's verse. The more moderate Formalists, the "Petersburg Group," shared a keen interest in the way in which historical processes have affected literature. The school as a whole was suppressed in 1930.

Forman, Milos (1932–). Czech-born film director. Forman, who was left an orphan by the Nazis during WORLD WAR II, went on to become the most prominent Czech director of his generation. He studied at the Prague film school. His first feature, *Talent Show* (1963), was a fictional story constructed out of various documentary film clips. *Loves of a Blonde* (1965) and *The Fireman's Ball* (1967), which were widely shown in the West during the loosened political atmosphere of PRAGUE SPRING, established Forman's international reputation. Following increased Soviet artistic repression, Forman immigrated to America in the 1970s. His highly successful Hollywood-based films include *One Flew Over The Cuckoo's Nest* (1975), *Hair* (1979), *Ragtime* (1980) and *Amadeus* (1985), which won the ACADEMY AWARD for best picture.

Forrestal, James V(incent) (1892–1949). American government official. Born in Beacon, New York, he attended Princeton, was an aviator in WORLD WAR I and became an investment banker during the 1920s. A supporter of President Franklin D. ROOSEVELT's program to regulate the stock market, he helped to draft the Securities and Exchange Act (1933) and entered government service as an administrative assistant to the president. He served as undersecretary of the Navy (1940–44) and secretary of the Navy (1944–47). With the merger of the War and Navy Departments into the Department of Defense in 1947, he was named the nation's first secretary of defense by President Harry S TRUMAN. Adamantly opposed to COMMUNISM, Forrestal was highly suspicious of post-World War II expansionism by the U.S.S.R. and repeatedly warned both Roosevelt and Truman. He later attempted to end inter-service squabbling by members of the military and to raise Defense Department appropriations in order to resist any possible Soviet aggression. Forrestal resigned in 1949 after policy disputes with Truman and the deterioration of his own health. Suffering from paranoia and severe depression, he was hospitalized, and committed suicide two months later.

Forrester, Maureen (1930–). Canadian contralto. Born in Montreal, Forrester studied voice and made her debut there in 1953. Debuts in Europe (1955) and the U.S. (1956) followed. *The New York Times* called her voice "darkly resonant . . . a superb voice of generous compass and volume." Her international career has included recitals at the EDINBURGH FESTIVAL and the Casals Festival in Puerto Rico, solo engagements with symphony orchestras, such as the New York Philharmonic, and opera roles with major companies. She is especially known for her interpretations of the works of MAHLER and Handel and has performed extensively in her native Canada.

Forssmann, Werner Theodor Otto (1904–1979). German surgeon and urologist. Forssmann was educated at the University of Berlin, where he qualified as a physician in 1929. He then worked in the 1930s as a surgeon in various German hospitals. After the war he practiced as a urologist at Bad Kreuznach from 1950 until 1958, when he moved to Dusseldorf as head of surgery at the Evangelical Hospital. In 1929 Forssmann introduced the procedure of cardiac catheterization into medicine. He was struck by the danger inherent in the direct injection of drugs into the heart (frequently demanded in an emergency). He proposed introducing a catheter through the venous system from a vein in the elbow directly into the right atrium of the heart. Drugs could then be introduced through this. After practice on cadavers and an unsuccessful attempt on himself made with the aid of a nervous colleague, Forssmann decided to do the whole thing himself. He consequently introduced a 26.5-inch catheter for its entire length, walked up several flights of stairs to the X-ray department and calmly confirmed that the tip of the catheter had in fact reached his heart. There had been no pain or discomfort. Further development was inhibited by criticism from the medical profession, which assumed that the method must be dangerous. Consequently it was left to Andre COURNAND and Dickinson Richards to develop the technique into a routine clinical tool in the 1940s; for this work they shared the NOBEL PRIZE in physiology or medicine with Forssmann in 1956.

Forster, E(dward) M(organ) (1879–1970). British novelist and critic. Born in London, Forster was named for his father, an architect, who died a year after Forster's birth. Forster was educated at Tonbridge school, which he detested, and at King's College, Cambridge, where he thrived under the influence of G.E. MOORE and Goldsworthy Lowes Dickinson, whose biography Forster wrote in 1934. In 1901, Forster was elected to the Apostles, the Cambridge intellectual society, and through his associations there later came in contact with the BLOOMSBURY GROUP. After Cambridge, he traveled in Italy and Greece and drew on these experiences in his early short stories and novels. In 1903, he began writing for the *Independent Review*, where he published his first short story in 1904. His first novel, *Where Angels Fear to Tread* (1905), satirized English tourists and established one of Forster's major themes—the inhibition of the English as contrasted with the sensuality and openness of other cultures. *The Longest Journey* (1907), *A Room with a View* (1908, filmed 1986) and *Howards End* (1910) followed, establishing him as an important modern novelist (see MODERNISM).

In 1912 and 1913 Forster traveled in India, and in 1913 he visited E. Carpenter in England. Carpenter's influence was brought to bear in *Maurice*—a novel portraying homosexuality—which Forster circulated privately at the time. It was published posthumously in 1971 and later filmed. Forster spent WORLD WAR I working for the Red Cross in Alexandria, Egypt. His last and most important novel, *A Passage to India* (1924), begun during the war, was highly critical of British colonialism; it also examined the ambiguous relationship between perception and reality. Some critics consider *A Passage to India* to be the most perfectly constructed English novel of the 20th century. Throughout his life, Forster, an outspoken liberal and humanist, fought censorship. He opposed the suppression of *The Well of Loneliness*, a novel about lesbianism by Marguerite Radclyffe Hall, and testified at the trial of the publishers of D.H. LAWRENCE's *Lady Chatterley's Lover*. He also gained some notoriety for saying that if he had to choose between his friends and his country, he would choose his friends.

For further reading:

Furbank, P.N., *E.M. Forster: A Life*. San Diego, Calif.: Harcourt Brace Jovanovich, 1981.

King, Francis, *E.M. Forster*. New York: Thames and Hudson, 1988.

Page, Norman, *E.M. Forster*. New York: St. Martin's, 1988.

Forsyte Saga, The. Three novels and two "interludes" by John GALSWORTHY published in 1922. The novels are *A Man of Property* (1906), *In Chancery* (1920) and *To Let* (1921). The interludes consist of the two short stories "The Indian Summer of a Forsyte," which was originally published in the collection *Five Tales* (1918), and "The Awakening" (1920). The *Saga* follows five generations of the Forsytes, a quintessential upper-middle-class Edwardian family. The *Saga* satirizes the rigid conventionality of the Forsytes' class and remains immensely popular as a portrait of Edwardian England. It has also been deemed by some as middlebrow soap opera. Two more Forsyte trilogies followed; in 1967 BBC television dramatized the first six novels.

Fortas, Abe (1910–1982). Associate justice, U.S. Supreme Court (1965–69). Fortas is best remembered as President Lyndon B. JOHNSON's unsuccessful choice for chief justice, and also for his later forced resignation from the Court. Fortas, a graduate of Southwestern College and Yale Law School, was a brilliant lawyer who, after a brief stint as a law professor at Yale, rose in federal posts at an early age. In 1946 Fortas started a Washington, D.C. law firm, later known as Arnold & Porter, and became wealthy representing large

U.S. Supreme Court Associate Justice Abe Fortas.

corporations. During this time he became a close associate of Senator Lyndon Johnson, who as president later appointed Fortas to the Supreme Court. In 1968, as Johnson was about to leave office, Earl WARREN, the presiding chief justice, retired. Johnson nominated Fortas as chief justice, but the nomination was attacked in the Senate because of Fortas' close ties to Johnson. Subsequently Fortas was forced to resign from the Court after it was disclosed that he had a financial relationship with a former client who was under federal investigation. He returned to private law practice.

Fortress Europe [German: *Festung Europa*]. Term used by the Germans in WORLD WAR II to describe the alleged invulnerable status of Europe provided by a defensive "wall." After 1942, as German defeats on all fronts escalated, the Nazi PROPAGANDA machine maintained that Allied attempts could never shatter the impenetrable walls of Fortress Europe provided by German defensive fortifications. These secure walls that were to shield Germany proved to be largely a fantasy. Only a few strategic sites had truly effective defenses. Most importantly, Fortress Europe had no roof, allowing Allied air forces to batter key German targets from the air.

47 Workshop. See George Pierce BAKER.

Fosse, Bob [Robert Louis Fosse] (1927–1987). American dancer, choreographer and director. Fosse became a major figure in Broadway musicals in the 1950s. He won a Tony award for the first Broadway show he choreographed, *Pajama Game* (1954). He won additional Tonys for, among other shows, *Damn Yankees* (1955), *Sweet Charity* (1966) and *Big Deal* (1986). In 1973 he won two Tony awards for *Pippin,* as well as an Oscar for *Cabaret* and an Emmy for a TV special with Liza Minnelli. In 1975 he had a massive heart attack, an experience on which he based the film *All That Jazz* (1979). He was working on a revival of *Sweet Charity* when he died of another heart attack.

Fossey, Dian (1932–1985). American naturalist. Fossey went to Africa in the 1960s to study the rare mountain gorilla in its Central African habitat. She established a research institute in Rwanda and campaigned to prevent the gorillas' extinction. Fossey was murdered in her cabin on December 26, 1985, possibly by poachers. Her life was dramatized in the film *Gorillas in the Mist* (1989), starring Sigourney Weaver.

For further reading:

Hayes, Harold T.P., *The Dark Romance of Dian Fossey*. New York: Simon & Schuster, 1990.

Foucault, Michel (1926–1984). French philosopher, psychologist, and social critic. He was one of the most learned and versatile French thinkers of the postwar era. He studied at the Sorbonne, earning degrees in philosophy and psychology, and went on to further graduate work in psychopathology at the University of Paris. During his subsequent teaching career, Foucault lectured at universities throughout Europe. Strongly influenced both by Marxism and by STRUCTURALISM (the theory that comparative cultural analyses should focus on the overall structures of information and belief), Foucault devoted many of his works to probing the psychological and economic assumptions that prevailed in France and other nations throughout history. His major works include *Madness and Civilization* (1961), *The Order of Things: An Archaeology of the Human Sciences* (1966) and the three-volume *The History of Sex* (1976–1984).

Fouche, Jacobus Johannes "Jim" (1898–1980). President of SOUTH AFRICA (1968–75). Fouche was first elected to the South African Parliament in 1941 as a member of the National Party. He served as defense minister from 1959 to 1966, during which time the country cut its ties to Britain and became an independent republic (1961). He was the republic's second president.

"Four Musketeers". Popular name for four French tennis champions of the 1920s. The four players were Jean Borotra, Jacques "Toto" Brugnon, Henri Cochet and Rene Lacoste. They dominated world tennis between 1922 and 1931, bringing the Davis Cup to France for the first time in 1927.

Fournier, Pierre (1906–1986). French cellist. Fournier's elegant and subdued manner of playing typified French musical style. His repertoire ranged from the unaccompanied sonatas of Bach to music written for him by such 20th-century composers as Bohuslav MARTINU and Francis POULENC. As much concerned with chamber music as with solo performance, he succeeded Pablo CASALS in the famous trio whose other members were violinists Jacques THIBAUD and pianist Alfred CORTOT.

Four Quartets. Four interrelated poems by T.S. ELIOT, published as a complete book in 1944. The four poems are "Burnt Norton" (1941), "East Coker" (1940), "The Dry Salvages" (1941) and "Little Gidding" (1942). Regarded by many critics as the crowning masterpiece of Eliot's poetic career, these symmetrical meditations on philosophical and religious subjects reflect Eliot's view of history, time and the nature of human experience. Originally conceived as a long poem loosely based on a scheme of the four seasons and four elements, it also contains autobiographical elements. It combines lyric, dramatic and narrative styles, successfully weaving its themes into an intricate formal pattern akin to that of the musical string quartet. *Four Quartets* is at once public, abstract, elegiac and optimistic.

Fourteen Points. Peace program formulated by U.S. President Woodrow WILSON and presented by him to a joint session of Congress on January 8, 1918. Through this idealistic yet practical plan, Wilson established himself as moral leader of the WORLD WAR I Allies and hoped to appeal to a wide variety of those involved. These included the more liberal forces in the Central Powers, the Allies, the people of the U.S. and the newly emerged Bolshevik government in Russia. The first five points were general and included the following: (1) rejection of secret diplomacy (the famous "open covenants openly arrived at"), (2) freedom of the seas, (3) removal of economic barriers to international trade to the greatest degree possible, (4) arms reduction as low as demands for domestic safety would permit, (5) fair adjustment of colonial claims taking into consideration self-determination and other factors. The next eight points concerned specific territorial issues. Point 14 called for the formation of an association of nations to provide for the political independence of each. Although many of these points were abrogated or compromised at the PARIS PEACE CONFERENCE (1919–20), the spirit of the Fourteen Points was, to some degree, maintained in the final settlement. Moreover, point 14 formed the basis for the establishment of the LEAGUE OF NATIONS.

Fowler, Alfred (1868–1940). British astrophysicist. Born in Bradford, Fowler attended the Normal School of Science (later the Royal College of Science). He joined the Solar Physics Observatory, London, becoming a professor of astrophysics in 1915. A cofounder of the International Astronomical Union (1919), he was its general secretary until 1925. Fowler was a research professor at the Royal Society from 1923 to 1934. His particular field of study was solar and stellar spectroscopy, and he was especially interested in spectrographic analysis, duplicating the light emissions of the sun and other stars in the laboratory. Among his discoveries were the presence of magnesium hydride in sunspots and carbon monoxide in comets' tails. Fowler was also active in the spectrographic analysis of atomic structure.

Fowler, William Alfred (1911–). American astrophysicist. Born in Pittsburgh, Pa., Fowler attended Ohio State University and the California Institute of Technology, where he has served as a professor of physics since 1946. Fowler's work mainly involved nuclear spectroscopy and nuclear physics, concentrating on the nature of energy-producing nuclear reactions in the immensely hot core of stars and the chemical elements synthesized thereby. His investigations in this area are outlined in a work cowritten by Fowler and Fred HOYLE entitled *Nucleosynthesis in Massive Stars and Supernovae* (1965). After the mid-1960s, Fowler's inquiries centered on fundamental questions that bear on the age and future of the universe, such as the amount of the elements of helium and deuterium present in the universe.

Fowles, John (Robert) (1926–). British novelist. Fowles was educated at Bedford School and New College, Oxford. He achieved recognition with his first novel, *The Collector* (1963, filmed 1965), a psychological thriller about a man who begins to collect human "specimens." Fowles experiments in his writing with varied styles and themes. *The Magus* (1966, revised 1977) bears traces of MAGIC REAL-

ISM; *Daniel Martin* (1977), of an experimental naturalism. His other works include *The French Lieutenant's Woman* (1969, filmed 1981 with screenplay by Harold PINTER), *Mantissa* (1982) and the nonfiction books *The Tree* (1979) and *The Enigma of Stonehenge* (1980).

For further reading:

Tarbox, Katherine, *The Art of John Fowles.* Athens, Ga.: University of Georgia Press, 1989.

Fox, Harold Munro (1889–1967). British zoologist. Born in London, Fox was educated at Cambridge University, where he was a fellow from 1920 to 1928. He served as professor of zoology at Birmingham University from 1928 to 1941 and at Bedford College from 1941 until his retirement in 1954. Fowler's earlier experiments concerned siphon growth in the sea squirt (*Ciona intestinalis*). His best-known work has involved investigations of invertebrate blood pigments, with emphasis on research into the relationship of water-borne oxygen and the synthesis of hemoglobin in the water flea (*Daphnia*) as it bears on the relative red or clear coloration of that tiny crustacean.

Fox, John (1907–1984). American newspaper publisher. Fox was best known as a leading crusader against COMMUNISM during the 1950s. With a fortune he amassed as a securities broker, he purchased the *Boston Post* (1952), which became a forum for his views. The paper failed in 1956. In 1958, testifying before a congressional committee, Fox accused President EISENHOWER's chief aide Sherman ADAMS of financial misconduct. Fox's testimony was not substantiated, but other testimony eventually led to Adams' resignation. In the 1960s, after losing his fortune, Fox became a JAZZ pianist in Boston's waterfront bars.

Fox, Sidney Walter (1912–). American biochemist. Born in Los Angeles, Fox attended the University of California and the California Institute of Technology. He held brief teaching posts at Berkeley and the University of Michigan but spent most of his early career as professor of biochemistry at Iowa State University (1947–54) and professor of chemistry at Florida State University (1954–64). In 1964 he became director of the Institute of Molecular and Cellular Evolution at the University of Miami. Fox's researches have led him to posit answers to questions involving the origin of life. From experiments (1958) that produced proteinlike amino acid polymers from the application of heat and the production of tiny spheres resembling bacteria from the cooling of these so-called protenoids, he has concluded that proteins were the first elements of life on earth.

Fox, Terry (1958–1981). Canadian popular hero. In 1977 Fox lost a leg to cancer. In 1980, fitted with an artificial limb, he attempted to run across Canada from coast to coast to raise money for cancer research and to show that people with cancer could still live active lives. His well-publicized run gained him the admiration of millions of people throughout Canada and the U.S. and raised more than $20 million. Fox's marathon was cut short at the halfway point when he was struck with lung cancer, and he died soon thereafter at the age of 22. His run was the subject of a TV movie.

Fox, Uffa (1898–1972). British designer of sailing yachts, better known (at least in England) as a sailor and frequent member of the crew of Prince Philip when he sailed in races. Fox was the designer of exceptionally fast racing dinghies and keelboats such as *Avenger* of 1928 and the racing class known as Flying Fifteen. It was *Coweslip* of this class, owned by Prince Philip, that brought special fame to Fox, leading to his reputation as a writer, lecturer, and broadcaster and making him something of a celebrity.

Foxx, Jimmie [James Emory Foxx] (1907–1967). American baseball player. Foxx was one of baseball's greatest hitters, driving in over 100 runs for 13 seasons. Known for his power at the plate, he led major league batters in all three categories—average, home runs and runs batted in—in his best year, 1932. As a fielder, he was known for his skill at first base, although he also played both sides of the battery as pitcher and catcher. Foxx began his carer with Connie MACK's Athletics, and later played for the Red Sox and the Cubs. He made a comeback during the war years, and pitched nine games in 1945. His lifetime batting average was .325, and he is ninth on the all-time home run list with 534. Known for his affability and generosity, Foxx was named to the Baseball Hall of Fame in 1951.

Foyt, A.J. (1935–). American race car driver. Foyt is considered one of the outstanding race car drivers of the 20th century; he holds the record for most wins (67) in the Indy car class. In his career he has driven in more Indianapolis 500 races than any other driver (33 consecutive years, beginning in 1959) and shares the record of four Indianapolis 500 victories (1961, '64, '67 and '77) with Al Unser Sr. He and Unser also share the record for most race victories in a season (10).

Fracci, Carla (1936–). Italian ballerina. Especially noted for such roles as Giselle and Juliet in the romantic ballets, Fracci is the first Italian ballerina in this century to garner an international reputation. She joined the La Scala Ballet Company in Milan in 1954, becoming prima ballerina in 1958, and has appeared as a guest artist with numerous other companies, most notably AMERICAN BALLET THEATRE. In 1969 she danced opposite Erik BRUHN in the film version of *Giselle,* and her television film, *Serata Con C.F.*, won the Golden Rose of Montreux Award in 1973. In addition, she has appeared in several ballets, such as *The Seagull* (1968) and *The Stone Flower* (1973), produced by her husband—theater director Beppe Menegatti—and choreographed by Loris Gai.

Fraenkel-Conrat, Heinz L. (1910–). German-American biochemist. Trained as a physician at the University of Breslau, he left Germany in 1934 to study at the University of Edinburgh, where he obtained a Ph.D. in 1936. He emigrated to the U.S., became a citizen in 1941 and joined the University of California, Berkeley in 1951 as professor of virology and of molecular biology. His extensive work on the tobacco mosaic virus (TMV) proved that viral RNA can, like DNA, be the transmitter of genetic information. Working with Wendell Stanley, he also outlined the complete 158–amino-acid-long chain of the TMV protein. He also did significant research on snake neurotoxins and wrote several virology texts.

Frame, Janet [Janet Paterson Frame Clutha] (1924–). New Zealand novelist and poet. Frame was born in Dunedin, New Zealand. Her first novel was *Owls Do Cry* (1957), followed by the more acclaimed *Faces in the Water* (1961), which, with its pessimistic and morbid tone, is characteristic of Frame's work. She draws on her own experiences with mental illness and hospitalization in that and subsequent works, such as *A State of Siege* (1966); *Intensive Care* (1970) and *The Carpathians* (1988). Frame's work is also noted for its intelligent portrayal of New Zealand geography. Her poetic works include *The Pocket Mirror* (1967), and she has also written the autobiographies *An Angel at My Table* (1984, filmed in 1991) and *The Envoy from Mirror City* (1985).

Frampton, Peter (1950–). English singer-guitarist. Despite his phenomenal success during the 1970s, he has never been able to dislodge the "teen idol" mantle that was hung on him early in his career. After short stints with the Herd and Humble Pie, two groups that never lived up to their apparent potential, Frampton formed Camel, the group that recorded such later Frampton trademarks as "Baby I Love Your Way" and "Show Me the Way." In 1976, he released *Frampton Comes Alive,* the most successful live pop album in history, with sales exceeding 15 million. His next album, *I'm in You,* was a mild follow-up success. He played the lead in the disastrous *Sgt Pepper's Lonely Hearts Club Band* movie, and his career was further impeded by a serious automobile accident in 1978. He continued to release albums throughout the 1980s but never approached his earlier success.

France. Western European country, officially called the French Republic, bordered by the English Channel to the north; GERMANY, SWITZERLAND and ITALY to the east; the Mediterranean Sea and SPAIN to the south, and the Atlantic Ocean to the west. At the turn of the century, France was strong and prosperous, with many colonies in Africa and Asia, although engaged in territorial disputes with Germany. At the outbreak of WORLD WAR I, Germany invaded France, which suffered huge losses of life and wealth during the war. In 1919 France and Germany signed the TREATY OF VERSAILLES, restoring to France the provinces of Alsace and Lorraine, which had been seized by Germany in 1871. Following the war, the Third Republic government was beset by economic strife and instability, and it directed its foreign policy toward weaken-

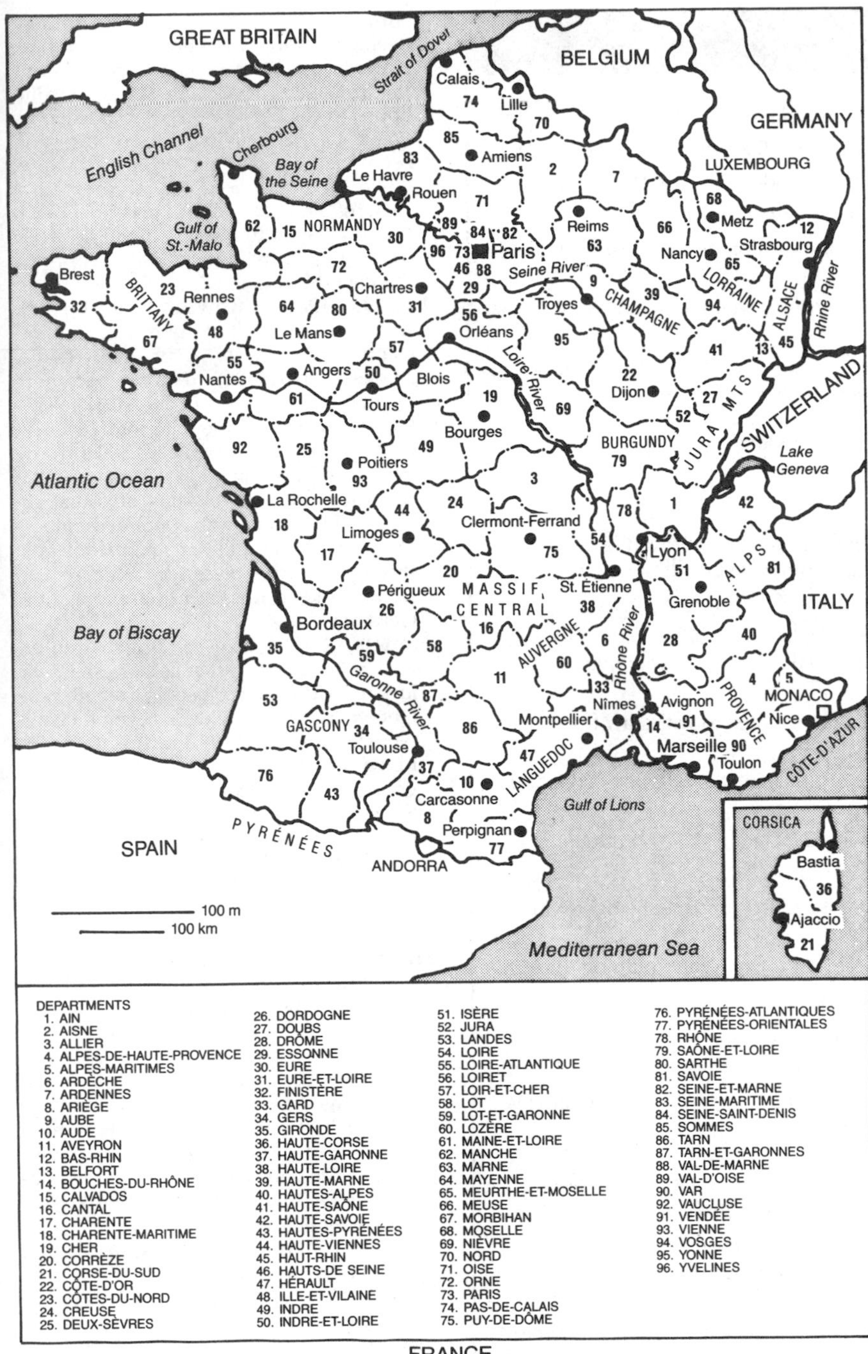

FRANCE

ing Germany and exacting postwar reparations from it. Adolf HITLER's Nazi Party rose to power, however, and France declared war on Germany after the Nazis invaded POLAND in 1939. In 1940 Germany, later joined by Italy, invaded and defeated France. The country was subsequently divided temporarily, with the northern part occupied by Germany and the south governed by Marshal Henri Philippe PETAIN, a French war hero, in VICHY. General Charles DE GAULLE formed the FREE FRENCH RESISTANCE movement to continue to fight the Germans. In 1944 Allied forces launched the INVASION OF NORMANDY on June 6, arriving in Paris on August 25 and effectively liberating France from German rule. A provisional government was established in Paris led by De Gaulle. In 1946 the constitution was revised to create the Fourth Republic, which changed the French colonial empire to the French Union and strengthened the National Assembly. De Gaulle resigned because it did not provide enough executive power. In a 1947 election—the first in which French women voted—Vincent AURIOL was elected president.

In 1946 revolution had begun in French INDOCHINA, which was later divided into CAMBODIA, LAOS and North and South VIETNAM. After much loss of life, the French withdrew from Indochina in 1954. That same year, the colony of ALGERIA began struggling for independence. Hoping to retain Algeria and prevent revolutions in the colonies of MOROCCO and TUNISIA, France granted the latter two independence. The continuing war in Algeria, however, was a divisive issue that led many French military personnel and Algerian settlers to threaten rebellion if the war ceased and independence was granted. In 1958 De Gaulle returned as prime minister, and his government drafted the new constitution of the Fifth Republic, of which he became first president. This constitution granted extensive executive power. In spite of opposition from rebellious French soldiers, France granted Algeria its independence in 1962 (see O.A.S.).

Although allied with the Western nations during the COLD WAR, De Gaulle strove to maintain a policy independent from the U.S. and NATO. Many people, however, were becoming disillusioned by De Gaulle's government. In 1968 Parisian students began a violent protest (see PARIS STUDENT DEMONSTRATIONS), which was joined by workers across the country and threatened to turn into civil war. De Gaulle managed to avert a crisis but was compelled to resign in 1969. His nationalist policies were largely maintained by his successors: George POMPIDOU and Valery GISCARD D'ESTAING.

In 1981 Socialist Francois MITTERRAND won a landslide victory over Giscard. Mitterrand's government nationalized some major industries and private banks. Mitterrand was reelected in 1986 and 1988. In 1985, *Rainbow Warrior,* a vessel of the Greenpeace environmental organization that was monitoring nuclear tests, was mined in Auckland Harbor, New Zealand, by the French secret service. Mitterrand later accepted responsibility for the event. France was a member of the UNITED NATIONS coalition and took part in the fighting against IRAQ during the PERSIAN GULF WAR (1990–91).

France, Anatole [Jacques Anatole Francois Thibault] (1844–1922). French novelist and critic. The son of a book dealer, France was educated at the College Stanislas in Paris. France began his literary career writing a column, "La Vie Litteraire" (The Literary Life), for the newspaper *Le Temps.* His first work of fiction—two short novels, *Jocaste* (Jocasta) and *Le Chat maigre* (The Famished Cat)—was published in 1879. But it was *Le Crime de Sylvestre Bonnard* (1881) that brought him success, which he maintained with *La Rotisserie de la Reine* (1893) and *Les opinions de M. Jerome Coignard* (1893). These social satires introduce variations on a prototypical France character (the bemused, scholarly professor), and they captured the mood of the country at the time. France's reputation gained him entree into the literary and social salon of Leontine Arman de Caillavet, for whom he later left his wife. France's work evidences his erudition and keen observation of French politics and society. Other

FRANCE

1906	Georges Clemenceau becomes prime minister.
1914-18	France suffers nearly 1,400,000 dead and 4,250,000 wounded in World War I.
1919	(June) Alsace-Lorraine returned to France under Treaty of Versailles.
1936	(May) Leon Blum elected as first socialist prime minister.
1938	(September) France agrees to German annexation of Czech Sudetenland in Munich Pact.
1939	(September) France declares war on Germany after German invasion of Poland; start of World War II.
1940	(June 22) Marshal Henri Philippe Petain signs armistice with Germany; Germans occupy 60% of France; collaborationist Vichy government established in unoccupied France; Gen. Charles de Gaulle forms alternative "Free French" government in London.
1942	(November) Germany occupies the rest of France.
1944	(Aug. 25, 1944) Allies liberate Paris.
1946	(Oct. 13) Constitution of France's Fourth Republic approved, allowing French colonies varying degrees of autonomy; De Gaulle serves as provisional president.
1949	France becomes founding member of NATO.
1951	France leads in formation of European Coal and Steel Community, forerunner of EEC.
1954	France suffers defeat at Dienbienphu and is forced to withdraw from Indochina.
1957	(March) France signs Treaty of Rome establishing the European Economic Community.
1958	(Oct. 5) Fifth Republic established, with De Gaulle as first president.
1960	(Feb. 13) France tests its first atomic bomb.
1962	Algerian independence granted despite terrorist campaign by right-wing French soldiers.
1963	(Jan. 14) De Gaulle vetoes Britain's request to enter the Common Market.
1965	France signs the Treaty of Brussels, setting up the EC.
1966	France withdraws from NATO; its headquarters are moved to Brussels.
1969	(June 15) Georges Pompidou, a Gaullist, is elected president.
1974	(April 2) Pompidou dies and Finance Minister Valery Giscard d'Estaing is elected president.
1979	(October) Giscard's administration is rocked by scandal when it is dicovered that as finance minister in 1973 he received $250,000 in diamonds from Emperor Bokassa of the Central African Republic.
1981	(May) Francois Mitterrand is elected the first socialist president of the Fifth Republic; later introduces economic austerity program.
1985	(July 11) Greenpeace ship *Rainbow Warrior* sunk by French frogmen on orders of the defense ministry; defense minister resigns and head of secret service is sacked.
1988	Mitterrand is reelected.
1989	(Jan. 1) Bicentennial celebration of the French Revolution commences with balloonists taking to the air and actors reading the Declaration of the Rights of Man in major towns.
1991	French forces participate in Operation Desert Storm to oust Iraq from Kuwait during Persian Gulf War.

important works include *Histoire contemporaire* (1897–1900), which consists of four novels; *L'Ile de pingouine* (1908) and *Les Dieux ont soif* (1912). France was awarded the NOBEL PRIZE for literature in 1921.

France, Battle of (1940). France's heavily fortified MAGINOT LINE afforded little security from GERMANY when, in June 1940, Nazi armies broke through north of the line as well as from Belgium into Brittany. A third force broke through at Champagne and attacked the line from the rear. Italy, having declared war on France (June 10, 1940), advanced from the south. The Allies had to retreat from eastern and central France, and on June 14 Paris fell without a fight, the French government fleeing to Tours, then Bordeaux. On June 22, 1940, France accepted German terms for armistice; aged General Henri Philippe PETAIN became premier, assisted by Pierre LAVAL—a Nazi collaborator—and set up a French government at VICHY, while Germans occupied northern and eastern France. Thousands of French troops escaped to continue fighting, while others joined the RESISTANCE to continue the covert struggle within France.

Francis, David Rowland (1850–1927). U.S. statesman. Starting as a grain merchant, Francis was mayor of St. Louis, Missouri (1885–89), before becoming Democratic governor of the state (1889–93). Secretary of the interior (1896–97) under President Grover Cleveland, he gained a presidential proclamation that set aside millions of acres of forest reserves. In 1916 he was appointed ambassador to RUSSIA, and remained at his post throughout the RUSSIAN REVOLUTION, trying to keep Russia in the war against Germany.

Francis, Dick (1920–). British author. Francis began his career as a steeplechase jockey. Riding for Queen Elizabeth, the Queen Mother, he won several championships. Retired from racing at age 36, he wrote a weekly racing column for the London *Sunday Express*. He then turned to novel-writing, achieving enormous popular success with a series of suspense novels set in the English racing world. His themes include greed, the lust for power and the need for family relationships.

Francis, Thomas, Jr. (1900–1969). American virologist. Born in Gas City, Ind., he attended Allegheny College and Yale University, receiving an M.D. in 1925. He was a researcher at the Rockefeller Institute (1925–38) and professor of bacteriology at the New York University College of Medicine (1938–41) before becoming professor of epidemiology at the University of Michigan (1941–69). From the mid-1930s to the mid-1950s Francis worked on the epidemiology of the influenza virus, detecting a strain of the first-discovered type (1934) and an entirely new type (1940). He was also active in developing flu vaccines. Francis gained wide public attention in 1954, when he evaluated the newly developed SALK polio vaccine trial.

Franck, James (1882–1964). German-American physicist. Born in Hamburg, he studied at Heidelberg and Berlin, receiving his doctorate in 1906. In 1913 he began a collaboration with Gustav **Hertz,** examining the interaction of electrons and atoms. Their discovery of quantized energy transfer in these interactions led to their being awarded the 1925 NOBEL PRIZE for physics. After distinguished service in WORLD WAR I, Franck accepted the chair in experimental physics at Gottingen, but fled Germany after the rise of HITLER. After a year in Copenhagen, he emigrated to the U.S. (1935), where he became a professor of physics at Johns Hopkins University (1935–38) and professor of physical chemistry at the University of

Francisco Franco in full regalia (ca. 1954).

Chicago (1938–49). In the U.S. Franck primarily investigated the physical chemistry of photosynthesis. He worked on the MANHATTAN PROJECT during WORLD WAR II and was responsible for the *Franck Report,* in which he and several other outstanding scientists argued against the use of the newly developed ATOMIC BOMB without first demonstrating its devastating effect on an unpopulated island.

Franco [L'Okanga La Ndju Pene Luambo Makiadi] (1939–1989). Zairean jazz guitarist and band leader. During his lifetime he was one of Africa's most popular and influential musicians. He was noted for creating the soukous style, a fusion of Afro-Cuban rhumba music with JAZZ, gospel, and African rhythms, and for lyrics that sometimes ridiculed Africa's ruling classes and offended the Zairean government. Following his death, however, Zairean President MOBUTU SESE SEKO declared an official four-day mourning period.

Franco, Francisco (1892–1975). Spanish general and head of the government of SPAIN. Born in El Ferrol in Galicia, Franco was a career army officer who became a brigadier general in 1926 at age 33. In 1934 he successfully suppressed a communist-led miner's revolt. The same year he was appointed chief of the Spanish Army. In 1936, as governor of the Canary Islands, he led the anti-socialist revolt that started the SPANISH CIVIL WAR. The Nationalists proclaimed him head of state, and by 1939 his regime, having won the civil war, received British and French diplomatic recognition. During World War II he led Spain on a fascist Italian model, under a single political party—the FALANGE. However, he maintained Spain's neutrality. After the war his regime received U.S. patronage but was opposed bitterly by intellectuals. In 1969 he nominated Prince JUAN CARLOS, grandson of ex-King ALFONSO XIII, to succeed him after his death. Franco resigned from the position of premier in 1973 but retained his functions as head of state until his death.

Frank, Anne (1929–1945). Jewish diarist of the HOLOCAUST. Her book, *The Diary of Anne Frank* (1947), which poignantly recounts the thoughts and experiences of a young Jewish girl living in hiding from the Nazis during WORLD WAR II, has been widely acknowledged as one of the spiritual classics of this century. A best-seller that has been published around the world, the *Diary* has also been successfully adapted to the Broadway stage (1956) and as a Hollywood film (1959). Frank, who fled with her family from Germany to Holland, went into hiding—along with her family and a few others—in a Dutch warehouse office from 1942 to 1944. In 1944, they were discovered by the Nazis. Frank died in the BERGEN-BELSEN CONCENTRATION CAMP. Her diary, which is most noteworthy for Frank's remarkably enduring faith in human nature, was discovered by her father after the war.

Frank, Leo. See LYNCHING OF LEO FRANK.

Frankenheimer, John (1930–). American motion picture and television director. Frankenheimer was born in New York, served in the Air Force in the early 1950s, and after his discharge joined other young men like Sidney LUMET at CBS to pursue a career in television. Quick, versatile, and technically adept in the new medium, he directed a religious series, "Lamp unto My Feet"; an interview series with Edward R. MURROW, PERSON TO PERSON; and a variety show, "The Garry Moore Show." His subsequent movies carry on this eclecticism and virtuoso technique. His best-known works include *The Manchurian Candidate* (1962), a surreal tale of brainwashing and assassination; *Seven Days in May* (1963), a political thriller; and *Grand Prix* (1966), a Cinerama racing epic. Less familiar, but no less full of quirky surprises, are *The Train* (1965), a WORLD WAR II thriller about protecting art masterpieces from invading Nazis; *French Connection II* (1975), a quirky sequel to the original; and *The Fourth War* (1990), an offbeat war movie that reflected the thaw in the COLD WAR tensions between East and West. *Seconds* (1966), arguably his finest, if most neglected film, nicely sums up his restless camera technique and nightmarish sense of mood and image. A man's search for lost youth and a new identity becomes an exercise in Kafkaesque horror—quite one of the scariest movies of the 1960s.

Frankenstein (1931). Prototype of the American horror film. Mary Shelley's 1818 novel had been filmed as early as 1910 by Edison, in a silent version that ran a scant 10 minutes. In 1931 UNIVERSAL Studios, cashing in on its recent success with *Dracula,* brought in writer/director Robert Florey and its new star, Bela LUGOSI, to make the first TALKING PICTURE version. Unhappy with the project, the studio transferred them to another film (*Murders in the Rue Morgue* [1932]) and brought in another team: director James WHALE and newcomer Boris KARLOFF. The results were superior to the rather static *Dracula,* as for the first time we see the archetypal horror formula assuming shape: the "creation" sequence ("It's alive!"); the old world atmosphere (via sets borrowed from Universal's ALL QUIET ON THE WESTERN FRONT); and the restless, torch-carrying locals storming the castle. Set designer Charles Hall twisted his interiors into the distorted shapes of German EXPRESSIONISM, Kenneth Strickfaden stitched the air with dazzling electrical effects, and makeup ace Jack Pierce devised the effective Monster makeup (reportedly after consulting with surgeons and pathologists). Above all, director James Whale infused the proceedings with a certain diabolical humor that has worn well over the years. Not even the numerous sequels, including *Abbott and Costello Meet Frankenstein* (1948) and Mel BROOKS's satiric *Young Frankenstein* (1974), can take the dark bloom off this eldritch rose.

For further reading:

Levine, George, and Knoepflmacher, U.C., ed., *The Endurance of "Frankenstein."* Berkeley: University of California Press, 1979.

Frankenthaler, Helen (1928–). American painter. Born in New York City, she studied with a number of artists, notably Hans Hofmann and Jackson POLLOCK. Influenced by art critic Clement GREENBERG and such painters as Pollock, Willem DE KOONING and Arshile Gorky, Frankenthaler developed a lyrical color-field technique that involves staining and saturating the canvas with color. Lyrical in mood, her works include *Mountains and Sea* (1952, Metropolitan Museum of Art, N.Y.C.) and *Arden* (1961, Whitney Museum of American Art, N.Y.C.).

Frankfurter, Felix (1882–1965). Associate justice, U.S. Supreme Court (1939–62). Born in Austria, Frankfurter was raised in poverty in New York City's lower East Side. He attended City University and Harvard Law School. After brief stints in private practice, the U.S. Attorney's Of-

U.S. Supreme Court Associate Justice Felix Frankfurter.

fice and the War Department, he returned to Harvard Law School as a professor for 25 years, interrupted by three years in various posts in Washington. Frankfurter was an active Zionist and also became involved in many controversial legal battles of the era, including the defense of SACCO AND VANZETTI. He was a founder of the AMERICAN CIVIL LIBERTIES UNION. He was also a close advisor of President Franklin D. ROOSEVELT, who appointed him to the Supreme Court in 1939 to replace Justice CARDOZO. Frankfurter generally supported NEW DEAL legislation. In later years he generally favored the doctrine of judicial restraint, which holds that the courts should not substitute their views for those of the elected legislatures.

For further reading:

Baker, Leonard, *Brandeis and Frankfurter: A Dual Biography*. New York: Harper & Row, 1984.

Simon, James F., *The Antagonists: Hugo Black, Felix Frankfurter & Civil Liberties in Modern America*. New York: Simon & Schuster, 1989.

Franklin, John Hope (1915–). U.S. educator and historian. With a Ph.D. from Harvard (1941), he taught on several college faculties before joining the Howard University staff in 1947. He was a Fulbright Scholar (1954) and a William Pitt Scholar (1962), both at Cambridge University. He became chairman of the history department at the University of Chicago in 1969. He was a trustee of the Chicago Symphony from 1976 to 1980. Considered one of the foremost historians of his time, he emphasized social, political and cultural history and biography in his writings and teachings. His writings include *From Slavery to Freedom: A History of Negro Americans* (1947), *The Militant South* (1956) and *The Emancipation Proclamation* (1963). He was named to the Oklahoma Hall of Fame in 1978.

Franklin, (Stella Maria Sarah) Miles (1879–1954). Australian novelist. Franklin first realized success with *My Brilliant Career* (1901). Written when she was 16, the novel depicts pioneer life in the Australian bush through the eyes of the young heroine who longs to escape it. In her lifetime, she was best known for *All That Swagger* (1936), also about the desolation of life in the bush; the filming of *My Brilliant Career* in 1980 led to a renewed interest in Franklin's work. Her other work includes *Some Everyday Folk and Dawn* (1909), which deals with women's suffrage. (See also WOMEN'S MOVEMENT.)

Franklin, Rosalind (1920–1958). British crystallographer and biophysicist. A graduate of Cambridge, Franklin worked for the British Coal Utilisation Research Associates from 1942 to 1947 and the Paris Laboratoire Centrale des Services Chimique from 1947 to 1950, when she returned to England. There she was a researcher at King's College (1951–53) and Birbeck College (1954–58). Franklin had an important part in the epoch-making discovery of the structure of DNA by James WATSON and Francis CRICK. Using X-ray diffraction photography, she showed that the DNA molecule's phosphates lay on its outside and provided information that indicated that DNA had a helical chain structure. Franklin's work and her alleged lack of cooperation with fellow-researcher Maurice Wilkins were described in Watson's book *The Double Helix* (1968). She also did important research on the structure of carbon and the tobacco mosaic virus.

Franz Ferdinand (1863–1914). Austrian archduke, after 1889 heir apparent to his uncle, Emperor Franz Joseph II. He was married to Sophie Chotek, a Czech countess. Because of her relatively low rank, their two sons were not granted the right of succession. Franz Ferdinand attempted to expand AUSTRIA-HUNGARY into a triple monarchy by adding Croatia. On a trip to Sarajevo in 1914, he and his wife were assassinated by the Serbian nationalist Gavrilo Princip—provoking Austria's declaration of war against SERBIA. This event was the spark that erupted into the conflagration of WORLD WAR I.

Franz Joseph II (1906–). Prince of LICHTENSTEIN. Becoming head of state of the small European principality in 1938, he oversaw Lichtenstein's development from a poor, rural country to a wealthy tax and banking haven with one of the world's highest per capita incomes. A keen sportsman, he served on the International Olympic Committee for more than 35 years. In 1984 he handed his executive powers over to his son, Crown Prince Hans Adam.

Franz Joseph Land [Russian: *Zemlya Frantsa Iosifa*]. Archipelago north of Novaya Zemlya in the Russian SSR, constituting the northern boundary of the Barents Sea. Found and named in 1873 by an Austrian expedition, Franz Joseph Land was scouted by several other polar expeditions including NANSEN'S, and has also been known as Fridtjof Nansen Land. Claimed by Russia in 1914, the archipelago was formally annexed in 1926 by the Soviet Union, which keeps the world's northernmost weather station here.

Fraser, James Earle (1876–1953). American sculptor. After studying art at the Art Institute of Chicago in 1894, Fraser moved to Paris to study at the Ecole des Beaux-Arts. His most famous work, *The End of the Trail*, depicting an exhausted Indian on horseback, was completed in 1896. In 1898 he became the student-assistant of famed sculptor Augustus St. Gaudens. As an artist Fraser was the recipient of hundreds of awards fron national and international organizations. Principal works of Fraser include a bust of Theodore ROOSEVELT on display in the U.S. Senate Chamber; two heroic figures, *Justice* and *Law*, in front of the Supreme Court building; statues of Albert Gallatin and Alexander Hamilton for the Treasury Building (all in Washington, D.C.); the Buffalo nickel; and monuments to Thomas Edison for the Edison Institute in Dearborn, Michigan.

Fraser, Malcolm (1930–). Prime minister of AUSTRALIA (1975–83). A member of the Australian LIBERAL PARTY, Fraser was educated at Oxford University. Returning to Australia, he entered politics and was elected to the Australian House of Representatives in 1955. He held various cabinet posts from 1966 to 1971. Fraser succeeded Gough WHITLAM as prime minister in 1975, following a budget crisis that brought down Whitlam's LABOUR PARTY government, and formed a ruling coalition with the National Party. He generally followed conservative economic and foreign policies. He was defeated by the Labour Party, led by Robert HAWKE, in 1983.

Frazier, Joe (1944–). American boxer, known as "Smokin' Joe." The world heavyweight champion from 1971 to 1973, Frazier was one of the most devastating fighters of his or any other time. He was discovered in Philadelphia by trainer Yank Durham, then worked his way up through the boxing ranks, taking on such opponents as Buster Mathis and Jerry Quarry, before defeating the champion Muhammad ALI in a 15-round unanimous decision at Madison Square Garden, New York, in 1971. Frazier lost his title to George FOREMAN two years later. In 1975 he again met Ali in one of the most vaunted fights of all time, the "thriller in Manila." Despite Frazier's superior power, Ali rallied to defeat him with a 15th-round TKO.

Frederick, Pauline (1918–1990). American radio and television news commentator. Frederick had her own news programs on three networks—ABC, NBC and National Public Radio—and served as NBC's UNITED NATIONS correspondent for 21 years. In 1976 she became the first woman to moderate a presidential debate—the one between Gerald R. FORD and Jimmy CARTER.

Frederika (1917–1981). Queen of GREECE (1947–64). Born in Germany, she was a member of an ancient German princely family. The stong-willed wife of King Paul, she intervened in Greek politics after her son King CONSTANTINE came to the throne in 1964; her activities helped pave the way for the overthrow of the monarchy in 1967. After Greece was officially proclaimed a republic in 1973, she went into self-imposed exile.

Freedom of Information Act. See SUNSHINE ACT.

Free French. Movement headed by General Charles DE GAULLE during WORLD WAR II as an alternative to the collaborationist VICHY regime. After the fall of Frence in 1940, de Gaulle headed RESISTANCE activities from exile in London, calling on his countrymen to resist the German occupation and organizing an army of French and colonial volunteers. By 1942 Free French troops numbered about 70,000 men, who participated in battles in Africa and in various naval engagements. After the Allied invasion of North Africa in 1942, a provisional Free French government was established in Algiers in 1943 (see NORTH AFRICAN CAMPAIGN). When Paris was liberated by Free French and other Allied forces in August 1944, the French government was moved to the capital. De Gaulle headed a provisional French government until the establishment of the Fourth Republic in 1946.

For further reading:

De Gaulle, Charles, *The Complete War Memoirs of Charles de Gaulle: 1940–1946.* New York: Da Capo Press, 1984.

free jazz. A term initially applied to the relatively open-ended improvisations of alto saxophonist Ornette COLEMAN and pianist Cecil Taylor. The term derived from Coleman's seminal recording, *Free Jazz* (1960), a sprawling, open-ended improvisation for two piano-less quartets that set the tone for the free jazz movement of the 1960s. Free jazz generally involves collective improvisation; also, although soloists often step forward, as in mainstream jazz, there is much more initiative and interaction among the others in the group. The abandonment of traditional song forms and harmonic structures associated with the mainstream is significant; in place of traditional sound ideals generally thought of as "beautiful" or "sonorous," avant-garde players, especially in the early years, incorporated wails, honks, shreiks and other "voice-like" sounds connoting anger and frustration. These emotive qualities were especially important to black American musicians who saw free jazz as a part of the larger CIVIL RIGHTS and BLACK POWER movements of the 1960s. In Europe, free jazz provoked controversy among both musicians and critics, who attacked its "free" aspect as license for an essentially undisciplined, musically illiterate, "anything goes" approach. Nonetheless, free jazz remains, especially in Europe, an important alternative to more mainstream styles; it has also provided a significant repertoire of gestures and even attitudes that have been incorporated into the music of such contemporary jazz artists as guitarists John SCOFIELD, Pat Metheny and John Abercrombie.

For further reading:

Litweiler, John, *The Freedom Principle: Jazz After 1958*. New York: William Morrow, 1984.

Free Officers. Army officers in EGYPT who overthrew King FAROUK in 1952.

Free Speech Movement (1964–65). The Free Speech Movement is the name given to a series of student-led demonstrations conducted on the campus of the University of California at Berkeley (1964–65). The central issue giving rise to the demonstrations was the ban placed by the university administration, headed by president Clark Kerr, on speech related to off-campus political issues being conducted on-campus at Bancroft Strip. The Free Speech Movement, which was led by student Mario Savio, became a cause celebre that received support from such luminaries as Norman MAILER and Bertrand RUSSELL. The Free Speech Movement ultimately prevailed by virtue of an overwhelming majority vote by the Academic Senate. More importantly, it became a paradigm of student protest in the 1960s.

Frei Montalva, Eduardo (1911–1982). President of CHILE (1964–70). A self-proclaimed radical reformer, Frei was the first Christian Democrat ever to lead a nation of the Western hemisphere. During his presidency he began an ambitious land distribution program but failed in his stated goal to give land to 100,000 poor farmers. He also started the nationalization of Chile's copper industry that was completed under his successor, Salvador ALLENDE GOSSENS. The hero of the democratic moderates, Frei was a leading opposition figure during the military government of General Augusto PINOCHET.

Frelimo [Frente de Libertacao de Mocambique]. Marxist liberation movement that waged a guerrilla war against the Portugese in MOZAMBIQUE from 1964 to 1974. The dominant political force in the country after independence.

Frenay, Henri (1905–1988). French politician. Frenay was one of the top leaders of the French RESISTANCE during WORLD WAR II. For a time he sought to challenge Charles DE GAULLE. Frenay created a national liberation movement, Combat, which he intended to be independent of the Anglo-Saxon powers and the communists as well as de Gaulle. After the war, he supported European federation.

French, Sir John Denton [1st Earl of Ypres] (1852–1925). British field marshal. A longtime army officer, French served in the Sudan (1884–85) and the SOUTH AFRICAN WAR (1899–1902) before becoming chief of the imperial general staff (1912–14). He was promoted to the rank of field marshal in 1913. During the first year of WORLD WAR I, French commanded the British Expeditionary Force in France and Belgium (1914–15), but was unable to coordinate with French forces and incurred heavy casualties in both the first and second battles of YPRES and the battle of Loos. Replaced by General Douglas HAIG in December, 1915, he returned to England, where he organized civil defenses. Later he was appointed lord lieutenant of Ireland (1918–21) and was made an earl upon his retirement in 1922.

French Community [La Communaute francaise]. Established in 1958 to succeed the FRENCH UNION, the French Community included FRANCE, its overseas departments and territories, and 12 African colonies given autonomy at the time (in 1958 GUINEA had voted for instant independence). In 1960 these countries were given independence and the option of leaving the Community; SENEGAL, GABON, CHAD, CONGO, the CENTRAL AFRICAN REPUBLIC and MADAGASCAR stayed; MALI, MAURITANIA, Upper Volta (now BURKINA FASO), Dahomey, NIGER and the Ivory Coast (now COTE D'IVOIRE) relinquished formal membership but continued a connection through special accords. The community's management was aimed at drafting common foreign, economic and military policies for its members, but the operation dwindled during the 1960s, eventually to be succeeded by bilateral agreements, fostered by powerful economic and cultural bonds, between France and the other community participants.

French Equatorial Africa [French Congo]. A former confederation of French colonies in West Africa that now make up the states of GABON, CONGO, CHAD and the CENTRAL AFRICAN REPUBLIC. The grouping was formed in 1910 and was a consolidated colony between 1934 and 1946; it became independent from the VICHY regime of defeated FRANCE in 1940. The capital, Brazzaville, became the nucleus of African operations for the FREE FRENCH in WORLD WAR II. In 1958 French Equatorial Africa disappeared when its constituent regions became autonomous members of the FRENCH COMMUNITY.

French Guiana [French: *Guyane Francaise*]. On the Atlantic coast of northeastern South America, it is an overseas region of FRANCE. During WORLD WAR II, French Guiana supported the VICHY government after the Nazi defeat of France, but in 1943 the FREE FRENCH assumed control. In 1958 French Guiana approved the constitution of France's Fifth Republic and chose to remain an overseas department, with its own representatives in the French parliament. It became a region in 1974. The local government during the 1980s was left-wing. Cayenne is the capital. (See also GUYANA.)

French Indochina War of 1946–54. After the Japanese invaders withdrew from French INDOCHINA at the end of WORLD WAR II, the French were not in a strong position to immediately reassert their authority. In the north, the VIET MINH, a political party led by HO CHI MINH, proclaimed the independent Democratic Republic of Vietnam. France agreed to recognize VIETNAM as a free state within the French Union, but negotiations dragged on. In December 1946, Viet Minh forces attacked French garrisons, and during the ensuing years guerrilla activity increased in the countryside. In 1949, a Vietnamese provisional government headed by Emperor BAO DAI was established and recognized by France, and in 1950 by the U.S. The communist-dominated Viet Minh rejected any remnant of French authority and consequently attacked French outposts along Vietnam's border with China, from whom they received substantial military aid.

In 1951, the Viet Minh created a common front with communist groups in Laos and Cambodia (Kampuchea) and became more and more aggressive. They were led by General VO NGUYEN GIAP, who launched an attack on March 18, 1954, against the strategic French stronghold at DIEN BIEN PHU in northwestern Vietnam. Giap's siege lasted 56 days; his Viet Minh troops continually attacked with artillery and mortar fire until the French defenders, short of ammunition, surrendered on May 7, 1954. Meanwhile, an international conference in Geneva was working out an agreement whereby the fighting would cease and the French would withdraw. The Viet Minh set up a government north of the 17th parallel, while Vietnamese noncommunists set up a government south of the

FRENCH GUIANA

demarcation line. The war was unpopular in France, most of whose citizens were relieved when it was over, in spite of their defeat and loss of influence in Southeast Asia. In July 1954, Vietnam was divided into the Democratic Republic of Vietnam (North Vietnam) and the Republic of Vietnam (South Vietnam). (See also VIETNAMESE CIVIL WAR OF 1955–65; VIETNAM WAR.)

French Polynesia. Overseas area of France, formerly known as French Oceania, comprised of nearly 105 islands in the South Pacific Ocean. The five main groups are: the Gambier Islands and the Marquesas, Society, Tuamotu and Tubuai, or Austral, Islands. Unpopulated Clipperton Island, 670 miles southwest of Mexico, is managerially a part of the region. Tahiti is the primary island, and the capital of the territory is Papeete on Tahiti. Some islands are volcanic; others are coral atolls; the citizens are mainly Polynesian. France claimed and annexed the island groups from 1842 to 1881. In 1903 the groups were united under a single administration as French Oceania (or Etablissements francaises de l'Oceanie); in 1946 they were reconsolidated as an overseas territory and renamed French Polynesia. The inhabitants voted in 1957 to remain connected to the FRENCH COMMUNITY, with representation in the French parliament. From 1966 to 1968 France conducted nuclear tests in the islands.

French Southern and Antarctic Territories. These islands lie in the southern Indian Ocean and cover a total area of 3,003 square miles. They include the extinct volcanoes Ile Amsterdam and Ile Saint-Paul, and Iles Kerguelen and Crozet. France also claims an area known as Terra Adelie in Antarctica as part of its Territories, a claim not recognized by the United States. Administered as dependencies of the former French colony of Madagascar from 1924 to 1955, the islands became a separate overseas territory in 1955. Scientific stations form the only permanent settlements.

French Union. Formed by the French Constitution of 1946, this was a federation of FRANCE, its overseas departments and territories, and the associated states of INDOCHINA, MOROCCO and TUNISIA. With the French Union allowing more automony to territories and protectorates, a number of them became ready for independence. The Union paved the way for a transition of France's colonial empire into the FRENCH COMMUNITY, which succeeded the Union in 1958.

French West Africa. A former federation of French colonies in West Africa that now comprise the states of BENIN, BURKINA FASO, GUINEA, COTE D'IVOIRE, MALI, MAURITANIA, NIGER and SENEGAL. Organized in 1895, the federation ended in 1958 when Guinea voted for immediate independence. The remaining constituent regions of French West Africa became autonomous constituents of the FRENCH COMMUNITY, achieving independence in 1960. (See also FRANCE.)

Freud, Anna (1895–1982). Austrian psychologist. Freud was the daughter of Sigmund FREUD, the founder of psychoanalysis, and she devoted much of her career to applying and defending the theoretical principles first articulated by her father. As a result of Nazi threats, Freud left Austria for Britain with her dying father in 1938. Over the next four decades, Freud became a major force in British psychology. Her highest achievement was the founding, in 1947, of the Hampstead Child Therapy Clinic in London. Freud specialized in the application of psychoanalysis to children. She also argued for the value of psychoanalytical insights in the interpretation of normal, as opposed to neurotic, behavior patterns. *The Ego and the Mechanisms of Defense* (1936) was her major work.

Freud, Sigmund (1856–1939). Austrian psychiatrist and founder of psychoanalysis. Freud is, beyond question, the most influential psychological theorist of the century, although his insights have been frequently misstated and oversimplified. Born of Jewish parentage in Moravia, Freud studied medicine in Vienna and Paris. In 1884 he studied under Josef Breuer, a Viennese physician who introduced Freud to the cathartic method of treating hysteria. This method, which focused on allowing patients to confront the root element of their abiding fears, became the essential starting point of psychoanalysis. In 1895 Freud and Breuer coauthored *Studies in Hysteria*. In 1900 Freud published a landmark work, THE INTERPRETATION OF DREAMS, which established the importance of the psychoanalytic movement. In *Three Essays on the Theory of Sexuality* (1905) Freud spelled out his insistence on the primal importance for personality development of unconscious sexual drives that emerge during infancy. In his later works, Freud analyzed cultural and religious issues and concluded that both artistic creation and religious belief were the result of sublimated sexual energy held in check by societal taboos. In 1938 Freud, who had been condemned by the Nazis, fled to London, where he died of throat cancer weeks after the outbreak of WORLD WAR II. Freud's ideas have had an enormous influence on 20th-century art, literature and social thought.

Freyssinet, Eugene (1879–1962). French structural engineer best known for his extraordinary constructions of reinforced concrete. Freyssinet designed vast twin airship hangars, built in 1916–21 at Orly Airport near Paris, using a continuous parabolic concrete arch with a span of 195 feet. The hangars were destroyed in 1944. Freyssinet was also the designer of various concrete bridges, including an arch bridge with a span of 430 feet over the

Seine at Pierre du Vauvray, built in 1922 and reconstructed in 1946, and of some buildings of the Gare d'Austerlitz in Paris of 1929.

Frick, Ford C. (1894–1978). Commissioner of baseball from 1951 to 1965. Frick was originally a newspaperman and then a radio announcer. He also served as president of baseball's National League for 17 years. He was elected to the Baseball Hall of Fame in 1970.

Fried, Alfred (1864–1921). Austrian journalist and pacifist. Fried ran a publishing company in Berlin and created the German Peace Society in 1892. Inspired by the first Hague peace conference in 1899, he devoted himself to promoting it and the cause of internationalism. He began publishing the *Annuaire de la Vie Internationale* (*Annual of International Life*) in 1905 and authored several books, notably, *Handbuch der Friedensbewegung* (*Handbook of the Peace Movement*, 1911). Fried was a joint recipient of the 1911 NOBEL PRIZE for peace along with Tobias ASSER.

Friedan, Betty (1921–). American feminist leader and author; one of the most prominent figures in the feminist movement since the publication of her landmark work, *The Feminine Mystique* (1963). In that work, Friedan captured wide public attention for her central thesis that women are culturally stereotyped in America as suited only to economically dependent and intellectually vacant lives as housewives and mothers. Friedan, who had for a time given up her own professional aspirations to live as a housewife in the suburbs, drew on her own surveys of a wide range of American women to support her then-controversial findings. In 1966, she founded the National Organization of Women (NOW) to serve as a lobbying and public opinion force on behalf of feminist political issues. In 1970, Friedan headed a nationwide Women's Strike for Equality. Her other books include *It Changed My Life* (1977) and *The Second Stage* (1981).

American author and leading feminist Betty Friedan (1983).

Friedman, Elizabeth S. (1894–1980). American pioneer cryptographer. Friedman helped decipher codes used by enemies of the U.S. during WORLD WAR I and WORLD WAR II. She also aided in the solving of international drug and liquor smuggling cases. Working with her husband, Col. **William Friedman,** she broke the top-secret Japanese **purple code,** which was used by Japanese diplomats before and during World War II.

Friedman, Herbert (1916–). U.S. rocket astronomy pioneer. After studying physics at Brooklyn College, Friedman did his graduate work at Johns Hopkins University in 1940. Joining the U.S. Naval Research Laboratory, he became involved in rocket astronomy during World War II and after the war was primarily concerned with RADAR detection devices and solar physics. In 1949 he directed a team that sent a V-2 rocket carrying scientific instruments into space, proving that X-rays emanated from the sun. During this same period, Friedman did pioneering work in ultraviolet mapping. Beginning in 1956 he began working with the Vanguard satellite development program, in an effort to continue his studies of X-rays and ultraviolet radiation from the sun. In 1960 he made the first X-ray photographs of the sun and made observations proving that neutral hydrogen is present throughout the solar system. Friedman was elected to the National Academy of Sciences in 1960 and has been awarded over 40 patents in the field of rocket and satellite astronomy. Recipient of the 1987 Wolf Prize in Physics, he is now retired from his position of superintendent of space science at the U.S. Naval Research Laboratory.

Friedman, Milton (1912–). American economist; leader of the monetarist, or "Chicago" school of economics. Friedman was born in New York City, the son of immigrants from Eastern Europe. He graduated from Rutgers University in 1932 and received his doctorate from Columbia University in 1946. After World War II he taught for two years at the University of Minnesota before joining the economics department of the University of Chicago, where he labored for the next three decades. In his 1957 book *A Theory of the Consumption Function,* Friedman introduced the extremely influential "permanent income hypothesis," which suggested, in contradiction to John Maynard KEYNES, that individuals base spending decisions on expected long-term income rather than on current income.

In 1963, Friedman, with his collaborator David Meiselman, continued his attack on Keynesian economics by arguing that money supply rather than government spending is the chief determiner of economic health. An economic adviser to Presidents NIXON and REAGAN, Friedman argued for a laissez-faire policy toward business and trade and played an important role in the creation of an all-volunteer Army and on other questions of public policy. He won the 1976 NOBEL PRIZE for economics. In 1977 Friedman retired from the University of Chicago and became a senior research associate at the Hoover Institution. In 1980 he published his best-selling book *Free to Choose,* which also became the basis of a television series. He was awarded the Medal of Freedom in 1988. (See also MONETARISM.)

Friedmann, Alexander Alexandrovich (1888–1925). Soviet astronomer. The son of a composer, Friedmann was educated at the University of St. Petersburg. He began his scientific career in 1913 at the Pavlovsk Observatory in St. Petersburg and, after war service, was appointed professor of theoretical mechanics at Perm University in 1918. In 1920 he returned to the St. Petersburg Observatory, where he became director shortly before his early death from typhoid at the age of 37. Friedmann established an early reputation for his work on atmospheric and meteorological physics. However, he is better known for his 1922 paper on the expanding universe. This arose from work of EINSTEIN in 1917 in which he attempted to apply his equations of general relativity to cosmology. Friedmann developed a theoretical model of the universe using Einstein's theory, in which the average mass density is constant and space has a constant curvature. Different cosmological models are possible depending on whether the curvature is zero, negative or positive. Such models are called "Friedmann universes." (See also BIG BANG THEORY.)

Friedrichshafen. City on Lake Constance, in the southeast German state of Baden-Wurttemberg. In 1908 it was chosen as the site of Count von ZEPPELIN's dirigible works, which were demolished in WORLD WAR II when Friedrichsafen was heavily shelled.

Friel, Brian (1929–). Northern Irish playwright. Friel has become an influential playwright in the British Isles by virtue of plays which probe the deep and persistent social, political and religious divisions between England and Ireland. In particular, Friel's plays have explored the violence and unrest that have persisted in his native NORTHERN IRELAND under British rule. His first play was *This Doubtful Paradise* (1959). Subsequent theatrical successes included *Philadelphia, Here I Come!* (1964), *Lovers* (1967), *The Freedom of the City* (1973), *Faith Healer* (1979), *Translations* (1980), and *Aristocrats* (1988). Friel also translated (1981) the classic play *Three Sisters* by Anton CHEKHOV.

Friend, Charlotte (1921–1987). American medical microbiologist. She was known for her important cancer research. In 1956 she discovered a virus that caused leukemia in mice; the **Friend virus,** as it came to be known, emerged as a major tool for study of the links between viruses and cancer.

Friends Service Council. Organization established by the Quakers in London in 1927. It was formed by merging the Friends Foreign Mission Association, which had been founded in 1868 to organize and operate schools, hospitals and Quaker societies abroad, and the Council for International Service, which was formed in 1919 to establish peace centers throughout the world. Headed from 1932 by Carl Heath, the FSC initially sponsored conferences that discussed problems brought on by the TREATY OF VERSAILLES, and interceded with governments to relieve persecuted minorities. After World War II, the FSC took over various relief activities that had been conducted by another Quaker organization during the war. Along with its U.S. counterpart, the AMERICAN FRIENDS SERVICE COMMITTEE, the FSC received the 1947 NOBEL PRIZE for peace. The FSC has continued its humanitarian work throught the world, operating relief camps for Palestinian refugees, aiding riot victims in INDIA, helping civilian victims of war in KOREA and VIETNAM, feeding people in famine-stricken Africa and conducting other relief and peace-related programs.

fringe theater. A general term for British experimental theater groups; first became a prominent usage in British theatrical circles in the 1950s, when the annual Edinburgh Drama Festival—which featured the best in accepted professional stage productions—became a stimulus for a number of alternative theatrical groups to perform their own experimental plays at the same time as the official festival productions. This informal competition between the "fringe" and the mainstream has continued to serve as an effective stimulus to British theater. A major playwright who emerged from the early "fringe" movement is Tom STOPPARD; subsequent "fringe" playwrights have included Howard Brenton and David HARE.

Frisch, Max (1911–91). Swiss novelist and playwright. Frisch, who began his career as an architect, achieved his first literary success with his play *When the War Was Over* (1949), which showed the strong influence of Frisch's close friend, the German playwright Bertolt BRECHT. In the 1950s Frisch turned his attention to fiction; his novel *I'm Not Stiller* (1954) earned international acclaim and enabled Frisch to devote himself full-time to writing. Frisch's most prominent themes are the pervasive nature of Nazi postwar guilt and the necessarily continuous struggle for political and personal freedom. His other novels include *Homo Faber* (1957), *Montauk* (1975), and *Man in the Holocene* (1979). Other plays by Frisch include *Andora* (1961) and *Biography: A Game* (1967). Frisch also produced several volumes of memoirs, most notably *Sketchbook 1946–49* (1977) and *Sketchbook 1966–71* (1974).

Friuli [German: Friaul]. In the ancient world, Forum Julii, a region on the Adriatic Sea south of Austria; now split between Slovenia in northwestern Yugoslavia and the Friuli-Venezia Giulia area of northeastern Italy. During WORLD WAR I the area was a battlefield; afterward, the victorious ITALY took all of old Friuli but had to cede the eastern section to YUGOSLAVIA after WORLD WAR II. The balance was united with Venezia Giulia as a region in 1947. Trieste was made its capital in 1954.

Social psychoanalyst Erich Fromm.

Poet Robert Frost.

Fromm, Erich (1900–1980). German-born psychoanalyst, social philosopher and humanist. Fromm obtained his Ph.D. from the University of Munich (1922) and also studied at Berlin's Psychoanalytic Institute. He started his own practice in 1925, and four years later began his lifelong teaching career. He emigrated from Nazi Germany to the U.S. in 1934, and subsequently lectured at Columbia, Yale, and other universities. Schooled in traditional Freudian analysis, he developed his own eclectic theories to explain human behavior. These theories stressed social and economic factors as well as unconscious drives. Fromm wrote some 20 books, including influential works on the theories of Karl Marx and Sigmund FREUD, the religious precepts of Judaism and Christianity, and the COLD WAR and the alienation of the individual.

Frost, Robert (Lee) (1874–1963). American poet. Frost dropped out of Dartmouth in 1892 to work as a mill laborer and teacher in Lawrence, Massachusetts. He attended Harvard, 1897–99; then moved to New Hampshire to farm and teach English. He lived in England briefly (1912–15) before returning to farm near Franconia, New Hampshire. Though his first poem appeared in 1894, his first success was in England with the publication of *A Boy's Will* (1913) and *North of Boston* (1914), written under the influence of his friend Edward THOMAS. Frost received the PULITZER PRIZE four times (1924, 1931, 1937, 1943) and was poetry consultant to the Library of Congress in 1958. Additional accolades included the Congressional Gold Medal awarded on his 88th birthday and more than 40 honorary degrees; he won a new, wide audience when he read at the inauguration of President John F. KENNEDY in 1961. Throughout his lifetime Frost cultivated the persona of a gentle, folksy, white-haired country farmer who wrote popular poems such as "Stopping by Woods on a Snowy Evening," "The Death of the Hired Man" and "Mending Wall," staples in every high school English class in the middle of the 20th century. However, his work and thought have more complex undercurrents than are at first apparent. While scholars and biographers have revealed a dark side to Frost's life and personality, he is universally acknowledged as a master craftsman and a major poet.

For further reading:

Pritchard, William H., *Frost: A Literary Life Reconsidered*. New York: Oxford University Press, 1984.

Thompson, Lawrence, *Robert Frost: A Biography*. New York: Holt, 1981.

Frunze, Mikhail Vasilevich (1885–1925). Russian BOLSHEVIK military leader. Having taken part in the Revolution of 1905, Frunze defeated the White Russian forces of Admiral KOLCHAK in 1919 and of General WRANGEL in 1920 during the RUSSIAN CIVIL WAR. During the intra-party struggle after the death of LENIN, Frunze sided with STALIN. He was appointed people's commissar of military and naval affairs in 1925 but died shortly thereafter.

Fry, Christopher (1907–). British playwright; achieved his greatest theatrical successes in the 1930s and 1940s. Fry was noted for his highly poetic and elevated style that dealt with romantic and mystical themes. His first play to gain attention was *The Boy With a Cart* (1937). In 1940, he was appointed director of the Oxford Playhouse, where his work was performed regularly throughout the decade. A number of leading British actors appeared in Fry's plays, including John GIELGUD in *The Lady's Not For Burning* (1948), Lawrence OLIVIER in *Venus Observed* (1950) and Edith EVANS in *The Dark Is Light Enough* (1954). Other plays by Fry include *A Phoenix Too Frequent* (1946), *The Firstborn* (1948) and *A Yard of Sun* (1970).

Fry, (Edwin) Maxwell (1899–1987). British architect. As a pioneer of modern architecture in Great Britain, his work included a housing project at Kensal Green in London that set new standards for its time. He was also involved in major architectural projects in British colonial West Africa, notably the design of the University of Ibadan in Nigeria. From 1951 to 1954, he was a member of the team of architects that worked with LE CORBUSIER on the design and initial construction of Chandigar, the new capital of the Punjab region of India.

Fry, Roger (Eliot) (1866–1934). British art critic, painter and author. Fry was educated at King's College, Cambridge, where as a member of the Apostles he became acquainted with members of the BLOOMSBURY GROUP, with which he would later be associated. Fry was a friend of and strong influence on Clive BELL. Fry wrote art criticism for the *Athenaeum* beginning in 1901, and helped found the *Burlington Magazine.* He worked at the Metropolitan Museum of Art in New York City from 1905 to 1910. Fry coined the term POST-IMPRESSIONISM, and presented a landmark exhibition of the style to a doubtful British public in 1910. Fry was named Slade Professor of Fine Art at Cambridge in 1933. His books include *Vision and Design* (1920), *Transformations: Critical and Speculative Essays on Art* (1926), and *The Arts of Painting and Sculpture* (1932). Virginia WOOLF wrote a biography of Fry which was published in 1940.

Frye, (Herman) Northrop (1912–1991). Canadian literary critic. Frye, who was educated at Oxford and taught for several decades at the University of Toronto, was one of the most influential literary critics of the post-World War II era. He is best known for his insistence on the underlying importance of myth and symbol as influences upon both creativity and formal literary structure. His major works include *Fearful Symmetry* (1947), a study of the British mystical poet William Blake, *Anatomy of Criticism* (1957), *Fables of Identity* (1963), and *The Well-Tempered Critic* (1967). In *The Great Code: The Bible and Literature* (1981), Frye argued for a pervasive shared symbolism between the Bible and the great works of Western literature.

Fuad I (1868–1936). First king of modern EGYPT (1922–36). The second son of Ismail Pasha, he was educated in Europe and succeeded his brother Hussein Kamil as sultan in 1917. He was proclaimed king in 1922, a year before Britain's recognition of his country's independence. In conflict with the WAFD party, he abrogated the existing constitution and introduced a new constitution in 1928, but was forced to restore the earlier document in 1935. Fuad was succeeded by his son FAROUK.

Fuchs, (Emil) Klaus (Julius) (1911–1988). German physicist and Soviet agent. Fuchs was active in the anti-Nazi underground movement before fleeing to France and later to England. He worked on the development of the ATOMIC BOMB in Britain and in the U.S. during WORLD WAR II. After the war, he helped direct nuclear research in Britain but also passed crucial nuclear secrets to the Soviet Union and was arrested for espionage in February 1950. Fuchs' case led to the exposure of a nuclear espionage ring that included Julius and Ethel ROSENBERG. Upon his release from prison in 1953 he flew to EAST GERMANY, where he became deputy director of the national nuclear research institute and a member of the central committee of the East German Communist Party.

Fuchs, Sir Vivien Ernest (1908–). British explorer and geologist. The son of a farmer of German origin, Fuchs was educated at Cambridge University, where he obtained his M.A. in geology in 1929 and his Ph.D. (1935). From 1929 he traveled on a series of expeditions as geologist, the first being the Cambridge East Greenland Expedition (1929). In 1947 he became a member of the Falkland Islands Dependencies Survey and in 1950 its director. As a result of his involvement with the survey, Fuchs led an expedition to Graham Land in ANTARCTICA (1948) to reassert the British claim to the territory, which was being challenged by Argentina. He was stranded on Storing Ton Island by bad weather until 1950. Fuchs is best known for the Commonwealth Trans-Antarctic Expedition he jointly led with Edmund HILLARY in the Weddell INTERNATIONAL GEOPHYSICAL YEAR (1957–58). Leaving Shackleton Base on the Weddell Sea on November 24, 1957, he reached the South Pole and met Hillary on January 19, 1958, then continued on to reach Scott Base, Victoria Land, on March 2. Fuchs was knighted in 1958.

Fuentes, Carlos (1928–). Mexican writer and diplomat. A liberal lawyer and political activist, Fuentes is one of Mexico's leading novelists and short story writers. His experimental novels are usually set in postrevolutionary Mexico and explore the mythology of his country's past and the social conditions of its present. His first work was a collection of surrealist stories, published in 1954. His first novel, *Where the Air Is Clear* (1958, tr. 1960), examined the lives of various inhabitants of Mexico City since the revolution of 1910. Fuentes achieved international acclaim with his novel *The Death of Artemio Cruz* (1962, tr. 1964). Fuentes' other fiction includes the novels *A Change of Skin* (1967, tr. 1968), *Terra Nostra* (1975, tr. 1976), *Distant Relations* (1980) and *The Old Gringo* (1985). He is also a playwright and essayist.

Fugard, Athol (1932–). South African playwright, actor and director; achieved worldwide fame for his searing plays depicting the physical and psychological horrors of APARTHEID. Fugard began his career as an actor in Cape Town in the 1950s. His first play was *No Good Friday* (1959), in which he also acted. His first major theatrical success was *The Blood Knot* (1961). In 1963 he founded his own theatrical troupe, the Serpent Players, which became a dominant force in South African theater. *Sizwe Bansi Is Dead* (1972) represented a shift for Fugard into a more experimental, improvisational mode of playwriting. Recent works include *Statements after an Arrest under the Immorality Act* (1972), *Dimetos* (1975), *A Lesson from Aloes* (1978) and the acclaimed *Master Harold and the Boys* (1982), which featured American actor James Earl JONES.

Fugitives and Agrarians (1920s-1930s). Literary movement by American writers of the South. The Fugitive literary movement—which was renamed the Agrarian movement in the 1930s—began in the years following World War I. John Crowe RANSOM, an eminent poet and literary critic, was teaching at Vanderbilt University. Among the students drawn to his classes were poet, critic and biographer Allen TATE and poet Robert Penn WARREN. Ransom inspired these writers and others to view the agrarian heritage of the South, along with its Confederate STATES' RIGHTS political background, as a vital cultural base for literary works. The Fugitives and Agrarians opposed industrialism and the policies of the NEW DEAL while promoting a new classicism for literature. *The Fugitive,* edited by Tate, was a major literary journal of the 1920s. Ransom went on to edit the influential *Kenyon Review* from 1938 to 1959.

Fulbright, J(ames) William (1905–). U.S. senator. Raised in Fayetteville, Arkansas, Fulbright graduated from the University of Arkansas in 1925, then studied at Oxford as a Rhodes scholar before earning a law degree at George Washington University. After serving as president of the University of Arkansas from 1939 to 1941, he was elected in 1942 to the U.S. House of Representatives and in 1944 to the U.S. Senate. In 1946, Fulbright sponsored the legislation establishing the foreign exchange program that bears his name. In 1959, he became chairman of the Senate Foreign Relations Committee. During the 1960s Fulbright urged the U.S. to reduce its expenditures supporting the COLD WAR with the Soviet Union and to concentrate its resources instead on domestic problems. In the early days of the VIETNAM WAR, he was a supporter of President Lyndon JOHNSON's policies, and it was Fulbright who introduced the TONKIN GULF RESOLUTION in the Senate on August 6, 1964, supporting the administration's use of force. However, beginning in 1966, he publicly questioned the wisdom of U.S. involvement in VIETNAM, and in 1967 his book *The Arrogance of Power* became a bestseller. In 1968, Fulbright denounced the Gulf of Tonkin Resolution. By 1970, when the resolution was repealed by Congress, Fulbright had emerged as a leading critic of the war. In 1974, after five full terms in the Senate, he was defeated by Arkansas Governor Dale Bumpers in the Democratic Senate primary.

Fuller, Loie (Mary Louise) (1862–1928). American dancer and choreographer. A self-taught dancer, Fuller created her first dance, *Serpentine Dance,* in 1891 after working as an actress, playwright and producer in the American theater for several years. Her 1892 solo dance debut at the Folies-Bergere in Paris was acclaimed. Hailed by the Impressionists and the ART NOUVEAU movement as an innovator for her experimentation with light, color, and stage devices, Fuller's choreographic style was characterized by improvised movement for the body clothed in masses of silk, which created a sculpted effect. She created 130 dances, including *Fire* (1895) and *Ballet of Light* (1908), founded a school in 1908, invented and patented costume designs, stage devices, and lighting machines, was honored by French scientists for her contributions to lighting theories, and inspired such artists as Toulouse-Lautrec and Auguste Rodin and the poet W.B. YEATS.

Fuller, R(ichard) Buckminster (1895–1983). Self-described "engineer, inventor, mathematician, architect, cartographer, philosopher, poet, cosmogonist, comprehensive designer and choreographer." He was best known for his 1947 invention of the **geodesic dome,** a sphere composed of triangles that provided maximum strength with great economy of materials. He designed many other innovative structures, including a futuristic three-wheeled automobile (1932) that was never built, and the DYMAXION House, a prefabricated glass-walled building that had rooms suspended from a pole. (Conceived in 1927, the first Dymaxion House was constructed in 1944.) Fuller, who attended Harvard but never graduated, wrote 25 books, held scores of patents, and received 39 honorary doctorates in fields ranging from the fine arts to engineering. In his later years, he dedicated himself to encouraging efficient use of resources; in the 1960s he had a cultlike following among those who saw his "alternative lifestyle" as a solution to modern ecological problems. He received the Presidential Medal of Freedom from President Ronald Reagan in 1983.

Fuller, Roy (Broadbent) (1912–). British poet and novelist. Fuller was a solicitor who in the 1930s began contributing poetry to *New Verse* and other left-wing literary journals. His first volume of poetry, *Poems,* was published in 1939. His early work shows the influence of W.H. AUDEN and Stephen SPENDER. His experiences in the Royal Navy during WORLD WAR II provided inspiration for the collections *The Middle of a War* (1942) and *A Lost Season* (1944). His later poetry, including *From the Joke Shop* (1975) and *The Reign of Sparrows* (1980), is more sarcastic and bitter in tone. Of his novels, which range from thrillers to children's books, perhaps most notable is *Image of a Society* (1956). Fuller was a professor of poetry at Oxford from 1968 until 1973, and has published the memoirs *Souvenirs* (1980), *Vamp Til Ready* (1982) and *Home and Dry* (1984). Fuller's son **John Fuller** (b. 1937) is also a noted poet and novelist. His works include the poetry collections *Cannibals and Missionaries* (1972) and *Lies and Secrets* (1979) and the novel *Flying to Nowhere* (1983).

Fulton. U.S. city in central Missouri's Callaway County, 25 miles north–northeast of Jefferson City. Fulton is the setting of Westminster College, where Winston CHURCHILL delivered his famous IRON CURTAIN speech on March 5, 1946. As a tribute, the college reproduced on its campus the London church of St. Mary the Virgin, Aldermanbury, conceived by Christopher Wren in 1677, as the Winston Churchill Memorial Library.

Funston, Frederick (1865–1917). U.S. Army officer. Educated at the University of Kansas, he received a Medal of Honor for his leadership of U.S. troops in the Philippines in 1899. Returning to the U.S., Funston commanded the Army departments of the Colorado, the Columbia, the Lake and California. His handling of the disaster of the 1906 SAN FRANCISCO EARTHQUAKE and fire further enhanced his national reputation. He served as the commander of U.S. forces along the Mexican border in 1916.

Furmanov, Dimitri Andreyevich (1891–1926). Russian writer. Originally a journalist, he wrote several "Sketches from the Front" after joining the Russian army in 1914 (see WORLD WAR I ON THE EASTERN FRONT). They were published in *Russkoye Slovo* in 1916. He joined the Communist Party in 1918 and served as a political commissar in CHAPAYEV's guerrilla forces. In 1923 he wrote the novel *Chapayev* about his experiences (filmed 1934). Other works include *Red Sortie* (1922), *Riot* (1923–25) and an unfinished novel, *Writers.*

Furman v. Georgia (1972). U.S. Supreme Court decision that temporarily overruled all state death penalties. By the 1970s some states had outlawed the death penalty as too cruel and unusual a punishment. However, other state courts sentenced prisoners to death for a variety of offenses. Petitioners challenged the Georgia death penalty statute by showing that the death penalty was inconsistently applied and fell most heavily on members of minority groups.

The Court did not hold that the death penalty was per se unconstitutional for being cruel and unusual, but reasoned that the states must have a formal procedure to ensure that the death sentence would be applied consistently, with ample opportunity for appeal.

Furtwangler, Wilhelm (1886–1954). German conductor, widely revered (with Arturo TOSCANINI) as one of the two greatest conductors of the 20th century. Furtwangler, the son of a distinguished archaeologist, was born in Berlin. After studying with Josef von Rheinberger, he was music director in Lubeck, Mannheim, and Frankfurt before succeeding Richard STRAUSS as Music Director of the Berlin State Opera in 1920. Two years later he became Music Director of the Berlin Philharmonic. During the 1920s through the 1940s, his mastery of the standard Austro-German repertoire—Beethoven, Brahms, Bruckner, and Wagner—became increasingly evident. He toured widely and conducted in the U.S., including a year as director of the New York Philharmonic (1937–38). He remained in Germany during WORLD WAR II; however, unlike his chief musical rival in Germany, Herbert von KARAJAN, Furtwangler was never a Nazi. Rather, he believed that he could serve the values of civilization by remaining in Germany and making the best of a bad situation. He defended Jewish musicians in the Berlin Philharmonic and also championed Paul HINDEMITH, whom the Nazis denounced. However, he was forbidden to conduct until 1948, when the Allies cleared him of Nazi sympathies. In later years, despite increasing deafness, he continued to conduct in Germany, Austria, and Switzerland. Furtwangler's contrasts with his great musical counterpart Toscanini are revealing. Whereas Toscanini was an implacable foe of FASCISM, Furtwangler tried to reconcile his distaste for politics with his devotion to German music. Toscanini's temper was notorious, while Furtwangler was reserved. Musically, Furtwangler's highly subjective interpretations, flexible tempi, and improvisatory performances contrast with Toscanini's tighter, more controlled performances. Toscanini sought to follow what he regarded as the letter of the score; Furtwangler strove to convey its spiritual qualities. Toscanini's influence on subsequent musicians and performance style has probably been greater; although many musicians have expressed admiration for Furtwangler, none have been able to duplicate his highly idiosyncratic performances. Initially indifferent and occasionally hostile to recording technology, Furtwangler nonetheless has left a rich legacy of records, including an incomparable *Tristan und Isolde* (1953) and a legendary radio recording of the *Ring* cycle (1953).

fusion jazz. Also known as jazz-rock, fusion jazz encompasses such amalgams as jazz-and-rock, jazz-and-blues and jazz-and-pop. First introduced in the 1960s, fusion was adopted by younger musicians (and audiences) who had grown up with both ROCK AND ROLL and jazz. It also reflected evolving technologies in the manufacture of musical instruments and recordings. For example, in fusion the electric bass guitar replaces the acoustic upright bass, various electronic keyboards substitute for the acoustic piano, and acoustic instruments such as the saxophone and trumpet are electronically amplified and modulated. Rhythmically, the fluid swing feel of jazz is discarded; instead of constant alterations between oscillating pulses of tension and release, the beat becomes metronomic, indeed, mechanistic, especially in groups of the 1980s using drum machines. Instead of supple walking bass lines, fusion tends to employ repeated ostinato figures. Harmonically, the traditionally sophisticated chordal changes associated with Tin Pan Alley and Broadway give way to simpler harmonic schemes, often borrowed from the MODAL JAZZ approach of saxophonist John COLTRANE.

The most important of the early fusion artists arose from the groups of trumpeter Miles DAVIS in the late 1960s and early

1970s. Keyboardists Herbie HANCOCK and Chick COREA, guitarist John McLaughlin and drummer Tony Williams all went on to establish notable solo careers as fusion group leaders. While much of fusion can be dismissed as commercially motivated, formulaic pap, the jazz-rock of such contemporary guitarists as John SCOFIELD, John Abercrombie and Pat Metheny embodies a genuine artistic quest for new sounds and new forms.

For further reading:

Gridley, Mark, *Jazz Styles*. Englewood Cliffs, New Jersey: Prentice-Hall, 1978.

Futurama. Name of the GENERAL MOTORS exhibit at the NEW YORK WORLD'S FAIR of 1939–40. Norman BEL GEDDES conceived and designed this famous exhibition pavilion to house a conveyer belt ride above an imagined world of the future (1960) created in model form, in which dramatic superhighways connected futuristic cities. The most popular exhibit at the fair, Futurama has often been credited as the key influence in the development of the superhighway network constructed after World War II.

future shock. A phrase coined by author Alvin Toffler in his book of the same title, 1970. The term soon spread into common usage in the U.S. It refers to the startling and disorienting impact experienced by a person who is confronted by ideals and behavior that differ markedly from the cultural norms which that person has previously lived by. Future shock can take place through a visit to a foreign land, or it can occur in one's own native country when one encounters an unfamiliar subculture therein. Future shock caused by the rapid pace of change is a particular feature of 20th-century life. It compels the person experiencing it either to hold fast to previously held cultural norms, or to adjust expectations and behavior in light of the new situation. As a result, future shock is often viewed as a helpful prelude to personal learning and growth on a major scale. The term is sometimes used interchangeably with **culture shock.**

futurism. Futurism was a theoretical movement that influenced literature, painting, theater and the arts in general in the early decades of the 20th century. The term "futurism" was coined by the Italian poet F.T. MARINETTI in a 1909 manifesto. Marinetti urged that artists should turn their backs on past eras of artistic creation and instead embrace the "dynamism" of the industrial era with its hectic urban pace of life and its machine-influenced asthetics. While Marinetti concentrated on the applications of futurism to poetic language, Italian painters such as Umberto Boccioni, Carlo CARRA and Luigi Russolo produced canvases filled with mechanical forms and the pulsing energy of the city. Russia was another country in which the influence of futurism showed itself strong, particularly in the work of poet Vladimir MAYAKOVSKY. In the 1920s, Marinetti continued to write on futurism and allied the movement with Italian FASCISM.

Gable, Clark [born William Gable] (1901–1960). Legendary American film actor. Born in Cadiz, Ohio, Gable began his show business career as a backstage handyman for a number of touring companies. He entered the HOLLYWOOD arena with bit performances in silent films during the 1920s, and by the early 1930s was a star. Cast mainly in he-man roles, he nonetheless won an ACADEMY AWARD for his sparkling comic performance in Frank CAPRA's *It Happened One Night* (1934). His best-known performance is undoubtedly that of Rhett Butler in the Civil War epic GONE WITH THE WIND (1939). Dubbed "the King of Hollywood," he appeared in some 65 films including *Red Dust* (1932), *Mutiny on the Bounty* (1935), *San Francisco* (1936), *The Hucksters* (1947), *The Tall Men* (1955) and *Run Silent, Run Deep* (1958). His rugged, straightforward style was last seen in *The Misfits* (1960), completed shortly before his death. Gable was married to the acclaimed comic actress Carole LOMBARD.

For further reading:
Essoe, Gabe, *The Complete Films of Clark Gable.* New York: Carol Publishing Group, 1986 (reissue).

Clark Gable, with costar Vivien Leigh, in his most famous role as Rhett Butler in Gone With the Wind *(1939).*

Gabo, Naum (1890–1977). Russian sculptor, painter and architect. Brother of Anton PEVSNER, he was born in Bryansk, Russia, lived in Germany and Norway during the RUSSIAN REVOLUTION and returned to his native country in 1917. While abroad, he studied medicine in Munich, but abandoned that career to study with the great art historian Heinrich Wolfflin. During this period he also met Wassily KANDINSKY and other modern artists and decided to devote himself to painting and sculpture. With his brother, he wrote the *Realist Manifesto* (1920), which stressed a new dynamism and proposed the inclusion of time and space into works of art. In Russia, Gabo was one of the founders of CONSTRUCTIVISM. His Constructivist sculptures are elegantly delicate abstract compositions, often employing plastic, nylon or metal in complicated geometric configurations. Gabo's non-political aesthetics clashed with Soviet art dogma, and he left Moscow in 1922. Gabo taught at the BAUHAUS in Berlin, until forced to flee by the Nazis in 1932. He moved first to England, then to the U.S., where he settled in 1946. Examples of his work can be found in many leading contemporary art museums, and he is known for a number of major architectural commissions, such as the U.S. Rubber Company Building in New York City.

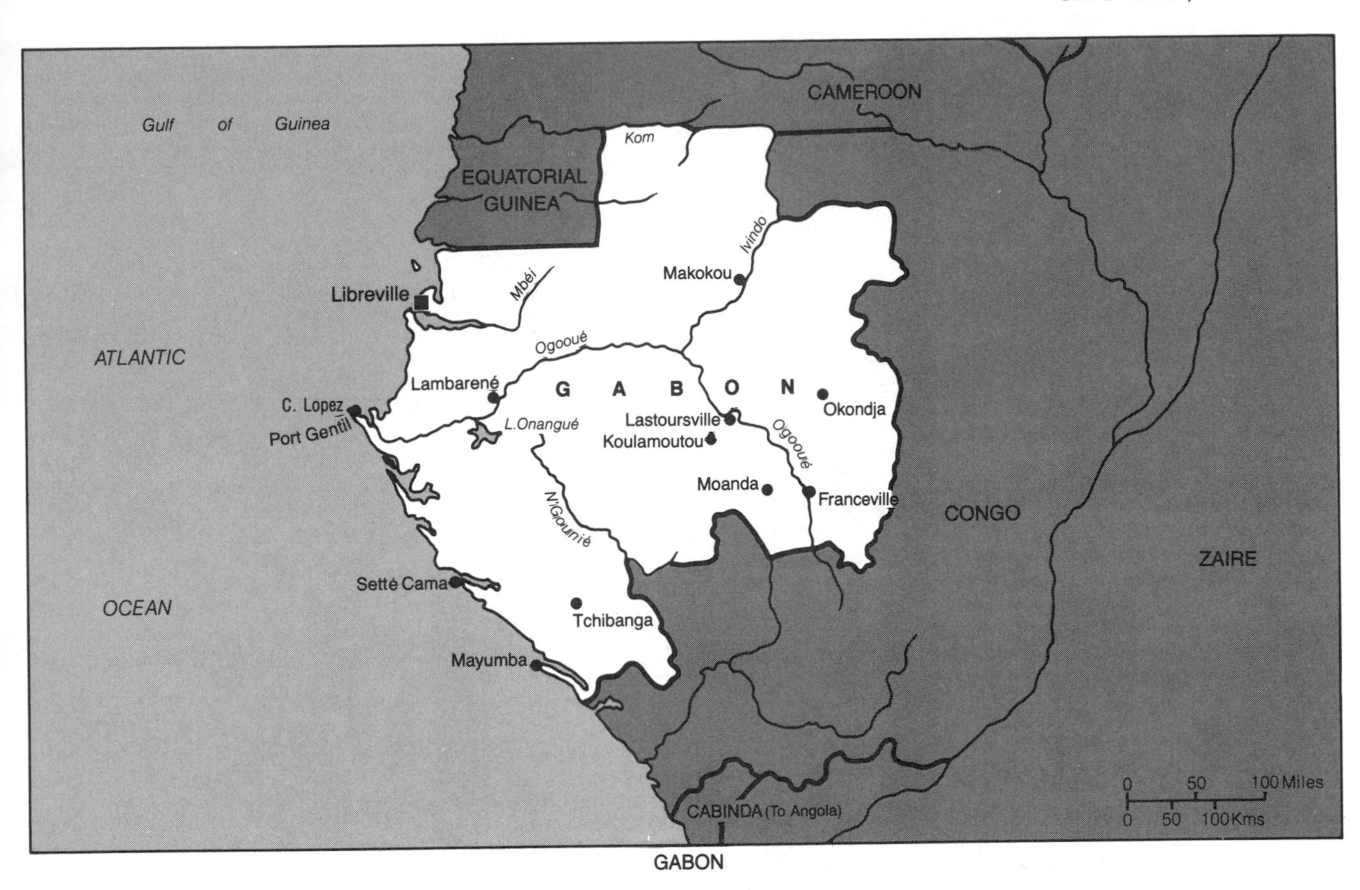

GABON

Gabon [Republic of Gabon]. Nation located on the west coast of Africa in the equatorial zone. Gabon covers an area of 103,062 square miles. A French colony until 1958, when it became an autonomous republic, Gabon achieved full independence in 1960. Leon M'ba was elected president in 1961, deposed by the military in 1964 and reinstated as president after French intervention. His successor, Albert-Bernard Bongo (1967–present), established a single-party government and maintained political and economic stability until the 1980s, when opposition groups formed a government in exile. In 1990, strikes, protests and continued opposition pressure pushed the government toward constitutional reform.

Gabor, Dennis (1900–1979). Hungarian-born British physicist. Gabor was educated in Budapest and Berlin, where he obtained his engineering doctorate (1927). After Adolf HITLER rose to power, he immigrated to Britain and became a British subject. In 1948 he jointed the faculty at the Imperial College of Science and Technology in London. He was later a staff scientist for the CBS. Gabor invented holography, a photographic method of reproducing three-dimensional images. He developed the system in 1948 by improving the resolution of the ELECTRON MICROSCOPE. (In 1960, other scientists achieved the same effect using laser beams.) For this invention, Gabor was awarded the 1971 NOBEL PRIZE for physics. He patented more than 100 other inventions.

Gabrilowitsch, Ossip (1878–1936). U.S. pianist and orchestra conductor who brought worldwide fame to the Detroit Symphony Orchestra. He gained a reputation as a brilliant concert pianist in Europe and visited the U.S. many times, directing leading orchestras before he settled down in Detroit in 1918. The Detroit Symphony Orchestra flourished under his conductorship.

Gaddis, William (1922–). American novelist. Largely unread and underrated, Gaddis' fiction is considered by some to be an important and original satire of American society. Gaddis began his career working as a fact checker at THE NEW YORKER from 1946 to 1947, during which time he became acquainted with writers of the BEAT GENERATION, such as Jack KEROUAC, who modeled the character Harold Sand in *The Subterraneans* on Gaddis. Gaddis' first novel, *Recognition* (1955), depicts Wyat Gwyon's deluded attempts to find integrity in the art world while surrounded by unethical liars and frauds. The book evidences Gaddis' own conflicting views about his Calvinistic upbringing. Gaddis worked in a variety of positions, bringing him closer to the corporate ideal of financial success at any cost, which he satirizes in *JR* (1975), written almost entirely in dialogue. *Carpenter's Gothic* (1985) is an even darker view of the subverted American spirit. Its publication revived interest in Gaddis and his first two novels were reissued. Gaddis contributed to many periodicals, among them *Harper's* and the *Atlantic*.

Gagarin, Yuri (1934–1968). Soviet cosmonaut and the first human being in space. Gagarin stunned the world on April 12, 1961, when he successfully orbited the Earth. Remaining in orbit for 89.1 minutes and traveling at a velocity that reached 17,400 miles an hour, Gagarin opened the door to space travel for humans. Although in a few short years his historic achievements would be eclipsed by a series of epic space voyages, he was truly the world's first space traveler. The son

Soviet cosmonaut Yuri Gagarin was the first human in space, orbiting the Earth on April 12, 1961.

of a carpenter born on a collective farm, Gagarin had lived with his family under German occupation for several years during World War II. While attending industrial technical school and studying to become a factory worker, he became interested in flying and joined an amateur pilot's club. Recommended for air force duty by one of the club's instructors, he joined the Orenburg air force school in 1955. For two years Gagarin served as a pilot with the Northern Fleet, based north of the Arctic Circle, then joined the cosmonaut corps and began training in October 1959.

After his historic space flight Gagarin found himself a popular and inspiring speaker. As a spokesman for the Soviet space program and its many successes, he charmed listeners around the world with his simple style and humility. Appointed commander of the cosmonaut team in 1961, he became deputy director of the cosmonaut training center in 1964. Yearning to get back into space, he managed to get himself assigned as a backup pilot for SOYUZ 3 and had just finished training when he was tragically killed in an aircraft accident on March 27, 1968. Today, a bronze statue of Gagarin welcomes visitors to Star City near Moscow, a symbol of the man, his accomplishment and his hold on the hearts of the Soviet people.

Gaiever, Ivar (1929–). Norwegian-American physicist. Gaiever studied electrical engineering at the Norwegian Institute of Technology. He did service with the Norwegian Army (1952–53) and worked as a patent examiner in the Norwegian Patent Office (1953–54). In 1954 he immigrated to Canada to take up the post of mechanical engineer with the Canadian General Electric Company, transferring to General Electric's Research and Development Center in Schenectady, New York, in 1956. He gained his doctorate in 1964 from the New York Rensselear Polytechnical Institute.

At General Electric, Gaiever worked on tunneling effects in SUPERCONDUCTORS, a phenomenon explored by Leo ESAKI. In 1960 he performed experiments with metals separated by a thin insulating film through which electrons tunneled, and found that if one of the metals was in the superconducting state, the current-voltage characteristics of such junctions revealed much about the superconducting state. This laid the foundation for Brian JOSEPHSON's important discovery of the **Josephson effect.** Gaiever, Josephson and Esaki shared the 1973 NOBEL PRIZE for physics for their various contributions to knowledge of the phenomenon of tunneling and superconductivity. Their work has had important application in microelectronics and in the precise measurement of electromotive force. Subsequently, Gaiever has also published work in the field of visual observation of the antibody-antigen reaction.

Gaitskell, Hugh (Todd Naylor) (1906–1963). British Labour politician. Gaitskell was educated at Winchester and at New

Hugh Gaitskell, leader of the British Labour Party from 1955 to 1963.

College, Oxford, where he became a socialist, influenced by the events surrounding the GENERAL STRIKE OF 1926. A lecturer in political economy at University College in London, Gaitskell was elected Labour M.P. in 1945. He served in the ATTLEE government as minister of fuel and power (1947–50), minister of economic affairs (1950) and chancellor of the exchequer (1950–51). In 1955, Gaitskell defeated Aneurin BEVAN and Herbert MORRISON for the leadership of the LABOUR PARTY, succeeding Clement Attlee. Gaitskell was a skilled parliamentarian and representative of the tradition of the Labour party, although his alterations of the NATIONAL HEALTH SERVICE alienated some of the party's left. He also opposed the party's position in favor of unilateral nuclear disarmament, and in 1961 persuaded the party to reverse its decision. Gaitskell died suddenly in 1963, but his enthusiasm had revitalized the Labour party and it prevailed in the 1964 elections.

Gaitskellites. British LABOUR PARTY members who supported the moderate policies of Hugh GAITSKELL in the late 1950s and early 1960s. Gaitskell was elected party leader in 1955 but was forced to abandon his idea of dropping Clause IV from the party constitution and was defeated on defense issues by unilateralists in 1960.

Galbraith, John Kenneth (1908–). Noted economist and author. Born and educated in Canada, Galbraith was a Harvard professor when he was brought to Washington, D.C., to serve in various government posts during World War II. An active liberal Democrat, he was an adviser to both Adlai STEVENSON and President John F. KENNEDY, who appointed him ambassador to INDIA during a critical period of Chinese-Indian border conflict. Galbraith was a prolific author throughout his career and is best known for three books: *American Capitalism* (1952), *The Affluent Society* (1958) and *The New Industrial State* (1967). Galbraith, trained as a Keynesian, argued that the free-enterprise system had its limits. Unlike many traditional economists Galbraith also emphasized the importance of political decisions in shaping the economic system. He said that the American government should assume responsibility for health, housing and other segments of the economy that were not effectively providing basic services for many Americans.

Gale, General Sir Richard (1896–1982). British military officer. As commander of the Sixth Airborn Division, he was one of the leaders of the Allied parachute troops at the INVASION OF NORMANDY during WORLD WAR II. For his role in the invasion, he was awarded the British Distinguished Service Order (DSO) and the American Legion of Merit. He also played an important role in the Allied counterattack during the BATTLE OF THE BULGE (December, 1944). After the war he commanded British forces in PALESTINE and in Egypt. He was aide-de-campe to Queen ELIZABETH II in the 1950s and was deputy supreme Allied commander in Europe for NATO (1958–60).

Galili, Israel (1911–1986). Israeli politician. Galili was a leader in establishing ISRAEL's arms industry, and was long active as a behind-the-scenes policy maker and conciliator in the Labor Party. He was said to have been especially influential in the government headed by Golda MEIR. In 1980, he was the principal architect of a compromise peace plan with JORDAN.

Gallant, Mavis (1922–). Canadian author. Born in Montreal, Gallant later lived in Paris. Her short story collections include *The Other Paris* (1956), *Overhead in a Balloon: twelve stories of Paris* (1987) and *In Transit: twenty stories* (1989). Novels include *Green Water, Green Sky* (1959) and *A Fairly Good Time* (1970). Gallant has been a frequent contributor to THE NEW YORKER, where many of her short stories first appeared.

Gallant Fox (1927–1954). Thoroughbred racehorse. The 1930 Triple Crown winner, Gallant Fox won 10 of 11 races during that campaign. The race he lost was responsible for one of the biggest payoffs in racing history, as he was upset as heavy

American economist and ambassador John Kenneth Galbraith.

favorite on a muddy track by 100–1 shot Jim Dandy in the Travers, who returned $20,000 on a two-dollar bet. Gallant Fox's stud career was perhaps even more outstanding, as his progeny included the 1935 Triple Crown winner Omaha and 1936 Horse of the Year, Granville.

Gallegos, Romulo (1884–1969). Venezuelan novelist and statesman. In self-imposed exile from the Venezuelan dictatorship (1931–35), he returned home and became minister of education. He was elected president of the nation in 1947, but was ousted in a coup less than a year later. He fled to Mexico, returning to VENEZUELA in 1958. As a novelist, Gallegos used modernist methods to portray the landscape of his homeland. An extremely prolific author, he began writing novels with *El ultimo solar* (1920, *The Last Manor*). His best known work is the novel *Dona Barbara* (1929, tr. 1931), a work about the Venezuelan plains. His other works include *Cantaclaro* (1931) and *Canaima* (1935).

Gallico, Paul (William) (1897–1976). American author. Gallico first made a name for himself as a sportswriter. At the age of 39, he turned to writing, publishing his first short stories in periodicals. His first novel, *The Snow Goose* (1941), was his only book to receive critical as well as popular acclaim; however, his popularity continued with his prolific output. He is perhaps best known for *Lou Gehrig: Pride of the Yankees* (1942, filmed as *Pride of the Yankees*, 1942) and *The Poseidon Adventure* (1969, filmed 1972). Other works include *Mrs 'Arris Goes to Paris* (1958), the first of a series about an English cleaning woman, and *Beyond the Poseidon Adventure* (1978) and *The House That Wouldn't Go Away* (1980), both published posthumously. Much of his fiction has been adapted for television and film.

Gallipoli Peninsula. In European TURKEY, a long and narrow point of land, aimed southwestward and lying athwart the DARDANELLES; perennially important because of its strategic position commanding the maritime commerce between the Mediterranean Sea and the Black Sea. In WORLD WAR I Allied British, Australian, French and New Zealand land and sea forces unsuccessfully stormed the Turkish forts in this area in 1915–16. Contemporaries, and later historians, blame First Lord of the Admiralty Winston CHURCHILL for the military disaster.

Galloway, William "Bill" (1877–1952). U.S. industrialist and catalog marketer. He put himself through college by selling pencils. This sales experience enabled him to become one of the first marketers through catalog solicitation. With his brother James he started Galloway Company at Waterloo, Iowa, to produce a complete line of farm machinery. Bill Galloway pioneered in marketing through catalog display and selective direct mailing. The company's manufacturing operations expanded quickly and encompassed a line of buildings almost a mile long, but internal disputes eventually brought the business down. The brothers started another business of manufacturing and distributing automatic humidifiers for furnaces. Galloway Park in Waterloo pays tribute to the pioneer Iowa industrialists.

Gallup, George H. (1901–1984). The American father of modern public opinion polling techniques. Gallup gained fame by predicting that Franklin D. ROOSEVELT would beat Alf LANDON in the 1936 presidential election, even though other pollsters predicted otherwise. Gallup survived a notable lapse when he incorrectly forecast that Thomas DEWEY would beat Harry S. TRUMAN in the 1948 election. Gallup's American Institute of Public Opinion, and later the Gallup Organization, came to set the standards for the polling industry around the world. He made polling a key tool of politics and business.

Gallup Poll. Public opinion poll originated by statistician and market research expert George GALLUP (1901–84). In 1935 Gallup, who was an advertising agency market researcher (1932–47), founded the American Institute of Public Opinion, and in 1939 he set up the Audience Research Institute, both with headquarters in Princeton, New Jersey. Based on sound scientific sampling methods developed by American business in the 1920s and refined by later pollsters, the Gallup Poll interviews a representative group of 1,500 people regarding their views on a given issue and, from their responses, extrapolates American public opinion on the question. The poll is supported by approximately 140 newspapers and some 20 surveys a year are conducted. The best known are the pre-election surveys carried out by the American Institute, which have been conducted yearly since 1936.

Galsworthy, John (1867–1933). British novelist, playwright and poet. Galsworthy was born in Surrey and educated at Harrow and New College, Oxford. Though called to the bar, he never practiced law. With a private income, Galsworthy was free to travel; during the course of one of his trips he became acquainted with Joseph CONRAD, who became a life long friend, and of whose work Galsworthy was an early champion. Galsworthy's first collection of short stories, *From the Four Winds*, was published in 1897; his first novel, *Jocelyn*, appeared in 1898. Both were published under the pseudonym John Sinjohn. These were followed by the short stories, *Villa Rubein*, in 1900, at which time Galsworthy became acquainted with the publisher Edward Garnett, who greatly encouraged Galsworthy in his work. Another source of encouragement was his future wife, Ada. Married unhappily when they met, she and Galsworthy lived together covertly until she was able to obtain her divorce. Her story and their relationship was the inspiration for Galsworthy's first major success, *The Man of Property* (1906), which was to become the first novel of THE FORSYTE SAGA, Galsworthy's best known work. The book not only tells the story of Irene and Soames Forsyte's unhappy marriage, but satirizes upper-middle-class life in Victorian England with its portrayal of the entire Forsyte family and their strict adherence to convention. It established Galsworthy's reputation. The other novels included in *The Forsyte Saga* (1922) are *In Chancery* (1920) and *To Let* (1921); and the short stories, "The Indian Summer of a Forsyte" (1918) and "The Awakening" (1920). However, Galsworthy published many other works of fiction between 1906 and 1920, including *Fraternity* (1909) and *The Dark Flower* (1913). Galsworthy's first play, *The Silver Box* (1906), established him also as a playwright of note. His realistic plays revolve around themes of social injustice. *Strife* (1909) examined the suffering of striking Welsh workers, while *Justice* (1910) reflected Galsworthy's crusade against solitary confinement of prisoners, and influenced Winston CHURCHILL's policy on prison reform. Galsworthy was offered a knighthood in 1917 which he refused. He was the founder of PEN in 1921. He was the recipient of the NOBEL PRIZE for literature in 1932. Galsworthy's work, though continually popular, has often been criticized as middlebrow, and he has been accused of inwardly admiring the very values his works purport to satirize. Other of his many works include the novels *The White Monkey* (1924), *The Silver Spoon* (1926) and *Swan Song* (1928), which further chronicle the Forsytes; and the plays *The Skin Game* (1920), *Loyalties* (1922) and *Old English* (1924).

Galtieri, Leopoldo Fortunato (1926–). Argentinean military officer, President of ARGENTINA. General Galtieri was leader of the controlling military junta in Argentina from 1979 to 1982, and was responsible for Argentina's seizure of the FALKLAND ISLANDS in 1982. Britain responded militarily, decisively defeating Argentina in the FALKLANDS WAR. Galtieri and other junta members were deposed by Argentinean democrats, accused of human rights violations and court-martialled. Galtieri was sentenced to 12 years in prison in 1986.

Gambia [Republic of Gambia]. Nation located on the west coast of Africa. Gambia is a separate enclave within the country of SENEGAL and occupies an area of 4,359 square miles. A British colony since 1888, the country achieved independence in 1965 and became a republic in 1970. Its president, Sir Dawda Kairaba Jawara (1965–present), formed a Senegambian Confederation with Senegal in 1982, primarily for economic reasons, but it was dissolved in 1989.

Gamow, George (1904–1968). Soviet-American physicist. Gamow, the son of a teacher, was educated at the University of Leningrad, where he obtained his doctorate in 1928 and later served as professor of physics (1931–34). Before his move to the U.S. in 1934 he spent long periods at Gottingen, Copenhagen and Cambridge, England, the major centers of the revolution then taking place in physics. In America he spent his career as professor of physics at George Washington University (1934–68) and then at the University of Colorado (1956–68).

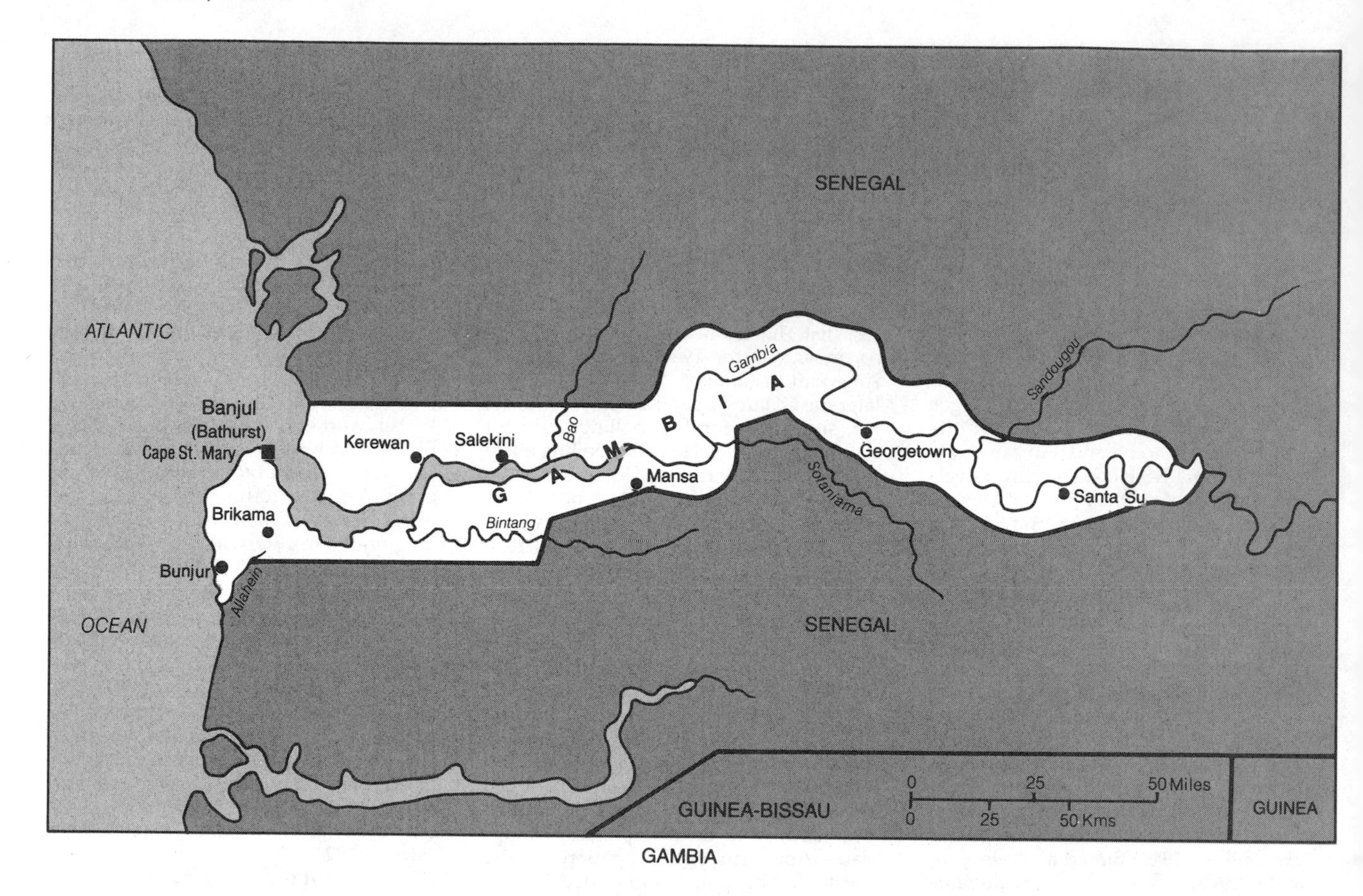

GAMBIA

Gamow made many contributions to nuclear and atomic physics, but is mainly noted for his work on interesting problems in cosmology and molecular biology. In cosmology he revised and extended the BIG BANG THEORY of the creation of the universe and first announced it in his famous "alpha beta gamma" paper in 1948, which he wrote in collaboration with Ralph ALPHER and Hans BETHE. A fuller account was later published by Gamow in his *Creation of the Universe* (1952). Gamow later moved from showing how the universe began to the no less interesting question of how life began. He was quick to see the significance of the DNA model proposed by James WATSON and Francis CRICK in 1953. The problem was to show how the sequences of the four nucleic acid bases that constitute the DNA chain could control the construction of proteins, which may be made from 20 or more amino acids. Gamow had the insight to see that the bases must contain a code for the construction of amino acids. Gamow also produced convincing arguments to show that the code was not overlapping. Gamow was widely known as one of the most successful popular science writers of his day. He wrote many books that conveyed to the general public much of the excitement of the revolution in physics that he lived through.

Gance, Abel (1889–1981). French film director and writer, one of the most important figures in the early development of the cinema. Gance was born in Paris to a physician father who wanted him to pursue a career in law. After abandoning early studies, however, Gance turned to acting and writing for the stage and for the medium still in its infancy, the motion picture. In 1911 he formed his own movie production company and made his first film, *La Digue*. Between 1915 and 1918 he made many films for the prestigious Film d'Art company, including the experimental *La Folie du Docteur Tube* (which distorted images through the use of mirrors and lenses). His first masterpiece, *J'accuse* (1919), was a pacifist statement made during WORLD WAR I with real soldiers under fire. (He remade it as a sound film in 1938 on the eve of World War II.) The two films upon which his reputation rests followed in the 1920s: *La Roue* (*The Wheel*) in 1923 and *Napoleon* in 1927. The first was a melodrama set against a railyard background. Technically astounding, it liberated the camera from the tripod and created a vast mosaic of thousands of shots intercut at times with dizzying rapidity. *Napoleon* may be regarded as the culmination of the era of SILENT FILM. An unabashed glorification of French spirit and art, it refined Gance's camera technique and presented an innovation, the Polyvision system, a triptych employing triple screen projection that anticipated Cinerama by 25 years. Excepting a few projects in the 1930s like *Beethoven* (1938), in which he experimented with montages of sound, Gance was tied to commercial projects and did little wholly creative work until his last original project, *Cyrano et d'Artagnan* (1963). Gance was a visionary whose finished work sometimes fell short of his grandiose ambitions. A member of the French movement known as The Seventh Art, he saw cinema as the marriage of feelings and machine.

For further reading:

Welsh, James and Steven Kramer, *Abel Gance*. Boston: Twayne, 1978.

Gander. City in Canada's province of Newfoundland that became well-known in the early days of transatlantic air travel; site of an international airport built by the British in 1939. During WORLD WAR II, Gander was the chief North American debarkation point for aircraft being ferried from the U.S. and Canada to the besieged island nation of Great Britain.

Gandhi, Indira (1917–1984). Prime minister of INDIA (1966–77, 1980–84). The daughter of Jawaharlal NEHRU (and unrelated to Mohandas K. GANDHI), she joined the CONGRESS PARTY in 1939. Minister for broadcasting and information from 1964 to 1966, on the death of Prime Minister Lal SHASTRI (1966) she was elected leader of Congress and became prime minister. Her premiership was marked by significant social and economic progress, but also by tension with PAKISTAN (see INDO-PAKISTANI WAR OF 1971) and increasing internal discontent over her assumption of almost dictatorial powers on the declaration of an emergency in 1975. In 1977 Congress was defeated for the first time by the Janata coalition, united only in their opposition to Mrs. Gandhi (see Mararji DESAI). Within a few months she was on the road back to power, win-

Indira Gandhi, daughter of Jawaharlal Nehru and prime minister of India from 1966 to 1977 and 1980 to 1984.

ning the election of 1980 with a promise of firm government, and demonstrating her popular appeal with ordinary people. She was assassinated in 1984 by Sikh extremists.

Gandhi, Mohandas K(aramchand) [aka Mahatma, or "great soul"] (1869–1948). Indian national leader who helped INDIA achieve independence through a campaign based on nonviolence and civil disobedience. Born at Porbandar on the western coast of India, Gandhi studied law in London in the late 1880s and returned home to practice as a barrister in Bombay. In 1907 he went to South Africa, where he conducted passive resistance campaigns in protest of the Transvaal government's discrimination against Indian settlers, who formed a minority in the region. He returned to India in 1915 and eventually emerged as leader of the CONGRESS PARTY, which called for India's independence from the UNITED KINGDOM. Shedding his Anglicized demeanor (both figuratively and literally) Gandhi adopted a simple, ascetic way of life. He organized a boycott of British goods (both as a symbolic protest of India's colonial status and in order to stimulate India's local industries). His nonviolent campaigns of civil disobedience to British rule provoked the British to imprison him on four different occasions (1922, 1930, 1933, 1942); he also went on hunger strikes to focus attention on, and gather sympathy for, his cause.

Gandhi worked with Britain's last two viceroys of India (WAVELL and MOUNTBATTEN) to plan his country's independence, which was granted in 1947. Acknowledging the demands of JINNAH and the Muslim minority, Gandhi accepted the partition of the colony into two separate nations, India and PAKISTAN. The following year Gandhi was assassinated by a Hindu fanatic who viewed Gandhi's acceptance of partition as a betrayal of the Hindu population. Many of Gandhi's followers regarded him as a saint; his doctrine of nonviolence had a direct and profound influence on Martin Luther KING Jr., leader of the CIVIL RIGHTS MOVEMENT in the U.S.

For further reading:

Brown, Judith, *Gandhi: Prisoner of Hope.* New Haven, Conn.: Yale University Press, 1990.

Nanda, B.R., *Mahatma Gandhi: A Biography.* Oxford: Oxford University Press, 1989.

Gandhi, Rajiv (1945–1991). Indian politician, prime minister of INDIA (1984–90). The grandson of Jawaharlal NEHRU and son of Indira GANDHI, Rajiv Gandhi was educated at Cambridge University and was subsequently a pilot in India. Following the death of his elder brother Sanjay in 1980, Indira Gandhi persuaded Rajiv to enter politics, hoping to groom him as her successor. Following her death in 1984, he won a record majority in the elections that year. Rajiv Gandhi identified domestic strife as his major problem and attempted to reduce tensions in Punjab, Assam and Gujarat, but was minimally successful, particularly in the Punjab, where Sikh militants revived their campaign for greater autonomy in 1986. Defeated in the 1990 elections, he was assassinated while campaigning in 1991.

"Mahatma" Gandhi (at right, with Jawaharlal Nehru in 1946) led India's struggle for independence.

Gang of Four. Four radical Chinese leaders—**Wang Hongwen, Zhang Chungqiao, Yao Wenyuan,** and CHIANG CH'ING, Mao's widow—who were publicly denounced following the triumph of moderates in 1976. A show trial was held following a PROPAGANDA campaign and the arrest of the four on a charge of trying to take control of the army. Jiang Qing was given a suspended death sentence in 1981. In Britain, the name "Gang of Four" was popularly given to four ex-LABOUR PARTY members—Roy JENKINS, Shirley WILLIAMS, William RODGERS, and David OWEN—whose decision to leave the party coincided with attacks on the Chinese Gang of Four. They formed the SOCIAL DEMOCRATIC PARTY in 1981.

Gann, Paul (1912–1989). U.S. real estate and automobile salesman who was coauthor (with Howard JARVIS) of California's PROPOSITION 13 tax revolt referendum. The referendum, which passed in 1978 by a vote of almost two to one, cut California property taxes in half and inspired similar tax revolt measures across the U.S. In 1987, Gann announced that he had contracted AIDS from a blood transfusion he received during emergency heart surgery in 1982.

Gapon, Father Georgi Apollonovich (1870–1906). Russian priest. He believed in police socialism and founded the Assembly of Russian Factory and Mill Workers in St. Petersburg in 1903, which was financed by police funds. A strike at the Putilov works in St. Petersburg began because of alleged victimization of assembly members and soon spread. Gapon decided to make an appeal to the czar. He promoted a petition that was revolutionary in its demands, and organized an illegal march of 200,000 to the Winter Palace. The police fired on the demonstrators, killing 130 people, and January 9, 1905, became known as BLOODY SUNDAY and saw the start of a year of revolutionary unrest. Evidence suggests that Gapon was an agent provocateur. He was murdered by his fellow revolutionaries.

Garbo, Greta [Greta Louisa Gustafsson] (1905–1990). Legendary Swedish-born movie star of the SILENT FILM era and the early years of TALKING PICTURES. Throughout her 19-year, 27-film career she specialized in playing glamorous seductresses who often became involved in tragic love affairs. Her movies included the silent *Flesh and the Devil* (1927) with leading man John Gilbert, with whom she was romantically involved; and the sound films *Anna Christie* (1930), *Mata Hari* (1931), *Grand Hotel* (1932), *Queen Christina* (1933), *Camille* (1936) and *Ninotchka* (1939). Garbo

Legendary film star Greta Garbo as she appeared in the title role of Queen Christina *(1933).*

was one of the highest-paid and most highly regarded stars of the 1930s; her performances generated acres of purple prose from writer-admirers attempting to explain her sphinx-like appeal. In the early 1940s, when WORLD WAR II cut off her European box-office (where much of her films' profits came from), Garbo took what was planned as a temporary sabbatical from films. The sabbatical eventually became permanent, and Garbo, who had always valued her privacy, became a famous recluse until her death.

For further reading:
Conway, Michael, *The Films of Greta Garbo.* New York: Citadel, 1968.
Gronowic, Antoni, *Garbo.* New York: Simon & Schuster, 1990.

Garcia, Jerry (Jerome John) (1942–). American ROCK AND ROLL songwriter, vocalist, and guitarist. Garcia, who is best known as the lead guitarist and primary public spokesman for the GRATEFUL DEAD, has been one of the most admired and influential rock guitarists of the past two decades. In the early 1960s, Garcia played guitar in folk, bluegrass and jug band styles before forging the blend of blues and psychedelic chord questing for which he became known in the late 1960s as the San Francisco-based Grateful Dead achieved national popularity. Garcia and lyricist Robert Hunter formed the primary songwriting team for the band. Garcia has combined his involvement with the Grateful Dead with outside solo projects and collaborative work with, among others, the bluegrass band Old and In the Way and with jazz saxophonist Ornette COLEMAN. In the early 1980s, Garcia successfully battled heroin addiction to return to top form in the Grateful Dead album *In the Dark* (1987), which featured the Garcia-Hunter hit *Touch Of Grey.*

Garcia Lorca, Federico (1898–1936). Spanish poet and playwright. Garcia Lorca is widely considered to be the most significant figure in Spanish literature of the 20th century. Born in Granada, Spain, to a wealthy family, Lorca showed himself early on to be gifted not only as a writer but as a painter and a musician as well. His first published book of verse, *Book of Poems* (1921), established him as an astonishingly evocative lyric poet with a gift for plain and moving utterance. Lorca also became a leading figure in the Spanish theater with plays such as *The Butterfly's Curse* (1920), *Mariana Pined* (1927), *The Shoemaker's Amazing Wife* (1930), *Blood Wedding* (1933), *Yerma* (1934) and the posthumously published *House of Bernarda Alba* (1945). Lorca's plays frequently dealt with the village-rooted lives of Andalusian peasants and the conflict between passion and honor. Lorca traveled abroad to New York and Argentina, among other locales, before returning to Spain in the early 1930s. He was murdered in 1936, during the SPANISH CIVIL WAR, by Nationalist partisans.

For further reading:
Gibson, Ian, *Federico Garcia Lorca: A Life.* New York: Pantheon, 1989.

Garcia Marquez, Gabriel (1928–). Colombian author. Garcia Marquez was born in Aracataca, and was raised in early childhood by his grandparents, the source of much of the Latin American myth and folklore which would later find its way into his writing. He was educated at the University of Bogota, and worked as a journalist beginning at the age of 18, moving to Bogota in 1954 to write full time for *El Espectador.* Eventually, he settled in Mexico City. Garcia Marquez's first important work of fiction, *La hojarasca,* (published in English as "The Leaf Storm," and included in *Leaf Storm and Other Stories,* 1972) was published in 1955, but it was not until *Cien anos de soledad,* (1967; *One Hundred Years of Solitude*) that he received international acclaim. The novel describes the decaying village of Macando as an metaphor for Latin America, and follows the descendants of the Buendia family over seven generations. The novel, with its flights into the supernatural and straightforward descriptions of magical events, is a hallmark of MAGIC REALISM. It also evidences the influence of William FAULKNER, and reflects Garcia Marquez's left-leaning political beliefs and his disgust at the manipulation of and corruption in Latin American politics. A personal friend of Fidel CASTRO, Garcia Marquez has nonetheless expressed reservations about the government in Cuba. Following the publication of *El otono del patriarca* (*The Autumn of the Patriarch,* 1975), a depiction through varying points of view of the decline of a despotic Latin American dictator, and *Cronica de una muerta anunciada* (*Chronicle of a Death Foretold,* 1981), the story of a murder, again portrayed through various viewpoints, Garcia Marquez was awarded the NOBEL PRIZE for literature in 1982. Other works include *In Evil Hour* (1979) and *Love in the Time of Cholera* (1988).

Colombian author Gabriel Garcia Marquez received the Nobel Prize for literature in 1982.

Garden, Mary [born Mary Davidson] (1874–1967). Scottish opera singer. Born in Scotland, Mary Garden grew up in Chicago and made her operatic debut in the title role of *Louise* in Paris in 1900. A member of the Opera-Comique from 1900 to 1907, she created the role of Melisande in the world premiere of Claude DEBUSSY's *Pelleas et Melisande* in 1902, a role which became her signature piece. She was principal soprano for the Manhattan Opera House (1907–1910), then became prima donna with the Chicago Opera (1910–30), serving briefly as the company's artistic director (1921–23). After a return to the Opera-Comique (1930–35), she gave recitals, served as vocal advisor to METRO-GOLDWYN-MAYER in HOLLYWOOD, and gave master classes in voice at the Chicago Musical College. She was renowned for her command of the French repertory, and achieved particular acclaim in the title roles in *Manon, Thais,* and *Salome.*

Gardiner, Baron Gerald Austin (1900–1990). British politician. Under Prime Minister Harold WILSON's Labour government, Gardiner held the post of Lord Chancellor of Great Britain from 1964 to 1970. During his tenure, capital punishment was ended, a cause he served as joint chairman of the National Campaign for the Abolition of Capital Punishment. He also oversaw the establishment of the Family Division of the High Court and the creation of the post of Ombudsman, which investigated complaints by citizens against the government. In 1981, he was the target of a failed assassination attempt by the IRISH REPUBLICAN ARMY.

Gardiner, Muriel (1901–1985). Psychoanalyst who specialized in the treatment of children. While studying medicine in Vienna in the 1930s, she joined the antifascist underground and helped hundreds of Austrians escape from the Nazis. The publisher of her 1983 memoirs suggested that she had been the model for the title character in the movie *Julia,* based on a key figure in Lillian HELLMAN's memoir *Pentimento.* Hellman denied the connection.

Gardner, Ava (Lavinia) (1922–1990). American actress. A farmer's daughter from North Carolina, Gardner was one of HOLLYWOOD's best-known stars from the 1940s through the 1960s. Early roles relied purely on her auburn-haired, green-eyed beauty, but she later won critical acclaim in such films as *Show Boat* (1951), *Mogambo* (1953), *The Barefoot Contessa* (1954), *On the Beach* (1959) and *The Night of the Iguana* (1964). Her marriages to actor Mickey ROONEY, band leader Artie SHAW, and singer Frank SINATRA garnered widespread media attention. Such attention led her to move to Europe, where she continued to act in movies and television films.

Gardner, Erle Stanley (1889–1970). American mystery writer. The most published American author of his time, Gardner had worked for two decades as a lawyer in California before beginning to publish short stories and novels. No prose stylist, Gardner's principal contribution to his craft was to redirect the mystery genre away from amateur sleuths and toward professionals. His most enduring character was lawyer Perry Mason. Gardner also published under various pen names, including A.A. Fair.

Gardner, John (1933–1982). American novelist, critic and teacher. Among Gardner's novels were *Grendel* (1971), *The Sunlight Dialogues* (1973) and *October Light* (1976; National Book Critic's Circle Award, 1976). In his controversial nonfiction book *On Moral Fiction* (1978) Gardner argued that "almost all modern work is tinny, commercial and immoral." He founded and headed the creative writing department at the State University of New York at Binghamton. He also wrote poetry, children's books, fairy tales and criticism. He was killed in a motorcycle accident.

Gargallo, Pablo (1881–1934). Spanish sculptor. Studying art in Barcelona, he visited Paris in 1906 and 1911–14, meeting PICASSO and falling under the influence of CUBISM. Gargallo began sculpting in stone, but soon turned to working in iron, becoming one of the first modern artists to use this medium for sculpture. From 1917 to 1924, he taught at the Escuela Superior de Artes Oficios in Barcelona, returning to Paris in 1924.

Garland, Hamlin (1860–1940). U.S. novelist who wrote about the difficult lives of farmers of the Midwest region. His early stories were published in 1891 as *Main-Travelled Roads*, followed by his first novel in 1893, *Prairie Folks*. His other novels include *Wayside Courtship* (1897) and his first autobiography *A Son of the Middle Border* (1917). He won the PULITZER PRIZE in 1922 for his second autobiographical novel *A Daughter of the Middle Border*. He also published a number of politically oriented works, collections of essays and verse, and occult fiction.

Garland, Judy [born Frances Gumm] (1922–1969). U.S. actress and singer. She started singing as a preschooler, and later became a stage actress. In 1935 she went under contract to METRO-GOLDWYN-MAYER and remained at MGM until 1950. She appeared in many films between 1936 and 1962, but perhaps is best remembered for her role in *The Wizard of Oz* (1939), for which she received a special ACADEMY AWARD. The tensions, demands and pressures of her acting career led to the cancellation of her MGM contract. She returned to the screen in 1954 with one of her greatest successes *A Star Is Born*. She was also involved in singing and concert tours, and is considered by many as one of the truly great personalities of the entertainment world.

Judy Garland as Dorothy in the screen classic The Wizard of Oz *(1939).*

Garland, William "Red" (1923–1984). American JAZZ pianist; was an influential figure during the 1950s. Garland accompanied such renowned musicians as Charlie PARKER, Miles DAVIS and Coleman HAWKINS.

Garmisch-Partenkirchen. Mountain town and alpine resort area in German state of Bavaria, 50 miles southwest of Munich. Site of the 1936 Winter OLYMPICS, it was said to have been reserved as a last retreat for Nazi leaders, until it fell to the Allies on April 30, 1945. Also the site of a resort for American servicemen stationed in Germany.

Garn, Jake (1932–). U.S. senator from Utah. Garn stirred up controversy when he flew as a civilian payload specialist aboard U.S. Shuttle mission 51–D in April 1985. As Republican chairman of the Senate Appropriations Subcommittee overseeing the NASA budget, Garn had been critical of Shuttle management; critics of NASA charged that their allowing him to fly was an effort to win him over. He was the first politician to fly in space. As a payload specialist, Garn served as a test subject for space-sickness experiments.

Garneau, Marc (1949–). Canadian astronaut and first Canadian citizen to fly in space. Garneau, a commander in the Canadian Navy, flew aboard U.S. Space Shuttle mission 41–G (October 5–13, 1984). As a civilian payload specialist, he spent his eight days in space working on scientific and medical experiments designed by Canadian scientists.

Garner, John Nance (1868–1967). American politician, vice president of the UNITED STATES (1933–41). Born in Red River County, Texas, Garner served in the Texas legislature (1898–1902) and House of Representatives (1903–1933) and won election as speaker of the House in 1931. Garner served as vice president during Franklin D. ROOSEVELT's first two terms, helping push through much of the early NEW DEAL legislation. He opposed Roosevelt's third-term candidacy and ran unsuccessfully against Roosevelt for the 1940 Democratic presidential nomination. He retired from politics in 1941.

Garvey, Marcus (1887–1940). The Jamaican-born Garvey was a flamboyant and controversial figure in black American politics from the end of WORLD WAR I through the mid-1920s. In 1914 he founded the Universal Negro Improvement Association, a black nationalist organization, in Jamaica. Moving to the U.S. a few years later, he established the association's new headquarters in the HARLEM district of NEW YORK CITY. Unlike W.E.B. DUBOIS (who believed in radical political action to solve racial and economic problems facing blacks) or Booker T. WASHINGTON (who believed in black self-improvement through education), Garvey saw little hope for blacks to achieve social and economic justice in the U.S. Rather, he advocated a "back-to-Africa" movement; at a 1920 convention he was elected president of the "Republic of Africa"—his name for the proposed African nation for black American settlers. By the early 1920s, he had gained several million followers, many of whom sent him money to help fund the movement. However, in 1925 Garvey was convicted of mail fraud. After two years in prison he was deported to Jamaica. His influence quickly declined, and he spent his final years in Britain.

Marcus Garvey, leader of the "back-to-Africa" movement, in uniform as the president of the Republic of Africa (1922).

For further reading:

Lawler, Mary, *Marcus Garvey*. New York: Chelsea House, 1989.
Stein, Judith, *The World of Marcus Garvey: Race and Class in Modern Society*. Baton Rouge: Louisiana State University Press, 1985.

Gascon, Jean (1920–1988). Canadian actor-director, a leading figure in both French and English theater in Canada. A native of Montreal, Gascon founded that city's influential Theatre du Nouveau Monde in 1951 and National Theater School in 1960. In 1969, he became the first native-born Canadian to be named artistic director of the Stratford (Ontario) festival, a post he held until 1974. From 1977 until his death, he was head of the theater program at Ottawa's National Arts Center.

Gass, William H(oward) (1924–). American author. Gass, a professor of philosophy, established himself with his acclaimed first novel, *Omensetter's Luck* (1966), which takes place along the Ohio River. Gass' work explores the nature of good and evil. Other works include the short stories *In the Heart of the Heart of the Country* (1968), and the essay collections *The World Within the Word* (1978) and *Habitations of the Word* (1985).

Gasser, Herbert Spencer (1888–1963). American physiologist. Gasser, the son of a country doctor, was educated at the United of Wisconsin and at Johns Hopkins University, qualifying as a physician in 1915. He then moved to Washington University, St. Louis, to take up an appointment as professor of pharmacology. Here he joined his old teacher Joseph ERLANGER in a famous collaboration that resulted in their sharing the 1944 NOBEL PRIZE for physiology or medicine for work on the differentiated function of nerve fibers. In 1931 Gasser was appointed to the chair of physiology at Cornell Medical School. Finally, in 1935, he was made director of the Rockefeller Institute in New York, a post he retained until his retirement in 1953.

Gastev, Alexei Kapitonovich (1882–1939). Russian poet and labor theorist. Gastev's poetry deals with industrialization, the necessity of building an "iron state," for which sacrifices are called. In his prose writings, Gastev expounded his theory of "mechanized collectivism," in which the workers synchronize their movements with the movements of machines, thus making individual thinking and a "normalized psychology" impossible. His reputation as a poet rests on his *Shockwork Poetry* (1918) and *A Stack of Orders* (1921). Gastev directed the Central Institute of Labor, but disappeared during the GREAT PURGE.

Gate Theatre. Dublin theatre company founded in 1928 by Hilton EDWARDS and Micheal MACLIAMMOIR which first performed in the Peacock Theatre, an adjunct of the ABBEY THEATRE, before establishing itself in the Rotunda Buildings in 1930. The aim of the Gate company was to create a world class theatre, and it differed from the Abbey in that it presented international works as well as Irish drama. Following World War II, Lord Longford, and later his widow Christine, Countess of Longford, ran the theatre, overseeing several renovations. The theatre continues to present the works of various small companies from Ireland and elsewhere.

GATT. An international body, established 1948, aimed at reducing tariffs and other restrictions and fostering free trade. As of the late 1980s, eighty percent of the world was covered by Gatt.

Gaudi I Cornet, Antonio (1852–1926). Spanish architect. Gaudi was trained at Barcelona University, and his best known works are found in that city; they include his Casa Batllo (1906), Casa Mila (1910) and Park Guell (1914), all of which have fantastical and highly complex elements. His monumental Church of La Sagrada Familia, begun in 1883 and continued throughout his career, remains incomplete. After World War II Gaudi's work received renewed attention, and in 1957 the MUSEUM OF MODERN ART mounted an exhibit of his designs.

Gaudier-Brzeska, Henri (1891–1915). French sculptor and artist. Gaudier-Brzeska, who added to his own the name of his beloved wife Sophie Brzeska, was a brilliant sculptor whose career was cut tragically short by his death in WORLD WAR I. His work was ardently championed by the American poet Ezra POUND, of whom Gaudier-Brzeska made a number of drawings and a famous bust. Gaudier-Brzeska emphasized that the beauty of a sculptural work is intimately related to the materials from which it is made. His sculptures, which did not adhere to the fixed credos of any artistic school, combined a number of contrasting geometric forms to produce a jarringly energetic whole that Pound termed a "form-fugue."

Gaullists. Political followers of General Charles DE GAULLE, although there is no precise definition of **Gaullism**. A short-lived mass movement under the Fourth French Republic centered on the **Rassemblement du Peuple Francais** (RPF), an authoritarian anti-communist party with Fascist tendencies; this movement enjoyed its greatest success in the late 1940s and early 1950s. The **Union de la Nouvelle Republique** (UNR) was formed from various Gaullist groups after the establishment of the Fifth French Republic in 1958. Gaullism survived the general's retirement in 1970, and provided a basis for support for his presidential successor, Georges POMPIDOU.

Gavaskar, Sunil Manohar (1949–). Indian cricketer. Gavaskar holds the all-time Test cricket records for most runs scored and most games played. He scored 10,122 runs for India from 214 innings in 125 Test matches from 1971 to 1987. Gavaskar also holds the record for most centuries (100 runs scored) in Test cricket, with 34. From 1976 to 1985, Gavaskar captained India 47 times, and in 1983 he led the team to its first World Cup victory.

Gavin, James Maurice (1907–1990). U.S. army officer. Gavin was one of the U.S.'s top combat leaders in WORLD WAR II. During the war he served in and eventually led the famous 82nd Airborne Division. Following the war, he rose to become the Army's chief of research and development. He was, however, a critic of several key Army policies, including its failure to pursue long-range missile technology and an overreliance on advanced hardware at the expense of conventional forces. He retired in 1958 with the rank of Lt. General and became a consultant with the Cambridge, Mass.-based industrial research firm of Arthur D. Little, Inc. In the early 1960s, he served a brief term as ambassador to FRANCE under President John F. KENNEDY. He was also the author of several books, including *War and Peace in the Space Age* (1958) and *Crisis Now* (1968).

Gaye, Marvin (1939–1984). Black American soul singer, popular from the early 1960s until his death. His string of hit records included "Can I Get a Witness" (1963), "Heard It Through the Grapevine" (1968), "What's Going On?" and "Sexual Healing" (1983 Grammy Award). Many of his songs featured social themes. Gaye was shot and killed by his father in a domestic dispute.

Gayoom, Maumoon Abdul (1937–). President of MALDIVES (1978–). Gayoom is considered an Islamic scholar and was educated at Cairo's al-Azhar University before serving as a research assistant in Islamic history at the American University of Cairo (1967–69). After his return to Maldives he served as minster of transportation and permanent representative of Maldives to the United Nations in the administration of Amin Ibrahim Nasir. As president, Gayoom has worked to diversify and modernize the economy, and has given high priority to improving the standard of living outside the capital. His extensive travels and active participation in numerous international forums have increased the nation's profile on the international scene.

gay rights movement. Political and social movement that seeks to win legal equality and economic opportunities for homosexuals. Since the 1960s the gay rights movement has campaigned to win societal acceptance of homosexuality as an "alternative lifestyle." The movement uses many of the same techniques, and was largely inspired by, the CIVIL RIGHTS MOVEMENT and WOMEN'S MOVEMENTS of the 1960s and '70s. The gay rights movement is sometimes dated from a police raid on a gay bar, the Stonewall Inn, in New York City in 1969, which led to increased political activism by gays. The advent of AIDS, which struck many gays in the 1980s, radicalized much of the gay community. Gay organizations such as Act-Up have held marches and demonstrations to demand government action. An annual "Gay Pride" march is held in San Francisco, and openly declared homosexuals and lesbians have been elected to political office. In 1989, Denmark became the first nation to allow civil marriage between homosexuals.

Gaza Strip. A strip of land (146 sq. miles) extending northeast from EGYPT and bordered by ISRAEL and the Mediterranean Sea. Temporarily occupied by Israel in the 1956 SUEZ CRISIS, and occupied again during the 1967 SIX–DAY WAR, it remains in Israeli possession and has become part of the controversy surrounding Israel's holding and settling of occupied territories.

Gdansk [German: Danzig]. Polish seaport on the Baltic Sea, just west of the mouth of the Vistula River; capital of Gdansk province. After WORLD WAR I the TREATY OF VERSAILLES restored its ancient status as a free city with its own legislature. But to provide a seaport for the newly recreated nation of POLAND, Danzig was made part of a Polish customs union under the jurisdiction of a high commissioner designated by the LEAGUE OF NATIONS—part of a strip of land barely 50 miles wide (the so-called **Danzig corridor**), with GERMANY proper to the west and the German province of East Prussia to the east. With the erosion of league authority after 1935, Danzig came under the influence, if not the control, of Nazi Germany. HITLER's call for the return of Danzig to Germany was a principal excuse for the German attack on Poland and a cause of the outbreak of WORLD WAR II. Danzig was annexed to Germany as the Hanseatic City of Danzig on September 1, 1939 (a small Polish garrison resisted until September 7). Retaken by the Soviets early in 1945, Danzig was soon returned by the Allies to Poland and its original name restored. Gdansk, largely destroyed during the war, has since been rebuilt; with nearby Gdynia, barely 20 miles away, it is one of the world's principal shipbuilding centers. In late 1970 rioting by workers here led to the fall of Polish Premier GOMULKA. By 1980 serious food shortages and labor discontent brought a strike at Gdansk's Lenin shipyards that led to the formation of the SOLIDARITY Labor Union, headed by Lech WALESA, movements to reform the Polish economy and political system—and, after a Gdansk Solidarity Congress (December 1981) called for a national vote of no-confidence in the government, the breakup of the union and the imposition of martial law.

Gehrig, Lou [Ludwig Heinrich Gehrig; The Iron Horse] (1903–1941). American baseball player. There is little dispute that Lou Gehrig was the greatest first baseman in history. He began his Yankee career at the age of 20, but his career began in earnest three seasons later when he filled in for an ailing Wally Pipp. Gehrig soon had a lock on the position that lasted 16 years and 2,130 consecutive games, a record that has never been approached. He posted a lifetime batting average of .340 with 493 home runs and 1,990 runs batted in. He led the league in home runs and runs batted in in several seasons and was a six-time All Star. He retired in 1939 after being diagnosed with

The greatest first baseman in the history of baseball, Lou Gehrig—"the Iron Horse"—played in 2,130 consecutive games.

amyotrophic lateral sclerosis, which came to be known as **Lou Gehrig's Disease**. His farewell address to fans at Yankee Stadium was one of the most moving and memorable events in baseball. Because of Gehrig's ill health, the entry requirements to the Hall of Fame were waived, and he was admitted that year. His life was recounted in the 1942 motion picture, *Pride of the Yankees*, starring Gary COOPER.

Geiger, Hans Wilhelm (1882–1945). German physicist; studied physics at the universities of Munich and Erlangen, obtaining his doctorate (1906) for work on electrical discharges in gases. Geiger then took up a position at the University of Manchester, where he worked with Ernest RUTHERFORD from 1907 to 1912. In that year he returned to Germany, and from then until his death held a series of important university positions, including director of the Physikalisch Technische Reichsanstalt in Berlin (1912) and professor of physics at Kiel University (1925). A pioneer in nuclear physics, Geiger developed a variety of instruments and techniques for detecting and counting individual charged particles. In 1908 Rutherford and Geiger, investigating the charge and nature of alpha particles, devised an instrument to detect and count these particles. The instrument consisted of a tube containing gas with a wire at high voltage along the axis. A particle passing through the gas caused ionization and initiated a brief discharge in the gas, resulting in a pulse of current that could be detected on a meter. This prototype was subsequently improved and made more sensitive; in 1928 Geiger produced, with W. Muller, a design for what is now known as the *Geiger-Muller counter*.

Gell-Mann, Murray (1929–). American theoretical physicist; graduated from Yale University in 1948 and gained his Ph.D. from the Massachusetts Institute of Technology in 1951. Gell-Mann spent a year at the Institute of Advanced Study in Princeton before joining the Institute for Nuclear Studies at the University of Chicago, where he worked with Enrico FERMI. In 1955 he went to the California Institute of Technology, where he became a full professor in theoretical physics in 1956. Gell-Mann's chosen subject was the theoretical study of elementary particles. His first major contribution in 1953 (at the age of only 24) was to introduce the idea of "strangeness." The concept came from the fact that certain mesons were "strange particles" in the sense that they had unexpectedly long lifetimes. Strangeness, as defined by Gell-Mann, is a quantum property conserved in any "strong" interaction of elementary particles. The search for order among the known elementary particles led Gell-Mann and Israeli physicist Yuval Ne'eman to advance, independently, a mathematical representation for the classification of hadrons (particles that undergo strong interactions). Gell-Mann felt that it should be possible to explain many of the properties of the known elementary particles by postulating even more basic particles (later to be called QUARKS, the name taken from *Finnegan's Wake* by James JOYCE). Quarks, together with their antiparticles, would normally be in combination as constituents of the more familiar nucleons and mesons. This idea challenged established thinking and has greatly influenced the direction of high-energy theory and experiment. Gell-Mann received the 1969 NOBEL PRIZE for physics, being cited for his "contributions and discoveries concerning the elementary particles and their interactions."

Gemini Program. American space program that launched 10 piloted flights in 1965–66, after two unmanned tests in 1964 and 1965. Called Gemini because of the two-man crew, this program followed the MERCURY PROGRAM and preceded the APOLLO PROJECT. It was designed to test the endurance of men in space (in preparation for lunar flights), to test the maneuvering ability of orbital spacecraft and to develop docking and rendezvous techniques needed for the later moon missions. The Gemini spacecraft consisted of two modules, a reentry or command module and a service module. The bell-shaped command module measured 11 ft. high, had a base diameter of 7.7 ft. and weighed just under 6,000 lbs. It was launched by a two-stage Titan 2 rocket with four retro-rockets, each with a thrust of 11,100 newtons (2,500 lbs.).

Highlights of the Gemini Program include Gemini 3, the first piloted mission, flown by Virgil I. (Gus) GRISSOM and John W. YOUNG and launched on March 23, 1965. During almost five hours of flight, it circled the Earth for three orbits. Gemini 4, launched on June 3, 1965, was flown by Edward H. WHITE II and James MCDIVITT. During the two-day flight, White made the first U.S. space walk. Gemini 6, launched on December 15, 1965, with Walter M. SCHIRRA and Thomas P. STAFFORD aboard, made the first U.S. space rendezvous, with Gemini 7, launched on December 4 with Frank BORMAN and James A. LOVELL aboard. The two capsules rendezvoused on December 15, coming within one foot of each other. Gemini 8, with Neil ARMSTRONG and David Scott, launched on March 16, 1966, was the first

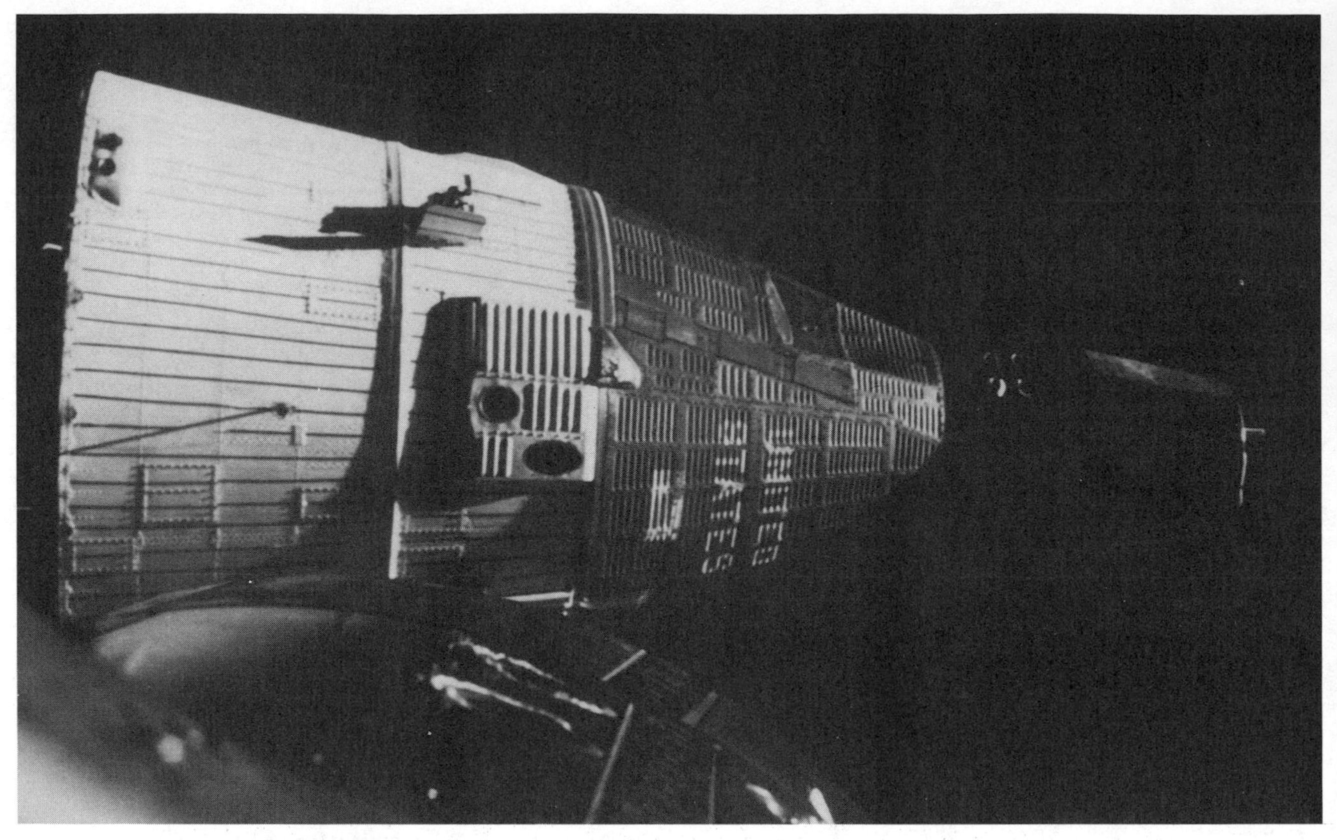

NASA's Gemini VII spacecraft, photographed in maneuvers approximately 160 miles above the Earth on Dec. 15, 1965.

to dock with another craft in space (an Agena target rocket). Later Gemini missions lengthened the time spent in space and the duration of space walks and vehicle dockings, and accomplished increasingly automated reentries.

Genda, Minoru (1904–1989). Japanese military and political leader. Genda was the general who planned JAPAN's December 7, 1941 attack on U.S. naval forces at PEARL HARBOR, Hawaii, that brought the U.S. into WORLD WAR II. He was widely credited with originating attacks by low-flying torpedo bombers, which caused extensive damage to the U.S. fleet during the battle. Following the end of the war, he was made a general in the Japanese air force and served as chief of staff (1959–62), after which he was elected to the upper house of Japan's parliament. In 1962, U.S. President John F. KENNEDY presented him with the Legion of Merit, the nation's highest foreign honor, for his role in rebuilding the Japanese air force and cooperating with the U.S. Genda made a controversial lecture tour of the U.S. in 1969; during the tour, he said that if Japan had possessed the ATOMIC BOMB during WORLD WAR II, it might have used it against the U.S. The remark sparked an uproar in Japan that forced him to resign as chief of the ruling Liberal Party's defense policy board, although he remained a member of parliament until 1986.

General Agreement on Tariffs and Trade. See GATT.

General Motors. American and international corporation (the largest manufacturing company in operation), primarily a builder of automobiles and related transport products. General Motors (GM) was founded in 1908 and gradually acquired various smaller automobile makers, including Chevrolet, Pontiac, Oldsmobile, Buick, and Cadillac. The diverse approaches to design by these firms were gradually brought together in an overall design program that was headed after 1925 by Harley EARL. Earl organized an intricate plan for sharing body components among the different brand names, with varied trim and detail giving each brand individuality. Changes in styling on an annual basis encouraged "planned obsolescence," leading consumers to buy new cars in greater numbers and at shorter intervals than might be required by actual wear. From 1959 to 1978, Bill Mitchell took over Earl's role and directed GM styling. Although overwhelmingly successful commercially, the GM approach to design has been criticized for what is seen by some as its neglect of functional and economic values in favor of size and glitter as sales features. The competition of European and Japanese imports has forced some adjustment in GM styling practice. Some GM products are now joint Japanese-American efforts. General Motors is also a major manufacturer of household appliances under the Frigidaire brand name, of trucks and buses, and of diesel railroad locomotives through its electromotive division.

General Strike of 1926. British labor strike of May 1926. The general strike was a culmination of several years of labor unrest, during which the miners' unions had garnered support from other industrial unions. It was triggered by the Samuel Report, a study of the mining industry by a royal commission released in March of 1926 which rejected nationalization and recommended a cut in wages. At the same time, mine owners supported longer hours for the workers. On May first, at a special meeting of the TRADES UNION CONGRESS (TUC), it was agreed to call out transport workers, printers, builders, heavy industrial workers and later engineers in support of the miners. Prime Minister BALDWIN's government responded by organizing volunteers to fill essential posts, recruiting special constables and using troops to maintain food supplies. Nine days later the TUC called off the strike. The miners unions stayed out until the following August. In July of 1927, the Trade Disputes Act was passed, which made general strikes illegal. It was repealed in 1946.

general theory of relativity. See Albert EINSTEIN.

Generation of 1927. Group of Spanish poets who were active between 1923 and the beginning of the SPANISH CIVIL WAR in 1936. United mainly by friendship, a tendency toward SURREALISM, an attitude of anguish over the contemporary world and an emphasis on aesthetic purity, they were a diverse group of individuals with distinct poetic styles. Among the members of the Generation of 1927 were Federico GARCIA LORCA, Rafael ALBERTI, Vicente ALEIXANDRE, Luis CERNUDA and Jorge GUILLEN. Many of their works were collected in the 1932 anthology *Poesia espanola contemporanea.*

Genet, Jean (1910–1986). French novelist and playwright; one of the major French authors of this century. Genet is also an unusual figure in the history of French literature due to his background as a convicted felon and a homosexual. He wrote his first novel, *Our Lady of the Flowers* (1944), while serving a jail sentence. This novel, which explores the complex psychological nature of homosexual relations within prison confines, won the attention of French intellectuals such as Jean-Paul SARTRE, who clamored successfully for Genet's parole. Other novels by Genet include *Miracle of the Rose* (1946) and *Thief's Journal* (1949). Genet also became a major figure in the THEATER OF THE ABSURD movement by virtue of his plays *The Maids* (1948), *The Balcony* (1956) and *The Blacks* (1958). He was also the subject of a full-length literary study by Sartre, *Saint Genet* (1952), which argued that Genet was the archetypal existential hero due to his having lived by his own value system.

genetic engineering. Popular term for various techniques that manipulate DNA, the nucleic acid (contained in the nucleus of cells) that transmits the inheritance of characteristics. Recombinant DNA is produced through gene-splicing, a technique in which molecules of DNA are removed from one organism and introduced into the genetic material of another organism. When inside a host cell, this recombinant DNA molecule replicates itself when the host divides, producing cloned cells with identical DNA structure. Gene-splicing is usually practiced on *Escherichia coli,* a common intestinal bacterium. A foreign gene is spliced into the plasmid, a circular piece of DNA that is the bacterial equivalent of a chromosome, and the *E. coli* goes on to produce cloned cells with the new genetic information. This technique has been used not only to study gene structure, but also to produce larger quantities of substances that are normally available only in extremely limited amounts. Substances produced by gene-splicing techniques include INSULIN, human growth hormone and INTERFERON. Other techniques of genetic engineering include nuclear transplants and cell fusion. It is hoped that one or more of the various genetic engineering techniques may ultimately be applied to the cure of human genetic diseases, and genetic engineering is one of the fastest-growing research fields in contemporary medicine.

Geneva. Swiss city at the southwest end of Lake Geneva; the Rhone River flows westward through the city and into France. Geneva was the seat of the LEAGUE OF NATIONS from 1920 to 1946, when the defunct league's buildings were taken over by the new UNITED NATIONS. The city is the UN's European headquarters, as well as international headquarters for the INTERNATIONAL LABOR ORGANIZATION (ILO), the WORLD HEALTH ORGANIZATION (WHO), the EUROPEAN ATOMIC ENERGY COMMUNITY (Euratom) and other international organizations. Geneva is city-of-choice for numerous international conferences, such as the START talks on nuclear arms reduction between the U.S. and the U.S.S.R.

Geneva Conventions. A series of international agreements reached to provide for the humane treatment of individuals in wartime. Those protected include the wounded, the sick, prisoners of war and civilians. The first of these treaties was signed by representatives of 16 countries convened in Geneva, Switzerland in 1864, and was recognized by all European nations, the U.S. and a number of countries in Asia and South America. Other such conventions were added in 1899, 1906, 1929, 1949 and 1977. The earliest agreements dealt mostly with combatants and with the international recognition of the role of the RED CROSS. Prompted by the phemonenon of total world war, later conventions extended the general laws of war and attempted to further protect civilians. They also forbade many kinds of racial and religious discrimination as well as such practices as the taking of hostages and the use of torture.

Gennadios, Bishop of Paphos (1910–1986). Cypriot Orthodox church leader. His support for the Greek Cypriot guerilla movement and opposition to Cypriot president Archbishop MAKARIOS III helped pave the way for the Turkish invasion of CYPRUS in 1974. Gennadios (also referred to as Yennadios) and two other bishops were defrocked in 1973 after they had proclaimed the defrocking of Makarios.

Gennep, Arnold van (1873–1957). French ethnographer and folklorist; a pioneer in the development of structured, analytical methods for the collection and preservation of folk material in France. Van Gennep devoted himself to field work and produced a large number of collections in his lifetime while influencing an entire subsequent generation of university-trained folklorists. Works by Van Gennep include *Rites of Passage* (1909), *Folklore of the Dauphine* (1933), *Folklore of Bourgogne* (1936) and the multivolume *Manual of Categories of French Folklore* (1943–1958). The methods of van Gennep exercised an influence on STRUCTURALISM.

Genovese, murder of Kitty. Infamous killing that occurred early in the morning of March 13, 1964. A young woman, Kitty Genovese, was fatally stabbed in the courtyard of her apartment building in the middle-class New York suburb of Kew Gardens. Assaulted several times, Genovese screamed repeatedly, but her cries for help were ignored by her neighbors, none of whom wished to become involved. Nearly 40 people watched or heard the attack, which went on for over half an hour. Finally, someone called the police, but by then it was too late to save Genovese. A much-publicized scandal at the time, the case has come to be emblematic of the apathy and anonymity of urban existence in the late-20th century.

Genovese, Vito (1897–1969). American gangster. Genovese began his career in crime early, working in the shadow of "Lucky" LUCIANO as a relatively minor MAFIA functionary in the 1920s. Charged with murder, Genovese fled to Italy in 1937, worked for the U.S. Army in 1944 and returned to New York in 1945. For the next decade he consolidated his position, engineering assassinations and emerging as a full-fledged Mafia don. Extremely important in the organized crime's narcotics operations, Genovese was implicated in a minor drug deal, arrested, tried and in 1959 sentenced to prison for 15 years. He allegedly continued to direct mob activities from his jail cell. He died while still in prison.

Gentile, Giovanni (1875–1944). Italian philosopher. Gentile is best remembered as the principal intellectual supporter of Italian FASCISM and the government of Benito MUSSOLINI. Gentile began his philosophical career as a neo-Hegelian theorist who emphasized the ideal nature of truth in *The Theory of Mind as Pure Act* (1916). He also worked closely with fellow Italian philosopher Benedetto CROCE and contributed to Croce's journal, *Critica.* In the 1920s, after Mussolini had assumed power, Gentile became politically active as a senator and as a minister of public instruction entrusted with major responsibility for the development of a revised Italian educational system. Gentile outlined his ideas in this sphere in *The Reform of Education* (1922). He met his death at the hands of anti-fascist partisans.

geodesic dome. See R. Buckminster FULLER.

George V (1865–1936). King of Great Britain (1910–1936). George V was the second son of EDWARD VII and Queen ALEXANDRA, and became heir to the throne when his elder brother, Albert Victor, died in 1892. In 1893, George V married his brother's fiancee, Mary of Teck, later Queen Mary. Their eldest son, later EDWARD VIII and Duke of Windsor, was born in 1894. Although torn by WORLD WAR I, and unsettled by the deposition of many European monarchs, the reign of George V was marked by an increasing affection between the British people and their sovereign, due in part to such gestures as his broadcasts in later years, but also because of his respect for the constitutional monarchy. George V dealt with restraint with the Parliament Act of 1911, the Irish Crisis of 1913–1914, BALDWIN'S succession to the prime ministry in 1923 and the formation of the NATIONAL GOVERNMENT in 1931. He was also the only British emperor of INDIA to visit there while sovereign. His Silver Jubilee in 1935 was the occasion of a moving display of popular loyalty to him. He died eight months later at Sandringham.

George VI [born Albert Frederick Arthur George]. King of the UNITED KINGDOM of Great Britain and Northern Ireland (1936–52). The second son of King GEORGE V and Queen Mary, he trained as a naval cadet. During WORLD WAR I he

Their Majesties King George VI and Queen Elizabeth of England in their first official photo (Feb. 8, 1937).

saw action at the Battle of Jutland as a Royal Navy officer. His service was interrupted by illness; however, before the war's end he joined the RAF and became a pilot. In 1920 he assumed the title of Duke of York. He married Lady Elizabeth Bowes-Lyon (later Queen Elizabeth the Queen Mother) of Scotland in 1923. Second-in-line to his brother David, the Prince of Wales (later EDWARD VII), he was seldom in the public eye during the first 41 years of his life. Shy and awkward, he was affected by a stammer which he eventually overcame. In 1936, when his brother (then king) abdicated the British throne to marry Mrs. Simpson, the Duke of York suddenly became king. Thrust into a role for which he had been thought unprepared, he quickly adapted to his new responsibilities and won the affection of the British people. Upon his coronation (1937) he assumed the name George. In 1939, on the eve of WORLD WAR II, he and his wife made an important state visit to Canada and the U.S. to win support for Britain; he thus became the first reigning monarch to visit the U.S. During the war he, the queen and their two daughters, Elizabeth and Margaret Rose, remained in London and shared the hazards of the Blitz with their subjects. (Buckingham Palace was hit several times by German bombs.) In the course of the war, he periodically visited British forces in North Africa, Italy, Malta, and Normandy. From the late 1940s he suffered from various illnesses, including lung cancer, and was forced to curtail his activities. Upon his death his elder daughter inherited the crown as ELIZABETH II.

For further reading:

Bradford, Sarah, *The Reluctant King*. New York: St. Martin's Press, 1990.

George, Stefan (1868–1933). German poet and literary critic; exercised a considerable influence on the German poets who emerged in the first decades of this century. George championed the classical poets of ancient Greece as a lasting standard for poetic excellence. He also applied the philosophical ideals of his countryman Friedrich Nietzsche in calling for a revived German humanism that would look to the poet as a central figure of societal guidance and inspiration. In his own verse, George dealt frequently with esoteric intellectual themes, as well as with his homosexual love affairs. His major volumes of poems include *Year of the Soul* (1897), *The Seventh Ring* (1907–11), and *The New Reich* (1928). While George was an ardent German nationalist, he was also a fierce opponent of NAZISM. In 1933, he chose exile in Switzerland after the rise of HITLER.

George-Brown, Lord [born George Alfred Brown] (1914–1985). British politician. The son of a truck driver, Brown worked as a union organizer before being elected to the House of Commons in 1945. In the 1950s, he was a member of the

GERMANY

Soviet Foreign Minister Molotov signs the German-Soviet Non-aggression Pact in Moscow (Aug. 23, 1939); standing directly behind him is Joachim von Ribbentrop and at the German's left is Joseph Stalin.

LABOUR PARTY's shadow cabinet, rising to deputy leader of the party under Hugh GAITSKELL. After Gaitskell's death in 1963, Brown was narrowly defeated by Harold WILSON in the contest for Labour leadership. Brown then served for two years as secretary for economic affairs before being named foreign secretary in 1966. He resigned in 1968 over a lack of consultation during a gold crisis. In 1970, he lost his seat in Parliament. In 1976, angered by legislation proposing closed shops, Brown resigned from the Labour Party. In 1981, he became a member of the centrist SOCIAL DEMOCRATIC PARTY.

Georgians. A term generally applied to authors who wrote during the reign of GEORGE V, 1910–1936, and specifically referring to the poets included in the five volume anthology *Georgian Poetry* (1912–1922). The name was coined by Edward Marsh, editor, who along with Rupert BROOKE, a contributor, conceived the series. Georgian poetry is traditional in form, and often celebrated nature and pastoral England. Critics—among them, the BLOOMSBURY GROUP—assailed its naivete and its irrelevance to the mood of post-World War I Britain, and the term took on a pejorative sense. Characteristic Georgian poets include Lascalle ABERCROMBIE, Walter DE LA MARE, John DRINKWATER, and Gordon Bottomley.

German Colonial Wars in Africa (1903–1908). Promoting white settlement to gain self-sufficiency for their African colonies, the Germans often dislodged native tribes by force. In 1903 the Hottentots revolted in German South West Africa (NAMIBIA), and the Herero tribe in 1904. Troops from Germany suppressed the rebels with much difficulty and bloodshed by 1908, killing 80 percent of the Herero and 50 percent of the Hottentots. Africans also revolted in German East Africa (now TANZANIA) and in CAMEROON in West Africa; all were brutally repressed and reduced to virtual slavery.

German Democratic Republic. See EAST GERMANY.

German-Soviet Non-aggression Pact. Also known as the Nazi-Soviet Pact and the Hitler-Stalin Pact, an agreement between Germany and the U.S.S.R. signed in Moscow on August 23, 1939, by Joachim von RIBBENTROP and Vyacheslav MOLOTOV. Its public provisions included pledges of neutrality if either country were to go to war, and a trade agreement. A secret clause defined spheres of interest for both countries in eastern Europe and the Baltics. A surprising agreement for the committed anti-communists of Germany and the equally committed anti-fascists of the Soviet Union, the pact was used by Germany to isolate Poland in preparation for its invasion of the country on September 1, 1939. The pact was honored by Hitler until June 1941, when German forces attacked the U.S.S.R.

Germany. Germany is located in north-central Europe and since 1990 covers an area of 138,003 square miles. The country entered the 20th century in a dangerous economic and political rivalry with Britain

GERMANY

1911	Agadir Crisis exacerbates tensions between Germany and Britain.
1914-18	Germany loses 1.7 million dead and 4.2 million wounded in World War I.
1918	Allied breakthrough on the Western Front leads to collapse of German forces; (Nov. 9) Kaiser Wilhelm II abdicates, German republic is declared; (Nov. 11) armistice ends World War I.
1919	(January) Left-wing uprising of "Spartacists" led by Rosa Luxemburg and Karl Liebknecht is put down; (June) Treaty of Versailles imposes harsh terms on Germany, including loss of territory, demilitarization and reparations; (July) Weimar constitution adopted.
1923	"Beer Hall Putsch" in Munich: Adolf Hitler leads unsuccessful attempt to seize power.
1925	Dawes Plan eases German reparations payments; Paul von Hindenburg becomes president.
1926	Germany joins the League of Nations.
1932	Nazis win 37% of the vote in national elections.
1933	(Jan. 30) President Hindenburg appoints Hitler chancellor of Germany; (March) Hitler assumes emergency powers following Reichstag fire, suspends Weimar constitution; Germany withdraws from League of Nations.
1934	(June) Hitler purges Nazi rivals in "Night of the Long Knives"; (August) death of Hindenburg; Hitler takes title of "Fuehrer."
1935	Nuremberg Laws deprive German Jews of civil rights.
1936	German forces occupy Rhineland; Germany forms "Axis" alliance with Italy, signs Anti-Comintern Pact with Italy and Japan.
1938	Germany demands and gains control of Sudetenland region of Czechoslovakia in Munich Pact (September); (Nov. 9-10) Nazis launch violent anti-Jewish pogrom on "Kristallnacht."
1939	(August) German Foreign Minister von Ribbentrop signs German-Soviet Non-Aggression Pact with Soviet Foreign Minister Molotov; (Sept. 1) German blitzkrieg invasion of Poland begins World War II.
1941	(June) Hitler launches surprise invasion of Soviet Union.
1942	(January) Wannsee Conference: systematic killing of Jews in concentration camps becomes official policy, unleashing the Holocaust; (October-November) German forces in North Africa decisively defeated by British.
1945	(May 7) Germany signs unconditional surrender; Germany partitioned into four zones of Allied occupation; (Nov. 20) war crimes trials open in Nuremberg.
1948-49	Soviets blockade Berlin; Western Allies supply city in Berlin Airlift.
1949	(May 23) British, French and U.S. occupation zones become Federal Republic of Germany. (Oct. 7) Soviet occupation zone proclaimed German Democratic Republic.
1990	(Oct. 3) East and West Germany reunited under the banner of the Federal Republic of Germany.

and France that culminated in WORLD WAR I, when the German empire fought against those countries and their allies. After Germany's defeat, Kaiser WILHELM II abdicated and a new government, the WEIMAR REPUBLIC, was formed with Friedrich Ebert (1919–25), then Field Marshal von HINDENBURG (1925–34), as president. The harsh terms of the VERSAILLES peace treaty (1919), coupled with the political weakness of the Weimar government and the effects of the world recession after 1929, led to the emergence of Adolf HITLER and his National Socialist German Workers' Party (Nazis), which embraced extreme nationalism and ANTI-SEMITISM (see also NAZISM). Hitler became leader of the new Third Reich, which replaced the Weimar government in 1933. During the next few years Germany rebuilt its military machine, then began to demand and gain territorial concessions from neighboring countries, notably CZECHOSLOVAKIA. German-speaking AUSTRIA was also annexed in the ANSCHLUSS (1938). Hitler's invasion of POLAND in 1939 started WORLD WAR II. Germany initially won quick victories and overran and occupied much of Europe, with dire consequences for the civilian populations. However, Hitler's fatal invasion of the Soviet Union and the entry of the U.S. into the war brought overwhelming forces to bear against Germany. The nation suffered devastating Allied bombing raids, while Hitler's war policy drained the country both economically and spiritually. Even while suffering military defeat, however, the Nazi regime was carrying out a horrific policy of genocide toward the JEWS of occupied Europe (see FINAL SOLUTION, HOLOCAUST). Germany's unconditional surrender (May 7, 1945) resulted in a four-power (U.S.S.R., U.S., U.K., France) occupation government and in the NUREMBERG WAR CRIMES TRIALS that eradicated the Nazi leadership. The Soviet Union's opposition to Western plans for eventual self-government led to the division of Germany into two states (1948–49): the Federal Republic of Germany, aligned with the West, and the German Democratic Republic, aligned with the Soviet Union. Germany was reunited as one country in Oct. 1990 under the name Federal Republic of Germany. In 1991, the Bundestag narrowly voted to restore Berlin as the nation's capital. Chancellor Kohl warned Germans against a resurgence of rampant nationalism. (For a history from 1949 to 1990 see separate entries for EAST GERMANY and WEST GERMANY.)

For further reading:

Craig, Gordon A., *The Germans*. New York: Dutton, 1989.

Eyck, Erich, *History of the Weimar Republic*. New York: Macmillan, 1970.

Gordon, John C., ed., *German History and Society, 1870–1920*. New York: St. Martin's, 1987.

Mau, Hermann, *German History, 1933–1945: An Assessment by German Historians*. New York: St. Martin's, 1987.

Shirer, William L., *The Rise and Fall of the Third Reich*. New York: Alfred A. Knopf, 1960.

Spielvogel, Jackson J., *Hitler and Nazi Germany: A History*. New York: Prentice Hall, 1988.

Gershwin, George (1898–1937). American composer who combined classical and jazz idioms to create enduring musical works. Gershwin was one of the great composers of popular and concert music in the 20th century. Gershwin published his first song in 1916 and achieved national recognition for his song "Swanee" (1919), as performed by Al JOLSON. He quickly rose above the run-of-the-mill, tin pan alley compositions of the day. Gershwin wrote the songs for five editions of *George White's Scandals* (1920–24), then composed the scores for several Broadway musicals, in collaboration with lyricist Ira GERSHWIN, his brother. Their musical plays included *Oh Kay!* (1926), *Funny Face* (1927) and *Of Thee I Sing* (1931). After the arrival of TALKING PICTURES, the Gershwin brothers also wrote songs for the movies, such as the Fred ASTAIRE films *Shall We Dance* (1937) and *A Damsel in Distress* (1937). Gershwin established his reputation as a composer of serious

The brothers Gershwin, composer George (left) and lyricist Ira, collaborated during the 1920s and '30s.

music with such works as RHAPSODY IN BLUE (1924), the symphonic poem *An American in Paris* (1928) and the folk opera PORGY AND BESS (1935), all of which have become musical classics. Among his enduringly popular songs are such standards as "Love Walked In," "But Not For Me," "They All Laughed," "Embraceable You" and "The Man I Love."

For further reading:

Jablonski, Edward, *Gershwin: A Biography.* New York: Doubleday, 1987.

Rosenberg, Deena, *The Brothers Gershwin: Their Lives and Work Together.* New York: Macmillan, 1989.

Gershwin, Ira (1896–1983). American song lyricist, noted for his distinguished collaboration with his brother George GERSHWIN during the 1920s and 1930s. Ira Gershwin put words to the music composed by his brother, creating such classic songs as *I Got Rhythm, Summertime, The Man I Love, S'Wonderful* and *Embraceable You,* among many others. The brothers' musical *Of Thee I Sing* (1932) was the first musical to win a PULITZER PRIZE for drama, and Ira Gershwin was the first lyricist to receive that honor. Their other musical collaborations included the Broadway show *Lady Be Good* (1924) and the operatic *Porgy and Bess* (1935). Gershwin also worked with his brother on a number of HOLLYWOOD films, and with other notable composers such as Harold ARLEN and Kurt WEILL, writing lyrics for *A Star Is Born, Cover Girl,* and *Lady in the Dark.* He is a member of the Songwriters Hall of Fame.

Gerstenmaier, Eugen Karl Albrecht (1906–1986). German diplomat. Gerstenmaier was post-war leader of WEST GERMANY's Christian Democrats and the architect of that country's reconciliation with ISRAEL. He was jailed under the Third Reich for his involvement in the 1944 army plot to kill Adolf HITLER. From 1954 to 1969, he was president of the lower house of the West Germany's parliament.

Gesell, Arnold L(ucius) (1880–1961). American psychologist. In the 1930s and 1940s, Gesell was a dominant figure in American psychology by virtue of his systematic studies of the nature and timing of intellectual and emotional development in children. In 1911, Gesell founded the highly influential Yale University Clinic of Child Development, which he served as director until 1948. Two of his major works, coauthored with F.L. Ilg, were *Infant and Child in the Culture of Today* (1943) and *The Child from Five to Ten* (1946). Subsequent generations of psychologists have criticized Gesell's findings due to his exclusive reliance on white, middle-class children as experimental subjects and his rigid insistence on developmental patterns that took little account of individual variations.

gestalt psychology. Originating in Germany in the early 1920s, gestalt psychology is a "school" that emphasizes "wholes"—that is, the organization, shape and unity of one's perception, behavior and experience. The German term *gestalt* means "pattern" or "form." Published studies on the organization of perception and the "phi phenomenon" by German psychologist Max WERTHEIMER (from 1912) established the gestalt school. Other leading gestaltists are Wolfgang KOHLER, Kurt KOFFKA, and Fritz and Laura PERLS. Gestalt psychology has had a profound impact on theories of learning because of its emphasis on perception as a dynamic system involving the interaction of all elements and human beings as active problem-solvers, not just passive responders to stimuli.

For further reading:

Crawford, Julia, *A Walk into Awareness: A Gestalt Approach to Growth.* Watercress Press, 1985.

Gestapo. Secret state police in Nazi GERMANY, officially known as the *Geheime Staatspolizei.* It was organized in 1933 by Herman GOERING as a Prussian political police force. Over the next few years the Gestapo came under the influence of Heinrich HIMMLER, who expanded it and took official control in 1936, the year it was absorbed into Himmler's ss (*Schutzstaffel*), which had been created as HITLER's personal guard. Three years later the Gestapo was combined with the SS's intelligence branch, the SD (*Sicherheitsdienst*), supervised by Reinhard Heydrich and, after Heydrich's assassination in 1943, by Ernst Kaltenbrunner. The Gestapo's daily operation was headed by Heinrich Mueller. Together, the SS, the SD and the Gestapo had enormous powers. The Gestapo's basic task was to eliminate all opposition to NAZISM in Germany and, after the start of WORLD WAR II, in occupied countries, a task it handled with ruthless and brutal efficiency. With virtually absolute power to arrest, torture, imprison in CONCENTRATION CAMPS or execute any person, its six sections handled all areas of possible opposition, from the religious to the political. Among its duties was the extermination of the JEWS, a subsection headed by the infamous Adolf EICHMANN. Gestapo membership from 1943 to 1945, the years of its greatest activity, has been estimated as between 30,000 and 50,000.

Getz, Stan (1927–91). American jazz musician, considered jazzdom's foremost tenor saxophone lyricist. Influenced by the flowing melodicism of Lester YOUNG, who had achieved fame with Count BASIE's band in the early 1940s, Getz fashioned an inimitable style marked by a light, vibrato-less sound and a sophisticated, indeed, elegant, diatonically based harmonic sensibility. A child prodigy, Getz made his first recording at the age of 16 as a sideman with trombonist Jack TEAGARDEN; important big band stints included Stan KENTON (1944–45), Benny GOODMAN (1945–46) and Woody HERMAN (1947–49). Getz's translucent and virtuosic ballad solo on Ralph Burns' "Early Autumn" (with Herman) established the young tenorist as a major figure and led to his dominance of the important jazz polls during the 1950s and 1960s; historically, by sustaining his lyrical approach in the face of the comparatively extroverted BEBOP revolution, Getz became a "leader" of the so-called "cool" approach that became centered in Los Angeles. In 1961, Getz achieved notable success with "Focus" (1961), a "third stream" amalgam of jazz improvisation and classically oriented scoring. A year later, he scored another hit with his adroit adaptation of the insinuating bossa nova rhythm from Brazil with composer/pianist Antonio Carlos Jobim, guitarist Joao Gilberto and singer Astrid Gilberto; their version of Jobim's "Girl from Ipanema" even made the pop music charts. Getz continued as one of jazzdom's most distinctive and satisfying soloists working primarily in small-group, acoustic settings. He also gained notoriety because of his widely publicized drug addiction and a landmark divorce case that went to the U.S. Supreme Court in 1990.

For further reading:

Palmer, Robert, "Stan Getz at 60," in *Jazz Journal International,* 1987.

GG-1 Locomotive. Electric locomotive with a striking streamlined shell designed by Raymond LOEWY. The GG-1 was developed in 1934 for use on the Pennsylvania Railroad's long distance electrified passenger and freight routes. Loewy's design made the locomotive appear smooth, elegant and fast even when standing still. A standardized type, it replaced a number of earlier smaller and slower electric locomotives. Some 139 were built between 1934 and 1943. The GG-1 was outstandingly successful, with many remaining in service into the 1970s.

Ghana [Republic of Ghana]. The nation of Ghana is located on the West African coast and covers an area of 92,133 square miles. Originally governed by Great Britain as the Gold Coast Colony, the country became independent in 1957, merging with British Togoland to form present-day Ghana. Under its first president, Dr. Kwame NKRUMAH, Ghana became a republic in 1960 and a socialist state in 1964. A military coup in 1966 brought successive military and civilian governments, none of which could maintain political or economic stability. Flight-Lieutenant Jerry Rawlings led a successful coup in 1981 and established a Provisional National Defense Council to bring about a democratization of the country. Though challenged by several coup attempts, a planned attack by American mercenaries and Ghanaian exiles in 1986, and student and labor protests, Rawlings had held on to power and continues to move toward economic and political reform.

For further reading:

Baynham, Simon, *Military and Politics in Nkrumah's Ghana*. Boulder, Colo.: Westview Press, 1988.

McFarland, Daniel M., *Historical Dictionary of Ghana*. Metuchen, N.J.: Scarecrow Press, 1985.

Ghelderode, Michel de (1898–1962). Belgian playwright. Ghelderode's plays were among the first works to point toward the dramatic movement that ultimately became known as the THEATER OF THE ABSURD. Ghelderode was especially well known for his adept black humor. He wrote over 50 plays, most of which were in a comic vein. Most notable among them were *Les Viellards* (1919), *Escurial* (1927), *Barabbas* (1928), *Fastes d'enfer* (1929), *Pantagleize* (1929), *Hop! Signor* (1935) and *Mademoiselle Jaire* (1934).

Gheorghiu-Dej, Gheorghe [born Gheorghe Gheorghiu] (1901–1965). Romanian communist leader, prime minister (1954–61) and president (1961–65) of ROMANIA. Gheorghiu began his career as a railway worker and became active in the outlawed Romanian Communist Party (1929). He was arrested and imprisoned in 1933 at Dej in Northern Transylvania. Escaping in 1944, he added the suffix "Dej" to his name. He quickly became involved in national politics. He was made secretary general of the Communist Party, and in March 1945 became economic minister in the new coalition government. After the communists proclaimed Romania a "People's Republic" (Dec. 30, 1947), Gheorghiu-Dej jockeyed for position within the party and ultimately eliminated his chief rivals in a 1952 purge. He was an early communist supporter of Soviet premier KHRUSHCHEV's call for PEACEFUL COEXISTENCE between the East and West. While favoring close relations with the Soviet Union, he managed to steer an independent course for Romania. On his death the mantle of leadership passed to his protege, Nicolae CEAUSESCU.

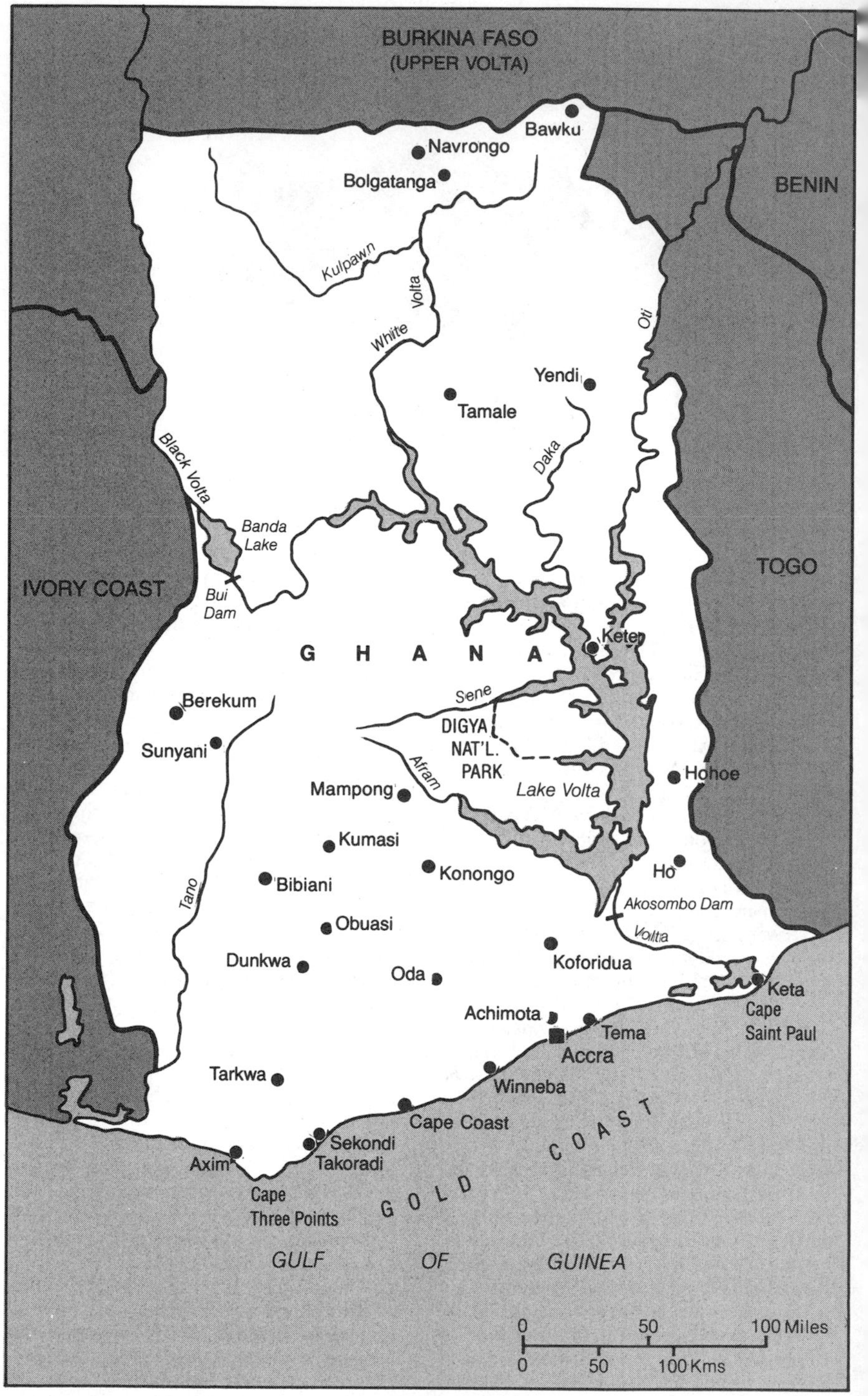

GHANA

Ghia, Giancinto (1887–1944). Italian designer and builder of automobile bodies. Ghia learned his skills in a Turin body shop and became known for his custom designs for luxury and sports cars. Since Ghia's death, his firm has carried on under the direction of Mario Boana. Ghia bodies have been developed for exotic Italian cars including the Maserati, but the best-known and most widely visible Ghia design is the special sport body developed for the VOLKSWAGEN Beetle chassis and engine, known as the Karmann Ghia. The firm was absorbed by Ford in 1972.

Giacometti, Alberto (1901–1966). Swiss sculptor and painter. Son of the impres-

GHANA

1901	Britain absorbs northern remnants of Ashanti empire into its Gold Coast Colony.
1903	First railroad completed.
1920	Gold Coast exports one-half of world's cocoa; spread of cocoa farming encourages breakup of tribes' communal land holdings into private plots.
1928	First deepwater port built at Takoradi.
1947	Moderate nationalists found Gold Coast Convention.
1949	Kwame Nkrumah founds radical Convention People's Party; campaigns for independence.
1957	Independence and merger with former British Togoland creates Ghana; Nkrumah first president.
1960	Ghana sends toops to Congo to assist Patrice Lumumba.
1961	Black American scholar W.E.B. DuBois assumes chair at university after renouncing American citizenship.
1964	Nkrumah declares "socialist single party state."
1965	Falling price of cocoa cripples economy.
1966	While on visit to China, Nkrumah ousted by military; completion of huge Akosambo hydroelectric project.
1969	Kofi Busia elected prime minister.
1972	Military coup.
1975	Economy worsens; migration to Nigeria increases; food imported as cocoa production continues.
1977	Doctors and lawyers go on strike; military agrees to elections.
1981	Second coup by Flight Lt. Jerry Rawlings leads to severe revolutionary government.
1982	Rawlings seeks ties with Cuba and Libya.
1983	Almost one million people forced back to Ghana from Nigeria.
1986	Exiles plot to overthrow Rawlings with American mercenaries.
1990	Ghana joins first modern inter-African peacekeeping force to end Liberian civil war.

sionist painter Giovanni Giacometti (1868–1933), he studied at the Ecole des Arts-et-Metiers in Geneva (1919). Traveling with his father to Italy in 1920, he spent two years there studying various historical art styles. Settling in Paris in 1922, he studied with the sculptor Antoine Bourdelle. Becoming associated first with CUBISM, then with SURREALISM, he produced his first important sculptures, such as the Surrealist-tinged *Palace at 4 A.M.* (1933, Museum of Modern Art, N.Y.C.). In the 1930s, Giacometti began to create the ghostly, elongated human figures with scarred and pitted surfaces, usually cast in bronze, for which he became famous. These strange and haunting sculptures project a kind of existential aloneness and, as such, have been hailed as emblems of 20th-century alienation. Monumental in feeling, whatever their size, these works have had a great influence on modern sculpture. Among them are *Walking Man II* (1960, Rijksmuseum Kroller Muller, Otterloo) and *Head of a Man* (1961, Hirshhorn Museum and Sculpture Garden, Washington, D.C.).

Giacometti, Diego (1902–1985). Swiss-born furniture designer and sculptor. For some 40 years, in a collaboration unique in 20th-century art history, Diego Giacometti harnessed his own creative energies to those of his older brother, world-renowned sculptor Alberto GIACOMETTI, who died in 1966. Diego sat constantly for his brother, and his head became almost a signature of Alberto's art. After his brother's death, Diego won fame in his own right as a creator of rough-hewn bronze furniture ornamented with bird and animal heads and foliage.

Giamatti, A(ngelo) Bart(lett) (1938–1989). American scholar who served as president of Yale University and as commissioner of Major League Baseball. Originally a noted literature professor, Giamatti became the youngest man in 200 years to be named president of Yale when he was selected to succeed Kingman Brewster in 1978 at the age of 40. He confronted a series of challenges ranging from a $10 million debt (which he eventually overcame) to a rancorous strike by members of a newly formed union of clerical and technical workers. A longtime baseball fan, he readily accepted an offer to serve as president of the National League upon his retirement from Yale in 1986. In September 1988, baseball owners voted to select him as commissioner of baseball, a post he took up on April 1, 1989. His five months as commissioner were dominated by the controversy surrounding Cincinnati Reds manager (and former superstar player) Pete ROSE, who was accused of betting on baseball. Eight days before his death Giamatti suspended Rose from baseball for life. Giamatti was widely admired for his committment to honesty, fairness and excellence.

Giancana, Sam "Momo" (1908–1975). American gangster. He began his criminal career early, first attracting notice as a gun runner for Al CAPONE in the mid-1920s. An active but not particularly slippery mobster, Giancana was arrested over 70 times and served a number of terms in jail. He rose to become an infamous MAFIA boss in Chicago, and was alleged to be involved in CIA plots to assassinate Fidel CASTRO during the 1960s.

Giannini, A(madeo) P(eter) (1870–1949). American banker who revolutionized the banking industry and instituted practices that became standard in the 20th century. Of Italian heritage, Giannini was a resident of San Francisco, California. In 1904 he founded a new bank, designed to serve ordinary citizens—Italian immigrants as well as others—in San Francisco. Loans from the Bank of Italy helped citizens rebuild after the 1906 SAN FRANCISCO EARTHQUAKE. Giannini was the first banker to open branch offices of his bank, and the first to advertise his services. By offering farm mortgages at reasonable interest rates, Giannini helped spur California agriculture; his loans to movie studios also helped the film industry. In 1930, the Bank of Italy was renamed the Bank of America National Trust and Savings Association. Giannini handed control of the bank to his son Lawrence Mario Giannini in 1936. Shortly after World War II, the Bank of America became the world's largest bank, with 538 branches and over $8 billion in assets by 1954. As BankAmerica Corp., it was still ranked number one in 1979, with $92 billion in assets, but it fell on hard times as THIRD WORLD nations defaulted on loans.

Giap, Vo Nguyen. See VO NGUYEN GIAP.

Gibbs, Sir Humphrey Vicary (1902–1990). British diplomat. The last British governor of Rhodesia (now ZIMBABWE), he was appointed to the post by Queen ELIZABETH II in 1959 and served until 1969. He spent the last four years of his tenure as a recluse in the governor's residence, following a unilateral declaration of independence by the white minority government of Prime Minister Ian D. SMITH in 1965. He was unable to leave the residence until 1969, when Smith declared Rhodesia a republic. He then retired to his 6,500–acre farm there.

Gibbs, William Francis (1886–1967). American naval architect, the primary designer in the firm of Gibbs and Cox. Gibbs was responsible for a large number of naval and merchant ships including the

OCEAN LINERS *America* and, his last great achievement, the *United States*. Gibbs was known for his obsessive concern with excellence and with matters of safety in passenger ships. His concern for fire safety led to many innovations in ship interiors aimed at the elimination of inflammable wood and textiles. The *United States* was the largest and most successful American passenger ship ever built. It established speed records for trans-Atlantic crossings that have never been exceeded. It was withdrawn from service and eventually scrapped when ship transportation declined as a result of the success of postwar airplanes, particularly jets, which made even the fastest ships seem unreasonably slow.

Gibraltar. The British colony of Gibraltar, which covers only two-and-a-third square miles, is a peninsula connected to SPAIN and jutting southward between Algeciras Bay on the west and the Mediterranean Sea on the east. Because it guards the narrow strait (Strait of Gibraltar) that links the Mediterranean and the Atlantic Ocean, Gibraltar has had tremendous strategic importance throughout history. Its harbor became a key naval base for the Allies during World Wars I and II. Friction over Spanish claims to the colony (dating from the 1300s) intensified during the 1960s, culminating in Spain's closing of the international land frontier between Spain and Gibraltar in 1969. Improved relations between Britain and Spain resulted in the 1985 reopening of the border and the scheduling of talks concerning the issue of sovereignty over Gibraltar.

Gibraltar Dispute. The British territory in southern SPAIN commanding the entrance to the Mediterranean, captured by Britain in 1704 and formerly a strategically important naval base, was claimed by Spain in 1939. The UN recognized the claim in 1963, with Britain asserting the wish of the population expressed overwhelmingly in a referendum was to remain British. The Spanish government closed the frontier in 1969, but, following discussions (1977–80) ended the blockade.

Gibran, Kahlil [Jubran Kahlil Jubran] (1883–1931). Lebanese poet, novelist, essayist, and painter. Gibran won an enduring worldwide fame for *The Prophet* (1923), a volume of inspirational poetry and prose in a highly spiritual vein. *The Prophet* has remained steadily in print over the decades and has been translated into over 20 languages. Gibran studied art with Auguste Rodin in Paris before immigrating to the U.S. in 1912. He wrote in both Arabic and in English. Gibran's works were especially influential in the American popular culture of the 1960s. Other books include *The Earth Gods* (1931), *The Garden of the Prophet* (1933), *The Death of the Prophet* (1933), *Tears and Laughter* (1947) and *Nymphs of the Valley* (1948).

Gibson, Bob (1935–). American baseball player. One of the most dominant pitchers of the modern era, Gibson was named the National League's Most Valuable Player in 1968, a year in which he turned

Pitcher Bob Gibson was inducted into the Baseball Hall of Fame in 1981.

in 13 shutouts and 15 consecutive wins for the St. Louis Cardinals. His postseason play was consistently stellar, and he won the deciding game in two World Series. He is second only to Whitey Ford in World Series wins and strikeouts. An excellent all-around athelete and fierce competitor, he won nine Gold Gloves for his fielding, and was also a rarity in that he was a good-hitting pitcher, with 24 home runs to his credit. He was named to the Hall of Fame in 1981.

Gibson, Walter (1897–1985). American writer. Under the pen name Maxwell Grant, Gibson chronicled the fictional adventures of Lamont Cranston, the wealthy playboy whose alter ego was the mysterious crime fighter known as "The Shadow." Gibson created the character in 1931, and his output of the stories eventually reached millions of words. The Shadow became the hero of one of the most popular radio shows of the 1930s, whereby the voice of Orson WELLES became known throughout America.

Gide, Andre (1869–1951). French novelist and essayist. Gide, who won the NOBEL PRIZE for literature in 1947, remains one of the most widely read French authors of this century. He was raised as a Catholic, and his work is filled with the tension that stemmed from his own rejection of traditional religious belief and his simultaneous discomfort with the absence of absolute values that was the hallmark of secular society. In his first major novel, *The Immoralist* (1902), Gide described, in a North African setting, the decadent embrace of sensuality by a protagonist who had left behind the psychological anchors of religion and marriage. *Strait is the Gate* (1909) further explores the conflict between Catholic belief and sensual temptation. In *Corydon* (1924), Gide defended his own homosexuality with reference to Greek societal ideals. *The Counterfeiters* (1926), his most famous novel, explores the nature of artistic creation and societal ethics. In *Return from the U.S.S.R.* (1936), Gide rejected the communist beliefs that had tempted him during the Depression era. *If It Die* (1936) is his autobiography.

***Gideon v. Wainwright* [right to counsel on arrest]** (1963). The 1963 landmark criminal case that established a constitutional right to counsel for all persons tried for a crime in the U.S., in both state and federal courts. Gideon was accused and convicted of breaking into and stealing money from a poolhall in Florida. He could not afford a private attorney and had none at trial; at the time, only persons accused of capital crimes received free court-appointed counsel. On appeal the U.S. Supreme Court held that in any criminal case, in either state or federal court, indigent parties must be provided with free counsel. Gideon's appeal was funded by the ACLU and was handled by Abe FORTAS, who was himself appointed to the Supreme Court a few years later. Because of the favorable appeal Gideon was retried and this time—with the help of an attorney—he was acquitted of all charges.

Giedion, Sigfried (1894–1968). Swiss-American architectural and design historian who played a significant role in the development and recognition of modern concepts in all aspects of design. Giedion studied art history in Zurich and Berlin and earned his doctorate under Heinrich Wolfflin at Munich. His 1938 lectures at Harvard formed the basis for his 1941 book, *Space, Time and Architecture*, one of the first works to place modern architecture in an historical context. It also created a new understanding and appreciation of the role of Baroque design in relation to MODERNISM. His *Mechanization Takes Command* of 1948 takes a similarly serious historical view of the development of utilitarian objects and is recognized as a basic work of design history. A number of other Giedion books deal with various aspects of art and architectural history. Giedion was among the founding members of the CIAM (International Congress of Modern Architecture).

Gielgud, (Sir) (Arthur) John (1904–). English stage and film actor and stage director. Gielgud is one of the most acclaimed stage actors of this century. He is especially well-known for his Shakespearean portrayals, in which he utilized his elegant profile and mellifluous voice to great effect. A great nephew of the famous English actress Ellen Terry, he was trained at the Royal Academy of Dramatic Art. He first won international fame for his portrayals of Hamlet and other Shakespearean leads while performing with the London-based Old Vic Company in the 1920s and 1930s. Gielgud also proved himself a deft comedic actor in the role of John Worthing in a 1930 performance of the Oscar Wilde classic, *The Importance of Being Earnest*. Gielgud remained active in the theater as both an actor and director in the decades that followed. From 1956 to 1964, he appeared worldwide in his one-man performance of Shakespearean soliloquies, *The Ages of Man*. In recent decades, Gielgud has appeared frequently as a film character actor and won a best supporting actor ACADEMY AWARD for his comedic role in *Arthur* (1981).

Gierek, Edward (1913–). Polish Communist Party leader (1970–80). Following food riots in 1970, Gierek replaced Wladyslaw GOMULKA as party leader. He attempted to raise living standards through production of more consumer goods. However, he encountered increasing opposition from dissident students and from the Catholic Church, which was encouraged by the election of Cardinal Wojtyla of Cracow as Pope in 1978 (see JOHN PAUL II). The emergence of the independent trade union SOLIDARITY in 1980 and further strikes raised doubts about his leadership, and he retired following a heart attack.

Gieseking, Walter (1895–1956). German pianist. Born in Lyons, France, of German parentage, Gieseking studied at the Hanover Conservatory, graduating in 1916. He made his debut in London seven years later, toured widely in Europe, and made his American debut in 1926. Thereafter, he made many successful tours, concertizing throughout the world. Noted for his rigorous precision, his brilliant technique and his wide repertoire, he was particularly skilled at performing French Impressionist works and was a great interpreter of the music of Claude DEBUSSY.

Gigli, Beniamino (1890–1957). Italian opera singer. Considered one of the great Italian tenors of the 1920s through the 1940s, Gigli first gained international attention when he won a vocal competition in Parma in 1914. Successful appearances throughout Europe followed, and eventually led to his American debut at the Metropolitan Opera as Faust in *Mefistofele* in 1920. After Enrico CARUSO's death in 1921, Gigli was principal tenor of the Met until 1932. Thereafter, he sang mostly in Europe, primarily as La Scala in Milan. Noted for the natural beauty of his voice and his technical mastery, he was best known for the title role in *Andrea Chenier*, Cavaradossi in PUCCINI's *Tosca* and Des Grieux in *Manon Lescaut*, and Nemorino in *L'Elisir d'Amour*.

Gilbert, Cass (1859–1934). American architect of major importance in the era of eclecticism. His best-known work is the Woolworth building (1911–13) in New York, for many years the tallest building in the world (760 feet). It is a modern office building of steel-frame construction, but its exterior design is based on medieval Gothic forms typical of the great cathedrals. Its lobby, rich with pseudo-Byzantine mosaics, is ornamented with "gargoyle" portraits of Woolworth and Gilbert. It was designated "the cathedral of commerce" and represented an outstanding effort to make the Gothic style applicable to tall, modern buildings. In contrast, one of his last works, the Supreme Court building in Washington, D.C. (1935), is modeled on a Roman Corinthian temple.

Gilels, Emil (Grigoryevich) (1916–1985). Soviet concert pianist, widely regarded as one of the giants of the keyboard in the decades after World War II. Gilels was one of the first outstanding Soviet musicians to be allowed to perform in the West. His 1955 U.S. debut was preceded by several European engagements. After that, he appeared regularly in both the U.S. and Europe, performing in solo recitals and with leading Western orchestras and conductors. Gilels combined a powerful technique with refined musical intelligence and sensitivity. He was especially noted for his performances of the masterworks of Beethoven and Brahms, and made numerous recordings.

Giles, Warren (1896–1979). American baseball executive. As general manager of the Cincinnati Reds (1936–48), Giles led the team from last place in the National League to the pennant in 1939 and World Series championship in 1940. He was later president of the Reds (1948–51) and president of the National League (1951–69).

Gilford, Jack [Jacob Gellman] (1907–1990). American actor. A comic actor in theater, films and television, he was blacklisted in the years following World War II. In an appearance before the HOUSE UN-AMERICAN ACTIVITIES COMMITTEE in 1956, he refused to answer questions as to whether he was a communist. He later said that it was 10 years before he was offered another film or television job. One of his best known roles was that of Hysterium in the theater and film versions of *A Funny Thing Happened on the Way to the Forum*. His other films included *Enter Laughing* (1967), *Catch-22* (1970) and *Cocoon* (1985). He was nominated for an ACADEMY AWARD for his performance in *Save the Tiger* (1973).

Gill, Arthur Eric Rowton (1882–1940). English artist, sculptor and type designer best known for his design of several modern typefaces. Gill studied at the Central School of Arts and Crafts in London and became known as an illustrator and book designer, working in a restrained and craftsmanly vocabulary within the developing idiom of MODERNISM. He was also a craftsman carver of architectural lettering on stone and so came to the design of typefaces for the Monotype Corporation. His Gill Sans, a modern sans serif face of 1928, has become a widely used modern typeface. Gill was also a religious and sociological thinker who combined concern for art and design with interest in social theory.

Gillespie, John Birks "Dizzy" (1917–). American jazz musician, bandleader and composer. Born in Cheraw, South Carolina, the son of a part-time musician, Gillespie played in the early part of his career with Teddy Hill, Edgar Hayes, Benny Carter and Cab CALLOWAY. At Minton's Playhouse in Harlem, Gillespie jammed with Charlie PARKER, Thelonius MONK and others, helping to invent the jazz style called BEBOP, a term that Gillespie is credited with coining. In the Forties, he composed many bebop and other modern standards, and he guest-starred with the bands of Lionel HAMPTON, Duke ELLINGTON and others. He formed and headed Billy ECKSTINE's orchestra in 1944, led his own big band from 1946 to 1950 and continued to perform in a variety of venues for the next four decades. Lauded as a virtuoso performer, a musical innovator and a great entertainer, Gillespie is recognized as the father of the modern jazz trumpet and one of the all-time jazz greats.

Jazz trumpeter and innovator Dizzy Gillespie performs at a tribute to Duke Ellington (June 30, 1974).

Gilliatt, Penelope (1932–). British novelist, story writer, film critic and screenplay writer. Gilliatt, an accomplished and versatile writer, remains best known in the U.S. for her long stint (1967–1979) as film critic for THE NEW YORKER, a position she shared with Pauline Kael. She has also published a number of critically acclaimed novels including *One by One* (1965), *A State of Change* (1967), *The Cutting Edge* (1978), and *Moral Matters* (1983). Her most noteworthy screenplay was for *Sunday Bloody Sunday*, a British film directed by John Schlesinger, which starred Peter Finch and Glenda JACKSON.

Gilmore, Mary Jean Cameron (1865–1962). Australian poet. One of the premier poets of Australia, Gilmore also taught and helped found an experimental socialist community in Paraguay in 1893. Her poetry collections include *Marri'd and Other Verses* (1910), *The Disinherited* (1941), *Pro Patria Australia and Other Poems* (1945) and *Verse for Children* (1955), one of many collections of juvenile poetry. Gilmore also wrote two volumes of autobiography, *Old Days, Old Ways: A Book of Recollections* (1934) and *More Recollections* (1935). She was named Dame Commander of Order of the British Empire in 1936.

Gil-Robles, Jose Maria (1899–1980). Spanish politician. A Christian Democrat, Gil-Robles led a conservative political coalition in the years before the SPANISH CIVIL WAR. At age 33 he was elected head of the Spanish Confederation of the Right. In 1935 he became minister of war. He was abroad when General Francisco FRANCO led the uprising against the Spanish republic. Gil-Robles remained in self-imposed exile for 17 years before returning to establish himself as a prominent critic of the Franco government.

Gilroy, (Sir) Norman T(homas) (1896–1977). Australian, Roman Catholic cardinal. Gilroy was elected to the college of cardinals in 1946, thereby becoming the first Australian-born cardinal in the history of the Catholic Church. He served in the Australian armed forces during World War II, then pursued theological studies in Rome and was ordained a Roman Catholic priest in 1923. From 1940 through 1971, Gilroy was the archbishop of Sydney, Australia. In 1969, he was knighted by Britain's Queen ELIZABETH II.

Gilruth, Robert Rowe (1913–). U.S. engineer and space scientist. Director of NASA's Project MERCURY from 1958 to 1961 and director of the Manned Spacecraft Center (now Johnson Space Center) at Houston from 1961 to 1972, Gilruth played a key role in shaping the early U.S. program for human space flight. An aerospace engineer with five doctoral degrees and numerous awards in his field, Gilruth continued to serve as a consultant to NASA after his retirement from the Manned Spacecraft Center in 1973. He was named to the National Space Hall of Fame in 1969 and the International Space Hall of Fame in 1976.

Ginastera, Alberto (1916–1983). Argentinian composer, known for his modern eclectic style. Ginastera's early nationalistic work in the late 1930s and 1940s combined folksong and dance with characteristic cultural rhythms. His later work was described as "neo-expressionist" (see EXPRESSIONISM). His operas, particularly *Bomarzo* and *Beatrix Cenci,* received wide attention for segments that were considered violent and sexually explicit. Ginastera also composed concertos, vocal and chamber music, and film scores. He received Argentina's national prize in 1940.

Ginsberg, Allen (1926–). American poet and diarist. Ginsberg is one of the most famous poets of modern times. He remains best known for his highly visible position of leadership—along with friends and fellow writers William BURROUGHS and Jack KEROUAC—in the BEAT GENERATION literary movement that burst into prominence in the 1950s. Ginsberg produced his best poems in that era, most notably *Howl and Other Poems* (1956), the title poem of which was unsuccessfully prosecuted as obscene. *Howl,* with its long, free-verse lines reminiscent of Walt Whitman, exemplifies Ginsberg's poetics of spontaneous composition with attention paid to the natural wanderings of the mind and the rhythms of breathing. Ginsberg was a key figure in the political protest and psychedelic exploration of the 1960s. His other major books of verse include *Kaddish and Other Poems* (1961), *Reality Sandwiches* (1963), *Airplane Dreams* (1969), *The Fall of America, Poems of These States* (1973), *Collected Poems* (1984) and *White Shroud* (1986). With William Burroughs he wrote *The Yage Letters* (1963).

Ginzburg, Alexander (1936–). Writer and dissident. An employee of the State Literary Museum, Ginzburg edited the journal *Syntaxis,* which expressed discontent with the Soviet way of life. In 1960 Ginzburg was prosecuted by the KGB in connection with this, and was convicted and given a sentence of two years in corrective labor camps. In 1964 the KGB charged Ginzburg with possessing "anti-Soviet" literature, but the case was dismissed. In 1967 Ginzburg and Yuri Galanskov were arrested on the grounds of anti-Soviet agitation and propaganda, and tried in 1968. Despite massive support at home and abroad, Ginzburg was sentenced to five years and Galanskov seven years hard labor.

Beat poet Allen Ginsberg reads to a crowd in Manhattan's Washington Square Park (Aug. 28, 1966).

Ginzburg, Natalia (1916–). Italian novelist and dramatist. Ginzburg published her early work under the pseudonym Alessandra Tournimparte. Her first book, *La strada che va in citta* (*The Road to the City,* 1942), consisted of two novellas—the title work and "The Dry Heart." It was with her third work, the novel *Tutti i nostri ieri* (1952, translated as *A Light for Fools,* 1956), noted for its ruefully comic treatment of tragic themes, that she began to receive international attention. Her dispassionate, contained style drew comparisons to that of Chekhov. Of her plays, perhaps best known is *The Advertisement,* first produced at the Old Vic in London in 1968 and winner of the Marzotto Prize for European Drama. Other works include the novels *Caro Michele* (1973, translated as *No Way* in 1974, and as *Dear Michael* in 1975) and *All Our Yesterdays* (1985).

Giolitti, Giovanni (1842–1928). Italian statesman, five-time premier (1892–93, 1903–05, 1906–09, 1911–14, 1920–21). Born in Mondovi in the Piedmont region, Giolitti was educated in Turin and began his career as a civil servant. He entered parliament as a Liberal in 1882, serving there until his death. As prime minister for a total of 11 years, longer than any other Italian except MUSSOLINI, he favored progressive reforms, introducing universal male suffrage (1912), social security and a variety of liberal agrarian, labor and social policies. In foreign policy, he led his nation into the Italo-Turkish war to conquer LIBYA (1911) and opposed Italy's entry into WORLD WAR I. By allowing Fascist candidates to stand for election in 1921, he opened the door to the rise of Mussolini, whom he at first supported but publicly condemned in 1924.

Giovanni, Nikki [Yolande Cornelia Giovanni] (1943–). American poet. Giovanni became an activist in the CIVIL RIGHTS MOVEMENT while attending Fisk University in the 1960s. Her early poetry, such as *Black Feeling, Black Talk* (1968) and *Re: Creation* (1970), reflects her political views and her anger at society's rejection of them, as well as the more universal themes of love and self-discovery. Her later works, while less embittered, continue to explore the search for one's identity. These include *Cotton Candy on a Rainy Day* (1978), which, as she has done with much of her poetry, Giovanni recorded; *Those Who Ride the Night Winds* (1983) and *Sacred Cows and Other Edibles* (1988). Giovanni has also written *Gemini: An Extended Autobiographical Statement on My First Twenty-five Years of Being a Black Poet* (1971), and published dialogues with James BALDWIN and Margaret Walker.

Gippius (Hippius), Zinaida Nikolayevna (1867–1945). Russian symbolist poet. Gippius was a member of the Religious

French General Henri Honore Giraud (left) takes his daily walk during his imprisonment by German forces (ca. 1940–41).

and Philosophical Society and wrote in a metaphysical vein. Leaving Russia in 1919 after the Russian Revolution, she continued writing poetry, plays, novels and short stories, many of which displayed bitter opposition to Bolshevism. Her most important novel is *The Devil's Puppet* (1911).

Giraud, Henri Honore (1879–1949). French general. A career military man, Giraud served in WORLD WAR I and was later (1922–25, 1930–36) a commander in MOROCCO. Early in WORLD WAR II he was captured by the Germans during the invasion of FRANCE in 1940. He made a bold escape in 1942, fleeing to unoccupied France, Gibraltar and finally North Africa, where he participated in the Allied landing and became commander-in-chief of French forces. After the assassination of Admiral DARLAN in December, 1942, he was also made French high commissioner in Africa. He and DE GAULLE cofounded the French Committee of National Liberation in June, 1943, but his deeply-rooted conservatism earned Giraud the distrust of most of the FREE FRENCH. Pressured by De Gaulle, he retired as commander-in-chief in April, 1944. After the war, he served in the Constituent Assembly.

Giraudoux, Jean (1882–1944). French playwright and novelist. Giraudoux, who also enjoyed a long and distinguished career as a diplomat, was one of the leading figures in French theater of this century. He began his writing career as a novelist, producing works including *Suzanne and the Pacific* (1921). But it was as a playwright that he made his real mark. Giraudoux combined an optimistic view of human nature with a subtle poetical style to produce works of warmth and humor that are still widely performed. His major plays include *Amphitryon 38* (1929), *Tiger at the Gates* (1937) and *The Madwoman of Chaillot* (1945).

Giri, V(arahagiri) V(enkata) (1894–1980). President of INDIA (1969–74). A militant trade unionist and pacifist, Giri organized and headed the Bengal-Nagpur railwaymen's union, which grew into a large national working-class movement. As president, between 1969 and 1974 he worked closely with Prime Minister Indira GANDHI. He endorsed several of her government's measures, including nationalizing the country's banks and ending the practice of paying stipends to the country's princes. However, his own radical proposals for ending poverty and unemployment in India went largely unheeded.

Girl of the Golden West. Popular stage play by David BELASCO that has been adapted to grand opera and the movies. It premiered in New York on November 13, 1905. The "Girl" is a tough young woman of the California mining camps: "She is used to flattery—knows exactly how to deal with men—is very shrewd—but quite capable of being a good friend to the camp boys." She gets caught in a deadly feud between Sheriff Jack Rance and desperado Dick Johnson. Attracted by the scenic potential of the play, filmmaker Cecil B. DE MILLE made the first movie version in 1914. Despite some innovative camera work and lighting, the results were generally bland; it failed to convey anything of the fatalistic worldview of the play. There have been three other movie versions: in 1923, with Sylvia Breamer in the title role; in 1930, the first TALKING PICTURE version, with Ann Harding; and a Sigmund ROMBERG musical version in 1937, starring Jeannette MacDonald and Nelson Eddy. The best known version of the play is the opera by Giacomo PUCCINI, *La Fanciulla del West.* Its premiere at the Metropolitan Opera in New York, December 10, 1910, was one of the most spectacular events in Met history. TOSCANINI conducted, Enrico CARUSO portrayed Dick Johnson and Belasco was on hand to supervise the production. Puccini biographer Mosco Carner reports the occasion was something special: "It represented a triumph for Puccini such as he had never enjoyed before or was ever to enjoy again."

Giroux, Andre (1916–). French-Canadian novelist and story writer. One of the major French language writers to emerge from Canada, Giroux was educated in the Quebec Academy and served in the provincial civil service before being named to the Quebec mission in Paris in 1963. Key themes in the fiction of Giroux include the hypocrisy of societal values and the psychological isolation of the individual. His major works include the novels *Au dela des visages* (1948, winner of the Prix David) and *La gouffre a toujours soif* (1953), and the story collection *Malgre tout, la joie* (1959, winner of the Governor General's Award).

Giscard d'Estaing, Valery (1926–). President of FRANCE (1974–81). A member of the National Assembly from 1956 to 1974, Giscard was leader of the Independent Republican Party, which supported the GAULLISTS after 1959 but retained its independence. Minister of finance under three successive prime ministers from 1962 to 1974, on the death of POMPIDOU (1974) Giscard was elected president, beating Gaullist and left-wing opponents. Though supported by Gaullists in the National Assembly, growing friction within the majority and alleged scandals, notably over gifts from Emperor BOKASSA of the Central African Empire, weakened his campaign for reelection in 1981 and led to his defeat by Francois MITTERRAND.

Gish, Lillian [Lillian de Guiche] (1896?-). American actress. Known as "the first lady of the silent screen," Gish has had a long and illustrious career in films, spanning more than eight decades. Her film debut was in D.W. GRIFFITH'S

Valery Giscard d'Estaing, president of France from 1974 to 1981.

two-reeler *An Unseen Enemy* (1912), and her association with the great director continued for more than 20 films, including the landmark *The Birth of a Nation* (1915), *Broken Blossoms* (1919) and *Orphans of the Storm* (1922). Gish struggled to find film roles in the 1920s and 1930s, due in part to salary disputes, the advent of sound films and a lack of interest on the part of the moviegoing public, which seemed to prefer the aggressively "modern woman" characterizations of Greta GARBO, Bette DAVIS and Joan CRAWFORD. But Gish found roles on Broadway and managed to win back her acclaim in films such as *Duel in the Sun* (1946) and *The Night of the Hunter* (1955). In the 1970s and '80s she continued to appear on screen, in *A Wedding* (1978) and *The Whales of August* (1987), among other films. In 1970 Gish was awarded a special ACADEMY AWARD "for her superlative and distinguished service in the making of motion pictures." Her sister and sometime costar Dorothy (who died in 1968) was also a respected film actress, although she never met with Lillian's phenomenal success.

Giulini, Carlo Maria (1914–). Italian-born opera and symphonic conductor known primarily for interpretations of the standard repertory. Giulini was born in Barletta in southern Italy. He studied the violin and played in many opera orchestras in the 1930s under such conductors as Richard STRAUSS, Wilhelm FURTWANGLER, and Bruno WALTER. In the early years of WORLD WAR II his anti-fascist sympathies drove him into hiding with the arrival of the Nazis in Italy. In 1950 he became conductor of the Milan Radio Orchestra and performed operas throughout Italy and abroad, making his first appearances in Britain and the U.S. in 1955. A number of appointments followed: permanent guest conductor of the Chicago Symphony Orchestra in 1969, principal conductor of the Vienna Symphony Orchestra in 1973–76, and conductor of the Los Angeles Philharmonic Orchestra in 1978. In later years he maintained a relatively limited repertoire and showned little interest in new composers. Giulini brings an almost mystical attitude to his interpretations, which critics have sometimes described as wayward and self-indulgent. He has been particularly praised for his performances of Mozart and Verdi operas and choral works and the symphonies of Bruckner and MAHLER.

For further reading:

Holmes, John, ed. *Conductors: A Record Collectors' Guide*. London: Gollancz, 1988.

Givenchy, Hubert Taffin de (1927–). French fashion designer known for quality design in a classic tradition stemming from Cristobal BALENCIAGA and emphasizing elegance over innovation. Hubert de Givenchy studied at the Ecole des Beaux-Arts and worked for designers Jacques Fath, Lucien Lelong, Robert Piguet, and Elsa Schiaparelli before opening his own house in 1952. His design was invariably refined and understated but perfectly cut, relying in part on a staff taken over from Balenciaga when his house closed in 1968. The ready-to-wear line designated Nouvelle Boutique has been added to Givenchy's couture production and is distributed throughout the world. The Givenchy name is now also attached to lines of eyeglasses, furs, home furnishings, men's shirts, perfumes, and sportswear under extensive licensing arrangements.

Gjellerup, Karl (1857–1919). Danish novelist and playwright. Gjellerup was a student of theology and philosophy, and his works evolved from naturalistic novels to contemporary dramas reflecting the influence of Ibsen. He is best known for the verse drama, *Brunhild* (1884), which was inspired by Richard Warner's *Ring* cycle. In what is considered to be a politically motivated move to strengthen allegiance between Denmark and Sweden and to emphasize the latter's neutral stance, Gjellerup was awarded the NOBEL PRIZE in literature along with Henrik PONTOPPIDAN in 1917. Gjellerup's other works include the play, *Die Opferfeuer* (The Sacrificial Fires, 1903), and the novels *Der Pilger Kamanita* (The Pilgrim Kamanita, (1906), and *Die Weltwandere* (The World Travelers, 1910).

Glackens, William (James) (1870–1938). American painter. Born in Philadelphia, he studied at the Pennsylvania Academy of the Fine Arts and subsequently became a successful illustrator for newspapers and magazines in his native city and New York City. He gained recognition as a member of the EIGHT OR ASHCAN SCHOOL, painting extremely realistic genre scenes and landscapes in a rather dark palette. Glackens traveled to Paris in the 1890s; taken with the work of the French Impressionists, particularly Renoir, he adopted a lighter, brighter color range after his return to the U.S. Characteristic of his later work is *Chez Mouquin* (1905, Art Institute of Chicago) and *Parade, Washington Square* (1912, Whitney Museum, N.Y.C.).

Glaser, Milton (1929–). Highly successful American graphic designer. Glaser studied at Cooper Union in New York and, on a Fulbright scholarship, with the Italian artist Giorgio Morandi in Bologna. His professional career began with the founding of Push Pin Studios (with Seymour Chwast and Edward Sorel) in New York in 1954. He established a reputation for the graphic redesign of magazine and newspaper formats, setting the standards for layout and typography at *New York* magazine, *Paris-Match, the Village Voice, New West* and *Esquire.* In addition, he has developed a wide variety of corporate identity programs (for Grand Union supermarkets, among others), packaging, and graphic materials. He is particularly known and highly visible through his design of posters for varied products, organizations, and events.

glasnost. Russian word that has been variously defined as "openness" or "speaking out." Glasnost, a policy initiated in the U.S.S.R. during the 1980s by Soviet leader Mikhail GORBACHEV, brought with it many new political, social and artistic freedoms. Under glasnost, censorship and repression of personal liberties were relaxed, bringing a new sense of openness to Soviet society.

Glass, Philip (1937–). American composer; highly influential and eclectic, best known for his role in establishing MINIMALISM as an important modern school of composition. But Glass has also shown the marked influence of JAZZ and ROCK AND ROLL themes in his more recent compositions. He graduated from the Juilliard School of Music in 1962 and studied with Nadia BOULANGER in Paris from 1964 to 1966. His pioneering involvement with minimalist compositions—which featured highly intricate and repetitive rhythms and frequently employed electronic synthesizers—won Glass international acclaim in the 1970s. He also achieved popular acclaim on the Broadway and London stage for his innovative musicals—*Einstein on the Beach* (1975), written in collaboration with Robert Wilson, and *Satyagraha* (1980), a portrayal of the difficult years spent by Mohandas K. GANDHI in South Africa.

Glazunov, Alexander Konstantinovich (1865–1936). Russian composer and conductor. He studied under Rimsky-Korsakov. In 1899 he was appointed professor of music at the St. Petersburg Conservatory, and in 1909 he was appointed director. Glazunov's musical output includes the ballets *Raymonda, Les Ruses d'Amour* and *The Seasons;* eight symphonies, choral music, orchestral works, piano and violin concertos, and chamber, vocal and instrumental music. Toward the end of his career, Glazunov became more interested in form and abstract music. He left Russia in 1928 and finally settled in Paris, where he died.

Gleason, Jackie (Herbert John) (1916–1987). American actor, comedian, musician, entertainer and television producer. Gleason was one of the leading show business figures of the 1950s and 1960s and a seminal figure in the new medium of television. Born into a poor Irish-American family in Brooklyn, New York, he began to pursue a career in small-time variety shows and nightclubs during the 1930s. In 1952, he inaugurated the weekly "Jackie Gleason Show," which ran on television until 1959 and then again from 1962 to 1970. On the show, Gleason excelled at creating comic characters, from the pompous Reginald van Gleason to the pathetic mute known as the Poor Soul. His classic television comedy series, "The Honeymooners" (1955–56), began as a sketch on the show and is still viewed by millions in reruns. In it, Gleason portrayed Ralph Kramden, a blustery, self-important but ultimately loveable New York City bus driver who was always looking to rise above his humble origins through some wildly improbable get-rich-quick scheme. Kramden shared his spartan tenement apartment (the main setting for most of the episodes) with his complaining, long-suffering, but devoted wife Alice (Audrey Meadows). Ralph's sidekick, sewer worker Ed Norton (Art Carney), often got the best of him through sheer good nature and luck. The show was notable for its memorable dialogue, inventive comic situations, improvisatory spirit and rich sense of humanity. It set a standard that few subsequent television "situation comedies" (among them, I LOVE LUCY, ALL IN THE FAMILY, and MASH) have been able to match. Gleason later won a best-actor award for his perfomance in the Broadway play *Take Me Along* (1959) and an ACADEMY AWARD nomination for his portrayal of pool shark Minnesota Fats in the film *The Hustler* (1961). The versatile Gleason, who epitomized the term bon vivant, was also a band leader and trumpeter. Although unable to read music, he composed a number of popular tunes, including his theme song, "Melancholy Serenade."

Gleiwitz incident. Attack on a German radio broadcasting station in the German (now Polish) border city of Gleiwitz (Gliwice) on August 31, 1939, by 12 men in Polish military uniforms. All 12 attackers were killed in the ensuing firefight. This incident, occurring some six miles from the Polish border, served as a pretext for HITLER'S invasion of POLAND the following day. It was later revealed that the attackers had been prisoners from a German CONCENTRATION CAMP ordered to perform the suicidal assault by the Nazi SS.

Glenn, John (Herschel), Jr. (1921–). U.S. astronaut, the first American to orbit the Earth. Glenn flew 59 Marine missions in the WORLD WAR II Pacific Theater during 1944 and 1945, and won several distinguished awards for his services in World War II and the KOREAN WAR. He completed test-pilot training in 1954 and made the first transcontinental supersonic flight in 1957 as a test pilot. After three years of rigorous training as part of Project MERCURY, Glenn circled the Earth three times in 4 hours and 36 minutes on February 20, 1962. Greeted by President Kennedy on his arrival at CAPE CANAVERAL and given one of New York's largest ticker-tape celebrations, Glenn became a national hero and was elected to the Senate in 1974 from his native state, Ohio. He was reelected in 1980 and 1986.

Ohio Senator John Glenn stands next to the Mercury spacecraft in which he orbited the Earth; Friendship 7 *is now on display at the Smithsonian Institute.*

Glennan, T. Keith (1905–). U.S. space administrator. Glennan became the first administrator of the National Aeronautics and Space Administration (NASA) when it was established October 1, 1958, and served in that position until January 20, 1961, when he was replaced by James E. Webb. He came to NASA from Case Institute of Technology, Cleveland, which he had headed since 1947; under his direction, Case had beome one of the top engineering schools in the country. After leaving NASA, Glennan returned to Case and stayed there until 1969. From 1970 to 1973, he served as U.S. ambassador to the International Atomic Energy Agency in Vienna. Early in his career, after receiving a degree in electrical engineering from Yale in 1927, he was studio manager of Paramount Pictures, Inc., and Samuel Goldwyn Studios.

Gliere, Reinhold Moritzovich (1875–1956). Russian composer. He studied in Kiev and Moscow and became professor of composition (1913) and director (1914) at the Kiev Conservatory, and professor of composition at the Moscow Conservatory (1920). He taught PROKOFIEV, KHACHATURIAN, Knipper and MYASKOVSKY. A prolific composer, his works include several symphonies, of which the best known is his number three, *Ilya Mouromets* (1909–11), the ballet *The Red Poppy* (1926–27) and a cello concerto. In his later works he used folk music from the U.S.S.R.

global warming. In the 1980s a series of unusually hot summers gave rise to fears that the Earth's climate was gradually becoming warmer. Some attributed this trend to carbon dioxide emissions from industrial plants and AUTOMOBILES and from the burning of RAIN FORESTS. If true, the global warming trend could lead to droughts, the melting of polar ice caps and a rise in sea levels. (See also GREENHOUSE EFFECT.)

Glubb, Sir John Bagot (1897–1986). British army officer. Glubb built JORDAN'S Arab Legion into one of the most effective fighting fores in the Middle East during WORLD WAR II. He joined the Arab Legion as second in command in 1930 and took formal command of it in 1939. He became known as Glubb Pasha, a title conferred upon him by Jordan's King ABDULLAH IBN HUSSEIN. He served as a close confidant to Abdullah until the king's assassination in Jerusalem in 1951, and remained commander of the legion until 1956. Growing militant Arab nationalism led to Glubb's dismissal by Abdullah's successor, King HUSSEIN, who expelled him from the country. After returning to England, he wrote many books about the Arab world.

Glueck, Eleanor Touroff (1898–1972). American criminologist. Glueck taught at Harvard Law School from 1928 to 1964. With her husband, **Sheldon Glueck,** she was a pioneer in the study of juvenile delinquency. In 1950 she published a controversial 10-year study, *Unraveling Juvenile Delinquency.*

Glushko, Valentin Petrovich (1906–1989). Soviet rocket pioneer. He became interested in the use of rockets for space travel while he was barely in his teens, and wrote to the Russian rocket pioneer Konstantin TSIOLKOVSKY about the subject in 1923. In 1929 he urged the Soviet government to develop a rocket propelled by liquid fuel. During the 1930s he worked on various rocket designs. After World War II he helped design a series of rocket engines that represented a major lead forward for Soviet missile technology. Among his achievements were the engine for the R-7, the world's first intercontinental ballistic missile, and engines for early Soviet manned and unmanned space flights.

Glyndebourne Festival. Held annually from May to early August at the Glyndebourne estate in Lewes, Sussex, England, the festival is devoted exclusively to opera, and is especially noted for performances of operas by Mozart and Richard Strauss. The estate owner, John Christie, built an opera house amid the celebrated gardens at a suggestion from his wife, soprano Audrey Mildmay; in 1934 the festival was inaugurated with a performance of Mozart's *The Marriage of Figaro*. A succession of distinguished conductors have guided the performances: Fritz Busch (1934–51), Vittorio Gui (1951–60), John Pritchard (1960–77) and Bernard Haitink (current). Since 1984 Sir Peter HALL has been the producer. Many of the world's great opera singers, such as Luciano PAVAROTTI, have performed there. The festival is also known for exciting productions of such recent operas as Oliver Knussen's *Where the Wild Things Are*.

Gmeiner, Herman (1919–1986). Austrian humanitarian. Gmeiner's SOS Children's Village became a haven for thousands of orphaned and abandoned children throughout the world. The movement grew from one village, which he founded in 1949 in the Tyrolean region of Austria, to more than 225 villages in 85 countries on five continents.

Gnessin, Michael Febianovich (1883–1957). Composer. Gnessin studied at St. Petersburg Conservatory and helped to found the Don Conservatory, becoming director in 1920. Later he was a professor at the Moscow and Leningrad conservatories. His compositions include an opera-poem *The Youth of Abraham* (1921–23), works for chorus and orchestra, including *Symphonic Monument, 1905–17* (1925), incidental music and folk song arrangements. After the revolution he set a poem by Sergei ESENIN to music for chorus and orchestra to commemorate the revolutions of 1905 and 1917.

Gobat, Albert (1843–1914). Swiss lawyer, politician, educator and peace advocate. He was active in the Interparliamentary Union in the 1890s. At the turn of the century he worked for arbitration as a means of solving international disputes. For this work he shared the second NOBEL PRIZE for peace with Elie DUCOMMUN in 1902. In 1906 he urged American President Theodore ROOSEVELT to attend a peace conference at The HAGUE, which Roosevelt did in 1907. Gobat directed the International Peace Bureau from 1906 to 1909 and unsuccessfully advocated French and German disarmament.

Gobbi, Tito (1913–1984). Italian opera singer. A baritone, Gobbi possessed great expressive range in both dramatic and comic roles and was considered one of the finest operatic actors of his generation. He made his debut in Rome in 1938 but did not achieve full recognition until the 1950s. He appeared regularly at New York's Metropolitan Opera from 1956 to 1976 and was also featured at Milan's La Scala and other leading European opera houses. Among his roles were Iago (in Verdi's *Otello*), Figaro (in Rossini's *Barber of Seville*) and the title characters in Mozart's *Don Giovanni*, Verdi's *Falstaff*, PUCCINI'S *Gianni Schicci* and BERG'S *Wozzeck*. His portrayal of Scarpia in Puccini's *Tosca* was considered definitive; he often played the role opposite Maria CALLAS and sang with her in a legendary 1953 recording of the work. After retiring from the stage he directed operas and was an influential singing teacher.

Godard, Jean-Luc (1930–). French filmmaker and critic, a leader (with Francois TRUFFAUT, Claude CHABROL and Jacques Rivette) of the NOUVELLE VAGUE in the late 1950s. Although he was educated in Switzerland and later at the Sorbonne, it was time spent watching films at Paris's Cinematheque Francaise that decided his future. After working as a critic, actor and writer in the circle of young enthusiasts grouped around Andre Bazin and the CAHIERS DU CINEMA, Godard created a sensation with his first feature, *A Bout de Souffle* (*Breathless*, 1959). With a script by Truffaut, this hommage to the gangster film was an iconoclastic experiment in loose-limbed film form and nervous, jump-cut continuity. Godard's mixture of leftist ideological polemic and comic-book slapstick made him the Bad Boy of the New Wave and the overnight darling of the cinema avant-garde. While critics John Simon and Susan SONTAG disagreed over his films ("infantile self-indulgence" and "nearly perfect work"), audiences were assaulted by the explicit atrocities of the Algerian War in *Le Petit Soldat* (1960), moved by the intensely personal feminist statement of *Vivre sa Vie* (*My Life to Live*, 1962), amused by the satiric comments on rebellious youth in *Bande a Part* (*Band of Outsiders*, 1964), scandalized by the explicit lyric sensuality of *Une Femme mariee* (*The Married Woman*, 1964) and puzzled by the Marxist image/word games of *La Chinoise* (1967). Sometimes he abandoned the "bourgeois" conventions of subject and story altogether, photographing words or punctuating his shots with gunshot sounds. Many critics feel that his later work abandoned the humor of his early films.

For further reading:

Roud, Richard, *Godard*. Bloomington: Indiana University Press, 1970.

Goddard, Paulette [Marion Levy] (1911–1990). American actress. A HOLLYWOOD film star of the 1930s and 1940s, Goddard was noted for her beauty and vivaciousness. Her two most memorable films were *Modern Times* (1936) and *The Great Dictator* (1940), made with her second husband, Charlie CHAPLIN. She eventually made more than 40 films, but her movie career began to fade in the early 1950s. In 1958, she married Erich Maria REMARQUE, author of ALL QUIET ON THE WESTERN FRONT, and retired to Switzerland, thereafter making only occasional film and television appearances.

Goddard, Robert H. (1882–1945). The "Father of American Rocketry," Goddard graduated from Worcestor Polytechnic Institute in 1908. He took his Ph.D. at Clark University three years later. An instructor in physics at Princeton (1912–13), he joined the Clark faculty in 1914 and was associated with the university until 1943. Fascinated with rockets all his life, he began testing them as early as 1908 and by 1914 had experimented with a two-stage rocket and various fuels. Highly individualistic and something of a loner, Goddard was a favorite target of the press, which saw his rocket experiments as fodder for sensational stories. After receiving a grant in 1916 from the Smithsonian Institution on the basis of a monograph outlining his ideas and research, he went on to publish his best known work, "A Method of Reaching Extreme Altitudes," in 1919. A "hands-on" experimenter, he continued his work with the use of liquid fuels for rocket propulsion throughout the 1920s, settling on a combination of gasoline and liquid oxygen. After firing his first liquid-fueled rocket in March 1926, he continued to work on improvements in their design. However, complaints from his New England neighbors and hurried visits by the local fire department every time he made a test were getting on Goddard's nerves.

In 1929, with the help of Charles LINDBERGH, he received a grant from the Guggenheim Foundation and moved his equipment to a testing range in New Mexico. Continuing to build his rockets and work on everything from combustion chambers to steering systems, Goddard launched a series of rockets from 1930 to 1935 that reached speeds of up to 550 miles an hour and heights of over a mile and a half. In a 1936 publication, *Liquid-Propellant Rocket Development*, he summarized his work up to that point. Still the U.S. government showed little interest other than to seek his assistance briefly during World War II to help in developing systems for jet-assisted takeoffs (JATO) of airplanes from aircraft carriers.

Largely unrecognized at the time of his death, he received a knowing tribute from German rocket scientist Wernher von BRAUN when, surprised at questions put to him about rocketry upon his arrival in America, von Braun wondered why the questioners had not asked Goddard. "Don't you know about your own rocket pioneer?" the German asked. "Dr. Goddard was ahead of us all." In 1960, government neglect came to an ironic end when the U.S. paid $1 million to God-

Robert Goddard, "the father of American rocketry," in his New Mexico workshop (1935).

dard's estate and the Guggenheim Foundation for infringements on many of the 200 patents dealing with rockets that Goddard had received during his lifetime. And, on July 17, 1969, as the APOLLO 11 astronauts prepared for their historic moon landing, *The New York Times* printed a formal retraction of its 1920 editorial ridiculing Goddard's claim that rockets would fly someday to the moon. Today, the Goddard Space Flight Center in Maryland bears his name.

Godden, Rumer (1907–). British novelist and poet. Born in Sussex, Godden spent much of her childhood in India, which was to figure prominently in her writing along with the influence of her Roman Catholic upbringing. Godden is perhaps best known for the novel, *The River* (1946) which she later adapted for film with the director Jean RENOIR for release in 1951. Of her many enormously popular works of fiction, several were adapted for film, notably, *Black Narcissus* (1939, filmed 1947). Other novels include *The Greengage Summer* (1958, filmed as *Loss of Innocence*, 1961), *The Battle of Villa Fiorita* (1961, filmed 1965) and *Five for Sorrow, Ten for Joy* (1979). Godden has also written several children's books, and her autobiography, *A Time to Dance, No Time to Weep* (1987).

Godel, Kurt (1906–1978). Austrian-American mathematician. Godel initially studied physics at the University of Vienna but soon turned to mathematics and mathematical logic. He obtained his Ph.D. in 1930 and the same year joined the faculty at Vienna. He became a member of the Institute of Advanced Study, Princeton, in 1938 and in 1940 immigrated to the U.S.. Godel was a professor at the institute from 1953 to 1976 and received many scientific honors and awards, including the National Medal of Science in 1975. In 1930 Godel published his doctoral dissertation, the proof that first-order logic is complete—that is, that every sentence of the language of first-order logic is provable or its negation is provable. The completeness of logical systems was then a concept of central importance owing to the various attempts that had been made to reveal a logical axiomatic basis for mathematics. Completeness can be thought of as ensuring that all logically valid statements, which a formal (logical) system can produce, can be proved from the axioms of the system, and that every invalid statement is disprovable.

In 1931 Godel presented his famous incompleteness proof for arithmetic. He showed that in any consistent formal system complicated enough to describe simple arithmetic there are propositions or statements that can be neither proved nor disproved on the basis of the axioms of the system—intuitively speaking, there are logical truths that cannot be proved within the system. Moreover, he showed (in his second incompleteness theorem) that the "consistency" of any formal system including arithmetic cannot be proved by methods formalizable within that system; consistency can only be proved by using a stronger system—whose own consistency has to be assumed. This latter result showed the impossibility of carrying out David HILBERT's program, at least in its original form.

Godel's second great result concerned two important postulates of set theory, whose consistency mathematicians had been trying to prove since the turn of the century. Between 1938 and 1940 he showed that if the axioms of (restricted) set theory are consistent, then they remain so upon the addition of the axiom of choice and the continuum hypothesis, and that these postulates cannot, therefore, be disproved by restricted set theory. (In 1963 Paul Cohen showed that they were independent of set theory.) Godel also worked on the construction of alternative universes that are models of the general theory of relativity, and produced a rotating-universe model.

***Godfather* Trilogy.** Acclaimed saga of a criminal MAFIA dynasty (although the term "Mafia" is avoided), directed by Francis Ford COPPOLA from stories by Mario Puzo. The narrative thread running through all three films (1972, 1974 and 1990) is the violent assumption of power by three generations of the Corleone family. Ambitions to "legitimize" the family's gangland activities preoccupy the aging Don Vito (Marlon BRANDO, in an Oscar-winning role) and then his son Michael (Al Pacino); but outside powers and internecine conflict displace family loyalties with greed and violence. The action ranges broadly over space and time, from Sicily and the poor immigrant neighborhoods of New York in the 1900s, to postwar America's posh estates and Nevada casinos, and finally to Vatican City. The tone is a counterpoint between the bright festivity of family ceremonies and a bitter chiaroscuro of treachery and deceit. But what had been fresh and fast in the first installment becomes brooding and complex in the second, and, in the opinion of many, terminally elegiac in the third. To date the trilogy has won 10 ACADEMY AWARDS and a place in the national vocabulary. Aside from Coppola's guiding hand, credit must also go to Ennio Morricone's music score, the performances by Pacino, Brando, James Caan and Robert Duvall (to name only a few), and the stunning cinematography by Gordon Willis.

Goebbels, (Paul) Joseph (1897–1945). German NAZI. Born at Rheydt in Westphalia, Goebbels attended the Univ. of Heidelberg, receiving a Ph.D. in literature and history. Rejected from service in World War I because of a congenital foot defect, he began to write articles for periodicals as well as several unsuccessful novels. Meanwhile, in 1922 he joined the National Socialist (Nazi) Party, and in 1926 HITLER appointed him Berlin's party leader. He was elected to the Reichstag in 1928, and when Hitler seized power five years later, Goebbels was named PROPAGANDA minister. This enormously powerful position gave him complete control over German media and arts, and with a singularly vicious shrewdness he dictated the content of the press, radio, literature, film, theater and the visual arts with the purpose of glorifying the Third Reich,

Joseph Goebbels, Nazi Party minister of propaganda.

pursuing the war effort and stressing Nazi ideology. A mesmerizing orator and a master of mass psychology, he staged huge rallies and candlelight marches where the Aryan myth was extolled and JEWS and intellectuals were excoriated. Goebbels remained completely loyal to Hitler until the fuhrer's suicide. Shortly thereafter as Russian troops entered Berlin, he and his wife poisoned their six children and the two then shot themselves. (See also NAZISM.)

Goering, Hermann (Wilhelm) (1893–1946). German Nazi leader. Born of a distinguished family in Rosenheim, Bavaria, Goering was a much-decorated WORLD WAR I hero and served as the last commander of Manfred von RICHTHOFEN's legendary air squadron. He studied briefly at Munich University (1920–21) and was an early convert to the National Socialist (NAZI) party, joining in 1922. A year later he was wounded in the Munich BEER HALL PUTSCH. Escaping to Sweden for four years, he returned to Germany and was elected to the Reichstag in 1928, becoming the legislature's president in 1932. After HITLER's accession to power in 1933, Goering became second only to his leader in the hierarchy of the Third Reich. His posts included German air minister, Prussian prime and interior minister and founder-head of the dreaded secret police, the GESTAPO. In 1936 he took over the direction of the four-year economic plan, becoming virtual dictator of all aspects of the nation's economy. In 1939 he was officially designated Hitler's successor and a year later he was awarded the specially-created rank of Reichmarshal. A vainglorious figure, enamored of smart uniforms and endless pageantry, he ultimately succumbed to morphine addiction and became increasingly reclusive. Responsible for Germany's total air war, he lost popularity as Allied bombings took their toll, and by 1943 he had lost much of his authority. In May 1945 Goering surrendered to U.S. forces. Found guilty of war crimes at the NUREMBERG TRIALS, he was sentenced to death, but managed to cheat the hangman by poisoning himself hours before his scheduled execution.

For further reading:

Irving, David, *Goering: A Biography*. New York: Morrow, 1989.

Hermann Goering, founder of the Gestapo, commander of the Luftwaffe and Marshal of the Reich.

Goeritz, Mathias (1915–1990). German-born architect and sculptor. Goeritz was educated both as a sculptor and an architect in his native Germany before leaving the country prior to World War II out of disapproval of the Nazi regime. He finally settled in 1949 in Mexico, where many of his greatest architectural works—which are frequently accompanied by his own large-scale abstract sculptures—now reside. These include the massive and sharp-edged *Towers of Satellite City* (1957, in collaboration with fellow architect Luis Barragan) and the cone-shaped *Automex Towers* (1967).

Goethals, George Washington (1858–1928). American civil engineer. Goethals graduated from the U.S. Military Academy at West Point in 1880. He served at various posts in the Army Engineer Corps (1882–05) and Army General Staff (1903–07) before being appointed chief engineer of the PANAMA CANAL in 1907. Despite numerous difficulties involving engineering problems, labor troubles, climate and yellow fever, he completed the project ahead of schedule. Goethals was the first governor of the Canal Zone (1914–16). Although retired from active duty in 1916, he was recalled in 1917. He served briefly as general manager of the Emergency Fleet Corporation (1917) and as acting quartermaster general and director of purchase, storage and traffic.

Goffman, Erving (1922–1982). Canadian-American sociologist. Goffman studied the hidden meanings of ordinary activities and transactions. In his books he argued that even an individual's most casual actions were actually performances calculated to establish a certain positive impression. Goffman held a Ph.D. from the University of Chicago (1953) and later taught at the University of California (1958–68) and the University of Pennsylvania (1968–82). Among his books are *Behavior in Public Places: Notes on the Social Organization of Gatherings* (1966), *Encounters* (1961) and *The Presentation of Self in Everyday Life* (1959).

Gogarten, Friedrich (1887–1967). German Protestant theologian; much influenced in his theological works by the writings of Karl BARTH and Martin BUBER. Gogarten began his career in 1917 by serving as a pastor at Stelzendorf. In 1931 he became a professor of theology at the University of Breslau, then moved on in 1935 to a similar position at the University of Gottingen, where he taught for nearly two decades. Gogarten held that true historical events were created only when an individual, in an attitude of unconditional faith, confronted the divine "Thou." His works include *Fichte als Religioser denke* (1914) and *Von Glauben und Offenbarung* (1923).

Golan Heights. Strategically important high ground in southern SYRIA overlooking Israeli territory, captured by ISRAEL in the Arab-Israeli War of 1967 (SIX–DAY WAR) and occupied since.

Gold, Herbert (1924–). American author. Gold's novels chronicle contemporary American life, often highlighting the difficulties in relations between men and women, and he is noted for his ability to reproduce idiom and spoken language. His early novels, such as *Birth of a Hero* (1951), are set in his native Midwest. Later novels shrewdly capture the mood of the West Coast. These include *He/She* (1980), *A Girl of Forty* (1986) and *Dreaming* (1988). Gold has also written the autobiographical novels *Fathers: A Novel in the Form of a Memoir* (1967) and *My Last Two Thousand Years* (1972).

Gold, H(orace) L(eonard) (1914–). Canadian-born science fiction writer and editor. Gold began his career in the 1930s as a science fiction writer, but in the 1940s he branched out into detective pulp fiction as well as writing for comic strips and radio. Science fiction always remained his first love, and Gold is best remembered as the founder and editor of *Galaxy*, a science fiction monthly that first appeared in 1950 and for 30 years was one of the most highly regarded magazines in the field. Gold edited *Galaxy* through the mid-1960s, encouraging a successful blend of satire and social sciences themes hitherto handled like lead bricks by the science fiction field.

Goldberg, Arthur J. (1908–1990). Associate justice, U.S. Supreme Court (1962–65). A graduate of Northwestern University and its law school, Goldberg became a well-known labor lawyer who represented the United Steelworkers and the Congress of Industrial Organizations (CIO) as well as other unions. In 1955 the CIO merged with the older American Federation of Labor to become the AFL-CIO;

Arthur J. Goldberg testifies before the U.S. Senate Rules and Administration Committee on the nomination of Nelson Rockefeller for vice president (1974).

Goldberg was a leading participant in the negotiations leading up to this historic merger. He subsequently served as special counsel to the AFL-CIO. He became President John F. KENNEDY's secretary of labor in 1961. In 1962 Kennedy nominated Goldberg to replace Felix FRANKFURTER on the Supreme Court, continuing the practice of appointing one Jewish member of the Court. Goldberg occupied the seat briefly. President Lyndon B. JOHNSON persuaded him to resign in 1965 to become U.S. ambassador to the UNITED NATIONS after the death of Adlai STEVENSON II. Goldberg later admitted that his resignation from the Court had been a mistake. After serving for three years he resigned as UN ambassador. After an unsuccessful run for governor of New York state he returned to private law practice until his death.

Goldberg, Rube (1883–1970). American cartoonist. Goldberg was born in San Francisco and worked for the *Chronicle* and *Bulletin* in that city before moving to New York in 1907 to draw for the *Evening Mail*. His whimsical, convoluted slapstick cartoons won him tremendous popularity, and his name entered the language as a term for a wacky, overly complex contraption for performing a simple task. Some of the many cartoon features and strips originated by Goldberg include *The Look-A-Like Boys, Foolish Questions, I'm the Guy* and *Boob McNutt*. Throughout the 1940s, Goldberg also drew political cartoons for the *New York Sun;* he won the PULITZER PRIZE in 1948 for his cartoon "Peace Today," which dealt with the issue of atomic weapons.

Golden Temple Massacre. On June 6, 1984, in an effort to suppress uprisings by extremist Sikh separatist groups, the Indian army invaded the Golden Temple, the holiest Sikh shrine, in Amritsar, Punjab. Between 800 and 1,000 were estimated killed, among them Jarnail Singh Bhindranwale, the fundamentalist leader of the Sikh extremists, and 48 Indian troops. The militant Sikhs, who had been using the temple as a bastion and refuge, had vowed in May to blockade all grain, water and power supplied from Punjab to the rest of INDIA. On June 1, 11 people had been killed in battle at the temple, and on June 2 the Indian government declared the state of Punjab a restricted area and brought in some 50,000 troops. Sikh uprisings, which had intensified that April, had since become increasingly violent, and Indian authorities applauded the attack. But it triggered a violent backlash by militant Sikhs in India and protests from Sikhs worldwide. The Indian government reopened the temple on June 25, and later announced a plan to overhaul the Punjab state administration to maintain peace. The assassination of Prime Minister Indira GANDHI by Sikh extremists on October 31 was regarded as an act of revenge for the Golden Temple Massacre.

Goldfield. Small village in U.S. state of Nevada that grew overnight from hamlet to a city of instant elegance, with theater, large hotel and fine residences—all courtesy of one of history's greatest gold rushes. Gold was discovered in 1902, the city transformed by 1903, ore production peaked by 1910 and the boom ended and the decline set in by 1918.

Goldie, Grace Wyndham (1905?–1986). BRITISH BROADCASTING CORPORATION producer. Goldie was a BBC television producer from 1944 to 1965 and played a key role in the development of political and public affairs broadcasting in Britain. She set the pattern for general election nights on BBC-TV in the general election of 1950 and was responsible for the development of such programs as "Press Conference," "Monitor" and "Panorama."

Golding, William Gerald (1911–). British novelist. Born in Cornwall, Golding was educated at Marlborough Grammar School and Brasenose College, Oxford, and published *Poems* (1934) while still a student. He worked for a time as a social worker, meanwhile writing plays and acting in a small London theater. In 1939 he began teaching English and philosophy at Bishop Wordsworth's School in Salisbury, where he remained, except for the years of World War II until 1961. Golding served in the Royal Navy during the war, and his experiences shaped his pessimistic view of human nature which is apparent in his writing. Golding's best-known work, THE LORD OF THE FLIES (1954, filmed 1963), a mythic tale of a group of boys abandoned on an island where they revert to savagery, was an immediate success and is still a part of most English curricula. Golding continued to explore the theme of man's inherent cruelty in the novels *The Inheritors* (1955), *Pincher Martin* (1956), *Free Fall* (1959) and *The Spire* (1964). Golding was awarded the NOBEL PRIZE for literature in 1983. Other works include the novels *Rites of Passage* (1980), which won the Booker Prize; *The Paper Men* (1984) and the essays *A Moving Target* (1982).

Goldman, Emma (1869–1940). Anarchist. She left Russia for the U.S. in 1885 and was politically active from about 1890 to 1917. She was imprisoned in 1893 for inciting a riot. After meeting Alexander Berkman in 1906, she became an active anarchist, was imprisoned in 1916 and in 1917; after two years in prison she was deported to Russia. She later lived in England and Canada and was involved in the SPANISH CIVIL WAR. Her writings include *Anarchism and Other Essays* (1911), *My Disillusionment in Russia* (1923) and an autobiography, *Living My Life* (1931). (See also ANARCHISM.)

Goldman, Nahum (1894–1982). Zionist leader who helped create the state of ISRAEL. Born in Lithuania, during his lifetime Goldman lived in several nations but never in Israel. He represented the Jewish Agency at the LEAGUE OF NATIONS in the 1930s. In the 1950s he was instrumental in negotiating the agreement under which WEST GERMANY paid Israel $827 million in post-war reparations. He headed the World Jewish Congress (1949–77) and the World Zionist Organization (1956–68). He was often outspoken in his opposition to Israeli government policies, and called on Israel to negotiate with the PALESTINE LIBERATION ORGANIZATION (PLO).

Emma Goldman, author and anarchist, with Alexander Berkman (July 9, 1917).

Goldmark, Carl Peter (1906–1977). Hungarian-American engineer and inventor. Although RCA Victor had demonstrated and released several 33.3 RPM, long-playing records in 1931, Goldmark conceived and invented the first commercially successful long-playing phonograph records (1948), utilizing the superior vinyl plastic instead of shellac; he was also instrumental in the development of color television. Born in Budapest, he immigrated to the U.S. in 1933 and joined the Columbia Broadcasting System (CBS) in 1936 as a technical engineer. Working in the CBS laboratory, he was credited with developing the first practical color television system, which was demonstrated in 1940. Goldmark's work in developing the modern long-playing record stemmed from his own interest in listening to recordings. The existing 78 RPM records could accommodate only four or five minutes of music per side. An entire symphony recording required several records, and the listener had to change the sides every few minutes. By contrast, a 33.3 LP could accommodate up to a half-hour of music on each side. Goldmark conceived a new stylus capable of cutting finer grooves on the long-playing 33.3 RPM disk, as well as the necessary turntable, tone arm and pick-up cartridge. All of these innovations became standard features and remained in use even after the advent of compact discs in the 1980s. Retiring from CBS in 1971 at the company's mandatory retirement age of 65, Goldmark formed Goldmark Communications Corp. in Stamford, Connecticut. Less than three weeks before his death in a car accident, Goldmark was awarded the National Medal of Science for developing communications sciences for education, entertainment and culture.

Goldwater, Barry (Morris) (1909–). American politician, 1964 U.S. presidential candidate and spokesman for the conservative wing of the REPUBLICAN PARTY. The heir to his family's Phoenix, Arizona department store, Goldwater entered politics after service in World War II and was elected to the U.S. Senate from Arizona in 1952. Building a reputation as a vigorous anti-communist and an opponent of big domestic social programs, he became a key spokesman for conservatives in the American South and West. By the fall of 1963 he was the leading contender for the Republican Party's 1964 presidential nomination, although he was reluctant to run. He officially announced his candidacy in January 1964. Opposing what he regarded as the liberal tendencies of most Democratic and Republican leaders, Goldwater insisted that he offered "a choice, not an echo." A bitter fight for the nomination against Nelson ROCKEFELLER split the Republican Party between its liberal and conservative wings. Answering his critics, Goldwater declared "extremism in the defense of liberty is no vice, and moderation in the pursuit of justice is no virtue." During the campaign, however, President Lyndon B. JOHNSON's forces successfully painted Goldwater as a dangerous extremist who would abolish social security and threaten world peace. Goldwater lost the election to Johnson in a landslide, with only 38.4% of the popular votes and six states. Although largely disavowed by the Republican Party and the country at large, Goldwater remained active in national politics and reentered the Senate in 1968. He was a HAWK on the VIETNAM WAR, but called for an end to the draft in favor of a volunteer Army. During the WATERGATE scandal, he at first supported President Richard M. NIXON. However, after the release of the White House tapes showing Nixon's involvement, Goldwater was instrumental in persuading the President to resign. The election of conservative Republican Ronald REAGAN as President in 1980 seemed to vindicate the views that Goldwater had espoused 16 years earlier. Ironically, Goldwater criticized Reagan on a number of issues. From being viewed as an extremist in many circles in the 1950s and 1960s, Goldwater grew into an elder statesman of the Republican Party in the 1970s and 1980s, earning the respect of his allies and opponents alike for his integrity and independence. He retired from the Senate in 1986. His biography is *Goldwater* (1988).

U.S. senator from Arizona Barry Goldwater was the Republican presidential candidate in 1964.

Goldwyn, Samuel [Samuel Goldfish] (1882–1974). American motion picture producer, one of the best known of the HOLLYWOOD moguls. Born in Warsaw, Poland, he immigrated to the U.S. as a teenager. By age 30 he was in Hollywood, where he co-produced the first full-length feature, *The Squaw Man* (1913). He teamed with the two Selwyn brothers to form Goldwyn Pictures (a name formed by combining the first syllable of his last name, Goldfish, and the last syllable of Selwyn); Goldfish subsequently adopted the name as his own. The name Goldwyn is best known as part of METRO-GOLDWYN-MAYER studios, but Goldwyn himself left MGM the year after it was founded to run his own production company. Among the films he produced are *Wuthering Heights* (1939), *The Best Years of Our Lives* (1946) and *Guys and Dolls* (1955).

Golkar. Official political party in INDONESIA during the SUKARNO era.

Gollan, Dr. Frank (1909–1988). American medical scientist. A polio victim, he was determined to find a cure for the disease. Gollan's isolation of the polio virus in 1948 aided other researchers in developing a vaccine. In the early 1950s, he invented the heart-lung machine for use in open-heart surgery.

Gollancz, Victor (1893–1967). British publisher, author, philanthropist. Although he founded a successful publishing house, Victor Gollancz, Ltd., in 1928, Gollancz is best known for his many campaigns to aid victims of injustice worldwide and for his political activities. In 1936 he founded the Left Book Club, which had a major impact on the development of the Labor political party. Establishing a committee to aid victims of the Nazis was just one of his humanitarian endeavors. He also wrote many books on religion, politics and music, and spearheaded campaigns for the abolition of capital punishment and for nuclear disarmament; he was knighted in 1965.

Gomez, Juan Vicente (1857–1935). Venezuelan dictator (1908–35). A meztizo from a cattle ranch in the Andes, Gomez became a guerilla leader in support of the revolutionary Cipriano Castro. He was Castro's vice-president, seizing control of the government for himself in 1908 while the erstwhile strongman was abroad. Sometimes assuming the title of president (1910–14, 1922–29, 1931–35), sometimes relinquishing it to others, Gomez nonetheless retained the reins of power for the next 27 years. His cunning and tyrannical rule was marked by absolute suppression of dissent by a ruthless secret police totally controlled by Gomez. However, the rule of "El Benemerito" ("The Meritorious One") was also characterized by political and economic stability. Gomez was able to pay VENEZUELA's huge debts and was instrumental in developing his nation's petroleum resources. He was also successful in setting up an array of public works projects that included a network of roads and railways. While amassing enormous wealth for himself and his large family, many of whom were made public officials, he was also responsible for bringing Venezuela into the modern world.

For further reading:

Clinton, Daniel J., *Gomez, Tyrant of the Andes*. Westport, Conn.: Greenwood, 1970.

McBeth, B. S., *Juan Vicente Gomez and the Oil Companies in Venezuela, 1908–1935*. Cambridge, U.K. and New York: Cambridge University Press, 1983.

Gompers, Samuel (1850–1924). American labor leader. Born in London, he immigrated to the U.S. with his parents in

Samuel Gompers, founder and president of the American Federation of Labor (AFL).

1863, becoming a cigarmaker that year and joining the local union a year later. He served as president of the Cigarmakers' Union (1874–81), before helping to found the Federation of Organized Trades and Labor Unions. Reorganized in 1886, the group was renamed the American Federation of Labor, and Gompers served as its first president (with the exception of the year 1895) until his death. Essentially conservative in his philosophy, Gompers built the AFL into the country's largest labor organization, encouraging improvements in wages, working conditions and hours, but avoiding political involvements and pronouncements. During World War I, he headed the War Committee on Labor and was a member of the Advisory Commission to the Council of National Defense, stressing the need for labor's loyalty to the war effort. His vigor and integrity made him the most influential and widely respected labor leader of his day.

Gomulka, Wladyslaw (1905–1982). Leader of POLAND's Communist Party from 1956 to 1970, Gomulka spearheaded the resistance to Soviet dominance of the Polish communist government. Active in the Communist Party from 1926, he organized the People's Guard RESISTANCE group during the WORLD WAR II German occupation. He was first secretary of the Communist Party from 1945 to 1949 but was imprisoned (1951–55) as the result of one of STALIN's purges. He returned to power in 1956 and initiated several reforms. However, widespread rioting over food prices coupled with his increased leaning toward more orthodox Marxism led to Gomulka's downfall in 1970.

Goncourt Prize. French literary award. The Academie Goncourt was established in the will of Edmond Goncourt (1822–1896), a 19th-century literary figure, to award the annual Prix Goncourt for prose. The Academie consists of ten individuals whose purpose is to recognize innovative, independent fiction with a cash award of 5,000 francs. The first award was made in 1903 to John Antoine Nau for *Force Ennemie* (1903).

Gone with the Wind. Novel and popular motion picture, set during and after the American Civil War. Margaret MITCHELL's novel was published in May of 1936; by September it had made publishing history as the fastest-selling book of all time, with 370,000 copies in print. A mammoth work, it spanned the South of Civil War and Reconstruction, presenting vivid characters like the dashing Rhett Butler and the (ultimately) indomitable Scarlett O'Hara. On January 13, 1939, HOLLYWOOD producer David O. SELZNICK ended months of suspense when he selected the virtually unknown British actress Vivien LEIGH to play Scarlett in his film version of the book opposite Clark GABLE's Rhett. Thirteen days later director George CUKOR yelled "Action." At year's end, on December 15, at a cost of $4.25 million, the finished film went into release through MGM and premiered at Loew's Grand Theater in Atlanta. It grossed an unprecedented $945,000 in a single week. It garnered 10 ACADEMY AWARDS, including best actress to Leigh, best supporting actress to Hattie McDaniel, best screenplay to Sidney Howard (with an uncredited assist from Ben HECHT) and best director to Victor Fleming (who had replaced George Cukor and who in turn was temporarily replaced by Sam Wood). The movie was a triumph of the studio system and stands today as a monument to Hollywood's Golden Age. In particular, the luxurious Technicolor photography (much of it shot by Lee Garmes) and the extensive use of stunning matte paintings and optical effects enabled a handful of incomplete sets to bloom into the improbable sumptuousness of everybody's dream of the Old South.

Gonzalez, Felipe Marquez (1942–). Premier of SPAIN (1982–). In 1964, while still at university, Gonzalez joined the then-illegal Spanish Socialist Workers Party (PSOE). In 1966, he graduated from Seville University Law School, and in 1970 he became a member of the executive committee of the PSOE, succeeding to the leadership of the party four years later. In 1977 the PSOE was legalized and became the largest party in the country. Following its landslide victory in the 1982 elections, Gonzalez became premier. Known as a moderate, he decentralized the government, improved social programs and brought Spain into the EUROPEAN ECONOMIC COMMUNITY. He was elected to a second term in 1986 and a third term in 1989.

Gonzalez, Julio (1876–1942). Spanish sculptor. Born in Barcelona, Gonzalez was trained in metalworking by his goldsmith father. The family moved to Paris in 1900, and Gonzalez soon met Pablo PICASSO, who introduced him to CUBISM and who was, in turn, tutored in ironworking techniques by the young Spaniard. He was a Cubist painter throughout the 1920s, turning to sculpture in the early 1930s. From that period on, he created the Cubist and Constructivist-influenced iron sculptures for which he is famous (see CONSTRUCTIVISM). Conceived as drawings in space, these semi-abstract works often suggest human figures. Considered one of the most innnovative sculptors of the 20th century, he was important in the development of such contemporary artists as David Smith and Anthony Caro. Among his best known works are *Woman Doing Her Hair* (1936, Museum of Modern Art, N.Y.C.) and *Montserrat* (1936–37, Stedelijk Museum, Amsterdam).

Gonzalez, Richard Alonzo "Pancho" (1928–). U.S. tennis player. Gonzalez dominated men's professional tennis throughout the 1950s. He won two U.S. singles titles and led the U.S. to a Davis Cup victory before turning professional in 1949. Speedy of both foot and serve, he won the U.S. professional title a record eight times, and was still able to defeat much younger opponents until he retired at the age of 41 in 1969.

Goodall, Jane (1934–). British zoologist known for her ground-breaking studies of the behavior of chimpanzees. Since the 1960s, Goodall has spent much time in Africa living in close contact with chimpanzees and observing their behavior. Her discoveries have greatly increased human knowledge of primates. Goodall's work became widely known through *National Geographic* magazine (see NATIONAL GEOGRAPHIC SOCIETY), and she is widely considered the world's foremost authority on these animals. (See also Dian FOSSEY.)

Goodhue, Bertram Grosvenor (1869–1924). American architect whose work developed from eclecticism toward a creative proto-MODERNISM, who is also known as a graphic and type designer of some importance. Trained as a draftsman in the offices of James Renwick (1818–95) in New York and in the Boston office of Ralph Adams CRAM (1863–1942), Goodhue became a specialist in Gothic-style eclecticism. Promoted to a partner in Cram, Goodhue & Ferguson, he remained with that firm until 1913. His major work during that period was St. Thomas Church in New York (1914), a large, handsome neo-Gothic work. He was chief architect for the 1915 Panama-Pacific exhibition in San Diego, California, working there in an eclectic Spanish style. His St. Bartholomew's Church (1919) in New York is an outstanding work in eclectic Byzantine style. As a graphic designer, Goodhue was influenced by the Arts and Crafts movement and the ideas of William Morris. Goodhue's last major work in architecture was the Nebraska State Capitol building (1922) in Lincoln, Nebraska.

Goodman, Benny (1909–1986). The "King of Swing"; one of jazzdom's transcendent figures. Acknowledged as the single most important force in popularizing the uncompromising big band jazz style that coalesced as the SWING ERA in 1935, Goodman's flawless clarinet solos and his highly disciplined big bands set still-peerless

Clarinetist Benny Goodman, known as "The King of Swing," was the first white bandleader to feature black musicians.

standards. Goodman was also the first prominent white band leader to feature black artists such as pianist Teddy WILSON, vibraphonist Lionel HAMPTON and guitarist Charlie Christian. Goodman received his first important training in his hometown of Chicago, from classical clarinetist Franz Schoepp, and is significant as the first jazz musician to attain unqualified success as a classical performer. In 1938, he recorded Mozart's Clarinet Quintet with the Budapest String Quartet. Goodman commissioned "Contrasts" by Bela BARTOK, which he premiered at CARNEGIE HALL in 1939; other clarinet concerto commissions were filled by Aaron COPLAND (1947) and Paul HINDEMITH (1947). Goodman's greatest recognition, however, was as a jazz artist whose small groups (the trios and quartets) and big bands were models of precision and virtuosic interplay. In spite of the swing era's demise in the mid-1940s, Goodman remained a highly successful performer whose ad hoc combos and bands reached audiences throughout the world during the postwar decades. *The Benny Goodman Story* (1956), starring Steve ALLEN, is a better than average HOLLYWOOD movie, with Goodman's clarinet swinging throughout the soundtrack. Goodman's papers and recordings are housed at Yale University.

For further reading:

Collier, James Lincoln, *Benny Goodman and the Swing Era*. New York: Oxford University Press, 1989.

Goodman, Paul (1911–1972). American author and social critic. Goodman's espousal of New Left causes won him a large following among American college students in the late 1960s. He was an early opponent of American involvement in the VIETNAM WAR (see ANTIWAR MOVEMENT). He published hundreds of articles and books in a wide range of intellectual disciplines.

"Goon Show, The". A comic British radio show that aired on the BBC from 1949 to 1960, the program was the brainchild of comedians Peter SELLERS, Spike MILLIGAN, Harry Secombe and Michael Bentine. The show was the most influential comedy program in British radio history, paving the way for such later comedy hits as the stage revue BEYOND THE FRINGE and the television program MONTY PYTHON'S FLYING CIRCUS. With its zany, off-the-wall humor, the show became a phenomenal success, achieving cult status.

Goossens, Leon (Jean) (1897–1988). English oboist. Goossens's career, spanning seven decades, helped redefine the potential of the oboe. Among the composers who dedicated works to Goossens were Benjamin BRITTEN, Francis POULENC and Sir Edward ELGAR. In the 1960s a serious car accident injured his teeth and lips, but within two years he returned to the concert stage after developing a new technique of lip control. His family included noted conductor Sir Eugene Goossens and the harpists Marie and Sidone Goossens.

Gorbachev, Mikhail (Sergeyevich) (1931–). Soviet political leader. Born near Stavropol, he studied law in Moscow, joined the Communist Party at the age of 20 and became a party leader in his native province. Coming to the attention of national party leaders, he was named to the party's Central Committee in 1971 and was put in charge of Soviet agriculture in 1978. A protege of Yuri ANDROPOV, he became the U.S.S.R.'s economic planner after his mentor was named Communist Party general secretary in 1982. After the death of Andropov (1984) and of his successor, Konstantin CHERNENKO (1985), Gorbachev became secretary general of the party—and, as such, leader of the Soviet Union. In 1988, he became chairman of the Presidium, functioning as president of the U.S.S.R. Later that year, the powers of the presidency were greatly expanded as a result of constitutional amendments proposed by Gorbachev himself, and in 1989 he was elected president (officially, chairman of the Supreme Soviet).

Soviet leader Mikhail Gorbachev, whose reforms led to profound changes in the U.S.S.R. after 1985.

Nothing in his background could have prepared the people of the U.S.S.R. for the sweeping changes Gorbachev would bring to the nation. Faced with a moribund economy, he instituted revolutionary changes in the communist system, announcing a restructuring (PERESTROIKA) and moving toward decentralization and privatization. At the same time, he called for an openness in government operation, a policy known worldwide as GLASNOST, and moved toward a more open and less repressive system of handling domestic affairs and matters of dissidence. This policy was extended to individuals and to the U.S.S.R.'s restive constituent republics, who were given widely increased autonomy (but some of whose calls for independence were met with violence in the early 1990s).

In international affairs, Gorbachev moved to improve relations with Western nations. Reducing defense spending and trying to bolster the failing economy, he called for increased trade and financial interaction, and in a series of meetings with U.S. President Ronald REAGAN (1985, 1986, 1988) successfully sought closer ties with the U.S. In 1987 Gorbachev and Reagan signed a treaty calling for the elimination of intermediate-range missiles, and in the following two years he withdrew Soviet troops from AFGHANISTAN. For these efforts, Gorbachev was awarded the 1990 NOBEL PRIZE for peace.

His domestic and foreign policy initiatives provoked criticism from both hardliners, who opposed any deviations from classic communist ideology and any rapprochement with the West, and reformers, such as Boris YELTSIN, who called for more rapid and revolutionary change and for greater freedom in the constituent republics. As he entered the 1990s, Gorbachev was faced with ever-increasing economic problems and with independence movements in the Baltic and other republics that threatened to split the nation. His use of force in LITHUANIA and LATVIA early in 1990 brought wide condemnation, and his leadership fell under increased criticism as the U.S.S.R. tottered on the brink of economic and political collapse.

With progressives like Foreign Minister Eduard SHEVARDNADZE quitting Gorbachev's government in protest of his shifting policies, it was uncertain whether or not the Russian leader might be drifting toward the old style of repressive dictatorship. On the international front, he continued to maintain close relations with the West, joining in the UN resolution (1990) that condemned his former ally, IRAQ, and calling for the use of force in the Persian Gulf.

Gordimer, Nadine (1923–). South African author. Gordimer's novels and short stories reflect her concern with South African politics and their effect on the human spirit. She is an active opponent of

APARTHEID. Her works include the short stories, *The Soft Voice of the Serpent* (1953), and the novels, *A Guest of Honor* (1970), *The Conservationist* (1974), which was awarded the Booker Prize jointly; and *Sport of Nature* (1987).

Gordon, Dexter (1922–1990). An American JAZZ tenor saxophonist, Gordon the was one of the pioneers of the BE BOP style. Throughout the 1940s, he played with the bands of Lionel HAMPTON, Louis ARMSTRONG and Billy ECKSTINE. In the 1950s, he became addicted to drugs and served a brief prison sentence before moving to Europe and becoming part of the American jazz community there. In 1986, he played the semi-autobiographical role of an aging jazz musician in the film *'Round Midnight*. The performance won him an ACADEMY AWARD nomination.

Gordon, Max (1903–1989). Founder of the Village Vanguard in New York City, one of the most influential JAZZ clubs in the U.S. After establishing the club in 1935, he helped promote the careers of many jazz greats and other performers, including the young Judy Holliday, Barbra STREISAND, Lenny BRUCE, and Woody GUTHRIE.

Gordon, Ruth [Ruth Gordon James] (1896–1985). A respected actress later in life, Gordon was in fact a highly successful playwright and screenwriter in the 1940s and 1950s. Between minor acting stints on Broadway and in film, she wrote—frequently in collaboration with husband Garson KANIN—*A Double Life* (1948), *Adam's Rib* (1949), *Pat and Mike* (1952) and several others. But it wasn't until she was 72 years old that she won public acclaim, winning the ACADEMY AWARD for best supporting actress for the occult-suspense film *Rosemary's Baby* (1968). This was followed in the 1970s and '80s by a string of "eccentric old lady" roles in films such as *Harold and Maude* (1971), *Where's Poppa?* (1978) and *My Bodyguard* (1980).

Gordon, Walter (Lockhart) (1906–1987). Canadian politician. In the 1950s Gordon chaired a royal commission on the Canadian economy and became an advocate of Canadian economic independence from the U.S. Finance minister under the Liberal government of Prime Minister Lester PEARSON from 1963 to 1965, his ideas on economic nationalism took root and became a major force in Canadian politics.

Gore, Sir (William) David Ormsby. See HARLECH, Lord.

Goremykin, Ivan Longinovich (1839–1917). Russian minister of the interior under Czar NICHOLAS II from 1895 to 1899 and chairman of the council of ministers in 1906 and again from 1914 to 1916. He was considered to have taken little action against RASPUTIN and was forced to resign.

Gorgas, William Crawford (1854–1920). American physician. Gorgas was born in Toulminville, Alabama, and received his medical degree from Bellevue Medical College in New York (1879). He was appointed to the U.S. Army Medical Corps the following year. In 1898, following the U.S. occupation of Havana in the Spanish-American War, he became the city's chief sanitary officer. Once Walter REED established the cause of yellow fever, Gorgas permanently rid the city of the disease by destroying mosquito breeding grounds and segregating patients. Gorgas became chief sanitary officer of the PANAMA CANAL Commission in 1904 and, despite administrative difficulties, successfully controlled malaria and yellow fever in the area, thus ensuring completion of the canal. He was appointed surgeon general of the Army in 1914 and, after 1916, was attached to the International Health Board.

Gorkin, Jess (1913–1985). American magazine editor. As editor of *Parade* magazine from 1949 to 1978, he guided it from a small Sunday magazine to the most widely circulated Sunday supplement in the U.S. Gorkin is credited with having originated the idea of a telephone **Hot Line** between Moscow and Washington; he proposed the idea in a *Parade* editorial in March 1960.

Gorky, Maxim [Aleksey Maximovich Pyeskov] (1868–1936). Russian novelist, autobiographer and essayist. Gorky, who first emerged as a major literary talent in the Imperial Russia of the 1900s, ended his career as the preeminent spokesman for culture under the Soviet regime of Josef STALIN. Gorky left his family home at age 12 and devoted long years to wandering, odd jobs and diverse human encounters. These years were recounted in his three-volume autobiographical series, *My Childhood* (1913), *My Apprenticeship* (1916) and *My Universities* (1922). Gorky, who as a young man was a protege of Anton CHEKHOV, scored his first major success with the play *The Lower Depths* (1902), which recounted the hardships of peasant life in realistic colloquial language and thus broke new ground in Russian theater. Gorky was a friend of Vladimir LENIN and enjoyed protected status after the RUSSIAN REVOLUTION of 1917. But his dissatisfaction with the new communist regime led to his voluntary exile from his homeland during the 1920s. In 1931 he returned to Russia, rendered praise to Stalin and articulated the theory of SOCIALIST REALISM that was to set the standard for publishable Soviet literature through the 1980s. In 1932, Gorky became the first president of the Union of Soviet Writers. The circumstances of Gorky's death remain unclear; there is a suspicion that he may have been a victim of Stalin.

Russian author Maxim Gorky articulated the theory of government-sanctioned "Socialist Realism" during the Stalin regime.

Gorlice. Polish town situated at the center of the country's petroleum industry, almost 60 miles southeast of Cracow. In the Dunajec Campaign of WORLD WAR I Gorlice was the scene of a May 1915 battle in which the Russians were driven back by Austro-German armies.

Gorodetsky, Sergei Mitrofanovich (1884–1967). Russian poet. His first book, *Yar* (1907), demonstrated his considerable promise as a Symbolist poet. His later work was disappointing. In 1912 Gorodetsky repudiated Symbolism, and together with Nicholas GUMILEV founded the Acmeist school (see ACMEISTS). After Gorodetsky had joined the Communist Party, he denounced any connection with the Acmeists, largely as a result of Gumilev's execution. His later collections of verse, *The Sickle* (1921) and *Mirolom* (1923), idealize the life of the Soviet workers.

Gorodok [Polish: Grodeck Jagiellonski]. Town in the Soviet Union's Ukraine, 16 miles west-southwest of LVOV. Formerly in Poland, Gorodok was an important Russian fortification in WORLD WAR I but nevertheless saw a Russian defeat on June 12, 1915.

Gorshkov, Sergei G(eorgievich) (1910–1988). Soviet admiral. As commander in chief of the Soviet Navy from 1956 to 1985, he transformed the U.S.S.R. from a nation with only a small coastal defense force into a nuclear-era sea power rivaled only by the United States. Many Western military experts regarded Gorshikov as a major contributor to modern naval strategy. His views were given seminal expression in his 1976 book *The Sea Power of the State*.

Gorz-Gradisca [Italian: Gorizia]. Former county and crownland of Austria, now Italy's Gorizia province, in the Friuli-Venezia Giulia region; on the Isonzo River, bordering on Yugoslavia. The scene of severe fighting during the Isonzo River campaign of WORLD WAR I, it was taken by the Italians in 1916, recaptured during the Austro-German Karst Drive of 1917, was taken again by Italy in 1918—and ceded to Italy by the 1919 Treaty of St. Germain. Following World War II, eastern Friuli was ceded to Yugoslavia (in 1947) but Gorizia remained Italian.

Gosplan. Acronym for State Planning Commission, founded in 1921, a group of government departments that plan and coordinate economic activities in the U.S.S.R. The Gosplan consists of three types of departments, according to regional differences and branches of the economy. The party leadership disap-

Klement Gottwald, communist president of Czechoslovakia from 1948 to 1953.

proved of Gosplan's first FIVE-YEAR PLAN, which provoked a wave of terror against some of those in charge. Since then, Gosplan has been directed by people from the party leadership. In 1960 responsibility for long-term economic planning was transferred to the *Gosekonomsoviet*, or state scientific economic council.

Gottwald, Klement (1896–1953). Czechoslovak communist leader, president of CZECHOSLOVAKIA (1948–53). Born into a peasant family in Moravia, Gottwald served in the Austrian army in WORLD WAR I. He joined the Czech Communist Party in 1921, becaming its secretary general in 1928. The following year he was elected to the Czech parliament. Gottwald spent WORLD WAR II in Moscow, where he edited a newspaper for Czechs in the Soviet Army. He became vice premier of Czechoslovakia after the war. When the Communist Party won 38 percent of the vote in the Czech elections of May 1946, Gottwald became premier, heading a coalition government. Two years later, with Soviet backing, he effected a coup d'etat and forced President Eduard BENES to accept a government composed entirely of Communists and their collaborators. In 1952, Gottwald purged his communist rival, party chief Rudolf Slansky, after charging him with treason and holding a show trial (see SLANSKY TRIAL). Gottwald was a strict Stalinist; ironically, he died after contracting pneumonia at Josef STALIN's funeral in Moscow (see STALINISM). Gottwald's rise to power has acquired notoriety in Czechoslovakia as a betrayal of democracy.

Goubau, Georg (1906–1980). German-born electronics engineer. A pioneer in microwave circuits, in the late 1940s Goubau developed an important message-transmission system for television and radio calls. This system enabled a single stand of wire to carry large volums of messages to isolated areas otherwise reached only by a coaxial cable. The invention was a milestone in the communications technology and foreshadowed the later development of FIBER OPTICS transmissions systems. Goubau wrote more than 60 scientific articles and received several awards for his scientific work.

Goudsmit, Samuel A(braham) (1902–1978). Dutch-born physicist. Goudsmit received his Ph.D. from the University of Leiden (1927), then immigrated to the U.S. He taught at the University of Michigan (1932–46) and Northwestern University (1946–48) before moving to Brookhaven National Laboratory (1948–70). In 1925 Goudsmit and George Uhlenbeck discovered that electrons in the nucleus of the atom rotate, thus becoming charged and creating a magnetic field. This discovery was important in understanding the structure of the atom. During WORLD WAR II Goudsmit worked on RADAR. In 1944 he became head of Project **Alsos,** a top-secret mission to find out if the Germans were making an ATOMIC BOMB. Goudsmit went to Europe with U.S. forces and inspected newly-captured areas for any evidence that the Germans were working on a bomb. He determined that they would not have an atomic bomb before the end of the war. Goudsmit was awarded the Medal of Freedom, and also received the National Medal of Science for his work.

For further reading:

Goudsmit, Samuel A., *Alsos*. New York: H. Schuman, 1947.

Mendelsohn, John (ed.), *Scientific and Technical Intelligence Gathering, Including the Alsos Mission*. New York: Garland Publishing, 1989.

Goudy, Frederic W. (1865–1947). American printer, typographer, and type designer known for a number of traditional roman typefaces. In 1903 Goudy set up the Village Press in a barn in Park Ridge, Illinois, where, with Will Ransom as a partner, he began to produce hand-printed books with bindings by his wife. His Goudy Old Style typeface of 1916 designed for American Type Founders is probably his best-known achievement, a classically elegant Roman face still frequently used. Garamont, Kennerly, and Goudy Trajan are other successful Goudy faces, the last based on the carved inscriptions on the Column of Trajan in Rome. Goudy was the author of a number of books on type and lettering and founded the magazine *Ars Typographica*. He won the Gold Medal of the American Institute of Graphic Arts (AIGA) in 1920.

Gould, Chester (1900–1985). American cartoonist. In 1931, while living in Chicago, Gould created DICK TRACY, the best-known of all comic strip detectives. The character was born out of Gould's hatred of such PROHIBITION-era gangsters as Al CAPONE. The strip was the first to present graphic violence. In the late 1950s, it was carried by close to 1,000 newspapers worldwide and read by 65 million people. Gould retired from drawing the strip in 1977.

Gould, Glenn (1932–1982). Canadian pianist and musical theorist, noted for his devotion to the music of J.S. Bach and for his musical and personal eccentricities. Some listeners believe Gould to have been one of the greatest musicians of the 20th century; others dismiss him as a crackpot. Born in Toronto, Gould was educated at the Toronto Royal Conservatory of Music, from which he graduated (the institution's youngest graduate ever) with high honors. He made his concert debut in 1947 playing Beethoven's Piano Concert No. 4 with the Toronto Symphony Orchestra; his first American performance was in Washington, D.C., in 1955. In 1956 he became the first North American pianist ever to play in the Soviet Union. Over the following decade, Gould built a substantial reputation through his concert appearances and recordings. However, increasingly ill at ease in the concert hall and convinced that a "perfect" performance could not be achieved in a "live" performance, after 1964 Gould refused to play in public. Thereafter, he made only recordings. The reclusive Gould also produced a documentary for Canadian television, "The Idea of North."

Gould's playing was marked by distorted tempi and idiosyncratic phrasing. He reportedly remarked that sound only interfered with music; his interpretations were attempts to get at the truth that he perceived behind the notes. At one early concert, conductor Leonard BERNSTEIN told the audience that he disagreed with Gould's interpretation of the piece they were about to play but thought that it deserved to be heard. Conductor George SZELL's remark about Gould was perhaps most telling of all: "That nut's a genius!" Gould's last recording was of Bach's *Goldberg Variations*—the first work he had ever recorded (1955).

Gould, Stephen Jay (1941–). American biologist and paleontologist. Born in New York City, Gould was educated at Antioch College and Columbia University. A working scientist with a clear and graceful prose style, he has been one of the country's most successful science popularizers. He has taught biology, geology and the history of science at Harvard since 1967, and is also the author of columns and essays that have appeared in many large-circulation magazines. In 1972 Gould and fellow-scientist Niles Eldredge posited a theory of evolution that suggested for numerous species a rapid evolution followed by a long period of relative genetic stagnation. This development, termed punctured equilibrium, remains a subject of intense scientific interest. Gould is the author of a number of books, some of them collections of his popular essays. Among his works are *Ontogeny and Phylogeny, The Panda's Thumb, The Flamingo's Smile* (1985) and *Wonderful Life* (1989).

Gowon, Yakuba (1934–). Head of the federal military government in NIGERIA (1966–75). An army officer involved in the successful coup against Tafawa BALEWA in 1966, Gowon succeeded the coup's initial leader, Major General Ironsi, who was killed a few months later. Between 1967 and 1970 Gowon's rule was dominated by civil war with the predominantly Ibo Eastern Region, which had proclaimed itself as independent BIAFRA. Economic difficulties led to another military coup in 1975, led by Brigadier Murtula Mohammed while Gowon was out of the country. Gowon retired to exile in the U.K.

GPU [Gosudarstvennoye Politicheskoe Upravleniye]. Abbreviation for "State Political Administration Soviet Security Service," which was founded in 1922, replacing the CHEKA. Its work was directed against the church, private entrepreneurs, KULAKS, the old intellectuals and former members of opposition parties. The GPU was also concerned with conflict within the party. In 1924 its name was changed to OGPU and in 1934 to NKVD before becoming the KGB in 1953. (See also SECRET POLICE.)

Grable, Betty (Elizabeth) (1916–1973). One of HOLLYWOOD's great glamour queens in the 1940s, Grable began performing at an early age. She studied ballet and tap dancing and—having lied about her age (she was only 13)—found work as a chorus girl in films and on Broadway. After being fired from four movie studios and a failed marriage with actor Jackie COOGAN, Grable suddenly became a national sensation as American servicemen's favorite pin-up girl during WORLD WAR II; she was also perhaps the prime beneficiary of the perfected Technicolor process in a string of successful musicals for 20TH CENTURY-FOX. Among her box-office smashes were films such as *Down Argentine Way* (1940), *Coney Island* (1943), *Pin-Up Girl* (1944), *The Dolly Sisters* (1945) and *How to Marry a Millionaire* (1953). In 1943 Grable married bandleader Harry JAMES.

Grace, Princess of Monaco [born Grace Kelly] (1928–1982). American-born film and stage actress. Grace Kelly began her career as a model, then acted on Broadway before turning to the movies and becoming one of the premier leading ladies of the American cinema in the 1950s. She projected a cool blonde elegance while bringing subtle emotionality to her roles. She remains especially well known for her roles in the Alfred HITCHCOCK films *Dial M for Murder* (1954), *Rear Window* (1954) and *To Catch a Thief* (1955) and won an ACADEMY AWARD as best actress for her role as the embittered wife of an alcoholic (played by Bing CROSBY) in *The Country Girl* (1954). Other films include *Fourteen Hours* (1951), *High Noon* (1952), *Mogambo* (1953), *The Bridges at Toko-Ri* (1955), *The Swan* (1956) and *High Society* (1956). In 1956 she left the cinema to marry Prince Rainier III of MONACO and became Princess Grace. She died in an auto accident in 1982. Her daughter, Princess Stephanie, has become an international celebrity.

Grade, (Baron) Lew [Lewis Winogradsky] (1906–). British impresario. The founder and chairman of Associated Television in Britain, Baron Grade created a show-business dynasty with his brothers Bernard and Leslie. After emigrating from Russia, he entered show business as a dancer, winning a World Charleston Competition (1926). A period as a talent agent led to his becoming a producer and establishing his own production company, now called the Grade Company (from 1985). He has produced such acclaimed films as *The Boys from Brazil* (1978) and *On Golden Pond* (1981), and such award-winning television specials as "Jesus of Nazareth" and "The Julie Andrews Show."

Ready for the ball, newly engaged Grace Kelly and Prince Rainier of Monaco exit her Manhattan apartment (1956).

Graebe, Herman (1901–1986). German engineer. As a civilian contractor for the Third Reich's Railroad Administration, he hired and protected hundreds of Jewish workers from the Nazis (see NAZISM) in WORLD WAR II. He subsequently became the only German to volunteer to testify for the prosecution at the NUREMBERG TRIALS. His testimony made his family's life in GERMANY untenable, and they moved to the U.S. in 1948. The Israeli government bestowed its highest honors on him in 1965.

Graf, Steffi (1969–). German tennis player. Graf became the first woman to permanently break the Evert-Navratilova domination of women's tennis. In 1982, she became the second-youngest player ever to reach the computer ranking system established in 1975. In 1986, she won her first singles championship and went on to win seven more that year, including victories over EVERT and NAVRATILOVA. In 1987, she won the French Open, her first grand-slam title. In 1988 she became only the third woman to complete a grand slam in a single season. She also won the 1988 Olympic championship.

Graf Spee. See Battle of the River PLATE.

Graham, Billy (William Franklin) (1918–). American Baptist clergyman and evangelist. Graham's personal charisma, religious fervor and skill at preaching have made him one of the most admired men in America and the best known evangelist worldwide. Ordained a Baptist minister in 1939, he gained national recognition during his 1949 crusade in Los Angeles. In 1950 he organized the Billy Graham Evangelistic Association and has conducted successful crusades around the world since then. Graham's message has also reached millions through radio, television and film programs, as well as through the print media. His many books include *Peace with God* (1953) and *How to Be Born Again* (1977).

For further reading:

Pollock, John Charles, *To All Nations: the Billy Graham Story*. New York: Harper & Row, 1985.

Graham, Martha (1894–1991). American dancer, choreographer, teacher and company director. Graham has been a major force in the founding and development of modern dance in America. She studied and danced with the Denishawn Dancers (1916–23), appeared in musical revues in New York City and taught at the Eastman School of Music before giving her first solo performance in 1926. She founded her School of Contemporary Dance in 1927, then formed her company and began regular performances in 1929. She developed a specific dance technique to express her "dance plays" which revolved around American and European myths. Often in collaboration with designer/sculptor Isamu NOGUCHI, composer Aaron COPLAND and musician Louis Horst, she has created over 160 works (dancing the lead role in many), including *Primitive Mysteries* (1931), *Letter to the World* (1940), *Appalachian Spring* (1944), *Seraphic Dialogue* (1955), *Clytemnestra* (1958), and *Lucifer* (1975). In 1973 she retired from dancing and thereafter focused on running her school and company. Such well-known dancers as Erick Hawkins and Merce CUNNINGHAM were trained by her. In 1976 Graham was awarded America's highest civilian honor, the Medal of Freedom.

Graham, Sheila [Lily Shiel] (1908?-1988). American writer. Born into poverty in a London slum, she immigrated to the U.S. in 1933 and became a newspaper columnist. Together with Louella Parsons and Hedda Hopper, Graham was one of a trio of Hollywood's most powerful gossip writers. Her affair with F. Scott FITZGERALD, who died in her arms in 1941, was the inspiration for her first book *Beloved Infidel*, published in 1958. She was the model for Kathleen, the heroine of Fitzgerald's novel *The Last Tycoon*.

Grainger, Percy (Aldridge) (1892–1961). Australian-American pianist and composer. Born in Melbourne, he was educated in Frankfurt. Greatly influenced by his friend Edvard Grieg, he took an interest in folk music, which was to become the abiding passion of his musical life. Grainger began his concert career in England in 1901, touring South Africa and Australia before settling in the U.S. (1914) and becoming a citizen. Grainger's light and spontaneous music is almost always based on folk themes, and he is best known for his settings of folk tunes from the British Isles. Among his works are *Irish Tunes from County Derry* (1909), *Song of Democracy* (1917) and *Suite on Danish Folksongs* (1937).

Gramsci, Antonio (1891–1937). Italian Marxist and political theorist. Educated at the University of Turin (1911–14), Gramsci was an associate of Palmiro Togliatti and became involved with the socialist politics of the 1920s. He was a cofounder of the newspaper *L'Ordine Nuovo* (1919) and of the Italian Communist Party (1921), which he headed from 1924. He served in the Italian Chamber of Deputies from 1924 to 1926, when he and other communists were arrested and jailed by the fascists. Remaining in prison until months before his death, Gramsci wrote the influential *Letters from Prison* (1947, tr. 1973) and *Prison Notebooks* (1948–57, tr. 1971).

Gran Chaco [Chaco]. Plains region of South America west of the Paraguay and Parana rivers; mostly in northern Argentina and western Paraguay but also in southern Bolivia. The present boundaries were settled upon in 1938—after the bloody CHACO WAR of 1932–35 between BOLIVIA and PARAGUAY.

Grand Coalition [German: *grosse Koalition*]. Term used in Central European politics to denote a coalition of two major parties, as opposed to a small coalition (*kleine Koalition*) of one major party and a minor party. Such a coalition, between the conservative Christian Democratic Union/Christian Social Union (CDU/CSU) and the Social Democratic Party (SPD) governed WEST GERMANY (1966–69) following the failure of the small coalition of CDU/CSU with the center-right Free Democratic Party (FDP). In 1969, the SPD and the FDP formed a small coalition and the Bundestag elected Willy BRANDT as chancellor. A grand coalition of the conservative OVP and the social democratic SPO governed AUSTRIA from 1945 to 1966.

Grand Couronne. Region of France east and northeast of NANCY. During a part of Germany's first campaign of WORLD WAR I (which they had foreseen as the only one necessary), the invaders attempted to capture Nancy from September 5 to 12, 1914, but were driven back by troops under French General De Castelnau.

Grandi, Dino (1895–1988). Italian fascist politician. He served as ambabsssador to Great Britain, justice minister and foreign minister under Benito MUSSOLINI. In 1943, he helped orchestrate Mussolini's downfall.

Grandma Moses [Anna Mary Robertson Moses] (1860–1961). American "primitive" landscape painter whose greatest measure of fame came during the last two decades of her long life. Actually, Moses despised the label, "primitive." "People come by the farm to look at the 'savage,'" she would laugh. "But my children are not amused." To put her longevity in perspective, she was five years old when President Lincoln was assassinated and 101 when astronaut Alan SHEPARD made his first manned space flight in 1961. She was a living link with a rapidly vanishing rural tradition. The titles of her more than 1200 paintings told the details of her idyllic childhood in Greenwich, New York, her years as farmwife and mother in the Shenandoah Valley, Virginia, and her last years in the tiny village of Eagle Bridge, New York—"Bringing in the Maple Sugar," "The Mailman Has Gone," "Joy Ride," "The Black Horses." "This whole paintin' business commenced when my arthritis flared up," she said in an article, "How I Paint" (1947). "I switched from yarn to paint for one reason only—you see, a needle is hard to hold. But you can get a good grip on a brush." Independent art agent Louis Calder one day found three of her tiny paintings in a local drugstore near Eagle Bridge, showed them to New York dealer Otto Kallir, and in 1940 Grandma had her first one-women show in New York. The critics argued, the viewers were delighted, she appeared on the covers of *Time* and *Life* magazines, Edward R. MURROW interviewed her on television in 1956, she met President TRUMAN, and she generally was astonished and delighted at all the fuss. When asked how she painted, she said simply, "From the top—down." However, there was no denying the masterful sense of form and organization and color.

Grange, Harold "Red" (1903–1991). Legendary American football player for the University of Illinois in the 1920s. Grange was popularly known as the "Galloping Ghost." In one of his most notable exploits, he scored four touchdowns and ran for 265 yards in the first 12 minutes of a game (against the University of Michigan in 1924). Grange joined the National Football League's Chicago Bears in 1925, giving the NFL a credibility it had lacked in its first few seasons. After a stint as a coach, he retired from the game in 1938 because of injuries. Grange tried a number of other pursuits (and even acted in a movie serial called *The Galloping Ghost* [1932]) and later became a radio and television commentator. He was a charter member of the Professional Football Hall of Fame in 1963.

Grant, Cary [born Archibald Leach] (1904–1986). British-born actor, one of the most popular film stars of the 20th century. In a HOLLYWOOD career that spanned more than three decades, Cary Grant was known as the personification of charm, wit and style. Born in Bristol, England, during the 1920s he alternated between British and American theater, mostly in musical comedy and vaudeville. He made his screen debut in 1932, and in 1933 was chosen by Mae WEST to play opposite her in *She Done Him Wrong*. The last of his 72 films was *Walk, Don't Run* (1966). Grant was equally adept as a leading man in screwball comedies as he was in suspense thrillers. He worked with most of the leading actresses of his time (he was especially effective opposite Katharine HEPBURN) and gave memorable performances directed by George CUKOR, Frank CAPRA, Howard HAWKS and Alfred HITCHCOCK. His most popular films included *The Awful Truth* (1937), *Bringing Up Baby* (1938), *His Girl Friday* (1940), *The Philadelphia Story (1940)*, *Suspicion* (1941), *Arsenic and Old Lace* (1944), *Notorious* (1946) and *North by Northwest* (1959). Grant retired at the height of his popularity and remained a legend. In 1970 he was given an ACADEMY AWARD for his "unique mastery of the art of screen acting."

Grant, Duncan (1885–1978). British artist and designer known for highly decorated work much at odds with the mainstream trend toward MODERNISM in the 1930s. Grant's work turned to textile and ceramic designs around 1912. In the 1920s and 1930s, he designed interiors, furniture, and such graphic materials as book jackets—always in an elaborately florid decorative vocabulary. Grant was associated with the BLOOMSBURY GROUP.

Grant, George (1897–1982). American politician. A Democrat from Alabama, Grant served in the U.S. House of Representatives from 1938 to 1965. He was best-known for his firm stance against "so-called civil rights legislation," which he considered anti-Southern. (See also CIVIL RIGHTS.)

Grant, George (1918–1988). Canadian philosopher and social commentator. An ardent nationalist, Grant lamented what he saw as the increasing U.S. dominance of Canada. He also addressed the dominance of technology, which he saw as destroying the human spirit. His books included *Lament for a Nation: The Defeat of Canadian Nationalism* (1965) and *Technology and Empire* (1969).

Grant, Maxwell. See Walter GIBSON.

Grant, William T. (1876–1972). American businessman and retailer, founder of Grant's department store chain. Grant opened his first department store in 1906 with fast-selling merchandise priced at 25 cents. In 1966, when he retired as chairman of the board at age 90, Grant's stores operated in 44 states and grossed $839.7 million. However, in the 1970s, new competition and financial loses forced W.T. Grant's to go out of business.

Granville-Barker, Harley (1877–1946). British theatrical actor, playwright, director and Shakespearean scholar. Granville-Barker was one of the leading forces in the British theater in the first decades of the 20th century. He first gained wide attention as an actor through his portrayal of Marchbanks in the premiere of *Candida* (1900) by George Bernard SHAW. From 1904 to 1907, Granville-Barker directed a number of premieres of Shaw's plays at the Royal Court Theatre in London. He also scored successes with his own plays, most notably *The Voysey Inheritance* (1905) and *The Madras House* (1910). Granville-Barker was also well-known for his productions of the works of Shakespeare, in which he insisted on a close adherence to the original text.

Grass, Gunter (1927–). German novelist, poet, playwright and essayist. Grass is one of the most prominent German authors of the latter half of the 20th century. He achieved international fame with his first novel, *The Tin Drum* (1959), which depicted the chaos and shame that dominated GERMANY during WORLD WAR II. That work drew from Grass' own difficult experiences as an adolescent boy attempting to survive in wartorn Germany. Other novels by Grass include *Cat and Mouse* (1961), *Dog Years* (1963), *Local Anaesthetic* (1969), *The Flounder* (1977) and *The Meeting at Telgte* (1979). Grass also achieved success as a playwright with *The Plebeians Rehearse the Uprising* (1966). *In the Egg and Other Poems* (1977) contains a representative selection of his verse. Grass has been active in postwar German politics as a supporter of the Social Democratic Party.

Grasso, Ella T. (1919–1981). American politician who was the first woman ever to be elected governor of a U.S. state without succeeding her husband in office. A Connecticut Democrat, Grasso held various state offices (1952–70) and served in the U.S. House of Representatives (1971–75). As governor of Connecticut (1975–80), she was in the mainstream of the Democratic political establishment, advocating liberal social programs while holding down state spending. She resigned from office halfway through her second term when she fell ill with cancer.

Grateful Dead, The. American rock and roll band. Since its formation in the mid-1960s in San Francisco during the rise of the psychedelic music era, the Grateful Dead has remained a powerful force in American ROCK AND ROLL. Indeed, the Dead—as the band is known by its fans—is one of the most popular live acts in rock history, and draws fans both young and old to its perpetually sold-out shows. While certain Dead personnel have changed over the years, the principal band members have remained guitarist and vocalist Jerry GARCIA, drummers Mickey Hart and Bill Kreutzmann, bassist Phil Lesh, and guitarist Bob Weir. Lyricist Robert Hunter has collaborated frequently with Garcia on Dead songs, while lyricist John Barlow has done the same with Weir. While live performance—and not recordings—remain the strength of the Dead, the band has produced a large number of albums. Notable among them are *Anthem of the Sun* (1968), *Live/Dead* (1970), *Workingman's Dead* (1970), *American Beauty* (1970), *In the Dark* (1987) and *Dylan and the Dead* (1988), a collaboration with Bob DYLAN.

Graves, Michael (1934–). American architect and designer known for his leading role in the development of the design direction generally called POSTMODERNISM. Graves was trained as an architect at the University of Cincinnati and at Harvard, graduating in 1959. He worked for a time in the office of George Nelson in New York and then, in 1960, went to Rome for two years at the American Academy on a Prix de Rome fellowship. In 1962 he returned to Princeton, N.J., to take a teaching post at Princeton University and to establish a practice. In the 1970s he became known as one of the New York Five (also informally called "The Whites"), a group recognized for their abstract and puristic work in a Late Modern vocabulary. Toward the end of the 1970s, raves pulled away from this group. Graves has completed a number of residential projects, shops, and showrooms and has been at work on designs for the expansion of the Whitney Museum in New York, which involves a major addition to the existing structure by Marcel BREUER. He has received many honors and awards, including seven Honor Awards from the American Institute of Architects and the Brunner Memorial prize from the American Academy and Institute of Arts and Letters. Two volumes titled *Michael Graves: Buildings and Projects* published in 1983 and 1988 document his work.

German author Gunter Grass (left) after receiving an honorary degree from Harvard University (June 17, 1976).

Graves, Morris (1910–). American painter. Born in Fox Valley, Oregon, he studied with Mark Tobey, who introduced him to the delicate calligraphic "white writing" he later employed in his ethereal paintings. Interested in the philosophies of the Orient, with an emphasis on Zen Buddhism, Graves traveled widely in the East and in Europe before settling in the wilds of Washington state. His first one-man show was held in Seattle in 1936. Graves' most memorable paintings contain the beautifully drawn, ghostly birds that have become emblematic of his enigmatic work. Among his characteristic works are *Bird Singing in the Moonlight* (1938–40), *Blind Bird* (1940), both in the collection of New York's Museum of Modern Art, and *Spirit Bird* (1954).

Graves, Robert (von Ranke) (1895–1985). British poet. Graves spent most of his life on the Spanish island of Majorca, taking up residence there in 1929. He was considered by many to be second only to William Butler YEATS among 20th-century authors of love poetry in English. Although he considered himself primarily a poet, Graves was also a distinguished prose stylist and a noted classical scholar, translator and historical novelist. He wrote well over 100 individual volumes. Some 40 years after their first publication, his two novels about the Roman Emperor Claudius, *I, Claudius* (1934) and *Claudius the God* (1934), became the basis for an extremely successful BBC miniseries in the 1970s. Among the best known of his other books were his 1929 autobiography *Goodbye to All That* and his highly speculative and controversial 1948 study of poetic myth, *The White Goddess*.

For further reading:

Graves, Richard Perceval, *Robert Graves*. New York: Viking Penguin, 1990.

Graves, Richard Percival, *Robert Graves: The Years with Laura, 1926–1940*. New York: Viking, 1990.

Seymour-Smith, Martin, *Robert Graves: His Life and Works*. New York: Paragon House, 1987.

Gray, Ellen (1878–1976). Irish-born interior, furniture, and architectural designer whose Paris-based career spanned a stylistic range from ART DECO to the MODERNISM of the INTERNATIONAL STYLE. Gray studied at the Slade School of Art in London before moving to Paris in 1902. After World War I, her work was extended to include the design of carpets in abstract patterns and interior design and decoration. She opened her own Paris gallery in 1922 to show her furniture, lamps, carpets, and lacquer work. Her work was admired by such leading modernists as J.J.P. Oud and LE CORBUSIER. Her furniture design used glass, mirror, ALUMINUM, and CHROMIUM-plated metal in geometric forms typical of the modernism of the 1930s. In spite of her outstanding work, Gray was largely forgotten after World War II; her name scarcely figures in most histories of the period. She was rediscovered in the 1960s and is now viewed as a significant figure in the development of modern design. Gray was a lively figure, known as a great beauty as well as an adventurous personality—an aviation enthusiast who made an English Channel crossing in a balloon in 1909 with the Hon. C.S. Rolls of Rolls-Royce fame.

Gray, Francine du Plessix (1930–). Franco-American journalist and author. Gray started her journalistic career working for United Press International, and later became a columnist for THE NEW YORKER. Grey's first books were non-fiction and include *Divine Disobedience: Profiles in Catholic Radicalism* (1970) and *Hawaii: The Sugar-Coated Fortress* (1972). Her first novel, *Lovers and Tyrants* (1976), is a highly-autobiographical collection of chronological pieces following the life of the heroine, Stephanie. The novel's theme, that women are held back by those who profess to love them, struck a feminist chord of the time, and was praised for its intelligent writing (see FEMINISM). Later works include the novel *World Without End* (1981) and the non-fiction, *Soviet Women: Walking the Tightrope* (1990).

Gray, Simon James Holliday (1936–). British playwright and novelist. Himself a lecturer in English, Gray is best known for his popular and acclaimed plays about academia and British middle-class life. These include *Butley* (1971), *Otherwise Engaged* (1975), and *Quatermaine's Terms* (1981), which was later serialized by the BBC. Gray also successfully adapted *The Idiot* by Dostoevsky for the National Theatre in 1970. Other works include the plays *Wise Child* (1967) and *The Common Pursuit* (1988).

Graziano, Rocky [born Thomas Rocco Barbella] (1921–1990). American boxer. For much of the 1940s and 1950s Graziano reigned as middleweight boxing champion, compiling a record of 67 wins, 10 losses and six draws from 1942 to 1952. Although he was not noted for his boxing skills or finesse, his brawling style made him a fan favorite. Three of his bouts, with Tony Zale in 1946, 1947 and 1948, were considered classics. In 1956, his autobiography *Somebody Up There Likes Me* was made into a film starring Paul NEWMAN. Graziano went onto a successful career as an entertainer and commercial spokesman. He was elected to the Boxing Hall of Fame in 1971.

Great Books Program. A foundation organized in Chicago in 1947 with Dr. Robert Maynard HUTCHINS, former president of the University of Chicago, as its chairman to promote the reading of a list of classics compiled by Mortimer J. ADLER. Groups formed across the country to read and discuss the works. The foundation, in conjunction with the *Encyclopaedia Britannica* Educational Corp. and the University of Chicago published a series, *Great Books of the Western World*, which was sold with a two-volume Syntopicon index. The series was edited by Hutchins and Adler.

Scenes like this, of unemployed in New York City, were common throughout the world during the Great Depression of the 1930s.

Great Depression. A worldwide economic crisis during the 1930s. In its magnitude and effects, the Great Depression is considered the 20th century's most severe peacetime crisis. Millions of people lost their jobs, their homes and their savings, and large segments of the economy came to a virtual standstill. The STOCK MARKET CRASH OF 1929 is generally considered to mark the beginning of the Great Depression, while the onset of WORLD WAR II is regarded as its end point. The causes of the Great Depression are not easily understood. Unsound business practices (notably, a widespread reliance on easy credit without the backing of actual wealth), high tariffs and agricultural dislocation as early as the boom period of the 1920s helped set the groundwork for economic depression. At the onset of the Depression, U.S. President Herbert HOOVER believed that the American economy would recover on its own without government intervention. As the Depression deepened, he created the Reconstruction Finance Corporation to provide loans to distressed banks and businesses. In 1932, Franklin D. ROOSEVELT was elected president of the U.S. on his promise to take decisive action to end the Depression. In his first HUNDRED DAYS in office he prompted Congress to enact far-reaching legislation—known collectively as the NEW DEAL—to provide public relief, create new jobs and stimulate business. Although the New Deal policies did help many Americans, the depression continued through the 1930s, affecting virtually every country in the world. In many areas economic weakness bred political turmoil. In GERMANY, the chaos of the Great Depression created conditions that brought Adolf HITLER to power, while in JAPAN the military gained strength. Thus, the anxieties of the Great Depression helped sow the seeds of World War II.

For further reading:

Garraty, John A., *The Great Depression*. New York: Doubleday, 1987.
Galbraith, John Kenneth, *The Great Crash of 1929*. Boston, Mass.: Houghton Mifflin, 1988.

Great Gatsby, The. Novel of 1925 by F. Scott FITZGERALD, considered a classic of 20th-century American literature. The novel is narrated by Nick Carroway, who tells the story of Jay Gatsby, who has mysteriously amassed a fortune and bought a Long Island estate, and is intent upon pursuing Daisy Buchanon, a distant cousin of Carroway. The novel depicts the extravagance and self-destruction of the wealthy during the JAZZ AGE in the U.S., and culminates in a murder. Many critics considered *Gatsby* to be Fitzgerald's best and most fully realized book.

Great Leap Forward. Chinese slogan for a series of radical changes in social and economic policy between 1958 and 1961 under MAO TSE-TUNG. Private consumption was cut and material incentives withdrawn. Massive agricultural communes were set up and serviced by light industrial and construction projects. The program failed following bad harvests and the withdrawal of Soviet technical aid.

Great Purge. A repressive wave of terror (1934–1938) by which STALIN aimed at eliminating the opposition. It was followed by a number of show trials that resulted in the arrest, exile or death of about 8–10 million people. In 1934, following the death of Sergei KIROV, which was used as the pretext for the purge, only former political opponents were arrested; but the number and range increased and the arrests became almost indiscriminate. Guilt was established by extracting confessions through torture. The charges made against "the enemies of the people" ranged from treason to sabotage and espionage. NKVD tribunals sentenced the prisoners to death or to long terms of imprisonment in corrective labor camps. Stalin justified the purge by stating that, as progress toward full socialism is realized, the class struggle must be intensified. The result of the purge was to give Stalin supreme power.

For further reading:
Conquest, Robert M., *The Great Terror: A Reassessment*. New York: Oxford University Press, 1990.
———, *Stalin and the Kirov Murder*. New York: Oxford University Press, 1988.

Great Society. Term for the 1960s U.S. domestic programs of the JOHNSON administration. The phrase comes from a speech delivered by President Johnson on May 23, 1964. Some Great Society legislation included: in 1964—the CIVIL RIGHTS ACT; the Revenue Act, which reduced taxes; the Food Stamp Act; the Economic Opportunity Act (also called "the War on Poverty"). In 1965—MEDICARE and MEDICAID; the sweeping Elementary and Secondary Education Act; the Higher Education Act, which provided student aid; the creation of the Department of Housing and Urban Development; and the VOTING RIGHTS ACT OF 1965. In 1968—the Housing and Urban Development Act.

Great Train Robbery. Popular name for the robbery of a Glasgow-to-London mail train on August 8, 1963. The robbery was executed by a gang of 20 to 30 masked robbers some 35 miles northwest of London and netted more than $7 million, making it the largest armed robbery to date. Detectives investigating the crime discovered the robbers' hideout, an isolated rural English cottage, on August 13. In 1964, 12 Britons were found guilty of involvement in the robbery and sentenced to prison terms ranging up to 30 years. However, only about $1 million of the stolen money was ever recovered.

Grechaninov, Alexander Tikhonovich (1864–1956). Russian composer. He studied at the St. Petersburg Conservatory under Rimsky-Korsakov and at the Moscow Conservatory with Vassily Ilich Safonov. In 1922 he made his first European tour. He lived in Paris from 1925 and finally settled in the U.S. His works comprise operas, including *Dobrynya Nikitich* (1902) and *Sister Beatrice* (1912), five symphonies, chamber music, Catholic church music, piano pieces, songs and folk songs. He intended his *Missa Oecumenica*, which was performed in Boston in 1944, to unite all creeds, both Eastern and Western.

Greco, Jose (1919–). Spanish dancer. Greco studied Spanish dance with "La Argentinita" (Encarnacion Lopez Julvez) and partnered her from 1943 to 1945. He subsequentlty partnered her sister Pilar Lopez from 1946 to 1948, before forming his own Spanish dance company in 1949. His company has toured the world, and he has appeared in many films and television productions. Greco has become one of the most influential and popular Spanish dancers in America as well as worldwide.

Greco-Turkish War of 1921–22. Turkish resistance to Allied dismemberment of the OTTOMAN EMPIRE, led by Mustafa Kemal ATATURK, included expelling the Greek army from western Anatolia. Granted the Smyrna (Izmir) region by the TREATY OF SEVRES (1920), the Greeks attempted to gain Thrace and much of Anatolia. Despite inadequate supplies, Greek forces advanced on Eskisehir, were repulsed (January and March, 1921), but moved towards Ankara. Seriously defeated at Sakarya River (August 24–September 16, 1921), they began a year-long retreat to Smyrna, which Ataturk's forces besieged and captured September 11, 1922, killing thousands of Greeks. The TREATY OF LAUSANNE (July 24, 1923) ended the war, forcing Greece to remove all occupation forces, return eastern Thrace and Turkish islands, and exchange Greece's Turkish minority people for Greek inhabitants of the Ottoman Empire.

GREECE

Greece (Hellenic Republic). Greece is located on the southern end of the Balkan peninsula in southeast Europe and covers a total area of 509,930 square miles, including over 1,400 Aegean and Ionian islands. During the BALKAN WARS (1912–13) the country acquired Crete to the south and the eastern Aegean islands. After fighting with the Allies during World War I, Greece entered a period of political turmoil, swinging from a monarchy under George II (1922–24) to a republic (1924–35) to restoration of the king (1935–40). German occupation of Greece during WORLD WAR II gave way to the GREEK CIVIL WAR between communists and pro-democracy forces, which ended with the restoration of the monarchy in 1946. Subsequent elections brought power struggles, military coups and the eventual exile of King CONSTANTINE II (1967). TURKEY'S invasion of CYPRUS in 1974 brought the end of military rule in Greece and in 1975 the adoption of a new constitution declaring a democratic republic. In 1981 Greece elected its first socialist government and joined the European Communities. Controversy over U.S. bases in Greece, a financial scandal involving government officials and another scandal surrounding powerful political leader George PAPANDREOU in 1988, plus a worsening economy, have dominated the political scene since 1983.

For further reading:
Clogg, Richard, *A Short History of Modern Greece*, 2nd ed. Cambridge: Cambridge University Press, 1987.
Woodhouse, C. M., *Modern Greece: A Short History*. London: Faber & Faber, 1986.

Greek Civil War. War of 1944–1949 between communists and pro-Western royalists in GREECE. In December 1944–January 1945, toward the end of WORLD WAR II, Greek communist guerrilla forces attempted to take over Greece, but were defeated. A British-arranged truce between leftists and moderates ultimately resulted in the restoration of the monarchy. In late 1946, communists reopened the war with support from ALBANIA, BULGARIA and YUGOSLAVIA. The Greek government, with British and American aid (the latter under the TRUMAN DOCTRINE), drove out the communist rebels with UNITED NATIONS support. The Greek com-

GREECE

1913	Greece acquires additional territory in Macedonia and Thrace following the Balkan Wars.
1917	Abdication of King Constantine I; Greece enters World War I on side of Allies.
1935	Restoration of monarchy under King George II.
1936	General Metaxas, named prime minister by George II, establishes fascist-style dictatorship.
1940	Greece repels attempted Italian invasion in World War II.
1941	Germany invades and occupies Greece.
1944-49	Civil War between communists and royalists; communists defeated.
1952	Greece joins NATO.
1964	Ascension of King Constantine II.
1967	Military coup brings right-wing colonels to power; constitutional rule suspended; Constantine II goes into exile after his failed attempt to depose the colonels.
1973	Monarchy formally abolished.
1974	War with Turkey over Cyprus leads to fall of military government; democratic government restored under Prime Minister Constantine Karamanlis.
1975	New constitution establishes a democratic republic.
1981	Greece joins European Community; socialist George Papandreou becomes prime minister.
1989	Papandreou steps down amid personal and political controversy.

munists announced the end of the war on October 16, 1949. About 50,000 combatants died in this conflict. The Greek Civil War was viewed as the first U.S. effort to halt the spread of COMMUNISM in the post-World War II era; it marked the opening phase of the COLD WAR.

Green, Henry [pen name of Henry Vincent Yorke] (1905–1974). British novelist. Widely admired by such contemporaries as Evelyn WAUGH and W.H. AUDEN, Green's work was little known in the U.S. until his early works were reissued in the late 1970's. His novels, which include *Blindness* (1926), *Back* (1946) and *Doting* (1952), explore all social classes and evidence Green's sensitivity to colloquial and idiomatic speech. *Loving* (1945), his most acclaimed work, depicts life in an Irish country house during the war. Green also wrote the autobiographical *Pack My Bags: A Self-Portrait* (1940).

Green, William (1873–1952). American labor leader. Born in Coshocton, Ohio, Green was a coal miner and a local miners' union leader while still a teenager, rising to become secretary-treasurer of the United Mine Workers of America (1912–24). In 1924 Green was elected to succeed the recently-deceased Samuel GOMPERS as president of the AMERICAN FEDERATION OF LABOR (AFL), a post he held until his death. During Green's period of leadership a rift between craft and industrial unions deepened, provoking a 1935 schism that resulted in the formation of the CONGRESS OF INDUSTRIAL ORGANIZATIONS (CIO). Green's labor movement philosophy is expressed in his book *Labor and Democracy* (1939).

green belt. Term, used in town planning, that describes a large tract of land around a city, on which building is not permitted. The green belt concept originated in the UNITED KINGDOM and was first put into practice after the end of World War II. British planners realized that cities ought not to spread out into the surrounding countryside through unlimited building, and that rural areas ought to be preserved. Relatively small NEW TOWNS were built in and around green belt areas to help relieve overcrowding in large existing cities, notably LONDON.

Greenberg, Hank (Henry Benjamin) (1911–1986). American baseball player. Greenberg led the American League in home runs five times while playing first base and outfield for the Detroit Tigers in the 1930s and 1940s. He was voted the American League's most valuable player in 1935 and 1940. In 1938, he hit 58 home runs, two shy of the 1927 record set by Babe RUTH. His career was plagued by injuries and interrupted by World War II, but his lifetime home run total was 331, with a lifetime batting average of .313. After his retirement in 1947, he held front-office jobs with the Cleveland Indians and Chicago White Sox. In 1956 Greenberg became the first Jewish player elected to the Baseball Hall of Fame.

Greene, Graham (1904–91). British novelist and man of letters. Greene is perhaps the preeminent British writer of the second half of this century. He is, beyond question, one of the most prolific and versatile writers of modern times, having created both serious novels and what Greene calls "entertainments," as well as screenplays, film criticism, political analyses, travel books, literary biographies, critical essays and an autobiography. Educated at Oxford, Greene converted to Roman Catholicism in 1926. The travails of political conscience and religious doubt are two recurring themes in his works. Major works of fiction by Greene include *Orient Express* (1933), *England Made Me* (1935), *The Power and the Glory* (1940), The Quiet American (1955), *Our Man in Havana* (1958), *The Honorary Consul* (1973), *The Human Factor* (1978), and *Monsieur Quixote* (1982). Greene has written two volumes of autobiography, *A Sort of Life* (1971) and *Ways of Escape* (1980). Greene was reportedly a candidate for the NOBEL PRIZE for literature on numerous occasions, but never received the award.

greenhouse effect. Term used to explain the theory of GLOBAL WARMING. According to many scientists, the greenhouse effect is caused by the buildup in the atmosphere of carbon dioxide from industry, agriculture and the burning of fossil fuels. The carbon dioxide causes heat from the sun to be trapped near the Earth's surface, much in the way that glass traps heat in a greenhouse. Scientific opinion as to whether there actually is a greenhouse effect is mixed. A UN report in 1990 concluded that the Earth's surface and lower atmosphere had warmed by 0.3 to 1.1 degrees Fahrenheit in the last century and could be expected to warm by another 2.7 to 8 degrees Fahrenheit in the next century. However, according to a study published in *Science* (March 30, 1990), microwave temperature data collected by U.S. weather satellites from 1979 through 1988 showed no evidence of a global warming from the greenhouse effect. If the "effect" proves valid, the greenhouse effect may have dire consequences for the Earth and its inhabitants in the next century.

Greenland. Bounded on the north by the Arctic Ocean and on the west, south and east by various arms of the North Atlantic, including Baffin Bay and the Greenland Sea, the island of Greenland covers 839,782 square miles—only 131,896 square miles of it free of ice. Ancient claims to the island by Denmark and Norway were resolved by the International Court of Justice in 1933, granting Denmark sovereignty. Greenland became an integral part of Denmark in 1953 and joined the various European Communities (EC), though its populace was opposed to this. Internal autonomy was achieved in 1979, resulting in the island's withdrawal from the EC in 1985. Recently, Greenland has been divided over the status of U.S. bases, established on the island during World War II.

Greenpeace. International organization known for its active efforts to protect the ocean environment and aquatic wildlife. Founded in Canada in 1969, Greenpeace has been at the forefront of the "save the whales" movement and worked for a worldwide ban on whale hunting. The group also attracted international attention in its efforts to stop the annual "cull" of baby seals off the coast of Newfoundland in the 1980s. Greenpeace does not rely solely on publicity to achieve its aims, but confronts hunters directly with its own fleet of boats. For example, in its "save the whales" campaign, Greenpeace boats mingle with boats of the hunting fleet and try to disrupt the hunt. Greenpeace became involved in an international incident in 1985 when one of its ships, the *Rainbow Warrior,* was sunk in Auckland harbor, New Zealand. The ship was about to sail into a nuclear test area in an effort to disrupt French atomic weapons testing in the South Pacific. It was subsequently revealed that French frogmen had sunk the ship on the orders of the French government, and the French defense minister was forced to resign.

Greens. Originally and principally, the German (originally West German) Ecology party, which first emerged as a political force in Bremen in 1979, when environmentalists and antinuclear groups won 5.9 percent of the seats in the Land (federal state) parliament. Greens were subsequently elected to other Land parliaments and to the BUNDESTAG, and similar parties had success in other West European countries. The **British Ecology Party** changed its name to the Greens in 1985.

Greensboro. U.S. city in north-central North Carolina, near Winston-Salem—scene of a 1979 anti-KU KLUX KLAN rally during which five participants were shot to death, allegedly by members of the Klan and the American Nazi Party.

Greenwich Village. Bohemian residential district of lower Manhattan in the U.S.'s NEW YORK CITY; extending south from 14th St. to Houston St. and west from Washington Square to the Hudson River. In recent decades "Greenwich Village" has come to signify three distinct areas: the West Village, roughly west of Seventh Avenue; Greenwich Village proper, west of Broadway; and the East Village, east of Broadway, also called the Lower East Side. An influx of foreign immigrants settled here after 1880, and by 1901 it was already famous as a hotbed of avant-garde artists, radicals and freethinkers. Its longtime reputation was reinforced in the Beat Era of the 1950s (see BEAT GENERATION) and the Flower-Power 1960s when the artists, poets and writers were joined by musicians, religious cultists, HIPPIES, homosexuals and just about anyone that the larger society considered different—all of it supported by cafes, galleries and clubs for jazz, folk and every other kind of music. Among the district's 20th-century residents were writers MILLAY, WHARTON, O'NEILL, DOS PASSOS, AUDEN, Dylan THOMAS; painters HOPPER and SLOAN; and journalist John REED.

Greer, Germaine (1939–). Australian author and feminist. Greer's controversial first book, *The Female Eunuch* (1971) brought her instant international celebrity and made her reputation as a leading figure in FEMINISM and the WOMEN'S MOVEMENT. The book argued that women's sexuality has been denied and misrepresented as passivity, and that the stereotypical feminine behavior societally imposed on women is essentially that of a eunuch. Her subsequent and varied works include *Sex and Destiny* (1984), *Shakespeare* (1986) and *Daddy, We Hardly Knew You* (1989). An English scholar, Greer was latterly a special lecturer at Newnham College, Cambridge.

Gregory, (Isabella) Augusta, Lady [nee Persse] (1852–1932). Irish playwright and patroness of the arts. An Irish nationalist instrumental in the IRISH LITERARY REVIVAL, Lady Gregory was a co-founder of the ABBEY THEATRE along with W. YEATS and J.M. SYNGE. Her many plays, which include *Spreading the News* (1904), *The Goal Gate* (1906) and *Dervorgilla* (1906) were written in Irish dialect and celebrated Irish tradition and folklore. She also translated the works of Moliere for the Irish theatre and collaborated with Yeats on numerous plays, including *Cathleen ni Houlihan* (1902). She successfully fought the censorship of Synge's PLAYBOY OF THE WESTERN WORLD and G.B. SHAW's *The Shewing up of Blanco Posnet.* Her house at Coole Park in County Galway was for many years a second home for some of IRELAND's leading literary figures. Lady Gregory recorded her memoirs of the early days of the Abbey in *Our Irish Theatre* (1913).

For further reading:

Kohfeld, Mary Lou, *Lady Gregory: the Woman Behind the Irish Renaissance.* New York: Atheneum, 1985.

Gregory, Cynthia (1946–). American ballerina. Known for her technical skill and purity of line in such classical ballets as *Swan Lake,* Gregory first danced with the San Francisco Ballet (1961–65). She joined AMERICAN BALLET THEATRE (ABT) in 1965 as a principal dancer and created roles in many ballets, including Alvin AILEY's *The River* (1971) and Rudolph NUREYEV's production of *Raymonda* (1975). Acclaimed as one of America's outstanding prima ballerinas, she dances in works from ABT's modern repertory, such as *Dark Elegies* and *Theme and Variations,* as well as in the classical ballets.

For further reading:

Gregory, Cynthia, *Cynthia Gregory Dances Swan Lake.* New York: Simon & Schuster, 1990.

Grenada. The most southerly of the Windward Islands in the eastern Caribbean Sea, Grenada has a total land area of 132.8 square miles, which includes the dependent islands of the Southern Grenadines to the north-northwest. Grenada attained full independence from Britain

U.S. soldiers hold prisoners at the Point Salines Airfield during the U.S. invasion of Grenada (Oct. 25, 1983).

in 1974, and Sir Eric Gairy became premier. His corrupt regime was overthrown in a bloodless coup in 1979 by left-wing rebels led by Maurice Bishop. Bishop's failure to draft a new constitution or to hold elections, as well as his growing alignment with CUBA, resulted in another coup in 1983 during which Bishop and his associates were murdered. A call for outside intervention led to the invasion of Grenada by troops from the UNITED STATES and other Caribbean countries in October 1983. Afterward, the constitution was restored, and elections were held in 1984. However, factional discord still plagues the government.

Grenfell, Joyce [Joyce Irene Phipps] (1910–1979). British actress and film comedienne. For more than 40 years, Grenfell was a popular fixture on stage, screen, radio and television. Her career included appearances in numerous revues, plays, one-woman shows, radio and television programs and international tours to Australia, Canada and the U.S. She also entertained Allied troops during WORLD WAR II. She used her long, toothy visage to create the character of a dotty, upper-class English spinster whom she made vastly popular with her audiences.

Gresley, (Sir) Herbert Nigel (1876–1941). British engineer known for the design of railroad locomotives, including streamlined types that achieved outstanding performance and speed. Gresley was in charge of locomotive design for the Great Northern Railway, and after World War I when British railway systems were reorganized, he became chief mechanical engineer for the newly created London & North Eastern Railway. In 1923, his design for a Pacific locomotive (with 4–6–2 wheel arrangement) became a new standard for both freight and passenger service. Beginning in 1932, a drive for speed records developed in English railroading, and in 1934, a Gresley Pacific pulling the *Flying Scotsman* reached a peak speed of 100 mph. The first streamlined Gresley Pacifics were of the A4 class of 1935, with the famous MALLARD setting a record speed of 126 mph in 1938. These locomotives were also notable for their reliability and performance in routine service in which they maintained high speeds over long runs in regularly scheduled service. Gresley was knighted in recognition of his achievements.

Gretzky, Wayne (1961–). Canadian ice hockey player. Born in Edmonton, Alberta, Gretzky is considered possibly the greatest player in the history of the game. He entered the National Hockey League in 1979 and played center for eight seasons for the Edmonton Oilers, leading them to four Stanley Cup championships. In 1988 he was traded to the Los Angeles Kings. On October 15, 1989, playing against his former team in his 780th game, he broke the NHL's all-time record for scoring points set by Gordie HOWE. Gretzky's lifetime record at the end of that game stood at 642 goals and 1,210 assists for a total of 1,852 points. Gretzky was the NHL's scoring leader every season from 1981 through 1987 (an NHL record) and won the Hart Trophy for most valuable player each of those years as well as in 1989, also a record.

Wayne Gretzky (left), considered by many to be the finest hockey player ever, in action.

Grey, Sir Edward [Viscount Grey of Fallodon (1916)] (1862–1933). British statesman. Educated at Oxford, he was elected to Parliament as a Liberal in 1885, becoming foreign secretary in the years preceding WORLD WAR I (1905–16). During this period, he supported France in the Moroccan crises of 1905 and 1912, concluded the ANGLO-RUSSIAN ENTENTE of 1907 and convened the London Peace Conference (1912–13) to negotiate an end to the BALKAN WARS. While hating the idea of war, the German violation of Belgian independence caused Grey in 1914 to urge Britain's entrance into WORLD WAR I. After the war, he championed the LEAGUE OF NATIONS and served as a special ambassador to the U.S. from 1919 to 1920.

Grey, Zane (1875–1939). American author of popular western fiction and nonfictional works on deep-sea and fresh-water fishing. After graduating from the University of Pennsylvania in 1896, Grey practiced dentistry before turning to writing. He published his first novel, *Betty Zane,* in 1904 and his famous *Riders of the Purple Sage* in 1912. Grey swiftly became a staple on national bestseller lists and his works have remained continuously in print.

Grierson, John (1898–1972). Motion picture producer, director and prominent leader in the British and Canadian documentary film movements. The son of a Scots schoolmaster, he studied philosophy at Glasgow University and social sciences in Chicago. Convinced that cinema presented an unparalleled mode of rhetoric and persuasion, he produced films about British trade and unity for the Empire Marketing Board (EMB). *Drifters* (1929) his first film, eschewed the romantic approach to picturesque fishing villages and replaced it with a contemporary "epic of steam and steel," depicting the modernization of the fishing trade. With his EMB Film Unit, an important group of rising young filmmakers, he produced over a hundred such films between 1930 and 1933. (After 1934 the Film Unit moved to the General Post Office and became known as the CROWN FILM UNIT.) In 1938 Grierson relocated to Canada, where he became film commissioner and the founder of the world-renowned Canadian Film Board. He continued throughout the postwar years to work tirelessly on behalf of the documentary film, forming International Film Associates in 1945, the Mass Communications and Public Information Department for UNESCO, and producing television documentaries in Scotland. By contrast to colleague Robert FLAHERTY (with whom he worked for a brief period in the early 1930s), Grierson placed document and ideology ahead of poetry and entertainment. "I look on cinema as a pulpit," he said in his numerous treatises and theoretical writings, "and use it as a propagandist." The working person was his constant subject and his sympathies with labor issues and problems frequently ran him afoul of the government agencies that employed him. It was Grierson who first coined the term "documentary"—in a 1926 review of Flaherty's *Moana*.

Griffes, Charles Tomlinson (1884–1920). American composer. Born in Elmira, N.Y., Griffes studied in Berlin, where he was a pupil of Engelbert Humperdinck, who encouraged his work as a composer. After returning to the U.S., Griffes taught music in a Tarrytown, N.Y., boys school until his death. Influenced by French and Russian music, he developed an impressionist style that later matured into an extremely individualistic mode of expression. His numerous compositions include the *Roman Sketches* (1915–16), piano pieces that include the well-known *White Peacock;* the orchestral work *The Pleasure-Dome of Kubla Khan* (1920) and the piano sonata (published 1921). Among his other works are chamber music, pieces for the theater and songs.

Griffin, John Howard (1920–1980). American author. In 1959 Griffin decided to get a firsthand picture of the treatment of blacks in the American South by posing as a black man. He temporarily altered his skin color by using chemicals and ultraviolet light, then traveled throughout the South for six weeks. He chronicled his experiences in the book *Black Like Me*, which sold more than a million copies over the next several years and was made into a film.

Griffith, Arthur (1872–1922). Irish statesman and nationalist. Griffith was a pivotal figure in the Irish HOME RULE movement. In 1905 he helped found SINN FEIN, a political party that advocated a separate Irish Parliament. When in 1916 he was elected to Parliament (British), he refused to serve. Instead he helped found the Irish revolutionary assembly, the DAIL EIREANN. He was imprisoned by the British several times (1916–18). In 1921 Griffith lead the delegation that negotiated the Treaty of Westminster, which created the Irish Free State.

Griffith, D(avid) W(ark) (1875–1948). America's greatest filmmaker during the SILENT FILM period and one of the most important influences on the course of international cinema. Raised in Louisville, Ky., under the influence of his father, a Civil War veteran, Griffith was steeped in the romance and chivalry of the Old South. Under the stage name of Lawrence Griffith he unsuccessfully tried acting and writing for the stage. Reluctantly, he turned to the new medium of motion pictures and gained a featured role in an Edwin S. Porter film, *Rescued from an Eagle's Nest* (1907). However, it was as a director, not an actor or writer, that Griffith soon made his way. From 1908 to 1913 he directed virtually all the short films for the popular BIOGRAPH COMPANY, forging a stock company that included Lillian and Dorothy GISH, and consolidating most of the technical and stylistic advances in the medium—dramatic use of close-ups, parallel editing, moving camera, historical reenactments, multiple-reel narratives and flashbacks. He brought a stinging satiric lash to the traditional forms of melodrama he knew from his itinerant years on the stage. His greatest international success and his most ambitious films come from the 1913–1924 period. He released through Mutual, UNITED ARTISTS, and PARAMOUNT classics like THE BIRTH OF A NATION (1915), *Intolerance* (1916), *Broken Blossoms* (1919), *Way Down East* (1920), *Orphans of the Storm* (1922), *America* (1924) and *Sally of the Sawdust* (1924); in 1919 he moved to his own production facility in Mamaroneck, N.Y. Often working from sketchy scripts and frequently with his favorite cameraman, G.W. ("Billy") Bitzer, Griffith produced a body of work that vaulted American cinema into worldwide prominence and prestige. Griffith's last years, however, saw a decline in his personal fortunes and an increasingly sophisticated audience impatient with his by-now "old-fashioned" style. Viewers laughed at his last film *The Struggle* (1931), a creaky drama of alcoholism. Except for an "honorary" ACADEMY AWARD in 1935 for his "distinguished creative achievements," Griffith spent his last years in relative obscurity. He died, bitter, lonely, and virtually forgotten, from a cerebral hemorrhage in a Hollywood hotel room at age 73.

Grigorenko, Pyotr Grigorevich (1907–1987). Soviet military hero and dissident. Grigorenko won distinction in WORLD WAR II, but was later critical of the Soviet establishment. In 1961 he was stripped of his rank of major general, and was later committed to a series of mental hospitals—standard punishment for political dissidents in the U.S.S.R. at that time. After being allowed to go to the U.S. for medical treatment in 1977, he was stripped of his Soviet citizenship.

Grimes, Martha (?–). American novelist. Like P.D. JAMES, Grimes followed the model established earlier in the century by Dorothy SAYERS, writing detective novels of literary merit. Her first 11 novels, whose titles are the names of pubs featured in the text, are set in an England both real and imagined. Rich in geographical and psychological detail, as well as wit, they explore human fallibility, familial relationships, childhood and the nature of good and evil. Grimes shows that trust is the basis of social order, although it can be exploited. She taught writing at Johns Hopkins University. Her books include *The Man With a Load of Mischief* (1981), *The Old Fox Deceived* (1982), *The Old Silent* (1989) and *The Old Contemptibles (1991)*.

Grin, Alexander [Alexander Stepanovich Grinevsky] (1880–1932). Russian writer. As a schoolboy Grin read avidly, although he was at times suspended from school for laziness. After a short time in the merchant marine he led a tramp's existence, and finally started a career as a writer. After fighting with the Red Army, ill and penniless he was rescued by Maxim GORKY. A chronic alcoholic, he spent the last few years of his life as a failed writer and geography teacher, turned to carving for a living, and died in poverty. His stories, frequently romantic and exotic in flavor, are underestimated by Soviet critics, but they convey the turmoil the Soviet Union was undergoing. His best known works include *The Ratcatcher* (1924), *Fantastic Tales* and *The Road to Nowhere* (1930).

Gris, Juan. Spanish painter. Gris was a key figure in the artistic school of CUBISM and was heavily influenced by Pablo PICASSO. Gris first came to Paris in 1906 and lived for a time as Picasso's neighbor. But Gris did not begin to paint until 1910. His first major painting, *Hommage a Picasso*, was shown at the influential *Salon des Independants* exhibition of 1912. Gris is considered representative of the "synthetic" phase of Cubism that followed after the initial "analytic" phase developed by Picasso and Georges BRAQUE. For Gris, the primary function of the artist was to transform the general concepts of the intellect and the imagination into unique yet comprehensible concrete forms. He was fond of comparing painting to mathematics and architecture in that it was a systematic means of representing the world and the evolving nature of human truth.

Grishchenko, Anatoly (1935–1990). Soviet aviator. He became a hero by flying his helicopter repeatedly over the site of the 1986 CHERNOBYL nuclear power plant disaster and dumping tons of sand and cement over the smoldering reactor. His actions were credited with helping to limit the effects of the disaster. He was given the SOVIET UNION's highest award for heroism. His death from leukemia was believed to have been radiation-induced.

Grissom, Virgil "Gus" (1926–1967). U.S. astronaut; one of the seven original MERCURY astronauts selected by NASA in April 1959. Grissom died in America's first major space tragedy, the APOLLO 1 fire on January 27, 1967—a tragedy waiting to happen. Grissom, who had flown a suborbital flight aboard Liberty Bell 7 (July 21, 1961) as part of the Mercury-Redstone series and a GEMINI flight with John YOUNG (March 23, 1965), had been apprehensive about Apollo 1. Over 20,000 test failures of the spacecraft cabin and engines had been recorded—and did not inspire confidence. A week before the fatal accident that took the lives of Grissom and fellow astronauts Roger CHAFFEE and Edward WHITE, Grissom had hung a lemon inside the cabin, signifying his opinion of the craft. Tragedy struck—sudden and deadly—during a routine simulated flight. With the three astronauts sealed inside the Apollo command module, a fire broke out, turning the cabin into a blazing, smoke-filled death trap, killing the three men in a matter of minutes. A board of inquiry confirmed the late Grissom's fears. Five factors, the board found, led to the tragedy: an abundance of inflammable materials that produced toxic gases inside the cabin; poorly designed and unprotected electric cables; unprotected tubing, which contained inflammable and corrosive coolant; lack of a suitable escape system for the crew; and the unsettling fact that no fire or emergency crews were even on duty at the time of the accident.

Griswold v. Connecticut (1965). U.S. Supreme Court case legalizing contraception for married adults. A Connecticut statute imposed an outright ban on the sale of contraceptives. The law was challenged all the way to the U.S. Supreme Court, which struck it down as contrary to the Constitution. Although there is no explicit language regarding sexual practices in the Constitution, the Court, through Justice William O. DOUGLAS' opinion, reasoned that the Bill of Rights created a right of personal privacy. Accordingly, the Court held that a state may not legally impose an outright ban on the sale or use of contraceptives by married adults. The Court later applied this right of privacy to legalize ABORTIONS in the controversial case ROE V. WADE (1973).

Grivas, George (1898–1974). Commander of the Greek Cypriot National Guard. A right-wing Greek army officer, Grivas initiated the guerrilla campaign in CYPRUS in 1953, creating a terrorist movement, EOKA. He was later given command of the Greek Cypriot National Guard, against Archbishop MAKARIOS's wishes.

Recalled to Athens in 1971, where he regarded Makarios' acceptance of Commonwealth membership as treason, Grivas later secretly returned to Cyprus (1971–74) and reorganized his followers against Makarios. His divisive legacy contributed to the disastrous coup and subsequent partition of Cyprus in the summer of 1975. (See also Greek-Turkish CYPRIOT WAR OF 1974.)

Grofe, Ferde (1892–1972). Popular American composer of *The Grand Canyon Suite* and architect of the modern "jazz orchestra" sound. His earliest musical training came from family members in his native New York City. Later in California he wrote arrangements of popular songs in JAZZ idioms for the Paul WHITEMAN Orchestra. His orchestration of George GERSHWIN'S RHAPSODY IN BLUE was performed (with Gershwin at the piano) in the legendary Whiteman concert, "An Experiment in Modern Music," in New York's Aeolian Hall, February 12, 1924. His remaining years were devoted to a handful of movie scores—including an early talkie epic, *King of Jazz* (1929); *Minstrel Man* (1944) for which he won an ACADEMY AWARD; and a science fiction thriller, *Rocketship X-M* (1950). He also wrote many popular orchestral suites, notably *The Mississippi Suite* (1925) and *The Grand Canyon Suite* (1931). (Several other suites, particularly the *Hudson River Suite* and *The Atlantic Crossing Suite,* are kitschy concoctions marred by the sound effects, respectively, of bowling balls and radio loudspeakers!) His most popular original composition was "On the Trail," from *The Grand Canyon Suite.* It suffered the fate of being adopted as the musical theme for Philip Morris cigarettes.

For further reading:

Jablonski, Edward, ed. *The Encyclopedia of American Music.* New York: Doubleday and Co., 1981.

Gromyko, Andrei Andreyevich (1909–1989). Soviet diplomat and political figure, foreign minister of the U.S.S.R. (1957–85). Gromyko served under every Soviet leader from Joseph STALIN to Mikhail GORBACHEV and played a leading role in the conduct of Soviet foreign policy in the post-World War II era. Born to a peasant family in Byelorussia, he joined the COMMUNIST PARTY in 1931 and quickly rose to become a diplomat in the foreign ministry. He was ambassador to the U.S. from 1943 to 1946 and headed the Soviet delegation to the 1944 DUMBARTON OAKS CONFERENCE on the foundation of the UNITED NATIONS. He was subsequently chief permanent Soviet delegate to the UN (1946–48), ambassador to Britain (1952–53) and deputy foreign minister. Named foreign minister in 1957, he played a largely subservient role to the outspoken Soviet leader Nikita KHRUSHCHEV. Under Khrushchev's successor, Leonid I. BREZHNEV, he began to exercise greater control over foreign policy, particularly after he was made a full member of the Politburo in 1973. He helped engineer detente agreements with the U.S. in the 1970s and defended the Soviet invasion of AFGHANISTAN in 1979

Andrei Gromyko, Soviet diplomat and foreign minister from 1957 to 1985.

and POLAND's martial-law crackdown on SOLIDARITY in 1981. Gromyko played a crucial role in Gorbachev's 1985 rise to power by nominating him as general secretary to the Soviet Communist Party. However, after assuming power, Gorbachev replaced Gromyko with the younger, more flexible Eduard A. SHEVARDNADZE, and relegated Gromyko to the largely ceremonial post of president. On Gromyko's death Gorbachev issued a lukewarm tribute and did not attend the funeral.

Gronchi, Giovanni (1887–1978). President of ITALY (1955–62). In 1915 Gronchi helped found the Italian Popular Party, the forerunner of the Italian Christian Democratic Party. He was an early proponent of the "opening to the left" in the early 1950s.

Grooms, Charles Roger [Red] (1937–). American artist. Born in Nashville, Tennessee, he studied at the Peabody Institute and Chicago Art Institute as well as with Hans Hofmann. His first one-man show took place in 1958, the same year he was involved in the HAPPENING *Burning Building.* Related to POP ART, his work is playful, figurative and often riotously funny. His large three-dimensional constructions of painted papier mache and wood are witty tableaux of various contemporary scenes filled with expressively distorted characters and their surroundings. They include *Discount Store* (1970), *Ruckus Manhattan* (1975) and *Tut's Fever* (1988), an ironic look at the motion picture on permanent display at the Museum of the Moving Image, New York City.

Gropius, Walter (1883–1969). German architect who founded the BAUHAUS school. Along with LE CORBUSIER and Ludwig MIES VAN DER ROHE, Gropius was the creator of architectural MODERNISM and the INTERNATIONAL STYLE. The son of a Berlin architect, he studied architecture in Munich and Berlin (1903–07), then worked with Peter BEHRENS (1908–10). After serving in WORLD WAR I, he became director of the schools of fine arts and applied arts in Weimar. Pursuing his theories about the relationship between art and design, Gropius merged the two schools to form the Bauhaus. He himself designed the Bauhaus building in DESSAU in 1925 and hired many of the faculty members. He directed the Bauhaus until 1928, when he resigned to set up a private practice in Berlin. After HITLER came to power, Gropius moved to England (1934), where he collaborated with Maxwell FRY in designing private houses and schools. In 1937 Gropius immigrated to the U.S., where he became a professor at Harvard. In this post he had an enormous influence on an entire generation of young American architects. Gropius was a prolific author and lecturer; among his best known books is the seminal *New Architecture and the Bauhaus* (1935).

For further reading:

Isaacs, Reginald, *Gropius: An Illustrated Biography of the Creator of the Bauhaus.* Boston: Bullfinch Press/Little, Brown, 1990.

Gropper, William (1897–1977). American painter and cartoonist. Born in New York City, Gropper was influenced in the development of his bitingly realistic style by his studies with Robert HENRI and George BELLOWS. In 1919 he began his career as a cartoonist for the New York *Tribune.* His left-wing views were soon illustrated by cartoons in such radical periodicals as *Rebel Worker* and *New Masses.* During the 1920s and 1930s he became a leading American realist, often treating themes of social injustice and class conflict. During this period, he created a number of important murals, including a series at the Department of the Interior Building, Washington, D.C. Intensely political and scathingly satirical, he also skewered the pompous and the corrupt in such paintings as *The Senate* (1935, Museum of Modern Art, N.Y.C.).

Groppi, James E. (1931–1985). American Roman Catholic priest. During the 1960s, Groppi served in a largely black neighborhood in his native Milwaukee. He drew national attention as a crusader for open housing. He led more than 200 marches and was arrested more than a dozen times. Later Groppi became active in advocating the rights of welfare recipients and American Indians. He was removed from the priesthood in 1976 for getting married.

Gross, Henry (1895–1986). American crime boss. Kingpin of a vast illegal gambling operation in the 1940s, Gross was convicted in 1951 of heading a multimillion dollar bookmaking ring. That case also led to the conviction of 22 policemen and the dismissal or resignation of 240 others. The scandal, which prompted major police reforms, also saw the departure of Police Commissioner William O'Brien and the resignation of Mayor William O'Dwyer. He committed suicide rather than go back to prison after his arrest on a heroin trafficking charge.

Grossman, Vasily Semyonovich (1905–1964). Russian writer. Grossman worked as an engineer in Donbas and Moscow. In 1934 his novel *Glyukauf* attracted the attention of Maxim GORKY, who published it. From 1941 to 1945 Grossman wrote stories and sketches for *The Red Star*, mostly about the war. After the war he turned his attention to writing a novel concerning the defense of STALINGRAD, and his play *If We Were to Believe the Pythagorians* (1946) was banned by authorities.

Grosz, George (1893–1959). German-American painter and graphic artist. Born in Berlin, Grosz attended the academies of Dresden and Berlin, where he became an illustrator of magazines and books. During WORLD WAR I he produced drawings and caricatures that depicted the brutality of war. Directly after the war (1919) he joined the DADA movement, and organized (1920) the First International Dada Fair. In the postwar years, he also attacked the degradation of German society and skewered the hypocritical bourgeoisie with jagged pen-and-ink drawings and (from 1924 on) scathing, acid-colored paintings unmatched in their satirical savagery. Among his best-known graphic portfolios is *Ecce Homo* (1923), containing incisive studies of high-and low-life in a morally repugnant German society. Faced with the rise of NAZISM, Grosz immigrated to the U.S. in 1932. He became a teacher at New York's Art Students League in 1933 and achieved U.S. citizenship in 1938. His work became more mellow and realistic for a while, but he again turned to subjects of corruption and ravaged humanity after the outbreak of World War II. His work is well represented in American museums. His autobiography, *A Little Yes and a Big No*, was published in 1946.

Grotewohl, Otto (1894–1964). German communist politician, first prime minister of the German Democratic Republic (EAST GERMANY) from 1949 to 1964. A politician during the WEIMAR REPUBLIC, Grotewohl kept a low profile during the Nazi period. He refounded the German Social Democratic Party in 1945, joined the communists under Soviet pressure and became prime minister in 1949.

Grotowski, Jerzy (1933–). Polish theatrical director. Grotowski has been one of the most influential directors of the post-World War II era, due to his striking theories as to experimental theatrical performance. He studied at the Cracow Theater School and first came to international prominence as a result of his work with actors in the 1960s at the Polish Theater Laboratory. Grotowski's approach elucidated in his book *Towards a Poor Theater* (1968), focused upon an intensity of dramatic presentation that was heightened through encouragement of improvisation on the part of the actors, as well as free-form participation by the audience itself. Settings and costumes were to be minimally utilized. In the 1970s, Grotowski worked with the Theater Laboratory in Poland. His theories much influenced the LIVING THEATER and the work of British director Peter BROOK.

Grottrup, Helmut (1916–1981). German rocket engineer. Of the group of rocketeers who had developed Germany's V-2 rocket at PEENEMUNDE, Grottrup was the only principal scientist to surrender to the Soviets instead of to the Americans at the end of World War II. After working for the Russians in Germany for a time, he was taken to the Soviet Union in the autumn of 1946. He returned to Germany in 1953, disappointed in the level of opportunity given him and feeling that his work for the Soviets had been neither appreciated nor worthwhile.

Group of Seven. Group of Canadian painters formed in 1920. They attempted to create a national art by depicting the grandeur of their nation's northern landscapes. Members of the Group of Seven included Frank Carmichael, Lawren HARRIS, A.Y. Jackson, Frank Johnson, Arthur Lismer, J.E.H. MacDonald and Frederick Varley. Influenced by the techniques of modern European art but rejecting the dominence of European subject matter, these artists created large canvases that are vividly colored and expressively painted. The group disbanded in 1931 but continued to influence later generations of Canadian painters.

Group Theatre. American theater movement headed by directors Harold CLURMAN, Cheryl Crawford and Lee STRASBERG. The goal of the Group Theatre, which was established in 1931 in New York City, was to present serious modern plays on the basis of quality alone, without regard to Broadway commercial concerns. Among the playwrights produced by the Group Theatre were Paul Green, Sidney Kingsley, Clifford ODETS and William SAROYAN. In 1941, due to funding difficulties and internal dissension, the Group Theatre disbanded. A similar theatrical movement, also called the Group Theatre, emerged in London in 1933, with Rupert Doone serving as principal director. The British Group Theatre staged plays by W.H. AUDEN, T.S. ELIOT, and Stephen SPENDER and often featured scores by composer Benjamin BRITTEN. It ceased production during World War II but was revived for a short time in the 1950s.

Grove, Robert Moses "Lefty" (1900–1975). American baseball player. An overpowering fastball pitcher, southpaw "Lefty" Grove finished his career with 300 wins. Over the course of 17 seasons with the Philadelphia Athletics (1925–33) and the Boston Red Sox (1934–41), he led the league in strikeouts seven consecutive times, earned-run average nine times and victories four times. In his early years he was famous for his inability to control either his pitches or his temper, and intimidated teammates and opponents alike. He was named to the Hall of Fame in 1947.

Groves, Leslie R(ichard) (1896–1970). American military engineer and administrator. Educated at the Massachusetts Institute of Technology and the U.S. Military Academy at West Point, by 1941 Groves was overseeing all U.S. military construction. From 1942 to 1947, he was the executive officer of the MANHATTAN PROJECT, responsible for coordinating the thousands of separate ultra-secret projects undertaken by the military, private corporations and universities that were necessary to the construction of the ATOMIC BOMB. In 1945, Groves was instrumental in the decision to drop the bomb, choosing the Japanese targets and training crews to perform the mission. In 1947, he organized the Armed Forces Special Weapons Project, which trained officers in the military aspects of atomic energy. He retired from the army in 1948 and became a business executive.

For further reading:

Groves, Leslie R., *Now It Can Be Told: The Story of the Manhattan Project*. New York: Da Capo Press, 1975.

Grozny. Capital city of the U.S.S.R.'s Chechen-Ingush Autonomous SSR; on a tributary of the Caucasus' Terek River, 50 miles from Ordzhonikidze. An oil-producing area of Russia since the "black gold" was discovered here in 1893, Grozny was a major strategic goal of the oil-hungry German invaders in WORLD WAR II. The Nazi advance was cut short by Soviet troops before they reached the city.

Gruen, Victor [born Victor Gruenbaum] (1903–1980). Austrian-born architect and community planner. Gruen pioneered the design for American suburban shopping centers in the 1950s. His major projects set the pattern for large-scale shopping mall development in the U.S. He later disavowed the shopping mall concept and blamed land developers for corrupting the idea by promoting uncontrolled suburban sprawl and automobile traffic congestion. Gruen also founded one of the U.S.'s leading architectural, planning, and engineering firms.

Gruentzig, Andres (1939–1985). German-born physician. In 1977, while working at a Zurich hospital, Gruentzig developed the revolutionary balloon catheter technique for cleaning arteries of fatty deposits. In 1980, the year he became a U.S. citizen, he also became a professor of cardiology and radiology at Emory University.

Grumiaux, Arthur (1921–1986). Belgian violinist. Grumiaux achieved world-wide fame through his stylish recordings and concert appearances. He often performed with pianist Clara Haskill, and their recordings of sonatas by Beethoven and Mozart came to be prized by collectors.

Grumman Corporation. American aircraft and aerospace manufacturer and defense contractor. It was founded by Leroy Grumman (1901–82) in 1929 as an aircraft-repair shop in a converted basement. The company expanded rapidly and was the first to make aircraft with folding landing gear. It also pioneered in the development of the collapsed wing. It manufactured the Hellcat fighters and Avenger torpedo bombers that played a pivotal role in the American victory in WORLD WAR II IN THE PACIFIC. The company later diversified; by the 1970s, it was largely dependent on defense and aerospace contracts, and in the 1980s was a major supplier of buses to American municipalities. The company is headquartered on Long Island, N.Y.

Grundgens, Gustav (1899–1963). German theatrical actor and director. Grundgens was a star of the German stage as a romantic actor in the 1930s, appearing in numerous plays by George Bernard SHAW and winning acclaim for his 1938 lead portrayal in *Hamlet*. Grundgens' startling successes at so early an age formed the inspiration for the novel *Mephisto* (1936) by Klaus Mann (the son of renowned German novelist Thomas MANN). After World War II, Grundgens worked both as a director and as an actor, starring as Mephistopheles in a touring production of Goethe's *Faust* in 1957–58. His death was an apparent suicide.

Grundig, Max (1908–1989). West German electronics pioneer. Grundig founded one of Europe's largest radio, television, and high-fidelity stereo equipment manufacturing companies, Grundig AG. The firm was regarded as a symbol of WEST GERMANY's post-World War II economic success. However, sales began declining in the late 1970s, due to increased competition from cheaper Japanese exports, and Grundig was forced into an alliance with N.V. Philips Gloeilampenfabrieken of the Netherlands.

Grunewald scandal. Controversy of 1951 involving Henry Grunewald, a notorious Washington, D.C., influence peddler, that rocked the administration of President Harry TRUMAN. Known as "the Dutchman," Grunewald was actually born in South Africa. After working as confidential secretary to Henry Marsh, an insurance executive, Grunewald started his own public relations and investigations firm. Among his services were uncovering unsavory information, peddling government influence and fixing tax bills. In 1951, a subcommittee of the House Ways and Means Committee investigated questionable practices at the Bureau of Internal Revenue (later the Internal Revenue Service). One witness testified that Grunewald, along with a former internal revenue commissioner and the chief counsel, attempted to fix his tax fraud case for a half-million-dollar payment. The hearings also revealed that the chief counsel had borrowed heavily from Grunewald. In 1953 Grunewald received a light sentence but was quickly back in court on charges that he had attempted to fix a company's taxes while he was on parole. Although convicted he won a new trial. The Dutchman died in 1958 while awaiting the retrial.

***Gruppe 47* [*English:* Group 47].** *Gruppe 47* was created in post-World War II GERMANY in 1947 by a diverse group of German writers who met initially to consider the founding of a literary journal. While the journal never came into being, *Gruppe 47* achieved prominence as a vital source of encouragement—through its annual autumn meetings in which manuscripts were read and discussed—for the postwar generation of German writers. Prominent writers who attended *Gruppe 47* meetings regularly or sporadically included NOBEL PRIZE-winning novelist Heinrich BOLL, poets Gunter Eich and Hans Magnus Enzenberger, and novelists Gunter GRASS, Siegfried Lenz, and Martin Walser.

Guadalcanal. Volcanic island in the western Pacific Ocean, 100 miles southeast of New Georgia; a part of the Solomon Islands. A protectorate of Great Britain's since 1893, it was captured by JAPAN in 1942 (see WORLD WAR II IN THE PACIFIC). U.S. Marines seized a newly built Japanese airfield on August 7, 1942, in the first of a hardfought series of land and naval battles known as the **Battle of Guadalcanal,** from August 7 to November 13, 1942. Henderson Field, the bone of bitter contention, is now an international airport.

Guadeloupe. Guadeloupe is a group of islands, including the larger islands of Basse-Terre and Grand-Terre, in the Caribbean Sea. Granted departmental status by France in 1946, the islands became a region of France in 1974 and were given greater autonomy in 1982. Recently, the elected councils of Guadeloupe have been pursuing independence from France.

Guam. Island and unincorporated U.S. territory in the western Pacific Ocean; largest and southernmost of the MARIANA ISLANDS group. Discovered by Magellan in 1521 it was a Spanish possession until captured by the United States in 1898, during the Spanish-American War. The Japanese captured the island in 1941, at the beginning of WORLD WAR II in the Pacific; retaken by U.S. forces in 1944, Guam became a base for air assaults on the Japanese home islands. In the 1960s the U.S. used it for air operations against VIETNAM and LAOS.

Guantanamo [Guantanamo Bay]. Harbor city in southeastern CUBA; the town is about 10 miles north of Guantanamo Bay. U.S. naval units landed here in 1898 during the Spanish-American War and have yet to leave. Often called the PEARL HARBOR of the Atlantic, "Gitmo" was leased by the U.S. in 1903 as a strategic naval station. Since 1960 it has been a bone of contention with the CASTRO government of Cuba, which has refused the token $5,000 annual rent from the U.S. and has pressed for surrender of the base.

Guare, John (1938–). American playwright. Guare is one of the most acclaimed of modern American playwrights. His plays fall into no fixed dramatic school, but rather are highly regarded for their poignant probing into the hopes and weaknesses of their characters. Guare first emerged in the 1960s with a series of Broadway successes including *A Day of Surprises* (1965), *The Loveliest Afternoon of the Year* (1966) and the acclaimed *The House of Blue Leaves* (1970). In 1973 he fashioned a musical version of Shakespeare's *Two Gentlemen of Verona.* His play *Rich and Famous* (1976) was adapted into a film starring Candace Bergen and Jacqueline Bisset. Guare's subsequent works include *Bosoms and Neglect* (1979) and *Six Degrees of Separation* (1990).

Guarnieri, Johnny (1917–1985). American musician; one of the major JAZZ pianists of the SWING ERA. A prolific recording artist, in 1940 he made a series of recordings with Artie SHAW on which he played what were considered to be the first jazz harpsichord solos. Guarnieri also

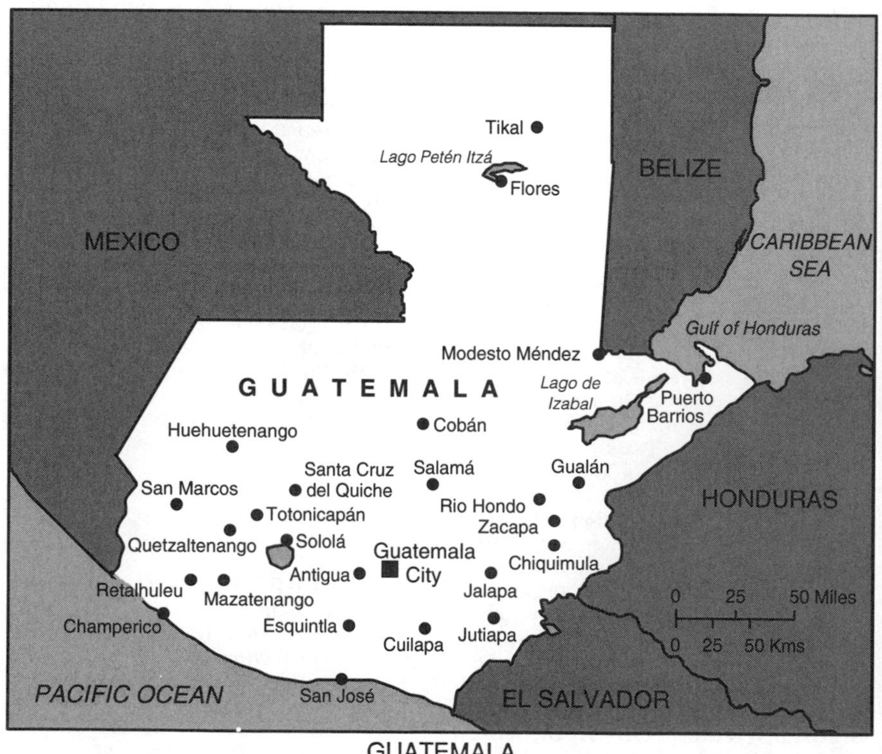

GUATEMALA

played with such noted musicians as Benny GOODMAN and Jimmy DORSEY.

Guatemala [Republic of Guatemala]. Covering an area of 42,031 square miles, Guatemala is located in Central America, just south of Mexico. The repressive government of General Jorge Ubico (1931–44) was followed by that of Juan Jose AREVALO BERMEJO, who initiated social, political and economic reforms. His successor, Colonel Jacobo ARBENZ GUZMAN, confiscated land owned by the U.S. Fruit Company, which resulted in a successful U.S.-backed coup in 1954. All reforms were rescinded. Since then Guatemala has been plagued by military coups and intense left-wing guerrilla activity, which has resulted in extreme military repression, massacre of suspected guerrilla supporters in the 1980s and international criticism for widespread human-rights violations. The current government, under President Mario Vinicio Cerezo Arevalo (since 1985), opened talks with the guerrilla leaders in 1987, but resolution of the conflict has not yet been achieved.

Gucci, Guccio (1881–1953). Italian leather worker and designer, the founder of the present firm that carries his name. Gucci opened a shop in Florence in 1904 producing saddles and, eventually, luggage. His sons enlarged the business and opened a shop in Rome in 1939. Shops in Paris, London and American cities followed. Gucci products are of generally high quality and distinguished design. In recent years Gucci has taken a strong turn toward high fashion and status appeal. The use of a monogram logotype and a decorative motif of thin red and green stripes makes Gucci products easily recognizable.

Guchkov, Alexander Ivanovich (1862–1936). Leader of the moderate liberals in Russia (1905–17). Founder and chairman of the Octobrist Party and president of the third state DUMA. In World War I he was chairman of the duma committee on military and naval affairs, and subsequently chairman of the nongovernmental central war industries committee. He became the minister for war and navy in the provisional government. He was a critic of the imperial regime and in March 1917 went to Pskov and secured the abdication of the czar. He left for Paris after the OCTOBER REVOLUTION.

Guderian, Heinz (1888–1954). German general. A career officer, trained in the Prussian tradition, he was commissioned in the infantry in 1908 and served with distinction in WWI. Specializing in armored fighting, he developed the highly-mobile *Panzerwaffe* (tank corps) that allowed GERMANY to pursue its devestating BLITZKRIEG attacks on Poland, Belgium and France in the early years of WORLD WAR II. He commanded a panzer army during the invasion of Russia in 1941, but was dismissed by HITLER for his failure to take Moscow. He was appointed inspector general of armored troops in 1943 and head of the general staff in 1944. In March, 1945, as the Red Army advanced on Berlin, Guderian was finally relieved of his duties by Hitler.

Guernica [Guernica y Luno]. Town in Spain's Vizcaya province, near Bilbao. Once the seat of the Basque parliament, Guernica was bombed in 1937 by German planes, acting on behalf of FRANCO's Nationalists during the SPANISH CIVIL WAR. The bombing indiscriminately killed men, women and children and was an early use of blanket air attacks on civilian targets with no other purpose than to terrify the enemy into submission. It shocked the world. The destruction was the subject of the great painting of the same name by Pablo PICASSO. By the artist's will, the painting was returned by New York City's MUSEUM OF MODERN ART in September 1981 to the Prado Museum in Madrid.

Gueudecourt. Village in France's SOMME department; taken by the British during a September 1916 battle, during WORLD WAR I.

Guevara, Ernesto "Che" (1928–1967). Latin American revolutionary. Born into a wealthy family in Argentina, Che became radicalized after witnessing American intervention in GUATEMALA in 1954. Guevara accompanied Fidel CASTRO to CUBA and played a prominent part in the guerrilla campaign (1956–59) that led to BATISTA's downfall. Minister for industries in Cuba (1961–65), he resigned and returned to the jungles of BOLIVIA to test his revolutionary theory. He was killed while leading a band of guerrillas against American-trained Bolivian troops in 1967.

GUATEMALA

1906	United Fruit Company develops banana plantations.
1917	Massive earthquake damages Guatemala City.
1920	Unionist Party overthrows dictator Estrada Cabrera after 22 years of rule.
1921	Liberal Party overthrows Unionists.
1925	Semi-feudal coffee plantations spread into highlands to be near Indian labor.
1930	Military coup.
1931	Jorge Ubico becomes dictator.
1938	Border with El Salvador defined.
1944	Revolution ousts Ubico; elections lead to progressive government under Jose Argualo.
1951	Progressive programs expanded under President Jacobo Arbenz; huge redistribution is begun of unused land, including major holdings of United Fruit Company.
1954	U.S. backs and participates in coup placing Colonel Castillo Armas in place; Arbenz programs are cancelled and all land returned to United Fruit Company.
1956	New constitution ratified.
1957	Military coup.
1963	Relations broken with Britain over claim to territory of Belize.
1965	New constitution.
1966	Elections held; Julio Cesar Mendez elected.
1967	Miguel Angel Asturias wins Nobel Prize for literature for stories based on Indian traditions.
1968	Church takes stand on social issues; Archbishop Casariggo kidnapped by right wing; violent leftist guerrillas active.
1976	Earthquake levels much of Guatemala City; 22,000 die.
1978	Leftist guerrilla activity increases; military mounts counter-terror campaign, massacring rural villages; massive migration of Indians results.
1979	Government announces "Four Year Development Plan."
1982	Military coup by Rios Montt voids elections.
1983	Military coup.
1984	Eugenia Tejada becomes first woman member of cabinet.
1986	Elections and new constitution.
1989	Guatemala City doubles in population since 1980.
1990	U.S. suspends military aid because of death squad activity by army.
1991	Election of Jorge Serrano reflects growing political power of conservative evangelical Christian movement.

Latin American revolutionary Che Guevara was an inspiration for radical students in the 1960s.

Che's rejection of both capitalism and orthodox communism made him a symbolic martyr for radical students throughout the world.

Guggenheim, Peggy [Marguerite Guggenheim] (1898–1979). American art collector and socialite. An expatriate millionaire who was the niece of philanthropist Solomon Guggenheim, Peggy Guggenheim assembled one of the foremost collections of modern art in her home on the Grand Canal in Venice. The collection included more than 250 works by BRAQUE, KLEE, MIRO, MONDRIAN, PICASSO, POLLOCK and other modern artists. It was valued at over $35 million at the time of her death. Guggenheim was also known for her flamboyant lifestyle.

Guided Democracy. Term given to the style of government of SUKARNO in INDONESIA.

Guild, Lurelle (1898–). American industrial designer, one of a group active in the 1930s who provided styling for manufacturers eager to boost sales in the difficult years of the GREAT DEPRESSION. A 1920 fine arts graduate of Syracuse University, Guild first worked in magazine illustration. He later claimed to have designed as many as a thousand products in a year. Such products as a Norge refrigerator and a May oil-burner, each styled in the manner known then as "modernistic," are typical of Guild's innumerable designs of the 1930s. His willingness to admit to "styling down" to a supposedly low level of public taste sets Guild apart from most of his competitors, who generally believed they were elevating public taste. His Electrolux vacuum cleaner of 1937 is probably his most famous design, with many thousands still in regular use.

Guillen, Jorge (1893–1984). Spanish poet, critic and teacher. Guillen was born in Castile and educated at the universities of Madrid and Granada. Like other members of the GENERATION OF 1927, he supported the Loyalist cause in the SPANISH CIVIL WAR. Imprisoned in 1936, he went into exile in 1938. He taught at Wellesley (1941-57) as well as McGill, Harvard, Princeton and Yale. Guillen devoted 47 years of work to *Anthologia: Aire nuestro* (1968), which incorporated *Cantico* (*Canticle,* four editions between 1928 and 1950), *Clamor* (*Clamour,* a trilogy published between 1957 and 1963) and *Homenaje* (1967, *Homage*). He received almost every international award except for the NOBEL PRIZE and was acknowledged in his lifetime as Spain's greatest poet. In 1972 the government of Madrid honored him with the first Cervantes Prize, the highest literary award of the world's Spanish-speaking nations. Guillen returned to Spain in 1977, two years after FRANCO's death.

Guillen, Nicolas Batista (1904–1989). Cuban writer. Widely considered CUBA's national poet, Guillen was deeply concerned with the black experience in the Caribbean. A communist, he fought on the Loyalist side in the SPANISH CIVIL WAR. He later supported Fidel CASTRO, was a deputy in the Cuban assembly and served as president of the National Union of Writers and Artists of Cuba. His 12 books of verse began with *Motivos de son* (1930, *Motifs of Sound*). Sensuous and rhythmic in character, his work incorporates elements of popular culture, incantations, dances and street cries. Other volumes of verse include *Songoro cosongo* (1931) and *Obra Poetica 1920–1958* (his complete poetry, published in 1973).

Guinea [Republic of Guinea]. Located on the west coast of Africa, Guinea covers an area of 94,901 square miles. A French colony since 1890, Guinea became independent in 1958. The elected president,

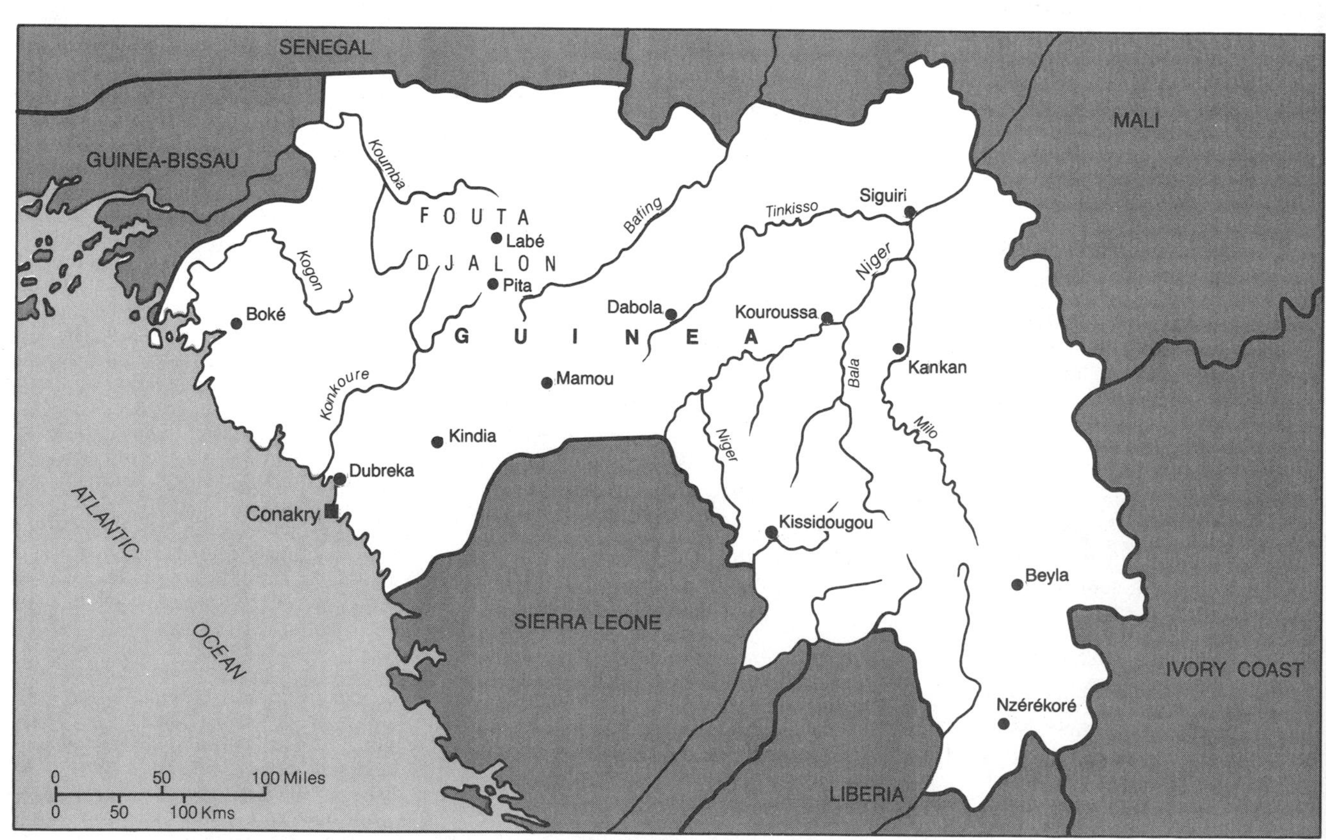

GUINEA

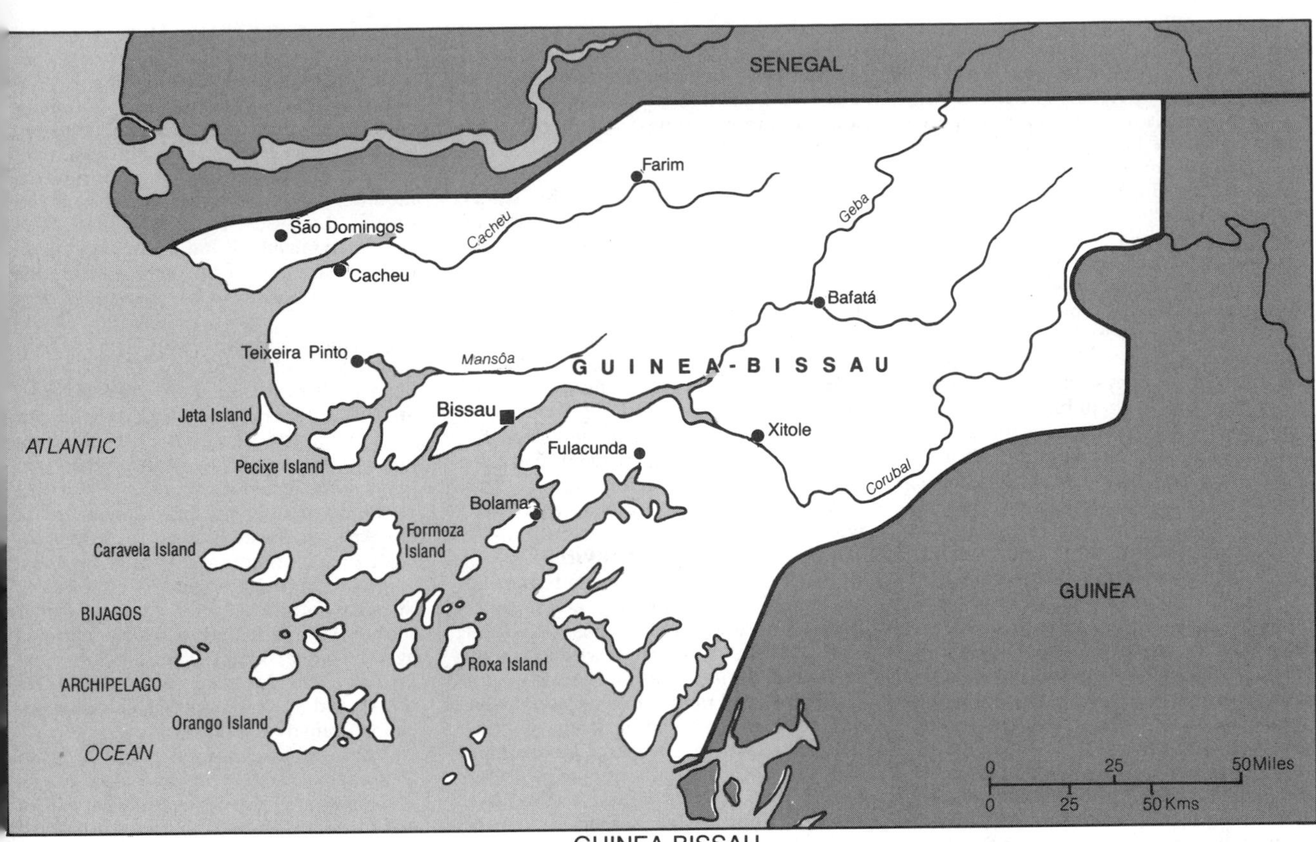

GUINEA-BISSAU

Ahmed Sekou Toure, governed from 1958 to 1984, putting down an attempted coup by Guinean exiles in 1970. Upon his death the military seized power, and Col. Lansana Conte became president. He foiled a coup attempt in 1985, which resulted in numerous executions, and was forced to endorse a return to a two-party system with an elected president and National Assembly after countrywide riots in 1988. In 1990 a new constitution was being written.

Guinea-Bissau. Small country on the west coast of Africa, between Senegal and Guinea; formerly known as Portuguese Guinea. Guinea-Bissau was a part of Portugal's colonial empire from the time explorers first reached its coastline in 1446. Five hundred years later, in the early 1960s, a rebellion against colonial rule began. By 1974, independence had finally come—as a result of the 1974 Happy Revolution in Portugal. Guinea-Bissau was the first Portuguese colonial possession in Africa to become free. Since that time the nation has been trying to deal with the legacy of its colonial past, develop its health care and educational system, and make the infrastructure improvements that are desperately needed. (See also GUINEA-BISSAUAN WAR OF INDEPENDENCE.)

Guinea-Bissauan War of Independence (1962–1974). Amilcar Cabral (1921–73), after founding the African Party for the Independence of Guinea and Cape Verde (PAIGC), attempted unsuccessfully to negotiate independence from the Portuguese. The PAIGC subsequently began a guerrilla campaign in late 1962. Bands established bases in the forest, while the Portuguese retaliated by bombing and raiding them. Tribalism and witchcraft threatened the rebels' unity until Cabral called a council and explained that the PAIGC was waging a dual revolution: against colonialism and out-moded beliefs. By 1973 it controlled two-thirds of Portuguese Guinea, and proclaimed independence as the Republic of GUINEA-BISSAU. Portugal refused recognition until 1974 when a military coup in Lisbon installed a new government. Luis de Almeida Cabral (b. 1931) became president after his brother Amilcar was assassinated in early 1973. Cape Verde Islands became an independent republic in 1975.

Guinness, Alec (Sir) (1914–). British theatrical and film actor. Known for his rich voice and for his ability to don the guises of varied characters, Guinness is one of the most acclaimed actors of modern times. He won fame both on the legitimate stage and in British and HOLLYWOOD films. Guinness began his career on the London stage in the 1930s, winning notice in productions by the Old Vic Company including a lead portrayal of Shakespeare's *Hamlet* (1938) in modern dress. After World War II, Guinness made notable appearances in his own stage adaptation of *The Brothers Karamazov* (1946), from the novel by Dostoyevsky, and in *The Cocktail Party* (1949) by T.S. ELIOT. Guinness began his film career in earnest in the late 1940s, appearing in a number of acclaimed movies, including the comedy *Kind Hearts and Coronets* (1949), and *The Bridge on the River Kwai* (1957), directed by David LEAN, for which he won an ACADEMY AWARD as best actor. His more recent projects include the *Star Wars*

One of the most versatile of British actors, Alec Guinness here portrays Julius Caesar in G.B. Shaw's Caesar and Cleopatra *in 1976.*

film trilogy (1977–83) and the role of spy George Smiley in television adaptations of the works of John LE CARRE.

Guinness Book of Records. *The Guinness Book of Records* is an annual authoritative compendium of facts, feats and exploits of the world and its inhabitants. Conceived by Sir Hugh Beaver (1890–1967), managing director of Guinness Ltd., it was first published in the United Kingdom in 1955. Norris and Ross McWhirter edited the first edition as well as many subsequent editions. The first U.S. edition was published in 1956. In 1974 *The Guinness Book of Records* gained a place within its own pages as the top-selling copyrighted book in publishing history, with sales of 23.9 million copies. Sales passed 60 million copies by 1989. By 1990 there were 262 editions in 35 languages; the first Soviet edition was also published that year.

Gulag Archipelago, The. Three-volume history of Soviet prison camps from 1918 to 1956 (published between 1973 and 1976) by Alexander SOLZHENITSYN, the 1970 recipient of the NOBEL PRIZE for literature. Solzhenitsyn, who was himself a longtime prisoner in Siberia during the reign of STALIN, created a unique blend of historical testimony and literary imagination in *The Gulag Archipelago*. Solzhenitsyn asserted in this work that a standard history of the camps was impossible, as too many of the millions who had suffered within them had died or were too afraid to recount their experiences. Thus Solzhenitsyn employed not only his own memories and the personal testimonies he had collected, but also literary metaphors and meditations on the meaning of so great a horror. *The Gulag Archipelago* was first published in Paris, after a copy of the manuscript had been smuggled out of the U.S.S.R. As a result of writing it, Solzhenitsyn was deported in 1974.

Gumilev, Nikolai (1886–1921). Russian poet. The son of a doctor, Gumilev studied at the University of St. Petersburg and the Sorbonne. He inaugurated two literary magazines, *Sirius* (1908) and *Apollon* (1909), the latter serving as a house organ for the ACMEISTS, a group of poets including Anna AKHMATOVA and Osip MANDELSTAM who opposed the neoromanticism of the Russian Symbolist school. Gumilev's first book of poetry was *The Path of Conquistadors* (1905). Other major collections include *Romantic Flowers* (1908), *Pearls* (1910) and *Foreign Skies* (1912). His poetry is characterized by regal flourishes of love, heroism and death. He attempted suicide in 1908. Then in 1910 he married Akhmatova, but they were divorced eight years later. Gumilev was shot by Soviet authorities in 1921 for "counter-revolutionary activity."

Gunnarsson, Gunnar (1889–1975). Icelandic novelist. A well-known figure in Iceland, Gunnarsson also lived in Denmark for many years, writing in Danish as well as Icelandic. He resettled in Iceland in 1939. Gunnarsson is best known for the tetralogy, *The Family Borg*, first published in 1927 which follows four generations of an Icelandic farm family, and for his historical novels of Iceland, such as *The Sworn Brothers* (1920). Other works include *Blackbird* (1929) and a five-volume autobiographical series, *The Church on the Hill* (1923–1928).

Gunther, John (1901–1970). American author. Gunther, who began his career as a news reporter, is best known for his "Inside" books, which include *Inside Europe* (1936), *Inside Latin America* (1941), *Inside U.S.A.* (1947) and the unfinished *Inside Australia* which was completed by William Forbis and published in 1972. The books are accessible, informative works combining history and journalism. Other non-fiction includes *Death Be Not Proud: A Memoir* (1949), *Inside Europe Today* (1961) and *Procession* (1965). Gunther has also written novels, including *The Lost City* (1964) and *The Indian Sign* (1970), which were not well received critically.

Gurdjieff, Georgei Ivanovitch (1877?-1949). Russian philosopher and spiritual teacher. Gurdjieff was one of the most fascinating and controversial spiritual teachers of this century. His written works, such as *Meetings with Remarkable Men* (1963), were all published posthumously. But Gurdjieff exercised his primary influence by face-to-face teaching encounters with his disciples and students, who included such eminent figures as the New Zealand short story writer Katherine MANSFIELD, the British essayist A.R. Orage, and the Russian philosopher P.D. Ouspensky. Gurdjieff was born at Alexandropol near the Russo-Persian border. As a youth, he traveled to Central Asia and other remote regions and came in contact with various spiritual masters who taught Gurdjieff a mode of personal development strongly influenced by Sufism. In the 1920s, Gurdjieff established himself at Fontainebleau, France, and attracted a number of disciples. Gurdjieff employed such means as verbal paradox, music, and disciplined physical labor to compel his followers to come to terms with their personality weaknesses and to attain to their higher selves.

Gurney, Ivor (1890–1937). English poet and composer. Born in Gloucester, Gurney studied with Sir Charles Stanford at the Royal College of Music (1911–14). He showed much promise as a composer, but WORLD WAR I interrupted his studies. Serving as a private on the Western Front, he was wounded in the arm and later gassed at PASSCHENDAELE (see WORLD WAR I ON THE WESTERN FRONT). In 1918, after suffering a nervous breakdown, he was discharged with "deferred shell-shock." Gurney published two wartime poetry collections, *Severn and Somme* (1917) and *War's Embers* (1919), but a third collection was rejected by his publisher. Returning to the Royal College of Music, he studied with Ralph VAUGHAN WILLIAMS but was unable to concentrate; he left the college and returned to an irregular life in Gloucestershire. During this time (1919–22) he wrote many fine poems and also composed songs, but he suffered increasingly from delusions, and in 1922 was committed to Dartford insane asylum, where he spent the rest of his life. Gurney's poetry was influenced by his wartime experiences and by his love for the Gloucester countryside; it is marked by subtle use of rhyme and by great imaginative resourcefulness. Largely unpublished during his lifetime, Gurney's work was rediscovered during the 1970s and 1980s. Gurney is now recognized as one of the most original British poets of the 20th century. His songs also have found a place in the repertoire.

For further reading:

Hurd, Michael, *The Ordeal of Ivor Gurney*. Oxford: Oxford University Press, 1978.

Guro, Elena [Eleonora Genrikhovna von Norenberg] (1877–1910). Russian Futurist poet. She was a professional painter who had graduated from the school of the Society for the Encouragement of the Arts, and was interested in French, German and Scandinavian literature. Guro is one of the most neglected of the early Russian Futurists. Her literary career started with *Early Spring* (1905), followed by *The Hurdy-Gurdy* (1909), *The Autumnal Dream* (1912), *The Baby Camels of the Sky* (1914) and other works. Her work remains unjustly overlooked.

Gustav Line. Stretching across Italy south of Rome, it was set up by the Germans as a main line of defense in WORLD WAR II. Bitterly defended, the key position of CASSINO, with the valley of the Liri River behind it, was reached by the attacking Allies in February 1944 but not taken by them until May.

Guthrie, Arlo (1947–). American folk and rock musician. The son of renowned folk singer Woody GUTHRIE, Arlo Guthrie burst into national prominence in 1967 due to the success of his album *Alice's Restaurant*. Its wry and rambling title song tells the story of a diffident 1960s rebel who refuses to kill for the U.S. Army and is ultimately arrested for littering. *Alice's Restaurant* became one of the anthems of the ANTIWAR MOVEMENT, and a film by the same title, directed by Arthur Penn and with Guthrie in a starring role, was produced in 1969. In the past two decades, Guthrie has recorded a number of albums, including a tribute to his father, and has joined with folk singer Pete SEEGER in a number of river clean-up campaigns.

Guthrie, Tyrone (1900–1971). English stage director. Noted for his inventiveness, Guthrie became famous for his direction of Elizabethan drama, especially the plays of Shakespeare. Initially, he was a director of the Scottish National Players (1926–27), then became director at the Cambridge Festival Theatre (1929–30) and the Old Vic (1933–34; 1936–37; 1951–52). In 1953 he founded the Shakespeare Festival in Stratford, Ontario, and subsequently served as one of the directors. In addition, he directed drama and opera in London and New York, and established a theater in Minneapolis in 1962, which bears his name and continues his theatrical legacy. Among his most important productions were *Hamlet* (Old Vic, 1938)

The music of folksinger and political activist Woody Guthrie has itself become a part of American history.

and *Troilus and Cressida* (Stratford, Ontario, 1954).

Guthrie, Woody (Woodrow Wilson) (1912–1967). American folksinger and political activist; widely considered the preeminent American folksinger of the 20th century. Certain of his songs of the 1930s—"This Land Is Your Land," "Hard Traveling," and "So Long, It's Been Good To Know Ya"—have become enduring classics of American popular music. Guthrie was born in Indian territory in Oklahoma and traveled widely during the 1920s and the GREAT DEPRESSION era. For a time he worked for a California radio station on which he performed his songs. Moving to New York City in the late 1930s, he performed with fellow folk singer Pete SEEGER, contributed pieces to the socialist *Daily Worker* and recorded a number of DUST BOWL ballad albums—containing both original material and old folk songs collected by Guthrie—for the Archive of American Folk Song. Guthrie died after a painful 13-year struggle with Huntington's Chorea. *Bound for Glory* (1943) and *Bound to Win* (1965) are autobiographical volumes; *Woody Says* (1975) is a posthumous collection. Singer Arlo GUTHRIE is his son.

Guttuso, Renato (1912–1987). Italian painter and Communist. He was perhaps the most commercially successful Italian painter of his generation. Most of his mature work was realistic or expressionistic in nature. Much of it dealt with political themes, from the execution of Spanish poet Federico GARCIA LORCA in 1936 to the student uprisings of 1968. Guttuso also served in the Italian Senate.

Guyana. Republic on the Atlantic coast of northeastern South America, bounded on the east and southeast by Surinam, on the south and southwest by Brazil and on the west by Brazil and Venezuela; formerly known as British Guiana. Its boundary with Venezuela, long a subject of controversy, became a serious issue in 1895, when U.S. Secretary of State Richard Olney took a threateningly "American" view in Venezuela's dispute with Britain. An arbitration award in 1899 upheld most British claims; and the boundary with Brazil was similarly arbitrated in 1904. With the outset of World War II, the U.S. leased sites for military and naval bases on the Demerara River and near Suddie. By 1966 the colony had achieved independence, and in 1970 it became a republic. Throughout the 1960s tension between East Indians, who control commerce, and blacks led to clashes and bloodshed, which subsided in the 1970s. International tensions were eased with the signing in 1970 of a 12-year truce with Venezuela and a mutual troop withdrawal agreement with Surinam. The Venezuela border controversy still simmers. In 1978 Guyana gained international notoriety as the scene of a mass suicide committed at JONESTOWN by followers of the U.S.-originated religious cult of the Reverend Jim Jones. The government has proved unstable, and in the 1980s the nation faced severe economic problems.

Guyanan Rebellion of 1969. Rebel bands invaded from Brazil, seized the towns of Lethem and Annai in southwestern Guyana (January 2, 1969), but were driven out by Guyanese Army forces within several days. Several policemen lost their lives. The invasion was apparently sponsored by Americans owning large cattle ranches in the region, wishing to establish a state they could control.

Gypsy Rose Lee (1914–1970). American entertainer. Born Rose Louise Hovick, Gypsy Rose Lee elevated the striptease to an art form and became the sophisticated queen of burlesque. Intelligent as well as beautiful, she became the toast of New York intellectuals. She starred in the ZIEGFELD FOLLIES in the 1930s and on Broadway *(Star and Garter)*, in addition to pub-

GUYANA

lishing a ghostwritten novel *(The G-String Murders)* and hosting her own national television talk show in the 1960s. A Broadway musical based on her life opened in 1959 (music by Jule STYNE and lyrics by Stephen SONDHEIM), was made into a film in 1962 and was revived on Broadway in 1990.

Gysi, Gregor (1948–). East German lawyer, leader of the East German Socialist Unity (Communist) Party following the ouster of Egon KRENZ, who in October 1989 replaced Erich HONECKER. A popular member of the reform wing of the party, he was nonetheless defeated by non-communists who favored reunification with WEST GERMANY in March 1990 in the first free elections in EAST GERMANY.

Habitat. International chain of stores owned by Terrence CONRAN that specializes in household goods (furniture, dishes, glassware, lamps, floor coverings, and so on) of reasonable price and excellent design. The majority of Habitat products have been specially designed for the firm. It is quite possible to furnish an entire apartment or house using only objects from a Habitat shop. Beginning with a single small shop in London in 1964, the Habitat chain reaches to France, Belgium, and Japan, and to the United States, where the stores are known as Conran's to avoid confusion with another firm.

Hadamar. Town in the German state of Hesse, 27 miles north of Wiesbaden; site of a Nazi CONCENTRATION CAMP during WORLD WAR II.

Haddad, Wadi (1928?-1978). Palestinian pediatrician, terrorist and cofounder (1966) of the Popular Front for the Liberation of Palestine. Haddad directed several prominent airliner hijackings, including the hijacking of an El Al plane to Algeria (1968) and the hijacking of a Lufthansa jet to Somalia (1977); he was also behind the hijacking of four airliners that resulted in three of the planes being blown up on a runway in Jordan (1970). He was also apparently linked to the Tel Aviv airport attack by the Japanese Red Army (1972).

Hadlee, Sir Richard John (1951–). New Zealand cricket player. Hadlee holds the all-time record for wickets taken in Test cricket at 413 in 86 Tests. A fast-medium bowler, Hadlee rarely gained his wickets through pace but relied on guile. A noted tactician, Hadlee came from a cricket family, his father Walter having captained New Zealand in the 1940s. Hadlee first played for New Zealand in 1973 and was an integral member of the side that gained its first victory ever in England at Wellington in 1977–78. Hadlee played English county cricket for Nottinghamshire, and his 105 wickets helped gain the championship in 1981. Hadlee retired in 1990, having taken 1,490 wickets in first-class cricket. He was knighted in June 1990 for his services to cricket.

Haganah. Protective force secretly formed by JEWS in PALESTINE in 1936 for defense of their communes against Arab attacks. Unlike purely terrorist organizations, it later became the nucleus of the Israeli army.

Hagen, Walter (1892–1969). U.S. golfer. He helped eliminate golf's elitist amateur image and turn it into a popular professional sport. A charismatic character who occasionally arrived at tournaments in a tuxedo, he was the leading golfer of the early 20th century, winning the U.S. Open in 1914 and 1919, the British Open four times between 1922 and 1929 and the PGA championship five times.

Hague, The [Den Haag; 's Gravenhage]. Capital city of the Netherlands' South Holland province; 4 miles from the North Sea and 33 miles from Amsterdam. Developed as a permanent site for negotiation between sovereign nations, it saw peace conferences in 1899 and 1907 that unsuccessfully attempted to solve the problems of fin de siecle Europe. In the 1920s The Hague became the seat of the **World Court** (now the **International Court of Justice)** as well as of various Dutch governmental bodies. During WORLD WAR II, Germans occupied the city from 1940 to 1945, in January 1945 launching V-1 rocket-bombs against advancing Allied troops.

Hague Conventions. International conferences convened by Czar NICHOLAS II; met May 18 to July 19, 1899, and June 15 to October 18, 1907, with the aim of "a possible reduction of the excessive armaments which weigh upon all nations" by "putting a limit on the progressive development of the present armaments." The first convention's achievements were limited but did include agreement on the use of gas, expanding bullets, the banning of explosives launched from balloons and the creation of a court of arbitration. The second convention reached agreement on a number of naval matters and on the employment of force to recover debts. A further convention was planned for 1915 but because of WORLD WAR I did not meet. The two conventions did influence the form of the LEAGUE OF NATIONS.

Hahn, Otto (1879–1968). German chemist. After obtaining his doctorate at the University of Marburg in 1901 Hahn studied abroad, first with William Ramsay in London and then at McGill University, Canada, with Ernest RUTHERFORD. Hahn returned to Germany in 1907, where he took up an appointment at the University of Berlin, being made professor of chemistry in 1910. Two years later he joined the Kaiser Wilhelm Institute of Chemistry where he served as director from 1928 to 1945.

Most of Hahn's career was spent in research on radioactivity. With Lise MEITNER he discovered a new element, protactinium, in 1917. He went on to define (1921) the phenomenon that arises when nuclei with different radioactive properties turn out to be identical in atomic number and mass. Hahn's most important work however, was done in the 1930s when, with Meitner and Fritz Strassmann, he made one of the most important discoveries of the century, namely nuclear fission. One of the strange features about Hahn's work was that he was repeating experiments already done and formulating hypotheses already rejected as nonsense or due to some contamination of the materials used.

Thus, when in 1938 Hahn bombarded uranium with slow neutrons and detected some strange, new half-lives, he assumed that the uranium had changed into radium, a close neighbor, with some undetected alpha particles. But when he tried to remove the radium all he could find was barium. This Hahn simply could not understand, for barium was far too low in the periodic table to be produced by the transmutation of uranium; and if the transformation was taking place it should be accompanied by the emission of a prodigious number of alpha particles, which Hahn could not have failed to detect. The thought that the heavy uranium nucleus could split into two lighter ones was too outrageous for him to consider seriously. He did realize that something of importance was going on. Appropriately enough it was his old collaborator Meitner, in exile from the Nazis in Sweden, and her nephew Otto Frisch, who made the necessary calculations and announced fission to the world early in 1939. Hahn received the NOBEL PRIZE for chemistry in 1944.

Haifa. Port and industrial center on the Mediterranean Sea coast of northern Israel. A port only since the 19th century, during World War II the Haifa area was one of the main Allied military supply bases in the Middle East. Iraqi Scud missiles hit Haifa during the PERSIAN GULF WAR (1991) but caused little damage.

Haig, Alexander (Meigs) (1924–). U.S. Army officer, presidential adviser and secretary of state (1981–82). A career Army officer, Haig rose through the ranks and, as colonel, commanded a brigade in VIETNAM (1966–67). Military adviser to President Richard M. NIXON from 1969 to 1973, General Haig became Nixon's White House chief of staff after the resignation of Robert Haldeman during the WATERGATE crisis and was a key figure in the White House during the final days of Nixon's presidency. Haig was subsequently commander in chief of American forces in Europe (1974–79) and supreme commander of NATO. He retired from the army with the rank of full general (four stars) to enter political life in 1979. He was appointed secretary of state by President Ronald REAGAN in 1981. When Reagan was shot by a would-be assassin, Haig made his famous "I'm in charge here" statement to the nation. As secretary of state, Haig's policy was often at variance with that of the president and other members of the administration, and Haig resigned after further differences with the president. He made an unsuccessful bid for the Republican presidential nomination in 1988.

Haig, Douglas [1st Earl Haig] (1861–1928). British field marshal. Born in Edinburgh, he was commissioned in the cavalry in 1885. Posted to the Sudan in 1898, he later served in the BOER WAR from 1899 to 1902. He was appointed an army corps commander in France at the outbreak of WORLD WAR I, becoming commander-in-chief of the British Expeditionary Force in 1915. Leading British troops during the bloody First Battle of the SOMME (1916) and Third Battle of YPRES (1917), Haig was widely held responsible for the appallingly high toll of British casualties in these engagements. Opposed by Prime Minister Lloyd GEORGE for wasting British lives, he nevertheless retained the loyalty of the British military. In 1918, Haig secured the appointment of Ferdinand FOCH as supreme Allied commander, and the two generals collaborated in the war's final campaigns. He was made a peer in 1919, and spent the rest of his life in activities for the British Legion and in soliciting aid for disabled veterans.

Field Marshal Douglas Haig, British commander in France during World War I.

For further reading:

De Groot, Gerard J., *Douglas Haig, 1861–1928*. Winchester Mass: Unwin Hyman, 1989.

Haile Selassie (1892–1975). Last emperor of ETHIOPIA. Haile Selassie ruled Ethiopia for half a century: as regent (1916), as king (1928–30) and as emperor (1930–74). His reign was interrupted for five years in May, 1936 following the Italian invasion of Ethiopia, which forced him into exile (see ITALO-ETHIOPIAN WAR OF 1935–36). In June 1936 he appealed to the LEAGUE OF NATIONS for aid against the Italian invaders but was refused. Selassie returned to Ethiopia in 1942 and began a series of modernization projects, including administrative reform, economic and judicial reorganization, the abolition of slavery and feudalism and the establishment of educational institutions. In 1963 he summoned the first meeting of the ORGANIZATION OF AFRICAN UNITY and devised the charter for the 38-member body, whose headquarters were in Addis Ababa. At his suggestion, the UNITED NATIONS set up the U.N. Economic Commission for Africa, also in Addis Ababa. However, he was unable to solve Ethiopia's social problems, and radicals in the country grew increasingly dissatisfied with his rule. Haile Selassie was overthrown in a 1974 coup by left-wing army officers, and died soon after under house arrest.

Haile Selassie.

Haiti [Republic of Haiti]. Covering an area of 10,712 square miles, Haiti comprises the western third of the Caribbean island of Hispaniola as well as several West Indian islets. Haiti has been plagued by dire poverty and political instability during most of the 20th century. The murder of President Guilliame Sam in 1915 led to United States intervention and administration of the country until 1934. Between 1946 and 1957 a succession of

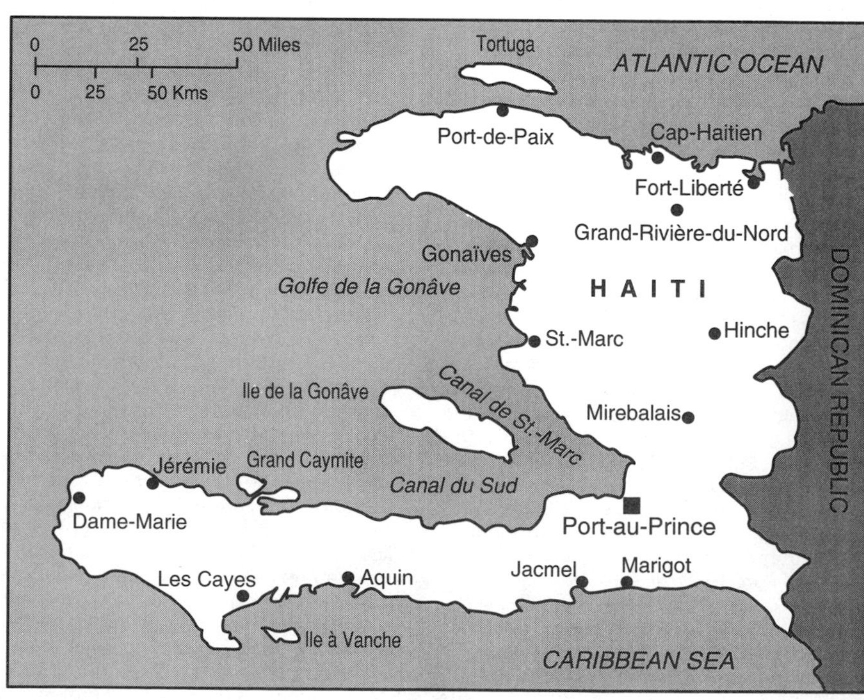

HAITI

presidents were either deposed or overthrown during coups. In 1957 Dr. Francois "Papa Doc" DUVALIER (1907–71) became dictator, creating a personal militia (the Ton-Ton Macoute) and declaring himself president-for-life (1964). Popular among a wide segment of the population, Duvalier brought a measure of stability; however, his personal charm belied his ruthlessness and corruption. Upon his death he was succeeded by his son, Jean-Claude "Baby Doc" Duvalier. The younger Duvalier was forced to flee the country in 1986 after food riots and increasingly violent demonstrations. A period of political upheaval followed until Rev. Jean-Bertrand Aristide, a leftist priest, was elected president in December 1990 in the first truly democratic election in Haiti's history. Over 100 people died in the unrest that followed a failed attempt to overthrow the Aristide government in January 1991.

For further reading:

Ferguson, James, *Papa Doc, Baby Doc*. Oxford: Basil Blackwell, 1987.

Haitian Revolt of 1915. With the country in chaos, Vibrun Guillaume Sam (d. 1915) seized control of HAITI's government in early 1915. A mob assassinated Sam, July 28, 1915 and in the subsequent anarchy U.S. Marines established order, protected foreigners and supervised elections. Phillippe Sudre Dartiguenave (1863–after 1922), the new president enforced a treaty (September 16, 1915) in which Haiti became a political and economic protectorate of the United States, with customs and police under American control.

Haitian Revolt of 1918–19. An American-supervised 1918 plebiscite adopted by the questionable vote of 98,225 to 768 established a new constitution in Haiti, since 1915 a ten-year protectorate of the U.S. Phillippe Sudre Dartiguenave (1863–after 1922) remained as president, while American officers ran the government and the gendarmerie revived the labor draft. In late 1918 Haitians led by Charlemagne Perlate (d. 1919) and Benoit Batraville (d. 1919) rebelled against the corvee and U.S. occupation. Between 20,000 to 40,000 poorly armed rebels believing themselves invincible through voodoo potions terrorized the region and attacked the capital, Port Au Prince. The gendarmerie crushed them with U.S. Marine and air support. Perlate and Batraville were executed and peace was restored. American occupation was later extended until 1934.

Halas, George (Stanley) "Papa Bear" (1895–1983). American athlete, football coach, and sports executive. Halas was a co-founder of the **National Football League,** owner of the **Chicago Bears** team franchise, and the winningest head coach in NFL history. After a brief stint with baseball's New York Yankees, Halas became player-coach of the Decatur (Ill.) Staleys of the American Professional Football Association. He bought the club and moved it to Chicago in 1921, renaming it the Chicago Bears. In 1922, he helped organize the NFL. He brought credibility to professional football by signing college star Red GRANGE in 1925. Halas coached for 40 years between 1920 and 1968, compiling a career record of 325 wins, 131 losses, and 31 ties. Under his leadership, the team also won six championships. Halas was inducted into the Pro Football Hall of Fame in 1963.

Haldane, John Burdon Sanderson (1892–1964). British geneticist. Haldane became involved in scientific research at an early age through helping in the laboratory of his father the physiologist John Scott Haldane. His interest in genetics was first stimulated as early as 1901, when he heard a lecture on Mendel's work, and he later applied this by studying inheritance in his sister's (the writer Naomi Mitchison) 300 guinea pigs. On leaving school he studied first mathematics and then the humanities at Oxford University. He served in WORLD WAR I with the Black Watch Regiment and was wounded at Loos and in Mesopotamia. Some work on gas masks, following the first German gas attacks, marked the beginning of his physiological studies.

In 1919 Haldane took up a fellowship at Oxford, where he continued research on respiration, investigating how the levels of carbon dioxide in the blood affect the muscles regulating breathing. He was next offered a readership in biochemistry at Cambridge, where he conducted some important work on enzymes. These experiments, and later work on conditions in submarines, aroused considerable public interest because he frequently used himself as a guinea pig.

In 1933 Haldane became professor of genetics at University College, London, a position he exchanged in 1937 for the chair of biometry. While at London he prepared a provisional map of the X sex chromosome and showed the genetic linkage between hemophilia and color blindness. He also produced the first estimate of mutation rates in humans from studies of the pedigrees of hemophiliacs, and described the effect of recurring deleterious mutations on a population. With the outbreak of the SPANISH CIVIL WAR, Haldane joined the Communist Party and advised the republican government on gas precautions. In the 1950s he left the party as a result of Soviet acceptance and promotion of Trofim LYSENKO. In protest at the Anglo-French invasion of Suez, Haldane immigrated to India in 1957, becoming an Indian citizen in 1961. He was director of the laboratory of genetics and biometry at Bhubaneswar from 1962 until his death. Haldane's books include *Enzymes* (1930), *The Causes of Evolution* (1932), abd *The Biochemistry of Genetics* (1954); he also wrote a number of books popularizing science.

Haldane, Richard Burden [Viscount] (1856–1928). British statesman. Born in Edinburgh, Haldane attended Gottingen University in Germany. He served as a Liberal member of Parliament from 1885 to 1911. As war minister from 1905 to 1912, he increased the efficiency of the British army, creating a general staff, a territorial army, an officers' training corps and an expeditionary force. In 1912 he traveled on a mission to Berlin, where he was unsuccessful in halting German naval rearmament and rejected a plea for British neutrality. He served as lord chancellor from 1912 to 1915 but was forced from public life at the outbreak of WORLD WAR I when his knowledge of German affairs caused him to be unjustly branded as pro-German. He briefly served again as lord chancellor in Ramsay MACDONALD's first Labour government in 1924. Also a noted academic philosopher, Haldane was later the chancellor of the University of Bristol. His writings include a number of works on philosophy and an autobiography (1929).

Halder, Franz (1884–1972). German general. A career army officer, Halder succeeded General Ludwig Beck as chief of the German general staff in 1938, just after the MUNICH PACT. Although opposed to HITLER's plans for European

HAITI

1915	U.S. Marines land to restore order after murder of President Guilliame Sam.
1934	U.S. Marines withdrawn.
1957	(September) Dr. Francois (Papa Doc) Duvalier is elected president.
1960	Roman Catholic archbishop, Msgr. Francois Poirier, is exiled.
1964	Duvalier declares himself president-for-life.
1971	(April) Papa Doc dies and is succeeded by his son Jean-Claude (Baby Doc) Duvalier.
1985	(December) Food riots break out in Gonaives and spread rapidly to the capital, Port-au-Prince.
1986	(Feb. 7) Baby Doc flees the country.
1990	(March) Supreme Court Justice Ertha Pascal-Trouillot assumes presidency; (Dec. 16) Jean-Bertrand Aristide wins landslide presidential election.
1991	(Jan. 7) A coup led by Tonton Macoutes attempts to prevent Aristide from assuming the presidency but is quickly crushed by the army; Aristide sworn in.

conquest, Halder engineered the German BLITZKRIEG victories against Poland, the Netherlands, Belgium, Luxembourg and France in 1939 and 1940. Hitler relieved Halder of his command in 1942. Halder was later arrested and imprisoned for his involvement in the plot to assassinate Hitler (July 20, 1944). He was freed by the Americans in April 1945.

Haley, Alex (1921–). American author. Haley became famous with the publication of the novel ROOTS (1976), which traces his ancestry back to Africa and follows his ancestors as they are captured and taken as slaves to the U.S. The book was adapted for television, becoming the first "miniseries," and its popularity was something of a media phenomenon. The book sparked an interest in genealogy, particularly among black Americans, whose history was obfuscated by the practice of slavery. Haley's other works include *The Autobiography of Malcolm X* (1965, written with MALCOLM X) and *A Different Kind of Christmas* (1988).

Haley, Bill (1927–1981). American guitarist, singer, band leader, and pioneer of ROCK-and-roll music. With his group, the Comets, Haley recorded such early rock and roll hits as "Shake, Rattle and Roll" (1954), "Rock the Joint" and "Crazy, Man, Crazy." The group's biggest hit, however, was "Rock Around the Clock" (1955), which was the theme song to the film *The Blackboard Jungle*. It was written by Haley, and sold 22.5 million copies over the next 15 years. Haley's performances throbbed with energy and exuberance and helped make rock and roll a major part of the American music idiom in the 1950s. Along with Elvis PRESLEY, Haley and the Comets were an important influence on the BEATLES and other prominent rock performers of the 1960s and 1970s. Although they are primarily thought of as a 1950s group, Haley and the Comets continued to perform successfully during the next two decades.

Haley, Sir William (John) (1901–1987). British journalist. In a career of nearly

Alex Haley, American author.

Bill Haley, pioneer rock-and-roll star and leader of the band "Bill Haley and the Comets" (1957).

five decades, Haley headed the *Manchester Guardian* (1939–43), the BBC (1944–52) and the *Times* of London (1952–66), as well as the *Encyclopaedia Britannica* (1968–69). While director general of the BBC, he broadened its cultural programming by instituting a Third Channel on radio in 1946. Perhaps his most memorable achievement as editor in chief of the *Times* was his banishment, in 1966, of birth, death and marriage notices from the front page; he replaced them with news.

Halfaya Pass [Nagb al-Halfayah]. Pass through a coastal range of hills in northwestern Egypt. Battles fought here in January and November 1942 earned it the WORLD WAR II nickname of "Hellfire Pass" from British soldiers.

Halifax. City on the Atlantic Coast of Canada's province of Nova Scotia. In 1917, during WORLD WAR I, a French ammunition ship exploded here, wrecking much of the city. During WORLD WAR II Halifax was the chief North American base for Allied supply ships.

Halifax, Edward Frederick Lindley Wood (1881–1959). British statesman. Lord Halifax began his political career as a Conservative member of Parliament (1910–25). He headed the Board of Education from 1922 to 1924 and the Board of Agriculture from 1924 to 1925, when he was created Baron Irwin. In the post of Viceroy of INDIA from 1926 to 1931, he negotiated with Mohandas GANDHI and advocated dominion status for the country. He succeeded his father as Viscount Halifax in 1934 and was appointed lord privy seal the following year. Serving as foreign secretary (1938–40) under Neville CHAMBERLAIN, he was at first a lukewarm supporter of the APPEASEMENT policy toward Nazi GERMANY. Halifax was considered as a possible successor to Chamberlain as prime minister, but declined the appointment in favor of Winston S. CHURCHILL. He remained foreign secretary for several months under Churchill, then served as ambassador to the U.S. from 1941 to 1951. Halifax was created an earl in 1944. His autobiography, *Fullness of Days*, was published in 1957. Halifax was also chancellor of Oxford University from 1953 until his death in 1959.

Hall, Edward T. (1914–). American anthropologist whose studies and writing had a direct influence on modern thinking about design and architecture. Hall's work became well-known with the publication of his books *The Silent Language* in 1959 and *The Hidden Dimension* in 1966. They report on his studies of the ways in which human interactions are influenced by such physical circumstances as the size and shape of spaces, placement of furniture, quality of light, color, and similar elements of the environment. When related to human life, the concept of territoriality, first studied as an aspect of animal behavior, has led to an awareness of the problems created by crowding in modern cities, buildings, and transport.

Hall, Gus (1910–). Secretary-general of the American Communist Party. The son of Finnish immigrants who were charter members of the American Communist Party, Hall himself joined the party at an early age. After serving in the Navy in World War II, he was imprisoned from 1949 to 1957 for conspiring to advocate the violent otherthrow of the U.S government. He was released in 1957, and in 1959 he became secretary-general of the party. In 1962, Hall refused to register the Communist Party with the federal government, as required by the McCarren Act, and in 1965 the United States Supreme Court ruled that the registration of individual members was unconstitutional. With the loosening of government restrictions, the party became more vocal throughout the 1960s, and Hall was nominated as the party's presidential candidate in 1972, 1976, 1980 and 1984.

Hall, Joyce Clyde (1891–1982). U.S. greeting card pioneer. He started selling postcards while still in school, and later started a wholesale business in postcards with his brother. In 1913 Hall became convinced that standard greetings could be printed to fit almost every occasion, and his philosophy provided the business pattern followed almost universally since. Hall devised marketing practices, such as the independent display rack. He invented the special occasion cards, and quickly Hallmark became the biggest name in the field. His company also sponsored quality radio and TV drama.

Hall, Peter (1930–). British theatrical director. Hall attended Cambridge University, where he began his theatrical career. His earliest work was at the Theatre Royal, Windsor, and the London Arts Theatre. In 1957 he founded his own company, the International Playwrights' Theatre. At the same time, he established a reputation as a Shakespearean director with his version of *Love's Labour's Lost* at Stratford-upon-Avon. From 1960 to 1968 he was managing director of the new ROYAL SHAKESPEARE COMPANY, creating an incomparable ensemble and staging plays at Stratford and at the Aldwych Theatre,

London. Among his most highly acclaimed productions were the *War of the Roses* cycle (1963) and *Richard III* (1964). Hall succeeded Laurence OLIVIER as director of the National Theatre in 1973, producing a wide range of plays until his departure in 1988. Among the best known were *Hamlet* (1975), Chekhov's *The Cherry Orchard* (1978) and Shaffer's *Amadeus* (1979).

Halleck, Charles A(braham) (1900–1986). American politician. A Republican from Indiana, Halleck was elected to 16 consecutive terms in the House of Representatives after winning a special election in 1935 to fill the remainder of the term of an incumbent who had died. He twice served as House majority leader, in 1947–48 and again in 1953–54. Although a conservative REPUBLICAN PARTY loyalist, he was frequently allied with conservative Southern Democrats. He parted company with them on the issue of CIVIL RIGHTS, supporting all major civil rights legislation in the late 1950s and early 1960s. Halleck became well known to U.S. television audiences in the 1960s as a participant with Illinois Republican Sen. Everett DIRKSEN in broadcasts attacking Democratic administration policies.

Haller, Fritz (1924–). Swiss architect and furniture designer known for the system of office furniture that bears his name. Haller has been in practice as architect and urban planner at Solothurn (near Basel), Switzerland, since 1949. He developed several steel-frame building systems currently used in Europe. In 1960 he developed a related system of office furniture using interchangeable steel tubes and connectors to form frames that carry shelves, work-tops, files and other storage elements. Haller has taught at the University of Southern California and at the University of Karlsruhe, West Germany. He is the author of *Integralurban; a Model,* a study of urban planning, and is the winner of several design awards.

Hallinan, Hazel Hunkins (1891–1982). American women's rights activist. She began her career as a member of the National Woman's Party in 1916, after chemical companies told her that they did not hire women. In 1917 she and other suffragists were arrested for chaining themselves to the White House fence and setting fire to its lawn. After the NINETEENTH AMENDMENT was passed in 1920 she moved to London, where she campaigned for British women's rights and wrote the "London Letter" column for the *Chicago Tribune.* (See also WOMEN'S MOVEMENTS.)

"Hallmark Hall of Fame." The most honored anthology series in the history of television. Hallmark Cards, Inc., had been founded by Mr. Joyce HALL in Kansas City in 1910. In the late 1930s and early 1940s he began sponsoring a radio series called "Tony Wons' Scrapbook." The "Hallmark Playhouse" debuted on radio in 1948 and featured such notables as Ronald Colman in "Around the World in 80 Days" and Herbert Marshall in "Lost Horizon." Hallmark moved to television in 1951 underwriting a series of 15-minute interviews hosted by Sarah Churchill (daughter of Winston); and then later on Dec. 24 of that year with the groundbreaking live telecast of the first original opera created for television, AMAHL AND THE NIGHT VISITORS. As the Hallmark-sponsored series moved into its "Golden Age" over the next thirty years—seen under a variety of names, like "The Television Playhouse" and, finally, "The Hallmark Hall of Fame"—it garnered many "firsts" for the medium. *Hamlet* (1953) was the first full-length Shakespeare on any network. That same year a re-broadcast of *Amahl* was the first color transmission (aired just two days after the FCC approved NBC's patented "color tine" process). *Kiss Me Kate* (1958) was the first color video tape telecast. The 1960 version of *Macbeth,* filmed in Scotland, lays claim to being the first made-for-television movie. *The Tempest* (1960) was the first classic drama to rank in the Top 10 television ratings. Most of the great actors of stage and screen have appeared—including Julie HARRIS in ten roles (including *Victoria Regina* in 1961), Katherine CORNELL in *There Shall Be No Night* (1957), James STEWART in *Harvey* (1972) and the team of Alfred LUNT and Lynne FONTANNE, in *The Magnificent Yankee* (1965). The series has won more than 56 Emmys, seven Peabody Awards, two Golden Globes, and numerous other distinctions. "I was convinced that the average American did not have the mind of a 12-year old," recalled Joyce C. Hall in his autobiography, *When You Care Enough* (1979), concerning his decision to sponsor these telecasts. "We wanted to reach the upper masses, not just the upper classes."

For further reading:

Hallmark Hall of Fame: A Tradition of Excellence. New York: Museum of Broadcasting, 1985.

Hallstein, Walter (1901–1982). German lawyer and statesman. Hallstein was a key figure in the molding of WEST GERMANY's foreign policy after WORLD WAR II. He developed the doctrine of severing ties with any government (except the U.S.S.R.) that recognized EAST GERMANY, but believed that it was important for West Germany to maintain diplomatic ties with the U.S.S.R. He was president of the commission of the EUROPEAN COMMUNITY (the Common Market, or EEC) from 1959 to 1967. In this post he worked for European unity.

halogen lighting. Lighting provided by a special type of incandescent lamp (bulb or tube in nontechnical language) that uses a tungsten-halogen filament to produce high-intensity light in a very small (often miniature) lamp. A special quartz glass outer bulb or tube is used to resist the very high heat and internal pressure of halogen lamps, so that the fixtures must be designed to protect against contact with the tube and any possibility of breakage. Halogen light is often used for special purposes, such as stage lighting, projectors, and instrument, dental, and airport lighting applications.

Halsey, William F(rederick, Jr.) "Bull" (1882–1959). American admiral. Born in Elizabeth, N.J., Halsey graduated from Annapolis in 1904. During WORLD WAR I, he was a destroyer commander, and he was a naval aviator after 1935. During WORLD WAR II, the tenacious "Bull" Halsey commanded the Allied forces in the South Pacific (1942–44), successfully directing the Solomon Islands campaign. Commander of the U.S. Third Fleet in 1944–45, he was in charge of naval activities in the Philippines, defeated the Japanese fleet at Leyte Gulf in October 1944 and directed the sea-based bombardment of JAPAN in July 1945. He became a five-star admiral, the Navy's highest rank, in 1945. He retired in 1947, the same year his memoirs, *Admiral Halsey's Story,* were published. (See also WORLD WAR II IN THE PACIFIC.)

Halston [born Roy Halston Frowick] (1932–1990). American fashion designer. Halston first became famous as the milliner who created the "pillbox" hat worn by Jacqueline KENNEDY during her husband's inauguration in 1961. He showed his first clothing designs in 1966 and established his own couture line two years later. His ready-to-wear line was established in 1972. The simple, clean lines of his designs were immediately popular and won him such friends and clients as Liza Minelli, Elizabeth TAYLOR, and Bianca Jagger. He sold his business and his trademark name in 1973, leaving him with little say as to the products that bore his name.

Hamburg. One of the largest ports in the world; a German cultural center and industrial city on the Elbe River, about 60 miles upriver from Cuxhaven, on the North Sea. The scene of communist rioting in 1923, since 1937 Hamburg has been coextensive with, and capital of, the state of Hamburg. During WORLD WAR II Hamburg was heavily bombed, so much so that much of the city today is brand new, while surviving buildings are identified as such by plaques. Many old churches were destroyed, but the baroque St. Michael's Church, built between 1750 and 1762, and the Church of St. Jacobi, begun in the 14th century, have survived. In 1989 Hamburg celebrated the 800th anniversary of its charter as a free city by Frederick Barbarossa.

Hameenlinna [Swedish: Tavastehus]. City in southwestern Finland's Hame province. During WORLD WAR I, Hameenlinna's fortress was held by Russia until Finnish troops recaptured it with German assistance. Composer Jean SIBELIUS was born here.

Hamilton, George Heard (1910–). American art historian, teacher and museum director. Educated at Yale University, Hamilton taught art history there and was a curator at the Yale Art Gallery (1936–66). He was a professor at Williams College (1965– 75), while serving as director of the Clark Art Institute, Williamstown, Mass. (1966–77). A specialist in European and American art of the 19th and 20th centuries, he is the author of

Dag Hammarskjold, secretary general of the United Nations (1959).

such books as *Painting and Sculpture in Europe, 1880–1940* (1967) and *Nineteenth and Twentieth Century Art (1970).*

Hamilton, Richard (1922–). British artist and art world figure. A forerunner of POP ART, Hamilton employs images from popular American culture in his works. Hamilton is probably best known for his 1956 collage *Just what is it that makes today's homes so different, so appealing?* He has also been involved in organizing various London art exhibitions.

Hamilton, Scott (1958–). American figure skater. The adopted child of university professors, Hamilton was diagnosed in early childhood with a growth-inhibiting disease. The disease abated when he took up skating at the age of nine. Never topping 5 foot 3 inches and 110 pounds, he won three consecutive world championships from 1981 to 1983. His ease with spectacular triple jumps made him a favorite entering the 1984 Winter OLYMPICS. While his performance in the short and long freeskating programs fell somewhat short, as he finished second to his longtime rival, Canadian Brian Orser, his compulsory figures were enough to give him the gold medal. After retiring from competition, Hamilton's insight into his sport led to a career as a skating commentator.

Hammarskjold, Dag (1905–1961). Swedish statesman, secretary-general of the UNITED NATIONS (1953–61). Hammarskjold was Sweden's deputy foreign minister from 1951 to 1953. Elected secretary-general of the UN in 1953, he was reelected in 1957. The dignity and impartiality with which he conducted UN affairs, especially during the SUEZ CRISIS, enhanced the standing of the organization. In 1960 his handling of the Congo crisis provoked hostility from the U.S.S.R. While seeking peace between the Congo and the secessionist province of KATANGA, Hammarskjold was killed in an airplane crash. He was awarded the 1961 NOBEL PRIZE for peace posthumously.

Hammer, Armand (1898–1990). American industrialist and Soviet expert. Born in New York City and trained as a physician, Hammer made his first visit to the U.S.S.R. in 1921 on a medical mission. Retaining an abiding interest in Soviet-American friendship, he had personal contacts with Russian leaders from LENIN to GORBACHEV. A gifted entrepeneur, he soon became involved in trading U.S. grain for Soviet furs and caviar. Over the years, Hammer headed successful businesses in fields ranging from whiskey to broadcasting, but his greatest fortune was made through his building of Occidental Petroleum Co. into a major international oil company. He was also a major philanthropist and noted art collector.

Armand Hammer, first capitalist to trade with the Soviet Union (1990).

Hammerstein, Oscar, II (1895–1960). American song lyricist and librettist best known for his collaborations with Jerome KERN and Richard RODGERS. Hammerstein was born in New York into a musical theater family. After abandoning law studies at Columbia University he embarked upon a series of notable collaborations with Herbert Stothart (*Wildflower*, 1923); Sigmund ROMBERG (*The Desert Song*, 1926, and *New Moon*, 1928); and Jerome KERN (*Show Boat*, 1927). The historic partnership with Richard Rodgers began with *Oklahoma* (1943) and included such landmark musical shows as *Carousel* (1945), *South Pacific* (1949), *The King and I* (1951), *Flower Drum Song* (1958) and their last, *The Sound of Music* (1959). In contrast to Rodgers' previous collaborator, Lorenz HART (to whom he was frequently and unfavorably compared), Hammerstein had a positive and romantic style. To quote one of his songs, he was "stuck like a dope with a thing called hope." The style emerged at its best in "Oh, What a Beautiful Morning," "Younger than Springtime," "Hello, Young Lovers" and "Billy's Soliloquy" (all with Rodgers); and at its worst in such saccharine ditties as "Happy Talk" and "Climb Ev'ry Mountain" (also with Rodgers). He wrote his autobiogra-

Oscar Hammerstein II (left) and partner Richard Rodgers celebrate the first anniversary of Carousel *and the third anniversary of* Oklahoma! *(April 21, 1946).*

phy, *Lyrics by Hammerstein*, in 1949, and died of cancer in 1960. He played an important part, wrote producer Max Gordon, in "laying the groundwork for what was to become America's undeniable contribution to the world's theatre."

For further reading:

Bordman, Gerald, *American Operetta*. New York: Oxford University Press, 1981.

Hammer v. Dagenhart (1918). U.S. Supreme Court decision striking down an early effort to ban child labor. During the early years of the century, young children were commonly employed in factories. Responding to popular outcries over this practice, Congress passed a federal Child Labor Law that outlawed the sale of goods produced by children working either more than six days a week or more than eight hours per day. The Supreme Court struck down the law as unconstitutional, however. The Court reasoned that manufacturing was not "commerce" and was outside the scope of Congress' regulatory authority. The case was not overruled until 1937 with the passage of the Fair Labor Standards Act, which severely limited the use of child labor in factories. (See also BAILEY V. DREXEL FURNITURE CO.)

Hammett, (Samuel) Dashiell (1894–1961). American novelist. Hammett's much-imitated fiction, beginning with *Red Harvest* (1929), is the origin of the tough, realistic genre of detective stories. His best known works include *The Maltese Falcon* (1930, filmed three times, most notably in 1941), which introduced the hard-boiled detective Sam Spade; and *The Thin Man* (1934, filmed 1934), which features Nick and Nora Charles. Hammett's writing was based on his own experiences as a private detective in the late teens. Following 1934, Hammett worked as a screenwriter in HOLLYWOOD. Among his credits is the screen adaptation for *Watch on the Rhine* (1943) by Lillian HELLMAN, who became Hammett's companion in 1930. During the MCCARTHY era, Hammett was jailed for refusing to testify in 1951. He was ill when he was released, and later impoverished as a result of increased scrutiny by the Internal Revenue Service.

Dashiell Hammett, author of The Thin Man *and other novels, testifying before Joseph McCarthy's Senate investigations subcommittee, refused to say whether he was or had been a communist (March 26, 1953).*

Hammond, John (1910–1987). American record producer. A JAZZ and BLUES aficionado, Hammond's legendary talent scouting abilities led him to such finds as Bessie SMITH, Billie HOLIDAY, Benny GOODMAN and Count BASIE. In 1933 he became American recording director of the English division of Columbia Records. There he used his private income as an heir to the Vanderbilt fortune to subsidize many recordings by such artists as Fletcher HENDERSON and Chick WEBB. A champion of racial equality, he was proud of his role in creating jazz's first integrated group—the Benny Goodman Trio. In later years, he signed Aretha FRANKLIN, Bob DYLAN and Bruce SPRINGSTEEN to Columbia Records.

Hampshire, Stuart (Sir) (1914–). British philosopher. Hampshire is one of the best known British philosophers of the post-World-War-II era, although he has been a clarifier and synthesizer of past ideas rather than an originator of a new philosophic system. Educated at Oxford, Hampshire taught there as well as at University College, London, and at Princeton University. The fields on which he has written include epistemology, philosophy of mind, aesthetics and metaphysics. One of his key ideas has been that different conditions apply to the certainty of a statement, depending on the particular class of statement under consideration. Major works by Hampshire include *Spinoza* (1951), *Thought and Action* (1959), *Feeling and Expression* (1960) and *Freedom of the Individual* (1965).

Hampton, Christopher James (1946–). British playwright. Hampton's first play, *When Did You Last See My Mother* (1966), was performed by the English State Company at the Royal Court Theatre, where Hampton was resident playwright from 1968 to 1970. There he wrote *Total Eclipse* (1968) and *The Philanthropist* (1970). Perhaps his best known work is *Les Liaisons Dangereuses* (1986, filmed 1989), which depicts a manipulative contest of seduction between a nobleman and lady in pre-revolutionary France. Hampton has also translated the works of CHEKHOV, Ibsen and Molire. Other works include *Savages* (1973) and *Tales from Hollywood* (1980).

Hampton, Lionel (1909–). American jazz musician and bandleader. Born in Louisville, Kentucky, Hampton performed in the early part of his career with Paul Howard, Les Hite, and Louis ARMSTRONG, playing drums, xylophone and vibraphone. He was a popular performer with Benny GOODMAN from 1936 to 1940, before founding his own band in 1941. One of the most popular and exciting big bands of the 1940s, Hampton's group survived until 1965, when he moved more into rhythm and blues and founded the Jazz Inner Circle sextet.

Hamsun, Knut [born Knut Pedersen] (1859–1952). Norwegian novelist. Hamsun first achieved acclaim with the novel *Sult* (*Hunger* 1890). Based on his own travails, the novel depicts a starving young writer attempting to establish himself. With its intense prose and hallucinatory passages, the novel has come to be regarded as a seminal modernist work. Important subsequent fiction includes *Mysterier* (*Mysteries* 1892), *Pan* (1894) and *Markens grode* (*Growth of the Soil*, 1917) Hamsun was awarded the NOBEL PRIZE for literature in 1920. Although he continued to write throughout his life, Hamsun's later works never received the attention of his early novels. He was an avid supporter of NAZISM during the 1930s and WORLD WAR II. After the war he was arrested by the Norwegian government and tried in 1947.

For further reading:

Ferguson, Robert, *Enigma: The Life of Knut Hamsun*. New York: Farrar, Straus & Giroux, 1987.

Hancock, Herbie (1940–). One of contemporary jazzdom's most visible and successful performers. While completing his education at Grinnell College in the late 1950s, Hancock returned to his hometown of Chicago on weekends to back such prominent jazz artists as Coleman HAWKINS. His successful recording debut as a leader in 1962 produced a hit song, "Watermelon Man," and an invitation to join Miles DAVIS's fabled quintet. With bassist Ron Carter and drummer Tony Williams, Hancock helped evolve a more open-ended and interactive approach to rhythm section playing that made the Davis fivesome one of the most influential groups of the 1960s. Following up the fusion experiments of Davis and groups like WEATHER REPORT, Hancock, since the late 1960s, has devoted much energy to various amalgams of rock, funk and jazz; his "Rockit" was a number-one pop hit in 1983. Hancock has made periodic returns to more conventional neo-bebop jazz settings, most significantly in his piano duos with Chick COREA. He has also scored feature films, including *Round Midnight* (1986), for which he won an ACADEMY AWARD. Among Hancock's original jazz standards are "Maiden Voyage," "Dolphin Dance," "Cantaloupe Island" and "Speak Like a Child."

For further reading:

Lyons, Len, *The Great Jazz Pianists: Speaking of Their Lives and Music*. New York: William Morrow, 1983.

Hand, Learned (1872–1961). American jurist. An honors graduate of both Harvard University and its law school, Hand was one of the best-known jurists of his day, although he was inexplicably never nominated to the U.S. Supreme Court. Hand favored the doctrine of judicial restraint, which requires courts not to substitute their views for those of the legislatures that make the laws. Under this doctrine courts should not make law or stretch laws beyond their intended purpose. Perhaps his best-known opinion was in DENNIS V. U.S. (1949), in which he upheld the convictions of 11 leaders of the U.S. Communist Party under the SMITH ACT. Hand's opinion was later upheld by the Supreme Court, which adopted his view that the government could bar political speech even when it did not incite violence. Hand's brother Augustus was also a prominent federal appeals judge.

Handke, Peter (1942–). Austrian playwright and novelist. Handke established himself as an unorthodox author with the plays, *Publikumsbschimpfung* (Offending the Audience, 1966), *Kaspar* (1968), which shows the influence of the philosopher Ludwig WITTGENSTEIN, and *Der Ritt ber den Bodensee* (1971). His works examine use of language and communication. His novels include *Across* (1986) and *Repetition* (1988).

Handl, Irene (1902–1987). One of Great Britain's most beloved character actresses, Handl excelled in comic portrayals of eccentric Cockneys. Although she did not turn to acting until her late 30s, she achieved quick success and emerged as a star of stage, cinema and television. Her biggest theatrical hit was *Goodnight Mrs. Puffin,* which ran for three years in the early 1960s. She was familiar to TV viewers for appearances in such comedy series as "For the Love of Ada" (1970–73) and "Never Say Die."

Handy, W(illiam) C(hristopher) (1873–1958). Noted American jazz composer. Handy initially studied organ and music theory, then cornet. His first significant professional experiences occurred at the turn-of-the-century with Mahara's Minstrels, first as a cornet soloist, later as the group's leader. In 1917 he moved to New York, where he supplemented his playing career with song writing; he also enjoyed some success as a music publisher. Though he continued performing into the 1940s, Handy's greatest significance was as a composer and collector of BLUES; his "Beale Street Blues" and "Memphis Blues" are among the most popular songs of the standard jazz repertoire. In 1928, a 17-minute film dramatized Handy's most famous and enduring composition, "St. Louis Blues"; the film is significant for the only cinematic appearance of legendary blues singer Bessie SMITH, who in the 1920s had helped popularize Handy's immortal tune; also important is the short film's status as perhaps the first widely released sound film to be based on a popular song and therefore a proto-forerunner of the music-video phenomenon. In 1957, Nat "King" COLE starred in a highly fictionalized biography of Handy, *St. Louis Blues.* Handy's autobiography is *Father of the Blues.*

Hanley, James (1901–1985). British author. Although Hanley never gained a large readership, he was regarded by some critics and fellow writers as one of the most important figures in 20th-century English literature. A number of his novels drew upon his youthful experiences as a seaman and led reviewers to compare him to Joseph CONRAD. Among the most acclaimed of his novels were *The Closed Harbor* (1952), *Levine* (1956), and *A Dream Journey* (1976). Although primarily a novelist, he probably achieved greater public recognition as a playwright. His plays were staged in London, New York, and elsewhere.

Hanoi. Capital of VIETNAM; on the Red River, about 75 miles upriver from the Gulf of Tonkin port of Haiphong. Occupied by France in 1883, Hanoi was the capital of French INDOCHINA from 1887 to 1946, a period of industrial development; during WORLD WAR II its Japanese occupiers were frequently bombed. From 1946 to 1954 Hanoi was the seat of the unrecognized (by France) Democratic Republic of Vietnam and a scene of heavy fighting between the French and the VIET MINH. After France threw in the colonial towel, Hanoi became the capital of **North Vietnam** and experienced a period of great industrial expansion—until the VIETNAM WAR of 1965–73. Heavily bombed by U.S. forces, its factories were dismantled and moved elsewhere but were speedily reconstructed after the war.

Hansberry, Lorraine (1930–1965). American playwright. Hansberry is best known for the celebrated play *A Raisin in the Sun* (1959, filmed 1961), which depicts a black family facing a moral dilemma involving racial prejudice. The title of the play was taken from a poem by Nikki GIOVANNI. Hansberry's life was tragically short, and the only other of her works she was to see performed was *The Sign in Sidney Brustein's Window* (1964), which concerns Jewish life in New York City.

Hanson, Duane (1925–). American sculptor. An influential New Realist, Hanson is known for his life-sized figures of ordinary Americans caught in moments typical of their everyday lives. Among his uncannily realistic sculptures are the 1970 works *Hard Hat* and *Woman with Dog* (Whitney Museum of American Art, N.Y.C.).

Hanson, Howard Harold (1896–1981). American composer, conductor and educator. Hanson studied music at the University of Nebraska, the Juilliard School and at Northwestern University, Chicago. His 1920 composition earned him the Prix de Rome, for a three-year advanced study period in that city. In 1924, Hanson became director of the Eastman School of Music, Rochester (1924–1964), and brought the school to national and international fame. He is considered one of the most influential teachers and composers of his time. Hanson founded the American Composers Concerts at Rochester, and wrote six symphonies, an opera and many other symphonic and choral works. He won a 1944 PULITZER PRIZE for his Fourth Symphony.

Hapoel Hamizrachi [Heb., The Mizrach Worker]. In ISRAEL, a religious—moderately orthodox—center-left party. It joined with MIZRACHI in 1956 to form the **National Religious Party**.

happening. Term for artistic event that emphasizes spontaneous developments. The term "happening" was coined in 1959 by conceptual artist Allan KAPROW to describe an artistic environment—whether in a public park or in a private art gallery—that allows participation by persons other than the artist in the creation of aesthetic works and moods. A key influence on the concept of a "happening" was the irreverent playfulness of the POP ART movement. Happenings featured artists painting, filming, and photographing on the spot; mass participation in the coloring of a canvas; dance and music; and any other activities that seemed to add to the joy and creativity of the situation. Happenings were as much philosophical statements on the stifled nature of societal behavior as they were aesthetic works of art. (See also BE-IN.)

Harare [formerly Salisbury]. Capital city of ZIMBABWE (formerly known as RHODESIA); in southeastern Africa. The largest city in Zimbabwe was founded in 1890 as a fort by the Pioneer Column, a mercenary force organized by Cecil J. Rhodes, a diamond-rich British imperialist and entrepreneur. The outpost was named for Robert Arthur Salisbury, then prime minister of Great Britain. Salisbury was the capital of the **Federation of Rhodesia and Nyasaland** from 1953 to 1963. In 1965, when Rhodesia unilaterally proclaimed its independence, Salisbury became the capital—and remained so when white political domination ended and the land was officially recognized as the African nation of Zimbabwe in 1979. In April 1982 Salisbury became Harare, to honor a 19th-century tribal chief.

Harbin [Haerhpin]. Major trading and industrial city of Chinese MANCHURIA, the capital of Heilungkiang province; on the Sungari River in northeastern China. Formerly known as Pinkiang, or Pingkiang, Harbin grew rapidly after China granted Russia a concession in 1896, and with the completion of a railroad to PORT ARTHUR in 1898. A Russian administrative headquarters from 1898 to 1905, Harbin was taken by China after Russia's defeat in the RUSSO-JAPANESE WAR, occupied by Japan from 1932 to 1945, seized again by the U.S.S.R. and finally taken by the Chinese communists in 1946.

Harburg, Edgar Y. "Yip" (1896–1981). American song lyricist. Harburg first gained notice with his words to the 1932 song, *Brother, Can You Spare a Dime,* a poignant account of a man's dreams and hardships during the GREAT DEPRESSION. During his career he wrote the lyrics to more than 30 other well-known songs, which were often marked by touches of romantic imagination and strong feelings of social justice. He collaborated with some of America's leading popular composers on scores of stage and film musicals, including *Finian's Rainbow* and, most notably, *The Wizard of Oz,* which won him an ACADEMY AWARD in 1939. Undoubtedly his most acclaimed song was "Somewhere Over the Rainbow," which made a star of Judy GARLAND.

hard-edge painting. Term for American painting developed in the late 1950s that uses large blocks of monochromatic color in sharp-edged geometrical forms. In these works, there is usually an interplay between positive and negative space, image and field. Artists who have used various forms of this style include Ellsworth KELLY, Alexander Liberman, Agnes Martin and Frank STELLA.

Hardie, (James) Keir (1856–1915). British labor leader and politician, revered as a major figure in the early history of the British LABOUR PARTY. The Scottish-born Hardie was a leading figure in the British labor movement from the 1880s until his death and was a cofounder of the Labour Party. He sat in Parliament from 1892 to 1895 and again (as M.P. for Merthyr Tydfil) from 1900 until his death. He was the first chairman (1906–7) of the parliamentary Labour Party and, more than anyone else, was responsible for establishing the party's identity and program in its early days. A committed pacifist and nonconformist, he opposed Britain's entry into WORLD WAR I.

Harding, Field Marshal Lord John (Allan Francis) (1896–1989). British army officer. Harding was the commander of British forces in North Africa during WORLD WAR II. As a brigadier general in 1940 he led Britain's Seventh Armoured Division, known as the "Desert Rats," in the battle of EL ALAMEIN, which turned the tide against the German forces in North Africa. After the war, he was appointed commander in chief of the British Army of the Rhine. He later served as governor of CYPRUS, where he was the target of death threats from a guerrilla group seeking unification with GREECE.

Harding, Warren G(amaliel) (1865–1923). Twenty-ninth president of the United States. Harding studied at Ohio Central College, began a journalistic career and built a strong Republican political base in Ohio. In 1899 he went to the state legislature and in 1904 became lieutenant governor. He lost a bid for the governorship but continued to rise politically. At the Republican national convention in 1912, he was chosen to present the nomination of William Howard TAFT. In 1914 he was elected to the U.S. Senate, where he had an undistinguished term. However, a group of his fellow Republican senators proposed his name for president at the Republican convention of 1920. When the convention became deadlocked, Harding was thought of as an ideal compromise candidate. He received the nomination on the tenth ballot and ran against Democrat James COX. The election of Harding was the first to be reported by radio.

Warren G. Harding, 29th president of the United States.

Harding had promised to form a cabinet of only the "best minds." In many instances he chose his administrative team well, but he also chose others with little civic responsibility. According to one source, "the [Harding] administration . . . was marked by one achievement, the Washington (naval) Conference" (1921–22). In August 1923, Harding became the first president to visit ALASKA. On this trip he received some notice of scandals in his administration, which had been kept from him until that time. On his way home, at San Francisco, Harding died unexpectedly under circumstances still not entirely clear. He was not to be troubled by the humiliating scandals that plagued the administration he left behind, including, but not limited to, the TEAPOT DOME SCANDAL (involving Secretary of the Interior Albert B. FALL and Attorney General Harry M. DAUGHERTY). (See also Calvin COOLIDGE.)

For further reading:
Trani, Eugene P., *The Presidency of Warren G. Harding*. Lawrence: Regents Press of Kansas, 1977.

Hardwick, Elizabeth (1916–). American author. Hardwick's fiction is noted for its insightful depictions of women and their roles within the family and for its cool, detached tone, which has been compared to that of Joan DIDION. Her novels include *The Ghostly Lover* (1945) and *Sleepless Nights* (1979). She has also published the collections of essays *Seduction and Betrayal: Women and Literature* (1974) and *Bartleby in Manhattan* (1983). Hardwick is a frequent contributor to THE NEW YORKER and other periodicals. She was the second wife of poet Robert LOWELL.

Hardy, Oliver. See LAUREL AND HARDY.

Hardy, Rene (1912–1987). French RESISTANCE leader during WORLD WAR II. After the war, Hardy's reputation was besmirched by charges that he had betrayed top Resistance leader Jean MOULIN to Klaus Barbie, the GESTAPO chief of Lyons. Hardy was twice tried for treason and twice acquitted. Nonetheless, many of his former Resistance colleagues continued to insist that he was guilty. In 1972 Barbie, then living in sanctuary in South America, said that Hardy had been a collaborator. Hardy, meanwhile, had become a successful novelist.

Hardy, Thomas (1839–1928). English novelist, essayist and poet. Hardy is one of the unquestioned great figures in the history of English literature. Although born

Thomas Hardy.

in the first half of the 19th century, his creative output and his influence extend well into the 20th. He earned his major renown for a series of intensely dramatic 19th-century novels set in his native Dorchester, which he renamed "Wessex" for fictional purposes. These include *Far From The Madding Crowd* (1874), *The Mayor of Casterbridge* (1886), *Tess of the D'Urbervilles* (1891) and *Jude the Obscure* (1896). In the late 1890s, spurred by bitter critical attacks on his novels but enjoying the financial security he had earned from them, Hardy resolved to devote the remainder of his writing career to poetry and poetic drama. He became, in the first three decades of the 20th century, a powerful practitioner in the standard metric forms of English verse, upholding tradition in the midst of the free verse literary revolution. The same pessimism and irony that pervades his fiction is also evident in his poetry. Among his key poetic works are the drama *The Dynasts* (1904) and the verse collection *Moments of Vision* (1917). Hardy's work has influenced many 20th century British poets and novelists, including the writers of the MOVEMENT of the 1950s, especially Philip LARKIN.

Hare, David (1947–). British dramatist and director. Hare was cofounder of the Portable Theatre in 1968, and acted as resident playwright at the Royal Court Theatre (1969–71) and the Nottingham Playhouse (1973). Sharply contemporary with a keen political edge, his plays include *Slag* (1970), *Fanshen* (1975), *Plenty* (1978), *A Map of the World* (1982), *Wetherby* (filmed 1985) and *Wrecked Eggs* (1986).

Harkness, Georgia E(lma) (1891–1974). American Methodist theologian and social critic; one of the most influential Methodist thinkers and educators of her era. Harkness emphasized the need for equal rights for women within the Methodist Church, although she did not herself seek ordination as a priest. In 1948 and 1954, Harkness served as a delegate to the ecumenical World Council of Churches. Beginning in 1950, Harkness also became an active opponent of nuclear armaments. Her writings include *Dark Night of the Soul* (1945) and *Women in Church and Society* (1971).

Harlan, John Marshall (1833–1911). U.S. Supreme Court associate justice (1877–1911); grandfather of John Marshall HARLAN II, who was later a Supreme Court associate justice. The elder Harlan, son of a U.S. congressman and a native of Kentucky, studied law at Transylvania University. Although a slaveowner, Harlan served as an officer in the Union Army during the Civil War. He was elected Kentucky's attorney general after the war and became prominent in the Republican Party. He was instrumental in securing the presidential nomination for Rutherford B. Hayes at the 1876 Republican convention and was later rewarded with his appointment to the Supreme Court. On the Court Harlan was known as a rustic who chewed and spat tobacco during Court sessions. He was also dubbed the "great dissenter" because of his opposition to many notable decisions, including *Plessy v. Ferguson* (1896), which upheld "separate but equal" public services along racial lines. However, Harlan outlasted many of his detractors, serving a remarkable 33 years on the Supreme Court.

Harlan, John Marshall, II (1899–1971). Associate justice, U.S. Supreme Court (1955–71). A graduate of Princeton University and a Rhodes Scholar, John Harlan was the grandson of John Marshall HARLAN, who served on the Supreme Court from 1877 to 1911. Harlan worked with a Wall Street law firm for many years, although he took leaves of absence to serve as an assistant U.S. attorney, special state assistant attorney general, and chief council of a state crime commission. He was appointed to the influential U.S. District Court for the Second Circuit in 1954. Several months later, President Dwight D. EISENHOWER nominated him to the Supreme Court. On the Court Harlan was generally known as a moderate. He resigned shortly before his death in 1971.

For further reading:

Clark, Floyd B., *The Constitutional Doctrines of Justice Harlan*. New York: Da Capo Press, 1969.

Harlech, Lord [Sir (William) David Ormsby Gore] (1918–1985). British diplomat. During the 1950s Sir David Gore led Britain's delegation at the UNITED NATIONS (UN). His career reached its peak when he served as Britain's ambassador to the U.S. during the administration of John F. KENNEDY. A close personal friend of the president, he reportedly exercised a restraining influence on Kennedy during the CUBAN MISSILE CRISIS (1962). In the 1970s he played a key role in British negotiations with its former colony RHODESIA. (See also ZIMBABWE.)

Harlem. Part of New York City's borough of Manhattan, its name derived from the original Dutch settlers of New York. In the early part of this century the migration of Southern blacks in search of better-paying jobs in the industrial North turned New York's Harlem into one of the largest black communities in the nation. From the 1920s through the 1940s, the HARLEM RENAISSANCE reflected black cultural life. After World War II the Hispanic population grew considerably in East Harlem. The economically depressed area is the home of the Abyssinian Baptist church, established in 1808 and headed for many years by Adam Clayton POWELL Jr. Harlem's historic Apollo Theatre stage still supports and encourages black theatrical talent. Poet Countee CULLEN, writer James BALDWIN and singer Billie HOLIDAY, among others, were residents.

Harlem Renaissance. Called by Langston HUGHES "that fantastic period when HARLEM was in vogue," the term Harlem Renaissance refers to an era of extraordinary artistic achievement by African-American writers and artists centered in the Harlem section of New York City. Ushered in by the JAZZ AGE and the successful black revue *Shuffle Along* (1921), the 1920s Harlem Renaissance saw the publication of important works by such authors as Hughes, Sterling BROWN, Countee CULLEN, Zora Neale HURSTON, Claude McKay, Jean Toomer, and many others. Harlem became a lively mecca for black artists and writers, and the movement symbolized a national mood of increased optimism and pride among black Americans. *The New Negro* anthology, edited by Alain Locke, remains an important document of the period and was mirrored in the "New Negro" social-political movement. There was increased activity by the NAACP under the leadership of W.E.B. DUBOIS, Marcus GARVEY'S Universal Negro Improvement Association, and the National URBAN LEAGUE. The GREAT DEPRESSION of the 1930s sent Harlem into a decline, together with the rest of the country, and African-Americans would not again capture such national attention until the CIVIL RIGHTS MOVEMENT of the 1950s and 1960s.

Harlow, Jean [Harlean Carpenter] (1911–1937). Hollywood's first "blonde bombshell," Harlow was the American film industry's greatest sex symbol of the 1930s. After running away from home at 16, Harlow became an extra in silent films in the late 1920s. Howard HUGHES caught sight of her beauty and cast her as the leading lady in his epic early talkie, *Hell's Angels* (1930). The hit led to several more films, at several more studios, including *Public Enemy* (1931, WARNER BROS.) and *Platinum Blonde* (1931, COLUMBIA). But it was in METRO-GOLDWYN-MAYER films such as *Red Dust* (1932) with Clark GABLE that she became a national sex goddess. Her magnificent career was cut short by tragedy, when she died of uremic poisoning during the filming of *Saratoga* (1937).

Harmon, Ernest N. (1894–1979). American military officer. Harmon was one of America's most decorated generals and among the U.S. Army's most daring and aggressive armored division commanders in WORLD WAR II. He commanded an invasion task force in North Africa and later led the "Hell on Wheels" 2nd Armored Division to victory in the BATTLE OF THE BULGE.

Harmon, Thomas Dudley "Tom" (1919–1990). American football player and commentator. While playing as a tailback with the Michigan Wolverines in the late 1930s, Harmon set a college record with 33 touchdowns, and scored 237 points in 24 games. He completed 101 of 233 passes for 1,399 yards and ran for a total of 4,280 yards, averaging 5.5 yards per carry. He won the Heisman Trophy, college football's highest award, in 1940 and was named the Associated Press male athlete of the year. After World War II he played professional football briefly for the Los Angeles Rams. He retired from the game in 1948, and went on to a successful career in radio and television sports broadcasting. He was the father of actor Mark Harmon.

Harmsworth, Alfred Charles William. See Lord NORTHCLIFFE.

Harmsworth, Esmond Cecil [Viscount Rothermere] (1898–1978). British newspaper publisher. Harmsworth was born into one of Britain's wealthiest and most powerful publishing families. He was the son of Harold Harmsworth (1st Viscount Rothermere, 1868–1940) and the nephew of Alfred Charles William Harmsworth (Lord NORTHCLIFFE). At age 21 Cecil Harmsworth became the youngest person ever elected to the House of Commons. He served in Parliament for 10 years, then entered the publishing business. He later inherited the family business and was publisher of the *Daily Mail* and the *Evening News*. He retired in 1971.

Harnwell, Gaylord P. (1903–1982). American atomic physicist and educator. During WORLD WAR II Harnwell headed the U.S. Navy Radio and Sound Laboratory at the University of California. In this post, he was responsible for the development of SONAR. He was president of the University of Pennsylvania from 1953 to 1970, expanding its enrollment, facilities and research programs.

Harriman, W(illiam) Averell (1891–1986). U.S. public official who advised Democratic presidents from Franklin D. ROOSEVELT to Lyndon B. JOHNSON, primarily as a diplomatic troubleshooter. Born in New York City, the patrician Harriman was heir to the Union Pacific Railroad fortune amassed by his father. By 1932 he had become chairman of the board of Union Pacific and had also embarked on a number of ventures in banking, shipbuilding and international finance. Along with Armand HAMMER, Harriman was one of the first Americans to seek business concessions from the Soviet government. In 1941, President Roosevelt sent Harriman to the U.S.S.R., where he remained until 1946, first as minister and then as ambassador. After serving briefly as ambassador to the U.K. (1946), Harriman became secretary of commerce in the TRUMAN administration. From 1949 to 1950 he helped administer the MARSHALL PLAN. During the KOREAN WAR he served as Truman's national security adviser. Harriman was elected governor of New York

W. Averell Harriman at a press conference on July 11, 1963, just prior to leaving for Moscow to represent the U.S. in nuclear test ban treaty talks.

in 1954 but was defeated in 1958 by Nelson ROCKEFELLER. He ran unsuccessfully for the Democratic presidential nomination in 1952 and 1956.

During the KENNEDY administration he served in several state department posts and in 1963 was a key figure in negotiating the NUCLEAR TEST BAN TREATY between the U.S. and the U.S.S.R. In 1965 President Lyndon Johnson appointed Harriman ambassador-at-large to handle Southeast Asian affairs. Harriman traveled around the world seeking international support for the U.S. policy in VIETNAM while sounding out the possibilities of a negotiated settlement of the war. When preliminary peace talks between the U.S. and North Vietnam opened in mid-1968, Harriman went to Paris as chief U.S. negotiator. He was succeeded by Henry Cabot LODGE after the election of Richard M. NIXON. Harriman subsequently criticized Nixon's handling of the war and the peace talks.

Harrington, Michael (1928–1989). American political scientist and writer. One of the most visible spokesmen for socialist ideals in the U.S., Harrington was co-chairman of the Democratic Socialists of America. His 1962 book *The Other America: Poverty in the United States* sparked a national debate on poverty with its assertion that there was an underclass of poor Americans who lived below the poverty line and who were ignored by government and society. The book was said to have inspired federal programs for the poor in the 1960s that became known as the War on Poverty. Harrington was widely respected by allies and opponents alike for his compassion, sincerity, and eloquence.

Harris, Arthur Travers "Bomber" (1892–1984). Marshal of the Royal Air Force who headed RAF Bomber Command during WORLD WAR II and directed the saturation bombing of German cities. Harris earned a reputation as a contentious and stubborn man. He defended the saturation bombing strategy against charges that it was wasteful and even immoral. Harris rejected arguments favoring precision bombing and claimed that his methods forced a concentration of German forces that would otherwise have been sent to the Russian front. His policy climaxed in the bombing of DRESDEN (April 1945), which destroyed the city and may have killed as many as 50,000 people.

Harris, Barbara (1951–). Reverend Barbara Harris became the first woman consecrated as a bishop in the Episcopal Church (February 11, 1989). Harris, a black CIVIL RIGHTS activist, had been ordained for the priesthood in 1980. However, she held no undergraduate degree and underwent no seminary training in theology. The controversial ordination was denounced as sacreligious by traditionalist members of the church.

Harris, Frank [pen name of James Thomas Harris] (1856–1931). Irish-born author and editor. Harris, who is best remembered for his sexually explicit three-volume autobiography, *My Life and Times* (1923–1927), was born in Ireland but at age 15 came to the U.S., where he worked at a variety of odd jobs including a stint as a cowboy. Harris then went to England, where he earned a law degree and established himself as a successful editor of the British *Saturday Review* from 1894 to 1898, during which time he befriended George Bernard SHAW and Oscar Wilde. He then returned to America to edit *Pearson's Magazine*, but his sympathy with the German cause during WORLD WAR I led to public criticism and spurred Harris to move to Europe; he spent most of his final years in France. *My Life and Times*, which was banned in both the U.S. and Europe, no longer shocks readers but does stand as an interesting social portrait of the Edwardian era. Other works by Harris include a biography of Oscar Wilde (1920) and a five-volume essay series of *Contemporary Portraits* (1915–1923) on famous friends and acquaintances.

Harris, Julie (Julia Ann) (1925–). American actress. Harris is one of the finest stage actresses in America. She first achieved critical acclaim for her role as the lonely tomboy in *The Member of the Wedding* (1950; repeating the role in the 1953 film version). Other major roles were Sally Bowles in *I Am a Camera* (1951; repeating the role in the 1955 film version) and Joan of Arc in *The Lark* (1955). Her most famous stage creation was the one-woman show *The Belle of Amherst* (1976), based on the life of Emily Dickinson. She has also appeared on television and in other motion pictures, most notably *East of Eden* (1955).

Harris, Lawren (1885–1970). An eminent Canadian landscape painter, Harris studied in Germany, returning to Toronto in 1907 to paint Impressionist-style canvases. After a tour of northern Ontario in 1918, he began to paint large panoramas of the Canadian wilderness. A member of the Canadian GROUP OF SEVEN, he also painted dramatic, somewhat stylized landscapes of the Canadian Arctic and Rocky Mountains.

Harris, Patricia Roberts (1924–1985). American lawyer, educator, administrator and CIVIL RIGHTS activist. Harris achieved a number of historic firsts for a black woman. In 1965 she became the first black woman to serve as a U.S. ambassador when President Lyndon B. JOHNSON named her ambassador to Luxembourg. Later she became the first black woman delegate to the UNITED NATIONS (UN). In 1969, she became the first black woman to serve as dean of a law school, a position she held briefly at Howard University. She was the first black woman member of a presidential cabinet when President Jimmy CARTER made her secretary of housing and urban development in 1977. She was later Carter's secretary of health, education, and welfare.

Harris, Roy Ellsworth (1898–1979). American composer. Harris started learning music while working as a truck driver, and then attended the University of California (1919–1929). His *Andante* (1926) brought him a Guggenheim Fellowship in Paris. His *When Johnny Comes Marching Home* (1935), a Civil War overture, gained wide attention. The completion of his *Third Symphony* in 1939 marked Harris as a leading American Classicist. He served on the faculty of Colorado College from 1948 to 1967. His work includes six symphonies, music for school bands, choruses, string and piano quintets, and piano solos. A recipient of numerous awards, he also won the prestigious Coolidge Medal for chamber music, from the Library of Congress in 1942.

Harrison, Sir Rex [Reginald Carey Harrison] (1908–1990). British-born actor. Harrison's 60-year career included more than 40 films and numerous plays. Among the films were *Blithe Spirit* (1945), *Anna and the King of Siam* (1946), *The Ghost and Mrs. Muir* (1947), *Cleopatra* (1963) and *Dr. Dolittle* (1967). He specialized in portraying urbane, sophisticated and somewhat eccentric characters and was best known for his portrayal of the waspish linguist Henry Higgins in *My Fair Lady*. Appearing in both the stage and film versions of the play, he won an ACADEMY AWARD and a Tony Award for his performances as Professor Higgins.

Harris-Tarnower affair. Widely-publicized 1980 murder of Dr. Herman Tarnower, a prominent cardiologist and the author of a best-selling diet book, by his mistress, Jean S. Harris, then headmistress of an exclusive girls' boarding school, in Purchase, N.Y. Distraught over Tarnower's affair with another woman, Harris shot him to death. In her trial she claimed that she had gone to his house to commit suicide but that the plan had accidentally backfired. Nonetheless, she was found guilty of second-degree murder. Sentenced to 15 years imprisonment in 1981, she applied her educational and administrative skills to organizing programs for inmates and their young children. Although her cause was championed by a number of feminists and others, repeated requests for her parole were refused.

Harsh, George (1908–1980). American-Canadian convict and war hero. In the late 1920s, Harsh was convicted of the "thrill killing" of a drugstore clerk in Atlanta, Georgia. He was pardoned in 1940, after serving 11 years. He served with the Royal Canadian Air Force (RCAF) in WORLD WAR II. Shot down over enemy lines and captured, he later helped plan the escape of 126 Allied soldiers from a German PRISONER OF WAR camp. This event was later the basis for the film, *The Great Escape.*

Hart, Gary (Warren) [born Gary Hartpence] (1936–). American politician. Born in Ottawa, Kan., Hart attended Bethany Nazarene College, Yale Divinity School and Yale Law School. He entered public life as an attorney for the Justice Department in 1964. In private practice from 1967 to 1974, Hart served as campaign director for George MCGOVERN in his unsuccessful bid for the presidency in 1972. He served as a Democratic senator from Colorado from 1975 to 1986. Hart gained wide attention during his unsuccessful bid for the Democratic presidential nomination in 1984, stressing "new ideas." He was considered the front-runner for the 1988 nomination. However, during the primaries, the press discovered that Hart was openly having an extramarital affair with a young model. Hart's personal judgment became a campaign issue, and Hart was forced to withdraw from the race. He later reentered the race briefly. His political career effectively ended, he returned to Colorado with heavy campaign debts.

Hart, Herbert L(ionel Adolphus) (1907–). British philosopher. Hart is one of the major thinkers on the philosophy of law in the 20th century. For decades he taught at Oxford University as its professor of jurisprudence. He defined his major task as a philosopher as the proper analysis of legal concepts. One of his major ideas is that all legal concepts are defeasible, that is, capable of being transformed and superseded if certain conditions exist. For example, a particular contract may meet all the standard legal criteria but is voidable if it is induced by fraud. Hart also argued that commonsense notions of causation should bear a great relevance to the exercise of punishment in the criminal law. Major works by Hart include *Causation in the Law* (1959), *The Concept of Law* (1961) and *Law, Liberty and Morality* (1963).

Hart, Lorenz (1895–1943). American song lyricist and librettist, best known for his musical shows with Richard RODGERS. While a student at Columbia University, Hart was already writing shows; and when he met a fellow Columbian, erstwhile composer Richard Rodgers, they immediately began working together—beginning with *Poor Little Ritz Girl* (1920) and ending with a revival of *A Connecticut Yankee* (1943). In all, the team wrote 28 shows and four film scores, including *Evergreen* (1930), *Jumbo* (1935), *On Your Toes* (1936), *Babes in Arms* (1937), *The Boys from Syracuse* (1938) and *Pal Joey* (1940). They ignored the stereotypes and hokum of Broadway formulas, injecting a full-scale ballet, "Slaughter on 10th Avenue," choreographed by George BALANCHINE, into *On Your Toes.* Hart's lyrics to *Pal Joey* were ahead of their time, so full of sex and illicit love that critics like Brooks ATKINSON rhetorically asked at the time, "Can you draw sweet water from a foul well?" While Hart's unpredictable, cynical nature lent an edginess to his finest songs, including "My Funny Valentine," "The Lady Is a Tramp" and "Falling in Love with Love," it may also have contributed to his chronic problems with alcohol. After a two-day drinking binge Hart died of complications from pneumonia in New York.

Hart, Moss (1904–1961). American playwright. Hart was a prolific writer for the theater who enjoyed steady popularity for over three decades. He remains best-known for his comedy collaborations with fellow American playwright George S. KAUFMAN. These included *Once In a Lifetime* (1930), *Merrily We Roll Along* (1934), and two oft-performed classics—*You Can't Take It With You* (1936), which won a Pulitzer Prize, and *The Man Who Came To Dinner* (1939). Hart then moved on to a solo career in which he wrote, among other plays, *Winged Victory* (1943), *Christopher Blake* (1946), *Light Up The Sky* (1948), and *The Climate of Eden* (1952). Hart also contributed to the text of numerous musicals, most notably *My Fair Lady* (1956) and *Camelot* (1960).

Hartack, William John "Bill" (1932–). Hartack was one of the most successful—and temperamental—jockeys in the history of American thoroughbred racing. Only the second jockey ever to win five Kentucky Derbys, Hartack was named the nation's leading jockey three consecutive years (1955–57). He had both strong principles and a hot temper, which led him to resign from the Jockeys' Guild over its treatment of another rider. The only rider of any prominence not to belong to the Guild, he was the first rider to post $2 million in winnings and, soon thereafter, the first to win $3 million. Although he never had a Triple Crown-winning mount, Hartack rode such notables as NORTHERN DANCER and Majestic Prince to victory in the Kentucky Derby and the Preakness. At the age of 40, He became the first jockey to win 4,000 races.

Hartal [*Hind.*, "shop" "bolt"]. Ceylonese (Sri Lankan) general strike organized by Marxists in 1953 in protest of rapid price rises, particularly of rice. Repressive measures were introduced, and there were clashes between government forces and strikers. Prime minister Senanayake, of the United National Party, was forced to resign, and the opposition Sri Lankan Freedom Party won the 1956 election. (See also SRI LANKA.)

Hartdegen, Stephen J. (1907–1989). Franciscan scholar and renowned biblical scholar. From 1944 to 1970, Hartdegen served as editor in chief of a group of scholars who produced the *New American Bible,* a translation from the ancient Hebrew, Greek, and Aramaic that supplanted the Douay bible, the official bible used in Roman Catholic churches in the U.S.

Hartigan, Grace (1922–). American painter. A member of the second generation of ABSTRACT EXPRESSIONISM, she was introduced to such seminal members of the movement as Willem DE KOONING and Jackson POLLOCK in the late 1940s, and had her first one-woman show in New York City in 1951. Her early work was sensuously abstract, and she soon turned to a style that incorporates figurative imagery into an abstract context. Her large canvases are usually characterized by vivid colors, strong lines and bold brushstrokes.

Hartog, Jan de (1914–). Dutch-born British novelist and playwright. Hartog, who was born in Haarlem, Holland, and ran away to sea at the age of ten, led an adventurous life that was frequently reflected in his fictional works. His earliest writings were in Dutch. During WORLD WAR II, Hartog served in the Dutch underground RESISTANCE, was badly wounded, and ultimately escaped to Britain, where he learned the English language so well that he began to write in it. His play *The Fourposter* won an Antoinette Perry Award during its Broadway run. But Hartog remains best-known for his popular and well-plotted novels, most notably *The Lost Sea* (1951) and *The Distant Shore* (1952).

Hartt, Frederick (1914–). American art historian and teacher. Hartt studied at New York University, and later taught at Smith College, N.Y.U., Washington University and the University of Pennsylvania. He was McIntire professor of Art History at the University of Virginia until 1984, when he retired. A specialist in the art of the Italian Renaissance, Hart is the author of such books as *History of Italian Renaissance Art* and *Michelangelo: The Complete Sculpture* (both, 1969).

Hartung, Hans (1904–). German-French painter. Born in Dresden, Germany, Hartung settled in Paris in 1935, fought with the Foreign Legion and became a French citizen. Influenced at first by German EXPRESSIONISM and KANDINSKY, Hartung evolved a distinctive abstract style that made him a leading figure in the School of Paris. Allied with COLOR-FIELD PAINTING, his untitled mature paintings feature cloud-like clusters of extremely thin calligraphic lines that seem to hover over luminously-colored grounds.

Harwell. Village in England's Oxfordshire, site of a World War II airfield and of the first English nuclear reactor.

Hasek, Jaroslav (1883–1923). Czechoslovakian novelist, story writer, and journalist. Early in his career Hasek was active as an anarchist and published widely in Czech political journals. During WORLD WAR I Hasek was a peripatetic soldier who served at various times in the Czech, Russian and Austrian armies. After the war Hasek composed a four-volume picaresque novel, *The Good Soldier Schweik* (1920–1923), that has been acclaimed as one of the great satires in world literature. Schweik, an infantry everyman, survives his war experiences—and the foolish, callous orders of his own officers—through simple peasant warmth, humor and guile. To many critics, Schweik is the archetypal portrait of the Czech people. A later collection of Hasek's work is *The Red Commissar* (1981).

Hasenclever, Walter (1890–1940). German playwright, novelist and poet. Hasenclever is best remembered as a figure in the Expressionist movement that dominated German theater in the years following World War I (see EXPRESSIONISM). His first major play, *The Son* (1916), focused on the difficult relationship between a father and son. Subsequent works included an adaptation of *Antigone* (1917), by the Greek tragedian Sophocles, and *Der Retter* (1919), an antiwar drama. Hasenclever then wrote comedies such as *A Man of Distinction* (1926) and *Marriages Are Made in Heaven* (1928). He committed suicide while imprisoned by the Nazis in France during WORLD WAR II.

Hass, Eric (1905–1980). American socialist politician. Hass was the U.S. Socialist Labor Party's candidate for president in the 1952, 1956, 1960, and 1964 elections. A lifelong Marxist, he was nonetheless a frequent critic of the U.S.S.R., which he claimed had distorted many of Karl Marx's political tenets.

Hassam, Childe (1859–1935). American painter and printmaker. One of the foremost American Impressionists, Hassam was born in Boston, Mass. and studied (1886) at the Academie Julien in Paris, where he was influenced by French Impressionist works. He returned to the U.S. in 1889, settling in New York City and joining (1898) "The Ten," a group of American Impressionists that included John Twachtman and Alden Weir. In 1913, Hassam exhibited in the ARMORY SHOW. His paintings include light-filled landscapes, people-filled cityscapes and lively interiors. Among his notable works are *Le Jour du Grand Prix* (1887, Museum of Fine Arts, Boston), *Isle of Shoals* and *Street Scene in Winter* (1901, both Metropolitan Museum of Art, N.Y.C.).

Hasselblad, Victor (1906–1978). Swedish inventor and industrialist. In the 1940s Hasselblad devised the high-quality **Hasselblad camera,** which was used by professional photographers throughout the world. Hasselblad cameras were also used on all U.S. space flights.

Hatch Act of 1939. U.S. legislation, sponsored by Senator Carl Hatch of New Mexico, that prohibited most federal officeholders in the executive branch from using their position to influence presidential or congressional elections. In 1940 the law was amended to include state and local employees whose salaries were derived even partially from federal monies. The amendment also limited the annual expenditures of political parties and the amount of individual campaign contributions.

Hatem, Dr. George [Shaffick Hatem] (1910–1988). American physician who devoted his career to public health efforts in China. Hatem arrived in China in 1933 and remained to treat venereal disease in Shanghai. After the communists took control in 1949, he helped organize the country's public health effort and was widely credited with eliminating syphilis and gonorrhea from China. The Chinese knew him as Ma Haide, meaning "virtue from overseas."

Hatfield. English town north of London, in Hertfordshire; a center of the aircraft industry since the 1930s, the famous Mosquito fighter plane was built here in World War II. Hatfield (formerly Bishops Hatfield, Kings Hatfield) is one of the postwar NEW TOWNS, created to ease overpopulation problems of London.

Hathaway, Henry [Henri Leopold de Fiennes] (1898–1985). American film director. Hathaway directed more than 60 HOLLYWOOD movies, specializing in westerns and crime dramas. His first major film was *Lives of a Bengal Lancer* (1935); subsequently he directed such well-known films as *Kiss of Death, The Desert Fox* and *13 Rue Madeleine* (1947). Six of his films starred John WAYNE, who won his only ACADEMY AWARD in Hathaway's western *True Grit* (1969). While not in the same league as his contemporaries, John FORD, Howard HAWKS and John HUSTON, Hathaway was considered a dependable director.

Hauptmann, Gerhart (1862–1946). German playwright, novelist, and poet. Hauptmann, who won the NOBEL PRIZE for literature in 1912, is one of the major figures in the history of German theater. He first made his reputation for stark, naturalistic treatments of such issues as poverty, the effects of heredity, and social pressures on individual freedom in plays such as *Before Dawn* (1889), *The Coming of Peace* (1890), *Lonely People* (1891) and *The Weavers* (1892), a study of an unsuccessful rebellion by the poor in the Silesian region of Germany in 1844. In his later work Hauptmann turned increasingly to fantastical Symbolist plots that utilized the supernatural. Noteworthy among these plays are *The Assumption of Hannele* (1893), *The Beaver Coat* (1893), *The Red Rooster* (1901) and *And Father Danced* (1906). Hauptmann was a fierce opponent of the Nazis, as evidenced by his four-part drama *Der Atriden* (1941).

Hausner, Gideon (1915–1990). Israeli politician. He served as ISRAEL's attorney general from 1960 to 1963, and led the prosecution of NAZI war criminal Adolf EICHMANN in 1961 and 1962. He later served in the Israeli Knesset (parliament) and as chairman of the Yad Vashem museum, which commemorated victims of the Nazi HOLOCAUST.

Haut-Zaire. Province (formerly Orientale) of northeastern ZAIRE; a post-independence stronghold of Patrice LUMUMBA, who, with Antoine Gizenga, attempted to set up a government at Kisangani (Stanleyville). The central government at KINSHASA (Leopoldville) regained control in 1962, only to face further unrest in 1964, 1966 and 1967.

Havel, Vaclav (1936–). Czechoslovak playwright, poet and essayist; president of CZECHOSLOVAKIA (1989–). Havel has emerged as one of the leading intellectual figures of the late 20th century and a major literary, political and moral force in Eastern Europe. He was born into a well-to-do family in Prague. Because of his "bourgeois" background, he was denied the right to attend university in communist Czechoslovakia. Instead, he served a stint in the military, then found work as a stagehand in Prague. Havel's interest in the theater quickly burgeoned; in 1963, at age 27, his first play was performed (*The Garden Party*, tr. 1969). He was subsequently enrolled at the Academy of Dramatic Arts in Prague, graduating in 1967. During the 1960s Hazel satirized the communist bureaucracy and the politics of conformity in Czechoslovakia in a series of plays. His work of this time borrows from the THEATER OF THE ABSURD. Havel was an active supporter of the PRAGUE SPRING reform movement of 1968. After the movement was crushed by the SOVIET INVASION OF CZECHOSLOVAKIA that summer, his work was banned by the hard-line regime that replaced the reform government of Alexander DUBCEK. However, he continued to write; his manuscripts were circulated privately and also produced in Western Europe. Havel was a founding member of the human rights organization CHARTER 77; because of his activities on behalf of this group, and because of his stature as a public figure who openly challenged the communist authorities, he was imprisoned from 1979 to 1982. He was rearrested during an anticommunist protest in January 1989 and released on parole that May. In November he formed a new opposition group, Civic Forum, and held talks on political reform and power-sharing with the Czechoslovak premier during a period of mass protest against communist rule. With the resignation of communist President Gustav HUSAK (December 10), the formation of an interim coalition cabinet and the promise of free elections, Havel announced his candidacy for the presidency.

On December 29 the Federal Assembly (parliament) unanimously elected Havel as Czechoslovakia's first noncommunist president in more than 40 years. During the first year of his presidency he was preoccupied with the difficult task of guiding Czechoslovakia's return to democracy. However, he has expressed his desire to return to private life and to writing. Among Havel's other plays are *The Memorandum* (1966; tr. 1967), *The Increased Difficulty of Concentration* (1968; tr. 1972), *Private View* (1975; tr. 1978) and *Protest* (1978; tr. 1980). *Disturbing the Peace: A Conversation with Karel Hvizdala* (published underground in Prague in 1986; tr. 1990) presents his thoughts on life, literature, politics and the Czechoslavak iden-

Vaclav Havel (left), renowned playwright and president of Czechoslovakia, meeting with Soviet Premier Mikhail Gorbachev in the Kremlin (Feb. 1990).

tity; *Letter to Olgo* (1988) contains his correspondence to his wife while he was imprisoned from 1979 to 1982.

Havemann, Robert (1910–1982). East German chemist and dissident. Havemann joined the Communist Party in 1932. During WORLD WAR II he took part in the RESISTANCE movement and was imprisoned by the Nazis. After the war he lived in East Germany but became an outspoken critic of TOTALITARIANISM. He was purged from the East German Communist Party in 1964, and was held under house arrest from 1979 until his death.

Hawaii. Fiftieth and last (to date) U.S. state; admitted to the Union in 1959, it is the only U.S. state not on the North American continent. The island of Hawaii is the largest of eight major and many lesser islands that lie over 2,000 miles southwest of San Francisco. The island of Oahu has the largest population and the most thriving economy; its principal city of Honolulu is the state's capital and largest city.

Queen Liliuokalani became ruler of what was formerly known as the Sandwich Islands in 1892 but was overthrown in 1893 during American-led agitation for governmental reform. In 1894, American business interests set up a republic and installed Sanford B. Dole as their president. U.S. President MCKINLEY favored annexation—accomplished in 1898. In 1900 Hawaii was made a U.S. territory.

On December 7, 1941, a well-prepared Japanese sneak attack on Oahu's PEARL HARBOR naval base (and other island military installations), dragged the U.S. into the already two-years-old WORLD WAR II. With the capture by the Japanese of the Philippines, Hawaii became the U.S.'s forward staging point for the Pacific theater of war. Afterwards, labor union attempts to improve working conditions led to major strikes in 1946, 1949 and 1959, but the postwar years and economical air travel also brought more tourists. They discovered a volcanic land of great cultural and ethnic diversity: Native Hawaiians (their population decimated in the 19th century) and mainland Americans (both black and white) were only a part of a Chinese, Japanese, Filipino, Korean, Portuguese, German and Puerto Rican mix. Continuing economic growth and increasing tourism have led to overcrowding in recent years, threatening the unique beauty of this Pacific paradise.

Hawke, Robert (James Lee) (1929–). Prime minister of AUSTRALIA (1983–). Born in Bordertown, South Australia, Hawke was educated at the University of Western Australia, from which he received bachelor's degrees in law and economics. He won a Rhodes scholarship to Oxford University in 1953, taking a bachelor of letters degree there in 1955. Active since 1958 in the Australian Council of Trade Unions as research officer and advocate, he was its president from 1970 to 1980. Concurrently, from 1972 to 1980, he served on the governing body of the International Labor Organization. From 1973 to 1978 Hawke was president of the Australian LABOR PARTY, which he had joined at age 17. In 1980 he was elected to parliament as representative of the federal electorate of Wills, later becoming the party's spokesman for industrial relations, employment and youth affairs. Early in 1983 Hawke was unanimously elected leader of the opposition. As Labor candidate for the office of prime minister, he led his party to victory and was sworn in on March 11, 1983. Hawke was reelected prime minister in 1984, 1987 and again in 1990 for a record fourth consecutive term.

Hawking, Stephen William (1942–). British astrophysicist, widely considered one of the most brilliant scientific minds since Albert EINSTEIN. A graduate of Oxford University, Hawking obtained his Ph.D. from Cambridge, where in 1977 he was appointed to the chair of gravitational physics. He subsequently held the seat of Lucasian Professor of Mathematics at Cambridge, a chair once held by Isaac Newton. Hawking has worked mainly in the field of general relativity and on the theory of BLACK HOLES. He is a leading authority on the BIG BANG THEORY. Hawking has been at the forefront of the search for a unified theory to account for, and reconcile, the general theory of relativity (which is concerned with the extraordinarily vast) and quantum theory (concerned with the extraordinarily tiny); such a theory, Hawking believes, would give "a complete description of the universe we live in." Hawking's book on the nature of time and the universe for the nonspecialist, *A Brief History of Time* (1988), was a phenomenal bestseller.

Since the early 1960s, Hawking has suffered from motor neuron disease, known as Lou Gehrig's disease, which has confined him to a wheelchair. In 1985 he underwent a tracheostomy operation, which left him unable to speak. However, a speech synthesizer and specially designed personal computer have allowed him to communicate his brilliant and complex concepts to the rest of the world.

Hawkins, Coleman (1904–1969). A native of St. Joseph, Missouri, Hawkins is significant for his pioneering role in establishing the tenor saxophone as a bona fide and primal voice in jazz. In the 1920s, during the early phase of his career with Mamie Smith's Jazz Hounds and Fletcher HENDERSON's big band, and then in the 1930s as an international jazz star in both Europe and the U.S., Hawkins perfected a robust sound, strong rhythmic drive and technical command that made his solos among the most exciting in jazz. His 1939 recording of "Body and Soul" was not only Hawkins' biggest hit, but also a declaration (and affirmation) that the tenor saxophone has arrived—an equal to the trumpet as the jazz world's most important "front-line" solo instrument. Throughout his career, Hawkins, unlike a number of his peers, welcomed innovations such as those spawned by the bebop revolution of the 1940s; but, although adapting newer elements that he deemed compatible with his overall style, Hawkins' rhythmic buoyancy, full-blooded tone and swinging inventiveness never faltered. Historically, Hawkins' muscular style is often contrasted to that of Lester YOUNG, whose lighter tone and more melodic improvisations had a profound influence on such 1950s "cool school" stylists as tenor saxophonist Stan GETZ. In actuality, virtually all saxophonists (and horn players) have been enriched by the contrasting yin and yang styles of Young and Hawkins, jazzdom's seminal pioneers of the tenor saxophone.

For further reading:

James, Burnett, *Coleman Hawkins*. New York: Hippocrene Books, 1984.

hawks. Term coined in the 1960s to describe American politicians who wished to continue, intensify or escalate the VIETNAM WAR. The term came to be applied generally to politicians taking an aggressive stance on foreign policy issues.

Hawks, Howard Winchester (1896–1977). American motion picture producer, writer and director. Hawks gew up in California studying mechanical engineering, working in the PARAMOUNT prop department, racing cars, and during WORLD WAR I, flying planes in the Army Air Corps. He began directing films in the mid-1920s. In the next 45 years his best work depicted professional groups in dangerous occupations: flying aces and air mail pilots in *The Dawn Patrol* (1930) and *Ceiling Zero* (1938); wacky scientists and journalists in the "screwball comedies" *Bringing up Baby* (1938) and *His Girl Friday* (1940); cattle drovers and gunslingers in the westerns *Red River* (1948) and *Rio Bravo* (1959); bombshells and weightlifters in the musical *Gentlemen Prefer Blondes* (1953); and racketeers and convicts in the gangster films *Scarface* (1932) and *The Criminal Code* (1931). The character groupings and dialogue in his pictures displayed an interlocking, machine-like precision. *His Girl Friday,* perhaps the fastest-talking movie of them all, snaps briskly along like a class sports car. *Only Angels Have Wings* (1930), by contrast, rolls by with the well-oiled, lordly deliberation of a Rolls Royce. Hawks was not interested in flashbacks, skewed camera angels or decorative cutting, preferring to be head-on, direct and functional. Famous for his insistence on autonomy—he refused to shoot while a producer was on the set—he wrote or supervised the writing of most of his films. Although Hawks received only one ACADEMY AWARD nomination during his career (for *Sergeant York* in 1941), in 1975 he received a special Award for lifetime achievement.

Hawley-Smoot Tariff Act. Protectionist legislation enacted in 1930 that brought U.S. tariffs to the highest level in history. Overall increases averaged approximately 5% but rates on agricultural raw materials increased from 30% to 50% in real terms. Sugar and textiles were given special protection. The act brought retaliation from other nations and led to a sharp decline in U.S. trade.

Haxell, Frank (1913–1988). British labor leader and the communist secretary general of one of Great Britain's most powerful labor unions, the Electrical Trades Union (ETU), forerunner of the Electrical, Electronic, Telecommunications and Plumbing Union (EETPU). Haxell headed the ETU from 1955 until his downfall in 1961, when he was removed from office after a High Court ruled that his election victory of 1959 had been rigged.

Hay, Gyula (1900–1975). Hungarian playwright. Hay scored his first major theatrical triumph with the play *Gott, Kaiser, Bauer* (1932), which was staged in Berlin by the renowned theatrical impressario Max REINHARDT. A politically controversial writer, Hay spent many years in exile from his native country. After his return, Hay was imprisoned in 1956 for his role in the 1956 HUNGARIAN UPRISING against Soviet authority. Other plays by Hay include *Tiszazug* (1945), *Das Pferd* (1964), a study of the Roman emperor Caligula, and *Gaspar Varros Recht* (1965), which featured an anticommunist theme.

Haya de la Torre, Victor Raul (1894–1979). Peruvian statesman and major spokesman for democratic political movements in Latin America for half a century. In 1924 Haya de la Torre founded the American Popular Revolutionary Alliance (APRA). Although it was anti-capitalist and Marxist in outlook, it did not favor Soviet-style communism. APRA called for a program of land, tax and educational reforms for landless peasants, urban laborers, Indians and other disadvantaged groups. On three occasions the military prevented Haya de la Torre from taking the presidency of PERU. He spent much of his life in exile, hiding and imprisonment. Nonetheless, his writings on economics and political theory had great influence throughout Latin America.

Haydee, Marcia [born Marcia Pereira de Silva] (1937–). Brazilian-born ballerina and ballet director. One of the great dramatic ballerinas of the 1960s and 1970s, Haydee danced at the Rio de Janeiro Teatro Municipal before joining Grand Ballet de Marquis de Cuevas in 1957. She became an internationally acclaimed prima ballerina after joining the Stuttgart Ballet (1961) where she created roles in John CRANKO's ballets, including Juliet in *Romeo and Juliet* (1962), Tatyana in *Onegin* (1965), and Kate in *Taming of the Shrew* (1969). She also has appeared with other companies, and created roles in Kenneth MACMILLAN's *Miss Julie* (1970) and Glen TETLEY's *Voluntaries* (1973), among others. In 1976 she was appointed artistic director of the Stuttgart Ballet.

Hayden, Robert E. (1913–1980). Black American poet. Hayden's work evoked Afro-American themes. He was the first black to hold the position of consultant in poetry to the Library of Congress (1978–80), and was also a member of the American Academy and Institute of Arts and Letters. He taught at the University of Michigan. His collections include *Words in Mourning Time* (1971) and *Angle of Ascent: New and Selected Poems* (1975).

Hayes, Helen [Helen Hayes Brown] (1900–). American actress. Born in Washington, D.C., Hayes made her stage debut there in 1905, first appeared in New York in 1908 and became a well-known child actress. She made her adult debut in *Dear Brutus* (1918). Her many notable performances have included roles in Kaufman and Connelly's *To the Ladies* (1922), SHAW's *Caesar and Cleopatra* (1925), ANDERSON's *Mary of Scotland* (1933) and the bravura title role in Laurence Houseman's *Victoria Regina* (1935–39). Hayes won an Academy Award in 1932 for *The Sin of Madelon Claudet.* She made her London debut in 1945, as Amanda in WILLIAMS' *The Glass Menagerie.* Other later roles included Norma Melody in O'Neill's *A Touch of the Poet* (1958) and Mrs. Antrobus in WILDER's *The Skin of Our Teeth* (1961). Among her films are *Arrowsmith* (1931), *A Farewell to Arms* (1933), *Anastasia* (1956) and *Airport* (1969). A beloved and widely respected figure, she is popularly known as the First Lady of the American Theater.

Hay-Herran Treaty. See COLOMBIA.

Haynes, Elwood (1857–1925). American inventor. Haynes was one of the pioneers in the development of the automobile. In 1893–94 he designed and constructed a horseless carriage, the oldest American automobile in existence and now on exhibit at the Smithsonian Institution. He was the first to use aluminum in automobile engines and was the inventor and builder of a rotary engine in 1903. Haynes discovered tungsten chrome steel and developed an alloy of cobalt and chromium for making cutting tools. The Haynes Stellite Company manufactured tools from 1912 to 1920 and developed **stainless steel,** which was patented in 1919.

Hays Code. Code of self-censorship adopted by the HOLLYWOOD film industry in self-defense against threatened government censorship. The Hays Code derived its name from Will H. Hays, a former chairman of the Republican National Committee who in 1922 was appointed by Hollywood studio owners to head a newly formed film standards organization, the Motion Picture Producers and Distributors of America, Inc. In the 1920s, Hays wielded little actual power over the content of films, but in the 1930s, as the public outcry over sexually suggestive movies (such as those starring Jean HAR-

LOW and Mae WEST) and violent gangster films increased, the Hays Code took on real teeth: The new enforcement policy was that films that violated the Code would not be distributed by the powerful studios or exhibited by the theaters they owned. The Code strictly limited the sexual content of films, tacitly forbade any religious controversy and demanded that, if evil was depicted powerfully, it should be punished to an equivalent extent—thus encouraging a predictable happy ending in which good emerged triumphant. In the 1950s, directors such as Otto PREMINGER helped to weaken the artistic shackles imposed by the Code. In the 1960s, the Code was replaced by the current rating system, which focuses on excluding younger audience members from scenes of explicit sex and violence.

Hayter, Stanley William (1901–1988). British-born abstract artist and printmaker; his Paris studio, Atelier 17, was widely regarded as the most influential print workshop of the 20th century. Many major artists, including Pablo PICASSO, Marc CHAGALL and Jackson POLLOCK worked under Hayter either in Paris or in New York City, where Atelier 17 was based in the 1940s.

Hayward, Max (1924–1979). British scholar and translator. Hayward specialized in contemporary Soviet literature, translating works by Boris PASTERNAK, Alexander SOLZHENITSYN and other authors who were banned or banished in their own country. His colleagues at Oxford and elsewhere regarded him as "the custodian of Russian literature in the West."

Hayworth, Rita [Margarita Carmen Cansino] (1918–1987). Mexican-American dancer and actress. Rita Hayworth was one of the most popular HOLLYWOOD film stars of the 1940s. Her career reached its peak in the years during and after World War II, when she shared pinup queen status with Betty GRABLE. She starred in a series of films that highlighted her lush beauty. Her screen persona was perhaps best realized in *Gilda* (1946), in which she played the title role, a seductress in black satin. Her second husband, Orson WELLES, directed her in another of her well-known films, *The Lady from Shanghai* (1948). In 1949 she left Hollywood to marry the third of her five husbands, Prince Aly Khan. She came back to Hollywood three years later, but never recaptured the glory of the war years. She later suffered from Alzheimer's disease.

Hazam, Louis (1911–1983). American television documentary writer and producer. Working for the National Broadcasting Company (NBC) from 1945 until 1966, Hazam was a pioneer in the field of broadcasting. He was credited with producing the first live telecast of a medical operation, the first telecast of the birth of a baby, and the first television report from the inside of a mental hospital. In 1956, his March of Medicine series became the first television program to receive an Albert Lasker Medical Journalism Award. He also received acclaim for

Rita Hayworth, Hollywood "love goddess," in a scene from the 1946 film Gilda.

his cultural productions, *Vincent Van Gogh: A Self-Portrait*, *Shakespeare: Soul of an Age*, and *Michelangelo: The Last Giant*.

Head, Edith (1907–1981). HOLLYWOOD costume designer. The most famous fashion designer in the history of the movies, Head was chief designer for PARAMOUNT PICTURES (1938–67) and UNIVERSAL (1967–81). During her long career she designed clothes for more than 1,000 movies and was nominated for 34 ACADEMY AWARDS. She won the award a record eight times, for *The Heiress* (1949), *All About Eve* (1950), *Samson and Delilah* (1950), *A Place in the Sun* (1951), *Roman Holiday* (1953), *Sabrina* (1954), *The Facts of Life* (1960) and *The Sting* (1973). She created screen wardrobes for such stars as Sophia Loren, Marlene DIETRICH, Elizabeth TAYLOR and Ingrid BERGMAN. Her clothes were also worn by the male and female leads in most of Alfred HITCHCOCK's Hollywood films.

Healey, Denis (Winston) (1917–). British politician. Born in London of Irish parents, Healey rose to become a senior figure in the LABOUR PARTY from the 1960s through the 1980s. He was a major in the commandos during WORLD WAR II, and entered Parliament in 1952. He was defense minister (1964–70) in the cabinet of Harold WILSON and chancellor of the exchequer (1974–79) under Wilson and his successor, James CALLAGHAN, who defeated Healey for the party leadership in 1976. In 1980 Healey again sought the leadership but was defeated by Michael FOOT. He served as deputy leader from 1980 to 1983. Although himself a leading moderate in the party, he was critical of the GANG OF FOUR moderates who left the party in 1981 to form the SOCIAL DEMOCRATIC PARTY (1981), and did not join them. Healey did not challenge Neil KINNOCK for the Labour Party leadership in 1983 but, as shadow foreign secretary, remained a respected and influential voice in the House of Commons.

For further reading:

Healey, Denis, *The Time of My Life*. New York: W.W. Norton, 1989.

Heaney, Seamus (1939–). Irish poet, critic, essayist and teacher. Heaney is widely considered to be the most important Irish poet since W.B. YEATS and one of the finest English-language poets of his generation. Born into a Catholic farming family in County Derry, NORTHERN IRELAND, Heaney was educated at Queen's University, Belfast, where his early work attracted favorable notice. His first book, *Death of a Naturalist* (1966), established him as an important poet; this reputation was confirmed by *Door into the Dark* (1969) and *Wintering Out* (1972). Full of closely observed details of Northern Irish country life, these books display the characteristic style and themes of his early period. With *North* (1975), Heaney addressed the ongoing civil strife in Northern Ireland, although in an oblique fashion. Around this time, partly to escape the turmoil and tensions of Belfast, Heaney moved to County Wicklow in Ireland, where he wrote most of the poems for his next book, *Field Work* (1979). In a country where the written word traditionally has had significant political implications, Heaney has been consistent in his refusal to reduce complex social and political issues to simple slogans or to endorse partisan causes. Heaney's more recent work, notably in *Station Island* (1985) and *The Haw Lantern* (1987), has often been allegorical and has drawn on the Divine Comedy of Dante and on the work of such contemporary central European writers as Czeslaw MILOSZ. Since the 1970s, Heaney has divided his time between Ireland and the U.S., where he teaches at Harvard University.

Hearst, Patricia (Campbell) (1954–). American heiress and kidnap victim. A scion of newspaper tycoon William Randolph HEARST, Patricia Hearst was kidnapped from her Berkeley, California apartment on February 4, 1974 by the Symbionese Liberation Army (SLA), a radical, anti-capitalist terrorist organization. As ransom, the SLA demanded that her father, Randolph Hearst, provide $400 million worth of food for California's poor; he eventually initiated a $2 million program. Two months after her abduction, Hearst announced that she had joined the SLA and changed her name to Tania. She was later seen on film taking part in an armed bank robbery. In another incident, she fired on a store to free SLA members Emily and Bill Harris, and the three fled to San Francisco. After sending a final taped message on June 7, 1974, Hearst went underground. On September 18, 1975, the FBI captured Hearst and the Harrises in San Francisco. Celebrated attorney F. Lee BAILEY represented her at her trial, contending that she had been brainwashed and was not responsible for her actions as Tania. On March 20, 1976, she was found guilty and sentenced to a total of 35 years in prison. After several attempts to appeal her conviction, Hearst's lawyers petitioned for and received presidential clemency from President Jimmy CARTER in 1979. Hearst later described how she had been kept in a closet, tortured and given propaganda by the SLA, and general public opinion is that she was indeed brainwashed. Hearst detailed her ordeal in the book *Every Secret Thing* (1982), and a film of her story was made in 1988. She married her former bodyguard, Bernard Shaw, in 1979.

Hearst, William Randolph (1863–1951). American editor and publisher. During the first half of the 20th century Hearst controlled one of the great communications empires in history. His first step in creating what would become the nation's largest newspaper chain was rebuilding the *San Francisco Examiner* (1887). His purchase of the *New York Journal* (1895) resulted in the famous newspaper war with Joseph Pulitzer's *New York World* during which the term "yellow journalism" was coined to describe their exaggerated journalistic style. Among the many magazines he owned were *Good Housekeeping, Cosmopolitan* and *Harper's Bazaar.* He bought or started papers in Chicago, Boston, Los Angeles and elsewhere. His empire also included Hearst News Service, King Features, radio stations and film companies. Hearst wielded power in politics, serving as New York Representative to Congress (1903–07); he ensured Franklin D. ROOSEVELT's 1932 presidential nomination and used his papers for political propaganda.

For further reading:

Swanberg, W.A., *Citizen Hearst*. New York: Scribner's, 1984.

Heartfield, John [born Helmut Herzfeld] (1891–1968). German artist and graphic designer known for his early and successful use of photomontage. Heartfield was a Berlin artist who, in the 1920s, became an active member of the DADA movement. His special contribution was the development of a montage technique in which photographs and other image materials are cut up and reassembled using a technique similar to collage. In the late 1920s and early 1930s, he used this technique to create propagandistic works attacking HITLER and the rise of NAZISM. By 1933 he was forced to leave Germany, staying briefly in Czechoslovakia before relocating in England where he changed his name (translating his German name into English) and continued his graphic work. Heartfield's role in 20th century design is based on his development and exploitation of the montage technique, which has become a widely used part of the vocabulary of modern graphic design.

Heart of Atlanta Motel, Inc. v. United States (1964). Unanimous U.S. Supreme Court decision that banned racial discrimination in the provision of public accommodations in restaurants and hotels. Although discrimination at facilities operated by state and local governments was outlawed in the early 1950s, private discrimination was still common in the early 1960s. The CIVIL RIGHTS ACT OF 1964 contained a controversial provision outlawing racial discrimination in public accommodations that were privately owned. The law was challenged as an unwarranted governmental regulation of private business. A unanimous Supreme Court upheld the law, reasoning that hotels and restaurants serve interstate travelers, and Congress also has the power to regulate local activities that may have a harmful effect on interstate commerce.

Heart of Darkness. Novella of 1902 by Joseph CONRAD. Notable both for its literary subtlety and for its examination of the contemporary human condition, *Heart of Darkness* is considered one of the supreme masterpieces of English-language fiction of the 20th century. Narrator "Marlow" (who both is and is not Conrad) recounts his journey up the Congo to find the trader Kurtz, who had disappeared earlier. The journey is not only geographic but also metaphorical, from certainty into doubt and back into self-knowledge. Conrad examines the ambiguous relation between civilization and barbarism and addresses themes of greed and colonialism. Kurtz's dying words—"The horror! the horror!"—may indicate Conrad's apprehension about the 20th century.

Heath, Edward (1916–). British statesman, prime minister of the UNITED KINGDOM (1970–74). Born at Broadstairs, Heath was educated at Chatham House School and Balliol College, Oxford. He served as an artillery officer from 1940 to 1946 and left the territorials in 1951 as a lieutenant colonel. A member of the CONSERVATIVE PARTY, he was elected to Parliament in 1950 and has sat in the House of Commons continuously since then. From 1955 to 1959 he held the influential post of Conservative chief whip. He entered the cabinet of Alec DOUGLAS-HOME as minister for trade and industry (1963–64). In 1965, he defeated Reginald MAUDLING and Enoch POWELL for the Conservative Party leadership. He became prime minister with the Conservatives' general election victory in June 1970.

A lifelong champion of European cooperation and unity, Heath led Britain into the EUROPEAN ECONOMIC COMMUNITY in 1973—the capstone of his political career. However, his government was less successful in domestic affairs and was marred by labor strife. His Industrial Relations Act (1971), designed to democratize Britain's trades unions and regulate strikes, was denounced by the unions. A coal miners' strike in late 1971–early 1972 led to power blackouts throughout Britain. Heath's attempt to impose limits on wage increases during an inflationary period led to further industrial action by the militant miners, and in January 1974 Heath put the nation on a three-day work week because of the resulting power crisis (see THREE-DAY WEEK). Seeking a mandate for his policies, Heath called a general election for February 1974 but failed to win a majority and resigned. The following year he was deposed as head of the party by Margaret THATCHER, who accused him of ineffectual leadership. After the Conservatives returned to power in 1979 he was a frequent critic of Thatcher's hard-line right-wing policies and allied himself with the so-called WETS within the party. Heath, a bachelor, is also known as a fine amateur conductor and yachtsman.

Hebert, Anne (1916–). Canadian poet and novelist. The daughter of a literary

British statesman Edward Heath (left) in a White House meeting with U.S. President Lyndon Johnson.

critic, Hebert was given a strict Catholic upbringing. Her struggles with the constraints of her faith are evident in her poetry, which includes *Le Songes en equilibre* ("Dreams in Equilibrium," 1942), *Le Tombeau des rois* (*The Tombs of the Kings*, 1953) and *In The Shadow of the Wind* (1984). Hebert has also written novels, which include *Kamouraski* (1970) and *Les Enfants du sabbat* (1975; *Children of the Black Sabbath* 1977); and plays, some of which are collected in *Le Temps sauvage, La Merciere assassinee, Les Invites au proces: Theatre* (1967).

Hecht, Ben (1893–1964). U.S. writer. He worked for CHICAGO newspapers and was a correspondent in Germany and the Soviet Union between 1918 and 1920. He produced his most famous play, *The Front Page* (1928), with Charles MacArthur. In 1923 he founded and edited for two years the *Chicago Literary Times*. In addition to plays, he wrote novels and short stories, and produced and directed many motion pictures. Other well-known works include *Twentieth Century* (1933) and *A Child of the Century* (1954). *The Scoundrel* screenplay won Hecht and MacArthur an ACADEMY AWARD in 1935. Hecht was also active in his support of Jewish refugees.

Hecht, Harold (1907–1985). American film producer. As a pioneering independent HOLLYWOOD producer, Hecht was considered largely responsible for breaking the grip of the studio system. In the late 1940s, he and actor Burt LANCASTER formed a partnership that over 15 years was responsible for a number of hits, including the ACADEMY AWARD-winning *Marty*. After production costs forced the dissolution of their partnership, Hecht went on producing on his own. In 1965, he made *Cat Ballou*, for which Lee Marvin won an Academy Award as best actor.

Heckel, Erich (1883–1970). German painter. Born in Dobeln, Saxony, Heckel studied architecture in Dresden (1904). In 1905 he, Ernst Ludwig KIRCHNER and Karl SCHMIDT-ROTTLUFF cofounded DIE BRUCKE. His earlier works are characterized by the slashing brushstrokes, angular forms, violent color and emotional drama of German EXPRESSIONISM. Heckel was a medical corpsman in World War I. He lived in Berlin from 1918 to 1934, when he was denounced by the Nazis and fled to Switzerland. He returned to Germany after the war and taught at the Karlsruhe Academy from 1949 to 1955. His later works often turned from figures, many of them nudes, to landscapes and became more gentle and meditative.

Hedayat, Sadeq (1903–1951). Iranian author and playwright. Hedayat's works, which include the novel *Buyf-i kur* (1936, translated as *The Blind Owl*, 1957) and the short story collections, *Zanda bi gur* (*Buried Alive*, 1930), *Se qatra kuhn* (*Three Drops of Blood*, 1932), and *Saage velgard* (*Stray Dog*, 1942), reflect his fundamentally hopeless and pessimistic world view. A significant figure in Iranian literature, Hedayat has also translated some of the works of KAFKA, among others, into Persian.

Martin Heidegger, German philosopher (1970).

Hedayat committed suicide in Paris in 1951.

Heidegger, Martin (1889–1976). German philosopher. Heidegger was one of the most influential of 20th-century philosophers. He concerned himself primarily with metaphysical and ontological questions on the nature of being and of ultimate reality and helped to establish EXISTENTIALISM as a major philosophical movement. Raised as a Catholic, Heidegger was educated at the University of Freiberg where he studied under the phenomenologist Edmund HUSSERL. After a period of intense thought and retirement in the Black Forest, Heidegger produced his major work, *Being and Time* (1927), which posited categories of authentic and inauthentic being and argued for angst as a major motivating force in human development. Heidegger was a member of the Nazi Party from 1933 to 1945 and was named rector of the University of Freiberg by the HITLER government. His refusal to repudiate his Nazi political beliefs after the war caused much controversy. Other works by Heidegger include *An Introduction to Metaphysics* (1953) and *What Is Philosophy?* (1956).

For further reading:

Neske, Gunther, and Emil Kettering, eds., *Martin Heidegger and National Socialism*. New York: Paragon House, 1990.

Heiden, Eric Arthur (1958–). American speed skater. In 1977, Heiden became the first American ever to win the men's all-around speed skating championship. His performances at the 1980 Lake Placid Olympics focused American attention on the little-watched sport of speed skating. He won gold medals in the 500–, 100–, 1500–, 5000– and 10,000–meter events, while setting a new record in each event. He retired after the 1980 Olympics to pursue a career in bicycle racing.

Heidenstam, Verner Von (1859–1940). Swedish poet and novelist. An important Swedish literary figure in his time, Heidenstam's reputation has not lasted, possibly, in part, due to the conservative and aristocratic bent of his later work. Heidenstam's lyric poetry includes, *Vallfart och vandringsar* (*Pilgrimage: The Wander Years*, 1888) and *Nya Dikter* (*New Poems*, 1915). His fiction includes *Endymion* (1889); the stories, *Korolinerna (The Charles Men*, 1897–1898), and the two-volume novel *Folkunga Tradet* (*The Tree of the Folkungs*, 1905–1907). Heidenstam was awarded the NOBEL PRIZE for literature in 1916.

Heifetz, Jascha (1901–1987). Lithuanian-born violinist. Heifetz was one of the most renowned violinists of the 20th-century. He achieved great success as a child prodigy in Europe before immigrating to the U.S. in 1917 with his parents at the onset of the RUSSIAN REVOLUTION. His October 1917 debut at New York City's CARNEGIE HALL became the stuff of musical legend. For the next 50 years he performed regularly in the U.S. and around the world. His playing was notable for tonal brilliance, technical perfection and fidelity to the written score. He recorded a memorable series of chamber music performances with pianist Artur RUBINSTEIN and cellist Gregor Piatigorsky. Heifetz retired from the concert stage in 1972, but continued to teach master classes at the University of Southern California until shortly before his death.

Heijermans, Herman (1864–1924). Dutch playwright and critic. Heijermans first achieved success with the play *Ahasverus* (1893), presented under the pseudonym Ivan Jelakowitch as he thought the Dutch favored foreign authors. Heijermans is best known for his later social dramas which include *Ghetto* (1899), *Op van Zegen* (1900, *The Good Hope* 1903), and *Eva Bonheur* (1917, translated as *The Devil to Pay*, 1925). Heijermans was also a theatrical critic, and wrote novels under the pseu-

Legendary violinist Jascha Heifetz.

donym Koos Habema, and short sketches using the name Samuel Falkland.

Hein, Piet (1905–). Danish designer, mathematician and poet-humorist well known for his small books of poems and cartoon sketches called "Grooks." Hein's design reputation is largely based on his remarkable invention of a new geometric shape, the super-ellipse, a form sharing some of the characteristics of the true ellipse, the oval, and the rectangle—it might be called a somewhat squared ellipse. It has been used as the plan layout for a traffic "circle" in central Stockholm, as the form for the top of a table manufactured by Bruno Mathsson, and, in three-dimensional form, to make the super-egg—a solid that has the peculiar property of being able to stand on end as readily as on its side.

Heinlein, Robert A(nson) (1907–1988). One of the world's most popular, prolific and influential writers of science fiction, Heinlein was voted an unprecedented four Hugo awards for best science fiction novel of the year. The awards, voted on by science fiction fans who are voting members of each year's annual world convention, were given for *Double Star* (1956), *Starship Troopers* (1959), *Stranger in a Strange Land* (1961) and *The Moon Is a Harsh Mistress* (1966). The best-selling *Stranger in a Strange Land* was regarded as a sort of "hippie bible" in the 1960s. In 1975, Heinlein was the first recipient of the Grand Master Award of the Science Fiction Writers of America, given for lifetime achievement. A graduate of the U.S. Naval Academy, Heinlein's Navy career was cut short by illness and followed by graduate studies in physics and mathematics, then a raft of different jobs and in 1939 his first story sale, to *Astounding* magazine. From then until his last novel, *To Sail Beyond the Sunset* (1987), Heinlein's matter-of-fact integration of technological innovation with a pugnaciously American frontier attitude that challenged all social ideas, in fast-moving but sometimes rambling plots, the whole carried forward by competent, no-nonsense men and women, yanked science fiction forever out of its pulp fiction straitjacket.

Heisenberg, Werner Karl (1901–1976). German physicist. Heisenberg was educated at the universities of Munich (where his father was a professor of Greek) and Gottingen, where in 1923 he obtained his doctorate. After spending the period from 1924 to 1926 in Copenhagen working with Niels BOHR, he returned to Germany to take up the professorship of theoretical physics at the University of Leipzig. In 1941 Heisenberg moved to Berlin where he was appointed director of the Kaiser Wilhelm Institute for Physics and where he played the key role in the German atomic bomb program. After the war he helped establish the Max Planck Institute for Physics at Gottingen, serving as director and moving with it to Munich in 1955, where he was also appointed professor of physics.

In 1925 Heisenberg formulated a version of quantum theory that became known as matrix mechanics. It was for this work (later shown to be formally equivalent to the wave mechanics of Edwin SCHRODINGER) that Heisenberg was awarded the 1932 NOBEL PRIZE for physics. In 1927 he went on to explore a deeper level of physical understanding when he formulated his fundamental "uncertainty principle": It is impossible to determine exactly both the position and momentum of such particles as the electron. He demonstrated this by simple "thought experiments." Like Max BORN, Heisenberg had found it necessary to introduce a basic indeterminacy into physics.

After his achievements in quantum theory in the 1920s Heisenberg turned his attention to the theory of elementary particles. In 1932, shortly after the discovery of the neutron by James CHADWICK, Heisenberg proposed that the nucleus consists of both neutrons and protons. He went further, arguing that they were, in fact, two states of the same basic entity—the "nucleon." As the strong nuclear force does not distinguish between them, he proposed that they were "isotopes" with nearly the same mass, distinguished by a property he called "isotopic spin." He later attempted the ambitious task of constructing a unified field theory of elementary particles. Although he published a monograph on the topic in 1966 it generated little support.

Unlike many other German scientists, Heisenberg remained in Germany throughout the war and the whole Nazi era. He was not a Nazi but thought it essential to remain in Germany to preserve traditional scientific values for the next generation. In 1935, when he wished to move to the University of Munich to succeed Arnold Sommerfeld, he was violently attacked by the Nazi Party press for refusing to compromise his support for the physics of Albert EINSTEIN. Eventually, the post went to the little-known W. Muller. With the outbreak of war in 1939 Heisenberg was soon called to Berlin to direct a program to construct an atom bomb. Heisenberg's exact role in the program is a matter of controversy. He has claimed that he never had any real intention of making such a bomb, let alone giving it to HITLER. As long as he played a key role he was, he later claimed, in a position to sabotage the program if it ever looked like being a success. He conveyed such thoughts to Niels Bohr in 1941 in Copenhagen, hinting that Allied physicists should pursue a similar policy. Bohr later reported that if such comments had been made to him they were too cryptic for him to grasp; he was rather under the impression that Heisenberg was trying to find out the progress made by the Allies. At any rate, when talking to German audiences Heisenberg was more inclined to explain the failure of the German atomic bomb program by the comparative lack of resources in the wartime economy after 1942. But by 1957 he was declaring publicly that he would not "in any way . . . take part in the production, the tests, or the application of atomic weapons."

Hejaz [Al-Hijaz]. Province along the Red Sea coast of western Saudi Arabia. Thousands of Islamic pilgrims visit its holy cities of Mecca and Medina annually. A railroad built from Damascus to Medina by the Ottoman Turks has been in disuse since the Turks lost their Arabian empire after WORLD WAR I. Husein ibn Ali, who gained independence for the province in 1916, was defeated by Ibn Saud of Nejd in 1924. The two provinces became a dual kingdom in 1926, and the single kingdom of SAUDI ARABIA in 1932.

Helgoland [Heligoland]. Resort island off the North Sea coast of Germany. Near the mouth of the Elbe River and the western end of the Kiel Canal (the great imperial naval base was at Kiel, on the Baltic Sea end of the canal) Helgoland was the almost inevitable site for several naval battles fought between Great Britain and Germany during WORLD WAR I. An early German defeat, on August 28, 1914, did much to discourage the Germans from leaving local waters to use their new, expensive fleet. The postwar TREATY OF VERSAILLES saw the dismantling of the island's fortifications, which were rebuilt under Adolf HITLER. Used by Germany as a naval base during WORLD WAR II, Helgoland was not surrendered to the Allies until May 5, 1945. In the British occupation zone, the island's fortifications were dynamited on April 18, 1947.

Heller, Joseph (1923–). American author. Heller achieved success with his iconoclastic first novel, CATCH 22 (1961, filmed 1970). Based on Heller's experiences as a bombardier in WORLD WAR II, the book depicts the absurdity of war and the system that promotes it. Its hero, Yossarian, who wants to be declared insane to get out of the war is told that if he is sane enough to want to leave, he cannot be discharged for insanity, and that is the catch of the title. Heller maintained his reputation satirizing modern life in such novels as *Something Happened* (1974), *Good as Gold* (1979) and *Picture This* (1988). In 1984 he was stricken with a rare, paralyzing disease which he chronicled in *No Laughing Matter* (1986). Heller has also written plays and screenplays.

Heller, Robert (1899–1973). American industrial designer whose work of the 1930s carried streamlining and MODERNISM (as related to ART DECO) to an extreme. Heller's best-known work is a streamlined electric fan designed in 1938 for the A.C. Gilbert Company. Although his 1933 building for radio station WCAU in Philadelphia has been destroyed, its interiors were a showcase of Art Deco interior design, while the street facade of blue cement with zig-zag trim in stainless steel symbolized the glamour of radio. However, conservative architects of that time and place found it offensive.

Heller, Walter W(olfgang) (1915–1987). American economist. Heller served as chairman of the Council of Economic advisers under two presidents, John F. KENNEDY and Lyndon B. JOHNSON. He held the post from the start of the Kennedy administration until the end of 1964, but continued to serve as consultant to Johnson until 1969. Heller was regarded as the architect of the historic tax cut of 1964 that led to an unprecedented boom in the U.S. economy. After he left office, he helped develop the theory of **revenue sharing,** under which state and local governments were deemed more efficient spenders of federal tax revenues than the federal government itself. Heller was a professor emeritus at the University of Minnesota.

Hellman, Lillian (Florence) (1905–1984). American playwright and memoirist. The New Orleans-born playwright studied at New York University, Columbia and Tufts. She worked as a manuscript reader and reviewer before her first Broadway success, *The Children's Hour* (1934). She began a tempestuous, lifelong relationship with mystery writer Dashiell HAMMETT in the early 1930s. Because she visited Russia in 1936 and 1945 and was active on the political left, she was called before the HOUSE UN-AMERICAN ACTIVITIES COMMITTEE in 1952 but refused to testify against her friends and colleagues. Her best-known plays include *The Little Foxes* (1939), *The Watch on the Rhine* (1941), *Another Part of the Forest* (1946) and *Toys in the Attic* (1960). Her memoirs appeared as *An Unfinished Woman* (1969), *Pentimento* (1973) and *Scoundrel Time* (1976). In her final years she engaged in a notorious public feud with novelist Mary MCCARTHY, who, in an interview on national television, had charged that Hellman was a liar.

For further reading:

Rollyson, Carl, *Lillian Hellman: Her Legend and Her Legacy*. New York: St. Martin, 1988.

Towns, Saundra, *Lillian Hellman*. New York: Chelsea House, 1989.

Wright, William, *Lillian Hellman: The Image, the Woman*. New York: Ballantine, 1988.

Helpmann, Robert (1909–1986). Australian dancer, choreographer, actor and director. As the principal male dancer for the Vic-Wells Ballet (1930–50), Helpmann danced classical, dramatic and comic roles with equal command and formed a celebrated partnership with Margot FONTEYN that contributed to the development of the ROYAL BALLET Company. He has choreographed works for several companies, and is noted for the unified dramatic effect of his creations, which include *Comus* (1942), *Hamlet* (1944), and *Elektra* (1963). An accomplished actor as well as dancer, he played leading roles in several Shakespearean plays, receiving special acclaim for his Hamlet. In addition, he appeared in the films *The Red Shoes* (1948) and *The Tales of Hoffman* (1951). He became co-artistic director of the Australian Ballet in 1965, and collaborated with Rudolph NUREYEV in filming the company's *Don Quixote* in 1973 in which he played the title role. Knighted by Queen ELIZABETH II in 1968, he retired in 1976 after producing the Australian Ballet's most popular work, *The Merry Widow*.

Lillian Hellman, American author and playwright, as she appeared in March 1970.

Helsinki Accords. The Helsinki Accords, a result of the Conference on Security and Cooperation in Europe, were signed by 33 European nations plus the U.S. and Canada, on August 1, 1975. Although the agreement does not have the legal status of a treaty, it served as a keystone of DETENTE. The accords implicitly recognized Soviet dominance of Eastern Europe while guaranteeing human rights in those nations, facilitating trade within Europe, and easing political and military tensions.

Hemingway, Ernest (1898–1961). Hemingway was one of the most famous American writers of the century. Born in Oak Park, Illinois, after high school he became a reporter in Kansas City. During WORLD WAR I he joined a volunteer ambulance unit in Italy, where he was wounded. Remaining in Europe after the war, he became part of the literary scene in Paris, associating with such American expatriate writers as Gertrude STEIN and F. Scott FITZGERALD. His first and perhaps most famous novel, *The Sun Also Rises* (1926), is a moving tribute to the "lost generation" of expatriate Americans whose beliefs were shattered by the war. Hemingway's World War I experiences inspired *A Farewell to Arms* (1929), considered a classic novel of the war despite its flaws. His writings reflected his many interests, including bullfighting and African big game hunting. After observing the SPANISH CIVIL WAR firsthand he wrote *For Whom the Bell Tolls* (1940). His WORLD WAR II reporting took him on many of the major Allied campaigns of WORLD WAR II IN EUROPE; his novel *Across the River and Into the Trees* (1950) is set during the war. Hemingway won a PULITZER PRIZE in 1953 for his novella *The Old Man and the Sea*, and the following year was awarded the NOBEL PRIZE for literature. Hemingway developed a type of laconic male character who typically faced violence and destruction with courage—what Hemingway called "grace under pressure." His deceptively simple prose style and his amoral outlook make Hemingway one of the leading figures of literary MODERNISM. He committed suicide by shooting himself at his home in Ketchum, Idaho.

Hempel, Carl G(ustav) (1905–). German philosopher. Hempel was trained in physics and mathematics and earned his doctoral degree at the University of Berlin in 1934. He was a member of the Berlin group of philosophers who contributed to the theories of the Vienna Circle—led by Rudolf CARNAP—that led to the formulation of the school of LOGICAL POSITIVISM. One of Hempel's key theories was that of a "translatability criterion" for truth: A statement was meaningful only if it was translatable into empiricist language. Hempel fled GERMANY and the Nazi regime in 1934 and ultimately came to the United States, where he taught at Princeton and Yale. Major works by Hempel include *Fundamentals of Concept Formation in Empirical Science* (1952) and *Aspects of Scientific Explanation* (1965).

Hench, Philip Showalter (1896–1965). American physician. Hench earned his M.D. from the University of Pittsburgh in 1920 and began work at the Mayo Clinic three years later. Over the course of his long career there, he researched a treatment for rheumatoid arthritis and was the first to use cortisone, developed by Edward KENDALL, to treat the condition. He shared the 1950 NOBEL PRIZE for physiology or medicine with Kendall and Tadeus Reichstein.

Henderson, Arthur (1863–1935). British statesman. Born in Glasgow, Scotland, at 12 Henderson was apprenticed to an iron molder. Becoming an iron worker, he was soon a leader in the labor union movement. In 1900, he was a cofounder of the Labour Representation Committee, the forerunner of the British LABOUR PARTY, and three years later he was elected to Parliament. He headed the 1906 conference that formally established the Labour party, acting as the party's parliamentary leader from 1908 to 1911 and 1914 to 1917, and as its secretary from 1911 to 1934. He held various posts in ASQUITH'S WORLD WAR I coalition government and was home secretary (1924) and foreign secretary (1929–31) in the Labour government of Ramsay MACDONALD. Losing his parliamentary seat in 1931, he became president of the World Disarmament Conference the following year. For the rest of his life Henderson devoted himself to his party and to the cause of world peace, and in 1934 he was awarded the NOBEL PRIZE for peace. His books include *The Aims of Labour* (1917), *Consolidating World Peace* (1931) and *Labour's Way to Peace* (1935).

For further reading:

Leventhal, F.M., *Arthur Henderson*. New York. St. Martin's, 1989.

Henderson, Edwin (1883–1977). American educator. Henderson was the first black instructor of physical education in the U.S.(1904). He was also active in the NATIONAL ASSOCIATION FOR THE ADVANCEMENT OF COLORED PEOPLE (NAACP). During the 1950s he served two terms as president of the NAACP's Virginia chapter.

Henderson, Fletcher (1897–1952). American bandleader-arranger. Like Duke ELLINGTON, Henderson was raised in an upper-middle class black family. He received early training in European classical music from his mother, a piano teacher who shunned blues, gospel and jazz forms as "unworthy." After graduation from Atlantic University as a chemistry major, Henderson moved to New York; unable to secure employment in his field because of racial prejudice, he became a song-plugger and music producer, putting together various acts for tour and club work. Soon, he became a bandleader. And by 1925, though he initially lacked any real jazz experience, his band featured such rising jazz talents as trumpeter Louis ARMSTRONG and saxophonist Lester YOUNG. Arrangements for Henderson's band, regarded as the prototype of the big swing bands that would dominate the 1930s, were made by Don Redman. When Redman departed, Henderson was forced to write much of his band's material. Fortuitously, Henderson's arranging gifts proved immense. Indeed, he was pivotal in establishing the basic format of the big band arrangement, featuring interplay between the reed and brass sections (sometimes in call-and-response dialogues, other times with one section playing background riffs behind the other), with improvised solos interspersed between the written passages. Though Henderson's lack of business acumen precluded his own large-scale success, his arrangements of tunes such as "King Porter Stomp" and "Down South Camp Meeting" helped catapult Benny GOODMAN to fame in the mid-1930s and, with Goodman, the entire big band swing phenomenon.

For further reading:

Schuller, Gunther, *The Swing Era: The Development of Jazz, 1930–1945*. New York: Oxford University Press, 1989.

Henderson, W(esley) Loy (1892–1986). U.S. diplomat. Henderson was one of the first career officers in the U.S. foreign service, ambassador to India and Iran. He was prominent in Middle East diplomacy in the decade following World War II, and was credited with having played a major role in preventing the communist takeover of GREECE in the late 1940s.

Hendrix, Jimi [James Marshall Hendrix] (1942–1970). American ROCK-AND-ROLL guitarist and vocalist. Hendrix is widely regarded as one of the greatest guitarists in the history of rock and roll. Hendrix learned his musical craft in the early 1960s, when he performed as a back-up musician for stars including B.B. KING, Little Richard, and Ike and Tina Turner. It was Keith Richard, guitarist for the ROLLING STONES, who brought Hendrix to the attention of music industry people capable of making him a star. Hendrix signed a recording contract in 1967 and had immediate success with his classic single "Hey Joe" (1967). That same year he performed with his band the Jimi Hendrix Experience at the Monterey Pop Festival—a performance preserved in the film *Monterey Pop* (1969)—and riveted the audience by burning his guitar for his finale. Hendrix died from a drug overdose in 1970. His noteworthy albums include *Are You Experienced* (1967), *Axis-Bold as Love* (1967), *Electric Ladyland* (1968) and *Rainbow Bridge* (1971).

Jimi Hendrix, rock singer and guitarist, performing on the Isle of Wight, England, a few days before his death on Sept. 18, 1970.

For further reading:

Murray, Charles S., *Crosstown Traffic: Jimi Hendrix and the Post-War Rock 'n' Roll Revolution*. New York: St. Martin's, 1990.

Heng, Samrin (1934–). Heng Samrin is president of CAMBODIA and leader of the country's official Communist Party. With little formal education, in the 1950s he became involved in illicit cattle trading across the Vietnamese border—the beginning of his contact with Vietnamese communists. He took up the revolutionary cause in 1959, then fled to the jungle in 1967 as Khmer communists escaped repression in Phnom Penh. Based in the eastern zone, near the Vietnamese border, in 1978 he joined the pro-Hanoi faction of the party. Samrin fled to Vietnam to escape POL POT's purges of cadres in the eastern zone. Shortly thereafter he returned to Cambodia with the Vietnamese invading force and became president of liberated Cambodia in January 1979.

Henie, Sonja (1912–1969). Norwegian-born skater and film star. Born to one of Norway's wealthiest families, Henie won an unequalled three OLYMPIC figure skating gold medals, in 1928, 1932 and 1936. Her popularity became so great during her skating career that police had to provide crowd control wherever she appeared. After winning 1,473 skating trophies, she signed with 20TH CENTURY-FOX. Her first film *One in a Million* (1936) was an enormous success, and a string of films whose plots revolved around skating followed. She retired from films in the 1940s. At her death she was worth an estimated $47 million.

Henri, Robert (1865–1929). American painter. Born in Cincinnati, Henri attended the Pennsylvania Academy of the Fine Arts, and continued his art studies in Paris from 1888 to 1891. Returning to teach in Philadelphia, he moved to New York City in 1900 and established his own school there nine years later. An advocate of a vivid and very American realism and an opponent of overly refined and mannered academic styles, Henri was a member of the group known as the EIGHT and its articulate spokesman. His bold, broad brushstroke was particularly effective in outstanding portraits, which include *Eva Green* (Wichita Art Museum), *Spanish Gypsy* (Metropolitan Museum, N.Y.C.) and *Young Woman in Black* (Art Institute of Chicago). At his school until 1912 and later at the Art Students League, Henri was an inspired and extremely influential teacher who numbered among his students George BELLOWS, William GLACKENS, Edward HOPPER, Rockwell Kent, George Luks and John SLOAN.

For further reading:

Homer, William I., *Robert Henri and His Circle*. New York: Hacker, 1988.

Henson, James "Jim" (1939–1990). Creator of the "Muppets" and a successful television and motion picture producer-director. Henson was born in Greenville, Miss., and after college landed his first television show, "Sam and Friends," on WRC-TV in Washington, D.C. He referred to his hand-operated characters as "Muppets"—a combination of the words "puppet" and "marionette." Such familiar characters as Kermit the Frog, Fozzie Bear, Miss Piggy and Cookie Monster were developed for the Children's Television Workshop program, "Sesame Street" (1969) and its spin-off "The Muppet Show," which began in London in 1976. Henson then starred his Muppets in three motion pictures, *The Muppet Movie* (1979), *The Great Muppet Caper* (1981) and *The Muppets Take Manhattan* (1984). Meanwhile, his company, Henson Associates, Inc., began a successful licensing campaign, a Saturday morning children's show, *The Muppet Babies* (1984) and two "serious" movie fantasies, *The Dark Crystal* (1982) and *The Labyrinth* (1985). He sold the rights to the Muppets to Walt Disney Enterprises for a reported $150 million in 1989. Henson's style adroitly blended gentle, positive humor for children with a satiric edge finely honed for the adults. He brought the tradition of hand-operated puppets as exemplified by his mentor, Burr TILLSTROM, into the modern age of robotic, remote- controlled technology. "In a sense the Muppets are more real than cartoon characters," he once remarked. "You can touch them. They really exist. Children feel closer to them. The appeal is to young and old because we all have fantasies about 'growing up.' We play at growing up, at the things that brighten or hurt us." It was characteristic of Henson that he kept his right hand upraised, close to his mouth, as he spoke. "Years of training do that," he explained. "Your hand is always ready for the Muppet. It's acting with the hand. Your whole performance is through the hand." Henson's voice, as he spoke, changed, perhaps unconsciously, into the familiar voice of Kermit the Frog. Henson died suddenly of pneumonia in 1990.

For further reading:
Katz, Ephraim, ed. *The Film Encyclopedia*. New York: Thomas Y. Crowell, 1979.

Henze, Hans Werner (1926–). German composer. Born in Gutersloh, he studied piano, percussion and composition, and was a student of Wolfgang Fortner and Rene Leibowitz. A British prisoner of war in World War II, he moved to Italy in 1953. Influenced by STRAVINSKY, HINDEMITH and BARTOK, he began writing twelve-tone music with his first violin concerto of 1947. Since the 1960s, Henze has modified that system into a more personal but no less dissonant style. He is probably best known for his operas, which include *King Stag* (1955), *Elegy for Young Lovers* (1961), *The Bassarids* (1965) and *La Cubana* (1973). Henze has also written six symphonies (1947–69), chamber music, orchestral works and vocal pieces.

Hepburn, Katharine (1907–). Celebrated American stage and motion picture actress. Hepburn has won four ACADEMY AWARDS, including for *Morning Glory* (1932), *Guess Who's Coming to Dinner* (1967) and *On Golden Pond* (1981). This Bryn Mawr-educated daughter of a distinguished New England family has had the uncanny knack of appearing in movies that parallel her own life and temperament. *A Woman Rebels* (1936), the story of a 19th-century feminist leader, could also have been a portrayal of Hepburn's suffragette mother. The events in *Stage Door* (1937) resemble her own attempts to break into Broadway. (*Holiday* [1938] allowed her to take on a role that she had understudied on the stage a decade earlier.) The men's clothes worn by her title characters in *Christopher Strong* (1933) and *Sylvia Scarlett* (1935) suggest her own fashion predilections. Her liberal political views surface in the politician's wife she portrays in Frank CAPRA's *State of the Union* (1947). Her 27-year personal and professional relationship with Spencer TRACY began with *Woman of the Year* (1942) and ended only with his death during the shooting of *Guess Who's Coming to Dinner?* (1967).

Katharine Hepburn performing in the film The Philadelphia Story *(1940)*

For further reading:
Katz, Ephraim, ed. *The Film Encyclopedia*. New York: Thomas Y. Crowell, 1979.

Hepworth, Cecil (1874–1953). Pioneering British motion picture director, producer, and inventor at the turn of the century. If first honors must go to Robert W. Paul as the Father of the British Film, Hepworth, lagging behind by only a few years, assumed the forefront of the British film industry for the first 15 years of the new century. The son of a noted lantern-slide lecturer, Hepworth designed and sold projector lamps. In 1898 he set up a company at Walton-on-Thames to process and make short films. Five years later at his own studio he began making short news films and trick films in the manner of MELIES and Paul. His production in 1905 of the six-minute "Rescued by Rover" (directed by Lewin Fitzhamon) was a spectacular success and, like the American *The Great Train Robbery* (1903), helped establish the narrative film as the most important form of cinema entertainment. "I have never in my life before or since witnessed such intense enthusiasm as these short, crude films evoked in audiences who saw films for the first time," he recalled in his autobiography, *Came the Dawn* (1951). In 1910 he patented an early system for the synchronization of image and phonographic sound, the Vivaphone. However, after 1914 his career went into decline; new developments in the industry overtook him as his own films, including *Annie Laurie* (1916) and *Boundary House* (1918), lapsed into routine formulas. In 1924 Hepworth declared bankruptcy and after 1927 he made no more feature pictures. His last years were spend directing short advertising films and trailers.

Hepworth, Dame (Jocelyn) Barbara (1903–1975). English sculptor. She studied at the Royal College of Art, London and absorbed Romanesque and Renaissance styles as well as stonecutting techniques in a 1924 study trip to Italy. Her work, carved directly in stone or wood, and later also cast in bronze, is simplified, abstract and organic. Often hollowed out and pierced, her sculpture has been compared to BRANCUSI, Henry MOORE and Jean ARP. After 1937, Hepworth often included color in her work and, after 1938, she also included string or wire into her compositions, giving the effect of abstract musical instruments. She is noted for several monumental public pieces, as in her work in the Royal Festival Hall, London, and she is particularly well represented in the Tate Gallery collection, London. Along with Moore and her husband Ben NICOLSON, she is considered one of the most important figures in British art (and in modern sculpture) in the 20th century.

Herbert, Frank (1910–1986). American science-fiction author. Herbert's epic novel *Dune* (1965) became an international best-seller and cult favorite. The lavish and expensive 1984 film version of the novel, although panned by U.S. critics, found success in Europe and Japan. *Dune* was the first book in what began as a trilogy and grew to six novels. Herbert was reported to have been working on a seventh at the time of his death.

Victor Herbert, Irish-American composer, cellist and conductor.

For further reading:
Touponce, William F., *Frank Herbert*. Boston: G.K. Hall, 1988.

Herbert, Victor (1859–1924). Irish-American composer, conductor and cellist. Born in Dublin, he studied at the Stuttgart Conservatory. He came to the U.S. in 1886 as a cellist for the Metropolitan Opera, N.Y.C. Herbert conducted various military bands and orchestras and was the conductor of the Pittsburgh Symphony Orchestra from 1898 to 1904, after which he devoted most of his time to composing. Famous for his light-hearted, melodious operettas, he is best known for *Babes in Toyland* (1903), *The Red Mill* (1906), *Naughty Marietta* (1910) and *Sweethearts* (1913) and for such songs as "Ah! Sweet Mystery of Life" and "Gypsy Love Song." He also wrote the grand operas *Natoma* (1911) and *Madeleine* (1914), music for the ZIEGFELD FOLLIES, orchestral pieces and a cello concerto.

Herbert, Zbigniew (1924–). Polish poet, essayist and playwright. Herbert is one of the finest postwar Polish poets. His verse is noteworthy for its taut, austere style that deals movingly with themes of war, loss, love, and the diminished meanings of faith and myth in a desacralized world. Herbert was born in Lvov, Poland and fought against the NAZIS in the underground RESISTANCE during WORLD WAR II, during which time he also began to write poetry. After the war, Herbert studied economics, law and philology at the universities of Krakow and Torun. In the 1950s he traveled in Western Europe, and he was Poet in Residence at the Free University of West Berlin in the late 1960s. His major volumes of verse include *The Chord of Light* (1956), *Hermes, Dog and Star* (1957) and *Study of the Object* (1961). *The Barbarian in the Garden* (1963) is a collection of travel essays. A volume of *Selected Poems*, including translations of

Herbert's verse by NOBEL PRIZE laureate Czeslaw MILOSZ, was published in English in 1968.

Herman, Woody (Woodrow Charles) (1913–1987). American musician. A JAZZ clarinetist and big band leader, Herman's career spanned five decades. He led a series of ensembles, generally called his "Thundering Herd," in a wide range of styles that reflected the continually changing character of popular music. Alumni of various "Herds" included such popular musicians as Stan GETZ, Milt Jackson and Terry Gibbs.

Hermosa. Town in Philippines province of Bataan, where savage fighting took place between invading Japanese and defending American and Filipino forces in January 1942, during WORLD WAR II.

Herriot, Edouard (1872–1957). French statesman. A moderate leftist, Herriot was an important figure in the political life of the Third and Fourth Republics and the leader of the Radical Socialist party of FRANCE. Elected mayor of Lyon in 1905, he held the office until 1941 and from 1945 until his death. Becoming a member of the senate in 1912 and of the chamber of deputies in 1919, he was a strong voice in opposing militarism and clericalism and promoting civil liberties and republicanism. Premier in 1924–25, he was responsible for withdrawing French forces from the Ruhr valley region and for recognizing the U.S.S.R. His unpopular stand in favor of paying war debts to the U.S. was the prime reason for the defeat of this government and for the failure of his next two terms as premier in 1926 and 1932. President of the chamber of deputies (1936–40), he opposed the VICHY government and was arrested in 1942. Deported to Germany in 1944, he was liberated the following year. Herriot served as president of the national assembly from 1947 to 1954. Also a noted man of letters, Herriot was the author of literary studies and a biography of Beethoven.

For further reading:

Jessner, Sabine, *Edouard Herriot and the French Republic*. Brooklyn, N.Y.: Haskell, 1974.

Herrmann, Bernard (1911–1975). American composer. Herrmann, who was educated at the Juilliard School of Music in New York, established himself as one of most important composers of HOLLYWOOD film scores. He showed a special talent for eery and ominous scores that effectively blended with the visual imagery of suspense master Alfred HITCHCOCK. Herrmann's auspicious debut as a film composer was the score for CITIZEN KANE (1941), the masterpiece of director Orson WELLES. Hitchcock films for which Herrmann composed music include *The Man Who Knew Too Much* (1956), *Vertigo* (1958), *North By Northwest* (1959) and *Psycho* (1960), the chilling score for which Herrmann remains best known. His last work was the score for *Taxi Driver* (1976) by director Martin SCORSESE.

Hersey, John (Richard) (1914–). American journalist and novelist. Hersey was born in China, and spoke the language fluently. He began his career as an assistant to Sinclair LEWIS and later began writing for TIME and LIFE magazines, serving as a war correspondent for them during WORLD WAR II. Hersey is best known for his journalistic novels about various countries during the war. These include *Man on Bataan* (1942), *A Bell for Adano* (1944, filmed 1945), which won a PULITZER PRIZE in 1946; *Hiroshima* (1946), which first appeared in *The New Yorker*, and *The Wall* (1950), a study of Poland under the Nazis. Later works include *Aspects of the Presidency* (1980), *The Call* (1985) and *Blues* (1987).

Hershey, Franklin Quick (1907–). American automobile designer best known for his work on the original (1955) Ford THUNDERBIRD, although a major portion of his career was spent with GENERAL MOTORS. Hershey studied at Occidental College in California before going to work for the California custom automobile design firm of Walter M. Murphy in 1927, where he remained (except for a brief period in 1928 at General Motors in Detroit) until the firm closed in 1931. He was briefly with Hudson before joining GM in 1932 to take charge of styling for Pontiac and later for Buick and overseas GM divisions. After World War II he returned to GM to work on Cadillac design and in the firm's experimental design studio. In 1953 he was placed in charge of styling at FORD. In 1956 he left automotive design to work for KAISER Aluminum and then, until his retirement in 1978, for Wright Autotronics in California. Hershey's work spanned a wide range of automotive design concepts, extending from the peerless custom body of the early 1930s through GM models of the 1930s and early 1940s to the elegant and greatly admired 1955 Thunderbird, a sports car of simple form. Surprisingly, he also directed the design of other Ford cars, such as the 1957 Fairlane 500, which typified the trend toward oversized fenders and heavy CHROMIUM trim.

Hertz, Gustav (1887–1975). German physicist. The nephew of 19th-century physicist Heinrich Hertz, Gustav Hertz was born in Hamburg, Germany. He attended the universities of Berlin and Munich and afterward taught in Berlin and Halle. In 1925, Hertz shared the NOBEL PRIZE for physics with his colleague James Franck, for "discovering the laws governing the impact of an electron on an atom." Beginning in 1928, he worked as an instructor at the Technical University in Berlin. From 1935, when he was forced by the Nazis to leave his teaching position, until the end of WORLD WAR II, he worked as an industrial physicist for Siemens. In the decade following the war, Hertz helped to develop the Soviet atomic bomb. From 1955 until his retirement in 1961, he was a professor at the Physics Institute in Leipzig.

Herut [Heb., The Freedom Party]. Extreme right-wing political group in ISRAEL, founded by Menachem BEGIN and a successor to the **Revisionist Party**. It was later a part of Gahal.

Theodor Herzl, founder of modern Zionism.

Herzl, Theodor (1860–1904). Founder of modern ZIONISM. A Hungarian Jew, Herzl studied law at the University of Vienna, receiving a doctorate in 1884. He became a journalist and was sent (1891) to Paris by the Viennese newspaper *Neue Freie Presse* and covered the Dreyfus Affair. His earlier experiences with anti-Jewish feeling coupled with the appalling ANTISEMITISM that he witnessed during the infamous trial turned Herzl against the idea of Jewish assimilation and convinced him that it was necessary for JEWS to have a nation of their own. He expressed this idea in the landmark work *The Jewish State* (1896), in which he suggested establishing this nation in the original Jewish homeland of PALESTINE. The following year Herzl convened the first World Zionist Congress in Basel, Switzerland, and he served as its president until his death. He worked tirelessly to promote Zionism and to secure both the necessary funding to realize his dream and the positive world opinion that would ease the way to a Jewish state. A year after the creation of ISRAEL, Herzl's body was moved from Vienna to Jerusalem.

Herzog, Chaim (1918–). President of ISRAEL (1983–). Herzog was born in Belfast, Ireland. He studied at the Universities of Dublin, London and Cambridge and at Hebron's yeshiva. He moved to PALESTINE in 1935, served as a British major during World War II and then on the Allied General Staff in Germany. He headed the Jewish Agency's security section (1947–48) and served as director of military intelligence (1948–50, 1959–62) and, from June 1967, as first military governor of the West Bank. He was Israel's ambassador to the United Nations from 1975 to 1978, became a Labor Party member of the Knesset in 1981 and was made president in 1983. A lawyer by training, he is the author of *Israel's Finest Hour*, *Days of Awe*, *War of Atonement* and *Who*

Stands Accused. He was awarded a KBE in 1970. Although Herzog has kept aloof from internal politics since becoming head of state in 1983, the series of presidential pardons he has granted to settlers and to members of the security service implicated in the killing of Palestinians has put him firmly on the right in Israel's political spectrum.

Herzog, Werner (1942–). German film director. Herzog is one of the most unique film directors of modern times. All of his films have an intensely visionary quality, and many critics have noted resemblances between his thematic concerns and those of the German Romantic writers of the 19th century. Herzog's first major film project, which was self-funded, was the satiric *Even Dwarfs Started Small* (1969). He achieved international fame for *Aguirre, the Wrath of God* (1975), which starred Klaus Kinski and dealt with greed and obsession in the age of the Spanish conquistadores. Subsequent films by Herzog include *Nosferatu the Vampire* (1979), *Woyzeck* (1979 and *Fitzcarraldo* (1982).

Hesburgh, Theodore M. (1917–). American educator. Hesburgh, who was ordained as a Roman Catholic priest in 1943, earned his doctorate from Catholic University in 1945. He was named president of Notre Dame University in 1952 and successfully transformed that institution from a strictly Catholic school to a secular university with a high academic standing. Hesburgh also entered the sphere of national politics through his appointment in 1957 by President Dwight EISENHOWER to the U.S. Commission on Civil Rights. Hesburgh remained on the Commission for fifteen years, served as its chairman from 1969 to 1972, and was instrumental in fostering the passage of major CIVIL RIGHTS legislation in the 1960s. Hesburgh was subsequently named by President Jimmy CARTER to the Overseas Development Council. In 1981, he was appointed by President Ronald REAGAN to the Select Commission on Immigration and Refugee Relief.

Heseltine, Michael (1933–). British politician. An Oxford graduate and a successful real estate developer and publisher, Heseltine entered politics as a moderate Tory. Elected to Parliament in 1966, he held several ministerial positions under Prime Minister HEATH. In Prime Minister THATCHER's government he was environment secretary (1979–83) and defense secretary (1983–86). After the inner city riots of 1981 he proposed a highly praised urban revitalization program. A leading figure in the CONSERVATIVE PARTY, Heseltine resigned from the government during the WESTLAND AFFAIR (1986). He helped force THATCHER's resignation in 1990 and served in the cabinet of her successor, John MAJOR.

Hess, Dame Myra (1890–1965). English pianist. Born in London, Hess studied at the Royal Academy of Music, London. She became a major soloist with her brilliant debut in London in 1907, playing Beethoven under the baton of Sir Thomas BEECHAM. Concertizing throughout Europe, the U.S. and Canada, she was known for her sensitive interpretations of the classical repetoire, particularly the works of Bach, Mozart and Beethoven. During WORLD WAR II she organized the famous luncheon concerts at the National Gallery, London, playing in many of them herself. For these performances, some occurring while bombs fell on London, Hess was made a Dame of the British Empire in 1941.

Hess, (Walter Richard) Rudolf (1894–1987). German Nazi official. An early member of the Nazi Party, Hess was Adolf HITLER's first great admirer, and in 1920 he became Hitler's political secretary and closest associate. He participated in the Munich BEER HALL PUTSCH (1923). During their subsequent term in prison, Hitler dictated his political tract MEIN KAMPF to Hess. In 1934, Hess was named deputy party leader, and was officially second only to GOERING behind Hitler in the hierarchy of the Third Reich. However, Hess was a naive man of limited intelligence and ability, essentially a dreamer rather than a doer. His influence waned with the rise of HIMMLER, GOEBBELS, and other more practical-minded Nazis. In 1941, on his own initiative, Hess made a solo flight to Scotland in a bizarre bid to end WORLD WAR II. He hoped that British leaders would negotiate with him and that this bold move would restore his flagging reputation in Germany. Instead, Hitler was infuriated by what he viewed as Hess' treason, while the British government refused to take Hess seriously. Hess was immediately imprisoned, and remained in British custody throughout the war. He was tried and convicted during the NUREMBERG WAR CRIMES TRIALS and sentenced to life imprisonment in SPANDAU PRISON in West Berlin. The last survivor of the 19 German officials convicted by the tribunal, by 1966 he was Spandau's only occupant, remaining there (at the insistence of the Soviet government) until his death, despite various appeals for his release. In the 1970s, he became an object of international attention when a British doctor claimed that the prisoner in Spandau was not Hess but a double. This charge was never proved.

For further reading:
Fest, Joachim, *The Face of the Third Reich: Portraits of the Nazi Leadership*, tr. Michael Bullock. New York: Pantheon, 1977.

Hesse, Hermann (1877–1962). German-Swiss novelist, poet and essayist. Winner of the 1946 NOBEL PRIZE for literature, Hesse is known for his psychological probing of the dichotomy between spirit

Rudolf Hess (right) greets Adolf Hitler at a Nazi congress in Nuremberg.

and flesh, art and life, emotion and intellect, independence and involvement, in his major works. His first successful novel, *Peter Camerzind*, was published in 1904. After World War I, Hesse produced his greatest works, which reflected his personal crises, his political views and his philosophical interests, especially in Confucianism and Buddhism. Important works include the novels *Siddhartha* (1922), *Der Steppenwolf* (1927) and *Das Glasperlenspiel* (1943); the poetry collection *Gesammelte Gedichte* (1952); and the volume of essays titled *Blick ins Chaos* (1920).

For further reading:

Mileck, Joseph, *Hermann Hesse: Biography and Bibliography*, 2 vols. Berkeley: University of California Press, 1977.

Heston, Charlton [Charlton Carter] (1923–). American film actor. Heston studied acting at Northwestern University and made his Broadway debut in *Antony and Cleopatra* (1947). Turning to the new media of television he became a respected actor in productions of *Julius Caesar* (1948), *Wuthering Heights* (1949), *Macbeth* (1949) and others. In the 1950s he starred in several films, including *The Greatest Show on Earth* (1952), but it wasn't until he portrayed Moses in Cecil B. DE MILLE's talkie remake of *The Ten Commandments* (1956) that he became known as America's leading actor in historical epics. Three years later he won the ACADEMY AWARD for best actor in the blockbuster remake of another silent hit, *Ben-Hur*. During his career Heston also had success in several offbeat roles; he played a Mexican narcotics officer in Orson WELLES' masterpiece *Touch of Evil* (1958) and an astronaut stranded in the future in the science fiction classic *Planet of the Apes* (1968).

Heyerdahl, Thor (1914–). Norwegian anthropologist and explorer. Heyerdahl became an international celebrity when he made his 4,100-mile raft journey across the Pacific Ocean in 1947. He developed a theory that ancient peoples migrated by sea as well as by land routes. To prove the feasibility of this theory, Heyerdahl and five others built a balsa-wood raft, called the *Kon-Tiki*, which was like the type used by early South American Indians, and traveled from Peru to Polynesia (1947). His 1969 attempt to further test his theory, by crossing the Atlantic from Morocco to South America in a papyrus boat, had to be abandoned.

Heyse, Paul (1830–1914). German author. Though a poet and playwright as well, Heyse is best known for his fiction, which includes the novellas *L'arrabbiata* (The Angry Girl, 1857) and *Bild der Mutter* (The Mother's Portrait, 1859), and the novels *Kinder der Welt* (*Children of the World*, 1873) and *Merlin* (1892). Heyse's romantic, lyric poetry was overshadowed by the Naturalists who followed him, and he is better remembered for his translations of Italian poets. His plays include, *Hans Lange* (1866) and *Maria von Magdala* (Mary of Magdala, 1899). Heyse was awarded the NOBEL PRIZE for literature in 1910, the first German writer to be so honored.

Heywood, Eddie (1915–1989). American JAZZ pianist, arranger, and composer. Haywood's sextet was one of the most popular jazz groups of the 1940s. A bout of severe arthritis forced his retirement in 1947; he then turned to composing such hits of the 1950s as *Land of Dreams, Soft Summer Breeze*, and *Canadian Sunset*. In his later years he suffered from Parkinson's disease and Alzheimer's disease.

Hezbollah. Iranian organization whose name means Party of God. Hezbollah, while not technically a political party exercises political influence through its supporters among IRP members of Parliament. It consists of organized street groups, allied to the clergy, that patrol large cities "in the name of the Imam," but represented the interests of the Ayatollah KHOMEINI during the 1980s. Criticized by Bani-Sadr as thugs, the Hezbollah were particularly active in the summer and fall of 1981 in battles with leftists. Hezbollah factions were also active in LEBANON and were believed responsible for some of the kidnappings of westerners there in the 1980s. (See also IRAN.)

Hidalgo Del Parral [Parral]. Transportation and mining center in northern Mexico's Chihuahua state; a hotbed of Francisco Madero's revolt of 1917, Parral was also where popular hero Pancho VILLA was assassinated in 1923.

Higashikuni, Naruhiko (1887–1990). Japanese monk. A member of JAPAN's imperial family, he became the country's first premier after World War II. He was the first member of the imperial family to head a cabinet, which he formed two days after the Japanese surrender on August 15, 1945. His government lasted less than two months. In 1947, he was deprived of his title and became a Buddhist monk.

Highland Park. Industrial suburb of U.S.'s Detroit; incorporated in 1917. FORD MOTOR COMPANY's first, innovative automobile production plant was established here in 1909; current world headquarters of CHRYSLER Corporation.

Highsmith, (Mary) Patricia (1921–). American novelist. Although they fall into the mystery genre Highsmith's novels have received acclaim from such critics as Brigid BROPHY for their psychological insight as well as their literary style. Perhaps best known in the U.S. is her first novel, *Strangers on a Train* (1950), which was filmed by Alfred HITCHCOCK in 1951. Highsmith's novels have a large following in Britain. Other of her many works include *The Talented Mr. Ripley* (1955, filmed as *Purple Noon* in 1961), the first of a series of novels featuring the repugnant anti-hero Ripley; *Found in the Street* (1986) and *The Animal Lovers Book of Beastly Murder* (1988). Highsmith originally published some of her early work under the pseudonym Clair Morgan.

Hilbersheimer, Ludwig Karl (1885–1967). German architect and town planner known as a teacher and writer who was influential in advancing BAUHAUS theory as it applied to urban planning. Hilbersheimer was trained in architecture and planning at the Institute of Technology at Karlsruhe in Germany and established his own practice thereafter in Berlin. From 1928 until 1932 he was at the Bauhaus, teaching architecture, construction, housing, and town planning. In 1938 he emigrated to the U.S. to become a professor of city planning at Illinois Institute of Technology in Chicago and, after 1955, director of the department of city and regional planning there. He was the author of many articles and a number of books, including *Groszstadt Architektur* (1927), *The New City* (1950) and *The Nature of Cities* (1955). Hilbersheimer's writing emphasizes historical study of urban forms, while his own approach to planning is highly theoretical, leading to abstract, geometric forms generated by studies of prevailing wind directions in relation to industrial pollution output and to the logical study of density, land use and circulation patterns. Although his proposals now seem overly mechanistic, Hilbersheimer's basic concepts remain significant for all modern urban planning.

Hilbert, David (1862–1943). German mathematician, generally considered one of the greatest of the 20th century. Hilbert studied at the universities of Konigsberg and Heidelberg and also spent brief periods in Paris and Leipzig. He took his Ph.D. in 1885, by 1892 was a professor and in 1895 moved to Gottingen to take up the chair that he occupied until his official retirement in 1930. Hilbert's mathematical work was wide-ranging; there were few fields to which he did not make some contribution and many he completely transformed. From 1885 to 1888 he solved the central problems of the newly created theory of invariants. He created entirely new methods for tackling problems, in the context of a much wider general theory. The fruit of this work consisted of many new and fundamental theorems in algebra. Much of his work on invariants was later applied to the new subject of homological algebra.

Hilbert next turned to algebraic number theory and probably his finest work. He produced not only a masterly account of number theory but also a substantial body of original and fundamental discoveries. The work was presented in *Zahlbericht* (1897) with an elegance and lucidity of exposition that has rarely been equaled. Hilbert moved to another area of mathematics and wrote a classic work, *Grundlagen der Geometrie* (1899, *Foundations of Geometry*), an account of geometry as it had developed in the 19th century.

In mathematical logic and the philosophy of mathematics, Hilbert is one of the major proponents of the formalist view, which had a formative impact on the development of mathematical logic. Hilbert aimed at formalizing as much of mathematics as possible and finding consistency proofs for the resulting formal systems. It was soon shown by Kurt GODEL that "Hilbert's program" could not be carried out, at least in its original form; but Godel's own revolutionary metamathematical work would have been inconceivable without Hilbert. Hilbert's contribution to mathematical logic was important, especially to the development of proof theory.

Hilbert also made notable contributions to analysis, to the calculus of variations and to mathematical physics. His work on operators and on "Hilbert space" (a type of infinite-dimensional space) was of crucial importance to QUANTUM MECHANICS. His considerable influence on mathematical physics was also exerted through his colleagues at Gottingen, who included Minkowski, Weyl, SCHRODINGER and HEISENBERG. In 1900 Hilbert presented a list of 23 outstanding unsolved mathematical problems to the International Congress of Mathematicians in Paris. A number of these problems remain unsolved, and the mathematics created in solving the others has fully vindicated his deep insight. Hilbert was an excellent teacher and during his time at Gottingen built the university into an outstanding center of mathematical research, which it remained until the dispersal of the intellectual community by the Nazis in 1933.

Hill 60. Hill in Belgian province of West Flanders, about three miles southeast of YPRES—a bloody battle site during the first spring of WORLD WAR I, between April 17 and May 5, 1915.

Hill 70. Hill in Pas-de-Calais department of northern France, 14 miles northeast of ARRAS. During WORLD WAR I occupied by Germany after fighting in September 1915; retaken by Canadian troops on August 15, 1917.

Hill 102 [Mamai Kurgan]. Hill in Russian city of Volgograd (formerly Tsaritsyn; STALINGRAD). In WORLD WAR II, occupied by the invading Germans in the summer of 1942, it soon became the scene of intense combat. The Russians struggled in vain to recapture the hill on September 14, at the beginning of the German army's 66–day siege of Stalingrad.

Hill 192. Strategically located hill in French province of NORMANDY, on the road from Saint-Lo to Bayeux; during the Allied invasion of France in WORLD WAR II, Hill 192 was part of a fierce U.S. offensive before capture on July 11, 1944.

Hill 304. Hill in the Meuse department of northeastern France, 10 miles from VERDUN. During WORLD WAR I the Germans attempted an advance on Verdun by way of Hill 304, in May 1916. In August 1917 fighting resumed and the French pushed the Germans out of the area.

Hill 516. See CASSINO.

Hill 609. Hill overlooking Mateur in northern Tunisia. In WORLD WAR II, occupied by Germany in December 1942, it was regained by Allied forces on May 1, 1943, after several days of bitter combat.

Hill, Lord Charles (1904–1989). British physician, politician and administrator. Hill became a household name in Britain during WORLD WAR II as the "Radio Doctor" who discussed medical problems in a homespun manner. He also served as secretary of the British Medical Association during negotiations preceding the establishment of Britain's NATIONAL HEALTH SERVICE (NHS). He was elected to Parliament as a Conservative in 1950 and served in several cabinet posts. After being appointed chairman of the Independent Television Authority (ITA), he was named chairman of the BRITISH BROADCASTING CORPORATION (BBC) in 1967.

Hill, Edwin C. (1884–1957). American author and radio commentator. From 1904 to 1923 he worked as a reporter for the *New York Sun*. He was director of the Fox News Reel (1923–24) and scenario editor for the Fox Film Corporation (1925–26). Hill was a feature writer for the *Sun* from 1927 to 1932, when he became a syndicated feature writer and radio broadcaster known for his "Human Side of the News."

Hill, Geoffrey (1932–). British poet. Hill was raised in Bromsgrove, Worcestershire, where his father was a police constable. Hill's first poems, published in the early 1950s while he was a student at Keble College, Oxford, attracted critical attention. His subsequent collections—*For the Unfallen* (1959), *King Log* (1968), *Mercian Hymns* (1972), *Tenebrae* (1979) and *The Mystery of the Charity of Charles Peguy* (1984)—have consolidated his reputation as perhaps the most important British poet of the second half of the 20th century. In his relatively small but extremely concentrated body of work, Hill addresses the brutal forces of history and the savagery of the human condition. His dense, formal, highly learned and allusive poetry is in many respects the verse equivalent of Simone WEIL's prose; the two writers share a similar visionary and uncompromising religious consciousness. Hill has taught successively at Leeds, Cambridge and Boston universities. A recipient of the Gregory Award (1961), Hawthornden Prize (1969) and Heinemann Award (1972), he is a Fellow of the Royal Society of Literature.

Hillary, Edmund (1919–). New Zealand explorer and mountaineer. Hillary became a mountain climber/explorer after WORLD WAR II, joining a New Zealand expedition to Garhwal, India, in 1951, then a British expedition to Cho Oyu, west of Mt. Everest, in 1952. During a 1953 expedition organized by the Royal Geographical Society and the Alpine Club, Hillary and his Sherpa guide Tenzing Norkay became the first people to reach the summit of Mt. Everest. He led the New Zealand contingent of the Commonwealth Trans-Antarctic Expedition, successfully completing the overland journey from the Ross Sea to the South Pole in 1958. Hillary's many books about his explorations include *No Latitude for Error* (1961). He became ambassador to India in 1985.

Hillenkoetter, Roscoe Henry (1897–1982). American naval officer and first director of the CENTRAL INTELLIGENCE AGENCY (CIA) (1947–50). A graduate of the U.S. Naval Academy (1919), he was a diplomatic courier in Europe in the mid-1930s. Before the U.S. became officially involved in WORLD WAR II, he was a naval attache to the VICHY government of France (1940–41), and also worked with the French RESISTANCE movement. Toward the end of 1941 he was transferred to the Pacific and was wounded in the Japanese attack on PEARL HARBOR (December 7, 1941). Later in the war he served as head of naval intelligence on Admiral NIMITZ's staff, then commanded a destroyer in the Pacific. In 1947 he was appointed director of the Central Intelligence Group, which evolved into the CIA, but was removed from his post by President TRUMAN in 1950. During the KOREAN WAR he commanded a Navy task force. He retired from the Navy in 1957 with the rank of vice admiral.

Hillman, Sidney (1887–1946). American labor leader. Hillman was born in Zagare, Lithuania, and immigrated to the U.S. in 1907, where he worked in the garment industry. He was the guiding spirit behind the formation of the Amalgamated Clothing Workers of America and became its first president in 1914. Hillman promoted union-management cooperation and pioneered in developing union health and welfare programs, cooperative housing, and banking. An advocate of industrial unionism, he was one of the founders of the CONGRESS OF INDUSTRIAL ORGANIZATIONS and served as its vice president from 1935 to 1940. He was co-director of the Office of Production Management from 1940 to 1942. Hillman was a strong supporter of Franklin D. ROOSEVELT and an influential figure in the Democratic Party. He was the founder of the American Labor Party in 1944 and helped create the World Federation of Trade Unions in 1945.

Hillsborough Accord (1985). Agreement between the UNITED KINGDOM and the Republic of IRELAND regarding the governing of NORTHERN IRELAND. The accord set up an Anglo-Irish intergovernmental conference to deal with political, security, legal and judicial matters affecting Northern Ireland, and to promote cross-border cooperation. Both governments pledged not to change the status of Northern Ireland without the consent of the majority of the people of Northern Ireland. In return, the Irish republic was given a consultative role in Northern Irish affairs. The agreement followed 15 months of secret negotiations and was the first of its kind since Ireland was partitioned in 1922. Although the accord was denounced by loyalist (Protestant) and republican (pro-IRA) extremists, it was widely regarded as a major step toward solving the complex sectarian conflict in Northern Ireland.

Hillsborough Stadium Disaster. On April 15, 1989, 95 British soccer fans were killed and nearly 200 injured when several thousand late-arriving fans surged into the stands at an important match between Liverpool and Nottingham Forest at Hillsborough Stadium in Sheffield. When 4,000 Liverpool supporters massed at one entrance to the already crowded stadium, orders were given to throw open an exit gate to allow the fans to enter. In the ensuing rush, fans already in the "terraces," or standing room, were pushed forward and those in the front were pushed up against metal fences. Eventually a gate to the field was opened and the injured and dying were treated on the field. Afterwards both government and popular demands were made to eliminate standing room; but the expense of stadium renovation, and the pull of tradition, put the issue to rest.

Hilton, Conrad (Nicholson) (1887–1979). Founder and chairman of Hilton Hotels Corp. and Hilton International. Conrad Hilton began in the hotel business in 1919, investing $5,000 in a Texas hotel. The business grew into a chain of hotels worldwide. At the time of his death, the business was valued at over $500 million. Located mainly in large cities and resorts, Hilton hotels generally provided a high standard of luxury, catering to executive business travelers and to well-off tourists. Many of Hilton's older hotels, such as the Waldorf-Astoria in New York, had been established by other owners; each of these hotels had its own distinct characteristics. However, after World War II, Hilton began the trend of building new hotels with identical architectural designs and standard features throughout the world.

Hilton, James (1900–1954). British novelist. Hilton is best remembered for the novels *Lost Horizon* (1933, filmed 1937), set in mystical Shangri-La in the Tibetan mountains, and *Goodbye, Mr. Chips* (1934, filmed 1939), the nostalgic story of a school master. In 1936 Hilton moved to HOLLYWOOD to work on screenplays. His film credits include the ACADEMY AWARD-winning *Mrs. Miniver* (1942). Hilton also wrote a mystery novel under the pseudonym Glen Trevor.

Hilton Hotels. See Conrad HILTON.

Himachal Pradesh. Himalayan state of northern INDIA, bordering on Tibet and China. Twenty-one former Punjab hill states were joined with it to form a union territory on April 15, 1948. Enlarged several times afterwards, the territory became a state in 1970. Largely underdeveloped, its capital is at the hill resort of Simla.

Himmler, Heinrich (1900–1945). German Nazi leader, head of the notorious SS (Schutzstaffel). Himmler was an early member of the Nazi Party, and took part in HITLER'S failed BEER HALL PUTSCH in Munich in 1923. During much of the remainder of the 1920s he was a chicken farmer. In 1929 he was appointed head of the party's SS organization, which then consisted of only 300 men. During the early 1930s he consolidated his power. After helping to liquidate Brownshirt leader Ernst ROEHM and other of Hitler's Nazi rivals on the NIGHT OF THE LONG KNIVES (June 30, 1934), Himmler was assured a leading position in the Nazi hierarchy. Two years later he was made head of the unified police forces within GERMANY and given the title Reichsfuhrer of the SS. Under his direction, the SS became virtually a state within the German state and made possible the Nazis' totalitarian control of all aspects of German life.

More than any other single individual, Himmler was responsible for putting into practice the so-called FINAL SOLUTION—the HOLOCAUST that saw the destruction of the JEWS of Europe. A cold and brutally efficient bureaucrat, Himmler administered the CONCENTRATION CAMPS from his Berlin headquarters. He was named minister of the interior in 1943. In the final days of the Nazi Reich, Himmler hoped to negotiate a peace settlement with the Allies and to succeed Hitler as leader of Germany at the war's end; however, his efforts were rebuffed by the Allies, who demanded Germany's unconditional surrender. Several weeks after the end of the war, Himmler was captured and arrested by British forces, on May 25, 1945. He committed suicide while in custody. (See also NAZISM.)

For further reading:

Breitman, Richard, *The Architect of Genocide: Himmler and the Final Solution*. New York: Knopf, 1991.

Hindemith, Paul (1895–1963). German composer. Born in Hanau, he studied at the Frankfurt Conservatory and began his career playing the viola and the violin. He was concertmaster for the Frankfurt Opera orchestra (1915–23), violist for the Amar Quartet (1922–29) and professor at the Berlin Hochschule (1927–37). When the Nazis came to power, his work was banned for its "decadent" modernism. Hindemith journeyed to the U.S. in 1937, becoming a professor of music theory at Yale University in 1940. He became an American citizen in 1946, but settled in Switzerland in 1953 to teach at the University of Zurich. One of the foremost composers of the early 20th century, he was extremely prolific and stylistically varied, usually employing the contrapuntal techniques of classical music in a contemporary idiom. His earlier compositions are usually atonal, while his later works display a tonality that has been dubbed **neoclassicism**. He is particularly known for his so-called *Gebrauchsmusic*, music written specifically for performance by amateurs.

Hindemith composed in nearly all of the musical genres: opera, chamber work, instrumental music, orchestral work, song, choral and others. His best known composition is the symphony (1934) derived from his opera *Mathis der Maler*. Among his other important works are the song cycle *Das Marienleben* (1923, 1948), the viola concerto *Der Schwanendreher* (1935), the ballet *Nobilissima Visione* (1938), the piano interludes and fugues of *Ludus Tonalis* (1942) and the choral and orchestral treatment of Whitman's *When Lilacs Last in the Dooryard Bloom'd* (1946).

Hindenburg, Paul von (1847–1934). German military and political leader. The son of a Prussian officer, Hindenburg entered the Prussian Cadet Corps at the age of 11 and was commissioned in the army in 1866. He first saw service in the Franco-Prussian War (1870–71), was appointed to the general staff in 1878 and retired from active service as a general in 1911. Recalled to command the army in East Prussia at the beginning of WORLD WAR I (1914), he won decisive victories over the Russians at Tannenberg, the Masurian Lakes and the eastern front (see WORLD WAR I ON THE EASTERN FRONT). Acclaimed as Germany's leading war hero, Hindenburg was appointed a field marshal and commander of the German armies in the East in 1914, then succeeded General Falkenhayn as commander-in-chief in 1916, with LUDENDORFF serving as first quartermaster-general. Together, they virtually ran wartime Germany, controlling policies at home, imposing harsh terms on Russia, strengthening the HINDENBURG LINE and mounting the 1918 offensive on the western front. The entry of the U.S. into the war in 1917 together with the counter-offensive of FOCH caused severe German reversals, and Hindenburg was forced to seek an armistice in October 1918. Subsequently Kaiser WILHELM II abdicated, but Hindenburg remained in command of the army until his retirement in July 1919. A monarchist, he nonetheless supported the new republican government and was elected president in 1925. In 1932, the elder statesman was returned to office, but, unable to cope with his nation's enormous political, social and economic crises, he appointed Adolf HITLER chancellor in January 1933. Increasingly senile and losing all real power, he remained the figurehead president until his death, when Hitler abolished the office.

For further reading:

Berman, Russell, *Paul von Hindenburg*. New York: Chelsea House, 1987.

Heinrich Himmler (left, front) inspects a prisoner-of-war camp in occupied Russia (ca. 1941).

Paul von Hindenburg, German military leader during World War I and later president.

Goldsmith, Margaret, *Hindenburg*. New York Ayer, 1972 (repr).

***Hindenburg* disaster.** Accident that destroyed the German dirigible *Hindenburg* at Lakehurst, N.J. on May 6, 1937. Designed by German aviation engineer Dr. Hugo Eckener and completed in 1936, the sumptuously outfitted *Hindenburg* was the world's first commercial aircraft to make regular transatlantic flights. Carrying over 70 passengers and a substantial cargo, and fitted out with private staterooms, lounges, a formal dining room and ship-like promenades, it made many 50-to-60-hour crossings during its almost two years of service. While most airships were inflated with helium, German airships at the time were filled with highly inflammable hydrogen gas because the U.S. refused to export helium to Nazi Germany. While landing at Lakehurst, the hydrogen ignited and the *Hindenburg* was destroyed in half a minute. Thirty-five passengers and crew and a member of the ground staff were killed in the conflagration. A radio news reporter covering the dirigible's landing captured the disaster in unforgettable commentary, and a motion-picture camera also recorded the event. Most authorities believe that electricity in the air was responsible (there was a lightning storm nearby), but some have claimed that the *Hindenburg* was sabotaged by anti-Nazi agents. In any case, the disaster destroyed public confidence in the dirigible and ended the commercial use of airships. The cause of the explosion has never been conclusively determined.

For further reading:

Boning, Richard A., *Horror Overhead*. Loft, Barnell Ltd., 1973.

Dick, Harold G., *The Golden Age of the Great Passenger Airships, Graf Zeppelin and Hindenburg*. Washington: Smithsonian Institution Press, 1985.

Hindenburg Line. Named for Field Marshal von Hindenburg, this fortified German defense line extended across northeastern France during WORLD WAR I. Consolidated in 1916, it was a locus for heavy fighting, particularly in 1917 and when it was finally breached in the fall of 1918.

Hine, Lewis (1874–1940). American documentary photographer particularly known for his dramatic interpretation of machine and other 20th-century industrial forms. Hine's earliest work documented the experience of immigrants arriving at ELLIS ISLAND. From 1908 to 1916 he worked for the National Child Labor Committee documenting working conditions in factories, workshops, and mines, with the goal of exposing little-known abuses. After World War I, his reputation for outstanding photography of industrial locations led to assignments from industry that accentuated the beauty of many mechanistic subjects. For example, from 1930 to 1931 he documented the men constructing the EMPIRE STATE BUILDING in New York in hundreds of striking photographs. Whether documenting the abuses of child labor or the drama of industry, Hine's work was always of fine technical and artistic quality, making him an important figure in the development of modern documentary photography.

Hines, Earl "Fatha" (1905–1983). American JAZZ musician, known as the father of modern jazz piano playing. He created the "trumpet style" of playing jazz piano while working with Louis ARMSTRONG in the 1920s, and established a place for piano as a solo instrument in jazz. Hines led big and small bands intermittently until his death, including a Chicago big band that launched the careers of vocalists Sarah VAUGHAN and Billy ECKSTINE.

Hinkle, Samuel F. (1900–1984). American research chemist and business executive. Hinkle played a major role in the growth of the Hershey Foods Corp. He began as Hershey's director in 1924, when the company was still a small candy manufacturer. By the time he became chairman (1962), Hershey was a giant food-products conglomerate. He retired in 1965. Hinkle developed the K, C and D rations issued to U.S. soldiers in WORLD WAR II.

hippies. Name first given in the 1960s to long-haired members of the era's COUNTERCULTURE. The precise derivation of the word "hippie" remains unclear, but one theory has it stemming from "hip," which was one of the favorite words of praise of the Beatniks of the 1950s, who exercised a tremendous influence on the hippies of the next decade. Indeed, many of

"Flower children" on top of a Volkswagen mini-bus during the Woodstock Music Festival (August 1969).

the literary heroes of the BEAT GENERATION—such as novelists William BURROUGHS and Jack KEROUAC and poets Allen GINSBERG and Gary Snyder—were highly popular with hippies as well. But the hippie phenomenon was based on more than a mere recycling of cultural trends. There were radically new factors at work in the 1960s. One of them was the research into the drug LSD being conducted by Harvard University psychology professor Timothy LEARY, who lost his academic position due to his enthusiasm for the drug's spiritual and psychological "benefits." Leary became a highly influential spokesman for hippies, who relished the Leary motto "Tune in, turn on, drop out." Hippies were also unique in their musical tastes, discarding the favored jazz of the 1950s beatniks for "psychedelic" rock such as that of the GRATEFUL DEAD, JEFFERSON AIRPLANE and other San Francisco-based groups. There were many superficial and faddish elements to the hippie phenomenon, such as love beads, day-glo posters and long hair.

Many hippie enthusiasms have transformed themselves, over the decades, into ongoing cultural influences in America, including: ecological awareness, nutritional consciousness and the value of organically grown foods, respect for Native American tribal traditions, widespread marijuana cultivation and use, and the entrepreneurial willingness to consider people-oriented forms of organizational structure in social and business contexts. Politically, hippies ranged from apolitical societal dropouts who went to live on isolated communes to fervent peace activists who contributed greatly to the strength of the ANTIWAR MOVEMENT. Hippie popularity in America and Europe reached its peak in the late 1960s with BE-INS in major urban parks that drew as many as 25,000 people in a single day. Hippies continue to carry on their freeform lifestyles—albeit in much smaller numbers—to the present day.

Hirohito (1901–1989). Emperor of JAPAN. The first member of the imperial family to travel abroad, Hirohito was appointed regent in 1921, shortly after a visit to Europe and the U.S. He succeeded to the Chrysanthemum Throne in 1926 upon the death of his father, Emperor Yoshihito (1879–1926). He married Princess Nagako Kuni in 1924, and his heir, AKIHITO, was born in 1933. A quiet, introspective and scholarly man, trained as a marine biologist, he apparently exerted little influence over political events in Japan during the 1930s and was not consulted during the military's drift toward WORLD WAR II or over its strategy during the war. However, in 1945 he was instrumental in persuading Japanese officials to accede to unconditional surrender and thus save the nation from total destruction. In 1946 Hirohito renounced the concept of imperial divinity as well as claims to all but ceremonial authority. The new Japanese constitution of 1946 proclaimed him a "symbol of the state and of the unity of the people," and he remained a beloved figure to the Japanese public.

Hirohito, emperor of Japan.

For further reading:

Kawahara, Toshiaki, *Hirohito and His Times: A Japanese Perspective*. New York: Kodansha/Farrar, Straus & Giroux, 1990.

Hiroshima. City and prefectural capital at the western end of Japan's Inland Sea. Founded in the 16th century, it grew in population and importance along with the railroad in the 19th century, also becoming a military headquarters. During WORLD WAR II it was devastated by the first ATOMIC BOMB dropped on an inhabited location (August 6, 1945). JAPAN surrendered eight days later, after another atomic bomb was dropped on NAGASAKI. Almost totally rebuilt, Hiroshima is a prosperous commercial center and hosts an annual world conference on the deterrence of nuclear weaponry.

Hirshfield, Morris (1872–1946). Polish-American painter. A self-taught primitive painter, Hirshfield began to paint when he was 65 years old. His entire output consists of 77 paintings, often of women or animals, created from 1937 until just before his death. His decorative, colorful, flat and highly patterned works are included in several museum collections, notably the Museum of Modern Art, N.Y.C.

Hiss, Alger. See HISS-CHAMBERS CASE.

Hiss-Chambers case. Confrontation between Alger Hiss (1904–) and Whittaker Chambers (1901–61) over Hiss' alleged membership in the Communist Party and espionage activities. A distinguished public official, the Baltimore-born Hiss attended Harvard Law School and worked for the Agricultural Adjustment Administration (1933–36) and the Justice Department (1935–36) before joining the State Department. There he rose quickly, becoming a key adviser at many international conferences, most importantly YALTA. Leaving the government in 1947, he was appointed president of the Carnegie Endowment for International Peace. His steady rise to eminence was halted in 1948 when Whittaker Chambers, a New York-born magazine editor and self-confessed communist agent during the 1930s, in testimony before the HOUSE UN-AMERICAN ACTIVITIES COMMITTEE (HUAC) accused Hiss of having been part of a communist underground. This accusation marked the beginning of a decades-long drama of denunciation and denial.

Soon Chambers expanded his testimony to include accusations that Hiss had provided him with secret State Department documents destined for transmittal to the Soviet Union. To prove his assertions, Chambers produced microfilms of the documents, supposedly typed on Hiss' Woodstock typewriter and then hidden in a hollowed-out pumpkin. These so-called "Pumpkin Papers" were handed over to the anticommunist California congressman Richard M. NIXON. Throughout all this, Hiss denied knowing Chambers, insisted that he had never been a member of the Communist Party and claimed that the evidence against him had been fabricated by a psychopathic liar. The statute of limitations for the charge of espionage had run out, so Hiss was indicted on two counts of perjury in 1949. The first trial resulted in a hung jury; the second found Hiss guilty. Sentenced to five years in prison, Hiss served 44 months, from 1951 to 1954.

The controversial Hiss-Chambers case caused a furor in American political circles. Hiss supporters claimed that he had been railroaded by MCCARTHYISM and accused the FBI of evidence tampering. Chambers allies applauded his courageous anticommunism. Each principal pressed his case in print, Chambers in *Witness* (1952) and Hiss in *In the Court of Public Opinion* (1957). While over 20 different books have examined the matter, the Hiss-Chambers controversy remained unresolved as the 20th century neared its end.

For further reading:

Chambers, Whittaker, *Witness*. Lanham, Md.: University Press of America, 1983.

Hiss, Alger, *Recollections of a Life*. New York: Arcade, 1989.

Weinstein, Allen, *Perjury: The Hiss-Chambers Case*. New York: Knopf, 1978.

Histadrut [Heb., Federation of Labor]. Organizational body of the Israeli trade-union movement.

Hitchcock, Alfred (Joseph) (1899–1980). British-born film director, known for his mastery of cinematic technique and screen suspense. In a career spanning half the century, Hitchcock directed scores of psychological thrillers, nightmares of menace and the macabre that became film classics. He became famous for planning every scene in advance, down to the smallest detail, and he pioneered new cinematic techniques. He made England's first talking picture, *Blackmail*, in 1929. Working in England in the 1930s, he won international acclaim for such spy thrillers as *The Man Who Knew Too Much* (1934), *The Thirty-Nine Steps* (1935), and *The Lady Van-*

Alger Hiss (right) and his attorney arrive at Federal Court in New York on Oct. 10, 1949, to ask for a change of venue in Hiss's second perjury trial

ishes (1938). In 1939 he moved to HOLLYWOOD, where he went on to make such stylish melodramas as *Rebecca* (1940), *Suspicion* (1940), *Lifeboat* (1944), *Notorious* (1946), *Strangers on a Train* (1951), *Rear Window* (1954), *Vertigo* (1958), and *North by Northwest* (1959). With *Psycho* (1960), Hitchcock's films became more overtly shocking and violent. He worked with such stars as Laurence OLIVIER, Ingrid BERGMAN, Cary GRANT, and James STEWART. He was nominated for five ACADEMY AWARDS for best director, but never won. He also hosted a popular weekly television show in the late 1950s and early 1960s.

Alfred Hitchcock, on the set of his movie Frenzy, *appears to be getting inspiration for his next picture (1972).*

For further reading:

Rothman, William, *Hitchcock: The Murderous Gaze.* Cambridge, Mass.: Harvard University Press, 1982.

Hitchcock, Henry-Russell (1903–1987). American architectural historian and teacher. Beginning in the 1920s, Hitchcock was a leading advocate of the INTERNATIONAL STYLE in architecture. He is believed to have coined the term.

Hitchings, George H(erbert) (1905–). American pharmacologist. Born in Hoquiam, Washington, he attended Washington State University and Harvard. He taught at Harvard and at Western Reserve before joining the Burroughs Wellcome Laboratory, Tuckahoe, N.Y., in 1942. His distinguished career spanned some 50 years of research at this lab. Along with his long-time collaborator Gertrude B. ELION, Hitchings made discoveries that had a fundamental impact on the development of various disease-fighting drugs. The two developed a central principle of contemporary pharmacology that is based on blocking the workings of nucleic acids (the chemical substances that control heredity and cell function) in diseased cells while allowing it to function in healthy cells. This discovery came about through the two scientists' study of the chemical components of nucleic acids. They applied the principle to the creation of various forms of chemotherapy, achieving their first success in the 1950s when, working with researchers at the Sloan-Kettering Institute, they produced the first effective drug against leukemia. During the next decades they worked on drugs to treat autoimmune, viral and infectious diseases and to fight organ rejection. Their studies led directly to the development of various modern drugs, including AZT for the treatment of AIDS. Hitchings and Elion were awarded the 1988 NOBEL PRIZE for physiology or medicine with Sir James Black.

Hitler, Adolf (1889–1945). Chancellor of GERMANY (1933–45). Along with Joseph STALIN, Adolf Hitler ranks as the most heinous of all 20th-century dictators. He plunged Germany and the world into a war that saw the destruction of ancient cities, the dismemberment of entire nations and the deaths of millions of sol-

Adolf Hitler at a ceremony in Brunswick to dedicate new Nazi flags (Oct. 18, 1931).

diers and civilians both in combat and through a calculated plan of extermination. Born at Brannau, Austria, across the Inn River from Germany, Hitler was the son of a minor government official and his young wife. He was raised near Linz, Austria. His father died when Hitler was in his early teens; soon thereafter Hitler left school. In 1907 he moved to Vienna with vague hopes of pursuing a career as an artist or architect. Rejected by the Vienna Academy of Fine Arts, he lived an aimless existence, living in doss houses and wandering the city as a malcontent. During this time he developed a fanatical belief in the superiority of the German-speaking people and a profound hatred of the JEWS (see ANTISEMITISM) and the institutions of bourgeois civilization. Obsessed by dreams of personal and national grandeur, he took to haranguing anyone who would listen to his ideas. He painted postcards to support himself but otherwise took no definite steps to improve his position in life. In 1913 he moved to Munich.

The outbreak of WORLD WAR I gave Hitler a focus for his discontented energy. He enlisted in the German army and served in the trenches on the Western Front (see WORLD WAR I ON THE WESTERN FRONT). During the war he was wounded and was also temporarily blinded by mustard gas. He received two Iron Crosses and reached the rank of corporal. Germany's defeat and the harsh terms imposed on the country by the TREATY OF VERSAILLES gave Hitler another cause to claim as his own. His life took a fateful turn in 1919 when he was hired as a police informer and assigned to report on the fledgling German Worker's Party, a minor political organization in Munich. Hitler joined the group as its seventh member and soon found that it gave him a platform from which to express his discontent with the state of the world. By 1921 he had gained control of the group and transformed it into a disciplined organization whose political aims matched his. The party name was changed to National Socialist German Workers' Party (abbreviated as NSDAP in German); the group soon became better known as the Nazi Party. Discovering his considerable power as an orator, Hitler expounded his philosophy of NAZISM to ever larger audiences. In 1923 Hitler, joined by World War I hero General Erich LUDENDORFF and some 2,000 Nazi storm troopers, attempted to seize control of the Bavarian government in the BEER HALL PUTSCH. The event proved a fiasco for the Nazis; Hitler was arrested and sentenced to five years in prison. There he dictated his political gospel MEIN KAMPF to his aide Rudolf HESS. Hitler served only nine months of his sentence before being released. He spent the following decade rebuilding the Nazi Party.

The beginning of the worldwide GREAT DEPRESSION, which caused economic and political chaos in Germany, gave Hitler an opportunity to emerge as a formidable politician. National elections in 1932 gave the Nazis the largest share of the vote, although not an absolute majority. With this backing Hitler maneuvered for the post of cancellor, claiming that he was the only political leader able to deal with the Depression and with the perceived menace posed to the middle and upper classes by German communists. The aging President HINDENBURG was ultimately persuaded to name Hitler chancellor on January 30, 1933. Although the leaders of the conservative German political establishment distrusted Hitler and indeed found him distasteful, they believed that they would be able to control him and, when necessary, remove him from office. The REICHSTAG FIRE (February 27, 1933) gave Hitler an excuse to suspend constitutional guarantees; he was, in effect, given dictatorial powers to cope with the perceived state of emergency. On the so-called "Night of the Long Knives" (June 30–July 1, 1934) he eliminated his chief rivals within the party, the left-wing Nazi Gregor Strasser and the SA head Ernst ROEHM; he also dissolved the SA. Upon Hindenburg's death a month later, Hitler proclaimed himself "Fuhrer" (leader) of the German people.

He quickly proceeded to suppress all remaining political opposition. This achieved, he worked to rebuild Germany's military might, ordering increased arms production, compulsory military service (March 1936) and the reoccupation of the Rhineland (March 1936)—all in violation of the Versailles Treaty. In the latter half of the 1930s, he systematically pursued his LEBENSRAUM foreign policy. He formed an alliance (the AXIS) with MUSSOLINI'S ITALY in 1936, annexed Austria in March 1938 (see ANSCHLUSS) and demanded and won the annexation of the German-speaking SUDETENLAND region of CZECHOSLOVAKIA in the MUNICH PACT (September-October 1938). In March 1939 he annexed the Czech regions (Bohemia and Moravia) of Czechoslovakia.

The NAZI-SOVIET PACT (August 1939) gave Hitler a free hand to invade POLAND (September 1939) without Soviet interference. However, upon the invasion of Poland, the UNITED KINGDOM and FRANCE, which had pledged to support Poland's independence, declared war on Germany. During the early part of the war Hitler enjoyed success as the Germans won victory after victory. The BLITZKRIEG tactics that had defeated Poland led to the capitulation of BELGIUM, the NETHERLANDS, FRANCE and NORWAY in 1940; BULGARIA and ROMANIA also fell into the Nazi fold. These successes emboldened him to pursue further conquests. His assault on Britain, however, failed to yield the island's submission (see BATTLE OF BRITAIN). Frustrated, Hitler turned his attention to his erstwhile ally, and attacked the Soviet Union. The difficulty of supplying the German forces over great distances, along with the tenacity of the Soviet defenders and the severity of the Russian winter, left the German armies in a fatal position. On December 19, 1941, Hitler made another costly mistake. Convinced of his genius as a military leader, he assumed direct command of Germany's army. From this point onward he ignored the advice of his generals, with dire consequences for Germany. Yet, even with military defeat inevitable, Hitler pursued his most terrible crime, the so-called FINAL SOLUTION to the Jewish problem—the extermination of Europe's Jews (see HOLOCAUST).

As Britain, the U.S.S.R. and other allies (now joined by the UNITED STATES) rallied against the German forces, Hitler became increasingly withdrawn and isolated from reality. German staff officers led by Count Claus von STAUFFENBERG attempted to assassinate Hitler on July 20, 1944. The Fuhrer was wounded but survived. Feeling betrayed by the German people who had failed to win the victories he expected of them, he decided that Germany deserved to be destroyed rather than surrender to the Allies. Trapped in his Berlin bunker as Soviet forces fought their way into the city, Hitler married his longtime mistress Eva Braun on April 30, 1945; shortly thereafter the couple committed suicide.

For further reading:

Payne, Robert, *Life and Death of Adolf Hitler*. New York: Hippocrene Books, 1990.
Toland, John, *Adolf Hitler*. New York: Ballantine, 1986.
Shirer, William S., *The Rise & Fall of Adolf Hitler*. New York: Random House, 1984.
Waite, Robert G., *The Psychopathic God: Adolf Hitler*. New York: NAL/Dutton, 1983.
Bullock, Alan, *Hitler, a Study in Tyranny*. New York: HarperCollins, n.d.

Hitler-Stalin Pact. See GERMAN-SOVIET NON-AGGRESSION PACT.

Hitler Youth [Hitler Jugend]. German youth organization of the 1930s and early 1940s. The Hitler Youth was formed to indoctrinate young Germans into the "ideals" of Adolf HITLER and to create the Nazis of the next generation. Like the Boy Scouts and other youth organizations in democracies, the Hitler Youth stressed outdoor and educational activities. However, it added the poison of NAZISM, crushing its members' individuality into unquestioning loyalty to the state and the Nazi Party. As an auxiliary arm of the party, the Hitler Youth Organization was active even before Hitler became chancellor in 1933. At the end of 1932, there were 110,000 members; by the end of 1936, that number had swelled to six million. The organization was led by a young idealist, Baldur von Schirach, whose parents had been born in the U.S. As the German army collapsed toward the end of the war, many teenage members of the Hitler Youth were pressed into military service, and many died in combat.

HIV. See AIDS.

Ho Ying-chin (1889–1987). Chinese military leader. A longtime associate of Gen. CHIANG KAI-SHEK, he served as Chinese minister of war from 1930 to 1944. He was commander-in-chief of the Chinese army when one million Japanese troops surrendered at Nanjing in 1945. Ho was among a dozen generals who fled mainland CHINA for TAIWAN in 1949 with Chiang Kai-shek after the communist victory in the CHINESE CIVIL WAR OF 1945–49. He then served as Taiwan's defense minister until 1958.

Hoaglund, Hudson (1899–1982). American neuroendocrinologist. Hoaglund pioneered in the study of brain waves and the use of the electroencephalogram, or EEG. In 1944 he co-founded the Worcester Foundation for Experimental Biology in Massachusetts, which developed the birth control PILL.

Ho-Chiang [Hokiang]. Formerly, a province of Chinese MANCHURIA created in 1945 by the Kuomintang Nationalists. Ho-Chiang became a part of Sung-Chiang province after the communist victory in the CHINESE CIVIL WAR OF 1945–49; five years later it was incorporated into Heilungkiang province.

Ho Chi Minh [born Nguyen Tat Thanh] (1890–1969). Vietnamese communist and nationalist leader, president of North Vietnam (1954–69). Born Nguyen Tat Thanh in central VIETNAM, he left Vietnam as a ship's steward, traveling to London (1912), where he worked as a hotel chef, and Paris (1917), where he wrote articles for socialist newspapers and was a founder of the French Communist Party. He lived in the U.S.S.R. from 1922 to 1925, becoming a member of the Comintern's Southeast Asia Bureau and studying Marxism and revolutionary techniques. He went on to China in 1925, organizing various communist groups. In China in 1938 he aided the communist revolution and planned his own country's struggle against colonialism, taking the name of Ho Chi Minh, "he who enlightens," in 1940. Ho returned to Vietnam at the beginning of WORLD WAR II after a 30–year absence and formed the VIET MINH, with which he began guerrilla war against the Japanese. Taking HANOI in 1945, he declared Vietnamese independence and became president, serving in that office until his death. Ho was the chief spokesman for the nationalistic aspirations of the Vietnamese people and fought for an independent and communist-led Vietnam, first against the French (1946–54) and, after the Geneva conference split the country in 1954, against the South Vietnamese and the U.S. Becoming less involved in governing after 1959, he remained the symbol of Vietnamese communism. (See also VIETNAM WAR.)

Ho Chi Minh, president of North Vietnam (1966).

Ho Chi Minh Trail. Popular name for the jungle supply route by which North Vietnam sent soldiers as well as arms, ammunition, food and other materiel into the South during the VIETNAM WAR. Construction of the strategic route was begun in 1959 and included existing mountain trails, incorporating them into a large network of roads. It was the work of over 30,000 troops and various other workers and measured over 12,500 miles. Beginning in 1965, repeated raids by U.S. bombers slowed the flow of men and supplies, but the North Vietnamese repaired the road constantly and the trail was never completely closed.

Hockney, David (1937–). English painter. Born in Bradford, he studied at the Royal College of Art, London. Considered one of the major figures in contemporary British art, Hockney is noted for his witty, realistic imagery and masterful draftsmanship. The artist, who has lived in Southern California for some years, is known for sunny, stylized scenes of contemporary life where POP ART elements mix with a highly personal style. He has also created a number of print series and has designed stage sets, such as those for England's Glyndebourne Opera.

Hodges, Gil (1924–1972). American baseball player and manager. Hodges was an outstanding first baseman with the Brooklyn (and L.A.) Dodgers (1948–61). Beloved by Brooklynites, he continued to make his home there after the close of his career. He closed out his playing days with the New York Mets in 1963. During his career he had 370 home runs, 1,921 base hits, 1,274 runs batted in and a .273 lifetime batting average. Following his retirement as a player, Hodges managed the Washington Senators (1963–67) and the New York Mets from 1968 until his death. In 1969 he guided the once-lowly Mets, who became known as the "Miracle Mets," over the favored Baltimore Orioles to victory in the World Series.

Hodgkin, Howard (1932–). English painter. Born in London, Hodgkin lived in the U.S. from 1940 to 1943. He studied at the Camberwell School of Art, London and the Bath Academy of Art, where he taught from 1956 to 1966. He later taught at various institutions, and in the late 1980s was Kress Professor at the National Gallery, Washington, D.C. His first one-man show was held in London in 1962. His early works concentrated on the figure in an interior, blending the abstract and the figural in a flat and brightly colored geometry. His importance to English painting was recognized when he was chosen to represent Great Britain in the Venice Biennale of 1984. Hodgkin's paintings have always been relatively small in scale and most are worked on over a period of years. In his recent work elements such as the figure, the interior and the landscape are inferred rather than stated in swags, dots and arcs of vivid colors that cover the wood panel of the painting and its frame.

Hodgson, William Hope (1877–1918). British writer of maritime romances and supernatural horror. An important transitional figure between Edgar Allan Poe and H.P. LOVECRAFT, Hodgson translated the materials of the gothic romance into the modern forms of science fiction. The son of a clergyman, he ran away to sea as a boy. In 1899 after eight years and three voyages around the world, he returned to Blackburn to establish a bodybuilding/physical culture academy and pursue a writing career. The bulk of his fiction, written in 1906–1914, may be categorized into three groups. *The Boats of the "Glen Carrig"* (1907), *The Ghost Pirates* (1909), and the short-story collection *Men of Deep Waters* (1914) are all nautical horror tales. The great novels, *The House on the Borderland* (1908) and *The Night Land* (1912), are dystopian nightmares of a future Earth wracked by war, holocaust, and extradimensional invasion by monstrous life-forms. The stories of a psychic detective named Carnacki pit 20th-century rationalism and technology against the traditional gothic apparatus of haunted houses and vengeful ghosts. Hodgson died in WORLD WAR I, killed in action near Ypres as an enlisted man in the Royal Field Artillery.

For further reading:

Sullivan, Jack, ed. *The Penguin Encyclopedia of Horror and the Supernatural.* New York: Viking Press, 1986.

Hoffa, James R(iddle) "Jimmy" (1913–1975). American labor leader. Born in Brazil, Indiana, Jimmy Hoffa moved to Detroit after his father's death and while still in his teens became actively involved in the teamster's union. Aligning himself with midwestern criminals, he strong-armed his way into enormous power in the union. In 1952 Hoffa became a vice-president of the union, and five years later he succeeded Dave Beck as its president (see BECK CASE). Intensively investigated by federal agencies, he was tried and found guilty of jury tampering and pension fraud, beginning a 13–year prison sentence in 1967. In 1971 Hoffa was pardoned by President Richard M. NIXON. After his release, in spite of a court order to stay out of union affairs until 1980, he apparently attempted to wrest control of the Teamster's from union president Frank FITZSIMMONS. On July 30, 1975 Hoffa left his home in Detroit and disappeared. He was widely assumed to have been murdered; his body has not been found.

Hoffman, (Abbott) "Abbie" (1936–1989). Radical American protest leader of the 1960s ANTIWAR MOVEMENT and founder of the Yippies (Youth International Party). Hoffman rose to national prominence as a defendant in the raucous CHICAGO SEVEN TRIAL (1969–70). The seven defendants had been charged with inciting a riot during the 1968 Democratic National Convention in Chicago. Hoffman and four other defendants were convicted following a trial that featured antics such as Hoffman stomping on a judicial robe, but the convictions were later overturned. In 1973 he was arrested on charges of selling cocaine to an undercover narcotics officer; before the case came to trial, he went into hiding and spent six years (1974–80) working as an environmental activist in upstate New York and as a food reviewer in Europe, using an alias. He surfaced in 1980 for a nationally televised interview with Barbara WALTERS and eventually pleaded guilty to a lesser charge that netted him a brief prison sentence. His death was an apparent suicide.

Hoffman, Dustin (1937–). American film and stage actor. Hoffman has been a major film star since his acclaimed debut as the confused Benjamin Braddock in *The Graduate* (1967), directed by Mike NICHOLS. His consistent stardom has been unusual in that Hoffman has more often appeared in character roles than in standard romantic leads. Hoffman began his career on the New York stage in the 1960s, winning an Obie Award for his performance in *The Journey of the Fifth Horse*. His successful films include *Little Big Man* (1970), in which he played a 112-year-old Indian survivor of Custer's last stand; *Papillon* (1973), in which he portrayed a nearsighted prisoner in a French penal colony; *All the President's Men* (1976), in which he appeared as reporter Carl Bernstein; and *Tootsie* (1982), in which he starred as a male actor who disguises himself as a female to get work. Hoffman won his first best actor ACADEMY AWARD for his role as a divorced father in *Kramer Versus Kramer* (1980) and his second for his performance as a man suffering from autism in *Rain Man* (1988).

Hoffman, Malvina (1887–1966). American sculptor. Born in New York City, Hoffman studied with Auguste Rodin. She executed a number of realistic portraits of important figures of her day such as Jan PADEREWSKI and John MUIR, and is noted for her bronze figures of dancers, such as *Pavlova gavotte*, and monumental public commissions such as *The Sacrifice* at Harvard University's War Memorial. Hoffmann is probably best remembered for a series of 100 anthropological portraits of the world's races she executed for the Hall of Man at the Field Museum in Chicago. She spent five years in travel and research preparing for this project and described it in her book *Heads and Tales* (1936). She was also the author of *Sculpture Inside and Out* (1939).

Hoffmann, Josef (1870–1956). Austrian architect and designer, a pioneer in the development of MODERNISM as expressed in the Werkstatte and Secession movements. Hoffmann was a pupil of Otto Wagner. After traveling in Italy, he returned to Vienna to work for Wagner from 1895 until 1899. He became a professor of architecture at the Vienna School of Applied Arts in 1899 and held that position until 1941. A member of the Secession, he helped found the Werkstatte in 1903. Hoffmann visited England in 1902 and was strongly influenced by the work of Charles Rennie MACKINTOSH. His work moved away from the curvilinear forms typical of Wagner's work and became more rectilinear with squares, cubes, and spheres appearing as favorite motifs. The Puckersdorf Sanatorium outside Vienna (1903–06) was a major example of the geometrically abstract direction in Hoffmann's work, while the special furniture designed for it carried the same themes. Hoffmann's major architectural masterpiece was the Palais Stoclet in Brussels (1905–11). It is a large town mansion in a geometrically austere style, with elaborate ornamentation inside and out. Much of its artwork is by Secessionist collaborators, including Gustav KLIMT and Carl CZESCHKA. Rich materials are used and detailing is elaborate, including special furniture, lighting fixtures, hardware, and textiles. Hoffmann's designs included work for Werkstatte craftsmen and for factory production in great variety. Hoffmann was the designer of Austrian pavilions at various exhibitions (Cologne in 1914, Paris in 1925, and Stockholm in 1930, among others), but it is his work of 1902 to 1910 that has attracted most interest in his career, particularly in recent years when the modernism of Secession work, with its characteristic ornamentation, has drawn increasing attention because of postmodern trends in both architecture and object design. Hoffmann remained active in both design and teaching, although few of his works were actually executed. Now much admired and collected, a number of his designs for furniture, metalwork, ceramics, and textiles are currently produced in reproduction.

Hofmannsthal, Hugo von (1874–1929). Austrian playwright, story writer, poet and opera librettist. Hofmansthal was a gifted and versatile writer who achieved his greatest successes as a playwright who combined a romantic sensibility with a deep moral intelligence. The first of his plays to win notice, *Death and the Fool* (1898), was a lyrical romance. *The Adventurer and the Singer* (1898) and several adaptations from classic Greek tragedies—*Elektra* (1903), *Oedipus and the Sphinx* (1905), *King Oedipus* (1907) and *Alcestis* (1909)—followed. His most acclaimed play was *Everyman* (1911), based on a famous medieval mystery play. Subsequent plays by Hofmannsthal include *The Difficult Man* (1921) and *The Tower* (1925), both of which deal with social issues. Hofmannsthal also won renown as a librettist for operas by Richard STRAUSS, including *Elektra* (1909), *Der Rosenkavalier* (1911), and *Ariadne auf Naxos* (1912). Hofmannsthal was a cofounder, in 1920, of the SALZBURG FESTIVAL.

Hofstadter, Robert (1915–1990). U.S. physicist. He won the NOBEL PRIZE in 1961 for his reasearch into the size and structure of the particles that make up the nucleus of the atom. The Royal Swedish Academy praised him for providing the first "reasonably consistent" picture of the nuclear structure of the atom, and for determining the size and shape of the proton and neutron. He taught at Stanford University from 1950 to 1985.

Hogan, (William) Ben(jamin) (1912–). U.S. golfer. The winner of more than 60 tournaments, he is considered one of the finest players in golf history. Known as "Bantam Ben" (he weighed only 135 pounds) he was a four-time winner of the U.S. Open. His most memorable Open win came in 1950, less than a year-and-a-half after a serious automobile accident left his future in doubt. He also won the PGA tournament twice, the Masters title twice and the British Open once.

Hogarth Press. See Virginia WOOLF.

Holiday, Billie [Eleanora Fagan, Eleanora Gough] (1915–1959). American jazz and blues singer, known as Lady Day; one of the great tragic figures in American jazz. The daughter of an unwed cleaning woman and a guitarist, Holiday was born in Baltimore, Maryland. She went to New York and by age 15 was singing in HARLEM nightclubs while living in poverty. Her rise was extraordinary; her talent was recognized almost immediately not only by the public but also by the greatest jazz musicians of the day. In the 1930s she sang with the bands of Benny GOODMAN, Count BASIE and Artie SHAW and performed with such greats as pianist Teddy WILSON and saxophonist Lester YOUNG; her partnership with Young ranks as one of the all-time great collaborations in jazz. Despite her professional success, her personal life was chaotic and insecure. Her later years were marred by heroin addiction and alcoholism, which took a sad toll on her health and her career.

At its peak, Holiday's voice was at once

Billie Holiday, blues and jazz singer.

casual and yet haunting; her uncanny phrasing and intonation, married to her life experience, gave her the ability to communicate the inner meaning of a given song. What Edith PIAF is to French ballad singing, Billie Holiday is to the blues. Among the songs for which she is best known are "I've Got My Love to Keep Me Warm," "The Very Thought of You," "These Foolish Things" and "Autumn in New York." Her autobiography is *Lady Sings the Blues.*

For further reading:

Kliment, Bud, *Billie Holiday: Singer.* New York: Chelsea House, 1990.

Hollister (Anabale), Gloria (1902–1988). American explorer. In 1931, Hollister set a woman's world record for ocean descent in a bathysphere. She was the chief assistant of famed oceanographer William Beebe on many of his voyages in the 1920s and 1930s. She also served with other expeditions of the New York Zoological Society.

Holloway, Stanley (1890–1982). A beloved showman of the now-vanished British music halls, Stanley Holloway worked in a fish market before becoming a singer. In the 1930s his comic monologues as "Sam Small of Lancashire" made him an instant sensation, and he recorded several novelty tunes. In the 1940s and '50s he appeared in films, notably as the gravedigger in Laurence OLIVIER's *Hamlet* (1948) and costarring with Alec GUINNESS in *The Lavender Hill Mob* (1951). But it was onstage that Holloway had his greatest triumph, as dustman and philosopher/drunk Alfred Doolittle in the LERNER and LOEWE musical *My Fair Lady* (1956). The show (and film, in 1964) featured his classic renditions of "With a Little Bit of Luck" and "Get Me to the Church on Time." In 1960 Holloway was awarded the Order of the British Empire. In 1980, when he was 90 years old, Holloway gave a "royal command performance."

Holly, Buddy [Charles Hardin Holley] (1936–1959). Rock and roll composer, vocalist, and guitarist. Holly is one of the great founding figures of ROCK AND ROLL. In addition to his performing excellence as lead guitarist and vocalist of his band, Buddy Holly and the Crickets, he also stands as one of the foremost songwriters in the history of rock and roll. His classic hits, all of which were recorded between 1956 and 1959, include "That'll Be The Day, "Everyday, "Peggy Sue", "Oh Boy, "Words of Love" and "Raining in My Heart". Holly was born in Lubbock, Texas in 1936 and learned the guitar at age twelve. He formed his first band while in junior high school and won national fame when "That'll Be The Day" hit Number One on the Billboard charts in 1957. He died in a famous 1959 plane crash that also took the lives of rock stars "Big Bopper" (J. P. Richardson) and Richie Valens. Paul MCCARTNEY, who purchased the rights to most of Holly's songs, is among the many stars of contemporary rock music who was deeply influenced by Holly's work.

Hollywood. A section of LOS ANGELES, CALIFORNIA, celebrated as the center of the American motion picture and television industries. In 1883 a Kansas prohibitionist, Harvey Wilcox, opened a real estate office seven miles from Los Angeles, subdivided a 120–acre tract and (at his wife's suggestion) filed the name "Hollywood" with the county recorder on February 1, 1887. Ten years later a post office was established, and the area became a sixth-class city. In 1910 it was annexed to Los Angeles, and its permanent boundaries were established in 1937: Doheny Drive on the west, the top of the Santa Monica Mountains on the north, the Los Angeles River on the east and Melrose Avenue on the south. The consistent, sunny weather and the area's distance from the New York film trusts encouraged filmmakers to establish studios there as early as 1907, when the Selig Polyscope Company arrived to shoot scenes for *The Count of Monte Cristo.* Although every major studio built production facilities in the area within the next 20 years, only COLUMBIA, PARAMOUNT and RKO were located within city limits (today, only Paramount). During the film industry's peak production years in the late 1930s, an estimated 750 features were made annually in Hollywood and environs.

Popular landmarks include Grauman's Chinese Theater (with its courtyard of celebrity footprints and handprints), the Griffith Park Observatory, the Hollywood Bowl, the Hollywood Hotel and the Brown Derby (the last two now closed or relocated). Hollywood has survived the crises of Depression, three wars, air pollution, the growing presence of drugs and prostitution, and the competitive inroads of radio, television and the recording industry—and continues as a symbol of the hope and heartbreak of the American Dream. Much of Tinseltown's colorful past has perished over the years, through greed and neglect, but recently there have been encouraging signs of change. The "Walk of Fame," for example, was instituted in 1960—emblazoning the names of famous entertainers onto brass stars and implanting them into the sidewalks of Hollywood Boulevard and Vine Street. (At a rate of one name per month, by 1991 the total had surpassed 2,000.) In 1978 the legendary "Hollywood" sign, built on the side of Mt. Cahuenga in 1924, was restored. And plans for a centralized Hollywood Museum are pending. But there are still no holly and no woods in Hollywood.

For further reading:

Torrence, Bruce T., *The First Hundred Years.* New York: Zoetrope, 1982.

Hollywood at War. When the U.S. entered WORLD WAR II (Dec. 1941), the HOLLYWOOD film industry was eager, but ill-prepared, to play a major role in the war. Working under the restrictions of the PRODUCTION CODE had forced filmmakers to eliminate most social and political commentary from films. The war called for Hollywood to be a soldier in a PROPAGANDA campaign to convince people that democracy was worth figh ing for.

Hollywood stood at the peak of its i fluence in 1941, averaging some 85 mi lion paid admissions in the U.S., an dominated the world market. In June 194 the U.S created an official propagand agency, the **Office of War Informatio** and appointed Elmer Davis as its directo OWI immediately opened a Hollywoo office, the Bureau of Motion Pictures, an began to work with studios to ensure tha films complemented U.S. war policy. government manual asked studios: "Wi This Picture Win the War?" Films wer to emphasize the war as a "people's war against FASCISM, stress unity among th Allies and point out the strengths of dem ocratic society. At the behest of the gov ernment the industry churned out film praising America's allies. *Mission to Mos cow* (WB, 1943) was the industry's tribut to STALIN, and *North Star* (Goldwyn, 1943 a salute to the heroic Russian people *The White Cliffs of Dover* (MGM, 1944 portrayed the British war effort; *Casa blanca* (WB, 1943) united U.S. and Frenc citizens; even China emerged as great democracy in *Dragon Seed* (MGM 1944).

Some of Hollywood's finest director left the comfortable confines of Holly wood to make documentary and propa ganda films for the War Department. Wil liam WYLER's *The Memphis Belle* (1944) John FORD's *The Battle of Midway* (1942 and John HUSTON's *The Battle of San Pietr* (1945) and *Let There Be Light* (1945) stood out. Perhaps the finest combination o documentary and propaganda film t emerge from the war was Frank CAPRA's series of films, *Why We Fight,* which told military recruits why America was fighting Germany, Japan and Italy and what they were preserving by so doing. Hollywood stars such as James STEWART, Tyrone Power, Douglas Fairbanks, Jr., Robert Montgomery and Clark GABLE entered the service and many others gave freely of their time to entertain troops and help raise money for the war effort. Hollywood emerged from the war as the premier mass entertainment force in the world, but would soon see its position collapse from the challenge of television and the rise of world-wide film production.

Hollywood Ten. Term coined to describe a group of American screenwriters and directors who were imprisoned and blacklisted following allegations before the HOUSE UN-AMERICAN ACTIVITIES COMMITTEE of communist affiliations. The committee had begun an "investigation" of HOLLYWOOD in the fall of 1947. Refusing to answer questions under the freedom of speech guaranteed by the First Amendment rather than the self-incrimination clause in the Fifth, they were voted in contempt of Congress on November 24, 1947. The following year they were tried in federal court, found guilty, and each sentenced to a year in prison. After the Supreme Court refused to review the convictions, they went to prison in the spring of 1950. The Ten were screenwriters Alvah Bessie, Herbert Biberman, Lester Cole, Ring LARDNER, Jr., John Howard Lawson, Albert Maltz, Samuel Ornitz, Adrian Scott, Dalton Trumbo, and director Edward Dmytryk. After their release, many were blacklisted by the film industry. Some could gain work only by using pseudonyms. The best-known example was Trumbo's "Robert Rich," the name under which he won an ACADEMY AWARD for best screenplay for *The Brave One* (1956). Ironically, those who went to the Federal Correctional Institution in Danbury, Connecticut, found that J. Parnell Thomas, former head of the HUAC committee that had condemned them, was also there, serving time for taking kickbacks.

Holm, Hanya (1898–). German-American dance teacher and choreographer. Through her teaching and lecture-demonstrations, Holm became one of the molders of the modern dance movement in America. She danced with Mary Wigman's company (1921–30), then opened the New York City branch of the Wigman School (1931), which became the Hanya Holm Studio (1936–67), one of the most important modern dance schools. In 1941 she founded the influential Center of the Dance in the West in Colorado Springs. She gained popular acclaim as a choreographer of such Broadway musicals as *Kiss Me Kate* (1948), *My Fair Lady* (1956) and *Camelot* (1960).

Holman, M. Carl (1919–1988). American poet, activist, editor and scholar described as the godfather of the CIVIL RIGHTS movement. President of the National Urban Coalition from 1968, Holman was noted for his adeptness at forming coalitions among diverse groups and individuals. He emphasized to blacks the importance of education, warning them that without it the next generation would become economically superfluous.

Holmes, Oliver Wendell, Jr. (1841–1935). Associate justice U.S. Supreme Court (1902–32). Arguably the greatest justice of the 20th century, Holmes was the son of the author-physician, Oliver Wendell Holmes, who was not only a leading poet, essayist and novelist but also a professor of anatomy at Harvard Medical School. Young Holmes was educated at Harvard, where he was class poet of 1861. After graduation he joined the Union Army, served in the Civil War and was wounded several times. After the war Holmes again enrolled at Harvard, but instead of following medicine, as had his father, he enrolled in the law school. A practicing lawyer, Holmes also taught law at Harvard. In 1881 his slim volume, *The Common Law*, containing a series of his public lectures, was published and immediately established Holmes as a legal philosopher of international reputation. He became an associate justice of the Massachusetts Supreme Court after Louis BRANDEIS was appointed to the U.S. Supreme Court, and he was later elevated to be the state's chief justice. Twenty-three years after, President Theodore ROOSEVELT tapped him for the U.S. Supreme Court. Justice Holmes was famous for short, well-reasoned majority and dissenting opinions. He applied the law equitably without favoritism or agenda. He served 29 years with distinction, retiring at age 90.

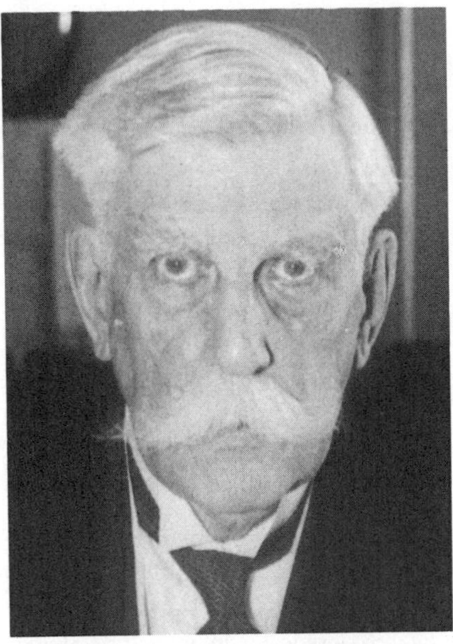

U.S. Supreme Court Associate Justice Oliver Wendell Holmes Jr. at age 90, shortly after he left the Court after nearly 30 years of service (Jan. 12, 1932).

For further reading:

Aichele, Gary, *Oliver Wendell Holmes, Jr.: Soldier, Scholar, Judge*. Boston: G.K. Hall, 1989.

Lerner, Max, ed., *The Mind & Faith of Oliver Wendell Holmes: His Speeches, Essays, Letters & Judicial Opinions*. New Brunswick, N.J.: Transaction Books, 1943.

Novick, Sheldon M., *The Honorable Justice: The Life of Oliver Wendell Holmes*. Boston: Little, Brown, 1989.

Holmes a Court, (Michael) Robert Hamilton (1937–1990). South African-born financier. He built a business empire in AUSTRALIA that made him that country's wealthiest man. He started out with a small textile mill and an ailing road haulage and engineering concern in 1973. By 1987, through a series of shrewd business and stock deals, his company was worth A$1.3 billion. He lost much of his fortune in the worldwide stock market crash of 1987, but had rebuilt it to A$700 million by 1990.

Holocaust. Name commonly used to describe the systematic mass murder of millions of JEWS in Nazi-dominated Europe, and the period when this took place. For Jews and many non-Jews alike, the Holocaust is regarded as the most horrific event in modern history. The Holocaust was more or less simultaneous with WORLD WAR II, but constitutes a separate event. It served no military purpose, but rather grew out of Adolf HITLER's intense ANTI-SEMITISM and his desire to "purify" the German Reich. Hitler's book MEIN KAMPF had outlined his contempt for the Jewish people; this virulent antisemitism became a cornerstone of NAZISM. Hitler's repeated insistence that the Jews were responsible for Germany's and the world's ills found a responsive chord among many Germans who sought a scapegoat for their problems. In the early 1930s, acts of intimidation against Jews in Germany became widespread. Nazis urged boycotts of Jewish businesses, and paramilitary storm troopers frequently attacked Jews, beating them and destroying Jewish property. After Hitler became chancellor in early 1933 many Jews, fearing the worst, fled Germany for the U.S., Britain and other countries. The majority, however, remained behind. In 1935 the Nazis enacted the **Nuremberg Laws** (1935), depriving German Jews of many of the rights of German citizens. On the evening of Nov. 9, 1938—***Kristallnacht*** ("night of broken glass")—Nazi thugs began a deliberate campaign of violence against Jews throughout Germany. Synagogues were burned, Jewish shops were looted and thousands of Jews were arrested. The German occupation of much of Europe during World War II brought millions of other Jews under Nazi jurisdiction. Initially, many of these Jews were confined to ghettos in the occupied countries. They were then systematically rounded up and transported to CONCENTRATION CAMPS, there to be used for slave labor or killed. Hitler's policy of exterminating the Jews—designated as "the FINAL SOLUTION to the Jewish problem"—was formalized at the **Wannsee conference** in January 1942. German killings of Jewish civilians continued up to the last days of the war. Although many of the Jews of Western Europe died, many were also sheltered or helped to escape by sympathetic gentiles in those countries, themselves victims of German occupation. The more numerous Jews of Eastern Europe—particularly in Poland and the Ukraine—were virtually wiped out. Over 90% of Poland's 3.5 million Jews died in concentration camps; at the war's end, only 4,000 Jews remained in Poland. Altogether, an estimated 6 million Jews died during the Holocaust; their suffering and the suffering of those who managed to survive this dark period cannot be measured.

For further reading:

Dawidowicz, Lucy S., *The War Against the Jews, 1933–1945*. New York: Free Press, 1986.

Gilbert, Martin, *The Holocaust: A History of the Jews of Europe During the Second World War*. New York: Henry Holt, 1985.

Rothchild, Sylvia, ed., *Voices from the Holocaust*. New York: NAL/Dutton, 1982.

Wiesel, Elie, *Dimensions of the Holocaust*, 2nd ed. Evanston, Ill.: Northwestern University Press, 1990.

Holst, Gustav (1874–1934). English composer. Born in Cheltenham, Gloucestershire, Holst was the son, grandson and great-grandson of musicians. He studied at the Royal College of Music, London, and later taught there from 1919 to 1924. At various times a church organist, trombonist and music school administrator, he organized British army musical activities in Greece and Turkey during WORLD WAR I. Early in his career, Holst was influenced by composers Richard STRAUSS and Ralph VAUGHAN WILLIAMS and folklorist Cecil Sharp; the latter two aroused his interest in English folk music. A composer of brilliant harmonic inventiveness, Holst is best known for his orchestral suite *The Planets* (1914–16), in which each movement corresponds to a planet of the solar system. The immense popularity of *The Planets* has tended to obscure the excellence of many of Holst's other compositions. These include the choral *Hymn of Jesus* (1917), the opera *A Perfect Fool* (1920–22), the *Choral Symphony* (1923–24), the symphonic poem *Egdon Heath* (1927) and the orchestral *Hammersmith* suite (1930).

For further reading:

Holst, Imogen, *Gustav Holst: A Biography*. 2nd ed. Oxford: Oxford University Press, 1969, 1986.

Short, Michael, *Gustav Holst: The Man and His Music*. Oxford: Oxford University Press, 1990.

Holt, John (1923–1985). American educator. Holt's landmark book *How Children Fail,* a diary based on his experience as a teacher, touched off a national debate on the failings of American education during the 1960s. The book and its sequel, *How Children Learn,* sold well over a million copies and were translated into 14 languages. Based on his conclusions, he founded the magazine *Growing Without Schooling* (1977), which was designed to help parents educate their children at home.

Holt, Victoria [Eleanor Burford Hibbert] (1906–). British novelist. Holt is best known for her gothic novels filled with plot twists and intrigue. *Mistress of Mellyn* (1960), *The Demon Lover* (1982) and *The Captive* (1989) are popular ones. Under the pseudonym Jean Plaidy she writes historical novels, which have received critical and popular acclaim. These include *Beyond the Blue Mountains* (1947), *Queen of the Realm: The Story of Elizabeth I* (1985) and *Victoria Victorious* (1986). Notable for her extraordinary prolificacy, Holt also has published under her maiden name, Eleanor Burford, and the pseudonyms Philippa Carr, Elbur Ford, Kathleen Kellow, and Ellalice Tate.

Holtby, Winifred (1898–1935). British author and feminist. Holtby left Oxford to serve with the WAAC in WORLD WAR I. Her experiences led her to a more international political stance, which, along with FEMINISM, figures in her journalism and novels. Her novels include *Anderby World* (1923), *The Land of Green Ginger* (1927) and *South Riding* (1936), which takes place in her native Yorkshire and is perhaps her best-known work. Holtby was a frequent contributor to the *Manchester Guardian, Time and Tide* and many other British periodicals. She is the subject of *Testament of Friendship* (1940), written by her friend Vera BRITTAIN.

Holyoake, Keith Jacka (1904–1983). Prime minister of NEW ZEALAND (1957, 1960–72). Holyoake was a farmer who then entered parliament as a Nationalist Party member in 1932. He later served as deputy prime minister and minister of agriculture from 1949 to 1957, when he briefly took over as prime minister when Sir Sidney Holland became ill. He was elected prime minister in 1960 serving until 1972. Holyoake was an advocate of multi-racialism, and outspoken against APARTHEID in SOUTH AFRICA and the regime of Ian SMITH in Rhodesia. He maintained close ties to the United States, and backed it by sending troops to VIETNAM in the 1960s. He was instrumental in the creation of the special trade relationship with Australia (NAFTA). Holyoake was governor-general from 1977 to 1980 when he became New Zealand's first knight of the garter.

Home, Lord. See Alec DOUGLAS-HOME

Home Rule. Movement in IRELAND, backed by the Liberals in Great Britain, seeking to establish a parliament in Dublin responsible for internal Irish affairs. The Home Rule Association was founded in 1870 by Isaac Butt (1813–1879) and gained momentum under the leadership of his successor Charles Parnell. Home Rule Bills introduced in the British Parliament under Gladstone (1886, 1893) were defeated. A third bill introduced in 1912 was opposed by Ulster Protestants, who feared potential domination by the Roman Catholic majority in the south of Ireland. By 1914 the issue of Home Rule had brought Ireland to the brink of civil war and led to the EASTER REBELLION (1916). In May 1921 six counties in northern Ireland obtained Home Rule with a parliament at Stormont, Belfast, forming the loyalist state of NORTHERN IRELAND. The remaining 26 counties negotiated for the status of a dominion with control over foreign affairs as well as internal and representation in the LEAGUE OF NATIONS, which was agreed to in December 1921. (See also DE VALERA.)

Honduran Civil War of 1909–11. Former Honduran president, Manuel Bonilla led his conservative supporters in revolt against liberal President Miguel R. Davila, who was placed in office by Nicaraguan dictator Jose Santos Zelaya after the HONDURAN-NICARAGUAN WAR OF 1907. The ensuing civil war was inconclusive, and in an armistice February 8, 1911, both sides agreed to abide by the forthcoming elections. Bonilla was elected president, October 29, 1911.

Honduran Guerrilla War of 1981– . Thousands of Salvadorans, Miskito Indians and anti-Sandinista Nicaraguans took refuge in Honduras, which feared conflict in their nations would exacerbate leftist struggle against the government. Cuban-trained Marxist guerrillas carried out urban terrorism, and police and military forces increased efforts to suppress them, prompting the U.S. to increase its military aid. The Honduras-based Nicaraguan Democratic Force (FDN) rebels continued raids into Nicaragua, heightening tensions with that country.

Honduran-Nicaraguan War of 1907. Jose Santos Zelaya, who became president of NICARAGUA through a liberal revolt in 1893, ruled as a dictator and meddled in the affairs of his neighbors. In 1903 Honduran conservative Manuel Bonilla overthrew the Honduran liberal government supported by Zelaya. Honduran rebels in 1906 attempted to oust Bonilla, getting Zelaya's support. Honduran troops invaded Nicaragua in pursuit of rebels, and Zelaya damanded war reparations. Honduras refused, and Nicaraguan forces invaded Honduras and on March 18, 1907 won the Battle of Namasigue, the first battle fought in Central America with machine guns. Nicaraguans occupied the Honduran capital, Tegucigalpa, Bonilla fled, and Zelaya named Miguel R. Davila as president. (See also HONDURAN CIVIL WAR OF 1909–11.)

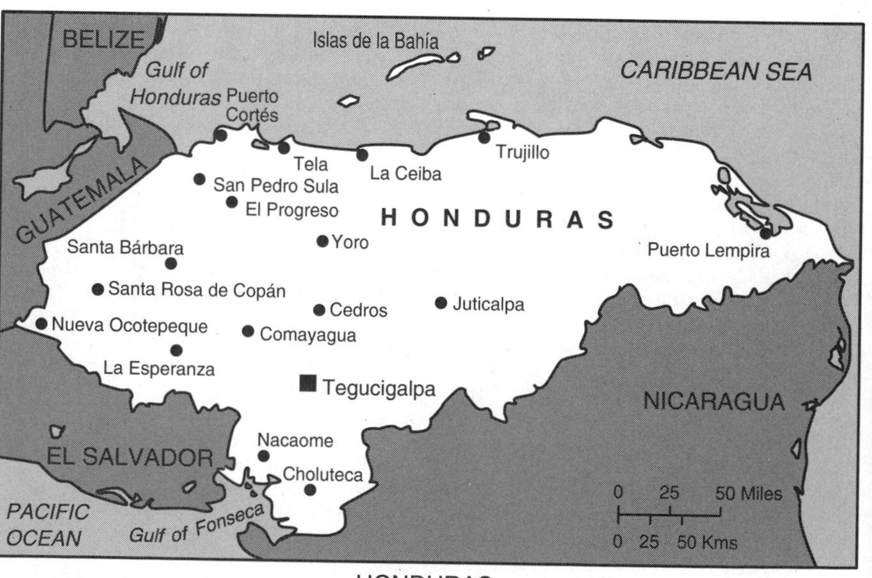

HONDURAS

HONDURAS

1900	American fruit companies establish huge holdings; build railroads and docks.
1903	U.S. Marines intervene to end political strife; install Miguel Davilla as president.
1923	Civil war; Marines return; U.S. sets policy of non-recognition of revolutionary governments; government formed by military-dominated PNH Party holds power for 31 years, despite challenges.
1931	"Sigatoka" blight damages banana crop; attempted revolution.
1943	Death of Froilan Turcios, novelist.
1948	PNH President Andino steps down.
1957	Liberal government elected; begins land reforms and social security programs.
1963	Military coup.
1969	Football war; border disputes with El Salvador erupt into two-week war after fans riot at a soccer match.
1971	First major north-south paved highway completed.
1974	Hurricane Fifi destroys three-quarters of banana crop.
1975	United Fruit Company admits $1.25 million bribe to "high government official" for relaxation of export duties.
1976	Continued border conflict with El Salvador seriously damages foreign trade; President Lopez overthrown by young officers who restart land reform.
1978	Political parties resume activity.
1980	Military government effectively ended by assembly elections.
1982	Liberal government elected; new constitution removes control of military from president; country joins in forming Central American Democratic Community.
1983	Contra rebels use Honduras as base to strike in Nicaragua; CIA conducts anti-Sandinista operations from Honduras.
1986	First succession of one elected government to another since 1929.
1987	Sixty percent of arable land owned by government, United Brands and Standard Fruit.
1990	"Banana War"; 600,000 workers threaten general strikes, win pay raise; UN troops disarm Contras; conservative Callejas elected president.

Honduras [Republic of Honduras]. Nation located on the Central American isthmus. Honduras covers an area of 43,266 square miles, including several islands off its Caribbean Sea coast and 288 islands in the Gulf of Fonseca off its Pacific coast. Politically unstable, Honduras was under the control of the military almost continuously from 1923 to 1975. Power was gained through numerous coups and maintained through rewritings of the constitution. The so-called Soccer War with EL SALVADOR, which began in 1969, was ostensibly over the outcome of a football (soccer) match but in reality was over economic issues. A 1980 treaty resolved the conflict but left Honduras weakened politically and economically. A return to a democratic government occurred in 1982 with the election of Roberto Suazo Cordova as president; all military political power was ended in 1984. Elections in 1990 brought Rafael Leonardo Callejas to the presidency, continuing the democratic process.

Hone, Evie (1894–1955). Irish painter and stained-glass designer. Born in Dublin, Hone studied in London with Walter Sickert and in Paris with Andre Lhote and Albert Gleizes. Her early work consisted mainly of abstract paintings executed in deep, jewel-like colors. Hone was strongly influenced by Georges Rouault in her painting and in the stained glass she created from 1933 until her death. Her most celebrated works are the *Crucifixion* and *Last Supper* windows at the Eton College Chapel (1942–52).

Honecker, Erich (1912–). East German communist political leader, secretary-general of the Socialist Unity (Communist) party (1971–89). Honecker joined the German Communist party in his teens, was arrested under HITLER in 1935, sentenced to 10 years in prison in 1937 and released at the end of WORLD WAR II. He was first secretary of the party's youth organization from 1946 to 1955. He joined the Central Committee in 1946 and the Politburo as candidate member in 1950 and as full member in 1958. Honecker succeeded Walter ULBRICHT as party leader in 1971. His policy was aimed at strengthening EAST GERMANY economically while repressing any challenges to the party's authority. He presided over East Germany's transformation into an industrial and military power second only to the U.S.S.R. in the WARSAW PACT. His hard-line leadership was successfully challenged in 1989 as East Germany's economy declined, tens of thousands of East Germans fled to the West and hundreds of thousands more took to the streets demanding an end to Communist rule. Honecker was ousted from his post on Oct. 10, 1989. Subsequent investigations revealed that he had led a lavish, privileged lifestyle at the expense of the East German people; he was put under house arrest, but because of ill-health he had not been formally tried for corruption as of March 1991. He later fled to the U.S.S.R.

Honegger, Arthur (1892–1955). French composer. Born in Le Havre of Swiss parents, he studied at the Zurich Conservatory and the Paris Conservatory. With Darius MILHAUD, Francis POULENC and three other young French composers, Honegger was a member of the 1920s group known as the SIX. Often polyphonic and polytonal, his music is strongly rhythmic and sharply dissonant. He is particularly noted for his theatrical works, such as the ballet *Judith* (1926), the oratorio *King David* (1921–23) and the film music for *Mayerling* (1935). His other works include the tone poem *Pacific 231* (1923), five symphonies, piano works, chamber music and songs.

"Honeymooners, The". See Jackie GLEASON.

Hong Kong. British crown colony located on the southeast coast of China. The territory of Hong Kong includes Hong Kong island (ceded to Britain in 1841) and adjacent islands, the Kowloon peninsula (ceded in 1860) and the New Territories (acquired by 99–year lease in 1898), which consist of a mainland area adjacent to Kowloon and 235 islands. The territory covers a total area of 414 square miles and is administered by Great Britain. The Japanese occupied Hong Kong during WORLD WAR II (1941–45), after which British rule resumed. Long a major center of trade, in the last third of the 20th century Hong Kong also became a leading center of manufacturing and international finance; along with JAPAN, it has taken a lead in the production of computers, radios, television sets, audio-video equipment and cameras. Historically an important center for refugees, Hong Kong experienced problems in the 1970s from increased illegal emigration from China, and in the 1980s from the arrival of huge numbers of Vietnamese BOAT PEOPLE. In 1989 Britain began a forced repatriation of the boat people to alleviate some of the problems. The Sino-British Joint Declaration of 1985 provides for China to regain sovereignty over Hong Kong on July 1, 1997. Fears over Hong Kong's future under Chinese rule have led to increased emigration from

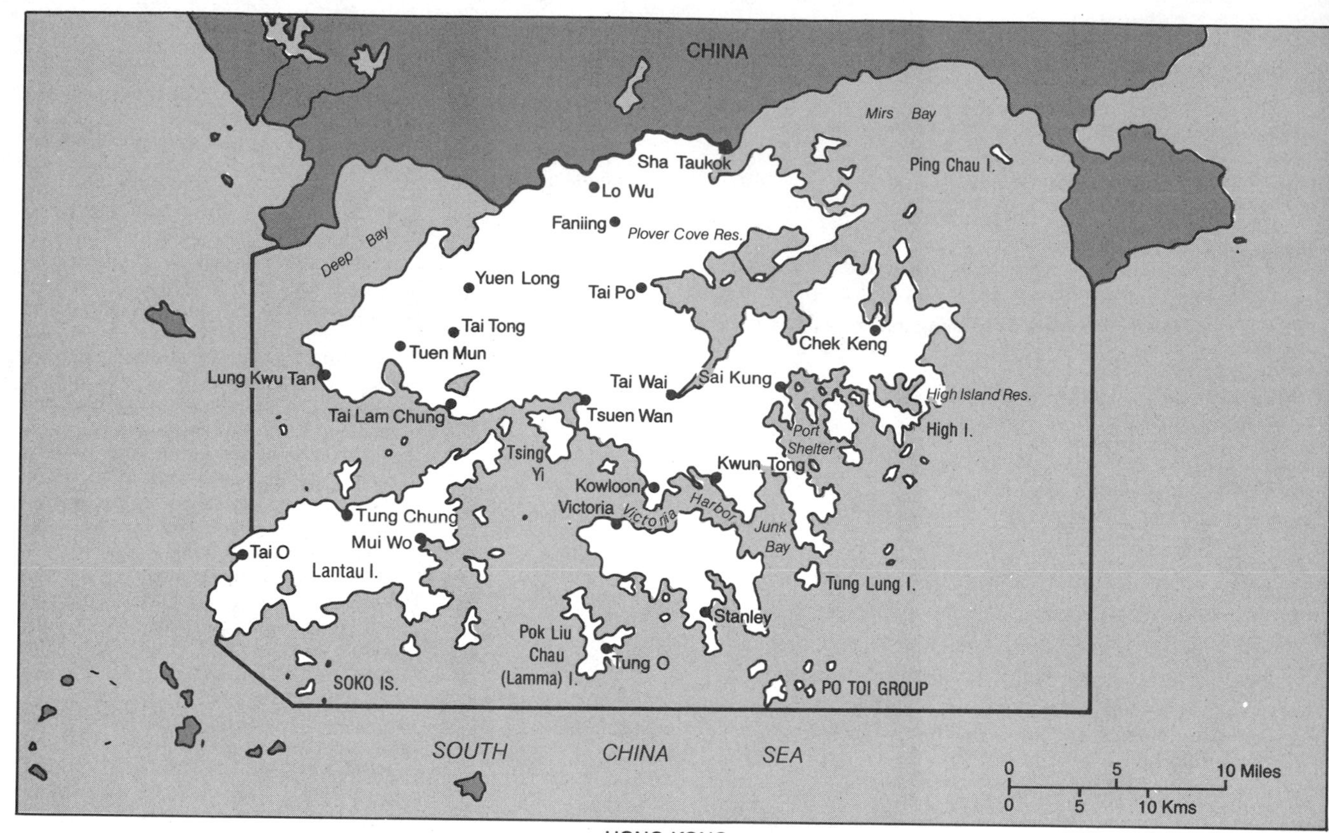

HONG KONG

HONG KONG

1898	British granted 99-year lease on land that would become Hong Kong City.
1911	First massive wave of refugees, fleeing Chinese revolution; University of Hong Kong founded; population reaches 500,000.
1927	Strikes; anti-foreign demonstrations; total boycott on trade with Britain.
1937	Second wave of refugees, fleeing Sino-Japanese War; population reaches 1,500,000.
1941	Japanese invasion; Europeans interned; almost 10% of population live on boats.
1949	Third wave of refugees, fleeing communist takeover of China; British abandon plans for self-government.
1950	Manufacturing initiates economic boom.
1955	Immense public housing program started.
1962	Famine on mainland leads to more refugees.
1967	Cultural Revolution on mainland fuels strikes and anti-British demonstrations.
1980	Wave of "boat people" refugees from Viet Nam.
1984	British agree to return Hong Kong to Chinese rule as of 1997; Hong Kong to retain democracy and capitalism for 50 years afterwards.
1989	Chinese suppress Democracy Movement in massacre at Tiananmen Square; Hong Kong residents agitate for resettlement to England.
1990	Population density reaches almost 14,000 per square mile; British begin forcibly returning boat people to Vietnam; estimated 62,000 people emigrate from Hong Kong.

the territory and pressure on Britain to admit the millions born in Hong Kong who can claim British passport rights under the British National (Overseas) category of immigration.

For further reading:

Morris, Jan, *Hong Kong*. New York: Random House, 1988.

Scott, Ian, *Political Change and the Crisis of Legitimacy in Hong Kong*. Honolulu: University of Hawaii Press, 1989.

Hood, Hugh (John Blagdon) (1928–). Canadian novelist. Hood began his writing career with the short stories *Flying a Red Kite* (1962) and the novel *White Figure, White Ground* (1964). He later devoted himself to writing the *romane-fleuve, Le Nouveau Siecle* (*The New Age*), which consists of the novels *The Swing in the Garden* (1975), *A New Athens* (1977), *Reservoir Ravine* (1979) and *Black and White Keys* (1981). Hoods' fiction reflects his socialist political views.

Hood, Raymond M. (1881–1934). American architect, one of many to work on the design of ROCKEFELLER CENTER, who moved toward MODERNISM at a time when eclecticism was the dominant direction in architecture in the U.S. A graduate of MIT, Hood was associated with J. Andre Fouilhoux and John Mead Howells. Together they won a competition for the design of the Chicago Tribune Building (1922), a neo-Gothic skyscraper with useless flying buttresses at its top. Under the influence of European modernism, Hood moved toward a noneclectic, modern style with details relating to ART DECO. His vertically striped Daily News and horizontally banded McGraw-Hill buildings (1930 and 1934), designed with Fouilhoux, exemplify this shift. Hood played a major role in the Art Deco design characteristics of Rockefeller Center (begun in 1932).

Hook, Sidney (1902–1989). American social philosopher. Hook was a prolific writer on politics, public policy and education. He described himself as a socialist and a "secular humanist," which he defined as someone who considered morality to be linked to human nature and separate from religious belief. Although a staunch anticommunist, he was also an early critic of the anticommunist crusade of Senator Joseph MCCARTHY in the 1950s. Hook taught at New York University from 1927 to 1969. In 1973 he became a senior research fellow at the Hoover Institution on War, Revolution, and Peace at Stanford University. His best-known books included *Toward the Understanding of Karl Marx: A Revolutionary Interpretation* (1933), *The Hero in History* (1943), and *Pragmatism and the Tragic Sense of Life* (1974).

Hoover, Herbert (Clark) (1874–1964). President of the United States (1929–33). One of the great humanitarians of the 20th century, Hoover had the misfortune to preside over the beginning of the GREAT DEPRESSION of the 1930s. Born into a Quaker family in Ohio, Hoover was orphaned at the age of eight and thereafter lived with various relatives. He attended Stanford University, graduating with a degree in geology (1895), and joined a London-based mining firm. During the next 20 years he worked as a mining engineer in some 14 countries, including Australia and China, where he supervised important mining projects and introduced new mining techniques. He formed his own consulting firm in 1908 and became a millionaire.

In London at the outbreak of WORLD WAR I, Hoover turned to public service and played a major role in humanitarian relief efforts. Heading the American Relief Committee and the Committee for the Relief of Belgium, he organized food relief for 11 million refugees in war-torn Belgium and northern France. When the U.S. entered the war in 1917, President Woodrow WILSON appointed him chairman of the Food Administration Board, responsible for food rationing and conservation efforts in the U.S. Hoover continued his overseas relief work after the war, helping to avert famine in defeated Germany and the massive famine in the U.S.S.R. in 1921.

Herbert Hoover, 31st president of the United States.

As secretary of commerce (1921–28) under Presidents Warren G. HARDING and Calvin COOLIDGE, Hoover modernized the Commerce Department. He reformed the bureaus of Foreign and Domestic Commerce and the Bureau of Fisheries. He declared the radio airwaves public property, and introduced radio station licensing. During his tenure, the number of commercial radio stations in the U.S. increased from two to several hundred. Hoover also called the first commercial aviation conference (1922) and the first national conference on highway safety (1923), promoted uniform manufacturing standards and supported child health and welfare activities and conservation programs.

One of the most energetic but self-effacing figures of the 1920s, Hoover was also one of the few high officials who were not implicated in the scandals of the Harding administration. With a reputation for integrity, brilliant administrative abilities and wide practical experience, Hoover was selected as the Republican presidential candidate in 1928. He defeated Al SMITH by the second-largest popular vote margin up to that time.

Hoover promised to bring high standards to government and pledged to end poverty and hunger in America. However, the STOCK MARKET CRASH OF 1929 intervened. Hoover established the Reconstruction Finance Administration to make loans to stricken businesses, adopted a budget designed to stimulate the economy, and urged the Federal Reserve Board to ease the money supply and lower interest rates. However, he refused to involve the federal government in direct relief, believing that the efforts of private business and individual initiative would best revive the economy. As his administration progressed, Hoover was severely criticized for appearing to favor big business while ignoring the plight of the ordinary citizen. His apparent lack of concern was reinforced by his cold, humorless manner and his inability to communicate his ideas convincingly to the people. His claim that "prosperity is just around the corner" was not taken seriously by the majority of voters, and he was soundly defeated by Democrat Franklin D. ROOSEVELT in the election of 1932.

Hoover remained a vocal critic of Roosevelt and the NEW DEAL, claiming that FDR's big-government programs threatened individual liberty and stifled initiative. He initially opposed the U.S. entry into WORLD WAR II, believing that the war was not America's concern. At war's end in 1945, acknowledging Hoover's expertise, President Harry S TRUMAN asked Hoover to again undertake famine relief efforts. In 1946 Hoover traveled over 50,000 miles, visiting 38 countries to determine how food could be distributed to the areas where it was most needed. His efforts helped save millions of Europeans and Asians from starvation. Hoover continued as an adviser to Truman. His Hoover Commission (1947–49) studied the organization of the executive branch of government and issued 273 recommendations to improve its efficiency; the majority of these recommendations were adopted. Hoover also advised President Dwight D. EISENHOWER on a number of issues, and won new respect as the elder statesman of the REPUBLICAN PARTY.

For more than a generation after his 1932 electoral defeat, Hoover was largely viewed as a heartless reactionary and do-nothing, a villain in 20th-century American history. However, historians have reevaluated Hoover's presidency and acknowledged his substantial positive accomplishments.

For further reading:

Nash, George H., *The Life of Herbert Hoover: The Engineer, 1874–1914*. New York: W. W. Norton, 1983.

———, *The Life of Herbert Hoover: The Humanitarian, 1914–1917*. New York: W. W. Norton, 1988.

Hoover, J(ohn) Edgar (1895–1972). American government administrator, director of the Federal Bureau of Investigation (FBI). Born in Washington, D.C., Hoover studied law at George Washington University, joined the U.S. Department of Justice in 1917, and from 1919 to 1921 worked extensively on the PALMER RAIDS. In 1924 he began his lifelong career as director of the Bureau of Investigation, which was renamed the FBI in 1935. During these years Hoover personified the FBI, both in its successes and its failures. At the time he took it over, the Bureau

J. Edgar Hoover, director of the Federal Bureau of Investigation (FBI) for 48 years.

was inefficient and scandal-ridden. Hoover quickly turned it into a crack policing agency, doing away with political appointments and recruiting improved staff, establishing centralized fingerprint and statistical files, developing a crime laboratory and founding a training academy. In the early 1930s he launched a war on "public enemies," engineering manhunts for high-profile criminals such as John DILLINGER, "Pretty Boy" FLOYD and "Baby Face" NELSON. This proved a highly successful public relations ploy but did little to dislodge the hold of organized crime, which Hoover had been criticized for largely ignoring. During WORLD WAR II, he was given the responsibility of protecting the U.S. from sabotage or subversion by enemy agents. In the COLD WAR era he renewed his earlier campaign against COMMUNISM by pursuing what he perceived as left-wing organizations and sympathizers with an obsessive tenacity that brought him charges of civil-rights violation and the prosecution of personal vendettas. During his many years in office serving under eight presidents, Hoover amassed tremendous personal power and became the subject of enormous controversy.

Hoover Dam. Formerly known as Boulder Dam, this immense engineering wonder was erected on the Colorado River, between Nevada and Arizona, between 1931 and 1936. Built by the U.S. Bureau of Reclamation, it is still one of the largest and most important hydroelectric power sources in the world and contributed greatly to the postwar growth of the southwestern U.S. Project workers founded Boulder City, Nevada.

Hope, Bob (Leslie Townes) (1903–). American entertainer, comedian and film star. Born in England, he moved with his family to Ohio at the age of four. One of the most popular entertainers on radio during the 1930s and 1940s and on TV beginning in the 1950s, he gained world renown for his seven "Road" movies (1940–53) costarring Bing CROSBY and Dorothy Lamour. During his career he made over 50 films. One of the most charitable figures in the performing arts, he made annual trips overseas to entertain American troops during WORLD WAR II, the KOREAN WAR, the VIETNAM WAR and in peacetime. He has continued to work in commercials and TV specials and, occasionally, still entertains troops. A personal friend of several U.S. presidents, he was awarded the Presidential Medal of Freedom in 1969. He has also received the Hersholt Award, an Emmy and an honorary ACADEMY AWARD.

Hopkins, Harry (Lloyd) (1890–1946). American public official and presidential adviser. Born in Sioux City, Iowa, Hopkins was trained as a social worker, and after college he settled in New York City. There, in 1931, he was appointed by then-governor Franklin D. ROOSEVELT as director of the Temporary Emergency Relief Administration. After Roosevelt became president, he made Hopkins chief of the Federal Emergency Relief Administration and the Civil Works Administration. Hopkins subsequently headed the WPA (1935–38) and served as secretary of commerce (1938–40). He was the key figure in administering NEW DEAL public assistance programs and in supplying jobs to some eight million workers. A close friend of Roosevelt, Hopkins was called on frequently by the president to serve as an emissary, confidant and adviser, particularly during WORLD WAR II. Administering the LEND-LEASE program in 1941, he also went on many wartime missions in London and Moscow. Despite ill health, he accompanied the president to all the major conferences of the war and helped shape peacetime alliances. After Roosevelt's death, at the request of President TRUMAN, the gravely ill Hopkins held talks with STALIN in 1945 regarding the UNITED NATIONS.

Hopkins, Sam "Lightnin'" (1912–1982). American country BLUES singer. Hopkins began his career in 1920 as a minstrel at Texas country fairs. He subsequently performed throughout the South and built a national reputation. After a hiatus of 15 years he regained prominence through appearances at New York's CARNEGIE HALL and the Village Gate club. Hopkins was one of the greatest and the last of the original blues performers. He was widely acclaimed by critics for his imaginative guitar playing, which exerted a major influence on ROCK guitar players.

Hopman, Harry (1906–1985). Australian tennis player; captain of Australia's Davis Cup team in 1938 and 1939 and again from 1950 to 1969. During the latter period, known as the golden age of Australian tennis, he worked with such great players as Rod Laver and John Newcombe. Hopman helped Australia capture the Davis Cup 15 times. He moved to Florida in the late 1970s to open an international tennis camp for young players.

Harry Hopkins, FDR's personal adviser.

Bob Hope entertaining troops in Korea.

Hopper, Edward (1882–1967). American painter. One of 20th-century America's finest realists, Hopper was born in Nyack, N.Y. He studied in New York City, with Robert HENRI, George Luks, Arthur B. Davies and others from 1900 to 1906. Hopper gained his first recognition through his early etchings. He traveled to Europe a number of times from 1906 to 1910, but was little affected by the new movements he encountered there. Hopper lived in New York City, exhibited at the ARMORY SHOW (1913), had his first one-man show at the Whitney Studio Club in 1919 and his first retrospective at the Museum of Modern Art in 1933. Hopper's paintings fall within the tradition of his teacher Henri and of the Ashcan School, but with a very personal approach. Painting his native New York or the landscapes of New England, he depicted slices of streets in cities or small towns strongly lit and shadowed with a cold light, often peopled with solitary figures, nearly always evoking a sense of profound loneliness and isolation. Unsentimental and starkly geometric, his best known works include *From Williamsburg Bridge* (1928, Metropolitan Museum, N.Y.C.), *House by the Railroad* (1925, Museum of Modern Art, N.Y.C.), *Early Sunday Morning* (1930, Whitney Museum, N.Y.C.) and *Nighthawks* (1942, Art Institute of Chicago).

Horenstein, Jascha (1898–1973). Russian-born conductor. Born in Kiev, Horenstein and his family moved to Vienna in 1904. He studied music there and in Berlin. In 1929 he was appointed director of the Dusseldorf Opera and conducted the company. In the 1930s he traveled and conducted throughout Europe. He settled in the U.S. in 1941, became an American citizen, and conducted in the U.S. and Latin America. After World War II Horenstein settled in Switzerland. A thoughtful and meticulous conductor, he was particularly known for his interpretations of the symphonies of Anton Bruckner and Gustav MAHLER.

Horne, Lena (1917–). American singer and actress. Known for her stylish interpretations of jazz and pop standards, Horne was born in Brooklyn, New York. While a teenager, she sang in a chorus at the famous Cotton Club in HARLEM. In the early 1940s she went to HOLLYWOOD, where she was featured in several all-black movies, most notably *Stormy Weather* (1943), whose title song became her signature tune, and also in several all-star musicals, where her own numbers could be neatly cut from the films when they played theaters in the South. The first black woman vocalist to be featured with a white band, Horne faced and fought discrimination for much of her career. She toured Europe and frequently appeared in nightclubs and on television variety shows in the 1950s and '60s.

Horney, Karen (1885–1952). German-American neo-Freudian psychoanalyst. Born in Hamburg, Germany, Karen Horney received her M.D. in Berlin in 1915. After World War I, she began work at the Berlin Psychoanalytic Institute. Horney took exception to many of the negative aspects of FREUD's theories, particularly those regarding women, and, like Alfred ADLER, went on to develop her own theories of personality and neurosis and to question key Freudian concepts and methods. Her books *Our Inner Conflicts* and *Neurosis and Human Growth* are considered landmark publications. Horney moved to the U.S. in 1932, and in 1941 she resigned from the New York Psychoanalytic Society and founded the Association for the Advancement of Psychoanalysis and the American Institute of Psychoanalysis.

Horniman, Annie (Elizabeth Fredericka) (1860–1937). British theatrical patron. A champion of modern drama, the wealthy Horniman founded Miss Horniman's Company of Actors. She financed a permanent home for the Irish National Theatre Company in the ABBEY THEATRE, Dublin. Though an admirer of W.B. YEATS, she had a difficult relationship with Lady GREGORY. Horniman withdrew her funding of the Abbey in 1910 when the theatre was kept open on the day of King EDWARD VII's funeral. She then focused on the Gaiety Theatre in Manchester, in which she had begun to invest in 1907. There she promoted new plays by local playwrights until 1921.

Hornsby, Rogers (1896–1963). American baseball player. Hornsby is a legend among baseball players and fans. He was the batting champion in the National League from 1920 to 1925, and again in 1928. Considered one of the greatest hitters of all time, his 1924 batting average of .424 still stands as a modern-day league record. He was player-manager for the St. Louis Cardinals in 1925 and 1926, leading the team to a winning World Series in 1926. He maintained a lifetime batting average of .358 from 1915 to 1933, won the most valuable player awards in 1925 and 1928, and was elected to the Baseball Hall of Fame in 1942.

Hornsby-Smith, Baroness (Margaret Patricia) (1914–1985). British politician; a prominent figure in the British House of Commons as Conservative MP for Chislehurst. Appointed parliamentary secretary to the ministry of health in 1951, she was, at 37, the youngest woman to hold office in any government. Hornsby-Smith held that post until 1957. When sworn of the Privy Council in 1959, she was the youngest woman ever to have received that honor.

Hornung, Paul Vernon (1935–). American football player. A stand-out running back at Notre Dame, Hornung was named winner of the prestigious Heisman Trophy in 1956. He turned professional with the Green Bay Packers and in 1960 set a season scoring record with 176 points. Under coach Vince LOMBARDI, he helped lead the team to three consecutive NFL championships (1960–62). Known for his relaxed approach to training, Hornung was suspended for the 1963 season for gambling on football games, although he never bet against his own team. His most memorable performance came in 1956, when he ran for five touchdowns.

Horowitz, Vladimir Samoylovich (1903–1989). Russian-born pianist whose technical brilliance and idiosyncratic interpretations placed him in the forefront of modern keyboard virtuosos. Born in Kiev, Horowitz studied with Felix Blumenfeld, a pupil of Anton Rubinstein. His friendship with the composer Alexander SCRIABIN confirmed his ambitions to specialize in music of the late Russian romantics. He left the U.S.S.R. in 1925 and three years later made his sensational CARNEGIE HALL debut with the Tchaikovsky 1st Piano Concerto (Thomas BEECHAM on the podium made his U.S. conducting debut). He immediately assumed his place among a galaxy of keyboard luminaries in New York including his great friend, Sergei RACHMANINOFF. He became best known for the speed and terrifying intensity of his Liszt and Rachmaninoff performances, although he also championed the icy fire of Scriabin and the poised clarity of Muzio Clementi and Domenico Scarlatti. His concert career, which made him the highest paid classical pianist in history, was frequently interrupted by "retirements" due to ill health and a high-strung temperament. His return to Moscow in 1986 was a spectacular media event and was broadcast live worldwide. He made more than 150 records and won more than 20 Grammy Awards. Since 1933 he was married to Wanda Toscanini, the daughter of conductor Arturo TOSCANINI.

For further reading:

Plaskin, Glenn, *Horowitz*. New York: William Morrow and Co., 1983.

Vladimir Horowitz performing in the U.S.S.R. for the first time in 61 years (April 1986).

Horrocks, Sir Brian (1895–1985). British military officer. Horrocks fought in WORLD WAR I. As a general in WORLD WAR II, he helped the British take North Africa from the Germans at the crucial battle of EL ALAMEIN (1942). He also played a major role in the June 1944 Allied D-day INVASION OF NORMANDY. He retired from active duty in 1949 and was knighted and given the important ceremonial post of Black Rod in the House of Lords. He was also a historian and a well-known British television personality.

Horthy de Nagybanya, Miklos (1868–1957). Hungarian admiral and political leader. An aide-de-camp to Emperor FRANZ JOSEPH from 1911 to 1913, Horthy de Nagybanya commanded the Austro-Hungarian fleet during WORLD WAR I. After Bela Kun became head of the Hungarian government in 1919, Horthy led a counterrevolution that ousted the Marxists. In 1920 he became regent and headed a nationalistic and conservative regime, guiding the country in the years between the two world wars and helping to recover some of the lands lost by HUNGARY in post-World War I settlements. He reluctantly joined WORLD WAR II on the side of GERMANY but continued to maintain ties with the Allies. In 1944, after Russian troops entered Hungary, Horthy unsuccessfully sued for a separate peace with the U.S.S.R. and was soon imprisoned by the Germans. Freed by U.S. troops, he testified at the NUREMBERG TRIALS (1946), and in 1949 he settled in Portugal, where he died.

Horvath, Odon von (1901–1938). German novelist and playwright. Horvath was one of the most critically admired German writers of his generation prior to his untimely death. He enjoyed a series of successes on the stage with socially poignant and romantic plays, including *Revolte auf Cafe* (1927), *Sladek* (1929), *Italienische Nacht* (1931), *Hin und Her* (1934) and *Der Jungste Tag* (1937). His novels include *Der Ewige Spiesser* (1930), *Ein Kind Unserer Zeit* (1938) and *Jegend Ohne Gott* (1938).

Hot Springs. U.S. village in West Virginia, near Warm Springs. The Japanese diplomats present in the U.S. at the beginning of WORLD WAR II were interned here shortly after their country attacked the U.S. fleet at PEARL HARBOR, Hawaii, on December 7, 1941.

Houdini, Harry [Ehrich Weiss] (1874–1926). Legendary American magician and escape artist. Born in Hungary, he later changed his name in honor of the French magician Houdin. In 1922 he went to New York City as a trapeze artist, and later began a magic act with his brother. On a trip to England, he mystified Scotland Yard with a staged escape and earned a wide reputation. He was particularly noted for his ability to escape from almost any seemingly impossible situation. He left instructions that, after death, he would return to a specific bridge in Chicago, and his followers have kept their vigil on that day each year—without result. He left his library of magic to the Library of Congress.

Harry Houdini, escape artist and magician.

Hounsfield, Godfrey (1919–). British engineer who developed the first commercially successful CAT SCAN machines in Britain. For this work, Hounsfield shared the 1979 NOBEL PRIZE in physiology or medicine with Alan Macleod CORMACK.

Houphouet-Boigny, Felix (1905–). African statesman, president of the Republic of the Ivory Coast (see COTE D'IVOIRE). Born in Yamoussoukro, Houphouet-Boigny was the son of a chief in the French colony of the Ivory Coast. He studied medicine in Paris, and returned to Africa to supervise his family's cocoa plantation and practice (1925–40). He entered politics and became chairman of the powerful African Democratic Rally in 1946. He served in the French National Assembly from 1946 to 1958. When the Ivory Coast attained autonomy within the FRENCH COMMUNITY in 1958, Houphouet-Boigny assumed the duties of president of the constituent assembly, and in 1959 he became the prime minister. Leading the country to full independence in 1960, he became president and was returned to that office in subsequent elections. He has maintained close ties to France in commercial and cultural affairs.

House, Edward Mandell (1858–1938). U.S. diplomat. A political adviser to several Democratic Texas governors (1892–1904), House was given the honorary title of "colonel." He assumed a major role in Woodrow WILSON's 1912 presidential campaign, and refused a cabinet post, choosing instead to help Wilson in a variety of political and administrative functions. As Wilson's chief agent in foreign affairs, he helped explore mediation alternatives with European countries in WORLD WAR I. As head of the U.S. mission, he was one of the signers of the TREATY OF VERSAILLES in June 1919. Because of disagreements about ratification of the treaty, and possible U.S. entry into the LEAGUE OF NATIONS, Wilson and House separated, never seeing each other again.

For further reading:

George, Alexander L., *Woodrow Wilson and Colonel House: A Personality Study*. New York: Dover, 1956.

Household, Geoffrey Edward West (1900–1988). British suspense novelist; best known for his classic psychological thriller *Rogue Male* (1939), in which an aristocratic English big-game hunter decides to stalk and assassinate an unnamed Central European dictator modeled on Adolf HITLER. It was later filmed by Fritz LANG as *Manhunt* (1941). Household described himself as a writer as "sort of a bastard by Stevenson out of Conrad."

Houseman, John [Jacques Haussman] (1902–1988). American actor and producer. In the 1930s he teamed with Orson WELLES on a series of projects. Their most famous collaboration was the 1938 radio production "War of the Worlds." He was best known for creating the role of Professor Kingsfield in the movie and television versions of *The Paper Chase*. Houseman's portrayal of the crusty law professor won him an Oscar in 1974 and led to a series of television ads for the Smith Barney investment firm. He also helped establish the Juilliard drama school and the Acting Company repertory group.

House Un-American Activities Committee (HUAC). Special committee of the U.S. House of Representatives established in 1938. At first called the Dies Committee, for its chairman, Texas Democrat Martin Dies Jr., it was formed to investigate fascist, communist and other "subversive" organizations in the U.S. It became a standing committee in 1945. For 30 years after the end of World War II, HUAC concentrated on ferreting out communists and left-wingers in a variety of American institutions and industries. In 1947 it investigated the film industry and condemned the HOLLYWOOD TEN. The following year, it shifted its efforts to investigating the State Department and conducted hearings regarding the HISS-CHAMBERS CASE. In 1950, HUAC sponsored a bill that became the McCarren Act, which, until some provisions were overturned by the courts, necessitated the registration of American communists as foreign agents, severely limiting their travel and preventing them from serving in government and certain strategic industries. As the RED SCARE of the 1950s lessened in intensity, HUAC gradually became less powerful. Renamed the Internal Security Committee in 1969, it was abolished in 1975.

Housman, Alfred Edward (1859–1936). English poet and scholar. Housman remains one of the most widely read of English poets. While he was by no means a prolific poet, a number of his rhymed, elegaic verses—reflecting as they do the sunset of Victorian England—have taken their place as beloved classics of the language. Poems from *A Shropshire Lad* (1896) *When I Was One-And-Twenty* and *To An Athlete Dying Young* have been memorized by generations of English schoolchildren. *Last Poems* (1922) is a representative collection of Housman's verse. Housman led a quiet, academic life, serving for most of his adult years as a Latin professor at Cambridge University.

Houston. U.S. port of entry near the Gulf of Mexico coast of southeastern Texas. Completion of the Houston Ship Canal in 1914 made Houston a deepwater port and led to a spectacular growth that was later augmented by the discovery of oil in the area and development of a shipbuilding industry during World War II. The U.S.'s Manned Spacecraft Center (now the JOHNSON SPACE CENTER) was built here in 1961. The city is also the site of the Astrodome, the first domed sports stadium in the U.S.

hovercraft. Invented by British engineer Sir Christopher Cockerell in 1955, the hovercraft is an air-cushion vehicle that can travel over water or flat terrain. It is technically an aircraft but resembles a boat. The hovercraft is lifted several feet off the ground by air pressure generated under the hull by propellers. The pressure is contained by a flexible rubber "skirt" around the hovercraft's hull. Following his patent of the hovercraft, in 1956 Cockerell formed his own company, Hovercraft Limited, and interested the British government in his invention. The first practical hovercraft was flown in 1959. Further refinements were made, and in 1968 the largest hovercraft ever built, the SR.N4, was introduced. This model, which can carry up to 600 passengers as well as automobiles, is in regular commercial service on the English Channel between Dover and Calais.

Hovhaness, Alan (1911–). American composer. Hovhaness, of Scottish and Armenian parentage, is noted for the variety of international influences in his musical compositions. Born in Massachusetts, Hovhaness studied at the New England Conservatory and at Tanglewood. From 1948 to 1952 he taught at the Boston Conservatory, after which he moved to New York and devoted many years to extensive travel. His compositions, which are often intensely melodic with a modal foundation, sometimes feature Eastern musical touches such as a repetition of single notes within a limited pitch and range. Major works by this prolific composer include *Lousadzak* (1944), *Khaldis* (1951), *Meditation on Orpheus* (1958) and *Mountains and Rivers without End* (1968).

Howard, Leslie (1893–1943). British film and stage actor and director. Howard was a gifted and sensitive leading man who made his mark in a number of memorable films of the 1930s. Howard served in the British Army in World War I and afterwards suffered from shell-shock, which led him to pursue an acting career on the stage to distract him from his difficult memories. He rapidly achieved reknown and made his Broadway debut in *Just Suppose* (1922); Howard's film debut came in *Outward Bound* (1930). He achieved stardom as the victimized lover of Bette DAVIS in *Of Human Bondage* (1934). Subsequent successes included *The Scarlet Pimpernel* (1935), *The Petrified Forest* (1936), *Pygmalion* (1938) and *Gone With the Wind* (1939), in which he played Confederate gentleman Ashley Wilkes. Howard disappeared at sea in 1943 during WORLD WAR II, when the plane he was flying in was shot down while he was on a diplomatic mission for Britain.

Howard, Robin Jared Stanley (1924–). British dance patron. Howard founded the London Contemporary Dance Theatre and helped popularize modern dance in England. He also established the Contemporary Dance Trust and the London Contemporary Dance School.

Howard, Roy (1883–1964). American newspaper reporter, editor and publisher. He began his career as a news reporter in 1902 for the *Indianapolis News*, and later worked in St. Louis, Cincinnati and New York. In 1907 he became the New York manager of United Press International Association, and finally its president from 1936 to 1952. In 1925 he became chairman of the Scripps-McRae newspaper chain, which later became Scripps-Howard—a leading newspaper conglomerate with over 30 papers. Founder of the conglomerate *New York World-Telegram and Sun*, he was its editor until 1960 and its president until 1962.

Howard, Trevor (1916–1988). British actor. Howard made the transition from theater to film in 1944 and appeared in more than 70 films, including such classics as David LEAN's *Brief Encounter* (1946) and Carol REED's *The Third Man* (1950). In 1962, he portrayed Captain William Bligh opposite Marlon BRANDO's Fletcher Christian in a remake of *Mutiny on the Bounty*.

Howe, Sir Geoffrey (1926–). British politician. A Conservative MP, Howe served as solicitor-general (1970–72) and minister for trade (1972–74) under Edward HEATH. Howe was a senior figure in the cabinet of Margaret THATCHER (1979–90). As her first chancellor of the exchequer (1979–83), he introduced strict monetarist policies (see MONETARISM). He served briefly as home secretary before becoming foreign secretary in 1983. In 1988 Howe was promoted to the nominal post of deputy prime minister, but his influence in the cabinet waned as a result of disagreements with Thatcher's European policy. Howe's dramatic resignation from the cabinet in October 1990 followed by his open criticism of Thatcher in the House of Commons led to Thatcher's ouster as leader of the CONSERVATIVE PARTY and as prime minister. Howe was the longest-serving member of Thatcher's cabinet.

Howe, George (1886–1955). American architect whose work moved from eclecticism to MODERNISM and who exercised considerable influence as an educator and spokesman for modern architecture. Howe was educated at Harvard and at the Ecole des Beaux-Arts in Paris. He joined the Philadelphia firm of Mellor, Meigs & Howe where he produced a variety of traditional houses and other buildings. After meeting William LESCAZE in 1929, Howe converted to modernism ideas and designed, with Lescaze as a partner, the Philadelphia Savings Fund Society building (PSFS 1932), the first excellent example of modern skyscraper design in America. Independently, Howe designed a handsome house with a strikingly cantilevered deck at Bar Harbor, Maine (1939), which was included in the MUSEUM OF MODERN ART exhibit and book *America Builds*. From 1950 to 1954 Howe was chairman of the architecture department at Yale University where he introduced Louis I. KAHN as a teacher and brought about reforms that made Yale a leading architectural school.

Howe, Gordon "Gordie" (1928–). Canadian athlete. Perhaps the greatest ice hockey player of all time, Howe retired holding every major record for scoring, endurance—and penalties. He was named the National Hockey League's Most Valuable Player six times and was leading scorer six times. Known for his quick and sneaky use of his elbows to intimidate lesser players, Howe was a complete athlete who amazed teammates and rivals alike with his stickhandling ability. He spent the first 25 years of his incredible career with the Detroit Red Wings. He was named to the Hockey Hall of Fame in 1972, but emerged from retirement in 1973 to join the WHA's Houston Aeros, where, at 45, he skated alongside his sons, Mark and Marty. Howe returned to the NHL with the Hartford Whalers in 1977 and finally retired in 1980.

Howe, Irving (1920–). American writer. A leftist social and literary critic, he is the author of such works as *William Faulkner: A Critical Study* (1952), *Politics and the Novel* (1957), *Decline of the New* (1970) and *Celebrations and Attacks* (1978). Winner of the National Book Award, his *World of Our Fathers* (1976) is an evocative history of New York's immigrant Jewish community. Howe has played a prominent role in liberal American periodicals as the founding editor (1953) of *Dissent* and writer for *The Partisan Review, The New Republic* and *The New York Review of Books*. Also a prolific editor, Howe is the author of the 1982 autobiography *A Margin of Hope*.

Hoxha, Enver (1908–1985). Albanian communist leader, first secretary of the Albanian Communist Party (1941–85). Hoxha was the longest-ruling communist leader of the 20th century. Educated in

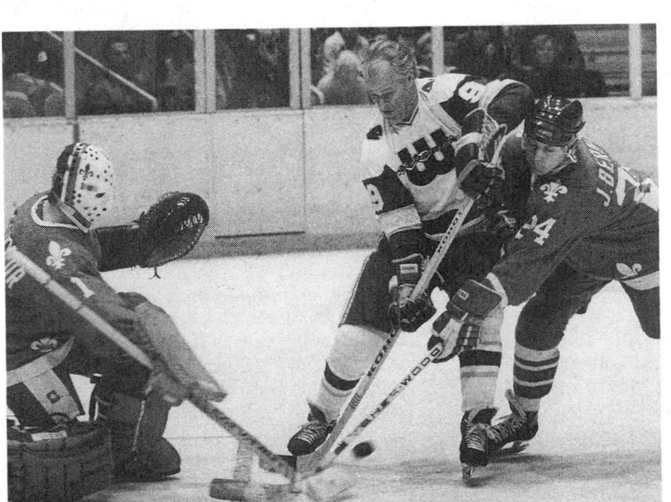

Gordie Howe (center), playing for the New England Whalers, attempts to score his 1,000th career goal.

France, he became a communist in the early 1930s. After his return to ALBANIA, he was a cofounder of the Albanian Communist Party and became its first secretary. During WORLD WAR II he was active in the RESISTANCE movement against the Italian occupation of Albania. With the establishment of a communist regime at the end of the war, he became Albania's premier and foreign minister. He held these posts until the early 1950s, when he resigned them to consolidate his power as party head. A strict Stalinist, Hoxha remained loyal to the U.S.S.R. until STALIN's death in 1953 (see STALINISM). He then severed diplomatic ties with Moscow and joined Peking in its ideological struggle against the Soviets. After the death of Chairman MAO TSE-TUNG he drifted away from China, though without severing diplomatic ties. He subsequently turned Albania into an even more isolated and secretive nation than it had been.

Hoyle, Sir Fred (1915–). British astronomer. Hoyle studied at Cambridge University, graduating in 1938. Hoyle lectured in mathematics at Cambridge from 1945 to 1958 when he became Plumian Professor of Astronomy. He also served as director of the Cambridge Institute of Theoretical Astronomy from 1967; he left Cambridge in 1973. He has held numerous research and visiting posts at such institutions as the California Institute of Technology, Cornell University, Manchester University and the Royal Institution in London. From 1954 to 1948 he was a staff member of the Mount Wilson and Palomar Observatories. He was one of the first to adopt the steady-state theory of Thomas Gold and Hermann BONDI and did much to introduce it to a wider audience in such works as *The Nature of the Universe* (1950); he was also one of the last to support the theory. He argued that violations found in the homogeneity of both space and time in the universe were more apparent than real, for they could be simply small-scale effects, whereas the steady-state theory was concerned with uniformities on the order of a billion light-years or more. Hoyle's contributions to cosmology and astrophysics have been numerous, deep and extensive. One of his main achievements was to show how elements heavier than hydrogen and helium could have been produced. With W.A. Fowler and Margaret and Geoffrey BURBIDGE, Hoyle gave in 1957 the first comprehensive account of how the elements are produced in the interior of stars.

A prolific writer on a wide variety of subjects, Hoyle has written a number of science fiction novels beginning with *The Black Cloud* (1957), has written on the history of a astronomy in *Copernicus* (1973), on archeo-astronomy in *From Stonehenge to Modern Cosmology* (1972), on the origin of disease in *Lifecloud* (1978) with Chandra Wickramnsinghe, and on questions of social policy in *Commonsense in Nuclear Energy* (1980). Such works are noted for their originality, rigor and a willingness to speculate and to argue in new and unexpected fields. He has also written a prodigious number of lectures, papers, textbooks and monographs, of which some of the most significant are his *Frontiers of Astronomy* (1955), *Astronomy and Cosmology* (1975) and, with J.V. Narlikar, various papers on gravity.

Hua Guofeng (1920–). Chinese political leader. A communist functionary and political disciple of MAO TSE-TUNG, he was minister of public security and deputy premier until the death of CHOU EN-LAI, becoming premier in 1976. When Mao died later that year, Hua also became the Communist Party chairman and head of the Military Affairs Commission. Responsible for the arrest of CHIANG CH'ING and the GANG OF FOUR, he was nonetheless criticized for his own political errors and personal cult of personality. In conflict with Deputy Premier DENG XIAOPING, he gradually lost leadership and power. In 1980 he was ousted as premier, the following year he lost the post of party chairman, and the year after that he was stripped of his seat on the politburo.

Huai-Hai, Battle of. Important engagement from November 1948 to January 1949, at the end of the CHINESE CIVIL WAR OF 1945–49. The battle is named for the two main defensive positions held by the Nationalists, the Huai River and the Lung Hai railway. The defeat of the Nationalist armies by overwelming communist forces led to the fall of Suchow on December 1. Destroying massive amounts of Nationalist supplies and severely undermining Nationalist morale, this battle opened the invasion route to Nanking and Shanghai, which were conquered by communist forces in the spring of 1949 and helped to seal the communist victory in the war.

Huang, Kechang (1903–1986). Chinese communist military officer. A survivor of the LONG MARCH of 1934–35, Huang was made chief of staff of CHINA's People's Liberation Army in 1958, although he was demoted the following year in a political struggle. In 1967 during the CULTURAL REVOLUTION, he was denounced as a rightist and remained in hiding for a decade.

Huang Ho River [Hwang Ho River; Yellow River]. Almost 3,000 miles long and of immense historical importance, this river rises in China's Tsinghai province and flows eastward through Kansu and Inner Mongolia, then south along the northern border of Honan. Its lower course has changed many times over the centuries and is vital to the farmlands of the Great Plains. In 1938 the Chinese diverted its course southward to deter Japanese invasion during the second SINO-JAPANESE WAR—a shift that cost nearly a million lives and was not rectified until 1947. Its perennial floods have earned it a reputation as "China's Sorrow."

Huascaran. Site of one of the worst natural disasters of this century. This mountain in the Ancash department of western Peru is the highest in the country and one of the highest in the Andes. In 1962 an avalanche rolled down its slope, burying the village of Ranrahirca, situated at its foot. But the worst was yet to come: In 1970 earthquakes destroyed 10 villages.

Hubbard, L. Ron (1911–1986). American writer. Hubbard's best-selling 1950 book, *Dianetics: The Modern Science of Mental Health,* became the basis for the Church of **Scientology,** founded by Hubbard in 1954. The church was based on a form of psychotherapy called "auditing" and not on the worship of a god. Hubbard lived on a huge yacht from 1968 to 1975, avoiding various law enforcement officials who had accused him of fraud and other crimes. In 1975 his church was the target of investigations by both the Internal Revenue Service and the Federal Bureau of Investigation.

Hubbell, Carl (Owen) (1903–1988). American baseball player. A star pitcher famed for his screwball, Hubbell won 253 games for the New York Giants between 1928 and 1943. He hurled five consecutive 20–win seasons and led the New York Giants to the World Series three times. Hubbell was named the National League's most valuable player in 1933 and 1936 and was an eight-time all-star. In a legendary feat in the second All-Star Game (1934), he struck out in succession five of the game's greatest hitters: Babe RUTH, Lou GEHRIG, Jimmie FOXX, Al Simmons and Joe CRONIN. He was elected to the Baseball Hall of Fame in 1947.

Hubble, Edwin Powell (1889–1953). American astronomer and cosmologist. Hubble was educated at the University of Chicago where he was influenced by astronomer George Hale. A good athlete, he was offered the role of Great White Hope in a match against black heavyweight champion Jack JOHNSON. Instead, he accepted a Rhodes scholarship to Oxford where, between 1910 and 1913, he studied jurisprudence, represented Oxford in athletics and fought French boxer Georges Carpentier. He practiced law briefly in America, but in 1914 returned to the study of astronomy at the Yerkes Observatory of the University of Chicago; he earned his Ph.D. in 1917. After being wounded in France in World War I he took up an appointment in 1919 at the Mount Wilson Observatory in California, where Hale was director and where he spent the rest of his career.

Hubble's early work involved studies of faint nebulae, which in the telescopes of the day appeared as fuzzy, extended images. After the powerful 100–inch telescope went into operation at Mount Wilson, he produced some of the most dramatic and significant astronomy of the 20th century. In 1923 he succeeded in resolving the outer region of the Andromeda nebula into "dense swarms of images which in no way differ from those of ordinary stars." Several of them were cepheids, which allowed him to determine their distance as the unexpectedly large 900,000 light-years. Between 1925 and 1929 he published three major papers showing that the spiral nebulae were at enormous distances, well outside our own galaxy, and were in fact isolated systems of stars, now called spiral galaxies.

In 1929 Hubble made his most significant discovery, announcing what came to be known as **Hubble's Law**. Using his own determination of the distances of 18 galaxies and the measurements of radial velocities from galactic red shifts carried out by Vesto Slipher and Milton Humason, he saw that the recessional velocity of the galaxies increased proportionately with their distance from us. It was this work that demonstrated to astronomers that the idea of an expanding universe, proposed earlier in the 1920s by Alexander FRIEDMANN and Georges LEMAITRE, was indeed correct. The expansion of the universe is now fundamental to every cosmological model. Hubble's Law was soon seen as containing the key to the size, age and future of the universe. Hubble also made a major contribution to the study of galactic evolution by producing the first significant classification of galaxies, a scheme that is still used as the basis for galactic classification.

Hubble space telescope. Astronomical instrument designed and constructed in the 1980s to orbit the Earth and, with its 94.5-inch mirror, to peer deeper into space and with a clarity 10 times greater than ever achieved by an Earth-based telescope. Launched by the space shuttle *Discovery* and deployed into an orbit 381 miles above Earth in 1990, the Hubble at first experienced problems with its antennas. After this was solved, the telescope began to send its first images back to Earth—pictures that were blurred due to an improper curvature in Hubble's primary mirror. Images from Hubble were still clearer than those from Earth-based astronomy but were only one-third as sharply focused as had been intended. The unexpected defect dashed hopes that Hubble might soon search for BLACK HOLES, distant quasars and possibly begin a calculation of the size of the universe, one of the telescope's chief objectives. In the early 1990s scientists were using computers in an attempt to improve the resolution of Hubble's images. However, it was thought that only hands-on intervention by a future space mission could introduce a lens alteration that would completely correct Hubble's visual imagery. Hubble's troubles caused critics to fault the management of the project by the NATIONAL AERONAUTICS AND SPACE ADMINISTRATION.

HUD scandal. Scandal involving loans made by the federal Housing and Urban Development (HUD) agency in the 1980s during the administration of President Ronald Reagan. One mission of HUD was to encourage the creation of low- and middle-income housing through the provision of subsidized loans to private developers. During the Reagan administration, HUD, under the lax stewardship of Samuel K. Pierce, used these monies as a political slush fund to reward major contributors to the Republican Party. Investigations revealed the misuse of these funds and also exposed extensive ineptitude and fraud in connection with several HUD programs. The investigations led to a number of criminal convictions, and Pierce resigned under a cloud of suspicion about his own complicity in the wrongdoing.

Hudson, H. Claude (1886–1989). Black American leader who helped found the NATIONAL ASSOCIATION FOR THE ADVANCEMENT OF COLORED PEOPLE (NAACP). Born to a family of former slaves in rural Louisiana, Hudson later went on to become the first black student to receive a law degree from Loyola University. He moved to Los Angeles in 1923 and eventually became one of the city's most respected black leaders.

Hudson, Rock [Roy Scherer Jr.] (1925–1985). American actor. Hudson's rugged good looks led him to superstardom under the old HOLLYWOOD studio system. He was twice voted the top box-office draw in the United States. His best known films were *Giant* (1956), for which he received his sole ACADEMY AWARD nomination, and *Pillow Talk* (1959), one of three romantic comedies in which he starred with Doris Day. In the 1970s, he became one of the first movie stars to make a successful transition to television when his series "MacMillan and Wife" ran for six seasons. His disclosure that he had been diagnosed as having AIDS helped to build worldwide awareness and increased public support to fight the disease.

Hudson, William H(enry) (1841–1922). Argentine-born English writer. Hudson was born into a family of Americans (of British descent) who had immigrated to Argentina to start a ranch. His early, active years in the Argentine countryside were to leave a lasting influence on Hudson, who at age 15 contracted rheumatic fever and was thereby compelled to adapt to the more secluded life of a writer. He moved to London in 1874 and lived in poverty for more than two decades until his writings—natural history essays, memoirs and fiction—began to win him first a critical and then a popular following. His best books include the story collection *The Purple Land* (1885), the novels *Green Mansions* (1904) and *A Shepherd's Life* (1910) and the nature study *Adventures Among Birds* (1913).

Hue. Ancient capital of the Annamese kings of INDOCHINA. This agricultural city, near the mouth of the Hue River in central Vietnam, was badly damaged during the FRENCH INDOCHINA WAR OF 1946–54, and was again a scene of heavy fighting in 1968, during the TET OFFENSIVE of the VIETNAM WAR, when most of the city, including the palaces and tombs of the old kings, was destroyed.

Huebner, Clarence R. (1888–1972). American army officer. Huebner commanded the famous U.S. 1st Division in campaigns in Sicily, France and Germany in WORLD WAR II. He served as commanding general of U.S. Army forces in Europe from 1947 to 1950, when he retired with the rank of lieutenant general.

Hufnagel, Charles Anthony (1916–1989). Heart surgeon. Hufnagel developed and implanted the first artificial human heart valve in 1952. He also participated in the first human kidney transplant operation (1947) and made a major contribution to the development of the heart and lung machine. In 1974, he was part of a three-doctor team that evaluated the health of President Richard M. NIXON (who was suffering from complications from an operation to treat his chronic phlebitis) and concluded that Nixon was too ill to testify at the WATERGATE conspiracy trial. Ironically, Hufnagel died of heart, lung, and kidney disease.

Hughes, Charles Evans (1862–1948). American statesman, presidential candidate, associate justice, U.S. Supreme Court (1910–16), chief justice (1930–41). A graduate of Brown University and Columbia University Law School, Hughes spent several years in private practice and later was special council to a state commission investigating business fraud. His success in this role led to his election as governor of his native New York (1907–10). A Republican, he was appointed to the U.S. Supreme Court in 1910 by President William Howard TAFT. However, he resigned in 1916 to run for president against Woodrow WILSON, who defeated him. Hughes served as secretary of state (1921–25) in the HARDING and COOLIDGE administrations. When Hughes was nominated for chief justice by President Herbert HOOVER, the nomination was opposed because of Hughes' past representation of big businesses. Despite his pro-business leanings, Hughes voted in favor of much of the NEW DEAL legislation. He retired in 1941 after serving as chief justice for 11 years.

For further reading:
Perkins, Dexter, *Charles Evans Hughes & American Democratic Statesmanship.* Westport, Conn.: Greenwood, 1978.

Hughes, Howard Robard (1869–1924). American inventor and industrialist. After working in the oil drilling business, Hughes invented a revolutionary cone-shaped drill bit (1908). He later founded the successful Hughes Tool Company, which manufactured his bits and other tools. He was the father of multi-millionaire aircraft pioneer Howard HUGHES.

Hughes, Howard Robard (1905–1976). American industrialist, aviator and film producer. Hughes studied at Rice Institute of Technology and California Institute of Technology, and inherited the family fortune at his father's death in 1925. He went to California to produce motion pictures. His *Two Arabian Knights* won an ACADEMY AWARD in 1928. He brought to fame stars like Jean HARLOW, Paul MUNI and Jane Russell. He founded Hughes Aircraft Company in 1933. In one of his personally designed planes he set a world speed record in 1935, flying at 352 miles per hour. In 1938 he completed a flight around the world in record time. Later he designed the world's largest airplane, which made only one short flight (1947), with Hughes at the controls. He also acquired controlling interest in Trans World Airlines (1959), and purchased major stock interest in Northeast Airlines.

After piloting his B-23 airplane from the West Coast, Howard Hughes arrives in Washington to attend a second round of Senate hearings on his wartime airplane contracts.

He bought enormous tracts of land in and around Las Vegas in the late 1960s, and was instrumental in development of that resort community.

Becoming a recluse in later life, he moved to Nicaragua and England and was widely followed by the media as one of the world's wealthiest and most mysterious figures. He was being flown from Mexico to Houston for medical treatment in early April 1976, when he died en route of liver failure.

For further reading:

Barlett, Donald L., *Empire: The Life, Legend and Madness of Howard Hughes*. New York: W.W. Norton, 1981.

Drosnin, Michael, *Citizen Hughes*. New York: Bantam, 1985.

Hughes, Langston (1902–1967). American author. Hughes dropped out of Columbia University and was traveling in Europe when his verse was discovered by Vachel LINDSAY in 1925. Subsequent praise for his work enabled him to graduate from Lincoln University in Pennsylvania in 1929, and he worked in New York City as a prominent member of the Harlem literary revival. His free-verse poetry is especially noted for its colloquial rhythms, as in "The Negro Speaks of Rivers" (1926) and "Weary Blues" (1926). His writings include novels and autobiographical works.

For further reading:

Mikolyzk, Thomas A., editor, *Langston Hughes: A Bio-Bibliography*. Westport: Greenwood Publishing Group, 1990.

Hughes, Richard (1906–1984). Australian foreign correspondent, historian and Far East expert. Based in Hong Kong, he covered the area for the London *Sunday Times* and wrote articles for *The Economist*, the *Sun* and *Herald* of Melbourne and the *New York Times*. He was one of two journalists permitted to interview British turncoat spies Donald MacLean and Guy BURGESS when they surfaced in Moscow in 1956. Hughes was a model for characters in spy novels by Ian FLEMING and John LE CARRE.

Hughes, Richard (Arthur Warren) (1900–1976). British author, poet and playwright. After a youth spent traveling and sometimes begging or performing for his keep, Hughes established his reputation with his first novel *The Innocent Voyage* (1929, published in Great Britain as *A High Wind in Jamaica*), which was adapted as a play in 1943 and a film in 1965. This, novel and his second, *In Hazard* (1938, published in Great Britain as *In Hazard: A Sea Story*) was a popular work. Critics consider *Human Predicament* a series that consists of *The Fox in the Attic* (1961) and *The Wooden Shepherdess* (1973), his most important work. Volume three was unfinished at Hughes' death. His other works include the poetry *Lines Written Upon First Observing an Elephant Devoured by a Roc* (1922), *Confessio Juvenis: Collected Poems* (1926), and the plays collected in *The Sisters' Tragedy and Other Plays* (1924, reprinted as *Plays*, 1966).

Hughes, Ted (1930–). English poet. Born and raised in Yorkshire, Hughes is perhaps the most prominent poet to have emerged in postwar England. He was named Poet Laureate in 1984, succeeding John BETJEMAN. Educated at Cambridge University, Hughes was married from 1956 to 1963 to poet Sylvia PLATH. Hughes' free verse style is marked by a taut, energetic use of language. He frequently employs violent imagery drawn from the struggle for survival in nature. His major volumes of poems include *The Hawk and the Rain* (1957), *Crow* (1970), *Gaudete* (1977) and *New and Selected Poems* (1982). Hughes has also written numerous children's stories and has translated a number of East European poets.

Langston Hughes, American author and poet, testifying before a Senate committee on March 26, 1953.

Hughes, William Morris (1864–1952). Prime minister of AUSTRALIA (1917–23). Born in London, Hughes immigrated to Australia in 1884. He founded the Waterside Workers' Federation in Sydney in 1893. In 1894 he was elected to the New South Wales parliament as a Labour MP and transferred to the first federal parliament in 1901. Hughes held office in the Labour government of 1904, was named attorney-general in 1910, and became prime minister in 1915. He left the LABOUR PARTY in 1917 after his military conscription proposals were rejected, but he continued to lead a National Coalition until 1923. Hughes was instrumental in establishing the United Australia Party in 1931. He subsequently served as minister for external affairs (1937–39), attorney-general (1939–41), and minister for the navy (1940–41). Hughes was an intelligent and gifted orator who often aroused controversy as prime minister with his opinionated and emotional stance. During WORLD WAR I, he was regarded as a strong wartime leader, but at the PARIS PEACE CONFERENCE in 1919 he offended many, particularly the Japanese, with his imperialistic attitudes.

Huie, William Bradford (1910–1986). American author and activist. An Alabama journalist and CIVIL RIGHTS crusader, Huie wrote more than 20 books, including the novel *The Revolt of Mamie Stover* and *The Americanization of Emily* (filmed, 1964). He was also the author of *He Slew the Dragon*, a controversial biography of Dr. Martin Luther KING Jr.'s convicted assassin, James Earl Ray, and *The Execution of Private Slovik*, about Eddie SLOVIK, the only U.S. serviceman put to death for desertion in the 20th century. During the 1960s Huie emerged as the arch-opponent of the segregationist policies of Alabama Governor George C. WALLACE. Huie was often a target of harassment, including cross-burnings.

Hull, Cordell (1871–1955). American statesman. Born near Byrdstown, Tennessee, Hull became a lawyer and Democratic member of the state legislature before his election to the House of Representatives, where he served from 1907 to 1921 and 1923 to 1931. A supporter and confidant of President Franklin D. ROOSEVELT, Hull resigned from Congress in 1933 to become Secretary of State, an office he held until 1944. He was particularly interested in international trade as a method of fostering worldwide accord, instituting the Reciprocal Trade Agreements of 1934 and the "good neighbor policy" toward Latin America. As WORLD WAR II broke out in Europe, Hull urged economic aid for the Allies. After the U.S. entered the war, he fostered coordination among the Allied powers, traveling to Moscow in 1943 to press for greater co-operation. An internationalist in the Woodrow WILSON mode, Hull was convinced that a new world peace-keeping organization was absolutely essential to the creation of a lasting peace. As a delegate to the 1945 San Francisco Conference, Hull was a prime architect of the UNITED NATIONS, a role that brought him the NOBEL PRIZE for peace later that year.

Hull, Field Marshal Sir Richard Amyatt (1907–1989). British army officer who succeeded Lord MOUNTBATTEN to become Britain's second chief of defense staff (1965–67). Hull helped determine the size and shape of Britain's post-World-War-II army and played a key role in setting British policy on the size of naval aircraft carriers in the mid-1960s.

Hull, Robert Marvin "Bobby" (1939–). Canadian hockey player. A left wing with the Chicago Black Hawks, Hull was the dominant scorer of the 1960s, leading the National Hockey League in goal-scoring seven times and points three times. His slapshot terrorized goaltenders, but his gentlemanly play won him the Lady Byng Trophy for good sportsmanship in 1966. A member of only one Stanley Cup winner, he lent instant credibility to the fledgling World Hockey Association by being the first name player to "jump" in 1972, signing with the Winnipeg Jets. When that league folded in 1979, he finished his career with the NHL Jets and Hartford Whalers, retiring in 1980. He was named to the Hockey Hall of Fame in 1983.

Hulme, T(homas) E(dward) (1883–1917). British literary critic and poet. Although he wrote relatively little and died tragically young, Hulme exercised a major influence on literary MODERNISM. Both his critical essays and his poems were greatly admired by T.S. ELIOT and Ezra POUND, among other notables. Hulme was a literary critic with a philosophical bent and austere, classical standards of aesthetics. He argued against the rhetorical excesses of Romanticism and favored a spare style in both prose and poetry. Hulme's admiration of what he termed hard, dry imagery influenced the poetic school of IMAGISM. Five brief poems by Hulme were published in 1912 in the literary journal *The New Age* under the ironic title *The Complete Poetical Works of T.E. Hulme.* Hulme was killed in WORLD WAR I. His major essays, edited by Herbert Read, were collected in two volumes, *Speculations: Essays on Humanism and the Philosophy of Art* (1924) and *Notes on Language and Style* (1929).

human engineering. One of several terms that describe the relationship of human users to mechanical and other industrial products. The fields of anthropometrics and ERGONOMICS, which emerged after World War II, overlap the concerns of human engineering, with the latter term increasingly used to describe all such studies.

Hume, George Basil. Roman Catholic Cardinal. Hume, a prominent Catholic religious leader in modern day Britain, first undertook monastic studies in 1941 at the Benedictine Abbey of St. Laurence. He joined the Benedictine Order in 1945 and was ordained as a priest in 1950. From 1963 to 1976 Hume served as abbot of Ampleforth before being elevated in 1976 as the archbishop of Westminster. He was also made cardinal in 1976 with St. Silvestro in Capite, Italy, as his titular church. Hume holds a curial membership on the Council on Christian Unity.

Humphrey, Hubert Horatio, Jr. (1911–1978). U.S. senator, vice president of the United States (1965–69). Humphrey graduated from the University of Minnesota in 1939, earned an M.A. from Louisiana University in 1940, and worked on a number of jobs, before he became state campaign director for Franklin D. ROOSEVELT's 1944 presidential campaign. In 1945 he was elected mayor of Minneapolis, then served as a U.S. senator from 1948 to 1964 and again from 1971 to 1978. A progressive Democrat, he became assistant majority leader of the Senate in 1961, and was instrumental in passing the historic CIVIL RIGHTS ACT OF 1964. In 1964 he was Lyndon B. JOHNSON's vice presidential running mate, then served as vice president from 1965 to 1969.

After Johnson declared his intention not to seek reelection in 1968, Humphrey announced his candidacy. He won the Democratic presidential nomination in 1968 in a race marred by violent protests against the VIETNAM WAR and the political establishment, and by the assassination of rival candidate Robert F. KENNEDY. He narrowly lost the election to Richard M. NIXON but continued to remain active in political life, later winning reelection to the Senate. Humphrey received numerous awards during his life. His protege, Walter MONDALE, served as vice president under President Jimmy CARTER and was the Democratic presidential candidate in 1984.

Senator Hubert H. Humphrey.

Hundred Days. The "Hundred Days" is a term used to denote the 1933 special session of Congress in which much of President Franklin D. ROOSEVELT'S NEW DEAL legislation was passed. When Roosevelt was inaugurated in March 1933 the U.S. economy had effectively ceased functioning and the country (with much of the world) was in the throes of the GREAT DEPRESSION. Roosevelt boldly called Congress into a special session that produced sweeping economic and social legislation, to aid victims of the Depression, and installed economic reforms. Roosevelt's unofficial advisers—his BRAIN TRUST—developed many of these programs. Banks were closed for a "bank holiday" and only solvent institutions were permitted to reopen, which rebuilt confidence in the nation's banking system. Congress also passed the Securities Act of 1933, regulating the issue of corporate stock; the NATIONAL INDUSTRIAL RECOVERY ACT (which established the NRA, the NATIONAL RECOVERY ADMINISTRATION), regulating business, including minimum wages and maximum hours; the CIVILIAN CONSERVATION CORPS (CCC), which put the unemployed to work in conservation projects; and the AGRICULTURAL ADJUSTMENT ADMINISTRATION (AAA) to aid farmers. In 1935 Congress approved another notable group of laws, including the WORKS PROGRESS ADMINISTRATION (WPA, later renamed the Work Projects Administration), the NATIONAL LABOR RELATIONS ACT and the SOCIAL SECURITY ACT. The 1935 session is known as the "Second Hundred Days."

Hung, Rham [born Pham Van Thien] (1913–1988). Vietnamese Communist political figure, premier of VIETNAM from June 1987 until his death. Hung had served for seven years as interior minister, supervising Vietnam's huge internal security system. He played key roles from 1960 to 1975 in the war against the U.S.-backed government of South Vietnam.

Hungarian Civil War of 1921. Former Austro-Hungarian Emperor CHARLES I, exiled in Switzerland since 1919, returned to regain his throne, calling on regent Nicholas HORTHY DE NAGYBANYA to step down in March 1921, but opposition to Charles was violent and he departed. He returned in October at Odenburg, Hungary and marched with troops on Budapest. Government troops repulsed them and arrested Charles, who was exiled to Madeira while the Hungarian Diet nullified all Hapsburg claims to the Hungarian throne.

Hungarian Revolution of 1918. Defeats and food shortages during World War I led Hungarian leftists and nationalists to agitate for independence from Austrian (Hapsburg) rule. The Hungarian diet called its troops home, Count Michael Karolyi (1875–1955) headed a liberal national council and Hungarians demanded an end to the war. Emperor CHARLES I made Karolyi premier (October 31, 1918) and a radical-socialist coalition came to power.

But the ethnic nationalism of Slovaks, Serbs, and Romanians threatened the state and Karolyi accepted peace terms with France, withdrawing Hungarian troops; Serb troops occupied the south, Romanians moved into Transylvania, and Czechoslavakian soldiers into Slovakia. The Austro-Hungarian monarchy had collapsed, and on November 16, 1918 the national council declared HUNGARY a republic.

Hungarian Uprising. Unplanned revolt by the people of Hungary against Soviet control of their nation and against their own communist government; occurred from October 23 to November 4, 1956. Hungarian students, workers and others gathered in Budapest on October 23 to demonstrate, demanding economic reforms, free elections, the withdrawal of Soviet forces and the reinstatement of Imre NAGY, the anti-Soviet premier who had been forced from office the previous year. Violence erupted when police fired on the peaceful demonstrators. As the uprising spread throughout the country, the Soviets at first seemed to favor cooperation with a new regime and a new party administration. Nagy was recalled as premier on October 24 and soon proclaimed his nation's neutrality, an end to Hungary's participation in the WARSAW PACT, an end to its one-party state and the release of the imprisoned anticommunist Cardinal Jozsef MINDSZENTY. Janos KADAR became party secretary. Meanwhile, revolutionary councils formed throughout the country seized its political institutions and factories in the name of the new Hungary, and Soviet forces began to withdraw. The changes were too

HUNGARY

1914	As part of Austro-Hungarian empire, Hungary enters World War I on the side of Germany and the Central Powers.
1918	(Nov. 16) Hungary becomes an independent republic after end of World War I.
1919	Bela Kun's Red Terror.
1920	Adml. Miklos Horthy becomes regent and refuses to allow King Karl to return to Hungary.
1944	(March 19) Germans occupy Hungary and begin exterminating Hungary's Jews and Gypsies; (Dec. 21) Stalin authorizes the formation in Debrecen of a provisional government comprising all the non-fascist parties.
1945	(April 4) The last German forces leave Hungary.
1947	Hungary signs peace treaty with Allied powers, giving up all territories acquired after 1937.
1948	(June) The Social Democrats are forcibly merged with the communists to form the Hungarian Workers' Party.
1949	Opposition political parties are outlawed; Roman Catholic primate of Hungary, Cardinal Jozef Mindszenty, sentenced to life imprisonment.
1953	(July) Imre Nagy becomes premier and introduces liberal and political reform.
1956	(Nov. 2) Soviet army invades Hungary; Nagy is executed; Janos Kadar is made premier.
1967	Jeno Fock becomes premier.
1968	The regime initiates a series of reforms known as New Economic Mechanism, decentralizing authority.
1989	(January) Law passed allowing formation of new political parties; (June) body of Imre Nagy exhumed and reburied after a state funeral on the 31st anniversary of his execution.
1990	(Mar. 10) Soviets agree to complete pullout from Hungary.
1991	(Mar. 31) Military alliance of the Warsaw Pact ends.

Patrons and clerks watch as members of Hungarian revolutionary forces take aim against Soviet secret police in Budapest (Nov. 2, 1956).

HUNGARY

drastic for Kadar, who left Budapest to form a new government in eastern Hungary and for the Soviets who, having massed their tanks, returned to the capitol on November 4 and ruthlessly destroyed the revolution. While Nagy called in vain for United Nations support, Hungarians fought in the streets. Within weeks, many thousands were killed, wounded or imprisoned, and some 200,000 Hungarians fled the country. Kadar took over and did institute some political and economic reforms, but Hungary's ties to the Soviet Union were not to be severed for over 30 more years.

For further reading:

Barber, Noel, *Seven Days of Freedom: The Hungarian Uprising, 1956*. Chelsea, Mi.: Scarborough House, 1974.

Laping, Francis, *Remember Hungary 1956: A Pictorial History of the Hungarian Revolution*. Medina, Ohio: Alpha Publications, 1975.

Hungary [Hungarian Republic]. A landlocked country in the Danube Basin of east-central Europe, Hungary today covers an area of 35,910 square miles. Once part of the Austro-Hungarian empire, it was reduced to its present size after the empire's defeat in WORLD WAR I. Plagued by economic woes and ethnic and class struggles, in 1920 Hungary was invaded by Romanian troops who overthrew a communist regime and placed in power Admiral Miklos HORTHY. He aligned the country with Nazi GERMANY, which occupied Hungary in 1944. After WORLD WAR II the communists gained control of the government, promoting industrialization and collectivization of agriculture. Poland's defiance of Soviet authority in 1956 led to huge demonstrations in Hungary demanding Soviet withdrawal. The Soviet army intervened, killing thousands of Hungarians and setting up a puppet government under Janos KADAR (see HUNGARIAN UPRISING). The previous reformist prime minister, Imre NAGY, was executed in 1958. Gradually the Kadar regime moved toward economic reforms and a loosening of repressive political controls, and by the 1970s Hungary was regarded as the most liberal country in the Eastern Bloc. Pro-democracy demonstrations in 1988–89 led to approval of the formation of a multiparty democratic system, and a transitional constitution was drafted. In Oct. 1989 Hungary was proclaimed a republic; Nagy was formally rehabilitated and his memory officially honored.

For further reading:

Hoensch, Jorg, *A History of Modern Hungary, 1867–1983*. White Plains, N.Y.: Longman, 1988.

Sugar, Peter F., ed., *A History of Hungary*. Bloomington: Indiana University Press, 1990.

Hunt brothers silver scandal. Commodities scandal in which the Hunt family of Texas attempted to manipulate the world's silver supply. The three wealthy Hunt brothers, Nelson, Herbert and Lamar, purchased silver commodities and made enormous profits as the price of silver skyrocketed. In March of 1980 the Hunts were either unwilling or unable to pay $100 million of margin calls from their commodity brokers, which caused panic selling in silver commodities. The price of silver dropped just as precipitously, from $52 to $10.50 an ounce, and the Hunts reportedly lost over $235 million. Although government investigations were conducted, no criminal charges were brought against the three brothers, who did, however, have to contend with lawsuits from a number of investors who claimed to have been harmed by their manipulations.

Hunter, Evan (1926–). American novelist and screenwriter. Hunter achieved success with his second novel *The Blackboard Jungle* (1954, filmed 1955), which reflected his experiences teaching at an inner-city vocational school in New York. His popular novels—among them *Mothers and Daughters (1961), Last Summer* (1968, filmed 1969), *Love, Dad* (1981) and *Lizzie* (1984)—often depict disenfranchised American youth. His screenplays include *Strangers When We Meet* (1960), based on his novel of the same name; *The Birds* (1963), based on a short story by Daphne DU MAURIER and directed by Alfred HITCHCOCK; and

The Chisholms (1980). Hunter has written a successful series of detective novels under the pseudonym Ed McBain and has also published under the names Hunt Collins and Richard Marsten.

Huntington, Anna Hyatt (1876–1973). American sculptor. Born in Cambridge, Massachusetts, Huntington studied at the Art Students League in New York City. Huntington is noted for her realistic studies of animals, such as the bronzes *Reaching Jaguar* (1926, Metropolitan Museum of Art) and *Fighting Elephants*. Among her public sculptures are an equestrian statue of Joan of Arc that stands on New York's Riverside Drive and a figure of El Cid, also in the city. Other large public pieces are located in Gloucester, Mass., Seville, Spain and Buenos Aires, Argentina.

Huntley, Chet (Chester Robert) (1911–1974). American news commentator. Known for his serious, straightforward demeanor, Huntley worked as a newsman for CBS and ABC, but it was for his stint with NBC from 1955 to 1970 that he is best remembered. During this time he co-anchored the **"Huntley-Brinkley Report,"** an evening news program, with David BRINKLEY. Huntley was later the anchor for syndicated news commentaries for Horizon Communications (1970–74). At its peak, the "Huntley-Brinkley Report" reached an audience of over 17,000,000 viewers.

Hurley, Patrick J. (1883–1963). American lawyer and diplomat. Hurley served as secretary of war under President Herbert HOOVER from 1929 to 1933. In a distinguished career as a diplomat, Hurley was the personal representative of the United States to the Soviet Union in November-December 1942 and to Egypt, Syria, Lebanon, Iraq, Iran, Palestine, Saudi Arabia, India, China and Trans-Jordan in 1943. He was the American ambassador to China in 1944. Among his many civic contributions, Hurley assisted in organizing the U.S. Chamber of Commerce in 1912. He negotiated an agreement between Mexico and five expropriated oil companies in 1940 and was the Republican candidate for U.S. senator from New Mexico in 1946 and 1948.

Hurley, Ruby (1909–1980). Black American civil rights activist. During the 1950s and 1960s, as an official of the NAACP, Hurley helped lead the CIVIL RIGHTS MOVEMENT in the American South. Known to her associates as "the queen of civil rights," she played a leading part in investigations of racial violence and in the legal struggles of black students who sought to enter previously all-white Southern universities.

Hurok, Sol (Solomon) (1888–1974). American impresario and theatrical manager. Born in Russia, he immigrated to the U.S. in 1906. He worked at a number of menial jobs before arranging concerts for various labor groups, his first attempts (1911) at putting together performances. During his career, Hurok presented thousands of artists and companies in performances and tours. Among the artists whose work he sponsored were the dancers Anna PAVLOVA and Isadora DUNCAN, singers Jan PEERCE and Marian ANDERSON, musicians Artur RUBINSTEIN, Andres SEGOVIA, Benny GOODMAN and Van CLIBURN, and such companies as the Comedie Francaise, the Old Vic, the Royal Ballet and the Bolshoi Ballet. His 1946 autobiography is titled *Impresario*.

Hurst, Fannie (1889–1968). American novelist. Born in Hamilton, Ohio, she graduated from Washington University in 1909. She is known for her popular sentimental tales, often of women in distress over romance or marriage. Her novels include *Stardust* (1919), *Lummox* (1923), *Back Street* (1931), *Imitation of Life* (1932) and *Anitra's Dance* (1934). Hurst was also the author of theater treatments and screenplays.

Hurston, Zora Neale (1901–1960). American author. Hurston began publishing short stories and essays while studying anthropology at Barnard College, in 1928 becoming that school's first black graduate. She then researched folk traditions and published ethnographic studies that include *Mules and Man* (1935) and *Tell My Horse* (1938). Winner of Rosenwald (1934) and Guggenheim (1936–37) fellowships, she became the most prolific black writer of the 1930s. Her novels include *Jonah's Gourd Vine* (1937) and *Seraph and the Suwanee* (1948).

For further reading:
Newson, Adele S., *Zora Neale Hurston: A Reference Guide*. Boston: G.K. Hall, 1987.

Husak, Gustav (1913–). President of CZECHOSLOVAKIA (1975–89). A leader of the 1944 Slovak uprising against the Nazis, after the war Husak held party and government posts until purged by STALIN. He was rehabilitated after a decade in prison; following the SOVIET INVASION OF CZECHOSLOVAKIA in 1968, he replaced the liberal Alexander DUBCEK as party secretary. A hardliner, he was made president of the country in 1975, holding the post until 1989, when he was succeeded by Vaclav HAVEL, the first noncommunist president of Czechoslovakia in four decades. In 1990, Husak was expelled from the Communist Party.

Hussein (1935–). King of JORDAN (1952–). Educated at the Sandhurst military academy in Britain, Hussein succeeded his father, who had been forced to abdicate because of his mental illness. A moderate, pro-Western Arab with close personal ties to Britain and the U.S., he took steps to modernize his country. Although unsympathetic to the left-wing Arab nationalism of Egyptian President NASSER, he allied Jordan with EGYPT and attacked ISRAEL in the SIX-DAY WAR (1967). Badly defeated, Jordan lost the WEST BANK and Jerusalem to Israel. The country became a haven for Palestinian refugees, and the PALESTINE LIBERATION ORGANIZATION (PLO) used Jordan as a base from which they launched guerrilla attacks on Israel without Hussein's approval. Hussein's attempts to control the guerrillas led to the JORDANIAN CIVIL WAR OF 1970–71; nevertheless, he was able to expel the PLO. He refused to endorse the **Camp David accords** (see CAMP DAVID TALKS), but sought to use his influence with the PLO and other Arab nations to work toward a peaceful solution of the Arab-Israeli conflict. King Hussein supported IRAQ during the PERSIAN GULF WAR (1990–91).

Hussein, Saddam (1937–). President of IRAQ (1979–). A Sunni Moslem, Saddam Hussein joined the BA'ATH Party in 1957. He was involved in the 1959 attempt on the life of Iraqi leader Abd al-Karim KASSEM. Sentenced to death, he escaped to Egypt, returning in 1964 to organize the civilian wing of the Ba'ath. He rose to become deputy secretary-general of the party in 1966 and vice-chairman of the Revolutionary Command Council in 1969. As president of Iraq, Hussein has fol-

King Hussein (left) meeting with PLO chairman Yasir Arafat in Amman, Jordan (Jan. 19, 1991).

Saddam Hussein, Iraqi dictator.

lowed an aggressive, militaristic policy aimed at making Iraq—and himself—the strongest power in the Arab world. A territorial dispute with neighboring IRAN led to Hussein's invasion of Iran and the subsequent bloody 8-year IRAN-IRAQ WAR, which ended in a stalemate. In this conflict, Hussein used poison gas on the Iranians and also against the Kurds of his own country. On August 2, 1990, Hussein launched a surprise invasion of KUWAIT, bringing that country under his control in a matter of days (see PERSIAN GULF WAR). Hussein was condemned by the UNITED NATIONS, and a multinational coalition of Arab and Western nations, led by the U.S. under President BUSH, sent forces to prevent an Iraqi invasion of SAUDI ARABIA. Comparing the Iraqi dictator to Adolf HITLER, Bush repeatedly called on Hussein to withdraw from Kuwait; despite a further buildup of U.S. and Allied forces and a U.N. deadline for withdrawal (Jan. 15, 1991), Hussein refused. On Jan. 16, the Allies launched a bombing campaign against military targets (**Operation Desert Storm**). Hussein responded by launching Scud missile attacks on Saudi Arabia and ISRAEL, but to little avail. Suffering a swift and humiliating defeat after the coalition's ground invasion of Kuwait and Iraq in late February 1991, Hussein was forced to sue for peace. With his army effectively detroyed and much of Iraq in ruins, Hussein's future was uncertain. Various Iraqi groups—disaffected soldiers, Shiite Muslims and Kurds—openly rebelled against Hussein, though as of mid-March 1991 he remained in power in Iraq. The name *Saddam* literally means "one who confronts."

For further reading:

Miller, Judith and Laurie Mylrole, *Saddam Hussein and the Crisis in the Gulf*. New York: Times Books, 1990.

Hussein bin Dato Onn (1922–1990). Malaysian politician, Prime Minister of MALAYSIA (1976–81). The country's third prime minister since independence, Hussein had replaced his brother-in-law, Abdul Razak, following Razak's death in 1976. He resigned in 1981 and selected Mahathir Mohamad to succeed him. The two men broke with each other in 1988 over Mahathir's attempt to purge his opponents in the ruling United Malays National Organization.

Husserl, Edmund (1859–1938). German philosopher. Husserl is regarded as the founder of the highly influential 20th-century philosophical school of PHENOMENOLOGY. Basically, phenomenology acknowledges that human thought is capable only of subjective, experiential analyses of reality—but it seeks to heighten the validity of such analyses by rigidly excluding personal value systems. Husserl, who taught philosophy at the Universities of Gottingen and Freiberg, wrote numerous books, including *Logical Investigations* (1900–1901), *Ideas* (1913), *The Phenomenology of Internal Time-Consciousness* (1928) and *Formal and Transcendental Logic* (1929). His writings greatly influenced Martin HEIDEGGER, Jean-Paul SARTRE and the development of EXISTENTIALISM.

Huston, John (1906–1987). American film director, writer and actor. The son of actor **Walter Huston**, John Huston's early years were full of restless travels and unfulfilled ambitions. He toured in vaudeville, rode in the Mexican cavalry, boxed, and studied painting in Paris. He collaborated on several successful screenplays before directing *The Maltese Falcon* (1941), one of the great directorial debuts in screen history. The film's cynical tone, claustrophobic interiors and ill-fated characters prefigured such later Huston classics as *The Treasure of the Sierra Madre* (1948, for which he won the best writer and best director ACADEMY AWARDS), *Key Largo* (1948), *The Asphalt Jungle* (1950), *The Misfits* (1960) and *Wise Blood* (1979). Humphrey BOGART was the quintessential antihero in several of Huston's early films, and won his only Academy Award in Huston's *The African Queen* (1951). Huston served in the Signal Corps during WORLD WAR II, producing two classic wartime documentaries—*The Battle of San Pietro* (1943), one of the screen's finest antiwar statements, and *Let There Be Light* (1946), which chronicled the effects of battle fatique on combat veterans, and which was suppressed by the government until 1980. Indeed, many of Huston's critical and box-office failures of the late 1950s and 1960s reveal inconsistencies of tone and technique. Yet he rebounded with a moving adventure film, *The Man Who Would Be King* (1975), adapted from a story by Rudyard KIPLING, and directed his daughter **Anjelica Huston** in an Academy-Award-winning performance in *Prizzi's Honor* (1985). He spent his last years in Mexico and Ireland but continued to work despite increasing ill-health, directing a faithful adaptation of James JOYCE's *The Dead* (1987) shortly before his own death.

For further reading:

John Huston: King Rebel. Los Angeles: Sherbourne Press, 1965.

Hutchins, Robert Maynard (1899–1977). American educator. Appointed president of the University of Chicago at age 29, Hutchins revolutionized American higher education with his belief that college students should be taught not vocational skills but to reason. Over the next five decades he frequently commented on educational and public policy issues. Leaving the university in 1951, he founded (1954) and headed the Center for the Study of Democratic Institutions, an organization studying social and political questions.

Hutton, Sir Leonard (1916–1990). English cricketer. In a playing career that lasted from 1934 to 1956 (with a six-year interruption for World War II), he scored a total of 40,000 runs, including 129 centuries. In 1938 he scored 364 runs against the Australian team—a record that stood for 20 years, In 1952, he was appointed the first professional captain of the English national team. The following year he led the team in regaining the Ashes trophy from AUSTRALIA for the first time since 1938, and retained it in 1954–55. Upon his retirement in 1956, he became a cricket commentator for the *Observer* and wrote three books about his experiences.

Hutton fraud case. Controversial cash management fraud case of 1985 that ended in the demise of the nation's fifth largest brokerage house. E.F. Hutton aggressively managed its cash by systematically writing checks larger than its account balances. This practice, which gave Hutton interest-free loans, is a crime called "check kiting." Additionally, Hutton deposited checks in more than one account to give the illusion of higher cash balances. As a result, various banks had losses totaling $10 billion. Although upper-level executives denied any involvement during a government investigation, the firm was eventually charged by the federal government with 2,000 counts of criminal mail and wire fraud. U.S. Attorney General Edwin Meese was criticized for declining to indict any individuals for the crimes. In 1985 the firm pleaded guilty and paid a $2 million fine. Later that year the SEC forced Hutton to reimburse $1 million in unpaid dividends to its customers. Hutton's venerable reputation was seriously eroded; despite a reorganization, the brokerage house continued its decline. In 1988 E.F. Hutton disappeared and was merged into Shearson Lehman.

Huxley, Aldous (1894–1963). British novelist, essayist and philosopher. Huxley was the descendant of an eminent British family that included the 19th-century Darwinian theorist Thomas Henry Huxley and the 20th-century biologist Julian Huxley. Huxley first gained literary renown for his witty, satiric novels of the 1920s, including *Crome Yellow* (1921), *Antic Hay* (1923), *Those Barren Leaves* (1925) and *Point Counter Point* (1928). During that decade he formed a close friendship with D.H. LAWRENCE with whom Huxley traveled in Italy and France. In 1932 Huxley published his most famous work,

BRAVE NEW WORLD, which marked his shift to a more somber, philosophical, novelistic style, further developed in *Eyeless in Gaza* (1936) and *After Many a Summer Dies the Swan* (1940). Huxley, who moved to the United States in 1938, assembled an anthology of worldwide mystical writings, *The Perennial Philosophy* (1945), and an influential study of consciousness expansion through mescalin, *The Doors of Perception* (1954). Huxley died in Los Angeles in 1963.

Huxley, Andrew Fielding (1917–). English physiologist. Huxley, a grandson of T.H. Huxley, graduated in 1938 from Cambridge University, receiving his M.A. there three years later. He is best known for his collaboration with Alan Hodgkin in elucidating the "sodium pump" mechanism by which nerve impulses are transmitted, for which they were awarded, with John Eccles, the NOBEL PRIZE for physiology or medicine (1963). He has also done important work on muscular contraction theory and has been involved in the development of the interference microscope and ultramicrotome. Huxley was reader in experimental biophysics at Cambridge (1959–60), and since 1960 has been Jodrell Professor of Physiology at University College, London. In 1980 he became president of the Royal Society.

Huxley, Sir Julian Sorell (1887–1975). English biologist. A grandson of noted Victorian biologist T.H. Huxley, and brother of novelist Aldous Huxley, Julian Huxley graduated in zoology from Oxford University in 1909. He did research on sponges at the Naples Zoological Station (1909–10) before taking up the post of lecturer in biology at Oxford (1910–12). From 1912 until 1916 he worked at the Rice Institute, Houston, Texas, where he met the famous American geneticist Hermann Muller. Before returning to Oxford to take up the post of senior demonstrator in zoology (1919–25) he saw war service in Italy. He was next appointed professor of zoology at King's College, London (1925–27), resigning from this post to devote more time to writing and research.

Huxley was a keen ornithologist. In the 1930s he was involved in the production of natural-history films, the most notable of which was the highly praised *Private Life of the Gannett* (1934). One of the leading popularizers of science of modern times (especially the years before and just after World War II), Huxley spent much of his life explaining advances in natural science to the layman and in advocating the application of science to the benefit of mankind. To many he is best remembered as a most capable and lucid educationalist, but Huxley was also eminent in many other fields.

In 1946 he was appointed the first director-general of UNESCO, a post he held for two years. As an adminsitrator, he also did much to transform the Zoological Society's collections at Regent's Park (London Zoo). Viewing man as "the sole agent of further evolutionary advance on this planet," he caused considerable controversy by advocating the deliberate physical and mental improvement of the human race through eugenics. Huxley's biological research was also extensive, including work on animal hormones, physiology, ecology, and animal (especially bird) behavior as it relates to evolution. He was president of the Institute of Animal Behavior and the originator of the term *ethology*, now used to define the science of animal behavior. He also introduced several other scientific terms, such as cline and clade. Huxley was knighted in 1958.

Hu Yaobang (1915–1989). Chinese political leader. He joined the Communist Party in 1933 and, following the communist revolution in 1949, held a series of party posts. Purged during the CULTURAL REVOLUTION of 1966, he was rehabilitated in 1973, became a member of the politburo in 1978 and was named to the chairmanship of the Communist Party in 1980. Widely regarded as a protege of DENG XIAOPING, Hu supported Deng's reform policies and was expected to succeed him. However, the student rebellions of 1986 forced his resignation early in 1987.

Hyde, Douglas (1860–1949). Irish playwright, author and first president of IRELAND (1938–45). A member of the Protestant Ascendancy, Hyde was a leading figure in the IRISH LITERARY REVIVAL, and committed to promoting the Irish language. He founded the Gaelic League in 1893 and was its president until 1915. His play *Casadh* (1901) was performed by the Irish Literary Theatre and was the first play in Irish professionally performed. Hyde served as vice president of the ABBEY THEATRE and often collaborated with Lady GREGORY and W.B. YEATS. Hyde's other works include *Love Songs of Connacht* (1893) and *A Literary History of Ireland* (1892). In recognition of his services to Irish language and culture, in 1938 he was elected Ireland's first president, a largely ceremonial but prestigious post.

hydrogen bomb. By far the most destructive weapon developed during the 20th century, the hydrogen bomb (H-bomb) can produce an explosion much more powerful than that of an ATOM BOMB. Whereas the atom bomb releases energy by fission, splitting the heavy uranium atom, the H-bomb produces its destructive force through the fusion of hydrogen atoms, the lightest atoms. Scientists recognized the theoretical possibility of hydrogen atom fusion as early as 1922. During WORLD WAR II, U.S. and Allied scientists concentrated on developing an atom bomb using uranium, which presented fewer technical problems (see MANHATTAN PROJECT). The Germans did preliminary work on a hydrogen bomb, attempting to produce the "heavy water" needed for the bomb in Norway. After the war ended, expert opinion in the West was split over the issue of whether to develop a hydrogen bomb. After the U.S.S.R. exploded its first atom bomb in 1949, President TRUMAN ordered work on the hydrogen bomb; the Soviets (whose research was led by physicist Andrei SAKHAROV) also raced to build a hydrogen bomb. The first H-bomb was tested by the U.S. on November 1, 1952, at the Pacific atoll of Eniwetok; it produced an explosion equal to 12 megatons (million tons) of TNT. The Soviets tested their bomb a few months later. Britain tested its first hydrogen bomb in 1957. American H-bomb tests during the 1950s at BIKINI

The mushroom cloud of a hydrogen bomb test dwarfs the warships surrounding it.

atoll and other sites proved the immense destructive force of the bomb.

During the 1950s, there was great fear throughout the world that there might be a Third World War between the U.S. and U.S.S.R., in which the use of H-bombs could cause destruction on an unprecedented scale. Radioactive fallout from H-bomb tests proved that the initial explosion wasn't the only danger of atomic warfare; the fallout from such a war could result in millions of other deaths over a long period of time. There were at least 500 H-bomb tests before the NUCLEAR TEST BAN TREATY of 1963 ended above-ground hydrogen bomb testing by the two superpowers and Britain. China and France, however, developed their own H-bombs in 1967 and 1968, respectively, and continued to test bombs above ground. Despite the nuclear non-proliferation treaty (effective in 1970) banning the development or acquisition of H-bombs by other nations, several other nations may possess the bomb or have the technology and materials necessary to build it. The apparent end of the COLD WAR and the easing of tensions between the U.S. and the U.S.S.R. has brought new hope that the H-bomb will never be used. However, there are fears that the bomb could fall into the hands of international terrorists.

Hyland, L(awrence) A. (Pat) (1897–1989). Pioneer in RADAR technology and aircraft communications equipment. As vice-president and chief executive of Hughes Aircraft Co. (1955–76), and president and chairman (1976–84) following the death of founder Howard HUGHES Hyland helped build the firm into the largest U.S. military electronics company and a leading builder of communications satillites.

Hynek, J(osef) Allen (1910–1986). U.S. astronomer. Hynek gained wide recognition during the more than two decades (1948–1969) he served as a consultant to a U.S. Air Force research project regarding unidentified flying objects. He came to believe that reports of UFO's were to be taken more seriously than the Air Force was willing to take them. In his 1972 book *The UFO Experience* Hynek coined the phrase, "close encounters of the third kind." He subsequently served as technical adviser on the 1977 Steven SPIELBERG film of the same name.

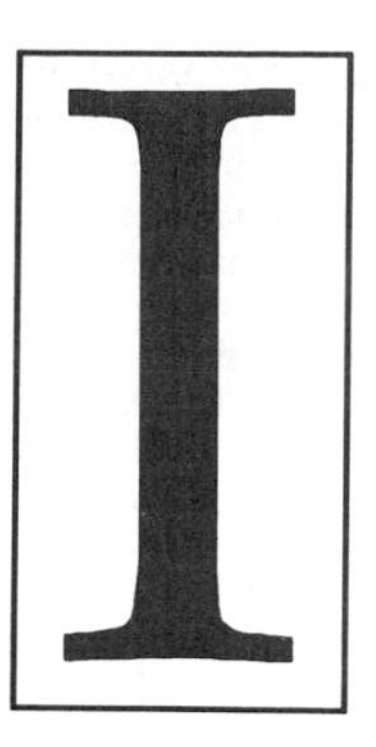

Iacocca, Lee [Lido Anthony Iacocca] (1924–). American automobile executive. An innovator in automotive engineering and marketing, Iacocca took over the financially distressed Chrysler Corporation in 1978 and was primarily responsible for transforming it into a profitable company by 1982. He began his career as a mechanical engineer, joined the Ford Motor Company and became a corporate vice president and general manager of the Ford division (1960) and president (1970). He introduced successful new models at Ford and introduced new fuel-efficient cars as head of Chrysler Corporation.

Ia Drang. Valley in northwestern South Vietnam, southwest of Pleiku, near the Cambodian border; site of the first major battle between the U.S.and North Vietnamese armies during the VIETNAM WAR. On November 14, 1965, 400 men of the U.S. First Batallion, Seventh Cavalry, were surprised in the Ia Drang Valley by more than 2,000 North Vietnamese troops. Although heavily outnumbered at first, the Americans were successfully reinforced, and the North Vietnamese disengaged, some retreating across the border into Cambodia and others fleeing into the jungle. On March 10, 1975, the North Vietnamese army launched their final offensive against South Vietnam from a few miles south of the Ia Drang Valley.

I Am a Camera. *I Am a Camera* is a title associated with Christopher ISHERWOOD and his famous fictional heroine, the cabaret performer Sally Bowles. In 1937 Isherwood published in the noted British literary journal *New Writing* a series of fictionalized character sketches based upon of his life in BERLIN in the early 1930s. These sketches, which were ultimately collected in *Goodbye to Berlin* (1939), included a piece on Sally Bowles, who makes a living as a cabaret artist by dint of her beauty and eccentric charm, even though she lacks any real theatrical talent. Sally and her Bohemian lifestyle were ultimately transposed by writer John VAN DRUTEN into a play, *I Am a Camera* (1951), which later formed the basis for the highly successful musical *Cabaret* (1968).

Iasi [Jassy, Yassy]. Moldavian capital city of Romania's Iasi district; during World War I, the temporary capital of ROMANIA. In WORLD WAR II, when Iasi was taken by Soviet forces in 1944, the city's large Jewish population was found to have been exterminated by the German occupiers.

Ibarruri, Dolores Gomez (1895–1989). Spanish Communist political figure and partisan known as "La Pasionaria." Ibarruri won fame with her impassioned oratory during the SPANISH CIVIL WAR (1936–39) in defense of the republican cause. She was one of the founders of the Spanish Communist Party in 1920. With the outbreak of the 1936 revolt by Fascist army commander General Francisco FRANCO and his troops, Ibarruri gave a renowned radio speech in which she told Spaniards, "It is better to die on your feet than to live on your knees! They shall not pass!" The last phrase, borrowed from the French slogan at VERDUN in WORLD WAR I, became the rallying cry of the republic. She left SPAIN in 1937 shortly before the republic fell to Franco, and fled to the U.S.S.R., where she lived until 1977. After Franco's death she returned to Spain and was elected to the Spanish parliament. At her death she was honorary president of the Spanish Communist Party.

Ibert, Jacques (1890–1962). French composer. He studied at the Paris Conservatory, where he was a student of Gabriel FAURE. He won the Prix de Rome in 1919, later returning to the Italian city as director of its French Academy from 1937 to 1955. Thereafter (1955–57), he directed the Paris Opera and the Opera Comique. Lively and melodic in the French tradition, his music proved to be quite popular with the public. His best known piece is probably *Escales* (*Ports of Call,* 1924), an orchestral suite that evoked his life while a French sailor in World War I. Other popular works are the orchestral *Divertissement* and the woodwind quintet *Trois pieces breves* (both 1930) and the concerto for saxophone (1935). Among his many other compositions are ballets, operas, songs, chamber music and symphonic poems.

IBM [International Business Machines]. Leading American international corporation. IBM was founded in 1914 when Thomas J. Watson Sr., a former executive of the National Cash Register Company, put together several small firms to create the Computing-Tabulating-Recording Company. The firm was a manufacturer of scales and time clocks, which gradually expanded into production of other types of business equipment. In 1924 the present name, International Business Machines Corp. (IBM), was adopted. Under Watson, IBM grew on the strength of an aggressive sales and service orientation. IBM's involvement with design began when Thomas J. Watson Jr. returned to the company in 1945 after service in World War II. He became president in 1952 and chief executive officer in 1956. Watson's acquaintance with architect and industrial designer Eliot Noyes led to his being given various design assignments and, eventually, general responsibility for all IBM design. Noyes was the designer of post-war IBM electric typewriters, including the 1961 Selectric model that became a virtual universal standard, while the punch card (now commonly known as an "IBM card") became a standard format for data storage and manipulation. As IBM entered into computer development (with the 1943 Harvard Mark I), the visual design of the enclosures and consoles gave IBM products an identity and air of quality that helped push the firm into a leadership role. Noyes' advice and influence brought about an extraordinary level of design quality in all IBM products. Marcel BREUER, Ludwig MIES VAN DER ROHE, Edward Larrabee Barnes, and Eero SAARINEN are among the architects who have designed for IBM. Charles EAMES was the designer of a number of IBM exhibits and produced a variety of educational films that aided understanding of the complex theories behind the function of IBM computer products.

Ibn Saud, Abd al-Aziz (ca. 1880–1953). Founder and king (1932–53) of SAUDI ARABIA. Born in Riyadh, Ibn Saud was a member of the Islamic Wahabi dynasty. During his youth, the Turkish-supported house of Rashid was in power, and he and his family were forced to live in exile in Kuwait (1891–1902). In 1902, Ibn Saud organized Arab resistance and, with his army, seized Riyadh. By 1912 he was in control of central Arabia, and in 1913 he expelled the Turks from eastern Arabia. In 1924–25, he defeated his rival Hussein Ibn Ali, captured the cities of Jedda, Medina and Mecca and proclaimed himself king of Hijaz and Najd. Solidifying his power over the Arabian peninsula, he renamed his kingdom Saudi Arabia in 1932. Ibn Saud granted oil concessions to American companies in the 1930s, and the riches that flowed from his nation's oil wells made it one of the wealthiest countries in the world. During World War II, he was officially neutral but favored the Allied cause. At his death in 1953, he was succeeded by his son Saud.

ICBM. An intercontinental ballistic missile (ICBM) is a land-launched missile that can deliver a nuclear warhead more than 3,000 nautical miles. American ICBMs include the Titan and Minuteman; Soviet ICBMs include the Sego, Sinner, Spanker, Satan, Stiletto and Sickle.

Iceland [Republic of Iceland]. The volcanic island of Iceland, covering an area of 39,758 square miles, is located in the North Atlantic Ocean approximately 186 miles northeast of Greenland, 559 miles west of Norway and 497 miles north of Scotland. In 1918 Iceland achieved full sovereignty but remained under the Danish Crown. After a friendly occupation by Britain and the U.S. during WORLD WAR II, the country declared its independence in 1944, and Sveinn Bjornsson became the first president. Iceland became a founding member of NATO in 1949. Conflict with Britain over fishing limits led to incidents at sea during the Cod War of 1972–76, which ended in compromise. Iceland declared itself a nuclear-free zone in 1985 after mounting opposition to the U.S./NATO base on the island.

Ickes, Harold (LeClaire) (1874–1952). American statesman and a leading figure in the NEW DEAL of the 1930s. Born in rural Pennsylvania, Ickes attended the University of Chicago, earning a law degree in 1907. A crusading reformer as a newspaper reporter and as a lawyer, he was extremely active in Progressive Republican politics in the midwest. In 1933 President Franklin D. ROOSEVELT appointed Ickes—an avid conservationist—secretary of the interior, a post he held for 13 years. "Honest Harold" reformed the notoriously corrupt department into a model of governmental efficiency, helping to conserve the nation's natural resources and opposing over-exploitation by private industry. As head of the PUBLIC WORKS ADMINISTRATION he oversaw the spending of some $6 billion on various public works programs. Following a political dispute, Ickes resigned from President TRUMAN's cabinet in 1946. His books include *The New Democracy* (1934), *The Autobiography of a Curmudgeon* (1934) and *The Secret Diary of Harold L. Ickes* (3 vols., 1953–54).

For further reading:

Watkins, T.H., *Righteous Pilgrim: The Life and Times of Harold Ickes, 1874–1952.* New York: Henry Holt, 1989.

White, Graham, *Harold Ickes of the New Deal: His Private Life and Public Career.* Cambridge, Mass.: Harvard University Press, 1985.

Idris Shah, Sultan (1924–1984). Ruler of the Malaysian state of Perak from 1963 until his death. In 1983 Idris Shah joined with other sultans to force the elected government to alter constitutional amendments aimed at limiting the powers of the rulers of the nine Malaysian states. At the time of his death he was the frontrunner in the election of Malaysia's next king.

Ilf and Petrov. Pseudonym of a literary partnership between Russian writers Ilya Arnoldovich Fainzilberg (1897–1937) and Yevgeny Petrovich KATAYEV (1903–42). In 1928 they published *The Twelve Chairs* and in 1931 *The Golden Calf,* both novels satirizing aspects of Soviet society. They also

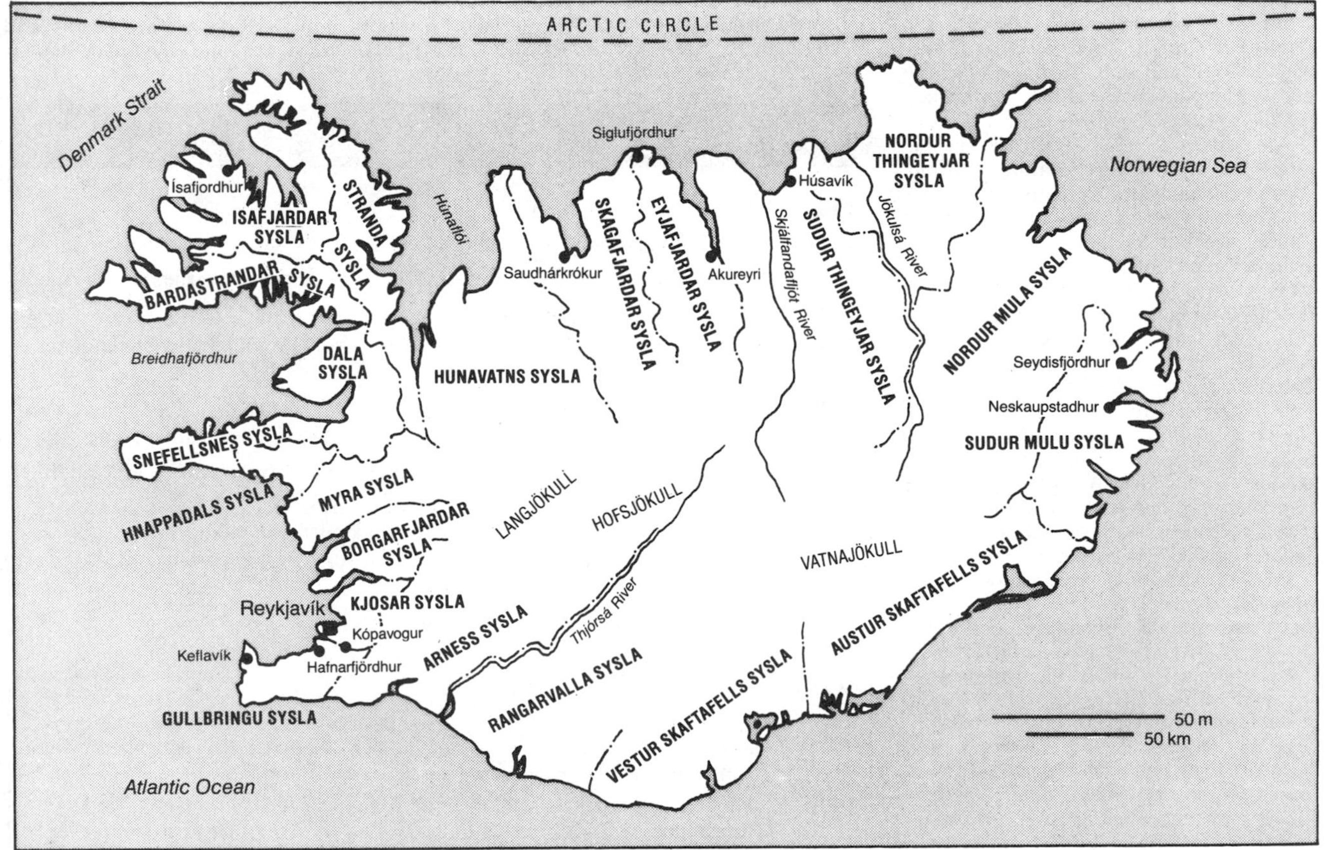

ICELAND

visited the United States and wrote *Little Golden America* (1936). Ilf and Petrov were frowned upon under STALIN, but their work later recovered its popularity.

Illia, Arturo (1900–1986). President of ARGENTINA (1963–66). A political moderate, Illia was elected in one of the freest elections in Argentina's history up to that time. He was overthrown by the military in a bloodless coup in 1966, however. He remained politically active thereafter, working to return Argentina to civilian government.

Illich, Ivan (1926–). Austrian-born educator and social critic. Illich, was ordained as a Roman Catholic priest in 1951, has become well known as a strident voice of dissent within the church, calling for increased social activism. Illich studied history and psychology at the University of Salzburg and earned his doctoral degree there in 1951. From 1951 to 1956, Illich was a priest in New York City, and from 1956 to 1960 served as vice-rector of Catholic University in Ponce, Puerto Rico. His major works include *Celebration of Awareness* (1970) and *De-Schooling Society* (1971).

"I Love Lucy". Innovative American television comedy series starring Lucille BALL. In its first six years of weekly half-hour shows (1951 to 1957), it never ranked lower than third in popularity among all television programs. (During its remaining four years the series was reduced to several one-hour specials, later rerun under the title, "The Lucille Ball/Desi Arnaz Shows.") The mix was unlikely—a Cuban bandleader (Desi), a redheaded, clownish wife (Lucy) and a mismatched married couple (Vivian Vance and William Frawley)—but superb scripts by writers Madelyn Pugh and Bob Carroll Jr. and Lucy's Chaplinesque antics captivated viewers in the 1950s as no show had done since Milton BERLE's "Texaco Star Theater" in the late 1940s. Among its innovations, largely at Lucy's insistence, was the decision not to broadcast live from New York but to film it in HOLLYWOOD with a three-camera process. Print quality was superior to that of kinescopes (film made from a picture tube image) and guaranteed the series a long life in syndication.

Ilyushin, Sergei Vladimirovich (1894–1977). Soviet aircraft designer. Ilyushin first became known for his Il-2 Stormovik, a dive bomber widely used by the Soviet Union during WORLD WAR II. He later worked on commercial aircraft, designing the jet airliner Il-62 (1962) and other airplanes used by the Soviet national airline Aeroflot. Altogether he designed more than 50 planes.

Imagism. American school of poetics, led by Amy LOWELL and Ezra POUND, which first emerged in the 1910s and has remained influential throughout the century. The central argument of Imagism was that the poetry of the Victorian and Edwardian eras had become clogged with excess verbiage, which was inserted by poets into their lines of verse simply for the sake of metrical completion. This excess verbiage did result in a superficial musicality, but it also diminished the vividness of poetic metaphor—the presentation of new and powerful sensual images to the reader—due to its tendencies toward vagueness and conventionality. Imagism called for spare, evocative poetic compositions that relied on an exactitude of verbal presentation in a free verse form. Major poets such as T.S. ELIOT, D.H. LAWRENCE and William Carlos WILLIAMS were highly influenced by Imagist theory.

Imagists, Russian. A postrevolutionary literary movement. Russian Imagism evolved more or less separately from Anglo-American IMAGISM. The Imagists founded the movement in 1919 as a successor to FUTURISM. Characteristics of Imagism are the primacy of the image, coarse language and pessimism; these features can be seen in Sergei ESENIN's *Confession of a Hooligan* (1920). In the first manifesto or declaration of Imagism, signed by Esenin, Ivnev, Mariengov and Shershenevich (1893–1942), the image was defined as "the naphthalene preserving a work of art from the moths of time." The movement, although in agreement with the ethic of the October Revolution, found itself unable to maintain an apolitical stance during the Civil War, and by 1927 it had disintegrated.

Ince, Thomas Harper (1882–1924). Prominent producer, director and writer in the SILENT FILM era. After an itinerant life with his actor parents, he began his film career in 1910 in New York directing Mary PICKFORD films for Carl LAEMMLE's Independent Motion Pictures Company. Moving to Los Angeles in 1912, he built a studio he dubbed "Inceville" upon 20,000 acres of land. There, he contracted for the cowboys, Indians and equipment of the "Miller 101 Wild West Show" to make the westerns that soon made him famous. Epic two-reelers like *War on the Plains* (1912) pioneered the modern western movie. Releasing through several distribution outlets in the next 10 years, Ince featured his top stars, William S. Hart and Charles Ray, in some of the finest outdoor dramas of the day, including *On the Night Stage* (1914), *Hell's Hinges* (1916) and *The Coward* (1916). His most important contribution to the movies lay in developing the shooting script system still used today and in personally supervising his various projects. He was convinced that it was the writer/producer, not the director, whose personal stamp should go on every film. His epics, like *Civilization* (1916), are of less interest today than his smaller, social-problem films, like the remarkably tough and poignant *The Italians* (1915), a gritty drama of immigrants come to grief in the New World. Ince's mysterious death during a yachting party in 1924 has never been adequately explained.

Inchon. City and port on the Yellow Sea coast of South Korea, 25 miles from SEOUL. Opened as a treaty port in 1883, it was expanded during the Japanese occupation (1904–45). In September 1950, during the KOREAN WAR, U.S.-led UN forces made a brilliantly successful amphibious landing here, following it up with an offensive northwards.

India [Republic of India]. Nation on the Indian sub-continent of southern Asia, covering an area of 1,222,396 square miles south of the Himalaya Mountains and between Pakistan and Myanmar; India is

INDIA

1906	Muslim League formed.
1913	Poet Rabindranath Tagore wins Nobel Prize.
1920	Mohandas Gandhi launches first civil disobedience campaign for self-rule.
1930	Gandhi makes salt, defying British.
1931	Gandhi represents Indian National Congress at Roundtable conference on constitutional reform in London.
1936	Jawaharlal Nehru becomes president of Indian National Congress.
1940	Muslim League calls for independent status in Muslim majority areas.
1942	British offer dominion status in exchange for support of war effort; Gandhi launches Quit India movement.
1947	Independence; Pakistan divided from India, igniting religious war.
1948	(January) Gandhi assassinated; discrimination against untouchables banned.
1952	First international birth control organization founded in Bombay.
1964	Nehru dies.
1965	War with Pakistan over Kashmir.
1984	Army assaults Golden Temple of Amritsar to suppress Sikh uprising; Prime Minister Indira Gandhi assassinated by Sikh bodyguards; succeeded by her son Rajiv Gandhi; poison gas leak devastates Bhopal.
1990	Hindus storm Babri Masjid mosque, claiming site is birthplace of god, Rama; final episode aired of *Mahabharata*, most popular tv program ever.

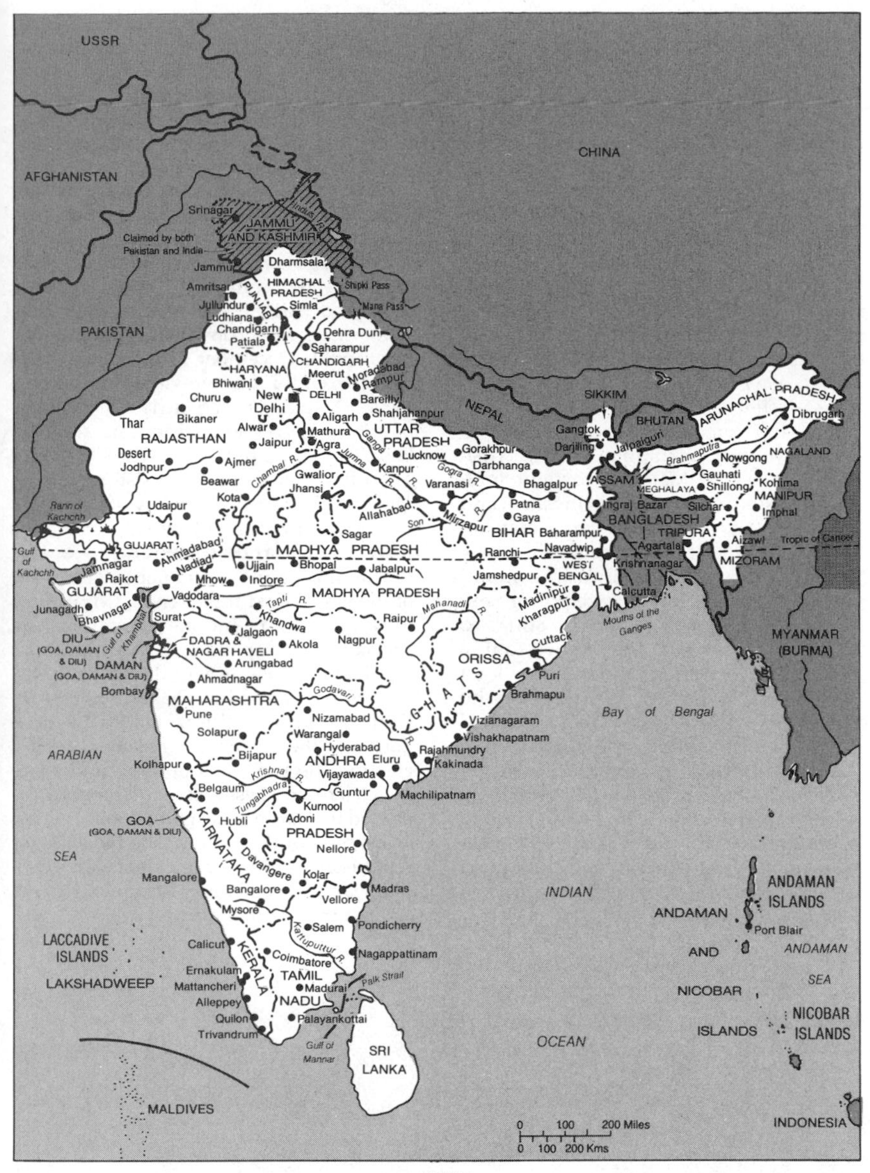

INDIA

the seventh largest country in the world. Centuries of British influence and rule in India ended in 1947 when the predominantly Hindu country was granted independence, after Mohandas GANDHI had made the nationalist movement a powerful force through his civil disobedience campaigns (1920–46). The last British governor-general, Lord Louis MOUNTBATTEN, partitioned British India into two states, India and PAKISTAN, to avoid religious conflict between Muslims and Hindus. Nevertheless, war between India and Pakistan over the disputed Indian state of Kashmir erupted in 1948 and ended in an unresolved ceasefire in 1949, only to explode again in 1965 (see INDO-PAKISTANI WAR OF 1947–48, INDO-PAKISTANI WAR OF 1965). A peace was achieved in 1966 through Soviet mediation. Under Prime Minister Jawaharlal NEHRU's leadership (1947–64) India adopted a new constitution and became a republic (1950). During his daughter Indira GANDHI's ministry (1966–77, 1980–84) India again fought with Pakistan over its support of an independent BANGLADESH (East Pakistan) in 1971, while Sikh militancy in the state of Punjab culminated in Mrs. Gandhi's assassination (1984). Though her son and successor, Rajiv GANDHI, granted some Sikh demands, violence continued throughout the 1980s. Political crisis continued with the resignation of Prime Minister Chandra Shekhar in March 1991 and attempts by Rajiv Gandhi to regain the post. Gandhi was himself assassinated in 1991. In foreign affairs, India has followed a non-aligned policy. Domestically, the problems of poverty, poor agriculture, high population density and friction between the various castes have continued to plague successive governments. (See also AMRITSAR MASSACRE, INDO-PAKISTANI WAR OF 1971, GOLDEN TEMPLE MASSACRE.)

For further reading:

Brass, Paul, *The Politics of India Since Independence*. Cambridge: Cambridge University Press, 1990.
Sharma, L.P., *History of Modern India, 1707–1947*. New York: Advent Books, 1990.
Singh, Anita I., *The Origins of the Partition of India, 1936–1947*. Oxford: Oxford University Press, 1987.

Indian Civil War of 1947–48. During 1947 efforts to arrange independence of a unified Indian sub-continent from Great Britain foundered when the Muslim League and the Indian National Congress failed to agree to a federal formula. Riots between Muslims and Hindus, endemic since the "Great Calcutta Killing" (August 16–20, 1946), erupted into civil war when partition into INDIA and PAKISTAN was announced August 14, 1947. At least 5,500,000 refugees moved between West Pakistan and western India, and 1,250,000 between East and West Bengal; rioting took at least a million lives, in part because Indian Prime Minister Jawaharlal NEHRU prevented British troops from intervening. War between India and Pakistan over KASHMIR (1947–48) exacerbated refugee conflicts. Mohandas K. GANDHI, Indian spiritual and nationalist leader, attempting to calm Hindu-Muslim tensions, was assassinated by a Hindu extremist. The shock restored order and unified the Indian government.

Indochina. Large peninsula in Southeast Asia, presently divided as the nations of BURMA, CAMBODIA (Kampuchea), LAOS, THAILAND, VIETNAM and West MALAYSIA. The 19th-century struggle for colonial empire saw the British in control of the western and southern sections (Burma and Malaysia); while Thailand, in the center and then known as Siam, retained its independence with some difficulty. The eastern part became French Indochina and consisted of the colony of Cochin China (south Vietnam) and protectorates over Tonkin (north Vietnam), Annam (central

INDOCHINA FOLLOWING THE GENEVA CONFERENCE, 1954

Vietnam), Laos and Cambodia. WORLD WAR II put an end to France's colonial empire. Although most of the region was reoccupied by France after the Japanese surrender at the end of the war, Vietnamese demands for independence from France were soon backed up by military action. The climax came in 1954 at DIEN BIEN PHU, a French military base in the northwest that fell to insurgent forces on May 7. That same year Laos and Cambodia gained their independence; and Vietnam, formed out of Annam, Cochin China and Tonkin in 1949–50, was partitioned into north and south sections—a division intended to be temporary. The major cities of Indochina are BANGKOK, HANOI, Haiphong, Ho Chi Minh City (SAIGON), KUALA LUMPUR, PHNOM PENH and RANGOON.

Indonesia, Republic of. Vast archipelago-nation of more than 13,000 islands, off the coast of Southeast Asia. After hundreds of years under Dutch rule and exploitation, the Netherlands East Indies (or Netherlands Indies) saw the beginnings of Indonesian nationalism and the push for independence in the early 20th century. But it took the Japanese invasion of WORLD WAR II to disrupt Dutch rule. After the Japanese occupiers surrendered in 1945, nationalist leader SUKARNO proclaimed independence; a spontaneous revolution against the returning Dutch finally led to the Europeans' relinquishing sovereignty to the U.S. of Indonesia late in 1949. Under Sukarno's leadership, Indonesia became a leader of the THIRD WORLD and by 1965 had developed close ties with China and the U.S.S.R. After an unsuccessful communist takeover attempt in 1965, Gen. SUHARTO led a right-wing coup, seized power and opened a campaign against the communists in Java and Bali, killing more than 100,000. In 1976 Suharto invaded Portuguese East Timor (also in the archipelago) and brutally eliminated all opposition. Since that unfortunate time, Indonesia has enjoyed generally favorable relations with the West, as a member of the ASEAN economic and political alliance. (See also NETHERLANDS.)

Indonesian-Malaysian War of 1963–66. In 1963 Indonesian "Lifetime President" Achmed SUKARNO refused to recognize the democratic federation of MALAYSIA, and urged Indonesians to crush it. Britain aided Malaysia to fight infiltrating Indonesian guerrillas in Sabah and Sarawak and Indonesian paratroops in Malaya. The war was financially costly for INDONESIA, and Indonesian communists (PKI) attempted to seize power September 30, 1965. General SUHARTO squashed the coup and carried out a bloody anti-communist purge; at least 300,000 leftists were killed. Sukarno, who had been supported by the PKI and had been friendly with communist China, failed to regain government control. Eventually he had to surrender all authority to Suharto, who became acting president in 1967 and was elected president in 1968. Malaysia and Indonesia ended hostilities by a treaty signed at Djakarta on August 11, 1966.

Indonesian War in East Timor (1975–). Rival factions contended for power in Portuguese Timor (East Timor). (West Timor, formerly Dutch, had become part of INDONESIA in 1950.) The Revolutionary Front for the Independence of East Timor (FRETILIN) called for independence, another faction for merger with Indonesia, a third for remaining with PORTUGAL. Civil war erupted August 1975, the Portuguese governor left, and FRETILIN gained control. Opposing groups requested Indonesian intervention, and Indonesia eagerly complied, capturing Dili, the capital, December 7, 1975, and driving FRETILIN fighters into the mountains. Despite UNITED NATIONS condemnation of aggression, Indonesia annexed East Timor on July 17, 1976. FRETILIN guerrillas continued to resist, and East Timor lay in ruins with many of its people starving in internment camps.

Indonesian War of Independence. Following the Japanese occupation (1942–45) of the Dutch East Indies (now INDONESIA) in WORLD WAR II, Indonesian nationalists proclaimed independence. Not recognizing the new government, Dutch and British soldiers landed at Djakarta to restore Dutch control. Fighting led to negotiations and the Cheribon Agreement (1946), creating the U.S. of Indonesia under the Dutch crown. Disagreements and disorder led to a large-scale Dutch police action arousing world opinion. The blockade of republican territory coincided with guerrilla warfare waged by Muslim extremists against both Dutch and republicans, and

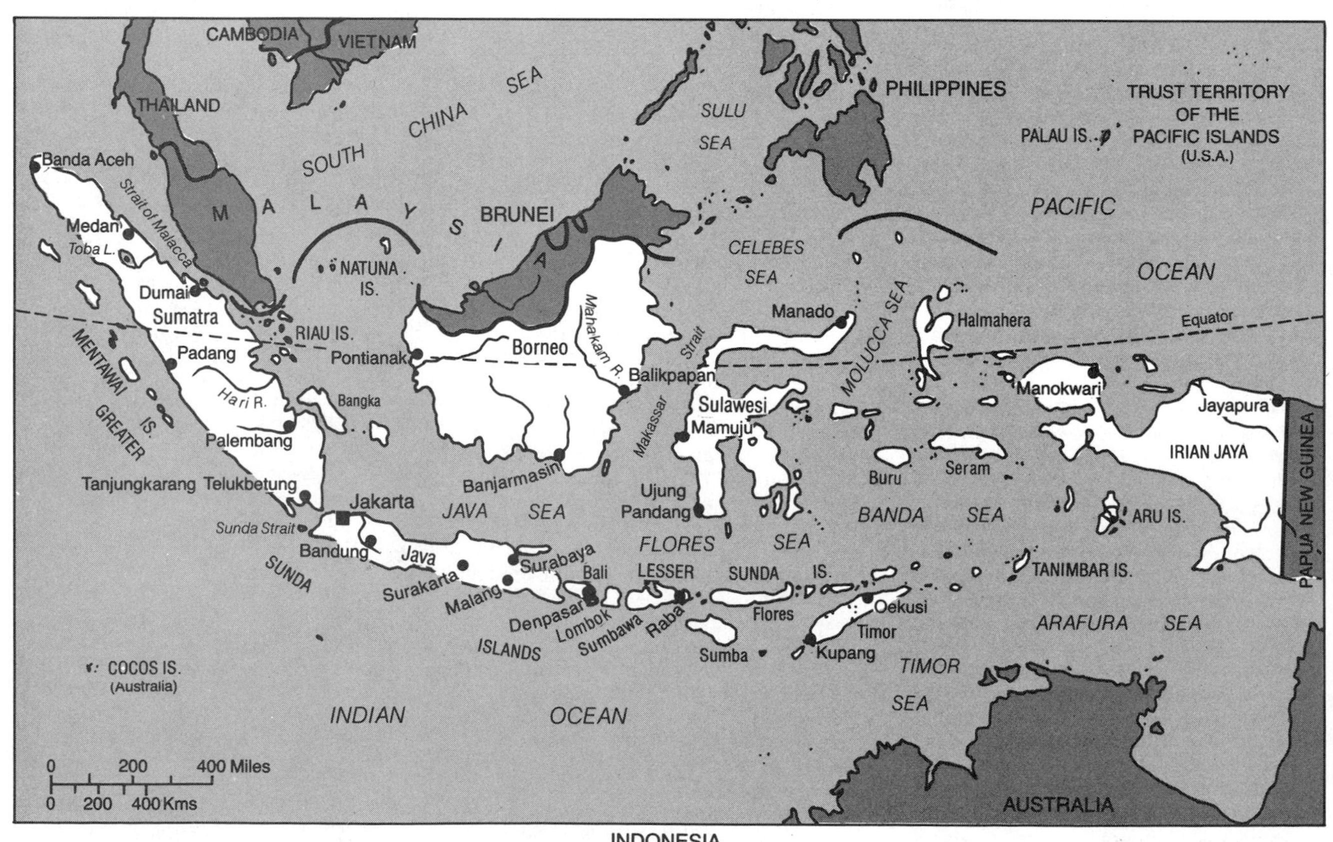

INDONESIA

INDONESIA

1901	"Ethical Policy" seeks better treatment of native populations under Dutch rule.
1910	Under the "Forward Movement," Dutch expand control through outer islands to reach present boundaries of Indonesia.
1927	Indonesians educated in Europe under Ethical Policy form groups of nationalist intellectuals; Sukarno founds Party National Indonesia.
1942	Japanese occupation; Sukarno cooperates, builds national power base.
1945	Three days after Japanese surrender, Sukarno declares independence; Dutch attempt at reentry meets guerrilla war.
1949	Federal republic established, with democratically elected parliament.
1954	Young officers mutiny in Sumatra.
1955	Afro-Asian conference at Bandung.
1956	Sukarno suspends parliament; begins "Guided Democracy" leading to martial law.
1962	Television introduced.
1963	Netherlands hands over West Irian (western New Guinea); Sukarno pursues friendship with China; influence of local communists grows; economy falters.
1965	Sukarno leaves UN; young communists within military attempt coup; General Suharto crushes it, and becomes real power in nation; 500,000 communists killed as CIA assists in round-up.
1967	Sukarno stripped of office.
1968	Suharto assumes presidency; "New Order" signals turn to West.
1969	Separatist guerrillas acting in West Irian.
1975	Indonesia invades newly independent Portuguese East Timor; over 200,000 residents killed; oil boom brings relative prosperity.
1976	Government officials charged with taking bribes from U.S. corporations; government oil company collapses.
1984	Muslims violently protest Suharto's attempts to secularize society.
1989	Fretelin guerrillas active in East Timor.
1990	Launches first communications satellite.

a communist uprising. The Dutch seized the republic's capital, Djakarta, and principal leaders, but resistance and United Nations condemnation continued. Indonesian and Dutch representatives met at The Hague (August 23–November 2, 1949), and the NETHERLANDS transferred full sovereignty to the U.S. of Indonesia with Achmed SUKARNO as president, Muhammed Hatta as premier. The state became the Republic of Indonesia in 1950.

Indonesian Wars of 1957–62. Continued Dutch rule of West New Guinea angered Indonesian President Achmed SUKARNO. INDONESIA claimed the area as West Irian, asking without success for the United Nations to resolve the dispute. In December 1957 Sukarno began a strike against Dutch businesses, expelled Dutch subjects and expropriated Dutch holdings. While the Dutch prepared New Guinean natives for self-determination and defense, Indonesia obtained warships and planes from the U.S.S.R. and in 1962 landed paratroops in West New Guinea to fight alongside rebel guerrillas against the Dutch. The U.S. and the United Nations sponsored negotiations to avert full-scale war. In an agreement of August 15, 1962, the NETHERLANDS transferred West New Guinea to UN control, which subsequently transferred it to Indonesia (1963).

Indo-Pakistani War of 1947–48. The partition into INDIA and PAKISTAN left the status of Jammu and KASHMIR undecided. An independent, largely Muslim kingdom bordering West Pakistan, Jammu and Kashmir was ruled by a Hindu Maharaja. Demands for democracy and revolts by Pathan Muslims against Hindu landlords encouraged Pakistan to attack, seizing Muzaffarbad and Uri in October 1947, advancing toward the Kashmiri capital of Srinagar. The Maharaja asked for India's help, receiving it October 27, when he ceded the state to India. Sikh troops pushed the invaders back, and Pakistan was about to send troops until its British officers threatened to resign. Then Pakistan transferred "volunteers" into the invaded area to hold it as Azad (free) Kashmir. The turmoil exacerbated Hindu-Muslim tensions in India, contributing to Mohandas K. GANDHI's (1869–1948) assassination by a Hindu extremist. Intervention by the United Nations resulted in a cease-fire and a de-facto boundary at the battle line; but Indo-Pakistani disputes over Kashmir continued.

Indo-Pakistani War of 1965. Hostility between INDIA and PAKISTAN increased after 1958 when General Mohammed AYUB KHAN seized power in Pakistan, signing a treaty with China that put Kashmir's Chinese boundaries into question. Indian and Pakistani forces first clashed (April 9–30, 1965) in the Rann of Kutch. In August and early September both sides crossed the Kashmiri cease-fire line, and on September 6 India launched a drive toward Lahore with 900,000 troops. Four-hundred-fifty Pakistani tanks were lost before the UNITED NATIONS arranged a cease-fire September 27, averting intervention by China. Mediation by Britain, the U.S. and the U.S.S.R. led to a conference in Tashkent (1966) in which promises of friendship, cooperation and a Kashmiri plebiscite were made; but Prime Minister Lal Bahadur SHASTRI died within hours of the conference. His successor, Indira GANDHI, fulfilled most of the promises, but intervening events prevented the plebiscite from being held.

Indo-Pakistani War of 1971. The Pakistani Civil War of 1971 forced more than 10 million refugees from East Pakistan (BANGLADESH) into West Bengal. INDIA appealed for international aid, but instead, the U.S., supporting PAKISTAN, cut off India's American credit. Pakistani warplanes attacked Indian airfields in Kashmir (December 3, 1971), and the next day India attacked both West and East Pakistan, recognizing Bangladesh's independence December 6. Indian forces captured Dacca, forced the surrender of Pakistan's forces in Bangladesh, and took 90,000 prisoners December 16; India established a cease-fire on both eastern and western fronts the following day. Pakistan lost over half its population and was on the verge of economic and military collapse. It finally recognized Bangladesh in 1974; the U.S. did so April 4, 1972.

Industrial Party. In the Soviet Union, an allegedly subversive group of the technical intelligentsia that was said to be wrecking the first Soviet FIVE-YEAR PLAN at capitalist instigation. The members were tried and condemned in 1930, together with a number of those considered sympathetic to them. (See also PURGES.)

Industrial Workers of the World [IWW]. Revolutionary union founded in 1905 by the Western Federation of Miners and other labor groups. Representing the principles of syndicalism, the organization was at first headed by Eugene DEBS and Daniel De Leon, with leadership soon passing to Vincent St. John and William Haywood. The IWW, whose members were known as Wobblies, aimed at organizing skilled and unskilled workers into one union, which, after a general strike, would topple capitalism and introduce a socialist industrial democracy. After 1908, it concentrated on organizing the unskilled. While meeting with strong opposition from local and federal government, the IWW amassed an impressive roster of membership, including agricultural, textile, dock, metal and lumber workers. It also made a special point of organizing both blacks and migrants. Membership reached a height of from 60,000 to 100,000 by the outbreak of World War I. Rejecting arbitration and collective bargaining, the IWW advocated direct action and conducted some 150 strikes. In the process, it was successful at achieving better working conditions and shorter hours for its members. In 1917 the Department of Justice arrested more than 200 Wobbly leaders for antiwar efforts. The RED SCARES of postwar America did much to discredit the IWW, and by the late 1920s it had ceased to be an important force in the American labor movement.

Indy, Vincent d' (1851–1931). French composer. He was a pupil and disciple of composer Cesar Franck, succeeding his master as president of the Societe Nationale de Musique. Also a follower of Richard Wagner, he did much to introduce the German composer's music to French audiences. He wrote noted biographies of both his mentors (1906 and 1930), as well as of Beethoven (1911). In 1894 d'Indy was one of the founders of the Schola Cantorum in Paris, teaching composition at the influential music school and directing it from 1911 until his death. His three-volume work *Cours de composition musicale* (1903, rev. 1950) embodies his teaching methods and philosophy. As a composer, he followed Franck's model in using recurring themes throughout various movements. His spare and contained compositions also employ plainsong and baroque elements. His most often-played works include the *Symphony on a French Mountain Air* (1887) and the symphonic variations *Istar* (1897). He also wrote three other symphonies, chamber music, piano pieces, choral works and the opera *Fervaal* (1897).

INF Treaty. The Intermediate-Range Force (INF) Treaty, signed by the U.S. and the Soviet Union in December 1987, was the first agreement between the two nations that eliminated an entire class of missiles. Under its terms, the U.S. agreed to destroy all CRUISE and Pershing II missiles and the Soviet Union agreed to eliminate all SS-20s; both types of missiles were intended primarily for deployment in Europe.

Inge, William (Motter) (1913–1973). American playwright. Inge was noted for such **"slice of life"** dramas as *Come Back, Little Sheba* (1950), *Picnic* (PULITZER PRIZE, 1953), *Bus Stop* (1955) and *The Dark at the Top of the Stairs* (1957). Many of his plays were made into successful films. He won the 1961 ACADEMY AWARD for best story and screenplay (written directly for the screen) for *Splendor in the Grass*.

For further reading:

Voss, Ralph F., *A Life of William Inge: The Strains of Triumph*. Lawrence: University Press of Kansas, 1989.

Inge, William R(alph) (1860–1954). British clergyman. Inge played a dominant role in the Anglican Church in the first half of this century. Educated at Cambridge University, he taught there and at Oxford University before becoming Dean of St. Paul's Cathedral in London, a position he held from 1911 to 1934. Inge achieved broad public recognition throughout Britain by virtue of his well-attended sermons and lectures, which frequently expressed a dour pessimism that earned Inge the nickname of "the gloomy Dean." Inge was also a prolific author. His major works include *Christian Mysticism* (1897), *Outspoken Essays* (1919), *Mysticism in Religion* (1948) and *Diary of a Dean* (1949).

Ingersoll, Ralph McAllister (1900–1985). American journalist and publisher. Ingersoll played a key editorial role in the development of magazines such as THE NEW YORKER, *Fortune*, TIME, and LIFE. He was best known as owner of the New York City newspaper *PM* (1940–48). Noted for its in-depth coverage of various issues with a liberal standpoint and for its policy of carrying no advertising, *PM* was the first major American newspaper to advocate U.S. entry into WORLD WAR II.

injection molding. Manufacturing technique in which PLASTIC in a semiliquid state is forced into a hollow mold where it hardens into the shape determined by the mold. The finished part is ejected from the mold ready for use or for whatever further finishing and assembly steps are required. While automatic machines can produce small injection moldings at high speed at relatively low cost, the high cost of the molds tends to limit use of the process to the production of objects and parts where demand can be expected to be high. Thermoplastics such as styrene and polyethylene are the usual materials used for injection molding to produce everyday objects such as plastic knives and forks, containers, and toys.

Inkatha. Zulu cultural and political organization in SOUTH AFRICA; led since 1975 by Chief Mangosuthu BUTHELEZI. Ostensibly, the group seeks to revive Zulu traditions and instill pride among Zulus. Some observers claim that Inkatha is supported by the white minority government only to fracture the anti-APARTHEID movement in South Africa. In the late 1980s and early 1990s, Inkatha members were involved in violent clashes with blacks from other tribes and with members of the AFRICAN NATIONAL CONGRESS.

Inner Mongolia [Inner Mongolian Autonomous Region]. Autonomous region of China bordering on Outer Mongolia and the U.S.S.R.; the capital is at Hu-Ho-Hao-T'e. Nominally under Chinese rule until 1911, it then became part of the Chinese Republic; in 1947, the first autonomous region established by the Chinese communist government. (See also MONGOLIA.)

Inonu. Village in Turkish province of Bilecik. During the GRECO-TURKISH WAR OF 1921–22, Greek offensives were twice halted at Inonu by Turks under Ismet Pasha, who, as a result of these victories, took the name of the village as his surname. As Ismet INONU he became president of Turkey in 1938.

Inonu, Ismet [born Ismet Pasha] (1884–1973). Turkish soldier and statesman. Inonu was born in Izmir. After a distinguished military career, he bacame ATATURK's chief of staff during the GRECO-TURKISH WAR OF 1921–22. He was first premier of the Republic of TURKEY (1923–38) and, after Ataturk's death, its second president (1938–50). He introduced free elections and a multiparty system in Turkey. After the 1950 elections, Inonu became leader of the parliamentary opposition. Under the Gursel government (1961–65), he was again premier, but resigned owing to lack of sufficient parliamentary support.

Institutional Revolutionary Party [*Partido Revolucionario Institucional*; PRI]. Mexican political party founded in 1929 as the National Revolutionary Party (*Partido Nacional Revolucionario;* PNR). The PNR was founded by former Mexican President Plutarco CALLES and joined regional and national leaders from the agrarian, labor, bureaucratic and military sectors. In 1933 the PNR established the practice of suggesting six-year plans for the country, which each subsequent president has adopted as his program. The party's national assembly changed the name to the Institutional Revolutionary Party (PRI) in 1946 to stress its continuing commitment to social and economic reforms. In 1963 the party created an Institute of Political, Economic and Social Studies (IEPES), which researches national needs and coordinates PRI and government policy. Since its inception, a core of party elite have selected PRI candidates. In 1964 its leader Carlos Madrazo attempted to establish open nominations and arrange party primaries. The National Executive Committee overrode him, however, and the party returned to its former practices in 1966. The PRI has traditionally dominated Mexican politics, and in 1985, in its lowest vote total ever, it still gathered 65% of the vote for the congressional district seats.

insulin. A natural substance produced by the pancreas and necessary for proper metabolism of glucose (sugar). Before the 20th century anyone whose pancreas stopped producing insulin developed diabetes mellitus and died. In 1921 Canadian Frederick BANTING extracted insulin from the pancreas of a dog and in January 1922 successfully treated a 14-year-old boy with diabetes mellitus. Insulin became commercially available by late 1922. A milestone 20th-century medical advance, insulin use has become routine and saved the lives of countless diabetes sufferers.

interferon. Any one of a naturally occurring protein family that functions as part of the body's defense mechanism by interfering with the multiplication of viruses within living cells. Discovered in 1957 by English scientist Alick Isaacs and his assistant Jean Lindenmann, interferons were subsequently produced by cells cultured outside the body. Recombinant-DNA technology and chemical synthesis commercially produced human interferons used to treat such diseases as shingles and certain types of cancer.

International. The First International was formed in London by Karl Marx in 1864; its aim was to coordinate working-class movements in different countries and thereby to establish international socialism. There were disputes between the Marxist and anarchist members, culminating in the final separation between Marx and Bakunin (1872). The movement was dissolved in 1876. The Second International was formed in Paris in 1889, comprising the radical parties of Austria, Belgium, Denmark, Germany, Spain, Sweden and Switzerland. A nonrevolutionary movement, it collapsed with the outbreak of World War I. The Third International (COMINTERN) was formed in Moscow by LENIN and the BOLSHEVIKS in 1917 and comprised the communist elements excluded from the Second International. Its aim was world revolution. A Fourth International was formed by TROTSKY in Mexico in the 1930s, and there was also a Fifth—the Situationist International—formed in 1954. There have been two revivals of the Second, nonrevolutionary Socialist International. The first (1923) ceased to operate in 1940. The second (1951) is the currently operative Socialist International. Its congress meets at least once every two years and its council, in which the Socialist Union of Central-Eastern Europe is represented, at least twice a year.

International Bank for Reconstruction and Development. See WORLD BANK.

International Committee of the Red Cross. A council of 25 Swiss citizens, with headquarters in Geneva, Switzerland, that acts as an administrative body coordinating the activities of individual Red Cross societies worldwide and of the Red Cross and wartime belligerents. The Red Cross grew from the work of Jean Henry Dunant, a Swiss humanitarian who aided the wounded in the battle of Solferino (1859). In 1863 the Geneva Public Welfare Society was formed and sponsored an international conference that laid the groundwork for the International Committee of the Red Cross (ICRC). The Red Cross became active in 1864, increasing its efforts in the Franco-Prussian War (1870–71) and the BALKAN WARS (1912–13). It grew in international scope, spreading to chapters around the world, including the founding of the American Red Cross in 1881. The organization assumed enormous importance with the outbreak of WORLD WAR I, when it trained volunteers, aided PRISONERS OF WAR and helped in repatriation. For its work the ICRC received the 1917 NOBEL PRIZE for peace. The organization again played a great role in humanitarian efforts during and after WORLD WAR II, helping PRISONERS OF WAR and attempting to aid victims of the HOLOCAUST. It received its second Nobel Prize for peace in 1944. Today, the Red Cross has a membership of about 100 million, with affiliates in 74 countries. It continues to provide services for victims of war and to assure the carrying out of the GENEVA CONVENTIONS. In addition, its services have been extended to many peacetime activities, including running blood banks, caring for disaster victims, aiding refugees and offering first-aid training. In 1963, its centennial year, the ICRC received a third Nobel Prize, this time shared with the LEAGUE OF RED CROSS SOCIETIES. Its emblem of a red cross on a white field (the reverse of the Swiss flag, replaced in Muslim countries by a red crescent and in Israel by a red star of David) remains an international symbol of humanitarianism and neutrality.

For further reading:

Willemin, G., *The International Committee of the Red Cross.* Hingham, Mass.: Kluwer Academic Publishers, 1984.

International Geophysical Year [IGY]. An international project (July 1, 1957–December 31, 1958) designed to study the geophysics of the Earth and its environment. The project was timed to coincide with increased sunspot activity. This enabled scientists to study the effects of sunspots on atmospheric magnetism and radio waves. More than 60,000 scientists from 60 nations were involved in research relating to the IGY. Some of the most important experiments were conducted by researchers stationed in ANTARCTICA. During the project, the first instrumented Earth satellites were launched, leading to the discovery of the VAN ALLEN radiation belts. Hugh Odishaw, the American scientist who coordinated the U.S. effort, called the IGY "the single most significant peaceful activity of mankind since the Renaissance and the Copernican Revolution."

International Labour Organisation. Specialized agency, originally created in 1919 by the TREATY OF VERSAILLES and affiliated with the LEAGUE OF NATIONS. Its original purpose was to establish international guidelines for improving labor practices, working conditions and standards of living for workers worldwide. In 1946 the International Labour Organisation (ILO) became an agency of the UNITED NATIONS. In its mission to improve the lives of workers, the ILO promotes standards for working hours, adequate wages, safe and disease-free working conditions, vacations, unemployment insurance, protection of women and children and other such matters and provides technical assistance for vocational and management training. The ILO consists of a general conference of representatives of its 151 member states (in 1985), a governing body and an International Labour Office; it is financed by its member states. In 1969 it was the recipient of the NOBEL PRIZE for peace. The U.S. withdrew from the ILO in 1977 because of the organization's criticism of ISRAEL and apparent favoring of leftist political movements; however, the U.S. rejoined the organization in 1980.

For further reading:

The International Labour Organisation in the United Nations Family. New York: United Nations, n.d.

Galenson, Walter, *The International Labor Organization: Mirroring the U.N.'s Problems.* Washington, D.C.: Heritage Foundation, 1982.

National Industrial Conference Board, Inc., Staff, *The Work of the International Labor Organization.* Buffalo, N.Y.: William S. Hein, 1983.

International Style. Term used to describe architectural design that is simple, functional, and unornamented, following the theoretical teachings of the BAUHAUS and the leading figures of MODERNISM of the 1920s and 1930s. While historic period design generally has been associated with national or regional traditions—as in French Gothic or Italian Renaissance styles—early modernism developed in France, Germany, the Scandinavian countries, and elsewhere in similar patterns, so that all such work can be considered truly international in character. The term was used as the title for an exhibition and related book at the MUSEUM OF MODERN ART in New York curated by Henry-Russell HITCHCOCK and Philip JOHNSON in 1932. Most of the work shown shared such characteristics as flat roofs, large glass areas, plain white walls, and an emphasis on the use of steel and concrete as building materials. The term has come to be associated with and applied to such designs, whereas other types of modern work (that of Frank Lloyd WRIGHT, for example) are not described by this term.

Interpretation of Dreams, The. Major theoretical work on the nature of dreams and the unconscious by Austrian psychiatrist Sigmund FREUD, the founder of psychoanalysis. In *The Interpretation of Dreams* (1900), Freud sought to establish a psychological technique for the interpretation of the "latent content" of dreams, that is, the unconscious drives, fears and obsessions that showed themselves in the "manifest content" of the dream itself. Freud outlined a theory of dream symbols that recurred frequently in the accounts of dreams offered by his patients. He further insisted on the importance of "condensation"—the transformation of "latent content" into the relatively brief dream narratives that could be consciously recalled by patients. Freud's basic tenet that dreams always contained a comprehensible psychical structure went against past medical dogma that had dismissed them as either hysterical symptoms or outright nonsense. As Freud's dream theories were not easily subject to empirical verification, they aroused considerable controversy. But *The Interpretation of Dreams* remains an influential classic of psychological thought. Freud himself thought it his most valuable work.

Intifada. Palestinian uprising in the form of riots against Israeli authority in the WEST BANK region. The intifada began on December 9, 1987, when a group of Palestinian youths ambushed some Israeli soldiers patrolling the area and began throwing stones. This activity was repeated in subsequent days, with more Palestinians taking part and violence spreading to other parts of the West Bank.

This Palestinian woman's son was arrested for stone-throwing in the Israeli-occupied Gaza Strip (1989).

Israeli soldiers responded by opening fire, and several Palestinians were killed or wounded. This pattern became an almost daily ritual; by December 1989, over 800 Palestinians and 44 Jews had died in the uprising. The Israelis claimed that the intifada was organized by the PALESTINE LIBERATION ORGANIZATION as a deliberate ploy to gain world sympathy for the Palestinian cause, and that Israel was justified in using armed force to maintain order. Whether or not the intifada was directly organized by the PLO, Israel was widely condemned for its handling of the situation. The worst day of violence came on October 8, 1990, when at least 17 Palestinians were killed on Jerusalem's Temple Mount. The following month, the UN unanimously adopted a resolution that referred to the occupied West Bank and GAZA STRIP as "Palestinian territories" and condemned Israel for its treatment of Arab civilians there.

Invisible Man. Novel by black American author Ralph ELLISON. *Invisible Man* (1952) is one of the most acclaimed American novels of this century. The winner of the National Book Award in 1953, *Invisible Man* remains a seminal imaginative text on racial prejudice and psychological alienation in America. It is also a stylistic tour de force that successfully captures on the page the precise lilt and lingo of 1950s HARLEM residents, BEBOP zoot suiters, West Indian immigrants, and a host of other American dialects. The unnamed protagonist of *Invisible Man* is a young black man who succeeds in educating himself despite the bigotry and cruelty he finds in white-dominated society. But despite this effort, he cannot find a place for himself in society either as a fervid black nationalist or as an assimilated black man acceptable to whites, and ends the novel hiding out in a sewer system.

in vitro fertilization. Method of fertilizing a human egg outside the body of the mother, creating a embryo that can then be transplanted into the mother's uterus and develop normally. The child produced by this technique of fertilization has been popularly called a "test-tube baby." The technique was developed by British physicians Patrick C. STEPTOE and Robert G. Edwards and was first used successfully in 1978. It was originally created for those cases of infertility in which the egg is produced normally but cannot be transmitted down the fallopian tube and into the uterus; it is now used in cases of low sperm count as well. The egg, or group of eggs, is removed from the mother's body, exposed to the father's sperm in a special culturing medium, fertilized and allowed to undergo several cell divisions before the tiny embryo is returned to the uterus. The technique has raised a number of ethical controversies but has provided an opportunity for thousands of previously infertile couples to have children.

Ioffe, Adolf Abrahmovich (1883–1927). Soviet revolutionary and diplomat, a supporter of TROTSKY. A member of the Menshevik Party, he joined Trotsky in Vienna in 1908. They both joined the BOLSHEVIKS in 1917. After the revolution he was one of the negotiators of the Russian-German TREATY OF BREST-LITOVSK, and he was made ambassador to Germany in 1918. He headed diplomatic missions to Geneva (1922) and China (1923). He remained a strong supporter of Trotsky in the power struggle after LENIN's death (1924). When Trotsky was defeated by STALIN, he committed suicide.

Ionesco, Eugene (1912–). French playwright and essayist. Ionesco, who won international fame with the premiere of his very first play, *The Bald Soprano* (1950), was one of the leading figures of the THEATER OF THE ABSURD and the most gifted comic playwright to emerge from within that movement. Ionesco was a master at crafting absurdist, nonsequitur dialogues that illustrated the fragility of language and of the social fabric itself. He adopted the existential outlook that society was based on arbitrary values and hence instilled a spirit of alienation in its citizens, who continued to hunger for meaning. This hunger was portrayed by Ionesco with a remarkably light touch, making his plays popular with theater audiences around the world. Other major plays by Ionesco include *The Lesson* (1951), *The Chairs* (1952), *Amedee, or How to Get Rid of It* (1954), *The New Tenant* (1955), *The Killer* (1959), *Rhinoceros* (1960), *Exit the King* (1962) and *A Stroll in the Air* (1963). *Notes and Counternotes* (1964) contains a selection of his essays on the theater.

Playwright Eugene Ionesco (1978).

Ipatyeff, Vladimir Nikolayevich (1867–1952). Russian chemist. He pioneered work on high-pressure catalytic reactions in hydrocarbons. He was made chairman of the government's chemical committee in 1914 and continued to work for the Soviet government after the revolution. He was, however, anti-communist and in 1927 he left the U.S.S.R. to settle later in the U.S. He is best known for his work during World War II, when his process for manufacturing high-octane gasoline from low-octane fuels was used to produce aviation fuel.

IRA. See IRISH REPUBLICAN ARMY.

Iran [Islamic Republic of Iran]. Iran encompasses an area of 646,128 square miles in southwest Asia. Known as Persia since ancient times, Reza PAHLEVI changed the country's name to Iran in 1935. For the first 26 years of this century Persia was ruled by the Oajar dynasty, a period marked by chaos and foreign intervention. After the shah was crowned in 1926, he introduced a modernization program, but his close relationship with Germany led Britain and Russia to invade Iran in 1941, forcing the shah to abdicate in favor of his son. The new shah, Muhammad Reza PAHLEVI, pursued economic and social reforms (called the White Revolution). The continued Westernization and secularization of Iran brought increased opposition, spearheaded by exiled Islamic Shi'ite leader Ayatollah KHOMEINI. The situation became so volatile that the shah fled Iran in January 1979, and Khomeini assumed power. He started the Islamic Cultural Revolution that prompted the Revolutionary Guards to storm the American Embassy in Teheran (November 1979), resulting in a hostage situation that lasted until January 1981. Historical claims to Iranian territory led neighboring IRAQ to invade Iran in 1980. The eight-year IRAN-IRAQ WAR was devastating, and Iran sued for peace in 1988 under provisions of a UNITED NATIONS plan. The U.S.'s covert involvement in the war surfaced in 1986 as the IRAN-CONTRA SCANDAL, involving secret arms deals with Iran in exchange for Iranian intervention to free American hostages in LEBANON. Since Khomeini's death in 1989, his successor

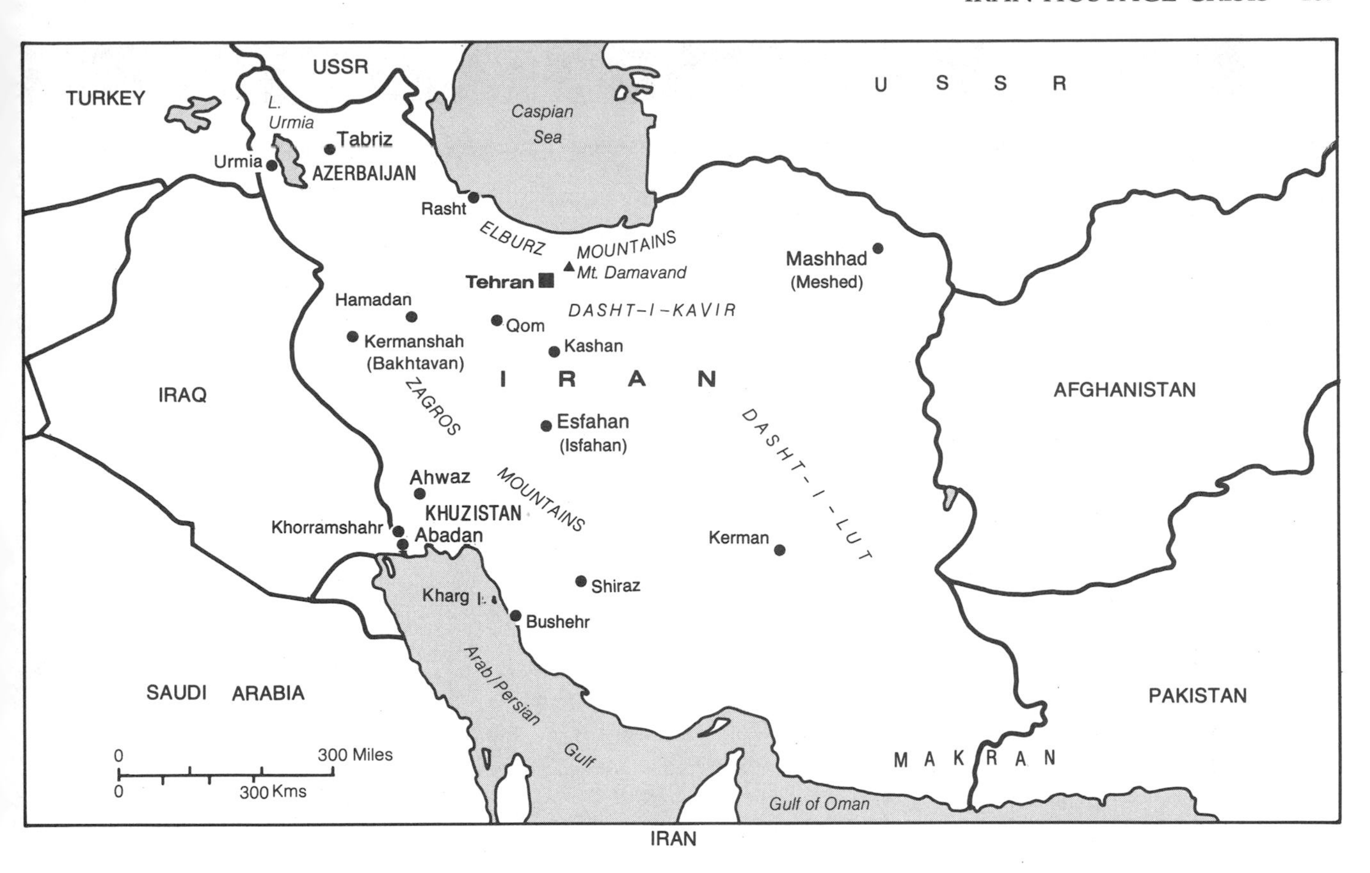

IRAN

Hashemi Rafsanjani has pursued a more moderate course. He declared Iran's neutrality in the UN-backed war against Iraq for its invasion of Kuwait in 1990, and tried to act as peacemaker during the conflict. (See also IRAN HOSTAGE CRISIS; PERSIAN GULF WAR.)

For further reading:

Avery, Peter, ed., *The Cambridge History of Iran. Vol. 7: From Nadir Shah to the Islamic Republic.* Cambridge: Cambridge University Press, 1990.

Ghods, M. Reza, *Iran in the Twentieth Century: A Political History.* Reinner, Lynne, 1989.

Wright, Robin, *In the Name of God: The Khomeini Decade, 1979–1989.* New York: Simon & Schuster, 1989.

Iran-Contra scandal. Political scandal that rocked the second term in office of President Ronald REAGAN. When Reagan came to office in 1981, the U.S. and IRAN were bitter adversaries. After the IRANIAN REVOLUTION OF 1979, Iran had held more than 50 American hostages for over a year. Reagan denounced Iran because of its support of terrorism but later funded the "Contra" movement, which was fighting a guerrilla war against the leftist Sandinista government of NICARAGUA. The Democrat-controlled Congress objected and voted to stop any financial support of the CONTRAS. In 1986 the press revealed that the U.S. government had secretly shipped arms to Iran and diverted the funds to a Swiss bank account controlled by the Contras in violation of Congress' ban. Highly publicized congressional investigations revealed that the prime movers in the scandal were Marine Lieutenant Colonel Oliver North and his boss, Vice Admiral John Poindexter. Also implicated was Robert "Bud" McFarland, the national security adviser. The hearings caused a sensation. Although President Reagan denied involvement and was never directly implicated, the scandal put his credibility and competence into question.

Iran hostage crisis. After Shah Muhammad Reza PAHLEVI of IRAN was forced to leave his country in January 1979, and

A bound and blindfolded American hostage is paraded before a crowd of Iranian students after the seizure of the American embassy in Teheran (1979).

IRAN

1907	Anglo-Russian agreement to protect foreign mineral interests effectively divides the country into three zones: Russian, British and neutral.
1914	Britain acquires controlling interest in the Anglo-Persian Oil Company.
1920	Gilan, an autonomous Soviet republic, is formed in the north of Iran.
1921	(Feb. 20) Col. Reza Khan takes over Gilan in a coup.
1923	Reza Khan becomes prime minister.
1926	Reza Khan is crowned Reza Shah Pahlevi.
1935	To curry favor with the Nazis, the shah changes the name of his country, Persia, to Iran—meaning "Aryan."
1941	Britain and Russia invade in 1941; Reza Shah Pahlevi abdicates in favor of his son Muhammed Reza.
1946	British and Russian occupation troops leave Iran; Azerbaijani dissidents establish independent republic and are put down by Iranian troops; Kurdish republic of Mahabad is proclaimed and suppressed by Iranian troops.
1952	With the support of Prime Minister Mohammed Mossadeq the Anglo-Iranian Oil Company is nationalized; relations with Great Britain are broken; shah dismisses Mossadeq but is forced to reinstate him; Mossadeq assumes complete control of the government; shah is forced to flee the country; in a countercoup, General Fazlollah Zahedi rallies army behind the shah and the shah is returned to power.
1954	Under a plan devised in Washington and London a consortium of oil companies is placed in charge of the AIOC (now called British Petroleum).
1955	Iran joins CENTO.
1957	SAVAK, the secret police, is established.
1960	Diplomatic recognition of Israel; Egypt breaks diplomatic relations as a result.
1963	Shah launches "White Revolution"; land reform and woman suffrage increased; Literacy Corps organized.
1967	Coronation of the shah.
1969	Dispute with Iraq over Shatt al-Arab erupts into open conflict.
1970	Iran accepts UN mediation on its claim to Bahrain.
1973	Oil industry is nationalized; Iran joins OPEC oil price hike.
1975	Restakhiz is made the sole political party.
1977	(October) Ayatollah Khomeini's son dies, sparking riots and strikes.
1978	(October) Khomeini's expulsion from Iraq to France highlights his position as opposition leader; strikes and demonstrations break out against the shah, country thrown into turmoil.
1979	(Jan. 16) The shah flees the country; (Feb. 1) Ayatollah Khomeini returns to Iran; (Nov. 4) Revolutionary Guards storm the U.S. embassy and take diplomatic personnel hostage.
1980	(Jan. 25) Abolhassan Bani Sadr elected as the first post-revolutionary president; Revolutionary Council disbands as Bani Sadr cabinet takes office; (March) nationalization of most medium- to large-size industries and financial institutions is begun; (Apr. 25) U.S. military attempt to rescue the embassy hostages fails; (Sept. 22) Iraq invades Iran, beginning bloody eight-year war.
1981	(Jan. 21) American hostages released; (June) impeachment proceedings commence against Bani Sadr; (July) Mohammed Ali Radjai named president; (August) Radjai and Prime Minister Bahonar killed in bomb attack launched by the Mujaheddin.
1985	U.S. offers arms deal to Iranians in an attempt to obtain release of American hostages in Lebanon.
1988	Iran sues for peace with Iraq on the basis of a UN resolution passed in 1987.
1989	(Feb. 14) Khomeini calls for the death of author Salman Rushdie for his book *The Satanic Verses*; (June) Khomeini dies; Hasemi Rafsanjani emerges as preeminent leader and is elected president.
1990	(Sept. 24) Iran states it will not violate UN trade sanctions imposed on Iraq for its invasion of Kuwait.

was subseqently admitted to the U.S. for medical treatment, tensions between the U.S. and Islamic fundamentalists within Iran greatly increased. On November 4, 1979, Iranian students, with the support of fundamentalists in the provisional government, seized the U.S. embassy in Teheran and held 63 members of the embassy staff hostage. The students demanded the return of the ousted shah for trial. The crisis received almost continual television and press coverage in the U.S. and virtually paralyzed the administration of U.S. President Jimmy CARTER. An American military rescue attempt failed disastrously on April 25, 1980, further exacerbating matters. The crisis and Carter's handling of it became a major issue in the 1980 U.S. presidential election and contributed to Carter's defeat by Ronald REAGAN in November 1980. Behind-the-scenes diplomacy and the payment of a substantial sum of U.S.-held Iranian assets finally secured the hostages' release, which the Iranians timed to coincide with Reagan's inauguration. Most Americans viewed the crisis as a manifestation of anti-American feelings and a test of U.S. strength. However, many Middle East experts interpreted the hostage-taking as part of a power struggle between hard-line Islamic fundamentalists and pro-Western moderates within the provisional government. The fundamentalist faction (led by Ayatollah KHOMEINI) gained the upper hand and purged the moderates, establishing an Islamic republic.

Iranian Revolution of 1979. IRAN's Shah Muhammed Reza PAHLEVI was opposed by Iranian liberals for his authoritarianism and by conservatives for his westernism. These groups collaborated in 1978 under exiled Muslim religious leader Ayatollah Ruhollah KHOMEINI until rioting forced the shah to flee in January 1979. Strikes, huge demonstrations, the neutrality of the army and the return of Khomeini to Iran brought down the government by February. Khomeini declared Iran an Islamic republic, establishing a revolutionary council to rule. Trials and executions of opponents ensued. The regime was approved overwhelmingly by a March 30, 1979, referendum, but the terror continued. Iran broke relations with the West and the Islamic world, and on November 4, 1979, militants seized U.S. embassy staff as hostages for the return of the shah's assets (see IRAN HOSTAGE CRISIS). Despite the shah's death (July 1980) the hostage crisis continued until Algerian mediation led to a U.S.-Iranian agreement freeing the hostages as Ronald REAGAN was being inaugurated as U.S. president (January 20, 1981). Khomeini's Islamic revolution continued in Iran.

Iran-Iraq War. Capping a long dispute over the Shatt-al-Arab waterway, and Ayatollah Ruhollah KHOMEINI's attempts to destabilize Iraq's government under President Saddam HUSSEIN, IRAQ invaded IRAN on September 21–22, 1980. With its well-equipped army it hoped for a quick victory. Iranian forces retaliated; Khomeini called for total mobilization and threatened oil shipments through the Strait of Hormuz. Despite massive offensives (Iraq had a 500,000-man army, Iran had 2 million), neither side was able to occupy enemy territory, and the war settled into a vicious, costly stalemate until 1988. Iraqi air attacks against tankers in the Persian Gulf led the U.S. to initiate an international naval patrol tilted against Iran, which was held responsible for terrorist attacks. Iraq also employed chemical warfare, and, after many failed attempts the UNITED NATIONS arranged a cease-fire in August 1988. (See also PERSIAN GULF WAR.)

Iraq [Republic of Iraq]. Iraq, encompassing the river valleys of the Tigris and Euphrates, was a birthplace of many of the civilizations of the ancient world. It is situated northwest of the PERSIAN GULF and is bordered by IRAN to the east, KUWAIT and SAUDI ARABIA to the south, JORDAN and SYRIA to the west and TURKEY to its north—an area of 167,881 square miles. Britain occupied the cities of BASRA and BAGHDAD during WORLD WAR I, and Iraq, carved out of the crumbled OTTOMAN EMPIRE, became a British mandate in 1920. The growth of nationalist feeling led to the termination of the mandate in 1932 and Iraq's acceptance as an independent country in the LEAGUE OF NATIONS. Britain again occupied Iraq during WORLD WAR II. The corrupt pro-British government that ruled after the war was overthrown and the royal family executed during the revolution of 1958. The new government of Abd al-Karim KASSEM was overthrown in 1963. Five years of war with Iraq's Kurdish minority ended with another coup, which brought Ahmed Hasan al-BAKR to power (1968). When Bakr resigned in 1979, Saddam HUSSEIN became president. Saddam invaded Iran (September 1980), claiming Iraqi rights to the Shatt-al-Arab waterway and the Iranian province of Khuzistan. The eight-year IRAN-IRAQ WAR was devastating for both countries and ended with a cease-fire in 1988. In August 1990 Saddam invaded and occupied Kuwait, at the head of the Persian Gulf, claiming historical rights to the territory. UN air forces, led by the U.S., attacked Iraq on January 16, 1991, after Saddam refused to withdraw from Kuwait. Six weeks of intensive high-precision bombing virtually destroyed Iraq's infrastructure; by the end of February 1991, Iraqi forces were in disarray and the nation was forced to accept a cease-fire on U.S. terms. Various rebel groups within Iraq subsequently turned against Hus-

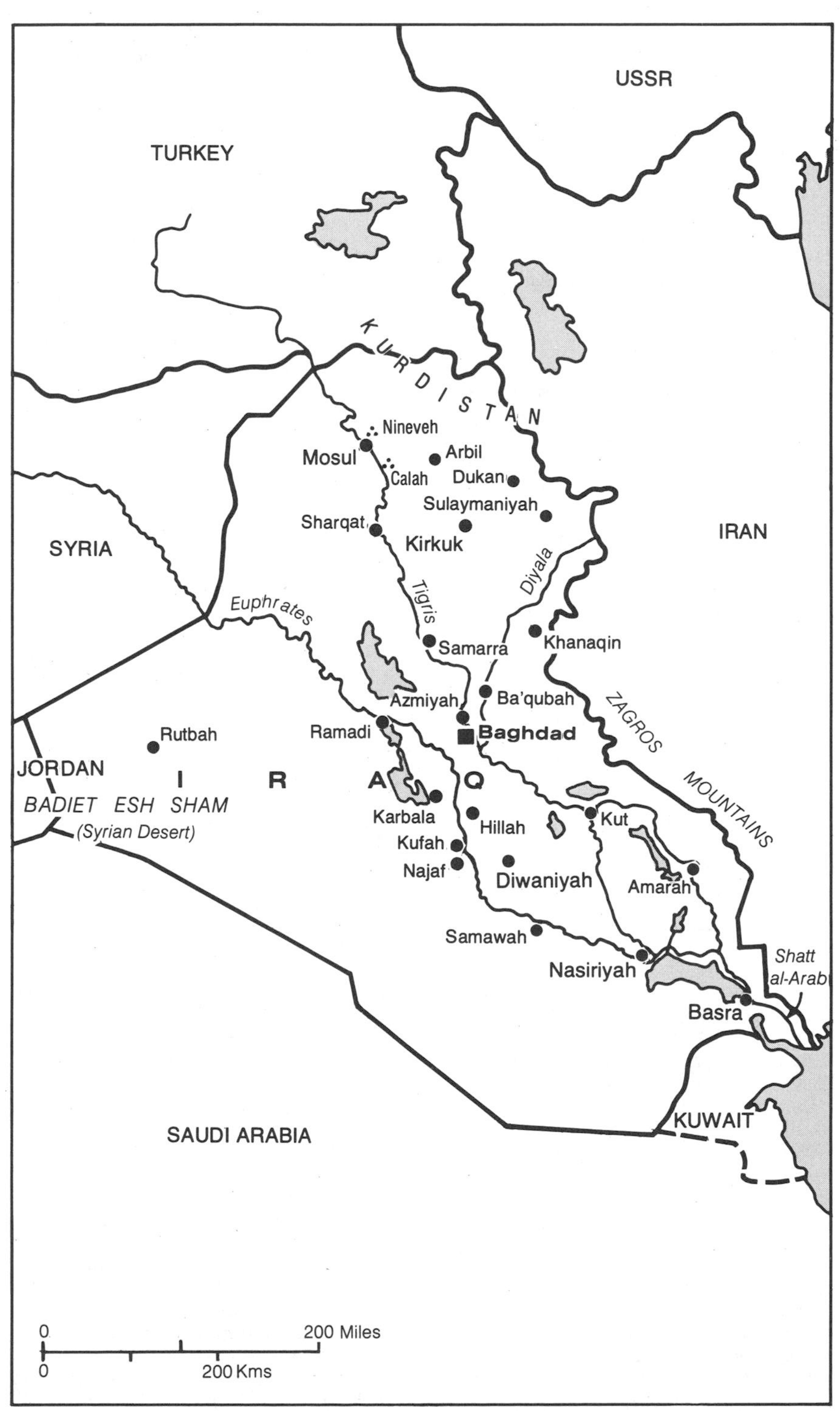

IRAQ

IRAQ

1914	(November) British occupy Shatt al-Arab waterway, removing it from control of Germany's ally, the Ottomans; modernize port at Basra.
1917	(March) British occupy Baghdad; promise postwar independence, encouraging a nationalist movement.
1920	San Remo Conference; League of Nations makes Iraq a British Mandate; Faisal I installed as king.
1923	Oil discovered.
1932	Nominal independence granted; British keep military bases.
1941	"Golden Square" officers group attempts anti-British, pro-German coup; Britain reoccupies.
1945	Pro-British prime minister installed; corruption rises.
1958	"Free Officers" group under Abd al-Karim stages coup; royal family and prime minister killed; U.S. lands Marines in Lebanon in response to this and other Arab nationalist activity.
1961	Death of Jawid Salim, creator of huge modern sculpture, "Monument to Revolution," in Baghdad.
1962	Nationalists agitate for union with Nasser's United Arab Republic; communists oppose.
1963	Nationalist coalition seizes power; massacres communists; coalition includes Ba'athists, who favor a pan-Arab, secular socialist state.
1964	Civil war with Kurds in northern Iraq.
1968	Ba'athists seize power after Arab defeat in Six-Day War; under Ahmed Hasan al-Bakr, country turns toward Soviets.
1972	Oil companies nationalized; price boom brings great wealth to government.
1974	Civil war with Kurds.
1978	Shiite Muslims (majority of population) oppose secular policies of Ba'athists; violent oppression of Shiites results.
1979	Ayatollah Khomeini leaves exile to foment Shiite revolution in Iran; vows to carry it to Iraq; Saddam Hussein succeeds Bakr.
1980	Saddam Hussein invades Iran; bloody eight-year war follows.
1988	Cease-fire with Iran.
1990	Iraq overruns Kuwait and declares annexation; U.S. organizes large force in Saudi Arabia and Turkey; issues ultimatum that Iraq pull back.
1991	After the heaviest aerial bombardment in history, U.S.-led forces invade Iraq; infrastructure of the country is destroyed; Hussein fails to draw Israel into war (and hence drive out Arab members of U.S. coalition); he remains in power despite Shiite and Kurdish rebellions; Kurds begin disastrous exodus into mountains of Turkey, where thousands die.

sein, and the country fell into civil strife. (See also PERSIAN GULF WAR.)

For further reading:

Farouk-Sluglett, Marion, and Peter Sluglett, *Iraq Since 1958: From Revolution to Dictatorship*. London: Routledge, Chapman & Hall, 1987.

Longrigg, Stephen, *Iraq, 1900–1950*. International Book Centre, 1968.

Ireland [Eire; Republic of Ireland]. Island nation in the Atlantic Ocean, 50 miles west of Great Britain. The Republic of Ireland occupies the south, central and northwest regions of the island of Ireland. Ireland entered the 20th century as part of the UNITED KINGDOM, represented in the British Parliament. Intermittently throughout the 19th century, the Irish had agitated for independence. In the late 19th century, two bills proposing HOME RULE for Ireland were introduced in Parliament but defeated; a third was passed in 1914. Northern Protestants, led by Sir Edward CARSON, were determined to defend the union with Britain by force. However, Home Rule was deferred for the duration of WORLD WAR I. Moderate Irish nationalists supported the British war effort. In April 1916, militant nationalist and left-wing elements, including SINN FEIN, launched the abortive EASTER RISING in DUBLIN under the leadership of Patrick PEARSE and James CONNOLLY; the British quickly suppressed the rebellion, but the subsequent execution of the 16 rebel leaders turned them into martyrs and led to increased public support for Irish independence. In the 1918 British general elections, Sinn Fein won 72 of the 105 Irish seats in the House of Commons; the Sinn Fein members refused to take their seats, but instead created a rebel Irish parliament, the DAIL EIREANN, in Dublin (1919).

Several years of guerrilla war followed as the rebels battled the constabulary, which was reinforced by the "Black and Tans." Under the Government of Ireland Act (December 1920), the six Protestant-dominated counties of Ulster were given their own home rule parliament. An Anglo-Irish Treaty (December 1921) created the **Irish Free State** as a self-governing dominion within the British COMMONWEALTH. NORTHERN IRELAND opted to remain with the U.K. The new Irish Free State consisted of 26 of the 32 Irish counties. The IRISH CIVIL WAR (1922–23) followed in the Free State between those accepting the treaty and a majority of Sinn Fein, led by Eamon DE VALERA and supported by the IRISH REPUBLICAN ARMY (IRA), who opposed the partition of Ireland. The pro-treaty side prevailed, and in 1927 de Valera took his Dail seat as leader of the new FIANNA FAIL party in opposition to a government led by the forerunner of the FINE GAEL party. Following Fianna Fail's election victory in 1932, de Valera became prime minister and brought in a new constitution (1937), still largely in force, which described the national territory as "the whole island of Ireland" and enshrined Roman Catholic moral and social precepts. Ireland remained neutral during WORLD WAR II (officially known as "the Emergency") and maintained Irish neutrality in the postwar era.

The 1948 elections brought to power a four-party coalition. The country subsequently adopted the name Republic of Ireland and left the COMMONWEALTH (1949). In the same year, British legislation guaranteed that Northern Ireland would not cease to be part of the U.K. without the consent of the Northern Irish parliament. De Valera was again prime minister (1951–54, 1957–59), then became president of the republic until his death in 1973. Under the Fianna Fail government of Sean Lemass (1959–66), Ireland achieved significant economic progress and established free trade with the U.K. The Fianna Fail government of Jack Lynch (1966–73) took the republic into full membership of the EUROPEAN COMMUNITY and the EUROPEAN ECONOMIC COMMUNITY, to the advantage of Irish agriculture. Successive Dublin governments sought a U.K.-Irish cooperative framework within which to address the conflict of aspirations between Protestants and Catholics in Northern Ireland, where escalating violence from the late 1960s had impelled the U.K. government to impose direct rule in 1972–73 and again from 1974. In August 1979, Lord MOUNTBATTEN was murdered by the IRA while visiting Ireland, and 18 British soldiers in Northern Ireland were killed the same day in a separate IRA attack. As a result Lynch (who had succeeded Cosgrave as prime minister in 1977) agreed to strengthen border security. In 1979 Charles Haughey (whose career had survived allegations of gun-running for the IRA in 1970) became Fianna Fail leader and prime minister, but elections two years later brought another Fine Gael/Labour coalition to power under Garret Fitzgerald. In November 1985 Fitzgerald and U.K. Prime Minister Margaret THATCHER signed an Anglo-Irish agreement (the HILLSBOROUGH ACCORD) giving Ireland a consultative role in Northern affairs in return for accepting that reunification could be achieved only with the consent of a Northern majority. Although Haughey had opposed the accord, he agreed to abide by it after he regained office in 1987.

Ireland faced serious economic problems in the 1980s—high inflation and unemployment. In the late 1980s, the new Haughey government intensified its predecessor's economic austerity program, seeking to reduce a huge budget deficit. In November 1990, Mary Robinson of the left-wing Labour Party became Ireland's first woman president (the official head of state) in an electoral upset.

For further reading:

Foster, R.F., *Modern Ireland, 1600–1972*. New York: Viking Penguin, 1990.

———, ed., *The Oxford Illustrated History of Ireland*. Oxford: Oxford University Press, 1989.

Lyons, F.S., *Culture and Anarchy in Ireland, 1890–1939*. Oxford: Oxford University Press, 1989.

Ireland, John (Nicholson) (1879–1962). English composer. Ireland studied at the Royal College of Music, London, where he later taught. He also served as a church organist in Chelsea (1904–26). His many influences include the scenic beauty of the Channel Islands, folk music, German romanticism and Celtic myth. He is most admired for the simple beauty of his over 70 songs, many of them set to poems by writers such as John Masefield, A.E. HOUSMAN and Thomas HARDY. Ireland's other works include chamber music, piano works including a concerto (1930), choral pieces and orchestral music such as the *Symphonic Rhapsody* (1920–21) and the *London Overture* (1936).

Irgun Zvai Leumi. Zionist terrorist organization founded in 1937. Operating in PALESTINE, the Irgun was led by Gideon Paglin (1923–) as its chief of operations and after 1943, with Menachem BEGIN as its commander. Its most notorious act of terrorism was the blowing up of the KING DAVID HOTEL in Jerusalem on July 22, 1946. The British administration was housed in the southwest wing of the hotel, which was completely destroyed, and 91 people were killed. Irgun claimed responsibility for over 200 terrorist acts against the British and the Arabs.

Irian Barat. A province of INDONESIA that comprises the western half of the island of NEW GUINEA and approximately 12 nearby islands; formerly known as Dutch, or Netherlands, New Guinea. Occupied by the Japanese during WORLD WAR II, it was not returned to Dutch control until 1949. Indonesian claims to the region led to a Dutch handover of the territory in 1963; Indonesia's sovereignty was recognized following a plebiscite in 1969.

Irish Civil War. See ANGLO-IRISH CIVIL WAR OF 1916–23.

Irish Free State. See IRELAND.

Irish Literary Revival. A resurgence in nationalist Irish literature that began in the latter decades of the 19th century and continued into the 1920s. Some Irish nationalists favored a "Gaelic revival" but were unsuccessful in reintroducing the Gaelic language. Most writers supported W.B. YEATS, who felt that a national literature could exist even though written in English. The beginnings of the movement occurred with a renewed interest in Irish folklore and culture evidenced by works such as *Love Songs of Connaught* by Samuel Ferguson (1810–1886) and *Literary History of Ireland* (1892) by Douglas HYDE. The same year Yeats' first play *The Countess Cathleen* (1892) appeared, thus launching a solely Irish drama separate from that of England. In 1899 Yeats and Lady GREGORY founded the Irish Literary Theatre to promote Irish drama. It became the Irish National Theatre Society, giving its first performance in 1902 of AE's *Deirdre* and Yeats' *Cathleen Ni Houlihan*. In the following year John Millington SYNGE's *In the Shadow of the Glen* and Padraic Colum's *Broken Soil* were presented. With the help of Annie HORNIMAN, the society found a home in the ABBEY THEATRE in 1904. Periodicals fundamental to the revival include *The Irish Statesman*, a literary review edited by AE, and the *Irish Review*, which was founded in 1911 by Colum, James STEPHENS, and Thomas MacDonagh. Other writers associated with the Irish literary revival include George MOORE, Sean O'CASEY, George Bernard SHAW and James JOYCE.

Irish Republican Army [IRA]. Nationalist organization whose goal is an independent and unified IRELAND. It was formed in 1919 by veterans of the 1916 EASTER REBELLION led by Michael COLLINS. Becoming the military arm of the SINN FEIN party, it fought the British Black and Tans; after the partition of Ireland and the formation of the Irish Free State

IRELAND

IRELAND

1904	W.B. Yeats and Lady Gregory found Abbey Theatre; Irish literary renaissance continues.
1905	Founding of Sinn Fein, independence movement; *Irish Independent* publishes first issue.
1916	Easter Uprising by Irish Republican Brotherhood crushed by British; 16 rebel leaders executed.
1918	After general election, Irish members of British Parliament refuse to report to London; convene as the Dail in Dublin (1919).
1920	British offer limited autonomy to both Northern and Southern Ireland; the south rejects it.
1921	Anglo-Irish Treaty: British agree to Irish Free State, with expanded autonomy; six counties of Northern Ireland remain within United Kingdom.
1922	Civil war between factions accepting Free State compromise and those demanding full independence; Yeats wins Nobel Prize for literature; James Joyce's *Ulysses* published in Paris, banned in Ireland.
1923	Fighting ends but IRA continues guerrilla struggle for independence; IRA outlawed.
1932	Eamon de Valera elected prime minister; begins cutting ties to Britain.
1937	Dail adopts new constitution, embodying Catholic stance on many moral issues.
1941	Ireland remains neutral in World War II to show displeasure with Britain.
1949	Independence declared; republic established; Ireland withdraws from Commonwealth.
1961	First television station.
1965	Anglo-Irish free-trade treaty.
1973	Legal ban on contraceptives relaxed.
1979	Lord Mountbatten assassinated by IRA in Sligo; IRA continues terrorist campaign for independent Northern Ireland.
1980	Population at one-half the level of 1840.
1985	Prime Minister Garret FitzGerald signs Anglo-Irish Agreement (Hillsborough Accord) on Northern Ireland with British Prime Minister Thatcher.
1990	President Lenihan brought down by scandal; Mary Robinson elected first woman president.
1991	Death of writer Sean O'Faolain.

in 1922, it refused to recognize a separate NORTHERN IRELAND and, as a secret terrorist organization, continued an armed struggle against the new government. The IRA's hit-and-run bombings and street fights were quite successful for about 10 years, but it was significantly weakened after former IRA supporter Eamon DE VALERA became head of the Free State in 1932. Its violent tactics and pro-German activities during WORLD WAR II further lessened the IRA's popularity. After the war, it was outlawed by both Irish governments but continued to operate and to perpetuate terrorist attacks throughout the 1950s. After a comparatively peaceful time in the 1960s, the IRA broke into two groups (1969), forming a moderate or official wing, which pursued political means, and a radical or provisional wing, which continued to use violent techniques. Subsequently, the provisionals mounted a campaign of terror in Northern Ireland, often concentrating on members of the British armed forces. In the early 1990s, the IRA continued to operate as an underground terrorist organization, and sporadic acts of violence perpetrated by its members continued in the two Irelands and England.

Iron Curtain. Term used to denote the boundary between Soviet-dominated Eastern Europe and the democratic West during the COLD WAR. The Iron Curtain was not so much a physical barrier between two geographical areas as a metaphor for the constraints on the movement of people and ideas that the communist regimes imposed on their citizens. The term was coined by Sir Winston CHURCHILL during a speech he delivered at Westminster College in Fulton, Missouri, on March 5, 1946. "From Stettin in the Baltic to Trieste on the Adriatic, an iron curtain has descended across the continent." Denouncing the "police governments" that the U.S.S.R. was establishing in Eastern Europe, Churchill added that "this is certainly not the liberated Europe we fought to build up." (See also BERLIN WALL.)

Iroquois Theater fire. Disastrous fire of December 31, 1903, that killed more than 500 patrons at the Iroquois Theater in Chicago. A matinee audience at the sumptuous theater was engulfed in flames after the stage caught fire and the asbestos safety curtain failed to function. Some were burned to death or died of smoke inhalation, but most of those killed were crushed or suffocated in the hysterical dash for exits. The death toll made the fire the worst single-structure fire in American history.

Irving, Clifford (1930–). American novelist and master literary forger. Irving began his writing career as a novelist and published three now-forgotten volumes of fiction. But he assured himself of a dubious immortality as the coauthor (with children's book writer Richard Suskind) of a forged autobiography of reclusive American billionaire Howard HUGHES, for which McGraw-Hill, the publisher of Irving's novels, paid Irving $765,000 in 1971. The autobiography manuscript (complete with notes in Hughes' handwriting, forged by Irving) was drawn both from library research and from illicit plagiarism of an unpublished work on Hughes's financial empire by journalist James Phelan, who was one of the first to point the finger at Irving as a forger. Deemed by many as the greatest literary hoax of the 20th century, the forged autobiography was never published and earned Irving, as well as Irving's wife (who deposited the advance check made out to Hughes in a false Swiss bank account) and coauthor Suskind, brief prison terms.

Irving, John (Winslow) (1942–). American novelist. Irving had already written three fanciful novels when he drew critical acclaim and national attention with *The World According to Garp* (1978, filmed 1982), which tells the story of novelist T.S. Garp, son of an iconoclastic single mother, Jenny Field. The book presents a dark side of modern life, but not without humor; and like Irving's subsequent fiction, imbues contemporary situations with traditional, romantic values. His other works include *The Hotel New Hampshire* (1981, filmed 1984), *Cider House Rules* (1985) and *A Prayer for Owen Meany* (1989).

Irwin, James (1930–). U.S. astronaut, popular public speaker and founder of the High Flight Foundation, a nonprofit religious organization. Irwin spent almost three days on the surface of the moon in 1971, but most recently has lead five expeditions to Mount Ararat in Turkey, searching for the remains of Noah's Ark. Irwin says that he experienced a religious revelation during his APOLLO 15 (July 26–August 7, 1971) flight; he resigned from NASA on July 1, 1972. Born in Pittsburgh, Pennsylvania, Irwin attended the U.S. Naval Academy at Annapolis, receiving a B.S. in 1951. After earning an M.S. in aeronautical engineering and instrumentation engineering from the University of Michigan, he entered the U.S. Air Force, serving as a fighter pilot. Irwin joined NASA in 1966, where he tested lunar module systems and served on the support crew for Apollo 10. As lunar command module pilot for Apollo 15, Irwin and fellow astronaut David Scott were the first astronauts to make use of the Lunar Rover, an electric car that carried them more than 18 miles on three moon excursions lasting a total of 21 hours.

Isherwood, Christopher (William Bradshaw) (1904–1986). British-born author. Educated at Cambridge, during the 1930s Isherwood was closely associated with poet W.H. AUDEN. The two collaborated on three verse plays and a travel book about China. Isherwood immigrated to the U.S. in 1939 and settled in California. He was best known for the stories he wrote in the 1930s about pre-Nazi BERLIN, which became the basis for the play and film *I Am a Camera* and the stage and screen musical *Cabaret*. These adaptations enabled him to give up the HOLLYWOOD screenwriting with which he had supported himself for a number of years. Isherwood was one of the first international figures to admit that he was homosexual, and in the 1970s became a leading spokesman for GAY RIGHTS. His autobiography, *Christopher and His Kind*, dealt candidly with homosexuality.

Iskander, Fazil (1929–). Soviet writer. Although born in Abkhazia, Iskander's stories and poetry are written in the Russian language. The plots of his stories are simple, and the style is conversational and witty, although this does not weaken the strong satire. Iskander's best-known novel is *The Goatibex Constellation* (1966), in which bureaucrats aspire to crossbreed an ordinary goat with a mountain wild ox, thus resolving the problem of food production in the Soviet Union and affirming Michurinist genetics.

Iskra Group. An unofficial body within the Social Democratic Workers' Party ("iskra" means "the spark"). It was organized by LENIN, Yuly Martov and Alexander Potresov in 1900. They aimed to unite the active Marxist members, and were successful in gaining control of local branches of the party. During the second party congress, which they organized, the group split; the more revolutionary faction formed the Bolshevik group. The Iskra provided Lenin with his first position of influence, and he also founded the newspaper of the same name, which after 1900 was published abroad.

Islamabad. Capital city of PAKISTAN, about eight miles northeast of Rawalpindi; erected on a barren site chosen in 1959 to be a new city and to replace KARACHI as the capital. After plans by several of the world's best known architects, Islamabad has distinct sections for government administration, diplomats, housing, light industry, etc.; it was first used as the capital in 1967.

isolationism. Diplomatic policy under which a nation maintains its rights and interests without alliances. The U.S. pursued a successful isolationist policy from 1800 until 1917, when it joined other countries to fight Germany in WORLD WAR I. After the war isolationism again dominated U.S. policy until WORLD WAR II and the ensuing COLD WAR made the policy untenable. The U.S. joined the UNITED NATIONS and established several defensive alliances, which have often entangled the country in foreign upheavals, such as the VIETNAM WAR. Cultural isolationism existed for much of the century in the U.S.S.R. and China.

Israel. Israel is situated in the Middle East along the eastern shores of the Mediterranean Sea; its area, as defined by the 1949 Arab-Israeli armistice, is approximately 8,017 square miles. Excluded are occupied territories in the GAZA STRIP, the WEST BANK and the GOLAN HEIGHTS, acquired during the SIX-DAY WAR in 1967. Sacred to Judaism, Christianity and Is-

ISRAEL

lam, the land has been a battleground for millennia. Carved out of the post-World War I ruins of the OTTOMAN EMPIRE, PALESTINE was administered by Britain under a LEAGUE OF NATIONS mandate (1922–47). Jewish immigration increased, as did Arab opposition; riots in 1929 progressed to sustained guerrilla warfare (1933 onward) between Arabs and JEWS. Attempts to partition the land into separate Arab and Jewish states failed (1937, 1947); Britain withdrew in 1947, leaving the country in a state of civil war. The state of Israel was proclaimed in 1948, with BEN GURION as the first prime minister. The problem of displaced Palestinian Arabs in the new state remained unresolved and led to the formation of the PALESTINE LIBERATION ORGANIZATION (PLO) in 1964. The PLO has launched repeated terrorist attacks against Israel and its primary ally the U.S. to force establishment of a Palestinian state. Israeli Prime Minister Menachem BEGIN signed the first peace treaty with an Arab country (Egypt) in 1979 (see CAMP DAVID TALKS). Israel invaded LEBANON in 1982 to destroy PLO bases but withdrew in 1986. Rapid Jewish settlement of the occupied West Bank led to the INTIFADA (Palestinian uprising), which began in 1987. Internal division within the current government led by Yitzhak SHAMIR has hampered resolution of the Palestinian question. During the PERSIAN GULF WAR between UN forces and Iraq (January-February 1991) Israel suffered Iraqi Scud missile attacks but remained uninvolved. After the war, U.S. President George BUSH announced a new peace initiative to resolve the ongoing Arab-Israeli dispute.

For further reading:

Magnum, *Israel: The First Forty Years*. New York: Macmillan, 1987.

Sachar, Howard M., *A History of Israel: From the Rise of Zionism to Our Time*. New York: Alfred A. Knopf, 1979.

———, *A History of Israel, Vol. 2: From the Aftermath of the Yom Kippur War*. Oxford: Oxford University Press, 1987.

Israeli War of Independence. See ARAB-ISRAELI WAR OF 1948–49.

Issigonis, Alec (1906–). British automotive engineer and automobile designer whose work includes some of the most important and innovative designs produced by the English motor industry. Issigonis was trained in London as an engineer and began work as a draftsman for Rootes Motors. He later joined Morris Motors and became that firm's chief en-

ISRAEL

1909	Tel-Aviv, the first modern all-Jewish city, is founded.
1917	(November) British Balfour Declaration calls for national Jewish home in Palestine but respects rights of Palestinians.
1922	Britain given League of Nations mandate over Palestine.
1929	As a result of increased Jewish presence, bloody riots break out in Jerusalem, Hebron and Safed between Jews and the indigenous Palestinian Arabs.
1946	Israeli terrorists bomb King David Hotel in Jerusalem, kill 91.
1948	Britain leaves Palestine; (May 14) State of Israel proclaimed in Tel Aviv; Egypt, Transjordan, Syria, Iraq and Lebanon invade Israel; Israel survives the war and adds territory to land granted by the UN; 780,000 Palestinians are displaced from their homes; Chaim Weizmann is elected first president and David Ben-Gurion first prime minister.
1949	Israel joins the UN.
1956	Suez War: Israel, with the backing of Britain and France, attacks Egyptian positions in Gaza and overruns the Sinai Peninsula, from which it withdraws after UN condemnation.
1960	Adolf Eichmann is kidnapped from Argentina and after a long trial is found guilty and hanged (1962).
1964	(January) Palestine National Council is formed advocating armed stuggle to liberate Palestine; (June) The Palestine National Council establishes the PLO.
1967	(June 5) Israel launches preemptive strike, beginning the Six-Day War; captures the Sinai Peninsula, Gaza, the West Bank and the Golan Heights, almost tripling the land under its control; (Nov. 22) UN Resolution 242 passed, calling for Israeli withdrawal from captured territory and "mutual respect for the sovereignty of all states within secure boundaries."
1969	(Mar. 17) Golda Meir becomes prime minister.
1972	Palestinian terrorists kill 11 Israeli athletes at the Olympic Games in Munich.
1973	(Oct. 6) Yom Kippur War starts when Eygpt and Syria attack Israel on the Jewish holy day. Cease-fire declared October 24.
1974	Golda Meir resigns and is replaced by Yitzhak Rabin.
1976	Israeli commandos free 110 hostages held at Entebbe Airport in Uganda by Arab terrorists.
1977	(May 13) Rabin steps down and is replaced by Menachem Begin, who favors Israeli settlement of the occupied territories; (Nov. 9) Anwar Sadat becomes the first Arab leader to visit Israel, address the Knesset.
1978	(Jan.) Israel attacks PLO bases in Lebanon in retaliation for PLO raids on Israeli border settlements; (Dec. 14) Israel annexes the Golan Heights.
1979	(Mar. 26) Anwar Sadat of Egypt and Menachem Begin of Israel sign Camp David Accords.
1982	(June 6) Israel invades Lebanon after an attempt to assassinate the Israeli ambassador in London; (Sept. 16) with Israeli complicity, Christian Falangist militiamen enter the Palestinian refugee camps of Sabra and Shatila and kill about 700; Israel begins phased withdrawal from Lebanon.
1984	(Aug. 31) Labor and Likud form a coalition, with Shimon Peres as prime minister.
1986	(Oct. 20) Yitzhak Shamir becomes prime minister.
1987	(Dec. 9) The *intifada* (Palestinian uprising) begins.
1990	(Aug. 12) Saddam Hussein links pull-out from Kuwait to withdrawal of Israel from occupied Arab lands.
1991	Israel hit by Iraqi Scud missiles during Persian Gulf War but does not enter conflict; U.S. Secretary of State James Baker launches new Arab-Israeli peace plan.

ISRAEL FOLLOWING U.N. PARTITION, 1947

gineer in 1961. His design (both engineering and appearance) for the Morris Minor of 1948 made it one of the most popular British cars of its era—it remained in production for twenty years. The Morris Mini of 1951 was an even more successful design, introducing the modern transverse engine and front-wheel drive in a small car. The Mini offered surprising space and comfort along with excellent economy and mechanical simplicity in a way that has made it immensely popular in a number of variations, including the sporty Mini Cooper. The Mini set a high standard for aesthetic design along with its technically advanced engineering. It remains in production in a somewhat updated form.

Istanbul [Byzantium; Constantinople]. Partly in Europe and partly in Asia, this ancient city in northwestern TURKEY is located on both sides of the Bosporus. A busy port and Turkey's largest city, it was here that in 1908 a revolt of the YOUNG TURKS called for a parliament for the entire OTTOMAN EMPIRE. Turkey fought with the CENTRAL POWERS—the losing side—in WORLD WAR I, and Constantinople fell to the Allies in 1918. Its centuries-old empire shredded to pieces, Turkey was declared a republic, and the capital was moved from Constantinople to Ankara by Kemal ATATURK in 1923. Istanbul (officially renamed in 1930) retains many notable signs of its past diversity and greatness, especially the church of Hagia Sophia, a masterpiece of Byzantine architecture.

Itala Films. Important early Italian motion picture studio, which helped vault that country's cinema to world prominence in the years before World War I. Founded in Turin in 1905 under the name "Rossi," Itala developed under the management of Giovanni PASTRONE into a successful operation, producing numerous short action pictures and short comedies (especially slapstick farces featuring the French actor "Cretinetti," the pseudonym of Andre Deed). Its most significant production, the feature *Cabiria* (1914), became, along with rival studio Cine's *Quo Vadis* (1913), the most influential movie in the world. It confirmed that the feature-length film was the wave of the future and heavily influenced the epic ambitions of the American director D.W. GRIFFITH. Itala quickly followed up *Cabiria*'s success with a series of historical vehicles for the strongman star, "Maciste" (Bartolomei Pagano), anticipating by decades the vehicles for later musclemen such as Steve Reeves and Arnold Schwarzenegger. At its height, Itala became part of the Unione Cinematografica Italiana, the most powerful film consortium in the world. The company went into decline when Pastrone retired and the Unione went bankrupt in 1923.

For further reading:
Fifty Years of Italian Cinema. Rome: Carlo Bestetti, 1954.

Italian Somaliland. Now a part of SOMALIA, this former Italian colony in East Africa extended from Cape Asir to the Kenya border; its capital was Mogadishu. A small protectorate, set up by the Italians in 1889, was enlarged by subsequent additions, until it became a state of Italian East Africa (which included ETHIOPIA and ERITREA) in 1936. Invaded in 1941 by the British during WORLD WAR II, it remained under their control until 1950; in 1960 it was joined with British Somaliland to form the independent republic of Somalia.

Italian Uprisings of 1914. A new, moderate conservative government being formed by Premier Antonio Salandra was faced with popular uprisings on June 7, 1914, in which radicals confronted strikebreakers, staged antidraft demonstrations, and began to take over Bologna, Ancona and other cities, with the Romagna declaring itself a republic. More than 100,000 soldiers were needed to restore order; but by July Italy was preoccupied with moves to declare neutrality, despite its alliance with Germany and Austria, in the imminent world war.

Italo-Ethiopian War of 1935–36. As early as 1928, Benito MUSSOLINI, fascist dictator of ITALY since 1922, had planned to avenge the Italian defeat in the Italo-Ethiopian War of 1895–96. In a blatantly underhanded way, he sought to convince the world of Italy's right to ETHIOPIA, appealing to the LEAGUE OF NATIONS—after altering treaty documents of 1887, 1896 and 1900 and a great power agreement of 1908. His ploy worked: The League of Nations suggested partition, but Ethiopia rejected the Hoare-Laval plan, which would have given Italy most of the country. In 1934, a bloody clash occurred between Italian and Ethiopian forces at Ualual, a disputed area on the Italian Somaliland border. As Italy slowly massed an invasion force, Ethiopia's Emperor HAILE SELASSIE pulled his troops back 20 miles from the Eritrean border; nonetheless, the Italians invaded Ethiopia, without declaring war, on October 3, 1935. Using aircraft and modern weapons, Italian forces slowly destroyed Ethiopia—so slowly, in fact, that it took seven months for the supposedly modern and superior armies of Generals BADOGLIO and Graziani to conquer the "inferior" Ethiopians. The Ethiopian capital of Addis Ababa was captured on May 5, 1936.

Haile Selassie fled and made a vain appeal for help to the League of Nations; Italy, however, had already called its own king "emperor of Ethiopia," had annexed Ethiopia and had united it with Eritrea and Italian Somaliland to form Italian East Africa. The Italians executed the archbishop of the Ethiopian Coptic Church, massacred monks and decimated Addis Ababa. Although it had failed to conquer the entire country, Italy occupied Ethiopia until 1941, when it was liberated by British, Free French and Ethiopian troops during WORLD WAR II. Haile Selassie regained his throne on May 5, 1941.

Italy [Italia]. Republic of southern Europe; a long, boot-shaped peninsula, it is bounded on the north by France, Switzerland, Austria and Yugoslavia. But most of its border is a water-lapped coastline touched on the east by the Adriatic Sea and on the west and south by the Mediterranean Sea. Also a part of Italy are the large islands of Sardinia and Sicily, the smaller islands of Capri, Ischia and Elba, and the Lipari Islands. After the late-19th-century occupation of Somaliland (now SOMALIA) and ERITREA on the Red Sea and an unsuccessful invasion of ETHIOPIA in 1896, Italy occupied LIBYA, across the Mediterranean on the coast of North Africa, in 1911. Italy joined the Allied WORLD WAR I effort in 1915, but only after a secret agreement that, if victorious, it would gain Austrian-held Trieste and desirable territories in Africa and the OTTOMAN EMPIRE (including more territory in Libya). A victorious postwar Italy saw the Christian Democrats and the Socialists develop into mass political parties that were largely ineffective in coping with postwar problems. Former socialist Benito MUSSOLINI (1883–1945) developed the theory of FASCISM and became leader of the movement. He and his BLACKSHIRTS marched on Rome in October 1922; King VICTOR EMMANUEL III named him premier, and

ITALY

by 1927 Mussolini ruled as dictator. Almost continuously at war in a barely pacified Ethiopia from 1935, Italy also intervened on the side of FRANCO and the FALANGE in the SPANISH CIVIL WAR.

As a partner in HITLER'S AXIS, Italy entered WORLD WAR II in June 1940, only to suffer humiliating defeats in Africa and in Greece, which was subsequently overrun by Germany. The Allies invaded Sicily on July 10, 1943. Mussolini was subsequently dismissed by King VICTOR EMMANUEL III and imprisoned, but he was rescued by German paratroops and established the Republic of Salo in northern Italy under German protection. As the war's devastation moved from south to north, all the way up the peninsula, many cities, including Naples, Rome, Genoa and Milan, suffered heavy bombing, although Rome was declared an open city and taken by the Allies without ground fighting. Mussolini was killed in April 1945 by partisans while trying to escape to Switzerland. Victor Emmanuel abdicated in May 1946 and Humberto II briefly became king, but on June 2 the Italians narrowly voted to replace the monarchy with a republic.

From 1948 until the early 1980s the Christian Democrats (a broad center-right party) were in power (with only two interruptions). Despite a proliferation of political parties, and numerous political crises resulting in frequent changes of prime ministers and cabinets, Italy's postwar democracy remained a stable force, enabling the country to rebuild after the war. The country has since enjoyed close cooperation with the rest of Western Europe and the U.S. In 1949 Italy was a founding member of the NORTH ATLANTIC TREATY ORGANIZATION (NATO). The country was also an original member of the EUROPEAN COAL AND STEEL COMMUNITY and, later, of the EUROPEAN ECONOMIC COMMUNITY (EEC). The long political monopoly of the Christian Democrats led to a measure of inertia and corruption in the late 1960s; the Italian Communist Party, the strongest communist party in Western Europe, has consistently proved an attractive alternative for a sizeable percentage of the Italian electorate. The Christian Democrats formed coalitions with other parties, including the Socialist, in order to exclude the communists from government. Extremist terrorism of the left and right in the late 1970s attempted to disrupt Italian society; trains and railroad stations were bombed, and in 1978 former Premier Aldo MORO was kidnapped and murdered by the notorious RED BRIGADES. Terrorism abated in the 1980s. For four years after the 1983 elections, the Socialist Party headed the government. Italy joined the coalition against IRAQ in the PERSIAN GULF WAR (1990–91), and Italian pilots flew sorties from Saudi Arabia during Operation Desert Storm. Italy remains a center of the traditional arts and culture, a main attraction of world tourism. Rome is the capital, and other major cities are Naples, Milan, Palermo and Genoa.

For further reading:

Barzini, Luigi, *The Italians*. New York: Macmillan, 1977.

Iturbi, Jose (1895–1980). Spanish-American pianist and conductor. Born in Valencia, he studied at the Paris Conservatory. Renowned for his interpretations of the music of Spain, he toured Europe and made his American debut in 1929, later settling in the U.S. He was a much sought-after concert artist, touring worldwide, playing with many of the foremost symphony orchestras and often performing with his sister, the pianist Amparo Iturbi (1898–1969). He conducted the Rochester Philharmonic Orchestra from 1936 to 1944. Iturbi was best known to the general public for his appearances in a number of American musical films during the 1940s.

Ivanov, Vsevolod Vyacheslavovich (1895–1963). Soviet writer. Ivanov is best known for his short stories and novels, notably *The Partisan* (1921) and *Armored Train 14–69* (1922), which described Soviet expansion into Siberia. A protege of Maxim GORKY, he used his wide experience as partisan fighter, sailor, actor and circus performer in his writing. His plays include *The Compromise of Niab Khan* and *Twelve Young Lads from a Snuffbox*. He published his memoirs, *Meeting with Gorky*, in 1947. His early work, with its vivid, naturalistic description that attracted Gorky's attention, is considered to be his best.

Ivanov, Vyacheslav Ivanovich (1866–1949). Russian symbolist poet. In 1903 Ivanov published a volume of lyric poetry, *kormchiye zvezdy*, which established him as leader of the St. Petersburg symbolist movement. *Cor Ardens* (1911) is considered his most important poetical work. He was also a philosopher and classical scholar. He was made professor of Greek at Baku University in 1921 and in 1924 immigrated to Italy, where he became a Catholic.

Ivanov-Razumnik (1878–1946). Pseudonym of Razumnik Valsilyevich Ivanov. He was a writer and critic and leader of

ITALY

1900	Umberto I assassinated by anarchist.
1907	Prince Borghese wins Peking to Paris auto race.
1915	Italy enters World War I on the side of the Allies.
1919	Vote granted to women; Mussolini publishes Fascist Manifesto.
1922	Mussolini leads fascist March on Rome; forms government.
1926	Mussolini abolishes all political opposition.
1929	The Lateran Treaties establish Italian recognition of the Vatican as a sovereign state.
1933	Toscanini boycotts German music festival to protest Nazi repression of artists.
1936	Italy conquers and annexes Ethiopia; Mussolini announces Axis pact with Germany.
1939	"Pact of Steel" with Germany.
1940	Italy enters World War II on Axis side; unsuccessfully attempts to invade Greece.
1943	Mussolini deposed; Italy signs armistice with Allies, declares war on Germany; Germans help Mussolini escape.
1945	Mussolini captured, tried and executed by partisans.
1946	King Victor Emmanuel III abdicates; Italian referendum narrowly rejects monarchy; Victor Emmanuel's son Humbert II also abdicates.
1959	Aldo Moro heads Christian Democrats.
1966	Floods devastate Florence.
1972	Michelangelo's *Pieta* vandalized.
1978	Red Brigade members kidnap and kill Aldo Moro.
1981	Pope John Paul II wounded in assassination attempt.
1982	Italy enjoys first World Cup Soccer victory; 100,000 demonstrate against Mafia.
1985	Rome airport bombed by terrorists.
1990	CIA-backed anticommunist network exposed; restoration of Sistine Chapel ceiling completed; Alberto Moravia dies.
1991	In Persian Gulf War, Italian forces fight in coalition to drive Iraq from Kuwait.

"The Scythians," an intellectual group that believed in Russia's destiny as a part-Asian nation. Before the revolution he wrote populist and revolutionary works; after the revolution his even stronger inclination toward the Left eventually brought about his arrest in the 1930s, as a "populist ideologist." He left the Soviet Union for Germany during the war and died in Munich. He wrote an account of his life, including his imprisonments and exile.

Ivens, Joris (Georg Henri Anton) (1898–1989). Dutch film maker. Ivens specialized in documentaries portraying the social impact of revolution, particularly in communist countries. His masterpiece was considered to be *The Spanish Earth* (1937), a documentary about the SPANISH CIVIL WAR that featured a commentary written and read by Ernest HEMINGWAY.

Ives, Burl (1909–). American folksinger and actor. Born in Illinois, Ives came out of a folksinging tradition. He traveled throughout the U.S., walking, hitchhiking and riding boxcars, before coming to New York City in 1937. Important in popularizing the folksong genre, he is remembered for his renditions of "The Foggy, Foggy Dew" and "The Wayfaring Stranger," which became the title of his radio show in 1940. Ives began acting in motion pictures in 1945, and won an ACADEMY AWARD for his performance in *The Big Country* in 1958. He is best known, however, for his role as Big Daddy in the Broadway production of Tennessee WILLIAMS' *Cat on a Hot Tin Roof* (1955) and in the film version that followed in 1958.

Ives, Charles (Edward) (1874–1954). America's first great pioneer in modern musical expression. Because of his abhorrence of publicity and reclusive nature, Ives allowed few works to be published or performed in his lifetime; only in his last years did musicians like Leonard BERNSTEIN and Leopold STOKOWSKI present world premieres of some of his major works. Ives was born in Danbury, Connecticut, and received his musical training and inspiration from his father, a bandmaster in General Grant's army. He graduated from Yale in 1898 and began a long and prosperous career in life insurance, establishing his own successful firm, Ives and Myrick, in New York in 1906. For the next 20 years Ives lead a double life, working by day in his Manhattan office and at night composing music at his farm in Redding, Connecticut. By 1917 he had completed four symphonies, hundreds of songs, two piano sonatas, and numerous other miscellaneous works. After a heart attack that year, Ives reconsidered his publishing proscriptions and released a huge volume of songs; later, he published his massive *Concord Piano Sonata*. At a time when most American composers still depended heavily upon the traditions of European academies and conservatories, Ives turned to the vernacular music styles of the New England Yankees. As if in response to Ralph Waldo Emerson's charge that American artists should "embrace the common," Ives evoked in his music the street bands of his youth. He quoted popular songs like "De Camptown Races" and "Old Black Joe." Years before the experiments by STRAVINSKY, BARTOK and SCHOENBERG, Ives utilized modernist idioms in his work—double aural images, dissonance, polyrhythms, and polytonalities. Ives composed little after 1918, choosing to live quietly at his farm with his wife of many years, Harmony Twichell. Only recently, it seems, has modern music caught up with Charles Ives. He died in New York City of complications following an operation in 1954.

For further reading:

Rossiter, Frank R., *Charles Ives & His America*. New York: Liveright, 1975.

Ivnev, Ryurik [Michael Alexandrovich Kovalev] (1893–?). Soviet writer who was a member of the Fellow-Traveler movement. His novels include *Neschastny angel* (1917) and *Geroy romana* (1928). In 1919 he was, with ESENIN, a founder of Imagist poetry. His later work depicted bohemian characters in Soviet society.

Ivory Coast. See COTE D'IVOIRE.

Iwo Jima. Largest of the Volcano Islands; in the western Pacific Ocean, 660 nautical

Composer Charles Ives.

The American flag is raised in victory at Iwo Jima (Feb. 23, 1945).

miles southeast of Tokyo. Iwo Jima was of strategic importance during WORLD WAR II because of its air base and its proximity to the Japanese main islands. The battle for control of the island—from February 19 to March 15, 1945—was one of the bloodiest in U.S. history. A memorable moment occurred on February 23, when men of the 28th Regiment of the Fifth Division of U.S. Marines scaled Iwo Jima's heavily fortified **Mount Suribachi** and planted the American flag on its summit. Administered by the U.S. until 1968, Iwo Jima was then returned to Japan.

***Izvestiya* [*News*].** Daily newspaper published by the Supreme Soviet Presidium; it was founded after the February 1917 Revolution as the organ of the Petrograd Soviet. It was published jointly by the central executive committee of Soviets and the Petrograd Soviet from August 1917, but became very similar to PRAVDA from October 1917. In 1918 publication was transferred to Moscow, and in 1957 the circulation stood at 1,550,000. However, under the editorship of Alexei Adzhubey (editor, 1959–64) the style of the newspaper changed, and it became an evening publication in 1960. It became and remains popular, and in the late 1970s the circulation was 8,600,000. A weekly supplement *Nedeliya (The Week)*, as of 1980 sold separately, is also published.

Izvolsky, Count Alexander Petrovich (1856–1919). Russian diplomat. As foreign minister he concluded a treaty with Britain resolving Anglo-Russian disagreements in the Middle East, but he was dismissed in 1910 following an unsuccessful agreement with Austria. In 1910 he was transferred to Paris, where he served as the Russian ambassador until 1917. He had sought Austrian help in 1908 in asserting Russia's right to use the DARDANELLES, but the resulting agreement strengthened Austria in the BALKANS at Russia's expense, and no aid was given in the Dardanelles question.

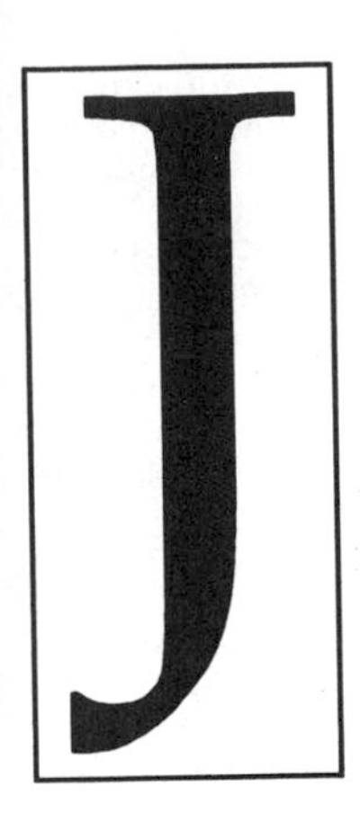

Jaccottet, Philippe (1925–). French poet, diarist, translator and literary critic. Jaccottet is one of the finest of the post-World War II generation of French poets. In his often lyrical verse, Jaccottet rejects the linguistic obscurity and experimentation of SURREALISM and other abstruse schools of French poetics in favor of a more emotionally direct expressiveness that takes in the beauty of nature and the fragility of civilized values in the nuclear age. Born in Switzerland, Jaccottet was educated at the University of Lausanne and is married to the artist Anne-Marie Hassler. His major books of poems include *Requiem* (1947), *Airs* (1967) and *Pensees sous les nuages* (1983).

Jackson, Alexander Young (1882–1973). Canadian painter. Born in Montreal, Jackson studied in the U.S. at the Art Institute of Chicago and later in Europe. Moving to Toronto in 1913, he joined the GROUP OF SEVEN in 1920. A landscape painter, he and his fellow group members specialized in panoramic canvases that portray the grandeur of Canada's vast wilderness. Jackson's autobiography, *A Painter's Country*, was published in 1958.

Jackson, Glenda (1936–). English actress. An outstanding actress of stage, screen and television, Jackson received international acclaim in the London and New York productions of Peter WEISS's play *Marat/Sade* (1964–65). Performing with the ROYAL SHAKESPEARE COMPANY she gained recognition for her roles in *Hedda Gabler* (1975) and *Antony and Cleopatra* (1978), among others. Title roles in Hugh Whitmore's *Stevie* (1977, about Stevie SMITH) and Andrew Davies's *Rose* (1980; Broadway, 1981) were personal triumphs. She has appeared in numerous films, receiving a best actress ACADEMY AWARD for *Women in Love* (1969). On television she triumphed as Elizabeth I in a BBC series.

Jackson, Henry M(artin) "Scoop" (1912–1983). U.S. senator. Jackson was born in Everett, Wash. After two years of private legal practice, he entered Democratic politics in 1935, was elected to the House of Representatives in 1940 and to the Senate in 1953. Thereafter, he served six terms. In domestic affairs, he was generally a liberal, maintaining close ties with organized labor and establishing a record as a dedicated environmentalist. In foreign affairs, he advocated large military expenditures from his seat on the Armed Services Committee, seeking to counter Soviet power. Jackson was a candidate for the Democratic nomination for president in 1972 and 1976.

Jackson, Jesse Louis (1941–). U.S. CIVIL RIGHTS leader and politician. Raised in the poor black section of Greenville, N.C., he starred on the basketball, football and baseball teams of all-black Sterling High School. An honor student and the college quarterback, he led the student protest in 1963 that resulted in the integration of Greensboro (North Carolina) theaters and restaurants. Jackson entered Chicago Theological Seminary in 1965. The same year he joined Dr. Martin Luther KING Jr. in his civil rights actions in SELMA, Alabama. Named head of the Chicago branch of Operation Breadbasket, he became its national director in 1967. He was ordained a Baptist minister in 1968. Jackson continued to gain national prominence and following, and in 1971 founded Operation Push (People United to Save Humanity) in Chicago.

He gained valuable support and experience in the field of politics in 1984 when he launched a campaign to win the Democratic presidential nomination. Again during the 1988 presidential primaries, Jackson received astonishing support, including from white voters, and received widespread press attention.

Jesse Jackson calls for unity in a speech to the 1988 Democratic National Convention.

Jackson, Mahalia (1911–1972). American gospel singer. She began making records in 1934, and later went on many concert tours in Europe and the U.S. She sang for President Eisenhower on his birthday in 1959, and at President Kennedy's inauguration in 1961. During the 1960s she became associated with the CIVIL RIGHTS MOVEMENT. She made eight records that sold over a million copies each.

Jackson, Michael (1958–). American pop singer; began his career with his brothers as one of the Jackson Five. The group recorded four consecutive number-one hits, including "ABC" and "The Love You Save." He recorded three top-five solo singles during the early 1970s, including the number-one "Ben," a love song to a rat sung in Michael's trademark falsetto. He made his film debut in 1978 playing the scarecrow in *The Wiz*, an all-black version of *The Wizard of Oz*. In 1979, his career began to skyrocket, with the album *Off the Wall* providing four top-10 hits. His 1982 release, *Thriller*, set new music industry standards for success, with seven top-ten hits and sales topping 40 million. Jackson's child-like beauty and vulnerability have made him a teen idol in two decades, albeit that appeal is widely rumored to have been assisted by extensive plastic surgery.

Jackson, Robert H. (1892–1954). Associate justice, U.S. Supreme Court (1941–

54). Jackson did not attend college but spent one year at Albany Law School in addition to studying law in a lawyer's office. He first gained attention as general counsel of the Internal Revenue Service. A loyal Democrat, he served President Franklin D. ROOSEVELT as assistant U.S. attorney general, solicitor general and attorney general. In 1941, Roosevelt elevated Jackson to the Supreme Court. During 1945–46, Jackson served as chief prosecutor at the NUREMBERG TRIALS. Jackson is credited with charging the Nazis with crimes against humanity.

Jackson apparently did not always get along with his fellow justices on the high court. Reputedly, two justices threatened to resign if President TRUMAN elevated Jackson to the position of Chief Justice. Jackson died in 1954 while still a member of the Court.

Jackson, Shirley (1919–1965). American writer of contemporary fantasy and horror. Jackson's works have been frequently adapted to movies and television. She was born in San Francisco and early in childhood developed an absorbing interest in witchcraft and the occult. After placing several stories in THE NEW YORKER magazine, she became an international sensation with *The Lottery* (1947), a violent tale of ritualized murder in a New England farming community. Although she continued to write disturbing tales of madness and horror—notably, the extraordinary *The Bird's Nest* (1954), a story of a women with multiple personalities; *The Sundial* (1958), an evocation of imminent global apocalypse; and *The Haunting of Hill House* (1959), a truly terrifying novel of the psychic investigation of a "haunted house"—she also wrote delightful accounts of her own husband and children, amusing stories of family life collected under the titles, *Life Among the Savages* (1953) and *Raising Demons* (1957). This duality is striking. She was, by turns, nondescript, thoroughly domestic, and essentially "normal;" and by others, withdrawn, paranoid, and increasingly the victim of barbituates and alcohol. Only half-jokingly, she referred to herself late in life as the only practicing witch in New England. "The very nicest thing about being a writer is that you can afford to indulge yourself endlessly with oddness, and nobody can really do anything about it. . . ," she wrote. Shortly before her death from a heart attack she wrote in her unfinished autobiographical novel, *Come Along with Me:* "How can anyone handle things if her head is full of voices and her world is full of things no one else can see?" Her husband, Stanley Edgar Hyman, published two posthumous collections of her work, *The Magic of Shirley Jackson* (1966) and *Come Along with Me* (1968).

For further reading:

Oppenheimer, Judy, *Raising Demons: The Life of Shirley Jackson*. New York: G.P. Putnam's Sons, 1988.

Jackson State shootings. Killing of two black students at Jackson State College, Jackson, Mississippi, by state lawmen on May 14, 1970. The shootings followed campus violence and were pictured as wanton killings by onlookers and as resistance to sniper fire by the police. A federal grand jury was convened later that year but failed to return any indictments. The shootings were viewed as emblematic of the campus unrest and civil rights strife that occurred in the U.S. during the late 1960s and early 1970s.

Jacobi, Lotte (1896–1990). German-American photographer. Born in Berlin, she was influenced by the artistic movements of her youth, using surrealist and cubist techniques in her many portraits. She was closely associated with Berlin's theatrical world in the 1920s and 1930s, creating strikingly original portraits of such figures as Bertolt BRECHT, Kurt WEILL and Lotte LENYA. Fleeing Germany for the U.S. in 1935, she settled in New York. There she continued portrait photography and, in the 1950s, began experiments with abstract "photogenics" and with the photographs, called "photograms," taken without benefit of a camera.

Jacobs, Walter L. (1896–1985). Business executive who founded America's first car-rental agency, which later became the Hertz Corp. In 1918, having acquired 12 Model T Fords, Jacobs started the Rent-A-Ford company in Chicago. In 1923 he sold the business to John D. Hertz, owner of a Chicago taxicab company. Jacobs remained with the company until 1960, serving as its president and chief operating officer.

Jacob's Pillow Dance Festival. The world-renowned Jacob's Pillow Dance Festival, located on 150 acres near Lee, Massachusetts became the first dance festival in the U.S. when it was established in 1941. In 1930 dancer Ted SHAWN bought the land as a summer rehearsal place for the Denishawn Dancers, then his Men Dancers. An interested group purchased the land, started a school, and established the festival (1941), with Shawn as director (1942–72). In 1942 the Shawn Theatre was built; it was the first theater in the western hemisphere to have a stage constructed exclusively for dance. Since its inception, the Festival has welcomed all kinds of dance. The American debuts of many European dancers and companies have taken place at this annual summer Festival, and over 300 new works have been premiered there. Since Shawn's death (1972), the Festival has had several directors; as of 1990, the director was Liz Thompson.

Jaehn, Sigmund (1937–). German cosmonaut-researcher and the first German in space. Jaehn flew aboard SOYUZ 31 (August-September 1978). An air force pilot, he had held an appointment at the Gagarin Air Force Academy in the U.S.S.R. before becoming an inspector for the general staff of the German Air Force.

Jaffa. Ancient seaport on the Mediterranean Sea coast of Israel, about 35 miles north of Jerusalem; it was merged with Tel Aviv in 1950. In WORLD WAR I British troops captured the city from Ottoman forces in November 1917; after the war it became part of Britain's LEAGUE OF NATIONS mandate for PALESTINE. In 1947 and 1948, during Israel's war of independence, fighting took place between mostly Arabic Jaffa and adjoining Tel Aviv, an Israeli city. Jaffa surrendered on May 14, 1948, when the independence of Israel was proclaimed.

Jagger, Mick (1943–). British ROCK-AND-ROLL songwriter and vocalist. Jagger has achieved international fame as the lead vocalist for the British rock band the ROLLING STONES. Jagger was born in Dartford, Kent, to a middle-class family and enrolled as a student in the London School of Economics in 1960. His love for American blues and rock music, notably Chuck BERRY and MUDDY WATERS, led Jagger to take up singing in 1962. His early gigs included guest spots with Alexis Korner's Blues Incorporated. In 1962 Jagger became a founding member of The Rolling Stones, and by 1963 he was a star in Britain. A 1964 Rolling Stones tour of the U.S. established Jagger on both sides of the ocean. Regarded as the "bad boy of rock and roll" because of his irreverent attitudes, Jagger is best known for his distinctive vocal style—insinuating and sneering, but also capable of great emotive power. He has also teamed with Keith Richard to write the majority of the Roll-

Mick Jagger, lead singer of the Rolling Stones, wails and struts for an audience of 90,000 at JFK Stadium in Philadelphia (1981).

ing Stones' hit songs, including the classic "(I Can't Get No) Satisfaction" (1965). Jagger recently released two solo albums, *She's The Boss* (1985) and *Primitive Cool* (1987).

Jajce Congress. Meeting held November 29–30, 1943, in the Bosnian town of Jajce. Consisting of Yugoslavian delegates to the Anti-Fascist National Liberation Committee, the Jajce Congress agreed to the postwar creation of a federated republic of YUGOSLAVIA. The Congress also established the committee as Yugoslavia's provisional government and gave communist partisan leader Josip TITO the title of Marshal. Exactly two years later, the Federal People's Republic of Yugoslavia was officially proclaimed.

Jamaica. Island republic in the West Indies, south of CUBA and west of HAITI; capital is Kingston. As a British colony, Jamaica experienced civil strife caused by poverty and British racial policies. This came to a peak in violent rioting in 1938, which brought about universal adult suffrage in 1944. Jamaica regained internal autonomy in 1953, and in 1958 joined the WEST INDIES FEDERATION. A campaign led by nationalist labor leader Sir Alexander BUSTAMENTE led to Jamaica's withdrawal from the Federation in 1961. In 1962, Jamaica became an independent member of the COMMONWEALTH with Bustamente as its first prime minister. Michael MANLEY of the People's National Party became prime minister in 1972 and instituted socialist reforms, but Jamaica's economy suffered, and some factions violently protested his government. In 1980, Edward P. Seaga, a conservative Labor Party member, defeated Manley and encouraged a return to capitalistic policy. Jamaica suffered in the recession of the early 1980s, but in 1984 Seaga responded with a series of reforms, including devaluation of the Jamaican dollar, which resulted in an increase in tourism, agriculture and manufacturing. Concurrent inflation, however, left many Jamaicans in poverty. In 1989, Manley was reelected, though on a more moderate platform than his previous administrations.

Jamalzade, Mohammed Ali (c.1895–). Iranian short story writer. Jamalzade received a progressive, Western-style education in Dijon and Lausanne, where he studied law. His father was a leading figure in the Iranian national revival. During World War I, he joined emigres in Berlin to fight against the Anglo-Russian occupation of Iran; thereafter he worked at the Iranian embassy in Berlin. In 1931 he took up permanent residence in Switzerland. His first book, *Yeki bud va yeki nabud* (1921, *There Once Was—Or Was There?*), gave a critical and realistic picture of Iranian life. He published no more books until 1941. *Dar ol-majanin* (1942, House of Fools), *Qualtashan Divan* (1946, *Dictator of the Imperial Office*) and *Sar o tahe yak karbas ya Esfahanname* (1956, *All of a Pattern, or the Book of Isfahan*) were longer works dealing with social themes. Jamalzade has also translated Schiller, Wilde and Anatole FRANCE.

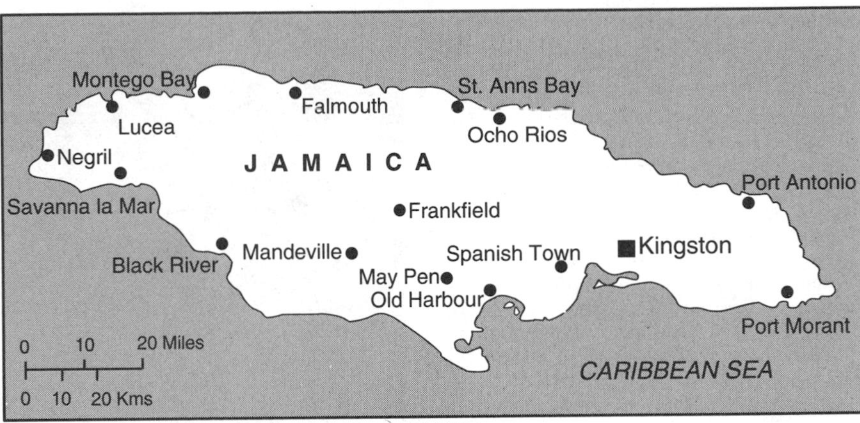

JAMAICA

JAMAICA

1907	Kingston leveled by earthquakes; governor of British crown colony resigns after misunderstanding leads to landing and rapid departure of U.S. Marines.
1916	Black Nationalist Marcus Garvey immigrates to U.S.
1930	Economic depression leads to rioting and strikes.
1939	Norman Manley founds People's National Party.
1940	U.S. granted military bases as part of Lend-Lease program.
1944	British allow internal self-government; first House of Representatives election is dominated by Jamaican Labour Party.
1945	Blight and wartime disruption of shipping discourage banana planting, lead to agricultural diversity and increased self-sufficiency.
1954	PLP purges leftist members and wins elections.
1958	Jamaica joins West Indian Federation.
1962	Full independence from Britain granted; secession from WIF; Bustamente of the JLP elected first prime minister; University of the West Indies chartered.
1965	International air routes make tourism an important industry.
1969	Jamaican dollar replaces the pound.
1970	Population down 15% from 1960, due to emigration.
1972	Michael Manley of the PNP elected; launches radical leftist programs, including land reform and ties to Cuba.
1975	Tourism slumps; oil prices rise; economy devastated.
1979	Prime Minister Manley refuses to accept conditions set by International Monetary Fund; denied desperately needed loans; middle-class emigration increases.
1980	Seven-hundred killed in election violence between PNP and JNP; Seaga of JNP elected.
1981	Seaga reverses Manley policies; seeks new ties with U.S.; encourages free enterprise; adopts IMF-backed austerity programs; singer Bob Marley dies; tourism up.
1988	Hurricane Gilbert leaves 20% of island's population homeless.
1989	Manley and the PNP, projecting a more moderate image, are reelected.
1990	Young & Rubicam, one of New York's leading advertising agencies, pleads guilty to bribing Jamaican officials in return for a large contract to promote tourism there.

James, C(yril) L(ionel) R(obert) (1901–1989). Trinidad-born political historian, literary critic, and cricket writer who was a leader of the pan-African movement. After moving to London in the 1930s, James became a Marxist and involved himself in several left-wing political causes. He rejected STALIN'S version of COMMUNISM, however, and allied himself with Stalin's exiled rival, Leon TROTSKY. After spending 15 years in the U.S., he was expelled in 1953 during a period of intense anticommunism (see MCCARTHYISM). He then traveled to Africa and became involved in the African independence movement. In 1958 he returned to Trinidad at the invitation of Chief Minister Eric WILLIAMS and later became secretary of the West Indies Federal Labour Party coalition. His books included *The Black Jacobins: Toussaint L'Ouverture and the San Domingo Revolution* (1938) and *Beyond the Boundary* (1963).

James, Harry (1916–1983). American trumpet player and bandleader. James began playing in bands at age eight. He played in the band of Benny GOODMAN from 1937 until 1939, when he started his own group. He added romantic ballad arrangements to his repertoire beginning in 1941 with *You Made Me Love You.* He helped launch the careers of singers Frank SINATRA, Dick Haymes, Helen Forrest, and Connie Haines. In 1943 he married film star Betty GRABLE and appeared in several films, which brought him more popularity. Along with Glenn MILLER, James developed and refined the big band sound known as swing, the most popular jazz style in the U.S. during World War II. (See also SWING ERA.)

James, Henry (1843–1916). American novelist whose works are remarkable for their subtlety, psychological penetration and stylistic care. One of the most influential figures in American literature, James was born in New York and educated abroad and at Harvard Law School. His father was a theological writer, and his older brother, William JAMES, became an eminent philosopher. James began his career contributing to periodicals. His first major novel, *Roderick Hudson* (1876), appeared in *The Atlantic Monthly* in 1875. James settled in England in 1875, and much of his work insightfully contrasts European worldliness with American naivete. Such novels include *Daisy Miller* (1879), *Portrait of a Lady* (1881), THE AMBASSADORS (1903), and *The Golden Bowl* (1904). Some of his fiction, including *The Spoils of Poynton* (1897) and *The Awkward Age* (1899), focuses more specifically on the nature of the English. James was a mentor and close friend to Edith WHARTON; a volume of their correspondence was published in 1989. In addition to a number of other novels, James also wrote short stories, the best known being *The Turn of the Screw* (1898); travel sketches; and plays. James became a British subject shortly before his death. A four-volume biography of James was written by Leon Edel between 1953 and 1972.

A somber portrait of American author Henry James.

James, M(ontague) R(hodes) (1862–1936). British medieval scholar and educator, commonly acknowledged as the 20th century's greatest master of the ghost story. The son of a Suffolk clergyman, James decided, after attending Eton and King's College, Cambridge, not to follow his father and brother into the Church. Rather, as Provost of King's College and, later, Eton, he pursued his scholarship of medieval manuscripts and architecture. He is best known today for his hobby—writing ghost stories for annual Christmas gatherings with his friends. The spectral tales first appeared in the collection, *Ghost Stories of an Antiquary* (1904) and in subsequent books, *More Ghost Stories of an Antiquary* (1911), *A Thin Ghost* (1919) and *A Warning to the Curious* (1926). Although the props and characters might seem at first glance rather cliched—haunted wells, yawning graves, vampires and ghosts—he has added some novel effects of his own. These include witchcraft on a tram car (*Casting the Runes*), a pair of haunted binoculars (*A View from a Hill*), and an inexplicable, "face of crumpled linen" of some haunted bedsheets (*Oh, Whistle, and I'll come to you, My Lad*). Yet the stories are set against careful and meticulous backgrounds of bookish, antiquarian lore; and they are written in a sober, refined narrative style. Notoriously reticent about his work, James best summed up his intent in the Latin inscription found on a certain ancient whistle in one of his stories: "Quis est este qui venit?" ("Who is this who is coming?") The answer was usually dreadful—and superbly memorable.

James, P(hyllis) D(orothy) (1923–). British novelist. Born in Oxford and educated at Cambridge University, she was an administrator in the NATIONAL HEALTH SERVICE from 1949 to 1968. In 1968 she transferred to the Home Office, where she worked as a senior civil servant in the police and criminal law departments. Her first book, *Cover Her Face* (1962), introduced readers to Scotland Yard detective Adam Dalgleish, who appears in most of her subsequent books. In 1979 she resigned from her job to write full time. James adapted the detective mystery genre (perfected in the 1930s by Dorothy L. SAYERS) to examine the social order in late-20th-century Britain. Her realistic novels transcend the customary limits of the mystery genre, and she is regarded as being in the mainstream of contemporary English literature. Several of her books have been adapted for television by the BBC. These include *The Black Tower* (1982), *A Taste for Death* (1986) and *Devices and Desires* (1989).

James, William. American philosopher and psychologist. James stands among the most original and influential thinkers that America has ever produced. He came from a remarkable New England family—his father, Henry James Sr., was a prominent theologian, and his brother Henry JAMES was one of the greatest American novelists. William James earned a medical degree from Harvard University in 1869 and went on to teach anatomy, physiology, psychology, and philosophy at Harvard. In 1884 James helped found the American Society for Psychical Research. His two-volume *Principles of Psychology* (1890) was a pioneering work in a then new field of social science. *Varieties of Religious Experience* (1902) remains a classic work on the nature and modalities of religious beliefs. James is best known for his formulation of the philosophy of **pragmatism,** which argues that we live in a pluralistic universe in which truth is relative and best measured by the extent to which it serves human freedom. James' key philosophical essays are contained in *Pragmatism* (1907) and *Essays in Radical Empiricism* (1912).

James Bond. Fictional British secret agent ("007") with a "licence to kill"; created by novelist Ian FLEMING, Bond first appeared in the novel *Casino Royale* (1954) and was subsequently featured in numerous feature films, beginning in the 1960s and continuing into the 1990s. James Bond was an immensely popular character; his far-fetched adventures bore little resemblance to actual espionage work but rather reflected male fantasies. Bond was first portrayed by actor Barry Nelson, on American television; in the movies, Bond was first portrayed by Scottish actor Sean CONNERY and afterwards by David Niven, George Lazenby, Roger Moore and Timothy Dalton.

Jameson, (Margaret) Storm [Mrs. Guy Chapman] (1891–1986). British novelist and feminist. As president of the English section of PEN from 1938 to 1944, Jameson worked tirelessly to rescue and assist writers from countries under Nazi occupation. Three of her finest novels stemmed from that period: *Cousin Honore, Europe to Let,* and *Cloudless May.* Perhaps her most important postwar work was her two-volume autobiography, *Journey from the North* (1969–70).

Janacek, Leos (1854–1928). Czech composer. Born in Moravia, his father was an organist and his earliest musical experience was as a choirboy. He began directing choirs as the age of 16 and later (1875–80) studied composition at Prague, Leipzig and Vienna. He moved to Brno in 1881, teaching and conducting there. He was a professor at Prague from 1921 to 1923. Janacek was an avid student and collector of Slavic folk music, and his work was influenced by its rhythms and melodies as well as by the inflections of the Czech language itself. He is particularly noted for his operas, including *Jenufa* (1904), *Katya Kabanova* (1921), *The Cunning Little Vixen* (1921) and *From the House of the Dead* (1930). Among his other works are the symphonic poem *Taras Bulba* (1915–18), the song cycle *The Diary of One Who Vanished* (1916–19) and the *Glagolitic Mass* (1926), as well as many orchestral, chamber, piano, vocal and choral compositions.

Janco, Marcel (1895–1984). Romanian-born Israeli painter and architect. Janco helped found the DADA movement in Switzerland in 1916. Together with Hans ARP, Tristan TZARA and other artists, Janco formulated an approach to art that abandoned traditional conventions in favor of art without preconceived ideas. This approach, DADAISM, was a forerunner of SURREALISM and modern ABSTRACT ART. Janco was best known for his abstract masks recalling the Japanese and Greek theater. In 1953 he founded Israel's first art colony, Ein Hod.

Janet, Pierre (Marie-Felix) (1859–1947). French psychiatrist. Janet was one of the pioneers of clinical psychiatry and a dominant figure in the administration of mental health programs in France. In the 1880s and 1890s, he served as the director of the prestigious Salpetriere clinic. For the first four decades of this century, he taught at the College de France. In papers written in the 1880s, Janet anticipated certain theories of Sigmund FREUD as to the unconscious symptomology of hysteria and other mental disorders. Janet also conducted researches into hypnosis and the clinical classification of mental illness. His major works include *Neuroses and Fixed Ideas* (1898), *The Mental State of Hysteria* (1911) and *Psychological Medicine* (1923).

Jan Mayen. Lonely volcanic island 300 miles east of Greenland, in the Arctic Ocean. Discovered by Henry Hudson in 1607, it bore his name until 1614, when a Dutch sea captain claimed it for his whaling company and for the NETHERLANDS. NORWAY formally annexed it on May 8, 1929.

Janson, H(orst) W(oldemar) (1913–1982). American art historian and teacher. Born in Leningrad, Janson studied at the universities of Hamburg and Munich and at Harvard, where he began his teaching career. He also taught at the Worcester Art Museum, Iowa State University and Washington University before becoming a professor of art history at New York University in 1949. One of America's most distinguished art historians, he is best known for his comprehensive survey, *History of Art* (1962), which sold more than 2 million copies internationally. Janson was also the author of such works as *Apes and Ape Lore in the Middle Ages* (1952) and *The Sculpture of Donatello* (1957).

Janssen, Werner (1899–1990). U.S. conductor and composer. A specialist in 20th-century music, in 1934 he became the first American-born conductor appointed to lead the New York Philharmonic orchestra. He later moved to Los Angeles, where he led his own Janssen Symphony (1940–52). He wrote scores for such films as *Blockade* (1938) and *The General Died at Dawn* (1936).

Japan. Japan entered the modern era in 1868 when young members of the military oligarchy installed Emperor Meiji on the throne and launched a vast program of industrialization and modernization. Japan opened its doors to Western influences and ideas, imported Western technologies and concluded friendship treaties with such countries as the U.S., Britain and the Netherlands. It was RUSSIA and

JAPAN

1904	(Feb.) Attacks Russia and declares war; wins territorial objectives in Korea and Manchuria.
1926	Accession of Emperor Hirohito.
1931	The Mukden incident of 1931, involving an explosion on the Manchurian Rail Line; results in annexation of Manchuria and army control of political power.
1932	(May) Prime Minister Takashi Inukai is assassinated, ending the last non-military-controlled government.
1936	Japan joins the Axis powers in a pact against the Soviet Union.
1937	(July) War with China erupts after Marco Polo Bridge Incident.
1941	(Dec. 7) Japan attacks Pearl Harbor in the U.S. Hawaiian Islands; (Dec. 8) U.S. declares war on Japan.
1942	Defeats at Midway Island and the Coral Sea break Japanese sea power.
1945	Philippines reconquered; (Aug. 6) Atomic bomb dropped on Hiroshima; (Aug. 8) Soviet Union declares war on Japan; (Aug. 9) Atomic bomb dropped on Nagasaki; (Aug. 14) Japan accepts the unconditional surrender terms of the Potsdam Declaration; (Sept. 2) Formal surrender signed; Gen. Douglas MacArthur becomes supreme commander of Allied forces occupying Japan.
1946	Demobilization and demilitarization are completed; civil and land reform commence.
1948	War Crimes Tribunal sentences 25 to death or life imprisonment; (Dec. 23) General Hideki Tojo is hanged.
1949	San Francisco Peace Conference promises full sovereignty to Japan by April 1952.
1952	Security treaty is signed with the U.S.
1955	Industrial output meets peak prewar levels.
1956	Japan admitted to the UN.
1960	Hayato Ikeda begins four-year term as prime minister.
1964	Tokyo Olympics; Eisaku Sato begins eight-year term as prime minister.
1970	EXPO '70, the first world exposition held in Asia, is hosted by the city of Osaka; United States returns Okinawa and Ryukyu islands.
1973	Oil embargo causes Japan to shift industrial focus from energy-intensive businesses such as steel and chemicals to high-tech areas such as consumer electronics.
1974	Prime Minister Kakuei Tanaka is implicated in the Lockheed scandal and is arrested for accepting a 500 million-yen bribe; Sato wins Nobel Prize for peace.
1986	To stem exports, Plaza Accord obliges Japan to accept a 40% upward valuation of the yen.
1988	Japan becomes the largest donor of foreign aid and largest supplier of foreign aid.
1989	(Jan. 7) Emperor Hirohito dies and is succeeded by his son Crown Prince Akihito.
1991	(April) Soviet President Gorbachev becomes first Soviet leader to visit Japan.

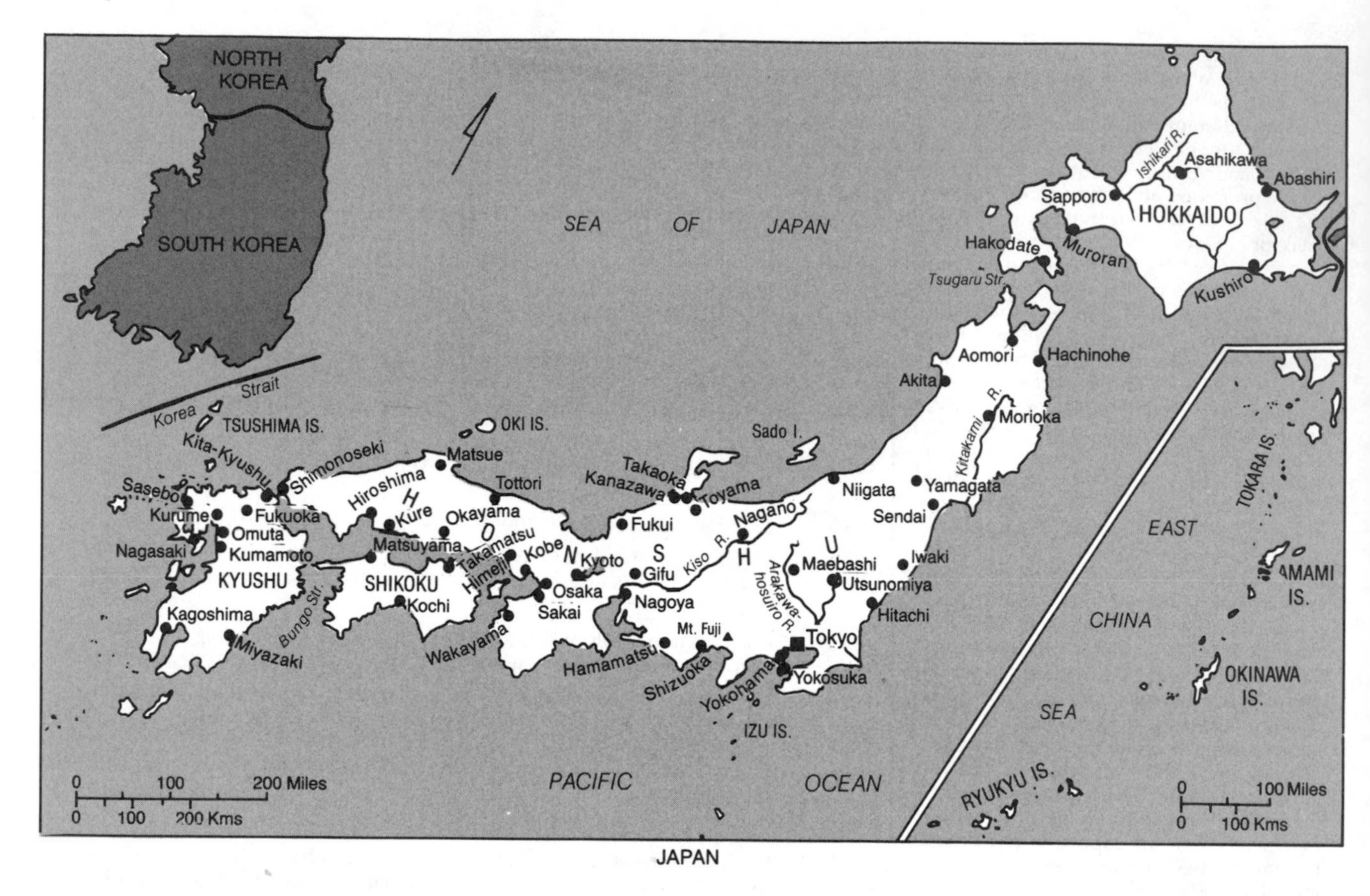

JAPAN

CHINA, however, that were to play a major role in Japanese foreign affairs between the 1890s and 1930s. The first Sino-Japanese War, over Korea, was fought in 1894–95; the RUSSO-JAPANESE WAR, over Manchuria, followed in 1904–05. Victorious in both encounters, Japan greatly increased its sphere of influence and gained tremendous military prestige. During WORLD WAR I, Japan was on the side of the Allies and became their major supplier of ammunition and ships. Its economic development was further enhanced by increasing demand from Asia and Africa, which could no longer rely on British and German exporters. The war also proved beneficial for Japan politically because, as an ally of Britain, it was asked to destroy German warships protecting German interests in China; this ultimately led to Japan's occupation of Shantung (now Shandong) province in China.

By 1922 Japan had been recognized as a major Asian power, and its navy had become the world's third largest after that of Britain and the U.S. The 1920s were a decade of rapid economic growth. An important step in the gradual democratization of Japan was taken in 1925 when the government enacted universal suffrage for males. Soon after the 1926 ascension to the throne of Emperor HIROHITO Japan was hit by the worldwide economic depression. The economic dislocations and discontent led to political violence (two prime ministers were assassinated in the early 1930s), to the rise of radical nationalistic groups and to the reemergence of the military, who felt that Japan should become "master of Asia." Without the knowledge of the country's political leaders, the Japanese armed forces took advantage of the political disarray in China and in 1931 invaded MANCHURIA. In 1932 the military proclaimed Manchuria an "independent" state, renamed MANCHUKUO, and installed a puppet government. The occupation of Manchuria was just the beginning of a protracted conflict between Japan and China, which escalated into another Sino-Japanese War in 1937 and lasted until 1945.

After signing military pacts with GERMANY and ITALY in 1940, Japanese military leaders began to plan an attack on the U.S. Pacific Fleet in order to prevent the United States from interfering with Japanese "liberation" of European colonies in East Asia (French INDOCHINA, British Malaya and BURMA and the Dutch East Indies). In April 1941 Japan concluded a nonaggression treaty with the Soviet Union to postpone any military encounter with that country. On December 7, 1941, Japanese bombers attacked PEARL HARBOR on Oahu and destroyed or severely damaged most of the U.S. ships and aircraft anchored there. Other U.S. military installations in the Pacific, including two airfields near Manila in the Philippines and bases on GUAM, MIDWAY and WAKE, were successfully attacked the same day. In January 1942 Japan captured the PHILIPPINES, and by the following spring it had conquered a vast area stretching from Malaya eastward to the Pacific islands of Wake and Guam and southward to the Dutch East Indies (present-day INDONESIA). U.S. armed forces soon struck back, and in early May 1942, in the battle of the CORAL SEA off New Guinea, stopped the Japanese expansion. The next three years saw a number of fierce battles (at Midway, GUADALCANAL, LEYTE GULF) and a steady American advance. In January 1945 the Philippines were recaptured. Meanwhile, in May 1945 peace in Europe was concluded, and the U.S. decided to use the newly developed ATOMIC BOMB to force Japan to surrender. Two bombs were dropped in August 1945, on HIROSHIMA and on NAGASAKI, causing the death of about 340,000 people. On August 14, 1945, Japan unconditionally surrendered to the Allied powers.

The U.S. military occupation of Japan, headed by Gen. Douglas MACARTHUR, lasted from 1945 to 1952. It was a period of far-reaching changes in Japanese society, politics and economy. Japan had lost over three million people during the war, and when the hostilities ended it was economically devastated, with most of its industry in shambles. The American occupation administration, working through a capable Japanese bureaucracy, set up a massive rebuilding course for the country. With huge amounts of American aid, and the Japanese tradition of hard work, the economic recovery was fast and impressive. Recovery was also helped by the KOREAN WAR of 1950–52, when Japan became the major base for the U.S., providing airfields, harbors, repair and medical services, ships and other materiel. Politically, the aim of the U.S. occupation was the demilitarization and democratization of Japan. After military leaders and others were executed for war crimes and acts of cruelty, the power of the military oligarchy was effectively broken.

In 1947 a new constitution was promulgated, renouncing the war, abolishing the divinity of the emperor and proclaiming the sovereignty of the people. The Japanese started to transform their country. Relations with the West were codified in a peace treaty in 1951. At the same time Japan concluded a bilateral security treaty with the U.S., which stipulated that U.S. armed forces would retain military bases in Japan and would assist Japan in case of aggression. Japan also normalized relations with its Asian neighbors. In 1965, diplomatic ties with South Korea were established, and in 1972 Japan established full relations with the People's Republic of China. A treaty for economic aid and investment between Japan and China was agreed upon in 1988. When Prime Minister TAKESHITA announced in 1988 that his government would spend U.S.$5 billion in foreign aid over the next five years (and thus become the world's largest donor of foreign aid), it became clear that Japan intended to play a global economic role, as befits a nation with the second largest GNP in the world.

For a short period in 1947 socialists controlled the government; otherwise, postwar Japan has been governed by conservatives. Two leading conservative parties, the Liberals and the Democrats, merged into a single party in 1955; since that time the LDP has been the predominant political force in Japan. Eisaku SATO, who served as prime minister from 1964 until 1972, was awarded the NOBEL PRIZE for peace in 1974 for his "reconciliation policy that contributed to a stabilization of conditions in the Pacific area." The first OLYMPIC GAMES to be held in Asia took place in Tokyo in the summer of 1964; six years later the Japan World Exposition was held in Osaka, and in 1972 Sapporo hosted the Winter Olympics. The thousands of visitors to these events were impressed by the highly developed Japanese technology, especially in transportation.

Kakuei TANAKA, Sato's successor, was in office during the first major oil crisis in 1973, which Japan withstood by making its industry more efficient and less energy-intensive. Politically, Tanaka fared worse. He had to resign in 1974; and in 1976 he was charged with, and later found guilty of, accepting bribes from the Lockheed Corporation. Tanaka was succeeded as prime minister by Takeo Miki, Takeo Fukuda, Masayoshi Ohira, Zenko Suzuki and in 1982 by Yasuhiro NAKASONE—who differed from the previous prime ministers by his forceful, almost flamboyant style, and his great international visibility. He visited the U.S., Australia, Southeast Asia and Europe, promoting political and economic ties. Domestically, he concentrated on restructuring government-run enterprises; on fiscal reform, aimed at eliminating the deficit; and on liberalization of the educational system. In 1987, Nakasone stepped down (after an unsuccessful bid for another term), and Noboru Takeshita became the new prime minister. Takeshita's political victory was overshadowed by a scandal involving many highly placed politicians and business executives who bought shares in a real estate company before they were publicly traded and thus made huge profits. The scandal eventually led to Takeshita's resignation. He was succeeded briefly by Sosuke Uno, who was himself forced to resign by another scandal. Toshiki Kaifu has been prime minister since August 1989.

Emperor Hirohito died in January 1989 and was succeeded by Crown Prince AKIHITO.

For further reading:

Beasley, W.S., *The Rise of Modern Japan.* New York: St. Martin's, 1990.

Dolan, Edward, *The New Japan.* New York: Franklin Watts, 1983.

Gibney, Frank, *Japan: The Fragile Superpower,* rev. ed. New York: NAL/Dutton, 1986.

Perkins, Dorothy, *The Encyclopedia of Japan.* New York: Facts On File, 1990.

Reischauer, Edwin O., and Shigeto Tsaru, eds., *The Kodansha Encyclopedia of Japan.* New York: Kodansha Ltd. USA, 1983.

Japanese-Americans, internment of. Forced detention of Americans of Japanese ancestry and resident aliens at the beginning of WORLD WAR II. After the Japanese attack on PEARL HARBOR (December 7, 1941), a wave of anti-Japanese sentiment swept the U.S. Lt. Gen. John L. DeWitt, security chief for the western U.S., alleged that Japanese-Americans posed a security threat. Convinced congressmen urged internment on President Franklin D. ROOSEVELT, who signed an executive order early in 1942 authorizing army relocation and detention of anyone considered dangerous. DeWitt established a military area in western Washington, Oregon and California and decreed that all people of Japanese origin be removed from it. With only a few days notice, some 120,000 Japanese-Americans were forced to sell what they owned and were removed to guarded barbed-wire-rimmed barracks in desolate parts of the West, where they were kept for two to three years. While most Americans were ignorant of this legal scandal, news of the internment gradually reached the public. In 1976 President FORD proclaimed that the detention had been wrong, and in 1988 a bill was passed that called for government apology and for the payment of $20,000 apiece to all survivors.

Young Japanese-Americans await baggage inspection at an assembly center in Turlock, California (May 2, 1942).

Jaray, Paul (1889–1974). Swiss engineer who pioneered in the development of automobile design using streamlined forms. As an engineer for the ZEPPELIN works, Jaray designed dirigible airships. In 1922 he patented an automobile design of streamlined form based on aerodynamics. Although he never designed a production car, his ideas have had a major influence on all modern automotive design.

Jaroslaw [Yaroslav]. City in POLAND's southeastern province of Rzeszow. In October 1914, during WORLD WAR I, the Russians enjoyed one of their all-too-few victories over the Germans; German and Austrian forces retook the city in May 1915. In 1919 Jaroslaw became a part of the new nation of Poland.

Jarrell, Randall (1914–1965). American critic and poet. Born in Nashville and educated at Vanderbilt Univesity, Jarrell was known as a vitriolic and even cruel critic. His friend Robert LOWELL said he was "almost brutally serious about literature." He taught at many colleges and universities and contributed to prestigious literary journals. In 1961 *The Woman at the Washington Zoo* won a National Book Award for poetry. He was a master of the modern plain style, where poetry resembles a colloquial mode of speech. One of his favorite themes was war: His most famous poem is a five-line lyric, "The Death of the Ball Turret Gunner." His best-known critical work is *Poetry and the Age* (1953).

For further reading:

Pritchard, William H., *Randall Jarrell: A Literary Life.* New York: Farrar, Straus & Giroux, 1989.

Jarry, Alfred (1873–1907). French playwright, novelist and poet. Although not a prolific writer, Jarry has exercised as great an influence on 20th-century theater as any playwright. Jarry's plays are the founding blocks of the THEATER OF THE ABSURD, and his overall oeuvre served to inspire both DADA and SURREALISM. Jarry, who began his literary career as a symbolist and an aspiring dandy, shocked Parisian theatrical circles with his raw absurdist play, *Ubu Roi,* which featured an obscenity-spouting monarch whose unending appetites and cynical lack of values made a mockery of all societal values. Riots broke out in the theater on the night of the first performance. Jarry's other works include a volume of poems *Days and Nights* (1897), the novel *The Supermale* (1902) and two further Ubu plays. Jarry coined the term **pataphysique**—loosely translated as the study of absurdity—which is still widely used in France.

Jaruzelski, Wojcieck (1923–). Polish general and communist prime minister (1981–89) and president (1989–90) of POLAND. Minister of defense from 1968 to 1983, Jaruzelski took office to restore order following the unrest (1980–81) that had arisen in fear of Soviet intervention. As prime minister, he initially made further concessions to the independent trade union SOLIDARITY. However, having also become leader of the Polish Communist Party, he proclaimed martial law in December 1981 and arrested Solidarity leaders, including union leader Lech WALESA. Some relaxation occurred the following year, but tension between the government and Solidarity led to sporadic outbursts of unrest throughout the 1980s. In 1989 Jaruzelski agreed to the relegalization of Solidarity and to far-reaching constitutional reforms, including free elections. He became president under the new governmental system (1989) but resigned at the end of 1990 after Walesa was elected president.

Jarvi, Neeme (1937–). Estonian conductor. Jarvi was born in Tallinn, Estonia and continued his music studies at the Leningrad State Conservatory, where he made his conducting debut at the age of 18. His first major appointment was Director of the Estonian Radio and Television Orchestra and the Tallinn Opera. A first prize at an international conducting competition in Rome in 1971 led to invitations to work with major orchestras throughout the world. He left the U.S.S.R. in 1980 and became a resident in America where he made his Metropolitan Opera debut with *Eugene Onegin* in the 1978–79 season. His subsequent principal appointments include principal conductor of the Gothenburg Symphony Orchestra and musical director of the Scottish National Orchestra. A prolific performer and recording artist, Jarvi has won special praise for his interpretations of composers once associated with his Gothenburg Symphony Orchestra, notably Jean SIBELIUS. A long-cherished project of great importance has been his recording of the complete orchestral works of fellow Estonian Edward Tubin.

For further reading:

Holmes, John, *Conductors: A Record Collectors' Guide.* London: Gollancz, 1988.

Jarvik heart. Artificial heart designed by the American physician Robert K. Jarvik. The first heart replacement intended for permanent implantation into a patient, the air-powered system is fitted with a disk-shaped pump, a power system, two ventricles and a system of air tubes. The Jarvik-7 was first used in a human recipient in 1982, when it was implanted in Barney Clark, who survived 112 days. Subsequent recipients had the heart implanted as a temporary or permanent measure, but there were a number of serious problems with blood clots and stroke.

Jarvis, Gregory (1941–1986). American astronaut, one of seven killed in the explosion of the space shuttle *Challenger* (January 28, 1986). He was an engineer with the Hughes Aircraft Co.

Jarvis, Howard (Arnold) (1902–1986). American politician. A leader of CALIFORNIA's tax revolt movement during the late 1970s, Jarvis cosponsored with Paul GANN PROPOSITION 13, the passage of which in 1978 led to a huge reduction in the state's property taxes. Californians rejected two of his three subsequent tax proposals.

Jaspers, Karl (Theodor) (1883–1969). German philosopher, psychiatrist and essayist. Jaspers was one of the leading influences upon the emerging philosophical school of EXISTENTIALISM. He began his career as a practicing psychiatrist at the University of Heidelberg hospital and produced a medical work, *General Psychopathology* (1913). But shortly thereafter Jaspers turned his primary attention to philosophy, which he believed represented man's unending search for ultimate reality. He emphasized the vital importance of individual freedom as opposed to socially conditioned values and behaviors. Forced into academic retirement by the Nazis, Jaspers continued his teaching career after World War II at the University of Basel in Switzerland. He forthrightly acknowledged a national German guilt for Nazi crimes and urged that serious attention be paid to the horrible lessons of recent history. Major works by Jaspers include the three-volume *Philosophy* (1932), *Reason and Existence* (1938) and *The Origin and Goal of History* (1949).

Jaures, Jean (1859–1914). French socialist writer, orator and political leader. Born of middle-class parents in Castres, he studied at Toulouse University, where he subsequently taught philosophy. He served in the chamber of deputies (1885–89, 1893–98 and 1902–14) and became a socialist; he was a leading supporter of Alfred Dreyfus. A noted writer and orator, he was founder (1904) and editor of the influential left-wing daily *L'Humanite.* In 1905, Jaures was successful in uniting the various factions of the socialist movement into a unified French Socialist Party. His was an idealistic socialism; he advocated economic equality through peaceful revolution and the separation of church and state while denouncing nationalism and ANTI-SEMITISM. A noted historian, he is remembered for his *Histoire socialiste de la Revolution francaise* (1901–07). As World War I approached, Jaures favored arbitration as an alternative to armed conflict. He was assassinated by a nationalist fanatic in 1914.

Java [Djawa]. Island in the Greater Sunda Islands group of Indonesia, southeast of Sumatra and south of Borneo. Two-thirds of INDONESIA's population lives on Java, although it is only the fifth-largest of the archipelago-nation's islands. The population includes Javanese, Sudanese, Madurese, Chinese and Arabs; people from India were the first colonizers and the Japanese were the last, occupying Java during WORLD WAR II. The Dutch tried to restore their rule after the war ended but had to fight Indonesian forces intent on winning independence, which they did by 1949. Jakarta is the nation's capital and largest city; Surabaja (Indonesia's major naval base) and Bandung (site of the BANDUNG CONFERENCE), both on Java, are the second- and third-largest cities.

Java Sea. Arm of the western Pacific Ocean, between the islands of Java and Borneo. An important naval battle was fought here between Japanese and Allied forces on February 27, 1942, early in WORLD WAR II. The Allies were defeated and JAVA was laid open to Japanese attack.

Javits, Jacob (Koppel) (1904–1986). American politician. The son of Jewish immigrants, Javits became a leader of the liberal wing of the REPUBLICAN PARTY. A U.S. senator representing New York from 1957 to 1981, he played a part in the 1973 War Powers Act, the creation of the National Endowment for the Humanities, and the 1974 Pension Reform Act. His age and ill health cost him his first and only electoral defeat in a 1980 primary contest.

Jaworski, Leon (1905–1982). American attorney. A graduate of Baylor University and the George Washington University School of Law, Jaworski made his reputation as a lawyer in Houston. Among his clients was then-Congressman Lyndon B. JOHNSON. Jaworksi also served as a prosecutor at the NUREMBERG WAR CRIMES TRIALS after World War II, and as president of the American Bar Association. Jaworski may be best remembered for his role as the special prosecutor during the investigation of the WATERGATE scandal that eventually forced the resignation of President Richard M. NIXON. Jaworski was appointed to the post after Nixon ordered the previous prosecutor, Archibald cox, fired in the infamous Saturday Night Massacre. Jaworski's investigation revealed wrong-doing at the highest levels and forced the resignation of both the U.S. Attorney General John MITCHELL and also President Nixon himself.

For further reading:

Griffith, Kathryn P., *Judge Learned Hand and the Role of the Federal Judiciary.* Norman: University of Oklahoma Press, 1973.

Schick, Marvin, *Learned Hand's Court.* Westport, Conn.: Greenwood, 1978.

Knappman, Edward, ed., *Watergate and the White House.* Books on Demand, n.d.

Kutler, Stanley I., *The Wars of Watergate: The Last Crisis of Richard Nixon.* New York: Knopf, 1990.

Jayewardene, Junius Richard (1906–). Jayewardene was elected the first president of SRI LANKA in 1978 and reelected in 1982. He led the country through the most difficult period of its postindependence, pursuing a carrot-and-stick policy toward Tamil moderates and militants until 1987. Under his rule military forces committed brutal atrocities against Tamil civilians. In 1987, in a remarkable change of policy, he signed an agreement with Indian prime minister Rajiv GANDHI, in which the Tamils were allowed a degree of regional autonomy and India effectively committed itself to maintain the unity of Sri Lanka. Jayewardene declined to seek a third term in 1988.

jazz. Jazz is generally thought to have developed from a fusion of elements present in the 19th-century musical heritage of Southern culture, specifically along the Mississippi River. A blend of European, Creole and traditional African rhythms, jazz drew upon the black field work songs, and spiritual and special funeral music. Other influences were the BLUES and RAGTIME. The first jazz records were made in 1917. Concerts given in New York City in 1917 by the ORIGINAL DIXIELAND JAZZ BAND led to the first official, critical acknowledgment of jazz. This group also played in London, England in 1919. Another famous jazz group was King OLIVER's Creole Band. Among the finest musicians who played with Joseph "King" OLIVER were saxophonist Sidney Bechet, and perhaps the greatest jazz soloist, cornetist Louis ARMSTRONG. From New Orleans, jazz spread to other cities like Memphis, St. Louis, Kansas City, Chicago, New York and to the West Coast. A number of styles emerged, often associated with a particular city or area. By the early 1930s, jazz had ceased to be strictly a Southern phenomenon and had become a long-established national and international tradition.

Jazz Age. Name commonly given to the 1920s, particularly in the U.S. and Britain. The jazz age generally coincides with PROHIBITION, the laissez-faire policies of Presidents HARDING and COOLIDGE, post-World-War-I prosperity and a hedonistic outlook on life prevalent among the leisured classes. The Jazz Age was largely a reaction to the cares engendered by the war and to the refined seriousness of the prewar era. For the wealthy, this period was marked by lavish parties and social events, fast cars and lighthearted liaisons—in short, a carefree attitude. The bouncy rhythms and flippant lyrics of contemporary jazz songs gave the era its name. The American novelist F. Scott FITZGERALD is regarded as the supreme chronicler of the Jazz Age; his novel THE GREAT GATSBY captures the high spirits and ultimate wastefulness of the age. The Jazz Age effectively ended with the STOCK MARKET CRASH OF 1929, which in turn brought on the GREAT DEPRESSION of the 1930s.

Jebel ed Druz [Jebel Druze; Djeb-el-Druze]. Area in southwestern SYRIA, bordering on Jordan; formerly a subdivision of Syria. Its capital of Es Suweida lies on the site of an ancient Roman town, about 50 miles south of Damascus. A region of plateaus and mountains, Jebel ed Druz is inhabited by the Druse Muslims, who also dwell in Israel, Lebanon and Jordan. The Druse' beliefs differ radically from those of both the Sunnites and Shiites. The Druse resisted France after the French were given a LEAGUE OF NATIONS mandate over Syria and LEBANON in 1920. Between 1925 and 1927, with the aid of Syrian nationalists, the Druse led a revolt against the French and captured Damascus. In 1944, with Syria independent, the Druse in Jebel ed Druz agreed to give up their autonomous rights. Since the late 1970s they have attempted to maintain their independence amid conflicts among Lebanese, Syrian and Israeli forces.

Jeffers, (John) Robinson (1887–1962). American poet. Son of a Presbyterian minister and scholar of biblical literature, Jeffers was born in Pittsburgh and educated at several colleges in the U.S. and at the University of Zurich. He did graduate work in forestry and medicine. After 1924, he built a stone house and tower near Carmel, California, where he lived in seclusion with his family. He termed his pessimistic philosophy "Inhumanism"; it called for a "recognition of the transhuman magnificence" and detachment from human concerns. After two minor volumes he made his name with *Tamar and Other Poems* (1924); the title poem is a long narrative of passion and incest based on an Old Testament story. *The Women at Point Sur* (1927), *Cawdor and Other Poems* (1928) and *Thurso's Landing and Other Poems* (1932). *Hungerfield and Other Poems* won a PULITZER PRIZE in 1954. His reputation has been controversial, in part due to his wartime isolationist stance. Many readers find his philosophy repugnant; others see him as an American prophet.

For further reading:

Everson, William, *The Excesses of God: Robinson Jeffers as a Religious Figure.* Palo Alto: Stanford University Press, 1988.

Jefferson Airplane. American ROCK-AND-ROLL band. Jefferson Airplane was the most commercially successful of the so-called psychedelic bands to emerge from the psychedelic rock scene that centered in SAN FRANCISCO in the late 1960s. The original members of the band, which released its first album *Jefferson Airplane Takes Off* in 1966, were vocalist Signe Anderson, vocalist and guitarist Marty Balin, bassist Jack Casady, drummer Spencer Dryden, and guitarists Paul Kantner and Jorma Kaukonen. Shortly after that album was released, vocalist Grace Slick replaced Anderson. The group's next album, *Surrealistic Pillow* (1967), reached number three on the Billboard pop album chart and featured two hit songs, "Somebody to Love" and "White Rabbit." Subsequent albums included *Crown of Creation* (1968) and *Volunteers* (1969). In the 1970s the group's name was changed to **Jefferson Starship** and issued an album that reached number one on the Billboard pop chart, *Red Octopus* (1975). With numerous personnel changes, Jefferson Starship—later simply Starship—issued recordings through the 1980s.

Jeffrey MacDonald case. Case arising from the brutal murders of Collette MacDonald, wife of Green Beret physician Jeffrey R. MacDonald, and their two young daughters on February 17, 1970. The killings, at MacDonald's Fort Bragg, North Carolina home, bore a resemblance to the earlier Charles MANSON slayings. MacDonald, who had been only superficially wounded, asserted that he and his family had been assaulted by a group of drug-crazed HIPPIES. Physical evidence pointed to MacDonald, but he was cleared in a 1970 court martial hearing. He later moved to California, where he practiced medicine. Through the persistence of his former father-in-law, a federal grand jury indicted MacDonald in 1975, and he was found guilty of murder in a 1979 trial. Sentenced to three consecutive life terms, he continued to protest his innocence.

For further reading:

McGinniss, Joe, *Fatal Vision.* New York: Putnam Publishing Group, 1983.

Jeffries, James J. (1875–1953). American prizefighter. Born in Carroll, Ohio, Jeffries began boxing in 1896. A powerful defensive fighter, he won the heavyweight championship in 1899 and defended his title six times before retiring undefeated in 1905. Touted by fight promoters as "the Great White Hope," he came out of retirement in 1910 to fight the black Jack JOHNSON; Johnson knocked Jeffries out in the 15th round of their championship bout at Reno, Nevada.

Jelgava [Yelgava; Mitau (German); Mitava (Russian)]. City on the Lielupe River in southern Latvia of the U.S.S.R. Occupied by German forces during WORLD WAR I, in October 1919 it was a headquarters for BOLSHEVIK troops until they were driven out by a Latvian and Lithuanian army. A part of independent LATVIA between 1920 and 1940, it was taken by the Soviet Union in 1940, reoccupied by Germany from 1941 to 1944 and reoccupied by counterattacking Russian forces in 1944.

Jellicoe, John Rushworth [1st Earl (1925)] (1859–1935). British admiral. A career naval officer, he entered the Royal Navy in 1872, was made a captain in 1897, vice admiral in 1910 and full admiral in 1915. In WORLD WAR I, he served as commander in chief of the Grand Fleet (1914–16), winning a Pyrrhic victory at the battle of JUTLAND. He was first sea lord (1916–17) and naval chief of staff at war's end. Jellicoe was governor general of New Zealand from 1920 to 1924.

Jenkins, Herbert (1907–1990). U.S. police chief. He held the post of police chief of Atlanta from 1947 to 1973. His policy of accommodating CIVIL RIGHTS leaders in the 1960s helped Atlanta's image as a Southern city that cooperated in the civil rights movement. He maintained order during sit-ins at lunch counters and gave police protection to "freedom riders." In

1967, he was the only Southerner appointed by President Lyndon B. JOHNSON to the National Advisory Commission on Civil Disorders. In 1968, he also provided a police escort for a KU KLUX KLAN march through one of the city's black sections, preventing conflict.

Jenkins, Roy (Harris) (1920–). British politician. Born in Wales, Jenkins is the son of a miner who became a union organizer and later an M.P. After leaving Oxford Jenkins served as an army captain in WORLD WAR II. He was elected to parliament in 1948. Jenkins was on the executive committee of the FABIAN SOCIETY from 1949 to 1961. A leading figure in the British LABOUR PARTY, he served as minister of aviation (1964–65), home secretary (1966–67, 1974–76) and chancellor of the exchequer (1967–70). Jenkins left Parliament in 1976 to serve as president of the EUROPEAN ECONOMIC COMMUNITY until 1980. In 1981 along with Shirley WILLIAMS, David OWEN and William RODGERS, he co-founded the SOCIAL DEMOCRATIC PARTY and served as its first leader until 1983. In a 1982 by-election, Jenkins was reelected to the House of Commons. He was elevated to the House of Lords in 1987. Jenkins is the author of biographies of Clement ATTLEE, Herbert ASQUITH and Charles Dilke.

Jensen, Alfred Julio (1903–1981). Guatemalan-born abstract painter who developed a highly distinctive style in his lushly colored, intricate-patterned canvases. Jensen was first associated with the abstract expressionists, then with the American avant-garde movement and the so-called "New York School." He began exhibiting in New York in 1952, and his paintings were displayed in major museums throughout the world.

Jensen, Georg Arthur (1866–1935). Best known of all Danish craft designers for his high-quality modern jewelry and silverware. Jensen was trained as a goldsmith and also studied sculpture at the Copenhagen Academy. Beginning in 1895 he worked in ceramics with Joachim Petersen. Some of his work was exhibited at the Paris Exhibition of 1900. In 1904 he opened a small shop in Copenhagen, offering jewelry and silver of his own design. As the business grew, it produced and sold designs of other Danish designers and craftsmen, eventually distributing a wide variety of Scandinavian products of high design quality, which combine the aesthetics of MODERNISM with traces of Nordic traditionalism. The firm is now international, with the New York shop well known as a primary showcase for Danish design.

Jensen, Johannes (1873–1950). Danish novelist. To support himself as a medical student at the University of Copenhagen, Jensen wrote a series of detective novels under the name Ivar Lykke. He also began work on his first serious novel, *Danskere* (Danes, 1896). With the publication of *Einar Elkoer* (1897), Jensen abandoned his medical studies. He first attracted critical acclaim with *Himmerlandsfolk* (*Himmerland People,* 1898), a collection of stories situated in his native Jutland, which he followed with several similar volumes. Jensen's best known work is the trilogy *Konages Fald* (*The Fall of the King,* 1901), which presents the life of Danish King Christian II, combining myth and realism. Between 1908 and 1922 Jensen published the six-volume *Den lange rejse* (*The Long Journey,* 1922–24), a fictional expression of his evolutionary theories, which begins in prehistoric Jutland, and ends with Columbus discovering the New World. Jensen then produced the 11-volume *Myter* (*Myths*) published between 1907 and 1944. Jensen was awarded the NOBEL PRIZE for literature in 1944. His other works include *Digte* (*Poems,* 1906) and *Andens Stadier* (*The Stages of the Mind,* 1928).

Jeritza, Maria (1887–1982). Czech-Austrian opera singer. A dramatic soprano, Jeritza made her debut as Elsa in Wagner's *Lohengrin* in 1910 and went on to huge successes in major roles at the Vienna Opera and New York's Metropolitan Opera over the next 25 years. She was a favorite soprano of both Richard STRAUSS and Giacomo PUCCINI. Strauss wrote the roles of Ariadne in his *Ariadne auf Naxos* and the Empress in *Die Frau ohne Schatten* for her. Her performances in the title roles of Puccini's *Tosca* and *Turandot* were considered definitive. Known for her brilliant voice, dramatic stage presence, and glamorous star quality, Jeritza was not only one of the greatest singers of her day but also an international celebrity.

Jersey. Largest and most southerly of the CHANNEL ISLANDS. In the English Channel, 15 miles from the coast of France's Normandy, Jersey was occupied by the Germans during WORLD WAR II, from 1941 to 1945; a part of the U.K. since the Norman Conquest, some 10,000 of its inhabitants had been evacuated to Britain. French is the official language of Jersey.

Jerusalem. Ancient city, sacred to three religions and capital of ISRAEL; 35 miles inland from the coast of the Mediterranean Sea and 13 miles west of the Dead Sea. The city is venerated by JEWS, Christians and Muslims. Inspired by the Zionist movement in the late-19th century, Jews began to settle once more in and around Jerusalem, until by 1900 they were the largest group in the city (see ZIONISM). During WORLD WAR I the city was captured by the British (Dec. 1917) from the Ottoman Turks, longtime rulers of PALESTINE. From 1922 until 1948 the city was under British rule as part of a LEAGUE OF NATIONS mandate. Exasperated by continuous Jewish-Arab conflict, Britain handed over its mandate to the UNITED NATIONS in 1947; the U.N. planned to partition Palestine between Jewish and Arab states and guarantee Jerusalem as a neutral city. On the expiration of the mandate in 1948, the Jews (emboldened by the informal BALFOUR DECLARATION of 1917, which pledged British support for a new Jewish state) and the Arabs went to war. JORDAN seized Jerusalem's old city, and the Israelis the new city, which they declared the capital of their new state of Israel. During the SIX-DAY WAR (1967) the old city was captured by Israel and integrated with the new, or Israeli, sector. Jerusalem as a whole was formally made the capital of Israel in 1980.

Jessner, Leopold (1878–1945). German theatrical director and producer. Jessner was one of the leading forces in German theater in the 1910s and 1920s, serving as a producer at prominent state theaters in Hamburg, Konigsberg, and Berlin. In particular, he fostered the rise of EXPRESSIONISM in German drama, championing the works of playwright Frank Wedekind, among others. Jessner also won renown for his adaptations of classic theatrical works by Shakespeare and Lessing. A Jew, Jessner fled Nazi Germany in 1933, going first to Palestine and then to the U.S.

jet engine. The jet engine is similar to the rocket engine, but takes oxygen from the atmosphere to burn its fuel, whereas the rocket engine carries its own oxygen. Jet engines generate greater thrust than piston-driven propellers; thus, jet planes can fly significantly faster. British engineer Frank Whittle patented the turbo-jet engine in 1930 and subsequently tested a successful jet engine on the ground. The first British jet aircraft, powered by Whittle's engine, flew in May 1941. German aviation engineer Ernst Heinkel developed a twin-engine jet fighter that flew in small numbers near the end of World War II. After the war, the British and Americans developed passenger jet aircraft. The late 1950s saw the dawning of the "jet age" with the introduction of long-distance passenger jets.

Jet Propulsion Laboratory [JPL]. NASA research laboratory in Pasadena, California. It was transferred from Army jurisdiction to NASA in 1958 and operated in conjunction with the California Institute of Technology. JPL managed the unmanned RANGER and SURVEYOR missions to the moon, as well as many later planetary missions, such as PIONEER missions to Jupiter and Saturn and VOYAGER missions to Jupiter, Saturn, Uranus and Neptune.

Jews. Jews are descendants of the Hebrews, a term including many Semitic, nomadic tribes of biblical times. Jews are not a separate race, but rather members of a religious or ethnic community drawn together by centuries of persecution and a minority status wherever they settled. Most Jews can trace their ancestry to either the Ashkenazim, which includes the Jews of central and eastern Europe, or the Sephardim, who were expelled from Spain and Portugal at the end of the 15th century. Currently, there is also an informal distinction between people of Jewish ancestry who associate themselves with the political aims and culture of the Jews but are not religious, and those who strictly uphold the practice of Judaism. Of the approximately 18 million Jewish people in the world, some 6 million live in the United States, about 3 million in ISRAEL and about 3 million in the Soviet Union. Other countries with significant Jewish populations include Argentina, Canada, France and the United Kingdom.

A renewed wave of anti-Semitism swept Europe toward the end of the 19th century. In Germany and Austria-Hungary, many sought to prove the inferiority of the Jews to the Aryans. In Russia, where Jews already had a diminished legal status, many were massacred during the POGROMS. Some 2 million Jews immigrated to the United States where they found their rights legally protected, although they still faced discrimination. In France, the Dreyfus Affair brought increased hostility toward the Jews. Theodor HERZL, a Jewish lawyer who reported on the Dreyfus case, was moved to form the World Zionist Organization and propose a separate Jewish homeland. In the early 1900s, Zionists began establishing colonies in PALESTINE. During WORLD WAR I, Great Britain seized Palestine from Turkey, then in 1917 issued the BALFOUR DECLARATION, which gave British endorsement to the formation of a Jewish state in Palestine. The LEAGUE OF NATIONS approved the declaration, and Palestine was made a mandated territory of Great Britain in 1920. In the face of much Arab opposition, many Jews immigrated to Palestine in the 1920s and '30s.

In 1933, Adolph HITLER came to power in GERMANY. His Nazi Party began disseminating vicious propaganda blaming the Jews for Germany's economic woes and proclaiming the superiority of the Aryan people. In 1935, German Jews were deprived of their citizenship. Many fled Germany, but many others, their property seized by the Nazis, were sent to CONCENTRATION CAMPS. Some, like Anne FRANK and her family, went into hiding. In 1941, Hitler proposed the FINAL SOLUTION, a systematic plan to exterminate all European Jews. Nazi firing squads murdered thousands of Jews, and concentration camps were outfitted with gas chambers for the mass annihilation of Jews. Approximately 6 million European Jews were killed during the HOLOCAUST in Nazi Germany.

Following WORLD WAR II, the decimated Jewish population renewed its efforts to form a state in Palestine but met continual opposition from the Arabs. In 1947, Britain urged the UNITED NATIONS to intervene. The U.N. proposed that Palestine be divided into an Arab state and a Jewish one, ISRAEL, which became independent the following year. Arab hostilities did not subside, however, and Israel was at war with its Arab neighbors in 1948, 1956, 1967 and 1973.

In the Soviet Union, Jewish culture and the practice of Judaism continued to be suppressed and the emigration of Jews restricted. Following years of protest, emigration laws began to ease in the early 1970s, and with the advent of PERESTROIKA, Jews regained many rights of expression and movement. American Jews—in this century, the most secure and successful—are concerned with the loss of their tradition and heritage as they become increasingly assimilated into American culture. Many maintain strong ties to Israel, which they consider their spiritual homeland. Jews continue to face discrimination, and fear the extremist, anti-Semitic organizations, such as the KU KLUX KLAN, in the U.S. and elsewhere.

Jhabvala, Ruth Prawer (1927–). British novelist and screenwriter. With her first novel, *To Whom She Will* (1955, published in the U.S. as *Amrita,* 1965), Jhabvala established her reputation as a perceptive chronicler of contemporary India, which she has maintained with a steady output of acclaimed fiction including, the novels *A New Dominion* (1972, published in the U.S. as *Travelers,* 1973), *Heat and Dust* (1975, filmed 1983), *Three Continents* (1987), and the short stories, *An Experience of India* (1971) and *How I Became a Holy Mother and Other Stories* (1976). In 1966 she became associated with the filmmaking team of director James Ivory and producer Ismail Merchant. She has adapted many of her novels for the screen and co-authored screenplays with Ivory. These include *Shakespeare Wallah* (1966) and *The Europeans* (1979), based on the novel by Henry JAMES.

Jigme Singye Wangchuk (1955–). King of BHUTAN. As a 17-year-old, he ascended the throne when his father died in 1972. He followed his father's policy of working with the National Assembly and moved to increase popular participation in economic planning.

Jimenez, Juan Ramon (1881–1958). Spanish poet. Jimenez published his first poetry in *Vida Nueva* (*New Life*) in 1899, where it attracted the attention of Ruben DARIO, among other notable Spanish-language writers, after which he devoted himself to writing poetry and later helped found the literary journals, *Helios* (*Helium*) and *Renacimiento* (*Renaissance*). His first volumes of poetry, such as *Almas de violeta* (*Violet Souls,* 1900) and *Ninfeas* (*Water Lilies,* 1900), now dated in their sentimentality, were still unique in their form and lyrical sensuality. He continually evolved in his style and scope. *Diario de un poeta recian casado* (*Diary of a Newlywed Poet,* 1917) is a hallmark in the use of free verse in Spanish poetry. Jimenez served as a cultural attache in the U.S. at the outbreak of the SPANISH CIVIL WAR; following FRANCO's rise to power in 1939, Jimenez decided to remain abroad, finally settling in Puerto Rico. He was awarded the NOBEL PRIZE for literature in 1956. Other works include *Animal de fondo* (*Animal of Depth,* 1949) and *Tercera antologia poatica* (*Third Poetic Anthology,* 1957).

Jinnah, Muhammad Ali (1876–1948). Founder of PAKISTAN. Born in Karachi, Jinnah studied law in England and was admitted to the bar there. Returning to India, he practiced law and entered politics as part of the Indian National Congress Party in 1906. Opposing Hindu dominance of the party and disapproving of the tactics of Mohandas GANDHI, Jinnah joined the Muslim League in 1913, becoming its president in 1916 and finally breaking with the CONGRESS PARTY in 1930. He reshaped the league into an organization that at first promoted parity between India's Hindus and Muslims. By the mid-1930s all the Muslim members of the Congress Party had joined the league, and a disillusioned Jinnah was calling for the partition of India and the creation of the independent state of Pakistan. During WORLD WAR II, Jinnah was an active supporter of the British, increasing his standing in British eyes. Muslim pressure and the bloody Hindu-Muslim riots of 1946 helped convince the Congress Party to accept the establishment of Pakistan in August 1947. Jinnah became the first governor general of Pakistan and died in office a little over a year later.

The great force of Muslim leader Muhammad Ali Jinnah is belied by the languid elegance of his pose (1945).

Jochum, Eugen (1902–1887). German conductor. Jochum held posts with various German orchestras between 1926 and 1949. Though he remained in Germany during WORLD WAR II, he did not join the Nazi Party. He founded the Bavarian Radio Symphony in Munich in 1949. After 1960 he concentrated on guest appearances with such major orchestras as the Berlin Philharmonic, Amsterdam Concertgebouw and London Symphony. His repertoire included the music of Bach, Mozart, Haydn, Schubert, Wagner, Richard STRAUSS, and Karl ORFF, among others. He recorded all the Beethoven and Brahms symphonies three times, and was the first conductor to record all of Anton Bruckner's symphonies. Jochum was one of the last representatives of the German romantic school of conducting. Like Wilhelm FURTWANGLER, he concentrated on the spiritual aspects of music, and his flexible tempos reflected a personal response to the composer rather than a literal reading of the score.

Joffrey, Robert [born Abdullah Jaffa Anver Beykhan] (1930–1989). American dancer, choreographer and ballet director. Founder and artistic director of the popular Joffrey Ballet, he was born in Seattle of Afghan descent. He trained as a dancer and joined Roland Petit's Ballet de Paris as a soloist in 1948. However, he found his metier as an impresario, company manager and choreographer when he launched his own company, which began as a raggle-taggle group that toured the U.S. in a loaned station wagon in 1956. His vision of hip, young, lithe Americana became widely admired and his company played an instrumental role in expanding the audience for ballet in general. Joffrey's style came to be known as strong, sleek, fast and sexy, with an athletic wit and a willingness to perform modern dance as well as ballet. His most important works include *Gamelon* (1962), *Astarte* (1967) and *Remembrances* (1973). In the 1980s Joffrey turned his attention to the past, embarking on ambitious revivals of rarely performed works of historical significance, by such choreographers as Vaslav NIJINSKY, Bronislava NIJINSKA and Frederick ASHTON. Following Joffrey's death, Gerald ARPINO became artistic director of the company.

Johannesburg. City in South Africa's southern Transvaal, about 300 miles northwest of the Indian Ocean port of Durban. Founded as a mining community in 1886 after the discovery of gold on the Witwatersrand, Johannesburg was occupied by victorious British forces in 1900 during the BOER WAR. It is South Africa's largest city and center of a gold-mining industry that employs large numbers of native blacks as labor. Under South Africa's APARTHEID racial laws, these laborers live mostly in SOWETO, a group of townships south of the city. Soweto has been the scene of serious racial riots and civil unrest.

John XXIII (1881–1963). Pontiff of the Roman Catholic Church (1958–63). Born Angelo Giuseppe Roncalli into an Italian peasant family and ordained in 1904, he rose through the echelons of Vatican diplomacy, becoming the VATICAN's first permanent observer at UNESCO, patriarch of Venice and, finally, Pope. As Pope John XXIII, he worked for world peace and favored the interchange of ideas with other religions. In 1962 he convened the SECOND VATICAN COUNCIL (also known as Vatican II), an ecumenical council that called for greater religious tolerance and Christian unity and brought about dramatic reforms within the Catholic Church.

John, Augustus (Edwin) (1879–1961). British painter. Born in Wales, he studied (1894–98) at London's Slade School of Art, where he was acclaimed for his phenomenal draughtsmanship. He journeyed to Paris and was influenced by the work of Puvis de Chavannes and PICASSO. John lived an exotic and bohemian life, from time to time tramping through Europe and living in gypsy caravans. He became a renowned portraitist, painting with verve and without flattery and numbering many of the important political, social, literary, artistic and theatrical figures of the day among his sitters. These included David LLOYD GEORGE, Queen ELIZABETH II, W.B. YEATS, Sir Jacob EPSTEIN, George Bernard SHAW and Tallulah BANKHEAD. Also a gifted etcher, John was the author of an autobiography, *Chiaroscuro* (1952).

John, Elton (Hercules) [born Reginald Kenneth Dwight] (1947–). British singer and songwriter. Paired with lyricist Bernie Taupin, Elton John dominated the pop charts in the 1970s. A rock pianist with classical training, his hit single "Your Song" (1970) was the first in an unbroken string of top-ten hits, culminating in the first album ever to debut at number one, *Rock of the Westies* (1975). Among his more critically acclaimed works were the double album *Goodbye Yellow Brick Road* (1973), and the autobiographical *Captain Fantastic and the Brown Dirt Cowboy* (1975). His performances have often included outrageous costumes and spectacular spectacles. The first rock star ever to tour the Soviet Union, he continued to achieve popular success through the 1980s and 1990s, and played to an record-breaking 600,000 people in New York's Central Park on September 13, 1980.

John Birch Society. Organization founded in the U.S. by Robert H.W. Welch Jr. in

Pope John XXIII (1960).

Pope John Paul II (1978).

1958. Named after Captain John Birch, who was killed by Chinese communists in 1945 and is considered the first hero of the COLD WAR, the society is strongly anticommunist and promotes ultraconservative causes. It has denounced most welfare programs and called for U.S. withdrawal from the UNITED NATIONS. The 100,000-member society is headquartered in Belmont, Massachusetts, and publishes several pamphlets and papers.

John Paul I (1912–1978). Pontiff of the Roman Catholic Church. Pope John Paul I has left an enduring memory as a man of great kindness and piety, even though his 34-day reign as Pope was the shortest since the 18-day rule of Pope Leo XI in 1605. Born Albino Luciani, he was raised in Forno di Canale (now Canale D'Agordo), a village in northeastern Italy. His father was a worker and a socialist, his mother a devout peasant. Luciani was ordained as a priest in 1936 and worked in the parish of his native village for a time before moving on to a teaching career. He served as vicar general from 1954 to 1958, when he was appointed bishop of Vittorio Veneto. In 1969 he became patriarch of Venice. One of his first acts in this prestigious office was to allow parishes to sell church jewels for the benefit of the poor and the handicapped. Throughout his years of service, Luciani emphasized the need to teach Christian truths simply, with respect for the needs of ordinary people. He was elected Pope in 1978.

John Paul II [born Karol Jozef Wojtyla] (1920–). Pontiff of the Roman Catholic

Church. John Paul II, who was elected Pope in 1978, is the first non-Italian Pope since the Dutch-born Adrian VI (1522–1523). John Paul II is a theological conservative who has sparked a great deal of controversy by his emphatic support of the traditional Catholic ban on artificial means of birth control. He has also insisted on theological conformity on the part of teachers in Catholic universities the world over; this has, at times, led to the withdrawal of teaching credentials for certain theologians. Politically, John Paul II has played a more liberal role, calling for a dedicated effort by all parts of the political spectrum to alleviate global poverty, and traveling to Latin America, the U.S. and Eastern Europe in order to emphasize the universal import of Catholic teachings. Born in Wadowice, Poland, John Paul II was ordained as a priest in 1946, was named archbishop of Krakow in 1964 and was elected to the college of cardinals in 1967.

Johns, Jasper (1930–). American artist. A major figure in contemporary American art, he was born in Allendale, S.C., studied at the University of South Carolina and settled in New York City in 1952. He burst on the art scene with his first one-man show in N.Y.C. in 1958. Influenced in subject matter by the commonplace objects used by Marcel DUCHAMP and the DADAISTS and by the painterly techniques of ABSTRACT EXPRESSIONISM, Johns became a precursor of the POP ART movement with his paintings of flags, targets, maps, letters and numbers. In these works, he sought to explore the relationship between the object portrayed and the image that portrays it, transforming ordinary subjects into art. His best known paintings include *Target with Four Faces* (1955, Museum of Modern Art, N.Y.C.) and *Flag on an Orange Field* (1957, Wallraf-Richartz Museum, Cologne). Johns is also noted for his graphics and for his brass castings of objects such as the beer cans portrayed in *Painted Bronze* (1964).

Johnson, Amy (1903–1941). British aviatrix. Johnson taught herself to fly and in 1929 became the first woman to hold an Air Ministry ground engineer's certificate. In 1930 she made a solo flight from Croydon, England to Darwin, Australia in 20 days, which brought her great celebrity. In recognition of this feat she was made a Commander of the British Empire. In 1931 she set a ten-day record flying from London to Tokyo, and in 1932, flew solo to Cape Town. From 1932 to 1938, she was married to the aviator Jim Mollison (1905–1959) and flew with him from London to the U.S. in 1932. During WORLD WAR II Johnson served in the Air Transport Auxiliary as a ferry pilot, and died in the line of duty when she bailed out before her aircraft crashed in the Thames estuary.

Johnson, Ben (1961–). Canadian sprinter who lost his Olympic gold medal after it was revealed that he had cheated by using steroids. Johnson blazed to fame in 1987 when he set a new world record time of 9.83 seconds for the 100–meter sprint at the 1987 World Championships. After he won the 100–meter race at the OLYMPIC GAMES, a routine drug test revealed that he had used illegal steroids; he was stripped of his gold medal and disgraced. The use of steroids by athletes subsequently became a major subject of concern.

Johnson, Dame Celia (1908–1982). British stage and screen actress. Johnson trained at the Royal Academy of Dramatic Art (RADA). Her long and distinguished career included roles in some of the best contemporary British films, modern plays and the classical repertory. Her films included *Rebecca* (1940), *In Which We Serve* (1942), *Brief Encounter* (1946) and *The Captain's Paradise* (1953). She gave acclaimed performances in plays by AYCKBOURN, CHEKHOV, SHAW and Shakespeare. She was awarded her title by Queen ELIZABETH II in 1981.

Johnson, Clarence L. ("Kelly") (1910–). American aeronautical engineer whose work has had an extensive influence on the design of modern aircraft and on all modern industrial design. Johnson was a graduate of the University of Michigan and began work for LOCKHEED in 1933. By 1938 he became chief engineer. The Lockheed P-38 fighter of 1941 was his first outstanding and original design. Later projects include the P-80 jet fighter, the U-2 spy plane and the C-130 Hercules military transport. His work is often credited with having had a strong influence on automotive design in 1952, when airplanelike tail fins appeared on American automobiles purely for style.

Johnson, Eyvind (1900–1976). Swedish novelist. On his own from the age of 13, Johnson educated himself by reading. His early novels, such as *Timans och rattfardigheten* (*Timans and Justice,* 1925), are strongly influenced by James JOYCE and Sigmund FREUD. Johnson began working a journalist, and during WORLD WAR II coedited *Et Handslag* (*A Handshake*) with Willy BRANDT for the Norwegian RESISTANCE. In Sweden Johnson is perhaps best known for the tetralogy, *Romanen om Olof* (*The Novel About Olof,* 1934–1937), which depicts the rise of the Swedish proletariat through one youth's development. Internationally, he is better known for *Strandernas svall* (1946), translated as *Return to Ithaca: The Odyssey Retold as a Modern Novel* in 1952, which began a series of novels emphasizing the repetition of history. Johnson was awarded the NOBEL PRIZE for literature in 1974 jointly with Henry MARTINSON. Of Johnson's 30 novels, only four have been translated into English.

Johnson, Hiram (1866–1945). U.S. politician. Johnson won election as governor of California in 1910 on a platform of political reform. During his administration he smashed the Southern Pacific Railroad machine, which had long dominated the statehouse, and passed the Public Utilities Act, which created one of the most effective systems of railroad control in the country. A founder of the Progressive Party, Johnson ran as vice president on the 1912 ticket headed by Theodore ROOSEVELT. In 1916 Johnson was elected to the Senate on the Progressive ticket. In the upper house he developed a reputation as an independent, reluctantly supporting U.S. entry into WORLD WAR I but criticizing Woodrow WILSON's foreign policy. Although he initially supported President HOOVER, he became increasingly critical of the administration, blaming it for much of the distress of the Depression. Johnson backed Franklin ROOSEVELT in 1932 but later refused to support FDR's foreign and domestic policy. He was one of the Senate's most consistent isolationists. Johnson was a leading candidate for the Republican nomination in 1920. When he lost the nomination to Warren HARDING, he refused offers of the vice presidential nomination; he served in the Senate until his death.

Johnson, Howard Deering (1896–1972). American ice cream maker and entrepreneur. In 1924, Howard Johnson bought a soda fountain in Wollaston, Mass., and started to sell his famous "28 flavors" of ice cream. Five years later, he began to license his name and products, creating the chain of Howard Johnson's restaurants. The firm flourished in the postwar years, and by 1964, when Johnson retired, it had grown into the largest food distributor in the United States.

Johnson, James Weldon (1871–1938). American author and promoter of civil rights. A graduate of Atlanta University, he was the first black admitted to the bar in Florida (1897). He also served as consul to Venezuela and Nicaragua. In 1901 Johnson moved to New York to collaborate with his brother on the lyrics for light operas and popular songs. Their "Lift Every Voice and Sing" was considered virtually a black national anthem. He taught creative literature at Fisk University from 1930 to 1938.

Johnson, John Arthur "Jack" (1878–1946). American boxer. Jackson fought his way through the ranks and, in 1908, became the first black world heavyweight champion. His flamboyant ways and lavish lifestyle led to his becoming the immediate subject of an outpouring of hate, which culminated in the search for a "great white hope" to take back the heavyweight crown. The searchers found former champion Jim JEFFRIES, whom Johnson decisively beat in 1910. In 1915 Johnson lost his title to Jess Willard in a bout held in the broiling sun of Havana, Cuba. Johnson's three marriages to white women aroused further racial prejudice, and he was harassed by federal authorities on a variety of trumped-up charges—including white slavery—which led him to flee to Europe to tour in theatrical shows. He returned to the U.S. in 1920, and served eight months of a one-year sentence at Leavenworth Penitentiary.

Johnson, John Harold (1918–). U.S. publisher. He started his Chicago-based publishing empire with emphasis on stories of black achievement. In 1942 he started *Negro Digest,* which changed its

Undated photograph of world heavyweight champion Jack Johnson.

title to *Black World* in 1970. Other Johnson magazines include *Ebony* (1945) and *Jet* (1951). Johnson was named Publisher of the Year in 1972. The company ranks first nationally in earnings among black enterprises.

Johnson, Lyndon Baines (1908–1973). Thirty-sixth president of the UNITED STATES (1963–69). Born near Johnson City, Texas, the son of a farmer, Johnson worked his way through teachers college and was a high school teacher before entering politics in 1932 as secretary to a Democratic congressman from Texas. Committed to the principles of the NEW DEAL, he became a protege of Sam RAYBURN, who successfully urged President Franklin D. ROOSEVELT to appoint him director of the National Yough Administration in 1935. He was first elected to the House of Representatives in 1937, serving there as an active supporter of Roosevelt's military and foreign policies until his election to the Senate in 1948. He was soon one of the nation's most powerful senators, becoming Democratic leader in 1953 and majority leader in 1954. A canny strategist and shrewd compromiser, he supported most of the programs of President Dwight D. EISENHOWER and was known for his moderate to conservative positions. He ran for the Democratic presidential nomination in 1960, but lost to John F. KENNEDY, who chose Johnson as his vice presidential running mate.

Lyndon Baines Johnson, 36th president of the United States.

Johnson was sworn in as president after the assassination of President Kennedy on November 22, 1963. As president, Johnson energetically endorsed the social programs promised by his predecessor and used his considerable political skills to see them enacted. Persuaded by Johnson, Congress passed a broad tax cut and the landmark CIVIL RIGHTS ACT OF 1964. Calling for what he called a GREAT SOCIETY, Johnson pressed for a vigorous domestic program that included a war against poverty and sweeping economic and social reform and legislation.

His domestic achievements were largely overshadowed by his troubles abroad, as Johnson became increasingly enmeshed in the VIETNAM WAR. After passage of the TONKIN GULF RESOLUTION, Johnson began the massive bombing of North Vietnam in 1965 and increased U.S. troop levels from some 20,000 to over 500,000. War costs increased, and many Great Society programs proved too expensive. Riots soon broke out in America's black ghettos, and the ANTIWAR MOVEMENT gained momentum across the country. Ailing and increasingly unpopular, Johnson announced that he would not run for reelection in 1968. He remained a powerful force in Democratic politics and saw to it that his chosen successor, Vice President Hubert HUMPHREY, was nominated for the presidency. Humphrey lost by a narrow margin to Richard M. NIXON, and Johnson retired to his Texas ranch in 1969. His memoirs, *The Vantage Point,* were published in 1971.

For further reading:

Caro, Robert A., *The Path to Power: The Years of Lyndon Johnson.* New York: Knopf, 1982.

Johnson, Martin (1884–1937). American explorer and writer. Johnson joined author Jack LONDON on the cruise of the *Snark.* He made well-known expeditions to the SOLOMON and NEW HEBRIDES islands (1914) and BORNEO (1917–19 and 1935). He and his wife Osa traveled around the world six times, wrote, lectured and gained a reputation as jungle experts, especially on Africa. They were famed for their motion pictures of their explorations, such as *Simba* and *Congorilla,* and also cowrote *Cannibal Land* (1917), *Camera Trails in Africa* (1924) and *Lion* (1929); Osa also wrote *I Married Adventure* (1940).

Johnson, Pamela Hansford (1912–1981). British novelist, playwright, and critic and wife of novelist C.P. SNOW. Although she did not achieve the same level of popularity as her husband, Johnson's work was highly regarded by critics. Among her 25 novels were *An Impossible Marriage* and *The Good Husband.*

Johnson, Philip (Cortelyou) (1906–). American architect. Born in Cleveland, Johnson attended Harvard University. He became one of the leading advocates of the new European architecture as the coauthor (with Henry-Russell HITCHCOCK) of *The International Style: Architecture since 1922* (1932) and as head of the department of architecture at the MUSEUM OF MODERN ART (1932–34, 1945–54). Johnson brought the INTERNATIONAL STYLE to the U.S. in his own buildings, designing a number of houses that were greatly influenced by MIES VAN DER ROHE. These include his own "glass house" (1949–50) and the Wiley house (1953), both in New Canaan, Connecticut. Johnson collaborated with Mies on the Seagram Building in New York City (1958), a great amber slab that is considered one of modern architecture's greatest skyscrapers. Johnson largely abandoned the International Style in the 1960s and produced such classically influenced buildings as the Sheldon Art Gallery, Lincoln, Nebraska (1963) and the New York State Theater at Lincoln Center (1964). In the 1970s he created innovative structures such as Pennzoil Place, Houston, Texas (1976) and the AT&T Building, New York City (1978), whose massive Chippendale-like broken pediment has been seen as an emblem of POSTMODERNISM.

Johnson, Robert (1912–1938). African-American blues composer, vocalist and guitarist. Johnson, who never reached a sizable audience outside his native Mississippi during his lifetime, achieved a posthumous reputation as perhaps the greatest songwriter and performer in the history of the blues. Contemporary musicians who have sung his praises (and performed his songs) include Eric CLAPTON and Bob DYLAN. Johnson ran away from home at an early age to learn guitar from blues master Son House. In the 1930s, Johnson performed in Mississippi with fellow blues greats Howlin' Wolf and Elmore James. His greatest recordings, featuring Johnson's heartrending, moaning vocals, include "Hellhound On My Trail," "Milkcow's Calf Blues" and "Terraplane Blues." Blues guitarist Robert Jr. Lockwood is his stepson.

Johnson, Walter (1887–1946). American baseball player. Elected to the Baseball Hall of Fame in 1936, Johnson ranks as one of the greatest fastball pitchers in history. While pitching for the Washington Senators from 1907 to 1927, he won 416 games. He set a career strikeout record of 3,508, and in 1913 pitched 56 consecutive innings without allowing a run. In his career, he pitched seven opening-game shutouts.

Johnson Space Center. NASA center at Clear Lake, Texas, near Houston. Originally known as the Manned Spacecraft Center, this site houses NASA Mission Control, which managed all manned space flights after lift-off from CAPE CANAVERAL Air Force Station (MERCURY, GEMINI and most unmanned missions) or from KENNEDY SPACE CENTER (APOLLO, SKYLAB and SPACE SHUTTLE missions). It was named for President Lyndon B. JOHNSON.

Johore [Johor]. A state of MALAYSIA, on the southern extremity of the Malay Peninsula, opposite SINGAPORE; its capital is at Johore Bahru. Occupied by Japan during World War II, Johore joined the Federation of Malaya in 1957 and became a part of Malaysia in 1963.

Joliot-Curie, Frederic (1900–1958). French physicist. Frederic Joliot, the son of a prosperous tradesman, was education at the School of Industrial Physics and Chemistry. In 1923 he began his research career at the Radium Institute under Marie CURIE, where he obtained his doctorate in 1930. He was appointed to a new chair of nuclear chemistry at the College de France in 1937 and, after World War II (in which he played an important part in the French RESISTANCE) was head of the new Commissariat a l'Energie Atomique (1946–50). In 1956 he became head of the Radium Institute.

In 1926 Joliot married the daughter of Marie CURIE, Irene, and changed his name to Joliot-Curie. In 1931 they began research that was to win them the NOBEL PRIZE for physics in 1935 for their fundamental discovery of artificial radioactivity (1934).

In 1939 Joliot-Curie was quick to see the significance of the discovery of nuclear fission by Otto HAHN. He confirmed Hahn's work and saw the likelihood of a chain reaction. He further realized that the chain reaction could only be produced in the presence of a moderator to slow the neutrons down. A good moderator was the heavy water that was produced on a largle scale only in Norway at Telemark. With considerable foresight Joliot-Curie managed to persuade the French government to obtain this entire stock of heavy-water, 185 kilograms in all, and to arrange for its shipment to England out of the reach of the advancing German army.

Joliot-Curie, Irene (1897–1956). French physicist. Irene Curie was the daughter of Pierre and Marie CURIE, the discoverers of radium. She received little formal schooling, attending instead informal classes where she was taught physics by her mother, mathematics by Paul Langevin, and chemistry by Jean Baptiste Perrin. She later attended the Sorbonne although she first served as a radiologist at the front during WORLD WAR I. In 1921 she began work at her mother's Radium Institute, with which she maintained her connection for the rest of her life, becoming its director in 1946. She was also, from 1937, a professor at the Sorbonne.

In 1926 Irene Curie married Frederic JOLIOT and took the name Joliot-Curie. In 1935 the Joliot-Curies won the NOBEL PRIZE for physics for their discovery in 1934 of articifial radioactivity.

Irene later almost anticipated Otto HAHN's discovery of nuclear fission but like many other physicists at that time found it too difficult to accept the simple hypothesis that heavy elements like uranium could split into lighter elements when bombarded with neutrons. Instead she tried to find heavier elements produced by the decay of uranium.

Like her mother, Irene Joliot-Curie produced a further generation of scientists. Her daughter, Helene, married the son of Marie Curie's old companion, Paul Langevin, and, together with her brother, Paul, became a distinguished physicist.

Jolson, Al [Asa Yoelson] (1886–1950). American stage and motion picture entertainer. A Russian immigrant, Jolson sang in a New York synagogue during his youth and also performed in VAUDEVILLE and blackface theaters. Popular entertainment won out, and at his peak in the early 1920s many people considered Jolson the greatest all-round performer in the world. It was his habit to interpolate into his shows any song that struck his fancy. Thus, during a performance of his hit show *Sinbad* (1918), he sang a little thing he had heard at a party, "Swanee"; the song's immediate success catapulted its composer George GERSHWIN into the big time. Jolson's film career did not spring full-blown from *The Jazz Singer*. He had been tested for the cameras many years previously; and he had made a sound short several months before beginning *The Jazz Singer*. His famous "throwaway" line—"You ain't heard nothing yet"—was actually a "signature" piece, already well known in his stage performances. And it was not *The Jazz Singer* so much as Jolson's immediate follow-up, *The Singing Fool* (1928)—with smash-hit songs "Sonny Boy," "There's a Rainbow Round My Shoulder" and "I'm Sittin' on Top of the World"—that really launched the TALKING PICTURES. In semi-retirement in the 1940s, Jolson found a new generation of admirers thanks to two less-than-truthful biographical films, *The Jolson Story* (1946) and *Jolson Sings Again* (1949), starring Larry Parks and utilizing Jolson's dubbed voice. Jolson died of a heart attack after a tour entertaining U.S. troops in Korea.

Back from Hollywood, singer Al Jolson arrives at Grand Central Station.

For further reading:

Geduld, Harry M. *From Edison to Jolson.* Bloomington: Indiana University Press, 1975.

Jones, Blanche Calloway [born Blanche Calloway] (1902–1978). American singer. Blanche Calloway first appeared in 1920 with the Earl "Fatha" HINES and Louis ARMSTRONG bands. In the 1930s she became the first woman to lead a major American dance band. After retiring as a singer in 1944, she became the first woman disk jockey in the American South. She was the sister of JAZZ bandleader and performer Cab CALLOWAY.

Jones, Bobby (1902–1971). U.S. golfer. His domination of the sport in the late 1920s and early 1930s was challenged only by Gene SARAZEN. In 1930, he won the U.S. Open, British Open, British Amateur and U.S. Amateur titles, completing an unprecedented "Grand Slam." He won the U.S. Open a total of four times, the British Open three times and the U.S. Amateur title five times. Although he retired at the age of 28, his influence on golf continued as he cofounded the Augusta National Golf Club. In 1934, he established the Masters Tournament, which rapidly became one of golf's most prestigious championships.

Jones, David (1895–1974). British poet, essayist and artist. Jones was born in Kent, England, but was strongly influenced by the Welsh ancestry of his family, an influence that shows in his poetic works. He served in the British army during WORLD WAR I, an experience that he drew upon in composing his literary masterpiece, *In Parenthesis* (1937), a haunting narrative blending of poetry and prose that explores wartime suffering along with the chivalric legends of King Arthur and the Welsh *Mabinogion.* Other works by Jones include *The Anathemata* (1952), *The Sleeping Lord* (1974) and *The Dying Gaul* (1978). Jones was also a gifted artist who produced engravings, watercolors and drawings to accompany his own writings as well as books by his contemporaries.

Jones, Hilary Pollard (1863–1938). U.S. Navy officer. Jones served in the Spanish-American War (1898) and commanded a cruiser division of the Atlantic Fleet during WORLD WAR I. He was commander-in-chief of the U.S. fleet from 1922 to 1923 and was a member of the U.S. delegation to the arms limitation talks in Geneva (1926–27).

Jones, James (1921–1977). American novelist. During WORLD WAR II he served in the Pacific and fought at GUADALCANAL.

His wartime experiences formed the background to his subsequent work as a writer. Jones is best known for his first—and many consider, his best—novel, *From Here To Eternity* (1951, filmed 1953) an expansive story that takes place on an army base prior to the bombing of PEARL HARBOR. This insightful, unsentimental study of masculine attitudes and interaction told in plain, blunt language won the National Book Award in 1951; the film won three ACADEMY AWARDS in 1953. Jones felt that the success of *From Here To Eternity* overshadowed his subsequent fiction, which includes *The Thin Red Line* (1962, filmed 1964), *The Ice-Cream Headache and Other Stories* (1968) and *Whistle*, edited by Willie Morris and published posthumously in 1978.

For further reading:

MacShane, Frank, *Into Eternity: The Life of James Jones, American Writer*. Boston: Houghton Mifflin, 1985.

Jones, James Earl (1931–). American stage and film actor. Born in rural Mississippi, Jones attended the University of Michigan. He first came to public attention in the early 1960s as a member of the New York Shakespeare Festival playing, among others, Caliban in *The Tempest* (1962) and the title role in *Othello* (1964) and returning as Lear in 1973. He became a star in the role of prizefighter Jack JOHNSON in *The Great White Hope* (1968; filmed 1970). Since then he has lent his superb acting skills and magnificent voice to such plays as *The Iceman Cometh* (1973), *Of Mice and Men* (1974), *Master Harold and the Boys* (1981) and *Fences* (1985) and to such films as *Star Wars* (1977, as the voice of Darth Vader), *Field of Dreams* (1989) and *The Hunt for Red October* (1990). He has also appeared in many television dramas, notably in the starring role of the early 1990s series "Gideon's Fire."

Jones, Jesse Holman (1874–1956). American financier and politician. Based in Houston, Texas, Jones became a millionaire lumber magnate and land developer. He served in different capacities under Presidents HOOVER and ROOSEVELT. His close ties to business made him a vital member of the wartime cabinet. He was a major figure in the rapid development of U.S. wartime industrial capacity and in the planning for postwar adjustments.

Jones, Peter (1930–1990). British sports commentator. As the BBC's senior sports commentator, Jones covered all major events, from the Wimbledon tennis championships to the OLYMPIC GAMES, but was best known as a football commentator. He was also called in to provide radio commentary for such major events as royal weddings and state openings of Parliament.

Jones, Spike [Lindley Armstrong] (1911–1964). American musician and bandleader. Spike Jones enjoyed a major success in show business in the 1940s and 1950s, when his madcap style of comical musical performance led to appearances by himself and his band on radio and on a regular television series. Jones was born in Long Beach, California, and first came to national attention with his recording of *Der Fuhrer's Face* (1942), a satirical attack on Hitler that featured a loud Bronx cheer. Jones toured the U.S. for many years with his band, the City Slickers, which featured such extemporaneous instruments as doorbells, pistols, hammers and anvils, and the "Latrinophone"—a toilet seat with catgut strings.

Jonestown massacre (Nov. 18, 1978). Mass suicide of members of the People's Temple religious cult, in the agricultural commune of Jonestown, Guyana. The group, led by Rev. Jim (James Warren) Jones (1931–78), an Indiana-born minister, began in Indianapolis in the late 1950s. With a predominately black congregation, Jones preached equality of social and racial status, favored apocalyptic predictions and made himself absolutely central to his flock's well-being. He and his growing band of followers moved to California in 1965, settling in San Francisco. As membership grew to the thousands, Jones expanded his activities to include social programs for the city's poor. In 1976 the popular preacher was named chairman of the San Francisco Housing Authority. However, word of his bizarre practices, including rigid and violent discipline, extortion of money and property, death threats and sexual misconduct, soon surfaced.

In 1977 Jones, together with several hundred cult members, fled to Guyana and settled on land Jones had acquired earlier. Some Temple members wrote relatives detailing the conditions of physical and psychological abuse under which they were forced to live abroad. On the basis of these complaints, Rep. Leo Ryan of California and an entourage of aides and press visited Jonestown in November 1978. After spending a night there, Ryan and his party, together with some residents who had decided to leave the commune, proceeded to the local airstrip, where they were set upon by an armed group of Jones' followers. In the ensuing gunfire, Ryan and four others were killed and a number wounded. After the ambush was revealed to Jones, he ordered his band to commit suicide by drinking a fruit punch laced with cyanide. Most followed the order without question; some resisted but were forced to consume the poison or

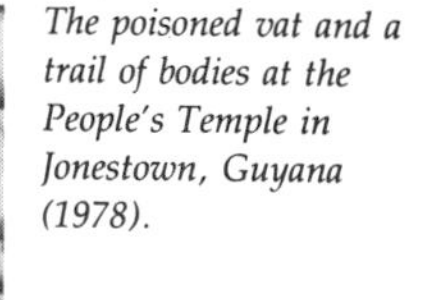

The poisoned vat and a trail of bodies at the People's Temple in Jonestown, Guyana (1978).

were shot; some escaped. Jones and several top aides shot themselves to death. Altogether, 911 died in the massacre.

Jong, Erica (Mann) (1942–). American novelist and poet. A native New Yorker educated at Barnard College, Jong published a well-received book of poems in 1971 before she burst on the scene with *Fear of Flying* (1973). This erotic feminist best-seller introduced her fictional alter ego, Isadora Wing, whose sexual exploits, marriages and divorces were later chronicled in *How to Save Your Own Life* (1977) and *Parachutes and Kisses* (1984). *Fanny, Being the True History of Fanny Hackabout-Jones* (1980) is a picaresque novel in the style of Fielding, Defoe and Cleland. *Serenissima: A Novel of Venice* (1987) follows its 20th-century heroine through a time warp similar to that of Virginia WOOLF's *Orlando*. Jong has also continued to produce poetry of indifferent quality. She has been much praised for her lusty humor and liberated fantasies and much derided for her tawdriness. It is safe to say, however, that she occupies a unique place in American literature.

Jooss, Kurt (1901–1979). German choreographer. Jooss was the first choreographer to successfully combine elements of modern dance with classical ballet. He introduced his new concepts with his ballet company in Essen, Germany, in the late 1920s and early 1930s. He fled to Britain after Adolf HITLER's rise to power, and did not return to his homeland until 1951. His ballets were noted for their compassion and social consciousness. His most famous ballet, *The Green Table* (1932), was perhaps the most acclaimed antiwar ballet ever choreographed.

Joplin, Janis (1945–1970). American rock-and-roll vocalist. Joplin was perhaps the greatest vocalist to emerge from the psychedelic era of the 1960s. Born and raised in Texas, she moved to San Francisco in 1966 and became the lead singer for a band, Big Brother and the Holding Company, which soon won international acclaim due to the sheer power and emotion of Joplin's bluesy, throaty vocals. *Cheap Thrills* (1968) remains a classic album of the era and features the hit single "Piece of My Heart."In 1969, Joplin pursued a solo career and released two noteworthy albums, *I Got Dem Ol' Cosmic Blues Again* (1969) and *Pearl* (1971), the latter including the hit single "Me And Bobby McGee." She died in 1970 from a heroin overdose. Posthumously released albums include *In Concert* (1972), *Janis* (1974), *Farewell Song* (1982) and *Janis Joplin in Concert* (1987).

Joplin, Scott (1868–1917). American pianist-composer; the preeminent exponent and popularizer of RAGTIME, a corruption of "ragged time," the popular pianistic form of the late-19th century that originated in the South and Midwest of the U.S. As developed by Joplin, the style typically set a highly syncopated, or "ragged," right-hand melody against a comparatively straightforward rhythmic pattern in the left-hand or bass. After initial successes playing "sporting houses" (brothels) in his native Texarkana, Texas, Joplin traveled throughout the Midwest scoring impressive triumphs, including the 1893 Chicago World's Fair. Joplin was the undisputed king of ragtime musicians. In addition to his spirited yet precise playing, Joplin became a prominent composer whose through-composed works included "Maple Leaf Rag," "The Entertainer" and "Gladiolus Rag." Royalties from his published rags enabled him to settle comfortably in St. Louis. However, a disastrous attempt to produce his ambitious opera *Treemonisha* (1911) broke Joplin's spirit, health and finances. In the 1970s, Joplin's rags enjoyed a huge revival by virtue of their use in the soundtrack of the hit motion picture, *The Sting* (1973), and due to the immensely popular recordings of pianist-musicologist Joshua Rifkin, who took to heart Joplin's admonition—"It is never right to play 'Ragtime' fast"—in performances clearly revealing the pristine, pre-jazz elegance of Joplin's original conception.

For further reading:

Blesh, Rudi, and Harriet Janis, *They All Played Ragtime*. New York: Alfred A. Knopf, 1958.

Jordan [Hashemite Kingdom of Jordan]. Jordan is located in the region of southwest Asia known as the Middle East and covers an area of 37,129 square miles, of which 2,565 square miles (known as the WEST BANK) are currently occupied by ISRAEL. For centuries a part of the OTTOMAN EMPIRE, modern Jordan took form in 1920 as **Transjordan,** a British sphere of influence. Autonomy was granted under Emir Abdullah in 1923, and full independence achieved in 1946. Now a constitutional monarchy, Jordan has been led by King HUSSEIN Ibn Talal since 1952. As a result of the 1967 SIX-DAY WAR, Israel occupied the West Bank of the Jordan River and East Jerusalem, both formerly held by Jordan. Tensions between the Jordanian government and the PALESTINE LIBERATION ORGANIZATION (PLO) led to the expulsion of the PLO in 1970–71. Hussein reconciled with PLO leader Yassir ARAFAT in 1983, while Jordan and Egypt formed a moderate Arab bloc to work for a solution to the issue of a Palestinian homeland. During the PERSIAN GULF WAR (1990–91) King Hussein supported the initial UNITED NATIONS resolutions condemning IRAQ for its invasion of KUWAIT. However, the majority of Jordanians (including its sizeable Palestinian refugee population) opposed military action by the allied coalition against Iraq, and Jordan lent its vocal support to Iraq's president, Saddam HUSSEIN. As a result, Jordan's ties with the U.S. and with other Arab nations who opposed Iraq were strained.

Jordan, Michael Jeffrey "Air" (1963–). American basketball player. Jordan has dominated every court he has played on since his high school days in North Carolina. Playing both guard and forward, the 6-foot 6-inch Jordan was a unanimous College All-American and Player of the Year in 1983 and 1984. Nicknamed "Air" for the improbable amount of time he seems to spend in mid-air, in his first year with the professional Chicago Bulls he averaged over 28 points per game, and was named the National Basketball Association's rookie of the year. He consistently ranks at the top of the league in steals and blocked shots and, in 1988, became the first player to be voted both the most valuable player and the defensive player of the year awards. His play has brought him numerous commercial endorsements, making him one of the country's most recognizable athletes.

Jordanian Civil War of 1970–71. After the SIX-DAY WAR 400,000 Palestinian refugees joined 700,000 others already in JORDAN. From Jordan some Palestinians conducted terrorist attacks against Israel. Adherents of Yasir ARAFAT'S PALESTINE LIBERATION ORGANIZATION (PLO) claimed Jordanian law did not apply to them; Israel staged retaliatory raids. King HUSSEIN, his regime threatened, resolved to destroy PLO power in Jordan, and after Palestinian hijackers flew airliners to Amman, Jordan's capital ("Black September," September 6–9, 1970), he declared martial law September 16. His troops surrounded refugee camps, disarming guerrillas and deporting militant leaders. By September 25 a cease-fire had been ar-

JORDAN

1918	Region of present-day Jordan gains independence from Ottoman empire.
1920	Jordan east of the Jordan River administered by Britain as Transjordan, a part of Britain's League of Nations mandate for Palestine.
1946	Jordan gains full independence.
1949	Transjordan renamed Jordan; annexes West Bank and East Jerusalem.
1952	Mentally ill King Tallal is deposed; his son Hussein declared king.
1967	Jordan loses West Bank to Israel in Six-Day War; 200,000 Palestinians seek refuge in Jordan.
1970	Jordanian army routs Palestinian guerrillas in a civil war; Hussein and Arafat truce.
1991	King Hussein supports Iraq in Persian Gulf War; aid from U.S. placed under review.

JORDAN

ranged by Arab heads of state, but battles against guerrilla bands continued until July 1971, when Palestinian bases were destroyed. Palestinian organizations subsequently moved to LEBANON.

Jorgensen, Christine [born George Jorgensen] (1926–1989). The first American transsexual to announce that she had undergone a sex-change operation. In Jorgensen's 1967 biography, the former army private said she had had a normal, happy childhood but, as an adult, had come to feel that she was a woman trapped in a man's body. Following the operation, which took place in Denmark in 1952, she became the focus of intense tabloid newspaper interest. She later starred in a nightclub act that featured her theme song, "I Enjoy Being a Girl."

Josephson, Brian David (1940–). British physicist. Josephson was educated at Cambridge University, where he obtained his Ph.D. in 1964. He remained at Cambridge and in 1974 was appointed to a professorship of physics.

His name is associated with the **Josephson effects** described in 1962 while still a graduate student. The work came out of theoretical speculations on electrons in SEMICONDUCTORS involving the exchange of electrons between two superconducting regions separated by a thin insulating layer **(Josephson junction)**. He showed theoretically that a current can flow across the junction in the absence of an applied voltage. Furthermore, a small direct voltage across the junction produces an alternating current with a frequency that is inversely proportional to the voltage. The effects have been verified experimentally, thus supporting the BCS theory of superconductivity of John BARDEEN and his colleagues. They have been used in making accurate physical measurements and in measuring weak magnetic fields. Josephson junctions can also be used as very fast switching devices in computers. For this work Josephson shared the 1973 NOBEL PRIZE for physics with Leo ESAKI and Ivar GAIEVER. More recently, Josephson has turned his attention to the study of the mind.

Jourdain, Francois (1876–1958). French architect and interior designer whose career extended from the ART NOUVEAU era through the MODERNISM of the 1930s. Jourdain was trained as a painter but after 1909 worked only as an interior and furniture designer. He was interested in low cost, prefabricated furniture of simple design. His work and publications of the 1920s were well known and influential since he was a strong champion of the austere, undecorated design vocabulary of the time. After 1945 he focused on historical writings about art and design.

Jouvet, Louis (1887–1951). French theatrical actor, director and producer. Jouvet was a major force in the French theater in the years between the two world wars. He served as director of several theaters, including a stint at the *Comedie des Champs-Elysee* from 1924 to 1934. Jouvet was noted for his popular touch in direction and production and was instrumental in first bringing the works of French playwrights Jean GIRAUDOUX and Jules ROMAINS to the attention of the French public. Jouvet also appeared as an actor in many of his own productions.

Joyce, James (Augustine Aloysius) (1882–1941). Irish novelist, short story writer and poet. Best known for his novel ULYSSES (1922), he is one of the towering figures of 20th-century literature and of MODERNISM. Born in DUBLIN, he was educated in Catholic schools and graduated from University College, Dublin (1902). After briefly studying medicine in Paris, he returned to Dublin, where, on June 16, 1904—the date on which he later set the events of ULYSSES—he met his future wife, Nora Barnacle. From 1905 on, he lived successively in Italy, Switzerland and France—in self-imposed exile from Ireland, a country he felt had rejected him. Moreover, he believed exile to be

Irish author James Joyce.

necessary for his art, which he felt should transcend the ties of family, country and religion. His first book of poems, *Chamber Music* (1907), was followed by a volume of stories, *Dubliners* (1914), the autobiographical novel *A Portrait of the Artist as a Young Man* (1916), and a play, *Exiles* (1918). After *Ulysses*, Joyce devoted nearly two decades to *Finnegans Wake*, a STREAM-OF-CONSCIOUSNESS dream book in which he transformed the English language by way of elaborate puns, soundplay and immense erudition.

For further reading:

Ellmann, Richard, *James Joyce*. New York: Oxford University Press, 1959.

Kenner, Hugh, *Dublin's Joyce*. Gloucester, Mass.: P.S. Smith, 1987.

Litz, A. Walton, *James Joyce*. New York: Twayne Publishers, 1966.

Joyner, Florence Griffith (1959–). American athlete. Joyner broke the world record for 100 meters (10.49 sec.) on July 16, 1988. At the OLYMPIC GAMES she won three gold medals: 100 meters, 200 meters (21.34 sec., another world record) and 4x100 relay. Her sister-in-law **Jackie Joyner-Kersee** (b. 1962) is also a world record-holder. She won the seven-event heptathlon in the 1988 Seoul Olympics with a record 7,291 points. Griffith-Joyner won a second Olympic medal in the long jump and holds the U.S. records for heptathlon, long jump and 100-meter high jump.

Jozsef, Attila (1905–1937). Hungarian poet. Born in Budapest, Jozsef spent his entire life in extreme poverty and used his poetry to protest the misery of the poor and express his own suffering. The influence of both Marx and Sigmund FREUD is evident in his work. At the age of three, he was abandoned by his father; at nine he attempted suicide; at 14 his mother died. His first volume, *Szepseg Koldusa*, appeared in 1922. In 1925 he was expelled from the University of Szeged for a revolutionary poem and left to study in Vienna and Paris. He joined the illegal Hungarian Communist Party in 1930 but was expelled in 1933 by Stalinists who attacked him as a fascist. Though he entered psychoanalysis in 1931 he was later hospitalized for severe depression. He committed suicide by throwing himself under a freight train. His poems began to be translated in the 1960s.

Juan Carlos I (1938–). King of Spain (1975–). The grandson of King ALFONSO XIII, Juan Carlos was named by dictator Francisco FRANCO as future king in 1969. Crowned in 1975, shortly before Franco's death, he encouraged the restoration of democracy in Spain and established himself as a constitutional monarch, with effective power in the hands of a prime minister.

Juba. Port city and capital of southern SUDAN's Equatoria province; on the White Nile River. Juba was the scene of a meeting in 1947 at which delegates from north and south agreed to unify Sudan (Africa's largest country) and prevent Great Britain from joining the south to its colony of UGANDA. Conflict between northern and southern elements led to a mutiny of southern forces here in 1955 and a civil war that lasted until 1969.

Jubaland [Transjuba]. Region of southwestern SOMALIA between the KENYA border and the Juba River. Once a province of Kenya, it was transferred by Britain to ITALY in 1925 and administered as a separate territory until July 1, 1926, when it was absorbed into Italian Somaliland.

Judson, Arthur (1881–1975). American impressario and concert manager. Judson was a major figure in the formative years of commercial recording and broadcasting in the U.S. He was a co-founder of the COLUMBIA BROADCASTING SYSTEM (CBS) and at one time was the sole owner of Columbia Records. From 1930 to 1935 he simultaneously managed the New York Philharmonic, the Philadelphia Orchestra, several summer concert series, and was president of Columbia Concerts Corp., a major booking agency.

July Days. Period of July 16–18, 1917, after the FEBRUARY REVOLUTION when Russian soldiers and civilians, in sympathy with the BOLSHEVIKS, tried to seize power from KERENSKY's provisional government in Petrograd. LENIN considered their rising inopportune. They received no significant support and the attempt failed. Bolshevik involvement was ascribed to pro-German sympathies and Bolsheviks in general were accused of treason. Lenin fled to Finland.

Jung, C(arl) G(ustav) (1875–1961). Swiss psychologist. Jung was one of the most famous psychological theorists of the 20th century. His most famous concept, that of the **Collective Unconscious**—a reservoir of inherited mental imagery and structure from which all members of the human race draw myth and meaning—has exercised a pervasive influence not only in psychology but also in philosophy and the arts. Jung received his medical degree in 1900 and began his professional career as a psychiatrist at the University of Zurich. In 1907 he met Sigmund FREUD and became closely associated with Freud's emerging school of psychoanalysis. But within a few years Jung broke with Freud over the latter's insistent emphasis on sexuality alone as the dominant factor in unconscious motivation. Jung subsequently developed his theories of the animus and the anima—the male and female elements of the unconscious psyche that must be brought into harmony. *Two Essays on Analytical Psychology* (1956) provides a useful introduction to Jung's thought. His *Memories, Dreams, Reflections* (1965) is a revelatory autobiography.

Carl Gustav Jung (1955).

"just-in-time" system. See Shigeo SHINGO.

Jutland [Jylland]. A peninsula, about 250 miles long, projecting into the North Sea from Germany; comprised of continental Denmark and the German state of Schleswig-Holstein. The only major fleet action of WORLD WAR I was fought by British and German DREADNOUGHTS and supporting vessels on May 31 and June 1, 1916, approximately 60 miles off Jutland's northwest coast. Although the British suffered heavy casualties and the loss of many smaller vessels, their capital ships (and Germany's) were largely undamaged; the smaller German fleet was forced to retreat, and Britain retained control of the North Sea. Winston CHURCHILL said of the victorious Admiral JELLICOE that he was the only man who could have lost the Great War in a single day. In Germany the BATTLE OF JUTLAND is known as the battle of Skagerrak.

Jutland, Battle of (1916). Part of British strategy against Germany in WORLD WAR I was to maintain a naval blockade in the North Sea to keep all shipping from German ports. Germany tested Britain's navy when its High Seas Fleet under Admiral Reinhard Scheer (1863–1928) sailed into Skagerrak, the sea passage between Jutland (Denmark) and Norway, May 31, 1916. British scouting squadrons encountered it and sustained severe losses. The British Grand Fleet under Admiral John R. JELLICOE arrived by evening, nearly entrapping the High Seas Fleet, but the Germans managed to escape in darkness and fog, losing only nine warships (out of 103) to the British loss of 14. Despite the heavier losses, the battle maintained British supremacy of the seas.

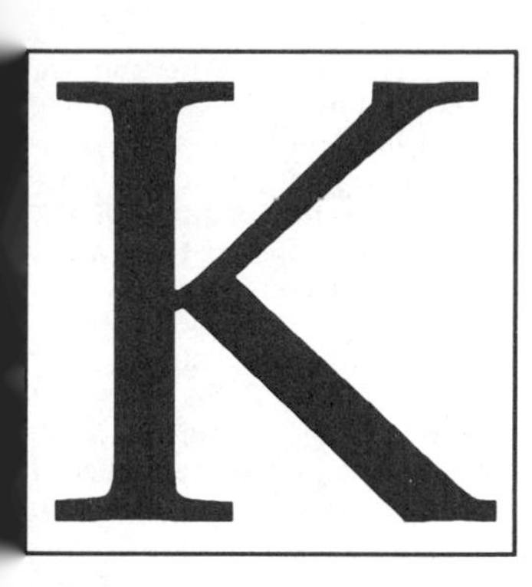

Kabalevsky, Dimitri Borisovich (1904–1987). Soviet composer, conductor and musicologist. He studied composition under Nicholas MYASKOVSKY and piano under SCRIABIN at the Moscow Conservatory. He taught at the conservatory from 1932, becoming a professor there in 1939. His works include the operas *Colas Breugnon* (1938), *Semya Tarasa* (1950) and *Nikita Vershinin* (1955). He has composed four symphonies, including his No. 1 in commemoration of the 15th anniversary of the Russian Revolution, three piano concertos, a violin concerto and a cello concerto, as well as many choral works, songs and piano works.

Kadar, Janos (1912–1989). Hungarian communist leader; he came to power in the wake of the 1956 HUNGARIAN UPRISING against Soviet domination and remained Hungarian Communist Party leader until 1988. During the uprising, he had initially sided with popular reformist Premier Imre NAGY but later negotiated in secret with Moscow and arranged to be installed as premier, supported by the Soviet invasion force. For years, Hungarians viewed him as a traitor to the uprising and to the reform movement. Nonetheless, in the early 1960s he initiated his own brand of economic and political liberalization, which made HUNGARY one of the most prosperous and tolerant members of the Eastern bloc and won Kadar a measure of grudging respect. His limited reforms eventually led to calls for more substantial changes, changes that Kadar was not prepared to make. As the Hungarian economy stagnated in the 1980s, he came to be viewed as an opponent of needed reform. He was replaced as party leader in May 1988 by Karoly Grosz and was given the figurehead position of party president; in early 1989 he was removed from this position due to failing health.

Kadet Party. Russian political party. The name was formed by the initials of the Constitutional-Democratic Party, which represented members of the bourgeoisie and petty bourgeoisie civil servants, army officers, shopkeepers and the like. It was founded in October 1905 and was headed by Pavel Miliukov, who advocated government on a constitutional basis to be attained by legal methods. He looked to Great Britain for a model of his ideas. Nearly all the ministers in the provisional government were Kadets. The party was suppressed in 1917.

Kaduna. Capital city of NIGERIA's Kaduna state, 140 miles southwest of Kano. Site of the January 1966 assassination of Sir Ahmadu Bello, northern premier and sultan of Sokoto, in an Ibo military coup that led to the secession of BIAFRA and subsequent civil war (1966–70).

Kaesong. North Korean city and district, 36 miles northwest of the South Korean capital of SEOUL. Intersected by the 38th parallel, it was the primary border crossing between NORTH KOREA and SOUTH KOREA from 1945 to 1951 and changed hands several times between UN and North Korean forces during the KOREAN WAR. Peace talks began here in 1951.

Kafka, Franz (1883–1924). Austrian novelist and short story writer. Born in Prague (then a part of the Austro-Hungarian empire) of a Jewish family, he studied law at the University of Prague and thereafter worked for most of his life in a government insurance office while writing in his off hours. Although his life was outwardly uneventful, he was tormented by phobias and dark obsessions. His novel *Amerika* (1927) was a fantasy of a country he never visited, and the novella *Metamorphosis* (1915) has its protagonist, Gregor Samsa, transformed into a giant cockroach. *The Trial* (1925) is a dreamlike novel of bureaucratic justice forever postponed, while *The Castle* (1926) concerns a royal summons that can never be fulfilled. Kafka also produced numerous other novellas, stories, parables and aphorisms. Most of his work was published only after his death, in spite of his request that his manuscripts be destroyed. His work prefigured that of such later writers as Albert CAMUS and Samuel BECKETT (see EXISTENTIALISM). The word "Kafkaesque" has become part of the vocabulary of the 20th century; it refers to the helplessness of the individual in the face of an absurd situation.

For further reading:

Citati, Pietro, *Kafka*. New York: Alfred A. Knopf, 1990.

Hayman, Ronald, *Kafka: A Biography*. New York: Oxford University Press, 1982.

Kafka, Franz, *The Diaries of Franz Kafka*. New York: Schocken, 1988.

———, *Letters to Felice*. New York: Schocken, 1984.

Kaganovich, Lazar Moyseyevich (1893–). Communist and disciple of LENIN. In 1911 Kaganovich joined the Bolshevik Party and played a prominent role in the leather workers' union. He assisted in organizing party affairs and rapidly advanced from post to post, including membership in the central committee from

Franz Kafka.

1924, head of party organization in the Ukraine (1925–28) and, from 1930, membership in the Politburo. He was in charge of the collectivization of agriculture from 1929 to 1934 and the party purge in 1933–34. He became one of STALIN's chief lieutenants, but in 1957, as a member of the "anti-party group," Kaganovich was expelled from the central committee and the Presidium. (See also ANTI-PARTY GROUP CRISIS.)

Kahn, Albert (1869–1942). American architect best known for his work on industrial buildings, often of outstanding modernist design. Kahn was born in Germany but came to the U.S. as a child. He worked for a Detroit architectural firm for some years before establishing his own office in 1902. Much of his work was for automobile manufacturers in the Detroit area. While the work tended to be conservative in ornamental detail, it excelled in the functional parts of factories where large glass areas and roof skylights generated forms related to those of more doctrinaire European modernists. The firm of Albert Kahn, Inc., was at its best with such works as the Chrysler Motor Company truck assembly plant building of 1936 near Detroit, with its dramatic structural trusses, or the Kellogg grain elevators in Battle Creek, Michigan. Kahn built projects around the world; there are many in the U.S.S.R. and even a few in China and Japan.

Kahn, Herman (1922–1983). American nuclear strategist, economic theorist and futurist. Kahn established a reputation as a strategist while working at the Rand Corporation in California from 1948 until 1961. He later founded and directed the **Hudson Institute,** a "think tank" at Croton-on-Hudson, New York, where a range of political, foreign policy and economic topics was explored. He believed that nuclear war was likely but survivable. He argued that nuclear deterrence was unworkable, and that policy planners must develop survival techniques. In economics he predicted that poverty and unemployment in the U.S. would disappear as a result of zero-inflation growth. He was consulted by every U.S. president from Harry S TRUMAN to Ronald REAGAN.

For further reading:

Kahn, Herman, *On Thermonuclear War.* Princeton: Princeton U. Press, 1961.

———, *Thinking the Unthinkable.* 1962.

Kahn, Louis I. (1901–1974). American architect and architectural educator whose influence far outstrips the extent of his executed work. Kahn was born in Estonia and studied art and architecture, the latter at the University of Pennsylvania in Philadelphia from 1920 to 1924, when the program there was oriented toward classical Beaux-Arts design. He worked for several Philadelphia firms and turned toward MODERNISM while working with George HOWE and Oscar Stonorov. Kahn was asked to teach at Yale by Howe in 1947. He stayed until 1957 and became known for his Yale University Art Gallery addition (1953) with its triangular, trussed structure visible as gallery ceilings. His Richards Medical Research Laboratories at the University of Pennsylvania, with all the service elements grouped in external towers, followed in 1957–61. Although a controversial work disliked by many of its users, it established his international reputation. From 1957 until his death he taught at the University of Pennsylvania in Philadelphia, where he is credited with becoming a major influence in developing the "Philadelphia school" of modernism. Kahn came to have an almost mystical power as an educator and architectural theorist in a way that went far beyond the seeming modesty of such works as his Unitarian Church (1963) in Rochester, New York, and his Salk Institute Laboratories (1965) in La Jolla, California. His last works included government buildings in Dacca, Pakistan (under construction at the time of his death) and the Kimbell Art Museum (1972) in Fort Worth, Texas. Kahn's design was generally simple in detail but powerful in form and full of complexities and subtleties that have made him one of the most admired and studied of all modern architects.

Kahn, Lord Richard Ferdinand (1905–1989). British economist. Kahn introduced the concept of the "multiplier" in an article in the *Economic Journal* in 1931. An associate of John Maynard KEYNES, he contributed to the discussions that formed the basis of Keynes' general theory of employment, interest, and money. He was also the author of *Selected Essays on Economic Growth* (1973) and *The Making of Keynes' General Theory* (1984).

Kahnweiler, Daniel-Henry (1884–1979). German-born art dealer and art historian. Kahnweiler was an early champion of the Cubist painters in his Paris gallery (see CUBISM). He met Pablo PICASSO in 1907 and was closely associated with him until Picasso's death in 1973.

Kaiser, Georg (1875–1945). German playwright. Kaiser was one of the leading figures in the rise of EXPRESSIONISM as a dominant force in German theater between the two world wars. His plays relied upon dramatic incident, sharp and rapid dialogue, and frequently dealt with the clash between individual freedom and the economic and social demands of the machine age. A highly popular voice in the theater, Kaiser was no longer allowed, after the rise of the Nazis in 1933, to have his works publicly performed. Kaiser's major work is his dramatic trilogy *The Coral* (1917), *Gas I* (1918) and *Gas II* (1920).

Kaiser, Henry John (1882–1967). American industrialist. Born in Sprout Brook, New York, Kaiser began in the construction business in 1913, becoming a leader in the road-paving industry. He became known as a builder of dams and bridges, participating in the construction of the Boulder (HOOVER) DAM (1936), Bonneville and Grand Coulee dams and the San Francisco-Oakland Bay Bridge. An important contributor to the war effort in WORLD WAR II, he and his companies produced enormous numbers of ships, planes and other military vehicles. After the war he headed Kaiser Industries (1945–67), presiding over the company as it prospered and grew to include steel, aluminum, cement and home-building. One of his few failures was the postwar automobile called the Kaiser-Frazer.

KAL 007. Early in the morning of September 1, 1983, a Korean Airlines Boeing 747 strayed from its normal flight path and was shot down by Soviet fighters. All 240 passengers and 29 crew members aboard the airliner, Flight 007 from New York to Seoul, Korea, were killed. The world was horrified; U.S. President Ronald REAGAN condemned the downing of the airliner and demanded an apology. The Soviets insisted that they had believed the plane was a military aircraft, and that the pilot had ignored their signals to identify himself. Some Americans speculated that flight KAL 007 had deliberately "strayed" into Soviet airspace to carry out a spying mission. The incident seemed to confirm President Reagan's assertion that the U.S.S.R. was an "evil empire."

Kaledin, Alexei Maksimovich (1861–1918). Russian Cossack leader and soldier. Kaledin served from 1914 in command of a cavalry division but opposed the military reforms of the provisional government and in 1917 was forced to resign. Returning to the Don region, he was elected hetman of the Cossacks and organized an anti-Bolshevik campaign, but he suffered many defeats and shot himself in February 1918.

Kalgoorlie. Australian goldmining town, providing about 75% of Australia's gold. Kalgoorlie is more than 300 miles northeast of Perth. The area has been mined since the 1800s. Production declined until 1929, when new mining techniques were introduced.

Kaline, Al (1934–). American baseball player. A 16-time All-Star, Kaline was known as Mr. Tiger, spending all of his 20-year career with Detroit. In 1955, he became the youngest player in American League history to capture the batting title. His average that year was .340, with 27 home runs and 102 runs batted in. Formidable on both offense and defense, his steady play in right field netted him 10 Gold Gloves. Kaline retired in 1974 and was named to the Hall of Fame in 1980.

Kalinin, Mikhail Ivanovich (1875–1946). Communist statesman, born at Tver (now Kalinin). An active revolutionary arrested many times after 1898, he became one of the first supporters of LENIN. He supported STALIN in the party struggle following Lenin's death. In 1919 he became chairman of the all-Russian executive committee of the Soviets and a member of the central committee. He was a member of the Politburo from 1926 and chairman of the Supreme Soviet of the U.S.S.R. from 1938 to 1946.

Kaliningrad [Konigsberg]. Soviet Baltic seaport on the Pregolya River, 80 miles east-northeast of Gdansk. Before WORLD WAR II Konigsberg was a part of German East Prussia and a major German naval base. Soviet troops captured it as they advanced toward Berlin at the end of the war. Under the POTSDAM agreement it was transferred to the U.S.S.R. and renamed in honor of communist statesman Mikhail Ivanovich KALININ.

Kalmyks [Kalmucks]. Mongol people of the Tibetan Buddhist faith living in the Kalmyk Autonomous Soviet Socialist Republic. They migrated from western China to Russia (Nogay Steppe) in the early 17th century. In 1920 a Kalmyk autonomous oblast was established and in 1933 it became an autonomous republic. Occupied in part by the Germans in 1942, it was thought that the Kalmyks had collaborated with the enemy; as a result they were exiled to Soviet Central Asia. Rehabilitation of the Kalmyks was announced in 1957 and they returned to their homes. In 1979 Kalmyks numbered about 150,000.

Kaltenborn, H(ans) V(on) (1878–1965). Pioneering radio news reporter. Born in Milwaukee, Kaltenborn attended Harvard University, then became a newspaperman, working on the *Brooklyn Eagle* from 1910 to 1930. While on the *Eagle* (1922), he began delivering current events talks on a New York City radio station (a "local" station, as were all the primitively powered stations of the time). Eight years later he began work at CBS as a news commentator, and in 1936 he traveled to Spain to report the SPANISH CIVIL WAR. Returning to New York, he continued to broadcast news bulletins along with running commentary, and was particularly noted for his broadcasts on the 1938 Munich crisis. Kaltenborn became famous for his quick, clipped delivery in a somewhat nasal voice and for an encyclopedic knowledge that allowed him to discourse on nearly any subject without preparation. His autobiography, *Fifty Fabulous Years,* was published in 1950.

Kamenev, Lev Borisovich (1883–1936). Soviet political figure; a prominent leader of the Bolshevik movement before the revolution. Although he opposed LENIN's seizure of power in 1917 he remained prominent in the party. Initially he supported STALIN against TROTSKY and later he supported Trotsky and ZINOVIEV. He was expelled from the party several times. Finally, in 1935, he was sentenced to five years' imprisonment; at a retrial in 1936 he was again sentenced and was executed.

kamikaze. Japanese for "divine wind," this term was used by the Japanese to describe the suicide air squadron that was formed toward the end of WORLD WAR II. It was an allusion to the typhoon that destroyed Kublai Khan's fleet before it could invade Japan in 1281. Kamikaze pilots attempted to crash their explosives-laden planes directly into Allied targets, mainly ships; a successful strike ensured their own deaths. The first attacks occurred at LEYTE GULF in November 1944, and they became a severe threat early in 1945. They were particularly devastating to Allied ships at OKINAWA. Largely because they came into use so late in the war, when Japanese defeat was all but assured, the kamikaze was of little importance in the outcome of the war.

Kamina. City in the southern Zaire province of SHABA (formerly KATANGA). After the Democratic Republic of the Congo became independent ZAIRE in July 1960, Katanga seceded, civil war began and Kamina was used by Belgian forces as a center of support for the secessionists. From 1960 to 1963 it was headquarters of the UNITED NATIONS force overseeing the withdrawal of foreign troops.

Kamranh Bay. See CAMRANH BAY.

Kandinsky, Wassily (1866–1944). Russian painter and art theorist. Widely considered the originator of purely ABSTRACT ART, he and his works have had enormous importance in the development of 20th-century painting. Born in Moscow, he was trained there as a lawyer, but abandoned the law to study painting in Munich in 1896. Traveling to Paris, he studied the work of the neoimpressionists, Gauguin and the Fauves. He exhibited at the Salon d'Automne (1904), at the Salon des Independants and with the German Expressionists of DIE BRUCKE (1907); in 1910 he founded the New Association of Munich Artists. The following year he painted his first nonrepresentational painting and articulated his ideas about the power of pure color and the relationship between art and music in his theoretical book *Concerning the Spiritual in Art* (1912). In 1911, along with Franz MARC and other artists, he founded the BLAUE REITER group. Kandinsky returned to Moscow in 1914, teaching and organizing museums and other artistic enterprises.

He settled in Germany again in 1921, taught at the BAUHAUS (1925–33) and wrote *Point and Line* (1926), a study that concentrated on the geometric in art. His paintings of the period tend to change from the brilliantly colored improvisations of his earlier work to more linear and geometrical compositions. In 1933, the Nazis closed the Bauhaus and denounced Kandinsky's art as degenerate. He moved to Paris, where he remained until his death. Kandinsky's paintings and drawings are represented in important museums

Two kamikazes hit the USS Bunker Hill *on May 11, 1945, leaving 372 dead.*

throughout the world. The Solomon R. Guggenheim Museum, N.Y.C., has an especially outstanding collection of his work.

Kanellopoulos, Panayotis (1902–1986). Greek politician. Kanellopoulos was briefly prime minister of GREECE in 1945 and again in 1967, when his caretaker government was overthrown after 18 days by the military coup that ushered in a period of rule by the GREEK COLONELS.

Kanin, Garson (1912–). American film and stage director, actor, playwright, screenwriter and novelist. Kanin enjoyed an unusually succesful and eclectic career in show business. But he is best remembered for his directorial and screenplay work in HOLLYWOOD. After working as both an actor and director on Broadway, Kanin came to Hollywood in 1938 and directed comedies including *The Great Man Votes* (1939), *Bachelor Mother* (1939), *My Favorite Wife* (1940) and *Tom, Dick and Harry* (1941). During WORLD WAR II, Kanin directed military documentaries, including collaborations with Sir Carol REED and Jean RENOIR. His play *Born Yesterday* (1946) was adapted into a successful film (1951). With wife Ruth Gordon, Kanin wrote the ACADEMY AWARD-nominated screenplay for *A Double Life* (1948). Kanin, again with Gordon, coscripted films for Katharine HEPBURN and Spencer TRACY including *Adam's Rib* (1949) and *Pat and Mike* (1952).

Kansas City Jazz. An influential style of American "Swing" jazz in the 1930s. Its major performers included Count BASIE, Pete Johnson, Mary Lou WILLIAMS, "Big Joe" TURNER and Jay MCSHANN. Many factors made Kansas City, Missouri, an active jazz center in the late 1920s and 1930s. It was a key intersection of the routes of many of the traveling bands of the time. New Orleans jazz was spreading north from the Crescent City. Locally, the notorious Pendergast political machine had created a wide-open town with many clubs and ballrooms and a large black population. "The jam session tradition really started in Kansas City," recalled Jay McShann. "You got cats from the north, south, east, and west; and everytime a new cat came to town, everybody would bring him down to the session and let him blow. It made for good times. . . ." Things really began to jump when Kansas City's leading jazz figure, Bennie Moten, absorbed the nucleus of the Blue Devils, an Oklahoma City jazz band that included bassist Walter Page, vocalist Jimmy Rushing, and pianist Count Basie. After Moten's death in 1935, the band became the Basie Band. Other groups that flourished at the time included the Andy Kirk band, Twelve Clouds of Joy. Young musicians were everywhere, at the Subway, the Reno Club, the Lone Star, the Sunset, mostly in areas around 18th and Vine. "Basie, Johnson, Williams, McShann, Turner—even the young Charlie 'Yardbird' Parker—all forged a distinctive, upbeat blues," says McShann "and we'd play all night until about six o'clock in the morning when the porter would come in to clean up. We'd just move over, do a little tastin', and then we'd start playin' again. Fellows headin' for work at that hour would come in with their lunch buckets and stay awhile. . . ." With the end of the decade, the departure for New York City of Basie and McShann, and the approaching war, the music scene declined in Kansas City, although that famous sound was now being heard worldwide.

Playwright Garson Kanin.

Kapek, Antonin (1922–1990). Czechoslovakian political leader. Kapek was the chief of CZECHOSLOVAKIA's Communist Party (1969–88) for the two decades following the Soviet invasion that crushed the PRAGUE SPRING reform movement. He rose to this post through the party ranks, at one point serving as a party boss in a machine factory. Kapek welcomed the Soviet invasion in 1968 and helped carry out the purges of reformers who had taken part in the Prague Spring movement under Alexander DUBCEK. In February 1990, following the "velvet revolution" that returned Czechoslovakia to democracy, Kapek was expelled from the Czechoslovak Communist Party. He apparently committed suicide.

Kapitsa, Pyotr Leonidovich (1894–1984). Soviet physicist. Educated at Leningrad and at Cambridge (under Lord RUTHERFORD), Kapitsa was assistant director of research in magnetism at the Cavendish Laboratory (1924–32) and Messel Research Professor at the Royal Society's Mond Laboratory (1932–35). He did important work on the magnetic and electrical properties of substances at low temperatures and also designed an improved plant for the liquefaction of hydrogen and helium. Kapitsa was detained in the U.S.S.R. in 1935, but later became director of the Institute for Physical Problems at the Academy of Sciences in Moscow. He was awarded the Stalin Prize for physics (1941 and 1943), and held the Order of Lenin. He was elected a Fellow of the Royal Society of Great Britain in 1929, the first foreigner in 200 years to gain membership. Kapitsa received the NOBEL PRIZE for physics (1978) in recognition of his lifetime scientific achievements. He was a strong advocate of the free exchange of scientific information.

Kaplan, Henry (1918–1984). American radiologist. Kaplan's pioneering work in research treatment was responsible for making Hodgkin's Disease one of the most curable forms of cancer. He was coinventor, with Edward Ginzton, of the **linear accelerator,** which enabled patients with cancer to receive high-dose radiation therapy. In 1969 he became the first physician to receive the Atoms for Peace prize, and in 1972 he was the first radiologist elected to the National Academy of Sciences.

Kapler, Aleksei Y. (1904–1979). Soviet screenwriter. Kapler was best known for his prewar films about LENIN, *Lenin in October* and *Lenin in 1918*. In 1943 he was sent into internal exile by Joseph STALIN, spending five of those years in Soviet prison camps (see GULAG).

Kapp Putsch. Nationalist conspiracy hatched by right-wing German politician and journalist Wolfgang Kapp (1868–1922), aimed at setting Kapp up as chancellor and restoring the monarchy. Supported by Erich LUDENDORFF and backed by General von Luttwitz (1859–1942) and his troops, the putsch occurred on May 13, 1920 when Luttwitz and his men took BERLIN and proclaimed a new government with Kapp at its head. The government of the WEIMAR REPUBLIC fled and quickly called a general strike, which, along with a lack of foreign support, soon destroyed Kapp's abortive regime. The putsch revealed the discontent and nationalism that seethed beneath the republican government's surface and was to find expression in the later triumph of Adolf HITLER.

Kaprow, Allan (1927–). American artist and art theorist. Born in Atlantic City, New Jersey, Kapro studied at Columbia with Meyer SCHAPIRO, Hans Hofmann (1947–48) and John CAGE (1956–58). Kaprow's early works were abstract expressionist paintings, and he had his first one-man show in New York City in 1953. In addition to painting he created experimental collages and assemblages, using a variety of nontraditional materials. Kaprow is best known as the creator of HAPPENINGS, works combining art and theater that he initiated in 1958 and that he and others continued to produce during the 1960s.

Karachi. Pakistani seaport. When the independent nation of PAKISTAN was created in 1947, Karachi was its first capital; in 1959, the capital was moved to Rawalpindi. The city was bombed and shelled during the INDO-PAKISTANI WAR OF 1971. Muhammad Ali JINNAH, the founder of Pakistan, is buried here.

Karajan, Herbert von (1908–1989). Austrian-born opera and symphonic conductor. Karajan's phenomenal musical gifts, flair for media exploitation, dramatic platform manner and controversial political

Conductor Herbert von Karajan.

associations made him into an international celebrity. Karajan was born in Salzburg and studied conducting under Bernhard Paumgartner. From 1928 to 1935 he conducted at Ulm, and from 1938 to 1944 he served as music director at Aachen, the youngest appointed conductor in Germany. A member of the Nazi Party, he remained in Germany during WORLD WAR II, and his career was championed by GOEBBELS. He was "denazified" in 1947 but political opprobrium, particularly in the U.S. and in Israel, dogged him the rest of his days. His peak creative period came with the Berlin Philharmonic Orchestra from 1955 to 1989 and with his many operatic performances in Milan and Vienna. Alternating a staggering series of recordings with a globe-trotting lifestyle, he was astute in exploiting the possibilities of every available medium: stereo LP record, film, television, video, and compact disc. He brought the famous juicy string sound and the burnished brass timbres of his orchestra to many recorded sets of Beethoven and Brahms symphonies, numerous Italian operas, and the lush sonorities of Richard STRAUSS and Peter Tchaikovsky. Despite a notorious ego and driving temperament, he was totally devoted to music, molding the BPO into the front rank of world ensembles.

For further reading:

Osborne, Richard, *Conversations with von Karajan*. New York: HarperCollins, 1990.

Karamanlis, Constantine. See Constantine CARAMANLIS.

Kardelj, Edvard (1910–1979). Yugoslav communist ideologist. Kardelj was an influential associate of President Josip TITO and served as a member of YUGOSLAVIA'S collective presidency. He favored socialist self-management and the nonaligned movement. He was viewed as Tito's probable successor, but died shortly before Tito.

Kardiner, Abram (1891–1981). Pychoanalyst. A student-patient of Sigmund FREUD for six months in 1921, Kardiner cofounded the first psychoanalytic training school in the U.S., the New York Psychiatric Institute (1930). He was a leading proponent of the so-called environmental school of psychiatry, which stressed the importance of social conditions to human behavior. In addition to several scholarly works, he wrote a popular account of psychoanalytical apprenticeship titled *My Analysis With Freud* (1977).

Karelia [Karelian Autonomous Soviet Socialist Republic]. An autonomous republic in the U.S.S.R.'s RSFSR, stretching from Finland to the White Sea and from the Kola Peninsula south to the Vologdia and Leningrad oblasts. As a result of the RUSSO-FINNISH WAR OF 1939–40 the western part, which had shared Finland's history, had nearly all of its territory absorbed by the Karelo-Finnish Soviet Socialist Republic (as it was known from 1940 to 1956). Finns and Germans occupied Karelia from 1941 to 1944 during WORLD WAR II, after which even more of the area passed to the Soviet Union.

Karjalainen, Ahti (1923–1990). Finnish politician. He was one of FINLAND'S most prominent politicians in the years after World War II. Although he served as prime minister from 1962 to 1964 and again in 1970–71, he was overshadowed by the 25-year presidency of Urho KEKKONEN, who served from 1956 to 1981. Karjalainen was a leading expert on trade with the U.S.S.R. Convicted of drunk driving in 1979, he was forced out of government.

Karlfeldt, Erik Axel (1864–1931). Swedish poet. Karlfeldt's work, little known outside of Sweden, celebrates nature and the lore of the Swedish peasantry. His collections include *Vildmarks—och käleksvisor* (*Songs of the Wilderness and of Love,* 1895), *Fridolins visor* (*Fridolin's Songs,* 1898) and *Fridolins lustgard* (Fridolin's Pleasure Garden, 1901). Beginning in 1907, Karlfeldt served on the Nobel Committee for literature and was subsequently offered the prize several times. He declined, becoming the first individual to do so. He was awarded the NOBEL PRIZE for literature posthumously in 1931.

Karloff, Boris [William Pratt] (1887–1969). British-born film and stage actor. One of the leading horror film actors of all time, Karloff has become indelibly identified with his role of the Monster in FRANKENSTEIN (1931), the film that made him a star. Karloff began his career on the Canadian stage and first came to HOLLYWOOD in 1921 where he worked as a bit actor in silent films throughout the decade. After his success in *Frankenstein,* Karloff became a ubiquitous figure in Hollywood horror films of the 1930s, including *The Mummy* (1932), *The Mask of Fu Manchu* (1932), the excellent *Bride of Frankenstein* (1935) and the disappointing *Son of Frankenstein* (1939). In the 1940s Karloff enjoyed a Broadway triumph as a killer on the run in the comedy *Arsenic and Old Lace.* His career declined in the 1950s, but Karloff enjoyed a comeback in the 1960s through his roles in the Roger CORMAN films *The Raven* (1963) and *A Comedy of Terrors* (1964). His last film was *Targets* (1967).

Karman, Theodore von (1881–1963). Hungarian-American aeronautical engineer and physicist. The son of an educator, von Karman was educated at the Royal Polytechnic University at Budapest, at Gottingen and at the University of Paris. After viewing an airplane flight in Paris in 1908, he developed an interest in aeronautical engineering. Von Karman moved to the United States, accepting a post at the Guggenheim Aeronautical Laboratory at the California Institute of Technology in Pasadena, (GALCIT). He became director the following year, and with Frank MALINA in the late 1930s, he developed the facility into the beginnings of what is now NASA'S JET PROPULSION LABORATORY. A pioneer in the theories of supersonic flight, von Karman later became chief consultant on the develpment of the Atlas, America's first operational intercontinental ballistic missile.

Karolyi, Count Mihaly (1875–1955). Hungarian statesman. Born in Budapest, Karolyi was a member of an ancient aristocratic family. A liberal with a taste foi reform, he entered parliament in 1905. During WORLD WAR I he was leader of the Independent Party, which supported the Allied cause. Appointed premier in 1918, he sought an armistice while attempting to mediate between political extremists of the left and right. When a republic was proclaimed in 1919, he was elected provisional president. Karolyi tried to initiate democratic reforms, but had little power. Finally, he was forced to cede the government to the communists and was supplanted by Bela KUN. He soon went into exile in England, returning to Hungary only after WORLD WAR II. He served as Hungarian ambassador to France from 1946 to 1949 but resigned in the face of disagreements with his increasingly totalitarian government. He spent his last six years as an exile in France.

Karpov, Anatoly (1951–). Soviet chess player. Karpov won the world individual championship for junior chess players in 1969, became an international grandmaster, and in 1975 became world champion. He held his title until 1985, when he was defeated by Gary KASPAROV. The two players resumed their rivalry in a championship match in 1990, and Karpov failed to regain his title.

Karsavin, Lev Platonovich (1882–1952). Russian historian and philosopher, brother of Tamara Platonovna KARSAVINA. In 1922 he was expelled from Russia and went to live in Germany. Later he was appointed professor of history at Kaunas University in Lithuania. He was arrested in 1948 and died in a Soviet CONCENTRATION CAMP. His works include *Philosophy of History* (1923).

Karsavina, Tamara Platonovna (1885–1978). Russian-born prima ballerina and star of Serge DIAGHILEV'S BALLETS RUSSES. The sister of Lev KARSAVIN, Karsavina made her debut in 1902 and became prima ballerina of the Maryinsky Theater in St. Petersburg. She joined the Ballets Russes at its inception in 1909 and remained closely associated with Diaghilev until his death in 1929. She had leading roles in the premieres of two of Igor STRAVINSKY'S works staged by Diaghilev in Paris. She was the first *Firebird* (1910) and the first ballerina-doll in *Petrouchka* (in which she danced with Vaslav NIJINSKY, 1911). She settled in London in 1918 and helped found the Royal Academy of Dance. After her retirement from the stage in 1933, she coached Margot FONTEYN and assisted the ROYAL BALLET.

Karsh, Yousuf (1908–). Armenian-born Canadian photographer. Karsh, who as a young boy survived the Turkish massacres of that country's Armenian population, emigrated to Canada in 1924 and established his first photographic studio in Ottawa in 1932. Karsh soon established himself as a leading portrait photographer of the great political, scientific and cultural figures of the age. In 1941, Karsh achieved popular fame for his striking portrait of a fierce-looking Winston S. CHURCHILL in *Life* magazine; Karsh elicited the expression from Churchill by snatching his cigar just before taking the picture. Karsh's photographs were collected in three volumes—*Faces of Destiny* (1946), *Portraits of Greatness* (1959), and *Karsh Portraits* (1976). *Search for Greatness* (1962) was his autobiography.

Kasavubu, Joseph (1910–1969). President of the Republic of the Congo (now ZAIRE, 1960–65). Mayor of Leopoldville (Kinshasha) in 1957, when the Belgian Congo became independent, Kasavubu became the first president, with LUMUMBA as prime minister. He remained in office during the civil war over the KATANGA secession until 1965, when he was replaced by MOBUTU following a military coup.

Kasdan, Lawrence (1948–). American film director, producer, and screenplay writer. Kasdan, who was educated at the University of Michigan, began his career as an advertising copywriter before selling his first screenplay in 1977. That same year, his screenplay for the film *Continental Divide* (1981) was purchased by Steven SPIELBERG, who recommended Kasdan to George LUCAS, who in turn hired Kasdan to write the screenplays for the blockbuster films *The Empire Strikes Back* (1980), *Raiders of the Lost Ark* (1981) and *The Return of the Jedi* (1983). Kasdan also emerged in the 1980s as a first-rate director with films including *Body Heat* (1981), *The Big Chill* (1983) and *The Accidental Tourist* (1988), all of which were written or cowritten by Kasdan as well.

Kashmir. After Britain granted independence to INDIA, this ancient princely state in the extreme north of India was claimed by both India and PAKISTAN. The conflicting claimed helped fuel the INDO-PAKISTANI WAR OF 1947–48. The region was formally partitioned in 1949; part of the region became the Indian state of Jammu and Kashmir, while part was given to Pakistan. The region has remained in dispute ever since. The INDO-PAKISTANI WAR OF 1965 was fought largely over the status of Kashmir; Pakistan also attacked Kashmir during the INDO-PAKISTANI WAR OF 1971.

Kasparov, Gary [born Garik Weinstein] (1963–). Russian chess master. Born in Baku, the capital of Soviet Azerbaijan, Kasparov took on a Russianized version of his maternal family's name after his father's death in 1970. A chess prodigy, he was solving complex chess problems at six and represented the U.S.S.R. at chess tournaments abroad by the age of 13. He became Soviet champion at 18 and world champion at 22, beating his arch-rival, the Russian grandmaster Anatoly KARPOV. A bold, passionate player, Kasparov also brought his passion to bear as a political dissident, actively opposing Soviet communism in the late 1980s. His many championship matches with Karpov have been seen as contests between the old-style Soviet regime as represented by Karpov and the radical change sweeping the U.S.S.R. as personified by Kasparov. In 1989 he and many of his family members were forced to flee the ethnic strife in Baku. Since then he has used Moscow as a home base. Traveling to various western cities, he promotes chess in an attempt to make the game a popular international sport and continues to criticize the communist system. He again defeated Karpov in an international match in 1990–91.

Kassem, Abdul Karim (1914–1963). Iraqi general and political leader. Born in Baghdad, he was trained in military institutions and became a career officer. He distinguished himself by his bravery in warfare against the KURDS and in the Palestine war (1948). Kassem was instrumental in the coup of July 1958 that overthrew King FEISAL II, and he became prime minister of the new republic that replaced the monarchy. He put down a communist uprising the following year, but his powers steadily waned, and he was overthrown in the BA'ATH Party coup of February 1963 and subsequently executed.

Kasserine Pass [Al-Kasrayn, Al-Qasrayn]. Mountain pass in Tunisia's Grand Dorsal chain, 130 miles southwest of Tunis, the scene of a decisive tank battle during the NORTH AFRICAN CAMPAIGN in WORLD WAR II. Driven westward into Tunisia after the German defeat by the British at EL ALAMEIN, German Field Marshal Erwin ROMMEL regrouped his forces and launched a daring counterattack. Tanks of his Afrika Korps captured the Kasserine Pass early on February 22, 1943. Four days later, however, U.S. forces under Gen. George S. PATTON dealt the Afrika Korps a mortal blow and recaptured the pass. This spelled the end of German domination of North Africa.

World champion chess player Gary Kasparov in a man-versus-machine match with the chess computer Deep Thought (1989).

Katanga Revolt (1960–63). On the granting of Congo independence by Belgium, the province of Katanga—encouraged by Union Miniere, a company with exclusive mining rights in the copper-and uranium-rich province—seceded from Congo on July 11, 1960, under Moise TSHOMBE. Using a white mercenary army to resist United Nations attempts to restore order, the Katanga rebellion lasted until January 14, 1963.

Kateyev, Valentin Petrovich (1897–1986). Soviet novelist and playwright. Among members of the older generation of Soviet writers, Kateyev was unusual in that he generally managed to avoid trouble with the Soviet authorities, while at the same time winning the respect of Western critics of Soviet literature. His reputation in the West rested largely on his lively satirical works dating from the 1920s, before SOCIALIST REALISM had become firmly entrenched as the dominant literary mode.

Katona, George (1901–1981). Hungarian-born economist and psychologist. Often called the dean of behavioral economists, Katona was the first to apply the study of consumer attitudes to economic forecasting. He taught at the University of Michigan (1946–72) and wrote more than a dozen books, including *The Mass Consumption Society*.

Katyn. Village in west-central Russia, approximately 12 miles west of Smolensk. Katyn was captured by the Germans in August 1941, during WORLD WAR II. On April 14, 1943, they announced the discovery of a mass grave of approximately 4,250 Polish officers in the woods near the village; the officers had all been tied and shot through the head. The Germans accused the Soviets of having murdered the soldiers in 1940, when the area had been under Soviet occupation. In 1944 a Soviet commission accused the Nazis of the crime. The International Red Cross tried to investigate the incident but was denied access to the site. In 1951–52, a U.S. congressional commission concluded that the Soviets were indeed responsible; in 1990, during the era of GLASNOST, the Soviets finally admitted culpability for the Katyn massacre. The Poles had apparently been among the cream of the Polish officer corps and, as such, had been marked for liquidation by STALIN.

Kauffer, Edward McKnight (1890–1954). American artist and graphic designer best known for his posters, especially those designed while he was living in England from 1914 until 1940. Kauffer studied painting in Paris, but came to notice in the 1930s for his poster designs beginning with an assignment by Frank Pick for the London Underground (subway). His book *The Art of the Poster* appeared in 1924 and his work in the field, using strong typography along with abstracted but recognizable illustrative imagery, was widely exhibited and received a variety of awards. He also designed books and book jackets. In 1940–41 he produced several graphic designs for the New York MUSEUM OF MODERN ART. He became inactive after the early 1940s, having designed over 250 posters and 150 book jackets.

Kaufman, George S. (1889–1961). American journalist, playwright and director. A towering influence on the American theater, Kaufman is also remembered for his caustic wit evident in his writing and his participation in the legendary Algonquin Round Table. Kaufman's plays include *Jacques Duval* (1920), *The Forty-niners* (1922) and *The Butter and Egg Man* (1925). He also collaborated on many successful plays with Edna FERBER and Moss HART, among others. His collaborations include *Dinner at Eight* (1932), *The Man Who Came to Dinner* (1939) and *Ninotchka* (1955). Kaufman was responsible for the production of 45 Broadway shows, many of which were adapted for film. He also directed classics such as *The Front Page* (1928), *Guys and Dolls* (1950), which he co-wrote and *Romanoff and Juliet* (1957).

Kaunda, Kenneth (1924–). President of ZAMBIA (1964–). Kaunda led the United Nationalist Independence Party in opposition to the Federation of Rhodesia and Nyasaland in 1960, which resulted in the end of the federation. Appointed Prime Minister of Northern Rhodesia in 1964 and having supervised the constitutional arrangements that won his country independence, he became president of Zambia 10 months later. Kaunda sought to hold in check militants opposed to the Ian SMITH regime in Rhodesia, but his strong hostility to racism led to periods of tension with Britain over this and other issues. He assumed autocratic powers in 1972 to prevent total breakup but, after a new constitution in 1973, his presidency was confirmed. He remained one of the most respected leaders of Africa and the Commonwealth, although by 1990 he faced significant internal opposition.

American playwright, producer and director George Kaufman.

Zambian President Kenneth Kaunda (1985).

Kautsky, Karl Johann (1854–1938). German socialist theorist. Born in Prague, he joined the Social Democratic Party in Vienna in 1875 and became private secretary to communist theorist Friedrich Engels in 1881. A loyal Marxist, he was founder and editor of the left-wing journal *Die neue Zeit* (1883–1917). He was largely responsible for the Erfurt program (1891), which linked the German Social Democratic Party with revolutionary Marxism, and he was a consistent opponent of Eduard Bernstein and his revisionist theories. Opposed to Germany's entry into World War I, he and Hugo Haase formed the Independent Social Democratic Party (1917–22). He bitterly denounced the BOLSHEVIKS in Russia, condemning their revolution (1917) as undemocratic and anti-Marxist. Kautsky settled in Vienna, where he rejoined the Social Democrats, living there until the eve of the Nazi occupation, when he fled (1938) to Holland. He was a prolific writer whose works include *The Economic Doctrines of Karl Marx* (tr. 1925) and *Ethics and the Materialist Conception of History* (tr. 1907). He also edited a four-volume history of the origins of World War I (1919).

Kawabata, Yasunari (1899–1972). Japanese author and playwright. Kawabata early evidenced his literary talent as a founder of an avant garde literary journal, *Bungei Jidai*, an advocate of the Neo-Sensualist movement. He experimented with surrealistic techniques, but his best known works are more traditional in style and characterized by a nostalgic despondency tinged with eroticism. Kawabata's numerous works include the novels *Izu no odoriko* (1925, translated as *The Izu Dancer* 1964), *Yaukiguni* (1937, translated as *Snow Country* 1957) and *Sembazuru* (1959, translated as *Thousand Cranes* 1959); he has also written short stories, plays and criticism. Kawabata was awarded the NOBEL PRIZE for literature in 1968. He committed suicide in 1972.

Kay, Hershy (1919–1981). American orchestrator, composer and arranger. Kay is best known for his ballet scores, many of which were commissioned by George BALANCHINE. He also made arrangements of Leonard BERNSTEIN's musicals and orchestrated popular Broadway shows such as *Evita, A Chorus Line* and *Barnum.*

Kaye, Danny [David Daniel Kaminski] (1913–1987). American comic actor and entertainer. Kaye became famous in 1940 in the Broadway show *Lady in the Dark.* His HOLLYWOOD film career began with *Up in Arms* (1944) and peaked with his acclaimed performance as *Hans Christian Andersen* (1952). His comic gifts were best displayed in *The Secret Life of Walter Mitty* (1947), in which he played a bumbling daydreamer. Beginning with a series of sold-out appearances at the London Palladium in 1948, he became perhaps the most popular American entertainer in postwar Britain. In the 1960s he hosted *The Danny Kaye Show* on U.S. television; later, he was known largely for his comic performances that raised millions of dollars for the United Nations International Children's Emergency Fund (UNICEF), and also for his burlesque conducting of symphony orchestras to benefit musicians' pension funds.

Kaye, Nora [born Nora Koreff] (1920–1987). American ballerina. Kaye was the first American dramatic ballerina to acquire an international reputation. She joined the AMERICAN BALLET THEATER (ABT) at its inception in 1939, and was primarily associated with this company. She also danced with the NEW YORK CITY BALLET. During her career some two dozen ballets were created for her. Prominent among these were Antony TUDOR's *Pillar of Fire* (1942) and Agnes DE MILLE's *Fall River Legend* (1948). Kaye retired from the dance stage in 1961, but subsequently worked with her husband, director-choreographer **Herbert Ross,** on several dance films, including *The Turning Point* (1977).

Kaye, Sammy (1910–1987). U.S. bandleader. During the Swing Era of the 1940s, Kaye led one of the country's most popular "sweet bands." A bandleader for over 50 years, he had more than 100 hit records. His band was particularly popular during World War II, when it performed live on Kaye's long-running radio show *Sunday Serenade.*

Kaysone Phomvihane (1925–). Laotian communist leader, Prime Minister of LAOS (1975). The son of a Vietnamese civil servant and a Laotian woman, Kaysone Phomvihane attended a lycee and law school in Hanoi. He was reputedly taught by the Vietnamese revolutionary, General VO NGUYEN GIAP. In 1955 he was a cofounder of the Laotian Communist Party, which he has since led. During the American bombing of Laos (approximately 1964–73), a part of the VIETNAM WAR, and for a couple of years thereafter, he and other PATHET LAO leaders lived in caves near the Vietnamese border. In 1975 he became prime minister of the newly formed Lao People's Democratic Republic, a post he still holds.

Kazan, Elia [born Elia Kazanjoglous] (1909–). American stage and film director. He was born in Istanbul, Turkey, to Greek parents. He immigrated to the U.S. in 1913, acted with New York's Group Theater in the 1930s and became a founding member of the Actors' Studio. Kazan was especially acclaimed for his powerful and realistic direction of the plays of Tennessee WILLIAMS, such as *A Streetcar Named Desire* (1947), and Arthur MILLER, such as DEATH OF A SALESMAN (1948). Among his many other stage successes were *The Skin of Our Teeth* (1942), *All My Sons* (1947) and *Tea and Sympathy* (1953). His films include *Gentleman's Agreement* (1947), *A Streetcar Named Desire* (1951), *On the Waterfront* (1954) and *East of Eden* (1955). Also a writer, he directed two films adapted from his own novels, *America, America* (1963) and *The Arrangement* (1969). More recently, he is the author of *The Anatolian* (1983), *An American Odyssey* (1989) and an autobiography, *A Life* (1988).

Kazantzakis, Nikos (1883–1957). Greek author. Considered modern Greece's greatest novelist, Kazantzakis was also one of the most controversial writers of his time. He was a philosophical writer greatly influenced by his teacher Henri BERGSON, Nietzschean theory and his birthplace of Crete. The latter became the central metaphor of his art, representing the dynamic of thesis, antithesis and final synthesis that he called the *Cretan Glance*. He gained international recognition with his novel *Zorba the Greek* (1946; tr. 1952). Other major works include the novels *Freedom or Death* (1954) and *The Last Temptation of Christ* (1960), and the epic poem *Odyseia* (1938; tr. *The Odyssey: A Modern Sequel*, 1958).

Kazin, Alfred (1915–). American critic. Born in Brooklyn, N.Y., he attended City College and Columbia University. His influential critical study of American prose, *On Native Grounds* (1942), established him as one of America's most important literary critics. Among his other critical works are *The Inmost Leaf* (1955), *Contemporaries* (1962), *Bright Book of Life* (1973) and *A Writer's America* (1988). A noted editor, teacher and memoirist, he is also the author of an evocative autobiographical trilogy, *Walker in the City* (1951), *Starting Out in the Thirties* (1965) and *New York Jew* (1978).

Keating Five scandal. In the late 1980s a real estate slump in the southwestern U.S. caused the collapse of many SAVINGS AND LOAN associations. Because the associations' deposits were federally insured, taxpayers ended up paying the huge losses. Ensuing lawsuits and government investigations showed that fraud and lax regulation were the cause of much of the loss. The case of Charles H. Keating Jr. was a striking example. Keating, a conservative Republican, had made large donations to the campaigns of a number of U.S. senators and/or to organizations that the senators supported. Interestingly, a few of Keating's donations were to well connected senators who were philosophically opposed to his own views. Five of these senators—Alan Cranston (California), John GLENN (Ohio), Denis DeConcini (Arizona), Don Riegle (Michigan) and John McCain (Arizona) later interceded with federal regulators on behalf of Keating. A 1990 Senate investigation of the so-called Keating Five revealed the connection between campaign contributions and improper influence on Capitol Hill.

Keaton, Buster (Joseph Francis) (1895–1966). American motion picture actor and producer. Keaton is considered one of the Big Five SILENT FILM actor-comedians, with Charles CHAPLIN, Douglas FAIRBANKS, Sr., Harry LANGDON, and Harold LLOYD. He was born in Piqua, Kansas, to a family of medicine show performers. His skills at rough-and-tumble acrobatic comedy—magician Harry HOUDINI dubbed him "Buster"—led to his first series of one-reel films with rotund funnyman Roscoe "Fatty" ARBUCKLE in 1917. Two years later Keaton teamed up with producer Joseph M. Schenck and for the next decade produced his finest work, numerous shorts and feature films that rank among the greatest of all silent-screen comedies. Many of the important Keaton themes emerged at this time—the dogged determination and triumph of "the little man" (*Our Hospitality*, 1923); the world as reality, fantasy and dream (shorts like *The Playhouse*, 1921, and features like *Sherlock, Jr.*, 1924); and man's uneasy relationship with machines (*The Navigator*, 1925, and *The General*, 1927). Contrasting with the ready grin of Fairbanks and Lloyd and the eager pathos of Chaplin and Langdon, Keaton's face was a mutely expressive mask, with barely a twitch of an eyelash to betray inner thoughts and feelings. Coupled to that face was a superbly coordinated body that contributed to chases and falls and a hair-raising sense of speed and danger (see the long, concluding chase in *Seven Chances*, 1925). In 1928 Keaton relinquished his customary complete control over his work and began releasing his pictures through MGM. A long decline began, further troubled by alcoholism and emotional and marital instability. Aside from a few flashes of his comic genius—some gag writing on Red Skelton films in the 1940s and a brief appearance with Chaplin in *Limelight* (1952)—he lapsed into obscurity. It was not until the late 1950s that a worldwide revival of interest in his work began at film festivals and on college campuses. At the time of his death from cancer in 1966, he was again acclaimed one of the masters of motion picture comedy.

Deadpan American silent film comedian Buster Keaton.

Keck, George Fred (1895–1980). American modernist architect who built a significant reputation in the 1930s before MODERNISM became widely accepted. Keck first won recognition as the designer of the futuristic House of Tomorrow in a village of model homes at the CENTURY OF PROGRESS EXHIBITION in Chicago in 1933. The house was a twelve-faceted, all-glass-walled circular pavilion placed on top of a base that included services, garage, and a hangar for the family airplane! At the 1934 fair Keck provided his Crystal House, also with walls of glass and a strikingly modern interior. His work thereafter for private clients was largely residential, including many midwestern houses of simple modern design. Most of his designs emphasized the concept of the solar house, which Keck developed by carefully studying patterns of the sun's path so that a maximum of winter sun aided heating and a minimum of summer sun penetrated the houses' windows. Orientation and placement of windows and overhangs for shading were planned to give maximum comfort and energy economy. It can be said that Keck is a precursor of the interest in solar heating that began in the 1970s.

Keeling Islands. See COCOS ISLANDS.

Kees, Weldon (1914–1955?). American author, painter and composer. Though virtually unknown during his lifetime, Kees wrote jazz compositions, did some painting and wrote fiction and poetry. Among his best known poems are "The Beach in August," "Early Winter" and "River Song." His fictional satire of scholarly life, *Fall Quarter*, originally written in the 1930s, was published in 1990. He disappeared in 1955 and is presumed a suicide.

Kefauver, Carey Estes (1903–1963). American politician. A Democratic U.S. congressman from Tennessee (1939–49), he was elected to the U.S. Senate in 1948. He gained national fame with the Kefauver Crime Committee (1950–51). In 1956 Kefauver ran unsuccessfully as the Democratic vice presidential candidate (with Adlai STEVENSON). He was the author of *Crime in America* (1951).

Kefauver investigation (1950–51). Televised U.S. Senate hearings into organized crime, chaired by Senator Estes KEFAUVER of Tennessee. The Senate Special Committee to Investigate Crime in Interstate

Commerce called hundreds of witnesses, including reputed mob bosses, corrupt policemen and politicians. The hearings, which gained wide attention because they were televised, made "taking the Fifth" part of the American vernacular after one witness refused to testify "on the grounds it might tend to incriminate me." The highlight of the hearings was the testimony of mob leader Frank Costello, who agreed to testify only if his face was not shown. The cameras focused on Costello's hands during his lengthy testimony. He was later sentenced to jail for contempt and tax evasion. Testimony also implicated former New York Mayor William O'Dwyer in the corruption. After the hearings' revelations, the FBI formally became involved in the fight against organized crime.

Keitel, Wilhelm (1882–1946). German field marshal. During WORLD WAR II, Keitel was chief of staff of the supreme command of German forces. On May 8, 1945, he signed the articles of surrender on behalf of the *Wehrmacht*. Keitel was condemned as a war criminal at the NUREMBERG TRIALS and was hanged.

Kekkonen, Urho K(aleva) (1900–1986). Finnish diplomat and politician. A dominant figure in Finnish politics for five decades, Kekkonen was first named FINLAND's minister of justice in 1936. He later served as prime minister five times before becoming president, a post he held from 1956 to 1981. He was regarded as the chief architect of his nation's special brand of neutrality, which evolved after World War II in response to Finland's need to maintain cordial relations with the Soviet Union while forging ties with the West.

Keldysh, Mstislav Vsevolodovich (1911–1978). Soviet scientist and mathematician. Keldysh was president of the Soviet Academy of Sciences from 1961 to 1975. In this post, he had responsibility for development of the Soviet space program and for all national scientific projects. His personal research was in computer science, rocketry and spacecraft.

Keller, Charles Ernest "Charlie" (1916–1990). American baseball player. Keller joined the New York Yankees in 1939 and quickly became their starting right fielder. Together with Joe DIMAGGIO and Tommy Henrich, he formed one of the most renowned outfields in baseball history. He later played for the Detroit Tigers. He appeared in the World Series four times, batting .306. He played 1,170 career games, with a .286 batting average. Retiring from baseball in 1952, Keller went on to a successful career as a horse breeder.

Keller, Helen Adams (1880–1968). American author. Keller lost her hearing and sight during an illness at 19 months of age. Under the tutelage of Anne Sullivan, she learned to speak, to use sign language, to read braille and to type. She graduated with honors from Radcliffe College in 1904. She wrote books, and made lecture tours to promote interest in the handicapped, and in the process became a world-famous inspiration for others. Her works include *The Story of My Life* (1903) and *Out of the Dark* (1913).

Kellogg, Frank Billings (1856–1937). American diplomat. A U.S. senator from Minnesota from 1917 to 1923, he became secretary of state in 1925 and served until 1929. He also served as special counsel for the United States and was a judge of the Permanent Court of International Justice from 1930 to 1935. He received the NOBEL PRIZE for peace in 1929.

Kellogg, Will Keith (1860–1951). American philanthropist and food products manufacturer. At the age of 14 he started selling brooms for his father. Later, he and his brother, who operated the Battle Creek Sanitarium, started experimenting with prepared cereal products of different kinds. In 1906 Will began the Kellogg business in cereals and started the prepared food era in America. He retired from active participation in the firm in 1929, and established the W.K. Kellogg Foundation in Battle Creek, Michigan. He invested most of his fortune in the foundation and supported endeavors he judged to be helpful.

Kellogg-Briand Pact. More formally known as the Pact of Paris, the agreement, signed August 27, 1928, renounced war as an instrument of national policy. The treaty, which arose out of negotiations between Aristide BRIAND, foreign minister of France, and Frank B. KELLOGG, U.S. secretary of state, called for the ratifying parties to use only peaceful means to settle disputes. By 1934 almost all the nations of the world had signed the pact, although many signed with certain limitations. Because it contained no provisions for enforcement, the pact proved ineffective. The treaty formed part of the basis for the war crime trials following World War II. (See also NUREMBERG TRIALS.)

Kelly, Charles E. (1920–1985). American World War II hero, popularly known as Commando Kelly. In 1943 he became the first enlisted man to receive the Medal of Honor in WORLD WAR II, for singlehandedly fighting off a German platoon in Italy in 1943. He wrote a book about his exploits, *One Man's War,* which was later made into a film.

Kelly, Ellsworth (1923–). American painter. Born in Newburgh, N.Y., Kelly studied at the Boston Museum School and the Academie des Beaux-Arts, Paris (1943–46), and continued to live in Paris until 1954. A leading exponent of HARD-EDGE PAINTING, he is known for grandly-proportioned canvases composed of large areas of vivid, flat color in abstract geometric shapes. Often named for the colors they contain, his paintings include *Blue Red Green* (1962, Walker Art Center, Minneapolis) and *Green Blue Red* (1964, Whitney Museum, New York City).

Kelly, Emmett (1898–1979). The most familiar clown in America. Kelly's forlorn and wistful characterization of a tattered hobo delighted audiences for more than 40 years. He appeared with Ringling Brothers and Barnum & Bailey Circus from 1942 to 1956, and with the Brooklyn Dodgers baseball team in 1957. He also made numerous television appearances. He was best known for a pantomime of sweeping the spotlight away.

Kelly, Gene (1912–). American actor, dancer, choreographer, film director. Kelly was one of the great popular dancers and innovative choreographers in motion pictures. He first gained attention in the Broadway musical *Pal Joey* (1941). He starred in several film musicals, including *On the Town* (1949) and *Singin' in the Rain* (1952). His innovations as director/choreographer are best seen in the films *An American in Paris* (1951) and *Invitation to the Dance* (1956). In the latter, unsuccessful film his dance sequences with animated characters made movie history.

Kelly, Grace. See GRACE, PRINCESS OF MONACO.

Kelso (1957–1983). Thoroughbred racehorse, widely considered the best racehorse of his time and one of the top American horses of the century. A gelding, Kelso captured the Gold Cup and the Horse of the Year title five times, from 1960 through 1965, a record no other racehorse has ever matched. During his career, he started 63 times, won 39 races, finished second 12 times, and third twice. He retired in 1965. His total earnings held the record for 13 years; at his death, he ranked fifth on the all-time earnings list.

Kempe, Rudolf (1910–1976). German-born opera and symphonic conductor, one of the greatest musicians of his generation. By contrast to the high-profile gloss of Herbert von KARAJAN and the mannered technique of Leonard BERNSTEIN, Kempe was a model of consistency and technique, sublimating himself to the service of the music. He was born in Niederpoyritz near Dresden, educated at the Orchestra School of the Saxon State Orchestra, and debuted as an opera conductor in 1933 with the Leipzig Opera. After a brief service as an infantryman in WORLD WAR II, he was named to several posts, including general music director of the Saxon State Theater in Dresden (1949–1952), conductor of the Bavarian State Opera in Munich (1952–1954), artistic director of the Royal Philharmonic Orchestra in 1964 (after the death of Sir Thomas BEECHAM), and chief conductor of the BBC Symphony Orchestra (1975). Never as well known in the U.S. as in Europe (although he occasionally conducted at the Metropolitan Opera in New York City), he built an exemplary reputation for opera—particularly German and Italian works—and for the works of orchestral composers as various as Frederick DELIUS and Richard STRAUSS.

Kendall, Edward Calvin (1886–1972). American biochemist. Born in South Norwalk, Conn., Kendall earned his Ph.D. from Columbia University in 1910. From 1921 to 1951, he was a professor of physiological chemistry at the MAYO Foundation. Kendall isolated the adrenal hormone later known as cortisone, which his colleague Philip HENCH demonstrated to be effective in the treatment of rheumatoid arthritis. For this work, Kendall shared the 1950 NOBEL PRIZE for physiology or medicine with Hench and Tadeus Reichstein.

Kendrick, Pearl L. (1890–1980). American microbiologist. Kendrick helped develop a whooping cough vaccine in 1939. The vaccine led to the virtual eradication of this childhood illness. Kendrick also developed the standard DPT shot, which provided combined protection against diptheria, whooping cough, and tetanus. She later worked as a consultant for the WORLD HEALTH ORGANIZATION (WHO) and started immunization programs in Mexico, India, Germany, the USSR, and South America.

Kennan, George F. (1904–). U.S. official and political analyst. Kennan graduated from Princeton University in 1925 and joined the diplomatic corps. After World War II, he was placed in charge of long-range policy planning for the State Department. In 1947, Kennan introduced the concept of "containment," the strategy of counteracting postwar Soviet expansionism with countermeasures aimed at preserving the status quo; Kennan believed that, in the face of vigilant, measured opposition from the West, the Soviet Union would eventually soften its foreign policy and liberalize its domestic controls. Many analysts believe that Kennan accurately predicted the outcome of the COLD WAR, more than 40 years later. Kennan went on to serve as U.S. ambassador to the Soviet Union and to Yugoslavia. In later years, he wrote and lectured widely on foreign policy. In 1989 he was awarded the Medal of Freedom.

Kennedy, Anthony M. (1936–). Associate justice, U.S. Supreme Court (1989–). A native of California, Kennedy is a graduate of Stanford University, the London School of Economics and Harvard University Law School. After several years in private practice in Sacramento, California Kennedy was appointed as a justice of the U.S. Court of Appeals for the Ninth Circuit. He was nominated to the Supreme Court by President Ronald REAGAN after Reagan's two previous nominees, Robert BORK and Douglas Ginsburg, failed to win approval. (Bork was rejected by the Senate based partly on his outspoken conservative views, while Ginsburg's nomination was withdrawn after it was revealed that he had smoked marijuana as a law student and professor.) In contrast, Justice Kennedy was confirmed without incident. On the bench Justice Kennedy was predictably conservative, generally helping to form a solid conservative bloc on the Court. However, in his first year on the Court he surprised many by siding with the liberal justices in overturning a Texas statute outlawing the desecration of the American flag on First Amendment grounds.

Kennedy, Jacqueline [nee Bouvier] (1929–). Born into a wealthy New York family and educated at Miss Porter's School, Vassar, the Sorbonne and George Washington University, Jacqueline Bouvier was an ideal wife for politician John F. KENNEDY, whom she married in 1953. After her husband became president in 1961, the elegant First Lady, dressed in Oleg Cassini gowns, BALENCIAGA suits and the "Pillbox" hats, designed by HALSTON, was emulated by women all over the world. Utilizing her knowledge of art and antiques, she undertook a renovation of the White House that was televised in the famous "A Tour of the White House with Mrs. John F. Kennedy" in 1962. During her tenure, Mrs. Kennedy was also an able ambassador for the U.S. and traveled widely, winning support for the Kennedy administration with her youthful beauty and finishing school charm. In 1963 she was voted the most admired woman in America, suffered the death of a newborn child and the terrible assassination of her husband, shot before her eyes in Dallas, Texas. Her stoicism as a young widow with two small children, Caroline and John, further endeared her to the American public. Her subsequent marriage to the Greek shipping magnate Aristotle ONASSIS in 1968 surprised her loyal fans. After his death in 1975, she established herself as an editor at the Doubleday publishing house in New York City and has since led a quiet life out of the public spotlight. She remains, however, a mysterious and fascinating figure to many and an enduring symbol of style and sophistication.

Kennedy, John Fitzgerald (1917–1963). Thirty-fifth president of the UNITED STATES (1961–63). Born in Brookline, Massachusetts, of Irish Catholic background, he was part of a well-known business and political family, the son of Joseph P. KENNEDY (1888–1969), a successful businessman and movie industry executive who had been ambassador to Great Britain, and the brother of Robert F. KENNEDY and Edward M. Kennedy. He attended Harvard University (1936–40) and enlisted in the Navy in 1941, distinguishing himself during WORLD WAR II as the commander of a PT boat in the Pacific. Kennedy entered politics as a congressman from Massachusetts (1947–53) and was a supporter of President TRUMAN's domestic policies but a critic of his relationship with China. He was elected to the Senate in 1952, and the following year he married Jacqueline Bouvier. He suffered from severe, war-related back problems in 1954–55 that to some degree hindered his active role in the Senate. During this period he wrote *Profiles in Courage* (1956), a series of biographical sketches of courageous American leaders that won him a 1957 PULITZER PRIZE. Kennedy was narrowly defeated for the vice presidential nomination in 1956 but won reelection to the Senate by a landslide in 1958.

An anticommunist in foreign policy and a liberal in domestic affairs, the charismatic and popular senator became the Democratic nominee for president in 1960. With Texan Lyndon B. JOHNSON as his running mate, he narrowly defeated his Republican opponent, Richard M. NIXON, to become the first Roman Catholic to be elected president and the youngest man ever to hold the office. He quickly initiated a domestic program (the New Frontier) that included tax reform, federal aid to education, increased civil rights and medical care for the elderly. He barely had time to fight for these programs when he was embroiled in crises abroad. His support of the failed Cuban BAY OF PIGS INVASION (1961) was largely criticized, but he was widely lauded for his resolute stand against the Soviets in the CUBAN MISSILE CRISIS (1962). In 1963 Kennedy was successful in working out a limited NUCLEAR TEST BAN TREATY with the U.S.S.R. In other foreign policy decisions, he established the PEACE CORPS to help the needy in developing countries and the ALLIANCE FOR PROGRESS to aid Latin America. He also increased the number of American advisers in South Vietnam from some 700 to about 16,000, thus adding to a U.S. presence that would soon escalate into the VIETNAM WAR. He continued to press for his domestic programs, proposing (1963) extensive civil rights legislation, but met with a good deal of resistance from Congress. Most of these programs were not acted upon until the Johnson administration.

Kennedy was shot to death in Dallas, Texas, on November 22, 1963. The apparent assassin was Lee Harvey OSWALD.

At 2:39 P.M., two hours and nine minutes after the assassination of her husband, Jacqueline Kennedy witnesses the swearing-in of Lyndon Johnson aboard Air Force One (Nov. 22, 1963).

John F. Kennedy, 35th president of the United States.

While the Warren Commission concluded that Oswald had been the killer and had acted alone, conspiracy theories about Kennedy's death abounded and flourish to this day. The death of the vital and eloquent young president, who had yet to fulfill his promise, caused shock and grief throughout the U.S. and the world.

For further reading:

Manchester, William, *One Brief Shining Moment: Remembering Kennedy.* Boston: Little, Brown, 1988.

Sorensen, Theodore C., *Kennedy.* New York: HarperCollins, 1988.

Kennedy, Joseph Patrick (1888–1969). U.S. ambassador to Great Britain. A successful businessman and movie industry executive, Kennedy served as chairman of the Securities and Exchange Commission (1934–35) and head of the U.S. Maritime Commission (1936–37) before his appointment as ambassador (1937–40). An opponent of U.S. intervention in European affairs, Kennedy supported Neville CHAMBERLAIN's negotiations with HITLER. He resigned in 1940 to return to business. Kennedy encouraged his sons to pursue political careers and was important in the election of John F. KENNEDY to the presidency in 1960.

Kennedy, Robert F(rancis) "Bobby" (1925–1968). American political figure. Born in Brookline, Massachusetts, he was a younger brother of John F. KENNEDY. He attended Harvard University and the University of Virginia Law School. After graduation in 1951, he worked as a lawyer for the Justice Department before becoming campaign manager for his brother's successful congressional bid. He was an assistant counsel for Sen. Joseph MCCARTHY's communist-hunting subcommittee from 1953 to 1956 and gained wide recognition as chief counsel for the Senate Rackets Committee, where he was instrumental in bringing to light the corruption in the Teamsters Union and of its leaders, James HOFFA and Dave BECK. He went to work for his brother again in 1960, this time managing the elder Kennedy's successful presidential campaign. A close adviser during his brother's adminstration, he was also appointed attorney general and won praise for his pursuit of organized crime and his enforcement of CIVIL RIGHTS legislation. After the president's assassination, he continued to serve in the cabinet but resigned to run for the Senate from New York in 1964. Elected, he was an outspoken advocate of social change and of the rights of the poor. From 1966 on, he also became a powerful critic of the VIETNAM WAR. He became a candidate for the Democratic nomination for president in 1968, winning a string of primary victories that culminated in the California primary of June 4. After a victory speech that evening, he was leaving a Los Angeles hotel when he was shot to death by a disaffected Jordanian immigrant named Sirhan Bishara Sirhan.

For further reading:

Schlesinger, Arthur M., Jr., *Robert Kennedy and His Times.* New York: Ballantine, 1985.

Kennedy Round. Long, complex negotiations to encourage world trade through reduction of tariffs on industrial and agricultural imports, particularly in the U.S. and Europe. These negotiations were prompted by President John F. KENNEDY's message to Congress on January 25, 1963. A final compromise was reached in Geneva on May 15, 1967.

Kenton, Stan (1911–1979). American bandleader-pianist-composer. Kenton began his career playing and writing for various West Coast theater and dance bands. He formed his first band in 1941, the Artistry in Rhythm Orchestra, which gained prominence with its large orchestral sound and precise ensemble playing. With the addition of arrangers like Pete Ruggolo and outstanding soloists such as alto saxophonist Art Pepper, Kenton's band dominated the jazz polls of the mid-1940s organized by such publications as *Down Beat* and *Metronome.* In 1949, Kenton appeared with the 20-piece Progressive Jazz Orchestra, which gave its name to the modern big band approach it represented. Kenton's most ambitious undertaking came in 1950–51 with the 43-piece Innovations in Modern Music Orchestra, with strings and an expanded wind section; though scoring successes with such large-scale compositions as Bob Graettinger's "City of Glass," the venture proved too costly to sustain. Thereafter, Kenton led a series of highly competent but more conventionally sized big bands.

Kenton's place in jazz history is somewhat ambiguous: On the one hand, he attracted a large and faithful following; on the other, he was often dismissed by the critics, especially in his more epic endeavors, as pompous and vacuous. What is indisputable is the large number of highly talented jazzmen he helped nurture, such as Stan GETZ and Maynard Ferguson. Kenton is similarly secure in his justly earned reputation as a pioneering jazz educator whose summer jazz camps introduced a new generation to the improvisational muse.

For further reading:

Lee, William F., *Stan Kenton: Artistry in Rhythm.* Los Angeles: Creative Press, 1980.

Kent State shootings. Shooting of student demonstrators protesting the VIETNAM WAR on the campus of Kent State University in Kent, Ohio on May 4, 1970. Students had gathered to protest the U.S. invasion of CAMBODIA on May 1, holding rallies on the Kent State campus and in town. On May 2, a state of civil emergency was declared by the mayor, who called for Ohio National Guard troops. The troops arrived that night as the ROTC building was burned. Tensions between students and troops escalated until the morning of May 4, when some 1,000 students gathered on campus. Refusing to disperse, the students taunted the guardsmen and hurled stones at them while the troops lobbed tear gas canisters at the students. Apparently believing that they were being shot at by a sniper, some of the guardsmen opened fire at 12:25 P.M., killing four students (two men and two women) and wounding 11. The shootings shocked the nation and set off a wave of demonstrations on campuses throughout the U.S. and abroad.

Kenya [Republic of Kenya]. Kenya, on the east coast of Africa, covers an area of 150,943 square miles. It became a British colony in 1920, but nationalist sentiment led to the formation of the Kikuyu Central Association (1928) with Jomo KENYATTA as leader. Pressure to restore land and political control to Africans brought about the violent MAU MAU uprisings from 1952 to 1960, during which the country was under a state of emergency. Kenya achieved independence in 1962, establishing a republic with Kenyatta as president (1963). Kenyatta's death brought Daniel arap Moi to the presidency in 1979. He maintained tribal balance in government and established close relations with the West. However, increased opposition to his policies led to an attempted coup (1982), student riots (1985, 1987), Muslim riots (1987) and detention of suspected rebels. Though Moi was reelected in 1988, the stability of the country has continued to deteriorate, with the murder of a government minister in 1990 igniting antigovernment riots.

Kenyatta, Jomo (1895?-1978). Kenyan nationalist leader, first president of KENYA (1964–78). A member of the minority Kikuyu tribe, Kenyatta was educated in a Christian mission school and began his public career in 1922 when he joined the Kikuyu Youth Association in Nairobi, the capital of Kenya, which was then a colony of Great Britain. As he rose in Kikuyu politics, he traveled to Europe in 1929 to protest British encroachment upon Kikuyu land. He returned to Europe in 1931 for a 15-year stay that included study at the London School of Economics. Upon his return to Kenya in 1946, Kenyatta

Kenyan President Jomo Kenyatta.

became head of the New Kenya African Union, a nationalist group seeking political rights for blacks. Although he favored reform by legal means, he was connected in many people's minds with the underground MAU MAU movement, which was responsible for acts of terror against whites and blacks from 1952 to 1955. He was jailed by the British during the 1952 emergency in Kenya and he subsequently was sentenced to seven years imprisonment. At the end of his term, Kenyatta was confined to his tribal village. After his release, Kenyatta headed the Kenya African National Union (KANU), which won a majority in elections in 1962 for an independent Kenyan parliament. Kenyatta became prime minister upon Kenya's independence in December 1963. The following year he proclaimed Kenya a republic and became its president. Under Kenyatta's administration, KANU became the sole legal political party, and few figures rose to challenge the president's leadership. He outlawed the Kenya People's Union in 1969 and detained those members who did not join KANU. After the assassination in that year of Tom MBOYA, widely regarded as Kenyatta's successor, talk of the president's replacement was discouraged and finally declared illegal in 1976. Under Kenyatta's leadership, the country followed a moderate, pro-West course, encouraging free enterprise and making Kenya one of the most prosperous countries in black Africa. While promoting foreign investment, Kenyatta also required that companies train and hire Africans, thus building up a native labor force capable of running the country's affairs. Despite great income disparity, urban unemployment and substantial corruption, Kenya's economic future was considered relatively promising compared with other African nations.

Kepes, Gyorgy (1906–). Hungarian-American painter, designer and art theorist. Born in Hungary, Kepes studied at Budapest's Academy of Fine Arts from 1924 to 1928. During his student days, Kepes began his photogram experiments, creating abstract images on photographic paper without benefit of camera. Emigrating to the U.S., he and Lazlo MOHOLY-NAGY cofounded the New Bauhaus in Chicago in 1937. In 1946 he went to the Massachusetts Institute of Technology where he became professor of visual design and director of the Center for Advanced Visual Studies. His works of art and his studies explored the emotional role of light and color in art, particularly in abstract images. His many books of art theory include *The Language of Vision* (1944) and *Structure in Art and Science* (1965).

Keppel, Francis (1916–1990). American educator. As U.S. Commissioner of Education from 1962 to 1966, he was a strong supporter of programs to improve the education of children from poor families and encouraged rigorous enforcement of the CIVIL RIGHTS ACT OF 1964 as it applied to education. He also played a major role in the creation of the National Assessment of Educational Progress, which

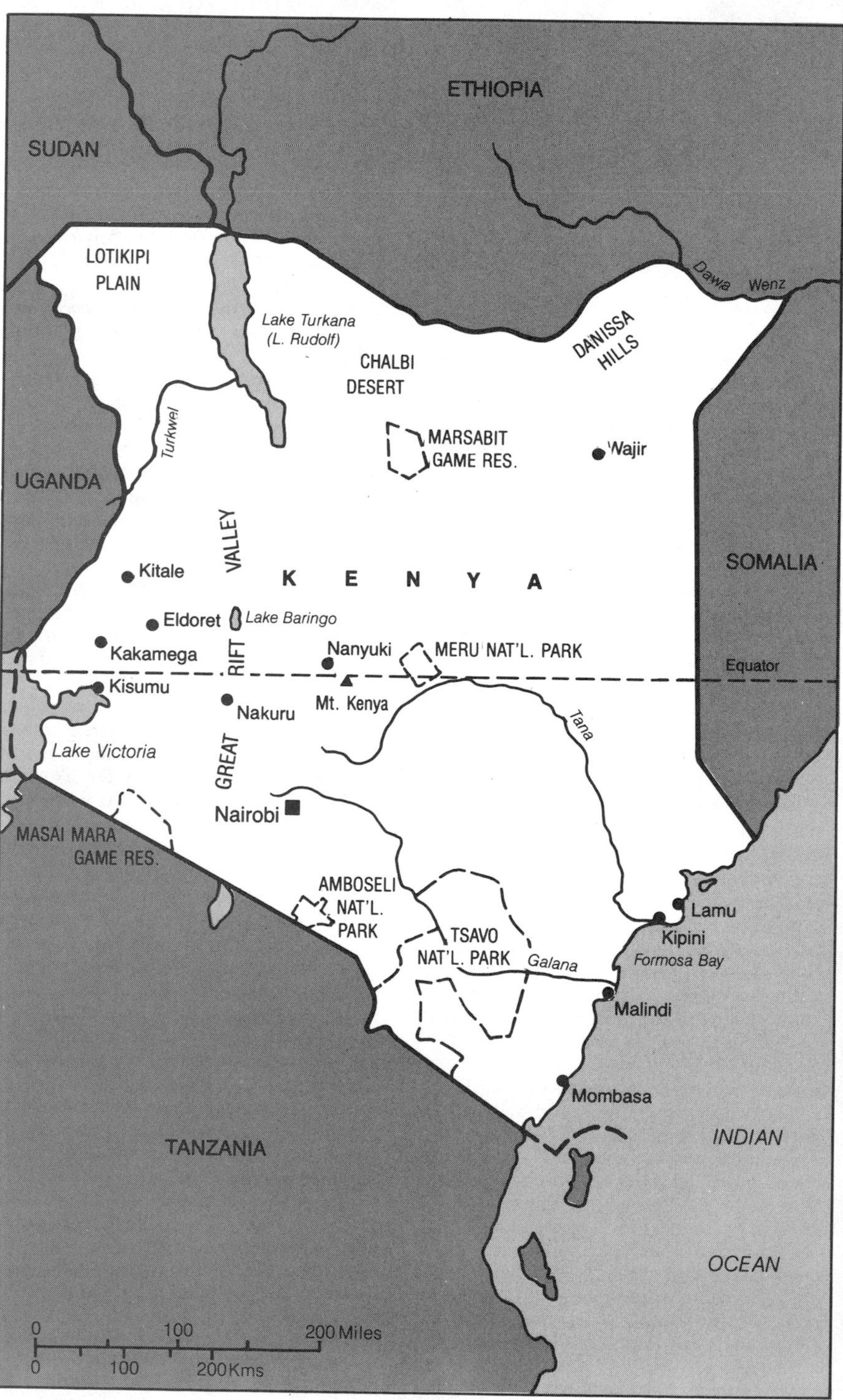

KENYA

KENYA

1920	Kenya becomes a British colony.
1952	Formation of Mau Mau anti-colonial terrorist movement; colonial government declares state of emergency, arrests nationalist leader Jomo Kenyatta.
1956	Mau Mau activity subsides; state of emergency lifted.
1960	Tom Mboya and Oginga Odinga form Kenya African National Union (KANU); British begin to prepare for Kenyan independence.
1961	Kenyatta released from detention.
1963	(June 1) Kenya gains self-government, with Kenyatta as prime minister.
1964	(Dec. 12) Kenya gains full independence, declared a republic with Kenyatta as president.
1969	Assassination of Tom Mboya.
1978	Death of Kenyatta; Daniel arap Moi becomes president.
1982	Attempted air force coup against Moi is foiled.
1990	Kenya's foreign affairs minister, a top government official, is found murdered; government bans demonstrations.

measured the effectiveness of education across the country. He later served as director of the education policy program of the Aspen Institute, and as an advisor the libraries, art centers, the WORLD BANK and developing nations.

Kerensky, Alexander Fedorovich (1881–1970). Russian statesman. A moderate socialist, Kerensky was elected to the fourth DUMA in 1912 and there led the Labor group of socialist peasant members. A brave opponent of the czarist government, he later joined the Socialist Revolutionary Party (see SOCIALIST REVOLUTIONARIES). He was a leading figure in the FEBRUARY REVOLUTION of 1917. During 1917 he held many government posts: minister of justice (February), minister of war and navy (May) and in July became prime minister. As prime minister he aimed to continue the war against Germany, but this undermined his popularity and in November he was ousted by the BOLSHEVIKS (see OCTOBER REVOLUTION). He lived the rest of his life in exile, first in France and then in Australia, and finally, from 1946, in the U.S.

Russian revolutionary and emigre Alexander Kerensky.

Kern, Jerome (David) (1885–1945). One of the prime architects of American popular song in the 20th century. As a boy in New York he preferred music studies at the New York College of Music to working in his father's business. Dividing his time between New York and London, he studied, worked for impresarios Charles Frohman and Florenz ZIEGFELD and finally had the chance to write his first musical score to a show, *The Red Petticoat* (1912). At a time when the American stage was dominated by European songs and shows, Kern wrote a series of small musicals for Broadway's Princess Theater, including *Very Good Eddie* (1915) and *Oh, Boy* (1917). He was soon an established figure in American musical theater, composing the songs and music for the landmark SHOW BOAT (1927). He moved to HOLLYWOOD in 1934 and wrote several original film scores, including *Swing Time* (1936), *High, Wide and Handsome* (1937) and *Cover Girl* (1944). His many collaborators were major figures in the business: Dorothy Fields, Johnny MERCER, E.Y. HARBURG, Ira GERSHWIN and Oscar HAMMERSTEIN II. Among his most distinguished melodies are "Look for the Silver Lining," "Make Believe," "Ol' Man River," "Smoke Gets in Your Eyes," "All the Things You Are" and "The Last Time I Saw Paris" (included in the score for the 1941 movie *Lady Be Good,* it won him an ACADEMY AWARD). Despite his classical training, Kern seldom strayed from song writing into the more traditional forms of "serious" music.

For further reading:

Freedland, Michael, *Jerome Kern.* New York: Stein and Day, 1978.

Kerner scandal. In 1973 Otto Kerner, a U.S. Federal Circuit Court judge and former governor of Illinois (1961–69), was convicted on 17 counts of conspiracy, fraud, perjury, bribery and income tax evasion committed when he was governor. He was sentenced to three years in prison and fined $50,000.

Kerouac, Jack (1922–1969). American novelist. Born Jean Louis Kerouac in Lowell, Massachusetts, he briefly attended Columbia University. A leader of the rebellious BEAT GENERATION of the 1950s, he is best known for the novel *On the Road* (1957), an autobiographical account of his travels throughout the U.S. in search of new sensation and a kind of drugged enlightenment. Similar in theme, his later works include *The Subterraneans* and *The Dharma Bums* (both 1958), *Big Sur* (1962) and *Desolation Angels* (1965). Kerouac also wrote poems and essays.

Kerr, Deborah (1921–). A veteran of 44 films between 1943 and 1969, Kerr was nominated for six ACADEMY AWARDS for best actress but never won. Born in Scotland, she achieved success in British films such as *Black Narcissus* (1947) before signing with METRO-GOLDWYN-MAYER in HOLLYWOOD. Although well-known for her portrayal of poised, well-bred women, steamy love scenes such as the one on the beach with Burt LANCASTER in *From Here to Eternity* proved her versatility. Other films include *The King and I* and *Tea and Sympathy* (1956), *Separate Tables* (1958), *The Sundowners* (1960) and *The Night of the Iguana* (1964).

Kerr, Walter (1913–). American drama critic and playwright. Kerr was a professor of theater at Catholic University in Washington before turning to criticism. He joined the New York *Herald Tribune* in 1951 and moved to *The New York Times* in 1966. His Broadway reviews influenced a generation of theatergoers. Other works include *How Not to Write a Play* (1956) and *Tragedy and Comedy* (1967). He also collaborated on the musical *Goldilocks* with his playwright-wife Jean Kerr.

Kersten, Felix (1899–1960). Estonian-born physiotherapist who acted as personal physician to WORLD WAR II Nazi SS chief Heinrich HIMMLER. Through his intercession with Himmler, Kersten prevented the deportation of 3 million Dutch citizens to Poland in 1941. According to the World Jewish Congress, his actions saved the lives of 60,000 JEWS.

Kesey, Ken (1935–). American writer. Born in La Junta, Colorado, Kesey became a COUNTERCULTURE hero in the 1960s with the publication of his uproarious and iconoclastic novel *One Flew Over the Cuckoo's Nest* (1962, filmed 1975). His reputation was enhanced by his advocacy of psychedelic drugs and by the antics of his "Merry Pranksters," a group of like-minded rebels who toured the U.S. and Mexico in a converted school bus. Their activities are described by Kesey in the novel *Ken Kesey's Garage Sale* (1973) and chronicled in Tom WOLFE's *The Electric Kool-Aid Acid Test* (1968). Kesey is also the author of *Sometimes a Great Notion* (1964) and *Demon Box* (1987).

Kesselring, Albert (1885–1960). German field marshal. Kesselring served as an artillery officer in WORLD WAR I. In WORLD WAR II, he was an important *Luftwaffe* commander, at one time or another in charge of air operations in Poland, the Western Front, central Russia and the Mediterranean. In 1943 he became supreme commander of German forces in Italy, and later that year, commander in chief of the West. In 1947, Kesselring was convicted of war crimes and sentenced to death, but his punishment was commuted to life in prison. He was released in 1952.

Keyes, Sidney (Arthur Killworth) (1922–1943). English poet. Keyes was a shy and frail child, and his early education took place mostly at home. At Queens College, Oxford, he displayed great brilliance and promise and was associated with the poet John Heath-Stubbs. He edited a literary magazine and founded a theater group that performed his play "Hosea." Following the publication of *The Iron Laurel* (1942), Keyes was mobilized and stationed in Tunisia. Shortly before his 21st birthday, he was killed on a reconnaissance patrol. *The Cruel Solstice* was issued posthumously in 1943. *Collected Poems* appeared in 1945; its introduction by Robert Penn WARREN praised Keyes for being the first English poet "to marry Continental symbolism to the English romantic tradition." His major influences were W.B. YEATS and Rainer Maria RILKE. He was one of three important English poets killed in WORLD WAR II, the others being Keith DOUGLAS and Alun LEWIS.

Keynes, John Maynard [1st Baron Keynes (1942)] (1883–1946). English economist. One of the most influential economic thinkers of the 20th century, he was born and educated at Cambridge. A member of the BLOOMSBURY GROUP, Keynes was a man of wide interests and great intelligence. He was a currency specialist in the India Office (1906–08) and served in the treasury (1915–19) before becoming the principal British financial representative to the PARIS PEACE CONFERENCE after World War I. He resigned in protest against the harshness of the terms imposed upon Germany, outlining his views in *Economic Consequences of the Peace* (1919), a book that won him international acclaim. While continuing to support a capitalist system, Keynes began to deviate from classical free economy concepts in 1929, supporting efforts by LLOYD GEORGE to create a program of government-sponsored public works and public employment. Keynes stressed full employment through cheap money, lowered interest rates and increased public and private investment.

His advocacy of active government intervention into the free play of the market and his belief that the unrestrained workings of that market would ultimately result in a depression were spelled out in his classic work *General Theory of Employment, Interest and Money* (1936). His economic and fiscal theories became generally accepted and were incorporated into such national policies as the American NEW DEAL. Keynes served as a consultant to the chancellor of the exchequer and was a director of the Bank of England during World War II. He was an important figure in the BRETTON WOODS CONFERENCE of 1944, establishing postwar monetary policies and creating a WORLD BANK (the INTERNATIONAL MONETARY FUND) to help developing countries. His many works include *Tract on Monetary Reform* (1923), *The End of Laissez Faire* (1926) and *Treatise on Money* (2 vols., 1930).

For further reading:

Blaug, Mark, *John Maynard Keynes: Life, Ideas, Legacy*. New York: Saint Martin's Press, 1990.

Mini, Piero V., *Keynes, Bloomsbury and "The General Theory."* New York: Saint Martin's Press, 1990.

Keyserling, Leon H. (1908–1987). U.S. government consultant. Keyserling helped draft major NEW DEAL legislation and served as a high-ranking official in federal housing programs. In 1949 he was named chairman of President Harry S TRUMAN's Council of Economic Advisers, a post he held until the end of Truman's presidency. After leaving government in 1953, he worked as a private consultant and lawyer and founded the Conference on Economic Progress, a nonprofit group devoted to public interest projects.

Kfar Sava [Kefar Saba, Kefar Sava]. Israeli city where the first Jewish settlement of the southern Sharon plain was made in 1903, six years before Tel Aviv (11 miles to the northeast). It faced great resistance from the OTTOMAN authorities at Constantinople. The city suffered severely in WORLD WAR I and in Arab riots in 1921, but it was reestablished in 1922.

KGB. Acronym for *Komitet Gosudarstvennoy Bezopasnosti* (Committee for State Security). The KGB has been the Soviet security service since 1953. It both enforces Communist Party rule at home and conducts espionage abroad. Despite the reforms of GLASNOST and PERESTROIKA under Mikhail GORBACHEV in the late 1980s, the KGB has remained a powerful force in the U.S.S.R. (See also SOVIET SECRET POLICE.)

For further reading:

Hingley, Ronald, *The Russian Secret Police*. New York: Simon and Schuster, 1971.

Khachaturian, Aram Ilyich (1903–1978). Soviet composer. Born in Georgia, he studied at the Moscow Conservatory (1923–34). His compositions were influenced by Armenian, Georgian and other folk tunes that he collected. His first symphony (1934) drew attention to his talent, and this was followed by a piano concerto (1936) and a violin concerto (1940). His best-known works are two ballets, *Gayane*, which includes the saber dance (1942), and *Spartacus* (1954, revised 1958). He also composed music for films and plays. For a short period he was under censure during the worst of the ZHDANOV "formalist" pressures. He received many awards, including the Order of Lenin.

Khe Sanh. Site of U.S. Marine base in the extreme northern corner of South Vietnam, near the Demilitarized Zone and the Laos border. On January 21, 1968, the North Vietnamese Army attacked the strategically located base and held it under siege, raising fears that Khe Sanh would become the military and public relations disaster for the Americans that DIEN BIEN PHU had been for the French. The siege was finally lifted on April 7, as the TET OFFENSIVE drew to a close, but the base was abandoned in June of that year as U.S. military plans changed. In the siege, 205 Americans had been killed, with official U.S. estimates of North Vietnamese dead placed at more than 10,000 men.

Khlebnikov, Velemir Vladimirovich (1885–1922). Russian poet and Slavophile. He was the founder of Russian FUTURISM, which aimed at shocking the reader and made an attempt at breaking with past conceptions of the use of words by creating a "trans-sense" language.

Khmer Rouge. Radical—and fanatical—Cambodian Marxist revolutionary political organization. Under the leadership of POL POT, the Khmer Rouge ruled CAMBODIA from 1975 to 1979 and conducted a bloody reign of terror. Pursuing a policy of radical social change, the Khmer Rouge tried to destroy Cambodia's old way of life and dealt ruthlessly with any and all potential opponents. The entire population of the capital, PHNOM PENH, was taken from the city and forced to work in the countryside; tens of thousands were executed, and as many as a million died from starvation and mistreatment. Khmer Rouge guerrillas still terrorize thousands of refugees in western Cambodia and Thailand while seeking to overthrow the Vietnam-backed government in Phnom Penh.

Khomeini, Ayatollah Ruhollah [born Sayyid Ruhollah Moussavi] (1900 or 1902–1989). Imam (spiritual leader) of IRAN (1979–89). Khomeini studied Islamic theology and law at the provincial center of Arak and moved in the early 1920s to the holy city of Qom. He became a teacher, wrote poetry and over 20 religious books, and delved into Islamic mysticism and even Western philosophy. Khomeini became known as a leading scholar in the 1930s and earned the title of ayatollah in the late 1950s. But it was not until the early 1960s that he emerged as the leader of the Shiite clergy's opposition to the shah's regime (see Reza PAHLEVI). He organized general strikes, boycotts and demonstrations to protest elements of the Shah's "White Revolution," or modernization programs, that the mullahs (clergy) deemed un-Islamic. Khomeini also led a campaign against diplomatic immunity for U.S. military personnel in Iran. Khomeini spent months in jail and almost a year under house arrest after calling in 1963 for the shah's overthrow. After a brief stay in Turkey, Khomeini settled in the Shiite holy city of Najaf in Iraq. Over the next 13 years he issued periodic proclamations against the shah that were widely circulated clandestinely in Iran. By 1970 he had broadened his attacks, speaking out against both the institution of the

Ayatollah Ruhollah Khomeini, Islamic leader of Iran.

monarchy and constitutional republicanism and calling instead for an Islamic state ruled by religious authorities.

In early 1978 a government-controlled newspaper published an article attacking Khomeini's character and implying he was a tool of foreigners and communists. The tactic backfired, leading to Moslem riots that spread across the country. After Khomeini refused an offer of amnesty from the shah, Iran prevailed upon Iraq first to place the ayatollah under house arrest and then to expel him. The move was a further miscalculation by Teheran: Khomeini set up new headquarters in a Paris suburb, where he had access to the international news media and could coordinate activities with his followers in Iran by telephone. After the shah fled into exile on January 16, 1979, Khomeini returned to a tumultuous welcome in Teheran on February 1. Under Khomeini, "modernists" were gradually shunted aside as an Islamic republic was declared and a constitution was approved by national referendum that consolidated the power of the clergy and made Khomeini Iran's supreme religious and political leader for life. Western music was banned, women's rights were curtailed, religious minorities were persecuted and uncounted thousands of people were executed.

Two of Khomeini's most widely touted slogans were "Death to America" and "Neither East nor West." Although revolutionary Iran steered a nonaligned course in world affairs, Khomeini reserved his special venom for what he called the "Great Satan"—the U.S. Khomeini's Iran provided the basis for the political humiliation of two successive American presidents. It was unclear if Khomeini gave prior approval to the militants who seized the U.S. embassy in Teheran and held its staff hostage for 444 days from November 4, 1979 to January 20, 1981 (see IRAN HOSTAGE CRISIS). But he refused to disavow the takeover, and did not consent to have the hostages go free until President Jimmy CARTER was leaving office. The seminal event of Iran under Khomeini was the IRAN-IRAQ WAR (1980–1988), which helped rally mass popular support around the revolutionary regime. In July 1988 after suffering hundreds of thousands of dead, and its economy a wreck, Iran accepted a United Nations-sponsored cease-fire. In early 1989, Khomeini denounced British author Salman RUSHDIE and his allegedly anti-Muslim book *The Satanic Verses* and called for Rushdie's assassination.

Khrennikov, Tikhon Nikolayevich (1913–). Soviet composer. He was a pupil of Shebalin at the Moscow Conservatory from 1932. His works include an opera, *The Brothers*, two symphonies, a piano concerto, piano works, music for plays and films, including incidental music for *Much Ado About Nothing*, and many songs, including some to words by Robert Burns. In 1948, acting in his capacity as secretary of the Union of Soviet Composers, he condemned many of his colleagues, including PROKOFIEV, for "formalism."

Khrushchev, Nikita Sergeyevich (1894–1971). Soviet politician, first secretary of the Central Committee of the Communist Party of the U.S.S.R. (1953–64). Khrushchev joined the party in 1918 while working as a locksmith in the Donets Basin. He became second secretary of the Moscow Party Organization in 1934, its first secretary in 1935 and first secretary of the Ukrainian Party Organization in 1938. Khrushchev took a prominent part in the GREAT PURGE. In 1939 he became a member of the Politburo and during World War II was an important political officer in the army. Toward the end of STALIN's rule Khrushchev was the party's chief agricultural expert, but his policy of "rural cities" was a disaster. After Stalin's death Khrushchev was first secretary of the central committee, proving to be the most powerful member of the "collective leadership." After denouncing Stalin in a four-hour secret speech at the 20TH PARTY CONGRESS of the CPSU in 1956, he pursued a policy of DESTALINIZATION with a degree of inconsistency. His plans for greater industrialized state farming eventually resulted in lower agricultural production. While Khrushchev's reforms improved the standard and quality of life in the U.S.S.R., they did not win him much popularity. In his dealings with the West, Khrushchev alternated peaceful gestures with threats, and his decisions led to the CUBAN MISSILE CRISIS with the United Sates in 1962. Khrushchev was forced out of office in 1964.

With fist raised, Soviet premier and cold-warrior Nikita Khrushchev addresses the General Assembly of the United Nations (1960).

For further reading:

Beschloss, Michael, *The Crisis Years: Kennedy and Khrushchev, 1960–1963*. New York: HarperCollins, 1991.

Khrushchev, Nikita, *Khrushchev Remembers*, 3 vols. Boston: Little, Brown, 1990 (vol. 3).

Kielce [Keltsy, Kel'tsy]. Polish city 85 miles north-northeast of Cracow; a part of Russia from 1818, it was given to the new state of Poland in 1919. Kielce was a German-Russian battle site in 1914–15; during WORLD WAR II four German CONCENTRATION CAMPS were sited here.

Kiel Mutiny (1918). GERMANY began to discuss a possible armistice with the Allies near the end of WORLD WAR I. At that time, the German navy was in a mutinous state. When the German High Seas Fleet was ordered to sail to the North Sea for a major battle against the British, the German sailors in Kiel refused to go and took up arms, setting off an open revolution throughout Germany (Oct. 29–Nov. 3, 1918). Only the U-boat crews remained loyal to Kaiser WILHELM II. Major revolts occurred in Hamburg, Bremen and Lubeck (Nov. 4–5) and spread to Munich (Nov. 7–8). Bavaria declared itself a democratic and socialist republic. The kaiser was forced to abdicate, and on Nov. 11, 1918, the armistice was signed and World War I ended.

Kiesinger, Kurt Georg (1904–1988). German politician, chancellor of WEST GERMANY from 1966 to 1969. As a Christian Democrat, Kiesinger led a government formed by a GRAND COALITION of Christian Democrats and Social Democrats. His past as a minor Nazi brought him much negative attention when he became a candidate for chancellor. He was slapped in the face by Nazi hunter Beate Klarsfeld at a conference in West Berlin in November 1968. After losing to Willy BRANDT in the 1969 election, he played only a minor role in West German politics, remaining a member of the Bundestag (Parliament) until 1980.

Kiesler, Frederick (1890–1965). Austrian theatrical designer who became part of the de STIJL movement in Holland in 1923. Kiesler's *Cite dans l'Espace*, a de Stijl utopian city of the future, was part of the Austrian exhibit at the 1925 Paris exhibition. From 1923 to 1960 he worked on the concept of a futuristic "Endless House" with curving, biomorphic forms. The house was never built but often published and exhibited. After coming to the U.S. in 1926, he designed the Film Guild

Cinema in New York in a style closely related to de Stijl thinking and established a reputation as both a sculptor and a designer of visionary and futuristic architectural projects. His *Art of this Century* gallery of 1942 was a strong expression of his personal aesthetic. From the 1940s until his death, Kiesler produced and regularly exhibited "Galaxies," sculptural works made by grouping flat, painted panels to form spatial environments. Lisa Phillip's 1989 book *Frederick Kiesler* is an inclusive survey of his achievements.

Kiev [Ukrainian: Kiyiv]. Capital and Dnieper River port of the U.S.S.R.'s Ukrainian SSR; about 470 miles southwest of Moscow. The city saw turmoil during the RUSSIAN CIVIL WAR of 1918–20. Kiev was the largest Soviet city captured by the Germans during WORLD WAR II, and suffered great privation. During the German occupation (1941–43) the SS was particularly active and killed at least 50,000 Jews here; much of the city was physically destroyed. (See also BABI YAR MASSACRE.)

Kilbrandon Report (November 1973). The successes of Scottish and Welsh nationalists in British parliamentary elections prompted the Kilbrandon inquiry and a report recommending elected assemblies in Wales and Scotland. A Scottish referendum on the issue on March 1, 1979, proved indecisive; on the same day, the Welsh overwhelmingly rejected the proposed devolution of power. (See also PLAID CYMRU.)

Killebrew, Harmon (Clayton) (1936–). American baseball player. Killebrew was one of the most dominant players of the 1960s, but his chance to break Babe RUTH's home run record was spoiled by injuries. His steady defensive play with the Washington Senators—later the Minnesota Twins—allowed his managers to use him at virtually any position. His hitting power was legendary, as his home run shots hit upper decks and sailed out of even the largest stadiums. An All-Star throughout his career, he had his best season in 1969, with 49 home runs and 140 runs batted in. Killebrew spent 1975, his last season, with the Kansas City Royals, and was inducted into the Baseball Hall of Fame in 1984. He had 573 lifetime home runs.

Killy, Jean-Claude (1943–). French skier. An Alpine racer with matinee-idol good looks and charm, Killy dominated international skiing during the late 1960s. He first came to prominence in 1964, when he won all three French Alpine championships—slalom, giant slalom and downhill—and led the French team to the world championship. During the 1968 Grenoble OLYMPIC GAMES in his native France, Killy became the focus of international media attention as he took all three Alpine gold medals. He retired from skiing after the games and turned to acting. Four years later, he began a career as a professional skier; he took the world professional championship in 1972.

Kilmer, (Alfred) Joyce (1886–1918). American poet. Born in New Brunswick, N.J., he worked on the *Standard Dictionary* before joining the U.S. Army at the outbreak of World War I. He is famous for the cloyingly sentimental poem "Trees" in *Trees and Other Poems* (1914). His other verse collections are *Summer of Love* (1911) and *Main Street and Other Poems* (1917). Kilmer wrote some powerful war poetry before being killed in action in France.

Kim Il (1910–1984). Korean communist leader. A member of the inner circle of early Korean revolutionaries, Kim Il joined the then-underground Communist Party in 1932 and fought Japanese colonial occupation. He was appointed first deputy premier of NORTH KOREA in 1959, premier in 1972 and vice president in 1976. He was also a member of the Central Committee of the Communist Party and of the National Administration Council.

Kim Il-sung (1912–). Communist leader of NORTH KOREA. Kim Il-sung joined the Communist Party in 1927. During World War II he was a guerrilla leader in Manchuria. After the war—and with Soviet support—he prevailed over opponents from other factions of the party and gradually became a supreme leader, the center of an extreme personality cult. He is extravagantly praised and called the "great leader," the "heaven-sent and talented leader" and so on. He also awarded himself a number of high orders and decorations, such as Hero of the Democratic People's Republic of Korea (two times) and the Order of National Flag First Class (three times). By designating his son as his successor, he is apparently attempting to found a communist dynasty.

Kiner, Ralph [born Ralph McPherran] (1922–). American baseball player. One of the great sluggers of the postwar years, Kiner led the National League in home runs from 1946 through 1952. The Pittsburgh Pirates tailored their left field line at Forbes Field to suit his (and Hank GREENBERG's) home run power, and that area of the park became known as "Kiner's Korner." The end of his career was hastened by back troubles, but he finished with 369 home runs, giving him a lifetime home run to at-bat ratio second only to Babe RUTH's. Kiner took the name "Kiner's Korner" for his talk and interview program when he began his successful broadcasting career with the expansion New York Mets in 1962. He was named to the Hall of Fame in 1975.

King, Billie Jean (1943–). U.S. tennis player. King's influence on and off the court is still felt in the world of tennis. A tireless fighter for the rights of women players, she brought the women's game to a wider audience and eventually helped to establish a separate women's tour. Winner of a record 20 Wimbledon titles, she won four U.S. Open singles titles, as well as an Australian and a French Open. Perhaps her best remembered match, however, was the super-hyped "Battle of the Sexes" in which she defeated the middleaged tennis great and self-proclaimed "male chauvinist pig" Bobby RIGGS.

King, Carole [born Carole Klein] (1942–). American singer-songwriter. With husband Gerry Goffin, King was one of the most important pop/rock composers of the 1960s. Together they penned such hits as "Will You Love Me Tomorrow," "Locomotion," "Some Kind of Wonderful" and "A Natural Woman." After the dissolution of their marriage and their professional partnership, King turned to performing. Her second album release, *Tapestry*, sold more than 14 million copies and was named album of the year. Hit singles from the album included "It's Too Late" and "I Feel the Earth Move." King has rarely performed live, and although she continues to release records, none of her later releases have approached the success of *Tapestry*.

King, Charles Glen (1896–1988). American chemist and nutritionist. In 1932, while on the faculty of the University of Pittsburgh, King isolated vitamin C from the juice of lemons. He was a professor of chemistry at Columbia University from 1941 to 1947.

King, Ernest (1878–1956). U.S. military officer. King was born in Lorain, Ohio, and graduated from the U.S. Naval Academy at Annapolis in 1901. He became a rear admiral in 1933. In 1941 King became commander of U.S. naval forces and was appointed chief of naval operations the following year. He was the only officer in U.S. history to occupy both posts. As commander of the greatest naval fleet in history, he directed the strategy that lead to the defeat of the Japanese navy. He was made admiral of the fleet in 1944.

King, Martin Luther, Jr. (1929–1968). American CIVIL RIGHTS leader. The son and grandson of black Baptist ministers in the Deep South, King was born in Atlanta, Georgia. He graduated from Morehouse College in 1948, then received

North Korean President Kim Il-sung (right) with Chinese President Li Xiannian in China (1987).

Civil rights leader Martin Luther King Jr.

a divinity degree from Crozer Theological Seminary in 1951 and a doctorate in 1955 from Boston University, where he met Coretta Scott, who became his wife. In 1954 King accepted a ministry at the Dexter Avenue Baptist Church in MONTGOMERY, Alabama. By December 1955, racial tensions there, which had focused on segregated bus seating, led him to form the Montgomery Improvement Association, the first of many organizations he formed to pursue a nonviolent resistance modeled on that led by Mahatma GANDHI in India. His leadership and his methods brought about integration of the Montgomery buses in 1956.

To broaden his civil rights activities King formed the SOUTHERN CHRISTIAN LEADERSHIP CONFERENCE in 1957. In 1959 he moved to Atlanta, where he became assistant pastor to his father at the Ebenezer Baptist Church. King first gained national fame for his civil rights demonstrations in BIRMINGHAM, Alabama, in 1963. There his followers were abused by police and King was arrested, leading to his *Letter from Birmingham Jail.* His most important demonstration was the MARCH ON WASHINGTON by 250,000 civil rights supporters on August 28, 1963, when he delived his "I Have a Dream" speech. For his nonviolent activities on behalf of civil rights, he was awarded the NOBEL PRIZE for peace in 1964.

In 1965 he led the Freedom March to SELMA, Alabama, for the cause of voting rights. The following year he brought his campaign to the North. During the later stages of his struggle, King opposed the VIETNAM WAR, arguing that it drained resources from the war on hunger and poverty. On the evening of April 4, 1968, King was assassinated in Memphis, Tennessee, where he had gone to lead a strike of sanitation workers. James Earl Ray, a white man, was later arrested and found guilty of the crime, although he has since claimed that a wider conspiracy was involved in the shooting. Despite later revelations of improprieties in King's personal life, for many people King remains one of the most revered Americans of the 20th century. His birthday, January 15, is celebrated as a legal holiday in most U.S. states.

For further reading:

Paterson, Lillie, *Martin Luther King, Jr., and the Freedom Movement*. New York: Facts On File, 1989.

Albert, Peter J. and Ronald Hoffman, eds.,*We Shall Overcome: Martin Luther King, Jr., and the Black Freedom Struggle*. New York: Pantheon Books, 1990.

Franklin, Robert Michael, *Liberating Visions: Human Fulfillment and Social Justice in African-American Thought*. Minneapolis: Fortress Press, 1990.

King, Riley B. "B.B." (1925–). American blues singer. Like so many blues singers of his era, King developed his style in childhood as a gospel singer. King and his guitar, Lucille, toured blues clubs throughout the Fifties and Sixties, without being able to cross over to a mainstream audience. In the late Sixties, younger audiences who were ready to discover the roots of rock music "discovered" B.B. King, and he began to achieve popular success with such albums as *Confessin' the Blues* (1966), *Blues Is King* (1967) and his biggest hit, *Live in Cook County Jail* (1971). The first blues singer to tour the Soviet Union, he continues to tour and receive world acclaim.

King, Stephen (Edwin) (1947–). American writer of the weird and the macabre, the most successful horror writer in the world. King was a struggling high school teacher in Maine living in a trailer when he published his first novel, *Carrie* (1974), a tale of a girl with telekinetic powers. Its modest success (13,000 copies sold in hardcover), coupled with the popular film adaptation by Brian DE PALMA in 1976 and the breakthrough publication of *Salem's Lot* in paperback that year (3,000,000 copies sold) quickly established King's preeminence in horror fiction. King is frankly derivative of the traditions in 19th-century gothic horror; and he peppers them with references to contemporary rock music and consumer culture. His diction is vulgarly realistic and his imagery is intentionally visceral and repellent, a modern extension of *grand guignol.* Some of his works, like *The Stand* (1978) and *It* (1986), are preoccupied with the cinematic effects of rapid crosscutting of scenes, shifts in points of view, alteration of time sequence, and so on; others like *The Shining* (1977) are authentic masterworks in the sheer excitation of terror; whereas others, like his best books, *The Dead Zone* (1979) and *Misery* (1987), are brooding psychological studies of psychotic states. In *Danse Macabre* (1981), a collection of essays on horror fiction, King described the writing process as a kind of "dance" in which the author searches out the private "phobic pressure points" of each reader. "We have emotional musculature just like we have physical musculature," he told an interviewer. "And our dark emotions need exercising, but society doesn't allow that. So, somebody has to take them for a walk and exercise them for you. And I guess I'm one of the guys who does that." Many of King's books have been adapted as motion pictures.

King, (William Lyon) Mackenzie (1874–1950). Canadian statesman, prime minister of CANADA (1921–30; 1935–48). Born in Kitchener, Ontario, he was the grandson of the 19th-century Canadian rebel leader William Lyon Mackenzie. King studied at the universities of Toronto and Chicago and at Harvard, becoming an expert in political economy and labor affairs. He helped to establish the Department of Labor during the Liberal administration of Wilfrid LAURIER and served as its deputy minister (1909–11) and minister (1909–11). In 1909 he also became a Liberal member of Parliament. During World War I, he did research on industrial relations for the American Rockefeller Foundation. In 1919 he succeeded Laurier as leader of the LIBERAL PARTY and became prime minister in 1921 after his party's victory in the national elections. Except for a two-month period, King served until 1930. He was the leader of the opposition during the Conservative administration of Richard Bedford BENNETT (1930–35) and was prime minister

Canadian Prime Minister Mackenzie King (right) at a press conference with U.S. President Franklin D. Roosevelt (center) and British Prime Minister Winston Churchill.

again after the Liberal victory of 1935, serving until he retired in 1948. Between the wars, King maintained an essentially isolationist position and pressed for Canadian autonomy within the BRITISH EMPIRE, while mediating between the English and French-speaking communities at home. He brought Canada into WORLD WAR II, forming a war cabinet, mobilizing public opinion in favor of the war and finally instituting conscription in 1944. Insisting upon the recognition of Canada's importance, he also maintained cooperation with Great Britain and signed joint defense agreements with the U.S. After the war, King was the head of the Canadian delegation at the 1945 San Francisco Conference that drafted the United Nations charter and at the 1946 Paris Conference.

For further reading:

Hardy, Henry H., *Mackenzie King of Canada: A Biography*. Westport, Conn.: Greenwood, 1970.

King David Hotel attack (July 22, 1946). Jewish guerrillas of the IRGUN ZVAI LEUMI organization blew up the King David Hotel, which housed the British administrative headquarters in JERUSALEM. The explosion caused 91 deaths.

King Kong. The giant ape King Kong made his first appearance in 1932, in a book of that title by Delos W. Lovelace, "novelized" from the screenplay of the forthcoming film *King Kong*, which was released in 1933. Directed by Merian C. Cooper and Ernest B. Schoedsack, the film starred Fay Wray as Ann, the woman Kong kidnaps in a variation on the beauty-and-the-beast theme. Featuring spectacular stop-motion special effects, the film was an instant sensation and is credited with saving the RKO studios from bankruptcy during the GREAT DEPRESSION. A remake of the film was made by Dino de Laurentiis in 1976, and a sequel, *King Kong Lives*, was released in 1986. Kong was also the star of two Japanese films, *King Kong vs. Godzilla* (1963) and *King Kong Escapes* (1967). An icon of popular culture, he has also been featured in a television cartoon show (1966–69), comic books and a variety of merchandise.

Kinnock, Neil (1942–). British politician. Born and educated in Wales, Kinnock worked for the Workers' Educational Association and was elected to Parliament as a Labour member in 1970 by a Welsh constituency. He served as shadow minister for education from 1979 to 1983. Despite his lack of government experience, Kinnock succeeded veteran Michael FOOT as leader of the LABOUR PARTY following the party's defeat in the 1983 general election. Originally in the left wing of the Labour Party, Kinnock was viewed as a compromise choice between the party's opposing factions and promised to follow a more moderate course. He instigated the ejection of the extreme left-wing Militant Tendency faction from parliament in 1986. Although a gifted orator, as leader of the Opposition, Kinnock proved an unequal opponent to Conservative Prime Minister Margaret THATCHER, and there

British Labour Party leader Neil Kinnock (1987).

was doubt both in and out of the party that he could lead Labour to a general election victory. Kinnock received attention in the U.S. in 1988 when Democratic presidential hopeful Joseph Biden was found to have plagiarized one of his speeches and was forced to withdraw from the campaign.

Kinsey Reports (published 1948, 1953). Research on human sexual behavior conducted by Professor Alfred Kinsey of Indiana University. Kinsey was a zoology professor who, in 1938, commenced what is regarded as the first major scientific study of the nature of human sexual preferences and patterns. The term "Kinsey Reports" refers to the two publications that summarized the findings of Kinsey and his researchers—*Sexual Behavior in the Human Male* (1948) and *Sexual Behavior in the Human Female* (1953). These books were deemed as degenerate and even as communist by MCCARTHY-era conservatives and religious fundamentalists. The basis for this furor, which led to cessation of funding for Kinsey's work by the Rockefeller Foundation and other agencies, was the statistical evidence put forward in the Kinsey Reports that indicated that human sexual behavior differed greatly from supposed established norms. For example, 37 percent of males were said to have had at some point a homosexual contact leading to orgasm. In addition, Kinsey pointed to partner insensitivity rather than biological incapability as the most frequent cause of female frigidity. At the time of his death, Kinsey was working on a book that was critical of sex laws in the U.S.. The Kinsey Reports are widely regarded as a pioneering effort toward an objective view of human sexuality. However, such notable public figures as anthropologist Margaret MEAD, theologian Reinhold NIEBUHR and critic Lionel TRILLING criticized the reports for ignoring the spiritual implications of sex.

Kinshasa. Capital city of ZAIRE; across the Zaire (Congo) River from Brazzaville, capital of Congo. It was developed as a trading center in the late 1800s by explorer Henry Stanley, who named it Leopoldville, after the Belgian king. It became capital of the BELGIAN CONGO in 1926. It was the center of the rebellion that led to independence from BELGIUM (1959). In 1966 the city was renamed after a tribal village located here before the Belgian outpost.

Kipling, Rudyard (1865–1936). British poet and author. Born in Bombay, India, Kipling was sent to England to be educated. He chronicled his unhappy childhood spent in a series of foster homes in the short story "Baa Baa, Black Sheep" (1888) and the novel *The Light That Failed* (1937). He completed his education at the United Services College in Devon. Unfit for military service because of poor eyesight, he returned to India to work as a journalist. His popular first collection of poems, *Departmental Ditties* was published in 1886; his first volume of short stories, *Plain Tales From the Hills* in 1888. Kipling continued writing prolifically and was received as a celebrity when he traveled to London in 1889. He married Caroline Balestier, with whose brother Kipling wrote the novel *The Naulahka* (1892). The Kiplings moved to Vermont where the Balestiers had property but returned to settle in England in 1896, though Kipling continued to travel throughout his life. Kipling's varied works depicted life in colonial India and reflected his conservative patriotism. *Barrack Room Ballads* (1892) includes the notable poems "Gunga Din" and "Mandalay." The poem "Recessional" celebrated Jubilee Day in 1897. *Kim* (1901), the novel considered to be his masterpiece, is an account of a boy and a Buddhist monk traveling in India. Kipling was the first English writer to receive the NOBEL PRIZE for literature, in 1907. He carried on a long correspondence with

British author Rudyard Kipling.

U.S. President Theodore ROOSEVELT and was influential in shaping Roosevelt's outlook in foreign policy. Kipling's reputation was to decline, partly due to its nationalistic jingoism—he coined the term "white man's burden"—and also because of what many considered to be its low-brow appeal. A resurgence in appreciation for his craftsmanship occurred when T.S. ELIOT edited a collection of his poetry for FABER & FABER in 1943. Later critics have also reevaluated Kipling's work and found more subtlety than he was earlier given credit for. Always popular were his works for children such as *The Jungle Book* (1894) and *Just So Stories* (1902). Other works include *Soldiers Three* (1890), *Captains Courageous* (1897) and an unfinished autobiography, *Something of Myself* (1937).

Kipnis, Alexander (1891–1978). Ukrainian-born operatic bass. Alexander Kipnis was best known for his Wagnerian roles and for his performances in Russian operas, particularly the title role in *Boris Godunov*. He was with the Chicago Civic Opera from 1923 to 1933, and sang over 100 performances at the Metropolitan Opera in New York from 1940 to 1945. He was a familiar figure in the great opera world of Europe and was also featured in numerous operatic and lieder recital recordings. His son **Igor Kipnis** (b. 1930) is a renowned harpsichordist and musicologist.

Kirchner, Ernst Ludwig (1880–1938). German painter and graphic artist, a leading exponent of German EXPRESSIONISM. At first a student of architecture, Kirchner began painting in Munich (1903–04) and Dresden (1905) and made a particular study of primitive art at the Dresden Museum of Ethnology. In 1905 he, Erich HECKEL and Karl SCHMIDT-ROTLUFF co-founded DIE BRUCKE. Influenced by the intensity of feeling and line in the paintings of Vincent Van Gogh and the intensity of color in FAUVISM, Kirchner was also shaped by Durer, Gothic woodcuts and Edvard MUNCH. His art exploits strong color contrasts and angular forms in the expressive portrayal of figures and landscapes. Moving from Dresden to Berlin in 1911, he captured the life of that city in acid-tinged portraits and street scenes. His paintings became increasingly bitter and tortured in colors that went from bright and pure in the early 1900s to dark and shadowy in works painted into the 1920s. Kirchner was also a master printmaker, producing some 2,000 powerful and often savage etchings, lithographs and, most notably, woodcuts. Drafted into the German army, he suffered an emotional breakdown in 1914 and moved to a sanatorium in Davos, Switzerland, remaining in the area for the rest of his life. Condemned by the Nazis for his "degenerate" art and in failing health, Kirchner committed suicide in 1938.

Kirgiz Soviet Socialist Republic. Constituent republic of the U.S.S.R., bounded by the Kazakh SSR, China, the Tadzhik SSR and the Uzbek SSR. The Kirghiz people resisted conscription under the czar in 1916 and then under the BOLSHEVIKS from 1917 to 1921. A famine in 1921–22 killed 500,000.

Kiribati. Republic in the western Pacific Ocean, on the equator and northeast of the Solomon Islands. Formerly known as the Gilbert Islands, the nation consists of the 16 former Gilbert islands, Ocean Island, some of the Line islands and some of the Phoenix islands. Great Britain proclaimed a protectorate over the Gilberts in 1892 and in 1915 combined them with the Ellice Islands into the Gilbert and Ellice Islands Colony. Ocean Island and some of the Line and Phoenix islands were then also included. In WORLD WAR II Japan occupied the Gilberts from 1941 to 1943. The U.S. Marines retook Tarawa atoll in a bloody battle in November 1943, while the Army regained Makin Island the same month. In 1971 the colony was given self-government, and at the start of 1976 the Ellice Islands (now TUVALU) were separated from the colony. On July 12, 1979, the Gilbert Islands and the others named above became independent as Kiribati, a member of the Commonwealth of Nations. Its inhabitants are Micronesian, and its chief exports are copra and phosphates.

Kirilenko, Andrei Pavlovich (1906–1990). Soviet politician. A long-time associate of Leonid BREZHNEV, in the 1970s Kirilenko was widely thought to be a leading candidate to succeed the Soviet leader. A member of the politburo, he retired from the body in 1982 and dropped from sight. Although the official explanation for his retirement was ill health, unofficial reports said that he had been disgraced by the defection of his son to the West.

Kirillin, Vladimir Alekseyevich (1913–). Soviet government official. A graduate of the power engineering institute, Kirillin gained membership in the COMMUNIST PARTY in 1937 and served in the Soviet army from 1941 to 1943. Kirillin's numerous posts include head of the department of science, high schools and schools (1954–55) and head of the ideologies department of the central committee (1955–63). From 1961 to 1966 Kirillin was a member of the central committee, and from 1963 to 1966 the chairman of the all-union society for the dissemination of political and scientific knowledge. In 1965 he became chairman of the Comecon committee for scientific-technological cooperation. Kirillin was decorated with various orders, medals and prizes.

Kirk, Alan Goodrich (1888–1963). U.S. Navy officer and diplomat. A graduate of the Naval Academy, Kirk served as gunnery officer aboard several ships, and was promoted to chief of staff for the commander of naval forces in Europe early in WORLD WAR II. He commanded the 1,000 ships in the INVASION OF NORMANDY, France. Admiral Kirk retired from the Navy in 1946, and served as U.S. ambassador to Belgium (1946–49), the U.S.S.R. (1949–52) and the Republic of China (1963).

Kirk, Russell (Amos) (1918–). American political writer. Kirk was one of the most eloquent writers in defense of the conservative tradition to emerge in postwar America. His first book, *The Conservative Mind* (1953), was his doctoral dissertation, but it won a wide readership by tracing a glowing intellectual tradition for CONSERVATISM that dated back to the 18th century and the English statesman Edmund Burke. Further, Kirk argued that the true basis of conservatism lay in defense of family, tradition, and community, and not in the support of big business and the free market. This latter view made Kirk a controversial figure within conservative circles. Kirk taught at Michigan State and other universities and lectured frequently throughout the country. His other books include *A Program for Conservatives* (1954) and *Confessions of a Bohemian Tory* (1963).

Kirkpatrick, Jeanne (1926–). U.S. public official. Originally a liberal Democrat, in the 1970s Kirkpatrick became a leading neoconservative and anticommunist. Her views attracted the attention of Ronald REAGAN, who appointed her U.S. ambassador to the UN (1981–85) when he took office. She criticized many UN programs as contrary to U.S. interests. She helped develop the Reagan administration's policies toward Latin America, condemning the Sandinista government in NICARAGUA and urging support for the CONTRAS. In the late 1980s Kirkpatrick was mentioned as a possible candidate for high office, but her support was limited.

Kirov, Sergei Mironovich (Kostrinov) (1886–1934). Soviet politician. He became a Bolshevik in 1905. His first task after the revolution was to establish soviet power in the Caucasus. From 1926 he was party secretary in the Leningrad area, and he became a Politburo member in 1930. Kirov gave support to STALIN but opposed Stalin's personal rule after the 17th party congress in 1934. His assassination in December 1934 began the witch-hunt that developed into the GREAT PURGE, which resulted in the judicial execution of over 100 suspected opponents of Stalin's regime.

For further reading:

Conquest, Robert, *Stalin and the Kirov Murder.* New York: Oxford University Press, 1988.

Kirst, Hans Helmut (1914–1989). German author. One of West Germany's most popular novelists, Kirst wrote a total of 46 books, many of which dealt with the experiences of soldiers in WORLD WAR II. (He himself had served in the German army throughout the war.) The English translations of his novels *The Lieutenant Must Be Mad* (1951), *Night of the Generals* (1962, filmed 1967), and the trilogy *08/15* (published in the mid-1950s) were highly popular in the U.S. and Great Britain. Critics argued, however, over whether his works were criticisms of Nazi Germany or merely adventure-thrillers with a wartime setting.

Kirstein, Lincoln (1907–). American writer and ballet director who was influential on the American and international ballet scene for over 50 years. Kirstein was responsible for bringing George BAL-

ANCHINE to the U.S. and for forming the School of American Ballet with Balanchine and E.M.M. Warburg (1934). He established the Ballet Society in 1946, from which the NEW YORK CITY BALLET (NYCB) evolved. Kirstein served as general director for NYCB from 1948 to 1991; he wrote many acclaimed ballet books, including *The New York City Ballet* (1974) and *Nijinsky Dancing* (1975). He was awarded the Medal of Freedom in 1984.

Kisangani. Congo River city in north-central ZAIRE, 750 miles northeast of KINSHASA; formerly known as Stanleyville. It was founded in 1883 on an island near its present location by Henry Morton Stanley, Anglo-American explorer and journalist who was heading an expedition for King Leopold II of Belgium. Attacked and burned by Arab slave traders, the present city dates from 1898. In the late 1950s Kisangani was the stronghold of Patrice LUMUMBA, who was the first prime minister of the Republic of the Congo, now Zaire, when it became independent in June 1960. After Lumumba was assassinated in February 1961, the city was the headquarters of Antoine Gizenga, who set up a government in competition with the central government in Kinshasa. He was put down; but in 1964, 1966 and 1967 Kisangani was again the site of unsuccessful revolts.

Kishi, Nobosuke (1896–1987). Japanese politician. Kishi was the dominant figure in pre-World War II Japanese industrial planning. During much of the war, he served as minister of commerce and industry and was responsible for economic mobilization. After the war he was arrested as a war criminal and imprisoned without trial until 1948. He began his political comeback in December 1956 and two months later became prime minister. He was forced to resign in 1960 after the passage of a revised version of the U.S.-Japan Mutual Security Treaty triggered mass protests. In retirement he continued to exercise considerable influence over the ruling Liberal Democratic Party. He was the brother of another prime minister, Eisakyu SATO, and the father-in-law of a leading prime ministerial contender, Shintaro Abe.

Kissinger, Henry (Alfred) (1923–). U.S. diplomat, foreign policy adviser and analyst and secretary of state (1973–77). Kissinger was arguably the most influential, and controversial, diplomat of his time. Born in Germany, he fled that country with his family and came to the U.S. when the Nazis came to power. Professor of government at Harvard from 1958 to 1971, he formed close ties with prominent U.S. politicians, including Nelson ROCKEFELLER, and was adviser to Richard M. NIXON during the 1968 presidential campaign. As White House national security adviser from 1969 to 1973, Kissinger played a more prominent role than the secretary of state, traveling on peace missions to the Middle East, Vietnam and southern Africa and negotiating with the U.S.S.R. in the Strategic Arms Limitation Talks (SALT). In 1971 he made a secret trip to

Henry Kissinger (1986).

the People's Republic of CHINA, paving the way for President Nixon's visit the following year and the normalization of relations between the two countries. Kissinger was also involved in negotiations to end the VIETNAM WAR. His statement just before the 1972 presidential election that "peace is at hand" helped build support for Nixon's candidacy, but Kissinger's credibility was questioned as talks—and the war—dragged on for another half-year. Kissinger was awarded the 1973 NOBEL PRIZE for peace with LE DUC THO (who refused to accept it) for concluding the PARIS PEACE ACCORD that ended the Vietnam War; the award caused much controversy.

He was appointed secretary of state in 1973, holding that office for the remainder of Nixon's presidency and throughout President Gerald FORD's administration. Kissinger practiced a conservative but pragmatic brand of diplomacy, concentrating on relations between the superpowers in terms of *realpolitik.* Although U.S. foreign policy took a different turn during the CARTER presidency, Kissinger was an influential if background figure during the REAGAN administration, in which several of his proteges served.

For further reading:

Hersh, Seymour, *The Price of Power: Kissinger in the Nixon White House.* New York: Summit Books, 1984.

Schulzinger, Robert D., *Henry Kissinger: Doctor of Diplomacy.* New York: Columbia University Press, 1989.

Kistiakowski, George Bogdan (1900–1982). Russian-born U.S. chemist. Kistiakowski emigrated to the U.S. in 1926 and worked briefly at Princeton before going to Harvard. He was named professor of chemistry at Harvard in 1937. During World War II he worked on the MANHATTAN PROJECT. As head of the Explosives Division at Los Alamos (1944–45), he developed the complicated trigger device used to detonate the first ATOMIC BOMB. After the war he was a leading member of the U.S. scientific establishment. He served as science advisor to President EISENHOWER from 1959 to 1961. Active in the movement for nuclear disarmament, he was later chairman of the Council for a Livable World and adviser to the U.S. Arms Control and Disarmament Agency.

Kitchen Debate. See Richard M. NIXON.

kitsch. Term used in design criticism to describe work of a deliberately tasteless, gross, and foolish sort. The Gillo Dorfles book of 1969, *Kitsch,* is the definitive study of the subject. It explains the obvious, popular attraction of objects and design elements that are silly, ugly, and insulting to both concepts of "high style" and serious theories of modernism. Gift and novelty shops thrive on the commercial distribution of kitsch trinkets, while kitsch themes often appear in housing, furniture, and accessories intended for the mass market. Post-modern theory continues to struggle with pop or kitsch elements in an attempt to bring about an accommodation between popular taste and serious design theory.

Kitt, Eartha (1928–). American singer. Born in Columbia, South Carolina, Kitt sang in New York and Paris before attracting widespread attention for her appearance in the 1952 Broadway revue *New Faces.* Known for the sultry sexuality of her renditions, which was considered somewhat shocking early in her career, Kitt's best-known songs include "C'est Si Bon," "Santa Baby" and "An Old-Fashioned Girl."

Kitty Hawk. Village in North Carolina, near Cape Hatteras. This otherwise obscure village became part of 20th-century history on Dec. 17, 1903, when the WRIGHT BROTHERS made the world's first successful flight in a powered heavier-than-air machine—the airplane. The Wright Brothers chose this part of the world for their glider and powered aircraft experiments because of the constant winds from the ocean; the deserted beaches and dunes were also ideal for such early aviation experiments.

Klammer, Franz (1953–). Austrian skier. Klammer is arguably the greatest downhill racer of all time. He won 22 races from 1974 to 1978, including six consecutive triumphs to best the old record held by Jean-Claude KILLY. His flying, wild run to win the downhill OLYMPIC gold in 1976 at Innsbruck in his native Austria may rank as one of the most thrilling moments in the history of any sport. Although Klammer was World Cup champion in 1977 and 1978, he was not selected to represent Austria in the 1980 Olympic games. He made a comeback in 1982–83, winning the World Cup championship once more.

Klee, Paul (1879–1940). Swiss painter. Combining sophisticated abstraction with an aura of childlike innocence, his delicate and dreamlike works are gentle monuments of 20th-century art. From a musical family, Klee was a violinist but finally decided to study art, entering the Munich Academy in 1900. He settled in Munich in 1906, became friendly with Wassily KANDINSKY and Franz MARC, and exhibited with the BLAUE REITER group. A trip to Tunisia in 1914 awakened the young artist to the possibilities of color and gave his work a new radiance. He taught at the BAUHAUS from 1922 to 1931 and at the Dusseldorf Academy from 1931 to 1933, when he was dismissed by the Nazis who considered his work degenerate. Klee defined his approach to art in his *Pedagogical Sketchbook* (1925, tr. 1964). He left Germany in 1933, returning to Switzerland where he spent the rest of his life. An extremely prolific artist, Klee created over 9,000 works—paintings, drawings and graphics—that are included in virtually all of the world's great museums. Some of his best known paintings are *The Twittering Machine* (1922, Museum of Modern Art, N.Y.C.), *Fish Magic* (1925, Philadelphia Museum of Art) and *Revolutions of the Viaducts* (1937, Kunsthall, Hamburg). Klee's works display a whimsy and fantasy, a witty personal language of signs and a poetic sense of mystery that are unique in all of modern art.

For further reading:

Braziller, George, *Paul Klee*. New York: George Braziller, 1962.

Kleiber, Erich (1890–1956). Austrian-born opera and symphonic conductor. A fierce individualist, on several occasions he clashed with repressive political regimes. He was born in Vienna. After hearing Gustav MAHLER conduct, he decided to pursue that career, and he made his debut at the German Theater in Prague in 1911. A quick succession of appointments followed—at Barmen-Elberfeld (1919–21), Duesseldorf (1921–22), Mannheim (1922–23), and the Berlin State Opera (1923). His service to the cause of new music reached its peak in these years; and he presented premieres of new works by Darius MILHAUD, Max Reger, Igor STRAVINSKY, Arnold SCHOENBERG, and Alban BERG.

His world premiere of Berg's WOZZECK in 1925 was a landmark event in the history of SERIAL MUSIC. Although not a Jew, he left Germany in 1935 protesting Nazi persecutions. He did not return until after the war and a number of guest posts in London, Prague, Amsterdam and Buenos Aires (becoming an Argentinian citizen in 1939). Dissatisfaction with the mix of art and propaganda in East Berlin led him to resign his post at the Berlin State Opera. He spent his last years conducting in London, Vienna, Cologne and Stuttgart. In his last decade he made many recordings for the Decca label, including a magnificent set of the complete symphonies of Beethoven, a composer whom he revered. Kleiber could be a difficult and tough disciplinarian. "A conductor must live in his house like a lion," he said, "with its claws deep in its prey." His son **Carlos Kleiber** (b. 1930) is also a highly acclaimed conductor.

Klein, Calvin (1942–). American fashion designer, a graduate of the Fashion Institute of Technology in New York, who has built a major national and international "name" reputation. The Calvin Klein stylistic direction shows the influence of Yves Saint Laurent but tends to have a more colorful, less subtle character. After five years as an apprentice designer with several large firms, Klein founded his own business in 1968 and built a name for apparel design that is simple, functional, and classic while at the same time recognizable and stylish. Klein designer jeans quickly became an international fad, and his name continues to make anything associated with it, such as Obsession perfume, a commercial success. He won a Coty design award in each of five consecutive years beginning in 1973.

Klemperer, Otto (1885–1973). German-born orchestra conductor, one of the last titans in the Austro-German tradition; born in Breslau and later studied in Hamburg, Frankfurt-am-Main, and in Berlin with Hans Pfitzner. The young Klemperer was encouraged in his conducting ambitions by Gustav MAHLER. After numerous conducting assignments, he settled into his first important post as director of the Kroll Opera in Berlin in the late 1920s. In addition to many standard works he also performed new operas by STRAVINSKY, SCHOENBERG and HINDEMITH. Because of his Jewish heritage, he was dismissed from the Berlin State Opera in 1933. In his subsequent travels through Austria, Switzerland and the U.S., he incurred a skull injury during a fall; and in 1939 an operation for a brain tumor left him partially paralyzed. Psychological affective disorders further impaired him at periodic intervals. And he was severely burned in a fire in 1959. But Klemperer always fought back from misfortune. He conducted the Los Angeles Philharmonic from 1935 to 1939, organized the Pittsburgh Symphony Orchestra in 1939 and became principal conductor of the Philharmonia Orchestra (later the New Philharmonia Orchestra) of London in 1959. His reputation with the Austro-German symphonic tradition of Beethoven, Brahms, Bruckner and Mahler grew. His seriousness, his imposing, monumental appearance, his big orchestral sound, his majestic (to some, laborious) tempi and his utter lack of flamboyance made him the venerated heir to musical traditions rooted in the 19th century. His recordings after 1954 on the EMI label have preserved that style and that sound for new generations.

Kliban, B(ernard) (1935–1990). American cartoonist. He was noted for his satirical drawings of fat, striped cats, who often engaged in uncatlike pursuits. His books included *Never Eat Anything Bigger Than Your Head & Other Drawings* (1975) and *Whack Your Porcupine* (1975). His cats appeared on merchandise ranging from greeting cards and calendars to bed sheets, launching an empire that reached $50 million in sales by the mid-1980s.

Klimt, Gustav (1862–1918). Austrian painter. A lifelong Viennese, he studied at Vienna's School of Decorative Art. He opened a mural studio with his brother in 1883, executing decorations at Vienna's Burgtheater and Kunsthistorisches Museum. Klimt was a cofounder of the Vienna secession, a group that rebelled against the academic art of the late 19th century, and served as its president from 1898 to 1903. The foremost exponent of *Secessionstil*, the Viennese version of ART NOUVEAU, he created works that were symbolic in theme, jewel-like in color, flatly decorative, richly patterned and rhythmically erotic. He continued to create works for public buildings, such as the ceiling murals at the University of Vienna, *Philosophy, Medicine* and *Jurisprudence* (1900–02)—whose sensual imagery caused a furor of criticism—and the mosaics for Josef HOFMANN's Palais Stoclet in Brussels (1905–09). However, his most celebrated works are his portraits and landscapes. Among his best known paintings are *The Kiss* (1907–08, Oesterreichische Galerie, Vienna, and 1909, Musee d'Art Moderne, Strasbourg) and *Hope I* (1903, National Gallery, Ottawa).

Kline, Franz (1910–1962). American painter, one of the chief figures in ABSTRACT EXPRESSIONISM. Born in Wilkes-Barre, Pennsylvania, Kline studied at Boston University (1931–35) and the Heatherley School of Fine Art in London (1937–38) before settling in New York City in 1938. A struggling painter during the 1940s, his early works were humorous sketches and realistic still lifes and city scenes. In the 1950s Kline developed the style that was to make him world-famous. In paintings such as *High Street* (1950), *Mahoning* (1956, Whitney Museum of American Art, New York City) and *Kupola* (1958) he filled huge canvases with heavy streaking black lines on a white field, developing a powerfully spare visual calligraphy that spoke of action, impulse, violence and disciplined gesture. Kline also taught at Black Mountain College (1952), Pratt Institute (1953) and the Philadelphia Museum School (1954). In the late 1950s he returned to color in large abstract works such as *Green Vertical* (1958) and *Copper and Red* (1959) that maintained much of the boldness and force of his earlier monochromatic compositions.

Klint, Kaare (1888–1954). Danish furniture designer and architect who had, as both teacher and designer, a broad influence on the development of the type of modern furniture called "Danish modern." Klint studied painting and architecture at the Copenhagen Academy. With his father P.V. Jensen Klint (1853–1930), Klint did extensive studies on human dimensions and developed storage furniture based on these studies. Beginning in 1924 he became a teacher of furniture design and craftsmanship at the Copenhagen Academy where he was also later a teacher of architecture. His teaching influenced a whole generation of Danish designers. His own work won many awards and appeared in a number of exhibitions. Klint's style was clearly modern but retained a respect for traditional values in structure and craftsmanship. His 1933 folding deck chair and knock-down Safari chair, both based on traditional models, are among his best known works.

Klyun, Ivan (1870–1942). Russian artist. He was a minor suprematist and a close friend of Kazimir MALEVICH (see SUPRE-

MATISM). His work is considered to show how the concern for ornamentation and beauty deteriorated into standard formulas after the Russian Revolution.

Knave of Diamonds. Society of painters, founded in Moscow in 1909 for exhibition purposes, by Michael LARIONOV and others. For two years the Knave of Diamonds was the leading movement of the Soviet avant-garde.

Knight, John S. (1895–1981). American publisher, founder of the Knight newspaper publishing empire. Starting with one local newspaper inherited from his father in Akron, Ohio in 1933, Knight went on to preside over Knight-Ridder Newspapers, which owned 33 daily newspapers nationwide, as well as three television stations and other subsidiaries. A fierce advocate of economic and editorial independence in journalism, he won the 1968 PULITZER PRIZE for distinguished editorial writing in his weekly "Editor's Notebook" columns.

Knipper-Chekhova, Olga Leonardovna (1870–1959). One of the most outstanding actresses of the first generation of the Moscow Art Theater. In 1901 she married Anton CHEKHOV. Knipper-Chekhova is especially remembered for her interpretation of the leading female roles of the plays of Chekhov, GORKY and Turgenev, as well as for her performance in plays by Moliere, Gogol and Griboyedov. She was awarded the Order of Lenin and twice received the Order of the Red Banner of Labor.

Knopf, Alfred A(braham) (1892–1984). American publisher, a pioneer in publishing translations of outstanding foreign authors, such as Knut HAMSUN, Franz KAFKA and Jean-Paul SARTRE, as well as in the publication of such influential American authors as Willa CATHER, John UPDIKE and H.L. MENCKEN. He founded Alfred A. Knopf, Inc., in 1915 and collaborated with assistant Blanche Wolf (who became his wife in 1916) to create a publishing house noted for high standards in the selection of titles, book design and printing quality. In 1924 he cofounded the *American Mercury* magazine with H.L. Mencken and George Jean Nathan. Though the Knopf company was sold to Random House in 1960, it has survived as a separate imprint. Knopf served as president of the company from 1918 to 1957 and as chairman of the board from 1957 to 1972. From 1972 until his death, he was chairman emeritus.

Koch, Frederick Henry (1877–1944). American dramatist and educator. A graduate of Harvard University, he joined the staff of the University of North Carolina in 1918. Considered the father of American folk drama, he founded the Carolina Playmakers. This group's playhouse became the first state-subsidized theater in America. Eleven volumes of folk plays appeared under his editorship.

Kodak. Coined brand name for the cameras developed by George EASTMAN that made photography a popular hobby through the use of his invention of roll film. With the slogan "You push the button, we do the rest," Eastman relieved the average camera user of the complexities of darkroom work. With the introduction of inexpensive box and folding cameras, Kodak quickly became synonymous with camera. On this basis the Eastman Kodak Company has become a major American and international corporation producing a vast variety of photographic and related and unrelated products.

Kodaly, Zoltan (1882–1967). Hungarian composer. Educated at the Budapest Hochschule, Kodaly later taught composition there and became its assistant director in 1919. As a lecturer at the University of Budapest (1931–33), a private music teacher and the author of books on musical pedagogy, he did much to improve the teaching of music in Hungary and introduced the "Kodaly Method" to the world. Second only to Bela BARTOK as Hungary's preeminent modern composer, like Bartok he was an avid collector of folk music and collaborated with his fellow-composer in its study. The melodies, rhythms and formal structure of this music is evident in his music, which is also strongly romantic in style. In addition to his most popular work, the opera (1926) and orchestral suite (1927) *Hary Janos,* Kodaly composed a symphony, an orchestral concerto, piano works, chamber music, songs, *Missa Brevis* (1945) and other choral works, theatrical music and many other works.

Kodama, Yoshio (1911–1984). Wealthy right-wing Japanese powerbroker who influenced major Japanese political figures. Kodama was the first person indicted by Japanese authorities in the LOCKHEED SCANDAL (1976). His conviction and prison sentence were being appealed at the time of his death.

Koestler, Arthur (1905–1983). Anglo-German author and journalist. Born in Budapest, Koestler was educated at the University of Vienna. He was a member of the German Communist Party from 1932 to 1938 and worked as a foreign correspondent. While reporting the SPANISH CIVIL WAR, Koestler was arrested and imprisoned under FRANCO, and in 1940 was arrested and interned under the VICHY government. After his release he moved to England and wrote his first book in English, *The Scum of the Earth* (1941), an autobiography. His best known work, DARKNESS AT NOON (1940), is a novel evidencing his rejection of COMMUNISM and TOTALITARIANISM, themes he elaborated on in his contributions to *The God That Failed: Six Studies in Communism* (1950). Koestler's later works, which include *The Roots of Coincidence* (1972), evidence his interest in philosophy and parapsychology. A lifelong advocate of euthanasia, Koestler, ill with leukemia and Parkinson's Disease, took his own life with a drug overdose. Other works include the political novels *Arrival and Departure* (1943) and *Thieves in the Night* (1946), and the nonfiction *The Trail of the Dinosaur and Other Essays* (1955) and *The Act of Creation* (1964).

Koffka, Kurt (1886–1941). German psychologist. Koffka, along with Wolfgang KOHLER and Max WERTHEIMER, was one of the key founders, in 1912, of GESTALT PSYCHOLOGY. The Gestalt school emphasized that human learning and perception was based upon the relatively rapid recognition and integration of structured wholes, as opposed to an instance-by-instance slow assemblage of isolated data. Gestalt psychology had a major influence on subsequent thinking in such diverse fields as psychotherapy, art criticism and aesthetics, and educational theory. Koffka taught at the University of Giessen from 1911 to 1924 before coming to America, where he served as a professor at Smith College from 1927 to 1941. His major works are *The Growth of the Mind* (1921) and *Principles of Gestalt Psychology* (1935).

Kogan, Leonid (Borisovich) (1924–1982). Soviet violinist. A graduate of the Moscow State Conservatory (1948), Kogan won first prize at the prestigious Queen Elizabeth International Competition in Brussels in 1951. He was acclaimed for his technical mastery and classical precision. He was a professor at the Moscow State Conservatory and performed frequently in the U.S.S.R. as well as Western Europe and the U.S.

Kohima. Battle site and capital of India's Nagaland state, 139 mi E of Shilleng. In March-June 1944 the Japanese took it, but the victory of Anglo-Indian forces here on June 30, 1944 stemmed the Japanese advance into India.

Kohl, Helmut (1930–). Chancellor of WEST GERMANY (1982–90) and of reunited GERMANY (1990–). Born in Ludwigshafen in the German Rhineland, Kohl attended the University of Frankfurt and earned his doctorate in political science from the University of Heidelberg. He joined the conservative CHRISTIAN DEMOCRATIC UNION and was elected to the Ludwigshafen city council. He went on to win a series of political posts that he was the youngest person ever to hold. Elected to the state parliament of the Rhineland Palatinate in 1959, he became minister-president of that state in 1969, and in 1973 was chosen as national chairman of the CDU. Elected to the Bundestag (national parliament) in 1976, Kohl served as leader of the opposition (1976–82) during the government of Helmut SCHMIDT.

Kohl was elected prime minster in 1982, forming a coalition government with the support of the Free Democrats. In his foreign policy, he was both pro-European and pro-American, keeping West Germany in the forefront of the EUROPEAN ECONOMIC COMMUNITY and NATO. Domestically, he followed a conservative economic policy favoring free enterprise, in contrast to the Social Democrats' emphasis on social programs. With the fall of the communist government of EAST GERMANY (1989–90), Kohl pushed for a quick reunification of the two Germanys under the existing West German constitution. In the first nationwide elections in the new, unified Germany (Dec. 2, 1990), he won an easy victory over his Social

West German Chancellor Helmut Kohl takes the oath of office for his third term (1987).

Democratic opponent, thus becoming the first chancellor of all Germany in more than 45 years. Kohl's critics have charged that he is unintellectual and unimaginative, but he has proven an astute, pragmatic and popular politician and a leading figure in the Western alliance.

Kohler, Wolfgang (1887–1967). German psychologist. Kohler, along with Kurt KOFFKA and Max WERTHEIMER, was one of the key founders, in 1912, of GESTALT PSYCHOLOGY. The Gestalt school emphasized that human learning and perception was based upon the relatively rapid recognition and integration of structured wholes, as opposed to an instance-by-instance slow assemblage of isolated data. Gestalt psychology had a major influence on subsequent thinking in such diverse fields as psychotherapy, art criticism and aesthetics, and educational theory. Kohler was the director of the Prussian Academy of Sciences in the Canary Islands from 1913 to 1920. His research on the learning capabilities of chimpanzees during this period was summarized in *The Mentality of Apes* (1917). Kohler fled Nazi GERMANY shortly after the rise of HITLER and came to the U.S. where he taught at Swarthmore College from 1935 to 1955. Other major works by Kohler include *Gestalt Psychology* (1929), *Dynamics in Psychology* (1940), and *The Task of Gestalt Psychology* (1969).

Kokkinaki, Vladimir (1904–1985). Soviet aviator. During the pre-jet era Kokkinaki held a number of aviation records, including the world altitude record. He made world headlines in 1939 when, on what was supposed to be the first nonstop flight from Moscow to New York, he ended up on Miscou Island in New Brunswick, Canada. The flight came to be known as "Moscow-Miscou."

Kokoschka, Oskar (1886–1980). Austrian painter, art theorist and dramatist. Kokoschka was a major figure in the Expressionist art movement. He became known for his psychologically intense canvases that evoked emotional depth through the use of uneven, nervous lines, formal distortion and jarring color contrasts. Kokoschka articulated his Expressionistic art theories in an influential essay, *On the Nature of Visions* (1912). He was influenced by the abstract art theories of Wassily KANDINSKY but continued to maintain that the objects and appearances of the real world were fundamental to painting. *Schriften 1907–1955* (1956) is a major collection of his writings on art.

Kokovtsov, Count Vladimir Nikolayevich (1853–1942). Russian politician. He served as state secretary (1902) and minister of finance (1906). In 1911 he became prime minister following the death of STOLYPIN but was dismissed in 1914 for taking a stand against corruption, especially as personified by RASPUTIN, and died in exile in Paris.

Kolbe, Georg (1877–1947). German sculptor. Beginning as a painter, Kolbe met Auguste Rodin and turned to sculpture, continuing to be influenced by Rodin's style throughout his career. His impressionist nudes, mostly executed in bronze during the 1920s, are his most highly regarded works. Many of them, such as *Standing Nude* (1926, Walker Art Center, Minneapolis), can be found in American collections. During the Nazi period, Kolbe turned to the creation of monumental figures of soldiers and athletes that correspond to Aryan ideals of masculinity.

Kolbe, Maksymilian Maria (1894–1941). Polish priest and saint. Kolbe was ordained in 1918. During the early 1930s he was a missionary in India and Japan, then returned to Poland where he founded a religious community near Warsaw. Early in WORLD WAR II, after the German invasion of POLAND (1939), Kolbe was arrested by the Nazis and eventually sent to AUSCHWITZ. There, in 1941, Kolbe sacrificed his life by taking the place of a fellow prisoner, Franciszek Gajowniczek, who was one of 10 persons randomly chosen to die of starvation; Gajowniczek survived the war and lived into his 80s. In 1982 Pope JOHN PAUL II elevated Kolbe to sainthood.

Kolchak, Admiral Alexander Vasilyevich (1873–1920). Russian naval commander and explorer; served with distinction in the RUSSO-JAPANESE WAR and with the Black Sea fleet during WORLD WAR I. Kolchak was leader of the anti-Bolshevik troops in Siberia (1918–20). He overthrew the Ufa Directory and was recognized by anti-Bolshevik organizations as representing a provisional government. Kolchak's early successes were followed by withdrawals; after the fall of Omsk in 1919 he retreated to Irkutsk and was taken prisoner, tried and executed.

Kollek, Teddy (1911–). Israeli politician, mayor of JERUSALEM (1965–). Kollek was born near Budapest, was raised in Vienna and immigrated to Palestine in 1936. He worked as intelligence liaison officer for the HAGANAH until 1945 and headed Haganah's New York office from 1947 to 1948 as chief arms buyer. He served as Israeli minister plenipotentiary in Washington (1951–52) and as director-general of the prime minister's office (1952–64). Kollek was chairman of the Israeli Tourist Board from 1956 to 1965 and is a founder and chairman of Jerusalem's Israel Museum. He was elected mayor of West Jerusalem in 1965 as the candidate of the Rafi Party with the support of Herut and the religious parties—defeating the Labor Party incumbent. Since 1967 Kollek has also administered East Jerusalem in place of Jordanian Mayor Rouhi al-Khatib. Kollek is renowned for his ability to reach compromises that enable the Israeli government to carry out its plans for the city without exacerbating Israeli-Palestinian tensions. Thus, in 1968, he ordered the erection of a memorial to the Arab war dead in East Jerusalem, in exchange for the Muslim authorities' unofficial consent to shifting all the Muslim graves in the city, which obstructed Israel's construction projects. In recent years Kollek has clashed with Jerusalem's Orthodox Jews, who have held mass demonstrations against him for extending secular leisure facilities and allowing a Mormon university to be built in the city.

Kollontay, Alexandra Mikhailovna (1872–1952). Russian politician and propagator of "free love." A BOLSHEVIK in the 1890s, Kollontay subsequently became a MENSHEVIK "liquidationist." After 1903, she lived in exile and joined the International Bureau of Women Socialists. From 1915 Kollontay assisted LENIN, and after her return to Russia in February 1917 she became a member of the Bolshevik central committee. Her interest in women's affairs found its outlet in 1920–21 when she was head of the women's department of the central committee. In 1921–22 she was secretary of the International Women's Secretariat of the COMINTERN. She continued her political career as a diplomat in Norway (1923–26 and 1927–30), Mexico (1926–27) and Sweden (1930–45). She developed the Bogdanovist approach to the question of relations between the sexes, and advanced the "winged eros theory," in which individuals in a socialist society should be free to associate with different persons of the opposite sex. Although Lenin disapproved, this theory was popular with others, since by making the family appear an outmoded institution, family ties were weakened. Her works include *The Workers' Opposition in Russia* (1923) and *Free Love* (1932).

Kollsman, Paul (1900–1982). American aeronautical engineer. Kollsman revolutionized AVIATION in the late 1920s when he invented the altimeter, which measures a plane's altitude while in flight.

Kollwitz, Kathe (Schmidt) (1867–1945). German graphic artist and sculptor. A resident of BERLIN, she was a socialist and pacifist whose themes were strongly political and social: poverty, war, human suffering and death. Her powerfully compassionate images were first recognized in her etching and lithograph illustrations based on Gerhardt HAUPTMANN's *The Weavers' Uprising* (1895–98). Kollwitz's other print series include the woodcuts in *War* (1902–08) and *Proletariat* (1925). She also is recognized for her portrayals of mothers and children and for her self-portraits. As a sculptor, she is particularly noted for her war memorial in the Rogevelt Military Cemetery in Belgium. Kollwitz was the director of the graphic arts department at the Berlin Academy in the early 1930s, but was dismissed when the Nazis came to power. Evacuated from Berlin in 1943, she settled in a German mountain village, where she died.

Kolmogorov, Andrei Nikolayevich (1903–). Soviet mathematician. From 1931 he has been a professor at Moscow University and, from 1939, a member of the Academy of Sciences. Kolmogorov is a leading international authority on the theory of probability, having put forward the widely accepted axiomatic theory, and is an authority on mathematical logic. He is also interested in cybernetics.

Komarov, Vladimir M. (1927–1967). Soviet cosmonaut. The first person to die during a space mission, Komarov plunged to his death on April 24, 1967, when the reentry parachute of his Soyuz 1 space capsule failed to deploy properly. Chosen for his skill to pilot the first manned flight of the new spacecraft, the Soviet cosmonaut had previously piloted Voskhod 1 on October 12–13, 1964, with design engineer Konstantin Feoktistov and aerospace physician Boris Yegorov aboard. His tragic death caused a delay in further SOYUZ flights for more than a year while an investigation ensued. Komarov graduated with honors from the Soviet Air Force secondary school in 1942 and was selected for cosmonaut training in 1960. A skilled parachutist who had made over 77 jumps, Komarov had once said "whoever has flown once, whoever has piloted an airplane once, will never want to part with either an aircraft or the sky."

Komenda, Erwin (1904–1966). German automotive engineer responsible for the body design of a number of famous, classic cars. Komenda worked for Daimler-Benz before joining PORSCHE in Stuttgart in the 1930s. He was the designer of the original VOLKSWAGEN Beetle, probably one of the the most widely recognized automotive designs ever developed—however controversial. His design for the 1949 Porsche, a somewhat plump and bulging streamlined form, was developed through study of aerodynamics rather than through aesthetic concerns. Komenda continued to develop Porsche body designs through the model 911 of 1963. Many critics would argue that the Porsche design has not been of equal quality since that time.

Komsomol [All-Union Leninist Communist Union of Youth]. A Soviet youth organization attached to and founded by the COMMUNIST PARTY in 1918, it now caters to the 14–28 age range. The Komsomol has worked closely with the party; Komsomol members participated in the RUSSIAN CIVIL WAR, collectivization and industrialization, and recently more than 70% of party recruits have come from the Komsomol. Komsomol members are encouraged to play a full part in sociopolitical life; membership and service also enhance employment and further education prospects.

Komsomolsk. Town situated 165 miles northeast of Khabarovsk on the Amur River. It was founded in 1932 by the KOMSOMOL, the communist youth movement. It has developed into a center for shipbuilding and sawmilling. Manufactures include steel, chemicals, wood pulp and paper. Population (1981): 274,000.

Konchalovsky, Peter (1876–1956). Russian painter. Expelled from Moscow College in 1909 for leftism, Konchalovsky exhibited paintings in the first KNAVE OF DIAMONDS exhibition. His *Portrait of Georgy Yakulov* is reminiscent of MATISSE's style, although later Konchalovsky was to be more influenced by Cezanne, in that his former predilection for color was replaced by a monochromatic palette.

Kondrashin, Kiril (1914–1981). Soviet-born symphony conductor. Kondrashin studied at the Moscow Conservatory (1931–36) and was later permanent conductor at the Bolshoi Theater (1943–56). He conducted for the American pianist Van CLIBURN at the 1958 Tchaikovsky Piano Competition in Moscow, and subsequently won acclaim in the West when he accompanied Cliburn on his triumphant return to America. In 1960 he was appointed music director of the Moscow Philharmonic and helped revitalize it. Feeling that his artistic freedom was being restricted, he defected to the West in 1978 and settled in Amsterdam.

Kondratenko, Roman Isidorovich (1857–1904). General in the Russian army who fought heroically in the defense of Port Arthur in 1904. Prior to Port Arthur, Kondratenko commanded the Seventh East-Siberian Infantry. Once at Port Arthur, he greatly increased its fortifications. (See also RUSSO-JAPANESE WAR.)

Koo, V(i) K(yun) Wellington (1887–1985). Chinese diplomat. Koo's career in international relations spanned more than 50 years. He was chairman of CHINA's delegation to the 1919 PARIS PEACE CONFERENCE and delegate to the LEAGUE OF NATIONS. During the 1920s he was briefly China's foreign minister and prime minister. During WORLD WAR II he was China's ambassador to the U.K. and afterwards was Nationalist China's ambassador in Washington. In 1945 he was acting chairman of the Chinese delegation at the San Francisco conference that created the UNITED NATIONS. A judge at the International Court of Justice at the Hague from 1957 to 1967, he was also the court's vice-president (1964–67). For many years a senior advisor to CHIANG KAI-SHEK, he continued as senior advisor to the president of the Republic of China in the U.S. after Chiang's death in 1975.

Kopelev, Lev Zinovyevich (1912–). Soviet author, critic, translator and literary historian. Graduating from the Moscow Foreign Language Institute in 1938, Kopelev pursued his studies before serving in World War II. He was expelled from the party in 1945 and sentenced to 10 years' imprisonment and five years' exile, but was released prematurely and rehabilitated. However, Kopelev was criticized for his role in the Human Rights Movement and expelled from the Writer's Union in 1965. His publications include *The Heart Is Always on the Left* (1960), *Myths and Truths of the American South* (1958) and *To Be Preserved Forever* (1976).

Korbut, Olga Valentinovna (1956–). Soviet gymnast. Korbut captivated the sports world with her Olympic performances. In the 1972 Munich games, she won three gold medals and a silver, and became the first person ever to do a backwards somersault on the uneven parallel bars. She is perhaps best remembered for her charm as well as her athleticism, as she broke free of the stereotype of the stolid, unemotional Soviet athlete, working the crowd and the camera with her petite charm, dazzling smile and innovative choreography. In 1976, a more grown-up Olga was able to capture only one individual medal, a silver on the balance beam, as gymnastics' next doll-like star, the unsmiling Nadia COMANECI, had already taken center stage. Korbut lives in the U.S., where she teaches gymnastics and devotes much of her time to raising funds for victims of the CHERNOBYL nuclear disaster.

Korchnoi, Victor (1931–). Soviet chess player. He was Soviet champion in 1960, 1962 and 1964 and is an international grandmaster. He left the U.S.S.R. in 1976.

Korda, Sir Alexander (1893–1956). Hungarian-born film director and producer. Korda made films in Bonn, Vienna, and HOLLYWOOD in the 1920s but achieved his greatest fame—as well as knighthood—for his work in Britain in the 1930s and 1940s. Korda was a major factor in bringing worldwide recognition to the British film industry through his direction of lushly produced and vividly acted historical epics such as *The Private Life of Henry VIII* (1933) and *Rembrandt* (1936), both of which starred Charles LAUGHTON in the title role. In subsequent decades, Korda turned his primary attention to producing films such as *Sinbad the Sailor* (1947), featuring Douglas Fairbanks, Jr., *The Third Man* (1949), directed by Sir Carol REED, and *Richard III* (1955), the Shakespearean adaptation by Sir Laurence OLIVIER.

Korea (pre-1953). Korea, a peninsula in northeast Asia, covers an area of 84,543 square miles. In 1904 it was conquered by Japan and in 1910 became a Japanese colony. After World War II the Allies partitioned Korea, with territory north of the 38th parallel occupied by the Soviet Union and territory south of the line occupied by American forces. By 1948 the COLD WAR had destroyed prospects for reunification of Korea, and the division of the country into the Democratic People's Republic in the north and the Republic of Korea in the south was formalized. Withdrawal of foreign troops brought armed conflict between the two states in 1948–49, which led to war in July 1950 when North Korean forces began a massive invasion of South Korea. UNITED NATIONS armies, predominantly composed of U.S. personnel, pushed the North Koreans back. Eventually, following a massive intervention by Chinese troops, the frontline was stabilized near the 38th parallel, and an armistice was signed on July 27, 1953. (For history after 1953, see separate

Maps showing the north and south boundaries of the demarcation zone are initialed during the Panmunjom cease-fire talks (Oct. 11, 1951).

entries for NORTH KOREA and SOUTH KOREA.)

For further reading:

Rees, Davis, *A Short History of Modern Korea*. New York: Hippocrene Books, 1988.

Koreagate (1977). Political scandal involving illegal South Korean influence peddling and bribery on Capitol Hill. House and Senate Ethics Committee investigations revealed that a number of congressmen had accepted gifts and contributions from Tongsun Park, a South Korean rice trader and influence peddler. The funds allegedly were paid in return for votes in favor of U.S. aid and the continuing presence of U.S. troops in South Korea. The investigations led to the indictment of Congressmen Hanna (California) and Passman (Louisiana), although only Hanna was convicted of taking bribes. A number of other congressmen were censured, and all charges were dropped against Tongsun Park, who testified at the hearings and cooperated with investigators.

Korean War (1950–53). In order to disarm Japanese forces that had occupied KOREA since 1904, the victorious Allies at the end of WORLD WAR II established the 38th parallel as a "temporary" dividing line between Soviet-occupied NORTH KOREA and

Members of an American convoy stop to rest during the frigid Korean winter.

U.S.-occupied SOUTH KOREA; later efforts by the UNITED NATIONS to reunite the country failed. On June 25, 1950, North Korean troops suddenly and without warning invaded South Korea; within two months they had pushed south almost to the tip of the Korean Peninsula, where South Korean defenses were thrown up in a perimeter around Pusan. Two days after the invasion, the UN had called on its members to help South Korea, and 15 did so. The international force was under the command of U.S. General Douglas MACARTHUR, who planned and executed a successful amphibious landing behind the lines at the Yellow Sea port of INCHON (September 15, 1950) and cut enemy supply routes. The North Koreans were driven northward and eventually back to the Yalu River (November 24, 1950), the boundary between CHINA and North Korea. UN forces, in two columns on each side of Korea's central mountain spine, planned to reunite Korea under southern control. But the plan was never realized because, on November 26, 1950, a large Communist Chinese army invaded the north in support of the North Koreans and helped them drive the UN forces south after much bitter fighting.

By January 1, 1951, a North Korean-Chinese army of about 485,000 men had forced MacArthur's 365,000 UN troops back to the 38th parallel. The South Korean capital of SEOUL fell into enemy hands, but a counteroffensive by UN forces retook the city on March 14, 1951. Both sides began a "talking war" to reach an accord; negotiations dragged on while fighting continued intermittently around the dividing line. MacArthur publicly advocated attacking and bombing Chinese bases in Manchuria, contrary to UN and American orders. On April 11, 1951, U.S. President Harry S. TRUMAN summarily dismissed MacArthur from command of UN and American forces in the Far East and appointed General Matthew B. RIDGWAY in his place. Offensives and counteroffensives were launched by both sides, which suffered heavy casualties.

Ridgway's truce negotiations, which hinged largely on the repatriation of prisoners, sick and wounded, broke down in October 1952; the UN forces had taken over 70,000 prisoners, and UN negotiators insisted that they be allowed to choose whether to return to the north or to stay in the south. The latter view ultimately prevailed, and three out of four prisoners remained in South Korea (21 American prisoners elected to stay with the communists). In April 1953, peace talks resumed and led to the signing of an armistice at PANMUNJOM on July 27, 1953; but no formal peace treaty has ever been concluded.

For further reading:

Blair, Clay, *The Forgotten War: America in Korea, 1950–1953.* New York: Random House, 1987.

Summers, Harry G., Jr., *Korean War Almanac.* New York: Facts On File, 1990.

Korngold, Erich Wolfgang (1897–1957). Celebrated symphonic, opera and motion picture composer. When Austrian-born Korngold arrived in HOLLYWOOD in 1934, he had already written operas and ballets as a teenager, collaborated with impresario Max REINHARDT on several Johann Strauss vehicles, and been acclaimed a "genius" and a "second Mozart" by Gustav MAHLER and Richard STRAUSS. It was at Reinhardt's invitation in 1935 that Korngold scored his first film for WARNER BROS., *A Midsummer Night's Dream.* In his subsequent 12 years in Hollywood he wrote 18 scores of a consistently high quality and achieved the enviable status of highest paid composer in the business. His greatest wish, however, was to return to the classical music world in Europe after World War II. Sadly, productions in his beloved Vienna of his most famous operas, *The Dead City* and *Die Kathrin,* were unsuccessful, and he had to return to Hollywood. His lasting legacy must surely be his film music. Particularly memorable is the brassy splendor of *King's Row* (1942), the dashing bravado of *The Adventures of Robin Hood* (1938) and *The Sea Hawk* (1940) and the lush sentiment of *The Constant Nymph* (1943). When accused by a film producer that his music had degenerated in quality over the years, Korngold snapped, "When I first came here, I couldn't understand the dialogue—now I can." Upon his death in Hollywood of a heart attack, a black flag—the traditional Austrian mark of mourning—appeared over the Vienna Opera House.

For further reading:

Thomas, Tony, *Music for the Movies.* Cranbury, N.J.: A.S. Barnes and Co., 1977.

Kornilov, General Lavr Georgevich (1870–1918). Russian soldier. Kornilov served in the RUSSO-JAPANESE WAR (1904–05) and in WORLD WAR I. He was captured by the Germans but made a spectacular escape. He was Petrograd military district commander in 1917 and was responsible for the arrest of NICHOLAS II and his family. As commander in chief of all Russian forces in August 1917, he believed that the provisional government was incapable of dealing with any threat from the BOLSHEVIKS. Mistakenly believing that Alexander KERENSKY was in agreement, he organized his troops to march on Petrograd but was arrested on Kerensky's orders. This action strengthened the Bolsheviks, and after the fall of Kerensky, Kornilov escaped to join the anti-Bolshevik forces of Anton DENIKIN on the Don, where he was killed in action.

Kornilov's Revolt (1917). Conservative Russian generals, backed by Alexander F. KERENSKY who had replaced Prince LVOV as premier in the provisional government, decided to form a military dictatorship to end the increasing anarchy and lack of army discipline after the FEBRUARY REVOLUTION. When Kerensky realized that General Lavr G. KORNILOV, whom he had appointed army commander in chief, aspired to become sole dictator, he declared him a traitor and dismissed him. In response, Kornilov dispatched his Cossack troops to Petrograd (now Leningrad), hoping to reform the soviet (revolutionary council) and the provisional government along more conservative lines. Kerensky withdrew his support for a rightist military takeover and sought help from the soviets' central committee and leftist forces. Workers, armed by the Bolsheviks and urged to resist Kornilov's threat to their revolution, persuaded the Cossacks to defect, and the counterrevolution collapsed after five days (September 9–14, 1917). Kornilov was arrested and jailed; he escaped from Petrograd after the BOLSHEVIK REVOLUTION, also called the October Revolution. (See also RUSSIAN REVOLUTION.)

Korovin, Konstant (1861–1939). Russian painter. Korovin is considered by many to be the first Russian artist to be influenced strongly by the impressionists, whose work he saw in Paris in 1885. Korovin's transposition of French Impressionist ideas brought about a complete

UN forces, withdrawing from the North Korean capital of Pyongyang, cross the 38th parallel (1950).

change in theatrical design in Russia. Appointed professor of the Moscow College in 1901, he supervised the work of almost all the avant-garde of the first decade of the 20th century.

Kosice incident. Bombing of the historic Slovakian city of Kosice in June 1941. It was assumed that the bombing had been carried out by Soviet aircraft, and the incident caused Hungary (Kosice was Hungarian from 1938 to 1944 and was called Kassa) to declare war on the U.S.S.R. The Soviet authorities subsequently denied that they had been responsible for the raid and maintained that it had been planned and executed by the Germans, who wished Hungary to join them in the Nazis' Russian campaign.

Kosinski, Jerzy (Nikodem) (1933–91). Polish-American novelist. Kosinski's impactful first novel, *Painted Bird* (1965), is a semiautobiographical account of his childhood in war-time Poland, when orphaned and homeless, he survived as he could. The book was published just eight years after he arrived in the U.S. having tricked the Polish authorities to emigrate. His next novel, *Steps* (1968), won the National Book Award in 1969. His work is often graphically brutal and violent. In 1982 Kosinski found himself at the center of controversy when *The Village Voice* published an article claiming that his books were written largely by assistants and secretaries. Kosinski denied the charges, and various members of the publishing community lined up on both sides. Other novels include *Being There* (1971, filmed 1979), *Pinball* (1982) and *The Hermit of 69th Street* (1988). Early in his career Kosinski also wrote anti-Communist nonfiction under the pseudonym Joseph Novak.

Kosygin, Alexei (1904–1980). Soviet politician, chairman (prime minister) of the Council of Ministers of the U.S.S.R. (1964–80). A member of the Central Committee of the COMMUNIST PARTY of the Soviet Union in 1939, Kosygin was minister for economic planning in 1956–57, rising to chairman of the state economic planning commission and first deputy prime minister in 1960. A leading figure in the ouster of Soviet leader Nikita KHRUSHCHEV in 1964, he succeeded Khrushchev as prime minister. He collaborated closely with Leonid BREZHNEV, but the latter became increasingly dominant. Kosygin partially attained his objective of decentralizing the control of industry and agriculture, but his hopes of producing more consumer goods remained largely unfulfilled. Ill health forced his resignation in 1980, and he died a few weeks later.

Koufax, Sandy (1935–). American baseball player. Widely considered one of the greatest pitchers in the history of baseball, Koufax pitched in 397 games from 1955 to 1966, all with the Brooklyn and Los Angeles Dodgers. A left-hander, in his early years in the game his pitching was often wild, but in the 1960s he mastered his overpowering fastball and virtually unhittable curve. During his career he pitched four no-hitters, including a perfect game. He struck out 2,396 batters

Los Angeles Dodger Sandy Koufax sets a new record in the 1963 World Series against the New York Yankees, striking out 15 batters.

in 2,325 innings. In 1963, when he led to Dodgers to a memorable World Series victory over the New York Yankees, he was named the National League's Most Valuable Player. His career record was 165 wins and 87 loses with an earned run average of 2.76. Koufax's career was cut short by arthritis. In 1972, at the age of 36, Koufax became the youngest person ever elected to the Baseball Hall of Fame.

Koussevitzky, Serge (1874–1951). Russian-born orchestra conductor and leader of the Boston Symphony Orchestra. In his time he was the most important and arguably the greatest of all Russian conductors. Born at Tver, near Moscow, in his youth he became a widely known double bass performer at the Moscow Philharmonic Society. He studied conducting at the Berlin School of Music, traveled extensively through Russia with his own orchestra and founded a Moscow publishing house, Editions Russes de Musique, to promote new music by STRAVINSKY, SCRIABIN, and PROKOFIEV. In 1920 he and his wife left Russia after the revolution. After a notable series of "Concerts Koussevitzky" in Paris, he replaced Pierre MONTEUX as conductor of the Boston Symphony Orchestra. There, despite poor relations with some of the players, notoriety as a bad score reader, reluctance to perform operas and other problems, Koussevitzky elevated the Boston Symphony to unquestioned stature as one of the greatest orchestras in the world. For 25 years he was one of the "Big Three" American conductors, along with Arturo TOSCANINI and Leopold STOKOWSKI. Certainly no conductor of his time meant more to American musical development. He sponsored new music by Aaron COPLAND, Walter PISTON, William SCHUMAN, and Roy HARRIS, for example; he took over the Berkshire Music Festival in Tanglewood, Mass., in 1937 and created a music school there in 1940. He led an acclaimed conducting class from which emerged such figures as Leonard BERNSTEIN. His notable series of RCA recordings still convey his unique nervous energy and glow, the unique lyric sheen of his RAVEL and DEBUSSY scores and—above all—unparalleled interpretations of the Russian masters.

Kovacs, Ernie (1919–1962). Zany American television personality, program host, writer, and movie actor, credited with many innovations in video programming. Kovacs was born in Trenton, New Jersey, of Hungarian immigrant parents. His professional career, which spanned little more than the decade of the 1950s, began with local television shows in Philadelphia in 1950, continued nationally on the CBS, NBC, Dumont, and ABC networks, and extended briefly into movie acting in HOLLYWOOD. He is best remembered for the series of Kovacs Specials, on ABC in 1961. By contrast with such other early television performers as Steve ALLEN and Sid CAESAR, who were still working essentially in a vaudeville tradition, Kovacs was defining the video medium itself, anticipating later video artists like Nam June Paix. He devised all manner of video chicanery from the very *effects* of the medium—the line-scan pattern, the "key" effects of camera switching and mats, picture compression and polarity reversals. He changed the nature of the television *event* as well. His first program, "3 to Get Ready" (1950), was the first morning talk show of its kind, defining television as an *audience-bound* event. He broke the medium's "fourth wall" for the first time, plunging beyond the studio set to the control room, outside corridors, the firescapes, and into the audience. His quick, pungent sketches, sudden noises, and satiric blackouts predated the formats of SATURDAY NIGHT LIVE and LAUGH-IN by a generation. An innovator, yes, but according to critic Jeff Greenfield, television's great subversive at the same time. Since his untimely death in a car crash in 1962, his work has been revived in tributes on public television in 1977 and at the Museum of Broadcasting in 1986. "Erratic," is the word he used to describe himself in his autobiographical novel, *Zoomar* (1957). "His comedy is too extreme and too frequently he gets his punch line from the grisly side of life."

Kozintsev, Grigory Mikhailovich (1905–1973). Soviet film director and script writer. Kozintsev began his career in film in 1920 in Kiev. In 1924, he was the director of the Lenfilm Studio in Leningrad. One of his best-known works is the *Maksim Trilogy*, which he produced at Trauberg. During World War II Kozintsev worked in the theater and produced *King Lear* (1941) and *Othello* (1943).

Kraft, Christopher C., Jr. (1924–). U.S. flight director. The most frequently heard voice during the early years of the U.S. space program, Chris Kraft was flight director on all the Project MERCURY flights and most of the GEMINI missions. His was the responsibility for controlling each mission from the ground, and he decided ultimately whether to launch or not and what to do if things went awry. Kraft began working for NACA in 1945, and in 1958 he became one of the original members of the space task group charged with developing the Mercury program. He was responsible for much of the mission and flight-control development and the design of the Mission Control Center at what is now the JOHNSON SPACE CENTER. Kraft also served as director of flight operations and became director of JSC in 1972, retiring in August 1982. (See also NASA.)

Krag, Jens Otto (1914–1978). Prime minister of DENMARK (1962–68; 1971–72). A Social Democrat, Krag led his country into the EUROPEAN ECONOMIC COMMUNITY (EEC) and resigned from office immediately after a referendum approved the step.

Kragujevac [Kragujevats]. City 60 miles south of BELGRADE, Yugoslavia. It has long been a stronghold of Serbian nationalism (see SERBIA). During WORLD WAR II it was occupied by the Germans, who exterminated 7,000 Serbian men and boys there in 1941

Kramer, Jack (1921–). American tennis player. Kramer won the U.S. National Doubles title while still a teenager (1940); he won again in 1941 and 1943. In 1946–47 he lead the U.S. Davis Cup team to victory. He won both the U.S. singles and doubles and the British singles and doubles that same year. In 1947 he turned professional and continued to win national and world titles until retiring as a player in 1954. Kramer then spent many years promoting the growth of professional tennis around the world.

Kramer, Stanley (1913–). American film director and producer. Kramer is best known as a creator of "message" films that take strong liberal stands on a range of social and political issues from racism to nuclear war. Born in New York City, Kramer worked as a B-movie screenwriter for METRO-GOLDWYN-MAYER studios before WORLD WAR II, during which he served in the armed forces. In 1948 he started Screen Plays, Inc., an independent production house that fostered memorable films including *Champion* (1949), *Cyrano de Bergerac* (1950) and *The Caine Mutiny* (1954). Kramer began directing his own films in 1955 and enjoyed a number of critical and popular successes including *On the Beach* (1959), a portrayal of a dying world after a nuclear war, and *Guess Who's Coming To Dinner* (1967), the story of an interracial marriage that featured Spencer TRACY's last film appearance. Kramer was less successful in the 1970s and has ceased filmmaking.

Krasin, Leonid Borisovich (1870–1926). Russian communist. Having become a member in 1890 of one of the earliest social democratic organizations in Russia, from 1900 to 1903 Krasin was a leading member of *Iskra*. From 1904 to 1905, Krasin opposed LENIN's methods in the party and had him expelled from the central committee. In 1905, however, with Lenin reinstated in favor, Lenin, Krasin and Bogdanov led the Bolshevik faction of the revolution. In 1909 he broke with Lenin. Krasin's important political positions include membership in the presidium of the supreme council of national economy, commissar for foreign trade, and ambassador to Britain twice and to France once. His technical skills and business acumen helped him to play a leading part in reorganizing the Soviet economy.

Krasner, Lee (1908–1984). American painter. Krasner was a leading figure in the so-called New York school of ABSTRACT EXPRESSIONISM. Her use of draftsmanship and color to celebrate the natural world showed the influence of MATISSE and Pablo PICASSO, as well as of her husband, Jackson POLLOCK. After Pollock's death (1956) she was slow to gain recognition in her own right; however, by the 1970s her work had won much international acclaim.

Krasnoye Selo. Soviet town outside LENINGRAD; the summer residence of Czar NICHOLAS II, it has two former palaces. The Germans occupied it from 1941 to 1944, while they had Leningrad under siege.

Kraus, Lili (1905–1986). Hungarian-born concert pianist renowned for her interpretations of the music of Mozart. Kraus had two careers, divided by three years during WORLD WAR II when she was held captive in a Japanese prison camp in the Dutch East Indies. A U.S. resident since the late 1960s, she retired from the concert stage in 1982.

Krebs, Sir Hans Adolf (1900–1981). German-British biochemist. Born in Germany, Krebs studied at the universities of Gottingen, Freiburg, Munich, Berlin and Hamburg, where he obtained an M.D. in 1925. He taught at Berlin's Kaiser Wilhelm Institute and the University of Freiburg, where he researched the production of urea in the liver, until the rise of NAZISM caused him to immigrate to England in 1933. While serving as a professor at Sheffield University (1935–54), he discovered in 1937 the Krebs cycle (or citric acid cycle), the chemical reactions in the later stages of the metabolism of food that provide much of the energy for living organisms. For this discovery, he was awarded the 1953 NOBEL PRIZE for physiology or medicine (with F.A. Lipmann). Krebs became a professor at Oxford in 1954, was knighted in 1958 and retired in 1967.

Kreisky, Bruno (1911–1990). Austrian politician. Born to a Jewish family, he was a lifelong socialist who was jailed for his activities in the 1930s. After the takeover of AUSTRIA by Nazi GERMANY in 1938, he fled to Sweden, where he remained until after World War II. He returned to Austria, entered the diplomatic service and was named foreign minster in 1959. In 1970, he became chancellor, a post he held until 1983. His tenure was marked by strong economic growth and prosperity. He pursued an active role for Austria in international affairs, but was criticized by ISRAEL for his evenhanded approach to Israel's Arab neighbors.

Kreisler, Fritz (1875–1962). Austrian violinist and composer. Kreisler is one of the legendary violin performers not only of the 20th century, but in the history of classical music. Born in Vienna, he was a musical prodigy, becoming the youngest student at the esteemed Vienna Conservatory at the age of seven. Among his teachers was the famed composer Anton Bruckner. By his teens Kreisler was an international star of the concert stage, on which he reigned for over six decades. Kreisler was also one of the great composers for the violin, although he sparked controversy by passing off his own compositions—in the early decades of his career—as "transcriptions" from earlier masters, in the hopes of thereby gaining for them a more respectful hearing. Kreisler's most famous compositions include *Liebesfreud*, *Caprice Viennois* and *La Gitana*.

kremlinology. Name derived from the Moscow Kremlin, where the Supreme Soviet of the U.S.S.R. holds its sessions. Kremlinology is the study of the policies of the Soviet government. It also implies gleaning information or clues about the conduct of Soviet politics, getting an indication of what goes on behind the facade of "monolithic unity" among the leaders. With the introduction of GLASNOST and other reforms by Mikhail GORBACHEV in the 1980s, kremlinology became a less obscure science.

Krenz, Egon (1937–). East German politician. Krenz was the communist leader who, on November 17, 1989, opened the BERLIN WALL and allowed East Germans free access to the West. Trained as a teacher, he spent most of his career as an administrator in the East German (GDR) Communist Party's youth movement. He was at the Soviet Communist Party's Central Committee College from 1964 to 1967. In November 1983 he was promoted to the East German Central Committee

Violinist-composer Fritz Kreisler.

Secretariat and also became a full member of the Politburo. Upon the resignation of Erich HONECKER (October 18, 1989), he became secretary general of the party and president of the GDR, promising reforms. However, he resigned (along with the entire Politburo) on December 3, 1989, as a result of continuing protests by the East German people against communist rule.

Kripalani, Jiwatram Bhagwandas (1888–1982). Indian political leader. In 1919 Kripalani became a disciple of Mohandas K. GANDHI. Kripalani worked closely with Gandhi over the next 28 years in the nonviolent struggle for INDIA's independence from Britain. He was president of the CONGRESS PARTY when India achieved independence (1947), but later broke with the party over differences with Jawaharlal NEHRU. He became an independent in 1957 and helped form the Janata Party, which came to power in 1977, temporarily ousting Indira GANDHI.

Krips, Josef (1902–1974). Austrian conductor. Born in Vienna, Krips studied at the Vienna Academy of Music with Felix WEINGARTNER. He began his musical career as a violinist, making his conducting debut in 1921. He served as the conductor of the Dortmund Municipal Theater (1925–26), music director at Karlsruhe (1926–33) and conductor of the Vienna State Opera (1933–38), and was a professor at the Vienna Academy of Music (1935–38). Because Krips had Jewish grandparents, he was forced to abandon his musical career after the German occupation in 1938. After World War II, Soviet authorities chose him to reconstruct Vienna's musical structure, a task he accomplished from 1945 to 1950. He was later the conductor of the London Symphony (1950–54), the Buffalo Philharmonic (1954–63) and the San Francisco Symphony (1963–70). Noted for the warmth and lyricism of his performances, he had a large repertoire that included the great Viennese and German classics as well as works by such modern composers as BARTOK, HINDEMITH and STRAVINSKY.

Krishnamurti, Jiddu (1895–1986). Indian philosopher and teacher. In 1929, Krishnamurti renounced all organized religions and ideologies, claiming that these tended to retard rather than advance self-awareness. With the aid of his supporters, he set up nonprofit foundations in California, England and India. He traveled around the world to deliver lectures stressing the importance of maximum self-awareness. Many of his 40-odd books were drawn from these lectures. He came to be regarded by many as an outstanding spiritual leader.

Kristallnacht. Nazi-directed anti-Jewish violence throughout Germany on the night of November 9, 1938. On that day, Ernst von Roth, a German official in Paris, died after being shot by a young Polish Jew. Using the incident as an excuse, Josef GOEBBELS, Nazi propaganda minister, ordered Nazis to commit acts of violence against German JEWS. Over the following 24 hours, more than 30,000 Jews were arrested, nearly 100 were killed and 36 were seriously injured. Seven thousand Jewish businesses were destroyed, and nearly 300 synagogues were burned. The name Kristallnacht, or "Night of the Broken Glass," is a reference to the windows of the Jewish-owned buildings.

Kroc, Ray A. (1902–1984). Founder and chairman of McDonald's Corp. Kroc opened his first McDonald's hamburger stand in Chicago in 1955. By 1983 more than 7,500 McDonald's franchise restaurants in 32 countries displayed the famous golden arches. Kroc's automating and standardizing techniques revolutionized the fast-food business and the American way of eating. Kroc also owned the San Diego Padres baseball team.

Kroeber, Louis and Theodora. American anthropologists. Alfred Louis (1876–1960) and Theodora Brown (1897–1979) Kroeber both wrote major works in the field of anthropology. Alfred exercised the broader influence, establishing the department of anthropology at the University of California in Berkeley in the early 1900s and teaching there until 1946. He wrote a widely used introductory text, *Anthropology* (1923), and did field work in Mexico and Peru. His later works include *The Nature of Culture* (1952) and *Style and Civilization* (1957). Theodora wrote two stylish and influential works, *The Inland Whale* (1959) and *Ishi in Two Worlds* (1961). Their daughter is science fiction writer Ursula K. LE GUIN.

Kronstadt Rebellion. An uprising among Soviet sailors in Kronstadt on the Gulf of Finland, March 7–18, 1921. The sailors, who had supported the BOLSHEVIKS in the OCTOBER REVOLUTION, demanded economic reforms and an end to Bolshevik political domination. The Red Army, led by Leon TROTSKY and Michael TUKHACHEVSKY, crushed the rebels, and Lenin's NEW ECONOMIC POLICY (1921) was introducted to relieve the privations that had given rise to the revolt.

Kruchenykh, Alexei Yeliseyevich (1886–1970). Futurist poet who began his career as a painter. Together with Velemir KHLEBNIKOV, Kruchenykh was the originator of "trans-sense" (or *zaumney*) verse. Although somewhat an outsider among postrevolutionary Futurists (see FUTURISM), he developed the Cubo-Futurist theory. His artistic output includes a "nonsense" play *Gli-Gli,* in which the senses of the audience were bombarded from all sides, and the opera *Victory Over the Sun* (1913), which—with its songs in Kruchenykh's language of the future, Kazimir MALEVICH's costumes and scenery representing partial objects and individual letters, and Matushin's quarter-tone music—constituted a landmark in theater.

Krupa, Gene (1909–1973). American JAZZ drummer and big band leader. Krupa is regarded as perhaps the greatest drum virtuoso in the history of jazz. His uniquely flamboyant style of playing emphasized his technical brilliance and unerring sense of rhythm. Krupa first gained national fame through his appearances in the 1930s with the Benny GOODMAN big band and trio. In 1938, Krupa formed his own big band, which continued—after a hiatus for World War II—through 1951. A Hollywood biographical film, *The Gene Krupa Story* (1959), featured actor Sal Mineo as Krupa.

Jazz drummer Gene Krupa.

Krupskaya, Nadezhda Konstantinovna (1869–1939). Russian communist educator and wife of LENIN. Educated at the Women's College in St. Petersburg, she aided Lenin in his revolutionary work and married him in 1898, accompanying him in his exile. After their return to Russia, Krupskaya was a member of the commissariat of education and developed and expounded the party's plans for education. She was later to become vice commissar of education and a member of the Central Committee of the Communist Party and the Presidium of the U.S.S.R. She died in the Kremlin on February 27, 1939.

Krutch, Joseph Wood (1893–1970). American author. After receiving his doctorate from Columbia University (1923), he became an editor of *The Nation* (1924–52). A noted literary critic, his works include *Comedy and Conscience After the Restoration* (1924), *The Desert Year* (1952) and *The Voice of the Desert* (1955). His *Measure of Man* (1954) won him a National Book Award.

Kuala Lumpur. Capital city of MALAYSIA, about 200 miles northwest of SINGAPORE. Capital of the **Federated Malay States** from 1895, it was held by Japan from 1942 to 1945, during WORLD WAR II; it became Malaysia's capital in 1963.

Kubelik, Jan (1880–1940). Czechoslovakian violinist. A prodigy, Kubelik entered the Prague Conservatory at the age of 12. He debuted in Vienna in 1898, and soon became a virtuoso performer throughout Europe. Beginning in 1901, he also made frequent tours of the U.S. Known for his brilliant, fiery style, he was acclaimed for his performances of the major violin concerto repertoire and for his superb interpretations of Paganini's compositions. Kubelik was also a composer, whose works include several violin concertos, a symphony and chamber music. He was the father of conductor Rafael KUBELIK.

Kubelik, Rafael (1914–). Czechoslovakian conductor. The son of violinist Jan KUBELIK, Rafael Kubelik studied at the Prague Conservatory (1928) and made his conducting debut in 1934. He was artistic director of the Czech Philharmonic Orchestra from 1942 to 1948. Emigrating to the U.S. in 1949 following the Communist takeover of CZECHOSLOVAKIA, he directed the Chicago Symphony Orchestra (1950–53) and became well known for his controversial introduction of new music to the orchestra's repertoire. He subsequently conducted the New York Philharmonic (1957–58) and the Royal Opera House orchestras, Covent Garden (1955–58). Chief conductor of the Bavarian Radio Symphony Orhestra from 1961 to 1979, he was briefly (1973) music director of New York's Metropolitan Opera. Kubelik is particularly known for his sensitive and lyrical performances of such Czech composers as Dvorak, Smetana and JANACEK, as well as for his performances of German orchestral classsics and the works of MAHLER and BARTOK. He made numerous recordings. Kubelik returned to Czechoslovakia for the first time in 1990, at the invitation of President Vaclav HAVEL.

Kubrick, Stanley (1928–). American film director. Kubrick is one of the most critically acclaimed film directors of the modern era, although his films have had a hit-and-miss record with film-going audiences. Born and raised in the Bronx, Kubrick was encouraged by his father to learn photography and became so skilled at it that he won a job with *Look* magazine upon graduating from high school. In the 1950s Kubrick made a series of self-funded small films before winning acclaim with the antiwar film *Paths of Glory* (1957), which starred Kirk DOUGLAS. Kubrick replaced director Anthony Mann to complete the filming of *Spartacus* (1962), which also starred Douglas. He then enjoyed a box office hit with *Lolita* (1962), based on the controversial novel by Vladimir NABOKOV. Kubrick's next project, *Dr. Strangelove or: How I Learned to Stop Worrying and Love the Bomb* (1964), remains a classic black comedy. *2001: A Space Odyssey* (1968) was alternately praised and reviled by critics, but most agreed that it set a new standard for visual splendor in filmmaking. Subsequent films by Kubrick include the darkly futuristic *A Clockwork Orange* (1971), *Barry Lyndon* (1975), *The Shining* (1980) and *Full Metal Jacket* (1986).

Kuibyshev [*formerly* Samara]. Soviet city on the Volga River, over 500 miles southeast of MOSCOW. In 1918 it was the center of the anti-BOLSHEVIK government (see WHITES; RUSSIAN CIVIL WAR). From 1941 to 1943 it was the seat of the Soviet government.

Kuiper, Gerard (1905–1973). Dutch-American astronomer. Born in the Netherlands, Kuiper earned his Ph.D. at the University of Leiden. After moving to the United States in 1933, he became an American citizen in 1937. Best known for his studies of our solar system, he had a long association with Yerkes Observatory, twice holding the position of director (1947–49 1957–60.) From 1960 until his death in 1973, Kuiper worked in a similar capacity at the Lunar and Planetary Laboratory at the University of Arizona. His theories of the origins of the planets, including the idea that stars and planets are products of condensation from interstellar gas clouds, helped to spark a renewed interest in our solar system. During the '60s and early '70s, he was closely linked with the American space program, instigating many planetary research projects.

Ku Klux Klan. American secret organization based on the idea of white supremacy. Organized in Pulaski, Tennessee in 1866 by Confederate veterans, its purpose was to oppose the former slaves. The organization spread throughout the South. Clad in long, hooded white robes, masked Klan members rode the countryside and employed violent measures in their supression of blacks. In 1869 the KKK was disbanded, but local organizations continued, largely in rural areas. The Klan's violent and overzealous activities prompted congressional legislation in 1870 and 1871. In 1915 a new organization, largely anti-Catholic and anti-Semitic, was founded—with the name Ku Klux Klan—in Stone Mountain, Georgia. This movement, active North as well South, used as its symbol a burning cross. It is estimated that the Klan's membership in the 1920s was between two to three million, but during the Depression of the 1930s, it lost most of its dues-paying members; by the early 1940s the organization disbanded. In 1964, as a result of the CIVIL RIGHTS ACT, there was a resurgence of the Klan. There have been sporadic KKK rallies in both North and South but Klan support is minimal.

Kulakov, Fyodor D. (1918–1978). Soviet communist politician. Kulakov was a member of the politburo and an apparent protege of Soviet leader Leonid BREZHNEV. Western Kremlinologists considered him a potential successor to Brezhnev, but he died before Brezhnev, at the relatively youthful age of 60.

kulaks. Term for wealthy peasants in Russia around the turn of the century and into the Stalinist era. Before the RUSSIAN REVOLUTION (1917) they were prominent in village affairs. After the revolution, they benefited from LENIN'S NEW ECONOMIC POLICY (NEP) until 1927, when STALIN raised their taxes and transformed their lands into collective farms. Stalin's collectivization program and his campaign against the kulaks resulted in the execution, starvation or exile of as many as 12 million of them.

Kuleshov, Lev Vladimirovich (1899–1970). Russian filmmaker and pioneering theoretician who founded the State Film School. Kuleshov was born in Tambov, Russia and received early training as a painter at the Fine Arts School in Moscow. A growing fascination with the motion picture—especially the work of the Americans D.W. GRIFFITH and Mack SENNETT—turned his interests toward that medium, and in 1918 he began writing the first substantial body of criticism and theory in Russia. After making a film, *Proyekt inzhenera Praita* (*Engineer Prite's Project*) in 1918, he began the formation

A gathering of the Ku Klux Klan.

of the First State Film School and in 1920 established the famous Kuleshov Workshop. Vsevelod PUDOVKIN and Sergei EISENSTEIN, among other important Soviet filmmakers, attended classes. Pudovkin conducted a series of "experiments" in montage theory and practice—the synthetic creation of events and ideas through the assemblage and alteration of film (scenes). Thus, his concepts of "creative geography," "creative anatomy," and "creative acting" (the "Mozhukin Experiment") were born. His most important films of the 1920s were *Neobychiniye priklucheniya Mistera Vesta v stranye bolshevikov* (*The Extraordinary Adventures of Mr. West in the Land of the Bolsheviks,* 1924), a satire on detective stories in the Sennett style, and *Pozakonu* (*By the Law,* 1926), an emotional tale of murder adapted from novelist Jack LONDON. Although Kuleshov fell out of favor due to his supposed "formalism" with the STALIN regime in 1935, he continued to direct the State Institute of Cinematography in Moscow after 1944. Before his death in 1970 he was "rediscovered" in several major retrospectives in the West. "The shot is a sign, a letter for montage," wrote Kuleshov in his treatise, *The Art of the Cinema* (1929). With him began the consideration of film as an expressive language.

Kulikov, Viktor Georgyevich (1921–). Soviet military official, and from 1942 a member of the COMMUNIST PARTY. Having served at the front during WORLD WAR II, Kulikov rose through various positions and responsibilities, and was made a member of the central committee in 1971. In 1977 he was appointed commander in chief of WARSAW PACT forces and marshal of the Soviet Union.

Kunayev, Dinmukhamed Akhmedovich (1912–). Soviet official. Kunayev joined the party in 1939 after graduating from the Institute of Non-Ferrous and Fine Metallurgy in Moscow in 1936. He pursued his career in science, rising to the position of chief engineer at *Altaypolymetall* combine, and was director of Leninogorsk Ore Board from 1936 to 1942. In 1949, Kunayev was made a member of the central committee of the Kazakh Communist Party. He was then elected to various governmental posts and in 1971 was made a member of the Politburo central committee.

Kundera, Milan (1929–). Czechoslovakian novelist. Kundera, who is one of the leading European writers of his generation, was a university student when the U.S.S.R. established its Communist regime in CZECHOSLOVAKIA in 1948. After working as a manual laborer and as a jazz musician, Kundera studied film and became a professor at the Institute for Advanced Cinematographic Studies in Prague. The publication of his first novel, *The Joke* (1968), coincided with the brief period of liberalization in 1968 known as PRAGUE SPRING. Shortly thereafter, the SOVIET INVASION OF CZECHOSLOVAKIA took place and Kundera lost both his teaching post and the right to publish his works. He immigrated to France in 1975. His major works of fiction include *Laughable Loves* (1974), *Life is Elsewhere* (1974), *The Farewell Party* (1976), *The Book of Laughter and Forgetting* (1980), *The Unbearable Lightness of Being* (1984, filmed 1988) and *Immortality* (1991).

Kung, Hans (1928–). Swiss theologian. Kung, a Roman Catholic, has emerged as one of the most brilliant and controversial theologians of the second half of this century. Ordained a Roman Catholic priest in 1954, he became a professor of theology at the University of Tubingen. In the 1960s, Kung was appointed by Pope JOHN XXIII as an official theologian of the SECOND VATICAN COUNCIL and produced numerous tracts in favor of increased ecumenicism on the part of the church. But Kung subsequently issued a challenge to papal authority with his book *Infallible? An Inquiry* (1970). In *On Being a Christian* (1974), Kung spoke out in favor of increased dissent within the church. He followed this with a similarly challenging work, *Does God Exist?* (1978). In 1979, Kung was censured by the Vatican and forbidden to teach under church auspices. He has been an outspoken critic of the traditionalist policies of Pope JOHN PAUL II.

Kuniyoshi, Yasuo (1893–1953). Japanese-American painter. Born in Okayama, Japan, Kuniyoshi emigrated to the U.S. in 1906, studying at the Los Angeles School of Art and the Art Students League in New York City, where he later taught from 1933 to 1953. He also taught at the New School and the Brooklyn Museum School. His richly figurative paintings, drawings and prints portray cityscapes, nudes and other human subjects in subdued tones and a style touched with SURREALISM and fantasy. His later works are brighter in color, but harsher in subject matter, concentrating on often grotesque figures in circus or carnival settings.

Kun's Red Terror (1919). Bela Kun established the Hungarian Communist Party December 20, 1918. When president Count Michael Karoly (1875–1955) resigned (March 21, 1919), Kun formed a coalition government, soon establishing a Communist dictatorship. Kun appealed to Hungarian nationalism, formed a Red Army and reconquered Slovakia from the Czechs. However, promised Soviet aid never materialized, nationalization of landed estates alienated the peasantry, while terror estranged the bourgeoisie. The Allies forced relinquishment of Slovakia, counterrevolutionaries attempted Kun's overthrow, and Romania, invading HUNGARY to protect newly acquired Transylvania, advanced on Budapest, the Hungarian capital. When his army refused to fight, Kun fled to Vienna, August 1, 1918. The Rumanians occupied and pillaged Budapest August 5–November 14. Admiral Nicholas HORTHY DE NAGYBANYA, leader of the counterrevolutionaries, entered Budapest and was appointed head of state, March 1920. He restored the monarchy, albeit separated from Austria.

Kuomintang. Chinese Nationalist Party, also known as the KMT, organized in 1912 by Sung Chiao-jen and led by SUN YAT-SEN. A successor to the earlier revolutionary group, the T'ung Meng Hui, its purpose was to promote democratic parliamentary government and social reforms. The KMT was suppressed by China's president, Yuan Shi-kai, and was returned to power on Yuan's death in 1916. As China's ruling party under Sun's leadership, the KMT accepted aid from the U.S.S.R., whose advisors exercised a great deal of control over the party's reorganization in the early 1920s. In a party congress held in Canton in 1924, the KMT officially adopted Sun's Three People's Principles: nationalism, democracy and a guaranteed livelihood. On Sun's death in 1925, leadership of the KMT was assumed by CHIANG KAI-SHEK, who led the NORTHERN EXPEDITION (1926) against the warlords in Peking. He expelled Russian advisors and Chinese communists from the party in 1927, beginning the struggle that ended in China's civil war. KMT troops captured Peking in 1928, and the party became the effective government of China during WORLD WAR II. By 1946 the KMT had betrayed its original democratic principles and had become a corrupt institution controlled by Chiang and his military oligarchy. It was defeated in the civil war, after which (1949) MAO TSE-TUNG and his Communist Party controlled China. When Chiang fled the mainland he brought his party with him, and the Kuomintang became the ruling party of TAIWAN. (See also CHINA.)

Kuprin, Alexander Ivanovich (1870–1939). Russian writer. Having served in the army for four years, he engaged in various professions before deciding to devote his life to literary pursuits. His first story, *Moloch,* was published in 1896, but *The Duel* (1916) was to bring him fame. Kuprin's novels include *Yama* (The Pit) (1927) and *Yunkera* (1933), although he is chiefly remembered for his collections of short stories, such as *The River of Life* (1916) and *Sasha* (1920). He was associated with GORKY's publishing enterprise, *Znanye,* and the Realist writers. Following the 1917 Revolution Kuprin lived in Paris, but he returned to the U.S.S.R. in 1938.

Kurds. Western Asian people who, with their neighboring Armenians, have suffered much throughout the 20th century. The Kurds are centered in Kurdistan, a region of mountains and plateau mainly in southeastern TURKEY, northwestern IRAN, northeastern IRAQ and northeastern SYRIA. The tribal Kurds were subjects of the OTTOMAN EMPIRE until WORLD WAR I. After the war they were promised autonomy, but that promise was never carried out. Since then various Kurdish rebellions have occurred but have been forcefully put down in Turkey, Iran and Iraq. In the 1980s Iraq's dictator Saddam HUSSEIN pursued a particularly brutal policy against the Kurds, killing perhaps tens of thousands, many with poison gas. After the PERSIAN GULF WAR, there was another Kurdish rebellion in northern Iraq. The

Turkish president, Turgut OZAL, expressed support for the Iraqi Kurds in 1991, and France urged UN action to stop their slaughter. The U.S. military subsequently provided shelter, food and protection for close to one million Kurdish refugees who had fled to the mountainous Iraq-Turkey border.

Kuril Islands. Island chain approximately 775 miles long, from the south Kamchatka peninsula to northeast Hokkaido, Japan; the Kurils are under the jurisdiction of the U.S.S.R. There are some 30 large islands and many smaller ones. In 1875 Japan exchanged SAKHALIN ISLAND (previously under joint Russo-Japanese control), for the Russian Kurils. Shortly before the end of WORLD WAR II the Soviets occupied the islands. The Kurils were granted to the U.S.S.R. at the YALTA CONFERENCE, but Japan has disputed the Soviet claim.

Kuropatkin, Alexei Nikolayevich (1848–1925). Russian general. Kuropatkin served in the Russo-Turkish War of 1877; following service in the Caucasus, he became minister of war in 1898. His campaigns in the early stages of the RUSSO-JAPANESE WAR were disastrous and brought about his resignation. He served in the first years of World War I, but in 1916 was appointed governor of Turkestan. He wrote *The Russian Army and the Japanese War* (1909).

Kurosawa, Akira (1910–). Japanese film director considered, with Kenji MIZOGUCHI and Yasujiro OZU, the greatest of that country's modern filmmakers. Kurosawa's work in the early 1950s helped "open up" Japanese cinema to the West. *Rashomon,* a tale of violence and rape told through multiple narrators, won the Grand Prix at the Venice International Film Festival in 1951. The most eclectic of the Japanese masters, Kurosawa has paid tribute to American western and gangster genres—*Shichinin no samurai* (*Seven Samurai,* 1954), *Yojimbo* (*The Body Guard,* 1960), and *Tengoku to jigoku* (*High and Low*), 1963; adapted Shakespeare's *Macbeth* (*Kumonosu-jo, Throne of Blood,* 1957) and *King Lear* (*Ran,* 1985); and ranged among subjects as diverse as martial arts (*Sugata Sanshiro,* 1943), nuclear war (*Ikimono no kiroku—I Live in Fear,* 1957) and police detectives (*Nora inu—Stray Dog,* 1949). He shaped the early career of Japanese superstar Toshiro MIFUNE. Scorning the traditional Japanese *enryo* (ceremonial reserve), his films are dynamically edited and dramatically composed. His mastery of widescreen, as in *High and Low* and *Akahiga* (*Red Beard*) is unrivaled. The recipient of an American ACADEMY AWARD for lifetime achievement (1989), Kurosawa is reverently addressed by his colleagues at Toho Studios as "Tenno"—"Emperor."

Kursk. Industrial city in western Russia, near Ukrainian border. During WORLD WAR II Kursk and its environs was the site of what many military historians regard as the greatest tank battle in history. This battle during the summer of 1943 resulted in a decisive Soviet victory that was perhaps the turning point of the war. From that point forward, the Germans were on the defensive. (See also WORLD WAR II ON THE RUSSIAN FRONT.)

Japanese film director Akira Kurosawa accepting an Academy Award.

Kushner, Rose (1929–1990). American journalist and psychologist. Kushner became a champion of the rights of breast cancer patients after discovering a lump in her own breast in 1974. She refused to undergo the then-standard procedure in which a cancerous breast was removed under general anesthesia before the patient was informed of the biopsy result. Her 1976 book *Why Me? What Every Woman Should Know About Breast Cancer to Save Her Life* described her experiences. Many of the controversial treatments she sought to implement, including less radical surgery and the use of hormonal therapy, later became common practice.

Kuskova, Ekaterina Dmitryevna (1869–1959). Russian journalist. She was the author of *Credo,* which advocated raising the living standards of the working people rather than following the main aim of orthodox Marxists, which was to overthrow the autocracy. In 1921 she was active in GORKY's famine relief committee, whose appeals to the world public resulted in the NANSEN and HOOVER relief missions. She was expelled from Russia in 1922, together with many leading intellectuals; she lived first in Prague and later in Geneva.

Kuwait. Located in western Asia at the head of the Persian Gulf, Kuwait covers an area of 6,879 square miles, including nine Gulf islands. Ruled by an emir of the Al Sabah royal family, Kuwait began the century as a protected state of Britain under the leadership of Emir Mubarak Al Sabah (1896–1915). The discovery of oil in 1938 led to a more direct British involvement in Kuwaiti affairs, until Kuwait gained full independence in 1961. A constitution and national assembly were established in 1962, but the assembly was dissolved in 1976 and again in 1986. The current emir, Shaikh Jabir al Ahmad al Jabir as Sabah, rules by decree. A founding member of the ORGANIZATION OF PETROLEUM EXPORTING COUNTRIES (OPEC) in 1960, Kuwait joined the UNITED NATIONS in 1963. In the 1980s Kuwait was affected by the IRAN-IRAQ WAR, enduring Iranian bombing and several terrorist attacks. Territorial claims by neighboring Iraq led to clashes with Kuwait in 1961 and 1973–74 and Iraq's invasion of Kuwait in August 1990. (See PERSIAN GULF WAR.) Attempts to negotiate an Iraqi withdrawal failed, leading to war. On January 16, 1991, American-led UN forces initiated an air attack against Iraq to forcibly remove it from Kuwait. A UN ground offensive launched on Feb. 21, Kuwait time, drove the Iraqis out of Kuwait in less than a week. Kuwait suffered greatly during the Iraqi occupation; 600 Kuwaiti oil wells burned out of control, creating an ecological and economic disaster.

Kuzmin, Michael Alekseyevich (1875–1936). Russian poet. A member of the Symbolist group, although his work is not considered part of the Symbolist school because his poetry is less solemn. Kuzmin's poems are often a blend of religious themes with a refined sensuality and are very carefully crafted. *Songs of Alexandria* (1906) is usually considered his best collection of verse. This was followed by *The Seasons of Love* (1907). Kuzmin also wrote scenarios for plays, ballets and operettas.

A young Kuwaiti girl waves the national flag to celebrate the liberation of her country from Iraqi invaders (1991).

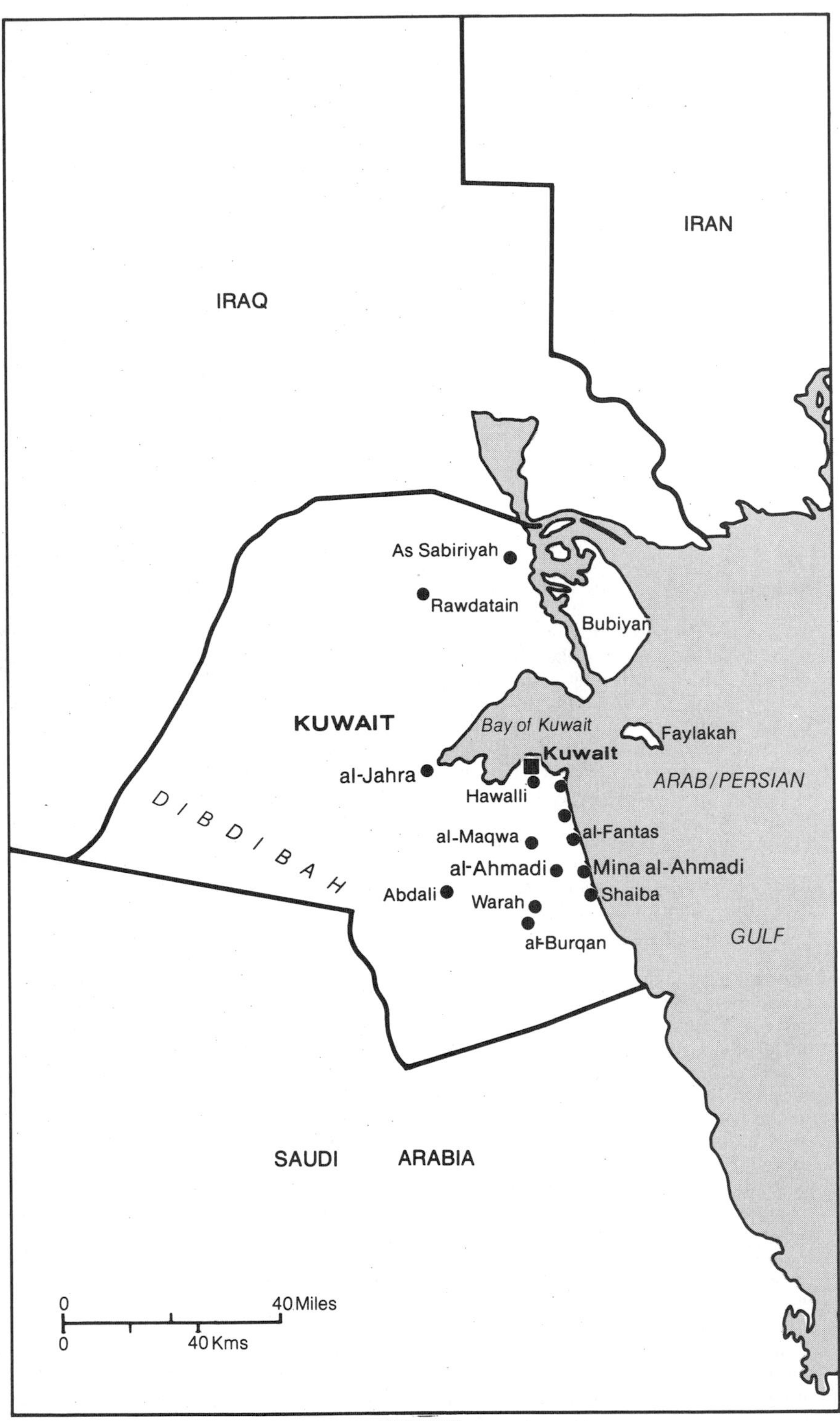

KUWAIT

In 1910 Kuzmin wrote *Concerning Beautiful Clarity*, a manifesto on poetry that marked the transition from Symbolism to ACMEISM.

Kuznets, Simon (1901–1985). Ukrainian-born economist. Kuznets emigrated to the U.S. in 1922 and did his most important work during a lengthy affiliation with the National Bureau of Economic Research. In 1971 while professor emiritus of economics at Harvard University, he was awarded the NOBEL PRIZE in economic science for his development of the concept of the gross national product (GNP).

Kuznetsov, Vasily V. (1901–1991). Soviet diplomat. He played a role in the negotiations surrounding several major international events of the 1960s, including the CUBAN MISSILE CRISIS of 1962, the SOVIET INVASION OF CZECHOSLOVAKIA in 1968 and the Sino-Soviet dispute. He served as first vice president under Leonid I. BREZHNEV and was also a nonvoting member of the politburo from 1977 to 1986.

Kwangtung [Guang-Dong, Kuang-Tong]. Southernmost province of CHINA, on Liaoning peninsula. The KUOMINTANG was formed here in 1912 by SUN YAT-SEN. Kwangtung was also the center of CHIANG KAI-SHEK's Nationalist forces in the 1920s.

Ky, Nguyen Cao (1930–). South Vietnamese military officer and political leader. Ky was drafted into the Vietnamese National Army (raised by the French to combat the VIET MINH insurrection) in 1950. After serving as an infantry lieutenant, he volunteered for pilot training and, after advanced training in France and Algeria, graduated as a fully qualified pilot in 1954. Rising to the rank of lieutenant general in the newly formed South Vietnamese Air Force, he was one of the Young Turks who seized power in 1965 to end the near anarchy that had followed the assassination of President Ngo Dinh DIEM two years earlier. Ky was elected by the Armed Forces Council to serve as prime minister. In 1966 Buddhists and other political factions demanded Ky's ouster; and protests, including immolations, took place in various cities, as they had under the Diem regime. The disturbances ended partly as a result of a government crackdown and partly because of a loss of support for the Buddhists among dissident elements of the military. Ky continued in the post of prime minister until the elections of 1967, when he became vice president of South Vietnam. He served in that position until 1971, when he chose not to run as an opposition candidate against President Nguyen Van THIEU. He reverted to the rank of air marshal in the air force. On April 29, 1975, during operation Frequent Wind, he flew from Saigon to join the U.S. evacuation fleet. (See also VIETNAM WAR.)

South Vietnamese Premier Nguyen Cao Ky (1965).

Labouisse, Henry R(ichardson) (1904–1987). U.S. diplomat. In the late 1940s, Labouisse was one of the principal organizers of the MARSHALL PLAN, the U.S.-backed program for the economic recovery of postwar Europe. From 1954–1958 he was director of the United Nations Relief and Works Agency for Palestinian Refugees. He was U.S. ambassador to Greece from 1962–1965. He returned to the United Nations in 1965 to head the United Nations International Children's Emergency Fund (UNICEF), a post he held until 1979.

Labour Party (Israel). Israeli political party formed in 1930. The Labour Party was originally called Maipai, from *Mifleget Poalei Yisrael* (Israel Workers Party). One of its organizers was David BEN-GURION, who became the first prime minister when ISRAEL became independent in 1948. He remained in power almost continuously until 1963, and Maipai repeatedly dominated the elections. In 1965 Ben-Gurion and his proteges, Moshe DAYAN and Shimon PERES left Maipai to form Rafi, which advocated more technocratic efficiency in government. Rafi rejoined Maipai in 1968 along with Achdut Haavodah, another political party previously associated with Maipai, to formally create the Israel Labour Party under Prime Minister Levi Eshkol. Upon his death in 1969, he was succeeded as party leader and coalition prime minister by Golda MEIR, who remained in office until 1974. The subsequent administration of Yitzhak RABIN was beset by corruption scandals and internal conflict. The Labour Party lost the 1977 elections and remained in opposition throughout the 1980's, except for a short-lived coalition with Yitzhak SHAMIR

Labour Party (New Zealand). NEW ZEALAND political party formed in 1916. The Labour Party entered its first general election in 1919. While it maintained policies favorable to farmers, the party gained prominence in the 1920s when New Zealand became increasingly urbanized. Labour won a majority in 1935 and remained in power until 1949 under the leadership of Prime Ministers Michael SAVAGE and Peter FRASER. During that time many relief and social welfare programs were instituted, including a state health care program in 1941. Labour came to power again in 1957 by a slim majority led by Prime Minister Sir Walter Nash, but he was unable to cope with a severe economic crisis, and the National Party was elected in 1960. From 1972 to 1975, Prime Ministers Norman Kirk and Wallace Rowling led Labour governments. After nine years of National administration, the Labour Party, led by David LANGE, was voted back into power in 1984.

Labour Party (United Kingdom). British political party formed in 1906. Labour party membership can be either individual or collective, and the party is comprised of a network of constituency associations overseen by 11 branch offices. At the national level are the national Executive Committee and the Parliamentary Labour Party (PLP) whose members act as shadow cabinet to the party.

Labour party philosophy reflects its socialist origins. It is strongly supportive of trade unions, government health and social welfare programs, and generally shares the political stance of the liberal faction of the American DEMOCRATIC PARTY. At various times the Labour party has advocated British withdrawal from the EEC, unilateral nuclear disarmament and abolition of the House of Lords and of private schools.

The Labour Party arose from the Labour Representation Committee that had been formed in 1900 by the FABIAN SOCIETY, the Independent Labour Party, and trade unions. Two Labour MPs were elected in 1900, and 30 in 1906. By 1922 it had become the second largest British political party. In 1924 and from 1929 to 1931, minority Labour governments held office with the support of the LIBERAL PARTY. In the 1945 elections, Labour won a sweeping victory and Clement ATTLEE became prime minister. He instituted a broad range of social reforms, including the creation of the NATIONAL HEALTH SERVICE. By the 1950 elections, however, Labour majority had dwindled, and the Conservatives returned to power in 1951. Subsequent Labour governments were from 1964 to 1970 under Harold WILSON and from 1974 to 1979, first under Wilson and then under James CALLAGHAN. The Labour Party has a history of factionalized squabbling between its left-wing and moderate elements. Beginning in the 1970s, the party's left gained prominence, taking control in 1980 when Michael FOOT became leader. In 1981 several moderate members left to form the SOCIAL DEMOCRATIC PARTY. Following Labour's stunning defeat in the 1983 general elections, Neil KINNOCK became party leader. Initially a member of the left of the party, Kinnock has become somewhat more moderate since 1983.

Labrador. The mainland portion of Canada's province of NEWFOUNDLAND; on the Atlantic coast of eastern Canada, north of the St. Lawrence River. After a long dispute between Quebec and Newfoundland over its western boundary, the British Privy Council transferred some of the area to Labrador in 1927. During WORLD WAR II Labrador provided valuable military bases for the Allies. In 1949 Labrador became Canada's 10th province. Iron, discovered in 1895, accounts for much of Canada's iron-ore production.

Labyrinth, The. WORLD WAR I fortification in France's Pas-de-Calais department, near Vimy Ridge. The Labyrinth was the site of fierce fighting from May 30 to June 19, 1915.

Lacan, Jacques (1901–1981). French psychologist, philosopher and literary critic. Lacan was a brilliant polymath who was jointly influenced by STRUCTURALISM, especially the works of linguistics theorists Roman Jakobson and Ferdinand de Saussure, and by the psychoanalytic theories of Sigmund FREUD. Lacan posed the theory that the structure of the unconscious resembled that of a language. He also argued that Freudian theory, while it discussed the nature of repression, had fallen victim to it by repressing its extreme significance. Lacan, who founded the Ecole Freudienne de Paris in 1963, was an unorthodox psychoanalytic practitioner who sometimes substituted 10-minute therapy sessions for the standard one hour encounter. His major essays are collected in *Ecrits* (1966). Other works by Lacan include *The Four Fundamental Concepts of Psychoanalysis* (1978) and *Speech and Language in Psychoanalysis* (1983).

Lacey, James Harry "Ginger" (1917–1989). British World War II fighter pilot. During the BATTLE OF BRITAIN (1940) Lacey shot down 18 enemy aircraft, more than any other pilot. Throughout the war, he shot down a total of 28 German Luftwaffe aircraft, including one that was returning from a bombing raid on Buckingham Palace.

Lachaise, Gaston (1882–1935). French-American sculptor. Born in Paris, Lachaise learned classical sculptural technique at the Ecole des Beaux-Arts, Paris. Emigrating to the U.S. in 1906, he executed sculptural details for the artists H.H. Kitson and Paul MANSHIP, working on such commissions as New York's Telephone and Telegraph Building and RCA Building. Lachaise is best known for his monumental figures of women. Powerful and voluptuous, these nudes seem to float pneumatically on tiny feet. They include the famous *Standing Woman* in the collection of the MUSEUM OF MODERN ART, New York City.

Lacoste, Robert (1898–1989). French socialist politician. Lacoste was best known for his opposition to the concept of Algerian independence in the late 1950s. His strong nationalist support of a French-controlled ALGERIA put him at odds with his own socialist party and eventually contributed to the downfall of France's Fourth Republic.

Lady Chatterley's Lover. Novel by D.H. LAWRENCE first published in Italy in 1928. An edited version was published in England in 1932; the full text was not published there until 1960. The book tells the story of Constance Chatterley who is married to Sir Clifford, an enfeebled intellectual wounded in WORLD WAR I and confined to a wheelchair. Lady Chatterley develops a satisfying and passionate relationship with the gamekeeper, Oliver Mellors. She becomes pregnant, and the novel ends with she and Mellors both seeking divorces and hoping for a life together. Lawrence contrasts the effete upper classes with the potency and earthiness of the lower. The novel's frank treatment of sexuality caused it to be banned as obscene in England. Its publication in 1960 caused the publishers, Penguin, to be embroiled in a prosecution under the Obscene Publications Act of 1959, and many authors, including E.M. FORSTER, spoke on behalf of the defense. Penguin was acquitted.

Laemmle, Carl (1867–1939). German-born motion picture producer and president of UNIVERSAL PICTURES. The diminutive Laemmle came to America in 1887 at age 13 and rose from errand boy at a New York drugstore to owner of his own company in 1907, a film distribution exchange called the Laemmle Film Service. Two years later, in defiance of the newly formed Motion Pictures Patents Company—a trust organized by Edison and others to put independent distributors and producers out of business—Laemmle founded the Independent Motion Picture Company of America (IMP), a forerunner of Universal Pictures. From his New York office he became one of the most powerful men in the film industry, not only defeating the trust in a court action in 1912, but also launching the "star system" and the feature-length film, among the most important innovations in film history. "Laemmle wasn't a brilliant aesthetic innovator," writes historian Neal Gabler, "but he had become a brilliant exploiter." After the opening in 1915 of the vast Universal City complex, a 230-acre municipality and studio facility in California's San Fernando Valley that cranked films out like a factory assembly line, he presided over operations until 1929, when he transferred power to his son, Carl Jr. The young Laemmle was one of 15 relatives eventually placed on the company payroll.

Laetrile [also called vitamin b-17, amygdalin]. Controversial chemical substance, claimed by some people to be a cure for cancer and by others to be a quack remedy. Laetrile occurs naturally in apricot pits, peaches, bitter almonds and other plants. It contains small amounts of the poison cyanide. In the 1970s laetrile was legally available in many countries but was banned in the U.S. by the Food and Drug Administration. Laetrile's promoters claimed that since there was no evidence that it was harmful, it should be legally available in the U.S. to patients who wanted it. The FDA said that numerous tests had indicated that laetrile was therapeutically worthless. The agency warned that cancer patients who put their faith in laetrile might be risking their lives by failing to receive orthodox medical treatment. Some authorities felt that laetrile's promoters were taking advantage of desperately ill people. Many cancer patients went to Mexico to receive laetrile treatment, and others obtained laetrile illegally in the U.S. In 1977 federal judges ruled that terminally ill patients should have the right to receive laetrile even if there was no proof that it could cure cancer. Most of the American medical establishment continued to question laetrile's effectiveness.

La Farge, Oliver (1901–1963). American author. La Farge won the PULITZER PRIZE in 1929 for his novel *Laughing Boy: A Navaho Romance,* which dramatized the painful effort of American Indians to adjust their age-old ways to the modern age. La Farge went on to serve as director for the Eastern Association on Indian Affairs (1930–32), and as president of the National Association on Indian Affairs (1933–37) and the American Association on Indian Affairs (1937–42).

Lafayette Escadrille. Renowned unit of volunteer American flyers in the French air service before the U.S. entered WORLD WAR I. It was reorganized in 1918 as the U.S.'s 103rd Pursuit Squadron. The escadrille (squadron) consisted of 38 flyers, only six of whom survived the war.

La Follette, Robert Marion (1855–1925). U.S. politician. A law graduate, he was elected district attorney and, later, to the Wisconsin House of Representatives as a Republican. In 1901 he was elected as the governor of Wisconsin; over a period from 1903 to 1905 many of his liberal reform policies were adopted. These included pensions for the blind, old age assistance, unemployment compensation and laws governing working conditions of children. He was one of the first to call on economic and other experts as government consultants. As a member of the U.S. Senate from 1906 to 1924, he became one of its most influential men. In 1909 he organized the National Progressive Republican League, from which Theodore ROOSEVELT adopted many of La Follette's liberal ideas. Later, he opposed American entry into WORLD WAR I, but supported most of Woodrow WILSON's policies. He also opposed the LEAGUE OF NATIONS and the World Court. In 1924 he ran unsuccessfully for president on the Progressive Party ticket (but gathered almost five million votes).

La Follette, Suzanne (1893–1983). American author and editor. A prominent conservative, La Follette founded several magazines, most notably the NATIONAL REVIEW. Among her books was *Concerning Women,* which argued for Civil Rights for women. She was an early anti-Soviet activist and served as secretary to the commission that investigated the Soviet-ordered assassination of Leon TROTSKY. She was a cousin of Senator Robert M. LA FOLLETTE.

Lagerkvist, Par (1891–1951). Swedish author and playwright. Lagerkvist first began publishing poetry in 1912, the same

Robert La Follette (1924).

year his first novella, *Manniskor* (*People*) was published. His early works were strongly influenced by modern painting, and rejected naturalism. The expressionist poetry collection, *Angest* (*Anguish*, 1916) reflects his pessimism and despair wrought by the events of WORLD WAR I. His early plays, which include *Den sista manniskan* (*The Last Man, 1917) and Himlens hemlighet* (*Secret of Heaven*, 1919) also evidenced an existential desperation. His later works were less stylized, humanistic outcries against FASCISM and evil. These include the poems, *Sang och strid* (*Song and Struggle*, 1940), the drama *Lat Manniskan leva* (*Let Man Live*, 1949) and the novel *Barabbas* (1950, filmed 1952), Lagerkvist's acclaimed and best known work. He was awarded the NOBEL PRIZE for literature in 1951. Later works include the novels, *Det heliga landet* (*The Holy Land*, 1964) and *Mariamne* (*Herod and Meriamne*, 1967).

Lagerlof, Selma (1858–1940). Swedish novelist. Lagerlof's first novel, *Gosta Berlings saga* (*The Story of Gosta Berling*, 1891), was published after it won a literary contest in a Swedish magazine. Its romantic style was unusual in a period of literary naturalism. Her many popular works, which include *Nils Holgerssons underbara resa genom Sverige* (*The Wonderful Adventures of Nils*, 1906), and *Tosen fran Stormyrtorpet* (*The Girl from the Marsh Croft*, 1907), are rich in Swedish folklore and myth. Lagerlof received the NOBEL PRIZE for literature in 1909. During WORLD WAR II, she donated the gold medal to a fund to benefit Finland, and was also instrumental in helping German intellectuals, such as Nelly SACHS, escape from Nazi GERMANY.

LaGuardia, Fiorello (Henry) (1882–1947). American politician known for his three terms as reform mayor of NEW YORK CITY. Popularly known as the "little flower," LaGuardia spent much of his childhood in the western U.S. and in Europe but returned to New York City, his birthplace, and graduated from New York University Law School. A reform Republican in a city dominated by Tammany Hall Democrats, LaGuardia was elected to Congress in 1916 and served (with the exception of the years 1919–1923) until 1933. He cosponsored the NORRIS-LAGUARDIA ACT (1932), a major labor law that protected the rights of striking workers. LaGuardia ran as a reformer for mayor of New York in 1929 but was defeated by Jimmy WALKER. In 1933, a year after he lost his congressional seat in the Democratic landslide, he was elected mayor of New York City on a "fusion" ticket after Walker resigned after investigations had exposed gross corruption in city government. Short, stout and often unkempt, LaGuardia was an energetic reform mayor who enjoyed broad support. He is popularly remembered for reading the comics on the radio during a prolonged newspaper strike.

For further reading:

Kessner, Thomas, *Fiorello H. LaGuardia and the Making of Modern New York*. New York: McGraw-Hill, 1989.

Fiorello LaGuardia, New York mayor.

Laika. Dog that became the first Earth creature to travel into outer space; the name Laika means "barker." On November 3, 1959, Laika was launched into orbit aboard Sputnik 2, the second artificial satellite launched by the Soviet Union (see SPUTNIK 1). Laika lived in space for 10 days before dying when her oxygen ran out. Laika's vital signs were monitored from the ground, Sputnik 2 thus providing the first information about the effects of space travel on living creatures. The flight of Laika showed that the Soviets were serious about sending people into space—and that the Soviets were ahead of the U.S. in the space race. In August 1960, Sputnik 5 carried two dogs, Belka and Strelka, into space; they returned to Earth safely, the first creatures to do so.

Laing, R(onald) D(avid) (1927–1989). Scottish psychiatrist. Laing's unorthodox theories about mental illness, particularly schizophrenia, made him a COUNTERCULTURE hero in the 1960s. His theories first gained recognition in 1960 with the publication of his first book, *The Divided Self: An Existential Study in Sanity and Madness*. Laing argued that schizophrenia was not a genetic or biochemical aberration but rather an avenue of escape from a family situation fraught with conflicting emotional demands. An outspoken critic of standard psychiatric treatments, which he claimed did more harm than good, he experimented with various alternative approaches, including the use of psychedelic drugs. He put his theories into practice at Kingsley Hall, a therapeutic community he set up in London in the 1960s. Eventually he became disenchanted with much of his early thinking about mental illness and admitted that many of his treatment methods had failed.

Lakehurst. Borough in east central New Jersey, U.S.A. In the mid-1920s the Lakehurst Naval Air Station became the U.S. terminal for transatlantic dirigibles. In 1929 the German airship *Graf Zeppelin* began a round-the-world voyage here, completing that journey at Lakehurst 21 days later. However, Lakehurst is best remembered as the place with the dirigible HINDENBURG suddenly exploded as it was attempting to land after a voyage from Germany (May 6, 1937).

Laker, Edwin Francis (1910–1980). American inventor. While serving as a major in the 82nd Airborne Division in WORLD WAR II, Laker developed the **Pathfinder** long-range bombing system. Bomber crews used this to find and mark targets with smoke or flares, which other aircraft then used as indicators to drop their bombs.

Lalique, Rene (1860–1945). French glass and jewelry designer. Born in the Marne, Lalique studied drawing and goldsmithing in Paris. Traveling to London (1878–80), he returned to Paris as a jewelry designer, cofounding a business to market his designs in 1884 and purchasing a jewelry workshop the following year. In 1891 Lalique began to work in glass. Starting to show his work at exhibitions in 1894, he was the recipient of many important awards, his success capped by his own pavilion at the Paris exhibition of 1925. Early in the 20th century he diversified into textiles, mirrors and other products, beginning to use engraved glass in jewelry in 1905 and adding pressed-glass perfume bottles to his roster in 1906. He opened his first glass factory in 1909, founding another in 1918. Lalique's innovative designs included various tablewares and light fixtures, and he was particularly famed for the elegant salon he designed for the luxury ocean liner NORMANDIE. Working at first in the ART NOUVEAU style, he developed a sleek, geometric design mode (employing plant, animal and abstract forms) that was the epitome of ART DECO.

Lamar, Joseph R. (1857–1916). Associate justice, U.S. Supreme Court (1910–16). Lamar, a native of Georgia, and a graduate of Bethany College, studied law at Washington and Lee University before his admission to the bar. In private law practice, he was also involved in politics and was elected to the Georgia legislature before being appointed to the state Supreme Court. In 1910 Lamar was appointed to the U.S. Supreme Court by President William Howard TAFT. A hard worker, Lamar died while serving on the Court in 1916.

L'Amour, Louis (Dearborn) (1908–1988). American author best known for his westerns. L'Amour wrote 101 books—86 novels, 14 story collections and one work of nonfiction, with sales nearing 200 million. *Hondo*, published in 1953, was his first and perhaps best known novel; it was made into a film starring John WAYNE. Many of L'Amour's other works were also adapted as feature films, including *Shalako, Stranger on Horseback* and *How the West Was Won; The Sacketts* was adapted for television. He was the only novelist honored with both a congressional gold medal (1983) and a presidential Medal of Freedom (1984).

Lampedusa, Giuseppi Tomasi Di (1896–1957). Italian novelist. An upper-class Sicilian, Lampedusa is best remembered for the novel *Il gattopardo* (*The Leopard*, 1955–56; filmed 1963), which describes the reactions of a noble family to the social and political landscape following Sicily's appropriation by Garibaldi in 1860.

Lancaster, Burt [Burton Stephen Lancaster] (1913–). American film actor. Born in New York City, Lancaster attended New York University but left to become a traveling acrobat. He served in World War II before making his acting debut on Broadway (1945). Moving to HOLLYWOOD, he won a role in *The Killers* (1946, adapted from an Ernest HEMINGWAY short story) and soon became a genuine star. Handsome and muscular, he was at first identified with swashbucklers, westerns and other action pictures, such as *The Flame and the Arrow* (1950), *Jim Thorpe—All American* (1951), *Apache* (1954), *Trapeze* (1956) and *Gunflight at O.K. Corral* (1957); in all of these he performed his own stunts. He also scored a hit as a romantic leading man in *From Here to Eternity* (1953) and showed his versatility in challenging dramatic roles in *All My Sons* (1948), *The Rose Tattoo* (1955), *The Rainmaker* (1957), *Elmer Gantry* (1960, ACADEMY AWARD), *The Birdman of Alcatraz* (1962), *The Leopard* (1963) and *The Swimmer* (1968). As he aged, Lancaster made a successful transition to character roles, as in Louis MALLE's *Atlantic City* (1980). He also created memorable supporting characters in *Local Hero* (1983), *Field of Dreams* (1989) and other films. While his performances are often mannered, they show his complete dedication to, and his impressive command of, the actor's craft. Lancaster has gradually been acknowledged as one of the finest film actors of his generation.

Lanchester, Elsa [born Elizabeth Sullivan] (1902–1986). British-born actress. After a successful stage career in London, Lanchester became one of HOLLYWOOD's most outstanding character actresses. Known for her talents in eccentric or comic parts, she scored a singular triumph in *The Bride of Frankenstein* (1935), a film in which she played both the title role and Frankenstein's creator, Mary Shelley. Her career was closely linked with that of her husband, Charles LAUGHTON, to whom she was married from 1929 until his death in 1962. They made a number of films together, most notably, *Witness for the Prosecution* (1957). After his death, she revealed that their marriage survived numerous homosexual liaisons on his part and affairs on hers. Her last film was *Murder by Death* (1976).

Land, Edwin H(erbert) (1909–1991). American inventor, scientist and industrialist. Born in Norwich, Connecticut, he attended Harvard University, but dropped out in 1932 to pursue his scientific interests on his own. Fascinated with polarized light, he began a series of inventions involving polarization and in 1937 founded the Polaroid Corporation. In 1943, Land conceived the idea for what was to be the most famous and successful of his many inventions (he held 533 patents): an instant camera that captured an image and developed it in a single-step process. He began marketing this Polaroid Land Camera in 1948 and introduced a color version in 1963. Land served as Polaroid's chairman until his retirement in 1981. Land was also a military adviser to the federal government and was an early advocate of the use of reconnaissance SATELLITES.

Landis, Kenesaw Mountain (1866–1944). American judge, first commissioner of professional baseball. In the early years of the century professional baseball and the World Series had caught the imagination of the American public. That same public was dismayed when it was revealed that several members of the Chicago White Sox had taken bribes to throw the 1919 World Series. The affair became known as the BLACK SOX SCANDAL. Judge Landis, a U.S. district court judge from Chicago, was enlisted to become the czar of baseball with broad powers to regulate the sport and banish those whose actions were not in the best interests of the game. Landis barred the errant participants for life and imposed a strict ban on gambling by ballplayers. Landis and those who followed established a tradition of a strong commissioner with sweeping powers to maintain the integrity of the sport.

Landon, Alf(red Mossman) (1887–1987). American politician. A banker and an oilman, Landon served as governor of Kansas (1933–1937). He was widely praised for economy in government operations during the GREAT DEPRESSION. Reelected in 1934, he gained national renown for his support of Kansas farmers in the depth of the Depression. He was the Republican nominee for president in 1936, but lost the election to the enormously popular Franklin D. ROOSEVELT. Landon's daughter, **Nancy Landon Kassebaum,** was later a U.S. senator.

Landowska, Wanda (1877–1959). Polish-French harpsichordist and pianist. Born in Warsaw, Landowska studied at the conservatory there and began her career as a pianist in 1891. She later taught piano at the Schola Cantorum, Paris (1900–12). Fascinated with the music of the baroque period, she turned her attention to the harpsichord, making her debut on the instrument in 1903. Landowska taught harpsichord at the Berlin Hochschule (1912–19) before establishing her own Ecole de Musique ancienne at Saint-Leu-la-Foret near Paris in 1919. She taught and gave renowned concerts of early music there until 1940, when World War II caused her to settle in the U.S. Here she continued her activities as teacher, performer and recording artist. The guiding spirit in the 20th-century revival of interest in the harpsichord, much admired for her Bach interpretations, she was also an inspiration to modern composers. Both Manuel de FALLA and Francis POULENC wrote harpsichord concertos expressly for her. Landowska and her husband, Henry Lew, were the authors of *Music of the Past*.

Alf Landon, 1936 Republican candidate for president.

Landsberg am Lech. City in Bavaria, 20 miles south of Augsburg, on the Lech River in Germany. Landsberg is where Adolf HITLER was imprisoned (1923–24) after his attempt to overthrow the Bavarian government in the BEER HALL PUTSCH (1923), and where he wrote MEIN KAMPF.

Lane, Sir Hugh Percy (1875–1915). Irish connoisseur and art collector. Born in Cork, Lane worked for a number of art dealers in London before opening his own gallery. In 1901, he commissioned John Butler YEATS to paint portraits of contemporary Irishmen, a project that was completed by Sir William ORPEN. He also organized various exhibits of Irish art, and participated in the foundation of Dublin's Gallery of Modern Art. In recognition of his services to Irish art, Lane was knighted in 1909. He was drowned in the torpedo attack on the LUSITANIA in 1915. The provisions of his will caused a bitter controversy in IRELAND. His collection, now split into two parts, is rotated every five years for alternate exhibition in Dublin and London.

Lang, Fritz (1890–1976). German-born director of fantasy and suspense movie thrillers. Lang entered the film industry in Berlin as a screenwriter and director in 1918. With his wife, screenwriter Thea von Harbou, he made some of GERMANY's most famous films in the 1920s, including the expressionist fantasies *Der Mude Tod* (*Destiny,* 1921), *Siegfrieds Tod* (*Siegfried's Death,* 1923), and *Metropolis* (1927); the visionary science fiction film *Die Frau im Mond* (*The Woman in the Moon,* 1929); the criminal conspiracy thrillers about "Dr. Mabuse" (1923); and the police procedural films *Spione* (*Spies,* 1928) and *M* (1931). After a hasty departure from Nazi Germany in 1933, Lang began a long career in America, where he became one of the architects of FILM NOIR, infusing the standard genres of the western (*The Return of Frank James,* 1940), romance (*Scarlet Street,* 1945), and gangster picture (*The Big Heat,* 1953) with his own unrelieved sense of darkness and paranoia. Disillusioned with HOLLYWOOD, Lang worked abroad after 1956, bringing the infamous "Dr. Mabuse" back for a final bow in *The 1000 Eyes of Dr. Mabuse* (1960).

Lang's central characters are usually victims or victimizers, either falling prey to their own obsessions (the child molester in *M*, the artist in *Scarlet Street*) or manipulating the world into their own insane images (the mad scientist Rotwang in *Metropolis* and Mabuse). In any case Lang's universe is closed to individual freedom—perhaps, significantly, like the motion picture set where Lang himself was able to exercise an almost despotic control.

For further reading:

Jensen, Paul M., *The Cinema of Fritz Lang*. New York: Ballantine Books, 1988.

Langdon, Harry (1884–1944). Generally regarded as one of America's greatest silent film comedians (along with CHAPLIN, KEATON and LLOYD), Langdon was born in Council Bluffs, Iowa. Working in his teens as a ticket seller, circus clown, acrobat and ventriloquist, Langdon was noticed by producer-director Mack SENNETT. The collaboration produced a few amusing short films, but it was not until Langdon met gagwriter (later director) Frank CAPRA and director Harry Edwards that his comic character of the "child with adult desires" developed. The three went on to make dozens of two-reel and three-reel comedy hits, including *Picking Peaches* (1924), and features, including *Tramp, Tramp, Tramp* (1926) and *Long Pants* (1927). With success under his belt, Langdon fired Capra and Edwards in order to write and direct his own films. The result was a string of critical and commercial flops. Langdon was never able to resurrect his early success; he continued to work in the 1930s but only in occasional featured roles. In 1944 Langdon died of a cerebral hemorrhage; his films have largely been forgotten by the public, but his strong influence can be detected in the style of Stan Laurel (see LAUREL AND HARDY), as well as other comedy stars.

Lange, David (1942–). Prime minister of NEW ZEALAND (1984–89). Born in Auckland, Lange graduated in law from the University of Auckland in 1966. He practiced as a lawyer, was a tutor at the University of Auckland and completed a postgraduate degree in law. Lange entered parliament at a by-election in 1977; became deputy leader of the LABOUR PARTY, then in opposition, in November 1979; and became leader of the party on February 3, 1983, upon the resignation of Sir Wallace Rowling. Following Labour's victory in the July 1984 election, he became New Zealand's youngest prime minister in this century. He stepped down as prime minister in mid-1989.

Lange, Dorothea (1895–1965). American photographer. Born in Hoboken, N.J., Lange took an early interest in photography and operated a portrait studio from 1916 to 1932. She became famous for her photographs taken during the GREAT DEPRESSION, stark works that record the time, place and character of the people portrayed with rare power. Photographs such as *Migrant Mother, Nipomo, California* (1936) reveal poverty and dignity in one powerful image. This work was part of a series Lange and her husband, the economist Paul Taylor, executed for the state of California, documenting the life of migrant workers. This project resulted in their book *An American Exodus* (1939). She worked for the Farm Security Administration (1935–42), on projects that studied rural America. After the outbreak of WORLD WAR II Lange created a series of documentary photographs that recorded the internment of JAPANESE-AMERICANS. She also contributed many photo essays to LIFE magazine.

Langemarck. Town in West Flanders, BELGIUM, 5 miles northeast of YPRES. A battlefield during WORLD WAR I, it is where poison gas was first used in battle (Apr. 22, 1915).

Langer, Suzanne K(naith) (1895–1985). American philosopher. Langer was one of the rare academic philosophers of the modern era to find a substantial popular readership. Her major work, *Philosophy in a New Key* (1942), which argued that all intellectual ideas are ultimately expressed in a symbolic mode, was reprinted many times and became a standard text in numerous undergraduate philosophy classes. Langer was educated at Radcliffe College, where she studied under the eminent philosopher Alfred North WHITEHEAD. Her other major works include *An Introduction to Symbolic Logic* (1937) and the three-volume *Mind: An Essay on Human Feeling* (1967–1982).

Langley, Samuel Pierpont (1834–1906). American scientist, inventor and aviation pioneer. In the 20th century, Langley is known for his efforts to fly the first motor-driven airplane. His interest in the possibility of powered flight dated to 1886, the year before he became secretary of the Smithsonian Institute in Washington, D.C. By 1903 he had designed and built a 60-foot-long aircraft with a wingspan of 48 feet. The plane was launched by catapult off a 70-foot ramp on the Potomac River, but crashed and was wrecked. Less than two months later (December 17, 1903) the WRIGHT BROTHERS made the first successful powered flight at Kitty Hawk, North Carolina. AVIATION experts have since recognized that Langley's plane crashed not because of any faulty design, but because of the catapult method of launching.

Lanham, Charles Truman "Buck" (1902–1978). A career U.S. Army officer, Lanham led the first American military unit to reach Paris (August 25, 1944) in WORLD WAR II. He was a friend of the writer Ernest HEMINGWAY and was said to be the model for the typical American soldier in Hemingway's novels. He retired with the rank of major general and was later chairman of Colt, the U.S. firearms manufacturer.

Lanphier Jr., Thomas G(eorge) (1890–1987). American fighter pilot. In WORLD WAR II, Lanphier flew 112 missions in the South Pacific. In April 1943 he shot down the airplane carrying the commander in chief of the Japanese Royal Navy, Adm. Isoroku YAMAMOTO, known as the architect of the attack on PEARL HARBOR.

Lansbury, George (1859–1940). British LABOUR PARTY leader. Lansbury joined the Social Democratic Federation in 1892 and served as a Labour Party member of Parliament (1910–12 and 1922–40). An articulate reformer, he was active in fighting against poverty and unemployment, and he vigorously championed woman suffrage. A pacifist, he also opposed World War I. One of the founders (1912) of the *Daily Herald*, he edited the paper until 1922. Commissioner of works from 1929 to 1931, he led the opposition to Ramsay MACDONALD's National Government from 1931 to 1935, when he resigned as

LAOS

1907	Most of Laos under French administration as part of French Indochina.
1940-45	Japan occupies Laos, ruling through the Vichy French government.
1950	Prince Souphanouvong forms communist-inspired Pathet Lao after contact with Ho Chi Minh in northeast Laos.
1954	Geneva Accords establish Laos as an independent, neutral nation under the rule of royal government and allot two "regroupment" provinces, adjacent to North Vietnam, to the Pathet Lao.
1960	Civil war begins between troops of the pro-western royal government and Pathet Lao.
1964	14-nation Geneva conference sets up coalition government with Prince Souvanna Phouma, a neutralist, as prime minister, anti-communist Prince Boun Oum and communist Prince Souphanouvong as cabinet ministers.
1971	South Vietnamese troops backed by U.S. bombers invade Laos to attack Ho Chi Minh Trail; CIA admits U.S. has 30,000-man army in Laos.
1975	Following American withdrawal and the subsequent fall of South Vietnam to the communists, King Savang Vatthana abdicates; Pathet Lao take control of Laos with the support of North Vietnamese troops.
1988	Two American MIA searchers arrested in Laos after offering $2.4 million for information; later claim that Laos still holds U.S. prisoners of war; charge is denied by Laotian authorities.

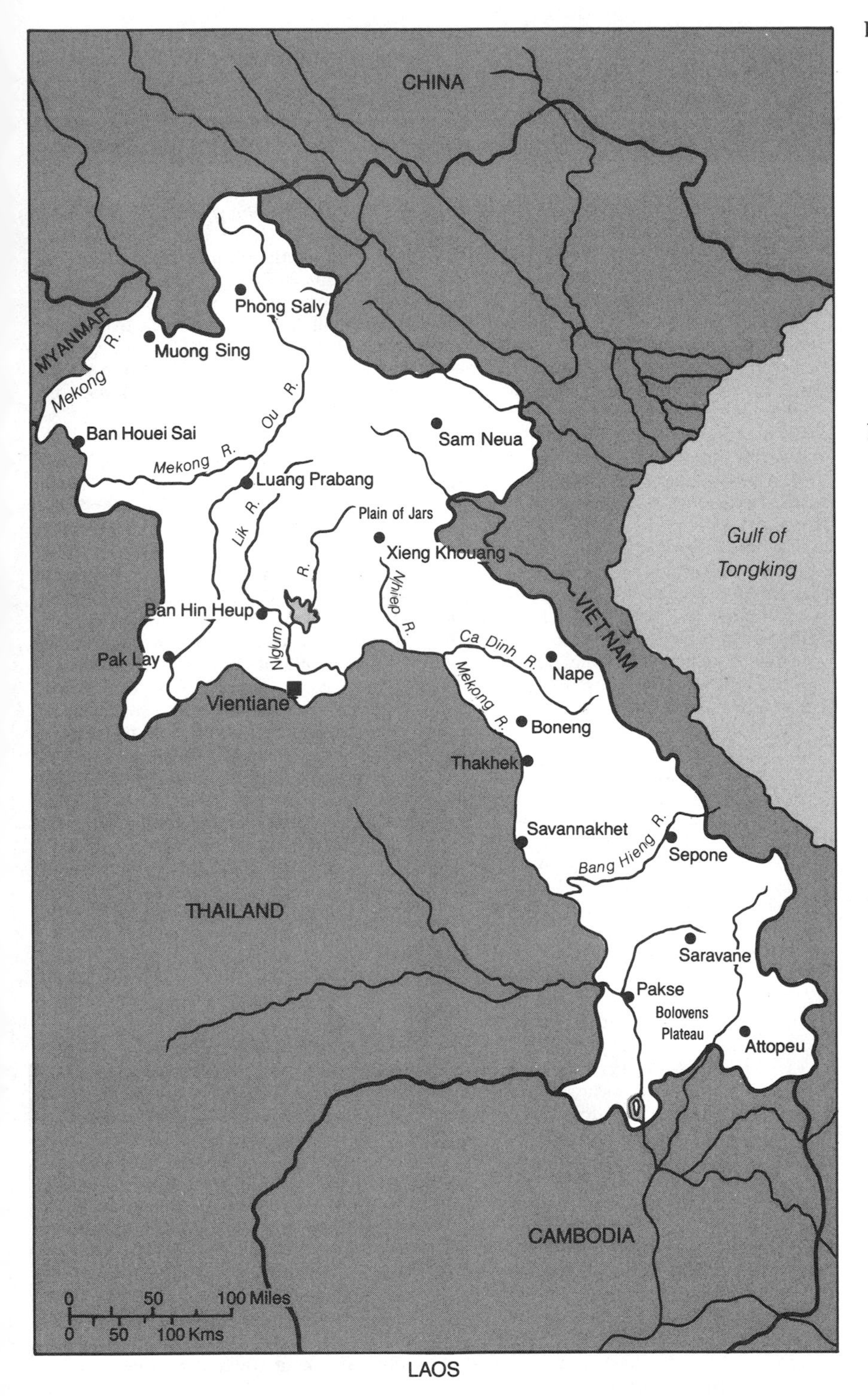

LAOS

party leader. Attempting to promote Anglo-German understanding and avoid another war, Lansbury advocated British disarmament and visited HITLER in 1937.

Lansing, Robert (1864–1928). U.S. secretary of state. Born in Watertown, New York, Lansing graduated from Amherst in 1886. An authority on international law, he frequently served as counsel for the U.S. in international disputes. Lansing succeeded William Jennings BRYAN as secretary of state in 1915. Because Woodrow WILSON conducted foreign policy with his close adviser Edward M. HOUSE, Lansing had little influence on the decision to enter WORLD WAR I, although he advocated participation in the struggle. Lansing worked in harmony with Wilson until the PARIS PEACE CONFERENCE, when he lost the president's confidence because of his view that the LEAGUE OF NATIONS was not important. When Lansing conducted cabinet meetings during Wilson's illness, the president requested his resignation.

Lansky, Meyer (1902–1983). American organized crime figure. Born in Poland, Lansky was reputedly the financial mastermind of organized crime in the U.S. for more than four decades. He began his criminal career in the 1920s during PROHIBITION, and formed a notorious crime syndicate with gangster "Lucky" LUCIANO. Lansky was said to have amassed a multimillion dollar personal fortune through illegal operations in gambling, bootlegging, loansharking, stock manipulation, and infiltration of legitimate businesses throughout the U.S. During his career, he was charged with many crimes, including tax evasion, assault and contempt of court; but he spent only two months of his life in prison.

Laos [Lao People's Democratic Republic]. Laos covers an area of 91,405 square miles on the Indochinese peninsula in southeast Asia (see INDOCHINA). Under French control since 1907, Laos was occupied by Japan during WORLD WAR II, then became a free state within the FRENCH COMMUNITY in 1946. Full independence was granted in 1953. The country suffered political instability during the next 20 years due to conflict between pro- and anti-Communist forces. The leftist political party's links with North Vietnam prompted the United States to initiate secret bombing raids into Laos to destroy North Vietnamese havens there (1964). In 1973 a ceasefire was signed; by 1975 the procommunists controlled the government and established the People's Democratic Republic. The country is still trying to draft a constitution.

La Pasionaria. See Dolores Gomez IBARRURI.

Lardner, Ring(gold Wilmer) (1885–1933). American short story writer and journalist. Lardner developed one of the unique voices in American literature—wry, colloquial, subtly incisive as to nuances of character. His best known volume of stories, *You Know Me, Al: A Busher's Letters* (1916), remains perhaps the finest fictional portrayal of baseball and its impact on American life. Lardner began his writing career as a journalist, covering sports for several years for newspapers in Chicago and New York. In the 1920s, he became a close friend of fellow writer F. Scott FITZGERALD. His tongue-in-cheek volume, *How to Write Short Stories* (1924), was typical Lardner with its bemused humility as to the nature of literary creation. Lardner also collaborated with George S. KAUFMAN on *June Moon* (1929) and other theatrical works. *Some Champions* (1976) is a posthumous selection of Lardner's stories.

Lardner, Ring (Wilmer), Jr. (1915–). American screenwriter and author. The son of noted sports and short story writer Ring LARDNER, Lardner began his film career as a press agent for David O. SELZNICK. His first screenwriting work came when he collaborated on rewriting *A Star Is Born* (1937). Other screenplays include *Woman of the Year* (1942), for which he won his first ACADEMY AWARD; *The Cincinnati Kid* (1965); and M*A*S*H (1970), for which he won his second Oscar. Lardner joined the U.S. Communist Party in 1937 and was among the HOLLYWOOD TEN who refused to testify to the HOUSE UN-AMERICAN ACTIVITIES COMMITTEE (HUAC) during its investigation of communist influence in Hollywood in 1947. Charged with contempt of court in 1950, he served 10 months in prison. Blacklisted, Lardner was unable to work in films again until 1965. In 1955 he published a book, *The Ecstasy of Owen Muir* in England, and in the late 1950s he wrote anonymously for television. In 1976 he published *The Lardners,* an account of his family.

Larionov, Mikhail Fyodorovich (1881–1964). Russian painter. Born in Teraspol, Larionov studied at the School of Painting, Sculpture and Architecture in Moscow. Interested in avant garde art, he took an important part in the introduction of new ideas from FRANCE and ITALY into Russian painting. With his wife, Natalya Goncherova, he founded the Rayonist movement in 1912, advocating color expressed in radiating light as the "guiding principle" of painting. This early doctrine influenced the development of abstract art in Russia, particularly on Kasimir MALEVICH and SUPREMATISM. Larionov settled in Paris in 1914 and abandoned painting in 1915 when he began an association with Serge DIAGHILEV that started with set designing and ended with the artist's involvement in all aspects of the BALLETS RUSSES.

Larkin, Philip (1922–1985). English poet, novelist and critic; a leading figure of THE MOVEMENT. Although hardly prolific, Larkin was one of the best known and most widely read English poets of his generation. Born in Coventry, he attended St. John's College, Oxford, during WORLD WAR II, where he knew Kingsley AMIS. After graduating he became a librarian; from 1955 until his death he was the librarian of the University of Hull. His first book was a slender collection of poems, *The North Ship,* influenced by YEATS. His two novels, *Jill* (1946; revised 1963) and *A Girl in Winter* (1947), explore the theme of adolescent loneliness in wartime England with great sensitivity. Larkin's literary reputation rests almost entirely on three poetry collections: *The Less Deceived* (1955), *The Whitsun Weddings* (1964) and *High Windows* (1974). Understated and carefully crafted, the poems in these books show the influence of Thomas HARDY. Moreover, they register the mood of provincial life in postwar England—a period of austerity and reduced expectations. Larkin's attitude to life is summed up in his famous statement, "deprivation is to me what daffodils are to Wordsworth." Larkin was also a noted jazz critic; his jazz reviews and articles were collected in *All What Jazz?* (1970).

Larsen, Leif Andreas (1906–1990). Norwegian sailor and WORLD WAR II hero. A member of the Norwegian RESISTANCE movement during the war, Larsen made 52 trips across the North Sea in fishing boats to smuggle arms, supplies and Allied agents into occupied NORWAY. He won 11 medals for bravery, making him one of the most highly decorated Allied naval officers of the war. His adventures were later retold in many books and films.

Lartigue, Jacques-Henri (1896–1986). French photographer. Little known until 1963, a retrospective at New York City's MUSEUM OF MODERN ART led to Lartigue being recognized as a major 20th-century photographer. His work provided a matchless chronicle of Parisian high society with photographs taken when he was a child being particularly memorable.

Lashley, Karl (1890–1958). American neuropsychologist. Lashley is best known for his research into the relationship between the brain's mass and its ability to learn. He taught at several universities between 1917 and 1955, including Harvard. He studied the relationship between behavior and brain damage in rats, and wrote *Brain Mechanisms and Intelligence* (1929).

Laski, Harold (Joseph) (1893–1950). British political scientist and economist. Laski attended Oxford University and had a distinguished teaching career at McGill University (1914–16), Harvard University (1916–20) and the London School of Economics (1926–50). A committed socialist, he was a member of the FABIAN SOCIETY and later became active in the British LABOUR PARTY, serving as its chairman in 1945 and 1946. Also holding a number of government posts, he was a prime figure in moving his country toward a peculiarly British socialism. He is best known as a prolific and influential author. Among his books are *Political Thought in England from Locke to Bentham* (1920), *Karl Marx* (1921), *Communism* (1927), *Democracy in Crisis* (1933), *Faith, Reason and Civilisation* (1944) and *The American Democracy* (1948). Laski's lively correspondence with his friend Justice Oliver Wendell HOLMES was published as *Holmes-Laski Letters* (2 vols., 1953).

Laski, Marghanita (1915–1988). British novelist, critic and radio personality; widely known as a broadcaster on "The Critics" and its successor, "Critics' Forum." One of her novels, *Little Boy Lost,* was the basis for a 1953 film about the displaced peoples of postwar Europe that starred Bing CROSBY. She wrote critical studies of such authors as Jane Austen, George Eliot and Rudyard KIPLING. A passionate amateur lexicographer, she was said to have contributed about a quarter of a million quotations to the four-volume supplement to the *Oxford English Dictionary,* the fourth volume of which was published in 1986.

Laskin, Bora (1912–1984). Chief justice of the Supreme Court of CANADA (1973–84). Laskin was appointed to the court in 1970. His written opinions, which often dissented from the more conservative opinions of his colleagues, were praised for their legal scholarship. In 1974 he wrote the unanimous opinion upholding the Official Languages Act, which upgraded the position of French in the Canadian Government.

Lasky, Victor (1918–1990). American journalist and author. An outspoken anti-communist, Lasky was a newspaper reporter and columnist, a Hollywood screenwriter and a lecturer for conservative organizations. His first book, *Seeds of Treason* (written with Ralph de Toledano), was based on the Alger HISS spy case of the late 1940s and became a best seller. His other books included *J.F.K., the Man and the Myth* (1963), and *It Didn't Start with Watergate* (1977), in which he showed the Democratic administrations also had been guilty of "dirty tricks."

Lassie. Perhaps the most famous canine star of all time, Lassie was featured in eight feature films and a long-running television series. Trained by Rudd Weatherwax, the first Lassie was a male collie named Pal, who appeared in *Lassie Come Home* in 1943, when the intended star, a female collie, was shedding too heavily to perform. Pal's male offspring later succeeded him in the role. The last Lassie movie, *The Magic of Lassie,* was released in 1978.

late modernism. Term that has come into use to describe and criticize current architectural and design practice and to designate work that continues to develop the ideas of MODERNISM, particularly the austere work of the INTERNATIONAL STYLE. While POSTMODERNISM tends to turn away from the ideas of the modern movement, introducing more decorative elements and often returning to historicism, the modernist direction survives and has also moved in the direction of greater complexity of form. The works of architects such as Charles Gwathmey and Robert Siegel, Richard Meier, and I.M. PEI with their strong loyalty to the modernist ethic, characterize the late-modernist direction.

Lattimore, Owen (1900–1989). American China scholar and writer. Born in Washington, Lattimore was educated in England and at Harvard. He then worked and studyed in China and elsewhere in Asia, becoming an expert on Asian affairs. He edited the *Journal of Pacific Affairs* (1934–41) and wrote a number of books on the Far East. During WORLD WAR II he served the U.S. government in several capacities, including advisor to CHIANG KAI-SHEK. In 1950 while he was director of the Walter Hines Page School at Johns Hopkins University, he was accused by Senator Joseph MCCARTHY of being "the top Soviet espionage agent in the U.S." A Senate Foreign Relations Subcommittee investigated the charges against Lattimore and concluded that they were "a fraud and a hoax." Nevertheless, he was indicted for perjury in 1952 in connection with his Senate testimony; a federal judge dismissed the indictment in 1955 for lack of evidence. His brother **Richard Lattimore** was a distinguished poet and classics scholar noted for his translations of Homer and other ancient Greek poets and dramatists.

For further reading:

Lattimore, Owen, *Ordeal by Slander*. Westport, Conn.: Greenwood, 1950 (repr. 1971).

Lattre de Tassigny, Jean de (1889–1952). French general. A prominent military figure during WORLD WAR II, Lattre de Tassigny commanded the Fifth Army in Alsace in 1939. The following year, he led the 14th Infantry in its attempt to repel the German invasion of France. He was arrested by the Germans in 1942, after having become the commander of the 17th Division in Montpelier, and sentenced to 10 years imprisonment. He escaped the following year, joining General GIRAUD and becoming a commander in French North Africa. In 1944 he led the First French Army in its landing in FRANCE, and fought northward until finally striking into GERMANY. Named inspector general of the army in 1945, he was posthumously granted the title of marshal of FRANCE.

Latvia. One of the Baltic Sea republics of the U.S.S.R., Latvia is located between ESTONIA and LITHUANIA in the northwest of the Soviet Union and covers an area of 24,704 square miles. The territory of modern Latvia was annexed to Russia by Peter the Great in 1709 and was controlled by German estate owners, called *Baltic Barons,* who served the Russian Czar. In 1918 Latvia declared its independence, but it did not gain international recognition until 1921. Karlis Ulmanis became dictator in 1934 after economic problems forced the suspension of democratic government. His failure to obtain German protection against Soviet encroachment led to Russian occupation and establishment of Latvia as a Soviet republic in 1940. Germany occupied the country from 1941 to 1944. Recent loosening of authoritarian control in the Soviet Union under the leadership of Mikhail GORBACHEV has led to Latvia's declaration of sovereignty and a movement toward full independence.

Latvian War of Independence (1919–20). After GERMANY's defeat in World War I, the Latvians proclaimed an independent state with Karlis Ulmanis (1877–1940) as prime minister. In early January 1919 Soviet forces invaded, seized the capital, Riga, and set up a Soviet government. German-Latvian troops with Allied approval forced the Soviets to withdraw in March 1919. By the TREATY OF VERSAILLES Germans were required to leave the area, but occupied Riga and were not expelled until November 1919, while the Soviets, again attempting a takeover, were evicted with Allied support by January 1920. By the Treaty of Riga, August 11, 1920 the Soviets recognized Latvian independence.

Lauder, Harry (1870–1950). Scottish entertainer. Primarily a comedian and singer, Lauder was one of the most popular music hall artists of the early 20th century and appeared widely in both Britain and the U.S. One of the most highly paid entertainers of his day, he was also a prolific songwriter as well as a novelist and short story writer. His popular songs included "I Love a Lassie" (1905), "Roamin' in the Gloamin" (1911) and "It's Nice to Get Up in the Morning" (1914). Lauder entertained British troops during WORLD WAR I and was knighted in 1919 for his aid to the war effort.

"Laugh-In". Zany American comedy-variety television series of the late 1960s. Its rapid-fire blackout sketches, burlesque gags and satiric pokes at contemporary America made it the number one program for two full seasons, 1968–70. It was a kind of "happening," a weekly push at the envelope of television propriety and censorship. Comedians Dan Rowan and Dick Martin presided over a cast of 40 regulars, each of whom appeared with a brief shtick, or tag, that became part of the national vocabulary: Arte Johnson had his gutteral "Verrrry Interesting!"; Ruth Buzzi her ferocious umbrella; Lily Tomlin her nasal snort; Goldie Hawn her jiggle; and announcer Gary Owens his outrageously overmodulated tonsils. Catchphrases were everywhere: "Sock it to me!" and "Here come da judge!" and "You bet your bippy!" are just a few examples. The show was like a quick mosaic of interchangeable pieces that changed pattern from week to week. A "Jock Wall" concluded each program, from which the faces of the cast popped in and out of little windows with quick one-liners. It ended its run in 1973. Six years later producer George Schlatter assembled a cast of unknowns and revived "Laugh-In" as a series of NBC specials. Although the show had grown stale and was dropped, at least one star was "discovered"—Robin Williams.

For further reading:
The Complete Directory to Prime Time Network TV Shows. New York: Ballantine Books, 1988.

Laughton, Charles (1899–1962). British film and theatrical actor. Laughton was one of the most gifted character actors in the history of the cinema. Educated at the Royal Academy of Dramatic Arts, Laughton achieved successes on the London and Broadway stages before appearing in his first HOLLYWOOD feature, *The Old Dark Horse* (1932), a horror film. He won widespread fame for his title role in *The Private Life of Henry VIII* (1933), a British film directed by Alexander KORDA. Returning to Hollywood, Laughton gave memorable performances in *The Barretts of Wimpole Street* (1934), *Ruggles of Red Gap* (1935), and *Mutiny on the Bounty* (1935), in which he played Captain Bligh opposite Clark GABLE as Fletcher Christian. One of Laughton's finest performances was as Quasimodo in *The Hunchback of Notre Dame* (1939). Laughton directed only one film, the classic thriller *The Night of the Hunter* (1955), starring Robert MITCHUM. His last film appearance came in *Advise and Consent* (1962). Laughton was married to the actress Elsa LANCHESTER.

Laurel and Hardy. The team of **Stan Laurel** (born Arthur Stanley Jefferson, 1890–1965) and **Oliver Hardy** (1892–1957) stands alongside the MARX BROTHERS as one of the greatest comedic ensembles ever captured on film. Both Laurel and Hardy enjoyed independent careers as comic actors in silent films, and in the 1910s Laurel served as an understudy for Charlie CHAPLIN. But they were teamed together in 1926 by film producer Hal Roach and enjoyed immediate success as evidenced by a series of over thirty silent shorts directed in the late 1920s by Leo McCarey, George STEVENS and others. With the transition to sound, Laurel and Hardy turned eventually to feature films and Laurel himself took over artistic responsibilities. The basic premise in their

Stan Laurel (left) and Oliver Hardy doing a little soft shoe (1936).

films was simple but had universal appeal: The thin, woebegone Englishman Laurel and the rotund, blustery American Hardy found themselves in circumstances they could neither control or understand. For all their good intentions, they were eternal victims of fate. Their performances were memorable because they combined outrageous slapstick pranks with genuine human pathos. The team won an ACADEMY AWARD for *The Music Box* (1932), a live action comedy short. Their classic comedy features include *Sons of the Desert* (1933), *Fra Diavolo* (1933), *Babes in Toyland* (1934), *Way Out West* (1937), and *A Chump at Oxford* (1940). In 1960 Stan Laurel was awarded a Special Oscar for his pioneering excellence in screen comedy.

Lauren, Ralph (1939–). American fashion designer whose career has vastly expanded from the introduction of wide necktie designs to designing clothing for men, women, and children, as well as the environments they inhabit. Born in the Bronx, Lauren studied business at New York's City College at night while holding a wide variety of jobs in clothing stores, including Brooks Brothers, where he found an affinity for classic, sports-oriented clothing. There are overtones of belonging to upper-class circles in his relaxed styling and in his own life-style (he owns a 10,000–acre ranch in Colorado). In addition to clothing, his business now includes designs for fragrances, home furnishing, and luggage. The restored Rhinelander Mansion in New York serves as a flagship for his vast network of Polo/Ralph Lauren shops. He was the recipient of a 1970 Coty Men's Wear Award, the year before he began designing women's clothing.

Laurier, Sir Wilfrid (1841–1919). Canadian statesman, prime minister of CANADA (1896–1911). Born in Quebec province, Laurier was educated at McGill University, became a lawyer and served in the Ottawa parliament as a Liberal member from 1874 to 1878. In the opposition to the Conservative government from 1878 to 1896, he was appointed Liberal leader in 1887. In 1896 Laurier became the first French-Canadian prime minister, and the following year he was knighted. His 15–year tenure has been called the "age of Laurier," an era in which a Canadian identity was forged. During this period the country grew enormously, its economy flourished and it opened its doors to some two million immigrants who helped develop the Canadian West and build the nation's huge railroad system. Laurier sought to create harmony between Canada's French and English-speaking citizens and to strengthen links with Great Britain and the U.S. His trade ties to the U.S. were central to his defeat in the 1911 elections. Leader of the opposition until his death, he supported Canada's 1914 entry into WORLD WAR I, but opposed conscription and resisted the formation of a coalition government in 1917. (See also LIBERAL PARTY–CANADA.)

Lausanne, Treaty of. Treaty signed in Lausanne, Switzerland in 1923 that established modern TURKEY's borders and settled a number of territorial problems that arose at the end of World War I. The earlier (1920) Treaty of SEVRES had virtually destroyed the defeated OTTOMAN EMPIRE. However, its provisions were rejected by Turkish nationalists led by Mustafa Kemal (later known as ATATURK), who forced new negotiations when they drove Greek troops out of Smyrna and overthrew the sultan. According to the new treaty, Turkey recovered Smyrna, eastern Thrace and some islands in the Aegean and resumed its control of the DARDANELLES, which were demilitarized. Turkey also renounced claims on former Ottoman Empire territories. A separate agreement between Greece and Turkey arranged for the forced exchange of minority populations from each signatory country.

Laval, Pierre (1883–1945). French statesman. Born in the Auvergne, Laval became a lawyer and entered politics as a Socialist deputy in 1914. He held a number of governmental posts, began moving to the right politically and was elected as an Independent senator in 1926. He served as premier from 1931 to 1932 and as premier and foreign minister from 1935 to 1936. In 1935 he and British foreign minister Sir Samuel Hoare formulated a plan to partition ETHIOPIA in order to stop the Italian invasion, a scheme that would have appeased MUSSOLINI by giving much of the country to its invader. Laval's government fell after public uproar over the plan caused its withdrawal. After the fall of FRANCE in 1940, Laval became vice-premier in the VICHY government, supporting close ties with Nazi GERMANY. He was dismissed on suspicion of attempting to overthrow Marshal PETAIN, but was reinstated in 1942. Facilitating Nazi policy, he nonetheless attempted to retain some distance from the Germans, a task in which he was largely unsuccessful. After the Allied invasion, the fleeing Germans arrested Laval in 1944, but he escaped to

Pierre Laval, French politician who collaborated with the Nazis.

Spain in 1945. He subsequently surrendered himself to the Allies, and was returned to FRANCE to face treason charges. Found guilty in a trial whose fairness was questionable and in which he eloquently defended himself, Laval was sentenced to death. After unsuccessfully attempting to commit suicide, he was executed.

Laver, Rod(ney George) (1938–). Australian tennis player. Best known for his Davis Cup play, Laver may be the last player to have made a worldwide reputation as an amateur. He won Wimbledon twice before turning professional and led Australia to four Davis Cups, winning all six of his singles event in 1960, 1961 and 1962. He relinquished his amateur status in 1963 and went on to win 71 championships in 17 countries, including two additional Wimbledons, and a 1969 Grand Slam. Laver was the first player to break the $1 million mark.

Lavin, Mary (1912–). Irish author. Though born in the U.S., Lavin moved to Ireland at the age of nine, and her writing evokes her enchantment with the Irish ambience. Encouraged to write by the playwright and Irish revivalist Lord DUNSANY, Lavin published her first collection of stories, *Tales from Bective Bridge* in 1942. Lavin was widowed and left with the management of a farm and three children, and remarried in 1969 after which she lived in Dublin and Meath. Her perceptive writing examines relationships, depicting the lives of both the Irish peasantry and the middle classes. Other works include the novels *The House in Cluew Street* (1945) and *Mary O'Grady* (1950) and the short story collection *The Shrine and other Stories* (1977).

Lavrenyov, Boris Andreyevich (1894–1952). Soviet author. Lavrenyov joined the army in 1915 and served as a cavalry officer in World War I. In 1921 he began to write seriously. In the early stages of his literary career Lavrenyov was attracted to FUTURISM, but he later came under the influence of ACMEISM. He was a member of the Leningrad literary group *Sodruzhestvo*. Lavrenyov's stories are romantic and his plots dynamic. Among his stories are the collections *Crazy Tales* (1925) and *The Forty-First* (1924). He also wrote the plays *Smoke* and *The Debacle* (1928). Much of his work recounts incidents from the Civil War and the days of WAR COMMUNISM.

Law, Andrew Bonar (1858–1923). British politician, prime minister of the UNITED KINGDOM (1923). Born in New Brunswick, Canada, Law emigrated to Scotland at the age of 12 and was educated at Glasgow High School. He was a successful iron merchant in Glasgow when he was first elected to Parliament in 1900 as a member of the CONSERVATIVE PARTY. He served as parliamentary secretary to the Board of Trade from 1902 to 1906, and gained support from party members who considered party leader Arthur BALFOUR too remote. In 1911 he succeeded Balfour as the leader of the Opposition, strongly supporting the Ulstermen in the Irish crisis of 1912–1914. At the outbreak of WORLD WAR I, Law supported the government and entered the ASQUITH coalition as colonial secretary, later becoming Chancellor of the exchequer and leader in the Commons under David LLOYD GEORGE from 1915 to 1919, and Lord Privy Seal from 1919 to 1922. Following Lloyd George's resignation in 1922, Law became prime minister, but was forced by an inoperable cancer to resign seven months later. Law's brief tenure set the pattern for British Conservatism between the two world wars.

Lawler, Richard (1895–1982). American surgeon who successfully performed the world's first kidney transplant operation (1950). Lawler performed the operation only once, saying that he "just wanted to get it started." He was nominated for the NOBEL PRIZE in 1970 for his pioneering surgery but did not receive the award.

Lawrence, D(avid) H(erbert) (1885–1930). English novelist, story writer, literary critic, travel writer, poet and painter. Lawrence is one of the greatest figures in 20th-century English literature. Indeed, there are few writers in the history of world literature who can equal Lawrence in terms of a versatility and excellence shown in so many writing genres. He was born in Eastwood, Nottinghamshire, the fourth child of a struggling coal miner who was a heavy drinker. Lawrence, who suffered from frail health for much of his life, was very close to his mother, who provided encouragement for his artistic career. He earned a scholarship to Nottingham University and briefly pursued a teaching career. The publication of his acclaimed first novel, *The White Peacock* (1911), launched him as a writer. His other major novels include *Sons and Lovers* (1913), *The Rainbow* (1915), *Women in Love* (1920) and the controversial LADY CHATTERLEY'S LOVER (1928), a frank and beautiful love story that was for a time banned in both Great Britain and the U.S. as pornographic. Lawrence also wrote vibrant short stories and lyric poetry, travel classics such as *Etruscan Places* (1932), and even attained posthumous renown for his expressionistic paintings completed in the 1920s. Lawrence married Frieda von Richthofen in 1914 and traveled with her through Europe, the U.S., Mexico and Australia in the final two decades of his life.

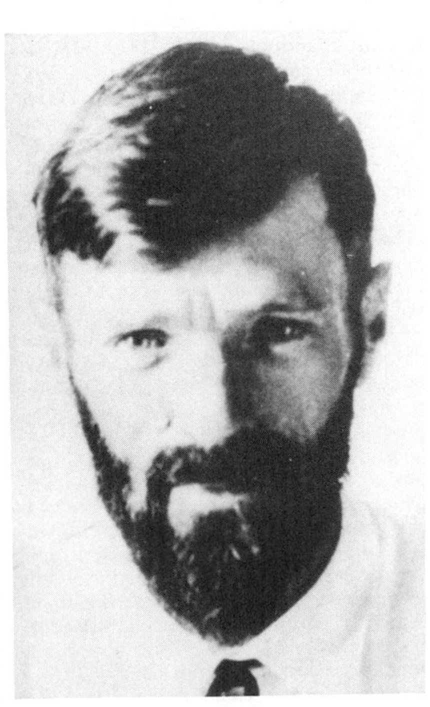

D.H. Lawrence.

Lawrence, Ernest Orlando (1901–1958). American physicist. Born in Canton, South Dakota, Lawrence earned his Ph.D. from Yale University in 1925. In 1930, while a professor at the University of California at Berkeley, he began experiments that eventually led to his invention of the cyclotron, a device in which atomic particles are accelerated by means of an alternating electric field in a constant magnetic field. Lawrence received the 1939 NOBEL PRIZE in physics for this work. Later, he played a key role in the development of the atomic bomb. Element 103, lawrencium, is named for him.

Lawrence, Gertrude [Gertrud Klasen] (1898–1952). British actress. Though she began her career performing in revues and musicals, Lawrence gained international acclaim in several Noel COWARD plays, most notably *Private Lives* (1930), which he wrote for her, and *Blithe Spirit* (1945). She also had personal triumphs in the Broadway musicals *Lady in the Dark* (1941) by Moss HART and Kurt WEILL and *The King and I* (1951) by Richard RODGERS and Oscar HAMMERSTEIN II.

Lawrence, Jacob (1917–). American painter. Born in Atlantic City, N.J., Lawrence studied at various schools and with various artists in New York City from 1932 to 1939. An African-American, he has explored the black experience in the U.S. in many of his figurative paintings. Flat, angular and decorative in style, often using tempera as a medium, Lawrence's work includes a number of painting cycles including *Harlem* and *Migration of the Negro* (1940–41). Lawrence is a noted teacher, and his work is included in collections such as the Whitney Museum of American Art and Museum of Modern Art, New York City, and the Phillips Collection, Washington, D.C.

Lawrence, T(homas) E(dward) [Lawrence of Arabia] (1888–1935). British soldier, adventurer, author and WORLD WAR I hero. Educated at Oxford, he participated in archaeological expeditions to the Middle East while still an undergraduate. He stayed in the region from 1911 to 1914, learning Arabic and working as an archaeologist. After the outbreak of World War I, he was posted to Egypt as a member of the British army's intelligence staff. In 1916, he joined the forces of the Arabian sheik Faisal al Husayn (later FAISAL I), becoming a leader in the Arab revolt against Turkish rule. His guerrilla tactics, striking at the Damascus-Medina railroad and fringe areas, were extremely successful in expelling the much larger Ottoman army from western Arabia and Syria (see OTTOMAN EMPIRE; WORLD WAR I IN MESOPOTAMIA). After the Arab forces took DAMASCUS in 1918, Lawrence returned to England. A delegate to the PARIS PEACE CONFERENCE after the war, he vainly fought for Arab independence. Thereafter, he was a research fellow at Oxford (1919) and a Middle Eastern advisor at the Colonial Office (1921–22).

T.E. Lawrence, British author and soldier.

Whether out of a sense of failure in the Arab cause, or from a desire from anonymity, Lawrence resigned from his post and in 1922 enlisted under the name of Ross as a mechanic in the Royal Air Force. His identity was discovered a year later and he joined the tank corps, later rejoining (1925) the RAF under the name of Shaw. His account of his Arabian adventures was privately printed in 1926 under the title *Seven Pillars of Wisdom*, later abridged to *Revolt in the Desert*. He died in a motorcycle accident near his home in Dorset on May 19, 1935. A man of intense contradictions, Lawrence remains one of the most legendary and enigmatic public figures of the 20th century. His exploits formed the basis of David LEAN's film, *Lawrence of Arabia* (1963).

For further reading:

Brown, Malcolm, *A Touch of Genius: The Life of T.E. Lawrence*. London: Dent, 1989.

Mack, John E., *A Prince of Our Disorder: The Life of T.E. Lawrence*. Boston: Little, Brown, 1978.

Wilson, Jeremy, *Lawrence of Arabia: The Authorized Biography of T.E. Lawrence*. New York: Atheneum, 1990.

Laxness, Halldor [Hallod r Guojdnsson] (1902–). Icelandic novelist. Laxness' early fiction, which includes the short stories *Nokkrar sogur* (*Some Stories, 1923*) and the novel *Verfarinn mikli from Kasmir* (The Great Weaver From Kashmir, 1927), reflects his conversion to Catholicism in 1923 and the influence of the surrealist movement. Influenced by Upton SINCLAIR on a trip to North America in the late twenties, Laxness became a socialist, and it is for his subsequent political fiction depicting the lower classes of Iceland that he is best known. These include the two-volume novel, *Salka Valka* (1931–1932), the first of his works to be translated into English; the two-volume *Sjolfstoett folk* (*Independent People,* 1934–1935), and the tetralogy *Heimsljos* (*World Light,* 1937–1940), which is considered his most important work. Laxness was awarded the NOBEL PRIZE for literature in 1955. Later works include the novel, *Brekkukotsannoll* (*The Fish Can Sing,* 1957) and the autobiographical *Skaldatimi* (*Poetic Age,* 1963).

Leach, Bernard (1887–1979). English master potter in the handcraft tradition, who reflected modernist directions in his works. Leach was born in Hong Kong and studied the traditional art and craftwork of China, Japan, and Korea, before moving to England in 1920. He established his own pottery at St. Ives in Cornwall where he produced individual works of high quality in terms of both craftsmanship and design. He eventually developed a range of basic designs that were handmade in considerable quantity and available for practical use. His shapes were generally simple and functional in a way that matched the developing taste of MODERNISM; his brush-painted decorations, where they occur, suggest a more self-conscious orientalism. His book, *A Potter's Book* (1940), is a standard text and manual in the field.

Leacock, Stephen (1869–1944). Canadian humorist, political scientist and man of letters. Although he was an admired professor of political science at McGill University (1901–36), Leacock gained fame as a gifted lecturer and after-dinner speaker, and as a writer of humor. As a speaker he was extremely popular in England and the U.S., often being compared to Mark Twain. His varied written works, including stories, histories, books on economics and political science, are noted for their biting humor. Among his many books are *Nonsense Novels* (1911) and *Sunshine Sketches of a Little Town* (1912).

League of Arab States. See ARAB LEAGUE.

League of Nations. International arbitration and peace-keeping organization established in 1919. U.S. President Woodrow WILSON was the chief architect of the League of Nations, and its formation was one of his FOURTEEN POINTS. He was, however, unable to persuade the U.S. Congress of its merits, and the U.S. never became a member. The League of Nations constitution was adopted at the PARIS PEACE CONFERENCE and recognized in post-World War I peace treaties. The League's headquarters were established in Geneva; its first secretary-general was Sir Eric Drummond (1876–1951), a British diplomat and later Earl of Perth. The League consisted of three branches: a council, the main peace-keeping arm composed of between 8 and 10 members; the assembly, in which all members participated; and the secretariat, which was its administrative staff. There were 42 original member-nations, including UNITED KINGDOM, CHINA, FRANCE, ITALY and JAPAN. GERMANY was a member from 1926 to 1933 and the UNION OF SOVIET SOCIALIST REPUBLICS from 1934 to 1940.

The League's aim was to provide collective security to member countries, in that all would come to the aid of a country attacked or threatened by war. It had no armed forces and would instead rely on economic sanctions to coerce errant countries. Its successes included settling conflicts in Latin America and the Balkans and providing assistance to Russian and Turkish refugees in the 1920s, but it proved ineffectual against more powerful or determined countries. When the League failed to recognize Japan's annexation of MANCHURIA, Japan withdrew from the organization in 1933. ITALY withdrew in 1937 after the League imposed sanctions on it over the Abyssinian War, and the U.S.S.R. was ejected in 1940 following its attack on FINLAND in 1939. As hostilities increased prior to World War II, most countries dismissed the League and operated independently. It was dissolved in 1946, and its functions were taken up by the UNITED NATIONS.

League of Red Cross Societies. Federation of national Red Cross societies that administers worldwide relief efforts. Headquartered in Geneva, Switzerland, it was founded in Paris after World War I. From its inception, the League's purposes included the prevention of disease, the encouragement of new national Red Cross organizations, the spreading of information regarding science and medicine and the coordination of national and international relief work. During its years of operation the League has participated in hundreds of relief, rescue and disease-prevention programs. In 1963 it was awarded the NOBEL PRIZE for peace, shared with the INTERNATIONAL COMMITTEE OF THE RED CROSS (ICRC). Today the League has a combined membership of some 250 million from approximately 144 national groups and is one of the three components of the International Movement of the Red Cross and Red Crescent, which also includes the ICRC and the various national Red Cross societies.

Leakey, Louis S(eymour) B(azett) (1903–1972). Anglo-Kenyan archaeologist and anthropologist. Born in Kenya to British missionary parents, Dr. Leakey is one of the best known anthropologists of the 20th century. His discoveries of early primate fossils in the Olduvai Gorge in east Africa helped shape the 20th-century view of human evolution. In 1959 he and his wife **Mary Leakey,** also a noted anthropologist, discovered fossils of *Zinjanthropus* (now called *Australopithecus boisei*), a close ancestor of humans. From 1961 to 1964 the Leakeys and their son **Jonathan Leakey** unearthed fossils of *Homo habilis,* the oldest known primate with human characteristics. Louis Leakey's theories about the age of humankind aroused much controversy. In 1972 his son **Richard Leakey** who directed the National Museum of Kenya, reported the discovery of a 2.6 million-year-old skull that bore a close resemblance to the skull of modern humans. Richard Leakey suggested that modern humans evolved from this creature rather than from *Austrolopithicus.* This finding raised further controversy. In 1975 Richard Leakey discovered the skull of *Homo erectus* (estimated at 1.6 million years old), and in 1984 he and another paleontologist discovered a virtually complete *Homo erectus* skeleton.

For further reading:

Leakey, Mary, *Disclosing the Past.* New York: McGraw-Hill, 1986.

Lean, David (1908–91). British film director. Lean earned a reputation as one of the leading directors in the cinema, primarily due to the epic grandeur and scope he instilled in classic films such as *The Bridge on the River Kwai* (1957) and *Lawrence of Arabia* (1962), both of which won the ACADEMY AWARD for best picture. Lean began his directorial career in the 1940s, first as an assistant to Noel COWARD and then as a director on his own film versions of the Coward plays, *Blithe Spirit* (1945) and *Brief Encounter* (1945). Lean went on to adapt two works by Charles Dickens to the cinema, *Great Expectations* (1946) and *Oliver Twist* (1948). *Lawrence of Arabia* (about T.E. LAWRENCE) vaulted Irish actor Peter O'Toole to world prominence. Subsequent films by Lean include *Doctor Zhivago* (1964), *Ryan's Daughter* (1970) and *A Passage to India* (1984). In the early 1990s he was working on a film version of Joseph CONRAD's novel *Nostromo.*

For further reading:

Anderegg, Michael A., *David Lean.* Boston: G.K. Hall, 1984.

Silverman, Stephen M., *David Lean.* New York: Abrams, 1989.

Lear, Norman (1922–). American television and motion picture producer/screenwriter, best known for ALL IN THE FAMILY. After serving with the Army Air Force in World War II, Lear worked for many years in television as a comedy writer; he and partner Bud Yorkin formed Tandem Productions, which produced a number of successful situation comedies depicting family life in the 1970s. ALL IN THE FAMILY began its 12–year run in 1971 (with spinoffs "Maude," 1972, and "The Jeffersons," 1975). "Sanford and Son" debuted in 1972, and "Good Times" first appeared in 1974. Another Lear company, T.A.T. Communications, developed several additional series, including "One Day at a Time" and "Mary Hartman, Mary Hartman" (both beginning in 1975). After leaving television in 1978, Lear pursued political, environmental and spiritual concerns in activist organizations like People for the American Way, Business Enterprise Trust and a multimedia conglomerate, ACT III. He later produced a new comedy series about what he called "today's lack of spiritual values"; he also produced several motion pictures for director Rob Reiner, who had earlier portrayed "Meathead" in "All in the Family."

For further reading:

Michaelson, Judith, "Divining the New Lear," *The Los Angeles Times Calendar.* December 2, 1990.

Lear, William Powell (1902–1978). American industrialist and inventor. Lear held patents on more than 150 inventions. He devised the automatic pilot, which became a standard feature on military, commercial and private aircraft. He also designed the first practical automobile radio and the eight-track stereo player. His small Lear Jet was designed for the corporate market and replaced other small propeller-driven aircraft as the most popular airplane model owned by businesses.

Leary, Timothy (Francis) (1920–). American psychologist and drug experimenter. Born in Springfield, Massachusetts, he received a B.A. from the University of Alabama (1942) and a Ph.D. from the University of California, Berkeley (1950). Leary began teaching at Harvard in 1958. There he and a colleague initiated a series of experiments with the hallucinogenic drug LSD, often using themselves and their students as subjects. Leary soon became a psychedelics evangelist, touting their revolutionary, consciousness-altering properties and helping to introduce them to influential members of the 1960s generation. His experiments caused friction with Harvard's administration and he was fired from his post early in the '60s. Having converted to Hinduism in 1965, Leary founded the League for Spiritual Discovery the following year. In 1967 he delivered a version of the anthematic 1960s line "Turn on, tune in, drop out." He was first arrested on a drug charge in 1965, and a subsequent 1970 arrest and conviction sent him into exile abroad and caused his 1973–76 imprisonment. With a somewhat softened message on drugs, Leary remained a COUNTERCULTURE spokesman into the 1990s.

Leavis, F(rank) R(aymond) (1895–1978). British author and critic. An enormously influential literary scholar and critic, Leavis was born in and educated at Cambridge, where he was influenced by I.A. RICHARDS, whose textual approach to literary criticism Leavis embraced and enhanced. He married Q.D. Leavis in 1929, another student of Richard's, whose *Fiction and the Reading Public* (1932) addressed the correlation between literature and literacy. From 1932 until 1953 Leavis was chief editor of *Scrutiny*, the controversial journal which was a forum for the NEW CRITICISM, and in which he attacked what he considered the dilettantish elitism of the BLOOMSBURY GROUP. Leavis' many groundbreaking works, which include *Mass Civilization and Minority Culture* (1930), *The Great Tradition: George Eliot, Henry James, Joseph Conrad* (1948), and *Dickens the Novelist*, written with Q.D. Leavis, (1970), purport that "ethical sensibility" is the most important criteria by which to judge an author. He offended many by criticizing literary lions such as Thomas HARDY and Charles Dickens. Leavis created additional furor by his caustic response to C.P. SNOW's lecture, Two Cultures, in *Two Cultures?: The Significance of C.P. Snow* (1962). Leavis taught at Cambridge until 1964.

Lebanese Civil War of 1958. Elected president of LEBANON in 1952, Camille CHAMOUN oversaw a predominantly Christian (Maronite) government that stressed closer ties to Europe and the U.S. Lebanese Muslims, who made up about half of the country's population, favored stronger economic and political relationships with the surrounding Arab nations. On May 9–13, 1958, Muslim groups openly rebelled against Chamoun's regime, rioting and fighting in the streets of Tripoli and BEIRUT, Lebanon's capital. The newly formed United Arab Republic (a political union of Egypt and Syria) had allegedly instigated the violence against the pro-Western policies of President Chamoun, whose government seemed on the verge of collapse as rebels under several Muslim leaders and Druse (Druze) chieftain Kamal Jumblatt overcame army troops. Refusing to resign, Chamoun appealed to the U.S. for help; U.S. President Dwight D. EISENHOWER ordered American forces from the Sixth Fleet to land near Beirut to support the government, as well as to protect American lives and to guard against a possible Egyptian-Syrian invasion of Lebanon (July 16–20, 1958). Within a month the Lebanese government and army, assisted by more than 14,000 U.S. troops, had control of the situation. General Fuad Chehab, a Maronite Christian, succeeded Chamoun as president on September 23, 1958; a new cabinet of four Christians, three Muslims and one Druse was formed. The U.S. backed the new government and completely withdrew its troops from Lebanon by late October that year.

Israeli armored personnel carrier on patrol in Lebanon's Bekaa Valley (May 1983).

Lebanese Civil War of 1975–90. LEBANON's various Muslim groups, principally the Shi'ite and Druse (Druze) sects, which make up about half the population, were never happy with the 1943 National Pact, which established a dominant political role for the Christians, especially the Maronites, in the central government. Further complicating the political climate was the presence of refugee Palestinian Muslims, living in camps or bases, particularly in the south, from which guerrillas of the PALESTINE LIBERATION ORGANIZATION (PLO) were carrying out attacks on neighboring Israel. Native Lebanese Muslims tended to sympathize with the PLO.

On April 13, 1975, a bus carrying many Palestinians was assaulted by Christian Phalangists and the passengers slain—triggering a long and bloody civil war. At first a leftist Muslim coalition fought rightist Christians; in early 1976, the PLO joined the Muslims after Christians raided a Palestinian refugee camp. ISRAEL supplied arms to Christians. With the backing of the ARAB LEAGUE of states, SYRIA sent 30,000 troops to restore order in Lebanon and to implement a peace plan (1976). Elias SARKIS, a Maronite Christian, was elected Lebanon's president and, with Syrian, Israeli, U.S. and Saudi support, attempted to establish authority. By 1977, Lebanon was divided into a northern section, controlled by Syrian forces, and a coastal section under Christian control, with enclaves in the south dominated by leftist Muslims and the PLO. Syrians and Christian militiamen were soon battling each other, and the Syrians shelled the Christian part of BEIRUT, Lebanon's capital. In retaliation for a Palestinian guerrilla terrorist attack on Israel, Israeli troops invaded southern Lebanon (March 14, 1978) to wipe out PLO bases and occupied the area as far north as the Litani River. The Israelis complied with a United

Nations demand for their withdrawal from the area, then occupied by a UN peacekeeping force (1978).

In 1980, Syria concentrated forces in central Lebanon's Bekaa (al-Biqa) Valley and later moved Soviet-made surface-to-air (SAM-6) missiles there. When the Phalangists (Christians) occupied the hills around Zahle near the strategic Beirut-Damascus highway, Syria launched a major offensive against them; Israeli jets intervened and attacked the Syrians and also bombed areas of Beirut in retaliation for PLO rocket attacks from Lebanon into northern Israel. A ceasefire went into effect on July 24, 1981, but it was temporary. To dispel the PLO, invading Israeli troops reached the outskirts of Beirut and forced the evacuation of PLO guerrillas in 1982.

Lebanon's Phalangist President-elect Bashir Gemayel (1947–82), chosen to succeed the retiring Sarkis, was assassinated on September 14, 1982; his brother, Amin Gemayel (b. 1942), a more moderate Christian leader, became president—just days before 328 Palestinian civilians would be massacred by alleged Phalangists at the SABRA AND SHATILA refugee camps in west Beirut (September 16–18, 1982). Afterward U.S. Marines and British, French and Italian troops arrived in Beirut as a peacekeeping force. A bomb blast killed more than 50 people at the U.S. embassy in Beirut on April 18, 1983. Israeli forces withdrew from Lebanon's Shuf Mountains, which the Druse under their leader Walid Jumblatt (b. 1947) occupied after heavy fighting against Christians and the Lebanese army. On October 23, 1983, and without warning, 239 Americans and 58 French died in separate, suicidal bomb attacks on U.S. and French military headquarters in Beirut.

At Tripoli, PLO leader Yasir ARAFAT and his loyalists were attacked and besieged by PLO dissidents, supported by Syria, for six weeks until they were evacuated by a U.N.-flag-flying Greek ship on December 20, 1983. U.S. warships off the coast bombarded Syrian and Druse positions. Faced with his country's disintegration into multiple ministates, President Gemayel sought national reconciliation talks to settle differences among political leaders—Phalangist, Maronite, Druse, Sunni, Shi'ite and others—in order to stabilize the government. U.S. Marines left Beirut in February 1984, with Lebanon still occupied in part by Syrian and Israeli troops and still divided by bitter feuds and warring factions. After Gemayel left office in 1988, Christian Gen. Michel Aoun refused to acknowledge the new Syrian-backed government. In March 1989 his forces began a bitter fight against the Syrians, and later, against Christian factions that supported the new government. This stage of the war consisted mostly of artillery shelling; the bloodshed continued and more areas of Beirut were reduced to rubble. Aoun finally surrendered in October, 1990. In the following months, calm returned to Beirut; Christians and Muslims both professed a sense of relief, and many observers believed that Lebanon had a chance to achieve a genuine peace.

Lebanon [Republic of Lebanon]. Lebanon covers an area of 4,014 square miles in southwest Asia, along the east coast of the Mediterranean. Part of France's LEAGUE OF NATIONS mandate for Syria in 1920, Lebanon became a semi-autonomous republic in 1926 and achieved full independence in 1944. The country fought with the Arab League against ISRAEL (1948–49). Internal stability was achieved for a period (1958–70) by maintaining a balance of political power between Christian and Muslim populations. The increased presence of the PALESTINE LIBERATION ORGANIZATION (PLO) by 1967 led to Israeli reprisal raids and eventual civil war between the PLO-leftist Muslim alliance and the Christians. As a result, Syrian forces occupied northern and eastern Lebanon in 1976, and Israel occupied southern Lebanon, withdrawing in favor of a UNITED NATIONS peacekeeping force (1978). Under President Amin Gemayel (1983–88)

LEBANON

LEBANON

1910	Lebanon becomes popular destination for European tourists; governed as a semi-autonomous province under shared French-Turkish control; internal power shared between representatives of Christian, Moslem and Druze communities.
1920	League of Nations formalizes French Mandate in Lebanon and Syria.
1926	Detached from Syria and made semi-autonomous republic by French, with Bechera al-Khoury as first president.
1943	Religious communities reach agreement to form government dominated by Christians, who are majority in population; independence granted.
1948	Lebanon joins Arab League attacks on Israel; accepts Palestinian refugees in large numbers.
1952	Corrupt al-Khoury forced to resign; Camille Chamoun assumes presidency.
1958	Nasserist Muslims revolt; U.S. President Eisenhower sends U.S. Marines at Chamoun's request to restore order.
1964	Under President Fuad Chebab, "Chebabist" Muslim-Christian alliance leads to period of calm; economic boom as Beirut becomes center of finance and trade in the Middle East.
1967	After the Six-Day War, PLO forces move to southern Lebanon, conduct raids on Israel.
1975	Despite new Moslem majority, Christians refuse to revise Agreement of 1943; frightened by Muslim demands and PLO strength, Christian militias attack Muslims; all-out civil war ensues.
1976	Syria and the Arab League intervene in Lebanese civil war.
1978	Israeli forces briefly occupy southern Lebanon; UN forces intervene after Israeli withdrawal.
1982	Israel again invades Lebanon, to wipe out PLO; Muslim refugees massacred by Israeli-backed right-wing Lebanese Phalangist militia; multi-national peace-keeping force intervenes; country divided into areas of military control, with little real authority for central government.
1984	Peace-keeping force withdraws after losing hundreds of soldiers in bombing attacks; Christians and Muslims each begin fighting among themselves; government is powerless as anarchy prevails.
1985	Israeli forces complete their withdrawal.
1990	General Aoun of Christian Militia occupies presidential palace; Glias Hrawi forms second government with Muslim backing; Syrian forces destroy Aoun's base; Hrawi proclaims "Second Republic" with new constitution reflecting Muslim majority but guaranteeing Christian and Druze rights
1991	Christian and Druze ministers quit new government and threaten new bloodshed.

reform attempts and proposals to remove foreign troops failed, and increasingly volatile factions within the Christian-Muslim schism proliferated. Militant Muslim groups began kidnapping Western nationals and holding them hostage (18 known hostages by 1987). There was a complete breakdown of government authority by 1988, resulting in Michel Aoun heading a transitional military government based in Christian east Beirut while a rival government formed by President Elias Hrawi was headquartered in Muslim west Beirut. Aoun finally surrendered in late 1990, and there was some hope for a meaningful political settlement of Lebanon's difficult problems. (See also LEBANESE CIVIL WAR OF 1975–90.)

Lebedev, Peter Nikolayevich (1866–1912). Soviet physicist. He studied at the Moscow Higher Technical School and at the universities of Strasbourg and Berlin and was appointed professor at Moscow University. He founded and built up the first large school of physics in Russia. Lebedev conducted research in Maxwell's electromagnetic theory and succeeded in proving the pressure of light on solids and gases. His *Experimental Research on Light Pressure* was published in 1901.

Lebensraum. German term meaning "living space," and the doctrine it described. The term *Lebensraum* was introduced as early as the 1870s, but the concept did not become part of German policy until the 1920s and 1930s, when Adolf HITLER argued that GERMANY's boundaries were too small to support the German population; therefore, Germany would have to conquer foreign territory in order to give the German people more "living space." Hitler considered the Slavic countries to the east of Germany—namely Poland and Russia—as Germany's destined "Lebensraum." In the NAZI mentality, the Slavic and Jewish people in these areas were inferior to the Aryan Germans. Germany thus had the right to occupy these lands and enslave or kill their people. The *Lebensraum* policy was carried out largely by Heinrich HIMMLER and the SS.

Le Bourget. French town about six miles outside Paris; the site of a major airport until its closure in 1969. The field gained the world spotlight when Charles LINDBERGH landed at Le Bourget on May 21, 1927, successfully completing his nonstop transatlantic flight.

Le Brocquy, Louis (1916–). Irish painter, graphic artist, and book and textile designer. Le Brocquy is one of the leading Irish artists of modern times, having won acclaim not only in his native land but also in England, America, and France. The latter country awarded him a Chevalier of the French Legion of Honor in 1975. Le Brocquy has painted tinkers and other figures out of Irish folklore, as well as numerous canvasses devoted to children. He is also renowned for his portraits of literary figures including countrymen Samuel BECKETT, James JOYCE and William Butler YEATS.

le Carre, John [David John Moore Cornwell] (1931–). British novelist known for his complex spy thrillers set during the COLD WAR. Educated at Oxford and Berne University, during the late 1950s he taught school at Eton and in Switzerland before joining the British foreign service. Ostensibly a member of the diplomatic corps in West Germany, he was actually an intelligence agent (1959–64). While in the Foreign Office he published two novels under the pen name John le Carre. These books attracted little notice, but his third, *The Spy Who Came in from the Cold* (1963), won international acclaim as a classic of the genre. The novel concerns the efforts of a British agent, Lemas, to discredit an East German official. However, like many of his subsequent books, it can also be read as a gloss on cold war morality and the decline of Britain as a world power. Throughout his writing, le Carre debunks the myth of the glamorous spy popularized by Ian FLEMING. George Smiley, the hero (or antihero) of many of le Carre's books (believed to be based on Sir Maurice OLDFIELD), is the antithesis of Fleming's suave hero, James Bond. In le Carre's world, the distinction between good and evil is often a matter of degree. Although his plots are meticulously detailed, le Carre is not interested primarily in the technical aspects of spycraft. Rather, he is concerned with the larger issues of loyalty, betrayal and faith. In this, in his careful prose style and in the doom-laden atmosphere of his novels, le Carre is the direct successor of Joseph CONRAD and Graham GREENE. Among le Carre's other books are *A Small Town in Germany* (1968), *Tinker, Tailor, Soldier, Spy* (1974), *The Honourable Schoolboy* (1977), *Smiley's People*

John le Carre (center) talks with director Sidney Lumet (left) and actor Maximillian Schell (right) on the set of The Deadly Affair *(May 10, 1966).*

(1980), *A Perfect Spy* (1986), *The Russia House* (1989) and *The Secret Pilgrim* (1991). (See also Kim PHILBY.)

For further reading:

Bloom, Harold, ed., *John le Carre.* New York: Chelsea House, 1987.

Le Corbusier [Charles Edouard Jeanneret-Gris] (1887–1965). Swiss-born architect. Le Corbusier was one of the most influential architects of this century. He was equally renowned for his theoretical writings and for his unique architectural projects, which were constructed in locales around the world. These latter projects included the Unite d'Habitation, a "vertical city" in Marseilles, and the Punjabi capitol complex at CHANDIGARH, India. Le Corbusier was closely associated with numerous painters influenced by the Cubist movement, including Fernand LEGER. In his writings Le Corbusier emphasized the need to plan for ideal cities of the future in which "modulor" man could function with efficiency and safety. His major works included *Towards a New Architecture* (1923), *The City of Tomorrow* (1925), and *When the Cities Were White* (1937).

Ledbetter, Huddie "Leadbelly" (1888–1949). American blues singer and composer. He started his career by playing guitar at dances. He was jailed three times for murder, attempted murder and assault charges between 1918 and 1939. Writer John A. Lomax met him in prison and assembled his songs into a book, *Negro Folk Songs as Sung by Lead Belly* (1936). After his release from prison, Ledbetter toured France in 1949.

Le Duc Tho [born Phan Dinh Khal] (1911–1990). North Vietnamese diplomat. A member of the North Vietnamese Communist Party Politburo from 1955 until his retirement in 1986, he negotiated secretly in Paris with U.S. national security adviser Henry KISSINGER in an effort to end the VIETNAM WAR. Those negotiations produced a ceasefire agreement and a withdrawal of U.S. troops, but fighting between North and South continued. The two men were jointly offered the NOBEL PRIZE for peace in 1973, but Tho declined on the grounds that "peace has not yet been established." He later directed the final military offensive by North Vietnam in 1975, which brought about the fall of the South Vietnamese government and the merger of the two nations under communist rule.

Led Zeppelin. British rock-and-roll band (1968–80). Led Zeppelin is one of the most commercially successful and musically influential bands in the history of ROCK AND ROLL. While many critics disdain the band's music, the Led Zeppelin sound—throbbing guitar and and thrashing rhythm section overlaid with melodramatic vocals—defined heavy metal in the 1970s and inspired a host of imitative bands who continue to perform to this day. The members of Led Zeppelin were John Bonham, drums; John Paul Jones, keyboards and bass; Jimmy Page, guitar; and Robert Plant, vocals. All ten Led Zeppelin albums went gold or platinum in total sales. The band's trademark anthem, "Stairway to Heaven" (1971), is considered one of the greatest rock-and-roll songs of all time.

Lee, Jennie [Baroness Lee of Asheridge] (1904–1988). British politician. A prominent member of the British LABOUR PARTY, Lee was the daughter of a Scottish coal miner. She was first elected to Parliament in 1928 at the age of 24, making her the youngest member of the House of Commons. Together with her husband Aneurin ("Nye") BEVAN, she was part of "Britain's first man-and-wife parliamentary team." She served as a member of the Labour Party's national executive committee from 1958 to 1970 and was elected party chairman in 1967 and 1968. In 1965, Prime Minister Harold WILSON gave her special responsibility for the arts, and, as arts minister, she helped found the OPEN UNIVERSITY program. After losing her parliamentary seat in 1970, she was named a life peeress.

Lee Kuan Yew (1923–). Prime minister of SINGAPORE; educated at Raffles College, Cambridge University (double first in law with star for special distinction) and the Middle Temple, London. In the early 1950s he was legal adviser to a number of trade unions in Singapore. Lee Kuan Yew helped found the PAP People's Action Party in 1954 and was elected to parliament in 1955. Prime minister of Singapore since 1959, he is widely recognized both within and outside Singapore as a man of outstanding intelligence, political skill and vision; but he is also seen as a man of ruthless determination who has found it increasingly difficult to tolerate opposition to his views. He remains the dominant figure in the political life of Singapore and one of Asia's most well-known political figures.

Lee Teng-hui (1923–). Lee became the first native-born president of TAIWAN in 1988. Educated in Japan, Taiwan and the United States, he received a Ph.D. in agricultural economics from Cornell University in 1968 and entered government service in 1972. He served as mayor of T'aipei from 1978 to 1981 and as governor of Taiwan province from 1981 to 1984, when he was named vice president. He automatically succeeded to the balance of Chiang Ching-kuo's term (until 1990), and he was confirmed as chairman of the ruling KUOMINTANG Party in July 1988.

LEF [Left Front Art]. Literary organization named after the journal founded by Vladimir MAYAKOVSKY in 1922. Descended from the Moscow Cubist-Futurists, the group's membership of 25 included Mayakovsky, V.V. Kamensky and Alexei Kruchenykh. In 1926 LEF abandoned revolutionary Futurism for a more "socially constructive" program. In 1929 the group became known as REF (Revolutionary Front of Art), and the following year it joined RAPP (All Russian Association of Proletarian Writers).

Left Opposition or Left Deviation. General term for the radical trend within the COMMUNIST PARTY opposing the policy of the majority of members. The left opposition was led by Nicholas BUKHARIN in 1918 and by Leon TROTSKY in 1923. Trotsky felt that Russian socialism could succeed only if there was a world revolution. The left opposition accordingly supported revolutionary movements abroad, while pursuing a militant socialist policy at home. It therefore opposed the NEW ECONOMIC POLICY, disagreeing with STALIN who believed that socialism could be achieved in the Soviet Union without a world revolution. In 1925, Grigory ZINOVIEV and Lev KAMENEV took over the leadership of the left opposition.

Left Socialist Revolutionaries. The heirs of the *narodnik* (see **Narodnaya Volya**) tradition, the Left Socialist Revolutionaries enjoyed the support of many of the peasants. One-time allies of the BOLSHEVIKS, their alliance foundered when the Bolsheviks strengthened the power of the army and police. The Left Socialist Revolutionaries, however, lacked clearly devised policies; although angered by the reintroduction of the death penalty, they kept their men in the CHEKA. They opposed LENIN over the Treaty of BREST-LITOVSK, in 1918; Muravev attempted to declare war on Germany and the Bolsheviks; and several groups of the Left Socialist Revolutionaries attempted to overthrow the Bolshevik leadership of the local Soviets in provincial towns. After the assassination of the German ambassador, Count Mirbach, Maria Spiridonova and other leading members were shot, and the Left Socialist Revolutionaries lost credibility and ceased to threaten the position of the Bolsheviks.

Leger, Fernand (1881–1955). French painter. Leger was deeply influenced by CUBISM, although he maintained a large degree of independence from all artistic movements during his lengthy career. He first came to prominence in the years prior to World War I after his canvasses were displayed at the *Section d'Or* exhibition of 1912, which also featured the work of numerous Cubist painters. Leger was fascinated with the possibilities of applying modern technology to artistic creation. He made a close study of architecture and became friends with LE CORBUSIER and the artists and craftsmen of the de STIJL movement. Leger's paintings also show the influence of the cinema and advertising art. His experience as an artilleryman during WORLD WAR I also showed itself in Leger's work and led him to theorize that machinery was the most successful and aesthetically significant of all human creations. In his later years Leger turned away from his abstract compositions to more figurative works.

Legion of Decency. Formed in the U.S. in 1933 by the Catholic Church, the Legion forced the film industry to adhere to a rigid moral code for all films; the church replaced it in 1966 with the National Catholic Office for Motion Pictures. Upset by what it considered to be an increasing number of immoral movies, like Mae WEST's *She Done Him Wrong* (1932), the Catholic Church launched its Legion of Decency campaign in 1933, led by Martin Quigley, owner of the industry trade paper *Motion Picture Herald*, and Archbishop John McNicholas of Cincinnati. The legion had two goals: to install a Catholic censor in Hollywood and to continue to pressure the industry to produce "clean" films. It achieved its first goal in 1934 when Will Hays, head of the Motion Picture Producers and Distributors of America (MPPDA), hired Joseph Breen, an active lay Catholic, as censor. Its second goal was successfully defended for almost 30 years.

From 1934 to 1936, Legion activities were centered in Chicago, where a "C," or Condemned, rating was initiated, forbidding Catholics to attend such films as *Anna Karenina* (MGM, 1935), *Laughing Boy* (MGM, 1934), *Of Human Bondage* (RKO, 1934) and *Girl From Missouri* (MGM, 1934). In 1936 Legion offices were moved to New York. Films were reviewed by the International Federation of Catholic Alumnae. A new rating system was developed that gave films an A-1 (Morally Unobjectionable), A-II (Morally Unobjectionable for Adults), B (Morally Objectionable in part) or C (Condemned). Each year the legion "pledge" was given by 20 million Catholics, who promised to avoid condemned and objectionable films. For three decades the legion quietly pressured Hollywood to alter hundreds of films. After an initial flurry of "C" ratings, the legion issued few because the industry began to rigidly enforce the motion picture code. There were notable exceptions. Howard HUGHES incurred the wrath of the legion when he released *The Outlaw* (1943), an oversexed story of outlaw Billy the Kid. Roberto ROSSELLINI's *The Miracle* (Tinia, 1948) was condemned as "sacrilegious and blasphemous" in 1950; it was banned in New York, but the U.S. Supreme Court overturned the decision and declared films protected under the First Amendment.

In a postwar climate of growing freedom of expression, the legion was seen as an anachronism. When the industry began to restrict audiences and rate its films in 1966—G for anyone, M for mature audiences, R restricted and X for adults only—the legion's influence began to wane.

Lego®. Plastic construction toy developed in Denmark that has outstanding design quality along with very rich play possibilities. Lego® is based on a modular plastic block studded on top with projecting disks that mate with a hollowed-out bottom so the blocks lock together. The system first appeared in 1947 and has gradually been expanded, with the addition of components in many shapes and sizes, all using the same connecting detail and all in modular sizes. In 1955 sets were introduced that make up particular toys (some very elaborate), but all using interchangeable components so that the toy can be used in a wide variety of ways as a child grows. The manufacturer, Lego System A/S of Billund, Denmark, does not give design credit to any individual, although the firm's founder, Godtfred Kirk Christiansen, appears to have developed the concept based on the children's wood blocks that the firm made previously. Many variations of Lego have appeared, and many imitations are now made. Lego® is a truly educational toy in both technical and aesthetic terms.

Le Guin, Ursula K. (1929–). American novelist, story writer, poet and essayist. Le Guin is best known for her science fiction novels, the most famous of which is *The Left Hand of Darkness* (1969), which depicted an alien planet on which female cultural values were dominant. She is the daughter of two well-known anthropologists, Alfred and Theodora KROEBER; an anthropological approach to customs and morals is one of the hallmarks of Le Guin's fiction. She is one of the most highly honored of science fiction writers—having won numerous Hugo and Nebula Awards—and her work in that genre has won the praise of mainstream critics as well. Other novels include *Wizard of Earthsea* (1968), *The Dispossessed: An Ambiguous Utopia* (1974), *The Lathe of Heaven* (1975) and *The Word for World Is Forest* (1976). *Orsinian Tales* (1976) is her best known story collection. *Always Coming Home* (1985) is a representative selection of stories, essays and poems.

Lehar, Franz (1870–1948). Austrian composer. Lehar was an extraordinarily popular composer of operettas during the early decades of the 20th century. His beautiful melodies and lilting waltzes typified the gaiety and joie de vivre of life in Vienna early in the century. His most well-known operetta, *The Merry Widow*, was first produced in 1905 and has enjoyed worldwide popularity with opera and light opera companies ever since.

Le Havre. City in Seine-Maritime department, on the Seine River estuary, FRANCE. Located on the English Channel, for much of the century, it and CHERBOURG were important ports for the great OCEAN LINERS that plied between France and the U.S. During WORLD WAR I tens of thousands of Allied soldiers from Britain and the U.S. disembarked here on their way to the trenches of the Western Front. The Belgian government fled here as the Germans occupied Belgium during WORLD WAR II. The Germans occupied Le Havre from June 1940 to September 1944, and it was heavily bombed by the Allies.

Lehmann, Lilli (1848–1929). German singer. The greatest Wagnerian soprano of her time and one of the great performers of Lieder, Lehmann also excelled in the French and Italian repertories, demonstrating her musical versatility and dramatic ability by mastering 170 roles in 119 operas. After performing with the Berlin Royal Opera, she made her New York Metropolitan Opera debut as Carmen in 1885. She thrilled Met audiences when she created the roles of Isolde in *Tristan and Isolde* (1886), Brunnhilde in *Siegfried* (1887) and Brunnhilde in *Die Gotterdammerung* (1888), for the first time in America. She gave lieder recitals after 1909; among her students was future opera star Geraldine FARRAR. Lehmann also taught at the Mozarteum in Salzburg, Austria (from 1926). Her annual appearances as singer and director at summer performances in Salzburg (1905–10) gave the impetus for the establishment of the annual SALZBURG FESTIVAL in 1920.

Lehmann, Lotte (1888–1976). German-born opera singer, recitalist and voice teacher, considered one of the great dramatic sopranos and *Lieder* singers of the early 20th century. After appearing with the Hamburg Opera (1909–14), Lehmann gained international fame with the Vienna Royal Opera, establishing herself as a great Wagnerian soprano in such roles as Sieglinde in *Die Walkure* and Eva in *Die Meistersinger*. She also became the foremost interpreter of female roles in Richard STRAUSS's operas, creating the role of the Dyer's wife in *Die Frau ohne Schatten* (among others) and emerging as the greatest Marschallin in *Der Rosenkavalier* of her generation. In the 1920s she began giving *Lieder* recitals, which continued even after her retirement from opera. In addition, she became a well-known voice teacher, helping to establish the Music Academy of the West at Santa Barbara, California. The recipient of many awards and honors, she became an American citizen in 1945.

Leica. Family of 33 mm cameras considered design classics, which are produced by the German optical firm of Ernst Leitz GmbH. of Wetzlar, Germany. The concept of the miniature camera using standard motion picture film was developed around 1913 by Oskar BARNACK, a technician employed by Leitz. In 1924 a commercial version of the camera was put into production, and improved versions were introduced in quick succession, adding refinements such as range-finder focusing, interchangeable lenses, and a full range of fast and slow shutter speeds. The design of the Leica, based on the technical vocabulary of quality optical instruments (such as the microscopes made by Leitz) and on close adherence to the functional demands of the camera, reached its high point with the models F and G of the 1930s. Acceptance by a number of famous photographers, such as Henri CARTIER-BRESSON and Walker EVANS, combined with awareness of the camera's technical excellence, made it extremely popular, and early models are now collected by a cult of admirers. Later models, including the post-World War II series M versions, have maintained Leica's high level of design excellence. Many similar cameras were developed to compete with the Leica, but none have reached the same level of popularity.

Leigh, Vivien [Vivien Mary Hartley] (1913–1967). British screen and stage actress. Leigh, renowned as one of the most ethereally beautiful actresses of the 20th century, remains best known for her starring role as Southern heroine Scarlet O'Hara in the 1939 film GONE WITH THE WIND, for which she won an ACADEMY AWARD for Best Actress. Leigh first rose to prominence in the British cinema in the 1930s, most notably through her starring role opposite Laurence OLIVIER—whom she married after leaving her first husband—in *Fire Over England* (1937). She also appeared frequently on the British stage, including a 1937 role as Ophelia opposite Olivier's Hamlet. After *Gone With The Wind,* Leigh became an international star, though recurrent physical and emotional problems limited her roles in the final decades of her life. Her subsequent films included *Waterloo Bridge* (1940), *That Hamilton Woman* (1941), *Caesar and Cleopatra* (1945), *Anna Karenina* (1948), a second Oscar-winning performance as Blanche du Bois in Tennessee WILLIAMS's *A Streetcar Named Desire* (1951), *The Deep Blue Sea* (1955), *The Roman Spring of Mrs. Stone* (1961) and *Ship of Fools* (1965).

Leighton, Margaret (1922–1976). British stage actress. Leighton came to prominence in the 1940s as an accomplished actress capable of playing the classic roles of the British theater. While a member of the renowned Old Vic company from 1944 to 1947, Leighton won acclaim for her roles as Raina in *Arms and the Man* by George Bernard SHAW, and as Regan opposite the Shakespearean King Lear of Laurence OLIVIER. Leighton subsequently appeared as Celia in *The Cocktail Party* (1950) by T.S. ELIOT and in three major Shakespearean roles—Rosalind, Ariel, and Lady Macbeth—at Stratford-upon-Avon (1952). Leighton continued to be active in both London and Broadway theatrical productions until her death.

Leinsdorf, Erich (1912–). Austrian-born opera and symphonic conductor renowned for his affiliations with the Metropolitan Opera and the Boston Symphony Orchestra. Leinsdorf is a latter-day adherent to the objective, antiromantic school of conducting. He was born in Vienna, graduated from the Vienna Conservatory, and assisted Bruno WALTER and Arturo TOSCANINI at the Salzburg festivals in the mid-1930s. In 1938 he immigrated to the U.S., where he reigned supreme for ten years at the Metropolitan Opera. He reached his zenith as Musical Director of the Boston Symphony in 1962–1969 succeeding, chronologically, Serge KOUSSEVITZKY and Charles MUNCH. His mastery of large forces and relentless discipline with players have made him an effective opera conductor. However, his methodical, calculating objectivity have not made him popular with many critics and performers. A man of great intellect with a thorough grasp of diverse subjects, he feels justified in altering or "adjusting" symphonic classics to his own standards. "I think these works should be edited in order to sound as well as they can sound," he told this writer. "They should not be done literally the way they have been orchestrated originally, because our orchestras are different, our halls are different, and our ears are different." He is well known for his advocacy of music of the so-called "second Viennese" school—Arnold SCHOENBERG, Alban BERG, and Anton WEBERN.

For further reading:

Schonberg, Harold C., *The Great Conductors.* New York: Simon and Schuster, 1967.

Lem, Stanislaw (1921–). Polish science fiction writer. Lem is the first major writer in this genre to have emerged from Eastern Europe. Currently regarded as one of the leading voices in science fiction, Lem was educated in his native Poland and earned a medical degree in 1946. He has enjoyed the rare distinction of seeing his science fiction stories published in mainstream literary periodicals such as the NEW YORKER. Lem has also been influential, through his essays in the Polish journal *Quarber Merkur,* as a stringent critic of the overall literary standards of the science fiction genre. Lem's major works of science fiction include *Solaris* (1970), *Memoirs Found in a Bathtub* (1977), *Memoirs of a Space Traveller* (1983) and *Imaginary Magnitude* (1984).

Lemaitre, Abbe Georges Edouard (1894–1966). Belgian astronomer and cosmologist. After serving in World War I, Lemaitre studied at the University of Louvain in Belgium from which he graduated in 1920. He then attended a seminary at Malines, and was ordained as a Roman Catholic priest in 1923. Before taking up an appointment at the University of Louvain in 1925, he spent a year at Cambridge, England, where he worked with Arthur EDDINGTON and a year in America where he worked at the Harvard College Observatory and the Massachusetts Institute of Technology. He remained at Louvain for the whole of his career, being made professor of astronomy in 1927. Lemaitre was one of the propounders of the BIG BANG THEORY of the origin of the universe. EINSTEIN's theory of general relativity, announced in 1916, had led to various cosmological models, including Einstein's own model of a static universe. Lemaitre in 1927 (and, independently, Alexander FRIEDMANN in 1922) discovered a family of solutions to Einstein's field equations of relativity that described not a static but an expanding universe. This idea of an expanding universe was demonstrated experimentally in 1929 by Edwin HUBBLE who was unaware of the work of Lemaitre and Friedmann. Lemaitre's model of the universe received little notice until Eddington arranged for it to be translated and reprinted in the *Monthly Notices of the Royal Astronomical Society* in 1931. It was not only the idea of an expanding universe, that was so important in Lemaitre's work, and on which others were soon working, but also his attempt to think of the cause and beginning of the expansion.

If matter is everywhere receding, it would seem natural to suppose that in the distant past it was closer together. If we go far enough back, argued Lemaitre, we reach the "primal atom," a time at which the entire universe was in an extremely compact and compressed state. He spoke of some instability being produced by radioactive decay of the primal atom that was sufficient to cause an immense explosion that initiated the expansion. This big bang model did not fit too well with the available time scales of the 1930s. Nor did Lemaitre provide enough mathematical detail to attract serious cosmologists. Its importance today is due more to the revival and revision it received at the hands of George GAMOW in 1946.

LeMay, Gen. Curtis Emerson (1906–1990). U.S. Air Force officer. In WORLD WAR II, LeMay pioneered precision daylight bombing of GERMANY and JAPAN. It was he who received President Harry S TRUMAN's order to drop nuclear bombs on HIROSHIMA and NAGASAKI in 1945. In 1948, he led the BERLIN AIRLIFT, which overcame a Soviet blockade of the city. He commanded the STRATEGIC AIR COMMAND from 1948 until 1957, when he was named Air Force vice chief of staff. From 1961 to 1965 he held the position of Air Force chief of staff. Following his retirement, in 1968 he was the controversial running mate of presidential candidate George WALLACE; he advocated the nuclear bombing of Vietnam.

Lemmon, Jack [John Uhler Lemmon III] (1925–). American actor. Educated at Harvard University, Lemmon served in the navy and returned to begin his acting career in Off-Broadway productions and television dramas. He made his movie debut opposite Judy Holliday in the comedy *It Should Happen to You* (1954). He later appeared in a number of films, his performance in *Mr. Roberts* (1955), winning a supporting actor ACADEMY AWARD. He became a major star through his association with director Billy WILDER, co-starring in *Some Like It Hot* (1959) and *The Apartment* (1960). His 1960s movies include the wrenching drama *The Days of Wine and Roses* (1962) and the hilarious comedy *The Odd Couple* (1968), the first of his many projects with actor Walter Matthau and writer Neil SIMON. His later films have included *The Prisoner of Second Avenue* (1975), *The China Syndrome* (1979), *Tribute* (1980) and *Mass Appeal* (1984). A kind of Hollywood "Everyman," Lemmon has distinguished himself in a wide variety of roles, from farce to melodrama, and continues to be an enduring movie star.

Lemnitzer, General Lyman L. (1899–1988). U.S. Army commander. Lemnitzer a WORLD WAR II hero who also served as a diplomat, helping to negotiate the surrender of Italian and German forces in Italy and Austria. Lemnitzer later commanded United Nations forces during the KOREAN WAR. In 1957 he returned to Washington and in 1960 was named chairman of the Joint Chiefs of Staff. His last post was as supreme Allied commander in Europe, a job he held until he retired from active duty in 1969.

Lemnos. Greek island in the northern Aegean Sea. Long a part of the OTTOMAN EMPIRE, it became a part of Greece in 1913 after the BALKAN WARS. During WORLD WAR I it was a British navy base before the DARDANELLES CAMPAIGN. (See also GALLIPOLI PENINSULA.)

Lemon, Bob (1920–). American baseball player and manager. One of the most consistent pitchers of the postwar era, Lemon posted 20–win seasons seven times. A fastballer, he was part of the Cleveland Indians' fearsome pitching staff of the 1950s that included Bob Feller and Early Wynn. He led the American League in strikeouts in 1950. A solid hitter, he was occasionally used in pinch-hit situations, and finished his career with 37 home runs. Upon his retirement in 1958, he stayed in baseball as a coach and scout. He returned to the major leagues in 1970 with the Kansas City Royals, and won Manager of the Year honors in 1971. In the late 1970s and early 1980s, he managed the tumultuous New York Yankees, replacing the often-hired-and-fired Billy Martin, and later being replaced by him. Later yet, he returned to replace Gene Michael, and was replaced by him in 1982. Lemon was named to the Hall of Fame in 1976.

LeMond, Greg (1962–). American cyclist. LeMond became the first non-European and only American to win the 2,500–mile, 22–leg Tour de France, in 1986. In April 1987 he was accidentally shot while hunting, and many believed his career was over. Nevertheless, he came back to win the Tour again in 1989 and was named "Sportsman of the Year" by *Sports Illustrated* magazine. In 1990 he won it for the third time, prompting the French sports paper *L'Etoile* to dub him "roi-soleil," the "sun king."

Le Mort Homme [Dead Man's Hill]. Dead Man's Hill near VERDUN in France was a strategic location in the defense of Verdun during WORLD WAR I. It earned its name on May 29, 1916, when it was overrun by the Germans after a bloody contest. The French did not recapture it until more than a year later (Aug. 20, 1917). Its military designation was Hill 295.

Lena Goldfield Massacre. In April 1912 workers in the Lena goldfield went on strike in order to obtain better living and working conditions and higher wages. About 5,000 protesters were confronted by troops, who fired on them, killing approximately 200 and wounding many others. As a result, the Russian work force became incensed, and during that year some 725,000 workers went on strike. The duma, also angered, called for an investigation of the massacre, which resulted in heavy criticism of the way in which the goldfield was managed.

Lendl, Ivan (1960–). Czechoslovakian-born tennis player. The son of two national tennis stars, Lendl became one of the top players of the 1980s. He won the U.S. Open singles championship three times from 1985 to 1987. He won the French Open twice and was Grand Prix Masters champion an unprecedented five times during the 1980s. His stern on-court demeanor prevented his ever becoming a crowd favorite, but tennis purists were enthralled by his powerful serve and forehand. Lendl moved to the U.S. in 1981.

Lend-Lease. Act proposed by President Franklin D. ROOSEVELT and passed by Congress on March 11, 1941, while the U.S. was still a neutral party in WORLD WAR II. The Lend-Lease Act allowed the president to transfer, lend or lease war materials to "the government of any country whose defense the president deems vital to the defense of the U.S." It permitted the immediate supply of arms, ships, machinery, food and services to Great Britain and China. The lend-lease program was soon extended to the U.S.S.R. and later to most of the Allied countries. It was also an important factor in pressing American industry to gear up for wartime production. From September 1942 the U.S. received "reverse lend-lease" from British COMMONWEALTH countries and the FREE FRENCH in goods and services supplied to U.S. troops abroad. By the time President Harry S TRUMAN ended the program on August 21, 1945 some $50 billion of lend-lease aid had been supplied to the Allies, with some $8 billion in "reverse lend-lease" given to the U.S. After the termination of lend-lease, American overseas aid was continued through the MARSHALL PLAN. Settlements of lend-lease debts were negotiated after World War II. The final settlement with the U.S.S.R. was concluded in 1972.

Lenin [Vladimir Ilyich Ulyanov] (1870–1924). Russian revolutionary, leader of the Bolsheviks and chief theoretician of Russian Marxism. He was born at Simbirsk into a middle-class family. His brother Alexander was hanged in 1887 for planning an attempt on Czar Alexander III's life, greatly influencing Lenin's early life. Lenin studied law at Kazan University, but was expelled for subversive activity. Having studied Marx extensively, he went to St. Petersburg and organized the League for the Liberation of the Working Class. As a result he was arrested in 1897 and exiled for three years to Siberia, where he married Nadezhda KRUPSKAYA. He continued his revolutionary activities abroad. In 1903, in London, Lenin became the leader of the BOLSHEVIK faction of the Russian Social Democratic Labor Party. He returned to RUSSIA for the 1905 Revolution. In 1907 he fled to Switzerland, and by means of underground organizations continued to mastermind the Russian revolutionary movement.

Vladimir Ilyich Lenin.

He was living in Switzerland during World War I and in March 1917 the Germans clandestinely arranged for Lenin to return home in a sealed train. Once in Petrograd, he turned his attention to the overthrowing of Alexander KERENSKY'S provisional government, and was appointed chairman of the council of people's commissars. The APRIL THESES were published, and during that summer he took refuge in Finland before returning to organize, with TROTSKY, the OCTOBER REVOLUTION. He secured peace with Germany by the Treaty of BREST-LITOVSK and in 1919 set up the COMINTERN to work toward world revolution.

Lenin and the Red Army fought until 1921 before defeating the WHITES. His position as chairman was strengthened, and Lenin became a virtual dictator. To restore the economy, he instituted the NEW ECONOMIC POLICY in 1921. Lenin's health, which had been failing since an assassination attempt in 1918, grew worse. Although he warned that STALIN should not be allowed to continue as secretary general of the COMMUNIST PARTY, Lenin's warning went unheeded. He died in 1924, and his body, now embalmed, lies in a mausoleum in Red Square.

For further reading:

Clark, Ronald W., *Lenin*. New York: HarperCollins, 1987.

Pipes, Richard, *The Russian Revolution*. New York: Knopf, 1990.

Leningrad. City in the northwest U.S.S.R., on the Gulf of Finland. Commonly called "the Venice of the North," Leningrad occupies both banks near the mouth of the Neva River as well as numerous small islands in the Neva. Built at the beginning of the 18th century under Czar Peter the Great as Russia's "window on the West," the city entered the 20th century as the capital of imperial RUSSIA; its name was then **St. Petersburg**. The unsuccessful RUSSIAN REVOLUTION OF 1905 against the rule of Czar NICHOLAS II broke out here. After Russia entered WORLD WAR I against Germany, the city's name was Russified; Petersburg became Petrograd (1914). The city figured prominently in the RUSSIAN REVOLUTION of 1917; V.I. LENIN arrived here from Finland to direct the BOLSHEVIKS, who deposed the KERENSKY government at the Winter Palace. With the Bolsheviks in control, the capital was transferred to Moscow (1918). After Lenin's death (1924) Petrograd was renamed Leningrad.

Within a few months after the German invasion of the U.S.S.R. began (June 22, 1941), HITLER's forces had reached Leningrad and virtually surrounded it. Thus began the SIEGE OF LENINGRAD. At least one million people died in Leningrad during the siege, which lasted for 872 days. The city was subseqently largely restored. Among Leningrad's many architectural and cultural treasures are the Winter Palace, the Hermitage Museum, and the Academy of Arts. Leningrad has always been noted for its literary heritage; in the 20th century it was home to poets Anna AKHMATOVA, Joseph BRODSKY and Osip MANDELSTAM as well as composer Dmitry SHOSTAKOVICH.

Leningrad, Siege of (1941–1944). Siege operation during WORLD WAR II. On June 22, 1941, the Germans put 500,000 troops over the Russian frontier, and by November 1941 elements of that army were outside Leningrad. The Soviet forces, weakened by the GREAT PURGE, were unprepared. Leningrad was besieged and 750,000 people eventually perished. On January 15, 1944, the Russians began to break out of the town, and on January 20 succeeded in cutting the German supply corridor to the Gulf of Finland. On January 27 the two-and-a-half-year siege—one of the most heroically defended in the history of warfare—ended.

For further reading:

Kochina, E. I., *Blockade Diary*. Ann Arbor, Mich.: Ardis, 1989.

Salisbury, Harrison E., *The Nine Hundred Days: The Siege of Leningrad*. New York: Da Capo, 1985.

Lenin Prizes. Lenin Prizes, established in 1925, are awarded yearly for outstanding work in science, technology, literature or the arts. There is also an International Lenin Peace Prize awarded for services to the "peace campaign." The award of a Lenin Prize carries a substantial sum of money and the title of "Laureate of the Lenin Prize." Lenin Prizes were originally established after LENIN's death, but were renamed Stalin Prizes in 1935; their title reverted in 1956. The awards are announced on Lenin's birthday and generally total 50, with an award of 75,000 rubles.

Lennon, John (1940–1980). British rock and roll composer, vocalist and guitarist. Lennon, who remains best known for his 1960s years in the BEATLES, was one of the greatest songwriters in the history of ROCK AND ROLL, as well as one of its most outspoken personalities. Born in 1940 to a working class LIVERPOOL family, Lennon took up the guitar at age 14 and, in 1955, began to play with fellow Liverpool teenager Paul MCCARTNEY. In 1958 the two formed a band named Johnny and the Moondogs that would transform into the Silver Beatles and then simply the Beatles. In the 1960s, Lennon and McCartney formed a songwriting team par excellence, drawing on their shared 1950s rock roots and their passion for studio experimentation. From "I Want to Hold Your Hand" (1964) to "Let It Be" (1970), Lennon-McCartney songs dominated and transformed popular music. In 1969, Lennon married Yoko Ono, with whom he would collaborate, after the breakup of the Beatles in 1970, on numerous musical projects. In the late 1960s, Lennon became a fervent antiwar spokesman and his song "Imagine" (1971) became an anthem of the peace movement. Lennon's final solo album *Double Fantasy* (1980), featured a Billboard number one hit song, "(Just Like) Starting Over". It was released just before the tragic murder of Lennon in New York City on December 8, 1980, which provoked worldwide mourning.

Lenya, Lotte [born Karoline Blamuer] (1898–1981). Austrian born actress and singer. While acting in BERLIN in the 1920s Lenya met the composer Kurt WEILL, whom she married. She appeared in many plays on which Weill collaborated with Bertolt BRECHT, including *Die Dreigroschen Oper* (THE THREEPENNY OPERA, 1927), in which she created the role of the prostitute, Jenny. She and Weill fled to the U.S. after Adolf HITLER came to power in GERMANY. After Weill's death she resumed her stage career on Broadway, winning a Tony Award for playing Jenny in a revival of *Threepenny Opera* (1955); she was also in *Cabaret* (1966). She also appeared in films, including *From Russia With Love* (1963), and supervised and sang on a series of recordings of Weill's music.

Leonard, Hugh [pen name of John Keyes Byrne] (1926–). Irish playwright, theater critic, and television and screenplay writer. Leonard worked as a civil servant before achieving success as a playwright in the 1950s. His first play, *The Big Birthday* (1956), was produced at the ABBEY THEATRE in Dublin and dealt with the social fabric of Irish life, as did subsequent plays including *A Leap in the Dark* (1957), *Madigan's Lock (1958), and The Passion of Peter Ginty* (1961), an adaptation of Henrik Ibsen's *Peer Gynt*. In 1959 Leonard began to write scripts for the BRITISH BROADCASTING CORPORATION while maintaining an active involvement in the theater. *Stephen D* (1962) is a stage adaptation of the writings of James JOYCE. Leonard focused on Anglo-Irish relations in the play *The Au Pair Man* (1968). Other plays by Leonard include *Da* (1973), *A Life* (1978), *Moving Days* (1981), and *Scorpions* (1983). *Home Before Dark* (1975) is his autobiography.

Leone, Sergio (1921–1989). Italian film director. Leone was best known for his "spaghetti westerns"—violent, low-budget movies set in the American wild west but produced in Italy and Spain. His westerns helped revive a genre that, at the time, was thought to be dead. He also made an international star of actor Clint EASTWOOD by featuring him in such films as *A Fistful of Dollars* (1964), *For a Few*

John Lennon with his wife Yoko Ono during their "Bed-In For Peace" in Montreal (May 27, 1969).

Dollars More (1965), and *The Good, the Bad, and the Ugly* (1966). Leone maintained that his movie violence was exaggerated because he "wanted to make a tongue-in-cheek satire of run-of-the-mill westerns." In 1984 U.S. film executives severely cut his last major project, an ambitious homage to American gangster films titled *Once Upon a Time in America.* Although the film had won awards in Europe, the truncated U.S. version received a lukewarm critical reception and popular response.

Leoni, Raul (1905–1972). President of VENEZUELA (1964–69). Leoni spent 30 years in exile after participating in the insurrection of 1921 while a student. He was later leader of the Accion Democratica party (1958–64). As president of Venezuela, he maintained the country's rapid economic growth and fostered political stability.

Leonov, Alexei (1934–). Soviet cosmonaut; an accomplished artist, the personable Leonov has been on two historic space missions. During his Voskhod 2 mission (March 18, 1965) he became the first human to walk in space when he spent 10 minutes outside the spacecraft commanded by fellow cosmonaut Pavel BELYAYEV. The successful Voskhod mission almost ended in disaster, when the cosmonauts missed their prime recovery area and were forced to land in the Ural Mountains, spending a freezing, snowy night aboard the spacecraft before rescuers could arrive. Leonov's second mission was as commander of the SOYUZ half of the historic APOLLO-SOYUZ Test Project (July 1975), which found the American and Soviet spacecraft linking up to share friendship and scientific experimentation in space. His flight engineer on the historic mission was Valery Kubasov, and after the mission the two Soviets joined their American counterparts in a worldwide speaking tour demonstrating the possibilities of U.S./Soviet cooperation in space. It was the only time that such a joint mission was flown.

Leonov, Leonid Maksimovich (1899–). Russian novelist. Having served in the Red Army, Leonov settled in Moscow and had his first work published in 1922. At the outset of his career he was a member of the Serapion Brotherhood (see SERAPION BROTHERS). At the same time, he was profoundly influenced by the writings of Dostoyevsky. Much of Leonov's work reflects his concern for universal ethical and moral problems and the fate of Russia. His novels include *The Badgers* (1924) and *The Thief* (1927). He was later obliged to conform to the demands of SOCIALIST REALISM, demands that he found easier to fulfill in plays rather than in novels. His psychological plays include *The Invasion* (1924) and *The Golden Carriage* (1954).

Leontief, Wassily (1906–). Born in Russia and educated in Germany, Leontief served as an adviser to the Chinese government before immigrating to the U.S. He joined the Harvard faculty in 1931. Leontief is best known for developing the input-output method of economic analysis used for national planning. He won the NOBEL PRIZE for economics in 1973.

Leopold III (1901–1983). King of BELGIUM (1934–51). When the Germans invaded Belgium early in WORLD WAR II (1940), Leopold surrendered to the Nazis instead of fleeing and establishing a government in exile, as his ministers had urged. Many Belgians regarded Leopold as a turncoat and collaborator for this act, and he left Belgium after the war. He returned in 1951 after a national referendum indicated that he would be accepted by his people. However, violent protests convinced him to abdicate in favor of his son Baudouin later that year.

Leopold, Aldo (1887–1948). American conservationist. Iowa-born, Leopold was a pioneering environmentalist. As an official with the United States Forest Service in the 1920s, he was instrumental in developing the science of wildlife management and he drafted the plan to set aside America's first wilderness area, Gila National Forest in New Mexico. He also taught at the University of Wisconsin and in 1935 was a founding member of the Wilderness Society. His credo as a naturalist is set forth in the autobiographical *A Sand County Almanac* (1949) and in the essays collected in *The River of the Mother of God* (1991).

Richard Loeb and Nathan Leopold during their trial for the murder of 14-year-old Bobby Franks (1924).

Leopold and Loeb case. One of the most sensational murder cases of the 20th century. Two wealthy Chicago teenagers, Nathan Leopold and Richard Loeb, planned what they conceived of as the "perfect murder" for the sheer excitement of committing the crime and getting away with it. On May 21, 1924, the two college students abducted and bludgeoned to death Loeb's distant cousin, 14-year-old Bobby Franks, and dumped his body in a drain pipe. Inept criminals, they were soon captured. In the widely publicized trial that followed, famous trial lawyer Clarence DARROW admitted their guilt but argued against putting them to death. Darrow was successful in his defense, and they were each sentenced to life plus 99 years for kidnap and murder. Loeb was killed in a prison brawl in 1926; Leopold was released in 1958 and died in 1971.

Lepeshinskaya, Olga Vasilyevna (1916–). Ballerina, graduated from the Bolshoi Theater School. One of the greatest Soviet dancers of her day, Lepeshinskaya's style is characterized by her virtuosity and strength. A member of the COMMUNIST PARTY since 1943, she has served on numerous boards and committees.

Lerner, Alan Jay (1918–1986). U.S. lyricist and playwright. Lerner's greatest successes were the product of a long-time collaboration with composer Frederick LOEWE. Their hit Broadway musicals included *Brigadoon* (1947), *Paint Your Wagon* (1951), and *Camelot* (1960). Their most successful work of all was *My Fair Lady*, which opened on Broadway in March 1956 and ran for more than 2,700 performances. Another collaboration, *Gigi* (1958), is regarded as one of the most fully realized of all film musicals.

Lescaze, William (1896–1969). American architect born in Switzerland, who is credited with introducing the INTERNATIONAL STYLE in America. Lescaze had studied with Karl Moser before coming to the U.S. in 1920. His best known work (in partnership with George HOWE) is the 1932 Philadelphia Savings Fund Society (PSFS) building, the first fully modern skyscraper anywhere, and one of the first examples of MODERNISM in American architecture. Lescaze seems to have been the leader in the design of the building (Howe's earlier work had been quite traditional), so a major share of the credit for its success is his. After the partnership with Howe ended in 1934, Lescaze con-

Alan Lerner (right) with his songwriting partner Frederick Loewe (October 1960).

tinued to practice architecture in New York, designing a number of modern townhouses (including his own on 48th Street), the Williamsbridge housing project in New York, and various other works including radio stations, office buildings, and a pavilion for the 1939 NEW YORK WORLD'S FAIR. Lescaze also designed furniture, lighting, and many small accessory products—all by-products of his architectural work.

Lesotho [Kingdom of Lesotho]. A landlocked country within the Republic of SOUTH AFRICA, Lesotho covers an area of 11,715 square miles. Originally known as Basutoland, the country became a British crown colony in 1884. Resisting incorporation into South Africa when that country was formed in 1910, Basutoland was granted a new constitution in 1960 and achieved independence as the Kingdom of Lesotho in 1966. Political tensions between King Moshoeshoe II and Prime Minister Chief Lebua Jonathan led to the declaration of a state of emergency in 1970 and the eventual overthrow of Chief Jonathan in 1986 in a military coup led by Major General Justin Lekhanya. In 1990 the king's powers were reduced, consolidating power in the hands of a military council headed by Lekhanya.

Lesser, Sol (1890–1980). Pioneer HOLLYWOOD film producer. Lesser started in the movie industry in 1907 as a producer of two-reel films. He went on to produce some 117 motion pictures, including a series of TARZAN films starring Johnny WEISSMULLER. Among his other credits were the ACADEMY AWARD-winning 1951 documentary *Kon Tiki*, *Our Town*, *The Red House* and *Stage Door Canteen*. Lesser was also credited with introducing new ideas in film merchandising that became standard practice, including previews and personal appearances by the stars.

Lessing, Doris [born Doris May Tayler] (1919–). British author. Lessing has emerged as one of the most important fiction writers since World War II. Her first novel, *The Grass Is Singing* (1950), achieved immediate critical and popular acclaim, and contains one of her recurring themes: the experience of living in Africa (she was raised in Southern Rhodesia, now ZIMBABWE). Other prominent themes include the individual's search for wholeness, FEMINISM, the battle of the sexes and, more recently, mental collapse and extrasensory perception. She most often uses a solitary, strong woman pushed to the breaking point as her protagonist. Among her many novels are *The Golden Notebook* (1962), considered one of her best, the five-volume series *Children of Violence* (1952–69) and *Memoirs of a Survivor* (1974). More recently she has embarked on a series of space-age fantasy books, such as *The Sirian Experiments* (1981), and was a guest of honor at the 1987 World Science Fiction Convention.

For further reading:

Whittaker, Ruth, *Doris Lessing*. New York: St. Martin's Press, 1988.

Lester, Richard (1932–). A controversial film director in the 1960s and '70s, Lester was born in Philadelphia, where he quickly

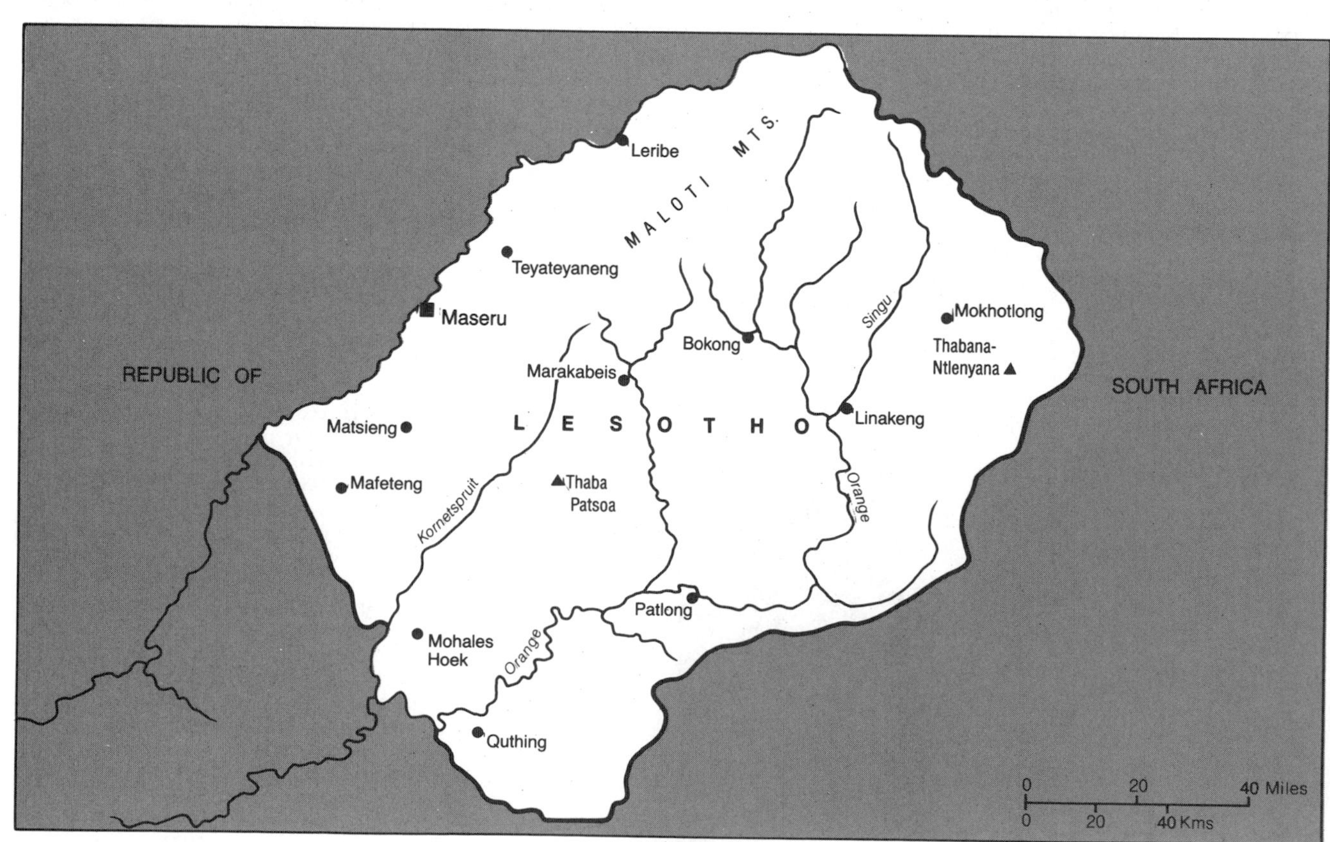

LESOTHO

advanced to director of a local television station. In the early 1950s he traveled throughout Europe and struggled to earn a living through writing and tuning pianos. Near starvation in 1955, Lester moved to England, where he met comedians Peter SELLERS and Spike MILLIGAN. Lester directed these two "Goons" in various shorts for British television, where he developed a reputation for broad comedy and satire. In 1964 and 1965 Lester's brand of humor clicked in two hilarious, off-the-cuff films featuring the BEATLES: *A Hard Day's Night* and *Help!* For the remainder of the decade Lester focused his creative energy on films with biting social satire, political commentary and black humor, such as *How I Won the War* (1967), *Petulia* (1968) and *The Bed-Sitting Room* (1969). Refusing to cater to studio demands, Lester struggled to find success in the early 1970s. But from the mid-1970s onward he returned to prominence with a series of entertaining adventure films, including *The Three Musketeers* (1974), *The Four Musketeers* (1975), *Robin and Marian* (1976), *Cuba* (1979) and *Superman II* (1980).

Letchworth. The English city of Letchworth, in Herts., 34 miles north of London, was Britain's first **garden city,** founded by Sir Ebenezer Howard in 1903.

Letelier, Orlando (1932–1976). Chilean official. Letelier had been CHILE's ambassador to the U.S. and was serving as President Salvador ALLENDE's defense minister when Allende was overthrown in a military coup in September 1973. Letelier was arrested at the time and, after his release in 1974, was exiled. He lived briefly in Venezuela, then moved to the U.S., where he was employed by the Institute for Policy Studies, a Washington, D.C., research group. Shortly before his death, Letelier had become outspoken in his criticism of the Chilean junta's civil rights violations under General Augusto PINOCHET. On September 10, Letelier's Chilean citizenship was revoked. On September 21, Letelier was killed when a bomb exploded under his car in Washington. His associate Ronni Karpen Moffitt was also killed in the blast. In 1980, the Federal District Court in Washington concluded that members of DINA, the Chilean national intelligence agency, had assassinated Letelier; in 1978, former DINA agent Michael Towley had confessed to planting the bomb, and in 1987, another former DINA agent, Armando Fernandez, also admitted involvement in the crime. Another arrest in the case was made in 1991.

Levesque, Rene (1922–1987). Canadian politician. Levesque entered politics as a Liberal with his 1960 election to the Quebec Legislative Assembly. He held a number of ministerial posts before being expelled from the LIBERAL PARTY in 1967 over the issue of Quebec sovereignty, which he had come to champion. He then formed the PARTI QUEBECOIS. He led the party to power in the 1976 election when he was elected prime minister of the province. In 1979 he pushed through a law, fiercely opposed by Prime Minister Pierre TRUDEAU, that formalized the status of French as Quebec's only official language and made English-language commercial signs illegal. Levesque resigned from the Parti Quebecois in 1985, ending his political career.

Rene Levesque, premier of Quebec (June 19, 1984).

Levi, Carlo (1902–1975). Italian novelist, essayist and painter. Levi earned a medical degree before turning to writing as a career. In the 1930s, he was exiled by the fascist regime of MUSSOLINI—which was displeased at his outspoken left-wing politics—to an isolated Italian village. This experience inspired Levi to write the novel *Christ Stopped At Eboli* (1945), a sensitive portrayal of life in an impoverished Italian village, which became an international best-seller. As a result, Levi became a major figure in the neorealism movement in postwar Italian literature. His subsequent novels include *The Watch* (1950) and *The Linden Trees* (1959). From 1963 to 1972, Levi served in the Italian Senate.

Levi, Primo (1919–1987). Italian Jewish author. Levi's autobiographical writings reflected his experiences as a survivor of the HOLOCAUST. During WORLD WAR II he served in the Italian RESISTANCE but was arrested and deported to AUSCHWITZ in 1943. His experiences there gave rise to his 1947 memoir, *If This Is a Man,* which became an international bestseller. Levi pursued his literary vocation while working as a chemist at a paint factory in Turin for 30 years. *The Periodic Table* (1975), one of his most highly-regarded works, fused his two callings, using the analogy of the chemical elements to analyze people and events. Levi committed suicide.

Levine, James (1943–). American conductor. Levine is best known as the principal conductor (since 1972) and musical director (since 1976) of the New York Metropolitan Opera. With George SZELL as his mentor, he became an apprentice conductor, then assistant conductor (1964–70) of the Cleveland Orchestra. In 1971 he made his Met debut conducting *Tosca.* He has appeared regularly at the SALZBURG FESTIVAL (since 1975) and has been a guest conductor with orchestras worldwide. Specializing in the Italian opera repertory, Levine has made many records of operas and symphonies.

Levine, Nat(han) (1900–1989). Early HOLLYWOOD film studio executive. Levine founded his own production company, Mascot Pictures, in 1927. The studio turned out some 500 serial reels, including films featuring the young John WAYNE and cowboy star Gene AUTRY, before merging in 1935 into the newly formed Republic Pictures, which Levine headed until 1937, producing low-budget feature films and serials.

Levison, Stanley (1912–1979). American lawyer, businessman and Jewish civic leader who played a prominent role behind the scenes in the CIVIL RIGHTS MOVEMENT of the 1960s. Levison was a key advisor to the Rev. Dr. Martin Luther KING Jr. and influenced the financial policies, strategy and tactics used by King and the SOUTHERN CHRISTIAN LEADERSHIP CONFERENCE.

Levi Strauss. American firm specializing in the production of utilitarian work pants, the famous "Levi's" that have become accepted as fashion items in modern times. The original Levi Strauss began his business in San Francisco during the 1850s' gold rush making tents for prospectors. In the 1960s Levi's became a popular form of informal dress and acquired a status that made the brand name important in the world of fashionable apparel.

Levi-Strauss, Claude (1908–). French anthropologist, the founder of STRUCTURALISM. Born in Brussels, Belgium, Levi-Strauss studied law and philosophy at the University of Paris (1927–32). He taught sociology at the University of Sao Paulo from 1935 to 1937, at which time he began anthropological field work in Brazil, researches which continued in 1938–39. He taught at the New School for Social Research, New York, from 1941 to 1945 and was France's cultural attache to the U.S. from 1946 to 1947. Director of the Ecole Pratique des Hautes Etudes, Paris, from 1950, he was elected to the chair of anthropology at the College de France in 1959. He was honored with election to the Academie Francaise in 1973. In formulating structuralism, he sought to analyze myths and kinship systems through a system of complicated mathematical and linguistic-based methods. The underlying structures thus discovered suggest, he posits, universal patterns of cultural behavior and uniform attributes of human logic. His methods and conclusions have been extremely influential, not only in anthropology, but in sociology, linguistics and literary criticism as well. Among his many works are *Elementary Structures of Kinship* (1949, tr. 1969), *Structural Anthropology* (1958, tr. 1963 and 1976), *Totemism* (1962, tr. 1963) and *Mythologies* (1964–71, tr. 1970–79).

Levy, Yisrael (1926–1990). Israeli activist. An underground fighter for Israeli independence in the 1940s, he was a member of the IGUN ZVAI LEUMI underground group headed by Menachem BEGIN. He helped carry out the 1946 bombing of the KING DAVID HOTEL in JERUSALEM, a luxury hotel that housed British headquarters, killing 91 people. After ISRAEL achieved independence, he led a quiet life as a stationery store owner.

Lewin, Ronald (1914–1984). British military historian. Critically acclaimed, Lewin was known for his books analyzing the leadership of Winston CHURCHILL and the strategies of field marshals Erwin ROMMEL of Germany and Bernard MONTGOMERY of Britain. Lewin served as chief of the BRITISH BROADCASTING CORPORATION's domestic radio service from 1957 to 1965. His most popular book was *Ultra Goes to War*, an account of Allied efforts to decode German secret messages during WORLD WAR II. (See also ENIGMA.)

For further reading:

Lewin, Ronald, *Churchill as Warlord*. New York: Stein and Day, 1973.

———, *Hitler's Mistakes*. New York: William Morrow, 1987.

Lewis, Alun (1915–1944). British poet. Lewis was born in Alberdare, a Welsh mining village, and educated at Aberystwyth University College and Manchester University. Lewis returned to Wales and taught for two years before deciding to enlist in 1940. His first volume of poetry, *Raider's Dawn*, was published in 1942. His first book of short stories, *The Last Inspection*, (1943), dealt with the tedium and drabness in the lives of soldiers in England waiting for assignment, themes which resurfaced in his most famous poem, "All Day It Has Rained." Lewis was posted to Burma in 1942, where he was killed in 1944. His lyrical poetry explores the themes of death and the fundamental isolation of the soldier and his resulting feelings of futility. Lewis' poetry shows the influence of Edward THOMAS. Other works include *Ha! Ha! Among the Trumpets* (1945), poetry; *In the Green Tree* (1948), a collection of letters and poetry; and *Selected Poetry and Prose* (1966), with an introduction by Ian Hamilton.

Lewis, Carl (Frederick Carlton) (1961–). American track and field star. Both of Lewis' parents were track stars, and he was already a standout by high school. Like so many American athletes, politics forced him onto the sidelines for the 1980 OLYMPIC GAMES. A winner of innumerable NCAA titles, he reached the world stage in 1983 in Helsinki, winning World Championship gold medals in the 100-meter dash, long jump and as part of a 400–meter relay team. The 1984 Olympics saw him win four gold medals in the 100-meter dash, 200-meter dash, 400-meter relay and the long jump.

Lewis, C(live) S(taples) (1898–1963). British literary critic, scholar and author. Lewis was a fellow of Magdalene College, Oxford and later a professor of Medieval and Renaissance English at Cambridge. An eminent scholar, Lewis has written distinguished works of criticism including *The Allegory of Love* (1936), *English Literature in the Sixteenth Century* (1954) and *An Experiment in Criticism* (1961). Outside of literary circles, he is best known for his popular fiction, fantasy and science fiction novels, such as *Out of the Silent Planet* (1938), which shows the influence of J.R.R. TOLKIEN; *The Screwtape Letters* (1940) and *The Lion, The Witch and the Wardrobe* (1950), which is the first of a series of children's books known as the *Chronicles of Narnia*. Lewis' writing reflects his abiding Christianity and explores moral dilemma in that context. He has also written *Surprised by Joy* (1955), an autobiography emphasizing his religious life.

Lewis, Jerry [Joseph Levitch] (1926–). American comedic actor and film director. Lewis, who was a leading HOLLYWOOD box office draw in the 1950s and 1960s, is best known for his cinematic slapstick style that combines physically distorted movements with psychological naivete verging on idiocy. To certain European film critics—most notably in France—he is one of the great clowns of the cinema. To most American critics, Lewis seems unduly obvious and obnoxious. Lewis first achieved film stardom in 1949 after forming a comedy team with straight man/crooner Dean Martin. Their first film, *My Friend Irma* (1949), was followed by fifteen more until Martin left in a highly publicized break-up in 1956. Lewis has since pursued a solo career in films, television, and nightclubs. His most highly regarded films, which he wrote and directed, are *The Ladies' Man* (1961), *The Nutty Professor* (1963) and *The Patsy* (1964). In recent decades, Lewis has become best known for his Labor Day telethons raising money for muscular dystrophy research.

Lewis, Jerry Lee (1935–). American rock-and-roll vocalist, pianist, and composer. Lewis is one of the founding fathers of the ROCK AND ROLL sound that burst into prominence in the U.S. in the mid-1950s. Lewis is especially well known for a flamboyant performing style that features his trademark pumping barrelhouse piano. Born in Louisiana, Lewis was exposed to both black blues and gospel and white country music as a youth. In 1956 he was signed to a contract by Sam Phillips of Sun Records in Memphis, Tennessee. Lewis enjoyed two massive hits in 1957—*Great Balls of Fire* and *Whole Lotta Shakin' Goin' On*. Lewis followed these up with *Breathless* (1958) and *High School Confidential* (1959), but the adverse publicity that stemmed from his marriage to a thirteen-year-old cousin seriously hampered his climb to stardom. In the 1960s and after, recording for several record labels, Lewis made a comeback as a country and western performer. He is still a crowd favorite today among both rock and country audiences. The film *Great Balls of Fire* (1989)—made with Lewis' cooperation—portrays his early success and subsequent downfall in the 1950s.

Lewis, John L(lewellyn) (1880–1969). American labor leader, president of the United Mine Workers of America (1920–60). Although highly controversial, Lewis was perhaps the single most important

John L. Lewis, president of the United Mine Workers (Sept. 8, 1936).

figure in the American labor movement in the 20th century. Born to Welsh immigrant parents in a coal mining community in Iowa, he quit school after the 7th grade and entered the mines at age 15. A man of commanding presence with a talent for oratory and a fondness for Shakespeare, Lewis considered going on the stage before deciding to pursue a career in the labor movement. In 1909 he moved to the coal fields of central Illinois, where he began to rise rapidly in the local hierarchy of the United Mine Workers of America (UMW). In 1911 he became a field representative of the American Federation of Labor (AFL), a job that enabled him to travel widely through the minefields and to build strong personal support within the UMW. As a result, he became UMW vice president in 1917, acting president in 1919 and president of the UMW—the largest union in the AFL—the next year.

In the years following WORLD WAR I, Lewis emerged as a dynamic but ambiguous figure on the national labor scene. A champion of industrial unionism, he headed an unsuccessful challenge to the conservative leadership of AFL president Samuel GOMPERS in 1921. At the same time, Lewis exemplified a tough, pragmatic business unionism. A Republican and a strong believer in free enterprise capitalism, he crushed the strong radical faction opposed to his leadership. With the advent of the NEW DEAL, Lewis took advantage of the NATIONAL INDUSTRIAL RECOVERY ACT (1933) to launch a massive organizing drive in the coalfields, recruiting 300,000 miners to the UMW in two months. Unsuccessful in persuading the AFL to open its membership to unskilled and semi-skilled workers, Lewis brought together the leaders of 10 other unions under the Committee for Industrial Organization (CIO) in 1935. The CIO began a sweeping organizing campaign in basic industries. After conflicts with AFL craft unions, it became the independent Congress of Industrial Organizations in 1936.

As head of both the UMW and the CIO, Lewis lent vital support to President Franklin D. ROOSEVELT'S 1936 reelection campaign. When WORLD WAR II began in Europe, Lewis opposed U.S. intervention and endorsed Wendell WILLKIE for president in 1940. Lewis resigned from the CIO presidency when Roosevelt won a third term. Following the Japanese attack on PEARL HARBOR, Lewis announced his support for the American war effort and joined other leaders in a no-strike pledge for the duration of the conflict. However, in 1943 he concluded that the government had taken advantage of the no-strike agreement to impose an unfair wage formula on workers, and he led a series of epic strikes in defiance of Roosevelt's threat to use federal troops to keep the mines in operation. Vilified by the press, Lewis nonetheless won a 35–hour work week and other benefits for UMW members.

After the war, Lewis was at odds with President TRUMAN'S labor policies. Beginning in April 1946, after talks between the UMW and mineowners broke down, Lewis led a national strike. Within a month coal shortages forced a national brownout, to save fuel, and cutbacks in auto and steel production; the government seized control of the mines. After a series of proposals and countermoves, the government found Lewis and the union guilty of civil and criminal contempt and imposed the heaviest fine in American history up to that time. Lewis's bitter feud with Truman continued. During the EISENHOWER administration (1953–61) Lewis pursued cooperation rather than conflict with the coal industry. He never again seriously used the threat of a strike. Rather, he encouraged the largest mineowners to introduce mechanization and close inefficient mines, even at the expense of massive miner unemployment. Lewis resigned the leadership of the UMW in 1960 and became president emeritus.

For further reading:

Dubovsky, Melvyn, *John L. Lewis: A Biography*. Champaign: University of Illinois Press, 1983.

Ziegler, Robert H., *John L. Lewis: Labor Leader*. Boston: G.K. Hall, 1988.

Lewis, Richard (1914–1990). British tenor. He was one of the first British singers to achieve worldwide fame in opera and concert performances. He appeared as Troilus in the world premier of William WALTON'S *Troilus and Cressida* (1955) and also sang leading roles in the first performances of *Midsummer Marriage* and *King Priam* by Michael TIPPETT.

Lewis, Sinclair (1884–1951). American author. He began his career as a newspaper reporter and later worked for the Associated Press. His first major work, *Main Street*, was published in 1920, and *Babbitt* appeared two years later. In 1926 he refused to accept the PULITZER PRIZE for his *Arrowsmith*. Residents of his hometown resented his depiction of small-town life, but accepted him after he won the NOBEL PRIZE for literature in 1930. His most notable later work was *It Can't Happen Here* (1935). His total output includes 22 novels and three plays.

Lewis, Wyndham (1884–1957). British writer and painter. Lewis, as both novelist and critic, was one of the key figures in the emergence of the modernist school of literature, which also included Lewis' friends T.S. ELIOT, James JOYCE and Ezra POUND. Lewis was also an important painter and the central theorist behind Vorticism, a school of British painting that flourished around the time of World War I. Lewis first gained attention as a writer in 1909 when his short stories were published in *The English Review*, an influential quarterly edited by Ford Maddox FORD. In the 1910s, Lewis edited *Blast*, which became the leading avant-garde journal of its time in Britain. His novels include *Tarr* (1918), *The Childermass* (1928), *The Apes of God* (1930), *The Vulgar Streak* (1941) and *Self-Condemned* (1954). As a critic, his most important works are *Time and Western Man* (1927), *Filibusters in Barbary* (1932) and *Men Without Art* (1914). Lewis authored several autobiographical volumes including *Blasting and Bombardiering* (1937).

Ley, Willy (1906–1969). German-American engineer and rocket pioneer. Born in Berlin, Ley studied at the University of Berlin and was on his way to becoming a zoologist when he chanced upon an early book on rocketry. From that moment the direction of his life was decided. One of the founders of the German Rocket Society he was also a writer whose popular books on rocketry captured the public's imagination. Although it was Ley who introduced Werner von BRAUN into the German Rocket Society, his conscience would not permit him to follow von Braun and others in their collaboration with the Nazis after Adolf HITLER came into power. After coming to the United States in 1935, he became a naturalized citizen in 1944. Although Ley had tremendous influence among science fiction writers and space buffs in the U.S., it was von Braun, bringing to the United States his experience with the V-2 rocket used by the Nazis, who became America's hope for a space future. Although he had fought for it and dreamed about it all of his life, Ley died three weeks before Neil ARMSTRONG and Edwin "Buzz" ALDRIN made their historic touchdown on the moon.

Leyte Gulf, Battle of the (Oct. 23–36, 1944). The decisive naval battle of WORLD WAR II IN THE PACIFIC. In a series of engagements U.S. naval forces, with air support, destroyed the Japanese fleet that had attempted to prevent the Allied landings on Leyte in the PHILIPPINES. The Japanese lost three battleships, four aircraft carriers, ten cruisers, nine destroyers and one submarine; the American naval losses were much lighter. Although fighting continued in the Pacific for another nine months, the U.S. victory at the Leyte Gulf gave the U.S. complete sea supremacy in the Pacific.

Lhasa [Lasa]. City and capital of TIBET, 250 miles northeast of Darjeeling, India. Capital of Tibet by the ninth century A.D., it later lost its position as capital but grew in religious importance. Made capital again in 1642, it was occupied by China in 1951. Following the Tibetan revolt of 1959, the Chinese destroyed many monastic institutions. Formerly a major Buddhist religious center, it was known for centuries as the Forbidden City because of its inaccessibility and the hostility of the Buddhist lamas. It was first visited by Europeans in 1904. It is the site of the former palace of the DALAI LAMA, parts of which were built in the eighth century.

Douglas MacArthur wades ashore at Leyte Gulf on Oct. 22, 1944, keeping his pledge to return to the Philippines.

Lhevinne, Josef and Rosina. Josef (1874–1944) and Rosina (1880–1976) Lhevinne were Russian-born pianists and music teachers. Both trained in piano in their native Russia—Josef earning a gold medal from the Moscow Conservatory in 1892 and Rosina winning a gold medal at the Kiev Conservatory in 1898. Josef also won the prestigious Anton Rubinstein piano competition in 1895. The two met when Josef was hired to give piano lessons to the young Rosina. They married in 1898. In subsequent decades, Josef became an internationally acclaimed piano soloist, while Josef and Rosina performed piano duets that established them as uniquely accomplished musical collaborators. In the 1910s, the couple lived in Berlin, but in 1919 they moved to the U.S. and became founding members of the faculty of the Juilliard School of Music in New York City. After Josef's death, Rosina continued to teach at Juilliard to the end of her life. Among her most famous pupils was pianist Van CLIBURN.

Li, Choh Hao (1913–1987). Chinese-born biochemist. Li spent more than 50 years in the University of California system. In 1971 while at the University of California at San Francisco, he synthesized the human pituitary growth hormone which he had discovered in the 1950s. In 1978 he discovered beta-endorphin, a powerful pain-killing substance produced in the brain. He was director of the laboratory of endocrinology at UCSF from 1983 until his death.

Liaquat, Ali Khan (1896–1951). First prime minister of PAKISTAN (1947–51). Liaquat was a leading member of the Muslim League in the 1920s and 1930s, working closely with Mohammad Ali JINNAH. After the partition of India and the creation of Pakistan in 1947, he became prime minister. Following Jinnah's death, he was the most powerful man in the new state. Criticized over his attempts to reduce tension with India and his refusal to declare Pakistan an Islamic state, he was assassinated by a fanatic in 1951.

Libby, Willard F(rank) (1908–1980). American chemist. Libby obtained his Ph.D. in chemistry from the University of California at Berkeley (1933). During World War II he participated in the MANHATTAN PROJECT that developed the ATOMIC BOMB. He worked at Columbia University under Harold UREY on the gaseous-diffusion method of separating uranium isotopes. Shortly after the war, at the University of Chicago, Libby discovered that radioactive carbon decayed at a predictable rate. Since all living organisms naturally absorb minute traces of this carbon (carbon-14), this meant that by measuring this carbon in dead organic archaeological and geological remains, the age of these remains could be determined. This technique, known as radiocarbon dating or **carbon-14 dating,** had immense implications for extending knowledge about the past and helped revolutionize archaeology, anthropology, and geology. For his role in developing radiocarbon dating, Libby was awarded the 1960 NOBEL PRIZE for chemistry. In addition to his other work, Libby also served on the Atomic Energy Commission (AEC) (1954–59).

Libedinsky, Yuri Nikolayevich (1898–?). Soviet author, one of the founders of the proletarian "October Group" in 1922. His short novel *A Week* (1922) won Libedinsky the party's favor, in spite of his nonproletarian origins. His next novel, *Tomorrow* (1923), implied that the Soviet Union should be rescued from the NEW ECONOMIC POLICY and was thus obviously less successful. Something of a political speculator, in his play *Heights* Libedinsky emphasized LENIN's warning that the party should not depend on officials trained by the czarist regime. He was expelled from the party in 1933 as a result of his novel *Birth of a Hero* (1930) but was later reinstated.

Dr. Willard Frank Libby working in his Chicago laboratory (Sept. 15, 1954).

Liberace [born Wladziu Valentino Liberace] (1919–1987). American pianist and entertainer. Liberace was known for his flamboyant showmanship and lavish costumes. Performing show tunes and popular arrangements of classical pieces, he became U.S. television's first matinee idol. In the 1950s his syndicated show was carried by a record number of stations. During this period he was said to have been the world's highest-paid entertainer, earning up to $400,000 a week in Las Vegas night clubs. He continued performing in Las Vegas after his show went off the air; he also toured and made occasional TV appearances. His death was believed to have been from complications resulting from AIDS.

liberalism. Philosophical and political doctrine that emphasizes individual freedom and stresses the goodness and rationality of human beings. In broad terms, liberalism is contrasted to CONSERVATISM. Supporting change in the status quo, liberalism traditionally upholds the idea of progress. In the U.S., political liberalism is generally associated with the DEMOCRATIC PARTY, although many Republicans have embraced the main tenets of liberalism, while there have also been conservative Democrats. Liberalism in the 20th century has largely centered around government as provider of individual freedom, and has asked the state to prevent the oppression of the individual and to provide decent conditions for all members of society. By supporting a government that intervenes in the national economy, liberals seek to provide for the economic and social welfare of the populace. This doctrine was instrumental in the creation of the WELFARE STATE in early 20th-century Europe and in providing an impetus for welfare state reforms in the U.S. The central figure in 20th-century American liberalism was undoubtedly President Franklin D. ROOSEVELT. His NEW DEAL programs, which encompassed the minimum wage, social security, welfare programs and progressive taxation, are all reflective of liberal thinking and have all become staples of the American social system. The liberal agenda in the last quarter of the 20th century includes racial and sexual equality, public education and equitable health care. While some liberals have embraced the principles of socialism, the degradation of individual rights that has been a feature of COMMUNISM in the 20th century makes many liberals extremely antagonistic to the principles and practice of Marxism.

For further reading:

Hartz, Louis, *The Liberal Tradition in America: An Interpretation of American Political Thought Since the Revolution.* San Diego: Harcourt Brace Jovanovich, 1991.

Pells, Richard H., *The Liberal Mind in a Conservative Age: American Intellectuals in the 1940s and 1950s*, 2nd ed. Hanover, N.H.: University Press of New England, 1989.

Liberal Party (Australia). Australian political party established in 1945. The Liberal Party was formed primarily by Sir Robert MENZIES, who became its first leader. He brought the non-Labour members of Parliament together and formed a mass organization to sustain them. The Liberal Party joined the coalition government formed by the Nationalist and Country Parties, and Menzies was prime minister from 1949 until 1966. The coalition remained in power until 1972. It was returned under Prime Minister Malcolm FRASER in 1975 following the controversial administration of Gough WHITLAM but was defeated in 1983.

Liberal Party (Canada). One of CANADA's two major political parties. The Liberal Party was formed when Canada gained dominion status in 1867. The party adopted free trade and anti-colonial policies. In English-speaking Canada the party's supporters included anticonservative, free-trade Ontario English (Clear Grits) and anglophone farmers. In French Quebec the party was largely based on anticlericalism. The party has a tradition of alternating Anglophone and Francophone leaders, many of whom became prime ministers. Twentieth-century Liberal prime ministers include Sir Wilfred LAURIER (1896–1911), William Lyon Mackenzie KING (1921–30, 1935–48), Louis ST. LAURENT (1948–57), Lester PEARSON (1963–68), Pierre Elliot TRUDEAU (1968–1979, 1980–1984). Although Laurier and King actively encouraged American investment, Trudeau sought a more independent Canada both economically and politically. In the second half of the century the party's power base was in central Canada, primarily Ontario.

Liberal Party (New Zealand). Former New Zealand political party. The New Zealand Liberal Party was dominant at the beginning of the century under the leadership of Prime Minister Richard Seddon. He left office in 1906, but the Liberals retained power until 1911. The Liberal Party took part in the wartime coalition government between 1915 and 1919 but went into decline after the war. Its leader, Sir Joseph Ward, restyled the party as the United Party in an effort to broaden its support. He was prime minister between 1928 and 1930. In 1935, the United Party joined with the Reform and Democratic Parties to form the NATIONAL PARTY.

Liberal Party (United Kingdom) [Liberal Democratic Party from 1988]. British political party established in 1877, known as the **Liberal Democratic Party** after 1988. Liberal policies occupy the moderate ground between the LABOUR and CONSERVATIVE parties. The Liberal Democratic Party advocates governmental decentralization, proportional representation in the House of Commons, reform of the House of Lords, and a mixed economy of nationalized industries and private enterprise. It also supports British membership in the EEC and NATO. The Liberal Party entered the 20th century as one of the two major British political parties, but began to decline early in the century due to its division on the question of Irish HOME RULE and to the advent of the Labour Party. Liberals came to power in 1906 under the leadership of Sir Henry CAMPBELL-BANNERMAN, whose government included David LLOYD GEORGE and Herbert ASQUITH, who succeeded him in 1908. The party was split by disputes between Lloyd George and Asquith during World War I, and its radical elements were absorbed by the Labour Party. The Liberal Party continued to dwindle between the wars, and has not held office since the National Coalition of World War II. Although it supported the minority Labour government in 1977 and 1978 (the so-called "Lib-Lab Pact"), Liberals held no cabinet seats in that government. In 1981 the Liberals formed an alliance with the new SOCIAL DEMOCRATIC PARTY, and they ran joint candidates in the 1983 general elections. Despite substantial support in the opinion polls, the Liberals failed to make significant inroads in the general elections. In 1988 the two parties merged to form the Liberal Democratic Party, with Paddy Ashdown as its leader.

Liberation Theology. The radical position initiated by many Catholic priests against oppressive regimes, especially in Latin America. It evolved in the 1960s and was expounded during the 1970s and 1980s despite the disapproval of the Vatican.

Liberec [German: Reichenberg]. City in CZECHOSLOVAKIA, 55 miles north-northeast of PRAGUE; founded in the 14th century. In the SUDETENLAND, it was the main center of Czechoslovakia's ethnic German population until after World War II. Agitation by pro-Nazi Czech-Germans in Liberec gave HITLER an excuse to demand the annexation of Czechoslovakia in 1938.

Liberia [Republic of Liberia]. Liberia is located on the west coast of Africa and covers an area of 42,988 square miles. The Republic of Liberia was established in 1847 by freed American slaves who had returned to Africa. Under President William Tubman (1944–71) foreign investment and citizen involvement in government were encouraged. His successor William R. Tolbert continued these policies but encountered protests when he instituted economic changes, resulting in riots that were violently suppressed (1979). In 1980 Tolbert was assassinated and army Sergeant Samuel K. Doe as-

LIBERIA

1926	Firestone Rubber Company begins operations in Liberia under the terms of a loan it made to the country; Liberian finances are brought under U.S. supervision.
1944	William Tubman inaugurated president; promotes foreign investment and local participation in government.
1947	Universal suffrage enacted.
1952	Firestone loan paid off 15 years before maturity.
1971	Tubman dies; William Tolbert ascends to the presidency.
1980	(April 12) Tolbert assassinated during coup led by Master Sergeant Samuel K. Doe; Doe suspends constitution and parliament and executes 13 leading officials of the former regime.
1985	(Oct. 15) Under allegations of election fraud Doe is elected president as head of the National Democratic Party of Liberia.
1988	(Oct. 10) William Kpolleh, leader of the Liberian Action Party, is imprisoned for plotting to overthrow the government.
1990	(July 30) Government troops massacre 300 to 600 men, women and children who have taken refuge in a Lutheran church in Monrovia; (Sept. 10) Doe is killed after being captured by rebel forces.

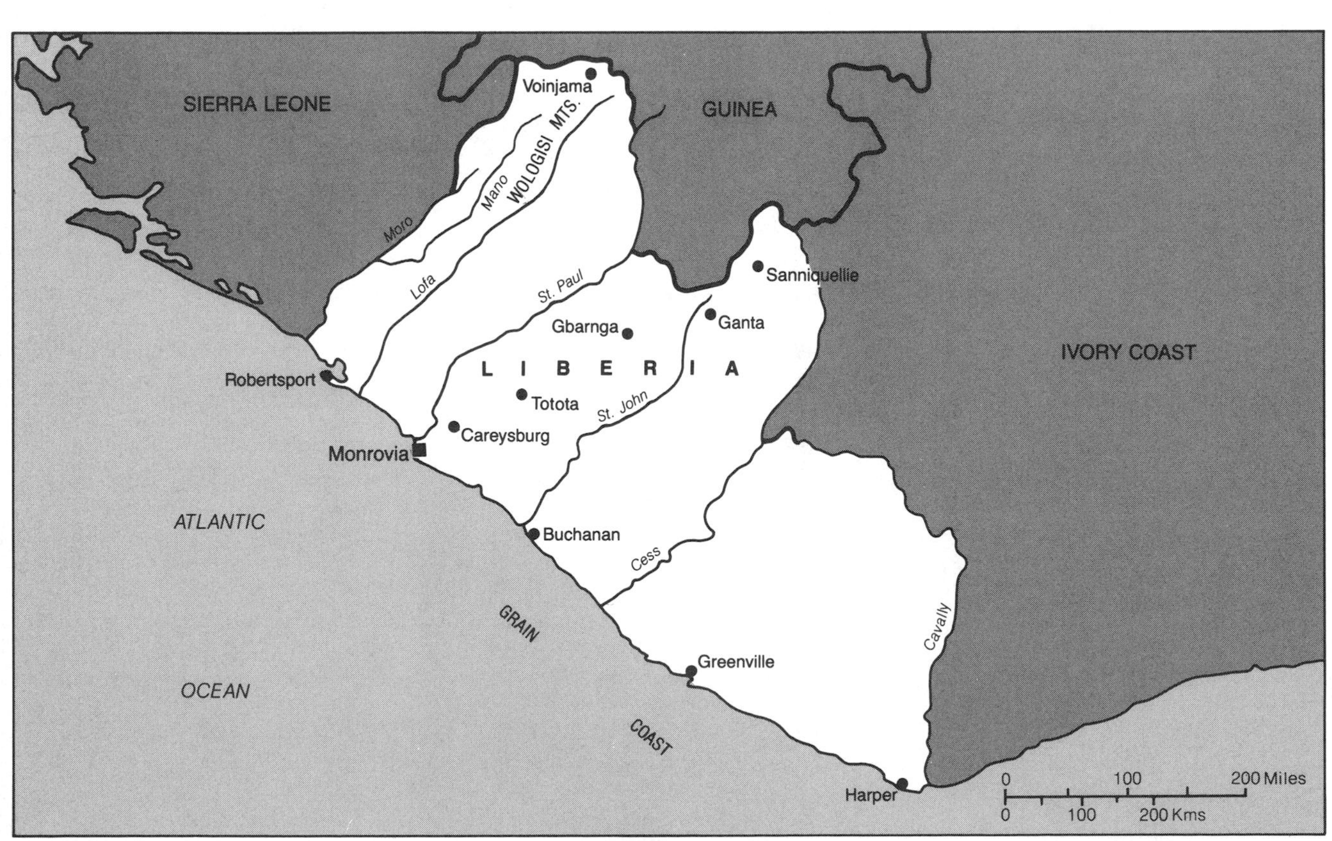

LIBERIA

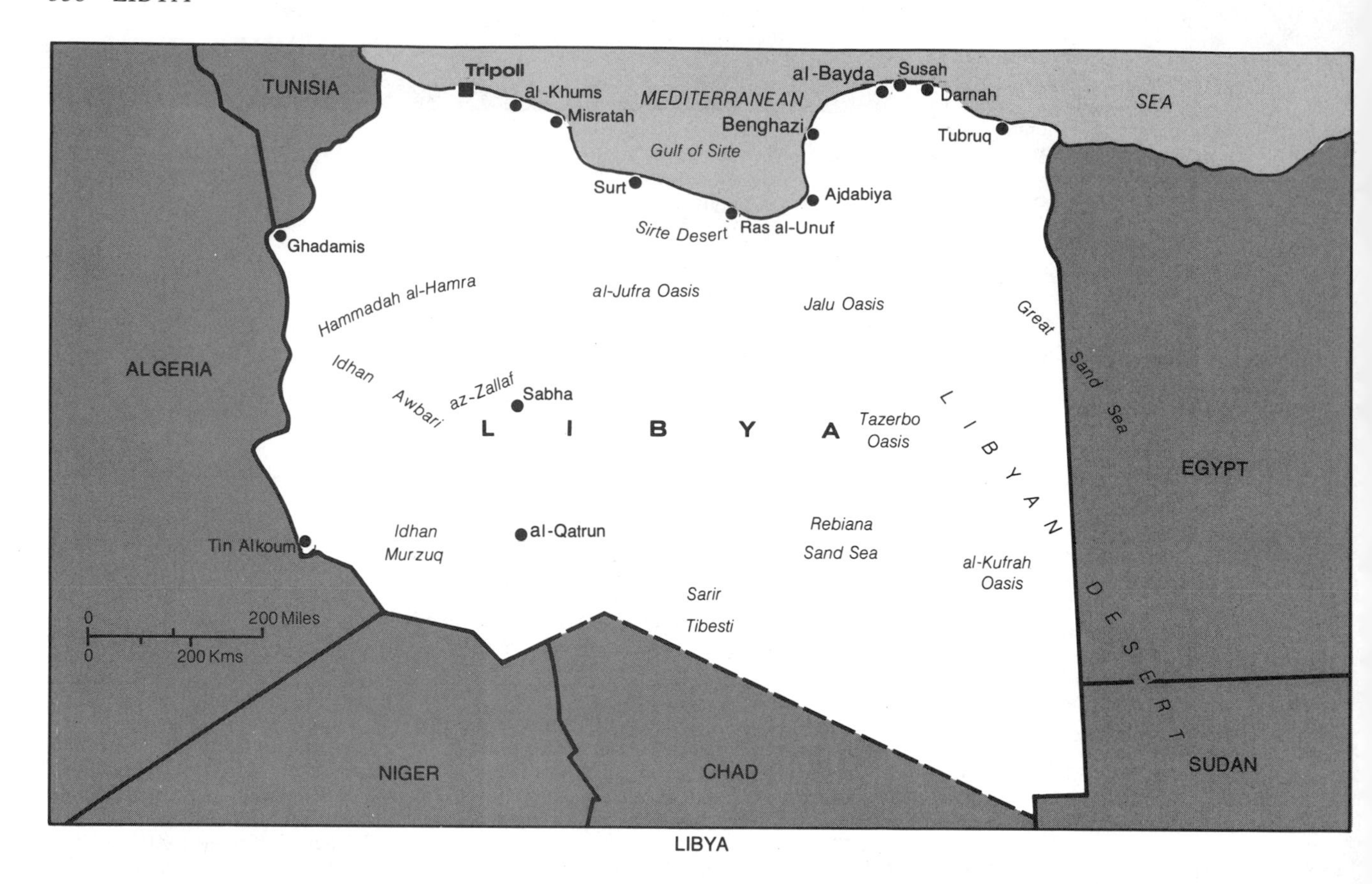

LIBYA

sumed power, gaining recognition and support from the U.S. A new constitution providing for universal adult suffrage without the qualification of property ownership was approved in 1984. Doe, who was elected president in 1985, survived several coup attempts before he was confronted with a bloody armed rebellion in northern Liberia (1990). The rebellion resulted in the deaths of partisans on both sides of the confrontation, and of many civilian deaths at the hands of both government and rebel forces. The situation degenerated into anarchy despite the attempts of neighboring African nations to intervene in the dispute. Doe himself was killed as the rebels moved into the capital. Afterwards, tensions continued between two rival rebel factions. There was a mass migration of Liberians into GUINEA and COTE D'IVOIRE.

Libya [Socialist People's Libyan Arab Jamahiriya]. Libya, located on the Mediterranean coast of north Africa, covers an area of 679,182 square miles. Part of the OTTOMAN EMPIRE since the 17th century, Libya was invaded by ITALY in 1911. The Turkish sultan relinquished all rights to the country in the 1912 peace settlement, and Italy secured its position through the strongarm tactics of Governor Giuseppe Volpi (1921–32) and colonization (1938–39). The British captured the capital of Tripoli during WORLD WAR II (1945). The victorious Allies permitted the Libyans to form an independent country, the United Kingdom of Libya, under King Idris in 1951. In 1969 a military coup led by Colonel Muammer el-QADDAFI deposed the king and set up a military regime with Qaddafi as head. He closed Western military bases (allowed by Idris since 1952) and espoused Arab nationalism. The new constitution of 1977 established the Socialist People's Libyan Arab Jamahiriya. During the 1980s Qaddafi was condemned for his assassination campaign against Libyan exiles and his promotion of worldwide terrorism. Ten-

LIBYA

1911	Italy seizes Libya from weakened Ottoman empire.
1938-39	30,000 Italian peasant farmers settled in Libya under Mussolini colonization policy.
1940-43	Italian and German forces use Libya as base of operations during World War II North African campaign.
1949	Libya is granted independence following Italy's defeat in World War II.
1951	United Kingdom of Libya proclaimed under King Idris (Muhammad Idris al-Mahdi al-Senusi).
1960s	Discovery of oil brings foreign investment, new wealth and social change.
1969	Coup led by Col. Muammer el-Qaddafi deposes King Idris; new Arab nationalist regime closes Western military bases, confiscates property of Jews and Italians.
1980	Libyan forces enter Chad; Qaddafi announces merger of the two countries; Libyan troops withdraw the following year.
1984	Britain breaks relations with Libya after Libyans fire on a crowd from their London embassy, killing a British policewoman.
1986	U.S. bombers raid Tripoli and Benghazi in retaliation for Libyan terrorist bombings.
1989	(January) U.S. Navy fighters shoot down two Libyan MIGs off Libyan coast; U.S. asserts that Libya is building chemical weapons factory with German assistance.
1991	Qaddafi releases international terrorist Abu Nidal from house arrest.

sions between Libya and the U.S. over Libyan support of terrorism culminated in the U.S. bombing of Tripoli and Benghazi in 1986.

Libyan-Egyptian War of 1977. Hostility between EGYPT and LIBYA increased April-May 1977 when demonstrators in each attacked the other's consulates. Colonel Muammer el-QADDAFI, Libyan head of state, accused Egypt of provoking a war, and despite Egyptian denials, ordered expulsion of the 225,000 Egyptian workers in Libya. Gunfire across their mutual border began a four-day war July 21, 1977 with tanks and warplanes, and some Libyan aircraft were destroyed on the ground by an Egyptian attack. Algeria's president intervened, mediating a cease-fire July 24; both sides had suffered heavy losses.

Libya Raid (April 14, 1986). On April 4, 1986, a U.S. serviceman was killed in a bomb explosion in a West Berlin discotheque. The attack was believed to have been carried out by Libyan-trained terrorists. In retaliation, U.S. President REAGAN ordered a military strike against suspected terrorist bases in Libya. U.S. F-111 bombers based in Britain carried out the mission. The raid was highly popular in the U.S., but international opinion was divided.

Lichine, Alexis (1913–1989). Russian-born wine expert. An internationally recognized authority, Lichine specialized in promoting French wines in the U.S. In 1951 he purchased the Chateau Prieure-Cantenac winery near Bordeaux, Franch, which he renamed the Chateau Prieure-Lichine. He also founded Alexis Lichine & Co., a wine shipping firm that he later sold to the British brewer Bass. His books *The Wines of France* (1951; later retitled *Alexis Lichine's Guide to the Wines and Vineyards of France*) and the *Encyclopedia of Wines and Spirits* (1967) were considered landmark reference books.

Lidice. Village in CZECHOSLOVAKIA, 10 miles west-northwest of PRAGUE. At the beginning of June 1942, during the German occupation of Czechoslovakia in WORLD WAR II, the Czechoslovak RESISTANCE assassinated Nazi official Reinhard Heydrich, the head of the German administration in Czechoslovakia. In retribution, the SS systematically destroyed the village of Lidice on June 9–10, 1942. Many villagers were burned in their homes. The surviving men were shot; women were deported to CONCENTRATION CAMPS and children went to German institutions. The obliteration of Lidice and its people became a symbol of Nazi barbarism. After the war a new village and a memorial were built.

Lie, Trygve (1896–1968). Norwegian statesman, secretary-general of the UNITED NATIONS (1946–53). A Social Democrat, Lie served in every Norwegian government from 1935 to 1946. Elected the first secretary-general of the UN, he was an early but unsuccessful advocate of the admission of communist CHINA to the UN. At the outbreak of the KOREAN WAR (1950) he took the initiative in organizing UN forces to assist SOUTH KOREA in checking aggression by NORTH KOREA. He resigned in 1953 and later reentered Norwegian politics.

UN Secretary-General Trygve Lie broadcasts on the United Nations Radio series "Price of Peace."

Lieb, Fred (1888–1980). American sportswriter and baseball historian. Lieb started his career in journalism in 1911. Active for nearly 70 years, he wrote more than a dozen books on baseball and covered some 8,000 major league games. It was Lieb who called Yankee Stadium "the house that Ruth built" (see Babe RUTH). He was the first sportswriter to be inducted into the Baseball Hall of Fame.

Liebes, Dorothy (1899–1972). Leading American designer of textiles, known for her typically modernist use of strong colors and unusual materials. Liebes' education was primarily academic, but in the 1930s she established a studio in San Francisco where she produced custom handweaves of simple design for designers and architects. In 1940 she became a designer for the production firm of Goodall Fabrics. As her reputation grew, she became a designer and consultant to a number of larger firms, including Sears Roebuck and DuPont. For many years she was the only textile designer with national public recognition.

Liechtenstein. Liechtenstein is an alpine principality of central Europe, tucked between Austria and Switzerland and occupying a total area of only 61.8 square miles; it is the fourth smallest country in the world. Neutral during both world wars of the 20th century, in 1919 Liechtenstein entrusted its external relations (previously handled by Austria) to neutral Switzerland, with which it established currency, customs and postal unions in 1921–24. Prince Franz Josef II succeeded his grand-uncle as ruler in 1938; the principality has since been governed by a coalition of the Patriotic Union (VU) and the Progressive Citizens' Party (FBP). Early in 1939 a plurality of 95% voted for continued independence and the Swiss link. In the postwar era Liechtenstein became increasingly prosperous as a financial center, achieving one of the world's highest per capita incomes. In August 1984 Prince Franz Josef transferred his executive powers to Crown Prince Hans Adam, while remaining titular head of state. Female suffrage was narrowly approved by referendum in July 1984; in February 1986 an environmentalist Free Voters' List (FW) just failed to win the 8% vote-share required for representation. Prince Franz Josef died in November 1989 and was succeeded by his son Hans Adam.

Lifar, Serge (1905–1986). Russian-born dancer and choreographer. He was the last world-famous dancer to emerge under the tutelage of Serge DIAGHILEV. He joined Diaghilev's BALLETS RUSSES in Paris in 1923 and two years later became the company's principal male dancer. Before that company disbanded in 1929, he created roles in a number of early ballets by George BALANCHINE, most notably *The Prodigal Son* and *Apollo*. He first tried his hand as a choreographer with Igor STRAVINSKY's *Le Renard*. From 1929 to 1945 and from 1947 to 1958, he served as ballet master of the Paris Opera Ballet. He greatly enlarged that company's repertory, restored technical standards and established the company's standards with the Parisian audience. He was also a prolific author of books on dance theory and dance history.

***Life* magazine.** American periodical. Started in 1936, *Life* magazine was conceived of by publisher Henry LUCE and his wife Clare Boothe LUCE. It was to be a large-format, inexpensive—its initial price was 10 cents an issue—photographic magazine. Its staff of photographers included Margaret BOURKE-WHITE and Alfred EISENSTADT, and it became known for its excellent photography, particularly for its stirring portraits of soldiers and war-torn Europe during WORLD WAR II. At its peak of popularity in the postwar years each issue sold 8 million copies worldwide. As the availability of televised images increased, the magazine foundered and eventually folded in the early 1970s but was later revived.

Likud. Alliance of various right-wing Israeli parties, which, under the leadership of Menachem BEGIN, won the general election of 1977, displacing the Israeli Labour Party for the first time in the country's history. Yitzhak SHAMIR later headed the Likud alliance.

Lillie, Beatrice Gladys [stage name of Constance Sylvia Munston, Lady Peel] (1898–1989). Canadian-born actress and comedienne, often called "the funniest woman in the world." Lillie emigrated to England in 1910 to study music, and soon began appearing in theatrical revues. During a 50-year career she appeared in numerous plays, musicals, and films in the U.S. and Britain, including *Auntie Mame, Around the World in Eighty Days, Thoroughly Modern Millie,* and *High Spirits*, a musical version of Noel COWARD's *Blithe Spirit*. Her one-woman show *An Evening with Beatrice Lillie* won her a Tony Award in 1953.

Lima Declaration. Document of Pan-American solidarity issued in Lima, Peru on December 26, 1938 by representatives of North and South American governments. Prompted by fascist incursions in Europe and by Japanese expansionism, it stated that a threat to the peace, security or territorial integrity of any republic in the Americas would be viewed as a threat to all of the American republics.

Limon, Jose (1908–1972). Mexican-American dancer, choreographer, and teacher. Limon studied with Doris Humphrey and Charles Weidman and joined their company in 1930. In 1946 he formed his own dance company with Humphrey as co-artistic director. The company received immediate acclaim as one of the outstanding modern dance troupes. Limon, himself, is one of the most influential and admired modern dance figures. He choreographed his most famous work, *The Moor's Pavane* in 1949. Other important works include *The Traitor* (1954) and *Missa Brevis* (1958). In addition to world tours with his company and yearly performances at the American Dance Festival at Connecticut College, he has taught at the Juilliard School of Music and various other colleges. After his death the Jose Limon Dance Company was in residence at the New York 92nd Street YM-YWHA.

Lin Biao (1908–1971). Chinese communist soldier and MAO TSE-TUNG's designated successor. Lin was a veteran of the LONG MARCH (1934–35), during which he commanded a communist army. He gained victories over CHIANG KAI-SHEK's KUOMINTANG troops in 1948 and carried the war victoriously into central CHINA in 1949. Created a marshal in 1955 and minister of defense in 1959, he assisted Mao in organizing the CULTURAL REVOLUTION of the mid-1960s. Marshal Lin was declared Mao's designated successor by the Ninth Party Congress in 1966 but was killed in an air crash in 1971 while fleeing from China after an unsuccessful attempt to seize power in Peking.

Lincoln Continental. Ford Motor Company luxury automobile of original and outstanding design, especially the models from 1939 to 1945. Henry FORD's son Edsel became interested in the design of expensive cars built in Europe and, after a 1938 trip abroad, asked Ford designers to design a customer model for his own use. He labeled the resulting car *Continental.* It was characterized by simple, unornamented forms, restrained streamlining, a long hood with simple radiator grille detailing, and a covered spare tire mounted at the back of the projecting trunk. The car was handsome and unique among American cars of the day. A decision was made to put the design into limited production. In 1941 a convertible version was added as an alternative to the closed original. The design has come to be regarded as one of the most striking classic designs Detroit automobile firms have produced. It remains a "collectors' item," exerting a strong influence on later automotive design. The Continental name has been used for a number of later designs that have attempted to recapture the quality of the original design.

Lincoln Division [of Ford Motor Company]. Division of Ford that produced cars using the Lincoln name. In this way Ford could launch a line of expensive luxury cars comparable to the Cadillacs and Chryslers of its competitors and at the same time minimize identification with the Ford reputation for economical, utilitarian vehicles. Lincolns were (and still are) big cars designed to appear costly and impressive.

Lincoln Zephyr. Model designation given to the Ford Motor Company automobile intended as a luxury car, which was slightly less costly than the luxury Lincoln. The Lincoln Zephyr of 1936 with a V-12 engine, used lines somewhat related to those of the Ford V-8s of 1933 and thereafter, but the body was given strongly streamlined forms, suggestive of those of the earlier Chrysler AIRFLOW but somewhat less radical and so less disturbing to the consumer public. The Zephyr is often viewed as the first American streamlined car to achieve even moderate public acceptance. Some of its forms and many of its mechanical elements were incorporated into the more elegant Lincoln Continental that appeared in 1939.

Lindbergh, Charles Augustus (1902–1974). American aviator. Born in Detroit, Michigan, Lindbergh was named for his father, a Republican congressman. Lindbergh attended flying school in Nebraska, and bought his first plane in 1923. He entered the U.S. Army Air Corps Reserve in 1925, and also flew as an airmail pilot. In 1927, enticed by a $25,000 reward being offered for the first nonstop solo transatlantic flight, Lindbergh won backing from a group of St. Louis businessmen, who funded the construction of a specially designed airplane, "The Spirit of St. Louis." Lindbergh took off from New York's Roosevelt Field on the morning of May 20, 1927. Thirty-three and a half hours later he landed at Bourget Field, Paris, and was welcomed by a rapturous crowd. The flight brought Lindbergh worldwide fame. Upon his return to New York he was hailed as "the lone eagle" and given the largest ticker-tape parade ever held up to that time. A long series of speaking engagements and receptions followed. In 1929 Lindbergh married Anne Morrow, the daughter of noted American banker and diplomat Dwight W. Morrow. They attempted to settle into a quiet family life, but in 1932 their infant son was kidnapped and murdered. A highly publicized investigation and trial ensued (see LINDBERGH KIDNAPPING CASE). To escape the constant attention of reporters and the curious public, the Lindberghs moved to England (1935). In 1938 the German government invited Lindbergh to inspect the Luftwaffe. Lindbergh was highly impressed by Nazi GERMANY and its military forces. (Some authorities have suggested that Lindbergh was actually an American spy, reporting to the U.S. government on the German military buildup.) Returning to the U.S. (1939), he became an outspoken advocate of American ISOLATIONISM and made public appearances for the

Charles Lindbergh standing before his plane, the Spirit of St. Louis.

AMERICA FIRST Committee. His view that the new world war was strictly a European affair which America ought to ignore angered many of his previous admirers. After JAPAN attacked PEARL HARBOR, however, Lindbergh supported America's role in WORLD WAR II and flew combat missions in the Pacific. He became a brigadier general in 1954 and was a consultant to the Defense Department and an advisor to Pan American Airways.

His autobiography, *The Spirit of St. Louis,* won a PULITZER PRIZE in 1953. In his later years, spent in Hawaii, Lindbergh was an active conservationist. Among his many accomplishments, Lindbergh was also the co-inventor (1936, with Alexis CARREL) of a so-called artificial heart that could pump nutrients through the human body. Lindbergh remains one of the most complex and fascinating figures of the 20th century. A man of great personal courage, he was also intensely private. Almost universally admired for his achievements in AVIATION, he was also criticized by many for his unorthodox political views.

For further reading:

Crouch, Tom D., ed., *Charles A. Lindbergh: An American Life.* Washington, D.C.: Smithsonian Institution Press, 1977.

Miller, Francis, T., *Lindbergh: His Story in Pictures.* Salem, N.H.: Ayer, 1979.

Lindbergh kidnapping case [*New Jersey v. Bruno Hauptmann*] (1932–36). Kidnapping and subsequent murder of the infant son of American aviator Charles

A. LINDBERGH, followed by a sensational trial. Lindbergh became a national hero after his solo transatlantic flight in 1927 in *The Spirit of St. Louis*. Two years later, he married the writer Anne Spencer Morrow, and the couple settled in rural Hopewell, New Jersey. The couple's bliss was shattered when their infant son Charles Lindbergh Jr. was kidnapped from his nursery during the night of March 1, 1932. In the following weeks, Lindbergh and the police followed numerous false leads in the hope of recovering the Lindbergh baby unharmed. After paying a ransom and receiving a note about the baby's whereabouts, their hopes were dashed when the baby's body was discovered on May 12, not far from their home. The nation was stunned and a massive manhunt eventually led to the arrest of Bruno Richard Hauptmann, a German immigrant.

Although there was only circumstantial evidence and Hauptmann maintained his innocence, he was convicted. After a series of unsuccessful appeals Hauptmann was executed in the electric chair. However, controversy still lingers about the actual facts of the crime. The Lindbergh case was one of the most sensational of the 20th century, and the glare of publicity that followed the Lindberghs forced them to leave the U.S. for several years.

Lindsay, (Nicholas) Vachel (1879–1931). American poet. Born in Springfield, Illinois, Lindsay attended Hiram College, the Art Institute of Chicago and the New York School of Art. During his early years, he walked the U.S. as a modern troubadour, selling his drawings and giving poetry readings to pay for his meals and his lodging. Lindsay's strongly musical and rhythmic poetry, often concerned with the American experience, is particularly effective when read aloud. Books that reflect his years of wandering include *Rhymes to Be Traded for Bread* (1912), *Adventures While Preaching the Gospel of Beauty* (1914) and *A Handy Guide for Beggars* (1916). Among his collected volumes of verse are *General William Booth Enters into Heaven* (1913), *The Congo* (1914) and *Collected Poems* (1930).

Link, Edwin A. (1904–1981). American inventor. In the 1930s Link invented the flight simulator, a mechanical device that simulated night conditions and was used for many years to train millions of military and commercial pilots, including some 50,000 WORLD WAR II pilots. He founded Link Aviation in 1935 and went on to design many other advanced aviation devices. Some of these were used to train the first astronauts. Link also developed equipment for deep-sea exploration, including the first submarine with an underwater exit hatch, and "The Shark," a protected television camera that could be lowered to depths that divers could not reach.

Lipatti, Dinu (1917–1950). Romanian concert pianist. Born into a musical family, Lipatti developed into a child prodigy. Encouraged by his godfather, composer Georges ENESCO, he attended the Bucharest Conservatory. When he placed second in an international competition in Vienna (1934), one of the judges, Alfred CORTOT, resigned from the jury in protest and invited Lipatti to study with him in Paris. Lipatti's budding career was curtailed by WORLD WAR II, which he spent in Switzerland. From 1944 to 1948, Lipatti was professor of piano at the Geneva Conservatory; during this period, through his recitals, concerts and recordings he won international recognition as a major artist, and was particularly renowned for his interpretations of the music of J.S. Bach and Frederic Chopin. In 1948 he was diagnosed as having leukemia; musicians around the world, including Yehudi MENUHIN and Igor STRAVINSKY, donated money for his treatment. Despite his illness, Lipatti remained active until his final months; his last recital was in the autumn of 1950. He died on December 2, 1950, at age 33. Many critics consider Lipatti's premature death a tremendous loss to 20th-century music and feel that, had he lived, he would have been one of the greatest pianists of the century. In the years since his death, his legend has grown.

Lipchitz, Jacques [Chaim Jacob Lipschitz] (1891–1973). Born in Lithuania, Lipchitz settled in Paris in 1909 and studied at the Ecole des Beaux-Arts. He soon became associated with cubist artists, reinterpreting the tenets of CUBISM in sculpted form in works such as *Man with a Guitar* (1916, Museum of Modern Art, New York City). In the 1920s he experimented with transparent sculptures and by the 1930s began to create monumental and powerful semi-abstract sculpture. Lipchitz lived in the U.S. during the early 1940s and returned to France after World War II. The large and rhythmic forms and the mingling of the allegorical and the contemporary in subject matter that characterize his mature style may be seen as early as *The Rape of Europe* (1941) and as late as *Peace on Earth* (1967–69). Lipchitz is widely considered to have played a pivotal role in the development of modern sculpture in the 20th century.

Li Peng (1928–). Prime minister of the People's Republic of CHINA (1988–). The son of a communist writer who had been executed by CHIANG KAI-SHEK in 1930, Li Peng was adopted at the age of three by ZHOU ENLAI. He studied engineering in the Soviet Union and is a nuclear expert. He began to rise in the political hierarchy in the late 1970s, and from the early 1980s on served in various ministerial posts. In November 1987 he became acting prime minister, and in April of the following year he was confirmed in this post at the seventh National People's Congress. He is a conservative technocrat and prefers a slower and more cautious approach in modernization efforts.

Lipinski, Edward (1888–1986). Polish economist. Lipinski twice served as director of POLAND's Institute of National Economy. In 1975 he resigned from the Communist Party and in 1976 helped found the Committee for Workers' Self-Defense. That group, known by its Polish initials KOR, was credited with helping pave the way for the formation of the SOLIDARITY free trade union confederation in 1980. At Solidarity's first national congress in 1981, Lipinski dissolved KOR, declaring it had outlived its usefulness.

Walter Lippmann (1969).

Lippmann, Walter (1889–1974). American journalist. Winner of two PULITZER PRIZES (1958, 1962), Lippmann was a dominant intellectual figure for four decades. In 1914 he helped establish the NEW REPUBLIC, serving as associate editor until 1917. He served as editorial page chief (1923–29) then editor (1929–31) of the *New York World*. He wrote his famous column, *Today and Tomorrow*, for the NEW YORK HERALD–TRIBUNE (1931–62), then for the *Washington Post* (1962–67). The column appeared in more than 250 newspapers worldwide. Lippmann was also the author of several books, including *Public Opinion* (1922) and *U.S. Foreign Policy* (1943). He retired in 1967.

For further reading:

Steel, Ronald, *Walter Lippmann and the American Century*. Boston: Little, Brown, 1980.

Lippold, Richard (1915–). American sculptor. Born in Milwaukee, Lipinski studied at the University of Chicago and the Chicago Art Institute (1933–37), becoming an industrial designer. His link with industry and architecture is clear in his elegant geometrical constructions of gleaming wire and sheet metal. Exquisitely engineered, these intricately constructed works are suspended in space and use the play of light as part of their design. Lippold has created a number of pieces for architectural installation, including *Orpheus and Apollo* at Avery Fisher Hall in Lincoln Center, New York City. Among his best known pieces are *Variation No. 7: Full Moon* (1949–50, Museum of Modern Art, New York City) and *Sun*

(Metropolitan Museum, New York City). Lippold also teaches art and was a professor at New York's Hunter College from 1952 to 1967.

Lipset, Seymour M(artin) (1922–). American sociologist. Lipset is one of the most admired and influential sociologists to have emerged in postwar America. He was raised in a working class New York Jewish family and came to know well the workings of the local printer's union to which his father belonged. This knowledge came to bear in one of Lipset's major works, *Union Democracy* (1956), in which he argued that not all organizations necessarily created elite leaderships—equality could lead to better decision making when a healthy level of disrespect prevailed. Lipset, who taught at Berkeley, Columbia, and Harvard universities, also sparked controversy in the 1950s by his analyses of the social origins of what he termed the "radical right"—a grouping of disaffected social groups who craved more status or feared losing what status they had and were thus deviant at root. *Political Man* (1960) argued that the delicate social and ideological balances necessary to maintain democracy were in danger of eroding. Lipset's later writings include *The Politics of Unreason* (1970).

Lispector, Clarice (1925–1977). Brazilian novelist and short story writer. Lispector was the daughter of Ukrainians who immigrated to Brazil shortly after her birth. She attended law school in Rio de Janeiro while working as a journalist. One year after graduation (1943) she published her first novel, *Perto do coracao selvagem* (*Close to the Savage Heart*). Because Brazilian writers of the 1940s were preoccupied with social problems and realistic fiction, critics were shocked by the poetic luminosity and introspectiveness of her prose; nevertheless the book won the Fundacao Graca Aranha prize. Her finest novel was *A Maca no escuro* (1961; tr. 1967 and reissued 1986 as *The Apple in the Dark*). In all she produced 15 volumes of fiction. Despite her high reputation in Latin America, her work is still difficult to obtain in translation.

Lissitzky, El(iezer Markovich) (1890–1941). Russian painter, designer and architect. Born in Smolensk, Lissitzky studied engineering at Darmstadt (1909–14), returning to Russia in 1919 to teach at the Vitebsk art school and becoming a professor at the Moscow Academy of Arts in 1921. Working closely with other members of the Russian avant garde, Lissitzky began (1919) to create abstract drawings and paintings using strong color and simple geometrical shapes that he named *Prouns*. When the Russian government manifested active disapproval of abstract art, he left the country and settled in GERMANY in 1922. There he helped to popularize SUPREMATISM and CONSTRUCTIVISM and added ideas from these movements to BAUHAUS philosophy. He returned to Moscow in 1928. Well represented in European and American museums, he was the author of a number of volumes including *Russia: The Reconstruction of Architecture in the Soviet Union*. (1930).

List, Eugene (1918–1985). American concert pianist. List gained international fame in 1945 when, while serving in the U.S. Army, he was asked to perform for Winston CHURCHILL, Harry S. TRUMAN, and Joseph STALIN at the POTSDAM CONFERENCE. Later he championed the music of the 19th-century American composer Louis Moreau Gottschalk. He also toured in "monster concerts" featuring performances by 20 or more pianists at a time, seated two to a keyboard.

Lithuania. One of the three Baltic Sea republics of the U.S.S.R., Lithuania is located in the northwest of the Soviet Union. After Lithuania declared its independence in 1918, invasion by Russian BOLSHEVIKS led to the Russo-Lithuanian War, which ended with the Treaty of Moscow in 1920. Recognized as a democratic republic in 1922, Lithuania continued to face conflict with GERMANY over the port of Memel (administered by Lithuania until HITLER's annexation in 1939) and with Poland over the city of Vilna (controlled by Poland until 1939). After the NAZI-SOVIET PACT of 1939, Lithuania's vulnerability to Soviet expansion led to a vote in 1940 to peacefully join the Soviet Union. Some liberalization under Soviet leader Mikhail GORBACHEV encouraged Lithuania to move toward independence (1988–89). However, a Soviet crackdown in late 1990 resulted in civilian deaths. On Feb. 9, 1991, Lithuania voted overwhelmingly (in a non-binding referendum) for independence, though Gorbachev refused to recognize the vote.

Lithuanian War of Independence (1918–20). Lithuania declared its independence (February 1918) when the Russian czar was overthrown. Soviet forces invaded, but were driven out by Germans. German troops withdrew after their World War I surrender, and Soviets invaded January 1919; the Poles intervened, driving the Soviets out. In December of that year the Lithuanian-Polish border, defined by the Allies, gave Vilnius to Lithuania. Fighting continued with the Soviets until they recognized Lithuanian independence in the Treaty of Moscow on July 12, 1920. Polish raiders, led by General Lucian Zeligowski (1865–1947) captured Vilnius, established a provisional government and by plebiscite demonstrated that a majority of its citizens wanted union with POLAND. Lithuanian relations with Poland were severed, but by 1922 Lithuania, minus Vilnius, had been recognized as a democratic republic.

At this protest in Vilnius, Lithuania, a rare group of pro-communist supporters resists the rising call for freedom from communist rule (March 27, 1990).

Little, Royal (1896–1989). U.S. business executive, credited with inventing the modern corporate conglomerate. The textile company Little founded in 1923 (which later became known as Textron, Inc.) showed little promise for expansion in the early 1950s, so Little branched out into other fields by acquiring a diverse range of companies. He stepped down as Textron chairman in 1960 and later founded a venture capital firm.

Little America. U.S. base on ANTARCTICA. Located on the Ross Ice Shelf, south of the Bay of Whales, it was established in 1928 by Commander Richard E. BYRD. Some 30 miles east, another U.S. base (Little America IV) served as a research station during the INTERNATIONAL GEOPHYSICAL YEAR (1957–58).

Little Review, The. American magazine. Founded in Chicago in 1914 by Margaret C. Anderson, the magazine was devoted to promoting the arts. Its home base was moved to San Francisco, New York and finally Paris before Anderson decided to cease publication in 1929. Foreign editors included Ezra POUND. The magazine presented reproductions of modern paintings and sculptures, and published the work of such writers as James JOYCE, Amy LOWELL, Sherwood ANDERSON, T.S. ELIOT, Marianne MOORE, Wallace STEVENS and W.B. YEATS.

Little Rock. Capital of the state of Arkansas, UNITED STATES. Little Rock became a center of world attention in 1957 when U.S. President Dwight D. EISENHOWER dispatched Federal troops here to enforce 1954 U.S. Supreme Court ruling against racial segregation in the public schools. (See BROWN V. BOARD OF EDUCATION.)

Litvinov, Maxim Maximovich [Meir Wallach] (1876–1951). Soviet diplomat and politician. Of Jewish background, Litvinov joined the Social Democratic Labor Party in 1898 and its Leninist faction in 1901. Having taken part in the 1905 Revolution, in 1907 he moved to London where he worked as a clerk. Named representative of the Soviet government in Great Britain after the 1917 Revolution, he was arrested and later exchanged for the British ambassador. Deputy foreign commissar in 1921–30 and 1939–46, Litvinov was foreign commissar from 1930 to 1939. He made a considerable impression at the LEAGUE OF NATIONS by advocating disarmament. Removed from the post in 1939, shortly before the pact with HITLER, he was appointed deputy foreign minister (1941–46) and was ambassador to Washington (1941–43).

Liu Bocheng (1892–1986). Chinese military leader. Known as the "one-eyed dragon" after losing an eye in battle, Liu led Communist forces during the SINO-JAPANESE WAR from 1937 to 1945. As the Communists fought for power in the late 1940s, he led the forces that captured Nanking. In 1955 he was named one of CHINA's 10 marshals, the highest military rank, and was elected to the Politburo a number of times.

Liu Shaoqi (1898–1974). Chairman of the People's Republic of CHINA (1959–69). Elected to the Central Committee of the Communist Party in 1927, Liu was appointed a political commissar during the LONG MARCH. A principal vice chairman of the party on the establishment of the Chinese People's Republic in 1949, Liu succeeded MAO TSE-TUNG as chairman (head of state) of the People's Republic. He lost his position as heir apparent to Mao during the CULTURAL REVOLUTION in 1966. Criticized for defending the importance of industrial workers instead of the primacy of the peasantry as a spearhead of the revolution, he was deprived of all his party offices in 1968. He disappeared from public life the following year.

Liverpool. Port city in Merseyside metropolitan county (formerly part of the county of Lancashire) on the right bank of the Mersey River, 3 miles from the Irish Sea. In the early part of the century Liverpool was one of the largest and busiest ports in the world, with more than seven miles of docks. However, the GREAT DEPRESSION of the 1930s, German bombing during WORLD WAR II, Britain's loss of empire and the decline of the British shipping industry all adversely affected Liverpool's fortunes. High unemployment and waterfront decay hit Liverpool in the second half of the century. The city's Toxteth district was the scene of rioting in the early 1980s. However, Liverpudlians (also called Scousers) are known for their liveliness and grit, and the waterfront has seen some refurbishment in the 1980s. The city draws tourists who come to visit the early haunts of the BEATLES, the rock musicians who grew up here and who changed the face of popular music in the 1960s. Liverpool's neogothic Anglican cathedral, begun in 1904 and still under construction, is planned to be the largest cathedral in England.

Living Theatre (1951–1970). Avant-garde theater group founded in 1951 by Julian Beck and Judith Malina, who served as the principal theorists and directors of the group. The Living Theatre quickly established itself in New York City as one of the leading Off-Broadway troupes. Its many experimental productions, which featured improvisation and modern re-settings of classic plays, included stagings of *The Connection* by Jack Gelber (1959) and a VIETNAM WAR era version of *Antigone* by the Greek dramatist Sophocles (1967). After extensive touring in Europe during the 1960s, the Living Theatre was dissolved in 1970.

Lleras Camargo, Alberto (1903–1990). Colombian politician. Lleras served as president of COLOMBIA (1945–46 and 1958–62). Following the establishment of the ORGANIZATION OF AMERICAN STATES in 1948, he served as the group's first president. He was instrumental in devising a 1957 coalition between his Liberal Party and the Conservative Party that helped end a widespread rural conflict known as "La Violencia." In 1961 he helped organize the Latin American Free Trade Association to help reduce tariffs in the region.

Llewellyn, Richard [pen name of Richard Dafydd Vivian Llewellyn Lloyd] (1907–1983). Welsh playwright and novelist. Llewellyn's first and best known novel, *How Green Was My Valley* (1939), became an international best-seller and was made into an ACADEMY AWARD-winning film (1941) directed by John FORD. It depicted life in a Welsh coal mining community.

Llewelyn-Davies, Richard [Lord Llewelyn-Davies] (1912–1981). Welsh architect and city planner. Head of the prominent British architectural firm of Llewelyn-Davies Weeks, he also taught at the University of London, where he was made head of the Bartlett School of Architecture in 1960. However, it was as a designer of NEW TOWNS after World War II that he won international fame. He designed Rushbrooke Village and Milton Keynes, among other new towns in Britain and elsewhere. His other works included London's Stock Exchange and the new wing of the Tate Gallery, and the Atlantic Richfield research complex in Philadelphia. He was made a life peer in 1963.

Lloyd, Harold (1894–1971). U.S. motion picture actor. Lloyd had already worked for the Edison Company before 1915, when he began appearing as "Lonesome Luke" in a series of one-reel comedies for Hal Roach. His enormous success guaranteed artistic control of his own films, and Lloyd went on to produce longer and feature-length comedies. He portrayed himself as a bumbling young man constantly getting into the most hair-raising situations. He was the highest paid actor of the 1920s, and renowned as one of the silent screen's most innovative performers and directors. Lloyd acted in some 500 films, some of the most popular including *For Heaven's Sake* (1926), *The Kid Brother* (1927) and *Speedy* (1928).

For further reading:

McCaffrey, Donald M., *Three Classic Silent Screen Comedies Starring Harold Lloyd.*

Screen comedian Harold Lloyd "hangs on" while a fan snaps a photograph.

David Lloyd George (Jan. 17, 1932).

Madison, N.J.: Fairleigh Dickinson University Press, 1976.

Lloyd George, David (1863–1945). British statesman, prime minister (1916–22); born in Manchester but raised in Wales. Lloyd George was apprenticed to a solicitor in 1878 and set up his own law practice six years later. He was elected as a LIBERAL PARTY member of Parliament in 1890 and served there for the next 55 years. He became president of the Board of Trade in 1905 and was appointed chancellor of the exchequer by Herbert ASQUITH in 1908. In the latter office, he carried out a number of significant social reforms, including the Old Age Pensions Act (1908) and the National Health Insurance Act (1911), both cornerstones of Britain's WELFARE STATE. In order to finance his pioneering programs, Lloyd George had new land and income taxes enacted in 1909 that proved extremely unpopular with the wealthy, powerful and conservative land-owning members of the House of Lords, who vetoed the tax package. The clash that followed led to the Parliament Act of 1911, which ended the House of Lords' veto power. After the outbreak of WORLD WAR I, Lloyd George remained chancellor until 1915 when he succeeded to the post of minister of munitions and then became minister of war in 1916.

Later in 1916 he joined with Conservatives to form a coalition that ousted Asquith, and Lloyd George succeeded him as prime minister. While frequently quarreling with his generals, he was a forceful and effective wartime leader and was instrumental in unifying Allied military forces under Marshal FOCH. After the war, he led the British delegation at the PARIS PEACE CONFERENCE (1919), where he tried to steer a moderate course between CLEMENCEAU's calls for retribution and WILSON's idealistic programs, and did much to shape the Treaty of VERSAILLES. At home, he dealt harshly with the Irish question but finally set up the Irish Free State in 1922. After the CHANAK CRISIS of that same year, the Conservatives withdrew from the coalition and his ministry fell. From 1926 to 1931 he was head of a severely weakened Liberal Party. Although he sympathized with German grievances and paid a friendly visit to HITLER in 1936, Lloyd George came to strongly oppose the MUNICH PACT and the policy of APPEASEMENT. He was made an earl shortly before his death.

For further reading:

Gilbert, B.B., *David Lloyd George: A Political Life: The Architect of Change 1863–1912.* Columbus: Ohio State University Press, 1987.

Lloyd Webber, Andrew (1948–). British composer. Andrew Lloyd Webber has established himself as one of the most successful composers in the modern musical theater. He first won international attention for a string of successes on which he collaborated with British lyricist Timothy Rice—*Joseph and the Amazing Technicolor Dreamcoat* (1968), *Jesus Christ Superstar* (1970), and *Evita* (1976). Webber then went on to compose the acclaimed musicals *Cats* (1981, based on humorous poems by T.S. ELIOT), *Starlight Express* (1984), and the phenomenally popular *Phantom of the Opera* (1987). His most recent musical is *Aspects of Love* (1989). Lloyd Webber founded the London-based Really Useful Company theatrical ensemble. Lloyd Webber's memorable melodies have earned him a fortune in royalties, but some critics charge that his works exploit surface effects and technical gimmickery at the expense of genuine emotional and intellectual depth.

Locarno Pact. Series of agreements signed on December 1, 1925 by representatives of the governments of Belgium, Great Britain, Czechoslovakia, France, Germany, Italy and Poland, all of whom met at Locarno, Switzerland. As a whole, the treaties dealt with various problems that were unsettled after World War I. The principal agreement, signed by France, Belgium and Germany and guaranteed by Britain and Italy, confirmed the French and Belgian borders with Germany and reaffirmed the demilitarization of the RHINELAND. Arbitration agreements regarding Germant's eastern borders were also signed. A diplomatic triumph for Great Britain's Austin CHAMBERLAIN, France's Aristide BRIAND and Germany's Gustav STRESEMANN, the Pact opened the way for Germany's entry into the LEAGUE OF NATIONS. The international harmony embodied in the Locarno Pact was shattered by HITLER's remilitarization of the Rhineland in 1936.

Lockerbie. See PAN AM 103.

Lockheed Aircraft Corporation. American firm founded in 1916 by Allan Lockheed (born Loughhead) in Burbank, California, to design and produce airplanes of advanced design. The single-engined, high-wing Lockheed Vega of 1927, designed by John K. NORTHROP, was one of the first truly streamlined airplanes, a monoplane without struts or wires. It was used by Amelia EARHART and Wiley POST in their pioneer flights and made Americans aware of the beauty possible in utilitarian forms. The Sirius of 1929 by the same designer was a low-winged design of similar styling, used by the LINDBERGHS in their early exploratory Arctic flights. The Orion introduced retractable landing gear and may be considered one of the most elegant of pre-World War II aircraft designs. The first Electra, a twin-engined, all-metal transport of 1934, was also an outstanding design, but was overshadowed by the success of the larger Douglas DC-3. The postwar Lockheed Constellation and Super-Constellation carried forward the firm's reputation for outstanding design with the remarkably elegant forms of fuselage and the striking triple-rudder tail, destined, however to become obsolete with improving technology. Lockheed continues to produce military aircraft and the 1011 transport jet.

Lockheed scandal (1975). Scandal involving bribes and kickbacks paid by LOCKHEED Corporation to obtain foreign contracts. In 1975 it was revealed that Lockheed, an aircraft manufacturer, regularly made payments to influence peddlers, foreign politicians and foreign military leaders as part of its sales strategy in marketing its planes overseas. A Senate investigation revealed that the payments were made with the knowledge of the corporation's senior managers. Revelation of the payments had far-reaching consequences. In Japan, Lockheed had made over $12 million in payments, including one to an aide close to Prime Minister TANAKA. In West Germany, Lockheed paid a kickback to the Christian Socialist Party, while in Italy the corporation made payments to members of the military. When it was revealed that Prince Bernhard, husband of Queen Juliana of the Netherlands, had secretly received $1 million, he resigned all his public offices in disgrace. These revelations caused the forced early retirement of a number of senior Lockheed executives.

Lockwood, Margaret (1916–1990). British actress. Her first well-known role was in the 1938 Alfred HITCHCOCK film *The Lady Vanishes.* She became one of the most popular actresses of the 1940s, appearing in such notable films as *Night Train* (1940), *The Stars Look Down* (1941) and *The Wicked Lady* (1945). In the 1960s and 1970s she appeared with her daughter Julia in the British television series "The Flying Swan." Her last film appearance was in 1976, in *The Slipper and the Rose.*

Loden, Barbara (1934–1980). American actress-director. Loden was the first woman to write, direct, and star in her own feature film. The film, *Wanda* (1970), about a drab, desperate Appalachian housewife, won the International Critics Prize at that year's Venice Film Festival. Loden was married to Elia KAZAN, who directed her on Broadway in a Tony Award-winning performance in Arthur MILLER's play *After the Fall.*

Lodge, David John (1935–). British critic and novelist. Born in London, Lodge was educated at University College, London. He taught and in 1976 became Professor of Modern English Literature at the University of Birmingham, then retired in the 1980s to write full time. Lodge's critical works *Language of Fiction* (1966), *The Nov-*

elist at the Crossroads (1971), *The Modes of Modern Writing* (1977) and *Working with Structuralism* (1980)—show his familiarity with many literary movements while professing his allegiance to realism. His early fiction, such as *Ginger, You're Barmy* (1962), which drew on his experiences in National Service in the 1950s, were anti-establishment satires. He turned to a more comedic style with *The British Museum is Falling Down* (1965) and *How Far Can You Go* (1980; published in the U.S. as *Souls and Bodies*), which explore the effects of social change on members of the Catholic Church. Other works include the academic satires *Changing Places* (1975); *Small World* (1984); and *Nice Work*, which lampoons both radical academic politics and Thatcherism.

Lodge, Henry Cabot (1850–1924). U.S. senator. Lodge graduated from Harvard in 1871 and from Harvard Law School in 1874. He received the first Ph.D. granted by Harvard in political science in 1876. Lodge had a successful career as a historian and editor before being elected as a Republican to the U.S. House of Representatives (1887–93), where he championed civil service reform. He served in the U.S. Senate from 1893 until his death. In the upper house Lodge helped draft the Sherman Antitrust Act (1896), the Pure Food and Drug Act (1906) and the Tariff of 1909. He was an ardent protectionist and an opponent of the direct election of senators and woman suffrage. A close friend of Theodore ROOSEVELT, he welcomed war with Spain in 1898 and supported the development of the armed forces. As chairman of the Senate Committee on Foreign Relations, Lodge bitterly opposed Woodrow WILSON's peace policy and led the successful fight against U.S. entry into the LEAGUE OF NATIONS after WORLD WAR I. Lodge played a major role in the Republican nomination of Warren HARDING in 1920.

Lodge, Henry Cabot, II (1902–1985). U.S. politician and diplomat. A Massachusetts Republican from a distinguished family, he was elected to the U.S. Senate in 1936 and reelected in 1942. He resigned his seat in 1944 to enter the army in World War II, the first senator since the Civil War to resign to fight in a war. After the war he was reelected (1946). In 1952 he was Dwight D. EISENHOWER's presidential campaign manager; that same year, ironically, he himself was defeated for reelection to the Senate by Democrat John F. KENNEDY. From 1953 to 1960, Lodge headed the U.S. delegation to the U.N. In 1960, he was Richard M. NIXON's vice-presidential running mate on the losing Republican ticket. He served as U.S. ambassador to VIETNAM (1963–64, 1965–67). After serving briefly as U.S. ambassador to WEST GERMANY, he was chief U.S. representative (1969) to the Paris peace talks on Vietnam. (See also VIETNAM WAR.)

Lodge, John Davis (1903–1985). American politician. Before entering politics, Lodge was a lawyer and then an actor. His most notable role was as Marlene DIETRICH's lover in *The Scarlet Empress.*

Henry Cabot Lodge II arriving in Paris for negotiations to end the Vietnam War (Jan. 25, 1969).

He began his political career as a member of the House of Representatives (1947–1951). He went on to become governor of Connecticut (1951–55) and U.S. ambassador to Spain (1955–1961), Argentina (1969–74) and Switzerland (1983–85). He was the brother of Henry Cabot LODGE II.

Loeb, William (1905–1981). American newspaper publisher. A maverick ultra-conservative, Loeb published New Hampshire's *Manchester Union Leader* and *New Hampshire Sunday News* and printed his editorials on the front page. Although his papers served a small state, from the 1950s through the 1970s he exerted great influence in national politics because every four years New Hampshire held the first presidential primary. The *Union Leader*, the only statewide paper in New Hampshire, was his forum for evaluating—and usually denouncing—the candidates in the first presidential primary every four years. His black-and-white right-wing views embarrassed many thoughtful conservatives and doomed many liberal causes. Loeb dubbed Dwight D. EISENHOWER "Doppy Dwight" and Gerald FORD "Gerald the Jerk" but staunchly supported Ronald REAGAN. In 1972 he dealt a fatal blow to Edmund MUSKIE's presidential campaign. In spite of his generally reactionary tone, Loeb also supported the labor movement, vigorously attacked waste and corruption, and probably printed more readers' letters than any other paper in the country.

Loesser, Frank (1910–1969). American lyricist and song writer, best known for his musical *Guys and Dolls* (1950). The fusion of popular and classical traditions was his specialty. Loesser, born in New York into a family of talented artists, struck out on his own, working odd jobs until he was signed by RKO Studios in HOLLYWOOD as staff lyricist. By the mid-1930s he was collaborating with composers Burton Lane, Hoagy CARMICHAEL and Victor Schertzinger on film songs like "Two Sleepy People" (*Thanks for the Memory*, 1938), "See What the Boys in the Backroom Will Have" (*Destry Rides Again*, 1939) and "Jingle, Jangle, Jingle" (*The Forest Rangers*, 1942). During his wartime service, Loesser began writing both lyrics and music; soon thereafter he had two Broadway smash hits, *Where's Charley?* (1948, an adaptation of an old farce called *Charley's Aunt*) and *Guys and Dolls* (1950, based on the underworld characters of Damon Runyan). Few shows could boast a more tuneful score. Critic Brooks ATKINSON wrote: "Every song defined a character . . . There was not a commonplace nor a superfluous song in the score." Perhaps Loesser's greatest achievement was *The Most Happy Fella* (1956), based on Sidney Howard's play *They Knew What They Wanted*, the story of a lovelorn California farmer and his mail-order bride. It was virtually a through-composed opera, juxtaposing arias like "Rosabella" with tuneful ditties like "Standing on the Corner." His last shows were *Greenwillow* (1960) and the brilliant *How to Succeed in Business Without Really Trying* (1961).

For further reading:

Laufe, Abe, *Broadway's Greatest Musicals*. New York: Funk & Wagnalls, 1977.

Loewe, Frederick (1904–1988). Austrian-born composer. Loewe immigrated to the U.S. in 1924, leaving behind a career in European operetta. Popular success eluded him until he teamed with lyricist Alan Jay LERNER in 1942. Their first hit Broadway musical was *Brigadoon* (1947), which was followed by *Paint Your Wagon* (1951). *My Fair Lady*, a musical version of G.B. SHAW's *Pygmalion*, was their biggest success, opening in March 1956 and running for more than 2,700 performances. Their last two major collaborations were the movie musical *Gigi* (1959) and the Broadway musical *Camelot* (1960).

Loewy, Raymond Fernand (1893–1986). French-born U.S. industrial designer. Loewy came to the U.S. after World War I and embarked on his career in 1929 when he redesigned the Gestetner duplicating machine in three days. That design was unchanged for decades. He was regarded as having pioneered the "streamlined" look that drastically altered the appearance of objects from toothbrushes to airplanes. Perhaps his single best known design was the Coca-Cola bottle, with another the interior of the SKYLAB space orbiter. His company, Raymond Loewy Associates, founded in 1945, was the world's largest industrial design firm.

Logan, Joshua (1908–1988). American playwright, director and producer. Winner of a PULITZER PRIZE in 1950 for coauthoring the musical play *South Pacific* with

Oscar HAMMERSTEIN II, Logan is best known as the director of such plays as *Charley's Aunt* (1940), *Annie, Get Your Gun* (1946), *Mr. Roberts* (1948), *South Pacific* (1949), *Picnic* (1953) and *Fanny* (1954). As a film director, his credits include *South Pacific* (1958), *Fanny* (1961) and *Camelot* (1967). It was Logan who encouraged James STEWART to become an actor.

Logical Positivism. School of philosophical thought that emerged in Vienna in the late 1920s. A major precursor of the school was Ludwig WITTGENSTEIN. The key figures in the creation of Logical Positivism were the members of what was termed the Vienna Circle—most notably Rudolf CARNAP, Hans Reichenbach, and Moritz Schlick. Philosophers in Berlin, such as Carl HEMPEL, and in England, such as A.J. AYER, also contributed to its development. The Logical Positivists viewed themselves as extending the criteria of science to the entire range of subject matters traditionally analyzed by philosophy. In this effort, statements were to be judged as meaningful only insofar as they were empirically verifiable. As a result, the idealist philosopher's claim of having special insights on issues of metaphysics, ethics and the philosophy of mind were disallowed. Ethical statements, such as "murder is wrong," were viewed as emotive or persuasive rather than verifiable assertions. Many Logical Positivists concluded that traditional philosophy as a whole had become largely meaningless. Logical Positivism had a considerable influence on the linguistic philosophy of later British philosophers such as J.L. AUSTIN.

Lo Jui-Ching (1906–1978). Chinese communist official. Lo took part in the LONG MARCH of 1935. During the 1950s he was minister of public security in the People's Republic of CHINA. He was later army chief of staff. During the CULTURAL REVOLUTION he was purged by the RED GUARDS and disappeared from public view until his rehabilitation in 1975. He returned to the Central Committee of the Chinese Communist Party in 1977.

Lombard, Carole [Jane Peters] (1908–1942). American film actress. The wife of actor William Powell and, later, of Clark GABLE, Lombard began acting in motion pictures at the Fox Studios in 1926 (see 20TH CENTURY-FOX). She gained fame for her beauty and her performances in "screwball" comedies. She appeared in such films as *No Man of Her Own* (1932), *My Man Godfrey* (1936) and *They Knew What They Wanted* (1940). She was killed in a plane crash while on a war bond sales drive.

For further reading:

Matzen, Robert D., *Carole Lombard: A Bio-Bibliography*. Westport, Conn.: Greenwood, 1988.

Lombardi, Vince (1913–1970). American football coach. Devoted equally to his players as individuals and to the team as a whole, the Brooklyn-born Lombardi was one of the most successful football coaches of all time. He began his pro career as a coach with the New York Giants in 1954 and joined the Green Bay Packers as head coach and general manager five years later. Often remembered for stating "Winning isn't everything, it's the only thing," he was also devoted to the ideal of equality among men both on and off the field, and refused to tolerate bigotry in any form. In the words of one of his players, "He's not prejudiced—He treats us all like dogs." Lombardi led his team, through nine frozen and muddy Wisconsin winters, to six conference championships and five league championships. He retired in 1968, only to reemerge as the coach of the Washington Redskins a year later, leading them to their first winning season in more than a decade. The Super Bowl Trophy is dedicated to his memory.

Lombardo, Guy (1902–1977). Canadian bandleader. Lombardo was born in London, Ontario. In 1917, he and three brothers formed a band called the Royal Canadians, with Guy as its leader. In 1924, the Royal Canadians began playing in the Midwestern U.S., and by 1928 they had begun to appear in New York City. In 1929, they started their tradition of playing at the Waldorf-Astoria Hotel on New Year's Eve, featuring their theme song "Auld Lang Syne"; these appearances, which were later televised for many years, continued until the time of Lombardo's death.

London. Capital of the UNITED KINGDOM and center of the former BRITISH EMPIRE; long considered the center of the English-speaking world. In the 20th century London has seen much change. Much of the city was destroyed by German bombing (the blitz) early in WORLD WAR II (see BATTLE OF BRITAIN). Later in the war, London was the target of German V-1 AND V-2 ROCKETS. The city has since been rebuilt; Prince CHARLES and many other critics believe that modern architects have done more to ruin London's appearance than did the German Luftwaffe. Numerous skyscrapers and ultramodern buildings have been built since the 1960s; the 619-foot Post Office Tower became Britain's tallest building in 1965 (but will soon be surpassed by a 55-story building on London's outskirts). Like other large cities, contemporary London has its share of social problems; the poverty-stricken Brixton district was hit by riots in 1981, and rioting occurred in central London in 1990 over the poll tax.

London, Artur (1915–1986). Czechoslovakian diplomat and author. He was deputy foreign minister during the early days of the communist regime in CZECHOSLOVAKIA. One of a number of leading officials put on trial for revisionism during a STALINIST-style purge in the early 1950s, he was sentenced to life in prison after confessing his guilt. London was released from prison in 1956 after Nikita KHRUSHCHEV's historic denunciation of STALIN, and moved to France in 1963. In 1969 he published *L'Aveu (The Confession)*, which gave a graphic account of the tortures inflicted upon him in prison to get him to confess. The book was translated into many languages and made into a 1970 film starring Simone SIGNORET and Yves MONTAND.

London, George [born George Burnstein] (1920–1985). Canadian-born opera singer, considered one of the greatest bass-baritones of his era. His international career began in 1949 in Vienna. He made his debut at New York's Metropolitan Opera in 1951 and appeared there regularly thereafter. At the Met he became the first North American singer to portray the title character in Mussorgsky's *Boris Godunov* (1953). His performance of Boris was universally acclaimed, and in 1960 he became the first non-Russian to perform the role at Moscow's Bolshoi Opera. London's singing career was cut short in 1967 when he developed a paralyzed vocal chord. He later held a number of artistic administrative posts in Washington, D.C.

London, Jack (1876–1916). American author. Drawing from his experiences during the Alaskan gold rush, London created several short stories and novels filled with adventure and rugged heroes, both men and dogs, who fight to survive against the forces of nature and civilization. He gained fame with three volumes of short stories, including *The Son of the Wolf* (1900). His novel *The Call of the Wild* (1903) has become an American classic. Other major novels include *White Fang* (1906), *The Sea Wolf* (1904) and *The Iron Heel* (1907), which best reveals his social and political beliefs. His most famous short stories are "To Build a Fire" and "The White Silence." London's work has had considerable influence on such American writers as Ernest HEMINGWAY.

For further reading:

Lundquist, James, *Jack London: Adventures, Ideas, and Fiction*. New York: Ungar, 1987.

Londonderry [Derry]. Port city in NORTHERN IRELAND, on the Foyle River, near the head of Lough Foyle, 60 miles northwest of Belfast. Londonderry is the second largest city in Northern Ireland. Although the population is predominantly Roman Catholic, Londonderry was included in the six Irish counties that chose to remain loyal to the UNITED KINGDOM.. The city was a British naval base during World Wars I and II. Since 1969 the Bogside district of Derry (as it is called by the Catholic population) has seen much violence between the IRA, on the one hand, and British troops and Protestant paramilitary groups on the other. The shooting of 13 unarmed demonstrators by British troops on BLOODY SUNDAY (1973) occurred here.

Lone Ranger, The. Riding his horse Silver and accompanied by his Indian companion Tonto, this masked crimefighter of the Old West was one of the premier heroes of 20th-century popular culture. The Lone Ranger made his debut in early 1933, on radio station WXYZ in Detroit; he was soon heard across America, with 2,596 adventures airing before the show was canceled in 1954. The Lone Ranger was also a syndicated comic strip from September 11, 1938 to April 1, 1984, with

Huey Long, governor and political "kingfish" of Louisiana.

a 10-year hiatus from 1971 to 1981. In addition, he starred in movie serials, feature films (including the 1981 release *The Legend of the Lone Ranger*), comic books, novels, his own pulp magazine, a long-running television series and animated cartoons.

Long, Huey Pierce (1893–1935). U.S. politician. Long was admitted to the Louisiana Bar in 1915 after only seven months of study at Tulane University. His first political victory was his 1918 campaign for the state railroad commission. He won election for state governor in 1928 as a Progressive Democrat. Long survived impeachment on bribery charges his very first year in office. Later, he launched a sweeping campaign to solidify his political strength by legislative programs popular with rural voters. Elected to the U.S. Senate in 1930, he retained his governor's seat, at times with the help of the National Guard, until he could turn it over to a loyal supporter. Finally Long claimed his Senate seat in 1932. In 1934 he returned to Louisiana to consolidate his power in the state. He abolished local government, gained total control of the legislature and effectively acted as dictator. He was assassinated by a political opponent in the Louisiana State Capitol.

"long count" fight. See Jack DEMPSEY.

Long March (1934–35). After holding off KUOMINTANG (Chinese Nationalist) troops in mountainous parts of Kiangsi in southern CHINA for more than a year, the Chinese communist army of 200,000 men escaped encirclement and started an orderly retreat (October 1934). Fighting along the way, they crossed southeast China to the west and then north to Shensi, a 6,000 mile trek over 18 mountain ranges, 24 rivers, a vast swamp and two enemy lines; about 50,000 men survived. The army was joined by about 50,000 along the way. CHU TEH (1886–1976) and MAO TSE-TUNG (1893–1976) led the Eighth Route Army, the largest force.

Longo, Luigi (1900–1980). Italian communist politician. Longo was among the founders of the Italian Communist Party (1922). He spent time in prison during MUSSOLINI's rule. During WORLD WAR II he became a guerrilla leader against the Germans. He was considered a superb organizer and rose through the party's ranks to become Communist Party secretary (1964–72). During his tenure the party gained credibility in Italian politics. However, Longo questioned the wisdom of working with the Christian Democrats—ITALY's governing party.

Long-Range Desert Patrol Group. British WORLD WAR II commando unit founded and led by Sir David STIRLING. Consisting of only 6 officers and 60 men, the group operated behind enemy lines in North Africa. They raided German airfields and ammunition depots, blowing up enemy planes and fuel while evading ROMMEL's Afrika Korps. After the war, the group evolved into the SPECIAL AIR SERVICES, a top-secret elite force specializing in anti-terrorist action.

Longworth, Alice Roosevelt (1884–1980). Elder daughter and last surviving child of President Theodore ROOSEVELT. She was a leading figure in Washington, D.C., society for nearly 80 years and was renowned for her beauty, charm, acerbic wit and influential political connections. Sometimes called "Washington's other monument," she was acquainted with and held outspoken opinions about virtually every important American political figure from President Benjamin Harrison to President Gerald FORD. Her husband, **Nicholas Longworth,** was speaker of the House of Representatives (1925–31).

Lon Nol (1913–). President of the Khmer Republic (CAMBODIA, 1972–75). A general who held various ministerial posts under Prince SIHANOUK, including prime minister (1966–67), Lon Nol headed the government after Sihanouk was deposed in 1970. He established close ties with the U.S. and South Vietnam, permitting their forces to operate in Cambodia. He assumed total power in the new republic in 1972 but fled in 1975 as communist KHMER ROUGE rebels marched on the capital.

Loos [Loos-en-Gohelle]. Town in Pas-de-Calais department of FRANCE, 3 miles from of Lens. The city was overrun by the Germans during their invasion of France early in WORLD WAR I. It was recaptured by the British after bloody fighting (Sept. 15–Oct. 13, 1915). The graves of many British soldiers are in this area.

Loos, Adolf (1870–1933). Austrian designer and architect. Loos practiced in Vienna where, for a time, he worked with Otto Wagner. He designed a number of houses and shops there, notably the Karntner Bar (1908), the Goldman & Salatsch shop (1910) and the Steiner house. Although his own designs employed some decorative detailing, Loos is well-known for his opposition to all decoration which he expressed in theoretical writings such as the essay "Ornament und Verbrechen" (1908; "Ornament and Crime"). Through his works and published writings Loos played an important role in the development of MODERNISM.

Loos, Anita (1893–1981). American screenwriter, playwright, novelist and social celebrity. Beginning her career as a child actress, Loos began writing plot outlines for films and eventually innovated the practice of writing screen captions for SILENT FILMS. Those she wrote for D.W. GRIFFITH's classic *Intolerance* (1916) were later lauded as classics of the genre. Among her 200-plus filmscripts were the highly acclaimed *San Francisco* (1936) and her adaptation of Clare Boothe LUCE's *The Women* (1939). She wrote several Broadway comedies, including *Happy Birthday* for Helen HAYES; and *Gigi,* an adaptation of the novel by COLETTE. She was probably most famous for the play *Gentlemen Prefer Blondes* (1926), later made into two movies and two musicals. (The 1953 film version made a star of Marilyn MONROE.) Loos' writing style was characterized by witty dialogue and a tendency to satirize romance.

Lopez Contreras, Eleazar (1883–1973). President of VENEZUELA (1935–41). Before assuming the presidency, Lopez served as minister of war under the dictator General Juan Vicente GOMEZ. He stepped in to lead the nation after Gomez's death.

Lopez Rega, Jose (1916?-1989). Argentinian politician. A leading right-wing figure, he was regarded as the power behind Isabel PERON when she served as president of ARGENTINA following the death of her husband, General Juan D. PERON (1974). He was forced to resign as minister of social welfare in 1975, following charges that he had siphoned off millions of dollars from the Argentine treasury and exerted a sinister influence on Isabel Peron, who had consulted him as an astrologer. At the time of his death, he was awaiting trial for his role in organizing Argentina's right-wing death squads in the 1970s.

Lopokova, Lydia (1892–1981). Russian prima ballerina. While still in her teens Lopokova gained fame dancing with Serge Diaghilev's BALLETS RUSSES, appearing opposite Vaslav NIJINSKY in *Carnival* during her first season (1910). After the RUSSIAN REVOLUTION she emigrated to Britain. Married to the British economist John Maynard KEYNES in 1925, she became a familiar and popular figure in English society.

Lorca, Federico Garcia. See GARCIA LORCA, Federico.

Lord of the Flies. Novel by William GOLDING published in 1954. The story depicts a group of upper-class school boys stranded on an island after an airplane wreck. Initially, they attempt to set up a democratic society, but soon degenerate into cruel savages acting out barbarian rites and rituals which eventually lead to the deaths of two boys. The mythic novel was Golding's response to *The Coral Island* by R.M. Ballantyne, a cheerful, boys' adventure story with the same initial premise, and it reflects Golding's pessimistic belief in the inherent cruelty and evil of man. The *Lord of the Flies* was an immediate success upon its publication in 1954, and is still part of the curricula in many

English departments. It was filmed by the British director Peter Brooks in 1963; a second film version was released in 1990.

Lord of the Rings. A famous trilogy of fantasy novels by philologist and Merton professor of English, J.R.R. TOLKIEN. The *Lord of the Rings* trilogy consists of *The Fellowship of the Ring* (1954), *The Two Towers* (1954), and *The Return of the King* (1955). The story these novels tell is begun in an earlier Tolkien novel, *The Hobbit* (1937), which introduces Bilbo Baggins, a hobbit who lives in Middle Earth. Hobbits are an ancient people who somewhat resemble humans in form and are by nature unobtrusive and peaceful, albeit capable of heroic valor should the need arise. The need does arise when Bilbo gains hold of a master ring that is sought by the evil Sauron of Mordor as part of his plan to conquer Middle Earth. The *Lord of the Rings* trilogy focuses on the quest of Frodo, Bilbo's heir, to destroy the ring by journeying to the far-off fire mountain Orodruin, where he can throw it into the cracks of doom. Many critics have seen Christian symbolism in the characters and events of the trilogy, although Tolkien himself was careful to disclaim any explicit allegorical interpretation.

Loren, Sophia [Sofia Villani Scicolone] (1934–). A stunning and apparently ageless film star, Loren has appeared on film for almost four decades. Born in Rome, Loren started as a walk-on in Italian films, worked her way to stardom and afterwards appeared in many American films, including *The Pride and the Passion* (1957), *Houseboat* (1958), *Desire Under the Elms* (1958) and *Arabesque* (1966). In 1961 she won an ACADEMY AWARD as best actress for her performance in the Italian film *Two Women;* her performance in *A Special Day* (1977) also received critical acclaim. She is married to the producer Carlo Ponti.

Lorenz, Konrad (1903–1989). German ethnologist. Lorenz was born in Vienna and received his M.D. from the University of Vienna in 1928, followed by a Ph.D. in zoology in 1933. Over the course of his distinguished academic career, he held a number of positions in European universities and received numerous awards, including the 1973 NOBEL PRIZE for physiology or medicine, which he shared with Karl von Frisch and Nikolaas TINBERGEN. Lorenz is known particularly for his work on individual and group behavior patterns, imprinting (rapid, virtually irreversible learning occurring during a critical period early in life) and aggression, which he believed to be partially innate in some animals, including man.

Lorre, Peter [born Lazlo Lowenstein] (1904–1964). Hungarian-born film and stage actor. Lorre is widely acknowledged as one of the great character actors in the history of the cinema. He began his career as a stage actor appearing throughout Central Europe—to no great acclaim—in the 1920s. But Lorre won international recognition for his powerful portrayal of a child murderer in the classic German film *M* (1931), directed by Fritz LANG. Lorre fled GERMANY after the NAZIS rose to power and, after a brief time in England during which he appeared in the film *The Man Who Knew Too Much* (1934), directed by Alfred HITCHCOCK, he came to America. In HOLLYWOOD, Lorre achieved fame for his portrayal of the Japanese detective Mr. Moto in a series of B-action films that appeared in the late 1930s. He then achieved film immortality for his supporting roles as Joel Cairo in *The Maltese Falcon* (1941) and Ugarte in *Casablanca* (1943). Lorre's career foundered in the 1950s, due in part to ill health, but he made a comeback in the 1960s through appearances in Roger CORMAN horror films such as *Tales of Terror* (1962) and *The Raven* (1964).

Los Alamos. Town in northwestern New Mexico, 35 miles northwest of Santa Fe. It was chosen in 1942 as the location for the Atomic Research Laboratory (see MANHATTAN PROJECT). Here the first ATOM BOMB was developed. After WORLD WAR II the first thermonuclear fusion HYDROGEN BOMB was also developed here. The Los Alamos Scientific Laboratory, operated by the University of California, is now a national historic landmark.

Los Angeles. City located on the Pacific Ocean coast of southern CALIFORNIA, United States. Los Angeles is, in many respects, emblematic of the contradictions of the 20th century and the modern world. Originally a Spanish mission settlement, Los Angeles grew rapidly after the coming of the railroads in the last quarter of the 19th century. It is now the second-largest city in the U.S. There is no identifiable city center; rather, greater Los Angeles is a collection of neighborhoods and municipalities that spread from the San Bernardino Mountains to the Pacific Ocean. Perhaps its most notable feature is the many miles of freeways that span the city. There is virtually no public transportation system; rather, citizens rely on their own automobiles to travel from place to place within Los Angeles.

In the early 20th century, its HOLLYWOOD suburb became the movie-making capital of the world and, later, the center of television program production. Despite its general wealth and the geographic and social mobility of Angelinos, the city has experienced many of the problems evident in other urban centers in the United States in the late 20th century, including crime, drug addiction and homelessness. Many of the city's blacks and Mexican-Americans have shared in the city's prosperity, but racial tensions have been evident. There was a major riot in the black suburb of WATTS in 1965. In 1991, in an incident captured on videotape, several white police officers stopped a young black and beat him severely, causing a national outcry and prompting a reexamination of race relations in Los Angeles.

Losey, Joseph (1909–1984). American film director. Losey was educated at Harvard and devoted his early career to stage direction, most notably the Broadway production of *Galileo Galilei* (1947). He then went to HOLLYWOOD; however, his left-wing political sympathies got him blacklisted during the MCCARTHY era (see MCCARTHYISM, HOLLYWOOD TEN). As a result, Losey moved to England, where he worked on films for several years under an assumed name before directing *Time Without Pity* (1957) under his real name. In the 1960s, Losey became a preeminent figure in the British film industry as a result of a series of artistic successes, including *The Servant* (1963), *Accident* (1967) and *The Go-Between* (1971), on which he collaborated with writer Harold PINTER. Subsequent films by Losey included *Mr. Klein* (1976) and *Don Giovanni* (1979). *Losey on Losey* (1968) is a selection from his writings on film.

Loss, Joe (Joshua Alexander) (1909–1990). British band leader. He was one of the most prominent figures in the big band era in Britain in the 1930s and 1940s. He remained popular for more than 50 years, and his band frequently performed on television and for royal social affairs, until the 1980s.

lost generation. Term coined by Gertrude STEIN that refers to the generation of expatriate American writers who lived and worked in Paris and other European capitals during the post-WORLD WAR I era. Besides Stein herself, other lost generation figures include Sherwood ANDERSON, Ernest HEMINGWAY and F. Scott FITZGERALD. (See also JAZZ AGE.)

Louganis, Gregory (1960–). American diver. Considered by many to be the greatest diver of all time, Louganis won 47 national and 13 world championships. His first Olympic medal came in 1976, when he won a silver medal in platform diving. He was expected to reach his athletic peak in 1980, when the U.S. boycott of the OLYMPIC GAMES kept him from competition. He won the 3-meter springboard and 10-meter platform gold medals in 1984; his final Olympic victories in 1988 made him the first diver in history to win those medals in successive OLYMPIC GAMES. The 1988 victories were hard-won, as Louganis hit his head on a diving board, then competed the next day with multiple stitches in his head. He retired from diving after the games to pursue an acting career.

Louis, Joe [born Joseph Louis Barrow] (1914–1981). American boxer, widely regarded as the greatest heavyweight champion of all time. The son of an Alabama sharecropper, Louis took the heavyweight title from James J. BRADDOCK in 1937 and held it until his first retirement in 1947—the longest reign of any champion in his weight class. Known as the "Brown Bomber" because of his vicious left jab and powerful right straight, Louis entered professional boxing in 1934, after two years as an amateur. His first loss came at the fists of German champion Max SCHMELING in 1936; Nazi propagandists seized on Schmeling's 12th-round knockout of Louis as proof of Aryan superiority over the black race. In their rematch on June 22, 1938, however,

Joe Louis, heavyweight boxing champion of the world from 1937 to 1947.

Louis knocked Schmeling out in the first round. He successfully defended his title a record 35 times. Besides defeating many second-rate challengers (on his so-called "Bum of the Month" tour), Louis also vanquished the top heavyweights of his day. After the second Schmeling fight, his most memorable victory came against Billy Conn on June 18, 1941; Louis dropped Conn in the 13th round of that spirited contest. He came out of retirement in 1950 to be beaten by then-champion Ezzard Charles and emerged from his second retirement in 1951, only to fall in his final fight to Rocky MARCIANO. In his 71 pro bouts, Louis had 68 victories, 54 by knockouts. In his later years, he suffered from financial difficulties and from health problems. Louis' triumphs and quiet dignity made him a national hero, particularly to black Americans.

Louis, Morris (1912–1962). American painter. A leading figure in COLOR-FIELD PAINTING, he was born in Baltimore and studied at the Maryland Institute (1929–1933). During the 1930s he joined other artists in executing projects for the WPA's Federal Arts Project. A resident of Washington, D.C., he taught at the Washington Workshop Center and the Corcoran School of Art (1952–1962). Louis is known for his vibrant, stained paintings created by pouring thinned pigment onto unprimed canvases. These large abstract works moved from the "veils" of the early 1950s to bursting "florals" and, in his last works, "stripes" such as *Pillars of Dawn* (1961, Wallraf-Richartz Museum, Cologne).

Love Canal. Highly publicized toxic waste site in Niagara Falls, New York; it focused public attention on the dangers of hazardous wastes. In 1978 residents in the area around a waterway named Love Canal were experiencing severe health problems. Neighbors brought suit against Hooker Chemical Company, the former owner of the land, and the matter drew national attention. Investigations revealed that the cause of their problems was the residue of the chemicals Hooker had dumped in the neighborhood years earlier. Although the extent of the danger was disputed, President Jimmy CARTER declared a state of emergency in the neighborhood. The inhabitants eventually moved elsewhere after the state of New York bought the majority of their homes, then bulldozed the structures. When Hooker Chemical was merged into Occidental Petroleum, Occidental agreed to compensate the former residents and also agreed to clean up the site.

Lovecraft, H(oward) P(hillips) (1890–1937). American writer, poet and essayist who was a major figure in 20th-century supernatural fiction. He spent most of his life in Providence, Rhode Island, one of several New England cities that served as a model for his legend-haunted fictional city, Arkham. Poor health and his reclusive nature reinforced his solitary pursuit of reading and writing. Never a prolific contributor to professional publications Lovecraft gained an enthusiastic following from his extensive work for amateur presses and as a consultant for other writers. Contemporary disciples such as Robert Bloch, Henry Kuttner and August Derleth—and later such masters as Brian Lumley and Ramsey Campbell—have all acknowledged his powerful influence. In his best stories—"The Colour Out of Space" (1927), "The Call of Cthulhu" (1928), the novels *At the Mountains of Madness* (1936) and *The Shadow over Innsmouth* (1936)—Lovecraft achieved a unique fusion of evolutionary theory and the type of science that appears in gothic horror tales, especially astronomy. He created a pattern of pseudomyth (the Cthulhu Mythos) that presented the world as a violent intersection of human and cosmic forces locked in a perpetual struggle. His dense and stilted style and rather archaic diction lent these lurid tales a peculiar dignity, elegance and expansiveness. Two years after his death August Derleth and Donald Wandrei established Arkham House, a press devoted to perpetuating Lovecraft's work. Lovecraft's work has been adapted extensively for television and films.

For further reading:

Long, Frank Belknap, *Howard Phillips Lovecraft: The Dreamer on the Night Side.* Sauk City: Arkham House, 1975.

Lovell, Sir (Alfred Charles) Bernard (1913–). British astronomer. Lovell was awarded his Ph.D. from the University of Bristol in 1936. In 1951, he was named director of the Jodrell Bank (now the Nuffield Radio Astronomy Laboratories), where he was instrumental in building the world's first large radio telescope, completed in 1957. In the coming decades, the telescope proved particularly valuable in the investigation of pulsars and quasars. Lovell was knighted in 1961.

Lovell, James (1928–). U.S. astronaut. "The moon is essentially gray, no color . . . looks like plaster of Paris, sort of gray sand" is how Lovell described the surface of the moon during the flyby flight of Apollo 8 (December 21–27, 1968). If, in the words of science fiction writer Robert Heinlein, "The moon is a harsh mistress," then we might wonder if such an unflattering description jinxed Lovell's next lunar mission. As commander of Apollo 13 (April 11–17, 1970), Lovell and his crewmates Fred Haise and Jack Swigert, gave the world some tense moments when an explosion aboard their spacecraft forced the three men into a dangerous and improvised return to Earth aboard the cramped and poorly equipped lunar module. A veteran of 30 days in space, in addition to his two APOLLO missions Lovell also piloted GEMINI 7 (December 4–18, 1965) and Gemini 12 (November 11–15, 1966). After retiring from NASA in March 1973 he entered private industry.

Lovestone, Jay (1898–1990). Lithuanian-born labor leader. Head of the American Communist Party in the 1920s, Lovestone later became a staunch anticommunist. He had advocated an independent party line in the U.S. and, as a result, was attacked by Soviet leader Joseph STALIN in a well-publicized argument in 1929. By 1940 Lovestone concluded that communism had become nothing more than a totalitarian conspiracy. He later served as international affairs director of the AFL-CIO, where he wielded considerable influence as the American labor movement's representative in international affairs.

Low, George M. (1926–1984). Vienna-born engineer who was a major force in the APOLLO space program. As a member of the NATIONAL AERONAUTICS AND SPACE ADMINISTRATION (NASA) and its predecessors from 1949 to 1976, Low helped draft the 1960 memo that suggested to President John F. KENNEDY that the U.S. could put a man on the moon by the end of the 1960s. After astronauts GRISSOM, WHITE and CHAFFEE were killed in a launch pad fire (Jan. 27, 1967), Low was charged with redesigning the Apollo spacecraft. He successfully drove the program to meet its end-of-decade deadline. In 1976 he became president of his alma mater, Renssaelaer Polytechnic Institute.

Lowell, Amy (1874–1925). American poet. The Lowell family occupies a special place in the history of American poetry. Amy Lowell was a descendant of the 19th-century poet James Russell Lowell, as well as an ancestor of the famous modern poet Robert LOWELL. Amy Lowell published her first verse at age 36, and soon became one of the most prominent American poets of her era, winning the PULITZER PRIZE in 1925 for her volume *What's O'Clock.* In the 1910s, Lowell worked together with Ezra POUND to draw attention to the poetic school of IMAGISM, which Pound soon began to call "Amygism" in wry tribute to Lowell's fervent leadership of the new literary movement. Lowell's other works include a two-volume biography of John Keats (1925). Her *Collected Poems* appeared in 1955. Glenn R. Ruhley has written a biography of Lowell, *The Thorn of a Rose* (1975).

Lowell, Percival (1855–1916). U.S. astronomer. Wealthy enough to pursue his own interests, Lowell was the world's most famous amateur astronomer, as well as founder of the Lowell Observatory at Flagstaff, Arizona, in 1894. He was also an important force in instituting the search that led to the discovery of the planet Pluto in 1930. Lowell is most famous, however, for his "observations" of "canals" on Mars. Inspired by the writings of Italian astronomer Giovanni Schiaparelli, Lowell believed that he saw a connecting pattern among the shifting patterns of dark and light material on the Martian surface (which we now know to be rock surfaces periodically exposed by wind-driven sand). He convinced himself that he was observing an intricate and elaborate network of artificial canals on the red planet. Not discouraged that other observers failed to report similar findings, Lowell wrote numerous articles and books in support of his observations, putting forth his romantic theories of an arid, dying planet populated by intelligent inhabitants who dug the canals to move water from its poles to the plains. Although Lowell was mistaken in his observations, his enthusiastic writings helped to keep popular interest in astronomy and the solar system alive in the age before spacecraft, and also influenced a generation of science fiction writers (see Edgar Rice BURROUGHS).

Lowell, Robert (Traill Spence, Jr.) (1917–1977). American poet. The scion of a Boston Brahmin line, Lowell was educated at Harvard (1935–37) and Kenyon College (1938–40). He was imprisoned as a conscientious objector during WORLD WAR II (1943–44) and later spent significant periods in mental hospitals. His turbulent marriages to three writers were well known: Jean STAFFORD (1940–48), Elizabeth HARDWICK (1949–72) and Caroline Blackwood (1972 to his death). *Lord Weary's Castle* (PULITZER PRIZE, 1947) and *The Mills of the Kavanaughs* (1957) focus on his conversion to Catholicism. *Life Studies* (1959) marked a breakthrough into more personal, less rhetorical poetry. *Notebook, For Lizzie and Harriet, The Dolphin* (Pulitzer Prize, 1973) and *Day by Day*, all published in the 1970s, represented an attempt to create a larger work along the lines of POUND'S CANTOS or BERRYMAN'S *Dream Songs*. Lowell is generally considered the father of the CONFESSIONAL POETS.

For further reading:

Hamilton, Ian, *Robert Lowell: A Biography*. New York: Random House, 1983.

Lowry, Malcolm (1909–1957). English novelist and short story writer. Lowry is best known for his novel UNDER THE VOLCANO (1947), which is an acknowledged classic of 20th-century literature. Lowry, who was educated at St. Catherine's College in England, interrupted his academic studies to go to sea and work for 18 months as a deckhand. This experience formed the basis for his first novel, *Ultramarine* (1933), which appeared when Lowry was 24. Despite this early success, Lowry endured subsequent years of poverty and neglect as a writer. He also battled his own chronic alcoholism. In 1936 Lowry visited Mexico, an important setting for many of his works. In 1939 he settled in Dollarton, British Columbia, where he built for himself a crude squatter's shack in which he lived with his second wife, the novelist Margerie Bonner and wrote in seclusion for more than a decade. Other novels by Lowry include *In Ballast to the White Sea* (1936), the unfinished *Lunar Caustic* (1968) and *Dark Is the Grave Wherein My Friend Is Laid* (1969). His *Selected Letters* were published in 1967.

For further reading:

Bareham, Tony, *Malcolm Lowry*. New York: St. Martin's, 1989.

Day, Douglas, *Malcolm Lowry: A Biography*. Oxford: Oxford University Press, 1973.

Loyalist. Term used to refer to Protestants in NORTHERN IRELAND who support the maintenance of the Union with Great Britain in opposition to those Catholics who wish to unite with the Republic of IRELAND.

LP records. See Carl Peter GOLDMARK.

LSD. See Timothy LEARY.

Lubin, Isador (1896–1978). American economist. Lubin was a leading member of President Franklin D. ROOSEVELT'S BRAIN TRUST and helped shape the NEW DEAL. As U.S. commissioner of labor statistics (1933–46), he supervised and made famous the CONSUMER PRICE INDEX.

Lubitsch, Ernst (1892–1947). German-born film director many of whose major works were produced in HOLLYWOOD. Lubitsch was one of the most stylish and sophisticated directors of comedy in the history of cinema. The phrase "the Lubitsch touch" became, in the 1930s and 1940s, synonymous with the subtle and refined handling of adult themes of love and betrayal in the elegant style of drawing room comedy. His best known film is *Ninotchka* (1939), which featured Greta GARBO in her first comedic role as a dour Russian communist agent who is induced to see the charms of Western bourgeois decadence by dapper Melvyn DOUGLAS. *To Be or Not To Be* (1942), starring Jack BENNY and Carole LOMBARD, was a parody of Nazi pretensions set in occupied Poland. Other Lubitsch films include *Monte Carlo* (1930), *Trouble in Paradise* (1932) and *The Merry Widow* (1934).

Lubumbashi [formerly Elisabethville]. City and capital of Shaba province, ZAIRE; it is Zaire's second-largest city. Established as a European settlement by Belgian colonists in 1910, Elisabethville was capital of the secessionist state of Katanga (now Shaba) from 1960 to 1965, when there was fighting between UNITED NATIONS forces and the rebels.

Lucas, George (1944–). American film director and producer. Lucas is one of the most popular filmmakers in the history of HOLLYWOOD. He is best known as the creator of the *Star Wars* trilogy—*Star Wars* (1977), which Lucas directed, *The Empire Strikes Back* (1980) and *Return of the Jedi* (1983) which he scripted and produced. The phenomenal box office success of these films, with their pioneering use of computer technology to create elaborate special effects, proved that blockbuster action and storytelling—without reliance on previously established big-name stars could capture the hearts and pocketbooks of audiences. Lucas' first directorial effort was a low budget science fiction film *THX 1138* (1970). His first critical breakthrough was the acclaimed *American Graffiti* (1973). He has also been associated with director-producer Steven SPIELBERG. Lucas now devotes his primary efforts to producing films.

Luce, Clare Boothe (1903–1987). U.S. editor, playwright and politician. Luce's career included the editorship of *Vanity Fair* (1933–1934) and the writing of hit plays, most notably *The Women* (1936). Her political career included two terms as a Republican congresswoman from Connecticut (1943–47) and service as U.S. ambassador to ITALY (1953–57). She was married for 32 years to media mogul Henry R. LUCE, the founder of the TIME magazine empire. After his death in 1967, she moved to Hawaii, where she lived until she returned to Washington in 1983. Long identified with the conservative wing of the REPUBLICAN PARTY, she served on President REAGAN'S Foreign Intelligence Advisory Board.

Luce, Henry R(obinson) (1898–1967). American editor and publisher. A titan of the publishing world, Luce founded TIME, the first modern news magazine, with Yale classmate Briton Hadden in 1923. He went on to successfully establish the business magazine *Fortune* (1930), the photojournalistic LIFE (1936) and *Sports Illustrated* (1954). His magazines reflected his personal views on politics and the free enterprise system. He also acquired radio and television stations and began publishing books under the Time-Life imprint. He was married to diplomat and playwright Clare Boothe LUCE.

For further reading:

Baughman, James L., *Henry R. Luce and the Rise of the American News Media*. Boston: G.K. Hall, 1987.

Luciano, Charles "Lucky" [born Salvatore Luciana] (1897–1962). American organized crime leader. Born near Palermo, Sicily, he emigrated to the U.S. (1906) and was soon arrested for shoplifting. By 1916 Luciano had become a member of New York's infamous Five Points gang; by the early 1920s he was an important figure in bootlegging. He subsequently assumed second-in-command status in the family of mob chieftain Giuseppe "Joe the Boss" Masseria. During a war (1928–30) between the Masseria factions and the opposing Maranzanos, Luciano solidified relations with younger gangsters in both camps. In 1931 Luciano was responsible for murdering both Masseria and Maranzano. Luciano then became the undisputed head of organized crime in New York and the leading figure in a new national crime syndicate that soon controlled bootlegging, prostitution, drugs, gambling, loanshark activities and labor racketeering. He prospered until 1936, when he was convicted on prostitution charges through the efforts of the crusading prosecutor Thomas E. DEWEY. Sentenced to 30 to 50 years imprisonment, he continued to control organized crime from his cell until his release in 1946, when he was deported to Italy. He wielded power from Cuba for a while but was returned to Italy, where his influence steadily waned.

Lucky Jim. Novel by Kingsley AMIS, published in 1954. It earned Amis a reputation as one of the ANGRY YOUNG MEN, and remains his most popular work. The story is set in a provincial British university where its lower-middle-class hero, Jim Dixon, is a lecturer. His radical, anarchist views expressed and reflected the discontent and anger of the young British leftists in the 1950s.

Ludendorff, Erich (1865–1937). German general. Commissioned in the infantry in 1882, Ludendorff was appointed to the Prussian general staff as a major in 1906. In the early days of WORLD WAR I, he led his troops in the capture of the Belgian citadel at Liege. Thereafter, he was named army chief of staff under HINDENBURG. Both became war heroes after the eastern front victories at Tannenberg and the Masurian Lakes (1914). As the war progressed, the two men made most of GERMANY's important military decisions, and from 1916 to 1918 Ludendorff exercised enormous power in civilian life as well. He was largely responsible for the beginning of unrestricted submarine warfare in 1917 and for the final offensive of 1918. When it failed, Ludendorff insisted on an armistice; after it was concluded, he fled to Sweden. Returning to Germany the following year, he engaged in antigovernment activity, supporting the KAPP PUTSCH (1920) and HITLER's "BEER-HALL PUTSCH" (1923). He was a National Socialist member of the Reichstag from 1924 to 1928. Although he broke with Hitler, he remained a vociferous supporter of "Aryan" rights and deplored Jews, Catholics and Freemasons alike.

Ludwigshafen am Rhein [Ludwigshafen]. City on the Rhine River, Germany. A center of German chemical production, it was bombed heavily by the Allies in WORLD WAR II. In 1948 there was a massive explosion that destroyed several chemical plants and killed a number of workers.

Lugosi, Bela [Bela Ferenc Dezso] (1882–1956). Hungarian-born film and stage actor. Although Lugosi was a working actor for more than four decades, his enduring fame stems from a single role with which he became permanently identified: the evil vampire, Count Dracula. Lugosi's portrayal of the caped Count in the classic 1931 film by Tod BROWNING—which followed Lugosi's successful Broadway run in the same role—typecast him forever after in macabre and horrific roles. Prior to his stardom as Dracula Lugosi had been a successful film and stage actor in both Europe and the U.S. to which he had emigrated in 1921. In the 1930s and

Gen. Erich Ludendorff, German military leader during World War I.

1940s, Lugosi appeared almost exclusively in horror films notably *The Black Cat* (1934), *Mark of the Vampire* (1935) and *The Raven* (1935). Lugosi's career declined in the 1950s, while his increasing psychological identification with the role of Dracula led to his being buried—pursuant to his own instructions—in his vampire cape.

Lukacs, Gjorgy (1885–1971). Hungarian writer, Marxist philosopher and literary critic. In 1918 Lukacs joined the Hungarian Communist Party. In 1930 he moved to Moscow and from 1933 to 1944 worked at the Institute of Philosophy of the Soviet Academy of Science. He exerted considerable influence on European communist thought and is noted for having formulated a Marxist system of aesthetics that opposes political control of artists and that defends humanism. Having returned to Hungary in 1945, Lukacs twice served as minister of culture. His publications include *Studies on Lenin* (1970) and *Solzhenitsyn* (1970, tr. 1971).

Lumet, Sidney (1924–). American motion picture and television director. As a child actor in Philadelphia and New York, Lumet appeared in many radio and Broadway plays. After service in World War II he began directing for some of the early CBS television dramatic anthology series, including "Omnibus," "Alcoa Theater," "Goodyear Playhouse" and "You Are There" and acquired a reputation for economical, efficient directing. His film career began with an adaptation of Reginald Rose's courtroom drama, *12 Angry Men* (1957). Half of his subsequent film projects derived from the theater—most notably Eugene O'NEILL's *Long Day's Journey into Night* (1964), Chekhov's *The Sea Gull* (1968), and *Equus* (1978), *The Wiz* (1979) and *Deathtrap* (1981). Many of his other films probe the gritty streets, tangled lives and police corruption of New York City. *Serpico* (1974) and *Prince of the City* (1981) were about cops who defy their peer groups to maintain their own code of morality; *Q&A* (1990) examined the opposite side of the same issue. Lumet's finest achievement may be *The Pawnbroker* (1965), starring Rod Steiger as Sol Nazerman, a Jew whose CONCENTRATION CAMP memories haunt his daily life. Its uncompromising harshness and brief nudity challenged—and defeated—HOLLYWOOD attempts to censor it. However, many audiences and critics have been put off by Lumet's rather humorless tone and his apparent lack of a consistent style.

For further reading:

Coursodon, Jean-Piere, ed. *American Directors.* New York: McGraw-Hill, 1983.

Lumiere brothers, the. Auguste (1862–1954) and Louis (1864–1948) Lumiere were

Film actor Bela Lugosi in his most famous role as Count Dracula (1931).

pioneers of French cinema and the movement known as the documentary. Sons of a photographer, they developed a dry-plate process that made the family's plant in Lyons Europe's leading manufacturer of photographic products. By 1894 they had invented the Cinematographe, which, unlike the Edison Kinetograph, was a portable, hand-cranked mechanism that combined the operations of camera, printer and projector. Within a year Louis had photographed on short lengths of film numerous actualities of French life—the arrival of a train, factory workers at the Lyons plant, fishermen with nets, the demolition of a wall—and shown them to members of the Societe d'Encouragement pour l'Industrie Nationale. On December 28, 1895—generally accepted as the birthday of world cinema—these images were projected before a paying audience in the basement of the Grand Cafe on the Boulevard des Capucines in Paris. This, a full four months before Edison's first projected films in New York City. Soon, the Lumieres dispatched an army of skilled photographers ("operators") around the world to shoot what later would be called newsreels showing the coronation of Czar NICHOLAS II in Moscow, the inauguration of President MCKINLEY, etc. After 1900 the brothers sold their filmmaking interests and devoted their time to invention and the manufacture of photographic processes (including a three-dimensional film process that Louis introduced in his 70s). Today, the Lumieres, especially Louis, are regarded as founders of cinema.

Lumumba, Patrice (1925–1961). First prime minister of the Republic of the Congo (now ZAIRE) in 1960. In the same year his party emerged as the largest in the national assembly, and the Belgians chose him to be the first prime minister, with KASAVUBU as president. During his four-month incumbency he faced various crises, notably the seccession of Katanga province (see KATANGA REVOLT). He was dismissed for seeking Soviet help, arrested by the army and handed over to Katanga rebels, who murdered him in 1961.

Lunacharsky, Anatoly Vasilyevich (1875–1933). Russian author, literary critic and politician. Deported in 1898 for revolutionary activities, Lunacharsky joined the Bolsheviks and worked on the party's journal *Vperyod.* Imprisoned during the 1905 Revolution, in 1909 he started a school for an elite of Russian factory workers on Capri; he was assisted by Maxim GORKY and Alexander Bogdanov. The three of them broke from LENIN, forming their own left-wing subfaction. In 1917 he joined Lenin and TROTSKY in Russia and was appointed people's commissar for education. A supporter of Bogdanovism during the 1920s, he introduced many innovations into the educational system. In 1933 he was appointed ambassador to Spain but died shortly after the appointment. The author of some 14 plays, Lunacharsky also produced many works of literary criticism.

Lunt and Fontanne. English-born actress **Lynn Fontanne** (1887–1983) and her husband, American actor **Alfred Lunt** (1892–1977), formed one of the most celebrated couples to act on the American stage in the 20th century. Married in 1922, over the next 40 years Lunt and Fontanne starred together in 27 plays. They scored their biggest hit with *O Mistress Mine,* which opened in New York City in 1946 and completed 451 performances. Among the playwrights with whom Fontanne and Lunt worked were Noel COWARD, Robert E. SHERWOOD, Terence RATTIGAN and Jean GIRAUDOUX; they also acted in G.B. SHAW'S *Arms and the Man* and Friedrich DURRENMATT'S *The Visit.* The couple won numerous honors, including a Presidential Medal of Freedom from Lyndon B. JOHNSON in 1964 and a special Tony award in 1970. Fontanne was praised for her elegant demeanor, sultry voice and comedic talents.

Lunts, Lev Natanovich (1901–1924). Soviet essayist and playwright. A member of the SERAPION BROTHERS, Lunts wrote the plays *The Apes Are Coming* and *The City of Truth,* a courageous anti-Bolshevik play. He emigrated and died abroad.

Lurcat, Jean (1892–1966). French artist and designer. Lurcat is known primarily for his important role in stimulating renewed interest in tapestry making in the 20th century. Lurcat created his first tapestry in 1917. By 1939, he had established a tapestry works in Aubusson that attracted international attention. Major tapestries by Lurcat include *Four Seasons* (1940), *Apocalypse Tapestry* (1948) and *The Song of the World* (1957–64). Lurcat was a highly versatile artist who also worked in theatrical set and costume design, lithography and book illustration.

Luria, Aleksandr R(omanovich) (1902–). Russian psychologist and neurologist. Luria was a prodigal figure in Soviet psychology. He earned degrees in medicine, education and psychology and, at an early age, pioneered techniques in the objective, experimental measurement of human emotions. As head of the department of neuropsychology at Moscow University he undertook considerable research on the function of language and how it relates to mental development. During World War II he improved techniques for brain surgery and postoperative recovery for trauma patients. His major works include *Higher Cortical Functions in Man* (1966), *The Mind of a Mnemonist* (1968), *The Working Brain* (1973), and *Basic Problems of Neurolinguistics* (1976).

Luria, Salvador Edward (1912–1991). Italian-American physician who shared the 1969 NOBEL PRIZE for medicine or physiology with Max DELBRUCK and Alfred D. Hershey. Luria was a professor at MIT from 1959 to 1978. In awarding the prize, the Nobel Foundation cited Luria's "discoveries concerning the replication mechanism and the genetic structure of viruses," which "set the solid foundation on which modern molecular biology rests." An ardent pacifist, Luria spoke out against the VIETNAM WAR (see ANTIWAR MOVEMENT). His outspokenness was apparently the reason behind his inclusion on a 1969 list of scientists who were barred from participating on advisory panels of the U.S. Department of Health, Education and Welfare.

Lurton, Horace H. (1844–1914). Associate justice, U.S. Supreme Court (1909–14). A native of Kentucky, Lurton was a graduate of the University of Chicago and Cumberland Law School. Lurton, a former Confederate soldier, was appointed as a Tennessee judge after his law partner became a U.S. senator. He was later appointed as a judge of the U.S. Court of Appeals for the Sixth Circuit by President Cleveland. During this time he also taught at Vanderbilt Law School. In 1909, President William Howard TAFT appointed Lurton to the Supreme Court. He died in 1914 after only five years on the Court.

Lusitania. British passenger ship. Hit by a German submarine torpedo, the *Lusitania* sank in the Atlantic off the south coast of Ireland on May 7, 1915. The Cunard luxury liner was unarmed but carried concealed munitions for the Allies. The sinking resulted in almost 1,200 deaths, among them 128 Americans. There was an immediate large-scale public outcry in the U.S., with some people calling for a declaration of war. President Woodrow WILSON asked GERMANY for reparations, which was denied. This incident caused public opinion to shift in favor of U.S. entry into WORLD WAR I on the side of the Allies.

Luthuli, Albert John (1898–1967). South African political and civil rights leader. Born near Bulawayo, a descendant of Zulu chiefs, he was educated at a Methodist mission school and taught there for 15 years. Appointed chief in 1936, he advocated the church's policy of non-violence in the struggle against racial discrimination. In 1945 he joined the AFRICAN NATIONAL CONGRESS, becoming president of the Natal branch in 1951 and head of the organization in 1952. Deposed as chief and restricted by the South African government in his political activities, he nonetheless headed a campaign of passive resistance against APARTHEID. In his efforts, Luthuli was influenced by his religious convictions and by the American CIVIL RIGHTS MOVEMENT. Arrested many times, he was banished to his village in 1959. In 1960 the government outlawed the ANC, and in 1962 Luthuli's statements were banned from publication. Luthuli was awarded the 1960 NOBEL PRIZE for peace. His autobiography *Let My People Go* was published two years later.

Lutoslawski, Witold (1913–). Polish composer. Lutoslawski was one of the major avant-garde composers of the postwar era. Strongly influenced by the atonal compositional techniques of modernists such as Bela BARTOK and Igor STRAVINSKY, Lutoslawski composed highly experimental works that occasionaly allowed for jazz-like improvisation by orchestral members. His major compositions include *Little Suite* (1951), *Concerto for Orchestra* (1954), *Funeral Music* (1958), *Venetian Games* (1961) and the choral composition *Three Poems by Henri Michaux* (1963).

The Lusitania*—and German U-boat 139, which sank her.*

Lutyens, Sir Edwin Landseer (1869–1944). English architect. Born in London, Lutyens studied at the South Kensington School of Art. Lutyens started his practice in 1889, designing a number of palatial country homes. Influenced by the Arts amd Crafts style, his beautifully-crafted houses represent a fusion of traditional English elements with a very personal approach. From domestic to public architecture, he executed a number of important projects that merge neoclassicism with mannerism. These include the plan for NEW DELHI, India (1912–1914), that city's imposing Viceroy's Palace (1920–1931) and Liverpool's monumental Anglican cathedral (1929–1941). He is also known for his war memorials, among which are the Cenotaph in London (1920), FRANCE'S Thiepval Memorial Arch (1924) and memorials at Manchester, England and Johannesburg, South Africa.

Luxembourg, Grand Duchy of. A landlocked country located in the northwest corner of Europe, covering an area of 998 square miles. Luxembourg's link with the Netherlands was severed in 1890, when the accession of a female to the Dutch throne impelled Luxembourg, where Salic Law applied, to choose a male sovereign from the House of Nassau. Salic Law was eventually revoked in 1912 to allow the accession of Grand Duchess Marie-Adelaide, whose sympathies for Luxembourg's German occupiers during WORLD WAR I attracted much criticism. Following an abortive republican coup attempt in early 1919, French pressure obliged Marie-Adelaide to abdicate in favor of her sister CHARLOTTE. Under the 1919 VERSAILLES TREATY Luxembourg was declared perpetually free of all ties with Germany, and in 1922 the Belgium-Luxembourg economic union was formed. Successive interwar governments were dominated by the Christian Social Party (CSV), although in 1937 the Social Democrats joined a coalition that enacted modern social legislation. During WORLD WAR II Luxembourg was again overrun by the Germans (1940) and annexed to the Third Reich (1942). Grand Duchess Charlotte and her ministers escaped to London. Her son, Prince Jean, was one of the first Allied soldiers to enter liberated Luxembourg in 1944. In the postwar era Luxembourg was a founding member of NATO (1949) and of the WEU (1955). It also joined the BENELUX economic union with Belgium and the Netherlands (1948) and the EUROPEAN COAL AND STEEL COMMUNITY, EUROPEAN ECONOMIC COMMUNITY and EURATOM (1951–58), rapidly achieving renewed prosperity on the basis of its large iron and steel industry.

Luxemburg, Rosa (1871–1919). German revolutionary leader and social theorist. Born in Russian Poland, she was involved in revolutionary activities from the age of 16. Forced to flee to Switzerland in 1889, she helped to found the Polish Socialist Party in 1892. Becoming a German citizen by marriage in 1898, she became a leader of the left wing of the German Social Democratic Party. A fiery orator and brilliant writer, she was part of the 1905 revolution in Russian Poland and was active in the Second INTERNATIONAL. Differing with more moderate German socialists, she and Karl Liebknecht founded the radical Spartacus League in 1916. Two years later it became the German Communist Party. Luxemburg was imprisoned during much of World War I (1916–18). After the SPARTACIST uprising in Berlin, she and Liebknecht were again arrested in 1919. While being transported to prison, both were murdered by German soldiers. Luxemburg's best known work is *Accumulation of Capital* (1913, tr. 1951).

Lvov. City in the Ukraine, U.S.S.R. Shortly after World War I Lvov was the capital of the short-lived West Ukrainian Democratic Republic. From 1919 to 1939 the city was part of POLAND. Annexed by the Soviet Union in 1939, it was captured by Germany after the German invasion of the U.S.S.R. (see WORLD WAR II ON THE

LUXEMBOURG

1912	Change in law allows female to succeed to the throne; Grand Duchess Marie-Adelaide becomes sovereign.
1914	German occupation; Marie-Adelaide is vocally sympathetic to German cause.
1919	Abortive Republican coup; Marie-Adelaide forced to abdicate in favor of her sister, Princess Charlotte; new constitution increases power of the elected government, decreases that of the monarchy; ties with Germany renounced in perpetuity.
1922	Economic union formed with Belgium.
1940	Second German occupation.
1944	(December) Battle of the Bulge; thousands of American soldiers buried on Luxembourg soil.
1948	"Benelux" economic union with Netherlands and Belgium.
1951	Membership in European Coal and Steel Community contributes to steel-making boom.
1963	One-thousandth anniversary as independent state.
1964	Charlotte abdicates in favor of her son, Prince Jean.
1967	Compulsory military service abolished; volunteer army under 1,000-strong established.
1968	"Explosion Scolaire"; rapid increase in school-aged children leads to education reform.
1975	Slump in steel-making leads government to encourage electronics and other industries.

RUSSIAN FRONT). During the German occupation, the SS exterminated Lvov's Jewish population.

Lvov, Prince Georgi Yevgenevich (1861–1925). Social reformer and statesman. Lvov was active in the ZEMSTVA movement and chairman of the All-Russian Union of Zemstvos. He formed a provisional government at the request of the provisional committee of the state duma in February 1917 following NICHOLAS II's abdication and was prime minister until KERENSKY replaced him in July of that year. He lived in exile in France after the Bolshevik seizure of power.

Lyautey, Louis Hubert (Gonzalve) (1854–1934). French soldier and colonial administrator. A career officer, educated at St. Cyr, he served in Algeria, Madagascar and Indo-China before being appointed French resident general in MOROCCO in 1912. He spent the next 13 years (with the exception of 1916–17, when he was war minister) as administrator of the protectorate. Lyautey maintained French control there during World War I and later was successful in a campaign against the Berber tribes of ABD EL-KRIM. As an administrator, he supported Arab traditions, helped to develop the economy, aided in the building of the port of Casablanca and extended the borders of the protectorate. Created a marshal of France in 1921, he resigned his colonial post in 1925.

lynching of Leo Frank. Infamous case of American ANTISEMITISM. In April, 1913 Mary Phagan, a 14–year-old employee of the National Pencil Co. in Atlanta, Georgia was found brutally raped and murdered. Although penciled notes accused a black, suspicions fell on Leo Frank, the 29–year-old, Brooklyn-born Jewish manager of the company. An air of clamorous antisemitism pervaded the 30–day trial of Frank, who was found guilty and sentenced to death. For the next two years, the verdict was appealed as far as the U.S. Supreme Court, but rejected by all. In 1915 Georgia governor John M. Slaton, who had been petitioned to save Frank and presented with evidence that he was innocent, commuted his sentence to life imprisonment. On August 17, 1915 a group of men entered the prison in which Frank was incarcerated, and abducted and hanged him.

Lyons, Joseph Aloysius (1879–1939). Australian statesman, prime minister (1931–39). Born in Tasmania, he taught school there for 13 years before entering the Tasmanian legislature as a Labour member in 1909. Serving as Tasmania's first Labour premier (1923–28), he was elected to the federal Parliament in 1929. He held cabinet posts until 1931, when he broke with the Labour Party over its economic policies and helped found the coalition United Australia Party. As prime minister, he was able to improve the nation's economy and expand its military forces in response to mounting threats from Japan.

Lysenko, Trofim Denisovich (1898–1976). Soviet agronomist and genetic theorist. Born in Karlovka, Lysenko attended the Kiev Agricultural Institute. During his early years at Odessa's Institute of Selection and Genetics, he worked on the vernalization of spring wheat, a moistening and cold treatment of seed that promotes early flowering. In the course of this work Lysenko became convinced that the acquired effects of vernalization could be inherited. From this faulty assumption, he went on to reject the accepted Mendelian theory of inheritance and to postulate the inheritance of acquired characteristics. This doctrine dovetailed with Marxist dogma regarding social and economic improvement, and Lysenko became a great favorite of STALIN. As president of the Lenin Academy of Agricultural Science (1938–56, 1961–62) and director of the Institute of Genetics of the Soviet Academy of Sciences (1940–65), he quashed all opposition and became the virtual dictator of Soviet genetics, with all teaching and textbooks in the U.S.S.R. forced to reflect his views. Lysenko's career faltered and his ruinous effect on Soviet biological science lessened after the death of Stalin in 1953. He was completely discredited in 1965 after the retirement of KHRUSHCHEV.

Lyulka, Arkhip (1908–1984). Soviet aircraft-engine designer. An expert in jet propulsion, Lyulka was credited with inventing the turbo-charging process used widely in WORLD WAR II fighter planes. He also supervised the production of the first Soviet jet engines, later designing the engines for most new Soviet civilian and military aircraft.

Maazel, Lorin (1930–). American conductor. Born in Neuilly, France, Maazel was brought to the U.S. as a child. A musical prodigy, he studied violin, piano and conducting and made his conducting debut at age seven; by the time he was 15, he had conducted most of the major orchestras in the U.S. After studying philosophy, music and fine art at the University of Pittsburgh, he turned to music full-time. He has been director of the Berlin Radio Symphony Orchestra (1965–75), New Philharmonia Orchestra (1970–72, 1976–80), Cleveland Orchestra (1971–82), Orchestre National de France (1977–82), Vienna State Opera (1983–84) and Pittsburgh Symphony Orchestra. In addition, he has served as guest conductor of other major orchestras throughout the world. Maazel is known for his superb baton technique, intellectual approach to music and polished performances. Particularly acclaimed for his interpretations of romantic works, he has an impressive repertoire that extends from Bach to STRAVINSKY, and has made many recordings.

Macao. Macao consists of a peninsula with a 0.21–mile-long border with CHINA, and two islands: the southernmost, Liha de Coloane, is connected to Liha da Taipa by a causeway, and Liha de Taipa is connected to the mainland of Macao by a bridge. The terrain is flat and essentially

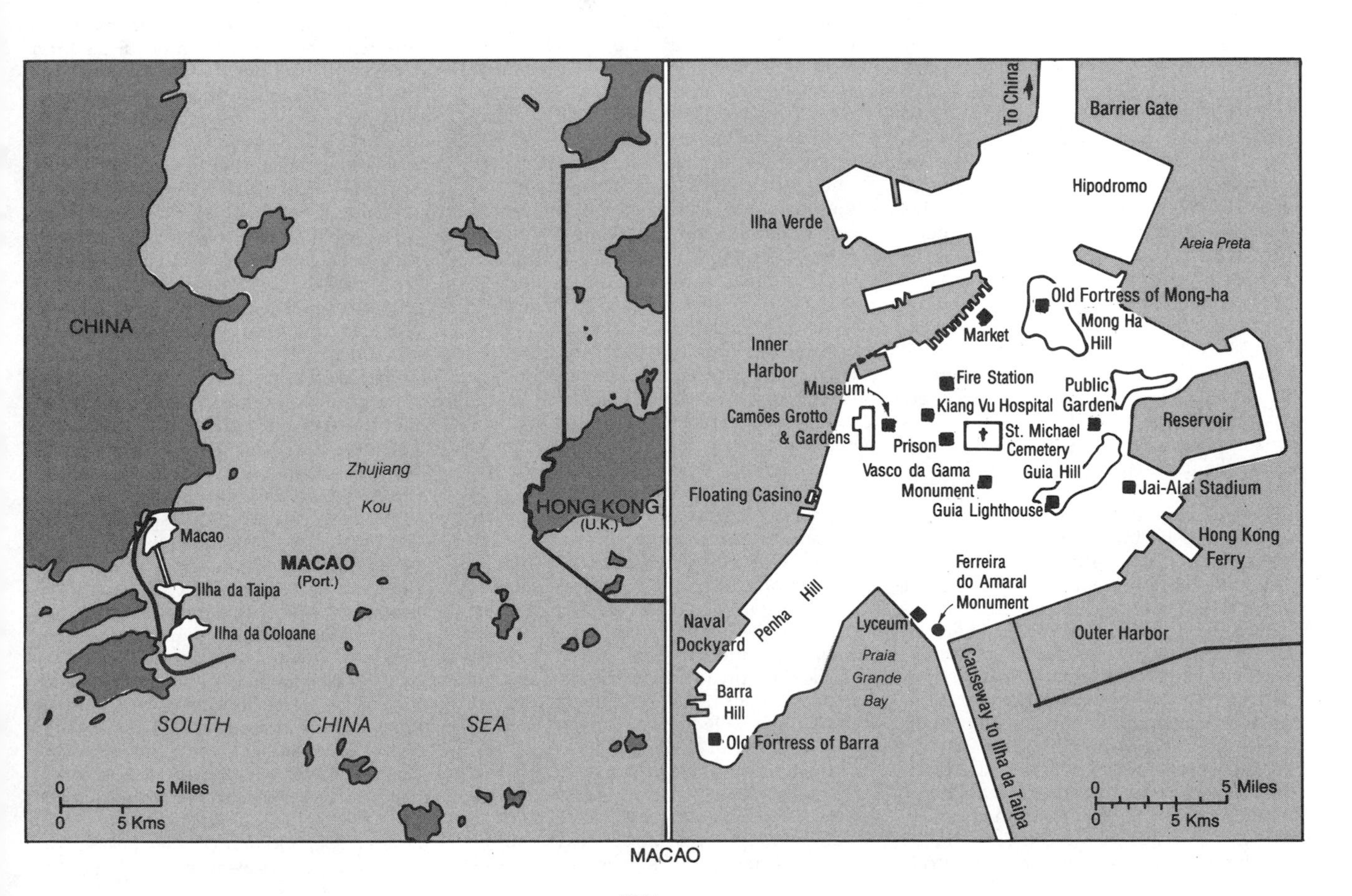

MACAO

urban. There is no land suitable for cultivation. The Portuguese colonized Macao in 1557 and for 200 years the territory flourished as one of the world's major East-West trading posts for silks, gold, spices and opium. Britain's occupation of nearby Hong Kong in the mid-19th century undermined Macao's position as a trading center. In 1848 the Portuguese declared Macao independent from China, an assertion not recognized by the Chinese until 1887. In 1951, Portugal proclaimed Macao an Overseas Province. Macao suffered widespread rioting at the height of the CULTURAL REVOLUTION in China during the mid-1960s. The protests unnerved the Portuguese and served to increase Beijing's influence in the territory.

Shortly after the 1974 Portuguese revolution, the new government offered to return Macao to Chinese rule. China turned the offer down but indicated that it had a comprehensive plan to resume sovereignty over both Macao and HONG KONG. In early 1976 Portugal promulgated an "organic statute" granting Macao greater autonomy and providing for a directly elected minority on the 17-member legislative assembly. In February 1979 Portugal and China established diplomatic relations, with Macao defined as "Chinese territory under Portuguese administration." Sino-Portuguese talks opened in Beijing in June 1986 and ended 10 months later in the signing of a formal agreement on the reversion of Macao to China in 1999. The agreement was based upon the "one country, two systems" principle that had formed the basis of China's negotiated settlement with the United Kingdom in 1984 concerning the future of Hong Kong. In elections in October 1988, three of the six directly elected seats on the legislative assembly were won by a pro-liberal grouping; the remaining seats were retained by the conservative Electoral Union group, which had gained four seats in 1984 elections.

MacArthur, Douglas (1880–1964). American general, widely considered one of the most brilliant military minds of the 20th century. Born in Little Rock, Arkansas, MacArthur was the son of a general and attended West Point, graduating at the head of his class in 1903. His early assignments took him to the PHILIPPINES and JAPAN, and he was an aide to President Theodore ROOSEVELT from 1906 to 1907. During WORLD WAR I he served with distinction in France: first as chief of staff of the 42nd (Rainbow) Division, then as commander of the 84th Infantry Brigade. After the war, promoted to the rank of brigadier general, he became superintendent of West Point (1919–22), where he raised military and academic standards. He held a variety of field commands from 1922 to 1930, when he was named a full general and appointed Army chief of staff, a post he held for the next five years.

MacArthur was appointed adviser to the U.S. military mission in the Philippines in 1935. He retired from the U.S. Army in 1937 and spent four years building the nascent Philippine military. With

U.S. Army General Douglas MacArthur, who commanded Allied forces in the Pacific in World War II and in the Korean War.

war imminent, however, he was recalled to active duty in 1941 by President Franklin D. ROOSEVELT as commander of American forces in the Far East. MacArthur valiantly defended the Philippines from Japanese attack until February 1942, when he was forced to retreat but vowed to return. He was awarded the Medal of Honor and immediately posted to Australia as supreme Allied commander in the Southwest Pacific. He masterminded a brilliant campaign in New Guinea and was successful in recapturing the Philippines (October, 1944–July, 1945), wading ashore with his troops in October 1944. In December of that year, MacArthur became the Army's first five-star general; the following April he was appointed commander of the U.S. Army in the Pacific. In this capacity, he accepted Japan's unconditional surrender on the U.S.S. MISSOURI on September 2, 1945. From 1945 to 1951 MacArthur directed the Allied occupation of Japan, modernizing and rehabilitating the defeated nation while introducing a new democratic constitution as well as democratic institutions and political practices. He antagonized many people in the U.S., however, with his austere and autocratic style. When fighting broke out in KOREA, he was appointed supreme UNITED NATIONS commander (June 1950). His typical strategic cunning was employed in the amphibious landings at INCHON, but he was surprised by the massive intervention of Chinese troops. Wishing to bomb CHINA and to check the spread of COMMUNISM in the Far East, MacArthur came into direct conflict with President Harry S TRUMAN, who relieved him of command on April 11, 1951. Returning to the U.S., perceived as a farsighted hero by conservatives and a dangerous demagogue by liberals, he gave a dramatic speech to Congress defending his aims and policies. His presidential ambitions were quashed by his failure to achieve the Republican nomination in 1952, and he then became a successful businessman. MacArthur published *Reminiscences* in 1964.

For further reading:

Schaller, Michael, *Douglas MacArthur: The Far Eastern General*. New York: Oxford University Press, 1989.

James, D. Clayton, *The Years of MacArthur: Triumph & Disaster, 1945–1964*. Boston, Mass.: Houghton Mifflin, 1985.

Langley, Michael, *Inchon Landing: MacArthur's Last Triumph*. New York: Random House, 1980.

Manchester, William, *American Caesar: Douglas MacArthur 1880–1964*. Boston, Mass.: Little, Brown, 1978.

MacBride, Sean (1904–1988). Irish lawyer, politician and diplomat. MacBride was the son of the famed Irish beauty and revolutionary Maud Gonne (who inspired much of YEATS' poetry) and Gonne's husband, **Colonel John MacBride,** who was executed for his part in the 1916 EASTER RISING. Following in his parents' footsteps, Sean MacBride was active in the IRISH REPUBLICAN ARMY from 1917 until 1937. He then joined the Irish bar and became Dublin's most successful trial lawyer. In 1946, he founded a radical nationalist party, Clann na Poblachta, which helped oust the FIANNA FAIL party two years later. From 1948 through 1951, he was the finance minister of the coalition government under which Ireland became an independent republic. He was a cofounder of AMNESTY INTERNATIONAL in 1961 and acted as secretary general of the International Commission of Jurists from 1963 to 1970. From 1974 to 1976 he was the U.N. commissioner for NAMIBIA. He shared the NOBEL PRIZE for peace with Japanese statesman Eisaku SATO in 1974 and was awarded the Soviet equivalent, the Lenin Prize, three years later.

MacColl, Ewan [born James Miller] (1915–1989). British folk singer and songwriter. He led the folk music revival in Britain in the 1950s and 1960s. He was also a cofounder, with Joan Littlewood, of the touring Theatre Workshop. One of his songs, "The First Time Ever I Saw Your Face," won a Grammy Award for American singer Roberta Flack in 1972.

MacDiarmid, Hugh [pen name of Christopher Murray Grieve] (1892–1978). Scottish poet and essayist. MacDiarmid, one of the greatest Scottish poets of the 20th century, was especially well-known for his effort to revive the neglected Scottish language. He was educated in his home town of Langholm, Scotland as well as in Edinburgh. His earliest writings were journalistic in nature, supporting left-wing political issues and cultural and political independence for Scotland. His first major work was the long poem *A Drunk Man Looks at the Thistle* (1926). Other volumes of MacDiarmid's verse include *To Circumjack Cencrastus* (1930), *First Hymn to Lenin and Other Poems* (1931), *Scots Unbound and Other Poems* (1932) and *In Memoriam James Joyce*. MacDiarmid was awarded the Foyle Poetry Prize and the Fletcher of Saltoun Medal, as well as an honorary doctoral degree from Edinburgh Uniersity. *Collected Poems* appeared in 1962; *Selected Essays*, in 1969.

MacDonald, Dwight (1906–1982). American essayist, critic and editor. He is known for his witty and acerbic writings on culture, politics and film. While a writer for *Fortune* magazine (1929–36), MacDonald became a committed socialist and Trotskyite. (See Leon TROTSKY.) A leading figure in American left-wing intellectual circles during the 1930s and 1940s, he was associated with the PARTISAN REVIEW from 1938 to 1943. A pacifist, he opposed WORLD WAR II, and in the 1960s was an outspoken critic of American involvement in the VIETNAM WAR. He was a longtime staff writer for THE NEW YORKER (1951–71) and a film critic for *Esquire* (1960–66).

MacDonald, J(ames) E(dward) H(ervey) (1873–1932). Anglo-Canadian painter and poet. Born in England, he emigrated to Canada in 1887. As a member of Canada's GROUP OF SEVEN, he sought to portray the natural splendors of his new homeland, painting north country panoramas in stylized forms and vivid colors. In his verse, MacDonald was strongly influenced by the 19th-century Americans Henry David Thoreau and Walt Whitman.

MacDonald, John D(ann) (1916–1986). U.S. author. Over the course of a 40-year writing career, he wrote dozens of books—most of them mysteries. His best-known character was the detective Travis McGee, a tough, cynical expert in salvaging who lived on a Florida houseboat. McGee appeared in 21 books published between 1964 and 1985. Each of those books bore a title that included a color.

MacDonald, Margaret (1865–1933). British-born artist-designer. She worked closely with her sister Frances MacDonald from 1894 until her marriage to Charles Rennie MACKINTOSH in 1900. MacDonald was educated at the Glasgow School of Art, where she met Mackintosh. Her reputation is based primarily on her watercolor paintings and book illustrations, as well as her collaboration in textile design with Mackintosh. After she and Mackintosh relocated to London in 1916, her work as a painter sustained them as his career tapered off in his later years.

MacDonald, (James) Ramsay (1866–1937). British Labour Party leader, Prime Minister of the UNITED KINGDOM (1924; 1929–35). MacDonald, born in poverty in the Scottish village of Lossiemouth, settled in England in 1886. An outspoken advocate of socialism, he joined the Independent Labour Party in 1894 and in 1900 became secretary of the newly formed LABOUR PARTY. He was elected Member of Parliament for Leicester in 1906 and then held the seat until 1918. MacDonald ably led the parliamentary Labour Party from 1911 until 1914, when his pacifist views cost him his influence at the outbreak of WORLD WAR I. Elected again in 1922 for Aberavon, he was re-elected leader of the parliamentary party, thereby heading the Opposition. In a general election called by Stanley BALDWIN, MacDonald became Britain's first Labour prime minister (January, 1924); he also served simultaneously as foreign secretary. Following the publication of the ZINOVIEV LETTER urging a communist overthrow in Britain, the Labour Party was accused of pro-communist sympathies, and the Conservatives were reelected to power in November, 1924.

MacDonald again became Labour prime minister from 1929 to 1931. However, the worsening financial situation caused a split in the party (see GREAT DEPRESSION). MacDonald resigned and then formed a coalition with the Conservatives and Liberals, known as the NATIONAL GOVERNMENT, which he headed from 1931 to 1935. Labour Party loyalists viewed MacDonald's formation of the National Government as a betrayal of Labour principles and felt that social ambition had wooed him away from his working-class origins. Although MacDonald maintained a Labour influence in foreign affairs and defense issues, the Conservatives dominated domestic affairs. MacDonald resigned in 1935 and was again succeeded by Baldwin. He remained in the cabinet as Lord President of the Council until his death on a vacation cruise. In his prime MacDonald was a skillful administrator with hopes for world peace through the LEAGUE OF NATIONS. His later years were troubled by declining health and disillusionment.

For further reading:

Marquand, David, *Ramsay MacDonald*. Savage, Md.: Rowman & Littlefield, 1977.

Morgan, Austen, *James Ramsey MacDonald*. New York: St. Martin's Press, 1988.

Ward, Stephen R., *James Ramsey MacDonald: Low Born Among the High Brows*. New York: Lang, Peter, 1989.

MacDonald, Ross [born Kenneth Millar] (1915–1983). American novelist, known for his detective stories featuring "Lew Archer." In a career spanning 32 years, MacDonald elevated the modern detective novel to the realm of literature. His early works were modeled closely after those of Raymond CHANDLER and Dashiell HAMMETT. He developed a distinctive style, however, in which he explored complex social and psychological relationships.

MacDowell Colony. In New Hampshire, a permanent summer retreat for writers, composers and artists. Originally a farm, it was purchased in 1896 by composer Edward MacDowell as a retreat. Following his death in 1908, a fund was formed and used to establish the colony. Considered a Mecca for creative artists, it is one of the longest-lasting art colonies in the country. The colony's distinguished roster of fellows includes poet Edwin Arlington ROBINSON, novelist Thornton WILDER, composer Leonard BERNSTEIN and artist Milton AVERY.

MacEntee, Sean (1889–1984). Irish nationalist and politician. MacEntee was a cofounder of the Irish Republic and the last surviving member of the first government established by the FIANNA FAIL party of Eamonn DE VALERA (see IRELAND). He fought against the British in the 1916 EASTER REBELLION and was sentenced to death but reprieved at the last minute and released from prison (with de Valera) under a general amnesty (1917). MacEntee was elected to the parliament of the Irish Free State in 1927. During his career he held a total of 27 posts in Fianna Fail governments, including those of finance minister and deputy prime minister. He retired in 1969.

Machine Art. Term used in art history and criticism to describe the relationship that developed in the 1920s and 1930s linking many modern artists with the increasing role of industrial machinery in production and its influence on products and the environment. The concept of the house as a machine for living was expressed by LE CORBUSIER, and artists such as Marcel DUCHAMP incorporated machine-made elements into their work. With the inclination of MODERNISM to turn away from ornament, the actual forms of machines and mechanical parts came to be seen as having aesthetic value in their own right. In 1934 the MUSEUM OF MODERN ART, New York City, mounted an exhibit entitled *Machine Art* in which such objects as springs, ball bearings and boat propellers were exhibited as art. Also shown were designed objects with strongly mechanistic character such as plumbing components, tools, instruments and utensils, as well as designed items with machinelike qualities such as clocks and furniture. In its effort to find an expressive quality suited to the technological nature of modern life, the Modern movement has had a continuing interest in the machine. The catalog of the *Machine Art* exhibit and the book *The Machine Age in America 1918–1941*—published in connection with an exhibition at the Brooklyn Museum dealing with this subject—are excellent reviews of the way mechanical devices have affected design and art.

Machito [born Frank Grillo] (1915–1984). Cuban-born bandleader. Machito moved to the U.S. in 1937 and pioneered the use of complex Latin rhythms in JAZZ in the early 1940s. His New York-based band, the Afro-Cubans, influenced such jazz greats as Dizzy GILLESPIE and Charlie PARKER. Machito's influence also extended through the Latin dance music known as Salsa, which was popular at the time of his death.

MacInnes, Helen (Clark) (1907–1985). Scottish-born novelist known for her stories of intrigue and espionage. MacInnes immigrated to the U.S. in 1937 with her husband, classics scholar Gilbert Highet. She began writing in the early 1940s. Several of her novels are set during WORLD WAR II, while others involve COLD WAR espionage. Her books were translated into 22 languages, and four were made into films, including the bestselling *Above Suspicion* (1941; filmed 1943), *The Venetian*

Affair (1963; filmed 1966) and *The Salzburg Connection* (1968; filmed 1972).

Mack, Connie (1862–1956). American baseball owner-manager. Mack began his 60-year baseball career as a catcher, primarily with the Pittsburgh Pirates. He became player-manager of the team in 1894 and retired from both positions two years later. In 1901 he took on the job of managing the Philadelphia Athletics (known as the A's), an entry in the newly formed American League. They quickly emerged as the team to beat, topping the league in six of its first 14 seasons. He led the A's to five World Series championships in nine fall classic appearances and went on to post a record 3,776 wins—and 4,025 losses. Mack was named to the Baseball Hall of Fame in 1937 and retired 13 years later in 1950, having managed the A's for 50 years.

Mack, Walter Staunton (1895–1990). U.S. businessman. Mack built Pepsi into the second-most popular soft drink in the U.S. after COCA-COLA. He served as president and chairman of Pepsi-Cola Co. (1951–83), helping to turn the small soft-drink firm into a major business through a combination of clever advertising and promotional activities. He resigned from the firm following a series of disputes with the board of directors over his promotional campaigns and went on to head several other companies.

Macke, August (1887–1914). German painter. Born in the Ruhr Valley, he studied at the Academy of Dusseldorf. He traveled to Paris several times from 1907 on and was deeply influenced by such French movements as CUBISM and FAUVISM and by the orphism of Robert DELAUNAY. In Munich in 1909 Macke met KANDINSKY and MARC; in 1911 he became a founding member of the BLAUE REITER group. A major figure in German EXPRESSIONISM, Macke employed luminous color and linear pattern in defining a very personal view of landscapes, cityscapes and figures. He traveled to Tunisia with Paul KLEE in 1914, producing subtly transparent watercolors in vividly heightened colors. His brilliant career was cut short on a battlefield in France during WORLD WAR I.

Mackenzie, Compton (1883–1973). British novelist and autobiographer. Mackenzie was one of the most widely read British fiction writers of the first half of the 20th century, and his novels continue to find a readership to this day. Educated at St. Paul's School and at Oxford University, Mackenzie began his writing career in the 1900s as a poet before enjoying success with his first novel, *The Passionate Elopement* (1911). Two other best-sellers followed quickly—*Carnival* (1912) and *Sinister Street* (1913–14). Mackenzie served in British naval intelligence during WORLD WAR I, an experience he chronicled in *Athenian Memories* (1931) and which formed the basis of two later novels, *Water on the Brain* (1933) and *Whisky Galore* (1947). Mackenzie was knighted in 1952.

Mackintosh, Charles Rennie (1868–1928). Scottish architect and designer. Born in Glasgow, he was trained as an architect. In the early 1890s, he became one of the first Britons to use the ART NOUVEAU style, employing it in decorative and graphic arts as well as in such architectural works as the Glasgow School of Art (1898–99), where he merged it with native Scottish traditions. Some of the finest of his Art Nouveau efforts are in the architecture, interior decor, furniture and murals of the four Miss Cranston's Tearooms in Glasgow (1896–1901). He is also noted for a number of turn-of-the-century Scottish country houses that updated the 17th-century manor style. These include Windyhill (1899–1901) and Hill House (1902–03). A participant in the Vienna Secession exhibition (1900), he influenced the development of 20th-century European architecture.

MacLeish, Archibald (1892–1982). American poet, playwright and statesman. Educated at Yale (B.A., 1915) and Harvard (LL.B., 1919), MacLeish gave up his law practice to join the LOST GENERATION of American expatriates in PARIS in 1923. His poems of this period show the influence of POUND, T.S. ELIOT and the symbolists. After his return home in 1928, he became an increasingly public figure, and his poetry reflected this sense of social commitment. A passionate critic of President Herbert HOOVER and an outspoken foe of NAZISM, MacLeish joined President Franklin D. ROOSEVELT'S NEW DEAL administration. He was librarian of Congress (1939–44), assistant director of the Office of War Information (1942–43) and assistant secretary of state (1944–45). He represented the U.S. in the organization of UNESCO and from 1949 to 1962 taught at Harvard. MacLeish won three PULITZER PRIZES for his poetry and drama: *Conquistador* (1932), *Collected Poems: 1917–1952* (1953) and *J.B.: A Play in Verse* (1959). *Collected Poems* also won the BOLLINGEN PRIZE and a National Book Award. His screenplay for *The Eleanor Roosevelt Story* received an ACADEMY AWARD in 1966. In his later years he also protested against MCCARTHYISM and the VIETNAM WAR.

For further reading:

Drabeck, Bernard A., ed., *Archibald MacLeish: Reflections*. Amherst: University of Massachusetts Press, 1988.

Falk, Signi L., *Archibald MacLeish*. New Haven, Conn.: New College and University Press, 1965.

[MacLeish, Archibald], *Letters of Archibald MacLeish, 1907–1982*. Boston: Houghton Mifflin, n.d.

American poet and playwright Archibald MacLeish.

MacLennan, (John) Hugh (1907–1990). Canadian writer. A novelist and essayist, he was the author of seven major fiction works. His novel *Two Solitudes* (1945) became a symbol of the conflict between English- and French-speaking Canadians. His other works include *The Watch That Ends the Night* (1959) and *The Colour of Canada* (1967).

MacLeod, Roderick (1892?-1984). British officer in WORLD WAR II. He organized two top-secret operations to mislead the Germans about Allied invasion plans. Using limited personnel and equipment to simulate large-scale troop movements, and leaking false information about these movements, MacLeod created "phantom armies" in Britain during 1943–44. The first ruse led the Germans to expect an invasion in Norway, where they diverted troops. The second caused the German high command to expect the D-DAY landings to come at CALAIS rather than NORMANDY as they actually did on June 6, 1944. Both deceptions played a significant rule in the success of the Allied INVASION OF NORMANDY.

MacLiammoir, Micheal [Micheal Wilmore] (1899–1978). Irish theatrical actor, set designer and playwright. MacLiammoir, one of the major figures in the 20th-century Irish theater, began his acting career as a child. He first achieved renown through founding, with Hilton EDWARDS, the GATE THEATRE in Dublin in the 1920s. MacLiammoir created striking set designs—influenced by the ART DECO style of artists Aubrey Beardsley and Leon BAKST—for more than 300 productions at Dublin Gate. He also appeared there as Romeo, Hamlet and Othello, among other leading roles. MacLiammoir achieved international success with three one-man shows: *The Importance of Being Oscar* (1960), a tribute to Oscar Wilde; *I Must Be Talking To My Friends* (1963); and *Talking About Yeats* (1970).

Macmillan, (Maurice) Harold (1894–1986). British statesman, prime minister of the UNITED KINGDOM (1957–63). Born in London, Macmillan was the grandson of the founder of the Macmillan publishing house. Educated at Eton and at Balliol College, Oxford, he served in the Grenadier Guards in WORLD WAR I and was wounded three times. A member of the CONSERVATIVE PARTY, he entered politics after the war and was elected to Parliament in 1924 for the constituency of Stockton. Except for two brief periods, he served in the House of Commons for the next 40 years.

Harold Macmillan, prime minister of the United Kingdom from 1957 to 1963.

In the 1920s Macmillan built a reputation as a leading progressive within the party. In the mid-1930s he joined Winston CHURCHILL in criticizing the foreign policy of the BALDWIN and CHAMBERLAIN governments—particularly Chamberlain's policy of APPEASEMENT toward Adolf HITLER'S GERMANY. He served in Churchill's government in 1940 as a junior minister before entering the cabinet in the special post of resident minister in North Africa. Later during WORLD WAR II he was also responsible for Britain's relations with her Allies in the Mediterranean and the Balkans, and served as liaison between Churchill and General Dwight D. EISENHOWER.

Minister of housing from 1951 to 1954, he subsequently served as defense minister (1954–55), foreign secretary (1955) and chancellor of the exchequer (1955–57). He succeeded Anthony EDEN as prime minister following Eden's resignation over the SUEZ CRISIS. Macmillan held office during a period of apparent economic prosperity, although there were some troubling signs in the British economy. In his famous WIND OF CHANGE speech (1960), Macmillan was the first British prime minister to publicly acknowledge and accept the fact that the BRITISH EMPIRE was no longer viable. He presided over the independence of a number of British colonies, mostly in Africa. Widely respected both at home and abroad, Macmillan reestablished good relations with the U.S. after the U.S. rebuke of Britain over the Suez affair. His personal friendships with U.S. Presidents Eisenhower and John F. KENNEDY helped maintain British prestige even after it was clear that Britain was no longer a world power. Macmillan resigned after the PROFUMO AFFAIR brought about domestic criticism of his government. In retirement, Macmillan was revered as an elder statesman. After turning down honors on several occasions, he accepted a life peerage as the Earl of Stockton in 1984.

For further reading:

Horne, Alistair, *Harold Macmillan*, 2 vols. New York: Viking Penguin, 1989.

Macmillan, Kenneth (1929–). British dancer, choreographer and ballet director. Macmillan, one of the major choreographers of the 20th century, began his career as a dancer with Sadler's Wells Theatre Ballet (1946) and Sadler's Wells Ballet (1948). After 1952 he worked for both companies and choreographed his first ballet, *Dances Concertantes,* in 1955. In 1958 he began working with ballerina Lynn Seymour, who became the inspiration for such ballets as *Baiser de la Fee* (1960) and the popular *Romeo and Juliet* (1965). Appointed resident choreographer of the Royal Ballet in 1965, he also served as director of the German Opera Ballet in Berlin from 1966 to 1969. He directed the Royal Ballet from 1970 to 1977, creating such works as the innovative *Anastasia* (1971), *Manon* (1974) and *Elite Syncopations* (1974) for that company. He became artistic associate of AMERICAN BALLET THEATRE in 1984 and has choreographed and staged his ballets for many other companies.

MacNeice, (Frederick) Louis (1907–1963). Anglo-Irish poet, playwright and translator. Born in Belfast, the son of an Anglican bishop, MacNeice attended Marlboro public school in England before going to Oxford in the late 1920s. At Oxford he was a prominent member of W.H. AUDEN'S circle and briefly shared the left-wing sympathies of Auden, Stephen SPENDER and C. DAY LEWIS. Ultimately, however, he was skeptical of all political systems. After graduating with a first in classics, he taught at Birmingham University and at Bedford College, University of London. From 1941 until his death he wrote and produced features, including numerous radio plays, for the BBC. MacNeice's poems view modern urban life through an introspective and ironic sensibility; the often playful lyricism of his work is matched by formal grace, moral intensity and philosophical seriousness. His translations of Aeschylus and Goethe are highly regarded. Somewhat shy, puritanical and conscious of his Northern Irish roots, MacNeice always felt distanced from the English society in which he moved, despite his success. During his lifetime he was overshadowed by Auden, but since his death his work has been reevaluated, and he is now regarded as a major literary figure in his own right, especially in Britain and Ireland. MacNeice's unfinished autobiography, *The Strings Are False,* was published posthumously in 1966, and his *Collected Poems* were issued the following year.

For further reading:

Longley, Edna, *Louis MacNeice: A Study.* London: Faber & Faber, 1989.

Marsack, Robyn, *The Cave of Making: The Poetry of Louis MacNeice.* New York: Oxford University Press, 1982.

Madagascar [Democratic Republic of Madagascar]. Madagascar, which comprises the main island and several smaller islets, is located in the Indian Ocean, off the southeast coast of Africa. France made Madagascar a colony in 1896, but Malagasy resistance flourished, resulting in brutal French suppression of riots in 1898–1904 and 1947–48. The country achieved autonomy in 1958, full independence in 1960. Philibert Tsirinana was president of the First Republic (1960–72) but resigned after protests and economic problems grew. An interim military regime dissolved parliament and closed foreign military bases. The present Democratic Republic was formed in 1975 with Didier Ratsiraka as president. He has moved the country toward socialism, but economic problems, regional rivalries, coup attempts and brutal suppression of demonstrations have plagued his regime. During the kung fu riots (1984, 1985) several people died as the government suppressed the martial arts cult. In 1987 many Indians and Pakistanis left the country in the face of prejudicial attacks.

Maeght, Aime (1906–1981). French printer, art dealer and art promoter. During half a century as an art dealer, Maeght promoted the careers of such leading European artists as Joan MIRO, Alberto GIACOMETTI, Georges BRAQUE and Henri MATISSE. He persuaded many of them to produce lithographs of their work in order to reach a broader public. In 1964 he founded the Foundation Marguerite et Aime Maeght, an innovative museum.

Mafia. Secret society of organized crime. Formed in medieval Sicily to fight French oppression of Italians, the name is an acronym of *Morte alla Francia Italia anela!* (Death to the French is Italy's Cry!). The organization evolved into a strongarm group with considerable local autonomy and assumed its criminal identity in 19th-century Sicily. There, in spite of regular campaigns against it (notably by Benito MUSSOLINI), it came to have the tremendous political and social control that it maintains to this day. The Mafia arrived in the U.S. with Sicilian immigrants in the late 1800s. The first killing in the U.S. that is attributed to the Mafia supposedly occurred in Louisiana in 1889 at the beginning of a waterfront war in New Orleans between Sicilian and Neopolitan gangsters. That war is said to have marked the Mafia's entry into big-time U.S. crime. The organization was soon operating in many large cities, often preying on the Italian immigrant community. During PROHIBITION (1920–33) the Mafia grew enormously, controlling the bootleg liquor business and running such enterprises as prostitution, loansharking, gambling and narcotics. As in Sicily, it has over time also taken control of a number of legitimate businesses in America, although their identity remains shadowy. The U.S. Mafia is comprised of a number of regional "families" operating in recognized territories. The American history of the group includes bloody struggles for the control of families as well as a

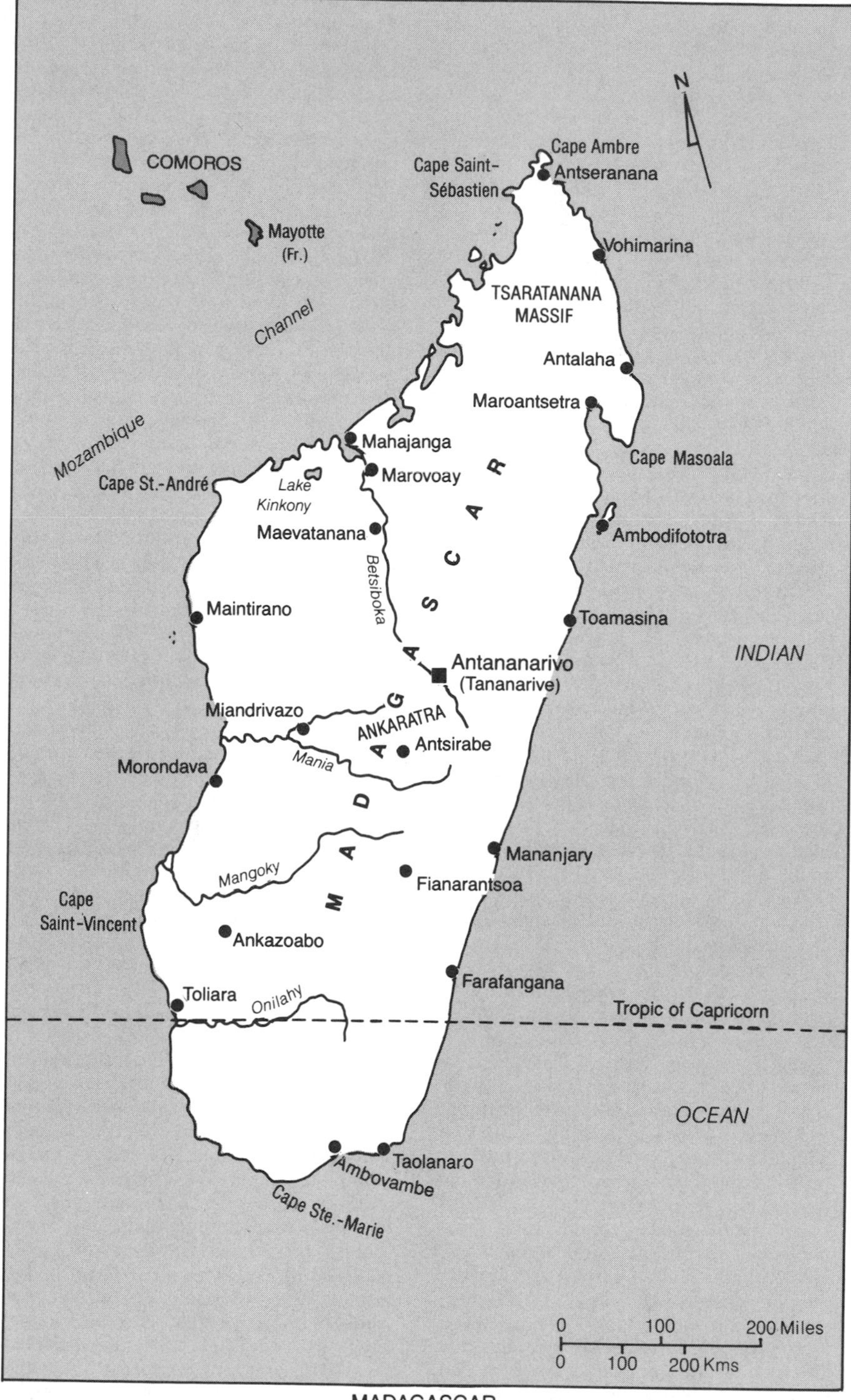

MADAGASCAR

modernization movement, which was largely engineered by "Lucky" LUCIANO, and which brought the Mafia closer to other, non-Italian factions of organized crime. Also referred to as the *Cosa Nostra* (Our Thing), it comprises an estimated 24 families and remains a dominant force in criminal activities in contemporary America.

Magic. Code name for material derived from the breaking of the Japanese diplomatic code, a feat accomplished by American cryptographic experts in 1940. The information produced by the Magic operation was vital to Allied success in a number of areas related to Axis activities. These included data on plans for Japanese KAMIKAZE attacks on U.S. warships, intelligence on German coastal defenses in the event of an Allied invasion of Occupied France, information on the development and locations of Germany's lethal V-2 rockets and facts about the spying activities in the U.S. of Spanish diplomats working for Japan.

For further reading:

Mendelsohn, John, ed., *Ultra, Magic and the Allies.* New York: Garland, 1989.

Magic Mountain, The. The most famous novel (1924) of German author Thomas MANN. Its central protagonist, Hans Castorp, is a young German burgher with solidly bourgeois values who has just completed his college studies and is planning, at the outset of the novel, to embark upon an engineering career. But the course of Castorp's life is changed when he goes to visit his tubercular cousin who is residing in a sanatorium high on a mountain—metaphorically, the "Magic Mountain" of the title. While paying his visit, Castorp himself is diagnosed by a physician as suffering from tuberculosis. As a result, his planned visit of three weeks extends on for seven years. In the course of his stay, Castorp grows spiritually as a result of his new, removed perspective of the world. He and his fellow tuberculosis victims, who engage in protracted philosophical dialogues on the declining state of European civilization, come to symbolize the detached helplessness of Western intellectuals confronted with historical forces that they can dissect and judge but never control. Mann's novel is thus a portrait of the conditions in Europe that led to WORLD WAR II.

magic realism—art. A style of figurative painting prevalent in the U.S. during the 1930s and, to a limited extent, in the 1940s and 1950s. Considerably influenced by the heightened sensibilities and distortions of SURREALISM, it is characterized by subject matter taken from everyday life. These images are elevated to the extraordinary by their portrayal in minutely precise details and excruciatingly brilliant light. Painters drawn to this style include Ivan Le Lorraine ALBRIGHT, Peter Bloom and Philip EVERGOOD. Among later practitioners of magic realism are the painters George TOOKER and Paul Cadmus.

magic realism—literature. Literary movement centered in Latin America. Magic realism is a school of fiction that calls for the narrative intermingling of realistic portrayals of social conditions along with mythic fantasy. A key precursor of magic realism was William FAULKNER, whose novels frequently drew upon the inner dreams and reveries of his characters while providing a detailed and realistic portrait of life in the American South. The generation of Latin American novelists that rose to prominence in the 1960s—notably Miguel Angel ASTURIAS of Guatemala, Julio CORTAZAR of Argentina, Carlos FUENTES of Mexico, Guillermo Cabrera Infante of Cuba and Gabriel GARCIA MARQUEZ of Colombia—became the key proponents of magic realism as a distinct literary school. *One Hundred Years of Solitude* (1970) by Marquez, with its family chronicle structure overlaid with fantasies and dreams, is perhaps the leading exemplar of the methods of magic realism.

Maginot Line. French fortification system running for 200 miles along the Franco-German border from Switzerland to Belgium. Consisting mainly of entrenchments and underground forts, it was built from 1930 to 1934 and was named for Andre Maginot (1877–1932), French minister of war during the first years of its construction. It was built to act as an impregnable barrier to German invasion—built by a militarily and emotionally exhausted France that was intent on using it as a deterrent to avoid another Great War. During WORLD WAR II, this fixed line was easily flanked by German armored forces, which advanced through Belgium in 1940. Its failure led to the fall of FRANCE in May of that year. The Maginot Line has come to be symbolic of fixed defensive positions that are open to mobile attack, and of the false sense of security that such lines can provide.

Magnitogorsk. Town 130 miles southwest of Chelyabinsk, on the Ural River in the Russian Soviet Federated Socialist Republic. It was built 1929–31 under the first FIVE-YEAR PLAN and is an important metallurgical center using magnetite iron ore from nearby Mount Magnitnaya. Other manufactures include machinery, cement, chemicals and clothing. Population (1981): 413,000.

Magritte, Rene (1898–1967). Belgian painter and art theorist. Magritte first won international attention in the 1920s as one of the most original painters in the school of SURREALISM. Heavily influenced by the metaphysical paintings of Giorgio de CHIRICO, Magritte developed a style laden with dreamlike imagery that was quietly poetic in tone, without the violent elements that marked much Surrealist painting of the period. Magritte sometimes painted verbal statements onto his canvasses to accompany his pictorial images, as in the case of his famous painting *The Wind and the Song* (1928–29), which portrays a pipe below which is written *"Ceci n'est pas une pipe"* (This is not a pipe). Other renowned canvasses by Magritte include *The Conqueror* (1925), *The Lovers* (1928) and *The Key of Dreams* (1930).

Mahathir bin Mohammad, Datuk Seri (1925–). Malaysian politician. Dr. Mahathir has served successively as prime minister, minister of home affairs and minister of justice (October 1987). He received a medical degree from the University of Malaya, Singapore, in the early 1950s and then began practice. He entered parliament after the 1964 federal election but lost his seat in the election of 1969. In the aftermath of the May 1969 riots, Dr. Mahathir led the campaign within the United Malays National Organization to force the resignation of Tunku Abdul RAHMAN; he was expelled from UMNO for breach of party discipline. Dr. Mahathir was soon restored to the party and returned to parliament in 1974. He became one of the three vice presidents of UMNO in 1975 and deputy minister in March 1976. He was elected president of the party in June 1981 and became prime minister of MALAYSIA the following month.

Mahfouz, Naguib (1911–). Egyptian novelist, playwright and screenwriter. A prolific author familiar to the Arab-speaking world, Mahfouz was relatively unknown to Westerners when he became the first Arabic writer to receive the NOBEL PRIZE for literature (1988). He first received acclaim for the novel *Madaq Alley* (1947) but is best known for *The Cairo Trilogy* (1956–57). Mahfouz's novels are realistic works generally portraying the lower and middle classes of Cairo. Mahfouz has been criticized in Arabic countries for his moderate stance toward Israel, and his books have been banned by religious leaders for what is perceived as his condemnation of Islam.

Mahler, Gustav (1860–1911). Conductor and composer most famous for his large-scaled, intensely romantic yet intricately-crafted symphonic works. In Arnold SCHOENBERG's words, he was "a man in a torment of emotion exerting himself to gain inner harmony." Born in Kalischt, Bohemia (then part of the Austro-Hungarian Empire), Mahler's musical precocity led to his enrollment in the Vienna Conservatory in 1875. Because his early efforts, including his First Symphony (1889) were rebuffed, he began a successful career as an opera conductor in, successively, Laibach, Olmuetz, Kassel, Prague, Leipzig, Budapest, and Vienna (where he served as Artistic Director at the Imperial Opera from 1897 to 1907). Driven, often ruthless in his quest for perfection, he virtually revolutionized modern operatic production. However, he seemed to live primarily for those times when he could escape the opera stage and spend his summers in Steinbach or Maiernigg or Toblach composing his ten symphonies. These works, in the judgment of historian David Ewen "are the last word in German Romanticism," struggling to convey in tones "the meaning of life and death, of the universe and nature, of eternal love and fate, of suffering, and resignation, and of resurrection." Mahler once told Jean SIBELIUS that "a symphony must embrace the world." His symphonies frequently drew upon songs he had composed to the texts of the Brentano-Arnim German folk poetry collection, *Das Knaben Wunderhorn* (*The Youth's Magic Horn*, 1805–08)—a strange world of talking animals, macabre jests, haunted forests and military marches.

Composer Gustav Mahler, whose immense symphonies reflect the angst of the 20th century.

In 1907 fate delivered three hammer blows to Mahler: the death of his daughter Maria, his departure from the Vienna Opera, and the medical diagnosis of a grave cardiac deficiency. He wrote: "At the end of my life, I must go back to living like a beginner and learn again how to stand." He underwent psychoanalysis with Sigmund FREUD, and in 1908 accepted the post of director of the Metropolitan Opera in New York City. During his few years in New York he conducted exceptional performances of operatic and orchestral works, but he returned to Vienna after wearying of disputes with musicians and with the Metropolitan's board.

In his final years Mahler composed a tryptich of "farewells" to the world—the Ninth Symphony, fragments of the Tenth Symphony, and the magnificent orchestral song-cycle, *Das Lied von der Erde* (*The Song of the Earth*, 1908). Set to texts by ancient Chinese poets, the work concludes with the famous "Der Abschied" ("The Farewell") to which Mahler penned these lines of his own: "My heart is peaceful, awaiting its hour. . . The beloved earth everywhere flowers and becomes green again." The final page, one of the most astonishing pages in all music, features an endless repetition by the voice of "Ewig" ("Forever") to a diaphanous background of clesta, flute and oboe. Mahler did not live to hear this work; and, acording to his wishes, not a word was spoken nor a note sung at his burial.

In the decades after his death, Mahler's music was championed by his main disciple, conductor Bruno WALTER and by a few others. However, his symphonies did not gain a secure place in the repertory until the 1960s, when Leonard BERNSTEIN's interpretations received wide critical and popular acclaim.

For further reading:

Mitchell, Donald, *Gustav Mahler*. Berkeley: University of California Press, 1980.

Mahler, Margaret S. (1897–1985). Hungarian-born American psychiatrist. She was clinical professor of psychiatry at Albert Einstein College of Medicine from 1955 until 1974. Her pioneering research into the psychological development of very young children led her to the conclusion that the foundation for adult character structure was laid in the first three years of life. These ideas were summarized in her 1976 book, *The Psychological Birth of the Human*.

Mahon, Derek (1941–). Northern Irish poet, editor screenwriter and translator; widely considered the direct successor to Louis MACNEICE. Born in Belfast, Mahon read classics at Trinity College, Dublin. He was later poetry editor for the *New Statesman* in London. His work reflects a profound historical awareness of the ironies of 20th-century existence. Technically, his poetry achieves a formal grace and perfection matched by few other poets of this century. Mahon's books include *Poems 1962–1978* (1979), *The Hunt By Night* (1982), *Antarctica* (1985) and *Selected Poems* (1991).

Mailer, Norman (1923–). American novelist, story writer, essayist and journalist. Mailer is one of the most acclaimed and controversial American writers of the postwar era. Raised in a Jewish family in Brooklyn, Mailer was educated at Harvard University and served in the U.S. Army during World War II. He drew upon his experiences of combat to write his acclaimed first novel, *The Naked and the Dead* (1948). Mailer's next two novels, *Barbary Shore* (1951) and *The Deer Park* (1955), were less successful with the critics and the public, but his essay *The White Negro* (1957) won praise as an astute analysis of race relations and alienation in America; it also revealed Mailer's affinity with the BEAT GENERATION. In the 1960s, his most important work was *The Armies of the Night* (1968)—an example of NEW JOURNALISM that earned Mailer a PULITZER PRIZE. His many subsequent works include *The Prisoner of Sex* (1971), an analysis of FEMINISM from the male perspective; *The Executioner's Song* (1979), a study of death-row prisoner Gary Gilmore that garnered Mailer a second Pulitzer Prize; and *Ancient Evenings* (1985), a historical novel set in Dynastic Egypt. Active in the ANTIWAR MOVEMENT during the VIETNAM WAR, Mailer has been involved in other liberal and radical causes. His stormy personal life has brought him much attention in newspaper gossip columns, but whether his work will have lasting literary value is a matter of debate.

Maillart, Robert (1872–1940). Swiss structural engineer. His work in reinforced concrete structures, particularly bridges, made Maillart one of the very few engineers to become internationally famous for the aesthetic qualities of his work. He was trained at the Zurich Technical College and worked for several established engineering firms before setting up his own practice in 1902. He became a specialist in the design of concrete bridges, designing more than 40 of increasingly elegant modernist form. The most famous of his works, all in Switzerland, are the Val Tschiel Bridge, near Donath (1952); the spectacularly beautiful Salginatobel Bridge with a 295-foot span and three-hinged arch, near Schiers (1929–30); the curving Schwandbach Bridge (1933); the bridge over the Thus, near Felsegg (1933); and the Arve Bridge at Vessy, Geneva (1936). Many of Maillart's bridges are in obscure places where local authorities were willing to accept his dramatically simple designs. Maillart also designed various other structures.

Controversial American author Norman Mailer, whose personal life has on occasion overshadowed his literary works.

Maillol, Aristide (1861–1944). French sculptor and graphic artist. He began as a painter, studying at the Ecole des Beaux-Arts in Paris. By 1903 he was associated with the Nabis. Maillol began to sculpt sometime between 1895 and 1900. His first sculptures were small-scale figures in wood or ceramic, but he quickly began much larger projects. His characteristic sculptures are larger-than-life female nudes—massive, idealized and sensuous. Strongly influenced by the classical Greek ideal, his style crystallized during a 1908 trip to Greece. At once strong and langorous, smoothly modeled and beautifully balanced, his nudes are often cast in bronze. Among his typical sculptures are *The River* (c. 1901, Museum of Modern Art, New York City) and *Pomona* (1910, Tuileries, Paris). Maillol is also known for the flowing linear quality of his woodcuts, many of which illustrated classical Greek and Roman poetry.

Majdanek. Site of a Nazi CONCENTRATION CAMP, located near Lublin, Poland, during WORLD WAR II. Jews, Poles, Russians and other people from Nazi-occupied Europe were sent to Majdanek during the early 1940s; as many as 1.5 million were killed in the camp's gas chambers.

Majlis [Iranian National Consultative Assembly]. Chief legislative body in IRAN under the shahs. The last shah dissolved the assembly in 1961, after it refused to pass his land reforms.

Major, John (1943–). British politician, prime minister of the UNITED KINGDOM (1990–). A quiet figure from a humble background, John Major seemed the least likely candidate to rise to the leadership of the CONSERVATIVE PARTY and the prime ministership. Born into a lower-middle-class family, he was raised in Brixton, a run-down district of London. He left school at 16 in order to help support his family and never attended university. He held a variety of odd jobs, including clerk, cement mixer and bus conductor. He also experienced unemployment and spent several months on the dole. Major's fortunes changed when he obtained a job with the district bank; he decided to pursue a career in banking and quickly gained his professional qualifications. He joined Standard Chartered Bank in 1965 and became an assistant to the bank's chairman,

British Prime Minister John Major, the youngest person to hold that position in the 20th century (1990).

who later served as chancellor of the Exchequer in the cabinet of Edward HEATH. Major entered politics in the late 1960s, serving in local government in South London from 1968 to 1971. An unsuccessful candidate for Parliament in 1974, he was elected to the House of Commons in the 1979 general election that swept Margaret THATCHER and the Conservatives into power. As a backbencher, he drew the notice of Thatcher, who made him a junior minister for social security (1986) and then chief secretary of the Treasury (1987). In June 1989 Major replaced Geoffrey HOWE as foreign secretary. Three months later Thatcher named him chancellor of the Exchequer upon the resignation of Chancellor Nigel Lawson. Conservative members of Parliament elected Major as party leader after Margaret Thatcher announced her resignation in November 1990. Major thus became, at age 47, the youngest British prime minister of the 20th century and the first postwar leader of a major country who did not have any personal memory of World War II. Some critics questioned whether he had sufficient experience to succeed; other observers, however, felt that his background would make him more sensitive to the everyday problems of ordinary people than Thatcher had seemed to be. He was expected to follow many of her policies but to take a more conciliatory view on several major issues, including the controversial community charge (poll tax) and the proposed monetary union with Europe. Major strongly supported the U.N. coalition action against IRAQ in the PERSIAN GULF WAR.

Makarios III (1913–1977). Archbishop of the Orthodox Church of Cyprus and president of the Republic of CYPRUS. The son of a poor shepherd, he studied theology in GREECE and the United States. Ordained in 1946, he became bishop of Kition in 1948 and archbishop in 1950. A leader in the struggle for ENOSIS (union) with Greece, he was elected president of Cyprus in 1959, 1968 and again in 1973. He survived several assassination attempts and a 1974 coup that resulted in a five-month exile in MALTA and the UNITED KINGDOM. He was unable to prevent Turkish occupation of much of northern Cyprus.

Makarov, Oleg (1933–). Soviet cosmonaut and design engineer. Encouraged by the experience of his friend and fellow design-engineer Konstantin Feoktistov in Voskhod 1, Makarov, of Sergei KOROLEV's design bureau, also applied to fly in space. As a result, he became one of the steady players in the Soviet program, making four flights in the position of flight engineer between 1973 and 1980. His first flight, aboard Soyuz 12 (September 1973) with Vasily Lazarev, was the first to follow after the tragedy of Soyuz 11, during which three cosmonauts suffocated because a valve leaked during reentry (to allow enough room for three they had worn no space suits). Makarov and Lazarev wore space suits in the redesigned Soyuz and their brief two-day mission went smoothly. Paired off again with Lazarev, Makarov was to visit Salyut 4 in a 60–day mission two years later. But luck was not with them; their Soyuz 18–A booster aborted shortly after launch on April 5, 1975. Their command module separated from the booster and careened back to Earth, landing the two in the mountains near the Chinese border. As the Soyuz plunged downward, the cosmonauts endured an agonizing pressure of 18 Gs, which may have caused internal injuries.

Makarov made it back onto the flight docket, and three years later he and Vladimir DZHANIBEKOV took Soyuz 27 (January 1978) up to the Salyut 6 space station that Makarov had helped design. After their one-week visit with Yuri Romanenko and Georgy Grechko, who were on a 30–day mission there, they returned in Romanenko and Grechko's Soyuz 26 spacecraft, leaving the fresh vehicle at the space station. November 1980 saw Makarov back at Salyut 6, this time on a repair mission with fellow cosmonauts Leonid Kizim and Gennady Strekalov. After 13 days, they had the station ready for its next long-duration crew, returning aboard their Soyuz T-3 craft, recently redesigned to accommodate three cosmonauts.

Speculation has it that, had the Soviets continued their lunar program, Makarov would have walked on the moon, but even without that opportunity, he made significant contributions as a cosmonaut and as senior engineer at the spacecraft bureau.

Makarov, Stepan Osipovich (1848–1904). Russian admiral in charge of defense during the RUSSO-JAPANESE WAR. Makarov went down with his flagship, the *Petropavlovsk*, outside Port Arthur.

Makarova, Natalia (1940–). Russian-born ballerina. After studying at the Kirov Ballet School in Leningrad, Makarova joined the Kirov Ballet Company in 1959. She won a gold medal at the Varna Ballet competition in 1965. In 1970 she chose to stay in the West at the conclusion of the Kirov's European tour and joined AMERICAN BALLET THEATRE that same year, making her debut in *Giselle*. Noted for an elegant style and expressiveness, her Giselle is considered the finest of the 1970s and early 1980s. She has been a guest artist with companies worldwide, most especially with the ROYAL BALLET in Britain. She has received acclaim for her dancing in such modern ballets as Antony TUDOR's *Jardin aux Lilas* and *Dark Elegies* as well as for the classical repertory.

Maklakov, Vasily Alexandrovich (1870–1957). Russian liberal and lawyer. A member of the second, third and fourth dumas, he acted as counsel for the defense for political cases during the 1905 Revolution. A member of the Constitutional Democratic Party, he was appointed ambassador to France by the provisional government in 1917. He subsequently acted as leader of the Russian emigres in Paris.

Malamud, Bernard (1914–1986). U.S. author. He was regarded as one of the most distinctive Jewish literary voices in postwar America. His works often reflected a concern with Jewish values and a belief in the nobility of ordinary people. His first novel, *The Natural*—an allegorical tale about the rise and fall of a baseball player—was published in 1952. Later novels included *The Assistant* (1957), *The Fixer* (1966) and *The Tenants* (1971). Some of his best-known short stories appeared in the collections *The Magic Barrel* (1958) and *Idiots First* (1963).

American author Bernard Malamud, whose novels explore the trials and tribulations of common people.

Malan, Daniel F(rancois) (1874–1959). South African political leader, prime minister of SOUTH AFRICA (1948–54). Trained as a clergyman, Malan was a pastor in the Dutch Reformed Church until World War I, when he became an editor of an Afrikaner nationalist newspaper. He officially entered politics in 1918 as a Nationalist member of Parliament and served as minister of the interior, public health and education in the government of J.B.M. Hertzog (1924–33). When the National Party won the 1940 election Malan became prime minister. In that office he was one of the main architects of APARTHEID. Fighting any movement toward racial integration, he urged the development of segregated black "homelands." Malan retired in 1954.

Malawi [Republic of Malawi]. Malawi covers an area of 45,735 square miles in southeast Africa. Originally a British colony known as Nyasaland (1907–53), the country joined Northern and Southern Rhodesia to form the Central African Federation (1953–63), before achieving independence in 1964. The country became a part of the COMMONWEALTH as the Republic of Malawi and elected Dr. Hastings Kamuzu BANDA president in 1966 (became president for life in 1971). Suspicions concerning the Banda government's responsibility for assassinations of opposition leaders living in Zimbabwe, as well as the deaths of possible successors, have been rampant. Tensions with Mozambique over Malawi's supposed aid to Mozambique rebel groups surfaced in the 1980s but were resolved in 1988.

Malaysia [Federation of Malaysia]. Comprising a total land area of 127,225 square miles in Southeast Asia, Malaysia consists of two separate sections, East (Sarawak and Sabah on the island of Bor-

MALAYSIA

1914	Britain gains control of Malay Peninsula.
1942	(February) Singapore falls to the Japanese.
1957	(Aug. 31) Malaya granted independence from Britain.
1963	(September) Malaya, Singapore, Sarawak and North Borneo join together to form the state of Malaysia.
1965	(Aug.) Singapore leaves the federation.
1969	(May) Race riots between Chinese and Malays break out and state of emergency is declared.
1981	Datuk Seri Dr. Mahathir Mohamad of the United Malays National Organization Party is elected prime minister.
1990	(Oct. 21) Mahathir is reelected.

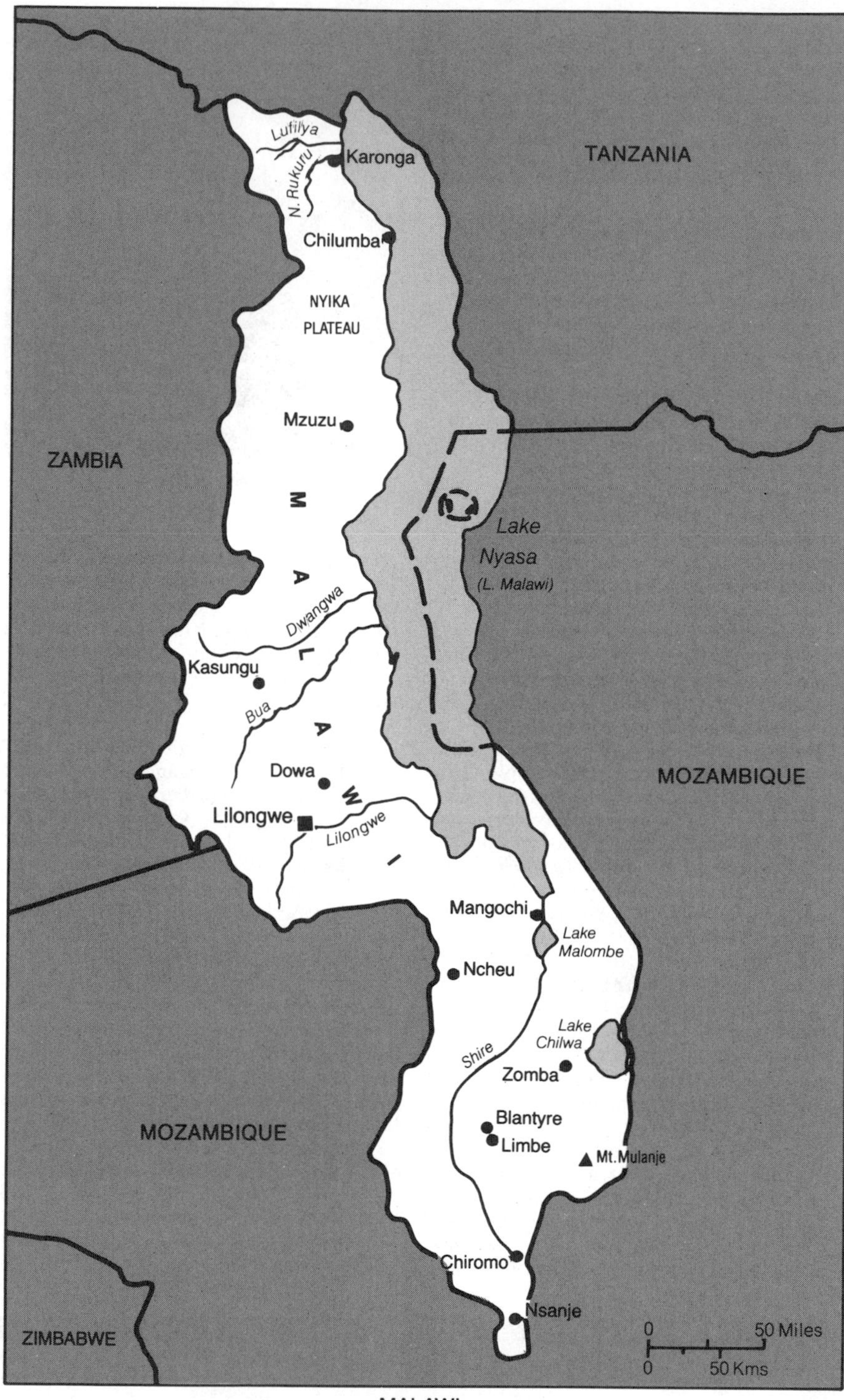

MALAWI

neo) and West Malaysia. In 1896 the states of Perak, Selangor, Negri Semilan and Pahang were united to form the Federated Malay States under British rule; by 1914 the remaining Malay states came under British control. Invaded by Japan in 1942, Malaysia returned to British control in 1946, then formalized its federation status in 1948. The country achieved independence in 1957 as the Federation of Malaysia. Tensions between the Malay population and the increasing number of Chinese and Indian immigrants led to political and economic unrest, resulting in declarations of a state of emergency in 1948 and again in 1969. Economic and human rights reforms have alleviated some problems, but opposition groups continued to press for more political freedom during the 1980s.

Malcolm X [born Malcolm Little] (1925–1965). American black militant. Born in Omaha, Nebraska, he moved east at 16, settled in New York City and became involved in the crime of Harlem's underworld. In prison from 1946 to 1952, he was impressed with the writings of Elijah MUHAMMAD and, after his release, joined the BLACK MUSLIM movement. Rejecting his "slave name," he changed it to Malcolm X, embraced black separatism and supported armed self-defense. Highly intelligent and a fiery orator, he quickly became the movement's foremost spokesman, winning it a host of new members. When an ideological split between Malcolm and Muhammad caused Malcolm's suspension as a minister in 1963, the firebrand left the Nation of Islam. Making the pilgrimage to Mecca in 1964, he proclaimed his conversion to orthodox Islam and founded a rival group, the Organization for Afro-American Unity. Forsaking the doctrine of racial separation, Malcolm advocated the struggle for radical social reform. In February 1965 he was shot and killed while addressing a public meeting in New York by assassins alleged to be Black Muslims. His book, *The Autobiography of Malcolm X* (dictated to Alex HALEY, 1964), has become an American literary and sociological classic.

Maldives. The Maldive archipelago comprises some 1,190 islands (202 of which are inhabited) in a chain of 20 coral atolls, covering an area of 116 square miles; in the Indian Ocean over 400 miles southwest of Sri Lanka. Protected from monsoon devastation by barrier reefs (faros), none of the islands rises above 5 ft. in elevation. Settled by its original Dravidian inhabitants perhaps as early as the 4th century B.C., the Maldives became a British protectorate in December 1887. The powers of the sultans were circumscribed by provisions of a 1932 constitution, and a short-lived modernizing regime set up a republic (1953–54)—before a coup restored the sultanate. Ibrahim NASIR, prime minister to the last of the sultans (from 1957) and effective leader of the country at the time of independence (July 26, 1965), became president when a referendum approved a republican constitution (November 11, 1968). He strengthened the powers of the presidency (1975) but then stood down and left the country (1978); Maumoon Abdul GAYOOM was elected to succeed him. Reelected for successive presidential terms (1983, 1988), Gayoom survived three attempted coups (1980, 1981, 1988), in each of which he saw the hand of his predecessor Nasir. The 1988 coup was suppressed only when Indian troops were dispatched to defeat the mercenaries, who apparently came from Sri Lanka. Meanwhile, Gayoom confirmed a nonaligned foreign policy practiced by his predecessor, who in 1957 had rejected a Soviet bid to lease the island of Gan. The Maldives joined the COMMONWEALTH as a special status member (July 1982) and became a full member on June 20, 1985.

Malenkov, Georgi Maximillianovich (1902–1988). Soviet politician. Malenkov succeeded STALIN as premier in March 1953 and was also, very briefly, first secretary of the COMMUNIST PARTY. He was alleged to have played a key role in the Stalinist purges in which millions of So-

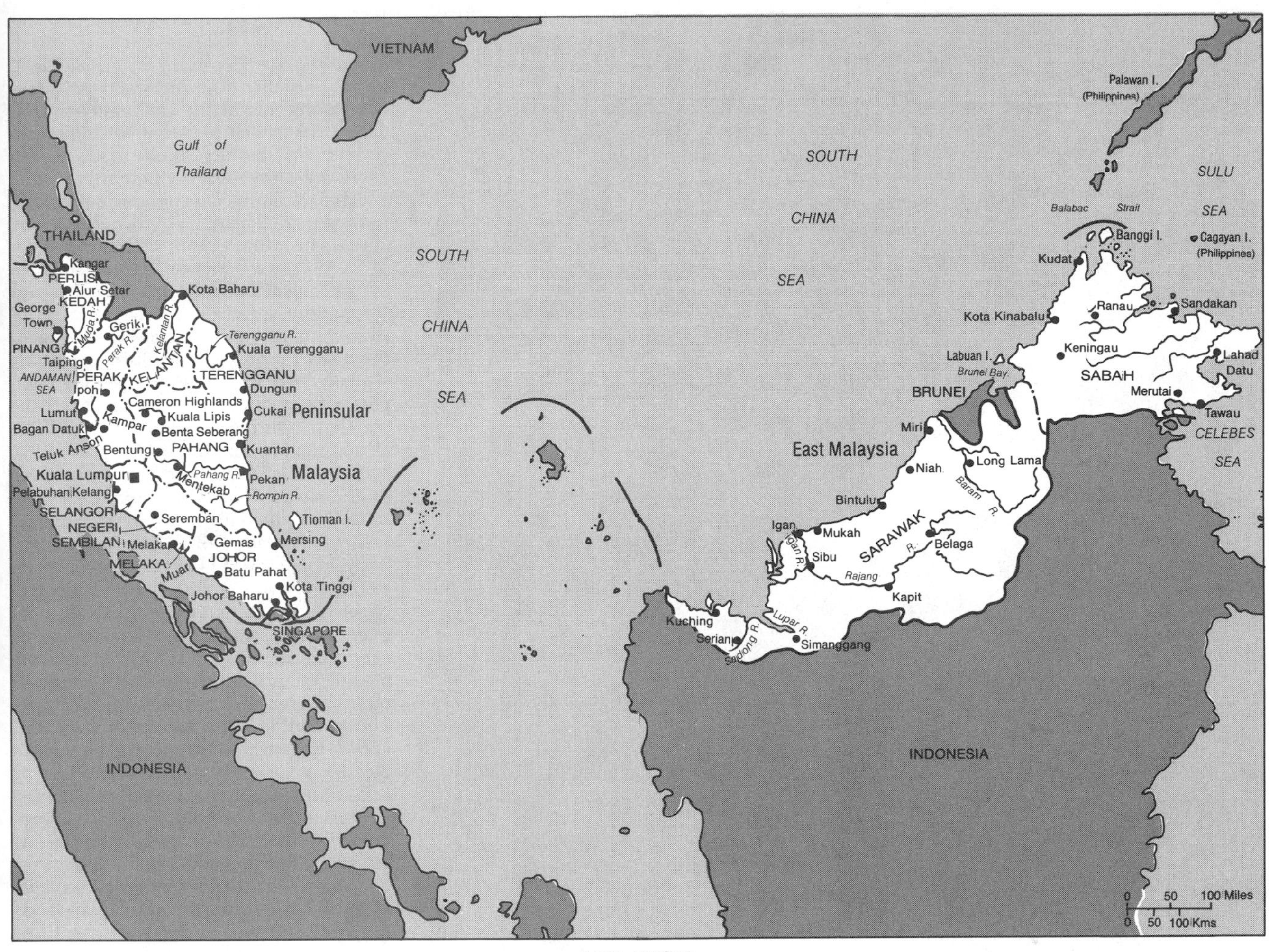

MALAYSIA

viet citizens died. His premiership was marked by a somewhat more conciliatory attitude toward the West and by attempts to increase the production of consumer goods. Nikita KHRUSHCHEV forced him from power in 1955. In 1957, Malenkov was removed from all important posts and banished to remote Kazakhstan in Central Asia to manage a hydroelectric plant.

Malevich, Kazimir (1878–1935). Russian artist, one of the first abstract painters. Influenced by IMPRESSIONISM, FAUVISM and CUBISM, in 1913 Malevich evolved his own abstract geometrical style, known as SUPREMATISM, in which only geometrical elements were used in construction. After teaching painting from 1919 to 1921 in Moscow and Leningrad, he traveled to Weimar, where he met Wassily KANDINSKY, and published his *The Non-Objective World.* Among his best-known paintings is the famous *White Square on a White Background.* Unfortunately his work met with official disapproval, and Malevich died in poverty in 1935.

Mali [Republic of Mali]. The landlocked country of Mali is located in western Africa and covers an area of 478,640 square miles. A French colony originally known as French Soudan (1920–58), the country was renamed the Sudanese Republic in 1958 and became an autonomous state within the FRENCH COMMUNITY. It united with the Republic of SENEGAL to form the Federation of Mali in 1959. When the federation became independent in 1960, Senegal seceded, and the Republic of Mali was declared. The first president, Modibo Keita, consolidated power in a one-party system but was overthrown in 1968 in a peaceful army coup. The new leader, General Moussa Traore, has maintained power by suppressing all protests. A brief war (December 25–29, 1985) with BURKINA FASO over a disputed border was resolved in 1986.

Malik, Charles Habib (1906–1987). Lebanese diplomat. A Greek Orthodox Christian, he helped draft LEBANON's 1943 constitution granting political hegemony to the Christian community. He was one of the last surviving signatories of the UNITED NATIONS Charter, which he helped draft in 1945. In 1958 and 1959 he was president of the United Nations General Assembly and was Lebanese ambassador to the U.S. (1953–55) and foreign minister (1956–58).

Malik, Yakov A(leksandrovich) (1906–1980). Soviet diplomat. During his career Malik served as the U.S.S.R.'s ambassador to the UNITED NATIONS (1948–52, 1968–76) and deputy foreign minister. He joined the COMMUNIST PARTY in 1938 and played a key role in negotiating the terms that ended the Berlin blockade in 1949 (see BERLIN AIRLIFT). He is best remembered, however, for the decision to boycott the U.N. Security Council in 1950. When the KOREAN WAR broke out, the U.S. took advantage of his absence to persuade the Council to send U.N. forces to SOUTH KOREA. A year later, Malik proposed a Korean truce; this led to talks between the two sides and an eventual cease-fire in 1953. Malik was regarded as one of his country's leading experts on the West. (See also COLD WAR.)

Malina, Frank J. (1912–1981). U.S. rocket pioneer and aeronautical engineer; his pioneering work on solid-fuel rockets helped set the stage for early U.S. rocket development. With aerodynamicist Theodore von KARMAN, Malina helped found what is now NASA's JET PROPULSION LABORATORY in California in the late 1930s. They researched high-altitude rockets and during WORLD WAR II they worked on jet-assisted takeoff (JATO) for propeller airplanes, using the same rocket principles. In 1945 von Karman and Malina tested

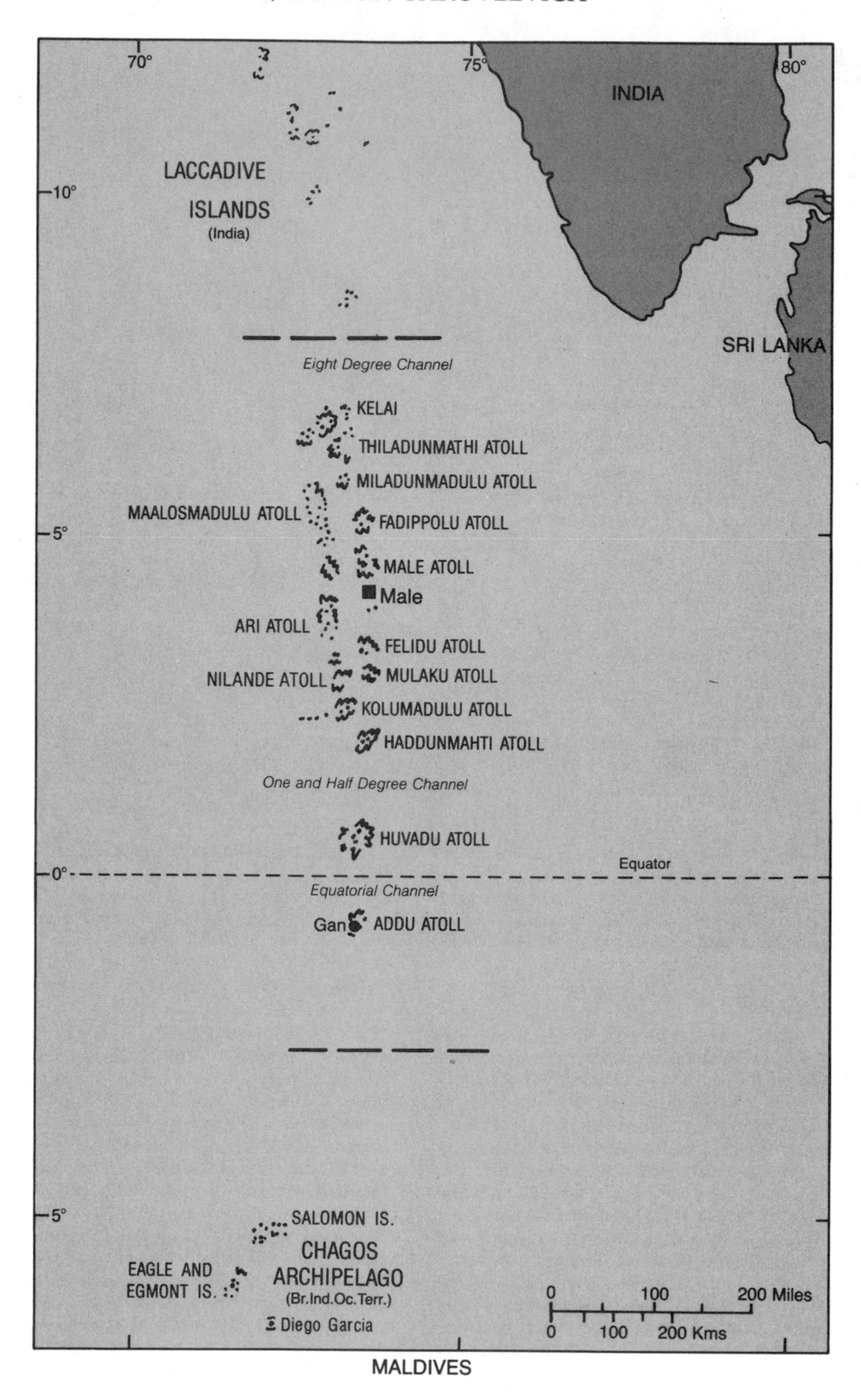

MALDIVES

the first WAC Corporal rocket, which they had designed for use as a high-altitude sounding rocket. It was one of the early predecessors of space-age rocket power in the U.S. Malina later left JPL to become head of the scientific research division of UNESCO in France, where he died.

Malinovsky, Rodion Yakovlevich (1898–1967). Soviet marshal. Having served with the French army in WORLD WAR I and having fought in the RUSSIAN CIVIL WAR, Malinovsky joined the party in 1926. In 1930 he graduated from the M.V. Frunze Military Academy. During WORLD WAR II, he proved to be a distinguished commander during the STALINGRAD offensive (1942). He then led the Southwest Army Group (1943) and the Second Ukrainian Army Group (1944), which occupied Rumania and Hungary. In 1945 he liberated Czechoslovakia and commanded the Transbaikalian Army Group in the brief war against Japan; in 1945–46 he commanded the Soviet forces in Manchuria. A candidate member of the party's central committee from 1952, in 1957 he was appointed minister of defense.

Malinowski, Bronislaw (1884–1942). Polish-born British anthropologist. Malinowski studied at the University of Cracow, from which he received a Ph.D. in physics and mathematics in 1908, as well as at the University of Leipzig and the London School of Economics. He performed field research in Africa, Melanesia and Mexico, and taught at the University of London from 1924 to 1942, in addition to lecturing at universities in America and throughout Europe. A brilliant descriptive ethnographer, Malinowski originated the theory of "functionalism," that is, that a culture should be studied as a complex whole that functions to satisfy its members' primary biological needs. He also argued against the judgmental 19th-century view that placed various cultures on a developmental ladder ranging from "savagery" to "civilization."

Mallard. Famous British railway locomotive. The *Mallard*, a blue streamlined steam locomotive, was designed by Sir Herbert Nigel GRESLEY in the late 1930s and remains the fastest railway steam engine ever built. In 1938, on the *Flying Scotsman* passenger run from London to Edinburgh, it reached a speed of 126 mph. The *Mallard* is now displayed at the National Railway Museum in York, England.

Malle, Louis (1932–). French motion picture director who sprang from the generation of the NOUVELLE VAGUE in the late 1950s. Unlike many of his colleagues—TRUFFAUT, GODARD, CHABROL, Rivette, Vadim—Malle has never stopped working and continues to make films of enormous variety and consistent quality. After studying at the Jesuit College at Fontainebleau he turned to filmmaking in 1951–52 and codirected with Jacques COUSTEAU the classic underwater documentary, *Le Monde de Silence* (*The Silent World*, 1956). His *Ascenseur pour l'Echafaud* (*Elevator to the Gallows*, 1957) and *Les Amants* (*The Lovers*, 1958) are regarded as early expressions of that movement, but Malle's work is difficult to categorize. While his color film *Zazie dans le Metro* (1960) is full of hijinks and chases, *Le Feu Follet* (*The Fire Within*, 1963), is a harrowing depiction in black-and-white of the last hours of a suicidal alcoholic. On the one hand, he closely observes contemporary life and poverty in his documentary *Calcutta* (1969), and on the other, lovingly recreates the period charm of the 19th century in *Viva Maria* (1965) and *Le Voleur* (*The Thief of Paris*, 1967). His controversial American film *Pretty Baby* (1978) is full of the lush imagery and sensuality of the New Orleans brothels; *My Dinner with Andre* (1981) explores the tensions between the imagination and reality in a dinner conversation between an intense theater director and a down-to-earth playwright. Malle's masterpiece is the autobiographical *Au Revoir, les Enfants* (*Farewell, Children*, 1988), a closely observed, poignant memoir of children growing up in Nazi-occupied Paris during World War II. "Of the New

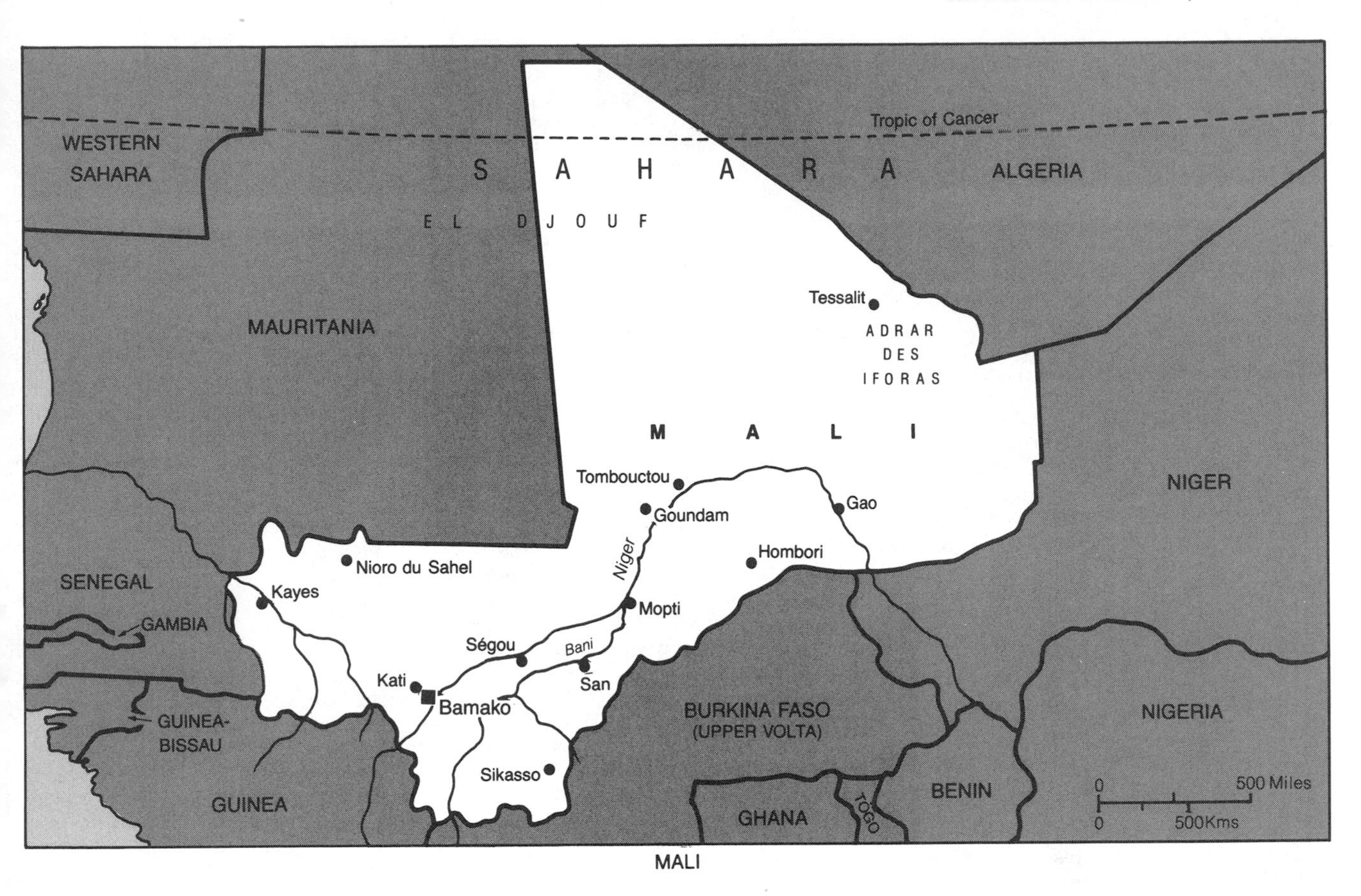

MALI

Wave survivors," writes historian John Baxter, "he is the most old-fashioned, the most erotic, and, arguably, the most widely successful."

Mallet-Stevens, Robert (1886–1945). French designer of furniture and architectural interiors, an important figure in the development of MODERNISM of the 1920s and 1930s. Mallet-Stevens was a student of the Ecole Speciale d'Architecture from 1905 to 1910 and an admirer of the work of such pioneers as Charles Rennie MACKINTOSH and Josef HOFFMANN. Beginning in 1912 he produced furniture and interiors in an early modern style, and his work gradually moved toward the modernism of the de STIJL movement with similarities to the early efforts of LE CORBUSIER. He designed pavilions for the Paris exhibitions of 1929 and 1937. Mallet-Stevens was a frequent contributor to journals dealing with modern design and wrote a book on modern stained glass.

Mallett, Jane (1899–1984). Canadian actress and comedienne. Mallett's career spanned nearly 60 years. Mallett played a leading role in the development of Canadian theater, film, radio and television and was active in major theatrical and broadcasting unions. In 1975 she received the Order of Canada and became one of the first to be awarded honorary membership in the newly independent Canadian Actors' Equity.

Malone, Richard Sankey (1909–1985). Canadian journalist. During his military career, Malone was one of the few members of the Allied forces to serve in all theaters of WORLD WAR II. He created the Canadian Army's public relations service and its newspaper, *The Maple Leaf.* He began as assistant general manager at the *Winnipeg Free Press* (FP) in 1936 and eventually became its publisher and editor in chief. From that base, he built the FP chain, acquiring newspapers throughout CANADA. Malone was publisher and editor in chief of one of FP's purchases, the *Toronto Globe and Mail,* from 1974 to 1978.

Malraux, Andre (1901–1976). French novelist, art critic, essayist and government minister. Malraux was a major figure in French letters and culture in this century. He began his career as a world traveler with leftist political leanings. Malraux participated in revolutionary activities in CHINA in the 1920s and fought on the Loyalist side in the SPANISH CIVIL WAR in the 1930s. His experiences in China were reflected in his first novel, *The Conquerors* (1928), as well as in his most famous novel, *Man's Fate* (1933). A subsequent novel, *Man's Hope* (1938), drew from his experiences in Spain. Malraux was a leader of the French RESISTANCE during WORLD WAR II and became a close associate of Charles DE GAULLE, who later named Malraux minister of culture (1959–69). *The Voices of Silence* (1951) is Malraux's major work of art criticism. *Antimemoirs* (1967) is his autobiography.

Malta [Republic of Malta]. Located in the central Mediterranean Sea, Malta consists of the islands of Malta, Gozo, Comino and the uninhabited islets of Cominotto, Filfa and St. Paul; total land area of 122 square miles. Governed by Great Britain since 1800, the ancient island was claimed by Italy during WORLD WAR II and endured heavy bombing by the Axis powers. Malta was granted self-government by Britain in 1947 and achieved full independence in 1964, though still maintaining defense and economic ties with Britain. The country became a republic within the COMMONWEALTH in 1974. Of strategic importance due to its proximity to the Suez Canal, Malta hosted British and NATO forces (1972–79), then proclaimed its neutrality and nonalignment (1979–80). During the presidency of Dom Mintoff (1971–84) Malta established relations with several communist and Arab countries.

Maltese Falcon, The (1929). American detective novel subsequently adapted into three different film versions for HOLLYWOOD. *The Maltese Falcon,* written by the renowned American mystery author Dashiell HAMMETT, has remained immensely popular with readers due its chiselled, laconic dialogue full of a wit and intelligence that was new to the mystery genre. Hollywood producers were naturally drawn to the novel, but the first two film adaptations—*The Maltese Falcon* (1931) and *Satan Met a Lady* (1936)—are eminently forgettable. The 1941 film version, written and directed by John HUSTON and starring Humphrey BOGART as detective Sam Spade, has become a classic and is regarded as one of the earliest examples of FILM NOIR. The basic plot of *The Maltese Falcon*—as Hammett wrote it and Huston adapted it—concerns the elusive quest for a black statue of a falcon that is filled with priceless jewels. Sam Spade is a tough, worldly-wise cynic who fends off the lies of seductive Brigid O'Shaughnessy (played by Mary Astor in the film) and the evil of the Fat Man (portrayed by Sydney Greenstreet) to solve the paradoxical mystery of the falcon while avenging the murder of his partner.

Malvinas. Spanish name for the FALKLAND ISLANDS, a British territory claimed by ARGENTINA and the scene of armed conflict between that country and Britain (1981) in which the latter was victorious. (See also FALKLANDS WAR.)

Malyshkin, Alexander Georgyevich (1892–1938). Soviet writer. After studying at St. Petersburg University, Malyshkin took part in the 1917 Revolution, joined the Red Army in 1918 and in 1920 was involved in the liberation of the Crimea. His first stories expose the injustices of the autocratic regime, but his *The Fall of Daiv* describes the Red Army. His best-known work is the novel *People from the Back of Beyond* (1937–38).

Mamet, David (1947–). American playwright. One of the finest contemporary dramatists, Mamet is particularly known for his dialogue. He taught theater at several universities, including the Yale School of Drama (1976–77), and was founder-director of the avant-garde St. Nicholas Theatre Company of Chicago (1973–76). His plays are frequently set in Chicago and focus on the underbelly of society (con artists, drifters) and the crucial interpersonal relationships that hold life together. He was greatly influenced by the improvisational comedy of the Second City Cabaret (in Chicago) where he worked for a while. Major plays include *Sexual Perversity in Chicago* (1975), *American Buffalo* (1976), *A Life in the Theatre* (1977), *Glengarry Glen Ross* (1984), for which he received the PULITZER PRIZE, and *Speed-the-Plow* (1987). Mamet has also made his mark as a screenwriter with such films as *The Verdict* (1982) and *The Untouchables* (1987).

For further reading:

Carroll, Dennis, *David Mamet*. New York: St. Martin's Press, 1987.

Mamoulian, Rouben (Zachary) (1898–1987). Russian-born film and stage director. Trained under VAKHTANGOV and STANISLAVSKY at the Moscow Art Theatre, he immigrated to America in 1926 and directed many notable plays for the Theatre Guild, including DuBose Heyward's *Porgy* (1927). He later directed the premiere of George GERSHWIN's operatic version, *Porgy and Bess* (1935). His first talking films for PARAMOUNT PICTURES, *Applause* (1929) and *City Streets* (1931), were acclaimed among the most innovative sound films of the day. In fact, all of his best films were distinguished by the imaginative use of image and sound—especially the horror classic *Dr. Jekyll and Mr. Hyde* (1932), the Jeanette MacDonald-Maurice Chevalier musical *Love Me Tonight* (1932), *Queen Christina* (with Greta GARBO, 1933) and the Technicolor *Becky Sharp* (1935). Mamoulian periodically returned to the Broadway stage, directing the premieres of such landmark productions as *Oklahoma* (1943), *Carousel* (1945) and *Lost in the Stars* (1949). His later films included *Summer Holiday* (1948), a musical version of Eugene O'NEILL's *Ah, Wilderness!*; and *Silk Stockings* (1957), a remake of *Ninotchka* starring Fred ASTAIRE.

For further reading:

Milne, Tom, *Mamoulian*. Bloomington: Indiana University Press, 1969.

Manchukuo. Name of the Japanese puppet state in Chinese MANCHURIA from 1932 to 1945. The Japanese had long coveted Manchuria, with its rich natural resources and raw materials. They seized the province with little resistance in the early 1930s while CHINA was in political turmoil (see CHINESE CIVIL WAR OF 1930–34). Henry PU-YI, who had been the last Manchu emperor of China, was installed as formal ruler of Manchukuo, but real power rested with the Japanese. Few governments recognized Manchukuo as an independent state, and it was returned to Chinese rule after WORLD WAR II.

Manchuria. Located in northeastern China, Manchuria became a part of China in 1903 and has been an autonomous area within China since 1924. Both Russia and Japan have dominated Manchuria at various times. In 1931 Japan seized several Manchurian cities and created the puppet state of MANCHUKUO, controlling the region until the end of WORLD WAR II. Soviet troops occupied Manchuria from August 1945 to April 1946. The Chinese communists gained control of Manchuria during the Chinese civil war (1945–49). Since the formation of the People's Republic of China (1949), relations with the Soviet Union have been tense, and both countries continue to keep troops massed along the Manchurian border.

Mancini, Henry (1924–). American composer and arranger. Born in Cleveland, Ohio, Mancini studied music at the Carnegie Institute in Pittsburgh and the Juilliard School in New York City. He then studied composition in Los Angeles and in 1952 became a composer-arranger for Universal-International film studios. Thus began a long, illustrious career creating memorable themes and scores for films and television. In 1958 Mancini won an Emmy for creating the jazzy theme for the "Peter Gunn" TV series. He received ACADEMY AWARDS for his scores for *Breakfast at Tiffany's* (which included song hit "Moon River") (1961) and *Victor/Victoria* (1982). Other well-known film scores Mancini has created include those for the *Pink Panther* films (1963, 1975), *Days of Wine and Roses* (1962), *Charade* (1963) and *Once Is Not Enough* (1976).

Mandela, Nelson (1918–). Black South African nationalist leader. Mandela practiced law until 1952, when his hostility to APARTHEID led him to join the AFRICAN NATIONAL CONGRESS (ANC). He traveled widely in SOUTH AFRICA in the 1950s, championing his ideal of a free, multiracial society. After the ANC was banned in 1961 he evaded arrest until 1962, when he was jailed for five years. In 1963 he was charged under the Suppression of Communism Act, and after an eight-month trial sentenced to life imprisonment. Although held in prison for over 25 years, he remained an important figure for black South Africans. During this time his wife **Winnie Mandela** continued to take an active part in politics, traveling widely at home and abroad and championing Mandela's causes despite restrictions imposed on her by the South African government. Many blacks and whites were suspicious of Winnie Mandela's motives and methods, however, especially after she was implicated in the murder of a young black man in the late 1980s. Nelson Mandela was released from prison by Prime Minister F.W. DE KLERK in 1990 and

Released after 25 years of political imprisonment, black South African leader Nelson Mandela appears at Soweto's Soccer City Stadium accompanied by wife Winnie (Feb. 13, 1990).

allowed to resume his activities. He subsequently traveled to Europe and the U.S. to publicize his cause, but tensions among several rival black groups in South Africa made it unclear whether Mandela could effectively unite the black opposition to apartheid.

Mandelstam, Osip (1891–1938). Russian poet. One of the foremost Russian poets of the 20th century, Mandelstam was the son of a Jewish leather merchant and grew up in Warsaw and St. Petersburg. He studied at the Sorbonne and the University of Heidelberg, then returned to St. Petersburg where he allied himself with the poets Anna AKHMATOVA and Nikolai GUMILEV. They christened themselves Acmeists in 1913, espousing the concrete and concise in poetry (see ACMEISM). Mandelstam's first book of poetry was *Stone* (1913). Due to the RUSSIAN REVOLUTION and his reluctance to serve its cause in his writing, his future work went unpublished or was circulated with great circumspection. After the revolution (1917), Mandelstam sought relative political freedom in the Crimea. In 1921 he married Nadezhda Khazina, who courageously preserved much of his poetry after his death. In the late 1920s Mandelstam concentrated on translating Italian poetry, and produced the lyrical prose works *The Noise of Time* (1925) and *The Egyptian Stamp* (1928). He was arrested in 1934 for an anti-STALIN poem and sent into internal exile in the provincial town of Voronezh for three years. In 1938 he was again officially condemned, and died soon after in a transit camp in Siberia. The hallmarks of Mandelstam's poetry are a detached tone, majestic language, an abundance of literary and historical allusions, and themes often revolving around art.

For further reading:

Brown, Clarence, *Mandelstam*. New York: Cambridge University Press, 1978.

Harris, Jane G., *Osip Mandelstam*. Boston: G.K. Hall, 1988.

Mandelstam, Nadezhda, *Hope Against Hope*, tr. Max Heyward. New York: Atheneum, 1970.

Manhattan Project [formally, Manhattan District Project]. Code name for the top secret American project to develop the atomic bomb during WORLD WAR II. During the 1930s, some scientists recognized the theoretical possibility of constructing an atomic bomb. Acting on the belief that Nazi Germany could develop such a bomb, Albert EINSTEIN wrote to U.S. President Franklin D. ROOSEVELT describing the destructive potential of such a weapon and urging a major research program so that the U.S. would be the first nation with the bomb. This letter spurred Roosevelt's decision to institute a crash program, later known as the Manhattan Project. U.S. Army General Leslie R. GROVES was appointed chief administrator. The project was carried out primarily at a facility in Oak Ridge, Tennessee, and, beginning in March 1943, at a "super" laboratory at Los Alamos, New Mexico. American physicist J. Robert OPPENHEIMER was director of the Los Alamos laboratory and persuaded top nuclear physicists to join the project. Among scientists engaged in the Manhattan Project were Oppenheimer's brother Frank OPPENHEIMER, Enrico FERMI, Edward TELLER, British physicist William George PENNEY and hundreds of others. Shrouded in secrecy, the Manhattan Project culminated in the successful test of the first atomic bomb on July 16, 1945. The atomic age had begun. Although highly controversial, the Manhattan Project is widely regarded as a model for any scientific project requiring the coordination of resources and energy to solve a particular problem.

For further reading:

Groves, Leslie R., *Now It Can Be Told: The Story of the Manhattan Project*. New York: Da Capo Press, 1975.

Rhodes, Richard, *The Making of the Atomic Bomb*. New York: Simon & Schuster, 1987.

Mankiewicz, Herman J. (1897–1953). American film producer and screenplay writer. Mankiewicz, the older brother of screenplay writer and director Joseph MANKIEWICZ, enjoyed considerable success in HOLLYWOOD both as a producer of commercial comedies and as a serious screenplay writer. He began his career as a New York theater critic in the 1920s contributing to the NEW YORKER, among other publications. Mankiewicz came to Hollywood in 1926 and, after a stint of writing titles for SILENT FILMS, came to prominence as the producer of the MARX BROTHERS films *Monkey Business* (1931), *Horsefeathers* (1932) and *Duck Soup* (1933). He also wrote the screenplays for numerous films, including *Dinner at Eight* (1933) and *The Pride of the Yankees* (1942). But Mankiewicz remains best known for his collaboration with Orson WELLES on the ACADEMY AWARD-winning screenplay for the classic film *Citizen Kane* (1941). Controversy continues over the question of whether Mankiewicz or Welles had the major hand in the screenplay.

Mankiewicz, Joseph L(eo) (1909–). American film director, producer and screenwriter. Mankiewicz, the brother of screenwriter and producer Herman J. MANKIEWICZ, became one of the most influential HOLLYWOOD directors of the 1940s and 1950s. He began his career as a journalist, then moved to writing English subtitles for German films, before coming to Hollywood in 1929. His early screenplays include *Million Dollar Legs* (1932) and *Our Daily Bread* (1934), a socially conscious—and controversial—film directed by King VIDOR. Mankiewicz also produced films, most notably *The Philadelphia Story* (1940). In the 1940s he took up directing his own scripts and, remarkably, won Oscars for Best Director and Best Screenplay in consecutive years for *A Letter to Three Wives* (1949) and *All About Eve* (1950). His career suffered from the commercial disappointment of *Cleopatra* (1963), but he later worked on the acclaimed mystery *Sleuth* (1972), starring Michael Caine and Laurence OLIVIER.

Jamaican Prime Minister Michael Manley.

Manley, Michael (1925–). Jamaican prime minister. Manley's father, **Norman Washington Manley,** was Jamaica's first prime minister and the founder of the People's National Party. Michael Manley was appointed to the Senate by his father in 1962. Five years later, he was elected to the House of Representatives. When his father retired in 1969, Manley succeeded him as leader of the People's National Party. In 1972, he began his first term as prime minister and attempted to introduce socialist reforms. He alienated the United States by his overtures to Fidel CASTRO and by the Jamaican government's acquisition of 50% of American and Canadian companies' Jamaican interests. He was reelected in 1976 but was unable to curb Jamaica's increasing unemployment. In 1980, Edward P. Seaga of the Jamaica Labor Party became prime minister. With a more moderate platform than he had maintained in the 1970s, Manley returned to power in 1989 when the People's National Party won 44 of the 60 seats in Parliament. Manley upheld the good relations with the U.S. established by Seaga, but also proposed a rebuilding of Jamaica's schools and tax breaks and incentives to small farms and businesses.

Mann, Frederick R. (1903–1987). U.S. industrialist and patron of the arts. He made his fortune in the early 1920s manufacturing cardboard boxes and became a leading supporter of classical music. The Mann Music Center in Philadelphia's Fairmount Park, home of the Philadelphia Orchestra's summer concerts, was named after him, as was the Mann Auditorium in Tel Aviv, home of the Israel Philharmonic. Mann was the first U.S. ambassador to BARBADOS (1967–69).

Mann, Thomas (1875–1955). German novelist, story writer and essayist. Mann, who was awarded the NOBEL PRIZE for literature in 1929, is widely regarded as one of the greatest German writers of the 20th century. Two of his most famous works are the novella DEATH IN VENICE (1911) and the novel THE MAGIC MOUN-

German author Thomas Mann received the Nobel Prize for literature in 1929.

TAIN (1924). Mann, whose brother Heinrich also became a renowned novelist, was raised in a middle-class bourgeois family whose values he depicted in his first novel, *Buddenbrooks* (1901). Over the next two decades, Mann devoted much of his energies to the novella and short story: *Tristan* (1902), *Tonio Kroger* (1903), *Felix Krull* (1911) and *A Man and His Dog* (1918) being prominent examples. In 1933, Mann, an outspoken opponent of the NAZIS, exiled himself from GERMANY and lived in California from 1930 until after the war. Other novels by Mann include the tetralogy *Joseph and His Brothers* (1933–43) and *Doctor Faustus* (1948).

Mann Act. U.S. law enacted in 1910 and aimed at abolishing the "white slave trade" (prostitution). The federal law bans the transportation of women across state lines for immoral purposes. Little used during the second half of the century, the first recorded prosecution under the act involved a celebrity. Heavyweight boxing champion, Jack JOHNSON, the first black American champion, was prosecuted under the act after he encouraged a white woman whom he later married to leave a brothel where she was working to travel with him to another state. After Johnson was convicted and sentenced to a year in jail, he fled the country but ultimately returned and served his sentence.

Manned Spacecraft Center. See JOHNSON SPACE CENTER.

Mannerheim, Carl Gustav Emil (1867–1951). Finnish military and political leader, president of FINLAND. Born of a wealthy and distinguished Finnish-Swedish family in Villnaes—in what was then the Russian province of Finland—he was trained as a soldier and commissioned in the Russian Imperial army (1889). He served in the RUSSO-JAPANESE WAR (1904–05) and by the outbreak of WORLD WAR I had attained the rank of general in the czar's army. He was a commander in the war, returning home in 1917, when Finland declared its independence. In 1918, after Finnish BOLSHEVIKS occupied Helsinki, Mannerheim organized a White counterforce and, with German help, drove the communists from Finland. He served briefly as regent of Finland and was defeated in the presidential elections of 1919. He was appointed head of the Finnish defense council (1931) and built the Mannerheim Line, an unsuccessful attempt to stem Soviet invasion, which occurred in 1940. He commanded Finnish forces in the RUSSO-FINNISH WAR (1939–40) and led his troops against the Soviets again during WORLD WAR II (1941–44). In 1944, he was appointed president of Finland and concluded an armistice with the U.S.S.R. He retired in 1946.

Manning, Olivia (1908–1980). British novelist best known for six novels that together comprise a series titled *Fortunes of War,* which Anthony BURGESS has called "the finest fictional record of [WORLD WAR II] produced by a British writer." Born in Portsmouth, England, Manning was raised in Ireland. Just before the outbreak of World War II she accompied her new husband to Bucharest, Romania, where he lectured for the BRITISH COUNCIL. As German forces invaded the Balkan nations, the couple fled first to Athens, then to Egypt and finally to Jerusalem, in Palestine. Following the war they returned to London, where Manning lived and wrote until her death. Her first novel, *Among the Missing,* was published in 1949, and several others followed during the 1950s. The three books in *The Balkan Trilogy* (the first part of *Fortunes of War*) appeared in 1960, 1962 and 1965, respectively; the six-novel series was completed in *The Levant Trilogy* (1977–80). *Fortunes of War* takes a somewhat feminist view of personal relations during the war, but its scope and richness have earned it comparison with such masterpieces as Tolstoy's *War and Peace* and DODERER's *The Demons.* Manning was awarded a CBE in 1976.

Manning, Timothy Cardinal (1909–1989). Roman Catholic archbishop of Los Angeles (1970–85). After being appointed to the post in Los Angeles, he worked to heal rifts that had opened between the diocese and the city's black and Hispanic Catholics. He was a liberal on social issues such as the VIETNAM WAR and the 1983 deportation of Salvadoran refugees, but conservative on theological issues such as ABORTION and birth control. He was elevated to cardinal in 1973.

Man O'War (1917–1947). Thoroughbred racehorse. Until SECRETARIAT, no modern racehorse was mentioned in the same breath as Man O'War. Bred by the Belmont family, the big chestnut made his racing debut in 1919 and won by six lengths. Although handicappers continued to increase the weight he was asked to carry, he knew defeat only once, and that was the result of an inexperienced starter operating the gate. He achieved international celebrity status as he shattered track records wherever he ran. Never a Triple Crown winner, as he was not entered for the Kentucky Derby, he won the Belmont by 20 lengths and set world and American records for the 1 3/8 miles at 2:14 1/5 (2:14:12). After winning 19 of his 20 races, Man O'War was retired as a three-year-old because the higher weights he would be asked to carry as a four-year-old increased the risk of injury. He was an outstanding stud, and many hundreds of successful racehorses can trace back to Man O'War on either side of their pedigree, including the great WAR ADMIRAL. Man O'War died of a colic attack at the age of 30. His memorial service was attended by thousands, and he was mourned by millions throughout the world.

Mansfield, Katherine [Katherine Mansfield Beauchamp] (1888–1923). British short story writer. Mansfield was born in New Zealand but moved to London in 1908. After a very brief marriage (1909), she became pregnant. Her first collection of stories, *In a German Pension* (1911), reflects her experience of giving birth to a stillborn child in Bavaria. In 1911 Mansfield met John Middleton MURRY, editor of *Rhythm* (to which she contributed short stories), and married him in 1918. They were friends of Frieda and D.H. Lawrence, with whom they founded the short-lived *Signature* magazine. Mansfield's other collections include *Bliss and other stories* (1920), *The Garden Party and other stories* (1922), and *Something Childish* (1924). Mansfield's original and sometimes ironic stories evidence the influence of Anton CHEKHOV. She died of tuberculosis in a sanitorium in France.

Mansfield, Mike (1903–). U.S. senator. A Democrat from Montana, Mansfield served a record 16 years as the majority leader of the U.S. Senate, from 1961 to 1977. He was particularly known for his influence in foreign affairs, and had a clear vision of the requirements of national security and balance-of-power relationships. He also served 10 years in the U.S. House of Representatives. He carried out foreign diplomatic assignments for Presidents Dwight D. EISENHOWER, John F. KENNEDY and Lyndon B. JOHNSON. He was appointed ambassador to Japan by President Jimmy CARTER, and retained the position under President REAGAN.

Manship, Paul (1885–1966). American sculptor. Born in St. Paul, Minnesota, he was educated at the St. Paul Institute of Arts, the Pennsylvania Academy of the Fine Arts and the American Academy at Rome, where in 1909 he was awarded the Prix de Rome. Manship used his rigorous academic training and his immersion in the art of ancient Rome and Renaissance Italy as inspiration for his muscular, realistic sculpture of human and animal figures, often drawing on classical mythology for subject matter. Usually working in bronze or marble, he produced many individual sculptures, such as *Dryad, Little Brother* (Metropolitan Museum of Art, New York City) and *Pronghorn Antelope* (Art Institute of Chicago), as well as major public commissions, including *Actaeon*

(Brookgreen Gardens, Georgetown, S.C.) and *Prometheus* (Rockefeller Center, New York City).

Manson, Charles (1934–). American mass murderer. Born in Cincinnati, Ohio, Manson was a habitual criminal who had served a number of terms in prison before setting up his notorious "family" commune in the California desert in the 1960s. His young hippie following, mainly women, believed that Manson was a godlike figure and subscribed to his bizarre, drug-riddled, and satanist-tinged apocalyptic philosophy. His complete control over this cult was exerted in the murders that he masterminded. At his direction, members of his group savagely killed seven people, including actress Sharon Tate, in two houses near Beverly Hills in August, 1969. The bloody details of the crimes were front-page news for months—as were the subsequent Los Angeles trials of Manson and four of his accomplices. Manson was found guilty of murder and in 1971 was sentenced to death. When California abolished the death penalty, his sentence was commuted to life imprisonment.

Manstein, Erich von (1887–1973). German soldier. A general during WORLD WAR II, he engineered the Nazi invasion of Western Europe and led conquering German troops into France. As commander of the 11th German Army, he defeated forces of the U.S.S.R. in the Crimea in 1941 and in 1942 was unsuccessful in efforts to relieve the troops of General Friedrich von Paulus at STALINGRAD (see WORLD WAR II ON THE RUSSIAN FRONT). A critic of HITLER's Russian campaign, von Manstein was dismissed from duty in 1944. Condemned to an 18-year prison sentence by a British court in 1949, he was freed in 1953.

Mantle, Mickey (Charles) (1931–). American baseball luminary. Born in Oklahoma, as a boy Mantle was groomed for baseball by his father, who named him in honor of Mickey Cochrane, a great catcher. Signed in high school by the New York Yankees, Mantle played in the minor leagues after graduation. In 1951 he was brought to New York as a centerfielder. Beginning in 1952, he hit over .300 in 10 of his 18 seasons. He was the American League's most valuable player in 1962. He hit 54 home runs in 1961 (the same year his teammate Roger MARIS hit 61 to break Babe RUTH's record by one), and played in 12 World Series. He retired in 1969. His autobiography is titled *The Mick*.

Man Who Was Thursday, The. G.K. CHESTERTON's best known novel, a seminal work in the history of the modern fantastic tale. Published in 1908 it is, by turns, a detective story, allegory, and (according to its subtitle) "nightmare" whose violently bizarre imagery and baffling ambiguity have been compared to Franz KAFKA. A young detective infiltrates a band of anarchists bent on destroying the world only to discover that each member, like him, is also a detective in disguise assigned to the same case. Meanwhile, the group's leader, the diabolically mysterious "Sunday," leads them all on a mad chase, ultimately revealing himself to be a Godlike entity who mocks their efforts. Man is born to search but not necessarily to understand, he says: "Since the beginning of the world, all men have hunted me like a wolf—kings and sages, and poets and law-givers, all the churches, and all the philosophers. But I have never been caught yet." Life, while not a sinister conspiracy, may yet turn out to be a cosmic prank. According to his *Autobiography* (1937) Chesterton wanted to vanquish with 20th-century optimism the pessimism and despair of the 19th century. However, this tour-de-force of paradoxes also implies any real meanings in life must remain secrets, hidden behind inscrutable masks.

Manzu, Giacomo (1908–). Italian sculptor. Born in Bergamo, he was apprenticed to a woodcarver in 1919, traveled to Paris in the late 1920s and settled in Milan in 1930. Aware of avant-garde movements in sculpture, he nonetheless chose representational works of classical antiquity and of such masters as Donatello and Rodin as his models. Mainly executed in bronze, his work is figurative, dignified and calm—often with a religious tone or subject matter. Among his many commissioned sculptures are the bronze doors at Salzburg Cathedral (1958) and the bronze *Door of Death* (1962) at St. Peter's Basilica in Rome.

Maoism. System of communism adopted in CHINA under MAO TSE-TUNG. Maoism envisions a more flexible political system than Marxism-Leninism and claims that self-reliance is more important than state authority—and that the concept of revolutionary momentum, as expressed in the CULTURAL REVOLUTION, is more important than the state machine. Various terrorist groups in the West professed themselves to be Maoist, but in China Maoism waned under Mao's successors, who were concerned most of all with modernizing the nation's economy.

Mao Tse-tung (1893–1976). Chinese political leader, founder of the People's Republic of CHINA. Born into a peasant family in Shao-shan, Hunan province, he studied the traditional Chinese classics and also received a modern Western education. He first encountered Marxism while working at Peking University and was soon converted to its doctrine. Mao was a founding member of the Chinese Communist Party (CCP) in 1921 and became its leader in Hunan. In a united effort with the KUOMINTANG, he organized peasant and industrial unions and became (1926) director of the Peasant Movement Training Institute. The CCP and the Kuomintang split in 1927. In the ensuing purge of communists, Mao fled to the countryside and, along with CHU TEH, formed a communist-led guerrilla army that operated in the hinterlands from 1928 to 1931. This stress on the rural areas, with support coming from the peasantry rather than from an urban proletariat, was to be the hallmark of the Chinese brand of communism that Mao pioneered.

Mao Tse-tung, founder of the People's Republic of China.

In 1931 Mao was named chairman of the newly created Soviet Republic of China, with headquarters in Kiangsi province. Battered by attacks from the Nationalist forces led by CHIANG KAI-SHEK, Mao led his Red Army in the epic LONG MARCH (1934–35), trekking 6,000 miles before reaching northern Shensi and establishing a new government at Yenan. After the XIAN INCIDENT of 1936, Mao and his communists again collaborated with the Nationalists, this time forming a united front against the Japanese that lasted from 1937 to 1945. After the war, the uneasy alliance again broke and civil war (1946–49) resulted in the rout of the Kuomintang by Mao's forces and the establishment (1949) of the People's Republic of China with Mao as chairman.

His slogan-captioned attempts at making a truly Chinese communist state began with the Hundred Flowers movement of 1956–57 in which intellectuals were encouraged to criticize the party. The second manifestation was in Mao's GREAT LEAP FORWARD (1958), a failed program that called for rapid industrial development and the total dismantling of private property. At the same time, Mao continued to struggle against domination by the U.S.S.R. Forced from his chairmanship in 1959, he was replaced by LIU SHAOQI. However, Mao soon regained primacy by means of the CULTURAL REVOLUTION, which peaked in the late 1960s and was spearheaded by his wife, CHIANG CH'ING. During this period, the "little red book" of Mao's maxims became the ultimate authority for political correctness, and Mao and his ideology were the objects of fanatical worship. Liu was ousted in 1968, and in 1969 Mao, who had continued as chairman of the Communist Party, chaired the Ninth Communist Party Congress. The following year he was named supreme commander of the nation and the army.

Mao consolidated his power during the 1970s, drawing further away from the U.S.S.R. and initiating ties with the U.S.

highlighted by a 1972 Peking meeting with President Richard NIXON. Mao is recognized as one of the most important Marxist theoreticians, and his writings have had particular influence throughout the THIRD WORLD. He succeeded in creating an enormous social revolution and in unifying his huge and once-fragmented nation. However, the excesses of Mao's government have caused some diminishing of his stature in his homeland in the years since his death.

Maowad, Rene (1925–1989). Lebanese politician, president of LEBANON (1989). A Maronite Christian from northern Lebanon, the moderate Maowad had been a member of Parliament since 1957 and had served as a cabinet minister three times. After the resignation of president Amin Gemayel in September of 1988, there were two rival interim premiers—General Michel Aoun, head of a military cabinet in Christian east Beirut that claimed to be Lebanon's sole legitimate government, and Selim al-Hoss, a Sunni Moslem in west Beirut. Following Aoun's declaration dissolving Parliament, 30 members of Parliament, most of them Christians, disputed his right to do so. Joining together with 27 deputies (mostly Moslem) they elected Maowad as Lebanon's 9th president in November 1989. Maowad was assassinated after only 17 days in office when a bomb exploded next to his motorcade on November 22, in Moslem west Beirut. No group claimed responsibility for the bombing. Another moderate, Elias Hrawi, was quickly elected president by Parliament on November 24, 1989.

Mao Zedong. See MAO TSE-TUNG.

Mapai [Miphlegeth Poalei Israel]. Israeli Workers' Party, founded in PALESTINE in 1930 and usually called the Labor Party. A moderate left-wing party, it dominated Israeli governments until the election of Menachem BEGIN in 1977.

Mapam. United Workers' Party, an Israeli socialist party far to the left of MAPAI, drawing much of its support from the kibbutzim.

Mapplethorpe, Robert (1946–1989). American photographer. Mapplethorpe was known for his dramatic, austere black-and-white photos, many with homoerotic or sadomasochistic content. Retrospectives of his work appeared at the Institute of Contemporary Art in Philadelphia, at the Whitney Museum of American Art in New York City, and elsewhere. In June 1989, the Corcoran Gallery of Art in Washington, D.C., announced that it had canceled a retrospective in order to avoid political controversy at a time when Congress was reviewing its annual appropriation for the National Endowment for the Arts, whose funds would have been used to underwrite the exhibit. The Washington Project for the Arts mounted the retrospective instead. In 1990, the Cincinnati Museum of Art and its director were tried but acquitted of obscenity charges after showing the same Mapplethorpe exhibit.

Maradona, Diego Armando (1960–). Argentine soccer player—the outstanding player of the 1980s. Maradona's hallmark was his phenomenal ball control and goal scoring abilities. A phenom, Maradona made his professional debut at 15 for Argentinos Juniors in 1975. His goal-scoring rate was astounding, gaining him adulation throughout his homeland. Astonishingly, he was omitted from Argentina's 1978 World Cup winning team, but rebounded from this disappointment to become the focus of the 1982 World Cup side. Following the tournament he joined Spanish giant Barcelona, but after an injury-filled tenure there he was traded to Napoli in Italy, where his career regained its momentum. He led Napoli to its first Italian championship, but his greatest triumph was the 1986 World Cup, where his virtuoso performances gained Argentina the championship. Napoli regained the Italian title in 1990, but injuries and harassment seemed to disenchant Maradona. During the 1990–91 season he missed training and games and in March 1991 was tested positive for drug use. In April the Italian authorities banned him from soccer for 15 months.

Maravich, (Peter) "Pistol Pete" (1948–1988). American basketball star. As a college basketball player, he was the greatest scorer in National Collegiate Athletic Association history. From 1968 to 1970, he scored a record 3,667 points for Louisiana State University. During his 10-year NBA career, he averaged 24.2 points per game. He led the league in scoring during the 1977 season and was inducted into the Basketball Hall of Fame in 1987. Throughout his career, he was known for his droopy socks and long hair.

Marble, Alice (1913–1990). U.S. tennis player. The top woman player of the late 1930s, she was credited with introducing the aggressive serve-and-volley style of play to women's tennis. She won the U.S. women's amateur singles title four times, in 1936, 1938, 1939 and 1940, and dominated the women's doubles championships with her partner Sara Palfrey Fabyan. She won the Wimbledon singles championship in 1939. In 1940, she turned professional, playing in exhibition matches and giving tennis clinics in the U.S. and abroad. In 1945, during the last months of World War II, she worked undercover as a U.S. intelligence agent in neutral Switzerland.

Marc, Franz (1880–1916). German painter. Born in Bavaria, he studied painting in Germany and became acquainted with modern art during trips to Paris in 1903 and 1909. In 1910 he met Auguste MACKE, who was to influence the expressionistic nature of his work. In 1911 he became a founding member of the BLAUE REITER group. Marc took the figures of animals, usually horses, as his primary subject matter, portraying them in an almost mystically evocative manner in richly vibrant colors and expressively rounded forms. Among his paintings in this genre are *Blue Horses* (Walker Art Center, Minneapolis) and *Yellow Horses* (1912, Staatsgalerie, Stuttgart). His later works depict nature in increasingly abstract shards of form and color, as in *Tyrol* (1913–14, Bavarian State Museum, Munich). Already one of Germany's leading expressionist painters by the beginning of WORLD WAR I, his career was cut short by his death in battle at VERDUN.

Marceau, Marcel (1923–). French mime. Marceau has received international acclaim as a mime performer, instantly recognizable in his most famous persona of the amiable, white-faced Bip in such sketches as the "tug-of-war." Influenced by the silent films of Charlie Chaplin, he began using wordless sketches while working as a teacher. As a solo performer he has appeared throughout Europe and the U.S. He established his own mime company in the late 1940s, which tours the world performing complete mime-dramas, such as the well-known drama based on Gogol's *The Overcoat* (1951).

Marcel, Gabriel (1889–1973). French philosopher and playwright. Marcel was one of the leading representatives of Christian existential philosophy. Educated at the Sorbonne, Marcel served in the RED CROSS during WORLD WAR I. The central event of his life was his conversion to Roman Catholicism in 1929—an event he described in his writings as breaking through to true freedom by means of religious faith. Marcel was a philosophical adversary of the atheistic existentialism of fellow French philosopher Jean-Paul SARTRE. His major works include *Metaphysical Journal* (1927), the two-volume *The Mystery of Being* (1951) and *The Existential Background to Human Destiny* (1963). Marcel also wrote a number of plays with Catholic themes that were widely produced in their era.

"March on Rome" (1922). In the summer of 1922 Italy was in chaos; the government couldn't cope with the fascists, who had seized power in Bologna, Milan and other cities. Benito MUSSOLINI, leader of the National Fascist Party, demanded the government's resignation. Premier Luigi Facta belatedly declared a state of siege when the fascists began to march on Rome (October 28, 1922), but King VICTOR EMMANUEL III refused to sign the martial law decree, dismissing Facta. Mussolini, arriving by railroad sleeping car from Milan, found only 25,000 of his BLACK SHIRTS occupying Rome, but thousands joined them next day, coming on special trains to cheer Mussolini. The king permitted him to form a government to reestablish order.

March on Washington. Massive civil rights rally held in Washington, D.C. on August 28, 1963. The march, organized by Rev. Martin Luther KING Jr., was attended by more than 200,000 people who gathered to demand immediate equality in jobs and full civil rights for American blacks. The demonstrators gathered in the morning at the Washington Monument, then marched down Constitution and Independence avenues to the Lincoln Memorial. There, almost completely filling the mall, they listened to addresses by the march's leaders, the most significant

More than 200,000 people participated in the civil rights march on Washington, D.C. (Aug. 28, 1963).

of which was Dr. King's eloquent speech in which he said "I have a dream."

Marciano, Rocky [Rocco Francis Marchegiano] (1923–1969). American boxer. An all-around athlete, Marciano gave up a professional baseball career for boxing. As an amateur, he won all but three of his 30 fights. He turned to a professional boxing career in 1947 and began his climb to the heavyweight title. During that struggle, he became only the second person to knock out Joe LOUIS. In 1952, he fought the titleholder, Jersey Joe Walcott, and knocked him out for the title. Over the next four years, Marciano's title was challenged six times, and six times Marciano defended the title successfully. He retired an undefeated champion with 49 wins, 43 of them knockouts. He met an untimely death in a plane crash.

Marconi, Marchese Guglielmo (1874–1937). Italian electrical engineer and inventor. Marconi, the second son of a prosperous Italian country gentleman and a wealthy Irishwoman, was educated in Livorno and Bologna. He studied physics under several well-known teachers and learned about the work on electromagnetic radiation of Heinrich Hertz, Oliver Lodge, Augusto Righi and others. Marconi became interested in using Hertz's "invisible rays" to signal Morse code and in 1894 began experimenting to this end at his father's estate. Although he was soon able to transmit radio signals over a distance of more than a mile, he received little encouragement to continue his work in Italy and was advised to go to England. Shortly after arriving in London in 1896 Marconi secured the interest of officials from the war office, the Admiralty and the postal service. He spent the next five years in demonstrating and improving the range and performance of his equipment—and in overcoming the prevailing skepticism. In 1897 he helped to form the Wireless Telegraphic and Signal Co. Ltd., which in 1900 became Marconi's Wireless Telegraphy Co. Ltd.

He achieved the first international wireless (i.e., radio) transmission, between England and France, in March 1899; this aroused considerable public interest and attracted attention in the world's press. In the same year the British navy's summer maneuvers, with several ships equipped with Marconi's apparatus, helped to convince the Admiralty and mercantile ship owners of the value of radio telegraphy at sea. In December 1901 Marconi for the first time transmitted radio signals in Morse code across the Atlantic, a distance of some 2,000 miles. Marconi created a sensation, becoming world famous overnight and silencing many of his critics from the scientific world, who had believed that radio waves could not follow the curvature of the Earth. But they did, and this phenomenon was explained by Arthur Kennelly in 1902 as being due to a reflecting layer—the ionosphere—in the Earth's atmosphere. Thus radio telegraphy became a practical system of communication, especially at sea. Marconi spent the rest of his life improving and extending his wireless and managing his companies.

Although a good deal of Marconi's work was based on the ideas and discoveries of others, he was responsible for some notable inventions. He held the first of all radio telegraphy patents based on the use of waves (1896); the elevated antenna (1894); patent 7777, which enabled several stations to operate on different wavelengths without mutual interference (1900); the magnetic detector (1902); the horizontal directional antenna (1915); and the timed-spark system of generating pseudocontinuous waves (1912). From about 1916, Marconi began to exploit the use of radio waves of short wavelength, which allowed a more efficient transmission of radiant energy. In 1924 the Marconi Company obtained a contract to establish shortwave communication between England and British Commonwealth countries; by 1927 a worldwide network had been formed.

Marconi was a plenipotentiary delegate at the 1919 PARIS PEACE CONFERENCE, and in 1923 he joined the Fascist Party and became a friend of MUSSOLINI. Marconi received several honorary degrees and many awards, which included the NOBEL PRIZE for physics jointly with Karl Braun (1909), and was president of the Royal Italian Academy in 1930. At the hour of his state funeral, all post office wireless

Inventor Guglielmo Marconi (right), the first person to transmit wireless signals, with David Sarnoff, president of RCA (1933).

telegraph and wireless telephone services to the British Isles observed a two-minute silence.

Marconi Scandal. British political scandal of 1912–13. When Britain's government ordered the British Marconi Company to build wireless stations throughout the Empire in 1912, cabinet ministers were rumored to have profited from their knowledge of the scheme by buying shares in the company. A committee report (1913) cleared attorney general Sir Rufus Isaacs, Lord Murray of Elibank and LLOYD GEORGE, then chancellor of the Exchequer, of corruption charges.

Marco Polo Bridge Incident. Clash between Chinese forces and Japanese troops on July 7, 1937. It occurred at the Marco Polo Bridge that crosses the Yungting River at Wanping in China's northern Hopeh Province. This incident marked the beginning of the Second SINO-JAPANESE WAR (1937–45). Provoked by the Japanese, who refused to negotiate, the action provided a convenient pretext for the Japanese occupation of Peking and Tientsin, while Chinese troops were forced to retreat to the south.

Marcos, Ferdinand (Edralin) (1917–1989). President of the PHILIPPINES (1965–1986). Marcos was born in Ilocos Norte province. He served in both the Philippine and U.S. armies in WORLD WAR II and emerged from the war as a highly decorated officer. Years later, Marcos dismissed persistent allegations that his war record had been fabricated. He claimed that the documentation of his military exploits had been destroyed in a fire. After spending 15 years in the Philippine legislature, Marcos was elected to his first term as president in 1965. He was reelected in 1969. In 1972, Marcos imposed martial law in the Philippines and adopted a new national constitution under which he became prime minister as well as president. The country remained under martial law until 1981. Marcos' grip on power in the Philippines began to weaken following the assassination in 1983 of Benigno Aquino, the nation's leading opposition figure, who was shot dead upon returning from exile. Marcos blamed the killing on a professional hit-man with ties to the communists, but the country's opposition movement accused the government of masterminding the murder. In the face of increasing unrest at home and new pressure from the U.S. to enact reforms, Marcos decided in November 1985 to call a snap election to test his popularity. The decision backfired when the opposition rallied around the presidential candidacy of Corazon AQUINO, who had assumed the mantle of leadership from her late husband. The subsequent elections, on February 7, 1986, were marred by fraud. Marcos declared himself victorious, but Aquino initiated a nationwide campaign of civil disobedience in an attempt to topple the government. Marcos' fate was sealed when the nation's two top military leaders resigned February 22 and threw their support to Aquino. Marcos left the country for Hawaii February 26 aboard a U.S. Air Force plane.

Ferdinand Marcos, president of the Philippines from 1965 to 1986, makes an inaugural speech shortly before being deposed (Feb. 25, 1986).

Marcuse, Herbert (1898–1979). German-born political philosopher and social critic. Marcuse taught at the Frankfurt Institute for Social Research before fleeing the Nazis in 1934. He immigrated to the United States, where, over the next four decades, he taught at Harvard, Yale, Columbia and other universities. Strongly influenced by both Marx and Freud, Marcuse argued that society suffered from psychological and economic repressions that could be alleviated only by revolution. Marcuse was a major influence on the New Left politics of the 1960s. His major works include *Reason and Revolution* (1941), *Eros and Civilization* (1955) and *One-Dimensional Man* (1964).

Mariana Islands, Northern [Commonwealth of the Northern Mariana Islands]. The Northern Mariana Islands lie in the North Pacific Ocean and cover an area of 184 square miles; the southern islands are limestone with fringing coral reefs, while the northern islands are volcanic. The capital is SAIPAN. Inhabited from 1500 B.C., the islands came under Spanish colonial rule in 1668. After losing the Spanish-American War of 1898, Spain ceded GUAM to the U.S. and sold the rest of the Marianas to Germany. With the outbreak of WORLD WAR I, JAPAN took possession of the German islands. In 1920 the LEAGUE OF NATIONS mandated control of Micronesia (which includes the Marianas) to Japan. In August 1944 Japanese forces in the Marianas were defeated by the U.S., and in 1945 the U.S. Navy assumed control of Micronesia. In 1947 the UNITED NATIONS established the Trust Territory of the Pacific Islands, a "strategic trust" under U.S. administration. In a plebiscite in June 1975 the people of the Northern Marianas voted to become a self-governing U.S. commonwealth territory separate from the rest of the Micronesian territories. The new status came into force in January 1978, elections for the territory's governorship and bicameral legislature having been held in December 1977. In 1984 the U.S. government entered into negotiations with landowners on Tinian Island over the use of their land for military purposes. In November 1986 the Northern Mariana islanders were granted U.S. citizenship. However, the UN Security Council had yet to officially terminate the UN trusteeship due to uncertainty over the future status of another Micronesian territory, Palau. The total population in 1989 was just over 21,000.

Marich, Man Singh Shrestha (1942–). Nepalese political leader, selected by King BIRENDRA to be prime minister in 1986. Shrestha was born an illegitimate child in a low-caste family of the Newar clan. At one time a member of the Nepali Communist Party, he was a high school headmaster before winning an uncontested election to the Rashtriya Panchayat.

Mariel Boatlift. Beginning in April of 1980, boatloads of Cuban refugees began leaving Mariel Harbor in CUBA to emigrate to the U.S. These freedom flotillas, as they came to be known, were headed mostly for Florida. The U.S. was having difficulties assimilating the influx of refugees, and U.S. Coast Guard blockades were expensive and largely unsuccessful. Some of the Cubans were contained in refugee and resettlement camps; others were confined in federal prisons to undergo expulsion hearings—a move ordered by President Jimmy CARTER in June. He also announced a plan in September to help Florida with its resettlement efforts, which included federal absorption of the costs of resettlement, prosecution of boat owners who attempted to profit from the refugees and relocation of some to a settlement camp in Puerto Rico. On September 26, the Cuban government closed Mariel Harbor, thus ending the boatlift—but some 125,000 Cubans entered the U.S. during its five-month duration.

Marin, John (1870–1953). American painter. An important early modernist, he was born in Rutherford, N.J. Marin studied architecture and worked as an architectural draftsman before turning to the study of painting at the Pennsylvania Academy of the Fine Arts from 1899 to 1901. Traveling to Europe in 1905, he was influenced by the work of James McNeill Whistler, and lived a meager existence abroad for five years. After he returned to the U.S. his work was first exhibited by Alfred STIEGLITZ (1909). He soon drew acclaim as a superb watercolorist and was recognized for his powerful use of the medium. Taking for his subject the skyline of New York City, the deserts of Taos, New Mexico and the seascapes of Maine, he painted with energy and expressiveness, employing bold brushstrokes, colors that are alternately subtle and vivid and an approach that mingled the abstract with the realistic. Marin's oils and watercolors are included in virtually every important collection of modern American art. (See also MODERNISM.)

Mariner probes. A series of U.S. planetary probes, launched from 1962 to 1973,

Cuban refugees leave Mariel harbor bound for Key West, Florida.

that greatly expanded our knowledge of the solar system. *Mariner 1* was launched on July 22, 1962, but was destroyed after veering off course following its launch. *Mariner 2* was launched on August 27, 1962, and flew by Venus in December of that year, measuring the Venusian temperature and confirming the existence of the solar wind. *Mariner 3* was launched on November 5, 1964, but failed to obtain the necessary velocity and headed for an unplanned orbit around the sun; communication with the craft was lost 10 hours after launch. *Mariner 4* was launched November 28, 1964, and passed by Mars in July 1965, returning photographs of the planet's surface. *Mariner 5* was launched June 4, 1967, and passed Venus in October of that year, measuring the Venusian temperature, testing its atmosphere and determining the planet's mass and diameter. *Mariner 6* was launched on February 24, 1969, and its twin *Mariner 7* was launched on March 27, 1969; they passed Mars in July and August, respectively, returning photographs and performing experiments testing the planet's temperature, atmosphere and size. *Mariner 9* was launched May 30, 1971, and entered Martian orbit in November of that year, returning more than 7,000 photographs of the planet before losing contact with Earth in October 1972. *Mariner 10* was launched November 3, 1973, flying by Venus in February 1974 and by Mercury in March and September 1974 and again in March 1975; the Mercury flybys resulted in the discovery of the planet's magnetic field. *Mariners 11* and *12* were renamed *Voyager 1* and *Voyager 2*. The latter was launched on August 20, 1977 and flew by Jupiter in July 1979, Saturn in August 1981, Uranus in January 1986 and Neptune in August 1989. *Voyager 1*, which was delayed by technical problems, was launched on September 5, 1977, and passed by Jupiter in March 1979, Saturn in November 1980 and Uranus in December 1985.

Marinetti, Filippo T(ommaso) (1876–1944). Italian aesthetic theorist, essayist and poet. Marinetti is best remembered as the principal ideologue for the right-wing, Italian segment of the multinational aesthetic movement known as FUTURISM. In his *Foundation and Manifesto of Futurism* (1908) and other writings, Marinetti argued for the aesthetic beauty of modern technology, pitted poetic diction against common language usage and held that nationalism and warfare were worthy of artistic exaltation. In the 1920s and after, Marinetti became a major spokesman for the fascist regime of Benito MUSSOLINI.

Marini, Marino (1901–1980). Italian sculptor. Beginning his career as a painter, he continued to paint and create prints while becoming an internationally known sculptor. Marini, influenced early in his career by classical Roman statuary, developed an intensely individualistic style that found its finest expression in figures of horses and riders. These powerful equestrian sculptures are exemplified by the monumental *Horse and Rider* (1952–53) in the collection of the Hirshhorn Museum, Washington, D.C.

Maris, Roger (Eugene) (1934–1985). American baseball player. In 1961, as an outfielder for the New York Yankees, Maris set an all-time single-season record of 61 home runs, breaking Babe RUTH's record of 60 set in 1927. He received much hostile media and fan attention from those who did not wish to see Ruth's record overturned. There were also those who would have preferred to see Maris' teammate Mickey MANTLE break the record. Maris played with the Yankees until 1966 when he was traded to the St. Louis Cardinals. He retired from baseball in 1968 with a career total of 275 home runs in the major leagues.

Maritain, Jacques (1882–1973). French philosopher. Educated at the Sorbonne and the University of Heidelberg, Maritain was a Protestant who converted to Roman Catholicism (1906) under the influence of the mystical poet Leon Bloy and an advocate of scientific materialism who was started on a path toward neo-Thomism by the philosophy of Henri BERGSON. He taught at a number of universities in France and the U.S. and was the author of over 50 books of philosophy and numerous scholarly articles. His applications of the philosophy of St. Thomas Aquinas to the contemporary world can be found in his works on metaphysics, politics, religion and aesthetics. Among his books are *The Degrees of Knowledge* (1932, tr. 1937), *True Humanism* (1936, tr. 1938), *Man and the State* (1951) and *On the Use of Philosophy* (1961).

Markelius, Sven (1889–1972). Swedish architect who introduced the vocabulary of MODERNISM through the INTERNATIONAL STYLE to Sweden. Markelius was trained at the Stockholm Technical College and Academy of Fine Arts. The concert hall at Halsingborg (1932) was his first major work. His simple and elegantly modern Swedish Pavilion at the NEW YORK WORLD'S FAIR OF 1939 brought him international notice. He was Stockholm's city architect and planner from 1944 to 1954 and was the primary planner of the satellite town of Vallingby near Stockholm, a much-admired example of advanced concepts in town planning. Markelius also often combined work in architecture with interior design. He was a member of the team that developed the design for the United Nations Headquarters building in New York; the interior of one of the council chambers there is a fine example of his work. Markelius' work combines the ideas of International Style modernism with a certain humane quality that is characteristic of the best of Scandinavian design.

Markert, Russell (1899–1990). U.S. choreographer. In 1916, he formed the high-kicking chorus line "The 16 Missouri Rockets." They were later billed as "The American Rockets" and were hired by showman Samuel (Roxy) Rothafel for the opening of RADIO CITY MUSIC HALL in 1932. Markert acted as director and choreographer for the troupe, which became known as the Radio City Musical Hall Rockettes, until his retirement in 1971.

Markham, Beryl (1902–1986). British-born aviator. She grew up in KENYA, where she learned to fly and became a bush pilot. She pioneered the scouting of elephants and other wild game from the air. The first person to fly solo across the Atlantic from east to west, her historic flight took place in September 1936 in bad weather. She took off from Abingdon, England and landed more than 21 hours later in a Nova Scotia bog. New York City, her intended destination, honored her with a ticker tape parade. Her historic flight was described at length in her memoirs, *West with the Night,* first published in 1943. Upon its rerelease in 1983, it was hailed by critics in Britain and the U.S. Also a professional horse trainer, she had six Kenya Derby winners.

For further reading:

Lovell, Mary S., *Straight on Till Morning*. New York: St. Martin's, 1987.

Markievicz, Countess Con(stance) [born Constance Gore-Booth] (1868–1927). Irish nationalist. A member of a prominent aristocratic Protestant family in the west of Ireland, Constance Gore-Booth married a Polish count in 1900. She became involved in radical Irish politics and participated in the EASTER REBELLION (1916). She was sentenced to death but pardoned and released from prison in 1917. The following year, as a SINN FEIN candidate, she became the first woman elected to the British Parliament but (along with the other victorious Sinn Fein candidates) refused to take her seat. Instead, she became a member of the new provisional Irish Parliament. W.B. YEATS celebrated Markievicz and her sister in his poem "In Memory of Eva Gore-Booth and Con Markievicz," although he later condemned her radical politics.

Markova, Alicia [Lillian Alicia Marks] (1910–). English dancer. One of the great Giselles of her time, Markova began her career as a member of Serge DIAGHILEV'S BALLETS RUSSES (1925–29). From 1930 to 1935 she danced with Ballet Rambert and Vic-Wells Ballet, becoming the first English ballerina to dance the classic roles while creating roles in many new ballets, such as Frederick ASHTON'S *Facade* (1931). As a ballerina with AMERICAN BALLET THEATRE (1941–46) she created many roles, including Juliet in Antony TUDOR'S *Romeo and Juliet* (1943). The Markova-Dolin Company, originally formed with Anton DOLIN in 1935, was reformed in 1945 and became the London Festival Ballet in 1950. Since her last performance in 1962, Markova has served as ballet director of the New York Metropolitan Opera (1963–69), visiting professor of ballet at the University of Cincinnati (1971–74) and first president of the London Festival Ballet (since 1986).

Marley, Bob [Robert Nesta Marley] (1945–1981). Jamaican reggae singer. With his group The Wailers, he helped establish the popularity of Reggae music in Britain and the U.S. during the 1970s. An outspoken advocate of Rastafarianism, he survived an assassination attempt in 1976.

Jamaican reggae star and Rastafarian spokesman Bob Marley.

Marne, First Battle of the (1914). In August 1914 German armies invaded Belgium and northeastern France, advancing to the Marne River within 15 miles of Paris. The French staged a desperate counterattack to the German right flank on September 6, 1914, which opened a gap in the German line. British and French troops advanced into the opening, attacking the other flank. The German armies, pushed further apart, retreated to the northern bank of the Aisne River, digging trench defenses and thus initiated the trench warfare of the next four years. The battle quashed German expectations of a quick and easy victory.

The **Second Battle of the Marne** began in late May 1918 when German forces began a powerful offensive against French positions, fighting their way to the Marne. After crossing the Marne on July 15, a German division was trapped and surrendered. On July 18, French, British and American troops under supreme Allied commander Marshal Ferdinand FOCH counterattacked; by mid-August the Germans were in full retreat and back to prewar German boundaries by September. They were soon to sue for peace.

Marquand, J(ohn) P(hilips) (1893–1960). American novelist. Born in Wilmington, Delaware, to an aristocratic New England family, he attended Harvard University, where he encountered the Boston Brahmins (who were to be the main subjects of his gently satirical novels). His earliest fiction was in the detective story genre, and he won fame with the character of the Japanese sleuth Mr. Moto. Marquand achieved acclaim as a serious novelist with the publication of *The Late George Apley* (1937), a novel of manners among Boston's best, brightest and richest, which was awarded a Pulitzer Prize. His other novels include *Wickford Point* (1939), *So Little Time* (1943) and *Point of No Return* (1949).

Marsalis, Wynton (1961–). Celebrated American jazz trumpeter who was a key participant in a series of dynamic events crucial to reenergizing the 1980s jazz scene. Marsalis, the younger brother of noted saxophonist Branford Marsalis and son of venerable pianist Ellis Marsalis, attained initial success at age 19 with Art BLAKEY and the Jazz Messengers. In 1981, his debut album as a leader led to the formation of his own group. Marsalis, like Benny GOODMAN, also won kudos for his classical playing. In 1984, he became the first musician to garner Grammy awards for jazz ("Think of One") and classical (Haydn/Hummel/L. Mozart Trumpet Concertos). Marsalis has been a vigorous spokesman for "authentic" jazz as embodied in the traditions of BEBOP and FUSION JAZZ, rock and rap. Also, Marsalis has insisted that jazz, "America's classical music," be accorded the same kind of respect tendered to European classical music. Through these varied activities, Marsalis has become a well-known media personality; indeed, his success has encouraged the promotion of a number of promising young jazz players, a phenomenon chronicled in a 1990 TIME magazine cover story. At the heart of Marsalis' success, though, is a commanding style in which his virtuosic technique and emotional depth are displayed with a neobebop vocabulary suggesting the dexterity of Clifford BROWN and the dramatic poignancy of Miles DAVIS.

For further reading:

Giddins, Gary, "Wynton Marsalis and

Jazz trumpeter Wynton Marsalis performing at Newport Jazz Festival (Jan. 6, 1985).

Other Neoclassical Lions," in *Rhythm-a-ning: Jazz Tradition and Improvisation in the 80's.* New York: Oxford University Press, 1985.

Marsh, Dame (Edith) Ngaio (1899–1982). New Zealand-born mystery novelist. She wrote 31 thrillers featuring a scholarly and charming detective, Chief Inspector Roderick Alleyn of Scotland Yard. In 1966 she was made a Dame of the British Empire by Queen Elizabeth II.

Marshall, George C(atlett) (1880–1959). American Army officer, diplomat and statesman. Born in Uniontown, Pennsylvania, Marshall attended the Virginia Military Institute and joined the Army in 1902. After service in the Philippines and the U.S., Marshall held high administrative and planning posts in France during WORLD WAR I and was an aide de camp to General John PERSHING (1919–24). He was stationed in China (1924–27), was assistant commandant of the Army Infantry School (1927–32) and headed several CIVILIAN CONSERVATION CORPS camps during the GREAT DEPRESSION. Having established a reputation for brilliant strategic and organizational skills, Marshall quickly rose to become assistant Army chief of staff and deputy chief of staff in 1938 and chief of staff in 1939, the year he was promoted to the rank of full general.

Warning of probable armed conflict ahead, he stressed military preparedness, significantly modernizing and enlarging the Army, urging the passage (1940) of the Selective Service Act and reorganizing the War Department. After the outbreak of WORLD WAR II, he became Franklin D. ROOSEVELT's military adviser, accompanying the president to the Allied summit conferences and proving himself a consummate diplomat. In military affairs, Marshall directed U.S. operations in both Europe and the Pacific, coordinating the North African and Sicilian campaigns, aiding the besieged U.S.S.R., helping to plan the cross-channel invasion of the European continent and urging the dropping of the ATOMIC BOMB on Japan. He was named General of the Army in 1944.

U.S. Army General George C. Marshall, architect of the "Marshall Plan" to rebuild post-World War II Europe.

Emerging from the war as a national hero, he retired from Army service in 1945. That year he became President TRUMAN's emissary to China, where he failed in an attempt to achieve a settlement of its civil war and a coalition between opposing Nationalists and Communists. In 1947, he was appointed Truman's secretary of state. In this post, he was successful in urging a firmer American policy toward the Soviet Union and in formulating and implementing the European Recovery Program, or MARSHALL PLAN, a comprehensive program of economic and technical assistance aimed at rebuilding war-torn Europe. In recognition of the plan's success, he was awarded the 1953 NOBEL PRIZE for peace. In poor health, Marshall resigned from office in 1949, but he was recalled to service (1950) after the outbreak of the KOREAN WAR as Truman's secretary of defense. During this period of service, he extended the draft and desegregated the armed forces. Marshall retired permanently in 1951, one of America's most respected military and diplomatic figures.

Marshall, Thurgood (1908–). First black justice of the U.S. Supreme Court (1967–91). A native of Baltimore and a graduate of Howard University Law School, Marshall became involved with the NAACP before World War II and headed the NAACP Legal Defense and Education Fund. In this position, he was at the very center of the U.S civil rights movement, coordinating the NAACP's legal challenges to segregation in voting rights, education and public accommodations. Marshall was chief counsel in the famous BROWN V. BOARD OF EDUCATION, in which the Supreme Court outlawed separate but equal schools. He was appointed a federal judge by President John F. KENNEDY and in 1967 was elevated to the Supreme Court by President Lyndon JOHNSON, who early in his career had supported segregation. Marshall joined the liberal wing of the Court and helped affirm much of the legislation of the era aimed at protecting minorities. In later years, as the Court grew more conservative, he became known for his liberal dissents and his public criticism of both politicians and potential nominees to the Court.

Thurgood Marshall was the first black to be appointed to the U.S. Supreme Court.

Marshall Islands. The Marshall Islands consist of two island chains of 30 atolls and 1,152 islands, including the former U.S. nuclear test sites of BIKINI and ENIWETOK; total land area is 70 square miles. The capital is Majuro. An influx of American and European whalers, traders and missionaries in the 19th century caused major social upheaval. Annexed by Spain in 1874, the Marshalls became a German protectorate in 1885. With the onset of WORLD WAR I, JAPAN took possession of the islands. In 1920 the LEAGUE OF NATIONS gave Japan a mandate to administer Micronesia, and in 1945, at the end of WORLD WAR II, the victorious U.S. Navy took control. In 1947 the UNITED NATIONS established the Trust Territory of the Pacific Islands, under U.S. control. From 1946 to 1958 the U.S. used Bikini and other atolls in the Marshalls to test nuclear weapons. Preparations for Micronesian self-government led to a referendum in July 1978 on a common constitution for the whole territory. The Marshallese voted against, and in 1979 the Republic of the Marshall Islands' separate constitution took effect. In 1982 over 1,000 dispossessed landowners from Kwajalein Atoll launched Operation Homecoming, a four-month protest against the U.S. military's use of the atoll as a missile testing range.

In October 1986 a Compact of Free Association between the Marshall Islands and the U.S. government came into effect: The Marshalls would be internally self-governing while the U.S. would retain responsibility for foreign relations and defense. The compact also ensured that the U.S. would maintain its military bases in the islands for at least 15 years and annually provide $30 million in economic aid. U.S. administration of Micronesia formally ended in November 1986, but the UN Security Council had yet to formally terminate the trusteeship owing to uncertainty over the future status of the Micronesian territory of Palau.

Marshall Plan. U.S. plan—formally, the European Recovery Program—for the reconstruction of Europe after WORLD WAR II. The plan was formulated by U.S. Secretary of State George C. MARSHALL and his aides, with suggestions from the European nations. At the end of the war Europe lay in ruins. Marshall recognized that, without a comprehensive package of U.S. aid, Europeans—victor and vanquished alike, stateless people and displaced persons—would continue to suffer from hunger, disease, a depressed economy and political instability. Moreover, Marshall was wary of the Soviet Union's intentions and believed that it was necessary to revive Western Europe economically and materially in order to prevent COMMUNISM from spreading further. He also believed that a revitalized Western Europe would stimulate U.S. production and trade. Marshall announced the plan during a commencement address at Harvard University (June 1947). "It is logical that the U.S. should do whatever it is able to do to assist in the return of normal economic health in the world, without which there can be no political stability and no assured peace," he said. "Our policy is directed not against any country or any doctrine but against hunger, poverty, depression and chaos." By the spring of 1948 Marshall had persuaded a majority in Congress to support the plan. The Marshall Plan provided $17 billion in assistance to 16 European nations between 1948 and 1952 and was perhaps the most ambitious international peacetime project ever attempted. Immensely successful, it helped restore prosperity to devastated areas of Europe, most notably WEST GERMANY. For his role in developing the European Recovery Program, George C. Marshall was awarded the 1953 NOBEL PRIZE for peace.

Martin, Frank (1890–1974). Swiss composer known for his contrapuntal techniques, and his use of harmony and stylized folk songs in his operas, ballets, instrumental and vocal works. A pianist and harpsichordist as well as a composer, Martin also taught at the Institute Jaques-Dalcroze (1927–38), was founder-director of the Technicum Moderne de Musique (1933–39) in Geneva and taught at the Cologne Hochschule fur Musik in the Netherlands (1950–57). His works include the oratorio *In terra pax,* which was specially commissioned to commemorate the end of WORLD WAR II (1945), and his opera *Der Sturm* (1952–54; *The Tempest*).

Martin, Glenn (1886–1955). U.S. airplane manufacturer. Educated at Kansas Wesleyan University, Martin began to build gliders in 1907 and by 1908 was experimenting with pusher type airplanes. He taught himself to fly and built one of the first airplane factories in the United States in 1909, in Wichita, Kansas. Martin later produced the first American-designed airplanes for Liberty engines and constructed Martin bombers.

Martin, Graham A(nderson) (1912–1990). U.S. diplomat. Martin, the last U.S. ambassador to South VIETNAM, after the fall of SAIGON (1975), was sharply criticized for having mishandled the evacuation of American personnel. Thousands of Vietnamese who had worked for the U.S. were left behind, together with hundreds of classified documents.

Martin, Joseph William, Jr. (1884–1968). U.S. politician. He was elected as a Republican to the Massachusetts state legislature (1912–17). In 1925 he won a seat in the U.S. House of Representatives where he served for 42 years. He was elected minority leader in 1939, and he was speaker of the House from 1947 to 1949 and 1953 to 1955. He created a strong Republican organization in the House, and opposed many of ROOSEVELT's and EISENHOWER's legislative programs.

Martin, Mary (Virginia) (1913–1990). American musical theater and film actress. She made her Broadway debut in 1938 in the Cole PORTER musical *Leave It to Me,* in which she sang the show-stopping "My Heart Belongs to Daddy." She starred in Richard RODGERS and Oscar HAMMERSTEIN II's *South Pacific* (1949). In 1954, she created on Broadway the role for which she is best known, that of PETER PAN; the musical was presented on television soon afterwards. She won a TONY AWARD for her performance in *The Sound of Music* (1959), as well as for *Peter Pan* and *Annie Get Your Gun.* Her son, Larry Hagman, starred in the television series "Dallas."

Martin, Steve (1945–). American comedian, film actor and screenplay writer. Martin is one of the major comedic talents of his generation. He began his show business career in the 1960s as a writer for television and won an Emmy for his scripts for *The Smothers Brothers Comedy Hour.* In the 1970s he turned to stand-up comedy and won national attention for his appearances on SATURDAY NIGHT LIVE. He recorded two Grammy award-winning albums, *Let's Get Small* and *Wild and Crazy Guy.* Martin's famous stand-up image featured a pure white suit, which he sometimes wore along with bunny ears. In the late 1970s, Martin turned to comedic film acting, a field in which he became preeminent. While maintaining great box office popularity, Martin is also highly regarded by critics for the genuine pathos he brings to many of his performances and for the diversity of roles and scripts he seeks out. Major films featuring Martin include *The Jerk* (1979), a tribute to Jerry LEWIS comedies; *Pennies From Heaven* (1981), a dark musical scripted by Dennis POTTER; *Dead Men Don't Wear Plaid* (1982), a witty spoof of FILM NOIR detective movies; *All of Me* (1984), for which he won a Best Actor Award from the New York Film Critics Circle; *Roxanne* (1987), a modern adaptation of *Cyrano de Bergerac; Dirty Rotten Scoundrels* (1988), in which he and Michael CAINE play a pair of con men; and *Parenthood* (1989).

American comedian Steve Martin, known for his madcap antics.

Martin-Artajo, Alberto (1904?-1979). Spanish diplomat. As SPAIN's foreign minister (1945–57), Martin-Artajo helped break the diplomatic isolation of Generalissimo Francisco FRANCO's regime after WORLD WAR II. In 1953 he won diplomatic recognition for Franco's government from the Vatican and the United States.

Martin du Gard, Roger (1881–1958). French novelist and playwright. Martin du Gard first achieved recognition with his second novel, *Jean Barois* (1913), a fictional portrait of the Dreyfus scandal. It was championed by Andre GIDE, who was to become a friend and correspondent. Martin du Gard is best known for the eight-volume roman fleuve, *Les Thibault* (the first six volumes were translated as *The Thibaults;* the latter two as *Summer 1914*). Published between 1922 and 1940, the novels depict the degeneration of society prior to WORLD WAR I by following two bourgeois families—one Catholic and one Protestant. Martin du Gard received the NOBEL PRIZE for literature in 1937. Other works include *Confidence Africaine* (*African Secret,* 1931); the play *Un Taciturne* (*A Silent Man* 1932), and the unfinished novel begun in 1940, *Les Souvenirs du colonel Maumort* (*The Memoirs of Colonel Maumort*).

Martinelli, Giovanni (1885–1969). Italian-American tenor. Born near Padua, Martinelli made his concert and operatic debuts in Milan in 1910. He first achieved recognition when Giacomo PUCCINI selected him as the lead tenor for the premiere of his THE GIRL OF THE GOLDEN WEST in 1911. Martinelli made his American debut in Philadelphia in 1913, and months later he sang for the first time at New York's Metropolitan Opera. For 32 seasons, Martinelli was the Met's principal tenor in the Italian and French repertories, singing some 50 leading roles.

Martinez Ruiz, Jose [Azorin] (1873–1967). Spanish writer. Born in Manovar, he studied law in Valencia, later becoming a noted and extremely prolific essayist, novelist and playwright. Influenced by ANARCHISM, he began as a leftist writer, but grew increasingly conservative as his career progressed. An important figure in the Generation of 1898, he was especially concerned with defining the nature of Spanish life and character. His compactly written essay collections include *El alma Castellana* (1900), *Castilla* (1912) and *Clasicos y modernos* (1913). Among his many novels are the autobiographical *La Voluntad* (1902), *Antonio Azorin* (1903) and *Las Confesiones de un pequeno filosofo* (1904), as well as the later experimental and surrealist works *Felix Vargas* (1928) and *Pueblo* (1930). His terse style and his concern with the continuity of Spanish history exercised an important influence on modern Spanish letters.

Martinique. Martinique is a Caribbean island with a total area of 425 square miles. Its mountainous terrain includes a dormant volcano, while the island's coastline is heavily indented and subject to hurricanes and flooding. The capital is Fort-de-France. Colonized by France in 1635, the island's capital, St. Pierre, was completely destroyed during a volcanic eruption of Mt. Pelee in 1902 that left only one survivor—a resident of the city's jail. In 1947 Martinique became a department of France. Demands for greater autonomy were expressed during the 1950s by the Parti Progressite Martiniquais (OOM), founded and led by Aime CESAIRE. Rioting in 1959 led to the French government devolving some of its powers in 1960, but a 1962 plebiscite produced a majority in favor of retaining departmental status. In 1974 Martinique also became a region of France and in 1982 was granted more autonomy. The left-wing parties, led by the PPM, succeeded in gaining a small majority on the new regional council, but the general council remained under the control of the right-wing and center parties. In 1986 the left-wing parties maintained their control of the regional council, but in elections to the general council in 1988, although they secured a majority of the seats for the first time, they failed to gain the presidency of the council.

Martins, Peter (1946–). Danish dancer, choreographer and ballet master. An outstanding male dancer from the mid-1960s to the mid-1980s, Martins later served as ballet-master-in-chief of the NEW YORK CITY BALLET (NYCB). He joined the ROYAL DANISH BALLET in 1965, then became a principal dancer with NYCB in 1969. He created roles in several ballets, including Jerome ROBBINS' *The Goldberg Variations* (1971) and George BALANCHINE's *Duo Concertant* (1972). Works choreographed for NYCB include *Calcium Light Night* (1978). In 1983 he became joint ballet-master-in-chief of NYCB (with Robbins) and was named sole ballet master in 1989.

Martinson, Harry (1904–1978). Swedish poet and novelist. Abandoned at an early age, Martinson fled from a number of foster homes before going to sea in his late teens. Forced by illness to return to Sweden in 1929, Martinson began publishing his first poetry, which was strongly derivative of KIPLING. With *Nomad* (1931), a collection of free verse, he began to establish his own voice. Subsequent poetry is steeped in primitivism. Martinson's fiction includes the autobiographical novels *Nsslorna blomma* (*Flowering Nettle*, 1935) and *Vgen ut* (*The Way Out*, 1936). His best-known works are the novel *Vgen till Klockrike* (*The Road*, 1948) and the epic poem *Aniara: En revy on Mnniskan i tid och rum* (*Aniara: A Review of Man in Time and Space*, 1956), which some consider to be his masterpiece, blaming the English translation for its lukewarm reception outside of Sweden. Martinson was a joint recipient of the NOBEL PRIZE for literature in 1974, along with Eyvind JOHNSON.

Martinu, Bohuslav (1890–1959). Czech composer. Martinu, who began his career as a violinist with the Czech Philharmonic (intermittently from 1913 to 1923), is known for his mastery of modern counterpoint and his lyricism inspired by Czech folk traditions. He first gained recognition with the choral/orchestral *Czech Symphony* (1918) and the ballet *Istar* (1921). From 1923 to 1940 he lived in Paris, and his compositions of this period reflect the influence of the French modernists. Martinu fled to the United States in 1941 and became visiting professor of music at Princeton University (1948–51). His best-known works include *Memorial to Lidice* (1943) and numerous chamber works, which were his forte.

Marvin v. Marvin (1976). Also known as the "palimony case," this 1976 trial established that an unmarried cohabitant could sometimes sue his or her partner after a romantic breakup and receive payments similar to alimony. The case involved the well-known actor Lee Marvin and his companion Michelle Triola, who had obtained the services of the flamboyant matrimonial attorney Marvin Michelson. The couple had cohabited, essentially as husband and wife, for a number of years, without benefit of wedlock, and later separated—at which point Michelle demanded a monetary settlement from the actor. Although married couples typically divide their marital property, the law at the time had no such provision for unmarried cohabitants: Living together outside marriage was considered to be against public policy. The Marvin case established that an unmarried cohabitant could receive a division of property on the showing that a formal or informal agreement existed to do so. However, Michelle had failed to prove that any contract to split property ever existed and she ultimately ended up with no damages. Although this was a California case, the concept of "palimony" quickly spread to a number of other states as well. A similar case involving actor William Hurt occurred in 1989.

Marx Brothers. Comedy stars of vaudeville, stage and screen. The Marx Brothers were five real-life brothers from a New York City tenement: **Chico** (Leonard) (1887–1961), **Harpo** (born Adolph, which later became Arthur) (1888–1964), **Groucho** (Julius Henry) (c. 1890–1977), **Gummo** (Milton) (c. 1893–1977) and **Zeppo** (Herbert) (1901–79). Encouraged by their mother, Minnie, and Uncle Al (Al Shean of the vaudevillian team "Gallagher and Shean"), the brothers toured with their comedy act under various names (including "The Three Nightingales") until they performed on Broadway in *I'll Say She Is* in 1924. This was followed by the Broadway hits *The Coconuts* (1925) and *Animal Crackers* (1928)—filmed in 1929 and 1930, respectively. Moving to HOLLYWOOD with the advent of TALKING PICTURES, for such classic films as *Monkey Business* (1931), *Duck Soup* (1933) and *A Night at the Opera* (1935), the team developed their own hilarious brand of farce, poking fun at convention and confounding audiences with non-sequiturs and double-entendres. Groucho became the leering, wisecracking pseudo-intellectual; Harpo, the mute clown; and Chico, the Italian con-artist. Zeppo appeared in a few early films as straight man but quit to become an agent; Gummo did not work in films. After the act split up in the early 1950s, Groucho went on to write several books and host the TV comedy quiz show "You Bet Your Life." Spurred by a Marx Brothers revival in the 1970s, Groucho went on a successful one-man tour and recorded the popular album *An Evening with Groucho.*

Marxism-Leninism, Institute of. Moscow's chief institution of study and research into the history and theory of communism. In 1931 the Marx-Engels Institute and the Lenin Institute merged to form the Marx-Engels-Lenin Institute; it served as a tool of Stalin during his lifetime. From 1953 to 1957 many of the main ideological policies of the party leadership allegedly were based on the findings of the institute.

Masaryk, Jan (1886–1948). Czechoslovak diplomat and foreign minister, son of Tomas MASARYK. Jan Masaryk attended the PARIS PEACE CONFERENCE of 1919–20 and was Czech minister (diplomatic envoy) to London from 1925 to 1928. He resigned after the MUNICH PACT (1938) ceded Czechoslovakia's SUDETENLAND to Germany. He spent WORLD WAR II in London as foreign minister and deputy prime minister of the Czech government-in-exile (1941–45). On the liberation of CZECHOSLOVAKIA he continued as foreign minister. Although unsympathetic to the increasingly pro-Soviet policy, he remained in office after the communist coup in 1948 but died a few days later after falling from a window in the Czech foreign ministry. His death has never been satisfactorily

Czechoslovak diplomat and Foreign Minister Jan Masaryk died under mysterious circumstances shortly after the communist takeover in 1948.

explained; many suspect he either committed suicide under duress or was murdered by the communists.

Masaryk, Tomas Garrigue (1850–1937). Czech philosopher and political leader, founding president of CZECHOSLOVAKIA (1918–35). Born in Moravia, he received a doctorate in 1876 and was a professor of philosophy at the Czech University, Prague from 1882 to 1914. An ardent democrat, he served in the Austrian parliament from 1891 to 1913 and again from 1907 to 1914. In 1900, he founded the Progressive (Realist) Party to advance his ideas of social reform, Czech equality and suffrage and the unification and protection of minorities. An early advocate of a federation of self-governing nationalities within the AUSTRO-HUNGARIAN EMPIRE, by the outbreak of WORLD WAR I he was supporting Czech independence. In 1914, he and Eduard BENES fled to London, where he formed a council that was recognized by the Allies in 1918 as Czechoslovakia's de facto government. During the war years, Masaryk traveled throughout Europe and the U.S., winning support and funding for the Czech cause. At the end of the war, the state of Czechoslovakia was established and Masaryk was elected its first president, winning reelection in 1920, 1927 and 1934. He was at least partially successful in creating a multicultural democracy and was revered throughout the world as a democratic leader. He was the father of Jan MASARYK.

"M*A*S*H". Popular anti-war television comedy series. Its run on CBS—from September 17, 1972 to September 19, 1983—coincided with a time of bitterly divided feelings in America toward the VIETNAM WAR and its aftermath. The members of the 4077th Mobile Army Surgical Hospital, working behind the front lines of the KOREAN WAR, were, with the exception of the gung-ho (but cowardly) Maj. Frank Burns (Larry Linville), all reluctant draftees coping with the horrors of war. Cast regulars for the first few seasons included Alan Alda ("Hawkeye" Pierce), Wayne Rogers ("Trapper John" McIntyre), Loretta Swit ("Hot Lips" Houlihan), Larry Linville (Maj. Burns), Gary Burghoff ("Radar" O'Reilly), McLean Stevenson (Lt. Col. Blake), William Christopher (Father Mulcahy), and Jamie Farr (Cpl. Klinger). Col. Blake was written out of the series in 1974 (his helicopter was shot down in the last episode that spring) and replaced by Col. Potter (Harry Morgan) for the remainder of the series. Other changes included the replacement of Trapper John by Cpt. B.J. Hunnicut (Mike Farrell) in 1975, and Maj. Burns by Maj. Charles Emerson Winchester (David Ogden Stiers) in 1977. Gary Burghoff, the only cast member who repeated his role from the original movie version by Robert ALTMAN, took his teddy bear and departed in 1979. In addition to series writer Larry Gelbart, Alda also wrote (and directed) some of the episodes. When the last original episode aired as a two-and-a-half-hour special on February 28, 1983, the entire nation tuned in—the largest audience ever to watch a single scheduled television program.

Tomas Masaryk, the architect of Czechoslovakian independence and the nation's first president.

Mason, James (1909–1984). British-born actor. Mason was noted for playing suave aristocrats and refined, romantic villains. His career spanned nearly half a century, and he acted in more than 100 films. He was nominated for ACADEMY AWARDS for his performances in *A Star Is Born, Georgy Girl* and *The Verdict*. Mason's other films include *The Seventh Veil, Odd Man Out, The Desert Fox* and *Lolita*.

Massey, Vincent (1887–1967). Canadian statesman. Born in Toronto, he was a teacher and government official before becoming president of his family business (1921–25). A supporter of the LIBERAL PARTY, he was CANADA'S first minister to the U.S. (1926–30) and high commissioner for Canada in Great Britain (1935–46). Massey was chairman of the Royal Commission on National Development in the Arts, Letters, and Sciences (1949–51) and chancellor of the University of Toronto (1947–52). From 1952 to 1959, he served as governor general of Canada, the first native-born Canadian to hold that post. His memoirs were published in 1963.

Massey, William Ferguson (1856–1925). NEW ZEALAND statesman, prime minister (1912–25). Born in Ulster, he emigrated to New Zealand in 1870, farming near Auckland and becoming the political spokesman for local dairy farmers. He entered the New Zealand parliament in 1894. Leader of the conservative Opposition Party (later the Reform Party), he became prime minister in 1912 and held the office until his death. An agrarian conservative, he supported moderate land reforms and suppressed his country's labor unions. A strong supporter of the British empire, he sent an expeditionary force to Europe at the outbreak of WORLD WAR I and served in the British war cabinet (1917–18). During the war, he participated in the coalition National government of the Reform and Liberal parties (1915–19). After the war, Massey opposed the movement to give New Zealand greater independence by making it a dominion within the empire.

Massine, Leonide (1895–1979). Russian-born choreographer and dancer whose ideas helped to shape 20th-century ballet. After training at the Imperial Ballet School in St. Petersburg, Massine joined Serge DIAGHILEV'S BALLETS RUSSES, winning immediate acclaim in Michael FOKINE'S *The Legend of Joseph* (1914). Massine's PARADE (1917), which he choreographed, is considered a milestone in modernist ballet. Other notable works choreographed by Massine include *La Boutique Fantastique, The Three-Cornered Hat, Gaiete Parisienne* and *Jeux d'Enfants*. The 1948 film *The Red Shoes*, which he choreographed and performed in, won Massine wide popularity.

Massing, Hede (1899–1981). Austrian-born actress who served as a spy for the Soviet intelligence network in the U.S. (1933–37), when she became disillusioned. Massing testified against Alger HISS at his second perjury trial in 1950. She was the only witness to corroborate the allegations by Whittaker CHAMBERS that Hiss, a former State Department official, had been a member of the COMMUNIST PARTY underground in Washington, D.C.

Masson, Andre (1896–1987). French painter and graphic artist. Born in Balagny, Masson studied at the Academie des Beaux-Arts, Brussels and Ecole des Beaux-Arts, Paris. His early work was influenced by CUBISM and by the painting of Juan GRIS in particular. After meeting Andre BRETON, Max ERNST and Joan MIRO in 1924, Masson became an exponent of SURREALISM—the style for which he is best known. His exploration of the subconscious led him to experiment with "automatic writing," and spontaneous drawing in which personal imagery is developed. Traveling to Spain in the 1930s, he painted bullfighters and other Catalonian themes, and when he visited the U.S. (1941–45), he explored African-American and American Indian imagery. Masson settled in Aix-en-Provence in 1947 and devoted himself to landscape painting. An extremely versatile artist, he is also known for his work as a book illustrator, sculptor, set and costume designer and writer.

mass production. Widely used term that describes the modern method of industrial production in which a large number of identical items are made by mechanized techniques. "Serial" production is a similar term, also referring to manufacturing based on the concept of the assembly line, where the object is moved (often by mechanized conveyors) past the work stations of individuals who perform particular repetitive tasks. The concept is based on the rationalization of production in which the steps of the manufacturing process are carefully analyzed and equipment is provided (often specially designed) so that each step can be accomplished with a minimum of handwork. Avoiding the delays and constant changes of task that are typical of craftwork increases efficiency and permits a maximum of mechanization that makes the manufacturing process as nearly automatic as possible.

The early enthusiasm for assembly-line production has been somewhat dimmed in recent years by recognition of the unfortunate consequences of monotonous, repetitive tasks for the individual worker. These effects also often lead to a decline in quality since pride in one's skill is negated when the demand for speed is the only significant work criterion. Recent efforts to organize work teams with greater responsibility for a total product and its quality have been introduced in some factories, including the classic assembly-line plant—the automobile factory. At the same time, automation in which human workers are entirely replaced by automatic machinery (robots) makes possible mass production without the costs of human labor. Computer control of automated production also makes possible the efficient manufacture of varied products on a single assembly line.

Masters, Edgar Lee (1869–1950). American poet. Born in Garnett, Kansas, Masters attended law school and was a practicing attorney in Chicago from 1892 to 1920. He owes his fame to one volume of poetry, *Spoon River Anthology* (1915), a series of epigrammatic free verse epitaphs that capture the character, triumphs and tragedies of the citizens of a typical American small town. Masters' other volumes of poetry include *Starved Rock* (1919), *Domesday Book* (1920) and *Illinois Poems* (1941). He was also the author of several novels and of such biographies as *Lincoln the Man* (1931), *Whitman* (1937) and *Mark Twain* (1938). His autobiography, *Across Spoon River*, was published in 1936.

Masters and Johnson. American sex researchers William Howell Masters (1915–), a gynecologist, and his wife, Virginia Eshelman Johnson (1925–), a psychologist, are pioneers in the field of human sexuality and the testing of various forms of sexual response. In the course of their work, they have exploded a number of widely held misconceptions about the nature of human sexuality. Masters and Johnson detail their researches in their volumes *Human Sexual Response* (1966), *Human Sexual Inadequacy* (1970) and *Homosexuality in Perspective* (1979). They have also done influential work in sex therapy and have an extensive training program for therapists at the institute they established in St. Louis in 1970.

Mastroianni, Marcello (Vincenzo Domenico) (1923–). A charming, handsome film star from Fontana Liri, Mastroianni is generally regarded as the leading Italian screen actor of his generation. On-screen from 1947, the "Italian Cary GRANT" has starred in more than 80 (primarily Italian) films, including *White Nights* (1957), *Where the Hot Wind Blows* (1958), *Divorce Italian-Style* (1962) and *Marriage Italian-Style* (1964). In America, he is best recognized in films directed by Federico FELLINI, such as *La Dolce Vita* (1960), *8 1/2* (1963), *City Of Women* (1981) and *Ginger and Fred* (1986).

Masuku, Lookout (1939–1986). African guerrilla leader. He was a leader in the struggle that led to the establishment of the black-ruled nation of ZIMBABWE in 1980. From 1980 to 1982, he was deputy commander of that country's national army. He was arrested in 1982 on charges of conspiring against Prime Minister Robert MUGABE's government. Acquitted in 1983, he was kept under detention until 1986.

Masursky, Harold (1922–). U.S. geologist-astronomer. Working with NASA since the U.S. Ranger series in the early 1960s, Masursky has specialized in studies of the surfaces of the moon and the planets of the solar system and has participated in almost every NASA planetary project since that time. As leader of the team that selected and monitored observations of Mars by the Mariner spacecraft, he also helped to select the Viking landing sites on Mars and is a member of the Venus Orbiter Imaging Radar Science Working Group. A familiar face at NASA press conferences, he has also been involved in NASA's Pioneer and Voyager projects. Masursky is a senior scientist with the U.S. Geological Survey. He took his degree from Yale University in 1951 and has received four medals from NASA for exceptional scientific achievement.

Mata Hari (1876–1917). Dutch spy. Mata Hari was the stage name of Margaretha Geertruida Zelle, a glamorous dancer from the Netherlands who settled in Paris. She entered Germany's secret service in 1907. During WORLD WAR I, she transmitted important military secrets to Germany that had been given to her by her many Allied officer lovers. In 1917 she was arrested, tried, convicted. She was executed by a French firing squad on October 15.

Mathewson, Christopher "Christy" (1880–1925). American baseball player. Mathewson's fadeaway curve, a forerunner of the screwball, made him one of the most successful and feared right-handers of his era. He spent most of his career with the New York Giants (1900–1916), where in 1905 he led the team to a World Series victory by pitching three shutouts in six days. He went to the Cincinnati Reds as a pitcher-manager (1916–18), but his pitching career was ended by WORLD WAR I, when he was gassed in France. He finished with 373 victories and 83 shutouts. Upon his return from the war, he was named president of the Boston Braves, a post he held until his death in 1925. Mathewson was among the first group of players named to the Baseball Hall of Fame, in 1936.

Mathias, Robert Bruce (1930–). American athlete. One of the greatest athletes of all time, Mathias was the only man ever to win the grueling Olympic decathlon twice. In high school, he starred in football and basketball, as well as track. Shortly after his high school graduation, he won his first Olympic gold medal as a decathlete. In the years before his next Olympic triumph, he starred as a fullback for the University of Southern California football team and also won four consecutive U.S. decathlon championships. Mathias went on from his athletic career to pursue his political aspirations and was elected to the U.S House of Representatives in 1966. (See also OLYMPIC GAMES.)

Mathieu, Georges (1921–). French painter. Self-taught, Mathieu began painting in 1942. Two years later, influenced by American ABSTRACT EXPRESSIONISM, he started to paint the large, lyrical and abstract works for which he is known. Extremely calligraphic in nature, his paintings are executed quickly in slashing strokes against a colored ground. A precursor of PERFORMANCE ART, he executed some of his works in front of an audience. Mathieu is also known for his posters and designs for the theater.

Mathis, Johnny (John Royce) (1935–). American popular singer. Born in San Francisco, Mathis joined Columbia Records in New York in 1956. He originally wanted to be a jazz singer, but Mitch Miller persuaded him to concentrate on ballads. A unique and haunting emotional quality made his voice unmistakable in such hits as "Misty" (1959), "The Shadow of Your Smile" (1960) and "The Twelfth of Never" (1961). "When a Child Is Born" was a No. 1 hit in Britain in 1976.

Matisse, Henri (1869–1954). One of the greatest French painters of the 20th century. After abandoning law studies in Paris, Matisse began to study painting with Gustave Moreau (1892). Soon, in work like the portrait *Green Stripe* (1905), he started working with the vibrant colors, complementary contrasts and spontaneous gestures of FAUVISM, the first real revolution in 20th century painting. Matisse strove to eliminate all traces of "illusion" in his images for the sake of a greater emphasis upon the two-dimensionality of color and shape. His great works, like *Dance and Music* (1909–1910), celebrate the writhing sensuality of color shapes; and *Red Studio* (1911) and *Harmony in Red* (1908) use vibrant color to unify areas of flat, decorative arabesques. Some of his later works, such as the *Bather by a River* (1917), achieve a more monumental grandeur and austerity. He was also a forceful sculptor. His relief bronzes include *Back I-IV* (1909–30). After moving to Nice, where he worked for most of the rest of his life, he turned increasingly to his famous "cut-out" techniques, organizing simple compositions from pieces of brightly colored paper. The culmination of his work came in his decorations for the Chapel of the Rosary at Vence (1949–51), a gift to the nuns who had looked after him during an illness. Despite a crippling arthritis, Matisse continued to work until his death.

Matisse, Pierre (1900–1989). Internationally known art dealer and younger son of artist Henri MATISSE. Born in France, he moved to the U.S. in 1925 and, with little encouragement from his father, arranged a series of exhibits and eventually established his own gallery in New York City. He helped popularize the works of such artists as Joan MIRO, Marc CHAGALL, and Jean DUBUFFET.

Matsuoka, Yosuke (1880–1946). Japanese diplomat and statesman. Born in JAPAN, Matsuoka went to Oregon at the age of 13 and later attended the University of Oregon. He joined the Japanese foreign service and served as JAPAN's chief representative to the LEAGUE OF NATIONS (1932–33), where he expressed his country's expansionist philosophy and withdrew from the organization. He was president of the South Manchurian Railway (1935–39). As Japan's foreign minister (1940–41), he concluded the AXIS Pact with GERMANY and ITALY (1940) and negotiated (1941) a nonagression agreement with the U.S.S.R. He was a strong supporter of Japan's entry into WORLD WAR II and opposed negotiations with the U.S. Indicted as a war criminal, he died before his trial.

Matsushita, Konosuke (1894–1989). Japanese manufacturing magnate, founder of Japan's Matsushita Electrical Industrial Co., the world's largest producer of consumer electrical goods. He rose from poverty to found his own firm (1918) based on his success with a new electric light socket. By the 1980s the company had sales of an estimated $41 billion and produced everything from electric rice cookers to video cassette recorders—many of which were sold under the brand name Panasonic. Matsushita was often regarded as the pioneer of the modern Japanese corporation, with its emphasis on *marugake* (strong social ties between a company and its employees).

Matta Echuarren, Roberto Sebastiano (1912–). Chilean painter. Usually known simply as Matta, he was born in Santiago. He moved to Paris, where in the 1930s he studied architecture with LE CORBUSIER. There he met Andre BRETON and other important figures in French SURREALISM. From 1938 to 1947 Matta painted in a Surrealist style, creating works with a strange otherworldly, almost cosmic aura. In 1939 he traveled to the U.S., where he met and was influenced by Marcel DUCHAMP. His later works are more abstract in nature, taking advantage of the linear designs of controlled spills and the atmospheric effects of deep color.

Matteotti Affair. Giacomo Matteotti (1885–1924), a leader of the Italian Socialist Party and an outspoken opponent of FASCISM, was murdered in June, 1924—apparently by fascist thugs. His death triggered antifascist demonstrations in the Italian parliament and pleas for the reestablishment of democracy. Italian leader Benito MUSSOLINI, who claimed ignorance and disapproved of the affair, reacted by banning socialist meetings and censoring the press. In 1926 several fascists were arrested for the murder, but they received little punishment. Antifascists subsequently invoked the affair to rally support. During WORLD WAR II, the Italian RESISTANCE movement formed Matteotti Brigades. A postwar investigation of the affair (1947) found a group of extremists over which Mussolini had little control responsible for the murder.

Matthews, Burnita Shelton (1894–1988). U.S. judge. Her 1949 appointment as a judge on the U.S. District Court for the District of Columbia reportedly made Matthews the first woman to serve as a federal district judge. By the time of that appointment, she had practiced law in Washington for three decades and had become known as a champion of women's rights. She continued hearing district court cases until 1983.

Matthiessen, F(rancis) O(tto) (1902–1950). American educator and literary critic. Matthiessen was a professor of history and English at Yale and later at Harvard. His critical works, which show the influence of Van Wyck BROOKS, include *The Achievement of T.S. Eliot: An Essay in the Nature of Poetry* (1935) and *American Renaissance: Art and Expression in the Age of Emerson and Whitman* (1941). He also wrote the biography *Sarah Orne Jewett* (1929).

Mauchly, John William (1907–1980). American engineer, co-inventor (with J. Presper Eckert Jr.) of the first electronic computer. Working with Eckert, Mauchly built ENIAC (Electronic Numerical Integrator And Computer) for the U.S. War Department in 1946. The computer took up 15,000 square feet and applied electronic speed to mathematical tasks for the first time. The two later designed the more advanced UNIVAC I computer (1951).

Maudling, Reginald (1917–1979). British politician. A member of the CONSERVATIVE PARTY, Maudling was first elected to Parliament in 1950 and held his seat until his death. He served in the governments of five prime ministers, notably as chancellor of the exchequer (1962–64) and home secretary (1970–72). He narrowly missed in two bids for party leadership—and the prime ministership—in 1963 and 1965.

Maugham, Syrie (1879–1955). Noted British interior designer and decorator. She was married for a short time to the writer Somerset MAUGHAM. Her individual style, developed in the 1930s, made use of pale, monochromatic colors and eventually moved toward all- (or nearly all) white schemes. Her firm, Syrie Ltd. established in the 1920s and began by producing work of the traditional eclectic character typical of decorators' taste of the time. As her style developed, Maugham often chose glass, mirror and silvered frames with otherwise largely white finishes. Although her white rooms often included furniture and details of traditional design character, these elements were often finished in white—reflecting her particularly personal way of working.

British author W. Somerset Maugham.

Maugham, W(illiam) Somerset (1874–1965). British novelist. Orphaned at the age of 10, Maugham was raised by his aunt and his uncle, a clergyman. He practiced medicine before turning permanently to writing. He recreated his austere childhood in the autobiographical novel *Of Human Bondage* (1915, filmed 1946), his best known work. The protagonist, Philip Carey, suffers from a club foot and later, while a medical student, from an obsessive, unrequited love for a rapacious lower-class woman. Maugham was traumatized by a childhood stutter. He established himself as a writer with his first novel, *Liza of Lambeth* (1897), which reflected his work as an obstetrical clerk in the slums of London and which was considered an example of the "new realism." It was the beginning of a successful and lucrative career, yet Maugham was always troubled by his status as a second-rate writer, a feeling he expressed in *The Summing Up* (1938). Other works include the novels *The Moon and Sixpence* (1919), *Cakes and Ale* (1930) and *The Razor's Edge* (1944) and the plays *The Circle* (1921) and *For Services Rendered* (1932). Also notable is the short story "Rain" (1921), which has been staged and was filmed four times.

Mau Mau. A society formed in 1948 among the Kikuyu tribe in KENYA, then a British colony. The Mau Mau sought the forcible eviction of white farmers from traditional Kikuyu lands by invoking ancient rituals and by murder. In 1952, following a violent Mau Mau uprising, Kenyan authorities responded with military force, declared a state of emergency and arrested Jomo KENYATTA as an instigator. The following year, the Mau Mau was responsible for the massacre of more than 80 people, the majority of whom were African. The Kikuyu and other tribes became disgusted with the rebellion, which was effectively subdued by 1954. The state of emergency was not lifted, however, until 1960. During the Mau Mau uprisings, an estimated 11,000 Kikuyu Mau Mau, 1,800 Africans opposed to them, 167 Kenyan security personnel and 68 Europeans—the original targets of the rebellion—were killed.

Mauritania [Islamic Republic of Mauritania]. Mauritania covers an area of 397,850 square miles in northwestern Africa. A French protectorate in 1903, Mauritania was incorporated into FRENCH WEST AFRICA in 1904 and became a French

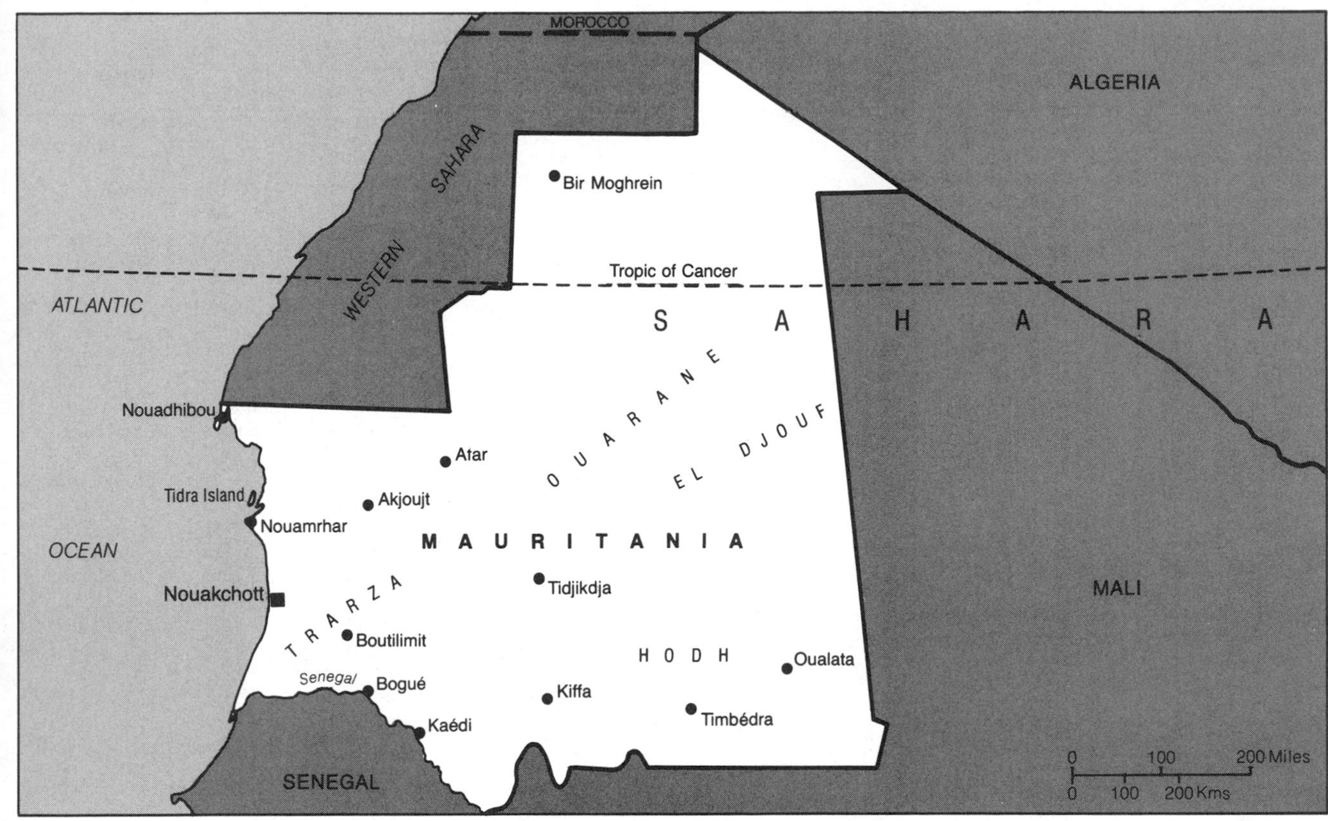

MAURITANIA

colony in 1920. Achieving autonomy within the French Community in 1958, the country declared its independence as the Islamic Republic of Mauritania in 1960. The resentment of the black African population toward the officially declared Arab identity of the country led to riots in 1966 and 1979. Tensions between Mauritania and MOROCCO over the status of the Saharan Arab Democratic Republic existed from 1976 to 1986, while internal political instability was the result of a series of military coups between 1978 and 1984. A bloodless coup in 1984 brought Colonel Moaouie Ould Sidi Mohamed Taya to power. His government has pursued a democratization policy. In 1989 a dispute with SENEGAL escalated into ethnic violence, resulting in hundreds of deaths and the expulsion of 40,000 black Mauritanians into Senegal.

Mauritius. Located east of Madagascar, Mauritius is comprised of a main island, 20 adjacent islets and the dependencies of the Agalega and Rodriques Islands and the Cargados Carajos shoals—a total land area of 718 square miles. Mauritius was under British control from 1810 to 1968 when the country achieved independence and became a member of the COMMONWEALTH. Ethnic tensions among the French Creoles, Muslims and immigrant Indian workers have dominated the political scene in Mauritius, resulting in periodic strikes and government crackdowns, a series of unstable coalition governments, and the formation of a left-wing political party. Anerood Jugnauth formed an alliance with several political groups and was elected prime minister in 1983 and again in 1987. Under his leadership the economy has improved, though there have been two attempts to assassinate him (1988, 1989).

Maurois, Andre [pen name of Emile Herzog] (1885–1967). French novelist, literary critic and biographer. Maurois was successful in a number of literary genres but remains best known for his romantic-style biographies that imaginatively recreated the psyches of his subjects. Maurois' many biographical studies include works on British Prime Minister Benjamin Disraeli (1924), the English poet Lord Byron (1930), and the French novelists George Sand (1952) and Honore de Balzac (1965). Maurois also wrote a number of popular novels, such as *The Silence of Colonel Bramble* (1918), and was an influential literary critic who was an early champion of the works of Marcel PROUST. His major autobiographical work is *Memoirs 1885–1967* (1970). He received the NOBEL PRIZE for literature in 1952.

Maurras, Charles (1868–1952). French political writer and critic. A literary and political conservative, he was a founder of the *Ecole romane,* a neoclassical movement in French letters. A monarchist and nationalist, he disseminated his views as editor of the *Action francaise* and by writing such books as *Enquete sur la monarchie* (1909) and *Mes Idees politiques* (1937). He was elected to the *Academie francaise* in 1938. A Nazi collaborator, he was expelled from the *Academie* and in 1945 was sentenced to life imprisonment. He was pardoned just before his death.

Maximalists. Small terrorist group of Russian populists that split off from the Socialist Revolutionaries in 1904. Having taken an active part in the RUSSIAN REVOLUTION OF 1905, they continued to organize violence, and in 1906 blew up Peter STOLYPIN's summer residence. As a result, many Maximalists were executed, and others escaped abroad. They worked with the BOLSHEVIKS after the latter's seizure of power in 1917, and were represented in the central executive committee. In 1920 the group disintegrated, and most of its members joined the Bolshevik Party.

Maxwell, Robert Ian [Jan Ludwig Hoch] (1923–). Czech-born British publisher, head of an information and communications empire that includes printing, publishing and cable television companies in 16 countries. His initial publishing success came with Pergamon Press (purchased in 1951), which filled a need for the dissemination of scientific information. Among the companies he owns are the Mirror Group Newspapers in England (since 1984), Macmillan, Inc. (since 1988) and the New York DAILY NEWS (since 1991). Maxwell has also been a LABOUR PARTY member of Parliament (1964–70) and was active in the Czech RESISTANCE during WORLD WAR II.

May, Elaine [Elaine Berlin] (1932–). American comedic actress, film director and screenplay writer. May first achieved success in show business in the 1950s,

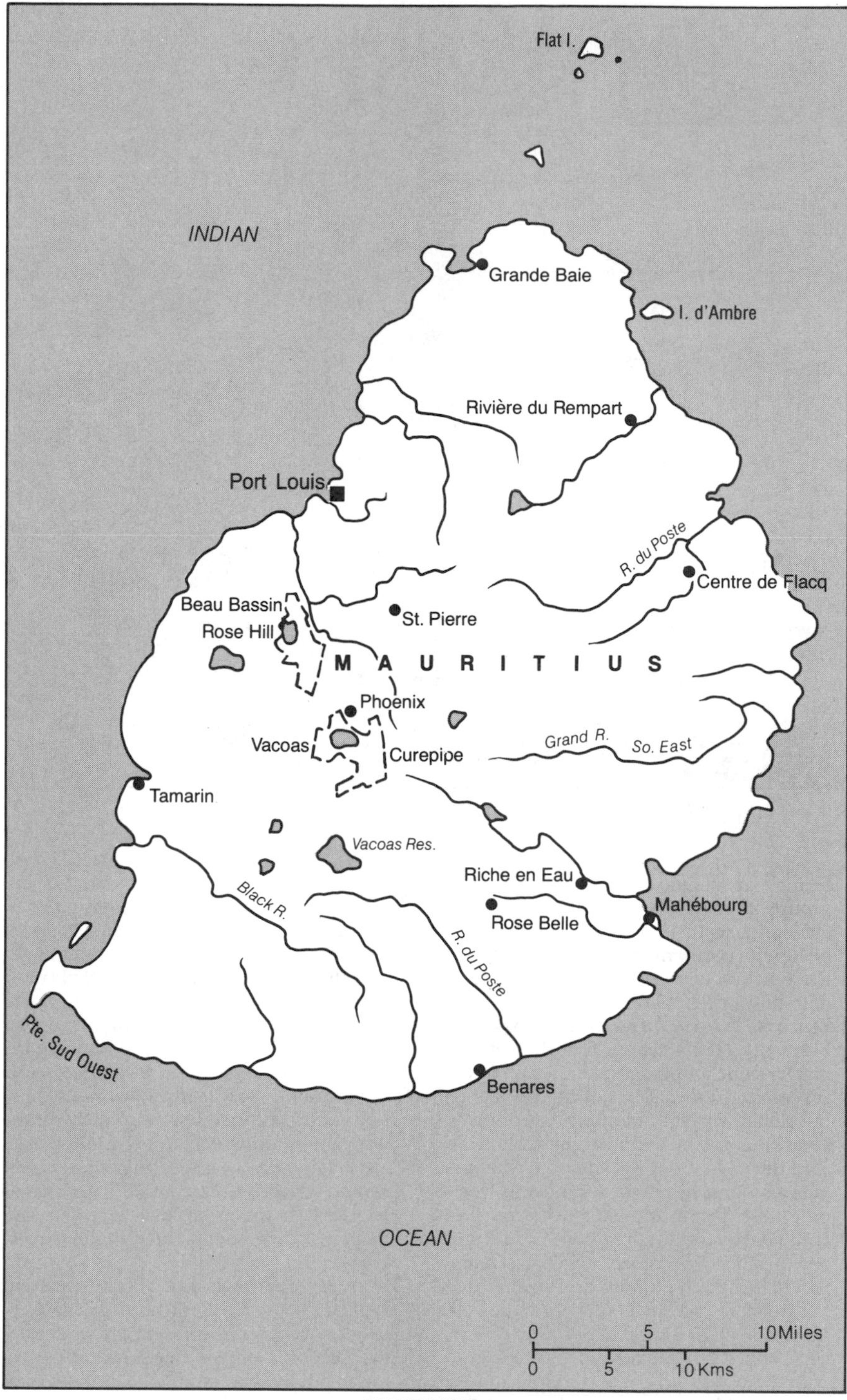

MAURITIUS

when she formed a stage comedy team with Mike NICHOLS. Together they enjoyed a Broadway hit with *An Evening with Mike Nichols and Elaine May* (1960). After the team broke up, May went on to become a pioneering figure in HOLLYWOOD as a woman who wrote, acted in and directed feature films. As an actress, she appeared in the comedies *Luv* (1967) and *Enter Laughing* (1967). One of her finest efforts—which May wrote, directed and costarred in with Walter Matthau—is the comedy *A New Leaf* (1971). Other films directed by May include *The Heartbreak Kid* (1972) and *Ishtar* (1987). She also cowrote the script for the hit comedy *Heaven Can Wait* (1978).

May, Rollo (Reese) (1909–). American psychologist. May studied to be a Congregational minister before turning to psychology and earning a Ph.D. in clinical psychology at Columbia University (1949). In his books he has explored the relationship between creativity and inner satisfaction. Many of his books, including *The Meaning of Anxiety* (1950), *Love and Will* (1969), *The Courage To Create* (1975) and *Freedom and Destiny* (1981), have become best-sellers. His humanistic approach to psychology has had a strong influence on the NEW AGE MOVEMENT.

Mayakovsky, Vladimir Vladimirovich (1894–1930). Russian poet. In 1908 Mayakovsky joined the Communist Party, and in 1911 he met some of the early FUTURISTS. His first collection of poems, *As Simple as Mooing* (1916), met with success. He wrote many poems about the revolution, including "150,000,000" (1920), in which President WILSON personifies capitalism. He also wrote satirical plays, including *The Bedbug* (1921). He was the leading representative of the Futurist school, and Mayakovsky had considerable influence on subsequent poets. Disenchanted with the party, he committed suicide in 1930; later he was eulogized by Stalin.

Maybray-King, Lord (Horace) (1901–1986). British politician. First elected to Parliament as a Labourite from Southampton (1950), in 1965 Maybray-King became the first speaker of the House of Commons from the LABOUR PARTY. He held the office until his retirement in 1970. He was made a life peer in 1971 and was a deputy speaker in the House of Lords until his death.

Mayer, Albert (1897–1981). American architect and city planner. Mayer cofounded the firm of Mayer, Whittlesey & Glass (1935) and was its senior partner. His views were influential in the creation of the U.S. Housing Authority (1937). An advocate of rationally planned urban expansion, he was the designer for many housing projects in the U.S. He gained international renown in the 1950s as the master planner for India's NEW TOWN CHANDIGARH.

Mayer, Arthur Loeb (1886–1981). Legendary American motion picture exhibitor and distributor, onetime head of publicity at PARAMOUNT PICTURES. Mayer would use any gimmick to fill a movie theater. His showings of double-feature horror films at New York's Rialto Theater earned him the epithet The Merchant of Menace. After WORLD WAR II he imported such outstanding Italian films as *Open City* and *The Bicycle Thief* and lectured on film history at colleges across the U.S.

Mayer, Louis B. (1885–1957). Russian-born motion picture pioneer and celebrated chief executive of MGM. Mayer followed his immigrant father's occupation of junk dealer in Boston until his company failed. In 1907 he took over the management of a theater chain and 10 years later formed his own production company, Louis B. Mayer Pictures. After the merger in 1924 that formed METRO-GOLDWYN-MAYER, he became vice president and general manager of the West Coast operation. At his peak in the 1930s and 1940s, Mayer was the epitome of the HOLLYWOOD mogul—ruthless, hardworking, paternalistic, staunchly conservative, vindictive toward his enemies, loyal to the point of indulgence to his friends—and obsessed with making movies. His annual salary of $1.25 million was the highest in the nation. Mayer's favorite among all his MGM pictures was *The Human Comedy* (1943), written by William SAROYAN. The film reflects Mayer's sentimental ideas, portraying an America of small towns and decent and industrious citizens, who, despite their differences, feel an almost spiritual sense of family. After years of infighting at MGM, Mayer was ousted in 1951 by former aide Dore SCHARY. He refused an opportunity to return as president of the company in 1957.

May Fourth Incident. Protest of May 4, 1919, by some 3,000 Chinese students in Peking. They had massed to demonstrate their disapproval of the continuation of internationally sponsored imperialism in CHINA, which was manifested at the PARIS PEACE CONFERENCE with the awarding of Germany's former concessions in Shantung province to Japan. The students marched to the legation quarter to present their grievances and then protested at the home of Ts'Ao Ju-lin (China's minister of communications and former vice foreign minister), where some were arrested. While the incident had little immediate importance, it triggered the MAY FOURTH MOVEMENT, which has been an important factor in the development of Chinese culture in the 20th century.

May Fourth Movement. Popular reform movement in CHINA that produced a virtual revolution in thought and culture from 1919 to 1921. It was sparked by the MAY FOURTH INCIDENT and early on resulted in a variety of strikes and anti-Japanese boycotts, which were influential enough to prevent Chinese delegates to the Paris Peace Conference from signing the TREATY OF VERSAILLES. As the movement escalated, it grew to include other aims beyond the elimination of Japanese imperialism in China. These included a program to improve literacy among the populace, an increased popularity of Western liberal ideas, the promotion of a vernacular literature and a widespread refutation of the traditional Confucian social hierarchy. This period of growing modernism also saw the beginnings of Chinese Marxism.

Mayo Clinic. Noted American medical facility at Rochester, Minnesota. Started in 1889, it is one of the largest and most widely recognized medical centers in the world. Founded by William Worrall Mayo and his two sons to care for surgical patients, the clinic's functions changed to those of a general medical center just before World War I. Over 200,000 patients are treated at the Mayo Clinic annually.

Mayotte. Island in the Mozambique Channel between Mozambique and Madagascar, forming part of the Comoro Archipelago and covering a total area of 145 square miles; the earliest inhabitants were a Melano-Polynesian people. In 1912 Mayotte was combined with the other Comoro Islands to form a dependency of France's colony of Madagascar. In 1946 the islands became a separate French overseas territory. Internal autonomy was granted in 1961. Elections to the Chamber of Deputies in December 1972 produced a strong majority for the coalition of parties in favor of independence. A referendum on December 22, 1974 resulted in a 96% majority throughout the Comoros for independence but not in Mayotte, where 64% voted against. In July 1975 the Comoran Chamber of Deputies unilaterally declared the islands independent, despite the protests of Mayotte. FRANCE remained in control of Mayotte and proposed a referendum on the island's future; held on February 8, 1976, it produced a 99% vote in favor of retaining links with France. The French government refused to consider making the island a department, but granted it the status of a territorial collective, a status between that of a department and an overseas territory. Following a Comoran coup in 1978 the new government offered to include Mayotte in a new federal system. Mayotte refused. In March 1987 there were outbreaks of rioting between the local population and illegal immigrants from the Comoros.

Mays, Benjamin E. (1895–1984). Black American educator and a champion of the CIVIL RIGHTS movement. Mays gained an international reputation while dean of the Howard University Divinity School (1934–40). From 1940 to 1967 he was president of Morehouse College, where his students included Martin Luther KING Jr. King later called Mays his "spiritual and intellectual leader." Mays also served on the Atlanta Board of Education (1969–81).

For further reading:

Mays, Benjamin E., *Born to Rebel: An Autobiography by Benjamin E. Mays.* Athens: University of Georgia Press, 1986.

———, *Quotable Quotes of Benjamin E. Mays.* New York: Vantage Press, 1983.

Mays, Willie Howard, Jr. (1931–). American baseball player. Undisputedly one of the greatest baseball players ever, Mays was a major figure during the glory years of New York baseball in the 1950s and 1960s. He was a brilliant fielder, with a career putout total of 7,095, a record that still stands. He led the New York Giants to the National League pennant in 1954 with a .345 batting average, and his outstanding fielding helped them win the World Series. Mays went with the team when they moved to San Francisco after the 1957 season. Although his play continued to sparkle, with another 50–home-run season, Mays was never as happy there as in New York. He finished his career with the New York Mets in 1973, with a career total of 511 home runs. He was named to the Hall of Fame in 1979.

When he retired from baseball in 1973, Willie Mays had a career total of 511 home runs.

Maysles, David (Peter) (1933–1987). U.S. filmmaker. He and his brother **Albert Maysles** (1933–) played key roles in the development of the documentary genre known as cinema verite, which used hand-held cameras, natural sound, and no scripts or staged sets. The best known of the brothers' films were *Salesmen* (1969), *Gimme Shelter* (1970, about the ROLLING STONES) and *Grey Gardens* (1975).

Maytag, Frederick Lewis (1857–1937). U.S. manufacturer. He converted his small business into a factory at Newton, Iowa, in 1907 to manufacture hand-operated washing machines. Four years later he introduced a motorized washing machine. A leader in the industry by the early 1920s, the company's management was taken over by Frederick's son in 1926. With its ongoing research and promotion, the company produced the first automatic washer in 1948 and continued to be a leading manufacturer of major appliances. The city of Newton still calls itself the "Washing Machine Capital of the World."

Mazowiecki, Tadeusz (1927–). Polish journalist and political leader, premier of

Charles and William Mayo, who founded the Mayo Clinic with their father William, receiving honorary degrees from Villanova University (June 3, 1937).

POLAND (1989–90). A leading Catholic intellectual, Mazowiecki was active in the SOLIDARITY movement during the late 1970s and the 1980s and was a trusted adviser to Lech WALESA. In 1989, when the Communist premier resigned under increasing pressure from Solidarity and the non-communist Polish majority, Mazowiecki was nominated for the post by Communist Party leader and president General Wojciech JARUZELSKI. Confirmed by the Polish parliament in a vote of 378 to 4 (with 41 abstentions), Mazowiecki became the first non-Communist premier in four decades. The momentous vote represented the first known democratic transfer of power away from a ruling communist party. It was an important milestone in the events of 1989 to 1990 that signaled the end both of the communist domination of Eastern Europe and of the COLD WAR. Mazowiecki faced considerable political and economic problems in governing Poland.

Mazursky, Paul (1930–). American film director, producer, screenplay writer and actor. Mazursky emerged as one of the most prolific directors in HOLLYWOOD during the 1970s and 1980s. His major successes have combined a deft comic touch with a substantive look at social issues of the day. Mazursky began his career in films with minor acting roles in the 1950s but scored a major commercial hit with his first directorial effort, the comedy about wife-swapping, *Bob & Carol & Ted & Alice* (1969). In the ensuing two decades, Mazursky produced, scripted and directed a host of films, most notably *Harry and Tonto* (1974); *An Unmarried Woman* (1978), which was one of the first films to examine the impact of divorce on women; *Moscow on the Hudson* (1984); *Down and Out in Beverly Hills* (1986); and *Moon Over Parador* (1988).

Mboya, Tom (1930–1969). Kenyan politician. A member of the Luo tribe, Mboya was educated at Ruskin College, Oxford before returning to Kenya to serve as treasurer of the Kenya African Union and as secretary of the Kenya Local Government Workers Union in the 1950s. He was among the first African members elected to the Kenya legislative council (1957), and he distinguished himself as a member of the Kenya African National Union (KANU)—the leading political party. After the country's independence in 1963, Mboya served as minister of labor, minister of justice and minister of economic planning under Jomo KENYATTA. He seemed destined for higher office but was assassinated in Nairobi (1969). Demonstrations following his murder brought Kenya close to civil war. A member of the Kikuyu tribe was found guilty of the killing and was hanged.

McAdoo, William Gibbs (1863–1941). U.S. politician. He was involved with organizing the Hudson and Manhattan Railways, which built tunnels under the Hudson River between New York and New Jersey. Later, he was appointed to the Woodrow WILSON cabinet as secretary of the treasury (1913–1918). Married to Wilson's daughter Eleanor (1914), he was chairman of the Federal Reserve Board and director general of U.S. railroads. McAdoo was elected senator from California and served in that capacity from 1933 to 1938.

McAnally, Ray(mond) (1926–1989). Irish character actor. He debuted at the ABBEY THEATRE in 1947 and appeared there in numerous Irish plays. Versatile and accomplished, he won praise over the years for his performances on stage, screen and television. He was seen by a wide international audience as the intractable papal envoy in *The Mission* (1986), the hearty working-class Yorkshireman Harry Perkins who becomes prime minister of Britain in the television production of *A Very British Coup*, and the smooth-talking con artist Rick Pym in the television adaptation of John LE CARRE's novel *A Perfect Spy*. He was also acclaimed for his portrayal of G.B. SHAW on the London stage in 1988.

McAuliffe, Anthony C. (1898–1975). McAuliffe was the American general who purportedly sent the reply "Nuts!" to a German ultimatum to surrender during the BATTLE OF THE BULGE (December 1944) in WORLD WAR II. At the time, he was acting commander of the 101st Airborne Division at BASTOGNE. (He was second-in-command to Major General Maxwell D. TAYLOR, who was attending conferences in Washington, D.C., when the battle started.) McAuliffe later commanded the 103d Infantry Division in the European campaign.

McAuliffe, (Sharon) Christa (1948–1986). American teacher who was killed in the explosion of the SPACE SHUTTLE CHALLENGER (January 28, 1986). She had been selected from more than 10,000 applicants to be the first civilian passenger on a U.S. space flight. A high-school social studies teacher from Concord, New Hampshire, she had planned to broadcast lessons from space on the Public Broadcasting Service to schoolchildren throughout the U.S.

McCain, John Sidney, Jr. (1911–1981). American naval officer. The son of a four-star admiral, during WORLD WAR II he commanded three SUBMARINES and sank 20,000 tons of Japanese shipping. He was decorated for his accomplishments. During the VIETNAM WAR he served as commander in chief of U.S. forces in the Pacific. McCain was a dedicated advocate of the importance of seapower to the national interest.

McCarren-Walter Act. Legislation codifying U.S. immigration laws. Passed in 1952 over the veto of President Harry S TRUMAN, the law maintained the national quota system of the 1924 New Quota Act but ended the earlier legislation's total ban on immigration of Asian and Pacific peoples. Provisions required elaborate screening of immigrants to keep out subversives and authorized the deportation of immigrants for communist and communist-front activities even after they had been naturalized.

McCarthy, Eugene (Joseph) (1916–). American politician. Born in Watkins, Minnesota, McCarthy later taught at the College of St. Thomas, St. Paul, Minnesota (1946–49). A Democrat, he entered politics in 1948 and served five terms in the U.S. House of Representatives (1949–59). McCarthy became a senator in 1959, establishing a liberal voting record and a reputation as a thoughtful, quiet intellectual. In 1966 he began to enunciate his opposition to President Lyndon B. JOHNSON'S VIETNAM WAR policy. In 1967 McCarthy announced his candidacy for the Democratic presidential nomination on a platform that supported a negotiated peace. Surrounded by a dedicated army of college students, McCarthy made surprisingly good showings in early primaries. His candidacy was one factor in Johnson's withdrawal from the race. McCarthy lost the nomination to Senator Hubert H. HUMPHREY. Retiring from the Senate in 1971, he returned to teaching. His subsequent attempts to reenter political life, including an independent bid for the presidency in 1976 and a run in a Senate primary in 1982, were unsuccessful.

U.S. Senator Eugene McCarthy, a contender for the Democratic nomination for the U.S. presidency in 1968. McCarthy's antiwar stance won him a wide following.

McCarthy, Joseph R(aymond) (1908–1957). American politician. Born in Grand Chute, Wisconsin, McCarthy studied law at Marquette University and, after practicing law in his home state, became a circuit judge (1940). After World War II service in the Marines, he entered politics in 1946 by defeating incumbent Wisconsin Senator Robert M. LA FOLLETTE Jr. for the Republican nomination and easily besting his Democratic rival. He was little noticed until 1950, when he accused the State Department of harboring communists. When asked for proof, McCarthy simply made new and more virulent accusations, making General George C. MARSHALL a particular object of scorn. Reelected in 1952, McCarthy gathered a loyal following around him and was soon appointed chairman of the Senate Permanent Investigations Subcommittee. Tapping into America's COLD WAR fears

In the early 1950s U.S. Senator Joseph McCarthy led a "crusade" to rid the U.S. of communists.

and wildly exacerbating them, he assumed great power and was responsible for the relentless pursuit of those he considered communists, subversives or fellow travelers and for the public disgrace of many. His attacks reached new heights in 1954 when his charges of communist infiltration into the U.S. Army provoked hearings that were broadcast on national television (see ARMY-MCCARTHY HEARINGS). As a result of the hearings, the Army was cleared and later that year McCarthy was condemned by the Senate. After this censure, his influence underwent a steep decline. McCarthy's activities inspired the term MCCARTHYISM, denoting violent and unfounded political attack.

McCarthy, Joseph Vincent ["Marse Joe"] (1887–1978). American baseball manager. McCarthy managed the legendary New York Yankees between 1931 and 1946. In that span, he led the Yankees to eight American League pennants and seven World Series titles. McCarthy was elected to the Baseball Hall of Fame in 1957.

McCarthy, Mary (Therese) (1912–1989). American novelist and critic. She was regarded as one of America's pre-eminent literary figures from the 1930s through the 1970s. Many of her works, including the memoir *Memories of a Catholic Girlhood* (1957) as well as the novel *The Group* (1963), about the lives of eight Vassar College graduates, were autobiographical. Her sharp-edged critical writings and comments often provoked other literary figures. She touched off a feud with Lillian HELLMAN after she declared in a television interview, "Everything she [Hellman] writes is a lie, including 'and' and 'the'." Hellman sued for libel but died in 1984 before the case could reach trial. In 1984 McCarthy received both the National Medal for Literature and the Edward MacDowell Medal for outstanding contribution to literature.

McCarthyism. Term derived from the behavior of U.S. Senator Joseph MCCARTHY in the early 1950s. It refers not only to McCarthy's activities, but also to the atmosphere in which he operated at the height of the COLD WAR. In his crusade against Communists and "subversives," McCarthy resorted to a variety of unethical tactics. These included making sensational and unsubstantiated charges against hitherto respectable citizens, claiming to have lists and statistics that supported his charges, and twisting witnesses' words to make them seem guilty or uncooperative. By assuming a patriotic, self-righteous stance, McCarthy made those who denied his charges seem guilty. While McCarthyism originally meant an unthinking right-wing attack against anything that vaguely smacked of COMMUNISM, the term has been expanded to encompass the cynical leveling of any kind of unfair political charges.

McCartney, (James) Paul (1942–). British rock and roll songwriter, vocalist, and bassist. Despite a solo career that has now lasted two decades, McCartney remains best known for his songwriting and vocals as a member of THE BEATLES. He and fellow Beatle John LENNON formed what many critics feel was the greatest songwriting team in the history of rock and roll. In 1970, after the breakup of The Beatles, McCartney released a highly successful eponymous solo album, *McCartney* (1970). In 1971 he formed the band Wings, which featured his wife, Linda, on keyboards and as an accompanying vocalist. There resulted a steady stream of singles hits by the ensemble Paul McCartney and Wings, including "My Love" (1973), "Live and Let Die" (1973), "Band on the Run" (1974) and "With a Little Luck" (1978). McCartney has also continued to pursue independent projects, making the hit song "Ebony and Ivory" (1982) in collaboration with Stevie WONDER and another hit, "Say Say Say" (1983), in collaboration with Michael JACKSON.

McCay, (Zenas) Winsor (1867–1934). American illustrator, cartoonist and pioneer of motion picture ANIMATION. Born in Spring Lake, Michigan, McCay spent 15 years working as a cartoonist for the *Cincinnati Commercial Tribune.* In New York after 1902, he began his famous comic strips *Dream of the Rarebit Fiend* (*New York Evening Telegram*) and *Little Nemo in Slumberland* (*New York Herald*). Both depicted the nightmares and fantasies of dreamers. These strips were more than just a popular art, writes biographer John Canemaker; they were "an anticipation of surrealist conceits in juxtapositions of fantastic occurrences in mundane settings, the instability of appearances, and the irrationality of life." Between 1908 and 1911 he hand-colored over 4,000 drawings on 35mm film for *Little Nemo* and in 1911 began touring the vaudeville theater circuits, showing his animated film and illustrating his monologues with hastily drawn sketches of his characters. In 1912 he created *The Story of a Mosquito* and in 1914 *Gertie the Dinosaur,* executing between 6,000 and 10,000 sketches each, on transparent rice paper. Lasting only a few minutes apiece, the films were timed so that the characters seemed to respond to McCay's on-stage "cues." His most ambitious animated film was *The Sinking of the Lusitania* (1918), a fervently anti-German response to the wartime tragedy (see LUSITANIA). After completing several more films, including another *Gertie* picture, McCay returned to newspaper cartooning on the *New York American.* Canemaker claims McCay was the first person to make and exhibit a hand-colored cartoon, the first to base a cartoon on a successful comic strip and the first to use the medium in a highly personal way.

McCloy, John J(ay) (1895–1989). U.S. lawyer and diplomat. He played key roles in a number of government and business operations. Among his most memorable assignments was that of U.S. high commissioner in Germany (1949–52); during that time he oversaw the creation of a democratic civilian government and supervised the disbursement of $1 billion in aid to the war-ravaged German economy (see MARSHALL PLAN). He also served as assistant secretary of war, president of the WORLD BANK, chairman of Chase Manhattan Bank and of the FORD FOUNDATION, and consultant to presidents KENNEDY, JOHNSON, NIXON, and FORD.

McCormack, John (1884–1943). Irish tenor. McCormack, who enjoyed great success both as an opera performer and as a singer of Irish popular songs, was the favorite vocalist of the great Irish novelist James JOYCE, who proclaimed McCormack to be an artistic genius. McCormack made his operatic debut in Italy (1906) and thereafter enjoyed success in both Europe and America, winning special praise for his role as Don Ottavio in Mozart's *Don Giovanni.* But while critics loved McCormack's voice, they found him a wooden actor—a verdict that McCormack himself did not dispute. After 1913 McCormack appeared strictly as a concert singer with a repertoire that drew from both opera and popular song; he was a favorite with audiences until his death. McCormack was made a papal count in 1928 and received many other honors. Many of his recordings have been remastered and remain available on LP records and compact discs.

Irish tenor John McCormack.

McCormack, John W(illiam) (1891–1980). American politician. A Democrat from Boston, Massachusetts, McCormack served in Congress for more than 40 years (1928–70), rising to the powerful position of Speaker of the House (1962–70). He was from an Irish family and was considered a model of the old-style big-city politician who tended to the needs, both great and small, of his home district. In Congress he was noted for his parliamentary skill and shrewd, temperate style, which helped him influence committee selection, shape legislation and control debate. As Speaker he helped formulate and steer through the House the outpouring of domestic legislation in the mid-1960s. (See also Lyndon B. JOHNSON, GREAT SOCIETY.)

McCormick, Frank Andrew "Buck" (1913–1982). American baseball player. He was first baseman for the Cincinnati Reds in the 1930s and 1940s. He was voted the National League's most valuable player in 1940, batting .309 that season with 19 home runs and 127 runs batted in. His career batting average was .299. He played in 652 consecutive games for Cincinnati between 1938 and 1942.

McCovey, Willie (Lee) (1938–). American baseball player. One of the most fearsome home run hitters of all time, McCovey was one of the few players to have homered in every National League stadium. His career, which stretched over four decades (1959–80), ended with a total of 521 home runs. He is perhaps best remembered for the hit he didn't get, a 1962 World Series line drive caught by Yankee Bobby Richardson that finished off the Giants' hopes in the bottom of the ninth inning of the seventh game. Traded to the San Diego Padres in 1974, he returned to the Giants for the remainder of his career in 1977. He retired in 1980, and was named to the Hall of Fame in 1986.

McCracken, James (1926–1988). American dramatic tenor; a mainstay of New York City's Metropolitan Opera Company in the 1960s and 1970s. In 1963, McCracken became the first U.S.-born singer to sing the title role in *Otello,* which remained his most celebrated role.

McCrea, Joel (1905–1990). U.S. actor. He appeared in more than 80 films, many of them Westerns, and specialized in playing calm, dependable heros. His best known Westerns included *Wells Fargo* (1937), *Union Pacific* (1939) and *Ride the High Country* (1962). He also starred in the Alfred HITCHCOCK thriller *Foreign Correspondent* (1940) and in such comedies as *Sullivan's Travels* (1941), *The Palm Beach Story* (1942) and *The More the Merrier* (1943). With the money he earned from acting, he was able to return to his first love, ranching, and built several large spreads in California.

McCullers, Carson (1917–1967). U.S. novelist. Partially paralyzed by a series of strokes while in her 20s, she was bound to a wheelchair during her last years. Her major works include *The Heart Is a Lonely Hunter* (1940), *The Member of the Wedding* (1946), *The Ballad of the Sad Cafe* (1951) and *Clock Without Hands* (1961).

American author Carson McCullers wrote her best known work, The Member of the Wedding, *in 1946.*

McCutcheon, John T. (1870–1949). American cartoonist. His first political cartoon work appeared during the political campaign of 1896. He traveled the world, visiting the Gobi Desert and Amazon River valley, and also covered the Boer conflict and the Mexican revolution of 1914. His cartoons reflectd his extraordinary background. He won the PULITZER PRIZE for cartoons in 1931. His writings include *Cartoons by McCutcheon* (1903) and *Mysterious Stranger and Other Cartoons* (1905). The *Chicago Tribune* has continued to reprint his "Indian Summer" cartoon on an annual basis, believing it to be typical of the Midwest heritage.

McDivitt, James (1929–). U.S. astronaut. Command pilot of Gemini 4 (June 3–7, 1965), McDivitt also commanded Apollo 9 (March 3–13, 1969), which was the first test in space of the lunar module. With David Scott in the command module, McDivitt and Rusty Schweickart moved into the lunar module, nicknamed "Spider," and ran tests in preparation for its future moon excursions. An Air Force pilot with 145 combat missions to his credit, McDivitt logged nearly 339 hours in space. He retired from NASA in 1972 to enter private industry.

McDonnell, James S., Jr. (1899–1980). American aircraft manufacturer, known for his innovation in aerospace invention and design. As chairman of the McDonnell Douglas Corporation, McDonnell built the company into one of the world's largest manufacturers of commercial jetliners, military aircraft, spacecraft, and missiles. (See also Donald Wills DOUGLAS.)

McEnroe, John (1959–). U.S. tennis player. As an 18-year-old amateur, he was the youngest man ever to reach the finals at Wimbledon. He dominated the world of tennis throughout the 1980s, and was only the second player to take the U.S. Open title three consecutive times (1979–81). He also won three Wimbledon singles titles, as well as doubles titles at both events. Known for his hot temper and undisciplined on-court antics, he only rarely let his emotions get the better of his game. He is married to actress Tatum O'Neal.

McEwen, John (1900–1980). Australian politician who served briefly as prime minister (1967–68). McEwen was known primarily for his leadership in international trade while trade minister. He was the architect of many trade treaties and opened up dozens of new export markets, including the U.S.S.R. and the People's Republic of CHINA, for Australian products. He worked to maintain Australia's close agricultural trade relationship with Britain and strongly opposed Britain's entry into the COMMON MARKET.

McGhee, Howard (1918–1987). U.S. musician. A JAZZ trumpeter, he was one of the first important big-band soloists to master the complexities of BEBOP. In the late 1940s and early 1950s he led his own small groups and, briefly, a big band. His career experienced a resurgence in the 1960s, when he made some of his best recordings.

McGovern, George S(tanley) (1922–). American political leader. Born in Avon, South Dakota, he attended Dakota Wesleyan University, served as a bomber pilot in WORLD WAR II, taught American history (1949–53) and earned his Ph.D. during his last year of teaching. A Democrat, he served in the House of Representatives (1957–61) and was director of President John F. KENNEDY's Food for Peace program (1961–62). Elected to the Senate in 1962, he compiled a liberal record and became an early and outspoken opponent of the VIETNAM WAR. The Democratic Party's nominee for president in 1972, he was overwhelmingly defeated by

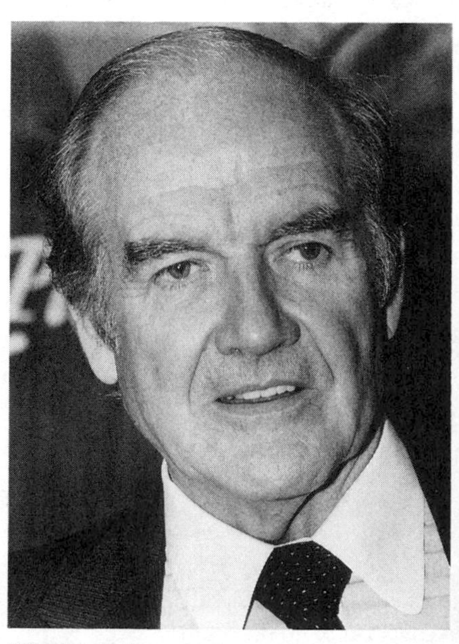

U.S. Senator George McGovern, the Democratic presidential candidate in 1972.

Richard M. NIXON. McGovern returned to the Senate but was defeated in a bid for reelection in 1980.

McGuckian, Medbh (1950–). Northern Irish poet. Born in Belfast, she was educated at Catholic schools and at Queens University, Belfast, where she was later the first female writer-in-residence (1986–88). She emerged in the 1980s with three collections and won several major prizes. Her work, highly lyrical and often surreal, explores the feminine subconscious. Her books include *The Flower Master* (1982), *Venus and the Rain* (1984) and *On Ballycastle Beach* (1988).

McIntyre, Oscar Odd (1881–1938). American newspaper columnist. He began his career in journalism as a feature writer in Missouri, and soon became a political writer and then the managing editor of the Dayton, Ohio, *Herald,* in 1906. His "New York Day by Day" was syndicated in 550 newspapers.

McIver, Loren (1909–). American painter. Born in New York City, she studied there at the Art Students League. Her pale, misty, poetic canvases depict forms on the margins of usual attention—such as fallen leaves, chalk scrawls or oil puddle rainbows marking city streets, cracks in the pavement or an ancient window shade. McIver's paintings include *Hopscotch* (1940, Museum of Modern Art, New York City) and *The Street* (Corcoran Gallery of Art, Washington, D.C.).

McKay, John (1922–1975). One of the top U.S. test pilots during the 1950s and early 1960s, McKay flew such advanced aircraft as the X-1 rocket plane, the Douglas Skyrocket and the X-15. After growing up in the West Indies, McKay returned to the United States and received his pilot's license at the age of 18. He flew combat missions for the U.S. Navy during World War II and after the war earned his B.S. in aeronautical engineering from Virginia Polytechnic Institute. Rejoining his old employer (NACA—The National Advisory Committee on Aeronautics) after graduation in 1950, he began his career as a test pilot at Edwards Air Force Base in California. McKay flew over 20 flights on the X-15 advanced rocket plane, reaching an altitude of 295,600 feet on one of his flights (September 28, 1965). Although by Air Force standards this should have qualified him as an astronaut, McKay was not awarded astronaut wings because he was a civilian. A crash landing during an X-15 flight on November 9, 1962, nearly ended his life, but McKay recovered to fly the plane again. His death in April 1975 was attributed to injuries suffered in that crash.

McKenna, Joseph (1843–1925). Associate justice, U.S. Supreme Court (1898–1925). A native of Philadelphia, McKenna moved to California at an early age. After passing the bar he became involved in politics and was elected to a number of offices, including the U.S. Congress. McKenna was appointed a judge of the U.S. Court of Appeals for the Ninth Circuit, and served one year as U.S. attorney general before being elevated to the Supreme Court to replace Justice Field, also of California. McKenna was ill-prepared for his work on the Court, and in his 26 years on the bench was seldom was entrusted with writing opinions.

For further reading:
McDevitt, Matthew, *Joseph McKenna.* New York: Da Capo Press, 1974.

McKenna, Siobhan (1923–1986). Irish actress. Her most acclaimed role was as the title character in George Bernard SHAW's play *St. Joan.* Her portrayal of Joan of Arc took London by storm in 1954 and had a similar effect on Broadway two years later. Among landmarks in her later career were her solo show *Here Are Ladies* (1970), an anthology of women as seen by various Irish writers, and her portrayal in 1977 of Sarah BERNHARDT. She began her stage career with Gaelic parts, and Irish audiences saw her in a Gaelic-language version of *St. Joan* that she herself had prepared. She also performed frequently at the ABBEY THEATRE.

McKinley, William (1843–1901). Twenty-fifth president of the UNITED STATES. After serving with distinction in the Civil War, he returned to Ohio to practice law. After serving in the House of Representatives as a Republican from 1876 to 1891 (except for a brief period), he was elected governor of Ohio in 1891 and 1893. McKinley won the Republican nomination for president in 1896. The early part of his presidency was relatively uneventful, but he later proved to be an able war president during the Spanish-American War (1898). He was the architect of the policies that acquired and governed the new territories coming under U.S. jurisdiction. On July 7, 1898, he signed the bill annexing Hawaii; the Treaty of Paris signed December 10, 1898, freed Cuba and ceded Guam, Puerto Rico and the Philippines to the U.S.; and on December 2, 1899, American Samoa was acquired by treaty. Reelected in 1900, his term had scarcely begun when he was shot in Buffalo, New York, on September 6, 1901; he died after nine days. He was greatly admired for his quiet efficiency, his integrity and a faultless private life. (See also Theodore ROOSEVELT.)

McLaren, Norman (1914–1987). Scottish-born Canadian filmmaker. He was one of the most inventive figures in the history of film ANIMATION. His career began in his native Scotland and continued in England, the U.S. and Canada. He eventually emerged as Canada's most admired film artist. For most of his career, he was associated with the National Film Board of Canada. His early experimentation at the fledgling NFB in the 1940s included making animation without a camera by drawing directly on clear acetate. Later he developed the technique of **pixillation**—live action seen in staggered single frames—for his cartoon *Neighbors,* about a deadly fight between two men over a flower on their property line. The 1952 ACADEMY AWARD given to the film was but one of more than 500 international awards McLaren won for about 60 short films he created in Canada.

McLuhan, (Herbert) Marshall (1911–1981). Canadian professor of English at University of Toronto (St. Michael's College). He developed theories about the role of the electronic media in mass popular culture. His books—including *The Mechanical Bride* (1951), *Understanding Media* (1964) and *The Medium Is the Message* (1967)—argue the thesis that print is an outmoded medium, too "linear" in its approach to reality, while television and other visual media override time and distance instantaneously—making the world a "global village." The advertising and broadcasting industries took up McLuhan's ideas with great enthusiasm, since they showed recognition and respect in a way not previously offered to these fields. McLuhan's name and his ideas were widely discussed in the 1960s and 1970s and exerted considerable influence in design fields, where understanding present and future developments is always important. McLuhan's work is now little read and discussed, although its basic message still has validity.

McMahon, Brien (1903–). American politician. Following graduation from Fordham and Yale universities, he practiced law and became a judge in Norwalk, Connecticut. He was elected to the U.S. Senate (1945–56), where he chaired the Joint Committee on Atomic Energy (1945–47) and authored the act that led to the formation of the Atomic Energy Commission.

McManus, George (1884–1954). American cartoonist. His famous comic strip *Bringing Up Father* appeared in over 700 papers around the world, in 27 languages. His other comic series include *Let George Do It* and *The Newly Weds and Their Baby Snookums.* He was awarded an honorary tribute in the *Congressional Record* of January 26, 1932.

McMillan, Edwin Mattison (1907–). American scientist. McMillan was a professor of physics at the University of California at Berkeley from 1934 to 1973. In 1940, working with Philip ABELSON, he discovered the first element heavier than uranium, element 93, which he named neptunium, after the planet Neptune. McMillan also predicted the discovery of element 94 (plutonium), which was later found by a team working under Glenn SEABORG; McMillan and Seaborg shared the 1951 NOBEL PRIZE for chemistry. In 1945, McMillan conceived the synchrotron, which was 40 times more powerful than the cyclotron developed by Ernest LAWRENCE.

McNair, Ronald E. (1950–1986). U.S. astronaut, one of seven killed in the explosion of the SPACE SHUTTLE CHALLENGER on January 28, 1986. He was a physicist and an expert on lasers. When he flew on a shuttle mission in 1984 he became the second African American in space.

McNamara, Robert Strange (1916–). U.S. secretary of state. McNamara taught business administration at Harvard (1940–43) and served in the Army Air Corps during World War II. He was an executive of the Ford Motor Company (1946–

60), where he was responsible for sweeping reforms in the managerial system and production techniques that led to the modernization of the firm. He became president of Ford in 1960 but resigned shortly thereafter to serve as secretary of defense during the KENNEDY and JOHNSON administrations. McNamara centralized decision making in the hands of the civilian secretary at the expense of the military secretaries and introduced modern management techniques to the department. He also shifted strategy away from nuclear weapons and high technology, strengthening conventional fighting capacity. An early advocate of escalating the VIETNAM WAR, McNamara resigned in 1968 after recommending that the president turn over major responsibility for ground combat to the South Vietnamese. He served as president of the WORLD BANK from 1968 to 1981.

McPherson, Aimee Semple (1890–1944). American evangelist. A highly flamboyant figure in the 1910s and 1920s, McPherson was one of the most successful of American evangelists. Billing herself as the "World's Most Pulchritudinous Evangelist," she founded the International Church of the Four-Square Gospel in Los Angeles, California, raised $1.5 million from her followers and built the 5,000-person capacity Angelus Temple to house her services, which featured faith healing and baptisms in the faith. In 1926, McPherson was apparently kidnapped, but, during a subsequent criminal obstruction of justice trial, facts emerged indicating that she had been trysting with a married lover during the month in question. While McPherson was ultimately acquitted, she never regained her former popularity.

McQueen, Steve (1930–1980). American film actor whose portrayal of tough, free-wheeling loners made him a national emblem in the 1960s. After training on the stage at the Neighborhood Playhouse and the Actors Studio in New York, he made his Broadway debut in *Hatful of Rain* (1955) and his screen debut in *Somebody Up There Likes Me* (1956). In 1958 he starred in a low-budget horror classic, *The Blob*, and landed the starring role in the television series "Wanted! Dead or Alive." During a 22-year movie career during which he made more than 24 films, he created an enduring character who lived on the outer fringes of society, surviving by quick wits, sturdy self-reliance and a quirky humor. Among his notable later films were *The Great Escape* (1963), *The Cincinnati Kid* (1965), *The Sand Pebbles* (1966), *The Thomas Crown Affair* (1968), *Bullitt* (1968) and *Papillon* (1973).

For further reading:

Bawden, Liz-Anne, ed., *The Oxford Companion to Film*. New York: Oxford University Press, 1966.

McReynolds, James C. (1862–1946). Associate justice, U.S. Supreme Court (1914–1941). A graduate of Vanderbilt University and the University of Virginia Law School, McReynolds established a successful law practice in Nashville, Tennessee. After an unsuccessful run for Congress he was appointed to the Justice Department by President Theodore ROOSEVELT and specialized in prosecuting antitrust cases. After returning to private practice he was appointed U.S. attorney general by President Woodrow WILSON in 1912, and in 1914 he was elevated to the Supreme Court. Although a Democrat, he took conservative positions on the bench. He reputedly would not sit next to either Justice BRANDEIS or CARDOZO, both of whom were Jewish. He retired in 1941.

McShann, James Columbus "Jay" (1916–). American jazz pianist and leading exponent of the KANSAS CITY JAZZ sound of the 1930s. Born in Muscogee, Oklahoma, Jay taught himself piano as a child. At the age of 20 he moved to Kansas City, Missouri, where he listened to and played with the emerging jazz greats of the time—Count BASIE, Joe TURNER, and Pete Johnson. "When I came to Kansas City, the town was wide open, jumpin', the joints staying open 24 hours a day," McShann told this writer. "I hadn't heard anything like it. I didn't want to go to bed; I was afraid I'd miss somethin'." In 1939 he formed his own big band and took his new discovery, Charlie "Yardbird" PARKER, to the Savoy Ballroom in New York City. But WORLD WAR II intervened; there was a subsequent decline in the popularity of the big bands; and by 1950 McShann was back in Kansas City to study at the Conservatory of Music (now part of the University of Missouri, Kansas City). He maintains an active schedule, still recording frequently for the Capitol, Atlantic, Black and Blue, and Sackville labels; and travels extensively to most of the top international jazz festivals. In 1988 he was the subject and dedicatee of a major Alvin AILEY ballet, *Opus McShann*. Today he is the last major survivor of the legendary Kansas City sound—a distinctive blend of improvisation, uptempo blues and a driving boogie-woogie beat. His signature piece, "Hootie's Blues," derives its name from jazz slang of the 1930s, referring to a state of intoxication, known as "getting hooted."

For further reading:

Keepnews, Orrin, and Bill Grauer, Jr., *A Pictorial History of Jazz*. New York: Crown Publishers, 1955.

Mead, Margaret (1901–1978). American anthropologist. Educated at Barnard College (B.A., 1923) and Columbia University (M.A., 1924; Ph.D., 1929), where she studied with Franz BOAS, Mead began her study of Pacific islands culture in the mid-1920s. *Coming of Age in Samoa* (1928), a best-seller that influenced several generations of students to enter the nascent field of anthropology, was followed by *Growing Up in New Guinea* (1930), *Sex and Temperament in Three Primitive Societies* (1935) and, most important, *Male and Female* (1949), an application of anthropological findings to the contemporary urban West. *An Anthropologist at Work* (1959) is a study of close friend and colleague Ruth BENEDICT; *A Rap on Race* (1971) is a dialogue with James BALDWIN; *Blackberry Winter: My Earlier Years* (1972) is her memoir. Although some colleagues critcized her methods, her broad-based, intuitive approach to cross-cultural analysis revolutionized the field. As prolific author and lecturer and a regular contributor to *Redbook* for 17 years, she became a popular celebrity as well as an intellectual and scholar.

American anthropologist Margaret Mead, whose work encouraged many students to enter the field of anthropological research.

For further reading:

Grosskurth, Phyllis, *Margaret Mead*. New York: Penguin, 1989.

Howard, Jane, *Margaret Mead: A Life*. New York: Fawcett, 1985.

Ziesk, Edra, *Margaret Mead*. New York: Chelsea House, 1990.

Means, Russell (1940–). American Indian activist. In 1972 Means participated in the week-long occupation of the offices of the Bureau of Indian Affairs—designed to dramatize grievances against the government's Indian policies. The following year he was one of the leaders of the 71-day armed occupation of Wounded Knee, South Dakota, organized to demand a Senate investigation of Indian treaties.

Meany, George (1894–1980). American labor leader. Born in New York City, Meaney became a plumber at 16 and began his union career in 1922. He swiftly moved from the Plumbers Union into the hierarchy of the AMERICAN FEDERATION OF LABOR (AFL), becoming president of the New York federation in 1934 and secretary-treasurer of the national union in 1940. He succeeded William GREEN as the union's president in 1952. Meany was an important force in the merging of the AFL and the CONGRESS OF INDUSTRIAL ORGANIZATIONS (CIO) in 1955. He became the AFL-CIO's first president and was reelected thereafter without opposition. A vocal anti-communist, Meany strongly supported American involvement in the VIETNAM WAR. He broke with the union movement's traditional support of Democrats, refusing to support the candidacy of George MCGOVERN in 1972 and later becoming a critic of the policies of President Jimmy CARTER.

Mechlin Incident. Popular name for an incident in the early days of WORLD WAR II. In late 1939 a German plane made a forced landing at Mechlin, on the eastern frontier of Belgium. When authorities arrived they found an officer aboard attempting to set fire to official papers. These were purported to be German general staff plans for the invasion of France, Holland and Belgium. The contents of these papers were sent to the French and British, both of whom concluded that they were bogus and that the whole incident was an attempt on the part of Germany to disseminate false military information.

Medawar, Sir Peter Brian (1915–1987). British zoologist. Born in Rio de Janeiro, Brazil, Medawar immigrated to Great Britain and attended Oxford University. Graduating in 1939, he continued there in research under Howard Florey and as a professor. Later (1947–51) he taught zoology at the University of Birmingham and comparative anatomy at University College, London (1951–62). Director of the National Institute of Medical Research in London until 1971, he was later affiliated with the Clinical Research Centre and a professor of experimental medicine at the Royal Institution. During WORLD WAR II he became interested in medical biology and he subsequently developed a concentrated fibrinogen used to heal damaged and grafted nerves. The war also precipitated Medawar's experiments on burns and the rejection of skin grafts, and he discovered that grafts were more or less successful depending on the genetic closeness of the donor and recipient. He and Sir Frank Macfarlane BURNET discovered acquired immunological tolerance, which later helped in the development of organ transplantation. For their discovery, Medawar and Burnet were awarded the 1960 NOBEL PRIZE for physiology or medicine.

Medellin Cartel. A powerful criminal organization of COCAINE producers and traffickers based in Medellin, COLOMBIA, the center of that country's illegal drug trade. Active in the late 1980s and into the 1990s, this violent cartel was believed responsible for about 80 percent of the cocaine smuggled into the U.S. The group assassinated Colombian judges, police officials, newspaper editors and others who opposed them. On August 18, 1989 cartel gunmen assassinated Colombian senator Luis Carlos Galan—a leading presidential candidate and opponent of the drug trade—at a campaign rally near Bogota. When President Virgilio Barcos announced an all-out war against the cartel, the cartel's paramilitary group, the Extraditables, threatened to escalate the violence and to kill 10 judges for each suspected drug trafficker extradited to the U.S. 550 lower-court judges in Bogata quit on August 25. After the arrest of a cartel financial adviser, nine bank offices in Medellin were dynamited and other bombings occurred in the days following. On August 30 a curfew was imposed in Medellin and nine other Colombian cities, and the U.S. ordered dependents of American diplomats to leave the country. In subsequent months, several cartel leaders were arrested and their property seized. Although the Medellin cartel suffered setbacks, it remained a dangerous criminal force.

Medicaid. American national health insurance for the needy who could not otherwise afford care, including all of those on public assistance. Like MEDICARE, the program was established in 1965. With its costs paid by the federal, state and county governments, it is administered by individual states, each of which must meet federal standards but also has a good deal of latitude in the services it provides. Medicaid plans usually provide for inpatient and outpatient hospital services; nursing home care; services by physicians, dentists and optometrists; X rays, drugs and other medical necessities.

Medicare. U.S. national health insurance for those aged 65 and over. Like MEDICAID, it was established in 1965 by amendments to Social Security. Managed by the Health Care Financing Administration of the Department of Health and Human Services, Medicare provides hospital insurance for most people 65 and over, along with supplementary medical insurance. In addition, it provides certain severely disabled people with health insurance. Medicare pays for a portion of hospital and nursing home care and for some health services administered at home. After paying a certain deductible amount, those covered by Medicare are entitled to 60 days of hospital care and, with a relatively small payment, to 30 more days thereafter. Medicare recipients are also eligible for 100 days of skilled nursing care, the first 20 days at no cost, the following 80 partly paid for by the recipient. Medicare also pays for physicians' services, prescription drugs and a number of other medical costs after a small yearly deductible, picking up 80% of "reasonable charges." Medicare is financed by a tax paid by workers and employers as well as by the self-employed as part of their Social Security payments.

Medici, Emilio Garrastazu (1905–1985). Brazilian general and politician. A career army officer, in 1969 he became BRAZIL's third military president since the 1964 overthrow of that country's civilian government. He remained in power until 1974.

Medina, Harold Raymond (1888–1990). American U.S. District Court judge who achieved fame in 1948 when presiding over the trial and conviction of 11 Communist Party members at the height of the anti-communist MCCARTHY era. Born in Brooklyn and educated at Princeton and at Columbia University Law School, Medina was a successful lawyer in private practice when in 1947 he was appointed a federal district court judge in Manhattan. In 1952 he was elevated to the prestigious federal Second Circuit Court of Appeals after the retirement of the Justice Learned HAND. Although Medina wrote hundreds of opinions in a remarkably long 33–year career on the bench, he is best remembered for the 1949 opinion convicting 11 communist leaders. At the time the country was involved in a rage of anticommunist sympathy, and the lengthy trial became a focal point with the judge the center of attention. Although Medina's opinion convicting the communist leaders under the SMITH ACT for advocating the overthrow of the federal government was upheld by the Supreme Court, the dissenting judges roundly criticized Medina's handling of the case as onesided. Medina retired in 1958, although he continued to hear cases until 1980 as a senior judge.

"Meet the Press". NBC public affairs program, the longest-running series on American network television. It was created by Martha Rountree and Lawrence Spivak in 1945 as a radio program. It moved to local television in Washington, D.C. in 1947 and was first telecast over the network later that year. Spivak, who had always appeared as a regular panelist, became the moderator in 1965 and served in that capacity for a decade. Replacements have included Bill Monroe, Marvin Kalb and Chris Wallace.

For further reading:

O'Connor, John E., ed., *American History/American Television: Interpreting the Video Past.* New York: Frederick Ungar, 1983.

Meier-Graefe, Julius (1867–1935). Hungarian-born writer and critic who was influential in encouraging and publicizing the ART NOUVEAU movement in the late 19th and early 20th centuries. Meier-Graefe was trained in engineering at Munich and Zurich and, in 1890, settled in Berlin. In 1893 he traveled in England and there met William Morris. Meier-Graefe later moved to Paris and met Samuel Bing (1895). The two worked together to found the Art Nouveau movement. In 1897 he founded the magazine *Dekorative Kunst* (published from 1897 until 1929 in Munich), which publicized Germany's Art Nouveau. After 1905 Meier-Graefe became somewhat disillusioned with the ideas of Art Nouveau and turned his attention to art criticism and history. In 1934 he left Germany to escape NAZISM and, in the last year of his life, applied for French citizenship.

Meighen, Arthur (1874–1960). Canadian statesman, prime minister (1920–21, 1926). Born in Ontario, he became a lawyer in Manitoba and entered politics as a Liberal-Conservative member of parliament in 1908. He was solicitor general (1913–16) and minister of both mines and the interior (1917–20) before becoming prime minister upon the resgination of Robert L. BORDEN in 1920. Defeated in the election of 1921, he became leader of the Conservative Party. He again became prime minister in 1926 but soon resigned. Meighen continued to be active in political life and served in the Canadian senate from 1932 to 1941.

Meiklejohn, William (1903–1981). HOLLYWOOD talent agent. He discovered such stars as Mickey ROONEY, Judy GARLAND

and a young radio sportscaster named Ronald REAGAN. Meiklejohn spent 60 years as a scout, 20 of them as talent chief at PARAMOUNT PICTURES.

***Mein Kampf* [*My Struggle*].** Book (1925–27) by Adolf HITLER, regarded as the bible of NAZISM. Hitler dictated *Mein Kampf* to his confidant Rudolf HESS while the two were serving a prison sentence for their part in the Munich BEER HALL PUTSCH (1923). Most readers have found *Mein Kampf* not only distasteful but also dull and unreadable. In a turgid, rambling style, Hitler rants against the JEWS (see ANTI-SEMITISM), the VERSAILLES TREATY and democracy, while extolling the virtues of the "Aryan race." Many, both in Germany and without, dismissed the book as the ravings of a crackpot. However, Hitler was remarkably honest and precise in stating his goals. Historians have speculated that, had the threats in *Mein Kampf* been taken seriously, the tragic consequences of Hitlerism might have been forestalled. Among other things, *Mein Kampf* called for the abolition of the WEIMAR REPUBLIC, the rebuilding of German military might, retribution against France and Russia for Germany's defeat in WORLD WAR I, German territorial expansion (see LEBENSRAUM) and the eradication of the Jews and other "inferior" peoples (see FINAL SOLUTION; HOLOCAUST).

Meir, Golda [born Golda Mabovitz] (1898–1978). Israeli political leader, prime minister (1969–74). Born in Kiev, Russia, she and her family immigrated to the U.S. in 1906, settling in Milwaukee. She married Morris Myerson in 1917 and moved to PALESTINE in 1921. She held important posts with the British-run Jewish Agency and the World Zionist Organization before and during World War II. After Israeli independence in 1948, she was ambassador to the U.S.S.R., labor minister (1949–56) and foreign minister (1956–66). In 1956 she took the Hebrew name Meir (light-giver). After the death of Levi Eshkol in 1969, she became interim prime minister and was elected to the post later that year. In October 1973, when the Egyptian and Syrian armies combined in a surprise attack, she rallied Israeli forces but was widely blamed for her nation's lack of military preparedness (see YOM KIPPUR WAR). Unable to form a government after Labor Party defeats in 1974, she resigned from office while retaining enormous personal popularity at home and abroad.

The government of Prime Minister Golda Meir supported large-scale development in Israel.

Meitner, Lise (1878–1968). Austrian-Swedish physicist. Meitner entered the University of Vienna in 1901, studied science under Ludwig Boltzmann and obtained her doctorate in 1906. From Vienna she went to Berlin to attend lectures by Max PLANCK on theoretical physics. Here she began to study the new phenomenon of radioactivity in collaboration with Otto HAHN, beginning a partnership that was to last 30 years. At Berlin Meitner met with remarkable difficulties caused by prejudice against women in academic life. She was forced to work in an old carpentry shop and forbidden by Emil FISCHER to enter laboratories in which males were working. In 1914, at the outbreak of WORLD WAR I, she became a nurse in the Austrian army, continuing to work with Hahn during leave periods. In 1918 they announced the discovery of the radioactive element protactinium.

After the war Meitner returned to Berlin as head of the department of radiation physics at the Kaiser Wilhelm Institute. Here she investigated the relationship between the gamma and beta rays emitted by radioactive material. In 1935 she and Hahn began work on the transformation of uranium nuclei under neutron bombardment. Following HITLER's annexation of Austria in 1938 she was no longer safe from persecution and, like many Jewish scientists, left Germany. With the help of Dutch colleagues she found refuge in Sweden, obtaining a post at the Nobel Institute in Stockholm. Hahn, with Fritz Strassman, continued the uranium work and in 1939 published results showing that nuclei were present that were much lighter than uranium. Shortly afterward Meitner, with Otto Frisch (her nephew), published an explanation interpreting these results as fission of the uranium nuclei. For this she received a share in the 1966 Enrico Fermi Prize of the Atomic Energy Commission.

Melba, Dame Nellie [Helen Porter Mitchell] (1859–1931). Australian operatic soprano. Born in a suburb of Melbourne, Melba studied in Paris with Mathilde Marchesi. She made her European operatic debut in Brussels in 1887 and her American debut at the Metropolitan Opera in 1893. Performing regularly at London's Covent Garden, New York's Metropolitan Opera and various European opera houses, she was acclaimed for such roles as Gilda in Verdi's *Rigoletto* and Violetta in PUCCINI's *La Traviata*. Made a Dame of the British Empire in 1918, she retired from the stage in 1926 and returned to Australia as president of the Melbourne Conservatory. Possessing a superb coloratura, Melba was noted for her pure tone throughout the operatic register, her perfect breath control and her birdlike trill. According to critic Irving Kolodin, her voice was "one of the most precious gifts that heaven ever put in a human throat." One of the leading celebrities of her time, Melba lent her name to such edibles as Melba toast and peach Melba.

For further reading:

Moran, William R., ed., *Nellie Melba: A Contemporary Review*. Westport, Conn.: Greenwood Press, 1985.

Melchior, Lauritz (1890–1973). Danish opera singer. Melchior was perhaps the greatest interpreter of the *Heldentenor* lead roles that proliferate in the Ring Cycle operas of the 19th-century composer Richard Wagner. Melchior made his debut as Tannhauser in 1918 and followed with portrayals of the Wagnerian heroes Siegfried, Lohengrin, Tristan and Parsifal. Melchior frequently appeared at the Bayreuth Wagnerian festival, as well as at Covent Garden in London and at the Metropolitan Opera in New York. He spent the last 20 years of his life in America, where he taught voice and continued to perform.

Melen, Ferit (1906–1988). Turkish politician. Melen held the posts of premier (1972–73) and defense minister of TURKEY (1971–72, 1975–77). Melen first became defense minister during one of Turkey's most violent periods, when the military struggled to control what Turks referred to as "the anarchy"—a period of extremist kidnappings, robberies and murders. The draconian countermeasures the military initiated succeeded only after martial law was declared and secretive courts-martial were held, harshly punishing thousands for allegedly attempting to impose a Soviet-style communist regime by terror.

Melies, Georges (1861–1938). French stage conjurer and pioneer in the narrative motion picture at the turn of the century. He was the son of a wealthy footwear manufacturer. Although he joined his brothers in the management of the family factory, his ambitions in painting and magic led him to sell his business interests in 1888 and purchase the Theatre Robert-Houdin. After enthusiastically viewing the program of films by the LUMIERE BROTHERS at the Grand Cafe in Paris in 1895, he developed his own camera and included his films in his stage programs. He utilized cinematic techniques of editing and superimpositions to transfer the effects and transformations of fairy pantomimes and magic shows to celluloid. At first they were simple "illusions," like *Escamotage d'une Dame* (*The Vanishing Lady*) in 1896. By the time he produced *Le Voyage dans la Lune* (*A Trip to the Moon*), however, they were elaborate story films with painted sets and machinery of his own design. These "artificially arranged scenes," as he called them, were made in his glass-enclosed studio in the garden of his Montreuil home—the first European movie studio—and released under the imprimatur of Star Films. At the peak of his success in 1903, he opened an American studio, where his brother, Gaston, made westerns. After the release of one of George's most ambitious films, *A la Conquete du Pole* (*The Conquest of the Pole*) in 1912, he went into decline. Failing fortunes forced him to sell his estate (1913), return to the variety stage (1915), declare bankruptcy (1923) and spend the remainder of his days running a toy concession at the Montparnasse railway station. His relative obscurity was relieved somewhat by the awarding of a Legion of Honor Medal and a pension in 1931. Melies' importance in the development of the story-film tradition can scarcely be exaggerated. His energies were indefatigable and his imagination unbounded. The motto of his Star Films company was characteristic: "The World Within Reach"—as was his comment on the making of *The Conquest of the Pole:* "Cook and Peary claimed to have reached the Pole. In fact, I don't think either one did. I said to myself, I'm going to go there."

For further reading:

Frazer, John, *Artificially Arranged Scenes: The Films of Georges Melies.* Boston: G.K. Hall, 1979.

Mellon, Andrew William (1855–1937). U.S. financier and cabinet member. Born in Pittsburgh, Mellon joined the family banking firm in 1874. He was active in developing the aluminum, coal and oil industries as well as in consolidating banking. By 1921, when Warren HARDING appointed him secretary of the treasury, Mellon was one of the wealthiest men in the U.S. As secretary, Mellon worked to lower taxes and reduce the national debt. He believed that business would prosper in proportion to a reduction in taxes; prosperity would then filter down to individual workers and farmers. During his tenure (1921–31), Mellon reduced the national debt by over $8 billion despite drastic tax cuts. Mellon did not foresee the GREAT DEPRESSION and emphasized retrenchment as a means to combat it. He resigned in 1932 and served as ambassador to Great Britain until 1933. In 1937 he donated his art collection, valued at $25 million, as well as funds for a museum to house it, to the U.S. The donation was the foundation of the National Gallery of Art, opened in 1941.

Memel, Insurrection at (1923). The predominantly German city of Memel (Klaipeda) in western LITHUANIA had been under Allied control since the end of World War I. Despite Lithuanian requests, the Allies established a French garrison in the city. On January 11, 1923, an insurrection engineered by the Lithuanians, whose troops occupied the district, forced out the French. The Allies protested but then decided to make Memel an autonomous region within Lithuania, and passed the Memel Statute on May 8, 1923, ratifying the decision.

Mencken, Henry Louis (1880–1956). U.S. author and philologist. He began his career as a reporter in Baltimore. In 1924 he founded the *American Mercury* with fellow critic George Jean Nathan, and served as

American journalist and social critic H.L. Mencken.

its editor through 1933. After visiting England Mencken became interested in American linguistics. The outcome of his research was the authoritative *The American Language* (1919), which was revised in 1921, 1923 and 1936; it was followed by *Supplement One* (1946) and *Supplement Two* (1948). Like George Bernard SHAW, Mencken was known for his insistence on correct usage of language. His other works include *Ventures into Verse* (1908) and the series of six collections of satirical essays called *Prejudices* (1919–27).

Mendelsohn, Erich (1887–1953). German-born architect associated with the development of MODERNISM through the unique expressionist character of some of his earlier work. Mendelsohn was trained at the Technical High School in Munich and was then active in theater design while coming in contact with artists of the expressionist BLAUE REITER group. After service in WORLD WAR I, he opened an office in Berlin (1919) and began work on a research laboratory for studies relating to EINSTEIN's theory of relativity. This led to his most famous work, the Einstein Tower at Potsdam, completed in 1924. It is an astronomical tower and observatory built in a flowing, sculptural form (intended for concrete construction but actually executed in brick and steel)—which is viewed by critics as expressionistic. Commissions that followed, for houses, industrial and commercial buildings, led to designs that were generally more reserved and related to the INTERNATIONAL STYLE. Mendelsohn's Department Store buildings in Stuttgart and Chemnitz, Germany, for the firm of Schoken are the best-known works of this period (1926–29), while his own house at Rupenhorn in Berlin (1930) is a fine example of his residential work, done in typically international-style terms. Mendelsohn visited the U.S. in 1924, studied the skyscraper architecture of the day and had a meeting with Frank Lloyd WRIGHT, which led to a continuing relationship. The atonal music of Arnold SCHOENBERG was also an ongoing source of stimulation for him.

In 1933 Mendelsohn left Germany for England, where he established a partnership with Serge Chermayeff. Together they designed the De La Ware Pavilion at Bexhill (1934–35). In 1939 Mendelsohn left for Palestine, where he had a number of commissions, but in 1941 he relocated to the U.S. and became a citizen in 1946. He was active as a lecturer and teacher and then designed the Maimonides Hospital (1946–50) in San Francisco. A number of residential and institutional projects followed; his last major work was the Mount Zion Community Center in St. Paul, Minnesota (1950–54).

In spite of his extensive achievements, Mendelsohn is usually viewed as a secondary figure somewhat outside the main life of modernist development. A recent resurgence of interest in his work has led to exhibition of his striking sketches, with their strongly expressionist qualities, and fresh interest in his unique style. Bruno Zevi's book *Erich Mendelsohn* (1985) is an excellent, compact summary of Mendelsohn's achievement.

Menderes, Adnan (1899–1961). Turkish statesman. Menderes studied law and entered politics in 1932 as a moderate critic of ATATURK. One of the founders of the reformist Democratic Party, Menderes became prime minister in 1950. He strengthened TURKEY's links with the West and sponsored its NATO membership in 1952. He also negotiated the CYPRUS agreement in 1959. Menderes was forced to rule dictatorially in April 1960 because of widespread disorders. His regime was overthrown in May 1960 by army officers under General Gursel. Sentenced to death, Menderes was hanged in September 1961.

Mendes-France, Pierre (1907–1982). French politician, premier of FRANCE (1954–55). A socialist from a middle-class Jewish family, he served in the national assembly (1932–40). He was arrested by the Germans shortly after they invaded France (1941) but escaped from a Nazi prison and joined Charles DE GAULLE'S FREE FRENCH forces. After the war he again served in the national assembly (1946–58). He was elected premier in June 1954 but held office for only seven months. During this short tenure he negotiated an end to the FRENCH-INDOCHINA WAR and began negotiations to grant independence to TUNISIA. He resigned in February 1955 after losing a vote of confidence over his policies on France's North African colonies. He remained in the national assembly until his unpopular opposition to de Gaulle led to his defeat in a general election. He returned to the assembly briefly from 1967 to 1968.

Mengelberg, Willem (1871–1951). Dutch orchestra conductor renowned in the first half of the century for his virtuosic performances with the Concertgebouw Orchestra of Amsterdam. He studied at the Cologne Conservatory in Germany and, upon his return to his native Holland in 1891, began his legendary 41-year association with the Concertgebouw. Among his other appointments was the co-conducting, with Arturo TOSCANINI, of the

New York Philharmonic (1927–28). During WORLD WAR II he collaborated with the Nazis, and his career subsequently declined. He was barred in 1945 by the Netherlands Honors Council from the musical life of that country. He spent his last years in virtual exile in Switzerland. Mengelberg has been called The Napoleon of the Orchestra, the supreme virtuoso of orchestral forces and effects. He loved the big, complicated scores of Gustav MAHLER (whom he met in 1902) and Richard STRAUSS (who dedicated his *Ein Heldenleben* to him in 1898); and he did not hesitate to adjust to his own satisfaction the presumed deficiencies of scores by Beethoven and others. Not even Serge KOUSSEVITZKY and Leopold STOKOWSKI surpassed him in the color and sensuous excitement of his performances. His legacy was not well preserved in recordings, however, and his reputation dwindled quickly after his death. As critic Harold C. Schonberg has observed: "Mengelberg was unfortunate enough to die in a period that looked down at his two greatest assets—virtuosity and romanticism."

For further reading:

Schonberg, Harold C., *The Great Conductors.* New York: Simon and Schuster, 1967.

Mengele, Josef (1911–1978?). Nazi war criminal. Known as "the Angel of Death," Dr. Josef Mengele was chief medical officer at AUSCHWITZ concentration camp in Poland, where he was responsible for deciding which prisoners would die immediately and which would be used for slave labor. He also conducted horribly cruel and scientifically worthless "medical experiments" on the camp's inmates. After the war, Mengele escaped to Argentina, where he was granted asylum. In 1960, faced with extradition to West Germany, Mengele escaped to Brazil and then to Paraguay, where he was reported to have drowned in 1978.

Mengistu Haile Mariam (1937–). President of ETHIOPIA (1977–91). Lt. Col. Mengistu took part in the coup that deposed Emperor HAILE SELASSIE in 1974. He became head of state in 1977 and began to reorganize Ethiopia along Marxist lines. The country was torn by insurrection in ERITREA, war with SOMALIA and a devastating famine in the mid-1980s that cost as many as one million Ethiopian lives. In May 1991, after rebel forces cut supply routes to the capital of ADDIS ABABA, Mengistu fled into exile in Zimbabwe.

Mennin, Peter (1923–1983). American composer. One of the leading American composers after World War II, he composed nine symphonies and a variety of concertos and chamber works that won high acclaim. In 1962 he became president of the Juilliard School of Music in New York. Under his direction, the size and reputation of Juilliard grew. He established Juilliard's Theater Center in 1968, the American Opera Center in 1970 and a permanent conducting program in 1972.

Menninger, Karl Augustus (1893–1990). U.S. psychiatrist. In the 1920s, with father **Charles Frederick Menninger** and brother **William Menninger,** he founded the Menninger Clinic and Foundation in Topeka, Kansas. He believed that emotional troubles could be eased by a sufficiently loving, caring environment. He also argued that crime was a result of mental and emotional illness and therefore advocated psychiatric treatment for prisoners. His 13 books and numerous magazine articles helped educate Americans about psychiatry. His books included *The Human Mind* (1930), *Love Against Hate* (1959) and *Whatever Became of Sin?* (1988).

Menninger Family. American psychiatrists. Dr. Charles F. Menninger and sons Drs. Karl and William Menninger founded the Menninger Foundation and Clinic in Topeka, Kansas. Dr. Charles Menninger (1862–1953) led his sons in pioneering the treatment of physical disorders in a community clinic setting. The clinic changed its total emphasis to psychiatry in 1941. William also served as chief consultant on psychiatry to the surgeon general of the United States Army during WORLD WAR II.

Menninger Foundation Clinic. Medical facility in Topeka, Kansas, established by Dr. **Charles F. Menninger** and his sons Drs. **Karl** and **William Menninger** in 1925 (see MENNINGER FAMILY). One of the world's leading psychiatric centers, it is part of the Menninger Foundation, a nonprofit organization. The clinic includes two psychiatric hospitals, a department of neurology, and internal medicine, neurosurgery, and outpatient and aftercare programs.

Menotti, Gian Carlo (1911–). Italian composer. Menotti is considered the foremost composer/librettist of modern, popular American opera. His first success was the one-act comic opera *Amelia Goes to the Ball,* staged at the Philadelphia Academy of Music in 1937. He received the PULITZER PRIZE for his operas *The Consul* (1950) and *The Saint of Bleecker Street* (1954). Menotti's most popular work, AMAHL AND THE NIGHT VISITORS (1951), became an annual Christmas event on television. His non-operatic works include the ballet *Sebastian* (1944), the symphonic poem *Apocalypse* (1951) and *The Halcyon* symphony (1976). In addition, he founded the Spoleto Arts Festival in Charleston, S.C., in 1977 and remained its artistic director until 1991.

For further reading:

Gruen, John, *Menotti: A Biography.* New York: Macmillan, 1978.

Mensheviks. Russian political party established in August 1917 at a congress of several social democratic groups. The Mensheviks proposed a proletarian party working with the liberals in order to replace the autocracy with a democratic constitution. Before 1917 "Menshevik" referred to the non-Leninist faction of the Russian Social Democratic Labor Party. Although the Mensheviks worked with the BOLSHEVIKS during the 1905 Revolution, and reunited with them the following year, relations were strained. The Mensheviks themselves were divided into the "liquidationalists," the "party-minded Mensheviks" of the center, the followers of Pavel Axelrod and the followers of TROTSKY. In 1922 the Mensheviks were suppressed, and in 1931 a show trial took place in Moscow. In 1920 a group of Mensheviks left Russia and settled in the United States.

Menuhin, Yehudi (1916–). American-born violinist, conductor, teacher and author. Born in New York City, Menuhin first made his mark as a child prodigy. He studied with Louis Persinger and Sigmund Anker and made his debut with the San Francisco Orchestra at the age of seven. Continuing his studies in Europe with Adolf Busch and Georges ENESCO, he debuted in Paris at age 10 and in 1929 appeared as a soloist with orchestras in Berlin, Dresden and London to great acclaim. He made a triumphant world tour during the 1934–35 season, then retired briefly to study his art. In subsequent years Menuhin became one of the world's most sought-after violin soloists, famous for his warm tone, intense playing and interpretive depth. A performer both of the classics and of modern music (BARTOK's "Sonata for Solo Violin" was written for him), Menuhin also explored a number of other musical traditions, such as Eastern music in collaboration with sitarist Ravi SHANKAR and JAZZ with French violinist Stephane Grappelli. He established a music festival at Gstaad, Switzerland (1959), directed England's annual Bath Festival (1959–68), founded the Menuhin School of Music at Stoke d'Abernon, Surrey (1963) and became president of the Trinity College of Music, London (1972). A gifted conductor, he has led his own chamber orchestras and guest-conducted major orchestras in Britain, Europe and the U.S. As a violinist, he has often performed chamber pieces with his sister, Hepzibah Menuhin (1920–81), and his son, Jeremy, both pianists. Menuhin has made numerous recordings as violin soloist,

Sir Yehudi Menuhin.

chamber musician and conductor. He became a British subject in 1985.

For further reading:
Menuhin, Yehudi, *Unfinished Journey*. London: Macdonald and Jane's, 1978.

Menzies, Sir Robert Gordon (1894–1978). Australian statesman, prime minister of AUSTRALIA (1949–66). Born in Jeparit, Victoria, he became a barrister in his home province, entered provincial government in 1928 and was elected to the Australian parliament in 1934. He served as attorney general (1935–39) in

Sir Robert Gordon Menzies, prime minister of Australia from 1939 to 1941 and again from 1949 to 1966.

the Joseph LYONS government, became prime minister upon Lyons' death in 1939 and lost his post in 1941. During his time out of office (1943–49), he led the parliamentary opposition to the Labor Party government and strove to create a coherent Liberal Party ideology. In 1949 a Liberal-Country Party coalition swept the Labor government from power, and Menzies again became prime minister. During his lengthy time in office, from 1949 to 1966, he was known for his anticommunist stance, for his development of a thriving Australian economy and for his establishment of strong ties with the U.S. and other Western powers.

Mercader, Ramon (1914–1978). Spanish laborer who assassinated exiled Soviet leader Leon TROTSKY in Mexico City in 1940, using a pickax. Mercader was convicted of the murder and imprisoned until 1961. Although Mercader always insisted that he had acted alone, the assassination was ordered by Soviet dictator Joseph STALIN, and the details were probably planned by Soviet agents of the NKVD.

Mercedes-Benz. German automobile produced by Daimler-Benz AG, which also manufactures trucks, locomotives and heavy machinery and is known for conservative design and high-quality standards. Karl Benz, one of the developers of the internal combustion engine, completed an early automobile in 1885. A rival firm, founded by Gottfried Daimler, named its 1902 model Mercedes after the daughter of its dealer-backer. In 1927 the two firms combined to produce the Mercedes-Benz model S, an elegant open car with a design based on racing car antecedents. Mercedes-Benz designs moved toward conservative, luxury models better known for engineering merit than for body styling until, in the post-World War II era, such adventurous designs as the 1954 300SL appeared—a design by Karl Wilfert known as Gullwing for its top-hinged, upward-opening side doors. In 1958 Bruno Sacco became a director of design for Daimler-Benz and was responsible for the reserved but elegant forms of the 1961 model 220SE and the 1963 230SL roadster. More recent Mercedes design has returned to a conservative image that emphasizes the role of the car as an affluent status symbol.

Mercer, John Herndon "Johnny" (1909–1976). American lyricist, composer and singer. Born in Savannah, Georgia, Mercer moved to New York in the late Twenties. By the mid-Thirties, he had earned a place among the most successful American lyricists. He eventually published more than 1,000 songs, working with the top composers of his day. As a singer, Mercer appeared on film and became popular on radio in the 1930s. He was also a cofounder of Capitol Records, in 1942. His songs include: "I'm an Old Cowhand" (1936), "Jeepers Creepers" (1938, with Harry Warren), "Come Rain or Come Shine" (1946, with Harold ARLEN), "In the Cool, Cool, Cool of the Evening" (1951, with Hoagy CARMICHAEL) and "Moon River" (1961, with Henry MANCINI).

Mercer, Mabel (1900–1984). British-American singer. Born in Burton-upon-Trent, Staffordshire, the daughter of an American father and a British music-hall singer, Mercer began performing at an early age. After World War I, she moved to Paris, where she appeared at BRICKTOP's from 1931 to 1938. Next she went to New York City, where she became popular at the Ruban Bleu. She sang at various clubs throughout the 1950s in New York, eventually opening her own establishment. She continued to perform into the 1980s, and received the American Medal of Freedom in 1983.

Merchant, Vijay (Madhavji) (1911–1987). Indian athlete; one of the greatest batsmen in the history of cricket and an

American astronaut John Glenn enters the Mercury-Atlas 6 spacecraft before lift-off at Cape Canaveral, Florida (Feb. 20, 1962).

elder statesman of the sport in India. In a career that ran from 1929 until 1951, Merchant's first class average of 71.22 ranked second only to that of Sir Donald BRADMAN's 95.14.

Merckx, Eddy (1945–). Belgian bicycle-racing champion. The dominant cyclist of the late 1960s and '70s, Merckx won the Tour de France five times (1969–72 and 1974), a record he shares with Jacques Anquetil and Bernard Hinault, both of France. Merckx also holds the record for the most wins in the sport's top events, with a total of 39 victories. He won the world professional road race title three times (in 1967, 1971 and 1974), a record he shares with Alfredo Binda of Italy and Rik van Steenbergen of Belgium. He won the Tour of Italy a record five times (1968, 1970, 1972–74), a mark he shares with Binda and Fausto Coppi of Italy. Merckx also holds the record for most wins in a season, 54, in 1971.

Mercury program [Project Mercury]. The Mercury program was the first U.S. manned spacecraft program. Seven pilots from the Navy, Air Force and Marines were chosen as the first U.S. astronauts; they were popularly known as the Mercury Seven. Several unmanned tests were made in 1960 and early 1961. The cramped quarters of the small Mercury capsule could carry one astronaut, strapped into a seat for the duration of the flight. The capsule was launched atop an Atlas rocket, originally designed as an Intercontinental Ballistic Missile (ICBM). The first two manned flights, in 1961, were short, suborbital flights to test the capsule's con-

THE MERCURY PROGRAM

1961	**May 5**	Alan Shepard makes 15-minute suborbital flight in Freedom 7.
	July 21	Gus Grissom makes 16-minute suborbital flight in Liberty Bell 7.
1962	**Feb. 20**	John Glenn completes three orbits in Friendship 7.
	May 24	Scott Carpenter completes three orbits in Aurora 7.
	Oct. 3	Wally Schirra completes six orbits in Sigma 7.
1963	**May 15**	Gordon Cooper makes 22-1/2 orbits in Faith 7.

trols. Four orbital missions followed. The Mercury astronauts became national heroes; one, John GLENN (the first American to orbit the Earth), later became a U.S. senator. One of the Mercury Seven, Deke SLAYTON, was grounded because of a heart problem and did not go into space during the Mercury program.

For further reading:

Wolfe, Tom, *The Right Stuff*. New York: Farrar Straus & Giroux, 1979.

Meredith, James (Howard) (1933–). American CIVIL RIGHTS activist. Born in Kosciusko, Mississippi, Meredith spent nine years in the Air Force before returning to his native state in 1960. In 1961 he applied to the all-white University of Mississippi and the following year became the first Afro-American to enter the institution. His court-ordered admission followed months of federal litigation, which ultimately desegregated "Ole Miss" and touched off rioting that brought National Guard and army troops to the campus. Meredith graduated in 1963, attended Columbia Law School and subsequently became a businessman in New York City. Continuing his involvement in the civil rights cause, he participated in demonstrations during the 1960s and was wounded while marching in Mississippi (1966). He unsuccessfully attempted to enter politics in the 1970s.

Merman, Ethel (1909–1984). American musical-comedy star. Merman was known for her booming voice and brash style. Her career spanned 50 years, and her perfect diction and pitch made her a favorite of many of the master composers and lyricists of her time. Her major successes on Broadway included leading roles in Cole PORTER's *Anything Goes*, Irving BERLIN's *Annie, Get Your Gun* and the Jule Styne-Stephen SONDHEIM musical *Gypsy*. She also starred in 14 movies, including *Alexander's Ragtime Band*. In 1972 she received a Tony Award for the entire body of her work.

Merrill, James (1926–). American poet. The son of the founder of the Merrill Lynch brokerage house, Merrill is acknowledged as one of the foremost poets of his time. He established himself as a lyric poet with his earliest volumes, such as *The Black Swan* (1946). With the publication of the volumes *The Fire Screen* (1969) and *Braving the Elements* (1972), Merrill was praised as the finest lyric poet in America, and he received the PULITZER PRIZE. He has also excelled as a narrative poet with such poems as *Days of 1971* (1972) and his three-part visionary epic published in one volume as *Changing Lights at Sandover* (1981). In addition, he has written dramas, such as *The Immortal Husband* (1956), and novels, including *The Seraglio* (1957).

Merritt, Abraham (1884–1943). American master of science fantasy during the Golden Age of the pulp magazine in the 1920s and 1930s. In contrast to the sober routines of his full-time job editing the popular magazine *American Weekly*, Merritt let his mind run wild in his spare time. His first great success, *The Moon Pool* (published first in *All-Story Magazine*, 1918) told of a gateway into the earth and the remnants of a Great Race that dwelt there. *The Face in the Abyss* (1923), which depicted a race of Snake Women in the Andes Mountains; *The Ship of Ishtar* (1924), which described a miniature sailing ship encompassing a cosmos of Good and Evil; and one of his finest stories, "Three Lines of Old French" (1918), which took a World War I infantryman back in history for a lesson in human immortality, followed. Two of his stories were adapted into movies—*Seven Footprints to Satan*, (1927) and *Devil Doll* (from *Burn, Witch, Burn!*) (1933)—although he disowned the results. Scorning orthodox religions, and something of a fatalist himself, Merritt questioned man's complacency in an unknowable, even hostile universe. "For in that vast crucible of life of which we are so small a part," he wrote in *The Metal Monster* (1920), "what other Shapes may even now be rising to submerge us?"

Merritt, H(iram) Houston (1902–1979). Pioneer neurologist and codeveloper (with Dr. Tracy J. Putnam) in 1936 of the anti-epilepsy drug Dilantin (diphenylhydantoin).

Merton, Thomas (1915–1968). American Trappist monk and spiritual writer. Merton, known as Father Lewis once he became a priest, was one of the most important spiritual writers of his time. After teaching English at Columbia University for a brief period, he entered the Catholic Church (1939), joining the Trappist order at Our Lady of Gethsemane monastery in Kentucky (1941). He was ordained a priest in 1949. Among Merton's many spiritual works are *Seeds of Contemplation* (1949), *No Man Is an Island* (1955) and *Mystics and Zen Masters* (1967).

Messerschmitt, Willy [Wilhelm Messerschmitt] (1898–1978). German aircraft designer, engineer and industrialist. Messerschmitt made and flew his own gliders at age 15. By age 26, he had formed his own aircraft manufacturing company. He was best known for the airplanes he produced for the Luftwaffe in WORLD WAR II. More than 30,000 of his ME-109 single-engine fighter planes were built; these fighters gave the Luftwaffe air supremacy during the early part of the war. Messerschmitt's ME-262 was the first operational combat jet. After the war, Messerschmitt was examined by an Allied denazification court (1948). The court found that he had been forced to build aircraft for the German war effort against his will. For the next 10 years, Messerschmitt and his company manufactured prefabricated houses and sewing machines. They resumed building airplanes in 1958.

Messiaen, Olivier (1908–). French classical music composer and critic. Messiaen was a highly original composer who led a 1930s movement, the Jeune France, that called for greater feeling and flamboyance in classical music, in contradistinction to the technical and intellectual emphases of the LES SIX school of the 1920s. During WORLD WAR II, Messiaen was imprisoned by the Nazis for two years. After the war, he taught at the Paris Conservatory for several decades. His major works include *Quartet for the End of Time* (1941), *Modes of Duration and Loudness* (1950), *Catalog of Birds* (1959) and *The Transfiguration* (1969).

American civil rights activist James Meredith was shot by a sniper while leading a march in Mississippi (1966).

Messiaen summarized his compositional methods in the two-volume work *The Technique of My Musical Language* (1944).

Messter, Oskar (1866–1943). German inventor, producer and motion picture director. His father ran an optical plant, and by 1896 young Oskar was adapting the American kinematograph and the French cinematographe into devices of his own for the recording, printing and projection of filmstrips. Technically, his greatest innovation was the Maltese Cross, a device that made it possible for a filmstrip to move intermittently through camera and projector. He is also credited with the first use in Germany of the close-up—as early as 1897. In 1910 he founded a company to manufacture film equipment, and in 1914 he began producing the German newsreel *Messter Woche* (*The Messter Weekly*), purportedly the first German newsweekly of its kind. Among his many commercial movies were *Salome* (1902), *Verkannt* (1910), *Richard Wagner* (1912) and *Ungarische Rhapsodie* (1913). He retired from active film production in 1917 when his company, Messter-Film, merged with Nordisk-Film and Viennese Sascha-Film to form the giant conglomerate Universum Film Aktien Gesellschaft (UFA).

For further reading:

Katz, Ephraim, ed., *The Film Encyclopedia*. New York: Thomas Y. Crowell, 1979.

metaphysical painting. Term coined by the Italian painter Giorgio de CHIRICO to define a kind of pre-SURREALIST painting that placed objects and figures in unexpected and mysterious juxtapositions. Conceived while de Chirico was in Paris from 1910 to 1915, it arose as a reaction against the dynamism of FUTURISM and exalted the stillness of classical antiquity, the architecture of ancient and Renaissance Italy and the validity of the dream world. Influenced by the philosophy of Nietzsche, Schopenhauer and Weininger, metaphysical painting attempted to portray a magically separate reality, defined by a raked perspective and inhabited by dramatic shadows, enigmatic figures, dressmakers' dummies, classical statuary and colonnaded buildings. The other important adherent of the style was the painter Carlo CARRA, with whom de Chirico founded the magazine *Pittura metafisica* in 1920.

Metaxas, Joannis (1871–1941). Greek general, statesman, dictator (1936–41). A career soldier commissioned in the army in 1890, he served in the Greco-Turkish War (1897) and the BALKAN WARS (1912–13). Appointed chief of the general staff in 1915, he was exiled to Italy in 1917 when Greece's entry into WORLD WAR I on the Allied side clashed with his pro-German sympathies. Returning in 1920, he led a coup attempt and was again exiled (1923–24). A leading royalist, he held a number of government posts from 1928 to 1936. In 1936, after the reestablishment of the monarchy, Metaxas was appointed prime minister. He assumed dictatorial powers later that year, dissolving parliament and suspending the constitution. When Greece was invaded by Italy in 1940, Metaxas aligned his country with the Allies and directed Greek RESISTANCE.

Metro-Goldwyn-Mayer. One of Hollywood's "Big Five" production/exhibition motion picture studios (along with WARNER BROS., RKO, TWENTIETH CENTURY-FOX and PARAMOUNT) and, arguably, the most prestigious. The complex history of its formation began with the establishment in 1912 of a theater chain by former nickelodeon and peep-show entrepreneur Marcus Loew. Needing more movie product, Loew acquired the Metro Picture Corporation in 1920 and Goldwyn Pictures Corp. and Louis B. MAYER Pictures in 1924. The new organization, Metro-Goldwyn-Mayer (MGM), was under the control of Louis B. Mayer as studio vice president and Irving THALBERG as vice president in charge of production. The years up to Thalberg's death in 1936 are generally considered MGM's peak period. Popular and prestigious pictures of that time include *Greed* (1924), *The Big Parade* (1926), *Ben Hur* (1927), *Flesh and the Devil* (1928), *Freaks* (1932), *Grand Hotel* (1932), *The Thin Man* (1934), *David Copperfield* (1935), *Mutiny on the Bounty* (1936) and *The Good Earth* (1936). By the mid-thirties MGM had 4,000 employees and 23 sound stages on its 117–acre lot in Culver City. An average of 40 features were made each year, costing approximately $500,000 each.

By the 1940s MGM's boast that it presented "more stars than there are in the heavens" seemed justified. Luminaries included Greta GARBO, Clark GABLE, the BARRYMORES, Jean HARLOW, Joan CRAWFORD, Spencer TRACY, Mickey ROONEY, Elizabeth TAYLOR, Judy GARLAND, William Powell and many others. Popular series included short-subjects—such as "Pete Smith Specialties," "Tom and Jerry" cartoons, and Hal Roach comedies—and feature programs—such as the Andy Hardy, TARZAN, and Dr. Kildare series. MGM also released the pictures of its British production company, Denham Studios under Michael Balcon, including *The Citadel* (1938) and *Goodbye, Mr. Chips* (1939), as well as numerous independently made movies—most notably, GONE WITH THE WIND (1939). A particularly noteworthy series of musicals appeared in the 1940s and early 1950s under the guidance of producers and filmmakers Arthur Freed, Stanley Donen, Vincente MINNELLI, and Gene KELLY—*Meet Me in St. Louis* (1944), *The Pirate* (1948), *On the Town* (1949), *An American in Paris* (1952), *Singin' in the Rain* (1953), *Seven Brides for Seven Brothers* (1955) and many others. After 1951 many changes affected the studio. The separation of MGM and the Loew's parent company was forced by government antitrust action. Following a bitter dispute between Mayer and Loew's president, Nicholas Schenck, Mayer was forced to resign and was replaced by his former production chief, Dore SCHARY. More corporate turnovers ensued. In 1969 Kirk Kerkorian bought the studio and began selling off the assets, disposing of the British studios and companies such as MGM Records. A public auction sold off many of the costumes and props. In 1979 MGM merged with United Artists, and the amalgamation has produced only sporadic releases, including the successful *Spaceballs* and *Moonstruck* (1988). At this writing Pathe International is negotiating a purchase of the studio.

For further reading:

Crowther, Bosley, *The Lion's Share: The Story of An Entertainment Empire*. New York: E.P. Dutton, 1957.

Metropolis. Prototype of the modern science fiction film. Directed by German filmmaker Fritz LANG in 1926 (and premiered in Berlin early in 1927), its futuristic architectural designs and special effects have had a profound effect on the genre. It was the most lavish and expensive film ever shot at the gigantic UFA studio complex in Berlin. Although it led to the virtual bankruptcy of that studio, and its absurd story of the revolt in the year 2000 of underground workers against their "topside" capitalist bosses was poorly received by the critics, there was no denying its spectacular visual and technical work. Cinematographer Karl Freund and set designers Otto Hunte and Karl Vollbrecht served up spectacular images of a divided world—above, the dazzling modern city of towers and flying machines (presided over by the despotic John Frederson), and below, the nightmarish world of gigantic machines and brain-washed workers (terrorized by the mad scientist, Rotwang). The hallucinatory images of the machines transforming into legendary monsters, the panic of the underworld citizens during a flood and the creation in Rotwang's laboratory of a robot remain unforgettable. The cutting of 7 of its original 17 reels for the American release (1927) accounts for the choppy, occasionally incomprehensible storyline of the release-prints available today.

Mexican Civil War of 1911. Francisco I. Madero (1873–1913), a U.S.-educated lawyer and liberal, called for the ouster of Mexican dictator Porfirio DIAZ and opposed him in the presidential election of 1910. Diaz had Madero arrested and, after the balloting, proclaimed himself the victor. On November 20, 1910 Madero and his supporters launched an armed revolt. Although the Porfirian army contained most of the outbreaks in 1911, Pascual Orozco maintained resistance in Chihuahua state, and in May, 1911 rebel forces under him and Francisco "Pancho" VILLA captured Ciudad Juarez. Thus encouraged, revolutionaries throughout MEXICO took up arms. With his own support crumbling, Diaz was forced to accept the Treaty of Ciudad Juarez stipulating his prompt resignation; Madero was elected president in October. But Madero could not control the forces he had unleashed, and the events of 1911 ushered in two decades of bloodshed. (See also MEXICAN REVOLT OF 1914–15.)

Mexican Civil War of 1920. Venustiano Carranza tried to dictate who would succeed him as president of MEXICO (see MEXICAN REVOLT OF 1914–15). He chose a little-known diplomat named Ignacio Bonillas, but Alvaro Obregon, who had helped put Carranza in office and served as his minister of war, felt the office should be his. Obregon's former comrade-in-arms, Adolfo de la Huerta, then governor of the state of Sonora, and General Plutarco Elias CALLES, chief of the Sonoran armed forces, called for Carranza's resignation. When Carranza sent federal troops into Sonora to break a labor strike, Huerta declared Sonora an independent republic. Obregon and Calles marched south, collecting arms and volunteer troops as they went. Finding no soldiers willing to oppose Obregon and his rebel army, Carranza fled from the capital, Mexico City, toward Veracruz aboard a train loaded with gold he had taken from the national treasury. En route, he learned that the governor of the state of Veracruz had joined the rebels; he then fled on horseback into the mountains, where he was betrayed and murdered. Obregon entered Mexico City unopposed; Huerta became provisional president and, after a special election, was succeeded by Obregon later in 1920.

Mexican Insurrections of 1926–29. Mexico's election of 1924 brought to the presidency Plutarco Elias CALLES, who implemented the previously unenforced anticlerical provisions of the 1917 constitution. In early 1926 officials of the Mexican Roman Catholic Church issued a condemnation of the provisions. Calles responded by closing Catholic schools, convents and seminaries; forcing the registration of priests; and accusing the Catholic hierarchy of treason. In mid-1926 Catholic laypersons retaliated by stopping all but their essential purchases, and soon the Catholic clergy ceased performing clerical functions. The *cristeros*, terrorists, whose cry was *Viva Cristo Rey* ("Long Live Christ the King"), took up arms against the anticlerical government and caused widespread destruction and murder in a dozen Mexican states. Although the Catholic hierarchy disavowed any connection with the *cristeros*, the government ordered the nationalization of church property, the deportation of several bishops, priests and nuns and the execution of a number of Catholics. Government forces crushed most of the *cristeros* by early 1928. Alvaro Obregon was elected president of Mexico on July 1, 1928. (He was assassinated later that month and was succeeded by Emilio Portes Gil, who was appointed provisional president.) The undisputed political power in Mexico still lay with Calles, even though in March 1929 another insurrection erupted under the leadership of politically and religiously discontented generals whose followers ravaged the country for about two months before the government restored order. Calles influenced the election to the presidency of Pascual Ortiz Rubio (1877–1963) in 1929; a half-hearted military insurrection against Ortiz failed; and Ortiz assumed office as Calles' puppet and continued his anticlerical policies.

Mexican Revolt of 1914–15. By a successful coup d'etat, Victoriano Huerta gained the presidency of MEXICO on February 18, 1913, overthrowing Francisco I. Madero. Huerta was opposed by the separate forces of Emiliano ZAPATA in the south, of Venustiano Carranza in the northeast, of Francisco "Pancho" VILLA in the north, and of Alvaro Obregon in the northwest. These four opposing forces increased their military activities until by the spring of 1914 they controlled about three-quarters of Mexico, confining Huerta and his followers to the areas around Mexico City, the capital, and Veracruz. U.S. President Woodrow WILSON refused to recognize Huerta's government, whose hostile acts resulted in American forces seizing and occupying Veracruz (April 21, 1914). When Villa's forces seized Zacatecas and Obregon's took Guadalajara and Queretaro, Huerta resigned as president. The rival leaders, Villa and Obregon, raced for the capital; Obregon arrived first and proclaimed his friend Carranza "First Chief" of Mexico. The leaders met at Aguascalientes to organize a government in late 1914, but Mexico was already torn by anarchy. Villa and Zapata occupied Mexico City, while Carranza and Obregon took control of Veracruz. Although Villa and Zapata had more troops and held about two-thirds of the country, Carranza was recognized by the U.S. and eight other nations in the Western Hemisphere as *de facto* president of Mexico. Carranza controlled the northeastern border with the U.S., across which he could purchase arms; he also had the expert military assistance of Obregon and the shrewdness to promise the people social reform. In early 1915, Obregon and his troops occupied the capital, forcing Villa to flee to the surrounding countryside. Villa and his forces were pursued to the town of Celaya, where Obregon employed military tactics developed in WORLD WAR I. His troops dug trenches and strung barbed wire around Celaya, and after a three-day battle in April 1915, they won a decisive victory over Villa, who retreated northward. Villa's men pulled up railroad tracks to prevent pursuit by their foes. Both Villa and Zapata continued guerrilla warfare against Carranza, who later became president officially. Obregon was appointed minister of war. (See also MEXICAN CIVIL WAR OF 1911; MEXICAN CIVIL WAR OF 1920; VILLA'S RAIDS.)

Mexico. North American republic bordered by the U.S. to the north, the Gulf of Mexico and the Caribbean to the east, GUATEMALA and BELIZE to the south and the Pacific Ocean to the west. Its capital is Mexico City. General Porfirio DIAZ took control of Mexico's government in 1876, and was its effective dictator for the next 34 years. His capitalist government favored the wealthy, and following a revolution, was toppled by Francisco I. Madero in 1910. Madero was himself overthrown and murdered in 1913 when Adolfo de la Huerta took power. The U.S. did not recognize his government, and landed troops in Veracruz in 1914, but ARGENTINA, BRAZIL and CHILE intervened to prevent a war. Following a raid in the U.S. by the revolutionary Francisco "Pancho" VILLA in 1916, the U.S. invaded northern Mexico in his pursuit, but failed to capture him. Venustiano Carranza initiated constitutional reforms in 1917. Following a brief civil war in 1920, a moderate, socialist government prevailed under the governments of presidents Alvaro Obregon and Plutarco Elias CALLES. In 1929, Calles founded the National Revolutionary Party, which was renamed the Institutional Revolutionary Party (PRI) in 1946, and which has peacefully dominated subsequent Mexican politics. Since 1946, internal Mexican policy has stressed industrialization which, while benefiting the upper and middle classes, did little for most of its rapidly increasing population. In the early 1980's, Mexico's eco-

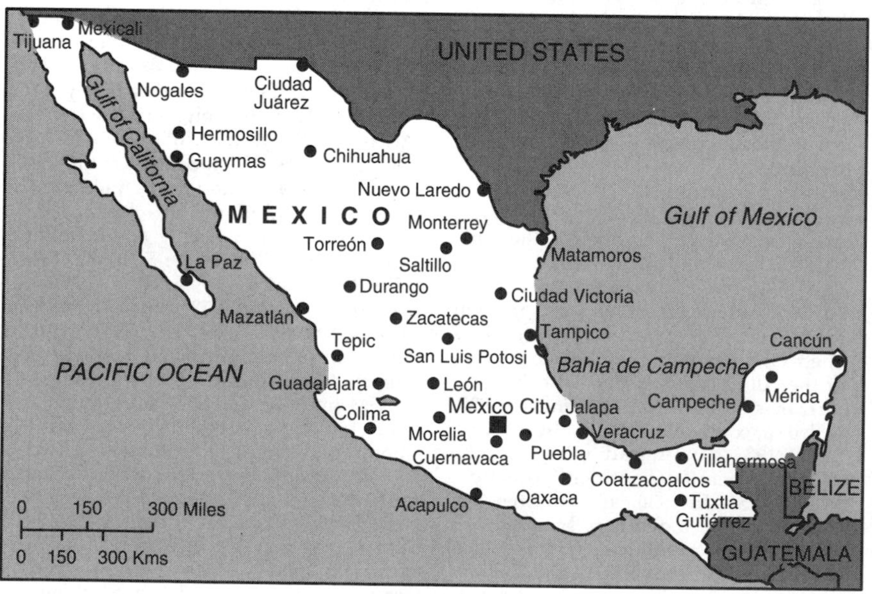

MEXICO

MEXICO

1911	Dictator Porfirio Diaz overthrown by Francisco Madero; guerrillas in the north, led by Pancho Villa, and peasants in the south, led by Emiliano Zapata, revolt, calling for social change and land reform.
1913	Madero is shot; General Victoriano Huerta seizes power; Madero's followers unite behind Venustiano Carranza, a state governor, to fight Huerta.
1914	Backing Carranza, U.S. President Woodrow Wilson sends Marines to occupy the port of Veracruz to prevent arms from reaching Huerta's army.
1915	U.S. halts gun supply to Villa and Zapata, who continue to fight Carranza.
1916	Villa forces raid Columbus, New Mexico, killing 18 Americans in revenge for U.S. interference in Mexico; American force of 4,000 searches for Villa in Mexico but does not find him.
1917	Revolutionary constitution adopted; it curtails the power of Roman Catholic Church, establishes state education, declares mineral and subsoil rights the property of the nation and promulgates social and labor reforms.
1919	Emiliano Zapata killed.
1920	Venustiano Carranza killed during revolt led by General Alvaro Obregon, who becomes president.
1923	Pancho Villa killed; Marxist painter Diego Rivera begins monumental revolutionary murals for the Ministry of Education and the Agricultural School, Chilpancingo.
1926-29	Cristero Rebellion led by militant Catholic priests protesting suppression of Church.
1929	National Revolutionary Party founded (PNR, named Mexican Revolutionary Party in 1938 and Institutional Revolutionary Party, PRI, in 1946); has held power ever since.
1938	U.S. and British oil companies expelled and their property expropriated during a period of accelerated reform under President Lazaro Cardenas.
1940	Exiled Bolshevik Leon Trotsky murdered in Mexico by Stalin's secret police.
1942-45	Mexico enters World War II on side of Allies; war supply exports expand economy dramatically.
1953	Women receive right to vote.
1957	Diego Rivera dies.
1968	Summer Olympics held in Mexico City.
1976	Economy suffering from worldwide recession, Mexico devalues currency twice to stabilize economy; after discovery of vast new oil deposits, accelerated production is planned.
1982	Close to bankruptcy, caused by rising interest rates and falling demand for oil, government announces it can no longer make payments on foreign debt.
1985	Earthquakes cause over 7,000 deaths and $4 billion in property damage.
1990	Debt-reduction pact is signed to reduce $54 billion debt to commercial banks; Japanese bankers write off 70% of $8.9 billion in loans; magazine *Proceso* prints names and locations of 57 U.S. Drug Enforcement agents working inside Mexico.
1991	U.S. President George Bush and Mexican President Carlos Salinas de Gortari negotiate free-trade agreement, pending ratification by U.S. Congress, against opposition of U.S. organized labor and environmental groups; pollution emergency declared in Mexico City, where respiratory illness is number-one cause of death.

nomic problems were exacerbated by a drop in oil prices. The peso was devalued in 1982, but in the following two years Mexico faced extreme unemployment and inability to pay its foreign debt. A devastating earthquake in Mexico City in 1985 worsened the situation. PRI claimed dominance of the 1985 elections, but there were charges of vote fraud. While a PRI candidate won the presidential election, opposition parties prevailed in the 1989 gubernatorial elections. Mexico, the fourth largest oil-producing nation, has benefited from the rising oil prices resulting from the IRAQ invasion of KUWAIT in 1990. Mexican foreign policy has traditionally been dominated by the U.S., but Mexico has criticized U.S. intervention in Central America, and also maintains ties with CUBA.

Meyer, Hannes (1889–1954). Swiss-born German architect known for his role at the BAUHAUS where he followed Walter GROPIUS as director (1928–30). Meyer was trained at the technical college at Basle and in Berlin. He began teaching at the Bauhaus in 1927 and also submitted an admired but unsuccessful entry to the Palace of the League of Nations competition held that year. After resigning from the Bauhaus, he worked in the U.S.S.R. (1930–36) and in Mexico (1939–49) where he was director of an institute for town planning. While at the Bauhaus, Meyer was the editor of eight issues of *Bauhaus* magazine published from 1928 to 1929. The 1965 book by Claude Schnaidt, *Hannes Meyer: Buildings, Projects and Writings,* is a comprehensive survey of his work.

Meyerhof, Otto Fritz (1884–1951). German-American biochemist. Meyerhof devoted the greater part of his academic life to the study of the biochemistry and metabolism of muscle and shared the NOBEL PRIZE for physiology or medicine with Archibald Hill in 1922. He held professorships at Kiel and Heidelberg universities, was director of physiology at the Kaiser Wilhelm Institute for Biology, Berlin, and was director of research at the Paris Institue of Biology. In 1940 he immigrated to America, where he joined the medical faculty of the University of Pennsylvania. Meyerhof demonstrated that the production of lactic acid in muscle tissue, formed as a result of glycogen breakdown, was effected without the consumption of oxygen (i.e., anaerobically). The lactic acid was reconverted to glycogen through oxidation by molecular oxygen, during muscle rest. This line of research was continued by Gustav EMBDEN and Carl and Gerty CORI, who worked out in greater detail the steps by which glycogen is converted to lactic acid—the **Embden-Meyerhof pathway**.

Meyerhold, Vsevolod Yemilyevich (1874–1942). Russian actor and director. Meyerhold worked with V.I. Nemirovich-Danchenko and Konstantin STANISLAVSKY at the Moscow Art Theater (1898–1902). In 1902 he founded the Society of New Drama in Russia. His method of production known as "biomechanics" involved reducing the actor to the status of a puppet under the control of the producer. He used a bare stage and stylized gestures. In 1920 he became head of theater in the People's Commissariat for Education. He founded his own theater in Moscow. Innovative and modernistic, he worked closely with Vladimir MAYAKOVSKY. In 1915 he made two films, now lost, *The Strong Man* and *Dorian Grey*, which are known to have influenced contemporary filmmakers. From 1920 Meyerhold had a working studio with student directors, including Sergei EISENSTEIN. Accused of Formalism, he was arrested in 1939 and "disappeared."

MGB. Russian abbreviation for Ministry of State Security. Name of the Soviet security service (1946–53), and responsible for internal security; the MGB replaced the NKVD and NKGB. Under BERIA's leadership and STALIN's orders the MGB became exceedingly powerful. Jewish intellectuals were harassed in 1949, and an operation was led against the former supporters of ZHDANOV. The wave of terror and the powerful position of the MGB reached its zenith with the discovery of the DOCTOR'S PLOT of 1952. Following the death of Stalin the ministry was once again subordinated to party control and was reorganized as the KGB (Committee of State Security).

MI5. British counterintelligence organization, created in 1909. MI5 was organized to fight subversion in Britain and to undertake counterintelligence operations abroad. During WORLD WAR I and WORLD WAR II, MI5 was successful in countering German spy networks in Britain. However, it was unable to prove that one of the top agents of MI6, Kim PHILBY, had long been a Soviet spy and had passed top secrets to the U.S.S.R. There were also allegations that MI5's director, Sir Roger Hollis, was a Soviet secret agent.

MI6. British intelligence agency, also known as the Secret Intelligence Service (SIS), founded in 1911. The British counterpart of the American OSS and, later, the CIA, MI6 operates under the highest secrecy. During the 1940s and 1950s one of MI6's top agents, Kim PHILBY, was a double agent for the Soviet Union.

Michener, James A(lbert) (1907?-). American novelist best known for his historical epics. There is uncertainty about the actual place and date of Michener's birth. He held a number of diverse jobs, including acting and sportswriting before his education and eventual position as a naval historian in the South Pacific. Michener's first work of fiction was *Tales of the South Pacific* (1947), which inspired the Rogers and Hammerstein musical *South Pacific* (1949, filmed 1958). His later novels are epic, often historical, adventures and include *The Bridges at Toko-Ri* (1953, filmed 1954), *Hawaii* (1959, filmed 1966, and as "The Hawaiians" in 1970), *Centennial* (1974) and *Alaska* (1988), among many others. Michener's nonfiction includes *The Bridge at Andau* (1957), *America vs. America: The Revolution in Middle-Class Values* (1969); he has also written on Japanese art.

Mickey Mouse. World-famous animated film character and ambassador for all Walt DISNEY enterprises. "The mouse that built an empire," as Disney described him, was born on a train somewhere between Chicago and Los Angeles in 1927. Disheartened by the failure of his "Alice" series of cartoons and by the loss of rights to the "Oswald Rabbit" character, Disney recalled his days in Kansas City as a youth when he shared his studio with a field mouse. That mouse (dubbed by his wife Lillian as "Mickey" contrary to Walt's wishes to name him "Mortimer") created a sensation at his first public appearance on November 18, 1928, in New York City's Colony Theater. *Steamboat Willie* (1928) not only launched the mouse but was an innovation in the new technique of synchronized-sound TALKING PICTURES. At a rate of 18 cartoons a year, Mickey soon became a national craze. With faithful Minnie and his arch-nemesis, Peg-Leg Pete, Mickey danced, tumbled, flew, and rode through slapstick adventures on screen and, after 1930, in the daily newspapers for King Features Syndicate. With all the trappings of success—an Oscar, the patronage of British aristocracy, his image in Madame Tussaud's—Mickey after 1940 became more of a entrepreneur than a movie star. He presented classical music to the public in FANTASIA (1940), opened the Disneyland theme park in 1955, the Walt Disney World park in 1971, hosted two television shows—"The Mickey Mouse Club" (1955) and "The New Mickey Mouse Club" (1977)—and lent his stature and image to all Disney-related activities. Before his retirement (albeit a temporary one) in 1953, Mickey made 120 cartoons in all. Walt Disney himself provided Mickey with a voice. And it is well known that Walt's mannerisms, sturdy individuality, occasional shyness all were adapted to Mickey's character. When Walt died in 1966, Mickey lived on, of course. But the edition of *Paris Match* magazine that appeared at the time displayed Mickey on its cover—with a tear in his eye.

Famed Walt Disney cartoon star Mickey Mouse with friend Pluto.

For further reading:

Bain, David and Bruce Harris, eds., *Mickey Mouse: Fifty Happy Years.* New York: Harmony Books, 1977.

Micronesia, Federated States of. The Federated States of Micronesia consist of four major island groups in the North Pacific Ocean with a total area of 271 square miles; its 607 islands vary geologically from mountainous terrain to coral atolls. Spain sold the Carolines, where Micronesia is situated, to Germany in 1899. At the outbreak of WORLD WAR I Japan took possession of the German Pacific colonies, and in 1920 the LEAGUE OF NATIONS mandated control of Micronesia to JAPAN. Truk Lagoon in the Carolines was one of Japan's most important bases during WORLD WAR II. The American Navy took command of Micronesia following Japan's defeat in 1945. In 1947 the United Nations established the Trust Territory of the Pacific Islands, under U.S. control.

Moves toward preparing Micronesia for self-government began in the 1960s. In a referendum in July 1978, of the six Trust Territory districts only four islands voted in favor of a common constitution. They became the FSM. In October 1982 the FSM and U.S. governments signed a Compact of Free Association, under which the FSM would be internally self-governing while the U.S. maintained responsibility for defense—primarily to deny access to other powers rather than to establish its own bases. U.S. administration of Micronesia formally ended in November 1986, but the U.N. Security Council has yet to officially terminate the trusteeship owing to uncertainty over the future status of the Micronesian territory of Palau.

Midway. Island group in the central Pacific, northwest of the Hawaiian Islands; site of critical WORLD WAR II naval battle between the American and Japanese navies. One of the decisive battles of the war, Midway (June 3–6, 1942) saw the destruction of the main Japanese carrier fleet and forced Japan into a defensive posture in the Pacific. Unaware that U.S. intelligence had broken Japanese military codes and therefore knew of his intentions, Admiral YAMAMOTO pressed ahead with his plans to seize Midway. The Japanese fleet, including four aircraft carriers and about 250 planes, was intercepted by a U.S. force including three carriers and about 350 aircraft, (plus those stationed on Midway itself). In ferocious dive-bomb attacks, American pilots destroyed all four Japanese heavy carriers, two cruisers, three destroyers, and 250 aircraft and killed 3,500 men; American losses were two ships, including the carrier *Yorktown*, 150 planes and 300 men. (See also WORLD WAR II IN THE PACIFIC.)

Mies van der Rohe, Ludwig (1886–1969). German architect and designer; one of the most acclaimed of 20th-century architects. His stylistic penchant for simplicity and clean elegance, as evidenced by his famous saying "less is more," shows itself in both his architectural projects and his furniture designs. He is an important figure both in the history of MINIMALISM and in the development of the international design school of architecture. Mies van der Rohe began his architectural career in 1907 without any formal training. In the early 1910s, he worked for the German-based architectural firm of Peter Behrens, a firm that also numbered among its architects Walter GROPIUS and LE CORBUSIER. From 1930 to 1933, Mies van der Rohe served as director of the BAUHAUS. After the Nazis came to power he remained in Germany for several years. In 1938 he fled to the U.S., where he spent most of the remaining years of his life. His most famous architectural works include the BARCELONA PAVILION (1929) in Barcelona, Spain, a largely glass structure without interior walls, and the Lakeshore Drive Apartments (1948–1951) in Chicago, Illinois.

For further reading:

Blake, Peter, *The Master Builders: Le Corbusier, Mies Van der Rohe, Frank Lloyd Wright*. New York: W.W. Norton, 1976.

Hochman, Elaine, *Architects of Fortune: Mies Van der Rohe and the Third Reich*. New York: Grove Weidenfeld, 1989.

Mifune, Toshiro (1920–). Popular Japanese motion picture actor who is frequently associated with the films of Akira KUROSAWA. He was born in Tsingtao, China, to Japanese parents. His appearance as the bandit in Kurosawa's landmark *Rashomon* (1950) led to a list of notable subsequent collaborations—as a psychologically disturbed police detective in *Stray Dog* (1949), a swashbuckling young *ronin* (masterless samurai) in *Seven Samurai* (1954), a murderous feudal king in *Throne of Blood* (1957), and an opportunistic swordsman in *Yojimbo* (1961). Beyond question he is the best known Japanese actor abroad, appearing in American films like *Hell in the Pacific* (1969) and *Midway* (1976),in which he portrayed Admiral YAMAMOTO. His abilities to convey an inner intensity as well as a flamboyant physicality are perhaps best fused in Kurosawa's *Red Beard* (1965), where he portrays a quiet, dedicated doctor whose work in the ghettos forces him to dispatch his enemies with some impressive techniques in judo and swordplay.

For further reading:

Katz, Ephraim, ed., *The Film Encyclopedia*. New York: Thomas Y. Crowell, 1979.

migrant labor. Body of transient or non-national laborers working in a foreign country. The term is usually specifically applied to the black labor force in SOUTH AFRICA, which was housed in barracks or hostels by employers and separated from their families. Elsewhere, Mexican (Chicano) laborers in the southwestern U.S. (generally referred to as **migrant workers**), Algerian workers in France and Turkish workers (called ***Gastarbeiters***) in Germany and Switzerland are also examples of migrant labor.

Mihailovic, Draza (1893–1946). Yugoslav military leader. Born in southern Serbia, he became an officer and served with the Serbian army during WORLD WAR I. After the fall of Yugoslavia (1941) during WORLD WAR II, Mihailovic organized the CHETNIKS (Serbian RESISTANCE forces), and was named minister of war by the Yugoslav government-in-exile. Meanwhile, a communist Resistance group under Josip Broz TITO was also fighting the Nazis, for the most part in Bosnia and Montenegro. As the war continued, Mihailovic, an ardent royalist and Serbian nationalist, opposed and finally fought Tito—and thus gradually lost Allied support. He was captured by Tito's partisan forces in 1946, tried for treason and sentenced to death. Although voices were raised throughout the world to protest his sentence, Tito considered him a threat to the nascent communist regime, and Mihailovic was executed.

For further reading:

Lees, Michael, *The Rape of Serbia: The British Rule in Tito's Grab for Power*. San Diego: Harcourt Brace Jovanovich, 1991.

Miki, Takeo (1907–1988). Japanese politician; first elected to the Japanese Diet in 1937 and reelected 19 times before his death, making him the parliament's longest-serving member. In the late 1930s, Miki sought to prevent JAPAN from becoming involved in a war against the U.S. After World War II, he rose to become one of the top leaders of the Liberal Democratic Party. When that party needed a candidate to refurbish its image following the 1974 resignation of Premier Kakuei TANAKA, it drafted Miki. He himself resigned from the premiership two years later in reaction to a poor showing by the Liberal Democrats in a parliamentary election.

Mikoyan, Anastas Ivanovich (1896–1978). Soviet communist official. Mikoyan joined the BOLSHEVIKS in 1915 and became a member of the POLITBURO in 1926. He served under every Soviet leader from LENIN to BREZHNEV and was in the front rank of the Kremlin hierarchy for nearly 50 years. His longevity was remarkable, considering the mortality rate of high-ranking officials during the rule of STALIN. He became deputy prime minister in 1937. He was later first vice chairman of the Council of Ministers (1955–64) and president of the Soviet Union (1964–65).

Milburn, Jackie (John) (1924–1988). English football (soccer) star and a member of Britain's most famous footballing family. Milburn gained widespread fame as a center-forward for Newcastle United and for England. After retiring from active play, he became a team manager and, later, a sportswriter.

Milestone, Lewis (1895–1980). Russian-born HOLLYWOOD film director. Milestone directed more than 30 films in a 40–year career and won ACADEMY AWARDS for *Two Arabian Knights* (1928) and *All Quiet On The Western Front* (1930), adapted from Erich Maria REMARQUE'S WORLD WAR I novel. His other film credits included *The Front Page* (written by Ben HECHT and Charles MacArthur), *The General Died at Dawn, Of Mice and Men* (adapted from John STEINBECK'S novel), *The North Star* (a WORLD WAR II film set in the U.S.S.R.), and *A Walk in the Sun*, a classic film about American G.I.s in ITALY during World War II. Milestone's directorial style was noted for its fluid camera technique, crisp dialogue, stong characterization, and vivid realism.

Milhaud, Darius (1892–1974). French composer. Born in Aix-en-Provence, he trained at the Paris Conservatory (1910–15) under Paul Dukas, Vincent d'INDY and others. He was a diplomatic aide to Paul CLAUDEL in Brazil (1917–18), coming into contact with Brazilian folk music, and later visited the U.S. where he became acquainted with JAZZ. Both forms were to influence his music. Returning to France, he became a member of the modernist group known as LES SIX. Milhaud taught composition at Mills College, Oakland, California, from 1940 to 1947, teaching thereafter at the Paris Conservatory. A prolific composer, he wrote over 400 works. He used polytonality to great effect in compositions noted for their decided rhythmic structure, excellent craftsmanship and expressive instrumentation. Milhaud is especially celebrated for his operas, including *Le Pauvre Matelot* (1930; libretto by Jean COCTEAU), *Christophe Colombe* (1930; libretto by Claudel), *Bolivar* (1943), *David* (1953) and *St. Louis, King of France* (1970–71; libretto by Claudel). His oeuvre also includes 12 symphonies, concertos, orchestral music, incidental music for plays, chamber pieces, choral works and songs.

Milland, Ray (1905–1986). Welsh-born actor. He was best known for his role as an alcoholic writer in the 1945 film *The Lost Weekend*, a performance that won him an ACADEMY AWARD for best actor. His 56–year career in Britain and the U.S. included numerous television roles and parts in almost 150 films, including *Dial M for Murder* and *Lady in the Dark*.

Millar, Richard William (1899–1990). American businessman. He was regarded as one of the pioneers in the development of Southern CALIFORNIA'S aerospace industry, and helped to forge strong links between the investment and aircraft communities. He served as president of Bankamerica Corp. before joining Northrop as chairman from 1947 to 1949. After a scandal involving illegal payments to political candidates, Millar was returned as chairman for 1975–76. He continued to serve as a board member until 1984.

Millay, Edna St. Vincent (1892–1950). U.S. poet. Her poem "Renascence" was given a literary prize by the publication *The Lyric Year* in 1912. After graduating from Vassar in 1917, she published the volume *Second April* in 1921. *The Ballad of the Harp-Weaver* (1922) was awarded the PULITZER PRIZE. Influenced by English poets Keats and Hopkins, she has written on a variety of New England subjects.

Miller, Arthur (1915–). American playwright. One of the most acclaimed American dramatists of the postwar period, he was born in New York City and educated at the University of Michigan, where he began writing plays. A profoundly serious writer, concerned with the morality of ordinary decisions and the tragic elements of everyday life, Miller scored his first big commercial success with *All My Sons* (1947, film 1948). His next box office triumph was the work widely considered his masterpiece, DEATH OF A SALESMAN (1949, film 1952). Winner of the PULITZER PRIZE, it is the story of Willy Loman, an ordinary man betrayed by the shallow values of the American dream. Miller's social conscience is clear in all his work, and is particularly in evidence in his Tony-winning *The Crucible* (1953), a drama set in the 17th-century Salem witch trials that serves as a parable of the effects of MCCARTHYISM. The Pulitzer Prize-winning tragedy *A View from the Bridge* (1955)

American playwright and two-time Pulitzer Prize-winner Arthur Miller poses with a copy of his autobiography.

details the breakdown of a Sicilian-American working-class family and *After the Fall* (1964) is a fictionalized view of Miller's troubled life with his second wife, Marilyn MONROE. His other plays include *Incident at Vichy* (1965), *The Price* (1968) and *The Creation of the World and Other Business* (1972). He is also the author of a novel, *Focus* (1945), the screenplay for *The Misfits* (1961), a short story collection and the television film *Playing for Time* (1980).

Miller, Glenn (1904–1944). American big band jazz bandleader, trombonist and arranger. Miller began his career as a trombone player and arranger for various 1930s jazz big bands, including the ensemble led by Jimmy and Tommy DORSEY. In 1938, he formed his own big band, which enjoyed a series of hits, including "Chattanooga Choo Choo," "In the Mood," "Moonlight Serenade" and "Tuxedo Junction." In 1942, Miller volunteered to become the leader of the U.S. Army Air Force band, based in Europe, which aired radio broadcasts to entertain the troops during WORLD WAR II. He died in a 1944 plane crash while en route from England to Paris.

Miller, Henry (1891–1980). American writer. Miller has been acknowledged by fellow writers as diverse as Norman MAILER, Isaac Bashevis SINGER and John UPDIKE as the leading force in this century in widening the boundaries of literature to include frank portrayals of lust and sexuality. Miller created a sensation with the publication of his classic first work, *Tropic of Cancer* (1934), an autobiographical novel that offered a lyric and bawdy portrayal of bohemian life in Paris. *Tropic of Cancer* was banned as obscene in the U.S. for nearly three decades, before a 1964 decision by the U.S. Supreme Court upheld its literary value. *Tropic of Capricorn* (1936) applied a similar approach to Miller's years of coming to manhood in his native Brooklyn. Miller proved himself a gifted literary critic and philosophical essayist in works such as *The Wisdom of the Heart* (1941), *The Time of the Assassins* (1946), and *The Books in My Life* (1952). *The Colossus of Maroussi* (1941) is a stirring account of Miller's travels in Greece just prior to World War II. *Sexus* (1948), *Plexus* (1963) and *Nexus* (1965) are a trilogy of autobiographical novels.

Miller, Izetta Jewel (1884?-1978). American actress and feminist. In the early 1920s Miller twice ran for the U.S. Senate from West Virginia, but was unsuccessful. She was the first woman in the American South to be nominated to run for national office by a major party (the DEMOCRATIC PARTY).

Miller, Jonathan (Wolfe) (1934–). British director. Although trained as a medical doctor, Miller has spent most of his life as a director in theater, television and opera. His first success was as coauthor and actor in the 1960 revue BEYOND THE FRINGE. He directed his first play, John OSBORNE's *Under Plain Cover*, in 1962. He is particularly noted for his innovative direction of Shakespeare's plays for television during the 1980s. An associate director of Britain's National Theatre from 1973 to 1975, Miller also served as artistic director of London's Old Vic Theatre from 1986 until March 1991. Among his notable productions are *King Lear* (1969), Chekhov's *Three Sisters* (1976) and Racine's *Andromache* (1988).

Miller, Perry (1905–1963). U.S. historian. Miller received his Ph.D. from the University of Chicago in 1931. He joined the Harvard faculty in 1931 and taught at that university until his death. A giant in the

American author Henry Miller's Tropic of Cancer *was banned in the U.S. for obscenity for 27 years.*

field of intellectual history, Miller wrote extensively on American Puritanism. His works argued that religion rather than economics was the primary motive for Puritan settlement in New England. Among his major works are *Orthodoxy in Massachusetts* (1933), *The New England Mind* (1939), *From Colony to Province* (1953) and *Errant into the Wilderness* (1956).

Miller, Stanley Lloyd (1930–). American chemist who tested the theory, first proposed by the Russian scientist Aleksandr OPARIN, that life on Earth arose out of a "primordial soup." In 1953, while working towards his Ph.D. at the University of Chicago, Miller published the results of an experiment whereby he produced a number of amino acids in an environment that simulated the early atmosphere of the Earth, which was believed to be similar to that of Jupiter and Saturn. To many scholars his famous paper, *A Production of Amino Acids under Possible Primitive Earth Conditions*, was evidence of the spontaneous origin of life. However, subsequent research has shown that for a single protein to develop from simpler amino acids, other principles would have to be involved. Miller has been a professor of chemistry at the University of California in San Diego since 1968.

Miller, William E(dward) (1914–1983). U.S. politician. Miller was best known as

"In the Mood"—the Glenn Miller Orchestra led by American "Swing" trombonist Glenn Miller.

the vice presidential running mate of Senator Barry GOLDWATER in the 1964 presidential elections. He served seven terms in the House of Representatives beginning in 1950. From 1960 to 1963 he was chairman of the Republican Congressional Campaign Committee.

Milligan, Spike (Terence Alan) (1918–). British humorist. Best known for his association with the hit radio program THE GOON SHOW. Milligan has had a tremendous impact on British humor. He made his radio debut in "Opportunity Knocks" (1949), then, in collaboration with Peter SELLERS, Harry Secombe and Michael Bentine, cowrote and performed in "The Goon Show" (1949–60). Famous for his zany, surrealistic and slightly skewed brand of humor, Milligan appeared in numerous television series and motion pictures and also on stage, most notably in *Treasure Island* (1961, 1973, 1974, 1975). In addition he has written many humorous works, including *Puckoon* (1963) and *The Looney: An Irish Fantasy* (1987).

Millikan, Robert Andrews (1868–1953). American physicist. In 1923 Millikan won the NOBEL PRIZE for physics for determining that the electric charge of an electron was always a simple multiple of the same basic electrostatic unit. In conjunction with this project, Millikan also attempted to demonstrate the validity of Albert EINSTEIN's description of the photoelectric effect, which was cited in his own Nobel award of 1905. Following Millikan's crowning achievement of 1923, he began a major study of cosmic rays, which would occupy him for the rest of his career. He argued that these rays were electromagnetic radiation photons, rather than charged particles, but his theory was later disproved by Arthur COMPTON.

Mills, Irving (1894–1985). U.S. composer and music publisher. In 1919 he cofounded a music publishing company called Mills Music that was to remain under his direction until 1965. He was best known for his association with Duke ELLINGTON, which began in 1926 and lasted until 1939. After discovering Ellington in a Broadway nightclub, Mills became his publisher and manager, as well as collaborating with him on such songs as "Mood Indigo" and "Sophisticated Lady." He also did much to advance the careers of other such well-known artists as Cab CALLOWAY, Hoagy CARMICHAEL and Milton BERLE.

Mills, John [Lewis Ernest Watts] (1908–). British actor. Mills has been one of Britain's finest stage and screen actors since the 1930s. His stage career began at the London Hippodrome in 1929 and has included leading roles in such varied works as *Charley's Aunt* (1930), Noel COWARD's drama *Cavalcade* (1931), *A Midsummer Night's Dream* (1939) and Brian Clark's *The Petition* (1987). In 1961 he made his New York stage debut in the title role of Terence Rattigan's *Ross*. Mills has also appeared in numerous films, including *Ryan's Daughter* (1971) for which he won a best supporting actor ACADEMY AWARD.

Mills, Wilbur (Daigh) (1909–). American politician. Born in Kensett, Arkansas, Mills was trained as a lawyer and was a probate judge before his election as a Democratic member of the House of Representatives in 1938. A protege of House Speaker Samuel RAYBURN, he was appointed to the prestigious Ways and Means Committee (1943) and assumed its chairmanship (1958). The House's foremost tax expert, he was a budget-balancing fiscal conservative who nonetheless supported various liberal reforms. He was extremely influential in molding the Tax Reform Act of 1969. Mills' distinguished political career ended in disgrace after his affair with a striptease dancer was revealed. Involved in a notorious incident at Washington's Tidal Basin with "the Argentine Firecracker" in 1974, he soon relinquished his post as committee chair. Mills retired from the House in 1977, later admitting his alcoholism.

Milne, A(lan) A(lexander) (1882–1956). English author. Although he wrote much fiction and drama for adults, Milne is best known for his whimsical portraits of childhood in his various children's books. He worked as a free-lance journalist (1903–06), then as assistant editor of the humor magazine *Punch* (1906–14) before becoming a full-time writer. In collaboration with illustrator E.H. Shepard, Milne created the memorable characters of Christopher Robin and Winnie-the-Pooh, among others, in the prose works *Winnie-the-Pooh* (1926) and *The House at Pooh Corner* (1928), and the books of verse *When We Were Very Young* (1924) and *Now We Are Six* (1927), which have become classics of children's literature. His works for adults include the novel *The Red House Mystery*.

For further reading:

Haring-Smith, Tori, *A.A. Milne: A Critical Biography*. New York: Garland, 1982.

Milne, David (1882–1953). Canadian painter. Born in Canada, he studied at the Art Students League, New York City (1904–07), and returned to Canada to paint. He is known for his fluid and sensitively rendered still lifes and landscapes, which are considered landmarks of Canadian painting.

Milstein, Nathan (1904–). Russian-American violinist. Born in Odessa, Milstein studied in his home city and at the St. Petersburg Conservatory with Leopold Auer. He began playing in Odessa at the age of 15 and followed this performance with a recital in Kiev, where he met and impressed the young Vladimir HOROWITZ. Shortly thereafter, the two began to give concerts together, sometimes joined by Gregor Piatigorsky. Given government permission to leave the U.S.S.R. for two years, Milstein debuted in Berlin in 1925 and made a stunning impact with his first Paris performance shortly thereafter. He made his first American appearance in 1929 and became a U.S. citizen in 1942. An acclaimed virtuoso with a large classical repertoire, Milstein was known for his phenomenal technique, sure yet delicate style and superb musicianship.

Mind of Adolf Hitler, The. In 1943, during WORLD WAR II, the OFFICE OF STRATEGIC SERVICES (OSS) commissioned psychoanalyst Walter Langer to write a comprehensive psychological profile of Adolf HITLER for use by top U.S. government officials. (Langer's brother, Harvard history professor William Leonard Langer, was chief of the OSS Research and Analysis Branch.) Langer studied the known details of Hitler's life and behavior and developed a psychoanalytic interpretation of the German leader. Among other things, Langer's top-secret report described Hitler as "a neurotic psychopath bordering on schizophrenia" and correctly predicted his suicide. The work later became a bestseller when it was declassified and published commercially under the title *The Mind of Adolf Hitler: The Secret Wartime Report*.

For further reading:

Langer, Walter. *The Mind of Adolf Hitler: The Secret Report*. New York: Basic Books, 1972.

Mindszenty, Jozsef (1892–1975). Hungarian Roman Catholic cardinal. He was ordained a priest in 1915, became a monsignor in 1937 and was appointed bishop of Veszprem in 1944 while the Germans occupied HUNGARY. Outspoken in his anti-Nazi views and his opposition to the persecution of Jews, he was arrested by Hungarian Nazis and imprisoned from 1944 to 1945. After World War II, he was named archbishop of Esztergom and primate of Hungary, becoming a cardinal in 1946. As opposed to communism as he was to fascism, he was again arrested in 1948, by the Hungarian government; charged with treason and currency offenses, he was convicted and sentenced to life in prison. Freed during the HUNGARIAN UPRISING of 1956, he took refuge in Budapest's American embassy when the revolt was crushed by the Soviets. He remained there as a symbol of opposition to communism, refusing to recognize the 1964 resumption of relations between the Vatican and Hungary. As stubborn as he was committed, Mindszenty finally left Budapest for Rome in 1971, but he remained anathema to the Hungarian regime. In 1974 Pope PAUL VI, in an attempt to improve relations between Hungary and the Vatican, officially removed Mindszenty as Polish primate.

Mingus, Charles (1922–1979). American bassist-composer, one of jazz history's towering giants. Growing up in Los Angeles, his first notable experiences were with such traditionalists as trombonist Kid ORY, trumpeter Louis ARMSTRONG and vibraphonist Lionel Hampton. After moving to New York, Mingus worked with such bebop giants as trumpeter Dizzy Gillespie and saxophonist Charlie PARKER. As a bassist, Mingus displayed a virtuoso technique and remarkably broad stylistic range; his thorough command of the major jazz styles was a hallmark of his composing as well. And, in works such as "Ysabel's Table Dance" (1957), "Fables of Faubus" (1959) and "Epitaph" (1962), one finds traces of jazzdom's var-

American jazz innovator and composer-bassist, Charlie Mingus.

ious traditions; also present are dark sonorities (achieved with low-pitched instruments), collective improvisations (an influence on the 1960s "free jazz" movement) and overlapping riff or ostinato figures. Mingus worked out the details of his music, where traditional distinctions between written and improvised sections were often blurred, in various "workshop" situations. His compositions were under constant revision in "performances" resembling rehearsals more than formal concert presentations. A temperamental iconoclast, Mingus lived much of his life in economic and emotional chaos. His sensational autobiography, *Beneath the Underdog,* was published in 1971.

For further reading:

Morgenstern, Dan, "Charles Mingus, 1922–1979," *Radio Free Jazz,* February 1979.

minimalism. Name for an aesthetic approach that minimizes consciously artistic and illusory effects. Minimalism emerged in the 1960s as a significant force, especially in the visual arts and in music. Painters such as Barnett Newman and Ellsworth KELLY employed flat colors and stark geometrical shapes in their canvases, while sculptors such as Carl Andre and Donald Judd displayed basic shapes and structures such as piled bricks and white-painted cubes. In music, minimalism showed itself in the simple melodic and harmonic progressions of composers such as Philip GLASS, Steven Reich and Terry Riley. In addition, minimalism influenced architectural design, although its key exponent in this field—MIES VAN DER ROHE—was a precursor rather than a follower of minimalism. In literature, the minimalist aesthetic played a tangential role in shaping French NOUVELLE ROMAN theory and also influenced the verse of Robert CREELEY and other American poets.

Minnelli, Vincente (1910–1986). American motion picture director. Recognized for his innovative use of color, he was best known for such film musicals as *Meet Me in St. Louis* and *Gigi,* for which he won an ACADEMY AWARD in 1958. He and his first wife, Hollywood legend Judy GARLAND, were the parents of movie star Liza Minnelli.

Minton, Sherman (1890–1965). Associate justice, U.S. Supreme Court (1949–56). A graduate of Indiana University and Yale University Law School, Minton served as Indiana public counselor before being elected to the U.S. Senate as a NEW DEAL Democrat in 1934. Defeated for reelection in 1940, he secured a federal post in Washington and was later appointed a justice of the U.S. Court of Appeals for the Seventh Circuit. He was appointed to the Supreme Court in 1949 by President Harry S. TRUMAN, with whom he had served in the senate. Despite his liberal background, Minton proved to be a conservative on the Court, especially in cases involving criminal law. He dissented in many civil liberties decisions in the WARREN Court, but supported the majority decision in BROWN V. BOARD OF EDUCATION. He resigned from the Court for health reasons in 1956.

Minutemen. Members of an extreme right-wing society founded in the U.S. in the 1960s to organize resistance to a feared Communist invasion. The organization had several hundred members, mainly in California and Illinois, and was declared subversive by the U.S. attorney general in 1965.

***Miranda v. Arizona* ["right to remain silent"]** (1966). Landmark American criminal case that established that criminal suspects must be informed of the constitutional right against self-incrimination when they are arrested. The Fifth Amendment of the U.S. Constitution provides that an individual accused of a crime cannot be compelled to testify against himself: The accused has the right to remain silent. The Supreme Court held that, on arrest, an individual must be informed of this right to remain silent before any interrogation may take place. In *Miranda,* the accused's conviction was reversed because he had been convicted based on a confession he had given without being informed of his rights. The rendition of the defendant's "Miranda rights" on arrest are familiar to viewers of television or motion pictures: "You have the right to remain silent; anything you say may be used in evidence against you in a court of law; you have the right to an attorney."

Mir Iskusstva [World of Art]. Movement in Russian art at the turn of this century. It took its name from the periodical founded by DIAGHILEV, which appeared from 1898 to 1904 and which published articles on modern Western European painting. At the same time, it also evaluated traditional Russian art. Diametrically opposed to the utilitarian idea that art should serve a socially useful function, the society advocated art for art's sake. It also organized several exhibitions to which the leading Russian artists of the day sent their work. Following the events of 1917, many of the *Mir Iskusstva* group emigrated. Among their number were Leon BAKST, Alexander BENOIS, Mstislav Dobuzhinsky, Michael LARIONOV and Nicholas ROERICH. Some of them collaborated with Diaghilev's BALLETS RUSSES.

Miro, Joan (1893–1983). Spanish-born artist. During the 1920s he was one of the leading Surrealist painters in Paris, along with Andre MASSON, Antonin ARTAUD, and Andre BRETON. Miro's work combined elements of CUBISM and Catalan primitive art and was often dominated by bright colors and abstract designs. A long collaboration with the potter Joseph Artigas resulted in major works, including the large ceramic murals at Harvard University and at the UNESCO building in Paris. As well as a painter, Miro was also an accomplished sculptor, printmaker, potter, and stage designer. His work particularly influenced American ABSTRACT EXPRESSIONIST painters such as Arshile Gorky, Robert MOTHERWELL, and Jackson POLLOCK. (See also SURREALISM.)

Mirza Ali Khan (1901?-1960). Fakir of Ipi, Pathan tribal leader (on the Pakistan-Afghanistan border). A Moslem religious fanatic, he led violent uprisings in 1931–32. He was later financed by Axis agents to keep an estimated 36,000 British troops occupied with tribal warfare in the region.

Mishima, Yukio [Kimitake Hiraoka] (1925–1970). Japanese novelist, short story writer, dramatist. The scion of a noble samurai family, after receiving a law degree from Tokyo Imperial University in 1947, Mishima worked briefly in the Finance Ministry. His semi-autobiographical *Confessions of a Mask* (1949) touches on his homosexuality and desire for an early and glorious death. Rejected for service in World War II because of his frailty, Mishima embarked on a regimen of strenuous body-building and samurai training. In 1968 he formed a private army of 83 youths, the goal of which was to return Japan to its prewar non-Western traditions. On November 25, 1970, an hour or two after delivering the final manuscript of his tetralogy to the publisher, Mishima and four of his soldiers took the commander of the Eastern Ground Self-Defense Forces as hostage and in view of 1,200 witnesses committed ritual seppuku (disembowelment) while crying "Long live the Emperor!" Mishima was a prolific, some said facile, writer. Among his works in translation are *Five Modern Noh Plays* (1957), *The Temple of the Golden Pavilion* (1959), *The Sailor Who Fell from Grace with the Sea* (1965), *Death in Midsummer and Other Stories* (1966) and *Thirst for Love* (1969). Mishima himself regarded *The Sea of Fertility: A Cycle of Four Novels* (1972–74) as the culmination of his work.

For further reading:

Nathan, John, *Mishima: A Biography.* Boston: Little, Brown, 1985.

***Missouri,* USS.** U.S. Navy Iowa-class battleship; commissioned on June 11, 1944, it is the last of the super-dreadnoughts built by the U.S. On September 2, 1945, in the presence of General Douglas MACARTHUR and other Allied officers, Japanese officials signed surrender papers aboard the *Missouri* in Tokyo harbor, ending WORLD WAR II. (The papers are now displayed in the Truman Library in Independence, Missouri.) In 1986, in an effort to restore American naval strength, the *Missouri* was re-outfitted and reactivated.

Mistral, Gabriela [Lucila Godoy Alcayaga] (1889–1957). Chilean poet, educator, stateswoman. Though she won her reputation as a poet with *Sonetos de la muerte,* which received the National Poetry Prize in 1914, Mistral had a parallel vocation first as a rural schoolteacher, later as director of schools throughout Chile and a university professor. The early suicide of her fiance after discovery of his embezzlement of funds had a profound effect on the tone and themes of her work, which expressed despair and loneliness as well as sympathy with oppressed peoples and sometimes reflected a religious sensibility. Mistral represented Chile as honorary consul in Brazil, Spain, Portugal and the U.S. Between 1922 and 1938 she worked with Mme. CURIE and Henri BERGSON in the LEAGUE OF NATIONS. In 1945 she became the first Latin American to win the NOBEL PRIZE. After World War II she was associated with a number of American universities. She died at her translator's home in Hempstead, N.Y. Her works include *Desolacion* (1922), *Ternura* (1924), *Tala* (1938) and *Lagar* (1954).

Mitchell, Clarence M. (1911–1984). Black American CIVIL RIGHTS activist. Mitchell was Washington lobbyist for the NATIONAL ASSOCIATION FOR THE ADVANCEMENT OF COLORED PEOPLE (NAACP) (1950–78). During much of the same period, he also lobbied for the Leadership Conference on Civil Rights. He first drew national attention in 1956, when he was arrested for refusing to use a blacks-only entrance to the Florence, North Carolina railroad station. He was instrumental in the passage of the CIVIL RIGHTS ACT OF 1964, the VOTING RIGHTS ACT OF 1965 and the Fair Housing Act of 1968. Mitchell was so influential among federal lawmakers that he was sometimes called the "101st senator." In 1980 he was awarded the presidential Medal of Freedom by President Jimmy CARTER.

Chilean poet Gabriela Mistral was the first Latin American to win the Nobel Prize for literature (1945).

Mitchell, Edgar (1930–). U.S. astronaut and the sixth person to walk on the Moon; Mitchell was lunar module pilot of Apollo 14 (January 31–February 9, 1971). Mitchell and fellow moonwalker Alan SHEPARD spent over 33 hours investigating the Moon's surface. A Navy pilot, he was one of 19 astronauts selected by NASA in April 1966; he retired from the Navy and resigned from NASA in October 1972. Strongly interested in ESP (extrasensory perception) and the paranormal, Mitchell, who had attempted an ESP experiment during his APOLLO flight, founded the Institute for Noetic Studies, in Palo Alto, California. The purpose of the institute is to continue studies into ESP and similar activities. In 1974, Mitchell's coauthored book, *Psychic Exploration: A Challenge for Science,* stirred up a brief flurry of interest among ESP believers.

Mitchell, Joan (1926–). American painter. She was born in Chicago and attended Smith College, Columbia University, the Chicago Art Institute School and New York University. She has lived in France since 1959 and has been greatly influenced by the work of Claude MONET and Willem DE KOONING. A member of the second generation of ABSTRACT EXPRESSIONISM, Mitchell is known for her large, lush and highly sophisticated canvases.

Mitchell, John Newton (1913–1988). U.S. attorney general (1969–72) and director of the Committee to Re-elect the President in 1972, Mitchell was one of President Richard NIXON's closest and most loyal advisers. The bugging of the offices of the Democratic National Committee in the WATERGATE apartment complex in 1972 and the scandal that followed led to his downfall. Mitchell spent 19 months in a federal prison, from 1977 to 1979, following his conviction for conspiracy, obstruction of justice and perjury.

Mitchell, Joni [born Roberta Joan Anderson] (1943–). Canadian folk and rock and roll songwriter, vocalist, and guitarist. Mitchell, who was raised in Alberta, Canada, turned to music while attending the Alberta College of Art. She moved to Detroit in 1965, signed her first record contract in 1967, and soon gained a reputation as a first-rate songwriter after her songs were covered by stars such as Johnny Cash and Judy COLLINS. Mitchell's own debut album, *Songs To A Seagull* (1968), was a critical and popular success due in large measure to her emotive and soaring voice. Her third album, *Ladies of the Canyon* (1970), featured her first hit single, *Big Yellow Taxi.* Other noteworthy albums by Mitchell include *For The Roses* (1972), *Court and Spark* (1974), *Mingus* (1979), her tribute to jazz giant Charles MINGUS, and *Dog Eat Dog* (1985).

Mitchell, Margaret (1900–1949). U.S. novelist. Interested in local history from an early age, she began to write for the *Atlanta Journal* in 1922 under the name Peggy Mitchell. In 1926 she started work on a novel based on stories told by family and friends. The outcome was *Gone with the Wind* (1936), which won a PULITZER PRIZE in 1937. It has since become one of the best-selling novels of all time and the basis of the immensely popular movie of the same name released in 1939.

Mitchell, Reginald (Joseph) (1895–1937). British aircraft designer. Mitchell designed some of the most innovative airplanes of the 1920s. His S-4 Floatplane (seaplane) won the prestigious Schneider Cup in 1927, 1929 and 1931. During the 1930s Mitchell visited GERMANY and witnessed the might of the Luftwaffe, the new German air force created by HITLER and GOERING. Realizing that war with Germany was probable and that the RAF was unprepared, he worked frantically to design a British fighter plane that could outmaneuver German fighters and shoot down German bombers. The product of his labors was the **Spitfire,** which first flew in 1936. Mitchell was already gravely ill and died the following year, before the fighter could prove itself in combat. The Spitfire helped give the RAF the edge in the BATTLE OF BRITAIN. Referring to "the few" (the Spitfire pilots) to whom so many owed so much, Prime Minister Winston S. CHURCHILL acknowledged Mitchell as the "First of the Few."

Mitchell, William "Billy" (1879–1936). American Army officer. In 1898, Mitchell dropped out of college and enlisted in the Army for the Spanish-American War. In 1915, he joined the aviation division of the Army Signal Corps and the following year was promoted from captain to major. With the U.S. entry into WORLD WAR I, Mitchell became an air officer of the American Expeditionary Forces, and in extensive combat he proved himself a talented air commander. In 1919, Mitchell was named assistant chief of the Air Service, in which capacity he became a vocal proponent of an independent air force and of enhanced air preparedness. By 1925, however, Mitchell's superiors had tired of his hectoring; they demoted him to colonel and transferred him to a much less visible position. That same year, when the Navy's dirigible *Shenandoah* was lost in bad weather, Mitchell made a statement to the press charging the Navy and the War Department with "incompetence, criminal negligence, and almost treasonable administration of the national defense." For this insubordination, he was court-martialed and given five years' suspension of pay and rank. Mitchell resigned from the Army in February 1926 and retired, although he continued to promote the supremacy of air power.

Mitchum, Robert (1917–). American actor. Raised in New York City, Mitchum worked at a number of odd jobs and joined a local theater group. He moved to Southern California and acted in a community theater before making his first film, a western, in 1943. The sleepy-eyed actor became the archetypical HOLLYWOOD tough guy in such movies as *The Big Steal* (1949), *The Racket* (1951), *Cape Fear* (1962), *Farewell, My Lovely* (1975) and *The Big Sleep* (1978), the latter two based on detective novels by Raymond CHANDLER. A versatile actor, he has also undertaken comedy roles in such motion pictures as *Two for the Seesaw* (1962) and dramatic parts in such films as David LEAN's *Ryan's Daughter* (1970). In the latter part of his career, Mitchum became well known for his performances in such 1980s television miniseries as *North and South, The Winds of War* and *War and Remembrance.*

Mitford sisters. English authors and daughters—Jessica (1917–), Nancy (1904–73), Unity (1914–48), Diana (1910–), Pamela and Deborah—of the 2nd Baron Redesdale. Jessica and Nancy have achieved international recognition as authors. Jessica is known for her journalistic exposes and her books that investigate controversial political and social issues. Her most famous works include *The American Way of Death* (1963); an anthology of her articles titled *Poison Penmanship: The Gentle Art of Muckraking* (1979); and her autobiography, *Daughters and Rebels* (1960). Nancy gained acclaim as a novelist, biographer and essayist. Her witty, often satirical novels about the English upper-class include *Love in a Cold Climate* (1949) and *The Blessing* (1959). Her major biographies include *The Sun King* (1966), about Louis XIV of France. As editor of a volume of essays, *Noblesse Oblige: An Inquiry into the Identifiable Characteristics of the English Aristocracy* (1956), she helped to introduce the classification of English society into "U" (upper class) and "Non-U" (non-upper class). Of the remaining sisters, Unity gained notoriety as a follower and friend of Adolf HITLER, and Diana married the leader of the British fascists, Sir Oswald MOSLEY. Deborah became the Duchess of Devonshire, and Pamela runs a large farm.

Mitterrand, Francois (1916–). President of FRANCE (1981–). Mitterrand entered politics in 1946 as socialist deputy for the Nievre department. He was a left-wing candidate against President DE GAULLE in 1965. After disagreement among the French socialist parties in the late 1960s, he recovered his political authority and was accepted as leader of the left throughout the 1970s. Again unsuccessfully contesting the presidency in 1974, in 1981 he defeated Valery GISCARD D'ESTAING with barely more than 50% of the vote. From 1981 to 1986 Mitterrand was backed by a socialist majority in the National Assembly; but, following the parliamentary elections of 1986, he had to share power with a Gaullist majority led by Jacques CHIRAC as prime minister. Mitterrand was reelected president in 1988. Despite his socialist background, he has proved a pragmatic leader, at times following an austerity program to deal with economic problems. A strong supporter of the EUROPEAN ECONOMIC COMMUNITY, Mitterrand allied France with the U.S.-led coalition in the 1991 war against Iraq, sending French combat forces to the region.

Mix, Tom (1880–1940). American motion picture actor. Mix claimed to have served in the Spanish-American War (1898), and became a cowboy in Oklahoma in 1906. He got involved in wild west shows, attracted the attention of movie makers and entered movies in 1910. His expert horsemanship made him a HOLLYWOOD star, and during the 1920s he was the leading box office draw. He appeared in more than 100 films, and made his last movie, *The Miracle Rider,* in 1935. During the 1930s he toured the country with his own wild west show. He died in an auto accident in the Southwest in 1940. The Tom Mix Museum is located in Dewey, Oklahoma.

Mizoguchi, Kenji (1898–1956). Japanese filmmaker. Born in Tokyo, Mizoguchi worked as a textile designer and newspaper illustrator before turning to filmmaking in the early 1920s. In addition to his distinguished body of 85 films—he was acknowledged as Japan's chief filmmaker during the 1940s—he also headed Japan's vast union governing all film production personnel. His reputation in the West was confirmed with *The Life of Oharu,* which won the Grand Prize at the Venice Film Festival in 1952. His postwar films, made with scriptwriter Yoshikata Yoda, actress Kinuyo Tanaka and the Daiei Films Studio, constitute an enduring string of masterpieces. His major themes include the ill-treatment of women (*Saikaku ichaidai onna, The Life of Oharu,* 1952) and the samurai epic (*Shin Heike monogatari, New Tales of the Taira Clan,* 1955). His extraordinary camera technique eschews traditional montage for the choreography of the moving camera and the revelation of the deep-focus shot. The viewer is both involved and distanced at the same time. *Ugetsu* sums up Mizoguchi's artistic and commercial priorities. The potter, Genjuro, abjures his crude wares for the more "artistic" creations inspired by his love for a spirit, the Lady Wakasa; he achieves a compromise between his commercial and elitist concerns. A revival of Mizoguchi's work was led in the 1960s by French NOUVELLE VAGUE artists Jean-Luc GODARD and Jacques Rivette.

For further reading:

Mellen, Joan. *The Waves at Genji's Door: Japan Through Its Cinema.* New York: Pantheon Books, 1973.

French President Francois Mitterrand meets with the emir of Kuwait in Paris (Sept. 25, 1989).

Mizrachi. Right-wing political party in ISRAEL; partner of HAPOEL HAMIZRACHI in the National Religious Party.

Mobutu Sese Seko [full name Mobutu Sese Seko Kuku Ngbendu Wa Sa Banga; born Joseph Desere Mobutu] (1930–). President of ZAIRE (formerly the Republic of the Congo, 1965–). Mobutu was educated at mission schools and later at the Institute of Journalism in Brussels. He served in the Congolese army (1956–58) and worked for the newspaper *L'Avenir* (1956–58). He joined Patrice LUMUMBA's nationalist movement in 1957 and was a delegate at the roundtable conference on the Congo in Brussels (1959–60). During the political crisis surrounding the struggle between Lumumba and Joseph KASAVUBU, Mobuto took power in the name of the army in Sept. 1960 until parliament was recalled in Aug. 1961. Col. Mobutu was promoted to major general in 1961, later rising to lieutenant general and commander-in-chief of the Congolese armed forces. He supported Moise TSHOMBE's leadership bid in 1964; but after intervening in the ensuing conflict between Tshombe and Kasavubu, Mobutu took power himself, becoming president of the Republic of Congo in Nov. 1965. He has remained in power and dominated the public life of Zaire ever since. Mobutu adopted his present name in Jan. 1972 as part of his Africanization policy. He is thought to have amassed enormous wealth; his fortune has been estimated at $5 billion and includes substantial property in Zaire and Europe. He was chairman of the OAU in 1967.

For further reading:

Elliot, Jeffrey M., *Mobutu Sese Seko: People, Politics, and Policy.* Washington, D.C.: Washington Institute Press, 1989.

Moch, Jules (1893–1985). French politician. A Socialist, Moch played a major role in French politics both before and after World War II. During his career he held such posts as minister of public works, minister of the interior and minister of defense. As interior minister, he took measures to crush a series of communist-led strikes in 1947 and 1948. His actions led to the permanent decline of the French Communist Party. In October 1949 he was premier of FRANCE for three days.

modal jazz. Popular jazz style originally appearing in the late 1950s. Instead of following the comparatively complex chordal patterns found in the standard tunes of Tin Pan Alley, Broadway and Hollywood that were typically favored by jazz players up to the 1950s, the modal approach employs a limited number of predetermined or modal scales based loosely on the classical modes (dorian, phrygian, etc.) first used by the ancient Greeks. Though providing the system's basic melodic and harmonic building blocks, modal scales are seldom deployed in their pure form; indeed, like the frequent alterations and harmonic "substitutions" found in the traditional diatonic approach, improvisers using modal strategies have added their own contrasting harmonic colors and ornamentations. The broad acceptance of the modal approach can be explained by its relative harmonic simplicity and its exotic and meditative overtones; indeed, some modal approaches are based on various Middle Eastern, Oriental and minor scales. Modality was introduced by pianist Bill EVANS and most significantly because of his widespread visibility, trumpeter Miles DAVIS; Evans' "Peace Piece" (1958), Davis' "All Blues" (1959) and saxophonist John COLTRANE's "Impressions" (1963) are prime examples of modal compositions found in the contemporary jazz repertory.

For further reading:

Kernfeld, Barry, ed., "Modal Jazz," in *The New Grove Dictionary of Jazz*. New York: Grove's Dictionaries of Music, 1988.

Model, Walther (1891–1945). German general. During WORLD WAR II, Model was chief of staff of German forces in Poland and France. He was also active on the Russian front, and following the invasion of NORMANDY, he was charged with stemming the Allied offensive. In April 1945, with his troops surrounded by Allied forces in the Ruhr, Model committed suicide.

modernism. General term to describe certain artistic and cultural movements; used by critics since midcentury. Modernism is a concept that eludes precise definition, most likely because it has been used by so many analysts in such disparate contexts that no precise definition can avoid being overly narrow. Fundamentally, modernism refers to the tendency of 20th-century art, literature and music to value innovation and reformulation over and above received cultural and aesthetic traditions. Artists whose work exemplifies the modernist approach include Pablo PICASSO in painting, James JOYCE in literature, Ezra POUND in poetry, Igor STRAVINSKY in music and Ludwig MIES VAN DER ROHE in architecture. Modernism is regarded by some critics as having reached an end in the 1950s and 1960s, at which time it was superseded by POSTMODERNISM. Other critics argue that modernism is better viewed as a pancultural phenomenon the essentials of which can be discerned in all eras of human civilization.

Modigliani, Amedeo (1884–1920). Italian painter. Born in Livorno, Modigliani settled in Paris in 1906 and remained there for the rest of his life. His early work was influenced by CUBISM, by the artists Pablo PICASSO and Paul Cezanne and by African sculpture. His first paintings were characterized by distorted figures and large areas of flat color. Under the influence of his friend, Constantin BRANCUSI, Modigliani produced a number of important sculptures, such as *Caryatid* (1914, Museum of Modern Art, New York City), notable for their stylized vertical forms. From 1915 on, he devoted himself to painting, and his mature work dates from that year until the year of his death. His haunting portraits and langorously sensual nudes are expressively elongated, graceful in line, glowing with rich color; their eyes slanted and almond-shaped, their faces individualized yet simplified and masklike. Unknown to all but his fellow artists, poor and ill with tuberculosis, he died at the age of 35. His works are included in important museum collections throughout the world.

Modjeski, Ralph (1861–1940). American engineer, the primary designer for a number of major bridges. Modjeski's best-known work is the Delaware River suspension bridge between Philadelphia and Camden, New Jersey—now known as the Benjamin Franklin Bridge. Modjeski worked as a partner in several firms over the years, including Modjeski & Cartlidge, designers of a steel railroad bridge over the Ohio River at Metropolis, Illinois (1914–17); Modjeski & Masters; and Modjeski, Masters & Chase. The Philadelphia-Camden bridge (1922–26) is sometimes referred to as the first truly modern suspension bridge, with its two cables and simple, X-braced towers. Paul CRET worked with the engineers as a consulting architect. The nearby Walt Whitman Bridge (1957) is similar but has a conceptually more modern structure and was built by Modjeski & Masters, working together with the firm of Ammann & Whitney.

Mogadishu Raid. Rescue operation carried out at the airport in Mogadishu, Somalia. Terrorists associated with the West German BAADER-MEINHOF GROUP had hijacked a Lufthansa airliner bound from Majorca to Frankfurt on October 13 in an attempt to extort money and free 13 prisoners. The pilot of the airplane was killed by the hijackers before the raid. A total of 86 passengers and crew members were freed by a squad of 28 West German commandos. Lasting less than a minute, the operation resulted in the death of three hijackers and the wounding of a hijacker, a commando and a hostage. Three imprisoned Baader-Meinhof leaders, including Andreas Baader, committed suicide in a West German prison hours after the rescue.

Mohieddin, Ahmed Fuad (1926–1984). Prime minister of EGYPT (1982–84). Mohieddin served as deputy prime minister under President Anwar el-SADAT and formed his first cabinet under President Hosni MUBARAK after Sadat's assassination. He was also secretary general of Egypt's ruling National Democratic Party.

Mohmand, Abdul Ahad (1959–). The first Afghan cosmonaut in space. Mohmand made his Soyuz TM-6 flight to the Mir space station (docking August 31, 1988) at a time when Soviet troops were withdrawing from his country. His weeklong stay was spent making photographic surveys of Afghanistan and beaming television broadcasts of good will. But the trip home on Soyuz TM-5 with Soviet veteran Vladimir Lyakhov nearly turned public relations into disaster, when guidance problems left the two cosmonauts stranded for 23 hours orbiting in space, their food and oxygen supply dwindling. Ground efforts to save them paid off, and they landed safely on September 7. Both were given awards for their courage.

Moholy-Nagy, Lazlo (1895–1946). Hungarian painter, sculptor, designer and photographer. Beginning as a law student, Moholy-Nagy became increasingly interested in art. In Berlin, he became a cofounder of CONSTRUCTIVISM, creating geometric sculptures of metal and translucent plastic and experimenting with photograms. In 1921 he met members of the de STIJL group and the bold geometic paintings he created in the early 1920s reveal his affinities with that group and with the Russian disciples of SUPREMATISM. An extremely influential teacher, he was a professor at the BAUHAUS from 1923 to 1928, coediting the school's publications with Walter GROPIUS. Settling in the U.S., he taught at the Chicago Institute of Design from 1938 to 1946. Moholy-Nagy showed his enormous versatility in such other works as films, stage sets and industrial designs. His books include *Painting Photography Film* (1925, tr. 1969) and *Vision in Motion* (1947).

Moiseiwitsch, Benno (1890–1963). Concert pianist; born in Odessa, Russia. Moiseiwitsch studied at the Black Sea port's Imperial Music Academy and in Vienna with the renowned Theodore Leschetitzky. In 1908 he moved to England, where he settled; he became a British subject in 1937, never returning to Russia. Moiseiwitsch was one of the most traveled virtuosos of his day, giving many concerts throughout Britain; he made his American debut in 1919 and made many recordings during the 1920s, '30s and '40s. His repertoire included music by Beethoven, Schumann and Chopin, as well as such 20th-century composers as POULENC, PROKOFIEV, STRAVINSKY and his friend RACHMANINOFF. During WORLD WAR II Moiseiwitsch was a frequent guest of British Prime Minister Winston CHURCHILL.

Moiseyev, Igor Alexandrovich (1906–?). Choreographer and founder of the State Folk Dance Ensemble. After graduating from the Choreographic School of the Bolshoi in 1924, from 1924 to 1939 Moiseyev worked as a dancer and choreographer at the Bolshoi Theater. Fascinated by the folk dances of the Soviet republics and wishing to create a national folk ballet, he founded the State Folk Dance Ensemble. The ensemble has toured extensively both abroad and in the Soviet Union, and has won much popularity. Moiseyev's dances include *Three Fat Men* (1935) and *The Snow Storm* (1959).

Mojahedin. Popular name of the Sazman-e Mojahedin-e Khalq-e Iran (Opposition Organization of the Crusaders of the Iranian People), an Iranian leftest political group. It was called the Islamic Marxists by the shah, a name that is still commonly used. It was formed in 1966 by a group of young militants and began military operations five years later. In violent opposition to the shah's regime, group members robbed banks, bombed offices, assassinated American military officials and attempted to hijack an Iranian airliner. The main opposition to the regime of Ayatollah KHOMEINI after it broke with him in 1981, the organization was brutally suppressed by his forces. By 1986 it had ceased to be an important factor in Iranian politics. Nonetheless, it remains the largest leftist group in Iran and continues underground activities in opposition to the ruling regime.

Moley, Raymond (1886–1975). Adviser to President Franklin D. ROOSEVELT and the leader of Roosevelt's BRAIN TRUST. It was Moley who coined the term NEW DEAL to describe Roosevelt's sweeping social reform program for dealing with the GREAT DEPRESSION. Moley broke with the President in 1936 when he could not reconcile himself with what he considered a radical trend in the New Deal.

Mollet, Guy (1905–1975). French statesman, premier (1956–57). A teacher and trade union leader, he took an active part in the RESISTANCE during the German occupation of France in WORLD WAR II. He was elected to the Chamber of Deputies in 1945 and served as secretary general of the French Socialist Party (1946–69). During the Leon BLUM government, he was minister of state (1946–47) and vice premier (1951). While premier, he supported the unity of Western Europe, sent French troops into Algeria to suppress a revolt (1956) and joined with Great Britain and Israel in invading Egypt during the SUEZ CRISIS (1956). Mollet subsequently served as minister of state under Charles DE GAULLE (1958–59).

Molotov, Vyacheslav Mikhailovich (1890–1986). Soviet communist official, a close aide of Joseph STALIN and a member of the Soviet leadership from 1921 to 1957. A nephew of composer Alexander SCRIABIN, he took the name Molotov ("the hammer") as a young revolutionary. As premier (1931–41), Molotov oversaw industrial and agricultural development. He helped implement Stalin's policy of forced COLLECTIVIZATION of farms, which led to famine in the UKRAINE. He also played a key role in the GREAT PURGE. As foreign minister (1939–49), he negotiated the GERMAN-SOVIET NON-AGGRESSION PACT with Joachim von RIBBENTROP (August 1939). After the German invasion of the U.S.S.R. in 1941, Molotov helped strengthen the Soviet alliance with the West. An opponent of Nikita KHRUSHCHEV, Molotov was expelled from the Politburo in 1957 after his failed attempt to oust Khrushchev. He was expelled from the COMMUNIST PARTY in 1962 but reinstated in 1984.

Molyneux, Edward (1891–1974). London-born Irish fashion designer. His career was based in Paris, where he catered to an elegant society of celebrities of the social and theatrical worlds. Molyneux was an art student in London when his fashion sketches were seen by Lady Duff Gordon (Lucile, as she was known in the world of fashion), who hired him as an artist and then as a designer for her Paris shop. After service in World War I, he opened his own house of fashion in Paris in 1919, beginning a long career of supplying simple elegance to such figures as Gertude LAWRENCE, whose Molyneux costumes in *Private Lives* made his work widely known and admired. He closed his firm in 1950 when he faced declining health, but, after a period of retirement in Jamaica, he recovered sufficiently to introduce a ready-to-wear line (1965) mass-produced under the name *Studio Molyneux*. His fame rests mainly on his simple, elegant designs of the 1930s.

Monaco, Principality of. Tiny principality on the Mediterranean Sea coast of southeastern France in the hills fronting the Cote d'Azur; it is the second smallest independent state in the world. Princely absolutism gave way to constitutional rule in 1911. France recognized Monaco's sovereignty in 1918 and 1919, subject to its acting "in complete conformity" with French interests. Occupied by the Italians (1940) and then by the Germans (1943), postwar Monaco reestablished itself as a major tourist center and, by virtue of economic union with France, became an integral part of the EUROPEAN COMMUNITY in the 1950s. Prince Rainier III succeeded to the throne in 1949 and on April 19, 1956, married U.S. film star Grace Kelly.

In the face of growing pressure for increased powers from the elected National Council (in particular, following the collapse in 1955 of Monaco's leading bank, the Societe Monegasque de Banque) Prince Rainier asserted his sovereign powers in 1959 by suspending the council. However, a revised constitution promulgated in 1962 guaranteed representative government and renounced royal divine right. Tensions with France over the principality's role as a tax haven were eased in 1963 by a convention placing certain Monaco-based companies under French fiscal law. Since 1963 the pro-Rainier National and Democratic Union group has dominated the National Council and won all 18 seats in the National Council in elections in 1978, 1983 and 1988.

Mondale, Walter F. (1928–). Vice president of the UNITED STATES (1977–81). A graduate of the University of Minnesota (1951) and of Minnesota Law School (1956), Mondale served as attorney general of Minnesota from 1960 to 1964. Active in the Democratic-Farmer-Labor Party of Minnesota, he gained national attention when he supported the cause of free legal counsel for indigent defendants in the case of GIDEON V. WAINWRIGHT (1963). When Mondale's mentor Hubert H. HUMPHREY vacated his U.S. Senate seat to run for vice president in 1964, Mondale was appointed as his replacement. Mondale was elected on his own in 1972. In 1976 Jimmy CARTER chose Mondale as the Democratic nominee for vice president. Mondale served as vice president of the U.S. from 1977 to 1981. The Democratic candidate for president in 1984, Mondale was the first candidate of a major party to choose a woman (Geraldine FERRARO) as his running mate. Advocating traditional liberal Democratic policies, they lost in the landslide reelection of President Ronald REAGAN and Vice President George BUSH.

Walter Mondale, vice president of the United States during the presidency of Jimmy Carter.

Mondrian, Piet (1872–1944). Dutch painter. One of the foremost geometric modernists, he was born in Amsfoot, Holland and studied at the Amsterdam Academy. His early work consisted of naturalistic landscapes. He became aware of avant-garde movements in art around 1908 and traveled to Paris in 1910, discovering the Cubist works of PICASSO and BRAQUE. In Paris (1912–14), Mondrian struggled with his own interpretation of Cubism and, returning to Holland began to create the rigorous geometrical work for which he is famous. In 1917 he and a number of other Dutch artists founded DE STIJL magazine and, with it, the movement that bears its name. Three years later, Mondrian explained his theories in the book *Neoplasticism*. The artist sought a plastic perfection through the use of intersecting straight lines meeting in right angles on vertical and horizontal axes and through a limitation of his palette to the primary colors of red, yellow and blue—along with black, white and gray. Through these purposely austere abstract means, he sought to express universal truths and to indicate the spiritual harmony of humankind and nature. Mondrian emigrated to the U.S. in 1940 and settled in New York City. Some of his finest compositions, such as *Broadway Boogie-Woogie* (1942–45), can be found in New York's Museum of Modern Art, as well as in the Gemeete Museum, The Hague and the Art Institute of Chicago. (See also MODERNISM.)

Monet, Claude (1840–1926). French painter. The paragon of Impressionism and a founder of the movement, Monet was born in Paris and spent his youth in Le Havre. There he struck up a friendship with the painter Eugene Boudin, who encouraged the young artist to paint in the open air—a practice which was central to his later style. Moving to Paris in 1859, Monet studied at the Academie Suisse and, after two years in the army, returned to the city to study painting. Living in appalling poverty, he persevered as a painter. At the same time, he became friendly with such artists as Camille Pissarro, Pierre Renoir, Paul Cezanne and Alfred Sisley. In the late 1860s Monet began to paint landscapes that reflected what were to be his lifelong concerns: the changing effects of light and color caused by variations in time and season. Studying the laws of optics, he developed a unique manner of capturing the phenomena of light as it is expressed in the forms, textures and hues of the landscape by breaking it down into its color components.

In 1872 Monet painted *Impression, Sunrise* (Musee Marmotton, Paris), a work whose title was soon assumed by the Impressionist movement. From 1872 to 1875, he painted river and garden scenes in which the forms of objects begin to dissolve in a shimmer of color and a flurry of brushstrokes. From 1876 on, he concentrated on a number of single subjects, such as the Parisian Gare Saint-Lazare. When his financial fortunes improved in the 1880s, Monet set about traveling through France, again painting the same subject in a series of views. These luminous, semi-abstract works are the culmination of his mature style. They include poplars, haystacks, the facade of Rouen Cathedral (1892–94) and the celebrated waterlilies (1899, 1904–25), which are lyrical masterpieces painted in his garden at Giverny. Among these *Nympheas* is the monumental triptych (c. 1920) in the Museum of Modern Art, New York City.

monetarism. A macroeconomic theory that arose in the 1960s; it views the money supply as central to understanding price levels and the economy's performance. Monetarists argue that although monetary policy cannot influence either output or employment in the long run, it does determine price levels, and accordingly affects both output and employment in the short-term. Accordingly, monetary policy has a direct affect on the stability of the economy. Monetarism was a reaction to Keynesian economics, which downplayed the role of the money supply in explaining the operation of the economy (see John Maynard KEYNES). In the U.S., economist Milton FRIEDMAN was a leading monetarist. Monetarist principles were followed by the FEDERAL RESERVE under Paul Volcker and Alan Greenspan during the REAGAN administration in the U.S. They were also applied by Margaret THATCHER's government in the U.K.

Mongolia [Mongolian People's Republic]. Mongolia comprises an area of 604,090 square miles in north-central Asia. With the support of Czarist Russia Mongolia broke from Chinese control and declared itself an independent monarchy in 1911, naming the Living Buddha of Urga as head of state. China occupied Mongolia (1919–20) after the Russian Revolution, but the Mongolians again declared independence in 1921, gaining military support from the newly formed U.S.S.R. The death of the Living Buddha brought a new Soviet-inspired constitution and the establishment of the Mongolian People's Republic (1924). The movement toward a socialist state brought slow collectivization of the economy (1928–1950s) and political purges (1922, 1939). During the presidency of Jambyn Batmonh (since 1984) Mongolia has slowly initiated some reforms, paralleling those taking place in the Soviet Union. In addition, peaceful demonstrations have occurred and new political organizations have formed (1989–90).

Moniz, Egas [born Antonio Caetanio de Abreu Freire] (1874–1955). Portuguese neurologist and political activist. Egas Moniz was educated at the University of Coimbra, where he gained his M.D. in 1899. After postgraduate work in Paris and Bordeaux he returned to Coimbra, becoming a professor in the medical faculty (1902). He moved to Lisbon in 1911 to a newly created chair of neurology, a post he retained until his retirement in 1944. At the same time he pursued a successful political career, being elected to the National Assembly in 1900. He served as ambassador to Spain in 1917 and in the following year became foreign minister, leading his country's delegation to the PARIS PEACE CONFERENCE. Egas Moniz achieved his first major success in the 1920s in the field of angiography (the study of the cardiovascular system using

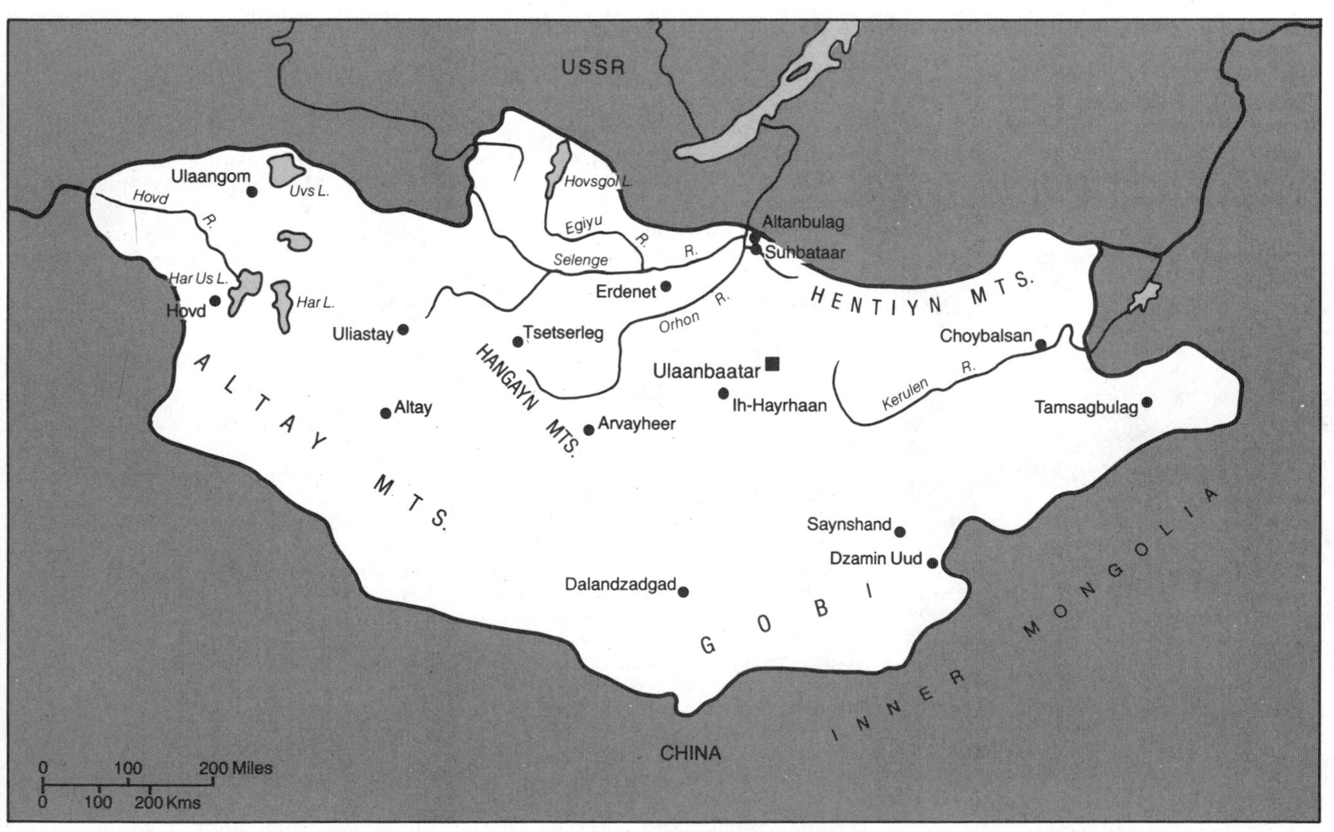

MONGOLIA

dyes that are opaque to X rays). In collaboration with Almeida Lima, he injected such radio-opaque dyes into the arteries, enabling the blood vessels of the brain to be photographed. In 1927 he was able to show that displacements in the cerebral circulation could be used to infer the presence and location of brain tumors; he published a detailed account of his technique in 1931.

Egas Moniz is better known for his introduction in 1935 of the operation called **prefrontal lobotomy**. It was for this work, described by the Nobel authorities as "one of the most important discoveries ever made in psychiatric therapy," that they awarded him the 1949 NOBEL PRIZE for physiology or medicine. The operation consisted of inserting a sharp knife into the prefontal lobe of the brain. It required the minimum of equipment and lasted less than five minutes. The technique was suggested to Egas Moniz on hearing an account of a chimpanzee that became less aggressive after its frontal lobes had been excised. Egas Moniz believed that a similar surgical operation would relieve severe emotional tension in psychiatric patients. He claimed that 14 of the first 20 patients operated upon were either cured or improved. The operation generated much controversy, since the extent of the improvement in the patients' symptoms was not easy to judge and the procedure often produced severe side effects.

Monk, Thelonius (Sphere) (1917–1982). American jazz pianist and composer. His original style—dissonant and rhythmically innovative—created a musical bridge between 1930s SWING and the BEBOP style of the 1940s. He became popular in the 1950s when he began recording his compositions, including "Round Midnight," "Ruby My Dear," "Well, You Needn't" and "Blue Monk." After 1957 he appeared regularly in New York nightclubs.

Monnet, Jean (1888–1979). French statesman and financier. At the age of 31, Monnet was assistant secretary general of the LEAGUE OF NATIONS. During WORLD WAR II he conceived the idea for LEND-LEASE. The Monnet Plan, which he authored in 1947, led to France's postwar economic recovery through participation in the MARSHALL PLAN. An architect of the EUROPEAN COAL AND STEEL COMMUNITY (1952), he also played a major role in the formation of the EUROPEAN ECONOMIC COMMUNITY (EEC, 1957), and later worked to establish a European monetary reserve fund with a single European currency. Monnet never sought or held elective office, but was a behind-the-scenes, moving force in European political life for much of the 20th century.

American jazz pianist Thelonius Monk was known for his innovative style, which helped to create the "bebop" style of the 1940s.

Monod, Jacques Lucien (1910–1976). French biochemist. Monod graduated from the University of Paris in 1931 and became assistant professor of zoology there in 1934, having spent the years immediately following his graduation investigating the origin of life. After World War II, in which he served in the RESISTANCE, he joined the Pasteur Institute, becoming head of the cellular biochemistry department in 1953. In 1958 Monod began working with Francois Jacob and Arthur Pardee on the regulation of enzyme synthesis in mutant bacteria. This work led to the formulation, by Monod and Jacob, of a theory explaining gene action and, particularly, how genes are switched on and off as necessary. In 1960 they introduced the term "operon" for a closely linked group of genes, each of which controls a different step in a given biochemical pathway. The following year they postulated the existence of a molecule, messenger RNA, that carries the genetic information necessary for protein synthesis from the operon to the ribosomes, where proteins are made. For this work Monod and Jacob were awarded the 1965 NOBEL PRIZE for physiology or medicine, which they shared with Andre Lwoff, who was also working on bacterial genetics. In 1971 Monod became director of the Pasteur Institute and in the same year published the best-seller *Chance and Necessity,* in which he argued that life arose by chance and progressed to its present level as a necessary consequence of the pressures exerted by natural selection.

Monroe, Harriet (1860–1936). American poetry editor and publisher. One of the most influential figures in the publication and development of modern poetry, she began as an art and drama critic for various CHICAGO newspapers and also wrote her own verse. Her greatest fame came as editor of *Poetry: a Magazine of Verse,* which she founded in 1912. Its contributors included almost every major American poet of the period, including T.S. ELIOT, Marianne MOORE and Ezra POUND, whose reputations were largely made through appearance in the magazine. Monroe particularly favored IMAGISM but included a wide variety of work in the magazine. With Alice Henderson she edited *New Poetry: An Anthology of Twentieth-Century Verse in English* (1917, rev. 1923, 1932). *Poetry* continues today with substantial but lessened influence. (See also MODERNISM.)

Monroe, Marilyn [Norma Jean Mortenson] (1926–1962). American motion picture actress who became a sex symbol in the 1950s. She was born in Los Angeles to a mother whose family had a history of mental disturbance and suicide (the identity of her father has never been established). After surviving abuse and neglect as a child, an unhappy first marriage (she was divorced in 1945) and tedious work in a wartime defense plant, she was discovered by pin-up photographers and HOLLYWOOD scouts. She changed her name to "Marilyn Monroe" and was in and out of the Fox and Columbia studios in a succession of bit parts. Finally, Fox signed her to a long-term contract in 1950, and by the time she married baseball hero Joe DIMAGGIO in 1954, she had made a thriller, *Niagara* (1952), a musical, *Gentlemen Prefer Blondes* (1953), and an adventure story, *River of No Return* (1954). At the height of her fame, when she had become the most sensational "sex goddess" in the movies, Monroe turned her back on Hollywood and, in a much publicized move, went to New York to study the famous "Method" with Lee and Paula STRASBERG. Her subsequent work in *Bus Stop* (1956), *Some Like It Hot* (1959) and her last film (scripted by playwright Arthur MILLER, her third husband), *The Misfits* (1961), showed greater range and subtlety. However, illness, depression, drug abuse and psychiatric problems cut short her promising career. She died in 1962 while filming *Something's Got to Give,* the victim of an apparent overdose of barbiturates. Monroe was a complex of contradictions and mysteries that, more than her obvious sex appeal, make her a continuing fascination.

For further reading:

Mailer, Norman. *Marilyn.* New York, Grosset and Dunlap, 1973.

Monroe, Marion (1898–1983). American child psychologist. With Dr. **William Gray,** she was co-author of the famous Dick and Jane series of school books that from the 1940s to the early 1970s introduced millions of American schoolchildren to reading. The books fell out of favor with educators in the late 1960s and early 1970s because of their perceived racist and sexist attitudes and stereotypes.

Montagu, Ewen (1901–1985). British espionage agent. Montagu led the British counterespionage unit responsible for a WORLD WAR II hoax to deceive the Nazis over landings in the Mediterranean. Code named **Operation Mincemeat,** the hoax (1943) involved floating ashore on the Spanish coast what seemed to be the dead body of a British officer. The body bore faked documents, indicating that Sardinia and GREECE were to be the targets for the next main Allied effort in the Mediterranean, providing cover for the real invasion in Sicily. The operation remained secret until 1953, when Montagu wrote about it in the book *The Man Who Never Was.* That account of the operation sold more than two million copies and was made into a film in 1956.

American film star Marilyn Monroe in a scene from The Seven Year Itch *(1955).*

Montale, Eugenio (1896–1981). Italian poet, critic, editor, translator and journalist. Although Montale produced only five volumes of poetry in 50 years, his citation for the 1975 NOBEL PRIZE for literature declared him to be "one of the most important poets of the contemporary West." He supported his poetry as an editor, translator, literary journalist and music critic. In the 1930s he was forced to resign his position as curator of a rare book collection because he refused to join the Fascist Party (see FASCISM). In 1947 he began a long association with the Milan daily newspaper *Corriere della sera.* His most important works are *Ossi di seppia* (1925, *Cuttlefish Bones*), *Le occasioni* (1939, *The Occasions*), *La bufera e altro* (1956, *The Storm and Other Things*). His poetry is marked by profound pessimism; it is highly subjective and symbolic. Along with UNGARETTI and QUASIMODO, he is associated with the movement known as **Hermeticism**. He is also a distinguished translator of Shakespeare, Hopkins, Thomas HARDY, Dickinson, Melville, T.S. ELIOT and Eugene O'NEILL.

For further reading:

Becker, Jared, *Eugenio Montale.* Boston: G.K. Hall, 1986.

Montana, Joe (1956–). American football player, considered by many sports aficionados to be the greatest quarterback of all time. Montana quarterbacked the San Francisco 49ers to their domination of the National Football League—and the Super Bowl—in the 1980s. Winner of four Super Bowls, in 1982, 1985, 1989 and 1990, Montana was named most valuable player of the championship game three times. He holds the Super Bowl career passing record with 1,142 yards and 83 completions, as well as the single-game mark of 357 yards.

Montand, Yves (1921–). Italian-born actor and singer. Montand began his career performing in vaudeville and in the Paris music halls before gaining fame in Marcel Carne's film *Les Portes de la Nuit* (1946). International acclaim and stardom came with his performance in *Le Salaire de la Peur* (1953). He has worked with several great directors, but his most important collaboration has been with Costi Costa-Gavras in the films *Z* (1968), *L'Aveu* (1970) and *Etat de Siege* (1973). He has made a few Hollywood films, most notably Vincente Minnelli's *On a Clear Day You Can See Forever* (1970) with Barbra STREISAND.

Montecassino. See CASSINO.

Montessori, Maria (1870–1952). Italian educator. The first Italian woman to receive an M.D., Montessori graduated from the University of Rome in 1894. In 1907 she became head of the new Casa dei Bambini in the Roman slums of San Lorenzo, and here Montessori put to work her revolutionary educational theories, which stressed light discipline, spontaneity and child-directed learning. In 1909 Montessori began to train others in her techniques, which became known as the Montessori Method, and in 1911, the first American Montessori school opened, in Tarrytown, New York. Soon similar institutions were established through the U.S. and Europe. Although Montessori was a controversial figure, many of her educational concepts have been incorporated into traditional schools throughout the world.

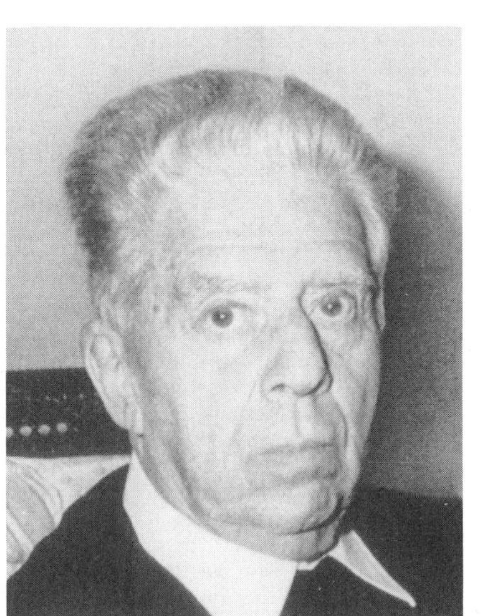

Italian poet Eugenio Montale received the Nobel Prize for literature in 1975.

Monteux, Pierre (1875–1964). The foremost French conductor of his generation. He was trained at the Paris Conservatory and became conductor in Paris of Serge DIAGHILEV'S BALLETS RUSSES (1912). During the next few years he conducted world premieres of some of the most important new music of this century, including Igor STRAVINSKY'S *Petrouchka,* LE SACRE DU PRINTEMPS and *Rossignol;* Maurice RAVEL'S *Daphnis et Chloe* and Claude DEBUSSY'S *Jeux.* Subsequently, he held numerous appointments in the U.S., including conducting at the Metropolitan Opera (1917–19), the Boston Symphony Orchestra (1917–19) and the San Francisco Symphony (1936–52). Rivaling Arturo TOSCANINI and Pablo CASALS in longevity, Monteux became music director of the London Symphony at the age of 86. Few conductors have been as universally beloved. Dapper and elegant, he was a superb technician and the most amiable of men. Critic Virgil THOMSON described his famous transparent sound as possessing "perfect balance" and "translucency." A model of tact, restraint and economy, Monteux insisted a conductor must not "overconduct" or make "unnecessary noises or gestures"; certainly he must never "worry" or "annoy" his players. A protean figure, he led an all-embracing life in opera, ballet and symphony.

For further reading:

Schonberg, Harold C., *The Great Conductors.* New York: Simon and Schuster, 1967.

Montgomery, Bernard Law [1st Viscount Montgomery of Alamein] (1887–1976). British field marshal. Educated at Sandhurst, Montgomery was commissioned in the Royal Warwickshire Regiment in 1908 and served with distinction on the western front during most of WORLD WAR I. In the years between the world wars, he held various staff and command posts in Britain and India. Probably the most important and popular British military commander in WORLD WAR II, "Monty" led an Expeditionary Force division in France from 1939 to 1940, and was involved in the evacuation of DUNKIRK. He was subsequently in charge of the commando raid at DIEPPE (1942) before being posted soon after to North Africa as commander of the Eighth Army. His military fame was assured there, as he commanded his troops in the spectacular victory over ROMMEL'S Afrika Korps at EL ALAMEIN (1942) and pursued the retreating German forces across Libya and Tunisia into Sicily and Southern Italy. Commanding the Allied ground forces in the invasion of NORMANDY, Montgomery and his troops swept through France and

"Monty"—British Field Marshal Bernard Law Montgomery, the hero of El Alamein.

into Germany during 1944 and 1945. His successes, however, were somewhat marred by his strategic disagreements with the Allied supreme commander Dwight D. EISENHOWER. Promoted to the rank of field marshal in 1944, he was created a viscount in 1946. In postwar Europe, Montgomery was commander of Great Britain's occupation forces in Germany (1945–46), chief of the British general staff (1946–48) and deputy supreme commander of NATO (1951–58). He was the author of a number of books on military history and published *Memoirs* in 1958.

Montgomery bus boycott. Struggle to end SEGREGATION on the public buses of Montgomery, Alabama. It took place from December 1955 until December 1956 and began when Rosa Parks, a black seamstress, was ordered to give up her seat on a bus to a white person. She refused and was arrested and jailed. Her action led to a boycott of the bus system by the black citizens of Montgomery. The boycott, led by the Rev. Martin Luther KING Jr., disrupted business as usual in the city. After a protracted struggle, it resulted in the desegregation of public transportation in Montgomery. This landmark event was one of the earliest victories of the CIVIL RIGHTS movement in the South.

The arrest of Rosa Parks for refusing to give up her bus seat to a white person started a boycott of the Montgomery, Alabama, bus system by black citizens (1955–1956).

Montherlant, Henri(-Marie-Joseph-Milon) de (1896–1972). French novelist, playwright and essayist. Born in Paris, by the time of World War II de Montherlant had become one of France's leading men of letters. He won the 1934 Grand Prix for *The Bachelors.* His 17 plays won popular acclaim and became part of the standard French theatrical repertoire. In 1960 he was elected to the French Academy. Like the American writer Ernest HEMINGWAY, early in his life de Montherlant was an active sportsman (and a bullfighter), and his works celebrate physical courage. Also like Hemingway, he committed suicide by shooting himself, apparently out of despondency over his failing health.

Montreux International Jazz Festival. The Montreux International Jazz Festival, established in 1967, continues to be one of jazzdom's most broad-based and significant forums. Presided over until the late 1980s by Claude Nobs, the jazzfest has typically presented a wide variety of jazz stylists over a 17–day period in July of each year. In the mid-1970s, the inclusion of popular music groups led to the deletion of "Jazz" in the event's title; by the late 1970s, "Jazz" was back in the festival's title and its center ring. In addition to featuring internationally known jazz groups playing everything from BEBOP to fusion, and big band to dixieland, the festival has spotlighted student groups, many from the U.S. It has enjoyed sponsorship from a variety of recording companies, a productive relationship that through the years has yielded a number of excellent recordings, especially those issued by the Pablo and Atlantic labels. There is a cooperative arrangement with a "sister" event in the U.S., the Montreux-Detroit Kool Jazz Festival.

Montserrat. A Caribbean island with a total land area of 39 square miles; it is a United Kingdom dependent territory. Between 1871 and 1956 Montserrat was administered as part of Britain's Federal Colony of the Leeward Islands, and between 1958 and 1962 it participated in the Federation of the West Indies. In 1960 a new constitution was granted, providing greater autonomy for the island. In 1978 the ruling Progressive Democratic Party (PDP) was defeated in elections by the opposition People's Liberation Movement (PLM), which won all seven seats in the Legislative Council. John Osborne, the leader of the PLM, became chief minister. The PLM won elections in 1983, and Osborne stated that he would be in favor of eventual independence for the territory. In June 1984 a state of emergency was declared after a strike by public service employees disrupted services. An early general election was held in August 1987 and again won by the PLM, which defeated the PDP and the more recent National Development Party.

Monty Python's Flying Circus. British comedy troupe and television show of the same name, noted for its bizarre sense of humor, ranging from surreal farce to sophisticated satire. The troupe was formed by a group of students at Cambridge University in the early 1960s as an amateur stage entertainment revue; the members were **Graham Chapman, John Cleese, Eric Idle, Terry Jones, Michael Palin** and **Terry Gilliam** (the only American-born member). They turned professional, and the show was broadcast by the BRITISH BROADCASTING CORPORATION (BBC) from 1969 to 1974. It was also repeated on public television in the U.S. and was a huge hit in both countries. The group also made several irreverant but good-natured films, including *Monty Python and the Holy Grail* (1978) and *The Life of Brian* (1979). Several of the members—notably Cleese, Idle and Palin—went on to successful careers in other films and television shows. Gilliam launched a spectacular career in the movies, directing *Time Bandits* (1981) and *Brazil* (1985, cowritten by Palin). Chapman died in 1989.

Moody, Helen Newington Wills (1905–). American tennis player. A player who combined thoughtful play with power, Moody dominated women's tennis throughout the 1920s and 1930s, winning her first U.S. championship at the age of 17 in 1923. She would win that title six more times, as well as an astonishing eight Wimbledon championships and four French championships. In 1928 and 1929, she took the women's Grand Slam, winning all three titles. She was named to the International Tennis Hall of Fame in 1959.

Moody, William H. (1853–1917). Associate justice, U.S. Supreme Court (1906–10). A native of Massachusetts, Moody graduated from Harvard University and briefly attended its Law School, leaving to read law in a law office in Boston. He became a prosecutor and is remembered for the unsuccessful prosecution of Lizzie Borden. He was elected to Congress in 1895 and was selected by President Theodore ROOSEVELT as secretary of the Navy and later as attorney general. Roosevelt appointed Moody to the Supreme Court. His nomination ran into opposition from business interests because, as attorney general, Moody had vigorously enforced the antitrust laws. In a highly unusual move he had personally argued in the antitrust case *Swift and Company v. United States.* Moody was forced to resign from the Court after only four years because of ill health.

Moody Blues, The. British rock and roll band, founded in 1964. The Moody Blues are best known for their successful blending of rock rhythms, orchestral string overlays and pop philosophy lyrics. The band enjoyed its greatest success with the album *Days of Future Passed (Dream)* (1967), which it recorded with the London Symphony Orchestra. The album featured the enduring hit single "Nights in White Satin." The personnel for this album were Graeme Edge, drums; Justin Hayward, vocals and guitar; John Lodge, bass; Mike Pinder, vocals; and Ray Thomas, flute and vocals. With occasional personnel changes, the band has remained together to the present day. Noteworthy albums include *In Search of the Lost Chord* (1968), *On the Threshold of a Dream* (1969) and *Octave* (1978).

Moon, Keith (1947–1978). British drummer who played in the rock group The WHO. Moon was one of the wild figures of the ROCK AND ROLL scene during the late 1960s and the 1970s. On one occasion, during a concert tour, he reportedly paid $400,000 to a hotel for damages caused by his antics. Another time, he drove his Rolls-Royce into a swimming pool. He died of a drug overdose.

Moon, Sun Myung (1920–). South Korean evangelist. Moon is best known as the founder and spiritual leader of the Unification Church (1954). Between 200,000 and 2 million people belong to the church worldwide. Most recruits are young people (derogatorily called "Moonies") who are encouraged to leave families and jobs in order to live in communes and work for the church. Due to conflicts with his business enterprises, Moon moved church headquarters from South Korea to the U.S. in 1973. He was convicted of income tax evasion in 1984 and sentenced to a prison term.

Moore, Archie [Archibald Lee Wright] (1913–). American boxer. Moore began boxing in 1936, but it wasn't until 1952 that he defeated Joey Maxim for the light-heavyweight title. In 1955 he sought the heavyweight title but was defeated by Rocky MARCIANO. The following year he tried again and was defeated by Floyd Patterson. He was able to successfully defend his light-heavyweight title until 1962. Moore registered 136 knockouts during his 220-bout career. Moore has also appeared in films—*The Adventures of Huckleberry Finn* (1959)—and written an autobiography, *Any Boy Can* (1971).

Moore, Brian (1921–). Irish-born novelist. Although he had written some early novels under the pseudonym Michael Bryan, Moore is best known for *The Lonely Passion of Judith Hearne* (1956; originally published in Britain as *Judith Hearne*, 1955; filmed 1987). This work depicts a lonely spinster who, thwarted in her last attempt for companionship, seeks solace in alcohol; it is typical of Moore's work with its themes of alienation and despair. Moore often calls upon his experiences as an emigre to Canada and later the U.S. in his subsequent fiction, which includes *The Luck of Ginger Coffey* (1960), *I Am Mary Dunne* (1968), *The Mangan Inheritance* (1979) and *Lies of Silence* (1990).

Moore, Colleen [Kathleen Morrison] (1902–1988). American actress who was a popular star of HOLLYWOOD silent films and early talkies. In a career that extended from 1917 to 1934, Moore achieved stardom through her portrayal of a flapper in *Flaming Youth* (1923), helping to touch off a craze for bobbed hair and short skirts; probably her greatest success was *Lilac Time* (1928). One of Hollywood's highest paid stars in the silent era, her personal favorite of her 100 or so films was *The Power and the Glory* (1933), in which she appeared opposite Spencer TRACY.

Moore, Dudley (1935–). British composer-songwriter, comedian and actor. Moore first gained notice in the revue BEYOND THE FRINGE (1960), for which he also wrote the songs. He went on to a second career as an accomplished jazz pianist and also formed a memorable partnership with Peter COOK in such classic films as *Bedazzled* (1967). In the U.S. he is best known for his starring roles in the hit film comedies *10* (1979) and *Arthur* (1981), in which he cultivated a bumbling but charming persona.

Moore, George Augustus (1852–1933). Anglo-Irish novelist. Moore studied painting in Paris, and his works show the influence of such French writers as Balzac and Zola. After returning to England he published *A Modern Lover* (1883). The novel's Bohemian subject matter caused it to be banned by circulating libraries in England, and Moore became an adamant opponent of censorship. Moore's other early novels include *A Mummer's Wife* (1885) and *Esther Waters* (1894), his best known work, which evokes his childhood home in County Mayo. Moore's later novels are of more epic proportions and include *The Brook Kerith* (1916) and *Heloise and Abelard* (1921). Moore was instrumental, along with W.B. YEATS, in the forming of the Irish National Theatre. Moore has also written the autobiographical *Confessions of a Young Man* (1888), *Memoirs of My Dead Life* (1906) and the three-volume *Hail and Farewell* (1911–14).

Moore, G(eorge) E(dward) (1873–1958). British philosopher. Moore, who was educated at Cambridge University and taught there for most of his adult life, was a highly influential philosopher who had a special fascination for the BLOOMSBURY GROUP. In his major work, *Principia Ethica*, Moore argued that ethical decisions hinged on a blend of idealism and utilitarianism. The idea of absolute good was an appropriate guide to right action in daily life. But right action, in turn, hinged upon moral obligations to others as well as the special value one assigned to aesthetic beauty and to personal joys such as friendship and love. Moore analyzed a variety of epistemological and ethical questions in *Philosophical Studies* (1922), in which his basic approach was to defend common sense as opposed to technical language analysis. Moore edited the influential British philosophical journal *Mind* from 1921 to 1947.

Moore, Gerald (1899–1987). English classical pianist. His career spanned a half century. Primarily a recital accompanist, he became celebrated as a virtuoso in that role. He was best known for his collaborations with singers. Among those he accompanied were Elisabeth SCHUMANN, John MCCORMACK, Victoria DE LOS ANGELES, Dietrich FISCHER-DIESKAU, and Janet BAKER. Moore retired from the concert stage in 1967.

Moore, Henry (Spencer) (1898–1986). British sculptor. During WORLD WAR II he became widely known in Britain for his drawings of people huddled together taking shelter in the London Underground during the blitz. He went on to become one of the most successful public sculptors of his age, and hundreds of his works came to grace parks, public squares and buildings throughout the world. His most characteristic subject was the reclining female. Many of his human figures had holes in them and small heads atop massive bodies. Among the best known of his works are the six-ton bronze sculpture completed in 1964 that decorated a fountain at Lincoln Center and the marble sculpture that decorates the headquarters of the UNITED NATIONS Educational, Scientific and Cultural Organization in PARIS.

Moore, Marianne (1887–1972). American poet. An indifferent student at Bryn Mawr (1905–09), where she was denied an English major, Moore burst onto the literary scene in 1915, when her first poems were accepted by the *Egoist* and *Poetry* magazines. Her originality, precise language, sharp and idiosyncratic vision and concentration of thought so impressed her literary peers that she was soon regarded as one of the leaders of the modernist movement in literature (see MODERNISM). Her position as editor of the *Dial* (1925–29) made her arguably the most powerful figure in modernist poetry in the 1920s. Her *Collected Poems* (1951) received the Bollingen Award, the PULITZER PRIZE and the NATIONAL BOOK AWARD. She went on to win virtually every prize and accolade offered to a poet in the U.S. In later years, her public image as a charming white-haired eccentric who appeared at Brook-

American poet Marianne Moore, a leading figure in the modernist movement in literature.

lyn Dodgers baseball games wearing a black tricorne hat overshadowed her reputation as a major poet.

For further reading:

Molesworth, Charles, *Marianne Moore: A Literary Life*. New York: Macmillan, 1990.

Moral Majority. See Jerry FALWELL.

Moral Re-Armament. See Frank BUCHMAN.

Morandi, Giorgio (1890–1964). Italian painter. Born in Bologna, he lived in that city for most of his life, never leaving his native country. Early in his career (1918–20) he was associated with the METAPHYSICAL PAINTING of the painter Giorgio de CHIRICO. In the early 1920s he created his own style of still-life painting. In these quietly poetic compositions, Morandi portrayed humble bottles, vases and jars in simplified shapes and in a severely limited palette, mainly earth tones. He was also a skilled etcher, again using still lifes for his subject matter.

Morante, Elsa (1918–1985). Italian novelist. Morante is one of the most highly regarded Italian novelists of the post-WORLD WAR II era. Her novels reflect a deep sense of historical awareness and a sensitivity to the need for love and to the ultimate fragility of the human psyche. While not prolific, Morante has so carefully crafted each of her novels as to gain them the status of modern classics. Morante first gained international attention with *Arturo's Island* (1957), an examination of the relationship between individualism and societal demands. *History: A Novel* (1974) is a penetrating study of the impact of World War II upon European culture. *Aracoeli* (1983) is a moving depiction of the difficulties of homosexual existence and the depth of a mother's love. Morante was at one time married to the Italian novelist Alberto MORAVIA.

Moravia, Alberto [born Alberto Pincherle] (1907–1990). Italian author. Moravia was perhaps the best known and most widely read Italian writer of his time. His books explored sex, alienation and other contemporary social issues. His first novel, *The Time of Indifference* (1929), was published when he was 21 years old. His subsequent works include *The Women of Rome* (1949; filmed 1956), *The Conformist* (1951) and *Two Women* (1958; adapted for the screen by Vittorio DE SICA and starring Sophia LOREN).

Moreau, Jeanne (1928–). French actress. Moreau, who is known for her sultry eroticism and wry humor, achieved international acclaim, particularly for her work in the films of Louis MALLE, Francois TRUFFAUT, and Luis BUNUEL. She began her career as a member of the Comedie Francaise (1948–52), then became the star of the Theatre National Populaire. Her first screen success came in Malle's *L'Ascenseur pour l'echafaud* (1957). Her performance in Roger Vadim's *Les Liaisons Dangereuses* (1959) made her a star. Other famous roles were in Truffaut's *Jules et Jim* (1961), Bunuel's *Le Journal d'une femme de chambre* (1964) and Malle's *Viva Maria!* (1965) with Brigitte BARDOT. She has also written, sung and recorded her own songs.

Moreell, Ben (1892–1978). American naval officer. During WORLD WAR II, Admiral Moreell organized and headed the U.S. Navy's Seabee construction battalions in the Pacific (see WORLD WAR II IN THE PACIFIC). After the war he was chairman and chief executive officer of Jones & Laughlin Steel Corp. (1947–58).

Morgan, J(ohn) P(ierpont) (1837–1913). U.S. financier. Morgan was born in Hartford, Connecticut, and educated at the University of Gottingen. In 1856 he entered his father's banking firm and by the end of the century had made the firm (known as J.P. Morgan & Co. after 1895) one of the most powerful banking houses in the world. Morgan was a major force in the centralization of industry and credit around the turn of the century. He also played a central role in the reorganization of U.S. railroads and in the marketing of government bonds. Morgan's personal influence helped stabilize financial conditions during the Panic of 1907. The financier was a target of the progressive Trust Busters. In 1904 the Supreme Court dissolved his Northern Securities Company, formed to control Western railroads, for violation of the Sherman Antitrust Act. The chief target of the 1912 Pujo investigation of the "Money Trust," Morgan emerged with his reputation and prestige unimpaired. A great philanthropist, he was a major benefactor of the Metropolitan Museum of Art. Morgan bequeathed his personal library to the public.

Morgan, J(ohn) P(ierpont), Jr. (1867–1943). U.S. businessman. The son of J.P. MORGAN, young Morgan became head of the house of Morgan after his father's death in 1913. As American agent for Great Britain in 1914, Morgan's banking firm raised huge amounts of money for the purchase of military supplies. The firm was not important in financing the war but handled most of the postwar loans, including those associated with reparations, while also sponsoring billions of dollars in domestic securities. A philanthropist, Morgan made large gifts to education and the arts.

Morgan, Thomas Hunt (1866–1945). American geneticist. Born in Lexington, Kentucky, Morgan earned his Ph.D. from Johns Hopkins in 1890. While a professor of experimental zoology at Columbia University (1904–28), he amended Mendel's laws of inheritance and developed the chromosome theory of genetics; he mapped individual genes, demonstrated genetic linkage and described the process of "crossing over," by which linkages are broken. In 1933, in recognition of his pioneering role as one of the founders of modern genetics, Morgan received the NOBEL PRIZE for medicine or physiology.

Morgenstern, Christian (1871–1914). German poet. Morgenstern contracted tuberculosis from his mother at an early age; due to his illness, he was forced to withdraw from the university. He moved to Scandinavia, where he translated the works of HAMSUN, STRINDBERG and Ibsen. His popular nonsense verse appeared as *Galgenlieder* (1905) and *Palmstroem* (1910). However, he was strongly influenced by Rudolf Steiner and anthroposophism and thus regarded his serious mystical verse as his greatest achievement. He also published lyric love poems in *Ein Sommer* (1899) and *Ich und Du* (1911), but he is best remembered as a master of wordplay and nonsense whose inventiveness rivals that of Edward Lear and Lewis Carroll.

Morgenthau, Hans Joachim (1904–1980). German-born political scientist, author and teacher. A Jewish exile from Nazi GERMANY, Morgenthau taught at the University of Chicago for 17 years. There he became one of America's most respected foreign policy analysts, known for writings that stressed national interest rather than world opinion in policy making. He was an early critic of American involvement in the VIETNAM WAR. He was also an outspoken critic of the U.S.S.R.'s treatment of JEWS and a strong advocate of nuclear arms control and DETENTE with the U.S.S.R.

Morgenthau, Henry, Jr. (1891–1967). U.S. secretary of the Treasury (1933–45). Born into a wealthy family, Morgenthau was a gentleman-farmer and a Hyde Park, N.Y., neighbor of Franklin ROOSEVELT. He assisted FDR's political comeback after Roosevelt was stricken with polio; and, after FDR became governor of New York, Roosevelt appointed his friend to a state post. Despite Morgenthau's lack of experience Roosevelt appointed him secretary of the Treasury when FDR went to the White House. Although a fiscal conservative, Morgenthau proved an active secretary and a major NEW DEAL figure. He was instrumental in financing the New Deal spending programs and in establishing a scheme to stabilize the world's monetary system. Toward the end of World War II his MORGENTHAU PLAN advocated a "pastoralized" Nazi Germany. After Harry TRUMAN became president on FDR's death in 1945, Morgenthau's influence waned and he resigned. He was critical of Truman for abandoning FDR's policy of cooperation with the U.S.S.R. In later years Morgenthau devoted himself to philanthropy, especially the United Jewish Appeal. He died at the age of 75 in 1967.

Morgenthau plan. Plan advanced toward the end of World War II by U.S. secretary of the Treasury Henry MORGENTHAU to "pastoralize" Nazi GERMANY after the war. German industry would be dismantled, and Germany would be turned into an agricultural nation. Industrial areas would be annexed by FRANCE and POLAND, and the nation itself would be split into separate northern and southern states. The plan also proposed separating German children from their parents by sending them to special Allied boarding schools. Proposed by Secretary Morgenthau at the QUEBEC CONFERENCE in 1944, the plan was originally accepted by U.S. President Franklin ROOSEVELT and British Prime Minister Winston CHURCHILL. However, they both dropped their support of the plan after the U.S. State Department and

The prominent Italian politician and former Prime Minister Aldo Moro was kidnapped and killed by Red Brigade terrorists in 1978.

British Foreign Office rejected it as unworkable because it would require heavy subsidies from the Allies. The Nazi propaganda office used the plan to encourage Germans to resist the Allied invasion to the bitter end.

Morison, Samuel Eliot (1887–1976). U.S. historian. He started his teaching career in 1915 at Harvard and became a full professor there in 1925. Two of his books, *Admiral of the Ocean Sea* (1942) and *John Paul Jones* (1959), won PULITZER PRIZES. He was commissioned by President Franklin ROOSEVELT to write the 15-volume *History of United States Naval Operations in World War II* (1946–62).

Morison, Stanley (Arthur) (1889–1967). English typographer and editor. Beginning his career on a printing journal in 1913, Morison went on to become the typographical adviser for Monotype Corporation (1922), cofounder and editor of *Fleuron* (1922–30) and typographical consultant to Cambridge University Press (1925). His greatest achievement is considered to be the creation of the typeface **Times Roman** in 1932. He wrote widely on the history of calligraphy, typography, printing and other subjects, and in 1945 he became the editor of *The Times Literary Supplement*.

Morley, Christopher (1890–1957). American author and editor. A Rhodes scholar, Morley began his career in publishing. He helped found *The Saturday Review of Literature* in 1924, for which he wrote until 1941, and served in an editorial capacity for many other journals and periodicals. Morley is best known for his popular novels which include *Parnassus on Wheels* (1917), *The Haunted Bookshop* (1919), *Kitty Foyle* (1939, filmed 1940) and *The Man Who Made Friends with Himself* (1949). Morley was also a poet, playwright and essayist; he also wrote the autobiography *John Mistletoe* (1931).

Moro, Aldo (1916–1978). Italian political leader. A prominent lawyer and Christian Democrat, he entered the constituent assembly in 1946, was elected to the chamber of deputies in 1948 and served as minister of justice from 1955 to 1957. Moro was also foreign minister (1965–66, 1969–72 and 1973–74) and prime minister (1963–68 and 1974–76). Considered an elder statesman in the Christian Democratic Party, he became its president in 1976, advocating rapprochement with the Communist Party. Moro was kidnapped on March 16, 1978, by the terrorist RED BRIGADES and was found shot to death on May 9, 1978. (See also ITALY.)

Moroccan War of 1907–12. The ALGECIRAS Conference (1906) stipulated that Moroccan territorial integrity was to be enforced by France and Spain although these two powers agreed to partition MOROCCO between them eventually. In 1907 Moroccans rioted against foreign workers in Casablanca and were crushed by French troops; but native opposition reemerged in 1908 when Sultan Abd-al Azziz IV was deposed by his brother. The new Sultan requested help to maintain order; in consequence Spanish troops suffered defeat by Rif tribesmen who attacked Fez, which the French then occupied (1909). Germany, protesting French actions, sent a gunboat to Morocco. War was averted when France ceded Congolese territory to Germany to gain recognition of French authority in Morocco. By the Treaty of Fez (March 30, 1912), the Sultan agreed to a French protectorate, and France and Spain then split Morocco into four zones with French rule over three of them.

Morocco. Coastal African nation, bordering the Mediterranean Sea on the north, the Atlantic Ocean on the west; it is north of Mauritania and west of Algeria.

In 1912 Morocco was made wholly a French protectorate, with the exception of a small Spanish territory in the north. The 1920s saw a period of almost constant

MOROCCO

1904	Secret agreement between France and Spain divides control of Morocco.
1906	Act of Algeria guarantees all major powers right to trade in the country.
1912	Rebellion against the sultan; French seize opportunity to send troops and proclaim protectorate; flood of French immigration begins.
1921	Abd el-Krim proclaims republic in the Rif Mountains; begins bitter five-year defense against French and Spanish.
1934	Plan of reform submitted to French by young nationalists.
1936	General Franco launches Spanish Civil War from base in northern Morocco.
1947	King Mohammed V leads independence struggle through Istiqlal Party.
1953	Mohammed exiled; terrorists fight French and Spanish.
1955	Death of Mohammed bin Ibrahim, great Arab poet.
1956	Independence granted by French; Mohammed returns; Spanish follow suit.
1959	Eleven-hundredth anniversary of Al-Qarawiyan University, probably the oldest in the world.
1961	Mohammed dies; his son crowned Hassan II; Morocco becomes world's leading source of phosphates.
1965	Student riots; Hassan assumes dictatorial powers; Arabic replaces French as language of law courts.
1977	Censorship "lifted," but laws against speaking ill of king, monarchy or Islam remain in force; political parties resume activity under these strictures.
1979	Polisario guerrillas wage independence struggle in Western Sahara; Hassan begins military buildup; price of phosphates drops; economy suffers.
1984	Hassan exempts drought-ridden farmers from taxation until the year 2000.
1986	Construction begins of fortified earthen wall 560 miles long in Western Sahara; Hassan and Peres make first Arab-Israeli meeting since 1981.
1988	UN organizes peace talks with Polisario forces; Moroccan political prisoners become focus of Western protests.
1989	Polisario mounts new offensive; "Arab Maghreb" economic union joins countries of northwest Africa.
1990	After killing 100 rioters at Fes, government agrees to wage hikes.
1991	Despite sending troops to join U.S.-led invasion of Iraq, government supports pro-Iraq general strike led by opposition parties.

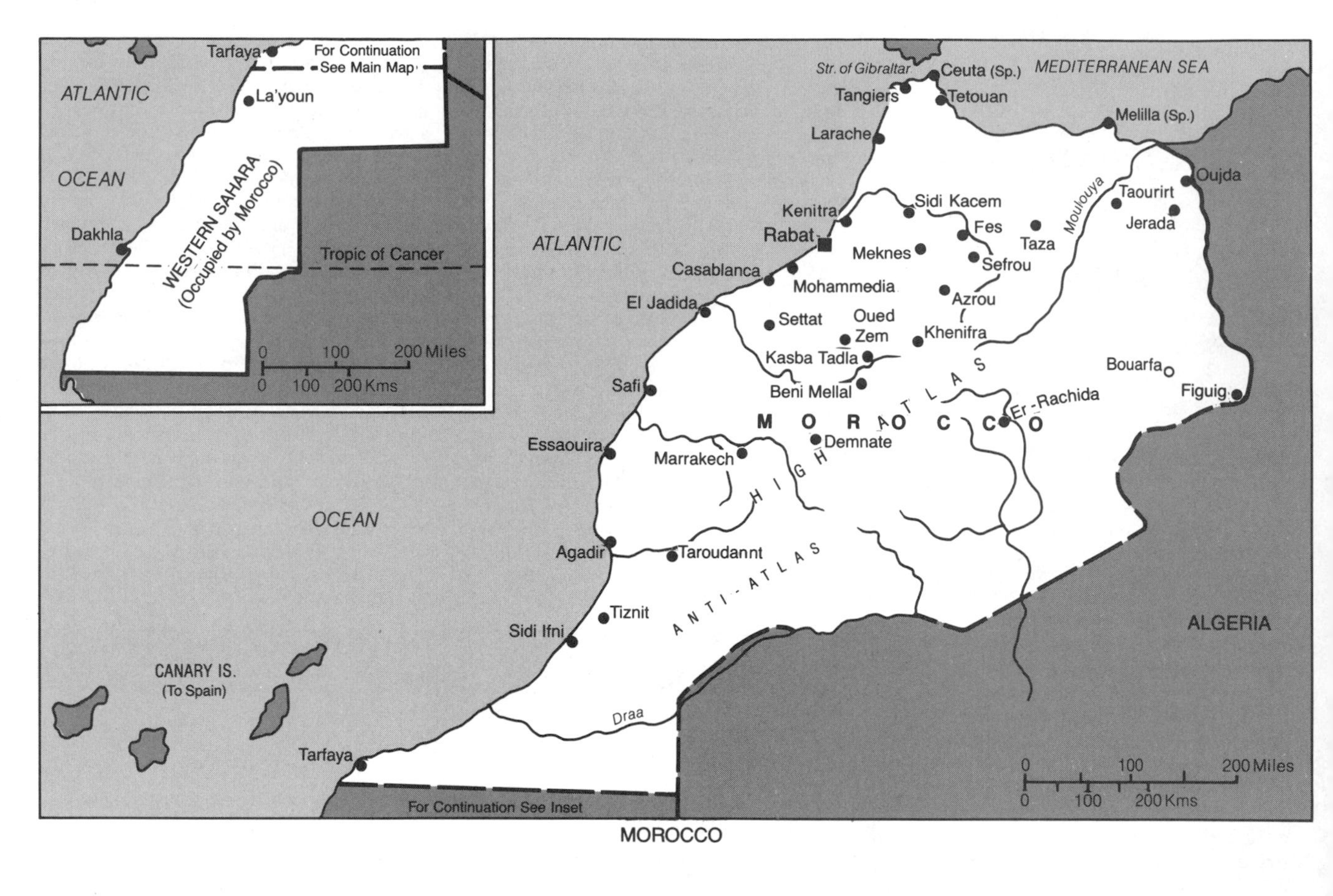

MOROCCO

revolt, but Moroccan independence did not come about until 1956, when Mohammed V established an independent monarchy. Absolute power was consolidated by his successor, Hassan II. In 1976 the oil-rich region of the Spanish Sahara in the southwest was taken over jointly with MAURITANIA, renouncing its claim in 1979 after fierce guerilla opposition, and Morocco regained full control of the territory.

Moro Wars (1901–13). The Moros, Muslim tribespeople of central and western Mindanao in the PHILIPPINES, traditionally had lived apart from Christian Filipinos. The Spanish, rulers until driven out by Americans in 1898, had left them alone. The Americans, however, wished them to be assimilated; the Moros resisted with sporadic outbreaks beginning in 1901. In 1903 they attacked American troops in central Mindanao; in 1906, 600 Moro rebels, taking refuge inside a volcanic crater in Jolo, were slaughtered by U.S. troops under General Leonard Wood, resulting in public indignation. The fighting ended after June, 1913 and the Moros were left in peace.

Morris (1961–1978). Famous "finicky" cat who starred in some 40 cat food commercials on American television during the 1960s and 1970s.

Morrison, Herbert (1906–1989). U.S. radio reporter. His emotional broadcast of the crash of the German airship HINDENBURG at Lakehurst, New Jersey in 1937 was recorded and made his voice familiar to millions.

Morrison, Herbert Stanley (1888–1965). British politician. The son of a London policeman, Morrison held a variety of jobs as he became involved in the London LABOUR PARTY, becoming its general secretary in 1915. He entered the London County Council in 1922 and through his abilities as an organizer became its leader (1934–40). Morrison was a member of Parliament (1923–24, 1929–31 and 1935–45). He also served as minister of transport (1931), and as minister of supply in Winston CHURCHILL's coalition government (1940), after which he served as home secretary until the end of the coalition. Morrison was instrumental in creating the National Fire Service and was involved in the development of the social services adopted after Clement ATTLEE came to power in 1946. Morrison was deputy prime minister and lord president of the council from 1945 to 1951 when he served briefly as foreign secretary. He attempted to succeed Attlee as party leader in 1955 but was defeated by Hugh GAITSKELL.

Morrison, Toni (1931–). American novelist. Beginning with *The Bluest Eye* (1969), which examines black self-hatred, Morrison's original fiction has explored the black experience in a racist culture, as well as universal themes of human interrelations. Subsequent novels include *Sula* (1973) and *Tar Baby* (1981). Morrison's work is both highly popular and critically esteemed. She was awarded the 1977 National Book Critics Circle Award for *Song of Solomon* (1977) and the 1988 PULITZER PRIZE for *Beloved* (1987). Educated at Harvard University, Morrison has been a member of the faculties of many American universities, including Princeton and Yale.

Morro Castle. On September 8, 1934, the passenger liner *Morro Castle* caught fire off the coast of New Jersey and beached at Asbury Park. One-hundred-thirty passengers were killed in the disaster, which, because of its proximity to New York, was thoroughly covered by newsreel camera crews.

Morse, David Abner (1907–1990). U.S. labor leader. He was acting U.S. secretary of labor in 1948, and director general of the UNITED NATIONS' INTERNATIONAL LABOR ORGANIZATION from 1948 to 1970. He was an advocate of an eight-hour working day, child labor laws, maternity leave, workers' compensation and improved safety regulations. In 1969, Morse accepted the NOBEL PRIZE for peace in behalf of the ILO.

Mortimer, John (Clifford) (1923–). British novelist and playwright. Mortimer trained and worked as a barrister before turning to writing. He is best known for the series "Rumpole of the Bailey," which centers on an eccentric barrister and his cases. These include *Rumpole and the Age of Miracles* (1989); early Rumpole books have been published in collections, such as *The Second Rumpole Omnibus* (1987). The series was successfully televised by the BBC. Mortimer's acute observations of life enrich his novels, which include *Summer's Lease* (1989), *Paradise Postponed* (1985) and its sequel *Titmus Regained* (1990). He is also known for his libertarian views and his stand against censorship. Other works include *A Voyage Round My Father* (1970), a biography of his father, and *Clinging to the Wreckage* (1982), an autobiography. Mortimer was formerly married to the novelist Penelope Mortimer.

Morton, Jelly Roll [La Menthe Morton] (1890–1941). American pianist-composer, ranks among jazzdom's true innovators by dint of his unique amalgamation of the different black musical styles he learned and performed in his native New Orleans—namely ragtime, instrumental blues, gospel songs, field hollers and minstrel show tunes. As a pianist, Morton is credited with "opening up" the through-composed ragtime of W.C. HANDY by interpolating sections designated for improvisation; Morton's "Grandpa's Spells" and "Kansas City Stomp" encapsulate the expanded ragtime approach that would be taken up in the 1930s by such piano virtuosos as Earl "Fatha" HINES. In ensemble works such as "Black Bottom Stomp" and "The Pearls," Morton proved that meticulous arrangements could include improvised sections without sacrificing clarity of form; the most significant examples of his group concept were recorded in 1926–27 by Morton's well-rehearsed and disciplined Red Hot Peppers. By the 1930s, given the whimsical nature of society's ever fickle and shifting musical tastes, Morton was considered passe. However, recordings made by folklorist Alan Lomax in 1938 revived Morton's career until ill health forced his retirement in 1940. Other classic Morton compositions include "Wolverine Blues," "Milenberg Joys" and the eponymous "Jelly Roll Blues."

For further reading:

Lomax, Alan, *Mister Jelly Roll: The Fortunes of Jelly Roll Morton, New Orleans Creole and "Inventor of Jazz."* New York: Duell, Sloan and Pearce, 1950.

Moscow Art Theater. Founded in 1898 by Konstantin STANISLAVSKY and Vladimir NEMIROVICH-DANCHENKO, the Moscow Art Theater achieved worldwide acclaim for its theatrical naturalism. Stanislavsky, who was in charge of stage direction, strove to strip the theater of commercialism and stereotyped mannerisms by concentrating on inner moods and emotions; in this he was influenced by the German Meiningen Company. The original ensemble was composed of amateur actors from the Society of Art and Literature. The theater performed plays by GORKY, ANDREYEV, Maeterlinck and HAUPTMANN, and in particular the works of CHEKHOV. The theater continued to flourish after the revolution. It has undertaken several international tours and has influenced theaters all over the world.

Moselle. Northeast department of FRANCE in Lorraine, south of Luxembourg, bordering the Saarland of West Germany on the east, the Bas-Rhin and Marche-et-Moselle divisions to the south. Its principal city is Metz, Thionville its capital. Annexed during the Franco-Prussian War in 1871, it remained part of GERMANY until the end of World War I, only to be reclaimed by the Germans in WORLD WAR II, between 1940 and 1944.

Moser, Koloman (Kolo) (1868–1918). Viennese artist, graphics and furniture designer. He was a founding member of the Vienna Secession movement. Moser had studied painting before becoming acquainted with Josef HOFFMANN, Gustav Klimt and Josef Olbrich. In 1898 he designed a stained-glass window for Olbrich's Secession Gallery. In 1899 Moser began to teach at the Vienna School of Applied Arts—a post he held until his death. During his career he designed furniture—often using decorative inlays—jewelry, toys and bookbindings. He also designed stained-glass for Otto Wagner's Vienna Kirche am Steinhof (1904), posters, and other graphics items, including an Austrian postage stamp of 1908. He was, with Josef Hoffmann, a founder of the Wiener Werkstatte. In his later years, Moser was chiefly active as a painter.

Moser-Proell, Annemarie (1953–). Austrian skiing champion. Known for her aggressive, risk-taking style, Moser-Proell joined the Austrian national ski team at age 15. Over the course of her career, she won 62 individual World Cup victories, more than any other woman. She also won a record seven World Cup downhill titles (1971–75, 1978–79) and won the overall World Cup title a record six times, in 1971–75 and again in 1979. From December 1972 to January 1974, she won 11 consecutive World Cup downhill races, a record. In the 1980 Winter OLYMPIC GAMES in Lake Placid, New York, Moser-Proell won a gold medal in the downhill. She announced her retirement from World Cup events that year.

Moses, Robert (1888–1981). American urban planner who transformed the landscape of NEW YORK CITY from the 1920s through the 1960s. A shrewd and aggressive bargainer known for his single-minded determination, he gained power within the state's public works system—at one point holding 12 positions simultaneously. He entered public service in 1919 under governor Alfred E. SMITH. For various periods between 1924 and 1968 his titles included among others, New York City parks commissioner, head of the State Parks Council and chairman of the Triborough Bridge and Tunnel Authority and of the New York State Power Authority. Although he was never elected to any public office (he was an unsuccessful candidate for governor in 1934), behind the scenes he wielded more actual power than many of the governors and mayors under whom he served. During his reign he oversaw the construction of 75 state parks, 11 bridges and 481 miles of highway around New York City. He was also responsible for the development of massive housing complexes, tunnels, playgrounds, beaches, zoos, civic centers and exhibition halls. Among his projects were Lincoln Center, the New York Coliseum, Shea Stadium, the Robert Moses Niagara Power Plant and the 1964–1965 World's Fair grounds. He held on to his power until the age of 80, when Governor Nelson ROCKEFELLER forced him to retire.

Moses exemplified the bigger-is-better approach to urban development in the 20th century. His monumental plans—often carried out at the expense of neighborhoods, tradition and human needs—contributed to the impersonality of the city. His projects in New York set an example that was repeated throughout the U.S. and in other parts of the world.

For further reading:

Caro, Robert A. *The Power Broker: Robert Moses and the Fall of New York.* New York: Alfred A. Knopf, 1974; Random House, 1975.

Mosley, Sir Oswald (Ernald) (1896–1980). British fascist leader. He began his political career as a Conservative member of Parliament in 1918, becoming an independent from 1922 to 1924, when he joined the Labour Party. A junior cabinet minister (1929–30), he resigned in a dispute over economic policies, and in 1931 founded the socialist New Party. Soon his views took a decidedly right-wing turn, and in 1932 he dissolved the New Party and founded the British Union of Fascists. When his first wife, Lady Cynthia Curzon died, he married (1936) Diana Guinness—a member of the MITFORD family, many of whom were active supporters of Adolf HITLER. Mosley began to stage fascist rallies and marches and to make violently anti-Semitic speeches. Mosley and his wife were interned in 1940 due to their espousal of the Nazi cause. They were released three years later. After the war, Mosley unsuccessfully attempted to revive his movement and his political career. His autobiography, *My Life*, was published in 1968.

Mosquito Coast [Miskito Coast, Mosquitia; Costa de Mosquitos] (Honduras and Nicaragua) A 40-mile-wide region extending from the San Juan River in the north into northeast HONDURAS, its name having been derived from the Mosquito (Misketto) Indians. In 1894 it was made part of NICARAGUA under the dictatorship of Jose Santos Zelaya, an issue that was not settled until 1960, when the International Court of Justice awarded the northern coastal region to Honduras. In the early 1980s, the Sandinista regime in Nicaragua was accused of having massacred the Indian population occupying both sides of the border with Honduras.

Mossadeq, Mohammed (1881–1967). Iranian political leader, prime minister of IRAN (1951–53). Born in Teheran, Mossadeq entered politics in 1914 and served as foreign minister from 1922 to 1924. When the shah assumed dictatorial powers in 1925, Mossadeq protested by retiring from political life. He returned to governmental affairs as a member of the Iranian parliament in 1942. A militant nationalist who objected to foreign interference in Iran's affairs, he opposed Soviet attempts to exploit the country's oil resources and spearheaded the movement to nationalize the British-owned Anglo-Iranian Oil Company. A fiery reformer and powerful speaker who was extremely popular with the Iranian people, he was appointed prime minister in 1951 after the passage of the oil nationalization act. Thereafter, Western technology experts withdrew from the country, rendering Iran powerless to produce the oil on which the country's economy and Mossadeq's promised social reforms rested. With the nation in political crisis, Mossadeq was dismissed by the shah in 1953 and was subsequently arrested. Imprisoned for three years, he spent the rest of his life under house arrest.

Motherwell, Robert (1915–91). American painter. Born in Aberdeen, Washington, he was educated at Stanford University and pursued graduate studies in philosophy and art history at Harvard and Columbia. He later taught art at a number of colleges. An articulate exponent of ABSTRACT EXPRESSIONISM, Motherwell edited the 15–volume series *Documents of Modern Art* from 1944 to 1961. His abstract works have titles that often allude to philosophical or political ideas. Motherwell paints large bold forms in strongly contrasting colors with slashing brushstrokes. Created as a reaction to the SPANISH CIVIL WAR, his best-known works are a series of more than 100 powerful paintings entitled *Elegy to the Spanish Republic* (1947–76).

Mothopeng, Zephania Lekoane (1913–1990). South African political activist. He joined the AFRICAN NATIONAL CONGRESS in his youth but split with the organization in 1959 to form the more militant Pan-African Congress. The group opposed power-sharing with whites and refused to join negotiations proposed by government President F.W. DE KLERK. Mothopeng was jailed several times between 1964 and 1988 for his activities.

Motown. American record company that was the wellhead of much of the important music of the 1960s. Motown artists included Smokey Robinson, the Temptations, Martha Reeves and the Vandellas, the Jackson 5, Stevie WONDER, the Four Tops and innumerable others. Founded in Detroit by paternal despot Berry Gordy, Motown became one of the most prominent black-owned corporations in the world. Gordy dictated artists' behavior on-and off-stage, including clothes, hair and choice of companions. Gordy was also reluctant to share financial information with the artists who were bringing in the revenue, and the label lost many artists in later years. Gordy's mark on the label's music is unmistakable, however, and the Motown sound instantly recognizable.

Mott, John (Raleigh) (1865–1955). American humanitarian and religious leader. Born in Livingston Manor, New York, he became an active member of the YMCA while an undergraduate at Cornell University, serving as national secretary of the organization's Intercollegiate Committee from 1888 to 1915. In 1888 he also became the director of the Student Volunteer Movement for Foreign Missions. In 1895 Mott founded the World's Student Christian Federation. As national executive of the American YMCA (1915) and general secretary of the National War Work Council (1916), he helped to raise some $200 million for WORLD WAR I relief efforts.

Mott became chairman of the International Missionary council in 1921 and president of the World YMCA in 1926. During WORLD WAR II he worked on numerous fund-raising campaigns to support the YMCA's many humanitarian programs. In 1946 he shared the NOBEL PRIZE for peace with Emily Greene BALCH. A leading Methodist layman and advocate of ecumenical efforts, he was named honorary president of the newly formed World Council of Churches in 1948.

For further reading:

Hopkins, C. Howard, *John R. Mott, Eighteen Sixty-Five to Nineteen Fifty Five: A Biography*. Grand Rapids, Mich.: William B. Eerdmans, n.d.

Mott, Sir Nevill Francis (1905–). British physicist; studied at Cambridge University, gaining his bachelor's degree in 1927 and master's in 1930. Mott never pursued a doctorate but from 1930 until 1933 was a lecturer and fellow of Granville and Caius College, Cambridge. Subsequently he moved to Bristol University as a professor of theoretical physics. In 1948 he became director of Bristol's physics laboratories but returned later to Cambridge as Cavendish Professor of Experimental Physics, where he served from 1954 until his retirement in 1971. Mott's work in the early 1930s was on the quantum theory of atomic collisions and scattering. With H.S.W. Massey he wrote the first of several classic texts, *The Theory of Atomic Collisions* (1934). Other influential texts that followed were *The Theory of the Properties of Metals and Alloys* (with H. Jones, 1936) and *Electronic Processes in Ionic Crystals* (with R.W. Gurney, 1940). Each marked a significant phase of active research. Mott also began to explore the defects and surface phenomena involved in the photographic process (explaining latent-image formation) and did significant work on dislocations, defects and the strength of crystals. By the mid-1950s, Mott was able to turn his attention to problems of disordered materials, liquid metals, impurity bands in semiconductors, and the glassy semiconductors. His models of the solid state became more and more complex and included an analysis of electronic processes in metal-insulator transitions, often called "Mott transitions." In 1977 Mott shared the NOBEL PRIZE for physics with Philip ANDERSON and John Van Vleck for their "fundamental theoretical investigations of the electronic structure of magnetic and disordered systems." Mott was knighted in 1962.

Moulin, Jean (1899–1943). Leader of the French RESISTANCE. A civil prefect in the French department of Eure-et-Loire when the Germans occupied France in 1940 during WORLD WAR II, Moulin was an active opponent of the Nazis, who imprisoned him. Released, he fled to London but returned to France and, from 1942 to early 1943, organized Resistance efforts, coordinated Resistance fighters in the north and south of France and united representatives of political movements, trade unions and political parties into a national Resistance council. Betrayed to the Germans, Moulin was captured on June 21, 1943 and, after nearly a month of torture by the GESTAPO, died on July 8, 1943.

Mountbatten, Lord Louis [Earl Mountbatten of Burma] (1900–1979). British naval officer, colonial administrator, member of the royal family; born Louis Francis Albert Nicholas Battenberg. As the last viceroy of INDIA, he guided that country's transition from Britain's largest colony to an independent nation and member of the COMMONWEALTH. A grandnephew of Queen Victoria, Mountbattan trained as a naval officer and served as a midshipman in WORLD WAR I. Early in WORLD WAR II he commanded a Royal Navy destroyer. He rose rapidly to become Allied Chief of Combined Operations in Southeast Asia, coordinating the Allied recapture of Burma from the Japanese. He also planned commando raids on German-held Europe before D-DAY. In 1947, as part of Britain's plan to grant India independence, Prime Minister ATTLEE appointed him viceroy. Mountbatten accomplished his task in five months, negotiating successfully with NEHRU and JINNAH despite many obstacles. Following independence, he was India's first governor-general. He later held the posts of commander in chief of NATO forces in the Mediterranean, first sea lord (head of the British navy) and chief of the British defense staff. In his later years he was an influential advisor to his grandnephew, Prince CHARLES. While vacationing in Ireland Mountbatten was killed by a bomb planted aboard his boat by IRA terrorists. After his death his cousin Queen ELIZABETH II changed the name of the royal family to Windsor-Mountbatten in his honor.

Lord Louis Mountbatten negotiated India's independence from Britain in 1947.

Moureu, Henri (1899–1978). French scientist and patriot. During WORLD WAR II Moureu foiled German plans to develop an ATOMIC BOMB by keeping the French supply of heavy water out of Nazi hands. He also foiled a German plan to destroy Paris with V-2 rockets. This he did by calculating the location of the German V-2 launching bases and passing this information to the U.S. Air Force, which destroyed them. Moureu was a member of the French Academy of Sciences.

Movement, The. Term coined to describe a group of British poets that coalesced during the 1950s, at about the same time as the rise of the ANGRY YOUNG MEN. The Movement first attracted attention with the publication of the anthology *New Lines* (1956), edited by poet, critic and Soviet expert Robert Conquest. Among the poets in this anthology were Philip LARKIN, Kingsley AMIS, Donald DAVIE and Thom Gunn. Reacting against the highly metaphysical and apocalyptic writing that characterized the work of Dylan THOMAS and other British poets during WORLD WAR II, the Movement poets addressed everyday British life in a plain, straightforward language and often in traditional forms. The Movement is widely considered to be the most significance influence in British writing after the war; some of the Movement poets continued to publish new work into the 1990s. However, the Movement has been criticized for what is perceived as its narrow, provincial outlook, especially in contrast to more ambitious work pursued by writers in Europe, North America and Latin America.

Moynihan, Daniel Patrick (1927–). American politician. Moynihan gained prominence as a member of Governor Averell HARRIMAN's staff in the 1950s. He served as assistant secretary of labor (1963–65) in the KENNEDY and JOHNSON administrations. During the 1970s he was ambassador to India and to the UN. As urban affairs adviser to President NIXON he caused a furor by proposing a policy of "benign neglect" toward welfare recipients. Elected to the U.S. Senate as a New York Democrat in 1978, he has supported a strong defense, criticized President REAGAN's Latin American policies and taken a liberal approach to domestic issues.

Mozambique [formerly: Portuguese East Africa]. East coastal African nation south of Tanzania, bordering Zimbabwe, Malawi, and Zambia to the west, South Africa to the south. Until recent times, the Portuguese dominated Mozambique for nearly 400 years, during which it had been used as a dumping ground for convicts, when Portugal's power waned in the 18th century, and later for slave trading, owing to heavy labor demands from Brazil in the late 18th and early 19th centuries. Actual control of the colony was wrested from Portugal for the most part, by renegade settler and native rebellions during the 19th century; the interior of Mozambique was not to be fully regained until 1920. The economy of the colony was successfully developed, by Portugal's utter exploitation of Mozambique's native population. Its capital, the town of Mozambique, was replaced in 1907 by Lourenco Marques, renamed Maputo in 1976.

After the outbreak of guerrilla warfare in ANGOLA in 1961, PORTUGAL begrudged the colony token reforms, but not until 1964 did the Mozambique National Liberation Front, FRELIMO, openly declare war against the colonial government, which mired Portugal in a rapidly escalating, costly war. In 1974 the government in Lisbon was overthrown, and the new regime moved quickly to negotiate with the rebels. In 1975 Mozambique became an independent nation, with Samora MACHEL, Fremlino's former leader, as the new socialist head of state. War was declared with RHODESIA, where border clashes were frequent in 1976, and ZIMBABWE guerillas operated out of Mozambique until 1979, when Rhodesia gained independence and emerged as the nation of Zimbabwe. It is estimated that 600,000 people died in the war. President Machel died in a suspicious plane crash (Oct.

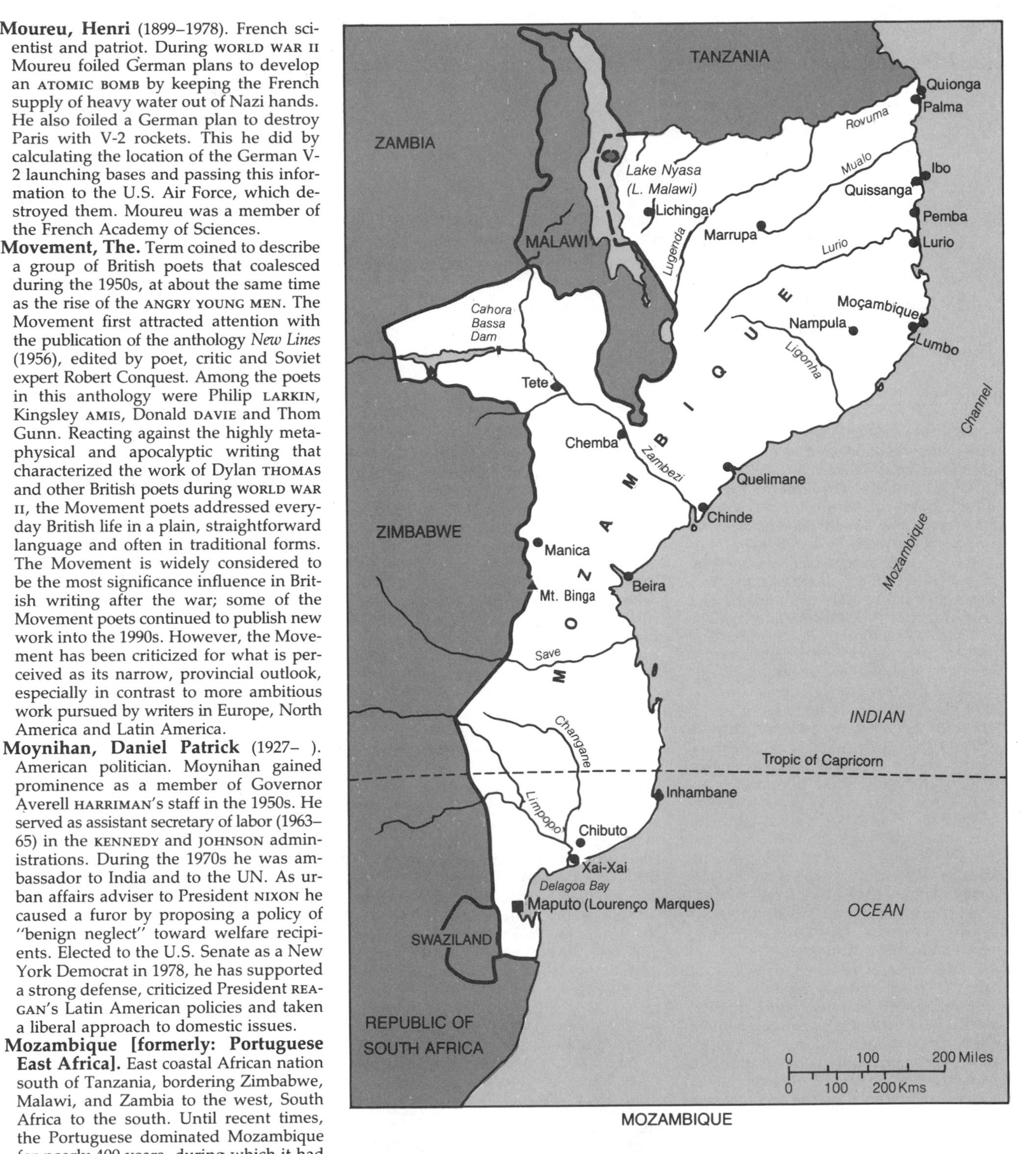

MOZAMBIQUE

MOZAMBIQUE

1951	Mozambique becomes a province of Portugal.
1964	Armed struggle against Portuguese commences.
1975	(June 25) Mozambique gains independence from Portugal; Samora Machel becomes ruler.
1976	Mozambique closes its border to Rhodesia in support of that country's guerrilla movement; the Rhodesian intelligence service forms and fosters the Mozambique National Resistance, which institutes terror campaign.
1986	(Oct. 19) Machel dies in mysterious plane crash and is succeeded by his foreign minister, Joaquim Chissano.
1989	(March) Joint UNICEF/Mozambican report estimates that 600,000 have been killed in the civil war and 494,000 have died of malnutrition.
1990	(Nov. 30) Mozambique legislature adopts new constitution designed to establish a Western-style democracy.

1986) and was succeeded by foreign minister Joaquim CHISSANO.

MPLA [People's Movement for the Liberation of Angola]. A socialist movement that fought alongside UNITA and FNLA between 1961 and 1975 to secure Angolan independence from Portugese rule (see ANGOLAN WAR OF INDEPENDENCE). After independence (November 10, 1975) it fought a civil war with UNITA and the FNLA for control of the country; it was aided by CUBA. Its People's Republic was eventually recognized as the true government of ANGOLA. (See also ANGOLAN CIVIL WAR.)

Mravinsky, Yevgeny Alexandrovich (1903–1988). Soviet conductor renowned for his interpretations of the Russian classics, particularly the symphonies of Tchaikovsky. Mravinsky led the Leningrad Philharmonic from 1938 until his death and was credited with transforming it into one of the world's great orchestras. Outside the U.S.S.R., he was known largely through his many recordings. He led the first performances of Dmitri SHOSTAKOVICH's fifth, sixth, eighth, ninth and tenth symphonies.

Mubarak, Hosni (1928–). President of EGYPT (1981–). Mubarak began his career in the Egyptian air force, rising through the ranks to become a squadron and then fighter brigade commander. After Egypt's defeat by ISRAEL in the SIX-DAY WAR (1967), Mubarak was appointed director of the Egyptian Air Academy. President NASSER appointed him air force chief of staff in 1969; in 1972 he was made commander-in-chief of the air force by President Anwar el-SADAT. In October 1973, during the ARAB-ISRAELI WAR OF 1973, he was promoted to lieutenant general; in 1975 Mubarak was appointed vice president of Egypt. He headed Egyptian delegations to the ORGANIZATION OF AFRICAN UNITY conferences in 1975 and 1976 and in 1981 was elected vice chairman and then secretary-general of Egypt's ruling National Democratic Party. In October 1981, following the assassination of Sadat, Mubarak was elected president of Egypt in a national referendum. Although lacking the charisma of his predecessors, Mubarak has proved a capable leader. Faced with serious economic and political problems at home and in the region, he has generally continued Sadat's pro-Western policies and is the leading Arab moderate in seeking peaceful coexistence rather than confrontation with Israel. Mubarak supported the U.S. coalition against IRAQ during the PERSIAN GULF WAR.

muckrakers. Name applied to American social and political critics writing during the first decade of the 20th century. The writers, most of whom wrote for mass circulation magazines such as *Colliers, McClure's* and *Everybody's,* attempted to expose political and business corruption as well as problems such as child labor and prostitution. The term was derived from a 1906 speech by Theodore ROOSEVELT in which he criticized the writers for an interest in turning up only filth. Among the most famous muckrakers were Lincoln STEFFENS, Ida TARBELL and Upton SINCLAIR. The muckrakers prepared the way for many of the social and political reforms of the Progressive period including child labor and pure food legislation, greater regulation of business and direct election of senators. The public lost interest in the writers after 1912, but their influence was long-lasting.

Hosni Mubarak, president of Egypt.

Zimbabwe Prime Minister Robert Mugabe calls for sanctions against South Africa in Dhaka, Bangladesh (Oct. 15, 1989).

Muddy Waters (1915–1983). American musician. The acknowledged king of the Chicago BLUES style of music, he was credited with having led the first electric blues-rock band using few players and maximum amplification. He began singing and playing guitar in the Mississippi Delta around 1930, and continued performing into the 1960s. He exerted a significant influence on modern popular musicians, including the ROLLING STONES.

Mugabe, Robert (1924–). African rebel leader, prime minister of ZIMBABWE (1980–). A member of the Shona tribe, Mugabe was educated at the University of South Africa and the University of London. He began his professional career as a teacher in the 1950s and his political career as a member of a group that opposed Rhodesia's white rule and favored independence. Detained by Rhodesian authorities in 1962, he fled to Tanzania and was a cofounder (1963) of the Zimbabwe African National Union (ZANU). Imprisoned by the Ian SMITH government from 1964 to 1974, he joined with Joshua NKOMO in 1976 and became joint leader of the Patriotic Front (PF).

Mugabe became ZANU's sole leader in 1975, and, as head of the Zimbabwe African National Liberation Army, he led a guerrilla war (1976–79) against the Rhodesian regime and the government of Abel Muzorewa. After the cease-fire, Mugabe and the ZANU-PF were victorious in the new nation's elections; and he became Zimbabwe's first prime minister. In 1987 a merger was negotiated between his ZANU-PF and Nkomo's opposition party, ZAPU. That same year, Mugabe engineered the passage of a new constitution under which he was appointed executive president and head of state.

Muggeridge, Malcolm (1903–1990). British journalist, author, social critic and television personality. Muggeridge was known for his caustic wit and iconoclastic views that frequently offended both the right and the left. Initially an admirer of Soviet COMMUNISM, he changed his mind after spending time there in the early 1930s as a journalist for the *Manchester Guardian*. He subsequently became a committed Christian. During WORLD WAR II, Muggeridge worked for British intelligence in Africa. From 1953 to 1957 he served as editor-in-chief of *Punch* and was credited with helping to sharpen the magazine's humor. After leaving *Punch* he turned to television journalism and book reviewing. His 1957 article, "Does England Really Need a Queen?" provoked a national controversy in Britain; he also ruffled feathers with his outspoken opinions on U.S. Presidents EISENHOWER and KENNEDY. In the 1960s Muggeridge became a leading voice of traditional CONSERVATISM and denounced the COUNTERCULTURE. His book *Jesus Reconsidered* (1969) described his spiritual journey. His other books include *Something Beautiful for God: Mother Teresa of Calcutta, Confessions of a Twentieth-Century Pilgrim* and *Chronicles of Wasted Time: An Autobiography*.

Muhammad, Elijah [born Elijah Poole] (1897–1975). American Black Muslim leader. Son of a Baptist minister, in 1923 he moved with his family to Detroit to find work. He experienced unemployment and welfare, and developed a bitter hostility to public assistance. In 1931, Wali Farad, the founder of Nation of Islam, renamed Poole as Muhammad. He was named Messenger of Allah in 1934 at Farad's disappearance. The Muslim faith grew under Muhammad's leadership and, after his death, continues to grow under the leadership of his son, Wallace.

Muir, Edwin (1887–1959). Scottish poet, essayist, novelist and translator. Muir is regarded by such critics as T.S. ELIOT as one of the finest English-language poets of the 20th century. Born on Orkney Island off the north coast of Scotland, Muir never received a university education, working instead at a series of dreary factory jobs through his 20s. By dint of self-education and his passion to write, he succeeded in establishing himself as an author of eminence. His most notable volumes of poetry are *Journeys and Places* (1937), *The Narrow Place* (1943), *One Foot in Eden* (1956) and the posthumous *Collected Poems* (1960). Muir's poignant *Autobiography* (1954) remains a classic of that genre. As a literary critic, he produced the influential *Structure of the Novel* (1928) and was invited to give the Charles Eliot Norton Lectures at Harvard University (1955–56), which were subsequently published as *The Estate of Poetry* (1962). Muir's best novel is *The Marionette* (1927). He and his wife Willa Muir were the first to translate the works of Franz KAFKA into English.

Elijah Muhammad, leader of the Nation of Islam, at the organization's annual convention in Chicago (Feb. 26, 1962).

Muir, John (1838–1914). American naturalist and conservationist. Born in Dunbar, Scotland, he immigrated to the U.S. in 1849, studied at the University of Wisconsin and moved to California in 1868. Devoted to the American wilderness, he traveled throughout the U.S., spending years studying the flora and geology of the Yosemite Valley and Alaska, where he discovered the Muir glacier. He also traveled extensively in Australia, India and Russia. Muir's love and respect for America's wild places helped to convince President Theodore ROOSEVELT to preserve wilderness areas in an extended national park system. Roosevelt also established (1908) the Muir Woods National Monument in California to honor the naturalist's achievements. Among Muir's books are *The Mountains of California* (1894), *Steep Trails* (1918) and the posthumously-published journals of *John of the Mountains* (1938).

Mujica Lainez, Manuel (1910–1984). Argentine novelist. Mujica was a leading figure in the Latin American school of MAGIC REALISM. His historical and fantastic novels were based on South American myths. Mujica Lainez's *Bomarzo*, banned by the Argentine government, made him known internationally and became a worldwide sensation as an opera with music by Alberto GINASTERA. He won Argentina's national prize for his 1957 novel *Invitados en el Paraiso*.

Mukden [*Chinese:* Shen-Yang]. Capital of China's province of Liao-ning, northeast on the Hun River, controlling north-south routes along the plain of south Manchuria. During the Russo-Japanese struggle for control of MANCHURIA it became a stronghold, first conquered by the Russians and then taken by the Japanese between Feb. 19 and March 10, 1905 after the battle of Mukden. In 1924 the warlord Chan Tso-Lin made it his headquarters during the CHINESE CIVIL WAR; he was assassinated there in 1928. On Sept. 18, 1931 a railroad was blown up, the so-called Mukden or Manchurian Incident, used by Japan to justify the invasion of Manchuria and the setting up of its puppet regime, MANCHUKUO. Under Japanese occupation from that time until 1945, Mukden was returned to Nationalist Chinese authority only to become a major battle site during the CHINESE CIVIL WAR OF 1945–49. In 1947–48, after ten months of heavy fighting and severe casualties, where thousands starved and the Nationalist force was annihilated, Mukden fell to communist forces on Nov. 1, 1948. It continued as a base for further conquest.

Mulder, Cornelius Petrus "Connie" (1925–1988). South African politician. Mulder almost defeated P.W. BOTHA for the prime ministership of SOUTH AFRICA in 1978. Shortly thereafter, his career in the ruling National Party was ruined by the exposure of his involvement in a secret influence-buying campaign. This scandal, known as "**Muldergate**," forced his resignation as minister of information. Later, he was forced to resign as leader of the National Party, and, finally as a member of the parliament. Mulder reentered politics in May 1987, when he was returned to Parliament as a candidate of the extreme right-wing Conservative Party.

Muller, Hermann Joseph (1890–1967). American geneticist. Muller is considered by some the most influential geneticist of the 20th century. Born in New York City, he earned his Ph.D. from Columbia University in 1916. He began to study mutations at a number of institutions, including the Rice Institute in Houston, Texas, the Berlin Institute for Brain Research, and the Moscow Institute of Genetics, before becoming in 1945 a professor of zoology at Indiana University, where he worked for the rest of his career. Among Muller's important contributions to genetics was his discovery in 1926 that X RAYS are capable of causing genetic mutations, which furthered research by allowing investigators to create mutations in the laboratory. Muller was awarded the 1946 NOBEL PRIZE for physiology or medicine.

Mullin, Willard (1902–1978). American sports cartoonist. Mullin's distinctive pen-and-ink drawings appeared in the *New York World-Telegram* (1934–66), *Life, Look,* the *Saturday Evening Post*, and many other publications. His best-known creation was probably the character "the Brooklyn Bum," who symbolized the Brooklyn Dodgers baseball team and their fans. In 1971 the National Cartoonists Society voted Mullin "The Sports Cartoonist of the Century."

Mulroney, (Martin) Brian (1939–). Prime Minister of CANADA (1984–). Born in Quebec, Mulroney received his law degree from Laval University in 1963. He became active in the PROGRESSIVE CONSERVATIVE PARTY while in college, after which he became a labor lawyer. He received national attention when he assumed presidency of the troubled Iron Ore Company in 1976, settled its labor disputes and turned a profit. He left the company in 1983 when he became leader of the Progressive Conservative Party. His party won the elections (1984) and he became prime minister. Mulroney had never held an elected office before and was the first leader of Canada to come

Brian Mulroney.

from Quebec in 90 years. In 1988 Mulroney signed a trade agreement with President REAGAN that aimed to reduce trade barriers between the U.S. and CANADA; the Liberal Party opposed it. In the elections later that year, the Progressive Conservatives maintained a majority, and Mulroney remained prime minister. In 1989 he proposed a budget targeting reduction in Canada's deficit by half by the year 1994.

Mumford, Lewis (1895–1990). American cultural critic, urban planner, historian, political commentator and self-described social philosopher. Born in New York City, Mumford attended City College (but did not graduate) and later took graduate classes at Columbia University and the New School for Social Research. In his writings and lectures, Mumford examined almost every facet of modern life, including architecture, science, technology, literature and city planning. Humanistic and antitechnocratic in his outlook, Mumford was an outspoken critic of architectural congestion and its dehumanizing influence. He published his first book, *The Story of Utopias,* in 1922 while also contributing to various journals. His writing led to his teaching an innovative course on American architecture at the New School. In 1923 Mumford helped found the Regional Planning Association of America. Beginning in the 1930s, he wrote a column, Sky Line, for The NEW YORKER, reviewing architecture and discussing the urban landscape of New York and other cities. Mumford is perhaps best known for the "Renewal of Life" series, which consists of *Technics and Civilization* (1933), *The Culture of Cities* (1938), *The Condition of Man* (1944) and *The Conduct of Life* (1951). These works follow the history of cities from the 10th century and set forth Mumford's ideas on the betterment of city life. Other important works include *The City in History* (1961), *Technics and Human Development*(1967) and *The Pentagon of Power* (1971). In 1986 Mumford was awarded the National Medal of Arts.

Munch, Charles (1891–1968). The most important French conductor of his generation, except only Pierre MONTEUX. Although he was born in Strasbourg, most of his early training and performing (as a violinist) was in Germany, where he was concertmaster of the Leipzig Gewandhaus Orchestra under Wilhelm FURTWANGLER. After refusing to become a German national, he moved to Paris and began to conduct the Straram Orchestra in 1932. Other positions followed—principal conductor with the Paris Philharmonic Orchestra and conductor of the Paris Conservatoire Orchestra. During WORLD WAR II he declined the directorship of the Paris Opera, refusing to collaborate with the Nazis. He was awarded the Legion of Honor after the war for his efforts on behalf of the French RESISTANCE. In 1948 he succeeded Serge KOUSSEVITZKY as conductor of the Boston Symphony Orchestra, remaining for the next 14 years. Not as temperamental as Koussevitzky or as authoritarian as George SZELL, Munch was most noted for his performances of the French repertoire—the ballets of RAVEL, POULENC and HONEGGER—and for his characteristic gentle humility and temperament. He conducted without a baton and usually from memory. "I came to conducting rather late," he said with whimsical candor in his book, *I Am a Conductor* (1954), "only because I am too stupid to do anything else."

For further reading:

Schonberg, Harold C., *The Great Conductors.* New York: Simon and Schuster, 1967.

Munch, Edvard (1863–1944). Norwegian painter; one of the most striking and influential painters of this century. Munch stands alongside Paul Cezanne, Vincent Van Gogh and James Ensor as one of the key founders of the artistic school of EXPRESSIONISM. He held that painting should go beyond the depiction of nature and render visible the intense states of the soul, thereby illuminating the nature of human existence. Munch's most famous painting, *The Cry* (1893), illustrates the expressionist method by its utilization of line and color to underscore the fear and terror experienced by an isolated, screaming woman on a bridge over swirling water. Munch produced large numbers of portraits and landscapes and was also a gifted woodcut artist.

Muni, Paul [Muni Weisenfreund] (1896–1967). Austrian-born character actor who was a major HOLLYWOOD star in the 1930s. Muni came to America with his family and first appeared in Yiddish theater in New York City. He debuted on Broadway in 1926 and soon moved into film, where he was quickly nominated for an ACADEMY AWARD as best actor for his performance in *The Valiant* (1929). His film career was established with *Scarface* (1931), in which he played a gangster resembling Al CAPONE. Muni subsequently gave notable performances in *The Story of Louis Pasteur* (1936), for which he won an ACADEMY AWARD for best actor; *The Life of Emile Zola;* and *Juarez* (1939). He played a Chinese in the 1937 film adaptation of Pearl BUCK's *The Good Earth* and starred in the classic *I Am a Fugitive from a Chain Gang* (1933). After the 1930s he acted mainly on Broadway and made few films; his final film appearance was in *The Last Angry Man* (1959).

Munich [*German:* Munchen] (West Germany). Capital of Bavaria, on the Isar River. The history of this industrial city is indelibly linked with that of Hitler's National Socialist Party, from 1919 until the end of WORLD WAR II. Nov. 8–9, 1923 was the date of the notorious BEER HALL PUTSCH, during which Hitler tried, unsuccessfully, to wrest control of the Bavarian government following a mass meeting in a beer hall. In Sept. 1938 Hitler signed the MUNICH PACT with France and Great Britain, which allowed him to annex the SUDETENLAND of CZECHOSLOVAKIA, an event that led directly to the outbreak of WORLD WAR II. Sustained Allied bombings largely destroyed Munich near the end of the war, but it since has been considerably rebuilt. Historic buildings may still be seen today.

Munich Olympics massacre. On September 5, 1972, during the 1972 summer OLYMPIC GAMES in Munich, Germany, Palestinian guerrillas of the BLACK SEPTEMBER organization attacked and occupied the Israeli athlete quarters. They killed two Israelis and took nine others hostage. German security forces subsequently attempted to rescue the hostages as they were being taken out of the country at Munich's airport. During the attempt, the remaining nine Israelis were killed, as were two Germans and five Palestinians.

Munich Pact. Agreement reached at the Munich Conference of September 29–30, 1938 by the heads of state of Germany (HITLER), Great Britain (CHAMBERLAIN), France (DALADIER) and Italy (MUSSOLINI). The agreement acceded to Hitler's demands by providing for Germany's occupation of the SUDETENLAND, a strategically important German-speaking region of Czechoslovakia. It also stipulated that plebiscites were to be held, which would have given residents a voice in the change, but the votes never took place. No Czech representative was present at the conference. Coming at a time of increased aggressive activity by Germany, the agreement was hailed by Chamberlain as a step toward peace in our time, and was simultaneously condemned by Winston CHURCHILL. The Munich Pact did not serve to halt, or even to slow Germany's march on Europe, and it is widely considered a blatant act of prewar APPEASEMENT—one that pushed Europe even closer to the brink of WORLD WAR II.

Munoz Marin, Luis (1898–1980). Governor of PUERTO RICO (1948–64). An early believer in Puerto Rican independence, Munoz later advocated economic association with the U.S. He helped found the Popular Democratic Party in 1938. As Puerto Rico's first elected governor, he implemented **Operation Bootstrap**. This program brought roads and schools to backward rural areas and helped diversify the island's economy.

The heads of state of Britain, Germany, Italy, and France signed the Munich Pact, allowing Germany to occupy the Sudetenland in Czechoslovakia (Sept. 30, 1938).

Munsey, Frank Andrew (1854–1925). U.S. magazine and newspaper publisher. *Munsey's Magazine* (1889) was the nation's first illustrated general-circulation magazine. He also pioneered the publication of mass-market, all-fiction magazines, printed on rough, wood-pulp paper and aimed at the general reading public; his editorial innovations and development of new writers and genres, like science fiction, drove the circulation of his magazines, like *Argosy* and *All-Story*, to unheard-of figures, creating a media form that splashily dominated U.S. newsstands for the first half of the 20th century. He eventually acquired a host of large-circulation newspapers in major U.S. cities. His practice of buying out competing newspapers made him a pioneer in newspaper consolidation.

Munson, Thurman (1947–1979). American baseball player. A star catcher, he was captain of the New York Yankees. He was the only Yankee ever to be named both American League rookie of the year (1970) and most valuable player (1976). An amateur pilot, he died when the private jet he was flying crashed near Canton, Ohio.

Muppets. See Jim HENSON.

Murder, Inc. Popular name for a group of professional killers who worked on assignment for organized crime during the 1930s. It originated as a gang in Brooklyn, N.Y., and came to be controlled by the labor racketeer Louis (Lepke) Buchalter, who expanded the organization's activities to cover the entire nation. Known to organized crime as the Troop, the group was also led by mobster Albert Anastasia. During its 10 years of operation, Murder, Inc., was responsible for somewhere between 100 and 500 killings of underworld figures—the most prominent of whom was probably "Dutch" SCHULTZ. Its activities were brought to light and ended in the early 1940s by the investigations of special prosecutor Thomas E. DEWEY, and many of the group were either convicted or killed. Later mob hits, which have continued to this day, have been executed on a less organized basis.

Murdoch, Iris [Alice Irene Murdoch] (1922–). British author, widely regarded as one of the most important English-language novelists of the 20th century. Born to an Anglo-Irish family in Dublin, she studied philosophy at Sommerville College, Oxford. After World War II she worked briefly for the UNITED NATIONS Relief Agency (UNRA). She later became a lecturer in philosphy at St. Anne's College, Oxford, and has published a study of Jean-Paul SARTRE and several works of philosophy. In the early 1950s she began writing fiction that explored such philosophical issues as good and evil, randomness and choice, and freedom and responsibility. Her plots are simultaneously gothic and witty; they usually involve a cast of eccentric characters in complex relationships. In Murdoch's world, love is both a disruptive and a healing force that has unforeseen dramatic consequences. Although Murdoch professes to be an agnostic, her more than 25 novels often reflect consciously religious concerns. Among her books are *Under the Net* (1954), *The Bell* (1958), *The Unicorn* (1963), *The Black Prince* (1973), *The Good Apprentice* (1984) and *The Message to the Planet* (1990).

For further reading:

Fletcher, *Iris Murdoch.* New York: Garland, 1990.

Bove, Cheryl B., *A Character Index and Guide to the Fiction of Iris Murdoch.* New York: Garland, 1990.

Murdoch, (Keith) Rupert (1931–). Australian-American communications magnate. Educated at Oxford, Murdoch began his career in Adelaide, Australia in 1953 when he inherited two modest-sized newspapers from his father. Returning to England in 1968, he started his British newspaper empire with the acquisition of *The News of the Week* (1968). His newspaper holdings grew to include London's three largest dailies, and he became famous for his shrill and often sleazy tabloids. In 1976 he began building his American holdings with the acquisition of *New York* magazine and the *New York Post* (later sold). He became a U.S. citizen in 1985. By the 1990s Murdoch controlled the world's first global media business encompassing television, publishing and entertainment. In Australia, he owned an airline, nine magazines and more than 100 newspapers; in Great Britain, five national newspapers, eight magazines and Sky T.V. (a four-channel satellite system); in the U.S., he had 10 magazines, seven television stations, two magazines, a book publishing house (HarperCollins, formerly Harper & Row) and the Fox television and motion picture conglomerate. Immensely successful yet beset by debt, Murdoch turned increasingly to innovations in electronic journalism.

Murmansk. Soviet city on the Barents Sea shore of the Kola Peninsula, capital of Murmansk oblast. Formerly a village prior to World War I and warmed by the Gulf Stream, an ice-free port was built in 1915–16, along with an inland railroad from Petrograd, now LENINGRAD, when the supply routes of the Russian Black and Baltic Seas were cut off by the CENTRAL POWERS. During the RUSSIAN CIVIL WAR from 1918 to 1920, occupying Allied forces used the Murmansk area as a base in their advance against the BOLSHEVIKS. It was bombed by Germany during WORLD WAR II, as a major supply base and port for Anglo-American convoys. Murmansk remains the largest city to date north of the Arctic Circle.

Murphy, Audie (1924–1971). American WORLD WAR II hero and movie actor. Attacked with his unit near Colmar, France, on January 26, 1945, Murphy used the machine gun on a burning tank destroyer to hold off six tanks and 250 enemy troops, killing about 50. Awarded more decorations during World War II than any other individual, including the Medal of Honor, Murphy later turned to acting and appeared in such films as *To Hell and Back* (1955). He made about 40 films, but by 1960 his popularity had faded. Turning to business he was unsuccessful and declared bankruptcy. He was killed in a light plane crash.

For further reading:

Graham, Don, *No Name on the Bullet: A Biography of Audie Murphy.* New York: Viking Penguin, 1989.

Murphy, Frank (1890–1949). American politician, associate justice of the U.S. Supreme Court (1940–49). A graduate of the University of Michigan and its Law School, Murphy served in WORLD WAR I. After additional legal studies in London and Dublin he returned to Michigan, where he served as an assistant attorney general and also worked in private practice before becoming a local judge. He had a long government career, serving successively as mayor of Detroit, governor general of the Philippines and governor of Michigan. A NEW DEAL Democrat, Murphy refused to use the state police against sit-down strikers, which reputedly cost him reelection as governor. Murphy was appointed attorney general and served in the post for one eventful year during which the Justice Department prosecuted Tom PENDERGAST, the Democratic political boss of Kansas City and a close associate of Harry TRUMAN. In 1939, President Franklin D. ROOSEVELT appointed Murphy to the Supreme Court. Although Murphy was reputedly less than enthused about his appointment, he became a strong liberal voice and champion of individual liberties. He died unexpectedly in 1949 while still on the Court.

For further reading:

Fine, Sidney, *Frank Murphy*, 3 vols. Ann Arbor: University of Michigan Press, 1975, 1979, 1984.

Murray, Sir (John) Hubert (1861–1940). Australian colonial administrator. Born in Sydney, the brother of Gilbert Murray, he was educated there and at Oxford University. He served in the BOER WAR and later practiced law in Australia. Appointed a colonial officer in Papua New Guinea in 1907, he became known for his humane treatment of the Papuans; the following year he was named the territory's lieutenant governor, a post he held until his death. His administration allowed economic development of the area without the enormous toll on its native population that was taken in many other colonial enterprises. Murray was knighted in 1925.

Murray, Les(lie Allan) (1938–). Widely considered the foremost Australian poet of his generation and one of the leading English-language poets of his time. Raised on a farm in New South Wales, in his mid-30s Murray began devoting himself solely to his writing. His interests are exceptionally wide-ranging, and his catholic tastes and knowledge are reflected in poems that are both intimate and all-encompassing. His books include *Poems Against Economics* (1972), *The Vernacular Republic* (1976) and *Dog Fox Field* (1990).

Murray, Phillip (1886–1952). American labor leader. A Scot by birth, Murray was a coal miner who rose to the presidency of the United Mine Worker's Union (UMW). The position was a powerful one because at the time coal was a vitally important fuel in the U.S. As head of the umbrella labor organization, the Congress of Industrial Organizations (CIO), he successfully led the drive to organize the steelworkers and later became president of the steelworker's union—the United Steelworkers of America.

Murrow, Edward R. (1908–1965). American radio and television newsman, war correspondent, and federal administrator. In the words of historian Daniel J. Leab, Murrow's verbal abilities "were coupled with a superb and dramatic sense of delivery as well as with a breadth and

American television news journalist Edward R. Murrow created his own style of investigative news reporting.

humanity of thought." He was born in Greensboro, North Carolina, traveled extensively as a young man in academic-related activities for the National Student Federation, and joined CBS in 1935. Soon after his assignment to Europe, war broke out. He was everywhere—flying combat missions, reporting from the concentration camps, and transmitting from the rooftops during the London Blitz: "It's a bomber's moon tonight. . ." After the war with partner Fred Friendly he developed the television investigative news program, SEE IT NOW. He was not afraid of controversy, and in a landmark "See It Now" broadcast he attacked the red-baiting tactics of Senator Joseph MCCARTHY in 1954: "We must not confuse dissent with disloyalty," he declared at the end of the show, glowering into the camera through a trail of cigarette smoke; "this is no time for men who oppose Senator McCarthy's methods to be silent." Although there were other television shows after the demise of "See It Now"—PERSON TO PERSON, for example, a live series of interviews by two-way hookup between Murrow in the studio and celebrities in their own homes—Murrow grew increasingly disenchanted with CBS. He left in 1961 to serve as director of the U.S. Information Agency in the KENNEDY administration. After a prolonged battle with lung cancer, he died in April 1965. Ironically, just ten years before, June 7, 1955, the chain-smoking Murrow had narrated a two-part television series on the relationship between cigarettes and cancer.

For further reading:

Barnouw, Erik, *Tube of Plenty: The Evolution of American Television*. New York: Oxford University Press, 1975.

Murry, John Middleton (1889–1957). British author and critic. While still a student at Oxford, Murry began editing *Rhythm*, a modernist magazine (see MODERNISM). He was later to serve as editor for *The Athenaeum* (1919–21) and *The Adelphi* (1923–30). In his editorial capacity he was to gain an influence over British literary life, publishing the authors Katherine MANSFIELD (whom he married in 1918); D. H. LAWRENCE (with whom Murry and Mansfield would publish the short-lived magazine, *Signature*); Virginia WOOLF; T. S. ELIOT; and VALERY—among others. Murry was an outspoken critic of the GEORGIAN poets, and his critical works include *Dostoevski* (1916), *The Problem of Style* (1922) and *Son of Woman, the Story of D.H. Lawrence* (1931). Following Mansfield's death in 1923, Murry—who married three more times—edited her works and wrote her biography in 1932. He also wrote the autobiography *Between Two Worlds* (1935).

Musa Dagi [Musa Dagh] (Turkey) West of Antakya, rising from the Mediterranean Sea, this southern mountain peak became a battleground for the Armenians' heroic struggle against the Turks during WORLD WAR I; depicted by Franz WERFEL in his novel *The Forty Days of Musa Dagh*.

Museum of Broadcasting, The. A nonprofit, public-access repository of more than 25,000 American television and radio programs located in midtown New York City. Sensing a need for a broadcasting archive, William S. PALEY, founder and longtime chairman of CBS Inc., conceived and funded the Museum in 1976. As of the early 1990s it operates on a $2 million annual budget deriving mostly from corporations, foundations, individual philanthropists and the small contributions of people using the facilities. Three-thousand hours of additional TV programming are added each year. Dozens of private viewing/listening cubicles enable visitors to review a wide range of fare, including HALLMARK HALL OF FAME, the ARMY-MCCARTHY HEARINGS, the Nixon-Kennedy Debates and the work of pioneering figures in broadcasting, such as Edward R. MURROW, Ernie KOVACS, Orson WELLES, Leonard BERNSTEIN, Lucille BALL, Sid CAESAR and others. All materials at the museum have been transferred to video tape, and the originals are preserved in fireproof, climate-controlled vaults. Activities include mounting traveling exhibitions, beaming seminars by satellite to college campuses, taping seminars for the permanent collection, presenting programs at the Manhattan location and sponsoring festivals at the Television Academy of Arts and Sciences in Los Angeles. A worldwide search continues for many lost television programs and newscasts, particularly material from the TRUMAN administration—the first administration to use television broadcasts. "What we have to do is come to terms with television as a creative force," said the museum's president Robert Batscha. "It has been a rich part of our lives and needs to be shared with future generations."

For further reading:

Bennetts, Leslie, "Where Watching TV Is Like Watching History," *The New York Times*, December 22, 1985.

Museum of Modern Art. Museum located in New York City that houses one of the world's premier collections of modern paintings, sculpture and other works of art. It was founded in 1929 by a group of prominent collectors in the city and was directed by Alfred H. BARR Jr. until his retirement in 1967. At first housed in rented facilities, the collection moved to its present location in 1945. Its building, designed in 1939 by Philip Goodwin and Edward Durell STONE, was enlarged by a new wing designed by Philip JOHNSON (1962–63). The nucleus of the museum's impressive collection is the Lillie P. Bliss bequest of 1934, which included a number of important Cezannes as well as other significant modern works. The museum's present permanent collection includes works from all of the major movements in European and American art during the late 19th and 20th centuries. The museum includes departments of painting and sculpture, architecture, film, prints and drawings. It also maintains an extensive reference library, as well as educational programs, loan and circulating exhibitions and programs for film and video.

Musial, Stan(ley Frank) ["Stan the Man"] (1920–). American baseball player. A St. Louis Cardinal for 22 seasons, Musial was one of the few athletes beloved by fans in every city. A three-time Most Valuable Player, he also led the National League in batting average seven times. He batted over .300 16 times. When he retired, he held more than 25 major league records. Upon his retirement in 1964, he began working for the Cardinals in an administrative capacity and continued to do so for over 25 years. Musial was named to the Hall of Fame in 1969, and in 1972 became the first non-Pole to be awarded Poland's Merited Champions Medal.

Musil, Robert (1880–1942). Austrian novelist. Trained first for the military and then as an engineer, Musil later studied philosophy, psychology and mathematics, earning a Ph.D. from the University of Berlin in 1908. The success of his first novel, *Young Torless* (1906), caused him to reject an academic career and to devote himself to writing. In this short fictional work, as well as in his long, unfinished novel, *The Man Without Qualities* (3 volumes, 1930–42), Musil reveals profound psychological and philosophical concerns in a style of great analytic subtlety. He was also the author of short stories, plays, essays and literary criticism. When the Nazis entered Vienna in 1938, Musil and his Jewish wife fled to Switzerland, where he spent his last years in poverty and obscurity.

Muskie, Edmund Sixtus (1914–). U.S. politician. After practicing law, he was elected to the Maine House of Representatives (1947–51), and in 1955 became the first Democratic governor of Maine in two decades. He served in the U.S. Senate from 1959 to 1980. He also served briefly as secretary of state in 1980–81.

Mussolini, Benito (1883–1945). Italian political leader who established FASCISM in ITALY; as Il Duce ("the leader"), he was the supreme authority in Italy from 1922 to 1943. Born in Predappio in Emilia Romagna, Mussolini was originally a journalist and a socialist and was active in the left-wing Italian opposition movement around the turn of the century. He spent several years in exile in Switzerland. Returning to Italy, he became a well-known figure in left-wing journalistic circles, editing a leading journal and writing articles in favor of left-wing causes. At the outbreak of WORLD WAR I (1914) he professed pacifism but soon after abruptly changed his views and urged Italy's entry into the war on the side of the Allies. He was immediately expelled from the Socialist Party. However, his editorials and speeches helped sway Italy to enter the war on May 24, 1915. He fought in World War I and was wounded.

Italian fascist leader Benito Mussolini.

After the war, Mussolini continued to espouse Italian nationalism and patriotism. He built a base of support among the working class and lower-middle-class, and organized a paramilitary group, known as the BLACK SHIRTS. During a period of domestic violence between socialist and fascist groups, Mussolini made a bold bid for power. He led his Black Shirts in the MARCH ON ROME and demanded that King VICTOR EMMANUEL III appoint him prime minister in order to restore order (1922); to his surprise, the king agreed. Mussolini subsequently consolidated his authority and on Jan. 3, 1925, he proclaimed Italy a fascist state, with himself as dictator. His authority was confirmed by a plebiscite in March 1929.

Mussolini was driven by visions of himself as a new Caesar who would restore Italy's greatness. In numerous speeches and decrees, he called on Italians to devote themselves to his national goals; at the same time, he quietly eliminated all political opposition. He also desired an overseas empire. On his orders Italy invaded and conquered ETHIOPIA (1935–36), not without resistance from the poorly armed Ethiopians. Although initially suspicious of German Chancellor Adolf HITLER, Mussolini met with the Fuhrer and formed an alliance with him—the Rome-Berlin AXIS, a term coined by Mussolini. The following year Mussolini joined Hitler and the Japanese government in the Anti-Comintern Pact; shortly thereafter he formally withdrew Italy from the LEAGUE OF NATIONS. When Hitler threatened CZECHOSLOVAKIA in 1938, Mussolini played the statesman and arranged a conference among Germany, France and Britain—the conference at which Neville CHAMBERLAIN signed the MUNICH PACT.

Mussolini brought Italy into WORLD WAR II on the side of his German ally—a disastrous move for Mussolini and Italy. Despite his long insistence on military glory and discipline, the Italian forces were ill-prepared for the world war and lacked Germany's armaments, organization and fighting will. After conquering ALBANIA, Italy suffered embarrassing reversals in its invasion of GREECE and in the NORTH AFRICAN CAMPAIGN in Libya. In both cases, Mussolini relied on German aid to salvage the situation. Following the Allied invasion of Sicily, Mussolini's Grand Fascist Council deposed Il Duce (July 24, 1943) and arrested him. On Sept. 12, 1943, he was rescued by a German SS commando team acting on Hitler's orders. He subsequently declared a new fascist republic in northern Italy, but this was little more than a puppet government beholden to Nazi Germany. As the Allies drove northward, Mussolini attempted to flee in disguise but was captured by anti-fascist Italian partisans and executed (Apr. 27, 1945).

For further reading:

Lyttle, Richard B., *Il Duce: The Rise and Fall of Benito Mussolini.* New York: Macmillan, 1987.

Smith, Denis M., *Mussolini.* New York: Alfred A. Knopf, 1982.

Mustard, Dr. William Thornton (1914–1987). Canadian surgeon. A pioneer in pediatric surgery, he was best known for an operation called the Mustard Procedure. This procedure involved rerouting the blood flow in hearts of children born with major blood vessels on the wrong side. He retired as chief of vascular surgery at Toronto's Hospital for Sick Children in 1976.

Muthesius, Hermann (1861–1927). German design theorist, writer and spokesman for design causes of the early Modern movement. Muthesius studied philosophy before training as an architect at the Berlin technical college. He worked for several architects before becoming an official architect for the Prussian government in 1893. In 1896 he was sent to the German Embassy in London to study and report on English design developments of the time. In articles published in Germany, Muthesius reported on the ideas and work of William Morris and the Arts and Crafts movement and on Charles Rennie MACKINTOSH. Back in Germany (1904 to 1905), he published the three-volume *Das Englishe Haus,* which brought the concepts of British domestic architecture and design to a German readership. Muthesius was an important figure in the formation of the DEUTSCHER WERKBUND (1907) and continued to encourage design quality through various roles in that organization. He exerted significant influence not only on the development of design and taste in Germany by introducing MODERNISM to that country in the 1920s but also on the character of German work since World War II.

mutual assured destruction [MAD]. Theory and strategy used to maintain the balance of power between the U.S. and the U.S.S.R. during the COLD WAR. The MAD theory held, paradoxically, that the large number of nuclear weapons in each nation's arsenal would prevent these weapons from ever being used, because both nations would be destroyed in any nuclear war.

Muzorewa, Abel (1925–). Zimbabwean churchman and political leader. Bishop of the United Methodist Church in Southern Rhodesia in 1968, he was founder and president of the African National Council in 1971. Muzorewa mobilized African opinion against the proposed Rhodesia settlement of 1971–72. A member of the executive council of the transitional government in Zimbabwe-Rhodesia (1978–80), he was considered by the British government and Rhodesian whites to be more conciliatory than his rivals. However, he was heavily defeated by Robert MUGABE in the 1980 election. Muzorewa's autobiography is *Arise and Walk.*

Myanmar. See BURMA.

Myaskovsky, Nicholas Yakovlevich (1881–1950). Polish-born Russian composer and teacher. Myaskovsky studied under Gliere, Lyadov and Rimsky-Korsakov before serving on the front as a military engineer (1914–18). In 1921 he was appointed professor at Moscow Conservatory. A prolific symphony writer, he was considered to be the foremost teacher of composition in Russia. Myaskovsky's works include 27 symphonies, two cantatas, 13 string quartets, songs, orchestral works and piano pieces.

Myer, Dillon S. (1891–1982). American government administrator. As director of the **War Relocation Authority** (1942–46), Myer supervised the internment of more than 100,000 Japanese-Americans during WORLD WAR II. However, he advocated the abolition of the agency and the return of Japanese-Americans to their homes. He was later cited by the Japanese-American Citizens League as a champion of human rights and common decency. After the war he served as commissioner of Indian affairs and as head of the Federal Public Housing Authority.

My Lai massacre. Atrocity that took place on May 16, 1968, in the South Vietnamese hamlet of My Lai during the VIETNAM WAR. A U.S. platoon headed by **Lt. William L. Calley** invaded the town, a supposed VIET CONG stronghold, rounded up its civilian population and shot to death 347 unarmed men, women and children. The incident came to light in 1969 and was then investigated by the Army. Although 13 officers and enlisted men were eventually charged with war crimes, only Lt. Calley was found guilty. Convicted on March 29, 1971, he was sentenced to life imprisonment. The verdict caused a great deal of controversy, and the incident helped to fuel the ANTIWAR MOVEMENT. Calley's sentence was eventually reduced to 10 years, and he was paroled in March 1974.

Myrdal, Alva (1902–1986). Swedish diplomat. A co-winner of the 1982 NOBEL PRIZE for peace, she first became known in the 1930s as a feminist, educator and sociologist. Later in her career, she held two major posts at the UNITED NATIONS. She also served as Sweden's ambassador to India, was a member of the Swedish Parliament and a cabinet minister. Her husband, Gunnar Myrdal, was Nobel laureate in economics (1974).

Myrdal, (Karl) Gunnar (1898–1987). Swedish economist and social scientist. His seminal work *An American Dilemma: The Negro Problem and Modern Democracy* (1944) left a deep mark on the history of race relations in the U.S. He helped draft many social and economic programs in Sweden and was also a vigorous advocate of land reform in South Asia. As a UNITED NATIONS official he was an early promoter of East-West detente, and as an economist he criticized orthodox ways of thinking and pioneered new ones. He was cowinner of the NOBEL PRIZE for economics in 1974. His wife, Swedish diplomat Alva Myrdal, was co-winner of the 1982 NOBEL PRIZE for peace.

NAACP. See NATIONAL ASSOCIATION FOR THE ADVANCEMENT OF COLORED PEOPLE.

Nabokov, Vladimir Vladimirovich (1899–1977). Russian author. An important and original voice in fiction and literary criticism, Nabokov left Russia in 1919, studying at Cambridge, in Berlin and in Paris before settling in the U.S. in 1940. Nabokov was a lecturer at Wellesley College and a professor of Russian Literature at Cornell University. Nabokov is perhaps best known for the controversial novel *Lolita* (1958), which depicts a middle-aged man's sexual obsession with a young girl. His writing is characterized by linguistic resourcefulness and perceptive narrative. His later works were written in English, which he translated to his native Russian. His other fiction includes *Mary* (1926), *Pale Fire* (1962) and *Look at the Harlequins!* (1974). Nabokov also wrote volumes of short stories and literary criticism, such as *Lectures on Literature* (1980) and his memoirs *Speak, Memory* (1967).

For further reading:

Boyd, Brian, *Vladimir Nabokov: The Russian Years*. Princeton University Press, 1990.

Bruccoli, Matthew J., Ed., *Vladimir Nabokov: Selected Letters, 1940–1977*. New York: Harcourt, Brace, 1990.

Nadelman, Elie (1882–1946). Polish-American sculptor. Born in Warsaw, he studied art in his native city and in Paris, where he lived from 1904–14. His work was exhibited in the U.S. at the Armory Show in 1913, and he emigrated to the U.S. the following year. Working mainly in metal or wood, he employed a number of styles in portraying the human form as simplified and often symbolic. His best known work is probably the elegantly jaunty bronze *Man in the Open Air* (c. 1915, Museum of Modern Art, New York City).

Nader, Ralph (1934–). American consumer advocate. Born in Winsted, Connecticut, Nader attended Princeton University and Harvard Law School. His role as a consumer activist began with his book *Unsafe at Any Speed* (1965), a study of defective automobile design and its relationship to accidents. This book and Nader's testimony before Congress (1966) were instrumental in bringing about the passage of the National Traffic and Motor Vehicle Safety Act of 1966. Two years later, the young lawyer organized a group of college interns in Washington, dubbed Nader's Raiders, into an investigative team. This group formed the nucleus of the Center for Study of Responsive Law—the first of many Nader-affiliated organizations that studied consumer problems and advocated various reforms. Other Nader organizations include the Center for Auto Safety, the Public Interest Research Group, Public Citizen, Congress Watch and various groups specializing in litigation, health research and tax reform. Nader was an important figure in the passage of the Wholesome Meat Act (1967), and he has been an outspoken critic of nuclear power and the abuses of private industry and public institutions. A hero to many and a villain to some, Nader maintains a spartan lifestyle and a selfless devotion to social and political causes.

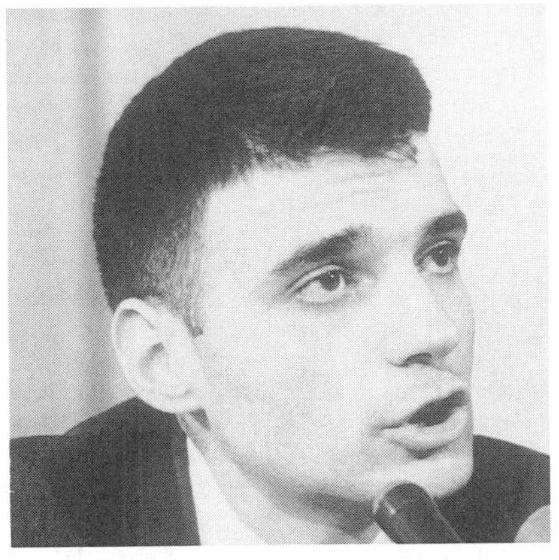

Consumer advocate Ralph Nader challenges the American auto industry before the Senate Government Operations Subcommittee (1966).

For further reading:

Peduzzi, Kelli, *Ralph Nader: Crusader for Safe Consumer Products and Lawyer for Public Interest*. Milwaukee, Wis.: Gareth Stevens Inc., 1990.

Nagaland. A state of northeastern INDIA, bordered by Burma to the east, Manipur to the south, and Assam to the north and west. A setting for missionary activity since 1840, British posts in Nagaland were raided by the Japanese during WORLD WAR II, who failed in their attempt to capture Kohima, its capital. Since the 1940s the spirited Naga people violently opposed Indian statehood, and in 1956–57 they fought viciously against government troops. In 1961 Nagaland was incorporated into India. Yet, the Nagas remain in favor of independence.

Nagano, Shigeo (1900–1984). Japanese industrialist and diplomat who helped shape JAPAN's post-WORLD WAR II foreign policy, domestic politics and economy. Nagano brought about the merger (1970) that made the Nippon Steel Corp. the world's largest steelmaker. Although a political conservative, he helped persuade Japanese businessmen to support the establishment of relations with CHINA and to cooperate with the U.S.S.R. on development projects in Siberia. He was president of the Japanese chamber of commerce from 1969 until his death.

Nagasaki. Port capital of Nagasaki prefecture, approximately 590 miles southwest of Tokyo. Nagasaki was the second Japanese city obliterated by the new ATOMIC BOMB, dropped by the U.S. on Aug. 9, 1945, near the end of WORLD WAR II.

Nagurski, Bronislau "Bronko" (1908–1990). American football player. Nagurski became a legendary running back and tackler with the University of Minnesota and the Chicago Bears in the 1920s and '30s. He helped lead the Bears to championships in 1932 and 1933, and by the time he retired, his name had become synonymous with gritty, dedicated play. In 1963 he was named a charter member of the Pro Football Hall of Fame.

The mushroom cloud from the second atomic bomb used in warfare floats over Nagasaki (Aug. 9, 1945).

Nagy, Imre (1896–1958). Hungarian political leader. Born in Kaposvar in southern HUNGARY, Nagy became a communist during WORLD WAR I. From 1930 to 1944 he lived in the U.S.S.R., where he became an agricultural specialist. Returning to Hungary in 1945, he was responsible for a number of major land reforms. Becoming premier in 1953, he moderated the harsh communist policies of his predecessors, placing greater emphasis on agriculture and less on heavy industry, eliminating forced collectivization and initiating a more liberal political climate. Nagy was removed from office in 1955 for his criticism of Soviet influence and his growing independence, and he was expelled from the Communist Party in 1956. He was reinstated (1956) as premier during the HUNGARIAN UPRISING as head of a coalition government. After Soviet forces quelled the rebellion, Nagy took refuge in the Yugoslav embassy. He later left under a false promise of safe conduct, was arrested and taken to Romania, where he was secretly tried for treason. In 1958, Janos KADAR announced that Nagy had been executed. Many Hungarians regard Nagy a national hero. In 1989 the Hungarian Socialist Workers (Communist) Party declared that Nagy's trial had been unlawful; on June 16, 1989, Nagy was reburied in a solemn nine-hour ceremony in Budapest, attended by an estimated 250,000 Hungarians.

Naipaul, Shiva (1945–1985). Author and journalist born in Trinidad. Like his older and better-known brother, V.S. NAIPAUL (also a writer), Shiva Naipaul made London his home base. He journeyed widely in the THIRD WORLD and wrote about it in a critical and often satirical manner. Among his half-dozen books were *North of South* (1978), dealing with Africa; and *Journey to Nowhere* (1980), an account of the mass suicide in JONESTOWN, GUYANA of the followers of Rev. Jim Jones.

Naipaul, V(idiadhar) S(urajprasad) (1932–). British novelist and essayist. Born in Trinidad, of Indian descent, Naipaul was educated at University College, Oxford, and settled in Great Britain in 1955. Naipaul's early fiction, most notably *A House for Mr. Biswas* (1961), takes place in Trinidad and depicts, in a sometimes comic, almost Dickensian fashion, the dissolution of a traditional way of life. His later works are darker and more political. They have been compared to the works of Joseph CONRAD because of their pessimistic portrayal of human nature and because of Naipaul's themes of exile and alienation. These include *In a Free State* (1971, Booker Prize), *A Bend in the River* (1979) and *Among the Believers* (1985). His fictional memoir, *The Enigma of Arrival* (1987), depicts the uneasy attempt of a West Indian to come to grips with English life. Naipaul has drawn considerable criticism from left-wing writers for his blunt criticisms of third-world social and political attitudes and for his disdain of fashionable left-wing ideologies. Naipaul's brother Shiva NAIPAUL was also a distinguished writer.

Nairobi. East African city and capital of Kenya. Only a waterhole in 1899, Nairobi began as a railroad depot on the Mombasa-Lake Victoria-Uganda line. In 1907 it was the seat of the British administration, and capital of Kenya Colony from 1920 to 1963, when it continued as capital of the independent state. In 1950 Nairobi was incorporated as a city, in which MAU MAU struggles for independence took place shortly thereafter. Today it is the commercial and cultural center of Kenya, with a population of more than 900,000.

Nakagusuku Bay [Buckner Bay]. Inlet in southeast OKINAWA Island, part of the Japanese Ryukyu islands of the Pacific Ocean. During the U.S. campaign against Okinawa in WORLD WAR II, a U.S. fleet stationed here suffered untold damage and heavy casualties from Japanese KAMIKAZE air attacks, from April to June 1945.

Nakasone, Yasuhiro (1918–). Prime minister of JAPAN (1982–87); by Japanese standards, an unusual politician because of his flair, eloquence and forcefulness in dealing with foreign leaders. In 1987 he picked Noboru TAKESHITA as his successor, and he continues to exert political influence as a leader of one faction with Japan's ruling Liberal Democratic Party.

Japanese Premier Yasuhiro Nakasone.

Namath, Joseph William "Joe Willie" (1943–). American football player. The most outstanding quarterback of the 1960s at both the college and professional level, the charismatic, green-eyed Namath was as well known for his taste in nightclubs as for his athletic ability. During his career at the University of Alabama, the Crimson Tide dominated college football, achieving a rare undefeated record in 1964. Signing with the New York Jets of the American Football League, he set into motion the process by which the NFL and the competing AFL would become one by giving the AFL the credibility it had lacked. Hobbled by serious knee injuries, Namath led the Jets to the AFL championship in 1969 and shocked the football world by "guaranteeing" a Jets win over the NFL champion Baltimore Colts. In a victory as memorable as Babe Ruth's called shot, the cool and confident Namath led the Jets to a stunning 16–7 victory over the Baltimore Colts and the forces of sports conservatism. He has gone on to a career as a commercial spokesman and sports commentator.

Namibia. Former German colony, mandated to SOUTH AFRICA by the LEAGUE OF NATIONS on December 17, 1920. In October 1966 the South West Africa People's Organization (SWAPO) launched a guerrilla campaign, which was stepped up in 1978 from bases in Angola and Zambia. In spite of the 1973 United Nations designation of SWAPO as the "sole authentic representative of the Namibian people," South Africa carried out a series of attacks on SWAPO camps in Angola. Despite a nonaggression pact signed by Angola and South Africa on February 16, 1984, SWAPO guerrilla activity in Namibia continued. In 1988 Angola, Cuba and South Africa signed an agreement providing for Namibian independence. Despite some pre-election violence, UN-supervised elections were held in November 1989. Namibia formally gained independence on March 21, 1991; SWAPO held a majority of seats in the new government.

Namos. Norwegian port town at the north head of Namsen Fjord. In 1940 British and German forces engaged heavily during WORLD WAR II. From April 14 to May 3 it was occupied by British troops on a mission to help free Norway from the German occupation of April 9, 1940.

Namur [*Flemish:* Namen]. Belgian industrial town and capital of Namur province, on the Meuse River in the south. Fortified against German attacks during WORLD WAR I, this strategically located town on the Meuse was captured nevertheless on Aug. 25, 1914, and again on May 16, 1940, after heavy fighting during WORLD WAR II.

Nanchang Uprising. Revolt (1927) against China's KUOMINTANG (KMT) government that occurred in the city of Nanchang, capital of Kiangsi province. After communist members of the KMT were ex-

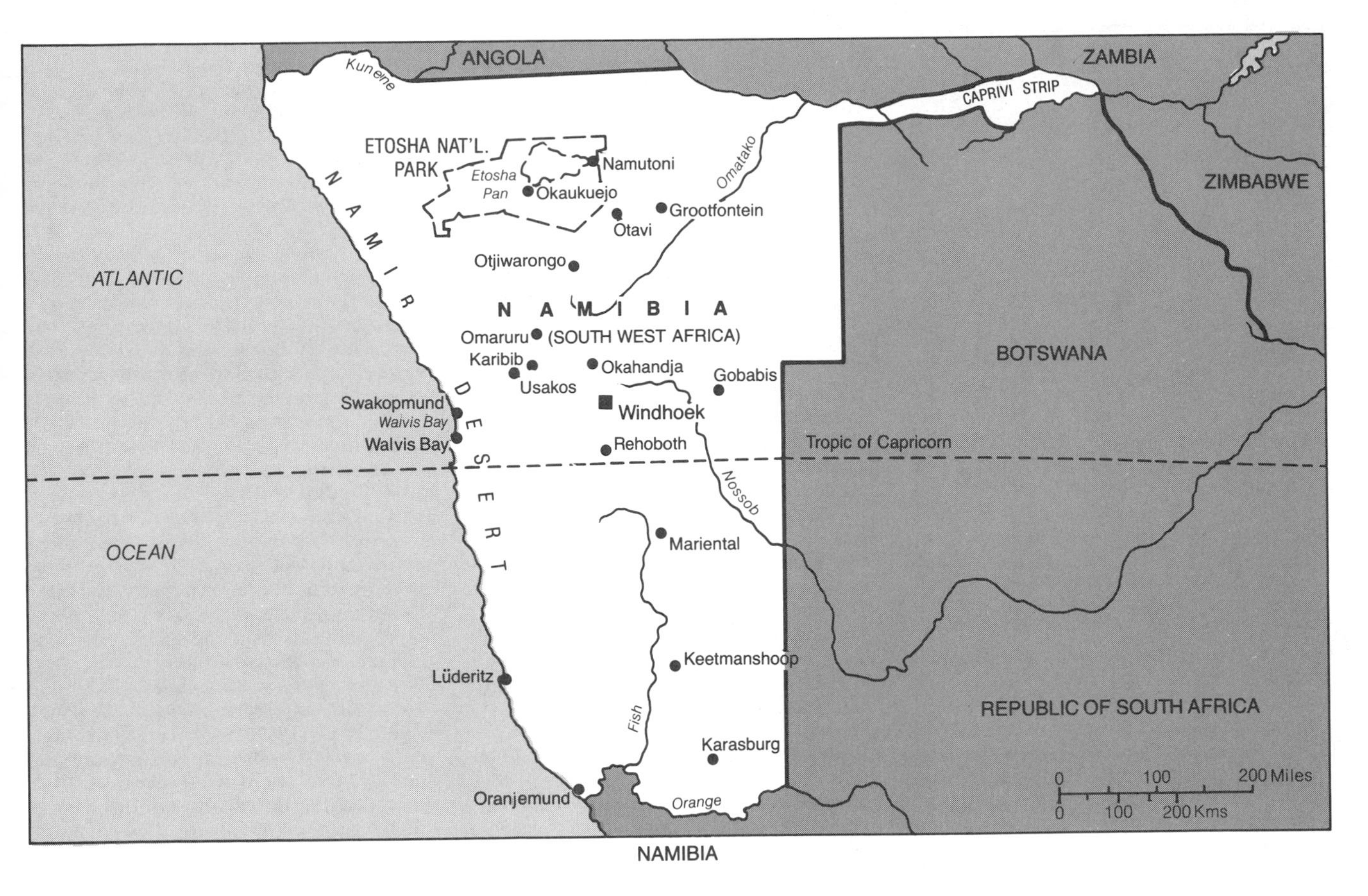

pelled in July, a garrison of some 30,000 communist soldiers under the leadership of CHU TEH rose against the government on August 1, 1927. They briefly founded a Chinese republic, before losing control of the city and fleeing west to eventually join MAO TSE-TUNG's forces. The Nanchang Uprising marked the birth of the People's Liberation Army—the military arm of what would become China's Communist government.

Nancy. Capital of Meurthe-et-Moselle department; on the Meurthe River, 178 miles east of Paris, France. Important as a rail center, it was heavily damaged during WORLD WAR I. After sustained air attacks during WORLD WAR II, it was liberated by U.S. forces on September 15, 1944.

Nanking, Rape of. Common term for the brutal treatment meted out to the inhabitants of the Chinese city of Nanking by the invading Japanese army during the SINO-JAPANESE WAR. Beginning on December 11, 1937, the terrible orgy of murder, torture and rape resulted in the death of hundreds of thousands of Chinese civilians and caused worldwide condemnation of the Japanese.

Nanning [Nan-Ning *formerly:* Yungning]. Capital of China's Kwangsi Chuang, approximately 360 miles west of Wuchow. Formerly a treaty port opened to the West in 1907, in 1949 the city of Nanning was taken by the communists to be used as a supply base in their war against the FRENCH in INDOCHINA, from 1946 to 1954. (See also VIETNAM.)

Nanook of the North. Classic American documentary film by Robert J. FLAHERTY. Its combination of ethnological documentation, poetic expression, and entertainment values has influenced generations of documentarists. An experienced explorer and cartographer for the Canadian railroads, Flaherty began taking portable cameras and developing equipment on his expeditions to Eskimo country around Hudson Bay. In 1916 he prepared a film documenting Eskimo life, but it was destroyed in a fire. Undaunted, he worked for another five years to finance a new film. In 1920, subsidized by Revillon Freres, he spent 16 months shooting the lifestyle and hunting activities of Nanook, the celebrated hunter of the Itivimuit tribe. Not only did the tribesmen willingly recreate their customs (some of them already outmoded) for the camera, but they became accomplished technicians in developing the film and servicing the equipment. Despite some manipulations and distortions—the natives had to learn anew how to build igloos, for example—the results were an impressive reaffirmation of a vanishing lifestyle threatened by industrial incursion. HOLLYWOOD, of course, had no idea what to do with such a film, so Pathe Distributors released it in July 1922—to immediate success and acclaim. *Nanook*, according to John Grierson, "first drew world-wide attention to the film's power of imaginative natural observation." Meanwhile, Nanook himself died of starvation two years later while deer hunting in the Ungava interior; years later, Flaherty's wife, Frances, recalled that once in Berlin she bought an "eskimo pie" confection depicting Nanook's face on the wrapper.

For further reading:

Griffith, Richard. *The World of Robert Flaherty*. London: Victor Gollancz, 1953.

Nansen, Fridtjof (1861–1930). Norwegian explorer, scientist, diplomat and humanitarian. Born near Oslo, Nansen studied at Christiana (now Oslo) University and embarked on his first expedition to the Arctic in 1882 while still a student. In 1888 he skied across GREENLAND, a journey chronicled in *First Crossing of Greenland* (1890). In order to prove his theory about the flow of ocean currents, he and his crush-resistant vessel, the *Fram*, anchored in the polar ice pack in 1893 and drifted, reaching Norway in 1896. In hopes of reaching the NORTH POLE, Nansen and a companion left the ship and traveled by sledge and skis to the northernmost point ever reached at that date. This expedition provided much useful scientific data about the Arctic Ocean and made Nansen a heroic figure at home and abroad. Named a professor at Christiana University in 1897, he also headed (1901) an International Commission for Study of the Sea and made a series of explorations in the North Atlantic from 1910 to 1914.

Nansen also launched a career as a statesman, working for the separation of NORWAY and SWEDEN in 1905. The following year, he was appointed Norway's first

Norwegian polar explorer and oceanographer Fridtjof Nansen.

minister to Great Britain, serving until 1908. After WORLD WAR I, Nansen became Norway's representative to the LEAGUE OF NATIONS. At the League, he was instrumental in providing relief to the victims of famine in Russia and in repatriating war prisoners. Becoming high commissioner for refugees in 1921, Nansen received the 1922 NOBEL PRIZE for peace for his humanitarian work. He was the author of many books both on the Arctic and on international relations.

napalm [acronym for naphthenic and palmitic acids]. A jellied gasoline used in flamethrowers and bombs. Napalm was used by both sides in the VIETNAM WAR—by the U.S. and South Vietnam primarily in the form of aerial bombs. The North Vietnamese and VIET CONG used it in flamethrowers, as in their massacre of the Montagnard villagers at Dak Son. Although fire has been used as a weapon since prehistoric times, napalm came into widespread use in WORLD WAR II, especially in flamethrowers used to destroy entrenched Japanese positions in the Pacific war. It was used extensively in the form of aerial bombs in the KOREAN WAR against Chinese and North Korean entrenchments. A favorite of television war coverage because of its vivid and awful display, use of napalm touched a primordial nerve among many Americans and aroused considerable controversy, including demonstrations against chemical companies that manufactured napalm.

Narain, Raj (1917–1986). Indian Socialist Party leader. His suit against then Prime Minister Indira GANDHI for electoral fraud (1975) precipitated a constitutional crisis that lasted nearly two years. When new elections were called in 1977, Gandhi was turned out of office and lost her parliamentary seat in Utar Pradesh State to Narain. Narain was briefly health minister in the administration of Prime Minister Morarji DESAI. He later led a fierce political revolt that toppled Desai in the summer of 1979 and replaced him with Charan Singh. After Gandhi swept back into power in 1980, Narain fell out with Singh and founded his own socialist party, which had few followers.

Narayan, Jayaprakash (1902–1979). Indian statesman. An early disciple of Mohandas K. GANDHI, he worked with Gandhi to free India from British colonial rule through nonviolent means. He founded the Congress Socialist Party (1934), organized strikes against the British and served several long prison terms for his actions. After India achieved independence (1947) he helped found the Indian Socialist Party. He was a leader of the coalition that temporarily toppled Prime Minister Indira GANDHI from power in 1977. Although Narayan never held elective office, he wielded great moral and political influence as a result of his campaigns for social justice.

Narayan, R(asipuram) K(rishnaswami) (1906–). Anglo-Indian novelist. Narayan writes in English, and his fiction explores the clash between Western ideology as imported by the British and the traditions of India. His first novel, *Swami and Friends* (1935), introduced the fictional town of Malgudi, which he has developed and peopled in subsequent works such as *The Financial Expert* (1952), *The Painter of Signs* (1977) and the short story collection *Malgudi Days* (1982). Other works include his memoir, *My Days* (1975), and *The World of Nagaraj* (1990).

Narvik. Norwegian port city on a peninsula in the Ofoten Fjord. Founded in 1887, it was taken by GERMANY in WORLD WAR II on April 9, 1940. Heavy fighting broke out between British and German naval vessels off its coast during the week of April 15, and from May 28 to June 9, 1940, the port was held by the British.

NASA. See NATIONAL AERONAUTICS AND SPACE ADMINISTRATION.

Nash, Ogden (1902–1971). American poet. Nash is known for his stylish light verse, in which he employed puns and other verbal antics as well as unconventional rhymes and irregular meter. His verse began appearing in the NEW YORKER and other publications in 1931. His collections include *The Private Dining Room* (1953), *You Can't Get There from Here* (1957) and *The Untold Adventures of Santa Claus* (1965).

Nash, Paul (1889–1946). British painter, designer and photographer. Educated at the Slade School of Art in London, Nash served in the British army during WORLD WAR I. After being invalided by a wound, he became an official war artist and earned praise for his sketches at the front lines. In the 1920s and 1930s, Nash worked as a painter and wood engraver, as well as in applied arts such as upholstery and glass design and photography. In all these areas, Nash provided a unique blending of symbolic and surrealistic elements. In the 1930s, he was a principal founder of "Unit One," an avant-garde group of British artists and architects. Nash again served as an official war artist during WORLD WAR II. *Outline: An Autobiography* (1949) was posthumously published.

Nashua (1952–1982). Thoroughbred racehorse. Bred at Claiborne Farm, Nashua was champion two-year-old of 1954, champion three-year-old and Horse of the

The horrifying aftermath of an accidental aerial napalm strike near Trang Bang, South Vietnam, on June 8, 1972.

Year the following year. Nashua's rivalry with his contemporary, the California-bred Swaps, began in the 1955 KENTUCKY DERBY, with Swaps taking the race by 1 1/2 lengths. Swaps returned home as Nashua went on to win the Preakness and Belmont. The two then met in a 1 1/4-mile match race at Washington Park, a race Nashua won by 6 1/2 lengths. As a four-year-old, he had an uneven campaign carrying heavy weights, but won the prestigious Jockey Club Gold Cup by 2 1/4 lengths, setting a 3:20 2/5 record in the process. He finished his career with 22 wins, four places, one show, finishing out of the money only three times. He retired to Spendthrift Farm, where he went on to become a successful sire, his progeny including the outstanding Damascus.

Nasir, Amin Ibrahim (1926–). Nasir became the first president of the independent Republic of MALDIVES in 1968. He had served as prime minister under Sultan Muhammad Amin Didi from 1957 to 1968, when the sultanate was abolished for the second time. Nasir eliminated the post of prime minister in 1975 and strengthened his powers; the following year he signed an agreement formally terminating the British military presence on the islands. After Nasir declined to stand for reelection in 1978, he left the country. He was later charged in absentia with misappropriation of government funds.

Nassau Agreement (December 18, 1962). An agreement between U.S. President John F. KENNEDY and U.K. Prime Minister Harold MACMILLAN on nuclear cooperation. Under the agreement, the U.S. would supply Britain with Polaris missiles for its submarines. The move antagonized French President DE GAULLE, who interpreted it as Britain's reassertion of its American rather than European loyalties. A month later, France vetoed Britain's entry into the EUROPEAN ECONOMIC COMMUNITY.

Nasser, Gamal Abdel (1918–1970). Egyptian political leader, first president of EGYPT (1956–70). Nasser was born near Asyut and educated at the Cairo Military Academy, graduating in 1938. A revolutionary from his youth, he was devoted to driving the British from Egypt. Nasser fought in the ARAB-ISRAELI WAR OF 1948 and was shocked by the Egyptian armed forces' inefficiency and corruption. He organized and led the anti-British republican group known as the FREE OFFICERS Movement that succeeded in ousting King FAROUK in 1952. In 1954 he toppled Gen. Muhammad Naguib, a relative figurehead, becoming Egypt's premier and, two years later, its president. Instituting a system called "Arab Socialism," Nasser confiscated the nation's great estates and nationalized (1956) the SUEZ CANAL. This action provoked the SUEZ CRISIS, a brief Anglo-French invasion of the canal and an Israeli invasion of the Sinai. The ensuing ARAB-ISRAELI WAR OF 1956 was halted by a UNITED NATIONS ceasefire, which left Nasser with increased prestige and popularity in the Arab world for his stand against Israel and the West. Nasser was

Egyptian President Gamal Abdel Nasser at the United Nations.

the head of the short-lived UNITED ARAB REPUBLIC (1958–61). He again came into conflict with Israel in 1967, when he precipitated the SIX-DAY WAR. Taking responsibility for the humiliating defeat, Nasser resigned but popular support quickly returned him to office. In 1970, Nasser succeeded in obtaining Soviet support for the massive ASWAN DAM project, for which the U.S. and Britain had refused to pay in 1956; it marked the apex of his career. Although increasingly dependent on Soviet support, he nonetheless was an important pan-Arabist and a hero to much of the THIRD WORLD. Nasser is widely considered one of the preeminent Arab leaders of the 20th century.

For further reading:

Vatikiotis, P.J., *Nasser and His Generation.* New York: St. Martin's Press, 1978.

Nasser, Lake. Lake in southeastern Egypt and northern Sudan created by the ASWAN High Dam, built in the 1960s for the production of hydroelectric power. Having flooded such important archaeological sites as ABU-SIMBEL, whose temple had to be elevated above the waters, nearly 90,000 people, mostly Sudanese, were relocated when the lake was formed.

Nast, Conde (1873–1942). American magazine publisher. Nast achieved success as advertising manager for *Collier's Weekly* between 1898 and 1905. In 1909, he acquired *Vogue,* then a small society periodical, and turned it into America's leading fashion magazine. He established a British edition of *Vogue* in 1916 and a French edition in 1920. By 1922, Nast's holdings included *Vanity Fair* and *House and Garden,* and he formed Conde Nast Publications, which continues to publish many periodicals. Nast also founded the Vogue Pattern Company in 1914 and published the *Vogue Pattern Book* in 1925. Nast was known as a lavish host to New York society.

Nation, The. American periodical founded in 1865. *The Nation,* a liberal weekly covering politics, philosophy and literature, has maintained its left-leaning, humanitarian stance throughout the shifts in American political thought. Frederick Law Olmsted, the architect of Central Park, proposed the formation of *The Nation,* which was established by Edwin Lawrence Godkin, who served as its editor from 1865 to 1881. *The Nation* was then owned by the *Saturday Evening Post* until 1918, when new editor Oswald Garrison Villard, son of the *Evening Post*'s late editor, severed *The Nation*'s ties with the paper. Villard was a founder of the NATIONAL ASSOCIATION FOR THE ADVANCEMENT OF COLORED PEOPLE, and *The Nation* was an early supporter of that organization as well as the AMERICAN CIVIL LIBERTIES UNION. It also espoused pacifism, opposed the TREATY OF VERSAILLES, backed the strikers and Wobblies and was sympathetic to the Russian revolutionaries. In the 1930s, *The Nation* advocated sanctions against the Nazi-Fascist AXIS, supported the Loyalists in the SPANISH CIVIL WAR and Franklin D. ROOSEVELT and his NEW DEAL. *The Nation* fought MCCARTHYISM in the '50s, opposed American intervention in VIETNAM in the '60s, and rallied against the conservative trend of the REAGAN administration. *The Nation* has rarely broken even—its circulation hovers around 25,000—and it is supported by patrons committed to the liberal cause.

National Aeronautics and Space Administration [NASA]. U.S. government agency that oversees advanced aeronautics; lunar, planetary and interplanetary spaceflights; and space probes, rockets and satellites. It was founded as an independent agency in 1958 and maintains headquarters in Washington, D.C. It has 10 major installations, including the John F. Kennedy Space Center, Cape Canaveral, Florida; the Johnson Space Center, Houston, Texas; the Goddard Space Flight Center, Beltsville, Maryland; the Marshall Space Flight Center, Huntsville, Alabama and the Jet Propulsion Laboratory, Pasadena, California, NASA has a staff of some 21,000 scientists, engineers and technicians. The agency grew rapidly in the 1960s and scored a triumph with its lunar-landing APOLLO missions. In 1973 it created America's first manned orbiting space lab, and in 1981 it launched the U.S.'s first manned space shuttle. After the explosion of the CHALLENGER shuttle in 1986, NASA's policies were widely investigated. Once held in the highest esteem, the agency was subjected to scrutiny and criticism, and its activities were to a large degree halted for two years. After management and safety reforms, NASA resumed manned space flight with the launch of the space shuttle *Discovery* in 1988.

National Association for the Advancement of Colored People [NAACP]. American CIVIL-RIGHTS organization. The oldest and largest organization of its kind, with a 1990 membership of some 400,000, it strives to eliminate discrimination against blacks and other minorities. Its membership is mainly black but also includes many whites and others. It was founded in 1910 by the merging of the NIAGARA MOVEMENT formed by W.E.B. DU BOIS and a group of prominent white liberals. With lawyer Moorfield Storey as its first president, much of the group's power was wielded by Du Bois, who edited its magazine *Crisis* from 1910 to 1934. During its early years, the organization worked successfully to pass antilynching laws and to stop lynching in the U.S. Its main thrust has always been change through legal and legislative action, a moderate stance that brought it criticism by more radical civil rights advocates. The NAACP played an important role in many legal battles, most memorably the landmark school desegregation case BROWN V. BOARD OF EDUCATION of Topeka (1954). Led by Roy WILKINS from 1955 to 1977, it also was important in obtaining passage of the CIVIL RIGHTS ACTS of 1957 and 1964 and the VOTING RIGHTS ACT OF 1965 and in winning extensions of the latter in the 1970s and '80s. In addition to litigation and lobbying, the NAACP runs voter registration drives, promotes education, acts to reduce poverty and hunger in the black community and protects the rights of black prison inmates. It is headquartered in Baltimore, Maryland.

National Bolsheviks. A political movement in Russia in the years following 1917. Although National Bolshevik supporters were not communists, they nevertheless regarded the BOLSHEVIKS as the party best qualified to govern Russia. During the 1920s they founded the "Change of Landmarks Movement," which flourished during World War II. Prominent among the National Bolsheviks were A.N. Tolstoy, General Alexei Alekseyevich Brusilov and B.D. Grekov.

National Education Association (NEA). An organization of professional educators in the U.S., the NEA is the largest group of its kind in the world with a membership (1990) of 1,600,000. Founded in 1857 as the National Teachers Association, it received a congressional charter in 1906. Its goals include the improvement of public education and the increase of salaries and benefits for teachers, administrators and other educators—from elementary school through college. It promotes these aims through professional activities, judicial and legislative efforts and collective bargaining. The NEA is headquartered in Washington, D.C., but has branches in every state and Puerto Rico and facilities for representing U.S. teachers abroad.

National Endowment for the Arts (NEA). Arts funding arm of the National Foundation on the Arts and the Humanities founded in 1965. The NEA's stated purpose is to encourage the development and preservation of the arts in the U.S. It consists of a chairperson and 26 presidentially appointed members, who award grants to individual artists, state and local arts agencies and nonprofit organizations. The NEA became embroiled in controversy in the late 1980s when its funding of a photography exhibit by Robert MAPPLETHORPE (which included homoerotic images) drew criticism from the right, led by Senator Jesse Helms. After much debate about obscenity, censorship and federal funding of the arts, Congress established an Independent Commission to determine if the NEA should be restructured or perhaps even abolished. In October of 1990, the House of Representatives passed a bill that included the requirement that artists funded by the NEA and convicted of violating local obscenity laws must return their grant money.

National Enquirer, The. Published by Generoso P. Pope Jr., who converted the paper in 1952 to a tabloid featuring the bizarre and the gory. By the mid-1960s, the paper had a circulation of nearly one million and was making huge profits. Pope again changed the formula in the late 1960s, putting the paper into supermarkets and featuring celebrities, UFOs and predictions by clairvoyants. In 1988, the paper had a circulation of over 4.5 million.

National Geographic Society. Scientific and educational organization. Popularly known through its monthly publication *The National Geographic Magazine*, the National Geographic Society also sponsors expeditions and research projects in a broad range of fields, including anthropology, geography and oceanography. The Society was founded in 1888 and now has more than 10 million members worldwide. Its notable projects include sponsorship of Richard BYRD and Robert PEARY's polar expedition and the first U.S. trek to the peak of Mount Everest. Its other publications include *National Geographic World, National Geographic Research, National Geographic Traveler*, maps and other educational support materials. It also produces popular television specials on nature, science and exploration.

National Government. Coalition that governed the UNITED KINGDOM from 1931 to 1935, during the GREAT DEPRESSION. LABOUR PARTY leader Ramsay MACDONALD, briefly prime minister in 1924, returned to office in 1929 as head of a Labour government. With the Depression crisis, MacDonald formed a coalition with the Conservatives and Liberals, who dominated the government. Angry Labour MPs denounced MacDonald.

National Health Service. The British National Health Service Act became law in 1946. Based on the recommendations of the BEVERIDGE REPORT, the act's intent was to provide free, comprehensive "cradle-to-grave" medical, dental and ophthalmological services to all Britons. The National Health Service came into being during the Labour government of Clement ATTLEE and had been a long-term goal of the LABOUR PARTY and the then minister of health, Ernest BEVIN. The program was an expensive one, and subsequent governments began imposing fees for some services. Margaret THATCHER's call for more private care and cutbacks in the Health Service in the 1980s resulted in real and threatened strikes by nurses and other health-care workers. In 1988 she fired the minister of health; created a new Cabinet position, secretary of state for health; and named Kenneth Clarke to the post. She planned a proposal by which doctors would operate within a budget and allot health services to their patients without exceeding it. The estimated cost of the National Health Service in 1988 was $41 billion, more than the British military budget.

National Industrial Recovery Act. Major NEW DEAL program, designed to regulate and revive industry; it was declared unconstitutional in 1935. When President Franklin ROOSEVELT assumed office at the height of the Depression, economic activity was at a standstill. The National Industrial Recovery Act was passed to revive the industrial sector. Modeled after the War Industries Board of World War I, it established industry codes designed to increase capital investment, end destructive competition and create jobs. The antitrust laws were suspended for two years, and trade, prices and labor practices were controlled by industry codes, while workers were guaranteed collective bargaining rights. To ensure job creation the NATIONAL RECOVERY ADMINISTRATION (NRA) and the Work Projects Administration (WPA) were created to carry out the act's provisions and to put people to work. In practice the system was not as successful as planned. Little new investment actually occurred and the law was criticized by a wide array of groups. While unions found the act harmful, so did the small business community, which feared the growth of government-supported monopolies. In 1935 in *Schechter v. United States*, which involved interstate commerce provisions of the act, the Supreme Court held the National Industrial Recovery Act to be unconstitutional. The Court reasoned that the act went far beyond the scope of Congress' power to regulate interstate commerce.

National Institutes of Health (NIH). An agency in the Public Health Service division of the U.S. Department of Health and Human Services. Originally started in 1887 as the Hygienic Laboratory at the U.S. Marine Hospital in Staten Island, New York, NIH took its present name in 1948; its laboratories are now located in Bethesda, Maryland. NIH conducts biomedical research, supports the training of research scientists and funds approximately 40 percent of health research in the U.S. It is comprised of 11 institutes, each specializing in health fields, such as aging, child health and human development and cancer research. It also includes the National Library of Medicine, the Fogarty International Center for Advanced Study in the Health Sciences and its research hospital—the Clinical Center.

nationalization. The process of assuming control and ownership of an industry on a national scale by a national government. This has happened in a number of countries and for a variety of purposes. Some governments, especially those in the THIRD WORLD, have nationalized vital industries to gain local control and keep profits in their own country. Other governments have tried nationalization to promote efficiency or to promote social goals such as increased employment or subsidization of certain goods. Utilities such as airlines, electric and gas generation and distribution, postal services and communication companies are commonly nationalized. Although FRANCE and the UNITED KINGDOM nationalized many industries, they later sought to divest these holdings to private ownership. Forced nationalization without compensation is known as "expropriation."

National Labor Relations Act [aka the Wagner Act] (1935). Landmark NEW DEAL legislation, sponsored by Senator Robert Wagner of New York, that established the right to collective bargaining and set up the **National Labor Relations Board,** a federal agency to oversee union elections. Although Congress legalized union membership and the right to peaceful picketing in the 1932 NORRIS-LAGUARDIA ACT, unions were still at a distinct disadvantage. The Wagner Act shifted this balance by providing a mechanism that enabled unions to hold certification elections under government supervision. The act also created the National Labor Relations Board (NLRB) with power to supervise elections and police "unfair labor practices"—such as interference with union organizing efforts, discrimination against union members and refusal to bargain in good faith with a duly-elected union representing workers.

National Labor Relations Board v. Jones & Laughlin Steel Corp. (1937). U.S. Supreme Court decision upholding a major NEW DEAL program. President Franklin D. ROOSEVELT's New Deal had run into a substantial roadblock when the Supreme Court overturned a number of the president's programs as unconstitutional. The Court had objected to New Deal programs as unwarranted governmental interference with private business. The NATIONAL LABOR RELATIONS ACT was a cornerstone of the New Deal, recognizing the right of workers to collectively bargain and establishing the National Labor Relations Board to supervise union elections. In a surprise decision, the conservative Supreme Court closely approved the legislation by a 5–4 margin. This marked the end of the Supreme Court's resistance to FDR's reform plans.

National Liberation Front [NLF]. The National Liberation Front was appropriately named, for it was a classic communist-front organization. Formed in Hanoi in December 1960, the NLF was designed to disguise its communist control and thus draw support from noncommunist South Vietnamese disaffected with their government. Many noncommunist members of the NLF thought they were working for southern independence, and the ANTIWAR MOVEMENT in the U.S. championed the NLF as the true representative of the South Vietnamese people. The NLF stressed land reform, expulsion of foreigners, unfairness of South Vietnam's tax system and other issues.

After the war the North Vietnamese freely admitted that the NLF was their own creation, totally controlled and directed from Hanoi. Betrayed and disillusioned, many southern NLF leaders have been purged or imprisoned or have fled into exile. (See also VIET CONG.)

National Party (New Zealand). New Zealand political party formed in 1935. During the GREAT DEPRESSION there were three conservative, anti-LABOUR parties in New Zealand: the Reform Party, the United Party and the Democratic Party. Their lack of unification contributed to Labour's stunning victory in 1935, after which the three parties' leadership called a convention to organize the National Party. It came to power in 1949 under the leadership of Sir Sidney Holland, who was prime minister until 1957, and again under Sir Keith HOLYOAKE (1960–72). From 1974 to 1984, National leader Robert Muldoon was prime minister. After the party's defeat (1984), Muldoon was succeeded by Jim McClay (1945–) as its leader.

National Public Radio. Based in Washington, D.C., National Public Radio provides programming to its noncommercial radio station members nationwide. Its news programming includes the acclaimed "All Things Considered" and "Morning Edition." It initially relied on the Corporation for Public Broadcasting for the majority of its funding; in 1981 they provided two-thirds of its $21 million budget. By 1983 NPR was close to bankruptcy but recovered by successfully seeking institutional donations. It then stopped depending on the Corporation for Public Broadcasting for support. The corporation now gives federal money directly to member stations, which pay higher rates to NPR for programming. By 1989 NPR was again solvent.

National Radio Astronomy Observatory (NRAO). The largest radio-astronomy observatory in the U.S. It is used by scientists throughout the country, funded by the National Science Foundation and operated by Associated Universities Inc. Founded in 1956, NBAO's many radio telescopes have detected radio waves given off by a huge number of objects in space—from the planets of our solar system to vastly distant quasars. With headquarters, scientific offices and computer facilities in Charlottesville, Virginia, the NRAO is responsible for radio telescopes in Socorro, New Mexico; Kitt Peak, Arizona and Green Bank, West Virginia. Its Socorro facility is the home of the Very Large Array, the world's most powerful radio telescope. It consists of 27 large mirrored reflectors, each 82 ft. in diameter and all operating as a single instrument. The Kitt Peak telescope, designed expressly to deal with extremely short radio waves, measures 39 ft. in diameter. The large Green Bay telescope, which with a diameter of 300 ft. was long the world's largest movable instrument of its kind, collapsed in 1988 and was completely destroyed. The other six smaller radio telescopes at the facility remain in operation. The NRAO is constructing another instrument, the Very Long Baseline Array Telescope. Scheduled for completion in 1992 and operated from Socorro, it will have 10 reflectors situated throughout the U.S. and in the Virgin Islands.

National Recovery Administration (NRA). U.S. government administrative bureau established in June, 1933 under the NATIONAL INDUSTRIAL RECOVERY ACT. One of President Franklin D. ROOSEVELT's earliest NEW DEAL creations, the NRA drew up and oversaw codes relating to fair competition in business and industry. These codes regulated prices, wages, working conditions, the construction of facilities and terms of credit. Administered by Hugh S. Johnson, it gained the cooperation of major industries throughout the U.S. The NRA was declared unconstitutional in May 1935 by a U.S. Supreme Court decision and it was subsequently abolished. A number of its provisions were enacted in later labor legislation.

National Review. Biweekly political magazine noted for its conservative outlook. The *National Review* was founded by William F. BUCKLEY Jr. in 1955, and has maintained its status as a leading journalistic forum for conservative political viewpoints. Buckley has edited the magazine since its inception, although in 1990 he announced his intention of turning over the primary editorial responsibilities to other hands in the near future. The *National Review* has frequently expressed opposition to government deficit spending, welfare programs and DETENTE with the U.S.S.R. and other communist regimes. The magazine has won a loyal following of subscribers and regular readers and has achieved commercial as well as critical success. (See also CONSERVATISM.)

National Rifle Association of America (NRA). Organization that promotes the shooting of rifles and pistols as a sport, in sharpshooting, hunting and other activities. Established in 1871, it sponsors competitions and chooses participants in international shooting events. With a membership that reached 3,000,000 by the early 1990s, the NRA also maintains a powerful lobby in Washington. The NRA opposes gun control and any other acts that it believes to provide unnecessary restrictions on the rights of gun owners and enthusiasts.

National Urban Coalition. American organization that works to solve urban problems. Founded in 1970 through the merger of the Urban Coalition and Urban America, it attempts to identify and publicize serious urban problems and to take steps to begin dealing with these problems. With representatives from business and labor as well as leaders from civic, community, religious and minority-rights groups, the organization deals with issues of employment, housing, education, economic well-being and health care for urban Americans. The National Urban Coalition is headquartered in Washington, D.C.

Native Dancer (1950–1967). Thoroughbred racehorse. Known as "the Gray Ghost," Native Dancer was an imposing gray colt who won all but one of his 22 races over the course of his brief career. Lightly raced but undefeated as a two-year-old, in his second season he lost only the Kentucky Derby, in which he was fouled. He went on that year to win the Preakness, Belmont, Arlington Classic and Dwyer and Travers Stakes. Asked to carry extraordinary weights as a four-year-old, his already weak ankles began to suffer and he was retired to stud. Among his outstanding descendants were Kauai King, NORTHERN DANCER and the brilliant Majestic Prince.

NATO. See NORTH ATLANTIC TREATY ORGANIZATION.

Natwick, Myron (1890–1990). U.S. animator. He created the curvaceous, Kewpie doll-faced cartoon character Betty Boop. The character first appeared in 1930 in a cartoon version of the song "Boop-Boop-a-Doop," sung by Helen Kane. Boop went on to star in a number of animated short films. Natwick also animated the character of Snow White in Walt DISNEY's full-length feature film, *Snow White and the Seven Dwarfs.*

Nauru [*formerly* Pleasant Island]. Independent island state west of KIRIBATI in the west Pacific Ocean, discovered in 1798. In 1888 it was claimed by Germany, and was made an Australian LEAGUE OF NATIONS mandate at the end of WORLD WAR I. From August 1942 through WORLD WAR II Nauru was occupied by the JAPANESE, and in 1947 became a trust territory of AUSTRALIA, UNITED KINGDOM, and NEW ZEALAND, gaining independence in 1968.

Nautilus. The world's first atomic-powered submarine, the U.S.S. *Nautilus* was launched in January 1954 and had its first sea trials a year later. It was developed largely through the advocacy of Admiral Hyman RICKOVER, who began supporting the idea of the nuclear-powered craft in the late-1940s. The 2,800–ton vessel was completed at a cost of some $55 million. It measures 323 feet long, can attain a speed of over 20 knots per hour when submerged and carries a crew of 105. In August 1958 the submarine made the first undersea crossing of the North Pole; later that month it set an east-west transatlantic record for submarines traveling from Portland, England, to New York.

Navarre, Henri (1898–1983). French general. Navarre was commander in chief of the French forces in INDOCHINA from 1953 to 1954, when the VIET MINH defeated the French at the battle of DIEN BIEN PHU, which marked the end of the French attempt to maintain control in Indochina.

Navratilova, Martina (1956–). Czechoslovakian-born U.S. tennis player. The daughter of avid tennis players, she won the Czech singles title three times from 1972 to 1974. In 1974, she defected to the U.S. Although she won nearly a quarter of a million dollars in prize money in 1975, a love of American junk food initially prevented her from reaching championship consistency. After 1977, when she began a stricter diet and training regimen, she achieved tennis superstar status. From 1978 to 1984 she won five Wimbledon singles titles, in addition to her six doubles titles. A two-time winner of the French Open, she did not win the U.S. Open until 1983, a feat she repeated in 1984.

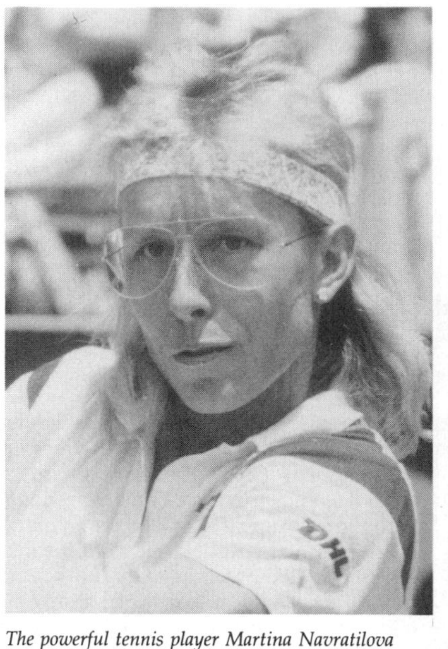

The powerful tennis player Martina Navratilova (1988).

Nazism. An ideology and a political movement that arose in GERMANY during the 1920s. Led by Adolf HITLER, crystallized in his National Socialist German Workers' Party (or Nazi Party), and at least partially defined in his book MEIN KAMPF, the movement ruled Germany from 1933 to 1945. The name "Nazi" was originally a derogatory abbreviation of the first word of the party's German name. Nazi ideology combined the pseudoscientific racism of such figures as the Comte de Gobineau (1816–82), Houston Stewart CHAMBERLAIN and the Nazis' own Alfred Rosenberg, with a powerful nationalism and sense of national destiny that demanded the unification of all German-speaking peoples. Violently anti-Semitic, it elevated the Germanic or "Aryan" race and placed the JEWS at the lowest end of the racial spectrum. A kind of FASCISM, it was authoritarian and totalitarian in character, allowing private property while suppressing individual rights.

Nazism arose as a result of the political, social and economic crises that befell Germany after the humiliation of its defeat in WORLD WAR I. Its extremist positions appealed to a people exhausted by war and disillusioned with the performance of postwar democracy. Promising order and prosperity to the German people and exalting discipline and power, Nazism condemned democracy, socialism and communism with equal fervor. The movement drew adherents from the military, the farmers, the urban middle class and the wealthy industrialist classes, and by the mid-1920s the party had some 20,000 members. It became more appealing and more powerful with the GREAT DEPRESSION, holding out promises of economic stability and glory for the German nation. By 1929 the Nazi Party had some 176,000 members, and in the 1932 elections it emerged as Germany's most powerful political party.

In 1933 Hitler was named chancellor, and Nazism became Germany's ruling ideology (with the Nazi Party as the nation's only legal political party). The Nazis took control of all aspects of German life, abolishing freedom of the press and speech and severely limiting civil liberties. Having established a private army in the 1920s, the Nazis expanded their military strength by creating a fearsome secret police force, the GESTAPO. They also established CONCENTRATION CAMPS, where they imprisoned Jews and other "enemies" of the Third Reich. Over the years, they murdered some six million Jews (see HOLOCAUST) and killed about five million others, including Gypsies, Slavs, homosexuals, communists and other political opponents of Nazism. In an attempt to build a German empire, the Nazis achieved ANSCHLUSS with Austria in 1938 and used strongarm political tactics and intimidation that same year against Czechoslovakia, annexing its German-speaking SUDETENLAND. When the Nazis entered Poland in 1939, WORLD WAR II was launched and Germany entered on a

The USS Nautilus, *the first nuclear-powered submarine, was also the first submarine to travel under the polar ice cap.*

A grim presage of the Holocaust, the Nazi sign reads "Germans! Defend yourselves! Do not buy from Jews!"

course that was to see its utter defeat in the war, marking the disintegration of Nazism. The Nazi Party was officially banned by WEST GERMANY's postwar constitution. Nonetheless, the movement and its ideology reappeared in neo-Nazi groups that occasionally sprang up in Europe and the U.S.

Nazi-Soviet Pact. See GERMAN-SOVIET NON-AGGRESSION PACT.

NBC [National Broadcasting Company]. One of the three major U.S. radio and television networks. The National Broadcasting Company was established in 1926; its stock was owned by RCA (Radio Corporation of America), Westinghouse and General Electric. RCA bought out the other two in 1930 to assume full ownership of the company. NBC established two national radio networks, the Red Network (with 25 stations) and the Blue Network (with six stations). During the GREAT DEPRESSION, NBC and its rival CBS provided news and entertainment programs to millions of radio listeners across the U.S. In 1943, the Federal Communications Commission ordered NBC to sell its Blue Network, which subsequently became ABC (the American Broadcasting Company). In the late 1940s and early 1950s, NBC pioneered programming in the new medium of television. NBC was especially known for its live drama and variety programs. In the 1960s, the network's news and documentary programs were noteworthy; NBC also programmed many new situation comedies and drama series. Live comedy returned to television in the 1970s via NBC's popular SATURDAY NIGHT LIVE program. By the 1980s, the NBC television network consisted of five NBC-owned stations plus some 210 affiliated stations; the NBC radio network included eight NBC-owned stations and about 300 affiliated stations.

"NBC White Paper". A notable series of investigative television documentaries. In its first real challenge to programs like CBS' SEE IT NOW, NBC lured Irving Gitlin from CBS to head the "creative projects" unit in NBC News. These network specials began with "The U-2 Affair" in November 1961 and included such other contemporary news subjects as "Angola: Journey to a War" (1961), "The Death of Stalin" (1963) and "Cuba: Bay of Pigs" (1964). Filmmakers like Robert Young and Albert Wasserman developed lightweight, portable 16mm cameras and sound equipment. This "cutting edge" technology enabled them to penetrate areas, from Angola to American slums, more easily and less obtrusively than had been possible with the old-fashioned 35mm camera equipment. By contrast to these probing contemporary investigations were programs like "The Real West" (1961), narrated by Gary COOPER, which used historic photographs to recreate a vanishing aspect of American culture.

For further reading:

The Complete Directory to Prime Time Network TV Shows. New York: Ballantine Books, 1988.

N'Djamena [*formerly* Fort-Lamy]. African city on the southwest border of Cameroon at the juncture of the Chari and Logone rivers. Named for a French explorer, Fort-Lamy was founded in 1900 as a base for the French conquest of central SUDAN, and later became a base for the FREE FRENCH during WORLD WAR II. A territorial capital since 1920, the city has been national capital of Chad since independence in 1960, and was renamed N'Djamena in 1973.

Neagle, Dame Anna [born Florence Marjorie Robinson] (1904–1986). British actress. She was regarded as the first lady of British cinema from the late 1930s through the early 1950s. She was Britain's number one box office draw throughout most of the 1940s. From 1943 until his death in 1977, she was married to Irish-born producer Herbert Wilcox, who produced and directed nearly all her films. Among her most successful performances were two as Queen Victoria in *Victoria the Great* and in *Sixty Glorious Years.* Her portrayal of a WORLD WAR II heroine of the French Resistance in *Odette* (1950) was regarded as her finest performance. Also active in the theater, she came to be listed in the GUINNESS BOOK OF RECORDS for her 2,062 performances in the London musical *Charlie Girl.*

Nearing, Scott (1883–1983). American pacifist and radical of the early 1900s. He had a doctorate in economics and taught at several universities early in his career but encountered difficulty because of his Marxist, antiestablishment views. In 1915 he lost his teaching post at the University of Pennsylvania when he spoke out against child labor. He lost another job when he was indicted for opposing U.S. participation in WORLD WAR I. He later became a leading environmentalist, dedicated to simple, rural living. His ideas about the environment, which he and his wife, Helen, put into practice on their farm in New England, attracted a large following in the 1960s. The Nearings wrote *Living the Good Life* (1954); Scott Nearing's autobiography is *The Making of a Radical* (1972).

Neave, Airey (1916–1979). British WORLD WAR II hero and politician. An RAF flier during the war, Neave was shot down over Germany and held as a PRISONER OF WAR in Germany's notorious Colditz Castle but managed to make a daring escape. After the war he was on the British prosecution team in the NUREMBERG TRIALS. He was elected to Parliament in 1953. A supporter of, and leading adviser to, Margaret THATCHER, he helped engineer her election to the leadership of the CONSERVATIVE PARTY in 1975. Neave took a particular interest in the problems of NORTHERN IRELAND, and it was widely assumed that he would become secretary of state for Northern Ireland in a Thatcher government. However, he was killed by a car bomb as he was leaving Parliament on March 30, 1979. The radical Irish National Liberation Army claimed responsibility for Neave's death.

Neel, Alice (1900–1984). American painter. The Pennsylvania-born expressionist painter spent most of her life in New York City. Highly individualistic in her style, she is noted for her psychologically acute and physically candid portraiture. Largely neglected during the postwar heyday of ABSTRACT EXPRESSIONISM, she was rediscovered in the late 1960s and 1970s and won a good deal of critical praise.

Negritude. Literary movement among black writers from French colonies in Africa that originated in Paris during the 1930s. Founded by the Guianan poet Leon Damas, it championed and celebrated the uniquenesss of black experience and talent. Leopold SENGHOR, later the founding father and first president of independent SENEGAL, was also a leader of the movement. Negritude was a consciousness-raising phenomenon that strongly influenced the black social and political revolution in the U.S. during the 1960s.

Negro leagues. American baseball leagues formed in the era when black players were banned from major league teams. The Negro National League was formed in 1920; the Negro American League followed in 1937. After Jackie ROBINSON joined the Brooklyn Dodgers in 1947, breaking baseball's color bar, many other black players began to play for major league teams, and the Negro leagues declined in importance. The last, the Negro American League, was disbanded in 1960. Stars of the Negro leagues included pitcher Satchel PAIGE; outfielder Cool Papa BELL; and catcher Josh Gibson, who held the Negro leagues' home run record.

Nehru, Pandit Jawaharlal (1889–1964). Indian statesman and nationalist, first prime minister of INDIA (1947–64). The son of attorney and journalist Motilal Nehru, Jawaharlal Nehru was born in Allahabad and educated in England at Cambridge University. After the AMRITSAR MASSACRE of 1919, he became active in the Indian Congress movement; with the support of Mohandas K. GANDHI, he assumed the presidency of the movement in 1929. In this position, Nehru was the chief architect of India's independence from Britain. Beginning in 1947, he served as the country's first prime minister, until his death in 1964. During his tenure, the pragmatic Nehru introduced industrial and social advances, guiding India to a role of leadership in the developing world. He was succeeded as prime minister by Lal SHASTRI, who was in turn succeeded by Nehru's daughter, Indira GANDHI.

For further reading:
Akbar, M.J., *Nehru: The Making of India.* New York: Viking Penguin, 1989.

Jawaharlal Nehru, the first prime minister of India, addresses the National Press Club in Washington, D.C.

Neill, A(lexander) S(utherland) (1883–1973). Scottish educator. A revolutionary, progressive educator, Neill is best known for establishing the independent, self-governing Summerhill School which was based on the premise of making "the school fit the child." A teacher at various schools (1903–21), he first founded a school near Salzburg, Austria, but moved it to Leiston in Suffolk, England, and called it the Summerhill School (1927). The school was coeducational and catered to children from higher-income families, mostly American. He published many books on education, and his ideas influenced the direction of education in both Britain and America.

Neizvestny, Ernst (1925–). Artist and sculptor. After studying at the V.I. Surikov State Institute of Arts, Neizvestny served in the Soviet army in 1942–45 and then worked as a sculptor at the studios of the U.S.S.R. Agricultural Exhibition. He became an influential figure among unorthodox Soviet artists. A member of the Artists' Union of the U.S.S.R. from 1953 to 1954 and from 1955 to 1957, in 1976 he was granted an exit visa to immigrate to Israel. His main works include *Mother* and *Great Mistakes.*

Nelson, George "Baby Face" [born Lester J. Gillis] (1908–1934). American gangster. Born in Chicago, the diminutive bankrobber and killer began his recognized criminal career at the age of 14, when he was sent to a juvenile home for auto theft. By 1929 he was working as a strong-arm man for Al CAPONE's gang. Arrested during a bank robbery in 1931, he escaped prison the following year and joined DILLINGER's gang. Nelson quickly affirmed his violent reputation by indiscriminately killing bank guards and bystanders. After Dillinger's death at the hands of the FBI in July, 1934, Nelson succeeded to the title of public enemy number one. He was killed by FBI agents during a shootout in Illinois four months later.

Nelson, Nate (1932–1984). Lead singer for the Flamingos (1954–62) and the Platters (1964–82). With the Flamingos he recorded the hit "I Only Have Eyes for You." His hits with the Platters included "Only You" and "Smoke Gets in Your Eyes."

Nelson, Ricky [Eric Hillard Nelson] (1940–1985). Ricky Nelson became a teenage singing idol for fans of ROCK AND ROLL during the 1950s. He appeared with his family on the long-running television show *The Adventures of Ozzie and Harriet.* By the time the show went off the air (1966), he had sold millions of records. Two of his biggest hits were "Mary Lou" and "Travellin' Man." In recent years, he had a more modest career as a country rock musician.

Nemerov, Howard (Stanley) (1920–91). American poet. Nemerov's first book of poetry, *The Image and Law* (1947), was critically acclaimed but derivative of T.S. ELIOT and other modernist poets. It was with *The Salt Garden* (1955) that he found his own voice. His realistic, romantic poetry often reflects an increasing concern with nature. Subsequent poetic works include *Inside the Onion* (1984) and *War Stories: poems about long ago and now* (1987). Nemerov's fiction, which shares with some of his poetry an ironic wit, includes *The Melodramatists* (1949) and *Stories, Fables and Other Diversions* (1971). Other works include *Figures of Thought: Speculations on the Meaning of Poetry and Other Essays* (1978) and *The Oak in the Acorn: On Remembrance of Things Past and on Teaching Proust, Who Will Never Learn* (1987). In 1988 he became the third poet laureate of the U.S. His sister was the photographer Diane ARBUS.

Nemirovich-Danchenko, Vasily Ivanovich (1848–1936). Author and journalist. He wrote prolifically, producing a vast number of narratives and novels directed at the general reader. Although superficial, his works are versatile and entertaining. They include *Personal Reminiscences of General Skobeleff* (1884), *The Prices of the Stock Exchange* (1914) and *Peasant Tales of Russia* (1917).

Nemon, Oscar (1905–1985). One of Britain's most accomplished sculptors, he was famed for his portrait busts and full-size sculptures. Nemon's subjects included Queen ELIZABETH II, Margaret THATCHER, Dwight D. EISENHOWER and Sigmund FREUD. He was best known for his more than 50 likenesses of Winston CHURCHILL, one of which was in the members' lobby of the House of Commons.

Nemtchinova, Vera (1899–1984). Russian-born ballerina. Nemtchinova became a star of Serge DIAGHILEV'S BALLETS RUSSES in the 1920s and went on to lead several other dance companies. Her most famous role was as the androgynous "Girl in Blue" in *Les Biches,* Bronislava NIJINSKA's 1924 ballet about French sexual and social mores. Nemtchinova was hailed both for her abilities as a classical dancer and as an experimental performer in the modern mold.

Nenni, Pietro (1891–1980). Italian socialist politician. Nenni's political career spanned seven decades. In 1922 he succeed Benito MUSSOLINI (who was then still a socialist) as editor of *Avanti,* a leading socialist newspaper. Strongly opposed to FASCISM, he was later imprisoned several times by Mussolini and spent a period in exile. He fought for the Loyalists in the SPANISH CIVIL WAR. After WORLD WAR II, he helped found the new Italian republic and served in its first government as deputy prime minister and foreign minister. He led ITALY's Socialist Party from 1949 to 1969. His political alliance with the Italian Communist Party and his opposition to the NORTH ATLANTIC TREATY ORGANIZATION (NATO) earned him a Stalin Prize for Peace in 1952. He broke with the communists, however, and renounced the award after the Soviet invasion of Hungary (1956; see HUNGARIAN UPRISING). In 1962 he allied his party with the Christian Democrats in a coalition that ruled Italy until 1976.

neoexpressionism. Term used for a revival and reinterpretation of 20th-century EXPRESSIONISM that flourished worldwide in the late 1970s, throughout the 1980s and into the 1990s. Rejecting passionless mimimalist abstraction, the movement draws its subject matter from the contemporary world in figurative images that are often violent, brutal, childlike and erotic. Among the many different artists who have been attracted to elements of the style are the Americans David Salle and Julian Schnabel and the Spaniards Sandro Chia and Francesco Clemente.

neorealism. Italian literary movement that began in the late 1920s and came to dominate Italian literature in the 1930s, 1940s and 1950s. Its major figures included Alberto MORAVIA, Cesare PAVESE and Ignazio SILONE. A major precursor in Italian letters was the 19th-century novelist and story writer Giovanni Verga. Neorealism saw itself as a liberating impulse that could enable writers to abandon pseudo-sophistication and ornate literary stylings in favor of a more direct vision of life that encompassed the hopes and sorrows of everyday men and women. The neorealists frequently set their works in smaller Italian towns and villages as opposed to such cosmopolitan centers as Rome. In their blunt vision of the social and economic hardships of the Italian people, they were antifascist and a source of concern to MUSSOLINI's government. Neorealism had a great influence on Italian film directors of the 1940s, such as Roberto ROSSELLINI and Vittorio DE SICA.

Nepal. Isolated central Asian kingdom bordering India in the northeast, Tibet and China in the north, landlocked by the Himalayan mountains. It was recognized as independent by GREAT BRITAIN in 1923. Nepal's Rana family held power as prime ministers from 1846 to 1950, and until 1956 Nepal exacted tribute from TIBET. After a successful democratic revolt in 1950, autocratic rule was replaced by constitutional government, later modified under the regime of King Mahendra in the 1960s. After his death in 1972 the king's son, Prince BIRENDRA, ascended the throne, and in May 1980 his monarchy and a parliament were ratified in Nepal's first election. The king has since vowed to establish a full-scale democracy. Having aided BRITAIN during WORLD WAR I, Nepal over the years has accepted financial aid from the U.S.S.R., China, and the U.S., though it remains essentially isolationist.

Neruda, Pablo [born Naftali Ricardo Reyes] (1904–1973). Chilean poet and diplomat. Neruda, who won the NOBEL PRIZE for literature in 1971, is one of the most widely read poets of modern times. His works are popular in all parts of the world, including China and the U.S.S.R. Neruda uses a variety of free verse forms—from short, epigrammatic poems to long-breath lines reminiscent of Walt Whitman. Born in Chile, the son of a railroad worker, Neruda studied for a career as a teacher. But his book of lyric poems, *Twenty Love Poems and a Song of Despair* (1924), proved a phenomenal success and set him on a career as a writer. Neruda also served in the Chilean diplomatic corps for many years, including stints as a consul in Burma, Singapore, Argentina (where he met Federico GARCIA LORCA) and Spain. A member of the Chilean Communist Party, Neruda ran as its candidate for the presidency of Chile in 1969 but then stepped aside in favor of Salvador ALLENDE. Other books of verse by Neruda include *Crepusculario* (1923), *Residence on Earth* (1933), *Canto General* (1950), *Elemental Odes* (1954) and *Extravagaria* (1958).

Nervi, Pier Luigi (1891–1979). Italian architect. Nervi was educated as a civil engineer, graduating in 1913. He had no formal training as an architect. Nonetheless, he went on to become an influential architect and winner of the 1965 gold medal of the American Institute of Architects. A pioneer in the structural and design use of concrete, in the mid-1940s he developed ferrocemento, a blend of mortar and steel-wire mesh. Using this material, he designed intricate buildings with soaring buttresses and swooping ceilings. Among his best-known buildings are the Turin Exhibition Hall (1949–50), the UNESCO building in Paris, the Palazzetto della Sport and other buildings for the 1960 OLYMPIC GAMES in Rome, and the Vatican Audience Hall.

Ness, Eliot (1902–1957). American law enforcement officer. Ness attended the University of Chicago and later joined the Justice Department. In 1928 he was put

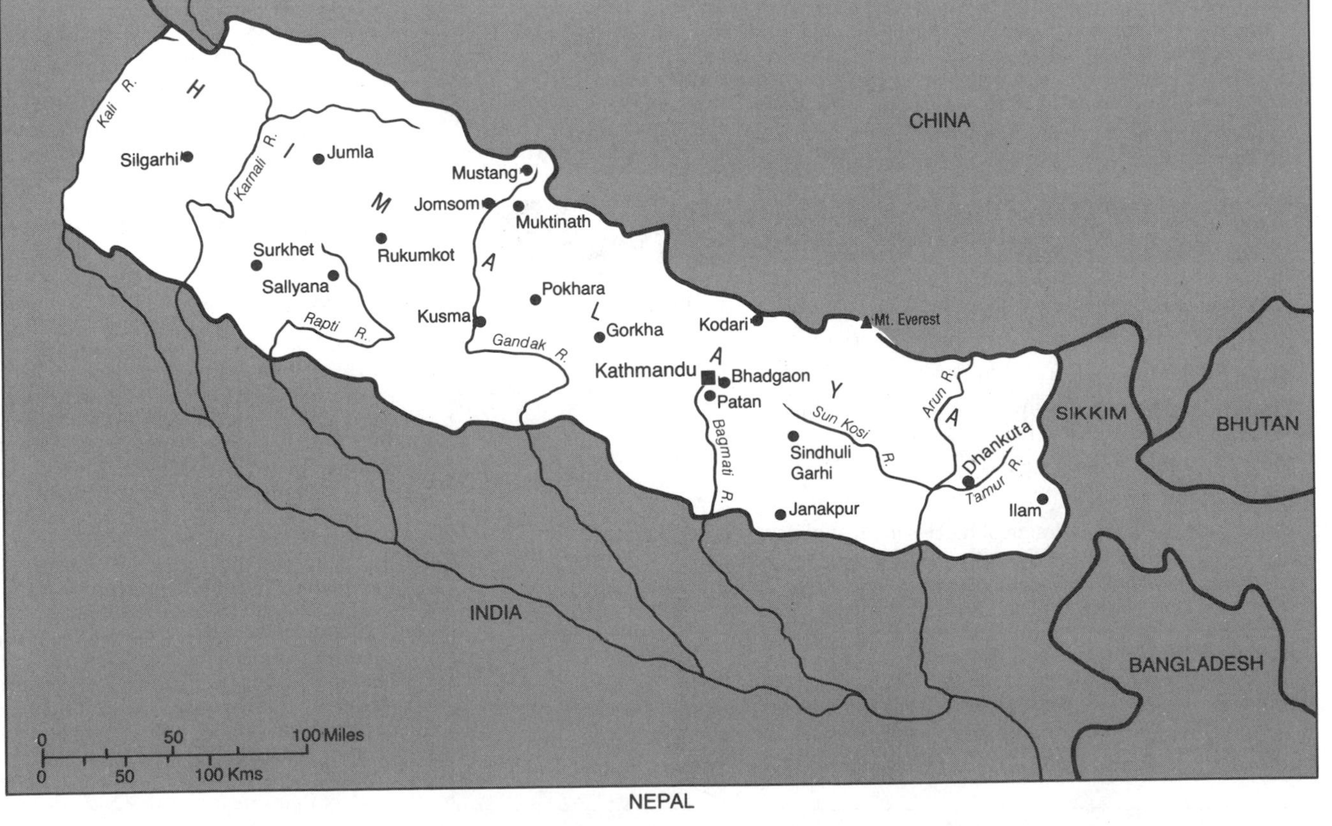

NEPAL

in charge of a hand-picked 10–man squad of incorruptible lawmen. Popularly known as the Untouchables, they were charged in general with fighting organized crime and in particular with eliminating Al CAPONE and his mob. They conducted a series of highly publicized brewery raids and distracted Capone while other agents ferreted out evidence of his income tax evasion, which led to his downfall. Ness was later named the Justice Department's chief investigator of PROHIBITION violations, first in Chicago, then in Appalachian moonshine territory. From 1935 to 1941 he was public safety director for crime-ridden Cleveland, Ohio and was credited with ridding the city of violence and corruption. He was federal director of the Division of Social Protection for the Office of Defense during WORLD WAR II, becoming a private businessman after the war. Ness' exploits were the subject of the popular television series *The Untouchables* during the 1950s and 1960s, and of a film by the same title (1989).

Netherlands, The. The Netherlands, popularly called Holland, lies on the North Sea coast of Western Europe and is bordered on the east by Germany and on the south by Belgium; the capital is Amsterdam but the seat of government is The Hague. A constitutional monarchy with a bicameral parliament, the sovereign is Queen Beatrix Wilhelmina Armgard (1938–), who became queen when her mother Queen Juliana, who had reigned since 1948, abdicated in 1980. Queen Beatrix was married in 1966 to Claus von Amsberg, a former West German diplomat, and gave birth to a son, Willem-Alexander Claus George Ferdinand in 1967—the first male heir to the throne since 1884. The monarch appoints a prime minister who is head of state and who chooses the cabinet; Prime Minister Ruud Lubbers was appointed in 1982.

The Netherlands had a firm tradition of neutrality and remained so during WORLD WAR I, but in WORLD WAR II it was invaded in 1940 by Nazi Germany. During the occupation, 104,000 Dutch Jews were deported and killed, but many were hidden and saved by other citizens. Following liberation in 1935, the Netherlands became a founder-member of the NORTH ATLANTIC TREATY ORGANIZATION (NATO), a member of the Western European Union and of the BENELUX customs union.

In 1949, the Netherlands granted independence to its East Indies colony after a four-year war. The new Republic of INDONESIA expanded in 1963 when the Netherlands ceded its western half of New Guinea to Indonesia, finally ending 300 years of Dutch presence in Asia. In 1975, SURINAME, on the northeast coast of South America, became independent. The independence of its former colonies resulted in some economic instability at home due to increased immigration homewards and resulting unemployment. In 1953, the Netherlands' economic problems were exacerbated by destructive flooding. The autonomous NETHERLANDS ANTILLES is the sole Dutch territory outside of the Netherlands. A new constitution, based on the constitution of 1815, was introduced in 1983. In 1985, after much controversy, Prime Minister Lubbers agreed to accept the deployment of U.S. CRUISE MISSILES on Dutch soil.

Netherlands Antilles [*formerly* Curacao]. Overseas territory containing the islands of Curacao, Bonaire, and Aruba off the coast of South America, as well as several northern Leeward Islands, in the West Indies, in the Caribbean Sea. Formerly a colony, it became a territory of the Netherlands in 1954, with Willemstad, on Curacao, as its capital. In 1969 it was the scene of civil strife, on Curacao.

Neto, Agostinho Antonio (1922–1979). Angolan physician and revolutionary leader, president of ANGOLA (1975–79). Born in a village near Luanda, Neto was the son of a white Methodist missionary and a black Angolan woman. He studied medicine in Portugal and received his degree in 1958. As a student in Lisbon, he became active in the movement to depose Portuguese dictator Antonio SALAZAR and was imprisoned several times. Escaping from house arrest in 1962, he assumed leadership of the Popular Movement for the Liberation of Angola (MPLA), a Soviet-backed independence group. The MPLA emerged victorious not only in its guerrilla war against Portugal, but also (with the aid of Cuban troops) in a subsequent civil war against two other nationalist organizations—Jonas SAVIMBI's National Union for the Total Independence of Angola (UNITA) and Holden Roberto's National Front for the Liberation of Angola (FNLA). Neto was proclaimed president of an independent Angola in 1975. He established a one-party state that favored the U.S.S.R. but sought ties with the West. Neto died in Moscow following surgery for cancer and was succeeded by Jose Eduardo DOS SANTOS.

Neuilly, Treaty of. Post-WORLD WAR I agreement concluded in 1919 between the Allies and BULGARIA. Part of western Thrace was ceded to Greece and small border areas were ceded to Yugoslavia. In addition, southern Dobrudja, acquired after the BALKAN WARS, was confirmed as Rumanian territory. Reparations were imposed, as was the restriction of the Bulgarian army to 20,000 men.

Neutra, Richard Josef (1892–1970). Austrian-born American architect, a pioneer in introducing modern architecture and design in the U.S. Neutra studied in Vienna with Adolf LOOS, and from 1921 to 1922 worked with Erich Mendelsohn before coming to the U.S. in 1923, where he met Louis Sullivan and worked briefly for Frank Lloyd WRIGHT. In 1926 Neutra moved to California where he established a successful practice designing houses in the INTERNATIONAL STYLE vocabulary of MODERNISM when such work was otherwise virtually unknown in the U.S. His Lovell ("Heath") house of 1927–29, with its white walls and bands of windows, established his style. It was included in New York's MUSEUM OF MODERN ART 1932 exhibition entitled *The International Style*. The desert house near Los Angeles for film director Josef Von STERNBERG, with walls of gleaming steel and large windows looking into a courtyard with a pool and curving walls (1936), is a striking example of the work that made him famous. Later work included schools and housing projects, such as the Channel Heights housing of 1946 at San Diego and the house of the same year for Edgar Kaufmann Sr. near Palm Springs, California. The massive Los Angeles County Hall of Records (1958), with automatically adjusting louvers for sun control, is an example of his later, large-scale work. Neutra's philosophy and design theories are set forth in his 1954 book *Survival Through Design*.

Neuve-Chapelle. French town 7 miles north of Bethune in Pas-de-Calais depart-

NETHERLANDS

1904	Dutch kill 541 Achinese in Sumatra; divide Timor island with Portuguese.
1914-18	Maintain neutrality during World War I.
1920	Permanent Court of Justice opens at The Hague.
1940	German troops invade, bomb Rotterdam; Dutch army surrenders, most of navy escapes to help Allies.
1945	Joins United Nations.
1947	Receives $1 billion in Marshall Plan aid.
1948	Queen Wilhelmina abdicates in favor of daughter Juliana; nationalist revolts intensify in Netherlands Indies (Indonesia); Dutch circle Jakarta, arrest Sukarno in defiance.
1949	Netherlands recognizes Indonesian independence.
1954	Suriname and Netherlands Antilles made self-governing, equal members of Dutch kingdom.
1990	Nearly completed Oosterscheldedam, world's most advanced sea barrier, holds off highest flood waters in 37 years.
1991	Lends non-combat support to Operation Desert Storm in Persian Gulf.

ment. It was occupied by the British from Mar. 10 to Mar. 13, 1915, close to the start of WORLD WAR I, and the scene of bloody battle. The British failed to take the ridge above the town, and lost 13,000 soldiers, owing to a barrage of heavy German artillery, among the first of the war. (See also NEUVILLE-ST.-VAAST.)

Neuve-Eglise [*Flemish:* Nieuwkerke]. Belgian village in the province of West Flanders, close to Ypres. During WORLD WAR I it became a battleground, after the third battle of Ypres, on April 12 and 13, 1918.

Neuville-St.-Vaast. French town 4 miles north of ARRAS in Pas-de-Calais department, near Vimy Ridge, where heavy fighting broke out between the British and the Germans in May 1915, near the start of WORLD WAR I. Completely destroyed, the town was rebuilt after the war.

Nevelson, Louise (1900–1988). American sculptor. Born Louise Berliawsky in Kiev, Russia, she came to the U.S. with her family at the age of five. She studied at the Art Students League in New York (1929–30) and at the Hans Hoffmann School in Munich (1931), subsequently serving as an assistant to Diego RIVERA in Mexico City (1932–33). She traveled widely in Europe and Latin America, returned to the U.S. and had her first one-woman show in New York in 1941. Her abstract sculptures are often composed of found objects, mainly planks, chair legs, balusters and other turned pieces of wood. Assembled into boxes painted in uniform tones of black, white or gold, they have a compelling and enigmatic presence. These compositions grew larger and more environmental as her career progressed. In the work of the 1960s and 1970s, Nevelson also made use of metals and Plexiglas. Her work is particularly well represented in the collections of New York's MUSEUM OF MODERN ART and Whitney Museum of American Art.

Nevins, Allan (1890–1971). American historian. Nevins earned a master's degree from the University of Illinois in 1913, after which he worked in New York City as a journalist. In 1928, he joined the history department of Columbia University, where he remained for three decades. During his long and fruitful career, Nevins wrote widely on American history, including his biographies of Grover Cleveland and Hamilton Fish, which won PULITZER PRIZES in 1932 and 1936, respectively, and his eight-volume history of the Civil War, *Ordeal of the Union* (1947–71). Nevins was also one of the founders of *American Heritage* magazine.

New Age Movement. The New Age Movement, which first won attention during the intense social change of the 1960s with its proclamations of a new Age of Aquarius, emerged in the 1980s and 1990s as a loosely defined but highly cherished label for a broad variety of spiritual, social and personal concerns. Basically, New Age refers to an open attitude toward such belief systems as pagan, occult, oriental and modern syncretistic movements; it considers them to be valid spiritual alternatives to the Judeo-Christian tradition. The New Age also posits the end of a past historical epoch dominated by war, nationalism and materialism; points to a new planetary union of peoples that will combine benign development with ecological awareness. Key, albeit disparate, figures in the development of New Age thinking include Joseph CAMPBELL, TEILHARD DE CHARDIN, Aleister CROWLEY, Fritz PERLS, E.F. Schumacher, D.T. Suzuki, and Alan Watts.

Newbery Medal. American children's literature award. The John Newbery Medal was established in 1922 and is awarded annually by the Children's Librarians Sections of the American Library Association to notable works of literature for children. It is named after John Newbery (1713–1767), one of the earliest publishers of children's books. The medal itself was designed by the American sculptor, Rene Chambellan and is contributed by Frederic G. Melcher, the editor of *Publisher's Weekly*. The first medal was presented to Hendrik Willem Van Loon for *The Story of Mankind* (1922).

New Britain [*German:* Neu-Pommern] (Papua New Guinea). Largest of the islands of the BISMARCK ARCHIPELAGO, in the southwest Pacific Ocean, first discovered by the British in 1700. In 1884 it was colonized by Germany, and during WORLD WAR I was taken by AUSTRALIA and retained as a LEAGUE OF NATIONS mandate from 1920 to 1941. In January 1942 it was claimed by the JAPANESE, whose positions here subjected it to heavy U.S. air raids and follow-up invasions from late 1943 to March 1944, and it remained the scene of intense conflict until the end of WORLD WAR II.

New Criticism. A term coined by poet and critic John Crowe RANSOM in *The New Criticism* (1941), which addresses the works of I.A. RICHARDS, T.S. ELIOT and William EMPSON, among others. The term's meaning has been stretched and blurred but generally it refers to literary interpretation based on close attention to the text and its nuance as well as emphasis on thematic organization. It rejects analysis of a work's background or its creator's motivation, focusing instead on each poem, story or novel as a self-contained work of art. Others associated with the New Criticism (not always willingly) include Robert Penn WARREN, R.P. Blackmur, and F.R. LEAVIS. The New Criticism was dominant in the academic study of literature from the 1940s through the 1960s but has since been largely supplanted by other critical approaches such as FEMINISM, DECONSTRUCTION and STRUCTURALISM.

New Deal. Economic and social reform program instituted by President Franklin ROOSEVELT in 1933. When Roosevelt assumed the presidency, the U.S. was in the depths of the GREAT DEPRESSION. Nearly one-quarter of the workforce had lost their jobs, and thousands of people, unable to pay their bills, had been thrown out of their homes and farms. FDR was elected with a mandate to deal with the crisis. His program was radical for its day: The government established social programs and became involved in the economy in an unprecedented manner. Programs like the Civil Works Administration (CWA), CIVILIAN CONSERVATION CORPS (CCC) and WORKS PROGRESS ADMINISTRATION (WPA) used borrowed money to put the unemployed back to work. FDR also established the Social Security system to provide a universal, social safety net. Many feared this massive expansion of government power, and the Supreme Court initially struck down many of the programs. Although the New Deal helped many, it was the mobilization for World War II that decisively brought the U.S. out of the Depression. However, the legacy of the New Deal endures—an expanded federal government that continues to play an active role in the social and economic life of the country.

New Delhi. Capital city of INDIA, five miles south of ancient Delhi on the Jumna River; built to replace CALCUTTA as the new British capital of INDIA. Begun in 1912 as an administrative center, it was designed on an imposing scale by Sir Edwin LUTYENS and others by order of King GEORGE V, with grand avenues and the impressive Government House for the viceroy taking 17 years to complete. In 1931 it was officially opened, but Britain withdrew soon thereafter, granting India its independence in 1948, also the year Mahatma GANDHI was assassinated here by a Hindu fanatic.

New Democratic Party (Canada). The third major Canadian political party behind the Liberals and Progressive Conservatives. The New Democratic Party is left-of-center and was formed in 1933 out of the United Farmers Party, the Socialist Party of Canada and various immigrant groups. Until 1961 the party was known as the Cooperative Commonwealth Federation. Its support has traditionally come from western farmers and working people in Ontario. To date, the party has been most successful at the provincial rather than the national level. During the 1970s the NDP controlled governments in the provinces of British Columbia and Saskatchewan. In 1990, the NDP shocked the nation as it took control of the government of Ontario, Canada's wealthiest and most populous province.

New Economic Policy. Economic policy practiced by the Soviet government in 1921–28, replacing the policies of WAR COMMUNISM (1918–21). It aimed at revitalizing the economy by allowing greater freedom in agriculture, industry and trade. In this, the government was successful and raised the national income above that of 1913. The NEP was followed by the first FIVE-YEAR PLAN.

Newfoundland. Province of eastern CANADA. Although Newfoundland had been an independent British colony since 1855, France did not cede its fishing rights until 1904. With fishing, paper production and iron ore, Newfoundland's economy was strong until the end of WORLD WAR I, when demand for its exports declined. After squabbling between Quebec and Newfoundland over Labrador, the British Privy Council established the current boundaries of the provinces in 1927. During the GREAT DEPRESSION, Britain responded to an appeal for help by suspending Newfoundland's internal government and reassuming control in 1934. In 1948 Newfoundland elected to become a part of Canada, and in 1949 Newfoundland and Labrador became Canada's 10th province.

New Georgia. Island group and chief island in the Solomon Islands archipelago, approximately 40 miles south of Choiseul Island. In 1942 it was seized by JAPAN and developed as a military base at Munda, and after fierce combat from June to August 1943 it was occupied by U.S. troops during WORLD WAR II. A former British protectorate, New Georgia gained independence in 1978 when it joined the nation of the SOLOMON ISLANDS.

New Hebrides. Island group in the southwest Pacific Ocean, east of Australia, discovered by the Portuguese in 1606. In the early 19th century British missionaries came to these islands, and by 1887 the group was placed under British-French rule to stop the enslavement of its native population for plantation labor in Australia. In 1906, New Hebrides became a condominium, and during WORLD WAR II it served as an important U.S. naval base, on ESPIRITU SANTO Island. The islands gained independence on July 30, 1980, as the Republic of VANUATU.

Newhouse, Samuel (Irving) (1895–1979). American publishing and broadcasting magnate. Described as "America's most profitable publisher," Newhouse began with a single newspaper in 1922 and went on to build a multimillion-dollar communications empire. By the 1970s his properties included 31 newspapers in 22 American cities, seven magazines, six television stations, five radio stations, and 20 cable television stations. His son S(amuel) I(rving) "Sy" Newhouse II inherited the business and added the distinguished publishing firm Random House to the Newhouse empire in 1980.

Ne Win, U (1911–). Ne Win has been by far the dominant figure in the political life of independent Myanmar (formerly BURMA). He was chief of the armed forces from 1948, deputy prime minister from 1948 to 1950, prime minister from 1958 to 1960, chairman of the Revolutionary Council from 1962 to 1974, president from 1974 to 1981 and chairman of the Burmese Socialist Program Party from 1962 to 1988. Ne Win has a retiring, self-effacing public persona; paradoxically, he exerts a most powerful charisma. It is widely believed that Ne Win has corruptly acquired vast wealth. This belief, allied to severely deteriorating economic conditions, fueled the unrest in mid-1988 that drove Ne Win to resign as chairman of the BSPP on July 12. He remains a powerful figure, and it is thought that he was the guiding hand behind the army coup of September 18, 1988.

New Journalism. Style of journalistic writing that first won wide popularity in the U.S. in the 1960s. New Journalism is a blending of factual reporting and imaginative interpretation that first flourished in such magazines as *Esquire* and *Rolling Stone* and weekly urban tabloids, such as the *Village Voice*—rather than in traditional daily newspapers. The best New Journalism pieces brought a freshness of style and an impassioned mode of analysis to subject matter—such as presidential elections—that had long been handled in a strictly objective format. Among the key practitioners of New Journalism during its emergence were Joan DIDION, Norman MAILER, Gay Talese, Hunter S. THOMPSON, and Tom WOLFE. The style has remained a staple of magazine writing ever since.

Newman, Arnold (1918–). American photographer. Born in New York City, Newman is highly acclaimed for his portraits of famous writers, actors, artists and political leaders. His photographic style is probing and sharply focused. He often poses his sitters in a setting that reflects their personalities and professions.

For further reading:

Newman, Arnold, *Arnold Newman in Florida*. Boston: David Godine, 1988.

———, *Arnold Newman: Five Decades*. Orlando, Florida: Harcourt Brace Jovanovich, 1986.

———, *The Great British*. Chicago: University of Chicago Press, 1980.

———, *One Man's Eye—The Portraits and Other Photographs of Arnold Newman*. 1974.

Newman, Barnett (1905–1971). American painter. Born in New York City, he studied at City College, Cornell University and the Art Students League. In the mid-1940s, he began to paint canvases that exploded spatial convention by interrupting flat fields of pure color with one or more narrow vertical stripes. *Stations of the Cross*, a series of paintings he did from 1958 to 1966, are severe black-and-white compositions in which vertical bands interact with a raw ground in completely two-dimensional space. Newman's later paintings, such as *Blue Midnight* (1970), contrast large areas of color on huge canvases, again separated and intensified by narrow stripes. Newman bridged the gap between ABSTRACT EXPRESSIONISM and COLOR-FIELD PAINTING—and was active in both movements. His works proved extremely influential on abstract painters of the 1960s and 1970s.

For further reading:

O'Neill, John P., ed., *Barnett Newman: Selected Writings and Interviews*. New York: Alfred Knopf, 1990.

Newman, Paul (1925–). American movie actor. Born in Shaker Heights, Ohio, he attended Kenyon College and was trained as an actor at the Yale School of Drama and the Actors Studio. His meteoric rise to fame began with his stage role in *Picnic* (1953). He achieved HOLLYWOOD stardom in *The Long Hot Summer* (1958). Handsome, gifted and possessed of extraordinary blue eyes, Newman gained fame for

American actor Paul Newman (1983).

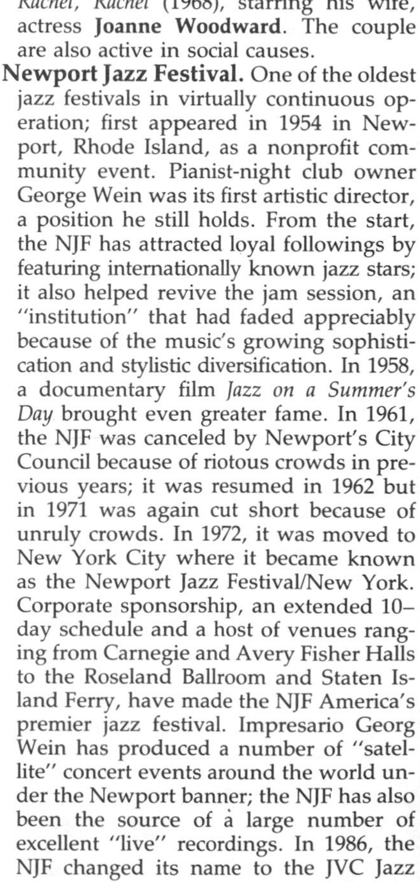

roles as ironic and self-reliant antiheroes in such movies as *The Hustler* (1961), *Hud* (1963), *Cool Hand Luke* (1967), *Butch Cassidy and the Sundance Kid* (1969), *The Sting* (1973), *Absence of Malice* (1981), *The Verdict* (1982) and *Blaze* (1989). He gave memorable performances in two dramas by Tennessee WILLIAMS: *Cat on a Hot Tin Roof* (1959) and *Sweet Bird of Youth* (1962). Newman received an ACADEMY AWARD for his reprise of *The Hustler*'s Fast Eddie in *The Color of Money* (1986). He is also a successful director whose credits include *Rachel, Rachel* (1968), starring his wife, actress **Joanne Woodward**. The couple are also active in social causes.

Newport Jazz Festival. One of the oldest jazz festivals in virtually continuous operation; first appeared in 1954 in Newport, Rhode Island, as a nonprofit community event. Pianist-night club owner George Wein was its first artistic director, a position he still holds. From the start, the NJF has attracted loyal followings by featuring internationally known jazz stars; it also helped revive the jam session, an "institution" that had faded appreciably because of the music's growing sophistication and stylistic diversification. In 1958, a documentary film *Jazz on a Summer's Day* brought even greater fame. In 1961, the NJF was canceled by Newport's City Council because of riotous crowds in previous years; it was resumed in 1962 but in 1971 was again cut short because of unruly crowds. In 1972, it was moved to New York City where it became known as the Newport Jazz Festival/New York. Corporate sponsorship, an extended 10–day schedule and a host of venues ranging from Carnegie and Avery Fisher Halls to the Roseland Ballroom and Staten Island Ferry, have made the NJF America's premier jazz festival. Impresario Georg Wein has produced a number of "satellite" concert events around the world under the Newport banner; the NJF has also been the source of a large number of excellent "live" recordings. In 1986, the NJF changed its name to the JVC Jazz Festival/New York to acknowledge its prime sponsor, the Japanese Victory Corporation.

For further reading:
Frankling, Ken, "George Wein's Long Run." *Jazz Times*, October 1985.

New Republic, The. American periodical founded in 1914. A liberal weekly, *The New Republic* was founded by William Straight, who married the wealthy Dorothy Whitney; the two financed the magazine and absorbed its losses. Under the editorship of Herbert Croly from 1914 until 1930, the magazine supported labor unions, woman suffrage and prison reform. It reluctantly abandoned its neutrality in WORLD WAR I but opposed the TREATY OF VERSAILLES, espousing "Peace without victory." Croly was succeeded by Bruce Bliven in 1930, and the magazine maintained its left-leaning stance, first supporting the socialist presidential candidate but later embracing Franklin D. ROOSEVELT. It accepted U.S. participation in WORLD WAR II. Henry A. WALLACE, former vice president to Roosevelt, became editor in 1946, and the magazine's circulation soared to nearly 100,000. In 1954, Dorothy Straight sold the magazine to Gilbert A. Harrison, and it went on to support the presidential bids of Adlai STEVENSON and John F. KENNEDY and later to assail the corruption of WATERGATE. In 1974, the magazine was sold again, to Martin Peretz, a lecturer at Harvard University, and has continued to uphold a moderate, liberal stance. Contributors to *The New Republic* have included Malcolm COWLEY, Margaret SANGER, Thomas WOLFE, John STEINBECK, Mary MCCARTHY and Delmore SCHWARTZ.

Newton, Huey P(ercy) (1942–1989). American black activist. In the late 1960s he cofounded the BLACK PANTHER Party, which advocated black self-reliance and self-defense against police racism and brutality. A charismatic symbol of black anger, Newton was dogged by frequent trouble with the law. When he was convicted in 1968 of voluntary manslaughter in the death of an Oakland, California policeman, "Free Huey" became a rallying cry among radicals and many college students. The conviction was overturned in 1970, and the charges were dismissed after two subsequent trials ended in hung juries. Later troubles stemmed from charges that he had murdered a prostitute, charges that were ultimately dropped. He was convicted in the early 1980s for weapons possession. In the meantime, he earned a Ph.D. in social psychology (1980) and entered a drug-abuse program in 1984. He was shot to death on a street in Oakland.

new towns. Urban planning concept for building entire "new towns" to relieve overcrowding in existing cities and provide a pleasant environment in which to live and work. The construction of new towns was legislated in the UNITED KINGDOM after World War II by the New Towns Act of 1946. New towns are designed to include residential and light industrial buildings, with ample shopping and leisure facilities for residents. New towns in Britain include Welwyn Garden City, Milton Keynes and Stevenage. (See also GREEN BELT.)

New Wave. Loosely defined and loosely organized movement in rock music that emerged in the 1970s. The New Wave, which became popular both in Britain and the U.S., embraced a number of highly disparate musical talents. It was united, however, by a reaction against both the superstar syndrome which had come to dominate rock and roll, as well as the heavy-metal emphasis that had emerged in the early 1970s (with bands such as LED ZEPPELIN). Instead, the New Wave musicians sought to pare rock down to its basic 1950s rhythm forms and to introduce new sounds, such as Reggae and minimalist electronic music. Major New Wave musicians and bands include The B-52s, The Cars, Elvis COSTELLO, Dave Edmunds, Nick Lowe, Graham Parker, The POLICE and Jonathan Richman.

New Wave. French film movement that began in the late 1900s. (See also NOUVELLE VAGUE.)

new world order. Term coined by U.S. President George BUSH to describe a post-COLD WAR realignment in international relations among the world's nations. Among the main tenets of the new world order is the assumption that the U.S. and the U.S.S.R. are no longer ideological enemies or military rivals; rather, the U.S. and the U.S.S.R. would cooperate to assure that other nations (notably those formerly under communist rule in Eastern Europe) achieve self-determination. The ideals of the new world order were first put to the test during the PERSIAN GULF WAR. In that conflict, the U.S.S.R. supported UNITED NATIONS resolutions to oust IRAQ from KUWAIT. Moreover, the U.S.S.R. did not oppose U.S. military efforts in the conflict.

New York City (United States) City and port at the mouth of the Hudson River on New York Bay, comprising the five boroughs of Manhattan, the Bronx, Brooklyn, Queens and Richmond (Staten Island), in southeast New York State. In addition to being the largest city in the U.S., for 200 years it has been one of the world's busiest ports, its leading financial center, foremost in entertainment and the arts, a premier manufacturing and commercial center, and a tourist mecca. The city also was a gateway for millions of immigrants who poured in through ELLIS ISLAND in the late 19th and 20th centuries, making New York perhaps the most illustrious "melting pot" in the world. The early 20th century witnessed the birth of New York's skyscrapers, and in 1904 the city opened one of the nation's first subway systems. Throughout alternating periods of corruption and political reform, the need for cooperation among the tri-state metropolitan region of New York, New Jersey, and Connecticut resulted in what now is the Port Authority of New York and New Jersey, established in 1921. Having suffered the ills of modern urbanization since WORLD WAR II, in 1975 New York was on the verge of bankruptcy. While the city's black and Hispanic population has increased, it lost population to its suburbs; city school and transportation systems have been severely strained, housing has deteriorated, and crime is on the rise. Despite its hardships, toward which most major U.S. cities are now tending, New York nevertheless reigns supreme for its historic architecture, national landmarks, including the Statue of Liberty, its museums, cultural institutions, colleges and universities, medical facilities, zoos, parks, churches and bridges, restaurants, music and theater, ROCKEFELLER CENTER, SoHo, Central Park, and Yankee Stadium. It is also the site of the UNITED NATIONS.

New York City Ballet. One of the great dance companies in the world, it emerged under its present name in 1948 as the resident company of New York City Center after 14 years of development, during which time it was known variously as American Ballet, Ballet Caravan and Ballet Society. With George BALANCHINE as artistic director, Jerome ROBBINS as artistic codirector and Lincoln KIRSTEIN as general manager, the company developed a classical style that is distinctly American. The company presented the first original full-length ballet created in America, Balanchine's *Midsummer Night's Dream* (1963), and staged a triumphant Stravinsky Festival in 1972 in honor of Balanchine's long-time musical collaborator, Igor STRAVINSKY. The repertory is dominated by the works of Balanchine, such as *Agon* (1957) and *Liebeslieder Walzer* (1960), and of Robbins, such as *Dances at a Gathering* (1969) and *The Goldberg Variations* (1971). Outstanding dancers associated with the company include Edward Villella, Maria TALLCHIEF, Suzanne FARRELL, Patricia McBride and Peter MARTINS. In 1964 the company took up residence at the New York State Theatre at Lincoln Center. After the death of Balanchine in 1983, Martins and Robbins became ballet masters in chief.

New Yorker, The. American magazine founded by Harold Ross in 1925. The magazine established itself as a sophisticated, satirical weekly notable not only for its humor, but also for its intelligent reporting. The many legendary American authors associated with the magazine's early days include Dorothy PARKER, James THURBER, E.B. WHITE, John HERSEY and the cartoonist Charles ADDAMS. The magazine maintains its literary standing, publishing fiction by John UPDIKE and Mavis GALLANT, among others. Since the editorial changes in the mid-1980s, however, when many long-time staffers left, some readers feel that its editorial quality has diminished. In 1985, *The New Yorker* was acquired by the publishing magnate S.I. NEWHOUSE.

For further reading:
Thurber, James, *The Years With Ross*. New York: AMS Press, 1957.
Gill, Brendan, *Here at the New Yorker*. New York: Carroll & Graf, 1975.

New York Herald-Tribune. American newspaper begun in 1924 and folded in

1966. The *Herald-Tribune* was formed by the merger of the *New York Herald* and the *New York Tribune,* whose owners, Ogden M. and Helen Rogers Reid, bought the *Herald* from Frank A. Munsey for $5 million. In its prime, the *Herald-Tribune* was noted for its typographical excellence, quality writing and incisive political and foreign reporting and commentary. Its reporters were considered the best in the country, and its political columnists included Walter LIPPMANN, Joseph Alsop and Roscoe Drummond. Its politics were consistently Republican except in 1964, when it supported Democratic presidential candidate Lyndon B. JOHNSON over Republican Barry GOLDWATER. The paper began to flounder following Ogden Reid's death in 1947 when his wife became president and their elder son, Whitelaw, editor. Mrs. Reid later withdrew, and her younger son Ogden became publisher and editor. In 1957, the *Herald-Tribune* was bought by John Hay Whitney, head of Whitney Communications Corporation, but his attempts to revive the paper were of little avail. The 114–day newspaper strike of 1962–63 proved disastrous; the paper steadily lost money and was forced to shut down three years later.

New York Times. American newspaper founded in 1851. Perhaps America's most venerated newspaper, the *Times* established its current reputation at the turn of the century under the leadership of Adolph S. Ochs, who had been appointed publisher and general manager in 1896. Ochs adopted the motto "All the News That's Fit to Print," installed the paper's vast, worldwide network of correspondents, emphasized international news and established the paper's policy of printing important speeches, papers and news conferences in their entirety. The *Times* was the only paper to publish the complete TREATY OF VERSAILLES, and it won a PULITZER PRIZE in 1918 for its comprehensive publication of wartime documents. It received another Pulitzer in 1972 for printing the PENTAGON PAPERS. The *Times* and its staff have won more Pulitzer Prizes than any other American daily. The *Times* pioneered the use of the wireless in news gathering, and on election night, 1928, its famous electronic bulletin board began circling the Times Tower in Manhattan's Times Square. This building, to which the paper had moved in 1904, was sold in 1961.

Following World War I, the paper characterized its editorial policy as independent and Democratic, yet it upholds a fairly conservative stance. It backed Republican presidential candidates in the '40s and '50s yet denounced MCCARTHYISM. In the 1960s, under executive editor A.M. Rosenthal, it endorsed Democratic candidates and published the entire Warren Commission Report following John F. KENNEDY's assassination. But it was unsympathetic to the student uprisings in 1968, and Columbia University students picketed the home of publisher Arthur Ochs "Punch" Sulzberger. While its revelation of the Pentagon Papers helped bring about an end to the VIETNAM WAR, the *Times* was second to the WASHINGTON POST in its coverage of the WATERGATE break-in. In the mid-1970s, though, it led the way in exposing abuses in the CENTRAL INTELLIGENCE AGENCY.

In 1978, it began running a four-section daily, with the third section devoted to a different topic each day. The *Times* has been criticized from both the right and the left for its political views and its economic position. In the 1980s, its shift toward more entertainment and "soft" news incurred censure; however, it retains its worldwide reputation with a nationwide circulation of approximately 873,000 daily and 1,430,000 Sunday, and also owns other papers, magazines, radio and television stations and book publishers.

New York Times v. Sullivan (1964). Landmark U.S. Supreme Court decision defining libel law and the right of the press under the First Amendment. In 1960 the *New York Times* ran a civil rights group's ad charging the Montgomery, Alabama, police with misconduct. Several statements in the ad were inaccurate, and a Montgomery court awarded the local police commissioner a $500,000 libel award against the newspaper. The *Times* appealed, and the case went to the Supreme Court. The Court absolved the *Times,* holding that if a public official or a "public figure" is libeled by a false report, the injured party must show that the press acted with actual malice in publishing the statement. Malice would consist of knowledge that the statement was false or reckless disregard of its falsity. A public figure is one who, although not a public official, is a party who has jumped or been thrust into the public limelight by news events.

New York Times v. United States. Popularly known as the Pentagon Papers case; the Supreme Court refused to halt the publication of stories in the *New York Times* and *Washington Post* based on material from a classified Pentagon study of the origins of the VIETNAM WAR. The Nixon administration had attempted to halt publication of these stories, claiming that their publication during the continuing Vietnam conflict would be detrimental to national security. The Supreme Court rejected this argument and held that, under the First Amendment, suppression of the material would be an illegal prior restraint of freedom of the press.

New York World's Fair of 1939. Held in Flushing Meadows, Queens (1939–40), this exposition included a number of American exhibits as well as national exhibits from various countries around the world. It took for its theme "Building the World of Tomorrow." Costing nearly $160 million, the Fair was symbolized by a 700 ft.-tall Trylon and a 200 ft.-diameter Perisphere. Among the better-known U.S. designers and architects who created sleek and streamlined exhibits for the 1939 World's Fair were Norman BEL GEDDES, Henry DREYFUSS, Raymond LOEWY and Walter Dorwin Teague. It was the last major World's Fair held until the Brussels Exposition of 1958.

New Zealand. Country in the South Pacific, 1,000 miles south of AUSTRALIA. Formerly a British colony, New Zealand became a dominion in 1907 and was granted independence by the Statute of Westminster in 1931. Its full independence as a commonwealth was confirmed by its parliament in 1947. New Zealand aided Britain and fought with the Allies in both WORLD WAR I and WORLD WAR II. New Zealand troops joined the UNITED NATIONS forces in KOREA in the 1950s, and a smaller contingent fought in VIETNAM in the 1960s. New Zealand has a history of progressive social reform, having passed legislation on the vote for women and on social security in the late 19th century. Beginning in 1935 under Prime Minister M.J. SAVAGE, the LABOUR PARTY introduced public works programs, aid to farmers as well as health care and social security enhancements to mitigate the effects of the worldwide GREAT DEPRESSION.

In the early 1970s under the administration of Labour Party Prime Minister Norman Kirk, New Zealand experienced some economic instability due to the energy crisis and GREAT BRITAIN's decision to enter the EEC. New Zealand began withdrawing what troops it had in Southeast Asia at this time. Kirk died in 1974 and was succeeded by his finance minister, Wallace Rowling. The economy worsened and the National Party was voted into power in 1975 with Robert Muldoon as prime minister.

The Labour Party returned to power in 1984, led by David LANGE, who proposed an antinuclear defense policy. Lange's government strained relations with the UNITED STATES by refusing entry into New Zealand's ports of any nuclear-powered vessel or vessel bearing nuclear arms. In 1985 *Rainbow Warrior,* a vessel of the GREENPEACE environmental organization that was monitoring nuclear tests in the area, was mined in Auckland Harbor—arousing much indignation. French Prime Minister MITTERRAND later admitted the French secret service was responsible. New Zealand's relations with the U.S. improved in 1987 when the National Party supported a bipartisan non-nuclear policy.

Ngala, Ronald G. (1923–1972). Kenyan political leader. A moderate nationalist, Ngala was involved in the movement for Kenyan independence in the late 1950s and early '60s. In 1960 with Daniel Arap Moi, he formed the Kenyan African Democratic Union, which was a rival to Jomo KENYATTA's more militant Kenya African National Union (KANU). Ngala led a coalition government in the early 1960s before independence. In 1964, following independence (December 12, 1963), Ngala announced that the KANU would support Kenyatta as president of the new republic. (See also KENYA.)

Ngoyi, Lillian (1911–1980). Black nationalist South African leader known as "the mother of the black resistance." From the

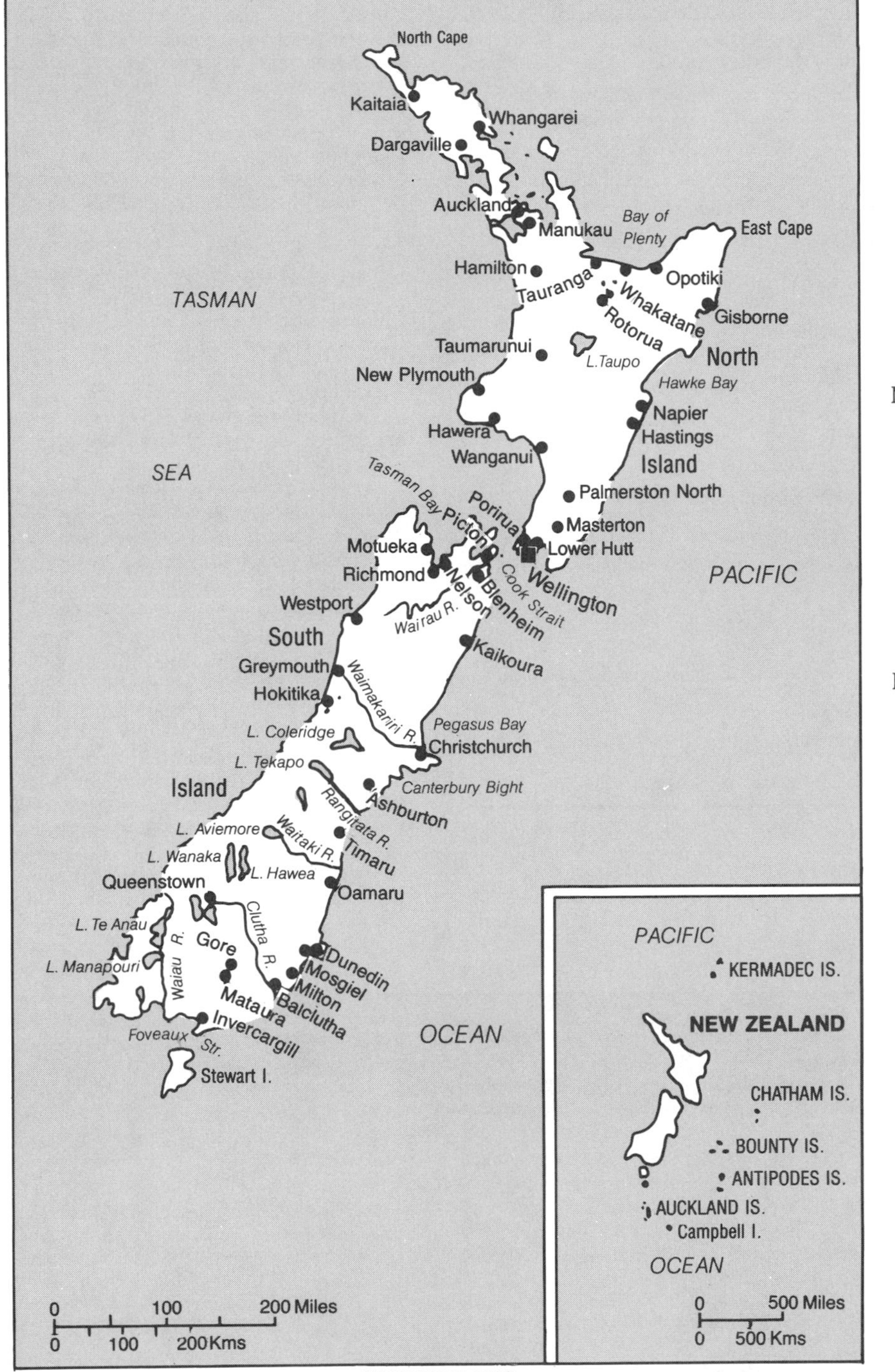

NEW ZEALAND

mid-1960s until her death, Ngoyi was declared a "banned person" by the South African government. Under the banning order, the government restricted her movements and contacts and forbade her to be quoted by newspapers. She was also one of the first persons to be confined under a 90-day detention law, spending 71 days in prison without charge or trial in 1963. (See also SOUTH AFRICA, APARTHEID.)

Nguyen Van Linh [born Nguyen Van Cuc] (1915–). Vietnamese communist leader. Nguyen Van Linh was elected secretary-general of the Vietnamese Communist Party in 1986. He joined the students' union of the Vietnam Revolutionary Youth Association in 1929 and was imprisoned in 1930 by the French for his resistance activities. He joined the ICP upon his release from prison in 1936 and founded a provisional party organization and many party bases in Haiphong. He was arrested again in 1941 after conducting revolutionary activities in central VIETNAM. After his release in 1945 he became secretary of the Saigon Party Committee and led the resistance against the French. From 1957 until 1960 he was acting secretary of the Central Party Commission for the South. In 1960 he was elected to the party central committee. Linh's party positions made him a major leader in southern resistance to the U.S.-backed regimes. He was appointed secretary of the Ho Chi Minh City Party Committee after reunification. He was reelected to the party central committee and appointed to the political bureau. Though originally a northerner, Linh has spent much time in the south. He has followed a reform policy and shown a willingness to experiment with free-market principles.

Niagara Movement. Pioneering organization formed by black Americans whose aim was to fight racial discrimination in the U.S. Led by W.E.B. DU BOIS, it was founded in 1905 and disbanded in 1910. The group was not particularly influential, but its ideas and programs were adopted by the NATIONAL ASSOCIATION FOR THE ADVANCEMENT OF COLORED PEOPLE (NAACP), an interracial group cofounded by Du Bois in 1909 that supplanted the Niagara Movement.

Nicaragua. Largest Central American nation, bordered by EL SALVADOR and HONDURAS to the north, by the Caribbean Sea on the east, by COSTA RICA on the south and the Pacific Ocean to the west. In 1909 a revolution broke out against the harsh presidency of Jose Santos Zelaya, and with help of the UNITED STATES, drove him from office. In 1912, U.S. Marines landed in Nicaragua to help quell rebellion against President Adolfo Diaz and to protect American investments, thus beginning an almost unbroken U.S. military presence in the country, which would continue until 1933. General Augusto Cesar SANDINO led rebels who were resentful of U.S. intervention. The U.S. helped establish a National Guard, which was led by Anastasio SOMOZA Garcia. After the departure of the U.S. Marines, Somoza had Sandino assassinated and later forced President Juan Sacasa out of office and assumed power. The Somoza family led a repressive and corrupt regime, aided by the U.S., toward whose interests they were friendly. In 1979 the Sandinista National Liberation Front (FSLN), with broadbased popular support, toppled the government of Major General Anastasio SOMOZA DEBAYLE, who fled the country. The Sandinistas established a junta to run the government. Initially moderate, the junta became increasingly left-leaning. In 1981 President REAGAN, charging that the Sandinistas had communist ties and were supplying arms to EL SALVADOR, revoked U.S. economic aid and set out to overthrow the government of Daniel ORTEGA, the revolutionary leader who became president in 1984. The CIA began covert operations, including mining Nicaraguan harbors, and the U.S. backed the counterrevolutionary CONTRAS, initially with the approval of Congress, and later illegally. In 1985 Reagan declared a trade embargo on Nicaragua, further destabilizing the economy. In 1988 the Sandinistas and the Contras negotiated a cease-fire, and elections were scheduled for 1990, when Violeta Barrios de CHAMORRO, a former publisher of *La Prensa* and a member of a prominent political family, was elected president.

Nicaraguan Civil War of 1909–12. In 1909 conservatives rebelled against the liberal dictator-president, Jose Santos Zelaya; two U.S. citizens aiding the rebels were executed, causing angry U.S. protests. Zelaya was forced to resign (December 16, 1909), and NICARAGUA was reduced to near anarchy. After a power struggle between conservative and liberal factions, the conservative Adolfo Diaz became provisional president (May 11, 1911), and requested U.S. aid. A treaty, to retire debts through American customs collection and provide loans from New York banks, was rejected by the U.S. Senate. It was, however, enacted by President William Howard TAFT as an executive order. A revolt by Nicaraguan liberals in July, 1912 was suppressed with aid from 2,500 U.S. Marines, who stayed to supervise elections; Diaz was elected. A U.S. legation guard of 100 remained in Nicaragua for 13 years.

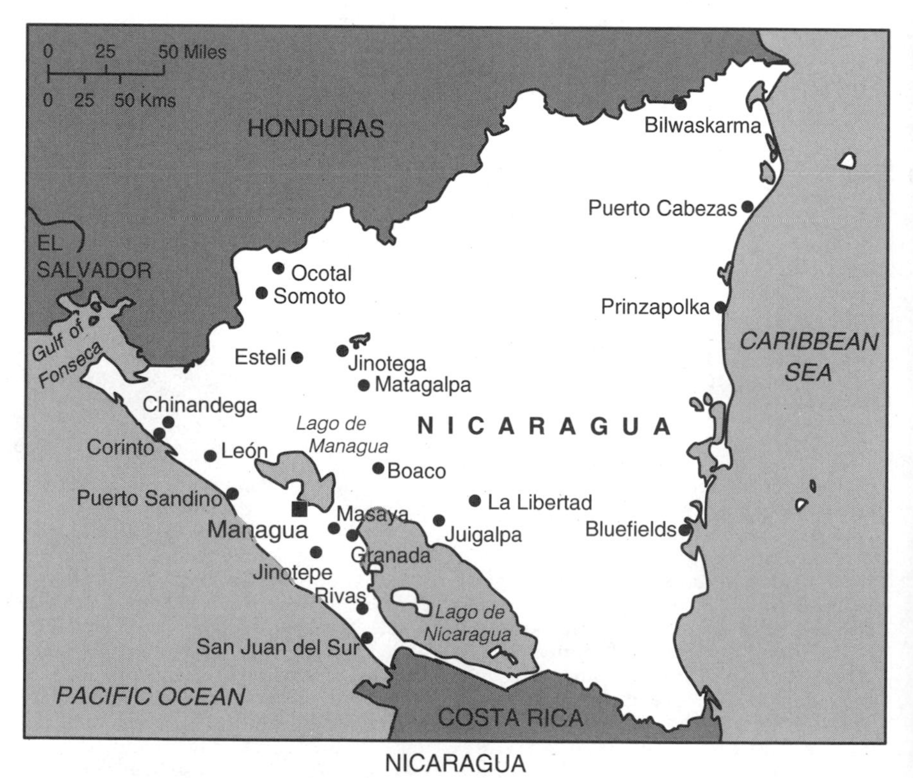

NICARAGUA

NEW ZEALAND

1907	New Zealand made a dominion under the British Crown.
1910	Refrigeration makes it possible for Britain to buy huge quantities of New Zealand meat and dairy products.
1914	Almost 10% of population volunteers to fight in World War I; almost 2% killed.
1926	Granted self-government within British Commonwealth.
1935	Labour Party creates world's first welfare state in response to Great Depression.
1936	National Party formed in opposition.
1944	Wartime conditions encourage self-sufficiency in manufacturing.
1947	Granted full independence.
1949	National Party wins elections.
1951	ANZUS alliance formed with Australia and U.S.
1952	New Zealand grants independence to Western Samoa.
1953	One of history's worst train wrecks kills hundreds at Tangiwai.
1967	Decimal currency adopted.
1984	Effectively leaves ANZUS alliance by refusing to allow nuclear-powered or -armed ships to enter its harbors.
1985	*Rainbow Warrior,* a ship belonging to Greenpeace environmentalist group, is blown up in Auckland harbor by French Secret Service; government begins programs to aid Maoris, islands' indigenous population.
1987	Maori recognized as an official language.
1990	Recession creates dissatisfaction with Labour government; National Party wins elections in landslide.

Nicaraguan Civil War of 1925–33. In 1925 a coalition government was elected; conservative Carlos Solarzano (fl. 1920s) became president, and liberal Juan Bautista Sacasa vice president, allowing U.S. Marines to depart after having been in the country for 13 years. On October 25, 1925 conservatives (General Emiliano Chamorro Vargas and Adolfo Diaz) seized power, ousting liberal Sacasa. Chamorro became president, despite U.S. disapproval, after Solarzano resigned in January, 1926. But when liberal rebels under General Augusto Cesar SANDINO seized U.S. property, U.S. forces intervened. Chamorro resigned in October, 1926, and Diaz was elected by the Nicaraguan congress, while Sacasa returned to establish a rival liberal government.

The resulting civil war was joined by Sandino when Diaz received the help of 2,000 U.S. marines. U.S. mediator Henry L. STIMSON induced rival leaders Diaz and liberal General Jose Maria Moncada to disarm, while the U.S. supervised elections. Moncada was elected president on November 4, 1928, but Sandino vowed to continue guerrilla warfare until the U.S. marines departed. When Sacasa was elected president in 1932, he persuaded Sandino to surrender after the marines withdrew (1933), but Sandino was assassinated by national guardsmen in 1934.

Nicholas, Grand Duke (1856–1929). Son of Grand Duke Nicholas and grandson of Czar Nicholas I. An army officer, com-

Sandinista guerrillas with captured Nicaraguan National Guards, some of whom had tried to escape by stripping off their uniforms to blend with civilians (1979).

missioned in 1872, he introduced major military reforms while serving in the Russo-Turkish War of 1877–78 and as inspector general of the cavalry (1895–1905). In 1905 he was appointed commander of the military district of St. Petersburg and first president of the imperial committee for national defense. He was commander in chief at the beginning of WORLD WAR I and then was sent to the Caucasus as viceroy of NICHOLAS II. He remained there until 1917. He was then reappointed commander in chief by the czar, but Prince Georgy LVOV, head of the provisional government, canceled the appointment. Nicholas then settled in France.

Nicholas II (1868–1918). Last czar of Russia (1894–1917). The eldest son of Alexander III, he assumed the throne in 1894, the same year he married Princess Alix of Hesse (ALEXANDRA FEDOROVNA). Dedicated to maintaining autocratic powers but possessing a limited understanding of the forces at work in his country, Nicholas suppressed all opposition. He refused pleas by moderates for political change in a Russia that was seething with discontent. His aggressive policies in the Far East were met with humiliating defeat in the RUSSO-JAPANESE WAR (1904–05), causing the monarch even greater unpopularity. This, coupled with domestic corruption, resulted in the RUSSIAN REVOLUTION OF 1905. Urged by Count Sergei WITTE, Nicholas agreed to set up a constitutional government and provide an elective DUMA. He soon reneged on his promises (1906), fired Witte and dissolved the Duma. His downfall began with the outbreak of WORLD WAR I. Taking command of the army in 1915, he all but abandoned domestic affairs to the superstitious czarina and her fanatical adviser Gregory RASPUTIN. Severe economic distress, food shortages and war weariness worsened the situation. Strikes and rioting erupted in Petrograd (now Leningrad) in February 1917, and Nicholas was forced to abdicate in March 1917 (see FEBRUARY REVOLUTION). Exiled first to Siberia and then to the Urals, the czar and his family were executed by the BOLSHEVIKS on July 16, 1918.

For further reading:

Massie, Robert K., *Nicholas and Alexandra.* New York: Macmillan, 1967.

Nichols, Mike [Michael Igor Peschowsky] (1931–). American comedian and theatrical and film director. Nichols is one of the leading current-day directors, having achieved triumphs both on the Broadway stage and in Hollywood films. After dropping out of the University of Chicago in the 1950s, Nichols briefly pursued a solo career as a standup comedian in New York City before returning to Chicago to join the renowned *Second City* comedy troupe. There, in 1957, he met fellow comedienne Elaine MAY. They teamed up for the Broadway hit *An Evening with Mike Nichols and Elaine May* (1960). Thereafter, Nichols turned his attention to directing on Broadway, winning Tony Awards for his work on *Barefoot in the Park* (1963) and *The Odd Couple* (1965). Other Broadway directorial efforts by Nichols include *The Real Thing* (1984)

NICARAGUA

1911	Nicaragua becomes a U.S. protectorate under the Knox-Castillo Treaty.
1934	General Anastasio Somoza Garcia, head of the national guard, becomes dictator under the National Liberal Party.
1956	General Somoza is shot and dies and is succeeded by his son Col. Luis Somoza Debayle.
1961	The Sandinista National Liberation Front (FSLN) is formed.
1967	General Anastasio Somoza, the younger brother of Luis, is elected president.
1972	An earthquake virtually destroys the capitol, Managua, and Somoza's control of foreign relief aid increases his power.
1979	(July) FSLN overthrows Somoza. Daniel Ortega Saavedra is later named as coordinator of the "provisional junta of national reconstruction."
1982	Contra attacks begin; (December) Financial support for the Contras is approved by the U.S. Congress.
1984	(Nov. 4) Ortega is elected president.
1990	(Feb. 25) Ortega is soundly defeated by Violetta Chamorro, the candidate sponsored by the 14-party National Opposition Union.

and a solo show by Whoopi Goldberg (1984). Nichols' films include *The Graduate* (1967), which launched the career of Dustin HOFFMAN; *Catch-22* (1969); *Carnal Knowledge* (1971), which starred Jack NICHOLSON; and *Working Girl* (1988).

Nicholson, Ben (1894–1982). British painter. Nicholson was internationally renowned for his abstract paintings, which were heavily influenced by CUBISM. At the same time, his canvases reflected the softer tones and representational techniques of the English landscape painting tradition. In the 1930s, Nicholson produced a series of all-white geometric "reliefs" carved out of wood that combined cubist montage techniques with pure abstract shapes. Nicholson, by virtue of both his technical excellence and his eclecticism, has remained a key influence on subsequent generations of British painters.

Nicholson, Jack (1937–). American film actor and director; one of the preeminent actors in HOLLYWOOD, renowned for both the diversity of his roles and the intensity and intelligence that he brings to their portrayal. Raised in New Jersey and California, he took his first job in Hollywood—errand boy at Metro-Goldwyn-Mayer—at age 17. His first screen role came in the Roger CORMAN cheapie *The Cry Baby Killer* (1958). After a decade of B-movie work with Corman and others, Nicholson emerged as a star in the Sixties cult hit *Easy Rider* (1969). Over the following decades, Nicholson consolidated his status as a great actor despite appearing in a fair number of box-office failures. His major successes incluude *Five Easy Pieces* (1970), *The Last Detail* (1973), *Chinatown* (1974), *One Flew Over the Cuckoo's Nest* (1975), for which he won an ACADEMY AWARD as best actor, *Terms of Endearment* (1983), for which he won a best supporting actor Oscar, *Prizzi's Honor* (1985) and *Batman* (1989). Nicholson also directed *Drive He Said* (1971) and *Goin' South* (1978). *The Two Jakes* (1990), a sequel to *Chinatown* that Nicholson starred in, won mixed reviews.

Nicklaus, Jack William (1940–). U.S. golfer. In 1988, Nicklaus was named "Player of the Century," a title that few would dispute. After winning the U.S. Amateur championship in 1959 and 1961, he turned professional in 1961. He won the U.S. Open in 1962. Five times PGA player of the year, from 1967 to 1976, he was named athlete of the decade for the Seventies. Golf's all-time money winner, among his 18 international titles are three British Opens, six Australian Opens and six Masters tournaments.

Niebuhr, Reinhold (1892–1971). American theologian, philosopher and social critic. Niebuhr was the foremost American Protestant theologian of this century. He exercised a considerable influence not only in church circles but also in the fields of domestic and foreign governmental policy. Niebuhr earned a degree in divinity from Yale University in 1914 and subsequently spent 13 years as a minister for a Detroit church. During this period, his numerous books and journalistic pieces advocated social activism on the part of the church and a left-wing approach to political issues. From 1928 to 1960, Niebuhr taught at the Union Theological Seminary in New York and became friends with many of the American political leaders of the era. After WORLD WAR II, Niebuhr became more conservative; during the COLD WAR, he championed an expansion of American power on the grounds of its relative moral superiority to communism. President Jimmy CARTER cited Niebuhr as a major influence on his own thought. Niebuhr's major works include *Moral Man and Immoral Society* (1932) and the two-volume *Nature and Destiny of Man* (1941–43).

Nielsen, Carl (August) (1865–1931). Danish composer. Nielsen is considered the father of the modern Danish school of composition, although his music was not widely performed until after his death. During his career he played violin in the Royal Chapel Orchestra in Copenhagen (1889–1905), conducted the Royal Opera in Copenhagen (1908–14) and directed the Danish Music Society (1915–27). He is particularly noted for his experimentation in harmony and his instrumental counterpoint. Major works include Symphony No. 3 (*The Expansive*, 1910–11) and Symphony No. 4 (*The Inextinguishable*, 1915–16) and for piano, the *Lucifer Suite* (1919–20).

Niemoeller, Martin (1892–1984). German Protestant minister and theologian. After serving as a U-boat commander in WORLD WAR I, Niemoeller became a Lutheran pastor in Berlin. At first sympathetic to Adolf HITLER and National Socialism, he quickly became a leader of the anti-Hitler movement in GERMANY. In 1933 he formed the pastors' Emergency League Against Hitlerism, a forerunner of the evangelical German Confessing Church. Arrested in 1937, he spent eight years in Nazi CONCENTRATION CAMPS. After his release at the end of the war (1945), he declared that the German people bore collective guilt for the war. He criticized the creation of the NORTH ATLANTIC TREATY ORGANIZATION (NATO) and the rearmament of WEST GERMANY. In 1948 he was one of the founders of the WORLD COUNCIL OF CHURCHES and served as one of its six presidents from 1961 to 1968. A pacifist, Niemoeller actively opposed the VIETNAM WAR and visited HANOI in 1967 to express his opposition to U.S. policies. Several months later he received the U.S.S.R.'s Lenin Peace Prize. In 1971 he was awarded Germany's highest honor, the Grand Cross of Merit.

Niger. Country in west-central Africa, landlocked by Libya and Algeria on the north border, Benin and Nigeria on the south, Upper Volta on the southeast, Mali on the west, and Chad on the east. Modern Niger did not become unified politically until late in the 19th century, when FRANCE made it part of its colonial African empire. Previously, the territory had been constantly under siege by warring tribes and rival states who competed for control of the region. Having overcome resistance by the Tuareg Arabs centered around Agadez, the French made Niger a territory in 1900, as part of their holdings in Upper Senegal-Niger.

In 1922 it was made a separate colony of FRENCH WEST AFRICA and remained under colonial rule until the end of WORLD WAR II, after which it was swept up in a great wave of African nationalism. It gained autonomy in 1958, and achieved complete independence under President Hammani DIORI. His leadership endured until the great Sahel drought brought famine and illness to his country from 1968 to 1974. That year, a coup led by Lt. Col. Senyi Kountche toppled the Diori government, and the military took power. Kountche himself survived several coup attempts. After his death Army Chief of Staff Col. Ali Saibou became president. After several people were killed during protests against austerity measures in 1990, the government was restructured.

Nigeria. West African country. The Federal Republic of Nigeria is bordered by Niger and Chad to the north, Cameroon to the east, the Gulf of Guinea to the south and Benin to the west. At the turn of the century, Nigeria consisted of two British protectorates: Northern and Southern. The two were joined in 1914 when Nigeria became Britain's largest African colony. Through the 1920s and '30s many Nigerians sought self-government, and in 1946 the country was divided into three regions—each with an advisory assembly consisting of Nigerian and British members. In 1954 a new constitution was adopted increasing the powers of the assemblies and making Nigeria a federation. It became a constitutional monarchy within the Commonwealth in 1960, and later an independent republic (1963). Dr. Nnambi AZIKIWE, formerly governor-general, was its first president; his political rival Abubakar Tafawa Balewa had been prime minister since 1957. In 1966 Tafawa Balewa was assassinated in a military coup led by Ibo officers from the oil-rich eastern region. Major General Johnson Aguiyi-Ironsi took power and attempted to abolish the federal system of government, but he was killed months later in a countercoup led by Colonel Yadubu GOWON, who assumed command. Following the massacre of thousands of Ibo in northern Nigeria, the military governor of the eastern region, Colonel Chikwuemeka OJUKWU, rejected Gowon's leadership and involved him in a dispute over oil revenues. In 1967 Odumegwu-Ojukwu declared the eastern region a separate Ibo state, BIAFRA, and a bloody civil war broke out. Biafra surrendered three years later.

Extensive reconstruction based on anticipated oil income ran aground, and in 1975, while Gowon was out of the country attending a meeting of the Organization of African Unity, a bloodless coup put Brigadier Murtala Mohammad in to power. He attempted some constitutional reforms and increased the number of states to 19, but he was killed in 1976 during an unsuccessful coup attempt. He was suc-

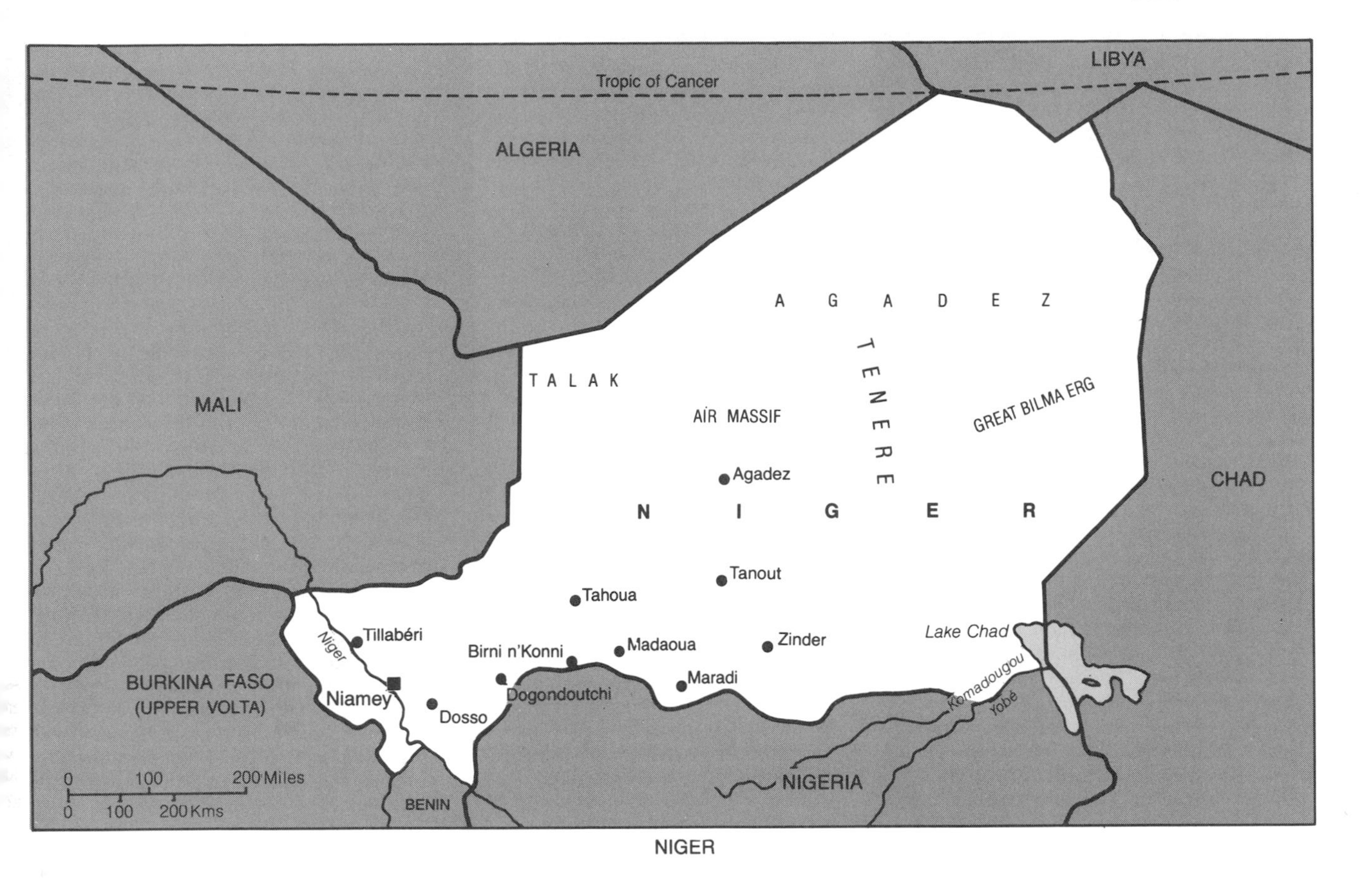

NIGER

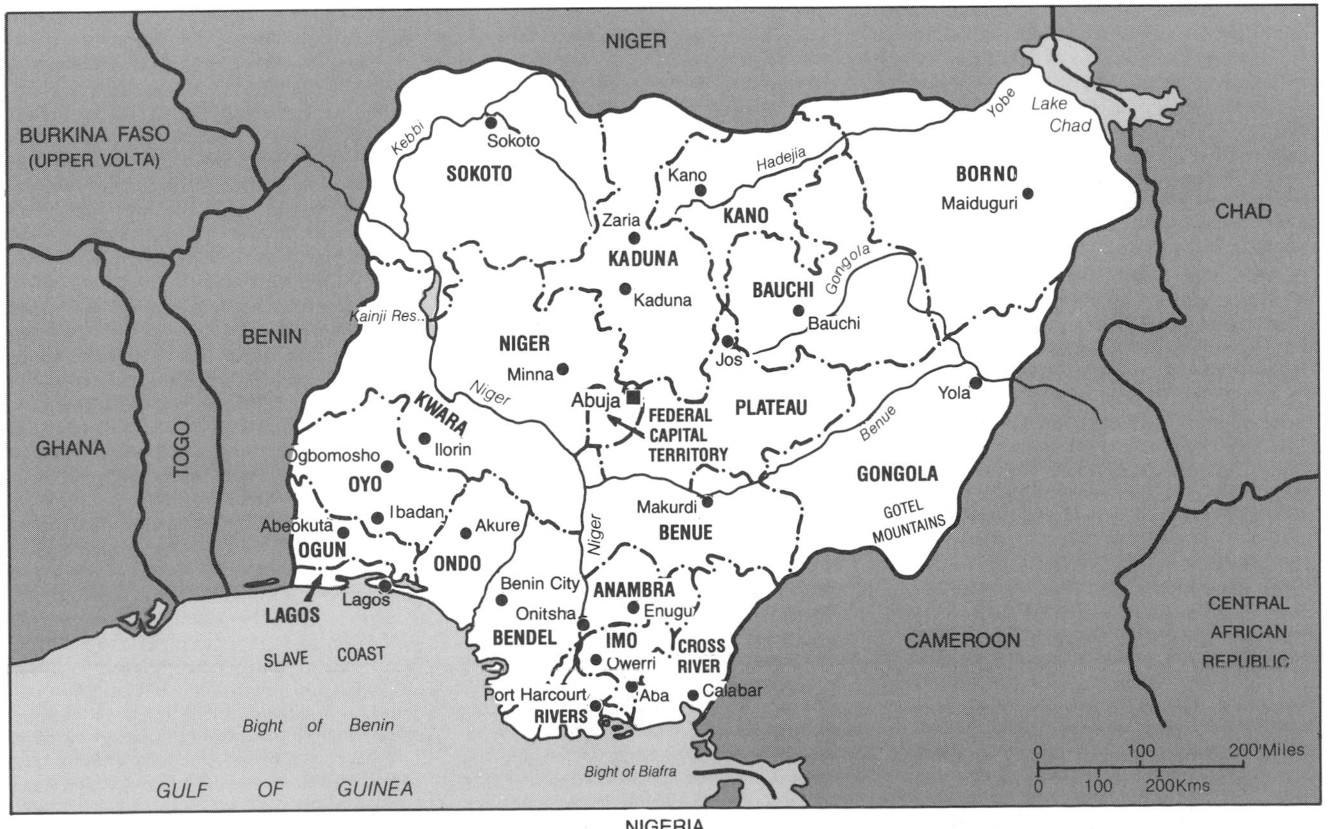

NIGERIA

NIGERIA

1914	British Protectorate of Northern Nigeria and British Protectorate of Southern Nigeria are joined to form colony of Nigeria.
1960	Independence.
1966	Ibo-led coup overthrows central government and kills regional premiers in the northern and western, non-Ibo regions; Ibo leader General Johnson Aguiyi-Ironsi abolishes federal system, establishes central government with mostly Ibo advisers; northern, Hausa-Fulani, army officers kill Aguiyi-Ironsi and seize government, making army Chief-of-Staff Yakuba Gowan head of state.
1967	Gowan divides country into 12 states to dilute power of larger tribes; the eastern Ibo tribal region refuses to be divided and attempts to secede as the independent nation of Biafra; three years of brutal civil war follow.
1985	Major General Ibrahim Babangida comes to power by internal military coup and promises return to civilian rule by 1992.
1989	Babangida overrules registration applications for 50 different political parties and creates a two-party system to dilute regional factionalism as a step toward civilian government.
1990	In advance of talks on reducing Nigeria's huge debt to Western commercial interests, President Babangida calls for reparations from Western countries for slave trade.

ceeded by General Olusegun Obasanjo, who announced a return to free elections and civilian government. In 1979 Shehu Shagari, leader of the National Party of Nigeria, was elected president, but the falling oil prices of the early 1980s destabilized his government. He was unseated in another bloodless coup and Major General Muhammadu Buhari assumed power. In 1985 Buhari was deposed by yet another nonviolent coup, and Major General Ibrahim Babangida, the army chief of staff, became head of the military government. Babangida quickly thwarted an attempted coup and announced a gradual return to a civilian, democratic government by 1992.

Nijinska, Bronislava (1891–1972). Dancer, choreographer and teacher and sister of Vaslav NIJINSKY. She studied at the Imperial Theater School, in St. Petersburg, and appeared with Nijinsky in the first season of the BALLETS RUSSES. She enjoyed the distinction of being the first woman choreographer and was called "La Nijinska" by DIAGHILEV. The most important ballets in her varied and brilliant career were *Les Noces* (1923), *Les Biches* (1924), *Les Comediens Jaloux* (1932) and *Pictures from an Exhibition* (1944). Her work as a teacher has been of the greatest significance.

Nijinsky, Vaslav (1890–1950). Ballet dancer and choreographer. Nijinsky trained at the Imperial Ballet School, in St. Petersburg, from 1900. His performance in *Le Pavilion d'Armide* by Fokine in 1907 attracted attention, and from 1909 he was the leading dancer in DIAGHILEV's BALLETS RUSSES in Paris, where he enjoyed enormous popularity, especially in *Le Spectre de la Rose* and *Petrushka*. Dismissed by Diaghilev, who was angered by Nijinsky's unexpected marriage in 1913,

Dancer Vaslav Nijinsky in Scheherazade *(1911).*

Nijinsky unsuccessfully attempted to form his own company. He continued to perform until 1919, when he suffered a nervous breakdown that permanently ended his career. He spent the remainder of his life in asylums in Switzerland and Britain. His unique powers of dancing earned him the title of *le dieu de la danse*, and he is remembered as one of the greatest male dancers.

Nikisch, Arthur (1855–1922). Hungarian violinist, pianist and conductor. A child prodigy, Nikisch began performing on the violin and the piano at age 8 and entered the Vienna Conservatory at 11. He started to conduct in 1878, later serving as the conductor of the Boston Symphony (1889–93), musical director of the Budapest Opera (1893–95), conductor of the Leipzig Opera (1879–89, 1905–06) and conductor of the Berlin Philharmonic (1895–1922). A frequent guest conductor throughout Europe and the U.S., Nikisch also made many appearances as a piano accompanist of lieder singer Elena Gerhardt. Noted for his superb technique and extraordinarily expressive hands, he excelled in interpretations of such German and Austrian masters as Beethoven, Brahms, Schubert and Schumann. In 1913 he made the first complete recording of a symphony (Beethoven's Symphony No. 5).

Nikolayev, Andrian (1929–). Soviet cosmonaut. The son of a farmer, Nikolayev attended the Marinsky-Posad Forestry Institute and worked as a lumberjack before being drafted into the Soviet army in 1950. Earning his wings as a pilot, he graduated from the Chernigov Higher Air Force School in 1954. After becoming a cosmonaut in 1960, he set an endurance record, of four days in space aboard Vostok 3 (August 1962). As commander of the Soyuz 9 mission (June 1970), he set a new record of 18 days in space, along with fellow cosmonaut Vitaly Sevastyanov. Nikolayev, who later married the world's first woman to travel in space, Valentina TERESHKOVA, has written two books, *Meeting in Orbit* (1969) and *Space, A Road Without End* (1979).

Niles, John Jacob (1892–1980). American folklorist, folksinger and collector of ballads and carols. His career spanned more than 70 years, from before WORLD WAR I until his death. He composed more than 1,000 ballads and carols and performed throughout the U.S. and Europe. He was credited with contributing to the revival of interest in American folk music.

Nilsson, Birgit (1918–). Swedish operatic soprano known for the clarity and power of her voice and for her brilliant interpretations of the heroines of Richard Wagner. Born on a farm near Malmo, Nilsson studied at Stockholm's Royal Academy of Music, graduating in 1946, the year she made her first operatic appearance. Nilsson sang at the Stockholm Opera from 1947 to 1951, in 1950 undertaking the first of the roles that would make her the most celebrated Wagnerian soprano of her generation. Her first important appearance outside Sweden was

Admiral Chester W. Nimitz, commander-in-chief of the U.S. Pacific Fleet and Pacific Ocean Areas (1945).

at England's GLYNDEBOURNE FESTIVAL in 1951, and she made her debut at the BAYREUTH FESTIVAL in 1954. She was widely acclaimed for her performance as Brunnhilde in Wagner's *Siegfried* at the Florence May Music Festival in 1956 and had a triumphant American debut with the San Francisco Opera as Brunnhilde in *Die Walkure* that same year. Nilsson also became known for her performance of the title role in *Turandot*, a part she first sang at her La Scala debut in 1958. Her first Metropolitan Opera performance was as Isolde in 1959. Nilsson was a guest soloist with many of the world's major opera companies and music festivals.

Nimitz, Chester William (1885–1966). U.S. naval commander. Nimitz graduated from the United States Naval Academy at Annapolis in 1905, and served as chief of staff to the commander of the United States Atlantic submarine force during WORLD WAR I. After the Japanese PEARL HARBOR attack, he was promoted to commander-in-chief of the Pacific Fleet. He planned the successful battles of Midway and the Coral Sea. The Japanese surrender was signed on his flagship, the U.S.S. MISSOURI, in Tokyo Bay on September 2, 1945. He was promoted to field admiral. From 1945 to 1947 he was chief of naval operations. After leaving government service he was a consultant on defense matters and edited, with E.B. Potter, *Sea Power, a Naval History* (1960).

For further reading:

Driskill, Frank A., *Admiral of the Hills: A Biography of Chester W. Nimitz.* Austin, Tx.: Eakin Press, 1983.

Nin, Anais (1903–1977). American author. Nin was born in Paris and became an American citizen in 1914. She later returned to France and was associated with the Villa Seurat group, which included Henry MILLER, when she began writing fiction in the 1930s. She is best known for her many published journals, beginning with *The Diary of Anais Nin, Volume I 1931–1934* (1966) and ending with the posthumously published Volume VII (1980). Their feminist perspective and search for self-knowledge and freedom caused her to be a much requested lecturer in universities across the U.S. There is much critical dispute about her fiction, although Edmund WILSON was an early champion of it in the U.S. Fictional works include *Winter of Artifice* (1939), *A Spy in the House of Love* (1954) and the erotic short story collection *The Delta of Venus* (1977).

1984. Novel by George ORWELL, written in 1948 and published in 1949. An impassioned warning about the dangers of totalitarianism and dehumanization, it depicts a bleak futuristic society headed by a mysterious and all-knowing dictator called "Big Brother" (believed to be modeled on Josef STALIN). In the world of the book, the state is all-important; all privacy and individual freedom have been abolished and all human activities are directed by the "thought police." The hero, Winston Smith, is a weak but decent man who yearns for a better existence. He finds brief happiness in a love affair with a young female member of the underground. However, they are discovered and arrested, and Smith is tortured, brainwashed and crushed. The book had an enormous impact on intellectuals around the world, and many of its catchwords—including "Big Brother," "Newspeak" (the Party's attempt to control thought by manipulating language) and "Doublethink" (the ability to cease to know what the Party has condemned)—have become part of the vocabulary of the late 20th century.

Nineteenth Amendment. Enacted in 1920, it gave the vote to women. Although nonwhites had been given the right to vote by the Fifteenth Amendment (1870), women did not gain that same right until much later. The woman suffrage movement arose in the late 19th century with the goal of universal woman suffrage. Although individual states had earlier allowed women to vote, it was not until 1920 that all states and the federal government were constitutionally required to allow women the vote.

Nirenberg, Marshall Warren (1927–). American biochemist. Nirenberg earned his Ph.D. from the University of Michigan in 1957, after which he began work at the National Institutes of Health in Bethesda, Maryland. Using Severo Ochoa's technique for producing artificial RNA, Nirenberg took a vital step in breaking the "genetic code" when he discovered that a uracil triplet in RNA was the code for the amino acid phenylalanine. For this work, Nirenberg shared the 1968 NOBEL PRIZE in physiology or medicine with Har Gobind Khorana and Robert Holley.

Nisei. Term for second-generation Japanese-Americans. (See also internment of JAPANESE-AMERICANS.)

Nishio, Suehiro (1891–1981). Japanese politician, founder of Japan's Democratic Socialist Party (1960). A left-wing activist, he was a labor leader in the early 1920s. In 1938 he was expelled from the Japanese Parliament because of his criticisms of the government's militarist policies. After the war he served as a member of the Japan Socialist Party but broke with the party when it opposed the security treaty with the U.S. in 1960.

Nixon, Richard M(ilhous) (1913–). Thirty-seventh president of the UNITED STATES (1969–74). Richard Nixon—the only U.S. president to resign from office—is perhaps the most complex and controversial American political figure of the postwar era. Born into a modest Quaker family in Yorba Linda, California, he developed a reputation as a brilliant debater in high school and was class president. He received a B.A. from Whittier College, graduating second in his class (1934); then earned a law degree from Duke University Law School (1937), where he placed third in his class. He returned to Whittier to start his own practice. At the outset of WORLD WAR II he worked for eight months in the Office of Price Administration (OPA), an experience that left him distrustful of government bureaucracy. From 1942 to 1945 he served as a noncombat Navy officer in the South Pacific.

Upon his return he entered REPUBLICAN PARTY politics and in 1946 won election to the House of Representatives from his California district. Nixon gained a national reputation as a strong anticommunist while a member of the HOUSE UN-AMERICAN ACTIVITIES COMMITTEE (HUAC). He was a prominent figure in the HISS-CHAMBERS case (1948–49), accusing State Department official Alger HISS of having been a communist agent. In 1950 he ran for the Senate against Helen Gahagan DOUGLAS. Portraying Douglas as pro-communist, he defeated her by a 680,000-vote margin. Regarded as a rising star in the Republican Party, Nixon became a national spokesman against the domestic and foreign policies of the TRUMAN administration. After Dwight D. EISENHOW-

Richard M. Nixon, 37th president of the United States.

ER'S presidential nomination, Thomas DEWEY successfully recommended Nixon for the vice presidency. Nixon's youth, his anticommunist reputation and his internationalist outlook were all considered assets. During the fall 1952 campaign, a political fund-raising scandal briefly jeopardized Nixon's fortunes, and some Republicans urged him to step down from the campaign. However, he survived the crisis after making an emotional half-hour appeal on national television—the so-called **Checkers speech,** in which he denied taking any gifts except one, a cocker spaniel named Checkers that had become the family pet. The Checkers speech gave a new boost to Nixon; moreover, it signaled the first significant use of television in national election campaigning. In November the Eisenhower-Nixon ticket won by a landslide.

Nixon was a highly visible vice president. He assumed many of Eisenhower's obligations as leader of the Republican Party and represented the administration in many overseas trips. During a tour of South America in May 1958 he was confronted by left-wing rioters in Lima, Peru and Caracas, Venezuela. His fortitude and calmness in facing physical danger earned him considerable admiration throughout the Western Hemisphere. Throughout his two terms he advocated a hard-line policy toward communist expansion. In July 1959 Nixon went to Moscow to open the American National Exhibition. The day after his arrival, Nixon and Soviet Premier Nikita KHRUSHCHEV engaged in an impromptu debate over the respective merits of capitalism and communism. The discussion took place in the model kitchen of the exhibition and became known as the **kitchen debate**. Many Americans believed that Nixon had bested the Soviet leader.

Nixon was the Republican presidential candidate in 1960, choosing U.N. ambassador Henry Cabot LODGE as his running mate; their Democratic opponents were Massachusetts Senator John F. KENNEDY and Texas Senator Lyndon B. JOHNSON. Nixon was better known and hoped to take advantage of his greater experience in national and international affairs. Believing it would be to his advantage, he agreed to debate Kennedy on national television—the first televised presidential debates in history. Four debates were scheduled. However, Nixon failed to come across well in the first debate (Sept. 26, 1960). He appeared haggard—he had recently been ill, and did not wear makeup; Kennedy, by contrast, looked healthy and confident. Television viewers gave Kennedy a clear edge in the debate, while radio listeners believed Nixon had done better. Many people believed that Nixon won the final three debates, but his candidacy had already been damaged. Kennedy's popularity surged, and he defeated Nixon—by only 113,000 votes out of 69 million, the smallest percentage difference in history.

Nixon retired to private life, joining a California Law firm and publishing his autobiographical *Six Crises* (1962). Later that year he ran for governor of California but lost to the incumbent, Pat Brown. Following this defeat, Nixon announced his withdrawal from politics and told reporters "you won't have Richard Nixon to kick around any more." He subsequently joined a New York law firm but campaigned for Republican candidates in other elections. Nixon made a triumphant return to politics when he won the 1968 Republican presidential nomination and then defeated Democratic candidate Hubert H. HUMPHREY and third-party candidate George WALLACE. Nixon's campaign platform called for an honorable end to the VIETNAM WAR and for a return to law and order at home.

His first priority as president was the "Vietnamization" of the war, shifting more responsibility for the ground fighting to the South Vietnamese while stepping up U.S. air bombings of North Vietnam and of Vietcong bases in LAOS and CAMBODIA. From 1969 to 1972 Nixon gradually withdrew 555,000 U.S. soldiers from Vietnam. However, mass protests against the war continued in the U.S. (see ANTIWAR MOVEMENT). Domestically, Nixon instituted "revenue sharing," a plan whereby the federal government directly transferred revenues to the states and localities. He also dealt with inflation through a multi-phase economic strategy that included wage and price controls. Nixon regarded foreign affairs as his main strength. During his presidency, he pursued a policy of DETENTE with the U.S.S.R. Nixon's greatest international triumph was a breakthrough in relations with the People's Republic of CHINA. His national security adviser, Henry KISSINGER, secretly flew to Beijing in July 1971 to begin negotiations with the Chinese. Nixon himself visited China in Feb. 1972 for an historic meeting with MAO TSE-TUNG and CHOU EN-LAI that laid the groundwork for formal relations between the two nations. Despite these successes, Nixon was frustrated by his inability to end the Vietnam War. On the eve of the 1972 presidential elections, Kissinger returned from talks with the North Vietnamese in Paris and announced that "peace is at hand." However, fighting continued until a formal ceasefire was announced on Jan. 23, 1973.

Nixon easily defeated his Democratic rival, George MCGOVERN, and was reelected in 1972. However, the WATERGATE scandal would cripple Nixon's administration and force the president to resign. Nixon and his staff were tied to a June 1972 break-in at the Democratic campaign headquarters in the Watergate apartment complex in Washington. The media and Congress began a highly publicized investigation of the break-in and the White House's role in a possible coverup. Nixon continued to deny any knowledge of the break-in, despite mounting evidence to the contrary, and his popularity plunged. Facing impeachment and a Senate trial, Nixon resigned in disgrace on Aug. 9, 1974. Nixon later acknowledged that he had made mistakes regarding the break-in but continued to deny any wrongdoing.

Nixon has been the subject of much personal and political analysis. His opponents cite what they see as his contempt for the Constitution and the democratic political process. His defenders point to his accomplishments in foreign affairs and claim that he was the victim of political persecution. After a period in relative seclusion, Nixon reemerged as something of an elder statesman. He has written several volumes of memoirs and political commentary. (See also Spiro AGNEW.)

For further reading:

Ambrose, Stephen E., *Nixon: The Education of a Politician, 1913–1962*. New York: Simon & Schuster, 1987.

———, *Nixon: The Triumph of a Politician, 1962–1972*. New York: Simon & Schuster, 1989.

Nadel, Laurie, *The Biography of Richard Nixon*. New York: Macmillan, 1991.

Wicker, Tom, *One of Us: Richard Nixon and the American Dream*. New York: Random House, 1991.

NKGB. Abbreviation for Norodny Komitet Gosudarstvennoy Bezopasnosti (People's Commissariat for State Security), which was the Soviet security force from 1943 to 1946. It was mainly concerned with "unreliable elements," many of whom were deported or sent to corrective labor camps. In 1946 the NKGB was renamed the MGB and, after the death of Stalin, the KGB.

Nkomati Accord. An agreement of March 1984 between SOUTH AFRICA and MOZAMBIQUE. South Africa promised not to support the Mozambique's rebel National Resistance Movement in return for Mozambique's undertaking not to back the outlawed AFRICAN NATIONAL CONGRESS' activities in South Africa. However, by 1986 the agreement appeared to be breaking down.

Nkomo, Joshua (1917–). Zimbabwean nationalist and guerrilla leader. A member of the Kalanga tribe, Nkomo was educated in South Africa. He began as a worker in the Rhodesian Railways and became active in the railroad union. A dedicated nationalist and opponent to white rule of RHODESIA, Nkomo was president of the AFRICAN NATIONAL CONGRESS (ANC) from 1957 to 1959. In exile from 1959 to 1960, he became president of the Zimbabwe African People's Union (ZAPU) in 1961 and was imprisoned from 1964 to 1974. After failed negotiations with Ian SMITH, Nkomo joined his ZAPU with Robert MUGABE'S ZANU, and the two became joint leaders of the Patriotic Front (PF) in its guerrilla warfare against the Rhodesian government (1976–79). After Zimbabwean independence and ZANU's victory in the subsequent elections, Nkomo joined Mugabe's cabinet. He was ousted in 1982 after allegations that he had attempted to lead a coup against the Mugabe regime. In 1987 the two leaders merged ZAPU and ZANU-PF, and the following year Nkomo rejoined Mugabe's cabinet.

Zimbabwean nationalist guerrilla leader Joshua Nkomo.

Nkrumah, Kwame (1909–72). Ghanaian statesman, president (1960–66). Born in what was then the western Gold Coast, he attended Achimota College in Accra, Lincoln University in Pennsylvania and the London School of Economics. A dedicated African nationalist and anticolonialist, he was active in student groups and soon founded (1949) the Convention's People's Party (CPP), which advocated self-government for the colony. Although he was imprisoned by the British from 1950 to 1951, his party won the colony's first general election (1951). Nkrumah then gained his freedom to become a member of parliament (1951) and then prime minister of Gold Coast (1954 to 1957) and of the newly renamed dominion of GHANA (1957 to 1960). When Ghana attained independence as a republic within the British Commonwealth (1960), Nkrumah became its first president. A respected pan-African leader, he opposed direct Western influence on the continent and was a participant (1961) in the Casablanca Conference, which codified African opposition to neocolonialism in the African Charter. He was a supporter of Patrice LUMUMBA in the Congo and an opponent of the government of SOUTH AFRICA. Becoming increasingly dictatorial at home, he quashed dissenters and established a one-party state. This, coupled with economic policies that led to a wild inflationary spiral and financial chaos (1965 to 1966), led to Nkrumah's increased unpopularity and to the military coup that deposed him in 1966. He fled, first to Guinea and then to Romania, where he sought medical treatment in 1972 and died later that year.

Ghanaian President Kwame Nkrumah.

NKVD. Abbreviation for Norodny Komitet Vnutrennykh Del (People's Commissariat of Internal Affairs), which was from 1934 to 1943 the Soviet security service in charge of police and civil registry offices and of the corrective labor camps. It was one of STALIN's main tools during the GREAT PURGE. In 1943 it was divided into two commissariats, the NKVD and the NKGB.

For further reading:

Conquest, Robert, *Inside Stalin's Secret Police: NKVD Politics, 1936–1939*. Stanford, Calif.: Hoover Institution Press, 1985.

Nobel Prize. Established in the will of Alfred Nobel (1833–1896), the Swedish chemist who made his fortune in the development of explosives, the yearly Nobel prizes go to individuals who have made outstanding contributions in the fields of physics, chemistry, physiology or medicine, literature and world peace. Nobel had stipulated that the winners in the fields of physics and chemistry be determined by the Royal Swedish Academy of Sciences; in medicine by the Karolinska Institute in Stockholm; for literature by the Swedish Academy in Stockholm; and for champions of peace by a committee of five elected by the Norwegian Storting (Parliament). He further asked that candidates of all nationalities be considered for the prizes. In 1900 the Nobel Foundation was established to carry out the intent of the will. The first Nobel Prizes were awarded on December 10, 1901. In 1968 the Bank of Sweden made a donation to establish an additional prize in economics. Called the Prize in Economic Sciences in Memory of Alfred Nobel, it was first awarded in 1969 and is presented on the same day as the other awards in a ceremony following their presentation in Oslo. The amount of the prize money has grown over the years, from a relatively small amount in 1901 to $700,000 in 1990. Apart from the monetary award, the Nobel Prize bestows the highest recognition of intellect and achievement on the recipient and commands worldwide attention and respect. The prize has often been criticized, however, because of the secrecy of the selection committees. In some years, the peace and literature awards have reportedly been influenced by political considerations.

Nobile, Umberto (1885–1978). Italian aviator and aeronautical engineer. General Nobile became the second person to fly over the NORTH POLE when he piloted the dirigible *Norge* over the spot two days after Admiral Richard BYRD made his historic flight (May 9, 1926). Nobile's passengers on this expedition included the Norwegian polar explorer Roald AMUNDSEN and the American explorer Lincoln ELLSWORTH. Two years later, Nobile attempted another such flight in a smaller airship, the *Italia*. However, he crashed in the Arctic. Amundsen quickly organized a rescue attempt, but his plane was lost at sea. Meanwhile, Nobile managed to survive and returned to Italy. The incident caused an international controversy. Nobile was accused of cowardice and recklessness and blamed for the deaths of Amundsen and 17 others, and his military career ended in disgrace. He spent the 1930s and early 1940s in the U.S. and the U.S.S.R. His rank of general was restored in 1945, and he lived to the age of 93.

Noble, Ray (1903–1978). British popular music composer and conductor. Noble composed such standards as "The Very Thought of You," "Goodnight, Sweetheart," "I Hadn't Anyone Til You" and "Cherokee." In the mid-1930s he was leader of an all-star American JAZZ band at the famous Rainbow Room at ROCKEFELLER CENTER in New York. He also performed frequently on radio, appearing on shows hosted by Edgar BERGEN, Jack BENNY and BURNS AND ALLEN.

Noel-Baker, Philip [born Philip John Baker] (1889–1982). British diplomat, statesman and pacifist. He was born into a British family from Canada; his parents were Quakers, and his father later became a Liberal member of parliament (1905). Educated in England and the U.S., he won honors in history (1910) and economics (1912) from King's College, Cambridge, receiving his M.A. in 1913. He was a conscientious objector to WORLD WAR I, but organized and commanded the Friend's Ambulance Corps and won awards for valor while serving in France and Italy. After the war he was an assistant to Robert CECIL at the PARIS PEACE CONFERENCE (1919) and helped draft the covenant of the LEAGUE OF NATIONS. He also worked with Fridtjof NANSEN on behalf of war refugees. In 1926 he published two books, *The League of Nations at Work* and *Disarmament*, which established him as an authority on disarmament. He was elected to Parliament for the LABOUR PARTY in 1929 and became parliamentary private secretary to the foreign secretary, Arthur HENDERSON. Defeated in the general election of 1931, he won another seat in 1936 and held it until his retirement in 1970.

During the 1930s Noel-Baker advocated sanctions against ITALY because of MUSSOLINI's invasion of ETHIOPIA (see ITALO-ETHIOPIAN WAR OF 1935–36). He also joined Winston CHURCHILL in warning of the dangers of NAZISM and militarism in HITLER's Germany. During WORLD WAR II he held posts in Churchill's coalition gov-

Nobel Prize winners of 1962: Francis Crick, Maurice Wilkins, John Steinbeck, James Watson, Max Perutz and John Kendrew.

ernment. He continued as an influential member of parliament after the war and helped negotiate the independence of INDIA. He also played an important role in establishing the UNITED NATIONS. He was awarded the 1959 NOBEL PRIZE for peace for his work in the League of Nations and the United Nations and for his commitment to international disarmament. Not only was Noel-Baker a distinguished statesman, he was also an outstanding athlete, competing in four OLYMPIC GAMES (1912, 1920, 1924, 1928) and winning a silver medal in the 1,500–meter run (1920). He changed his name to Noel-Baker in 1923, adding his wife's family name to his. He was made a life peer as Baron Noel-Baker of Derby in 1977.

No Exit. Play (1944) by French author Jean-Paul SARTRE. *No Exit,* written during the German occupation of FRANCE, is a dark portrayal of the limitations of human goodness and the difficulties of collective resistance to evil. The play illustrates the existential outlook of Sartre in the 1940s, as exemplified in more abstract terms in his philosophical magnum opus BEING AND NOTHINGNESS. The straightforward plot of *No Exit* concerns a group of randomly chosen persons who find themselves in Hell, which has taken the form of a comfortable room from which exit is impossible. The tortures of Hell are seen to be of these people's own devising, as each in turn seeks futilely to manipulate the others for the sake of selfish personal needs.

Noguchi, Isamu (1904–). American sculptor. Born in Los Angeles, he lived in Japan from the age of 2 to 14. Returning to the U.S., he was a premedical student before studying at New York City art schools and apprenticing with Gutzon BORGLUM. He traveled to Paris on a Guggenheim grant and studied with Constantin BRANCUSI from 1927 to 1929. During the 1940s Noguchi designed a variety of striking sets and costumes for the Martha GRAHAM dance company and developed his sculptural style in various free-standing abstract pieces. He is best known for the sculptures he created from the 1950s on—large abstract works, often in stone, that are designed in conjunction with architecture. Smooth, still and graceful presences, his works are elegant blends of Eastern and Western traditions, many designed for outdoor sculpture gardens and playgrounds. Among his public projects are the Garden of Peace at the UNESCO building, Paris (1956 to 1958), the Billy Rose Art Garden, Jerusalem (1965) and the entrance to the Museum of Modern Art, Tokyo (1969).

Noland, Kenneth (1924–). American painter. Born in Ashville, North Carolina, he studied at Black Mountain College and at the Zadkine School in Paris. Associated with both COLOR-FIELD and HARD-EDGE PAINTING, Noland experimented with the use of stained colors of equal pictorial value on unprimed canvas. He is particularly noted for his huge images of vividly colored targets and chevrons, painted in the late 1950s and early 1960s. Later works employed large horizontal stripes or plaid designs in a more muted tonal range.

Nolde, Emil (1867–1956). German painter. Born Emile Hansen, he was trained as a furniture craftsman, studied art in Munich, Dachau and Paris and changed his name to Nolde, the town in which he was born. An early exponent of EXPRESSIONISM, he exhibited with DIE BRUCKE from 1906 to 1907. A solitary and deeply individualistic painter, he soon left the group to pursue his own singular imagery. Nolde is known for expressionistically distorted paintings filled with violent color combinations. He was particularly brilliant in capturing religious images that mingle the demonic with the mystical. Typical of these paintings are *The Last Supper* (1909, Statens Museum, Copenhagen) and *The Prophet* (1912, National Gallery, Washington, D.C.). Nolde also used his expressionist technique to great effect in powerful landscapes, still lifes, figure paintings and portraits. He was also a master of the watercolor and of graphic arts, executing many important etchings, lithographs and woodcuts. Like many other modernists, Nolde was condemned by the Nazis. Forbidden to paint, he retired to his farm and executed a monumental series of watercolors entitled *Unpainted Pictures* (1938 to 1945).

Nono, Luigi (1924–1990). Italian composer. Born in Venice, Nono was a student of Bruno Maderna and learned twelve-tone technique from Hermann SCHERCHEN (see SERIAL MUSIC). Married to the daughter of Arnold SCHOENBERG, whose compositions strongly influenced him, Nono became an important figure in contemporary music during the 1950s. A leader of the Italian Communist Party in Venice, he has composed a number of extremely political pieces, such as *Intolerance* (1960) and *A Specter Rises over Europe* (1971). Nono has also experimented with taped sounds and electronic music.

Noordung, Hermann [Potocnik] (1892–1929). Austrian army captain. Writing under the pen name "Hermann Noordung," Captain Potocnik of the Austrian reserve was a graduate engineer. Little else is known about his personal life, but his visionary writings about space, published in 1928, explored the concept of space stations from an engineering perspective in a way no one else had. He envisioned a 164–foot long wheel-shaped craft that would spin on its axis to produce artificial gravity. Noordung inspired many more recent concepts, including Gerard K. O'Neill's wheel-shaped "space colony." The Noordung space station also included a bowl-shaped power station and a cylinder-shaped observatory.

Noriega Morena, Manuel Antonio. See PANAMA.

Norman, Jessye (1945–). American opera singer. An impressive interpreter of both soprano and mezzo-soprano roles in the French, German and Italian repertories, Norman is famous for her rich, powerful voice and precise diction. She made her debut as Elisabeth in Richard Wagner's *Tannhauser* with the Deutsche Opera in Berlin in 1969. Her New York Metropolitan Opera debut, first as Cassandra then as Dido in Berlioz's *Les Troyens,* was a triumph (1983). Other major roles include Aida and Ariadne in *Ariadne auf*

Naxos. In addition, Norman is well known as a *lieder* singer, especially for her interpretations of songs by Wagner and Richard Strauss.

Normandie. French ocean liner designed to be the largest, fastest and most beautiful passenger ship in the world. The *Normandie*'s maiden voyage in 1935 established a transatlantic speed record but created even more interest through its extraordinary design, both technical and visual, external and internal. The *Normandie* incorporated innovations in turboelectric propulsion machinery and hull design developed by Russian-born architect and engineer Vladimir Yourkevitch. It presented an unusual and striking visual appearance, with streamlined forms for portions of its superstructure and its three giant funnels. It was widely viewed as outstandingly beautiful externally. Internally, the passenger accommodations were a lavish showcase of French ART DECO design of the 1930s. Jean Dupas, Rene LALIQUE, Emile-Jacques Ruhlmann, Raymond Subes and Louis SUE were among the distinguished artists and designers whose work was represented on the *Normandie,* although many others with lesser-known names also had major roles. Although larger and faster ships were built after the *Normandie,* she captured the imagination of the public in a way that has made her the ultimate example of the ocean liner. Early in 1942 the vessel was at one of New York City's Hudson River piers, being converted into a troopship for World War II duty, when a fire broke out; after burning for several days, the ship capsized when too much water was pumped into the wrong compartments. Years later it was revealed that the fire had been set by Mafia hitman Albert Anastasia in an effort to shake down the U.S. government into appealing for organized crime's aid in keeping Nazi saboteurs out of New York Harbor.

Normandy, Invasion of. On June 6, 1944, the Allies, directed by supreme Allied commander General Dwight D. EISENHOWER, invaded the European mainland across the English Channel. Thousands of troop ships, amphibious craft and warships transported British, French, American, Canadian and other Allied troops across the stormy English Channel to NORMANDY in northwestern France. Before the invasion, the Allied air forces and navies had bombarded strong German fortifications along the French coast. Nonetheless, U.S. forces encountered stiff resistance on Utah and Omaha beaches; to the east, British and Canadian troops fought resolutely for the German-defended port of Caen. The hedgerow terrain of Normandy was fairly easy to defend, and the Germans made the most of it. By the end of July 1944, however, after seven weeks of intense fighting, Allied bridgeheads were established and the invasion had succeeded. The Allied armies were united along the coast. In early August 1944, the U.S. Third Army broke through German lines in the west into Brittany, south to the Loire River, and then east toward Paris. A German attempt to split the American forces failed, and instead a British force driving from the south trapped the German Seventh Army and wiped it out. (See also WORLD WAR II ON THE WESTERN FRONT.)

General Eisenhower talks to American paratroopers before the Allied invasion of Normandy.

Norris, George William (1861–1944). U.S. politician. In 1912 Norris began a 30–year career as Republican U.S. senator from Nebraska, and prided himself on his independence from party domination. He supported Franklin D. ROOSEVELT in his four presidential campaigns, and worked tirelessly for the establishment of the TENNESSEE VALLEY AUTHORITY. Norris secured appropriation for a series of dams for conservation and power in the Platte Valley in Nebraska, creating what became known as the "Little TVA." He led the fight in the Senate for passage of the NORRIS-LAGUARDIA Anti-Injunction Act (1932).

Under heavy Nazi machine-gun fire, American soldiers leave a Coast Guard landing boat and move toward the Normandy shore (June 6, 1944).

Norris, Kathleen (1878–1966). American novelist. Norris is best known for her more than 80 works of romantic fiction, beginning with *Mother* in 1911, and her numerous short stories originally published in women's magazines. Norris described her fiction as depicting conventional heroines with simple virtues. Other novels include *Certain People of Importance* (1922), which is considered her best work, and *Family Gathering* (1959). Norris was also a feminist and pacifist dedicated to worldwide disarmament. She spoke at a rally for world peace in Madison Square Garden in 1932.

Norrish, Ronald George Wreyford (1897–1978). British chemist. Norrish was educated at Emmanuel College, Cambridge. His studies were interrupted by WORLD WAR I, in which he served in the Royal Artillery in France. In 1918 he was captured by the Germans and spent a year as a PRISONER OF WAR. He received his undergraduate degree in 1921 and his Ph.D. in 1924. He was later a professor and director of physical chemistry (1937–65) at Cambridge. During WORLD WAR II he headed government research on the suppression of gun flash. From 1949 to 1965 he worked with his former student George Porter on flash photolysis and kinetic spectroscopy. These methods allowed researchers to observe and investigate very fast chemical reactions for the first time. For this work, Norrish and Porter shared the 1967 NOBEL PRIZE for chemistry with Manfred EIGEN.

Norris-LaGuardia Act. Anti-injunction act of 1932 that was a major advance for organized unions in the U.S. During the infancy of the American labor movement, unions were viewed with mistrust—and by the courts as conspiracies and illegal restraints of trade under the Sherman Antitrust Act. Employers could seek an injunction in federal court to ban even peaceful strikes, picketing and boycotts. The anti-injunction act was named after its cosponsors in Congress, Fiorello LAGUARDIA and George NORRIS. The act restricts federal courts in issuing injunctions against a union that is engaged in a peaceful strike against an employer. It was the first step in establishing organized labor's right to organize, strike and collectively bargain.

Norstad, General Lauris (1907–1988). American Air Force officer. A West Point graduate, Norstad was assistant chief of intelligence for the U.S. Army Air Corps during WORLD WAR II. He helped coordinate air support for the Allied landings in North Africa and Sicily; later in the war he helped direct the bombing campaign against Japan, including the dropping of the ATOMIC BOMB on HIROSHIMA and NAGASAKI. After the war, Norstad helped establish the Air Force as a separate branch of the U.S. armed forces. Commander of the NORTH ATLANTIC TREATY ORGANIZATION from 1956 to 1963, he headed Allied forces in Europe during the BERLIN crisis of 1961, when East Germany built the BERLIN WALL. As NATO commander, he urged organization members to strengthen conventional forces as a defensive "ground shield" while holding nuclear retaliatory power in reserve. Norstad resigned from the Air Force in January 1963 over a policy dispute with President John F. KENNEDY.

North African Campaign. In North Africa (1940–1943) during WORLD WAR II, the AXIS sought to seize the SUEZ CANAL to control the Mediterranean. Large tank battles occurred along Egyptian and Libyan shores. In September, 1940 Italian forces penetrated Egyptian territory but were repulsed and later destroyed. The German Afrika Korps, under General Erwin ROMMEL replaced the Italians in March 1941, forcing the British out of Libya. The British Eighth Army counterattacked in November, driving the Germans westward. In May, 1942 Rommel took the offensive, routing the British in the battle of Gazala-Bir Hakim (May 28–June 13, 1942), pushing them 250 miles into Egypt. The British established a defensive line from El Alamein on the coast to the Qattara Depression, which Rommel was unable to breach. On October 23, 1942 the British Eighth Army under General Bernard L. MONTGOMERY attacked, broke through German lines and forced Rommel on a long retreat into Tunisia. The battle of El Alamein was decisive, boosted Allied morale and led to the surrender of Axis forces in North Africa on May 12, 1943.

North American Air Defense Command [NORAD]. Coordinator of air defenses of the United States and Canada. NORAD, headquartered deep within Cheyenne Mountain near Colorado Springs, Colorado, controls all American and Canadian air defense forces through a $65 million combat operations center completed in 1965.

North Atlantic Treaty Organization [NATO]. Military alliance established under the terms of the North Atlantic Treaty, signed in Washington, D.C., on April 4, 1949, to provide for the mutual defense of member nations—originally, Belgium, Canada, Denmark, France, Iceland, Italy, Luxembourg, the Netherlands, Norway, Purtugal, the U.K. and the U.S. They were joined by Greece and Turkey in 1952, West Germany in 1955 and Spain in 1982. NATO's principal goal is to develop individual and collective capacity among Atlantic Community nations to resist armed attack and, regarding an attack on one as an attack on all, to take whatever action is deemed necessary under Article 51 of the UN Charter. It also aimed at settling disputes by peaceful means and at promoting various kinds of political, social and economic ties among its members. Aimed mainly at protecting Western nations from the Soviet bloc, which came to be represented by the WARSAW PACT, it was the most important Western military organization formed in response to the COLD WAR.

With headquarters in Brussels, Belgium, NATO is run under the auspices of the North Atlantic Council (its policy-making and coordinating body), headed by a secretary general. NATO's military force was formed in 1950 under its first commander, General Dwight D. EISENHOWER; its headquarters, the Supreme Headquarters Allied Powers in Europe (SHAPE), is also located in Brussels. NATO's Military Committee recommends defense actions to the council's military arm, the Defense Planning Committee (DPC). Consisting of military representatives from each member country (except France, which withdrew from the Military Committee in 1966 while remaining a member of the council), the DPC has its headquarters in Washington, D.C. NATO maintains three separate commands: the Atlantic Ocean Command, the European Command and the Channel Command. In addition, North American questions are handled by the Canada-U.S. Regional Planning Group. With the disbanding of NATO's rival organization, the communist WARSAW PACT, in 1991, NATO announced it would halve its forces.

For further reading:

Cook, Don, *Forging the Alliance: NATO, 1945–1950*. New York: William Morrow, 1989.

Northcliffe, Viscount [Lord Alfred Charles William Harmsworth] (1865–1922). British journalist and newspaper publisher. Born near Dublin, he was raised in London. His journalistic efforts started in boyhood, and by 1880 he had founded *Answers to Correspondents*, a successful weekly magazine featuring information, puzzles and games. In 1894 he and his brother Harold Harmsworth (later Viscount Rothermere), with whom he had collaborated on *Answers*, purchased the London *Evening News*, thus launching his career in newspapers. In 1896 he founded the morning *Daily Mail*, selling it at a halfpenny—half the price of other newspapers—and thus beginning the modern British daily. The *Daily Mirror*, an illustrated tabloid, followed in 1903 and the *Continental Daily Mail* was founded in Paris in 1905. In 1908 he gained control of the failing *Times*, restoring it to journalistic eminence. During WORLD WAR I, he pressed for vigorous leadership in England's conduct of the war, and his support of LLOYD GEORGE in 1916 helped to topple the ASQUITH government. Northcliffe transformed English popular journalism by introducing the blaring headline and the brightly written story and by initiating such features as the gossip column, serial and women's page. In addition, his publicity-seeking led him to finance Arctic exploration, automobile driving and aviation. Through his newspapers, Northcliffe exercised enormous influence on British public opinion and public policy.

French, U.S., and British NATO representatives meet.

Northern Dancer (1961–1990). Canadian thoroughbred racehorse. Northern Dancer enjoyed an outstanding racing career, posting wins in the Kentucky Derby and the Preakness, and winning 14 of his 18 starts. Northern Dancer's career as an athlete, however, was far overshadowed by his career as one of the greatest sires in thoroughbred history. Three of his colts won the Epsom Derby in England—the most famous being Nijinsky II, who went on to a brilliant career at stud that rivaled that of his sire. A grandson of NATIVE DANCER, Northern Dancer sired 635 offspring who won nearly 500 stakes races—primarily in Europe—by the time of his death at the age of 29 from colic. Certainly the greatest Canadian-bred horse in history, he was returned to his native land for burial.

Northern Expedition (1926–28). To reunify CHINA, Kuomintang forces under CHIANG KAI-SHEK set out northward from their capital, Canton (July 1926). By spring 1927 they controlled all provinces south of the Yangtze river, and Honan north of it. Kuomintang success came in part from having soldiers who were trained not to prey on civilians and in part from propaganda. A widening rift within the movement, however, caused Chiang to resign his command, while dismissing Russian advisers and expelling the communists. Chiang resumed command in the spring of 1928, and the northward push continued. Northern armies were defeated, a sympathetic general captured Peking, the capital, and China was reunited (June, 1928). The capital was then moved south to Nanking.

Northern Ireland. A part of the UNITED KINGDOM of Great Britain and Northern Ireland; often called Ulster, it is comprised of six of the nine counties of that historic province in northeastern IRELAND: Antrim, Armagh, Down, Fermanagh, Londonderry and Tyrone. BELFAST is the capital. In recent years Northern Ireland has been torn by violence between the Protestant majority (wishing to to remain a part of the United Kingdom) and the Catholic minority (demanding union with the Republic of Ireland). Thousands of British troops maintain, or attempt to maintain, the public peace, while the Catholics' illegal IRISH REPUBLICAN ARMY (IRA) and the Protestants' Ulster Defense Force both disrupt public order with acts of terrorism.

In the late-19th century proposals were made for Irish self-government via HOME RULE, an early slogan of Irish nationalists. But Northern Ireland feared that this would lead to domination by the island's Catholic majority. Northern Ireland was by then more industrialized than the perennially depressed south and so had more economic ties with England. The threat of civil war simmered for decades, until in 1920 Great Britain enacted the Government of Ireland Act, which gave Home Rule separately to the two sections and thus officially created Northern Ireland. But the Irish Free State, established in the south in 1922, refused to recognize this partition. Violence began and has continued, off and on, ever since.

In 1968, Bernadette Devlin and others organized a protest movement (modeled on the U.S. CIVIL RIGHTS MOVEMENT) calling for equal rights for Northern Irish Catholics. Protestants responded with violence, and British troops arrived specifically to protect the Catholic minority. However, relations between the British army and the Catholics soon soured. The BLOODY SUNDAY Massacre occurred in January, 1972, when British troops killed 13 Catholics demonstrating in Londonderry. This led in March to the suspension of the Protestant-ruled Northern Irish government by the London authorities. A coalition government of Protestants and Catholics was formed in 1973, but it collapsed in May, 1974, after a general strike called by Protestant extremists. London once again took direct control. In the late 1970s Mairead CORRIGAN and Betty WILLIAMS attempted to bring about a peaceful solution; they received little more than the 1977 NOBEL PRIZE for peace for their efforts at reconciliation. The 1985 HILLSBOROUGH ACCORD, signed by the U.K. and Ireland, gave the Irish Republic an advisory role in the governing of Northern Ireland. Many viewed the accord as the most promising and constructive step toward peace in Northern Ireland, but extremist unionist leaders (notably Ian PAISLEY) denounced it.

A hooded member of the Provisional IRA waves a submachine gun during an anti-British "Troops Out" rally in Belfast, Northern Ireland.

For further reading:

Ward, Alan J., ed., *Northern Ireland: Living with the Crisis.* Westport, Conn.: Greenwood, 1987.

Northern Rhodesia. Country in central Africa, formerly a British protectorate, now the republic of ZAMBIA. The explorations of the Scottish missionary David Livingstone first sparked European interest in the region, and by 1890 the British South Africa Company, founded by Cecil Rhodes, who later named Rhodesia, sent agents to garner treaties from the local tribal chieftains. Using these treaties as a pretext, Great Britain sent troops in 1891 to claim the territory, and met with fierce opposition from Lunda and Ngoni warriors, who bitterly fought colonial British rule. By 1911 Great Britain had the Northeast and Northwest parts of Rhodesia shored up, combining them as a single protectorate, Northern Rhodesia. In the early 1920s heavy deposits of copper were discovered in Northern Rhodesia, which touched off a mining boom that by 1930 had created towns and cities whose populations almost entirely consisted of black and white workers drawn from various regions in southern Africa. As the natives of Northern Rhodesia strove for improvements, segregation and racial discrimination were imported from SOUTH AFRICA, and there were riots and strikes in 1925, 1940, and 1956.

The first great wave of African nationalism that followed in the wake of WORLD WAR II was unsuccessful, however, in preventing the formation of the Federation of Rhodesia and Nyasaland, dominated by a white ruling class. The first leader of the nationalist political movement was Harry Nkumbala; in 1958 Kenneth KAUNDA became prominent. Two years later, in 1960, an attempt was made by Great Britain to transfer power gradually into the hands of Northern Rhodesia's African majority and was met with fierce white resistance from a community of 70,000. In 1964, however, after the first open election Kuanda became prime minister, and on October 24, 1964 Northern Rhodesia became the independent Republic of Zambia, with Kuanda as its president.

North Korea [Democratic People's Republic of Korea]. North Korea, covering an area of 46,528 square miles, is located in the northern half of the Korean Peninsula in northeast Asia. The Communist Korean Worker's Party (KWP) established the Democratic People's Republic of Korea in 1953 after the signing of the armistice ending the KOREAN WAR. The country has been ruled since 1958 by KIM IL-SUNG, who has kept control through a strong personality cult and a personally constructed communist ideology known as Juche. During the first two seven-year plans, dependence on imports from the West for rapid development of heavy industry led to huge foreign debts by 1976. The third seven-year plan (1987–93) involves more realistic growth expectations. Good relations have been maintained with China and the Soviet Union, but relations with South Korea have been tense, with only a slight improvement since 1988.

For further reading:

Rees, Davis, *A Short History of Modern Korea.* New York: Hippocrene Books, 1988.

North Pole. Northernmost end of the earth's axis, and one of the great conquests of explorers and adventurers. American Adm. Robert E. PEARY reached it first on April 6, 1909 after a series of unsuccessful attempts in the race to the North Pole. In 1926 Adm. Richard E. BYRD and Floyd BENNETT were the first to reach it by air, and in 1958 the atomic-powered NAUTILUS submarine was the first to reach the North Pole underwater. In 1960 another U.S. submarine, the *Skate,* arrived at the surface of the pole following the *Nautilus* route. The first successful foot dogsled expedition crossed over the pole in 1968 and 1969, and in 1971 Italy's Guido Monzino faithfully retraced Peary's footsteps. Naomi Uemura of Japan was the first man ever to reach the North Pole alone by dogsled in 1978, and in 1977 the Soviet icebreaker *Arktika* arrived here, followed in 1979 by a Soviet team on skis. An international expedition led by Will Stegner traveled to the pole in the 1980s.

Northrop, John Howard (1891–). American chemist. Between 1930 and 1935, Northrop and several colleagues at the Rockefeller Institute of Medical Research succeeded in isolating a number of enzymes, crystallizing them and revealing their protein nature. These experimental findings confirmed James B. Sumner's 1926

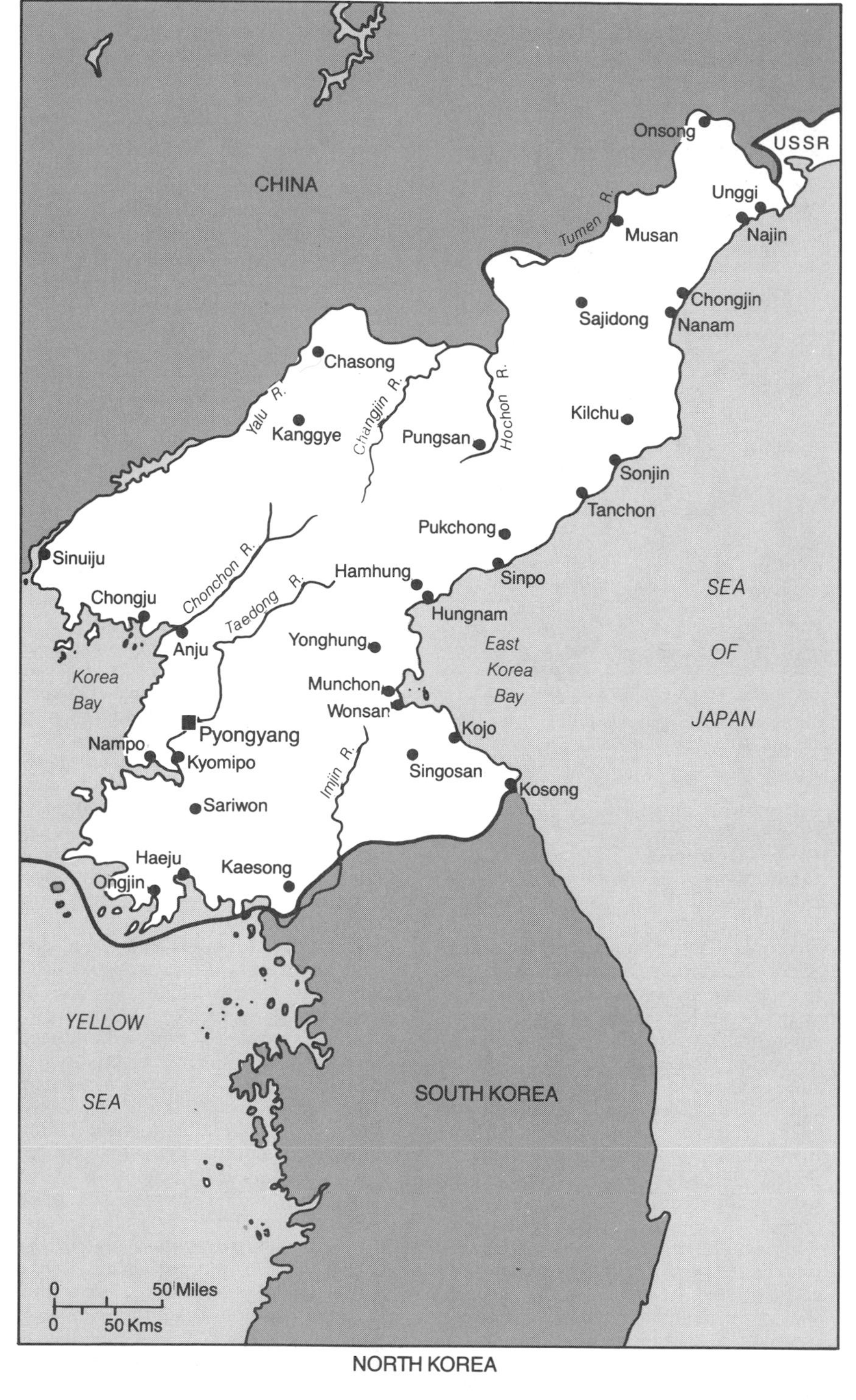

NORTH KOREA

report that the enzyme urease also appeared to be a protein, a theory that had been rejected in favor of the assertion by the influential German chemist Richard Willstatter that enzymes were unlike any known organic compound. Building on Northrop's findings, another Rockefeller Institute colleague, Wendell Stanley, would be the first to isolate a bacterial virus, in 1939. For their preparation of enzymes and virus proteins in pure form, Northrop and Stanley shared the 1946 NOBEL PRIZE for chemistry.

Northrop, John Knudsen (1895–1981). American pioneer aircraft designer, cofounder of the Lockheed Corp. (1927) and founder of the Northrop Corp. (1939). He designed and built the Lockheed Vega (1927), the aircraft used by Amelia EARHART in her historic solo transatlantic flight in 1932. He also designed several important military airplanes. Among these were the A-17 attack plane, early Navy dive bombers, the WORLD WAR II P-61 night fighter (known as the Black Widow) and the boomerang-shaped Flying Wing.

North Trial. Trial (1989) of Oliver North, a Marine colonel and member of President Ronald REAGAN's National Security Council who was implicated in the IRAN-CONTRA SCANDAL. The Reagan administration supported a rebel group, dubbed the CONTRAS, who opposed the leftist Sandinista regime in NICARAGUA. When Congress cut off all funding of the Contras, individuals in the Reagan administration arranged for the sale of arms to Iran and the diversion of the profits to the Contras. At the time the Iranian regime was unpopular because it had seized several hundred U.S. hostages during the fundamentalist revolution that had deposed the shah of IRAN. (See IRAN HOSTAGE CRISIS.)

North was implicated in the arms deal. North became a national celebrity when his secretary revealed that he had shredded numerous incriminating documents during a congressional investigation of the matter. Although North was convicted on three of 12 criminal counts, two of these were later thrown out. North was viewed by both the jury and a large segment of the public as a scapegoat for high administration officials who may have participated in the arms transfer and subsequent diversion of funds to the Contras. North's critics viewed him as a maverick who considered himself above the law; his supporters claimed that North had acted out of patriotism.

Norway. Northern European country on the Scandinavian Peninsula, bordered on the north by the Barents Sea, the northeast by Finland and the Soviet Union, the east by Sweden and the west by the Atlantic Ocean. Norway entered the 20th century under the Swedish crown, but with its own Storting, or Parliament. In 1905 a peaceable agreement was reached by which Norway would become independent under its own monarch. Prince Carl of DENMARK was elected King Haakon VII, and he ruled until his death in 1957 when he was succeeded by his son, OLAV V. Norway remained neutral during WORLD WAR I and attempted to do so during WORLD WAR II, but it was invaded by Germany in 1940 and occupied until 1945. Norway made its merchant fleet available to the Allies during the war. The experience of the occupation led Norway away from its neutral stance, and it joined NATO in 1949 but refused to allow NATO bases or nuclear weapons on its territory. During the years of the COLD WAR, Norway managed to maintain amicable relations with the U.S.S.R. without alienating its Western allies. Norway joined the EUROPEAN FREE TRADE ASSOCIATION (EFTA) in 1960 and was accepted into membership of the EUROPEAN COMMUNITY in 1972, but Norwegian voters rejected the referendum. Norway began exploiting North Sea oil fields in the 1970s and has been prosperously producing petroleum and natural gas.

Norway, German Invasion of. Although Norway had proclaimed its neutrality at the beginning of WORLD WAR II, the Germans invaded on April 9, 1940.

NORTH KOREA

1905	Russo-Japanese War ends; at peace conference Theodore Roosevelt OK's Japanese takeover of Korea.
1910	Japanese annexation completed; emperor's abdication ends 518-year dynasty; use of Korean language banned; place names and surnames changed to Japanese; workers conscripted and property given away to Japanese citizens.
1945	Japanese driven out; land north of 38th parallel occupied by Soviets.
1948	Democratic People's Republic of Korea formed; division from South Korea formalized.
1950	North Korea invades South, overruns the country; American-led counterattack sweeps to Chinese border; Chinese enter war and drive UN forces back to 38th parallel.
1953	Cease-fire leaves heavily fortified border at 38th parallel; no North-South treaty signed.
1958	Kim Il-Sung consolidates power within Communist Party; promotes "Juche" self-reliance for nation, begins creation of intense personality cult around himself, which approaches deification.
1959	Last land removed from private ownership.
1965	Kim Il-Sung successfully avoids taking sides in Sino-Soviet rift; maintains ties but also independence.
1967	Kim Il-Sung criticized during Cultural Revolution; relations with China cool.
1968	Seizure of U.S.S. *Pueblo*; crew imprisoned.
1971	Purchase of Western technology leads to heavy foreign debt.
1975	Fall of Saigon ends period of eased tension with South Korea.
1976	Default on foreign debt; two U.S. soldiers killed at border.
1979	Reunification talks deadlock.
1984	Kim Chong Il groomed to succeed his father as president.
1990	Japan apologizes for crimes of colonial period; signs agreement covering already active trade with North Korea.

Lt. Col. Oliver North testifies before a joint House-Senate committee investigating the Iran-Contra affair (1987).

Their warships seized control of the major harbors, while the Luftwaffe bombed airfields and radio stations, and troops swiftly occupied the cities—aided by Nazi sympathizers (see Vidkun QUISLING). Norwegians resisted, British submarines sank Nazi warships, a landing force temporarily drove the Germans out of Narvik and an Anglo-French force aided in fighting Germans around Oslo, Norway's capital. The Germans responded with blitzkrieg tactics. Norway's King Haakon VII (1871–1957) and his cabinet escaped to London, along with many Norwegian ships and Norwegians who later joined the RESISTANCE movement. (See also Lief LARSEN.)

Nouveau Roman ["new novel"]. French literary movement that gained prominence in the 1950s and 1960s. Major writers associated with the Nouveau Roman movement included Michel BUTOR, Alain ROBBE-GRILLET, Nathalie SARRAUTE and Claude SIMON. The major critical text produced by the movement was Robbe-Grillet's *For A New Novel: Essays on Fiction* (1963). Writers in the Nouveau Roman movement declared that the traditional mainstays of fictional technique—dramatic plotting, moral and psychological analysis of character and elegant style—were out of date and inappropriate for the modern consciousness. Writers, they said, ought not to invent dramatic significance for the events of life but should rather depict them in a matter-of-fact style that reflected their essentially random sequence. Fiction could thus become a means of pointing the reader toward the possibility of freely constructing one's individual life out of the dictates of one's own taste or conscience.

Nouvelle Vague [New Wave]. Term for a French film movement inspired by a "new wave" of directors of the late 1950s and early 1960s; now used to characterize any new movement in any national cinema. Given its initial impetus by the film writers for the journal CAHIERS DU CINEMA, the movement generally espoused an admiration for American cinema, a personal style in direction and an informal approach to filmmaking, with a preference for shooting out in the streets or in real houses, often using a hand-held camera. The first important film of the *nouvelle vague* was Claude CHABROL's *Le Beau Serge* (1959). Several critically acclaimed as well as commercially successful new wave films followed, including Francois TRUFFAUT's *Les Quatre Cents Coups* (*The 400 Blows,* 1959), Alain RESNAIS's *Hiroshima Mon Amour* (1959) and Jean-Luc GODARD's *A Bout de Souffle* (*Breathless,* 1960).

Novaes, Guiomar (1896–1979). Brazilian concert pianist. A child prodigy, Novaes gave her first public performance at age eight and later won a scholarship to study in Paris (1909). Her debuts in London (1912) and New York (1915) established her as one of the finest pianists of her generation. She was especially known for her performances of works by Chopin and Schumann. Her final New York appearance was in 1972.

Novaya Zemlya. Two U.S.S.R. islands between the Barents and Kara seas in the Arctic Ocean, north of the Arctic Circle. In the late 1970s these large islands were the site of Soviet thermonuclear testing, and contained scientific stations and other settlements.

Novello, Ivor [David Ivor Davies] (1893–1951). British composer, author and actor. A matinee idol on stage and screen during the 1920s, Novello first gained fame with his 1914 song "Keep the Home Fires Burning" (composed to a poem by Lena Guilbert Ford), which became one of the most popular songs of WORLD WAR I. After the war he appeared in movies and on stage; he turned to writing for the theater in the 1930s and '40s. Among his successful musicals are *Glamorous Night* (1935) and *Perchance to Dream* (1945). In 1955 the Songwriter's Guild of Great Britain initiated the Ivor Novello Awards to honor achievement in popular and light music.

NORWAY

Novokuznetsk [formerly Stalinsk]. Town situated in the Russian Soviet Federated Socialist Republic 115 miles south-southeast of Kemerovo, on the Tom River. Founded in 1617 by the Cossacks, it developed in the 20th century into an important transportation and industrial center with one of the largest iron and steel works in the world. Manufactures include locomotives, machinery and metal and aluminum products, chemicals and cement. Population (1981): 551,000.

Novosibirsk [*formerly* Novonikolaevsk] (U.S.S.R.). Capital city 390 miles east of Omsk, Novosibirsk oblast, Russian SFSR. It was originally a Trans-Siberian Railway crew construction settlement in 1896, later to become capital of Western Siberia. Dismantled factories from the West were sent here during WORLD WAR II, after which it became itself a center for developing industry. (See also SIBERIA.)

Novotny, Antonin (1904–1975). First Secretary, Czechoslovak Communist Party (1953–68) and president of CZECHOSLOVAKIA (1957–68). Novotny joined the Czechoslovak Communist Party shortly after it was formed in 1921. When the communists won key government positions after WORLD WAR II, Novotny organized the communist control of the Czech police. A hard-line Stalinist, he played a key role in crushing opposition to the communist takeover of the government in 1948 (see STALINISM). He took a prominent part in the spy trial and execution of Rudolf Slansky and was made a member of the Politburo. The SLANSKY TRIAL was held in 1952. Novotny was a major ally of Klement GOTTWALD, and after Gottwald's death he became the leader of the Czech communist hard-liners and of the party itself. It 1957 he also succeeded the more reform-minded Antonin Zapotocky as president of Czechoslovakia. Thus he held the two top positions in Czechoslovakia until he was deposed during the PRAGUE SPRING (1968) by Alexander DUBCEK and the reformers. Novotny failed to regain his prestige even after the SOVIET INVASION OF CZECHOSLOVAKIA ousted the reformers and restored a more orthodox communist regime.

***Novy Mir* [*New World*].** Monthly literary magazine, first published in January 1925 in Moscow. Many well-known works, such as A. Tolstoy's *Peter the First* (1929–45) and Mikhail SHOLOKHOV's four-volume *The Quiet Don* (1937–40), and numerous sketches by Leonid Leonov, Alexander Tvardovsky, Konstantin Simonov, Konstantin Fedin, Fedor Gladkov and Yury Trifonov have been serialized in *Novy Mir*—as was SOLZHENITSYN's *One Day in the Life of Ivan Denisovich.*

Noyce, Robert Norton (1927–1990). American inventor. In 1957, he founded the Fairchild Camera and Instruments Corp. in what was to become CALIFORNIA's Silicon Valley. Two years later, with Jack Kilby, he was awarded a patent for the integrated circuit. In the 1970s and 1980s, the device, also known as the silicon microchip, became the basis for such products as the personal COMPUTER, the pocket calculator and the programmable microwave oven.

Noyes, Alfred (1880–1959). British poet. Noyes firmly resisted MODERNISM, embracing the traditional style in his poetry, which includes *Drake* (1908) and *Tales of the Mermaid Tavern* (1913). Life at sea is a recurring theme in Noyes' work, but in the ambitious *The Torchbearers,* a trilogy appearing between 1922 and 1930, he celebrates men of science. Noyes, who taught at Princeton from 1914 to 1923, also wrote plays, novels and an autobiography, *Two Worlds for Memory* (1953).

nuclear magnetic resonance [NMR]. Medical diagnostic technique in which radio waves are passed through a body in an electromagnetic field. First used in 1973 and widely employed since the early 1980s, the test allows researchers to create images of interior organs and to detect and analyze changes in the structure and function of those organs. Since it does not rely on X RAYS, like the CAT SCAN, NMR imaging has been considered a safe procedure for the patient.

Nuclear Non-proliferation Treaty. Treaty, signed in 1968 by over 60 nations, that was designed to stop the spread of nuclear weapons. The agreement provided that nuclear-weapons states signing the treaty would act immediately through the United Nations to provide or support immediate assistance to any non-nuclear-weapon signatory of the treaty that came under nuclear attack or threat of nuclear attack.

Nuclear Test Ban Treaty. A U.S., Soviet and British agreement (August 5, 1963) to end nuclear tests in the atmosphere, in space and underwater; concluded after five years of negotiations. Underground testing was permitted to continue. France and China refused to accept the treaty, but over 90 other nations signed in the following two years. The nuclear test ban treaty was the first major international treaty of its kind between the superpowers in the nuclear age.

Nuremberg [Nurnberg]. Bavarian city, formerly in West Germany, on the Pegnitz River, 92 miles northwest of Munich. It was headquarters for HITLER's National Socialist Party in the 1930s, and after the so-called **Nuremberg laws** were in effect, along with other anti-Semitic propaganda, it served as the main industrial and political center of the Nazi war effort. Massive Nazi rallies were staged at the immense Nuremberg Stadium (see NUREMBERG RALLIES). The city was heavily bombed by the Allies in the course of WORLD WAR II. Afterwards, it was the site of judicial hearings on international war crimes, the NUREMBERG TRIALS, which set a symbolic, legal precedent for the individual right to disobey unjust orders, and his or her guilt by carrying them out. A Hohenzollern castle, medieval churches, and parts of the old city wall are still intact, but the old interior city was completely rebuilt.

Nuremberg Rallies. Series of annual Nazi Party meetings held each September from 1933 through 1938 near the Bavarian city of Nuremberg. Organized by Joseph GOEBBELS and other Nazi chiefs, they were highly theatrical PROPAGANDA exercises. Each rally featured athletic events, impressive torchlight processions and inflammatory speeches—and ended with a speech by Adolf HITLER at the Nuremberg stadium designed by Albert SPEER. During the 1935 rally, Hitler announced the so-called **Nuremberg laws,** which deprived JEWS of civic rights, closed professions to them and forbade the marriage of Jews to non-Jews. The German filmmaker Leni RIEFENSTAHL documented the 1934 Nuremberg Rally in her spectacular film *The Triumph of the Will* (1936).

Nuremberg Trials. Trials in 1946 of high-ranked Nazi politicians and German military officers following WORLD WAR II. After the Nazi defeat U.S., Russian, British and Provisional French leaders decided to try Nazi leaders for crimes against peace, for planning and waging the war, for war crimes, including needless killing of civilians, the use of slave labor and the destruction of cities, towns and villages, and for crimes against humanity—the deportation and genocide of the Jews and other groups in Europe. The individual defendants included 24 top Nazis; among them were Hermann GOERING, Rudolf HESS, Joachim von RIBBENTROP, Albert SPEER, Field Marshal Wilhelm KEITEL and Martin BORMANN, who was tried in absentia. Adolf HITLER, Joseph GOEBBELS and Heinrich HIMMLER were not tried, as they had all committed suicide in the closing days of the war.

The trial judges included Francis Biddle (U.S.), Henri Donnedieu de Vabre (France), General Nikitchenko (U.S.S.R.) and Lord Justice Lawrence (U.K.). U.S. Supreme Court Justice Robert JACKSON was one of the prosecutors. The defendants argued that they were merely following lawful orders. Most but not all of the defendants were found guilty; several, including Goering, were sentenced to death. Hess was given life imprisonment and others received lesser terms.

Nureyev, Rudolph (1938–). Russian-born dancer, choreographer and ballet director. Internationally acclaimed as the greatest male dancer of the 1960s and early 1970s, Nureyev has shown astounding virtuosity and a charismatic stage presence in more than 100 roles in the classical and modern dance repertory. After studying at the Kirov Ballet School in Leningrad, he joined the Kirov Ballet in 1958 and scored a personal triumph during its Paris visit in 1961. He was granted political asylum in 1961 and has

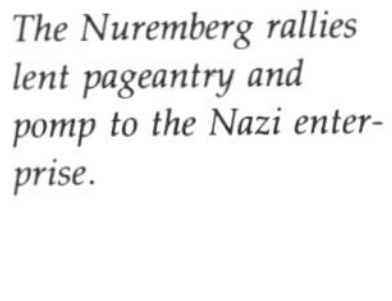

The Nuremberg rallies lent pageantry and pomp to the Nazi enterprise.

NORWAY

1901	First Nobel Prize for peace awarded in Christiania.
1905	Norway demands its own foreign service to handle affairs of world's leading merchant fleet; after a brief war, union with Sweden dissolved; Haakon VII is king.
1913	Suffrage for women.
1914	Economic boom as neutral Norway supplies Allies with food and raw materials.
1918	Merchant fleet at half of prewar level due to sinkings by Germany.
1925	Christiania reverts to original name—Oslo.
1928	Prince Olav wins Olympic gold medal in sailing.
1935	Labor government, elected in the face of 25% to 33% unemployment, begins 30-year hold on government; creation of a welfare state.
1940	Germans invade; Haakon VII leads government-in-exile from London; Olav organizes armed resistance.
1945	Vidkun Quisling, leader of puppet government during occupation, is executed; border with U.S.S.R. created.
1949	Joins NATO but rejects bases and nuclear arms to avoid angering Soviets; Trygve Lie is first secretary-general of UN.
1957	Haakon VII dies; prince crowned Olav V.
1965	Non-socialist coalition assumes control of government.
1970	Norway's second university founded at Bergen.
1972	Voters reject membership in European Economic Community.
1975	North Sea oil and gas fields stimulate economy.
1981	Government-owned computer company implicated in scandal for selling equipment to U.S.S.R.
1990	Brundtland elected for third time as voters again reject EEC membership.
1991	Kaci five assumes leadership of Conservatives; leaders of three out of four major parties, one-third of Storting (parliament) and one-half of cabinet, are women.

View of the defendants' dock at the Nuremberg Trials (c. 1945–46).

Tanzanian President Julius Nyerere (1985).

since danced with many companies worldwide. As a guest artist with Britain's ROYAL BALLET (1962 to mid-1970s) he formed a legendary partnership with Margot FONTEYN. He is famous for his interpretation of heroic roles in such ballets as *Petrushka, Marguerite and Armand* and Kenneth MACMILLAN's *Romeo and Juliet*—as well as for creating roles in such modern works as Rudi van DANTZIG's *The Ropes of Time* (1970) and Martha GRAHAM's *Lucifer* (1975). He has choreographed and staged many works, including *Nutcracker* (1967) and *Don Quixote* (1966; film version, 1973) and starred in the television film *I Am a Dancer* (1972). He became an Austrian citizen in 1982. Since 1983 he has been director of the Paris Opera Ballet.

Nurmi, Paavo (1897–1973). Finnish athlete. Popularly known as the Flying Finn, Nurmi was one of the greatest track stars of the 20th century. He set 20 world records from 1920 to 1932 and won nine gold and three silver medals in the OLYMPIC GAMES of 1920, '24 and '28. He set records in runs of from 1 to 10 miles and from 1,500 to 20,000 meters. His running career was effectively ended in 1932 when he was barred from the Olympics for accepting expense money and compromising his amateur standing.

Nye, Gerald (Prentice) (1892–1971). U.S. senator. After a newspaper editing career in Wisconsin and North Dakota, Nye became involved in populist politics. In 1926 he was elected a Republican senator from North Dakota. He served in the U.S. Senate until 1944 where he opposed corruption in politics, monopolies, price-fixing and banking, and worked for farm interests. He generally defended President Franklin D. ROOSEVELT'S NEW DEAL. As the chief spokesman for the Peace Lobby in Congress, his efforts had revealed the profiteering of munitions makers during WORLD WAR I. He was most instrumental in passage of the Neutrality Act of 1935 and in opposing LEND-LEASE.

Nyerere, Julius Kambarage (1922–). Tanzanian political leader, president (1964 to 1985). The son of a Butiama chief, he was born at a village on Lake Victoria and attended Makerere University College in Uganda and Edinburgh University. He taught at various mission schools and founded the Tanganyika African National Union (1954) to promote self-rule. After the party's overwhelming victory in the 1960 election, Nyerere became the colony's chief minister and pursued a Christian socialist agenda. When Tanganyika achieved independence in 1961, he became its first prime minister and, after it became a republic the following year, he was elected its first president. Nyerere engineered the union of Tanganyika and Zanzibar into the Republic of TANZANIA (1964). He won reelection in Tanzania's subsequent presidential elections.

Nyswander, Marl (1919–1986). American psychiatrist. In the 1950s, she became one of the first members of her profession to advocate treating drug addiction as a medical problem. She and Dr. Vincent Dole, whose research group she joined in 1964 and whom she married in 1965, were credited with developing the methadone maintenance method for treating heroin addiction.

Oak Ridge. City (pop. 27,662) in Anderson County in the east-central part of Tennessee. Located on a 59,000–acre tract of federal land, it was built to accommodate the WORLD WAR II Atomic Energy Program (the MANHATTAN PROJECT); its personnel reached a wartime high of 70,000. The site was chosen for its seclusion and also because it provided the necessary resources and transportation via the Louisville & Nashville, and Southern Railroads. Government engineers started construction of Oak Ridge (originally named the Clinton Engineer Works) in 1942 and completed it in two-and-a-half years under tight security. In 1944 its plants began to process uranium. By the early 1950s, although activity had been greatly reduced from wartime, Oak Ridge still had processing plants, an atomic energy field office and an atomic laboratory where training and research was carried on. The government began offering its land and homes for private purchase in 1956, and Oak Ridge was incorporated as a city in 1959. Present manufactures include tools, dies, metal fabrication and electroplating. The city is the home of the American Museum of Science and Energy and the Oak Ridge Associated Universities.

O.A.S. [*Organisation de l'Armee Secrete*]. A secret army made up of dissident members of the French army in ALGERIA (1961–62). Led by General Raoul SALAN and supported by French settlers in Algeria, the group launched a terrorist campaign aimed at preventing DE GAULLE's Algerian policy, thwarting Algerian independence and, ultimately, bringing down France's Fifth Republic. The O.A.S. engaged in terrorist activities against Algeria's Muslims, and it was unsuccessful in a variety of attempts to assassinate de Gaulle. It ceased to pose a threat after the capture of Salan and other leaders, and the revolt was ended. (See also ALGERIAN WAR OF 1954–62.)

For further reading:

Harrison, Alexander, *Challenging De Gaulle: The O.A.S. and the Counterrevolution in Algeria, 1954–1962.* Westport, Connecticut: Greenwood, 1989.

Oates, Joyce Carol (1938–). American novelist. Oates's naturalistic fiction often explores deviance and violence in contemporary American settings. Such works include, *Them* (1969), *Wonderland* (1971) and *Because It Is Bitter and Because It Is My Heart* (1990)—the title of which was taken from a poem by Stephen Crane. An extremely prolific author, Oates has also written several neo-gothic novels, such as *A Bloodsmoor Romance* (1982), and mystery fiction under the pseudonym Rosamond Smith. She has written non-fiction, short stories, and edited the *Ontario Review* with her husband, Raymond J. Smith.

Oberth, Hermann (1894–1989). Hungarian mathematician, rocket theorist and experimenter. Rocket pioneer, Oberth never left as big a mark as his two contemporaries, Konstantin TSIOLKOVSKY and American Robert GODDARD. The son of a physician, he became interested in astronautics while recuperating from wounds suffered while serving in the Austro-Hungarian army during WORLD WAR I. The government wasn't interested in listening to his ideas; and after the war, in 1922, his attempt to obtain his Ph.D. with a dissertation on rocket design was also rejected. Turning to his own greatly limited resources, he published *The Rocket into Interplanetary Space*, partly at his own expense. The book, which also included one of the first detailed discussions of orbiting space stations, was a popular success, and in 1929 he published his major work *The Road to Space Travel.* A theorist rather than a hands-on engineer or inventor, Oberth nevertheless began to build up a following in Germany, and in 1938 he joined the faculty of the Technical University of Vienna and became a German citizen. Although he worked for a while with von BRAUN and for the Nazis at PEENEMUNDE, the association was uneasy, as were his later years spent with von Braun in the United States. In 1958, after three years in the U.S., he retired and returned to Germany.

Obote, Milton (1924–). Ugandan politcal leader. Obote was a member of the Uganda National Congress from 1950 to 1962. When UGANDA became independent in 1962, Obote, head of the majority Uganda People's Congress (UPC), became prime minister. He soon suspended the constitution, deposed the president, assumed all executive power himself and used the military to quell opposition. In 1971 military commander Idi AMIN seized control. After a nine-year exile in Tanzania, Obote returned (1980) and, in a disputed election, became president. In 1985 he was deposed by a military coup and exiled to Zambia.

O'Brien, Conor Cruise (1917–). Irish critic, playwright and diplomat. O'Brien's first critical work, *Maria Cross: Imaginative Patterns in a Group of Modern Catholic Writers* (written under the pseudomym Donat O'Donnell, 1952) was much admired by Dag HAMMARSKJOLD, to whom O'Brien became a special representative. A leading member of the FINE GAEL Party, he also served as IRELAND's representative at the UNITED NATIONS (1955–61) and as minister of posts and telegraphs (1973–77) in the cabinet of Prime Minister Liam Cosgrave. He was also editor of the British Sunday newspaper, the *Observer.* O'Brien has written widely on politics and the arts. His plays, perhaps best known of which is *Murderous Angels: A Political Tragedy and Comedy in Black and White* (1970), present the world political arena as drama. He addressed issues of international diplomacy in *To Katanga and Back: A UN Case* (1962) and *The United Nations: Sacred Drama* (1968). Among his other varied works are *The Idea of the Modern in Literature and the Arts* (1968), *Literature in Revolution* (1972) and *God Land: Reflections on Religion and Nationalism* (1988).

O'Brien, Edna (1932–). Irish author. Born in the West of Ireland, she attended the Pharmaceutical College in Dublin. After marriage at age 20 and the birth of two sons, she moved to London. *The Country Girls* (1960) is her first novel and the first of a trilogy (completed with) *The Lonely Girls*, 1962, and *Girls in Their Married Bliss*, 1963) that follows the lives of two convent-bred Irish girls, Cathleen Brady and Bridget Brennen, who escape to Dublin and eventually move to London. O'Brien's writing reflects her rejection of the constraints of her Catholic upbringing. Though she is cynical about relations between the sexes, her fiction is exuberantly sensual. Other works include *A Pagan Place* (1971), *Johnny I Hardly Knew You* (1977) and *Tales for the Telling: Irish Folk and Fairy Tales* (1986). O'Brien has also published collections of short stories and has written plays and television scripts.

O'Brien, Flann [pen name of Brian O Nuallain] (1912–1966). Irish novelist, widely considered one of the greatest and most original comic writers of the 20th century. Nolan worked for the Irish civil service and wrote a brilliant satirical column in the *Irish Times* for 27 years under the pseudonym Myles na gCopaleen (literally, "Myles of the Little Horses"). His first novel, *At Swim-Two-Birds* (1939), was largely ignored at the time of its publication but has since come to be regarded as a masterpiece. The book shows the influence of James JOYCE, who championed it, and is an innovative pastiche of Irish culture and folklore. *The Third Policeman* (written in 1940 but not published until 1966), in which the central character is dead and in which a policeman's molecules become intermixed with those of his bicycle—so that each takes on some characteristics of the other—is also highly regarded. His other fiction includes *An Beal Bocht* (1941), written in Gaelic and published in English as *The Poor Mouth* (1973); *The Dalkey Archive* (1964); and *The Hard Life* (1962). Few other writers have matched O'Brien's ear for dialogue, his brilliant wordplay, philosophical outlook and sense of the absurd.

O'Brien, Lawrence Francis, Jr. (1917–1990). U.S. political strategist. A Democrat, he directed the successful senatorial and presidential campaigns of John F. KENNEDY. He was Kennedy's liaison to Congress and helped win passage of many of Kennedy's New Frontier programs, such as the CIVIL RIGHTS ACT of 1964 and MEDICARE. He went on to serve as postmaster general (1965–68) and as chairman of the Democratic National Committee (1968–69 and 1970–72). It was his office at the WATERGATE building that was broken into in 1972 by burglars seeking to wiretap his conversations, an event leading to the eventual resignation of President Richard M. NIXON. He left politics to serve as commissioner of the National Basketball Association, overseeing its merger with the American Basketball Association.

O'Casey, Sean (1880–1964). Irish playwright. Born into a lower-middle-class Protestant family, O'Casey described himself as educated in the streets of Dublin. In his early years he held a number of menial jobs, was involved in James Larkin's labor movement and joined the Irish Citizen Army. O'Casey's early dramas realistically portrayed lower-class life in Dublin and the violence that can spring from it; they also explore themes of patriotism. In 1923 his first mature play, *The Shadow of a Gunman*, was staged at the ABBEY THEATRE; it was followed by *Juno and the Paycock* (1924), perhaps his greatest play. *The Plough and the Stars* (1926), set during the EASTER RISING, provoked rioting when it was performed at the Abbey because it portrayed Irish republican revolutionaries as less than noble. He moved to England in 1927. After his antiwar play *The Silver Tassie* (1928) was rejected by W.B. YEATS, O'Casey ended his association with the Abbey. He experimented with EXPRESSIONISM in such later plays as *Within the Gates* (1933) and *The Bishop's Bonfire* (1955).. These works were never as well received as his earlier, realistic plays. O'Casey also wrote six acclaimed volumes of autobiography beginning with *I Knock at the Door* (1939); *Sunset and Evening Star* (1954) is the last.

For further reading:

Krause, David. *Sean O'Casey: the Man and His Work.* New York: Macmillan, 1975.

ocean liners. The 20th century saw the rise, glory and eventual decline of the great ocean liners. The North Atlantic route between Northern Europe and North America was the most popular and glamorous. But ocean liners also plied other seas and traveled to other destinations. Some ships sailed regularly between Europe and South America, Africa or Australia. For the first part of the century, ocean liners were the only way to travel across oceans. But these ships were not just a means of travel; they were expressions of national pride and prosperity. The industrial nations of Europe vied with one another to build the largest, fastest and most luxurious liners. The British White Star liner TITANIC (launched 1912) was to be not only the greatest ship of its time, but also the embodiment of a new technological age. When it struck an iceberg and sank on its maiden voyage (Apr. 14–15, 1912) with the loss of some 1,500 lives, it was a stark lesson in the limits of technology. However, the *Titanic* disaster led to new safety regulations and improved designs for ships.

In 1921, new U.S. immigration laws restricted the number of immigrants who could enter the U.S. The new law had a profound effect on the international shipping business. Despite their much-publicized luxury, ocean liners had been designed to capitalize on the immigrant trade, carrying huge numbers of European immigrants westward to the U.S. in small, cramped third-class quarters ("steerage"). After the new law came into effect, shipping lines modified their vessels and changed their appeal. Instead of concentrating on transporting immigrants to the U.S., liners began carrying large numbers of well-to-do American tourists to Europe. The 1930s was the heyday of the ocean liner. The two great liners of the day were Cunard's QUEEN MARY (launched 1936; 80,774 tons) and CGT's (French Line) NORMANDIE (launched 1935; 79,280 tons). Both ships vied for the "Blue Riband," representing the speed record for the fastest voyage across the Atlantic. The *Queen Mary* and the *Normandie* were the first ships able to cross the Atlantic in less than four days.

During WORLD WAR II, many ocean liners (including the *Queen Mary* and her newer sister ship, *Queen Elizabeth* (launched 1940), were pressed into service as troop ships. Some of these liners survived the war; others were torpedoed or otherwise sunk by the enemy. A few were accidentally destroyed while being converted, either at the beginning of the war or after the war.

Ocean liners remained the primary means of intercontinental travel throughout the 1950s. *Queen Mary, Queen Elizabeth* and many smaller ships regularly carried thousands of passengers between Europe and North America, and between these continents and destinations in South America, Africa, Asia and Australia. In 1958, however, transatlantic passenger jet service was introduced, and more and more passengers began to fly rather than take the liners. Regular ocean liner service continued through the 1960s and into the 1970s, and new ships were introduced, but the passenger shipping companies began to feel the pinch of increased competition from the airlines and increased operating costs. By 1990, there was no regular year-round transatlantic passenger ocean liner service. New cruise liners thrived by carrying passengers to the West Indies and other vacation destinations.

For further reading:

Braynard, Frank O., *Fifty Famous Liners.* New York: W.W. Norton, 1982.

Brinnin, John Malcolm, *Beau Voyage: Life Aboard the Last Great Ships.* New York: Dorset Press, 1988.

Miller, William H., *Famous Ocean Liners.* New York: Harper Collins, 1987.

———, *Liner.* New York: HarperCollins, 1987.

Ochab, Edward (1906–1989). Polish communist official. He served as party leader for seven months in 1956, a time of intense anti-Soviet feeling. In 1964 he became chairman of the Polish Council of State, the collective presidency of POLAND. He resigned four years later in protest against a communist-led ANTI-SEMITISM campaign that forced some 20,000 Polish Jews to emigrate.

Ochoa, Severo (1905–). Spanish-American biochemist. Ochoa was one of the first to demonstrate the role of high-energy phosphates in the storage and release of the body's energy. Of great significance was his isolation of the bacterial enzyme polynucleotide phosphorylase in 1955, while investigating the process of oxidative phosphorylation. He then used this enzyme to catalyze the formation of ribonucleic acid (RNA) from appropriate nucleotides. This procedure was later used in the synthesis of artificial RNA. His pivotal achievement enabled subsequent researchers to decipher the genetic code.

In 1959, Ochoa shared the NOBEL PRIZE for physiology or medicine with Arthur Kornberg, who synthesized deoxyribonucleic acid.

O'Connor, Donald (1925–). Hollywood actor-dancer. O'Connor was born into a family of circus performers and worked as a child in VAUDEVILLE. He made his film debut at age 11 in *Melody For Two* (1937). Although he made many low-budget musicals during the 1940s, it was a non-musical role playing opposite a talking mule named *Francis* that boosted his career and lead to a starring role in the classic musical film *Singin' In the Rain* (1952) with Debbie Reynolds and Gene KELLY. During the 1950s O'Connor appeared in the musicals *Call Me Madam* (1953) and *There's No Business Like Show Business* (1954). He also starred in five films and a TV series featuring Francis, the talking mule. After the 1950s O'Connor made few film and TV appearances.

O'Connor, (Mary) Flannery (1925–1964). American author. After graduating from Georgia College (B.A., 1945), O'Connor went to the University of Iowa Writer's Workshop (M.F.A., 1947). She published her first story, "The Geranium" (1946), and first novel, *Wise Blood* (1953). Despite constant illness, there followed *A Good Man Is Hard to Find and Other Short Stories* (1955), her acclaimed *The Violent Bear It Away* (1959) and other stories, including "Judgment Day" and "Parker's Back." O'Connor's highly polished fiction, often comic and misunderstood, presented characters tortured over the meaning of their lives.

O'Connor, Frank [Michael O'Donovan] (1903–1966). Irish author. O'Connor is perhaps best known for his short stories, which include the collections *Bones of Contention* (1936), *Traveller's Samples* (1951) and *Domestic Relations* (1957), and which present the middle and lower-middle classes of IRELAND, often situated in his native County Cork. O'Connor was also a champion of Irish literature and wrote *A Short History of Irish Literature: A Backward Look*, translated many Gaelic works into English and edited the anthology *A Book of Ireland* (1959). Other works include the novel *The Big Fellow* (1937) and the autobiographies *An Only Child* (1961) and *My Father's Son* (1969). In the latter part of his life, O'Connor lived mostly in the U.S. and taught at Harvard and Northwestern universities. His critical works include *The Lonely Voice: A Study of the Short Story* (1962).

O'Connor, Sandra Day (1930–). O'Connor is the first woman to serve on the U.S. Supreme Court. A native of west Texas, she graduated from Stanford University and its law school. Although graduating at the top of her class, O'Connor was rejected by a number of large law firms and first worked as a deputy county attorney in California, and was later in private practice, before becoming an Arizona assistant attorney general. A Republican active in politics, O'Connor was appointed and then elected to the Arizona state senate, eventually rising to the

Sandra Day O'Connor, U.S. Supreme Court associate justice.

position of majority leader. She was next elected a local judge and later appointed to the Arizona Court of Appeals. In 1981 O'Connor was a surprise appointment to the Supreme Court by President Ronald REAGAN. On the bench O'Connor was generally a member of the conservative block, sometimes voting against legislation favoring women and minorities. She proved a champion of STATES' RIGHTS against the federal government.

For further reading:

Horner, Matina S., ed., *Sandra Day O'Connor*. New York: Chelsea House, 1990.

Woods, Harold, *Equal Justice: A Biography of Sandra Day O'Connor*. Minneapolis: Dillon Press, 1985.

October (November) Revolution. After an abortive attempt by the BOLSHEVIKS (a radical Marxist party) to seize power from the provisional government in Petrograd (now Leningrad) in July 1917, Bolshevik leader Vladimir I. LENIN fled to Finland, and Russian socialist Alexander F. KERENSKY succeeded the liberal Prince LVOV as premier (see RUSSIAN REVOLUTION; FEBRUARY REVOLUTION). A reactionary coup attempt failed (see KORNILOV'S REVOLT) but weakened Kerensky's power; support for the Bolsheviks increased as the Russians, exhausted and suffering severe privations from WORLD WAR I, grew suspicious of military and governmental leaders. In early November 1917 (late October by the Old Style calendar), soviets, or revolutionary councils, throughout RUSSIA voted to form a Soviet government that would end the war and establish citizen-run industries and farms.

Bolshevik leader Leon TROTSKY took over the military revolutionary committee at Petrograd, where the troops voted to obey only the committee's orders. Kerensky demanded rescission of the vote and sent soldiers on November 6, 1917 (October 24, O.S.), to shut down the Bolshevik press in Petrograd. The Bolsheviks, along with sympathetic troops and the workers' Red Guards, marched upon and peacefully took over the government buildings and public utilities. While Kerensky gathered his forces to oust the Bolsheviks, his ministers at the Winter Palace surrendered in the face of Bolshevik armed might. Then Kerensky's troops marched to Gatchina near Petrograd, and there the pro-Kerensky committee of public defense ordered the military-school trainees to arrest the military revolutionary committee and to attack Bolshevik or Soviet-held areas. The Bolsheviks withstood this assault and took charge of the military schools. Trotsky moved to Gatchina, where his troops defeated government forces in two days; Kerensky then fled abroad. Lenin became president of a Council of People's Commissars, the name of the new government, in which Trotsky and Joseph STALIN (1879–1953) were chief commissars. The Bolsheviks soon took Moscow after bloody street fighting, and within a month they controlled the country. In January 1918, Lenin dissolved the freely elected, socialist-dominated national assembly, thereby ending Russia's only attempt at democracy. (See also RUSSIAN CIVIL WAR.)

For further reading:

Chamberlain, William H., *The Russian Revolution, 1917–1921. Vol. 1: 1917–1918: From the Overthrow of the Tsar to the Assumption of Power by the Bolsheviks*. Princeton, N.J.: Princeton University Press, 1987.

Pipes, Richard, *History of the Russian Revolution*. New York: Alfred A. Knopf, 1990.

Octobrists. Members of the "Union of October 17," a political party founded in November 1905 with the aim of ensuring the implementation of the promises made in NICHOLAS II's manifesto of 1905, which granted a constitution. The party was led by Alexander Ivanovich GUCHKOV and Michael Vladimirovich RODZYANKO, and the party won 12 seats in the first duma, 32 in the second, 150 in the third and 97 in the fourth. In the third and fourth dumas the Octobrists had an overall majority. They joined the "progressive bloc" in 1915 and took part in the provisional government of 1917.

O Dalaigh, Cearbhall (1911–1978). President of the Republic of IRELAND (1974–76). A noted lawyer, O Dalaigh became a judge in 1953, and was chief justice of Ireland's Supreme Court from 1961 to 1973.

Oder-Neisse Line. Boundary along the rivers Oder and Neisse between POLAND and GERMANY; provisionally agreed upon by the U.S., U.K. and U.S.S.R. at the YALTA and POTSDAM conferences. The new boundary gave Poland a fifth of Germany's 1938 territory and a sixth of its population. WEST GERMANY did not officially recognize the Oder-Neisse line until November 18, 1970, as a part of Chancellor Willy BRANDT'S OSTPOLITIK reconciliation policy.

Odets, Clifford (1906–1963). American playwright. Known for his social protest dramas of the 1930s, Odets was born in Philadelphia, became an actor and joined the GROUP THEATER (1931). Turning from acting in plays to writing them, he created the short, working-class drama *Waiting for Lefty* (1935). Immediately acclaimed for his powerful play, Odets followed it with his first full-length drama, *Awake and Sing!* (1935)—a tale of travail and rebellion in an impoverished Jewish family; it is widely considered his best work. His most popular play, *Golden Boy* (1937) tells of a young man who gives up the violin for a more lucrative career in the brutal world of prizefighting. His other plays include *Clash by Night* (1942), *The Big Knife* (1949), *The Country Girl* (1950) and *The Flowering Peach* (1954). Odets spent the latter part of his life as a HOLLYWOOD screenwriter.

O'Donnell, Peadar (1893–1986). Irish author and political activist. He fought for Irish independence with the IRISH REPUBLICAN ARMY and later helped organize the small Irish group that joined the International Brigade to fight in the SPANISH CIVIL WAR. He cofounded *The Bell,* a major literary magazine during WORLD WAR II, with Sean O'FAOLAIN. Early in his career he wrote such acclaimed novels as *Islanders* and *The Kife,* chronicling the lives of Irish peasants. *The Big Window* (1954) is widely regarded as his finest novel.

Odum, Howard Washington (1884–1954). Sociologist and author. Odum developed regional analysis to reflect the social life of the Southern Negro. At the University of North Carolina (1920) he began pioneer work in social science, founding the departments of public welfare and sociology, establishing the journal *Social Forces* and developing the university's Research Institute. Under President Herbert HOOVER he prepared the influential report *Recent Social Trends* (1933). Author of many books, including *Rainbow Round My Shoulder* (1928) and *Southern Regions of the United States* (1936), Odum also earned a Master Breeders Award for work with cattle.

Oerter, Al (Alfred Adolph) (1936–). American athlete. Oerter won the OLYMPIC gold medal for the discus throw in 1956, 1960, 1964 and 1968. This is an Olympic record—he is the only individual to have won four consecutive titles in the same event. In 1962 he broke the 200-foot barrier by throwing the discus 200 feet 5 inches. He was also national Amateur Athletic Union (AAU) champion six times.

O'Faolain, Sean (1900–1991). Irish novelist and short story writer. O'Faolain was a member of the IRISH REPUBLICAN ARMY and studied at Harvard University prior to the publication of his first collection of short stories, *Midsummer Night Madness and Other Stories* (1932). His fiction affectionately satirizes his Irish characters, and laments the lost cause of Irish nationalism. O'Faolain wrote three novels, *A Nest of Simple Folk* (1934), *Bird Alone* (1936) and *Come Back to Erin* (1940), many biographies, and the non-fiction, *The Irish* (1947). His autobiography, *Vive Moi!* (1964), recounts his experiences in the IRA and contains lyrical descriptions of the Irish countryside. *Collected Stories* was published in 1981.

Office of Strategic Services. American intelligence agency during WORLD WAR II; forerunner of the peacetime CIA. On June 13, 1942, President Franklin D. ROOSEVELT replaced the Office of Coordinator of Information with the OSS. William "Wild Bill" DONOVAN was named head of the new civilian agency, whose mission was to direct intelligence operations and related covert activities. During the war, the OSS proved extremely useful to the Allies. Its activities in North Africa were credited with ensuring the success of the Allied landings there. OSS agents also worked extensively with RESISTANCE groups throughout Europe, fought behind enemy lines and provided Allied planners with a steady stream of invaluable intelligence on enemy troop movements, battle plans and other topics of vital concern. The OSS was disbanded on September 20, 1945; it was succeeded in early 1946 by the Central Intelligence Group, which in July 1947 became the Central Intelligence Agency (CIA).

O Fiaich, Cardinal Tomas (1923–1990). Irish religious leader. As Roman Catholic primate of all Ireland since 1977, he headed the Catholic Church both in the Republic of IRELAND and in predominantly Protestant NORTHERN IRELAND. He was an outspoken critic of the IRISH REPUBLICAN ARMY's attempt to end British rule in Northern Ireland and, at times, of Britain's administration there.

O'Flaherty, Liam (1897–1984). Irish author and nationalist. A political influence as well as a literary one, O'Flaherty helped form the Irish Communist Party before writing his first novel, *The Neighbor's Wife* (1923). His fiction often depicts rural life in Ireland and reflects his own political struggles. O'Flaherty's writing generally lacks subtlety. His stories are often overwritten and crudely constructed. Nonetheless, they made a powerful impact. Perhaps his best-known novel is *The Informer* (1925), which was filmed by John FORD in 1935, but critics point to *Famine* (1937) as his most important book. In Ireland he is equally lauded for his short stories, which include *Spring Sowing* (1924) and *Two Lovely Beasts* (1948). He has also written three lively volumes of autobiography, *Two Years* (1930), *I Went to Russia* (1931) and *Shame the Devil* (1934).

Ogaden. Region in ETHIOPIA's Harar province, bordering SOMALIA. Claimed by ITALY as a protectorate in 1891, Ogaden was recaptured by Menelik II in the same year. Coveted by MUSSOLINI, he contrived a 1934 dispute at Walwal as a pretext for invading Ethiopia. (See also ITALO-ETHIOPIAN WAR OF 1935–36.) In 1948 Ogaden was restored to Ethiopia and remained the subject of boundary disputes between Somalia and Ethiopia since 1960. After a major Ethiopian offensive with the aid of CUBA and the Soviet Union in 1978, Somali troops were withdrawn, but Ethiopian forces continued to be opposed by the rebels.

Ogdon, John (1937–1989). British pianist. A champion of 20th-century and late Romantic-era works, he was praised for his virtuosic technique and his unusual programming. He won the Liszt Prize in BUDAPEST in 1961 and shared first place in the 1962 Tchaikovsky Competition with Vladimir ASHKENAZY. His career was curtailed by acute schizophrenia.

O'Hara, John (Henry) (1905–1970). American author. O'Hara is best known for his short stories, a great many of which were first published in the NEW YORKER and later published in various collections, including *The Doctor's Son* (1935). O'Hara's tone was tough and sophisticated, and his works were noted for their frank treatment of sexuality. His novels include *Appointment in Samarra* (1934); *Butterfield 8* (1935, filmed 1960); *Pal Joey* (1940), which was adapted into a musical that was filmed in 1957; and *A Rage to Live* (1949). His subsequent works lacked the impact of his early fiction.

O. Henry [William Sydney Porter] (1862–1910). O. Henry was the pen name of the American short-story writer William Sydney Porter. Born in Greensboro, North Carolina, he settled in Texas in 1882, working at a number of jobs and becoming the editor of a humor magazine. Accused of embezzling while a teller at an Austin bank, he protested his innocence but fled to Honduras and South America to avoid arrest. Returning in 1897, he was tried and convicted and served three years in a federal penitentiary. There he began writing and selling his short stories. After his release, he moved to New York City (1902), where he flourished as an author, contributing pieces to many popular magazines. Intricately plotted, his famous stories usually involve everyday people and situations subjected to ironic twists and surprise endings. Often artificial and sentimental, they are nonetheless beautifully drafted, colorful and often deeply felt. Over 700 in number, his stories were collected in such volumes as *Cabbages and Kings* (1904), *The Four Million* (1906), *The Voice of the City* (1908) and *Opinions* (1909).

Ohno, Talichi (1912–1990). Japanese engineer. Ohno developed the just-in-time manufacturing system, which Toyota adopted in the 1950s. The system, in which inventories of parts were kept intentionally low in order to reduce costs and increase flexibility, helped transform the company into the third-largest auto manufacturer in the world. Ohno's system was widely adopted by manufacturers in many other industries around the world.

oil embargo, Arab. In October 1973, the Arab oil-producing states imposed an oil embargo against the UNITED STATES because of its support of ISRAEL in the ARAB-ISRAELI WAR OF 1973. LIBYA ordered a complete halt in shipments of crude oil and petroleum products to the U.S. on October 19; SAUDI ARABIA followed suit the following day, and BAHRAIN, Dubai, KUWAIT and QATAR cut off their exports to the U.S. on October 21. U.S. oil companies estimated that by October 26, shipments of oil from the Arab countries had been cut by about 4 million barrels per day, or about 20% of the prewar flow.

The NETHERLANDS was also targeted by the embargo, and on October 30 imposed a ban on Sunday pleasure driving. Gasoline prices rose significantly in the U.S. The crisis continued into 1974 but was eased as the Arab nations resumed oil shipments. The embargo and its effects showed the danger of U.S. dependence on imported oil and the necessity for conservation. This lesson was reinforced during the energy crisis of 1979 and again during the PERSIAN GULF WAR (1990–91).

Oise River. River, rising in the mountains of Ardennes, south Belgium, flowing southwest through the north of France, where it meets the Seine River near Pontoise. The Oise is an important transportation route connecting to other rivers by a series of canals, and is navigable for most of its 186–mile length. At the end of WORLD WAR I the armistice was signed on its banks at Compiegne, on November 11, 1918. On June 22, 1940, Adolf HITLER demanded that FRANCE capitulate to GERMANY on the same spot. Important WORLD WAR II battles were fought along its banks, the Oise-Cambre Canal forming a natural battle line.

Oistrakh, David (1908–1974). Soviet violinist. A graduate of the Odessa Conservatory (1926), he first won international attention during the 1930s when he won several important competitions and began to make recordings. He began teaching at the Moscow Conservatory in 1934 and from 1937 until his death held the rank of professor. He received the Stalin Prize in 1942. He first performed in the U.S. in 1955 and thereafter appeared frequently there and in Western Europe. Oistrakh was considered not only the finest Soviet violinist of his generation but was also widely regarded as one of the top half-dozen players in the world. He excelled in the violin concertos and sonatas of the great classical and romantic composers and made many recordings.

For further reading:
Schwartz, Boris, *The Great Masters of the Violin: From Corelli & Vivaldi to Stern, Zukerman & Perlman*. New York: Simon & Schuster, 1985.

Ojukwu, Chukwenmeka (1933–). President of BIAFRA (1967–70). An army officer who served in the UN peacekeeping force in Congo in 1962, Ojukwu became military governor of Eastern Nigeria in 1966. The following year he proclaimed the province as the independent Republic of Biafra. He led Biafra's rebellion against federal NIGERIA from 1967 until Biafra's defeat in 1970. He then fled to the Ivory Coast (now COTE D'IVOIRE).

O'Keeffe, Georgia (1887–1986). U.S. artist. O'Keeffe was a leading figure in American art for seven decades. Her paintings were noted for their stunning use of color and the subtle eroticism with which she invested such objects as flowers, skyscrapers and animal skulls. Her first major exposure as an artist came in 1916, with a one-woman show mounted by pioneer photographer Alfred STIEGLITZ, whom O'Keeffe married eight years later. He continued to present her work

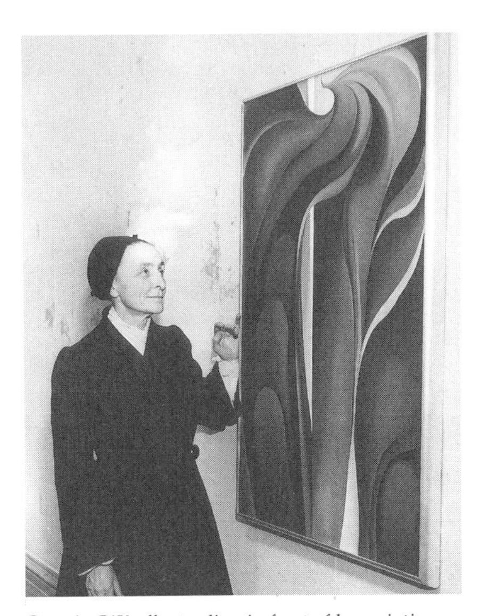

Georgia O'Keeffe standing in front of her painting Jack In The Pulpit *at the Art Institute of Chicago (Jan. 18, 1943).*

in one-woman shows until his death in 1946. O'Keeffe drew inspiration from New Mexico, which she first visited in 1929 and made her permanent home after her husband's death.

Okies. Derogatory term referring to Oklahomans who moved to California during the DUST BOWL.

Okinawa. Agricultural island in the Ryukyu Islands chain, 350 miles southwest of Kyushu in the north Pacific Ocean. From April 1 to June 21, 1945, U.S. Marines staged a successful amphibious assault to establish air bases here during WORLD WAR II. Close to mainland JAPAN, costly damages were inflicted on U.S. ships by KAMIKAZE air attacks in one of the bloodiest campaigns of the war. In 1972 the U.S. returned Okinawa to Japan but retained several military bases.

Oklahoma! Landmark American musical show by RODGERS and HAMMERSTEIN. It opened at the St. James Theatre on March 31, 1943, and ran for 2,248 performances. It was directed by Rouben MAMOULIAN, choreographed by Agnes DE MILLE, and starred Alfred Drake as Curly. This first collaboration between Rodgers and Hammerstein was not, as has been claimed, the first "serious" musical on Broadway (*Show Boat* achieved that distinction), or the first to feature a ballet (*On Your Toes*, 1936, had the "Slaughter on 10th Avenue" ballet), or the first to achieve literary distinction (*Of Thee I Sing*, 1931, had won a PULITZER PRIZE as a drama); but it was a revolutionary integration of songs, dance, and action that signalled, in historian Abe Laufe's words, "the change in the whole concept of musical theater." The source materials were Lynn Riggs' comedy, *Green Grow the Lilacs* (1931), a folksy play about ranchers and cowboys set in Indian territory (now called Oklahoma) in 1907. When the musical version opened in New Haven it was entitled *Away We Go*. There were predictions of failure: no musical had ever opened so quietly, or had a character killed on stage, or had waited 45 minutes before bringing on the chorus girls, etc. But with some revisions and a new title, *Oklahoma!* (the exclamation point was added during a tryout in Boston), it was a smash on Broadway. Hit songs included "Oh, What a Beautiful Mornin'," "Surrey with the Fringe on Top," "People Will Say We're in Love," the mournfully satiric "Pore Jud," and, of course, the title song (which became Oklahoma's state song in 1953). The motion picture version, starring Gordon McCrae as Curly, was directed in 1955 by Fred Zinneman.

For further reading:
Ewen, David, *The Complete Book of the American Musical Theater*. New York: Holt, Rinehart and Winston, 1970.

Olav V (1903–1991). King of NORWAY (1957–91), son of King Haakon VII. Olav was born at the British royal estate in Sandringham, England, and attended the Norwegian Military Academy and Oxford. In 1929 he married Princess Martha of Sweden. When Hitler's troops invaded Norway in 1940, Crown Prince Olav, the king and parliamentary leaders held out in the Norwegian forests before fleeing to exile in England. He took an active part in the RESISTANCE movement, helping to build and commanding (1944) a free Norwegian army. A national symbol of resistance to Nazi occupation, he aided in the Allied liberation of his country and returned home in triumph in 1945. Olav became regent in 1955 and king in 1957. He was succeeded by his son, Crown Prince Harald.

Oldenburg, Claes (1929–). American sculptor. Born in Stockholm, he spent his childhood in Chicago, graduated from Yale University (1950) and attended the Chicago Art Institute School (1952–55). In 1956 he settled in N.Y.C. and began to create sculptures of objects from the everyday world in plaster or papier-mache. A leader of the POP ART movement, Oldenburg is noted for his witty versions of the commonplace in unexpected materials and sizes. He is best known for his soft sculptures, such as *Soft Typewriter* (1963) and *Soft Toilet* (1966), and for his jumbo-sized renditions of common objects, such as the *Lipstick Monument* (1969) at Yale University.

Oldfield, Sir Maurice (1915–1981). British intelligence officer. Oldfield spent four decades in the British intelligence service and worked under Kim PHILBY, the Soviet double agent who betrayed the West's secrets for 20 years. Known for his reserved manner and dry wit, Oldfield is believed to have been the inspiration for George Smiley in John LE CARRE's spy novels and also of the spy chief "M" in Ian FLEMING's James Bond books.

Olduvai Gorge. East African ravine 150 miles northwest of TANZANIA's Mt. Kilimanjaro, where the ancient fossil skull of *Homo habilis*, 1.75 million years old, was discovered by British anthropologist L.S.B. Leakey in 1959. The site of rich fossil beds, discoveries have since been made, and anthropological explorations continue.

Oliver, Joe "King" (1885–1938). Like the best of jazzdom's first generation of innovators, King Oliver received his first important experiences in various New Orleans brass and dance bands. In 1918, after winning fame as a distinctive Dixieland cornet stylist in his native new Orleans, Oliver moved upriver to Chicago, where he attained even greater success at the helm of King Oliver's Creole Jazz Band and Dixie Syncopaters. During this productive Chicago period (1920–27), Oliver nurtured the talents of such jazz notables as reedmen Barney Bigard and Albert Nicholas, trombonist Kid ORY, pianist Lil Harden (Armstrong) and most prominently, fellow cornetist Louis ARMSTRONG, who named Oliver his idol and mentor. Celebrated stints at venues such as the Royal Garden Cafe and Lincoln Gardens enabled aspiring white musicians to "study" Oliver's approach firsthand. In 1923, Oliver's influence was further extended through a series of landmark recordings, the first such series by a black group, regardless of genre. Significant Oliver compositions include "Sugar Foot Stomp" and "West End Blues"; as a cornetist, Oliver's approach was noted for its wa-wa-effects, mute tricks and clipped, syncopated style.

For further reading:

Williams, Martin, *King Oliver*. New York: A.S. Barnes, 1961.

Oliver, Sy (Melvin James) (1910–1988). American jazz musician and composer. Oliver's work with the Jimmie Lunceford and Tommy DORSEY orchestras made him one of the most influential figures of the BIG BAND era. After World War II, he pursued a career as a freelance arranger and musical director. Oliver appeared at the Rainbow Room with his own nine-piece band from 1974 until his retirement in 1984.

Olivier, Giorgio Borg (1911–1980). Prime Minister of MALTA (1966–71). He was a dominant figure in Maltese life for more than 30 years. A nationalist, he guided the island to independence from Britain in 1964. Under his government, Malta began a program to change its economy from one based on revenue earned from British military bases to one that relied mostly on manufacturing and tourism.

Olivier, Laurence (1907–1989). British actor, widely considered the most distinguished actor of his generation. Olivier began acting professionally as a teenager and by the 1930s was regarded as one of the foremost classical theater actors of the day, along with John GIELGUD and Ralph RICHARDSON. His appearance in such HOLLYWOOD films as *Wuthering Heights* (1939) and Alfred HITCHCOCK's *Rebecca* (1940) made him a movie star as well. He also directed and starred in film adaptations of Shakespeare's *Henry V* (1945), *Hamlet* (1948) and *Richard III* (1956), remarkable for his physical energy and his psychological insight. Returning to the stage, he broke new ground in 1958 by playing the second-rate vaudeville performer Archie Rice in John OSBORNE's drama *The Entertainer*—a role he recreated on film two years later. As a veteran theater actor-manager, he was the obvious choice to head Britain's ROYAL NATIONAL THEATRE following its official opening in 1963; he served as artistic director until he was replaced by Sir Peter HALL in 1973. In failing health in his later years, he returned to movie roles and television productions in order to earn money. His later projects included the films *Marathon Man* (1976) and *The Boys from Brazil* (1978), as well as a television adaptation of Evelyn WAUGH's *Brideshead Revisited.* An early marriage (to Jill Esmond) had broken up when he began a widely publicized but scandalous affair with the actress Vivien LEIGH in the late 1930s; the couple married in 1940, but the marriage gradually disintegrated due to Leigh's advancing mental illness. Olivier later married the actress Joan Plowright. He was knighted in 1947 and elevated to a life peerage in 1970.

Laurence Olivier (1948).

Olson, Charles (1910–1970). American poet, essayist and educator. Olson, one of the most influential American poets of the postwar era, was educated at Wesleyan, Yale and Harvard. After working for a time as a government bureaucrat, Olson shifted his energies, in the 1940s, to writing and teaching. He first received literary acclaim for *Call Me Ishmael* (1947), a study of Herman Melville that blended history, geography and economics with more standard forms of literary analysis. As a poetic theorist, Olson was markedly influenced by Ezra POUND. This influence showed in Olson's essays *Projective Verse* (1950) and *Human Universe* (1951), which called for a spoken, direct language in poetry, with lines to be measured by the natural rhythms of human breathing. Olson was a key founder of the Black Mountain School of poetry, which also included, among others, Robert CREELEY and Robert DUNCAN. The movement took its name from Black Mountain College in North Carolina, where Olson taught from 1948 to 1956. *The Maximus Poems* (1960) is Olson's major volume of poetry.

Olympic Games. In ancient Greece, the Olympic Games were a celebration of amateur sportsmanship, held from 776 B.C. to 393 A.D. Resumed on an international basis in 1896, the first modern games were held in Athens. A host of events—including archery, equestrian competitions and canoeing—were gradually added to the traditional track and field contests. Women were allowed to compete in the games beginning in 1912, and winter sports were added with the Chamonix games in 1924. Despite the avowed spirit of amateur and individual, not national, competition, the games have always had political overtones. From Nazi objections to the American team's Jewish and black competitors (particularly Jesse OWENS) in 1936, to the tragedy of Israeli athletes murdered by terrorists in 1972, security—and nationalism—has seemingly increased with each round of games. (See also MUNICH OLYMPICS MASSACRE.)

Omaha Beach. Code name for the west central coastal region of France's NORMANDY during WORLD WAR II. On D-DAY, June 6, 1944, U.S. troops landed here under intensive air and naval cover, opening a major invasion of Nazi-held Europe. After prolonged and bitter fighting, the Allies eventually gained a foothold on the European continent.

O'Malley, Walter F. (1903–1979). U.S. baseball executive. The colorful O'Malley owned the Brooklyn (and Los Angeles) Dodgers from 1950 until his death, building the team into one of major league baseball's most successful franchises. During his tenure, the Dodgers won 10 National League pennants and four World Series. However, the team's New York fans never forgave him for moving the Dodgers from Brooklyn to the West Coast (making it the first major league team in California) in 1958.

Oman [Sultanate of Oman]. Oman covers an area of 82,008 square miles on the southeastern coast of the Arabian peninsula, and includes the islands of Masirah, Kuria Maria, and Daymaruyat plus the tip of the Musandam peninsula. Though Oman was ostensibly a British protectorate since 1798, power struggles based on the geographical and religious divisions between the coastal region governed by Hindu sultans and the interior ruled by Muslim imams occurred until a 1920 agreement which ushered in three decades of peaceful coexistence. In the mid-1950s the imam, with support from Saudi Arabia, started a revolt, but was defeated by the British-backed sultan. Sultan bin Taymur (ruled 1932–70) was replaced in 1970 during a palace coup by his son, Sultan Qabus, who changed the country's name to the Sultanate of Oman. Rebellion in the province of Dhofar (1960s-1975) was quelled, resulting in the province being governed as a separate entity. A founding member of the Gulf Cooperation Council (1981), Oman has promoted peace among the Gulf states.

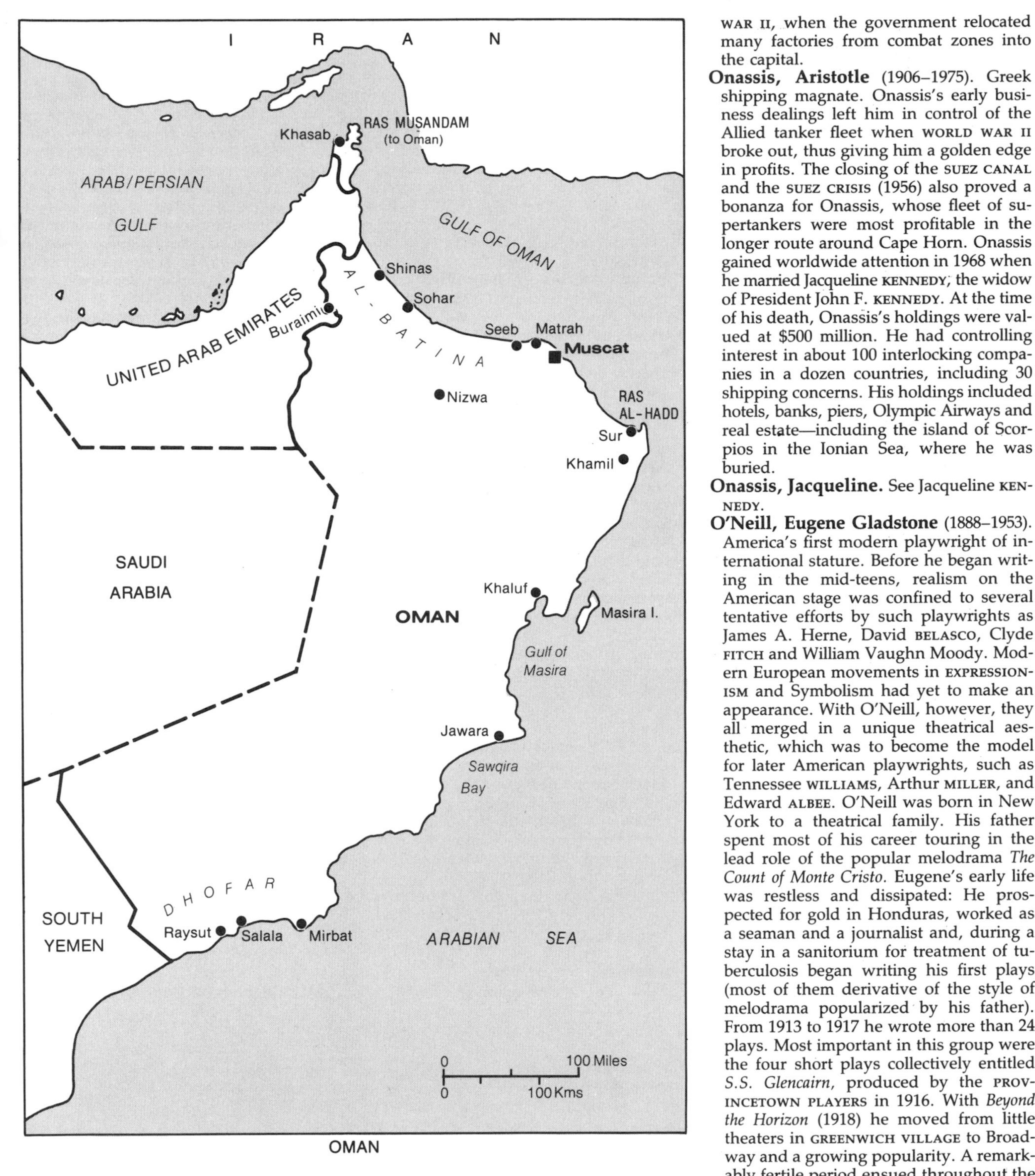

OMAN

Omega workshops. British effort of 1913–21 to recreate in a 20th-century context some of the design-craft philosophy of the arts and crafts movement. Leading spirit Roger FRY drew into it such personalities as Vanessa BELL, Duncan GRANT and Wyndham LEWIS. The workshops produced various items of furniture, pottery, textiles, stained glass and a few complete interiors, but the effort appears to have been handicapped by an amateurish, dilettante level of performance that kept its productions decorative and trivial. Dissension among the participants led to its collapse in the 1920s.

Omsk. City and capital of the Russian SFSR's Omsk oblast, at the junction of the Om and Irtysh rivers. Anti-Bolshevik headquarters to the armed forces of Adm. A. V. KOLCHAK during the RUSSIAN CIVIL WAR (see also WHITES), Omsk later became a center for industry during WORLD WAR II, when the government relocated many factories from combat zones into the capital.

Onassis, Aristotle (1906–1975). Greek shipping magnate. Onassis's early business dealings left him in control of the Allied tanker fleet when WORLD WAR II broke out, thus giving him a golden edge in profits. The closing of the SUEZ CANAL and the SUEZ CRISIS (1956) also proved a bonanza for Onassis, whose fleet of supertankers were most profitable in the longer route around Cape Horn. Onassis gained worldwide attention in 1968 when he married Jacqueline KENNEDY, the widow of President John F. KENNEDY. At the time of his death, Onassis's holdings were valued at $500 million. He had controlling interest in about 100 interlocking companies in a dozen countries, including 30 shipping concerns. His holdings included hotels, banks, piers, Olympic Airways and real estate—including the island of Scorpios in the Ionian Sea, where he was buried.

Onassis, Jacqueline. See Jacqueline KENNEDY.

O'Neill, Eugene Gladstone (1888–1953). America's first modern playwright of international stature. Before he began writing in the mid-teens, realism on the American stage was confined to several tentative efforts by such playwrights as James A. Herne, David BELASCO, Clyde FITCH and William Vaughn Moody. Modern European movements in EXPRESSIONISM and Symbolism had yet to make an appearance. With O'Neill, however, they all merged in a unique theatrical aesthetic, which was to become the model for later American playwrights, such as Tennessee WILLIAMS, Arthur MILLER, and Edward ALBEE. O'Neill was born in New York to a theatrical family. His father spent most of his career touring in the lead role of the popular melodrama *The Count of Monte Cristo.* Eugene's early life was restless and dissipated: He prospected for gold in Honduras, worked as a seaman and a journalist and, during a stay in a sanitorium for treatment of tuberculosis began writing his first plays (most of them derivative of the style of melodrama popularized by his father). From 1913 to 1917 he wrote more than 24 plays. Most important in this group were the four short plays collectively entitled *S.S. Glencairn,* produced by the PROVINCETOWN PLAYERS in 1916. With *Beyond the Horizon* (1918) he moved from little theaters in GREENWICH VILLAGE to Broadway and a growing popularity. A remarkably fertile period ensued throughout the decade of the 1920s. *Anna Christie* (1921) won a PULITZER PRIZE. He experimented with Expressionist techniques in *The Emperor Jones* (1920) and *The Hairy Ape* (1921); with the masks and choruses of the Greek Theater in *The Great God Brown* (1928) and *Lazarus Laughed* (1928); and with devices of the stock melodrama, like the aside, in *Strange Interlude* (1928). However, his subsequent work in the 1930s—the trilogy *Mourning Becomes Electra* (1929–31), the nostalgic comedy of *Ah, Wilderness!*

Eugene O'Neill

(1933), *The Iceman Cometh* (1930) and *Long Day's Journey into Night* (1939)—subsumed experimental techniques, melodrama and realism into a unified vision. Characters and situations were frankly autobiographical, drawing extensively from O'Neill's own family. The themes of displaced persons, dysfunctional families, dreams as mechanisms for coping with sordid life and alienation from history predominated. He called his method supernaturalism, by which he meant going beyond realism by using symbolism in a realistic way. (He detested what he called the photographic plays of his contemporaries.) Thus, for example, the character of Yank in *The Hairy Ape* is both a man and a representation of mankind; the site of Harry Hope's saloon in *The Iceman Cometh* becomes, in Act 2, an evocation of The Last Supper; and so forth. After a failed production of *A Moon for the Misbegotten* (1943), O'Neill wrote no new plays. He died in 1953 of a lifelong nervous disorder, which brought about a loss of motor control.

For further reading:

Clark, Barrett H., *Eugene O'Neill: The Man and His Plays.* New York: Dover Publications, 1947.

O'Neill, Ralph A. (1897–1980). American pilot and commercial airline pioneer. A fighter pilot during WORLD WAR I, O'Neill was credited with shooting down 11 German planes. He flew in MEXICO in the 1920s and trained Mexican pilots who helped put down a revolt against President Alvaro Obregon. He began flying passengers between Miami and Buenos Aires in 1928, setting a six-day flying record that stood until 1936.

O'Neill, Lord Terence Marne (1914–1990). Irish politician. From 1963 to 1969, he served as prime minister of NORTHERN IRELAND. While in office, he worked to improve relations between the Roman Catholic minority and the Protestant majority. He offered important concessions to Catholics, including the establishment of an ombudsman to oversee the fairness of government policies. In 1965, he became the first prime minister of Northern Ireland to meet with a prime minister of the Republic of IRELAND. Their efforts were criticized both by Catholics and his own Unionist Party. He was forced to resign in 1969, and was made a life peer in 1970.

Onizuka, Ellison (1946–1986). U.S. astronaut, one of seven killed in the explosion of the SPACE SHUTTLE CHALLENGER on January 28, 1986. The Hawaiian-born aerospace engineer became the first Asian-American in space when he flew on a shuttle mission in 1985.

Oparin, Alexander Ivanovich (1894–1976). Soviet biochemist. Oparin studied plant physiology at the Moscow State University, where he later served as professor. He helped found the Bakh Institute of Biochemistry, which the Soviet government established in 1935. Oparin became director of the institute in 1946. As early as 1922, Oparin was speculating on how life first originated; he made the then controversial suggestion that the first organisms must have been heliotropic—that is, they could not make their own food from inorganic materials but relied upon organic substances. This questioned the prevailing view that life originated with autotropic organisms that (like present-day plants) could synthesize their food from simple inorganic materials. Oparin's view gradually gained acceptance in many circles. Oparin did much to stimulate research on the origin of life and organized the first international meeting to discuss the problem in Moscow in 1957.

op art [abbreviation for optical art]. Op art was a movement and a style that developed in Europe and the U.S. during the 1960s. Its guiding principle was the exploitation of various phenomena of visual perception in color or black and white. Op art images appear to vibrate with violently contrasting but tonally similar color, move backward and forward from the picture plane in geometric constructs, pulsate in concentric circles or shimmer with moire patterns. Much op art attempted to recreate the effect of psychodelic trips. Artists who were active in the movement include Victor de Vašarely, Richard Anusziewicz and Bridget Riley.

OPEC. See ORGANIZATION OF PETROLEUM EXPORTING COUNTRIES.

Open University. An experimental university for adults opened in January of 1971 and located in Milton Keynes, Buckinghamshire, England. Its goal was to provide access to higher education to a broad range of people; there were no academic prerequisites for admission. To extend its reach, courses were conducted by correspondence, supplemented by television, and by seminars and study groups held at various locations across the country.

Operation Barbarossa. See BARBAROSSA.

Operation Bootstrap. See Luis MUNOZ MARIN.

Operation Coronet. See OPERATION OLYMPIC.

Operation Desert Shield. See PERSIAN GULF WAR; H. Norman SCHWARZKOPF.

Operation Desert Storm. See Saddam HUSSEIN; PERSIAN GULF WAR; H. Norman SCHWARZKOPF.

Operation Dynamo. See Sir John FISHER.

Operation Mincemeat. See Ewen MONTAGU.

Operation Olympic. Code name for a planned U.S. invasion of JAPAN (at the island of Kyushu) in WORLD WAR II. Operation Olympic was scheduled for November 1945; a second invasion near Tokyo (**Operation Coronet**) on the island of Honshu was planned for March 1946. U.S. analysts estimated that perhaps 1 million American lives would be lost in the invasions. Japan's surrender on September 2, 1945, following the destruction of HIROSHIMA (August 6) and NAGASAKI (August 9), made the invasions unnecessary.

Operation Overlord. Code name for the Allied invasion of NORMANDY (June 6, 1944) in WORLD WAR II.

Operation Paperclip. U.S. plan that brought German scientists to the United States at the end of WORLD WAR II. Fearing that German military and scientific secrets would fall into the hands of the U.S.S.R., the joint chiefs of staff ordered General Dwight D. EISENHOWER to "preserve from destruction and take under

Maj. Gen. Walther Dornberger (left), Lt. Col. Herbert Axter, Wernher von Braun (with cast) and Hans Lindenberg (Austria, May 3, 1945). These German scientists were taken to the U.S. after World War II in Operation Paperclip.

your control records, plans, documents, papers, files and scientific, industrial and other information belonging to . . . German organizations engaged in military research." The plan was supervised by U.S. Chief of Technical Intelligence Holger N. TOFTOY. Among the Germans brought to the U.S. in this sensitive and controversial operation were many who had worked on the V-2 rocket at PEENEMUNDE. American critics were incensed that those who had helped HITLER develop weapons of war used against the Allies were suddenly part of the U.S. scientific establishment. Ironically, these engineers came to play a crucial role in developing the U.S. space program. They included Walter DORNBERGER and Wernher von BRAUN.

Ophuls, Marcel (1927–). German-born film director. Ophuls, who is the son of the renowned film director Max OPHULS, accompanied his father to the U.S. in 1941 and ultimately became an American citizen. But in 1950 Ophuls returned to France, where he worked as an assistant to numerous directors, including his father and John HUSTON. After directing features for French television, Ophuls achieved international recognition for *The Sorrow and the Pity* (1969), a powerful documentary on French ANTI-SEMITISM and collaboration with the Nazis during WORLD WAR II. Subsequent political documentaries by Ophuls include *A Sense of Loss* (1972), on NORTHERN IRELAND and *Memory of Justice* (1976)—which portrayed military atrocities in Europe during WORLD WAR II, during the 1950s in ALGERIA, and in VIETNAM.

Ophuls, Max [born Max Oppenheimer] (1902–1957). German-born film director. Ophuls was a brilliant and well-traveled director who made films throughout Europe and in HOLLYWOOD. He began his career as a theatrical actor and director in Germany before becoming a French citizen in 1934. After making films in Italy and the Netherlands, Ophuls evaded the Nazis by going to Hollywood in 1941, where his greatest successes were *Letter from an Unknown Woman* (1948) and *The Reckless Moment* (1949). Ophuls then returned to France, where he made a number of films, including *La Ronde* (1950), *The Earrings of Madame de . . .* (1953) and *Lola Montez* (1955), a sweeping and sentimental historical epic on the life of a 19th-century romantic adventuress that is regarded as Ophuls' masterwork.

Oppenheimer, Frank (1912–1985). U.S. nuclear physicist. During WORLD WAR II he worked on the development of the ATOMIC BOMB in the MANHATTAN PROJECT, headed by his older brother, J. Robert OPPENHEIMER. At the time, his left-wing views aroused concern in the government that he and his brother were security risks. In 1949 after testifying before the HOUSE UN-AMERICAN ACTIVITIES COMMITTEE that he had been a member of the American Communist Party in the 1930s, he was fired from his teaching position at the University of Minnesota. He later became a cattle rancher in Colorado. In 1969 he founded the Exploratorium, a San Francisco museum with exhibits that help even young children grasp the basic principles of science.

Oppenheimer, J(ulius) Robert (1904–1967). American physicist, best known as the father of the ATOMIC BOMB. Born in New York City, he attended Harvard (B.A., 1925), Cambridge and the University of Gottingen (Ph.D., 1927). Collaborating with Max BORN, he did significant work on the quantum theory of molecules. From 1929 to 1942, Oppenheimer taught theoretical physics at the University of California (Berkeley) and the California Institute of Technology (Pasadena). At both schools, he studied quantum theory and nuclear physics and did experimental research on the positron, while winning a reputation as a brilliant and inspirational teacher and acquiring a corps of dedicated assistants. Oppenheimer first became interested in the possibility of an atomic bomb in 1939, and in 1941 he began research into the problems of nuclear fission at the Lawrence Radiation Laboratory, Berkeley. This work was continued during WORLD WAR II, when he acted (1942–45) as director of the top-secret atomic energy research program known as the MANHATTAN PROJECT—at a remote site in LOS ALAMOS, New Mexico. Gathering around him some of the greatest minds in nuclear physics, Oppenheimer and his colleagues worked tirelessly in a successful effort to create the bomb. In 1945, he was one of a panel of scientists who advised its use against Japan. After the bomb was dropped, he became a strong adherent of the international control of atomic energy.

In 1947 Oppenheimer returned to academia as director of the Institute for Advanced Study at Princeton. At the same time, he remained an adviser to the State Department and the Pentagon, and that same year he was appointed chairman of the General Advisory Committee (GAC) to the Atomic Energy Commission (AEC).

J. Robert Oppenheimer puffs on his pipe as he surveys an atomic bomb test site in Alamogordo, New Mexico (Sept. 9, 1945).

In this capacity, Oppenheimer at first opposed research on a HYDROGEN BOMB but reversed his position in 1951. However, his early opposition to the fusion bomb, his stand on arms control, his left-wing political connections and his sometimes lofty attitude soon brought him into conflict with the MCCARTHYISM of the 1950s. Faced with allegations that the scientist was a security risk, President EISENHOWER suspended Oppenheimer's security clearance in a controversial 1953 decision. After an appeal failed to restore the clearance, Oppenheimer devoted himself to his Princeton activities and to work on the spiritual and intellectual ramifications of nuclear physics. A man of undoubted integrity and loyalty, he was the most notorious scientific victim of McCarthyism. In 1963 Oppenheimer was awarded the government's prestigious Enrico Fermi Award.

Oran. Algerian commercial port, 225 miles west of Algiers on the Gulf of Oran of the Mediterranean Sea. An important economic center and naval base in the 19th century, Oran was held by the VICHY government of France during WORLD WAR II, and was captured by the Allies at the start of the North African Campaign on Nov. 10, 1942. Most of its European populace fled in the 1950s, owing to violent French terrorist and Algerian nationalist activities. (See also ALGERIA; ALGERIAN WAR OF 1954–62.)

Orangemen. Members of the **Orange Order,** an Irish society formed in Ulster in 1795 to uphold Protestantism. The name is taken from William III, Prince of Orange, who defeated James II at the Battle of the Boyne in 1690. The society is bitterly anti-Catholic. It maintains the Ulster Unionist Party and has branches outside NORTHERN IRELAND, particularly in Liverpool and Glasgow. The society organizes annual summer marches—notably the march in Belfast on July 12—to celebrate William's victory at the Boyne and to demonstrate the Protestant and LOYALIST presence in Northern Ireland.

Orbison, Roy (1936–1988). U.S. singer-songwriter. In the early 1960s, Orbison was one of the world's most popular recording artists. He favored an introspective musical style that wedded rockabilly and dramatic ballads. His career first took off in 1960 with a recording of "Only the Lonely." Between 1960 and 1964 he was the top-selling male singer in the world, with such songs as "Running Scared," "Crying," "Blue Bayou and "Oh, Pretty Woman." The death of his first wife in 1966, followed by the deaths of two of his children in 1968 and by problems with alcohol and drugs, temporarily ended Orbison's performing career. He began a successful comeback effort in 1987, the year he was inducted into the Rock and Roll Hall of Fame.

Order No. 1. An order issued by the Petrograd Soviet of Workers' and Soldiers' Deputies on March 14, 1917. It stated that military affairs should be administered by elected committees. This order, which stripped officers of much of their power, contributed to the eventual collapse of the Russian army.

Ordzhonikidze, Grigory Konstantinovich (1866–1937). Georgian communist. He joined the BOLSHEVIKS in 1903, and in 1912 he was made a member of the central committee. After spending some years in prison and banishment, Ordzhonikidze was appointed extraordinary commissar of the Soviet government in southern Russia. Once Soviet government in Georgia was established, he merged Armenia and Azerbaijan with Georgia, thus establishing the Transcaucasian Federal Republic. Chairman of the central control commission in 1926, in 1930 he was made a Politburo member and chairman of the supreme council of national economy. Having played an important part in organizing and developing Soviet industry during the first FIVE-YEAR PLAN, in 1932 Ordzhonikidze was made commissar for heavy industry. He disagreed, however, with STALIN's industrial policy and thus fell from favor. He died in mysterious circumstances at the time of the GREAT PURGE.

Orel [Orlov, Oryol]. Capital of the Russian SFSR's Orel oblast, on the Oka River, 200 miles south of Moscow. During the RUSSIAN CIVIL WAR in 1919, the northernmost point reached by Gen. DENIKIN's White Army. An important railroad junction, it was taken over in WORLD WAR II by the Germans on Oct. 3, 1941, only to be later recaptured by the Soviets in 1943, when it was nearly destroyed during the battles of Kursk and Orel as the entire central front was cleared of German control.

Oren Affair. In 1952, while visiting CZECHOSLOVAKIA, prominent Israeli leftist Mordechai Oren was arrested and summoned to testify against Rudolf SLANSKY, the Communist Party secretary general who was on trial for treason. Accused of treason himself, Oren was sentenced to 15 years in prison in 1953. He was released in 1956 during Czechoslovakia's de-Stalinization period. (See STALIN, STALINISM.) After returning to ISRAEL, he claimed that he had been forced to confess what never happened. In the 1960s the Czechoslovak government formally cleared Oren.

Orff, Carl (1895–1982). German composer and music educator. Born in Munich, he attended the city's Academy of Music and was cofounder (1924) and teacher at its Guntherschule. Fascinated by the primitive in music and with the combination of music, dance and text, he initiated an influential teaching method that mixed rhythmic games, melodic exercises, chant, gymnastics and dance. Orff's method was outlined in his popular text *Das Schulwerk.* Extremely interested in early music, he incorporated its lively rhythms and monodic forms into his own compositions. His most popular work is *Carmina Burana* (1937), a vigorous setting of secular medieval texts for choir and vocal soloists. It forms the first part of a trilogy that also includes *Catulli Carmina* (1943) and *Trionfo di Afrodite* (1953). Prior to 1937, Orff composed a variety of orchestral, chamber and vocal music. After that date, he composed exclusively for the theater in such works as the operas *Die Kluge* (1941–42), *Prometheus* (1968) and *Play from the End of Time* (1973). From 1961, he was head of the Orff Institute at the Mozarteum Music Academy in Salzburg.

Organisation de l'Armee Secrete. See O.A.S.

Organization for Economic Cooperation and Development (OECD). International organization that succeeded the ORGANIZATION FOR EUROPEAN ECONOMIC COOPERATION (OEEC) in 1960. With headquarters in Paris, it is made up of Australia (1971), Austria, Belgium, Canada, Denmark, Finland (1969), France, West Germany, Greece, Iceland, Ireland, Italy, Japan (1964), Luxembourg, the Netherlands, New Zealand (1973), Norway, Portugal, Spain, Sweden, Switzerland, Turkey, the U.K., the U.S. and Yugoslavia (which has special status). It is an attempt by the leading industrial nations to promote high economic growth in member states and to assist in the economic growth of the developing countries. The OECD is an important research organization, studying and debating such international questions as balance of payments, agriculture, energy and technology. Headed by a secretary-general, its organizational structure employs a council and an executive committee.

Organization for European Economic Cooperation (OEEC). International organization established in 1948 as a coordinating group for MARSHALL PLAN aid. It aimed at reconstructing Europe and at achieving a sound European economy through the cooperation of its members. Its original 16 member states were Austria, Belgium, Denmark, France, Greece, Iceland, Ireland, Italy, Luxembourg, the Netherlands, Norway, Portugal, Sweden, Switzerland, the U.K. and Turkey. They were joined by West Germany in 1955 and Spain in 1958. The U.S. and Canada later became associate members. This organization provided a framework for the EUROPEAN ECONOMIC COMMUNITY or Common Market. In 1960 it was superseded by the ORGANIZATION FOR ECONOMIC COOPERATION AND DEVELOPMENT.

Organization of African Unity. An international group of African states founded in Addis Ababa, Ethiopia, in 1963. Its goals include promoting the unity and solidarity of African nations; guaranteeing the independence and territorial integrity of its members; coordinating political, economic, cultural, health, scientific and defense policies among its members and eliminating colonialism. Heads of the member states meet on an annual basis, the Council of Ministers meets every six months and separate commissions concentrate on varying subjects. The organization was successful in mediating border disputes between Algeria and Morocco (1965) and between Somalia and Ethiopia and Somalia and Kenya (1965–67) but failed in an attempt to settle the Nigeria-Biafra civil war (1968–70). While it had a membership of 50 in the early 1990s, it failed to command the respect it had in its earlier days.

Organization of American States (OAS). Regional organization of Western Hemisphere states formed to promote peace, justice and solidarity; to strengthen political cooperation among its members; to encourage hemispheric economic development and to defend the sovereignty and independence of its member nations. It was established by treaty at a meeting in Bogota, Colombia, in April 1948 and was officially founded in 1951. With a membership of 32 countries, it has headquarters in Washington, D.C. The OAS is built on the earlier International Bureau of American Republics, established in 1890, and its successor, the Pan-American Union, founded in 1910, which became the Secretariat of the OAS. It is made up of a General Assembly, which meets annually in member nations, a Permanent Council and a Meeting of Consultation of Ministers of Foreign Affairs. Four other councils consider such issues as economic and social conditions, education, legal matters and human rights. The organization is overseen by a secretary-general, elected by the assembly for a five-year term. The OAS has taken stands against Cuba, which was expelled from active membership in 1962 and boycotted by the OAS from 1964 to 1975. In more recent years, the organization has rebelled against the strong role traditionally played by the U.S. in Latin-American affairs.

Organization of Petroleum Exporting Countries (OPEC). Organization established in 1960 to coordinate oil policies in member states, all Third World petroleum-producing nations; original members were Iran, Iraq, Kuwait, Saudi Arabia and Venezuela. Qatar joined in 1961, Indonesia and Libya in 1962, Algeria in 1969, Abu Dhabi (now in the U.A.E.) in 1967, Nigeria in 1971 and Ecuador and Gabon in 1973. The original intent of OPEC was to guard against oil price cuts and overproduction by companies in the U.S. and Europe. In the 1970s, it pressed for petroleum rate increases and succeeded in raising oil prices by more than 100% before the end of the decade, thus creating severe oil shortages. At the beginning of the 1980s, large-scale production of oil by Saudi Arabia and energy-preserving policies initiated by many oil-importing nations caused an oil surplus and led to problems in OPEC. As widely varying prices for oil held sway, the organization strove to maintain a standardized pricing structure.

Original Dixieland Jazz Band. The Original Dixieland Jazz Band, often considered the first white jazz band, was formed during WORLD WAR I in New Orleans by cornetist-leader Nick LaRocca, clarinetist Larry Shields, trombonist Eddie Edwards, drummer Tony Sbarbaro and pianist Henry Ragas (later replaced by J. Russell Robinson). Achieving success in Chicago in 1916, the ODJB was brought to New York in 1917 for a sen sational stand at Reisenweber's Restaurant, where it successfully capitalized on the wartime vogue for jazz dancing; the group continued as a major attraction until breaking up in 1925. The ODJB is also significant for being the first jazz band to record phonograph records. As for its historical significance, the ODJB is the subject of still heated controversy. Some experts dismiss it as derivative of black New Orleans music; others, including LaRocca, argue that the ODJB deserves greater credit for its "innovations." The truth, as Gunther Schuller eloquently chronicles in *Early Jazz* (1968), lies at some point between these extremes. What is incontrovertible, however, is the significant role played by the ODJB in popularizing the Dixieland style throughout the U.S. and Europe.

For further reading:

Brunn, H.O., *The Story of the Original Dixieland Jazz Band.* Baton Rouge: Louisiana State University Press, 1960.

Orkin, Ruth (1921–1985). American photographer. Orkin's work on celebrities and street life regularly appeared in LIFE, *Look* and other major magazines during the 1940s, 1950s and 1960s. In the early 1950s, she and her husband Morris Engel made *The Little Fugitive*, a film that was credited with influencing the French NOUVELLE VAGUE (new wave) cinema.

Orlando, Vittorio Emmanuele (1860–1952). Italian statesman, premier (1917–19). A law professor in Palermo, he was elected to parliament in 1897 and held several cabinet posts from 1903 to 1917. Appointed premier after Italy's defeat at Caporetto, he helped to rally his nation for ultimate victory in WORLD WAR I. Orlando was one of the "Big Four" (with Georges CLEMENCEAU, David LLOYD GEORGE and Woodrow WILSON) at the 1919 PARIS PEACE CONFERENCE. He quarreled bitterly with Wilson over Italy's territorial demands, dramatically leaving the conference only to return a month later. Failing in his efforts, Orlando resigned the premiership. An opponent of MUSSOLINI's fascist government, he resigned from parliament in 1925. After the defeat of the fascists, he became a leader of the Democratic Union and served as president of the constituent assembly (1946–47) and as a senator from 1948 until his death.

Orlov, Yuri Alexandrovich (1893–1966). Soviet paleontologist and member of the Academy of Sciences from 1960. Having graduated from Petrograd University in 1917, Orlov taught at Perm, Leningrad and Moscow. He was named head of Moscow's department of paleontology in 1942. He edited the *Paleontology Journal* (1959–66) and was chief editor of the 15-volume *Basic Paleontology*. He was awarded the Order of Lenin and various other medals.

Ormandy, Eugene [born Jeno Blau] (1899–1985). Hungarian-born American conductor. Trained in BUDAPEST as a violinist, Jeno Blau came to the U.S. in 1921 on the liner *Normandie*, from which he took his new name. He played briefly in a theater orchestra before becoming its conductor and made guest appearances with other orchestras. He conducted the Minneapolis Symphony (1932–36). In 1936 he became co-director of the Philadelphia Orchestra with Leopold STOKOWSKI and was named sole musical director in 1938. Under his guidance, the orchestra retained the celebrated richness of sound that Stokowski had done much to cultivate. Over the years, Ormandy led the orchestra on numerous foreign tours, including a historic visit to China in 1973. Between 1936 and 1986 he made almost 600 recordings. When he retired in 1980, he had been head of a single orchestra longer than any other conductor in the 20th century. Although critics sometimes complained that his interpretations were slick, Ormandy was an extremely knowledgeable musician. He had a wide repertoire but was best known for his performances of music of the romantic period.

O'Rorke, Brian (1901–1974). English designer known for his work on boat and airplane interiors. Trained in engineering and architecture, O'Rorke established his own design firm in London in 1929. His most distinguished work was the interior design of the Orient Line passenger vessels *Orion* and *Orcades* of the 1930s. These ships were remarkable for their sensibly functional, handsome interiors at a time when the more excessive ART DECO was the norm for ocean-liner interior design. O'Rorke also worked on railroad and airplane interiors, providing straightforward and appropriate design for a number of transport projects, including the interior of the Vickers Viking airplane of 1946.

Orpen, Sir William (Newenham Montague) (1878–1931). Irish portrait, landscape and genre painter. Born in County Dublin, he studied art at Dublin's Metropolitan School, where he later taught (1902–14), and at London's Slade School. Perhaps the most influential and popular Irish painter of his day, he was knighted in 1918. He is best known for his sketches of everyday life in Ireland, scenes of WORLD WAR I (being an official war artist from 1917–18) and portraits of prominent Irish figures. His works are in major Irish museums as well as such collections as the Tate Gallery, London; Metropolitan Museum, New York City and Carnegie Institute, Pittsburgh.

Orr, Robert Gordon "Bobby" (1948–). Canadian hockey player. In many ways, Orr was the artist who put the finishing touches on the modern game of hockey. While there had been earlier rushing defensemen, Orr orchestrated his team's movements from the blueline when he was not carrying the puck across himself, as he won the league's scoring title three times. The Boston Bruins of the early 1970s became known as the "Big Bad Bruins" as they dominated the league with their explosive scoring and their fists. Plagued throughout his career by bad knees, Orr was an All-Star throughout that career and won the Norris Trophy as best defenseman eight times. He was named to the Hockey Hall of Fame in 1979.

Ortega Saavedra, Daniel (1945–). Nicaraguan guerrilla and political leader, president of NICARAGUA (1945–90). Active in various underground resistance movements against the regime of Anastasio SOMOZA, Ortega was a member of the National Directorate of the FSLN (Sandinista Liberation Front), 1966–67 and im-

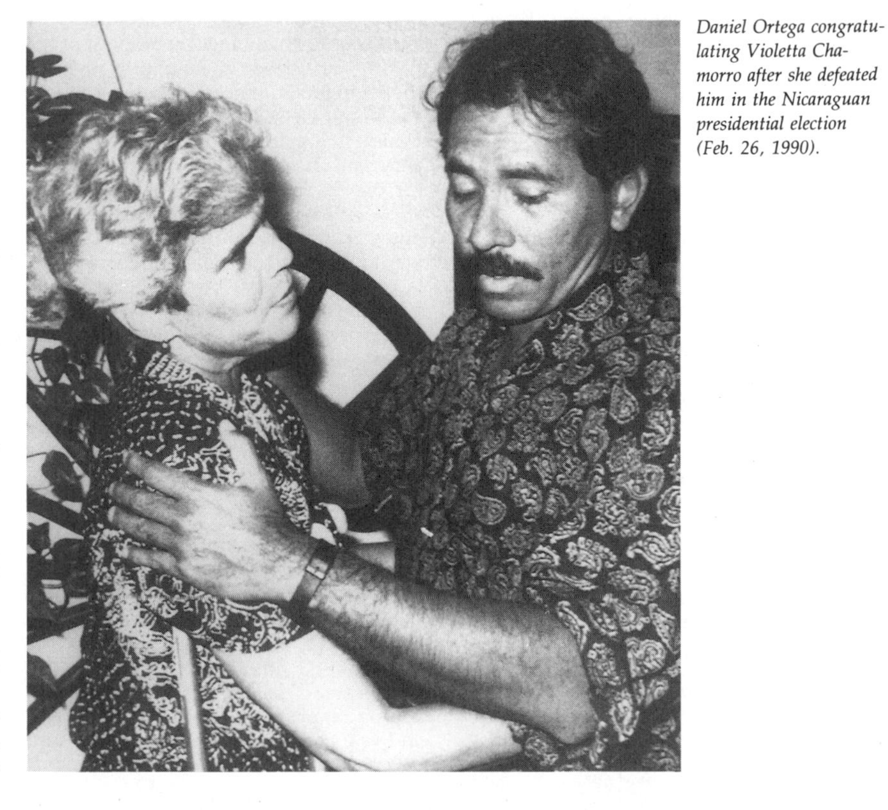

Daniel Ortega congratulating Violetta Chamorro after she defeated him in the Nicaraguan presidential election (Feb. 26, 1990).

prisoned from 1967 to 1974. He resumed his position with the FSLN and became involved in further revolutionary activities. He fought a two-year military offensive that overthrew the Somoza regime in 1979. He was subsequently a member of the Junta of National Reconstruction and became president in 1981. Ortega developed close relations with CUBA. As he became increasingly intolerant of those who did not follow his party line and espoused Marxist revolutionary doctrine, the non-communist members of the junta either resigned or were forced out of the junta. Many of his onetime associates denounced his rule, and some joined the CONTRAS, who were attempting to overthrow Ortega. Ortega was also denounced by the REAGAN administration in the U.S., which gave support to the Contras. In the late 1980s Ortega agreed to hold free elections under a plan that called for the Contras to lay down their arms. Ortega was predicted to win easily, but he was upset on Feb. 25, 1990, by Violetta CHAMORRO, the candidate of the 14–party National Opposition Union. Ortega remained in the government as defense minister.

Ortega y Gasset, Jose (1883–1955). Spanish philosopher, sociologist, literary critic and politician. Ortega was one of the preeminent Spanish men of letters of the 20th century. He held the chair of metaphysics at the University of Madrid for several decades and served as a member of the Spanish parliament. After the SPANISH CIVIL WAR and the rise of FRANCO's fascist regime in the 1930s, Ortega went into exile, ultimately settling in Portugal. Ortega was known for his ardent defense of classicism and the humanities, as well as for his fear that the working class, in gaining political power, would threaten the ultimate values of Western civilization. His major works include *Meditations on Quixote* (1914), *The Dehumanization of Art and Other Essays* (1925) and *Revolt of the Masses* (1930).

Ortiz, Peter J(ulien) (1913–1988). U.S. military hero. He was a highly decorated U.S. Marine Corps veteran whose exploits were the subject of two films: *13 Rue Madeleine* (1946) and *Operation Secret* (1952).

Orton, Joe (Kingsley Orton) (1933–1967). British playwright and actor. Orton left school to begin acting at 16. His dark comedies, starting with *Entertaining Mr. Sloane* (1964), frequently focused on sexual perversion, corruption and violence and created a sensation based partly on shock value. Other works include *Loot* (1965), *The Ruffian on the Stair* (1967) and *What the Butler Saw* (1969), which was performed posthumously. Orton was beaten to death by his lover and companion, who then committed suicide.

Orwell, George [pen name of Eric Arthur Blair] (1903–1950). British novelist, essayist and journalist. Born to a middle-class English family in Bengal (then part of Britain's Indian empire), he was educated at Eton and afterward spent five years with the Indian Imperial Police in Burma—an experience that later provided the background for his first novel, *Burmese Days* (1934). During the GREAT DEPRESSION he worked at a variety of jobs, often leading a hand-to-mouth existence. His experiences of this time, which gave him a profound sympathy with the poor and unemployed and intensified his commitment to socialism, are recounted in his nonfiction works *Down and Out in Paris and London* (1933) and *The Road to Wigan Pier* (1937). In 1936 he went to Spain to report on the SPANISH CIVIL WAR; he soon joined the fight against the Fascists (see FASCISM). He described his experience and perceptions in *Homage to Catalonia* (1939), an incisive account of the war that criticized the infighting amongst the various Republican factions. The war confirmed Orwell's hatred of TOTALITARIANISM and increased his distrust of COMMUNISM. These attitudes are apparent in his two most important novels, ANIMAL FARM (1945), an allegorical satire of the RUSSIAN REVOLUTION; and 1984 (1949), a warning about the bleak outcome of totalitarianism. These two political works have had an enormous influence on other writers and thinkers and have been subject to much literary and political analysis.

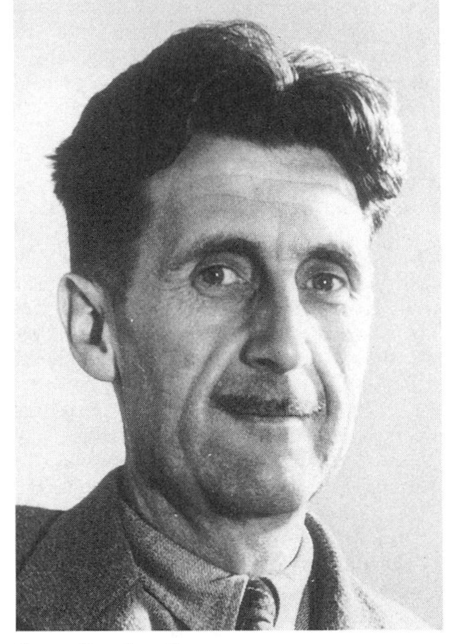

George Orwell, author.

During WORLD WAR II, Orwell served as literary editor for the British LABOUR PARTY journal, *Tribune* (1943–45), and broadcast for the BRITISH BROADCASTING CORPORATION. He wrote numerous essays and articles, many of which can be found in *Collected Essays, Journalism and Letters* (1968). His other, more conventional novels include *A Clergyman's Daughter* (1935), *Keep the Aspidistra Flying* (1936) and *Coming Up for Air* (1939). A complex and often contradictory figure, Orwell stands as one of the most original and uncompromising writers of his time—and as a champion of human liberty and decency.

For further reading:

Coppard, Audrey, and Bernard Crick (eds.), *Orwell Remembered*. New York: Facts On File, 1984.
Crick, Bernard, *George Orwell: A Life*. Boston, Massachusetts: Little, Brown, & Co., 1980; rev. 1982.
Stansky, Peter, and William Abrahams, *Orwell: The Transformation*. New York: Knopf, 1980.

Ory, Edward "Kid" (1886–1973). Kid Ory is the most famous exponent of the New Orleans "tailgate" trombone style, with its roughhewn syntax of growls, glissandi and other "vocalizations," the latter often achieved with various mutes. Between 1912 and 1919, Ory led one of the most influential bands in New Orleans; among his sidemen were noted trumpeters King OLIVER and Louis ARMSTRONG, as well as clarinetists Johnny Dodds, Sidney Bechet, Jimmie None and George Lewis. Ory was also a key figure in the prolific Chicago jazz scene of the 1920s, where he participated in the landmark "Hot Five" recordings with Louis Armstrong. After retiring to run a successful California chicken ranch in the 1930s, his career was revived due to a 1944 radio broadcast with Orson WELLES. In 1954, his Dixieland standard, "Muskrat Ramble," attained hit status with newly fitted lyrics; he also had an acting and playing role in *The Benny Goodman Story* (1955). Ory's pioneering style exerted profound influence both in his early years in New Orleans and during the post-World War II traditional jazz revival.

For further reading:

Williams, Martin, *Jazz Masters of New Orleans*. New York: MacMillan, 1967.

Osaka. Capital of JAPAN's Osaka prefecture, 27 miles west of Kyoto, 20 miles east of Kobe, in south Honshu on Osaka Bay. One of the most ancient cities in the Orient. It received a city charter in 1889, and during WORLD WAR II became an important center for developing industry. As a consequence, the city was a natural target for deadly U.S. air attacks, from 1944 to 1945. Today a center of Japanese theater and culture, it also was the site of the 1970 World's Fair.

Osborne, John (James) (1929–). British playwright and actor. Osborne, who began his career acting in provincial repertory companies, is best known for the play *Look Back in Anger* (1956). Its domestic realism and its lower-class antihero caused Osborne to be categorized as one of the ANGRY YOUNG MEN. His early work, which also includes *The Entertainer* (1957, filmed 1960), *The World of Paul Slickey* (1959) and *Luther* (1961), is credited with changing the course of British drama. *A Patriot for Me* (1966) was originally censored because of its homosexual theme but was revived successfully in 1983. Many critics feel that Osborne's later works, such as *West of Suez* (1971) and *Watch It Come Down* (1975), are increasingly cranky in tone and lack the impact of his early plays.

For further reading:

Osborne, John, *A Better Class of Person: An Autobiography*. New York: Dutton, 1981.

Oslo [*formerly:* Christiana]. Capital of Norway in Akershus county at the north end of Oslo Fjord. First captured by Sweden in 1716, it later replaced Bergen as the commercial center of Norway in the 19th century, beginning a cultural renaissance that was soon followed by a wave of nationalism. As a result, Norway split with Sweden in 1905. The city was renamed Oslo in 1925, and was given over to the Nazis by Vidkun QUISLING's group on April 9, 1940. Oslo remained under German occupation until the end of WORLD WAR II.

OSS. See OFFICE OF STRATEGIC SERVICES.

Ossietzky, Carl von (1889–1938). German author and pacifist. Born in Hamburg, he was a fledgling poet when distaste for German militarism led him to cofound the German Peace Society in 1912. Service in WORLD WAR I deepened his antiwar sentiments, and in 1920 he became the secretary of the German Peace Society. Settling in Berlin, he became the editor in chief of the antimilitarist weekly *Weltbuhne* in 1927. Jailed briefly for publishing an article that criticized the government for allowing the development of paramilitary organizations, he was again imprisoned in 1932 for printing a piece that exposed Germany's secret rearmament. After the REICHSTAG FIRE (1933), Ossietzky was again imprisoned—this time by the Nazis: first in Berlin, then in two CONCENTRATION CAMPS. Suffering from a heart condition and tuberculosis, he was transferred to a prison hospital in 1936—the same year he was awarded the NOBEL PRIZE for peace. Subsequently, the German government decreed that no citizen could accept a Nobel Prize. Ossietzky died two years later in the prison hospital.

Ostend [Oostende]. An important Belgian commercial and fishing port on the North Sea in the province of west Flanders, Ostend stood as one of Europe's most fashionable social centers until WORLD WAR I, when it was overrun by the Germans and used as a submarine base. During WORLD WAR II the port was bombed heavily by the Allies.

***Ostpolitik* [German, "eastern policy"].** Policy of the German Federal Republic (WEST GERMANY) developed by Kurt KIESINGER and practiced by Willy BRANDT and others as an attempt to normalize relations with communist countries other than the U.S.S.R., including recognition of the German Democratic Republic (GDR). With the reunification of GERMANY in 1990, West Germany seemed to have far surpassed the original goals of *Ostpolitik*.

Oswald, Lee Harvey (1939–1964). Presumed assassin of U.S. President John F. KENNEDY. Born in New Orleans and raised in poverty, he was by all accounts a loner. He served in the U.S. Marine Corps but received an undesirable discharge (1959). He then lived in the U.S.S.R. for 2–1/2 years, marrying a Soviet woman, Marina Nicholaevna. Apparently disillusioned with the U.S.S.R., he returned to the U.S. in June 1962 with his wife and infant daughter and became involved in pro-CASTRO activities. He separated from his

Lee Harvey Oswald being escorted into Dallas police headquarters.

wife in 1963 and moved to Dallas, where he found a low-paying job in the **Texas School Book Depository,** from where, as far as can be determined, he fired the shots that killed President Kennedy. Shortly after leaving the building, he also shot and killed a Dallas police officer, **J. D. Tippitt,** who had stopped him for questioning. Oswald was captured soon thereafter. He met his own death two days later on November 24 as police were taking him through the basement of Dallas's municipal building to be transferred from the city jail to the county jail. As millions watched on television, Jack RUBY, a Dallas nightclub owner, sprang from a crowd of reporters and fired a .38–caliber revolver point blank at Oswald, who died within hours. From the time of his arrest until his own death, Oswald never admitted any connection with the Kennedy assassination; his defiant words upon his arrest were "Mister, I shot nobody." Because of Oswald's death, the evidence against him could not be presented in court. Although the Warren Commission later reported that Oswald acted alone in the assassination, conspiracy theories claiming Cuban and Mafia involvement in the assassination persisted.

Oswiecim. See AUSCHWITZ.

Ott, Mel(vin Thomas) (1909–1958). American baseball player. Ott became a regular with the New York Giants at the age of 19, and remained with the club throughout his 22–year career. A perennial All-Star, he was the first player in the National League to reach the 500–home-run plateau. His popularity in New York led to him being named player-manager of the Giants in 1942. He retired from the managerial post in 1948, one year after the end of his playing career. He was named to the Hall of Fame in 1951.

Ottoman empire. The once powerful Ottoman empire lasted for hundreds of years, until it met its fate in the first quarter of the 20th century. By the turn of the century, its size, power, wealth and stability had declined greatly from its height in the 1500s. It was widely regarded as "the sick man of Europe." At this time, its territory had been reduced to present-day TURKEY and regions mainly in the Middle East and on the Arabian peninsula under Turkish rule. The Sublime Porte was threatened by Russia, by Arab independence movements and by the YOUNG TURKS, who demanded modernization and reform. In 1908, the Young Turks forced Sultan ABDUL HAMID II to restore constitutional rule. The empire was allied with GERMANY in WORLD WAR I. During the war, the British occupied much of the Ottoman territory in PALESTINE and present-day IRAQ. This occupation, combined with Arab uprisings (assisted by Col. T.E. LAWRENCE, "Lawrence of Arabia") ended Turkish domination of the region. The Treaty of SEVRES (1920) recognized the independence of the non-Turkish peoples of the Middle East. Meanwhile, the Turkish nationalist Kemal ATATURK assumed power (1920), abolished the sultanate (1922) and declared Turkey a republic (1923), thus formally dissolving the Ottoman empire.

Outerbridge, Paul, Jr. (1891–1959). American photographer whose work ranged from rather sentimentalized commercial images to still lifes with an abstract and documentary quality and powerful design impact. Outerbridge became involved in photography during his military service in WORLD WAR I. In 1921 he entered the school operated by Clarence H. White in New York to learn pictorial and commercial photography. *Collar,* produced on his first commercial assignment in 1922, is a still life showing a man's collar resting on a checkerboard background in a way that makes the image abstract and elegant while still totally realistic. Other work included city scenes, details of mechanical parts, and such common objects as a wine glass or tin box, beautifully contact-printed on platinum paper, making each image an expressive design. His role in the history of modern photography points toward the work of Berenice ABBOTT and Walker EVANS, whose work gave documentary photography a place in both design and art.

Ovando Candia, Alfredo (1918–1982). President of BOLIVIA (1969–70) and co-president (1965–66). Ovando organized the 1967 military offensive against Ernesto "Che" GUEVARA, in which the revolutionary was killed.

Owen, David (Anthony Llewellyn) (1938–). British politician. Educated at Cambridge, Owen practiced as a neurologist before entering Parliament as a Labour member in 1966. As foreign secretary (1977–79) in the government of James CALLAGHAN, he was instrumental in negotiating an agreement with Rhodesian leader Ian SMITH, Bishop Abel MUZOREWA, Robert MUGABE and Joshua NKOMO to bring about the peaceful transfer of power to the black majority (see ZIMBABWE). A leading moderate in the LABOUR PARTY, Owen was one of the GANG OF FOUR who left the party in 1981 to found the SOCIAL DEMOCRATIC PARTY (SDP). In 1983 Owen succeeded Jenkins as party leader. Owen opposed the SDP's decision to merge with the LIBERAL PARTY in 1987 and stepped down from his post. Without a party, his political future was uncertain. Owen is the author of *Face the Future* (1981).

Owen, Wilfred (1893–1918). British poet and military hero. Owen, who was killed in action on the western front one week before the end of WORLD WAR I, is regarded by many critics as the finest poet to have written of that war, as well as one of the greatest elegaic poets in the history of the English language. Educated at the University of London, Owen enlisted in the British army in 1915 despite ill health. Invalided in 1917 and suffering from shattered nerves, Owen met fellow British poet Siegfried SASSOON while in a hospital in Scotland. Sassoon, who saw to the publication of Owen's posthumous *Poems* (1920), was a major influence on Owen, as was Robert GRAVES. Owen returned to active service, won the Military Cross for combat bravery in October 1918 and was killed the following month. His notable poems include "Strange Meeting" and "Anthem for Doomed Youth." Owen's *Collected Poems* (1931) featured an introduction by Edmund Blunden.

Owens, Jesse (1913–1980). Black American track and field star. Jesse Owens is considered one of the greatest athletes of the 20th century and ranks as one of the all-time greats in track and field events. When in his early 20s, he had achieved fame as a sprinter, hurdler and long-jumper of unsurpassing grace. In his sophomore year at Ohio State University, he broke five world records and tied a sixth, all within 45 minutes of competition. He was best known for his memorable performance at the 1936 OLYMPIC GAMES in BERLIN, where he won four gold medals (in the 100– and 200–meter dashes, the broad jump and the 400–meter relay). The feat was made more dramatic by the presence of Adolf HITLER in the stadium. Before the games, Hitler had proclaimed Aryan racial superiority and mocked American black athletes as members of an inferior race. Despite his Olympic triumphs, Owens did not receive official U.S. recognition of his feats until 1976, when he was awarded the Presidential Medal of Freedom. After his career as an amateur runner, he became a well-known public speaker and operated his own public relations and marketing firms.

***OXFAM* [Oxford Committee for Famine Relief].** Privately funded British relief agency founded in Oxford, England, in 1942, to feed the children in GREECE during WORLD WAR II. Its scope broadened as it aided refugees worldwide following the war. In the 1960s OXFAM changed its focus to improving agriculture and food production in developing and THIRD WORLD countries, providing staff, equipment and training to people so that they could control their own production. In the 1970s OXFAM organizations were formed in the U.S., CANADA, BELGIUM and AUSTRALIA. In addition to continued agricultural support, OXFAM provides emergency assistance in areas stricken by natural disasters.

Jesse Owens prepares for a sprint.

Oxford Group. Established at Oxford in the 1920s, the Oxford Group was the British equivalent of Frank BUCHMAN'S MORAL RE-ARMAMENT in the U.S. This evangelical movement aimed at changing social conditions through personal religious action.

Ozal, Turgut (1927–). Turkish statesman. After graduating in electrical engineering, Ozal taught at the Middle East Technical University at ANKARA. A member of the right-wing Motherland Party, Ozal was formerly a member of the religious National Salvation Party. In 1967 he became undersecretary of the State Planning Organization. Ozal also worked for the WORLD BANK. He served as the minister of state (1980–82) and has been prime minister since 1983. With strong background in economic policy, he sponsored TURKEY'S application for membership in the EUROPEAN COMMUNITY in 1987. He survived an assassination attempt in 1988, and a defeat in a March 1989 referendum regarding local elections. He strongly supported the UNITED NATIONS actions against IRAQ after Iraq's 1990 invasion of KUWAIT.

Ozawa, Seiji (1935–). Japanese-born conductor known for his sensitivity to tempo, tone and balance. Ozawa was influenced by his mentors, KARAJAN and BERNSTEIN. He made his Western conducting debut at New York's CARNEGIE HALL in 1961. From 1970 to 1976 he was musical director of the San Francisco Symphony Orchestra. He has appeared at the SALZBURG FESTIVAL and at Covent Garden and conducted operas at La Scala and Paris. Since 1968 he has been principal conductor of the New Japan Philharmonic Orchestra, and from 1973 he has served as musical director of the Boston Symphony Orchestra.

Ozu, Yasujiro (1903–1963). Japanese filmmaker. Ozu is ranked with Kenji MIZOGUCHI and Akira KUROSAWA as the greatest of modern Japanese filmmakers. He has been called "the most Japanese" of all directors. The Tokyo-born filmmaker has won the Japanese equivalent of six ACADEMY AWARDS. By contrast with the more flamboyant work of his famous protege, Kurosawa, Ozu reveals character primarily through dialogue, not action. His main subject is the strain of contemporary life upon the integrity of the family. He began in the movies as an assistant cameraman for the great Japanese studio, Shochiko Motion Picture Company (with which he was associated the rest of his life). His "home dramas," such as *Ochazuke no aji* (*The Flavor of Green Tea over Rice*, 1952), *Tokyo monogatari* (*Tokyo Story*), and *Ukigusa* (*Floating Weeds*), display a fascinating formal design. He places his camera in the *tatami* position, approximately the point-of-view from a kneeling position three feet above the floor. He eschews such transitional devices as fades and dissolves. Dialogue and action are intercut with shots of static views—trees, hallways, windows, street signs, etc. The entire effect is a spare simplicity, serene calm and repose. Yet the emotional charge of those lingering shots through doorways—such as the last view of an old man abandoned by his family in *Samma no aji* (*An Autumn Afternoon*, 1962)—is overwhelming. "What remains after an Ozu film is the feeling that, if only for an hour or two, you have seen the goodness and beauty of everyday things and everyday people," says biographer Donald Richie. Ozu's tombstone displays the single character for *mu*—a term translated as "nothingness"—which in Zen philosophy also means "everything."

For further reading:

Richie, Donald, *Ozu: His Life and Films.* University of California Press, 1974.

Pacific Islands, Trust Territory of the. Several island chains in the western Pacific under U.S. administration; includes the CAROLINES (as well as the Palaus), the MARSHALLS and the MARIANAS (except GUAM), in Micronesia. A Japanese LEAGUE OF NATIONS mandate from 1919 to 1945, in 1944 the islands were seized by the U.S. during WORLD WAR II; in 1947 they became a trust territory with the approval of the UNITED NATIONS. The trusteeship ended in 1990.

Pact of Paris. See KELLOGG-BRIAND PACT.

Paderewski, Ignace Jan (1860–1941). Polish pianist, composer and statesman. Born in Kurylowka in Russian Poland, Paderewski began playing the piano at an early age. He entered the Warsaw Conservatory in 1872 and later studied with Theodor Leschetizky. Paderewski debuted in Vienna in 1887, in Paris in

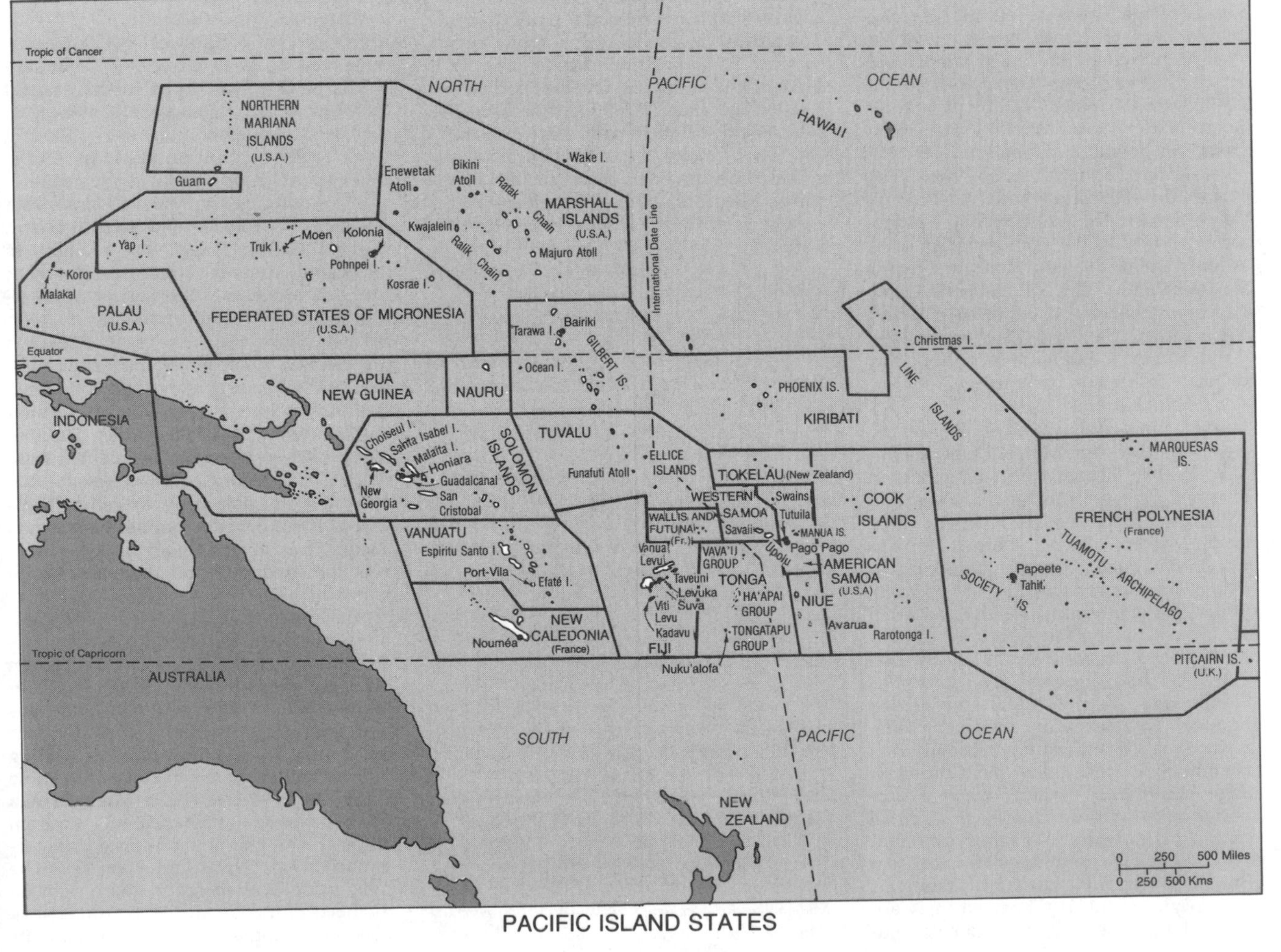

PACIFIC ISLAND STATES

1888 and in the U.S. in 1891. His technical virtuosity and brilliant style soon made him the most celebrated and beloved pianist since Franz Liszt. Also a composer, he wrote orchestral pieces, an opera, a cantata, songs and chamber music, as well as piano pieces, notably the well-known Minuet in G. Touring repeatedly and commanding huge fees, he donated much of his fortune to Poland, mainly in the form of aid to refugees and musicians. Paderewski was a passionate Polish nationalist and patriot. After World War I, when the new Polish state was proclaimed in 1918, he briefly served as its ambassador to Washington and shortly afterward became his country's prime minister. In this capacity, he signed the VERSAILLES Peace Treaty and served until 1920. Retaining an interest in Polish affairs, he later devoted most of his time to music. But in 1940–41 he was head of POLAND's government-in-exile during the Nazi occupation.

For further reading:

Drozdowski, Marian M., *Ignace Jan Paderewski: A Political Life in Outline*. New York: Hippocrene, 1983

Page, Ruth (1899–1991). American dancer, choreographer and ballet director. A dynamic performer who gained international acclaim in solo concerts and with such companies as Anna PAVLOVA's classical ballet and Serge DIAGHILEV'S BALLETS RUSSES, Page was one of the first choreographers to create works based on American themes. Her most famous ballet in this vein was *Frankie and Johnny* (1938) in collaboration with Bentley Stone. Some of her most popular ballets were based on operas and operettas, such as *Vilia* (1953), adapted from *The Merry Widow*. In 1928 she created the role of Terpsichore in the world premiere of Igor STRAVINSKY's *Apollo*, as choreographed by Adolph Bolm. She founded the Chicago Opera Ballet in 1956, which became Ruth Page's International Ballet (1966–69), then the Chicago Ballet (1972–present). Rudolph NUREYEV made his New York City debut with her company in 1962.

For further reading:

Martin, John, *Ruth Page: An Intimate Biography*. New York: Marcel Dekker, 1977.

Page, Walter Hines (1855–1918). American author, publisher and ambassador. After attending Duke University, Randolph-Macon College and Johns Hopkins University, Page began his literary career in 1880 as a reporter for the *Gazette* in St. Louis. In later years he either reported for or edited the *New York World*, the *Raleigh State Chronicle*, the *New York Evening Post*, the *Forum*, the *Atlantic Monthly* and *World's Work*. In 1900 Page joined Frank N. Doubleday in establishing Doubleday-Page, a publishing company that later became Doubleday and Company. Page became an early and active supporter in Woodrow WILSON's presidential campaign, and when Wilson was elected, he appointed Page ambassador to Great Britain. Throughout most of his tenure as ambassador (1913–18), Page strongly advocated that the U.S. abandon its neutrality in WORLD WAR I and join the side of Great Britain. On this issue Page was at constant odds with President Wilson.

Pagis, Dan (1931–1986). Israeli poet. A scholar of medieval Hebrew literature, Pagis spent three years during WORLD WAR II in a NAZI CONCENTRATION CAMP. He emigrated to ISRAEL in 1946. His poetry was regarded as a significant literary response to the HOLOCAUST.

Pahlevi, Muhammad Reza [Shah of Iran] (1919–1980). Shah of IRAN (1941–79); son of Reza Khan, he succeeded to the throne after his father was deposed by British and Soviet pressure. His long rule was interrupted in 1953 after an uprising led by Prime Minister Muhammad MOSSADEQ. He was soon reinstated, with the secret participation of the U.S., and assumed even greater powers of control over the government and the people of Iran. In 1963 the shah began a campaign of modernization that included land reform, the emancipation of women and the promotion of public education. However, as revenue from the nation's oil industries swelled, the shah's government became increasingly corrupt and his own royal extravagance as an ostentatiously uniformed international jet-setter became more extreme. The country suffered from inflation and economic distress, and the shah was opposed both by Muslim fundamentalists and by liberals, all of whom resented the repressive enforcement methods of his brutal secret police, SAVAK. Demonstrations in 1978 led to the full-scale revolution that deposed the shah in 1979 and brought the Ayatollah Ruhollah KHOMEINI to power. Ill with cancer, the shah fled Iran and (after brief stays in Morocco, the Bahamas, Mexico and the U.S.) finally found asylum in Egypt, where he died soon after.

Muhammad Reza Pahlevi's official coronation portrait (Oct. 28, 1967).

For further reading:

Lenczowski, George, ed., *Iran Under the Pahlavis*. Stanford, Calif.: Hoover Institute, 1978.

Shawcross, William, *The Shah's Last Ride*. New York: Simon & Schuster, 1989.

Pahlevi, Reza Shah [born Reza Khan] (1878–1944). Shah of IRAN (1925–41); a career army officer and one of the organizers of a 1921 coup d'etat, after which he became war minister and later (1923) prime minister. A strong leader who forged a powerful army, Reza Khan was successful in ousting Russian (1921) and British (1924) forces from their occupation of parts of Persia. Assuming broad powers, he deposed the last ruler of the Qajar dynasty in 1925 and proclaimed himself shah. He moved to modernize Persia, restructuring the government and the armed forces; promoting industrialization; establishing new schools, hospitals, networks of roads and the Trans-Iranian Railroad; and reducing the role of the clergy in government and law. Changing his name, he became the founder of the Pahlevi dynasty. And in 1935 he changed the name of his country—from Persia to the Nazi-endorsed Iran. During World War II his pro-German sympathies prompted the British and Soviet governments to reoccupy Iran; in 1941 he abdicated in favor of his son, Muhammad Reza PAHLEVI. Three years later he died in exile in South Africa.

Paige, Leroy "Satchel" (1906?-1982). American baseball player. A legendary pitcher, Paige was noted for his fastball and his variety of curveball pitches, as well as his longevity in the sport. Starting in baseball's Negro Leagues in the 1920s, Paige spent his prime playing years there, prior to entering the Major Leagues as a 42–year-old "rookie" with the Cleveland Indians (1948). Paige was brought to Cleveland a year after the Brooklyn Dodgers broke the color barrier with second baseman Jackie ROBINSON. Despite his late beginning, the 6–foot-33–inch pitcher was a deceptive, powerful addition to the Major Leagues and completed a relatively long career when he retired in 1965, while in his late fifties. The first black pitcher in major league baseball, Paige's birth records were so obscure that even he was able only to estimate his date of birth. Some authorities have added as much as a decade to his age. Paige was inducted into the Baseball Hall of Fame in 1971.

Paine, Thomas (1921–). U.S. space administrator. Best known in recent years as the chair of the National Commission on Space and before that as administrator of NASA from 1968 to 1970, Paine has had a strong impact on the U.S. space program. Charged in 1985 with setting out the nation's goals in space, the Paine Commission consisted of more than a dozen space-age luminaries, ranging from Nobel Prize–winning physicist Luis ALVAREZ to X-1 pilot Charles YEAGER. The publication of their report came right on the heels of the January 1986 CHALLENGER disaster, giving all the more impact to its bold visions. They called for an ambitious agenda of exploration, development, and eventual settlement of new worlds in the next 50 years, "from the highlands of the Moon to the Plains of Mars." From October 1968 to September 1970, when Paine served as acting administrator and then as NASA's third administrator, the first seven manned APOLLO missions were launched. It was a time when the nation was galvanized by the excitement of seeing 21 astronauts orbit the Earth over the span of two years, with 15 of them traveling to the Moon and four of them walking on its surface.

Paisley, Ian (Richard Kyle) (1926–). Northern Irish politician and Protestant clergyman. A fundamentalist minister, Paisley founded the Free Presbyterian Church of Ulster in 1951 and the Martyrs' Memorial Free Presbyterian Church in 1969. In both the pulpit and the political arena, he is an outspoken activist against Catholic dominance in Ulster and against interference in NORTHERN IRELAND from either Britain or Dublin. Paisley entered Parliament as a Protestant Unionist member in 1970. A year later he helped form the Democratic Unionist Party, which has become Northern Ireland's second largest party. Paisley won a seat in the European Parliament in 1979, to which he was reelected in 1984, although he consistently opposed British membership in the EUROPEAN ECONOMIC COMMUNITY. He denounced the 1985 HILLSBOROUGH ACCORD designed to foster cooperation from all parties on Northern Ireland. Although ostensibly opposed to violence, Paisley has earned a reputation as a demagogue; he has organized numerous Protestant protests, and his rhetoric is widely seen as a divisive force in the province. In 1988, when Pope JOHN PAUL II visited Northern Ireland, Paisley interrupted him, calling out "antichrist," and was subsequently ejected from the European Parliament.

Pakistan. Country in south Asia; bordered by Afghanistan on the north and west, China on the northeast, India on the east and southeast, Iran on the southwest and the Arabian Sea on the south. Pakistan, scene of countless invasions over the centuries, is approximately 90% Muslim, and its official language is Urdu. From 1857 to independence in 1947 it was a part of British INDIA; in 1956 it became a republic in the British Commonwealth. Formation of the Muslim League in 1906 led to increased demands for Muslim political freedom in the face of India's dominant Hindu population. By 1930 a national separatist movement had evolved, led by the poet and statesman Muhammad Iqbal, and in 1940 Muhammad Ali JINNAH took over as leader of the Muslim League, later serving as Pakistan's first head of state in 1947.

The abrupt division of British India into the new nations of Pakistan and India caused bloody riots and warfare among hundreds of thousands of Hindus and Muslims, who uprooted themselves to be among their own people. At independence, West Pakistan (present-day Pakistan) was separated from East Pakistan (now known as BANGLADESH) by approximately 1,000 miles of territory under India's jurisdiction. Further, in 1947–48 divided Pakistan went to war with India over the mountain provinces of JAMMU and KASHMIR; disputes erupted again in 1965, but in December 1972 a boundary was firmly established.

PAKISTAN

Growing dissatisfaction in East Pakistan accused the government of favoring the West; although the East won a majority in parliament in December 1970, its legislature was not allowed to convene. In March 1971 East Pakistan declared itself independent as Bangladesh. West Pakistani troops were unsuccessful in their attempts to crush the rebellion, and they were defeated when India entered the war in December (see INDO-PAKISTANI WAR OF 1971). In February 1974, Pakistan was forced to recognize independent Bangladesh. Further tension broke out on the Pakistani border in December 1979, during the Soviet invasion of neighboring

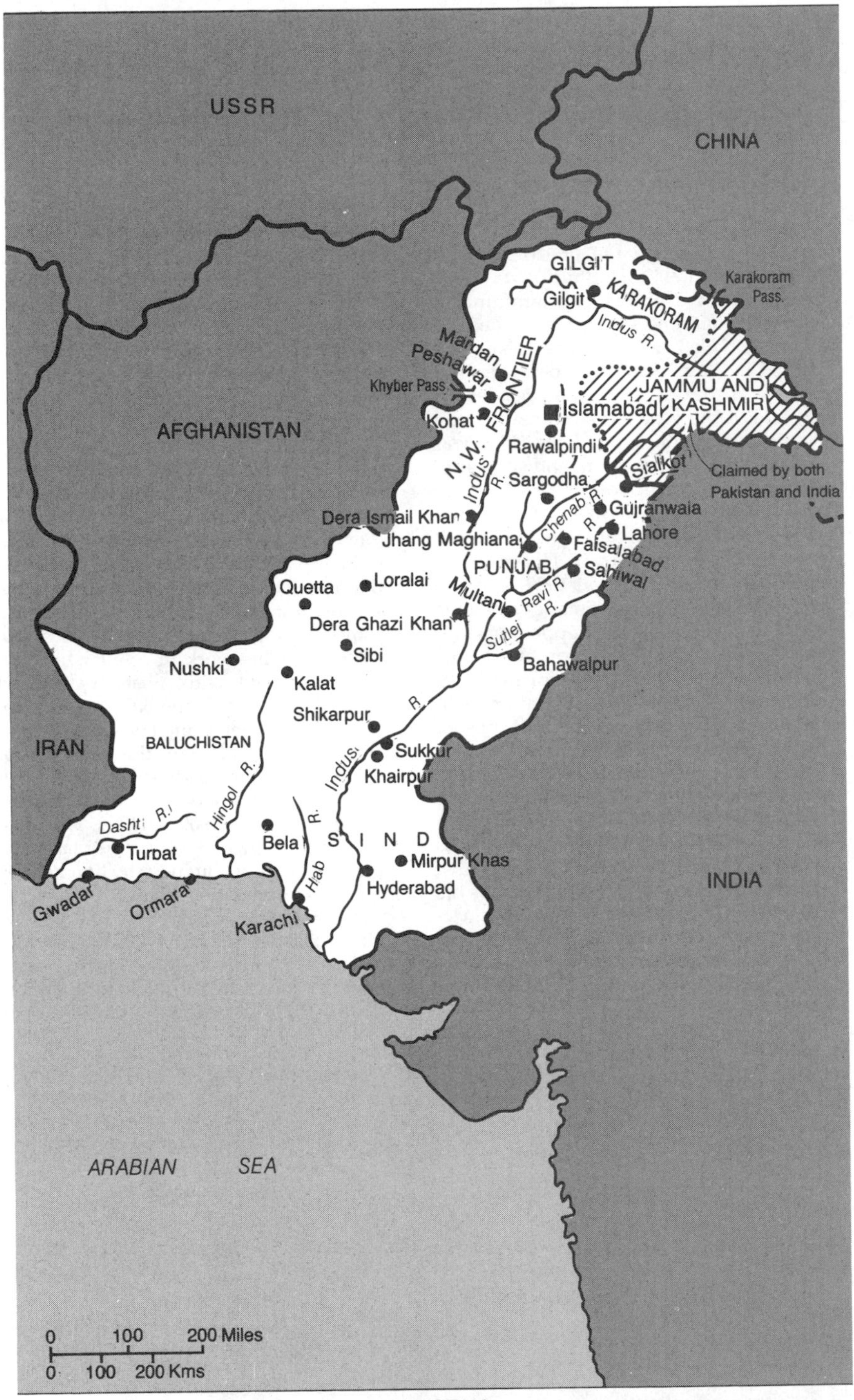

AFGHANISTAN. Zulfiqar Ali BHUTTO, leader of the Pakistan People's Party, became president in Dec. 1971; with the introduction of a new constitution (1973), he became prime minister. Bhutto followed a policy of Islamic socialism, strengthening relations with other Islamic (mainly Arab) countries and nationalizing key industries. He won reelection in 1977 but was overthrown in a coup led by Gen. Zia al-Haq, who assumed the presidency and declared martial law. Bhutto was executed. Because of his anticommunism, Zia received strong support from the U.S. Zia was killed when his airplane exploded in Aug. 1988. Bhutto's daughter, Benazir BHUTTO, was elected president at the end of the year but faced severe economic and political problems. She was defeated in a 1990 election, and soon after charged with corruption.

Pal, George (1908–1980). HOLLYWOOD producer-director of animated and science fiction films. Born in Hungary, he immigrated to the U.S. in 1939. Early in his film career he was primarily a cinema cartoonist. His series of "Puppetoons" for PARAMOUNT in the 1940s won him a special ACADEMY AWARD (1943) for his innovations in "stop-motion" animation techniques. In the 1950s he became one of Hollywood's foremost masters of science fiction and fantasy films. He won eight Academy Awards for the productions of such classics as *Destination Moon* (1950), *When Worlds Collide* (1951), *War of the Worlds* (1953) and *The Seven Faces of Dr. Lao* (1964). Perhaps his greatest achievement was his adaptation of H.G. WELLS's *The Time Machine* (1960), which he also directed and for which he realized many of the cinematic implications embedded in the original book.

For further reading:

Hickman, Gail Morgan, *The Films of George Pal*. Cranbury, New Jersey: A.S. Barnes, 1977.

Palade, George Emil (1912–). Romanian-American physiologist and cell biologist; educated at Bucharest University, he was a professor of physiology during World War II. Palade immigrated to America in 1946, becoming a naturalized citizen in 1952. He worked at the Rockefeller Institute for Medical Research, New York, becoming professor of cytology there (1958–72). In 1972 he became director of studies in cell biology at Yale University's medical school. Although Palade's work has been primarily concerned with studies of the fine structure of animal cells, he has also investigated the nature of plant chloroplasts. His discovery of small bodies called "microsomes," which function independently of the mitochondria (of which they were previously thought to be a part), showed them to be rich in ribonucleic acid (RNA) and therefore the site of protein manufacture. The microsomes were subsequently renamed ribosomes. For his work in cellular biology, Palade received, with Albert CLAUDE and Christian DE DUVE, the NOBEL PRIZE for physiology or medicine (1974).

Palanan. City in Luzon, the PHILIPPINES. Palanan was the headquarters of the Filipino revolutionary General Emilio Aguinaldo from 1900 to 1901. Aguinaldo's capture by U.S. forces on March 23, 1901, ended the Filipino rebellion against the U.S. occupation that followed the Spanish-American War.

Palar, Lambertus N. (1902–1981). Indonesian statesman and diplomat, prominent in INDONESIA's struggle for independence. Palar served as Indonesia's chief delegate to the UNITED NATIONS from 1950 to 1953. Later he was ambassador to India, Canada and the U.S. A leading spokesman for the non-aligned nations of Asia and Africa, he denounced "neocolonialism," called for neutral and nuclear-free zones and advocated strong sanctions against SOUTH AFRICA because of that nation's policy of APARTHEID.

Jewish children on their way to Palestine after being liberated from the Buchenwald Concentration Camp (June 5, 1945).

Palawan. Agricultural island in the southwestern PHILIPPINES. During their occupation of Palawan in WORLD WAR II, the Japanese massacred U.S. PRISONERS OF WAR on the island.

Palchinsky, Peter Ioakimovich (1875–1929). Russian engineer and politician. During World War I Palchinsky was a leading member of the central war industries committee. Following the 1917 FEBRUARY REVOLUTION he was appointed the provisional government's deputy minister of trade and industry and defended the Winter Palace against the BOLSHEVIKS. A technical expert of GOSPLAN, he was accused of sabotage and shot at the beginning of the PURGES. He was said to have founded the underground league of engineering organizations.

Palestine. Though there is no official Palestinian state at present, historically the biblical land of Palestine covered the general area of the modern State of ISRAEL and its occupied territories of GAZA and the WEST BANK. Part of the OTTOMAN EMPIRE, Palestine became a British Mandate after WORLD WAR I until its partition into Arab and Jewish zones by the UNITED NATIONS in 1947. The Palestinians, Arabs who trace their origins to the biblical Palestine, have fought against Jewish settlement of the area, especially after the State of Israel was established in 1948. Feeling dispossessed of their land, thousands left during the Israeli War for Independence (see ARAB-ISRAELI WAR OF 1948–49) and are scattered throughout the Middle East, with large numbers in JORDAN and the Israeli-occupied territories. Attempts to settle the problems of Palestinian displacement have failed, and Arab-Israeli tensions have escalated with wars in 1956, 1967, 1973, and 1982. The situation has been exacerbated by the PALESTINE LIBERATION ORGANIZATION (PLO; founded 1964), which has used terrorist attacks to push for Palestine's liberation, and by the INTIFADA, which broke out in the occupied territories in 1987. In 1988 the PLO acceded to a 1967 UN resolution, thereby implicitly recognizing Israel, renouncing terrorism, and accepting a two-state solution based on Israeli withdrawal from the occupied territories. Although the PLO also declared the independent state of Palestine (recognized only by Arab states), the problem of a Palestinian homeland remains unresolved.

Palestine Liberation Organization (PLO). Coordinating organization, including several separate Arab groups, that aims at the "liberation" of PALESTINE from the Israeli regime and the creation of a homeland for Palestinians. It is widely considered the political spokesman and military arm of the Palestinian people.

PALESTINE

1917	British Balfour Declaration promising a national home for Jews in Palestine encourages Jewish immigration.
1922	Britain is given League of Nations mandate over Palestine.
1948	Britain leaves Palestine; (May 14) State of Israel proclaimed in Tel Aviv.
1948-49	Israeli war of independence drives 780,000 Palestinians from their homeland.
1964	Palestine National Council (PNC), "a parliament-in-exile," is formed and establishes the Palestine Liberation Organization.
1987	Intifada (uprising) breaks out.
1988	(November) PNC votes to support UN resolution 242 (1967), which recognizes Israel and calls for Israeli withdrawal from the West Bank of Gaza. It also declares the existence of an independent state of Palestine with Jerusalem as its capital; (December) with the PLO's renunciation of terrorism, dialogue is opened with the U.S.
1990	(June 20) Diplomatic dialogue with PLO is suspended by the U.S. after the PLO fails to condemn an abortive speedboat raid on Israeli beaches.

Founded in 1964, it is dominated by the Al Fatah guerrillas led by Yasir ARAFAT, who was named PLO head in 1969. The UNITED NATIONS recognized it as the legitimate Palestinian government in 1974. The group was forced out of Jordan in 1971, moving to BEIRUT, LEBANON, until expelled by the Israeli invasion of 1982. PLO members now inhabit a number of Arab countries, notably Syria and Tunisia. The group has engaged in many acts of terrorism throughout the world in attempts to further its cause, but claims to have largely abandoned violence in favor of political action.

Paley, William S. (1901–1990). U.S. broadcast entrepreneur. He created the CBS network out of a handful of ailing radio stations he purchased in 1928. The network branched out into television in the 1950s and was the dominant force in U.S. broadcasting into the 1970s. He signed such popular performers as Lucille BALL, Jack BENNY, Jackie GLEASON and Ed SULLIVAN, as well as newsmen Edward R. MURROW, William L. SHIRER, Howard K. Smith and Eric SEVAREID. CBS produced such popular successes as "Gunsmoke," "I LOVE LUCY," "The Mary Tyler Moore Show," ALL IN THE FAMILY and M*A*S*H*. Paley was a noted socialite and art collector, as well as a powerful, and often ruthless, businessman.

Palme, Olof (1927–1986). Swedish premier. Born into an aristocratic family, Palme attended Kenyon College in Ohio and in 1951 earned a law degree at the University of Stockholm. In 1969, after serving in parliament and as a government minister, Palme became leader of the Social Democratic Party and then premier. For the next two decades he dominated Swedish politics. On the international scene, he was a vocal critic of the U.S. role in VIETNAM as well as of the Soviet invasion of CZECHOSLOVAKIA. On the domestic front, Palme levied high taxes to provide generous medical, educational and recreational programs for Swedish citizens. On February 28, 1986, Palme was assassinated by an unknown gunman as he and his wife were leaving a Stockholm movie theater, shocking Sweden and the world. An unemployed laborer named Carl Gustav Christer Pettersson was convicted of the crime, but his conviction was later overturned by a court of appeals.

Palmer, Arnold (1929–). U.S. golfer. A dominant golfer from the 1950s to the 1980s, he is one of the greatest golfers of all time. In 1981 the PGA championship trophy was renamed the Arnold Palmer Award. As golf became a popular televised sport, viewers watched Palmer's fans, dubbed "Arnie's Army," follow him through every round. His 60 tour victories included four Masters titles and a 1959 U.S. Open. The winner of 19 foreign titles, he played on six Ryder Cup teams and seven World Cup teams.

Palmer, Geoffrey (1942–). NEW ZEALAND politician; educated at the Victoria University of Wellington (B.A. in political science, 1964; LL.B., 1965) and the University of Chicago (doctor of laws, 1967). Before entering parliament, Palmer practiced as a solicitor and taught at Victoria University, the University of Iowa and the University of Virginia. He entered the House of Representatives at a by-election in August 1979 and became deputy leader of the LABOUR PARTY in February 1983. Palmer became deputy prime minister in 1988, heading the ministries of justice and the environment as well. He became prime minister in mid-1989.

Palmer Raids. See RED SCARE.

Pan, Hermes [Hermes Panagiotopulos] (1910–90). U.S choreographer. He created the dances for all but one of the 10 films starring Fred ASTAIRE and Ginger ROGERS in the 1930s and 1940s; among the films were *Flying Down to Rio* (1933), *Top Hat* (1935) and *Swing Time* (1936). He won an ACADEMY AWARD in 1937 for *A Damsel in Distress*. His other films included *Kiss Me Kate* (1953), *Cleopatra* (1963) and *My Fair Lady* (1964).

Panama [Republic of Panama]. Covering an area of 30,185 square miles, Panama is located on the southern part of the Central American isthmus which joins North and South America. Much of Panama's history in this century has been dominated by its relationship with the UNITED STATES and the importance of the PANAMA CANAL (completed in 1914). With U.S. support Panama became independent from Colombia in 1903. Opposition to U.S. influence led to revisions of the Canal Treaty (originated in 1903) in 1936 and 1955 revoking U.S. rights of intervention in Panamanian affairs. Anti-U.S. sentiment led to riots in 1959. Politically unstable, Panama had elected governments overthrown in 1941, 1949, 1951, and 1968. Colonel Omar TORRIJOS came to power in 1968, initiating reforms and negotiating new Canal treaties with the U.S. which abolished the Canal Zone and paved the way for transition of the Canal to Panamanian control by the year 2000. General Manuel Antonio Noriega Morena, who rose to power in the 1980s, was accused of political fraud and assassination, and of ties to drug smuggling. Attempts to remove him from power culminated in the U.S. military invasion in 1989 and the installation of Guillermo Endara as president. Noriega surrendered in 1990 and is awaiting trial on drug charges in Miami, Florida.

Panama Canal. Canal across the Isthmus of Panama, connecting the Caribbean Sea and the Atlantic Ocean with the Pacific Ocean. Some 50 miles long, the Panama Canal is one of the engineering marvels of the 20th century. It is also of immense strategic and commercial importance. The French attempted to dig a canal across Panama in 1881, but this effort failed because of disease (malaria), poor planning and lack of funds. The U.S. obtained rights to dig a canal in 1901; when Colombia (of which Panama was then a part) refused permission to continue in 1903, U.S. President Theodore ROOSEVELT encouraged a successful Panamanian independence movement. Under the Hay-Bunau-Varilla Treaty between the U.S. and Panama, the U.S. obtained the 10-mile-wide PANAMA CANAL ZONE in exchange for $10 million and an annual rent of $250,000. Meanwhile, U.S. Army doctors Walter REED and William C. GORGAS took measures to eliminate the mosquitos whose transmission of yellow fever and malaria had plagued the earlier French effort. U.S. construction of the canal began in 1904. Because the sea level is not the same on the Atlantic and Pacific ends of the canal, three sets of locks had to be constructed to raise and lower ships as they pass from one ocean to the other. The canal was officially opened on Aug. 15, 1914.

The U.S. ownership of the canal has often been a source of friction between Panama and the U.S. The PANAMA CANAL TREATY (1977) provided for the return of the Canal Zone to Panama; the canal is to be turned over to Panama in 1999. The

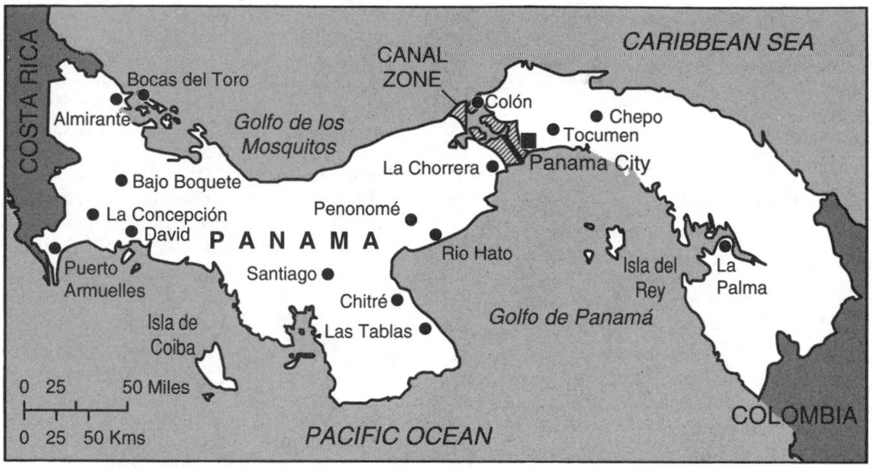

PANAMA

U.S. exercised its right to protect the canal when U.S. forces invaded Panama in December 1989 to arrest Panamanian strongman Manuel Noriega. (See also PANAMA.)

Panama Canal Zone. A strategically significant ribbon of territory 10 miles wide, stretching along both sides of the PANAMA CANAL. The zone was created in 1903 and assigned to U.S. supervision by treaty, but the surrounding country of PANAMA complained about this arrangement as early as 1926. American control of the zone was a sore point for Panamanian nationalists. In a move that caused controversy in the U.S., President Jimmy CARTER formally transferred the Canal Zone to Panama in 1978; complete shifting of jurisdiction and control is scheduled to be accomplished by 1999.

Panama Canal Zone Treaty. Agreement of September 7, 1977, between U.S. President CARTER and Panamanian General Torrijos that the U.S. would evacuate its five-mile-wide zone (on each side of the PANAMA CANAL) on January 1, 2000.

Panamanian Revolution of 1903. By the Hay-Herran Treaty, COLOMBIA was to lease the U.S. land across the isthmus of Panama to build a canal. Colombian president Jose Manuel Moarroquin favored this action, but the Colombian congress rejected the treaty. Phillippe Jean Bunau-Varilla, who held canal-building rights, organized a revolt in PANAMA against Colombia on November 3–4, 1903. The rebels proclaimed independence, the U.S. cruiser *Nashville* deterred landing of Colombian troops to suppress the uprising, and U.S. President Theodore ROOSEVELT recognized Panamanian independence on November 6, 1903 and received Bunau-Varilla as its minister. On November 18, 1903, the U.S. and Panama signed the Hay-Bunau-Varilla Treaty, giving the U.S. a lease in perpetuity of a 10–mile-wide strip of land across the isthmus for payments to Panama of $10 million, plus $250,000 annually.

Pan American World Airways [Pan Am]. American airline, founded in 1927 by Juan TRIPPE. In the first few decades of its existence, Pan Am established important international air routes and made long-distance passenger air travel an everyday reality. In the late 1950s it was one of the first airlines to introduce jet service, and it was the first airline to have the BOEING 747 jumbo jet in regular service (1970). Following the deregulation of the U.S. airline industry in the 1980s, Pan Am suffered financial losses and was forced to retrench its service.

Pan Am 103. On December 21, 1988, Pan American Flight 103 crashed near the village of Lockerbie, Scotland. All 244 passengers and 15 crew members aboard the 747 jumbo jet were killed in the crash, which also claimed the lives of 11 people on the ground. The flight had originated in Frankfurt, Germany, had stopped over at London's Heathrow Airport and was headed for Kennedy Airport in New York City when the disaster occurred. British and U.S. investigators soon established that the crash was caused by a plastic bomb hidden inside a radio cassette recorder placed in passenger luggage. It was further disclosed that the U.S. government had alerted airlines, airports and embassies in Europe of a threat to bomb Pan Am planes flying from Frankfurt to the U.S. during this period, but that authorities had not informed the flying public. After the crash, responsibility was claimed by a pro-Iranian group calling itself the Guardians of the Islamic Revolution; investigators later identified a group called the Popular Front for the Liberation of Palestine–General Command as the likely criminals. The disaster provoked a tightening of airline security for U.S. airliners operating abroad. The bombing of Pan Am flight 103 is regarded as one of the most heinous of the many terrorist attacks on innocent civilians in the late 20th century.

Pandit, Vijaya Lakshmi (1900–1990). Indian diplomat. She was the sister of the first prime minister of INDIA, Jawaharlal NEHRU. When the country gained its independence from Britain in 1947, Nehru appointed her ambassador to the U.S.S.R, a post she held from 1947 to 1949. She then served as ambassador to the U.S. from 1949 to 1952. She was the first woman to serve as president of the UNITED NATIONS General Assembly (1953–54). From 1954 to 1961 she was India's high commissioner to Britain. During the 1970s, she became alarmed by the authoritarian character of her niece Indira GANDHI's rule and became a staunch critic of the regime.

Panferov, Fedor Ivanovich (1896–1960). Russian author. His four-volume novel *Bruski* (1931–37) brought him renown. The novel *The Mother River Volga* (1953) was an early critical work in the post-Stalin period. It incurred displeasure, and he was dismissed from the editorship of the literary journal *Oktyabr* and expelled from

PANAMA

1903	Independence from Colombia.
1914	Panama Canal completed; U.S. accorded "sovereign rights" in Canal Treaty.
1925	U.S. troops land to protect U.S. interests during strikes and rent riots.
1936	Canal Treaty revised, rent paid to Panama increased, right of U.S. intervention revoked.
1959	Riots in Panama City protest U.S. flag flying in Canal Zone and not Panama flag.
1972	Brigadier General Omar Torrijos is vested with virtually unlimited power as "Supreme Leader of the Panamanian Revolution."
1980	Former shah of Iran is granted asylum, triggering demonstrations and student violence; shah is persuaded to leave for Egypt.
1988	General Manuel Antonio Noriega, head of Panama Defense Forces, indicted on drug charges in U.S.; President Eric Arturo Delvalle ousted by National Assembly after attempt to dismiss Noriega.
1989	Noriega captured in U.S. invasion of Panama; a Democratic Opposition Alliance candidate who lost election when results were annulled by Noriega, Guillermo Endara, is installed as president with U.S. support.

the Writers' Union but was reinstated in 1958.

Pankhurst, Emmeline Goulden (1858–1928). British suffragist. With her husband, the barrister Richard Pankhurst, she founded the Women's Franchise League in 1889. When the LIBERAL PARTY failed to support women's rights, she formed (1903) the more militant Women's Social and Political Union. Joined in the movement by her daughters Christabel Harriette Pankhurst (1880–1958) and (Estelle) Sylvia Pankhurst (1882–1960), she and other members engaged in a number of militant actions to further the cause. Repeatedly arrested, she used hunger strikes as a tactic. After the outbreak of WORLD WAR I, she devoted herself to the war effort. She moved to Canada after the war, returning to England in 1926. A revered figure in Great Britain, she died while running for election to Parliament a few weeks after full voting rights had been granted to women.

Panmunjom. Village in SOUTH KOREA on the border with NORTH KOREA. Panmunjom was the site of the peace negotiations that ultimately brought the cessation of hostilities in the KOREAN WAR. The truce ending the fighting was signed here on July 27, 1953.

Panofsky, Erwin (1892–1968). German-American art historian. Born in Germany, he received a Ph.D. from the University of Freiburg and taught at the University of Hamburg from 1921 to 1933. Panofsky fled Germany and emigrated to the U.S., where he became a professor of fine arts at New York University and in 1935 joined the faculty at the Institute for Advanced Study, Princeton, New Jersey. One of the most important art historians of the 20th century, he took an early interest in the Italian Renaissance and gradually turned his attention to Northern European art of the 15th and 16th centuries. A rigorous scholar, he was intensely concerned with the iconography of the various periods he studied. Among his many works are *Studies in Iconology* (1939, 2nd ed. 1962), *Albrecht Durer* (1943, 4th ed. 1955), *Early Netherlandish Painting (1953) and Renaissance and Renascences in Western Art* (1960).

Papadopoulos, George (1919–). Greek military officer and political leader. A career officer, Papadopoulos attained the rank of colonel and was a member of the military junta that seized control of the Greek government in 1967. Resigning from the army, Papadopoulos became premier later that year and soon established himself as a harsh and dictatorial ruler. He became regent in 1972, abolished the monarchy and created a republic the following year and named himself president. An unpopular ruler, he was ousted by yet another military coup late in 1973.

Papagos, Alexander (1883–1955). Greek military and political leader, prime minister (1952–55). A career officer, commissioned in 1906, he was appointed minister of war (1935) and army chief of staff (1936). Commander in chief of the Greek army in WORLD WAR II, he repelled invasion by Italy in 1940, but his forces were defeated by Germany in 1941. After the war he directed the 1949 campaign against communist guerrillas. Again appointed chief of the armed forces in 1950, he resigned to form the conservative Greek Rally Party and became prime minister in 1952. During his term in office, Papagos strengthened Greek ties with the West.

Papal States. See the VATICAN.

Papandreou, Andreas (1919–). Greek political leader. Son of George PAPANDREOU, who served as GREECE's premier from 1963 to 1967, Papandreou immigrated to the U.S. in 1940, where he served in the Navy and taught economics at the University of Minnesota and the University of California until returning to Greece in 1959. After his father became premier he renounced his U.S. citizenship and held several government posts, eventually enduring imprisonment and self-imposed exile when his father was overthrown in 1967. He returned to Greece in 1974 and founded a new political party that espoused controversial socialist ideas and opposed U.S. influence and military presence. He was elected premier in 1981, but lost the 1989 election because of charges of misconduct and a marital scandal.

Andreas Papandreou (1982).

Papandreou, George (1888–1968). Greek statesman, three-time premier (1944–45, 1963, 1964–65). Born in Salonika, he became a lawyer and entered political life as an antiroyalist moderate socialist. He served as a member of parliament and was interior minister (1923), was exiled briefly in 1926 and then served in a number of government posts. Again exiled in 1936, he was active in the resistance movement and headed a Greek government-in-exile from 1944 to 1945. Returning to GREECE after WORLD WAR II, he held office in various Social Democratic cabinets from 1946 to 1952. In 1961 he formed the liberal Center Union Party, serving as premier for 55 days in 1963 and again becoming premier the following year. Disputes with King CONSTANTINE II led to his dismissal in 1965. In 1967, after a military coup d'etat, Papandreou was arrested and briefly imprisoned. Constantly at odds with the government, he was placed under house arrest a number of times thereafter until his death.

Papanin, Ivan Dmitriyevich (1894–1986). Soviet polar explorer. He joined the CPSU in 1919. In 1931 he took part in his first polar expedition, and in 1937 led the North Polar Drift Expedition. In the following year he was appointed head of the Northern Sea Route Administration. Papanin's publications include *Life on an Icefloe* (1947) and *Northern Sea Route* (1952).

Papen, Franz von (1879–1969). German politician. A military attache to Washington (1913–15), he was posted to Turkey during World War I, after which he began his political career. A Catholic Center Party member of the Prussian parliament from 1921 to 1932, he was appointed chancellor by Paul von HINDENBURG in 1932 but was soon succeeded by Kurt von Schleicher. Remaining close to Hindenburg, Papen was instrumental in persuading the aging president to name Adolf HITLER as chancellor in 1933, while Papen himself was appointed vice chancellor. Afterward, he served as German ambassador to Austria (1936–38), helping to prepare for the ANSCHLUSS. For the duration of WORLD WAR II he was ambassador to Turkey. Tried at the NUREMBERG WAR CRIMES TRIALS (1946), von Papen was acquitted, but he was later imprisoned by a German denazification court. He was freed in 1949. Von Papen's memoirs were published in 1952 (Eng. tr., 1953). (See also GERMANY.)

Papp, Joseph [Joseph Papirefsky] (1921–). American theatrical director and producer. Born in New York City, Papp was trained at the Actor's Lab in Los Angeles. Since the 1950s he has been one of the most innovative and influential figures in American theater. In 1954 he founded the New York Shakespeare Festival, and in an attempt to make Shakespearean plays available to the general public he staged a variety of productions in Central Park from 1957 to 1962. In 1967 Papp founded the Public Theater, and in 1973 he was appointed director of the Vivian Beaumont and Mitzi C. Newhouse theaters at Lincoln Center. Papp has been responsible for introducing a wide array of new playwrights, directors and actors in Broadway and off-Broadway productions. Among his most memorable plays are *Hair* (1967), a musical version of *Two Gentlemen of Verona* (1971), *That Championship Season* (1972), *A Chorus Line* (1975) and *Pirates of Penzance* (1980).

Papua New Guinea. Nation in the southwestern Pacific Ocean, east of Indonesia and north of the northeastern tip of Australia. It occupies the eastern half of the island of New Guinea as well as a number of adjacent islands, including Bougainville in the Solomon Islands and New Britain in the Bismarck Archipelago. Much of this tropical country is mountainous and heavily forested, with exotic fauna and flora. In 1906 British New

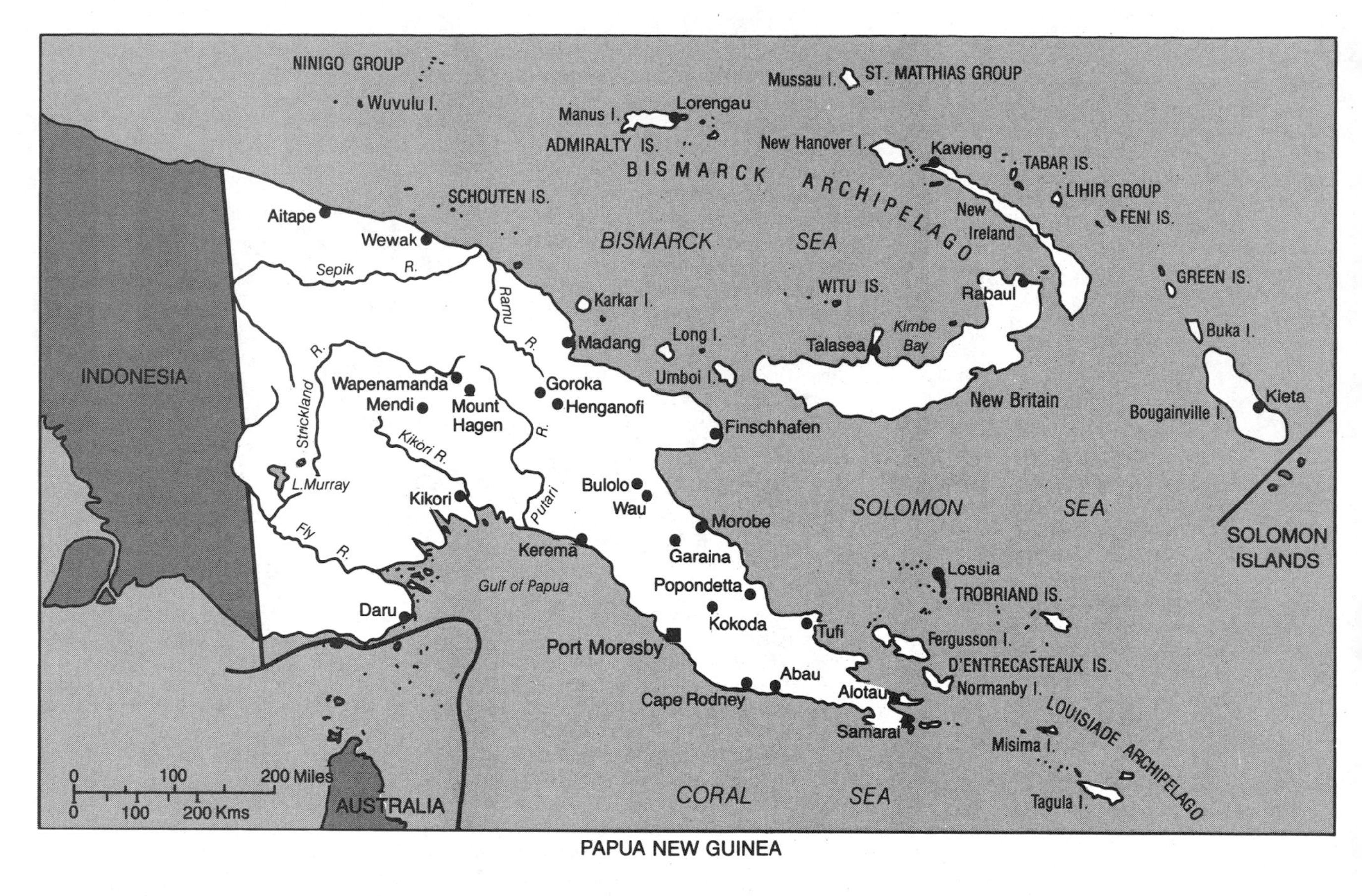

PAPUA NEW GUINEA

Guinea became the Territory of Papua, as control was transferred to newly independent Australia. With the outbreak of WORLD WAR I, Australia also took control of German New Guinea, and in 1920 this became a LEAGUE OF NATIONS Mandated Trust Territory under Australian trusteeship. Following Japanese occupation during WORLD WAR II, the eastern half of New Guinea reverted to Australian control as a single colony, the Territory of Papua and New Guinea. In 1963 INDONESIA took control of Dutch New Guinea and incorporated it into the Indonesian state as the territory of Irian Jaya. Papua New Guinea achieved self-government in 1973 and full independence in 1975, with a parliamentary system of government. The country has been ruled by a series of unstable coalitions composed of political parties based on patronage rather than ideology. At independence Papua New Guinea faced serious secessionist threats. Problems of law and order led to the declaration of states of emergency in PORT MORESBY (the capital) in 1979 and 1985, and in the Highlands (where there was severe ethnic unrest) in 1979. Unrest resurfaced on Bougainville island in late 1988, when local landowners demanded compensation for damage done to their land by the island's giant copper mine. Over 80% of the population of 3,800,000 is Papuan; less than 15% is Melanesian, while Polynesian, Chinese and European minorities comprise the remainder.

Parade. Landmark French cubist ballet, the collaboration of impresario Serge DIAGHILEV, composer Erik SATIE, designer Pablo PICASSO and choreographer Leonide MASSINE. Begun in 1915, it was premiered by the BALLETS RUSSES at the Theatre du Chatelet in Paris on May 18, 1917. The stage action depicts the street efforts by a number of circus performers—magicians, acrobats, cowboys and animals—to lure passersby into the show. Even if the pedestrians on stage are ultimately unimpressed by it all, the production itself exploded like a grenade in the face of the ballet world. Subsequent performances were jeered, and Satie almost came to blows with a hostile critic. Singled out for derision were Picasso's nine-foot-tall, wooden Cubist sculpture; costumes that included mobile skyscrapers; and Satie's use of sound effects in the orchestra—typewriters, police sirens and airplane engines. (See also CUBISM.)

For further reading:

Dictionary of Modern Ballet. New York: Tudor Publishing, 1959.

Paraguay [Republic of Paraguay]. Located in central South America, Paraguay covers an area of 157,006 square miles. From 1900 to 1935 Paraguay suffered economic chaos and violence from power struggles between two opposing political parties. Paraguay was united only when it defeated Bolivia during the CHACO WAR (1932–35), fought over Bolivia's attempt to control the upper Paraguay River. The untimely death of popular president Marshall Jose Felix Estigarribia (1939–40) led to the provisional presidency of General Higinio Moringo, which ended in the 1947 revolts, leaving thousands dead. After six presidents in as many years, General Alfredo STROESSNER became dictator in 1954, establishing economic and political stability during his 35–year rule. He was overthrown in 1989, and new elections were held, bringing General Andres Rodriguez to the presidency.

Paramount Pictures. One of HOLLYWOOD's "Big Five" production/exhibition motion picture studios (along with METRO-GOLDWYN-MAYER, WARNER BROS., RKO and 20TH CENTURY-FOX). In 1912 Adolph ZUKOR, a furrier turned entrepreneur, incorporated the Famous Players Film Company, which successfully launched a series of prestige movie adaptations of popular stage plays, including *Queen Elizabeth* with Sarah BERNHARDT. In 1916 Famous Players merged with the Jesse L. Lasky Feature Play Company, which boasted a roster of stage and screen talent including David BELASCO, Samuel GOLDWYN, and Cecil B. DE MILLE. (The Lasky/De Mille *The Squaw Man* [1913] had been one of the first feature-length movies made in the Hollywood/Los Angeles area.) The distribution network for Famous Players-Lasky was Paramount, formed in 1914 by W.W. Hodkinson. By 1917 other production companies began releasing through Paramount, including Artcraft, which had two of the biggest movie stars in the world under contract, Mary PICKFORD and Douglas FAIRBANKS. Acquisition of more movie theaters began in the 1920s. Zukor took over the business operations in New York City and Jesse Lasky oversaw the

BOLIVIA
Mayor Pablo Lagerenza
General Eugenio A. Garay
Fuerte Olimpo
BRAZIL
Mariscal Estigarribia
Puerto Casado
Dr. Pedro P. Peña
Puerto Pinasco
Pedro Juan Caballero
P A R A G U A Y
Concepción
Pozo Colorado
Paraguay River
San Pedro
Salto del Guairá
ARGENTINA
San Estanislao
Asunción
Caaguazú
Paraguarí
Villarrica
Abaí
Caazapá
San Juan Bautista
Pilar
Encarnación
0 75 150 Miles
0 75 150 Kms

PARAGUAY

productions in Hollywood. In 1930 the corporate name became the Paramount Publix Corporation. Although Paramount was by now one of the biggest studios in the U.S., GREAT DEPRESSION–related difficulties forced it into bankruptcy in 1933. Lasky was forced out. Zukor became chairman of the board when it was reorganized in 1935 as Paramount Pictures. The 1930s and '40s were Paramount's peak period as the studio continued the policy originated by Famous Players of utilizing talent developed in other media, radio, recording, vaudeville and the legitimate stage. Top directors included Ernst LUBITSCH, Rouben MAMOULIAN, Josef von STERNBERG, and Billy WILDER. Stars included Mae WEST, Jeanette MacDonald, the MARX BROTHERS, W.C. FIELDS, Bing CROSBY, Gary COOPER, and Martin and LEWIS. Some of the most successful pictures were Preston STURGES comedies (*The Lady Eve*, 1941), musicals (*Holiday Inn*, 1942) and the Crosby-Hope "Road" pictures (*Road to Zanzibar*, 1943). Later releases included several Alfred HITCHCOCK pictures (*Vertigo*, 1958, and *Psycho*, 1960); the Francis Ford COPPOLA GODFATHER series; the "Star Trek" series; and the Indiana Jones series. In 1949, along with other major Hollywood studios, Paramount was forced by government action to divest itself of its theater chains. Gulf and Western Industries acquired the studio in 1966.

For further reading:
Eames, John Douglas, *The Paramount Story*. New York: Crown Publishers, 1985.

Paris. Capital city of FRANCE. Located on the Seine River, Paris has long been the premier city of France and one of the leading cultural and intellectual centers of the world. In the 20th century it was host to numerous artistic and literary movements and the site of many historic events. The PARIS PEACE CONFERENCE (1919), attended by international leaders and diplomats, formally ended WORLD WAR I and shaped the postwar world. Between the two world wars, Paris was home to many famous expatriate writers, among them Ernest HEMINGWAY and James JOYCE. Such literary and artistic movements as CUBISM and SURREALISM flourished here. The city's cafes and salons attracted painters, poets, philosophers, filmmakers, actors and other creative personalities. Paris life darkened during WORLD WAR II, when the city was occupied by the Germans (1940–44). However, Paris survived the war with only minor damage. It was never bombed, and it escaped destruction when German officers disobeyed HITLER's order to burn the city as the Allies advanced toward it in the summer of 1944. NATO headquarters was located here from 1950 to 1967, when French president DE GAULLE withdrew France from the organization. The city saw tumult during the PARIS STUDENT DEMONSTRATIONS (1968) that challenged the authority of the French government, and the city has seen occasional acts of international terrorism. Less violent but no less vociferous controversies over architectural and cultural matters have been a familiar feature of Parisian life in the late 20th century—the outcry over the futuristic designs of the POMPIDOU CENTER and the La Defense building complex, the debate over the artistic control of the new Bastille Opera house. Despite new construction, encroaching commercialism and the high cost of living, Paris remains, as Hemingway once called it, "a moveable feast."

Paris de Bollardiere, Jacques Marie Roch Andre (1907–1986). French pacifist. He was a hero of the French RESISTANCE during WORLD WAR II who became a general in the French army. He caused an uproar in 1957, when he asked to be relieved of his command in ALGERIA to protest the torture of Algerian rebels. In 1961 he retired from active duty and began to emerge as an outspoken pacifist. His participation in a 1973 protest expedition to France's South Pacific nuclear testing site of Mururoa led to his being struck from the French army reserve list.

Parish, Mrs. Henry (Sister) II (1910–). Leading American interior decorator best known for the development of an informal or casual style in large and often elaborate residential projects. Parish (widely known by the familiar "Sister," as she was called by her family) began practice in 1933 without formal training, taking on projects for friends and, as her reputation grew, for many wealthy and well-known clients. Her style was eclectic, her rooms comfortably cluttered with a profusion of antiques and accessories. During the 1960s she took on the redecoration of the White House for the KENNEDYS, working toward historic restoration with the use of appropriate antiques and decorative elements. Since 1962, Mrs. Parish has continued in practice, with Albert Hadley as a partner, in the firm of Parish-Hadley Associates, Inc.

Paris Peace Accord (1973). A cease-fire agreement intended to end the VIETNAM WAR. The pact was formally signed on January 27, 1973, by representatives of the four parties directly involved in the conflict—the U.S., North Vietnam, South Vietnam and the VIET CONG. The battlefield truce went into effect at 8 A.M., January 28, Saigon time. The pact also called for the withdrawal of all American troops from South Vietnam, the communist release of all U.S. PRISONERS OF WAR and a four-nation commission to police the truce. It did not provide a political solution to the conflict, but allowed North Vietnamese troops to remain in the South and called for an eventual reunification of the country "through peaceful means." The pact was worked out by U.S. national security advisor Henry KISSINGER, North

PARAGUAY

1904	Argentine-backed liberals take control from Brazilian-backed Colorado Party.
1932	Chaco War; Bolivia attempts conquest of huge jungle area with rumored oil reserves and access to navigable rivers; Paraguay holds out against an army three times the size of its own; economy is exhausted.
1935	Treaty with Bolivia; Paraguay gains territory, grants access to rivers.
1936	Army ejects liberals.
1939	War hero General Estigarribia elected; begins building state-dominated society in line with national traditions of authoritarianism.
1940	Estigarribia killed in plane crash.
1944	Paraguay allows wide activity by Axis powers, but still receives massive U.S. military aid.
1945	Declares war on Axis, just prior to end of war.
1947	Liberals revolt; thousands killed.
1954	After six presidents attempt to govern in six years, General Alfredo Stroessner seizes power; establishes brutal dictatorship.
1959	Invasion of exiles from Brazil and Argentina crushed; agreement with Japan brings settlers to forested regions.
1960	Stroessner cements ties with U.S., which aids development projects.
1961	Friendship Bridge completes first direct road link to Atlantic ports.
1973	World's largest hydroelectric project completed at Itaipu, in partnership with Brazil.
1980	Former Nicaraguan dictator Somoza, granted asylum by Stroessner, is assassinated in Asuncion; relations with Nicaragua broken off.
1987	Under pressure from Catholic Church and U.S., Stroessner relaxes martial law.
1989	Military coup overthrows Stroessner; free elections put General Rodriguez, coup leader, in power.

Vietnamese foreign minister LE DUC THO and other negotiators at the Paris peace conference over a number of months. (Kissinger and Le Duc Tho were subsequently awarded the 1973 NOBEL PRIZE for peace. The choice met with much controversy.) Kissinger and Le Duc Tho initialed the plan on January 23. That day, U.S. President Richard M. NIXON announced the end of the war, calling the peace plan "an honorable agreement." South Vietnamese president Nguyen Van THIEU simultaneously announced the pact in South Vietnam but expressed doubt about the permanence of the agreement. Many historians believe that the Paris agreement was intended solely to allow an orderly, face-saving U.S. withdrawal from VIETNAM and to create the semblance of a peaceful solution. The last American troops were withdrawn on March 29, 1973. In January 1975 the North Vietnamese launched their final offensive, capturing SAIGON and forcing South Vietnam to surrender (April 30). The North Vietnamese thus achieved the victory they had sought from the beginning of the war.

U.S. Secretary of State William P. Rogers signs the agreement ending the Vietnam War at the Hotel Majestic in Paris (Jan. 27, 1973).

David Lloyd George, Vittorio Orlando, Georges Clemenceau and Woodrow Wilson in front of the Hotel Crillon, during the Paris Peace Conference (May 27, 1919).

Paris Peace Conference. Multi-national post-WORLD WAR I congress held by the victorious countries, 27 in all, led by the "Big Four"—Great Britain's LLOYD GEORGE, France's CLEMENCEAU, Italy's Orlando and the U.S.'s WILSON. It convened on January 18, 1919 and held its last session on January 16, 1920. The results of this often tumultuous and conflict-ridden conference were embodied in a number of treaties that officially terminated the war and fixed postwar settlement terms for each of the defeated nations. They were the VERSAILLES TREATY (Germany), St. Germain (Austria), Neuilly (Bulgaria), Trianon (Hungary) and SEVRES (Turkey). The most significant of these, the Versailles Treaty of May 1919, forced Germany to admit its guilt in the war; severely limited German rearmament; ceded territory (Alsace and Lorraine restored to France, Prussian Poland and a majority of West Prussia to Poland); provided for many of the reparations demanded by France; placed the Saar and the Rhineland under allied occupation and called for a number of plebiscites in freed territories. The Paris Peace Conference largely rejected Woodrow Wilson's FOURTEEN POINTS, but it did accept his proposed LEAGUE OF NATIONS, which was officially approved in April 1919. The conference was marred by the squabbling of countries that sought their own national goals rather than a reasoned consensus and by the forced lack of participation of the defeated powers, who came to bitterly resent terms that were not agreed upon by all the parties but dictated by the victors to the vanquished.

Paris Peace Treaties. Post–WORLD WAR II treaties signed in Paris on February 10, 1947, between the Allies and the principal European supporters of Germany. They were the result of a 21-nation Allied conference that began in July 1946. In separate documents, treaties were signed between the Allies and Italy, Rumania, Hungary, Bulgaria and Finland. Terms of the treaties included the ceding of some territory by Italy, Finland and Hungary, colonial losses by Italy, the creation of Trieste as a free city and various border agreements. These terms were not harsh, largely because the nations involved had made separate peace agreements with the Allies and had opposed Germany by the time WORLD WAR II ended.

Paris student demonstrations. Protest demonstrations held by French students in the spring of 1968 to protest the government's large expenditure on the military and lack of funding for education and social programs and to demand curriculum reform. A massed group of students demonstrated on the Left Bank on May 2 and was attacked by police. Rioting ensued, with the students supported by workers, who staged the longest general strike in French history. The ferment did not cease until late June and almost destroyed the Gaullist government and the Fifth Republic. As a result of the demonstrations, the students were promised reforms and the workers were given a large pay increase.

Park Chung Hee (1917–1979). Korean general and politician; president of SOUTH KOREA (1963–79). Park began his military career in the Japanese army in WORLD WAR II. At the war's end he joined the South Korean army. Rising to major general, in 1961 he led a coup that deposed the South Korean government. Park was elected president in 1963 and pursued a successful policy of economic modernization. However, intolerant of any dissent, he declared martial law in 1971 and imprisoned opposition leaders. A failed assassination attempt in 1974 killed his wife. In 1979 he was assassinated by the head of the Korean Central Intelligence Agency during a meeting.

Parker, Bonnie. See BONNIE AND CLYDE.

Parker, Charlie "Bird" (1920–1955). American alto saxophonist. Charlie Parker is a prime exemplar of the archetypal and inspired jazz virtuoso. His advanced technique, soaring sound and constant quest for extending jazzdom's basic theme-and-variation approach led him to the sophisticated, post–World War II style best known as BEBOP. Parker's musical roots were in Kansas City, whose easy-going, bluesy swing was based on slightly altered repetitions of "riffs," or motifs. His unique contribution came with his capacity to invent ever new and complex motivic variations at innovatively brisk tempos; also significant was his ability to swing with a freeflowing yet insistent momentum. Indeed, throughout the 1950s, Parker's transcendent solo style became the benchmark against which other improvisors were measured.

Historically, Parker and his fellow boppers are pivotal because of their role in transforming jazz from an essentially popular, big band dance music to a small group affair in which inspired, sound-of-surprise virtuosity became the prime value. Parker also contributed to the repertory of jazz standards with "Ornithology," "Now's the Time" and "Scrapple from the Apple." In the conformist postwar period of the late 1940s–50s, Parker became a major cult figure, a larger-than-life icon whose genius was seen as expressed not only in his music, but also in an unorthodox and tragic lifestyle influenced by drug and alcohol addiction. Parker's story is the subject of two important films, the documentary *Celebrating Bird* (1987) by Gary Giddins, and Clint EASTWOOD's docu-drama feature, *Bird* (1988).

For further reading:

Giddins, Gary, *Celebrating Bird: The Triumph of Charlie Parker*. New York: William Morrow, 1987.

Charlie Parker warming up before performing at the International Jazz Festival in Paris in 1949.

Parker, Dorothy [born Dorothy Rothschild] (1893–1967). American poet, short story writer and one of the outstanding satirists and wits of her generation. While working as the drama critic for *Vanity Fair* magazine (1917–20) and theater critic/book reviewer for The NEW YORKER (1927–33), she became a legendary figure in the New York literary scene, noted for her acid quips and wry comebacks. A member of the famous Round Table of wits at the Algonquin Hotel during the 1920s and '30s, she soon established a reputation for plangent lyrics and ironic short stories, all beautifully crafted literary miniatures. Among her poetry collections are *Enough Rope* (1926), *Death and Taxes* (1931) and *Deep as a Well* (1936). Her short story collections include *Laments for the Living* (1930) and *After Such Pleasures* (1933), which contains "Big Blonde," her single most famous story. Parker was also a playwright, screenwriter and correspondent. Her *Collected Stories* were published in 1942, the *Collected Poetry* in 1944.

For further reading:

Douglas, George H., *Women of the Twenties*. Saybrook, N.Y.: Saybrook Publishing Co., 1989.

Frewin, Leslie, *The Late Mrs. Dorothy Parker*. New York: Macmillan, 1986.

Meade, Marion, *Dorothy Parker: What Fresh Hell Is This?* New York: Random House, 1987.

Parker v. Brown (1942). U.S. Supreme Court decision upholding a California marketing scheme for raisin producers. Although individual states may regulate the sale of food and other products within the state, they may generally not regulate in a way that fixes prices or that unfairly discriminates against out-of-state products. In this case, the Supreme Court approved California's raisin marketing scheme, which seemed to illegally fix raisin prices charged by in-state producers. The Court reasoned that some types of state regulation are valid even if they do result in some price-fixing.

Parks, Gordon (1912–). American photographer and filmmaker. After working as a photographer for the Farm Security Administration and for Standard Oil, Parks worked as a staff photographer for *Life* magazine from 1948 to 1968. In 1969, he directed the film based on his novel *The Learning Tree*, and in 1971 he began making his *Shaft* detective films, making him the first black director of major Hollywood releases.

Parks, Rosa. See MONTGOMERY BUS BOYCOTT.

Parra, Nicanor (1914–). Chilean poet. Educated at the University of Chile, Brown and Oxford, Parra has had a career as a teacher of mathematics and physics. His first book was *Cancionero sin nombre* (1937), but he achieved his fame with *Poemas y antipoemas* (1954), which has been translated both as *Antipoems* (1960) and *Poems and Antipoems* (1967). As an "antipoet"—a freewheeling iconoclast who seeks to deflate the intellectual pretensions of poetry as a form—Parra's influence and stature in Chilean letters are second only to Pablo NERUDA, his collaborator for the prose work *Discuros* (1962). His *Obra gruesa* (1969) has also been translated as *Emergency Poems* (1972).

Parri, Ferruccio (1889–1981). Italian politician. During the 1930s Parri played a leading role in the underground opposition to Benito MUSSOLINI. He later led the largest Italian partisan group in the guerrilla war against German occupation at the end of WORLD WAR II. He founded the short-lived Action Party and was named premier of ITALY in June 1945. His six-party coalition lasted only five months before two of the groups withdrew in protest over his plan to dismantle some large corporations. He was later a founding member of the Italian Republican Party. In 1963, as an independent leftist, he was appointed senator for life.

Parrish, (Frederick) Maxfield (1870–1966). American painter known for his murals and commercial illustrations. "The work of no American artist," writes Coy Ludwig, "was . . . more familiar in the United States during the first three decades of this century than that of Maxfield Parrish." Born in Philadelphia, Parrish traveled widely during his youth and received artistic encouragement from his father, entering the Pennsylvania Academy of Fine Arts in 1892. From his studio, "The Oaks," in New Hampshire he took advantage of the flourishing print media of the day. Around the turn of the century he began producing the numerous book illustrations, calendars and posters that quickly established him as one of America's most prominent illustrators. His most famous book illustrations include those for Kenneth Grahame's *Dream Days* (1900), Eugene Field's *Poems of Childhood* (1904) and *The Arabian Nights* (1907). He regularly worked for such major magazines as *Harper's Weekly*, *Scribner's Magazine* and *Collier's*. His elegant whimsies contributed to the advertising of products such as Jello-O, Fisk tires and General Electric Mazda Lamps.

Parrish also dominated the art-print market. *Garden of Allah* (1918) and *Daybreak* (1922), for example, made him, as reported by TIME magazine in 1936, one of the three most popular artists in the world (with Van Gogh and Cezanne). His extraordinary murals, including the 18 panels he painted for the Curtis Publishing Company in Philadelphia, are among his most significant achievements. His work is distinguished by monumental, draped figures, Greco-Roman architectural elements—particularly pillars—luminous light (particularly the color blue) and a determined theatricality that balances the graceful with the grotesque. "My theory is that you should use all the objects of nature . . . as stage properties on which to hang your idea." He worked until his 91st year, when arthritis forced him to lay aside his brushes.

For further reading:

Ludwig, Coy, *Maxfield Parrish*. New York: Watson-Guptill Publications, 1973.

Parris Island. Island off the southern coast of South Carolina, U.S.A. It is the site of a U.S. Marine Corps training base, established in 1915.

Parrot's Beak. Region in southeastern CAMBODIA (Kampuchea). During the VIETNAM WAR, the North Vietnamese used the region as a military staging area for raids on SAIGON and the Mekong Delta. In April 1970 U.S. President Richard M. NIXON ordered an "incursion" into the region to destroy the North Vietnamese bases and supply lines; this operation, carried out by South Vietnamese and U.S. troops, lasted until June 30, 1970. The invasion and bombings set off renewed protests by the ANTIWAR MOVEMENT in the U.S.; one of these protests led to the KENT STATE SHOOTINGS.

Parsons, Talcott (1902–1979). American sociologist and social theorist. Parsons' 46-year teaching career at Harvard University (1927–73) helped to mold three generations of sociologists. His theory of human behavior, once described as "vast and tangled, a veritable jungle of fine distinctions and intertwining classifications," was not fully understood by many sociologists.

Parti Quebecois (Canada). Separatist political party in the province of Quebec, CANADA. The Parti Quebecois (or PQ) rose to power in Quebec in the 1970s behind its energetic leader, Rene LEVESQUE. The separatist movement had gained momentum and some credibility when Charles DeGaulle, president of France, announced "Vive Quebec Libre" during a visit to Montreal. However, once in power the party's referendums to begin negotiations to secede from Canada were twice rejected by provincial voters, and the party lost the next election to the Liberals. A newer generation of PQ separatists may prevail where the older generation failed, because of voter disappointment with the rejection of the so-called Meach Lake agreement that would have given Quebec a special status within the Canadian federation.

Partisan Review. American literary quarterly, founded in 1934. The *Partisan Review* has long been one of the leading "little magazines" of America, but it exercised an especially great influence from the 1930s to the 1950s, when its liberal-to-left political viewpoints and its combination of sociological analysis and literary criticism made it an intellectual focal point. Coedited by Philip Rahv for over 30 years, its leading writers included critic Lionel TRILLING, poets Randall JARRELL and Delmore SCHWARTZ, and fiction writer Saul BELLOW.

Partisans. Armed bands offering resistance behind enemy lines. The term is particularly applied to Tito's communist guerrillas in YUGOSLAVIA during WORLD WAR II. (See also WORLD WAR II IN THE BALKANS.)

Partsalides, Dimitrios (1901–1980). Greek politician. Born in the Turkish port of Trabzon, Partsalides went to GREECE as a refugee after the GRECO-TURKISH WAR OF 1921–22. He became involved in the Greek communist movement in the 1930s. During the GREEK CIVIL WAR (1946–49) he was designated prime minister by the communist insurgent movement but never actually held the post.

Pascin, Jules [born Julius Pincas] (1885–1930). American painter. Born in Vidin, Bulgaria, Pascin first became known for the sketches he did around 1903 for Munich's satirical newspaper *Simplicissimus.* He moved to Paris in 1905, settled in the U.S. and became a citizen in 1914. Pascin traveled widely and was a well-known bohemian figure in Paris, where he again settled in 1922 and where he committed suicide eight years later. He was a splendid draftsman, and his sensuous paintings have an elegant line and pastel tonality. Among his characteristic works are *Young Woman in Red* (1924, Musee d'Art Moderne, Paris) and *Ginette and Mireille* (1929, Petit Palais, Paris). Pascin was also a talented printmaker and book illustrator.

Pasic, Nikola (1845–1926). Serbian statesman. He was trained as an engineer but soon turned to politics and was elected to the Serbian parliament in 1878. That year he formed the Serbian Radical Party, a group dedicated to the creation of a greater Serbia, which he headed for the rest of his life. Exiled from 1883 to 1889, he returned and became premier of Serbia in 1891, the first of many times he was to serve in that office. He was extremely powerful in Serbia during the years preceding WORLD WAR I and led the country throughout it. After the 1917 overthrow of the Russian monarchy, which he had supported, Pasic negotiated the formation of the Kingdom of the Serbs, Croats and Slovenes (later YUGOSLAVIA). A delegate at the PARIS PEACE CONFERENCE, he was the increasingly conservative premier of Yugoslavia during most of the years from 1921 until his death.

Pasolini, Pier Paolo (1922–1975). Italian director and writer. Often controversial, Pasolini was a gifted film director and writer who focused on the seamier side of life and used nonprofessionals to play his characters. He published his first novel, *Ragazzi di vita* (*Children of Light*), in 1954 and wrote his first screenplay, for *Woman of the River,* in 1955. In 1961 he directed his first film, *Accattone.* International acclaim came with his award-winning film *The Gospel According to St. Matthew* (1964). Pasolini's evocation of the sensuality and richness of the medieval world was seen in *The Decameron* (1971), *The Canterbury Tales* (1972), and *The Arabian Nights* (1974). He was murdered in 1975.

An American officer and a French partisan during World War II (1944).

For further reading:
Friedrich, Pia, *Pier Paolo Pasolini.* Boston: G.K. Hall, 1982

Passchendaele. Village situated on a ridge eight miles east of the Flemish town of Ypres in southwestern Belgium. It was the farthest point reached by British and Canadian troops in the third Battle of YPRES (July–November, 1917). Troops under the command of General Douglas HAIG seeking to advance into Belgium managed to capture only the village and ridge, a total gain of 5 miles. This campaign, in which Germany used mustard gas for the first time, cost Allied forces a staggering 300,000 casualties and was the summit of the war's horrors for the British and Canadians. Germany suffered approximately 260,000 dead and wounded. Bloody and fruitless as it proved to be, the fighting at Passchendaele did divert German attention from the beleagured French forces and helped to prevent a German victory. (See also WORLD WAR I.)
For further reading:
Paschall, Rod, *The Defeat of Imperial Germany: 1917–1918.* Chapel Hill, N.C.: Algonquin Books, 1989.
Slowe, Peter, *Fields of Death: Battle Scenes of the First World War.* Phoenix, Az.: Phoenix Books, 1990.

Passero, Cape. Cape in southeastern Sicily where British forces landed on July 10, 1943, at the beginning of the Allied invasion of Sicily during WORLD WAR II.

Pass Laws. Legislation in SOUTH AFRICA requiring black South Africans to carry passbooks (internal passports) at all times. Instituted in the 1950s, the laws severely restricted blacks' freedom of movement and were a source of black discontent. The pass laws were repealed in 1986.

Pasternak, Boris (1890–1960). Russian poet and novelist widely acknowledged as one of the greatest Russian writers of the 20th century. The son of the noted portrait painter Leonid Pasternak and his wife, pianist Rosa Pasternak, Pasternak grew up in a comfortable Moscow household. His parents entertained such famous figures as Leo Tolstoy, Rainer Maria RILKE and Aleksandr SCRIABIN, who made a lasting impression on the young Pasternak. Educated in Russia and at Heidelberg, he studied art, music and philosophy before turning to literature. His first collection of poetry was *A Twin in the Clouds* (1914), but it was his third volume, *Sister, My Life* (1922), that established his reputation, which he was to maintain with many subsequent poetic works. Pasternak experienced the RUSSIAN REVOLUTION as an observer rather than as a participant, and for most of his life he remained as apolitical as he was prudent. During the 1920s and into the early '30s he received official approval to go with his critical acclaim. However, following differences with Joseph STALIN in the mid-1930s, Pasternak was unable to publish his own work for several years. (Stalin's apparent respect for and fear of Pasternak, whom he could have easily destroyed, remains one of the fascinating mysteries of the Soviet dictator's behavior.) During this time he occupied himself with translating the works of Shakespeare, Shelley and others into Russian. Sometime after WORLD WAR II Pasternak began writing the work for which he is best known in the West, the novel DOCTOR ZHIVAGO. The manuscript was smuggled into Italy for publication in 1957. Awarded the NOBEL PRIZE for literature in 1958, Pasternak was denounced by the Soviet government and forced to refuse the award. *Doctor Zhivago* remained unpublished in the U.S.S.R. until 1987. Yevgeny Pasternak, the author's son, accepted his father's Nobel Prize medal at a ceremony in Stockholm on December 10, 1989. Among Pasternak's other books is *Safe Conduct* (1931).
For further reading:
Fleishman, Lazar, *The Poet and His Politics.* Harvard University Press, 1990.
Barnes, Christopher, *A Literary Biography, Vol I, 1890–1928.* New York: Cambridge University Press, 1990.

Boris Pasternak, one of Russia's greatest literary figures, was forced to renounce the Nobel Prize.

Pastrone, Giovanni (1883–1959). Italian motion picture pioneer, director and producer at the turn of the century. Born in Montechiaro d'Asti, he began his film career in one of Italy's first studios, Rossi (later ITALA FILMS), in Turin. Quickly he distinguished himself as both a studio manager and a filmmaker. He created a chain of movie theaters throughout Italy to show the Itala product; and with his one-reel *La caduta di Troia* (*The Fall of Troy*) displayed the traits that would make him world famous—a flair for spectacle and skill at handling crowds. His most important film was the feature-length *Cabiria* (1914), a landmark mixture of historical spectacle and revolutionary camera work that had an enormous impact upon the epic ambitions of American director D.W. GRIFFITH. Made under the nominal imprimatur of esteemed Italian playwright Gabriele D'ANNUNZIO, it established Italy as the dominant country in film production at the time. Its central character, the strongman "Maciste" (Bartolomei Pagano), starred in several subsequent Pastrone-directed vehicles. Under the pseudonym "Piero Fosco" he also directed several intimate chamber dramas, including *Hedda Gabler* (1919). He was Italy's first great impresario/filmmaker. Today he is less well-known for his technical innovations, which included camera supports and projection lamps. He left Itala Films in 1919 and retired from the business, devoting the rest of his life to medical research.
For further reading:
Weinberg, Herman G., ed., *Fifty Years of Italian Cinema.* Rome: Carlo Bestetti, 1954.

Patasse, Ange (1937–). Prime minister (1976–78) of the Central African Empire under Emperor BOKASSA. Patasse held a variety of cabinet posts from 1965 until he became prime minister in 1976. Ousted in July 1978, he formed an opposition council in exile in Paris. He later opposed President Kolinba and was again forced into exile. (See also CENTRAL AFRICAN REPUBLIC.)

Pathet Lao. Communist guerrilla movement in LAOS. From 1954 to 1973 the Pathet Lao were involved in a civil war against pro-American, royalist army officers. Following the ceasefire of 1973 a royalist-communist coalition government held office until the communist victory in VIETNAM (1975) led to a complete communist takeover of Laos.

Pathfinder. A long-range bombing system developed and used during WORLD WAR II. (See also Edwin Francis LAKER.)

Paton, Alan (Stewart) (1903–1988). South African author. Paton was educated as a physicist and mathematician at the University of Natal and subsequently taught at various South African institutions. Paton established his reputation with his first and best-known novel, CRY, THE BELOVED COUNTRY (1948; filmed 1951), which was an early and eloquent plea for racial equality in SOUTH AFRICA. This was followed by *Too Late the Phalarope* (1953, adapted as a play, 1965), another successful social commentary in which a young, white South African is imprisoned because of his love affair with a black woman. Paton wrote many works of nonfiction, including *The Land and People of South Africa* (1955) and the autobiography *Towards the Mountain* (1980), before his next novel, *Ah, But Your Land Is Beautiful,* appeared in 1981. The novel, which depicts the beginning of the antiapartheid movement, includes details about the Liberal Party of South Africa, of which Paton was founder and president from 1958 to 1968, when it was banned. A second volume of autobiography, *Journey Continued,* was published in 1988.

Patsayev, Viktor (1933–1971). Soviet cosmonaut. Patsayev served as test-engineer on the ill-fated Soyuz 11/Salyut 1 mission. After an exciting 23–day mission aboard the new space station, the Soviet space program seemed to be up and running after years of frustration. But a valve in the crew's SOYUZ reentry capsule leaked during descent, sucking the atmosphere out of the cabin almost instantly. Patsayev and fellow cosmonauts Georgy

DOBROVOLSKY and Vladislav VOLKOV were all dead when rescuers rushed to open the spacecraft at its landing site on the Russian steppe.

Patterson, Floyd (1935–). American boxer. In 1952, Patterson won an Olympic gold medal as a heavyweight. He then turned professional and began the three-year climb that would lead to a shot at the title left open by Rocky MARCIANO's retirement. He took the title in 1956 and successfully defended it until a 1959 loss to Ingemar Johansson of Sweden. The following year, Patterson became the first man ever to retake the title as he defeated Johansson in a rematch. He lost the title for the last time to Sonny Liston in 1962 but continued to fight until he was defeated by Muhammad ALI in 1972.

Patterson, William A. (1899–1980). American pioneer in the commercial aviation industry. Patterson was the first president of United Airlines (1934–66) and helped build the company into what at the time was the world's largest private airline. He introduced a number of major innovations that transformed passenger flying from a hazardous adventure into a routine occurrence. In the 1930s he introduced the use of female flight attendants and guaranteed monthly pay for pilots. In the 1950s he made United the first airline to commit itself to the jet aircraft.

Patton, George S(mith), Jr. (1885–1945). American general noted for his exploits during WORLD WAR II. Born into a distinguished military family in San Gabriel, California, he attended West Point, was commissioned in 1909 and commanded a tank brigade in France during WORLD WAR I. A swashbuckling figure and daring tactician, he became a master of armored warfare. During World War II he was a corps commander (1942–43) in the invasions of North Africa and Sicily. As commander of the 3rd Army (1944–45) after the invasion of NORMANDY, Patton spearheaded the brilliant sweep of American troops from Normandy, through France and into Germany. He was instrumental in stopping the German offensive in the battle of the BULGE (December 1944–January 1945) and relieving the besieged American troops at BASTOGNE. He later sped across the Rhine, through Germany and into Czechoslovakia. Briefly military governor of Bavaria at the end of the war, he headed the 15th Army in 1945 but was fatally injured in an automobile accident soon after his appointment. Patton's brilliant record was somewhat marred by a much-publicized incident in which he slapped a combat-weary soldier during a hospital visit, an incident for which he later apologized. His unfavorable views on the U.S.S.R., then a U.S. ally, were also outspoken and controversial. Patton's memoirs, *War as I Knew It,* were published posthumously in 1947; his wartime service was later the basis of the motion picture *Patton* (1970).

Gen. George Patton.

For further reading:

Blumenson, Martin, *Patton: The Man Behind the Legend—1885–1945.* New York: William Morrow, 1985.

Farago, Ladislas, *Patton: Ordeal and Triumph.* New York: Astor-Honor, 1964.

———, *The Last Days of Patton.* New York: Berkley, 1986.

Peifer, Charles, Jr., *Soldier of Destiny: A Biography of George Patton.* Minneapolis, Minnesota: Dillon Press, 1988.

Wallace, Brenton G., *Patton and His Third Army.* Westport, Conn.: Greenwood, 1979.

Paul VI, Pope [born Giovanni Montini] (1897–1978). Pontiff of the Roman Catholic Church. Montini was born in Concesio, Italy, the son of a member of the Italian parliament who also edited a Catholic newspaper. Ordained as a priest in 1920, he was papal secretary of state from 1924 to 1954 and was subsequently named Archbishop of Milan. In 1958 he became a cardinal. Montini—taking the name Paul VI—succeeded Pope JOHN XXIII in June 1963 and oversaw the final work of the ecumenical SECOND VATICAN COUNCIL that had been initiated by his papal predecessor. Paul VI broke with historical tradition by becoming the first pope to travel to non-European nations—including visits to Israel and India in 1964, the UNITED NATIONS headquarters in New York City in 1965, a tour of Latin America in 1968 and missions to Uganda in 1969 and Australia and the Philippines in 1970. As to matters of dogma, Paul VI was conservative on the controversial issue of birth control but advocated a liberalized usage of the vernacular in church ritual. He died of a heart attack in 1978.

Paul, Robert William (1869–1943). Pioneering British motion picture director, producer and inventor at the turn of the century. Born in Highbury, England, he studied engineering. Learning about the Edison recording and peep-show devices (the Kinetoscope and Kinematograph) used in America, he devised similar machines himself—the first such machines in England. A year later, in collaboration with Great Britain's first cameraman, Birt Acres, he began experimenting and filming actualities and music hall acts. The effects of fast, slow and reverse motion, he claimed, were inspired in part from a novel by his friend H.G. WELLS, *The Time Machine.* By 1895 Paul was making short films in the first British film studio, located in North London, and projecting them in music halls with his own patented Theatrographe (later renamed the Animatographe). *The Twins' Tea Party* (1897) contains an early use of the close-up. A trick film called *The Motorist* (1905) has a simple plot where, in Paul's words, a motor-car eludes a pursuing policeman by climbing up the side of a house and "goes motoring right across the clouds, makes a friendly call on the sun. . . then resumes its cloudy journey, and reaches the planet Saturn." He made his last film, *The Butterfly,* in 1910 and then, disinterested in the growing sophistication of story films, retired from the business and spent his remaining years in instrument making.

Linus Pauling delivering a statement at the "Hiroshima Peace Summit" on Aug. 6, 1986.

For further reading:

Chanan, Michael, *The Dream That Kicks: The Prehistory and Early Years of Cinema in Britain.* London: Routledge and Kegan Paul, 1980.

Pauli, Wolfgang (1900–1958). Austrian-Swiss physicist; educated at the University of Munich, where he obtained his Ph.D. in 1922. After further study in Copenhagen with Niels BOHR and at Gottingen with Max BORN, Pauli taught at Heidelberg before accepting the professorship of physics at the Federal Institute of Technology, Zurich. Apart from the war years, which he spent in the U.S. at the Institute of Advanced Studies, Princeton, Pauli remained at Zurich until his death and was respected for his deep insight into the newly emerging quantum theory. His initial reputation was made in relativity theory with his publication in 1921 of his *Relativitatstheorie.* His name is mainly linked with two substantial achievements. The first, formulated in 1924, is known as the "Pauli exclusion principle." It follows from this that as an electron can spin in only two ways, each quantum orbit can hold no more than two electrons. Once both vacancies are full, further electrons can fit only into other orbits. With this principle the distribution of orbital electrons at last became clear, that is, it could be explained and predicted in purely quantum terms. For his introduction of the exclusion principle, Pauli was awarded the 1945 NOBEL PRIZE for physics. Pauli's second great insight was in resolving a problem in beta decay—a type of radioactivity in which electrons are emitted by the atomic nucleus.

Pauling, Linus (Carl) (1901–). American chemist. Born in Portland, Oregon, he attended Oregon State Agricultural College and received a Ph.D. from the California Institute of Technology in 1925, teaching there until 1964. His early research dealt with the nature of chemical bonding and molecular structure, as he applied the quantum theory to chemistry. His ideas were published in the landmark scientific study *The Nature of the Chemical Bond* (1939). Pauling also conducted research on biological molecules. In 1940 he and Max DELBRUCK introduced a molecular-based theory of antibody-antigen reactions, and later that decade he did extensive studies of sickle cell anemia. Using magnetic measurements, he studied the hemoglobin molecule, work that later led to extensive explorations of the helical structure of proteins conducted with R.B. Corey. In 1954 Pauling was awarded the NOBEL PRIZE for chemistry in recognition of his work on chemical bonding. After WORLD WAR II, he became increasingly concerned with the dangers of radioactivity and nuclear testing, and actively campaigned against the U.S. testing program. He has also been a committed and vocal proponent of world disarmament and international peace, concerns he expressed in *No More War* (1958). He became one of the few individuals to win two Nobel Prizes when he was awarded the Nobel Prize for peace in 1962. In the 1960s Pauling developed an interest in the biological effects of large doses of vitamin C, advocating its use in preventing the common cold. He continued to conduct research on vitamin theory throughout the 1970s.

Pavarotti, Luciano (1935–). Italian tenor; one of the greatest bel canto singers of this century and perhaps the most popular tenor since Enrico CARUSO. Pavarotti was born in Modena and was originally a school teacher. After winning the first prize in the Concorso Internationale in Reggio Emilia, Pavarotti debuted in that city as Rodolfo in PUCCINI's *La Boheme*, a role that is one of his finest. He made his first appearance at Covent Garden in the same part in 1963 and at the Metropolitan Opera in 1968. His performances in the 1960s and '70s opposite soprano Joan SUTHERLAND were especially memorable. Specializing in the great lyric tenor roles, he is a featured singer at the Met, at La Scala and at many other major opera houses throughout the world. Among his other notable roles are Edgardo in *Lucia di Lammermoor*, Nemorino in *L'Elisir d'Amore*, Tonio in *The Daughter of the Regiment*, the duke in *Rigoletto* and Riccardo in *Un Ballo in Maschera*. A romantic leading man despite his considerable bulk and his wooden acting, Pavarotti is known as "the King of the High Cs." He is an enormously popular figure, with legions of loyal fans even among the non-operagoing public, and has starred in numer-

Luciano Pavarotti performing in Donizetti's L'Elisir d'Amore *at London's Royal Opera House in March 1990.*

ous television specials. In addition to singing in many opera recordings, he has also made solo albums featuring operatic selections, Neapolitan songs and Christmas music. Some critics have questioned his taste and dismissed his many galas and television extravaganzas as contrived media events. Nonetheless, Pavarotti has been almost universally acclaimed for the lyrical purity of his voice and the stylistic verve of his performances.

Pavese, Cesare (1908–1950). Italian novelist, poet, translator, editor. Pavese was educated in Turin; he graduated in 1930 with a thesis on Walt Whitman, whose influence was evident in *Lavorare stanca* (1936, *Hard Labor*). After 1933 he was an editor and reader for a publishing house. In 1935 he was imprisoned by the fascists; confinement and solitude were prominent themes in his work. His first novel, *Paesi tuoi* (1941, *Your Country*) portrayed Piedmontese peasants, whereas his second, *La spiaggia* (1942, *The Beach*), was a portrait of the bourgeois Italian Riviera reminiscent of F. Scott FITZGERALD. His best novel was *La luna e ifalo* (1950, *The Moon and the Bonfires*). His work reflects a transitional age as the rural Italian countryside gives way to modern technological urbanism. He translated his favorite book, *Moby-Dick*, as well as works by John STEINBECK, James JOYCE and Gertrude STEIN. Not long after his receipt of the prestigious Strega Prize, he committed suicide in a Turin hotel room. Many of his writings were published posthumously.

For further reading:

Lajolo, Davide, *An Absurd Vice: A Biography of Cesare Pavese*. Newton, N.J.: New Directions, 1983.

O'Healy, Anne-Marie, *Cesare Pavese*. Boston: G.K. Hall, 1988.

Pavlov, Ivan Petrovich (1849–1936). Russian physiologist; discoverer of the conditioned reflex. In 1870, Pavlov entered the University of St. Petersburg (now Leningrad), where he studied chemistry and animal physiology. In 1883, he received his M.D. from the Medico-Chirurgical Academy, where he continued to work for virtually the rest of his life. Until 1902, Pavlov studied blood pressure and respiration in dogs and the animal's digestive system; for the latter work he received the 1904 NOBEL PRIZE for medicine or physiology. From 1902 until his death, Pavlov conducted his famous research on conditioned reflexes, a term he coined. Working again with dogs, Pavlov demonstrated that the animals had learned to associate certain stimuli (such as their attendant) with their feedings and had come to exhibit the same physiological responses to these stimuli as to the food itself. That is, the dogs demonstrated a learned, or conditioned, reflex in addition to their store of innate, or unconditioned, reflexes. Through these experiments, Pavlov believed he had established the fundamentally physiological nature of psychological phenomena, although he was never able to adequately explain the exact mechanism of the connection.

Pavlova, Anna Pavlovna (1881–1931). Russian prima ballerina. Having trained under Per Christian Johansson and Paul Gerdt at the Imperial Theater School, Pavlova danced with the Maryinsky Theater in 1899 and was made prima ballerina in 1906. In 1909 she joined DIAGHILEV's

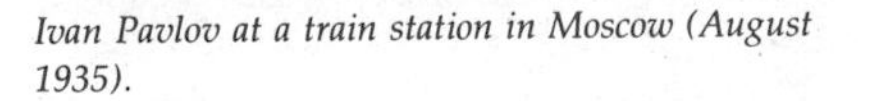

Ivan Pavlov at a train station in Moscow (August 1935).

Anna Pavlova, prima ballerina.

BALLETS RUSSES, but in 1911 she left the company after becoming a traditionalist and rejecting the innovations of Diaghilev. She settled in London, formed her own company and toured extensively with it. She is considered one of the greatest prima ballerinas of all time.

Payne, Melvin Monroe (1911–1990). U.S. scientific research director. He served as an executive director and scientific research director with the NATIONAL GEOGRAPHIC SOCIETY for 55 years and was also the society's president (1967–76) and chairman (1976–87). He was chairman of the society's committee for research and exploration (1975–89), in which he supported such research as the underwater expeditions of Jacques-Yves COUSTEAU, Louis LEAKEY's search for early man in East Africa and Jane GOODALL's study of wild chimpanzees.

Payton, Walter Jerry (1954–). American football player. One of the greatest running backs of all time, Payton initially planned on a career in music, taking up football late in high school. During his college career at Jackson State University, he scored a record 464 points in an abbreviated 3-1/2 year career. In 1975, he was drafted by the Chicago Bears, who went on to compile their first winning record in a decade. Two years later, Payton set a single-game rushing record with 275 yards, and later that year was named the league's most valuable player. He is near or at the top in all rushing categories, including touchdowns scored.

Paz, Octavio (1914–). Mexican poet, critic, essayist, diplomat. Although Paz was born and educated in Mexico City, his world travels have immersed him in many different cultural traditions. He published his first poems at the age of 17. In 1937 he visited Spain and was strongly affected by the SPANISH CIVIL WAR. In 1943–45 he traveled in the U.S. on a Guggenheim fellowship. In 1945 he met Andre BRETON and the surrealists in Paris (see SURREALISM). He entered the diplomatic service and was posted to San Francisco, New York, Paris, Tokyo, Geneva and Delhi. In the early 1970s he taught at Cambridge and Harvard. *Sun Stone* (1957) and *Blanco* (1966) are recognized as his finest poetry. His many influential prose works include *The Labyrinth of Solitude* (1950; revised 1959), *The Bow and the Lyre* (1956), *Quadrivium* (1965), *Alternating Current* (1967) and *Conjunctions and Disjunctions* (1969). Although he has left-wing sympathies, Paz has been extremely critical of the U.S.S.R. and Cuba. Paz was awarded the NOBEL PRIZE for literature in 1990.

For further reading:

Wilson, Jason, *Octavio Paz*. Boston: G.K. Hall, 1986.

Peace Corps. Independent agency of the U.S. government, established by President John F. KENNEDY in 1961. The Peace Corps sends American volunteers to third-world countries that request its services. These volunteers teach basic skills and give advice about such subjects as agriculture, engineering and nutrition. Often, volunteers directly participate in construction projects, planting and harvesting, or in the provision of medical care. Since it was founded, more than 80,000 Americans—many of them recent college graduates—have served two-year terms in the Peace Corps.

peaceful coexistence. Term referring to the state of relations between socialist and capitalist countries. At the Allied Supreme Council at Cannes in 1922 the Allies endorsed Georgy Chicherin's coexistence thesis, stating that each nation should choose its own system of government and economy. KHRUSHCHEV pursued a foreign policy of so-called peaceful coexistence, acknowledging the existence of noncommunist social systems, but believing that communism would ultimately triumph.

Octavio Paz, Mexican poet, essayist and diplomat (February 1988).

Peacock, Andrew (1939–). Australian politician. Educated at Melbourne University, Peacock entered the House of Representatives in 1966 as the Liberal member for Kooyong. He held ministerial office in the closing years of Liberal domination in the late 1960s and early 1970s and again when the LIBERAL PARTY regained power in 1975. Between 1975 and 1980 he was minister of foreign affairs. When the Liberals lost power in 1983, Peacock succeeded Malcolm FRASER as Liberal leader; in 1985 he was removed by John Howard, after a bitter party feud, but in May 1989 returned to leadership of the Liberal Party. (See also AUSTRALIA.)

Peake, Mervyn L(aurence) (1911–1968). British writer, poet and artist. Peake remains best known as a writer of Gothic fantasy literature. His most famous work is the Gormenghast trilogy—*Titus Groan* (1946), *Gormenghast* (1950) and *Titus Alone* (1959)—which recounts the memories of Titus, the aging 77th earl of Groan, as he sits in his slowly crumbling ancestral castle. Critics have rated the Gormenghast trilogy as the only serious rival, in fantasy literature, to the *Lord of the Rings* trilogy of J.R.R. TOLKIEN. Peake was born in China, the son of a British medical missionary. He was educated at Oxford. In addition to his fantasy fiction, Peake was a poet whose volumes include *The Glassblowers* (1950) and *The Rhyme of the Flying Bomb* (1962). He was also a renowned book illustrator who illustrated his own works and produced illustrated editions of *The Rime of the Ancient Mariner* by Samuel Taylor Coleridge (1943) and *Treasure Island* by Robert Louis Stevenson (1949).

Pearl Harbor, Japanese attack on (December 7, 1941). At 7:55 A.M. on Sunday, December 7, 1941, a swarm of Japanese aircraft swooped out of the sky and attacked the U.S. naval and air bases at Pearl Harbor on Oahu Island, HAWAII. This attack was a complete surprise, although tensions between the U.S. and Japan had been building up for some time (see WORLD WAR II). No one was prepared to do battle early on a Sunday morning in Hawaii, and for two hours the Japanese planes, aided by SUBMARINES and midget submarines, wreaked havoc on the U.S. fleet. Of the eight battleships present, three were sunk, another capsized and the remainder badly damaged; three cruisers, three destroyers and five other vessels were sunk or seriously damaged; and 247 planes, 175 of which were destroyed on the ground, were lost. Only 29 of the 360 Japanese planes were shot down before the rest returned to their distant aircraft carriers. About 4,500 persons were killed or wounded, including

The U.S.S. Arizona *in her death throes after the Japanese attack on Pearl Harbor (December 7, 1941).*

2,300 U.S. military personnel. The next day the U.S. Congress declared war against Japan; U.S. President Franklin D. ROOSEVELT declared that December 7, 1941, was a "day that shall live in infamy." (See also WORLD WAR II IN THE PACIFIC.)

Pears, Sir Peter (1910–1986). British tenor. Pears was a founder member of the English Opera Group and an active director of the Aldeburgh Festival, which he cofounded with Benjamin BRITTEN and Eric Crozier in 1948. Britten created some of Pears' most notable roles, in such works as *Peter Grimes, Billy Budd,* and *Death in Venice.* They were professional partners from the 1930s until the composer's death in 1976. Pears also participated in the premiers of such major nonoperatic works by Britten as the *Serenade for Tenor, Horn and Strings,* and the *War Requiem.* He was also an outstanding interpreter of music by other 20th-century British composers and of music by classical masters ranging from Heinrich Schuetz to Franz Schubert.

Pearse, Patrick Henry [Padraig Pearse] (1879–1916). Irish nationalist and revolutionary. Born in Dublin, Pearse was the son of an Englishman and an Irish woman. He was educated in law but became interested in Irish language and culture, which had been suppressed by the British. He became a schoolteacher and also edited *An Claidheamh Soluis,* the journal of the Gaelic League. In his writings, Pearse developed the idea of blood sacrifice, calling for the Irish to shed their blood in order to achieve independence from the British. In 1913 Pearse became active in the paramilitary Irish Volunteers. He directed the group during the 1916 EASTER RISING against British rule and proclaimed IRELAND's independence from the steps of the General Post Office in Dublin. After the rebellion was put down he was tried by a military court and executed. Pearse is considered a martyr and national hero by many Irish, but his romantic ideas about the necessity of violence have been widely blamed for contributing to the allure of the IRISH REPUBLICAN ARMY and for impeding a peaceful solution to the troubles of NORTHERN IRELAND.

Pearson, Drew [Andrew Russell Pearson] (1896–1969). American journalist. As a staff member of the Baltimore *Sun,* Pearson became known in 1931 for his article "The Washington Merry-Go-Round," on which he collaborated with Robert Allen. In 1932 the two started a column of the same name that specialized in exposing the private lives of public figures and unearthing government corruption. The enormously popular but not always completely accurate column was syndicated in 350 newspapers by 1942. Pearson conducted an exclusive interview with Soviet Premier Nikita KHRUSHCHEV in 1961; and Pearson's influence was manifest when his exposure of the financial misconduct of Senator Thomas DODD led to Senate hearings and Dodd's eventual censure. When Pearson died in 1969, his column was the most widely read in the U.S. He was succeeded by columnist Jack ANDERSON.

Pearson, Lester (Bowles) (1897–1972). Canadian diplomat and statesman, prime minister of CANADA (1963–68). Born in Ontario, he attended the University of Toronto and Oxford. Entering the diplomatic service, he held a variety of posts and served as ambassador to Washington (1944–46). During his tenure in the U.S., he was Canada's advisor at the conferences at DUMBARTON OAKS (1944) and San Francisco (1945), playing an important part in the establishment of the UNITED NATIONS and leading Canada's UN delegation from 1946 to 1956. Also serving as Canada's secretary of state for external affairs from 1948 to 1957, he became the first Canadian to win the NOBEL PRIZE for peace (1957) in recognition of his efforts in mediating the SUEZ CRISIS of 1956. An important figure in the COMMONWEALTH OF NATIONS, Pearson was also important in the formation of the NORTH ATLANTIC TREATY ORGANIZATION (NATO). He led the oppositon in the Canadian parliament from 1958 to 1963 and after the Liberal victory in 1963 became prime minister, serving in that office until 1968. His books include *Democracy in World Politics* (1955), *Words and Occasions* (1970) and three volumes of memoirs (1972–75).

Peart, Lord (Frederick) (1914–1988). British politician, LABOUR PARTY minister of agriculture, and leader of the House of Commons under Prime Minister Harold WILSON. During the 1970s Peart reversed his opinion and came to believe that British involvement with the COMMONWEALTH nations was less important than British participation in the EUROPEAN COMMUNITY. In 1976 he was appointed leader of the House of Lords, becoming the first parliamentarian since Benjamin Disraeli to have been leader of both houses.

Peary, Robert Edwin (1856–1920). American explorer. Peary is famous for his discovery of the North Pole in 1909. A civil engineer in the U.S. Navy by profession, Peary made his first expedition to Greenland in 1891 accompanied by Matthew Henson, who was his assistant on all his Arctic expeditions. He discovered new land and proved that Greenland is an island. He failed twice to reach the North Pole (1898–1902; 1905–06) before achieving his goal in 1909. He led 24 men who guided 19 sledges pulled by 133 dogs over 400 miles of drifting ice flows. Finally on April 6, Peary, Henson and four Eskimos reached the Pole. A later controversy over whether Frederick A. COOK had reached the Pole first was settled in Peary's favor.

For further reading:

Weems, John, *Peary: The Explorer and the Man.* Los Angeles: J.P. Tarcher, 1988.

Peasants' Union. Russian organization established in 1905 as a result of populist activity. The union demanded that land be nationalized, and that it be used only by those who till it. Its members disagreed as to whether to use peaceful or violent methods to achieve their aims, and the union disintegrated in 1906.

Pechstein, Max (1881–1955). German painter. He began his career as an apprentice to a decorative artist in 1896 and later taught art in Dresden. An Expressionist, he joined DIE BRUCKE in 1906. An interest in the exotic in art prompted him to visit the South Seas in 1913–14. A member of the Prussian Academy of Arts from 1922 to 1933, he was expelled by the Nazis, who condemned him as a "degenerate" artist and forbade exhibition of his work. Pechstein taught at the Berlin School of Fine Arts from 1945 until his death. His work is bold in color and composition, but less dramatic and more decorative than that of his fellow German Expressionists. He is also well-known for his graphics and for the stained glass and mosaics that he executed late in his career. (See also EXPRESSIONISM.)

Peckham, Rufus W. (1838–1909). Associate justice, U.S. Supreme Court (1895–1909). A native of Albany, New York, Peckham did not attend college but was privately educated. Peckham was the

Admiral Robert Peary (November 18, 1909).

product of a politically-active family and the son of a prominent judge; after admission to the bar he became a lawyer in his father's Albany law firm. Active in politics, Peckham was elected to the New York Supreme Court and next to the Court of Appeals, New York's highest court. In 1895, President Grover Cleveland, who as governor of New York had known Peckham, appointed the judge to the U.S. Supreme Court. Interestingly, Peckham's brother, Wheeler, had been nominated for the Court one year earlier but had been rejected by the Senate. On the Court Peckham proved a conservative and died while still on the Court, after 17 years of service.

Pedersen, William (1938–). American architect. Educated at the University of Minnesota and the Massachusetts Institute of Technology and a winner of the Rome Prize in Architecture, he is the chief design architect at Kohn Pedersen Fox in New York City. He is known for contextual buildings that relate strikingly to their environments, relating them to their setting and their streets, and emphasizing human and social elements in their designs. He is best known for two office high-rise buildings on Wacker Drive in Chicago and for the Cincinnati headquarters for Proctor & Gamble.

Peenemunde. Village on Usedom Island, on the Baltic Sea, at the mouth of the Peene River, in northeastern Germany. Peenemunde was a top-secret German rocket research facility during WORLD WAR II. Germany's leading rocket scientists, including Wernher von BRAUN, Walter DORNBERGER and Hermann OBERTH worked at Peenemunde developing the V-1 AND V-2 rocket bombs. An Allied bombing raid on Aug. 18, 1943, killed many scientists and set back the German rocket program. At the war's end many of the German scientists were taken to the U.S. in OPERATION PAPERCLIP. Peenemunde itself was captured by the Soviets in April 1945 and later was part of EAST GERMANY.

Peerce, Jan [Jacob Pincus Perelmuth] (1904–1984). American operatic tenor and concert performer. Born in New York City, Peerce gained his earliest musical experience singing in a synagogue choir; he also studied violin and became an accomplished performer during his teens. However, his fame came as a principal singer at RADIO CITY MUSIC HALL (1932–40) and as a singer on the radio. In 1938 he made the first of many appearances with conductor Arturo TOSCANINI when he sang the tenor solo in Beethoven's *Ninth Symphony* with the New York Philharmonic. He made his opera debut as the Duke in *Rigoletto* with the Columbia Opera Company in 1938 and his Metropolitan Opera debut as Alfredo in *La Traviata* in 1941. For the next 26 years he sang with the Met and was guest artist with major opera companies in Europe, appearing in such roles as Edgardo in *Lucia di Lammermoor* and Rodolfo in *La Boheme*. He has also appeared in films, including *Carnegie Hall* (1947) and on Broadway as Tevye in the musical *Fiddler on the Roof* (1971).

Pegler, (James) Westbrook (1894–1969). American newspaper columnist. Born in Minneapolis, Minnesota, Pegler was a working journalist by the age of 16. He wrote for the United Press for many years, then, in 1933, began writing his *New York World-Telegram* column "Fair Enough," in which he caustically attacked public figures. Ultra-conservative, Pegler lambasted Franklin D. ROOSEVELT and his NEW DEAL policies; yet he also showed his hatred for European fascists. In 1941, Pegler won a PULITZER PRIZE for his exposure of racketeering in labor unions. From 1944 to 1962 he wrote for King Features Syndicate and from 1962 to 1964 for the JOHN BIRCH SOCIETY publication *American Opinion*. In 1954, he lost a highly publicized libel case to writer Quentin Reynolds.

Peguy, Charles (Pierre) (1873–1914). French poet. Peguy, a Roman Catholic, was one of the major French poets of the first decades of this century. Raised in abject poverty, Peguy succeeded in winning academic scholarships and thereby educating himself to take a major role in French literary life. In 1900 he founded the journal *Cahiers de la Quinzane*, which became the leading French literary quarterly of its era. An ardent patriot, Peguy wrote several lengthy prose poems that combined nationalistic fervor and Catholic piety. Some of these were translated into English as *Basic Virtues* (1943) and *Men and Saints* (1944). Peguy was killed during WORLD WAR I at the Battle of the MARNE.

For further reading:
Hill, Geoffrey, *The Mystery of the Charity of Charles Peguy*. New York: Oxford University Press, 1984.

Pei, I(eoh) M(ing) (1917–). Chinese-American architect. Born in Canton, he emigrated to the U.S. in 1935, studied at the Massachusetts Institute of Technology and Harvard University, where he taught from 1945 to 1948, and became an American citizen in 1954. In 1948 he moved to New York City, where he executed a number of major projects for Webb and Knapp. In 1955 he opened his own firm. His influential works, in which buildings are sensitively integrated into their surroundings, include Mile High Center, Denver (1956); Place Ville Marie, Montreal (1963); and Kips Bay Plaza apartments, New York City (1960–65). Noted for their monumentality, simplicity and beauty, Pei's other commissions include the National Center for Atmospheric Research, Boulder (1967); two buildings at M.I.T. (1964; 1970); the Everson Museum of Art, Syracuse, New York (1968); the East Building at the National Gallery of Art, Washington, D.C. (1978); the Bank of China Building, Hong Kong; and the Fragrant Hill Hotel, Beijing. One of his best known and most controversial structures is Le Grand Louvre in Paris (1989). This set of three glass and steel pyramids, one large and two subsidiary, covers an underground visitors' center, stores and other facilities in the courtyard of the world-renowned Louvre Museum.

Pei, Mario (1901–1978). Italian-born linguist and educator. Pei, who was born in Rome, came to the U.S. as a youth and was educated at the City College of New York. A facility for languages led Pei to make the study of the history of human languages his special scholarly province. His major works include *The Story of Language* (1949), a widely read general survey, and *Words in Sheep's Clothing* (1969). Pei taught at Columbia University for over three decades and also served as a special adviser on language training for U.S. Army personnel.

Pei, Wenzhong (1904–1982). Chinese archaeologist. In 1929 he discovered the skull of Peking Man, estimated to be half a million years old. The discovery furnished the first strong evidence of man's evolution from less-advanced life forms.

Peking [Beijing]. Capital city of the People's Republic of CHINA and its political and cultural center, as well as an important industrial and financial hub. At the turn of the century, European diplomats and military forces in Peking were besieged by Chinese nationalists during the BOXER REBELLION (June-Aug. 1900). An international military force fought its way into the city to relieve the European garrison. Various rival factions gained and lost control of Peking during the civil wars that followed China's creation as a republic in (1911). The MARCO POLO BRIDGE INCIDENT (July 7, 1937) the occurred just outside the city sparked the SINO-JAPANESE WAR OF 1937–45. The communists captured Peking in January 1949, declaring victory in the CHINESE CIVIL WAR OF 1945–49. MAO TSE-TUNG'S RED GUARDS virtually controlled the capital during the CULTURAL REVOLUTION of the late 1960s and early '70s. In February 1972 U.S. President Richard M. NIXON became the first American leader to visit Peking; his meeting with Mao and Premier CHOU EN-LAI led to the establishment of formal relation between the two countries. Turmoil hit the capital again in 1989 as hundreds of thousands of students and workers in the DEMOCRACY MOVEMENT demanded political reform. These demonstrations culminated in the TIANANMEN SQUARE MASSACRE (June 3–4) and the arrest and trials of the dissident leaders.

Pele [Edson Arantes do Nascimento] (1940–). Brazilian soccer player. Considered to be the greatest soccer player ever, Pele is the only person to have played on three World Cup-winning teams (1958, 1962 and 1970). Discovered by Brito, a former Brazilian international player, Pele joined the Santos club in 1956 at 16. The following year he starred in Brazil's first World Cup triumph, scoring two goals in the final. During his career with Santos and Brazil (1956–1974), he scored 1,216 goals in 1,254 games, the highest goal scoring rate in soccer history; his 1,000th goal was scored on November 19, 1969. Pele first played for Brazil in 1957; he retired from international play following the 1970 World Cup victory having scored a record 97 goals for Brazil. He played his final club game for Santos on October 2,

Pele, whose soccer skills amazed fans throughout the world.

1974, but came out of retirement in 1975 to play for the New York Cosmos of the North American Soccer League. Pele retired on October 1, 1977, having scored 1,281 goals in 1,363 games.

Pelee, Mount. Volcano on island of MARTINIQUE in the West Indies. Mount Pelee erupted in 1902 and 1929. The 1902 eruption destroyed the entire town of Saint Pierre, along with all of its 40,000 inhabitant—except for one, a prisoner in the local jail.

Pellan, Alfred (1906–). Canadian painter. Born in Quebec, he lived in Paris from 1926 to 1940, when he returned to Canada to paint and teach. Fully versed in Europe's modernist movements, he developed a style that combined CUBISM and SURREALISM. An extremely influential figure in Canadian art, he is particularly known for his large murals in various public buildings.

Pelli, Cesar (Antonio) (1926–). American architect. Born in Argentina, he studied at the University of Illinois. He has devoted himself to a public architecture that "celebrates life," creating large buildings that have a feeling of great lightness and an inherent humanity. From 1968 to 1976 he headed the architectectural design division of Gruen Associates in California. Among the outstanding works of this period are the 1967 headquarters of Comsat in Clarksburg, Virginia and of Teledyne in Northridge, California. In 1977 he opened his own office in New Haven, Connecticut and became the chairman of the department of architecture at Yale. Among his notable later buildings are the World Financial Center, New York City, the Northwest Center, Minneapolis and the Pacific Design Center, Los Angeles.

Penderecki, Krzysztof (1933–). Polish composer. Associated with the avant-garde movement, Penderecki developed a highly individual style of composition in which he utilizes all resources of sound, such as shouting and striking the piano strings with mallets. He developed his own system of optical notation, using symbolic ideograms to indicate the desired sound. He has taught at the Superior School of Music in Cracow (1958–66), the Folkwang Hochschule fur Musik in Essen, West Germany (1966–68), and part-time at Yale University (since 1973). His best known work is *Threnody in Memory of the Victims of Hiroshima* (1959–60). Other important works include the choral-orchestral piece *The Resurrection of Christ* (1971).

Pendergast, Thomas Joseph (1872–1945). American politician and Democratic Party leader. He rose to power as a political boss in the Missouri Democratic Party after serving in various state positions. He aided in Harry TRUMAN's U.S. Senate victory (1934), but was imprisoned in 1939 after being convicted for income tax violations; his political machine collapsed.

Pendray, G. Edward (1901–1987). One of the founders of the American Interplanetary Society (later called the American Rocket Society). A science reporter for the *New York Herald Tribune*, Pendray was also a fellow member of the British Interplanetary Society, elected a few months after the society was formed in 1933. After visiting Europe in 1931 and observing the work of the German Rocket Society a month after it had successfully launched it first liquid-propellant rocket, Pendray urged the AIS to follow suit. The American Interplanetary Society launched its first liquid-propellant rocket May 14, 1933. The rocket cost a grand total of $30.60 with an additional cost of $28.80 for launch expenses. But Robert GODDARD, working independently, had already beaten the AIS to the punch and, by the time of the AIS launch, was already working on more advanced models of the liquid-propellant rocket.

Penguin Books. Penguin Books, Ltd., was founded by Allen Lane in England in 1935. American Penguin was established in 1939 with Ian Ballantine as manager. Noted for its inexpensive quality paperbacks and its focus on literary classics, American Penguin began domestic production of its books during WORLD WAR II with the help of Kent Enoch. When Ballantine left to form Bantam Books, Enoch formed a partnership with Victor Weybright and asserted American Penguin's independence from Lane's parent company, becoming the New American Library of World Literature. Lane reincorporated as Penguin Books, Inc., in 1951 in New York. Upon his death in 1970, the British Penguin was acquired by S. Pearson and Son. American Penguin acquired two-thirds of Viking Press in 1975, becoming Viking Penguin, Inc.

penicillin. Generic term for a group of antibiotic agents that were the first to be used in the treatment of bacterial infections in human beings. The effect of penicillin on bacteria was first observed by Sir Alexander FLEMING in 1929, but the substance did not become widely useful in clinical treatment until after it had been purified by various biologists, notably H.W. FLOREY and E.B. CHAIN, in 1941. Penicillin was first obtained from the *Penicillium notatum* molds observed by Fleming but is now more frequently produced from large, aerated fermentation vats of *P. chrysogenum*. Penicillin works by breaking down the walls of bacterial cells and is effective against many gram-positive bacteria. Penicillin has been used to treat syphilis, meningococcal meningitis, gas gangrene and pneumococcal pneumonia, as well as many staph and strep infections. Although some gram-negative bacteria, such as those causing gonorrhea, are susceptible to penicillin, most gram-negative infections cannot be treated by the antibiotic. However, such synthetic versions of the antibiotic as ampicillin, methicillin and oxacilin have been used against both kinds of bacteria. The use of penicillin is limited by its tendency to cause allergic reactions in some people and by the ability of a number of micro-organisms to become penicillin-resistant.

Penkovsky, Oleg (1919–1963). Soviet double agent. After serving in World War II, Penkovsky went to work for Soviet military intelligence. In 1961, he became a double agent for the West and began to pass top-secret information concerning Soviet military strategy and preparedness. His activities exposed in 1963, Penkovsky was tried by Soviet officials and sentenced to death. The information he provided is credited with helping to determine American responses to Soviet actions during the BERLIN WALL and the CUBAN MISSILE crises in the early Sixties.

Penn, Irving (1917–). American photographer. Born in Plainfield, New Jersey, Penn attended the School of Industrial Art in Philadelphia from 1934 to 1938. On the staff of *Vogue* magazine since 1943, he is best known for his dramatically stylish high fashion photography. His work has been exhibited at a number of leading museums, notably the Metropolitan Museum of Art and the Museum of Modern Art, New York City.

Penney, J(ames) C(ash) (1875–1971). American department store tycoon. Penney founded J.C. Penney Company, Inc., in 1902. The company eventually operated more than 2,000 domestic and foreign retail outlets, including 1,700 stores in the U.S.

Penney, William George (1909–1991). Creator of the British ATOMIC BOMB. A mathematician and physicist who specialized in measuring the force of explosions, Penney was sent by the British to work with the U.S. team that was assembling the world's first atomic bomb in LOS ALAMOS, N.M., in 1944. Following its use of two atomic bombs against Japan in 1945, the U.S. ended its atomic weapons research collaboration with the British in 1946. Penney returned to England, where he began from scratch to design the first British atomic bomb, successfully tested in 1952. He later became director of the British government's Atomic Weapons Research Establishment. He was made a life peer in 1967.

Penrose, Roland (1900–1984). British art patron. A champion of SURREALISM and of surrealist and other modern artists, Penrose was known for his biographies of Pablo PICASSO (1960), Joan MIRO (1970) and Man RAY (1975). He organized major expositions for the MUSEUM OF MODERN ART in New York City and the Tate Gallery in London. Penrose also founded and directed the Institute of Contemporary Art in London.

Pentagon Papers. See NEW YORK TIMES V. UNITED STATES.

Pepper, Claude (Denson) (1900–1989). American politician. A liberal Democrat from Florida, Pepper's congressional career began in the Senate, where he served from 1937 until 1951. During his Senate years, he was a close ally of President Franklin D. ROOSEVELT and a passionate advocate of such NEW DEAL programs as Social Security, health care insurance and minimum wage legislation. In 1951 he lost a bitter Democratic primary contest to a former protege who branded him "Red Pepper" for his supposedly pro-Soviet attitudes. Pepper returned to Congress in 1962, serving in the House of Representatives. In his later years he was a champion of legislation on behalf of the elderly. Shortly before his death, President George BUSH awarded him the U.S. Medal of Freedom, the nation's highest civilian award. At the time of his death he was the oldest member of the U.S. Congress. Congress voted to have his body lie in state in the Capitol Rotunda, an honor usually granted only to U.S. presidents and national heroes.

Percy, Walker (1916–1990). American author. Percy's novels portrayed the spiritual despair of upper-middle-class life in the post-World War II American South. Trained as physician and psychiatrist, he published his first book in 1961. That book, *The Moviegoer,* won him a National Book Award for Fiction. His later works included *The Thanatos Syndrome* (1987), *Love in the Ruins* (1971), *The Last Gentleman* (1966) and *The Second Coming* (1980).

Perekop, Isthmus of. Isthmus between the Crimean peninsula and the mainland of the U.S.S.R. In 1920, during the RUSSIAN CIVIL WAR, the Red Army won a major victory here over General Piotr WRANGEL and the WHITES.

Perelman, S(idney) J(oseph) (1904–1979). American humorist, author and scriptwriter. Perelman's brilliant talent for wordplay, spoofs and madcap comedy helped shape American humor in the 20th century. He wrote parts of the early MARX BROTHERS movies *Monkey Business* (1931) and *Horse Feathers* (1932). Among his other credits were numerous essays, books, and plays. He wrote the book for the 1943 Broadway musical hit *One Touch of Venus* as well as the script for the ACADEMY AWARD-winning film *Around the World in Eighty Days* (1956). He also contributed short humor pieces to THE NEW YORKER magazine.

Peres, Shimon (1923–). Israeli political leader, vice premier and foreign minister (1986–), prime minister (1984–86). Peres was born in Poland and immigrated to Palestine in 1934. He was educated at a youth village and at Tel Aviv University. During the 1948 war he was put in charge of naval supplies and then of major arms purchases. After a brief stint in the U.S. as head of an arms-purchasing mission for the Israeli Defense Ministry, he served

Shimon Peres during his term as prime minister of Israel

as its director-general (1952–59). He was deputy minister of defense from 1959 to 1965. In 1965 Peres followed his mentor, David BEN GURION, into the breakaway Rafi Party but later rejoined Labor and served as minister of communications and transport (1970–74). He was minister of defense from 1974 until Labor's 1977 election defeat. In 1984 he became prime minister in the government of national unity but handed over the post to Yitzhak SHAMIR in late 1986. Although Peres ratified the construction of further WEST BANK settlements during his term in office, his strong political overtures toward King HUSSEIN of Jordan marked a new development (expectedly curtailed by the government leadership rotation). An organization man with a flair for international public relations, Peres is renowned for his vision of ISRAEL as a technological power. He was the driving force behind the establishment of Israel's aircraft industry and its nuclear reactor in Dimona, and he is committed to the development of the country's electronics industry. Peres speaks fluent French and was the architect of the "French connection," leading to the secret pact with France and Britain before the Suez War and to Israel's acquisition of an unprecedented military arsenal. He was awarded the Legion of Honor by the French government in 1957.

perestroika [Russian for "restructuring"]. Shortly after he came to power in 1985, Soviet leader Mikhail GORBACHEV acknowledged that the U.S.S.R. faced grave economic problems. Under its traditional Marxist-Leninist policies, which emphasized central planning and control of all phases of production and distribution, the Soviet economy had stagnated. The country was burdened by a lethargic bureaucracy, inefficient state-run industries, poor quality of manufactured goods, lack of consumer products, food shortages and a generally low standard of living. Gorbachev stressed the need for wide-ranging economic reforms, some of which ran counter to the accepted Marxist-Leninist economic doctrine. These included opening the economy to market forces, allowing competition and a limited amount of private ownership. Gorbachev's program of *perestroika* was hailed in the West as a sign of movement away from the U.S.S.R.'s hard-line communist past, although Gorbachev seemed reluctant to abandon Marxist principles altogether. Given the continuing decline of the Soviet economy and the possibility of economic and political upheaval, many economists wondered whether Gorbachev's reforms would be too little and too late to revive the nation's economy. Boris YELTSIN and other reformers claimed that Gorbachev's approach was too cautious; they pushed for more radical reforms. As of early 1991, the fate of *perestroika* was uncertain.

For further reading:

Afanasiev, Yuri, *Perestroika and the Soviet Past*. New York: W.W. Norton, 1991.

Gorbachev, Mikhail S., *Perestroika: New Thinking for Our Country and the World.* New York: HarperCollins, 1988.

Kagarlitsky, Boris, *Farewell Perestroika: A Soviet Chronicle.* New York: Routledge, Chapman and Hall, 1990.

Perez Alfonzo, Juan Pablo (1904–1979). Oil minister of VENEZUELA and cofounder of the ORGANIZATION OF PETROLEUM EXPORTING COUNTRIES (OPEC). Perez drafted the revolutionary policies that led to the nationalization of the Venezuelan oil industry in 1976.

Perez de Cuellar, Javier (1920–). Peruvian diplomat, UN secretary-general (1982–). Perez de Cuellar held various posts from 1944 to 1978. He represented Peru at the UNITED NATIONS from 1971 to 1975 and was president of the Security Council in 1974. He served as undersecretary-general for special political affairs from 1979 to 1981. As secretary-general, in August 1988 he succeeded in negotiating a ceasefire between Iran and Iraq, ending the bloody IRAN-IRAQ WAR OF 1980–88. In January 1991 he went to Baghdad in a last-ditch effort to persuade Iraqi leader Saddam HUSSEIN to withdraw Iraqi forces from Kuwait by the UN deadline of January 15, 1991. Hussein rebuffed Perez, and UN coalition forces lead by the U.S. subsequently initiated OPERATION DESERT STORM against Iraq.

performance art. Art form utilizing live performance as a medium. While the term "performance art" first came to prominence in the 1960s, the cabaret performances of DADA artists in the World War I era constitute the real beginning of performance art as an accepted cultural form. Performance art views itself as a form of visual art that uses human movement and theatrical effects, as well as spoken lines and music. In the 1960s, performance art played a key role in the HAPPENINGS of the era. Performance art is often a vehicle for social protest.

Perkins, Frances (1882–1965). American public official and U.S. Secretary of Labor. As part of his NEW DEAL reform program aimed at pulling the U.S. out of the GREAT DEPRESSION, President Franklin D. ROOSEVELT envisioned a stronger role for organized labor. The president shocked many by appointing Frances Perkins as secretary of labor in 1933, the first woman to be appointed to a cabinet post. Perkins had previously served as New York state's industrial commissioner under then-Governor Roosevelt. In her influential post Perkins lobbied for strong labor legislation and oversaw the revitalization of the Department of Labor to enforce the new statutes. She served for the duration of the Roosevelt administration.

For further reading:

Mohr, Lillian H., *Frances Perkins: That Woman in FDR's Cabinet!* Croton-on-Hudson, NY: North River Press, 1979.

Perkins, Maxwell (1884–1947). Legendary American book editor. Born in New York City, he was educated at Harvard University and worked as a reporter for the *New York Times* before becoming an editor at Charles Scribner's Sons in 1910. There he became famous as an advocate of contemporary U.S. fiction. A sensitive reader with a superb ear for language and an uncanny ability to shape a brilliant but undisciplined manuscript into literature, he was important in editing and publishing the works of such eminent American writers as F. Scott FITZGERALD, Ernest HEMINGWAY, J.P. MARQUAND and Thomas WOLFE.

For further reading:

Cowley, Malcolm, *Unshaken Friend: A Profile of Maxwell Perkins.* New York: Rinehart, Roberts, 1985.

Wheelock, John H., ed., *Editor to Author: The Letters of Maxwell E. Perkins.* New York: Macmillan, 1987.

Perlman, Itzhak (1945–). Israeli-born concert violinist. Left permanently crippled from poliomyelitis at the age of four, Perlman overcame his handicap to become probably the best known violin virtuoso of his generation. After appearances on the "Ed SULLIVAN Show" (1959) and winning the Leventritt competition at CARNEGIE HALL in 1964, he performed with several orchestras, including the New York Philharmonic. Perlman toured the United States in 1965–66 and Europe in 1966–67. He has made many acclaimed recordings, often in collaboration with pianist Vladimir ASHKENAZY, violinists Isaac STERN or Pinchas Zukerman or conductor Zubin Mehta. He received a Grammy in 1978 for his album of Vivaldi's *The Four Seasons.* In addition, Perlman teaches and performs at the Aspen Music Festival in Colorado and serves on the faculty of Brooklyn College School of the Performing Arts (since 1975). He has been featured in numerous television specials.

Perls, Frederick Solomon and Laura Posner. Married couple, both German-born, who were the key founders of the psychological school of GESTALT psychotherapy. Fritz (1894?-1970) and Laura Perls (1905–1990) met as university students in Frankfurt in 1930. They left Germany in 1933 to escape the emergent Nazi rule and, after a stay in South Africa, went to the U.S. in 1948. In the late 1940s and 1950s, they combined to produce a number of writings (sometimes published with only Fritz listed as the author) that established gestalt psychotherapy as a leading influence on therapeutic practice in America and Europe. They also founded the New York Institute for Gestalt Therapy in 1952. The gestalt approach rejected the psychoanalytic emphasis on early childhood trauma to focus instead on the present-time patterns of perception and emotional attachments of patients. The Perls borrowed from the gestalt perception researches of German psychologist Kurt Goldstein as well as from EXISTENTIALISM and the theatrical acting-out techniques of psychodrama. Fritz became a widely known figure in the 1960s for his teaching work at the Esalen Institute in California.

Peron, Eva (Duarte de) ["Evita"] (1919–1952). Argentinian political figure. Born Eva Duarte, she was a well-known actress before marrying Juan PERON in 1945. After Peron was elected president in 1946, the glamorous Evita, a superb public speaker, became the virtual coruler of ARGENTINA. The unofficial minister of health and labor and founder of the Eva Peron Social Aid Foundation, she was influential in securing voting rights for women and in providing educational and social reforms. She was particularly popular with Argentina's poor, many of whom regarded her as a near saint. Opposed by the military, she failed in an attempt to become vice president in 1951. Her death from cancer a year later was an enormous blow to Peron's first regime. Eva Peron's legend was perpetuated in the musical *Evita* (1976) by Tim RICE and Andrew LLOYD WEBBER.

For further reading:

Barnes, John, *Evita, First Lady.* New York: Grove Weidenfeld, 1989.

Fraser, Nicholas, *Eva Peron.* New York: W.W. Norton, 1985.

Peron, Juan Domingo (1895–1974). Two-time president of ARGENTINA (1946–55, 1973–74). Born in Buenos Aires, Peron became a professional military officer and, in travels to Germany and Italy, was impressed by the fascist regimes there. In 1943 he was an important figure in the right-wing coup that toppled President Ramon S. Castillo. After the installation of Edelmiro Farrell as president, Peron first became secretary of labor and social welfare, then minister of war and vice president, thereby assuming the most powerful position in the ruling military junta. His support of labor unions and social reform won him widespread, almost fanatical support among Argentina's workers. When the leaders of a 1945 coup imprisoned him, mass demonstrations by the *descamisados* ("shirtless ones")

Eva Peron and Juan Peron in their home in Buenos Aires just before attending a gala celebration (May 25, 1951).

organized by his second wife, Eva Duarte PERON, won his release. He was subsequently elected president in the 1946 landslide. Peron's massive reform program, known as PERONISMO, was a mixture of strong nationalism and a fascist-influenced TOTALITARIANISM in which all opposition was quashed. His attempt to provide economic stability and self-sufficiency to the nation lost momentum in the late 1940s and early '50s, as demand for Argentinian wheat and beef waned and the economy lagged. The death of the enormously popular Eva in 1952 further weakened his position, disputes with the Roman Catholic church led to his excommunication in 1955 and that same year he was deposed by a military coup. Fleeing the country, he settled in Spain in 1960. The hold of *peronismo*, which had united workers, nationalists, industrialists and the military, remained strong and Peron continued to direct it from exile. In 1971 he returned to Argentina, and two years later he was again elected president. He died in office nine months later and was succeeded by his vice president, his third wife, **Isabel Martinez de Peron**. She was overthrown in a military coup in 1976.

***Peronismo* [also called *justicialismo*].** Political, economic and social program pursued by Argentinian dictator Juan PERON between 1946 and 1955. In some ways similar to FASCISM, it involved a five-year economic plan, extensive government control of economy and society and an end of British influence on the economy.

Perret, Auguste (1874–1954). French architect and engineer whose work moved French architecture toward MODERNISM early in the 20th century. Perret was born in Brussels and joined his father and brothers in the family construction firm. He was a student at the Ecole des BEAUX-ARTS in Paris and first became known for his 1903 apartment house at Paris' 25 bis, rue Franklin, a building that expresses its reinforced concrete frame externally, while incorporating decorative tile ornament of an ART NOUVEAU character. The Theatre des Champs Elysees of 1911–13 was completed by Perret with visible concrete framing. The emphasis on structure in these works places them in a historical line that leads directly to modernism. The church of Notre Dame du Raincy (1922–23) uses concrete framing with walls largely filled by modern stained glass—a striking and much imitated approach to a modern form of ecclesiastical architecture. His plans for the postwar rebuilding of Le Havre (1949–56) were among his last works. Perret's strong influence was extended by his role as a teacher in several ateliers and schools, including, in 1940, at the Ecole des Beaux-Arts.

Perry, Fred(erick John) (1909–). British tennis player. A world-renowned player during the 1930s, Perry was the first player to win all four grand slam tournaments (although not in the same year)—he won Wimbledon (1934–36), the U.S. Open (1933–34), the French Open (1935) and the Australian Open (1934). He was the first non-American to win the U.S. Open and the first Britisher to win the French and Australian Opens.

Perse, Saint-John [born Marie-Rene Alexis Saint-Leger Leger] (1887–1975). French poet and diplomat. Born in the West Indies, he and his family moved to France in 1899. A career diplomat, he was posted to the French embassy in Beijing, served at the 1921 arms limitation talks in Washington, D.C., and was secretary-general of the French Ministry of Foreign Affairs from 1933 to 1940. A staunch opponent of FASCISM, he went into self-imposed exile in the U.S. from 1940 until the end of WORLD WAR II. His poetry is at once arcane and lyrical, difficult and evocative. Perse published his first poem in 1909. It was followed by the volumes *Eloges* (1911, tr. 1944) and *Amitie du Prince* (1921). He attracted his first significant critical attention with the publication of *Anabase* (1924), a symbolic history of humanity that was translated as *Anabasis* by T.S. ELIOT in 1930. His other volumes of verse include *Exil* (1944, tr. 1949), *Vents* (1946; *Winds*, 1953) and *Amers* (1957; *Seamarks*, 1958). Widely considered one of the most original poets of the 20th century, he was awarded the NOBEL PRIZE for literature in 1960.

Pershing, John Joseph "Black Jack" (1860–1948). American general, commander in chief of the American Expeditionary Force in WORLD WAR I. A graduate of the Military Academy at West Point

Gen. Pershing at general headquarters, Chaumont, France (Oct. 19, 1918).

(1886), Pershing served in several Indian wars and in the Spanish-American War. He was adjutant general in the Philippine Islands (1906–13) and defeated the Philippine Moros in 1913. In 1916–17 he commanded the U.S. raid into Mexico against Pancho VILLA (see VILLA'S RAIDS). In 1917 President Woodrow WILSON chose Pershing to command the American forces in Europe. His army was never totally self-sufficient, but the Americans distinguished themselves in several major engagements, and Pershing returned to a

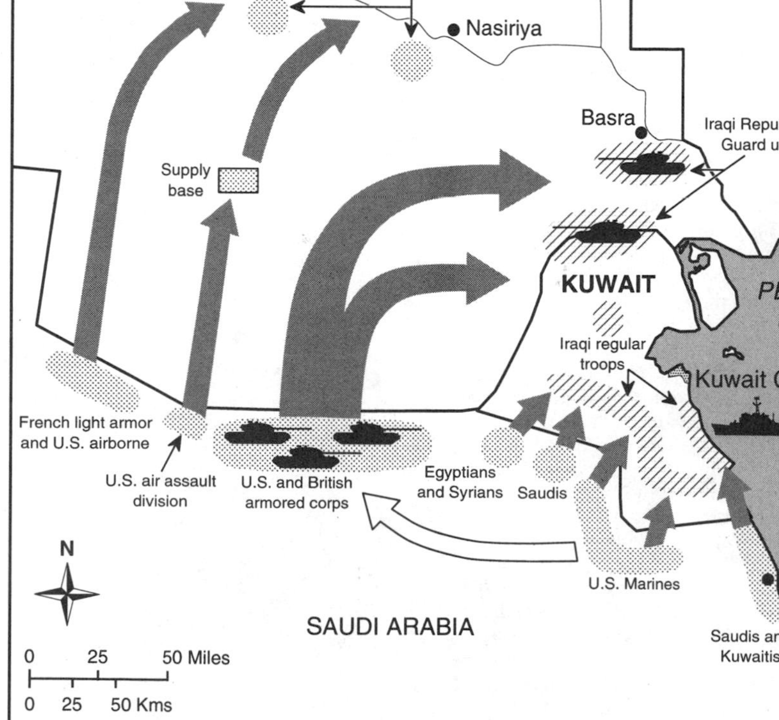

PERSIAN GULF WAR

Iraqis stand amid the rubble west of Baghdad's Al-Ahrar bridge following an Allied bombing raid (Feb. 20, 1991).

hero's welcome in the U.S. in 1919. That year he was named General of the Armies, the first American general to hold that rank. Pershing later served as Army chief of staff (1921–24). He won the PULITZER PRIZE for his memoirs *My Experiences in the World War* (1931).

Persia. See IRAN.

Persian Gulf [Arabian Gulf]. During the 20th century the Persian Gulf region has gradually become one of the most sensitive parts of the world, both economically and militarily. The gulf itself is an arm of the Arabian Sea, extending some 600 miles from the Shatt el-Arab delta to the Strait of Hormuz. Its maximum width is approximately 200 miles. The oil-rich nations of BAHRAIN, QATAR, the UNITED ARAB EMIRATES, SAUDI ARABIA, KUWAIT, IRAQ and IRAN all have some coastline on the gulf. Much of the oil exported from these countries is transported by tankers through the gulf. At the turn of the century, Britain was a dominant force in the region. An international agreement in 1907 formally recognized the gulf as part of the British sphere of influence. The realization in the 1930's that the gulf region contained the largest petroleum reserves in the world made the Persian Gulf a vital shipping lane. Regional conflicts in the last quarter of the century have made the gulf a center of world-wide attention. The Islamic revolution in Iran (1979), the Soviet invasion of AFGHANISTAN (1979), the IRAN-IRAQ WAR OF 1980–88 and Iraq's invasion of Kuwait (1990) and the subsequent PERSIAN GULF WAR (1991) all emphasized the Western and Japanese dependence on imported oil and underlined the strategic importance of the Persian Gulf.

Persian Gulf War. Conflict (1990–91) between IRAQ and an allied coalition sponsored by the UNITED NATIONS and largely directed by the UNITED STATES. On August 2, 1990, on the orders of its dictator Saddam HUSSEIN, Iraq launched a surprise invasion of the small neighboring country of KUWAIT. Kuwait was quickly overwhelmed and occupied, and Iraq announced that Kuwait was no longer an independent country but a province of Iraq. The occupying Iraqis systematically plundered the country. A number of nations, including the U.S., denounced the invasion and called for Iraqi troops to withdraw. The U.S. swiftly sent armed forces to SAUDI ARABIA to deter an Iraqi attack on that country; the U.S. operation, involving some 250,000 troops, was dubbed **Operation Desert Shield**. Other nations in the coalition who sent troops to the region included the UNITED KINGDOM, FRANCE, EGYPT and SYRIA; Saudi Arabia, as the host country for the coalition forces, also provided major facilities and manpower. The coalition forces were under the command of U.S. General Norman SCHWARZKOPF. In the following months, the UN passed a series of resolutions calling for Iraq's total withdrawal from Kuwait and imposing sanctions on that country. In November 1990, President BUSH ordered more U.S. forces to the region, bringing the total of U.S. troops in Operation Desert Shield to some 500,000.

Bush also won international support for a UN resolution imposing a deadline of January 15, 1991, for the withdrawal of all Iraqi forces from Kuwait. If the Iraqis did not comply, the resolution authorized the U.S. and its allies to use force to remove them. After debate, the U.S. Congress also authorized the president to use force if necessary. Despite negotiations, including last-minute diplomatic moves by the U.S.S.R. (which supported the resolution) to persuade Iraq to withdraw, Hussein refused to budge. Hussein warned that there would be dire consequences if his forces were attacked, implying the use of chemical weapons. Less than 17 hours after the UN Security Council's deadline expired, the U.S. and its allies—notably Britain and France—launched a massive air and missile assault on Iraq (Jan 16, 1991).

This attack was code-named **Operation Desert Storm**. Using high-technology equipment in combat for the first time—CRUISE MISSILES, laser-guided "smart" bombs and other ordnance—the Allies achieved rapid air superiority and scored hits against key military targets in Iraq. Although the Iraqis shot down several Allied aircraft, they otherwise put up little resistance; much of the Iraqi air force fled to Iran or to bases in the north. Hoping to bring ISRAEL into the conflict and split the Western-Arab coalition, Iraq also intermittently launched Soviet-built Scud missiles against Israel (as well as against Saudi Arabia). However, these did not cause any military damage, and the U.S. successfully persuaded Israel not to counterattack.

After six weeks of round-the-clock bombardment, the Allies launched a multipronged ground offensive against Iraqi

A destroyed Iraqi tank stands in front of some of the hundreds of oil well fires burning out of control in Kuwait (March 9, 1991).

forces in Kuwait and in Iraq (Feb. 24). The Allies swifly outflanked and overwhelmed the Iraqis; by the third day of the invasion, more than 50,000 Iraqis had surrendered. Hussein's much-vaunted Republican Guards—the elite Iraqi forces—failed to slow the Allied advance. However, the Iraqis did set fire to hundreds of oil wells in Kuwait and (earlier) also dumped millions of gallons of crude oil into the Persian Gulf. These acts served no military purpose but caused the worst environmental contamination in history. Kuwait was liberated on February 27, and a ceasefire took effect on February 27–28. The destruction of Kuwaiti oil wells and Iraq's plundering of the country left Kuwait's infrastructure severely damaged. In the aftermath of the war, meanwhile, various rebel groups in Iraq attempted to overthrow Saddam Hussein, but by the beginning of April 1991 Hussein seemed to have the upper hand against opponents of his regime.

Persian Revolution of 1906–9. Persia was in financial straits when the ailing shah succumbed to popular pressure for a constitution, signing the Fundamental Law in 1906, establishing a constitutional monarchy. He died soon after, succeeded by his son, Muhammed Ali (1872–1925). Using a Persian Cossack brigade formed with Russian help, Ali prorogued the assembly. A second assembly developed an absolutist constitution, without abrogating the previous one. Ali's reactionary prime minister was murdered, however, and a liberal prime minister upheld the 1906 document until his arrest in December 1907. The assembly was dispersed by Cossacks in June 1908. A third assembly abolished the 1906 constitution, after which Muhammed Ali attempted to rule absolutely. Rebellions erupted in Tabriz (1908), Rasht and Isfahan (1909), and despite Russian aid, Bakhtiari tribesmen and troops from Rasht captured Teheran in July 1909, forcing Ali's abdication in favor of his 12-year-old son, Ahmed Mirza (1898–1930).

Persian Revolution of 1921. Persia was on the verge of collapse, its ruler corrupt, when Reza Khan PAHLEVI (1877–1944), an army officer, led cossacks in a coup d'etat on February 21, 1921. Pahlevi made himself minister of war and commander in chief and gained control of the country. He introduced reforms, remodeled the army, induced the Russians to withdraw their troops (1921) and Britain as well (1923), became prime minister (1923) and, after gaining dictatorial powers, had the shah deposed (1925). In late 1925 he changed his name to Reza Shah Pahlevi and founded the Pahlevi dynasty.

Persichetti, Vincent (1915–1987). American composer. As a composition teacher, he was long associated with New York City's Juilliard School of Music. Working in an essentially conservative idiom, he composed nine symphonies, much chamber and choral music, as well as a great deal of music for wind band. Many of his works were first performed by the Philadelphia Orchestra, and his music for chorus and for band came to be favored by youth ensembles.

"Person to Person". Innovative American television interview program of the 1950s. Edward R. MURROW hosted the first six years of the show, from October 1953 to June 1959; and Charles Collingwood took over until the show's demise in September 1961. By contrast to Murrow's news-oriented SEE IT NOW program, "Person to Person" was a relaxed, informal visit via live television into the homes of celebrities. Wreathed in cigarette smoke, Murrow would sit in the studio before a wall screen and converse with celebrities conducting tours of their homes. The range of guests was amazing—politicians and world leaders like Fidel CASTRO and then-Senator John F. KENNEDY, scientists like Margaret MEAD, authors like John STEINBECK, and entertainers like Marilyn MONROE. For all its avowed informality, the complexities of the live transmissions were enormous and Murrow frequently seemed ill at ease. Purportedly, he did the show to ensure that *See It Now* could remain on the air. "To do the show I want to do," he once said, "I have to do the show I don't want to do." The series was seldom controversial, concludes historian Erik Barnouw, and depended upon "a *Vogue* and *House Beautiful* appeal, along with a voyeuristic element." Needless to say, its ratings were always much higher than those of "See It Now."

For further reading:
The Complete Directory to Prime Time Network TV Shows. New York: Ballantine, 1988.

Pertini, Alessandro "Sandro" (1896–1990). Italian politician, president of ITALY (1978–85). A hero of WORLD WAR II, Pertini was a founder of the Italian Socialist Party. As president of Italy, he was widely hailed for restoring credibility to the Italian government following a period marked by urban terrorism, economic troubles and corruption.

Peru. Western South American nation, bordered by ECUADOR and COLOMBIA on the north, BRAZIL and BOLIVIA on the east, CHILE on the south, and the Pacific Ocean on the west. Its capital is Lima. Peru emerged from the 19th century involved

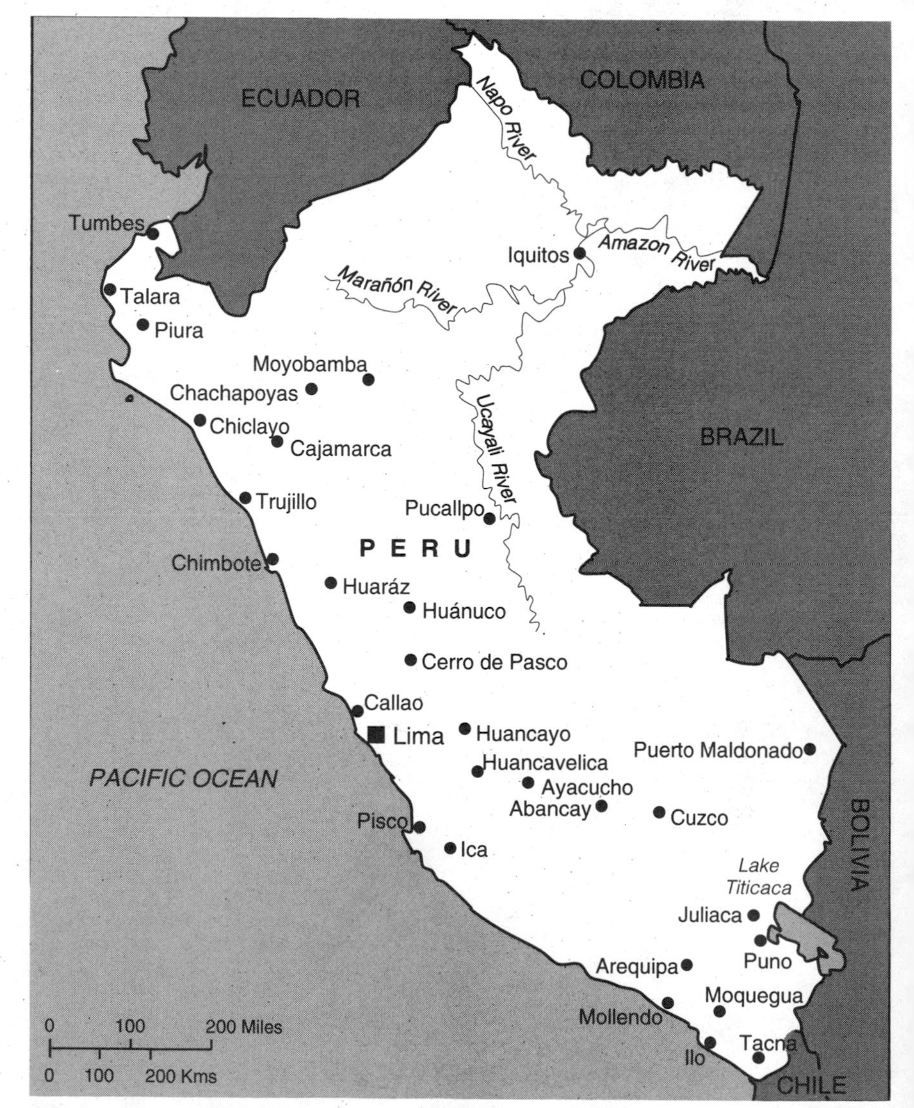

PERU

PERU

1919	Augusto Leguia becomes president and gives U.S. companies extensive rights to exploit Peruvian mineral and oil deposits.
1924	The American Revolutionary Popular Alliance is formed (APRA).
1931	Military junta led by Colonel Lui Sanchez Cerro takes over the country.
1956	Former President Manuel Prado (1939-45) becomes president and through austerity measures helps create economic stability.
1968	General Juan Velasco Alvarado in a self-styled military junta seizes power and institutes land reforms and nationalizes U.S. assets.
1975	General Francisco Morales Bermudez takes over the country and institutes austerity measures in hopes of obtaining aid from the International Monetary Fund.
1985	Alan Garcia, head of APRA, is elected president. As triple-digit inflation devastates wages and civil war is threatened, Garcia declares a state of emergency.
1990	(June 10) Alberto Fujimori, an agricultural engineer of Japanese descent who had no previous political experience, defeats novelist Mario Vargas Llosa, also a political novice, for the presidency.

in border disputes with its neighbors. In the early 1900s its politics were dominated by Augusto B. Leguia, who was president from 1908 to 1912 and again from 1919 to 1930. A virtual dictator, Leguia courted U.S. investments, with little regard for the economic welfare of the Peruvian people. During the 1920s a new political party, APRA (American Popular Revolutionary Alliance), was formed to fight imperialism and to better the treatment of the Indian population. By the 1940s it had taken hold, and in 1945 a free election was held. The elected government was toppled in 1948 in a military coup led by General Manuel Odria. APRA was temporarily banned, and Odria served as president from 1950 to 1956, when Manuel Prado, who had served as president from 1939 to 1945, was reelected. The moderate Fernando Belaunde Terry was elected in 1963 but was overthrown in a coup led by General Juan Velasco Alvarado in 1968. Velasco installed a military junta that was deposed in a bloodless coup in 1975 by his premier, General Francisco Morales Bermudez, who promised a gradual return to civilian government. In 1980 elections were held and Beluande Terry was reelected. His government faced increasingly dire economic conditions and threats of a border war with Ecuador, but he managed to last out his term. In 1985 Alan Garcia Parez became president. A young Social Democrat, Garcia Parez set out to clean up the government and boost the economy by limiting its payment of foreign debt and price controls. In 1987 he announced his intention to nationalize Peru's banks. Garcia Parez voiced support for the Sandanistas and was critical of U.S. policy in Central America. Peru continued to struggle with its economy—in 1987 and '88 there were widespread worker's strikes—and with Maoist insurgents such as the Sendero Luminoso guerrillas. Peru is also a major grower of coca, which is used to produce COCAINE. In 1990 Garcia Parez was succeeded by Alberto Fujimori, who refused U.S. military aid and is attempting to replace coca crops with other agricultural production.

Perutz, Max Ferdinand (1914–). Austrian-British biochemist. In 1937 Perutz began investigating the structure of hemoglobin, the oxygen-carrying protein of the blood. He set up the molecular biology laboratory at Cambridge University in 1946; seven years later, Perutz was still hard at work trying to find an underlying regularity in the structure of protein molecules. In 1953 he seized upon a solution by applying the isomorphous replacement technique, which alters the diffraction patterns of a molecule, making it easier to compute the positions of atoms. This technique allowed him to determine the structure of hemoglobin, which contains some 12,000 atoms. In 1962 he was awarded the NOBEL PRIZE for chemistry, along with his colleague John C. Kendrew, who conducted X-ray studies of the muscle protein myoglobin. After receiving the NOBEL PRIZE, Perutz further refined his model of the hemoglobin molecule, depicting how oxygen is transported in the blood.

Pervukhin, Mikhail Georgievich (1904–1978). Deputy premier of the Soviet Union and member of the ruling POLITBURO (1952–57). A member of the Anti-Party group opposed to Nikita S. KHRUSHCHEV, Pervukhin was removed from office by Khrushchev on June 22, 1957. (See also ANTI-PARTY GROUP CRISIS.)

Pessoa, Fernando (1888–1935). Portuguese poet and literary critic. Pessoa stands as the major Portuguese literary figure to emerge in the modern era. Relatively little of his work was published in his lifetime, and his critical reputation has grown slowly but steadily. Born in Lisbon, Pessoa was educated in South Africa after the death of his father. While there Pessoa became fluent in English. He wrote noteworthy verse in both Portuguese and English. A poetical technique for which Pessoa is especially noted is the use of heteronyms, or alternative authorial personalities, resembling the verse personae of Ezra POUND. As a literary critic, Pessoa was influenced by the tenets of FUTURISM. His books of verse include *Antinous* (1918), *Inscriptions* (1920) and *Mensagem* (1935).

Petain, Henri Philippe (1856–1951). French army officer and head of France's VICHY government during WORLD WAR II. A graduate of the military academy at St. Cyr, he was commissioned in the infantry in 1878 and subsequently taught at the Ecole de Guerre. In WORLD WAR I he became a military hero, stopping German advances at the battle of VERDUN (1916). Appointed commander in chief of the French forces in 1917, he was promoted to the rank of marshal the following year. After the war he was posted to MOROCCO, where he joined Spain in the campaign against ABD EL-KRIM (1926). After the fall of FRANCE in 1940, Petain was recalled from his post as ambassador to Spain and made vice premier. Succeeding Paul REYNAUD as premier, he concluded an armistice with GERMANY and assumed the title of chief of state in the new Vichy government of occupied France. Petain sought an "honorable" collaboration with Germany in order to protect French citizens and prisoners, but his status as hero crumbled as harsh fascist policies were brought to bear. At the end of 1941 he dismissed Prime Minister Pierre LAVAL, who urged total collaboration with the Nazis. However, the following year, at the Germans' insistence, he was forced to recall Laval to office. Laval assumed the bulk of power and Petain became a virtual figurehead. After the defeat of Germany in 1945, Petain was tried for treason, found guilty and sentenced to death. That penalty was commuted to life imprisonment by Charles DE GAULLE, and Petain died in prison.

For further reading:

Paxton, Robert O., *Vichy France: Old Guard and New Order*. New York: Columbia University Press, 1982.

Marshal Henri Philippe Petain in court as his treason trial opened (July 23, 1945).

Peter II (1923–1970). King of YUGOSLAVIA (1934–45). Yugoslavia's second and last king, he succeeded to the throne under the regency of his cousin, Prince Paul, after the assassination of his father, King Alexander. Peter assumed power in 1941 after a coup d'etat overthrew the regency. Weeks later he was forced to flee his country for England when GERMANY invaded Yugoslavia (see WORLD WAR II IN THE BALKANS). After the war, in 1945 TITO's communist regime abolished the monarchy and deposed Peter. The ex-king settled in the U.S., where his autobiography, *A King's Heritage*, was published in 1955. He died in the U.S. 15 years later.

Peter, Paul & Mary. American folk group. Comprised of Peter Yarrow, Paul Stookey and Mary Travers, the group's roots are in the protest movement of the 1960s, even as their political activism continues today. Their early albums, such as *Peter, Paul & Mary* (1962) and *In the Wind* (1963), influenced such artists as Bob DYLAN. Among their hit singles in the early 1960s were such songs as "If I Had a Hammer" and "Puff the Magic Dragon," a perennial children's favorite. They had an unexpected number-one hit in 1969 with the romantic ballad "Leaving on a Jet Plane." In more recent years, members of the group have continued to be active in such issues as political repression in El Salvador, as well as touring widely.

Peter Pan. Long-running fantasy play by Sir James BARRIE about a boy who refused to grow up and ran away to a life of adventure in the Never, Never Land. The play has been an international success since its first English production on December 27, 1904, with Nina Boucicault in the title role. The first American production quickly followed on November 6, 1905, with Maude ADAMS. It has been estimated that in its first 50 years in England alone the play was presented over 10,000 times. The genesis of the play is long and complex. It contains scenes and characters from Barrie's boyhood in Kirriemuir and Dumfries, Scotland. Peter himself was a composite of the four children of Arthur and Sylvia Davies, whom Barrie had met in Kensington Gardens in 1898 and with whom Barrie remained closely associated the rest of his life. The character first appears by name in Barrie's novel for adults, *The Little White Bird* (1901), and was later developed in 1903 under the title, *The Great White Father*. The title was changed from the 1904 premiere.

The central roles of Pan and Captain Hook have attracted numerous stage and screen luminaries over the years. Traditionally, Peter has been played by an actress, and the list includes Maude Adams, Margaret Lockwood, Jean Arthur, Mary MARTIN and gymnast Cathy Rigby. Since Gerald Du Maurier first played Hook, the role has been taken on by the likes of Charles LAUGHTON, Alastair Sim, Boris KARLOFF and Cyril Ritchard. Barrie rewrote the play in novel form in *Peter and Wendy* in 1911. In America producer Herbert Brenon adapted it for the movies in 1924 with Betty Bronson in the title role. Subsequent versions include a musical version by Leonard BERNSTEIN in 1950, the Walt DISNEY animated film in 1953 and the Mary Martin television/stage musical in 1954, which has undergone several revivals with other actresses.

For further reading:
Green, Roger Lancelyn, *Fifth Years of Peter Pan*. London: Peter Davies, 1954.

"Peter Principle". A rule that states that every employee tends to rise to his or her level of incompetence, then remain there. The principle was set forth and popularized in the satirical best-selling book, *The Peter Principle: Why Things Always Go Wrong* (1969) by Canadian educator and psychologist Peter J. Laurence. The book explained that if an employee does a good job, he or she is repeatedly promoted until he eventually reaches a level where he cannot do the work—and there he or she remains. Although the "Peter Principle" was conceived tongue-in-cheek, it undoubtedly has a large element of truth.

Peters, Roberta [Roberta Peterman] (1930–). American coloratura soprano. Born in New York City, Peters spent her teenage years studying voice, languages, dancing and drama. By age 19 she had learned 20 opera roles. Her first professional appearance and Metropolitan Opera debut came unexpectedly when, with six hours notice, she sang the role of Zerlina in *Don Giovanni* (1950). Over the next quarter century Peters excelled in the bel canto repertory at the Met. Her most distinguished and often-sung roles (in addition to Zerlina) included Gilda in *Rigoletto*, Queen of the Night in *The Magic Flute* and Despina in *Cosi fan tutte*. Peters has also won the Bolshoi medal (usually given to Russian artists only), sung at the White House six times, been a highly successful recitalist and made numerous recordings and TV appearances.

Petersburg Soviet. Because St. Petersburg was the center of the FEBRUARY REVOLUTION, the St. Petersburg Soviet carried out the role of a national Soviet for a few months but relinquished this role in June to an All-Russian Congress of Soviets. After this, in theory at least, it became solely a local city Soviet. Its voice and directorate was the executive committee that the delegates elected.

Peterson, Forrest (1922–). U.S. test pilot. Peterson flew the X-15 in five flights between 1960 and 1962 to a top altitude of 101,800 feet and was the only Navy pilot to fly the experimental rocket plane. Having spent four years in the program, Peterson left in 1962 to pursue what became a highly successful career in naval aviation, during which he served as captain of the aircraft carrier USS *Enterprise*, commander of the Sixth Fleet's Carrier Group Two and vice chief of naval operations for air at the Pentagon. He retired in 1980.

Petlyura, Semyon Vasilyevich (1879–1926). Ukrainian patriot who worked tirelessly to gain independence for the UKRAINE. In 1905 Petlyura helped found the Ukrainian Social Democratic Workers' Party. Having served in the Russian army in World War I, in 1917 he joined the Ukrainian central council, and was minister of defense in the first Ukrainian government. In 1920 he fought not only the Red Army in the north but also the anti-Soviet forces of General Anton Ivanovich DENIKIN. He spent some months in Warsaw, but after the peace of Riga he moved his government to Paris and was assassinated by a communist agent.

Petri, Elio (1929–1982). Italian film director and a leader of the neo-realist movement in cinema. His 10 films satirized Italian society and challenged the established political order. Among his best known films were *The Working Class Goes to Heaven*, which shared the Grand Prize at the 1972 CANNES FILM FESTIVAL, and *Investigation of a Citizen Above Suspicion*, which won the 1970 ACADEMY AWARD for best foreign film.

Pevsner, Anton (1886–1962). Russian Constructivist artist. Having spent a year at the St. Petersburg Academy of Art in 1910, Pevsner went to Paris and then Norway, where he painted in the Cubist style. In the early 1920s Pevsner began working on constructions and, together with his brother Naum GABO, joined the antiproductionist group Inkhuk.

Pevsner, Nikolaus (Bernhard) (1902–1983). German-born British architectural historian and critic. He established his career at the University of Gottingen. When Adolf HITLER became chancellor in 1933, Pevsner escaped from NAZI GERMANY to England, where he lectured at Cambridge and Oxford universities and at the University of London. He was best known for editing the monumental 46–volume series, *The Buildings of England* (1951–74).

P-40. See FLYING TIGERS.

Pham Van Dong (1906–). North Vietnamese official. Born in the French protectorate of Annam, which later became part of North Vietnam, Pham Van Dong was a close associate of HO CHI MINH both before and after the FRENCH INDOCHINA WAR OF 1946–54. During the VIETNAM WAR, he served as minister of foreign affairs and later as prime minister of North Vietnam. In July 1976, he was named prime minister of the newly unified Socialist Republic of VIETNAM.

Phao Sriyanond (?-1960). Thai army leader of the 1947 coup that restored Field Marshal Pibul Songgram to power in THAILAND. He served as chief of the Thai national police from 1947 to 1957. In 1957 he was exiled by Field Marshal Thanarat for alleged secret dealings with the government of communist CHINA. He spent the remainder of his life in Switzerland.

Phat Huynh Tan (1913–1989). Vietnamese communist leader. He was the chief theoretician of the VIETCONG, the communist-led political movement in South Vietnam that was backed by North Vietnam during the VIETNAM WAR. Following the communist victory in South Vietnam (1975), he became one of the few South Vietnamese to hold a leadership position in the HANOI government.

phenomenology. School of philosophical thought that emerged in the early 1900s. Phenomenology—literally, the study of phenomena—has had a tremendous influence on psychology, sociology, theology, historical analysis and literary criticism in the 20th century. The key figures behind its formulation in the first decades of this century were three Germans—historian Wilhelm Dilthey, philosopher Edmund HUSSERL and sociologist Max Scheler. Phenomenology borrowed from 18th-century philosopher Immanuel Kant the notion of phenomena (perceived and experienced reality) as being distinct from noumena (ultimate reality). Phenomena alone may be comprehended by human observers. The method of phenomenology emphasized that the task of an intellectual observer was to achieve a reconstructive identification with the phenomena under study, with the understanding that perfect objectivity was impossible while blatant bias was to be shunned. Phenomenology had a major influence on EXISTENTIALISM.

Philby, H(arold) A(drian) R(ussell) "Kim" (1912–1988). British-born Soviet spy, considered the most notorious double agent of the COLD WAR, if not of the 20th century. Philby was educated at Cambridge University in the early 1930s and recruited there as a Soviet KGB agent in 1933. He joined the British intelligence agency M16 at the outbreak of World War II, becoming head of the service's anti-Soviet section in 1944. This key post enabled him to pass top secret information to Moscow. In the late 1940s Philby betrayed a secret Anglo-American plan to overthrow the communist government of ALBANIA. In 1949, he became M16's liaison officer with the U.S. CENTRAL INTELLIGENCE AGENCY and was thus in an ideal position to compromise every M16/CIA operation against the Soviet Union. In 1951, he warned fellow Cambridge graduates and Soviet spies Guy BURGESS and Donald MACLEAN that they were under suspicion, giving them time to defect to the Soviet Union. The CIA believed that Philby was the "third man" in the spy ring, but M15, the British counterintelligence unit, was unable to prove any connection. Philby's activities were not fully exposed until he himself defected to the Soviet Union in 1963 just before his planned arrest. In Moscow, Philby continued his life as a KGB general; he never expressed regret for his treason.

For further reading:

Knightley, Phillip, *The Master Spy: The Story of Kim Philby*. New York: Random House, 1990.

Philippine election of 1986. Historic election that led to the fall of the regime of President Ferdinand MARCOS. Marcos had made an apparently impromptu announcement of upcoming elections while being questioned on an American news program. The election was held as promised, amid allegations of widespread fraud, with Corazon AQUINO, the widow of assassinated opposition leader **Benigno Aquino,** as Marcos' main challenger. Both Marcos and Aquino claimed victory, but independent observers declared that Aquino had actually won the election. Less than three weeks later, U.S. President Ronald REAGAN called on Marcos to resign and offered him a haven in the U.S. On February 25, Marcos and Aquino each held their own inauguration ceremonies. Several hours later, Marcos went into exile. His 20-year reign as president was brought to an end after two leading military allies resigned from their posts—Lieutenant General Fidel RAMOS and Defense Minister Juan Ponce Enrile. The departure of Marcos, his wife **Imelda Marcos** and their entourage was widely hailed by Filipinos who felt that the Marcos regime had been thoroughly corrupt.

Philippine Insurrection of 1899–1902. The Philippines led by Emilio Aguinaldo had declared independence from Spain on June 12, 1898, but Spain ceded the islands to the U.S. by the treaty of Paris. Aguinaldo refused U.S. control, establishing an independent government under the Malolos constitution. Hostilities

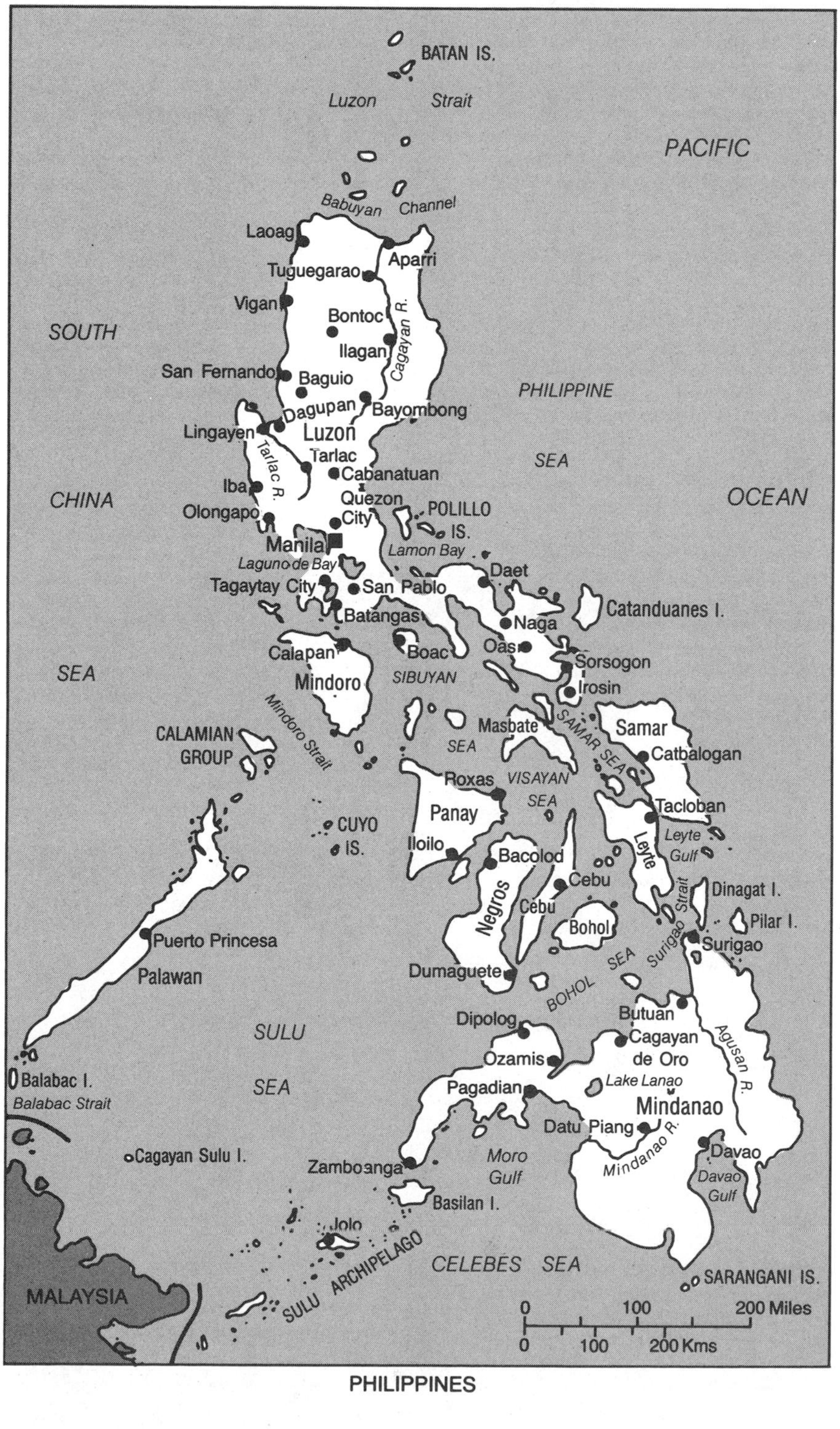

PHILIPPINES

Supporters of Corazon Aquino outside the presidential palace hold a sign declaring her victorious in the presidential election (Feb. 24, 1986).

against American rule began February 4, 1899. After several battles, American forces pushed the Filipinos back from Manila, capturing their capital at Malolos. Aguinaldo carried on guerrilla war until captured on March 23, 1901. The guerrilla war continued until May 6, 1902, when civil government was established under American control with William Howard TAFT as the first governor.

Philippines [Republic of the Philippines]. The Philippines consist of 7,100 islands which cover a total land area of approximately 115,800 square miles in the west Pacific Ocean about 497 miles off the southeast Asian coast. Formally ceded to the United States under terms of the Treaty of Paris which ended the Spanish-American War, the country became the Commonwealth of the Philippines in 1935. JAPAN invaded the country in 1941, exploiting and brutalizing the people until U.S. forces liberated the country in 1944. The Republic of the Philippines was declared in 1946. After two decades of one-term presidents, Ferdinand MARCOS became president in 1965. During the next 20 years he crushed all opposition and quelled insurrections by communist and Muslim guerrilla groups. He was ousted in 1986 with the election of Corazon AQUINO, widow of opposition leader Benigno Aquino who had been murdered on his return to the country in 1983. A new constitution was approved in 1987. The Aquino government continued to battle guerrilla groups and survived several attempted coups, the most serious of which occurred in 1989.

PHILIPPINES

1898	Philippines ceded to U.S. after Spanish-American War.
1899	Philippine nationalists who fought with Americans against Spanish in the Spanish-American conflict now fight U.S. domination in the Philippine-American War.
1941-45	Japan invades and subjects Philippines to brutal occupation.
1945	U.S. forces invade Philippines and liberate Manila.
1946	Republic of Philippines proclaimed independent sovereign state.
1965	Ferdinand Marcos wins presidency; attendant economic stagnation, rampant inflation and endemic corruption fuel popular opposition to his administration.
1972	Marcos imposes martial law.
1983	Prominent opposition leader Benigno Aquino returns from exile and is shot dead in the airport terminal as he disembarks plane.
1986	Under U.S. pressure, Marcos calls election, is defeated by Corazon Aquino, widow of Benigno; Aquino vows to recover national assets looted by Marcos and his allies, wipe out corruption and affirm civilian supremacy over military.
1987	One hundred thousand people visit Malacanang Palace to view luxury goods abandoned by Marcos family, among which are 1,060 pairs of Imelda Marcos' shoes.
1989	Ferdinand Marcos dies in exile in Hawaii.
1990	Earthquake on island of Luzon kills 1,621 people; President Aquino asks U.S. Congress for aid; Imelda Marcos charged with stealing $200 million from Philippine treasury, is acquitted in U.S. Federal Court for lack of evidence.

Phillips, Rev. Channing E. (1928–1987). American CIVIL RIGHTS activist. A United Church of Christ clergyman, he was Washington D.C.'s Democratic national committeeman from 1968 to 1972. He became the first black nominated for president by a major political party when the Washington delegation to the 1968 Democratic National Convention nominated him as its favorite son candidate in place of the slain Robert F. KENNEDY.

Phnom Penh. Capital city of CAMBODIA (Kampuchea). An ancient and historic center of Cambodian culture, Phnom Penh has suffered greatly during the 20th century. It was occupied by the Japanese during WORLD WAR II. During the CAMBODIAN CIVIL WAR OF 1970–75, it was threatened by the communist rebels (KHMER ROUGE). Much of the population fled before Phnom Penh fell to the Khmer Rouge in April 1975. Later, the Khmer Rouge removed most of the remaining population and forced them to work in the countryside. In 1979 the Khmer Rouge was routed by the Vietnamese, who set up a pro-Vietnamese government in the city. Phnom Penh subsequently regained a semblance of normality.

Phoenix Islands. Group of eight uninhabited islands north of Samoa in the central Pacific Ocean. The Phoenix islands were claimed by Britain and the U.S. in the early 19th century. In 1939 the two nations agreed to jointly administer two of the islands, Canton Atoll and Enderbury, for 50 years. The remaining islands became part of the British Gilbert and Ellice Islands Colony. They are now part of KIRIBATI. Attempts to settle three of these islands in the late 1930s and early 1940s failed.

Phony War [German: *Sitzkrieg*]. Term given to a brief period in WORLD WAR II that followed Germany's BLITZKRIEG attack on Poland. Lasting from late 1939 until early 1940, the Phony War (also known as the "Sitzkrieg") was a time of inaction during which the French and British maintained a defensive position behind the MAGINOT LINE and the U.S.S.R. turned its attention to the RUSSO-FINNISH WAR. Given over to strategizing, this period of military malaise was ended by Adolf HITLER'S invasion of NORWAY on April 9, 1940, and the subsequent replacement of Neville CHAMBERLAIN with Winston CHURCHILL as British prime minister on May 10.

photojournalism. Technique of journalistic reporting that relies heavily on incisive and exemplary photographic images. While photography has served as a component of journalism since the mid-19th century, it stepped to the forefront only in the 20th century. The first key development of the modern era was German inventor Alfred Korn's 1907 technique of sending photographic images by wire. By the 1920s, German magazines such as the *Munchner Illustrierte Presse* (MIP) had won an audience by letting photographs do much of the narrative work in their articles. In the U.S., this approach was successfully emulated by two magazines founded in the mid-1930s, LIFE and *Look.* Photojournalists who have won renown for their work since the 1930s include Margaret BOURKE-WHITE, Robert CAPA, Walker EVANS and W. Eugene Smith.

Photo-Secession. A loose-knit group of American photographers formed at the beginning of the 20th century by Alfred STIEGLITZ. As propounded in 1902 in its journal *Camera Work,* the general mandate was the promotion of the higher forms of photography as a fine art. At the time, argues historian William Innes Homer, American photography was "embarrassingly awkward," a collection of stereotypical studio portraits and "superficial imitations of the conventions of painting." Photo-Secession's original members included Edward STEICHEN, Gertrude Kasebier, Clarence H. White, Joseph T. Keiley, Frank Eugene and Alvin Langdon COBURN. There were many exhibitions over the next few years, notably in "291," Stieglitz' famous exhibition space on Fifth Avenue. Dissension soon eroded the ranks of the society. Stieglitz grew increasingly dissatisfied at those members whose pictorial effects imitated with soft-focus lenses the hazy effects of Impressionist paintings. He demanded that photography pursue the course of a "straight," unmediated expression. Other members were disgruntled at Stieglitz' increasing use of the exhibition space for contemporary painters. By the time the group sponsored the International Exhibition of Pictorial Photography in Buffalo in 1910, a schism with Stieglitz was imminent. After his withdrawal, the Photo-Secessionists organized a "second" Secession, the Pictorial Photographers of America, in 1916. Its gradual dissolution came, writes Homer, from a preponderance of "bland, soft-focus pictorialism."

For further reading:
Homer, William Innes, *Alfred Stieglitz and the Photo-Secession.* Boston: Little Brown and Co., 1983.

Piaf, Edith [Giovanna Gassion] (1915–1963). French singer. *Piaf* is the French word for sparrow, and this adopted name became the symbol of Edith Piaf's immense popularity with the French people. She was known as The Little Sparrow because of her slight build and plaintive singing style that could wring the heights of emotion from the ballads that dominated her musical repertoire. In the 1940s and '50s, at the height of her fame, Piaf was a familiar figure not only in her native land but also in England and the U.S. She was admired not only by her fans but by literati such as Jean COCTEAU. Her life was in many ways a tragic one, marred by failed marriages and drug abuse. The hit Broadway play *Piaf* (1980), written by Pam Gens and starring Jane Lapotaire, was a musical re-creation of her legend.

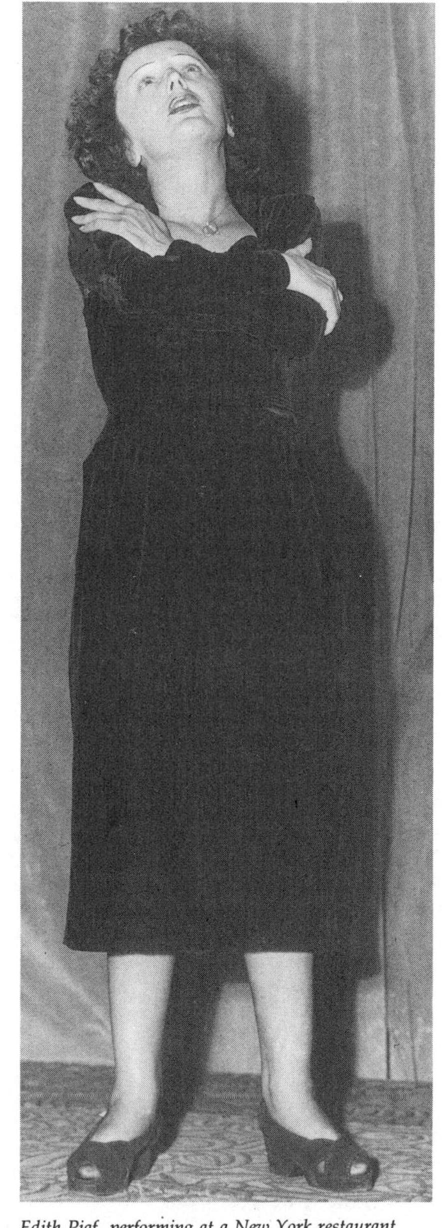

Edith Piaf, performing at a New York restaurant (Oct. 28, 1949).

Pablo Picasso (July 8, 1965).

Piaget, Jean (1896–1980). Swiss psychologist, renowned for his ground-breaking studies of child development and theories of human intelligence. Piaget was initially interested in the natural sciences, and received his doctorate in science in 1918. However, he became increasingly fascinated by the question of how children learn and by the 1920s had shifted his energy to this as-yet undeveloped field. He theorized that all children learned by passing through a series of distinct intellectual stages and that each child was a significant agent in that process. He also proposed that each child, starting from birth, was constantly constructing and reconstructing his own model of reality, revising his conceptions of the world around him through his own self-discoveries. Piaget was active in research for more than 60 years; during this time he exercised a profound influence on the field of child psychology in Europe and the U.S. He wrote more than 50 books and monographs and received honorary degrees from more than 30 universities. He worked at the universities of Geneva (1929–54), Lausanne (1938–51) and the Sorbonne (1952–63).

Picasso, Pablo (1881–1973). Spanish-born painter, sculptor and potter, widely regarded as the greatest visual artist of the 20th century. Trained at an early age by his Spanish painter father, Picasso moved to PARIS as a young man and spent most of his life there and in the Midi region of France. In the early 1900s, Picasso produced noteworthy portraits during what are known as his Blue and Rose Periods. With fellow painter Georges BRAQUE, Picasso founded the highly influential artistic movement known as CUBISM in the late 1900s. His famous painting, *Les Demoiselles d'Avignon* (1907)—which depicts five women in diverse geometric poses and incorporates the influence of African art—is regarded as the first true cubist painting. Picasso's painting styles continued to evolve throughout his career, ranging from strong realism to extreme abstraction. In the 1940s, he produced a series of "found object" sculptures. In the 1950s and after, he devoted considerable energy to his pottery works in the Midi.

For further reading:

Lyttle, Richard B., *Pablo Picasso: The Man and the Image*. New York: Macmillan, 1989.

Penrose, Roland, *Picasso: His Life and Work*. Berkeley: University of California Press, 1981.

Podoksik, Anatoly, *Picasso*. New York: Harry N. Abrams, 1990.

Richardson, John, *A Life of Picasso: Volume I: 1881–1906*. New York: Random House, 1991.

Piccard, Auguste (1884–1962). Swiss physicist. A pioneer in the exploration of the atmosphere and the ocean floor, Piccard taught in the U.S. and Switzerland before becoming professor of physics at Brussels Polytechnic (1922–56). To explore the atmosphere he developed a pressurized cabin attached to a balloon; he successfully tested it in 1931, ascending approximately 11 miles into the atmosphere. Next he designed a maneuverable craft to explore the ocean deeps, which reached a depth of about a mile when tested in 1948. A second craft descended to 2.5 miles in the Mediterranean. It was later sold to the U.S. Navy and used to plumb the Marianas trench in the Pacific (seven miles deep) in 1960.

Piccolo, Lucio (1903–1969). Italian poet. A native son of Palermo, Piccolo led a relatively isolated life at his home in Sicily and often focused on Sicilian subjects. *Nove liriche* (*Nine Poems*) was privately printed in 1954. He owes his critical discovery to Eugenio MONTALE's praise of his 1956 *Canti barocchi* (*Baroque Songs*). Other works include *Gioco a nascondere* (1960, *Hide and Seek*) and *Plumela* (1967). His poems are filled with rich and exotic imagery and attempt to achieve a sense of timelessness.

Pickford, Mary (1893–1979). The most popular motion picture star in screen history. She was a rare combination of dramatic actress, comedienne, entrepreneur and businessperson. Born Gladys Smith in Toronto, she toured with various theater road companies as "Baby Gladys," the primary breadwinner in her family. By the age of 16 she had not only conquered the Broadway stage (winning over producer David BELASCO to star in his *The Warrens of Virginia*) but had begun appearing in short films directed by D.W. GRIFFITH for the BIOGRAPH company. The next seven years consolidated her position as the number-one box-office star

Mary Pickford, star of the silent screen.

and highest paid contract player in the business. "The Little Girl with the Curls," as her fans dubbed her, became "The Girl with the Cash-Register Brain," as her boss at Famous Players, Adolph ZUKOR, described her. She went from $40 a week at Biograph to $10,000 a week in 1916. With the creation that year of the Pickford Film Corporation, she became the first star to produce her own pictures and win a degree of control over her work. These were the years of her quintessential image, a radiant, sprightly little girl with plenty of courage and daring. With her favorite directors, Marshall Neilan and Maurice Tourneur, she made many classics, including *Poor Little Rich Girl* (1917), *Pride of the Clan* (1916) and *Daddy Long Legs* (1919); and some genuine masterpieces such as *Rebecca of Sunnybrook Farm* (1917) and *Stella Maris* (1918). After her marriage to Douglas FAIRBANKS Sr. in 1920 and her involvement in the founding of UNITED ARTISTS, her work began to change. Bigger budgets and more mature roles produced *Dorothy Vernon of Haddon Hall* (1925), *The Taming of the Shrew* (1929) and *Coquette*, for which she won an ACADEMY AWARD as best actress in 1929. Her famous curls were cut off for that role, creating a sensation with the press and the public. After making *Secrets* in 1933, she retired from acting and devoted the rest of her life to business affairs, charitable activities, a book of memoirs (*Sunshine and Shadow*, 1955) and presiding over Beverly Hills society at her home, Pickfair, with her third husband, Charles "Buddy" Rogers. Before her death in 1979 she donated more than 50 of her Biograph-period films to the American Film Institute and received a special Academy Award in 1975 in recognition of her contributions to American film.

For further reading:

Herndon, Booton, *Mary Pickford and Douglas Fairbanks*. New York: W.W. Norton and Co., 1977.

Pierlot, Hubert (1883–1964). Belgian statesman. A member of the Catholic Party, he was prime minister in 1940 when Germany invaded BELGIUM. Attempting to flee to France, he was arrested later that year, but escaped to London, where he presided over a government in exile. There he continued to oppose Germany and to maintain Belgium as an Allied power. He returned to Brussels in 1944, forming a National Union government and resigning the following year.

Piggott, Lester (1935–). British jockey. Piggott is widely regarded as the leading British jockey of the 20th century. Born to a father who was a steeplechase rider and a mother from a racing family, Piggott scored the first of his record seven Epsom Derby wins in 1954 when he was only 19. He was the British champion jockey in 1960, and continuously from 1964 to 1971. His best year was 1966 when he booted home 191 wins. Always popular with racing fans for his intense style, his rough riding tactics rendered him less so with his fellow jockeys. His 3,000 wins over 25 years included victories in the Irish Sweepstakes, the Arc de Triomphe and the Washington International. In the 1980s, Piggott ran afoul of the law and served a prison term for tax evasion. However, he made a spectacular comeback when he won a major race in the 1990 Breeders' Cup at Belmont at age 55.

"Pig War" (1905–09). SERBIA, in an attempt to reduce dependence on Austria-Hungary, imported French (instead of Austrian) munitions and established a customs union with BULGARIA, making Austrian goods uncompetitive. AUSTRIA responded by closing off Serbian pork imports. Serbia refused to bow, pressuring for a trade outlet on the Adriatic Sea through Austrian administered BOSNIA-HERZEGOVINA, and was supported by Russia. War between RUSSIA and Austria was averted by a German ultimatum (1909) demanding cessation of Russian aid to Serbia. Austria and Serbia developed a new commercial treaty, but Serbia covertly agitated among Slavs in newly Austrian annexed Bosnia-Herzegovina, contributing to the start of WORLD WAR I.

Piliniszky, Janos (1921–1981). Hungarian poet. Pilinszky's work describes the horrors of CONCENTRATION CAMPS and daily life in GERMANY during WORLD WAR II.

For further reading:

Pilinszky, Janos, *Crater: Poems 1974–1975*. London: Anvil Press, 1978.

———, *The Desert of Love*. London: Anvil Press, 1988.

Pill, the. Method of oral contraception that became widely available in 1961. Early forms of the pill contained artificial forms of the female hormones estrogen and progesterone. Taken for 21 days during a menstrual cycle, they suppress the production of the pituitary hormones that normally cause ovulation. The lack of ovulation prevents the possibility of pregnancy. More recent versions of the pill have contained only the progesterone-like hormone. It does not prevent ovulation but does prevent fertilization. The contraceptive pill is extremely popular because of its ease of use and comparative safety. However, it has been shown to cause some health risks, including cardiac or cardiovascular problems, and blood clots in some women who smoke, are overweight or are above the age of 35. Among the less serious side effects that the pill may produce are nausea, headache and weight gain.

Pilnyak, Boris [B.A. Vogau] (1894–1937). Russian writer. Pilnyak's novel *The Naked Year* (1922) was the first novel to deal with the revolution and its effects on Russian life. Pilnyak became disillusioned with the regime, and the publication of *Mahogany* (1929) caused him to be expelled from the author association. His novel about the FIVE-YEAR PLAN, *The Volga Flows into the Caspian Sea,* was an attempt to reinstate himself in official favor. He survived the purges by publicly denouncing his "antirevolutionary" writings.

Pilsudski, Jozef (1867–1935). Polish soldier and nationalist leader. Pilsudski began his political career agitating against Russian rule of POLAND. At age 20 he was sent to Siberia for several years as punishment for his anti-Russian activities. Returning to Poland (1892), he founded and edited a socialist-nationalist newspaper. During the RUSSO-JAPANESE WAR (1904–05) he went to Tokyo to appeal for Japanese aid for a Polish revolt against RUSSIA, but this mission failed. At the start of WORLD WAR I he organized a force of some 10,000 Polish volunteers to fight alongside the Austrians against Russia. However, he earned the mistrust of the Germans, who interned him in 1917. He returned to newly-independent POLAND at the end of the war (1918). With the title of Marshal he assumed command of all Polish troops and was made provisional head of state. He successfully defended Poland against a Soviet invasion (1919–20). He retired as head of the army in 1923 but led a military coup three years later (May 12–15, 1926) after a breakdown of the democratic government. He was officially prime minister from 1926 to 1928 and again briefly in 1930; but as minister of war from 1926 on, he remained the virtual dictator of Poland until his death. Pilsudski was one of the first European leaders to recognize the dangers of NAZISM, but his warnings went largely unheeded.

For further reading:
Jedrzejewicz, Waclaw, *Pilsudski: A Life for Poland*. New York: Hippocrene Books, 1990.

Pimen, Patriarch (Sergei Izvekov) (1910–1990). Russian religious leader, primate of the Russian Orthodox Church (1971 to 1990). Pimen was the first patriarch to be educated under the Soviet system and was widely regarded as a compliant supporter of the Soviet government. Throughout his tenure, he was criticized in the U.S.S.R. and abroad for bowing to pressure from the Kremlin on issues ranging from the selection of priests to the approval of church doctrine. In March 1988 he was the target of protests by religious dissidents who urged him to step aside to make way for a younger leader, who might be more willing to take advantage of the religious liberalization permitted by President Mikhail GORBACHEV.

Pinhiero de Azevedo, Jose Baptista (1917–1983). Portuguese naval officer and politician. He was a member of the ruling **Junta of National Salvation,** a coalition of leaders who governed PORTUGAL following a military coup in April 1974 that ousted the authoritarian government of Premier Marcelo Caetano. Pinheiro de Azevedo served as premier in a provisional government from September 1975 until June 1976, when he oversaw the country's first democratic elections in 48 years.

Pink Floyd. British ROCK and roll band. Pink Floyd, which achieved great commercial success in the 1970s, was founded in London in 1966. Featuring a psychedelic style, the original lineup of musicians included Syd Barrett, vocals and guitar; Roger Waters, bass; Richard Wright, keyboards; and Nick Mason, drums. Pink Floyd enjoyed its first British hit with the single "Arnold Layne" (1967). In 1968 David Gilmour joined the band as a replacement for Barrett. Pink Floyd became known for its dramatic and inventive use of large-scale sound systems, electronic music and vocal choruses. Its album *The Dark Side of the Moon* (1973) remained on the American album charts for over a decade—the longest run in recording history. Its 1979 album *The Wall* featured the hit single "Another Brick in the Wall."

Pinochet, Augusto (1915–). A career Chilean army officer, Pinochet rose to general and was commander in chief of CHILE's armed forces from 1973 to 1980. He led the right-wing coup that deposed President Salvador ALLENDE in 1973. President of the Government Council of Chile (1973–74), he subsequently became president of Chile in 1974. An authoritarian though not totalitarian leader, he followed a strict policy of repression against opponents of his regime. In October 1988 a referendum calling for new elections was adopted by popular vote; Pinochet agreed to abide by the result. A democratic civilian government was elected in 1989, and Pinochet stepped down upon the inauguration of the new president, although he remained as commander in chief of the army.

Augusto Pinochet, president of Chile (1988).

Pinter, Harold [born Harold Da Pinta] (1930–). British playwright, screenplay writer and theatrical director. Pinter is the leading British playwright of the postwar era, with a unique gift—for which admiring critics coined the term "Pinteresque"—for portraying psychological anguish through subtly revelatory dialogue. His first success, the one-act play *The Room* (1957), was followed by several acclaimed full-length plays including *The Birthday Party* (1958), *The Dumb Waiter* (1958), and *The Caretaker* (1960), which was adapted into an acclaimed British film, titled *The Guest* (1964), featuring Alan Bates, Donald Pleasance, and Robert Shaw. A more recent play, *Betrayal* (1978), was adapted by Pinter himself into screenplay form for the film *Betrayal* (1982), starring Jeremy Irons, Ben Kingsley, and Patricia Hodge and concerning a tortured love triangle. Pinter has written frequently for films—including the screenplay for *The French Lieutenant's Woman* (1981)—while continuing his involvement with the theater. He is married to the British writer Lady Antonia Fraser.

Pinza, Ezio (1892–1957). Italian bass opera singer and actor. Pinza was considered one of the greatest bass voices of the opera stage from the 1920s to the 1940s. He was a regular performer with the Metropolitan Opera in New York, although he toured regularly in Europe and South America as well. Pinza appeared often in Verdi basso roles and also triumphed in the lead role of Mozart's *Don Giovanni.* Late in his career, Pinza turned to less demanding vocal roles in Broadway musicals and enjoyed great success in Richard RODGERS and Oscar HAMMERSTEIN II's *South Pacific* (1949). He thereafter enjoyed a brief HOLLYWOOD career in films such as *Tonight We Sing* (1953).

Pioneer. Early U.S. spacecraft and program, developed in response to the Soviet Luna missions, which had orbited and photographed the moon at close range. Pioneer 1, which attained an altitude of 70,171 miles, was launched on October 11, 1958. A month later, the launch of Pioneer 2 failed; Pioneer 3, launched on December 6, reached an altitude of 63,580 miles. Pioneer 4, launched March 3, 1959, completed the first lunar fly-by at a distance of 37,300 miles from the moon. The Pioneers were succeeded by the RANGER missions, but continued to be used into the '70s for long-range probes to Jupiter, Saturn and beyond.

Pioneers. Group for young Soviets between the ages of 10 and 14 to 15 years, founded as an auxiliary to the KOMSOMOL in 1922. The aim of the movement is outlined in the Komsomol statute: It should make its members "convinced fighters for the Communist Party cause, inculcate in them the love of labor and knowledge, and assist the formation of the younger generation in the spirit of communist consciousness and morality."

Regular meetings are held; visits are arranged to places of revolutionary interest; and Pioneers parade and take part in summer camps. Pioneer activities often provide a useful addition to the school curriculum. Those wishing to join must take the Pioneer oath and undertake to obey the Pioneer laws. Nearly all children in this age range are Pioneers.

Piotrovsky, Boris B. (1907?–90). Russian archaeologist and museum director. Piotrovsky was one of the leading archaeologists of the 20th century. His most famous project was the discovery, in 1939, of remains of the ancient civilization of Urartu in what is now Armenia. Through his excavations in Karmir Blur in Armenia, Piotrovsky unearthed an Urartu fortress and town. During his career, he published over 200 scholarly works. In 1964 he was named director of the Hermitage, the famous LENINGRAD museum that houses one of the world's great collections of art and archaeological artifacts. Piotrovsky was an honorary member of numerous Western academies of science, including those of France and England.

Pirandello, Luigi (1867–1936). Italian playwright, actor, story writer, novelist and literary critic. Pirandello, who won the NOBEL PRIZE for literature in 1934, was a prolific and versatile writer who remains best known for his works for the stage. An important precursor of the Theater of the ABSURD movement, Pirandello was a theatrical pioneer in dealing with existential themes including the tenuous nature of sanity, the loss of secure personal identity in modern society and the absurd cruelties occasioned by political ambition. He was also influential by virtue of his discarding of standard dramatic plot structure. Pirandello's first success came with the play *Right You Are (If You Think So)* (1917). His major theatrical works include *Enrico IV* (1922), *The Man with a Flower in His Mouth* (1923), *Lazarus* (1929) and the trilogy of *Six Characters in Search of an Author* (1922), *Each in His Own Way* (1924) and *Tonight We Improvise* (1929).

Pire, Jules (1878–1953). Belgian general and WORLD WAR II RESISTANCE leader. At the time of the Nazi invasion of BELGIUM in May 1940, Pire was an infantry commander. Joining the forces resisting Germany, Pire entered the Belgian Legion in 1941 and was widely known by the code name "Pygmalion." In collaboration with other Resistance groups, he executed a number of important sabotage raids in 1944. Leading the underground Belgian army, he aided British and American troops in the liberation of Belgium in September 1944, preventing the retreating German army from destroying such key installations as the port facilities at Antwerp and protecting Belgian armored divisions that were actively supporting Allied activities.

Piro, Frank "Killer Joe" (1920–1989). American dancer and dance instructor who taught popular dance steps to scores of high-society figures. Among Piro's students were the Duke and Duchess of WINDSOR (see EDWARD VIII), Luci Baines Johnson (daughter of Lyndon Baines JOHNSON), and Dame Margot FONTEYN. He also helped popularize many of the discotheque-style dances of the 1960s and '70s. He was known as "Killer Joe" for his ability to outlast any partner on the dance floor.

Piston, Walter (1894–1976). American composer and teacher. As a composer, Piston is noted for his sophisticated, balanced, neoclassical style and his use of harmony and counterpoint. As a teacher, he was admired for his musical knowledge and ability to inspire such students as Leonard BERNSTEIN. He taught music at Harvard University from 1926 until he retired in 1960. His most famous compositions include Symphony No. 3 (1947) and Symphony No. 7 (1960), for which he received PULITZER PRIZES, and a Viola Concerto (1957) and String Quartet No. 5 (1962), for which he received New York Music Critics Circle Awards.

Pitney, Mahlon (1858–1924). Associate justice, U.S. Supreme Court (1912–22). A graduate of Princeton University, Pitney practiced law with his father until his election to Congress in 1894. However, he resigned his seat, was elected to the New Jersey state senate and was next appointed to the New Jersey Supreme Court. In 1912 Pitney was nominated to the U.S. Supreme Court by President William Howard TAFT. He was generally a conservative on the bench and resigned in 1922 for health reasons.

Pius X (1835–1914). Roman Catholic Pope. Born Giuseppe Sarto in Riese, Italy, Pius X reigned from 1903 to 1914. As Pope, he condemned religious modernism, reformed the Church's system of religious instruction, opposed anticlerical laws in Italy and France, and began the process of recodifying canon law and retranslating the Bible. Renowned for his concern for the poor, Pius X was canonized a saint in 1954 by Pope PIUS XII.

Pius XI (1857–1939). Roman Catholic Pope. Achille Ratti, born in Desio, Italy, reigned as Pope from February 6, 1922, to February 10, 1939. As Pope, Pius XI promoted missionary activities, criticized laissez-faire capitalism and denounced MUSSOLINI and HITLER. In 1929, he signed with Italy the Lateran Agreement, which granted independent status to Vatican City and recognized Catholicism as Italy's official religion.

Pius XII [Eugenio Pacelli] (1876–1958). Pontiff of the Roman Catholic Church (1939–58). Born in Rome, Pacelli was ordained a Roman Catholic priest in 1899 and entered the papal diplomatic service in 1901, serving in various capacities therein for 38 years. He became both a cardinal and a papal secretary of state in 1930. Pacelli became acquainted with German politics as a nuncio to the WEIMAR REPUBLIC during the 1920s, and in 1933 he negotiated a diplomatic agreement between the Vatican and the newly formed Nazi government. In 1939 he was elected as pope and took the name Pius XII. During WORLD WAR II Pius XII failed to make any public protest against the Nazi genocide efforts against the Jews, thereby earning a great deal of public criticism. After the war Pius XII condemned the new communist regimes in Poland, Romania, Hungary and Yugoslavia.

Plague, The. Novel (1947) by French NOBEL PRIZE-winning author Albert CAMUS, widely regarded as one of the great novels of this century. Written in post-WORLD WAR II France, it shows the influence of the painful occupation of France by the Nazis, during which time Camus was active in the French RESISTANCE. The story is set in the Algerian city of Oran, in which a plague (interpreted by many critics as symbolizing the invading Nazi forces) has broken out. As the city is cordoned off and dwindles in population and resources, the inner resources of each resident are tested. Some, such as heroic Dr. Bernard Rieux, give themselves over to helping their fellow humans and succeed in spiritually transcending their formerly shallow lives to become, in the terms of Camus' existential philosophy, saints without a God. Other persons retreat into selfishness and are likened unto the rats that scamper in the plague-ridden streets. (See also EXISTENTIALISM.)

Plaid Cymru. Welsh name for the Party of Wales, or Welsh Nationalist Party, formed by intellectuals who merged several small groups in August 1925. Its program favors Welsh language and culture. It gained publicity with involvment in the terrorist bombings of a Royal Air Force (RAF) base in 1938. In 1966 disillusionment with the LABOUR PARTY gained Plaid Cymru its first House of Commons seat, which increased to three by 1974. The party is also represented in local governments and councils. After the defeat of Welsh autonomy in the 1979 referendum, the party lost ground, but managed to retain two seats in Parliament in that year's election. Its members are mostly from the middle class, favoring a moderate economic program and opposing English-language signs and migration to Wales by wealthy English people.

Planchon, Roger (1931–). French stage director, actor and playwright. Planchon is best known as an innovative theatrical visionary who succeeded, in his native land, in drawing substantial popular and critical attention to productions staged outside of Paris. His own theater, first founded in Lyon in 1950 and subsequently located in Villeurbanne as the Theatre National Populaire, has become one of the leading centers of French drama. Influenced by Antonin ARTAUD and Bertolt BRECHT, Planchon has tended to avoid the classic French theater repertoire in favor of innovative stagings of modern European playwrights as well as iconoclastic reinterpretations of Shakespeare. His own plays include *Bleus, blancs, rouges* (1967), *Le Cochon noir* (1974) and *Gilles de Rais* (1976).

Planck, Max Karl Ernst Ludwig (1858–1947). German physicist. Planck is the originator of quantum theory and therefore the father of 20th-century physics. He received his Ph.D. in 1879 from the

University of Munich, and from 1889 to his retirement in 1928, he was affiliated with the University of Berlin. In 1900, while investigating the radiation given off by hot bodies, Planck discovered that the radiation was not emitted consistently over all wave lengths, as predicted by classical physics, but in "jumps"; this led him to suggest that energy was released in small packets, or quanta. Planck's revolutionary theory was soon put to the test by other researchers, including Albert EINSTEIN, who used the quantum theory to explain the photoelectric effect in 1905; Niels BOHR, who based his model of the hydrogen atom on the principle in 1913; and Arthur COMPTON, who used it to investigate X-ray scattering in 1923. In 1918, Planck won the NOBEL PRIZE for physics.

Plante, (Joseph) Jacques (Omer) (1929–1986). French-Canadian athlete. He was one of the greatest goaltenders in the history of the National Hockey League. During his 17–year career he played with five teams but was best known as the goalie of the Montreal Canadiens in the 1950s, when the team won five successive Stanley Cups. His career goals against average was 2.37, with 82 shutouts. He won the Vezina Trophy seven times for the lowest goals against average. He emerged from a three-year retirement in 1968, lending credibility to the expansionist St. Louis Blues. He was the first modern goaltender to wear a face mask and was one of the first to establish the modern style of roaming beyond the goal crease.

plastics. Plastics are synthetic materials that can be turned into a variety of usable products through such processes as heating and molding. As a result of their molecular structure (plastic molecules are called polymers), plastics soften when heated but become rigid when cooled, and are tough and lightweight. The term "plastic" is derived from the Greek "plastikos," meaning "to form." In 1910 American chemist Leo H. Baekeland made the first completely synthetic plastic, called BAKELITE. The plastics industry exploded after 1920 with the growth of the chemical industry and development of necessary equipment for its manufacture. Such raw materials as cellulose, coal and petroleum products are combined with a variety of chemicals and additives to make durable plastic. Plastics can be made by molding, extrusion, lamination, casting and foaming, and are used in everything from rigid foam for refrigerator insulation and flexible foam for clothing to nylon films for medical use.

Plate, Battle of the River. Naval engagement between the British and Germans that took place on December 13, 1939, in the early part of WORLD WAR II. The German pocket battleship *Graf Spee*, which had already sunk nine Allied ships, was sighted in the South Atlantic by a British cruiser squadron under the command of Commodore Henry Harwood (later admiral). The three-ship squadron inflicted considerable damage on the German vessel, which was forced into Montevideo for repairs. Meanwhile, a large naval force gathered at the Plate estuary. The Germans were forced to scuttle the *Graf Spee* off the coast of Uruguay on December 17, rather than face the British ships. The Battle of the River Plate was the first direct encounter between British and German forces during the war, and was an important naval victory and morale-booster for the British.

Plath, Sylvia (1932–1963). American poet. The daughter of an elderly German-American entomologist who died when she was eight, and of an ambitious mother, Plath was a star student in high school. In the summer of 1954, along with Anne SEXTON, she studied with Robert LOWELL at Boston University. Plath's autobiographical novel *The Bell Jar* (1961) describes her years at Smith College (B.A., 1955), an unhappy stint as a guest editor for *Mademoiselle* in 1953, and her hospitalization after her first suicide attempt. She attended Newnham College, Cambridge, where she married the poet Ted HUGHES in 1956. In 1959 she settled in England. She published only two books before her suicide at the age of 31, but her posthumous *Ariel* (1965) stunned the literary world with its starkly powerful and horrific imagery. Her poetry continued to appear for a decade while her reputation and influence burgeoned, particularly among Feminists (see FEMINISM). Plath is considered among the strongest and most original of the CONFESSIONAL POETS, although her work continues to stir controversy.

For further reading:

Stevenson, Anne, *Bitter Fame: The Life of Sylvia Plath.* Boston: Houghton Mifflin, 1989.

Wagner-Martin, Linda, *Sylvia Plath: A Biography.* New York: Saint Martin's Press, 1988.

Sylvia Plath, whose works have influenced a generation of poets, critics and readers.

Platonov, Sergei Fedorovich (1860–1933). Russian historian and professor at St. Petersburg University. A specialist on the Time of Troubles, Platonov protested loudly at the falsification of history by the Soviet authorities. As a result he was dismissed from the Academy of Sciences and banished. His publications include the textbook *A History of Russia* (1925).

Playboy of the Western World, The. Play (1907) by the Irish playwright John Millington SYNGE. Though it is now acknowledged as a classic, *The Playboy of the Western World* was a highly controversial play when it was first performed, sparking riots by audiences in Dublin in 1907 and in New York City upon its American premiere in 1911. What aroused the audience so was the bold portrayal of its protagonist, the randy and charismatic Christy Mahon, who wins the heart of the lovely Pegeen Mike and the esteem of an entire Irish village due to his false bragging as to how he murdered his tyrant of a father. When Christy's father—still alive and healthy—arrives in search of his son, Christy feels compelled to try to kill him to save his honor. But a murder attempt pursued in their own environs leads the once-admiring villagers to call for Christy's death. Christy's father begs for clemency, however, and he and his son depart from the village reunited in spirit. The central theme of *Playboy* is the ease by which people are swayed by superficial appearances and assumptions.

Player, Gary Jim (1935–). South African golfer. Arnold PALMER, Jack NICKLAUS and Gary Player had a virtual lock on tournament play during the 1960s. In 1959, at the age of 23, Player became the youngest player ever to win the modern British Open, an event he was to capture again in 1968 and 1972. He twice won the U.S. Masters at Augusta: first, in a thrilling one-stroke victory over Arnold Palmer and again 13 years later. Despite his preference for playing in Europe, Asia and Africa, Player finished his career sixth on the American career earnings list.

Plekhanov, Georgi Valentinovich (1857–1919). Russian politician. When the organization *Zemlya i Volya*, of which Plekhanov was a member, split into violent and nonviolent factions, Plekhanov became leader of the new, nonviolent *Cherny Peredel* (*Black Repartition*). Having become a Marxist in Western Europe, in 1883 he founded the Liberation of Labor group. Collaborating with LENIN, Plekhanov at first supported the BOLSHEVIKS, but in 1903 joined the MENSHEVIKS, and in 1910 he established the faction of "party-minded" Mensheviks. He played a unique part in converting the Russian intelligentsia to Marxism. After the FEBRUARY REVOLUTION of 1917, Plekhanov set up the right-wing Social Democratic organization Unity, but died shortly after the Bolshevik seizure of power.

Plisetskaya, Maya (1925–). Russian ballerina. Having studied at the Bolshoi School, Plisetskaya is considered one of the greatest ballerinas of her time. She is noted particularly for her interpretation of the role of Odette-Odile in *Swan Lake*.

Ploesti [Ploiesti]. City in ROMANIA. Some 35 miles north of Bucharest, Ploesti is a major oil drilling and refining center. The Germans invaded Romania in WORLD WAR II largely in order to obtain access to the plentiful oil supply and petrochemical products of the region. Allied bombing raids on the refineries (beginning in Aug. 1943) caused much damage.

Plomley, Roy (1914–1985). British radio personality who created and hosted what was believed to be the world's longest-running radio series, "Desert Island Discs," broadcast on the BBC since 1942. Each week, he asked his guest celebrities to choose eight records, one book and one luxury item they would like to have with them if marooned on a desert island. He would then chat with them about their lives and intersperse the conversation with recordings of their musical selections. Over the years he had close to 1,800 guests on the show, including Princess Margaret and Prime Minister Margaret Thatcher.

PM. See Ralph McAllister INGERSOLL.

Poalei Agudas Yisrael [the Agudas Workers of Israel]. Left-wing, ultra-religious Israeli political party.

Pocket Book. American publishing company, founded 1939 by Robert F. de Graff (1895–1981). It was the first U.S. publisher to specialize in paperback editions. Beginning with 10 inexpensive reprints, it marketed these books by selling them at newsstands, in grocery stores and drugstores for 25 cents apiece. Pocket Book revolutionized the U.S. publishing industry and opened the way for what became a standard practice in the publishing and bookselling industry. By the time de Graff retired in 1957, Pocket Book's annual sales totaled $15 million.

Podhoretz, Norman. See COMMENTARY.

Podoloff, Maurice (1890–1985). American sports executive. Podoloff was president of the Basketball Association of America (BAA) from 1946 to 1949 and, from 1949 until his retirement in 1963, first president of the National Basketball Association (NBA). That league was created through a merger of the BAA and the old National Basketball League. Only 5 feet 2 inches tall himself, he never played basketball but was one of the game's great innovators. He invented the 24-second clock and the six-foul rule and implemented the use of professional referees. He was responsible for the NBA landing its first TV contract in 1954.

Podvoysky, Nicholas Ilich (1880–1948). Soviet politician. Having joined the Social Democratic Labor Party in 1901, Podvoysky later adhered to its BOLSHEVIK faction. He was the owner of a publishing house specializing in Social Democratic literature before World War I. Following the FEBRUARY REVOLUTION of 1917, he was a member of the executive branch of the first legal Bolshevik St. Petersburg committee and chairman of the military commission of the central committee and of the military revolutionary committee of the Petrograd Soviet. After the seizure of power, Podvoysky set about the task of organizing the Red Army. In spite of the fact that he served as a commissar in the RUSSIAN CIVIL WAR, he fell out of favor and from the 1930s was relegated to serving on the staff of the Marx-Engels-Lenin Institute.

pogrom [devastation]. An attack on JEWS and Jewish property, especially in the Russian empire. Russian pogroms, which were condoned by the government, were particularly common in the years immediately after the assassination of Alexander II in 1881 and again from 1903 to 1906, although mob persecution of Jews continued until the 1917 Russian Revolution.

Poincare, Raymond (1860–1934). French statesman, president of FRANCE (1913–20). A Parisian lawyer, he was a member of the chamber of deputies from 1887 to 1912, holding various cabinet posts, and served as a senator from 1903 to 1913. He became premier and foreign minister in 1912. Perceiving the threat of war from Germany, he strengthened ententes between France and both Russia and England, while attempting to prepare his nation for hostilities. Becoming president in 1913, he extended service in the military to three years. During WORLD WAR I he supported a personal and political foe, Georges CLEMENCEAU, as head of the government in order to secure French unity. After the war Poincare called for stringent punishment of Germany and felt that the terms of the TREATY OF VERSAILLES were overly lenient. Leaving the presidency, he once more served as a senator from 1920 to 1929. Again named premier and foreign minister in 1922, he attempted to force continued German reparations by sending French troops into the RUHR in 1923. Forced out of office in 1924, he returned in 1926 during a period of financial crisis and carried out policies that stabilized the franc. He retired in 1929.

Pointe-Noire. Congo port city on the Atlantic Ocean, 230 miles southwest of Brazzaville. Founded in 1883, Pointe-Noire developed into a commercial seaport between 1934 and 1939, with a railroad completed in 1948. In 1950 Pointe-Noire was capital of France's Middle Congo, itself a part of French Equatorial Africa; in 1958 the capital was moved to Brazzaville.

Poitier, Sidney (1924–). American actor and director. Known for his subtle and powerful performances, Poitier was the first black American to become a major HOLLYWOOD star. Born in Florida of Bahamian parents, he received his training at the American Negro Theater in New York in the late 1940s. Poitier broke into film in the 1950s, starring in several important pictures dealing with racism: *Cry, the Beloved Country* (1952, based on the novel by Alan PATON), *The Blackboard Jungle* (1955) and *The Defiant Ones* (1958), which earned him an ACADEMY AWARD nomination as best actor. He won the best actor award for his performance in *Lilies*

POLAND

POLAND

1905	Pilsudski begins revolutionary activity in Russian-occupied areas; forced to flee.
1916	Germans create puppet government as Russians retreat; Pilsudski and others oppose it.
1917	Polish National Committee formed in Switzerland is recognized by Allies.
1918	As Germans and Austrians surrender, republic is proclaimed; first Polish state since 1772.
1919	Pilsudski abandons attempt to form socialist government in favor of Paderewski, who becomes first premier.
1921	Treaty of Riga ends war with Bolsheviks; gains Poland much territory.
1924	Construction of new port begins at Gdynia.
1926	Severe depression; Russian-German treaty causes fears; Pilsudski seizes power and institutes limited dictatorship.
1935	Pilsudski dies; military government continues.
1939	Secret Nazi-Soviet agreement leads to invasion from West, then East; first shots of World War II fired at Danzig (Gdansk).
1941	Nazi death camp at Auschwitz/Birkenau begins extermination of between one and three million Jews, Gypsies, Poles and others.
1943	Graves of 4,300 Polish officers found in Katyn Forest; Soviets blame Nazis; at Teheran Conference, Roosevelt and Churchill secretly agree to Stalin's demand for Poland.
1944	Soviet army delays entering the capital until Warsaw Uprising is crushed by Germans; 200,000 die.
1945	Boundaries shifted west at Potsdam Conference; U.S. and Britain recognize Soviet-installed government.
1949	Government, now openly communist, begins period of severe Stalinist repression.
1956	Worker protests crushed; Gomulka assumes power and begins limited Stalinization.
1970	Strikes at Gdynia and Gdansk lead to Gomulka's ouster.
1979	Visit of Polish-born Pope John Paul II stirs religious and nationalist feelings.
1980	Czeslaw Milosz wins Nobel Prize for literature; strikes in essential ports and coalfields force legalization of unions; Solidarity, a union of all trades, is formed; electrician Lech Walesa becomes leader.
1981	With up to 10 million Solidarity members demanding free elections, General Jaruzelski imposes martial law and arrests union leaders.
1983	International sanctions lead to lifting of martial law but contribute to rapid decay of Polish economy; Solidarity continues underground; Nobel Prize for peace to Walesa.
1988	As economy crumbles, wave of strikes questions communist ability to govern.
1989	Solidarity relegalized; Jaruzelski agrees to sweeping changes: free-market economy, elections, press freedom; Solidarity gains control of new parliament; Mazowiecki becomes first noncommunist prime minister in Eastern Europe since 1945.
1990	Communist Party disbanded; republic proclaimed; Solidarity splits as Walesa defeats Mazowiecki for presidency; many Poles express dissatisfaction with Solidarity and ruined economy by voting for maverick Polish-Canadian businessman Tyminski; Soviets admit Katyn Forest massacre.

of the Field (1963). In 1967 he played leading roles in three hits: a schoolteacher in inner-city London in *To Sir, with Love;* a black detective from the North investigating a murder in the deep South in *In the Heat of the Night;* and a man about to enter an interracial marriage in *Guess Who's Coming to Dinner*. In the 1970s he directed and costarred in several films with Bill COSBY. After an absence from the screen, he reemerged in 1988, directing and starring in the chase thriller *Shoot to Kill*.

For further reading:

Bergman, Carol, *Sidney Poitier*. New York: Chelsea House, 1989.

Marill, Alvin H., *The Films of Sidney Poitier*. New York: Carol Publishing Group, 1978.

Poland. Eastern European nation bordered on the north by the Baltic Sea, the east by the SOVIET UNION, the south by CZECHOSLOVAKIA and the west by GERMANY. Divided among Russia, Prussia and AUSTRIA after 1795, Poland did not gain independence until 1918 under the leadership of Jozef PILSUDSKI, who had led Polish forces in WORLD WAR I for Austria against Russia. In 1920, taking advantage of Russia's internal upheaval, Poland fought for and regained additional territory, which was ceded in a 1921 treaty. In August of 1939 NAZI Germany and the U.S.S.R. signed a treaty containing a covert agreement to divide Poland between them. In September the German invasion of Poland was quickly followed by a Soviet invasion from the east. Poland fell and WORLD WAR II began. Wladyslaw Raczkiewicz formed an exile government in Paris, which moved to London when France was occupied in 1940. In 1941 Germany attacked the U.S.S.R. and took all of Poland. Polish communists fought alongside the Soviets. The Poles formed

Gen. Wojciech Jaruzelski (left) and Solidarity leader Lech Walesa sit together during the first session of Poland's newly created senate (July 3, 1989).

an alternate government in 1944, the Polish Committee of National Liberation, which the Soviets recognized. Declaring itself the Provisional Government of Poland, it moved to Lublin, where it was joined by some of the exiled government from London. The Allies recognized it at the YALTA CONFERENCE in 1945. A 1944 treaty between Poland and the U.S.S.R. established their border at the CURZON LINE, but Poland gained territory from Germany to the west in an Allied agreement after the war, so the country was effectively shifted westward and millions of Poles resettled. Elections in 1947 established a "people's republic" in Poland, and in 1952 a new constitution was adopted, thus beginning a repressive, STALINIST government with close ties to the U.S.S.R. Poland's government also sought to abolish the Roman Catholic church. In 1956, following strikes and riots over food shortages and Soviet control, Wladyslaw GOMULKA was elected leader of the United Workers Party. Gomulka eased restrictions on private farming and released Cardinal Stefan WYSZYNSKI, who had been imprisoned in 1953. Strikes again broke out in 1970, and Gomulka was succeeded by Edward GIEREK. Opposition to his government mounted through the decade and peaked in 1979 after the first of three visits by Polish-born Pope JOHN PAUL II. In 1980 a strike that started in the Gdansk shipyards spread to all industries, and the government conceded workers' the right to strike. Lech WALESA formed the SOLIDARITY (*Solidarnoa*) union. It sought workers' rights and liberties. In 1981, following a national strike for a five-day work week, Premier Pinkowski was replaced by General Wojciech JARUZELSKI. Martial law was imposed, Solidarity banned and its leaders arrested. The U.S. responded by initiating economic sanctions. In 1982 curfews were eased and further rioting occurred. Lech Walesa was released from prison and martial law suspended. Following another conciliatory visit by the pope in 1983, the government granted amnesty to political prisoners, releasing 35,000 of them in 1984 on the 40th anniversary of the People's Republic, the remainder were released in 1986. The U.S. loosened its sanctions, which were lifted in 1987. Martial law ended in 1984, but many restrictions were still in force. Food shortages continued, and opposition to the government grew. Following widespread strikes in 1988, the government was forced to recognize Solidarity and allow it to participate in elections in 1989, when Solidarity-backed candidates won overwhelmingly in parliament. The Polish government, still facing shortages, has announced programs to restructure the economy, including plans to privatize industries. Walesa was elected president in 1990.

Polanski, Roman (1933–). Polish actor and director. Polanski is widely considered one of the most original and disturbing film directors of his generation; both his movies and his personal life have generated much controversy. Born in Paris, Polanski grew up in Crakow, Poland. A survivor of the HOLOCAUST, he later attended the Polish Film School at Lodz (1954). During the late 1950s he wrote, directed or acted in several short films. His first feature, *Knife in the Water* (1962), brought Polanski international notice. He subsequently moved to England, where he directed *Repulsion* (1965) and *Cul de Sac* (1966). His first HOLLYWOOD film was *The Fearless Vampire Killers* (1967), a horror film spoof. It was followed by *Rosemary's Baby* (1968), a suspense thriller about witchcraft in New York City that became a popular hit and is regarded as a classic of its genre. The following year Polanski's wife, actress Sharon Tate, was murdered by Charles MANSON. The sensationalism and publicity surrounding the case drove Polanski to seek refuge in England, where he directed a controversial adaptation of Shakespeare's *Macbeth* (1971). Polanski's *Chinatown* (1974), starring Jack NICHOLSON, was an acclaimed mystery in the FILM NOIR style. *The Tenant* (1976), in which Polanski also acted, was a morbid psychological drama. Shortly thereafter Polanski was arrested in California for statutory rape. While awaiting trial he jumped bail, fled the U.S. and settled in France. His subsequent relationship with actress Nastassia Kinski, whom he directed in *Tess* (1981, an adaptation of Thomas HARDY's *Tess of the D'Urbervilles*) also caused considerable comment. His later films include *Pirates* (1986) and *Frantic* (1988).

For further reading:
Wexman, Virginia W., *Roman Polanski*. Boston: G.K. Hall, 1985.

Police. U.K. rock group; formed in 1976 by bassist Sting (Gordon Sumner), guitarist Andy Summers and drummer Stewart Copeland. They stirred little interest in the then punk-dominated music scene until all three dyed their hair blond. Their music was more cerebral than that of their peers, with a pronounced THIRD WORLD influence. Their breakthrough album, *Outlandos d'Amour*, included the hit "Can't Stand Losing You." Although they claim to still exist as a group, all have pursued solo careers since the early 1980s. Their last number-one hit as a group was "Every Breath You Take" in 1983. Sting's solo career included a critically dismissed Broadway appearance in *Threepenny Opera* and film work in *Dune* and *The Bride*. He has made many concert appearances on behalf of Amnesty International, as well as ecological causes.

political correctness ["pc"]. A controversial concept, and the term used to describe it, that surfaced in many American universities in the late 1980s and early 1990s. "Political correctness" or "pc" was especially prominent in humanities departments at Duke and Stanford universities, among other institutions. Faculty members who advocated "political correctness" generally saw the classroom as a forum for instilling "progressive" or "correct" political ideals in their students. PC advocates criticized traditional courses in Western literature and civilization as biased, and instead favored a "multicultural" approach to history and literature. Political correctness aimed at a larger criticism of Western society, which was viewed as controlled by white males at the expense of women and minorities. On some campuses, faculty members whose courses did not conform to so-called "politically correct" ideologies were denounced as racist or sexist and were often denied tenure. Critics of political correctness viewed it as a latter-day left-wing version of MCCARTHYISM. The term was used derisively by those who saw it as an extremist attempt to rewrite history and stifle intellectual debate. President George BUSH weighed in against the idea of political correctness in an address at the University of Michigan in the spring of 1991.

For further reading:
Kimball, Roger, *Tenured Radicals: How Politics Has Corrupted Our Higher Education*. New York: HarperCollins, 1990.

Pollard, Fritz (Frederick Douglas) (1894–1986). American athlete and coach. In 1916, after a sensational season as a halfback for Brown University, Pollard became the first black to be named to an all-American college football team. He was the only black head coach of an NFL team, until Art Snell was named a head coach in 1989.

Pollock, Jackson (1912–1956). American painter. After finishing school in the West, Pollock moved to New York City and enrolled in the Art Students League (1930–33). Pollock was interested in abstract art. His paintings became splotches and splashes and drippings and textures, said by some critics to be thoroughly controlled. His paintings started the art movement that later became known as the "action school." Beginning in 1973 his paintings brought the highest prices ever paid for contemporary art. His *The Search* was sold in 1988 for $4,840,000.

For further reading:
Frank, Elizabeth, *Jackson Pollock, 1912–1956*. New York: Abbeville Press, 1983.
Naifeh, Steven, *Jackson Pollock: An American Genius*. New York: Crown, 1989.

Pol Pot [born Saloth Sar] (1928–). The notorious leader of the Cambodian KHMER ROUGE was born in Kompong Thom province, the youngest of seven children in a family that could be classified as "rich peasants." He attended a Catholic primary school in Phnom Penh and Norodom Sihanouk High School in Kompong Cham City. In 1949 he received a scholarship for a two-year technician's course at the Ecole Francaise de Radioelectricite in Paris. There Pol Pot joined a small group of Cambodian students in the "Marxist Circle." He returned to Phnom Penh in 1953 and later joined the Vietnamese-Khmer UIF cell in the eastern zone. In 1955 he returned to Phnom Penh and became involved with the Khmer People's Revolutionary Party or KPRP. Throughout the 1950s he gained increasing control over party activities in the city. After the murder of party leader Tou Samouth in 1962 (perhaps by the Pol Pot faction), he became acting secretary-general of the party. The struggle then returned to the countryside to garner strength for the eventual takeover of the country in April 1975. Pol Pot became prime minister in 1976, and his faction orchestrated policies of execution and forced labor from 1975 to 1979. He retreated in 1979 to the Thai border with an estimated 35,000 remaining Khmer Rouge troops. Though rumored to be ill (he has not appeared in public for years), he and his forces have remained the major threat to stability in CAMBODIA.

Polya, George (1887–1985). American mathematician. As professor emeritus of mathematics at Stanford University, Polya was one of the leading research mathematicians of his time. Among his most important contributions to modern mathematics were the elaboration of the concept of "random walk" in probability theory and the formulation of a crucial theorem in combinational analysis that came to be known as the Polya enumeration theorem. He was also the author of one of the all-time mathematical best-sellers, *How to Solve It*, a book that presented practical approaches to effective problem solving.

Pompidou, Georges (1911–1974). French political leader and president of FRANCE (1969–74). Originally a teacher, Pompidou served in WORLD WAR II until the fall of France (1940), when he returned to teaching. A member of the RESISTANCE, he joined Charles DE GAULLE's staff in 1944. He became affiliated with the Rothschild bank in 1954, serving as its director. A trusted aide to De Gaulle, he became the principal adviser to the new president of the Fifth Republic in 1958 and was appointed premier in 1962. Pompidou played a strong role in settling the strikes and strife of 1968. However, de Gaulle did not reappoint him as premier in July of that year. After De Gaulle resigned in 1969, Pompidou was elected president. During his five-year tenure in office, he attempted to deal with France's economic problems by initiating such stern measures as a price freeze and devaluation of the franc. In foreign policy, he drew closer to other European nations and rejected De Gaulle's opposition to Great Britain's entry into the EUROPEAN ECONOMIC COMMUNITY.

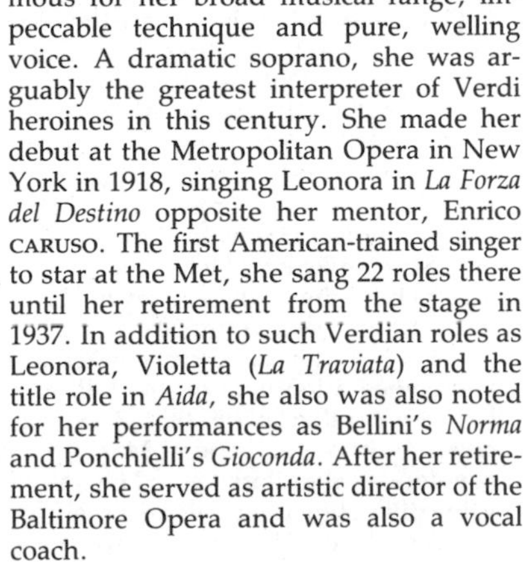
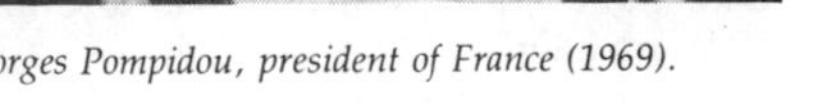
Georges Pompidou, president of France (1969).

Pompidou Center. The popular name of the Centre National d'Art et de Culture Georges Pompidou; also known as Beaubourg, for the Paris district in which it is located. Originally suggested by President Georges POMPIDOU in 1969 and named in his honor, the structure was completed in 1978. Designed by the Italian-British architectural team of Renzo Piano and Richard Rogers, the building caused a sensation during its first years due to its bold industrial design, which exposes its tubular steel framework and sports enormous, brightly painted utility pipes, brilliant red elevators, and escalators in clear plastic tunnels. The center eventually became a Parisian landmark and now houses a museum of modern art, a reference library and research centers for music and industrial design.

Ponge, Francis (1899–1988). French poet; considered the last of the original generation of French surrealist poets, he was a precursor of French novelists such as Michel BUTOR and Alain ROBBE-GRILLET. Ponge was known for his "thing-poetry"—lengthy, detailed descriptions of objects, directed toward a restoration of the power and purity of language. His works included *Les Parti pris des Choses* (The Voice of Things) and *Le Savon* (Soap), an exhaustive prose poem on the subject of "soap." SARTRE described Ponge's poems as among "the most curious and perhaps the most important of the age." A visiting professor at Columbia University in 1967, he was a recluse for the last 20 years of his life.

Ponnelle, Jean-Pierre (1932–1988). Opera director and designer. In New York Ponnelle's work was generally received unsympathetically, particularly his versions of Wagner's *Flying Dutchman* in 1979 and Massenet's *Manon* in 1986. His productions have been seen in nearly every important opera house in the world, as well as at the BAYREUTH and SALZBURG FESTIVALS.

Ponselle, Rosa [born Rosa Ponzillo] (1897–1981). American opera singer famous for her broad musical range, impeccable technique and pure, welling voice. A dramatic soprano, she was arguably the greatest interpreter of Verdi heroines in this century. She made her debut at the Metropolitan Opera in New York in 1918, singing Leonora in *La Forza del Destino* opposite her mentor, Enrico CARUSO. The first American-trained singer to star at the Met, she sang 22 roles there until her retirement from the stage in 1937. In addition to such Verdian roles as Leonora, Violetta (*La Traviata*) and the title role in *Aida*, she also was also noted for her performances as Bellini's *Norma* and Ponchielli's *Gioconda*. After her retirement, she served as artistic director of the Baltimore Opera and was also a vocal coach.

Pontoppidan, Henrik (1857–1943). Danish novelist. Pontoppidan's realistic novels depict the social fabric of Denmark in his time and reflect his advocacy of a more democratic society. His three major works are the trilogy *Det Forjoettede Land* (*The Promised Land*, published between 1891 and 1895), the octateuch *Lykke-Per* (*Lucky Peter*, published between 1898 and 1904) and the pentateuch *De Dodes Rige* (*The Kingdom of the Dead*, published between 1912 and 1916). With Karl GJELLERUP, Pontoppidan received the 1917 NOBEL PRIZE in literature. Pontoppidan also published five volumes of memoirs, *Drengeaar* (Boyhood Years, 1933), *Hamskifte* (Sloughing, 1936), *Arv og Goeld* (Inheritance and Debt, 1938), *Familieliv* (Family Life, 1940) and *Undervejs til mig selv* (On the Way to Myself, 1943).

Pool, Ithiel de Sola (1917–1984). Communications theorist and political scientist. A professor at the Massachusetts Institute of Technology, Pool was one of the first social scientists to use computer models extensively in research on human behavior. He explored the effects of various modes of communication on society and politics. His book *Candidates, Issues and Strategies* discussed computer simulations of voting behavior used in John F. KENNEDY's 1960 presidential campaign. His *American Business and Public Policy* was considered the standard reference work in the field of social communication. Pool was a fellow of the American Academy of Arts and Sciences.

pop art. Term coined in the 1950s by the British critic Lawrence Alloway. It came to define a movement beginning in the late 1950s and flourishing in the '60s, largely in the U.S., that reacted against the sometimes pretentiously serious ABSTRACT EXPRESSIONISM by portraying objects from the everyday world in flat, colorful and impersonal images. Pop artists found their subjects in commercial products such as soup cans and soda bottles, comic strips, advertising art and food. They exalted the surface of things, eschewing the plumbing of artistic depths to celebrate the transitory objects of ordinary life with flashy immediacy. The fusion of high and popular culture that pop art represented has had enormous influence on the arts and attitudes of the later 20th century. Among the important figures of the pop art movement are Roy Lichtenstein, Claes OLDENBURG, James Rosenquist and Andy WARHOL.

Popeye. The creation of E.C. Segar, Popeye the sailor made his first appearance on January 17, 1929, in the King Features syndicated comic strip *Thimble Theater;* he has been syndicated continuously ever since. Popeye appeared in his first animated cartoon in 1933, and more than 450 of these were made, most of them by Max Fleischer. In both the comic strip and the cartoons, Popeye has only average powers until he eats spinach, which gives him extraordinary strength; he uses his powers mostly to battle his archenemies Brutus (also known as Bluto), the Sea Hag and Alice the Goon. Other notable characters include Olive Oyl, Popeye's girlfriend; Swee'pea, his adoptive son; and Wimpy, the perennial moocher. The live-action motion picture *Popeye* was released in 1980, starring Robin Williams in the title role.

Popov, Dusko (1912–1981). Yugoslav-born double agent for Britain during WORLD WAR II, code-named "Tricycle." He passed Nazi secrets to London and gave false information to Berlin. In 1941 he gave an unheeded warning to the U.S. about Japanese plans to bomb the U.S. Navy base at PEARL HARBOR. In 1944 he helped divert German troops from the site of the Allied landing in NORMANDY. The author of a book of memoirs, *Spy, Counter Spy,* he was also thought to be one of the models for Ian FLEMING's fictional spy hero, JAMES BOND.

Popovich, Pavel (1930–). Soviet cosmonaut and author of a biography of Yuri GAGARIN, *It Couldn't Have Been Otherwise* (1980). Popovich made his only space flight aboard the Soviet spacecraft Vostok 4 (August 12–14, 1962). The mission was designed to pass within five miles of Vostok 3 (August 11, 1962), which had been launched the previous day. Besides his book on Gagarin, Popovich has published an autobiography, *Takeoff in the Morning* (1974), and a book of memoirs, *Testing Space and on Earth* (1982).

Popper, Hans (1903–1988). Viennese-born pathologist. As a young physician in Austria, Popper conducted pioneering biochemical research. After immigrating to the U.S. in 1938, he was based in Chicago for two decades before moving to New York City. He was known internationally as the founder of hepatology, the study of the liver and its diseases.

Popper, Sir Karl Raimund (1902–). Austrian-British philosopher. While a professor of logic and scientific method at the London School of Economics, from 1949 to 1969, Popper's insight into the basic procedure of science was fully formulated. His view was that science begins, not with observation, but with problems. The problems are then addressed by developing hypotheses, or "conjectures," as Popper called them, which can hold up to repeated attempts to prove them false. Popper's belief, which has found significant support among working scientists, is that it is impossible to select among competing conjectures the one that is "true," but that science consists of ardent attempts at refutation, and accepts only those conjectures that survive these attempts.

Popular Front. Coalition governments made up of leftist and centrist elements that arose in the mid-1930s. In FRANCE, a Popular Front of socialists, communists and radical socialists led by Leon BLUM governed from 1936 to 1938. Created to preserve the Third Republic against the incursions of FASCISM, the Popular Front enacted a variety of social, labor and economic reforms. It was ultimately overturned by conservatives. In SPAIN, a Popular Front coalition of republicans, socialists, communists and syndicalists won the national elections of 1936. This government formed the republican core during the SPANISH CIVIL WAR (1936–39). A democratic-leftist Popular Front government also led CHILE from 1938 to 1946, instituting many important social reforms.

Porgy and Bess. Musical show by American composer George GERSHWIN that blended the idioms of black folk music and the forms of traditional grand opera. Dubose Heyward's novel, *Porgy* (1925), and the subsequent THEATRE GUILD stage version (1927) told the story of the ill-starred love between the lame Porgy and the faithless Bess, set against the background of Catfish Row (based on Cabbage Row in Charleston, South Carolina). Intrigued by the story's musical possibilities, composer George Gershwin collaborated with librettist Ira GERSHWIN and Heyward, spending many weeks living and researching the life and music of the blacks on Folly Island, near Charleston. The opera, directed by Rouben MAMOULIAN, premiered at the Theatre Guild's Alvin Theatre on October 10, 1935, with a mostly black cast, including Todd Duncan as Porgy, Anne Brown as Bess, and John Bubbles as Sportin' Life. The initial critical reception was mixed. Black composer Duke ELLINGTON deplored Gershwin's "lampblack Negroisms"; and other critics like Virgil THOMSON attacked its presumed white chauvinism. With the 1942 revival (five years after Gershwin's death) the opera began its real success. In the 1950s it toured Europe, the Near East, the Soviet Union, and Latin America. Producer Samuel Goldwyn made a movie version in technicolor in 1959. And since 1970 it has entered the repertoires of many opera companies, including the Metropolitan Opera. In the concert hall arranger Robert Russell Bennett's symphonic suite (composed for conductor Fritz REINER in 1941) has been a popular staple. According to biographer David Ewen, Gershwin did not directly quote Negro melodies but assimilated folk idioms into his own musical expression, claiming to bring this musical tradition for the first time to the legitimate stage. Many blacks today continue to question the validity and the success of that assertion. The lyrics to the show's standards, like "It Ain't Necessarily So," "Summertime," and "I Got Plenty o' Nuttin'," were the results of a close collaboration between Ira Gershwin and Dubose Heyward.

Pork Chop Hill, Battle of. Colloquial name for Hill 255, situated on the eastern side of the Iron Triangle along the Yokkokchon River, in Korea; site of fighting during the KOREAN WAR. Pork Chop Hill was successfully held by UN forces against attacks from the Chinese army in November 1952 and March and April 1953. On July 6, 1953, Chinese forces attacked again and gained a foothold on the hill, which UN counterattacks on July 7, 8 and 9 failed to dislodge. General Maxwell TAYLOR decided that Pork Chop Hill's tactical value did not justify additional casualties, and on July 10–11, the UN forces evacuated. Two weeks later, the war ended, and Pork Chop Hill became part of the Demilitarized Zone separating North from South Korea.

pornography and obscenity. "Pornography" is sexually explicit written or visual material. "Obscenity" refers to something that is offensive to modesty or decency. The U.S. legal system has devoted considerable attention to defining these terms and determining the extent to which governments can control material with sexually explicit content. On the one hand, the U.S. Constitution's First Amendment unequivocally provides that "no law" may abridge freedom of speech. However, legislatures and the courts have attempted to balance First Amendment rights against majority sensibilities. Generally, U.S. courts upheld state and federal laws banning obscene materials—the courtroom test for obscenity being whether the material tended to deprave and corrupt. By 1957 the Supreme Court had adopted a standard that a work was obscene and not constitutionally protected if an average person using community standards found the dominant theme appealed to the prurient interest. In 1973 the Court refined this test. Material could be banned as obscene only if it was totally without redeeming value, and taken as a whole lacks serious literary, artistic, political or scientific value.

Porsche, Ferdinand (1875–1951). Automotive engineer, designer and manufacturer known for his development of the original VOLKSWAGEN and the sequence of sports cars that carry the Porsche name. Responsible for many automotive designs of the 1920s when he was employed by Daimler-Benz, Porsche established his own firm with his son Ferdinand ("Ferry") Porsche II in Stuttgart, where he worked on the Volkswagen design in the 1930s. The first Porsche car was produced in 1949 by a factory in Austria, with a body designed by Erwin KOMENDA using elements of the regular Volkswagen. It was marketed in 1952 as the Porsche 356 and quickly became a classic, although its bulbous, aero-dynamic design was sometimes criticized as clumsy. The Type 911 was introduced in 1964 with a somewhat modified body design. Successive designs for Type 912, the Targa, and the mid-engined 914 built the reputation of the Porsche as a prestigious status symbol as well as a sports car of outstanding performance.

Port Arthur. City in northeastern CHINA, at the southern end of the Liao-tung peninsula. In 1898 Russia obtained a lease on the peninsula. Port Arthur subsequently figured prominently in the RUSSO-JAPANESE WAR (1904–05). A Japanese surprise attack on Port Arthur (Feb. 8, 1904) trapped Russia's Pacific fleet here. The Japanese laid siege to Port Arthur and captured it on January 2, 1905. The city remained under Japanese control until the end of WORLD WAR II, when it became the headquarters of a joint Sino-Soviet administration. It was turned over to China 10 years later.

Porter, Cole (1891–1964). Celebrated American lyricist and song writer. Porter came from a wealthy Indiana family, studied law at Yale, served in the French Foreign Legion, studied music under Vincent D'INDY at the Schola Cantorum in Paris and, in general, lived the life of a playboy-dilettante. By the late 1920s, he had turned increasingly to show music. Early works, like "You Do Something to Me" (from *Fifty Million Frenchmen,* 1929), "What Is This Thing Called Love?" (from *Wake Up and Dream,* 1929) and "Night and Day" (from *Gay Divorce,* 1932), displayed Porter's trademarks: unexpected chromatics, intricate rhythms and ingeniously naughty lyrics. He wrote the scores to more than 20 shows, including *Anything Goes* (1934) and *Kiss Me Kate* (1948); six motion pictures, including *Born to Dance* (1936) and *The Pirate* (1948); and one television musical, *Aladdin* (1958). Cary GRANT portrayed him in the movie *Night and Day* (1947), which failed to come to terms with the facts of his life and the quirky, mercurial, sometimes hedonist aspects of his temperament. A 1937 horseback riding accident left Porter with two crushed legs and damage to his nervous system, necessitating 30 operations over the next 20 years. After a leg was amputated in 1958 he no longer wrote songs, living as a virtual recluse until his death.

For further reading:

Jablonski, Edward, ed., *The Encyclopedia of American Music.* New York: Doubleday and Co., 1981.

Porter, Katherine Anne (1890–1980). American novelist and short story writer. Porter's elegantly crafted writing won critical acclaim for more than 40 years. Her literary work, which bore the influence of her Deep South upbringing in Texas and Louisiana, often evoked dark, brooding themes: the sense of the past, the collusion between good and evil and the reality of self-betrayal. Her most famous work was the bestselling 1962 novel *Ship of Fools,* which was made into a film. She won the PULITZER PRIZE and the National Book Award in 1966 for her short fiction, *The Collected Stories of Katherine Anne Porter;* among her other works were *Noon Wine, The Old Order, Flowering Judas, Pale Horse, Pale Rider, Maria Concepcion* and *Hacienda.*

Porter, William Sydney. See O. HENRY.

Port Moresby. Capital of PAPUA NEW GUINEA. Established as a British settlement in 1873 by John Moresby several years later it became the capital of British New Guinea. During WORLD WAR II it was a major Allied military and naval base. Because of its strategic location between the Japanese forces and Australia, the Japanese hoped to capture it and use it as a jumping-off point for an invasion of Australia. However, the Japanese offensive (Dec. 1942–Jan. 1943) against Port Moresby was successfully repulsed. (See also WORLD WAR II IN THE PACIFIC.)

Portsmouth, Treaty of. Treaty negotiated September 5, 1905, at Portsmouth, New Hampshire, U.S., ending the RUSSO-JAPANESE WAR. It was mediated by U.S. President Theodore ROOSEVELT. MANCHURIA was evacuated by both countries and was returned to CHINA. The defeated Russians turned over south SAKHALIN ISLAND and their leases over PORT ARTHUR and the Liaotung Peninsula to JAPAN. Japan superseded RUSSIA as the leading power in KOREA and adjacent areas. President Roosevelt's mediation confirmed the status of the U.S. as a world power.

Portugal. Portugal covers an area of 34,308 square miles along the Atlantic coast of the Iberian peninsula in southwest Europe, and includes the semi-autonomous Azores and Madeira Islands. King Carlos' assassination in 1908 led to instability, insurrection, and the declaration of a Republic in 1910. Heavy losses during WORLD WAR I brought renewed turmoil which only stabilized with the election of General Antonio Carmona as president in 1928. Under the dictatorship of Antonio de Oliveira SALAZAR (1932–68) Portugal stayed out of WORLD WAR II, became a founding member of NATO (1949), joined the UNITED NATIONS (1955), witnessed social reforms, and engaged in costly wars to retain its African colonies (see ANGOLAN WAR OF INDEPENDENCE). A bloodless coup in 1974 toppled Salazar's successor, Marcello CAETANO, and brought General Antonio Ramalho Eanes to the presidency. His government recognized the independence of former Portuguese colonies, and restored full civilian government by 1982. In the 1986 election Antonio Soares be-

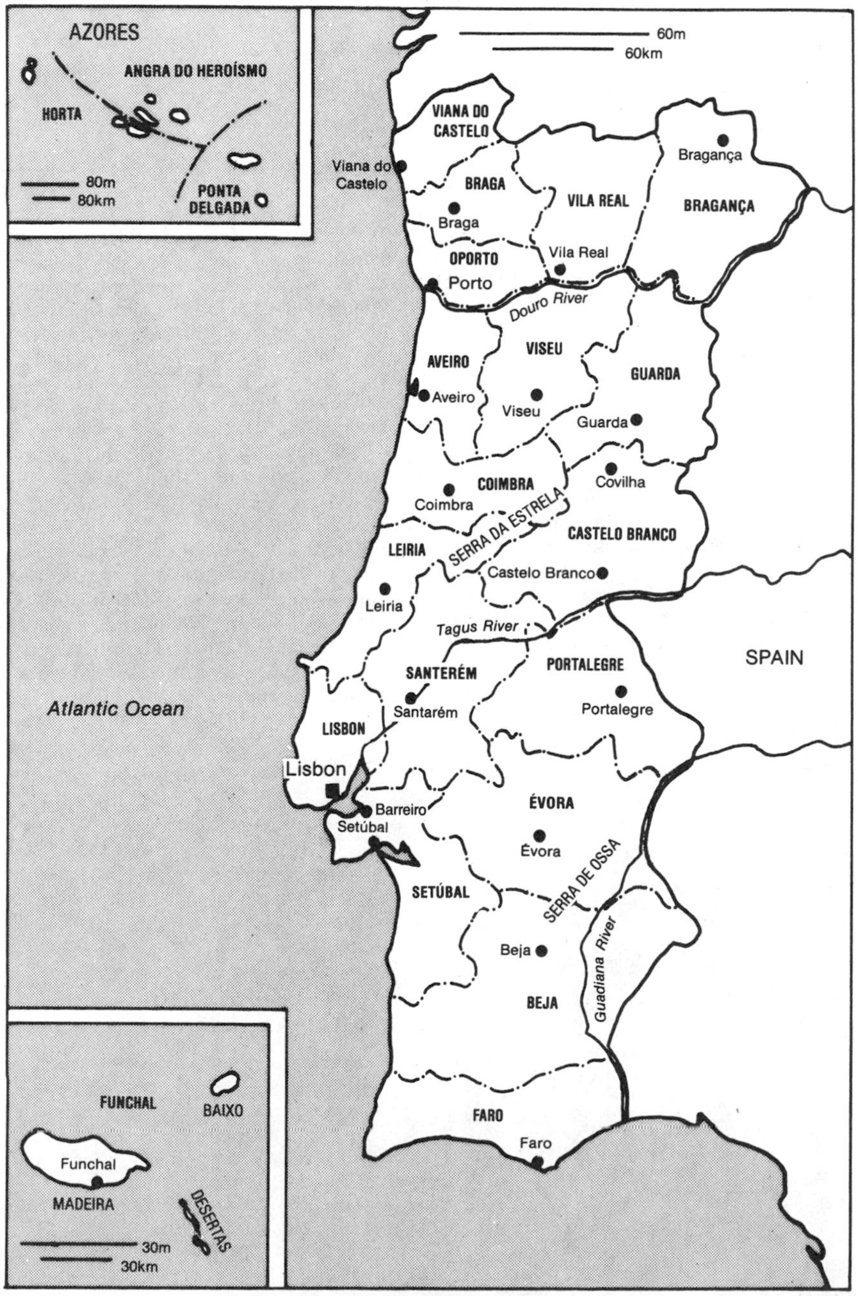

PORTUGAL

PORTUGAL

1910	(Oct. 5) Republic of Portugal declared.
1911	Manuel de Arriagas is elected Portugal's first president.
1916	Germany declares war on Portugal.
1932	Oliveira Salazar becomes prime minister and suppresses opposition parties.
1949	Becomes founding member of NATO.
1968	Salazar vacates the premiership and is succeeded by Marcello Caetano.
1974	(Apr. 25) Leftist army officers seize power in a coup and Antonio de Spinola is named president.
1974-75	Portugal grants independence to its colonies, Guinea-Bissau, Mozambique, Cape Verde, Sao Tome and Principe and Angola.
1976	(April) In assembly elections General Antonio Ramalho Eanes becomes president and Mario Soares becomes prime minister.
1982	Full civilian government restored.
1986	(Jan. 1) Portugal becomes a member of the EC.
1987	(July) Cavaco Silva is the first president elected with an overall assembly majority since the 1974 revolution.
1989	Fire destroys the old Chiado district in Lisbon.

came Portugal's first civilian president in 60 years.

Pospelov, Pyotr N. (1898–1979). Soviet propagandist, principal theoretician of the COMMUNIST PARTY of the Soviet Union, and editor of PRAVDA. He was one of the most durable figures in the Kremlin. He survived the Stalinist PURGES of 1936–37, de-Stalinization and KHRUSHCHEV's own downfall.

Post, Wiley (1899–1935). American aviator. Post began flying in 1924 by investing money received from insurance for the loss of an eye in an accident. He won the Chicago-Los Angeles Air Derby in 1930 flying the *Winnie Mae*. From his home in Oklahoma City, he served as an aerial navigation instructor and adviser for the U.S. Army. Post set many records in his career. He made the first around-the-world flight between June 23 and July 1, 1931, with Harold Gatty as navigator. He and Gatty wrote about their experience in *Around the World in Eight Days* (1931). Post and his passenger, humorist Will ROGERS, were killed when their plane crashed near Point Barrow, Alaska.

postimpressionism. Term coined in 1910 by the British art critic Roger FRY to refer to the work of various French painters who worked from about 1880 to 1910. While differing widely in stylistic approach and technique, the postimpressionist artists were united in their rejection of the aesthetics of Impressionism. Major figures in the group include Cezanne, Gauguin, Toulouse-Lautrec and Van Gogh. The term has also been used to describe the neoimpressionist work of Seurat and Signac.

Wiley Post (left) with his navigator, Harold Gatty.

postmodernism. Ill-defined term that refers to the fragmented philosophical and aesthetic influences from the past that continue to influence—often in unexpected and bizarre ways—much of late-20th-century culture. The central idea behind postmodernism is that art and philosophy have, over the past two millennia, already explored all the major creative possibilities open to them. Postmodern culture, which is generally held to have come to the forefront in the 1950s and '60s, merely reassembles past ideas into old-new juxtapositions that pay homage to those ideas but also place them in an ironic or absurdist light. The artist and philosopher Marcel DUCHAMP anticipated many of the key insights of postmodern aesthetics. Postmodernism has found expression in virtually all the creative arts as well as in architecture and design.

***Potemkin* mutiny.** Mutiny that occurred on the Russian battleship *Potemkin* in the Black Sea while anchored off Odessa on June 14, 1905. The mistreated sailors killed the captain and most of the officers, then put the ship out to sea but eventually surrendered. The mutiny and the brutal reprisals that ended the incident are best known as the subject of the classic film *The Battleship Potemkin* (1925) by the pioneering Soviet filmmaker Sergi EISENSTEIN.

Potsdam Conference. The last great Allied summit meeting of WORLD WAR II, held from July 17 to August 2, 1945, at Potsdam, Germany. The U.S. delegation was led by President TRUMAN, the U.S.S.R. by Premier STALIN and the British by Prime Minister CHURCHILL (replaced by his successor, Clement ATTLEE). The conference reaffirmed and clarified agreements already reached at the YALTA CONFERENCE regarding a defeated GERMANY. It stipulated that Germany would not have a central government but would be administered in four Allied zones: American, British, Russian and French. It decentralized the German economy, agreed upon German disarmament and settled on the punishment of Nazi war criminals. The conference also established a council of foreign ministers to pass on matters of peace settlements and draft peace treaties. The POTSDAM DECLARATION of July 26 also issued an ultimatum to JAPAN, promising destruction of the nation if unconditional surrender was not forthcoming. Disagreements at Potsdam between the Soviets and the Western allies over German reparations, boundaries and unification and over the nature of Eastern Europe and the Mediterranean region were portents of the coming COLD WAR.

Potsdam Declaration. Ultimatum to Japan issued on July 26, 1945, as a part of the WORLD WAR II POTSDAM CONFERENCE. In it the U.S., Great Britain and China demanded JAPAN's unconditional surrender and, without mentioning the existence of an ATOMIC BOMB, threatened the complete destruction of Japan if the declaration was not acceded to. It also explained Allied intentions in postwar Japan, including the dissolution of the

Wary Allies—Stalin, Truman and Churchill at the Potsdam Conference.

Japanese empire, the demobilization of the nation's military forces, the prosecution of war criminals, the occupation of the country and the creation of a democratic form of government. Japan did not accept the declaration until the U.S.S.R. joined the Allies in the Asian war. HIROSHIMA and NAGASAKI were destroyed by U.S. nuclear attacks and Emperor HIROHITO called for surrender.

Potter, (Helen) Beatrix (1866–1943). British illustrator and author. Throughout a lonely childhood, Potter amused herself by sketching nature. Her talent was brought to bear in a series of children's books beginning with *The Tale of Peter Rabbit* (1901), which she had published herself. Her third book, *Squirrel Nutkin* (1903), was professionally published and brought her great success. The delicately illustrated books, which include also *The Tailor of Gloucester* (1902) and *Johnny Town-Mouse* (1918), continue to be enormously popular with children and adults worldwide. Potter kept a journal in an elaborate code, which was finally deciphered and published as *The Journal of Beatrix Potter* in 1964. Her home at Sawrey in the Lake District is open to the public.

Potter, Dennis (1935–). British television and film writer, playwright and novelist. Potter, educated at Oxford University, has earned international fame for his unique plays written for the medium of television. His best known teleplays are *Pennies from Heaven,* adapted into a 1981 film starring Steve MARTIN and scripted by Potter, and *The Singing Detective,* which made its debut on the BRITISH BROADCASTING CORPORATION in 1986. Both of these works are marked by an eerie blend of stock melodramatic conventions and intensely private fantasies that dominate the lives of the lead characters. Other works by Potter include the play *Waiting for the Boat* (1984) and the novel *Blackeyes* (1988).

Potteries. District around Stoke-on-Trent in Staffordshire, England, famous for the manufacture of china and pottery. The Wedgwood firm is located here. The district was the setting for Arnold BENNETT's "Five Towns" novels.

Poujadists. Followers of Pierre Poujade, founder of a right-wing political movement (*Union de Defence des Commercants et Artisans*) violently active in FRANCE between 1954 and 1958. The movement's membership was petit-bourgeois and its ideology antisocialist, anti-intellectual and anti-European. It won 52 seats in the National Assembly in 1956 but declined after Charles DE GAULLE returned to politics and the Fifth Republic was founded.

Poulenc, Francis (1899–1963). French composer and pianist. Born in Paris of a well-to-do musical family, he began to study the piano as a small child. Influenced by the style and the aesthetics of Eric SATIE and the poetry of Jean COCTEAU, Poulenc was a member of the post-impressionist musical group Les SIX. His music combines wit, clarity, directness and lyricism. Many of his finest works are intimate piano pieces and songs. From 1936 on he composed sacred music, and in 1944 he began writing operas. Among his best known religious music is the Mass in G (1937). His most celebrated opera is *Dialogue of the Carmelites* (1957). Poulenc also wrote ballet music, concertos, chamber pieces and choral works.

Poulter, Thomas C. (1897–1978). American scientist, inventor and explorer. Poulter was second in command on Admiral Richard BYRD's second expedition to the Antarctic (1933–35). He led the expedition that saved Byrd's life after Byrd had spent part of the winter alone. As an inventor, Poulter held more than 75 patents, including ones for antisubmarine devices and for seismic methods of discovering oil. He was later a research consultant for Stanford Research International in California and established its laboratory for the study of biological sonar and its application to the blind.

Pound, Ezra (Loomis) (1885–1972). American poet, critic and translator. Born in Hailey, Idaho, Pound was educated at Hamilton College and the University of Pennsylvania, where he met W.C. WILLIAMS and Hilda Doolittle (HD). In 1907 he went to Europe, settling first in England, where he was briefly an informal secretary to YEATS; then in Paris, where he knew Gertrude STEIN and HEMINGWAY; and finally in 1925 in Italy. Pound was a charismatic literary entrepreneur whose grand vision and generous support of major writers such as JOYCE, ELIOT and Marianne MOORE placed him at the forefront of literary MODERNISM. He created both Vorticism and IMAGISM. *A lume spento* (1908), *Personae* (1909), *Lustra* (1916) and especially *Hugh Selwyn Mauberly* (1920) broke the static mold of GEORGIAN verse with a voice both shockingly modern and classically serene. In 1925 he began publishing his most important and controversial work, the CANTOS, on which he continued to work until his last years. A scholar of wide, if sometimes sketchy, erudition, Pound drew on Anglo-Saxon, Oriental, French Provencal and Italian Renaissance traditions.

Increasing megalomania led to an obsession with the economic theory of SOCIAL CREDIT and to ANTI-SEMITISM. An admirer of MUSSOLINI and FASCISM, during WORLD WAR II Pound made radio broadcasts for the Fascists in Italy. Indicted for treason *in absentia* in 1942, he was arrested by U.S. forces toward the end of the war and committed to St. Elizabeth's Hospital in Washington in 1946. In 1949 a violent controversy erupted over his receipt of the BOLLINGEN PRIZE. After his release in 1958, he returned to Italy and entered on a period of bitter, self-enforced silence. To this day the great poet who was also a traitor to his country arouses mixed emotions.

For further reading:

Ackroyd, Peter, *Ezra Pound.* New York: Thames & Hudson, 1987.
Carpenter, Humphrey, *A Serious Character: The Life of Ezra Pound.* Boston: Houghton Mifflin, 1988.
Cookson, William, *A Guide to the Cantos of Ezra Pound.* New York: Persea, 1985.

Ezra Pound, whose poems and pronouncements alike generated immense controversy.

Poveda Burbano, Admiral Alfredo (1925–1990). Ecuadoran politician. In 1976, he headed a military junta that seized control of ECUADOR from another military dictator, Gen. Guillermo Rodriguez Lara. The country's last military dictator, his government wrote a constitution in 1978. The government gave up power the following year to elected president Jaime Roldos.

Powell, Adam Clayton (1908–1972). Black American congressman and CIVIL RIGHTS activist. The son of a clergyman, the flamboyant Powell was one of the most outspoken and controversial figures in the American civil rights movement. He was widely admired for his fiery oratory on behalf of civil rights causes, but many critics considered him a demagogue (see DEMAGOGUES). A Democrat, he represented New York's Harlem district in the House of Representatives from 1945 to 1969. He served as chairman of the House Committee on Education and Labor (1960–67). In 1960 he was involved in a widely publicized lawsuit by a woman he accused of being a "bag woman" for police graft. Thereafter he maintained a home on the island of Bimini in the Bahamas. In 1967 a House committee unseated him on charges of misusing public funds, but he was reelected in a special election. He returned to Congress in 1969 but was fined $25,000 and deprived of his seniority. That year the Supreme Court overturned his expulsion from the House of Representatives. He was defeated for reelection in 1970.

For further reading:

Alexander, E. Curtis, *Adam Clayton Powell, Jr.: A Black Power Political Educator.* New York: ECA Associates, 1983.

Jakoubek, Robert, *Adam Clayton Powell, Jr.* New York: Chelsea House, 1989.

Mwadilifu, Mwalimu I. (ed.), *Selected Speeches, Sermons and Writings of Adam Clayton Powell, Jr., 1935–71.* New York: ECA Associates.

Adam Clayton Powell, U.S. congressman and civil rights activist.

Powell, Anthony (1905–). British novelist, essayist and memoirist. With his contemporaries Graham GREENE and Evelyn WAUGH, Powell is one of the most acclaimed and widely read of modern British novelists. He has been an influential figure in British letters both as a novelist and by virtue of his work as an editor and literary critic. During the 1930s Powell worked in publishing in London and was briefly a scriptwriter in HOLLYWOOD. During this time he wrote several interesting but minor novels. He served in WORLD WAR II. His magnum opus is the 12–volume novel sequence, A DANCE TO THE MUSIC OF TIME, whose individual volumes appeared from the early 1950s through the mid-1970s. In addition, Powell has published a four-volume autobiography—*Infants of the Spring* (1976), *Messengers of the Day* (1978), *Faces in My Time* (1980) and *The Strangers All Are Gone* (1982). Conservative in outlook, Powell's writings focus on the transformations in the political and social fabric in Britain from the 1920s to the modern era.

Powell, Colin L. (1937–). American soldier and public official, chairman of the Joint Chiefs of Staff during the PERSIAN GULF WAR. Born in the HARLEM district of New York to parents who had emigrated from Jamaica, Powell was educated at public schools in Harlem and the Bronx. He attended City College, where he was a member of the Reserve Officers Training Corps and was graduated at the top of his ROTC class as a cadet colonel. In 1962 he was sent to VIETNAM, where he saw a tour of duty as a military adviser. Later, while maintaining his military affiliation and rising through the ranks, Powell held a series of sensitive posts in the administrations of Jimmy CARTER and Ronald REAGAN. He was an assistant to Defense Secretary Caspar Weinberger; in 1986 he was appointed deputy national security adviser, becoming national security adviser the following year. In 1988 he was promoted to four-star general and assigned to head the U.S. Army Forces Command. In 1989, he was named chairman of the Joint Chiefs of Staff, thus becoming the first black to hold the highest post in the U.S. military. In this capacity, he came to international prominence as a key adviser to President George BUSH during the PERSIAN GULF WAR. Powell initially counselled against direct military action, but after Bush's decision to go to war, Powell supported the president's action and worked closely with Defense Secretary Dick Cheney and General H. Norman SCHWARZKOPF in military planning. A political independent, Powell is widely admired for his industriousness and sound judgment and has been mentioned as a potential candidate for national political office.

Powell, (John) Enoch (1915–). British politician. Powell was educated at Trinity College, Cambridge, and served there as a classics don from 1934 to 1938. After serving as a professor of Greek at the University of Sydney, Australia, he joined the army and rose to the rank of brigadier by the end of WORLD WAR II. A member of the CONSERVATIVE PARTY, Powell was elected to the House of Commons in 1950 and subsequently served as parliamentary secretary to the ministry of housing and local government in 1955, financial secretary to the treasury from 1957 to 1958, and minister for health from 1960 to 1963 under Harold MACMILLAN. Powell opposed Britain's entry into the EUROPEAN ECONOMIC COMMUNITY. His highly-publicized views, including a call for Britain to curtail non-white immigration, caused much controversy. Powell left the Conservative Party in 1974 but returned to Parliament as an Ulster Unionist. He was re-elected in 1979 and 1983. Powell, who is also a poet, published *Collected Poems* in 1990.

Powell, Lewis Franklin Jr. (1907–). U.S. Supreme Court associate justice. Powell was born in Suffolk, Virginia, and received both his B.A. and his law degree from Washington and Lee University, the latter in 1931. President Richard NIXON appointed Lowell to the Supreme Court in 1971, to replace Hugo BLACK. A pragmatist who shunned extreme positions, Powell generally sided with the Court's conservatives on business and criminal law issues and with the liberals on social issues such as ABORTION, civil liberties and separation of church and state. In June 1987, Powell retired from the Court, sparking a furor over who would be his successor. On July 1, President Ronald REAGAN nominated Robert BORK to the Court, but after an acrimonious battle, the Senate refused to confirm Bork. Reagan's second choice, Douglas Ginsburg, withdrew his name from nomination after it was reported that he had experimented with marijuana. Finally, in February 1988, Anthony KENNEDY took Powell's seat on the High Court.

Powell, Michael (1905–1990). British film director, writer and producer. His films were noted for their quirky, imaginative style and sense of magic. Those works included *The Thief of Bagdad* (1940), *The 49th Parallel* (1940), which won an ACADEMY AWARD, *The Life and Times of Colonel Blimp* (1943), *A Matter of Life and Death* (1946) and *The Red Shoes* (1948). Together with his screenwriting collaborator Emeric PRESSBURGER, he formed the Archers production company in 1942.

Powellites. Wing of the British CONSERVATIVE PARTY that supported Enoch POWELL in the late 1960s. Associated with MONETARISM, anti-EUROPEAN ECONOMIC COMMUNITY and anti-immigration positions, Powell was expelled from the Conservative Party and became an Ulster Unionist Member of Parliament in October 1974.

Powers, John A. "Shorty" (1922–1980). American Air Force officer. Powers became widely known in the early 1960s as "the voice of Mission Control" who described the early U.S. space flights over radio and television and coined the popular phrase, "everything is A-OK." Because of his close association in the public mind with the MERCURY project astronauts, the public came to regard him as the "eighth astronaut."

Powys, John Cowper (1872–1963). British author. Although he also wrote poetry and essays on a variety of topics, Powys is best known for his idiosyncratic historical novels, which frequently evoke the Dorset countryside where he was raised. His first novel was *Wood and Stone* (1915), but his first major success came with *Wolf Solent* (1929). His best known work is *A Gastonbury Romance* (1932), an ambitious historical novel influenced by myth and legend. He also produced a notable *Autobiography* (1934). Later works include *Porius* (1951) and *The Brazen Head* (1956). There are conflicting critical assessments of Powys's ability as a writer. Powys's two brothers were also men of letters. **Llewelyn Powys** (1884–1939) was an essayist and novelist whose work includes *The Pathetic Fallacy* (1928). **T(heodore) F(rancis) Powys** (1875–1953) was the author of *Mr. Weston's Good Wine* (1927).

Poznan. Polish industrial city on the Warta River, 167 miles west of Warsaw. From June 28 to 30, 1956, the city was the site of the Poznan riots, in which workers dissatisfied with living conditions, the presence of Soviet troops, and the policies of the Polish government, broke out in armed rebellion. Although official government figures listed approximately 50 killed and 400 wounded, Western witnesses reported 200–300 dead. The riots resulted in the installation of a more liberal government under Wladyslaw GOMULKA.

pragmatism. See William JAMES.

Prague. Capital city of CZECHOSLOVAKIA, situated on the Vltava River. Prague's history in the 20th century in many ways mirrors and encapsulates that of Europe, particularly central Europe. In 1918, after WORLD WAR I, it became the capital of the new Czech republic. Occupied by the Germans in 1939, before the start of WORLD WAR II, during the war it escaped the bombing that devastated many European cities. It was liberated by the Soviet army in 1945. Prague was the scene of the communist takeover of Czechoslovakia and the mysterious death of Jan MASARYK in 1948; the PRAGUE SPRING of 1968; and a focal point of Czech resistance to the SOVIET INVASION OF CZECHOSLOVAKIA in August of that same year. In 1977, Czech dissidents formed the human rights group CHARTER 77 in Prague. In 1989, the city was the site of popular mass demonstrations against the communist government. In 1990, its citizens celebrated the end of more than 40 years of communist rule. Prague retains many of its original, pre-20th-century architectural features.

Prague Spring. Term used to characterize a series of economic and political reforms in CZECHOSLOVAKIA, and the period during which they occurred. The Prague Spring developed under the guidance of Alexander DUBCEK, who had been named first secretary of Czechoslovakia's Communist Party on January 5, 1968. It also coincided with the ouster of hardline communist President Antonin NOVOTNY (Mar. 22, 1968), who had long kept Czechoslovakia in the grip of STALINISM. At a conference in Brno (Mar. 16, 1968), Dubcek promised the "widest possible democratization" for the country, including the relaxation of censorship. He promised to build "socialism with a human face" and to "bring in new people

On August 21, 1968, Soviet tanks rolled into Wenceslas Square in Prague, ending the Prague Spring.

who can carry out the new policies." The Prague Spring reforms also included greater independence for the government, the courts, trade unions and economic enterprises. On April 5, 1968, the Communist Party leadership adopted a plan of liberal economic reforms. In a speech to the Czechoslovakian parliament on April 24, 1968, Premier Oldrich CERNIK announced that noncommunists would be allowed to participate in the government. That same day, Dubcek announced that "we cannot go back and we cannot go halfway," and warned that "moving along unexplored paths . . . requires caution and courage." At the same time, he assured the Soviet Union that Czechoslovakia would remain its ally in the WARSAW PACT. A wave of hope swept through Czechoslovakia. However, the sudden SOVIET INVASION OF CZECHOSLOVAKIA (Aug. 20–21) brought the Prague Spring to an abrupt end. Despite the reimposition of a hardline communist government, the promises of the Prague Spring remained alive during the next 20 years and were realized in Dec. 1989, when the communists were finally swept out of power.

Prairie School. Group of architects who developed an early form of MODERNISM in the American Midwest between 1890 and 1914. The early works of Frank Lloyd WRIGHT (who called his residential designs "Prairie Houses") are the best known examples of the style, but it also includes the designs of Louis Sullivan and a number of associates and followers of Sullivan and Wright—a body of work with its own distinctive character, quite different from European modernism. Like modernism, the Prairie School is nontraditional and strives for an organic union of strong, simple forms. But unlike orthodox modernism, it makes considerable use of ornament, often based on naturalistic forms suggestive of ART NOUVEAU and earlier Victorian styles. The best known Prairie School figures (aside from Sullivan and Wright) are George G. Elmslie, George W. Maher, Walter Burley Griffin and Marion Mahoney, who was the wife of Griffin.

Pravda. The official organ of the Communist Party Central Committee in the Soviet Union. Founded in opposition to the establishment by the BOLSHEVIKS in 1912, *Pravda* ("truth") has a circulation of about 12 million and is read daily by more than 90% of COMMUNIST PARTY members. The paper's value in informing the Soviet public is secondary to its role in shaping the "new Soviet man" and providing the most authoritative Kremlin interpretation of current events. It has followed a rigid format since its inception, with reports of worker productivity, official speeches, party proceedings and economic news appearing on the front page, while domestic and international news is found in the back. In the era of GLASNOST, *Pravda* has addressed such previously off-limit topics as high-level corruption, the Soviet presence in AFGHANISTAN, the nuclear disaster at CHERNOBYL, drug problems and other social ills, though disinformation continues. The paper is governed by an "Index of Information Not To Be Published in the Open Press," and is censored once before printing and once before distribution (the censor's number appears at the foot of the back page of every edition).

Prayer Book Controversy. A modernized Book of Common Prayer was approved by the Episcopal Church of the U.S. in 1979. The new prayer book replaced the standard 1928 version, which was based closely on the original 16th-century book. The decision to adopt the 1979 version climaxed a long, emotionally charged controversy within the three-million member church. It upset traditionalists and caused many members to quit in protest. The new book was seen by its advocates as an attempt to adapt the language and liturgy of the Episcopal Church to changes in the contemporary world. Critics argued that the book lacked the richness of language, depth and beauty of thought of the version it was to replace. A similar controversy also raged in Britain during the 1980s over a similar revision of the prayer book. There, the effort to maintain the traditional liturgy was carried on by the Prayer Book Society.

Prebisch, Raul (1901–1986). Argentine economist. He helped shape economic development throughout the developing world. In the 1950s he headed the United Nations Economic Commission for Latin America. As director of the U.N. Conference on Trade and Development in the 1960s, he won important trade preferences for THIRD WORLD countries and helped obtain increased funding for various regional development banks. Most recently he had been an economic advisor to Argentine President Raul ALFONSIN.

Predappio. Village near Forli in southeastern Emilia-Romagna, Italy. Predappio was the birthplace—and is the final burial place—of Italian dictator Benito MUSSOLINI.

prefrontal lobotomy. See Egas MONIZ.

Prem, Tinsulanonda (1920–). Prem was a career military man before serving as prime minister of THAILAND from 1980 to 1988. He was educated at Chulachomklao Royal Military Academy in Bangkok and began his military career as a sublieutenant in 1941. He became the commander of cavalry headquarters in 1968, then assistant commander in chief of the Royal Thai Army in 1977. In 1977 he was appointed minister of interior and in 1979 minister of defense. Prem began his tenure as prime minister in 1980 and served the longest of any civilian prime minister before he declined to accept a fourth term after general elections in July 1988. He retired from the army before heading the government, thus acting as a civilian, nonpartisan leader. The balance he struck between the political parties and the military enabled him to sustain a fragile democracy throughout his tenure. He thwarted two coup attempts (1981, 1985), thus diluting the military's influence on mainstream politics.

Preminger, Otto (1906–1986). Austrian-born movie producer and director. He achieved great success in the U.S. film industry, despite his tempestuous temper and his choosing to work outside the HOLLYWOOD studio system. He emigrated to the U.S. from Vienna in 1935 and achieved a measure of success on Broadway before making his first American film, the murder mystery *Laura* (1944). He challenged the industry's Production Code Office and the Roman Catholic church when he produced *The Moon Is Blue,* a 1953 adaptation of a mild Broadway sex comedy. The U.S. Supreme Court ultimately ruled that local censorship boards could not block the showing of the film. Other notable Preminger films were *Carmen Jones* (1954), *The Man with the Golden Arm* (1955), *Anatomy of a Murder* (1959), *Exodus* (1962) and *Advise and Consent* (1962).

Prendergast, Maurice (1859–1924). American painter. Born in St. John's, Newfoundland, Canada, he spent his youth in Boston. He traveled to Europe in 1886, studying art in Paris (1891–94) and coming under the influence of such modernist movements as neoimpressionism and symbolism. Throughout his life Prendergast made frequent visits to Europe, traveling to various countries then returning to New York City. He joined with other artists in the formation of the EIGHT in 1908 and was an organizer of the ARMORY SHOW in 1913. Working in oil and watercolor, Prendergast evolved a tapestry-like postimpressionist style that employed lively brushstrokes and rich color in capturing landscapes and figures. He was particularly adept at portraying open-air promenades, as in his *Central Park* (1901) in the collection of the Whitney Museum of American Art, New York City

Presley, Elvis (Aaron) (1935–1977). American singer, performer and film star. One of the most popular entertainment figures of the 20th century, Presley helped establish ROCK AND ROLL as a dominant musical force. Born in Tupelo, Mississippi, as a child he sang gospel tunes in his neighborhood church. In 1953, while working as a truck driver in Memphis, Tennessee, he recorded two songs for his mother. These recordings led to his discovery by Memphis-based Sun Records, which launched Presley's career as a white singer who could blend country, gospel and black rhythm and blues. "Heartbreak Hotel" (1956) was the first Presley song to reach number one on the musical charts. Over the next two decades, he recorded numerous hits, including "Don't Be Cruel," "Hound Dog," "Jailhouse Rock," "Love Me Tender" and "Are You Lonesome Tonight." He also starred in over 20 films and in several television specials. The victim of his own spectacular success, Presley was plagued by personal problems, including drug addiction, and he died at age 42. His phenomenal popularity, however, continued after his death.

Elvis Presley during a concert in 1973.

Pressburger, Emeric (1902–1988). Hungarian-born British screenwriter. His widely acclaimed films made in collaboration with director Michael POWELL included *A Canterbury Tale* (1944), *Black Narcissus* (1947) and their most famous effort, *The Red Shoes* (1948). Pressburger won an ACADEMY AWARD for best original story for *49th Parallel* (1941), considered one of the most effective Allied PROPAGANDA films of WORLD WAR II.

Presser, Jackie (1926–1988). U.S. union leader. Presser was president of the International Brotherhood of Teamsters from 1983 until his death; his predecessor, Roy WILLIAMS, was convicted of conspiring to bribe a U.S. senator. Presser faced federal charges of using union funds to pay organized-crime figures for work they had not performed. The Justice Department filed suit asking that the union's leaders be replaced by a court-appointed trustee. In 1986, the White House Commission on Organized Crime concluded that neither Williams nor Presser would have become president without the help of Anthony "Fat Tony" Salerno, reputed head of the New York-based Genovese crime family. Salerno was later acquitted on charges of rigging union elections.

Prevert, Jacques (1900–1977). French poet and screenwriter. Prevert was the most popular poet of his time in France. He is noted for his precise use of language, his gruesome images and the use of humor to underscore his social and political ideas. Initially influenced by the surrealists, he was first published in the surrealist monthly, *Commerce*. Major poetry collections include the immensely popular *Paroles* (1946), *Lumiere d'homme* (1955) and *Imaginaires* (1970). In addition, Prevert wrote many screenplays, such as the acclaimed *Le Crime de Monsieur Lange* (1935) and *Les Enfants du paradis* (1944).

Previn, Andre [born Ludwig Andreas Priwin] (1929–). American conductor, pianist and composer. Born in Berlin, he began studying music at the age of six and by the age of eight he was an accomplished pianist. He and his family fled Hitler's Germany for Paris, where young Previn studied at the Paris Conservatory for a year, and emigrated to the U.S. in 1939, settling in Los Angeles. He studied with Mario CASTELNUOVO-TEDESCO, composed film music, played the piano and conducted a youth orchestra while still a teenager. Previn became a U.S. citizen in 1943. His first celebrity was as a JAZZ pianist, and in 1945 he began a series of popular jazz recordings. He also achieved success as a composer and arranger of film music, winning ACADEMY AWARDS for the arrangements for *Gigi* (1958), *Porgy and Bess* (1959), *Irma La Douce* (1963) and *My Fair Lady* (1964). During the 1960s Previn's interest turned mainly to classical music. He became the permanent conductor of the Houston Symphony Orchestra (1967–69), the London Symphony Orchestra (1969–79), the Pittsburgh Symphony Orchestra (1976–84) and the Los Angeles Philharmonic (1984–89). He is particularly proficient in his interpretations of such Russians as Tchaikovsky, RACHMANINOFF, SHOSTAKOVICH and PROKOFIEV and of the music of British composers VAUGHAN WILLIAMS, WALTON and BRITTEN. In addition to a lively career as a soloist, Previn has also composed a number of orchestral works, chamber pieces, piano preludes, concertos for various instruments and other music.

Price, Florence Beatrice Smith (1888–1953). Composer. Graduating from the New England Conservatory in 1906, Price taught at Shorter College (1906–10) and at Clark University (1910–12). After further study at Chicago Musical College and the American Conservatory, she won several competitions, including the Wanamaker Prize (1931–32), and in 1933 premiered her *Symphony in E Minor* with the CHICAGO SYMPHONY, the first by a black woman with a major orchestra. Price's works drew on black spirituals and other tunes, avoided jazz and kept in the mainstream of late European romanticism. Her songs were popularized by Marian ANDERSON and others.

Price, H(enry) Ryan (1912–1986). British racehorse trainer. During the 1950s, Price sent out a succession of champion jumpers from his stables at Findon. In the 1970s, he proved to be equally adept at training horses to win prestigious races on the flat.

Price, Leontyne [Mary Violet] (1927–). American singer. Acclaimed for her passionate artistry and the remarkable range of her rich soprano voice, Price first gained

Leontyne Price.

recognition for the role of Bess in George GERSHWIN'S PORGY AND BESS, when it toured the U.S. and Europe in 1952–55. She made her Metropolitan Opera debut as Leonora in Verdi's *Il Trovatore* (1961) and became a leading prima donna of the company until her retirement in 1985. Price was particularly admired for her interpretation of Verdi heroines, especially Aida, and she created the role of Cleopatra in Samuel BARBER'S *Antony and Cleopatra*, which opened the new Metropolitan Opera House at Lincoln Center in 1966. In addition, she was the first black woman to sing with La Scala Opera Company in Milan (1959).

Price, T. Rowe (1898–1983). American investment expert. A pioneer in the field of investment counseling, research and analysis, Price was largely responsible for popularizing the "growth stock" concept of investment that advocated making long-term investments in small, well-managed companies. He founded his own investment counseling firm, T. Rowe Price Associates, in 1937. From the early 1950s through the 1960s his name was synonymous with growth stock mutual funds.

Pride, Admiral Alfred Melville (1897–1988). American aviator. A pioneer of naval aviation, Pride served on the original crew of the U.S. Navy's first aircraft carrier. During WORLD WAR II he played a major role planning the invasion of OKINAWA and the Japanese home islands (the latter superseded by the dropping of the ATOMIC BOMB on Japan). From 1947 to 1951, he was chief of the Navy's Bureau of aeronautics.

Priestley, J(ohn) B(oynton) (1894–1984). British novelist, dramatist, essayist, broadcaster and critic. "JBP" was considered the last of a line of distinguished "men of letters" in England that extended back through G.K. CHESTERTON to such 19th-century luminaries as Charles Dickens and George Meredith. Priestley was born at Bradford, Yorkshire—a region in which many of his stories are located—

and educated at Trinity Hall, Cambridge. His first book was a volume of verse, *The Chapman of Rhymes* (1918), written during his wartime service. After working as journalist and commentator throughout the 1920s, he achieved his first spectacular success with *The Good Companions* (1929), an enormous novel about a picaresque troupe of traveling performers. He wrote many stage plays and travel books in the next decade, including two brilliant chronicles of travel throughout his own country and the American Southwest—respectively, *English Journey* (1934) and *Midnight on the Desert* (1937). During WORLD WAR II he was a tireless supporter of the Allied cause in his writings and BBC broadcasts and for many years thereafter continued to write works of fiction, cultural history, *belles-lettres* and philosophy. The image he affected of a rather crusty, pipe-smoking sage celebrating the vanished values of Merrie Olde England is misleading. In truth Priestley was something of a pessimist and a mystic. What he called "the muddle of life" and "the density of evil" haunt his best books, such as the tragic *Angel Pavement* (1930) and the grim account of war-torn England, *Black-Out in Gretley* (1942). A dark, bittersweet tang flavors the adventurous *Faraway* (1932) and the nostalgic *Lost Empires* (1965). His preoccupations with precognition, time travel and the supernatural surface in such plays as *I Have Never Been Here Before* (1937). As for his alleged hearty patriotism, it was really qualified by a sense of rootlessness: "I am too restless to develop any loyalty even to a place I really enjoy," he wrote in *Midnight on the Desert*. Elsewhere, he observed that most Englishmen "stagger under their inheritance." And yet he always retained a youthful, wide-eyed wonder about the world around him—his most endearing trait. On his 79th birthday he said he felt like a youth who had been kidnapped off the street and "rushed into a theater and made to don the grey hair, the wrinkles and the other attributes of age, then wheeled on stage. Behind the appearance of age I am the same person, with the same thoughts, as when I was younger."

For further reading:

Atkins, John, *J.B. Priestley: The Last of the Sages*. New York: Riverrun Press, 1981.

Prigogine, Ilya (1917–). Belgian chemist. In 1955 Prigogine produced a seminal work, *Thermodynamics of Irreversible Processes*, in which he argued that a true thermodynamic equilibrium is rarely attained and that a serious limitation in classical thermodynamics is that it is restricted to equilibrium states and reersible processes. Prigogine was most interested in the thermodynamics of nonequilibrium systems, a subject that had been approached somewhat by Lars Onsager. In a radical departure, Prigogine developed the equipment to deal with these states, which he called "dissipative structures." This led to his exploration of such structures in biological processes, in 1975. In 1977 he was awarded the NOBEL PRIZE for chemistry for his work in this area.

Prima, Louis (1911–1978). American JAZZ trumpeter and bandleader. In 1940 Prima composed the jazz classic *Sing Sing Sing*, which became a standard of Benny GOODMAN. With Keely Smith, his wife and nightclub partner for eight years, he recorded *That Old Black Magic*, which hit the top of the record charts in 1961.

Primo de Rivera, Miguel (1870–1930). Spanish general, prime minister of SPAIN (1923–30). A career army officer, Primo de Rivera served in Cuba and the Philippines during the Spanish-American War, just before the turn of the century, and later in Spanish Morocco. He rose to major general (1910) and then lieutenant general (1919), becoming a leading public figure. During a period of political turmoil, King ALFONSO XIII called on Primo to establish a military government (1923). Under the slogan "Country, Religion and Monarchy" Primo suspended the parliament, declared martial law and assumed dictatorial powers. He resigned office in 1930, shortly before his death. His son **Jose Antonio Primo de Rivera** (1903–36) founded the FALANGE, based on Miguel Primo de Rivera's ideas.

Primrose, William (1903–1982). Scottish-born violist. He was a member of the London String Quartet (1935–37), then moved to the U.S. where he joined the NBC Symphony, playing first viola (1937–42). Thereafter he concentrated on a solo career. He taught at several universities and conservatories. Widely considered the greatest violist of his time, Primrose was renowned for his consummate musicianship and sweetness of tone.

Prince, Harold (Hal) (1928–). American director and producer. One of America's foremost directors, Prince has directed and/or produced 46 musicals, plays and operas in the U.S. and Britain since he first produced *The Pajama Game* in 1954. He has won 16 Tony Awards for the directing of *Cabaret* (1966), *Sweeney Todd* (1979), *Evita* (1980) and *The Phantom of the Opera* (1987), among others. He has directed and produced several Stephen SONDHEIM musicals, including *A Little Night Music* (1973) and *Pacific Overtures* (1976). He also produced such shows as *Damn Yankees* (1955) and *Fiddler on the Roof* (1964), directed revivals of plays by Eugene O'NEILL and others, and served on the National Council for the Arts.

Prinz, Joachim (1902–1988). German-born rabbi; president of the American Jewish Congress from 1958 to 1966 and a leader in CIVIL RIGHTS causes. One of the founding chairmen of the 1963 March on Washington led by Dr. Martin Luther KING Jr., Prinz fought racism and bigotry in New York as well as the South.

prisoners of war. Also known as POWs, they are members of a military force captured by the enemy during war. Prisoners may be taken by surrender or captured during battle. Until the 19th century, prisoners of war were considered booty, and many were enslaved, ransomed or killed. However, through humane regulations promulgated in the late 19th and the 20th centuries, POWs are protected from mistreatment by a number of international agreements, most importantly the Hague Conventions and the GENEVA CONVENTIONS. A POW is required only to inform his captors of his name, rank, serial number and birthdate. POWs are entitled to living quarters in safe and inspected camps, to receive adequate food and medical care, to be paid for work and to receive and send mail. These and other rules are regulated and insured by the international RED CROSS. Despite the elaborate precautions enacted to protect prisoners of war, harsh treatment has been prevalent in many modern conflicts, particularly WORLD WAR II, the KOREAN WAR and the VIETNAM WAR.

Pritchard, Sir John Michael (1921–1989). British conductor. Among other posts, he was musical director of the London Philharmonic Orchestra (1962–66) and chief conductor of the BRITISH BROADCASTING CORPORATION (BBC) Symphony Orches-

German prisoners of war in a French POW camp during World War I.

tra (1982–89). He specialized in the operas of Mozart and Donizetti.

Pritchett, (Sir) V(ictor) S(awdon) (1900–). British author and critic. An accomplished novelist and short story writer, Pritchett is probably best known for his literary criticism. He was a newspaper correspondent before achieving recognition as a writer with such works as *Claire Drummer* (1929), *Elopement into Exile* (1932) and *Mr. Beluncle* (1951). His fiction is peopled with eccentric characters; his style is witty and ironic. His critical works include *The Living Novel* (1947) and *The Myth Makers* (1979). He also contributed to the *New Statesman* and the *New York Review of Books* and lectured widely.

Pritikin, Nathan (1915–1985). American nutritionist. Self-taught and with no medical credentials, Pritikin developed a diet that he claimed could, together with proper exercise, prevent and even reverse heart disease and other ailments. He developed his diet after having been diagnosed a heart disease victim in 1957. In addition to being low in fat and cholesterol, the diet prohibited salt, sugar, alcohol and caffeine. Pritikin promoted the controversial diet through several best selling books and at three "longevity centers," which attracted thousands of high-paying clients.

privatization. Selling of nationalized industries and other parts of the public sector to private businesses and individuals. Privatization was a hallmark of the THATCHER government in Britain during the 1980s and of France under CHIRAC beginning in 1986.

Production Code, the. Written by Father Daniel Lord, S.J., and adopted by the MPPDA in 1930 as a guideline (HAYS CODE) for the producers of the U.S. motion picture industry, the code controlled the content of U.S. films for more than three decades. Part of the Hays Office (MPPDA) system of self regulation, the code assumed that movies could "uplift" or "degrade" audiences. Therefore, a basic premise of the code was that films uphold, not question or challenge, the basic values of society. The sanctity of home, marriage and church was to be upheld. Law was not to be belittled or ridiculed. From 1930 to 1933 the code was enforced but not with the severity that industry critics demanded.

In 1934, under pressure from the Catholic LEGION OF DECENCY, a new Production Code Administration was created, and a Catholic censor, Joseph I. Breen, was appointed director by Will Hays. No film could be produced or shown in the U.S. without the approval of Breen and his PCA staff. Studios had to submit scripts to Breen, who rigidly enforced the code. For example, he banned Mae WEST's early films from the screen and so censored her after 1934 that her screen appeal was greatly diminished. Breen demanded that films stress moral values and conservative politics. In U.S. movies adultery was punished, divorce shown as wrong and actresses clothed from head to toe. The code was also used to limit social and political commentary. Breen refused an MGM request to film the Sinclair LEWIS novel *It Can't Happen Here* in 1937 and used his authority to alter films that dealt with sensitive topics like unemployment, housing, racism and drug addiction.

In the late 1940s Breen used the Production Code to fight a new openness in cinema that emerged after the war. He tried to ban *The Bicycle Thief* (1948) because it showed a young boy urinating and contained a scene in a brothel. He refused a PCA seal for Otto PREMINGER's *The Moon Is Blue* because of its cavalier attitude toward sexual relationships. But Breen's dominance was now limited by changing public attitudes, the deregulation of the industry by the federal government, by the rise of television and the determination of independent producers to challenge Breen's authority. Breen retired in 1954 and was replaced by his assistant Geoffrey Shurlock. By the late 1960s the industry moved from the self-censorship imposed under the Production Code to an industry rating system—G, for general audiences; M, for mature fans; R, restricted to over 16; and X for adults—that allowed audiences to choose the type of movies they wanted.

Profumo Affair. Sensational British political scandal. In 1963 it came out that the Conservative war minister John Profumo had been involved with a prostitute, Christine Keeler, who had also associated with a Soviet naval attache. Profumo initially denied the allegations, but later admitted that he had lied and resigned from the ministry, the Privy Council, and Parliament. Following a government investigation, it was announced that there had been no breech of national security from the affair, but the highly publicized scandal contributed to the CONSERVATIVE PARTY's defeat in the 1964 elections.

Progressive Conservative Party (Canada). One of the four major Canadian political parties, the Progressive Conservative Party (formerly known as the Conservative Party) dominated in the early years after confederation in 1867. The party advocated strong ties to Britain and a wariness of the U.S. The party also appealed to conservatives in French-speaking Quebec. It became the Progressive Conservative Party when it merged with the Progressive Party, which had broad support in the prairie provinces. World War I created a crisis for the party because French-Canadians objected to conscription. The party never regained its support in Quebec, which has remained a Liberal Party stronghold. Although LIBERAL PARTY prime ministers have been in power for most of the latter half of the century, Brian MULRONEY, a PC from Quebec, became prime minister in 1986.

progressive movement. Movement that advocated political and social reforms in the UNITED STATES in the early 1900s. The progressive movement was largely a reaction to urban corruption and to abuses by business monopolies. Theodore ROOSEVELT, a Republican and U.S. president from 1901 to 1909, was a leading progressive. In 1912, disappointed with the conservative policies of his successor, William Howard TAFT, Roosevelt unsuccessfully ran for the presidency as candidate of the newly formed, progressive **Bull Moose Party**. Another Progressive Party, centered in the American midwest and favoring farmers and workers, formed in 1924. Its presidential candidate, the fiery U.S. Senator Robert LA FOLLETTE, waged a credible campaign but carried only Wisconsin, his home state.

Prohibition. Period between 1919 and 1933 when the manufacture, sale or transport of alcoholic drinks was prohibited in the U.S. Public drunkenness had always been a problem in the U.S. and by 1920 an active temperance movement led by the Anti-Saloon League had succeeded in banning alcoholic drinks in a number of states. Following World War I, the movement received a boost when the idea was promoted that drinking alcohol was unpatriotic because many German-Americans were involved in the trade. The 18th Amendment to the U.S. Constitution banned the manufacture and sale of alcoholic drinks, including beer and wine. But bootleggers began to manufacture and

Federal agents destroying a seized cache of liquor barrels.

distribute illegal alcoholic beverages, which were dispensed in speakeasies. Many otherwise law-abiding citizens simply ignored the ban. Distribution was soon taken over by organized crime figures such as Al CAPONE, and gang warfare broke out. The DEMOCRATIC PARTY platform in the election year of 1932 proposed to repeal the "Great Experiment"; ROOSEVELT won and in 1933 the 21st Amendment made the sale of alcoholic beverages once again legal in most of the U.S.

Prokofiev, Serge [Sergei Sergeyevich Prokofiev] (1891–1953). Soviet composer. Born in the Ukraine, Prokofiev began composing at age five and later studied with Reinhold GLIERE and at the Saint Petersburg Conservatory with Rimsky-Korsakov. A brilliant pianist and conductor, he left the U.S.S.R. in 1918, shortly after the RUSSIAN REVOLUTION. He toured the world and settled in Paris during the 1920s, only returning permanently to the U.S.S.R. in 1936. Although he generally enjoyed the approval of the Soviet authorities, in 1948 Prokofiev (along with Dmitri SHOSTAKOVICH and Aram KHACHATURIAN) was accused of "formalism" and personally reprimanded by Joseph STALIN. Prokofiev's early works are innovative and restrained, combining lyricism with dissonance, melodic beauty with abrupt rhythmic effects. His later pieces are more simplified and accessible. All his compositions, however, are very distinctive in style, often treating Russian themes. Among Prokoviev's works are seven symphonies—most notably the First (the *Classical Symphony,* 1916–17) and the Fifth (1944), two violin concertos, five piano concertos, various piano pieces and numerous chamber works. His vocal compositions include the operas *The Gambler* (1915–16), *The Love for Three Oranges* (1921) and *War and Peace* (1953). His dramatic cantata *Alexander Nevsky* (1939) was used as the score for Sergei EISENSTEIN's film of the same name. Also a superb composer for the ballet, Prokofiev's works in this genre include *L'enfant Prodigue* (1929), one of several ballets he created for DIAGHILEV'S BALLETS RUSSES, and *Romeo and Juliet* (1938). Among his best known works is the symphonic fairy tale *Peter and the Wolf* (1936).

For further reading:

Robinson, Harlow, *Sergei Prokofiev: A Biography.* New York: Viking Penguin, 1987.

Prokosch, Frederic (1908–1989). American author. His best selling first novel, *The Asiatics* (1935), won wide acclaim for its profile of a young American making his way from Beirut, Lebanon to China. His other works included *The Seven Sisters* (1962), *The Missolonghi Manuscript* (1968) and *Voices* (1983), a memoir of his encounters with such figures as T.S. ELIOT, James JOYCE, and Gertrude STEIN.

propaganda. Manipulation of public opinion and behavior in favor of or in opposition to an idea or cause through a number of means, from the use of rhetoric and symbols to written or broadcast messages. The term is generally used in a negative fashion. The word is derived from the *Congregatio de propaganda fide* (Congregation for the Propagation of the Faith), a Roman Catholic missionary agency established in 1622. With the growth of means for disseminating information after the Industrial Revolution, propaganda assumed a great deal of importance and has been an influential part of life in the 20th century. Propaganda differs from education in its deliberately one-sided view of a given issue; only that information is disseminated that will support the propagandists' argument and denigrate the opinions of their opponents. Propaganda was used with considerable success in the BOLSHEVIK movement of the early 20th century, and it is evident in V.I. LENIN's *What Is to Be Done?* (1902), in which he stressed "agitprop," a combination of agitation and propaganda in support of communist revolution. Later in the century propaganda was an important tool of the fascist movements of Adolf HITLER, whose information minister Joseph GOEBBELS was a master propagandist, and of Benito MUSSOLINI. During WORLD WAR II propaganda was an important weapon for both sides of the conflict, and it was extensively used by both the Axis and the Allies, the latter producing material under the auspices of the Office of War Information. In the contemporary era propaganda in printed communications, on the radio and particularly on television has been used for many purposes, from promoting systems of government, to attempting to elect candidates, to selling commercial products through advertising. Moreover, the effectiveness of propaganda campaigns has been increasingly quantified through the use of public opinion surveys. At the same time, a more sophisticated audience seems somewhat better able to distinguish between the efforts of propagandists and those with honestly differing opinions.

Allied propaganda during World War II told civilians about the Nazi enemy.

Proposition 13. Proposal on a statewide referendum in CALIFORNIA that called for a cut in property taxes. Passed by a large margin, Proposition 13 signaled a widespread backlash against high taxes and massive government spending in the U.S. This wave of popular anti-tax feeling helped Ronald REAGAN win the 1980 presidential election.

protectionism. Government economic policy that seeks high tariffs on imported goods in an effort to reduce foreign imports and protect domestic producers and manufacturers. The issue of protectionism has stirred much political debate in the 20th century. Advocates of protectionism (generally supporters of the labor movement) say that protectionist policies protect domestic jobs and help prevent a trade deficit. Opponents say that imposing high tariffs only causes foreign countries to impose similar restrictions on imports, thereby slowing the economy and hurting the very workers the tariffs are meant to help. The HAWLEY-SMOOT TARIFF ACT (1930), enacted at the beginning of the GREAT DEPRESSION, raised U.S. tariffs to their highest levels ever; foreign governments retaliated with similar tariffs, thus damaging world trade and deepening the Depression. In the 1980s, some U.S. politicians have called for protectionist tariffs to stem the flow of imports from Japan.

Proton booster. Soviet "D-Class" launch vehicle, designed to lift heavy loads such as the SALYUT and Mir space stations. It was the first Soviet booster not developed directly from a military rocket. Introduced in July 1965, it is an enlarged version of the smaller "A-class" booster used to launch all three SPUTNIK satellites, as well as VOSTOK, VOSKHOD, SOYUZ, and Progress missions. In the late 1980s the U.S.S.R. began promoting the Proton launcher for use by the rest of the world as a commercial launch vehicle.

Protopopovs, the. Soviet skaters, Lyudmilla Belousova and Oleg Protopopov. This husband and wife ice skating team won two Olympic gold medals for pairs figure skating: at Innsbruck in 1964 and at Grenoble in 1968. Known for their elegant and sophisticated style, the Protopopovs also won several European championships.

Proust, Marcel (1871–1922). French novelist, story writer and essayist. Proust is generally recognized as the greatest French novelist of the 20th century on the strength of his sequence of seven novels, REMEMBRANCE OF THINGS PAST. Born to a Catholic father and a Jewish mother, Proust suffered from poor health as a child and was a near invalid during his early teens. Nonetheless, he went on to graduate from the Sorbonne and to serve in the French army. In the Parisian society of the 1890s Belle Epoque, Proust established a reputation for himself as a dandy. His first volume of stories, *Pleasures and Days* (1896), won him only a small readership. In the 1900s Proust published a great deal of literary criticism. He was very close to his mother, and her death in 1905 spurred him, the following year, to retire from society and devote himself to literature. Dogged by failing health, Proust devoted the final 15 years of his life to *Remembrance of Things Past*, writing in a cork-lined room to keep out the noises of the Parisian streets.

Marcel Proust, whose prose masterwork Remembrance of Things Past *captured the texture of human experience.*

Prouve, Jean (1901–). French designer and architect. Educated in Nancy, Prouve began executing design commissions in 1918, becoming known for his modernist metal furniture. Associated with LE CORBUSIER in the late 1920s, he was a founder of the Union des Artistes Modernes. He stopped designing in 1950, devoting himself thereafter to architecture. As an architect, he is best known for a series of public buildings in the modern idiom notable for their sophisticated engineering.

Provincetown Players (1916–1921). American theatrical ensemble of playwrights and actors. The Provincetown Players were well-known for their willingness to premiere socially controversial works by new and experimental playwrights. The most famous figure to emerge from the Provinceown Players milieu was Eugene O'NEILL, whose classic play *Desire Under the Elms* was first produced by an offshoot of the Players—the Playwrights' Theatre—in 1924. While the Players first appeared at the Wharf Theater in Providence, Rhode Island, the ensemble moved to GREENWICH VILLAGE before resettling in the Provincetown Playhouse in 1918. The Provincetown Players disbanded in 1921.

Provisional Government. Government formed by Russia's DUMA in February 1917 in Petrograd upon the collapse of the autocracy. The provisional government promised to form a constitutional assembly and to hold free elections. It abolished the secret police and granted religious freedom. Many of its leaders were of a conservative outlook, although KERENSKY was a moderate socialist. Because of the war effort grave problems, such as redistribution of land and the rights of non-Russian people to self-government, could not be resolved. As a result, discontent continued to grow. At the same time as the provisional government, the Soviet of workers' deputies had been established; this had the support of industrial workers and socialists, and in October 1917 they overthrew the provisional government.

Prunariu, Dumitru (1952–). Romanian cosmonaut-researcher; the first of his countrymen to fly in space when he served as cosmonaut-researcher aboard the Soviet Soyuz 40 mission (May 1981). Prunariu and Soyuz commander Leonid Popov spent one week of their eight-day mission linked to the Salyut 6 space station with its inhabitants Vladimir Kovalenok and Viktor Savinykh.

PSFS Building. Headquarters of the Philadelphia Savings Fund Society, built in 1932 and generally regarded as the first truly modern skyscraper office building; among the first large buildings in the INTERNATIONAL STYLE to be built in the U.S. It was designed by William LesCaze and George Howe and is remarkable for the consistency and excellence of its overall concept and details. The black granite base contains an austerely geometric banking room with a windowed, rounded corner. Above is a 28–story, tower office block with columns exposed along the sides and front, cantilevered forward. A highly successful building, it remains in fine condition and in regular use for its intended purposes.

Public Works Administration [PWA]. U.S. government agency, established in 1933 during the first HUNDRED DAYS of President Franklin D. ROOSEVELT's adminstration. Part of the NEW DEAL, the PWA was one of the most visible government programs during the GREAT DEPRESSION. As its name suggests, the PWA was responsible for public works. It put thousands of people to work on construction projects throughout the U.S. Numerous public buildings, including many post offices, schools, courthouses and other government facilities were built by the PWA; many of these buildings remained in use toward the end of the century. (See also WORKS PROGRESS ADMINISTRATION.)

Puccini, Giacomo (1858–1924). Italian composer and one of the most popular operatic composers of the late 19th and early 20th centuries; born in Lucca, Italy of a distinguished musical family. A precocious musician, Puccini began his musical studies as a child, attending the Instituto Musicale and later studying (1880–83) at the Milan Conservatory. His first opera, the one-act *Le Villi* (1884), met with some success, but it was not until the production of his third work, *Manon Lescaut* (1893), that Puccini became a celebrated and successful composer. His finest works are generally acknowledged to be *La Boheme* (1896), *Tosca* (1900), *Madama Butterfly* (1904) and *Turandot*, which was not quite finished at the composer's death and which premiered at La Scala in 1926. Lesser works include *La Fanciulla del West* (1910) and *Il Trittico* (1918). In his operas, Puccini combined such traditional features of Italian opera as arias and love duets with such Wagnerian innovations as leitmotivs and complex dramatic characterizations. To this mixture he added

Giacomo Puccini, Italian opera composer (1924).

superb melodies, lush orchestration, exotic settings and erotic tension mingled with sentimentality.

For further reading:

Carner, Mosco, *Puccini: A Critical Biography*, 2nd ed. New York: Holmes and Meier, 1977.

Greenfeld, Howard, *Puccini: A Biography*. 1980.

Pudovkin, Vsevelod Illarionovitch (1893–1953). Soviet filmmaker and theoretician. With colleagues Lev KULESHOV, Sergei EISENSTEIN and Dziga VERTOV, he stood at the center of the great decade of Soviet filmmaking in the 1920s. He was born in Penza and educated in physics and chemistry at Moscow University. In 1920 he entered the State Film School and two years later worked with Kuleshov in the famous "Kuleshov Workshop." Pudovkin's most important films were made in the second half of the decade, *Mat* (*Mother*) in 1926, *Konyets Sankt-Peterburga* (*The End of St. Petersburg*) in 1927 and *Potomak Chingis-khan* (*The Heir to Genghis Khan*, or, *Storm over Asia*) in 1928. Nominally, like Eisenstein's films, they are all concerned with issues of Soviet revolution, but, again like Eisenstein, their chief distinction lies in their applications of film shots to make "the all-inclusive discovery and explanation of the interrelationships of the phenomena of real life." The "linkage" of shots, Pudovkin argued, is the foundation of film art, the building from raw pieces of celluloid a "filmic space and time." The art of film acting, as a consequence, must differ radically from stage technique. The actor must work in brief time-space fragments, becoming a "material" of "equal and undifferentiated value" with other components of cinema, and subject to the same manipulations. Despite these theoretical formulations, however, Pudovkin's films display more compassion, poetic sensibility and interest in individual personalities than do Eisenstein's. After sustaining injuries in a car wreck in 1935, Pudovkin returned to cinema, directing a number of historical films and appearing in others such as Eisenstein's *Ivan Groznyi* (*Ivan the Terrible*) in 1944. His major theoretical works, *Film Technique* and *Film-Acting* (1926), first appeared in translation in 1933.

For further reading:

Dart, Peter, *Pudovkin's Films and Film Theory*. New York: Arno Press, 1974.

***Pueblo* incident.** Capture of the U.S.S. *Pueblo*, a navy electronic and radio intelligence-gathering ship, off the eastern coast of NORTH KOREA on January 23, 1968, and its aftermath. The vessel, under Commander Lloyd M. Bucher, was fired on, boarded and seized by ships from the North Korean navy and removed to the port of Wonson. The U.S. demanded release of the ship and its crew together with an apology, maintaining that it had been in international waters at the time of its capture. The North Korean government held the ship and men hostage for 11 months. The U.S. finally acceded to North Korean demands, and in December 1968 it signed an admission of intrusion into North Korean waters, which it disavowed before the signing, and an apology. With this and the promise not to engage in further spying, the ship and crew were released. Afterward, Bucher and others on the *Pueblo* charged that they had been tortured and forced to sign false confessions. The ship's captain gave his version of the events in *Bucher: My Story* (1970).

Puente, Tito [Ernesto Antonio Puente Jr.] (1923–). American musician, bandleader, composer and producer. A virtuoso timbales player, Puente also plays the vibes, sax, piano, bongos and conga. His first band, the Piccadilly Boys, formed in 1947 and soon became the Tito Puente Orchestra. He was a leader of the big band mambo and chachacha styles of the 1950s. As a member or leader of other groups specializing in Latin rhythms, he has toured Europe, produced many records and won two Grammy Awards, for *Tito Puente and His Latin Ensemble on Broadway* (1983) and *Mambo Diablo* (1985). His many compositions include the hit "Oye Cano Va."

Puerto Rico. The Commonwealth of Puerto Rico is an island covering 3,514 square miles in the Caribbean Sea. The terrain is mostly mountainous, with a coastal plain in the north. The capital is San Juan. American troops invaded the centuries-old Spanish island in May 1898 and in December the island was ceded to the U.S. It became an unincorporated U.S. territory and U.S. citizenship was granted to Puerto Ricans in 1917. Many islanders, however, wanted greater internal self-government and economic and social reforms, a policy advocated by the Partido Popular Democratico (PPD). The PPD gained a majority in the Senate in elections in 1940 and the first elections to the post of governor in 1947 were won by the PPD's leader, Luis MUNOZ MARIN. Puerto Rico was granted a new constitution in 1952 when it became a commonwealth in association with the U.S. Under the PPD administration a program of investment and industrialization developed the island's economy and improved social conditions. In 1967 a plebiscite produced a majority in favor of commonwealth status, rather than statehood, with only a very small minority in favor of independence.

The PPD remained in power until 1968 when it was defeated by the Partido Nuevo Progressista (PNP), which favors statehood. Luis A. Ferre became governor. In 1972 the PPD was returned to power with Rafael Hernandez Colon elected governor. The PNP's candidate for governor, Carlos Romero Barcelo, won in the 1976 elections, but in 1980 the PNP lost its majority in both houses of the Legislative Assembly, although Romero Barcelo retained the governorship. Internal factionalism within the PNP led to divisions in the party over Romero Barcelo's leadership. In 1984 Romero Barcelo was defeated by Hernandez Colon for the governorship, and the PPD maintained its majority in the assembly. Hernandez Colon retained the governorship in the election held in November 1988, defeating Baltasar Corrada del Rio of the PNP by a narrow margin.

Pugwash Conferences. See Cyrus EATON.

Puig, Manuel (1932–1990). Argentinian novelist. Puig, who was best known for his novel *The Kiss of the Spider Woman* (1979), which was adapted into a highly successful HOLLYWOOD film starring William Hurt and Raul Julia, grew up highly enamored of the film medium that would spread his fame. As a young boy living in a remote region of the Argentine pampas, Puig used films to escape from his culturally narrow environment. After studying philosophy at the University of Buenos Aires, Puig went to Rome in 1955 where he studied film technique. His first novel, *Betrayed by Rita Hayworth* (1971), portrayed the commingling of Hollywood fantasy and the bleak realities of Argentine life. In *The Kiss of the Spider Woman*, two prisoners—one a political radical, the other a homosexual—bide their prison sentence time and reveal their souls through retelling the romantic plots of old movies. Other novels by Puig include *Heartbreak Tango: A Serial* (1973) and *Eternal Curse on the Reader of These Pages* (1985).

Pulitzer Prize. American award for journalism, letters and music. The annual Pulitzer Prizes were established in 1915 in the will of the Hungarian-American newspaper publisher Joseph Pulitzer, who also established the Columbia University School of Journalism, which confers the prizes. The prizes are bestowed on American citizens who distinguish themselves in the field of letters (including history, biography, poetry, drama and fiction, music) and journalism (including reporting, photography and criticism). The prizes, originally $1,000, are now $3,000, except for public service in journalism, which is given a gold medal. The first Pulitzer Prizes were awarded in 1917. The Pulitzer Prize is widely regarded as the most prestigious American award in these fields.

Punk Rock. Hard-edged musical style that constitutes a performing sub-genre of ROCK AND ROLL. Punk rock first came to attention in both Britain and America in the mid-1970s. The first major punk rock song is generally considered to be "God Save the Queen" (1977) by the British-based group the Sex Pistols, which featured scathingly raw and sneering vocals by lead singer Johnny Rotten and unsophisticated but intensely hard-driving guitar and percussion work. Other major bands that influenced the punk rock style include the Buzzcocks, the Ramones and James White and the Blacks. While punk rock musical creativity dwindled by the early 1980s, the basic punk rock style continued to hold its popularity with a new generation of rock audiences.

"Purple Code". See Elizabeth S. FRIEDMAN.

Purser, Sarah (1848–1943). Irish painter, designer and stained-glass artist. She studied in Ireland, France and Italy, returning to Dublin in 1878. In addition to creating her own works, she was also an important force in the promotion of native Irish art. In 1924 she founded the Friends of the National Collections of Ireland, and in 1930 she secured from the government sumptuous Dublin quarters to house the Lane Collection and the Modern Art Gallery.

Purvis, Melvin (1903–1960). American law enforcement officer. Born in South Carolina, Purvis became a lawyer and joined the FBI in 1927. He was appointed to the FBI's Chicago office in 1932, and for the next three years he presided over the hunt for and apprehension of such public enemy criminals as "Pretty Boy" FLOYD, "Baby Face" NELSON and, most notably, John DILLINGER, whom he and his agents gunned down in 1934. Apparently in conflict with FBI director J. Edgar HOOVER, Purvis resigned from the Bureau in 1935. During WORLD WAR II he worked for the U.S. Army War Crimes Office and after the war returned to the practice of law.

Pusan. City in southeastern South Korea; site of major battle between UN forces and the North Korean People's Army (NKPA) early in the KOREAN WAR. Korea's largest port, Pusan served as a beachhead for UN forces, and from early July through mid-September 1950, the NKPA attempted to dislodge the allies from their toehold. However, the UN forces managed to hold off the North Koreans, while reinforcements and supplies arrived through the port. On September 16, the battle finally ended as UN troops broke out of the perimeter and took the offensive following the Allied invasion at INCHON. The Allies suffered more than 19,000 casualties, including over 400 dead; however, the successful defense of Pusan proved a decisive factor in the UN forces' eventual victory.

Puskas, Ferenc (1926–). Hungarian-born soccer player. Puskas was the dominant player on the outstanding Hungarian national team of the early 1950s. A natural goalscorer, Puskas won his first cap at age 18 in August 1945. He was captain of the Hungary team that won the 1952 Olympic gold medal. Puskas's most memorable performance came at Wembley Stadium, England in 1953 when he scored two goals in Hungary's 6–3 thrashing of England, their first-ever home loss. In a return match in 1964 in Budapest, Hungary won 7–1; Puskas scored two again and established himself as the world's best player. This was the pinnacle of Puskas' career. In the 1954 World Cup in Switzerland, Puskas was injured and Hungary lost to West Germany 3–2 in the final. During the 1956 HUNGARIAN UPRISING, Puskas was touring with his team, Honved, and decided not to return home. He eventually settled in Spain, and joined the European Champions, Real Madrid. He joined forces with the legendary Alfredo di Stefano and led Real to its fifth European Championship in 1960. Puskas played for Spain in the 1962 World Cup and retired in 1966.

Pu-yi, Henry (1906–1967). Last emperor of CHINA (1908–12), who reigned under the name Hsuan-t'ung. Born in Beijing, a grand-nephew of the dowager empress, he succeeded to the throne as a small child. The republican revolution forced his abdication in 1912, and he remained in the Forbidden City under government support and warlord influence until 1924. In 1925 he fled to the Japanese concession in Tientsin, living there until 1931. He became the figurehead emperor of the Japanese puppet state of MANCHUKUO (Manchuria) in 1934. Captured by Soviet troops in 1945, he was imprisoned in Siberia for five years, testifying at the war crimes trial in Tokyo in 1946. Turned over to the People's Republic of China in 1950, he remained in prison until granted amnesty in 1959. After political "reeducation," he became a private citizen in Beijing. His life was the subject of Bernardo BERTOLUCCI'S ACADEMY AWARD-winning 1987 film *The Last Emperor*.

PWA. See PUBLIC WORKS ADMINISTRATION.

Pyatakov, Grigory L. (1890–1937). Politician and leader of the left wing of the Ukrainian Communist Party. In December 1918 Moscow ordered that a concealed Soviet government be set up in Kursk under Pyatakov. Pyatakov accordingly set up a Soviet regime and invaded the UKRAINE with Red troops. In 1937, however, he was tried at the "anti-Soviet Trotskyite Center" trial.

Pyle, Ernie (1900–1945). American journalist. Pyle held a variety of newspaper posts in New York and Washington, D.C., during the 1920s and 1930s. In 1935 he become a syndicated columnist and roving reporter. However, his career reached its zenith during WORLD WAR II, when he became perhaps the best known and most widely read war correspondent. He accompanied American troops on the front lines, covering the war in North Africa, Europe and the Pacific in his regular column. Pyle did not report the course of the war in strategic terms but, rather, chronicled the day-to-day existence of ordinary GIs. He won the 1944 PULITZER PRIZE for his reporting. Pyle was killed by Japanese machine gun fire on April 18, 1945, on the island of Iishima, near OKINAWA.

Pym, Barbara [Mary Crampton] (1913–1980). British novelist. Born in Shropshire and educated at Oxford, Pym worked for a time at the International African Institute in London. Her keenly observed satirical novels of provincial English life, including *Excellent Women* (1952), *Less Than Angels* (1955), *Quartet in Autumn* (1977) and *A Few Green Leaves* (1980), are reminiscent of the work of Jane Austen. Pym enjoyed modest success during the 1950s, but in 1961 her publishers dropped her from their list. Her reputation rose again in the late 1970s when Lord David CECIL and Philip LARKIN both cited her as one of the most underrated writers of the 20th century.

American war correspondent Ernie Pyle, who wrote about the lives of average GIs at the front.

Pynchon, Thomas (1937–). American novelist. Pynchon is highly reclusive, and few facts concerning the last 30 years of his life are known. In his youth he served in the U.S. Navy, graduated from Cornell University and worked for a brief time as a technical writer for Boeing Aircraft. Since the publication of his acclaimed first novel, *V* (1963), Pynchon has been regarded as one of the most dazzling and difficult fiction writers of modern times. He possesses a detailed knowledge of both literature and modern technology and combines the vocabulary and insights of both fields to create a richly woven verbal tapestry filled with baroque allusions and imagery. Two of his central themes are the elusive nature of paranoia and the pervasive presence of entropic forces in a world that is losing its structured coherence. Pynchon has written only three other novels,—*The Crying of Lot 49* (1946), *Gravity's Rainbow* (1973), which won the National Book Award, and *Vineland* (1990)—but his work is meticulously conceived and forms a monumental whole.

Qaddafi, Muammer el- (1942–). Libyan nationalist and revolutionary leader. A bedouin Arab, Qaddafi received a traditional Koranic education, then attended high school, from which he was expelled for nationalist political activity. He subsequently studied history at the University of Benghazi (1962–63), then attended the Libyan Military Academy and the British Royal Signal Corps School at Beaconsfield, England. In 1965 he was commissioned as a signal corps officer in the Royal Libyan Army. He led the 1969 revolution and was promoted by 11 fellow members of the Revolutionary Command Council to be commander-in-chief, with the rank of colonel. He served as prime minister and defense minister from January 1970 until 1972, when he relinquished the former post. In 1976 he chaired the first General People's Congress (GPC) and was elected general secretary of the GPC secretariat in 1977. His *Green Book* (1976) called for revolutionary Arab socialism. Qaddafi has sought to project himself as the champion of the Arab people but was condemned by the REAGAN administration as a sponsor of international terrorism; the U.S. raid on LIBYA in April 1986 was in retaliation for Qaddafi's previous terrorist actions, as well as a warning to deter him from further terrorism. Qaddafi has gained Libya the capability to produce chemical weapons but has lost credibility among Arab moderates.

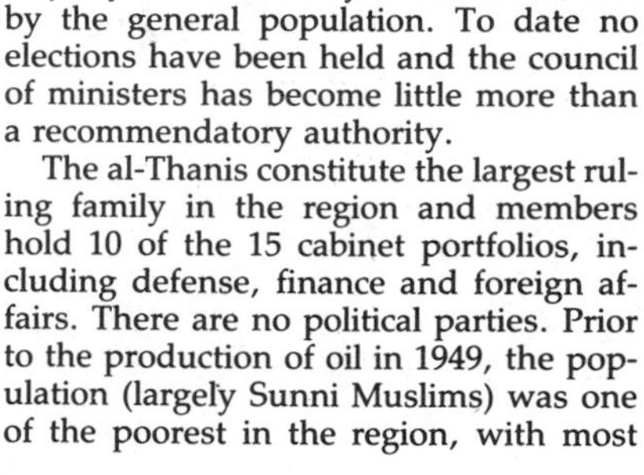

Colonel Muammer el-Qaddafi led the military overthrow of the Libyan monarchy in 1969.

Qantarah, Al [El Kantara]. Town on the east bank of the SUEZ CANAL, in northeastern Egypt. Qantarah was the western terminus of a rail line to PALESTINE that was built during WORLD WAR I for the British Expeditionary Force. The town was captured by Israel during the SIX-DAY WAR (1967) and returned to Egypt in 1974.

Qatar, State of. On the eastern coast of the Arabian Peninsula, the state is comprised of the Qatar peninsula and several offshore islands; Bahrain lies to the northwest. Qatar came under British influence in 1869, and under a treaty signed in 1916 Britain gained effective control over Qatar's foreign relations, together with responsibility for security and commercial privileges. This protectorate status continued until Qatar gained independence in 1971. In 1972 a palace coup occurred when Shaikh Khalifa ibn Hamad al-Thani ousted his cousin, Shaikh Ahmad. A year before independence, Qatar promulgated a written constitution that provided for a council of ministers and an advisory council. It stipulated that the former was to be appointed by the ruler and that a majority of the advisory council be elected by the general population. To date no elections have been held and the council of ministers has become little more than a recommendatory authority.

The al-Thanis constitute the largest ruling family in the region and members hold 10 of the 15 cabinet portfolios, including defense, finance and foreign affairs. There are no political parties. Prior to the production of oil in 1949, the population (largely Sunni Muslims) was one of the poorest in the region, with most livelihoods dependent upon fishing and pearling. Petroleum production and export together with the nationalization of both major oil producers, Qatar Petroleum Company and Shell Oil of Qatar, have led to the government providing considerable investment for infrastructural development. Qatar has been a member of the Gulf Cooperation Council since its inception in 1981 and is a member of the Organization of Arab Petroleum Exporting Countries and OPEC. The historic territorial dispute with Bahrain over the Hawar islands flared up in 1986 when Qatari troops briefly occupied Fasht al-Dibal, a coral reef that was being reclaimed from the sea by Bahrain. It was later destroyed by agreement of both parties.

Qiao Guanhua [Chaio Kuan Hua, Chiao Kuan-hua] (1908–1983). Chinese communist political leader. During the early 1970s he played a key role in the normalization of relations between the PEOPLE'S REPUBLIC OF CHINA and the U.S. He headed China's first delegation to the UNITED NATIONS. With Henry KISSINGER, Qiao drafted the **Shanghai communique** during U.S. President Richard NIXON'S 1972 visit to China. He was foreign minister from 1974 until 1976, when he was dismissed following the arrest of the GANG OF FOUR. He then played no public role for several years, but shortly before his death in 1983 he was appointed advisor to the People's Association for Friendship with Foreign Countries.

Qom [Kum, Qum]. Iranian city 75 miles south of Teheran. A Shi'ite Muslim pilgrimage center and the site of the shrine of Fatima, an important saint of the Shi'ites. In the 1970s Qom became known as the seat of the Ayatollah KHOMEINI, the religious and political leader of Iran.

Quango [Quasi-Autonomous Non-Governmental Organisation]. A body in Britain that has the power to spend public money but is not under direct governmental control.

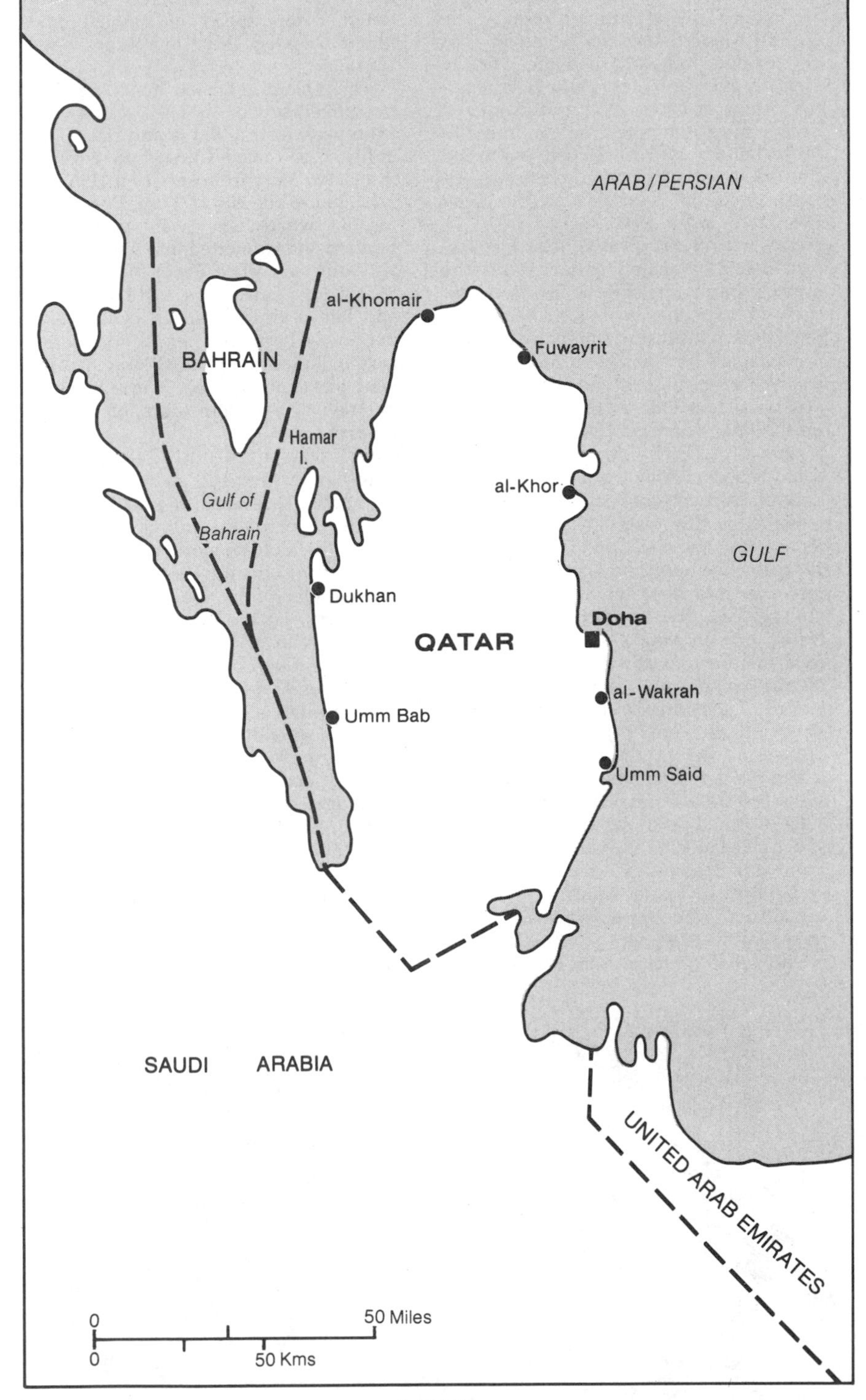

QATAR

Quant, Mary (1934–). British fashion designer and retailer, a key figure in the rise of British fashion in the 1950s and 1960s. Quant studied art at Goldsmith's College in London, where she met Alexander Greene, who became her partner in 1955. (They were married two years later.) The first Quant shop, *Bazaar*, opened in London in 1955 on the King's Road; it introduced a modern youth-oriented concept in display and marketing as well as in the actual garments offered for sale. Quant helped Britain rise to a position of leadership in the fashion world with the introduction of the miniskirt in 1964.

Quantico. Town on the Potomac River near Fredericksburg, Virginia, U.S.A. Quantico is best known as the site of a U.S. Marine Corps training base, established in 1918.

quantum mechanics. Branch of physics that deals with matter and energy on an atomic and sub-atomic level. The quantum theory was first formulated in 1900 by Max PLANCK. According to this theory, energy (light, for example) does not travel in a continuous wave, as was previously thought, but is formed by infinitely small bits ("quanta") pulsing in rapid succession. Albert EINSTEIN (1905), Niels BOHR (1913) and (all in the mid-1920s) Max BORN, Werner HEISENBERG, Paul DIRAC, Pascal Jordan, Erwin SCHRODINGER and Louis DE BROGLIE all made important contributions to the field of quantum mechanics; Heisenberg introduced the **uncertainty principle** as a fundamental law of quantum mechanics. This 20th-century branch of science has revolutionized human knowledge of matter and energy.

quark. Subatomic particle, believed to be the smallest elementary particle—1,000 times smaller than a proton. Physicists believe that quarks are the basis of protons and neutrons. The existence of quarks was first suggested by Murray GELL-MANN and George Zweig in 1964. The name is taken from a word coined by James JOYCE in *Finnegans Wake* (1939). Quarks can be classified as "charmed" or "strange," among other terms.

Quasimodo, Salvatore (1901–1968). Italian poet, critic and translator who won the NOBEL PRIZE for literature in 1959. After completing his studies to become an engineer, Quasimodo joined the Ministry of Public Works in 1928. His first collection, *Acque e terra* (1930, *Waters and Land*) recalled his Sicilian childhood. In 1938 he abandoned his technical trade, and in 1941 he became a professor of literature. Though his early poems showed the influence of symbolism and Hermeticism, over the years his language became simpler and his themes more public and socially committed. Of particular note are *Giorno doppo giorno* (1947, *Day after Day*), *La vita non e sogno* (1949, *Life Is Not Dream*), *La terra impareggiabile* (1958, *The Incomparable Land*) and *Dare e avere* (1966, *To Give and to Have*). He also translated ancient Greek and Latin poetry, Shakespeare, Moliere, NERUDA and CUMMINGS.

Quayle, Sir (John) Anthony (1913–1989). British theater, film and television actor. Noted for the wide range of his work—from classical drama to Shakespeare to war movies—he began acting with the Old Vic Company in London but left the theater to enlist in the military in WORLD WAR II. After the war he joined the Shakespeare Memorial Theatre Company (now the ROYAL SHAKESPEARE COMPANY) in Stratford-upon-Avon and served both as an actor and as the group's director (1948–56). He also founded the touring Compass group in 1984. Among his best known films were *The Wrong Man* (1957), *The Guns of Navarone* (1961) and *Lawrence of Arabia* (1963). He was nominated for an ACADEMY AWARD in 1970 for his portrayal of Cardinal Wolsey in *Anne of a Thousand Days*, a historical film about Henry VIII and Anne Boleyn. He was knighted in 1985.

Quebec. Province of eastern CANADA and one of the four founding provinces of the dominion (1867). Although French authority ended in 1763, French culture has remained dominant; in 1974 French was made the sole official language in the province. A group advocating independence arose in the 1960s, but in a referendum in May 1980 Quebec voted against secession. The secession movement revived in the late 1980s. (See also PARTI QUEBECOIS, Rene LEVESQUE.)

Quebec Conferences. Two talks held in Quebec during WORLD WAR II between U.S. President Franklin D. ROOSEVELT and British Prime Minister Winston CHURCHILL, with the participation of their military staffs. The first, code-named "Quadrant," was held in August, 1943 and involved plans for the NORMANDY landings, Southeast Asia campaigns and the war in Italy. The second, code-named "Octagon" and held in September, 1944, concerned the naval war in the Pacific, the Allied advance into Germany, operations in the Philippines and the MORGENTHAU PLAN.

Queen, Ellery [pen name of Frederic Dannay and Manfred B. Lee]. Both the author and his celebrated American detective creation, "Queen" was an amateur sleuth, radio-TV-film star, magazine editor, anthologist and chronicler of the history of detective fiction. From *The Roman Hat Mystery* (1929) to *A Fine and Private Place* (1971), his 35 novels and numerous short stories ranged from exercises in pure deduction (*The Chinese Orange Mystery*) to complex psychological dramas (the justly famed "Wrightsville" cases, including *Calamity Town* and *Ten Days Wonder*). Queen himself changed from a snobbish, intellectual dandy to a probing and vulnerable observer of human truths and foibles. He has been portrayed in the movies, radio and television by Lew Ayres, Ralph Bellamy, William Gargan and George Nader. As editor and anthologist, he is without peer. *Ellery Queen's Mystery Magazine* began in 1941 and to date has published the work of virtually every luminary in the field. After the deaths of Lee in 1971 and Dannay a decade later, the magazine continued in other hands. In 1941 Queen published the finest anthology of crime fiction extant, *101 Years' Entertainment: The Great Detective Stories of 1841–1941*.

Queen Mary. British-flag OCEAN LINER, considered by many to have been the greatest passenger ship of the 20th century. In 1926, the board of directors of the Cunard Steamship Company ordered a new flagship. The *Queen Mary* was to be the largest, fastest and most glamorous passenger ship in the world. Work on the liner began on December 1, 1930, at the John Brown shipyard at Clydesbank, Scotland. After the project had been delayed for two years because of the GREAT DEPRESSION, the *Queen Mary* was christened and launched on September 26, 1934; further outfitting was required before the ship departed on her maiden voyage from Southampton, England, to New York on May 27, 1936. Her main rival on the transatlantic route was the elegant French liner NORMANDIE. Cunard launched a slightly larger sister ship, the *Queen Elizabeth*, in 1938. At the outbreak of WORLD WAR II, the *Queen Mary* was refitted as a troop ship. During the war, she sailed 600,000 miles and carried nearly 900,000 Allied personnel. On one voyage she carried 15,000 soldiers—the largest number of passengers ever carried on any ship. British Prime Minister Winston CHURCHILL made three secret wartime transatlantic crossings on the *Queen* to attend Allied conferences in North America. Adolf HITLER ordered her sunk, but her top speed of more than 31 knots allowed her to elude enemy U-boats.

The *Queen* returned to transatlantic passenger service in 1947. Competition from passenger jetliners and rising operating costs forced Cunard to withdraw the *Queen Mary* from service in 1967. She was sold to the city of Long Beach, California, where she was permanently berthed and converted into a luxury hotel and museum. The *Queen Mary* weighs 81,237 tons, measures 1,019.5 feet long and had a cruising speed of 28.5 knots per hour. During her heyday, her passengers included many of the most prominent statesmen, authors, musicians, industrialists and film stars of the 20th century.

Queen Maud Mountains. Mountain range in ANTARCTICA south of the Ross Ice Shelf. Discovered in 1911 by Norwegian explorer Roald AMUNDSEN, the range boasts three of the world's great glaciers: Amundsen, Liv and Thorne.

Queens. One of the five boroughs of NEW YORK CITY, on the western end of Long Island. With the construction of the Queensborough Bridge in 1909, connecting Queens with the borough of MANHATTAN, and a railroad tunnel in 1910, Queens expanded rapidly. It was twice the site of a World's Fair, in 1939–40 and 1964–65 (see NEW YORK WORLD'S FAIR OF 1939). It also has two major airports, John F. Kennedy International (formerly Idlewild) and La Guardia. The New York Mets baseball team, established in 1962, have played at Shea Stadium in Queens since 1964.

Quemoy incident. Quemoy, a Nationalist Chinese-held island six miles off the

The Queen Mary *arrives in New York Harbor (June 20, 1945) carrying thousands of U.S. soldiers returning from the European theater.*

Red Chinese mainland, was a base for Nationalist raids against the communist mainland from 1953 to 1958. In August–September 1958 it was bombarded and threatened with invasion by the communists. A U.S. fleet moved in with supplies and a guarantee of military assistance.

Queremistas [Sp., *queremos Getuilo,* "we want Getuilo"]. Supporters of Getuilo Vargas in the 1945 Brazilian presidential election. Getuilo was dictator from 1937 to 1945 and from 1951 to 1954, when he committed suicide.

Quick, Armand J. (1894–1978). American pathologist. An authority on blood clotting, Quick was considered one of the 20th century's leading specialists on blood diseases. In 1932 he developed the prothrombin time test, also known as the Quick test, which was used to regulate the dosage of blood-thinning drugs and in diagnosing liver diseases.

Quisling, Vidkun (1887–1945). Norwegian politician, infamous as a traitor and Nazi collaborator during WORLD WAR II. Graduated from the Norwegian military academy with the highest honors ever awarded up to that time, he was a military attache in Finland and Russia (1918–21), and later in the 1920s worked with Fridtjof NANSEN on famine relief in the UKRAINE. A fervent anticommunist, he served as NORWAY's minister of defense (1931–33); shortly thereafter, he founded the fascist National Unity (*Nasjonal Samling*) Party, which failed to win popular support. In the late 1930s he formed close ties with German Nazi leaders. He proclaimed himself prime minister after the German invasion of Norway (1940), and was officially recognized as such by the Germans in 1942. He formally allied Norway with Germany in 1943, but the Norwegian population remained firmly anti-Nazi. After the war he was tried for high treason by a Norwegian tribunal, found guilty and executed. The name "Quisling" has entered the 20th-century vocabulary as an eponym for "traitor."

Norwegian dictator and Nazi sympathizer Vidkun Quisling is arraigned for high treason (May 26, 1945); he was later executed.

quiz show scandal. Television scandal that revealed in 1959 that many TV quiz shows were actually rigged. During the 1950s, quiz programs had emerged as one of the most popular types of television show. The "$64,000 Question" competed with "Twenty-One" as contestants attempted to turn their knowledge into an instant fortune. The industry's image was tarnished when revelations emerged that many of the big winners were provided with the answers in advance. Producers and sponsors manipulated the shows to boost their ratings and sales. Perhaps the best known casualty of the scandal was Professor Charles Van Doren of Columbia University, who not only was publicly humiliated but also lost his university post when his complicity in the scheme was exposed. Adding to the air of corruption at the time was the "payola" scandal in which disc jockeys at a number of radio stations were bribed by record companies to promote certain recording artists.

Qumran. Village in PALESTINE; on the northwestern shore of the Dead Sea. Qumran, in the WEST BANK region, was part of JORDAN until it was occupied by ISRAEL in 1967. The village was inhabited by a group of religious Jews, probably Essenes, from the second century B.C. until the Romans destroyed it in 68 A.D. In 1947 a shepherd discovered a group of ancient manuscripts in a nearby cave. Archaeologists subsequently uncovered more manuscripts of the same origin. These turned out to have been written by the sect, and came to be known as the **Dead Sea Scrolls**—one of the major archaeological finds of the 20th century.

R

Raanana. Settlement on Israel's Plain of Sharon, northeast of Tel Aviv, where Zionists established a large reception camp for Jewish immigrants in 1921, as well as an Orthodox Jewish children's community. (See also PALESTINE; ZIONISM).

Rabaul. Port town on the northeast shore of New Britain Island, in the Bismarck Archipelago of the western Pacific Ocean; a part of PAPUA NEW GUINEA. Rabaul was founded in 1910 as the capital of German New Guinea; from 1920 to 1941 it was the capital of the Territory of New Guinea. In January 1942 it was captured by the Japanese, who hoped to use it as an air and naval base for their attack on Australia, which never materialized (see WORLD WAR II IN THE PACIFIC). The town was hit by Allied air raids but rebuilt after the war.

Rabi, I(sidor) I(saac) (1898–1988). American physicist. Born in Rymanow in the Austro-Hungarian Empire, Rabi immigrated to the U.S. with his family shortly after his birth. He grew up on New York City's Lower East Side and in Brooklyn. Rabi studied electrical engineering, chemistry and physics, receiving his B.S. in chemistry from Cornell University (1919) and his Ph.D. in physics from Columbia (1927). A postgraduate fellowship enabled him to work with Niels BOHR, Werner HEISENBERG, Wolfgang PAULI, Erwin SCHRODINGER and Otto Stern in Denmark and Germany in the late 1920s. Rabi was particularly interested in the new field of quantum mechanics, which explained many phenomena not explained by classical physics. He returned to Columbia in 1929 and was associated with the university for the remainder of his career. During World War II he played a major role in the development of RADAR. He received the 1944 NOBEL PRIZE for physics for his discovery and measurement of the radio-frequency spectrum of atomic nuclei whose magnetic spin had been disturbed. This work eventually led to the development of extremely precise atomic clocks and of nuclear magnetic resonance imaging for medical diagnosis. After the war Rabi became an advocate for nuclear arms control. From 1952 to 1956 he was chairman of the general advisory committee to the Atomic Energy Commission. He later headed President EISENHOWER's science advisory council, served on the U.S. delegation to UNESCO and worked for the establishment of an international physics laboratory, CERN, in Geneva.

Rabin, Yitzhak (1922–). Israeli politician, prime minister (1974–77). Born in Jerusalem, Rabin attended agricultural college (1936–40) before taking part in the Allied invasion of Syria in 1941. He was a member of the HAGANAH and an Israeli Defense Force (IDF) commander in the 1948 war. He was the head of the IDF's Tactical Operations Branch (1950–52) and, after graduating from the British Staff College, served successively as head of the IDF's training department (1954–56), head of the Northern Command (1956–59), deputy chief of staff (1960–64) and chief of staff (1964–68). The IDF's victory in the 1967 war brought him international acclaim, and he left to become ISRAEL's ambassador to Washington in 1968. Upon returning to Israel in 1973 he joined the Labor Party and served as its leader from 1974 to 1977; he was appointed prime minister after its 1974 election victory. He resigned in 1977 after being implicated in a minor infringement of foreign currency regulations, but remained active in politics and was appointed minister of defense by the Labor-led government of national unity in 1984. He gained immediate popularity by his skillful withdrawal of the IDF from LEBANON, but was criticized by dovish Israelis for continuing his predecessor Ariel SHARON's strong-arm policy against WEST BANK Palestinians. In March 1986 Rabin publicly berated Prime Minister Shimon PERES for advocating unilateral West Bank autonomy. Condemning the proposal as "excessive talk about a concept which nobody can define," he provoked a major crisis within the Labor leadership, which exposed the long rivalry between the two men.

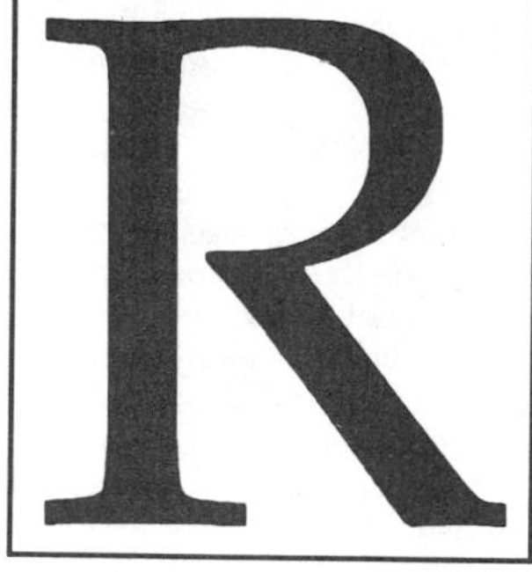

American physicist I.I. Rabi received the Nobel Prize for physics in 1944.

Raby, Albert (1933–1988). U.S. CIVIL RIGHTS leader. A former schoolteacher, Raby helped lead the fight against segregation in Chicago's school system. In 1966, Raby played a key role in convincing Martin Luther KING Jr. to bring his civil rights movement to Chicago. He later managed Harold Washington's 1983 campaign to become the city's first black mayor.

Rachmaninoff, Sergei Vasilyevich (1873–1943). Russian composer and pianist. From an aristocratic family, Rachmaninoff studied at the Moscow Conservatory (1885–92) and quickly established a career as a virtuoso pianist and composer. Touring Scandinavia during the 1917 RUSSIAN REVOLUTION, he never returned to his homeland but settled first in Switzerland and then in the United

Russian pianist and composer Sergei Rachmaninoff.

States, where he supported himself by extensive concertizing. One of the greatest pianists of the 20th century, Rachmaninoff also won popular acclaim for his romantic compositions, which are marked by sensuous tonality, rich melody and a melancholic mood. His work includes three symphonies, four piano concertos, the *Rhapsody on a Theme of Paganini* for piano and orchestra, and numerous works for solo piano as well as songs, operas and choral pieces. Rachmaninoff's music has been performed and recorded widely in the West and in the U.S.S.R.

Rackham, Arthur (1867–1939). English illustrator and watercolorist. One of the leading illustrators of the early 20th century, he is famed for his teeming, sinuously linear, delicately colored and brilliantly imagined illustrations of children's classics. These include Grimm's *Fairy Tales* (1900), *Rip Van Winkle* (1905), *Peter Pan* (1906), *Alice in Wonderland* (1907) and *A Christmas Carol* (1915). Rackham also created notable illustrations for Izaak Walton's *The Compleat Angler* (1931) and Poe's *Tales of Mystery* (1935).

radar. A system for locating a distant object by bouncing radio waves off its surface; the name is an acronym for "*ra*dio *d*etection *a*nd *r*anging." Developed independently in several countries during the 1930s, it was first put into practical operation by Sir Robert Watson-Watt. Radar sends electromagnetic wave pulses toward an object by means of a transmitter; the waves reflect off the target and the returning waves are picked up by a receiver, amplified and converted into images displayed on a cathode ray tube. Usually used to detect aircraft, radar gives information on a target's position, distance, direction, movement and shape. Radar employing long waves was first used in England early in WORLD WAR II. However, these wide beams proved inaccurate and were soon replaced by the accuracy of narrow microwaves produced by a cavity magnetron, a generating device invented (1940) by Sir John T. Randal and Henry A. Boot. By 1940 the British coast bristled with radar installations whose antennae were directed toward enemy countries. Radar was an enormously important defensive and offensive tool for Allied land and naval forces in World War II and was also used by the Germans after 1942 to target antiaircraft guns. Systems were greatly improved and refined after the war. Today, radar continues to be used in many weapons systems and in defensive early warning installations, but is also widely employed in peacetime applications. It is routinely used by commercial airliners and traffic controllers, by weather forecasting systems, in surveying and navigating, and as a guidance tool for rockets and satellites. Radar technology is also the basis for radio astronomy.

For further reading:

Bowen, E.G., *Radar Days*. New York: Taylor & Francis, 1987.

Page, Robert M., *The Origin of Radar*. Westport, Conn.: Greenwood, 1979.

Radek, Karl Bernardovich [Sobelsohn] (1885–1940?). Russian author and politician. Born in Poland of Jewish ancestry, he became a journalist and supported the German Social Democratic Party from 1904. He was imprisoned several times, fought in the RUSSIAN REVOLUTION (1917) and tried to organize a communist revolution in Germany (1918–19). He was a member of the presidium of the Communist International (1919–23), but his influence declined when the Comintern proved ineffective. He became head of the Sun Yat-Sen Communist University for Chinese students in Moscow (1923–27) until he was expelled from the Communist Party (1927) on a charge of having supported TROTSKY, and was banished to the Urals. He was rehabilitated and wrote for *Izvestiya*. He also helped draft the 1936 constitution. In 1937 he was sentenced to 10 years' imprisonment for treason and is thought to have died in prison.

radio. Radio is the transmission of electromagnetic waves from a source to a receiver. In 1901 MARCONI transmitted the letter "S" across the Atlantic; in 1904 John A. Fleming developed the vacuum electron tube; and in 1913 Edwin Armstrong patented the circuit that made long-range reception possible. By 1910 ship to shore radio communication was commonplace. The German army first used radio for entertainment during WORLD WAR I. The first commercial station in the U.S., KDKA, was established in Pittsburgh, Pennsylvania, in 1920. During the 1920s the number of radio stations, broadcasts and receivers increased dramatically. A new news and entertainment medium came into being. In 1932 radio transmissions were received from the Milky Way Galaxy. During WORLD WAR II radio technology was used in the development of RADAR. Radio changed every aspect of 20th-century life—industry, science, sports and entertainment.

Radio City Music Hall. Theater forming a part of New York City's ROCKEFELLER CENTER complex of office buildings; regarded as one of the major masterpieces of the ART DECO style. The original architects were Reinhard & Hofmeister; Corbett, Harrison & MacMurray; and Hood & Fouilhoux, with the last team responsible for the overall original design of Rockefeller Center (1931–33). The Music Hall is discreetly imbedded within the RKO Building in such a way that it has no clear external identity, except for its corner entrance and marquee; but the interiors, designed with Donald DESKEY in charge of decoration, are a finely preserved showcase of 1930s design. The main auditorium is a vast space seating 6,250, with stage and orchestra pit elaborately equipped with elevators, turntables and other mechanical devices. The lobbies, grand stairway and many lounges and smoking rooms are distinguished examples of Art Deco idiom. The Music Hall has been a popular success and tourist attraction since its opening, as much for its design as for the films and stage shows offered there. The popular Rockettes chorus line has been a fixture at Rockefeller Center for many years.

Radio Station WHA. Claimed as the world's oldest, the station was developed in the laboratories of the department of physics of the University of Wisconsin at Madison. When the station started a broadcasting service in 1915, clear broadcasting signals were received as far away as the Great Lakes Naval Station in northern Illinois. In 1922 WHA received a federal license to broadcast and is considered to be the world's oldest continuously operated radio station. When it first went on the air its tubes were hand-blown by local glassmakers and fitted for broadcast by local craftsmen. The station was the first educational radio station and broadcast the first music appreciation program to be sent across the airwaves.

Raft, George (1895–1980). American film actor. He was best known for his portrayal of cool, tough-guy characters in HOLLYWOOD gangster films of the 1930s and '40s. Between 1929 and 1967 he appeared in 105 movies, many of which were low-budget melodramas such as *Scarface*, *They Drive by Night*, *Each Dawn I Die* and *Souls at Sea*. In his heyday he was one of Hollywood's highest-paid stars. However, he turned down the leading roles in *High Sierra*, *The Maltese Falcon* and *Casablanca*—roles that were subsequently played with great success by Humphrey BOGART, who soon eclipsed Raft as Hollywood's leading romantic tough guy. A frequenter of gambling casinos, Raft was rumored to be involved in organized crime; in 1965 he was convicted of tax evasion.

ragtime. Popular American musical form originating in the 19th century; characterized by a syncopated melody set against a rhythmically foursquare bass. Its greatest vogue occurred between 1890 and 1914. Ragtime began in the Midwest, probably the result of improvisations by black pianists and banjo players playing in saloons and sporting houses. It was influenced by dance music, marching band music and ballads combined with African, Caribbean and American rhythms. Sedalia and St. Louis, Missouri, were two important early centers of ragtime. The ragtime written in these cities came to be known as the Missouri style, characterized by lyrical melodies and easy tempos. For years the form was transmitted aurally. The first published rag—"Mississippi Rag" by William H. Krell, a white bandmaster—appeared in 1897. The great popularity of ragtime was partly due to the fact that music in printed form and on piano rolls was widely available. For example, the "Maple Leaf Rag" by Scott JOPLIN, one of the most successful ragtime composers, sold over a million copies shortly after it was published in 1899. Besides Joplin, other composers in the Missouri style were New Jersey-born Joseph E. Lamb (1887–1960) and James Scott (1886–1938), who was based in Kansas City. As the popularity of the form spread, other ragtime styles emerged in other parts of the country. While ragtime was eclipsed by JAZZ about 1914, it enjoyed a revival in the late 1960s and 1970s with the rediscovery of the music of Scott Joplin and other ragtime composers.

For further reading:

Waldo, Terry. *This Is Ragtime*. New York: Da Capo Press, 1984.

Gammond, Peter, *Scott Joplin and the Ragtime Era*. New York: St. Martin's Press, 1975.

Jasen, David A. *Rags and Ragtime: A Musical History*. New York: Seabury Press, 1978.

Rahman, Sheikh Mujibur (1920–1975). Prime minister of BANGLADESH (1972–75). Leader of the Awami League, he campaigned for the independence of East Bengal from PAKISTAN. Arrested several times and charged with treason in 1971, he was released upon Indian military intervention against Pakistan (see INDO-PAKISTANI WAR OF 1971). He returned to a hero's welcome on the establishment of the independent republic of Bangladesh at the end of 1971. As prime minister, the problems of creating a socialist state and parliamentary democracy in a desperately poor country proved too much, and Rahman assumed dictatorial powers in 1975. Later that year the army staged a coup, and he was murdered.

Rahman, Tunku Abdul (1903–1990). Malaysian statesman. The son of a sultan, he was educated at Cambridge and became a barrister (lawyer). He entered the Kedah state civil service in 1931 and was a cofounder of the nationalist United Malay National Organization in 1945. Named chief minister of Malaya in 1955, he was elected prime minister of an independent Malaya in 1957 and became prime minister of the newly created Federation of MALAYSIA in 1963. Fiercely anticommunist, he was adept at mediating among the various peoples of Malaysia to create a national consensus. Stresses on the system led to ethnic riots in 1969, and Rahman retired the following year. He later became a revered elder statesman and spoke out against the repressive regime of Prime Minister Mahathir bin Mohamad.

Rahner, Karl (1904–1984). German-born theologian. One of the most prominent Roman Catholic theologians of the 20th century, Rahner played a key role in the reforms of the SECOND VATICAN COUNCIL during the early 1960s. A member of the Jesuit order, he was regarded as progressive on most church issues. He developed a transcendental theological philosophy aimed at lessening the rigidity of the traditional Christian faith. Strongly influenced by the German existentialist philosopher Martin HEIDEGGER, Rahner published more than 4,000 works, including 30 books.

Raid on Entebbe. See ENTEBBE, RAID ON.

Raid on Tokyo. Bombing raid conducted by U.S. Army planes commanded by James DOOLITTLE on April 18, 1942. It was carried out by 16 B-25 Mitchell bombers launched from the aircraft carrier U.S.S. *Hornet*. Although the strike had to be carried on during daytime instead of at night, as originally planned, Doolittle and Admiral William HALSEY decided to go ahead. Thirteen bombers hit Tokyo and three others bombed Nagoya, Osaka and Kobe. Because of the distances involved, none of the planes could reach friendly airfields. One landed in the U.S.S.R. and the others crash-landed or bailed out over China. In the process five U.S. airmen were killed and eight were captured by the Japanese. While the raid caused little serious physical damage to its targets, it was an enormous propaganda success in the U.S., boosting morale that had been depressed by the Japanese attack on PEARL HARBOR the previous December.

rain forests. In the late 20th century, the fate of Earth's rain forests became a matter of grave concern. The human development of rain forest areas in economically depressed THIRD WORLD countries threatens one of Earth's largest, most important natural habitats. The South American rain forests alone may contain half of all living species. Using slash-and-burn methods, settlers are clearing huge areas of forest in a futile effort to make the land suitable for farming; in other areas, indiscriminate logging has taken its toll: In Brazil alone, some 4 million acres of forest vanishes every year. Consequently, thousands of species are being lost, while soil erosion threatens to create new desert. Massive forest fires spew carbon dioxide into the atmosphere, contributing to the GREENHOUSE EFFECT.

Rains, Claude (1889–1967). Anglo-American film actor, best known for his portrayals of suave villains. Born in London, Rains began as a child actor at age 11, and moved to the U.S. in 1914, where he was successful on the stage and later in radio. His first film success was as the title character in *The Invisible Man* (1933), adapted from the novel by H.G. WELLS. After his acclaimed portrayal of King John in *The Adventures of Robin Hood* (1938), Rains played a corrupt senator in Frank CAPRA's *Mr. Smith Goes to Washington* (1939) and a roguish Nazi collaborator in CASABLANCA (1942), earning two ACADEMY AWARD nominations. He was nominated twice more for his performances in *Mr. Skeffington* (1944) and in Alfred HITCHCOCK's *Notorious* (1946). He also starred in a remake of *The Phantom of the Opera* (1943) and played supporting roles in *Lawrence of Arabia* (1962) and *The Greatest Story Ever Told* (1965).

Rajasthan [Rajastan]. This state of northwestern INDIA, with its capital at Jaipur, was created in 1948 (as the Union of Rajasthan) out of several former principalities of the old region of Rajputana; in 1956 other areas were added to the state. Although Rajasthan borders on Islamic PAKISTAN, about three-quarters of its inhabitants are Hindu.

Rajk, Lazlo (1909–1949). Hungarian communist leader. Born near Budapest, he became a communist as a university student and fought from 1936 to 1939 with the International Brigade in the SPANISH CIVIL WAR. Returning to HUNGARY in 1941, he became active in the Communist Party, then an illegal organization. During WORLD WAR II, he resisted German occupation as a member of the underground. After the war he became Hungary's minister of the interior (1946–48) and foreign minister (1948–49). In 1949 he was charged with conspiring with TITO to overthrow the Hungarian government. While the evidence presented was clearly fabricated, he confessed and was hanged. In 1956 the Hungarian government admitted that the conviction had been in error and "rehabilitated" Rajk as a political figure.

Rajneesh, Bhagwan Shree [born Chandra Mohan Jain] (1931–1990). Indian guru. He began his career in India, where he took the name Bhagwan (god) and preached a combination of free love and Eastern mysticism. He emigrated to the U.S. in 1981 and set up a commune near the tiny town of Antelope, Oregon, outraging local residents. In 1985 he pleaded guilty to violating immigration laws by arranging sham marriages between U.S. followers and foreign disciples. He was deported in 1985 and returned to India in 1986.

Rakosi, Matyas (1892–1971). Hungarian communist leader and prime minister of HUNGARY (1949–53, 1955–56). Active in the communist opposition between the two world wars, Rakosi was sentenced to life imprisonment in 1935. He was released in 1940 to go to Moscow, where he led a committee of Hungarian communists. From 1945 he led the party and the government, presiding over the establishment of a Stalinist regime (see STALINISM). Replaced by the more liberal NAGY in 1953, by 1955 Rakosi had regained control of the party. His repressive methods contributed to the unrest that led to the HUNGARIAN UPRISING OF 1956. In an attempt to appease the Hungarians the U.S.S.R. persuaded him to resign.

Rakovsky, Khristian Georgyevich (1873–1938). Communist leader and diplomat, of Bulgarian origin. Because of his involvement with the socialist movement, Rakovsky was not able to enter Sofia University, but studied abroad. In 1900 he was an officer in the Romanian army, but in 1907 he was expelled from Romania. After the communists came to power in Russia, Rakovsky was made a member of the All-Russian Central Executive Committee, and in 1919 of the Central Committee of the Communist Party. The chairman of the council of people's commissars of the Ukraine, he occupied several diplomatic posts, including Soviet ambassador to France (1926–27). He was, however, expelled from the Communist Party in 1927 as a result of his support of TROTSKY. He was readmitted in 1935 and was a departmental head of the People's Commissariat of Health. In 1937 he was dismissed, and in 1938, arrested. He was sentenced to 20 years' imprisonment, and it is believed that he died in a concentration camp.

Ram, Jaglivan (1908–1986). Indian politician. The acknowledged leader of INDIA's more than 100 million untouchables, he was born to an untouchable family in Bihar. In 1931 he joined the Congress Party, which under the leadership of Mohandas GANDHI and Jawaharla NEHRU was the main force behind India's drive to independence. He was a member of nearly every Indian cabinet since that time. He served in the first government as minister of labor and went on to serve twice as minister of agriculture and also as railway minister. From 1970 to 1974 and from 1977 to 1979, he was minister of defense.

Rama IX [Bhumibol Adulyadej] (1927–). King Rama IX of the Chikri Dynasty is THAILAND's longest-reigning monarch. Crowned May 5, 1950, he spent much of his young life in Switzerland, where he was educated at the Ecole Miremont in Lausanne and the Ecole Nouvelle de la Suisse Romande. He succeeded his elder brother, Ananda Mahidol, on June 9, 1946, after Ananda was found dead in the palace from a gunshot wound. Whether the death was an accident, suicide or murder has never been determined. The king is highly respected not only because of his title but also because of his unending defense of and assistance to Thailand's rural poor.

Ramadi [Rumadiya]. Euphrates River town in central Iraq, 60 miles west of Baghdad—the starting point of a cross-desert highway to the Mediterranean Sea. During WORLD WAR I British forces defeated the Turks here in a major battle, on Sept. 28–29, 1917. It was hit by allied air raids during the PERSIAN GULF WAR (1991).

Rambert, Marie [Cyvia Rambam] (1888–1982). Ballet dancer, teacher, producer. Born in Poland, Rambert began dancing in Paris. After a season with Serge DIAGHILEV'S BALLETS RUSSES, she moved to London where she taught dance and encouraged works by new choreographers. In 1926 she produced Frederick ASHTON's first ballet *A Tragedy of Fashion.* She founded Ballet Rambert in the mid-1930s and spent 30 years producing works by new choreographers and guiding the careers of young dancers. She was knighted in 1962 for her contribution to the development of British ballet.

Ramgoolam, Sir Seewoosagur (1900–1985). Mauritian diplomat. Ramgoolam was a physician who became the first prime minister of MAURITIUS after that small Indian Ocean island gained independence from Britain in 1968. He led a succession of coalition governments until his administration was swept out of office in the general election of 1982. He held the largely ceremonial office of governor general until his death.

Ramos, Fidel (1928–). Philippine general and secretary of defense; perhaps the most loyal supporter of President AQUINO. Ramos graduated from the U.S. Military Academy at West Point in 1950; he earned a master's degree in civil engineering from the University of Illinois in 1951 and also possesses other military degrees. Ramos ascended through army ranks to become chief of the Philippine constabulary in 1972. He became vice chief of staff of the army in 1981 and chief of staff in 1986. He loyally supported Aquino against attempted coups and was widely considered an honest and disciplined military man, though not without presidential ambitions. He was appointed secretary of defense in January 1988 after the resignation of Rafael Ileto. In 1990, after Aquino declared that she would not seek reelection, Ramos announced that he would run for the presidency.

Rampal, Jean-Pierre (1922–). French flutist. Born in Marseilles, Rampal first studied flute with his father, a professor at the Marseilles Conservatory of Music. He then studied at the Paris Conservatory and in 1945 joined the Paris Opera Orchestra where he was first flutist from 1958 to 1964. In the late 1940s Rampal also began to tour and to make recordings. His records have won numerous Grand Prix du Disque awards. He first toured the U.S. in 1958 and has returned regularly ever since. He enlarged the flute repertoire by resurrecting forgotten music of the Baroque era and also by adapting for flute compositions originally written for other instruments. In the 1990s, he continues to be enormously popular, giving over 150 concerts per year and filling concert halls the world over.

Ramsey, (Sir) Alf(red) (1920–). English soccer player and manager. Ramsey is best known as the mastermind of England's World Cup triumph in 1966. Although his greatest success came as a manager, Ramsey also enjoyed a successful playing career. He was a "polished" right back for Southampton and Tottenham Hotspur, and played 32 times for England. On his retirement, Ramsey joined Ipswich Town as manager and led the team from the obscurity of the second division to the first division championship in 1961–62. Following his success at Ipswich, Ramsey was appointed manager of England. Ramsey's innovative tactics and leadership qualities were well suited to international soccer. He introduced the 4-4-2 formation to English football, and his "wingless wonders" won the World Cup in 1966, defeating West Germany 4–2 in the final. He led England in its unsuccessful defense of the World Cup in 1970 and was dismissed as manager following England's failure to qualify for the 1974 World Cup finals. Ramsey was knighted for his services to soccer.

Ramsey, Arthur Michael (1904–1988). British religious leader. Ramsey held the post of Archbishop of Canterbury (spiritual head of the Church of England and leader of the worldwide Anglican communion) from 1961 to 1974. A progressive social activist, Ramsey called on Great Britain to do away with nuclear weapons, spoke out against the VIETNAM WAR and opposed curbs on minority immigration into Britain. He also supported abolition of the death penalty and of criminal penalties against homosexuals. In 1966, he met with Pope PAUL VI in Rome in what was the first official visit to a Pope by a head of the Anglican Church in 400 years. Upon his retirement in 1974, he was made a life peer and took the title of Lord Ramsey of Canterbury.

Ramu [known as the "Wolf Boy"] (c. 1960s-1985). In 1976 a wild boy was discovered in the jungle in India, walking on all fours and in the company of three wolves. After examining him, Indian zoologists concluded that he had been raised by wolves. He was placed in a home for paupers run by Mother TERESA, winner of the 1979 NOBEL PRIZE for peace. He learned to bathe and dress himself but never learned to speak. The case gained worldwide attention.

Rand, Ayn (1905–1982). American novelist. Rand was born in Russia and became an American citizen in 1931. Her loathing of the Soviet revolution led her to develop a philosophy of almost rabid capitalism. Her best-selling novels have been greeted with derision on the one hand and various cult followings on the other. Her first major novel was *The Foun-*

American author and social critic Ayn Rand.

tainhead 1943; filmed 1949), which portrayed an iconoclastic architect fighting conventional attitudes. Her best-known novel, *Atlas Shrugged* (1957), presents the archetypical Rand hero, John Galt, an individualist fighting against "non-productive people" and struggling toward his own ends. *The Virtue of Selfishness: A New Concept of Egoism* (1964) awarded her the status of a leader of the popular intellectual movement "objectivism," and she was in much demand as a lecturer. Other works include *We the Living* (1936) and *The Ayn Rand Lexicon: Objectivism from A to Z* (1984), a posthumous collection of earlier works. She also wrote plays and film scripts.

Randolph, A(sa) Philip (1889–1979). American labor leader and CIVIL RIGHTS activist. The son of a Methodist preacher, Randolph moved to New York to study at City College. There he was strongly impressed by the socialist ideas of Eugene V. DEBS. Randolph organized and published the black radical journal *The Messenger;* through this influential vehicle he promoted black causes, including the affiliation of black workers with labor unions. In 1925 he created and administered the Brotherhood of Sleeping Car Porters, which became affiliated with the AMERICAN FEDERATION OF LABOR (AFL) in 1936; and he was president of the National Negro Congress in the 1930s. In 1941 he threatened to lead a march on Washington, D.C., to protest the exclusion of blacks from industrial war work, which led to President Franklin D. ROOSEVELT's creation of the Commission on Fair Employment Practices. He was director of the 1963 MARCH ON WASHINGTON that led to increased jobs and civil rights for blacks.

For further reading:

Pfeffer, Paula F., *A. Philip Randolph, Pioneer of the Civil Rights Movement.* Baton Rouge: Louisiana State University Press, 1990.

Anderson, Jervis, *A Philip Randolph: A Biographical Portrait.* New York: Harcourt Brace Jovanovich, 1974.

American labor leader and civil rights activist A. Philip Randolph founded the first black labor union in 1925.

Ranger. A precursor to the APOLLO program, which was designed to land men on the moon, the Ranger series of unmanned spacecraft was initiated to relay from the moon's surface information needed for a manned landing. From August 1961 to March 1965, a series of Ranger spacecraft, managed by the JET PROPULSION LABORATORY in Pasadena, California, were launched. Ranger 7, one of the most successful, sent back more than 4,000 close-up images of the moon. Unfortunately, of the nine missions launched, only the last three were successful, and the program was replaced by the Lunar Orbiter series in August 1966.

Rangoon. Capital and largest city of MYANMAR (formerly Burma); on the Rangoon River, near the Gulf of Martaban. Rangoon was heavily damaged and occupied by Japan from 1942 to 1945, during WORLD WAR II.

Rank, Otto [born Otto Rosenfeld] (1884–1939). Austrian psychologist. Rank was born in Vienna and earned a doctorate in philology from the University of Vienna in 1912. He began to study psychoanalysis under Sigmund FREUD in 1905 and went on to serve as Freud's personal secretary. From 1912 to 1924 Rank edited two different psychoanalytic journals and became one of the leading factors behind the growth in influence of psychoanalysis. Rank was the director of the International Psychoanalytic Institute of Vienna from 1919 to 1924. A Jew, he left Austria to escape the Nazis and spent the final years of his life in Paris and New York. His major writings include *Art and Artist* (1907), *The Myth of the Birth of the Hero* (1909) and *The Trauma of Birth* (1924), which Freud regarded as heretical to his own theories due to its emphasis on the birth experience itself as a factor in the creation of neurosis.

Rankin, Jeannette (1880–1973). U.S. congresswoman. Rankin initially worked as a seamstress, gaining knowledge of social conditions. After working for woman suffrage on the West Coast in 1910, she led a similar successful campaign in Montana in 1914. In 1916 Rankin became the first woman ever elected to the U.S. House of Representatives. She opposed U.S. entry into WORLD WAR I and WORLD WAR II. She declined to run for reelection in 1942, but continued a private career as an ardent feminist (see FEMINISM). In the 1960s she founded a cooperative homestead for women in Georgia and protested against the VIETNAM WAR.

Ransom, John Crowe (1888–1974). American poet and critic. A teacher at Vanderbilt for 23 years, Ransom was the editor and the eldest of the Southern poets who contributed to *The Fugitive* from 1922 to 1925. Ransom was a former professor of the group's other leaders, Allen TATE and Robert Penn WARREN. Ransom originated the phrase NEW CRITICISM, a type of literary study closely associated with this group, and encouraged the polemic *I'll Take My Stand* (1930), a statement of agrarian ideals central to the thought of the new Southern writers. Later he went to Kenyon College as professor of poetry. In 1939 he was founder and editor of the *Kenyon Review.* Ransom is best remembered for the poems "Bells for John Whiteside's Daughter" and "Here Lies a Lady."

For further reading:

Young, Thomas Daniel, *John Crowe Ransom.* Austin, Texas: Steck-Vaughn Co., 1971.

———, *Gentleman in a Dustcoat: A Biography of John Crowe Ransom.* Baton Rouge: Louisiana State University Press, 1976.

Rapacki Plan. Polish Foreign Minister Rapacki proposed on February 14, 1958, a ban on the manufacture and deployment of nuclear weapons in Czechoslovakia, Poland, and East and West Germany, to be guaranteed by joint NATO-WARSAW PACT inspection. A renewal of the suggestion at the U.N. on October 2, 1958, met with U.S. and British rejection, as the U.S.S.R. would retain its conventional weapons superiority.

Rapallo. Italian town on the Ligurian Sea, near Genoa. In the **Treaty of Rapallo** (Nov. 12, 1920), Italy and Yugoslavia agreed to establish RIJEKA (Fiume) as a free state, although a protofascist expedition led by Italian poet, adventurer and aviator Gabriele D'ANNUNZIO had seized the city in 1919. In another treaty (between Germany and the U.S.S.R., Apr. 16, 1922) Germany became the first government to recognize the Soviet government. This treaty renounced all claims stemming from the war, canceled prewar debts and formalized trade arrangements between the two nations. Among its secret provisions, the treaty allowed Germany to develop (in the U.S.S.R.) weapons that it was forbidden to have by the Treaty of VERSAILLES.

Rashid bin Said al Maktum, Sheik (1914–1990). Arab diplomat. In 1971, he cofounded the United Arab Emirate, a collection of seven sheikdoms in the PERSIAN GULF. He served as vice president of the UAE, while his brother-in-law Sheik Zayid bin Sultan Al Nuhayyan, ruler of Abu Dhabi, served as president. Previously, the sheikdoms had been ruled separately as the Trucial States under an agreement with Great Britain.

Rasputin, Grigory Yefimovich (1872–1916). Siberian peasant who exerted a pernicious influence at the court of Czar NICHOLAS II and on political affairs in RUSSIA in the years leading up to the RUSSIAN REVOLUTION. Although without education, Rasputin allegedly possessed hypnotic powers, which he did not hesitate to exploit, and claimed to be able to work miracles, preaching that physical contact with him had a healing effect. As a youth Rasputin had been influenced by the *Khlysty* (Flagellants) sect. In 1903 Rasputin arrived in St. Petersburg as a *starets* (holy man) and as such gained access to the highest circles of society. He exercised virtually unlimited influence on Czarina ALEXANDRA by using hypnotism to stop the hemophiliac czarevich's bleeding. She viewed him as a divine missionary, sent to save the dynasty. The church denounced him as an impostor, and in 1912 he was sent back to Siberia. In 1914 he returned, and by 1915, when the czarina was left in charge of domestic affairs, Rasputin's influence was vast, and many of the more capable ministers were dismissed. He continued his dissolute habits until his assassination by Prince Yusupov in 1916.

For further reading:

De Jonge, Alex, *The Life and Times of Grigorii Rasputin.* New York: Dorset Press, 1988.

Fuhrmann, Joseph T., *Rasputin: A Life.* Westport, Conn.: Greenwood, 1989.

Rathbone, Basil (1892–1967). Anglo-American actor. Rathbone, who is perhaps best remembered in the U.S. for his portrayals of SHERLOCK HOLMES beginning with *The Hound of the Baskervilles* (1939), was born in South Africa and educated in England. He began his career as a Shakespearean stage actor; his first film in England was *The Fruitful Vine* (1923). Soon thereafter he went to HOLLYWOOD, where he made *Pity the Chorus Girl?* (1924) and other silent films while continuing to act on stage. With the advent of sound, Rathbone, with his cultivated accent, came into his own appearing opposite Norma Shearer in *The Last of Mrs. Cheyney* (1929) and as detective Philo Vance in *The Bishop Murder Case* (1930). Following his role in *David Copperfield* (1935) he settled in Hollywood playing a series of cerebral villains as well as making 14 Sherlock Holmes films. In the 1960s he took on a few unfortunate roles trading on his villainous image, the last of which was *Hillbillys in a Haunted House* (1967). Other important films include *Anna Karenina* (1935), *The Dawn Patrol* (1938) and John FORD's *The Last Hurrah* (1958).

Rathenau, Walther (1867–1922). German industrialist, statesman and social theorist. Born in Berlin, the son of Emil Rathenau (1838–1915), he succeeded his father as president of a vast electrical trust. He organized GERMANY's war economy during WORLD WAR I and, after the war, served as minister of reconstruction (1921) and foreign minister (1922). In the latter office, he worked for reconciliation with the Allies, attempted to comply with reparation obligations and signed the Treaty of RAPALLO with the U.S.S.R. An advocate of a moderate decentralized social democracy and a Jew, he was despised by anti-Semitic nationalists. Several of these fanatics assassinated him in Berlin on June 24, 1922. His books include *In Days to Come* and *The New Society* (both 1921).

Rattigan, Sir Terence (Mervyn) (1911–1977). British playwright. Rattigan's early plays, beginning with *French Without Tears* (1936), were popular comedies. With *Winslow Boy* (1946), the story of a father defending his son against an accusation of theft, he established himself as an author of serious drama, a reputation he was to maintain in his subsequent works, such as *The Browning Version;* (1948); *Ross* (1960), which was based on the life of T.E. LAWRENCE; and *Cause Celebre* (1977), which focused on an actual murder trial. In the preface to *Collected Works* (1953), Rattigan introduced "Aunt Edna," an archetypical, middle-brow theatergoer. Many critics—particularly those enamored of "the kitchen sink" dramatists—complained that Rattigan's work was middle brow as well. His popularity was undiminished, and his works continue to be revived.

Ratushinskaya, Irina (1954–). Russian poet and dissident; perhaps the last in a long line of distinguished poets who were persecuted under Soviet COMMUNISM during the 20th century. She studied physics at the University of Odessa, where she also began writing poetry and first encountered difficulties with the authorities. After graduation she taught physics and mathematics. In 1980 she and her husband, also a physicist, were denied emigration visas. Arrested for "anti-social" activities in 1982, she was sentenced to seven years hard labor in the GULAG, to be followed by five years of internal exile. In prison she secretly wrote numerous poems that were circulated in Samizdat. In 1986 PEN organized an international campaign for her release. The Soviet authorities released her on October 9, 1986 (the eve of the Reykjavik Summit), as a goodwill gesture. She and her husband immigrated to Britain, where she continued to write and also lectured about her experiences. Her books include *No, I'm Not Afraid* (1986), *Beyond the Limit* (1987), *Grey Is the Color of Hope* (1988) and *Pencil Letter* (1989).

Rau, Lady Dhanvanthi Rama (1893–1987). Indian feminist. A leading advocate of birth control, she was named president of the International Planned Parenthood Federation in 1963. She continued to serve as president emeritus after she resigned the post in 1971. She was the mother of author Santha Rama Rau.

Rauff, Walter Herman Julius (1907–1984). Nazi war criminal. An SS colonel, Rauff was accused of supervising the killing of thousands of Eastern European JEWS in mobile gas chambers during WORLD WAR II. He was said to have personally designed and directed the "Black Raven" vans in which victims were locked and asphyxiated with exhaust fumes. Possibly 250,000 people died in the vans, which were used before HITLER's death camps were completed (see CONCENTRATION CAMPS, HOLOCAUST). Rauff escaped from a British POW camp in 1946 and settled in Chile in 1958. The Chilean government refused numerous requests to extradite him to stand trial.

Rauschenberg, Robert (1925–). American painter. Born in Port Arthur, Texas, he studied at the Kansas City Art Institute, the Academie Julian in Paris, Black Mountain College with Josef ALBERS and New York's Art Students League. He has had an important role in various artistic and cultural movements of the mid-century U.S., including HAPPENINGS, POP ART, environmental art and the experimental theater. His most celebrated paintings of the 1950s are his COLLAGE "combines," works that mix a painterly abstraction with everyday objects such as clocks, tires and even stuffed animals. Among the best-known of these are *Gloria* (1956, Cleveland Museum of Art) and *Monogram* (1959, Moderna Museet, Stockholm). His work of the 1960s, such as *Kite* (1963), combines silkscreened images of the popular culture with painted elements, often on large scale. Interested in many facets of the arts and in contemporary technological developments, Rauchenberg has served as a designer for the dancer/choreographer Merce CUNNINGHAM and in 1966 was a cofounder of Experiments in Art and Technology (EAT).

For further reading:

Kotz, Mary Lyn, *Rauschenberg/Art and Life.* New York: Abrams, 1990.

Ravel, Maurice (1875–1937). Important French composer who was second only to Claude DEBUSSY in his position as chief architect of modern French music. His *Bolero* (1928) and *Pavane pour une Infante Defunte* (*Pavane for a Dead Princess,* 1899) are among the most popular of all modern compositions. He was born in Cibourne in the Basque region of France. At the Paris Conservatory, while less conspicuously radical than his immediate predecessor, Debussy, he nonetheless startled his teachers with his experiments in bold harmonic explorations; and he gained added notoriety through his association with the progressive musical group *Apache* (which included as members Igor STRAVINSKY and Manuel de FALLA). The range of his compositions was extraordinary. His ballet *Daphnis et Chloe* (1912), arguably his greatest work, was a highlight in the series of BALLETS RUSSES performances from the DIAGHILEV-

French composer Maurice Ravel, who, along with Claude Debussy, was a leading figure in French musical impressionism.

FOKINE-NIJINSKY triumvirate. The piano works *Jeux d'Eau* (1902) and *Miroirs* (Mirrors, 1905) probably influenced the impressionist cast of Debussy's later piano music. The *Tzigane* (1924) and the *G major Piano Concerto* (1932) outrageously satirize, respectively, gypsy music and American JAZZ; while the weird *La Valse* (1920) virtually destroyed traditional waltz styles. Like Debussy, Ravel revolted against the Wagner hegemony; however, unlike Debussy, Ravel rarely employed the whole-tone scale and hardly ever abandoned tonality. Ravel was the most meticulous of craftsmen and retained a fastidious respect for classical form all his life. As a result, according to critic Virgil THOMSON, "his work presents fewer difficulties of comprehension than that of any other great figure in the modern movement." He was the master of twilight enchantment—the needlepoint sorcery of the *F major Quartet* and the *Ma Mere l'Oye* (1910)—and fantastic humor—the ragtime dialogue between a black Wedgwood teapot and a Chinese cup in *L'Enfant et les Sortileges* (*The Dream of a Naughty Child*, 1925). He died of a brain tumor in 1937, several years after a debilitating automobile accident.

For further reading:
Orenstein, Arbie, *Ravel: Man and Musician*. New York: Columbia University Press, 1975.

Ravensbruck. Village in the German state of Brandenburg, the site of an infamous CONCENTRATION CAMP for women during the Nazi regime of the 1930s and early 1940s.

Ravera, Camilla (1889–1988). Italian politician; postwar Italy's first woman senator-for-life and one of the founding members of the nation's COMMUNIST PARTY in 1921. A major figure in Italy's WOMEN'S LIBERATION MOVEMENT, Ravera spent five years in prison and eight years in internal exile during the fascist era.

Rawlings, Marjorie Kinnan (1896–1953). American author. A graduate of the University of Wisconsin (1918), Rawlings' early work was as a journalist. All her novels had a Southern background, particularly in the backwoods of Florida, except for her final novel, *The Sojourner* (1953), which had a northern setting. In 1938 she wrote *The Yearling*, which won the PULITZER PRIZE in 1939 and has become an American classic. Her other works include *South Moon Under* (1933), *Golden Apples* (1935) and *Cross Creek* (1942).

Ray, Man (1890–1976). American painter and photographer. Ray is best known as the only American artist to make a substantial contribution to SURREALISM and to be welcomed into its European circles. Born in Philadelphia, he was raised in New York City and worked there for a time as an advertising illustrator, becoming familiar with graphic art processes. In 1914 he became involved with a circle of American painters including Joseph Stella. In 1915 came a decisive meeting between Ray and Marcel DUCHAMP, who introduced Ray to the aesthetics of DADA. Ray emigrated to Paris in 1921, where he won renown both as a painter and as the inventor of the "Rayogram"—a photographic technique in which objects or persons are positioned so as to cast evocative shadows on light-sensitive paper. For this mechanistic innovation, Ray was dubbed the "machine-poet" by his fellow Surrealists. One of his most famous paintings is *L'Etoile de Mer* (1928). *Self-Portrait* (1963) is his autobiography. *Man Ray: Photographs* (1982) is a major collection of his work in that medium.

Rayburn, Samuel Taliaferro (1882–1961). American politician. Raised on a Texas farm, Rayburn taught school and became a lawyer in Bonham. Developing an interest in politics, he started his career as a state legislator (1907–12) and became speaker of the Texas House of Representatives in 1911. He set a record for tenure when he was elected as a Democrat to the U.S. House of Representatives for 24 consecutive terms (1913–61). Appointed chairman of the Commission on Interest and Foreign Commerce in 1931, he helped design President Franklin ROOSEVELT'S NEW DEAL program and coauthored six important laws to support it. Rayburn was speaker of the House from 1940 to 1947, 1949 to 1953 and 1955 to 1961. He became one of the strongest speakers in U.S. history. Highly regarded for his integrity and lack of pretension, he was extremely successful in dominating, indirectly, the legislative process and committee assignments through personal relationships with powerful committee chairmen. He was President Harry S. TRUMAN'S chief supporter in Congress and one of his closest advisers. Except for civil rights measures, he backed much of Truman's domestic program and eventually supported his foreign policy as well. During the 1950s he worked with the EISENHOWER administration to defeat Republican isolationist measures. Although a supporter of Lyndon JOHNSON for president in 1960, he worked with the KENNEDY administration on much of its initial legislation.

Sam Rayburn held the powerful post of speaker of the U.S. House of Representatives (1940–47, 1949–53, 1955–61).

For further reading:
Hardeman, D.B., *Rayburn: A Biography*. Austin, Texas: Texas Monthly Press, 1987.
Champagne, Anthony, *Congressman Sam Rayburn*. New Brunswick, New Jersey: Rutgers University Press, 1984.

RCA Corporation. American communications corporation established in 1919. RCA was incorporated in Delaware and later moved to 30 Rockefeller Plaza in New York City. A month after incorporating, it acquired the Marconi Wireless Telegraph Company, a British-dominated company that owned most of the commercial radio communication facilities in the U.S. RCA entered the field of broadcasting in 1926 when it bought WEAF, now WNBC (New York), from AT&T. NBC was incorporated that year, with RCA owning 30% of the stock; Westinghouse Electric Corporation, 20%; and General Electric, 50%. RCA would later own NBC entirely. RCA grew into a giant multinational corporation whose operations extended far beyond broadcasting and included the production of SATELLITES and SEMICONDUCTORS. In 1986, RCA and its subsidiary NBC were acquired by General Electric (GE) for $6.4 billion.

Read, Sir Herbert Edward (1893–1968). British poet and critic. Born in Leeds, Read served in France during WORLD WAR I, the formative event of his life. He was later a professor of fine art. His early poetry collections, such as *Songs of Chaos* (1915) and *Naked Warriors* (1919), showed a strong Imagist influence (see IMAGISM). Later poetry, including that in *The End of the War* (1933) and *Collected Poems* (1966), is more esoteric and deemed inaccessible by some. A friend of T.S. ELIOT, Read was an influential figure in the British critical and literary establishment from the 1930s until his death. His critical works include *The True Voice in Feeling* (1953) and *Essays in Literary Criticism* (1969). He also wrote on the arts, notably in *Arts and Industry* (1934) and *Education through Art* (1943), and frequently championed new artistic movements. He recollected the war in such works as *In Retreat* (1925) and his life in the autobiography *The Contrary Experience* (1963). His son, Piers Paul Read (b. 1941), is a novelist.

Reader's Digest. American periodical. *Reader's Digest* was conceived by De Witt Wallace, whose marriage to heiress Lila Bell Acheson brought him the backing to begin publishing the magazine in 1922. Its original intent was to present edited versions of articles from other magazines to save readers' time, but as its popularity grew, Wallace adopted the odd practice of paying other magazines to accept stories that he would then edit for use in the *Digest*. It eventually included original material as well. Aimed at the American middle class, the magazine has been criticized for its unintellectual, platitudinous style and subject matter, but by the mid-1950s it had the highest circulation of any magazine in the world. The Reader's Digest, Incorporated empire came to include record clubs, condensed-book clubs and many other assets in addition to the magazine.

Reagan, Ronald Wilson (1911–). American actor, politician and fortieth president of the U.S. (1981–89). His family moved to Dixon, Illinois, while Ronald was a boy. Following participation in football at Eureka College, he graduated from the Illinois school in 1932. His very successful career as a sportscaster at radio station WHO in Des Moines, Iowa, coupled with his handsome good looks, attracted the attention of HOLLYWOOD, where he had a successful career as a second-rank leading man. His most-remembered movie was *Knute Rockne—All American* (1940). He served in WORLD WAR II as an Air Force captain.

He began a successful administrative career in 1947 as president of the Screen Actors Guild, serving until 1952 and again in 1959. He kept his name before the public in occasional screen roles and on television programs, and was a widely heard radio commentator. Changing from a liberal Democrat to a moderate Republican in 1962, he took an interest in politics, beginning with the unsuccessful campaign of Barry GOLDWATER for president in 1964 (the same year in which Reagan made his last screen appearance, in Don SIEGEL's *The Killers*). Two years later, after a meteoric rise in politics, Ronald Reagan was elected governor of CALIFORNIA. Soon to become the most populous state in the Union, California provided an important opportunity for an aspiring politician. Reagan was reelected in 1970. His successes in meeting California's budget, reducing the bureaucracy, eliminating the state deficit and reducing social services, were the most noted aspects of his administrations.

Retiring as governor in 1974, he began to put his extraordinary administrative and public relations experience to work in a run for the presidency. He made a strong bid in 1976, but lost the Republican nomination to Gerald FORD. Nominated in 1980, Reagan won a landslide victory over Jimmy CARTER, opposing all the Carter liberal policies and accusing him of gross ineptitude.

Ronald Reagan, fortieth president of the United States (1981–1989).

Minutes after Reagan was inaugurated, on January 20, 1981, the 52 Americans who had been held hostage in Iran for 444 days were flown to freedom, following an agreement to return a portion of Iran's frozen assets. On March 30, the president was shot in the chest by John Hinckley, Jr., as he walked to his car after an address at the Washington Hilton. On August 5, in one of his boldest strokes, he fired striking air traffic controllers, who had defied his back-to-work order. His dispatch of a task force to lead the invasion of Grenada in 1983 greatly increased his general popularity.

On the domestic front, his administration was dominated by so-called "Reaganomics." This economic program called for substantial tax cuts and reduced spending for domestic programs. With the help of a bipartisan coalition in Congress, he succeeded in programs to cut the budget and reform Social Security. His economic policies and their successes were credited by many economists with reducing inflation, and Reagan remained a firm believer in his economic theories. He also was ever-vigilant in his program to build up the armed forces, which he felt had been dangerously weakened during the Carter administration.

In 1984 Reagan and Vice President George BUSH were nominated by the Republicans and won a landslide victory over Walter MONDALE. At age 73 Reagan became the oldest person ever to hold the office of president. Surgery in 1985 and 1987 was followed by swift recovery, remarkable for a man of his age.

During most of his first term, Reagan had referred to the Soviet Union as an "evil empire." He was a firm advocate of U.S. support for arming Europe in defense of that empire. However, during his second term, he apparently concluded that his military program had brought the Russian leaders to a change of heart, and the administration began arms control discussions. Reagan's summit meeting with Soviet leader GORBACHEV in November 1985 failed to reach general agreement, but the Reagan-Gorbachev meeting in early 1988 resulted in a draft treaty to reduce nuclear arms in Europe. Later that year in Moscow, the two leaders signed the treaty, which was ratified by the appropriate legislatures in each country.

During the early part of his second term, the president received some of the highest popularity ratings in the history of the office—spurred on by low unemployment, a strong economy and low interest rates. He continued to be strong in support of the Central American countries, providing help to EL SALVADOR against the insurgents there and successfully promoting support of the CONTRA rebels in NICARAGUA. That support was undercut by the actions of some of his administrators in selling arms to IRAN, monies from which sale were diverted to aid for the Contras. This Contra scandal substantially lessened his national support and international stature, making the balance of his second term a period of uncertain accomplishment.

For further reading:

Noonan, Peggy, *What I Saw at the Revolution: A Political Life in the Reagan Era.* New York: Random House, 1990.

Schieffer, Bob, *The Acting President: Ronald Reagan and the Men Who Helped Him Create the Illusion That Held America Spellbound.* New York: Dutton, 1989.

Schwartzberg, Renee, *Ronald Reagan.* New York: Chelsea House, 1990.

Reaganomics. Term used somewhat derisively to refer to the economic policies of the REAGAN administration in the U.S.

recession. A downturn in the business cycle that is milder than a slump or depression. The U.S. economy weathered a number of recessions after World War II. A recession is typically characterized by two successive quarters of negative growth in the Gross National Product (GNP), and an overall decline in business activity. Although postwar recessions have varied in severity they have averaged about 11 months in length. The recession of 1974 was severe in some regions but mild in others.

Recruit Scandal [Japan]. Bribery scandal (1988–89). Recruit Co. (a multi-company conglomerate) made cash available to and sold unlisted, expensive stock in Recruit Cosmos (real estate affiliate) to high-ranking government officials. The stock later traded publicly at much higher rates, creating large profits for officials involved. Prime Minister TAKESHITA NOBORU was implicated and resigned in April 1989. In July 1989, Takeshita's Liberal Democratic Party was defeated for the first time in 34 years and lost its majority in the Diet (parliament).

Red Army. Bolshevik army whose task was to protect the Soviet Union from its external enemies. The workers' and peasants' Red Army was formed by LENIN on January 28, 1918, from the workers' militia, the Red Guards. At first consisting of proletarian volunteers, conscription was introduced during the RUSSIAN CIVIL WAR; at this stage the army was under TROTSKY. The Red Army was demobilized at the end of the Civil War and the war with Poland, although a core of half a million men was retained. Owing to the party's commitment to war as a means of bringing about revolution, expansion was rapid during the 1920s and 1930s; and in the latter decade ranks were reintroduced and officers' privileges reinstated. At first during WORLD WAR II the Red Army was fighting mainly a defensive war, but from 1943 the army embarked on offensive operations. Following the war its name was changed to Soviet Army, and it was reorganized along traditional Russian lines. In 1981 there were about 187 divisions, of which some 100 were at combat readiness, with a total force of about 1.8 million.

Red Army Faction. Radical wing of the BAADER-MEINHOF terrorist group.

Red Brigades [Brigate rosse]. Left-wing Italian urban terrorist organization, active from the early 1970s into the early 1980s. The Red Brigades waged a violent campaign against the political and business establishment of ITALY, using much the same methods as their German counterpart, the BAADER-MEINHOF GROUP—bombings, kidnappings and assassinations. Their most infamous act, the kidnapping and murder of former Italian Prime Minister Aldo MORO in spring 1978, gave rise to public revulsion and tough new antiterrorist measures.

Red Cross. See INTERNATIONAL COMMITTEE OF THE RED CROSS; LEAGUE OF RED CROSS SOCIETIES.

Redding, J. Saunders (1906–1988). U.S. author and historian; one of the founders of the academic discipline of Afro-American studies. In 1949, Redding became one of the first blacks to teach at an Ivy League institution when he was appointed a visiting professor of English at Brown University, his alma mater. In 1970, he became the first black professor on Cornell University's faculty of arts and sciences.

Redding, Otis (1941–1967). American singer. Born in Dawson, Georgia, the son of a Baptist minister, Redding became one of the preeminent male rhythm-and-blues singers of the Sixties. He had his first major success in 1963 with "These Arms of Mine," which he also wrote. In 1967, he was at the height of his career following his performance at the Monterey Pop Festival and his nomination as top male singer by *Melody Maker.* On December 10 of that year, he and four members of his band were killed when their chartered plane crashed into Lake Monona in southern Wisconsin. Early in 1968, Redding's "(Sittin' on) The Dock of the Bay," which he had recorded shortly before the accident, made it to number-one on both the pop and the rhythm-and-blues charts.

Redford, Robert (1937–). American film actor. Born Charles Robert Redford in Santa Monica, California, the handsome blond actor is one of America's authentic superstars. He attended the University of Colorado, quitting to travel and paint. Returning to the U.S. in 1957, he decided on a career as a theatrical scene designer and enrolled in Pratt Institute and the American Academy of Dramatic Arts. He began working as an actor in 1959 and scored his first success in Neil SIMON's *Barefoot in the Park* (1963; filmed 1967). Since then he has starred in such film hits as *Butch Cassidy and the Sundance Kid* (1969) and *The Sting* (1973), playing lovable rogues with Paul NEWMAN as his partner in crime; *The Candidate* (1972), *All the President's Men* (1976) and *The Natural* (1984). Some of his best roles have been under the direction of Sydney Pollack. These include *Jeremiah Johnson* (1972), *The Way We Were* (1973), *The Electric Horseman* (1978) and *Out of Africa* (1985). Redford was also the director of *Ordinary People* (1980) and *The Milagro Beanfield War* (1987). A liberal activist, he has been particularly concerned with environmental issues.

Redgrave, Sir Michael (Scudamore) (1908–1985). British actor. One of the leading British actors of his generation, he first made his reputation in the mid-1930s in Shakespearean roles on the London stage. His first film performance, in Alfred HITCHCOCK's *The Lady Vanishes* (1938), made him an overnight movie star. He appeared in 34 other films, the last in 1971. On stage his portrayal of the title character in CHEKHOV's *Uncle Vanya* was considered definitive. Suffering from Parkinson's disease, he made his last appearance in a major theatrical production as a speechless, wheelchair-bound invalid in Simon GRAY's *Close of Play* (1979). Redgrave was the father of two well-known actresses, **Lynn Redgrave** and Vanessa REDGRAVE; his son Colin was also an actor.

Redgrave, Vanessa (1937–). British actress. The daughter of distinguished actor Sir Michael REDGRAVE and sister of actress Lynn Redgrave, Vanessa Redgrave was born in London. She studied at the Central School of Speech and Drama in that city and made her stage debut at the Frinton Summer Theatre in July 1957. Although her vocal left-wing politics and public support of the PALESTINE LIBERATION ORGANIZATION have occasionally received more attention than her acting, Redgrave has enjoyed a remarkable career both on the stage and on film. She won the *Evening Standard* Award for Best Actress of the Year on London's West End twice, in 1961 for *The Lady from the Sea* and in 1966 for *The Prime of Miss Jean Brodie.* She was nominated for best actress ACADEMY AWARDS three times, for her performances in *Morgan!*, *The Loves of Isadora* and *Mary, Queen of Scots.* She won an Academy Award for best supporting actress for *Julia.*

Red Guards. Term used to describe the radical students and other cadres who carried out MAO TSE-TUNG'S CULTURAL REVOLUTION in CHINA in the late 1960s. The Red Guards disrupted life at all levels and threw the nation into chaos. Brandishing Mao's *Little Red Book* and imbued with a fanatical spirit, they denounced, harassed, arrested, tried and punished those whom they considered enemies of Mao and the revolution. Victims of the Red Guards included educators, intellectuals, artists and writers and Communist Party bureaucrats. Perhaps 400,000 people died at the hands of the Red Guards; many more were imprisoned or forced to work on collective farms as part of their political "reeducation." At the height of the Cultural Revolution, there were an estimated 11 million Red Guards. The Guards were disbanded after Mao's death in 1976.

Red Scare. Wave of fear of political radicalism that swept the U.S. in the wake of the RUSSIAN REVOLUTION (1917). It culminated in the so-called **Palmer Raids** that occurred during the tenure of Alexander Mitchell Palmer as U.S. attorney general (1919–21). Peaking in 1920, roundups conducted in 33 American cities resulted in the arrests of thousands of citizens and aliens alleged to be "Reds" (communists, socialists, anarchists and other radicals) who were charged with attempting to overthrow the government by force and violence. Several hundred aliens, including Emma Goldman, were subsequently deported.

Red Shoes, The. Classic English film made in 1948 that focuses on the obsessions and ambitions of the ballet world. The film is famous for its romanticism, visual impact, special effects and imaginatively filmed ballet sequences, and had an effect on such major dance films as *An American in Paris* (1951). Based on a Hans Christian Andersen fairy tale, *The Red Shoes* was written and directed by Michael POWELL and Emeric PRESSBURGER, and starred dancers Moira Shearer, Robert HELPMANN and Leonide MASSINE, as well as actors Marius Goring and Anton Walbrook.

Reed, Carol (Sir) (1906–1976). British actor and film director. Reed was among the foremost British directors of his generation. He began his career as a film and theater actor in the 1930s. Reed's feature-length directorial debut came with *Night Train to Munich* (1940), a political thriller. During WORLD WAR II, Reed devoted himself to documentaries on the war effort. Following the war, he directed *Odd Man Out* (1947) and *The Fallen Idol* (1948). Next came his most critically acclaimed film, *The Third Man* (1949). Starring Orson WELLES and Joseph Cotten, and utilizing a brilliant screenplay by Graham GREENE, *The Third Man* masterfully explored post-war despair and intrigue in Vienna. Subsequent films directed by Reed include *The Agony and the Ecstasy* (1965), a treatment of the life of Michelangelo starring Charlton HESTON, and *Oliver!* (1968), a musical that won the ACADEMY AWARD for best picture, while Reed was honored with the award for best director.

Reed, Henry (1914–1986). English author. His radio plays, produced for the BBC's Third Programme, were regarded as among the wittiest and most accomplished works of their kind. He was also author of two of the most memorable poems to have emerged from WORLD WAR II, *Judging Distances* and *Naming of Parts.* These poems appeared in his collection *The Lessons of War* (1970).

Reed, John (1887–1920). American journalist who covered the war in Eastern Europe, becoming a close friend of LENIN. He was an eyewitness of the 1917 OCTOBER REVOLUTION and wrote his account *Ten Days that Shook the World* (1919). In 1919 he organized the Communist Labor Party in the U.S. and was founder and first editor of the *Voice of Labor.* For a short period he was the Soviet consul in New York. He left the U.S. for Russia, where he died of typhus and was buried in the Kremlin wall. Other works include *The War in Eastern Europe* (1916) and *Red Russia* (1919).

Reed, Stanley (1884–1980). U.S. Supreme Court justice (1938–57). Reed was named to the Supreme Court by President Franklin D. ROOSEVELT and wrote more than 300 opinions on a broad range of issues, including social welfare, civil rights and the regulatory powers of the federal government. His decisions often defied prediction. However, he was noted for his support of NEW DEAL legislation and his restrained view of civil liberties. Reed regularly voted to uphold federal economic and social welfare laws and thus helped to legitimize the expansion of government regulatory powers that occurred during the 1930s. Previous to his Court appointment, Reed served as counsel of the Federal Farm Board (1929–32) and as general counsel of the Reconstruction Finance Corporation (1932–35). He was U.S. solicitor general from 1935 until his appointment to the Supreme Court in 1938.

Reed, Walter (1851–1902). American Army pathologist and bacteriologist. Reed obtained his medical degree from the University of Virginia (1869) before he was 18. He was commissioned in the Army Medical Corps in 1875 and began to specialize in bacteriology. In 1900 he headed a commission to investigate the causes and mode of transmission of an epidemic of yellow fever among American troops in Havana, Cuba. He and other doctors conducted a series of daring experiments using human volunteers. The results of the experiments proved the fever was caused and transmitted by a virus carried by a certain type of mosquito. Shortly before Reed's death, Harvard conferred on him an honorary degree of A.M., and the University of Michigan gave him the degree of LL.D. The Army Medical Center in Washington, D.C., is named in his honor.

For further reading:
Bean, William Bennett, *Walter Reed: A Biography*. Charlottesville: University Press of Virginia, 1982.

regionalism. A movement in American painting during the GREAT DEPRESSION of the 1930s that celebrated the sturdy, homespun values and people of the Midwest. It was a timely confluence of many artistic, social and political factors. In reaction to the flood of modern European art on the market, there was a growing desire to support an indigenously American form of art. Anxiety over the depression and growing distrust of urban centers because of the stock market crash (1929) stimulated a yearning for a return to a simpler life closer to the soil. It all began with an exhibition at the Kansas City Art Institute in 1933 by New York art dealer Maynard Walker (a native Kansan). "American Painting Since Whistler" comprised 35 paintings, featuring prominently work by John Stewart Curry, a Kansas commercial illustrator; Grant WOOD, an Iowa painter; and Thomas Hart BENTON, a Missouri mural painter. The December 24, 1934, issue of *Time* magazine picked up on the story, displaying Benton's self-portrait on the cover and a full-color illustrated article inside, "The U.S. Scene." It was the first time a major American periodical had given so much attention to living artists. It proclaimed Curry, Wood, and Benton as the leading painters of the American scene. Nine months later an article by Thomas Craven in *Harper's Monthly*, "Our Art Becomes American: We Draw Up Our Declaration of Independence," confirmed the movement now dubbed "regionalism." The ensuing decade tended to stereotype both the artists and their work. What had originally been a satiric view of middle western subjects now seemed to soften and mellow. As Tom Benton admitted: "Grant Wood became the typical Iowa small towner, John Curry the typical Kansas farmer, and I just an Ozark hillbilly. We accepted our roles." The movement lost its momentum (if not its public favor) with the transfer of public attention from local to international issues during WORLD WAR II. Wood died of liver cancer in 1942 and Curry of a stroke in 1946. Benton himself barely survived a heart attack in 1952. Attacks on regionalism's supposed "antiartistic" aims and essentially fascist narrowness of ideology in such magazines as *The Magazine of Art* after 1946 further weakened its position in the art world.

For further reading:
Adams, Henry, *Thomas Hart Benton: An American Original*. New York: Alfred Knopf, 1989.

Regle du jeu, La [The Rules of the Game]. French film acknowledged as Jean RENOIR's masterpiece and regularly included in *Sight and Sound* magazine's annual poll of the Ten Best Movies of all time. It culminated a great sequence of masterpieces from Renoir's peak phase in the 1930s (including *Le Crime de M. Lange* and *La Grande Illusion*). The exteriors were shot in the late winter and spring of 1939 in the Chateau de la Ferte-Saint-Aubin; and the interiors were shot at the Billancourt Studios in Joinville. Although Renoir called his story (freely derived from de Musset and Beaumarchais) a "divertissement," it conveyed so bitter a view of French society that it was censored for its initial release in 1939. (The film was not restored to its original form until 1959.) The story of an outing at a country estate of a disparate group of aristocrats, citizens, and servants is essentially an ensemble piece that, in part, was improvised. It achieves great complexity by its balance of humor and pathos, compassion and satire, artifice and reality. By turns, there are the tender love scenes between the tragic Octave (Renoir himself) and the ambivalent Christine (Nora Gregor); the delicious "vaudevilles" of the amateur theatricals at the estate; and the brutal savagery of the celebrated "rabbit hunt" sequence. This rondelay of love and cruelty was perfectly captured by the mobile camera and deep-space compositions of cinematographer Jean Bachelet. All is flux. Relationships shift, change, and realign again. The continual revelation of layered meanings through repeated viewings is exhilarating. A favorite quotation of Renoir's applies: "In nature nothing is created, nothing is lost, everything is transformed."

For further reading:
Sesonske, Alexander, *Jean Renoir: The French Films, 1924–1939*. Cambridge: Harvard University Press, 1980.

Rehnquist, William H(ubbs) (1924–). Associate justice, U.S. Supreme Court (1971–86), chief justice (1986–). A graduate of Stanford, Harvard and Stanford Law School, early in his career he was a clerk to Supreme Court Justice Robert H. JACKSON. A conservative Republican, he was appointed to the highly visible position of chief legal counsel for the Justice Department under President Richard M. NIXON. He became an eloquent spokesperson for the Nixon administration's positions, some of which were highly controversial. He was nominated to the Supreme Court by President Nixon in 1971; in 1986 President Ronald REAGAN nominated him to fill the vacancy in the chief justice's seat after Warren BURGER's resignation. There was significant opposition to his nomination, although it ultimately proved successful. On the Court, Justice Rehnquist has been a consistent conservative, although often in dissent. In later years, a larger conservative block on the Court allowed the Rehnquist Court to issue more conservative rulings, significantly cutting back the rulings issued by the Court during the WARREN and Burger years.

Reich, Wilhelm (1897–1957). Austrian psychiatrist. After graduate and postgraduate work at the University of Vienna, Reich trained in psychoanalysis under FREUD. In 1927, he published *The Function of Orgasm*, in which he argued that the release of sexual tension is necessary for personal health. In the late 1920s, Reich became a politically active Marxist. He moved to Berlin in 1930 but was forced to flee Nazi Germany in 1933. He continued his work, now on character structure and political psychology, in Scandinavia before leaving Europe for the U.S. in 1939. In America, Reich conducted his research on "orgone," or sexual energy. He and his colleagues at the Orgone Institute designed an "orgone accumulator," a box that they claimed could cure many diseases, including cancer, by concentrating orgonismic energy from the atmosphere. The government declared Reich's therapy a fraud, and he was sentenced to two years in prison, where he died of a heart attack.

Reichstag fire. Fire that destroyed Germany's parliament building on February 27, 1933, a month after Adolf HITLER became chancellor. Blaming the conflagration on communist terrorists, Hitler succeeded in passing legislation that gave him dictatorial powers and suspended civil rights. The police arrested a Dutch worker, Marinus van der Lubbe, along with a number of communist leaders including Georgi DIMITROV. In the subsequent trial, van der Lubbe was found guilty and executed, while the communists were judged to be not guilty. Opponents of the Nazis alleged that the fire had been set by them

German Chancellor Adolf Hitler used the burning of the Reichstag (Feb. 27, 1933) as an excuse to pass legislation giving him dictatorial powers.

to ensure the passage of anticommunist laws. However, later evidence suggested that van der Lubbe alone was responsible for the fire.

Reilly, Sidney [born Sigmund Rosenbloom] (1874–1925). Russian-born British secret agent. Reilly, "ace of spies," was a legendary yet shadowy figure who is widely considered to have been the first modern intelligence agent. His activities spanned the first quarter of the 20th century. Of Jewish origin, he emigrated to Britain and offered his services to the foreign office. In the years leading up to WORLD WAR I he was reputedly involved in espionage activities in Germany, where he attempted to obtain secret plans for German battleships. He developed business interests in Russia which gave him access to high officials. After the RUSSIAN REVOLUTION he worked to keep Russia in the war against Germany. Soon after the BOLSHEVIK (OCTOBER) REVOLUTION he organized a plan to overthrow LENIN and replace the Bolshevik government with a White Russian government headed by himself, but this was thwarted. He spent the next several years working with White Russian emigre organizations in Europe and the U.S. In 1925 he returned to Russia to expose the Trust, a reputed counterrevolutionary group, as an organization controlled by the CHEKA (secret police) designed to funnel funds from the West and lure anti-Bolshevik emigres back to Russia, where they would be arrested. Reilly himself was arrested by Feliks DZERZHINSKY, head of the Cheka, apparently on the direct orders of STALIN. He was subsequently executed. However, learning of the secret Trust, the suspicious Stalin ordered its members arrested and executed; Dzershinsky himself was a victim of this early purge. Even though he lost his life, Reilly had thus succeeded in his final mission.

For further reading:
Lockhart, Robin B., *Reilly: Ace of Spies*. New York: Penguin, 1984.

Reiner, Carl (1922–). American comedian, comedy writer and director of television and film. Reiner has worked in show business for more than 40 years and with some of HOLLYWOOD's funniest talent: Sid CAESAR, Dick Van Dyke, Mel BROOKS and Steve MARTIN. Beginning in the 1940s by adlibbing humorous doubletalk in Army productions of *Hamlet*, Reiner moved on to television revues in the 1950s, until he became a comedy star on Sid Caesar's Emmy-award-winning program "Your Show of Shows" (1950–54, known as "Caesar's Hour" 1954–57) during the "Golden Age of Television Comedy." Reiner served the show in various roles including sketch writer, straight man and even creating oddball characters with funny accents. On the show, Reiner also teamed up with Mel Brooks to create the classic comedy routine "The Two Thousand Year Old Man," which was made into a successful album. Reiner created another television hit, "The Dick Van Dyke Show" (1961–66), which launched the careers of stars Dick Van Dyke and Mary Tyler Moore; he also costarred in this pioneering "sitcom for adults." In the late 1960s and '70s Reiner's brilliance for comedy continued to flourish, as he shifted his talents to writing, directing or starring in several accomplished films, including *It's a Mad, Mad, Mad, Mad World* (1963), *The Russians Are Coming, the Russians Are Coming* (1966), *The Comic* (1969) and *Oh God* (1977). Several other of his film projects have achieved cult status, such as *Where's Poppa?* (1970) and his fruitful collaborations with comedian Steve Martin, such as *The Jerk (1979), Dead Men Don't Wear Plaid* (1982) and *All of Me* (1984). Reiner's son Rob (1945–) is also a major Hollywood talent, acting in the hit television show ALL IN THE FAMILY and directing such films as *This Is Spinal Tap* (1984), *Stand By Me* (1986), *The Princess Bride* (1987) and *When Harry Met Sally* (1989).

Reiner, Fritz (1888–1963). Hungarian-born orchestra conductor who brought the Chicago Symphony Orchestra to world prominence at mid-century. Reiner was born in Budapest where at age 10 he studied with Bela BARTOK. Despite family pressure to become a lawyer, he pursued a conducting career, leading the Dresden Court Orchestra from 1914 to 1922 and succeeding Eugene Ysaye at the Cincinnati Symphony in the U.S. from 1922 to 1931. He became an American citizen in 1928 and held many posts during the next 25 years—head of the opera and orchestral departments at the Curtis Institute during the 1930s, music director of the Pittsburgh Symphony Orchestra from 1938 to 1948, conductor of the Metropolitan Opera from 1949 to 1953 and (most significantly) music director of the Chicago Symphony Orchestra during its peak period from 1953 to 1962. Comparisons with Arturo TOSCANINI are inevitable: His baton technique was minimal but legendary in its precision; his mood was irascible and he frequently bullied his players; and he rejected "romantic," effusive interpretations of music in favor of a no-nonsense, objective approach. In addition to his beloved Viennese classics, Reiner was especially renowned for his performances of Bartok, Paul HINDEMITH and Richard STRAUSS.

For further reading:
Schonberg, Harold C., *The Great Conductors*. New York: Simon and Schuster, 1967.

Reinhardt, Ad(olph) (1913–1967). American painter. Born in Buffalo, New York, he studied art history at Columbia University with Meyer SCHAPIRO and at New York University's Institute of Fine Arts. A theorist and teacher, he taught at Brooklyn College from 1947 until his death. His early works are geometric in character and employ strong color contrasts. In the 1950s his work became quieter and tended toward symmetrical monotones. In the 1960s he developed the "black paintings" for which he is best known. These canvases appear totally black at first glance, but further scrutiny reveals a subtle geometry in an extremely close tonal range.

Reinhardt, Max [Max Goldmann] (1873–1943). Austrian theatrical director and producer. Reinhardt was one of the most important and influential figures in the development of the modern theater in Europe. He began his theatrical career as an actor (1890–1900), becoming well-known for his performances at Berlin's Deutsches Theater. He managed his own theater (1902–05) and took over directorial duties at the Deutsches Theater in 1905. His many productions there set the standard for European experimental theater, and he initiated such practices as including the audience in the production. Reinhardt became known for his spectacularly rich productions, filled with large casts, elaborate costumes and masterful sets. He was just as adept in staging the works of great masters, such as Sophocles, Shakespeare and Goethe, as he was in producing and directing works by contemporaries, such as Luigi PIRANDELLO and George Bernard SHAW. In 1919 Reinhardt opened the massive Grosses Schauspielhaus in Berlin, and the following year he initiated the Salzburg Festival, where he staged a yearly production of *Everyman*. Among his greatest successes were GORKY's *The Lower Depths* (1903), *Oedipus Rex* (1910), *The Oresteia* (1919), *Danton's Death* (1920), *A Midsummer Night's Dream* (1934; film, 1935) and *Six Characters in Search of an Author* (1940). The coming of the Nazis caused Reinhardt to flee Germany in 1933. He settled in the U.S., continued his theatrical career on the New York stage and the Hollywood screen, and became an American citizen in 1940.

Reisman, David (1909–). American sociologist. Reisman taught sociology at the University of Chicago from 1946 to 1958. His scholarly book, *The Lonely Crowd: A Study of the Changing American Character* (1950), about the trend toward individual isolation and depersonalization, was a bestseller and became a classic of sociology. He taught at Harvard (1958–80) and specialized in the sociology of higher education.

Reitsch, Hanna (1912–1979). German flyer. One of the most famous women pilots of the 1930s, Reitsch won many awards for setting altitude and endurance records and during World War II flight-tested the robot-controlled V-1. She piloted what may have been the last German airplane out of besieged Berlin in April 1945 and, as a favorite of Adolf HITLER, is believed to have been one of the last people to see him alive.

relativity, theory of. See Albert EINSTEIN.

Relay. Two early experimental communications satellites built by RCA for NASA. Both were launched in three-stage Thor-Delta rockets from Cape Canaveral (see CAPE KENNEDY); *Relay 1* blasted off on December 13, 1962, and *Relay 2* was launched on January 21, 1964. Both were designed to transmit either one television channel, 300 one-way voice channels or 12 two-way telephone channels, receiving and retransmitting signals between the U.S., Europe, Japan and South America. The 170–lb. aluminum satellites were tapered octagons, 33 inches high and 29 inches in diameter at their broad ends. Their 11 watts of power were produced by some 8,200 solar cells on each exterior. *Relay 1* had an orbit with an apogee of 4,612 miles and a perigee of 819 miles with an angle to the equator of 47.5 degrees and a period of 186 minutes. *Relay 2*'s orbit had an apogee of 4,606 miles and a perigee of 1,298 miles at an angle of 46 degrees to the equator and a period of 195 minutes. Both operated until their power was shut off, *Relay 1* in February 1965 and *Relay 2* seven months later.

Remagen. Rhine River town in Germany's Rhineland-Palatinate, about 20 miles north of Koblenz. Remagen secured a place in 20th-century history as the location of the Ludendorff Bridge (built during World War I). This was the only Rhine River bridge still standing when the advancing Allies reached the river early in 1945, near the end of WORLD WAR II. After fierce fighting the Allies captured the bridge on March 8, 1945. This victory enabled the Allies to cross the river in force and with heavy equipment, thus numbering the days of HITLER's Reich.

Remarque, Erich Maria (1898–1970). German-American author. Most famous for his powerful anti-war novel *All Quiet on the Western Front* (1929), Remarque used the theme of the horrors and chaos of war and its aftermath in all subsequent works. The catalyst for his writing was his stint in the German army during WORLD WAR I. After the war he worked at various jobs including teacher and auto worker. He left Germany in the 1930s when the Nazis rose to power. In 1947 he became an American citizen. Other major novels include *The Road Back* (1931), *Arch of Triumph* (1946), *A Time to Love and a Time to Die* (1954) and *The Night in Lisbon* (1964).

For further reading:

Owen, C.R., *Erich Maria Remarque: A Critical BioBibliography.* Atlantic Highlands, New Jersey: Humanities Press, 1984.

Remembrance of Things Past. Seven-volume novel sequence (1913–1927) by French writer Marcel PROUST. *Remembrance of Things Past* stands among the supreme achievements of 20th-century literature. The central theme of the sequence, which was initiated with *Swann's Way* in 1913, is the intricate individual consciousness of time's passing and its implications for human endeavors and for the ultimate event of death. *Remembrance of Things Past* was conceived by Proust when he was 38, and his relatively late arrival to artistic maturity is reflected in the poignancy with which all the characters of the sequence review lives filled with time squandered and opportunities lost. Memory alone—in all its vividness, beauty and anguish—has a restorative power for the human soul. Love and jealousy are seen as inextricably intertwined. On the social scale, *Remembrance of Things Past* depicts the transformation of French society from aristocratic reign to the economic dominance of the untitled bourgeoisie.

Remizov, Alexei Mikhailovich (1877–1957). Writer. Expelled from Moscow University, he spent the next few years at Penza, Ust-Sysolsk and Vologda. In 1904 he was released from police surveillance and settled in St. Petersburg. He organized the satirical Great and Free House of Apes, of which he was "chancellor," and sent most Russian writers and publishers handwritten charters, stating their position in the House. By World War I Remizov was head of a new school of fiction. His *Mala* and *The Lament for the Ruin of Russia* (1917) convey conditions in Petrograd (Leningrad) from 1914 to 1921. His work, however, is extremely varied in style and content. His prose consists of contemporary stories, the best known of which is *The Story of Ivan Semyonovich Stratilatov* (1909), legends, folk stories, dreams and plays. His verse is less successful. In 1921 Remizov emigrated and settled in Paris.

Remy, Colonel. See Gilbert RENAULT.

Renault, Gilbert (1904–1984). Renault was one of FRANCE's most decorated heroes of the RESISTANCE against the Germans during WORLD WAR II. Best known by his wartime pseudonym, Colonel Remy, he was the principal organizer of the FREE FRENCH intelligence network, which provided the Allies with valuable information on German troop movements before D-DAY. Renault's autobiography, *Memoirs of a Secret Agent of Free France,* was highly acclaimed when it was published in the U.S. in 1948. He was also a film director and writer.

Renault, Mary [Mary Challans] (1905–1983). British novelist. Renault is best known for her popular historical novels, which bring 20th-century insights and knowledge to bear on ancient events, frequently in Greece or Asia Minor. Her novels include *The King Must Die* (1958) and *The Bull from the Sea* (1962), both based on Theseus, legendary king of Athens; *The Persian Boy* (1972), which evokes the reign of Alexander the Great; and *The Friendly Young Ladies* (1985).

Reno. U.S. city, in the state of Nevada, about 20 miles north of Lake Tahoe. Reno's 20th-century renown derives from its status as a center of gambling (legalized here in 1931) and quick divorce.

Renoir, Jean (1894–1979). French director, widely acclaimed as France's greatest filmmaker. Renoir was born in Paris, the second son of Impressionist painter Auguste Renoir. A growing passion for the cinema led to his first directorial effort, *La Fille de l'Eau* (1924). By the time he filmed his early talkies, *La Chienne* and *Boudu sauve des Eaux* (*Boudu Saved From Drowning,* 1932), he had gained a measure of artistic independence, which he stubbornly fought to maintain the rest of his long career.

His greatest creative period came in the late 1930s with *Le Crime de M. Lange* (*The Crime of M. Lange,* 1936), a drama of collectivism and working-class solidarity (eloquent of Renoir's leftist sympathies with the POPULAR FRONT); *La Grande Illusion* (*The Grand Illusion,* 1937), a drama of relationships in a World War I prison camp; *La Bete humaine* (*The Human Beast,* 1938), a melodrama of trains and murder adapted from Emile Zola; and his masterpiece, LA REGLE DU JEU (*The Rules of the Game,* 1939),

French film director Jean Renoir helps actress Ingrid Bergman adjust her makeup.

a dark-humored indictment of a world poised on the brink of war. Renoir's war years were spent in HOLLYWOOD where he became an American citizen. His last works included a meditation on the artifices of theater and film, *Le Petit Theatre de Jean Renoir* (1971), and an autobiography, *Ma Vie et mes films* (*My Life and My Films*, 1974). Before his death in 1979 he received a lifetime achievement ACADEMY AWARD. The range of his achievement makes him difficult to categorize. There is the sparkling humor of the "Arizona Jim" episodes of *M. Lange*, the deeply felt, sensitive, almost documentary observation of nature in *Partie de campagne* (*A Day in the Country*, 1937) and the grim, blunt depiction of the savagery of man in the famous "rabbit hunt" sequence in *The Rules of the Game*. His awesome camera technique was perfectly wedded to his humanistic aims. Andre Bazin hailed Renoir as the spiritual godfather of the so-called French NEW WAVE in the 1950s. His deep-focus frame, moving camera and long takes "permitted everything to be said without chopping the world up into little fragments, that would reveal the hidden meanings in people and things without disturbing the unity natural to them." Ultimately there are no villains and heroes in Renoir's world, no easy labels of praise or blame.

For further reading:

Lyon, Christopher, ed., *The International Dictionary of Films and Filmmakers*. New York: Macmillan, 1984.

Republican Party. American political party founded in 1854; one of the two major political parties in the UNITED STATES. The philosophy of the Republican Party is generally more conservative than that of the DEMOCRATIC PARTY. Republicans tend to support a free rein to business interests, opposing government regulation in the economy and federally funded social programs. They have traditionally been unsupportive of organized labor and of organizations seeking change in society.

The Republican National Committee serves as a coordinator of the national conventions and assists in campaigning and fund raising, at which, since the 1970s, it has become more effective and organized than its Democratic counterpart.

With the exception of Woodrow WILSON's presidency (1913 to 1921), Republicans controlled the presidency from 1900 to 1932 and dominated both the House and the Senate for most of that time. After Franklin ROOSEVELT'S NEW DEAL, the Republican Party went into decline. By 1960 it was in such disarray that some observers predicted its demise.

Following 1969 it began to gain strength. The Republican Party had traditionally been divided between moderates and conservatives, but beginning with the Barry GOLDWATER's nomination in 1964, the conservative faction gained party dominance. The party's credibility was damaged during Richard NIXON's administration by the WATERGATE affair, but following the tax revolts of the late 1970s it gained support among those opposed to government spending. Ronald REAGAN'S election in 1980 brought renewed vigor to the party, and his support of the Moral Majority brought fundamentalist religious groups, many of which were traditional southern Democrats, to the Republican side. Reagan's personal popularity overshadowed the IRAN-CONTRA SCANDAL, and Republicans prevailed at the 1988 elections when George BUSH succeeded him. However, despite its successes in retaining the presidency, the Republican Party remained the minority party in both houses of Congress.

Republics, Constituent. The UNION OF SOVIET SOCIALIST REPUBLICS was formed by the union of the Russian Soviet Federated Socialist Republic, the Ukrainian Soviet Socialist Republic, the Belorussian Soviet Socialist Republic and the Transcaucasian Soviet Socialist Republic. The Treaty of Union was adopted by the first Soviet congress of the U.S.S.R. on December 30, 1922. In May 1925 the Uzbek and Turkmen Autonomous Soviet Socialist Republics and in December 1929 the Tadzhik Autonomous Soviet Socialist Republic were declared constituent members of the U.S.S.R., becoming union republics.

At the eighth congress of the Soviets, on December 5, 1936, a new constitution of the U.S.S.R. was adopted. The Transcaucasian Republic was split into the Armenian Soviet Socialist Republic, the Azerbaijan Soviet Socialist Republic and the Georgian Soviet Socialist Republic, each of which became a constituent republic of the union. At the same time the Kazakh Soviet Socialist Republic and the Kirghiz Soviet Socialist Republic, previously autonomous republics within the Russian Soviet Federated Socialist Republic, were proclaimed constituent republics of the U.S.S.R.

In September 1939 Soviet troops occupied eastern Poland as far as the CURZON LINE, which in 1919 had been drawn on ethnographic grounds as the eastern frontier of Poland, and incorporated it into the Ukrainian and Belorussian Soviet Socialist Republics. In February 1951 some districts of the Drogobych Region of the Ukraine and the Lublin Voyevodship of Poland were exchanged.

On March 31, 1940, territory ceded by Finland was joined to that of the autonomous Soviet socialist republic of Karelia to form the Karelo-Finnish Soviet Socialist Republic, which was admitted into the union as the 12th union republic. On July 16, 1956, the Supreme Soviet of the U.S.S.R. adopted a law altering the status of the Karelo-Finnish Republic from that of a union (constituent) republic of the U.S.S.R. to that of an autonomous (Karelian) republic within the Russian Soviet Federated Socialist Republic.

On August 2, 1940, the Moldavian Soviet Socialist Republic was constituted as the 13th union republic. It comprised the former Moldavian Autonomous Soviet Socialist Republic and Bessarabia (the latter ceded by Romania on June 28, 1940), except for the Bessarabia districts of Khotin, Akerman and Ismail, which, together with northern Bukovina, were incorporated in the Ukrainian Soviet Republic. The Soviet-Romanian frontier thus constituted was confirmed by the peace treaty with Romania, signed on February 10, 1947. On June 29, 1945, Ruthenia (Sub-Carpathian Russia) was by treaty with Czechoslovakia absorbed in the Ukrainian Soviet Socialist Republic.

On August 3, 1940, Estonia, Latvia and Lithuania were incorporated in the Soviet Union as the 14th, 15th and 16th union republics. The change in the status of the Karelo-Finnish Republic has reduced the number of union republics to 15.

After the defeat of Germany it was agreed by the governments of Great Britain, the U.S. and the U.S.S.R. (the Potsdam agreement) that part of East Prussia should be ceded to the U.S.S.R. The area, which includes the towns of Konigsberg (renamed Kaliningrad), Tilsit (renamed Sovyetsk) and Insterburg (renamed Chernyakhovsk), was joined to the Russian Soviet Federated Socialist Republic by a decree of April 7, 1946.

By the peace treaty with Finland, signed on February 10, 1947, the province of Petsamo (Pechenga), ceded to Finland on October 14, 1920, and March 12, 1946, was returned to the Soviet Union. On September 19, 1955, the Soviet Union renounced its treaty rights to the naval base of Porkkala-Udd and on January 26, 1956, completed the withdrawal of forces from Finnish territory.

In 1945, after the defeat of Japan, the southern half of Sakhalin island, and the Kuril Islands, were, by agreement with the Allies, incorporated into the U.S.S.R. Japan, however, asked for the return of the islands of Etorofu and Kunashiri as not belonging to the Kuril Islands proper. The Soviet government informed Japan on January 27, 1960, that the Habomai Islands and Shikotan would be handed back to Japan on the withdrawal of American troops from Japan.

Resistance. Movement among citizens of the countries occupied by Germany in WORLD WAR II in opposition to the Nazis. The model for Resistance organization and activity can been said to have been provided by French General Charles DE GAULLE and his followers. According to De Gaulle himself, there were three stages in the development of the Resistance: (1) the establishment of an information network to benefit the Allies; (2) the sabotage of the enemy war machine and rejection of compromise with occupying authority; (3) the organization and training of military forces (in the case of France, the FREE FRENCH) to attack German troops as the Allies advanced and the promotion of a climate hospitable to the restoration of the nation when the enemy was defeated. As the war progressed, individual Resistance groups ranged from small cells to large armies. Organized networks specialized in obtaining military or economic information, providing aid and escape routes for prisoners, maintaining caches of arms, producing propaganda, engaging in sabotage and mounting guerrilla attacks. At the end of the war Resistance groups cooperated closely with the liberating armies in mopping up the retreating German forces. After the war members of the Resistance were swift and often violent in punishing those who had collaborated with the Germans.

Resnais, Alain (1922–). French film director. Resnais was one of the leading directors of the NOUVELLE VAGUE that dominated the French cinema of the late 1950s and 1960s. He won great acclaim for his very first film, *Night and Fog* (1956), a documentary on the Nazi CONCENTRATION CAMPS. In his later imaginative films, Resnais experimented with flashback and memory to convey the emotional complexity of his characters. These films include *Hiroshima mon Amour* (1959), *Last Year at Marienbad* (1961, screenplay by Alain ROBBE-GRILLET), *Providence* (1977) and *La Vie est un roman* (1982).

Resnik, Judith (1949–1986). U.S. astronaut, one of seven killed in the explosion of the SPACE SHUTTLE CHALLENGER on January 28, 1986. A research scientist, she held an electrical engineering degree and was also a classical pianist. She became the second American woman in space when she flew on a shuttle mission in 1984.

Respighi, Ottorino (1879–1936). Italian composer. Respighi is regarded as a master of orchestration who successfully blended evocative melodies and rich harmonies in his works. In 1900 he became first viola with the Imperial Opera Orchestra in St. Petersburg, Russia, and was greatly influenced by his composition teacher Rimsky-Korsakov. He toured as a concert violinist (1903–08), then taught at the Accademia di Santa Cecilia in Rome from 1913 onward. Respighi's most famous works were two symphonic poems that powerfully evoke the Italian scene: *La fontane di Roma* (1917; *The Fountains of Rome*) and *I pini di Roma* (1924; *The Pines of Rome*). One of his innovations was the insertion of a recording of a singing nightingale in the score of the latter piece.

Reunion. Reunion is an island in the Indian Ocean, more than 400 miles east of Madagascar. A French colony until 1946, the 969–square-mile island then became an overseas department of FRANCE, but in practice was not integrated with metropolitan France. From 1959 onwards the influential local communist party has campaigned for autonomy for the island. Communists dominate the Anti-Colonialist Front for the Self-Determination of Reunion (FRACPAR, or FRA), formed in 1978. A regional council was elected for the first time in February 1983.

Reuther, Walter (1907–1970). American labor union leader. Born in Wheeling, West Virginia, Reuther attended Wayne State University in Detroit. In 1936 he was elected president of the United Automobile Workers (UAW) Local 174 in that city. With his brother Victor, Reuther led the first of the large-scale sit-down strikes, at the Kelsey-Hayes plants in Detroit, and late in 1936 the strike spread to the General Motors plant in Flint, Michigan. In 1937 both GM and Chrysler Motors recognized the UAW as the workers' bargaining agent.

With the end of World War II, Reuther demanded a 30–percent pay raise for GM workers to compensate them for lost overtime and premium pay for war-related work. When the company refused, he led the first major strike of the postwar period, a 113–day walkout of 200,000 GM workers (Nov. 21, 1945–Mar. 13, 1946). This strike helped precipitate strikes in the steel, electrical, meatpacking and other industries, but in the end the workers won an increase of only 18.5 cents an hour. Reuther's aggressive prosecution of the strike won him support among UAW radicals, however, and in 1946 he was elected president of the union. In 1951 he was elected president of the Congress of Industrial Organizations (CIO), and was instrumental in effecting that union's merger with the AMERICAN FEDERATION OF LABOR (AFL) in 1955. In the following years, Reuther was frequently at odds with AFL-CIO chairman George MEANY. In 1968 the UAW withdrew from that organization, claiming that the parent group was moribund and undemocratic. In May 1969 the UAW merged with James HOFFA's International Brotherhood of Teamsters, and the group assumed the name Alliance for Labor Action. On May 9, 1970, Reuther and his wife, May, were killed when their chartered plane crashed in Michigan.

Reverdy, Pierre (1889–1960). One of the leading French lyric poets of the century. His powerful and imagistic verse shows the influence of CUBISM, which first emerged as a theory of painting. In the 1910s Reverdy became a leader of a poetic school of Cubism that also included fellow French poets Guillaume APOLLINAIRE, Blaise CENDRARS, Jean COCTEAU and Max Jacob. Reverdy also emphasized the need for a "poesie brut," or brutal poetry, that would reject conventional structures and appearances to bring out the true underlying forms of experience. After a brief involvement with SURREALISM in the 1920s, Reverdy chose to follow a life of religious contemplation, retiring to the Abbey of Solesmes in 1926. *La Lucarne Ovale* (1916) and *Plupart du Temps* (1945) are representative volumes of his verse.

Revueltas, Jose (1914–1976). Mexican novelist, story writer, essayist, playwright. Revueltas, who is best known for his prose fiction, was one of the most influential Mexican writers to emerge in the middle decades of this century. A lifelong political activist, he was strongly influenced by Marxism but also drew from the insights of Freudian psychoanalysis and surrealist aesthetics. His most highly regarded novel is *The Stone Knife* (1943), which utilizes cinematic narrative techniques in dealing with the lives of six rural workers attempting to flee from a life-threatening flood. Revueltas also published two noteworthy story collections, *God on Earth* (1944) and *Sleep on Earth* (1960).

Rexroth, Kenneth (1905–1982). American poet. Born in South Bend, Indiana, he settled in San Francisco and there, as a cofounder of the San Francisco Poetry Center, with Allen GINSBERG and Lawrence FERLINGHETTI, was associated with the early development of the BEAT GENERATION. An autodidact, he taught himself a number of languages and was devoted to Oriental poetry. His translations include *One Hundred Poems from the Japanese* (1956). His own poetry exhibits an almost Oriental delicacy of image combined with a highly developed Western social conscience. Rexroth's many verse collections include *In What Hour* (1940), *The Phoenix and the Tortoise* (1944), *In Defense of the Earth* (1956) and *New Poems* (1974). He was also the author of a verse play, a number of volumes of essays and of *An Autobiographical Novel* (1966).

Reyes, Alfonso (1889–1959). Mexican poet, essayist, educator and diplomat; one of the leading Mexican men of letters of this century. Reyes was especially well-known for his elegant essays that sought to reconcile and blend the cultures of pre-Columbian and modern-day Mexico. A classicist by temperament, Reyes remained somewhat apart from all literary movements but emerged as a major poet with *Pulse* (1921). In the 1920s and 1930s, Reyes served as the Mexican ambassador to Argentina and Brazil. He also held numerous university teaching positions in his native land. Major collections of his essays include *Criticism and the Roman Mind* (1963) and *Mexico in a Nutshell and Other Essays* (1964).

Reykjavik. Largest city, port and capital of ICELAND. On the island's southwest coast, it became the official capital in 1918. The U.S. leased nearby Keflavik field during WORLD WAR II. Strategically important, Reykjavik helped the Allies achieve domination of the seas and the convoy lanes during the Battle of the North ATLANTIC. Homes and buildings in the city are heated by steam obtained from nearby hot springs.

Reymont, Wladyslaw (Stanislaw) (1868–1924). Polish novelist and essayist. Reymont won the NOBEL PRIZE for literature in 1924 and remains one of the leading Polish novelists of this century, although he is little read by modern-day Western readers. Largely self-educated, he held a wide array of odd jobs in his youth and drew heavily from those experiences in his novels, most of which are written in an intensely realistic style. His magnum opus is the four-volume sequence *The Peasants* (1904–1909), which portrays the struggle of a father and a son who strive to work the land while in conflict over their love for the same woman. Other novels by Reymont include *The Commedienne* (1896) and *The Promised Land* (1899).

Reynaud, Paul (1878–1966). French statesman. A lawyer, he was elected to the chamber of deputies in 1919, holding various cabinet posts from 1930 to 1940. He succeeded Edouard DALADIER as premier during WORLD WAR II (1940) and was unsuccessful in attempts to rally France's war efforts. Shortly thereafter he was obliged to surrender leadership to Marshal Henri PETAIN, who imprisoned him later that year. Deported to Germany in 1942, he was released in 1945. After the war Reynaud was France's finance minister (1948) and vice premier (1953).

Reynolds v. Sims (1964). U.S. Supreme Court decision that established that federal courts can intercede in the drawing of state legislature electoral district boundaries. Although non-whites were enfranchised, they were largely excluded from elective office by clever drawing of election district boundaries to favor white candidates. Election districts typically differed greatly in population. For many years the federal courts would not allow challenges to electoral district boundaries or reapportionments because the issue was thought to be a political question. In the case BAKER V. CARR, the Supreme Court first rejected the hands-off stance, and in *Reynolds* the Supreme Court squarely held that state legislative reapportionment could be challenged in the federal courts. Following this decision, several successful challenges were brought, especially in the South.

Rhapsody in Blue. Landmark American composition for piano and orchestra that advanced the cause of "popular jazz." Bandleader Paul WHITEMAN and composer George GERSHWIN spent barely a month (from January to February, 1924) preparing an *American Rhapsody* for an announced concert of "Experimental Music" at New York's Aeolian Hall on February 12 of that year. The debut performance of the now-retitled *Rhapsody in Blue* (title suggested by the composer's brother, Ira) featured an orchestration by Ferde GROFE, Gershwin at the piano and Whiteman's modest orchestra. Although the program also featured music by the popular Zez Confrey ("Kitten on the Keys") and Victor HERBERT, the Gershwin contribution stole the show and created a sensation, launching him as a "serious" composer. It was encored at CARNEGIE HALL on April 21, 1924. When the symphonic concert version was prepared in 1926—the one heard today—Grofe again did the orchestration. Although specialists quibble about the music's merits as "concert hall jazz" (just as they also dispute such claims about certain contemporary works by Darius MILHAUD and Aaron COPLAND), there is no questioning the vitality of its eclectic, and enduring, blend of American vernacular idioms with European classical styles. When the work was performed (by Oscar Levant) in a HOLLYWOOD biopic of Gershwin, *Rhapsody in Blue* (1945), it was inflated into an extravaganza of Technicolor sight and sound out of all recognition.

For further reading:

Jablonski, Edward, ed., *The Encyclopedia of American Music.* New York: Doubleday and Co., 1981.

Rhee, Syngman (1875–1965). President of South Korea (1948–1960). Rhee was in exile in the U.S. from 1912 to 1945, acting as spokesman for Korean independence from Japan. He returned to Korea in 1945 with U.S. support and was elected South Korea's first president following the division of Korea. He was a strong leader in the KOREAN WAR, but his increasingly dictatorial style provoked unrest and riots, which led to his resignation in 1960. He retired in exile to Hawaii.

Rheims [Reims]. City in the Champagne region of northeastern France, about 80 miles east-northeast of Paris. On May 7, 1945 (known as **V-E Day**), Germany signed an unconditional surrender at Allied headquarters in Rheims, officially ending WORLD WAR II in Europe. The city was severely damaged during both world wars.

Rhine, Joseph B(anks) (1895–1980). American psychologist, known as "the father of parapsychology. Shortly after receiving his doctorate in botany (1925), Rhine became interested in psychic phenomena and went to Duke University to study psychology. After joining the Duke faculty in 1930, he helped open the new field of parapsychological research. He shocked the scientific world with the results of his controversial studies of unexplained human behavior. Rhine's pioneering experiments in clairvoyance, mental telepathy and other psychic occurrences led to his theory of extrasensory perception (ESP) and made ESP a common term in the vocabulary of the 20th century.

Rhineland. The part of GERMANY west of the Rhine River, centered around Cologne. In general, the Rhineland is taken to include those parts of the German states of North Rhine-Westphalia, Rhineland-Palatinate, Hesse and Baden-Wurttemberg in the Rhine valley. After WORLD WAR I, the region was made a demilitarized zone by the Allies, who did not withdraw until 1930. Defying the terms of the Treaty of VERSAILLES of 1919 and the LOCARNO PACT of 1925, the HITLER government remilitarized the region from 1936 and built the SIEGFRIED LINE, an extensive chain of almost impenetrable fortifications.

Rhine River. A principal waterway of Europe that rises in the Swiss Alps and flows for over 800 miles before emptying into the North Sea; contiguous to Austria, Switzerland, Germany, France and the Netherlands. Opened to international navigation in 1868, the victory of the Allies over Germany in WORLD WAR I enabled them to reassert the Rhine as the historic boundary between France and Germany—and to reward France with the left-bank provinces of ALSACE and LORRAINE. Before WORLD WAR II the Rhineland was the site of the German SIEGFRIED and French MAGINOT defensive lines, which played an important part in the early stages of the war. In March 1945 U.S. troops succeeded in crossing the Rhine at REMAGEN. The Rhine is famous in legend and rhyme, but it has lost much of its romantic lustre in modern times. It has suffered considerable pollution as factories along the river have dumped their waste products into the water.

Rhodes. Greek island that was the medieval stronghold of the Knights of St. John of Jerusalem. Largest of the Aegean Sea's Dodecanese islands, it was taken by Italy from the Ottoman Turks in 1912 and formally ceded to GREECE in 1947.

Rhodesia [Southern Rhodesia]. Now known as ZIMBABWE, this landlocked country of south-central Africa—bordered by Zambia on the north, Mozambique on the east, Botswana on the west and South Africa to the south—bore until 1980 the name of 19th-century capitalist adventurer Cecil Rhodes, who in 1890 led European and South African colonists here under the aegis of his British South Africa Company.

Rhys, Jean [Ella Gwendolwn Rees Williams] (1890–1979). British author. Rhys began her career as a chorus girl in London, an experience she would recount in the novel *Voyage in the Dark* (1934). In 1919 she moved to Paris and married her first husband. Her first book was *The Left Bank: Sketches and Studies of Present-Day Bohemian Paris* (1927), to which Ford Maddox FORD wrote the introduction. Her other early works include *Postures* (1928), *After Leaving Mr. Mackenzie* (1930) and *Good Morning, Midnight* (1939). Rhys returned to England and did not write again until an radio dramatization of *Good Morning, Midnight* brought her back into the public eye. Later works include *Wide Sargasso Sea* (1966), which was set in Dominica where Rhys was born; two short story collections, *Tigers are Better Looking* (1968) and *Sleep it Off, Lady* (1976); and the unfinished autobiography *Smile Please* (1979).

Ribbentrop, Joachim von (1893–1946). German foreign minister (1938–45) under the Nazis. A cavalry officer during WORLD WAR I, he was later a wine merchant. He

German Nazi Foreign Minister (1938–1945) Joachim von Ribbentrop.

joined the Nazi Party in 1932, becoming chief foreign policy advisor to Adolf HITLER the following year. Ambassador to Great Britain from 1936 to 1938, he returned to Berlin to assume the post of foreign minister. An enthusiastic supporter of the Nazi regime, he helped to cement the Anglo-German naval agreement (1935), was influential in forming the Anglo-Berlin Axis (1936) and played a leading role in securing the NAZI-SOVIET PACT (1939). Indicted at the NUREMBERG TRIALS, he was found guilty of war crimes and hanged.

Rice, Elmer [Elmer Leopold Reizenstein] (1892–1967). American playwright. Rice was one of the most prolific American playwrights of this century. At the peak of his fame, in the 1920s and 1930s, he was one of the leading voices in the American theater whose plays always reflected a strong concern for freedom and social justice. *The Adding Machine* (1923), which borrowed techniques from the European school of dramatic EXPRESSIONISM, concerns the plight of a futuristic protagonist, Mr. Zero, who is replaced at his job by a computer. *Street Scene* (1929), which won the PULITZER PRIZE for drama, deals with the pressures of life in a New York tenement. Rice helped to found the Dramatists' Guild in 1937 and also served during that period as a regional director for the Federal Theater Project.

Rice, Tim(othy Miles Brandon) (1944–). British lyricist. Rice established himself at a precociously young age as perhaps the leading lyricist in the British musical theater. His lyrics are often optimistic and passionate in tone, featuring a humorous touch that veers away from hard-edged satire. Rice is best known for his string of successful collaborations with British composer Andrew LLOYD WEBBER, including *Joseph and the Amazing Technicolor Dreamcoat* (1968), *Jesus Christ Superstar* (1970) and *Evita* (1976).

Rich, Adrienne (1929–). American poet and feminist theorist. Born in Baltimore, she attended Radcliffe College. At first interested in an elegant precision of verse, as evidenced in her volume *A Change of World* (1951), she emerged as a poet-activist whose works have mirrored the significant social conflicts of her time and her own growth in relation to them. Her poetry has dealt with movements for black rights, against the war in Vietnam and, most significantly, with the women's movement, for which she is widely considered an articulate spokesperson. Rich mingles the personal and the feminist in poems that define the quality of women's lives in *Diving into the Wreck* (1973), winner of the 1974 National Book Award; *A Wild Patience Has Taken Me This Far* (1981); *The Dream of a Common Language* (1978); *Time's Power* (1989); and other volumes of verse. She is also the author of such essays as *On Lies, Secrets and Silence* (1979) and the powerful and candid study of motherhood, *Of Women Born* (1976).

Rich, Bernard "Buddy" (1917–1987). American jazz musician, often hailed as "the world's greatest drummer." He rose from his vaudeville beginnings as Baby Traps to play for the bands of Artie SHAW and Tommy DORSEY before starting his own band after WORLD WAR II. He then toured with trumpeter Harry JAMES. In 1966 he again formed his own band, with which he worked sporadically for the rest of his life. He was known not only for his virtuosic drumming but for his fiery temper and caustic wit.

Richard, Joseph Henri Maurice "Rocket" (1921–). Canadian hockey player. Known for his flashing eyes and reckless style, the Rocket was one of the most explosive goal scorers of his—or any—era. A perennial all-star at right wing, he was a Montreal Canadien for 19 seasons, and provided much of the firepower for the Canadiens' dynasty. In 1944, he scored 50 goals in 50 games, a feat that has been equaled numerically only in a post-expansion, diluted league. The team won five consecutive Stanley Cups (1956–60), and Richard finished his career with 82 playoff goals. He was named to the Hockey Hall of Fame in 1961.

Richard, Marthe (1889–1982). French patriot. During WORLD WAR I she was involved in dangerous espionage work behind German lines. For this she was awarded the Legion of Honor in 1933. During WORLD WAR II she ran an underground network that smuggled downed Allied fliers out of France. A member of the Paris Municipal Council in 1946, she succeeded in passing a law that closed France's bordellos. The law is still known by her name.

Richards, Sir Gordon (1904–1986). Britain's dominant jockey for three decades until his retirement in 1954. Richards was champion jockey 26 times and rode more than 4,800 winners, including 14 Classic races. In 1953, he rode his only Epsom Derby winner. He was also knighted that year, the only jockey to receive that honor.

Richards, I(vor) A(rmstrong) (1893–1979). British critic and poet. Richards was educated at Magdalene College, Cambridge, where he later became a fellow, and spent several years at Harvard teaching and studying linguistics. Richards was enormously influential on a generation of poets and critics, among them William EMPSON, who was his student at Cambridge, and he is credited with creating a receptive attitude toward MODERNISM. His insistence on careful textual study laid the groundwork for the NEW CRITICISM. Richards' critical works include *Principles of Literary Criticism* (1924), *Science and Poetry* (1926) and the seminal *Practical Criticism: A Study of Literary Judgment* (1929). His poetry was collected in *Internal Colloquies: Poems and Plays* (1972).

Richards, (Isaac) Viv(ian Alexander) (1952–). Antiguan cricketer. One of the greatest batsmen in cricket history, Richards is noted for his aggressive approach and masterly improvisation at the crease. Through 1990, he had represented the West Indies a record 111 times, his first selection coming in 1974. During his tenure with the team the West Indies has dominated world cricket in both "tests" and "one-day" varieties. Richards scored 7,990 runs (1974–90) in test matches, including 24 centuries, one of which is the fastest of all time (56 balls v. England on April 15, 1986). He was appointed West Indies captain in 1980, a position he still held in 1990. Richards' success in "one-day" cricket is unparalleled. He has scored the most runs (6,501), the highest individual score (189 v. England on May 31, 1984) and taken the most catches by a fielder (99). Richards plays for his native Antigua in West Indies domestic cricket; he has also played for Somerset and Glamorgan in England.

Richardson, Dorothy Miller (1873–1957). British novelist. While working as a journalist, Richardson became acquainted with H.G. WELLS, who encourage her to write fiction. *Pointed Roofs* (1919) was the first of a series of autobiographical novels that she called *Pilgrimage;* the last volume was *March Moonlight* (1967), published posthumously. Richardson utilized the technique of STREAM OF CONSCIOUSNESS in her idiosyncratic fiction, which is written from a feminist perspective. Virginia WOOLF was an early champion of Richardson's work, and August Wilson brought about a revival of interest in it in the late 1960s.

Richardson, Sir Ralph (David) (1902–1983). Eminent British stage and film actor. His career spanned more than 60 years. He debuted as Lorenzo in *The Merchant of Venice* in 1921, then acted in modern and Shakespearean roles in provincial theaters before moving to London's West End in 1926. He was highly regarded for his portrayal of Falstaff in parts I and II of Shakespeare's *Henry IV* at London's Old Vic Theatre in the 1940s. From 1944 to 1947 he was joint director of the Old Vic, and in 1947 he was knighted for his efforts to revitalize that theater. Later in his career he received acclaim for his appearances with Sir John GIELGUD in the 1970s in David STOREY's *Home* and Harold PINTER's *No Man's Land;* he was active in the theater until the year of his death. He also made memorable screen appearancs in *The Fallen Idol* (1948), *The Heiress* (1949), *Breaking the Sound Barrier* (1952) and *Doctor Zhivago* (1964). Richardson was greatly admired for his distinctive theatrical voice and his ability to combine comic eccentricity with pathos.

Richardson, Tony [Cecil Antonio Richardson] (1928–). British theatrical and film director. Richardson is one of the few directors to have scored equal successes in his theater and film work. He first came to prominence through his directorial work at the Royal Court Theater in London in the 1950s, where he staged the premieres of two famous plays by British playwright John OSBORNE, *Look Back in Anger* (1956) and *The Entertainer* (1958), the latter starring Laurence OLIVIER. Richardson also directed an acclaimed production of *The Chairs* (1957) by French playwright Eugene IONESCO. His subsequent theatrical productions—many of which reached Broadway—included *The Seagull* (1964) by Anton CHE-

KHOV and Shakespeare's *Hamlet* (1969) with Nicol Williamson in the lead role. Richardson created an enduring critical and popular success with his direction of the film *Tom Jones* (1963), based on the bawdy 18th-century novel by Henry Fielding, which starred Albert FINNEY and earned four ACADEMY AWARDS.

Richberg, Donald Randall (1881–1960). American public official. Richberg was a Chicago attorney who specialized in railroad and labor legislation. In 1933 he helped draft the NATIONAL INDUSTRIAL RECOVERY ACT, for which he served as adviser and chief administrator. He was the author of numerous books including *Government and Business Tomorrow* (1943) and *Labor Union Monopoly* (1957).

Richier, Germaine (1904–1959). French sculptor. Educated in Montpellier and Paris, she was a student of the sculptor Emile Antoine Bourdelle from 1925 to 1929 and lived in Switzerland from 1939 to 1945. Influenced by her teacher, by the SURREALIST movement as well as by the horrors of WORLD WAR II, she developed a style that employed slender, distorted figures in openwork forms that express the terrors of war and death.

Richland. U.S. city on the Columbia River in Washington state; settled in 1892, incorporated in 1910. Hanford remained primarily a farming community until WORLD WAR II. The U.S. government obtained thousands of acres of land and between 1943 and 1945 built the Hanford Works nearby, for research and production of the ATOMIC BOMB (see MANHATTAN PROJECT). The production of atomic weapons has since remained the major industry. Radioactive contamination from the Hanford plant has been held responsible for a high incidence of cancer, and other health problems, in area residents.

Richler, Mordecai (1931–). Canadian novelist, critic and screenwriter. Highly regarded by his peers, Richler remains largely unknown to the general public. He began his career as a journalist, first in Canada, then in Paris and London. His first two novels, *The Acrobats* (1954) and *Son of a Smaller Hero* (1955), expressed the feelings of isolation of JEWS in Canada. Perhaps his best-known novel is *The Apprenticeship of Duddy Kravitz* (1959), a coming-of-age novel that is found on the reading lists of many Canadian schools. Richler's acerbic and controversial nonfiction includes *Hunting Tigers under Glass: Essays and Reports* (1969) and *Notes on an Endangered Species and Others* (1974). Other fiction includes *Cocksure* (1968) and *Joshua Then and Now: A Novel* (1980). *Perspectives on Mordecai Richler* appeared in 1986.

Richter, Burton (1931–). American physicist. After earning his Ph.D. from the Massachusetts Institute of Technology in 1956, Richter began his work in the physics of subatomic particles at the Stanford Linear Accelerator Center, where he designed the Stanford Positron Electron Accelerating Ring (SPEAR). In 1974, using SPEAR, Richter and his coworkers observed a new elementary particle, which they called "psi." A group of researchers under Samuel Ting at the Brookhaven Laboratory on Long Island simultaneously discovered the same particle, which they labeled "J." (It is now known as the "J/psi.") Richter and Ting shared the 1976 NOBEL PRIZE for physics.

Richter, Curt Paul (1894–1988). American psychobiologist credited with originating the idea of the "biological clock." The Johns Hopkins University Medical Institution, where he had been a faculty member, said that Richter had introduced the phrase in a 1927 paper on cyclical internal mechanisms. In other work, Richter demonstrated that human biology was strongly influenced by learned behavior.

Richter, Hans (1888–1976). German-American artist. Born in Berlin, he was involved with many of the important avant-garde movements of the early 20th century, including de STIJL, CUBISM, DADA and CONSTRUCTIVISM. In 1918 he and the Swedish painter Viking Eggeling began to create abstract paintings on scrolls, work that eventually led him to the making of abstract films such as *Rhythmus 21* (1921). The rise of Hitler caused him to flee Germany in 1932, when he settled to Switzerland. In 1945 he immigrated to the U.S., where he subsequently taught at Brooklyn College. Richter is best known for the film *Dreams That Money Can Buy* (1944–47), an experimental work made in collaboration with Marcel DUCHAMP, Max ERNST and Fernand LEGER that explores the fantasy lives of a number of psychiatric patients.

Richter, Karl (1926–1981). German conductor, harpsichordist and organist known for his interpretations of the music of Bach. Founder and director of the Munich Bach Chorus and Orchestra, he played a major role in the Bach and Handel revival in the 1950s and 1960s. Although he was not part of the early music/original instruments movement, he helped pave the way with his performances that followed the score without embellishment. He made over 100 recordings, primarily of masterworks of the Baroque period.

Richter, Sviatoslav (Teofilovich) (1914–). Soviet pianist, considered by many to be one of the greatest virtuosos of the latter half of the 20th century. Born near Kiev, Richter was raised in Odessa. He studied at the Moscow Conservatory (1937–44) under Heinrich Neuhaus. In 1940, while still a student, he gave the world premiere of Serge PROKOFIEV's Piano Sonata No. 6, to great acclaim. He was quickly recognized as a major virtuoso pianist and as a leading interpreter of Prokofiev's piano music. His fame spread to the West, although he did not play outside the IRON CURTAIN until 1960, when he performed in Finland and North America. Richter's playing combines virtuosic technique with lyricism, although his performances are sometimes considered wayward. He has received many high honors in the U.S.S.R. and prizes in the West, and has made numerous recordings.

Baron Manfred von Richthofen, the German World War I flying ace known as the "Red Baron" (ca. 1917).

Richter scale. A gauge of the magnitude of an earthquake and of the energy released by it; developed in the 1930s by American seismologist Charles F. Richter. During a quake, ground motion is recorded by a seismograph; the readings are then calibrated onto the Richter scale. The numbers on the scale increase geometrically rather than arithmetically. For example, an increase from magnitude 4.0 to 5.0 means that the ground motion of the latter reading is 10 times greater. An earthquake of magnitude 2 is considered the smallest normally felt by human beings. Slight damage begins to occur from an earthquake of 3.5 magnitude, and anything over 5 is considered a serious quake. Contrary to popular assumption, the upper limit of the scale is not 10 but is theoretically infinite. However, the highest reading ever recorded is 8.9, in a quake off the coast of Japan in 1933.

Richthofen, Manfred, Baron von (1892–1918). German WORLD WAR I aviator. A master of the dogfight, he was credited with shooting down an amazing 80 Allied airplanes from 1916 to 1918. Known as the "Red Baron" for the crimson Fokker triplane he flew, the German ace was killed when his plane was shot down by Allied fire on April 21, 1918. Von Richthofen's sister Frieda was married to the English novelist D.H. LAWRENCE.

Rickenbacker, Edward Vernon "Eddie" (1890–1973). American aviator, business executive. At the age of 16, young Rickenbacker was a well-known auto racer, setting several speed records. Volunteering for the American Air Force, he became America's most celebrated aviation ace in WORLD WAR I by destroying 26 German aircraft. He received the Congressional Medal of Honor. Gaining experience as an executive of several commercial airline companies, he became president of Eastern Airlines (1938), which he built into one of the most important airlines in the country. In 1942 he was appointed special representative of the

American World War I flying ace Capt. Edward Rickenbacker (ca. 1919), who later founded Eastern Airlines.

secretary of war to inspect air bases in the Pacific theater of war. His B-17 was shot down while over the Pacific, and Rickenbacker survived on a raft for 22 days; he wrote about this experience in his book *Seven Came Through* (1943).

Rickey, (Wesley) Branch (1881–1965). American baseball executive. Rickey had a relatively undistinguished career as a catcher for the St. Louis Browns and the New York Yankees before becoming a coach for the Browns. He was named president of the St. Louis Cardinals organization in 1917, and in 1920 he began a number of farm teams for the Cardinals, a system that became standard in major-league baseball. As general manager for the Brooklyn Dodgers (1942–50), Rickey became famous for ending segregation in big league baseball by hiring Jackie ROBINSON in 1947. General manager for the Pittsburgh Pirates from 1950 to 1955, he was posthumously (1967) voted into the Baseball Hall of Fame.

Rickey, George (1907–). American sculptor. Born in South Bend, Indiana, he moved to Scotland at the age of six. He studied widely, notably at Oxford, the Academie Andre Lhote in Paris and New York University, and met many of the leading figures of the European modernist movements. Returning to the U.S. in 1930, he became a teacher and concentrated on painting, turning mainly to sculpture in 1950. Rickey is a leading figure in the "kinetic art" movement. His mature work, executed in metal, is CONSTRUCTIVIST in emphasis and employs geometrical forms and blades that move gently in response to air currents. He is especially noted for his large architectural works, such as his commission for the Lincoln Center for the Performing Arts in New York City.

Rickover, Hyman George (1900–1986). U.S. admiral; father of the nuclear navy. Born in Makow, Russia (now a part of Poland), Rickover immigrated to the U.S. in 1916 and graduated from the U.S. Naval Academy in 1922. During WORLD WAR II, he served as head of the electrical section of the Navy's Bureau of Ships. In 1946, he was assigned to the atomic submarine project at Oak Ridge, Tennessee, where he played a crucial role in convincing the Navy that nuclear sea power was both feasible and militarily essential. He directed the planning and building of the world's first nuclear-powered ship, the NAUTILUS, which was launched in 1954. Promoted to rear admiral in 1953, vice admiral in 1958 and admiral in 1973, he retired in 1982.

Riddell, Robert F. (1902–1984). Canadian army officer. Riddell was known for his heroic exploits in the Arctic. In a legendary display of endurance in the Great White North he tracked down and killed the Mad Trapper of Rat River, who had murdered a Mountie. In 1924 Riddell was part of a group that set up the first radio station inside the Arctic Circle, at the coastal village of Aklavik.

Riddle, Nelson (Smock) (1921–1985). American bandleader, composer and arranger. Riddle became well-known in the 1950s for his song orchestrations for Frank SINATRA. His distinctive arrangements, which borrowed elements from JAZZ and BIG BAND music, were known for their smooth and dusky sound. Among his original compositions was the theme for the 1960s television series "Route 66" and the 1975 Academy-Award-winning score for *The Great Gatsby*. In 1983 he collaborated with Linda RONSTADT on the album *What's New?*, which sold more than 3.5 million copies.

Ride, Sally (1951–). U.S. astronaut; a much-publicized space traveler when, as the first American woman in space, she made her historic U.S. Space Shuttle flight aboard STS-7 (June 18–24, 1983). After a second flight aboard U.S. Space Shuttle mission 41–G (October 5–13, 1984), the publicity-shy Ride moved to the administrative end of NASA and was instrumental in issuing the so-called "Ride Report" in 1987, which recommended future directions and missions for the space program, including renewed development of lunar flights, an eventual lunar base and manned missions to Mars. Ride retired from NASA in August 1987 to become a research fellow at Stanford University.

Ridgway, Matthew Bunker (1895–). U.S. Army general. Born in Fort Monroe, Virginia, Ridgway attended West Point, graduating in 1917. In June 1942, Ridgway succeeded General Omar BRADLEY as commander of the 82nd Infantry Division, elements of which engaged in the invasion of Sicily, the attack on Salerno and the invasion of NORMANDY. In August 1944, Ridgway assumed command of the XVIII Airborne Corps, whose troops played an important role in the BATTLE OF THE BULGE. During the KOREAN WAR, Ridgway was appointed commander of the Eighth Army in December 1950, and was credited with revitalizing that force; in the following April he replaced General Douglas MACARTHUR as commander of the United Nations forces in Korea. In 1953, Ridgway was made chief of staff of the army; he retired in 1955.

Riefenstahl, Leni (1902–). German movie director and actress. Noted primarily as a director of Nazi PROPAGANDA films, Riefenstahl began her career as an actress in such films as *The Holy Mountain* (1927) and *The White Frenzy* (1931). She formed her own production company in 1932 and directed her first film, *The Blue Light*, that same year. From 1933 to 1938 she directed and produced a number of propaganda films for Adolf HITLER, whom she greatly admired. Her masterpiece, *Triumph of the Will* (1934), is arguably the most powerful propaganda film ever made. *Olympia* (1938), a two-part documentary film of the 1936 Berlin OLYMPICS, is another of her films. Blacklisted by the Allies at the end of WORLD WAR II, she did not work again until 1952 when she directed *Tiefland*. Ironically, in the 1970s and 1980s she won new fame for her photographs of primitive peoples.

Riegel, Byron (1906–1975). American biologist and pathologist. Riegel was a pioneer in steroid chemistry. He led the research team that developed the first oral contraceptive. He was considered an authority on vitamin K and drugs related to anticancer and antimalarial agents.

Rietveld, Gerrit Thomas (1888–1964). Dutch furniture designer and architect. Born in Utrecht, he was the son of a cabinetmaker, who began designing furniture as a youth and also studied architecture. As a designer, his piece de resistance was his red-blue wooden armchair of 1918, a work that revolutionized furniture design with its angular forms and openwork patterns and that greatly influenced later BAUHAUS designs. From 1919 to 1931 he was a member of de STIJL and contributed a number of articles to its eponymous magazine. His most notable architectural achievement was the 1924 Schroder House in Utrecht, a three-dimensional expression of De Stijl aesthetics that is closely related to the work of Piet MONDRIAN. Rietveld was a founding member of the International Congress of Modern Architecture in 1928 and thereafter continued to work in architecture and furniture design, producing his celebrated zigzag chair in 1934. During the postwar de Stijl revival of the 1950s, he also executed a number of important architectural projects, notably the Otterlo sculpture pavilion (1954).

Rif War of 1919–26 [Abd el-Krim's Revolt]. In 1919 the Spanish possessions in northern Morocco were being attacked in two sectors: in the east by the Rif (Riff), Muslim Berber tribes under chieftain ABD EL-KRIM, and in the west by Moroccans under the brigand Ahmed ibn-Muhammad Raisuli. The Spanish high commissioner of Morocco, Damaso Berenguer, achieved success against Raisuli, but General Fernandez Silvestre met disaster at the hands of Abd el-Krim. Silvestre and some 12,000 Spanish troops (out of a total of 20,000) were slain by the Rif at the Battle of Anual on July 21, 1921. This forced Spain's withdrawal from the eastern sector, where Abd el-Krim set up the "Republic of the Rif," with himself as president, and prepared to drive out the French and control all of Morocco. With a well-equipped force of 20,000 Rif, he moved south and captured many French blockhouses on the way to Fez in 1925. The French and Spanish, putting aside their rivalry in Morocco, formed an alliance to counter Abd el-Krim. Spain's dictator Miguel PRIMO DE RIVERA personally led a large Spanish-French expeditionary force, which landed at Alhucemas Bay on Morocco's Mediterranean coast in September 1925, and began advancing on Abd el-Krim's headquarters, Targuist. From the south a 160,000–man French army led by Marshal Henri P. PETAIN moved rapidly northward, squeezing the fiercely fighting Rif troops into the area north of Taza (1925). Faced with defeat by superior forces, Abd el-Krim surrendered on May 26, 1926; he was exiled to the island of Reunion. At a Paris conference (June 16–July 10, 1926), France and Spain restored the borders of their Moroccan zones, which had been set by a 1912 treaty.

Riga. Port city and capital of LATVIA (the U.S.S.R.'s Latvian Republic); During WORLD WAR I Germany seized Riga from czarist Russia in 1917. The following year LATVIA declared its independence here; but in 1940 the country was absorbed into the Soviet Union. After renewed German occupation in WORLD WAR II, it was recaptured by the Soviets in 1944. In the late 1980s and early '90s, it once again became a center of Latvian nationalism.

Riggs, Bobby (1918–). American tennis player and self-proclaimed male chauvinist. While Riggs will remain in the tennis record books for such feats as his 1939 sweep of the Wimbledon singles, doubles and mixed doubles championships, he will be remembered for the challenge he posed to women's tennis in the early 1970s. He claimed that women's tennis was a sham, and that no female player could beat him. His claim seemed to hold up as the first to respond to his challenge, Margaret Court (see Margaret Court SMITH), went down 6–2, 6–1 to the 55-year-old Riggs. Riggs' 1973 match at the Houston Astrodome with the best player in women's tennis, Billie Jean KING, became a publicity extravaganza, televised nationwide to an audience of 50 million. In a triumph for "women's lib," King defeated Riggs 6–4, 6–3, 6–3.

Right Opposition. In the U.S.S.R., opposition to the COMMUNIST PARTY by those who stress compromise and cooperation with noncommunists. The Right Opposition of 1928–29 was led by Nicholas BUKHARIN, Alexei RYKOV and Michael Tomsky.

Riis, Jacob (1849–1914). Danish-American journalist and social reformer. Born in Ribe, Denmark, he immigrated to the U.S. in 1870. Seven years later he became a police reporter for the New York *Tribune*, working there until 1888, when he joined the staff of the *Evening Sun*, where he was a reporter until 1899. His stories and photographs of the wretched lives faced by immigrants on New York's Lower East Side were extremely important in raising the consciousness of U.S. and in provoking legislation to improve conditions. He again wrote of these squalid living conditions in his book *How the Other Half Lives* (1890), which was followed by other volumes including *The Children of the Poor* (1892), *Children of the Tenements* (1903) and *Neighbors: Life Stories of the Other Half* (1914). Riis captured the attention of Theodore ROOSEVELT, with whom he founded a New York settlement house, and whom he profiled in *Theodore Roosevelt the Citizen* (1904). His autobiography, *The Making of an American*, was published in 1901.

Rijeka [Fiume]. Croatian port city on the Adriatic coast of Yugoslavia, about 40 miles southeast of Trieste; a part of AUSTRIA-HUNGARY at the beginning of the century. Because of its large Italian population, it was claimed by Italy after WORLD WAR I but instead was awarded to the new nation of YUGOSLAVIA. Seized by a freebooting corps under poet and flier Gabriele D'ANNUNZIO in September 1919, an agreement at RAPALLO nevertheless made Fiume a free state. But a fascist coup in 1922 toppled the local government and let in Italian troops. The Treaty of Rome (1924) left Fiume Italian but gave Yugoslavia the Fiume suburb of Susak. The post-WORLD WAR II peace treaty with Italy (1947) put Fiume firmly into Yugoslav hands. United with Susak, it became a major industrial city, commercial center and port, officially dubbed Rijeka.

Rijksmuseum. Dutch national museum, located in Amsterdam. An institution of international repute, it originated as the Great Royal Museum founded by Louis Napoleon Bonaparte in 1808, was renamed and moved to the Trippenhuis in 1815 and opened in its present quarters designed by P.J.H. Cuypers in 1885. The museum is famous for its superb collection of 17th-century Dutch paintings by such masters as Frans Hals, Jan Vermeer and Rembrandt. It also has a fine selection of Dutch primitives and landscapes. The Rijksmuseum boasts an excellent collection of European sculpture and is renowned for its drawings and prints, including one of the world's greatest representations of Rembrandt's graphic work.

Rilke, Rainer Maria (1875–1926). Czech-born poet, novelist, story writer and essayist. Rilke is the most beloved and critically esteemed German-language poet of this century. Two of his poetical works, the *Duino Elegies* (1922) and the *Sonnets to Orpheus* (1922)—both written while Rilke was living in a small stone tower in Muzot, Switzerland—are regarded as masterpieces both in terms of their lyrical beauty and their spiritual insight.

Rilke was born in Prague in 1875. After an unhappy stint in the military school to which he was sent by his parents, Rilke avoided formal education but steeped himself deeply in all areas of the humanities. His first poems and stories appeared in the 1890s. The novella *The Lay of the Love and Death of Cornet Christoph Rilke* (1899) is a major work of this period. In 1901 he married Clara Westhoff. Together with their daughter Ruth, they moved to Paris in 1902, where both husband and wife studied with the sculptor Auguste Rodin. The marriage did not last, and Rilke sought out solitude for the remaining decades of his life. His *New Poems* (1907, 1908) influenced an entire generation of German poets. During WORLD WAR I Rilke briefly served as an office bureaucrat for the German army. In 1919 he moved to Switzerland, where he lived for the remainder of his life. His *Letters to a Young Poet* (1934) remains a popular inspirational work.

Rin-Tin-Tin (?–1932). Saved from a World War I trench by American Captain Lee Duncan, Rin-Tin-Tin went on to become the preeminent animal star of the silent movie period. Duncan brought the male German shepherd to HOLLYWOOD, and in 1922 the dog appeared in his first feature, *The Man from Hell's River*. Throughout the 1920s, Rin-Tin-Tin was WARNER BROS.' biggest star, and his popularity continued until his death in 1932. Another Rin-Tin-Tin starred in a television series of that title in the 1950s.

Riopelle, Jean Paul (1923–). Canadian painter. Born in Montreal, he is Canada's leading abstract painter. Associated with the modernist *automatiste* group in Montreal, he settled in Paris in 1947. There he created a totally nonrepresentational style, painting monumental canvases of mosaiclike strokes executed in vibrant jewellike color. He is known for his oil paintings and for works in such media as ink, pastel and watercolor.

Ripley, Elmer Horton (1891–1982). American basketball star and coach. Ripley was a leading professional player (1908–30) in the early years of the sport. From 1922 to 1953 he coached some of the top college teams, including Yale, Columbia, Notre Dame and Army, bringing Yale the Ivy League championship in the 1932–33 season. He later coached the Harlem Globetrotters (1953–56), the Israeli Olympic team (1956) and the Canadian Olympic team (1960). He was inducted into the Basketball Hall of Fame in 1972.

***Rite of Spring, The* [Le Sacre du Printemps].** One of the most famous and (in its day) notorious of all modern ballets. First produced by the BALLETS RUSSES it was a collaboration among some of the greatest figures of the contemporary ballet stage, composer Igor STRAVINSKY, impresario Serge DIAGHILEV, and choreographer/dancer Vaslav NIJINSKY. The premiere at the Theatre des Champs-Elysees in Paris on May 29, 1913 created a veritable riot. Such an uproar arose from an outraged audience that Nijinsky fled to the wings and conductor Pierre MONTEUX could not hear the orchestra. The ballet's "pictures of pagan Russia" began with a series of primitive fertility rites connected with the advent of spring and concluded with a sacrificial ritual in which a chosen virgin literally dances herself to death. It was shocking stuff, all right; but that initial notoriety was amplified by the choreography and music. The movements of the dancers were heavy, lumpy, and earth-bound. The Stravinsky music was insistently percussive and dissonant, the rhythms erratic and unpredictable. "The end of the music was greeted by the arrival of gendarmes," Monteux wrote of the premiere. "Stravinsky had disappeared through a window backstage, to wander disconsolately along the streets of Paris." Quickly the music world recovered itself and the ballet was readily accepted in Diaghilev's 1920 version with choreography by Leonide MASSINE. Although there are frequent revivals worldwide, the ballet is best known through the concert suite by Stravinsky. Moviegoers remember it as a sequence in Walt DISNEY's *Fantasia* where the music, rearranged and altered, accompanied the ponderous lumberings of gigantic dinosaurs. It was only an animated cartoon, but Stravinsky purportedly wept. Today *The Rite of Spring* is a staple of the orchestral repertoire, and there are numerous recorded versions, including one conducted by Stravinsky himself.

For further reading:
The Dictionary of Modern Ballet. New York: Tudor Publishing, 1959.

Ritsos, Yannis (1909–1990). Greek poet. After the defeat of the Greeks by the Turks in the GRECO-TURKISH WAR OF 1921–22, Ritsos's wealthy family suffered financial ruin. His mother and brother died of tuberculosis, and his father and sister became insane. His personal tragedies were intensified by social problems in Greece. Ritsos embraced socialism and looked toward the Soviet Union. In 1936 one of his most famous poems, "Epitaphios," was included in a public book burning by the Metaxas dictatorship. In 1948 he was exiled to a camp in the Greek islands. His books were banned until 1954. After the GREEK COLONELS' coup d'etat in 1967 he was again deported; even after his release from the camps, he was kept under house arrest and his works banned until 1972. Ritsos was a prolific writer, and his works have been translated into dozens of languages. The poems, set to music by Mikis Theodorakis, became an anthem for progressive forces in Greece.

Ritt, Martin (1914–1990). U.S. film and television director. Noted for his socially conscious dramas, Ritt was blacklisted in Hollywood during the anticommunist MCCARTHY era of the 1950s. He later took a darkly comic look at the McCarthy years in his 1976 film *The Front*. His other films include *Hud* (1963), *Sounder* (1972) and *Norma Rae* (1979).

Rivera, Diego (1886–1957). Mexican painter. The foremost modern Mexican muralist was born at Guanajuato and studied with the popular painter Jose Guadalupe Posada and other Mexican artists. Traveling in Europe from 1907 to 1910 and 1911 to 1921, he was influenced by the work of such Old Masters as Giotto, El Greco and Goya as well as by his friendships with Cezanne and PICASSO. In Europe he also became politicized, deciding that art should be created for the masses and preferably be situated on the walls of public buildings. He returned to Mexico in 1921 to paint the murals about which he had philosophized, exploring the history and social struggles of his native land in bold figurative images. Murals from this period include those in the Ministry of Education in Mexico City and the Agricultural School in Chilpancingo. Visiting Moscow from 1927 to 1928, he was inspired to even greater revolutionary fervor, returning to paint such overtly ideological murals as those at the National Palace (1929–55) and the Palace of Cortes, Cuernavaca (1929–30). His works in the U.S. include frescoes in the San Francisco Stock Exchange (1931), murals of industrial America in the Detroit Institute of Arts and a mural in ROCKEFELLER CENTER, New York City, the latter destroyed by its sponsors because it included a portrait of LENIN. Drawing on archaeological and folk sources, boldly linear and richly colored, Rivera created an indigenous style that has enormously influenced his country's art and gained him an international reputation.

Rivers, Thomas Milton (1888–1962). American virologist. A graduate of Emory College (1909) and Johns Hopkins (1915), Rivers began research in 1918 on a form of pneumonia that accompanied measles. Working with the Rockefeller Institute for Medical Research (1937–55), he performed pioneer viral research on flu, chicken pox and polio, and managed the research projects leading to the SALK antipolio vaccines.

Riyadh [El Riad, Riad]. Capital city of SAUDI ARABIA, inland about 235 miles from the Persian Gulf. Between 1891 and 1902 it came under the control of the Rashid family; it was reconquered by IBN SAUD, who established it as the headquarters from which he extended his rule over Saudi Arabia. In 1991, during the PERSIAN GULF WAR, Riyadh was a target of scud missiles fired from IRAQ.

Rjukan. Town on the Mane River of Telemark county, in southern NORWAY. Rjukan was occupied by the Germans during WORLD WAR II. After the war, it was revealed that a local plant producing heavy water had been destroyed by Norwegian commandos in February 1943 to halt the Nazi effort to develop the first ATOMIC BOMB.

RKO Radio Pictures, Inc. One of Hollywood's "Big Five" production/exhibition motion picture studios (along with METRO-GOLDWYN-MAYER, 20TH CENTURY-FOX, PARAMOUNT PICTURES and WARNER BROS.). It was the only major studio born directly out of the TALKING PICTURE revolution. RKO's roots were in the Film Booking Office (FBO) of America, a small production/distribution company whose chief star was Strongheart the Dog. In 1926 Joseph P. KENNEDY acquired FBO and joined forces a year later with David SARNOFF, the president of Radio Corporation of America (RCA). Sarnoff needed a showcase for his new optical sound system, trademarked "Photophone." Theaters controlled by the vaudeville circuit of Keith-Albee-Orpheum were added to the conglomerate in 1928. The giant $300 million corporation was named the Radio-Keith-Orpheum Corporation and the famous radio tower adopted as its logograph. In 1931 David O. SELZNICK became production chief, but after a series of notable releases, including *What Price Hollywood?* (1932), *A Bill of Divorcement* (1932) and *King Kong* (1933), he was replaced by Merian C. Cooper in 1933. Less stable than its competitors, RKO remained in a perpetual state of chaos the rest of its corporate life. A succession of studio heads came and went, including B.B. Kahane, Samuel Briskin, Pandro S. Berman and tycoon Howard HUGHES. The Hughes years sowed the seeds of the studio's downfall with aborted projects, disastrous releases such as *The Conqueror* (1956) and general corporate disarray. Hughes sold the studio to General Teleradio, Inc., in 1955, which in turn released the film library to television. In 1957 Desilu Productions bought the RKO lot for its television production. Despite its checkered history, RKO is remembered for a splendidly diverse output. The ASTAIRE/ROGERS musicals, from *Flying Down to Rio* (1933) to *The Story of Vernon and Irene Castle* (1939), were some of the brightest films of the 1930s. During the WORLD WAR II years a remarkable series of horror films emerged from the Val Lewton unit, including *The Cat People* (1943) and *The Body Snatcher* (1944). The immediate postwar years saw several notable films under the short-lived tutelage of production chief Dore SCHARY—*Crossfire* (1947), *They Live by Night* (1947) and *Out of the Past* (1947). A number of important stars and filmmakers built their reputations at the studio—Orson WELLES, George CUKOR, Katharine HEPBURN, composer Max STEINER, Edward Dmytryk, Robert MITCHUM and many others. RKO remains in existence as a corporate entity of General Tire, RKO General Inc. It has abandoned the motion picture field in favor of broadcasting and cable television.

For further reading:
Jewell, Richard B. and Vernon Harbin, *The RKO Story*. New York: Arlington House, 1982.

Robbe-Grillet, Alain (1922–). French novelist and literary critic. Robbe-Grillet is best known as the foremost theoretician and practitioner of the NOUVEAU ROMAN. His approach to the novel, as outlined in his critical work *For a New Novel: Essays on Fiction* (1963), is to adjure standard dramatic plotting and psychological analysis of character in favor of flat, nonjudgmental depictions of the random events of everyday reality. Life, according to Robbe-Grillet, is neither overtly meaningful nor patently absurd but rather simply is. Novels by Robbe-Grillet include *The Erasers* (1953), *Jealousy* (1957), *In the Labyrinth* (1959) and *Recollections of the Gold*

Triangle (1978). His novels influenced the directors of the French cinematic Nouvelle Vague on the 1960s, especially Alain RESNAIS. Robbe-Grillet wrote the screenplay for Resnais's *Last Year in Marienbad* (1961).

Robbins, Fredrick Chapman (1916–). American virologist and pediatrician. Having earned his M.D. at Harvard, Robbins practiced at Children's Hospital, Boston, for two years prior to joining the Army. During WORLD WAR II he served in the Mediterranean Theater where he was chief of the viral and rickettsial section of the 15th Medical General Laboratory. Joining J.F. ENDERS and T.H. Weller (1948) in research at Children's Hospital, he helped produce polio cultures that led to new vaccines, diagnostic techniques and identification of other viruses. In 1954 he shared the NOBEL PRIZE in physiology and medicine with Enders and Weller for breeding the poliomyelitis virus in tissue culture.

Robbins, Harold (1916–). American novelist. Robbins is known for his many best-selling novels, which are rife with sex and violence and the conflicts of the wealthy and glamorous. Robbins' first novel, *Never Love a Stranger* (1948), drew on his own experiences as an orphan on the streets of New York and created controversy with its graphic sexuality. Of his many works, perhaps most acclaimed was *A Stone for Danny Fisher* (1951). Other titles include *The Carpetbaggers* (1961), *The Betsy* (1971) and *Piranha* (1986). Several of his books have been adapted into films.

Robbins, Jerome (1918–). American dancer, choreographer and director. One of the foremost choreographers for the American musical theater and classical ballet, Robbins began his career as a dancer in Broadway musicals (1938–40). He joined the AMERICAN BALLET THEATRE in 1940 and choreographed his first ballet, *Fancy Free,* for that company (1944). His successful adaptation of this ballet to a musical comedy, *On the Town* (with Betty COMDEN and Adolph Green), led to his choreographing the shows *Billion Dollar Baby* (1946) and *High Button Shoes* (1947). During his long association with the NEW YORK CITY BALLET, he was associate artistic director (1949–59) and joint ballet master-in-chief (1983–89), and choreographed such works as *Afternoon of a Fawn* (1953) and *Dances at a Gathering* (1969) for the company. In 1957 he collaborated with Leonard BERNSTEIN to create the landmark musical *West Side Story,* and won two ACADEMY AWARDS for the film version (1962). He also directed and choreographed many other Broadway musicals, including *The King and I* (1951), *Peter Pan* (1954), *Funny Girl* (1964) and *Fiddler on the Roof* (1964), and toured Europe with his own company, Ballets: USA, in 1958 and 1961.

Robbins, Lionel Charles (1898–1984). One of the most distinguished British economists of the 20th century. Although initially conservative, he later embraced the liberal theories of John Maynard KEYNES. Robbins served with Keynes on the British delegation to the BRETTON WOODS CONFERENCE that set post-World War II monetary policy. He wrote several books; *An Essay on the Nature and Significance of Economic Science* (1935) was considered the most influential. In the early 1960s he headed a committee on higher education; the **Robbins Report** (1963) had a major effect on expanding the British college and university system. Robbins taught at the London School of Economics (1929–61).

Roberts, Elizabeth Madox (1881–1941). American novelist. Born in Perryville, Kentucky, she attended the University of Chicago. She began her literary career as a poet but is remembered primarily for her movingly accurate portraits of life in rural Kentucky told in a language that recalls poetry in its lyricism and rhythmic beauty. Her novels include *The Time of Man* (1923), *Jingling in the Wing* (1928), *The Great Meadow* (1930) and *Black Is My Truelove's Hair* (1938). Roberts also wrote a number of volumes of short stories.

Roberts, Owen J. (1875–1955). Associate justice, U.S. Supreme Court (1930–45). An honors graduate of the University of Pennsylvania and its law school, Roberts became an assistant attorney general after a brief time in private law practice. He returned to private practice, building a successful corporate law practice. He interrupted his private career twice, once as a special attorney general in Philadelphia and later in Washington, D.C., investigating the corruption in the Harding administration. Roberts was appointed to the U.S. Supreme Court in 1930 by President Herbert HOOVER and continued to serve throughout Franklin D. ROOSEVELT's administrations. Although a conservative Republican, Roberts wrote a number of groundbreaking opinions, including the opinion in *Cantwell v. Connecticut* (1940) that set aside on First Amendment grounds a Connecticut conviction for preaching in public. In *Wickard v. Filburn* (1942), he expanded federal regulation of interstate commerce by upholding the regulation of grain grown within one state. He dissented in KOREMATSU V. UNITED STATES, which upheld the detention of JAPANESE-AMERICANS during World War II. After his resignation from the Court in 1945, Roberts became dean of the University of Pennsylvania law school and remained active in public life until his death.

Roberts, Richard (1911–1980). American nuclear physicist and microbiologist. Roberts was the principal contributor to the discovery of delayed neutrons, the basis for atomic reactors. His experiments with electronic vacuum tubes aided in the construction of the proximity fuse, a bomb-detonating device that was of important use in WORLD WAR II. As a microbiologist, he discovered the key chemical synthetic processes by which cell duplication occurred.

Robertson, Oscar (1938–). American basketball player. In high school, Robertson led his team to a 45–game winning streak. The first college player ever to be named player of the year for three consecutive years, he was drafted in 1960 by the Cincinnati Royal of the National Basketball Association. Before beginning his pro career, he was co-captain of the U.S.' gold medal Olympic team. He remained in Cincinnati for 10 years, where his playmaking as a guard made him an all-star for virtually the entire decade (1961–1969), and led the league in assists seven times. Robertson finished his career in Milwaukee and retired with totals of 26,710 points, 9,887 rebounds and 2,931 assists.

Robeson, Paul (1898–1976). American singer, actor and political activist. Born in Princeton, New Jersey, the son of a minister who had been a slave, Robeson began his distinguished career as a scholar-athlete at Rutgers University, then attended Columbia University Law School, graduating in 1923. While practicing law he first became involved in the theater and soon left the legal world to devote himself to acting. Becoming associated with the PROVINCETOWN PLAYERS in 1924, he won acclaim for his performances in a number of plays by Eugene O'NEILL, highlighted by his creation of the title role in *Emperor Jones* (1925; film, 1933). Robeson also used his magnificent bass-baritone voice in concert performances, making his debut in 1925. Performing in Jerome KERN'S SHOW BOAT (1928; film, 1936), he created a sensation with his rendition of "Ol' Man River." He was also famous for his interpretations of spirituals and for his performances of songs in over 20 languages. As an actor, he was particularly noted for his performance of the title role in *Othello* (London, 1930; Broadway, 1943–45). Throughout his life Robeson championed leftist causes, calling for uncompromising civil rights and lauding the U.S.S.R. as a friend to black people. These stands brought him into conflict with the prevailing anticommunism of the late 1940s and 1950s. A controversial figure, Robeson was blacklisted, denied a passport (1950) and brought before the HOUSE UN-

Black American actor, singer, athlete and Rhodes scholar Paul Robeson was blacklisted in 1950 for his political activities.

AMERICAN ACTIVITIES COMMITTEE (1956). When his passport was renewed in 1958, he left the country, lived in the U.S.S.R. and Europe, and returned to the U.S. in 1963. His final years were spent in seclusion.

For further reading:

Duberman, Martin B., *Paul Robeson: A Biography*. New York: Knopf, 1989.

Robeson, Susan, *The Whole World in His Hands: A Pictoral Biography of Paul Robeson*. New York: Carol Publishing Group, 1981.

Robinson, Bill ["Bojangles"] (1878–1949). American dancer. Perhaps the best known tap dancer the U.S. ever produced, he began performing in night clubs and eventually reached the Broadway stage. Moving on to HOLLYWOOD, Robinson made a total of 14 films. Among the most successful were those in which he starred with Shirley TEMPLE, including *The Little Colonel* and *The Littlest Rebel* (both 1935) and *Rebecca of Sunnybrook Farm* (1938). Famed for his grace, showmanship, inventiveness and versatility, as well as for his sheer endurance, Robinson continued dancing well into his mid-60s, becoming the model for several new generations of American tap dancers.

For further reading:

Haskins, Jim, and N.R. Mitgang, *Mr. Bojangles: The Biography of Bill Robinson*. New York: William Morrow, 1988.

Robinson, Brooks (1937–). American baseball player. One of the premier third basemen ever to play the game, Brooks Robinson was an All-Star in 15 of the 23 seasons he played for the Baltimore Orioles. A 16–time Gold Glove, he stills holds virtually every fielding record for third basemen, including putouts, assists and fielding percentage. He finished his career with a .263 batting average, finishing over .300 only once, in 1964. That year he was named the American League's most valuable player, with 28 home runs and 118 runs batted in. Robinson retired in 1975 and went on to become an Orioles' broadcaster. He was inducted into the Baseball Hall of Fame in 1983.

Robinson, Edward G. (1893–1973). American film actor. Born Emanual Goldenberg in Bucharest, Romania, he emigrated to the U.S. the age of nine and grew up on New York City's Lower East Side. Attending the American Academy of Dramatic Arts, he began his acting career in 1913. Robinson made his Hollywood mark as the quintessential gangster. His first such role was in a Broadway play, *The Racket* (1927), but he soon made his way to the West Coast. In 1930 he established himself as king of the tough guys with his portrayal of Rico Bandello in *Little Caesar* (1930). Robinson's other movies included *A Slight Case of Murder* (1938), *Double Indemnity (1944) and Key Largo* (1948). He also played character roles in such films as the biographical *Dr. Ehrlich's Magic Bullet* (1940) and the psychological drama *The Woman in the Window* (1944). His last part was a supporting role in *Soylent Green* (1973).

Robinson, Edwin Arlington (1869–1935). American poet. Born in Head Tide, Maine, and educated at Harvard, he is a major figure in the poetry of the U.S. He was intimately acquainted with the residents of his hometown of Gardner, Maine, eventually transmuting it into the "Tilbury Town" of his early verse. The inhabitants of this small fictional hamlet were the subject of the brief and telling psychological portraits that are Robinson's best-remembered poems. These include "Miniver Cheevy," "Richard Cory" and "Luke Havergal." Virtually unknown at the beginning of his career, he published his first volume of verse, *The Torrent and the Night Before* (1896), at his own expense. A shy, reclusive figure, he moved to New York City in 1899 and lived in some financial difficulty until President Theodore ROOSEVELT, an early admirer, secured him a position at the New York customs house (1905–09). With the publication of *The Man Against the Sky* (1916), he achieved significant critical acclaim and thereafter was able to support himself through writing. Deeply serious and often symbolic, his later volumes include such long narrative poems as *Avon's Harvest* (1921), the PULITZER PRIZE-winning *The Man Who Died Twice* (1924) and *Amaranth* (1934) as well as such lengthy Arthurian tales as *Lancelot* (1920) and *Tristram* (1928), also awarded a Pulitzer Prize.

Robinson, Frank (1935–). American baseball player. Frank Robinson began his career in left field with the Cincinnati Reds in 1956. That year he was named to the All-Star team and was rookie of the year. He remained with the Reds for the next 10 seasons, and was named most valuable player a second time before being traded to the Baltimore Orioles. Robinson responded by leading the Orioles to a pennant and a World Series title in 1966, as he took the batting title with a .317 average and 49 home runs. He was traded to the Los Angeles Dodgers in 1970, the California Angels the following year, and in 1975 became playing manager of the Cleveland Indians. He retired as a player in 1976 and went on to coach for a number of teams before returning to the Orioles as a coach in 1986. He was named manager of that club in 1988. He was elected to the Hall of Fame in 1982.

Robinson, Jackie [John Roosevelt Robinson] (1919–1972). American baseball player. In the spring of 1947, baseball changed forever when Branch RICKEY signed Jackie Robinson to a Brooklyn Dodgers contract. The first black to play in the Major Leagues, Robinson's competitive drive and personal pride helped carry him through a rookie year filled with taunts and difficulties. Named rookie of the year, he spent 10 more seasons in the Dodger infield. His hitting and base running helped bring the team six league championships and a World Series championship. Robinson's best year, 1949, saw him hit .342 and steal 37 bases, making him the league leader in both categories as well as being named most valuable player. After his retirement in 1956, Robingson devoted himself to political and CIVIL RIGHTS work. He was named to the Baseball Hall of Fame in 1962.

For further reading:

Allen, Maury, *Jackie Robinson: A Life Remembered*. New York: Franklin Watts, 1987.

Alvarez, Mark, *The Story of Jackie Robinson*. New York: Simon & Schuster, 1990.

Golenbock, Peter, *Teammates*. San Diego: Harcourt Brace Jovanovich, 1990.

Robinson, Joan [born Joan Maurice] (1903–1983). British economist. A socialist, Robinson taught at Cambridge University from 1931 to 1971. She collaborated with John Maynard KEYNES, helping him formulate the theory of full employment. She questioned traditional economic assumptions and made significant contributions to theories of international trade and the economics of growth and development.

Robinson, Joseph Taylor (1872–1937). American politician. A lawyer, Robinson

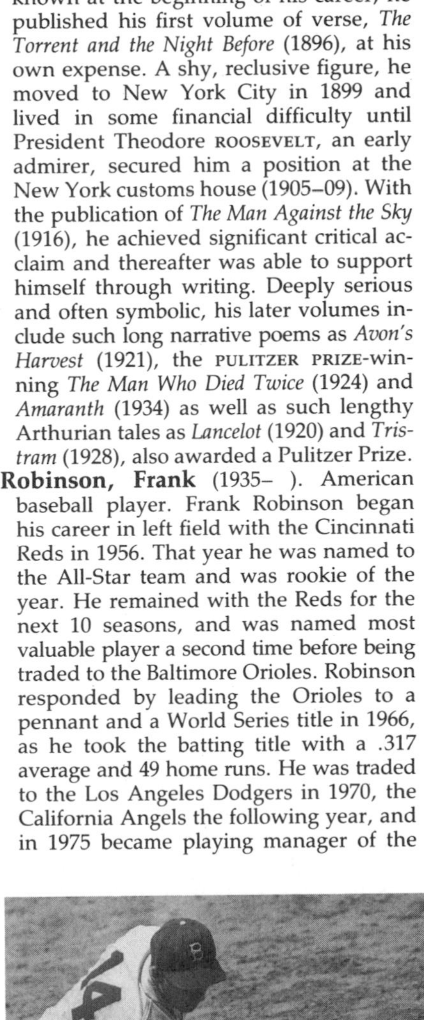
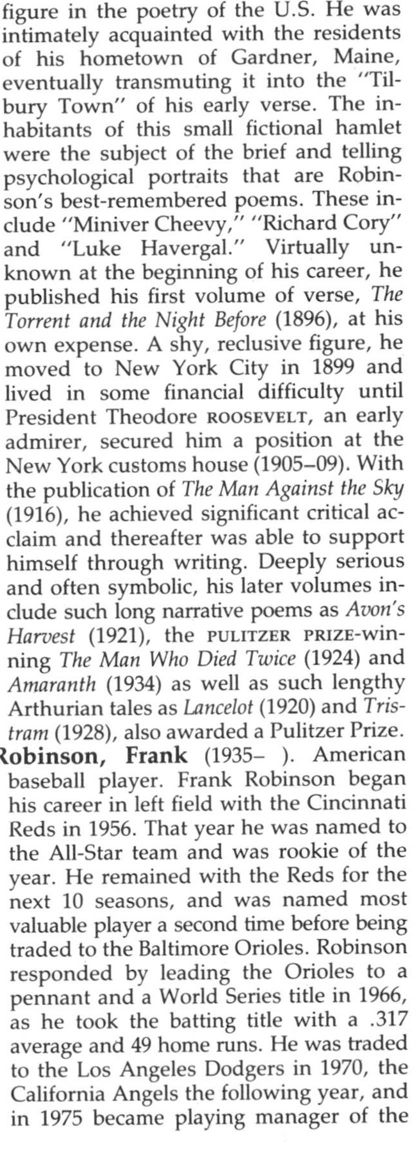
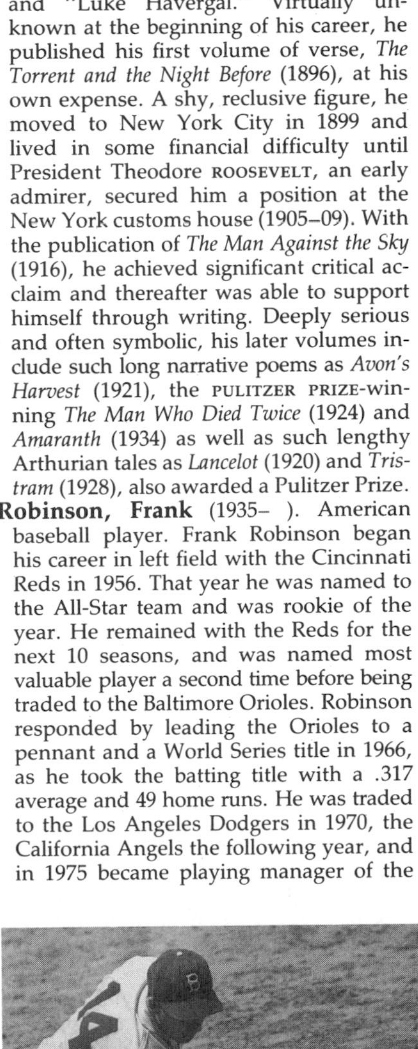

The first black man to play baseball in the Major Leagues, Jackie Robinson steals home plate (July 2, 1950).

began his political career as a U.S. congressman from Arkansas (1903–13). He served two months as governor of the state before he was elected to fill a vacancy in the U.S. Senate (1913–37). He was Democratic minority leader of the Senate from 1923 to 1933 and majority leader from 1933 to 1937. In 1928 he was the unsuccessful candidate for vice president on the ticket with Alfred E. SMITH. Robinson played a leading role in the passage of many NEW DEAL measures and was cosponsor of the Robinson-Patman Act in 1936, which legislated against price discrimination. He led the unsuccessful fight for Franklin D. ROOSEVELT's Supreme Court reorganization.

Robinson, (Esme Stuart) Lennox (1886–1958). Irish playwright. Robinson is known for his many varied patriotic dramas and comedies depicting Irish life. These include *The Clancy Name* (1911), *Patriots* (1912) and *Church Street* (1955). A friend of W.B. YEATS, Robinson was manager of the ABBEY THEATRE and in 1923 became its director, which he remained until his death. He was coeditor of *The Oxford Book of Irish Verse* (1958) and wrote *The Irish Theatre* (1939) and *Ireland's Abbey Theatre. A History* (1951).

Robinson, Rubye Doris Smith (1942–1967). American CIVIL RIGHTS activist. As a sophomore at Spelman College in 1960, she joined a sit-in campaign and helped found the Student Nonviolent Coordinating Committee (SNCC). In 1963 she became administrative assistant to SNCC executive secretary James Forman, and until 1967 served as SNCC's main administrative and logistical planner. By 1964 she had begun advocating Black African nationalism and a greater say by women within the SNCC. In 1966 she became the SNCC's executive secretary, supporting the BLACK POWER movement launched in 1966 by James MEREDITH and Stokely CARMICHAEL.

Robinson, Sugar Ray [born Walker Smith] (1920–1989). Five-time world champion middleweight boxer. Many boxing experts believe that, "pound for pound," he was the best boxer ever. During a career that lasted from 1940 to 1965, he posted a record of 175 wins (with 110 knockouts) and 19 losses (with only one knockout). He was noted for his boxing artistry and his knockout skills. He won the world welterweight championship in 1946 and the middleweight championship in a bout with Jake LaMotta in 1951. Although he lost the middleweight title several times, he regained the crown with fights against Randy Turpin (1951), Carl (Bobo) Olson (1955), Gene Fullmer (1957) and Carmen Basilio (1958). He was elected to the Boxing Hall of Fame in 1967. In his last years he suffered from Alzheimer's disease and diabetes.

Robinson, William (Billy) (1884–1916). Pioneer aviator and aircraft experimenter. Robinson developed one of the first radial air-cooled airplane engines. Receiving permission to fly mail from Des Moines to Chicago, he began the first authorized air mail flight in 1914. When he overshot Chicago, possibly on purpose, he landed in Kentland, Indiana, breaking the nonstop flying distance record, with a flight of 390 miles in four hours and 44 minutes. He lost his life in an attempt to break another aviation record. He had previously reached altitudes of over 14,000 feet, but in attempting to surpass the record of 17,000 feet, he lost control and plummeted to his death.

robot. Robots are machines that can be COMPUTER-programmed or guided by remote control to perform a variety of tasks. The word "robot" was coined in 1920 by Czech playwright and novelist Karel CAPEK. Prominent in 20th-century science fiction, robots are often portrayed as ominous mechanical beings that have superhuman strength and minds of their own. In reality, robots bear little resemblance to their fictional counterparts, and they do only what they are programmed to do (although the application of artificial intelligence may allow robots to mimic human behavior). Refined in the late 20th century, robots perform work in settings that would be deadly for humans, such as under the sea or in outer space. Robots have also been used to handle radioactive materials, both routinely and at the damaged THREE MILE ISLAND and CHERNOBYL reactors. Japanese AUTOMOBILE manufacturers were among the first to employ robots to perform high-precision assembly line work.

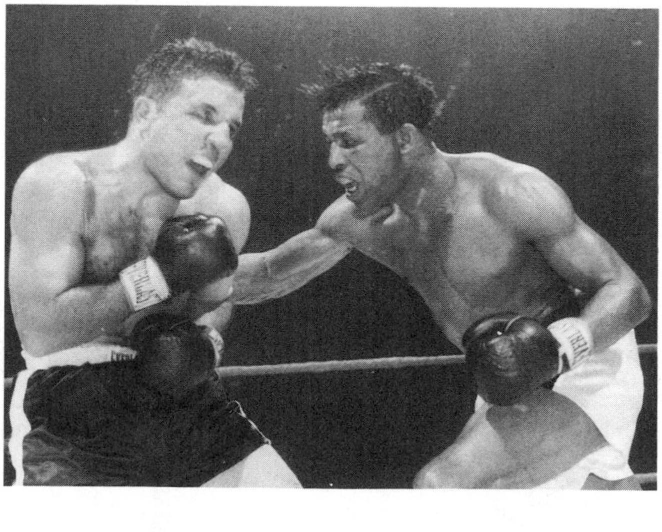

Sugar Ray Robinson (right) defeated Jake LaMotta in this fight to gain the world middleweight boxing title (Feb. 15, 1951).

Robson, Mark (1913–1978). Canadian-born film director. Robson first gained prominence in 1949 with *Champion* and *Home of the Brave,* and went on to direct many other films. Oddly, he specialized in two genres that had little in common: war adventure films aimed at male audiences and "soap opera" potboilers geared to predominantly female audiences. In the former category were *The Bridges at Toko-Ri* (1954) and *Von Ryan's Express* (1965), while films in the latter category included *Peyton Place* (1957) and *Valley of the Dolls* (1967). Such movies were box office hits, although they were generally dismissed by critics.

Rochet, Waldeck (1905–1983). French communist. As leader of the French Communist Party from 1964 to 1972, he steered the party toward a policy of greater independence from the U.S.S.R. He brought about an alliance with socialists and other leftists to support Francois MITTERAND in the 1965 presidential election. In 1968 he led the French communists to condemn the SOVIET INVASION OF CZECHOSLOVAKIA.

rock [rock and roll]. An original American musical form that saw much of its early development in the South before being modified by influences from other parts of the country and abroad (particularly England). Rock and roll had its origins in the late 1940s as a kind of heavily accented music, with debts to JAZZ, BLUES and popular music played primarily by black musicians. Known as "rhythm and blues" (its politest designation) because of its blues roots, it was also labeled "race" music, and many pop music radio stations throughout the country refused to play it. This contempt was to follow rock and roll well into the 1960s as society sought, vainly and often hysterically, to "stop this trash." Led by the increasingly popular recordings of such performers as Fats DOMINO, Chuck BERRY and "Little Richard" Penniman, rhythm and blues built up an increasingly avid audience among both white and black teenagers.

In 1954, about the time the term "rock and roll" began to appear, a new wave burst upon the public. Elvis PRESLEY made his first recordings in Memphis with Sun Records. A year later, Bill HALEY and the Comets' "Rock Around the Clock" reached the top of the pop charts, and a new era in popular music had begun. These early years, in which the raucous new music vied for popularity with the traditional productions of Eddie Fisher and Doris Day, saw the spectacular rise of Presley with such hits as "Heartbreak Hotel" (1955), "Hound Dog" and "Don't Be Cruel" (both 1956), an appearance on "The Ed SULLIVAN Show" and a three-picture movie deal.

Rock had taken the country by storm and much of this early activity was generated in the South. As it grew, it drew upon other existing forms, such as COUNTRY AND WESTERN MUSIC, to produce a hybrid form, "rockabilly," a term derived from "rock" and "hillbilly" to indicate a combination of elements taken from both. Among the best known examples are "That's All Right" (1954) by Presley and "Blue Suede Shoes" by Carl Perkins, another Sun Records singer. Other performers, such as Jerry Lee LEWIS and Charlie Rich, shared a similar background.

Rock and roll music played over British and West European radio stations became equally popular abroad, aided by the success of the film *Rock Around the Clock*, with Bill Haley and Alan Freed, who is generally credited with first applying the term "rock and roll" to the new music. As the 1950s drew to a close the first wave of rock, which had started in the South was now firmly entrenched throughout the Western world. In the 1960s American-influenced British groups, particularly the BEATLES and the ROLLING STONES, were to return the favor with the "British invasion" that began in 1964. Thereafter, rock was truly an international affair.

For further reading:

Carlin, Richard, *Rock and Roll: 1955–1970.* New York: Facts On File, 1988.

Rockefeller, John Davison, Jr. (1874–1960). U.S. businessman and philanthropist; the only son of oil magnate John D. Rockefeller, he took over management of his father's interests in 1911. During their lives, father and son gave over $3 billion to various scientific, cultural and educational institutions. Among his most notable philanthropies were the restoration of Williamsburg, Virginia, the establishment of Rockefeller University and the Rockefeller Foundation as well as the donation of the site for the United Nations headquarters in New York City. He helped plan ROCKEFELLER CENTER, completed in 1939.

Rockefeller, Nelson Aldrich (1908–1979). American politician, governor of the state of New York (1958–73) and vice president of the U.S. (1974–77). The grandson of John D. Rockefeller I, the Standard Oil magnate, Rockefeller was born into one of America's wealthiest families. He entered government service in 1940 when he became coordinator of inter-American affairs in the State Department. He was named assistant secretary of state for Latin America in 1944. In these posts he helped formulate and carry out President Franklin D. ROOSEVELT's "Good Neighbor" policy. In 1950 Rockefeller served under President Harry S TRUMAN as chairman of the International Development Advisory Board on aid to underdeveloped countries. In the administration of Dwight D. EISENHOWER he was undersecretary of the Department of Health, Education and Welfare from 1953 to 1955, when he became a special assistant to the president for foreign affairs. Rockefeller entered elective politics in 1958, defeating incumbent W. Averell HARRIMAN for the governorship of New York. He served for four successive terms and became a national political figure. As governor, he initiated massive welfare programs. He also started drug rehabilitation programs, reorganized New York's transportation system and constructed lavish public works projects. To carry out these programs, he increased taxes, instituting a state sales tax and income tax. His handling of an uprising at Attica state prison (1971), in which 42 prisoners and guards were killed, was heavily criticized.

The leader of the liberal wing of the REPUBLICAN PARTY, Rockefeller long harbored presidential aspirations. He sought the Republican nomination for president in 1960, 1964 and 1968, but each time was rejected by the party as too liberal. In 1974 Gerald FORD, who had succeeded Richard M. NIXON as president following the WATERGATE SCANDAL, chose Rockefeller as his vice president; confirmed by the House and Senate, Rockefeller was sworn in on December 19, 1974. As vice president, he headed a special commission (the Rockefeller Commission) that investigated allegations of illegal activities by the CIA. He also made recommendations regarding the administration's domestic and economic policies. Because of opposition from the conservative wing of the Republican Party, Rockefeller withdrew from consideration as Ford's running mate in the 1976 presidential campaign. He retired to private life at the end of his vice presidential term. Rockefeller's four brothers were also prominent. **John D. Rockefeller III** (1906–78) was a philanthropist; **Laurence Rockefeller** (1910–) was a philanthropist and conservationist; **David Rockefeller** (1915–) was president and chairman of Chase Manhattan Bank; **Winthrop Rockefeller** (1912–73) served two terms as governor of Arkansas.

For further reading:

Underwood, James E., *Governor Rockefeller in New York: The Apex of Pragmatic Liberalism in the United States.* Westport, Conn.: Greenwood, 1982.

Rockefeller Center. New York City complex of skyscraper office buildings, admired both as a popular tourist attraction and as an early example of a coherently planned, urban high-rise grouping. Beginning during the GREAT DEPRESSION in 1931, Rockefeller interests bought out all the structures on three entire city blocks in the heart of a midtown Manhattan where few large buildings existed. A team of architects developed a coordinated design for a group of 13 large buildings, planning a midblock private street (Rockefeller Plaza), a central garden walk leading to an open sunken plaza, and individual skyscraper buildings. The architects were Reinhard & Hofmeister; Corbett, Harrison, & MacMurray; Hood & Fouilhoux; and, after World War II, Carson & Lundin. The buildings are of varying height, with the 850-foot RCA building at the center. All have similar external materials, detailing and slablike forms with setbacks typical of the skyscraper design of the ART DECO era. The project included underground pedestrian shopping areas and truck delivery access, but not the originally intented opera house. There were two large movie theaters (only one, RADIO CITY MUSIC HALL, survives), the radio studios of NBC, many shops and restaurants and some 10 million square feet of office space. Many works of art, sculpture, bas-reliefs and murals are incorporated, including work by a number of leading artists of the 1930s.

Although the architecture of the individual buildings may now seem undistinguished, the coordinated planning of the project and the massing of the group have been greatly admired. Since 1960, Rockefeller Center has been extended, with additional buildings adjacent to it on the north and west (across Sixth Avenue); the newer buildings are of indifferent design quality, though well-related to the concept of the original project. This complex remains a major attraction for visitors to New York and is a continuing example of the value of coordinated architectural planning in contrast to the usual chaos of major urban real estate development. Rockefeller Center was sold to Japanese investors in 1989.

American politician Nelson Rockefeller served as governor of New York state from 1958 to 1973 and vice president of the U.S. from 1974 to 1977.

Rockingham, John (1911–1987). Canadian soldier. One of CANADA's most decorated military officers, he was a hero of the NORMANDY campaign during WORLD WAR II. He led Canadian soliders in KOREA under the UNITED NATIONS flag during the first year of the KOREAN WAR.

Rockne, Knute (1888–1931). Football coach. Rockne excelled in football as a student at Notre Dame University, winning a crucial game with Army in 1913 through the then unused forward pass—a turning point in football strategy. After graduation in 1914, he became a chemistry instructor and assistant football coach at Notre Dame, and head coach in 1918. As head coach for 13 years he led his teams in winning 105 games with only 12 losses and five ties and made Notre Dame a leading football center of the U.S. He revolutionized football theory, stressed offense, developed the precision backfield, called the "Notre Dame shift," perfected line play and other strategy. Among

"All-American" college football coach Knute Rockne's strategies and "pep" talks have become sports legend.

the famous stars he developed were the "Four Horsemen of Notre Dame," the most famous of all backfields. He was noted for his ability to exemplify values and ideals and inculcate qualities of leadership among his "boys." He died tragically in an airplane crash. One of his several books on football was *Coaching, the Way of the Winner*.

For further reading:
Riper, Guernsey V., Jr., *Knute Rockne: Young Athlete*. New York: Macmillan, 1986.

Rockwell, Norman Perceval (1894–1978). American painter famous for his magazine and book illustrations. Born in a shabby brownstone in New York, Rockwell dropped out of high school at 16 to study art full-time. He preferred the Art Students League to the more prestigious National Academy, which had discouraged his pretensions to be an illustrator. Renting a studio once owned by painter Frederic Remington, he quickly established a reputation for children's subjects in such popular magazines as *St. Nicholas, American Boy* and *Boy's Life*. In later years he worked for LIFE, *Look* and *American Artist*. His real ambition, however, was to paint covers for the *Saturday Evening Post*—"the greatest show window in America for an illustrator," he said in his autobiography, *My Adventures As an Illustrator* (1960). From 1916 to 1963 he enjoyed an uninterrupted relationship with the *Post*, painting 322 covers. Here was the Rockwell vision America remembers, an apple-cheeked, ingenuous view of rural life, with barefoot boys and gap-toothed girls, soda-jerks and Boy Scouts, loving grandmas and quaint village characters. "I paint life as I would like it to be," he wrote. "Maybe as I grew up and found that the world wasn't the perfectly pleasant place I had thought it to be, I unconsciously decided that, even if it wasn't an ideal world, it should be and so painted only the ideal aspects of it."

The care and meticulous precision of his work is legendary. Even to those disposed to dismiss his anecdotal, realistic style, his technique and draughtsmanship are impressive. His zeal for "authenticity" led him to use as models his friends and neighbors in the towns of Arlington, Vermont, and Stockbridge, Massachusetts. Perhaps the archetypal image among his *Post* covers is a self-portrait that appeared October 8, 1938: The artist sits with his back to us and scratches his head, puzzling what to make out of the blank canvas before him.

For further reading:
Meyer, Susan E., *The Great Illustrators*. New York: Harry N. Abrams, 1978.

Rodchenko, Aleksandr Mikhailovich (1891–1956). Russian painter. Associated with MALEVICH, Rodchenko founded the Russian nonobjectivist movement, an abstract style closely related to his mentor's SUPREMATISM. His best-known painting is probably *Black on Black* (1918; Tretyakov Gallery, Moscow), an artistic answer to Malevich's celebrated *White on White* (1918; Museum of Modern Art, New York City). He is also known for the constructions he created in collaboration with the constructivist Vladimir TATLIN.

Rodeo. Classic American ballet. First performed by the Ballet Russe de Monte-Carlo at the Metropolitan Opera in New York on October 16, 1942, it brought together the talents of choreographer Agnes DE MILLE, composer Aaron COPLAND and scenic designer Oliver Smith. Subtitled "The Courting at Burnt Ranch," it is set in the American Southwest and tells the story of the tomboyish Cow Girl in love with the Head Wrangler. She discards her rope and boots for a girlish frock, becomes the belle of the local ball and is eventually carried off by the Champion Roper.

Incidents of riding, roping and a square dance (complete with a "caller") alternate with sentimental episodes. Agnes de Mille appeared as the Cow Girl. "The beauty and genuiness of 'Rodeo' reside precisely in the apparent casualness of its American expression," wrote dance critic George Amberg. The same can be said for Copland's score, a catchy, rambunctious evocation of cowboy tunes and dance rhythms. The ballet is best known today for the orchestral suite Copland wrote in 1945.

Rodgers, Richard (1902–1979). Celebrated American composer of Broadway, ballet, the movies and television. Rodgers' shows revolutionized the American musical theater, breaking away from the line of light American musical comedies to establish a more operatic musical drama. Rodgers enjoyed a comfortable boyhood in New York, where he had ample opportunity for musical studies and theatergoing. While at Columbia University, he met the two songwriters with whom his career would be most closely associated, Lorenz HART and Oscar HAMMERSTEIN II. After a few shows of only middling success (*Poor Little Ritz Girl,* 1920), Rodgers and Hart hit their stride with several *Garrick Gaieties* revues and many subsequent successes, from the late 1920s through the early 1940s. These included *A Connecticut Yankee* (1927), *Evergreen* (1930), *Jumbo* (1935), *On Your Toes* (1936), *Babes in Arms* (1937), *The Boys from Syracuse* (1938) and *Pal Joey* (1942). Among Rodgers and Hart's hit songs were "Dancing on the Ceiling," "Little Girl Blue," "My Funny Valentine," "Johnny One Note" and "Bewitched." The two also wrote the film music for *Love Me Tonight* (1933), which featured "Isn't It Romantic," and *Hallelujah, I'm a Bum* (1933).

Rodgers switched partners in 1943, collaborating with Oscar Hammerstein II on *Oklahoma!* It was the first of their many blockbusters, including *Carousel* (1945), with "You'll Never Walk Alone" and "If I Loved You"; *South Pacific* (1949), with "Some Enchanted Evening" and "This Nearly Was Mine"; *The King and I* (1951), with "Getting to Know You," "Hello, Young Lovers" and "We Kiss in a Shadow"; and *The Sound of Music* (1959), with "Climb Every Mountain" and "My Favorite Things." After Hammerstein's death in 1960, Rodgers wrote both words and music to *No Strings* (1962). His other compositions include ballet music (the "Slaughter on 10th Avenue" number for *On Your Toes*) and the scores for television's "Victory at Sea" (1952–53) and "Winston Churchill: The Valiant Years" (1960). His autobiography, *Musical Stages,* was published in 1975.

For further reading:
Jablonski, Edward, ed., *The Encyclopedia of American Music*. New York: Doubleday and Co., 1981.

Rodgers, William (1928–). British politician. As a Labour member of Parliament, Rodgers served as transport minister and junior minister in defense from 1974 to 1979 and Labour government and shadow defense minister from 1979 to 1980. In 1981 Rodgers was a cofounder, along with Shirley WILLIAMS, Roy JENKINS and David OWEN, of the SOCIAL DEMOCRATIC PARTY. Rodgers lost his seat in Parliament in the 1983 general elections.

Rodnina, Irina (1953–). Soviet skater. Rodnina won three Olympic gold medals in the pairs skating competition, partnered by Aleksei Ulanov at Sapporo in 1970, then by Aleksandr Zaitsev at Innsbruck in 1976 and at Lake Placid in 1980. She also won 10 world championships. She and her partner had a dazzling style full of complicated leaps.

Rodrigo, Joaquin (1901–). Spanish composer. Although he has been blind since childhood, Rodrigo became a gifted composer noted for the use of traditional Spanish rhythms in his works. He became a professor of music history at Madrid University in 1946. His works include the famous *Concierto de Aranjuez* for guitar and orchestra (1940), the *Concierto Andaluz* for four guitars and orchestra (1967) and the *Concierto como un divertimento* for voice and orchestra (1979–81).

Rodzyanko, Michael Vladimirovich (1859–1924). Russian president of the DUMA. Having supported the autocracy's suppression of the 1905 Revolution, he unsuccessfully opposed the idea that Czar NICHOLAS II should take command of the army. With Alexander Guchkov he led the Octobrists, a party of right-wing liberals who constituted the majority party in the third and fourth dumas.

Roehm, Ernst (1887–1934). Leader of the Nazi Sturm Abteilung (SA, or storm troopers). Roehm served as a captain in the German army in WORLD WAR I. In September 1930, he became chief of staff of the Nazi paramilitary group known as the SA, or "Brownshirts," building the organization into an effective instrument of mass terror. However, tension between Roehm and Hitler rose steadily over the next three years, as Roehm called for the creation of a military state. To appease his more moderate supporters in the army and in the business community, Hitler agreed to destroy the Brownshirts as well as the radical political wing of the Nazi Party. On June 30, 1934, the "Night of the Long Knives," the ss under Heinrich HIMMLER and the special police under Hermann GOERING murdered an estimated 500 to 1,000 of these elements, as well as others who were deemed enemies of the party. Roehm was shot by SS officers in Stadelheim Prison.

Roerich, Nicholas Konstantin (1874–1947). Russian artist. Traveling through his native country (1901–04) and central Asia (1923–28), he became known for his numerous exotic landscapes and figure studies. He was particularly acclaimed for the designs he executed for the MOSCOW ART THEATRE and the DIAGHILEV ballet, notably the stage sets for STRAVINSKY'S 1913 RITE OF SPRING. Also an amateur archaeologist, he traveled to the U.S., where New York City's Roerich Museum was established to house his paintings and collection of artifacts.

Roethke, Theodore (1908–1963). American poet. Roethke was born in Michigan, where his father was a horticulturist. Roethke's poetry is rich in nature imagery, evoking growth and also the inevitability of decomposition and decay. His first volume of poetry was *Open House* (1941). Other works include *The Lost Son* (1948), *I Am! Says the Lamb* (1961) and the posthumous volumes, *The Far Field* (1964) and *Selected Poems* (1969), an exuberantly sensual collection compiled by his wife, Beatrice. Roethke's work has been likened to that of Blake and was an influence on Sylvia PLATH.

Roe v. Wade (1973). U.S. Supreme Court decision legalizing ABORTION in most cases. The case proved extremely controversial because opponents of abortion contended that the Court had, in effect, condoned the murder of the unborn. Although abortion had at one time been a medical decision for doctors, by the 1970s many states had outlawed the practice. The Court held that women have a constitutional right to an abortion; according to the Court's ruling, this right springs from the right to privacy implicit in the Fifth and Fourteenth Amendments. The Court reaffirmed the view that abortion is a medical procedure to be decided upon by a physician and patient. The Court voted 7–2; the majority opinion was written by Justice Harry BLACKMUN. The Court did allow states to regulate abortion during the later stages of pregnancy, however. Abortion continued to be an extremely sensitive political issue through the 1970s and 1980s and into the 1990s, with activists polarized on both sides. (See also WEBSTER V. REPRODUCTIVE SERVICES.)

Rogers, Carl R(ansom) (1902–1987). American psychologist. An extremely influential figure in the field, he developed the client-centered approach to psychotherapy. Unlike the standard psychoanalytic approach, this allowed the patient a major say in determining the course of treatment. Rogers was also a founder of **humanistic psychology** and was instrumental in the encounter group movement that emerged in the 1960s. His book *On Becoming a Person* (1961) became a bible for the human potential movement.

Rogers, Ginger [Virginia Katherine McMath] (1911–). Actress, comedienne and dancer. Rogers is best remembered for her dancing in 1930s musicals with Fred ASTAIRE. After a brief career as a band singer and some experience on Broadway, Rogers went to HOLLYWOOD. She appeared in such pictures as *Flying Down to Rio* (1933), *Top Hat* (1935) and *Bachelor Mother* (1939). She won an ACADEMY AWARD as best actress in 1940 for *Kitty Foyle*.

For further reading:

Croce, Arlene, *The Fred Astaire and Ginger Rogers Book*. New York: Dutton, 1987.

Rogers, Roy [Leonard Slye] (1911–). American singing cowboy and actor. Known as the "King of the Cowboys," Rogers began his career with the Pioneer Trio in Grade-B Western movies. His breakthrough role came in 1938 in *Under Western Skies*, and he went on to star, with his horse Trigger, in more than 100 such films. In 1947 he married singer **Dale Evans.** Rogers and Trigger joined Evans and her horse Buttermilk to appear in such films as *Hollywood Canteen* (1944); *Son of Paleface* (1952) was Roy and Trigger's last movie. Roy and Dale starred in a hit 1950s television series whose theme song was "Happy Trails to You." In more recent years, the couple has become involved in charity and religious work.

Rogers, Will(iam Penn Adair) (1879–1935). American humorist. Born in Oolagah, then Indian Territory, now Oklahoma, he grew up on his family's prosperous ranch, worked as a cowboy and began his career as a rodeo entertainer. He was a rider and trick roper in Wild West shows around the world before returning to the U.S. in 1880. Settling in New York City, he began to work in VAUDEVILLE, supplementing his skills at the lariat with down-home banter. From this beginning grew the homespun humor that made Rogers one of America's most beloved entertainers. After working at the ZIEGFELD FOLLIES (1915–17), he moved on to HOLLYWOOD, where he made his first film in 1918. The following year he began a syndicated newspaper column that featured disarmingly simple and insightful analyses of current events. The "cowboy philosopher" continued to dispense his witty brand of rural wisdom in movies, radio shows and books until he and Wiley POST were killed in an airplane crash near Point Barrow, Alaska.

Rohde, Gilbert (1894–1944). Pioneering American industrial designer whose career in the 1930s was an important factor in introducing MODERNISM to the U.S. Rohde became familiar with cabinetmaking in his father's shop. He worked as a furniture illustrator for several New York stores before making a trip in 1927 to Paris, where he became familiar with the Moderne styles of the 1920s. In 1929 he opened his own design office, working on interiors and producing modern furniture designs at a time when modernism was largely unknown in America. In 1930 he established a relationship with Herman Miller, Inc., that was central to both his career and that furniture company's growth. His designs were clearly modern, although they incorporated decorative elements that now seem to imply ART DECO directions, with much use of exotic wood veneers, glass, mirrors and chrome details. He developed the concepts of modular and sectional furniture and applied the modular idea to office furniture in his Executive Office Group (EOG). Rohde developed various exhibit designs for the NEW YORK WORLD'S FAIR OF 1939. He was briefly the director of the short-lived Design Laboratory School, a project sponsored by the WPA from 1935 until 1938. He was also head of the industrial design program at the New York University School of Architecture from 1939 until 1943.

Rohlfs, Christian (1849–1938). German painter. Living at Weimar until 1900, he painted in an Impressionist manner and taught for 30 years at the Weimar Art School. Moving to Hagan, he was an instructor at the Folkwang School, where he was influenced by a 1902 exhibition of Van Gogh's works as well as by his friendship with the German Expressionist Emil NOLDE. His style altered to a gentle version of EXPRESSIONISM, and he gradually abandoned oil painting in favor of tempera, watercolor and woodcuts. He is best known for his late paintings, delicately beautiful floral works that he produced while living in Switzerland from 1927 until his death.

Rohmer, Eric (1920–). French film director and critic. Rohmer is a much admired director of subtle, delicate films on questions of everyday morality and the nuances of sexual attraction. He began his career as a writer for CAHIERS DU CINEMA, of which he became the editor after the death of Andre Bazin in 1958. Rohmer was ousted as editor in 1963, as *Cahiers* struggled to balance aesthetics and politics. His feature debut as a director came with *The Sign of the Lion* (1959), an evocation of Paris in August. But his major films—under the group title *Six Moral Tales*—are *La Boulangere de Monceau* (1963), *La Carriere de Suzanne* (1963), *La Collectioneuse* (1966), *My Night At Maud's* (1968), *Claire's Knee* (1970) and *Love in the Afternoon* (1972). In each of these films Rohmer focuses on the telling discrepancies between words and deeds while refraining from making definitive moral judgments on his characters. His many subsequent films have been in a similar vein.

Rohmer, Sax [pen name of Arthur Henry Sarsfield Ward] (1883–1959). British author. Although also a playwright and songwriter under his own name, Rohmer is best known as the author of the popular series of adventure books featuring the clever criminal Fu Manchu. These include *The Insidious Dr. Fu Manchu* (1913), *The Mask of Fu Manchu* (1932) and *Emperor Fu Manchu* (1959). In addition to the more than 30 Fu Manchu books, Rohmer also wrote two other detective series featuring Gaston Max and Paul Harley.

Roh Tae Woo (1932–). Elected president of the Republic of KOREA in 1987 and head of the Democratic Justice Party, Roh was educated at the Korean Military Academy and the U.S. Special Warfare School. He fought in the KOREAN WAR and rose in the ranks of the Korean army, becoming commanding general of the 9th Special forces Brigade in 1974, commander of the Capital Security Command in 1979 and commander of the Defense Security Command in 1980. He was made a four-star general in 1981 and retired from the army in July of the same year. In 1981 he entered the cabinet as minister of state for national security and foreign affairs. In 1982 he was appointed minister of sports and minister of home affairs. He has held a number of other positions outside the government, including the presidencies of the Seoul Olympic Organizing Committee, the Korean Amateur Sports Association and the Korean Olympic Committee.

Rokossovsky, Konstantin Konstantinovich (1896–1968). Marshal of the Soviet Union. Of Polish origin, Rokossovsky joined the Red Army in 1919 and became a member of the Bolshevik Party. During WORLD WAR II he was an outstanding Soviet commander. He acted with great heroism at the battles of Moscow (1941–42), STALINGRAD (1942–43), Kursk (1943) and in Belorussia and at the battle for Berlin (1944–45). In 1944 he became a marshal and commanded the Soviet forces in Poland. In 1949 he was transferred to the Polish army. He became minister of defense and a member of the Politburo of the Polish Communist Party. In 1956 he was dismissed by Wladyslaw GOMULKA and was appointed a deputy minister of defense of the U.S.S.R.

Rolland, Romain (1866–1944). French novelist and playwright. Rolland is best remembered as a practitioner of the *Roman Fleuve*, exemplified by his major work, the 10–volume *Jean Cristophe*, which was published between 1905 and 1912 and which follows the family of a musical genius based loosely on Beethoven. Rolland was also interested in music and the theater; his first literary works were play cycles, such as the interrelated *Saint Louis* (1897), *Aert* (1898) and *Le Triomphe de la raison* (*The Triumph of Reason*, 1899). Largely because of *Jean Cristophe*, Rolland was awarded the NOBEL PRIZE for literature in 1915, in spite of some controversy due to his pacifistic position regarding WORLD WAR I, which he expressed in the essay collection, *Au-dessus de la melee* (*Above the Battle*, 1915). Other works include *Michelangelo* (1915), *I Will Not Rest* (1935) and *The Journey Within* (1947).

Rolling Stones. British ROCK AND ROLL band, founded in 1963. The Rolling Stones, who are often billed on their concert tours as "The Greatest Rock and Roll Band in the World," have many fans and critics who support that claim. Since their first singles hit, "It's All Over Now" (1964), the Stones have enjoyed phenomenal popularity. The band lineup—which remained remarkably stable through the early 1990s—originally included Mick JAGGER, lead vocalist; Brian Jones, guitar; Keith Richard, guitar and vocals; Ian Stewart, piano; Charlie Watt, drums; and Bill Wyman, bass. In 1969, after the accidental death of Jones, Mick Taylor replaced him on guitar. Taylor was subsequently replaced by Ron Wood in 1974. Jagger and Richard, who have written all of the band's original material since 1965, have both attained the status of international celebrity. Among the many Rolling Stones classic hits are "(I Can't Get No) Satisfaction" (1965), "Ruby Tuesday" (1967), "Let's Spend the Night Together" (1967), "Jumping Jack Flash" (1968), "Honky Tonk Women" (1969), "Brown Sugar" (1971), "It's Only Rock and Roll" (1974) and "Start Me Up" (1981).

Rolvaag, Ole Edvart (1876–1931). Norwegian-born educator and author. Rolvaag is best remembered for *Giants in the Earth* (1927), an epic of early life on the South Dakota prairies. He was educated at St. Olaf College in Northfield, Minnesota, where he later returned to serve as professor and head of the department of Norwegian language and literature. He resigned in August 1931 to write full-time but died only a few months later.

Romagne-Sous-Montfaucon. Village in northeastern France, about 20 miles northwest of Verdun. More than 14,200 soldiers killed in WORLD WAR I are interred at U.S. military cemetery here—the largest U.S. military cemetery in France.

Romaine, Paul [born Burton Bleamer] (1905–1986). American book dealer. He was a close friend of Ernest HEMINGWAY, whom he met in PARIS in the mid-1920s while both were part of the expatriate American scene there. Targeted for prosecution in 1963 as a seller of the bawdy 18th-century novel *Fanny Hill*, he became the central figure in one of the last major obscenity trials in the U.S. His conviction was later overturned by the Illinois Supreme Court.

Romains, Jules [pen name of Louis Farigoule] (1885–1972). French novelist, dramatist and poet. Romains worked on an epic scale and spent 15 years (1931–46) writing his masterpiece, *Men of Good Will*. One of the longest and most intricate of modern novels, it contained 3 million words and some 400 characters. It spanned 25 years of French history in minute detail. Romains also founded a philosophy called **unanism,** which defined man in the context of his familiar, religious and social groups. He was elected to the French Academy in 1946.

Romanenko, Yuri (1944–). Soviet cosmonaut; one-half of the Romanenko/Grechko Soyuz 26 (December 10, 1977) mission to the Soviet space station SALYUT. He was also part of the eight-day SOYUZ 38 (September 18, 1980) mission to that station and a long-duration mission to MIR in 1987. During their 1977–78 stay aboard Salyut 6, Romanenko and Grechko gained international fame by staying in space for a then record-breaking 96 days. The mission has sometimes been referred to as "the flight of the classics," since "Grechko" and "Romanenko" are Ukrainian for "Greek" and "Roman." In 1987, Romanenko set yet another record, 326 days aboard the Mir space station, the previous record had been 237 days, set by Leonid Kizim, Vladimir Solovyov and Oleg Atkov aboard Salyut 7 in 1984. During Romanenko's marathon he went outside the station for several EVAs with fellow cosmonaut Alexander Laveikin, once to clear the docking area for a 27–ton astrophysical module, and a second time to erect a third solar panel for the space station.

Romania. The nation of Romania covers an area of 91,675 square miles in southeastern Europe; its name and its Latin-derived language are a mark of its ancient status as a part of the Roman empire. In 1877 Romanians declared full independence from the Ottoman Turks and in 1881 Karl of Hohenzollern-Sigmaringen was crowned King Carol I. Neutral at the outset of WORLD WAR I, Romania fought with the Allies from 1916 and gained Transylvania (from Hungary), Bessarabia (from Russia) and southern Dobrudja (from Bulgaria) under terms of the postwar peace settlement (1920). The Iron Guard, Romania's homegrown fascist movement, dominated a corrupt political establishment in the 1930s. Neutral once again, at the beginning of WORLD WAR II, Romania was forced to restore almost all of its territorial gains to the Soviet Union, Bulgaria and Hungary. King CAROL II abdicated in 1940, and Romania swiftly became an AXIS ally. In August 1944 King Michael declared war on Germany; a postwar peace treaty in 1947 restored all of Transylvania to Rumania. Also in 1947, King Michael (1940–47) was forced to abdicate by a radical left-wing government, and the People's Republic was formed. Internal power struggles led to political purges (1948–50) and the establishment of a communist government that nationalized industry and collectivized agriculture. Romania joined the WARSAW PACT, yet maintained its independence from the Soviet Union. Nicolae CEAUSESCU, who became president in 1967, amassed a huge foreign debt during the 1970s, which led to privation and protests by 1987, when he tried to reduce the debt. His policy of

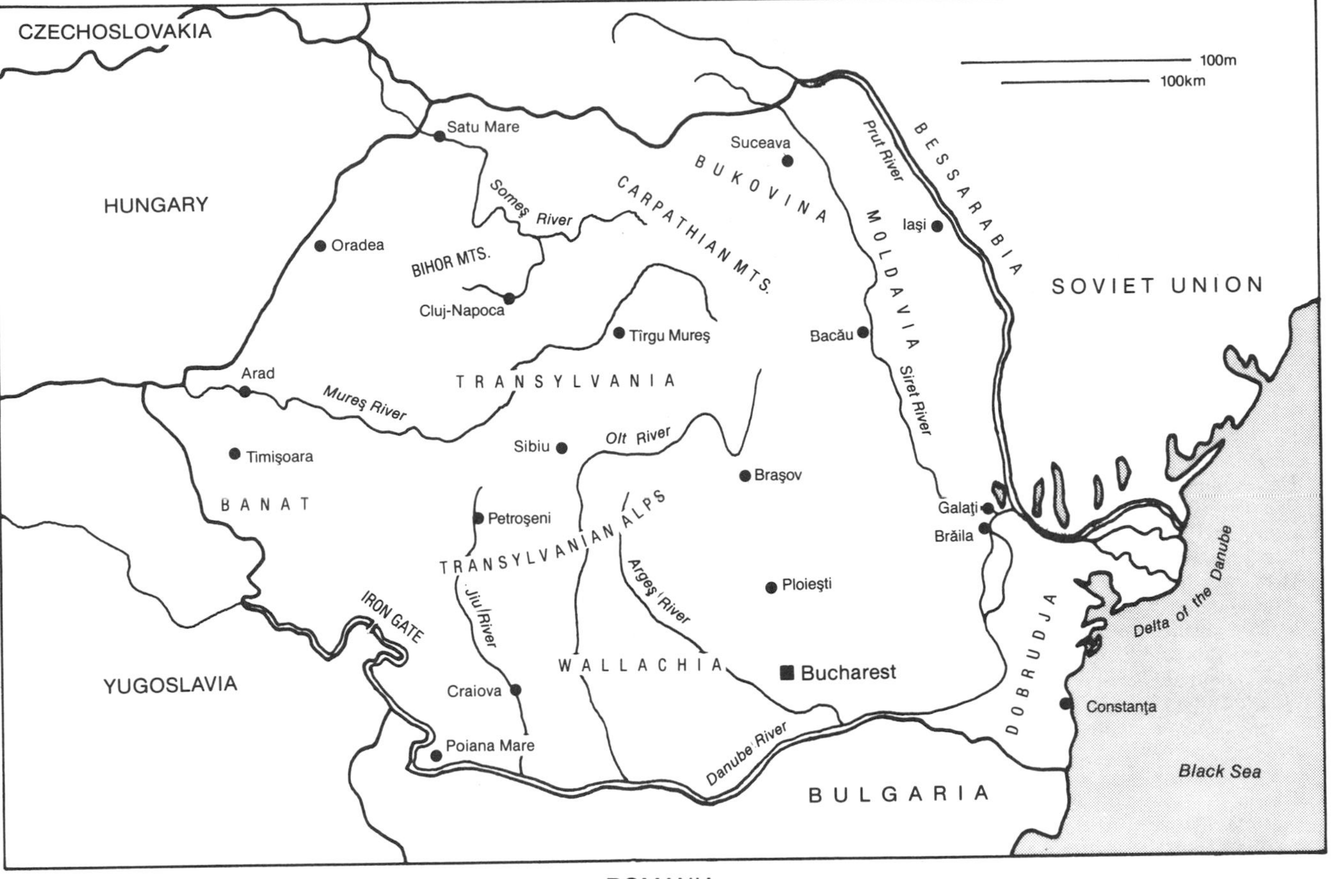

ROMANIA

ROMANIA

1919	Gains Transylvania, Bessarabia and southern Dobrudja in post-World War I peace settlement, doubling size of country.
1940-45	During World War II Romania fights first on the German side, then on the side of the Allies.
1947	Democratic parties are purged; King Michael forced to abdicate; Communist People's Republic is declared.
1958	Withdrawal of Soviet troops negotiated.
1967	Nicolae Ceausescu assumes presidency during which he outlaws birth control to increase population; borrows heavily from West then imposes harsh austerity measures on population to reduce foreign debt.
1988	Ceausescu announces systemization policy under which 7,000 villages will be demolished and inhabitants resettled in agro-industrial centers.
1989	Anti-government demonstrations begin in city of Timisoara and spread to Bucharest despite authorities' armed efforts to suppress them; Defense Minister Vasile Milea commits suicide rather than obey Ceausescu order to open fire on demonstrators; Ceausescu and his wife Elena try to flee but are captured and executed after a military tribunal finds them guilty of genocide, corruption and destruction of the economy.
1990	Provisional government President Ion Iliescu brutally suppresses student-led anti-government rioting when, answering Iliescu's nationally broadcast call, 10,000 miners from Jiu Valley region pour into Bucharest, armed with axe handles and iron bars, occupy the city, beat at random anyone suspected of anti-government proclivities and wreck the offices of the opposition and only independent, mass-circulation newspaper.

systemization, which involved the destruction of thousands of rural villages and resettlement of the population in agro-industrial centers, brought massive demonstrations in 1989. Ceausescu attempted to flee but was captured, found guilty of genocide and corruption by a military tribunal, and executed on December 25, 1989. A new government has promised reforms and moved toward free elections. (See also Gheorghe GHEORGHIU-DEJ.)

Romanov, Panteleymon Sergeyevich (1884–1938). Russian author. While his short sketches give a picture of life during the RUSSIAN CIVIL WAR and the period of the NEW ECONOMIC POLICY, many characters of his novels are recognizable descendants of the 19th-century "superfluous man." His most important novel, *The New Table of Commandments* (1928), however, deals with a Soviet marriage. In 1927 Romanov met with official disapproval, and was forbidden to publish, although the ban was later lifted.

Romberg, Sigmund (1887–1951). Hungarian-born composer best known for his American operettas. Despite an engineering background in his native Hungary, Romberg found in America more opportunities for composing. From 1914 to 1917 in New York he wrote many knockabout songs for musical revues of the Shubert brothers. However, it was with *Maytime* (1917) and *Blossom Time* (1921) that he discovered his true metier, operetta. Romberg described the form, which had its genesis in the late-19th century work of Franz Lehar and Gilbert and Sullivan, as "light comedy opera" that "leaned toward the operatic rather than the jazz type." He believed that audiences wanted "a better class of music" than they found in popular musicals. *The Student Prince* (1924), *The Desert Song* (1926) and *New Moon* (1928) had rich musical scores that demanded operatically trained voices. Romberg's rousing choral numbers ("Drinking Song," "The Riff Song" and "Stout-Hearted Men"), lyrical serenades ("Softly, As in a Morning Sunrise") and magnificent duets ("One Alone") brought a classical prestige to the Broadway stage. At least two love songs, "One Flower Grows Alone in Your Garden" (from *The Desert Song*) and "Overhead the Moon Is Beaming" (from *The Student Prince*) achieve a searing intensity quite distinct from anything currently on the American stage. However, this kind of work was, in the words of a critic, "so many brave St. Georges against the dragonfly, Jazz." Even if operettas would soon be dismissed as old-fashioned, Romberg successfully adapted to a more contemporary kind of musical, *Up in Central Park* (1945), and had his own radio show in the 1940s, "An Evening with Romberg."

For further reading:

Bordman, Gerald, *American Operetta.* New York: Oxford University Press, 1981.

Rome, Treaty of. Treaty signed on March 25, 1957, by Belgium, France, Italy, Luxembourg, the Netherlands and West Germany that established the EUROPEAN ECONOMIC COMMUNITY (EEC, also known as the Common Market) and the European Atomic Energy Community (EURATOM). The EEC aimed at forming a united European economy by eliminating internal tariffs, setting uniform external tariffs and establishing free movement of people, capital and goods within the member states. EURATOM aimed at integrating the nuclear power efforts of the member countries and creating a commonality of practices and markets in nuclear materials.

Romero, Oscar (1917–1980). Roman Catholic archbishop in EL SALVADOR. Following the seizure of power by a military junta in 1979, the highly respected Romero had often spoken out on behalf of human rights and the poor and against extremists of both the Right and the Left. Above all, he had advocated an end to political violence in the strife-torn nation. On March 24, 1980, Romero was killed by a single bullet while saying Mass in a small chapel in San Salvador. No gunman was identified, but the widespread assumption was that the archbishop had been killed because of his continuing criticism of El Salvador's government. Rioting followed the assassination, in which more than 30 people were killed and another 400 were injured.

Rommel, Erwin (1891–1944). German field marshal. Rommel joined the army in 1910, was commissioned an officer in 1912 and

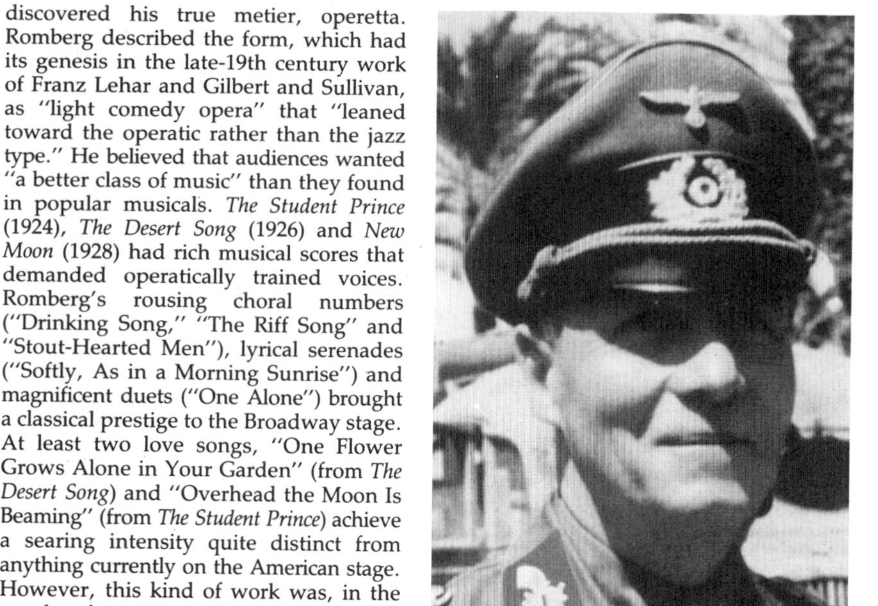

German Field Marshal Erwin Rommel earned the nickname "The Desert Fox" for his leadership of the German Afrika Korps during World War II.

served with distinction during WORLD WAR I. He attracted Adolf HITLER's attention between the wars and was made a general in 1939. After commanding an armored division in the attack on France (1940), he was assigned to North Africa, becoming (1941) leader of Germany's crack Afrika Korps. A skilled and intuitive strategist, he scored a string of successes that earned him a promotion to field marshal and the name "the desert fox." Pushing into Egypt, he was defeated in November, 1942 at the decisive battle of EL ALAMEIN. In 1943 Rommel was appointed a commander in northern France, where he was serving at the time of the Allied invasion at NORMANDY in June 1944. He was severely wounded in a strafing attack the following month. Known to be disillusioned with Hitler's leadership, Rommel was implicated in the plot to overthrow the Fuhrer. He was forced to commit suicide by taking poison on October 14, 1944.

Romulo, Carlos P(ena) (1899–1985). Filipino diplomat. One of the signatories of the UNITED NATIONS charter, Romulo was the PHILIPPINES chief delegate to the UN from 1945 to 1954. As a UN delegate, he was one of the leading champions of the interests of newly independent third world countries. In 1949, he became the first Asian president of the General Assembly. He was a leader at the BANDUNG CONFERENCE of Asian and African nations in 1955. Twice the Philippines' foreign minister, he served in that capacity from 1950 to 1952 and from 1968 to 1984.

Ronchamp. Location of, and therefore the usual informal name for, one of LE CORBUSIER's most important works, generally regarded as a key masterpiece of modern architecture—the chapel of Notre Dame du Haut near Belfort in the French Vosges. Built in 1950–55 to replace a structure destroyed during World War II, it marks the architect's abandonment of the strictly geometric forms of his earlier INTERNATIONAL STYLE work in favor of a strongly sculptural, organic, even expressionistic direction. It is a concrete structure, with curving walls and a curved, overhanging, hollow concrete roof, suggesting the shape of an airplane wing or, some say, the form of a traditional nun's hat. The internal space is small but dramatically lit by stained glass windows of Le Corbusier's own design. There is an outdoor chancel for open-air services held for pilgrimage congregations. The site also includes a small hostel to accommodate visitors in simple and austere style.

R. 101 disaster. Deadly crash of the British airship R. 101 on a hillside near Beauvais, France, on its maiden flight on October 5, 1931. Filled with inflammable hydrogen gas, the 777–foot-long R. 101 went up in flames after its crash, killing 48 passengers, including Air Minister Lord Thomson, and crew. This disaster marked the end of British interest in dirigibles, either for military or commercial purposes. The Germans, however, actively continued their ZEPPELIN program until the crash of the ill-fated HINDENBURG in 1937.

Ronne, Finn (1899–1980). Norwegian-born polar explorer. Finn accompanied Admiral Richard Evelyn BYRD on Byrd's second Antarctic expedition in 1923. Altogether he took part in 14 major U.S. expeditions, including nine trips to ANTARCTICA. During his career he traveled some 3,600 miles by skis and dog sled, more than anyone else in history, to chart the SOUTH POLE.

Ronstadt, Linda Marie (1946–). American singer. Her first hit came in 1967 with the Stone Poneys, singing "Different Drum." Her stylistic range is remarkable, as she has recorded successful albums in such genres as pop-rock, country and big band. Her first solo hit came in 1970 with "Long Long Time." Her most successful year on the rock charts was 1974, with top-five singles "You're No Good" and "When Will I Be Loved." In the 1980s she turned to the works of George GERSHWIN and Irving BERLIN in BIG BAND arrangements by Nelson RIDDLE on the albums *What's New* and *Lush Life*. In 1988, she celebrated her Mexican roots with the Spanish-language album *Canciones de Mi Padre*.

Rontgen, Wilhelm Conrad (1845–1923). German physicist. After an early education in the Netherlands, then study at the Federal Institute of Technology, Zurich, Rontgen received his doctorate in 1869. He held various university posts, including professor of physics at Wurzburg (1888) and professor of physics at Munich (1900). Rontgen researched into many branches of physics, including elasticity, the specific heat of gases, capillarity, piezoelectricity and polarized light. He is chiefly remembered for his discovery of X RAYS, at Wurzburg on November 8, 1895. The discovery immediately created tremendous interest. It did not solve the contemporary wave-particle controversy on the nature of radiation, but it stimulated further investigations that led, among other things, to the discovery of radioactivity. It also provided a valuable tool for research into crystal structures and atomic structure, and X rays were soon applied to medical diagnosis. Unfortunately, it was very much later before their danger to health became understood; both Rontgen and his technician suffered from X-ray poisoning. Although Rontgen was subjected to some bitter attacks and there were attempts to belittle his achievements, his discovery of X rays earned him several honors, including the first NOBEL PRIZE for physics (1901).

Rooney, Mickey [Joe Yule] (1922–). American actor. Rooney is best known for his role as Andy Hardy in the film series about the Hardy family (1937–47) and for the film musicals *Babes in Arms* (1939) and *Strike Up the Band* (1940) in which he starred with Judy GARLAND. He scored his first feature film triumph as Puck in the 1935 film of *A Midsummer Night's Dream.* He made the difficult transition from child to adult roles, earning particular acclaim for his strong character roles in several television specials and for his comic skill in the revue-like musical *Sugar Babies* (all in the 1980s). He won a special ACADEMY AWARD for *Boys' Town* in 1938.

For further reading:

Marx, Arthur, *The Nine Lives of Mickey Rooney*. New York: Berkeley Publishing, 1988.

Roosevelt, Eleanor (1884–1962). American humanitarian and first lady. Born in New York City, she was a niece of Theodore ROOSEVELT and married her distant cousin Franklin D. ROOSEVELT in 1905. Although naturally shy, she became active in politics in 1921 when her husband was stricken with polio. As the wife of the governor of New York and, later, of the president, she tranformed the role of first lady into a position of visibility and power and became one of the most active

Eleanor Roosevelt, wife of President Franklin D. Roosevelt, was a noted humanitarian and diplomat in her own right.

and admired women in the U.S. Involving herself in a number of causes, she supported CIVIL RIGHTS for minorities, women's rights, housing and employment reform, international understanding and other causes through speeches, a radio program and a daily newspaper column. During WORLD WAR II she was assistant director of the Office of Civilian Defense (1941–42) and traveled throughout the world to further the Allied cause.

After her husband's death in 1945, she continued her work as a delegate to the UNITED NATIONS (1945–52, 1961–62), as a drafter of the UN Declaration of Human Rights and as chairman of the UN Commission on Human Rights (1947–51). Among her autobiographical books are *This Is My Story* (1937), *On My Own* (1958) and *The Autobiography of Eleanor Roosevelt* (1961).

For further reading:

Lash, Joseph P., *Eleanor: The Years Alone*. Norton, 1972.

Hareven, Tamara, *Eleanor Roosevelt: An American Conscience*. Da Capo, 1975.

Roosevelt, Franklin Delano (1882–1945). 32nd President of the U.S. (1933–45), he served during an era of crisis, dealing with the complex problems of the GREAT DEPRESSION and leading the nation during WORLD WAR II. Born at Hyde Park, New York, of an old and distinguished American family, he was educated at Harvard and at Columbia Law School. A lifelong Democrat, he entered politics in 1910 as a New York state senator. In 1912 he fought vigorously against Tammany Hall-supported candidates and for the nomination of Woodrow WILSON, and was awarded the post of assistant secretary of the navy, serving from 1913 to 1920. Roosevelt was the vice-presidental candidate on the unsuccessful 1920 ticket of James COX. The following year he was stricken with poliomyelitis. His career apparently over, Roosevelt refused to give up, pursuing a course of rigorous physical therapy and eventually walking with the assistance of leg braces. He supported New York Govenor Alfred E. SMITH for the presidency in 1924 and 1928. When Smith secured the nomination in 1928, he urged Roosevelt to run for the governor's office. Smith lost, but Roosevelt was victorious. During his four years in Albany, he initiated a number of social reforms that were to serve as a prelude to his legislative program in the White House and assembled the BRAIN TRUST advisors who would counsel him during his presidency. Roosevelt was nominated by the Democrats in 1932 and easily defeated President Herbert HOOVER. He was inaugurated in the midst of a national banking crisis, with some 13 million Americans unemployed.

In his address, he told his audience that "the only thing we have to fear is fear itself," and he immediately began a campaign to deal with the GREAT DEPRESSION during the famous HUNDRED DAYS (March-June 1933), inaugurating programs that entailed the expenditure of vast public funds in the pursuit of eco-

Franklin Delano Roosevelt, 32nd president of the United States (1933–1945), led the nation through some of the darkest days of the 20th century.

nomic recovery. Roosevelt's NEW DEAL measures included banking regulation, the abandonment of the gold standard, bank deposit insurance, the passage of the SOCIAL SECURITY Act and the Wagner Labor Relations Act and the creation of a number of powerful federal agencies whose mandate was to provide relief to suffering Americans and to revivify the American economy, with emphasis on restructuring agricultural, business and labor practices. These agencies included the Federal Emergency Relief Administration, Civil Works Administration, PUBLIC WORKS ADMINISTRATION, WORKS PROGRESS ADMINISTRATION, NATIONAL RECOVERY ADMINISTRATION, AGRICULTURAL ADJUSTMENT ADMINISTRATION, SECURITIES AND EXCHANGE COMMISSION, Home Owners Loans Corporation, CIVILIAN CONSERVATION CORPS and TENNESSEE VALLEY AUTHORITY. He also initiated the "fireside chats," radio broadcasts in which he informed the public of his intentions and actions. Roosevelt's massive efforts toward curing the ills of the depression resulted in his overwhelming victory in the 1936 election.

However, opposition to New Deal measures, particularly in the business community, hardened during his second term. When the Supreme Court invalidated a number of New Deal measures, Roosevelt attempted to restructure the Court (1937), but failed. Nonetheless, New Deal programs did much to ameliorate the desperate economic and social situation, and in 1937 Roosevelt secured the passage of new labor legislation that ensured a 40-hour week and minimum wages for many industries. Concentrating on domestic recovery, Roosevelt established a foreign policy that promoted a "good neighbor policy" toward Latin America. His most notable action was probably the recognition of the U.S.S.R. in 1933. He attempted to maintain American neutrality, but by 1938 he was speaking out strongly against the aggression of Germany and Japan. When World War II broke out in Europe, Roosevelt speeded up a program for national armament, seeking to make the U.S. an "arsenal of democracy." Winning an unprecedented third term in 1940, he gradually moved the country toward war. In 1941 LEND-LEASE was initiated and the ATLANTIC CHARTER was signed. After the Japanese attack on PEARL HARBOR (December 7, 1941), the U.S. was plunged into the war. Along with Prime Minister Winston CHURCHILL, Roosevelt did much to shape Allied military strategy. With little debate over war policy, Roosevelt was elected to a fourth term in 1944, with Harry S TRUMAN as vice president. As the tide of battle turned in favor of the Allies, Roosevelt participated in a number of international conferences with Churchill, STALIN, CHIANG KAI-SHEK and others, meetings that did much to plan the postwar world. After the YALTA CONFERENCE (February 1945), an exhausted Roosevelt traveled to Warm Springs, Georgia, where he died suddenly on April 12. His presidency was one of the most exceptional in the history of the U.S.

For further reading:

Alsop, Joseph, *Franklin Delano Roosevelt: A Centenary Remembrance 1882–1945*. New York: Viking, 1982.

Miller, Nathan, *FDR: An Intimate History*. Garden City, N.Y.: Doubleday, 1983.

Schlesinger, Arthur M., Jr., *The Age of Roosevelt*, 3 vols. Boston: Houghton Mifflin, 1957–1960.

Roosevelt, Theodore (1858–1919). Twenty-sixth president of the U.S. (1901–09). A dominant figure in American political life from the turn of the century to the beginning of WORLD WAR I, he was born in New York City of a wealthy and distinguished New York family. Frail in health, he pursued physical fitness with zeal while cultivating a sharp intellect. He attended Harvard University, graduating in 1880. An independent and progressive Republican, he entered politics as a member of the New York State Assembly (1882). The deaths of his mother and his wife in 1884 caused him to retire to a Dakota Territory ranch for two years. Returning to New York City in 1886, he ran unsuccessfully for mayor and became an important figure in the state's Republican Party. At the same time he became known for his writings, including biographies and the historical *Winning of the West* (1889–96). He served as a progressive-minded member of the Civil Service Commission (1889–95) before becoming head of the New York City police board (1895–97) and assistant secretary of the Navy (1897–98). At the outbreak of the Spanish-American War (1898), he organized a volunteer cavalry division known as the Rough Riders and won fame for his service in Cuba. Returning to the U.S. as a heroic colonel, he was nominated for governor and won a closely contested race. As governor (1899–1900) he was entirely too progressive to suit Republican

Theodore Roosevelt, 26th president of the United States (1901–1909).

boss Thomas Collier Platt, who, in an attempt to rid the state of Roosevelt, engineered a scheme to have him nominated for vice president on the Republican ticket for 1900. Elected, he was spared vice presidential obscurity with the assassination of President MCKINLEY in 1901.

A vivid character, a bluff and powerful speaker, a robust outdoorsman and a spokesman for the ordinary citizen, "T.R." soon became an immensely popular leader. A progressive activist, he took on the abusive power of the large corporations in his "trust-busting" efforts by initiating about 40 lawsuits against the largest of the nation's business monopolies. An ardent conservationist, he also supported land reclamation, irrigation and the expansion of forest reserves. In foreign policy Roosevelt was aggressive and vigorous, particularly in relation to Latin America. He intervened in a Panamanian civil war (1903) and was active in promoting the building of the PANAMA CANAL the following year. His popularity resulted in a landslide victory in the 1904 elections. Highlights of his second term were his mediation of the RUSSO-JAPANESE WAR in 1905, for which he won the 1906 NOBEL PRIZE for peace, and the passage of the Pure Food and Drug Act of 1906. His hand-picked successor, William Howard TAFT, became president in 1909, and Roosevelt retired. However, disputes with the new president drew him back into politics. He was unsuccessful in seeking the 1912 Republican presidential nomination, and subsequently formed a progressive third party (popularly known as the Bull Moose party). When Roosevelt split the Republican vote, Woodrow WILSON was elected. Roosevelt resumed his Republicanism and remained an important force in the party and the nation until his death.

Root, Elihu (1845–1937). American statesman. Born in Clinton, New York, Root practiced law in New York City and served as U.S. attorney for the southern district of New York from 1883 to 1885. A Republican, he was secretary of war from 1899 to 1904 under Presidents William MCKINLEY and Theodore ROOSEVELT, modernizing the Army and, in 1901, founding the Army War College. As Roosevelt's secretary of state (1905–09), he was instrumental in securing improved relations with Latin America and an agreement (1908) with Japan and in negotiating arbitration treaties with various European countries. Root, who declined to run for office, was appointed senator from New York in 1909 and served until 1915. He participated in the Hague Tribunal and played a vital role in negotiating the North Atlantic Coast Fisheries Arbitration of 1910. In 1912 Root was awarded the NOBEL PRIZE for peace in recognition of his efforts to promote world peace. He strongly supported American participation in the LEAGUE OF NATIONS and was a drafter of the constitution for the World Court.

Roots. The most watched dramatic show in television history. An estimated 100 million viewers (nearly half the population of America) saw the first telecast of the eight episodes in January 1977. Alex HALEY's massive 850–page novel traced his own roots back to 1750 in Gambia, West Africa, with the birth of "Kunta Kinte." Subsequent generations of the family were slaves in America from the Revolution through the Civil War. The story ended as Tom, the great-grandson of Kunta, began a new life in Tennessee. This "miniseries" format "allowed television to achieve the thematic power and narrative sweep ordinarily reserved for film." While there were some isolated incidents of racial unrest following some of the episodes, a survey of the NAACP claimed, in general, that the series stimulated black-history awareness and education in schools and colleges. The series garnered an unprecedented 37 Emmy nominations and received 9 Emmys. Alex Haley received a National Book Award and a special PULITZER PRIZE.

For further reading:

The Complete Directory to Prime Time Network TV Shows. New York: Ballantine Books, 1988.

Rorem, C. Rufus (1894–1988). U.S. economist; his early advocacy of prepaid health care and group medical practice led to the founding of Blue Cross and Blue Shield. Rorem's radical proposals began to be put into practice when he became head of the American Hospital Association in 1937. He was the father of composer Ned Rorem.

Rorschach test. One of the best known of all psychological tests, devised by German psychologist Hermann Rorschach. Consisting of a series of abstract inkblot shapes, as well as a separate series of chromatic patterns, it is designed to test the perceptual and analytic tendencies of the test subject. It is administered via the free response of the subject as to what he or she "sees" in the shapes and patterns displayed. Rorschach set forth the research findings on which his test is based in *Psychodiagnostics: A Diagnostics Test Based on Perception* (1942). It is frequently used to this day as a measure of the subconscious contents of the psyche.

Rose, Billy [William Samuel Rosenberg] (1899–1966). American producer and lyricist. A showman who produced revues, musicals, Aquacades and expositions, Rose began his career as a lyricist, writing songs for such revues as the *Charlot Revue of 1926*. In 1929 he collaborated with Edward Eliscu and Vincent Youmans on the score for the show *Great Day*, writing lyrics for such songs as "More Than You Know" and "Without a Song." After producing a series of revues on Broadway, he produced the hit shows *Jumbo* (1935) and *Carmen Jones* (1943). The comedienne Fanny BRICE was his first wife.

Rose, Pete (1942–). American baseball player and manager. Pete Rose's legacy may be that of the greatest player never named to the Baseball Hall of Fame. Rookie of the year in 1963, Rose led the Cincinnati Reds' "Big Red Machine" to four National League championships and two World Series victories from 1970 to 1976. His aggressive level of play gave him the nickname "Charlie Hustle," and he was as hated in opposing ballparks as he was beloved in his own. He hit close to or over 200 hits a season 12 times and reached the .300 mark in nine consecutive seasons. An outstanding outfielder, his fielding accuracy reached record heights in 1974, with a .992 percentage. During his last season with the Reds, 1978, he had hits in 44 consecutive games, a league record. The following year he joined the Philadelphia Phillies, and the team went on to win the World Series in 1983. After a brief stint in Montreal, he rejoined the Reds as player-manager in 1984. Upon retiring as a player in 1986, Rose stood at the top of the major league all-time hit list, ahead of longtime leader Ty COBB. However, years of rumor about his gambling problems caught up with Rose, and in 1989 baseball Commissioner A. Bart GIAMATTI banned Rose from baseball for life for having bet on games, stating that Rose's actions were detrimental to the game of baseball. Rose was subsequently convicted of tax evasion and served a prison term. Although he was declared ineligible for the Baseball Hall of Fame in 1991, Rose's bat remained on display at Cooperstown.

Rosenberg, Harold (1906–1978). American art critic. Born in New York City, during the 1940s and '50s he was one of the chief admirers and theorists of ABSTRACT EXPRESSIONISM and the coiner of the phrase "action painting." The art critic for *The New Yorker* magazine and a contributor to many other periodicals, he was known for his intellectually rigorous analyses of contemporary art. Among his books are *The Tradition of the New* (1959), *The Anxious Object* (1966) and *Art on the Edge* (1975).

Rosenberg, Isaac (1890–1918). English poet and painter. Born in Bristol, he grew up in London and studied art at the city's Slade School from 1911 to 1914. Establishing some reputation as an artist, he exhibited at the Whitechapel Gallery. Enlisting in the British army in 1915, he fought in WORLD WAR I. His finest poems are considered to be his elegiac verses that describe his wartime experiences. A promising career was cut short when he was killed in battle in France. His *Collected Poems* were published posthumously in 1922.

Rosenberg Trial (1951). Sensational U.S. treason trial in which Julius and Ethel Rosenberg were sentenced to death for passing atomic secrets to the Russians. In 1949 the Soviet Union detonated its first atomic bomb, only four years after the first U.S. bomb. U.S. intelligence implicated Julius and Ethel Rosenberg, along with Martin Sobel, as having passed atomic secrets to the Russians.

Although the U.S. and the Soviet Union were still officially postwar allies, the trio were tried for treason in 1951 at the time of the KOREAN WAR and at the height of the anti-left MCCARTHY hysteria. The ensuing treason trial generated daily headlines and resulted in the Rosenbergs being sentenced to death and Sobel to 30 years in prison. The verdict was controversial; many liberals believed the pair innocent or deserving of a much lighter penalty. However, the third volume of Nikita KHRUSCHCHEV's memoirs, published posthumously in 1990, confirmed that the Rosenbergs had indeed been Soviet spies and had passed U.S. atomic secrets to the grateful Soviets.

Ross, Diana (1944–). American singer and actress. Ross began her singing career as the lead performer with a group called "The Supremes." The original Supremes were Jean Terrell, Diana Ross and Florence Ballard. By 1964 the group had received seven gold records in less than two years. It was the first group to have five consecutive records reach the top of the best-seller charts. As her fame grew the group's name changed to "Diana Ross and the Supremes." She eventually decided to do solo work and continued her successful career. Ross starred in such motion pictures as *Lady Sings the Blues* (1972), *Mahogany* (1974) and *The Wiz* (1984). She has been the recipient of a certificate from Vice President Hubert HUMPHREY for her efforts on behalf of President JOHNSON's Youth Opportunity Program, and citations from Mrs. Martin Luther King Jr. and Reverend Ralph ABERNATHY for contributions to the SOUTHERN CHRISTIAN LEADERSHIP CONFERENCE. Ross won a Grammy award as top female singer in 1972 and was named female entertainer of the year and given the Image award for best actress by the NAACP.

Ross, Harold. See THE NEW YORKER.

Ross, Sinclair (1908–). Canadian novelist. Born near Prince Albert, Saskatchewan, he was a banker until his retirement in 1968. His reputation rests on his first novel, *As for Me and My House* (1941), a bleak picture of the loneliness of life on the Canadian prairie written in diary form that has become a classic of modern Canadian literature. He has written three other novels, *The Well, Whir of Gold* and *Sawbones Memorial*, as well as the short story collections *The Lamp at Noon and Other Stories* (1968) and *The Race and Other Stories*.

Rossellini, Roberto (1906–). Italian movie director. Rossellini was the first director to draw international attention to the neorealist style of filmmaking. He received international acclaim for his film *Roma, Citta Aperta* (1945). Other important neorealist films were *Paisa* (1947) and *Germania, Anno Zero* (1947). His reputation was enhanced by such films as *Viaggio in Italia* (1952) in which he directed his wife Ingrid BERGMAN. He has also directed for the theater and television.

Ethel and Julius Rosenberg were tried and executed for treason for passing atomic secrets to the Soviet Union in 1951.

For further reading:
Brunette, Peter, *Roberto Rossellini*. New York: Oxford University Press, 1987.

Rostropovich, Mstislav (1927–). Russian cellist and conductor. Born in Baku, Azerbaijan, of a musical family, he and his family moved to Moscow in 1931, and he attended the Gnessin Institute and the Moscow Conservatory. There he studied composition under Dimitri SHOSTAKOVICH, who became a close friend and a great influence on his career. He made his professional debut at the age of 13. Winning the World Festival cello competition in Budapest (1949) and the International Competition in Prague (1950), Rostropovich quickly became one of the U.S.S.R.'s most acclaimed soloists. His first appearance outside U.S.S.R. was in Florence in 1951, and he soon began an active touring schedule that made him a worldwide reputation for his superb musicianship. His made his first appearance as a conductor in 1961, and he has maintained an active career in conducting. Rostropovich has excelled as a soloist in the entire range of classical cello works, and as a conductor he has stressed such Russian composers as PROKOFIEV and Shostakovich in his repertoire. Essentially apolitical, he incurred the displeasure of Soviet authorities when he sheltered Aleksandr SOLZHENITSYN in his country home in 1970. Under increased musical strictures, he and his wife, the noted soprano Galina VISHNEVSKAYA, and children fled the U.S.S.R. in 1974. In 1976 he was appointed music director of the National Symphony Orchestra, Washington, D.C., and in 1978 he and his wife were stripped of their Soviet citizenship. They have remained as exiles but with the thawing of the COLD WAR were able to return to the U.S.S.R. on a musical tour in 1990.

Roszak, Theodore (1907–1981). Polish-born sculptor best known for his work in welded steel, which often evoked an emotional response through its powerful, sometimes violent images. Roszak was the center of a controversy in 1960 when the eagle he designed for the U.S. embassy in London was pronounced "gaudy" and too big for its sober, subdued surroundings.

Russian conductor, cellist and exile Mstislav Rostropovich performs in front of the Berlin Wall (Nov. 11, 1989).

Rota, Nino (1911–1979). Italian composer best known for his many motion picture scores. A child prodigy in his home town of Milan, Rota composed an oratorio at the age of 11. Later he studied at the Santa Cecilia Academy in Rome and the Curtis Institute in Philadelphia. Although he wrote many orchestral and stage works in his lifetime, including four symphonies and eight operas, his movie scores secured his reputation. He has been associated with some of the world's greatest filmmakers, including Luchino VISCONTI (*Il Gattopardo/The Leopard*, 1963), Franco ZEFFIRELLI (*Romeo and Juliet*, 1968) and Francis Ford COPPOLA (the first two *Godfather* films, 1972 and 1974). His long and brilliant association with Federico FELLINI, beginning with *Lo Sceicco bianco* (*The White Sheik*, 1952) and concluding with *Prova d'Orchestra* (*Orchestra Rehearsal*, 1979), produced his most memorable scores. His buoyant, tuneful melodies provide a counterpart to the many parades, circus acts and strutting characters of the Fellini world. Like the painted face of actress Giulietta Masina in pictures like *La Strada* (*The Road*, 1954) and *Le Notti di Cabiria* (*Nights of Cabiria*, 1956), Rota's music holds up the promise of a bright, brittle gaiety; but ultimately, in the words of a Fellini character, it delivers a "very sad song."

For further reading:
Katz, Ephraim, ed., *The Film Encyclopedia*. New York: Thomas Y. Crowell, 1979.

Roth, Philip (1933–). American novelist. Roth was raised in an Orthodox Jewish household, and his religious background is reflected in his fiction, which wryly presents the angst of contemporary American life, often controversially. Roth first achieved success with *Good-bye, Columbus* (1959). *Portnoy's Complaint* (1969), perhaps his most notorious book, revealed a man's discussions with his psychiatrist. Roth has also written a series of novels following the life of imaginary novelist Nathan Zuckerman, including *My Life as a Man* (1974), *The Anatomy Lesson* (1983) and *Deception* (1990).

Rothko, Mark (1903–1970). American painter. Born in Dvinska, Russia, he emigrated to the U.S. in 1913. He attended Yale University (1921–23) and the Art Students League (1925), where he studied with Max Weber. Subsequently he was heavily influenced by SURREALISM. In the early 1940s he created pale canvases filled with biomorphic forms. By the late 1940s his work had become completely abstract. Perhaps the most lyrical practitioner of ABSTRACT EXPRESSIONISM, he is best known for his large and luminous compositions in which irregular rectangles of color appear to float against a glowing ground. Rothko had a rather mystical approach to his work, viewing his paintings as tools for meditation and expressions of emotion, not as mere formal exercises. He committed suicide on February 25, 1970.

Rothschild, Lord (Nathaniel Mayer Victor) (1910–1990). British baron. The third baron of Rothschild, the famous European banking family, he was a zoologist and business executive. He headed the UNITED KINGDOM's Central Policy Review Staff, known as the Whitehall "think tank," in the early 1970s and later went on to serve as an executive with Royal Dutch Shell. After his former friend Anthony BLUNT was exposed in 1979 as having been the "fourth man" in the BURGESS-MACLEAN-PHILBY Soviet spy ring, Rothschild was also accused of having been a member of the group. He denied the charge, and Prime Minister Margaret THATCHER declared that there was no evidence to support the accusation.

Roth v. United States (1957). U.S. Supreme Court decision defining First Amendment protection for obscene material. Roth, convicted of selling and mailing obscene literature in violation of a federal statute, protested that the enforcement of the law violated his First Amendment free speech rights. The Supreme Court held that obscene materials are not protected by the First Amendment.

A divided Court also announced a test to determine if a work was obscene: Would an average person consider that its dominant theme appealed to the prurient interest? Fifteen years later the Court relaxed this test to the following: Would the average person, applying contemporary local standards, find that it appeals to the prurient interest; and, if it depicts in a patently offensive way sexual activity specifically defined by state law, that it lacks any serious redeeming value? Despite this definition, the line between freedom of speech and obscenity remained a point of contention, as demonstrated in the 1989 MAPPLETHORPE controversy and similar cases. (See also PORNOGRAPHY AND OBSCENITY.)

Rotterdam. Netherlands port city on the Nieuwe Maas, about 15 miles from the North Sea. On May 14, 1940, during Germany's BLITZKRIEG conquest of Western Europe, much of Rotterdam was flattened by German bombers—even though the NETHERLANDS had already surrendered to Germany. Modern Rotterdam, built after the war, is one of the largest and most modern ports in the world.

Roussel, Albert (1869–1937). French composer. Born in the north of France, he served in the navy before studying (1898–1907) with Vincent d'INDY at the Schola Cantorum, where he became a professor (1902–14). His first compositions, such as the symphonic *Le Poeme de la foret* (1904–06) and the opera-ballet *Padmavati* (1918), were executed in an Impressionistic style. Influenced by his study of 18th-century music and by STRAVINSKY, his later works stress a neoclassical approach and are also often touched with Oriental motifs, styles and rhythms. His mature works, notably the last three of his four symphonies and the ballet *Bacchus et Ariane* (1931), exhibit a delicate melodic sense mingled with elegant dissonances. His many other compositions include orchestral pieces, chamber music, choral works and songs.

Rowan, Carl T. (1925–). American journalist and government official. Rowan was born in Tennessee and in 1944 was among the first blacks to receive a Navy commission. Following World War II, he attended Oberlin College and the University of Minnesota and in 1950 became a reporter for the *Minneapolis Tribune*. Rowan's books, based on his travels and on reporting assignments, include *South of Freedom* (1952), *The Pitiful and the Proud* (1956) and *Go South to Sorrow* (1957). In 1961, President KENNEDY named Rowan deputy assistant secretary of state for public affairs, and in 1963, ambassador to Finland. In 1964, President JOHNSON appointed him chief of the United States Information Agency (USIA), but Rowan resigned the following year after charges that USIA's VOICE OF AMERICA was biased in favor of the administration. Rowan returned to journalism, producing popular syndicated columns, providing television commentary, contributing to READER'S DIGEST and lecturing.

Rowe, James H. (1909–1984). Influential aide to President Franklin D. ROOSEVELT during the 1930s' NEW DEAL era. Rowe was one of the idealistic Harvard-educated lawyers who formed Roosevelt's BRAIN TRUST. He served on scores of federal boards and commissions. He later advised Adlai STEVENSON and Hubert HUMPHREY in their unsuccessful presidential bids and was credited with helping to place Lyndon B. JOHNSON on the ticket as John F. KENNEDY'S vice presidential running mate in 1960.

Roy, Maurice Cardinal (1905–1985). Roman Catholic primate of Canada (1956–81). Roy was long regarded as a leader of the moderate progressive wing of his church's hierarchy. Named archbishop of his native Quebec in 1947, he was designated a cardinal by Pope PAUL VI in 1965. From 1967 to 1977 he headed two VATICAN agencies, the Council of the Laity and the Pontifical Commission on Justice and Peace.

Royal Ballet. Britain's national ballet company. Founded by Ninette de VALOIS and Lilian Baylis in 1931 as the Vic-Wells Ballet, it became Sadler's Wells Ballet in 1940 and the Royal Ballet in 1956. De Valois served as its director until 1963 and was succeeded by Sir Frederick ASHTON (1963–70), Sir Kenneth MACMILLAN (1970–77), N. Morrice (1977–86) and Anthony DOWELL (since 1986). Internationally acclaimed, the company has its own school, a home theater at Covent Garden Opera House, and balances classical tradition with original choreography. *The Sleeping Beauty* (first mounted in 1946) has become its signature work. Other famous ballets presented by the company include Ashton's *Symphonic Variations* and *The Dream*, and Macmillan's *Romeo and Juliet* and *Manon*. Dancers associated with the company include Dame Margot FONTEYN, Rudolph NUREYEV, Antoinette Sibley and Anthony Dowell.

For further reading:

Bland, Alexander, *The Royal Ballet—The First 50 Years*. London: Threshold Books, 1981.

Royal Danish Ballet. One of the oldest ballet companies in the world (established 1748), the Royal Danish Ballet was dominated during the 19th century by August Bournonville, who created a series of ballets that form the Danish classical repertory and established the excellence of Danish male dancing. The company declined after Bournonville's death but experienced a second flowering under the direction of Harald Lander (1932–51). Lander gave the company an international repertoire and gained it international recognition. The directors that followed Lander have struggled to maintain the Bournonville ballets and style while developing a contemporary repertory. Outstanding 20th-century Royal Danish dancers include Margot Lander, Borge Ralov, Henning Kronstam, Erik BRUHN, Peter MARTINS and Peter Schaufuss.

Royal National Theatre. A theater complex in London consisting of three theaters, performance and exhibition space, restaurants, and shops that was established in 1962 with Sir Laurence OLIVIER as director of its board. Subsequent directors are Peter HALL, Richard Eyre and David Aukin. The idea for the theater was a long time in being realized. In 1907 the Shakespeare Memorial National Theatre Committee was established. In 1944 a site on the South Bank of the Thames was found, and in 1976 the Lyttelton, Olivier and Cottesloe theatres began to open. "Royal" was added to the name in 1988. The repertory company presents both traditional and modern, experimental drama.

Royal Shakespeare Company. A British theater company established in 1960 under the direction of Peter HALL. The company achieved success in 1963 with its production of the *The Wars of the Roses* cycle of Shakespeare's works, but it presents the works of other traditional and modern playwrights as well. The company, which has had many eminent theatrical personalities among it ranks, has performed in Stratford and London as well as touring internationally. In the 1980s the company went to Broadway with an adaptation of Dicken's *Nicholas Nickleby*, Hugo's *Les Miserables* and an unfortunate presentation of Stephen KING'S *Carrie*.

Royce, Josiah (1855–1916). American philosopher. Born in Grass Valley, California, Royce studied at the University of California and received his doctorate from Johns Hopkins University in 1870. Royce taught at the University of California until 1882, when he joined the faculty at Harvard, where he taught for the rest of his life. Royce was the foremost American idealist of his day. He combined idealism and nationalism in a peculiarly American way, taking into consideration both history and science and stressing action as well as thought. He posited an absolute God, an all-knowing cosmic purpose, in an absolute self, an absolute mind and an absolute community, which deserves humanity's loyalty. Royce saw mankind as a part of the logos and thus able to know reality beyond itself. His ideas were very influential in the religious and ethical thought of his era. Among his books are *The World and the Individual* (1900–1901), *The Philosophy of Loyalty* (1908) and *Modern Idealism* (1919).

Ruanda-Urundi. A colonial territory in central Africa that was formerly known as Belgian East Africa but has now been divided into the independent states of RWANDA and BURUNDI; the capital was at Usumbura (now Bujumburu). The area became part of German East Africa in the early 20th century. In 1916, during WORLD WAR I, it was taken by BELGIUM. In 1924 the LEAGUE OF NATIONS assigned the territory to Belgium as a mandate. In 1946 Ruanda-Urundi was made a trust territory of the UNITED NATIONS. The two nations of Rwanda and Burundi were created when the territory was granted independence on July 1, 1962.

Rubbra, Edmund (1901–1986). British composer. He produced a great deal of symphonic, chamber and vocal music in an essentially conservative idiom distinguished by its use of polyphony. His 11 symphonies formed the core of his work.

Rubin, Jerry (1938–). American political activist. Rubin became involved in the Vietnam ANTIWAR MOVEMENT in Berkeley, California, in 1964. He was very adept at organizing and gaining media attention for antiwar rallies. In 1968 Rubin's Yippie (Youth International) Party demonstrated during the Democratic National Convention in Chicago; Rubin and others were arrested. Media coverage of confrontations between the police and the demonstrators overshadowed the convention. (See also CHICAGO 7 TRIAL.)

Rubinstein, Arthur (1887–1982). Legendary Polish concert pianist; one of the most popular pianists of the 20th century, during his lifetime his fame was equaled only by that of Vladimir HOROWITZ, whose style and personality were very different. Born in Lodz (in Russian Poland), as a young man Rubinstein spent much time in Paris and Berlin and toured widely in Europe and North and South America.

Polish-American concert pianist Arthur Rubinstein, famous for his unaffected interpretations of the classics.

Although a prodigy, Rubinstein did not gain acceptance as a great pianist until the 1930s. He was one of the first pianists to take advantage of the new medium of electronic recording, and during his long career he recorded virtually his entire repertoire. His interpretations of the music of Chopin are regarded as definitive; his performances of Beethoven and Brahms, among other composers, were exceptional. Stylistically, Rubinstein's playing was remarkable for its effortless lyricism and lack of romantic affectation, yet also for its great warmth, subtlety and expressiveness; in many ways, he was the first truly modern pianist. He gave concerts until the age of 90.

Ruby, Jack [born Jacob Rubinstein] (1911–1967). American nightclub operator, assassin of Lee Harvey OSWALD. Ruby was a shadowy figure in Dallas, Texas, a feature of local nightlife with reputed connections to organized crime. Allegedly a great admirer of President John F. KENNEDY, he shot the president's alleged killer on November 24, 1963, as Oswald was being escorted to an armored truck in the basement of the Dallas municipal building. Ruby has often been accused of implication in one of any number of assassination plots. However, he steadfastly denied this as well as any previous connection with Oswald. Convicted of murder, Ruby died in prison while awaiting retrial on appeal.

Rudel, Hans Ulrich (1916–82). German bomber pilot during WORLD WAR II. Rudel was one of the most decorated German soldiers of the war. He flew 2,500 missions in a Stuka dive-bomber, mostly on the Russian Front (see WORLD WAR II ON THE RUSSIAN FRONT). He was credited with destroying 519 tanks, 150 gun emplacements, and 800 combat vehicles. He continued to espouse Nazi doctrines for many years after the war.

Rudolph, Wilma (1940–). American athlete. Born into a poor family in St. Bethlehem, Tennessee, Rudolph was stricken with a childhood illness that left one leg crippled. With physical therapy, she made a full recovery, and at age 16 she had secured a place on the 1956 U.S. Olympic track team, where she was a member of the bronze-medal-winning relay team. In the 1960 Olympics, Rudolph won three gold medals—in the 100 meters, the 200 meters and again in the relay—earning her the nickname "the Black Gazelle." Rudolph set three records in 1961, for the 60- and 220-yard dashes and for the 400-meter relay. That year she was named the Associated Press female athlete of the year and was awarded the Sullivan Memorial Trophy by the AAU as oustanding amateur athlete of 1961. In later years, Rudolph became a coach and teacher and was active in youth charities.

Millions watched on television as nightclub owner Jack Ruby shot Lee Harvey Oswald, the alleged assassin of President John F. Kennedy, on November 24, 1963.

Ruffian (1972–1975). Thoroughbred racehorse. The greatest filly of her time, Ruffian seemed destined to become one of the greatest racehorses of all time. The winner of five straight races as a two-year-old, she was named the champion filly of 1974. In 1975, the big black filly reeled off five more wins, including New York's triple distaff crown. The bringing together of Ruffian and that year's leading colt, Foolish Pleasure, in a match race at Belmont generated enormous interest. While the two horses were head-to-head, Ruffian stumbled. Her right foreleg was broken, and her gallant attempt to keep running damaged the leg irreparably. Attempts were made to save her, but the filly thrashed about and caused herself further damage. Ruffian was put down and is buried in the infield at Belmont.

Ruffing, Charles "Red" (1904–1986). U.S. athlete. His baseball career spanned 22 seasons ending in 1947. Considered the best-hitting pitcher of his era, he spent 15 seasons with the New York Yankees. His lifetime regular season record was 273 victories and 225 defeats, with four consecutive 20–win seasons. His career batting average of .269 included eight seasons over .300. He was elected to the Baseball Hall of Fame in 1967.

Ruggles, Carl (1876–1971). American composer. Born in Marion, Massachusetts, he attended Harvard University. Like his friend Charles IVES, Ruggles was an American original who rejected traditional musical forms. A conductor of small orchestral and chamber groups and a teacher at the University of Florida at Miami (1937–46), he was careful and self-critical, creating a comparatively small oeuvre. Dense and vigorous, his complexly atonal compositions include works for the piano and voice as well as chamber music and orchestral pieces. Among his better-known works are the orchestral *Men and Mountains* (1924), the tone poem *Sun-Treader* (1932) and the piano piece *Evocations* (1934–43).

Ruhr. German river that flows westward into the Rhine at Duisburg. The name Ruhr often also refers to the valley itself, GERMANY's industrial heartland. The Ruhr valley includes such centers of industry as Bochum, Dortmund, Duisburg and Essen. Huge coal and steel empires were developed here by the Krupp and Thyssen families during the 19th century. From 1923 to 1925 the Ruhr was occupied by Belgian and French forces during a dispute over Germany's postwar reparations payments. Adolf HITLER used the French occupation as an excuse to rise against the WEIMAR REPUBLIC in his unsuccessful BEER HALL PUTSCH of 1923. The Ruhr was the primary center of Germany's war production during WORLD WAR II. As such, it was heavily bombed by the Allies; the cities of the region suffered great damage. After the war, the Ruhr remained under the control of the Western Allies until

1954, when it was turned over to WEST GERMANY.

Rule, Elton Hoert (1916–1990). American executive. Rule was president of ABC (American Broadcasting Company) from 1973 to 1983. His pioneering use of miniseries, made-for-TV movies and Monday Night Football helped the once-ailing company become the dominant U.S. television network in the 1970s.

Rumor, Mariano (1915–1990). Italian politician. A Christian Democrat, Rumor held the post of premier five times between 1968 and 1974. He served during turbulent times in ITALY and had to contend with economic crises, student protests, labor unrest and terrorism from extremists of the both the left and the right. In 1976 he was investigated for possible involvement in the LOCKHEED SCANDAL. The U.S. aircraft maker had admitted bribing Italian officials to help ease negotiations over a large airplane contract. Rumor denied the charges and was narrowly exonerated by parliament.

Runcie, Robert (1921–). Archbishop of Canterbury (1979–90) and spiritual leader of the Anglican Church. Runcie was known for his outspoken liberal political views, which sometimes clashed with the policies of Tory Prime Minister Margaret THATCHER. In particular, Runcie called for a less strictly materialistic approach to economic issues and the plight of the poor. Runcie parted company with his predecessor, Archbishop Donald COGGAN, by insisting that the ordination of women as priests was a reform for which the Anglican Church was not yet ready. Prior to his election as archbishop, Runcie had been bishop of St. Albans and a professor of theology at Cambridge University.

Rundstedt, Karl Rudolf Gerd von (1875–1953). German military commander during WORLD WAR II. Rundstedt led the BLITZKRIEG in Poland (1939), the French campaign in 1940 and the Russian campaign in 1941. He was supreme commander in the West from 1942 to 1945. Rundstedt led the German counteroffensive, known as the Battle of the BULGE, in 1944. The British held him as a possible war criminal after Germany's defeat, but he was released in 1949 because of poor health. (See also Battle of FRANCE; WORLD WAR II ON THE EASTERN FRONT; WORLD WAR II ON THE WESTERN FRONT.)

Runyon, Damon (1884–1946). American author. Runyon began his career as a sports writer and brought the immediacy of reporting to his colorful fiction, which painted a racy picture of New York's underworld during the 1920s and '30s. His short stories, such as "Guys and Dolls" (1931), have been collected into such works as *The Damon Runyon Omnibus* (1944) and *The Best of Damon Runyon* (1966), and many of them have been adapted into plays and films.

Ruschi, Augusto (1916–1986). Brazilian naturalist. His work included cataloging 80% of known species of Brazilian hummingbirds. He became a hero in his country for defending a nature preserve against deforestation and encroaching coffee farms. His death from cirrhosis of the liver came less than six months after his widely publicized announcement that Amazonian Indian treatments had cured him of progressive liver failure, which he said had come from handling poisonous toads. At least one British medical specialist had attributed Ruschi's condition not to toads but to the cumulative effect of treatment with antimalarial agents.

Rushdie, Salman (1947–). British novelist. A Moslem, Rushdie was born in Bombay, India. His family emigrated to Pakistan in 1964, and he was educated at King's College, Cambridge. He remained in England, initially to pursue a career as an actor. Rushdie's first novel, *Grimus* (1975), did not impress readers or critics. He established his reputation with *Midnight's Children* (1981), which won the Booker Prize, among other awards. Rushdie's fiction is associated with MAGIC REALISM and is rich in Moslem imagery. Rushdie received a peculiar notoriety with the publication of ***The Satanic Verses*** (1988). A critically acclaimed story of the struggle between good and evil, the book contains two chapters, "Mahound" and "Return to Jahiliya," that many Moslems deem to be a blasphemous and obscene mockery of the origins of Islam. On February 14, 1989, the Ayatollah KHOMEINI pronounced a death sentence on Rushdie, urging Moslems to execute not only him but the publishers of the book. A day later an aide to Khomeini offered a million-dollar reward for Rushdie's death, and he was forced into hiding. Many bookstores, fearful of attack, stopped selling the book, and his publishers were hesitant about releasing a paperback edition, causing much outcry about freedom of speech and censorship. The book was banned in several countries, among them Pakistan, India and Egypt, and violent protests in these countries caused several deaths. Rushdie attempted to appease his critics with the essay "In Good Faith" (1990) and issued an apology in which he reaffirmed his respect for Islam. However, Iranian clerics did not repudiate their death threat. While in hiding, Rushdie published *Haroun and the Sea of Stories* (1990).

For further reading:

Appignanesi, Lisa, and Sara Maitland (eds), *The Rushdie File*. Syracuse, N.Y.: Syracuse University Press, 1990.
Pipes, Daniel, *The Rushdie Affair*. New York: Carol Publishing Group, 1990.
Weatherby, W. J., *Salman Rushdie, Sentenced to Death*. New York: Carroll & Graf, 1990.

Rushworth, Robert (1924–). U.S. military flier and test pilot who made more flights in the X-15 rocket plane than any other pilot. During one of his 34 flights, on June 27, 1963, Rushworth reached an altitude of 55 miles (285,000 feet), earning astronaut status by the Air Force definition. Over the course of his career he flew 50 different aircraft, logging more than 6,500 hours of flying time. Rushworth started out in 1943 as a U.S. Army enlisted man. He trained as an aviation cadet and became a pilot in 1944, after which he flew combat missions in China, Burma and India. He left the military in 1946 to get a degree in mechanical engineering, but by February 1951 he was back in the Air Force, earned an M.S. in aeronautical engineering in 1954 and became a test pilot. From 1957 to 1966 he flew experimental aircraft and rocket planes at Edwards Air Force Base, earning a Distinguished Flying Cross for a tricky landing of the X-15. In 1966 he went back to combat duty, this time in VIETNAM. On returning to the states in 1969, he served as commander of several test centers.

Rusk, (David) Dean (1909–). U.S. secretary of state (1961–69). After teaching political science in the 1930s and serving in World War II, Rusk followed his mentor George C. MARSHALL into the State Department. He was named assistant secretary of state for Far Eastern affairs in 1950 and, under Dean ACHESON, played an important role in the formulation of policy during the KOREAN WAR. In 1952 Rusk left the State Department to become head of the Rockefeller Foundation. President John F. KENNEDY appointed him secretary of state in 1961, and he retained that post under President Lyndon B. JOHNSON. Rusk advocated worldwide economic cooperation and military opposition to communist expansion, becoming a prominent apologist (with Robert MCNAMARA) for the escalation of the VIETNAM WAR. In 1970 he became a professor of international law at the University of Georgia.

For further reading:

Halberstam, David, *The Best and the Brightest*. New York: Random House, 1972.

Rusk, Howard Archibald (1901–1989). American physician, a pioneer in the science of medical rehabilitation. His interest in rehabilitation began while he was in charge of the Army Air Force Convalescent Training Program in WORLD WAR II. During the war he helped develop programs to rehabilitate soldiers using both physical and psychological means. Many of his techniques became part of standard medical practice around the world. Rusk received numerous awards, including three Albert Lasker Awards, the Distinguished Service Medal and the French Legion of Honor. The Howard A. Rusk Institute of Rehabilitative Medicine was named for him. He was also a president and chairman of the World Rehabilitation Fund, which he founded in 1955.

Ruska, Ernst (1906–1988). German electrical engineer credited with the development of the ELECTRON MICROSCOPE in 1931. Ruska received belated recognition for that achievement when he shared the NOBEL PRIZE for physics in 1986..

Russell, Bertrand A(rthur William) [3rd Earl of Russell] (1872–1970). British philosopher, mathematician and social critic. Russell, who won the NOBEL PRIZE for literature in 1950, was one of the most influential and widely read philosophers of this century. He was born into an aristocratic British family and educated at

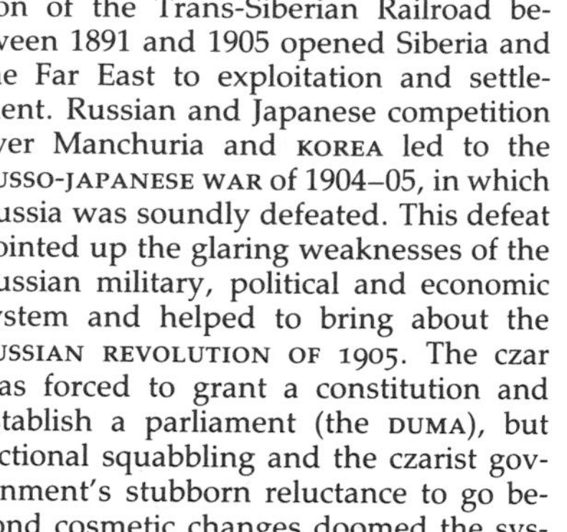

British philosopher and mathematician Bertrand Russell, who received the Nobel Prize for literature in 1950, seen here on his 90th birthday (1962).

Cambridge University, but for most of his life Russell advocated political and social beliefs—such as pacifism and left-wing economic reforms—that went contrary to his class and background. Russell's first great work, completed in collaboration with Alfred North WHITEHEAD, was the three-volume *Principia Mathematica* (1910–13), which asserted that mathematics was essentially an extension of philosophical logic. In 1916, during WORLD WAR I, Russell was dismissed from the faculty of Cambridge University for his pacifist beliefs. In the final decades of his life, Russell was active in the antinuclear weapons movement. His major works included *Why I Am Not a Christian* (1927), *Marriage and Morals* (1929) and *The History of Western Philosophy* (1945).

Russell, Bill (William Fenton) (1934–). American basketball player. Russell is generally acknowledged to be the greatest basketball player of all time, and was so voted by the Professional Basketball Writers Association. After leading his college team at the University of San Francisco to two championships, he was drafted by the Boston Celtics and remained with them for his entire career (1956–1969). At center, Russell was named most valuable player five times, and the team won 11 championships. During the last three years of that span, Russell also coached the team to two championships and was the first black coach in league history. His totals as a player included 21,620 rebounds and 14,522 points. He went on to coach the Seattle Supersonics (1973–1979). He was named to the Basketball Hall of Fame in 1974.

Russia. Former European-Asian empire, supplanted and expanded by the UNION OF SOVIET SOCIALIST REPUBLICS. The name is also applied to the U.S.S.R.'s RUSSIAN SOVIET FEDERATED SOCIALIST REPUBLIC. At the turn of the century, under Czar NICHOLAS II, the Russian empire stretched from the German and Austro-Hungarian borders in the west to the Pacific Ocean on the east, including the vast but sparsely populated north Asian territory of SIBERIA. Much of present-day Poland was under Russian control. In 1894 Russian had entered into an alliance with France and an arrangement with Great Britain; this alliance was formalized as the TRIPLE ALLIANCE in 1907. Meanwhile, the construction of the Trans-Siberian Railroad between 1891 and 1905 opened Siberia and the Far East to exploitation and settlement. Russian and Japanese competition over Manchuria and KOREA led to the RUSSO-JAPANESE WAR of 1904–05, in which Russia was soundly defeated. This defeat pointed up the glaring weaknesses of the Russian military, political and economic system and helped to bring about the RUSSIAN REVOLUTION OF 1905. The czar was forced to grant a constitution and establish a parliament (the DUMA), but factional squabbling and the czarist government's stubborn reluctance to go beyond cosmetic changes doomed the system to failure.

In August, 1914, Russia was drawn into WORLD WAR I, ostensibly as a defender of Slavic peoples in the Balkans and elsewhere. However, the nation was as ill-prepared for this war—if not more so—than it had been for the war with Japan. Russia's advantage in manpower was offset by the nation's inability to properly arm, feed and train its soldiers. Moreover, much of the leadership was incompetent. The Russian army suffered catastrophic defeats at the hands of Germany and Austria-Hungary. Mass discontent in the ranks, fueled by the bitter conditions of warfare and by resentment against the aristocratic officer corps and the apparently callous czarist government, led to desertion and to the spread of revolutionary propaganda. On the home front, food shortages developed. Revolution broke out in February 1917, and Nicholas abdicated on March 15 (see FEBRUARY REVOLUTION). A provisional government was organized; in May it admitted socialists and in July made Alexander F. KERENSKY its head. Historians speculate that, had this government made peace with Germany, it might have survived and guided Russia on a democratic path. However, it insisted on carrying on the unpopular war, while economic conditions continued to deteriorate. The disciplined, well-organized BOLSHEVIKS, under V.I. LENIN and Leon TROTSKY, staged a coup in late October (old style calendar; early November, new style) and the Kerensky government collapsed (see OCTOBER REVOLUTION). The Bolsheviks consolidated their control of the government and reached a peace agreement with Germany in the treaty of BREST-LITOVSK. In

RUSSIA

1902	Socialist Revolutionary Party founded.
1903	V.I. Lenin splits Social-Democratic Party into Bolshevik and Menshevik factions.
1904-5	Russo-Japanese War.
1905	(Jan. 9) Czar's troops kill 100 demonstrators in Bloody Sunday massacre in St. Petersburg; (May) Japanese destroy Russian fleet at Tsushima; (Aug.) Treaty of Portsmouth (mediated by U.S. President Theodore Roosevelt) ends Russo-Japanese War; assassination of Grand Duke Sergei; Revolution of 1905 suppressed; (Oct.) Czar Nicholas grants civil liberties and limited representative government.
1906	First Duma (representative assembly) sits.
1906-11	The Stolypin era; agricultural reforms; Rasputin gains influence over Czar Nicholas and Czarina Alexandra.
1907	Anglo-Russian Entente.
1911	Assassination of Stolypin.
1912	Lena goldfield massacre; first issue of *Pravda*.
1914	Russia mobilizes for war; (Aug.) enters World War I against Germany and Austria; (Aug. 26) Russian army routed at battle of Tannenberg; (Sept.) Russians suffer huge losses at Masurian Lakes.
1916	Aristocrats murder Rasputin.
1917	(Feb.) Outbreak of Russian Revolution, abdication of Czar Nicholas II; formation of provisional government under Kerensky; (Oct.) Lenin and Bolsheviks seize power.
1918	Russia withdraws from World War I in Treaty of Brest-Litovsk; Czar Nicholas II and the royal family murdered on Lenin's orders; Lenin proclaims "Red Terror."
1918-21	Russian Civil War and War Communism.
1921	Lenin institutes New Economic Policy.
1923	Union of Soviet Socialist Republics formed.

1918 the czar and his family were executed. Despite opposition from various anti-Bolshevik forces (see WHITES), including Western troops, the Bolsheviks prevailed, eventually bringing Russia under their authority (see RUSSIAN CIVIL WAR) and establishing the COMMUNIST PARTY as the sole power in the new Union of Soviet Socialist Republics.

Russian Civil War of 1918–21. In 1918, several months after the popularly elected Russian assembly was disbanded as a counterrevolutionary body (see OCTOBER REVOLUTION), civil war broke out between the ruling BOLSHEVIKS (or communists) and the anti-Bolshevik WHITES. It was triggered by a clash between Czech troops (in transit through Siberia) and the Bolsheviks, whose punishment of the Czechs provoked the Czechs to raid Siberian villages. Taking advantage of the situation, the Whites began battling the Bolsheviks' newly formed Red Army and successfully took almost all of Siberia. During the struggle, Czar NICHOLAS II and his entire family were murdered at Ekaterinburg (Sverdlovsk) in July 1918. A month later, British, French, Japanese and American troops, in support of the Whites, landed at Vladivostok on the Sea of Japan, while British and American forces disembarked at Archangel on the Arctic's White Sea and helped a new provisional government to establish itself there. Through these foreign efforts, Bolshevik rule was eliminated east of the Ural Mountains.

However, the Red Army under Leon TROTSKY waged fierce battles and ultimately defeated three White armies from the Caucasus, Baltic and Siberian areas. The Czechs withdrew, but the other foreign powers continued to furnish troops and supplies to fight the communists. Terrorism and assassinations increased on both sides, and communist distrust of non-Bolsheviks was hardened. After peace negotiations failed, a White army advanced toward Moscow, reaching Orel, about 200 miles to the south; and another White force came within 10 miles of Petrograd (Leningrad). But the Red Army turned them back and won a victory at Novorossisk on the Black Sea. After the western Siberia city of Omsk, headquarters of the anticommunist forces of Admiral Alexander V. KOLCHAK, fell to the Reds in November 1919, and the foreign forces withdrew from the war, the Whites were gradually crushed as they fought in hostile territory. The bloody civil war, which also saw the KRONSTADT REBELLION, ended with the communists firmly in control of the government and the country (including Siberia) by 1921. (See also DENIKIN; FINNISH WAR OF INDEPENDENCE; RUSSO-POLISH WAR OF 1919–20; WRANGEL.)

Russian Revolution (1917). The revolution of March and November (Old Style February and October) 1917 that overthrew the Russian monarchy and established the world's first communist state. It began with the FEBRUARY REVOLUTION, when riots over shortages of bread and coal in Petrograd (formerly St. Petersburg) led to the establishment of the Petrograd Soviet of workers' and soldiers' deputies, dominated by the MENSHEVIKS and Social Revolutionaries, and of a provisional government of DUMA deputies, which forced NICHOLAS II to abdicate. The failure of the provisional government, under Prince George LVOV and then KERENSKY, to end Russia's participation in WORLD WAR I and to deal with food shortages led to the demand of the BOLSHEVIKS under LENIN for "all power to the Soviets." The Bolsheviks, who had gained a majority in the Soviet by September, staged the OCTOBER (or Bolshevik) REVOLUTION, seizing power and establishing the Soviet of people's commissars. The new government made peace with Germany in early 1918 but almost immediately faced opposition at home. In the subsequent CIVIL WAR (1918–21) the Red Army was ultimately victorious against the anticommunist WHITE but with the loss of some 100,000 lives. In addition, some two million Russians emigrated.

For further reading:
Pipes, Richard, *The Russian Revolution*. New York: Knopf, 1990.

Russian Revolution of 1905. An insurrection in RUSSIA. It was an expression of the widespread discontent that foreshadowed the RUSSIAN REVOLUTION of 1917. It began on BLOODY SUNDAY, January 22, 1905, when a group of striking workers, led by Father GAPON, marched peacefully to the Winter Palace in St. Petersburg only to be met by gunfire. The massacre precipitated nationwide strikes, uprisings and mutinies (including the mutiny on the cruiser *Potemkin*). By October Russia was gripped by a general strike, which with the establishment of the St. Petersburg Soviet (workers' council) dominated by the MENSHEVIKS, including TROTSKY, forced Emperor NICHOLAS II to promise a constitutional government (see DUMA). The revolution was substantially crushed by the end of December.

For further reading:
Ascher, Abraham, *The Revolution of 1905: Russia in Disarray*. Stanford, Calif.: Stanford University Press.

Russian Social Democratic Labor Party. Founded in 1898 as the Social Democratic Labor Party, the party consisted of orthodox Marxists, revisionists and trade unionists. Although the party split into BOLSHEVIKS and MENSHEVIKS at the second party congress in 1903, it was later formally reunited, but both factions continued to exist. In 1919 the Bolsheviks no longer used the name of Russian Social Democratic Party, but the Mensheviks opted to retain it.

Russian Soviet Federated Socialist Republic [RSFSR]. The largest of the 15 republics of the UNION OF SOVIET SOCIALIST REPUBLICS (U.S.S.R.). With such cities as Moscow (the capital of the RSFSR

Russian soldiers during the Russian Revolution (1917).

as well as of the U.S.S.R.) and LENINGRAD, it is the political, social, economic and cultural nerve center of the Soviet Union. Stretching some 5,000 miles from eastern Europe and the Baltic Sea across northern Asia (SIBERIA) to the Pacific Ocean, it contains more than half the population of the Soviet Union and more than three-quarters of its land. The BOLSHEVIKS established the RSFSR in January 1918. In 1922 the RSFSR was formally united with the UKRAINE, Belorussia and Transcaucasia to form the Union of Soviet Socialist Republics. By virtue of its plentiful natural resources and its location in the heartland of the old Russian empire, the RSFSR became highly industrialized during the 20th century. In the late 1980s, with various ethnic groups throughout the U.S.S.R. demanding autonomy, the Russian republic became the center of a resurgent Russian nationalism. Communist maverick politician Boris YELTSIN was elected president of the republic and challenged the authority of the central Soviet government.

Russki, Nicholas (1854–1918). Russian soldier. He studied at the staff college in St. Petersburg and was made a general (1896). In 1914 he was posted to the southwestern front, and in September he defeated the Austrians at Rawa Ruska near Lvov. Later he was reassigned to the western front, and he prevented HINDENBURG from breaking through near Lodz. He is believed to have been killed by the Bolsheviks in 1918.

Russo-Finnish War of 1939–40. On the outbreak of WORLD WAR II, Soviet Russia demanded FINLAND lease a naval base on the Hanko Peninsula, demilitarize its Mannerheim Line fortifications and cede several islands. Finland refused and about 1 million Soviet troops invaded. From November 30, 1939, to March 12, 1940, 300,000 Finnish troops and international volunteers held off the Soviets, using the Finnish winter to advantage. At Suomussalmi the Finns nearly annihilated two Soviet divisions. They were unable to halt the incessant Soviet assaults, however. Aided by heavy artillery and air bombardments, the Soviets breached the Mannerheim Line in February 1940. The Finns sued for peace when the Soviets pushed on toward on Vyborg on March 12, 1940, ceding the Karelian isthmus and Vyborg (Viipuri). In June 1941 the Finns joined the German invasion of the U.S.S.R.

Russo-Japanese War. War (1904–05) arising from the conflict of Russian and Japanese aspirations in Asia. RUSSIA refused to withdraw from MANCHURIA, despite having agreed to do so in 1902, and also wished to gain concessions in KOREA. Alexander Bezobrazov's timber company began work on the Korean side of the Yalu River, and in 1904 the Russian fleet was attacked by the Japanese at PORT ARTHUR. In May 1905 the Japanese virtually destroyed Russia's Baltic fleet at Tsushima. Britain's proposal of American mediation was accepted. At the peace conference, presided over by Theodore ROOSEVELT, in Portsmouth, New Hampshire, Russia ceded Port Arthur, the southern line of the Chinese Eastern Railway and the southern half of Sakhalin Island to JAPAN.

Russo-Persian War of 1911. After the Persian Revolution of 1906–09, Russia sent troops to Kazvin in northern Persia to protect its interests there, in violation of the Anglo-Russian agreement of 1907. William Morgan Shuster, an American serving as Persian treasurer, clashed with Russia, which supported an attempted coup by the former shah and demanded Shuster's removal; the parliament refused. The Russians committed atrocities in Tabriz, took over Azerbaijan and advanced on Teheran. Persia's regent governing for the minor Ahmed Shah enacted a coup, closed down the assembly and accepted Russia's demand.

Russo-Polish War of 1919–20. As German troops withdrew from POLAND after WORLD WAR I, Soviet troops advanced westward. Polish forces under General Jozef PILSUDSKI pushed the Soviets back into the UKRAINE. The Allies approved an eastern Polish border within Russia, but Pilsudski, seeking to seize the Ukraine, allied with anti-Soviet Ukrainians under Simon PETLYURA, capturing Kiev on April 25–May 7, 1920. A Soviet counterattack drove the Poles out, and Soviet troops were threatening Warsaw by August. With aid from the French under General Maxime WEYGAND, Polish armies defeated Soviet troops under Mikhail Tukacheveski in September, 1920 along the Niemen River. An armistice ended fighting on October 12, 1920, and by the Treaty of Riga (March 18, 1921) Poland's territorial claims eastward were accepted by the U.S.S.R.

Rustin, Bayard (1910–1987). American civil rights leader. He was one of the foremost theorists and practitioners of the CIVIL RIGHTS MOVEMENT. A close advisor to the Reverend Martin Luther KING Jr. since the 1950s, Rustin was a principal organizer of the 1963 Washington, D.C., march and rally at which King delivered his "I have a dream" speech (see MARCH ON WASHINGTON, 1963). A socialist, pacifist and Quaker, he remained a lifelong believer in nonviolent protest. He favored a coalition approach to achieving social change, involving alliances with labor, white liberals, Jews and other minorities, an approach often criticized by other black leaders. Rustin, who was openly gay, urged black leaders to adopt a more active role in the fight against AIDS (acquired immune deficiency syndrome).

Ruth, George Herman "Babe" (1895–1948). American baseball player. The greatest home run hitter of his time, Ruth discovered baseball while at St. Mary's Industrial School in Baltimore. After gaining experience with a local, minor league team, he signed with the Baltimore Orioles and was later sold to the Boston Red Sox as a pitcher. He pitched 29–2/3 scoreless World Series innings for them, and had a 94–46 overall record, but by 1918 he had been shifted to the outfield so that he could hit every day. Sold to the New York Yankees in 1920 for $125,000, Ruth began the 14 seasons of home run hitting that established him as the "Sultan of Swat." He broke the home run record in three consecutive seasons (1919–21), hit 60 home runs in 154 games in 1927, led the American League in home runs for 12 seasons and hit 50 or more home runs in four seasons—all records. His career total of 714 home runs was the record until it was surpassed by Hank AARON in 1974. Less well known is that fact that Ruth set a lifetime record of 2,056 bases on balls. Somewhat notorious for his rowdy nightlife, Ruth was fined for misconduct several times, and after his retirement in 1935 he failed to attract the job of team manager that he desired. He became the second player to be elected to the Baseball Hall of Fame (1936).

New York Yankees legend Babe Ruth hit 714 home runs in his illustrious career.

For further reading:

Wagenheim, Kal, *Babe Ruth: His Life and Legend*. New York: Praeger Publishers, 1974.

Smelser, Marshall, *The Life that Ruth Built: A Biography*. New York: Quadrangle/New York Times Book Co., 1975.

Rutherford, Ernest (1871–1937). New Zealand-born British physicist. One of the century's most influential scientists, Rutherford revolutionized our understanding of atomic physics. Born near Nelson, New Zealand, he received his B.A. from Canterbury College, in Christchurch, in 1892, his M.A. the following year and a B.S. in 1894. Rutherford next entered Cambridge University as a research student for J.J. Thomson at the prestigious Cavendish Laboratory and assisted in the research that led to Thomson's discovery of the electron. From 1898 to 1907, Rutherford taught at McGill University in Montreal, where he performed landmark experiments in radioactivity, including those marking the discovery of alpha and beta particles. In 1907, Rutherford accepted a post at Manchester University in England. The following year he was awarded the NOBEL PRIZE for chemistry. In 1911 he presented a new model of the atom, still generally accepted, that called for a mass of positively charged particles in the center with negatively charged electrons orbiting about the periphery. Rutherford moved in 1919 to Cambridge University, where he headed the Cavendish Laboratory until his death. He headed the Royal Society from 1925 to 1930, and he was elevated to the peerage in 1931.

Rutledge, Wiley B(lount) (1894–1949). Associate justice, U.S. Supreme Court (1943–49). A graduate of the University of Wisconsin, Rutledge graduated from the University of Colorado Law School after his education had been interrupted by tuberculosis and financial difficulties. After a brief time in private practice he became a law professor. Rutledge was appointed by President Franklin D. ROOSEVELT to the U.S. Court of Appeals for the District of Columbia and was elevated to the U.S. Supreme Court in 1943. His career on the Court was cut short when he died unexpectedly in 1949.

Rwanda. Rwanda, a landlocked country just south of the equator in east-central Africa, has a total area of 10,167 square miles. Rwanda, together with BURUNDI, came under the colonial rule of Germany, and the two were merged in 1899 and renamed Ruanda-Urundi. Troops from the adjoining Belgian Congo occupied the colony during WORLD WAR I (1916). After the war Belgium was given a LEAGUE OF NATIONS mandate to rule Ruanda-Urundi; in 1946 it was made a UN trusteeship. A Hutu revolution in 1959 demolished the monarch and the power of the rival Tutsi. Hundreds of people were killed and many Tutsi fled Rwanda, which became a republic in 1961 and fully independent on July 1, 1962, when the Hutu-led Parti du Mouvement de l'Emancipation Hutu (PARMEHUTU) came to power under President Gregoire Kayibanda.

Up to 20,000 Tutsi were reportedly killed by Hutu following border raids in December 1963. Kayibanda was overthrown in a bloodless military coup (July 5, 1973) and former Defense Minister General Juvenal Habyarimana became president. In 1975 Habyarimana formed a new ruling party of civilian and military members, the Mouvement Revolutionnaire National pour le Developpement (MRND). Rwanda returned to constitutional government in 1978. Habyarimana was reelected in 1983 and again in 1989. Tensions have simmered between central and northern Hutu; northern elements took the upper hand in government, which remains civilian-military. Ethnic tensions in Burundi (August 1988) sent 38,000 Hutu refugees fleeing to Rwanda; most returned.

Ryan, (Lynn) Nolan (1947–). American baseball player. Known as "The Myth" during his four years with the New York Mets, his early years were plagued by lack of control and blister problems. In the worst deal in Met history (if not in baseball history), Ryan (along with two other players) was traded to the California Angels for Jim Fregosi in 1971. In California, he began to achieve mastery over his astonishing fastball, and became the first righthander since Bob Feller to strike out 300 batters in a season. He signed with the Houston Astros in 1979, and later remained in his native Texas as he signed with the Rangers in 1988. Clocked at over 100 miles per hour, Ryan is baseball's all-time strikeout leader with over 5,000—1,000 more than the second-highest total, held by Steve Carlton. Ryan pitched his sixth no-hitter in 1990, at the age of 43. That year he also reached the milestone of 300 wins. An astute businessman, Ryan owns a bank, a town and several ranches throughout Texas, but continues to play—and best—players half his age. He pitched an astonishing seventh no-hitter in May 1991.

Ryder, Robert E(dward) D(udley) (1907–1986). British naval officer. Ryder became a hero during WORLD WAR II when he led a raid on the French port of St. Nazaire (March 1942). One of the boldest combined operations of the war, the raid was totally successful in its main objective, to inflict enough damage on the port's huge Normandie Dock to prevent it from being used by the German battleship *Tirpitz.*

Rykov, Alexei Ivanovich (1881–1938). Russian member of the militant wing of the Social Democratic Labor Party and of its Bolshevik faction. Rykov worked as an underground agent in RUSSIA but broke with LENIN in 1910 to become leader of the "party-minded BOLSHEVIKS," a subfaction that was more tolerant toward the MENSHEVIKS. After the OCTOBER REVOLUTION in 1917 he advocated a coalition government of all socialist parties. Chairman of the supreme council of national

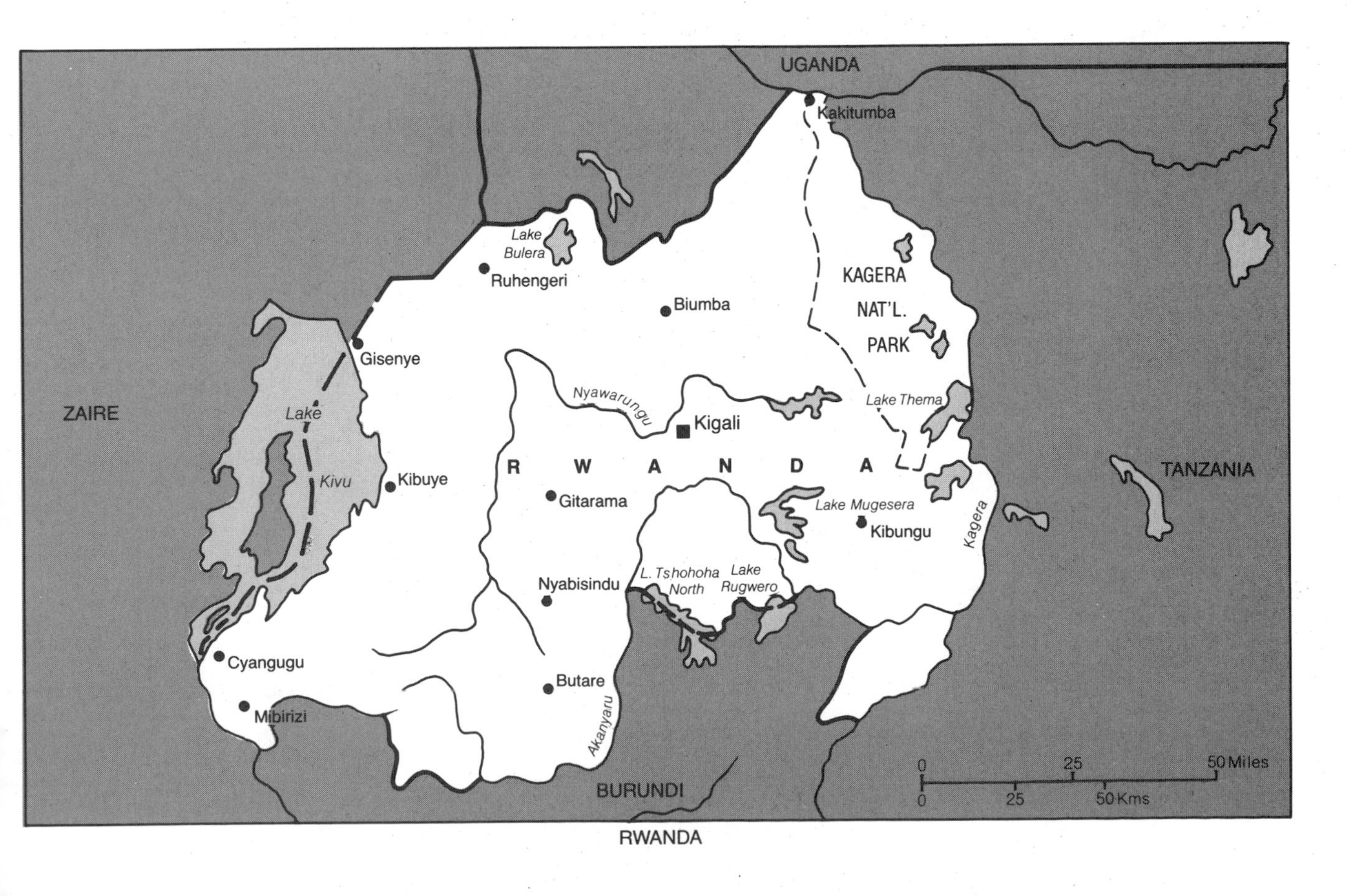

economy in 1918–20 and 1923–24, in 1921–24 he was deputy chairman of the council of people's commissars, and later chairman. A member of the Politburo, he became a leading member of the RIGHT OPPOSITION. He was executed following the last show trial of the GREAT PURGE.

Ryskind, Morris (Morrie) (1895–1985). American comedy writer. Ryskind collaborated with playwright George S. KAUFMAN on a series of MARX BROTHERS stage and screen hits, including *Cocanuts, Animal Crackers* and *A Night at the Opera.* He share the 1932 PULITZER PRIZE for drama with Kaufman for the musical *Of Thee I Sing.* A socialist in his youth, he later became a staunch anticommunist. In 1947, he testified before the HOUSE COMMITTEE ON UN-AMERICAN ACTIVITIES on communist infiltration of the Screenwriters Guild. He went on to become a member of the JOHN BIRCH SOCIETY and to write a politically conservative column for the *Los Angeles Times* from 1960 to 1971.

Ryun, James Ronald "Jim" (1947–). American track and field star. Ryun was born in Wichita, Kansas, and was the first athlete to break the four-minute mile while still in high school. Although he held many world records during the 1960s and in 1966 was named sportsman of the year by *Sports Illustrated,* he never won an Olympic medal. A fall during the 1968 Olympics ended his chance for a medal. After retiring as an active competitor, Ryun founded the Jim Ryun Distance Running Camps to help develop young runners, and was active in philanthropic causes. (See also OLYMPIC GAMES.)

S

Saarinen, Eero (1910–1961). Finnish-born American architect whose varied and imaginative work in both furniture design and architecture was a significant part of the design scene in the 1950s. The son of famous Finnish architect Eliel SAARINEN, who relocated in the U.S. in 1923, Eero Saarinen grew up at Cranbrook Academy where his father was a principal teacher. He planned to become a sculptor and studied in Paris from 1930 to 1931, but returned to study architecture at Yale. He graduated in 1934 and worked briefly for Norman BEL GEDDES before returning to Cranbrook. Saarinen worked there with Charles EAMES and won two first prizes with him in the 1940 Organic Design in Home Furnishing competition, organized by the MUSEUM OF MODERN ART in New York. As an architect, Saarinen began in partnership with his father in 1936 and often worked with Robert F. Swanson as associate or partner (from 1944 to 1947). In 1939 Saarinen, Swanson, and Saarinen won a national competition for a never-built Smithsonian Gallery of Art for Washington, D.C. A number of distinguished schools, a 1942 church in Columbus, Indiana, and the music shed at Tanglewood, Massachusetts, were among the projects completed before the death of the elder Saarinen.

Thereafter, Eero carried on the practice in his name alone, with Joseph Lacy, John Dinkeloo and Kevin Roche as partners. The General Motors Technical Center (1948–56) at Warren, Michigan, is designed in a severe INTERNATIONAL STYLE. In later work, Saarinen took pride in developing a unique design direction for each project, never adapting a personal style to be applied to every project. Nevertheless, all his buildings share a quality that might be described as sincerity, a directness and simplicity along with a certain poetic sensibility. Important works in a sculptural vocabulary include MIT's Kresge auditorium (a huge spherical triangle touching the ground at only three points) and a cylindrical, brick chapel (1953–55) in Cambridge, Massachusetts, as well as the Yale Hockey Rink (1953–59) in New Haven and the TWA passenger terminal (1956–62) at Kennedy Airport in New York. More restrained are the CBS tower (1965) in New York and the John Deere office building (1965) in Moline, Illinois, which were both completed after Saarinen's death. One of his last designs, the main building of northern Virginia's Dulles International Airport (completed 1963) combines the restrained and the sculptural directions in his work with a vast, curving, cable-suspended roof hanging between sloping concrete supports.

Saarinen, Eliel (1873–1950). Leading architect of the national Romantic movement in Finland who built a second career in a more modernist direction after relocating in the U.S. in 1923. Born in Rantasalmi, Finland, Saarinen was trained at the Helsinki Polytechnic. His early work was done in partnership with Herman Gesselius and Armas Lindgren, themselves leaders in Finnish architecture of the early 20th century. Their offices and houses in Hvittrask are fine examples of the Romantic style at its best. Saarinen alone was responsible for the executed design of the Helsinki Railway Station (1910–14), a building that brought him international fame. His second-prize design in the 1922 competition for the Chicago Tribune Building received critical acclaim and led to his coming to the United States. He became associated with Cranbrook Academy in 1925, designed its buildings and taught architecture there, eventually becoming its president (1932–46). Frequently, he designed interiors, furniture, lighting fixtures and other decorative elements for his buildings, working in a vocabulary that combined MODERNISM, a craft orientation, and a decorative style relating to the ART DECO work of the 1930s. He practiced alone and then in partnership with his son Eero SAARINEN, producing a number of distinguished buildings, such as a 1942 church in Columbus, Indiana, and the shed at Tanglewood, Massachusetts, which combined the rigors of INTERNATIONAL STYLE modernism with a delicacy and charm that stemmed from the Scandinavian Romantic movement of his early career.

Saarland. Small German state between the French frontier and the German state of Rheinland-Pfalz; drained by the Saar River, its capital is Saarbrucken. The Saar became the tenth state of the Federal Republic of Germany (WEST GERMANY) in 1957. After GERMANY's defeat in WORLD WAR I, the Treaty of VERSAILLES (1919) assigned the Saarland's coal mines to France for 15 years. The region was returned to Germany's Third Reich in 1935. After HITLER claimed France's Lorraine in 1940, he combined the two regions under the name Westmark. Heavy fighting between the Allies and Germans took place along the Saar River in December 1944. The Saarland fell within the French occupation zone after the war.

Saba, Umberto (1883–1957). Italian poet. Born in Trieste under the Austro-Hungarian Empire, Saba was trained as a clerk and primarily self-educated. His first verses appeared in 1911 and 1912. Saba was a close friend of Italo SVEVO, who shared his profound interest in Freud. Due to his Jewish heritage, during WORLD WAR II he was forced to close the small antiquarian bookshop that supported him to live in exile in France and Italy, where he was sheltered by Eugenio MONTALE, among others. The definitive 1961 edition of his *Canzoniere* (*Songbook*) comprised three volumes, corresponding to the poems of his youth, maturity and old age. A lyric autobiography, it was continually revised over the years. *Storia e cronistoria del Canzoniere* (1948, *History and Chronicle of the Songbook*) is a systematic self-criticism of his own poetry.

Sabin, Albert (Bruce) (1906–). Polish-American microbiologist. Born in Bialystok, Russia (now Poland), Sabin immigrated to the U.S. with his family in 1921 and was naturalized in 1930. He attended

Dr. Albert Sabin holds a vial of his new live-virus polio vaccine (1959).

New York University, receiving an M.D. in 1931. Becoming a medical researcher, he was on the staff of the Rockefeller Institute before becoming a member of the college of medicine at the University of Cincinnati in 1939. He was appointed research professor of pediatrics there in 1946. Sabin is known for his development of an oral live-virus vaccine against poliomyelitis. Mass field tested in 1959, the vaccine has now largely replaced the earlier killed-virus vaccine developed by Jonas SALK. It gives a stronger and longer-lasting immunity than the earlier vaccine and protects against both paralysis and infection. Sabin concentrated on cancer research in his later work.

Sabkhat Al-Kurziyah. Lake in north-central Tunisia. A decisive battle of the NORTH AFRICAN CAMPAIGN of WORLD WAR II took place here in April and May 1943. Allied forces accepted the surrender of the Axis forces in North Africa here on May 12, 1943.

Sabra and Shatila Massacre (September 16, 1982). Following the PLO evacuation of BEIRUT, Lebanese Christian militiamen attacked the Sabra and Shatila refugee camps in west Beirut and killed hundreds of the inhabitants. ISRAEL came under international criticism for the attacks because the Christian militia were considered its allies, and Israeli complicity was suspected. Israel itself conducted an investigation into the atrocities, which led to the resignation of several Israeli military officers who had been stationed in the region. Israeli Defense Secretary Ariel SHARON was also forced to resign.

Saburov, Maksim Zakharovich (1900–). Soviet communist functionary. He joined the party in 1926 and volunteered for work suppressing armed resistance to the regime. He studied at the Sverdlov Communist University (1923–26) and then studied engineering at Moscow University. From 1941 to 1944 and 1949 to 1955 Saburov was chairman of Gosplan. He was chairman of the state economic commission from 1955 to 1956 and a first deputy prime minister from 1955 to 1957. In 1952 he was a member of the central committee and its presidium. As a result of accusations of membership in the antiparty group, in 1957 he was removed from positions of governmental responsibility. Since then he has worked as deputy chairman of the committee for the economic cooperation of the Soviet bloc countries and as a factory manager.

Sacco and Vanzetti Case. Long, controversial U.S. criminal case in which two Italian-born American anarchists were convicted of murder and executed after lengthy, well-publicized legal appeals and international protests about the conduct of the trial. In May 1920, Nicola Sacco and Bartolomeo Vanzetti were arrested and charged with the armed robbery and murder of two employees of a shoe factory in South Braintree, Massachusetts. The evidence at trial was not substantial, and the trial judge made a number of prejudicial rulings at the trial, in which they were convicted and sentenced to the electric chair. Alarmed at the possible miscarriage of justice extensive appeals were taken and the pair received support and publicity among liberals and immigrants in the U.S. At the time the U.S. was caught up in a hysterical anti-Red campaign led by Attorney General Palmer, who had presidential ambitions. Critics charged that the pair were convicted without evidence merely because they were avowed anarchists. The case also received considerable attention in the U.K. and in Europe. The legal appeals lasted six years, and in a highly unusual move the governor of Massachusetts appointed a commission headed by the president of Harvard University to review the judicial process. The commission sustained the trial verdict, though it criticized the conduct of the trial judge. Despite protests and street demonstrations Sacco and Vanzetti were executed in August 1927. The execution provoked more demonstrations both within the U.S. and abroad.

Sachs, Nelly (1891–1971). German-born Jewish poet. As a young girl, Sachs began corresponding with the novelist Selma LAGERLOF, who was later instrumental in helping Sachs and her mother flee Nazi GERMANY in 1940. Although Sachs had written traditional, romantic poetry as a young woman, she is best known for work written after she escaped to Sweden. These collections include *In den Wohnungen des Todes* ("In the habitations of death," 1946) *Und Niemand weiss weiter* ("And No One Knows How to Go On," 1957) and *Flucht und Verwandlung* ("Flight and Transformation," 1959). Her poems recall the horrors of the HOLOCAUST and the suffering of the Jewish people, often with mystic imagery. Sachs also wrote the plays *Eli: Ein Mysterienspiel vom Leiden Israels* (*Eli: A Mystery Play of the Sufferings of Israel*, 1951) and *Zeichen im Sand* (*Marks in the Sand* 1962), among others. Sachs shared the 1966 NOBEL PRIZE for literature with S.Y. AGNON.

Sachsenhausen. Village in eastern Germany's state of Brandenburg, about five miles north of Berlin. It was infamous as the site of a Nazi CONCENTRATION CAMP, established during the 1930s. In April 1945, as the Soviet army advanced toward BERLIN, the German authorities evacuated the camp and forced its 40,000 inmates—many near death—to march out of the path of the Soviet juggernaut.

Sackville-West, Vita (Victoria Mary) (1892–1962). British poet and novelist. Sackville-West portrayed her childhood home in Kent in *Knole and the Sackvilles* (1922) and in her best-known novel, *The Edwardians* (1930). Her poetry includes *The Land* (1926), which won the Hawthorn-don Prize, and *Collected Poems* (1933). Sackville-West met Virginia WOOLF in 1922. The two became lovers, and the relationship was the inspiration for Woolf's *Orlando* (1928). Sackville-West's life-style and unconventional relationship with her husband Nigel Nicolson, whom she married in 1913, have been much written about—notably by their son, Nigel Nicolson, in *Portrait of a Marriage* (1973).

Sadat, (Mohammed) Anwar el- (1918–1981). President of EGYPT (1970–1981). The son of a poor government clerk and his half-Sudanese wife, Sadat was one of 13 children. He received his earliest education from an Islamic cleric and earned a lifetime reputation for piety. He graduated (1938) from the Royal Military Academy, which had previously been reserved for the aristocracy. During WORLD WAR II he was imprisoned by the British for opposing their policy in Egypt. He later joined the FREE OFFICERS movement and took part in the coup against King FAROUK led by Gamal Abdel NASSER. He subsequently held a variety of posts leading to the vice presidency (1969) and succeeded to the presidency on Nasser's death (1970). During Nasser's rule, Sadat had been widely regarded as a weak figure and was dismissed by some critics as "Nasser's poodle." Many thought he would be merely an interim president, but he quickly consolidated his power. In 1972 he reversed Nasser's policy of close ties to the U.S.S.R. and expelled the Soviet military

Egyptian President Anwar Sadat shortly before his assassination (1981).

advisers from Egypt. Like Nasser, he initially took a hard line against ISRAEL. He coordinated the Arab surprise attacks on Israel in October 1973, which resulted in a disastrous defeat for Egypt (see ARAB-ISRAELI WAR OF 1973). With the intercession of U.S. Secretary of State Henry KISSINGER'S SHUTTLE DIPLOMACY, he agreed to terms for a disengagement with Israel in January 1974. Efforts for a more comprehensive peace made only limited progress until 1977, when Sadat boldly followed up Israeli hints and made a sudden surprise visit to JERUSALEM to meet with Israeli Premier Menachem BEGIN and address the Knesset. This action initiated the peace process that led to the CAMP DAVID ACCORDS of 1978, sponsored by U.S. President CARTER. For his role in establishing peace with Israel, Sadat shared the 1978 NOBEL PRIZE for peace with Begin. But while Sadat won enormous respect in the U.S. and other Western nations, many Arabs denounced him as a traitor to the Arab cause. The peace with Israel, the erratic pace of economic progress and the Westernization of some segments of Egyptian society were accompanied by increasing Islamic fundamentalist unrest. Sadat responded with a widespread crackdown on Muslim extremists in September 1981. On October 6, while he was reviewing a military parade in Cairo, a small band of commandos in the parade dismounted from their truck and fired into the reviewing stand, killing Sadat and several other officials. Sadat was regarded as a complex man, a humble autocrat of unusual flexibility, whose unquestioned dignity and undeniable warmth made him a formidable politician and world statesman.

Sadler, Barry (1941–1989). American singer-songwriter. While serving as a U.S. Special Forces medic in VIETNAM during the VIETNAM WAR, he wrote and recorded "The Ballad of the Green Berets." This tribute to the special forces became the number-one song in the U.S. for five weeks in 1966. In 1988, while training anticommunist Nicaraguan CONTRA guerrillas in Guatemala, he was shot in the head and paralyzed. He subsequently died as a result of wounds.

Sadler's Wells Royal Ballet. Sister company of Britain's ROYAL BALLET. Formed in 1945 as the Sadler's Wells Theatre Ballet to perform in operas at that theater, it became the touring company of the Royal Ballet in 1955. Still based at Sadler's Wells, it adopted its present name in 1977. In 1989 the company moved its base to the Hippodrome Theater in Birmingham. Classical, modern and experimental works are performed. Choreographers, such as John CRANKO and Kenneth MACMILLAN, created their first works for this company.

Sagan, Carl (1934–). One of the best known astronomers in America, Sagan has done much in his many television appearances to put astronomy and the space program before the American people. He received his Ph.D. at the University of Chicago in 1960 and in 1968 became associate professor of astronomy and director for planetary studies at Cornell University. Although Sagan's primary interests are planetary surfaces and atmospheres, an area in which he has done much respected scientific work, he has also done pioneering studies in the possibilities of extraterrestrial life. A vocal and untiring advocate of both the romantic and popular sides of science, Sagan is the author of many popular books, including two outside the field of astronomy, *The Dragons of Eden* and *Broca's Brain.*

Sagan, Francoise [Francoise Quoirez] (1935–). French novelist, playwright and screenwriter. Sagan made a sensation with her first novel, *Bonjour Tristesse* (*Hello, Sadness,* 1954; filmed 1958). Written when she was 18, the novel was critically acclaimed as well as a *succes de scandale* for its dispassionate tone and depiction of a young woman breaking up her father's affair. Her second novel, *Un Certain Sourire* (*A Certain Smile,* 1956; filmed 1958), enjoyed similar success, but her subsequent fiction was never as successful or admired. Later works include *Incidental Music: Stories* (1983) and *Avec mon meilleur souvenir* (1984). Sagan has also written plays and screenplays of her own novels as well as those of others.

Sagdeyev, Roald (1933–). Soviet scientist. As head of Russia's Institute for Space Research (IKI) Sagdeyev is credited with breathing new life into the Soviet space program in the early 1970s. Under his direction the program not only became more open but also realized such spectacular successes as the Venera 9 and 10 projects to Venus and the Vega mission to Halley's Comet.

Sahel. Region of Africa south of the Sahara, with the savannas to the south. The nations of MALI, NIGER, CHAD and SUDAN fall largely within the Sahel. The Sahel has been the site of much human misery during the latter half of the 20th century. In the late 1960s, a prolonged drought devasted local agriculture and brought severe famine to the region.

Sahl, Mort (1927–). Born in Montreal but raised in Los Angeles, California, Sahl was one of the most influential stand-up comedians of the 1950s and '60s. After working at an Alaskan Air Force Base and graduating from the University of Southern California in 1950, Sahl began to perform stand-up in San Francisco. In contrast to the "normal Vegas comic," Sahl developed a unique style that used a casual, free-form technique, which included stream of consciousness, ad-libs, political commentary and his trademark prop—a rolled up newspaper. Labeled a "Will Rogers with fangs," Sahl mercilessly remarked about presidents (Eisenhower, Nixon and Kennedy), politicians (McCarthy) and virtually anyone else in the public eye. In the 1970s Sahl focused his attention on writing for television and film, performing with less regularity. In 1988 he had a brief but successful one-man show on Broadway. Today Sahl is acknowledged as the leading influence on comedians Lenny BRUCE, Woody ALLEN and countless others.

Saigon [Ho Chi Minh City]. Former capital city of the former South VIETNAM; on the right bank of the Saigon River, north of the Mekong River delta. Originally a settlement of the Khmer people, its history dates back many centuries. It was the capital of French INDOCHINA from 1887 to 1902. As a result of long French settlement in the 19th and 20th centuries, Saigon's architecture is more European than Asian. After the French withdrawal, Saigon became the capital of the new nation of South Vietnam in 1954. During the VIETNAM WAR it served as the command headquarters for U.S. forces in the country. It was infiltrated and attacked by the VIET CONG during the TET OFFENSIVE (1968). When the North Vietnamese broke through South Vietnamese lines in April 1975, panic struck Saigon as thousands of Vietnamese attempted to flee the city. The U.S. organized a hasty evacuation for U.S. personnel and as many endangered South Vietnamese (those who had worked closely with the U.S.) as it could accommodate. The city fell to the communists on April 30, 1975. The victorious North Vietnamese renamed Saigon after the venerated communist leader, HO CHI MINH.

For further reading:

Butler, David, *The Fall of Saigon.* New York: Simon & Schuster, 1985.

Saint Christopher and Nevis. Located at the northern end of the Leeward Islands chain of the West Indies, the federation is comprised of St. Christopher (more commonly known as St. Kitts, [6.5 square miles]) and Nevis (36 square miles). The two islands are divided by a 2-mile-wide sea strait known as the Narrows. Both islands are volcanic in origin and are dominated by mountains that rise to 3,793 feet (at Mount Misery on St. Kitts) and 3,232 feet on Nevis. Over 75% of the population of 40,000 live on St. Kitts. The British joined Anguilla administratively to the other two islands in 1816. Universal suffrage was granted in 1951 and in 1967 the territory attained full internal self-government. Robert Bradshaw, leader of the ruling Labour Party, became premier. In 1967 Anguilla declared itself independent of St. Kitts. British troops intervened in 1969 and in 1971 the island reverted to being a British dependent territory; it was formally separated from St. Kitts-Nevis in 1980.

Bradshaw died in May 1978 and was succeeded by Paul Southwell, who also died a year later. New premier Lee Moore called elections for February 1980, but the Labour Party lost and was replaced by a coalition of the People's Action Movement (PAM) and the Nevis Reformation Party (NRP), which sought greater autonomy for Nevis. Dr. Kennedy Simmonds of the PAM became premier and then prime minister on the attainment of full independence from Britain on September 19, 1983. The PAM-NRP coalition remained in power after winning general elections in 1984 and 1989, in spite of the PAM achieving a clear majority of seats in the National Assembly.

St. Denis, Ruth [born Ruth Dennis] (1879–1968). American dancer, choreographer and teacher. A founder of the American modern dance movement, St. Denis achieved fame as a choreographer/dancer with her work *Radha* in 1906. After successful solo dance tours of Europe (1906–09) and America (1909–10), she teamed with, and married, Ted SHAWN (1914). They founded Denishawn School and Dance Troupe (1915) where such great dancer/choreographers as Martha GRAHAM got their start. She also founded the dance department at Adelphi College (1938), appeared at the JACOB'S PILLOW DANCE FESTIVAL (1949–55) and gave lecture/dance performances throughout the country. Among her famous choreographic works, many of which are based on Eastern religions and cultures, are *Cobras, Nautch* and *Incense.*

For further reading:

Shelton, Suzanne, *Divine Dancer: A Biography of Ruth St. Denis.* Garden City, N.Y.: Doubleday, 1981.

Sainte-Adresse. Town near the port of Le Havre, in northern France. During WORLD WAR I Sainte-Adresse served as the headquarters of the Belgian government, which had fled there when the Germans occupied BELGIUM.

Sainte-Mere-Eglise. Town in northern France, approximately 20 miles inland from the Channel port of Cherbourg. During the early hours of the Allied invasion of NORMANDY (June 6, 1944), U.S. paratroopers raided this town, capturing it on June 10, 1944.

Saint-Exupery, Antoine de (1900–1943). French aviator, novelist, travel writer and children's book author. Saint-Exupery was educated at a Jesuit college in Le Mans and at the College of Saint Jean in Fribourg. He served in the French Air Force from 1921 to 1923 and flew in Morocco. Saint-Exupery remained in North Africa as a pilot for the Air Mail Service, which experience formed the basis for his first book, *Courrier Sud* (1929). He next moved to Argentina, where he headed an air mail service there. His writing career was established wth the international success of his novel *Night Flight* (1931), which dealt with the tragic death of a mail pilot. Saint-Exupery attempted to set a time record for a flight from Paris to Saigon but crashed in the Arabian desert; the story of his survival is recounted in *Wind, Sand and Stars* (1939). *The Little Prince* (1943) is his classic children's story. He died in 1943 while serving as a reconnaissance pilot over North Africa for the American forces during WORLD WAR II.

Saint-Goban. Village in the Aisne department of northern France; during WORLD WAR I, an important fortification point on Germany's HINDENBURG LINE until October 1918.

St. Jacques, Raymond [James Arthur Johnson] (1930–1990). American actor. He helped lower racial barriers for other black actors with his performances in numerous films and television shows. His films include *Black Like Me* (1964), *The Pawnbroker* (1965), *The Green Berets* (1968) and *Cotton Comes to Harlem* (1970). He also appeared on the TV Western series "Rawhide" in the 1960s and in the mini-series "Roots" (1977).

Saint Jean de Maurienne Agreement. A secret agreement reached in April, 1917 by representatives of the British, French, Italian and Russian governments regarding post-World War I territorial arrangements. It promised to give Italy a part of Turkey, but was never implemented. In 1918 the BOLSHEVIK government of Russia revealed the understanding, leading to Greek and Turkish distrust of Italy.

Saint John's. Since 1946, the capital city of Canada's province of NEWFOUNDLAND, on the Atlantic coast of the Avalon Peninsula. Closer to Europe than any other North American city, it was here that MARCONI'S first transatlantic wireless message was received in 1901. In 1919, Alcock and Brown took off from Saint John's on the first nonstop (but not solo) transatlantic flight.

Saint Kitts-Nevis. See SAINT CHRISTOPHER AND NEVIS.

St. Laurent, Louis Stephen (1882–1973). Canadian political leader, prime minister of CANADA (1948–57). Born in Compton, Quebec, St. Laurent attended Laval University and was a well-known corporate lawyer before entering political life in 1941. He was minister of justice, attorney general and minister of external affairs (the latter post, 1946–48) during the administration of MacKenzie KING. In 1948 he succeeded King in the post of LIBERAL PARTY leader and became prime minister in November of that year. While St. Laurent was in office, Canada assumed a larger role on the world stage, Newfoundland became a province (1949), the Old Age Security Act was enacted (1951) and the ST. LAWRENCE SEAWAY was agreed upon and partially constructed. As the country swung to the Conservatives, the Liberals failed to obtain a majority in the 1957 election, and St. Laurent was succeeded as prime minister by John G. DIEFENBAKER. He retired as party head in 1958 and returned to his law practice.

Saint Laurent, Yves (1936–). French fashion designer sometimes regarded as the "king of fashion" for his enormous success based on design that is practical, charming or pretty while still expressive of haute couture style. Saint Laurent was an art student in Paris when, at the age of 17, he won a fashion sketch contest staged by the International Wool Secretariat. At 19 he was employed by Christian DIOR, becoming head designer for that house on Dior's death in 1958. With the support of an American financial backer, he opened his own firm in 1962, established his ready-to-wear line, Rive Gauche, in 1966 and added men's wear design in 1974. His work is known for its practical qualities, along with a certain glamour and occasional exotic touches based on oriental art and gypsy and African motifs. His name and YSL initials have became a recognized brand name, licensed with vast commercial success to cosmetics, linens, perfumes (including the popular Opium and Y), sweaters and other products. Saint Laurent was honored with a retrospective exhibit of his work in 1983 at the Costume Institute of the Metropolitan Museum of Art in New York.

Saint-Laurent-Sur-Mer. Town on the bay of the Seine River, eight miles northwest of Bayeux. For two weeks in June 1944 it was the busiest harbor in Europe, courtesy of the Allied invaders of NORMANDY in WORLD WAR II. A large artificial harbor, towed by the invasion fleet from England, was later greatly damaged by a severe gale—but not until it had successfully landed a great deal of ordnance, artillery and heavy-duty war materiel.

St. Lawrence Seaway. International waterway along a part of the boundary between the U.S. and Canada; a link between the Great Lakes and the Atlantic Ocean, the seaway is comprised of a system of locks, dams and canals on the St. Lawrence River and channels that connect the river with the Great Lakes. Measuring 2,342 miles in length, it was opened in 1959. The seaway allows large oceangoing ships passage to such inland cities as the U.S.'s Buffalo, Chicago, Detroit and Milwaukee, and Canada's Montreal, Hamilton, Thunder Bay and Toronto. It accommodates vessels up to 730 feet long, with a cargo capacity of up to 28,000 tons. Of great commercial importance, the seaway handles annual traffic of approximately 50 million short tons (45 million metric tons). It also provides for hydroelectric facilities.

Saint-Lo. Capital town of northwestern France's Manche department, 34 miles west of Caen and a major objective of the Allies after the NORMANDY landings in June 1944. The ancient Briovera (or Laudus) was attacked by U.S. troops on July 7 and captured on the 18th, after heavy bombing. With one end of the German line successfully breached, the Allies began their advance across France.

Saint Louis Symphony. Founded in 1880, the symphony of St. Louis, Missouri, has the distinction of being the second oldest in the United States. Among its distinguished conductors was Rudolph Ganz, one of America's most noted music educators, who was also a distinguished composer. In St. Louis, Ganz introduced concerts for children. TIME magazine, in its annual evaluation for 1988, described the St. Louis Symphony as second only to the CHICAGO SYMPHONY in musical quality. This distinction has come about mainly through the efforts of its current conductor, Leonard Slatkin, who is also known as a masterful advocate of contemporary American classical composers.

Saint Lucia. Saint Lucia, the second largest island in the Windward group of the West Indies, is situated in the East Caribbean 24 miles south of Martinique and 20 miles north of Saint Vincent. Ownership of the island alternated between Britain and France many times before it was finally ceded to Britain in 1814. Universal suffrage was introduced in 1951 and full internal autonomy in 1967. Elections in 1974 were won by the ruling United

Workers' Party (UWP), led by John Compton; it campaigned for full independence, which was attained on February 22, 1979. The UWP was defeated in elections held shortly afterwards by the St. Lucia Labour Party (SLP), led by Allan Louisy. In May 1981 Louisy was forced to resign, leading to the collapse of the SLP government in January 1982 amid strikes and demonstrations. Fresh elections were won overwhelmingly by the UWP, and Compton returned as prime minister. In elections held in 1987 the UWP was returned to power, but with a majority of only one seat over the SLP. Compton called a new election for later the same month, hoping to obtain a more decisive mandate, but the distribution of seats remained the same.

Saint Martin [Sint Maarten]. One of the Leeward Islands, in the West Indies east of Puerto Rico, divided between the Dutch and the French. Dutch Sint Maarten is in the south of the island; it is associated with the NETHERLANDS ANTILLES. The French section is associated with GUADELOUPE. Marigot is the capital of the French Saint Martin, while Dutch-speaking Philipsburg is the chief town of Sint Maarten. A popular tourist destination, the island is visited by many cruise ships.

Saint-Mihiel. French town on the Meuse River in Lorraine. In the WORLD WAR I Battle of Saint-Mihiel (September 12–14, 1918), U.S. soldiers under General John PERSHING overwhelmed the German defenders and captured the town. This was the first major U.S. action of the war.

Saint-Nazaire. French port in Brittany, on the Loire River estuary about 30 miles from Nantes. After the surrender of France early in WORLD WAR II, it became a base for German U-boats. It was raided by British commandos in 1942. The German installation in Saint-Nazaire was a target of heavy Allied bombing. Although the Allies liberated the surrounding areas of France by August 1944, the German garrison in Saint-Nazaire only surrendered with the end of the war in May 1945.

Saint-Pierre. See MARTINIQUE.

Saint Pierre and Miquelon. St. Pierre and Miquelon—93 miles square—are islands in the North Atlantic Ocean that are a relic of France's once-mighty New World empire. The terrain is mostly barren rock; the capital is St. Pierre. The first permanent settlement was established in 1604. The importance of France's last possessions in North America is that they allowed the French to exploit the rich fishing grounds of Newfoundland. Fishing for cod allowed the islands to prosper until the introduction of factory ships and frozen fish facilities reduced the importance of the islands' harbors. Saint Pierre and Miquelon, off the coast of Canada's Newfoundland, became an overseas territory of France in 1946 and in 1976 was made a department, against the wishes of many of the islanders. General strikes and unrest over departmental status intensified during the late 1970s and early 1980s. In 1976 Canada declared a 200–mile economic interest zone around its shores, prompting the French to declare a similar zone around Saint Pierre, although the Canadians recognized only a 12–mile limit. In 1987 it was agreed to take the dispute to the International Court of Justice. However, in October negotiations over future fishing quotas broke down, and French vessels were banned from Canadian waters. In April 1988 several fishermen and island politicians were arrested by Canadian authorities for fishing in Canadian waters. The total population of the islands is 6,300.

Saint-Quentin. French city on the SOMME River, 80 miles northeast of Paris. During WORLD WAR I it was the scene of a decisive British breakthrough of the German lines (September-October 1918). Routed, demoralized and in dire economic shape, Germany was soon forced to seek an armistice.

Saint Radegund. Village in Upper Austria, about 30 miles north of Salzburg; site of a memorial to Franz Jagerstatter, a local resident who in 1943 refused to be drafted into the German army. Arrested by the Nazis, Jagerstatter was taken to Berlin and executed.

Saint-Tropez. Town on the Mediterranean Sea coast of southeastern France's Riviera. Originally a fishing port, the town began attracting wealthy tourists and the "smart set" in the 1920s. Favored by expatriate Americans, it is the setting of F. Scott FITZGERALD's novel *Tender Is the Night*. In WORLD WAR II Saint-Tropez suffered damage during Allied landings in August 1944. In the latter part of the 20th century, Saint-Tropez has developed a reputation as a sophisticated playground of the international jet-set.

St. Valentine's Day Massacre. Sensational gangland execution that occurred in a Chicago garage on St. Valentine's Day, 1929. Dressed in police uniforms, gunmen in the employ of Al CAPONE machine-gunned seven men connected with the gang of George "Bugs" Moran. It was one of the most vicious and violent crimes of a vicious and violent era. The massacre was thought to have been perpetrated in reprisal for a whiskey hijacking, and it effectively wiped out an important Capone rival.

Saint Vincent and the Grenadines. The Windward Islands nation of St. Vincent and the Grenadines lies in the East Caribbean, 93 miles west of Barbados; it has a total area of 150 square miles, most of it being the chief island, St. Vincent. Universal suffrage was introduced in 1951 and full internal self-government in 1969. Elections in 1972 resulted in the People's Political Party (PPP) and the St. Vincent Labour Party (SVLP) each winning six seats in the House of Assembly. The balance of power was held by an independent, James Mitchell, who joined the PPP to form a government with himself as premier. Mitchell's government collapsed in 1974 and was replaced after elections by a coalition of the PPP and SVLP, whose leader, Milton Cato, led the country to full independence from Britain on October 27, 1979. Discontent at the government's record and failure to improve the economy led to its defeat in 1984 by the New Democratic Party (NDP), founded by Mitchell. Mitchell became prime minister and strengthened the NPD's position by polling 71% of the vote and winning all 15 seats in the House of Assembly in elections in May 1989.

Saipan. Volcanic island in the MARIANAS of the western Pacific; under U.S. control, a part of the UN-established Trust Territory of the Pacific Islands. A Spanish possession from 1565 to 1899 and German from 1899 to 1914, in 1920 the 47–square-mile island was mandated to JAPAN with the other Marianas by the LEAGUE OF NATIONS. Its air base was a prime U.S. target in WORLD WAR II. The strategic surprise of the American invasion in June 1944 caught the Japanese unprepared (and also lured the Japanese Combined Fleet out of Philippine waters). The lessons learned by Japan's doomed garrison were put to use in the later defense of IWO JIMA and OKINAWA—to the misfortune of the Americans. Total American casualties on Saipan were over 14,000, while 24,000 Japanese were killed or committed suicide—and only 1,780 were taken prisoner (more than half of them Korean). The U.S. used Saipan as a base for attacking the Japanese mainland.

Sakdal Uprising (1935). Sakdal, meaning "accuse" in Tagalog, a major Philippine language, signified the anger of the landless peasants in central Luzon. Many joined the Sakdal movement led by Benigno Ramos calling for lower taxes, land reform and independence. As a party, the Sakdals drew many votes in the 1934 Philippine elections. On May 2, 1935, armed Sakdals seized government buildings in 14 towns in Luzon. Government troops quickly suppressed the rebellion, Ramos escaped to Japan and the party was declared illegal.

Sakhalin. Long, narrow island off the Pacific coast of the U.S.S.R.; separated from the Soviet mainland by the Tatar Strait, Sakhalin's eastern shores are bordered by the Sea of Okhotsk. North of the Japanese main island of Hokkaido, it was colonized by both Russia and Japan in the 18th and 19th centuries. The population became mostly Russian after 1875. Sakhalin was a penal colony for common criminals as well as a place of exile for political opponents of the czarist government; the noted Russian author Anton CHEKHOV visited Sakhalin and wrote about the conditions there. Sakhalin also served as a center of Russian commercial interests in the Far East. Following its defeat in the RUSSO-JAPANESE WAR, Russia ceded the southern part of Sakhalin to Japan. This territory was returned to the U.S.S.R. after WORLD WAR II.

Sakharov, Andrei Dmitrievich (1921–1989). Soviet nuclear physicist, dissident and human rights activist. Possibly the most brilliant nuclear physicist of the 20th century, Sakharov played a key role in the Soviet development of the HYDROGEN BOMB in the late 1940s and the '50s. As

Andrei Sakharov (right center) and Yelena Bonner with Polish Solidarity leader Lech Walesa (left) and French Premier Michel Rocard (left center) (1988).

such, he held a leading position in the Soviet scientific community. However, he eventually became alarmed by the threat of radioactive contamination from nuclear testing and the threat of nuclear war. Increasingly opposed to the Soviet government's policies, he spoke out against human rights abuses and other failures of the Soviet system. Following the international publication of an article titled "Thoughts on Progress, Peaceful Co-Existence and Intellectual Freedom" (1968), he was shunned by the Soviet establishment. He received the 1975 NOBEL PRIZE for peace for his efforts on behalf of human rights. After he criticized the Soviet invasion of Afghanistan, he and his wife, Yelena Bonner, were exiled to the closed city of Gorky in 1980. There they were frequently harassed by the KGB and were forbidden to communicate with other dissidents and with Westerners. In 1987 they were released on the order of Soviet leader Mikhail GORBACHEV. In the new atmosphere of GLASNOST, Sakharov was hailed by many for his courage and his moral stance, although hard-liners reviled him. He continued to press for political, social and economic change. In April 1989 he was elected to the new Congress of People's Deputies, where he led a reform group. He died of a heart attack on December 14, just after taking part in an important debate in the Congress.

For further reading:

Sakharov, Andrei, *Memoirs*. New York: Alfred Knopf, 1990.

Saki [pen name of Hector Hugh Munro] (1870–1916). British author of macabre and wryly amusing short stories. He was born in Akyab, Burma, the son of an inspector-general for the Burma police. After a boyhood in English boarding schools, later police service in Burma and travel through the Balkans as a London press correspondent, his satiric columns and short stories began appearing under the pen name "Saki" (the name of the cupbearer in *The Rubaiyat of Omar Khayyam*) in the *Westminster Gazette* and *Morning Post*. Volumes of the stories were *Reginald* (1904), *Reginald in Russia* (1910), *The Chronicles of Clovis* (1911), *Beasts and Super-Beasts* (1914) and two posthumous works, *The Toys of Peace* (1923) and *The Square Egg* (1924). These are stories that, in the words of a Saki character, "are true enough to be interesting and not true enough to be tiresome." They depict a familiar world of overstuffed drawing rooms, gossipy garden parties, amateur theatricals, lonely railway carriages and exclusive club rooms—invaded by fierce society matrons, foppish young men, inveterate liars and murderous animals. No sentiment whatever can exist in these savage conditions. Only predators survive—those who, like the great ferret "Sredni Vashtar," lay "special stress on the fierce, impatient side of things." There are the wolves of "The Interlopers," the were-beasts of "Gabriel-Ernest" and "Music on the Hill," the wicked "romancers" of "The Open Window" and "A Defensive Diamond," and the witches of "The Peace of Mowsle Barton." Were vicious struggles for survival ever portrayed more grimly—yet more comically—than in "The Strategist?" It is, ultimately, a fatalistic vision. "After all," says Reginald, one of Saki's bright young men, "life teems with things that have no earthly reason." Was there, then, a terrible symmetry (or inevitability) about the sniper's bullet that killed Munro on November 14, 1916, while serving in the trenches with the Royal Fusiliers?

For further reading:

Sullivan, Jack, ed., *The Penguin Encyclopedia of Horror and the Supernatural*. New York: Viking Press, 1986.

Salam, Abdus (1926–). Pakistani physicist. Salam helped establish the International Center for Theoretical Physics in Trieste, to assist physicists from developing countries. His own work concerns the behavior and properties of elementary particles, for which he received the 1979 NOBEL PRIZE for physics, in conjunction with Sheldon Glashow and Steven WEINBERG. Through independent work, these three physicists each contributed to a theory that explained weak and electromagnetic interactions, including the phenomenon of neutral currents and their strengths. This "theory" was first confirmed in 1973 at the European Organization for Nuclear Research.

Salam al-Khalidi, Anbara (1897–1986). Lebanese author. A translator and pioneer campaigner for Arab women's rights, in 1927 she became the first Arab woman in greater SYRIA to unveil her face in public. This act necessitated her retirement into private life for a time. In 1929 she married Ahmad Samih al-Khalidi, who at that time was the foremost Arab education official in PALESTINE. The couple collaborated on historical and educational studies. Her books included the first translations into Arabic of Homer's *Odyssey* and Virgil's *Aeneid*.

Salan, Raoul (1899–1984). French soldier and rebel leader. A WORLD WAR II veteran, General Salan was one of FRANCE'S most decorated soldiers. During the war, he serviced in the FREE FRENCH forces in FRENCH WEST AFRICA. He was later with the French army in INDOCHINA (1945–53). However, Salan is remembered as the man who twice brought France to the brink of civil war during the ALGERIAN WAR OF 1954–62. He was senior French officer in Algiers (1956), and in 1958 became commander-in-chief of the French forces in ALGERIA. His defiance of civilian authority over the Algerian issue in 1958 helped General Charles DE GAULLE topple the Fourth Republic and come to power as the first president of the French Fifth Republic. However, Salan soon disagreed with De Gaulle over France's Algerian policy. In 1960, Salan formed the OAS (ORGANISATION DE L'ARMEE SECRETE, or Secret Army Organization) and waged a terrorist campaign to try to kill De Gaulle and prevent Algerian independence. Captured in 1962 and sentenced to life imprisonment, he received amnesty with other plotters in 1968 and was fully pardoned and reinstated in the army in 1982 by President Francois MITTERRAND.

Salazar, Antonio de Oliveira (1889–1970). Portuguese statesman and dictator (1932–68). Born in a village near Lisbon, he was educated at a seminary, studied law at Coimbra University and became a professor of economics there. He served briefly in the chamber of deputies in 1921 and as finance minister in 1926. Recalled to office in 1928 by General Antonio de Carmona, he assumed complete control of Portuguese finances and soon was able to deal with the nation's chronic economic crises. Becoming premier in 1932, he assumed dictatorial powers. The following year he promulgated a new constitution that governed under fascist-like corporate principles (see FASCISM). He suppressed all dissent and maintained a large army and a vigilant secret police. His foreign policy sought ties with Spain, Great Britain and the U.S. During WORLD WAR II he kept Portugal neutral while maintaining cordial relations with the Allies. He instituted a series of domestic reforms after the war. His latter years were largely spent in a vain attempt to suppress rebellion in Portugal's African colonies. He was succeeded as premier by Marcello CAETANO in 1968 while in a coma following a stroke. Government officials never told him that he had been replaced, fearing that the news might kill him, but kept up a charade of meeting with him as if he were still in power. Salazar continued to live in the chief of state's official residence until his death.

Salinger, J(erome) D(avid) (1916–). American novelist and short story writer. Salinger, who in the 1950s and '60s was widely read by American youth and attained a virtual cult status, has earnestly sought seclusion from the public eye. Hence relatively little is known about his life. Salinger was raised in New York City and educated at various schools including a military academy, much like Holden Caulfield, the protagonist of A CATCHER IN THE RYE (1951), his most famous novel. Salinger served in the American infantry during WORLD WAR II and was decorated for bravery. In the decade following the war, Salinger's stories appeared frequently in the NEW YORKER magazine. Many of them concerned members of the fictional Glass family, all of whom were brilliant and extraordinarily sensitive to the everyday horrors of modern life. Salinger's other major works are *Nine Stories* (1953), *Franny and Zooey* (1961) and, in tandem, *Raise High the Roof Beam, Carpenters and Seymour: An Introduction* (1963).

Salisbury. See HARARE.

Salk, Jonas (Edward) (1914–). American microbioligist. Born in New York City, Salk received his M.D. from New York University Medical School in 1939. He researched the influenza virus at the University of Michigan, becoming an assistant professor of epidemiology there in 1946. In 1947 he moved to the University of Pittsburgh, where he was appointed professor of bacteriology in 1949. There he began work on the vaccine for poliomylitis that would be the first such vaccine proved effective against the disease

Dr. Jonas Salk, developer of the first vaccine against poliomyelitis (1955).

and that would make him a national hero in the U.S. His formulation, a formaldehyde-killed vaccine, was extensively field tested in 1953 and 1954. It was used throughout the world until it was largely supplanted by Albert SABIN's live-virus vaccine in 1960. In 1963 he became director of the Salk Institute for Biological Studies at the University of California, San Diego. His later researches concentrated on the search for an AIDS vaccine.

Salomon, Erich (1886–1944). German photographer. A pioneer of PHOTOJOURNALISM, during the 1920s he used the newly developed small camera with innovative ingenuity. He became famous for his candid photographs of participants at international diplomatic conferences, some made with permission, some without. Many of these early "snapshots" are included in his volume *Beruhmte Zeitgenossen in unbewachten Augenblicken* (Famous Contemporaries Caught Off-Guard, 1931). A Jew, Salomon escaped from Nazi Germany to the Netherlands in 1933. Later captured, he was deported to the CONCENTRATION CAMP at AUSCHWITZ, where he died.

SALT. The SALT (Strategic Arms Limitation Talks) I Treaty, signed May 26, 1972, by the U.S. and the Soviet Union, was the first agreement by those nations to limit their offensive nuclear weapons. As such, it was a highlight of DETENTE. The pact prohibited either country from building any new ICBM or submarine-based missile launchers for a period of five years. The SALT II Treaty, signed on June 18, 1979, further limited the number and type of offensive nuclear weapons the two countries were allowed to keep in their arsenal.

Salt March. Two-hundred-mile march (1930) by Mohandas K. GANDHI and his followers to the sea to make salt from seawater, in defiance of a British ban on the Indian manufacture of salt. As part of his nonviolent campaign to achieve Indian self-sufficiency, Gandhi challenged the monopoly and the salt tax. Setting out on March 12, he reached the sea and made salt on April 5. He was arrested on May 4. Anti-British rioting followed later that month in Bombay and elsewhere.

Salyut. The name given to the first seven Soviet space stations. The name means "salute" and honors Soviet cosmonaut Yuri GAGARIN, the first human in space. The first Salyut was launched April 19, 1971. Salyut 7, launched April 19, 1982, was "retired" though still orbiting when the MIR space station was launched in 1986.

Salzburg Festival. Annual summer music festival held since 1920 in the town of Mozart's birth; suspended during World War II. Mozart festivals given in Salzburg from 1877 to 1910 attracted worldwide attention, especially when soprano Lilli Lehmann performed (1905–10). Richard STRAUSS, Max REINHARDT, Hugo von HOFMANNSTHAL and Franz Schalk founded the expanded festival in 1920. From 1957 until his death in 1989, Herbert von KARAJAN served as artistic director. Many of the great musicians of the world have appeared at the festival, including conductor Arturo TOSCANINI, composer-conductor Richard Strauss, and singers Marilyn Horne and Frederica VON STADE. The scope of the festival has broadened to include works by composers other than Mozart, such as Benjamin BRITTEN and Samuel BARBER.

Samaroff, Olga [born Olga Hickenlooper] (1882–1948). American concert pianist and teacher. Samaroff (a name she adopted because it sounded more European than her own maiden name) made her concert debut in 1905, appearing with the New York Philharmonic at CARNEGIE HALL. She appeared with all the major American orchestras, and was once married to conductor Leopold STOKOWSKI. She taught piano at the Juilliard Graduate School of Music from 1925 until her death.

Sambre River. The Sambre River rises in France's Aisne department and flows northeastward to join the Meuse River at Namur in Belgium. In the 20th century it was the site of an important British victory in November 1918, as WORLD WAR I was drawing to a close.

Samil Independence Movement (1919–20). JAPAN annexed KOREA against its will in 1910, and after WORLD WAR I Koreans argued unsuccessfully at the Paris Conference for their right of self-determination. On March 1, 1919, cultural and religious leaders signed a "Proclamation of Independence" in SEOUL, the capital. The independence movement spread rapidly, and in the following year over 1,500 peaceful demonstrations involving about 2 million people were held throughout the country. Japanese police and military harshly suppressed the demonstrators, killing or wounding 23,000, arresting 47,000 and imprisoning 5,000. The Japanese carried out minor reforms, permitting limited self-governance. Today, March 1 commemorates the demonstrators' patriotism in both South and North Korea.

samizdat. Term coined by Soviet dissenters for the system of preparing and circulating writings, usually in typescript form, so as to avoid official censorship. Though this phenomenon appeared on a large scale in the late 1950s during the period of DESTALINIZATION, the word itself dates from the mid-1960s. It is a parody of the official acronym *Gosizdat* (State Publishing House) and means "self-publishing" or "do-it-yourself publishing." In *samizdat*, materials are circulated on the chain-letter principle. Typescript copies of the original text are passed on to trusted colleagues who in turn make further copies and hand them on to their friends to do likewise.

The authors and distributors of *samizdat* often operate under conditions of great difficulty and risk arrest and imprisonment in the event of discovery. Two articles of Soviet law specifically prescribe terms of imprisonment for citizens who seek to express their opinions in ways disapproved of by the authorities. Article 190–1 of the Russian Soviet Federated

Socialist Republic Criminal Code, "dissemination of fabrications known to be false which defame the Soviet state and social system," and Article 70 of the same code, "anti-Soviet agitation and propaganda," carry maximum penalties of three and 12 years' imprisonment respectively.

Samizdat has become a permanent feature of Soviet life in the post-Stalin period. It has provided an alternative, unofficial and uncontrolled channel of communication. *Samizdat* provides a forum for opinions, as well as a source of information on political, national, religious and literary themes that cannot find expression in the official press and publishing. It is not limited to the larger Russian cities but is also well developed in some of the non-Russian republics of the Soviet Union, particularly in Lithuania and the Ukraine. A striking feature of *samizdat* is the wide range and volume of its material. The range of subjects varies from petitions, protests and statements to complete novels, e.g., PASTERNAK'S DOCTOR ZHIVAGO, and lengthy historical works, e.g., SOLZHENITSYN'S THE GULAG ARCHIPELAGO. Perhaps the most outstanding achievement of *samizdat* has been the appearance between 1968 and 1980 of over 50 issues of the journal *A Chronicle of Current Events*, the mouthpiece of the human rights movement in the U.S.S.R. The *Chronicle* reports on human rights violations throughout the Soviet Union and is noted for its objectivity and accuracy.

The practice of circulating uncensored material privately has a long tradition in Russia. It can be traced as far back as the 1820s when the poet Pushkin, the playwright Alexander Sergeyevich Griboyedov and others are known to have privately distributed manuscripts of works disapproved of by the censors. The practice flourished in the second half of the 19th century as various revolutionary groups, and later political parties and national movements, emerged. It continued after the Bolshevik seizure of power in October 1917, and the creation of a new system of censorship. By the mid-1930s, however, the practice was effectively stamped out everywhere except in the labor camps, and it did not begin to reappear until after STALIN's death in 1953.

Samoa, American. American Samoa is a group of five volcanic islands and two coral atolls in the South Pacific Ocean that cover a total of 77 square miles; the capital is Pago Pago. In 1872 the Americans, in their search for a strategic harbor for their navy, gained exclusive rights from the High Chief of the Polynesian inhabitants to use the harbor of Pago Pago on Tutuila, the main island in the eastern group. Rivalries among Germany, Britain and the U.S. eventually led to a convention between them, whereby the U.S. acquired Eastern Samoa. The territory, which became known as American Samoa in 1911, was administered by the U.S. Navy from 1900 to 1951, after which the U.S. Department of the Interior took over. American Samoa remains an unincorporated territory of the U.S.; its people are U.S. nationals, but not citizens. The 1960 constitution, combining traditional practices with the needs of a modern state, gives American Samoans self-government, with certain powers reserved to the U.S. secretary of the interior. A non-voting delegate is elected to the U.S. House of Representatives. In 1978 Peter Tali Coleman became the first popularly elected governor; he was succeeded in 1984 by A.P. Lutali. A revised constitution, drawn up in 1986, excludes commoners and women from voting but has yet to be ratified by the U.S. Congress.

Samsonov, Alexander Vasilyevich (1859–1914). Russian general. Samsonov commanded the army that invaded East Prussia in August 1914 and was defeated by Generals LUDENDORFF and von HINDENBURG at the battle of Tannenberg; two Russian corps were destroyed and three others were reduced to half their size in one of the most decisive Allied defeats of WORLD WAR I. Samsonov committed suicide.

Sandburg, Carl (1878–1967). American poet and biographer. A major American poet, he was born in Galesburg, Illinois, the son of Swedish immigrants. A laborer by the age of 13, he fought in the Spanish-American War and returned to his hometown to attend a local college. Graduating in 1902, he traveled across the U.S., worked on various newspapers and published his first poetry in 1904. Secretary to Milwaukee's socialist mayor from 1910 to 1912, he settled in Chicago in 1913, writing for a number of newspapers until the late 1920s. Little attention was paid to his poems until 1914, when they began to appear in Chicago's *Poetry* magazine. His reputation was established with the publication of *Chicago Poems* (1916) and was augmented by his next volume, the PULITZER PRIZE-winning *Cornhuskers* (1918). Sandburg's other books of verse include

American poet Carl Sandburg on his 84th birthday (Jan. 6, 1962).

Smoke and Steel (1920), *Good Morning, America* (1928), *The People, Yes* (1936), *Complete Poems* (1950, PULITZER PRIZE, rev. ed. 1970) and the posthumous *Breathing Tokens* (1978). Writing with profound concern of the American experience and the American worker in unrhymed Whitmanesque free verse, his simple and vigorous language transformed ordinary life into a poetry that has influenced the course of American verse. Deeply interested in the history of the U.S., Sandburg was the author of an epic six-volume biography of Abraham Lincoln (1926–39). He also wrote a novel, *Remembrance Rock* (1948); a collection of folk songs, *The American Songbag* (1927); children's tales that include *Rootabaga Stories* (1922); and the autobiographical *Always the Young Strangers* (1953).

Sandino, Augusto Cesar (1893–1934). Legendary Nicaraguan rebel and patriot. Opposed to the military government that deposed an elected civilian government in a 1925 coup, Sandino led rebel forces in the NICARAGUAN CIVIL WAR OF 1925–33. Sandino demanded that U.S. marines who had been sent to NICARAGUA be withdrawn unconditionally. Sandino stopped fighting in 1933, after the U.S. forces left Nicaragua, and was pardoned by the newly elected government. However, the following year he was murdered in Managua by members of the national guard, which had opposed Sandino's forces in the war. In the 1970s his name was taken by the rebels who opposed the rule of SOMOZA; they called themselves the **Sandinistas**. (See also Daniel ORTEGA SAAVEDRA.)

Sanford, Edward T. (1865–1930). Associate justice, U.S. Supreme Court (1923–30). A graduate of the University of Tennessee and Harvard Law School, Sanford was in private practice in Tennessee when he was enlisted by the Justice Department to help in Theodore ROOSEVELT's antitrust-enforcement actions. In 1908 Roosevelt appointed Sanford a U.S. District Court judge. In 1923 Sanford was appointed to the U.S. Supreme Court by President Warren G. HARDING. Although he was generally a conservative on the Court, he wrote the majority opinion in *Gitlow v. New York* (1925), the first case to extend free speech protection of the First Amendment to the states as well as the federal government. He died in 1930 while still on the Court.

San Francisco. U.S. city on the coast of west-central CALIFORNIA; on a narrow peninsula between the Pacific Ocean and San Francisco Bay. The SAN FRANCISCO EARTHQUAKE (April 18, 1906) and a subsequent fire destroyed much of the city, but San Francisco was soon rebuilt. The opening of the famed Golden Gate Bridge (1937) and the less romantic but equally important San Francisco-Oakland Bay Bridge (1936) helped put the city on the map of the 20th century. In the early 1940s the city was a major port of embarkation and supply for the U.S. war effort in the Pacific (see WORLD WAR II IN THE PACIFIC). Over the years, the city's interesting geography, attractive architecture and moderate climate, along with a pervasive "laid-back" tolerant attitude, has drawn writers, artists, musicians and others. During the 1960s San Francisco's Haight-Ashbury district was perhaps the COUNTERCULTURE capital of the world, attracting numerous HIPPIES and others in search of an "alternative lifestyle." Yet the city has also prospered economically as a center of service industries, including banking, finance and insurance.

San Francisco earthquake. Disastrous earthquake that struck the city of San Francisco at 5:13 A.M. on April 18, 1906. It resulted from a violent movement of the San Andreas Fault. The quake, which measured 8.3 on the RICHTER SCALE, lasted less than a minute. It toppled structures throughout the city, cracked gas and water mains and caused widespread destruction. Even more devastating was the three-day-long fire that, sparked by the quake, almost completely razed San Francisco.

Sanger, Frederick (1918–). British biochemist. Sanger was awarded his Ph.D. in 1943 from Cambridge University, where he worked throughout his career. In 1955, he established the amino-acid structure of insulin, which had earlier been isolated by F.G. BANTING and C.H. Best. This discovery, which led to the synthesis of artificial insulin, won Sanger his first NOBEL PRIZE in chemistry, in 1958. In 1977 Sanger and his group used original techniques to map the complete DNA of the virus Phi X 174. For this revolutionary research, which led to the creation of genetic material in the laboratory, Sanger was awarded his second Nobel Prize in chemistry, which he shared with Walter Gilbert and Paul Berg.

Sanger, Margaret [Margaret Higgins] (1883–1966). American social reformer and a pioneer of the birth control movement in the U.S. Born in Corning, New York, Sanger studied nursing and was a pupil of Havelock ELLIS. As a public-health nurse, she was a witness to the terrible problems created, on the one hand, by overly large families, and on the other, by botched abortions. Convinced of the necessity of family planning, she began a campaign of education and in 1914 founded the National Birth Control League. In 1915 she was arrested for sending informational material on birth control through the mails. The following year she opened a birth-control clinic in Brooklyn and was again arrested. Gradually winning over both the public and the legal system, Sanger organized birth-control conferences, was founder-president of the National Committee on Federal Legislation for Birth Control from 1923 to 1937 and became the first president of the International Planned Parenthood Foundation in 1953. Her autobiography was published in 1938.

San Marino, Republic of. San Marino is a landlocked republic on the slopes of Monte Titano in east-central Italy, 12 miles west of the Adriatic Sea. The world's smallest republic, it has a total area of 24 square miles and is divided into nine castles or districts. San Marino claims to be the world's oldest republic. San Marino volunteers fought for ITALY in WORLD WAR I and from 1923 the republic came under the domination of MUSSOLINI's fascist regime. In WORLD WAR II, San Marino followed Italy in declaring war on Britain (1940) but abolished the fascist system and declared its neutrality shortly before Italy's surrender (September 1943). A year later San Marino declared war on Germany after German forces entered its territory and captured its 300–man army. The postwar party structure reflected Italy's. A Communist/Socialist (PCS/PSS) coalition (1945–57) was followed (1957–73) by one between the Christian Democrats (PDCS) and the Independent Social Democrats (PSDIS). By virtue of its economic union with Italy, San Marino became an integral part of the European Communities in the 1950s. Women obtained the vote in 1960 and became eligible for election in 1973. In June 1986, the Christian Democrats and the Communists, as the two largest parties, formed a grand coalition, which was returned to power in the May 1988 elections.

San Miniato. Tuscan town about 20 miles from Florence, Italy; in July 1944, during WORLD WAR II ON THE ITALIAN FRONT, its inhabitants were massacred by retreating Germans.

San Remo. Ancient port and resort town on the Gulf of Genoa, 27 miles east of Nice. An international conference here (April 19–26, 1920), ratified the decisions made the previous May at the PARIS PEACE CONFERENCE. The decisions made at San Remo led to the Treaty of Sevres.

San Roman, Jose Alfredo Perez (1931–1989). Cuban-American co-commander of the U.S.-trained Cuban exile force that failed in its attempt to invade CUBA at the BAY OF PIGS in April 1961. San Roman was taken prisoner together with 1,100 of his men; they were freed 20 months later, after the U.S. supplied Cuba with $53 million in food and medical supplies. After returning to the U.S. he served in the U.S. army and worked as a truck driver. He committed suicide.

San Sebastian. Spanish provincial capital on the Bay of Biscay. The **San Sebastian Pact**, a republican manifesto calling for the abolition of the Spanish monarchy, was signed here in 1930.

Santa Cruz de Tenerife. Port and capital city of the Canary Islands' Tenerife province. Here General FRANCO organized the uprising against the republican government that developed into the SPANISH CIVIL WAR.

Santa Cruz Islands. Remote island group in the southwestern Pacific Ocean, north of the New Hebrides. During a naval battle here on October 26, 1942, the U.S. aircraft carrier *Hornet* was destroyed by the Japanese. U.S. forces, however, won the battle. (See also WORLD WAR II IN THE PACIFIC.)

Santayana, George (1863–1952). Spanish-born American philosopher and literary critic. Santayana, who taught at Harvard from 1889 to 1912 before spending the remainder of his long life in a secluded Italian villa, was acclaimed as one of the great literary stylists of his age. Indeed, the beauty of his writing came to supersede the influence of Santayana's eclectic philosophy, which was an unsystematized blend of skepticism, Epicureanism and Platonic humanism. Santayana was at his best as an appreciator of the arts, and *The Sense of Beauty* (1896) remains a major work in the field of aesthetics. His five-volume magnum opus, *The Life of Reason: Phases of Human Progress* (1905–06), studies creative evolution within human civilizations. Metaphysical works by Santayana include *Skepticism and Animal Faith* (1923) and the four-volume *The Realms of Being* (1927–40). A novel, *The Last Puritan* (1936), was a surprising best-seller. The three-volume *Persons and Places* (1944–53) was Santayana's autobiography.

Santmyer, Helen Hooven (1895–1986). American author. Her mammoth novel, *And Ladies of the Club,* about life in a small midwestern town, turned her into a celebrity at age 88. The book shot up the best-seller lists after being published commercially in 1984 (Ohio State University Press had brought out a limited edition in 1982). She had worked on the book for more than 50 years while working as an English professor, college dean and librarian.

Santo Domingo. Capital, largest city and chief port of the Dominican Republic. Devastated by a Caribbean hurricane in 1930, it was rebuilt and renamed Ciudad Trujillo for then-dictator Rafael TRUJILLO Molina; its former name was restored in 1961. The U.S. sent troops here in 1965 to restore order during a leftist rebellion and civil war.

Sanusi Revolt of 1915–17. The Sanyusiyah brotherhood, Sufist and puritanical Muslims, established themselves in eastern LIBYA, fighting against French expansionism in the Sahara and Italian colonization in Libya. They attacked British forces in the Egyptian desert during WORLD WAR I, and in November 1915 the British needed reinforcements to stop them. A British offensive February-March 1916 drove them to the Suva Oasis. In 1917 the British pushed them back to Libya, where they antagonized the Italians. Sanusis gained control of Libya after WORLD WAR II, when their leader became IDRIS I. Idris reigned until deposed in 1969 by Muammer EL-QADDAFI.

Sao Tome and Principe. Two main islands, Sao Tome and Principe, and the rocky islets of Caroco, Pedras, Tinhosas and Rolas, comprise this democratic republic situated in the Bight of Biafra, off the coast of West Africa. Cocoa was introduced by the Portugese in the 19th century, but production declined after 1905, when an international boycott was imposed over the conditions of virtual slavery suffered by plantation laborers. In 1960 a nationalist liberation group was set up, which reorganized itself in 1972 as the Movimento de Libertacao de Sao Tome e Principe (MLSTP), under the

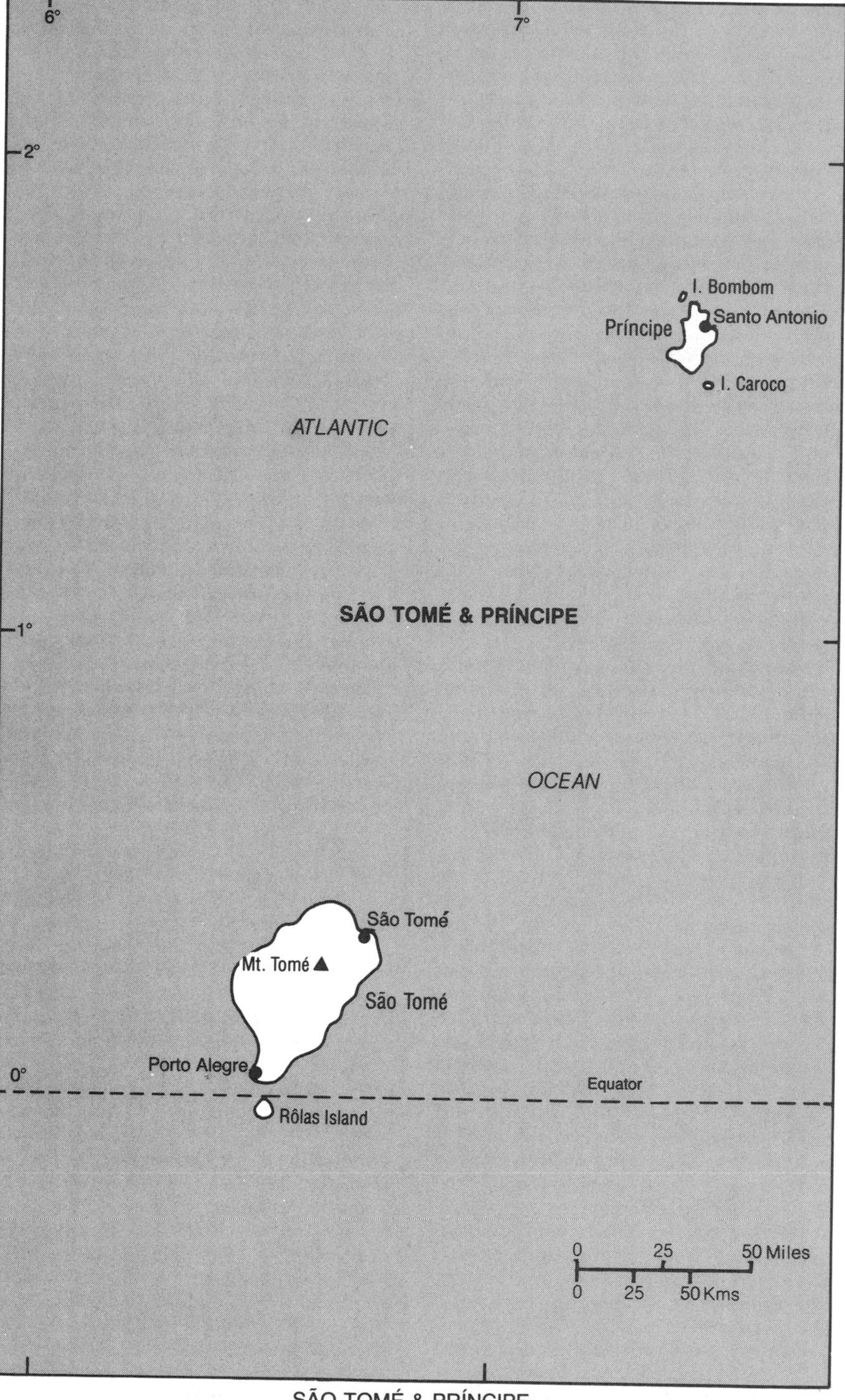

SÃO TOMÉ & PRÍNCIPE

leadership of Dr. Manuel Pinto da Costa. After the armed forces' coup in Portugal in April 1974, the MLSTP was recognized as the sole representative group. When independence was achieved on July 12, 1975, da Costa became the first president. In 1978 a coup attempt by foreign mercenaries was suppressed. In late 1984 President da Costa proclaimed the islands to be nonaligned; in 1985, the ministers of foreign affairs and planning, supporters of cooperation with the Soviet Union, were dismissed. Major constitutional changes were announced in October 1987, providing for the election by universal suffrage of the president and the national people's assembly. In March 1988 an invading force of 46 armed men unsuccessfully attempted to seize police headquarters near the capital, on Sao Tome. During their trial, which began in July 1989, the would-be invaders, among them Cape Verdeans and Angolans, admitted that they had been trained in South Africa.

Saragat, Giuseppe (1898–1988). Italian politician. A prominent figure in the history of Italian socialism, Saragat was president of ITALY from 1964 to 1971. A staunch anticommunist, he tried to keep the Socialist Party, then led by Pietro NENNI, from strengthening its ties to the communists. In 1947, he broke with Nenni and founded his own party, the Socialist Party of Italian Workers, which later became the Social Democratic Party. Before his election to the presidency, he served as foreign minister in the center-left administration headed by Christian Democrat Aldo MORO.

Sarajevo. Capital city of Yugoslavia's BOSNIA AND HERZEGOVINA, 125 miles southwest of Belgrade. Under Austrian rule from 1878, Sarajevo became a center of the Serbian nationalist movement. It can truly be said that the 20th century started here—on June 28, 1914—when Hapsburg heir Archduke FRANZ FERDINAND and his wife were assassinated in an open carriage on the streets of Sarajevo by a Serbian nationalist. This fateful act sparked the conflagration that was WORLD WAR I. Sarajevo became a part of the new state of YUGOSLAVIA in 1918. The city was the focus of happier attention in 1984, when it hosted the winter OLYMPIC GAMES.

Sarawak. Malaysian state on the northwestern side of the island of BORNEO. A British protectorate from 1888, it was occupied by Japan in WORLD WAR II. After the war it was ceded to the UNITED KINGDOM as a crown colony (1946). Sarawak was a center of anti-Malaysian rebellions prior to the formation of MALAYSIA in 1963. Kuching (formerly called Sarawak) is its capital.

Sarazen, Gene [born Eugene Saraceni] (1902–). American golfer. Sarazen was one of the leading players of golf's first golden age, in the 1920s and 1930s. In 1922, he won the U.S. Open and PGA tournaments. He went on to win the PGA title twice more, along with an additional U.S. Open title and a British Open. In 1935, he won the Masters Tournament in a memorable playoff with Craig Wood. Sarazen represented the United States on six Ryder Cup teams.

Sargent, John Singer (1856–1925). American painter. Born in Florence, Italy, of American parents, he was raised in Europe and educated in Italy, France and Germany. He studied with Carolus-Duran in Paris, traveled widely and made his first journey to the U.S. in 1876. He first exhibited his work in the Salon of 1878. By the time he moved to London in 1884, he had already established a reputation as a virtuoso portraitist. He remained in London for most of his life, portraying fashionable society figures with a remarkably painterly bravado. The style and elegance of his portraits was enhanced by his amazing facility for capturing textures with his sweeping brushstrokes. Among his best-known portraits are *Mme. X* (Metropolitan Museum of Art, New York City) and *Isabella Stewart Gardner* (Gardner Museum, Boston). Spending a good deal of his time in the U.S. in the 1890s, he was commissioned to paint a mural series, *The History of Religion,* for the Boston Public Library, a project he finally completed in 1916. At the beginning of his career and after 1910, Sargent also produced a number of superb watercolor landscapes done in a highly personal impressionistic style.

Sargent, Sir Malcolm (1895–1967). British conductor and organist. A dapper and dashing figure, Sargent was immensely popular with the British concert-going public even though he was not considered a great musician. He was effective in conducting large-scale choral works and championed British music. Sargent began his career as an organist for a London church, but he turned to conducting in 1921. He held a number of prominent musical posts before becoming the director of the BBC Symphony in the 1950s. Sargent also taught conducting at the Royal College of Music. During WORLD WAR II, he conducted morale-boosting concerts during the Nazi air raid Blitz on LONDON. He was knighted in 1947.

Sarikamis. Town in northeastern Turkey where the Russians decisively defeated the Turks in an important battle of WORLD WAR I in December 1914.

Sarkis, Elias (1924–1985). Lebanese lawyer and diplomat. Sarkis served as presidential chief of staff from 1958 to 1966, and governor of the Central Bank from 1968 to 1976. He held the office of president of LEBANON from 1976 to 1982. A Maronite Christian, he was unable to stem fighting among that country's religious factions. He left office at the end of his six-year term and settled in FRANCE.

Sarnoff, David (1891–1971). American businessman, pioneer of the broadcasting industry. Born in Uzlian, Russia, he immigrated to the U.S. with his family in 1900, settling in New York City. He worked as a cablegram messenger boy and, after teaching himself Morse code, became a telegraph operator for the Marconi Wireless Telegraph Co. while also attending Pratt Institute. He first received public notice for broadcasting the first news of the sinking of the S.S. TITANIC in 1912. Four years later Sarnoff outlined to the Marconi management his idea for a radio receiver. When the Radio Corporation of America (RCA) absorbed Marconi in 1921, Sarnoff became RCA's general manager. The company soon began to manufacture radios on a mass basis. In order to increase the market for these receivers, RCA, under Sarnoff's direction, organized (1926) the first successful commercial radio network in the U.S., the National Broadcasting Company (NBC). He became RCA's president in 1930 and chairman of the board in 1947. Sarnoff was also a leader in the development of American television. He set up an experimental station in 1928 and 12 years later launched a commercial channel. A brigadier general during WORLD WAR II, he was communications consultant to General Dwight D. EISENHOWER. He retired as chief executive officer of RCA in 1966 and was succeeded by his son, Robert W. Sarnoff, but remained board chairman until his death.

Saroyan, William (1908–1981). American novelist, playwright and songwriter. Raised in an Armenian-American community in Fresno, California, he moved to San Francisco during the GREAT DEPRESSION of the 1930s and quickly established his reputation as a prolific writer with an ascerbic wit. Famed for the rapid pace of his writing, he was also possessed of a rapid-fire temper that caused him to break with HOLLYWOOD over the production of his novel *The Human Comedy* (1943) and to refuse the 1939 PULITZER PRIZE for his play *The Time of Your Life* because he resented "wealth patronizing art." In addition to his novels, plays and songs, Saroyan's output also included more than 400 short stories. A romantic nonconformist, he called the Associated Press five days before his death to leave a posthumous statement: "Everybody has got to die, but I have always believed an exception would be made in my case. Now what?"

Sarraute, Nathalie [born Nathalie Tcherniak] (1900–). Russian-born French novelist and literary critic. Sarraute commenced her literary career relatively late in life, having worked as an attorney through her late 30s. But she became one of the pioneers of the NOUVEAU ROMAN (New Novel) literary movement in France. Her first published work, *Tropisms* (1938), a collection of short sketches, rejected the traditional literary conventions of plot and moral analysis, instead focusing on the small, instinctual life responses—tropisms—of her characters that revealed their true, unconsciously motivated life. Subsequent novels by Sarraute, written in a similar vein, include *The Planetarium* (1959), *The Golden Fruits* (1963), *Do You Hear Them?* (1972) and *Fools Say* (1976). *The Age of Suspicion* (1956) is a collection of her critical essays, while *Childhood* (1984) is a partial autobiography.

Sartre, Jean-Paul (1905–1980). French philosopher, novelist, playwright and literary critic. Sartre, who was awarded the NOBEL PRIZE for literature in 1964 but declined it in protest of the values of bourgeois capitalist society, was perhaps the most influential French writer of this century. His first major work was the novel *Nausea* (1938), in which the existential nothingness of daily existence was vividly portrayed. In 1943 came BEING AND NOTHINGNESS, Sartre's major philosophical work. His play *No Exit* (1944) explores the manipulative fears and greed that cause unhappiness in human relationships. After the war, Sartre produced a series of novels, notably *The Age of Reason* (1945), that probed the dilemmas of French life during the Nazi occupation. *Questions of Method* (1957) and *Critique of Dialectical Reason* (1960) sought to blend Marxism and EXISTENTIALISM, to the widespread displeasure of both camps. Sartre composed a number of major critical studies, including *Baudelaire* (1947) and *Saint Genet* (1952) (on Jean GENET). Sartre was the longtime lover and companion of Simone DE BEAUVOIR and was also, in the 1940s, closely linked to fellow existentialist Albert CAMUS.

Sasebo. Port city on the Japanese main island of Kyushu, on Omura Bay. Its deep harbor made it ideal as the chief Japanese base during the RUSSO-JAPANESE WAR (1904–05). The U.S. bombed the city heavily in 1944–45, during WORLD WAR II. Sasebo later became the site of an important U.S. Navy base. It also saw anti-U.S. demonstrations by Japanese left-wing radicals.

Sassoon, Siegfried (Lorraine) (1886–1967). British poet and pacifist. Alhough he had written earlier poetry, Sassoon's first major works were written during WORLD WAR I, in which he served as a lieutenant on the Western Front. Shocked by the savagry and the enormous casualties of the war, he produced poetry with a desolate air that railed against complacent patriotism. Sassoon encouraged the work of Wilfred OWEN, whom he met while both were recuperating in Scotland in 1917. Published in *Counter-attack* (1918), Sassoon's verse was not immediately popular with a public still entrenched in wartime nationalism and enamored of the GEORGIAN poets. His work began to receive acclaim in the 1920s, when *Satirical Poems* (1926) appeared; collections of his works were published in 1947 and 1961. He also wrote the acclaimed, semiautobiographical novels *Memoirs of a Fox-Hunting Man* (1928), *Memoirs of an Infantry Officer* (1930) and *Sherston's Progress* (1936), which were later collected into *The Complete Memoirs of George Sherston* (1937); and the autobiographies *The Old Century and Seven More Years* (1938), *The Weald of Youth* (1942) and *Siegfried's Journey* (1945). His diaries were published in 1981 and 1983, edited by R. Hart-Davis.

Satanic Verses, The. See Salman RUSHDIE.

satellite. The first artificial Earth satellite, SPUTNIK I (launched by the U.S.S.R. on October 4, 1957), has been followed by hundreds of other Soviet, U.S., European and Asian satellites. By the early 1960s, satellites such as TELSTAR and RELAY had begun to revolutionize global communications. Placed in geostationary orbits, they relay telephone, radio or television signals from one part of Earth to another. The INTELSAT (international satellite network), founded in the 1970s, provides international telecommunications service. Weather satellites have made reliable forecasting possible and can track weather patterns over a period of time. LANDSAT satellites provide photographs that help scientists to understand the effects of various types of land use on Earth's fragile ecosystem. Both the U.S. and Soviet use reconnaissance or "spy" satellites.

Satherly, Arthur "Uncle Art" (1889–1986). American executive. Born in Britain, he immigrated to the U.S. in 1913 and became involved in the early development of the recording industry through his work with Thomas EDISON. A pioneer in that industry, he helped launch the careers of such major country music performers as Gene Autry, Tex Ritter and Roy ROGERS.

Satie, Erik (1866–1925). Parisian composer who, with DEBUSSY and RAVEL, was the chief architect of modern French music. Born and raised in Honfleur, in the Calvados region of France, he learned early to thumb his nose at the excesses of post-Wagnerism and the pretentiousness of Impressionism. It was his firm conviction, recounts Virgil THOMSON, "that the only healthy thing music can do in our century is to stop being impressive." Forsaking the Paris Conservatory after only one year, the 20–year-old youth lived in virtual poverty, working as a pianist in Montmartre cafes, where he wrote musical polemic in a small newspaper and forged an important friendship with Claude Debussy. Satie's characteristic blend of pop tunes, unusual harmonies, austere textures, sardonic humor and bizarre titles marked early piano works like the *Gymnopedies* (1888), the *Gnossiennes* (1890) and the *Pieces en forme de poire* (1903) for critical abuse as well as the praise of Debussy and Ravel. At the age of 40 he returned to musical studies at the Schola Cantorum and subsequently produced his most important works: the collaboration with PICASSO, COCTEAU and DIAGHILEV of the landmark Cubist ballet, PARADE (1917); the setting for voice and orchestra of Plato's dialogues, *Socrate* (1918); and experiments in film music—*Musique d'ameublement* or "furniture music," per Satie—for *Relache* (1924). Before his death from cirrhosis of the liver in 1925, he had been adopted as a mentor by the young composers of LES SIX. An inspection of his reclusive quarters after his death revealed dozens of shiny blue suits, an out-of-tune piano, hundreds of umbrellas and an inscription on the wall, "This house is haunted by the devil." (See also CUBISM.)

For further reading:

Myers, Rollo H., *Erik Satie*. New York: Dover Publications, 1968.

Sato, Eisaku (1901–1975). Prime minister of Japan. After graduating from Tokyo University in 1924, Sato held a number of government positions before being elected to the House of Representatives (the lower house of the Diet, or parliament) in 1949. In 1953, he was made secretary-general of the Liberal Democratic Party. From 1958 to 1964, Sato held a number of cabinet posts, before succeeding Ikeda Hayato as party leader and prime minister in November of that year. Sato remained in office until July 1972, making him the longest-serving premier in the nation's history. During his tenure, Japan became a major economic power and relations with Southeast Asia and the U.S. were strengthened. In 1974 Sato won the NOBEL PRIZE for peace for his anti-nuclear stance.

Saturday Evening Post. American weekly periodical begun in 1821. The *Post* was established as a Saturday magazine of miscellany with no illustrations. By 1897, it faced bankruptcy, but was purchased by Cyrus H.K. Curtis who installed George Horace Lorimer as editor. The magazine, which was written to appeal to a middle-brow audience, became famous for its romantic fiction, mysteries, Western serials and illustrations of archetypal American life by Norman ROCKWELL. By the 1920s, the magazine was a success. Contributors included Agatha CHRISTIE, J.P. MARQUAND, William FAULKNER, Ben HECHT, Stephen Vincent BENET, Dorothy THOMPSON and Will ROGERS. Despite that eclectic group of writers, the magazine's policy was Republican, conservative and isolationist. In 1962, the *Post* began to lose money, and it was shut down in 1969. It was later revived as a nine-times-a-year publication and achieved a circulation of 467,000, but never regained the immense popularity of its heyday.

"Saturday Night Live." Late-night American comedy/variety series. It pre-

SAUDI ARABIA

miered on NBC on Oct. 11, 1975. Producer Lorne Michaels and the original cast—Chevy Chase, Jane Curtin, John Belushi, Dan Aykroyd, Gilda Radner, Garret Morris and Bill Murray (who joined the show in 1977)—concocted a "live," weekly 90 minutes of topical satire, slapstick comedy and music. In a sense, it became the LAUGH-IN of the 1970s, taking the irreverent pulse of its day. Popular comic trademarks included Chase's bumbling pratfalls, Aykroyd's fast-talking sleazoids, Murray's crooning lounge lizards, Belushi's Samurai characters, and the glorious antics of the "Blues Brothers" (Aykroyd and Belushi). There were "The Coneheads" (interplanetary goons), the "Week-End Update" newscasts (hosted by Chase and Jane Curtin), and the "Wild and Crazy Guys" (Aykroyd and frequent guest Steve MARTIN). A "second generation" of comics took over after 1980, including Eddie Murphy, Billy Crystal, Martin Short and Randy Quaid. Later series regulars included Dana Carvey, Jon Lovitz, and Dennis Miller. Some things have always been a part of the format over the years—the use of unlikely guest hosts each week (politicians like New York Mayor Ed Koch, sports figures like Yankees owner George Steinbrenner, consumer advocate Ralph NADER) and the distinctive voice of announcer Don Pardo.

For further reading:
The Complete Directory to Prime Time Network TV Shows. New York: Ballantine Books, 1988.

Saudi Arabia. Saudi Arabia is located on the Arabian Peninsula of southwestern Asia and covers an area of 829,780 square miles. In 1902 Abd al-Aziz IBN SAUD began a 30–year campaign during which he conquered all of present-day Saudi Arabia and established the Kingdom of Saudi Arabia in 1932. The country has been a dominant force in Middle East politics, supporting the monarchists during the civil war in North Yemen (1962–67), supporting IRAQ in the IRAN-IRAQ WAR and attempting to mediate a peace in LEBANON (1980s). In 1975 King Faisal was assassinated, and his brother became King Khaled, although the real power was held by another brother, Fahd, who eventually became king in 1982. Fanatic fundamentalists occupied the Great Mosque at Mecca in 1979 but were removed in bloody fighting. In 1980 a Shia Muslim revolt was quelled and reforms initiated. During the 1987 haj to Mecca there were violent clashes between Iranian pilgrims and Saudi forces. After Iraq's invasion of KUWAIT (1990), King Fahd asked for U.S. help to defend his country against Iraqi aggression (see PERSIAN GULF WAR). Saudi Arabia became the base of operations for the successful UNITED NATIONS-backed action against Iraq (August 1990–February 1991).

SAUDI ARABIA

1902	Abd al-Aziz takes city of Riyadh in daring night raid; governs through "Wahhabi" principles, seeking to purify Islam through return to traditional practice.
1912	Abd al-Aziz founds Ikwhan ("Brothers"); Wahhabi missionaries and shock troops spread movement among Berber tribes.
1926	Conquest of peninsula complete; al-Aziz becomes King Saud of Saudi Arabia, a new kingdom based on "Sharia" (Koranic law).
1929	Battle of Sabila; Saud eliminates extremists of the Ikwhan.
1937	Standard Oil of California strikes world's largest oil fields; sets up Arabian-American Oil Company in partnership with Saud.
1945	Formation of the Arab League.
1953	King Saud dies.
1956	Relations with France and Britain broken over their invasion of Egypt.
1957	Saud II forms "King's Alliance" with monarchs of Jordan and Iraq.
1960	Saudis found Organization of Petroleum Exporting Countries (OPEC).
1961	World Muslim League formed in Mecca; Saudis support Yemeni monarchists against secular Nasserist rebels; slavery made illegal; social security system begins distributing oil wealth.
1964	Saud abdicates in favor of brother Faisal, judged more competent to handle immense oil wealth while preserving traditional values.
1967	Secular states of Egypt and Syria defeated in Six-Day War; Saudi prestige increases among Arabs.
1970	Islamic Conference founded; Faisal creates world political network.
1973	Faisal supports Arab assault on Israel with money; engineers pan-Arab oil embargo against U.S. in effort to force Israelis out of occupied Palestine, holy city of Jerusalem.
1974	Share in Aramco increased to 60%.
1975	Faisal assassinated by family members.
1977	Princess of royal family beheaded for adultery.
1979	Shiite Muslims take over Grand Mosque at Mecca until killed.
1981	Support for Iraq in war with Iran; Saudis re-cement U.S. ties, become largest buyer of U.S. arms.
1983	New push toward self-sufficiency in agriculture.
1990	As secular Iraq overruns monarchist Kuwait, Saudis allow build-up of massive U.S.-led force on Saudi soil; Western troops segregated from Saudi citizens; King Fahd holds Arab members of coalition in line with anti-Iraq policy.
1991	Saudi troops take part in assault on Iraq; first modern military operation; joins new regional alignment with Egypt, Syria and U.S.

Sauguet, Henri (1901–1989). French composer. His simple but elegant works made him one of France's most important composers of the 1920s. He wrote the music for 14 ballets, eight theatrical productions, and 35 films as well as numerous vocal and instrumental works, including the opera *La Chartreuse de Parme.*

Savage, Michael Joseph (1872–1940). Prime minister of NEW ZEALAND (1935–40). Born in Australia, he became a gold miner and labor leader. In 1907 he immigrated to New Zealand, where he continued his union activities and in 1933 became a founding member of the LABOUR PARTY. Holding the post of Labour's parliamentary leader from 1933, he formed New Zealand's first Labour government after the party's victory in the 1935 elections. He was reelected in 1938. During his terms in office, Savage instituted various social and educational reforms, enacted social security legislation and helped to revive a flagging economy. A popular leader, he died in office.

Savak. Iranian secret police under the shah, dispersed after the Islamic IRANIAN REVOLUTION OF 1979. Many former Savak members were murdered by the people in revenge for crimes of torture and murder.

Savary, Alain (1918–1988). French politician. During WORLD WAR II Savary was in the French RESISTANCE and was a leader in the government formed just after Liberation. He was a member of the National Assembly and held ministerial posts under Charles DE GAULLE and in other governments. A prominent socialist, he was secretary general of that party from 1969 to 1971. Savary served as education minister from 1981 until he was forced to resign in 1984 after a lengthy public uproar over his proposals to reform the country's private school system.

Savimbi, Jonas (1934–). Angolan military and political leader. Savimbi studied at universities in Lisbon and Lausanne before returning to ANGOLA. There he joined Holden Roberto's fledgling nationalist movement. In 1962 he was involved in the evolution of this group into the National Front for the Liberation of Angola (FNLA). After conflicts with Roberto, he left the FNLA and formed his own group, the National Union for Total Independence of Angola (UNITA), in 1966. In the ANGOLAN CIVIL WAR that began in 1975, Savimbi was defeated in his quest to control Angola by Agostinho NETO's Popular Movement for the Liberation of Angola (MPLA). Continuing his struggle throughout the 1970s and '80s, he has been supported with political and material aid from South Africa and Western countries including the U.S. In 1990 there were allegations that Savimbi's forces had slaughtered elephants in Africa in order to raise money by selling their tusks. At the same time, the rebels and the government were engaged in negotiations aimed at bringing about a peaceful solution to the civil war.

savings & loan scandal. During the 1980s, the administration of President Ronald REAGAN adopted deregulation of industry as a national priority. Financial institutions were largely deregulated and both banks and savings and loan associations became far more aggressive in offering attractive returns to savers—and in accepting far more risky loans. When many borrowers defaulted and real estate values plummeted in the Southwest and elsewhere a number of savings and loan institutions failed. The problem was so severe that the federal program for insuring savings and loans—the FSLIC—was nearly insolvent and had to be merged into the FDIC. Investigations of the scandal uncovered many sharp operators, and also favoritism and systematically lax regulation of the S&Ls. The scandal also resulted in the so-called Keating Five investigation of five U.S. senators who were accused of improperly using their influence over regulators on behalf of Charles Keating, an S&L executive. (See also KEATING FIVE SCANDAL.)

Savitskaya, Svetlana (1948–). Soviet cosmonaut. The second Soviet woman to fly in space, Savitskaya and fellow cosmonauts Leonid Popov and Alexandr Serebrov, flew the Soyuz T-7 mission (August 19, 1982) to link up with the Soviet space station SALYUT 7. During her second flight aboard a SOYUZ spacecraft, the Soyuz T-12 (July 17, 1984), she became the second woman in space, performing 3.5 hours of extravehicular activity (EVA).

Sawchuk, Terrance Gordon "Terry" (1929–1970). Canadian hockey player. A Calder Trophy winner as National Hockey League rookie of the year with the Detroit Red Wings in 1950, Sawchuk was one of the most enigmatic of that enigmatic breed, goaltenders. A quiet, intense man who played most of his career in the pre-mask era, his face was a road map of scars and lacerations. His goals against average stayed below 2.00 during his first five years in the league. He won the Vezina Trophy four times as the league's best goalie, and led the Toronto Maple Leafs to an upset Stanley Cup victory in 1967. His astounding 103rd shutout came with the New York Rangers, the last stop on what had become a peripatetic career. Sawchuk died that offseason during a shoving match with a teammate. He entered the Hockey Hall of Fame in 1971.

Saw Maung (1928–). Burmese general; began his military career after 1945, rising through the ranks to become head of the Southwest Command in the early 1980s. Saw Maung became minister of defense in 1988 and led the September 1988 army coup. He subsequently became head of the Myanmar (see BURMA) government.

Sayers, Dorothy L(eigh) (1893–1957). British novelist, essayist, medieval scholar and anthologist. She is best known for her stories about the amateur detective Lord Peter Wimsey. In the words of historian Howard Haycroft, she held "pre-eminence as one of the most brilliant and prescient artists the genre has yet produced." The daughter of a clergyman-schoolmaster, Sayers grew up in the fen country of East Anglia (the location of her most famous Wimsey novel, *The Nine Tailors*, 1934). After taking top honors in medieval literature in Somerville College, Oxford, she taught at Hull High School for Girls and worked for an advertising agency in London. Her detective stories about the eccentric Lord Wimsey and his independent-minded Harriet Vane, Miss Climpson (leader of a group of female detectives) and Montague Egg (a traveling salesman) were acclaimed and secured her a modest independence. Her translations of Dante in the 1950s were hailed in academic circles. Publicly flamboyant, privately secretive, her fiction alone reveals her inner loneliness. Her alter ego, the spinster Miss Climpson, who appears in several Wimsey stories, is resourceful, formidable—but essentially alone. "I'd never been treated as a woman," Sayers confided once, "only as a kind of literary freak . . . I loathe being deferred to." (Her illegitimate son, Anthony, remained a carefully kept secret all her life.) She never relaxed her high standards in detective fiction. In the initiation ritual she wrote for London's Detective Club, of which she became a member in 1919, she made prospective members swear that they "play fair" with their readers; otherwise, she admonished, "May your Pages swarm with Misprints and your Sales continually Diminish. Amen."

For further reading:

Brabaon, James, *Dorothy Sayers*. New York: Scribner's, 1981.

Sazonov, Sergei Dmitriyevich (1861–1927). Russian diplomat and statesman. Sazonov started working for the foreign ministry in 1883 and in 1910 was appointed foreign minister. He attempted to ease relations with Germany, but relations with Great Britain deteriorated. He eventually forced the Germans to relinquish command of Turkish troops in Constantinople. After the assassination of Archduke FRANZ FERDINAND, Sazonov pressured the czar to agree to complete mobilization. He was dismissed in 1916 as a result of his view that an autonomous POLAND should be created. In 1917 he was appointed ambassador to London and then acted as foreign minister for Admiral A.V. KOLCHAK.

Scalia, Antonin (1936–). Associate justice, U.S. Supreme Court (1986–present). A graduate of Georgetown University and Harvard Law School, Scalia practiced with a large Cleveland law firm before becoming a law professor at the University of Virginia. He worked in the NIXON administration, eventually becoming head of the White House office of Legal Counsel. He returned to teach at the University of Chicago Law School where he became known as a leading conservative legal scholar. President Ronald REAGAN appointed Scalia to the U.S. Court of Appeals for the District of Columbia, whose judges at the time were known as being extremely liberal. In 1986 President Reagan appointed Scalia to the Supreme Court. On the Court Scalia helped forge a solid conservative majority that rejected the judicial activism of the prior 50 years. He indicated his fundamental opposition to ABORTION in a separate majority opinion in WEBSTER V. REPRODUCTIVE SERVICES (1989). Scalia was noted for his careful legal scholarship.

Scandinavia. Historic region in northern Europe, consisting of DENMARK, NORWAY and SWEDEN. Strictly speaking, FINLAND is not part of the region, although it is often considered to be so because of its geographic proximity to these other nations. ICELAND too is sometimes referred to as part of it because Iceland's people are of Scandinavian descent. Norway and Sweden occupy the Scandinavian Peninsula. After almost a century, the union of Norway and Sweden was ended peacefully in 1905, and in 1918 Iceland gained independence from Denmark. Germany seized Denmark and Norway by force (April 1940) during WORLD WAR II, while Sweden remained neutral; Finland was dominated by the U.S.S.R. Iceland's union with Denmark ended entirely in 1944. The Scandinavian nations are known for having pioneered the modern WELFARE STATE.

Scapa Flow. Sea basin surrounded by the Orkney Islands (principally Mainland and Hoy), off the north coast of Scotland. During both World Wars, Scapa Flow was the site of an important British naval base. The British naval vessel *Vanguard* was torpedoed here in 1917. In October 1939, in the opening days of WORLD WAR II, the *Royal Oak* was sunk by a German U-boat, causing a temporary closing of the base. On June 21, 1919, the bottom of Scapa

Flow turned into a naval museum when the officers and crew of the interned German High Seas Fleet opened the underwater valves of their ships and sent them to Davy Jones' Locker. The Scapa Flow naval base was closed permanently in 1956.

Scargill, Arthur (1938–). British union leader. Scargill, a miner from Yorkshire, became president of the National Union of Mineworkers (NUM) in 1981. A radical Marxist, he aroused much controversy, and even the LABOUR PARTY, traditionally friendly to unions, sought to distance itself from his rhetoric. Scargill led the NUM through the year-long coal miners strike of 1984–85, in which the union was ultimately unsuccessful. The strikers hoped to persuade the state-owned British Coal Board to abandon its plans to cut back in workers and close old mines; after the strike some 70,000 workers were laid off and 67 mines closed. Some NUM members opposed to Scargill's extremism broke from the NUM and formed the Union of Democratic Mineworkers.

Schacht, Hjalmar (Horace Greeley) (1877–1970). German financier. A successful banker, Schacht became commissioner of currency of the WEIMAR REPUBLIC in 1923. In this post he managed to stabilize GERMANY's currency and put an end to the enormous inflation that had plagued the nation. He simultaneously served as president of the Reichsbank (1923–30), Germany's leading financial institution, before resigning because of his opposition to Germany's continuing reparation payments. At the beginning of the Nazi era, Schacht continued to serve the German government, again becoming president of the Reichsbank in 1933 and helping to finance Germany's rearmament. In 1934 he was also appointed minister of economics, but resigned the position in 1937 after a series of disagreements with Hermann GOERING. Opposing Adolf HITLER's enormous rearmament program as inflationary, Schacht was removed from the Reichsbank in 1939. Increasingly opposed to Nazi policy, he was accused of involvement in the plot to assassinate Hitler and jailed in 1944. Tried for war crimes at NUREMBERG in 1946, he was acquitted and went on to hold various posts in German finance. Schacht wrote an autobiography, *Confessions of the Old Wizard* (1953, tr. 1956).

Schaeffer, Rev. Francis August (1912–1984). Evangelical theologian and leading scholar of fundamentalist Protestantism. Ordained as a Presbyterian, Schaeffer and his wife in 1955 founded *l'Abri* (*The Shelter*), a chalet and spiritual center in the Swiss alps. Schaeffer attracted thousands of students and intellectuals by teaching a reasoned rather than an emotional approach to religion. *L'Abri*, eventually expanded to six countries, including the U.S. Schaeffer's 23 philosophical books included the 1976 bestseller, *How Should We Then Live?*

Schaffner, Franklin (James) (1920–1989). American stage, television, and film director. In the 1950s and early '60s he directed many major television productions, including "Person to Person" with Edward R. MURROW. He also directed the successful Broadway adaptation of Allan DRURY's *Advise and Consent* (1960). As a film director, he specialized in large-scale historical dramas and adaptations of popular novels. He received a total of 28 ACADEMY AWARD nominations for such films as *Planet of the Apes* (1968), *Nicholas and Alexandra* (1971), *Papillon* (1973) and *The Boys from Brazil* (1978). His 1970 film *Patton* won a total of seven Academy Awards, including best picture and best director.

Schapiro, Meyer (1904–). American art historian. Born in Lithuania, he immigrated to the U.S at the age of three, grew up in New York City and attended Columbia University, receiving a Ph.D. and teaching there from 1928. A partisan of modernist movements from the 1930s and an important critic of contemporary art, he has been one of the most influential of all American art historians. In addition to social, psychological and aesthetic analyses of 19th- and 20th-century art, Schapiro has also done significant research in early Christian and medieval art. He is known for such essays as "The Nature of Abstract Art" (1937) and "Leonardo and Freud" (1956), as well as many books, including studies of Van Gogh (1950) and Cezanne (1952).

Schary, Dore (1905–1980). HOLLYWOOD film writer and movie producer, playwright and political activist. Failing as a playwright and actor on Broadway in the 1930s, Schary set out for Hollywood. His fortunes rose after he won an ACADEMY AWARD for the original story of *Boys Town* (1938). He was briefly production chief at RKO, where he specialized in socially conscious movies including *Crossfire* (1947), an expose of ANTI-SEMITISM in the U.S., and *The Boy with Green Hair* (1948), an antiwar film. As production chief at METRO-GOLDWYN-MAYER (1948–56) he continued his two-pronged policy of presenting entertainment vehicles and "message" films, balancing musicals such as the classic *An American in Paris* (1951) and *Seven Brides for Seven Brothers* (1954) with serious dramas such as *The Blackboard Jungle* (1955), a realistic treatment of urban juvenile delinquency. In 1956 he wrote his finest play, *Sunrise at Campobello,* about Franklin D. ROOSEVELT; four years later he adapted it for the screen. A lifelong political activist, during the 1950s Schary fought MCCARTHYISM and the blacklist in Hollywood. He produced or oversaw the production of some 250 movies and wrote more than 40 screenplays.

For further reading:

Schatz, Thomas, *The Genius of the System: Hollywood Filmmaking in the Studio Era.* New York: Pantheon Books, 1988.

Schaufuss, Peter (1949–). Danish dancer and ballet director. Schaufuss joined the Royal Danish Ballet in 1965, then became, successively, a principal dancer with the NEW YORK CITY BALLET (1974–77) and the National Ballet of Canada (1977–83). He has also been a guest artist with several other dance companies, and is especially noted for his productions of August Bournonville's *La Sylphide* (London Festival Ballet, 1979) and *Napoli* (National Ballet of Canada, 1981). He won the silver medal at the Moscow Ballet Competition in 1973. Since 1984 he has been artistic director of the London Festival Ballet.

Schecter Poultry v. U.S. (1935). Unanimous U.S. Supreme Court decision holding that segments of the NEW DEAL'S NATIONAL INDUSTRIAL RECOVERY ACT (NRA) were unconstitutional. A cornerstone of President Franklin D. ROOSEVELT's New Deal program, the NRA sought to regulate competition within ailing industries by setting up "fair competition" codes. The Court held the Act impermissibly regulated activities that were not within Congress' power and also gave the president too much power in designing the codes. The case marked the first salvo in the conservative Supreme Court's opposition to FDR's New Deal program.

Scheidemann, Philipp (1865–1939). German official. Elected to the Reichstag in 1903, Scheidemann proclaimed the WEIMAR REPUBLIC in 1918. He served as chancellor of the new republic for five months before resigning in protest of the punitive TREATY OF VERSAILLES that ended World War I. Scheidemann held other elected positions before fleeing the Nazis in 1933. (See also NAZISM.)

Schenck v. United States (1919). U.S. Supreme Court decision that defined the limits of free speech. The famous opinion, written by Justice Oliver Wendell HOLMES, upheld enforcement of the Espionage Act of 1917 against an attack on the statute as a violation of the First Amendment's protection of free speech. Holmes announced that the concept of free speech was not absolute and that words were not protected when they created a clear and present danger. The opinion contains Holmes' famous admonition that the First Amendment would not protect a man who falsely shouts "fire!" in a theater and thereby causes a panic.

Scherchen, Hermann (1891–1966). German conductor. Scherchen was one of the most ardent and influential interpreters of modern classical music. He was a special champion of the composers of the Viennese Expressionist school—Alban BERG, Arnold SCHOENBERG and Anton WEBERN—and frequently conducted premieres of their works. Scherchen began his career as a violist with the Berlin Philharmonic from 1907 to 1910. But he soon turned to full-time conducting, being named in 1928 as musical director of the Konigsberg Philharmonic Orchestra. With the rise of the Nazis, Scherchen fled Germany in 1933. He spent most of his remaining years in Switzerland, where he was active not only as a conductor but also as a teacher and as a pioneer in the development of electronic-acoustical music.

Schiele, Egon (1890–1918). Austrian painter. An expressionist, he was strongly influenced by Gustav KLIMT. Like Klimt, he took the erotic for much of his subject matter, was often criticized for his works and even jailed for obscenity in 1912. Filled with a lonely, haunted angst, his figures are defined by a jagged and delicate linearity and often vibrant colors. While much of his work is highly sexual in nature and reflects a deep interest in Freudian psychology, it conveys more of a sense of anxiety than of sensuality. He was also a talented portraitist and is noted for his almost frighteningly direct self-portraits. He and KOKOSCHKA were the leaders of Austrian EXPRESSIONISM, and his promising career was cut short by his death in the influenza epidemic of 1918.

Schindler, Alma (1879–1964). Pianist, memoirist and wife, successively, of Gustav MAHLER, Walter GROPIUS and Franz WERFEL. Schindler was one of the leading female figures in fin de siecle Vienna. The daughter of painter Anton Schindler, she was highly trained in piano and musical composition. During her marriage to Mahler, she exercised a considerable influence on his compositions; Mahler composed the so-called "Alma theme" in the opening movement of his Sixth Symphony as her musical portrait. She published a selection of Mahler's letters (1924) and later wrote a memoir (1940) of him. After Mahler's death in 1911, Schindler was married to Gropius and Werfel.

Schirra, Walter (1923–). U.S. astronaut; a veteran of the APOLLO program, Schirra has also flown MERCURY and GEMINI spacecraft. As pilot of the Mercury-Atlas 8 (October 3, 1962) during the early days of the American space program, Schirra's six-orbit nine hour and 13 minute space flight helped pave the way for the next U.S. step into space, the Gemini program. On the two-man Gemini-Titan 6-A mission (December 15–16, 1965), Schirra and Thomas STAFFORD added a lighthearted note by reporting the sighting of a UFO resembling Santa Claus; and they concluded their report with Schirra giving an off-key rendition of "Jingle Bells." The Apollo 7 mission (October 11–22, 1968) was conducted in a more serious vein. In the course of 11 days in space, Schirra and astronauts Donn Eisele and Walter Cunningham had the unenviable job of proving the controversial Apollo spacecraft qualified for flight after the tragic launchpad fire that killed Gus GRISSOM, Roger CHAFFEE and Edward WHITE on January 27, 1967.

Schlemmer, Oskar (1888–1943). German painter. Born in Stuttgart, he studied there with Adolf Hoelzel. He became acquainted with avant-garde art in Berlin, soon developing a personal style of modernism that emphasized geometrically streamlined and machine-like human figures. He was an influential teacher at the BAUHAUS from 1921 to 1929, heading the sculpture and theater departments. At this time he also concentrated on stage design and is particularly noted for his *Triadic Ballet* (1922) with music by Paul HINDEMITH. As a sculptor, he created Constructivist-like reliefs in mortar and wire. An art teacher in Berlin from 1932 to 1933, he was dismissed by the Nazis, and spent his last years as a manual laborer.

Schlieffen Plan. Master plan for GERMANY's strategy in WORLD WAR I prepared by Field Marshal Alfred, Graf von Schlieffen, chief of the German general staff from 1891 to 1905. The plan assumed a two-front war that could be won by swiftly defeating France, provoking the surrender of the Western Allies, and by then attacking Russia with the full force of the German military machine. It required Germany to engage in a bold flanking movement through Belgium and Holland into France. In a modified and somewhat weakened form, prepared by Schlieffen's successor, H.J.L. von Moltke, the plan was attempted at the outbreak of WORLD WAR I in 1914. It was unsuccessful due to France's delaying defense, Russia's military might, Germany's lack of organization and other factors. The concept of the lightning strike embodied in the Schlieffen Plan was later used by the Nazis in their *blitzkriegs* at the beginning of WORLD WAR II.

Schlumberger, Jean (1907–1987). French designer. One of the foremost jewelry designers of the 20th century, he achieved international renown through his association with Tiffany & Co. in New York City. His clients included some of the world's most glamorous women. In 1957 he set the legendary Tiffany diamond, the largest canary diamond in the world.

Schmeling, Max(imilian) (1905–). German boxer. Schmeling was the first European in the 20th century to win the heavyweight championship of the world. He began his career as European light-heavyweight champion and German heavyweight champion, came to the U.S. in 1928 and took the world championship two years later. His most memorable fights are his 12-round knockout of Joe LOUIS in 1936, and Louis' return of the favor, in 1938. Schmeling left the U.S. after Nazi boosterism made him unpopular. He later renounced NAZISM and returned to boxing. He retired after World War II, in 1948, with a record of 55–15, with 38 knockouts.

Schmidt, Helmut (1918–). Chancellor of WEST GERMANY (1974–82). An economist, Schmidt joined the German Social Democratic Party (SDP) in 1946 and was elected to the Bundestag in 1953. In 1965 he became chairman of the SDP and was later minister of defense (1969–72) and of finance (1972–74) in the cabinet of Willy BRANDT. He succeeded Brandt as chancellor in 1974 and was reelected in 1976 and 1980. Schmidt followed a pragmatic course, distancing himself from Brandt's OSTPOLITIK policy and favoring closer ties with the Western alliance.

Schmidt, Mike (1949–). U.S. baseball player. Schmidt was considered by many to be the greatest ever at third base; in his best year, 1980, he had 48 homers, 121 runs batted in and a .286 average. That season he was named the National League's most valuable player, an honor he won three times, as well as the World Series most valuable player. His career total of 548 home runs in 18 seasons ranked seventh on the career list, and he won the Gold Glove award for fielding 10 times. He retired from the Philadelphia Phillies in 1989, with career statistics of 1,595 runs batted in, 2,234 hits, 1,883 strikeouts and 1,506 runs.

Schmidt-Rottluff, Karl (1884–1976). German painter. Born in Saxony, he studied architecture in Dresden, where he met the artists HECKEL and KIRCHNER and, with them in 1905, cofounded the Expressionist group DIE BRUCKE. His vigorously rhythmic and emotionally dramatic oils, often landscapes or portraits, are composed of simple forms executed in blocks of intense, flat colors. He is also noted for his many extremely powerful woodcuts. Schmidt-Rottluff settled in Berlin in 1911, was forbidden to paint by the Nazis and became a professor of art in postwar East Berlin.

Schmitt, Harrison (1935–). U.S. astronaut and the first scientist to walk on the moon. Schmitt flew on the Apollo 17 (December 7–19, 1972) lunar landing mission, the last of the APOLLO series. A geologist, he spent three days on the lunar surface with astronaut Eugene CERNAN while command module pilot Ronald Evans orbited above. The mission, which made extensive use of the Lunar Rover, was one of the most scientifically successful of the Apollo series. Schmitt resigned from NASA in 1975 and in 1976 was elected to the U.S. Senate from the state of New Mexico.

Schnabel, Artur (1882–1951). Austrian-Polish born pianist and composer best known for his authoritative interpretations of the music of Schubert and Beethoven. Schnabel studied with Leschetizky in Vienna and in the 1920s and 1930s became one of the foremost performers and teachers in Berlin. His cycles of the complete Beethoven piano sonatas were legendary. He repudiated the romantic virtuoso piano tradition of the day. According to one of his students, pianist Claude Frank, "Schnabel thought of himself as a musician rather than a pianist. He was completely at the service of the music itself. He made you forget the notes—and there were many wrong ones in his performances—and listen to the music." Pianist-commentator Abram Chasins remarked that "Schnabel could be so careless about technical details that a performance or a recording would sound more like a 'priva rista' reading than a prepared execution. . . . [Yet] his art was a fighting faith. He was perpetually vigilant against attempts to serve expediency or compromise." Schnabel himself said, "I am a simple musician." But he said it with the air of an emperor. Schnabel single-handedly resurrected the piano sonatas of Franz Schubert, which had been all-but-forgotten. He also helped restore the sonatas and concertos of Mozart to the standard repertoire.

For further reading:

Chasins, Abram, *Speaking of Pianists*. New York: Alfred A. Knopf, 1967.

Schneider, Alan [born Abram Leopoldovich] (1917–1984). Russian-born American stage director. Schneider was considered one of the most important directors in contemporary theater. In his 40–year career, he was closely associated with the works of Samuel BECKETT, Edward ALBEE, Harold PINTER and Bertolt BRECHT. He directed the American premiere of Beckett's WAITING FOR GODOT (1956). Schneider won a Tony Award for his 1962 Broadway production of *Who's Afraid of Virginia Woolf?*

Schneiderman, Rose (1882–1972). Polish-born American labor leader. In the early 1900s she organized the Women's Trade Union League. She served as the league's president for many years. During the GREAT DEPRESSION of the 1930s she was a member of President Franklin D. ROOSEVELT'S BRAIN TRUST. She was later secretary of the New York State Labor Department.

Schneiderman, William V. (1905–1985). Prominent American Communist. Born in czarist RUSSIA, he immigrated to the U.S. at the age of two and became a naturalized citizen. He later headed the Communist Party of California for 25 years. In 1939 a federal judge ruled that he had lied about his party affiliation when he became a citizen and should be deported. The U.S. Supreme Court reversed this decision in 1943 after Wendell WILLKIE, the 1940 Republican presidential candidate, argued on Schneiderman's behalf. In 1952 Schneiderman and 13 other communists were found guilty of advocating the violent overthrow of the U.S. government and were given fines and prison sentences; however, retrials were ordered and the indictments were later dropped for lack of evidence.

Schnitzler, Arthur (1862–1931). Austrian playwright and novelist. The son of a prominent Viennese Jewish doctor, he was trained as a physician and practiced medicine during the earlier part of his career. A sophisticated observer of fin-de-siecle society in Vienna, he gained fame for the sparkling wit, ironic vision and psychological insight he brought to bear in lively portrayals of the many sides of love and human sexuality. His first recognition came with the play *Anatol* (1893, tr. 1911), an episodic account of a playboy's erotic adventures. His other dramas include *Liebelei* (1895, tr. 1907), *Reigen* (1900, tr. *Merry-Go-Round,* 1953), an erotic romp that became a successful French film as *La Ronde* in 1950, and *Der einsame Weg* (1903, tr. *The Lonely Way,* 1915). Schnitzler dealt with the theme of ANTI-SEMITISM in his play *Professor Bernhardi* (1912, tr. 1927) and focused on various social problems of his day in other works. He also wrote a number of novels, including the autobiographical *The Road to the Open* (1908, trans. 1923), and short stories, such as *None but the Brave* (1901, tr. 1926).

Schoenberg, Arnold (1874–1951). Viennese-born composer, leader of the New Viennese School, whose innovations in atonality and nontonal serial techniques profoundly influenced modern music in

Composer Arnold Schoenberg at home in Santa Monica, California.

this century. He studied with Alexander Zemlinsky in Vienna. His first major works, while solidly within the Wagnerian, late romantic tradition, stretched tonal ambiguity almost to the breaking point—*Verklaerte Nacht* (*Transfigured Night,* 1899) and *Pelleas und Melisande* (1905). The public hostility that had greeted these works turned to outright brawls and riots with the premieres in London, Berlin and Vienna of later works that finally broke with tonality, the chilling *Pierrot Lunaire* and the landmark *Five Pieces for Orchestra* (both in 1912). Schoenberg worked to bring order and discipline to this free tonality with the dodecaphonic system, a jaw-breaking word designating compositions based on a series of notes, or "row," containing all the 12 chromatic tones in a succession chosen by the composer. "Ich fuehle Luft von anderem Planeten," prophetically sang the soprano voice introduced at the end of the *Second String Quartet* (1908)—"I feel air from another planet." By the time the *Third String Quartet* was premiered in 1927, nothing like this music had been heard before. However, during the later years of Schoenberg's American residence—he left Germany in 1933 out of distaste for the Nazi regime—he maintained what Leonard BERNSTEIN called "a rocky romance with tonality." Works such as *The Ode to Napoleon* (1942) flirted with tonal systems; while the numerous late transcriptions of Strauss and Brahms were quite traditional tonal works. Schoenberg himself admitted that "the longing to return to the older style was always vigorous in me." (And we recall that the last piece in *Pierrot Lunaire* yearned for the "alter Duft aus Maerchenzeit"—the "ancient fragrance of once-upon-a-time.") Disciples Anton von WEBERN and Alban BERG carried on his torch; and most subsequent composers have had to grapple with his influence. Some, like Igor STRAVINSKY, ultimately accepted it; and others, like Bernstein, finally rejected it.

For further reading:

Schoenberg, Arnold, *Style and Idea.* New York: Philosophical Library, 1950.

Scholz, Jackson (1897–1986). American athlete. He was once considered the world's fastest human. In 1924 he earned the gold medal for the U.S. in the 200–meter run in the Paris OLYMPIC GAMES. His loss to British runner Harold Abrahams in the 100–meter run was depicted years later in the film *Chariots of Fire* (1981).

Schouten Islands [Misore Islands]. Island group off IRIAN BARAT, the western part of the island of NEW GUINEA; comprised of Biak, Numfor and other islands. The Schouten Islands were on the U.S. force's itinerary during the U.S. island-hopping campaign in WORLD WAR II IN THE PACIFIC. U.S. forces took Biak on May 27, 1944, after severe fighting; Numfor was secured on July 6. After years of dispute, this area was taken over by INDONESIA in May 1963.

Schrodinger, Erwin (1887–1961). Austrian physicist. Schrodinger was educated in Vienna at both the gymnasium and the university, where he obtained his doctorate in 1910. After serving as an artillery officer in World War I, he taught at various German-speaking universities before he succeeded Max PLANCK as professor of physics at the University of Berlin in 1927. In 1933 Schrodinger's bitter opposition to the Nazis drove him into his first period of exile, which he spent in Oxford, England. Homesick, he allowed himself in 1936 to be tempted by the University of Graz in Austria, but, after the ANSCHLUSS in 1938, he found himself once more under a Nazi government, which this time was determined to arrest him. Schrodinger had no alternative but to flee. Fortunately, the prime minister of Ireland, Eamon DE VALERA, himself a mathematician, was keen to attract Schrodinger to a newly established Institute of Advanced Studies in Dublin. Working there from 1939 Schrodinger gave seminars that attracted many eminent foreign physicists (as well as the frequent presence of De Valera) until his retirement in 1956, when he returned to Austria.

Starting from the work of Louis DE BROGLIE, Schrodinger in 1925–26 developed wave mechanics, one of the several varieties of quantum theory that emerged in the mid-1920s. He was deeply dissatisfied with the early quantum theory of the atom developed by Niels BOHR, and complained of the apparently arbitrary nature of a good many of the quantum rules. Schrodinger took the radical step of eliminating the particle altogether and substituting for it waves alone. His first step was to derive an equation to describe the behavior of an electron orbiting an atomic nucleus. Schrodinger eventually succeeded in establishing his famous wave equation, which when applied to the hydrogen atom yielded all the results of Bohr and de Broglie. It was for this work that he shared the 1933 NOBEL PRIZE for physics with Paul DIRAC. Despite the considerable predictive success of wave mechanics, there remained problems for

Schrodinger, when the probabilistic interpretation of Max Born soon developed into a new orthodoxy. Schrodinger found such a view totally unacceptable, joining those other founders of quantum theory, EINSTEIN and de Broglie, in an unrelenting opposition to indeterminism entering physics.

In 1944 Schrodinger published his *What is Life?*, one of the seminal books of the period. It influenced many talented young physicists who, disillusioned by the bombing of HIROSHIMA, wanted no part of atomic physics. Schrodinger solved their problem by revealing a discipline—free from military applications—that was significant and, perhaps just as important, largely unexplored. He argued that the gene was not built like a crystal but that it was rather what he termed an "aperiodic solid." He went on to talk of the possibility of a "code" and observed that "with the molecular picture of the gene it is no longer inconceivable that the miniature code should precisely correspond with a highly complicated and specific plan of development." Such passages, written with more insight than that contained in most contemporary biochemical works, inspired a generation of scientists to explore and decipher such a code.

Schultz, "Dutch" [born Arthur Flegenheimer] (1902–1935). American gangster. Born in the Bronx, New York, Schultz was a minor criminal until the mid-1920s, when he organized a gang and strong-armed his way into the control of the Bronx beer trade. He quickly enlarged his operations to include the Harlem numbers racket. An erratic, savage and miserly mobster, he was quick to have his opposition gunned down and acquired a reputation for violence beyond even the usual gangland standards. After his gunmen's murder of Vincent "Mad Dog" Coll in 1932, Schultz reigned supreme in New York City crime under the protection of Tammany Hall boss Jimmy Hines. When special prosecutor Thomas E. DEWEY began to investigate organized crime in 1935, Schultz argued that he should be killed. Syndicate mobsters disagreed and hired assassins from MURDER, INC. to do away with the Dutchman. Ambushed in Newark, New Jersey, he lingered for two days before succumbing.

Schuman, William (1910–). American composer, educator and administrator. Born in New York, Schuman studied composition with Charles Haubiel and attended the Teacher's College at Columbia University. He earned a B.A. in 1935 and an M.A. in 1937. He taught at Sarah Lawrence College from 1935 to 1945. His work *American Festival Overture* was performed by the Boston Symphony in 1939. This led to performances in Boston of his Third and Fifth symphonies, with Schuman conducting. His Fourth Symphony was performed in Cleveland in 1942. In 1945 Schuman became president of the Juilliard School of Music in New York. He left Juilliard in 1962 to become president of the Lincoln Center for the Performing Arts, a post he held until 1969.

Schumann, Elisabeth (1885–1952). German-American singer. A soprano, Schumann was known equally for her work in the opera house and on the concert stage. Born in Merseburg, Thuringia, Germany, she debuted with the Hamburg Opera in 1909 and sang with that company for a decade, enjoying special success in her Mozart roles. Schumann made her Metropolitan debut in 1914, as Sophie in *Der Rosenkavalier* (probably her most famous role) by Richard STRAUSS. She performed for two decades for Strauss at the Vienna State Opera, also enjoying triumphs during this period at the SALZBURG FESTIVAL (1922–35), the Zurich Mozart Festival (1917) and Covent Garden (1924). During these years, she also made guest appearances throughout Europe and in South America. In 1938, Schumann moved to the U.S. with her husband, Karl Alwin, and their son, Gerd; that year she joined the faculty of the Curtis Institute of Music in Philadelphia, where she taught for the rest of her life. In 1944 she became an American citizen. She died in New York City on April 23, 1952.

Schumann-Heink, Ernestine (1861–1936). Austrian-American opera singer. A contralto, Schumann-Heink made her operatic debut on October 13, 1878, as Azucena in the Dresden Opera's production of *Il Trovatore*. In the years before World War I, she sang at the Hamburg Municipal Opera, Berlin's Kroll Opera, Covent Garden in London, the BAYREUTH FESTIVAL, and the Metropolitan Opera in New York. In 1903–04, Schumann-Heink made a triumphal concert tour of the U.S., and in 1905 she became an American citizen. After her "farewell" tour in 1926, she appeared mostly in concerts and on the radio, also appearing in the 1935 film *Here's to Romance*. She died in Hollywood on November 17, 1936.

Schuschnigg, Kurt von (1897–1977). Austrian political leader. A nationalist and supporter of the Hapsburg restoration, Schuschnigg served as AUSTRIA's minister of justice from 1932 to 1934 and its minister of education from 1933 to 1934. After the assassination of Engelbert DOLLFUSS in 1934, Schuschnigg became chancellor, heading a semi-fascist regime. When Adolf HITLER demanded absorption of Austria through ANSCHLUSS, Schuschnigg countered with a call for an Austrian plebescite. His struggle against Hitler was successful until 1938, when he was forced to resign and was replaced by Nazi Arthur SEYSS-INQUART. Schuschnigg was arrested after the Germans entered Austria in March 1938 and imprisoned until 1945. He testified for the prosecution at the NUREMBERG TRIALS (1946) and was subsequently a professor in the U.S. (1947–67).

Schwartz, Delmore (1913–1966). American poet. Schwartz is perhaps best known for the ambitious poetic work *Genesis, Book I* (1943), which explores the experience of an American of Russian-Jewish descent living in New York City. *Vaudeville for a Princess* (1950) is a later collection of poetry and prose. Schwartz also wrote the short story collection *The World Is a Wedding* (1948), which revolves around middle-class Jewish life. Schwartz taught at Harvard University from 1940 until 1947. He served as editor of PARTISAN REVIEW and became poetry editor of the NEW REPUBLIC in 1955, serving also as an occasional film critic for them. His later years were spent in obscurity. He was the model for the fictional title character in Saul BELLOW's *Humbolt's Gift*.

Schwarzkopf, Elisabeth (1915–). German opera singer. Schwarzkopf began her opera career as a coloratura in such roles as Zerbinetta in *Ariadne auf Naxos* at the Charlottenburg Opera in Berlin, but became a lyric soprano after World War II, gaining fame for her roles in the operas of Mozart and Richard STRAUSS. She made her American debut in 1955 with the San Francisco Opera. One of her most distinguished roles, the Marschallin in *Der Rosenkavalier*, was preserved in a famous recording and film of the production with conductor Herbert von KARAJAN at the Salzburg Festival in 1960. She was also renowned for her *Lieder* singing, giving recitals and making recordings of the art songs of Gustav MAHLER and Franz Schubert, among others. In 1953 she married record producer **Walter Legge**, director of EMI and founder of London's Philharmonia Orchestra. She has given master classes in opera and *Lieder* singing around the world since 1976.

Schwarzkopf, H. Norman (1934–). American general who led the allied coalition forces against IRAQ during the PERSIAN GULF WAR (1990–91). Born in Trenton, New Jersey, Schwarzkopf was the son of the chief investigator of the LINDBERGH KIDNAPPING CASE. He grew up in New Jersey and in Tehran, IRAN, where President Franklin D. ROOSEVELT had sent his father to advise the shah. The younger Schwarzkopf consequently developed a life-long interest in the Middle East. He graduated from the U.S. Military Academy at West Point in 1956 and later earned a master's degree in guided missile engineering from the University of Southern California. He served two tours of duty in the VIETNAM WAR and was twice wounded. In 1983 he commanded the U.S. invasion of GRENADA. That year he was also assigned to develop contingency plans for the U.S. military in the event of a crisis in the PERSIAN GULF region. In 1988 he became head of the Central Command, responsible for U.S. military forces in the Middle East, Africa and the Persian Gulf. When IRAQ invaded KUWAIT in August 1990, Schwarzkopf commanded the U.S. forces ordered to SAUDI ARABIA by U.S. President George BUSH in **Operation Desert Shield**. He was made supreme commander of all the coalition forces in the region—more than a half million soldiers, sailors and fliers, the largest military force assembled since World War II. With the chairman of the Joint Chiefs of Staff, General Colin POWELL, and other military leaders, Schwarzkopf devised a plan of attack to drive the Iraqis from Kuwait with a minimum of allied casualties. He directed **Operation Desert Storm,**

Persian Gulf War triumvirate Gen. Colin Powell, Defense Secretary Dick Cheney and Gen. H. Norman Schwarzkopf in Riyadh, Saudi Arabia (1991).

which began on January 17, 1991 (local time) with an air bombardment of Iraq that lasted six weeks. The ground phase of the war was launched on February 24, 1991; Schwarzkopf's forces liberated Kuwait in less than a week. Known affectionately to his troops as "Stormin' Norman," Schwarzkopf gained great respect for his expressed concern not only about the success of the allied mission but about the safety of his troops and of Iraqi civilians. These qualities, along with his plain-spoken and avuncular nature, made Schwarzkopf a national hero. The swift and overwhelming allied victory, achieved through a bold but meticulously planned strategy with very few U.S. casualties, further enhanced Schwarzkopf's reputation as a military commander.

Schweinfurt. German city on the Main River in northwestern BAVARIA. The center of the German ball-bearing industry, during WORLD WAR II it was the target of numerous Allied bombing raids between 1942 and 1945. Schweinfurt was well defended by the Luftwaffe and anti-aircraft emplacements, and many Allied planes were shot down.

Schweitzer, Albert (1875–1965). German theologian, philosopher, musicologist, organ player, doctor and humanitarian. Schweitzer, who won the NOBEL PRIZE for peace in 1952, became a world-famous figure in his later years as a result of his dedicated work as a doctor and Christian missionary at a hospital that he constructed and administered in Lambarene in French Equatorial Africa (now the nation of Gabon). Schweitzer turned to the study of medicine only in 1905, having already established himself both as a theologian of note and as a scholar and virtuoso interpreter of the organ works of Johann Sebastian Bach. Schweitzer, who earned doctoral degrees in both philosophy and theology, wrote *The Quest of the Historical Jesus* (1906) in defense of a faith-oriented approach to Jesus that rejected historical evidence as a criterion of belief. His *J.S. Bach* (1908) remains a major musicological work that asserted for the first time the importance of pictorial imagination in Bach's compositions. A commitment to serve humanity led Schweitzer to give up his comfortable role as a scholar at the University of Strasbourg and to move to Africa in 1913, where he spent most of his remaining years. An absolute reverence for life became the hallmark of Schweitzer's philosophy. *My Life and Thought* (1933) is his autobiography, while *The Light Within Us* (1959) is representative of his later writings.

Schwitters, Kurt (1887–1948). German artist best known for his work in collage, a technique he developed into an important modern abstract art form. Schwitters was trained in conventional painting at the Dresden Academy and began his career painting traditional portraits. His inclinations toward the DADA movement suffered a setback when he was refused membership in the 1918 Club Dada in Berlin. He developed his own, similar direction with the name *Merz* and began to create his *Merzbilder*, "trash pictures," made by pasting together bits of paper and other miscellaneous items, often picked up from the street. He also constructed *Merzbau*, abstract conglomerations of scrap materials that reached room size, anticipating the "environments" created by some conceptual artists of the 1980s. With the rise of NAZISM in the

The penetrating gaze of Albert Schweitzer, humanitarian and Nobel laureate (1952).

1930s, Schwitters was forced to relocate, first in Norway and then in England. His work has had a continuing influence in the development of modern art and design, with a particularly strong impact on graphic design, where collage techniques have been used in such commercial work as advertising layout.

Sciascia, Leonardo (1921–1989). Italian novelist. Sciascia's first work to appear in English, *Le parrocchie di Regalpetra* (1956, translated as *Salt in the Wound*) was a book of essays depicting an imaginary town in Sicily. Its portrayals of Italian politics and the Mafia established themes to which Sciascia would often return. His novels, which have been described as intelligent suspense stories, include *Mafia Vendetta* (1963), *Candido, or A Dream Dreamed in Sicily* (1979) and *La sentenza memorabile* (1982).

scientology. Quasi-religious movement founded by pulp writer L. Ron HUBBARD in 1952. Hubbard, who became extremely wealthy (and reclusive) after the success of his legally established Church of Scientology, began as a writer for the now-vanished pulp fiction magazines, selling stories in every genre, from westerns to detective, but garnering most of his fame in the science fiction field. It was the leading monthly *Astounding* that first published Hubbard's articles on dianetics—a theory of allegedly "clear" mental health through the elimination of repressed past traumas—which formed the fundamental basis of scientology. Scientology extracts a great deal of money from its ardent followers, and the practices of the Church of Scientology have been closely investigated in Great Britain and Canada, among other countries.

Scissors Crisis. Name given to the economic crisis of 1923–24 in the Soviet Union. Prices of farm produce were falling, while those of industrial goods were rising. As a result, the standard of living of the peasants was falling; to offset this, the government took measures to keep prices of industrial products artificially low.

Scobee, Francis R(ichard) "Dick" (1939–1986). American astronaut who was the commander of the space shuttle CHALLENGER when it exploded on January 28, 1986. A combat pilot in the U.S. Air Force in the VIETNAM WAR, he logged more than 6,500 hours of flight in 45 types of aircraft. He served on a shuttle crew in 1984.

Scofield, John (1951–). American electric guitarist. Scofield typifies the younger group of virtuosic post-bop, jazz musicians whose musical roots range from BEBOP and the MODAL JAZZ of John COLTRANE to ROCK AND ROLL and rhythm and blues. Initially influenced by the urban blues guitar styles of B.B. King, Albert King and Chuck BERRY, Scofield broadened his horizons through studies at the Berklee School of Music in Boston (along with the University of North Texas in Denton, at the top of the new breed of jazz schools that began appearing after World War II). Engagements with mainstream artists such as baritone saxophonist Gerry Mulligan and trumpeter Chet

William Jennings Bryan (right) with Clarence Darrow at the Scopes trial in 1925.

Baker led to work with the jazz-rock fusion groups of drummer Billy Cobham and keyboardist George Duke. A stint in the early 1980s with jazz legend Miles DAVIS propelled Scofield to international fame. Since the mid-1980s, Scofield has toured and recorded mostly under his own name. Stylistically, like such fellow modern jazz guitarists as John Abercrombie and Pat Metheny, Scofield has evolved a highly personal and galvanizing style forged from virtuosic alloys of post-bebop harmonics, blues, rock and even country.

For further reading:

Milkowski, Bill, "John Scofield: All Shades of Blue," *Down Beat*, 1987.

Scopes Trial. Infamous landmark judicial case that took place in 1925. In March of that year, the Tennessee legislature passed a statute that prohibited public schools from teaching theories of evolution that differed from accepted biblical accounts. In July, John Scopes, a Dayton physics teacher, was put on trial for defying the statute by presenting Darwin's theory of evolution in his classroom. The American Civil Liberties Union came out in Scopes' defense and obtained the services of a distinguished lawyer, Clarence DARROW, to argue Scopes' case. Populist and perennial presidential candidate William Jennings BRYAN argued for the prosecution. The trial was dramatic, drawing international attention. Although Darrow insisted the statute was a violation of the separation of church and state, Scopes was convicted. He was later released by the state supreme court on a technicality.

For further reading:

Ginger, Ray, *Six Days or Forever?: Tennessee vs. John Thomas Scopes.* New York: Oxford University Press, 1974.

Scorsese, Martin (1942–). American film director. Scorsese is one of the major American film directors of the modern era. His films often deal with the dark side of American culture—its obsessions with violence and status—but Scorsese has also displayed an elegaic and even a comic sensibility. Educated at New York University film school, Scorsese scored his first critical success with *Mean Streets* (1973), a drama set in his native Little Italy district in New York City. The film helped make actor Robert DE NIRO a star. Scorsese and De Niro have collaborated several times since in films including *Taxi Driver* (1976), a chilling study of urban alienation and violence; *Raging Bull* (1979), the story of boxer Jake La Motta, and *Goodfellas* (1990), a look at life within organized crime. *The Last Waltz* (1978) is a documentary of the final rock concert by The BAND. *After Hours* (1985) is an absurdist comedy about New York night life. *The Last Temptation of Christ* (1988), based on the novel by Nikos KAZANTZAKIS, drew the ire of religious fundamentalists for its recognition of the human, sensual side of Christ's being.

Scott, Charles S., Sr. (1932–1989). American CIVIL RIGHTS attorney. In 1951 he helped lead the fight to integrate public schools by bringing a lawsuit against the Topeka, Kansas, school board on behalf of a black elementary-school student, Linda Brown. The case eventually went to the Supreme Court as BROWN V. BOARD OF EDUCATION. The court's 1954 decision in favor of Brown produced the landmark ruling that declared racial segregation in public schools unconstitutional.

Scott, Francis Reginald (1899–1985). Canadian politician, lawyer and poet. In the 1920s he was one of Canada's leading modernist poets (see MODERNISM). In the 1930s he helped found the Cooperative Commonwealth Federation, a democratic socialist party; he later served as its national chairman (1942–50). He was an authority on Canadian constitutional law. In the 1950s he was a member of legal teams that argued and won three landmark cases before Canada's Supreme Court. He served as dean of McGill University's school of law (1961–64). During his career he published several volumes of poetry. His *Collected Poems* (1981) won the prestigious Governor General Award.

Scott, Hazel (1920–1981). American pianist and singer, born in Trinidad. She was best known as an outstanding JAZZ performer but was equally outstanding as a BLUES and classical musician. A child prodigy, she enrolled in New York's Juilliard School of Music at age eight. She later starred in clubs, on Broadway and in films, including *The George Gershwin Story*. In 1945 she married U.S. representative Adam Clayton POWELL Jr.; they divorced in 1960. She often performed in support of various CIVIL RIGHTS groups. On one occasion, she appeared before the HOUSE UN-AMERICAN ACTIVITIES COMMITTEE (HUAC) to defend her civil rights activities.

Scott, Sir Peter Markham (1909–1989). British naturalist, painter, author and television personality, the son of Antarctic explorer Robert Falcon SCOTT. He was a founder, in 1961, of the World Wildlife Fund (later renamed the World Wide Fund for Nature) and designer of its panda logo. He was a celebrated painter of wildfowl and founder of the Wildfowl Trust (later renamed the Wildfowl and Wetlands Trust); he was also a passionate advocate of the existence of the Loch Ness Monster. He wrote 18 books on natural history and one autobiography, illustrated 20 other books and hosted the long-running BRITISH BROADCASTING CORPORATION (BBC) series "Look." He was knighted in 1973.

Scott, Robert F(alcon) (1868–1912). British explorer and naval officer. Scott is remembered as the leader of one of the most tragically ill-fated expeditions in the history of geographic exploration. He first explored the Antarctic region in the early 1900s as a member of a Royal Navy expedition. In 1910, he became the leader of a second expedition that had as its primary goal becoming the first to reach the SOUTH POLE. After lengthy prepara-

British polar explorer Robert Falcon Scott.

tions and grueling effort, the Scott expedition reached the Pole on January 17, 1912—only to find a flag planted there on December 14, 1911, by a Norwegian expedition led by Roald AMUNDSEN. Fierce blizzards led to the death of all members of the Scott expedition in March 1912, as they were attempting to return to civilization. Scott's diaries of the expedition, found on his person, were published in 1913. The British film *Scott of the Antarctic* (1948) dramatized the story of this expedition. Scott has long been revered as a model of quiet English self-sacrifice, but later research has suggested that he was motivated largely by vanity, was ill-prepared for his trek to the Pole and needlessly endangered the lives of his companions.

Scotto, Renata (1935–). Italian coloratura soprano. Born in Savona, Scotto studied at the Verdi Conservatory in Milan and made her debut there in 1954 as Violetta in *La Traviata*. Roles at La Scala (Milan), Covent Garden (London) and the Vienna State Opera followed. Scotto made her U.S. debut in 1960 as Mimi in *La Boheme* at the Chicago Lyric Opera. In 1965 she debuted at the Metropolitan Opera in New York performing Cio-Cio-San in *Madama Butterfly*. During the next decade Scotto played leading coloratura roles at opera houses around the world. She specialized in the Italian bel canto repertoire and was known for the agility of her high register and elegant phrasing of legato passages. She also appeared in Metropolitan Opera telecasts and has recorded extensively.

Scottsboro case. Notable legal case that established that under U.S. law persons facing the death penalty have a constitutional right to counsel, time to prepare for trial, and a right to a fair jury. The case involved a series of trials. Lasting six years, it gained international attention and helped focus attention on the legal inequality of blacks and whites in the American South.

In 1931 nine young blacks (subsequently known as the "**Scottsboro Boys**") were tried in state court in Scottsboro, Alabama, on charges that they raped two white women in a freight car. The accused were given an attorney only at the last minute, and the initial trial was held only six days after their arrest. The nine were tried and convicted by an all-white jury. (Blacks were excluded from juries throughout the South at the time.) The Scottsboro Boys were all either sentenced to death or to 75 to 99 years of jail for the conviction. However, the convictions were appealed to the U.S. Supreme Court, which twice reversed the trial court's convictions because of procedural errors at trial. After a retrial, five of the accused were dismissed as defendants. Four others were paroled in the 1940s, long after one of the women had admitted that no rapes had occurred. The last surviving defendant, Clarence Willie Norris, was officially pardoned by the state of Alabama in 1976. The Scottsboro cases established a constitutional right to an attorney in a capital case and the right to an integrated jury.

Scoville, Herbert "Pete," Jr. (1915–1985). American military expert. A physical chemist by training, from 1948 to 1955 he worked on the development of nuclear weapons as technical director of the defense department's Armed Forces Special Weapons Project. From 1955 to 1963 he served as deputy director for research and technology in the CENTRAL INTELLIGENCE AGENCY (CIA). While holding that post he became convinced of the need to control nuclear weapons. After leaving the CIA, he served for six years as assistant director of the Arms Control and Disarmament Agency, his final government position. From 1969 on, he campaigned tirelessly for arms control through books, articles, lectures and frequent appearances on Capitol Hill.

Scriabin, Alexander Nikolayevich (1872–1915). Composer of piano and orchestral music. In 1888 he entered the Moscow Conservatory and from 1898 to 1903 he taught there. He married pianist Vera Isakovich in 1897. From 1900 on, he was interested in mystical philosophy, and the end of his First Symphony was designed to be a glorification of art as religion. Theosophical ideas inspired his *Le Divin Poeme* (1905) and *Poeme de l'estase* (1908). He eventually viewed himself as a messiah who would reunite Russia with the Spirit. He devised a "liturgical act," which made use of poetry, dancing, colors and scents, as well as music, in an attempt to induce a "supreme final ecstasy." His music became progressively more idiosyncratic.

Scribner's. American monthly magazine from 1887 to 1939. Established by Charles Scribner's Sons, the New York publishing house, *Scribner's* was a celebrated literary magazine presenting fiction, poetry, biography, varied essays and criticism. Its contributors included Henry JAMES, Stephen Crane, Edith WHARTON, Jacob A. RIIS, S.S. Van Dine, Ernest HEMINGWAY, Thomas WOLFE, F. Scott FITZGERALD, Clarence DARROW, Lewis MUMFORD and Edmund WILSON. It was illustrated by N.C. WYETH and Maxfield PARRISH, among others, and its cover was designed by Stanford White. Its circulation reached a peak of 200,000 in 1910, but it went into decline shortly thereafter. An attempt to appeal to a broader audience in the early '30s was unsuccessful, and by 1936 its circulation had dropped to 40,000. In 1937, *Scribner's* was sold to Harlan Logan Associates, but after two years of financial struggle the magazine was discontinued.

SDS. See STUDENTS FOR A DEMOCRATIC SOCIETY.

Seabiscuit (1933–1947). American race horse. Purchased in 1936 for $7,500, the ill-tempered, half-crippled Seabiscuit went on to become the leading money winner of his time. A come-from-behind winner, he seemed to toy with his adversaries in the stretch, letting them smell victory before snatching it away again. He was ridden primarily by the oft-injured Johnny Pollard and the legendary George Woolf. Pollard was aboard for the horse's legendary match race victory over the great War Admiral at Pimlico. Seabiscuit twice lost the Santa Anita Handicap by inches,

Sheriff Charles McComb stands by as attorney Samuel Leibowitz confers with his clients, the "Scottsboro boys" (1935).

but in 1940, in the final race of his career, he won it and became the greatest money-winner of the time.

Seaborg, Glenn T(heodore) (1912–). American chemist. In 1939 Seaborg became an instructor at the University of California at Berkeley. During WORLD WAR II he went to Chicago as one of the principal figures in the development of the ATOMIC BOMB in its initial phases, at the University of CHICAGO. Returning to Berkeley he became chancellor of the university in 1958. In 1961 President John F. KENNEDY asked him to serve as head of the Atomic Energy Commission, a post he retained until 1971. Seaborg was the first scientist to head the AEC. He represented the U.S. at atomic and other scientific conferences, and served on numerous scientific and educational boards. Upon leaving the AEC, he returned to the University of California at Berkeley. He shared the 1951 NOBEL PRIZE for chemistry. He is the discoverer of nine elements, a unique achievement for which he received the Enrico Fermi Award in 1959.

Seale, Bobby (1937–). American black activist. Born in Dallas, Texas, he studied at Merritt College in Oakland, California, where he met Huey NEWTON. The two founded the BLACK PANTHERS in 1966, with Seale as chairman. Active in the ANTI-WAR MOVEMENT, he was indicted in 1969 as one of the "Chicago Eight" for his participation in demonstrations at the 1968 Democratic convention. A mistrial was later declared and charges were dropped. In the early 1970s Seale led the Panthers away from armed struggle and toward self-help programs. In 1973 he ran for mayor of Oakland, losing but receiving a very respectable vote total. He left the party shortly after the election. His autobiography, *A Lonely Rage,* was published in 1978.

search-and-destroy. An operational term used in the VIETNAM WAR. It was adopted by the MACV (U.S. Military Assistance Command Vietnam) in 1964 to describe operations designed to find, fix in place and destroy enemy forces and their base areas and supply caches. Originally intended to delineate one of the basic missions performed by South Vietnamese military forces, the term became widely used by U.S. forces later in the war. Public repugnance toward the brutality implied by the term in addition to vivid media accounts of destruction of Vietnamese villages helped undermine support for the war.

Searle, Ronald (1920–). English cartoonist. Educated at the Cambridge School of Art, he was a Japanese PRISONER OF WAR during WORLD WAR II. He is well-known for witty drawings, executed in a delicately linear style, that have appeared in such periodicals as the NEW YORKER and *Punch*. He has also been involved in films, as the creator of the mischievous female students of St. Trinian's School who became the subjects of several English comedies and as the designer of animation sequences for *Those Magnificent Men in Their Flying Machines* (1965) and *Scrooge* (1970). His cartoons have been included in such collections as *Forty Drawings* (1946), *Searle's Cats* (1968) and *Searle's Zoodiac* (1977).

Sears, Roebuck & Company. American department store and mail-order chain. It began in 1886 as a watch-selling sideline of Minnesota-born railroad worker Richard Warren Sears. The business prospered and he soon started the R.W. Sears Watch Company. Sears moved from Minneapolis to Chicago in 1887 and was joined by Indiana-born Alvah Curtis Roebuck. The company produced its first mail-order catalog, a 32-page affair, in 1891. Two years later the company name was changed to Sears, Roebuck & Company. By 1920 the company's sales volume had grown to $245 million. Offering an almost incredible range of goods, often to rural Americans whose opportunity for shopping was severely limited, the catalog supplied necessities and luxuries to millions of Americans and became one of the country's greatest retailing success stories. While it has undergone many changes, the Sears stores and catalog have survived and prospered into the final decade of the 20th century.

SEATO [South East Asia Treaty Organization]. Conceived by Secretary of State John Foster DULLES as a kind of Southeast Asian NATO, SEATO was founded in 1954. It included the U.S., Britain, France, Australia, New Zealand, Pakistan, Thailand and the Philippines. A separate protocol extended SEATO's protection to nonmember states South Vietnam, Laos and Cambodia. For the U.S. the purpose of SEATO was to provide a framework for building stable states to contain communist expansion. While Australia, New Zealand, Thailand and the Philippines assisted U.S. efforts in South Vietnam by dispatching of combat forces, other SEATO nations did not share American concerns. Because of these major political differences, SEATO was relatively ineffective and was disbanded in 1977.

Seattle. Largest city in U.S. state of Washington, and the most important commercial and industrial center in the Pacific Northwest. With the Alaska Gold Rush, Seattle became an important commercial center at the turn of the century. The opening of the PANAMA CANAL in 1914, coinciding with WORLD WAR I, led to the expansion of the port. In WORLD WAR II Seattle became a center of the aircraft industry; it is still the headquarters of the Boeing Aircraft Corporation. Seattle also figures prominently in the history of the American labor movement. In 1919 the radical Industrial Workers of the World (IWW) organized a general strike here.

Seattle Slew (1974–). American thoroughbred racehorse. Purchased at public auction for only $17,500, in 1977 Seattle Slew went on to become the first Triple Crown winner since SECRETARIAT. The son of Bold Reasoning was the first horse in racing history to head into the three races undefeated. The heavy favorite going into the Kentucky Derby, his lackluster performance while winning led to criticism of both the horse and his rider, Jean Cruguet. They went on, however, to win the Preakness in the second fastest time ever and the Belmont in masterful fashion.

Seberg, Jean (1939–1979). American film actress. Born in Marshalltown, Iowa, she had her first role as the star of Otto PREMINGER's *St. Joan* (1957) and was later seen in *Bonjour Tristesse* (1958). The crop-haired actress became famous for her performance as an American gamine in the Jean-Luc GODARD's New Wave classic *Breathless* (1959). Her later films included *The Five-Day Lover* (1960) and *Lilith* (1964). Hounded for her radical political views, the actress settled in Europe. Often-married (once to author Romain Gary) and psychologically troubled, she committed suicide at age 40.

Second Front. Allied invasion of the European mainland requested by Joseph STALIN in 1941 to take the enormous pressure of German attack off the U.S.S.R. The U.S. was involved in the Pacific war and European attention was focused on the African campaign. Early in 1942 requests for a second front were widespread in Europe and the U.S. However, coordination of efforts, sufficient planning for such a large enterprise and naval difficulties prevented the Allies from acting until a second front was finally agreed upon at the QUEBEC CONFERENCE of August, 1943. It was accomplished on June 6, 1944, with the NORMANDY landing.

Second or Great Boer War. The discovery of gold in 1886 drew the British to the Transvaal, exacerbating British-Boer tensions and leading finally to declaration of war against Great Britain by the Transvaal and the Orange Free State in October, 1899. Boer forces scored initial successes, seizing Kimberly, Mafeking and Ladysmith. In 1900 heavy British reinforcements under Field Marshal Lord Frederick Roberts, and General Lord Horatio Kitchener turned the tide, seizing BLOEMFONTEIN, capital of Orange Free State, on March 13, 1900, and occupying the country. The British invaded Transvaal, captured JOHANNESBURG and Pretoria in May-June 1900 and crushed battlefield resistance. The British annexed the Boer states, but it took Lord Kitchener two years of bitter fighting and repression to quell guerrillas led by Jan SMUTS, Louis BOTHA and Christaan de Wet. By the Treaty of Vereeniging (May 31, 1902) British sovereignty was recognized by the Boers in exchange for an indemnity and other concessions.

Second Sex, The. Nonfiction work by Simone de BEAUVOIR, published in France in 1949 as *Le Deuxieme Sexe* and translated into English in 1953. A probing analysis of traditional attitudes toward women and of their inferior social status, it became a virtual text for the women's movement and made its author one of the authentic heroes of contemporary FEMINISM.

Second Vatican Council. See VATICAN II.

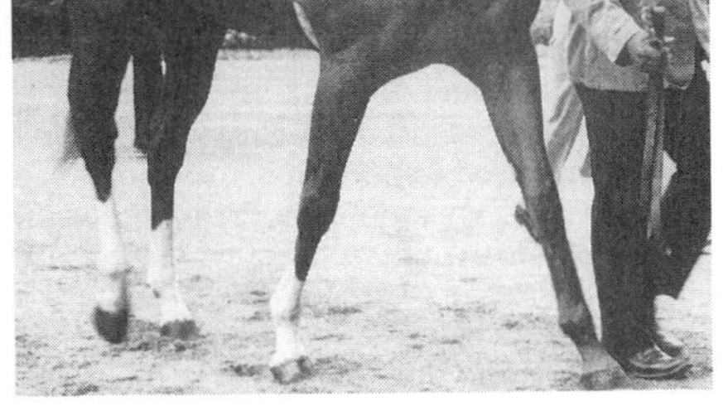

Triple Crown winner Secretariat, jockey Ron Turcotte up, on his way to set a world record in the 1973 Marlboro Cup.

Secretariat (1970–1989). Throrougbred racehorse, affectionately known as "Big Red" and widely considered "the horse of the century." The Kentucky-bred son of Bold Ruler and Somethingroyal, in 1973 he became the first horse since 1948 to win American racing's Triple Crown. In doing so, he set two track records that still stood at the time of his death. The chestnut colt ran the 1-1/4-mile Kentucky Derby at Churchill Downs in 1:59 2/5 minutes and ran the 1-1/2 Belmont Stakes in 2:24 minutes. The latter record, which produced a spectacular 31-length win, was more than two seconds faster than any other winning Belmont time. Secretariat won 16 victories in 21 career starts and earned $1,316,808 before being retired to stud after his three-year-old season. He sired more than 40 stakes winners. He was put down by lethal injection at Claiborne Farm in Paris, Kentucky, suffering from laminitis, a degenerative hoof disease.

secret police, Soviet. From 1917 to 1922 the Soviet security service was known as the CHEKA (All-Russian Extraordinary Commission for Combating Counter-Revolution and Sabotage). This was reorganized as the GPU (State Political Administration) in 1922 and as the OGPU (United State Political Administration) in 1923. In 1934 the OGPU was succeeded by the NKVD (People's Commissariat for Internal Affairs), in 1943 by the NKGB (People's Commissariat for State Security), in 1946 by the MGB (Ministry for State Security) and in 1953 by the MVD (Ministry of Internal Affairs). Since 1954 the Secret Police has been known as the KGB (Committee for State Security).

The secret police has directed its energies against the church, private traders, KULAKS, the intelligentsia and any who disagree with the regime. It became a particularly sinister and powerful tool under YEZHOV during the GREAT PURGE in which 8 to 10 million people perished. The KGB is also responsible for foreign espionage. It is now part of the U.S.S.R. council of ministers, and it is estimated that it has half a million employees.

Securities and Exchange Commission [SEC]. The Securities and Exchange Commission was established by Congress in 1934 to oversee enforcement of the federal securities laws that were passed in 1933 and 1934. Congress concluded that a major cause of the Stock Market Crash of 1929 and the Depression was a lack of regulation in the securities markets. Headed by Joseph P. Kennedy (father of John F. KENNEDY) and later by William O. DOUGLAS, who was to become a Supreme Court justice, the SEC quickly became the federal government's preeminent regulatory agency.

The SEC has responsibility for requiring public disclosure of facts and financial data by firms issuing securities and also by companies whose shares are publicly traded. The SEC regulates the stock exchanges as well as the activities of stock brokers, dealers and investment advisors, investigates and prosecutes securities fraud, and also oversees takeovers and proxies. The SEC has been especially vigorous in prosecuting "insider trading"—the misuse of inside information by those with access to confidential corporate information.

Seeckt, Hans von (1866–1936). German general. Born of a military family in Schleswig, he was commissioned in 1885 and joined the general staff at the century's end. During WORLD WAR I, he commanded German forces in Poland, Turkey and the Balkans. After the war, as the head of the army (Reichswehr) from 1919 to 1926, he was effective in circumventing restrictions placed on the German military by the TREATY OF VERSAILLES. Training troops outside the formal army, which was limited to 100,000 men, and secretly acquiring forbidden weaponry, von Seeckt rebuilt the German army into a formidable fighting force. From 1930 to 1932, he was a member of the Reichstag, and he ended his military career as a military advisor to CHIANG KAI-SHEK in China from 1934 to 1935.

Seefried, Irmgard (1919–1988). German-born Austrian soprano; best known for her interpretations of operas by Wolfgang Amadeus Mozart. Although Seefried spent most of her career with the Vienna State Opera, she also performed as a recital and concert singer. Critics praised the clarity of her voice and the warmth of her interpretations.

Seeger, Alan (1888–1916). American writer, known mainly for his WORLD WAR I poem "Rendezvous" and for his own death in the war. Born in New York, he lived in Mexico as a child and later went to Harvard. In 1912 he went to Paris, where he led a bohemian life. He joined the French Foreign Legion at the outbreak of World War I, and his war poetry became enormously popular because of its heroic and patriotic sentiment. Seeger and his entire unit were mowed down by German machine guns at the battle of the SOMME on July 4, 1916. Reported in American newspapers, his death helped stir American public opinion against Germany and toward involvement in the war at a time when the U.S. was officially neutral. "Rendezvous," containing the line "I have a rendezvous with death," was memorized by a generation of American school children.

Seeger, Charles L. (1886–1979). American musicologist. Seeger introduced and taught the first U.S. course in musicology (1912–19) at the University of California at Berkeley. He was the father of folk-singer Pete SEEGER.

Seeger, Pete (1919–). American folk music composer, guitarist and vocalist. Seeger is one of the most important figures in 20th-century American folk music. He has been a performer and composer since the 1930s, when he developed an enduring friendship with fellow folk musician and social activist Woody GUTHRIE. Seeger, who served in the U.S. military during World War II, in 1955 declined to answer questions on communist activities before the House Committee on Un-American Activities. He was convicted for contempt—a conviction that was overturned in 1962. Among Seeger's major folk compositions are "If I Had A Hammer," "Where Have All the Flowers Gone?," "Kisses Sweeter Than Wine," "I'll Sing Me A Love Song" and "The Happy Whistler." He was also a co-lyricist of the protest anthem "We Shall Overcome." In the 1950s, Seeger was a member of the popular folk group the Weavers, which enjoyed such hits as "Goodnight, Irene" and "On Top of Old Smoky." In recent years, Seeger has been active in Hudson River clean-up efforts.

"See It Now". Innovative television program of the 1950s, the prototype for the modern television news documentary. Coproducers Edward R. MURROW and Fred W. Friendly adapted the format of their successful weekly radio show, "Hear It Now"—a "magazine of the air"—into a half-hour television series that premiered on CBS on Sunday afternoon, November 18, 1951. It went into a prime-time slot, 6:30 P.M., for the 1952–53 season; thereafter, until its demise in July 1958, it was irregularly scheduled (provoking Gilbert Seldes to quip that it should be called "See It Now and Then"). The technology was new; program number one demonstrated the capabilities of the newly developed transcontinental coaxial cable and microwave networks (which meant that Murrow could "cue" the Atlantic and Pacific Oceans on two different monitor screens). Coverage included visits with troops in Korea, natural disasters like floods and interviews with personages like Winston CHURCHILL and Arnold TOYNBEE. And there were forays into what Murrow called "the hard, unyielding realities of the world in which we live": the Milo Radulovich program (1954) discussed nuclear energy and the atomic bomb; and the Joseph MCCARTHY segment (1954) openly attacked his anticommunist "witch-hunts." Although programs like this cost CBS the support of sponsors like Alcoa, a far greater threat proved to be a new kind of prime-time program that soon would push "See It Now" off the air. It must have been with a chill of impending doom that Murrow watched the premiere on the night of June 7, 1955, of the first of the big-time game shows, "The $64,000 Question."

For further reading:

O'Connor, John E., ed., *American History/American Television*. New York: Frederick Ungar, 1983.

Seferis, George (1900–1971). Greek poet and diplomat. Seferis, who won the NOBEL PRIZE for literature in 1963, is one of the greatest figures in Greek literature of this century. His verse, which frequently deals with classical themes, was markedly influenced by MODERNISM, and most particularly by the poetic styles of T.S. ELIOT and of Serferis' countryman Constantine CAVAFY. Seferis was a career diplomat who served in numerous posts, including ambassador to London from 1947 to 1962. Seferis first won fame as a poet with the publication of *Mythistorema* (1935), the poems of which treat the intertwining of history and myth.

Segal, George (1924–). American sculptor. Born in New York City, he attended New York University and Rutgers. His first one-man show was held in New York in 1956. One of the "New Realists" of the early 1960s, Segal is best known for life-sized cast-plaster figures of ordinary people frozen in everyday moments, often with props such as window- or doorframes. Displaying an unusual sense of immediacy, some of his works remain in the rough plaster while others are cast in bronze and often finished in a white patina resembling the original plaster. Typical works are *Bus Driver* (1961, Museum of Modern Art, New York City) and *Restaurant Window* (1967, Walraff-Richartz Museum, Cologne). Many of his later bronzes are designed for site-specific architectural installation; among these are *Commuters* at the Port Authority Bus Terminal, New York City, and *Gay Liberation*, created for a park in Greenwich Village, New York City.

Segovia, Andres (1893–1987). Spanish classical guitarist. Over the course of an eight-decade career, he came to be regarded as the most important performer and teacher in the history of the guitar. In the early 1900s he more or less invented classical guitar technique on his own. Later, through transcription of early contrapuntal music, he showed the possibilities of the guitar as a concert instrument and was largely responsible for the 20th-century resurgence of interest in the instrument. The repertory for the guitar was greatly expanded by the music of composers inspired by Segovia's virtuosity. He continued to fill concert halls worldwide when he was well past his 90th birthday.

segregation. Separation of the races by law and custom. It can be seen in one of its most extreme manifestations in South Africa's APARTHEID. In the U.S., segregation of blacks from other Americans had its genesis in slavery. It was codified after the Civil War by the restrictive Black Codes. By the beginning of the 20th century, segregation of African-Americans was entrenched in American society, written into law in the Southern states and often a matter of established practice in the rest of the country. The beginning of the century also marked the beginning of many organized efforts to secure CIVIL RIGHTS for black Americans and to reverse segregation. Through the efforts of W.E.B. DU BOIS and others, the NATIONAL ASSOCIATION FOR THE ADVANCEMENT OF COLORED PEOPLE (NAACP) was formed in 1909, and this organization has been in the forefront of the fight against segregation ever since. The thrust toward ending segregation, particularly the legal sort found in the South, gathered momentum in the 1930s. By the beginning of World War II President ROOSEVELT ordered an end to segregation in defense plants; the Fair Employment Practices Act (1947) barred discrimination in hiring based on race or national origin, and President TRUMAN forbade (1948) segregation in the military. Perhaps the most important milestone in the integration struggle during this century was the decision in the 1954 Supreme Court case BROWN V. BOARD OF EDUCATION, in which the Court ruled against segregation in the public schools. Further inroads were achieved in the 1960s, a decade that saw unprecedented violence and struggle in the fight against segregation and for civil rights, with the passage of the CIVIL RIGHTS ACT OF 1964, the VOTING RIGHTS ACT OF 1965 and the Fair Housing Act (1968). While the civil rights struggles of the 1960s subsided, issues regarding segregation and integration, whether de jure or de facto, continued to be important in the closing decades of the 20th century.

Seifert, Jaroslav (1901–1986). Czechoslovakian poet. Seifert was a prolific poet whose style underwent several changes during a lengthy writing career that began in earnest in the 1920s. His earliest volumes, such as *City in Tears* (1921) and *All Love* (1923), reflected both Seifert's enthusiasm for the RUSSIAN REVOLUTION of 1917 and the experimental poetics of dadaism and SURREALISM. But by 1929 Seifert had rejected the Stalinist turn of Soviet communism. In the 1930s his poems became more direct and lyrical, with less linguistic experimentation. *Eight Days* (1937) is representattive of this period. The Nazi conquest of CZECHOSLOVAKIA led to censorship, but Seifert continued to write poems that expressed the anguish of his conquered homeland, as in *The Stone Bridge* (1944) and *Helmet of Clay* (1945). In the decades following WORLD WAR II, Seifert continued to write while adding his voice to those who protested the Soviet rule of Czechoslovakia. In 1956 he wrote of the impact of Soviet censorship: "If a writer is silent, he is lying." In 1969 Seifert became president of the Czechoslovakian Writers Union but resigned shortly thereafter in protest of Soviet restrictions on artistic freedom. His later volumes include *The Casting of Bells* (1967) and *An Umbrella from Picadilly* (1979). Seifert's work was virtually unknown in the West until he won the NOBEL PRIZE for literature in 1984. (See also DADA.)

Guitar virtuoso Andres Segovia (1952).

Seine River. French river that flows through PARIS. It rises in the Plateau de Langres of France's Cote d'Or department and flows for 482 miles, emptying into the English Channel near LE HAVRE. After the Germans under General von Kluck advanced past the MARNE and toward Paris at the beginning of WORLD WAR I, the Allies hastily threw up a defensive line along the Seine east of Paris. Von Kluck had originally planned to encircle the city, but the Allied action foiled this plan.

Selfridge, Harry Gordon (1864–1947). American-born merchant. Selfridge became a partner in the Marshall Field Company and manager of its retail store in CHICAGO before selling out his interest in 1904. With several partners he bought the firm of Schlesinger and Mayer and changed the name to H.G. Selfridge and Company. This store was sold to Carson, Pirie, Scott and Company of Chicago in August of 1904. Selfridge traveled to London in 1906 and organized Selfridge and Company Ltd., wholesale and retail merchants, and built one of the largest stores in Europe. He became a naturalized British citizen on June 1, 1937.

Sellafield. British nuclear power plant on the coast of Cumbria in the Lake District. Originally called Windscale (see WINDSCALE ACCIDENT), it had a history of problems and leaked radioactivity into the atmosphere in the late 1950s. Antinuclear activists continue to point to Sellafield as a lesson in the dangers of nuclear power.

Sellers, Peter (1925–1980). British actor. Sellers became one of the leading comedic actors in films through his rare combined mastery of physical comedy, verbal delivery and outlandish disguise. He first came to prominence in the 1950s in a series of British-made comedies including *The La-*

dykillers (1955) and *The Mouse That Roared* (1959). Sellers appeared in multiple roles in *Dr. Strangelove: Or, How I Learned to Stop Worrying and Love the Bomb* (1964), the classic black comedy by Stanley KUBRICK. In the 1960s and '70s, Sellers made a highly popular series of films in which he portrayed the bumbling French gendarme, Inspector Clouseau; these included *A Shot in the Dark* (1964) and *The Pink Panther Strikes Again* (1976). One of Seller's most acclaimed roles was in *Being There* (1980) as Chance, the near-idiot gardener for a wealthy Washington mansion whose sole interest is television and who becomes, by a series of flukish events, an influential political and media figure.

Selma. Industrial city and county seat of Dallas County, Alabama; on the Alabama River, some 50 miles west of Montgomery. In 1965 Selma was the scene of important CIVIL RIGHTS demonstrations led by Dr. Martin Luther KING Jr. King had gone to Selma at the beginning of the year to organize a black voter registration drive. Many demonstrators, including King, were arrested as the local authorities attempted to bar blacks from registering. The KU KLUX KLAN also opposed the civil rights movement and tried to intimidate the organizers with violence. King planned a march from Selma to Montgomery to call national attention to the civils rights movement. On March 7, state troopers broke up a march, using tear gas, night sticks and whips on the marchers. One protester, Rev. James Reeb of Boston, died two days later from injuries. President Lyndon B. JOHNSON condemned the brutality, and there was a national outcry. A second march was turned back by police, but a third attempt was successful. After reaching Birmingham on March 25, King told his followers that Selma had become "a shining moment in the conscience of man. If the worst in American life lurked in the dark streets, the best of American instincts arose passionately from across the nation to overcome it." The events that occurred in Selma helped persuade Congress to pass the VOTING RIGHTS ACT OF 1965.

Selye, Hans (1907–1982). Austrian-born endocrinologist who established a clear link between stress and illness. In 1932 he immigrated to Canada, where he founded and directed the International Institute of Stress in Montreal. He conducted numerous studies on the physiological effects of stress. He reported his findings in some 33 books and 1,600 articles.

Selznick, David O. (1902–1965). American motion picture producer, best known for GONE WITH THE WIND. Selznick was the son of Lewis J. Selznick, a pioneer film producer of the 1910s and 1920s; his elder brother Myron was one of the top talent agents in HOLLYWOOD. David began his own career as an assistant story editor at MGM in 1926, working for his father's former partner, Louis B. MAYER, whose daughter he married. He then moved to Paramount, where he became an associate producer, and to new studio RKO, where he was named vice president in charge of production and was responsible for *King Kong* (1933), among other films. Selznick returned to MGM in 1933, replacing an ailing Irving THALBERG as the studio's production chief; he produced some of MGM's glossiest blockbusters, including *Dinner at Eight* (1933), *David Copperfield* (1935) and *A Tale of Two Cities* (1935).

In 1936 he formed his own independent company, Selznick International, and perfected his "hands on" policy of filmmaking, overseeing through his famous memos every detail of a picture. Whether he made a satiric melodrama (*A Star Is Born*, 1937), a Civil War romance (*Gone With the Wind*, 1939), wartime homefront epic (*Since You Went Away*, 1944) or supercharged western (*Duel in the Sun*, 1946), his priorities were the same: "Our mission is to discover the nature of the demand and meet it as best we can." A persistent wooer of talent, he lured Alfred HITCHCOCK to Hollywood and produced four of his pictures, including *Rebecca* (1940) and *Notorious* (1946). He courted actress Phyllis Isley, signed her to a contract, changed her name to Jennifer Jones, married her and got her an ACADEMY AWARD for his *Song of Bernadette* (1943). The great American public proved fickle in the end and generally stayed away from his last picture, *A Farewell to Arms* (1957).

For further reading:

Haver, Ron, *David O. Selznick's Hollywood*. New York: Alfred Knopf, 1980.

semiconductors. Semiconductors are materials that have some electrical conducting properties but also some resisting properties. Silicon is the most widely used semiconductor. Semiconductors have myriad and important applications in modern electronics and communications technology. They are essential components in COMPUTERS. (See also SUPERCONDUCTORS; TRANSISTOR.)

semiotics. The study of signs—broadly defined as any agreed-upon set of signifiers, from written letters to hand signals to visual symbols—as products of human culture and as means of communication. Semiotics has emerged as a major field of intellectual endeavor in the 20th century, although past thinkers including Saint Augustine and John Locke had written on the subject of signs and their meaning. Pioneering writers on semiotics in this century include the American philosopher Charles Pierce and the Swiss linguistics theorist Ferdinand de Saussure. Saussure stressed the terms "signifier" (the form of the sign) and "signified" (the idea expressed), while Pierce drew attention to the "interpretant," a new sign created by the interaction of the first two. Semiotics has been applied to literary criticism as a means of highlighting the role of fixed language rules in literary creation. The French critic Roland BARTHES has been particularly influential in this area by his emphasis on the creative role of the reader in comprehending the text. Semiotics has often been linked to STRUCTURALISM as an intellectual method, in that both seek out structures that govern diverse individual expression.

Sendak, Maurice (1928–). American children's book illustator and writer. Born in Brooklyn, he is known for unsentimental books that convey the world of childhood with all of its angers and terrors. A brilliant draftsman, he has worked in a number of styles, from the broad grotesques of *Where the Wild Things Are* (1963), winner of the 1964 Caldecott Medal, to the delicately linear black-and-white drawings of *Higglety Pigglety Pop!* (1967). Both these books were written and illustrated by Sendak, as were such works as *The Nutshell Library* (1962), *In the Night Kitchen* (1970) and *Outside Over There* (1981). In addition, he has illustrated such books as Isaac Bashevis SINGER's *Zlateh the Goat and Other Stories* (1966) and *The Juniper Tree and Other Tales from Grimm* (1973). A fascination with the theater has led him to write the libretto and design the sets for an opera version of *Where the Wild Things Are* and the musical version of *Really Rosie* as well as to create the costumes and sets for new productions of Mozart's *The Magic Flute* and JANACEK's *The Cunning Little Vixen*.

Sendic, Raul (1924–1989). Uruguayan revolutionary. He was the founder of the leftist Uruguayan guerrilla group known as the Tupamaros; the group, formed in 1962, was one of the first leftist insurgency movements in Latin America. Its activities ranged from robbery on behalf of the poor to kidnappings, assassinations and bombings. Two of the group's most notorious actions were the 1971 kidnapping of the British ambassador and the 1970 kidnapping and murder of a U.S. advisor. This latter case formed the basis of the COSTA-GAVRAS film *State of Seige*. Sendic served more than 13 years in prison and was one of the last political prisoners released following URUGUAY's return to civilian rule in 1985. On his release, he reorganized the Tupamaros as a political party.

Senead Eireann. Irish senate, consisting of 49 members elected by the universities and panels of candidates representing Irish society and 11 nominated by the TAOISEACH. Elections must take place within 90 days of the dissolution of the DAIL EIREANN.

Senegal. Senegal occupies an area of 75,729 square miles on the west coast of Africa; it is bordered by Mauritania, Mali and Guinea and totally surrounds Gambia. At the beginning of the century, Senegal was part of the Federation of FRENCH WEST AFRICA. Briefly incorporated into the independent Mali Federation, the country seceded and declared the independent Republic of Senegal in 1960, with Leopold SENGHOR as the first president (1960–81). In 1968 the French aided Senghor in controlling growing student and labor unrest, which stemmed from a worsening economy. His successor, Abdou Diouf (1983–), has had to deal with increasing economic and social problems as well as a secessionist movement by the prosperous province of Casamance.

SENEGAL

1960	(June 20) Becomes independent from France as part of the Mali Federation; (Aug. 20) Secedes from the federation and becomes the Republic of Senegal with Leopold Senghor as president.
1963	(Mar. 7) New constitution created strengthening Senghor's political power.
1966	Legally recognized opposition parties no longer exist.
1973	Catastrophic drought strikes Sahel.
1975	All political prisoners are released.
1976	New constitution allows for up to three opposition parties.
1981	(January) Senghor retires and names Abdou Diouf as president.
1988	Diouf elected president for the second time.

Senegambia. Confederation agreed upon by the West African countries of SENEGAL and GAMBIA on December 17, 1981.

Senghor, Leopold Sedar (1906–). African statesman and poet, president of SENEGAL (1960–80). Senghor was a leading figure in the movement for African independence in the 1950s and 1960s, and is also internationally regarded as a literary figure. He was educated in Dakar and Paris, where he studied philosophy and pursued an academic career in the 1930s. He turned to politics after World War II and was elected as a deputy for Senegal in the French Constituent Assembly. Senghor subsequently helped to frame the constitution giving each French West African territory its own assembly and more deputies in the French parliament. He served as a deputy himself until 1958. Originally a member of the French Socialist Party, he left it in 1948 to start his own party, the Bloc Democratique Senegalaise. This party evolved into the Union Progressiste Senegalaise (UPS). Senghor was minister-councillor for cultural affairs, education and justice in the French government in 1959–60. In 1959 he became president of the federal assembly of the Mali Federation of Senegal and Sudan; after the federation split in 1960, he became president of the Republic of Senegal. He was reelected in 1963, 1968, 1973 and 1978. Retiring in 1980, he was succeeded by his prime minister, Abdou Diouf. In addition to his political career, Senghor pursued an active literary career and philosophical interests as a poet and theorist of NEGRITUDE and African socialism.

For further reading:

Spleth, Janice, *Leopold Sedar Senghor*. Boston: G.K. Hall, 1985.

Sennett, Mack [Michael Sinnott] (1880–1960). Celebrated American motion picture producer, best known for his "Keystone Comedies." Born to working-class Irish immigrants in Quebec, he shifted from common laborer to stage actor when he began working in New York burlesque. As "Mack Sennett" he appeared in and wrote many BIOGRAPH movie shorts in 1910–1911 for D.W. GRIFFITH. For his own new production company, Keystone, he gathered together associates from his Biograph days—Ford Sterling, Fred Mace and Mabel Normand—and developed new stars, like Roscoe "Fatty" Arbuckle, Chester Conklin, Mack Swain, Charles CHAPLIN, to make the frenetic, hyper-kinetic slapstick comedies that made his reputation. By the time Keystone was absorbed into the Triangle Film Corporation in 1915, Sennett was supervising bigger-budget, two-reel comedies that depended less and less on slapstick. After Triangle foundered in 1918, Sennett spent the next 20 years dabbling in features, Harry LANGDON comedies and sound shorts for W.C. FIELDS and Bing CROSBY (1932). In 1936 he received a special ACADEMY AWARD for his comic contributions to film. Broke and embittered near the end of his life, Sennett could still write in his autobiography, *King of Comedy* (1954): "I believe I have associated intimately with

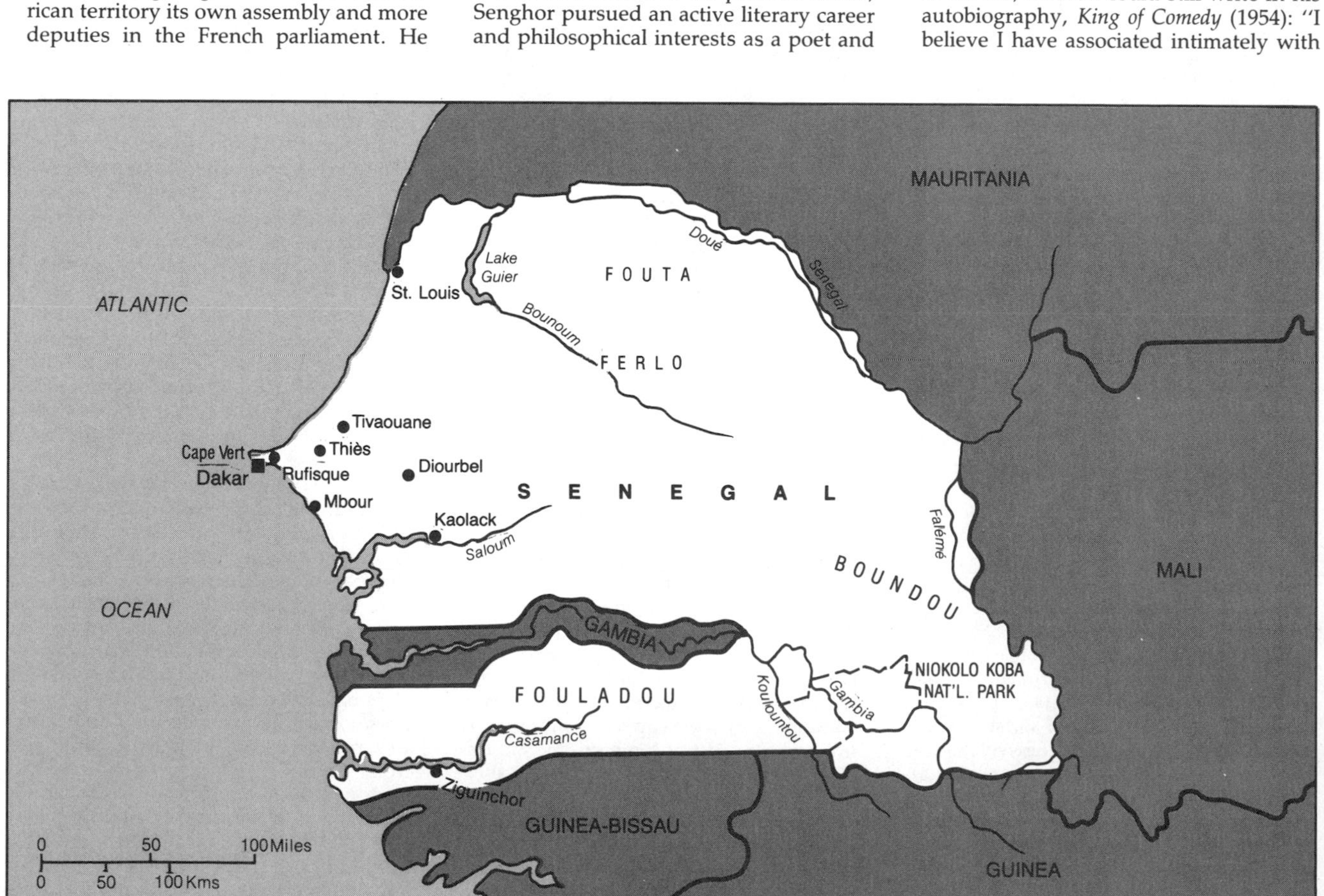

SENEGAL

more fools than any man living, a blessing for which I thank God."

For further reading:

Sennett, Mack, *King of Comedy*. New York: Doubleday and Co., 1954.

Seoul. Capital of SOUTH KOREA; inland about 40 miles from the port of INCHON. Seoul is the industrial, commercial and cultural center of the country. Until 1910, when KOREA was occupied by the Japanese, it was the capital of the Korean Yi dyansty. Modernized during the period of Japanese rule (1910–45), Seoul became the headquarters of the U.S. military government at the end of WORLD WAR II. On August 15, 1948, it became capital of the Republic of Korea (South Korea). Three days after North Korean communist forces swept across the 38th parallel at the outbreak of the KOREAN WAR, Seoul was captured by the communists and occupied (June 28–Sept. 29, 1950). Although the North Koreans were driven out, they recaptured the city the following year and again occupied it from January 4 to March 14, 1951, before UN forces drove them out for good. The UN subsequently based its military command headquarters in Seoul. The city suffered much damage but was rebuilt after the war. Seoul has been the site of many student protests—some of them violent—against the South Korean government and the U.S. presence in the country.

Serafimovich. Don River town in the Volgograd oblast of the U.S.S.R.'s Russian Republic. In November 1942, near the end of Germany's unsuccessful 66–day siege of STALINGRAD (now Volgograd), the first Soviet counteroffensive took place here. The successful Serafimovich counterattack led to the surrender of the German forces in this zone three months later. (See also WORLD WAR II ON THE RUSSIAN FRONT.)

Serapion Brothers. A group of 12 young Russian writers who were fellow travelers and who had met in Petrograd in 1921. They took their name from E.T.A. Hoffmann's "Storyteller and Hermit." They rejected the idea that their literature should be in any way associated with propaganda, thus incurring the suspicion of party critics. Frequently original in style and form, as a group the Serapion Brothers are characterized by their irreverence and wit. Perhaps the most promising of them, Led Lunts, died at the age of 23; others, such as Konstantin Fedin, Nicholas Tikhonov and Venyamin Kaverin, later adopted the party line on literature.

Serbia. Former kingdom in the Balkans region; subsequently the largest and most influential of the six constituent republics that formed YUGOSLAVIA. After centuries of domination by the Ottoman Turks, the Serbs forced them out of most of their ancestral lands in 1829. Thereafter, the Karageorge and Obrenovic families fought each other for control of the government. In 1903 King Alexander was assassinated, ending the Obrenovic line of succession. Peter I, a member of the Karageorge family, ascended the throne. He strengthened the parliament and revived Serbia's economy. Peter I and Serbia guided the formation of the Balkan League, an alliance of Montenegro, BULGARIA and GREECE designed to offset the power of AUSTRIA-HUNGARY and the waning OTTOMAN EMPIRE. With Russian assistance the league defeated Turkey in 1912 in the First BALKAN WAR. However, Serbia turned against its former ally Bulgaria in 1913, in the Second Balkan War. When Crown Prince FRANZ FERDINAND, heir to the Austro-Hungarian throne, was assassinated by a Serbian nationalist at SARAJEVO (June 28, 1914), the empire slapped Serbia with an ultimatum that led to the start of WORLD WAR I. Serbia was occupied by the Central Powers in November 1915. Following the end of the war in 1918, Serbia became part of the Kingdom of the Serbs, Croats and Slovenes, renamed Yugoslavia in 1929. From 1941 to 1945, during WORLD WAR II, Serbia was a puppet state of Nazi GERMANY. King PETER II, last of the Karageorges, spent the war in exile and lost his throne when Yugoslavia became a republic on November 29, 1945. Despite Yugoslav leader TITO's efforts to balance power evenly among the six Yugoslav republics, Serbia remained politically dominant. Anti-Serbian demonstrations and moves for greater autonomy by the other republics have threatened to break up Yugoslavia.

Sergio, Lisa (1905–1989). Pioneer radio broadcaster in Benito MUSSOLINI's Italy who immigrated to the U.S. and became a commentator on American radio. During her years on Italian radio, she sang and translated Mussolini's speeches into English and French until she was fired in 1937 for making changes in PROPAGANDA commentary. Faced with arrest, she escaped to the U.S. and became a dedicated anti-fascist. (See also FASCISM.)

serial music. General term frequently applied to the various non-tonal systems employed by Arnold SCHOENBERG and his followers to replace Western traditions of tonal music. After the turn of the century, composers like Gustav MAHLER, Igor STRAVINSKY and Bela BARTOK pushed tonal ambiguity almost to the point of no return, to what Leonard Bernstein later called "the tonal crisis." Schoenberg, whose *Pierrot Lunaire* (1912) had achieved complete atonality, devised systems to impose order upon the 12 equal tones of the chromatic scale. His theory of the "twelve-tone row," or dodecaphonic system, consisted of a preconceived constellation of 12 tones where no single tone could be repeated until all 11 others had sounded. Schoenberg's ideas were carried to extremes by his disciple Anton von WEBERN. In works like the *Orchestral Variations* he devised a 12–tone *color* system in which no given instrument could play two successive notes until the other instruments had made their appearance. He abandoned the essentials of harmony and counterpoint completely and replaced the row with multiple possible sequences so the music could not be reduced to any given sequence of 12 notes. Webern, in turn, influenced post-World War II composers like Pierre BOULEZ and Karlheinz Stockhausen who have gone on to develop concepts like the "technique of groups"—the serial treatment of entire sections of sonorous material. Other developments include experimentation by John CAGE in electronically produced music and in the chance accumulations of notes and noise.

For further reading:

Ewen, David, *Modern Music: From Wagner to Webern*. New York: Chilton Co., 1962.

Serkin, Rudolf (1903–91). Austrian-American concert pianist. Born in Bohemia, Serkin made his first public appearance at age five and at nine he went to Vienna to study piano. At the age of 12, he debuted as a soloist with the Vienna Symphony Orchestra, and from 1919 to 1920 he studied composition with Arnold SCHOENBERG. After meeting Adolf Busch (later his father-in-law), he lived with the violinist and his family in Berlin and performed with him in a series of memorable joint recitals and in ensembles with other musicians. Serkin made his U.S. debut in a sonata recital with Busch in 1933, and first appeared as a soloist here three years later. After the outbreak of World War II in Europe, Serkin and his family immigrated to the U.S. He became a member of the faculty at Philadelphia's Curtis Institute of Music, serving as its director from 1968 to 1975. In 1949 he cofounded Vermont's Marlboro School of Music and acted as director of the summer Marlboro Music Festival. Serkin's repertoire centered on the music of Mozart, Beethoven, Schubert, Mendelssohn, Schumann and Brahms. He was known for his strong technique and his poetic, subtly nuanced interpretations.

Serling, Rod. See THE TWILIGHT ZONE.

Service, Robert William (1874–1958). Canadian poet. Service is best remembered for his ballads such as "The Shooting of Dan McGrew," which were inspired by the rough frontier life he observed during the gold rush to the Yukon in 1895. Service's collections include *Songs of a Sourdough* (1907), *Rhymes of a Rolling Stone* (1912) and the autobiographical *Ploughman of the Moon* (1945) and *Harper of Heaven* (1948).

Sessions, Roger (1896–1985). American composer. Considered one of the foremost American composers of the 20th century, he was known for the uncompromising rigor of his musical thinking. Early in his career he composed complex neo-classical scores influenced by Igor STRAVINSKY. Later, after befriending Arnold SCHOENBERG, he adopted the 12–tone or SERIAL MUSIC style that Schoenberg had pioneered. Among Sessions' works were nine symphonies, a violin concerto, a piano concerto, two operas, and a concerto for orchestra for which he won the 1982 PULITZER PRIZE for music. A noted theoretician and teacher, Sessions taught at Princeton University (1953–65), the University of California at Berkeley, and at the Juilliard School of Music. Many of his students went on to become well-known composers.

Seton, Anya (1916–1990). U.S. author. She was a best-selling author of historical and biographical novels. Among her most popular works were *Dragonwyck,* which was made into a 1946 film starring Vincent Price, and *Foxfire,* made into a 1955 film starring Jane Russell.

Seuss, Dr. [pen name of Theodore Seuss Geisel] (1904–). American children's book author and illustrator Dr. Theodore Seuss Geisel, known to the world as Dr. Seuss, was born in Springfield, Massachusetts. He has written over 50 delightfully nonsensical tales including works that have become children's classics, such as *Horton Hears a Who* (1954), *The Cat in the Hat* and *How the Grinch Stole Christmas* (both 1957). His words and rhymes are intended to help preschoolers to recognize and pronounce syllables, and his bold and fanciful cartoon illustrations are designed to enchant. He is also a cartoonist, using the pen name Theo Le Seig for these works.

Sevareid, Eric (1912–). American journalist. Sevareid began his career as a reporter for the *Minneapolis Journal* and later worked for the Paris edition of the *New York Herald-Tribune.* In 1939, he was summoned to London by Edward R. MURROW and asked to join CBS News. Sevareid was the last reporter to broadcast from Paris before the German occupation in 1940. In his long association with CBS News, Sevareid covered every presidential election from 1948 to 1976 and a variety of beats in the United States and abroad. In 1964, he began appearing on the CBS Evening News, for which he continued to serve as a consultant following his retirement in 1977.

Sevastopol. Black Sea port city of the U.S.S.R. on the Crimean Peninsula. Strategically located, Sevastopol became an important Russian naval base in the 19th century. Sailors of the Russian navy mutinied here during the RUSSIAN REVOLUTION OF 1905. During the RUSSIAN CIVIL WAR Sevastopol was the headquarters of the White Army under General WRANGEL (see WHITES). During WORLD WAR II the Germans besieged Sevastopol from October 1941 to July 1942 and finally occupied it; the Soviets retook the city May 19, 1944.

Severini, Gino (1883–1966). Italian painter. He was educated in Rome, where he met modernist artists such as Giacomo BALLA and Umberto Boccioni, and settled in Paris in 1906. During his years in France he formed close ties with members of the Parisian avant garde and associated himself with CUBISM. He was in France in 1910 when he signed the Futurist manifesto. Becoming associated with FUTURISM and strongly influenced by Seurat and neoimpressionism, Severini embraced the Futurist aesthetic of motion, while adding to it a uniquely delicate touch and decorative approach. His happy, sequin-spattered canvas *Hieroglyph of the Bal Tabarin* (1912; Museum of Modern Art, New York City), which was exhibited in the first exhibition of Futurist work held in Paris in 1912, is a characteristic example of his work.

Seveso. Industrial town in northern Italy, a suburb of Milan. On July 10, 1976, an explosion at a chemical factory in Seveso released a cloud of chemicals, including five pounds of the highly toxic chemical dioxin, into the atmosphere. Hundreds of people were hospitalized, and the entire population was evacuated from the contaminated area around the town. (See also BHOPAL DISASTER.)

Sevres, Treaty of. Post-WORLD WAR I treaty that led to the dissolution of the OTTOMAN EMPIRE. Signed on August 10, 1920, in a suburb of Paris, the treaty dismissed all of TURKEY's territorial claims in Arab Asia and North Africa; the Ottomans were also forced to grant independence to Armenia and autonomy to Kurdistan. GREECE was given territory in Thrace, the Aegean and the Anatolian west coast, and was given the administration of Smyrna for five years. Turkish nationalists rejected the treaty, and it was superceded by the Treaty of LAUSANNE in July 1923.

The cat in the hat, created by Dr. Seuss (1972).

Sewell, Joe (1898–1990). American baseball player. An infielder in the 1920s and '30s, Sewell established a record by striking out only 114 times in the course of a 14–year career. He was noted for his ability to hit any ball that entered the strike zone. His career batting average was .312, with a career-high .353 in 1923. He was elected to the Hall of Fame by the veterans committee in 1977.

Sexton, Anne (Harvey) (1928–1974). American poet. The poems in Sexton's first books, *To Bedlam and Part Way Back* (1960) and *All My Pretty Ones* (1962), were begun as therapy after a nervous breakdown led to her hospitalization. She was influenced by Robert LOWELL, whose workshop in poetry she attended with Sylvia PLATH and Maxine Kumin, to break the academic and formal constraints common to American poetry in the 1950s. Her poems are notable for their fresh and startling imagery and their unconventional, often FEMINIST as well as personal, themes. *Live or Die* won a PULITZER PRIZE in 1966. After her divorce in 1974, her writing became more religious and despairing, and she committed suicide. *The Death Notebooks* (1974), *The Awful Rowing Towards God* (1975) and *45 Mercy Street* (1976) were published posthumously.

Seychelles. Located in the Indian Ocean, almost a thousand miles northeast of Madagascar, the Republic of Seychelles is comprised of 115 islands and islets dispersed over 250,900 square miles of ocean, with a total land area of 175 square miles. The Seychelles became a British crown colony in 1903. The political influence of plantation owners was unchallenged until the emergence of nationalist parties in the 1960s. James Mancham's Seychelles Democratic Party was by 1974 seeking independence. Mancham formed a coalition government in 1975 with his more radical rival, France-Albert Rene of the Seychelles People's United Party, leading the country to independence (June 28, 1976)—with Mancham as executive president and Rene as prime minister.

Rene, increasingly critical of Mancham's international jet-set image, overthrew him in June 1977. He launched a social reform program and sought to diversify from excessive dependence on tourism. Rene's party, retitled the Seychelles People's Progressive Front, became sole party under the June 1979 constitution. Mancham was accused by Rene of backing unsuccessful coup attempts involving mercenaries (April 1978, November 1979, November 1981). The last of these, launched from South Africa, led to the trial and imprisonment there of its organizer, Colonel "Mad Mike" Hoare. Tanzanian troops supported the Rene regime and suppressed a mutiny in August 1982. In 1984, exiled opponents formed a Seychelles National Movement, whose president, Gerard Horeau, was assassinated at his London home (November 30, 1985).

Seyss-Inquart, Arthur (1892–1946). Austrian political leader. A Nazi, Seyss-Inquart was appointed chancellor of AUS-

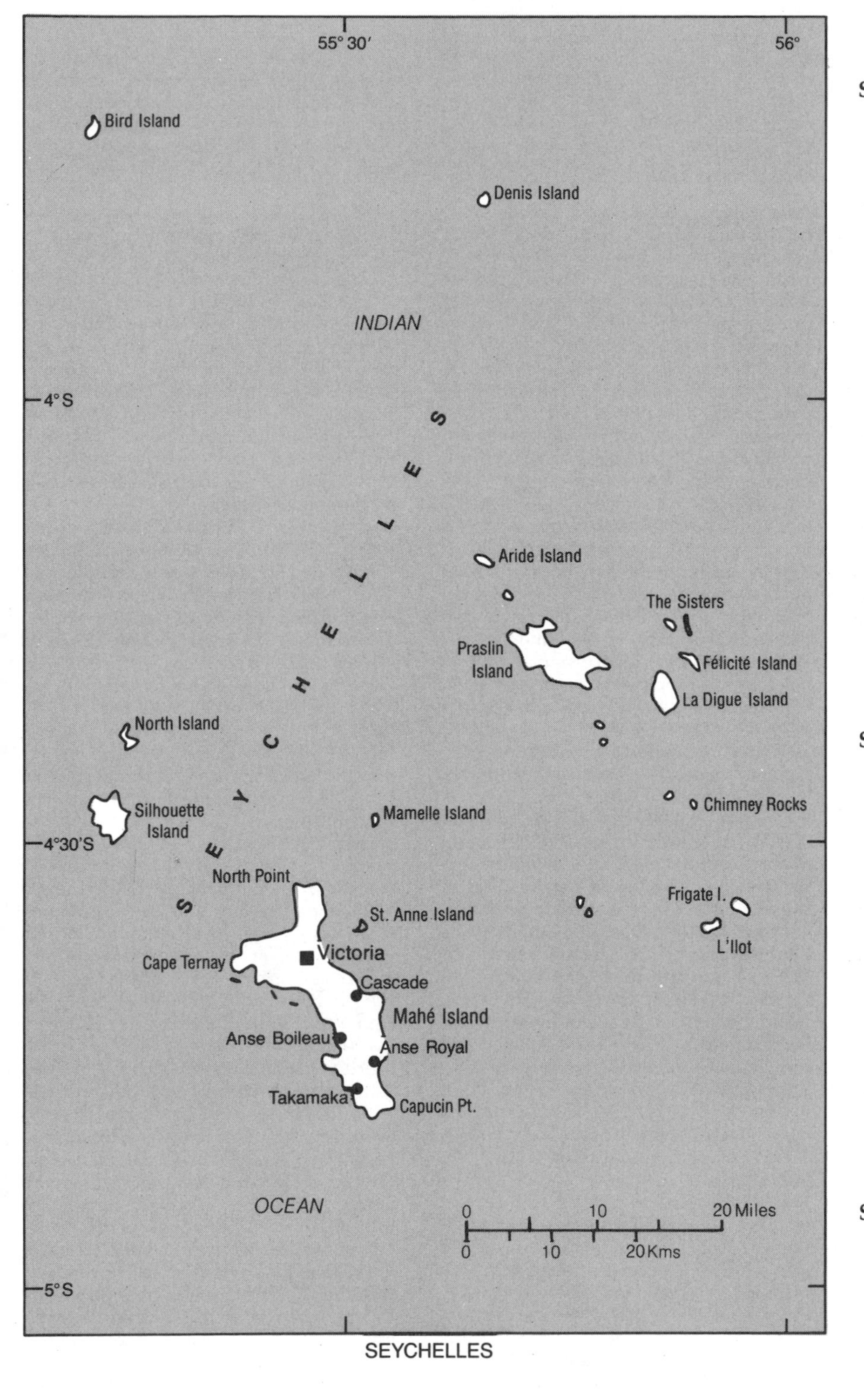

SEYCHELLES

TRIA in March 1938 after the Germans forced the dismissal of Kurt von SCHUSCHNIGG. A few days after German troops entered the country, only hours after Seyss-Inquart's appointment, ANSCHLUSS was proclaimed and he became Austria's governor. A year later he was named deputy governor-general of occupied POLAND. Seyss-Inquart was appointed to the post of German high commissioner of the occupied NETHERLANDS in 1940, and he proved relentless in his hunt for Dutch JEWS, thousands of whom were deported and sent to Nazi CONCENTRATION CAMPS. In 1945 he was arrested by Allied troops. Sentenced to death by the NUREMBERG WAR CRIMES TRIALS, he was hanged in 1946.

Shaba. Copper-rich, southern province of ZAIRE. Known as **Katanga** in 1960, the province seceded from newly independent Zaire and declared itself independent (see KATANGA REVOLT). A UN force intervened, but the rebels, who were supported by Belgian mining interests, were not routed until 1963. (See also Moise TSHOMBE.)

Shackleton, Ernest Henry (1874–1922). English explorer, innovative and persistent and endowed with outstanding leadership qualities. Shackleton made full use of technological advances and media coverage during his polar expeditions. After several years in the merchant marine, he joined Captain Robert Falcon SCOTT's 1901 Antarctic expedition. Leading his own expedition to ANTARCTICA in 1907, he discovered the Beardmore Glacier, crossed the Polar Plateau to within 97 miles of the South Pole and took the first motion pictures of Antarctica. In addition, some of his group reached the South Magnetic Pole. His 1914 expedition to cross the Antarctic continent failed when his ship was crushed by the ice, a misfortune that allowed Shackleton to etch his name forever into the annals of personal heroism. He led his entire party almost 200 miles across the ice, then with a few companions crossed almost 800 miles of rugged seas, crossed the craggy island of South Georgia to a whaling station and eventually managed to rescue every last member of his expedition. Shackleton died during his last journey to explore the islands of the sub-Antarctic.

Shaeffer, W.A. (1867–1946). Inventor, manufacturer. As a jewelry store operator in Fort Madison, Iowa, Shaeffer toyed with the idea of a better writing instrument. He devised a means of pulling ink into a rubber container in the handle of the pen, using a lever and suction. This ink was then delivered in a continuous flow to the pen point. This relatively simple 1912 invention revolutionized writing and resulted in the founding of the Shaeffer pen manufacturing factory. The pens have carried the Shaeffer name around the world. The business, one of the largest of its kind, has been continued by three generations of Shaeffers, who have managed to keep pace with modern developments in writing instruments of all kinds. The company is known for profit sharing and other employee considerations. (See also Ladislao BIRO.)

Shaffer, Peter Levin (1926–). British playwright. With the production of his first play, *Five Finger Exercise* (1958), Shaffer was cited as the most promising British playwright of that year. He maintained his reputation with *The Private Ear* and *The Public Eye*, a joint production in 1962, and *Black Comedy* (1965). Perhaps his best known plays are *Equus* (1973; filmed 1977), a psychological drama examining the relationship between a repressed psychiatrist and his patient; and *Amadeus* (1979; filmed 1987), a study of the nature of creativity in the conflicts between the composers Mozart and Salieri. Other works include *The Royal Hunt of the Sun* (1964) and *Lettuce and Lovage* (1988). Shaffer's twin brother, Anthony, is also a playwright whose works include *Sleuth* (1970) and *Murderer* (1975).

Shahn, Ben (1898–1969). American artist. Born in Lithuania, this important social realist immigrated to the U.S. in 1906. He worked as a lithographer until 1930, becoming known for a series of paintings and drawings executed from 1931 to 1932 that express his outrage over the SACCO-VANZETTI CASE. One of the best known of these is *The Passion of Sacco and Vanzetti* in the collection of New York City's Whitney Museum of American Art. Shahn's concerns were overwhelmingly political and social, his approach liberal and humanistic. His keen graphic sense led him to create many notable posters and to use the mural as a medium, working with Diego RIVERA on murals at Radio City in 1933 and creating murals at the Bronx Post Office, New York City, from 1938 to 1939. Taking an interest in photography, he produced memorable images of the poverty of rural America while working for the Farm Security Administration from 1933 to 1938. Deeply affected by World War II, in the 1940s he created a moving series of paintings dealing with war-torn Europe. While remaining figurative, his last works tend to be less political and deal with subjects in a more abstract manner.

Shalamov, Varlam (1907–1982). Russian writer and poet. Shalamov was arrested in 1937 for declaring that Ivan BUNIN, an expatriate writer and Nobel laureate, was a classic of Russian literature. For this crime he spent 17 years in the Kolyma labor camps in Eastern Siberia (see GULAG). He recounted his experiences in *Kolyma Notes*, autobiographical short stories, which found their way to the West. In the 1970s Shalamov was forced to denounce the publication of his own works abroad.

Shamir, Yitzhak (1915–). Prime minister of ISRAEL (1983–84, 1986–). Shamir immigrated to Palestine in 1935 and studied law in Jerusalem. He joined the Irgun in 1937 but left it for Lehi (the STERN GANG) in 1940 and became part of that group's leading triumvirate after Stern's assassination in 1942. Shamir was twice exiled

Israeli Prime Minister Yitzhak Shamir (1990).

by the mandate authorities but escaped and returned to Israel in 1948. He spent most of the next 17 years abroad as a senior Mossad operative. In 1965 he became a businessman and in 1970 joined his old Irgun rival Menachem BEGIN's Herut Party. Shamir was elected to the Knesset in 1973 and served as its speaker from 1977 to 1980, a period during which he campaigned against the CAMP DAVID agreements on the grounds that they gave too much to Egypt in exchange for too little. He served as foreign minister for three years from 1980 and took over as prime minister after Begin's resignation in 1983. He failed to lead the Likud to victory in the 1984 elections, but managed to form a coalition with Labor, which had won a narrow majority. The agreement provided for a handing over of the premiership to him halfway through the government's term in office, which occurred in October 1986. The taciturn premier, a strong supporter, on security grounds, of the Greater Israel movement, announced upon taking office that he saw as his main task "the consolidation of the Jewish presence in all parts of the Land."

Shanghai. Major Chinese port, about 13 miles upriver from the mouth of the Huang P'u River. Shanghai is CHINA's largest city (and one of the largest cities in the world) as well as the nation's gateway for international trade, its financial hub and a leading industrial center. Long China's most cosmopolitan city, during the first half of the century its residents included many western nationals—businesspeople, diplomats and their families. Taken by Nationalist Chinese forces in 1927 during their campaign to unify China, it was the target of Japanese bombing raids in 1932. This unprecedented bombing of civilians shocked the world, and Japan was internationally condemned. Heavy fighting recurred in 1937 as the Japanese returned to the offensive (see SINO-JAPANESE WAR OF 1937–45). IN 1941, WITH WORLD WAR II keeping the Europeans busy, Japan occupied Shanghai's foreign settlement and brought the entire city under Japanese control by the end of the year. The U.S., the U.K. and France renounced their claims to the city and it was restored to China at the end of the war. One of the last Nationalist strongholds on the mainland, Shanghai fell to the communists in May 1949 (see CHINESE CIVIL WAR OF 1945–49).

Shankar, Ravi (1920–). Indian sitar player-composer. Shankar might have spent his career in relative obscurity as a lecturer at the University of California, had not BEATLE George Harrison sought him out as a sitar instructor for the song "Norwegian Wood." Rock quickly embraced the sitar's haunting and exotic sound during the late Sixties, but almost as quickly the instrument became associated with rock's idea of mysticism—which had drug-related overtones. Shankar then returned to the relatively obscure life of the sitar virtuoso. He recorded *The Sounds of India* and *The Genius of Ravi Shankar*, as well as *Live at Monterey* (1967).

Shankar, Uday (1902–1977). Indian dancer, choreographer and teacher. A leading Hindu dancer, Shankar combined classical Indian dance with a modern dance idiom and captured the attention of Western audiences with his charismatic, often erotic performances. The brother of musician Ravi SHANKAR, he initially worked with his father as a painter and producer in the theater. He devoted himself to dance after staging and dancing in Anna PAVLOVA's ballet *Radha-Krishna* (1924). He toured Europe and the U.S. with Pavlova (1924–28), then returned to India and formed his own company with which he frequently toured in Europe, the U.S. and India. Backed by British and American funding, he established the Uday Shankar Indian Culture Center to research, film and teach classical dance and music (1938). Though closed during WORLD WAR II, the center reopened in 1965.

Shannon, Del [born Charles Westover] (1939–1990). American singer-songwriter. Shannon created hits such as "Runaway" (1961) and "Keep Searchin'" (1965). The British duo Peter and Gordon also had a hit with his song "I Go to Pieces" in the mid-1960s. He made several attempts to regain his early popularity in the 1970s and 1980s, but none of those efforts was commercially successful.

Shansi. Chinese province bordering on Inner Mongolia. From the CHINESE REVOLUTION OF 1911–12 until the communist takeover of 1949, this ancient region was ruled as an independent fiefdom by the warlord Yen Hsi-Shan. Partially occupied by the Japanese during the SINO-JAPANESE WAR OF 1937–45, the strategically located province was at the mercy of communist guerrillas during the 1940s.

SHAPE [Supreme Headquarters, Allied Powers in Europe]. NATO headquarters in Brussels.

Shapley, Harlow (1885–1972). American astronomer. Shapley was born in Nashville, Missouri, and earned his Ph.D. in astronomy from Princeton in 1913. In 1921, he left the Mount Wilson Observatory in California to become head of the Harvard College Observatory, where he worked until 1952. By 1920, Shapley had determined the size and structure of the Milky Way Galaxy as well as the approximate position of our solar system within it; for this he received the nickname "the modern Copernicus." Under Shapley's leadership, the Harvard Observatory became a leading center of astronomical study and the site of important research on galaxies, binary stars and related phenomena.

Sharon, Ariel (1928–). Israeli military and political figure. Born in Palestine, Sharon caught the eye of senior HAGANAH commanders, while still a boy, by organizing retaliatory raids against local Bedouin tribes. In the 1948 war Sharon, a gifted tactician, was made a battalion commander at the age of 20. Wounded in the battle for Latrun, he became convinced that only military training and aggressive action could make Israel secure;

in 1953 he was given the chance to prove this by being put in charge of the newly formed "Unit 101," which gained notoriety when it killed 69 Jordanian men, women and children in a retaliatory raid. A few months later Sharon was promoted by Chief of Staff Moshe DAYAN to command the IDF's paratroop battalion. Under Sharon's command the paratroopers tried but failed to hold the Mitla Pass in the 1956 war. Sharon was relegated to military teaching jobs until 1962, when he was given command of the IDF's armored brigade. The newly appointed chief of staff, Yitzhak RABIN, promoted him to head of staff of the Northern Command in 1964 and to head of IDF training in 1966. In the 1967 war Sharon for the first time commanded a full division, and defeated an Egyptian armored brigade in the battle of Abu Aguila. After the war Sharon was given the task of stamping out opposition in the GAZA STRIP, a task his force performed with a harshness that aroused public disquiet in Israel.

In the 1973 war Sharon managed to forge a bridgehead across the Suez Canal but quarreled so violently with other senior officers that they demanded his dismissal. Sharon retired with the rank of major general and sat as a Knesset member for the Likud Party (1973–74). He was adviser to Labor Prime Minister Yitzhak RABIN (1975–77) and served as Likud minister of agriculture (1977–81), when he channeled massive resources to West Bank settlements. Appointed minister of defense in 1981, he commanded Israel's 1982 invasion of Lebanon. In 1983, found by the Kahan Commission "personally responsible" for the SABRA AND SHATILA MASSACRE, he was demoted to minister without portfolio by Prime Minister Menachem BEGIN. He was appointed minister of trade and industry in the government of national unity in 1984. Sharon is a charismatic figure whose vitriolic attacks on fellow politicians have especially endeared him to development-town voters. In recent years he has widened his power base by wooing Likud Party activists. He was narrowly defeated by Yitzhak SHAMIR in the Herut leadership contest and is a possible successor to Shamir.

Sharp, George G. (1874–1960). English-born American naval architect; founder of the still-active firm of George G. Sharp, Inc., which has been responsible for the design of more than 1,500 ships, including a number of outstandingly innovative designs. Sharp was educated in Scotland and came to the U.S. in 1902. He worked for a number of shipbuilding organizations in positions of increasing importance until 1916, when he was appointed chief surveyor of the American Bureau of Shipping. In 1920 he founded his own firm in New York. The 1939 Panama Line passenger ships *Ancon, Cristobal* and *Panama* were notable for their innovative design, for their striking appearance and for their interiors (with decorative design by the office of Raymond LOEWY), which used only fireproof materials throughout. The Sharp firm was also responsible for many wartime designs. In the 1950s and 1960s, Sharp developed the first cellular containerships and the first roll-on/roll-off (RO) ships, which greatly improved the efficiency of cargo loading and unloading operations; both types are now in general use worldwide. The first nuclear-powered merchant ship, the N.S. *Savannah*, a ship of handsomely streamlined form that was eventually converted to an ocean research vessel, was designed by the Sharp firm. The firm continues to be a leading designer of merchant and naval ships for both U.S. and foreign clients.

Sharpeville massacre. Shootings that occurred in Sharpeville, South Africa, a black township near Johannesburg, on March 21, 1960. An estimated 20,000 unarmed demonstrators, organized by the Pan-Africanist Congress, were protesting the pass laws, APARTHEID legislation that required black South Africans to carry passbooks at all times, when police opened fire. About 70 protestors were killed and another 190 were wounded. The Sharpeville massacre remains one of the most violent single incidents in the struggle against apartheid.

Sharqat. Village on the Tigris River, near ancient Ashur. In October 1918, the British won their final victory of WORLD WAR I IN MESOPOTAMIA at Sharqat. They subsequently signed an armistice with the rapidly crumbling Ottoman Turks on October 30.

Shastri, Lal Bahadur (1904–1966). Indian statesman, prime minister (1964–66). Born in Benares, Shastri joined Mohandas K. Gandhi's CONGRESS PARTY in 1920, and participated in numerous nonviolent protests, for which he was imprisoned on several occasions. He was elected to the central legislature in 1952, serving as minister of railways until 1956, as minister of commerce and industry (1957–61) and as minister of home affairs (1961–63). He succeeded the ailing Jawaharlal Nehru as prime minister in 1964. After the INDO-PAKISTANI WAR OF 1965, Shastri met with President AYUB KHAN and signed a peace agreement. However, he suffered a heart attack and died the following day.

Shaw, Artie [born Arthur Arshawsky] (1910–). American JAZZ clarinetist and big band leader. Shaw became one of the most popular big band leaders of the late 1930s and early 1940s. Born in New Jersey, he worked for numerous bands in the 1920s and early 1930s as a clarinet sideman. His perfect clarinet technique, featuring a catchy, swinging style, made Shaw a highly popular performer. In 1937, he formed his own big band and enjoyed numerous hits through 1942, including "Begin the Beguine," "Star Dust" and "Moonglow." Shaw served in the United States Navy during WORLD WAR II and led an overseas service big band. He gave up performing in 1955 and turned to theatrical and film production in the 1960s. His eight wives included Hollywood actresses Lana Turner and Ava Gardner.

Shaw, George Bernard (1856–1950). Anglo-Irish playwright and critic. A leading figure in 20th-century theater, Shaw was born in Dublin and moved to London in 1876 where he began to write and to educate himself at the British Museum. He wrote five unsuccessful novels, which include *Cashel Byron's Profession* (1886) and *An Unsocial Socialist* (1887), and ghosted articles of musical criticism, later writing under his own name for such publications such as *Dramatic Review, The World* and *The Star*. His criticism was later collected into *Shaw's Music* (1981, three volumes). He became a drama critic for *The Saturday Review* in 1895, and in his opinionated, controversial articles he championed Ibsen. These articles were collected in *Our Theatres in the Nineties* (1932, three volumes). A vegetarian who eschewed alcohol and tobacco, Shaw was also a socialist and a member of the FABIAN SOCIETY. While serving on its executive committee from 1885 to 1911, Shaw trained himself in public speaking and gave lectures on its behalf as well as contributing to and editing *Fabian Essays in Socialism* (1889). Shaw's first play, *Widower's Houses* (1892) as well as several subsequent ones, including *Arms and the Man* (1893) and *Mrs. Warren's Profession* (1899), were not well received initially. It wasn't until *John Bull's Other Island* (1904) that he achieved critical and popular success. Shaw's plays, carried largely by dialogue, presented contemporary moral dilemmas with characteristic "Shavian" wit. Shaw was an extremely prolific writer and his many important works include *Man and Superman* (1903); *Major Barbara* (1905, filmed 1941); *Pygmalion* (1913), which evidences his interest in language, and was adapted into the successful musical *My Fair Lady* (1956); *Heartbreak House* (1920) and *Buoyant Billions* (1948). Shaw was awarded the NOBEL PRIZE for literature in 1925. Other works include *The Intelligent*

George Bernard Shaw.

Woman's Guide to Socialism and Capitalism (1928) and *Everybody's Political What's What* (1944). Shaw married Charlotte Payne-Townshend in 1898 and remained with her until her death in 1943, although it was evidently only a companionable marriage of convenience, and he was occasionally linked with other women.

Shaw, Irwin (1913–1984). American popular novelist. Shaw first won acclaim for his play *Bury the Dead* (1936); his short stories of the 1930s and 1940s also won critical praise, and his World War II novel *The Young Lions* (1948) found a wide readership. Thereafter he was known as a bestselling novelist. His later books include *Rich Man, Poor Man* (1970), which was made into a television miniseries, and *Evening in Byzantium* (1973).

Shawn, Edwin Myers "Ted" (1891–1972). American modern dancer. Originally a divinity student, Shawn was introduced to the study of dance as therapy after an illness. In 1914, he met and married Ruth ST. DENIS, also a dancer, and together they founded the Denishawn School in Los Angeles in 1915 and later moved the school to New York City. The couple ended their personal and professional association in 1930. In 1941 he founded the JACOB'S PILLOW DANCE FESTIVAL near Lee, Massachusetts, as a summer residence/theater for his dancers and developed it into an internationally important dance center.

For further reading:

Shawn, Ted, *One Thousand and One Night Stands*. New York: Da Capo Press, 1960.

Terry, Walter, *Ted Shawn, Father of American Dance: A Biography*. New York: Dial Press, 1976.

Shcharansky, Anatoly (1948–). Soviet mathematician and dissident. A leading Jewish dissident during the 1970s, Shcharansky was convicted in 1978 of espionage, treason and "anti-Soviet agitation." His case attracted much attention in the West, mobilizing human rights advocates. His supporters maintained that the charges were brought because he was an outspoken critic of Soviet policy toward Jews. He was released as part of a Soviet-American swap of alleged spies in 1986. Currently residing in Israel, Shcharansky continues to champion human rights.

Shcherbitsky, Vladimir Vasilievich (1918–1990). Soviet politician. Known as a hard-liner, Shcherbitsky had been a member of the POLITBURO since the days of Leonid I. BREZHNEV. As long-time chief of the Ukrainian Communist Party, he was accused of suppressing information about the radiation damage from the CHERNOBYL nuclear power plant accident in the Ukraine in 1986. He was ousted from both posts in September 1989 as part of a shake-up orchestrated by Soviet leader Mikhail GORBACHEV.

Sheed, Francis Joseph (1897–1981). Anglo-American Roman Catholic lay theologian, writer, lecturer and publisher. Sheed founded the English publishing company Sheed & Ward in 1926 and later opened a New York branch. He published the works of major British philosophers, historians, and church apologists. His best-known book, *Theology and Sanity*, became a standard theological text. He was the father of the American novelist **Wilfred Sheed**.

Sheeler, Charles (1883–1965). American painter. Born in Philadelphia, Sheeler attended that city's School of Industrial Art and the Pennsylvania Academy of the Fine Arts, studying under William Merritt Chase. He traveled to Europe with his teacher, and was influenced by the vivid color of FAUVISM. His early work was exhibited in the 1913 ARMORY SHOW. Sheeler is best known for paintings produced after World War I, executed in a kind of cool American CUBISM, with sleek, streamlined, volumetric shapes and subjects drawn from architecture and machinery, as well as land- and seascape. Also a skilled photographer, his style is thought to be partially derived from his immaculately photographed barns, towers and Shaker furnishings. The clean abstraction of the work of Sheeler and his contemporary Charles Demuth has been termed "precisionism" by art historians. Among his characteristic paintings are *American Landscape* (1930, Museum of Modern Art, New York City) and *California Industrial* (1957).

Sheen, Archbishop Fulton (John) (1895–1979). American Roman Catholic clergyman, radio and television evangelist and author. In his heyday Sheen was one of the best known church figures in the United States. He became the first regular preacher over national radio in the 1930s on "The Catholic Hour." He later conducted the popular 1950s television series "Life Is Worth Living." He wrote more than 60 books and pamphlets, taught philosophy at Catholic University and served as bishop of Rochester, New York for three years before his retirement in 1969. A traditionalist, he was famous for his attacks on communism and Freudian psychoanalysis. He also espoused causes of social justice.

Shehu, Mehmet (1913–1981). Premier of ALBANIA (1954–81). A hard-line Communist, Shehu was the closest aide of Albanian Communist leader Enver HOXHA. He survived many purges and was known for his fiery temper. His death was reportedly a suicide.

Shelepin, Alexander Nikolayevich (1918–). Communist official. Having studied in Moscow, Shelepin joined the party in 1940, and worked in the Komsomol apparatus; in 1958 he was appointed first secretary of its central committee, and became a member of the party central committee. He was chairman of the committee of state security (KGB) from 158 to 1961. He was removed from the leadership, and thus eliminated as a potential opponent to BREZHNEV, in 1975.

Shelley, Norman (1903–1980). British radio actor. In 1940 during the BATTLE OF BRITAIN in WORLD WAR II, Shelley was enlisted by the British government to deliver a radio broadcast version of Winston CHURCHILL's famous "We Shall Never Surrender" speech. Churchill had made the speech to Parliament, but it was not recorded. Shelley imitated Churchill's voice with such uncanny accuracy that his recording helped rally the all-but-defeated nation against Germany and stirred American public opinion. The use of Shelley remained one of the war's best-kept secrets and was not disclosed until 1979.

Shelley v. Kramer (1948). U.S. Supreme Court decision outlawing private, racially restrictive covenants. During the first half of the century it was common for real estate deeds to bar the sale of the property to black Americans or members of other minority groups. Although the law forbade racial discrimination, private agreements upheld it. In 1948 the Supreme Court held that while the states did not have the power to ban such private agreements, the Fourteenth Amendment barred the states from permitting their court systems to enforce these racially restrictive covenants. By its decision the Court made these covenants unenforceable.

Shen Congwen [born Shen Yuehuan] (1902–1988). Chinese novelist; one of the most widely anthologized modern writers in English-language collections of Chinese literature. His works produced a vivid picture of life in the Chinese countryside during the chaotic warlord era of the 1920s and 1930s. *Long River*, regarded by many critics as his finest novel, appeared in 1943. In the ensuing decade, he became a victim of politics, being denounced by communists and KUOMINTANG supporters alike. His books were banned in Taiwan, while mainland publishing houses burned his books and destroyed the printing plates. It was not until 1978 that the Chinese government began reissuing his works, although in very limited editions.

Shensi. Province of north-central China, bordering on Inner Mongolia. From 1935 until final victory in 1949, it was the stronghold of the Chinese communists.

Shepard, Alan (1923–). U.S astronaut. On May 5, 1961, Shepard became the first American in space when he took a 15.5 minute suborbital flight for 304 miles reaching an altitude of 116 miles before landing in the Atlantic. The flight was short and sweet and effective. America had its first man in space. Shepard later recounted that the flight happened so fast that he managed only a 30–second glimpse out of the spacecraft's small window. Shepard got a better view of space 10 years later, when as commander of APOLLO 14 (January 31–February 9, 1971) he spent two days on the surface of the moon. The only one of the original MERCURY astronauts to fly to the moon, Shepard was born in East Derry, New Hampshire, the son of a career Army officer. Although his father had attended West Point, Shepard earned his B.S. from the United States Naval Academy in 1944. After service in World War II he attended the U.S. Navy Test Pilot School at Patuxent River in 1950, serving as an instructor from 1951 to 1953. After retiring from NASA and the Navy in 1974, Shepard entered the private sector. In 1971 he served as a delegate to the 26th UN General Assembly.

Shepard, Sam (1943–). American playwright and film actor. Shepard first burst into theatrical prominence in the 1960s when he wrote a series of striking one-act plays—*Cowboys* (1964), *Rock Garden* (1964), *Chicago* (1965), and *Icarus' Mother* (1965)—that dealt movingly with the decline of the free-roaming American West and the advent of technology. *Rock Garden* was subsequently incorporated into the Kenneth Tynan Broadway hit *Oh, Calcutta!* Shepard moved on to full-length plays including *La Turista* (1966), *Operation Sidewinder* (1970), *The Tooth of Crime* (1972), *The Curse of the Starving Class* (1977), the PULITZER PRIZE winning *Buried Child* (1978), *Seduced* (1979), *True West* (1980), *Fool For Love* (1983) and *A Life of the Mind* (1986). He has also won acclaim as a film actor through his dramatic roles in *The Right Stuff* (1983) and *Country* (1984), in which he co-starred with his wife, Jessica Lange.

Shepherd, General Lemuel Cornick, Jr. (1896–1990). U.S. military leader. He was a decorated veteran of World War I, World War II and the Korean War. In 1945, he led the last land battle of World War II, defeating Japanese troops on the island of OKINAWA. Commandant of the U.S. Marine Corps from 1952 to 1955, he was the first head of the Marines to serve as a member of the Joint Chiefs of Staff.

Sheppard case. Sensational pair of murder trials during the 1950s and 1960s involving Cleveland surgeon Sam Sheppard who was accused of murdering his wife. After Marilyn Sheppard was found dead in her suburban Cleveland home her husband was arrested for her murder. Sam Sheppard, who confessed during the trial to having an extramarital affair, alleged that he had been knocked unconscious by his wife's assailant. The murder trial attracted wide attention, especially in Cleveland where emotions were inflamed by the local press. Sheppard was convicted and was sentenced to life in prison in 1954. Sheppard's supporters continued their efforts on his behalf, and he gained a new trial in 1966 after the U.S. Supreme Court threw out the first conviction because of the trial's carnival atmosphere. Sheppard was ultimately acquitted but his life deteriorated. After a divorce and a medical malpractice suit he briefly became a professional wrestler before his death in 1970.

Sherlock Holmes. Without question the world's most famous consulting detective, whose adventures link the picturesque milieu of Edwardian England with modern 20th-century police methods and technology. As recorded by colleague Dr. John H. Watson (and published by literary agent Sir Arthur Conan DOYLE), Holmes and Watson battled crime in 56 short stories and four novels that have been dubbed affectionately by their fans "The Canon," or "The Sacred Writings." The pair first met in a chemistry laboratory in St. Bartholomew's Hospital in the pages of *Beeton's Christmas Annual* (December, 1887)—where the novel *A Study in Scarlet* was originally printed. Popular enthusiastic response was delayed, however, until after the publication of another novel, *The Sign of Four* (in the February, 1890 *Lippincott's Monthly Magazine*), plus a cycle of 12 short stories in *The Strand Magazine* from 1891 to 1892. Artist Sidney Paget's illustrations helped popularize Watson's famous description of Holmes as a tall man with an excessively lean figure, sharp and piercing eyes, and a thin, hawk-like nose. The 221B Baker Street lodgings, under the watchful eye of the landlady (later identified as Mrs. Hudson), likewise became a matter of public record. The short stories were collected in *The Adventures of Sherlock·Holmes* (1892), *The Memoirs of Sherlock Holmes* (1894), *The Return of Sherlock Holmes* (1905), *His Last Bow* (1917) and *The Case-Book of Sherlock Holmes* (1927). Stage and screen impersonations began with William Gillette's play, *Sherlock Holmes* (1899) and continued in British silent films of Eille Norwood (1920), the Goldwyn Pictures adaption (1920) with John BARRYMORE, the Basil RATHBONE series for 20TH CENTURY-FOX and UNIVERSAL in the late 1930s and '40s, and the British Jeremy Brett television plays in the 1980s. So fully drawn was Holmes' eccentric manner and towering intellect that it has been the conviction of millions of readers that he really existed. That attitude is carried on today by Holmesian organizations, such as The Baker Street Irregulars (founded in America, 1933), The Sherlock Holmes Society of London (also 1933) and The Adventures of Sherlock Holmes (founded in America, 1970). Affiliated with these groups are hundreds of other societies around the world. Today the sole surviving child of Doyle—Dame Jean Conan Doyle—guards the Holmes copyright, which, while it has expired in Great Britain, still obtains in America. "I've grown up with an affection for this character," she told this writer in 1988. "And I hate to see it denigrated by those taking advantage of the lapsed copyright." Meanwhile, Holmes is doubtless still at work bee-keeping on the Sussex Downs. And, somewhere in the vaults of Cox and Company on Charing Cross Road, London, exists that battered tin box, which someday will be unearthed and will reveal to a startled world yet a new series of three-pipe problems.

For further reading:

Starrett, Vincent, *The Private Life of Sherlock Holmes*. New York: Pinnacle Books, 1975.

Sherriff, R(obert) C(edric) (1896–1975). British playwright and novelist. Sherriff was a gifted and entertaining writer who enjoyed long-term success with the British public both through his fiction and his plays. He first made his mark with his play *Journey's End* (1928), an incisive portrayal of life in the trenches during WORLD WAR I. Sherriff continues to be best remembered for his plays, which include *Badger's Green* (1930), *Home at Seven* (1950), *The White Carnation* (1953), *The Long Sunset* (1955) and *The Telescope* (1957).

Sherwood, Bobby (1914–1981). American JAZZ trumpeter, band leader, composer, and musical arranger of the BIG BAND era. In the 1930s Sherwood was an arranger and conductor for the radio shows of Bing CROSBY and Eddie Cantor. He also worked for Hollywood film studios, writing musical arrangements for stars such as Fred ASTAIRE, Judy GARLAND, Jeanette MacDonald and Nelson Eddy. As a trumpeter, he played with important jazz figures including Artie SHAW, Zoot SIMS, and Stan GETZ.

Sherwood, Robert E(mmet) (1896–1955). American playwright. Born in New Rochelle, New York, Sherwood attended Harvard, becoming a magazine writer, a film critic from 1920 to 1928 and an editor at *Life* from 1924 to 1928. He achieved success with his first play, the comedy *The Road to Rome* (1927), but became best known for dramas such as *The Petrified Forest* (1935), *Idiot's Delight* (1936), *Abe Lincoln in Illinois* (1938) and *There Shall Be No Night* (1941), the last three of which all won PULITZER PRIZES. During WORLD WAR II, Sherwood served with the Office of War Information and was a speech writer for Franklin D. ROOSEVELT. He wrote of the President and his advisor Harry HOPKINS in the biographical *Roosevelt and Hopkins* (1948), another Pulitzer prize winner. Also active in films, Sherwood was the recipient of an ACADEMY AWARD for his moving script *The Best Years of Our Lives* (1946).

Shestov, Led [Led Isakovich Schwartzmann] (1866–1938). Russian writer. Of Jewish origin, he studied for the bar and turned to literature late in life. His first book, *Shakespeare and His Critic Brandes* (1898), contains an attack on positivism and rationalism, and later works, such as *Dostoyevsky and Nietzsche* and *The Philosophy of Tragedy* (1901), illustrate his profound lack of belief in Idealism. He spent many years abroad studying the history of philosophy and mysticism. Opposed to the Bolsheviks, in 1917 Shestov settled in Paris.

Shevardnadze, Eduard (1928–). Soviet foreign minister. Shevardnadze joined the COMMUNIST PARTY OF THE U.S.S.R. as a young man and began to advance in the party bureaucracy in his native Georgia, holding the posts of minister of internal affairs and secretary general there. In 1976, he was appointed to the Central Committee of the national party and in 1978 was named to the Politburo. In July 1985 he was named Soviet foreign minister. Over the next five years, Shevardnadze played an important role in drafting foreign policy, in improving Soviet relations with China and Japan, and in conducting arms control negotiations with the U.S. In addition, he worked doggedly but unsuccessfully to find a negotiated settlement of the war in Afghanistan. On December 20, 1990, Shevardnadze abruptly resigned as foreign minister, saying he believed the Soviet Union to be on the verge of succumbing to a right-wing dictatorship.

Shikanai, Nobutaka (1911–1990). Japanese media entrepreneur. He built the Fujisankei Communications Group into JAPAN's largest media and entertainment conglomerate before turning it over to his son-in-law in 1989. He often generated controversy with his right-wing views, and with such actions as paying former U.S. President Ronald REAGAN and his wife Nancy $2 million to visit Japan in 1989. He was also a collector of modern art who built one of the most famous museums in Japan.

Shiki, Masaoka [Masaoka Tsunenori] (1867–1902). Japanese poet, essayist, critic. Shiki abandoned his studies at Tokyo Imperial University for a career as a journalist. Although he contracted tuberculosis, he continued to work as a war correspondent during the Sino-Japanese War of 1894–95. Thereafter, he was bedridden and in continual pain. Shiki is known as a reformer of the traditional forms of Japanese poetry, the haiku and the tanka, and as the best haiku writer of modern times. He introduced colloquial speech and contemporary subjects to the tradition. He published several influential studies, including *The Essence of the Haiku* (1895) and *Buson: The Haiku Poet*. The latter served to popularize the work of the 18th-century poet and painter Buson. Shiki's collected works comprise 22 volumes.

Shimazaki Toson (1872–1943). Japanese writer. Shimazaki began his literary career as a poet, but achieved greatest recognition as a novelist and has been an extremely influential figure in 20th-century Japanese fiction. His classic work *Hakai* (1906, trans. *The Broken Commandment*, 1974) is a work of profound social concern that is considered Japan's first naturalistic novel. His later fiction is largely autobiographical in character.

Shin Bet. Israeli security service.

Shingo, Shigeo (1090–1990). Japanese industrial management specialist. While with the Toyota Motor Co., he and Taiichi OHNO developed the "just-in-time" manufacturing system, whereby inventories were kept deliberately low to reduce costs and increase flexibility. He was also credited with promoting the "poka yoka" system of mistake-proofing, which provided feedback to managers to help them identify production problems.

Shinn, Everett (1873–1953). American painter. Born in Woodstown, New Jersey, Shinn attended the Pennsylvania Academy of the Fine Arts. Settling in New York City, he became the youngest member of the realist group known as The EIGHT. Unlike other Ashcan School figures who tended to paint grim urban scenes, Shinn gravitated toward bustling panoramas of contemporary street life and theatrical tableaus painted in a vivid, Impressionist-influenced style. His exuberant theater scenes include *London Hippodrome* (1902, Art Institute of Chicago) and *London Music Hall* (Metropolitan Museum of Art, New York City). Shinn is also known for his lively murals and magazine illustrations.

Shinwell, Lord (Emanuel) (1884–1986). British politician. A combative veteran of Britain's trades union movement, Shinwell became a leading LABOUR PARTY politician and held three successive cabinet posts as minister of fuel and power, war secretary and minister of defense, in the government headed by Prime Minister Clement ATTLEE. After serving for many years in the House of Commons, Shinwell gave up his seat in 1970 and entered the House of Lords as a life peer. He became disillusioned with Labour's leftward drift in the 1970s and from 1982 sat in the Lords as an independent. His 100th birthday, in October 1984, was celebrated in grand style by the House of Lords, and he became the first centenarian to address either house of Parliament.

Shipov, Dimitri Nikolayevich (1851–1920). Liberal politician. Chairman of the Moscow *Zemstvo*, Shipov organized unofficial congresses of *zemstvo* representatives in the 1890s and 1900s. In 1905 he was one of the founders and 10 leaders of the OCTOBRIST Party, and in the following year, a leader of the party of peaceful renovation.

Shirer, William L. (1904–). American journalist and author. Shirer began working for the Paris edition of the NEW YORK HERALD-TRIBUNE and later served in Paris as correspondent for the *Chicago Tribune*. In 1937, he was hired by William R. MURROW for CBS, where he worked as a commentator until 1947. Shirer reported on the ANSCHLUSS and the German army's invasion of France. He was also a columnist for the *New York Herald-Tribune* from 1942 to 1948. Shirer is the author of the acclaimed *Berlin Diary* (1941) and *The Rise and Fall of the Third Reich* (1960), which won a National Book Award.

Shklovsky, Iosif Samuilovich (1916–1985). Soviet astrophysicist. Widely known for his speculations on alien life, Shklovsky led the U.S.S.R.'s search for extraterrestrial intelligence. As a theoretical researcher, he was the first scientist to propose an explanation for the strange light emanating from the Crab Nebula.

For further reading:

Shklovsky, Iosif S. with Carl Sagan, *Intelligent Life in the Universe*. Oakland, Calif.: Holden-Day, 1966.

Shkoder. Town and province of ALBANIA, between the Drin River and Lake Scutari. Montenegrin troops threw out the Ottoman Turks in 1913, only to see the BALKAN WAR peace settlement award the area to Albania. A battle zone during WORLD WAR I, it was occupied by Austria from 1916 to 1918.

Shlonsky, Abraham (1900–1973). Israeli poet and translator. Born in Russia, Shklovsky moved to Palestine in 1921, becoming one of the leading modernist poets writing in the Hebrew language. Shlonsky is also known as an editor and as a sensitive translator, rendering the work of European masters such as Shakespeare and Pushkin into Heb[illegible]w.

Shockley, William Bradford (1910–1989). American physicist known for his invention of the TRANSISTOR and for his controversial theories on black's. In 1956 Shockley shared the NOBEL PRIZE for physics with John BARDEEN and Walter H. BRATTAIN for the work they did at Bell Laboratories on the invention of the transistor. In the 1950s the device revolutionized all forms of electronics, from high technology to consumer goods, by allowing the development of faster, better, smaller and cheaper products. In the 1970s, however, Shockley began to alienate his colleagues and anger the public with his assertions that blacks were genetically inferior to whites and should be encouraged to volunteer for sterilization. He sued the *Atlanta Constitution* after a 1980 column in the newspaper compared his suggestion to Nazi experiments in GENETIC ENGINEERING. He eventually won his case, but was awarded only $1 in damages. At the time of his death, Shockley was professor emeritus of electrical engineering at Stanford University.

Shockworkers' Movement. From 1927 to 1935 Soviet workers were encouraged by trade unions to become "shockworkers" (*udarniki*), a particularly dedicated kind of worker who, according to the Communist Party, actively directed participation in economic construction.

Shoemaker, Willie (1931–). William Lee Shoemaker—better known as "Willie," "Bill" and "The Shoe"—is widely considered the greatest jockey in the history of American racing. Twenty-five ounces at birth, the diminutive Shoemaker never topped 95 pounds, but he had a legendary ability to guide thoroughbred racehorses across the finish line in first place without needing to use a forceful whip hand. He rode the first of his 8,833 winners in 1949, and his last in 1990, winning $123 million in purses. In those 41 years, he won the Kentucky Derby four times, the Preakness twice and the Belmont five times. At the age of 54, he became the oldest rider ever to win the Derby. Perhaps his most famous Derby ride was the one he lost in 1957: riding Gallant Man to seeming victory, Shoemaker misjudged the Churchill Downs finish line and began to rein in his mount with 1/16 of a mile remaining in the race. In 1990, Shoemaker retired to pursue a career as a trainer. An automobile accident in 1991 left him paralyzed.

Sholokhov, Mikhail Alexandrovich (1905–1984). Soviet author. Born in a small Cossack village in the Don Region, Sholokhov was educated in Moscow and worked as a teacher, clerk and journalist. In 1920 he started to publish sketches and joined several literary circles. The start of his literary career was boosted by Alexander Serafimovich's help. In 1926 Sholokhov is thought to have begun his famous trilogy, *Tales of the Don*, although it has been alleged that he did not in fact write it. *The Quiet Don* was published in 1926–40, *And Quiet Flows the Don* in 1934 and *The Don Flows to the Sea* in 1940. A member of the Communist Party from

Soviet composer Dmitri Shostakovich.

1931, he was elected to the Soviet Academy of Sciences, and later to the central committee of the Soviet Union. From 1946 he served as a deputy to the Supreme Soviet. He was awarded the NOBEL PRIZE for literature in 1965. He later launched an attack on Andrei SINYAVSKY. (See also SOCIALIST REALISM.)

Shostakovich, Dmitri Dmitrievich (1906–1975). Dmitri Shostakovich is widely regarded as the most significant Soviet composer of the 20th century. A graduate of the Petrograd (Leningrad) Conservatory (1926), Shostakovich first won attention with his graduation piece, the 1st Symphony (1926). His career subsequently mirrored the tumultuous history of the U.S.S.R. and the dilemma of an artist torn between serving the dictates of a mass ideology and his own personal vision. Shostakovich alternately found himself acclaimed as a great "people's artist" and denounced for straying from the dictates of the Communist Party. The quality of his music often reflects its political content: His "public" works tend to be trite and bombastic, while his more personal music is often searing and intense. His 2nd and 3rd symphonies, celebrating events in Soviet history, were well received, but his 4th was banned because of its originality, as was his opera *Lady MacBeth of Mtsensk* (1934). His official reputation was restored with the stirring 5th Symphony (1937), among the most popular of his 15 symphonies. His 7th ("Leningrad"), composed during the World War II SIEGE OF LENINGRAD, was acclaimed as a portrayal of that city's beleaguered defenders. However, his 8th Symphony (1943) was attacked by ZHDANOV at the 1948 Communist Party Congress, and STALIN himself accused Shostakovich (along with PROKOFIEV and KHACHATURIAN) of "formalism." Likewise, his 13th Symphony ("Babi Yar," 1962), a choral setting of poems by Yevtushenko, was criticized by KHRUSHCHEV and banned because of its implications of Soviet ANTISEMITISM. Among his most enduring works are the 10th Symphony (1953) and 8th String Quartet (1962). His son **Maksim Shostakovich** was a noted conductor who emigrated to the West.

For further reading:

MacDonald, Ian, *The New Shostakovich.* Boston: Northeastern University Press, 1990.

Show Boat. Classic Broadway musical show, one of the landmarks of the modern stage. Novelist Edna FERBER had never seen a show boat (or the Mississippi River, for that matter) when she began the story in 1924. It recounted the adventures of the show boat *Cotton Blossom,* and a gallery of diverse characters, including the comic Cap'n Andy, the lovely Magnolia, the dashing gambler Gaylord Ravenal, the black ship's hand, Joe (originally "Jo"), and the tragic mulatto Julie. The Broadway musical adaptation by composer Jerome KERN, librettist Oscar. HAMMERSTEIN II, and producer Florenz Ziegfeld made theater history at its premiere at the Ziegfeld Theater in New York, December 27, 1927. Contrasting with the typically light and fluffy musical show of the day, *Show Boat* had controversial subject matter—miscegenation, alcoholism and desertion—and an unusually tight integration of song and story. "Old Man River," "Make Believe," and "Can't Help Lovin' That Man" became standards. Actress Helen Morgan was an overnight success as Julie, and revivals in 1929 and 1932, respectively, made stars of Irene DUNNE as Magnolia and Paul ROBESON as Joe. There have been three movie versions, two for Universal in 1929 and 1936, and one for MGM in 1951. However, according to the show's historian, Miles Kreuger, it was not until an EMI/Angel recording in 1989 that the original version was restored. "Many songs were cut over the years," Kreuger says, "as were most of the racial (some would say racist) vernacular common to the time period depicted in the story. Unlike other classics, *Oklahoma!* and *Carousel,* for example, there has been no 'original' version extant until now." While the model for Ferber's show boat, the *James Adams Floating Theatre,* sank in 1928, happily the musical show, freshly refurbished, continues to sail on.

For further reading:

Kreuger, Miles, *"Show Boat:" The Story of a Classic American Musical.* New York: Oxford University Press, 1977.

Shriver, (Robert) Sargent (1915–). American public official. Born in Westminster, Maryland, Shriver attended Yale University, graduating from its law school in 1941. He served in WORLD WAR II and was a magazine editor before becoming a business associate of Joseph P. KENNEDY, whose daughter, Eunice, he later married. Business manager for his brother-in-law John F. KENNEDY's presidential campaign, Shriver became the first director of the PEACE CORPS (1961–66). He also held the office of director of the Office of Economic Opportunity under President Lyndon B. JOHNSON from 1964 to 1968. He was ambassador to France from 1968 to 1970. After vice-presidential nominee Thomas EAGLETON withdrew from the campaign in 1972, Shriver became George MCGOVERN's running mate in his unsuccessful bid for the presidency.

Shukairy, Ahmed (1907–1980). First head of the PALESTINE LIBERATION ORGANIZATION (PLO). Shukairy worked in the ARAB LEAGUE (1951–57) and served as SAUDI ARABIA's ambassador to the UNITED NATIONS (1957–62). A leading hard-line opponent of Arab peace with ISRAEL, he was elected head of the PLO when it was created in 1964. He held the post until after the disastrous Arab losses to Israel in the SIX-DAY WAR (1967).

shuttle diplomacy. Mediation between conflicting parties, which involves constant travel by a representative from one antagonist to the other in order to achieve a settlement. Alternatively, the representative may be a third party, as was the case with Henry KISSINGER and Philip Habib on behalf of the U.S. in attempting to mediate in the Arab-Israeli conflict.

Sibelius, Jean (Julius Christian) (1865–1957). Finnish composer. Born in Tavastehus, Sibelius abandoned the study of law for music. He was educated at the conservatories of Helsinki, Berlin and Vienna. His early compositions reflect the influence of late-romantic German composers and of Tchaikovsky. Many of these works, including *En Saga* (1892), *The Swan of Tuonela* (1893), *Finlandia* (1900) and the First (1899) and Second Symphonies (1902) employ Finnish folk music or embody national themes. Coinciding with the rise of Finnish nationalism, these compositions came to be regarded as anthems of the Finnish resistance to Russian rule; they established Sibelius as FINLAND's leading composer and one of its foremost citizens. In 1897, the Finnish government awarded Sibelius a lifetime grant that allowed him to devote his time to composing. Sibelius' output includes seven symphonies, a violin concerto (1903), tone poems, chamber works and music for theater. His later symphonies, with their austere textures and mysterious sense of

Finnish composer Jean Sibelius.

foreboding, rank among the most original musical accomplishments of the 20th century. Sibelius gave up composing after his tone poem *Tapiola* (1926) and spent the remaining 30 years of his life at his country home (Jarvenpaa), as an international but secluded celebrity. For many years, musicians and audiences speculated about an "eighth symphony" that Sibelius was supposedly composing, but this work never materialized. A 1935 poll identified Sibelius as American audiences' favorite composer; later, his reputation went into decline, except in Finland and Britain. Sibelius is now widely regarded as one of the most significant symphonic composers of the 20th century.

For further reading:

Abraham, Gerald, ed., *The Music of Sibelius*. New York: Da Capo, 1975.

Layton, Robert, *Sibelius*, rev. ed., Lanham, Md.: Littlefield, Adams & Co., 1978.

Siberia. Geographically a part of Asia, politically most of Siberia belongs to the U.S.S.R.'s Russian Republic. This northern third of Asia, from the Ural Mountains to the Pacific Ocean, saw little settlement by Russians until construction of the Trans-Siberian Railroad (1891–1905). An autonomous government, formed in 1918 after the RUSSIAN REVOLUTION of 1917, was overthrown by the counterrevolutionary Admiral KOLCHAK. With the aid of an Allied Expeditionary Force, Kolchak's WHITES held Siberia until 1920, when it came decisively under communist control. During WORLD WAR II entire industrial plants were moved from European Russia to Siberia to escape capture and destruction by the invading Germans. Siberia has long been a dreaded place of political exile and imprisonment—first under the czars and subsequently under the communists. During the rule of STALIN, Siberian labor camps were swelled with prisoners numbering into the millions—many of whom did not survive to return to their homes.

Sicily. A part of ITALY, this largest island of the Mediterranean Sea took a big beating during WORLD WAR II. Invaded by the Allies on July 9–10, 1943, the island was in Allied hands by mid-August (see WORLD WAR II ON THE ITALIAN FRONT). Unfortunately, it has never fully recovered from that short period of destruction; official indifference to the problems of southern Italy, and the pervasive malaise of MAFIA-influenced corruption, have not helped matters.

Sidra Crisis, Gulf of. On August 19, 1981, a pair of U.S. Navy F-14 jet fighters downed two Libyan SU-22s in the Mediterranean Sea over the Gulf of Sidra, about 60 miles from the Libyan coast. Libya claimed that part of the Gulf of Sidra as its territory, and Libyan leader QADDAFI had proclaimed a "line of death" protecting the area. The U.S. considered the area international waters. The confrontation occurred in the final hours of a two-day U.S. Navy military exercise in the Mediterranean and in the northern part of the Gulf of Sidra.

Siegfried Line. German defense system in the west, running from the Swiss border to Kleve in North Rhine-Westphalia, opposite the Netherlands. Set up by Nazi Germany in the 1930s, it was named after the hero of Wagner's Ring Cycle—reflecting Adolf HITLER's devotion to Wagner, Teutonic legend, and the dream of greater German glory. The Siegfried Line ran more or less parallel to the Rhine River and, in its southern reaches, faced France's MAGINOT LINE. It was not breached by the Allies until the last months of WORLD WAR II. A popular British wartime song scoffed at this much-vaunted symbol of German military might, promising that the Allies would "hang out our washing on the Siegfried Line."

Sienkiewicz, Henryk (1846–1916). Polish novelist, short-story writer and essayist. A prolific writer, Sienkiewicz had a strong Polish and Roman Catholic outlook on life. He was highly regarded during his lifetime, and received the NOBEL PRIZE for literature in 1905. Today he is mainly remembered for his historical novel, *Quo Vadis?* (1896), and for a trilogy of novels about 17th-century Poland.

Siepi, Cesare (1923–). Italian bass. Born in Milan, Siepi won a national vocal competition at 18 and made his operatic debut in 1941. During World War II, he escaped conscription into the German army by fleeing to Switzerland. He returned to Italy in 1945 and began singing at La Scala when the Milan opera house reopened in 1946; he made his Metropolitan Opera debut in 1950. Spending over two decades at the Metropolitan, Siepi became one of the company's principal bassos and was particularly noted for his performances of the title roles in *Don Giovanni, The Marriage of Figaro* and *Boris Godunov*, as well as Mephistopheles in *Faust*. After his concert debut in Verdi's *Requiem* (1951), he also made numerous appearances in recital.

Sierra Leone. Sierra Leone, bordered by Guinea and Liberia, covers an area of 27,692 square miles on the West African coast. Originally a British crown colony, it was granted independence in 1961 and

French actress Simone Signoret (1959).

became a republic within the COMMONWEALTH in 1971. Economic problems and rioting led President Siaka Stevens (1971–85) to declare a state of emergency in 1977 and again in 1981. A new constitution, providing for a one-party state, was approved in 1978. Economic instability has continued to plague the country during the presidency of General Joseph Momoh (1985–), and an economic state of emergency was imposed in 1987 after strikes by public employees.

Signoret, Simone [Simone Kaminker] (1921–1985). One of France's most renowned actresses, over the course of a career that spanned four decades, Signoret won the 1960 ACADEMY AWARD for best actress for the film *Room at the Top*. She gave other notable performances in such films as *Diabolique, Ship of Fools* and *Madame Rosa*. She married actor-singer Yves MONTAND in 1951. Their left-wing political activities prevented them from entering the U.S. during the 1950s. During the last decade of her life, she also published several books, the last of which, *Adieu, Voldia*, was a best-seller.

Sihanouk, Norodom (1922–). Prince of CAMBODIA. Son of the late King Norodom Suramarit and Queen Kossamack Neareath, Sihanouk has been on-and-off head of the CGDK coalition government of

Chinese Premier Deng Xiaoping (left) welcomes Cambodian Prince Norodom Sihanouk to Beijing (1987).

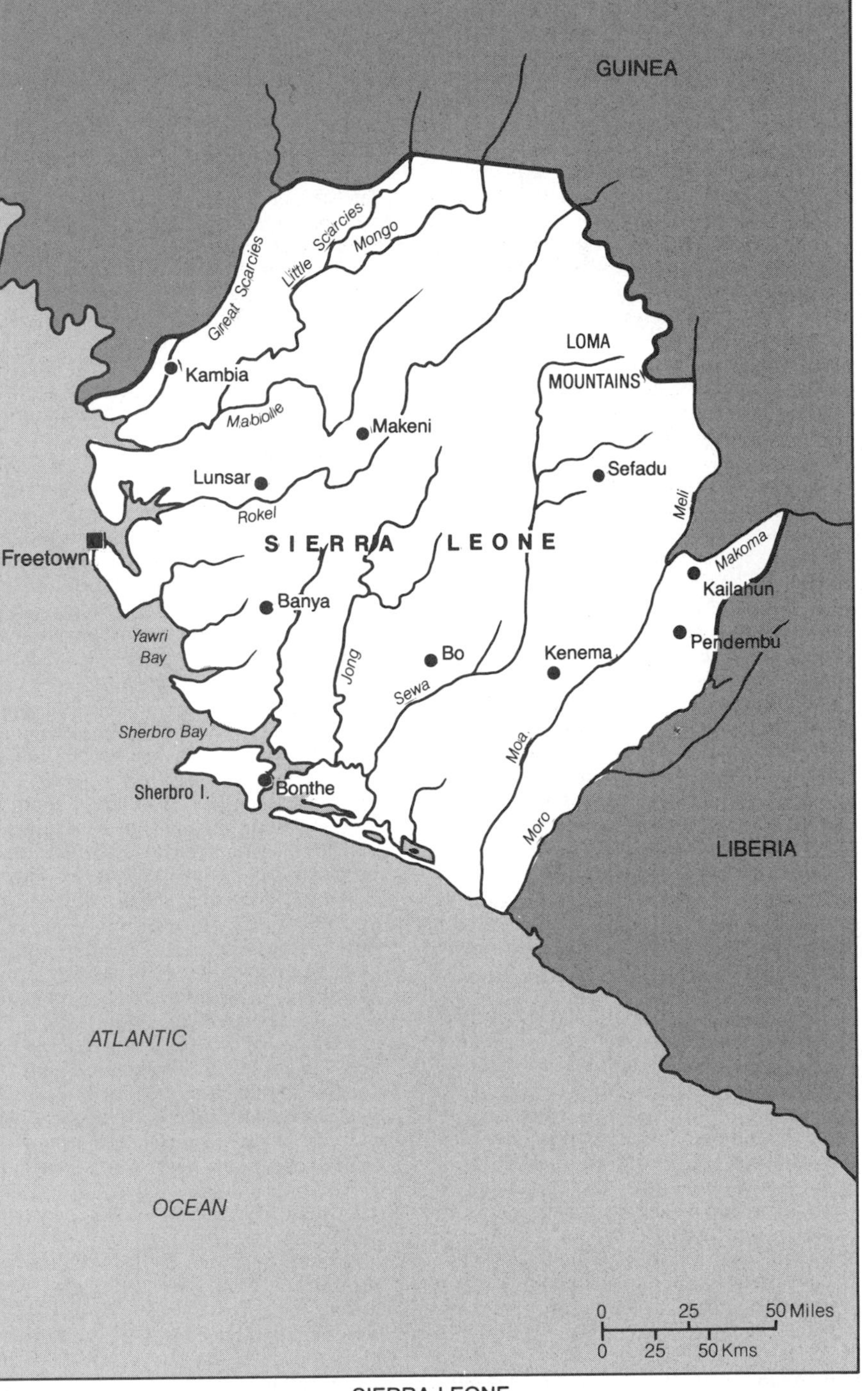

SIERRA LEONE

Democratic Kampuchea since it was formed in 1982. He was educated in Saigon and Paris and in 1941 became king. Frustrated at restrictions on the monarchy's power, he abdicated in 1955 and assumed the positions of prime minister and minister of foreign affairs. He was elected head of state after the death of his father in 1960. His conservative government followed a neutralist path throughout the 1960s, seeking to avoid becoming embroiled in the Vietnam conflict. In 1970 Sihanouk was deposed by Marshal LON NOL and took up residence in Beijing, where he formed the FUNC in alliance with the Khmer Rouge. He was restored as head of state when the KHMER ROUGE captured PHNOM PENH in 1975 but resigned a year later and spent four years under house arrest in the capital. In 1982 he became head of the CGDK; known for his volatile personality, he has since resigned several times. Sihanouk's resignation on January 30, 1988, was interpreted as a ploy to strengthen his position in negotiations with the Phnom Penh government. While Sihanouk remains a highly revered figure among the Cambodian population and would undoubtedly hold a position in a reconciliation government, he would be a figurehead without any real power.

Sikkim. Tiny Himalayan country tucked between China to the north, Nepal to the west and India to the south. Officially a Buddhist state, it was a British protectorate until the partition of British INDIA in 1947. A treaty made it an Indian protectorate; in 1975 Sikkim's ruler was pressured into accepting a constitution that reduced his power and made Sikkim an associated state of India.

Sikorski, Wladyslaw (1881–1943). Polish general and statesman. Born in Galicia, Sikorski studied engineering at the universities of Cracow and Lvov. He fought in WORLD WAR I, and in the postwar period held a number of cabinet posts (1922 to 1925). Distrusted by Premier PILSUDSKI for his democratic sympathies, he was retired from the army in 1926 and dismissed from public service two years later. After Germany's conquest of Poland in 1939, Sikorski escaped to France, became premier of the Polish government in exile and organized an army that, under his command, fought on the side of the Allies during WORLD WAR II. In 1941 he restored Poland's diplomatic relations with the U.S.S.R., but broke them off again after the KATYN massacre. He was killed in an airplane crash at Gibralter while on a trip to inspect Polish forces in the Mediterranean.

Sikorsky, Igor Ivanovich (1889–1972). Russian-American engineer. Sikorsky was born in Kiev and emigrated to the U.S. in 1919. In 1913 he had produced the Bolsche, the first multi-engined airplane. He is best remembered for his design and production of single-rotor helicopters, which he began producing in the U.S. in 1940.

silent film. A general term designating the years of cinema history before the advent of the TALKING PICTURE—from the first experiments in photography and projection in the mid-1890s to the adoption of mechanically synchronized sound by the industry after 1927. The descriptive terms used for the medium during these years tell a "rags to riches" story, as the sneering epithets of "flickers" and "galloping tintypes" were replaced by more stuffy terms, like "photoplay."

In many important ways the silent film period developed and consolidated the practices and effects used in modern cinema. By 1915, with the epoch-marking appearance of D.W. GRIFFITH'S THE BIRTH OF A NATION, the movies were making the transition from a hand-me-down orphan of the theater—slavishly imitating the business practices and entertainment formulas of the popular stage and vaudeville (the exhibition house circuits, the "star system," the wholesale takeover of the most popular stories and plays)—to an autonomous and powerful industry, boasting of huge, vertically integrated studios and theater chains, internationally known performers like Charles CHAPLIN and Mary PICKFORD and a growing critical acceptance in newspapers and magazines. With the last great silent pictures, like *Napoleon* (Abel GANCE, 1927), *The Passion of Joan of Arc* (Carl DREYER, 1928), *The General Line* (Sergei EISENSTEIN, 1929) and *The Crowd* (King VIDOR, 1928), the film medium had fully matured. Not only were technical processes familiar today already being exploited—color, 3–D, wide screen, experiments in synchronized sound, hand-held cameras and telephoto lenses, artificial lighting, etc.—but also the aesthetic foundations of image and montage were being formulated by poets and thinkers like Vachel LINDSAY and Hugo Munsterberg in America, Louis Delluc in France and Lev KULESHOV in Russia.

But, as historian Kevin Brownlow has observed, the silent film was not merely a prologue to the modern sound film; rather, it was a medium with its own unique identity. Without dialogue and with limited use of intertitles as a substitute and for commentary, the burden of storytelling and characterization had to be borne by gesture, pantomime, movement and sophisticated pictorial effect devices (split-screen, dissolve, superimposition, etc.). Further, before the standardization after 1928 of a 24–frame-per-second film speed (necessary for the new, synchronized-sound systems of motor-driven cameras and projectors), cinematographers captured the action by hand-cranking their cameras, varying from 12 to 28 frames per second. This flexibility, says Brownlow, "allowed the cameraman to slow down or speed up the action during shooting, sometimes *within the shot*." The results are seen, most typically, in the slapstick "fast motion" chases of the Keystone Kops and the surreal "slow motion" dream sequences of Rene CLAIR and Abel GANCE.

Each country made its own contribution to the silent film. By 1905 France, Great Britain and America were making popular documentary and narrative films, seen in the work of the LUMIERE BROTHERS and Georges MELIES, Cecil HEPWORTH and Edwin S. Porter. Denmark and Italy led the field by 1913 in elaborate spectacles and costume pictures. America dominated world markets during World War I with the ambitious productions of Griffith and the star vehicles of Chaplin and Pickford. In the 1920s Germany and Russia achieved their own golden ages with the Expressionist drama of Fritz LANG and the revolutionary masterpieces of Eisenstein and PUDOVKIN. And in France Rene Clair and Abel Gance made movies in the SURREALISM and DADA modes.

The term "silent film" is misleading, since from the very beginning most motion pictures—including animation, newsreels and short subjects—had some kind of sound/musical component. Mood-inducing music was performed during the filming; "live" actors frequently spoke their lines from positions behind the screen during projections; adapted and original scores were written for most of the pictures; and musicians—ranging from pianists to full symphony orchestras—accompanied performances with scores specially composed for a given program. Most countries experimented with mechanically synchronized sound.

Tragically, sporadic and careless restoration of silent films has left us little of their original beauty and power. Some commentators, forced back upon their recollections, envelop the period with hazy nostalgia and false romanticism. Others, viewing today's oft-duplicated prints struck from deteriorating negatives projected at the wrong speeds (and sans music), encounter only shadows of shadows, gesticulating images mutely pleading for our attention. The reality in both instances was far different, concludes Brownlow: "The silent film was not only a vigorous popular art, it was a universal language—Esperanto for the eyes."

For further reading:

Brownlow, Kevin, *The Parade's Gone By*. New York: Alfred Knopf, 1968.

Silesia. A region of east-central Europe now divided among GERMANY, POLAND and CZECHOSLOVAKIA. A Prussian province until WORLD WAR I, most of Silesia was given to the new nation of Poland after the war. Nazi Germany took it back during WORLD WAR II, until the Red Army rolled through in 1945. The POTSDAM CONFERENCE of 1945 confirmed Polish sovereignty over most of Silesia, but postwar Polish-German tensions saw a major exodus of Silesia's German-speaking peoples to the west. In 1972 West Germany renounced all claims to Silesia. The region contains considerable coal and iron deposits.

Silkin, John (Ernest) (1923–1987). British LABOUR PARTY politician. As a member of Parliament, Silkin represented Deptford in southeast London from 1963 until his death in 1987. Silkin was chief government whip from 1966 to 1969. Between 1969 and 1979, he served as minister of public buildings and works, minister of planning and local government and minister of agriculture.

Silkin, Lord (Samuel Charles) (1918–1988). British attorney general from 1974 to 1979 during the WILSON and CALLAGHAN governments. Silkin was a LABOUR PARTY member of Parliament for many years. In 1975 he advised the Wilson government to attempt to halt the publication of the *Crossman Diaries* by the *Sunday Times*. He also declined to prosecute Post Office workers threatening to boycott mail destined for SOUTH AFRICA. He refused to allow a private prosecution of what would have been an illegal strike, a position that was ultimately vindicated.

Silkwood, Karen (1946–1974). American nuclear safety advocate. A laboratory technician at the Kerr-McGee Corporation plutonium plant in Cimarron, Oklahoma, Silkwood began investigating safety practices and regulations at the plant, and became an active labor organizer. In November 1974, Silkwood discovered she had been contaminated by radiation whose source was plutonium found in her apartment. She was killed in an automobile accident on November 13, 1974, while on her way to meet with a reporter from *The New York Times* and a union official to present her allegations of safety violations. Many felt that the plutonium had been planted in her apartment to intimidate her, and that Kerr-McGee may have been responsible for her death. In 1979 a federal jury in Oklahoma City awarded $10.5 million in damages to her estate, ruling that her contamination had resulted from Kerr-McGee's negligence. Silkwood's death and the subsequent lawsuit galvanized labor and environmental groups, and gave rise to a growing antinuclear movement. The film *Silkwood* (1983) dramatized her story.

Sillanpaa, Frans Emil (1888–1967). Finnish novelist. Sillanpaa's first major novel was *Mark Heritage* (1919) which reflected his impressions of the 1918 Finnish Civil War. He is best remembered for the acclaimed *The Maid Silja* (1931). Sillanpaa was editor of *Panu*, a literary journal, and wrote many short stories and novels about Finnish life. He was awarded the NOBEL PRIZE for literature in 1939.

Sillitoe, Alan (1928–). British author. Sillitoe began writing with the encouragement of Robert GRAVES, whom Sillitoe met while traveling in Majorca with American poet Ruth Fainlight, whom he later married. Sillitoe's first volume of poetry was *Without Beer or Bread* (1957); his first novel *Saturday Night and Sunday Morning* (1958, filmed 1960). With its provincial setting, the novel drew comparisons to the work of the ANGRY YOUNG MEN, although Sillitoe's hero was firmly routed in the working class, not rising above it. The acclaimed title story in the collection, *The Loneliness of the Long Distance Runner* (1959, filmed 1962) tells the story of a rebellious Borstal boy. Other works include the novels, *Her Victory* (1982) and *Out of the Whirlpool* (1987); and the poetry collections, *Storm and Other Poems* (1974) and *Barbarians and Other Poems* (1974). Sillitoe has also written plays and screenplays.

Sills, Beverly [born Belle Miriam Silverman] (1929–). American opera singer. Sills is one of the most popular opera personalities and one of the great coloratura sopranos, especially noted for her bel canto singing and her acting ability. She made her debut in 1947 with the Philadelphia Civic Opera. She has been most closely associated with the New York City Opera, making her debut with that company as Rosalinde in *Die Fledermaus* in 1955. Her 1966 performance as Cleopatra in Handel's *Giulio Cesare* made her a superstar. Already acclaimed as a great diva, she finally debuted in opera houses worldwide after 1967, and made her Metropolitan Opera debut in 1975. Among her most famous roles are Lucia in *Lucia di Lammermoor*, the three British queens in the Donizetti operas (*Roberto Devereux*, *Maria Stuarda*, *Anna Bolena*), and all three soprano roles in *Les Contes d'Hoffmann*. In 1980 she retired from singing and became director of the New York City Opera (until 1989), revitalizing the repertory and reviving classic Broadway musicals. In addition she has made recordings, appeared on television specials and served on the Council of the National Endowment for the Arts.

Silone, Ignazio (1900–1978). Italian novelist, essayist, and autobiographer. Silone is one of the major figures in Italian literature of this century. His major novels, written in a powerfully realistic style, reflect Silone's strong commitment to social justice. Orphaned at an early age, Silone was raised in poverty and early on was drawn to Communist Party politics. In the 1920s and '30s, after MUSSOLINI rose to power, Silone was forced to live in exile from Italy, spending time in Russia and Switzerland. In 1931, due to the repressions of STALINISM, Silone left the Communist Party and moved toward a broader humanism that reflected ultimate spiritual values without taking on religious beliefs. Silone became internationally famous in the 1930s through the success of his novels *Fontamara* (1933), which portrayed the impact of Fascist rule on an Italian village, and *Bread and Wine* (1937). *Emergency Exit* (1965) is a collection of autobiographical essays.

Silvers, Phil [Phil Silversmith] (1912–1985). American comic actor. Silvers was best known for his role as the conniving Sgt. Ernie Bilko in one of the most popular television shows of the 1950s, "The Phil Silvers Show" (originally "You'll Never Get Rich"). The show ran from 1955 to 1959 and continues to appear in syndication. He also appeared in a number of films and Broadway shows. In 1972, Silvers made his last Broadway appearance in a revival of the musical *A Funny Thing Happened on the Way to the Forum*, for which he won a Tony award. The show's run was cut short after he suffered a stroke; thereafter, his career was limited mostly to guest appearances.

Simenon, Georges (1903–1989). Belgian novelist. Simenon was best known as the creator of Paris police detective Inspector Maigret. An extremely prolific author, he wrote each of his books in a matter of days. Altogether he turned out 84 Maigret mysteries, 136 other novels, more than 1,000 articles and short stories and 200 pseudonymous novellas early in his career. According to his American publisher, during his lifetime more than 600 million copies of his books were sold around the world in 47 languages. His non-Maigret novels, many of which won critical praise, were generally psychological dramas that ended in tragedy.

Simler, George B. (1921–1972). American Air Force officer. In 1965 in the early stages of America's involvement in the VIETNAM WAR, Simler was director of all American air flight missions in Southeast Asia. He subsequently held that authority over all American air missions throughout the world (1967–69). In 1970 he was appointed head of the Air Force Air Training Command. At the time of his death in a jet crash in Texas, he held the rank of lieutenant general.

Simon, Carly (1945–). American singer-songwriter. As a singer terrified of live performance, Carly Simon's success has rested solely on her recorded performances. Her first major success came in 1971 with the top-10 "That's The Way I've Always Heard It Should Be." Her second album, *Anticipation*, solidified her position as one of the leading solo artists of the Seventies and provided the number-one hit "You're So Vain." Her marriage to folk-rock performer James Taylor coincided with a leveling off in her career, although they scored a hit with the duet "Mockingbird." After their marriage ended, Simon had a string of successes with songs she wrote for films, including "Nobody Does It Better," written for the James Bond film *The Spy Who Loved Me*, "Let the River Run" for *Working Girl* and "Coming Around Again" for *Heartburn*.

Simon, Claude (1913–). French novelist. Simon, who won the NOBEL PRIZE for literature in 1985, first won international acclaim in the 1950s as a leading practitioner of the NOUVEAU ROMAN, which deemphasized traditional plot and characterization in favor of direct portrayals of existential reality. Simon, who as a youth studied painting and was greatly influenced by the aesthetic theories of painter Raoul DUFY, has emphasized that he approaches writing with an emphasis on artistic composition of language. His major novels include *The Wind* (1957), *The Flanders Road* (1961), *The Battle of Pharsalus* (1969), *Triptych* (1973) and *Georgics* (1981). Simon served in the French RESISTANCE during WORLD WAR II.

Simon, Sir John Allsebrook [1st Viscount Simon] (1873–1954). British barrister and statesman. Born in Manchester, Simon studied at Oxford and became a barrister in 1899. He was elected to Parliament as a Liberal in 1906, serving until 1918, and again from 1922 to 1931. He was solicitor general from 1910 to 1913, attorney general from 1913 to 1914 and home secretary from 1915 to 1916, resigning over his opposition to WORLD WAR I conscription. He fought in France from 1917 to 1918. Simon took part in the LABRADOR boundary settlement in 1926, and from 1927 to 1930 he was chairman of the commission on Indian affairs that issued the SIMON REPORT. He returned to the Ramsay MACDONALD cabinet as foreign secretary (1931 to 1935), and later was home secretary (1935 to 1937) and chancellor of the exchequer (1937 to 1940). One of the strongest supporters of the APPEASEMENT policy toward Germany, in 1935 he became the first British cabinet member to visit Adolf HITLER.

Simon, (Martin) Neil (1927–). American playwright and screenplay writer. Simon is one of the most popular comedic writers in the history of show business. The author of over 20 hit Broadway plays, Simon has also become a major force in HOLLYWOOD through his film adaptations of his plays as well as his original screenplays. Simon began his career in the 1950s as a comedy writer for numerous television shows including *Caesar's Hour* and *The Phil Silvers Show*. He scored his first Broadway success with *Come Blow Your Horn* (1961), then followed with many more plays that he adapted into films such as *Barefoot in the Park* (1967), *The Odd Couple* (1968), *Plaza Suite* (1971), *Last of the Red Hot Lovers* (1972), *The Prisoner of Second Avenue* (1975), *The Sunshine Boys* (1975), *Chapter Two* (1979), *Brighton Beach Memoirs* (1986) and *Biloxi Blues* (1988). The latter three constitute an autobiographical trilogy by Simon that blends his comic touch with serious dramatic shadings. Original screenplays by Simon include *Max Dugan Returns* (1983) and *The Slugger's Wife* (1985). He won the 1991 PULITZER PRIZE for his play *Lost in Yonkers*.

Simon and Garfunkel (1957–70). American folk and rock music singing duo. Paul Simon and Art Garfunkel first performed together in 1957 as "Tom and Jerry" at fraternity parties and other unglamorous venues. But in the mid-1960s, they emerged as major stars. Simon was far and away the major musical force in the duo, writing the songs, performing on guitar and handling the bulk of the lead vocals. Their major hits included "The Sounds of Silence" (1966), "Homeward Bound" (1966), "I Am a Rock" (1966), "Scarborough Fair" (1968), "Mrs. Robinson" (1968, which became hugely famous through its use in the Mike NICHOLS film *The Graduate*) and "Bridge Over Troubled Water" (1970). In 1970, Simon broke off the partnership with Garfunkel to pursue a highly successful solo career that has included the acclaimed albums *Graceland* (1987) and *The Rhythm of the Saints* (1990).

Simonov, Konstantin Mikhailovich (1915–1979). Soviet novelist, poet and war correspondent. Much of Simonov's work chronicled the battles of the Soviet Army during World War II (see WORLD WAR II ON THE RUSSIAN FRONT). In the West, his best known work was the novel *Days and Nights* (1944), an epic account of the SIEGE OF STALINGRAD that was a bestseller in the U.S. In 1956 he publicly defended the work of Anna AKHMATOVA and Isaac BABEL, which was banned at the time.

Simon Report. Report issued in 1930 by the Indian Statutory Commission, which met from 1927 to 1930 under the Chairmanship of Sir John SIMON. It was critical of then-current governmental systems, recommended indirect election to a central Indian legislature and urged more responsible government. Its recommendations were strengthened in London meetings of 1931 to 1932, which supported the establishment of an Indian Federation. Many of the criticisms embodied in the Report were addressed in the India Act of 1935.

Simons, Arthur D. (1919–1979). American military officer. As a colonel in the Green Berets, Simons led a raid into North VIETNAM in 1970 in an unsuccessful attempt to free American PRISONERS OF WAR. He received the Distinguished Service

Cross from President NIXON. After retiring he helped two American engineers escape from IRAN in early 1979. (See also IRAN HOSTAGE CRISIS.)

Simplon Pass. In southwestern Switzerland, an alpine pass running from Brig in Switzerland to Iselle in Italy. Its roadway, constructed by Napoleon I, fell into disuse after the completion in 1906 of one of the engineering marvels of the century, the **Simplon Railway Tunnel**. The 13-mile-long tunnel was the longest in the world, until the construction of the ENGLISH CHANNEL TUNNEL, scheduled for completion in the 1990s.

Simpson, Louis [Aston Marantz] (1923–). American poet. Simpson was born in Jamaica but was educated and later taught in the U.S. Simpson's first collection, *The Arrivistes: Poems, 1910–1949,* (1949) was praised for its portrayal of contemporary themes and ideas in traditional poetic forms. Beginning with *A Dream of Governors* (1959), he began to experiment more with the structure of his poetry and its imagery. Other works include *At the End of the Open Road* (1963), poems; *North of Jamaica* (1972), an autobiography; and *A Revolution in Taste: Studies of Dylan Thomas, Allen Ginsberg, Sylvia Plath and Robert Lowell* (1978). Simpson was awarded the PULITZER PRIZE for poetry in 1964.

Simpson, O(renthal) J(ames) (1947–). American football player. The dominant college running back of the late 1960s, Simpson led the University of Southern California Trojans to a Rose Bowl victory in 1968. That same year, he ran for a record 1,309 yards and was awarded the Heisman Trophy. Choosing to play with the Buffalo Bills of the American Football League, he gave the league an added dose of credibility, bringing it one step closer to parity with the older National Football League. In 1973, he rushed for a record-breaking 2,003 yards. His record of 23 touchdowns in a single season has stood for more than 15 years. His lifetime total is 11,236 yards rushing over 11 seasons. After retiring from the game, Simpson became a commercial spokesman, actor and sports commentator.

Simpson, Wallis Warfield. See Duchess of WINDSOR.

Simpson, William Hood (1888–1980). American army officer. In 1916 Simpson took part in General John J. PERSHING's expedition into Mexico against the Mexican revolutionary leader Pancho VILLA. In WORLD WAR II, General Simpson was commander of the U.S. Ninth Army when it thrust into the heart of GERMANY in 1944 to 1945. He was known for his unusual tactical knowledge and sound military judgment.

Sims, John Haley "Zoot" (1925–1985). Jazz saxophonist. A leading jazz performer, Sims' career spanned more than 40 years from the 1940s into the '80s. At first he was associated with the BIG BANDS of Benny GOODMAN, Woody HERMAN, and Stan KENTON. From the mid-1950s on he worked primarily as a freelancer, appearing in clubs and festivals all over the world. He made more than 40 recordings as a featured performer.

Sinai Peninsula. Triangular-shaped peninsula in northeastern EGYPT, between the Gulf of Suez on the west and the Gulf of Aqaba on the east. The region is primarily desert. At the beginning of this century it was under the control of the khedive of Egypt, who owed nominal authority to the Ottoman sultan but was under British influence. The Sinai was a battlefield during the ARAB-ISRAELI WARS of 1956 and 1973 as well as the SIX DAY WAR of 1967; during these wars, it was contested by ISRAEL and Egypt. In 1974 UN troops stood between the Egyptian-occupied east bank of the Gulf of Suez and Israeli armies. In accordance with the CAMP DAVID agreements of 1978, all Israeli forces had gradually withdrawn by 1982. (See also CAMP DAVID TALKS.)

Sinatra, Frank [Francis Albert Sinatra] (1915–). American JAZZ and popular music singer and film actor. Sinatra, whose nicknames include "The Voice" and "The Chairman of the Board," is one of the greatest show business stars of the 20th century. As a vocalist, he is ranked as one of the finest jazz and pop stylists ever and is especially noted for his impeccable phrasing and his ability to "swing" a tune. Born in Hoboken, N.J., Sinatra began his career as a vocalist in the 1930s. He achieved stardom after joining the Harry JAMES band in 1939, and in 1940 he moved to the Tommy DORSEY big band. By 1942, Sinatra was the adored favorite of his young, female "bobby-soxer" fans. Among his many hit songs from the 1940s to the present are "Come Rain or Come Shine," "I'll Never Smile Again," "In the Wee Small Hours," "I've Got You Under My Skin," "The Lady is a Tramp," "Strangers in the Night," "New York, New York," "My Way" and "There Are Such Things." Sinatra also enjoyed a long and successful film career that included musicals such as *On the Town* (1949)

"Ol' blue eyes"—Frank Sinatra performs at Radio City Music Hall (1990).

Author Upton Sinclair (1942).

and *Guys and Dolls* (1955) and dramatic films such as *From Here to Eternity* (1953)—for which he won an ACADEMY AWARD for best supporting actor—*Some Came Running* (1958) and *The Detective* (1968). Although his voice has deteriorated somewhat through the years, Sinatra remained active through his 75th birthday, and the passage of time has only confirmed his classic status.

Sinclair, Upton Beall (1878–1968). American author. An ardent socialist with unfulfilled political ambitions, Sinclair gained fame when he turned from the dime novels he wrote to pay his way through college, to the composition of a Chicago stockyard expose, *The Jungle* (1906). The book was an enormous popular success, brought about reform of the labor conditions Sinclair abhorred, and enabled him to establish and support the socialist commune Helicon Home Colony in Englewood, N.J. Never concerned with aesthetic matters of the literary craft, Sinclair wrote journalistic novels intended to expose and correct particular social inequities. His other works include *The Moneychangers* (1908), *King Coal* (1917), *Boston* (1928), which was about the SACCO-VANZETTI case, and *Plays of Protest* (1912). His *Dragon's Teeth* (1942) won a PULITZER PRIZE in 1943

For further reading:

Harris, Leon A., *Upton Sinclair, American Rebel.* New York: Crowell, 1975.

Yoder, Jon A., *Upton Sinclair*. New York: Ungar, 1975.

Singapore. Singapore, at the southern tip of Southeast Asia's Malay Peninsula, is comprised of the main island of Singapore and 57 smaller islands. Connected to the mainland by a causeway, the republic covers a total land area of 239 square miles. Under British rule from 1867, the strategically important island became a successful free port. Britain constructed naval bases on Singapore after World War I. Nevertheless, in WORLD WAR II Singapore's sea-oriented defenses were overcome by a carefully planned overland attack down the Malay Peninsula, and the country was occupied by Japan in 1942. With the restoration of British control in

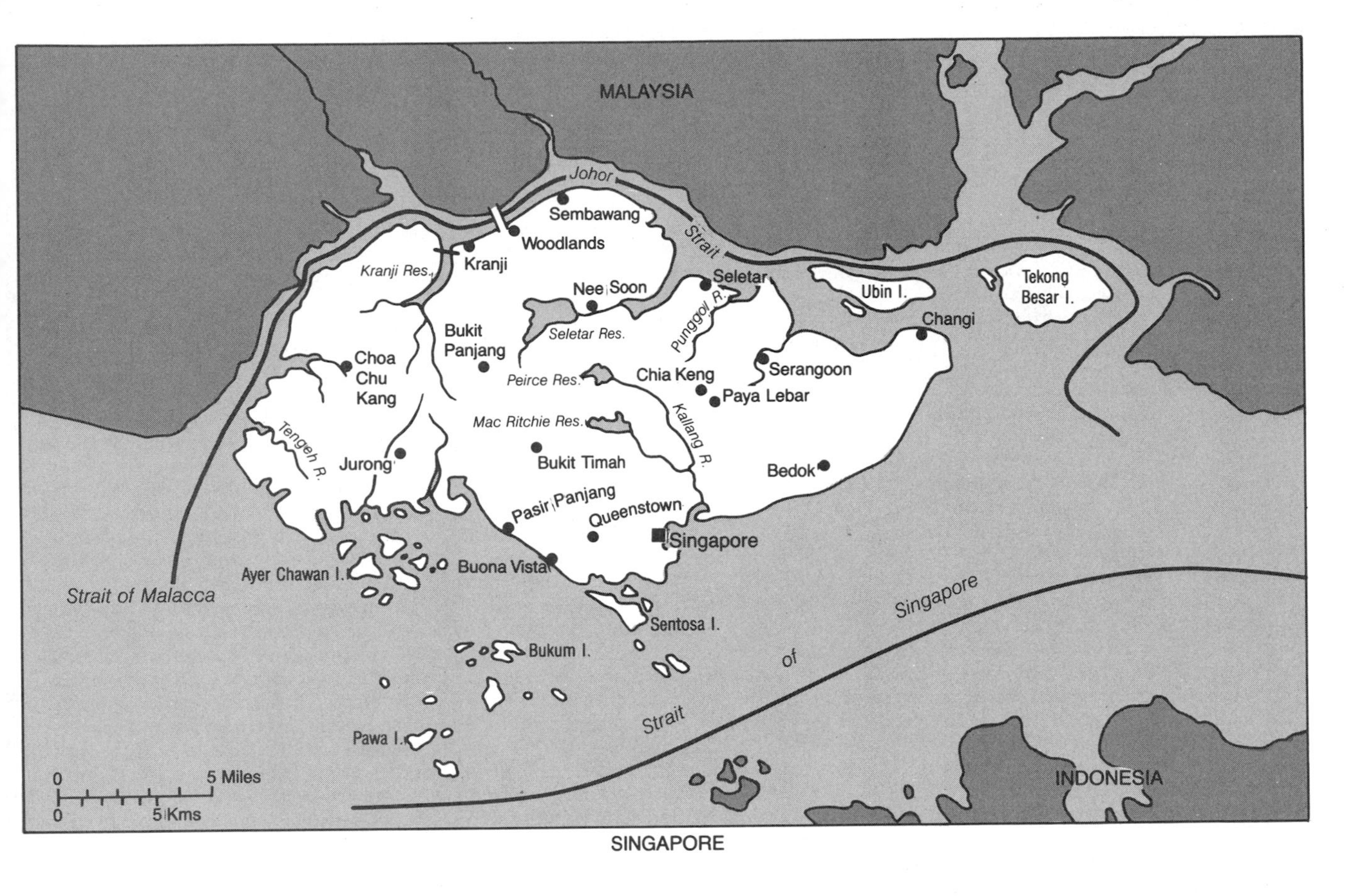

SINGAPORE

1945, Singapore became a crown colony, then a self-governing state in 1959. A state within the Federation of Malaysia from 1963 to 1965, Singapore gained independence as a republic within the Commonwealth in 1965. LEE KUAN YEW has served as prime minister since 1959, guiding the country to increased economic prosperity while countering opposition demands for more political freedom.

Singer, Isaac Bashevis (1904–). Yiddish author. Singer immigrated to New York from Poland in 1935 and began his career as a journalist for the *Jewish Daily Forward*, a Yiddish language periodical which published his early short stories. His first novel published in English was *The Family Moskat* (1950). Singer's fanciful novels and short stories detail the lives of Polish Jews in various periods of history as well as the present and examine the role of the Jewish faith in their lives. Other works include the novels *The Magician of Lublin* (1960), *Shosha* (1978) and *Enemies: A Love Story*, and the short story collections *A Friend of Kafka* (1970), and *The Death of Methuselah* and *Other Stories* (1988). Singer received the NOBEL PRIZE for literature in 1978.

Sinkiang. Large, autonomous area of western CHINA, between Tibet on the south and the Soviet Union on the west. Between 1917 and 1942 it was under Soviet influence. Established as a Chinese province in 1942, it saw rebellion and civil war in 1944–45 but in 1949 yielded to the victorious Chinese communists as they drove the Nationalists from the mainland of China. (See also CHINESE CIVIL WAR OF 1945–49.)

Sinn Fein [Ir., "ourselves alone"]. Irish nationalist movement founded by Arthur Griffiths in 1902, originally with the aim of securing independence from Britain. Griffiths was succeeded by more militant leaders, including James CONNOLLY and Padraig PEARSE, who organized the 1916 EASTER RISING in Dublin. In the latter half of the century, and especially after the outbreak of sectarian strife in NORTHERN IRELAND in 1968, Sinn Fein was influential as the political wing of the IRISH REPUBLICAN ARMY (IRA).

Sino-Japanese War of 1937–45. In the 1930s Japan had extended her influence into China north of the Great Wall. In July 1937 shots exchanged at the Marco Polo Bridge north of Peking soon escalated into an undeclared war. Japanese bombers attacked northern cities; her fleet attacked Shanghai. The capital, Nanking, fell December 1937; Hankow became the new capital. Canton and Hankow were captured in 1938, and the capital moved to Chungking. The Japanese controlled all the coastal ports, railroads and major cities of China by 1938. By 1941, with the U.S. in the war, the Allies flew supplies to Chungking "over the hump" of the Himalayas. With a new air force, aided by the U.S., the Chinese bombed Japanese strongholds, while in the north, Communist guerrillas harrassed the Japanese occupation. The Japanese failed to occupy the Chinese countryside or to establish a successful puppet government. Russia entered the war August 8, 1945, soon liberating Manchuria. By Japan's surrender, September 2, 1945, many coastal areas had been retaken by Chinese forces.

Sino-Soviet Treaty of 1945. Agreement signed by China and the U.S.S.R. The treaty's key terms included the U.S.S.R.'s promise of aid to the national government, Soviet recognition of Chinese sovereignty in Manchuria, Chinese recognition of an independent Outer Mongolia (if a plebescite showed that this independence had popular support), China's agreement to open-port status for the city of Dairen and its granting to the U.S.S.R. of a free lease to half of the city's port facilities. This treaty was largely an expansion and a clarification of various agreements reached at the YALTA CONFERENCE, in which China had not been a participant.

Sinyavsky, Andrei (Donatevich) (1925–). Soviet author. Sinyavsky, while a literary critic at the Gorki Institute of World Literature in Moscow, first began attracting attention in the West with the publication of the essay "On Socialist Realism" in the French magazine *L'Esprit* in 1959. The essay assailed the notion of art as an instrument of propaganda. It was first published unsigned, but later reprints appeared under the pseudonym **Abram Tertz**. His first works of fiction to appear in the West were *The Trial Begins* (1960), a black comedy originally published as *Sud Idyot* and *Sad Idzie* (1959),

Fantasticheskie Povesti (1961; *Fantastic Stories,* 1963), and *The Makepeace Experiment* (1964), published originally as *Lyubivom.* In 1965 Sinyavsky, along with author Yuli DANIEL, was arrested for his pseudonymous writings. In 1966 they were brought to trial and charged with writing anti-Soviet propaganda. Sinyavsky was sentenced to seven years in a labor camp. The case caused a worldwide uproar, as it was the first time that a writer had been held criminally responsible for the possible interpretations of a work of literature. Many authors from around the world pled Sinyavsky's cause to Soviet Premier KOSYGIN, yet he remained in prison where he began writing what would become *A Voice from the Chorus* (1976; originally *Golos iz khora,* 1973). In 1973 Sinyavsky was allowed to immigrate to Paris where he had been offered a position at the Sorbonne. His later works include the novel *Goodnight!* (1989).

Sirica, John J(oseph) (1904–). Federal District Court judge who gained national prominence during the WATERGATE scandal. Sirica graduated from Georgetown University Law School, having worked his way through school as a boxing coach. He worked as a U.S. attorney in Washington, D.C., and later entered private practice. Politically active, he was appointed to the federal bench by President Dwight D. EISENHOWER. An able judge, he was known as "Maximum John" because of his often harsh sentences. In 1972 Sirica was thrown into the spotlight when as chief judge of the District Court he presided over the trial of seven operatives of President Richard M. NIXON's reelection committee who had broken into Democratic headquarters at the Watergate apartment complex. In a highly publicized trial the judge aggressively asked questions from the bench and after their convictions he sentenced the defendants provisionally on the condition that they cooperate with investigators. The defendants did in fact cooperate, which implicated others including U.S. Attorney General John Mitchell, who along with President Nixon was ultimately forced to resign.

For further reading:

Kutler, Stanley I., *The Wars of Watergate: The Last Crisis of Richard Nixon.* New York: Knopf, 1990.

Woodward, Bob, and Carl Bernstein, *All the President's Men.* New York: Simon & Schuster, 1974.

Sirk, Douglas [born Detlef Sierck] (1900–1987). German-born film director. Sirk was known for his HOLLYWOOD melodramas, including *Magnificent Obsession* (1954) and *Written on the Wind* (1956). After finishing *Imitation of Life* (1959) he left Hollywood and returned to Europe, where he resumed a career in the theater. His films eventually developed a cult following, especially in Europe.

SIS. See MI6.

Sisson, C(harles) H(ubert) (1914–). English poet, essayist and translator. Born in Bristol and educated at the universities of Bristol (1934), Berlin and Freiburg (1934–35) and the Sorbonne (1935–36), Sisson enjoyed a long career as a civil servant. He published no poetry until well into middle age, declaring that "one should speak, whether in prose or verse, because one has something to say, and not otherwise." Much of his work is politically critical and satirical, though he has also written on religious and moral themes. His piercing wit and mordant tone are the greatest pleasures of his verse; in that vein he has described his work as "no more than an ironic contribution to a hopeless situation." His poetry includes *The London Zoo* (1961), *Numbers* (1965), *Metamorphoses* (1968) and *Anchises* (1976). His *Collected Poems* appeared in 1984. Sisson has translated Horace, Catullus, Dante and Heine.

Sister Carrie. Published in 1900, this century's first masterpiece of unflinching realism and now regarded as a landmark in the development of the modern American novel. The story of its writing and hostile reception has become the stuff of literary legend. Theodore DREISER was a struggling young journalist in New York at the turn of the century when he first devised the story of Carrie Meeber, an 18–year-old Chicago factory worker who is seduced and taken to New York by her lover, a thief named Hurstwood. Dreiser knew both the milieu and the characters well. The first he derived from his repertorial assignments in the squalid Bowery, the great hotels and the glittering Broadway theaters. The latter he drew from the experiences of his sister, Emma, who had eloped to New York with her lover, a married man who had stolen money from a Chicago saloon. The bulky manuscript was accepted by Doubleday, Page & Co. but, presumably due to its sensational subject matter and scrupulous detail, its subsequent circulation and sale was restricted to barely 650 copies. Dreiser, bruised and depressed by its hostile critical reception, went into a decline that lasted almost seven years. The real reputation of the book begins with its second publication in 1907 by the new firm of B.W. Dodge. Measured against the occasionally forced tone of Stephen Crane and the melodramatic excess of Frank Norris, *Sister Carrie* remains an astonishing achievement. The contrasting fortunes of Hurstwood and Carrie create powerful, oscillating rhythms built upon relentlessly moving events. Two such different fates, seemingly delicately balanced and intertwined, are actually forged together in likenesss of cold steel. They are victims of the urban flux, writes Dreiser, to "the blare of sound, a roar of life, a vast array of human lives." The novel was adapted in 1952 into a tepid screen version starring Jennifer Jones and Laurence OLIVIER.

For further reading:

Moers, Ellen, *Sister Carrie—The Two Dreisers.* New York: Viking Press, 1969.

Sitwells, The. Notable English literary family comprised of **Dame Edith Sitwell** (1887–1964) and her brothers **Sir Osbert Sitwell** (1892–1969) and **Sir Sacheverell Sitwell** (1897–1988). Dame Edith began writing poetry at an early age, and shared with her brother Osbert a scathing contempt for the GEORGIAN poets. They were advocates of MODERNISM, and from 1916 to 1921 edited the periodical *Wheels.* Dame Edith's first volume of poetry was *The Mother and Other Poems* (1915), and her subsequent works and theatrical personality made her a well-known literary figure. Her only novel, *I Live under a Black Sun* (1937), was not a success, but her war-inspired poetry, which includes *Street Songs* (1942) and *The Shadow of Cain* (1947), were highly acclaimed. Her poem "Masquerade" provided the text to William WALTON's musical piece of the same name.

Sitzkrieg. See PHONY WAR.

Six, Les. Group of six young French composers who, just after World War I, united in opposition to the IMPRESSIONISM of composers such as Claude DEBUSSY and Maurice RAVEL. Inspired by the writings of Jean COCTEAU and the compositions and musical philosophy of Erik SATIE, Les Six included Georges AURIC, Louis Durey, Arthur HONEGGER, Darius Milhaud, Francis POULENC and Germaine Tailleferre.

Six, the. Name given to the original member states (Belgium, France, West Germany, Italy, Luxembourg and the Netherlands) of the EUROPEAN ECONOMIC COMMUNITY (EEC) before the admission of Britain, Ireland and Denmark in 1973.

Six Counties. The counties of NORTHERN IRELAND: Antrim, Armagh, Down, Fermanagh, Londonderry and Tyrone. With Cavan, Donegal and Monaghan, they originally formed the province of Ulster, but in 1923 these three were made part of the Dominion of IRELAND, while the other six remained part of the UNITED KINGDOM.

Six-Day War (1967). In May 1967 EGYPT's President Gamal Abdel NASSER (1918–70) demanded (and obtained) the removal of a United Nations emergency force (UNEF) from Egyptian territory. Shortly afterward, Nasser ordered a shipping blockade of the Strait of Tiran, effectively closing the Israeli port of Elat on the Gulf of Aqaba. By this time Syrian, Egyptian and Israeli forces had mobilized along their respective borders, along which guerrilla raids had taken place frequently since the end of the ARAB-ISRAELI WAR OF 1956. Suddenly, on June 5, 1967, Israeli warplanes attacked and bombed two dozen Arab airfields, destroying more than 400 Egyptian, Syrian and Jordanian planes on the ground. Israeli land forces invaded the SINAI PENINSULA, JERUSALEM's Old City, JORDAN'S WEST BANK, the GAZA STRIP and the GOLAN HEIGHTS and occupied these areas when the war ended with a UN-sponsored ceasefire on June 10, 1967. (See also ARAB-ISRAELI WAR OF 1973.)

"60 Minutes". American documentary television series begun in 1969. CBS's "60 Minutes" introduced the "news magazine" format, in which a mixture of hard and soft news stories are presented in discrete segments. "60 Minutes" focuses on controversy and the exposing of corruption in government and business. The show's news team has included Mike

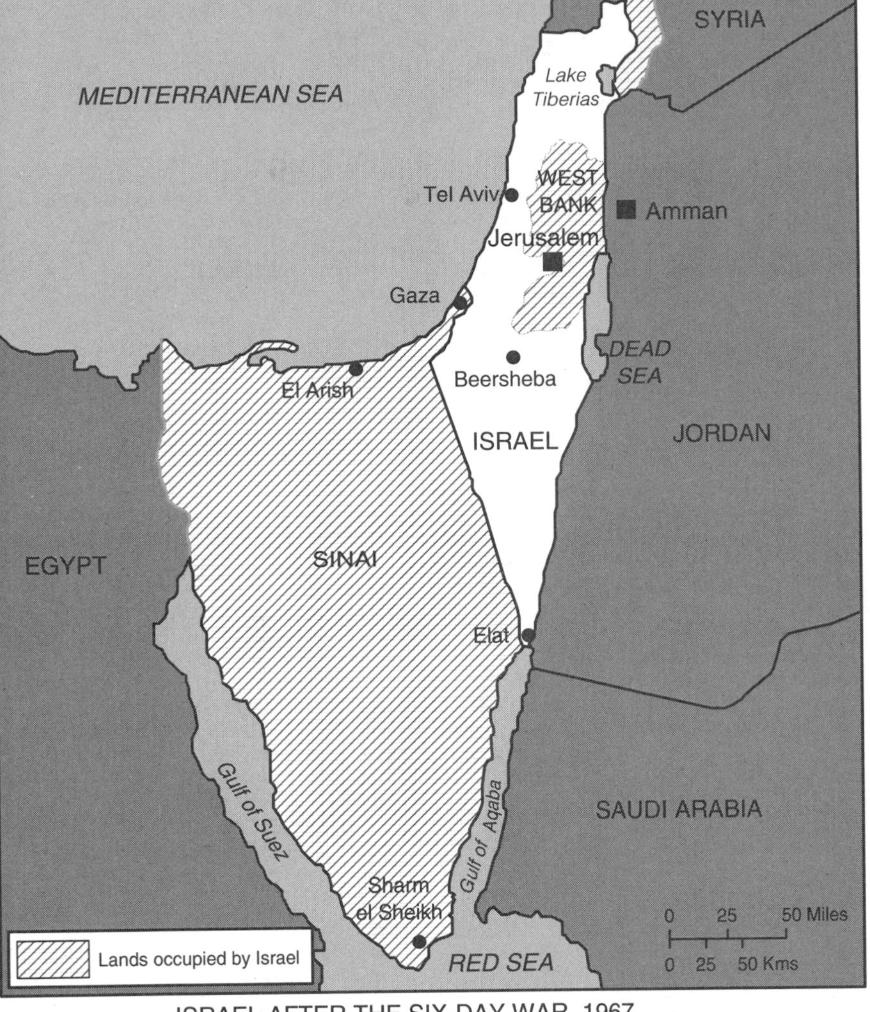

ISRAEL AFTER THE SIX-DAY WAR, 1967

Wallace, Morley Safer, Harry Reasoner, Dan Rather and Diane Sawyer. Since its inception, "60 Minutes" has been enormously popular and is seen by upwards of 23 million people a week.

Skardon, William James "Jim" (1904–1987). British counterespionage agent. Skardon gained a reputation as one of MI5's most formidable interrogators. He was involved in almost all the important spy cases of his time, but probably achieved his greatest success with the interrogation that drew a confession from the atom spy Klaus FUCHS in 1950.

Skidmore, Owings & Merrill. American architectural firm founded in 1936 by Louis Skidmore, Nathaniel Owings and John O. Merrill. Skidmore and Owings were chief design consultants on the 1933 Chicago Exposition, and one of the most influential forces in post-World-War-II architecture. The firm is known for its skyscrapers in the INTERNATIONAL STYLE. Its "glass box" designs became the standard pattern for office buildings throughout the 1950s and 1960s, beginning with Lever House in New York (1952). Other notable buildings by Skidmore, Owings & Merrill include the U.S. Air Force Academy in Colorado Springs (1954–62) and the John Hancock Center (1970) and Sears Tower (1974) in Chicago.

Skinner, B(urrhus) F(rederic) (1904–1990). U.S. psychologist. He was a pioneer in the field of behaviorism, seeking to explain even complex human behavior as a series of conditioned responses to outside stimuli. He created the so-called Skinner box, an enclosed experimental environment for laboratory animals. Among his books were *Walden Two* (1948) and *Beyond Freedom and Dignity* (1971).

Skvorecky, Josef (1924–). Czechoslovakian novelist and story writer. Skvorecky, who immigrated to Canada in the early 1970s, remains a major literary figure in his native land despite his nearly two decades in exile. Skvorecky and his wife established a Czechoslovakian publishing house in Canada, while widespread translations of his novels and stories have earned for Skvorecky an international reputation as well. Educated at Charles University in Prague, Skvorecky first came to prominence with *The Cowards* (1958), a satirical novel that attacked the petty greed of the officials who established the Communist regime in CZECHOSLOVAKIA after World War II. *The Cowards* was banned by that very regime two weeks after it was published. *The Emoke Legend* (1963) and *The Bass Saxophone* (1969) were subsequently allowed to be published in his native land, but ongoing censorial pressures led Skvorecky to emigrate. His later novels, which combine wry humor and a committed humanism, include *The Engineer of Human Souls* (1983) and *Dvorak in Love* (1986).

Skylab. U.S. space station; in service for two years, it was manned by three teams of astronauts in 1973 and 1974. Unmanned for the following five years, it crashed to Earth in 1979.

Slansky trial. Trial on charges of treason of Rudolf Slansky, vice premier of CZECHOSLOVAKIA and Communist Party secretary, and 13 other party officials. The show trial, held from November 17 to 30, 1952, with fabricated evidence and heavily antisemitic overtones, resulted in the conviction and hanging of 11 of the accused, including Slansky. It was the greatest communist purge outside the U.S.S.R. and coincided with a period of enormous ANTI-SEMITISM by Josef STALIN inside the U.S.S.R.

Slayton, Donald "Deke" (1924–). One of the original seven MERCURY astronauts selected in 1959, Deke Slayton was grounded by a heart problem and didn't have a chance to fly until his APOLLO-SOYUZ Test Project flight, July 15–24, 1975. During that well-publicized flight, a joint mission and link-up in space between the U.S. and U.S.S.R., Slayton and fellow astronauts Thomas STAFFORD and Vance Brand docked with a Soviet Soyuz spacecraft and spent two days sharing quarters and conducting experiments with Russian cosmonauts Alexei LEONOV and Valery Kubasov. After unlinking and spend-

American psychologist and author B.F. Skinner (1954).

ing five more days in space alone, the Apollo spacecraft accidentally filled with deadly exhaust gas on its return splashdown. Slayton's lungs were severely burned, and the three-man Apollo crew came near to losing their lives. Apollo-Soyuz was Slayton's only space flight, but during it he logged a total of nearly nine days in space.

Slim, William Joseph (1891–1970). British field marshal. In Burma during WORLD WAR II, Slim commanded Britain's "forgotten army" of British and Indian troops, who swept the Japanese from the Indian frontier in one of the most arduous campaigns of modern warfare. Slim was knighted in 1944 and served as chief of the British Imperial Staff from 1948 to 1952. From 1953 to 1960, he was governor-general of Australia.

Sloan, Alfred Pritchard, Jr. (1875–1966). President of General Motors Corporation. Sloan was born in New Haven, Connecticut, but grew up largely in Brooklyn, New York. He received an engineering degree from the Massachusetts Institute of Technology in 1895. Sloan was president of the Hyatt Roller Bearing Company from 1898 to 1916, when he sold it to William Durant, founder of GM. Sloan was president of the resulting GM subsidiary, United Motors Corporation, until 1919, when that company was dissolved and he was named a vice president and director of GM. In 1923, Sloan succeeded as president of GM Pierre S. du Pont, who had himself succeeded Durant in 1920. During his presidency, which extended until 1937, Sloan, in his methodical, unostentatious way, drastically reorganized GM and guided it to undisputed first place among auto manufacturers worldwide. He served as chairman of the board of GM until 1956, when he retired. The term "Sloanism" refers to GM's policy, under Sloan, of offering a diversity of products to the consuming public, as opposed to Henry FORD's policy of offering a single, mass-produced model.

Sloan, John (1871–1951). American painter. Born in Lock Haven, Pennsylvania, Sloan studied at the Pennsylvania Academy of the Fine Arts with Robert HENRI. He became an illustrator, working in Philadelphia on the *Inquirer* and the *Press* and continued to create newspaper illustrations after he moved to New York City in 1904. A member of The EIGHT, he was an early social realist who excelled in portrayals of the crowded streets of New York City. A social and artistic activist, he was art director of the radical magazine *The Masses* from 1912–1914 and a founder and president of the Society of Independent Artists from 1918 to 1944. He was also an influential teacher at New York City's Art Students League, his long tenure lasting from 1916 to 1937. Characteristic paintings include *McSorley's Bar* (Detroit Institute of Arts) and *Wake of the Ferry* (Phillips Collection, Washington, D.C.). Sloan was also a skilled etcher, whose graphic subject matter—mainly street scenes and nudes—are also typical of his paintings.

Slot, The. During WORLD WAR II, the usual route taken by Japanese supply ships and planes en route to their outposts on GUADALCANAL in the SOLOMON ISLANDS. The northwest-to-southeast open-water passage received its name from U.S. forces who hotly contested control of the "Slot" between August 1942 and January 1943.

Slovakia. Historic region and a state of eastern CZECHOSLOVAKIA. Until WORLD WAR I a part of AUSTRIA-HUNGARY, in 1918 the Slovak National Council declared Slovakia independent of Hungary and incorporated with the Czechs to form the new country of Czechoslovakia. Between the wars, the Slovaks consistently complained that their autonomy was being slighted by the Czechs. After the MUNICH PACT of 1938 and the dismemberment of Czechoslovakia, Nazi Germany installed Slovak patriot and fascist Father Jozef TISO as ruler of the "independent" rump state of Slovakia. Although an Axis ally during WORLD WAR II, a pro-Allied underground joined oncoming Soviet forces in 1944 to help force out the Germans. By 1948 Slovakia was once again a part of Czechoslovakia but retained its own government agencies; the central government controlled defense, foreign policy, taxation and finance. After the demise of the communist regime and the election of a democratic government under President Vaclav HAVEL, a Czech, the Slovaks agitated for independence and threatened to break up the Czechoslovak republic.

Slovenia. A constituent republic of YUGOSLAVIA since 1946. In 1918, Slovenia, then a part of AUSTRIA-HUNGARY, became part of the new Kingdom of the Serbs, Croats and Slovenes (Yugoslavia). During WORLD WAR II it was divided among the fascist regimes of GERMANY, HUNGARY and ITALY.

Slovik, Eddie (1921–1945). American Army private executed for desertion (January 31, 1945) during WORLD WAR II—the first such execution since 1864. In 1944, assigned to an infantry regiment and shipped overseas, Slovik deserted, returning the next day with a written vow to do so again. The Army had been plagued with some 40,000 desertions in Europe during the war. Many other deserters had been convicted, but their death sentences had been commuted. It was felt that the Army intended to make an example of Slovik, whose past criminal record may have influenced their choice. It failed as a deterrent, largely because the Army kept the execution secret; even Slovik's wife was unaware of the cause of his death until 1953 when the documentation was declassified. The public was informed in 1954 when journalist William Bradford HUIE published *The Execution of Private Slovik*. In 1977 Slovik's widow appealed for a reversal of his conviction, maintaining that he had been unfairly singled out and she petitioned for a $70,000 payment plus interest on his National Service Life Insurance policy. Her appeal was rejected by the secretary of the Army, and the case was referred to the Justice Department. In 1987 Slovik's remains were exhumed from a war criminals' grave in France and reburied in Detroit.

Smersh [*Smert' Shpionam* (Death to Spies)]. Acronym for a division of the Soviet security organ that eliminated real, suspected or potential opponents to the Soviet government. Most of its targets had lived for a while outside the control of the Soviet regime during World War II as civilian deportees, refugees or prisoners of war. Smersh favored large-scale arrests, executions or deportation.

Smith, Alfred E(manuel) (1873–1944). American political leader. Born into a poor immigrant family on New York City's Lower East Side, Smith became active in Democratic city politics and was elected to the New York State Assembly (1904–15). In 1913 he became speaker of the Assembly, and in 1918 he was elected governor of New York. He was defeated in his bid for reelection in 1922, but was returned to office in 1924, and again in 1926. Smith proved a popular, reformist governor, and in 1928, with the assistance of Franklin D. ROOSEVELT, he became the first Roman Catholic candidate for president, but was defeated by Herbert HOOVER. Smith retired to private life, becoming president of the company that built and operated the EMPIRE STATE BUILDING as well as editor of *New Outlook* magazine (1932–34). His memoirs, entitled *Up to Now*, were published in 1929.

Smith, Bessie (1898–1937). American singer. Called the "Empress of the Blues," Smith was a famous black singer who made 150 recordings during her career. A student of sorts of the first great female blues singer, "Ma" Rainey, Smith rapidly developed a style of her own and came to be regarded as one of the greatest blues singers of her time. She sang with such famous instrumentalists as Benny GOODMAN, Fletcher Henderson and Louis ARMSTRONG. Some of her most famous record-

Alfred E. Smith, the first Roman Catholic to run for president of the United States.

Blues singer Bessie Smith.

ings include "Jailhouse Blues" and "Cold in Hand Blues." Smith was seriously injured in an automobile accident in 1937, and it is said that she died of her injuries because a nearby hospital refused to care for her because of her race.

For further reading:

Brooks, Edward, *The Bessie Smith Companion*. New York: Da Capo Press, 1983.

Albertson, Chris, *Bessie*. Scarborough House, 1974.

Smith, Cyrus Rowlett (1899–1990). American aviator and business executive. Smith was head of American Airlines from 1934 until 1968, building it into one of the world's major airlines. Although he resigned from the company in 1968 to become secretary of commerce under President Lyndon B. JOHNSON, he was called back as chairman in 1973 to 1974 to help restore the company's economic vitality.

Smith, Ellison DuRant (1864–1944). American politician. Smith was an important organizer of the Southern Cotton Association in New Orleans in 1905. Smith's political career began with his election to the Louisiana House of Representatives (1896–1900). In 1908 he was elected as a Democrat to the U.S. Senate, where he remained until his death. A Southern agrarian, Smith opposed high tariffs, hard currency and big business. He played little role in passage of the NEW DEAL farm programs, despite his position as chairman of the Senate Agriculture Committee, and opposed wages and hours laws as well as President Franklin D. ROOSEVELT's war policies.

Smith, Gerald L.K. (1898–1976). American clergyman, editor and lecturer. Born in Pardeeville, Wisconsin, Smith came of a long line of fundamentalist preachers and became the minister of a Shreveport, Louisiana church in 1928. In the 1930s Smith turned his considerable oratorical skills to the support of Huey LONG. After Long's assassination in 1935, Smith's views became increasingly fanatical and right-wing. An opponent of the labor movement and of President Franklin D. ROOSEVELT'S NEW DEAL, he was a supporter of the pro-Nazi and antisemitic views of Father Charles COUGHLIN and a booster of what he called "true Americanism." In 1937 he founded the **Committee of One Million** to oppose communism and five years later he established the right-wing monthly *The Cross and the Flag*, which he edited. In 1947 he established the Christian Nationalist Crusade, an organization that he headed until his death. (See also DEMAGOGUES.)

Smith, Holland McTyeire (1882–1967). U.S. Marine officer. He earned the nickname "Howlin' Mad" as a general in the Marines. He pioneered methods of amphibious warfare, and commanded forces in the Gilbert, Marshall and Marianas Islands campaigns during WORLD WAR II. Smith was commander of the Fleet Marine Force in the Pacific from 1944 to 1945.

Smith, Ian (1919–). Prime minister of RHODESIA (1964–78). Smith first came to prominence during WORLD WAR II as a SPITFIRE fighter pilot in the BATTLE OF BRITAIN. A member of the Southern Rhodesia legislature from 1948 to 1953, he was a member of the federal parliament from 1953 to 1962, founder of the Rhodesian Front Party in 1962 and prime minister from 1964 to 1978. He declared independence for Southern Rhodesia unilaterally in 1965 (see UDI). After unsuccessful talks with British Prime Minister Harold WILSON aboard HMS *Tiger* in 1966 and HMS *Fearless* in 1968, Smith declared Rhodesia a republic in 1970. Forced by guerrilla war and external pressures to negotiate an internal settlement, he sought agreement with black moderates led by Bishop Abel MUZUREWA, forming a joint black and white government in 1978. Smith became minister without portfolio in the Zimbabwe-Rhodesia government under Muzorewa in 1979 and came to London for talks that finally settled the Rhodesia crisis. He returned as one of the white members of the first parliament of independent ZIMBABWE following the election won by Robert MUGABE, but was suspended from parliament in 1987.

Smith, James H., Jr. (1909–1982). American WORLD WAR II bomber pilot and assistant secretary of the Navy (1953–56). In a highly pubicized incident in 1953, Smith reinstated a Navy official who had been accused of having Communist leanings. Smith thus became one of the first officials of the EISENHOWER administration to resist MCCARTHYISM. He later headed the U.S. foreign aid program as chairman of the International Cooperation Administration (1957–59).

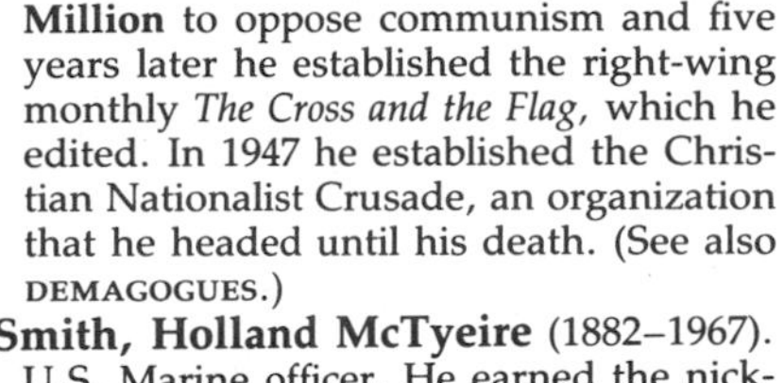
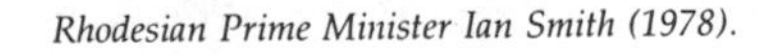

Rhodesian Prime Minister Ian Smith (1978).

Smith, Kate (1909–1986). American singer. Smith's stirring rendition of Irving BERLIN's song *God Bless America* made her a symbol of U.S. patriotism. She acquired the rights to *God Bless America* from Berlin, and her lusty rendition turned the song into a second national anthem during WORLD WAR II, when she traveled thousands of miles to entertain servicepeople and sell war bonds. Her theme *When the Moon Comes Over the Mountain,* was one of 3,000 songs she recorded. She experienced a curious resurgence of popularity in the early 1970s when hockey's Philadelphia Flyers began to win whenever they substituted her recording of *God Bless America* for the national anthem. She even sang in person before several critical games, as the team went on to win two championships.

Smith, Lillian (1897–1966). American author and civil rights activist. She cofounded *The North Georgia Review* in 1936. As *South Today* it became the first white-run Southern journal to publish the work of blacks. Her novels include *Strange Fruit* (1944) and *Killers of the Dream* (1949), which condemned racism. Her *One Hour* exposed the McCarthy hysteria of the 1950s (see MCCARTHYISM), while *Our Faces, Our Worlds* (1964) celebrated the CIVIL RIGHTS MOVEMENT. A friend of Dr. Martin Luther KING Jr., Smith was also on the executive board of the CONGRESS OF RACIAL EQUALITY (CORE).

Smith, Maggie (1934–). British actress. An outstanding actress of both stage and screen, she has performed with the Old Vic Company, the National Theatre and the Stratford (Ontario) Festival, as well as in numerous West End and Broadway plays. In Britain she has won four best actress awards, including one for Hedda Gabler (1970) and one for *Virginia* (1981), while in the U.S. she won the 1990 Tony Award for *Lettice and Lovage*. Her many films include Oscar-winning performances in *The Prime of Miss Jean Brodie* and *California Suite*. She has also won many other acting awards, and was made a Dame Commander of the Order of the British Empire (D.B.E.) in 1989.

Smith, Margaret Court (1942–). Australian tennis player. The rangy (5 feet 8 inches) Court was known for her strong serve and ground strokes, which helped her win seven consecutive Australian championships (1960–1966). At the peak of her career she won the French and U.S. Opens (1962) and Wimbledon (1963). In recent years, Court has been outspoken in her political views, decrying the presence of lesbians on the professional tour.

Smith, Michael J. (1945–1986). American astronaut who was the pilot of the space shuttle CHALLENGER when it exploded on

January 28, 1986. A U.S. Navy officer, Smith served as a combat pilot in the VIETNAM WAR and was decorated.

Smith, Stevie [Florence Margaret Smith] (1902–1971). British poet and novelist. Smith's poetry, which includes the collections *A Good Time Was Had by All* (1937), *Not Waving but Drowning* (1957) and *Scorpion* (1972), became increasingly popular after her retirement as a secretary in 1953, when she began giving poetry readings in her home in London. Her work, while on the surface witty and droll, carries an underlying sense of isolation and an obsession with death. She would often illustrate her poems with idiosyncratic *faux-naif* drawings, many of which can be found in *Some Are More Human than Others* (1958) and *Me Again: The Uncollected Writings of Stevie Smith, Illustrated by Herself* (1981). Smith was awarded the Chomondeley Award in 1966 and the Queen's Gold Medal for Poetry in 1969. She also wrote three clever novels, *Novel on Yellow Paper* (1936), *Over the Frontier* (1938) and *The Holiday* (1949). *Stevie*, an acclaimed film based on her life and starring Glenda JACKSON was released in 1981.

For further reading:

Spalding, Frances, *Stevie Smith: A Biography*. New York: W.W. Norton, 1991.

Smith, Walter Wellesley "Red" (1905–1982). American sportswriter. Smith's impeccable and distinctive style combined with an integrity and wide-ranging knowledge that extended far beyond the sports arena gained him thousands of devoted readers and the respect of his peers. He began his career as a society news reporter in 1927, but soon switched to covering sports for the *St. Louis Star* (1928–36) and later the *Philadelphia Record* (1936–45). Moving to New York, he wrote for the *Herald Tribune* (1945–66) and also started a column that by 1972 was syndicated in 500 U.S. and foreign newspapers. In 1976 he won a PULITZER PRIZE for Distinguished Commentary. During his last ten years he was the chief staff sportswriter of *The New York Times* and was considered the dean of American sportswriters.

Smith, William French (1917–1990). U.S. attorney general. From the 1960s he was a friend and legal adviser to Ronald REAGAN. As president, Reagan appointed him attorney general in 1981, a post he held until 1985. During his tenure as head of the Justice Department, he presided over a shift to a more conservative agenda that included stronger attacks on organized crime and illegal drugs. Some critics saw a weaker enforcement of civil rights and antitrust laws during Smith's tenure.

Smith Act (1940). Controversial federal law prohibiting advocacy of the forcible or violent overthrow of the American government. Passed during the early days of World War II and before the U.S. entered the conflict, it was aimed at conspiracies by wartime subversives against the government. In later years it was used against leftists and suspected communists. The act was challenged in the case of DENNIS V. UNITED STATES (1951) as a violation of the First Amendment's protection of free speech. The Supreme Court upheld the statute, reasoning that a conspiracy to advocate the overthrow of the government would create a peril even if no action is imminent.

Smith and Dale. American VAUDEVILLE comedy team comprised of Joe Smith (1884–1981, born Joe Sultzer) and Charlie Dale (1881–1971, born Charles Marks). The two comedians started their partnership in 1898, playing in vaudeville theaters and Bowery saloons in New York. They went on to win wide acclaim for classic comedy sketches such as *Hungarian Rhapsody*, *Dr. Kronkheit*, *The New School Teacher* and *Venetian Knights*. In the early 1930s they starred in several HOLLYWOOD films. They remained active into the 1960s, appearing in nightclubs and on television. Smith and Dale helped establish the pattern of the deadpan straightman and his antic sidekick, a pattern followed by such later comedy teams as ABBOTT AND COSTELLO, Bob HOPE and Bing CROSBY, and Jerry LEWIS and Dean Martin. Smith and Dale were the models for the two aging vaudeville comedians in Neil SIMON's play *The Sunshine Boys* (1972, filmed 1975).

Smuts, Jan (Christiaan) (1870–1950). South African soldier and statesman. Born in the Cape Colony, he was educated at Victoria College, Stellenbosch and Cambridge. Smuts became a lawyer (1895) and was appointed state attorney in 1898. During the BOER WAR, he headed Boer commando forces in the Cape Colony (1901–02). Convinced of the necessity of Anglo-Boer cooperation, he and Louis BOTHA cofounded the moderate *Het Volk* Party in 1905. In 1910 Smuts played a leading role in the establishment of the Union of SOUTH AFRICA; he served as its minister of the interior and mines (1910–12), finance (1912–13) and defense (1910–19). In 1916 he commanded Allied forces in their campaign against the Germans in East Africa. He served in the British war cabinet from 1917 to 1918 and represented South Africa at the VERSAILLES peace conference of 1919. A confirmed internationalist, Smuts was instrumental in creating the LEAGUE OF NATIONS. Returning to South Africa, he succeeded Botha as prime minister in 1919, serving until 1924. He was minister of justice under Gen. James Hertzog (1933–39) and again became prime minister upon the outbreak of WORLD WAR II. Declaring war on Germany, he sent economic aid to Great Britain, and his forces fought in a number of campaigns in Africa and Italy.

After the war, he was South Africa's representative at the 1945 conference that drafted the UNITED NATIONS charter. Smuts' moderating views on racial segregation were at variance with the prevailing views of white South Africans and largely accounted for his defeat by the National Party in the 1948 general elections. A man of great intellectual accomplishment, Smuts was also an evolutionary theorist, a botanist and a philosopher. He was noted for his powerful and thoughtful speeches and was the author of a number of books. The seven-volume *Selections from the Smuts Papers* was published between 1966 and 1973.

Smyslovsky, Boris (1897–1988). White Russian general. Smyslovsky commanded the First Russian National Army in the ranks of the German Wehrmacht during WORLD WAR II. His unit was the first Russian force to fight with HITLER against STALIN after the German invasion of the U.S.S.R. in 1941. A member of the Russian Imperial Guard before the Bolsheviks seized power in 1917, Smyslovsky believed only the NAZIS were capable of defeating the Soviets and restoring the old regime. After the war he acquired Argentine citizenship under an assumed name.

Smyth, Henry (1898–1986). American physicist. During WORLD WAR II, while at Princeton University, Smith's involvement in ATOM BOMB research led him to write the U.S. government's official report on the development of the bomb, *Atomic Energy for Military Purposes*. The **Smyth Report,** as it was known, was published in 1945, shortly after the atomic bombings of HIROSHIMA and NAGASAKI. He was on the U.S. Atomic Energy Commission from 1949 to 1954, and from 1961 to 1970 was U.S. representative to the International Atomic Energy Agency.

Snead, Samuel Jackson (1912–). U.S. golfer. "Slammin' Sam" Snead was one of the dominant golfers of the first half of the century. Although he is credited with 135 victories, he never won the U.S. Open, finishing second several times. A four-time winner of the Vardon Trophy, awarded by the PGA for the lowest average score in its events, he won the Masters Championship in 1949, 1952 and 1954, and the Professional Golfers' Association championship in 1942, 1949 and 1951.

Snedden, Sir Billy (Mackle) (1926–1987). Australian politician. A leader of Australia's LIBERAL PARTY, Snedden held a number of senior posts after entering the federal House of Representatives in 1955. During that tenure, he served as attorney general (1963–66), leader of the house (1966–70), minister of labor (1969–71) and treasurer (1971–72). He was Liberal Party leader in opposition from 1972 to 1975, and was speaker of the house for seven years until retiring in 1983.

Sneh, Moshe (1909–1972). Israeli communist politician. Sneh was commander-in-chief of HAGANAH, the underground guerrilla movement formed to gain Israel's independence. Sneh was later a member of the Knesset and a leader of Israel's small Communist party. He broke with the Kremlin after the Soviets gave aid to the Arabs during the SIX DAY WAR of 1967.

Snider, Duke [Edwin Donald Snider] (1926–). American baseball player. Duke Snider is acknowledged as one of the three great center fielders in New York during the 1950s, along with Willie MAYS and Mickey MANTLE. Snider's play for the legendary Brooklyn Dodgers made him the dominant home run hitter of the 1950s. A graceful fielder with a strong arm, he was named a National League All-Star six times. The only man to hit four home runs in two World Series, he appeared in six fall classics with the Dodgers. He went with the team when they moved to Los Angeles in 1958, although the configuration of that park was not complementary to his style as a hitter. He was signed by the Mets in 1963, and spent his last season, 1964, with the Giants. He was named to the Hall of Fame in 1980, and wrote a best-selling autobiography in 1988.

Snow, C(harles) P(ercy) [Baron Snow of Leicester] (1905–1980). British novelist, essayist, and physicist. Snow was a brilliant and versatile figure, earning a degree in physics at Cambridge University and working in scientific circles, at the same time establishing himself as one of the leading British novelists of his generation. His major literary work was the eleven-volume novelistic series, *Strangers and Brothers,* that appeared between 1940 and 1970 and chronicled the values and failings of the British intelligentsia and of the middle class. Snow, who held government advisory posts during both WORLD WAR II and the 1960s LABOUR PARTY era, was knighted in 1957 and became a member of the House of Lords. His most controversial work, the essay *The Two Cultures and the Scientific Revolution* (1960), decried the growing gap in knowledge and sympathy between the artistic and scientific communities.

Snow White and the Seven Dwarfs. The first full-length animated feature film and a milestone in the career of Walt DISNEY. He always had been fascinated with the Brothers Grimm story (he had seen a live-action Marguerite Clark film in Kansas City in 1915 during his boyhood) and in 1934 began planning an animated version. Dissatisfied with the cost inefficiency of producing only short cartoons (and aware these brief formats allowed little time for character development) he defied all the nay-sayers and proposed a feature-length project. It took four years. All the studio's technical resources were lavished on the picture: the newly developed multiplane camera added three-dimensional illusion, "rotoscoping" photographed live-action actors and transferred the images to drawings, and unusually vivid color, music, and pacing imparted a freezing horror to the scenes with the Wicked Queen. "Character animation, as we called it, came into its own here," recalled veteran Disney animator Frank Thomas. "We were each assigned a particular character and a handful of particular situations. We had to *become* our drawings, just like an actor becomes his part. We acted them out, learned our lines, and made faces into our mirrors." As a result, dwarfs like "Dopey," "Grumpy," and "Doc" have become a part of the modern cultural vernacular. Songs like "Whistle While You Work," "One Song," and "Some Day My Prince Will Come," by Frank Churchill and Leigh Harline, have become standards. And the picture, after its unprecedented five weeks at the RADIO CITY MUSIC HALL (December 1937–January 1938) won a "Special" Oscar accompanied by seven miniature Oscars (see ACADEMY AWARDS). The box office success saved the Disney studios from financial ruin and spawned a host of imitations from rival studios, including the spoof, "Coal Black and de Sebbin Dwarfs" from WARNER BROS. (which, for obvious reasons, is seldom seen today). However, not everyone joins in the acclaim. Because of the horror sequences the picture was banned in Great Britain. And fairy tale authority Bruno BETTELHEIM deplored such "ill-considered additions to fairy tales" as Disney's differentiation of each dwarf, which made it difficult to grasp "the story's deeper meaning." He may have a point, since few today can remember *all* seven dwarfs.

For further reading:

Maltin, Leonard, *The Disney Films.* New York: Crown, 1972.

Soames, Lord (Arthur Christopher John) (1920–1987). British diplomat. A military hero during WORLD WAR II, in the early 1950s Soames served as parliamentary secretary to his father-in-law Sir Winston CHURCHILL. He held office under five subsequent conservative prime ministers. From 1968 to 1972, as ambassador to FRANCE, he played a key role in ensuring Great Britain's entry into the EUROPEAN COMMUNITY. His four-month stint as governor of RHODESIA in the period leading up to that colony's independence from Great Britain and emergence as the country of ZIMBABWE in 1980 was regarded as his greatest achievement.

Sobers, Gary [Sir Garfield St. Aubrun Sobers] (1936–). Jamaican cricketer. Widely regarded as cricket's best all-rounder, Sobers excelled as both a batsman and bowler. In 93 test matches for the West Indies, Sobers scored 8,032 runs and bagged 235 wickets. His most notable achievement was his innings of 365 not out, the highest score in test cricket, which Sobers scored for the West Indies v. Pakistan in Kingston, Jamaica on 27 February-1 March 1958. Sobers set another cricket milestone on August 31, 1968 when he became the first batsman to score the maximum 36 runs off a six-ball over, playing for Nottinghamshire v. Glamorgan in the English County Championship. Sobers began his test career in 1954 and first captained the West Indies in 1965. Overall Sobers captained the West Indies 39 times and played 93 tests, 1954–74. Sobers career began in his native Jamaica in 1953 and he later played for Nottinghamshire in English county cricket. His career totals in test and first class cricket were 28,315 runs and 1,043 wickets. A fine fielder, Sobers recorded 109 catches in test cricket. Following his retirement, Sobers was knighted for his services to cricket.

Sobhuza II (1899–1982). King of SWAZILAND (1900 to 1982). Sobhuza became king at the age of one and was the longest-reigning monarch of any country in the 20th century. Known to his people as "the Lion," he seized absolute power after Swaziland gained independence from Britain in 1969. He encouraged foreign investment and kept peace with neighboring SOUTH AFRICA and MOZAMBIQUE.

Sobibor. Nazi CONCENTRATION CAMP in German-occupied Soviet territory (now within Poland) during WORLD WAR II. In June 1941 HITLER authorized the execution of all communists and Jews caught behind German lines. Sobibor was created in April 1942 to exterminate Jews captured during the German advance into Russia. At its peak the camp was capable of liquidating up to 20,000 victims per day. The only successful mass escape from a concentration camp occurred at Sobibor.

Sobukwe, Robert Mangaliso (1924–1978). South African black nationalist leader. Sobukwe founded and led the banned Pan African Congress. He was an advocate of passive resistance. He was imprisoned for three years in connection with the 1960 SHARPVILLE MASSACRE, in which police opened fire on him and other blacks protesting the use of identity cards. After his three-year jail term expired, he was held an additional six years under a special amendment to the Suppression of Communism Act that later became known as the "Sobukwe Clause." After his release from prison he was put under a five-year banning order that was renewed in 1974.

social credit. A political movement that advocated a redistribution of wealth by increasing workers' purchasing power. The movement originated with Clifford Hugh Douglas, a Scot who theorized that national income could be increased by increasing worker purchasing power, this by socializing the banking system (to ease credit) and by the payment of national dividends to workers. The workers' increased purchasing power would stimulate production, which would in turn increase the money supply. Social credit theories gained some support during the GREAT DEPRESSION of the 1930s, but never became national policy in any country.

Social Credit Party (Canada). Canadian political party with a strong following in British Columbia. The Canadian Social Credit Party was most successful at the provincial level in British Columbia where W.A.C. BENNETT and his son Bill Bennett, both of Kamloops, B.C., presided over the province's government for the majority of the years after World War II. The Social Credit Party stressed free enterprise and close association with the U.S., views opposed by the NEW DEMOCRATIC PARTY (NDP), which advocated a socialistic approach. On the national level, the Social Credit Party also attracted a following in Quebec.

Social Democratic Party [SDP]. British political party founded in 1981 by the so-called "gang of four"—David OWEN, Shirley WILLIAMS, Roy JENKINS and William RODGERS. These four leading moderates in the LABOUR PARTY objected to the leftward turn the Labour party had taken, and saw the SDP as an alternative for disillusioned Labour supporters. The SDP's stance was a moderate, reformist social democratic one. In 1981 it formed an alliance with the LIBERAL PARTY. Although the party enjoyed some success in by-elections and showed significant support in opinion polls, its candidates failed to make substantial headway in the general elections of 1983 and 1987. In 1988 the SDP was dissolved, its members merging with the Liberal Party to form the **Liberal Democratic Party**.

Socialist International. See INTERNATIONAL.

Socialist Realism. The "basic method" of art and literature. Although works of Socialist Realism existed prior to 1930, in 1934 the doctrine was officially adopted at the first all-union congress of Soviet writers. Accordingly, art should be the truthful, historically concrete presentation of reality in its revolutionary development and must also assist with the ideological remaking and education of writers in the spirit of socialism. Thus all art was constrained by the duty to base it on Marxist-Leninist philosophy.

Socialist Revolutionaries. Political party founded in 1902 by the leaders of revolutionary populism. It was led by Viktor Chernov and Nicholas Avksentev. It demanded socialization of the land, a federal state structure and self-determination for non-Russian peoples. One section of the party, the Left Socialist Revolutionaries, having supported the Bolsheviks in 1917, played a part in the Bolshevik government until the Treaty of BREST-LITOVSK of 1918. In 1922 the Bolsheviks suppressed the party.

Social Security Act of 1935. Landmark U.S. law that created a universal safety net for working Americans by establishing old age pensions, unemployment insurance, and survivor and disability benefits. Prior to 1935 the federal government was not involved in the social welfare area. The lack of programs was especially acute during the GREAT DEPRESSION of the 1930s when millions were out of work and many of the aged had lost their savings in bank failures and the stock market crash. The Social Security Act contained help for three groups: the aged, the unemployed, and women and children. The act provided old age pensions for those who had worked and contributed; unemployment compensation benefits, administered by the states; and increased health services for the needy. The system was to be funded through both employee and employer contributions. The program was administered by the Social Security Administration, which would also oversee the later MEDICARE program, providing hospitalization of senior citizens.

Soderblom, Nathan (1866–1931). Swedish Lutheran clergyman and theologian. Soderblom, who won the NOBEL PRIZE for peace in 1930, is best remembered for his ardent devotion to the cause of ecumenism. His greatest achievement was the organizing of the Universal Christian Conference on Life and Work in Stockholm in 1925. The success of this conference led ultimately to the creation, in 1948, of the WORLD COUNCIL OF CHURCHES. Soderblom, who taught for many years at the University of Uppsala, was a popular teacher who sparked a renewed interest in Christianity amongst the youth of his native land. His writings include *Christian Fellowship* (1923) and *The Church and Peace* (1929).

Sokolnikov, Grigory Yakovlevich (1888–1939). Russian politician. In 1905 Sokolnikov was a member of the Bolshevik faction of the Social Democratic Labor Party. In 1910 he disagreed with LENIN's treatment of the MENSHEVIKS. A member of the central committee following the February Revolution, he was later in charge of nationalizing the banks. Chairman of the third Soviet delegation, he was a commissar in the Red Army during the RUSSIAN CIVIL WAR, people's commissar of finance (1921–26) and ambassador to Great Britain (1929–32). He was imprisoned in 1937 and died two years later.

Solidarity [Solidarnosc]. Polish trade union. Unofficial strikes by workers in POLAND's coalfields and shipyards in the summer of 1980 forced the government to permit the formation of independent trade unions. Solidarity was officially formed on Sept. 22, 1980 by Lech WALESA, an electrician at the Lenin Shipyard in Gdansk, POLAND. In the following months, the union's membership swelled and, together with the Catholic Church, Solidarity became a potent force against communism in Poland, claiming 10 million members. On Dec. 12, 1981, Solidarity called for a national referendum on free elections. The following day Prime Minister JARUZELSKI declared martial law, banned Solidarity and arrested its leaders. However, Solidarity continued to operate underground, with many members showing open but peaceful defiance of the government. Solidarity was re-legalized in April 1989. In free elections in June 1989, Solidarity members won many seats in the new National Assembly. In August, 1989, journalist Tadeusz MAZOWIECKI was elected Prime Minister of Poland. However, many Solidary supporters were dissatisfied with the pace of change and with deteriorating economic conditions, and the movement split into two factions. Mazowiecki led the intellectual wing, while Walesa was favored by rank-and-file workers. After his defeat in a three-way election for the presidency of Poland in 1990, Mazowiecki threw his support to Walesa, who was subsequently elected.

Solomon [born Solomon Cutner] (1902–1988). British pianist; known by his first name alone, he created a stir as a child prodigy from his first appearances. Solomon went on to a major career as a mature concert artist whose technical gifts were matched by his intellectual understanding of his repertory. In his later years he focused particularly on Mozart, Beethoven, Schumann and Brahms. His career was cut short in the late 1950s after he suffered a stroke.

Solomon Islands. Scattered over 249,000 nautical square miles of the south-western Pacific Ocean between New Guinea and Vanuatu, the Solomon Islands archipelago consists of several hundred islands with a total land area of 10,980 square miles. The six main islands are GUADALCANAL, Malaita, New Georgia, San Cristobal (now known as Makira), Santa Isabel and Choiseul. The larger islands are typified by densely forested mountain ranges with deep river valleys, ringed by narrow coastal plains, supporting the bulk of the population, and coral reefs. Most of the outer islands are small, evolving coral atolls. The abuses of labor recruiters led Britain in 1893 to establish a protectorate over the southern Solomons; in 1900 Britain acquired the northern Solomons from Germany. Commercial development began early in the 20th century with the development of the copra industry on a large scale, until a fall in prices in the 1920s. During WORLD WAR II the Japanese occupied the main islands from 1942 to 1943, until Allied forces drove them out after fierce fighting. Anti-government movements, notably Marching Rule, emerged in the postwar period. But after their decline and a lessening of the political tension that had hampered development and administration, there was a gradual increase in the establishment of local government councils. In 1976 self-government was introduced and "Solomon Islands" was officially adopted in place of "British Solomon Islands Protectorate." The country became indepen-

Solidarity members demonstrate against Gen. Wojcieck Jaruzelski's Soviet-backed presidential candidacy (1989).

dent on July 7, 1978, as a constitutional monarchy within the Commonwealth, with the governor-general as the British monarch's representative. A cyclone caused widespread destruction in 1986. In a scandal over the allocation of cyclone-damage aid, Prime Minister Sir Peter Kenilorea resigned in late 1986 and was succeeded by Ezekiel Alebua, a colleague from the ruling Solomon Islands United Party. The Alebua government was decisively defeated at a general election in February 1989 and was replaced by a government led by Solomon Mamaloni, the leader of the People's Alliance Party.

Solomon R. Guggenheim Museum. Located in New York City, one of the most important museums in the U.S. specializing in the collection and display of modern art. Founded in 1939 as the Museum of Non-objective Art, the importance and visibility of the institution were vastly enhanced when it moved into its present building, a major late work of Frank Lloyd WRIGHT. This building, completed in 1959, is a unique and striking design in reinforced concrete, having as its main exhibit space a spiral ramp wound around a skylit central space that runs the full height of the building. Wright died before the building was completed so that some details may not be quite as he intended. Although the architecture is often criticized as so strong as to overpower the works exhibited there, the museum is still one of Wright's masterpieces as well as one of the most exciting New York City buildings. The museum later required more space, and considerable controversy developed over the Gwathmey, Siegel & Associates' addition.

Solti, Sir George (1912–). Hungarian-British conductor. Born in Budapest, Solti studied piano with Bela BARTOK, Zoltan KODALY and Ernst von DOHNANYI at the Liszt Academy, graduating in 1930. He entered the music profession as an opera coach. In 1936 he assisted Arturo TOSCANINI at the SALZBURG FESTIVAL and in 1938 made his conducting debut at the Budapest State Opera. After spending World War II in Switzerland, Solti was appointed director of the Munich State Opera (1946–52) by the American military government. He subsequently served as director of the Frankfurt Opera (1952–61), the Royal Opera at Covent Garden (1961–71) and the Chicago Symphony Orchestra (1971–90), among other posts. He became a British subject and was knighted in 1972. Solti became widely known in the late 1950s, when he began recording the complete *Ring* cycle of Richard Wagner. This widely hailed set established high sonic and technical standards for the new medium of stereophonic recording, and it is still considered one of the most impressive opera recordings ever made. Likewise, some critics considered the Chicago Symphony under Solti to be the finest orchestra in the world. Solti is known for the intensity, brilliance and precision of his performances, which emphasize the dramatic rather than the lyrical aspects of the music. He was most effective leading large-scale symphonic and operatic works, and championed such 20th-century composers as Bartok, Gustav MAHLER, Richard STRAUSS, Igor STRAVINSKY and Arnold SCHOENBERG. Solti made numerous recordings and has won more Grammy Awards than any other classical musician.

Solzhenitsyn, Alexander Isayevich (1918–). Russian dissident novelist, memoirist and historian who chronicled the horrors of STALINISM in several important books. Solzhenitsyn has been regarded as the conscience of the Soviet Union in the 20th century. He studied mathematics and physics at Rostov University, as well as obtaining a degree in literature. During World War II Solzhenitsyn served in the Red Army as a gunner and artillery officer at the front, for which he was decorated. In February 1945 he was arrested in Konigsberg by SMERSH on the grounds that he had criticized STALIN; he then spent eight years in labor camps. Released in 1953, Solzhenitsyn spent three years in internal exile. During this time he suffered from stomach cancer but recovered after treatment. He subsequently taught in a secondary school in Ryazan. In 1962, with KHRUSHCHEV's approval, he was permitted to publish *One Day in the Life of Ivan Denisovich,* an account of life in the Soviet GULAG, in the journal *Novy Mir.* This work established his reputation. However, in 1968 he was attacked in the *Literaturnaya Gazeta.* He won the NOBEL PRIZE for literature in 1970, but was expelled from the writers' union that same year and arrested and deported in 1974, following the publication in Europe of the first volume of the GULAG ARCHIPELAGO. Solzhenitsyn eventually settled in Vermont, U.S. As well as denouncing Soviet communism, Solzhenitsyn has also been highly critical of western materialism. In the late 1980s, the GORBACHEV government announced that Solzhenitsyn was free to return to the U.S.S.R., but as of early 1991 he had

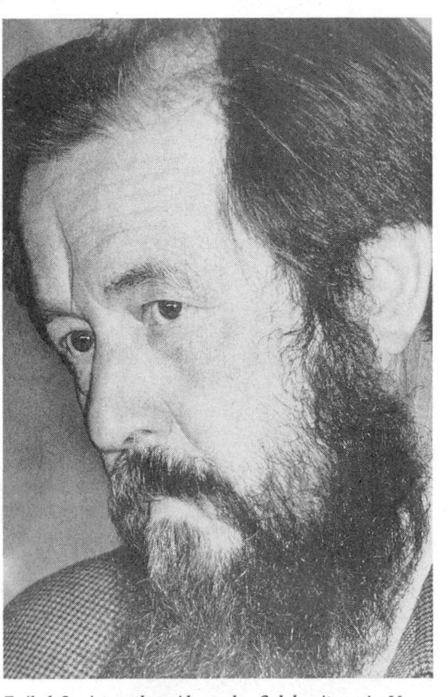

Exiled Soviet author Alexander Solzhenitsyn in Vermont (1975).

refused this invitation. In 1990 Solzhenitsyn also refused a literary prize for the *Gulag Archipelago* offered by the Russian Republic, saying that "the phenomenon of the Gulag has not been overcome either legally or morally. . . . This book is about the suffering of millions and I cannot reap an honor from it." Solzhenitsyn's other works include *Cancer Ward* (1968), *The First Circle* (1968), *August 1914* (1971, tr. 1972) *The Oak and the Calf* (1975, tr. 1980) and *From Under the Rubble.*

For further reading:

Scammell, Michael, *Solzhenitsyn: A Biography.* New York: W.W. Norton, 1986.

Somalia [Somali Democratic Republic]. Somalia, located on the Horn of Africa, covers an area of 246,136 square miles. Northern Somalia became a British pro-

SOMALIA

1948	Ethiopia regains Ogaden region from Somalia.
1960	Britain and Italy each grant independence to their Somali territories, which reunify to form a republic.
1964	War with Ethiopia for Ogaden region; first national elections.
1969	Major General Mohammed Siyad Barre comes to power in military coup; adopts policy of "scientific socialism," governing through a Revolutionary Council of 25.
1981	Somali National Movement (SNM) is formed in opposition to Barre regime and, with other rebel groups, undertakes guerrilla war against the government from bases in Ethiopia.
1988	Fighting over Ogaden region ends when Ethiopia and Somalia sign peace agreement.
1990	Siyad Barre's bodyguards kill 65 at soccer match, shooting into crowd that booed and threw stones as Barre made pre-game speech; in the continuing civil war, rebels approach capital and Barre is forced to flee his palace.

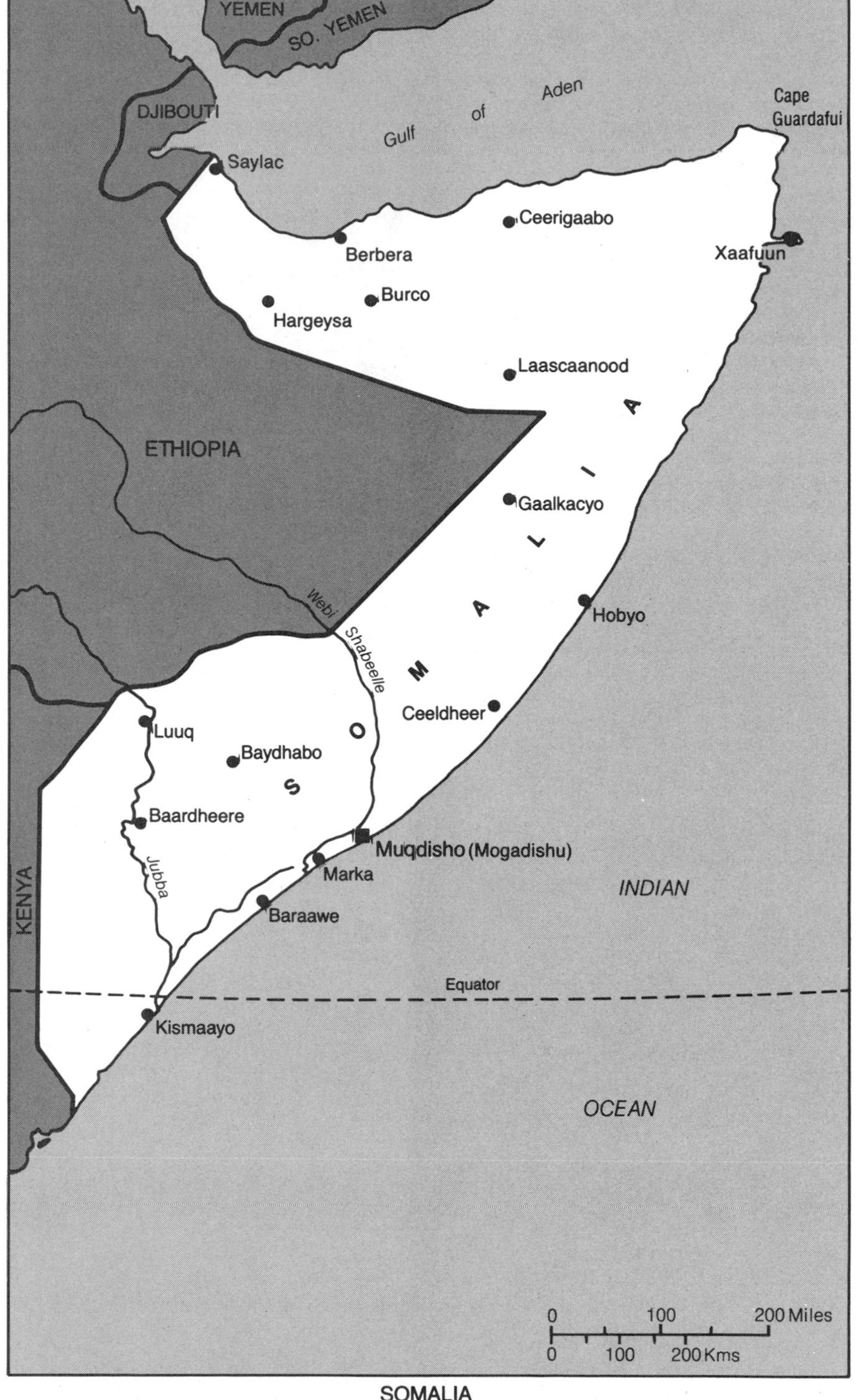

SOMALIA

tectorate in 1885; southern Somalia became an Italian protectorate in 1889, then a UNITED NATIONS trusteeship in 1950. Northern and southern Somalia were unified when full independence was gained in 1960, but ethnic rivalries erupted. President Shermakhe was assassinated in 1969, and the subsequent military coup brought Major General Mohammed Siyad Barre to power. In 1964 and 1977 Somalia went to war with its biggest neighbor, ETHIOPIA, over claims to the Ogaden region—resulting in a defeat in 1978 that led Barre to shift allegiances from the Soviet Union to the United States. Opposition groups carried on a guerrilla war from bases in Ethiopia until 1987, when they occupied northern Somalia and a full-scale civil war erupted. The rebels captured the capital and overthrew the government early in 1991, but the political situation remained uncertain.

Somerville and Ross. Collective pen name of Irish authors Edith Onone Somerville (1858–1949) and Violet Florence Martin (1862–1915). Somerville and Ross were second cousins who first met in 1886 and subsequently began collaborating on writing fiction. Their combined voice was seamless, and their fiction, while reflecting their Protestant Ascendancy backgrounds, humorously chides their social class. Much of their work, such as *The Real Charlotte* (1894), depicts the decline of the Big House. They are perhaps best remembered for the popular stories *Some Experiences of an Irish R. M.* (1899), which was successfully adapted for television by the BBC in the 1980s. After Martin's death in 1915, Somerville, who claimed to be in communication with her, continued writing less successfully as Somerville and Ross, though *The Big House of Inver* (1925) is notable in its depiction of the decline of a social institution.

Somme, Battles of the. Two important WORLD WAR I battles that were fought near the Somme River in northwest France. The First Battle of the Somme took place from June 24 to November 13, 1916. It pitted the forces of the British Fourth Army and the French Sixth Army against an entrenched German force along the Somme. It was intended to dislodge the highly fortified Germans from their positions and to relieve pressure on the French at VERDUN. Following week-long artillery fire, the Allies attacked on July 1, led by the British under Field Marshal Sir Douglas HAIG. Terrible casualties were taken by the British, who suffered 60,000 casualties and 19,000 dead on the first day alone, and who lost over 400,000 men (the French lost almost 200,000) during the twenty weeks of successive attacks. The cost to Germany too was catastrophic, with casualties amounting to about 600,000. The battle proved indecisive, with the German positions only slightly changed but the objectives at Verdun largely achieved. However, the enormous losses sustained by Germany at the Somme and at Verdun have been considered the beginning of the end of the German cause. The Second Battle of the Somme took place from March 21 to April 5, 1918. In an attempt to inflict a decisive defeat on the Allies before the arrival of U.S. forces, German troops under General Erich LUDENDORFF attacked along a 60-mile front. Early German successes against the British (again under Haig) and the French were reversed when French reserves under general Ferdinand FOCH counterattacked. This battle also took a terrible toll, with the Allies and the Germans each suffering almost 250,000 casualties.

Somoza Debayle, Anastasio (1925–1980). President of NICARAGUA (1967–72, 1974–79). The Somoza family controlled Nicaragua for 45 years; Anastasio Somoza was the last of the Somozas to hold office. His imposition of martial law in 1972, suppression of opponents and violations of human rights led the U.S. to abandon its support for Somoza, despite the risk of a takeover by left-wing Sandinista guerrillas. Somoza fled the country in 1979 as Sandinista troops marched on the capital. He was assassinated in 1980.

sonar. System used to locate underwater objects by means of echoing sound waves; an acronym for "*so*und *n*avigation *a*nd *r*anging." It was first developed by Allied scientists during WORLD WAR I as a device for locating submarines and icebergs. In essence, sonar is the same system used by marine animals, notably porpoises, to locate their prey. The sonar device generates pulses of underwater sound waves through a transmitter. When an echo from a submerged object or the bottom of a body of water returns it is picked up by a hydrophone receiver, passed through an amplifier and, converted into electrical impulses, displayed. This display may be in the form of a stylus writing on a strip of moving paper, may be shown on a cathode-ray tube, or it may be broadcast as sound through a loudspeaker. The time elapsed between the sending of the sound and the return of its echo indicates the depth of the object or ocean floor. Sonar is used for the detection of submarines and for communication between submarines; also employed by commercial and sport fishermen as a locator for schools of fish, and in marine seismology, archaeology and exploration.

Sondheim, Stephen (1930–). American composer and lyricist. An outstanding composer/lyricist of the American musical, Sondheim first gained recognition as a lyricist for *West Side Story* (1957). Among successful musicals for which he wrote both music and lyrics are *Company* (1970), *Follies* (1971), *A Little Night Music* (1973) and *Sweeney Todd* (1979), each of which won a Tony Award. He is known for the operatic nature of his scores and for his experimentation, such as in the Kabuki-like *Pacific Overtures* (1976); *Sunday in the Park with George* (1984), inspired by a Georges Seurat painting; and *Into the Woods* (1987), based on fairy tales.

For further reading:
Zadan, C., *Sondheim & Co.* New York: Harper Collins, 1974.

Sonneborn, Rudolf Goldschmid (1898–1986). American industrialist and Zionist leader. Sonneborn developed a small family business into a flourishing concern dealing with petroleum specialty products. Active on behalf of the Jewish community in PALESTINE from as early as the end of World War I, he did much to assist Jewish refugees in Europe during WORLD WAR II. After the creation of Israel in 1948, he was in the forefront of campaigns that raised hundreds of millions of dollars for the new state.

Son of Sam killings. Series of eight attacks in New York City from July 1976 to August 1977, in which six young persons were killed and another seven were wounded. For more than a year, New York City was terrorized by the pseudonymous killer, who signed himself "Son of Sam" in letters to newspapers and who claimed that "Sam" was forcing him to commit the crimes. The shootings, which ranged over the Bronx, Queens and Brooklyn and which were all committed with a .44–caliber pistol, were mostly directed at young women or at couples parked in cars. Finally, on August 10, 1977, a 25-year-old mailman and former auxiliary policeman named David Berkowitz was apprehended. He pleaded guilty and was sentenced to 30 years in prison, the harshest penalty allowed under law.

Sontag, Susan (1933–). American intellectual, critic, essayist, novelist, short story writer and film maker. Sontag studied at Berkeley, Chicago, Harvard and Oxford and has at various times been a lecturer in English, philosophy, and religion. She is probably best known for *Against Interpretation* (1966), which argued that the proper response to art is intuitive not intellectual. *Trip to Hanoi* (1968) voiced her opposition to the VIETNAM WAR. *Styles of Radical Will* (1969) explored ways of altering one's consciousness for aesthetic purposes. Other works include *On Photography* (1977), *Illness as Metaphor* (1978) and *Under the Sign of Saturn* (1980). In *AIDS and Its Metaphors* she explored the effects of AIDS on social thought. Neither her experimental films or her novels—*The Benefactor* (1963) and *Death Kit* (1967)—have been as successful as her criticism. Sontag's influential essays appear regularly in leading cultural periodicals, and she is widely esteemed as an intellectual leader in matters of aesthetic taste and moral judgment.

Sony. Japanese manufacturer of consumer electronic products, known for its high standards of both technical quality and design. The firm was founded immediately after World War II as TTK (an abbreviation of the Japanese for Tokyo Telecommunications Engineering) by Masaru Ibuka and Akio Morita. In 1955 the firm marketed the first transistor radio, the TR-55, under the Sony brand name, beginning a flow of miniaturized electronic products. The 1959 portable television, TV5–303, made TV compact and convenient. The Trinitron color TV tube of 1968 introduced a new level of color picture quality and began a sequence of TV products of good design quality that have become internationally known. The 1979 Walkman cassette tape recorder introduced the pocketable hi-fi music system. Although Sony designers remain anonymous, the quality of Sony design has been a major factor in the success of the firm's products.

Soong Ching-ling (1892–1981). Chinese stateswoman and a leading figure in the People's Republic of CHINA, often called the "conscience of China." Educated in the U.S. (1908–13), shortly after her return to China (1913) Soong succeeded her older sister as the secretary of the nationalist revolutionary leader SUN YAT-SEN. She married Sun (1914) while they were in temporary exile in Japan. After Sun's death (1925), she was critical of the policies of his successor, CHIANG KAI-SHEK. In 1927 she resigned from the KUOMINTANG, which Sun had established, and spent two years in the U.S.S.R. Thereafter she lived quietly in Shanghai, moving to HONG KONG (1937) after war broke out with JAPAN. She returned to Shanghai at the end of the war (1945). Although she supported the Communists under MAO TSE-TUNG, she was not herself a member of the Communist party. After 1949 she served in a number of high posts in the People's Republic of China and was held in high esteem by the Chinese. A month before her death she was named honorary chairman of China, the nation's highest tribute.

Soong Mei-ling [Madame Chiang Kai-Shek] (1897–). Soong Mei-ling was a member of the wealthy and influential Soong family in Shanghai. She was trained in sociology at Wellesley College in the United States and was married to CHIANG KAI-SHEK from 1927 until his death in 1975. Her son Chiang Ching-Kuo (1910–88) succeeded his father as head of the KUOMINTANG Party. Although she held few official posts, she served as her husband's adviser and became internationally known while traveling widely to seek support for the Kuomintang cause. In 1988 she joined other conservative mainlanders in an unsuccessful attempt to block LEE TENG-HUI's confirmation as head of the Kuomintang.

Sopwith, Sir Thomas Octave Murdoch (1888–1989). British aircraft designer. A pioneer in the field of aircraft design, Sopwith was best known for his WORLD WAR I Sopwith Camel fighter plane. The Sopwith Camel was considered the most maneuverable of all World War I aircraft and shot down more enemy aircraft than any other Allied plane. Canadian flying ace Captain Roy Brown was piloting a Sopwith Camel when, in 1917, he shot down Germany's best-known fighter pilot, Baron Manfred von RICHTHOFEN, the "Red Baron." Although Sopwith was forced to liquidate his original aviation company after the war's end, he later helped found Hawker Aircraft Co., which produced the world's first vertical-take-off-and-landing aircraft, the Hawker Harrier jump jet.

Souers, William Sidney (1892–1973). American naval officer and intelligence officer. Souers spent WORLD WAR II in naval intelligence in the U.S., attaining the rank of rear admiral (1943) and the post of deputy chief of Naval Intelligence (1944). After the war President TRUMAN appointed him director of the new Central Intelligence Group (1946), the forerunner of the CENTRAL INTELLIGENCE AGENCY (CIA). Souers was subsequently first executive secretary of the National Security Council (1947–50) and an advisor to Truman during the Korean War.

Soupault, Philippe (1897–1990). French writer and poet. Soupault was one of the founders of the Surrealist movement in the early 1920s (see SURREALISM). Together with Andre BRETON and Louis ARAGON, he founded the review *Litterature*, which became a major vehicle for young intellectuals of the day. With Breton he wrote *Les Champs Magnetiques (Magnetic Fields)*, a poem which was considered to be the first surrealist text.

Souphanouvoung (1909–). Prince of LAOS. Born into the Lao royal family, Souphanouvoung became president of the Lao

People's Democratic Republic in 1975. The prince has always enjoyed national prominence because of his royal blood. He received his higher education in Paris, and joined an Indochinese engineering corps in Vietnam upon his return. He began his revolutionary activities in 1944, was a member of the Lao Issara government that fled to Thailand after World War II, and became chairman of the Lao Resistance Front in 1950. Souphanouvoung was the chief spokesman for the PL and its chief negotiator with the RLG for over two decades. In 1962 he was named deputy prime minister in the second coalition government. After the 1975 takeover he held the president's post until late 1986 when he fell ill and resigned. His actual political power within the Pathet Lao has often been a subject of debate. Some consider him a figurehead, manipulated by the Vietnamese and their chosen Lao leaders because of his name and traditional status. However, his picture hangs next to that of KAYSONE PHOMVIHAM, cabinet chairman, in all public areas in Vientiane.

Soustelle, Jacques Emile (1912–1990). French diplomat and anthropologist. While serving as governor general of ALGERIA in the mid-1950s, he became convinced that the colony should remain French. This conviction clashed with Gen. Charles de Gaulle's 1959 decision to grant Algeria independence, and Soustelle quit the government. In 1962, he joined a secret army that conducted a campaign of assassination and sabotage in an effort to keep Algeria French. He was charged with "attempts against the state," and fled the country. In 1968, after a general amnesty was declared, he returned to devote himself to politics and the study of pre-Colombian culture. He was named to the Academie Francaise in 1983.

Souter, David (1939–). Associate justice, U.S. Supreme Court (1990–). A graduate of Harvard University and Harvard Law School, and a Rhodes Scholar at Oxford University, David Souter spent the majority of his legal career in public service. After a brief time in private practice he became an assistant deputy attorney general in his native New Hampshire, rising to become the state attorney general in 1976. Two years later he became a state judge and was soon appointed to the Supreme Court of New Hampshire. In 1990, Souter was named to the U.S. Court of Appeals for the First Circuit. Two months later he was President George BUSH's surprise choice to fill the Supreme Court seat left vacant by the resignation of William BRENNAN. During his confirmation hearings, Souter avoided giving his personal views on particular controversial issues, including ABORTION; conservatives hoped that he would prove to be the deciding vote necessary to overturn ROE V. WADE.

South Africa [Republic of South Africa]. Located at the southernmost point of the African continent, South Africa occupies an area of 476,094 square miles. In 1910 the Union of South Africa was established as a dominion under the British Crown. After World War II, it sought independence from Britain and became a republic in 1961. Legislation to preserve white supremacy led to introduction of the policy of APARTHEID in 1948. The apartheid policy created 10 homelands to preserve the identity of various African ethnic groups, but the homelands had no rights or power. Opposition to apartheid was led by the AFRICAN NATIONAL CONGRESS (ANC) headed by Nelson MANDELA, who was imprisoned in 1963 for committing sabotage. Stringent measures were taken and discriminatory laws passed to keep the South African blacks powerless. Uprisings in 1976, the death of black leader Steven BIKO in 1977, and the violent repression of riots in 1984 and 1985, brought international condemnation and the imposition of trade sanctions (1986–87) by several Western countries. Archbishop Desmond TUTU emerged as a leader against apartheid. President P.W. BOTHA introduced some reforms during his tenure (1983–89), and his successor, F.W. DE

SOUTH AFRICA

1902	Transvaal and Orange Free State reabsorbed into British colony with end of Second Boer War.
1907	Mohandas Gandhi leads first non-violent protests in response to racial inequality.
1910	South Africa becomes a dominion under the British Crown; Jan Smuts and Louis Botha are first leaders.
1919	Southwest Africa mandated to South Africa by League of Nations.
1927	Native Administration Act—early step in legal codification of white supremacy.
1939	Assembly narrowly votes to declare war on Germany.
1944	Nelson Mandela joins African National Congress.
1948	National Party comes to power behind philosophy of "Apartheid"; begins to enact mass of laws defining the state and individual rights in racial terms.
1951	Bantu Authorities Act divides African population along tribal lines, to discourage unity.
1955	ANC signs anti-apartheid "Free Charter."
1960	ANC and other groups protest "pass laws" that control people's movements; police kill 67 demonstrators at Sharpeville; ANC banned, begins guerrilla war; Mandela goes underground.
1961	Under Voerster of the National Party, independent republic is declared; British Commonwealth is abandoned.
1963	Mandela jailed for life.
1966	Voerster assassinated; UN revokes mandate for Southwest Africa (Namibia); SWAPO guerrillas there wage war for independence from South Africa.
1968	Christiaan Barnard performs first heart transplant.
1974	UN ambassador stops attending sessions.
1976	Soweto riots; "tribal homelands" created.
1977	Death of Steve Biko in police custody creates international outrage.
1980	Border skirmishes and raids into neighboring nations allied with ANC.
1981	Unsuccessful peace talks with SWAPO.
1984	New constitution replaces prime minister with president; Desmond Tutu wins Nobel Prize for peace.
1988	Minor reforms announced, but extremely violent protests lead to "state of emergency" and severe repression; this leads to economic sanctions by many nations; unsuccessful crackdown on anti-apartheid groups; sanctions damage economy.
1989	New President de Klerk begins desegregation; opens talks with ANC.
1990	ANC legalized; Mandela and others released; Mandela makes triumphal world tour; violence between members of ANC and Inkatha Zulu, a tribal organization; troops withdrawn from Namibia, which achieves independence.
1991	Despite ANC requests, Western nations begin lifting sanctions.

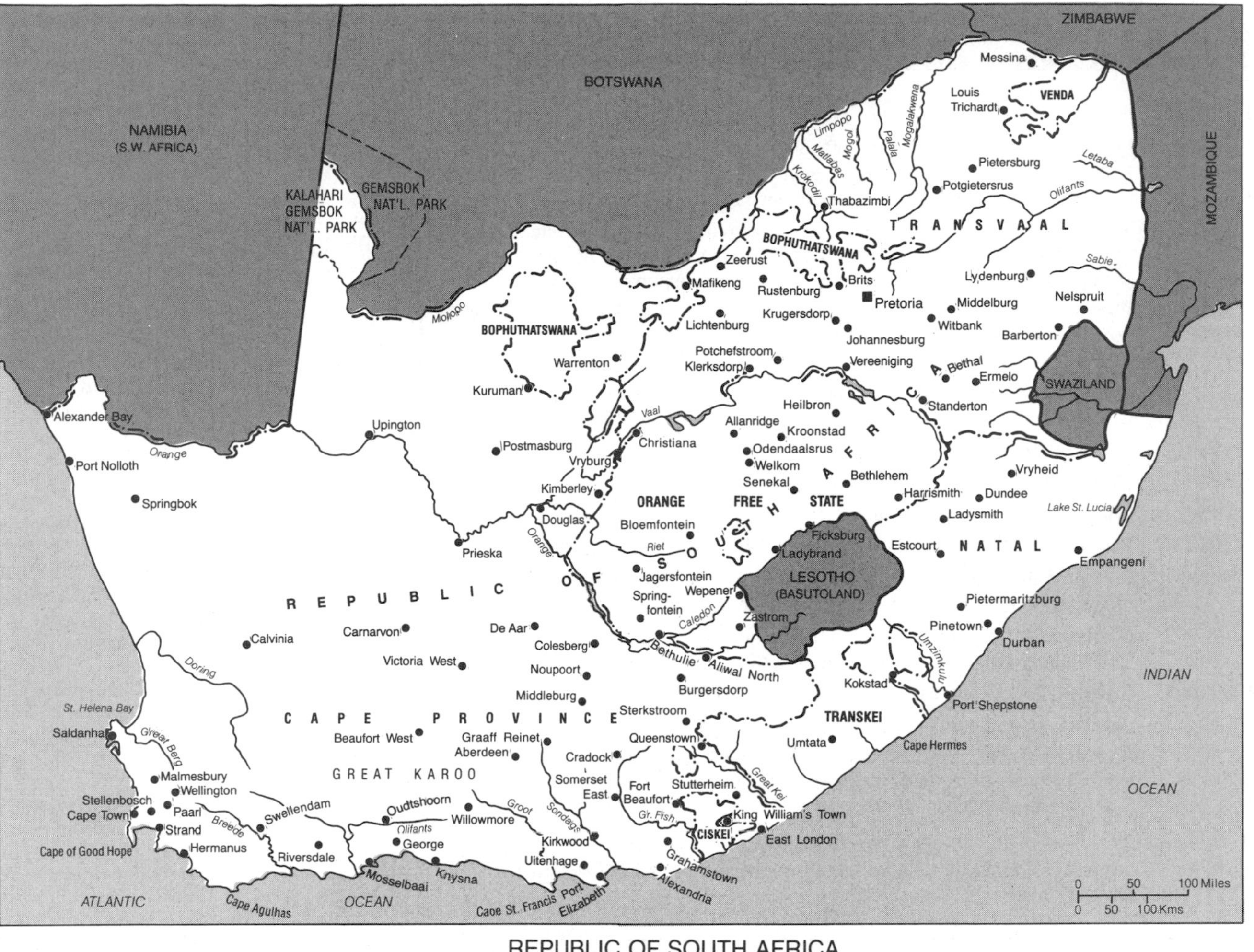

REPUBLIC OF SOUTH AFRICA

KLERK, moved toward negotiations with black leaders, releasing Mandela in 1990 and lifting restrictions on the ANC and other anti-apartheid groups. However, white supremacists continue to work against black enfranchisement, while blacks fight among themselves.

South Arabia, Federation of. Federation formed by 1963 merger of Britain's colony of ADEN with its protectorate, the Federated Emirates of the South. The federation collapsed and British forces withdrew in 1967, after which Aden and South Arabia merged to form the independent South Yemen, now part of YEMEN.

South East Asia Treaty Organization. See SEATO.

Southern Christian Leadership Conference [SCLC]. American civil-rights organization. Founded in 1957 by Martin Luther KING Jr., it was headed by him until his assassination in 1968. Its aims are to achieve equal rights for blacks through nonviolent protest and to sponsor community development. From its beginning, the leadership has largely been made up of black Protestant clergymen. It first gained wide attention for its 1963 campaign to desegregate public facilities in Birmingham, Alabama. The SCLC is perhaps best known for organizing the massive 1963 MARCH ON WASHINGTON, which mobilized some 250,000 Americans in the CIVIL RIGHTS cause. Its voters' rights campaigns were highlighted by the 1965 conflict between demonstrators and police in Selma, Alabama, which brought world attention to the plight of blacks in the South. The organization was headed by Rev. Ralph ABERNATHY from 1968 to 1977, but its influence, prestige and membership dwindled after Dr. King's death. Its headquarters are in Atlanta, Georgia.

Southern Rhodesia. See ZIMBABWE.

South Korea [Republic of Korea]. Covering an area of 38,015 square miles, the Republic of KOREA is located on the southern half of the Korean Peninsula in northeast Asia. The corrupt government of South Korea's first president, Syngman RHEE (1948–60), was overthrown in 1960, but the unstable Second Republic that replaced it fell victim to a military coup in 1961, bringing to power General PARK CHUNG HEE (1962–79). Though his regime brought economic success, it also introduced an authoritarian constitution (1972) and practiced coercion. After Park's assassination in 1979, subsequent popular uprisings led to a declaration of martial law. Chun Doo Huan became president in 1980, lifting martial law (1981) and im-

South Africa's new equation, President F.W. de Klerk and A.N.C. leader Nelson Mandela, in Cape Town (1990).

SOUTH KOREA

1904	Japan annexes Korea.
1910	Formally made a colony of Japan.
1945	Following the defeat of Japan, Korean territory north of the 38th parallel is occupied by Soviet troops and southward by American forces.
1948	The country's division is formalized by formation of the Republic of Korea in the south and the Democratic People's Republic in the north with both governments claiming sovereignty over the entire peninsula; Syngman Rhee is elected president.
1949	Soviet and U.S. troops begin withdrawal.
1950	(July 25) North Korea invades South Korea; (September) U.N. forces land amphibious forces at Inchon, outflanking the North Koreans; (November) Chinese volunteers enter the war, driving UN forces back.
1953	(July 27) Armistice signed.
1960	(April) Rhee overthrown by popular revolt.
1961	(May 16) General Park Chung Hee emerges as leader.
1963	Park, as member of the Democratic Republican Party, is elected president.
1972	Park procalims martial law and is elected to a six-year term by the new electoral body, the National Conference for Unification.
1979	(October 26) Park is assasinated by the head of his secret police; (Dec. 12) Military coup takes over government.
1980	(August) Presidency assumed by Chun Doo Hwan.
1981	(January) Martial law is lifted.
1987	(October) New democratic constitution is approved; (November) South Korean jetliner destroyed by agents of North Korea; (December 16) Roh Tae Woo is elected president.
1988	Summer Olympic Games held in Seoul.
1991	Soviet President Mikhail Gorbachev becomes first Soviet leader to visit South Korea.

proving human rights in response to foreign pressure. His successor, ROH TAE WOO (1987–), undertook reforms and established a new democratic constitution in 1987 in response to proposals to move the coming OLYMPIC GAMES (held in Seoul in 1988) because of unrest in Korea. By the end of 1990, there was a movement toward talks between the two Koreas.

For further reading:
Rees, Davis, *A Short History of Modern Korea*. New York: Hippocrene Books, 1988.

South Pole. At 90 degrees south latitude and 0 degrees longitude, this is the south end of the Earth's axis, on the continent of ANTARCTICA. In 1909 the British explorer Sir Ernest SHACKLETON came within 97 miles of the Pole. On December 14, 1911, it was reached for the first time by an overland expedition led by Norwegian explorer Roald AMUNDSEN; the expedition of British explorer Robert F. SCOTT, which arrived over a month later, perished on its return journey. On November 29, 1929, Americans Richard E. BYRD and Bernt Balchen were the first to fly over the pole. Scientific exploration continued throughout the century. A 1958 COMMONWEALTH expedition led by Vivian FUCHS was the first to cross Antarctica by land via the South Pole. In 1990 an international team led by American adventurer Will Stegner traversed the Pole by dogsled.

Southwell-Keely, Terry (Terence Hugh) (1908–1985). Australian journalist; chief of staff at the *Sydney Morning Herald* until 1955, when he became publicity chief of Ampol and promoted the oil company by organizing many sporting events, including popular fishing contests. He originated the Walkley Award for Journalism and also spearheaded a drive to popularize the technique of mouth-to-mouth resuscitation.

Souvanna Phouma, Prince (1901–1984). Laotian political leader. Souvanna served as prime minister of LAOS intermittently from 1951 to 1975, when Marxist PATHET LAO rebels took power and established the Lao People's Democratic Republic. A neutralist, he attempted to establish a coalition government incorporating pro-Western elements and the communist insurgents, who were led by his half-brother, Prince SOUPHANOUVOUNG. Souvanna also served as ambassador to France (1958–60).

Soviet Far East. See FAR EASTERN REPUBLIC.

Soviet Union. See UNION OF SOVIET SOCIALIST REPUBLICS.

Soweto uprising. In June 1976 a group of students staged a march through the black township of Soweto (outside Johannesburg, SOUTH AFRICA) to protest the government's Bantu education program. Police opened fire, killing several marchers, and unarmed students retaliated by throwing bottles and stones. The official count at week's end was 176 killed, 1,139 wounded and 1,298 detained. The protest spread. A march of 20,000 to 40,000 produced more deaths. The uprising galvanized black political activity and led to the Black Consciousness Movement and other organizations.

Soyinka, Wole (1934–). Nigerian dramatist, novelist and poet. Born in Abeokuta, the son of a well-to-do Yoruba couple, Soyinka attended University College, Ibadan, and Leeds University. As a student he wrote his first two important plays, *The Swamp Dwellers* and *The Lion and the Jewel*, both of which examine the conflict between tradition and change in contemporary Africa. Returning to Nigeria in 1960, he wrote a number of plays including *The Trials of Brother Jero*. Soyinka's first novel, *The Interpreters* (1965), explores the lives of Europeanized Nigerians. Accused of conspiring with Ibo rebels during the BIAFRA rebellion, he was imprisoned (1967–69), an experience he movingly described in *The Man Died* (1972). Soyinka's other plays include *The Bacchae, Death and the King's Horseman* and *Opera Wonyosi*, an adaptation of BRECHT's *Threepenny Opera*. He is the author of poetry including *A Shuttle in the Crypt* (1972) and of the autobiography *Ake: The Years of Childhood* (1981). In 1986 Soyinka became the first African to be awarded the NOBEL PRIZE for literature.

Soyuz. A Soviet spacecraft originally designed to carry three cosmonauts. First used in 1967, the first mission ended in the deaths of its three cosmonauts. Its name, meaning "union," indicates its main mission, to provide transportation to and from a space station, where it could dock during missions aboard the station. The descendants of this spacecraft, the Soyuz TM series, were still being flown in the late 1980s.

Wole Soyinka, Nigerian author and Nobel laureate (1986).

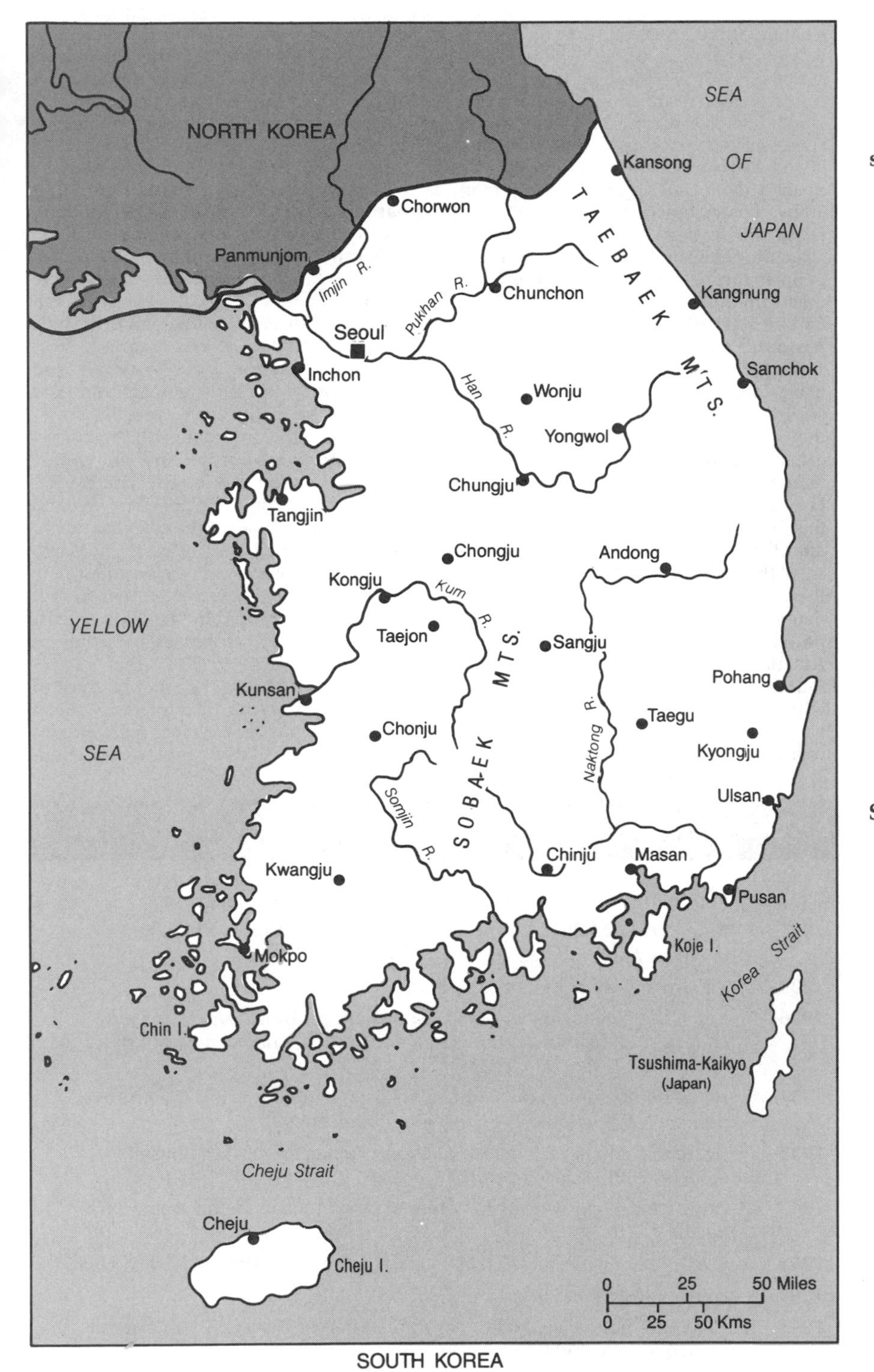

SOUTH KOREA

Spaak, Paul-Henri (1899–1972). Belgian statesman and political leader. A major figure in international affairs of the post-WORLD WAR II period, Spaak helped write the charter of the UNITED NATIONS and served as first president of the General Assembly (1946). He was regarded as one of the founders of the EUROPEAN ECONOMIC COMMUNITY (EEC). He helped create the NORTH ATLANTIC TREATY ORGANIZATION (NATO) and was its secretary-general from 1957 to 1961. Spaak served in 17 Belgian governments, including six stints as foreign minister. He also held presidential posts in the EUROPEAN COAL AND STEEL COMMUNITY, the Council of Europe, and the ORGANIZATION FOR EUROPEAN ECONOMIC COOPERATION.

Spaatz, Carl (1891–1974). U.S. military officer. After Pearl Harbor Spaatz served as chief of the Air Force Combat Command and in 1942 became head of the U.S. Eighth Air Force. He led the Allied Northwest African Air Forces and the Mediterranean Allied Air Forces in 1943. Spaatz commanded the U.S. Strategic Air Force in Europe during 1944–45. In that post he secured air superiority over Germany by concentrating attacks on vital industrial targets. In 1945–46 Spaatz commanded the U.S. Strategic Air Force in the Pacific.

space medicine. Sometimes referred as "bioastronautics," space medicine has been classified as a separate medical field since the early 1960s. Every aspect of the physical and psychological conditions encountered in space flight is studied by the specialists at the Aerospace Medical Center, San Antonio, Texas. Sophisticated tests, examinations and training are provided for astronauts and are designed to meet all conditions and problems that might be encountered in space. These include human reactions to acceleration forces, cosmic rays and weightlessness. Instruments-carrying astronauts have recorded their brain waves, respiration and blood pressure along with other data needed to prepare for future flights into space. Specialists in space medicine have developed personal life-support systems, which provide astronauts with food, oxygen and water so that they may perform "space walks" outside the safety of the space capsule. Among future problems confronting space medicine specialists are management of illness in space and ways of providing the necessary exercise and entertainment needed for mental health on long voyages through space.

Space Shuttle. American spacecraft. Unlike the manned spacecraft used in previous U.S. space programs (MERCURY, GEMINI and APOLLO) administered by NASA, the space shuttle can land on a runway and can be reused on subsequent missions into space. The shuttle's roomy cabin can accommodate up to eight astronauts, and a large payload bay enables the shuttle to carry satellites into space. The space shuttle program was intended not only for space exploration and for conducting space experiments, but it was also conceived partly as a commercial enterprise: private communications companies would pay NASA to carry their telecommunications satellites into space aboard the shuttle. Some of the shuttle missions have also been secret military missions, presumably involving testing of components for the STRATEGIC DEFENSE INITIATIVE program. The first shuttle, *Columbia,* was launched into space with two astronauts on April 12, 1981 and returned to Earth on April 14. Over the next four-and-a-half years, another 23 successful missions were carried out aboard NASA's four space shuttles (*Challenger, Discovery* and *Atlantis* having joined *Columbia* in the program). However, the scheduled 25th flight of the shuttle program ended in tragedy when the *Challenger* exploded moments after launch on January 28, 1986; the seven crew members were killed (see CHALLENGER DISASTER). The remaining shuttles were grounded and there was an investigation into the disaster. The shuttle program resumed on September 29, 1988, when the *Discovery* was launched into orbit. Apart from the *Challenger* disaster, the space shuttle program has been plagued by numerous delays, mounting costs, and an inability to deliver on expectations. The program continued into the 1990s, but some members of Congress and many people in the space business have questioned the wisdom of using manned spacecraft to do what unmanned craft can do perhaps more safely, cheaply and efficiently.

Spaggiari, Albert (?-1989). French bank robber. Spaggiari masterminded the 1976 robbery of the Societe Generale Bank in Nice, France that became known as "the heist of the century." Together with a gang of 20 associates, he tunneled into the bank and made off with about $9 million in cash, gold and jewelry. He was caught and jailed, but escaped from a magistrate's office in March 1977. Thereafter, he evaded the authorities and lived in an undisclosed location. He died of lung cancer; his body was found at his mother's house in Hyeres, France.

Spahn, Warren (1921–). American baseball player. Arguably the best lefthanded pitcher of all time, Spahn led the Braves for 18 years. He earned immortality in the jingle "Spahn and Sain and pray for rain," referring to the fact that the Braves had only two reliable pitchers. He won 20 games 12 times and was an All Star 14 times. He moved with the Braves from Boston to Milwaukee, and led the team to the pennant in 1957, when he was 36, and won a World Series game, as the Braves defeated the Yankees. He threw his first no-hitter in 1960 at age 39, and followed with another at the age of 40. He was sold to the Mets in 1964, and finished his major league career with the Giants in 1965. He continued to pitch in the minor leagues until he retired in 1967. He was named to the Hall of Fame in 1973.

Spain. Spain occupies an area of 194,846 square miles and shares the Iberian Peninsula of southwestern Europe with Portugal; it includes the Canary and Balearic Islands (in the Atlantic Ocean and Mediterranean Sea) and the municipalities of Ceuta and Melilla on the North African coast of Morocco. After the dictatorship of General PRIMO DE RIVERA (1923–30) and the abdication of King ALFONSO XIII in 1931, Spain had a brief period as a republic (1931–36) before General Francisco FRANCO exported a military rebellion from Spanish Morocco to Spain. The resulting SPANISH CIVIL WAR (1936–39) galvanized international support—for either the socialist government or Franco's pro-fascist forces. When Barcelona and Madrid surrendered in 1939, Franco became dictator (1939–75). Spain remained neutral during WORLD WAR II in spite of Axis pressure for Franco to support the Germans and the Italians, who had materially aided his cause in the civil war. Conflict with Britain over Spanish claims to GIBRALTAR led to the closing of the Spain-Gibraltar border in 1969; it was reopened in 1985, after the two countries agreed to discuss Gibraltar's sovereignty (see GIBRALTAR DISPUTE). The 1973 assassination of the prime minister by militant Basque separatists brought several executions in 1975, resulting in international condemnation of the Franco government. Upon Franco's death (1975) his chosen successor JUAN CARLOS became king and introduced a new constitution, declaring Spain a democratic, parliamentary monarchy. Spain joined NATO in 1982 but voted to remain outside the military structure (1986) and to reduce U.S. forces in Spain (present since 1953). The government continues to face terrorism from the Basque separatist movement.

Spandau Prison. Built as a fortress in the 16th century, in the 20th century Spandau gained notoriety as the prison in which Nazi war criminals were incarcerated after the NUREMBERG TRIALS of 1945–46. Located in Berlin, Spandau was administered by France, the United Kingdom, the U.S. and the U.S.S.R., the four powers that had occupied and divided GERMANY after that country's defeat in WORLD WAR II. With the death in 1987 of Hitler crony Rudolf HESS, the last Nazi inmate, Spandau was razed.

Spanel, Abram Nathaniel (1901–1985). American businessman. In 1932 Spanel founded the International Laytex Corp., which would later be known as the International Playtex Corp. He was one of the first industrialists to install air conditioning for his workers and to provide them with such benefits as paid health and life insurance. For nearly four decades, he disseminated his liberal views through paid editorial advertisements in dozens of newspapers. He retired as Playtex's chairman in 1972. A prolific inventor, he held more than 2,000 patents.

Spanish Civil War (1936–39). Military revolt against the unstable socialist Republican government of SPAIN. The Nationalists, as the rebels were called, were led by General Francisco FRANCO. All Europe took sides in this ideological struggle between democracy and tyranny, freedom and FASCISM. Nazi GERMANY and fascist ITALY supplied bombers and land forces to the Nationalists, and the Soviet Union and the International Brigades—volunteers from Europe and the United States—supplied and fought with the Republicans. During 1936 the Basques and Catalans, and much of the east and north, held out against Franco's forces. On March 5, 1939, the Republican government flew to exile in France, and later that month Madrid was captured by the Nationalists. There were over half a million casualities in this civil war.

Spanish Sahara. On the Atlantic coast of northwestern Africa, this former Spanish colony became an overseas province of Spain in 1958. It was granted indepen-

SPAIN

1923	Imposition of military dictatorship by General Primo de Rivera.
1931	King Alfonso abdicates in favor of the Second Republic, which introduces universal adult suffrage.
1933	Right-wing Falangist Party founded.
1936	Jose Calvo Sotelo, leader of the fascist National Bloc, is assassinated, causing military intervention; Francisco Franco is named head of state; Spanish civil war commences.
1937	Aerial bombardment of Guernica by German planes marks the first-ever use of massive civilian bombing for military ends.
1939	(March) Nationalists are victorious and Franco establishes himself as dictator, with Nazi sympathies.
1947	Law of Succession allows for return of monarchical rule upon Franco's death.
1953	U.S. military bases allowed in Spain with the signing of the Pact of Madrid.
1969	Franco closes the border with Gibraltar.
1973	(Dec. 20) Basque separatist kills Prime Minister Admiral Luis Carrero Blanco in a Madrid bomb explosion.
1975	(Nov. 20) Franco dies; Juan Carlos ascends to the throne.
1976	(July 20) Adolfo Suarez Gonzalez becomes prime minister; National Movement is disbanded and political parties and trade unions are legalized.
1978	(December) New constitution approved declaring Spain to be a democratic parliamentary monarchy.
1979	Basque country and Catalonia become autonomous communities.
1981	(Feb. 23) Attempted coup by members of the civil guards is foiled by the intervention of King Juan Carlos.
1982	(May) Becomes 16th member of NATO.
1989	(Oct. 29) Gonzales is elected prime minister for a third term.

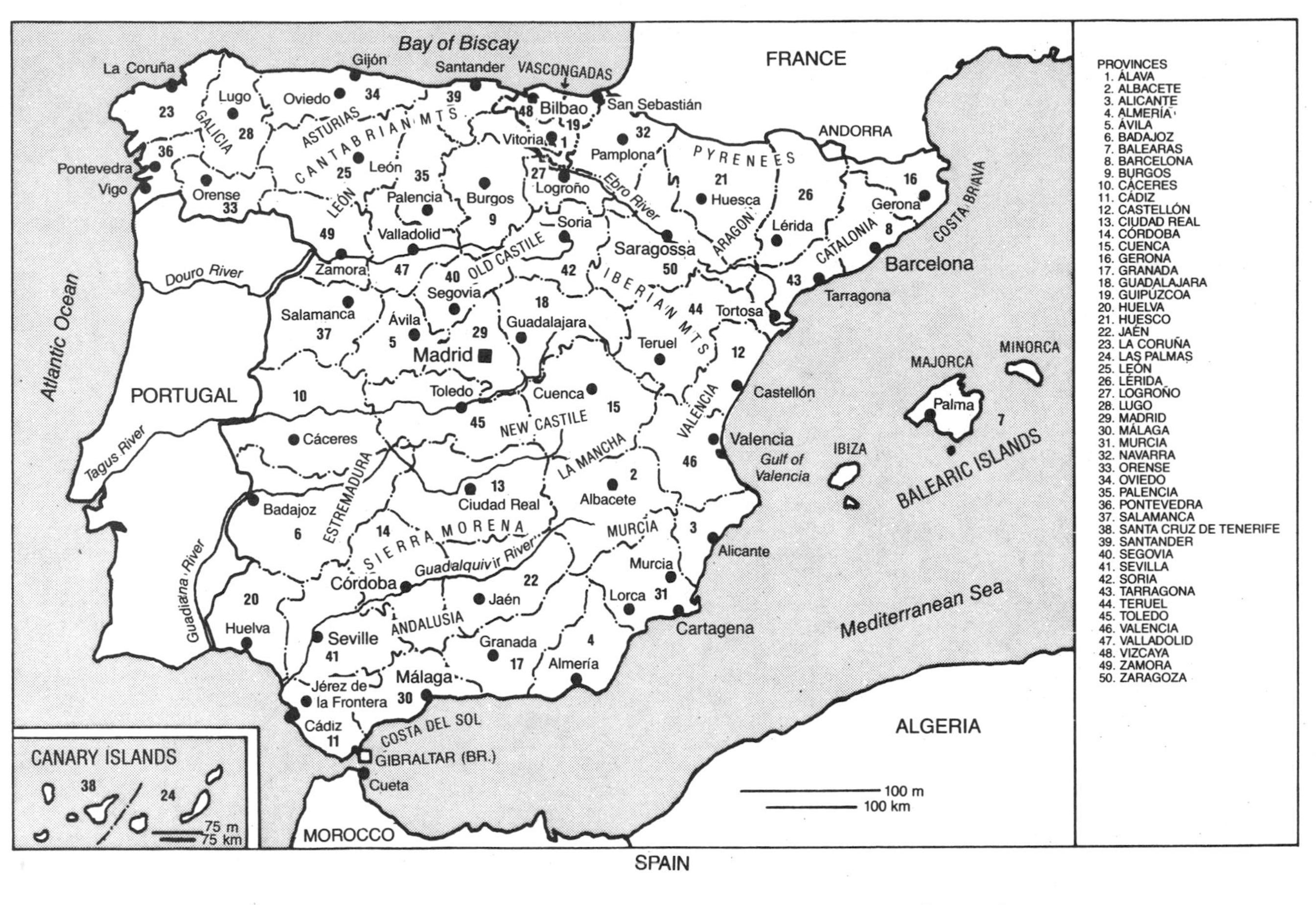

SPAIN

dence in 1976. (See also WESTERN SAHARA.)

Spark, Muriel (1918–). British novelist and story writer. Born and educated in Edinburgh, Scotland, Spark spent several years in Africa, the setting for many of her early short stories. Returning to Britain, she edited the Poetry Society's *Poetry Review* (1947–49). After winning the *Observer* fiction competition in 1951, she devoted herself to her writing. Her books, including *Memento Mori* (1959), *The Prime of Miss Jean Brodie* (1961, filmed 1969), *Loitering with Intent* (1981) and *A Far Cry from Kensington* (1988), are spare, witty and elegant, often tinged with surrealism, and reflect her concerns as a convert to Catholicism. Spark has also written poems and plays. In her later years she lived in Italy.

Spanish Republican planes bomb a rebel bridge over the Guadalquivir River (1936).

Sparkman, John J(ackson) (1899–1985). American politician. A Democrat from Alabama, Sparkman served in the U.S. House of Representatives for 10 years before winning a special election to the Senate in 1946. He supported the creation of the TENNESSEE VALLEY AUTHORITY, President Franklin D. ROOSEVELT'S NEW DEAL programs, and President Harry S TRUMAN'S FAIR DEAL proposals. However, he opposed most civil rights legislation. Sparkman was Adlai E. STEVENSON'S vice presidential running mate in the 1952 presidential election. Sparkman remained influential in the Senate until his retirement in 1979, chairing the important Senate Foreign Relations Committee as well as an earlier committee on banking, housing and urban affairs.

Sparkman & Stephens. U.S. firm of naval architects noted for the design of sailing yachts. The company was established in New York in 1928 by Olin and Roderick STEPHENS and Drake Sparkman. With Olin Stephens as its leading designer until his retirement in 1979, the firm designed many cruising and racing yachts, including a series of America's Cup winners. *Freedom,* a 135–foot luxury yacht built in Italy in 1986 with an all-aluminum hull, is a fine example of recent work of the firm.

Sparkman & Stephens designs have set a high standard in both performance and aesthetics for modern sailing craft.

Spartacists. Also known as the Spartacus Party, an organization of radical German socialists. Drawing its name from the leader of a Roman slave revolt, the group was founded in 1916 under the leadership of Karl Liebknecht and Rosa LUXEMBURG. They advocated a classical Marxist dictatorship of the proletariat, opposing the government of WILHELM II and, after the emperor's fall in 1918, the moderate socialist government that followed. They were active propagandists, occasionally engaging in acts of terrorism. The Spartacists became the new German Communist Party after a 1918–19 meeting. They organized a revolt and a general strike in Berlin early in 1919. It was quickly put down by military action and both Liebknecht and Luxemburg were arrested and killed.

Spassky, Boris (1937–). Russian journalist and chess player, he studied at the Leningrad State University faculty of journalism and worked as a trainer at the Leningrad section of the voluntary sport society. Spassky has played in numerous international chess tournaments; in 1956 he was the U.S.S.R. grand master, the international grand master and world chess student champion. He was world champion from 1969 to 1972.

Speaker, Tris(tram) (1888–1958). American baseball star. Considered one of baseball's all-around greats, especially in defense, Speaker began his professional career as an outfielder with the Boston Red Sox (1907–15), continuing with the Cleveland Indians (1916–26), then with Washington in 1927 and Philadelphia in 1928. His lifetime batting average was .344. He was elected to baseball's Hall of Fame in 1937.

Special Air Services [SAS]. Elite commando and anti-terrorist unit in the British Army. The Special Air Services evolved out of the World War II LONG-RANGE DESERT PATROL GROUP established by David STIRLING. Operating in tight secrecy during the 1980s the SAS was involved in hostage crises, seiges and raids on terrorist headquarters. In their most daring action on May 5, 1980 the SAS stormed the Iranian embassy in London, which had been taken over by terrorists, and rescued hostages held there. Members of the group took part in an 1987 ambush in NORTHERN IRELAND in which eight members of an IRA bombing squad were killed. The SAS was also responsible for the controversial killing in Gibraltar (March 6, 1988) of three unarmed IRA agents who were apparently planning to plant a bomb to kill British soldiers in the colony. Critics charged that the SAS operated as if it were above the law and said that the terrorists could have been arrested rather than shot. The group's motto is "Who Dares Wins."

special theory of relativity. See Albert EINSTEIN.

Speer, Albert (1905–1981). German architect and administrator who served as minister of armaments and war production in the government of Adolf HITLER during WORLD WAR II. As a young architect in BERLIN, Speer joined the NAZI Party in 1931. He was one of the few people to gain Hitler's complete confidence—possibly because Hitler himself had been an aspiring architect and regarded the young Speer as a son. Hitler appointed Speer his chief state architect. In this capacity, Speer undertook several massive building projects, designing the stadium where the NUREMBERG RALLIES were later held as well as the new chancellery building. In 1942, as the war began to turn against Germany, Speer was appointed minister of armaments and war production. Despite a shortage of labor, equipment and material, Speer actually managed to increase industrial output. After Hitler's suicide he served as economics minister in the short-lived interim government established (May 1945) by Admiral DOENITZ. In the NUREMBERG TRIALS (1946) Speer was charged with having used millions of people, including PRISONERS OF WAR, in forced labor. He pleaded guilty—the only important Nazi leader to do so. Sentenced to 20 years imprisonment, he served his full term in SPANDAU PRISON. After his release in 1966 he wrote three controversial books describing his experiences as Hitler's trusted confidante and his time in prison. In the first of these (*Inside the Third Reich*, 1970), he described his growing disillusionment with Hitler and disclosed his abortive attempt near the end of the war to assassinate the fuhrer. Readers sympathetic to Speer held him up as an example of how an intelligent and well-meaning person can be seduced by power. To his critics, however, Speer was merely a self-serving and manipulative opportunist whose war crimes were inexcusable.

Spellman, Francis J(oseph) (1889–1967). Roman Catholic cardinal and archbishop of New York. Spellman was the most visible and powerful Catholic clergyman in America from the 1940s through the 1960s. Ordained as a priest in 1916, he became archbishop of New York in 1939 and was elected to the college of cardinals in 1946. Highly conservative politically, Spellman was an outspoken supporter of Senator Joseph MCCARTHY, even after the latter's condemnation by the United States Senate in 1954. Spellman was also an ardent supporter of the Vietnam War, a stance that brought him into conflict with his superior, Pope PAUL VI.

Spence, (Sir) Basil (1907–1976). British architect. Spence remains best known for his designing of the rebuilt Coventry Cathedral—a design that was commissioned in 1951 and completed in 1962. Spence retained the steeple of the original cathedral as the only major vertical ascent in his design, which included much creative integration of older sections of the cathedral as well as modern touches such as sawtooth-styled side walls. Spence first came to prominence in the 1930s as a designer of large country houses in Scotland. In the final decades of his life, Spence and his architectural firm specialized in university site projects and also designed the chancellery of the British Embassy in Rome (1971).

Spencer, (Sir) Stanley (1891–1959). English painter. Spencer is one of the major figures in 20th-century British painting. His canvasses, which often deal with spiritual themes, have been compared—in terms of their simplicity and luminosity—to the pictorial works of William Blake. Spencer studied art in the Slade School in London and was an official war artist for the British government in both WORLD WAR I and WORLD WAR II. His most famous painting is *The Resurrection: Cookham* (1924), which utilizes his native village as the setting for the resurrection of Christ. In the 1930s, Spencer earned the ire of the British public for a series of erotically explicit canvasses. His younger brother Gilbert was also a painter.

Spender, Sir Stephen (Harold) (1909–). British poet, editor, literary journalist, critic and translator. While a student at Oxford, Spender came under the influence of AUDEN. In 1930 he accompanied ISHERWOOD to Germany; *Poems* appeared in 1933. Spender was the most politically-active member of the Thirties Generation, and his writings reflected his belief in the coming of a new world order. *Forward from Liberalism* (1937) argued for COMMUNISM as a means of defeating FASCISM in Europe. In 1939–41 he served as editor, with Cyril CONNOLLY, of *Horizon;* from 1953–67 he was an editor of *Encounter.* After World War II he published little poetry, and overall his reputation as an intellectual has overshadowed his poetry. In 1962 he was made a CBE (Commander, Order of the British Empire).

For further reading:

Weatherhead, A.K., *Stephen Spender and the Thirties.* Lewisburg, Pa.: Bucknell University Press, 1975.

Spengler, Oswald (1880–1936). German historian and philosopher. Spengler was one of the most influential historians of this century. He achieved international recognition and a wide readership upon the publication in two volumes of his magnum opus, THE DECLINE OF THE WEST (1918, 1922). Spengler taught at numerous German universities. Despite his aversion to the Nazi movement, Spengler was falsely hailed as a precursor of Nazi philosophy by Josef GOEBBELS.

Spielberg, Steven (1947–). American filmmaker. Spielberg began making short films in 8mm at age 10 and by the age of 16 had made *Firelight*, a prototype of the later *Close Encounters of the Third Kind* (1977). After haunting the precincts of UNIVERSAL Studios he won the support of a producer to make a 20–minute short, *Amblin,* whose success got him a contract to direct episodes for the television series "Colombo" and "Night Gallery." His television movie *Duel* (1971) was shot in only 16 days and was hailed by critic Pauline Kael "one of the most phenomenal debut films in the history of the movies." Spielberg's major films are distinguished by a staggering camera tech-

Film director Steven Spielberg (1989).

nique and uncanny ability to cut on action. The early works are essentially chase films: the Texas police chase of Goldie Hawn in *Sugarland Express* (1974); the stalking of a small boat by a Great White shark in *Jaws* (1975). And everybody chases everybody in the three "Indiana Jones" films. In such later works as *The Color Purple* (1985) and *Empire of the Sun* (1987) Spielberg shows more attention to integrating character and relationships into the action. As a producer, he has had a magic touch with successes like the three *Back to the Future* pictures, *Poltergeist* (1982) and THE TWILIGHT ZONE (1983), his tribute to the classic television series (for which he directed the "Kick the Can" segment). The riotous *Who Framed Roger Rabbit?* (1988), produced by Spielberg in association with Walt Disney Studios, combined live actors with animated characters. Although justly renowned for such virtuoso sequences as the toys running amok in E.T. and the jitterbug dance in *1941*, Spielberg can also deliver effective, quiet moments—like the chilling "shark monologue" of Robert Shaw in *Jaws* and the whimsical "trick-or-treat" scene in *E.T.*

For further reading:

Sinyard, Neil, *The Films of Steven Spielberg*. London: Bison Books, 1986.

Spillane, Mickey [Frank Morrison] (1918–). American writer. Spillane began his career while still in college, as a contributor to pulp magazines. He went on to redefine the detective genre with his hard-boiled heroes Mike Hammer and Tiger Mann. Sexist, sadistic and crude, the books found an audience around the world. His works include the best-selling *I, the Jury* (1947), *My Gun Is Quick* (1950) and *Kiss Me Deadly* (1952). In later years, Spillane became something of a personality and star of award-winning beer commercials.

Spitfire. Famous single-engine propeller fighter plane designed by Reginald MITCHELL in the 1930s and used by the Royal Air Force (RAF) to defend the UNITED KINGDOM during the BATTLE OF BRITAIN in WORLD WAR II.

Spitsbergen. Large island and archipelago north of the Arctic Circle and 360 miles north of NORWAY; officially became a part of Norway on August 14, 1925. Arctic explorers like NOBILE and BYRD used Spitsbergen as a jumping-off point for many of their expeditions.

Spitz, Mark Andrew (1950–). U.S. swimmer. Arguably the greatest swimmer of all time, Spitz set 35 world records. A dedicated swimmer from a young age, early in his career he was frequently booed by his own teammates for his conceit. He won five gold medals in the 1967 Pan American Games and made a respectable showing in the 1968 Olympic Games, with two gold team medals and individual medals for second and third. He perfected his style while on the team at Indiana University and led that team to four national championships from 1969 to 1972. In the 1972 Olympic Games, he won an astonishing seven gold medals. In the late 1980s, he began preparing for an Olympic comeback.

Spock, Benjamin (McLaine) (1903–). American pediatrician, psychiatrist and antiwar activist; studied medicine at Yale and Columbia in the 1930s and served as a U.S. Navy psychiatrist during World War II. Spock achieved nationwide fame with the publication of his immensely influential *The Common Sense Book of Baby and Child Care* (1946), which has since been republished in numerous editions and stands as the all-time best-selling book by an American author. In the 1960s, Spock became national cochairman of the Committee for a Sane Nuclear Policy (SANE) and actively opposed the VIETNAM WAR. In 1968, Spock and other defendants were charged with conspiracy to aid and abet draft evaders. After a highly publicized trial, the case against Spock was ultimately dismissed. In 1972, Spock ran for president as the candidate of the pacifist People's Party. Spock's autobiography is *Spock on Spock: A Memoir of Growing Up with the Century* (1989).

American swimmer Mark Spitz at the 1972 Summer Olympics.

Spoleto Festivals (Italy and USA). The Festival of Two Worlds in Spoleto, Italy was founded by composer Gian Carlo MENOTTI in 1958. One of the most comprehensive international arts festivals, it is held annually from late June to mid-July and presents all types of music, ballet, theater, art exhibitions and poetry readings. The festival has gained a reputation for providing a venue for new talent, such as composer Nino ROTA who premiered his opera *Napoli Milonaria* there. In 1977 Menotti founded the *Second World* festival—Spoleto Festival USA—in Charleston, South Carolina. Held annually from late May to early June, this international festival is also devoted to all the arts. Performers who have appeared there include vocalist Johanna Meier, conductor Clayton Westerman and the Dance Theater of Harlem.

Springer, Axel (1912–1985). West German publisher. Springer headed Axel Springer Verlag, one of Western Europe's biggest publishing empires. The group's flagship newspapers were the conservative *Die Welt* and *Bild Zeitung*, a sensational tabloid with the largest circulation in Western Europe. The company also published magazines and books and in the mid-1980s began to branch out into television. Known for his strong opposition to communism and left-wing terrorism, Springer was a strong proponent of German reunification and an outspoken friend of Israel.

Springsteen, Bruce (1949–). American rock-and-roll singer, composer, guitarist, and band leader. Springsteen is one of the most passionate and popular performers in the history of ROCK AND ROLL. Raised in New Jersey, he played in bar bands in his home state and in New York City before being signed to a contract by Columbia Records producer John HAMMOND in 1972. Springsteen's first album, *Greetings from Asbury Park, New Jersey* (1973), earned him critical comparisons to Bob DYLAN but was not a great commercial success. With the album *Born To Run* (1975), Springsteen found a wide audience for himself and his now consolidated back-up group, the E Street Band, featuring guitarist Steve Van Zandt and saxophonist Clarence Clemons. Springsteen has been a steady hit-maker ever since, with albums including *The River* (1980), *Nebraska* (1982), *Born in the U.S.A.* (1985) and *Tunnel of Love* (1989). In 1989 Springsteen finally broke with the E Street Band. Critics and fans alike are awaiting the new Springsteen sound of the 1990s.

Spruance, Raymond Ames (1886–1969). U.S. Navy officer. He earned his commission at Annapolis in 1906. After meritorious service at the battle of MIDWAY during WORLD WAR II, he commanded the invasion of the MARSHALL ISLANDS. He retired from the Navy as an admiral and commander-in-chief of the Pacific fleet.

Sputnik. First artificial satellite, launched by the Soviet Union. The Soviet news agency Tass astounded the world by announcing on October 5, 1957, that the U.S.S.R. had successfully launched "the first artificial earth satellite" on the previous day. *Sputnik* whose Russian name means "something that is traveling with a traveler" (the traveler in this case being the earth), was a 23-inch aluminum sphere weighing 184 pounds and fitted with four steel antennae emitting continuous radio signals on two frequencies over the next 21 days. It traveled at approximately 18,000 miles per hour in its orbit about 560 miles above the earth's surface.

Despite the satellite's minute size, *Sputnik*'s effects were far reaching. The launching deeply wounded Western pride, especially since *Sputnik* was nine times heavier and orbited twice as high as the Vanguard Project satellite then under development in the U.S. It also resulted in an unprecedented emphasis on science in education and defense, as American policymakers sought to regain technological superiority over the Soviet Union. In reaction to the *Sputnik* launching, President EISENHOWER signed into law in July 1958 legislation for the creation of a National Space and Aeronautics Agency, thereby joining the "space race" that culminated with the American landing of a man on the moon in July 1969.

The Soviet Union followed up the success of *Sputnik 1* with the launching of the 1,121-pound *Sputnik 2*, containing a small dog, on November 3, 1957; the dog, named LAIKA, survived in space for ten days, proving that living organisms could survive in that environment. (See also EXPLORER.)

***Spycatcher* affair.** See Peter WRIGHT.

Square Deal. President Theodore ROOSEVELT's personal political philosophy that later became the platform of the Progressive Party. Roosevelt stood for American citizenship and patriotism, family values, hard work and material success and also Christian brotherhood. TR first used the phrase "square deal" during a tour of the West, and it almost immediately became a popular expression.

Sri Lanka [Democratic Socialist Republic of Sri Lanka]. Sri Lanka—one large island and several smaller islets collectively called Adam's Bridge—is located off the southeast coast of the Indian subcontinent and covers a total land area of 25,325 square miles. Originally called **Ceylon,** the island country was ruled by Britain until achieving independence in 1948. Sri Lanka's history has been dominated by conflicts between the Hindu Tamils of the north and the Buddhist Sinhalese of the south. The Tamil minority suffered repression during the 1950s, while riots in 1977 left many dead. Ceylon changed its name to Sri Lanka and became a republic in 1972. A state of emergency has existed since 1983 because of Tamil guerrillas fighting to force creation of a separate Tamil state. With the agreement of the Sri Lankan government, INDIA sent forces into Tamil territory to subdue the rebellion in 1987, withdrawing in 1990.

SS [*Schutzstaffel*]. Elite military corps of the NAZI Party. The SS was created in 1925 through the merger of Hitler's shock troops, the *Stosstuppe,* and a right-wing guard organization called the *Stabswache.* At first a small group that protected Nazi leaders and defended the Party against attack, it was vastly enlarged and turned into a rigorously disciplined force under the leadership of Heinrich HIMMLER, who became its head in 1929. Under Himmler, membership in the SS grew to 50,000 and they adopted the infamous uniforms with their runic double-"S," death's head insignias and black shirts. In 1934 the SS destroyed Ernst ROEHM's Storm Troops (*Sturm Abteilung,* or SA) in the bloody "NIGHT OF THE LONG KNIVES." After this purge, the SS became Germany's major police force and by 1939 the country was divided into various SS areas, each under the direction of an SS officer-police chief. As WORLD WAR II progressed, the SS became increasingly powerful, with the extermination of the Jews and other "enemies of the Reich," the supervision of imported forced laborers and the running of CONCENTRATION CAMPS all under SS control. In addition, the SS had special units known as the *Waffen* SS within the regular German military forces. Noted for their reckless bravery and ruthless brutality, at the height of the war they numbered 38 divisions with some 900,000 men.

SST [supersonic transport]. Although Chuck YEAGER broke the sound barrier in 1947, the first supersonic passenger jet did not enter service until 30 years later. A U.S. SST project was cancelled in 1971 because of lack of government funds; the Soviet Tupolev Tu-144, which entered service in 1977, was withdrawn from service in 1983 because of financial and technical problems. The Anglo-French *Concorde* flies on London-Washington and Paris-Washington routes operated by British Airways and Air France, respectively. The *Concorde*'s top speed is over 1,500 mph; it makes the transatlantic flight in under 4 hours.

Stafford, Jean (1915–1979). American novelist and short story writer. Raised in Colorado, Stafford later lived in Boston. She won a PULITZER PRIZE (1970) for her *Collected Stories*. She was the first wife (1940–48) of the poet Robert LOWELL.

Stafford, Thomas (1930–). U.S. astronaut. The soft-spoken Stafford, nicknamed "Mumbles" by his fellow astronauts, made four space flights between 1965 and 1975. His missions included copiloting Gemini 6-A (December 15–16, 1965) with Walter Schirra; commanding Gemini 9-A (June 3–6, 1966) with Eugene Cernan; commanding Apollo 10 (May 18–26, 1969) with Cernan and John Young; and commanding the American participants in the APOLLO-SOYUZ link-up mission (July 15–24, 1975). He logged over 21 days in space.

Stagg, Amos Alonzo (1862–1965). American football's "Grand Old Man." Stagg coached football at the University of CHICAGO for 41 years. After he retired from the Chicago post at the age of 70, he coached at the College of the Pacific from 1933 to 1946 and at Susquehanna University from 1947 to 1952. Stagg developed many new football techniques, including the tackling dummy. He became even more famous as the oldest active coach in the United States and as the coach with the greatest number of coaching seasons.

Stalin, Joseph Vissarionovich (Dzhugashvili) (1879–1953). Dictator of the U.S.S.R. and leader of the world communist movement. Along with his near-contemporary Adolf HITLER, Stalin stands as one of the most ruthless and destructive figures of the 20th century. During his rule, Stalin's reach extended into virtually every aspect of life in the Soviet Union, and millions of Soviet citizens perished as a result of Stalin's decrees. The son of a Georgian shoemaker, he was

SRI LANKA

1948	Independence; newly formed state under United National Party (UNP) strips 800,000 Tamil plantation workers (of Indian origin) of citizenship and suffrage rights.
1954	Sri Lankan Freedom Party (SLFP) demands Sinhala be made country's sole official language and its united front organization—Mahajana Eksath Peramuna (MEP)—wins majority in National Assembly; proclamation of Sinhala as official language met with wave of Tamil civil disobedience; violent anti-Tamil pogroms follow.
1972	Ceylon renamed Sri Lanka.
1983	State of emergency declared in response to mounting security threats posed by Tamil guerrillas fighting for a separate state—Eelam—in the north and east of island.
1987	Unable to overcome militant Tamil groups, most importantly the Liberation Tigers of Tamil Eelam (LTTE), the Sri Lankan government allows Indian forces to enter the north and east regions of the country to disarm and quell rebels.
1990	After protracted dispute over formula for withdrawal of Indian troops policing Tamil areas, India finally withdraws; hundreds die in ethnic violence as civil war continues.

SRI LANKA

RYKOV's help he defeated Zinoviev and Kamenev in the struggle for power. MOLOTOV, VOROSHILOV, Kaganovich, Ordzhonikidze and KIROV then helped him to defeat Bukharin and Rykov's RIGHT OPPOSITION. From 1929 to 1934 he ruled with them, assuming the position of leader until they opposed him. This provided the catalyst for abandoning collective leadership and for instigating the GREAT PURGE. With Stalin as official head of government in 1940 and chairman of the state defense committee, a reign of terror ensued.

Stalin's refusal to believe numerous intelligence reports of an impending German invasion in 1941 gave Hitler's armies a toll-free ticket that led them to the outskirts of Moscow and ensured a long and bitter war. Generalissimo during WORLD WAR II, he outwitted CHURCHILL and ROOSEVELT. He became increasingly obsessed with problems of security. He was jealous, anti-Semitic, chauvinistic and xenophobic, while demanding to be treated as a virtual demigod by all. He died in 1953, just as he was launching another purge. (See also DOCTORS' PLOT.)

For further reading:

Laqueur, Walter, *Stalin: The Glasnost Revelations.* New York: Scribners/Stewart, 1990.

Tucker, Robert C., *Stalin in Power: The Revolution from Above, 1928–1941.* New York: W.W. Norton, 1990.

Stalingrad, Siege of (1942–43). In May and June of 1942 German tanks, dive-bombers and other forces were approaching the lower Volga River and the Caucasus. Having crossed the Don River, they reached the outskirts of Stalingrad and besieged the city. By mid-November 1942, the British victory at EL ALAMEIN and the Allied pursuit of the defeated Germans resulted in no more reinforcements for the German army near Stalingrad. Fresh Russian reinforcements were brought in, and on November 20 Yeremenko broke the enemy line. The Russians launched a great thrust from the north, and Marshal von Manstein was forced to retreat. The encircled Germans under General von Paulus surrendered on February 2, 1943, having sustained a loss of 200,000 men. (See also WORLD WAR II ON THE RUSSIAN FRONT.)

For further reading:

Craig, William, *Enemy at the Gates.* New York: Ballantine, 1974.

Stalinism. Name given to Stalin's political theorizing and rule of the U.S.S.R., the

German troops invade Stalin's Soviet Union.

expelled from the Tbilisi Theological Seminary in 1898, as a result of his interest in the revolutionary movement. He then joined the Russian Social Democratic Party and, in 1903, its BOLSHEVIK faction. Having worked in the underground movement in Transcaucasia, he was made part of the Bolshevik central committee by LENIN and ZINOVIEV. Banished to Petrograd after the February Revolution of 1917, Stalin edited the party's newspaper, *Pravda*. Stalin served as commissar for nationalities and commissar for worker-peasant inspection (1919–23) and became a very close collaborator of Lenin. During the CIVIL WAR he served as a commissar for nationalities.

In 1922 he was appointed secretary-general of the central committee, although Lenin, nurturing misgivings about Stalin's suitability for this position, was planning to remove him from it. Lenin's death prevented this, and Stalin's political career continued unchecked. Together with Zinoviev and KAMENEV he defeated TROTSKY, and then with BUKHARIN and

Eastern European Bloc countries and the world communist movement. Based on Marxism, Leninism and national Bolshevism, STALIN with the help of MOLOTOV, ZHDANOV and VYSHINSKY added such doctrines and ideas as the existence of the state under full communism, SOCIALIST REALISM in the arts, the concept of building socialism in one country, the people's great love for the Communist Party, their unanimous support of Stalin, and the security organs to eliminate "misguided" dissenters. CONCENTRATION CAMPS were much in use, especially during Stalin's GREAT PURGE. Some aspects of Stalinism became obsolete, particularly after KHRUSHCHEV's secret report to the 20th Party Congress; others, such as the role of the Communist Party, remained. Forms of Stalinism were practiced by communist leaders in several eastern-bloc countries, including Enver HOXHA of ALBANIA and Nicolae CEAUSESCU of ROMANIA.

For further reading:

Medvedev, Roy, *Let History Judge: The Origins and Consequences of Stalinism,* rev. ed. New York: Columbia University Press, 1990.

Tucker, Robert C., *Stalin in Power: The Revolution from Above.* New York: W. W. Norton, 1990.

Stambolisky, Alexander (1879–1923). Bulgarian political leader. Born into a well-to-do peasant family, Stambolisky studied agriculture in Germany and became a leader of the Agrarian Party. Leading the opposition to Czar FERDINAND, he was imprisoned during World War I for his opposition to Bulgaria's entry into the war as an ally of Germany. After his release he served as president of a short-lived republic (1918). When BORIS III succeeded Ferdinand, Stambolisky became premier (1919) and by the following year he had become the virtual dictator of Bulgaria. Hostile to both liberal and communist doctrine, he instituted a peasant dictatorship and embarked on a campaign of agrarian reform. He was assassinated in a 1923 coup by right-wing forces who opposed his associations with Yugoslavia.

Stanford-Tuck, Robert (Roland) (1916–1987). British airman. A celebrated WORLD WAR II flying ace, Stanford-Tuck became a highly decorated wing commander by the time he was 25. He fought the German Luftwaffe in the 1940 BATTLE OF BRITAIN. Shot down over occupied FRANCE in 1942, he remained a German PRISONER OF WAR until early 1945. After his retirement from the Royal Air Force in 1949, he pursued a career in mushroom farming.

Stanislavsky, Konstantin Sergeyevich (1865–1938). Russian director, actor, teacher. One of the great theorists of 20th-century theater, Stanislavsky influenced theater worldwide with his emphasis on a realistic acting style and naturalism in scenic design. In the U.S. his theories on acting led to the development of method acting. Initially an actor, he became cofounder of the Society of Literature and Art in 1888, then cofounder of the Moscow Art Theater in 1898. He achieved his first success as a director in 1891 with a production of Leo Tolstoy's *The Fruits of Enlightenment.* His greatest triumphs were as director of the plays of CHEKHOV. His influence outside Russia came primarily as a result of his books, including *An Actor Prepares* (1926) and *Building a Character,* and the teachers trained by him.

For further reading:

Benedetti, Jean, *Stanislavski.* New York: Routledge, 1988.

Stanwyck, Barbara [born Ruby Stevens] (1907–1990). American actress. Stanwyck appeared in more than 80 films, playing a variety of strong-minded, warm-hearted women. They included classic films such as *Stella Dallas* (1937), *The Lady Eve* (1941), *Double Indemnity* (1944) and *Sorry, Wrong Number* (1948). At the height of her film career, in 1944, the Bureau of Internal Revenue listed her $400,000 as the highest of any woman in the U.S. One of the first films stars to make the transition to television, she portrayed Victoria Barkley, in the "Big Valley" western series from 1965 to 1969, and won three Emmy Awards for her work. Although she never won any of the four Academy awards for which she had been nominated, she was given an honorary ACADEMY AWARD in 1982.

Stargell, Willie [Wilver Dornell Stargell] (1940–). American baseball player. A member of the Pittsburgh Pirates for 20 years, Stargell began a string of 13 consecutive home run seasons in 1976. A seven-time All Star, his best season came in 1979 as he led the Pirates to World Series victory, batting .400, with three home runs. He shared regular season National League Most Valuable Player honors, but stood alone as League Championship Series MVP and World Series MVP. A fearsome power hitter, he was responsible for the only two blasts ever to sail completely out of Dodger Stadium. He was named to the Hall of Fame in 1988.

Stark, Harold R. (1880–1972). American admiral. Stark was chief of naval operations in the Pacific at the time of the Japanese attack on PEARL HARBOR (December 7, 1941). He was relieved of his command and made commander of U.S. forces in European waters.

Starker, Janos (1924–). Hungarian-American cellist. Born in Budapest, Starker began playing the cello at the age of seven, later studying at the Franz Liszt Academy. After service in World War II, he was named (1945) principal cellist of the Budapest Philharmonic and the Budapest Opera Orchestra. He left Hungary the following year, touring throughout Europe, and immigrated to the U.S. in 1948. There he became first cellist for the Dallas Symphony (1948–49), the Metropolitan Opera Orchestra (1949–53) and the Chicago Symphony (1953–58). In 1958 he left orchestral playing in order to concentrate on his career as a soloist, and he also became a professor of music at Indiana University. Starker made his New York debut in 1960, and has since appeared throughout the world, averaging some 80 concerts a year. Known for his tonal richness and fine musicianship, he has largely concentrated on the works of Bach, Beethoven and Brahms and has performed a good deal of modern music.

START [Strategic Arms Reduction Talks]. Long-term, ongoing negotiations between the UNITED STATES and the UNION OF SOVIET SOCIALIST REPUBLICS, concerning nuclear armaments, bombers, ballistic missiles and space weapons (see STRATEGIC DEFENSE INITIATIVE). The fourth round of START was held in GENEVA, Switzerland in 1986. Although Mikhail GORBACHEV's proposal for a worldwide ban on all nuclear weapons by the year 2000 was rejected, by 1991 much progress had been made toward arms reduction.

Star Wars. Popular name (often with derisive connotations) for the STRATEGIC DEFENSE INITIATIVE (SDI) proposed by U.S. President Ronald REAGAN in 1983; the name is derived from a popular 1977 science fiction film of the same title.

Stassen, Harold Edward (1907–). Former Minnesota governor, candidate for the Republican nomination for president in 1948, 1952 and 1964. Continuing, as late as 1988, to announce his candidacy for the top post—without much hope of selection—he became known as the "perennial candidate." Stassen was an attorney in Dakota County before being elected governor of Minnesota in 1938. He was reelected twice and resigned early in this third term to serve in the Navy. While governor, Stassen gained national attention by supporting a labor law that provided a "cooling-off" period before striking. After service in WORLD WAR II Stassen was a delegate to the conference in San Francisco that founded the UNITED NATIONS. He was appointed president of the University of Pennsylvania in 1948. He served until 1953 when he resigned to serve as a mutual security administrator and then as a foreign operations administrator, controlling American aid to many countries. Stassen attempted to win the nomination for governor of Pennsylvania in 1958, but lost. In 1987, at the age of 80, Stassen again announced his intention to run for the presidency, in 1988, but made little headway beyond the announcement.

State Conference in Moscow. Conference convened by Alexander KERENSKY in order to unite the state power with all organized forces in the country. Over 2,000 people were invited from different sectors of the population. It opened on August 25, 1917, at the Bolshoi Theater. The conference met with BOLSHEVIK disapproval, and the main result of the conference was to sharply split the revolutionaries into left and right.

states' rights. A doctrine whereby the states claimed all powers not reserved by the U.S. Constitution for the federal government. The assertion of this doctrine caused many clashes between the states and the federal government, culminating in the Civil War of 1861–1865. The states based their claim on the Tenth Amendment, which states, "The powers not delegated to the United States by the Constitution, nor prohibited by it to the States, are reserved to the States respectively, or to the people."

The defeat of the Confederacy effectively crushed the doctrine of states' rights, although it resurfaced in the 20th century during the period of desegregation in the 1950s and 1960s. State governors such as Orval E. FAUBUS of Arkansas and George C. WALLACE of Alabama made states' rights statements, and Southern state legislatures passed a number of laws to try to circumvent federal desegregation policies. During this period federal troops were called out several times to assist the desegregation process. Although over 200 years the U.S. government has effectively consolidated its power, it is unlikely that the concept of states' rights will ever completely disappear.

Statute of Westminster. British statute adopted in 1931 delineating the status of dominions. Responding to resolutions of the Imperial Conferences of 1926 and 1930 brought about by stirrings of independence in the Commonwealth, the Statute of Westminster decreed that dominions were, "autonomous communities . . . united by a common allegiance to the Crown, and freely associated as members of the British COMMONWEALTH OF NATIONS."

Stauffenberg, Count Claus Schenk von (1907–1944). German aristocrat and military officer. A staff officer in WORLD WAR II, Stauffenberg was wounded in battle and considered a genuine war hero. Disillusioned with Adolf HITLER's leadership as Germany's situation in the war became desperate, Stauffenberg took the leading role in the July 20, 1944 attempt to assassinate the fuhrer. After the bomb he had planted failed to kill Hitler, Stauffenberg himself was executed by German soldiers.

Stavisky Affair. French financial scandal of 1933–1934. In December 1933 the financier Serge Alexandre Stavisky was found to have been issuing worthless bonds for the municipal pawnshop of Bayonne. He fled to Chamonix, where he committed suicide in January 1934. After his death it was widely alleged that he had been protected by corrupt and influential officials and the premier, Camille Chautemps, was forced to resign. Rightist groups such as the ACTION FRANCAISE continued to agitate, alleging that Stavisky had been murdered in a government cover-up. Bloody rioting broke out in Paris in February 1934, toppling the government of Edouard DALADIER, and was followed by a general strike. The threatened Third Republic was saved by the formation of a coalition by Gaston Doumergue (1863–1937). However, the scandal had the effect of bringing the republic and the parliamentary form of government itself into lasting disrepute and of fostering right-wing ideology in France.

Stead, Christina Ellen (1902–1983). Australian novelist. Born and educated in Australia, Stead moved to London in 1928, and later traveled and lived in Europe and America with the American political economist William J. Blake, whom she eventually married. She returned to Australia permanently in 1974. Stead's first work was the collection of gothic stories, *The Salzburg Tales* (1934), but it is for the acclaimed novel, *The Man Who Loved Children* (1940), a sardonic portrait of an American family, that she is best known. Other novels include *House of All Nations* (1938), *Dark Places in the Heart* (1966, published in Britain as *Cotter's England*, 1967); and *Miss Herbert (The Suburban Wife*, 1976). Her fiction reflects her left-wing and feminist viewpoints, as well as her abhorrence of the tyranny of egotism.

Stealth. Term used to describe military aircraft (both fighters and bombers) designed so that they are virtually undetectable by enemy RADAR. The U.S. military began developing Stealth technology in the 1970s, during the CARTER administration. The Stealth program was top secret, and the first Stealth aircraft—the B-2 bomber, designed and manufactured by Northrop—was not seen by the public until 1988. Stealth aircraft saw their first wartime use during the PERSIAN GULF WAR (1991), in which the U.S. Air Force flew 40 Lockheed F-117A Stealth fighter-bombers in combat without a single loss.

Steber, Eleanor (1914–1990). American singer. An outstanding soprano with the Metropolitan Opera (MET) during the 1940s and 1950s, Steber also gave recitals in the U.S. and Europe and appeared at the major European music festivals. She made her Met debut as Sophie in *Der Rosenkavalier* in 1940, and became particularly noted for her roles in such Mozart operas as *The Marriage of Figaro* and *The Magic Flute*. She also starred in revivals of the musicals *Where's Charley?* and *The Sound of Music* (1966–67) at Lincoln Center for the Performing Arts, and conducted master voice classes at the Juilliard School of Music, among other schools.

Steel, David (Martin Scott) (1938–). British politician. Steel, a Scot, entered Parliament in 1965 as a Liberal, representing Roxburgh, Scotland. He succeeded Jeremy THORPE as LIBERAL PARTY leader in 1976. Steel formed an agreement with the Labour government in 1977 and 1978 (the "Lib-Lab Pact"), and an alliance with the SOCIAL DEMOCRATIC PARTY (SDP) in 1983. He was strongly in favor of his party's decision to merge with the SDP (1987), and stepped down in 1988 to allow new leadership for the new party.

Steeleye Span. British folk-rock group formed in 1968; members were Tim Hart, guitar and dulcimer, Ashley Hutchings, bass, Maddy Prior and Gay Woods, vocals, and Terry Woods, guitar, mandolin and vocals. The band's pedigree was similar to that of other successful folk-rock groups of the time, including FAIRPORT CONVENTION. Steeleye Span achieved a high level of commercial success for a folk-oriented group, even as their personnel shifted with virtually every album. Their best-selling albums came in the mid-'70s, and included *Below the Salt*, *Parcel of Rogues* and *Now We Are Six*.

Steffens, (Joseph) Lincoln (1866–1936). American journalist and autobiographer. Steffens was one of the most influential American journalists in the first three decades of the 20th century. He first came to national prominence in the 1900s as a leading investigative reporter of the type labeled—in a speech by a displeased President Theodore ROOSEVELT—as "muckrakers." Steffens, while writing for the *New York Post* and other publications in the 1900s, focused on political corruption in American cities. He published three influential books on this theme: *The Shame of the Cities* (1904), *The Struggle for Self-Government* (1906) and *The Upbuilders* (1909). In the 1910s and 1920s, Steffens traveled widely and worked as a foreign correspondent. Late in life he wrote his *Autobiography* (1931), which is still regarded as an American classic in that genre.

Steichen, Edward (1879–1973). American photographer, one of the American pioneers of photography practiced as a conscious art form. An early associate of photographer Alfred STIEGLITZ, Steichen was also the brother-in-law of poet Carl SANDBURG. In the 1900s, Steichen contributed celebrity photographic portraits—e.g., tycoon J.P. Morgan—to various periodicals. In the 1920s and 1930s, he broadened his focus to include fashion photography for *Vogue* and *Vanity Fair*.

Photographer Edward Steichen positions himself for a shot during World War II (c.1943).

From 1947 to 1962, he served as director of the department of photography of the New York-based Museum of Modern Art. It was there, in 1955, that Steichen organized the famous photographic exhibit *The Family of Man* (also published in book form).

Stein, Gertrude (1874–1946). American author and patron of the arts. Born in Pennsylvania and educated at Radcliffe, Stein studied under William JAMES and George SANTAYANA. In 1902 she moved to Paris, where she began collecting the works of young artists. She established an artistic and literary salon at her home in the rue de Fleurs, where artists Pablo PICASSO, Henri MATISSE, and Juan GRIS and writers Ernest HEMINGWAY, Sherwood ANDERSON and Ford Maddox FORD among others frequently gathered during the 1920s and '30s. In 1907 she met Alice B. Toklas, who became her life-long companion and secretary. Stein later wrote *The Autobiography of Alice B. Toklas* (1933), Stein's own memoirs written as if by Toklas herself. Stein's first novel, which she wrote during the period when she sat for Picasso's portrait of her, was *Three Lives* (1907). Other works include *The Making of Americans* (1945), an attempt at the history of her family; *Tender Buttons* (1914), a poetic work in her repetitive, STREAM-OF-CONSCIOUSNESS style; *Wars I Have Seen* (1945), a description of occupied Paris during WORLD WAR II; and a play, *Four Saints in Three Acts*. Though remembered almost as much for who she was as for what she wrote, Stein was an important innovator in the use of language and a major practitioner of literary MODERNISM. She coined the famous phrase "the lost generation."

For further reading:

Brinnin, John Malcolm, *The Third Rose: Gertrude Stein and Her World*, Reading, Mass.: Addison-Wesley, 1987.

Steinbeck, John (Ernst) (1902–1968). American novelist, story writer, playwright, essayist and screenplay writer. Steinbeck, who won the NOBEL PRIZE for literature in 1962, was a prolific, versatile and moving writer. He is best remembered for *The Grapes of Wrath* (1939), a novel widely considered to be a 20th-century classic. Set largely in the Oklahoma dustbowl during the GREAT DEPRESSION of the 1930s, *The Grapes of Wrath* recounts the efforts of the impoverished Joad family to move to California in hopes of a better life. Steinbeck studied at Stanford University, though he dropped out before earning a degree. His first novel was *Cup of Gold* (1929), but he first earned acclaim with *Tortilla Flat* (1935), set in the hills above Monterrey, California, a region Steinbeck also described in *Cannery Row* (1945). *Of Mice and Men* (1937), a novel about the sad lives of two migrant workers, one of whom is mentally retarded, was successfully adapted for the Broadway stage by Steinbeck in collaboration with George S. KAUFMAN. Steinbeck dealt with nature and ecology in *Sea of Cortez: A Leisurely Journal of Travel and Research* (1941). The novel *East of Eden* (1954) and the nonfiction *Travels With Charlie in Search of America* (1962) are the most famous of Steinbeck's later works.

Author Gertrude Stein on her 1935 visit to California.

Novelist John Steinbeck the day he won the Nobel Prize for literature in 1962.

Steinberg, William (1899–1978). German-American conductor. Born in Cologne, Steinberg was a musical prodigy on the violin and piano and made his first appearance as a conductor at thirteen. After studies at Cologne University, he became (1920) the assistant to Otto KLEMPERER. He conducted the German Theater, Prague (1925–29) and the Frankfurt Opera Orchestra (1929–33) before being forced out by the Nazis. In 1934 he assembled a group of other Jewish musicians into the Jewish Culture League and performed for Jewish audiences for the next two years. Leaving Germany in 1936, he fled to Palestine, where he assembled, trained and conducted the Palestine Symphony Orchestra (now the Israel Philharmonic). In 1937 Steinberg took the post of assistant to Arturo TOSCANINI at the NBC Symphony, and he became a U.S. citizen in 1944. He served as music director of the Buffalo Symphony Orchestra from 1945 to 1952 and of the Pittsburgh Symphony from 1952 to 1976, developing it into one of the country's most noted orchestras. Steinberg was known for his intensely precise musical interpretations and the pure beauty of his sound.

Steindler, Arthur (1878–1959). Austrian-born surgical pioneer, one of a pioneer team of medical men who made the Medical Center of the University of Iowa known worldwide for its excellence. Dr. Steindler became one of the world's most distinguished orthopedic specialists. He was responsible for the development of many of the techniques used universally today, including methods of bone care, treatment, straightening, grafting, lengthening and other orthopedic practices.

Steinem, Gloria (1934–). American feminist and magazine editor. Educated at Smith College, Steinem began her journalism career in the 1960s as a freelance writer for several New York-based magazines, including *Esquire, Vogue* and *New York*, for which she wrote a liberal political column, *The City Politic*, that first brought her national attention. By the late 1960s, Steinem was focusing on FEMINISM as her key political interest. In 1971, she was a founding member—along with Bella Abzug, Shirley Chisholm and Betty FRIEDAN—of the National Women's Political Caucus. That same year, Steinem was a key force behind the establishment of the Women's Action Alliance. In 1972, Steinem became editor of *Ms.* magazine, a major national feminist journal for which she has continued to edit and write. She has also become active as a patron and sponsor of feminist-inspired artistic, cultural and political events. (See also WOMEN'S MOVEMENTS.)

Steiner, Max (1888–1971). The dean of American film composers; his music for *Gone with the Wind* (1939) remains the most familiar of all movie scores. Born in Vienna, Austria, to a prosperous family (his father managed the prestigious Theater an der Wien), Steiner studied composition and orchestration with Felix WEINGARTNER and Gustav MAHLER at the Imperial Academy of Music. His interests in musical theater drew him to London, Paris and finally to New York in 1914. After 15 years orchestrating and conducting Broadway shows for Victor HERBERT, Jerome KERN and George GERSHWIN, he went to HOLLYWOOD in 1929 to adapt Ziegfeld's *Rio Rita* to the screen. At RKO, in addition to arranging such musicals as the Fred ASTAIRE-Ginger ROGERS series, he composed his first important film scores for *Bird of Paradise* (1932) and *King Kong* (1933). His most productive period was at WARNER BROTHERS, where he averaged eight scores a year (150 films in all), including many of the Humphrey BOGART, Errol FLYNN and Bette DAVIS vehicles. He won ACADEMY AWARDS for his music for

The Informer (1935), *Now, Voyager* (1943) and *Since You Went Away* (1944). *Casablanca* demonstrates his use of classical techniques, including permutations upon a designated main theme ("As Time Goes By"), the assigning of leitmotifs to characters and situations, the use of "descriptive" and mood-enhancing music to complement the story, and a superb sensitivity for string writing. Steiner biographer Tony Thomas: "It was Steiner more than any other composer who pioneered the use of original composition as background scoring for films."

For further reading:
Thomas, Tony, *Music for the Movies*. Cranbury, New Jersey: A.S. Barnes, 1977.

Steinmetz, Charles (1865–1923). German-American electrical engineer. In 1889, Steinmetz immigrated to the U.S. From 1893 to 1923, he worked for the General Electric Company in Schenectady, New York; beginning in 1902 he also taught at Union College in that city. Steinmetz explained the power loss resulting from magnetic resistance and demonstrated that alternating current could partially compensate for that loss, thereby hastening the commercial use of alternating current. Although Steinmetz's reputation rests primarily on his theoretical work, he was also awarded 200 patents.

Stella, Frank (1936–). American painter. Born in Malden, Massachusetts. Stella studied at Princeton University, and became a prominent figure in the New York art world during the 1960s. His early 1960s work mainly consisted of large minimal black paintings of angular "pinstripes" that contrasted strongly with Abstract Expressionist work in their measured formalism and pictorial restraint. Later in the decade, he produced polychrome striped works in metallic pigments, often on shaped canvases. Later, his style moved into shaped works with complicated curvilinear forms that jut into space and richly colored and patterned surfaces.

Stengel, Charles Dillon "Casey" "The Old Professor" (1889–1975). American baseball player and manager. Casey Stengel was one of the most colorful characters in the history of baseball. His wit perhaps obscured the fact that he was one of the greatest managers ever. Stengel played outfield from 1912 to 1925, much of that time with the Brooklyn Dodgers. He went on to manage that team from 1934 to 1936, and later several other teams. It was not until 1949 that he joined the New York Yankees, an association that would become legend. He managed the team to five consecutive World Series championships. In 1960 he was fired by the Yankees but returned to baseball two years later with the New York Mets. The team owed much of its reputation as New York's Amazin's to Stengel's verbal dexterity. A fast-talking master of the non sequitor, he was able to deflect interest from the team's utter fecklessness to its loopy charm. He retired in 1965 and was named to the Hall of Fame a year later. Stengel died during the league championships in 1975. His funeral was delayed one week—until an off-day—so that all of baseball could attend.

Stenmark, Ingemar (1956–). Swedish skier. A slalom and giant slalom specialist, Stenmark became a folk hero in Sweden for his come-from-behind performances on the slopes. First overall in the World Cup from 1976 to 1978, he was first in the giant slalom six times in the late 1970s and early 1980s, and first in slalom from 1975 to 1981 and again in 1983. World Champion in giant slalom and slalom in 1978, and slalom in 1982, he is best remembered for his 1980 OLYMPIC performances at Lake Placid. Both the slalom and giant slalom were vintage Stenmark, as he turned in cautious first runs and thrilling, seemingly reckless runs in the second round, and took the gold medal in both events. He was not permitted to take part in the 1984 games, as a result of his turning "professional."

Stephanopoulos, Stephanos (1898–). Prime Minister of GREECE (1965–1966). Having served as finance minister and foreign minister, Stephanopoulos succeeded George PAPANDREOU as prime minister after the latter resigned in a political crisis with King CONSTANTINE. However, he was unable to govern effectively and resigned after 17 months in office. The following year the GREEK COLONELS seized power in a coup.

Stephens, James (1882–1950). Irish author. Stephens' first work was the poetry collection, *Insurrections* (1909), but it is for the prose fantasy, *The Crock of Gold* (1912) that he is best remembered. Written in the Irish vernacular, it depicts a whimsical world of fairies and humans. His novels include *The Charwoman's Daughter* (1912) and *Dierdre* (1923). *Irish Fairy Tales* (1920), which was illustrated by Arthur Rackham, is one of many collections of short stories. *Collected Poems* was first published in 1923, and was revised and reissued in 1953. Stephens became a popular radio personality, broadcasting stories and poems.

Stephens, Olin J. (1908–). U.S. naval architect best known for the design of sailing yachts, including a number of highly successful racing craft. Stephens designed his first 6–meter racing yacht, *Thalia*, in 1926, after only one term at MIT. In 1928 he established the firm of SPARKMAN & STEPHENS with his brother Roderick and Drake Sparkman as partners. *Dorade*, a yawl of 1930, established a new standard for sailing yachts, with successes in a Bermuda race and a transatlantic race shortly after she was built. In 1937, Harold S. Vanderbilt asked Stephens to work with Starling Burgess on the design of the America's Cup yacht, *Ranger*, built with a steel hull. A succession of winning America's Cup racers followed, including *Columbia; Constellation; Courageous; Freedom*, a 1980 winner; and *Intrepid* (often viewed as Stephens' greatest design). *Finisterre* of 1955, a 39–foot centerboard design, established a modern standard for yachts designed for equal success in racing and extended cruising. Stephens retired in 1979, but the firm remains active.

Stephenson, Tom (1892–1987). The man to whom British long-distance walkers are indebted for the creation of the **Pennine Way**. In 1935 Stephenson's newspaper article, "Wanted, a Long Green Trail," fired the first salvo in a campaign that eventually led to the creation of the Pennine Way in 1965. In 1948 Stephenson became secretary of the **Ramblers' Association,** serving for 21 years.

Stephenson, Sir William S. "Wild Bill" (1896–1989). Canadian-born millionaire industrialist and spy master. After the outbreak of WORLD WAR II, Prime Minister Winston CHURCHILL sent Stephenson to the U.S., where he served as a link between Churchill and President Franklin ROOSEVELT. Stephenson helped organized the U.S. wartime intelligence operation, the Office of Strategic Services (OSS), a forerunner of the CIA. His wartime adventures were related in the 1979 best-seller, *A Man Called Intrepid*.

For further reading:
Stephenson, William, *Intrepid's Last Case*. Guilford, Conn.: Ulverscroft, 1984.

Stepinac, Aloysius (1898–1960). Yugoslavian prelate. Stepinac was appointed archbishop of Zagreb in 1937. He served in the Croatian state council during World War II, in a government established by the nationalistic terrorists known as the USTASE. After the war he was convicted of collaboration and imprisoned until 1951, when he was ordered to remain in his native city of Krasic. Marshal TITO opposed Stepinac while the Vatican treated him as a persecuted figure and elevated him to cardinal in 1953. This disagreement over Stepinac was an important factor in the gulf between the Yugoslavian government and the Roman Catholic Church.

Steptoe, Patrick Christopher (1913–1988). British obstetrician-gynecologist. With Cambridge University physiologist Robert Edwards, Steptoe pioneered the first in vitro ("test-tube") fertilization procedure. In 1978, he delivered the world's first TEST-TUBE BABY by cesarean section in northern England.

Sterba, Richard (1898–1989). American psychoanalyst. He touched off a major international musicological controversy with the 1945 publication of *Beethoven and His Nephew: A Psychoanalytic Study of their Relationship* (1945), written with his wife, Editha. The book argued that Beethoven had been a repressed homosexual whose inner conflicts had resulted in sadistic attempts to control his nephew, Karl. Although their theory was later at least partially discredited, the Sterbas were widely acknowledged to have helped lay the groundwork for the later popular school of musical psychobiography.

Stern, Curt (1902–1981). German-born geneticist. After receiving his doctorate in zoology from the University of Berlin (1923), Stern spent two years as a post-doctoral fellow at Columbia University in New York. There he worked with a group of scientists who virtually developed the modern science of genetics, discovering many of the fundamental rules of heredity. He returned to Berlin in 1928, but fled to America when Adolf HITLER came to power (1933). During WORLD WAR II he worked on the MANHATTAN PROJECT that developed the ATOMIC BOMB, and pioneered the study of the effects of radiation on living organisms. He was an advisor to the Atomic Energy Commission when it was formed in 1945. He taught at the University of California, BERKELEY (1947–70) and wrote *The Principles of Human Genetics* (1949), which remained a standard textbook for two decades.

Stern, Isaac (1920–). American violinist. Born in the U.S.S.R., as an infant Stern came to the U.S. with his family and settled in San Francisco. He entered the San Francisco Conservatory at ten, made his debut as a soloist with the San Francisco Symphony the following year, and his New York debut at Town Hall in 1937. After this he began a series of brilliant worldwide tours, and by the early 1940s he was acclaimed as one of the world's master violinists. Noted for his exquisite tone and superb musicianship, he has performed as a soloist with every major orchestra and at every important music festival. He has also become known for his many chamber music performances, particularly with the Istomen-Stern-Rose Trio, which he cofounded. His repertoire is extensive, including not only classic violin pieces, but 20th-century music as well. He has premiered works by composers such as Paul HINDEMITH, William Schuman and Leonard BERNSTEIN. Stern has maintained close musical ties with Israel, where he often performs, is an officer of the America-Israel Cultural Foundation and a cofounder of the Israeli Music Center. Stern is also closely associated with CARNEGIE HALL in New York City. When the hall was threatened with demolition in the late 1950s, Stern organized a movement to save it. He has subsequently served as president of the Carnegie Hall Corporation and has been a leading figure in numerous events connected to Carnegie Hall.

Sternberg, Josef von [born Josef Sternberg] (1894–1969). Austrian-born Jewish film director. Von Sternberg is primarily remembered for his richly textured films of the 1930s that starred Marlene DIETRICH. The aristocratic "von" of his name was added on as a show business touch during von Sternberg's early years in HOLLYWOOD, during which he worked as an assistant director. Von Sternberg made his directorial debut with *The Salvation Hunters* (1925), then followed up with a series of gangster films including *Underworld* (1927) and *Thunderbolt* (1929). But he won international fame with *The Blue Angel* (1930) in which von Sternberg introduced Dietrich to cinema audiences in the seductive role of Lola Lola for which she is best remembered. Several more films with Dietrich followed—*Morocco* (1930), *Dishonored* (1931), *Shanghai Express* (1932), *Blonde Venus* (1932), *The Scarlet Empress* (1934) and *The Devil Is a Woman* (1935). Each film featured innovative backlighting and glamorous costuming, but von Sternberg's preference for atmosphere over plot led to his commercial decline. His last film was *Anatahan* (1953).

Stern Gang [*Lohamei Herut Yisrael*, Fighters for the Freedom of Israel]. Jewish guerrilla group founded by Avraham STERN. It operated in PALESTINE in the mid-1940s, and was responsible for the assassination of Count Folke BERNADOTTE, the United Nations mediator in Palestine in 1945.

Stettinius, Edward R. (1900–1949). U.S. government official. Born into a prominent New York City family, Stettinius went to work in Washington as a lobbyist for General Motors. In 1938, he was named chairman of the board of U.S. Steel, but in 1939 he resigned that post and in 1940 joined the National Defense Advisory Commission, the first of a number of government appointments over the next few years. In 1944, President Franklin D. ROOSEVELT appointed Stettinius secretary of state, and in 1945, the new president, Harry S TRUMAN, named him first U.S. ambassador to the UNITED NATIONS. Stettinius resigned in 1946 after a disagreement with then-Secretary of State James BYRNES. He died of a heart condition three years later.

Stevens, George (1904–1975). Prestigious American motion picture director. A native Californian, Stevens traveled as a youngster in his parents' touring theater company. He worked as a cameraman in the 1920s and photographed many LAUREL AND HARDY comedy shorts, including the classic *Big Business* (1928). After serving an apprenticeship directing comedy shorts for RKO and UNIVERSAL, he debuted as a director of "A" films with the delightful *Alice Adams* (1935), starring Katharine HEPBURN. After several top-notch genre pieces, including the ASTAIRE-ROGERS musical *Swing Time* (1936) and the swashbuckling adventure *Gunga Din* (1939), he served in WORLD WAR II as a lieutenant colonel in the Army Signal Corps. His film unit covered, among other events, the liberation of the DACHAU inmates. He entered his most successful decade in the 1950s with several big-budget epics, including *A Place in the Sun* (a 1951 adaptation of DREISER's *An American Tragedy*), the classic western *Shane* (1953), the "modern" western *Giant* (1956) and the epic *The Greatest Story Ever Told* (1965). Increasingly, Stevens' drive for perfection, outsized budgets and interminable running times strangled the life out of his films. As historian Andrew Sarris concludes: "All in all, his little movies have outlasted his big ones."

For further reading:

Coursodon, Jean-Pierre, ed., *American Directors*. New York: McGraw-Hill, 1983.

Stevens, John Paul, III (1920–). Associate justice, U.S. Supreme Court (1975–). A native of Chicago and a graduate of the University of Chicago and Northwestern Law School, Stevens served as a law clerk to Justice Wiley RUTLEDGE after law school. After practicing antitrust law in Chicago, Stevens was appointed to the U.S. Court of Appeals for the Seventh Circuit by President Richard M. NIXON in 1970. In 1975 President Gerald FORD appointed Stevens to the U.S. Supreme Court. Although he has been termed a moderate judge, a more apt description might be a maverick with no ideological agenda. However, he proved a staunch defender of both CIVIL RIGHTS and civil liberties, often providing the decisive fifth vote in close decisions.

Stevens, Rise [Rise Steenberg] (1913–). American singer. An acclaimed mezzo-soprano, she performed at major opera houses worldwide, in movies and on network radio programs. She made her debut at the Prague Opera in the title role of *Mignon* in 1936, and made her Metropolitan Opera debut in the same role in 1938. In 1945 she appeared as *Carmen*, which became her most famous role. She also starred in the film version of the operetta, *The Chocolate Soldier* (1941), and in a revival of the musical *The King and I* at Lincoln Center for the Performing Arts (1964). From 1975 to 1978 she served as president of Mannes College of Music.

Stevens, Robert T(en Broeck) (1899–1983). American secretary of the Army (1953 to 1955). Heir to the textile firm of J.P. Stevens and Co., he entered the family business after serving in WORLD WAR I. During the GREAT DEPRESSION he served on the NATIONAL RECOVERY ADMINISTRATION (NRA), and was director of the Federal Reserve Bank of New York (1934–53). During WORLD WAR II he was director of purchases in the office of the Quartermaster General. Following the election of Dwight D. EISENHOWER as president, Stevens, a Republican, was appointed secretary of the Army. He became famous for his televised confrontations with Senator Joseph MCCARTHY during the ARMY-MCCARTHY SENATE HEARINGS in 1954. During the hearings, he denied McCarthy's allegations of communist infiltration in the Army, and condemned the senator's tactics. Stevens' firm stand was the beginning of McCarthy's downfall. Stevens resigned from his post for personal reasons (1955) and returned to business.

Stevens, Siaka (Probyn) (1905–1988). Sierra Leone politician. Stevens led the West African nation of SIERRA LEONE for 17 years, first as prime minister and then as president. Stevens became prime minister in 1968 after a military coup and assumed the presidency in 1971. He retired from the presidency in 1985, becoming one of only a few black African leaders to give up power voluntarily.

Stevens, Wallace (1879–1955). American poet and essayist. Stevens is regarded as one of the greatest English-language poets of the 20th century, although his literary career was relatively slow in unfolding and he won real fame late in life. Born in Reading, Pennsylvania and educated at Harvard University, Stevens wrote his earliest poems for the *Advocate*, an undergraduate journal. He subsequently pursued a legal and business career and ultimately became a vice president with the Hartford Accident and Indemnity Company. He published his first volume of poems, *Harmonium* (1923), at age 44. His later volumes include *The Man with the Blue Guitar* (1937), *Transports of Summer* (1947), *The Auroras of Autumn* (1950), *Collected Poems* (1954) and *Opus Posthumous* (1957). One of the most original figures in 20th-century American letters, Stevens is neither a popular nor an easy poet. Although his work includes elements of symbolism and SURREALISM, he cannot be placed in any literary school. His poems rarely deal with subjects in the "real world," but are usually meditations on the imaginative intellect. They are marked by recurring and startling images, unexpected turns of thought, and a highly musical and formal diction. *The Necessary Angel* (1951) is a volume of literary essays. Stevens won the BOLLINGEN PRIZE for poetry in 1950 and the PULITZER PRIZE in 1955.

Stevenson, Adlai Ewing, II (1900–1965). American statesman. After studies at Princeton and Harvard, Stevenson received his law degree from Northwestern University. His first public office was in the AGRICULTURAL ADJUSTMENT ADMINISTRATION from 1933 to 1934. During WORLD WAR II he was a special counsel to Secretary of the Navy Frank Knox. After the war, Stevenson was an alternate delegate to the UNITED NATIONS. In 1948 he was elected governor of his home state, Illinois, on a reform Democratic ticket—with the largest plurality in the state's history to that point. He is credited with spearheading 78 "clean-up" measures. In 1952 he was drafted as the Democratic candidate for president, despite the fact that he refused to campaign for the nomination. However, as the nominee he did campaign vigorously, in a manner said to have been "marked by eloquent speeches whose wit and civility were often memorable." He was defeated then and again in 1956 by Dwight D. EISENHOWER. In that campaign he was hampered by what some considered his overly intellectual approach to national issues, as contrasted to Eisenhower's more homey touch. Stevenson served as one of the U.S.'s most notable ambassadors to the United Nations, from 1961 until his death.

Adlai Stevenson, U.S. ambassador to the UN and two-time Democratic presidential candidate.

For further reading:

McKeever, Porter, *Adlai Stevenson: His Life and Legacy*. New York: William Morrow & Co., 1989.

Stevenson, Sir (Aubrey) Melford (Steed) (1902–1987). British judge who often attracted public attention for his outspoken comments from the bench. Stevenson became a barrister in 1925 and was a judge from 1957 until his retirement in 1979. As a lawyer, his best-known client was Ruth Ellis, who in 1955 became the last woman to be hanged in England.

Stevenson, William Edwards (1900–1985). American lawyer and diplomat. During WORLD WAR II, Stevenson directed American Red Cross operations in England and North Africa. In 1947 he was named president of Oberlin (Ohio) College, a post he held until 1960. Under President KENNEDY, he served as ambassador to the PHILIPPINES. He headed The Aspen Institute in Colorado from 1967 to 1970.

Steward, Julian Haynes (1902–1972). American anthropologist. Steward received his Ph.D. at the University of California (1929) and went on to teach at numerous universities around the country. He was a noted expert on cultural evolution in the United States and worked at the Smithsonian Institution. While there, in the Bureau of American Ethnology, he edited the seven-volume *Handbook of South American Indians* (1946–59). Some of his other works include *Area Research, Theory and Practice* (1950) and *Theory of Culture Change* (1955).

Stewart, "Jackie" John Young (1939–). Scottish auto racing driver. Stewart began his career in 1954 as a garage mechanic, working his way up to racing mechanic, and then driver, in 1961. He was named to the British national motor team in 1965, and in 1969 won the South American, Spanish, Dutch, French, British and Italian championships. Awarded the Order of the British Empire in 1972, Stewart retired in 1973, after the death of a teammate, with a total of 27 Grand Prix championships. He went on to a career as a racing commentator.

Stewart, James (1908–). American film and theater actor. Stewart, one of the most popular actors in HOLLYWOOD history, has enjoyed a lengthy career and the adoration of fans and critics alike. After graduation from Princeton University, he joined the University Players, a theater ensemble that also included Henry FONDA. Stewart moved to Hollywood in the 1930s and emerged as a leading man with a gift for light comedy in films such as *You Can't Take It With You* (1938) and *Mr. Smith Goes to Washington* (1939), both directed by Frank CAPRA. He won a best actor Oscar for *The Philadelphia Story* (1940). During World War II Stewart served in the Army Air Force as a bomber pilot. He returned to Hollywood, reuniting with director Capra in *It's A Wonderful Life* (1946), a box-office dog in its day but now considered a movie classic. In the 1950s and 1960s, Stewart shifted to tougher roles in such westerns as *Winchester 73* (1950) and *Bend of the River* (1952). He also starred in the Alfred HITCHCOCK thrillers *Rear Window* (1954), *The Man Who Knew Too Much* (1956) and *Vertigo* (1958). *Harvey* (1950) demonstrated once again his talent for light comedy. In recent decades, Stewart has made only brief and infrequent film appearances, as in *The Shootist* (1976) and *The Big Sleep* (1978).

Stewart, Potter (1915–1985). American jurist. During his tenure as a Supreme Court Justice (1958–81), Stewart often provided the pivotal swing vote. During his first 11 years on the court, he often dissented from many of the liberal rulings under Chief Justice Earl WARREN. Afterward, he came to occupy the decisive center of the more conservative court under Chief Justice Warren E. BURGER.

Stickley, Gustav (1857–1942). American designer and furniture maker. In 1898, Stickley founded a furniture company in Eastwood, New York, to produce his designs, which were inspired by the English Arts and Crafts movement. Also known as "Mission Style," Stickley's simple oak pieces became widely popular. In 1901, he began publication of *The Craftsman* magazine to promote his design concepts as well as his progressive social ideas. Stickley's company declared bankruptcy in 1915, but his work continued to exert a strong influence on other early 20th-century architects and designers, including Frank Lloyd WRIGHT.

Stieglitz, Alfred (1864–1946). American photographer and editor widely regarded as the father of modern photography. Born in Hoboken, New Jersey, and educated in mechanical engineering and photochemistry in Karlsruhe and Berlin, Stieglitz returned to New York in 1890 and founded the influential journal *Camera Work*, the most important organ of the PHOTO-SECESSION movement. He promoted modern art in America, establishing in New York an exhibition space for advanced American and European art called "291" (after its Fifth Avenue address). Between 1908 and 1917 he presented important shows of photographers and painters—members of the Photo-Secession and modern painters such as MATISSE, PICASSO and BRANCUSI. After World War I Stieglitz continued to support the work of native artists, particularly of his wife, Georgia O'KEEFFE. Concludes historian William Innes Homer, "Stieglitz elevated American photography to a respected international position, performing his task so well that the American School became preeminent the world over."

For further reading:

Homer, William Innes, *Alfred Stieglitz and the Phtot-Secession*. Boston: Little, Brown and Co., 1983.

Stijl, de ["the style"]. Dutch art movement of a severe nonfigurative character, also known as neoplasticism. It was formally initiated, along with a journal of the same name in 1917, by a group of artists, architects and poets. Led by Dutch artists Theo van DOESBURG and Piet MONDRIAN, the movement stressed the elimination of all ornamental flourishes in favor of strict geometric compositions and the use of primary colors, black and white. This austere doctrine and the images it produced had worldwide influence, and the movement continued until 1931 (the magazine closed in 1928). It proved especially applicable to architecture, where it was important in the work of J.J.P. Oud, Gerrit RIETVELD, Walter GROPIUS and the BAUHAUS movement in general. Its strong, clean lines and pure color also influenced a wide range of visual expression, from posters to packaging and advertising.

Still, Clifford (1904–1980). American painter. Still was one of the founders of the artistic school of ABSTRACT EXPRESSIONISM that came to prominence in America in the 1940s and '50s. He was known for his fiercely independent and uncompromising views on artistic matters and the need for American painters to develop a unique style that was free of European tradition. Born in North Dakota, Still was educated in Washington State and taught at the California School of Fine Art (now the San Francisco Art Institute) from 1941 to 1949. In 1950 he moved to New York City, where the Abstract Expressionist movement began to flourish. Despite his own prominence, Still was highly critical of artists who sought to become self-conscious leaders of artistic movements.

Still, William Grant (1895–1978). American composer, arranger and conductor. Still was best known for his *Afro-American Symphony* (1931). He studied with the French composer Edgar VARESE. In 1936 he became the first black to conduct a major U.S. orchestra when he led the Los Angeles Philharmonic at the Hollywood Bowl. Still also arranged JAZZ scores for W.C. HANDY and Paul WHITEMAN, and provided musical arrangements for films, radio, television and the stage.

Stilwell, Joseph W(arren) (1883–1946). American general. Born in Palatka, Florida, Stilwell attended West Point and was commissioned in the army in 1904. He served in World War I and spent three tours of duty in CHINA during a period of 13 years. With the outbreak of the war, Stilwell was again posted in China, where in 1942 he was named chief of staff to General CHIANG KAI-SHEK and commander of American forces in the China-Burma-India theater of battle. He was defeated in Burma and retreated to India late in May 1942. There he regrouped his forces and struggled to retake Burma, a task that was eventually accomplished in 1945. In the meantime, however, Stilwell's frequent clashes with Chiang, whom he constantly criticized, had provoked his 1944 recall to the U.S. The outspoken general, popularly referred to as "Vinegar Joe," spent the rest of the war commanding American forces on OKINAWA.

Stimson, Henry Lewis (1867–1950). American statesman. Born in New York City, Stimson attended Yale University and Harvard Law School and became a successful Wall Street lawyer. After failing as the Republican gubernatorial candidate in 1910, he became (1911–13) President TAFT's Secretary of War and served in World War I. He was governor general of the Philippines from 1928 to 1929 and was recalled to be Herbert HOOVER's Secretary of State (1929–33). In this post he pressed for disarmament as chairman of the U.S. delegation to the London Naval Conference (1930–31) and the Geneva Disarmament Conference (1932). Opposing the Japanese invasion of Manchuria (1932) he refused to recognize their puppet regime in a treaty policy known as the Stimson Doctrine. He was appointed Secretary of War a second time by President Franklin D. ROOSEVELT, serving from 1940 to 1945. An energetic and effective secretary, he organized U.S. armed forces, advocated an allied invasion across the English Channel, advised the president on nuclear affairs and was an important voice in the debate over dropping the ATOMIC BOMB on Japan. His autobiography, *On Active Service in Peace and War,* was published in 1948.

For further reading:
Hodgson, Godfrey, *The Colonel: The Life and Wars of Henry Stimson, 1867–1950*. New York: Alfred Knopf, 1990.

Stirling, Sir (Archibald) David (1915–1990). British commando, founder of the Long-Range Desert Patrol Group and the SPECIAL AIR SERVICES. During WORLD WAR II IN NORTH AFRICA, Colonel Stirling formed the Long-Range Desert Patrol Group and led them in daring raids behind ememy lines. Stirling was so successful that the Germans dubbed him "the Phantom Major." Captured by the Germans, he escaped, was recaptured, and spent the remainder of the war in Colditz Castle, Germany's top-security Prisoner of War camp. For his exploits Stirling was decorated for bravery. After the war Stirling left the army and went to Rhodesia. He founded the Capricorn Africa Society, a group that promoted racial harmony. He later directed Watchguard International, Ltd., a security firm that trained and advised security units for Arab and African countries. Stirling was knighted by Queen ELIZABETH in 1990.

For further reading:
Cowles, Virginia, *The Phantom Major*. New York: Harper, 1958.

Stitt, Sonny (1982–1982). American alto saxophonist. Stitt was one of the most prolific recording artists in JAZZ history. Stitt's musical style was often compared to that of Charlie "Bird" PARKER. A week before Parker's death in 1955, Parker reportedly told Stitt, "Man, I'm handing you the keys to the kingdom."

Stock, Frederick (1872–1942). German-born orchestra conductor. Stock came to Chicago in 1895 to join the CHICAGO SYMPHONY ORCHESTRA as principal viola. He served as the assistant director for several years, and in 1903 became the musical director and conductor of the Chicago Symphony. Stock, a naturalized citizen of the United States in 1919, conducted several performances of Wagnerian opera for the Civic Opera Company of Chicago in 1923. He was the general music director for Chicago's Century of Progress Exposition in 1933. Stock's compositions include a symphony, two concert overtures, a tone poem for orchestra and a concerto for violin and orchestra. He was renowned for his support of modern composers, presenting world premieres of works by many composers well known today. Stock was the symphony's conductor until his death.

Stockhausen, Karlheinz (1928–). German composer and music theorist. Stockhausen studied at the University of Cologne and was a composition student of Frank Martin in Cologne (1950–51) and of Olivier MESSIAEN and Darius MILHAUD in Paris (1951–53). An innovative avant-gardist, he met and collaborated with Pierre BOULEZ and worked with the tape-recorded and variously altered sounds of "music concrete." Stockhausen has been associated with various modern musical idioms, including the 12–tone system and serial, electronic and aleatory music, in which performer improvisation is encouraged. His compositions have often been termed difficult, exploiting as they do, dissonant and percussive effects as well as experiments with tone, volume and duration. Among his works are *Gruppen* (1955–59), *Klavierstuck XI* (1956), *Telemusik* (1966) and *Sirius* (1975–76).

stock market crash of 1929. Disastrous collapse of stock prices on the U.S.'s national stock exchanges, signaling the start of the GREAT DEPRESSION of the 1930s. For many years, the value of American corporate stock had climbed as the economy expanded. Speculators often bought stock on margin—borrowing their broker's money to buy the stock in anticipation of quick profits and a quick return of the borrowed money. For various reasons, the decade-long market boom collapsed in little more than a week (Oct. 24–29). The value of thousands of stocks plummeted as panicked sellers dumped their stocks; by December 1, 1929 New York Stock Exchange shares had lost an estimated $26 billion from their highest value on September 3. The crash disillusioned many business leaders and the economy started on a severe and painful economic contraction that lasted nearly a decade.

stock market crash of 1987. Collapse of stock prices that was similar to the STOCK MARKET CRASH OF 1929 but whose consequences were less severe. In 1987, the U.S. stock market had been through an almost unprecedented seven-year "bull market." The bubble burst on October 19, 1987, when prices on the New York Stock Exchange plunged over 508 points, almost a 23% drop in value. The London and Tokyo stock exchanges experienced similar crashes during the same week.

Interestingly, the 1987 crash was more severe than the 1929 crash from both an absolute and percentage view. However, the market rebounded later in the year, and the recession in 1990–91 seemed only indirectly related to the 1987 crash.

Stockwell, General Sir Hugh (1903–1986). British military officer. Stockwell commanded Britain's land forces in the 1956 Anglo-French invasion of the Suez Canal Zone (see SUEZ CRISIS). After that campaign, he was military secretary to the secretary of state for war from 1957 to 1959 and deputy supreme commander of NORTH ATLANTIC TREATY ORGANIZATION (NATO) forces in Europe from 1960 to 1964.

Stoica, Chivu (1908–1975). Premier of ROMANIA (1955–61). A communist revolutionary, while in his mid-20s Stoica was sentenced to 15 years hard labor for his role in a railway strike (1933). He was released after the communists gained power in 1944, and later became a member of the ruling Politburo in communist Romania. He was dismissed from the Central Committee and the presidium by Nicolae CEAUSESCU in 1969.

Stokowski, Leopold (1882–1977). Flamboyant American conductor of Polish and Irish descent. Stokowski brought the Philadelphia Orchestra to world prominence between 1912 and 1936. He was born in London and studied composition at Oxford with Charles Stanford. His first major post was in America with the Cincinnati Symphony Orchestra from 1909 to 1912. After his stint with the Philadelphia Orchestra he organized the All-American Youth Orchestra in 1939 and toured South America. His numerous subsequent associations included positions with the Hollywood Bowl in 1945, co-music director (with Dmitri Mitropoulos) of the New York Philharmonic from 1945 to 1950 and founder in 1962 of the American Symphony in New York. With Arturo TOSCANINI and Serge KOUSSEVITZKY, Stokowski was the most famous American conductor of his time. He personified the public image of the artist, keeping the spotlight on his aureole of fluffy white hair and long, white fingers (he scorned the baton), and keeping his colorful private life in the newspaper headlines. He appeared in the movies—as himself, of course—most notably co-starring with Deanna Durbin in *100 Men and a Girl* (1937) and with Mickey Mouse in FANTASIA (1940). An inveterate tinkerer, he experimented with innovative microphonic techniques. Critic Virgil THOMSON summed up the intellectual establishment's contempt for "Stokie," accusing him of "distorted interpretations" and "lapses of musical taste"—references to his notorious orchestral transcriptions of Bach organ works and his "retouchings" of other scores. However, his services to new music were significant. He conducted the American premieres of Gustav MAHLER's Second and Eighth Symphonies, Igor STRAVINSKY'S LE SACRE DU PRINTEMPS, Alban BERG'S WOZZECK, and Charles IVES' Fourth Symphony. "There are millions who find solace in music," this showman/charlatan/genius wrote, without batting an eye, in *Music for All of Us* (1943). "It opens for them the sun-batched gates of inspiration." He remained active well into his eighties.

For further reading:
Schonberg, Harold C., *The Great Conductors.* New York: Simon and Schuster, 1967.

Conductor Leopold Stokowski (1944).

Stolypin, Peter Arkadyevich (1862–1911). Russian statesman. As a liberal conservative, he failed to win the approval of either the extreme right or the radicals. From 1906 Stolypin was minister of the interior and chairman of the council of ministers. While firmly suppressing the 1905 Revolution, he wished to carry out liberal reforms. Under his agrarian reforms of 1906–11, peasants were permitted to leave village communities, settle in separate farms, buy land, and were encouraged to settle in less populated areas. In 1907 Stolypin altered the electoral system by imperial decree. He was assassinated by a Socialist Revolutionary terrorist in 1911.

Stone, Edward Durell (1902–1978). American architect. Stone's first successes were the interior of the RADIO CITY MUSIC HALL and the MUSEUM OF MODERN ART (with Philip L. Goodwin) in New York. Among his best known designs were the U.S. Embassy in New Delhi, India, the General Motors Building and the Huntington Hartford Gallery in New York, the State University of New York campus in Albany, and the John F. Kennedy Center for the Performing Arts in Washington, D.C.

Stone, Harlan Fiske (1872–1946). Associate justice, U.S. Supreme Court (1925–41); chief justice (1941–46). A native of New Hampshire and a graduate of Amherst and Columbia University Law School, Stone served as U.S. attorney general (1924–25) under President Calvin COOLIDGE (who was one class behind him at Amherst). As attorney general, Stone helped restore integrity in the federal government during the investigation of the TEAPOT DOME SCANDAL of the HARDING administration. After only a year, Coolidge named Stone to the Supreme Court. President Franklin D. ROOSEVELT later nominated him as chief justice on the retirement of Charles Evans HUGHES. Stone was a supporter of "judicial restraint," deferring to congressional intent. Although a conservative, he voted to uphold NEW DEAL legislation passed by Congress. Stone served for 22 years and died on the bench.

Stone, Irving [born Irving Tennenbaum] (1903–1989). American author. Stone pioneered and specialized in the genre known as the biographical novel. Many of his heavily researched, voluminous works in that genre became best-sellers, beginning with the first, *Lust for Life* (1934), based on the life of Dutch painter Vincent van Gogh. Perhaps the best known of his biographical novels was *The Agony and the Ecstasy* (1961), based on the life of Michelangelo.

Stone, I(sidore) F(einstein) (1907–1989). American journalist and author. A liberal iconoclast, Stone published the muckraking newsletter *I.F. Stone's Weekly* from 1953 through 1968. He used the newsletter as a vehicle to attack MCCARTHYISM, racism, the nuclear arms race and American involvement in the VIETNAM WAR. Although his principal sources of information were newspapers and official documents such as the records of congressional debates and obscure committee hearings, he thoroughly combed them and, in the process, uncovered several major instances of government wrongdoing. He was among the first to challenge the factual basis of the Gulf of TONKIN Incident (1964) that led to escalated U.S. involvement in Vietnam. When he was in his 70s he learned classical Greek in order to do research for a best-selling book, *The Trial of Socrates* (1988), in which he criticized Socrates for preaching against Athenian democracy.

For further reading:
Patner, Andrew, *I.F. Stone: A Portrait.* New York: Anchor Books, 1990.

Journalist I.F. Stone (1983).

Stone, Marshall Harvey (1903–1989). American mathematician. Stone's eminent and influential work integrated diverse areas of abstract mathematics, including analysis, algebra and topology. As chairman of the mathematics department at the University of Chicago (1945–52), he helped make the department one of the foremost in the U.S. He was also an emeritus professor at the University of Massachusetts. In 1983 he received the National Medal of Science.

Stoneham, Horace Charles (1904–1990). American sports entrepreneur. As owner of the New York—later San Francisco—Giants from 1936 to 1976, Stoneham was one of the last of the old-time baseball owners who were involved in every aspect of the business. He took over as president of the team following the death of his father, Charles A. Stoneham, and steered the team to four pennants and one world championship in New York. When attendance at the Polo Grounds dwindled, he moved the team to California in 1958. The Giants won one more pennant under Stoneham's ownership in 1962.

Stonehouse, John (1925–1988). British politician. Stonehouse was a cabinet minister from 1967 to 1970 and Labour member of Parliament from 1957 to 1974. His commercial failures and impending bankruptcy led him to fake his own death by drowning in 1974. He fled to Australia, where two months later he was arrested and extradited to the U.K. to stand trial on charges of theft, fraud and deception. He also wrote three novels, all thrillers.

Stoppard, Tom (Straussler) (1937–). Czechoslovakian-born British playwright. Stoppard is regarded by many critics as the most gifted comic playwright to have emerged in Britain in the postwar era. He first won acclaim with *Rosencrantz and Guildenstern are Dead* (1966), which borrowed from the techniques of THEATER OF THE ABSURD in presenting the confusion of two minor characters from Shakespeare's *Hamlet* as they view the tangled goings on in Hamlet's family. *Jumpers* (1972) parodied the linguistic tangles of modern philosophy. *Every Good Boy Deserves Favor* (1977) was a sharply satiric look at political oppression in Eastern Europe. Other plays by Stoppard include *The Real Thing* (1982) and *Hapgood* (1988). He also wrote the screenplay for the film adaptation of John LE CARRE's *The Russia House* (1990).

Storey, David (Malcolm) (1933–). British novelist and playwright. Storey's first novel, *The Sporting Life* (1960), reflected his experiences as a professional rugby player which he later recalled in the play *The Changing Room* (1971). Much of his early fiction reflects the influence of D.H. LAWRENCE. As a playwright Storey established himself with *In Celebration* (1969), in which the educated sons of a miner return home and face their feelings of discontent and alienation there. Storey is the son of a miner in Wakefield. His other varied plays include *The Contractor* (1970), *Home* (1970) and *Mother's Day* (1976). His later novels include *Pasmore* (1972) and *Saville* (1976), which won the Booker Prize that year. Storey's works often evoke the isolation and insecurity incurred by class mobility.

Stout, Rex (Todhunter) (1896–1975). American mystery novelist. Born in Noblesville, Indiana, Stout moved to New York City and became the founder-director of the Vanguard Press. During a long career that began in the pulp magazines of the 1910s, Stout created over 70 detective novels, 46 of them featuring the chubby and sedentary gourmet sleuth Nero Wolfe. These books include *Fer-de-Lance* (1934), his first mystery tale, *Too Many Cooks* (1938), *If Death Ever Slept* (1957), *Royal Flush* (1965) and *Three Aces* (1971).

Stout, William Bushnell (1880–1956). American aeronautical engineer. Stout sold the Stout Metal Aircraft Company to FORD MOTOR COMPANY in 1925, but remained as a vice president and general manager during the development of the FORD TRIMOTOR transport plane from a single-engine transport. Stout founded Stout Air Services in 1926, the first company in the U.S. to provide passenger service exclusively. The airline flew between Detroit and Grand Rapids, Michigan. With the development of the Trimotor, Stout moved the airline from Detroit to Cleveland in 1927 and added a Detroit to Chicago route. Stout opened the Stout Engineering Labs in 1929 for research and development in aeronautics. His company developed and built the all-metal Sky Car, a new type of airplane for private owner use, and, under contract to the Pullman Car and Manufacturing Company, developed a high-speed Railplane. Stout's last major invention was a fiberglass automobile with its engine in the rear.

Strachey, (Evelyn) John (1901–1963). British official and author. After graduating from Oxford, where he was active in socialist politics, Strachey was elected as a Labour member of Parliament in 1929. He resigned in 1931 but was elected again in 1945, and he served in the chamber until his death, holding a variety of cabinet posts. Strachey was known as a prominent theoretician of the Labour cause, and he published many books on politics, including *The Coming Struggle for Power* (1932), *The Nature of the Capitalist Crisis* (1935), *The End of Empire* and *On the Prevention of War* (1962).

Strachey, Lytton (1880–1932). British biographer and critic. Born to a prominent army family, Strachey was educated at Trinity College, Cambridge, where he met Virginia WOOLF and others with whom he would later associate in the BLOOMSBURY GROUP. Strachey's first work is the vibrant *Landmarks in French Literature* (1912). With *Eminent Victorians* (1918), which consisted of biographical essays on Florence Nightingale, Cardinal Manning, General Charles George Gordon and Dr. Thomas Arnold, Strachey achieved fame and notoriety, for he incorporated satire, psychological analysis and telling anecdotes. The book marked a turning point in the history of biography. Subsequent works include *Queen Victoria* (1921), which some regard as his masterwork, and the popular *Elizabeth and Essex: A Tragic History* (1928), which some critics deemed salacious and facetiously called Strachey's only work of fiction.

Strand, Paul (1890–1976). American photographer, member of the PHOTO-SECESSION, and documentary film-maker. His was an objective vision of "unadorned" nature. In the words of mentor Alfred STIEGLITZ, "His work is brutally direct and devoid of flim-flam." He was born in New York in 1890. The gift of a Brownie camera at age 12 confirmed his photographic ambitions and soon he was studying with Lewis HINE and Stieglitz. His exhibition at Stieglitz' "291" gallery in 1916 (and subsequent notice in the important journal, *Camera-Work*) brought something new to American photography. The views of city streets and people were candid and fresh. The face of a blind beggar expressed all the crushing forces of urban poverty. A white picket fence starkly outlined against grey buildings had all the affirmative power of beauty located in a despairing world, Strand spent much of his time in the 1920s and 1930s working with cinematography. He shot location footage for HOLLYWOOD studios and made some of the first movie documentaries in America, including the classic *Manhattan* (1921), a view of the abstract designs of the city; *The Wave* (1936), an record of a fishermen's strike in the Bay of Vera Cruz; and (with collaborators Ralph Steiner and Pare Lorenz) *The Plow That Broke the Plains* (1936), a document of agricultural problems in Depression America made for the federal Resettlement Administration. Committed to the social problems of his times, he formed his own documentary company, Frontier Films, from 1937 to 1942. However, a growing distaste for post-war MCCARTHYISM led him to leave the country in 1950 and relocate in Paris, where he returned to still photography. He stubbornly insisted that the artist maintain "a real respect for the thing in front of him"—a credo as spare and moving as the images he produced.

Strang, William [Lord Strang, 1954] (1893–1978). British diplomat. Strang accompanied Prime Minister Neville CHAMBERLAIN on his visits to HITLER prior to WORLD WAR II (see MUNICH PACT). During the war, he was Britain's representative on the European Advisory Commission, which planned the terms of Germany's surrender. Later he was permanent undersecretary of state for four years (1949–53) until his retirement.

Strasberg, Lee (1901–1982). American teacher of "method" acting. Born in Austria-Hungary, Strasberg emigrated to the U.S. at an early age and studied acting with two disciples of Konstantin STANISLAVSKY. He joined the Theater Guild in 1924 as an actor and stage manager. In 1948 he became artistic director of the new New York Actors Studio, remaining active in that role until his death. At the Actors Studio, Strasberg exerted a major influence on American theater, teaching student actors such as Marlon BRANDO, Marilyn MONROE, Robert DE NIRO, Ellen BURSTYN, Joanne Woodward, Paul NEWMAN, Jack NICHOLSON and Dustin HOFFMAN.

Strasbourg. A French-German city in France's Bas-Rhin department; on the Ill River, two miles short of its meeting with the Rhine. Known for its distinguished cultural and historical heritage, it is the primary city in Alsace (see ALSACE-LORRAINE). Strasbourg changed hands between FRANCE and GERMANY several times during the 20th century. As Strassburg, it entered the 20th century under German rule, having been seized by Germany during the Franco-Prussian War (1870–71). France regained it in 1919, after Germany's defeat in WORLD WAR I. It was again occupied by Germany in 1940 and returned to French jurisdiction at the end of WORLD WAR II. Today it is the site of the European parliament.

Stratas, Teresa [Anastasia Strataki] (1938–). Canadian-born opera singer known for her intense characterizations. An acclaimed singing actress in opera since the late 1950s, Stratas was born in Toronto to a Greek immigrant family. She made her debut as Mimi in PUCCINI's *La Boheme* in 1958 with the Toronto Opera. She made her Metropolitan Opera debut in a small role in *Manon* (1959), but achieved prominence in 1961 when she replaced the lead soprano in a performance of *Turnadot*. Other outstanding roles include Marguerite in *Faust*, Violetta in *La Traviata* and Sardula in the U.S. premiere of Gian Carlo MENOTTI's *The Last Savage*. In addition, she has starred in several movies, including *Eugene Onegin* and *Otello*.

Strategic Air Command [SAC]. Long-range bomber and missile force of the United States Air Force. Headquartered at Offutt Air Force Base in Omaha, Nebraska, SAC has been called the "headquarters of the nation's peace-keeping force" since its founding in 1946. SAC's combat-ready air forces, including an estimated 1,300 jet bombers and tanker airplanes (1990), can be mobilized within seconds of a warning. Bombers can be dispatched within 15 minutes. An airborne command plane, one of several in the air at all times, would be able to direct attacks if the gound command post was destroyed.

Strategic Arms Limitation Treaties. See SALT.

Strategic Defense Initiative [SDI]. Controversial U.S. anti-missile defense system. Nicknamed "Star Wars," the Strategic Defense Iniative was launched by U.S. President Ronald REAGAN on March 23, 1983, when he announced plans to build a land and space based defensive shield against enemy ballistic missiles. The proposed system would use such high technology as lasers, microwave devices, particle beams and projectile beams to destroy missiles high above the earth. Proponents of the system view it as a historic breakthrough that could make nuclear weapons themselves obsolete. Critics of SDI argue that it is a violation of the 1972 Anti-Ballistic Missile Treaty between the Soviet Union and the United States, that it would create a dangerous new arms race, and that it is in any event technologically unfeasible. Despite President George BUSH's support for SDI, development of the program lost some momentum during his administration. Funding for the program was cut substantially, and the initial plan to use laser systems was largely abandoned in favor of less expensive, more promising space-based interceptors called "Brilliant Pebbles," small orbiting rockets that would use impact rather than explosive force to destroy the missiles.

Strater, Henry (1896–1987). American realist painter. Strater was part of the Lost Generation of Americans with artistic aspirations who converged on Paris after WORLD WAR I. There he associated with future literary giants such as the poet Ezra POUND, and novelists F. Scott FITZGERALD and Ernest HEMINGWAY. He illustrated Pound's CANTOS and was the basis of a character in Fitzgerald's novel *This Side of Paradise*.

Strauss, Franz Josef (1915–1988). West German politician; premier of the West German state of BAVARIA and one of the leading politicians of post-1945 WEST GERMANY. After the defeat of Nazi Germany Strauss cofounded the conservative Christian Social Union, which he later led for 25 years. He played a major role as the architect of West German rearmament while defense minister from 1956 to 1962. He was forced to resign in 1962 after he pressed treason charges against *Der Spiegel* magazine for printing an article critical of the German military. He was finance minister from 1966 to 1969 and became one of the most eager pursuers of trade and contacts with EAST GERMANY, the U.S.S.R. and other communist countries.

Strauss, Lewis Lictenstein (1896–1974). American statesman. An advocate of the development of the HYDROGEN BOMB, he served on the Atomic Energy Commission from 1946 to 1950 and later was its chairman (1953–58). Strauss was appointed secretary of commerce by President Dwight EISENHOWER in November 1958, but the Senate refused to confirm the nomination in June 1959.

Strauss, Richard (1864–1949). German composer and conductor; one of the towering musical figures of the 20th century. An outstanding composer of opera and orchestral works, he had achieved recognition as a composer by age 18. From 1885 to 1924 he served as conductor for various European orchestras, including the Munich Opera and the Vienna State Opera. A series of successful symphonic poems, including *Macbeth* (1886–88) and *Don Quixote* (1886–97), led to the staging of the major one-act operas *Salome* (1905) and *Elektra* (1909). His successful collaboration with poet and librettist Hugo von HOFMANNSTHAL produced several full-length operas including *Der Rosenkavalier* (1911) and *Ariadne auf Naxos* (1912). *Der Rosenkavalier*, in which he pays homage to Mozart—the Mozart of *The Marriage of Figaro*—is generally regarded as his masterpiece and is widely considered one of the greatest operas of the 20th century. Strauss was also a founder of the SALZBURG FESTIVAL (1920).

German composer Richard Strauss (1927).

Strauss' activities during the Nazi era have been a matter of controversy. He was initially willing to go along with NAZISM, but later fell out of favor with the Nazi leadership because of his collaborations with the Jewish writers von Hofmannsthal and Stefan ZWEIG and because of his antiwar attitudes. He was officially "denazified" by a court in 1948. A final burst of creative genius during his later years produced such works as the one-act opera *Capriccio* (1942), the orchestral piece *Metamorphosen* (1945) and the haunting *Four Last Songs*. Despite dissonant passages in many of his works, especially his later operas, Strauss never abandoned tonality; his music, influenced by Richard Wagner, has been described as both romantic and post-romantic.

For further reading:

Kennedy, Michael, *Richard Strauss*. London: Rowman & Littlefield, 1976.

Stravinsky, Igor Fedorovich (1882–1971). Russian-born composer whose influence upon the course of modern music has been lasting and profound. Stravinsky was born in Oranienbaum near St. Petersburg. Despite his avowed interest in music, he was forced by his father into law studies and had to continue his music studies in private. Gaining the influence of composer Nikolai Rimsky-Korsakov, he presented his first works in a private concert in 1907. Ballet impresario Sergei DIAGHILEV heard his *Feu d'Artifice* (*Fireworks*) two years later and promptly commissioned new works for his BALLETS RUSSES. *L'Oiseau de Feu* (*The Firebird*, 1910), *Petrouchka* (1911), and the notorious Le Sacre du Printemps (THE RITE OF SPRING, 1913) created a sensation and subse-

Soviet-born composer Igor Stravinsky.

quently have become cornerstones in the modern ballet repertoire. The percussive, dissonant "neo-primitivism" and Russian nationalism of these works, including *Le Chant du Rossignol* (*The Song of the Nightingale,* 1917) and *Les Noces* (*The Wedding,* 1917) were gradually replaced after 1919 by a more spare, neo-classical style. *L'Histoire du Soldat* (*The Soldier's Tale,* 1918), for example, was severely scored for only seven instruments, three performers, and a narrator and was full of contrapuntal techniques. *Pulcinella* (1920) was derived from the music of the 18th century composer, Pergolesi. This style continued later in America (where after 1939 he remained as a citizen) in *The Symphony in Three Movements* (1946), the ballet *Orpheus* (1948), and the opera *The Rake's Progress* (1951). However, at the age of 70 Stravinsky embarked upon the last phase of his career. A ballet, *Agon* (1957) and an opera, *Noah and the Flood* (1962), embraced the dodecaphonic and serial techniques derived from Arnold SCHOENBERG. Stravinsky's last years were full of international honors, a recording project for Columbia Records, and the tireless efforts on his behalf by his protege, Robert Craft. "Stravinsky tried to keep musical progress on the move," said Leonard BERNSTEIN, "by driving tonal and structural ambiguities on and on to a point of no return." New techniques of "polytonalities" and asymmetrical rhythmic patterns freshly stimulated the ear like, in Bernstein's words, "an ascerbic, needling cold shower." Sometimes criticized as cold, emotionless and detached, Stravinsky was nonetheless wholly devoted to his art. Perhaps he may be compared to the puppet Petrouchka in the ballet of that name—a bundle of sticks and rags that concealed a passionate human heart.

For further reading:

Van den Toorn, Pieter C., *The Music of Igor Stravinsky.* New Haven: Yale University Press, 1983.

streamlining. Widely used term for design work in which concepts of aerodynamics are applied to generate forms based on forms first developed for aircraft. For example, a bulletlike nose and a tapering tail were found to improve the flight characteristics of dirigibles and were later introduced in the design of airplanes. As these forms became visible in the 1930s, many industrial designers began to use them for strictly visual appeal. At first, streamlining was most often applied to moving vehicles, such as locomotives, whole trains, automobiles and ships. As streamlined forms became equated with newness and functional excellence, they were adopted for less logical objects—furniture, office machines, toasters and even, in a famous design by the firm of Raymond LOEWY, a pencil sharpener. As a design theme of the 1930s and early 1940s, streamlining has acquired a certain quality of nostalgia, bringing it to recent popularity, even (or perhaps especially) in its more absurd applications—the clocks, toasters and radios now regarded as collectible.

stream of consciousness. Literary technique that came into special prominence in the 20th century. The term *stream of consciousness* refers to the attempt by fiction writers to capture the sense of a character's interior world by directly depicting the thoughts, feelings and sensory impressions of that character. The writer, in using this technique, steadfastly avoids all authorial comments of an exterior or omniscient nature. The most famous practitioner of the stream-of-consciousness technique is James JOYCE, who explored its possibilities fully in ULYSSES (1922) and *Finnegans Wake.* Other pioneering stream-of-consciousness works include *To the Lighthouse* (1925) by Virginia WOOLF, *The Sound and the Fury* (1929) by William FAULKNER, and UNDER THE VOLCANO (1947) by Malcolm LOWRY. The stream-of-consciousness technique was subsequently practiced widely by other fiction writers.

Streep, Meryl (1951–). American motion picture actress celebrated for the diversity of her many roles. Performing was always a part of Streep's life, from opera training and high school theatrics to a major in drama at Yale and performances at the Yale Repertory Theater. After winning a Tony Award for her role in a revival of Tennessee WILLIAMS' *27 Wagons Full of Cotton* (while serving a stint in the 1976 New York Shakespeare Festival), she began her movie career in *Julia* (1977). A political pundit in *The Seduction of Joe Tynan* (1979), a lesbian in Woody Allen's *Manhattan* (1979), the doomed Karen SILKWOOD in *Silkwood* (1983), the novelist Isak DINESEN in *Out of Africa* (1987) and an accused murderess, Lindy Chamberlain, in *Cry in the Dark* (1988)—this succession of highly varied roles has displayed her almost chameleon-like ability to get into a character. She has had ACADEMY AWARD nominations for almost every film, winning the best actress award for *Kramer vs. Kramer* (1979) and *Sophie's Choice* (1985).

For further reading:

Katz, Ephraim, *The Film Encyclopedia.* New York: Thomas Y. Crowell, 1979.

Streisand, Barbra (1942–). American singer and actress. Streisand first achieved success in the Broadway play *I Can Get It for You Wholesale* in 1963. She was nominated for a Tony for her performance, and co-starred with actor Eliot Gould, who became her first husband. Her career mushroomed: Streisand won a Grammy for her first album, an Emmy for her first television special, and tied with Katherine HEPBURN for an ACADEMY AWARD for her first film, *Funny Girl* (1968). Other films include a remake of the film *A Star Is Born* (1976), for which she co-wrote and recorded the ACADEMY AWARD-winning song, "Evergreen"; *Yentl* (1983), which she also cowrote, produced and directed; and *Nuts* (1987).

Stresa Conferences. Two historic conferences held in the northern Italian resort town of Stresa during the 1930s. The first, held from September 5–20, 1932, was a meeting concerning European economic cooperation that included representatives from 15 countries. The second, from April 11–14, 1935, was a conference held by the prime ministers, foreign ministers and staffs of France, Great Britain and Italy. Convened to solidify the three old Allies' opposition to HITLER's rearming of Germany in contravention of the TREATY OF VERSAILLES, it was the last pre-World WAR II meeting at which Italy was still in the Allied camp.

Stresemann, Gustav (1878–1929). German statesman. Born in Berlin, Stresemann received a doctorate in economics in 1900, and was a founder (1902) and director of the League of German Industrialists. He entered political life in 1907 as the youngest member of the Reichstag. An ardent nationalist and supporter of the German monarchy in World War I, he moderated his views after his nation's defeat. He felt that Germany's best chance of regaining its national status in Europe was to accept the harsh and unpopular terms of the Treaty of Versailles. As chancellor (1923) and foreign minister (1923–29), he did his best to mitigate these crushing terms and to bring Germany back as a respected member of the community of nations. He succeeded in evacuating the French from the industrial RUHR in 1924 and assented to two significant reparations agreements, the DAWES PLAN (1924) and the YOUNG PLAN (1929). Stresemann was a prime architect of the LOCARNO PACT (1925) and in 1926 was successful in securing Germany's admittance to the LEAGUE OF NATIONS as a great power. A signatory of the Kellogg-Briand Pact (1928), he and his French counterpart Aristide BRIAND were awarded the 1926 NOBEL PRIZE for peace.

Strijdom, Johannes Gerhardus (1893–1958). South African politician, prime minister (1954 to 1958). Born in the Cape Province, Strijdom attended universities at Stellenbosch and Pretoria and became a Transvaal lawyer. He entered politics as a Nationalist member of parliament in 1929, and by the mid-1930s had become a leader of the extreme Afrikaner faction of the party. As prime minister, he was a fanatical supporter of apartheid who segregated universities, disenfranchised the so-called Cape coloreds and presided over the infamous Treason Trial of 156 supporters of the Freedom Charter.

Strindberg, (Johann) August (1849–1912). Swedish playwright, novelist, and essayist. Although Strindberg explored many writing genres, it is as a dramatist of exceptional vision and emotional power that he is best remembered. In his earliest plays he was strongly influenced by the social realism of Norwegian playwright Henrik Ibsen. But Strindberg soon moved on to concentrate on the psychic depths of his characters, who were often locked into unhappy marriages. Strindberg employed poetic language and a stark sensual realism that anticipated the Expressionist movement in the European drama of the 1920s (see EXPRESSIONISM). Strindberg's best known plays include *The Father* (1887), *Miss Julie* (1889), *Till Damascus* (1900), *A Dream Play* (1905), *The Storm* (1907) and *The Ghost Sonata* (1908).

Stritch, Samuel Alphonsus (1887–1958). Catholic cardinal. Ordained a Roman Catholic priest in 1910, he served in many official positions in Tennessee, Ohio and Illinois before being named a cardinal in 1946. As head of the diocese of Chicago, the largest in the country, he became increasingly influential. He was the first American ever to be appointed to the Roman Curia, the principal governing body of the Roman Catholic Church. Shortly before his death, he was appointed head of all Catholic mission work.

Stroessner, Alfredo (1912–). Dictator of Paraguay. The son of a German immigrant to Paraguay, Stroessner became a general in the army, then assumed power in a coup in 1954. After a one-party election, he was elected president that year. Reelected in seven successive ballots widely considered to be rigged, Stroessner controlled the country for the next 35 years, making him the longest-ruling head of state in the Western Hemisphere. During his tenure, Paraguay became a notorious haven for international fugitives, and his regime was widely criticized for violations of human rights and suppression of political dissent. In 1989, Stroessner was ousted in a coup by General Andres Rodriguez, the second-ranking officer in the Paraguayan armed forces.

Stroheim, Erich von (1885–1957). Austrian-born film director, actor, screenplay writer, and set designer. Von Stroheim is one of the legendary figures of the cinema. He is remembered both as the archetypal Prussian officer in numerous films from the 1910s to the 1950s (one 1918 film advertisement billed him as "The Man You Love To Hate") and as one of the most gifted and extravagant directors of the Silent Film Era of the 1920s. After a brief tour of active duty in the Austrian army during World War I, von Stroheim immigrated to America and found work in HOLLYWOOD as an actor and as an assistant director under D.W. GRIFFITH. Von Stroheim made his own directorial debut with *Blind Husbands* (1918) and went on to make a series of sexually sophisticated films including *Foolish Wives* (1921) and *Merry-Go-Round* (1922). His films were commercially successful, but von Stroheim earned the ire of Hollywood producers for his chronically over-budget productions. His critical masterpiece is the epic-length *Greed* (1924), which was never released as von Stroheim edited it but remains a cinematic landmark for its breathtaking vision, notably a climactic scene shot in Death Valley. When the silent era ended, von Stroheim could no longer find work as a director, though he continued to act in numerous films including *Sunset Boulevard* (1950).

Stromgren, Bengt (1907–1987). Swedish-born astronomer. Stromgren grew up in Denmark and pursued his scientific career there and in the U.S. In 1940 he succeeded his father in the directorship of the Royal Copenhagen Observatory. He later directed the University of Chicago's Yerkes Observatory in Wisconsin. He gained international recognition for his research and theories on stellar matter and interstellar space.

structuralism. Diverse school of thought that has influenced anthropology, linguistics, literary criticism and philosophy. The two essential premises of structuralism are (1) that social and aesthetic phenomena do not have inherent meaning but rather can be sensibly defined only as parts of larger governing systems; and (2) that the true meaning of these phenomena can be revealed only when these larger systems are recognized and understood. Structuralism is related in approach to SEMIOTICS, the study of meaningful signs within systems. Major figures in the development of structuralism include the linguist Ferdinand de Saussure, the anthropologist Claude LEVI-STRAUSS and the literary critic Roland BARTHES. De Saussure utilized structuralism to probe the underlying structures of all languages, where Levi-Strauss applied it to explain ritual beliefs in alternative cultures and Barthes drew from it to place literary works within the dominant cultural forces of their time. (See also DECONSTRUCTION.)

Struve, Peter Bernardovich (1870–1944). Economist and sociologist. Of German origin, Struve was one of the main theorists of Marxism in Russia in the 1890s. In 1898, he drafted the Social Democratic Labor Party's manifesto, but then changed allegiance and became leader of the Liberal Constitutional movement. In 1905 he joined the Constitutional Democratic Party and was an important member of the *Vekhi* movement.

Student, Kurt (1890–1978). German general who developed the paratroop assault tactics used in WORLD WAR II. Student planned the 1943 air rescue mission that freed Benito MUSSOLINI from his captors, enabling the Italian dictator to remain in power for one more year.

Students for a Democratic Society. Radical left-wing student organization, formed in the U.S. in the mid-1960s. Active in the ANTIWAR MOVEMENT, the SDS urged resistance to the draft and a redistribution of political power. In April 1968 the SDS organized the student takeover of campus buildings at Columbia University, and in August of that year led demonstrations at the Democratic National Convention in Chicago. Critics of the SDS charged that its members sought to disrupt society rather than make it more democratic. Among prominent SDS leaders were Mark Rudd and Tom Hayden.

Sturges, Preston [born Edmund Preston Biden] (1898–1959). American screenwriter and director known for his screwball and romantic comedies in the 1940s. Sturges worked unsuccessfully as an inventor, composer and cosmetics salesman before gaining success as a playwright with the hit Broadway comedy *Strictly Dishonorable* (1929). After his other theater productions received only lukewarm receptions, Sturges turned to HOLLYWOOD screenwriting. He scripted more than a dozen successful films, including *The Power and the Glory* (1933) and *Thirty-Day Princess* (1933). In 1940 he was given the opportunity to direct his original script, *The Great McGinty* (originally titled *Down Went McGinty*). The film was a critical and commercial success, and Sturges went on to win the ACADEMY AWARD for best screenplay. Given free reign as writer-director, Sturges followed with a string of sparkling comedies—*Christmas in July* (1940), *The Lady Eve* (1940), *Sullivan's Travels* (1941), *The Palm Beach Story* (1942), *The Miracle of Morgan's Creek* (1942) and *Hail the Conquering Hero* (1943)—that featured his personal blend of slapstick, biting satire and clever dialogue. However, these successes were followed after the mid-40s with a succession of flops, apart from the comedy *Unfaithfully Yours* (1948). His repeated efforts to return to film and the theater failed, and Sturges died an alcoholic. In the 1980s and '90s, Sturges' films have enjoyed revivals and received new critical and popular attention.

Sturgis, Russell (1836–1909). American architect, critic and author. One of the first to recognize and promote the work of architect Frank Lloyd WRIGHT, Sturgis was a graduate of the Free Academy (Now City College) of New York. He designed many buildings, including the Mechanics Bank of Albany, N.Y., Flower Hospital in New York City, and a Yale University chapel. In the early 1900s he wrote and edited books about architecture, art history and art appreciation.

Sturmer, Boris Vladimirovich (1848–1917). Prime minister of RUSSIA. A previous master of ceremonies at court, Sturmer was appointed prime minister in 1916. He was also in charge of the ministry of foreign affairs. A puppet of RASPUTIN, he was not liked and was dismissed from the duma on November 23, 1916.

Stuttgart Exhibition (1927). Also known as the *Weissenhofsiedlung*, an architectural exhibition commissioned by the *Deutsche Werkbund*, a group of German artists and industrialists. It marked an early mile-

stone in the career of the architect Ludwig MIES VAN DER ROHE, who prepared the plan for the exhibition, selected architects to design over 30 buildings and himself created an important block of housing for the show. Other architects involved in the project included Walter GROPIUS, LE CORBUSIER, Peter BEHRENS and J.J.P. Oud. This exposition was an important event in the establishment of modern architecture as a viable style.

Styer, Wilhelm (1893–1975). American military officer. Styer commanded the U.S. Army in the western Pacific during World War II (see WORLD WAR II IN THE PACIFIC). Later in the war he also played a role in the development of the ATOMIC BOMB, acting as a liaison betweem the War Department and scientists involved in the MANHATTAN PROJECT. After the end of the war, he headed a military tribunal that found the Japanese commander in the Philippines, General Tomoyuki Yamashita, guilty of war crimes.

Styne, Jule (1905–). British-American composer. Born in London in 1905, Styne moved to Chicago with his family at the age of eight. As a child, he performed on the piano with the Chicago Symphony Orchestra and elsewhere, and as a teenager he played with his own band at the Bismark Hotel. His first hit, "Sunday," was published in 1926. Styne had a long and fruitful collaboration with lyricist Sammy CAHN, but he worked with others as well, including Stephen SONDHEIM. Styne has dozens of stage and film credits, including *Gentlemen Prefer Blondes* (1949; film 1953), *Gypsy* (1959, revived 1989; film 1962); and *Funny Girl* (1964; film 1968).

Styron, William (1925–). American novelist and essayist. Styron is one of the most acclaimed and widely read of modern American fiction writers. Born in Virginia, Styron was educated at Duke University and served in the U.S. Marine Corps. He enjoyed great success with his first novel, *Lie Down in Darkness* (1951), an introspective tale of a woman's suicide that employed the STREAM OF CONSCIOUSNESS technique as developed by William FAULKNER and James JOYCE. Styron won a PULITZER PRIZE for a later novel, *The Confessions of Nat Turner* (1967), a fictionalized treatment of a 19th-century slave revolt in Confederate Virginia. However, the novel also aroused some controversy. *Sophie's Choice* (1979) dealt with the psychic turmoil of a woman who had survived the HOLOCAUST. Other novels by Styron include *The Long March* (1953) and *Set this House on Fire* (1960). He recounted his personal struggle with depression in *Darkness Visible: A Memoir of Madness* (1990).

submarine. After a century of tinkering, the submarine had come into practical use by the early 1900s. France, Britain and the U.S. all had submarines, but Germany was the first to see the craft's potential as a naval weapon. At the outbreak of WORLD WAR I, Germany had twice as many long-range submarines as Britain. These slow-moving, diesel-powered vessels had to surface regularly, but battery-powered electric motors allowed them

A German submarine in rough seas.

to operate underwater and sink Allied ships with their torpedoes. German submarines were effective against Allied shipping in the North Atlantic in WORLD WAR II, while U.S. submarines struck at Japanese supply lines in the Pacific. Submarine technology made its greatest leap with the introduction of the nuclear-powered submarine in the 1950s (see NAUTILUS). Nuclear submarines could remain at sea for months without refueling and could stay submerged for days. With high-tech equipment and such weapons as the nuclear-armed Polaris and Poseidon missiles, they were a formidable strategic resource.

Sudan. Located south of Egypt and north and west of Ethiopia, Africa's largest country covers an area of 967,243 square miles. Once known as the Anglo-Egyptian Sudan, the vast country was controlled from Egypt by the UNITED KINGDOM from 1898 to 1956, when independence was granted. Conflict between the economically undeveloped Christian south and the dominant Muslim north erupted into civil war in 1956. Colonel Joafar el Nemery, who came to power in 1969 in a bloodless coup, brought a temporary end to the war by granting limited autonomy to the Christian south in 1972. However, his introduction of Islamic law in 1983 rekindled the rebellion and led to his overthrow in 1985. A state of emergency was declared in 1987, and the army took control in 1989. Attempts by former U.S. President Jimmy CARTER to mediate a peace broke down, and the

SUDAN

1898	Anglo-Egyptian force defeats Islamic Mahdist uprising after long struggle.
1925	British develop cotton plantations and irrigation.
1936	ASHQIPA nationalist party formed.
1955	Black non-Islamic troops in south rebel against northern Islamic commanders; form Anya Nya—"snake venom"—movement.
1956	British grant independence in the midst of civil war and economic decay.
1958	General Abboud takes power.
1965	Elections held; el-Mahdi of People's Party elected.
1966	Cotton price drops; economy in ruins.
1969	Colonel Nemery takes power, forms one-party government; civil war continues.
1972	Addis Ababa Agreement; temporary stop to civil war.
1983	Nemery introduces traditional Koranic law ("Sharia"); south rebels again under U.S.-educated Colonel Garang.
1984	Drought leads to widespread starvation.
1985	Food riots in Khartoum; Nemery deposed by troops.
1986	Elections; el-Mahdi returns from exile to win; civil war intensifies.
1989	Coup by General al-Bashir; Jimmy Carter leads unsuccessful talks with rebels; locusts damage food crops; freak rains ending drought destroy mud houses, leave 1 million homeless in Khartoum; U.S. airlifts food.
1990	Government and rebels stop food shipments, create "man-made famine" to reduce each other's supporters.
1991	U.S. closes embassy due to Bashir pro-Iraq stance; Bashir agrees to UN food airlift.

SUDAN

Christian south continued to push for secession.

Sudetenland. Region in central Europe, currently within the nation of CZECHOSLOVAKIA. Although the population of the Sudetenland included many German-speaking people, the region was assigned to Czechoslovakia when that nation was formed in 1918. In the 1930s, German Chancellor Adolf HITLER claimed the Sudetenland as German territory and demanded that Czechoslovakia turn it over to the Nazi Reich. Hitler's demand provoked an international crisis, complicated by pro-Nazi demonstrations in the Sudetenland itself. Italian dictator MUSSOLINI arranged a conference in Munich at which Germany, Italy, France and the United Kingdom discussed the fate of the Sudetenland (1938). In the MUNICH PACT, France and the U.K. turned the Sudetenland over to Germany in return for Hitler's pledge that he would not seek any more territory. Czechoslovakia was effectively partitioned. The following year (1939) Hitler went back on his word as German troops occupied PRAGUE and much of the rest of Czechoslovakia. After the war, Czechoslovakia expelled over three million German-speaking inhabitants from the region.

Sue, Louis (1875–1968). French architect and designer, a prominent figure in the ART DECO design of the 1920s and 1930s. Sue was trained as a painter in Paris and also became active as an architect after 1905. He visited Austria in 1910, becoming aware of SECESSION design of the period. In 1912 he set up his own studio in Paris, designing textiles, furniture and ceramics. In 1919 he was a partner (with Andre Mare) in establishing the Compagnie des Arts Francais, devoted to the production of design based somewhat on neoclassical origins, in opposition to the emerging MODERNISM of the time. The firm exhibited at the 1925 Paris Exhibition and designed various Paris shops before achieving special note with its interiors of the French liner *Ile-de-France* in 1928. Sue also designed the Deauville suite on the liner NORMANDIE of 1935. His interior design was featured in the 1937 Paris Exhibition pavilion of the Societe des Artistes-Decorateurs. His 1938 interiors for the Paris house of Helena Rubinstein mixed Art Deco modernism with African art and antiques in a lavish fashion that was somewhat surrealistic in effect. Sue retired in 1953.

Suez Canal. Major ship canal across the Isthmus of Suez in northeastern EGYPT. Along with the PANAMA CANAL, it is one of the most important artificial waterways in the world. More than 100 miles long, the Suez Canal connects the Mediterranean Sea with the Gulf of Suez and the Red Sea and, eventually, the Indian Ocean. The canal thus allows ships traveling between Europe and Indian Ocean ports (as well as ports on the PERSIAN GULF) to avoid the lengthy route around Africa in favor of a quicker and more direct route.

Constructed by the French between 1859 and 1869, the Suez Canal was opened in 1869. The 1888 Convention of Constantinople declared the canal to be a neutral facility operated by the Suez Canal Company. The canal remained open throughout WORLD WAR I and WORLD WAR II; during both wars, it was controlled by the Allies and used for Allied shipping. In 1956, it was nationalized by Egyptian President Gamal Abdel NASSER, provoking the SUEZ CRISIS as the UNITED KINGDOM and FRANCE attempted to seize the canal militarily (see ARAB-ISRAELI WAR OF 1956). The canal remained closed for several months, reopening in April 1957 under Egyptian control. During the SIX-DAY WAR (1967) and the ARAB-ISRAELI WAR OF 1973, the Suez Canal was in the war zone as ISRAEL battled Egypt for control of the region. Several ships were sunk or trapped in the canal. The canal did not reopen until 1975.

Suez Crisis. Following the Egyptian nationalization of the strategically important SUEZ CANAL on July 26, 1956, Britain,

FRANCE and ISRAEL secretly agreed for Israel to attack Egypt through Sinai, while Britain and France occupied the Canal Zone on the pretext of separating the combatants. Israel attacked on October 29. Britain and France began air attacks on Egyptian air force bases on October 31 and landed paratroops at Port Said and Port Fuaz at the mouth of the canal on November 5. These actions provoked intense domestic and international criticism of the two nations. The U.S. refusal to support Britain and France forced a cease-fire on November 6 and the deployment of a United Nations Emergency Force. The Suez crisis confirmed Britain's decline internationally and pushed NASSER closer to the U.S.S.R. British Prime Minister Anthony EDEN resigned in disgrace two months later.

Suharto (1921–). President of INDONESIA (1968–). Born in a village near Yogyakarta, central Java, Suharto underwent basic military training at cadet schools in the early 1940s. He served in several companies and regiments during the war of independence against the Dutch from 1945 to 1949. During the 1950s and first half of the 1960s Suharto rose through the army command, attaining the rank of major general. He assumed leadership of the army in the immediate aftermath of the September 30, 1965, attempted coup and was raised to the rank of general in July 1966. With the removal of SUKARNO from power in March 1967, Suharto was appointed acting president. He was inaugurated as president on March 27, 1968, and was reelected to that position in 1973, 1978, 1983 and 1988. Essentially unchallenged, he dominated Indonesian political life throughout that period.

Sukarno (1901–1970). Indonesian statesman, first president of the republic of Indonesia (1945 to 1966). Born in eastern Java, Sukarno was educated at Dutch schools and studied engineering. As a student he was active in a club that resisted cooperation with the Dutch colonial powers. By 1928 the club had become the Indonesian Nationalist party, and Sukarno had emerged as its leader. During the 1930s the young firebrand was jailed and exiled a number of times. He cooperated with the occupying Japanese forces during World War II, simultaneously working with the independence movement. At the end of the war in 1945, he declared the nation independent and proclaimed himself president. Following a neutralist policy, he hosted the Afro-Asian BANDUNG CONFERENCE in 1955. Becoming increasingly authoritarian, the following year he announced a "guided democracy." In 1959 he dissolved the parliament and in 1963 he proclaimed himself president for life. His foreign policy took an increasingly pro-Communist tack, and he was implicated in a Communist plot against the Indonesian military in 1965. A military counterattack by General SUHARTO eventually resulted in Sukarno's forced retirement in 1966.

Sullivan, Ed (1902–1974). American newspaper columnist and television variety show host. Sullivan was one of the best known celebrities of his era, through both his Broadway beat column, *Little Old New York*, for the New York *Daily News*, and his high visibility as host of the "Ed Sullivan Show" on the CBS television network. The show ran from 1948 to 1971 and featured early television appearances by Elvis PRESLEY and the BEATLES, among other stars. Sullivan, who first joined the *Daily News* in 1932, was the delight of comic impressionists who enjoyed miming his stiff, hunched posture and his trademark line—"really big show."

Sukarno, president, premier, supreme commander of the armed forces, leader of the revolution against the Dutch (1966).

Sullivan, Louis (Henry) (1856–1924). American architect. Widely considered the first architectural modernist in the U.S., Sullivan was born in Boston and studied briefly at the Massachusetts Institute of Technology and at the Ecole des Beaux-Arts, Paris. He is best known for his adage "form follows function," the idea that the outward form of a structure should express its utilitarian function. This dictum forms the philosophical cornerstone of the modernist movement in architecture. Sullivan is noted for his designs of early skyscrapers in which an architectonic and functionalist modernism is embellished by gorgeously organic decorative ornament. Settling in Chicago in 1879, he joined the firm of Dankmar Adler and in 1881 became a partner. There he produced such important designs as the Auditorium Building (Chicago, 1886–89), the Wainwright Building (St. Louis, 1890), the Stock Exchange Building (Chicago, 1893–94) and the Guaranty (now Prudential) Building (Buffalo, 1894–95). Sullivan ended his partnership with Adler in 1895. He produced his last major building, the Schlesinger-Meyer department store (now Carson Pirie Scott), Chicago, from 1899 to 1904.

Going against the tide of the then fashionable neo-classicism, he found it increasingly difficult to obtain clients and concentrated his efforts on less important projects, located mainly in medium-sized midwestern cities. There he created a beautiful series of small banks, notably the National Farmers' Bank (Owatonna, Minnesota, 1907–08) and the Merchants' National Bank (Grinnell, Iowa, 1914). Sullivan was the most influential figure in the development of modern architecture in the U.S. He envisioned a thoroughly American design in the democratic tradition, one that employed the materials of contemporary technology in an organic way and that expressed a profound connection with nature. His architectural philosophy was enunciated in such books as *Kindergarten Chats* (1918) and *Autobiography of an Idea* (1924) and was brought to fruition later in the 20th century by a number of disciples and pupils, notably Frank Lloyd WRIGHT.

American impresario Ed Sullivan (1965).

Sully-Prudhomme, Rene (1839–1907). Essentially a 19th-century figure, the French philosophical poet Sully-Prudhomme received the first NOBEL PRIZE for literature in 1901. The Swedish Academy awarded the prize in recognition of his "excellent merit as an author, and especially of the high idealism, artistic perfection, as well as the unusual combination of qualities of the heart and genius to which his work bears witness." His work is now largely forgotten, but his name is memorialized by the Sully-Prudhomme Prize that he established for young French poets with his Nobel Prize money.

Summersby, Kay [Kay Summersby Morgan] (1909–1975). Confidential secretary, driver and confidante to General Dwight D. EISENHOWER during WORLD WAR II. Summersby was a member of the British Women's Auxiliary Corps and met Eisenhower in England while he was Supreme Commander, Allied Forces in Europe. Their relationship was a closely guarded secret throughout the war. In 1973 it was rumored that Eisenhower at one time wished to divorce his wife, Mamie Dowd Eisenhower, and marry Summersby, but Summersby denied this. Nonetheless, this footnote in history remained a subject of speculation in the popular press and in books through the 1970s and the 1980s and was the subject of a 1978 television movie.

Summerskill, Edith C(lara) (1901–1980). British feminist, social reformer and physician. A member of the LABOUR PARTY, Summerskill was an MP from 1938 to 1961, and briefly chaired the Party (1954–55). Among the feminist causes she successfully championed were equal financial status for married women, the right of a married woman to keep her maiden name and the availability of painless childbirth methods. She also campaigned to improve health care. She developed her own general practice among the London poor and was largely responsible for the founding of the Socialist Medical Association. This, in turn, helped bring about the NATIONAL HEALTH SERVICE (NHS) after World War II.

Sun Also Rises, The. Novel by Ernest HEMINGWAY published in 1926, and as *Fiesta* in Great Britain in 1927. Often cited as Hemingway's finest and most important novel, *The Sun Also Rises* tells the story of the American expatriate journalist Jake Barnes. Wounded and rendered impotent during the war, he is unable to consummate his love affair with Lady Brett Ashley. They travel to Spain, where the vacuity of their lives is set off against the backdrop of the festivities surrounding a bull fight. In Hemingway's terse prose, the novel expressed the malaise and sense of hopelessness following WORLD WAR I, and it is typical of his fiction with its stalwart hero and depictions of fishing and bull fighting as masculine moral contests.

Sunay, Cevdet (1899–1982). President of TURKEY (1966–73). Sunay played a key role in maintaining a parliamentary democracy when strife between military and political leaders forced the resignation of Premier Suleyman DEMIREL's government in 1971.

Sunday, Billy (William Ashley) (1863–1935). American evangelist and prohibitionist. Sunday, a minister of the Chicago Presbytery, ordained April 15, 1903, is said to have preached to more people than any other man in Christian history before the age of mass communication. He is further given credit for being the single greatest factor in causing the decline of the saloon in the United States. Between 1904 and 1907 Sunday received from 1,000 to 5,000 converts per month. He galvanized evangelistic meetings in major cities across the country, during which he was known to jump over the pulpit, tear his hair and occasionally roll on the floor, while still delivering sermons with sincere warmth. Sunday began life in the Midwest as a very successful professional baseball player from 1883 to 1890 with Chicago, Pittsburgh and Philadelphia teams and is credited with developing the bunt.

Sun Ra [Herman "Sonny" Blound] (1914–). American keyboardist-composer-band leader. Sun Ra exemplifies what might be called free-form, postmodern jazz. Achieving early prominence as a pianist-arranger with big band leader Fletcher HENDERSON in the late 1940s, Sun Ra moved to Chicago where his Myth-Science or Solar Arkestra became a key part of that city's thriving avant-garde music scene. By the 1960s, his eclectic approach had consolidated; like much of the period's new music, there were juxtapositions of old and new, with traditional big band and Dixieland elements mixing freely with various electronic effects and open-ended improvisations. Sun Ra has also incorporated mixed media strategies by utilizing modern dance as well as slide and light shows; exotic costuming and musical motifs loosely derived from Egyptian and astronomical sources add yet another dimension to his concert and club appearances, which some have bracketed as PERFORMANCE ART. In spite of having had little sustained work, Sun Ray has kept the Solar Arkestra together by dint of his charismatic personality and vision. Though his greatest influence has been on the European avant-garde, Sun Ra is significant as an emblem of the idiosyncratic fusions of musical, theatrical and literary sources characterizing so much of what is described under the rubric of contemporary "postmodern art."

For further reading:
Litweiler, John, *The Freedom Principle: Jazz After 1958*. New York: William Morrow, 1984.

Sunshine Act [Freedom of Information Act]. During the administration of President Richard NIXON, it was revealed that the federal government had systematically maintained files on American citizens suspected of being disloyal. Both the FBI and the CIA were involved in domestic surveillance of citizens. After the WATERGATE scandal and the end of the VIETNAM WAR, public opinion demanded access to these files. The 1976 Freedom of Information Act allows citizens and businesses to request copies of government records. Certain records are exempted, including those that touch on trade secrets of businesses and national security. Citizens can not only learn if federal agencies maintain any files pertaining to them, but also receive copies of such files. This law has also been used successfully by scholars and researchers. The U.S. government and a number of states have "sunshine" or "open meeting" laws that require all governmental meetings to be announced in advance and open to the public. A "sunset law" is a provision—in any act that empowers a government body—requiring a government body to automatically go out of existence unless the legislature specifically votes to reinstate it. The act is intended to promote more efficient government by eliminating nonessential bodies and agencies.

Sun Yat-sen [born Sun Wen] (1867–1925). Chinese revolutionary leader. The father of the Chinese republic was born in Hsiang-Shan, Kwangtung Province. The son of fairly well-to-do peasants, he attended a church school in Honolulu (1879–82) and was strongly influenced by Christianity. He studied medicine in Canton and Hong Kong, where he practiced for a short time. Devoted to the overthrow of the Ch'ing Dynasty, Sun fled CHINA in 1895 after a failed revolt. He toured the world, picking up the support of expatriate Chinese and studying contemporary Western social and political theories. In 1905, in Japan, he founded the T'ung-meng hue (Alliance Society), a revolutionary league. Two years later he issued a manifesto containing the first published version of his Three Principles of the People (San-min chu-i). These cornerstones of his political ideology were nationalism, democracy and the livelihood of the people. When revolution broke out in China in 1911, Sun was elected provisional president of the newly formed Chinese Republic. Within months he resigned in favor of YUAN SHIH-K'AI, who was able to stabilize the republic through his political power. As Yuan's imperial ambitions surfaced, Sun's associate Sung Chiao-jen organized a rival party, the KUOMINTANG, and Sun became its leader. In 1913 he led an unsuccessful revolt against Yuan and fled to Japan. Returning to China in 1917, he became president of a rival government in Canton in 1921. In 1924, he began a policy of cooperation with the communists and received aid from the U.S.S.R. in hopes of attaining full national authority and uniting the country. Two years after his death the communists and the Kuomintang split, each claiming to be Sun's true political heir. Today, Sun Yat-sen is a revered national hero in China, and his tomb in Nanking is a national shrine.

Sun Yefang (1907–1983). Chinese economist. Sun Yefang's advocacy of economic incentives and price mechanisms in the People's Republic of CHINA under MAO TSE-TUNG led to his imprisonment at the beginning of the CULTURAL REVOLUTION (1966). However, following the death of Mao and the arrest of the GANG OF FOUR, his ideas won official acceptance and helped form the basis of DENG XIAOPING's economic modernization program.

Sun Yun-hsuan (1930–). Sun Yun-hsuan succeeded Chiang Ching-kuo as prime minister of TAIWAN in 1978. Trained as an engineer at Harbin Polytechnic Institute, he worked at power plants in China, the United States, Nigeria and Taiwan, where he was president of the Taiwan Power Company from 1962 to 1964. He served in the cabinet as minister of communications (1967–69) and economic affairs (1969–78) before becoming prime minister. He retired in 1984 after suffering a stroke.

superconductors. Superconductors are materials that conduct electricity without any resistance. There are no known naturally existing superconductors; in most materials, superconductivity can occur only at extremely low temperatures. The basic principles of superconductivity were discovered by American physicists John BARDEEN, Leon N. COOPER and John Robert Schrieffer, who shared the 1972 NOBEL PRIZE in physics for their work. Superconductors have important applications in electromagnetics and, potentially, in sophisticated electronic circuitry.

Superman. The first and most influential comic book hero made his first appearance in 1938, in DC Comics' *Action Comics #1*. The creation of Jerry Siegel and Joe Shuster, Superman was a native of the doomed planet Krypton who had been sent to Earth as an infant and raised in the midwestern town of Smallville by foster parents Jonathan and Martha Kent. As an adult, "Clark Kent" moves to the nearby city of Metropolis, where he becomes a reporter on the *Daily Planet*, working alongside colleagues Perry White, Jimmy Olsen and Lois Lane. In his hidden life as a crime-fighting superhero, Superman fights the forces of evil, utilizing the extraordinary powers he enjoys on Earth, including flying, X-ray vision and super strength. He is impervious to bullets and is susceptible only to kryptonite, a piece of Krypton that has survived the planet's explosion. Besides comic books, Superman has performed his feats in novels, on radio, in movie serials, in animated cartoons, on television and in feature-length motion pictures.

supply-side economics. An economic theory stressing the importance of the aggregate supply of goods and services in influencing prices and employment in the economy. Supply-side economics was a reaction to Keynesian economics, which focused attention on the demand side. Supply-side theories were applied to the U.S. economy by President Ronald REAGAN, who radically lowered taxes with the goal of increasing savings and investment without an increase in inflation. Proponents of the supply-side theory used the **Laffer curve** to theorize that tax cuts could pay for themselves by increasing incentives and production, which would generate additional tax revenues. Although liberals and many Democrats attacked the tax cut as a boon to the wealthy, supporters argued that the **"trickle down"** effect of the tax cut would benefit the entire economy.

Suppression of Communism Act (1950). South African legislation banning the Communist Party, defining all persons advocating political, industrial, social or economic change as "Communists." The justice minister was empowered to impose banning orders on individuals, limiting their rights to publish, speak or meet others, and effectively providing for house arrest.

Suprematism. Abstract art movement of an extreme geometrical character that was created by the Russian painter Kasimir MALEVICH in 1913. At first it was built solely on the square, while later its elements increased to encompass the square, circle, triangle and cross, all flatly painted on pure canvas. It was important in the U.S.S.R. until 1921, when the government turned against abstract art movements. The austere concepts of suprematism were largely spread by the BAUHAUS publication (1927) of the German translation of its manifesto, Malevich's *Non-Objective World*, and the movement was an important influence on the development of European modernism. Perhaps the best-known suprematist work is Malevich's *White on White* in the collection of the Museum of Modern Art, New York City.

Supremes, the. See Diana ROSS.

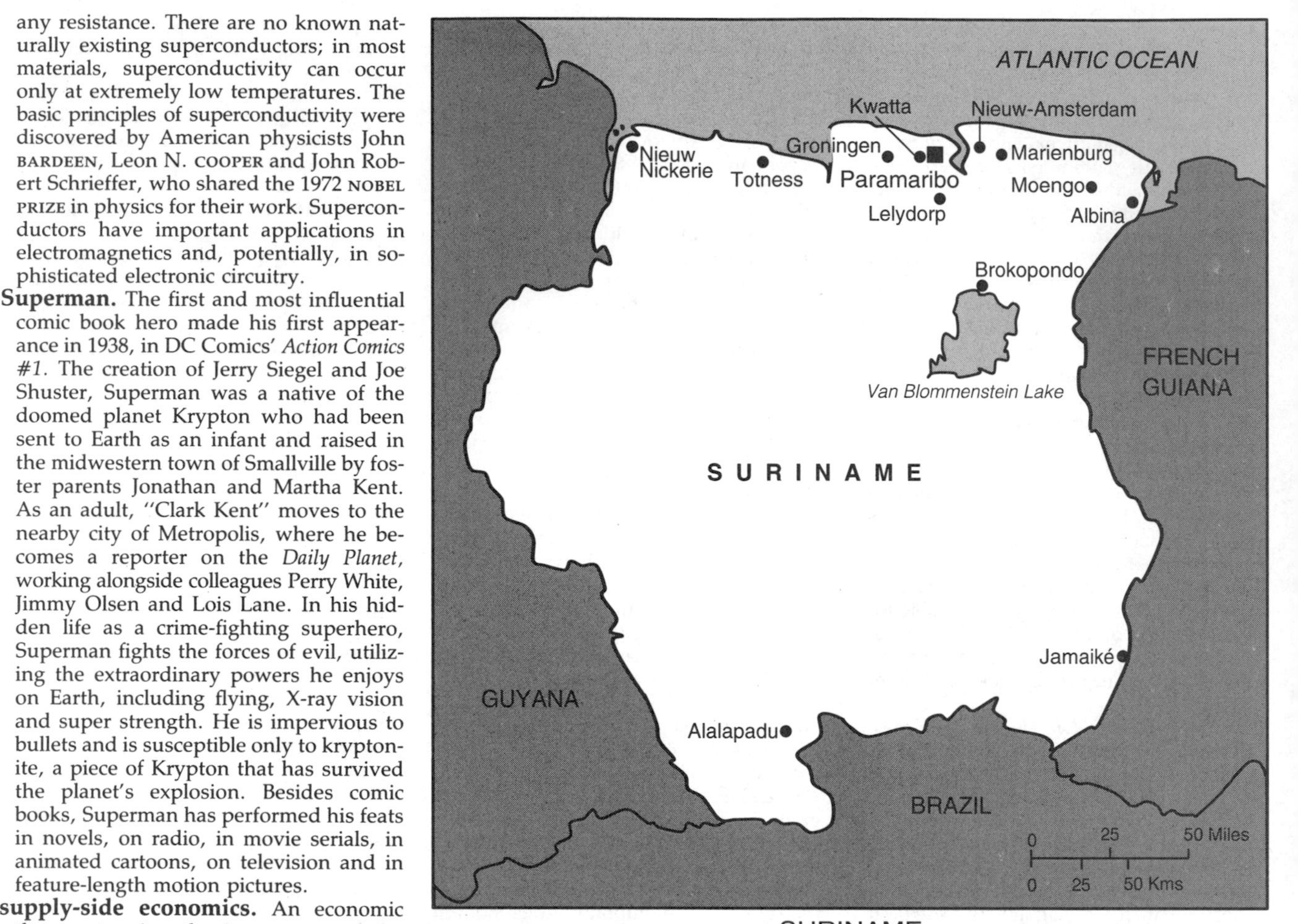

SURINAME

Suriname. Suriname covers an area of 63,022 square miles on the Atlantic coast of northeastern South America. A Dutch possession since 1677, the former Dutch Guiana became an equal member of the "Tripartite Kingdom" of the NETHERLANDS in 1954. Coalition governments, formed among political parties that had developed around racial identity, governed the country between 1958 and 1969. Full independence was granted in 1975. A military coup in 1980 brought Desi Bouterse to power. He dissolved the legislature and dismissed the president. Subsequent power struggles between political and military groups resulted in strikes and demonstrations and the killing of several prominent citizens. A new constitution was introduced in 1987, and a gradual transition to democracy is underway.

surrealism. Movement in art and literature that attempted to liberate artistic expression from convention and reason. Founded in Paris in 1924 by Andre BRETON, whose *Manifeste du surrealisme* (Manifesto of Surrealism) was published that year, surrealism built on the foundation laid by such post-World War I movements as CUBISM, FUTURISM and DADA. However, it replaced the revolutionary nihilism of Dada with a more positive philosophy that attempted to rejuvenate esthetic expression. As a literary movement, surrealism is concerned more with creating novel combinations of words than in the literal meanings of those words. In literature, surrealism appeared principally in France, where its adherents included Louis ARAGON, Robert DESNOS, and Paul ELUARD, Henri Michaux, Benjamin Peret, Jacques PREVERT and Philippe Soupault, as well as the filmmaker Jean COCTEAU. In Britain, poet Dylan THOMAS was strongly influenced by the surrealists, and in America, the work of E.E. CUMMINGS and William Carlos WILLIAMS also shows elements of surrealism. In the visual arts, the influence of surrealism was more widely felt, becoming dominant in the 1920s and '30s. Artists such as Salvador

DALI, Max ERNST, Rene MAGRITTE, Joan MIRO, Andre MASSON and Yves TANGUY embraced surrealism, and their works demonstrated the fantastic imagery, dream-like symbols, incongruous juxtapositions and spontaneity characteristic of the movement. Although surrealism managed to survive World War II, it never regained the prominence it enjoyed in the prewar years.

Surveyor. Following the RANGER and Lunar Orbiter series, the Surveyor program launched seven exploratory probes to the moon between May 1966 and January 1968. Beginning with Surveyor 1, five of the probes succeeded in making the soft landings on the surface of the moon that would be essential to the future manned APOLLO missions. They sent back valuable geological, scientific and engineering data, including over 10,000 photographs from one mission alone. In another first, Surveyor 6 succeeded in lifting off from the moon's surface and moving 10 feet to a new location.

Susskind, David (Howard) (1920–1987). American television, motion picture, and theater producer. Susskind was one of America's earliest and best-known TV talk-show hosts. He set up his own production company in 1952, and by the late 1950s was producing more live television than the three U.S. networks combined. Over the years his productions won numerous awards. Susskind took to the airwaves himself as an interviewer in 1958 with "Open End," a late-night New York City talk show without set time limits. In 1976 "Open End" became "The David Susskind Show," a two-hour program eventually carried by 100 stations; it remained on the air until 1986. Susskind continued to focus on serious issues—although in a combative manner that was not universally admired—long after other talk shows had veered to entertainment.

Sutherland, George (1862–1942). Associate justice, U.S. Supreme Court (1922–38). Born in Britain, Sutherland graduated from Brigham Young University and attended the University of Michigan Law School for one year before starting to practice law in Utah. After serving as a state senator he was elected to the U.S. House of Representatives and then to the Senate in 1904. In the Senate Sutherland proved a reactionary, opposing the passage of both the Clayton Antitrust Act and the Federal Trade Commission Act. His own REPUBLICAN PARTY failed to put him up for reelection in 1916. Sutherland stayed in Washington and helped Warren G. HARDING in his successful presidential campaign. Sutherland was rewarded with several government posts and in 1922 Harding appointed him to the Supreme Court. Sutherland was predictably conservative on the Court, opposing much of President Franklin D. ROOSEVELT'S NEW DEAL legislation during the 1930s. He retired in 1938 after Roosevelt's unsuccessful COURT-PACKING ATTEMPT.

Sutherland, Graham (Vivian) (1903–1980). British painter. Sutherland gained fame in the 1930s as a landscape painter; his landscapes reflected both a sense of romanticism and aspects of SURREALISM. During WORLD WAR II he was commissioned to record scenes of wartime Britain. The result was a body of powerful work depicting the violence and destruction of the war. After the war, he gained new acclaim as a portrait painter. His notable works of this period included portraits of Somerset MAUGHAM, Helena Rubenstein, and Lord BEAVERBROOK. Sutherland became embroiled in controversy when Sir Winston CHURCHILL publicly criticized Sutherland's 1955 portrait of him.

Sutherland, Joan (1926–). Austalian opera singer. Acclaimed for her large, beautiful voice and her bel canto singing, Sutherland is one of the outstanding coloratura sopranos of the second half of this century. Originally trained as a Wagnerian soprano, she became a coloratura under the guidance of her husband, conductor **Richard Bonynge**. She made her London debut at Covent Garden in 1952, but it was her electrifying performance as Lucia in Franco Zeffrelli's production of *Lucia de Lammermoor* in 1959 that made her famous. In 1960 she made her American debut with the Dallas Opera in Handel's *Alcina*, another role for which she is known. Other famous roles include Marie in *The Daughter of the Regiment*, Donna Anna in *Don Giovanni*, and the title role in *Norma*. In addition, she has made several critically-acclaimed recordings, performed on television, and appeared at the Glyndebourne and Edinburgh Festivals. Her partnership with the Italian tenor Luciano PAVAROTTI was legendary. Sutherland was made a Dame of the British Empire in 1979 and retired from the operatic stage in 1990.

Sutton, Willie ["the actor"] (1901–1980). American bank robber and prison escape artist of the 1930s and 1940s. Sutton was noted for his meticulously planned bank robberies, which he often pulled off while wearing ingenious disguises. His criminal career spanned 35 years, ending in 1952; he estimated that he robbed close to $2 million. He spent more than half his life behind bars.

Sverdlov, Yakov Mikhailovich (1885–1919). Russian politician. He joined the Social Democratic Labor Party in 1901 and from 1902 to 1917 acted as a professional revolutionary for the BOLSHEVIKS. In 1913 he was made part of the central committee. Following the February Revolution Sverdlov was the chief organizer of the party and became chairman of the All-Russian Central Executive Committee of the Soviets. He was a close collaborator of LENIN.

Australian opera singer Joan Sutherland acknowledges applause at her final performance at the Sydney Opera House (1990).

Svevo, Italo [pen name of Ettore Schmitz] (1861–1928). Italian novelist. Svevo, who has become recognized as one of the leading Italian novelists of the century, owes his present renown largely to the championing of his work by James JOYCE. In the 1910s the expatriate Joyce served as an English tutor to Svevo, who was unhappily devoting himself to a business career. Two previous novels by Svevo—*A Life* (1892) and *As a Man Grows Older* (1898)—had received negative reviews and Svevo had concluded that he was not destined to write. But with Joyce's encouragement, Svevo produced his most famous work, *Confessions of Zeno* (1923), an intricate comic novel revolving around the central protagonist's attempts to quit smoking. The novel, which was among the first works of literature to make major use of Freudian psychoanalytical themes, received international acclaim. *Further Confessions of Zeno* (1969) appeared posthumously.

Svoboda, Ludvik (1895–1979). President of CZECHOSLOVAKIA (1968–75). A career army officer, Svoboda became a hero of WORLD WAR II by forming and leading a Czech unit within the Soviet army. He did not emerge onto the political scene until 1968. During the PRAGUE SPRING of that year he was chosen to replace Antonin NOVOTNY as president of Czechoslovakia. As a war hero, he had credibility both with the reformers (led by Alexander DUBCEK) and with the Soviets and hardliners. During the SOVIET INVASION OF CZECHOSLOVAKIA soon thereafter, he went to Moscow to negotiate with Soviet leaders. Svoboda was the only political figure of the Prague Spring to survive the post-invasion purges of the Czechoslovak Communist Party, in which some 400,000 Czechs lost their party membership. Svoboda was reelected president in 1973 but resigned due to illness two years later and was replaced by Communist Party secretary Gustav HUSAK.

Swanson, Gloria [born Gloria Josephine May Svensson or Swenson] (1899–1983). Legendary American film star of the 1920s. Swanson began her film career in the 'teens, but achieved real stardom in a series of SILENT FILMS for Cecil B. DE MILLE. A highly publicized series of marriages and divorces in the late 1920s, the near-bankruptcy incurred by the unfinished *Queen Kelly* (1928), and the difficulties of the transition to sound led to her retirement from the screen in the mid-1930s. A comeback in Billy WILDER'S *Sunset Boulevard* (1950) brought her one of her greatest roles, the neurotic fading movie star Norma Desmond. Her later years were spent promoting cosmetics and health foods. Swanson appeared in over 60 movies as well as in numerous television programs and some stage plays. She was reportedly the first actress to make over $1 million a year. Small of stature, she nonetheless imparted a grand presence on the screen. "I am big," says her character in *Sunset Boulevard*, "it's the pictures that got small."

For further reading:

Swanson, Gloria, *Swanson on Swanson: An Autobiography*. New York: Random House, 1980.

SWAPO [South West African People's Organization]. Founded in 1960 by Sam Nujoma and Herman Toivo Ja Toivo. In 1920 NAMIBIA was mandated by the LEAGUE OF NATIONS to SOUTH AFRICA, which later attempted to integrate it into its other territories. In 1966 SWAPO began mounting guerrilla actions against South African military units, following a United Nations resolution revoking South Africa's mandate. In 1971 the UNITED NATIONS recognized SWAPO as "sole authentic representative of the people of Namibia." SWAPO was excluded from the independence negotiations and process in the 1970s, and a National Assembly and Council of Ministers were instituted by South Africa. Conflict between South Africa and SWAPO continued through the 1980s. In 1989 SWAPO won 57.3 percent of the vote in UN-supervised elections to determine the future of Africa's last colony.

Swart, Charles (1893–1982). First president of the Republic of SOUTH AFRICA (1961 to 1967). Before South Africa withdrew from the British Commonwealth, Swart served as minister of justice (1948–59) and governor general (1959–61). He helped draft a number of the nation's APARTHEID laws.

Swaziland [Umbuso Weswatini]. The landlocked kingdom of Swaziland in southern Africa, less than 100 miles from the Indian Ocean, covers a total area of 6,702 square miles. Britain assumed sovereignty in 1894, and in 1903 the governor of the Transvaal was empowered to administer Swaziland. In 1906 those powers were transferred to a high commissioner for Basutoland, Bechuanaland and Swaziland. Limited self-government was granted in 1963. The British resisted South African pressure for incorporation within SOUTH AFRICA, and the Imbokodvo (Grindstone) National Movement, formed by King SOBHUZA II, won all 24 seats in the House of Assembly in 1967, as a kingdom was proclaimed under British protection. Full independence was achieved on September 6, 1968. Swaziland maintained close links with South Africa in the 1970s and joined the South African Customs Union; the Swazi government signed a secret nonaggression pact with South Africa in February 1982 and expelled several AFRICAN NATIONAL CONGRESS members. Nevertheless, the South Africans launched a raid in June 1986 on the Swazi capital of Mbabane, killing three ANC members. In 1973 and 1977 King Sobhuza II dismissed parliament and abolished the

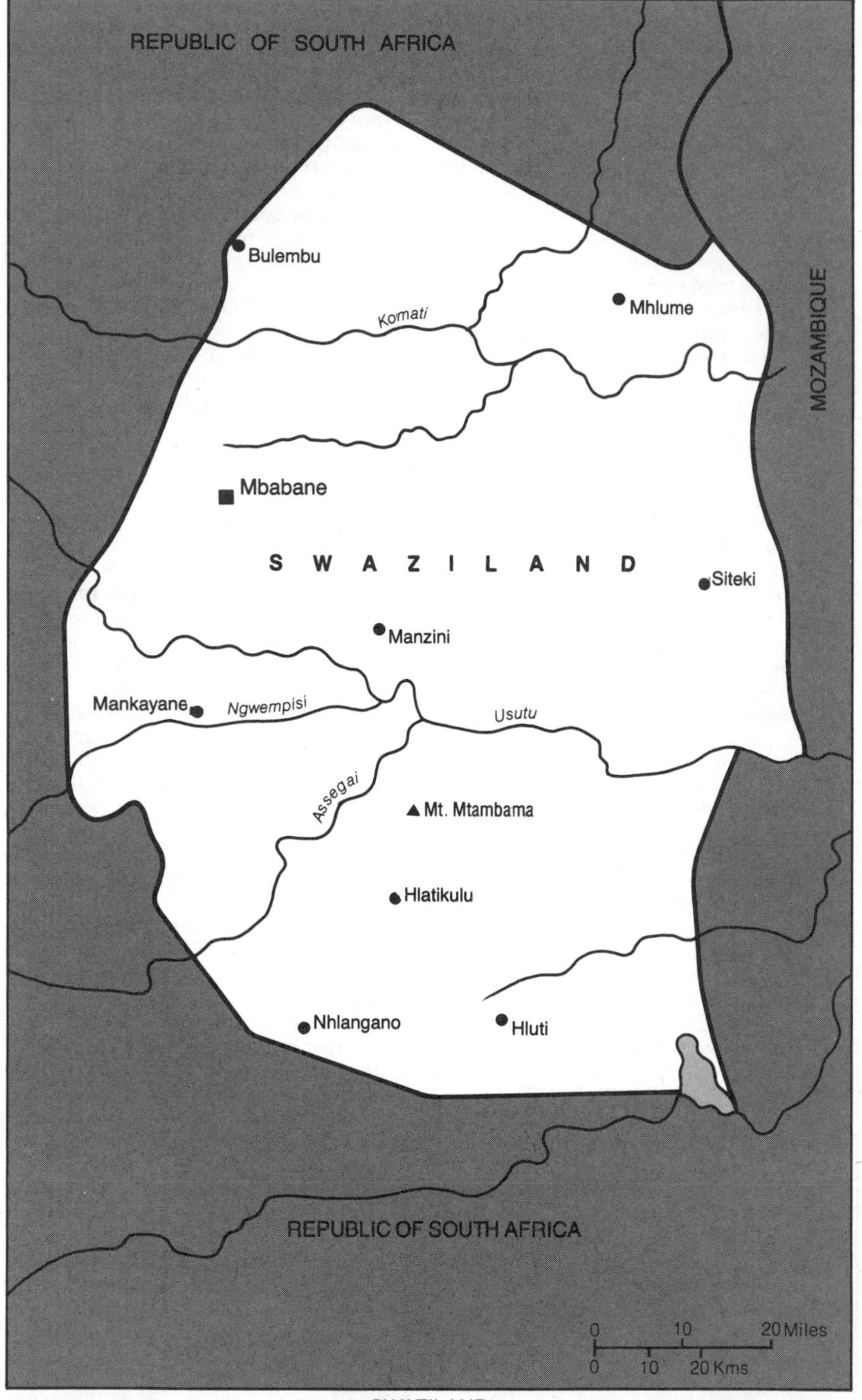

SWAZILAND

constitution, only to replace it with a new one two years later. Sobhuza II died in August 1982 and was succeeded by his teenage son, Prince Makhosetive. A power struggle ensued between the traditionalists and the modernists, which continued through the 1980s. Makhosetive was crowned as Mswati III on April 25, 1986.

Sweatt, Heman (1913–1982). African-American whose lawsuit against the state of Texas led to a landmark 1950 Supreme Court decision challenging the doctrine of "separate but equal" education for blacks. Sweatt brought suit after being denied admission to the all-white University of Texas Law School in 1946. The Supreme Court ordered him admitted.

Sweden. Sweden covers an area of 172,786 square miles on the Scandinavian Peninsula of Northern Europe. Neutral during both World Wars, Sweden was criticized by the Allied powers during those wars for its continued trade with Germany. The Social Democratic Party, which dominated successive governments from 1932 to 1976, made Sweden one of the most

SWEDEN

1919	Universal adult suffrage introduced.
1932	Social Democrats under Per Albin Hansson take power.
1949	The Riksdag passes the new Freedom of the Press Act.
1969	Olof Palme becomes prime minister.
1973	Carl XVI Gustav succeeds his grandfather Gustav VI.
1975	Implementation of constitutional measures that reduce the monarch to ceremonial functions and create a unicameral Riksdag with a three-year term.
1986	Palme is shot dead on a Stockholm street and is succeeded as prime minister by Ingvar Carlsson.

SWEDEN

affluent countries in the world, as well as the most advanced WELFARE STATE. Sweden joined the UNITED NATIONS as a nonaligned country and became a founding member of the Nordic Council (1953) and EFTA (1959). In 1975 Sweden initiated a constitutional reform that limited the monarchy to ceremonial functions. Prime Minister Olof Palme was murdered in 1986; the governments formed by his successor, Ingvar Carlsson, have been plagued by political scandals and economic problems.

Swing Era, The. The Swing Era, extending from the early 1930s to the late 1940s, was named for the type of popular music associated with the period. "Swing" music was played by instrumental ensembles typically ranging from 12 to 16 musicians, a repertory based largely on tunes from Tin Pan Alley, Broadway shows and Hollywood movies, and a subtly insinuated pulse where all four beats of the measure were given approximately equal weight. Growing out of the New Orleans-and Chicago-styled jazz groups of "The Roaring Twenties," these larger instrumental units typically included four to five saxophones (usually "doubling" on clarinet), three to four trombones and four to five trumpets; the rhythm section, by the mid-1930s, included piano, guitar (replacing banjo), string bass (replacing tuba) and drums. It was a period of virtuoso soloists (trumpeters Harry JAMES and Roy Eldridge, for example) and "star" leaders both black (Fletcher HENDERSON, Duke ELLINGTON, Count BASIE) and white (Benny GOODMAN, Glenn MILLER, Woody HERMAN, Stan KENTON). Popularized by new media such as network radio and the sound film, Swing Era big bands kept America dancing during the GREAT DEPRESSION of the 1930s and the war years of the 1940s. In the mid-1940s, Swing bands began to fade due to war-inflated traveling expenses and the public's growing affection for crooners like Frank SINATRA. Today, the big band sound resounds on "oldies" radio broadcasts and in traveling "ghost" bands playing the repertoires of such Swing Era favorites as Miller, Herman and Ellington. Big bands have also become important training grounds for nurturing young improvisers in the burgeoning jazz education movement.

For further reading:

Simon, George T., *The Big Bands*. New York: Macmillan, 1967.

Switzerland [Swiss Confederation]. Situated in central Europe, the landlocked Alpine country of Switzerland covers an area of 15,939 square miles. One of the most prosperous and politically stable countries in the world, Switzerland has become a center for international banking. After declaring its neutrality in 1815, the country reaffirmed its non-belligerent status during both World Wars, playing a humanitarian role through the work of the International Red Cross (founded in Geneva in 1864). Switzerland maintains observer status at the UNITED NATIONS, participating in many

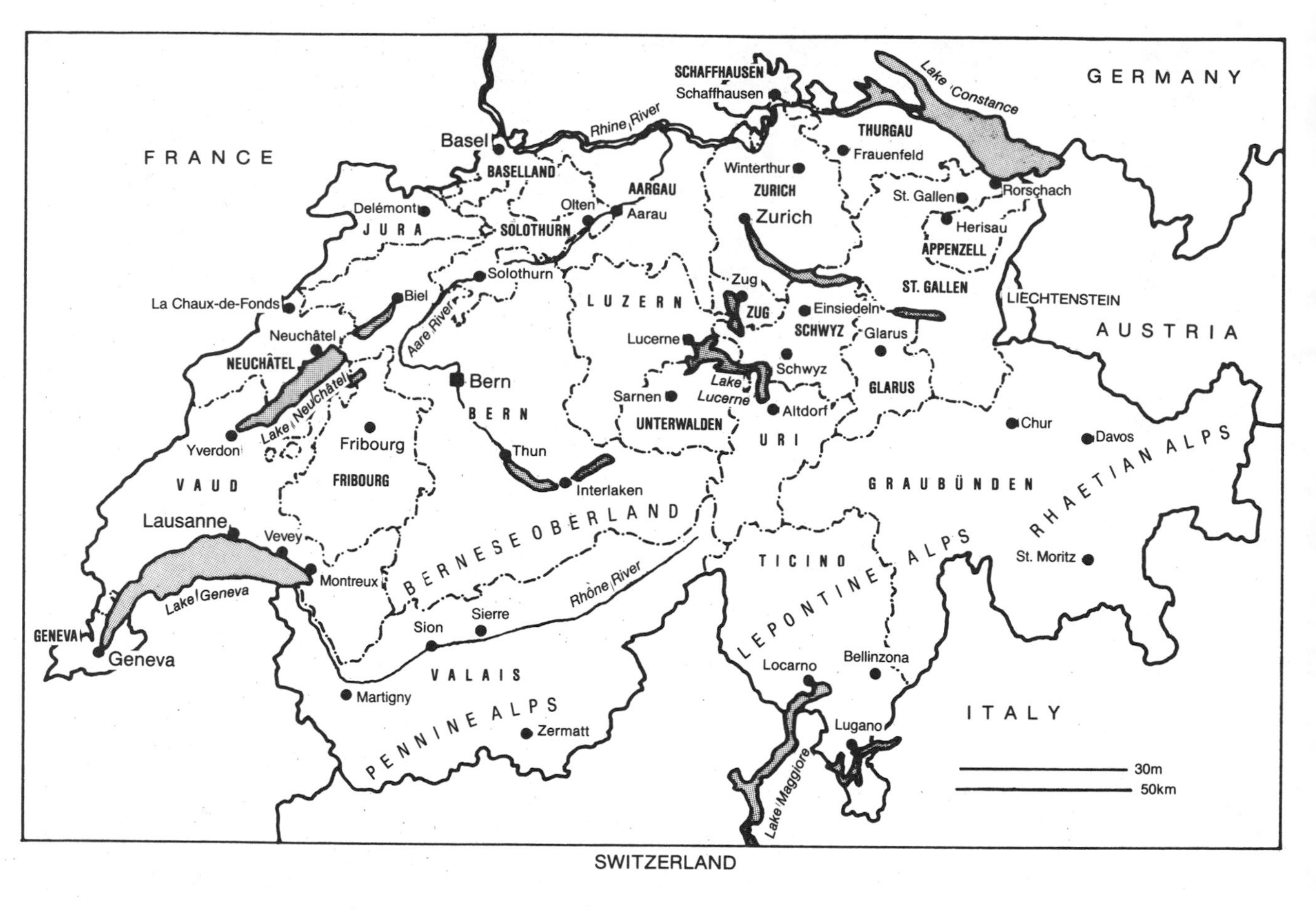

SWITZERLAND

UN agencies, and was a founding member of EFTA (1959). Restrictions on foreign workers and alien residents were imposed after the 1967 and 1971 elections, which brought increased power to radical right-wing groups demanding such curbs. Women were given the right to vote in federal elections in 1971.

Symington, (William) Stuart (1901–1988). American politician, Democratic senator from Missouri (1953–76). Symington entered government service in 1945 when President Harry S TRUMAN appointed him chairman of the Surplus Property Administration. When the Air Force was formed in 1947, he was named its first secretary. During the ARMY-MCCARTHY HEARINGS in 1954, he emerged as a strong opponent of Sen. Joseph R. MCCARTHY. In 1956 and 1960 he ran unsuccessfully for the Democratic presidential nomination. Although he had long supported a strong U.S. military force, in the 1960s he became increasingly critical of military spending and the U.S. presence in VIETNAM. He retired from the Senate in 1976.

Syndicate, The. New York-based organization of theatrical producers and businessmen who at the turn of the century controlled the American popular stage. As a result of the Panic of 1893, the theater establishment, like other businesses, was on the verge of economic collapse and crippling unemployment. As had happened with the forming monopolies in oil, tobacco and rubber, the theaters formed their own trust. This so-called Syndicate dominated the artistic and business practices of the stage from 1896 to 1915, growing from just 33 theaters to thousands of houses and hundreds of traveling companies nationwide. This was the age of the touring show. The Syndicate brought badly needed order to theater construction, traveling-circuit management and play production. It centralized control of the star system, exploiting the talents of such contemporary luminaries as Maude ADAMS, Henry Irving and De Wolfe Hopper, and encouraged such blockbuster productions as *Ben Hur* (1899) and the ZIEGFELD FOLLIES. Of the six organizing producers—Sam Nixon, Fred Zimmerman, Al Hayman, Marc Klaw, Abe Erlanger and Charles Frohman, only Frohman was directly involved in theatrical production. Klaw was the legal brains behind the operations, and Erlanger provided the business acumen. The relative merits of the Syndicate continue to be debated. On the positive side, it increased employment and standardized house conditions. It toughened copyright protections against the infringing new medium, the motion picture. It introduced business operations of binding contracts and promotions that are in use today. It invested heavily in theatrical real estate and construction. On the other hand, it enforced a monopoly over producers and players, blackballing such recalcitrants as actress Minnie Maddern Fiske

SWITZERLAND

1901	Albert Einstein becomes citizen.
1920	First session of League of Nations meets in Geneva.
1971	Women gain right to vote in national elections; constitutional article accepted on protection of environment.
1984	Elizabeth Kopp is first woman member of Federal Council.
1986	Thirty tons of toxic wastes released into Rhine in fire at Sandoz company warehouse in Basel; spill considered worst environmental disaster in Europe in decade; voters reject Swiss membership in UN.
1990	Outlaws money-laundering; tightens immigration laws, including banning seekers of political asylum from working for first three months of stay.

and producer David BELASCO. Priorities in box-office draw encouraged a standard in artistic mediocrity that resisted experiment and change. After 1905 the Syndicate faced formidable competition from the new Shubert organization of theater houses. After the 1915 death of Charles Frohman, the Syndicate declined and gradually lost control to its rival. Meanwhile, the Little Theater movement encouraged the local control of theater houses and play production.

For further reading:

Meserve, Walter J., *An Outline History of American Drama*. Totowa, New Jersey: Littlefield, Adams and Co., 1970.

Synge, (Edmund) John Millington (1871–1909). Irish playwright. Following his education at Trinity College, Dublin, Synge traveled to Paris, where he lived the bohemian life of a struggling and impoverished writer. There in 1896 he was befriended by the poet W.B. YEATS. Yeats urged him to abandon Paris and go to the Aran islands off the west coast of Ireland. Synge did so, spending his summers there between 1898 and 1902, and was transformed into a major artist. He subsequently wrote six remarkable plays imbued with a deep sympathy for the Irish peasantry and the rhythms of natural Irish speech. In 1906, with Yeats and Lady Augusta GREGORY, he became a director of the ABBEY THEATRE, where most of his work was first performed. His plays include *In the Shadow of the Glen* (1903), *Riders to the Sea* (1904, adapted as an opera by Ralph VAUGHAN WILLIAMS, 1937) and *The Tinker's Wedding* (1908). His masterpiece was THE PLAYBOY OF THE WESTERN WORLD (1907), which caused riots when it was first performed at the Abbey. Synge suffered from Hodgkin's disease and was unable to complete his last play, *Deirdre of the Sorrows* (1910). While they aroused controversy, Synge's ironic, realistic and poetic plays enormously influenced subsequent Irish theater.

Syria [Syrian Arab Republic]. Syria is located on the Mediterranean Sea coast of the Middle East and covers an area of 71,480 square miles. Ruled from Constantinople by the Ottoman Turks until the collapse of the OTTOMAN EMPIRE at the end of WORLD WAR I, Syria became a French Mandate of the LEAGUE OF NATIONS in 1920. Nationalist sentiments led to riots and strikes until the country gained independence in 1946. After several coups in the 1950s and early 1960s political control was seized by the BA'ATH Party (Arab Socialist Renaissance Party) in 1963. Ba'ath military leader Hafiz al-ASSAD seized power in 1970 and has remained president ever since. Uprisings led by Sunni Islamic fundamentalists challenged Assad's rule from 1976 to 1982. In 1976 Syria intervened in the LEBANESE CIVIL WAR and continues to maintain a presence there, although pressure to oust Syria has intensified since 1989. Syria mounted a major military operation in 1987 to end the fighting in BEIRUT. Syria's anti-Israel stance and sponsorship of radical Palestinian factions have created tensions with the United States. Syria has been widely condemned for its human rights abuses and identified as a sponsor of international terrorism. However, Syria supported the UNITED NATIONS sanctions against IRAQ for its invasion of KUWAIT (1990) and joined the United States and other countries in the successful war to oust Iraq (Aug. 1990–Feb. 1991).

Szabo, Gabor (1941–1982). Hungarian guitarist. A freedom fighter, Szabo fled Hungary after the Soviet Union crushed the HUNGARIAN UPRISING (1956) and settled in the U.S. He wrote moody pieces that blended American JAZZ and ROCK AND ROLL rhythms with melodies from Hungary, India and South America. His virtuosity and distinctive melodic style strongly influenced American jazz artists.

Szell, George (1897–1970). Hungarian-born orchestra conductor who at midcentury brought the Cleveland Symphony Orchestra to world prominence. Szell was regarded as one of the finest technicians in the post-TOSCANINI era of conducting. He was born in Budapest and trained in Vienna, conducting his first concert at age sixteen. After studying with Max Reger in Leipzig and with the encouragement of Richard STRAUSS, he succeeded Otto KLEMPERER at the Strasbourg Municipal Theatre in 1917. Other posts included conducting at Darmstadt (1921–1924), Duesseldorf (1922–1924), Berlin (1924–1929) and Prague (1927–1937). During a visit to the U.S. in 1939 World War II broke out and he decided to stay, becoming a citizen in 1946. He became Principal Conductor of the New York Metropolitan Opera from 1942 to 1946 and that year went to the Cleveland Symphony Orchestra, where he remained until his death. His tenure with the orchestra made it one of the greatest ensembles in the world. Like Arturo TOSCANINI and Fritz REINER, Szell stressed absolute fidelity to the score. Scorning showmanship and "romantic" interpretation, he demanded clear articulation and a perfect balance among sections. "It is perfectly legitimate to prefer the hectic, the arhythmic, the untidy," he said, "but to my mind great artistry is not disorderliness." His great series of recordings for CBS-Epic attest to

SYRIA

1918	British-Arab force drives Turks from Damascus; Prince Faisal calls for Syrian nation.
1920	Treaty of San Remo; League of Nations mandates Syria to France; agitation for independence begins.
1926	Lebanon separated from Syria and made independent.
1936	General strike against French rule.
1941	British and Free French defeat Vichy French at Damascus.
1946	French grant independence; Shukri al-Kuwatly is first president.
1948	Syria defeated in attack on Israel.
1949	Military coup.
1957	Election of Ba'ath Party—pan-Arab, secular socialist movement.
1958	Syria forms United Arab Republic with Egypt.
1962	Nasser seeks Egypt-Syria merger; anti-Nasser coup in Damascus; UAR dissolved.
1963	Anti-Nasser wing of Ba'athists takes power.
1967	Golan Heights lost to Israel in Six-Day War; relations with U.S. broken.
1970	Moderate Ba'athists under Assad take power.
1973	Attacks Israel; fought to standstill.
1976	Troops occupy Lebanon; assert traditional ties with Syria.
1977	Sadat visits Israel; Assad breaks ties.
1979	Violence between Sunni Moslems and minority Alewite sect—now powerful through Assad's membership.
1980	Assad supports Iran in war on Iraq; nearly joins war.
1982	Sunni fundamentalist uprising crushed.
1985	Abu Nidal conducts international terror campaign from Damascus.
1989	Soviet aid declines.
1990	Syrian troops participate in Beirut peace arrangements; Assad calls for "Holy War" against Israel; joins U.S.-led force opposing Iraqi occupation of Kuwait.
1991	Assad hints at recognition for Israel; joins U.S.-led regional defense plan with Egypt and Saudis.

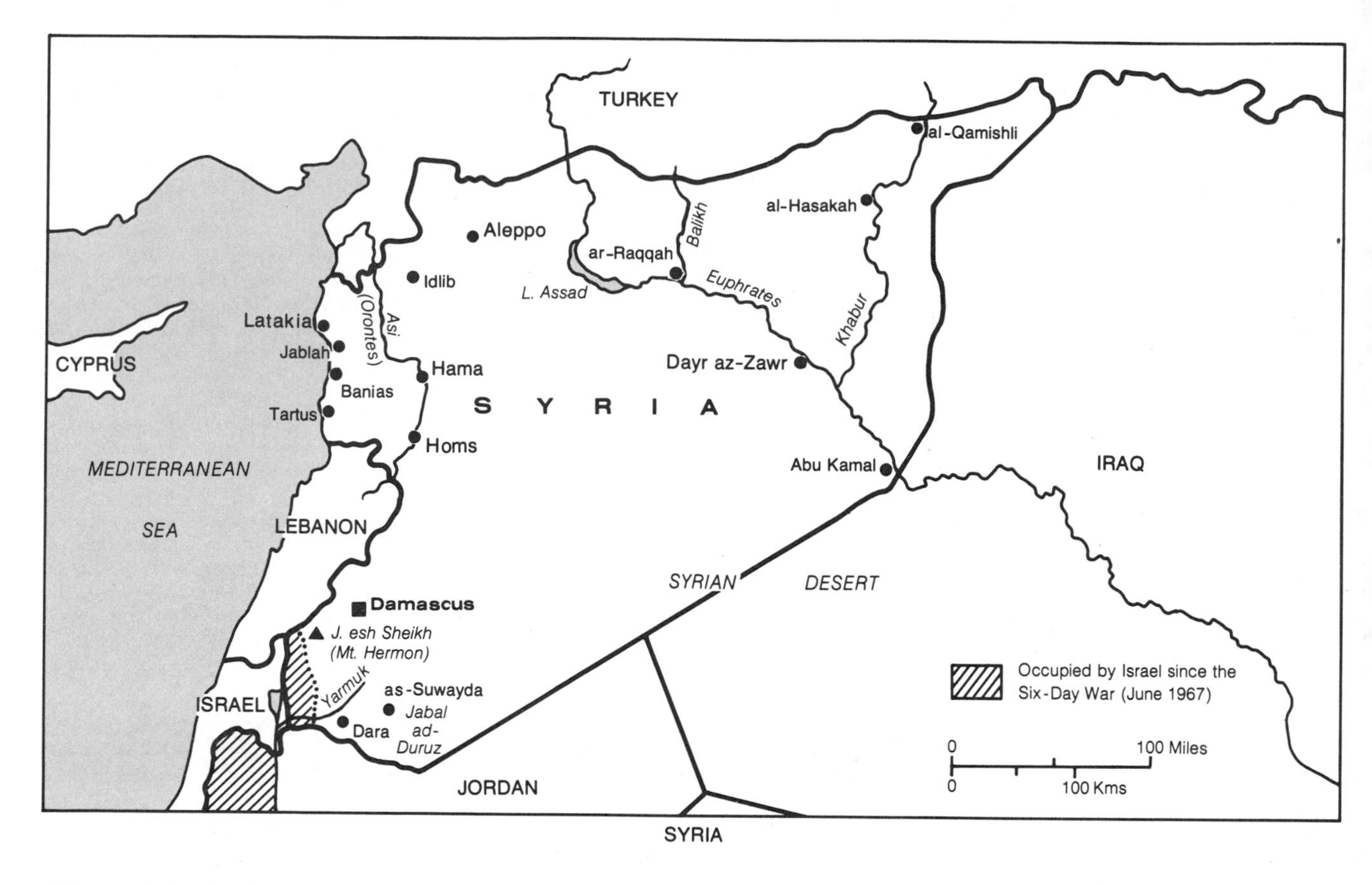

his sensitivity for the works of Haydn, Mozart and Beethoven, although he performed relatively little the French, Russian and modern repertoire. In particular there were notable cycles of Schumann symphonies, the Beethoven piano concertos (especially with pianist Leon Fleischer) and works by William WALTON and Antonin Dvorak.

Szent-Gyorgyi, Albert (1893–1986). Hungarian-born biochemist. Szent-Gyorgyi won the 1937 NOBEL PRIZE for medicine or physiology for his isolation of vitamin C. Although he remained in Hungary during World War II, he spent much of the war in hiding because of his anti-Nazi activities. He came to the U.S. in 1947 and assumed the post of director of research at the Institute of Muscle Research. In 1954 he won an Albert Lasker Award for his research on heart muscle contraction. He received a number of grants for cancer research, but his "bioelectronic" theory of cancer did not gain wide acceptance.

Szeryng, Henryk (1918–1988). Polish-born violinist; a leading exponent of the Romantic school of violin playing. While serving with the Polish government-in-exile during WORLD WAR II he had occasion to go to Mexico, where he decided to settle. He became a Mexican citizen in 1949, later traveling on a diplomatic passport as Mexico's cultural and good will ambassador.

Szigeti, Joseph (1892–1972). Hungarian-American violinist. Born in Budapest, Szigeti was the child prodigy of a violin teacher. He studied with Jeno Hubay and made his professional debut at the age of 11. He performed widely in Germany and made his first tour of Europe in 1912. A superb musician, he was skilled in the classical repertoire and became known for his performances of work by contemporary composers, many of whom, including BARTOK, BLOCH, BUSONI and PROKOFIEV wrote works especially for him. He made his American debut with the Philadelphia Orchestra in 1925. Szigeti and his wife fled Europe after the fall of France. They settled in California, and he became an American citizen in 1951. In the U.S. he was particularly known for his radio concerts and for his many recordings. His autobiography, *With Strings Attached,* was published in 1947.

Szilard, Leo (1898–1964). Hungarian-American physicist. Szilard was born in Budapest and received his doctorate from the University of Berlin in 1922. In 1934, while working in London, he discovered the principle of the nuclear chain reaction, and in 1939, he confirmed the feasibility of using uranium to generate a nuclear reaction. Having immigrated to the U.S. in 1938, the following year Szilard persuaded Albert EINSTEIN to write a letter to President Franklin D. ROOSEVELT, urging him to authorize development of an ATOMIC BOMB. Roosevelt agreed, and the MANHATTAN PROJECT was begun. In 1942, while working on the bomb, Szilard and Enrico FERMI created the first self-sustaining nuclear reactor. One of the first to recognize the potential of atomic energy, Szilard later regretted his work on the MANHATTAN PROJECT, and he became one of the first advocates of nuclear disarmament. After the war, Szilard changed the focus of his research to molecular biology.

Szold, Henrietta (1860–1945). Zionist and educator. Szold pioneered the landmark Baltimore School for Immigrant Workers (1891) and was editor of the Jewish Publication Society of America (1892–1916). In 1912 she was the founder of Hadassah, the world's largest Zionist movement. The first woman elected a World Zionist executive, she directed Youth Aliyah Bureau (1933–45), the world movement to rescue young European Jewish children from the Nazis, and strove for Arab-Jewish cooperation through common social programs. (See also JEWS; ZIONISM.)

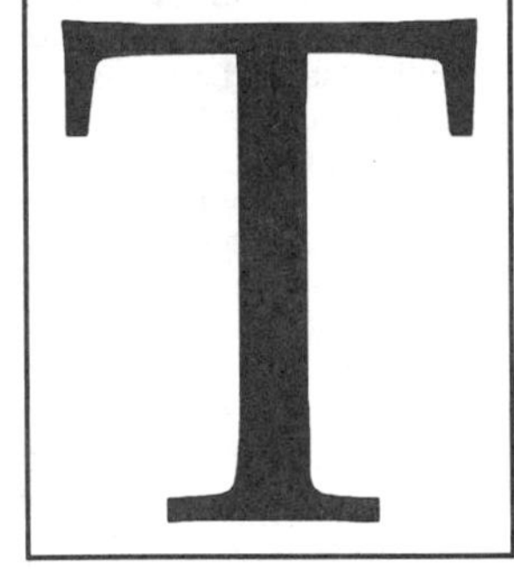

Taft, Robert Alphonso (1889–1953). U.S. senator, son of President William Howard TAFT. Robert Taft practiced law in Ohio and served in the state legislature. He was elected to the U.S. Senate in 1938. A foe of big government, he opposed F.D. ROOSEVELT on a number of his programs and became the leader of the conservative Republicans. His influence in Congress was so great that he blocked many of President Harry S TRUMAN'S FAIR DEAL measures, turning Truman into an unforgiving foe. Although he was an isolationist before WORLD WAR II, Taft favored the UNITED NATIONS. He was coauthor of the TAFT-HARTLEY ACT, regulating labor practices—considered his principal legislative accomplishment. Taft opposed U.S. entry into the NORTH ATLANTIC TREATY ORGANIZATION (NATO). He considered the Truman administration to be soft on communism and supported the early investigations of Senator Joseph MCCARTHY concerning communist infiltration into government. Taft was so thoroughly in tune with his party's line that he became known as "Mr. Republican." He unsuccessfully sought the Republican nomination for president in 1940 and in 1948.

In 1952, he was considered to be the most likely Republican nominee for the office. However, the candidacy of Dwight D. EISENHOWER brought on a long struggle with Taft supporters that almost split the party. After losing the nomination of 1952 to Eisenhower, he loyally supported the Republican ticket. Taft became the majority leader in the Senate and worked closely as an Eisenhower adviser. Some authorities consider Robert Taft to have been one of the most influential senators in U.S. history.

Taft, William Howard (1857–1930). Twenty-seventh president of the UNITED STATES and 10th chief justice of the U.S. Supreme Court. Upon graduation from Yale in 1878, Taft attended Cincinnati Law School and took a law degree in 1880. He began the practice of law in Cincinnati and almost immediately took an active part in local Republican politics, holding several minor public offices before being appointed to serve on the superior court of Ohio (1887–90). In 1890 his selection by President Benjamin Harrison as U.S. solicitor general brought him into national political prominence.

Beginning in 1892, he was presiding judge of the sixth federal circuit court of appeals and spent eight years on that bench. He gained a reputation as serving conservatively but effectively in the post. Although considered anti-labor, his decisions were based on what he thought were the proper limits of labor actions, and he opposed such practices as secondary boycotts and violence.

In 1900, as president of the U.S. commission to the PHILIPPINES he began at once to organize an efficient civilian government there, continuing his effective administration when he became the first U.S. governor of the Philippines. He was particularly successful in improving relations between the Philippine people and the United States. In 1904 President Theodore ROOSEVELT appointed Taft secretary of war, and they became close friends, with Taft as one of the president's most cherished advisers. He was a prime mover in the organization of the PANAMA CANAL construction.

William Howard Taft, 27th president of the United States, later served as chief justice of the Supreme Court.

Personally chosen by Roosevelt as his successor, Taft had little difficulty in the election of 1908. The parcel post system, the postal savings bank and the Department of Labor were among the innovations of his administration. Principal accomplishments were a trade agreement with Canada and arbitration treaties with France and Britain. However, the Senate failed to ratify any of these. His antitrust actions were more numerous than Roosevelt's, but failed to attract much attention. Increasingly attuned to the conservative wing of the REPUBLICAN PARTY, he approved the Payne-Aldrich Tariff Act of 1909, which made few concessions to tariff reduction, because Taft felt it was the best politically possible act. But this angered the Progressive Republicans, and his growing conservatism led him to fall out of favor with Theodore Roosevelt. Roosevelt fought Taft for the Republican presidential nomination in 1912. Failing to get the nod, which went to Taft, Roosevelt organized his own Progressive Party (popularly called the Bull Moose Party) and ran for president. The Republican Party was split, and the Democrats won one of the closest elections in American history. Taft retired to private life, teaching law at Yale University.

In 1921 he was appointed to the post of chief justice of the Supreme Court by President Warren G. HARDING. He made substantial contributions to the administrative procedures of the Court, inaugurating methods that managed to eliminate the backlog of cases on the docket. In 1925 he was instrumental in the passage of the Judges' Act. This permitted the courts more discrimination in accepting cases.

One of his important opinions came in BAILEY V. DREXEL FURNITURE CO. (1922), in which he concurred with the majority that Congress had exceeded its authority to the extent of a loss of state sovereignty. In *Adkins v. Children's Hospital* (1923), he demonstrated his more liberal side, upholding a women's minimum wage law in the District of Columbia. His majority opinion in *Myers v. United States* (1926) clarified and extended the power of the president to remove executive officeholders. Taft resigned as chief justice early in 1930, due to poor health, and died a month later. William Howard Taft is the only person in U.S. history to have served as both president and chief justice.

Taft-Hartley Act [Labor-Management Relations Act] (1947). Congressional act, sponsored by Senator Robert A. TAFT and Representative Fred A. Hartley. The Taft-Hartley Act regulates organized union activity. In 1935 Congress passed the NATIONAL LABOR RELATIONS ACT (NLRA), also known as the Wagner Act, which recognized the right of workers to bargain collectively through unions and also established the National Labor Relations Board to investigate "unfair labor practices" by employers. After World War II, a rash of major strikes turned both public and congressional opinion against organized labor. The result was the Taft-Hartley Act whose passage was vigorously opposed by the union movement. The Taft-Hartley Act, passed by Congress over President Harry S TRUMAN's veto, amended the NLRA by defining as prohibited such "union unfair labor practices" as the closed shop, which requires union membership as a precondition of employment, secondary boycotts of an employer's suppliers or customers, and jurisdictional strikes. The Landrum-Griffin Act (1959) imposed additional restrictions on union activities.

Tagore, Rabindranath (Sir) (1861–1941). Indian poet, story writer, philosopher, playwright, educator and statesman. Tagore, who won the NOBEL PRIZE for literature in 1913, is the greatest literary figure to have emerged from the Indian subcontinent in this century. His prolific output included over 100 volumes of poetry, some 50 dramas, 40 works of fiction, and numerous spiritual and philosophical studies emphasizing the age old wisdom of his native land. Tagore was born in Calcutta, the son of a wealthy Brahmin. In 1878 he went to study law in England, but then gave up his studies to return to India to write and to devote himself to the growing nationalist movement there. *Gitanjali* (1912), a volume of poems, won him international acclaim, and Tagore subsequently made lecture tours of both England and the U.S. In 1915 Tagore was knighted but surrendered the title to protest the British suppression of the Punjab riots. *Sadhana: The Realization of Life* (1914) is Tagore's best known philosophical work.

Tairov, Alexander Yakovlevich (Kornblit) (1885–1950). Actor and director. He studied law at St. Petersburg University, and had wide experience in the theaters of St. Petersburg, Moscow and Riga. In 1914 he founded the Kamerny Theater in Moscow. In 1946 he was dismissed as the artistic director, and in 1949 he ceased to produce plays there. He particularly stressed the need for form and technique on the part of the cast.

Taiwan [Republic of China]. Taiwan—comprised of the island of Taiwan (also known as Formosa), the P'eng-hu Lien-tao Islands and the islands of Lau Hsu, Lu Tao, Quemoy, Matsu and a few small islets—is located off the southeast coast of CHINA and covers a total land area of 13,965 square miles. Ruled by JAPAN from 1895 to 1945, Taiwan reverted to China after Japan's defeat in WORLD WAR II. Rebellion against Chinese rule was brutally suppressed in 1947. After communists occupied China's mainland in 1949, Generalissimo CHIANG KAI-SHEK brought his defeated Nationalist KUOMINTANG forces to

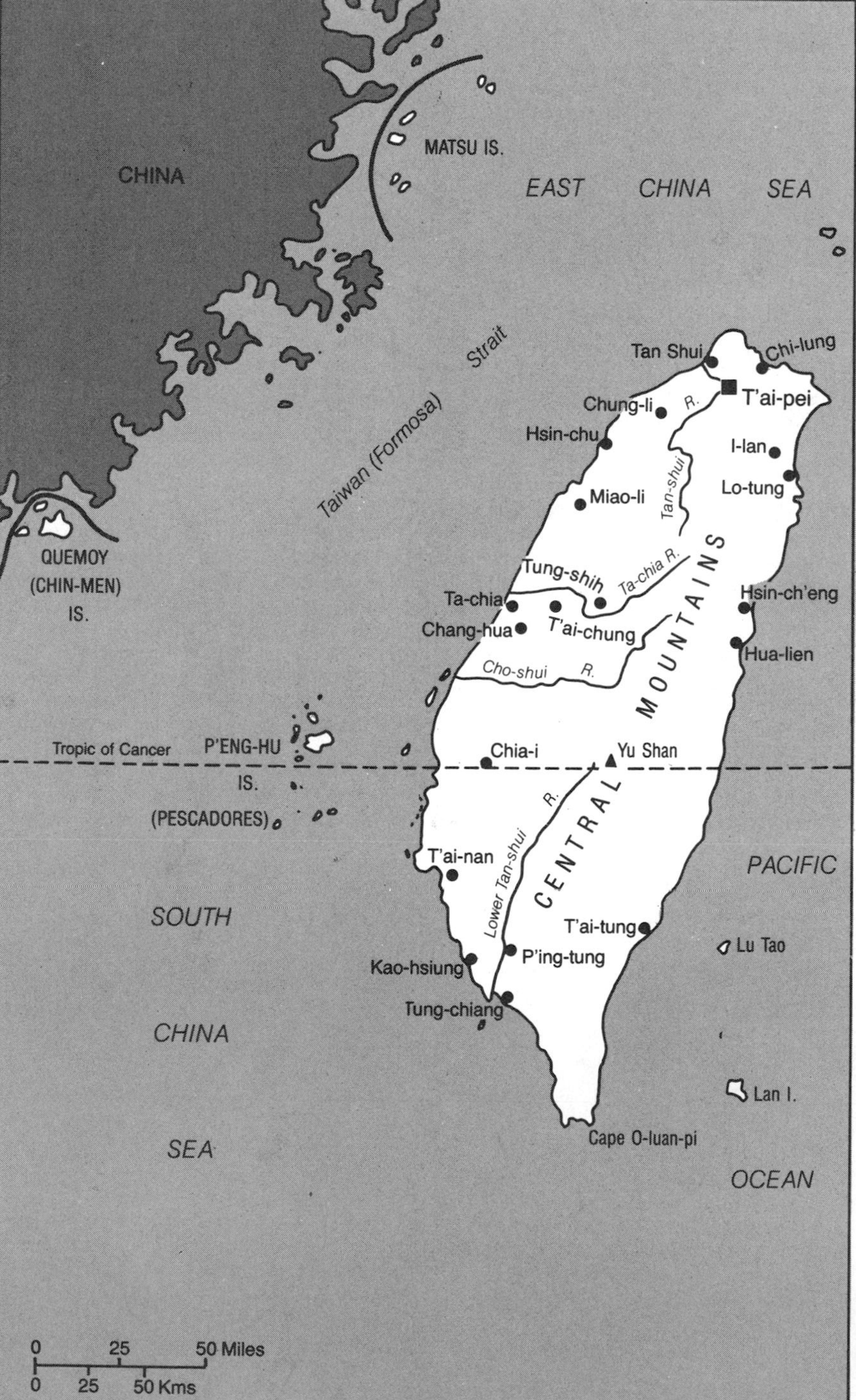

TAIWAN

TAIWAN

1945	After Japan's defeat Taiwan reverts back to China.
1947	(February) Taiwanese revolt against Chinese Nationalist rule is crushed.
1949	The Nationalist Kuomintang forces flee to Taiwan and establish the Republic of China under Chiang Kai-shek; Chiang establishes martial law and bans other political parties.
1951	(January) U.S. announces that it will recognize only Taiwan as the legal representative of China.
1971	UN General Assembly votes to unseat Taiwan and replace it with the People's Republic of China.
1975	Chiang Kai-shek dies and his son, General Chiang Ching-kuo, succeeds him.
1979	(Jan. 1) U.S. announces its recognition of the People's Republic of China and that it is terminating its mutual defense treaty with Taiwan; (April) U.S. passses an act providing for Taiwan security in absence of diplomatic relations.
1986	(September) The Democratic Progress Party is formed in contravention of martial law.
1987	(July) Chiang announces the replacement of martial law by a new national security law.
1988	(January) Chiang Ching-kuo dies and is suceeded by Lee Teng-hui, his vice president—the first native Taiwanese to be appointed head of state.
1989	(December) In national elections the Nationalist Kuomintang Party suffers its first electoral defeat to the Democratic Progress Party.
1990	(March) Amid protest, President Lee, the only official candidate, is reelected for a six-year term by the National Assembly.

Taiwan. He established the Republic of China, which was officially recognized by the United States as the only legal Chinese government (1951). The Taiwan government represented China in the UNITED NATIONS until the People's Republic of China was given that right in 1971, thereby excluding Taiwan from the world body. Chiang Kai-shek's son, Chiang Ching-Kuo, became president in 1978 (reelected in 1984) and proceeded to open informal relations with the People's Republic in 1987–88. Along with Japan, HONG KONG and SOUTH KOREA, Taiwan has become a major force in international trade; consumer electronics products manufactured in Taiwan are exported to the U.S. and other countries.

Takeshita, Noboru (1924–). Prime minister of Japan from late 1987 until his resignation in mid-1989, Takeshita comes from the affluent family of a sake brewer in the Shimane prefecture, near the Sea of Japan. He attended Waseda University in Tokyo and in 1944 took a course in KAMIKAZE pilot training; before he finished it, the war was over. In 1951 he was elected to a seat in the local assembly and in 1958 became an LDP member of the national House of Representatives. Known since his youth for an ability to compromise, Takeshita began to move up in the party hierarchy and held a number of government posts. He was Eisaku Sato's chief cabinet secretary in 1971, and twice he served as minister of finance (1979–80, 1982–86). In July 1986 Takeshita became secretary-general of the LDP and a year later he formed his own faction, which superseded the Tanaka faction. In October 1987 he was elected the 12th president of the LDP and in November 1987 he became Japan's 17th postwar prime minister.

Tal, Mikhail Nakhemyevich (1936–). Soviet chess player. Born in Latvia, he won his first Soviet chess championship in 1957, winning it again in 1958, 1967, 1972, 1974 and 1978. In 1960 he defeated BOTVINNIK to become world chess champion, the youngest man to hold the title (Gary KASPAROV broke the record 25 years later). Despite ill-health brought on by kidney problems, Tal won a reputation for his quickness, confidence, love of complexity and crushing, aggressive game.

Talaat, Mehmed (1874–1921). Turkish statesman. Born in Salonika (now Thessaloniki, Greece), Talat worked as the chief clerk at the Salonika Post Office. There he formed the "Society [later Committee] of Union and Progress" together with other opponents of the reactionary regime of Sultan ABDUL HAMID II. This society soon recruited army officers who led the YOUNG TURK rebellion in 1908. Always favoring nationalism over liberalism, Talaat, with the army generals ENVER BEY and Ahmed DJEMAL, dominated Turkish politics until Turkey's defeat in WORLD WAR I (1918). He also served as the interior minister during World War I.

Taliesin. Frank Lloyd WRIGHT home near Spring Green, Wisconsin; designed by him to follow the contour of a hill. It was built of brown stucco and limestone, quarried nearby. Wright called it "an example of the use of native materials and the play of space relations, the long stretches of low ceilings extending outside over and beyond the windows, related in direction to some feature in the landscape." In later years the structure gave its name to and became a part of Wright's larger activities through his foundation and his Taliesin Fellowships for architectural apprentices.

talking pictures. Generic label applied in the late 1920s to motion pictures with synchronized sound. Although there had been many earlier experiments in synchronizing sound to moving images—by recording sound either on cylinders (Edison's "Kinetophone") or on the film strip (Lee DE FOREST's "Phonofilm")—it wasn't until the introduction in 1926 of the WARNER BROS. "Vitaphone" process, a sound-on-disc method developed in association with Western Electric, that the "talkie" revolution really began. *Don Juan,* a John BARRYMORE swashbuckler with a synchronized-sound background score, attracted only mild attention when it premiered in August 1926. But on October 6, 1927, Al JOLSON's *The Jazz Singer,* featuring a synchronized score and a handful of talking sequences, created a sensation. Within the next few months another Jolson vehicle, *The Singing Fool,* and the "all-talking" feature, *The Lights of New York,* convinced everybody that sound was no mere novelty but the next, inevitable step in the evolution of the industry.

Virtually overnight, every studio in America and abroad scrambled to retool their operations. Significantly, Warners was the only major studio to use the sound-on-disc system. Although the recorded sound quality was exceptionally good, there were problems. "We couldn't record loud sounds, for example," recalled Warners sound engineer Bernard Brown. "Our valve-springs would stick together and give us overload. Synchronization between projector and phonograph in the theaters was very tricky. And it was difficult to edit sound in wax."

Meanwhile, the other major studios in America and abroad considered several sound-on-film options. William FOX, Warners' most powerful rival, opted for a sound-on-film process called "Movietone," which derived from pioneering photoelectric technology by inventors Lee DE FOREST and Theodore Case. Like other sound-on-film systems, it recorded sound patterns on the edge of the film strip, scanned them during projection through a light-sensitive photoelectric cell, and converted them into electric impulses—which were transformed back into sound waves and amplified with loudspeakers. Movietone was introduced throughout 1927–29 with a pioneering program of sound newsreels (such as a document of the LINDBERGH flight), numerous short musical subjects and its first all-talking feature, *In Old Arizona.* A new studio, RKO, was formed in 1929 to take advantage of RCA's "Photophone." In Europe, a German system, "Tobis-Klangfilm," became widely used.

Between 1928 and 1930 a smothering sea change swept over the motion picture. "King Mike," as the new technology was called, brought the once fluid and dramatic SILENT FILM to a grinding halt. Film crews buried themselves alive in stuffy, insulated sound studios. Noisy cameras (and their operators) disappeared into soundproof booths. Actors (newly imported from the Broadway stage) froze into static tableaux near the all-important fixed microphones. Dialogue seemed to die in this airless void. Some formerly successful superstars, like John Gilbert, failed in the new medium—a problem not of vocal quality but of distorting microphones. The mere novelty of sound quickly palled.

Not surprisingly, the talkies stirred up heated debate among artists, critics and viewers. While H.G. WELLS hailed them as the "art form of the future," G.B. SHAW sniffed that they were merely a regression to the theatrical past. Critic George Jean Nathan was merely gloomy, pronouncing the new talkies "cold corpses." But French filmmaker Rene CLAIR, for whom sound "had driven poetry off the screen," was also one of the handful of directors to demonstrate the real possibilities of sound-image combinations. His *Sous les Toits de Paris* (*Under the Roofs of Paris*, 1929) showed how sound could be recorded and mixed separately from the image montage.

In America that same year more breakthroughs came in the use of boom mikes, blimped cameras and multiple-channel sound mixing in early talkies like Victor Fleming's *The Virginian* and Rouben MAMOULIAN's *Applause*. And in an important 1928 manifesto Russian theoreticians Sergei EISENSTEIN and Vsevelod PUDOVKIN published their principles of asynchronous sound, describing the potentials of sound-image counterpoint. In practice and in theory, the talkies were here to stay.

For further reading:

Walker, Alexander, *The Shattered Silents: How the Talkies Came to Stay*. New York: William Morrow and Co., 1979.

Tallchief, Maria (1925–). American ballerina. Of American Indian descent, Tallchief danced with the Ballet Russe de Monte Carlo (1942–47), then with Ballet Society and NEW YORK CITY BALLET (1948–65). She was married to George BALANCHINE (1946–52) and became most closely identified with his ballets, creating roles in such works as *Firebird* (1948) and *Allegro brillante* (1956). As the principal ballerina, she was regarded as the most technically brilliant American-born ballerina of her time. She also appeared as a guest artist with other dance companies, and founded the Chicago City Ballet in 1981.

Talvela, Martti (Olava) (1935–1989). Finnish operatic bass. Talvela was considered one of the greatest interpreters of the title role in Modest Mussorgsky's *Boris Godunov*. The physically imposing Talvela appeared frequently at the Metropolitan Opera in New York City and at the Bayreuth Festival in Germany. He was elected director of the Finnish National Opera shortly before his death from a heart attack.

Tamayo-Mendez, Arnaldo (1942–). Cuban cosmonaut-researcher aboard SOYUZ 38 (September 1980). With fellow cosmonaut Yuri Romanenko, he spent eight days in space, seven of them linked with the Soviet SALYUT 6 space station and cosmonauts Leonid Popov and Valery Ryumin. Tamayo-Mendez was the first black and the first Hispanic to fly in space.

Tambo, Oliver (1917–). South African anti-apartheid leader and head of the AFRICAN NATIONAL CONGRESS (ANC) since 1967. Born in South Africa and educated at the University of Fort Hare, Cape Province, Tambo's political involvement in the protest against APARTHEID began in 1944, when he and Nelson MANDELA helped to found the ANC Youth League. In a legal partnership with Mandela from 1951 to 1960, Tambo was banned from attending ANC meetings from 1954 to 1956, when he was arrested on treason charges. The charges were dropped in 1957, and Tambo became deputy president of the ANC the following year. Tambo was again banned from attending meetings in 1959, went into exile in London in 1960 and was later based in Zambia. With Mandela's incarceration in 1964, Tambo became the foremost spokesman for the ANC, accepting no compromises in his demands for unambiguous majority rule in South Africa. Although the ANC formed alliances with the South African Communist Party, Tambo himself is not a member of the Communist Party. In December 1990, partially disabled from a stroke he suffered the year before, Tambo was allowed to return to South Africa. Tambo has on several occasions addressed the United Nations, which has referred to him as "the legitimate representative of South African people," and his speeches and articles are collected in *Oliver Tambo Speaks: Preparing for Power* (1988).

Tanaka, Kakuei (1918–). Prime minister of Japan. Tanaka became wealthy in his own construction company before being elected to the House of Representatives (the lower house of the Diet, or parliament) in 1947. In 1972, after holding several cabinet and party posts, he was named president of the ruling Liberal Democratic Party (LDP) and prime minister of the nation. Two years later, Tanaka was forced to resign from office after being accused of accepting approximately $2 million in bribes from the Lockheed Corporation in exchange for arranging the purchase of that company's planes for All Nippon Airways. In 1976, despite his indictment on the charges, Tanaka and his codefendants were reelected to the Diet; throughout his long trial the ex-premier remained one of the most powerful politicians in Japan, leading the largest faction within the LDP. Convicted in 1983, he was sentenced to four years in prison and fined $2 million. In 1985 Tanaka suffered a stroke, and in 1989 he announced his retirement from the Diet.

Tandy, Jessica (1909–). British-born American stage and film actress. Tandy has enjoyed a long and distinguished stage career, the highlight of which was her Broadway triumph as Blanche du Bois in the premiere of *A Streetcar Named Desire* (1947) by Tennessee WILLIAMS. In recent years she has enjoyed equal success in films with acclaimed roles in *Cocoon* (1985) and, most notably, *Driving Miss Daisy* (1989), for which she won an ACADEMY AWARD as Best Actress. Tandy made her stage debut in London in 1927 and her Broadway debut in 1930. She starred in stage productions in both countries over the following decades. With her second husband, actor Hume Cronyn, she appeared in several plays, including *A Day By The Sea* (1955) by N.C. Hunter and *Three Sisters* (1963) by Anton CHEKHOV.

Tanganyika. Former colony in East Africa; it now comprises the mainland portion of the nation of TANZANIA. From 1891 until World War I Tanganyika was a German protectorate within German East Africa. British forces gained control of the area during the war; after the war the LEAGUE OF NATIONS assigned it to the UNITED KINGDOM as a mandate. Tanganyika gained full independence in 1961, and in 1964 merged with ZANZIBAR to form Tanzania.

Tanguy, Yves (1900–1955). French painter. Born in Paris, Tanguy spent his early years as a merchant seaman. A friend of Jaques PREVERT, he was immersed in the artistic milieu of early 20th-century PARIS, but he did not begin to paint until the day in 1923 when he saw a painting by Giorgio de CHIRICO in a gallery window. Self-taught, Tanguy went on to create a dreamlike personal vision, and in 1925 he joined the newly formed Surrealist group (see also SURREALISM, DADA). His characteristic paintings are delicately tonal imaginary landscapes of indefinite space and mist in which strange biomorphic forms bend and float. Tanguy moved to the U.S. in 1939, settling in Connecticut (1942) and becoming a U.S. citizen in 1948.

tank. Armored military vehicle, armed with a large shell-firing gun and machine guns; propelled on steel treads. Barbed wire and the machine gun gave the defense the advantage in WORLD WAR I trench warfare. Cavalry, which in previous wars had been used for swift offensive thrusts, was rendered obsolete. The tank, the first offensive weapon capable of breaking through trench defenses, first saw action in September 1916 in the battle of the SOMME. The tank came into its own with the German BLITZKRIEG in WORLD WAR II. German Field Marshal Erwin ROMMEL and U.S. General George S. PATTON were brilliant exponents of tank warfare. The greatest tank battle in history occurred in 1943 at Kursk in the U.S.S.R., where the Soviets decisively defeated the Germans. Tanks have been used in virtually every major war since World War II, and have proved especially effective when used with air support in quick-moving desert warfare, as in the SIX-DAY WAR (1967) and the PERSIAN GULF WAR (1991).

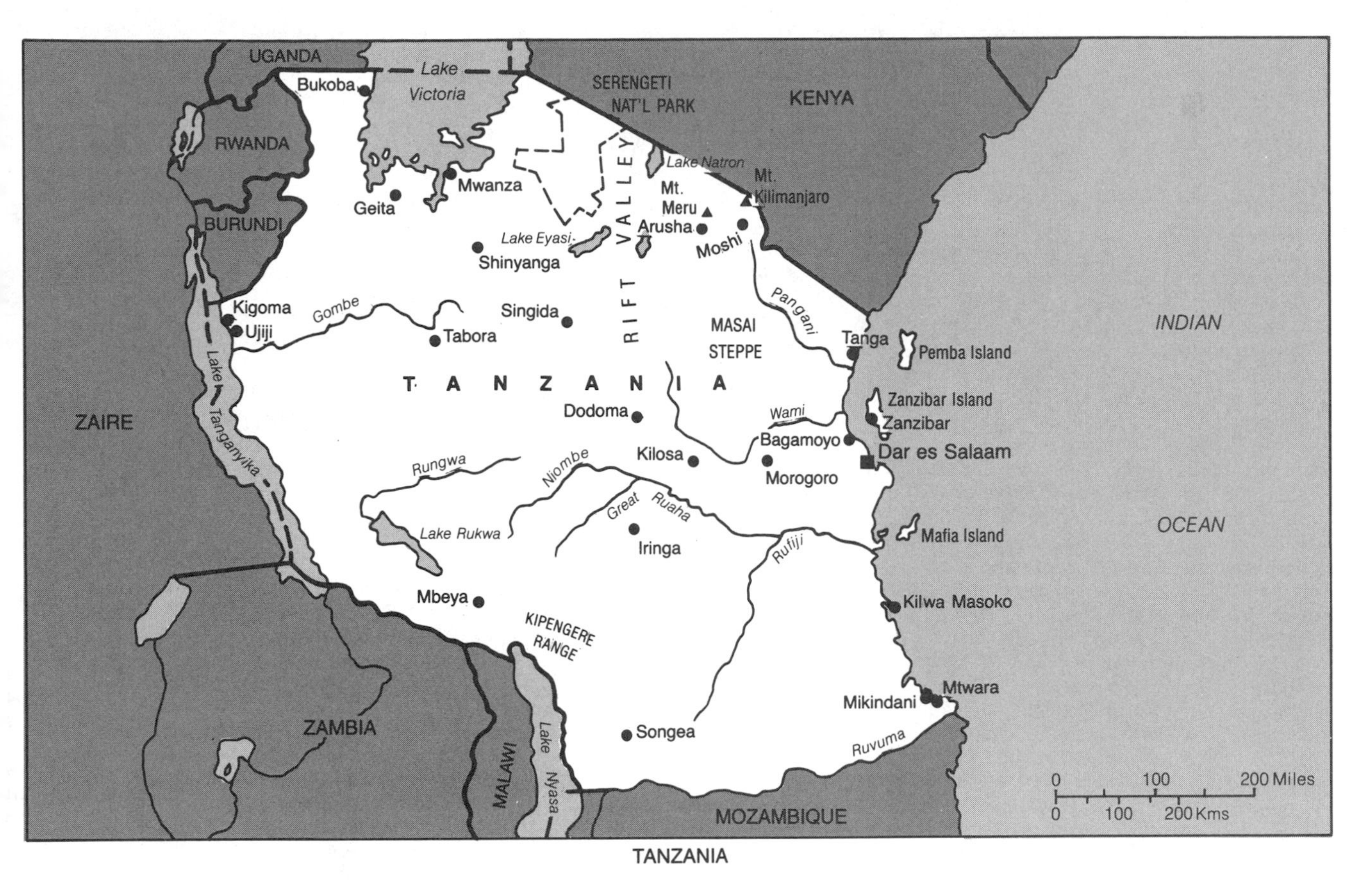

TANZANIA

Tan-Zam Railway. Chinese-aided project of the mid-1960s to provide landlocked ZAMBIA with a rail route to the sea through TANZANIA, avoiding dependence on the white regime in RHODESIA during the period of UDI.

Tanzania [United Republic of Tanzania]. On the east coast of Africa just south of the equator, Tanzania covers an area of 364,805 square miles that includes the island territories of Zanzibar, Pemba and Matia. Formerly known as **Tanganyika,** the country was a German colony from 1884 until the end of WORLD WAR I, when it became a British Mandate under the LEAGUE OF NATIONS. After World War II, Tanganyika was designated a UNITED NATIONS Trust Territory under British control, until achieving independence in 1961. The island of Zanzibar united with Tanganyika in 1964 to form the United Republic of Tanzania. Under the leadership of its first president, Dr. Julius NYERERE (1962–85), Tanzania supported the liberation movements of other countries in southern Africa and repulsed an invasion by UGANDA in 1978, maintaining armed forces in that country until 1981.

TANZANIA

1961	Gains independence under Prime Minister Julius Nyerere; Louis Leakey finds oldest human bones.
1962	Nyerere elected first president of Republic of Tanganyika by overwhelming majority of population.
1964	Sultan of Zanzibar deposed and republic proclaimed; Zanzibar Act of Union with Tanganyika formally creates Tanzania.
1978	Uganda President Idi Amin's forces invade Tanzania; Tanzania pushes back Ugandan forces and, in turn, invades Uganda, remaining until Amin regime overthrown.
1980	Nyerere is reelected president; Zanzibar granted new constitution under which it will elect own president.
1983	Human Resources Deployment Act authorizes government to round up vagrants, unemployed people, and resettle them forcibly in productive sectors.
1989	Bans trade in ivory.

Taoiseach. Official title of the prime minister of IRELAND.

Tarbell, Ida (1857–1944). American journalist and biographer. Tarbell won renown in the 1900s as one of a group of socially conscious investigative reporters who became known—after a speech by President Theodore ROOSEVELT that bitterly attacked their alleged negative methods—as "muckrakers." Tarbell's chief work was a two-volume expose on the monopolistic tactics of John D. Rockefeller and fellow oil industry magnates, *The History of the Standard Oil Company* (1904). By the 1920s, Tarbell had mellowed in her attitudes toward American business, and she wrote admiring biographies of entrepreneurs Elbert H. Gary (1925) and Owen Young (1932).

Tardieu, Jean (1903–). French playwright, poet, and art critic. Tardieu has been an influential force in both French theater and poetry for much of the 20th century. Raised in an artistic family, Tardieu studied at the Sorbonne in Paris. Although he wrote plays early on, Tardieu first achieved literary success with his poems. Volumes such as *The Hidden River* (1933), *Accents* (1939) and *Petrified Days 1942–1944* (1947–1948) were marked by strong, pulsing rhythms and striking imagery that showed the influence of SURREALISM. During WORLD WAR II, Tardieu served in the French RESISTANCE. After the war he returned to playwriting. Tardieu's plays are generally short and resemble poetic monologues or dialogues rather than full-scale dramas. His spare language, black humor and absurdist themes have led critics to see Tardieu as an influence on the THEATER OF THE ABSURD. *Chamber Theater I* (1955) and *Theater II: Plays for Acting* (1960) contain the best of his theatrical works. *About Painting That is Abstract* (1960) is his best known work of art criticism.

Tarkenton, Fran(cis Asbury) (1940–). American football player. By the time he retired in 1978, Tarkenton held virtually every passing record in professional football. As quarterback for the University of Georgia, he led his team to an Orange Bowl in his senior year. He began his professional career with the Minnesota Vikings and completed 17 of 23 passes in his first start. A few years later, in 1967, he was benched in a coaching dispute and was traded to the New York Giants. Tarkenton led the Giants for five years and then returned to Minnesota for the final six years of his career. Over his career he gained 47,003 yards and completed 3,686 passes. He has gone on to a career in motivational speaking.

Tarkington, (Newton) Booth (1869–1946). Novelist and dramatist. Tarkington is best remembered for *Seventeen* (1916), portraying the joys and problems of adolescence. He also presented a cross-section of life in his hometown of Indianapolis in such works as the 1918 PULITZER PRIZE-winner *The Magnificent Ambersons* (1918). His best work is considered to be *Alice Adams* (1921), which brought him a second Pulitzer in 1921. Among his other honors were the gold medal of the National Institute of Arts and Sciences and the Theodore Roosevelt Memorial medal. He served in the Indiana House of Representatives from 1902 to 1903.

Tarzan of the Apes. This century's best-known version of the "noble savage" myth, Tarzan may be rivaled only by SHERLOCK HOLMES and PETER PAN as modern literature's most popular and recognizable figure. The first four books in Edgar Rice BURROUGHS' 24–volume series—*Tarzan of the Apes, The Return of Tarzan, The Beasts of Tarzan* and *The Son of Tarzan* (published in hard covers between 1914 and 1917)—tell most of the story: A baby is born to an English couple stranded in Africa. After their deaths he is raised by a female ape, Kala, and becomes a great chief in the ape tribe. Upon learning of his human ancestry, he journeys to England, France and America in search of both a bride and an aristocratic title. Finally, he returns to his African estates in "Waziri Country" as an English nobleman with his wife and son. The character, known variously as "Tarzan" ("white-skin" in the ape tongue), "John Clayton" and "Lord Greystoke" by the English, and simply as "M. Jean C. Tarzan" by the French, first appeared in the pages of *The All-Story Magazine* (October 1912). Until Burroughs' death in 1950, scarcely a year passed without a new, ever more bizarre Tarzan adventure. Through two world wars he battled Germans, Japanese and communists. He discovered many lost races, hunted bizarre animals and even penetrated the earth's core. Once, he auditioned—and was turned down—for the role of "Tarzan" in a HOLLYWOOD movie (*Tarzan and the Lion Man,* 1933). Burroughs chafed as the character assumed an independent life in the movies, radio, newspaper cartoon strips and elsewhere. The complex, intelligent man who had a good deal to love and hate about both civilization and the jungle was being reduced to an illiterate, barely articulate lout in a loin cloth. (However, Burroughs admitted that some of the early Johnny Weissmuller pictures for MGM, especially *Tarzan and His Mate* [1934] were rattling good adventures—and indeed they were.) Meanwhile, the growing suspicion that Tarzan was indeed a real person has been "confirmed" by author Philip Jose Farmer's biography, *Tarzan Alive* (1972). Burroughs, more ambivalent on this point, simply wrote in 1927 that Tarzan "is an interesting experiment in the mental laboratory we call imagination."

Tarzan (Johnny Weissmuller), Jane (Maureen O'Sullivan) and the chimpanzee Skippy, as Cheeta, portray the jungle family (1936).

Tashkent Agreement. Temporarily successful mediation (January 1966) by Soviet Premier KOSYGIN between prime ministers SHASTRI of INDIA and AYUB KHAN of PAKISTAN over the KASHMIR dispute, following armed conflict between the two states in 1965. (See also INDO-PAKISTANI WAR OF 1965.)

TASS [Telegraphic Agency of the Soviet Union]. The official Soviet news agency, founded in 1925. The agency deals with news both at home and abroad. It is attached to the council of ministers, and its work is carefully controlled by the propaganda department.

Tate, Allen (1899–1979). American poet, critic and teacher. A graduate of Vanderbilt University in Tennessee (1922), he was associated with John Crowe RANSOM and Robert Penn WARREN. He helped found and edit the journal *The Fugitive* (1922–25) and was later editor of the influential *Sewanee Review.* With Ransom, he helped establish the NEW CRITICISM. He was president of the National Institute of Arts and Letters in 1968 and received its National Medal for Literature in 1976. His best known poem, "Ode to the Confederate Dead," is widely considered a minor masterpiece.

Tati, Jacques [born Jacques Tatischeff] (1908–1982). French actor, director and screenwriter. Tati is considered a comic master of the French cinema. As an actor he was best known as Monsieur Hulot, the bungling character he played in his 1953 film *Mr. Hulot's Holiday.* His film *Mon Oncle* won the 1958 ACADEMY AWARD for best foreign film. Tati once said that his films were meant to proclaim "the survival of the individual in a world that is more and more dehumanized."

Tatlin, Vladimir (1885–1953). Artist and founder of CONSTRUCTIVISM. After an unhappy childhood, at the age of 18 Tatlin ran away to become a sailor and traveled to Egypt. This had a profound influence on his art. After studying at the Penza School of Art and at the Moscow College of Painting, Sculpture, and Architecture, Tatlin worked as a free-lance painter, and sent works to the Union of Russian Artists and the Union of Youth exhibitions. He later contributed works to the KNAVE OF DIAMONDS (1913). In the same year, he journeyed to Berlin with some Ukrainian singers and played the accordion with them at the Russian Exhibition of Folk Art. With the proceeds, he went to Paris and visited Picasso. From 1913 to 1914, Tatlin began to explore the possibility of "painting relief" and became known as the founder of Constructivism.

Tatum, Art (1909–1956). American jazz pianist. Tatum was one of the transcendent influences in the history of jazz. His technical accomplishments were unexcelled; his authority over the entire range of the keyboard, the delicate lightness of touch and capacity to spin out endless variations on the standard repertory of popular Broadway, Hollywood and Tin Pan Alley tunes made him the envy of his peers. He also was able to incorporate elements from the other great jazz pianists of his day—Thomas "Fats" WALLER, Earl "Fatha" HINES and Teddy WILSON—without substantially altering his virtuosic and swinging lyricism. Having established his reputation in an essentially solo context, in 1943 Tatum, influenced by the successful piano trio of Nat "King" COLE, formed his own trio with bassist Slam Stewart and guitarist Tiny Grimes (later replaced by Everett Barksdale); the trio format is the one that gave rise to perhaps his greatest improvisatory flights, though his extensive solo recordings for impresario Norman Granz in the 1950s are also of import. Tatum has been an important influence for such varied modern jazz stylists as Bud Powell, Lennie Tristano and Herbie HANCOCK.

For further reading:
Taylor, Billy, *Jazz Piano: History and Development*. Dubuque: Iowa, William C. Brown, 1982.

Tauber, Richard (1892–1948). Austrian tenor. Born in Linz, Tauber studied at the Hoch Conservatory in Frankfort. Beginning his musical career as a conductor, he made his singing debut in Chemnitz, Germany in 1913 as Tamino in *The Magic Flute*. A popular *bel canto* tenor, he appeared throughout Europe and made his American debut in 1931. Tauber was noted for his operatic roles, particularly in works by Mozart, for his masterful lieder interpretations and for his performances in various operettas, many of them by his friend, the Austrian composer Franz LEHAR. He became famous for his role as Prince Sou-Chong in Lehar's *Das Land des Lachelns* (*The Land of Smiles*). Tauber fled Austria in 1938, settling in London and becoming a British subject in 1940. Today he is also remembered as the personification of Viennese elegance and charm.

Taussig, Helen Brooke (1899–1986). American physician. She is recognized as the founder of pediatric cardiology. In the 1940s, she and Dr. Alfred Blalock developed the successful "blue baby" operations, a surgical procedure that eventually saved the lives of thousands of children born with congenital heart defects. In 1959, she became the first woman to be made a full professor at the Johns Hopkins Medical School. In the early 1960s she played a key role in preventing the repetition in the U.S. of an epidemic of major birth defects in Europe among babies born to women who had taken the tranquilizer thalidomide. In 1965, she became the first woman to be elected president of the American Heart Association.

Taylor, A(lan) J(ohn) P(ercival) (1906–1990). British historian. His most controversial book was *The Origins of the Second World War* (1961), in which he argued that HITLER had not been solely responsible for WORLD WAR II but had merely taken advantage of opportunities. He was the author of 29 books, including *The Struggle for Mastery in Europe, 1848–1918* and *English History, 1914–45* for the Oxford History of England series. He was well-known as a columnist for the *Sunday Express*. Although he taught at Oxford for 25 years, he was never made a professor.

Taylor, Billy (1921–). American jazz pianist and educator. As a prime exponent of the post-bebop modern piano style, Taylor (since 1952) has most often displayed his supple keyboard skills at the helm of various editions of the Billy Taylor Trio. As an educator committed to spreading the gospel of jazz, Taylor helped establish the model Jazzmobile program, which since 1965 has taken the sounds of jazz to New York City's inner-city youth. As a broadcaster, Taylor achieved fame as leader of an 11–piece jazz band for television's "David Frost Show" (1969–72); in 1981, he began hosting jazz features for CBS's "Sunday Morning" with Charles Kuralt. In 1975, Taylor earned a D.Mus.Ed. from the University of Massachusetts-Amherst; his *Jazz Piano: History and Development* (1982), a standard text, is informed by scholarly precision and a wealth of experience going back to his days as house pianist at New York's fabled Birdland, where the young Taylor backed such jazz luminaries as Charlie PARKER, Dizzy GILLESPIE and Roy Eldridge. The pianist's efforts on behalf of "America's classical music" have made Taylor jazzdom's most visible and effective spokesman, both as a panelist for the National Endowment for the Arts and as a keynote speaker for the International Association of Jazz Educators.

For further reading:
Lyons, Len, "Billy Taylor" in *The Great Jazz Pianists: Speaking of Their Lives and Music*. New York: William Morrow, 1983.

Taylor, Cecil P(hilip) (1929–1981). Scottish playwright. Taylor was both a popular and a critically acclaimed playwright whose works were performed primarily by regional companies in the British Isles, as opposed to the major West End theaters in London. In part this reflects the Scots—as opposed to English—perspective that informs the political themes of several of his plays. Taylor is best known for his play *Good* (1981), which explores the process by which a liberal German professor decides to work in AUSCHWITZ, the Nazi death camp. Other plays by Taylor include *Lies About Vietnam* (1969), *Schippel* (1974), *And a Nightingale Sang . . .* (1979), and *Bring Me Sunshine, Bring Me Smiles* (1982).

Taylor, Elizabeth [born Elizabeth Cole] (1912–1975). British novelist. Taylor worked as a governess and a librarian before her marriage in 1934. With her first novel, *At Mrs. Lippincote's* (1945), she established her reputation as a shrewd observer of the British middle class. Her other acclaimed novels, which include *A Wreath of Roses* (1950), *In a Summer Season* (1961), *Mrs. Palfrey at the Claremont* (1972), and the posthumously published *Blaming* (1976), portray the inward lives and longings behind her characters' facades. Taylor's short story collections include *Hester Lilly* (1954), *A Dedicated Man* (1965) and *The Devastating Boys* (1972).

Taylor, Elizabeth (1932–). American film actress. Born in London to American parents, Taylor and her family settled in Los Angeles just before the outbreak of World War II. She had her first screen role at the age of ten and became a star after her performance in *National Velvet* (1944). The violet-eyed beauty has played a wide variety of roles during her long career. Her most notable motion pictures include *Father of the Bride* (1950), *A Place in the Sun* (1951), *Giant* (1956), *Cat on a Hot Tin Roof* (1958) and *Butterfield 8* (1960: ACADEMY AWARD). A favorite of gossip columnists, Taylor is as celebrated for her private life as for her movie roles. She has been married seven times, twice to Richard BURTON, with whom she costarred in two of her most memorable films, *Cleopatra* (1963) and *Who's Afraid of Virginia Woolf* (1966; Academy Award). In the latter part of her career, she has worked mainly in the theater and in television.

For further reading:
Walker, Alexander, *Elizabeth: The Life of Elizabeth Taylor*. New York: Grove Weidenfeld, 1991.

Taylor, Glen H(earst) (1904–1984). American politician. Taylor was U.S. senator from Idaho (1945–51) and vice presidential candidate on Henry A. WALLACE's Progressive Party ticket (1948). Taylor first gained attention for his colorful show business act as "The Singing Cowboy" in the 1920s and 1930s. Elected to the senate as a Democrat, he supported liberal domestic legislation and CIVIL RIGHTS and opposed big business and the TAFT-HARTLEY ACT. He also opposed President Harry S TRUMAN's foreign policy, especially Truman's policy toward the U.S.S.R. He denounced the TRUMAN DOCTRINE, the MARSHALL PLAN and the NORTH ATLANTIC TREATY ORGANIZATION and demanded an end to the COLD WAR. During the election of 1948, conservatives and liberals alike portrayed both Taylor and Wallace as dupes of the communists. Taylor's 1950 Senate reelection bid was defeated when he lost Idaho's Democratic primary. Taylor subsequently retired from politics and entered private business.

Taylor, Maxwell Davenport (1901–1987). Military officer. A 1922 graduate of the U.S. Military Academy at West Point, New York, he helped organize the first Army airborne division, the 82nd, in the early years of WORLD WAR II. He was cited for bravery when he chose to cross enemy lines at great personal risk just 24 hours before the Allied invasion of Italy (1943), to discuss with Italian leaders the possible seizure of Roman airfields. He also led the 101st Airborne Division in assaults on Normandy and the Netherlands. In 1953 he served as commanding general of the 8th Army and directed the UNITED NATIONS forces in KOREA; in 1955 was appointed Army chief of staff; in 1962, chairman of the Joints Chiefs of Staff; and in 1964, U.S. ambassador to SOUTH VIETNAM. Urging President Lyndon B. JOHNSON to increase U.S. participation in the war with North Vietnam, he was one of the most important factors in expanding that unpopular conflict.

Taylor, Paul (1930–). American dancer, choreographer and company director. Taylor has performed with various modern dance companies, including those of Merce CUNNINGHAM (1953–54) and Martha GRAHAM (1955–61), creating roles in many of the latter's works, such as *Clytemnestra* (1958) and *Embattled Garden* (1958). Since 1954 he has directed his own company, which has performed throughout the world. A major figure in modern dance in America, Taylor creates works characterized by a classical orientation, use of humor and often touches of the macabre. Some of the best known of his over 50 works include *Three Epitaphs* (1956), *Aureole* (1962) and *Esplanade* (1975). He has received many awards including best choreographer at the Paris Dance Festival (1962) and L'Order des Arts et des Lettres (1984).

Taylor, Robert [born Spangler Arlington Brugh] (1911–1969). American film actor. Born in Nebraska, Taylor studied at Pomona College in Southern California. His first screen appearance was in 1934, and he attained stardom after playing the lead in *Magnificent Obsession* (1935). Known mainly for his handsome profile but a versatile actor as well, Taylor starred in such vehicles as *His Brother's Wife* (1936), *Camille* (1937), *Yank at Oxford* (1938), *Waterloo Bridge* (1940), *Bataan* (1943) and *Quo Vadis* (1951).

Taylor, Telford (1908–). American attorney and author. After working in Franklin ROOSEVELT's administration, Taylor entered the Army during World War II. Promoted to brigadier general, he was chief U.S. prosecutor during the NUREMBERG TRIALS of Nazi war criminals. After the war, Taylor taught law at Columbia University and Cardozo law schools and published a number of books, including *Nuremberg and Vietnam* (1970), in which he criticized U.S. policy in Southeast Asia; *Courts of Terror*, about Soviet Jews; and *Munich: The Price of Peace*, about the APPEASEMENT of HITLER.

Teagarden, Jack (1905–1964). Jazz trombonist, vocalist and big band arranger. Teagarden is renowned as one of the greatest JAZZ trombonists of all time. His trademark full-toned sound showed a marked BLUES influence. Teagarden began his career in the 1920s working as a sideman for numerous bands throughout the Southwest. He moved to New York in the late 1920s and began recording with various bands. In 1939, he formed his own big band, which had as its theme song "I Gotta Right to Sing the Blues," a tune that Teagarden also recorded with the Benny GOODMAN big band. From 1947 to 1951, Teagarden toured with the Louis ARMSTRONG All-Stars. He remained active as a band leader and sideman until his death.

Teague, Walter Dorwin, Sr. (1883–1960). American industrial designer, one of the leaders in the development of the profession in the 1920s and the 1930s. Teague was a student at the Art Students League of New York before starting work as a professional illustrator. In 1927 his name was given to an Eastman KODAK representative as a possible source of some sketches for a name camera. Teague insisted on a far more thorough study of the project, leading to a long-standing relationship with Kodak and the launching of his own design firm. In his 1940 book, *Design This Day*, he outlined his philosophy relating traditional aesthetic theory to the concepts of MODERNISM as he had encountered it in Europe on a 1926 visit. Early work of the Teague office often combined a touch of ART DECO decorative form with straightforward functionalism. The famous Kodak Baby Brownie camera of 1935 was a simple molded box of black plastic (then a new material), but its rounded corners and parallel ribbing made it modernistic, to the delight of purchasers who made it an immense commercial success. Later designs for Kodak included the tiny Bantam Special (1936), a gleaming, streamlined miniature camera in black and polished aluminum, and the 620 Special, a larger roll film camera incorporating both a coupled range finder and a coupled exposure meter, a remarkable innovation in 1939. Work for other clients eventually included New Haven Railroad passenger cars, NEW YORK WORLD'S FAIR exhibits for Ford and U.S. Steel, and a very visible standard service station design for Texaco. Teague came to be regarded as one of the four leaders of the industrial design profession along with Norman BEL GEDDES, Henry DREYFUSS and Raymond LOEWY. In 1944 he became the first president of the Society of Industrial Designers.

Teapot Dome Scandal. In 1922, during the administration of President Warren G. HARDING, Secretary of the Interior Albert FALL leased naval oil reserve lands at Teapot Dome, Wyoming, to oil producers Harry Sinclair and E.L. Doheny, without competitive bidding and after accepting loans of hundreds of thousands of dollars. Fall resigned in 1923 and joined Sinclair Oil. Indicted after a Senate investigation, in 1929 he was convicted of taking a bribe, and imprisoned (1931–32). The event cast a continuing shadow on the memory of the Harding administration.

For further reading:

Bates, James L., *The Origins of Teapot Dome: Progressive Parties and Petroleum*. Westport, Conn.: Greenwood, 1978.

Teasdale, Sara (1884–1933). American poet. Excessively sheltered early in life by her parents, Teasdale published, while traveling with a chaperone, *Sonnets to Dues and Other Poems* (1907) and *Helen of Troy and Other Poems* (1911). These brought her some critical attention, and following her marriage in 1914 she broke away from her family to lead a more daring, although never entirely happy, life as a poet. She received the 1918 PULITZER PRIZE for *Love Songs* (1917), and she published several other collections before taking her own life.

Teatro Grottesco [theater of the grotesque]. Italian theater movement. The Teatro Grottesco emerged during WORLD WAR I in an effort to lead Italian theater away from the grand rhetoric and unquestioning nationalism of then dominant Italian playwright Gabriele D'ANNUNZIO. The name *Teatro Grottesco* came from the subtitle of a 1916 play, *The Mask and the Face*, by the Italian playwright Chiarelli. Plays staged by the Teatro Grottesco questioned societal values and surface appearances. A leading playwright of the movement was Rosso di San Secondo.

Tebaldi, Renata (1922–). Italian opera singer. Tebaldi was regarded as an outstanding lyric and spinto soprano during the height of her career in the 1940s and 1950s. She gained national attention in Italy when she sang at a concert organized by Arturo TOSCANINI for the reopening of La Scala in 1946. In 1950 she made her La Scala opera debut in *Aida*, viewed as one of her finest roles. She sang in opera houses worldwide and made many excellent recordings before her retirement in the early 1970s. Other famous roles include Mimi in PUCCINI's *La Boheme*, Desdemona in *Otello* and the title roles in *Tosca* and *Madame Butterfly*. Tebaldi's famous rivalry with soprano Maria CALLAS was largely the creation of the press.

Tedder, Arthur William [1st Baron Tedder of Glenguin] (1890–1967). British air marshal. A career military man, Tedder fought in the infantry and the Royal Air Force (RAF) during WORLD WAR I. As chief of the British air forces in the Middle East from 1941 to 1943, he was instrumental in driving German forces out of Tunisia. Tedder was appointed commander in chief of Britain's Mediterranean Air Command in 1943. From 1943 to 1945 he was deputy commander of all the allied invasion forces, giving valuable air support to the NORMANDY invasion and subsequent advances. The much-decorated strategist was raised to the peerage in 1946. In the postwar years he served as air chief of staff (1946–50) and became chancellor of Cambridge University in 1950. His memoirs, *With Prejudice*, were published in 1966.

Teheran Conference. WORLD WAR II meeting held in Teheran, Iran, from November 28 to December 1, 1943, by U.S. President Franklin Delano ROOSEVELT, British Prime Minister Winston CHURCHILL and Soviet Premier Joseph STALIN and their staffs. The conference strengthened three-power ties and featured strategy talks regarding the conduct of the war in Europe, including plans for the

Allied invasion of FRANCE. During the conference, Stalin again pledged to fight against JAPAN after the end of the conflict with GERMANY. The powers also agreed to guarantee an independent IRAN.

Teilhard de Chardin, Pierre (1881–1955). French Catholic theologian and paleontologist; one of the most unique thinkers among 20th-century theologians. After being ordained as a Jesuit priest in 1911, Teilhard went on to earn a doctorate in paleontology from the Sorbonne. After a brief teaching stint at the Institute Catholique in Paris in the mid-1920s, he was ordered by his Jesuit superiors—who mistrusted his attempts to reconcile evolutionary theory and traditional theology—to refrain from teaching in France and to restrict himself to scientific writings only. Teilhard obeyed these restrictions, spending the bulk of his remaining years in China and there participating in the discovery of the paleontological remains of Peking Man. His influential theological works, such as *The Phenomenon of Man* (1955), were all published posthumously. In them, Teilhard expresses optimism for the survival of the human species and argues for regarding the planet Earth as worthy of holy reverence.

television. Electronic communications medium that has had a profound effect on life in the 20th century. The first television system was patented by Paul Nipkow in Germany in 1884. The first workable television set was produced by Scottish inventor John Logie BAIRD in 1926. In the U.S. General Electric began television tests that same year and in 1928 produced the first television play, *The Queen's Messenger*. During the 1930s great technological advances occurred: In the U.S. the RCA CORPORATION spent millions on research; a crude television service was developed in Germany; and in Great Britain a camera tube known as Emitron was developed. In 1937 the BBC produced the first outside broadcast—the coronation procession of GEORGE VI. NBC began experimental broadcasts in 1931 and in 1939 broadcast the opening of the NEW YORK WORLD'S FAIR. NBC was granted the first commercial television license in the U.S. in 1941. World War II interrupted the development of commercial television. In 1950 9% of U.S. households had a television; by 1960 87% owned a TV. Correspondingly, attendance at movies declined, RADIO lost listeners and libraries reported a drop in book circulation. The first communications SATELLITE, TELSTAR, was sent into orbit in 1962, allowing millions around the globe to witness the funeral of John F. KENNEDY via live TV and satellite in 1963. The ability of television to bring news, sports and entertainment events live to a world wide audience has made the world in the 20th century a "global village."

Teller, Edward (1908–). Hungarian-American physicist. After completing his doctorate in physical chemistry at the University of Leipzig in 1930, Teller studied with Niels BOHR, the distinguished Danish physicist. He left Germany when the Nazis came to power and became an American citizen in 1941. During WORLD WAR II Teller worked on the MANHATTAN PROJECT, which developed the atomic bomb, and from 1949 to 1951 he was an assistant director of the science laboratory at Los Alamos, N.M. During the 1950s he taught physics at the University of California. In 1954 he became an associate director of the Atomic Energy Commission's Lawrence Livermore Laboratory in Livermore, California.

During the 1950s Teller became a leading scientific spokesman for the maintenance of U.S. atomic weapons superiority. He believed that American supremacy was the only means of countering what he viewed as an aggressive Soviet arms policy. Described by *Newsweek* as "the principal architect of the H-bomb," Teller was a leading advocate of that weapon's development. In the 1954 AEC security hearings, he testified against granting J. Robert OPPENHEIMER a security clearance, claiming that Oppenheimer's opposition to the H-bomb project had delayed its development. Teller opposed the three-year moratorium on atomic testing that ended in September 1961 when the U.S.S.R. resumed atmospheric explosions, and he favored the renewed U.S. testing, which began later that month. Calling nuclear test ban negotiations "dangerous," he said they "have helped the Soviets" and "have impeded our own testing."

During the August 1963 Senate hearings on the NUCLEAR TEST BAN TREATY, Teller was the most influential scientist to testify against ratification. His principal objection was to the ban's prohibition of atmospheric tests, which were necessary for the further development of antiballistic missiles (ABMs). Teller feared that the Soviets had a lead in ABM production and that the treaty might enable them to increase that lead. Warning that current detection techniques would be ineffective for policing the agreement, Teller also believed that the treaty would inhibit the military's ability to respond in case of war since it stipulated that atomic weapons could be used only three months after repudiation of the agreement. Teller's views were rejected by Gen. Maxwell TAYLOR, Glenn SEABORG and other military and government officials who testified in support of the treaty. President KENNEDY rebutted many of Teller's objections in a news conference in late August and signed the treaty in October. In addition to his call for atomic superiority, Teller believed that the threat of international communism required an aggressive American stance in other areas.

Telstar. First privately owned communications satellite to orbit the Earth, it was built by the American Telephone & Telegraph Co. and its Bell Telephone Laboratories and blasted into orbit on July 10, 1962. A 170-pound, 34.25-inch-diameter sphere, it was launched from CAPE CANAVERAL by NASA, in the nose of a three-stage booster rocket. Its orbit had an apogee of 5,636 miles, a perigee of 593 miles at an angle of 44.8° to the equator, with a period of 158 minutes. *Telstar I* had one transponder to receive and retransmit signals and was powered by over 3,500 solar cells on the outer part of the sphere and nickel-cadmium batteries in its interior. It ceased to operate on February 21, 1963 and was followed by *Telstar II*, which was launched later in 1963 and rendered inoperable in May 1965. Both *Telstar* satellites were capable of processing six telephone calls or one television channel. The first *Telstar* transmitted the first transatlantic TV broadcast, and the second transmitted the first such color-TV program. Both *Telstars* gathered important information on the effects of radiation on satellite communications.

Temin, Howard Martin (1934–). American molecular biologist. Temin's years of research into the two classes of viruses, those with DNA and those with RNA genes, led to his discovery in 1970 of the enzyme known variously as reverse transcriptase or RNA-directed DNA polymerase, which he deduced was capable of producing a sequence of viral replication outside of the Central Dogma of molecular biology, as it was then known. This reaction was also discovered independently by David BALTIMORE. For this, Temin and Baltimore shared the 1975 NOBEL PRIZE for physiology or medicine, along with Renato DULBECCO.

Temple, Shirley (1928–). American actress and diplomat. Born in Santa Monica, California, Shirley Temple became the most popular child star in HOLLYWOOD history. Her earliest work was in one-reel comedy shorts in 1931. Signed to a TWENTIETH CENTURY-FOX contract after her role in the feature-length *Stand Up and Cheer*

Shirley Temple and Bill "Bojangles" Robinson in a scene from their 1935 motion picture The Little Colonel.

(1934), she quickly became the studio's biggest star. A talented singer, dancer and actress with blond ringlets, a sparkling smile and irresistible dimples, she cheered Depression-era audiences in such films as *Little Miss Marker* (1934), *The Little Colonel* (1935), *Captain January* (1936, in which she sang her trademark "On the Good Ship, Lollipop"), *Wee Willie Winkie* (1937) and *Rebecca of Sunnybrook Farm* (1938). She made several films in the 1940s, including *Since You Went Away* (1944), but could never recapture her earlier superstar status; Temple retired from the movies after *A Kiss for Corliss* (1949). As Shirley Temple Black (she married businessman Charles Black in 1950), she became active in Republican politics. She served as a delegate to the United Nations in 1969, was American ambassador to Ghana from 1974 to 1976 and U.S. chief of protocol in 1976. Her autobiography, *Child Star*, was published in 1988; in 1989 she was named U.S. ambassador to Czechoslovakia.

Temple, William (1881–1941). British theologian and archbishop of Canterbury. Temple, whose father Frederick Temple also served as archbishop of Canterbury (1896–1902), was a highly influential figure in the religious life of Britain. Educated in philosophy at Oxford University, Temple was named bishop of Manchester (1921–29) and archbishop of York (1929–42) before becoming archbishop of Canterbury in the final years of his life (1942–44). As a Christian socialist with a widely respected pulpit, he helped attain greater respectability for the British LABOUR PARTY. In addition, his theological works, such as *Nature, Man and God* (1934) and *Christianity and the Social Order* (1942), were influential in bringing a broader, international ecumenism to the Anglican Church.

Ten Boom, Corrie (1892–1983). Dutch writer and religious activist. During WORLD WAR II Ten Boom and her family sheltered JEWS from the NAZIS in the NETHERLANDS. The Ten Booms were credited with saving more than 700 Jews from German CONCENTRATION CAMPS; she herself was finally arrested and sent to a concentration camp. Her wartime experiences formed the basis for her co-authored bestselling book, *The Hiding Place* (1974), and a movie of the same name produced in association with the American evangelist Billy GRAHAM.

Tennessee Valley Authority [TVA]. Independent federal agency established to control flooding, develop and promote navigation, and produce electrical power along the course of the Tennessee River and its tributaries. First proposed in the 1920s as a solution to the problem of what to do with the wartime Muscle Shoals project in Alabama, it was redrafted and set up by President Franklin D. ROOSEVELT in 1933. Construction of the first project, Norris Dam on the Clinch River near Knoxville, was begun in the fall of that year. Unique among federal agencies because its headquarters are in the region instead of in Washington, D.C., it has jurisdiction over a drainage area of nearly 41,000 sq. mi., including parts of Tennessee, Kentucky, Virginia, North Carolina, Georgia, Alabama and Mississippi. An early model for other river development plans, the TVA system operates 32 major dams, 21 of them constructed by the TVA and the remainder purchased from, or operated for, private companies. The production and sale of electric power was highly criticized by privately-owned power companies who charged that the TVA was exempt from taxation and not obligated to make a profit.

In 1960 the TVA was allowed to issue up to $750 million in bonds for its proposed power capacity increase in lieu of having to apply to Congress for appropriations. Along with dominating the economic life of the Tennessee Valley as far as power production (109.8 billion kilowatts were generated in 1974) and river traffic, the system has also been responsible for the establishment of recreational facilities and the control of malaria in the region, and has been involved in numerous land and wildlife conservation programs (1.5 million acres of land reforested by 1975).

For further reading:

Thurman, Sybil, ed., *A History of the Tennessee Valley Authority*. Knoxville, Tenn.: S.B. Newman, 1983.

Callahan, North, *TVA: Bridge Over Troubled Waters*. South Brunswick, N.J.: A.S. Barnes, 1980.

Teresa, Mother [born Agnes Gonxha Bojaxhiu] (1910–). Roman Catholic nun and missionary. Born in Skopje (then within the Ottoman Empore, now part of Yugoslavia) of Albanian parents, Mother Teresa joined the Sisters of Loreto in 1922, studied English in Dublin and embarked for CALCUTTA, India, in 1929. There she taught high school until 1948 and became fluent in Bengali and Hindi. In 1946 she received "a call within a call" to leave the convent and "help the poor, while living among them." Two years later she received permission from the archbishop of Calcutta and began her work outside the convent, adopting a white sari for her habit and becoming an Indian citizen. In

Mother Teresa, a tireless comforter of the poor and sick of Calcutta and the world (Feb. 6, 1989).

1950 she started a new order, the Missionaries of Charity, whose vows included giving free service to the poorest of the poor. She established a home for the dying in 1954 and soon after founded an orphanage for abandoned children. Beginning in 1965 she opened centers, hospitals, schools and orphanages in many countries. In 1979 Mother Teresa was awarded the NOBEL PRIZE for peace. In 1990 she resigned temporarily as superior general of her order because of ill health, but resumed her activities soon thereafter. The Missionaries of Charity now numbers hundreds of sisters of many nationalities working throughout the world, and Mother Teresa is considered a model of selfless devotion to her fellow human beings.

Tereshkova, Valentina (1937–). Soviet cosmonaut and the first woman to fly in space. Tereshkova, an accomplished parachutist, faced her mission with little training and considerable courage. On June 16, 1963, her tiny VOSTOK 6 capsule was lifted into orbit to the great roar of its boosters. There she spent three days circling the Earth, completing 48 orbits. In one mission she outshone all six American MERCURY astronauts who had flown

Valentina Tereshkova (right), the first woman to go into space, with the Marchioness of Lothian, founder of the Woman of the Year Luncheon, after a press onference in London (1984).

up to that time, and her call sign "Chaika" ("Seagull") caught the imaginations of women everywhere whose vision encompassed more than traditional homemaking and motherhood. She made television broadcasts from space and kept in constant radio contact with Valery BYKOVSKY, who was flying Vostok 5 at the same time. The American space program did not put a woman in space until June 18, 1983, a decision that brought criticism and charges of sexism. Ironically, the Soviets have included only one other woman in their space program, Svetlana SAVITSKAYA, in 1982 and 1984.

Terkel, "Studs" (Louis) (1912–). American journalist and writer. Born in New York City, Studs Terkel has been a sportswriter, actor, playwright and newspaper reporter. A superb interviewer, he is particularly noted for his oral histories of important eras in 20th-century America, including *Hard Times: An Oral History of the Great Depression in America* (1970) and *The Good War: An Oral History of World War II* (1986). Among Terkel's other books are *Division Street, America* (1966) and *Working People Talk About What They Do All Day and How They Feel About What They Do* (1974). A lively, street-smart, voluble man, he has become a familiar feature in the popular media, moderating his own radio and television shows, and participating in numerous televised documentaries such as PBS's *The Civil War* (1990).

Terry, Luther Leonidas (1911–1985). American physician. As surgeon general of the U.S. from 1961 to 1965, Terry was responsible for the historic government report linking cigarette smoking to lung cancer and other diseases. Upon its release in 1964, the report bolstered anti-smoking efforts throughout the world. In 1965, at Terry's urging, Congress introduced the requirement that cigarette packages carry a health warning. Six years later he helped obtain a ban on cigarette ads on radio and television.

Terry, Walter (1913–1982). American writer and lecturer on dance. A graduate of the University of North Carolina, Terry studied dance with Alicia Markova and Martha GRAHAM, among others. He served as dance critic of the *Boston Herald* (1936–39), the *New York Herald Tribune* (1939–42, 1945–67), and *Saturday Review* (from 1967). He also directed the JACOB'S PILLOW DANCE FESTIVAL in 1973, and has lectured on dance and served as a dance consultant. He has written many dance books, including *The Ballet Companion* (1968), *Miss Ruth—The More Living Life of Ruth St. Denis* (1969) and *Frontiers of Dance: The Life of Martha Graham* (1975).

Terry-Thomas [born Terry Thomas Hoar Stevens] (1911–1990). British comedian and actor. Terry-Thomas specialized in playing slightly demented English dandies and cads, first winning fame in Britain in the television series "How Do You View?" in the 1950s. His gap-toothed grin, mustache, cigarette-holder and upper-class accent became his trademarks. He later moved to HOLLYWOOD and starred in films such as *It's a Mad, Mad, Mad, Mad World* (1963), *Those Magnificent Men in Their Flying Machines* (1965) and *How to Murder Your Wife* (1965).

Tertz, Abram. See Andrei SINYAVSKY.

Test Ban Treaty. See NUCLEAR TEST BAN TREATY.

"test-tube babies". See IN VITRO FERTILIZATION.

Tetley, Glen (1926–). American dancer and choreographer. Tetley has danced with a number of ballet and contemporary dance companies, including those of Hanya Holm (1946–51), Martha GRAHAM (1958), and AMERICAN BALLET THEATRE (1960). In 1962 he choreographed his first dances, most notably *Pierrot Lunaire,* for his own group. Then in 1964 he joined the Netherlands Dance Theatre as dancer/choreographer, eventually becoming as artistic advisor (until 1970). He succeeded John CRANKO as director of the Stuttgart Ballet in 1974, creating one of his most popular ballets, *Voluntaries,* for that company in honor of Cranko. He resigned the directorship in 1976 and continued to work as a freelance choreographer until becoming the artistic advisor for the National Ballet of Canada in 1987.

Tet Offensive. "Tet" is a traditionally celebrated Vietnamese holiday. It had been customary during the VIETNAM WAR to observe a cease-fire during the Tet holidays and 1968 was no exception; in fact the NATIONAL LIBERATION FRONT (North Vietnam's front organization for the VIET CONG) had publicly called for scrupulous observance of the Tet cease-fire. While intelligence reports had been received that the North Vietnamese Army (NVA) and Viet Cong might take advantage of the holiday to launch an attack, there was no feeling that a major offensive was imminent. On January 30, 1968 the Tet holiday began, but shortly after midnight several cities were attacked and by noon on January 30 all U.S. units were placed on maximum alert. At 3:00 A.M. on January 31 the North Vietnamese and Viet Cong launched what has become known as the Tet Offensive. Simultaneous attacks were made on Hue and other major cities, towns and military bases throughout Vietnam. One assault team got within the walls of the U.S. embassy in Saigon before they were destroyed. Television footage of this attack received widespread attention in the U.S. Initial media reports stated that U.S. and South Vietnamese Army forces had been surprised and defeated.

But it was not the U.S. that was defeated on the battlefield. It was the North Vietnamese Army and especially the Viet Cong. Their "general offensive and general uprising" had been a tactical disaster. Not only had their military forces been resoundingly defeated, but their ideological illusion that the South Vietnamese people would flock to their banner during the "general uprising" proved false. From Tet 1968 on, the NVA realized it would not be able to attain its political objective with guerrilla forces and increasingly the war became an affair for the regular forces of the NVA. But if the U.S. had won tactically, it suffered a fatal strategic blow. False expectations had been raised at home that the war was virtually won. Public opinion had turned against the war in October 1967 and the events of Tet confirmed that disenchantment. The Tet Offensive cost the government and the military the confidence of the American people. Not only did the American public turn further against the war, but the commander-in-chief, President Johnson, seemed psychologically defeated by the Tet Offensive. Challenged within his own party for renomination and with public support slipping away, he thereafter publicly announced that he would not seek reelection. Although the war continued for another seven years, the war for the support of the American people was lost on January 30, 1968. From that point on, the problem was not how to win the war but how to disengage.

For further reading:

Oberdorfer, Don, *Tet! The Turning Point of the Vietnam War.* New York: Da Capo, 1983.

"Texaco Star Theater". Popular variety show in the early years of American television. During its peak years on NBC—from June 8, 1948, to the end of the 1951 season—it became a national obession as millions clustered around any available set on Tuesday evening to watch the clownish Milton BERLE ("Uncle Miltie") and his burlesque antics. Relying on his vaudeville experience, Berle helped launch the standard television variety formula. "I suggested to the powers at Texaco a show in which I would serve as host," he writes in his autobiography, "do some of my routines and introduce guest stars, who would do their specialities, and then I would mix it up with them for some comedy." The show originated live from Studio 6B in the RCA Building at Rockefeller Center in New York City. Four men dressed in Texaco uniforms stepped in front of a curtain, singing "Oh, we're the men of Texaco/We work from Maine to Mexico," after which Berle emerged in an outlandish costume (a pilgrim, a caveman, frequently a woman) and presided over a divine kind of madness—taking pratfalls with the acrobats, singing silly duets with guests like Elvis PRESLEY and dodging hundreds of thrown pies and squirting seltzer bottles. A Nielsen rating in late 1950 revealed that a little over 60% of TV-equiped homes were tuned in to the show, and historian Arthur Wertheim credits a 1950–51 boom in the sale of TV sets to the shows's incredible popularity. As early as 1952 the format began to change, Berle's aggressive persona was softened and ratings began to drop. In the mid-1950s Berle was replaced as host by a succession of entertainers, like Jimmy DURANTE and Donald O'Connor. The show finally succumbed in the mid-1960s, a victim of changes in audience tastes.

For further reading:

The Complete Directory of Prime Time Network TV Shows. New York: Ballantine Books, 1988.

Texas. U.S. Navy battleship. Built in 1911–12, the *Texas* was 573 feet long with an extreme beam of 93 feet 3 inches. Capable of reaching a speed of 21 knots and outfitted with 14-inch guns, the *Texas* was the first ship ever to launch a plane from its deck (1919), an event that led to the development of the aircraft carrier and radically changed the tactics of naval warfare. The *Texas* served in WORLD WAR I and WORLD WAR II before being decommissioned in 1948.

Texas School Book Depository. See Lee Harvey OSWALD.

Tey, Josephine [pen name of Elizabeth Mackintosh] (1896–1952). Scottish playwright and novelist. Tey is perhaps best known for her series of mystery novels featuring Scotland Yard Inspector Alan Grant. These books include *Ms. Pym Disposes* (1946) and *The Singing Sands* (1952). *A Shilling for Candles* (1936) inspired Alfred HITCHCOCK's 1937 film *Young and Innocent*. Under the pseudonym Gordon Daviot, Tey was also a successful playwright. Her plays include *Richard of Bordeaux* (1933, produced in 1932), *The Laughing Woman* (1934) and *The Little Dry Thorn* (1953, produced in 1947).

Teyte, Dame Maggie [born Margaret Tate] (1888–1976). English soprano. Born in Wolverhampton, Teyte studied at the Royal College of Music in London and privately in Paris. She made her debut at a Mozart festival in Paris in 1905. From 1908 to 1910, she appeared with the Opera Comique, Paris, where she became renowned for the role of Melisande in *Pelleas and Melisande*. She made her debut in London in 1909 and in the U.S. in 1911, was a member of the Boston Opera Company (1915–17) and made extensive tours of the U.S. Beginning in 1932, she became one of the BBC's principal radio artists. During World War II, she sang for Allied troops and in Myra HESS's National Gallery concerts in London. Teyte became well known for her recordings of French songs and performed in U.S. tours during the 1940s. Her final operatic performance took place in 1951, and her last U.S. tour in 1954. In 1957 Teyte was made a Chevalier of the Legion of Honor by France and a Dame of the British Empire by England.

TGV [Trains a Grande Vitesse]. French high-speed train—the fastest scheduled passenger train in the world. The TGV was inaugurated on September 27, 1981, on the Paris-Lyons route, making the run in two hours. The electric-powered TGV cruises at 160 miles per hour on specially welded rails. The soundproofed train includes 10 passenger cars, with 386 seats. In the first two months of operation, TGVs carried one million passengers—an average of 13,000 per day. TGVs have since been added to the Paris-Marseilles and the Paris-Bordeaux runs. Previously, the fastest train was Japan's Bullet Train, at 130 mph.

Thailand. Thailand, wedged between BURMA, LAOS and CAMBODIA, is a part of the Indochina Peninsula in Southeast Asia and covers an area of 198,404 square miles. Known as Siam until 1939, the country was ruled as an absolute monarchy until a bloodless coup in 1932 established a constitutional monarchy. Under Prime Minister Phibun Songkhram (1939–44), Thailand pursued an anti-Western policy and collaborated with the Japanese invasion of the country in 1941. Phibun was overthrown in 1944 but regained control in 1948. From the 1950s to the early 1970s the military held power. In 1971 the military government collapsed in the face of social problems, protests and the withdrawal of the king's support. The new democratic government failed, and the military took control again in 1977. By 1979 Thailand was embroiled in problems associated with VIETNAM's occupation of Cambodia. A bloodless coup in 1991 deposed another civilian prime minister and returned Thailand to military rule.

Thalberg, Irving G. (1899–1936). Legendary American motion picture producer; credited by biographer Bob Thomas not only for inventing the big-studio system that kept American movies supreme throughout the world, but also for his "unceasing pursuit of quality." The Brooklyn-born son of German parents suffered rheumatic fever throughout his childhood and never finished high school. From 1918 to 1923 he worked for film mogul Carl LAEMMLE, rising from private secretary to production head of UNIVERSAL PICTURES in Los Angeles. The fresh-faced "Boy Wonder" was precocious, tough and an astute judge of story material. From 1924 until his death in 1936 he supervised production at MGM under the management of Louis B. MAYER, helping to shape the studio into the most successful operation in the film industry. Obsessed with filmmaking at all levels, closer to home he guided the career of his wife, actress **Norma Shearer,** to five ACADEMY AWARD nominations (she won once, in 1930). His personally supervised prestige projects included the von STROHEIM-directed *Greed* (1924), the epic *Ben Hur* (1927), the GARBO-Gilbert vehicle, *Flesh and the Devil* (1927), the maritime epic *Mutiny on the Bounty* (1935), the oversized *Romeo and Juliet* (1936) and the adaptation of Pearl BUCK's *The Good Earth* (released posthumously in 1937).

Although some of his power was curtailed when he was replaced as production chief in 1933 by David O. SELZNICK, Thalberg retained to the end his own independent production unit. He initiated the "sneak preview" concept. He subjected scripts to endless rewrites, employing such notable writers as F. Scott FITZGERALD. And some of his projects ran against the glossy MGM grain—the horrific but poignant *Freaks* (1933) and the zany MARX BROTHERS film *A Night at the Opera* (1935). Although he worked in the most visible business in the world, he jealously guarded his own privacy, refusing to use his name on a film's credits. ("I want to make it perfectly clear that my name should be on nothing," he once said, "not even my parking space.") However, anonymity was not to be. His name is inscribed on the "Irving G. Thal-

THAILAND

1910	Death of King Chulalangkorn after 42-year reign; Siam is the last uncolonized state in southeast Asia.
1932	Westernized Siamese revolt to form constitutional monarchy, but military under Colonel Phahon emerges with power.
1939	Marshal Phibun, admirer of Hitler, stages anti-Western, anti-Chinese campaign; "Thailand" adopted as name.
1941	Phibun collaborates with Japanese takeover.
1944	Japanese collapse; civilian government set up.
1946	King Ananda dies mysteriously.
1948	Business leaders fear communist threat; Phibun regains power.
1954	SEATO headquartered at Bangkok.
1955	Television introduced.
1957	Marshal Sarit imposes dictatorship.
1963	New constitution; buildup of U.S. bases adds to prosperity; builds tourism.
1969	Limited parliamentary elections.
1973	Massive student demonstrations lead to democratically elected government, which begins leftist programs and seeks ties with China, Viet Nam.
1976	Military reasserts control.
1977	Campaign to stimulate foreign investment.
1979	Flood of refugees from Kampuchea.
1983	Amnesty for outlawed communists.
1988	Peaceful change of governments through free elections.
1991	U.S. stops aid after military coup.

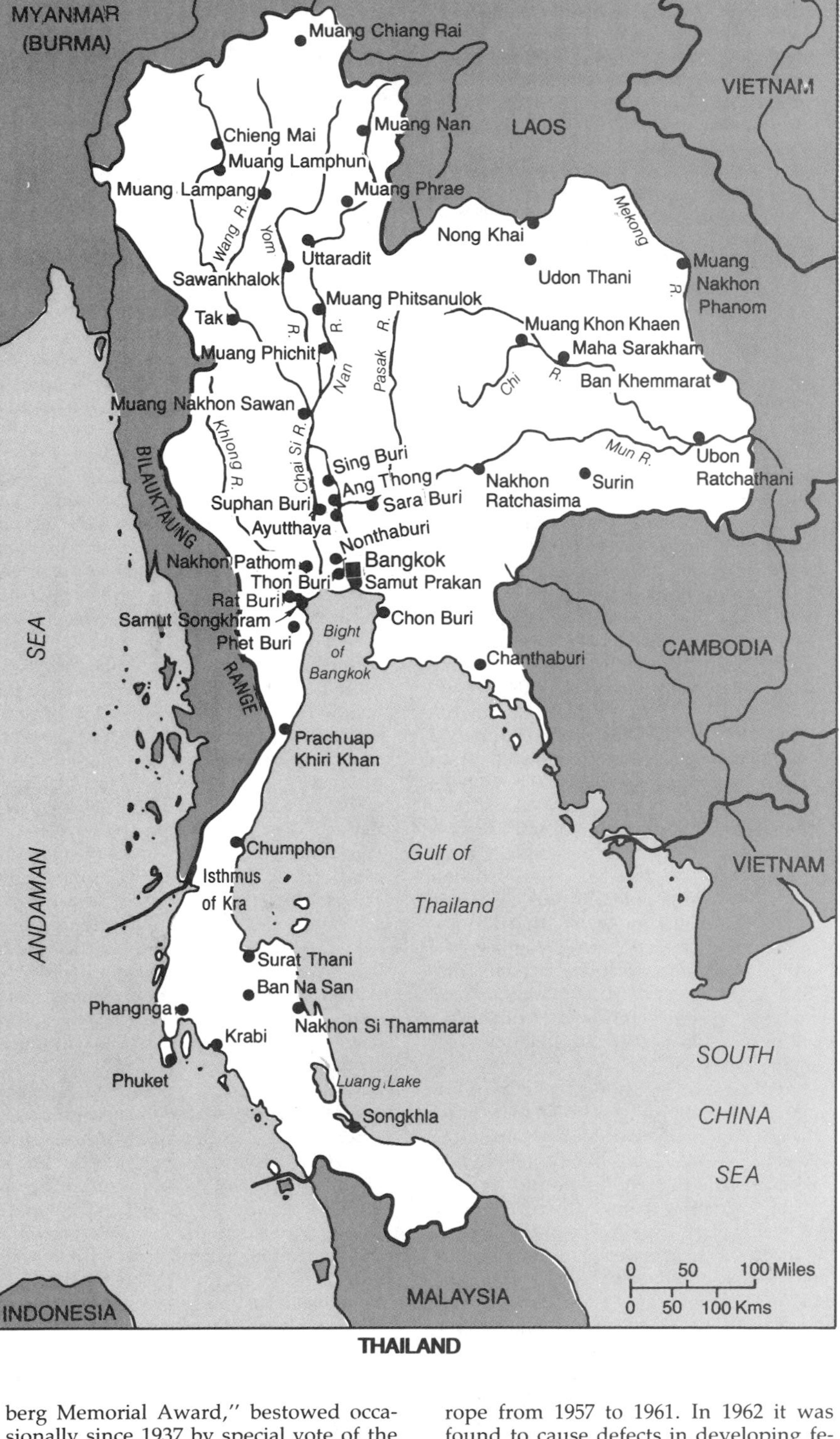

THAILAND

berg Memorial Award," bestowed occasionally since 1937 by special vote of the academy. He was the model for the characters of "Miles Calman" and "Monroe Stahr" in Fitzgerald's *Crazy Sunday* and the unfinished novel, *The Last Tycoon* (1940).

For further reading:

Thomas, Bob, *Thalberg: Life and Legend*. New York: Doubleday, 1969.

thalidomide. A drug, used as a sedative, to induce sleep and to prevent nausea in pregnancy, and widely marketed in Europe from 1957 to 1961. In 1962 it was found to cause defects in developing fetuses leading to severe malformations at birth. Its use was particularly widespread in West Germany and Great Britain, where it was given official approval. The most severe of the birth defects was phocomelia, the development of short and often useless hands and feet. Before it was removed from the market in 1962, the drug had deformed or killed between 8,000 to 10,000 babies in 20 countries. The drug was never officially approved in the U.S., but had been distributed in sample form and given to many American women.

Tharp, Twyla (1941–). American dancer and choreographer. A graduate of Barnard College, Tharp studied dance with Merce CUNNINGHAM and Alwin Nikolais, among others, and debuted with the Paul TAYLOR Dance Company in 1963. In 1965 she formed her own company and began to choreograph works for other companies as well as for her own. Her works are a blend of popular dance forms (jazz, social dance) and formal ballet technique, and she often uses popular music by composers such as Fats WALLER and the BEACH BOYS for her dances. Her best known works include *Eight Jelly Rolls* (1971), *Deuce Coupe* (1976) and *Push Comes to Shove* (1976) which she created especially for Mikhail BARYSHNIKOV and AMERICAN BALLET THEATRE (ABT). She also choreographed and directed the Broadway musical *Singin' in the Rain* (1985). She has disbanded her company, and has since become affiliated with ABT.

Thatcher, Margaret Hilda [born Margaret Hilda Roberts] (1925–). British politician, CONSERVATIVE PARTY leader and prime minister of the UNITED KINGDOM (1979–90). The daughter of a Grantham, Lincolnshire grocer, Thatcher was educated as a research chemist at Somerville College, Oxford, but subsequently pursued a career in politics. Elected to Parliament (1959) as a Conservative, she gained wide attention as minister for education (1970–74) in the cabinet of Edward HEATH when she abolished free milk for schoolchildren. In 1975 she ousted Heath in an acrimonious contest for party leadership. Four years later she won a landslide victory (May 3, 1979) over James CALLAGHAN and became the first woman prime minister in British history. She was re-elected in 1983 following the British victory in the FALKLANDS WAR, and again in 1987. In 1988 she became the longest-serving prime minister in the 20th century. A staunch supporter of the free market, Thatcher undertook an ambitious plan to revitalize Britain's economy and curtail the WEL-

Margaret Thatcher, British prime minister throughout the 1980s.

FARE STATE. Pursuing strict monetarist policies and dominating both her own cabinet and Parliament, she cut public spending, sold off unprofitable nationalized industries to private investors, and curbed the power of the trade unions (see also NATIONALIZATION, PRIVATIZATION). She also cut personal income tax rates significantly, but more than doubled Britain's value-added tax (VAT). Her measures resulted in a rise in the standard of living for many Britons; however, high unemployment, recurring inflation, and social unrest in the inner cities persisted, and her confrontation with the coal miner's union (1984–85) caused much bitterness. In her foreign policy Thatcher was nationalistic and anti-communist but pragmatic. She was the first Western leader to meet with Soviet leader Mikhael GORBACHEV and to recognize his significance. Often critical of the EUROPEAN ECONOMIC COMMUNITY (EEC), Thatcher enjoyed warm relations with U.S. President Ronald REAGAN. Thatcher's introduction of a flat-rate "community charge" or poll tax to replace local property taxes ("rates") proved highly unpopular and provoked riots in 1990. Her government suffered another setback in October 1990 when Thatcher publicly denounced a plan for the monetary integration of Europe, which all other EEC nations—and many Conservatives—supported. Sir Geoffrey HOWE, a longtime Thatcher supporter and senior Conservative official, resigned from the cabinet, sparking a revolt by back-bench MPs who felt that Thatcher no longer represented the majority of the party. After failing to defeat MP Michael HESELTINE in a party leadership vote, Thatcher announced her resignation (November 1990). She was succeeded as party leader and prime minister by her chancellor of the exchequer and protege, John MAJOR. Thatcher was subsequently awarded the Order of Merit by Queen ELIZABETH II. One of the most important if most controversial political figures of her time, Thatcher exerted immense influence on the course of Britain in the 1980s, on general notions of government, politics and economics, and on the Western Alliance.

For further reading:

Harris, Kenneth, *Margaret Thatcher*. Boston: Little, Brown, 1988.

Minogue, Kenneth, and Michael Biddiss, ed., *Thatcherism: Personality and Politics*. New York: St. Martin's, 1987.

Hughes, Libby, *Madam Prime Minister: A Biography of Margaret Thatcher*. Minneapolis: Dillon Press, 1989.

Jenkins, Peter, *Mrs. Thatcher's Revolution: The Ending of the Socialist Era*. Cambridge: Harvard University Press, 1988.

Kavanaugh, Dennis A., *The Thatcher Effect: A Decade of Change*. New York: Oxford University Press, 1989.

Young, Hugo, *The Iron Lady*. New York: Farrar, Straus & Giroux, 1989.

Thatcherites. Supporters of British Conservative Prime Minister Margaret THATCHER and her radical right-wing policies. They include the DRIES.

Thaw case. Sensational 1906 murder trial of playboy millionaire Harry K. Thaw, who shot prominent architect Stanford White in the roof garden restaurant of the old Madison Square Garden in New York. White had a reputation for seducing young women, including the 16-year-old Evelyn Nesbit. Thaw, known as a lecherous womanizer, was later married to Nesbit, who was a popular actress on Broadway. He regularly beat his young wife and during one of these episodes, Nesbit revealed to him details of her earlier relationship with White. Some time later, while the couple was attending a musical at the Garden's roof restaurant, Thaw spotted White, calmly walked up to him and shot him dead in front of a startled crowd. In the ensuing, highly publicized murder trial, the defense portrayed White as a deviant who seduced young girls after having them pose on the red velvet swing in his hideaway. Although the first trial resulted in a hung jury, a second jury found Thaw insane. After being committed to a mental hospital he was temporarily released. However, he was recommitted after horsewhipping a teenage male sexual partner. Thaw was released years later and died in 1947.

Theater of the Absurd. A style of playwrighting that became dominant in Europe after World War II and flourished worldwide throughout the 1950s and 1960s. Major playwrights who have been grouped under the "Absurd" rubric include Samuel BECKETT, Friedrich DURRENMATT, Jean GENET, Eugene IONESCO, Luigi PIRANDELLO and Tom STOPPARD. Theater of the Absurd is noted for its acceptance of the existential viewpoint that life has no meaning beyond what each individual arbitrarily applies to it (see EXISTENTIALISM). It holds that all laws and societal mores are relative and favors comic situations in which characters are mocked for their shallow ideals and hypocrisies and lauded when they show the simple courage to live according to their own inner dictates. Dramatic pathos arises from the sense of despair all must ultimately face when absolute truths are found lacking. As to stage presentation, the conventions of realism are usually flouted by spare, stylized set designs that emphasize a sense of alienation between the individual and his environment.

Theater of the Grotesque. See TEATRO GROTTESCO.

Theatre Guild. American production company. The Theatre Guild was formed in New York in 1919, originally based in the Garrick Theatre, moving to its own Guild Theatre in 1925. The guild distinguished itself producing innovative American and foreign drama. Important early productions include George Bernard SHAW's *Heartbreak House* (1920), Henrik Ibsen's *Peer Gynt* (1923) and Elmer RICE's *The Adding Machine* (1923). The Guild also presented the musical *Oklahoma!* (1943). Guild actors include Helen HAYES, Alfred LUNT and Lynne FONTANNE and Alla Nazimona. The Theatre Guild was incorporated into the American National Theatre and Academy in 1950.

Theiner, Georg (1927–1985). Czech writer; editor of the *Index on Censorship* issued by Writers and Scholars International. Born in Prague, he fled to Britain following the Nazi invasion of CZECHOSLOVAKIA. Theiner returned after the war, working for the official Czech news agency. He lost his job in 1948 when he refused to join the Communist Party. His dissent eventually landed him in a forced labor camp in the Siberian coal fields, until 1953. Following the Soviet invasion of Czechoslovakia in 1968, he returned to London where he spent the rest of his life.

theosophy. Group of occult, mystical and spiritualist teachings. While the general term has long referred to theories on the divinely inspired structure of the universe, in modern usage it means the teachings of the Theosophical Society founded in New York in 1875. The society's principal leader at that time was Helena Petrovna Blavatsky, a Russian-born charlatan with remarkable imaginative and analytical powers who wrote massive theoretical tomes, including the multi-volume *The Secret Doctrine* (1888), which became a mainstay text of the theosophical movement. While Blavatsky was ultimately shown to have used false mechanisms to create so-called "spiritual" effects—such as sudden letters from secret Himalayan Masters—the influence of her teachings has endured. Theosophy is a highly eclectic blend of Eastern Brahmanism and Buddhism with Western spiritualism and occult traditions such as astral travel. In the 20th century, the Theosophical Society has endured many schisms and divisions. One theosophical sect, the Star in the East, held forth Jidda KRISHNAMURTI as world savior during the 1920s. But in 1929, Krishnamurti dissolved the sect and renounced his savior role, going on to become a highly influential philosopher and thinker.

Thibaud, Jacques (1880–1953). French violinist. Born in Bordeaux, Thibaud studied violin at the Paris Conservatory (1894–96). He made his concert debut in Paris in 1898, and debuted in the U.S. in 1903. He fought with distinction in WORLD WAR I, returning to the concert stage after the war to tour virtually every major city in the world. He was noted for his work as a guest artist and for his chamber music performances, particularly in trios with Pablo CASALS and Alfred CORTOT. Acclaimed for his interpretations of Mozart and the composers of the French school, Thibaut was an exponent of the classic French violin technique, emphasizing stylistic elegance over bravura performance. A member of the RESISTANCE movement during WORLD WAR II, he remained active as a performer during and after the war. He was killed in an airplane crash en route to a concert in Indochina.

Thieu, Nguyen Van (1923–). Vietnamese general and politician, president of South Vietnam (1967–75). Commissioned in the infantry, he distinguished himself in action against the VIET MINH. When

Nguyen Van Thieu, president of South Vietnam throughout much of the Vietnam War (March 27, 1970).

the South Vietnamese Army was established in 1959, Thieu was appointed commander of its 21st Infantry Division. He also served as commandant of the National Military Academy. After graduating from the U.S. Command and General Staff College at Fort Leavenworth, Kansas, in 1947, Colonel Thieu commanded the South Vietnamese Army First Infantry Division from 1960 to 1962, when he was appointed to command the Fifth Infantry Division near Saigon. During the coup that overthrew President Ngo Dinh DIEM in November 1963, Colonel Thieu led one of his regiments in an attack on the barracks of the presidential bodyguard. Promoted to brigadier general, Thieu was appointed commander of IV Corps. To end the near anarchy that followed the assassination of President Diem, General Thieu took part in a coup by Air Vice Marshal Nguyen Cao KY in December 1964. A civilian government was installed and Thieu, now a major general, became part of a 25–man Armed Forces Council. In June 1965 another coup resulted in a 10–man military National Leadership Committee, which elected General Thieu as chairman and chief of state and Air Marshal Ky as premier. When elections were held in 1967 the situation was reversed. Thieu was elected president and Ky vice president. Ky chose not to run against Thieu in 1971, and Thieu was reelected to the presidency, although charges of a rigged election surfaced.

Pressured by the United States to agree to the PARIS PEACE ACCORD in 1973, which left the North Vietnamese Army (NVA) in control of large segments of the country, President Thieu's position was further undermined when the U.S. Congress cut promised military aid and especially when, after an open NVA attack on Binh Long Province in November 1974, President FORD failed to honor U.S. guarantees to uphold the terms of the Paris Accords. With four NVA corps closing in on Saigon and all hope of outside assistance gone, President Thieu resigned and on April 25, 1975, flew to Taiwan. He now resides in Great Britain.

Third International. See COMINTERN.

Third World. Term in use in the second half of the 20th century; refers to former colonies, now independent. "First World" nations are the industrialized, democratic Western countries, such as the U.S., Canada, Britain and France. The "Second World" consisted of communist nations behind the IRON CURTAIN. Third World nations are mainly in Africa, Asia and Latin America.

Thomas, Charles Allen (1900–1982). American physical chemist. During WORLD WAR II Thomas was part of the MANHATTAN PROJECT team that developed the ATOMIC BOMB. He later served on a panel recommending international control of atomic power for peaceful purposes. He was president (1950–60) and board chairman (1960–65) of the giant Monsanto Chemical Corp. He also served as president and board chairman of the American Chemical Society and was a founding member of the American Academy of Engineering.

Thomas, D(onald) M(ichael) (1935–). British novelist and poet. Thomas was educated at Oxford and learned Russian while training for the British Foreign Service. His extensive knowledge of Russian literature has been a major influence on his own creative work. As a poet Thomas has published several volumes of original verse including *Two Voices* (1968), *Logan Stone* (1971), *Love and Other Deaths* (1975), *The Honeymoon Voyage* (1978), *Dreaming in Bronze* (1981) and *Selected Poems* (1983). He has also translated the verse of the renowned 20th century Russian poet Anna AKHMATOVA. But Thomas has earned his primary fame as a novelist whose best known work, *The White Hotel* (1981), features an intensely realized Russian milieu. Other novels by Thomas include *The Flute Player* (1979), which is dedicated to the spirits of persecuted Russian poets including Akhmatova and Boris PASTERNAK, as well as *Birthstone* (1980) and *Ararat* (1983).

Thomas, Dylan (1914–1953). Welsh poet and story writer. Thomas is one of the legendary figures of 20th-century English poetry. Not only was he an exceptionally gifted lyric poet, but he also possessed a melodic voice that made him a great favorite both on BRITISH BROADCASTING CORPORATION radio programs and on poetry reading tours in Great Britain and the U.S. Thomas was born in the Welsh seaport town of Swansea. He received little formal education but described himself as being deeply steeped as a child in both Welsh folklore and the Bible. After working at a variety of odd jobs, including hack journalism, he achieved early fame as a lyric prodigy in the 1930s. *The Map of Love* (1939) is a representative selection of his early poems and prose. Thomas' writing style bears traces of romanticism, symbolism and SURREALISM,

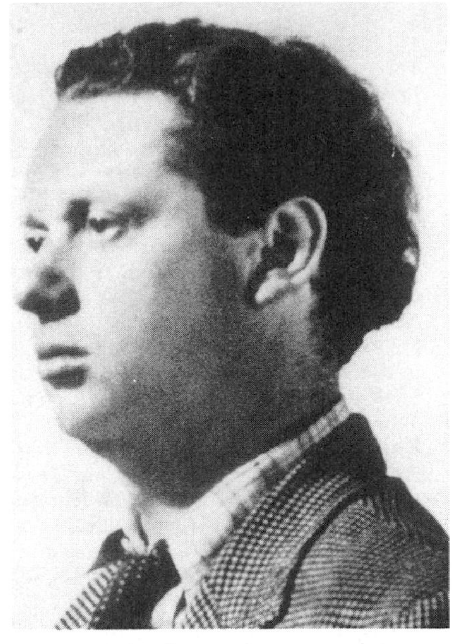

Welsh poet Dylan Thomas.

but is wholly idiosyncratic. In the 1940s and 1950s, Thomas became a highly public figure due to his radio work and readings. With his Irish wife, Caitlin, he lived in the Welsh fishing village of Laugharne; they had three children. But Thomas drove himself to an early death through alcohol, collapsing at the age of 39 during a reading tour in New York City. Thomas' larger-than-life public image has tended to obscure the true value of his work, and critics are divided over his ultimate significance. *Portrait of the Artist as a Young Dog* (1940) and *Adventures in the Skin Trade* (1955) contain the best of his stories. His *Collected Poems* (1960) has remained a perennial favorite.

Thomas, Edward (1878–1917). British poet and prose writer. Of Welsh parentage, Thomas was educated at St. Paul's School, London, and at Lincoln College, Oxford. Sensitive and moody, he made a meagre living as a free-lance writer and reviewer for various journals and newspapers. His evocative essays on the pre-World War I English countryside capture a now-vanished way of life. In 1913 he met Robert FROST, who was then living in England. Thomas was the first major critic to recognize Frost's importance. Frost, in turn, encouraged Thomas to write poetry himself. In the remaining few years of his life Thomas wrote 140 poems, many of which rank among the finest English poems of the 20th century; only six were published during his lifetime. At age 37, Thomas enlisted in the British army ("the Artists' Rifles") in WORLD WAR I and was killed in action during the battle of ARRAS, April 9, 1917. Although his work is not widely known outside the British Isles, it has greatly influenced many later British and Irish writers, including Philip LARKIN and Seamus HEANEY.

For further reading:

Thomas, Edward, *Collected Poems*. London: Faber & Faber, 1979.

———, *A Literary Pilgrim in England*. New York: Oxford University Press, 1980.
Thomas, R. George, *Edward Thomas: A Portrait*. Oxford: Oxford University Press, 1985.

Thomas, Howard (1909–1986). British broadcasting innovator. Thomas was long a major figure in the field, first at BBC, where during World War II he created "The Brains Trust," and later in independent television. For ABC, one of the original "big four" companies when independent television started in 1955, he created the immensely popular and stylish tongue-in-cheek spy series, "The Avengers." From 1974 to 1979 he was chairman of Thames Television.

Thomas, Lowell (Jackson) (1892–1981). American broadcaster, author and world traveler. As a foreign correspondent during WORLD WAR I, he met the British soldier T.E. LAWRENCE and accompanied him on several missions. Thomas' subsequent book, *With Lawrence in Arabia* (1924), was a highly romanticized account of Lawrence's exploits; it made both Thomas and Lawrence world famous—and also embarrassed Lawrence. Thomas' career as a radio news broadcaster spanned nearly half a century from 1930 to 1976. During this period, his voice was one of the most familiar in America. He was not an intellectual or a tough investigative reporter; his easy-going accounts of the day's events, he acknowledged, were not intended to "destroy the digestive system of the American people." His radio career was paralleled by several others. Millions of Americans got their first glimpse of foreign lands through his colorful travelogues. He made trips to regions in Alaska, Africa, India and other parts of the world that few Westerners had visited at the time. His explorations resulted in dozens of books, newsreels, slide shows and television programs that made Thomas wealthy.

Thomas, Norman (Mattoon) (1884–1968). American socialist leader. Born in Marion, Ohio, Thomas attended Princeton University and Union Theological Seminary. After his graduation in 1911 he became pastor of the East Harlem Presbyterian Church, New York, and did social work in this poverty-stricken area of the city. He became a pacifist and was a founder (1917) of the organization that became the AMERICAN CIVIL LIBERTIES UNION. In 1918 Thomas joined the Socialist Party and ceased his religious activities. He ran unsuccessfully for governor of New York in 1924 and 1938 and as mayor of New York in 1925 and 1929. At the death of Eugene V. DEBS in 1926, Thomas assumed the leadership of the Socialist Party. Subsequently, he continued his quixotic attempts to achieve electoral office, running for the presidency every four years from 1928 to 1948. An opponent of both fascism and communism, he opposed American entry into World War II and subsequent Soviet expansionism. In the postwar world, he advocated controlled international disarmament and in 1957 was a cofounder of the Committee for a Sane Nuclear Policy. During the 1950s, he was an outspoken opponent of MCCARTHYISM, and in the 1960s he strongly denounced the VIETNAM WAR. Throughout his career, Thomas acted as conscience and gadfly, criticizing America's social inequities and its two major political parties. Among his books are *Socialism of Our Time* (1929), *The Test of Freedom* (1954) and *Socialism Reexamined* (1963).

Thomas, R(onald) S(tuart) (1913–). Welsh poet and priest. For most of his adult life, Thomas ministered to a small Anglican parish on the rural Lleyn Peninsula in north Wales. Since his first book, *The Stones of the Field* (1946), Thomas has quietly grown to become one of the most original and authentic poets of the 20th century. Much of his later work is collected in *Selected Poems 1946–1968* (1973), *Later Poems* (1983) and *Counterpoint* (1990). Thomas' work frequently deals with the dissolution of the traditional way of life in rural Wales and addresses the central issue of religious faith in a relentlessly secular age.

Thomas, William (1863–1947). American sociologist. After graduating from the University of Tennessee in 1884, Williams taught English there and at Oberlin College. From 1894 to 1918 he taught sociology at the University of Chicago. He spent the rest of his life researching and writing, and produced important theories dealing with man's relationship with his environment. He divided man's behavior into four areas that became his well-known "four wishes" theory. His published works include *Source Book of Social Origins* (1909), *The Unadjusted Girl* (1923) and *The Polish Peasant in Europe and America* (1918–19).

Thomaz, Americo (1894–1987). Portuguese politician. After a career as an admiral and naval minister, in 1958 Thomaz became PORTUGAL's president in elections that were widely regarded as rigged by the dictator and prime minister Antonio SALAZAR. "Reelected" twice, Thomaz was ousted as president in an almost bloodless left-wing coup in 1974.

Thompson, Daley (1958–). British decathlete. Between 1978 and 1987, Thompson won every decathlon he completed; his string was broken when he placed ninth at the World Track and Field Championships that year. Thompson was only the second man in history (after Bob Mathias) to win two Olympic gold medals in the event (in 1980 and 1984). In 1983, he won the world championship, and in 1986 he won his third straight Commonwealth decathlon as well as the decathlon at the European Track and Field Championships.

Thompson, Dorothy (1894–1961). American foreign correspondent, newspaper columnist and radio commentator. Thompson, who enjoyed her greatest influence and readership in the 1930s, was one of the leading journalistic voices against HITLER and Nazi ANTI-SEMITISM. She strongly urged an interventionist position for the United States in the late 1930s, when an isolationist stance toward Europe was favored by the bulk of public opinion. British Prime Minister Winston CHURCHILL lauded Thompson for her efforts in obtaining American military and economic aid for Great Britain during WORLD WAR II. Thompson, who attended Syracuse University, began her journalistic career in the 1920s and married American novelist Sinclair LEWIS in 1928 (they divorced in 1942). Her thrice-weekly column was featured in the *New York Herald-Tribune* from 1936 to 1941 and syndicated nationally through 1958.

Thompson, Hunter (1939–). American journalist and political essayist. Thompson emerged in the 1960s as one of the leading practitioners of the NEW JOURNALISM, a style of reportage that emphasized subjective opinion and personal involvement in the story being reported upon. Thompson, to whom the adjective "gonzo" (meaning crazed or outlandish) is frequently applied, is the most controversial of the New Journalists because of the vituperative extremes of his style and the anarchistic flavor of his political viewpoints. Many of his journalistic pieces first appeared in *Rolling Stone*. His major books include *Hell's Angels* (1966), *Fear and Loathing in Las Vegas, A Savage Journey to the Heart of the American Dream* (1972) and *Fear and Loathing: On the Campaign Trail '72* (1973). Thompson continues as a prolific journalistic, although his influence declined with the shift in political mood from the 1960s to the 1990s. He is caricatured as "Uncle Duke" in the Garry Trudeau comic strip *Doonesbury*.

Thompson, Joe (1887–1980). American model sculptor whose clay works helped revolutionize automobile design. Thompson was among the first craftsmen in the industry to work extensively with clay in transforming sketches into three-dimensional automobile designs. He went on to create the first models for the Model A FORD, the Pontiac, the Opel and the LINCOLN-ZEPHYR.

Thompson, Mickey (1928–1988). American auto racer. Thompson became famous in the 1950s as the "Speed King," when he set the first of his nearly 500 speed and endurance records. In 1960, driving a four-engine streamlined car across Utah's Bonneville Salt Flats, he became the first person to go 400 miles per hour on land. In later years, he became a racing promoter.

Thompson, Milton (1926–). NASA test pilot; flew various experimental craft, including the X-15 (14 times). Thompson was scheduled to fly the Dyna-Soar X-20 rocket plane, but it never got off the drawing boards. He did, however, pioneer flight of a wingless "lifting body" aircraft in 1963 that was a distant precursor of the Space Shuttle.

Thomson, Sir Joseph John (1856–1940). British physicist and head of Oxford's Cavendish Laboratory; best known for his research on cathode rays. His discovery of the electron in 1897 revolutionized physics. He also initiated the research that led F.W. ASTON to develop the mass spectrograph, which identifies a substance's chemical components by separating ions according to mass and charge. Thomson won the 1906 NOBEL PRIZE for physics for his work on the conduction of electricity through gases.

Thomson, Roy Herbert [1st Baron of Fleet] (1894–1978). British newspaper publisher. Born in Canada, Thomson bought a small radio station in 1931 and a weekly newspaper in 1933. After building a chain of radio stations and newspapers in Canada, he emigrated to Britain in 1953. There he continued to expand his holdings and acquired the prestigious *Sunday Times* (1962) and London *Times* (1967). His empire included 285 publications as well as radio and TV stations on four continents.

Thomson, Virgil Garnett (1896–1989). Prominent American composer and influential music critic. The polarities of Thomson's life and work were marked by two cities, Paris and Kansas City. They were the only places he "felt at home," he said; and they inspired, on the one hand, Thomson's wit and elegance, and, on the other, his homespun simplicity and common sense. He was born in Kansas City, Missouri, where as a boy he played the organ at Calvary Baptist Church services. After a brief stint in WORLD WAR I in the Military Aviation Corps, he relocated to Harvard and later to Paris, where he began lifelong friendships with sometime collaborators Pablo PICASSO, Jean COCTEAU, Ernest HEMINGWAY and Gertrude STEIN (with the latter he wrote two operas, *Four Saints in Three Acts*, 1928, first performed in 1934; and *The Mother of Us All*, 1947). Back in New York in the mid-1930s Thomson wrote the score for the Orson WELLES/Negro Theater Project adaption of *Macbeth* (1936). For filmmaker Pare Lorentz he wrote the scores for two important documentary films about American land reclamation projects, *The Plow That Broke the Plains* (1936) and *The River* (1937). In 1938 Thomson's ballet, *The Filling Station*, became the first successful ballet on American themes and the first performed by American dancers. In these and many other works Thomson fused modern harmonic practices with American folk music idioms like cowboy songs, Cajun tunes and jazz. The Baptist hymn, particularly "How Firm a Foundation, Ye Saints of the Lord," appears everywhere in his work and is the basis for one of his finest orchestral works, *Symphony on a Hymn Tune* (1928, premiered in 1945).

Meanwhile, he was beginning a career as a music critic. In the fall of 1940 he succeeded Lawrence Gilman as music critic of the *New York Herald Tribune* where, until his retirement in 1954, he was a powerful, outspoken—frequently astringent—champion of new music. (See his anthologies of collected criticism, *The Musical Scene* [1946] and *Music Right and Left* [1951].) His later years were full of honors: the French Legion of Honor; the PULITZER PRIZE (for his music score to Robert FLAHERTY's *The Louisiana Story* [1949]); and the National Medal of the Arts, among others. Sporadically he left his New York Chelsea Hotel residence to visit his favorite cities, Paris and Kansas City. To the last he remained tough and uncompromising about his art and his criticism. "I don't get into feuds with artists or composers," he said during one of his last interviews. "I get into feuds with management. I'm an artist. I defend the artist." He died in his sleep in New York City on September 30, 1989.

For further reading:

Thomson, Virgil, *Virgil Thomson*. New York: Da Capo Press, 1967.

Thornton, Charles B. "Tex" (1913–1981). American business executive. Thornton won fame during WORLD WAR II as the inventor of a "statistical control" system to monitor the military's global resources. He then went on to apply his organizational and management skills in the civilian world as one of the so-called "Whiz Kids" who reorganized the ailing FORD Motor Company in the mid-1940s. In 1953 he acquired a small microwave tube company and turned it into the huge conglomerate **Litton Industries**. He remained chairman and chief executive officer until his death. As head of Litton he devised the modern concept of conglomerates, buying small, prosperous companies that did not lead in their fields, thus avoiding violation of monopoly laws.

Thorpe, James Francis "Jim" (1888–1953). American athlete. Great-grandson of the American Indian chief Black Hawk, Thorpe started his athletic career at the Carlisle Indian Industrial School, Pennsylvania, where he played on the football team from 1908 to 1912. Thorpe was voted All-American in 1908, 1911 and 1912. He participated in the 1912 OLYMPIC GAMES in Stockholm, Sweden. He played professional baseball with the New York Giants in 1913, 1914 and from 1917 to 1919. In 1920 he became the first president of the American Professional Football Association. In 1932 he was voted the greatest football player of the first half of the 20th century.

For further reading:

Van Riper, Guernsey, Jr., *Jim Thorpe: Olympic Champion*. New York: Macmillan, 1986.

Jim Thorpe, American athlete.

Wheeler, Robert W., *Jim Thorpe: World's Greatest Athlete*. Norman: University of Oklahoma Press, 1981.

Thorpe, Jeremy (1929–). British politician. Thorpe was leader of the LIBERAL PARTY from 1967 to 1976, when a former male model claimed to have had sexual relations with him and Thorpe was forced to step down. In 1978 he was arrested for conspiracy to murder the model. Although he was later acquitted, the THORPE TRIAL brought an end to his political career.

Thorpe trial. In 1978, Jeremy THORPE, a former leader of the British LIBERAL PARTY, was arrested for conspiring to murder a former male model, Norman Scott. Scott had created a political scandal for Thorpe in 1976 by claiming to have had sexual relations with him. The murder plot was first revealed in 1977 when a former airline pilot, Andrew Newton, told a reporter that he had been paid to kill Scott by a Liberal Party fund-raiser. Newton claimed he had lost his nerve and shot Scott's dog instead. Arrested along with Thorpe were David Holmes, a former deputy treasurer of the Liberal Party, and two businessmen, George Deakin and John le Mesurier. All were acquitted following a trial in 1979, although Thorpe's political career was effectively ended.

Thousand Days, War of a (1899–1903). Bitter political struggles between liberals and conservatives disrupted COLOMBIA, and when Manuel Sanclemente (1820–1902) was elected president by the conservatives in 1898, wrangling within the Conservative Party emboldened the liberals to revolt in 1899. Vice President Jose Manuel Marroquin (1827–1908), a conservative, ousted Sanclemente on July 31, 1900, and became President. Three years of violent clashes between armed liberals and conservatives dragged Colombia into economic ruin. Marroquin's troops finally suppressed the liberal rebels, restoring order June 1903, after an estimated 100,000 Colombians had been killed. Later that year, PANAMA, with U.S. help, successfully established its independence from Colombia.

Three-Day Week. The result of economic crisis in Britain in 1973 following an increase in the cost of oil and overtime bans by coal miners, power-workers and railway workers. These resulted in the declaration of a state of emergency by Edward HEATH's Conservative government on November 13, 1973. Strict controls were introduced on domestic and industrial consumption of electricity. From January 1, 1974 until early March of that year, electricity could only be supplied to industry on three specified days a week; thus, many businesses cut their work-week to three days. An election was called in March to test support for the government policy; the Conservatives lost.

Three Mile Island accident. Critical, nonfatal accident at the Three Mile Island nuclear power plant, on the Susquehanna River, near Harrisburg, Pennsylvania, U.S.A. On the morning of March 28, 1979, a malfunction in the primary and emergency core cooling systems of the plant's No. 2 reactor resulted in the formation of a giant hydrogen gas bubble in the reactor vessel. The level of the cooling water surrounding the uranium fuel rods in the reactor fell, exposing the tops of the rods and causing intense heat. Authorities feared that a "meltdown" of the uranium fuel core could occur; such a meltdown would release lethal radioactivity over a wide area and cause many deaths and long-term contamination. There was also the possibility that the gas bubble might explode. Nuclear engineers worked to cool the uranium fuel core and finally managed to shut down the reactor on April 27. During the accident, the plant released radioactive gases, and the governor advised pregnant women and preschool children within a five-mile radius of the plant to leave the area. The mishap was later investigated by a presidential commission, which urged fundamental changes in the way reactors were built, operated and regulated. The commission's report acknowledged that the Three Mile Island accident was "the most severe accident in U.S. commercial nuclear power operating history." The Three Mile Island accident focused worldwide attention on the possible dangers of nuclear power, and led to mass demonstrations against nuclear power, although officials continued to assert that nuclear power was safe. Amazingly, the accident occurred only two weeks after the release of a controversial movie, *The China Syndrome*, about a meltdown at a nuclear power plant. (See also CHERNOBYL DISASTER; WINDSCALE ACCIDENT.)

***Threepenny Opera, The* [*Die Dreigroschenoper*].** German musical play by Bertolt BRECHT featuring songs by Kurt WEILL. From the time of its debut performance in Berlin in 1928, *The Threepenny Opera* has stood as a classic work of the 20th-century theater. It was Brecht's first major success as a playwright and features his unique blend of black humor and incisive social commentary. It also went against the long tradition of musical theater as comedic or light in tone, with Weill's fiercely dramatic score highlighting Brecht's social message. The basic plot of *The Threepenny Opera* concerns the marriage, criminal conviction and ultimate pardon of "Macheath," a robber who reflects the greed and opportunism that reflects society as a whole. The play warns that good persons find it difficult to hold out against the enticements of a corrupt society—a prescient view, given the rise of the NAZIS in GERMANY four years after the play's opening.

Three Stooges, The. Perhaps the century's most violent practitioners of slapstick comedy, the Stooges began in vaudeville with three members: mop-haired Moe Howard (born Moses Horwitz, 1897–1975), his greasy-haired brother Shemp (born Samuel Horwitz, 1895–1955) and Ted Healy (born Charles Earnest Nash, 1896–1937). Before the trio began to make films, changes took place: Shemp was replaced by his heavyset, bald brother Curly (born Jerome Horwitz, 1903–1952); Healy left, due to differences with the other members, and in stepped frizzy-haired comedian Larry Fine (born Louis Feinberg, 1902–1975). With these three members—Larry, Moe and Curly—the boys wreaked havoc on the movie screen in more than 200 short comedies and a handful of B-movies from 1933 to 1965, including *Pop Goes the Easel* (1935), *Dutiful But Dumb* (1941), *Hold That Lion* (1947) and *Spooks* (1953). While the boys maintained an enormous popularity throughout their careers (particularly among younger audiences), their wild, often abusive antics—eye-poking, face slapping, fists in the belly, vocal yowls—offended many and amused few critics. When Curly suffered a stroke in 1946, brother Shemp—who had worked successfully solo in films—returned to the Stooges until his death in 1955. Joe Besser (1907–1988) then joined the group for a period. In the late 1960s and early '70s ex-burlesque comic Joe DeRita (born Joseph Wardell, 1909–) performed sporadically with Moe and Larry, but the Stooges officially disbanded when Larry died in 1975.

Thresher. On April 10, 1963, the nuclear-powered U.S. Navy SUBMARINE U.S.S. *Thresher* sank during deep diving tests in the North Atlantic. The entire crew of 126 men was killed—the worst submarine disaster in U.S. history. It was presumed that a piping system failure had caused the engine room to flood. There were fears that the ship's nuclear reactor could leak and contaminate the ocean, but Vice Admiral Hyman RICKOVER assured the public that there was "no radioactive hazard." The *Thresher* had been commissioned in 1961 and was the first of its class of nuclear submarines.

Throckmorton, John L(athrop) (1913–1986). American general. Throckmorton was deputy commander of U.S. forces in VIETNAM (1964–65), and commanding general of the Third Army (1967–69). He was placed in command of federal and state troops during the 1967 riots in DETROIT, at which time he instructed National Guardsmen to unload their weapons, an order that later subjected him to congressional criticism.

Thunderbird. Name given to a semi-sports car model introduced by the FORD Motor Company in 1955. At the time, interest in European sports cars was increasing, and the absence of any American products in the field had attracted considerable comment. When GENERAL MOTORS introduced the CORVETTE in 1953, Ford was under competitive pressure to produce an equal. The original model approached the concept of European competition with a streamlined body. A porthole-like rear quarter "opera window" and a "continental" spare tire displayed at the rear cluttered the design with styling elements that detracted from its simplicity. In 1958 a four-seat model was introduced, not really a sports car in concept, but still popular with American car buyers. Earlier models, virtual symbols of the popular taste of the 1950s, are now collected and referred to affectionately as "T-Birds."

Thurber, James (1894–1961). American humorist, cartoonist and playwright, considered one of America's greatest humorists since Mark Twain. Thurber regarded his boyhood in Columbus, Ohio, as the prime source for all his later ideas and attitudes. The colorful characters in his family were the models for his comic essays and stories collected in *My Life and Hard Times* (1933) and *My World and Welcome to It* (1942). The strong-minded female relatives, particularly, seem to have left him with a permanent distrust—albeit an affectionate one—of women; and an injury to one eye (which was subsequently removed) reinforced his solitary ways and wry, detached manner. He moved to New York in the mid-1920s where he began a persistent assault on that edifice of sophisticated humor, *The New Yorker* magazine. He placed some essays in 1927 and soon was working on the popular column, "The Talk of the Town." With office mate, humorist E.B. WHITE, he collaborated on his first successful book, *Is Sex Necessary?* (1929), providing also a number of highly idiosyncratic cartoons (described by White as depicting "the daily severity of life's mystery"). The Thurber world was full of implausible animals, affectionate dogs, harried husbands, ferocious wives and an almost surreal humor. For the rest of his life, Thurber would be identified with *The New Yorker* essays and drawings. Among

James Thurber, magazine humorist (left), receiving the Art Directors Club Medal from journalist Lowell Thomas (March 29, 1939).

his other works are two plays, *The Male Animal* (1940) and *A Thurber Carnival* (1960); and several collections of relatively serious fantasies like *Fables for Our Time* (1939). He began to lose the sight in his one remaining eye in 1940. "The imagination doesn't go blind," he wrote. "When I write now. . . I am not handicapped by vision." If he had a personal credo, it was best expressed in the foreword to his last book, *Lanterns and Lances* (1960): ". . . Let us not look back in anger, or forward in fear, but around in awareness."

For further reading:
Holmes, Charles, *The Clocks of Columbus.* New York: Atheneum, 1972.

Tiananmen Square Massacre. Violent military crackdown of June 3–4, 1989, on students and workers in the DEMOCRACY MOVEMENT that occurred in the huge Tiananmen Square, in the center of Beijing, People's Republic of CHINA. The violence came two weeks after the government declared martial law and warned the students to call off their protests. Tensions had been increasing for several days before the massacre. On June 1, Chinese authorities banned all press coverage, photographs and videotapes of any demonstrations in the city or of army troops enforcing martial law. The following day, June 2, the official Communist Party newspaper announced that army troops had taken up positions at "10 key points" in and around the capital. That evening, more than 100,000 people turned out for a rally in support of the students. Shortly after midnight on June 3, between 2,000 and 10,000 unarmed soldiers headed toward Tiananmen Square in an effort to remove the students; however, they were blocked by students and workers and retreated. On the afternoon of June 3, police and troops began to fire tear gas and beat protestors in various parts of the city. Around midnight, dozens of tanks and armored personnel carriers and armed soldiers launched a direct assault on the protesters. Accounts of the crackdown varied; Western observers estimated that as many as 5,000 civilians were killed and 10,000 injured; the Chinese government reported that very few had been killed or injured. After the massacre, troops cordoned off the square to prevent any further protests. During the following weeks, Chinese authorities arrested hundreds of pro-democracy activists in Beijing and throughout the nation. Communist PROPAGANDA portrayed the Tiananmen Square massacre as a heroic action by the army to save China from turmoil; pro-democracy activists and many foreign governments condemned the event as wanton slaughter. In 1991 the Chinese government reiterated that it had been justified in using force to restore order, and warned that it would do so again in similar circumstances.

Tibbett, Lawrence (Mervil) (1896–1960). American opera singer and actor who was one of the foremost stars of the Metropolitan Opera between 1925 and 1950. Tibbett was a leader in the movement to popularize opera in radio, movies and television. Born in Bakersfield, California, as "Tibbet" (he added the final "t" later), he first pursued an acting career with Tyrone Power Sr.'s Shakespearean company. After a stint in the Navy during World War I he began a singing career and, contrary to prevailing traditions in operatic singing, chose to study in New York rather than abroad. His sensational performance at the Met as a last-minute replacement in the role of "Ford" in Verdi's *Falstaff* in 1925 became the stuff of opera legend. It launched a busy career that embraced 52 roles and 644 performances until his retirement in 1950. Today, he is most remembered for his Verdi roles, like Amonasro in *Aida,* Iago in *Otello* and the title roles in *Rigoletto* and *Simon Boccanegra* (the latter generally considered his finest achievement). In modern opera he created the roles of Brutus Jones, in Louis Gruenberg's adaptation of Eugene O'NEILL's *The Emperor Jones* in 1933, and Eadgar in Deems Taylor's *The King's Henchman* in 1927.

His flamboyant style and charismatic personality was ideally suited to HOLLYWOOD, where he was the first major opera star to make feature-length TALKING PICTURES, most of them operetta-derived projects like *The Rogue Song* (1930) and *The New Moon* (1930). His best film, *Metropolitan* (1935), was a knowing wink at the pretensions and absurdities of grand opera. "Too much opera is still trying to make the people adapt themselves to it," he was fond of saying, "instead of adapting itself to them." In his efforts to take music to as many people as possible, he worked indefatigably in live radio and television. He fought tirelessly for the rights of performing artists, forming the American Guild of Musical Artists, Inc. (AGMA) in 1936 and serving as its president until 1953. He died from injuries sustained in an auto accident.

For further reading:
Farkas, Andrew, ed., *Lawrence Tibbett: Singing Actor.* Portland, Oregon: Amadeus Press, 1988.

Tibet [Xiang Autonomous Region]. Located in southwestern China, Tibet covers an area of 463,300 square miles. A distinct ethnic and linguistic group from the Chinese, the Tibetans have struggled for autonomy during the 20th century. Britain unsuccessfully attempted to exert influence in 1904, after Francis Younghusband led an expedition to the region. Tibet declared its independence in 1911, but Communist China reasserted Chinese suzerainty over Tibet in 1950, promising internal autonomy but actually threatening Tibetan culture when troops invaded and established a new government. An anti-Chinese revolt in 1959 led to the flight of the 14th Dalai Lama (the religious and political leader of Tibet) to India, and a period of violent repression followed. In 1965 China assimilated Tibet as an autonomous region. Further uprisings occurred in 1987, 1988 and 1989.

***Tiger* Talks.** A meeting, December 2–4, 1966, on the Royal Navy cruiser HMS *Tiger* off Gibraltar between British Prime Minister Harold WILSON and Rhodesian Prime Minister Ian SMITH to reach a settlement of RHODESIA's Unilateral Declaration of Independence (see also UDI). The talks failed as did further ones on HMS *Fearless* in October 1968 through Smith's refusal to accept unimpeded progress toward black majority rule.

Tikhomirov, N.I. (1860–1930). Russian rocket pioneer. As early as 1894, Tikhomirov had started experiments that would become the first practical research in Russian rocketry. By 1912 he had presented his plans for development of a liquid-propellant rocket to the minister of the Russian navy, and he continued to submit proposals over the coming years. The uneasy political climate following the RUSSIAN REVOLUTION left his work all but unnoticed, until finally, in 1919, he caught the attention of officials, having made a direct appeal to LENIN in May of that year. Two years later, the Revolutionary Military Council set up a research laboratory for the study of rocket propulsion. With his assistant, V.A. Artemiev, Tikhomirov's lab officially opened on March 1, 1921, in Moscow. The lab concentrated on solid-fuel propellants and performed tests between 1923 and 1925, moving to Leningrad in 1925. By 1928, Tikhomirov's laboratory had become the GDL (Gas Dynamics Laboratory), with an official affiliation with the Soviet Military Research Council. The work of the GDL that ensued became the foundation from which today's Russian rocketry was to develop.

Tikhomirov, Vasily (1876–1956). Dancing teacher. He was a pupil of Paul Gerdt and became a teacher at the BOLSHOI school of ballet in 1896. He taught many leading dancers and was considered one of the best teachers of his time.

Tikhonov, Nicholas Semyonovich (1896–1979). Russian poet. He was influenced at various stages in his career by Nicholas GUMILEV, Vladimir MAYAKOVSKY and Boris PASTERNAK. He became chairman of the Writers' Union in 1944, but he was removed by Andrei ZHDANOV in 1946 and replaced by Alexander FADEYEV. He received the Order of Lenin and the Stalin Prize for his work and in the 1950s was one of those who instigated a critical campaign against Pasternak. His first publications, two collections of poems, were *The Horde* (1922) and *Meade* (1923).

Tikhonravov, Mikhail K. (1900–1974). Russian rocket pioneer. Designer of the first hybrid, solid-liquid-propellant rocket, Tikhonravov saw his concept take off in a successful test, GIRD 09, on August 17, 1933. The rocket was built by a team that included Sergei KOROLEV, who was to become unquestionably the greatest figure in Soviet rocket design. During its test, GIRD 09 reached a height of 1,312 feet and the event was recorded with fervor: " . . . starting with this moment Soviet rockets must fly over the Union of Republics . . . rockets must conquer space!"

Tilden, Bill [William Tatem Tilden II] (1893–1953). American tennis player. During his career, Tilden dominated the game of tennis as no one had before. In

1920, he became the first American ever to win Britain's Wimbledon championship, a title he won three times. He won the American National Turf Court Championship seven times, and was ranked number one in the world from 1920 to 1929. He was a dramatic and flamboyant player, who abhorred the snobbery inherent in the game at the time, and helped broaden tennis's appeal beyond the country club set. He turned professional in 1931 and gave exhibition matches. Tilden was arrested for contributing to the delinquency of male minors twice before he died, impoverished, in 1953.

Tillich, Paul (1886–1965). German-born theologian and philosopher. Tillich was one of the leading theological figures of 20th-century EXISTENTIALISM. After ordination into the Evangelical Lutheran Church, he served as a chaplain for German forces during WORLD WAR I. During the Weimar Republic of the 1920s, he was active as a religious socialist. In 1933, Tillich fled the NAZI regime to come to the United States, where he taught at Harvard University and the University of Chicago, among other institutions, and was highly influential in shaping academic disciplines for the study of religion. His major works include the three-volume *Systematic Theology* (1951–1963) and *The Courage to Be* (1952).

Tillstrom, Burr (1917–1985). American puppeteer. Tillstrom created *Kukla, Fran and Ollie,* one of the most popular U.S. TV shows of the 1950s. The show, which featured a cast of puppets known as the Kuklapolitan Players, ran live for more than 10 years. It was hosted by singer-actress Fran ALLISON, who was the only human member of the cast. Tillstrom, who was never seen on the show, did all the puppets' voices. From 1971 to 1979 he, Allison and the puppets hosted the CBS Children's Film Festival.

***Time*.** American periodical. *Time,* a weekly news magazine, was founded in 1923 by Henry LUCE and his former college friend, Briton Hadden, who died in 1929. *Time,* which they had originally intended to call *Fact,* began by culling news from *The New York Times,* but became enormously successful and soon had news bureaus worldwide. It became known for its annual "Man of the Year" issue, and it also featured articles on the arts and society, many of which have evolved into separate publications such as *People* magazine. The magazine is the flagship of the huge Time-Life, Incorporated publishing empire.

Timoshenko, Semyon Konstantinovich (1895–1970). Marshal of the Soviet Union. Of Ukrainian origin, Timoshenko commanded a division in Semyon BUDENNY's first cavalry army during the RUSSIAN CIVIL WAR and commanded RED ARMY units during the 1939–40 war with Finland. In 1940 he was appointed commissar for defense and was responsible for the introduction of stricter army regulations. His work as commander on the Western Front following the German invasion of the Soviet Union was not particularly successful. He later commanded a number of military districts and retired in 1960.

Tinbergen, Nikolaas (1907–1988). British zoologist. After gaining a Ph.D. in zoology (1932) at Leiden University, Tinbergen taught there until 1949, becoming a professor of experimental biology. He then joined Oxford University, where he helped to originate the Animal Behaviour Research Group, within the department of zoology, becoming first reader (1962) and then professor of animal behavior (1966). Like Konrad Lorenz, Tinbergen exercised considerable influence in establishing the comparatively new science of ethology. His work (like Lorenz's) emphasizes the importance of field observations of animals under natural conditions, though amplified by laboratory experiment designed to trigger responses under controlled conditions. His studies embrace both vertebrate and invertebrate animals, from arctic foxes, seals, sticklebacks and sea birds to digger wasps, butterflies and snails—investigating such topics as animal camouflage and warning colors, and social, courtship and mating behavior. One of Tinbergen's most important theses is his belief that a study of aggression in animals could lead to a greater understanding of such behavior in man and perhaps provide some means of modifying it and its effects. His work in relating ethology to the human condition led to his being awarded, jointly with Lorenz and Karl von Frisch, the NOBEL PRIZE for physiology and medicine in 1973. His most influential publication, *The Study of Instinct* (1951), presents a summary of the work of ethologists in the first half of the 20th century.

Tiomkin, Dimitri (1899–1979). Russian-born composer of motion picture scores. Tiomkin studied composition at the St. Petersburg Conservatory of Music and later in Berlin, under Alexander GLAZUNOV and Ferrucio BUSONI; he performed in cinema theaters and music halls as a pop pianist and arranger. In 1928 he gave the European premiere of GERSHWIN's *Concerto in F* in Paris. After moving to HOLLYWOOD he composed his first original film score for *Resurrection* (1931). When an accident to his right hand cut short a concert career, he turned exclusively to film composing. His long association with director Frank CAPRA began in 1937 with *Lost Horizon* and subsequently included *Mr. Smith Goes to Washington* (1939), *Meet John Doe* (1941) and *It's a Wonderful Life* (1946). His ACADEMY-AWARD-winning scores for *The High and the Mighty* (1954), *The Old Man and the Sea* (1958) and *High Noon* (1951) only begin to suggest his amazing range. There was the simplicity of *High Noon*'s folksy ballad, "Do Not Forsake Me, Oh My Darling"; the inflated drive of his "big" scores for *Duel in the Sun* (1946) and *The Alamo* (1960); the weird, horrific effects of *The Thing* (1951); and several suspenseful scores for Alfred HITCHCOCK (including *Shadow of a Doubt,* 1943, and *Dial M for Murder,* 1954). His autobiography, *Please Don't Hate Me,* appeared in 1960. Although the quality of Tiomkin's scores varied from project to project, he remained faithful to the classical traditions in which he was trained. Accepting his Oscar in 1955 for *The High and the Mighty,* he said: "I would like to thank Beethoven, Brahms, Wagner, Strauss, Rimsky-Korsakov."

For further reading:

Thomas, Tony, *Music for the Movies.* Cranbury, New Jersey: A.S. Barnes, 1977.

Tippett, (Sir) Michael K(emp) (1905–). British composer and music critic. Tippett, one of the best known British composers of this century, was strongly influenced by the modernist composing techniques of Igor STRAVINSKY. Educated at the Royal College of Music in London, Tippett went on to compose popular works that included *Concerto for Double String Orchestra* (1939) and the antifascist oratorio *A Child for Our Time* (1943), which reflected Tippett's pacifist views as a conscientious objector during WORLD WAR II. Later works by Tippett include *The Midsummer Marriage* (1952) and *The Mask of Time* (1984). His musical writings include *Moving into Aquarius* (1959) and *Music of the Angels* (1980).

TIROS. Acronym for Television and Infrared Observation Satellite, the name given to each of ten weather satellites that were launched by NASA between April 1, 1960 and July 1, 1965. Using television cameras, sun-angle and horizon scanners, infra-red sensors, tape recorders and radios, they examined and recorded the earth's cloud cover, storms and other weather phenomena. Constructed of aluminum and stainless steel, the 270–lb. cylindrical satellites were 19" high and 42" in diameter and were powered by exterior solar cells and interior nickel-cadmium batteries.

Tirpitz, Alfred von (1849–1930). German admiral. Born in Kustrin, he joined the Prussian navy as a cadet in 1865. He soon became an expert in torpedoes and from 1871 on supervised the development of this newly invented weapon for the German navy. Appointed German naval minister in 1897, he began to build a major fleet of battleships, a program that was a source of constant antagonism to Great Britain. He was named grand admiral in 1911. At the outbreak of WORLD WAR I, Tirpitz encouraged the building of a German submarine fleet and supported unrestricted submarine warfare. Frustrated in his efforts to implement this submarine policy, he resigned in 1916. His wartime memoirs were published in 1919. Tirpitz later organized a right-wing nationalistic political party and was a deputy to the Reichstag from 1924 to 1928.

Tiso, Josef (1887–1947). Slovak political leader. Born near Bratislava, he was ordained a priest in 1910. A Slovak nationalist, Tiso was instrumental in building the Slovak People's Party, a separatist political group. He served as minister of health (1927–29) in the Czechoslovakian coalition government. Tiso succeeded to the leadership of the People's Party in 1938 and that year became premier of the

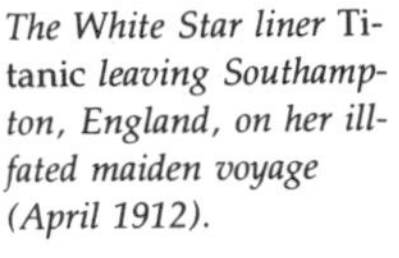

The White Star liner Titanic *leaving Southampton, England, on her ill-fated maiden voyage (April 1912).*

autonomous Slovak Republic created under the provisions of the MUNICH PACT. He proclaimed an independent republic of SLOVAKIA with himself as president in 1939, accepting the status of a German protectorate later that year and siding with the Axis powers during WORLD WAR II. After the war, he went into hiding in Austria, where he was arrested in 1945. Tried as a war criminal, he was found guilty, sentenced to death and hanged on April 18, 1947.

Titanic. British OCEAN LINER that, in one of the most famous disasters of the 20th century, struck an iceberg and sank on April 14–15, 1912. On its maiden voyage from Southampton to New York, the liner, which was the largest (900 feet long, 11 decks high) and most luxurious ship afloat and had been called unsinkable, collided with an iceberg in the North Atlantic. Of the over 2,200 aboard some 1,500 were killed. Contributing to the terrible loss of life was the fact that the lifeboats carried by the liner were insufficient to hold all those aboard and that a nearby ship, the *Californian,* did not respond to the *Titanic*'s SOS call. Later inquiries found that the ship had been traveling much too fast for the icy conditions, which were unusual that far south, and thus was unable to avoid the collision.

***Titanic,* discovery of the.** In September 1985 scientists from the Woods Hole Oceanographic Institute in Massachusetts located the wreckage of the legendary ocean liner TITANIC, which sank in 1912. The ship rested 12,500 feet beneath the surface of the Atlantic Ocean, about 500 miles south of Newfoundland. On July 13, 1986, these scientists, led by Robert D. Ballard, explored the *Titanic* from the *Atlantis II* research ship. Their three-man *Alvin* submarine allowed them to roam the liner and its surroundings for a total of 33 hours over 11 dives, ending July 24, 1986. Close viewing was made possible by the *Jason Jr.,* a robot camera that was able to enter the *Titanic* and explore below decks. The camera was tethered to the *Alvin* by a cable and operated from the submarine by remote control. The expedition took 57,000 photographs and 140 videotapes. The wreck of the *Titanic* was found to be broken into two sections and badly rusted. But many goods from the ship were still intact and were well preserved. No human remains were found. The most remarkable discovery was that, contrary to expectations, there was no long gash along the ship's side. Ballard said it seemed that the *Titanic* had not been torn open by the iceberg with which it collided, but instead had ground against it. The ship's steel plates had probably buckled, forcing their rivets to pop and opening seams that allowed the ship to flood.

Tito, Josip Broz (1892–1980). Yugoslav political leader, president of YUGOSLAVIA (1953–80). Born Josip Broz near the Croatia-Slovenia border, he served with the Austrian infantry in WORLD WAR I and was captured by the Russians in 1915. Escaping in 1917, he joined the BOLSHEVIK revolutionaries at Petrograd and subsequently fought with them during the RUSSIAN CIVIL WAR (1918–21). He returned to Croatia in 1920, becoming a metal worker in Zagreb and a prominent trade union leader. Broz joined the illegal Yugoslav Communist Party, adopting the code name "Tito." Captured by the police in 1928, he was jailed from 1929 to 1934. A member of the politburo from 1934, he was assigned the task of revivifying Yugoslavia's Communist Party. After GERMANY invaded Yugoslavia in 1941, Tito became a leader of the PARTISANS in their resistance to NAZI occupation. With the support of the Allies, who repudiated rival resistance leader Draza MIHAILOVIC, Tito was appointed the official head of a new Yugoslav federal government in 1945.

Virtual dictator of the nation, Tito was elected head of a communist-led National Liberation Front government later in 1945, and he quickly proclaimed Yugoslavia a republic and forced the abdication of King PETER II. An advocate of Yugoslav independence, Tito broke with the U.S.S.R. in 1948 and led his nation in a non-Soviet-bloc communist regime. Maintaining his status as a nonaligned country, he established friendly relations with Eastern European states and was usually on cordial terms with Western powers and other nonaligned countries as well. While he achieved a measure of reconciliation with the Soviets in 1955, he was by no means an apologist for all of their policies, and he condemned the armed Russian interventions in HUNGARY (1956) and CZECHOSLOVAKIA (1968). On the home front, he worked toward increased participation in government by the workers and greater economic decentralization. Elected president of Yugoslavia in 1953, he became president for life in 1974 and served in that office until his death in 1980.

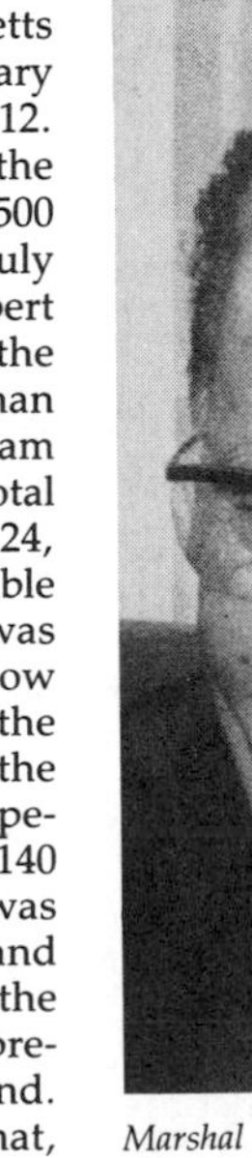

Marshal Josip Tito, Yugoslavian ruler (1968).

Titov, Gherman (1935–). Soviet cosmonaut. Titov's sole space flight aboard VOSTOK 2 (August 6, 1961) was the second orbital flight to be performed by a human. Titov spent 24 hours orbiting the Earth, a then record-breaking 17 times.

Titterton, Sir Ernest William (1916–1990). British nuclear scientist. Titterton helped build the country's first ATOMIC BOMB. After Britain began nuclear testing in AUSTRALIA in the early 1950s, he became an adviser to the Australian government. In the 1980s he was criticized for having concealed information from the Australian government in order to further Britain's interests.

Tjader, Cal (1925–1982). American JAZZ vibraphonist and percussionist. Tjader was known for his light touch and his original style of Latin-influenced music. He was a prolific performer. After starting his own sextet in the mid-1950s, he turned out albums at breakneck speed. He won a Grammy in 1981 for "La Onda Va Bien."

"Toast of the Town, The". American television's most famous variety show. Every Sunday night, from June 20, 1948, to June 6, 1971, "The Toast of The Town" (renamed "The Ed Sullivan Show" in 1955) brought to American homes the strangest mix of jugglers, rock stars, classical artists and theater and film luminaries this side of the June Taylor Dancers. SULLIVAN, a columnist for the New York *Daily News,* brought together a typically eclectic group of guests for the first program: the comedy team of Martin and Lewis, concert pianist Eugene LIST and theater showmen RODGERS and HAMMERSTEIN. No matter that critics complained of the weird blend of talent and Sullivan's awkward presence; or that nightclub comics wickedly lampooned his stiff, peculiar mannerisms and strangled voice—the show worked. And worked. And worked. It was even the affectionate butt of the 1960 Broadway musical, *Bye Bye Birdie,* which contained a hushed and reverential choral number—"Ed Sullivan." To play Sullivan was to make headlines; and many luminaries made their television debuts here—Charles LAUGHTON, Bob HOPE, the BEATLES and Walt DISNEY. In a peculiar quirk of fate a full-hour edition was devoted to Disney on February 8, 1953. A year later Disney began his own television hour on ABC in competition with Sullivan. Eventually Disney surpassed his rival as the longest-running prime-time network show in history. That's show business.

For further reading:

The Complete Directory to Prime Time Network TV Shows. New York: Ballantine Books, 1988.

Tobruk. A port on the Mediterranean Sea in northeastern Libya, about 50 miles from the Egyptian border; during WORLD WAR II, Tobruk was the object of fierce fighting between German and British forces. A valuable supply base, Tobruk was captured from its Italian garrison by British forces on January 22, 1941. In late March of that year, ROMMEL pushed the British forces back to the Egyptian border, but he failed to retake Tobruk; under siege from April 10, the city finally fell to the Germans on November 28, 1941. Rommel withdrew in December, then advanced once more in January 1942 but was repulsed at Gazala. He attacked again on May 28, and finally succeeded in retaking Tobruk on June 21. The port remained in German hands until after the battle of EL ALAMEIN, in October and November of 1942.

Toftoy, Holger N. (1902–1967). U.S. military officer. As chief of technical intelligence for Army ordnance in Europe, Toftoy was responsible for OPERATION PAPERCLIP, which brought Wernher von BRAUN and approximately 129 German scientists and engineers to the United States after WORLD WAR II. Known as "Mr. Missile," Toftoy was continuously on the scene in the early development of guided missiles, including the Redstone missile, which was one of the pioneering rockets used in the U.S. space program. He served for four years as commanding general of Redstone Arsenal in Huntsville, Alabama (1954–58), prior to his retirement in 1960.

Togo. Togo, wedged between Ghana and Dahomey, covers an area of 21,921 square miles on the Gulf of Guinea in western Africa. Part of the German colony of Togoland from 1894 to 1914, the country became a LEAGUE OF NATIONS Mandate known as French Togoland in 1922, then a UNITED NATIONS Trust Territory in 1946. In 1956 French Togoland became an autonomous republic within the FRENCH COMMUNITY; in 1960 it became completely independent. The assassination of the first president, Sylvanus Olympio, during a coup in 1963 led to another coup, which brought current president General Etienne Eyadema to power in 1967. Terrorist attacks in 1985–86, which implicated the involvement of neighboring countries, brought French and Zairean troops to the aid of Togo. International allegations of mistreatment of political prisoners, coupled with internal discontent, pressured Eyadema to initiate some reforms.

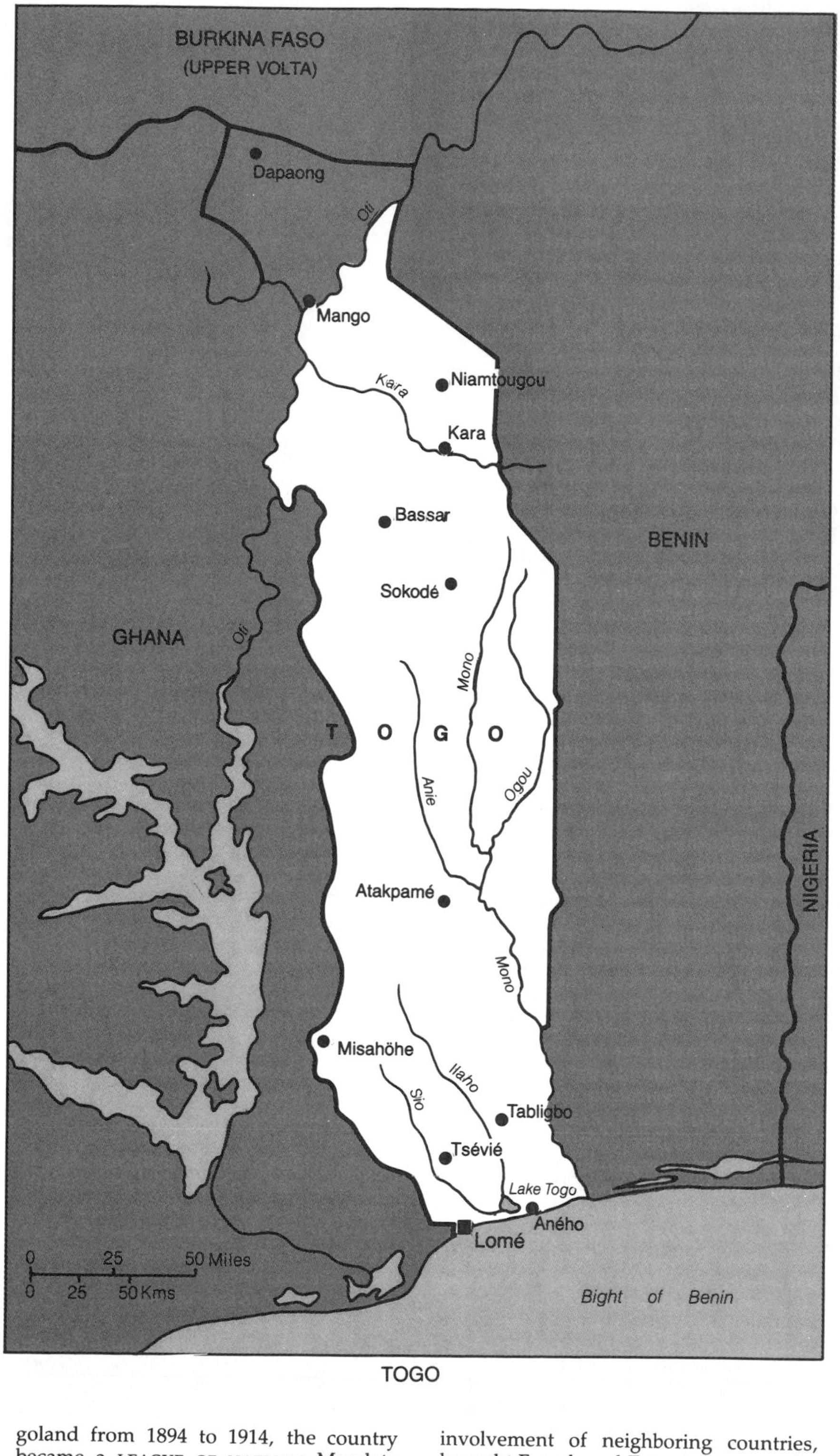

TOGO

Tojo, Hideki (1884–1948). Japanese general, political leader and prime minister of wartime JAPAN (1941–44). Born in Tokyo, Tojo attended Japan's military college and was military attache to GERMANY after WORLD WAR I. The leader of Japan's militarist party from 1931 and a leading

Hideki Tojo, Japanese general and prime minister during World War II.

advocate of armed Japanese expansionism, he became war minister in 1940 and was instrumental in forging his nation's alliances with Germany and ITALY. Becoming prime minister in 1941, Tojo authorized the attack on the U.S. fleet at PEARL HARBOR and urged his country's offensive thrusts throughout Asia. He remained Japan's wartime leader until repeated defeats forced him to resign in 1944. After the war, Tojo was arrested (1945) as a war criminal, tried before a military tribunal, found guilty and hanged.

Tokyo Rose (1916–). Japanese-American propaganda broadcaster. Iva Ikuko Toguri d'Aquino was born in Los Angeles to Japanese parents. Visiting Japan when WORLD WAR II broke out, she was stranded in Tokyo. In 1942 she began work at the Domei news agency, soon moving to Radio Tokyo. There she became one of 13 women announcers whose task it was to try to demoralize American troops stationed in the Pacific. Broadcasting music and chat that urged the men to surrender or return home, the seductive-voiced announcer was nicknamed "Tokyo Rose" by her GI listeners. Returning to the U.S. in 1948, she was convicted of treason the following year, but claimed she had been forced to make the broadcasts. Released from prison in 1956, she was formally pardoned by President Gerald FORD in 1977 and her U.S. citizenship was restored.

Tolkien, John R(onald) R(euel) (1892–1973). English fantasy novelist and literary scholar. Tolkien is ranked by many critics and readers as the greatest fantasy writer of the 20th century. His most famous work is THE LORD OF THE RINGS trilogy, comprised of the three novels *The Fellowship of the Ring* (1954), *The Two Towers* (1954) and *The Return of the King* (1955). Tolkien, who was educated at Oxford University, also taught at that university for many years and wrote noteworthy scholarly studies of medieval English literature, such as *A Middle English Vocabulary* (1922). He was also good friends with fellow scholars and writers C.S. LEWIS and Charles Williams, both of whom also wrote in the fantasy vein. Tolkien described his *The Silmarillion* (1977) as an attempt to create a mythology for his native England.

Toller, Ernst (1893–1939). German playwright and poet. Toller was a leading figure in the expressionist school of German drama, as well as a vivid and fiercely political poet. He is best remembered for his plays, which combined intense emotionality with leftist political didacticism. Two of his early plays, *The Inner Change* (1919) and *Masses and Man* (1920), led to Toller being imprisoned as a communist. Subsequent plays by Toller focused on the themes of working class revolt and individual struggle and martyrdom. These include *The Machine Wreckers* (1922), *Hoppla!* (1927), *Draw the Fires!* (1930) and *The Blind Goddess* (1932).

Tolstoy, Count Aleksey Nikolayevich (1883–1945). Russian novelist, playwright and NATIONAL BOLSHEVIK. He rose to fame as a NEOREALIST before the 1917 Revolution, and supported the WHITES during the CIVIL WAR. He emigrated, but as a member of the Change of Landmarks organization, Tolstoy returned to Russia. At first, as a FELLOW TRAVELER, he was regarded with suspicion, but by the mid-1930s, he was regarded as a loyal Stalinist and did much to create the STALIN cult. He is also remembered for his trilogy on the intelligentsia between 1914 and 1921, *The Road to Calvary* (1920–41).

Tombaugh, Clyde William (1906–). American astronomer who discovered the planet Pluto. Raised on a Kansas farm, Tombaugh developed an early interest in astronomy. As a teenager, he studied Mars and Jupiter through homemade telescopes and sent drawings of his observations to the Lowell Observatory in Arizona. The observatory hired him to photograph the then-unknown planet that

Aleksey Tolstoy, Russian author and playwright (1945).

lay beyond Neptune. On Feb. 18, 1930, at age 24, Tombaugh discovered the planet, Pluto—the first planetary discovery since 1846. Tombaugh received the Jackson-Gwilt Medal and Gift of the Royal Astronomical Society of Great Britain in 1931. During his long career he constructed 10 reflecting telescopes and made several thousand visual and photographic observations through the large Lowell telescope. He was also a professor at New Mexico State University, where he taught astronomy, geology and meteorology. He continued to lecture into his 80s.

Tonga. The Kingdom of Tonga consists of an archipelago of some 172 islands (36 permanently inhabited) in the southwest Pacific, 404 miles east of FIJI and 1,863 miles northeast of Sydney, Australia; total area is 289 square miles. In 1900 Tonga signed a Treaty of Friendship and Protection with Britain in order to ward off German advances; under the treaty, Tongan foreign policy was conducted through a British consul. King George Tupou II died in 1918 and was succeeded by his daughter, Queen Salote Tupou III. During WORLD WAR II she placed Tonga's resources at the disposal of the Allies. On the queen's death in 1965 her son, Prince Tungi, became King Taufa'ahau Tupou IV. Tonga and Britain signed a new Treaty of Friendship in 1958; complete independence from Britain came in 1970, when Tonga also joined the COMMONWEALTH. Although the 1987 general election indicated areas of discontent, overall political power has remained with the king's appointees and the nobility, who together constitute a permanent majority within the legislature. The king's 70th birthday in July 1988 was marked by official celebrations. Elections in February 1990 resulted in several prominent pro-democracy commoners entering the legislature.

"Tonight Show, The". Popular American late-night television talk/variety show, which since 1954 has shaped the nighttime viewing habits of several generations of viewers. The prototype was the short-lived "Broadway Open House," which appeared at 11:00 P.M. on weeknights from 1950 to 1951 on the NBC network. Sylvester "Pat" Weaver, NBC programming chief, brought in newcomer Steve ALLEN and the show, retitled the "Tonight" show premiered on September 27, 1954. Allen's relaxed manner, talent for ad-libbing and sketch comedy and quick eye for young talent—which would include bandleader Skitch Henderson and singers Steve Lawrence, Eydie Gorme and Andy Williams—immediately established the format that would survive generally unchanged to this day. After Allen left to do his own show in 1956 successors included Jack Lescoulie ("America after Dark," 1957) and Jack Paar ("The Jack Paar Show," 1957–62). Then on October 2, 1962, the calm and unflappable Johnny CARSON took over and the show was renamed, "The Tonight Show Starring Johnny Carson." Characters and sketches like "Carnack the Magnificent" (who first appeared in 1964) and "The Mighty Carson Art Players" (which first appeared in 1966) quickly became a part of the national vernacular. In May 1972 the show moved permanently from New York City to Burbank, California. The early episodes of the original "Tonight" show have been lost. A man in charge of the NBC storage facility emptied out all the kinescopes of the shows and burned them in the late 1950s.

For further reading:

The Tonight Show—The Complete Directory to Prime Time Network TV Shows. New York: Ballantine Books, 1988.

Tonkin Gulf Resolution. On August 2, 1964 the U.S. destroyer *Maddox*—on patrol in international waters in the Gulf of Tonkin off the coast of North VIETNAM—was attacked by North Vietnamese torpedo boats. The attack was repulsed. On August 4 the *Maddox,* joined by the destroyer *Turner Joy,* again reported an attack by North Vietnamese torpedo boats. Using these incidents as a *casus bellum,* President JOHNSON asked Congress for a resolution empowering him to "take all necessary measures to repel an armed attack against the forces of the U.S. and to prevent further aggression." On Aug. 7 the so-called Gulf of Tonkin Resolution (officially the Southeast Asia Resolution) passed the Senate by a vote of 88 to 2 and the House by a unanimous voice vote of 416 to 0. Some have claimed that the Congress was misled by the Gulf of Tonkin Resolution and did not intend to grant the President a *de facto* declaration of war. On March 1, 1966, long after the bombing of North Vietnam had begun and American ground combat forces had been committed to battle, Senator Wayne Morse introduced an amendment to repeal this resolution. This amendment was defeated in the Senate by a vote of 92 to 5. On August 18, 1967, President Johnson repudiated the Gulf of Tonkin Resolution as the legal basis for the war in VIETNAM and fell back on his authority granted by Article II of the Constitution as Commander-in-Chief of the Armed Forces. The Gulf of Tonkin Resolution was terminated by Congress in May 1960, but U.S. combat involvement in Vietnam continued until the PARIS PEACE ACCORDS (January 1973). (See also VIETNAM WAR.)

Tooker, George (1920–). American painter. Born in Brooklyn, New York, Tooker studied at Harvard and the Art Students League. An American SURREALIST, the artist takes for his subject the anonymity and unease of contemporary urban life. Immaculately realistic and preternaturally still, often painted in egg tempera, his works portray round-headed, flat-faced, almond-eyed figures in enigmatic and vaguely threatening situations. Among his characteristic paintings are *The Table, The Subway* (Whitney Museum, New York City) and *Mirror II* (Addison Gallery, Andover, Massachusetts).

Torrijos, Omar (Herrera) (1929–1981). Panamanian military and political leader. A career officer, Torrijos had attained the rank of lieutenant colonel by 1968, when he and Colonel Boris Martinez led the coup that toppled PANAMA's President Arnulfo ARIAS MADRID. The following year Torrijos was responsible for sending Martinez into exile; he took control of Panama, at the same time elevating himself to brigadier general. Panama's de facto leader from 1969, he was officially named chief of state in 1972. Torrijos became a strong and often repressive leader. He instituted a number of reforms in his country's economy, taking land from Panama's powerful oligarchy and distributing it to the hitherto landless, and in its social practices, by such innovations as birth control education. An advocate of Panama's right to the PANAMA CANAL, he negotiated with U.S. President Jimmy CARTER and was responsible for the 1978 canal treaties. In 1978 he resigned as president, but retained control over the country as head of the National Guard until his death in a plane crash on July 31, 1981.

Torvill and Dean. British ice dancers. **Jayne Torvill** (1957–), a former insurance clerk, and **Christopher Dean** (1958–), a former policeman, were granted £14,000 by the Nottingham City Council to help with their training. They repaid that loan by going on to become the greatest ice dancing team in the history of the sport. At the Helsinki World Championships in 1983 they posted their first unbroken string of 6.0s for artistic impression, scoring 5.9s for technical merit. In 1984 at the Sarajevo Winter OLYMPICS, their stunning interpretation of RAVEL's *Bolero* pushed the limits of the sport, for which they received 12 6.0s of a possible 18. The team went on to their fourth world championship, followed by a career as professional skaters.

Toscanini, Arturo (1867–1957). Italian-born opera and symphonic conductor. During his 68–year career, Toscanini was the most famous conductor in the world. Born in Parma, Italy, he graduated from the Parma Conservatory in 1885 as a cellist. His conducting career began during a South American tour with an orchestra; as a last-minute replacement, he conducted *Aida* from memory. Many appointments followed: principal conductor at La Scala, Milan, for 16 years; conductor of the New York Philharmonic-Symphony Orchestra for seven years; and leader of the NBC Symphony for 17 seasons. He conducted at many world premieres, including PUCCINI's *La Boheme* (1896), *La Fanciulla del West* (*The Girl of the Golden West*) (1910), *Turandot* (1926) and Pietro Mascagni's *Pagliacci* (1892). With the NBC Symphony, formed in 1937 by David SARNOFF, president of the Radio Corporation of America (RCA), he reached millions of people by radio and through numerous studio recordings. No greater testament to his abilities as an opera conductor can be found than the fact that he was the preeminent Verdi conductor in Italy and the preeminent WAGNER conductor in Germany. However, his fierce opposition to FASCISM and NAZISM led him to refuse to appear in both countries during WORLD WAR II. Although small in stature, his intense eyes, expressive hands and phenomenal musical memory placed him in absolute control of any orchestra. He was the embodiment (and the subsequent public image) of the "superstar" musician, although he said he rejected personal interpretations in favor of absolute fidelity to the score.

Italian conductor Arturo Toscanini, a relentless musical perfectionist.

For further reading:

Horowitz, Joseph, *Understanding Toscanini: How He Became an American Culture-God and Helped Create a New Audience for Old Music.* New York: Knopf, 1987.

Sachs, Harvey, *Toscanini.* New York: Harper & Row, 1978.

Schonberg, Harold C., *The Great Conductors.* New York: Simon and Schuster, 1967.

totalitarianism. Type of government in which the state controls all aspects of its citizen's lives. Totalitarianism is not an ideology, but rather a means for assuring that an ideology, such as COMMUNISM, can achieve its ends without opposition. A peculiarly 20th-century development, it allows no scope for private life; the individual exists only to serve the state. Totalitarian governments attempt to control all forms of thought through relentless PROPAGANDA. Even the discoveries and conclusions of science will appear to underwrite the ideology of the party or state. The U.S.S.R. under STALIN, Cambodia under POL POT and the KHMER ROUGE, and Nazi Germany are prime examples of totalitarian regimes. George ORWELL's novel 1984 paints a chilling portrait of a totalitarian society, while *The Origins of Totalitarianism* by German philosopher Hannah ARENDT provides a perceptive analysis of totalitarianism. Despite the crushing power of totalitarian regimes, with their omnipresent secret police, and the immense human suffering that they have caused, 20th-century history suggests that such systems collapse through their own internal weaknesses.

Tourette, La. Convent (monastery) at Eveux near Lyons in France designed (1957–60) by LE CORBUSIER, one of his most distinguished works in the post-World War II style often called New BRUTALISM. Forming a hollow square, the building is made up of a church on one side and a U-shaped group of monastic buildings around a central courtyard. Le Corbusier is said to have studied the medieval Cistercian monastery of Le Thoronet, making it a basis for the utter simplicity and austerity of his design, which relies entirely on the geometry of its proportions (based on Le Corbusier's modular system) to achieve a sense of extraordinary beauty and serenity in a structure of rough concrete (*"beton brut"*). The monks of the monastery have now relocated in accord with changing ideas of their religious duties, and the building has become a study and research center.

Towle, Katherine A. (1898–1986). American college dean from 1948 to 1953, Towle served as the first director of the women's marines as part of the regular U.S. Marine Corps. She was the first woman dean of students at the University of California, BERKELEY, a post she held from 1961 to 1965. In 1964 she signed an order limiting political activity at the Berkeley campus that touched off the tumultuous FREE SPEECH MOVEMENT.

Townes, Charles Hard (1915–). American physicist. A graduate of Furman University (1935) and California Institute of Technology (1939), he worked during WORLD WAR II with RADAR and microwave spectroscopy. He taught physics at Columbia University (1948–59), where he wrote a paper on maser and laser power in 1958. He was vice president and director of research of the Institute of Defense Analysis (1959) and joined the University of California staff in 1967. He shared the NOBEL PRIZE for physics (1964) with Russians Nikolai Busov and Alexander Prochorov for work in quantum electronics and oscillators and amplifiers, leading to maser and LASER technology.

Townsend, Francis Everett (1867–1960). American physician. While practicing medicine in southern California during the Depression, Townsend formulated a scheme for a national retirement pension. Called the "Townsend Plan," it would have provided $200 per month to retirees over the age of 60 who would agree to spend the money the month it was received; the funds were to be raised by a 2% sales tax on business transactions. The Townsend Plan gained millions of advocates, but it was obviated by the SOCIAL SECURITY ACT OF 1935.

Toynbee, Arnold J(oseph) (1889–1975). British historian. Toynbee was one of the most influential historians of this century. His magnum opus was the 12–volume *A Study of History* (1934–1961), in which Toynbee examined the entire course of recorded world history and concluded that each and every dominant civilization was subject to an all but inevitable cycle of triumphant early struggle, vigorous growth and stagnant decline. Educated at Oxford University, Toynbee was a member of British Intelligence during WORLD WAR I and attended the postwar Paris peace conference. He taught for many years at the University of London. *Experiences* (1969) is his autobiography.

Toyota. JAPAN's largest AUTOMOBILE manufacturer, and the third largest in the world. Founded in 1933, in the mid-1950s it revolutionized manufacturing with the **just-in-time** system. Toyota sales were mainly domestic until the early 1970s, when the Arab OIL EMBARGO and the soaring cost of gasoline caused many Americans to turn to smaller, more fuel-efficient cars. Toyota now exports more than half the cars it makes in Japan and also operates assembly plants in several foreign countries, including the U.S.

Tracy, Spencer (1900–1967). American film and theater actor. Tracy is one of the legendary figures of American film, a craggy leading man who won over audiences and critics by virtue of his remarkable acting ability. Tracy began his acting career on the stage in the 1920s, scoring a Broadway hit as a prisoner on death row in *The Last Mile* (1929). He moved on to HOLLYWOOD where he continued to be typecast as a gangster until his dramatic breakthrough in the film *The Power and the Glory* (1933). Tracy won his first best actor ACADEMY AWARD for his role in *Captains Courageous* (1937) and his second for his portrayal of Father Flanagan in *Boys Town* (1938). In the 1940s and 1950s he was teamed with Katharine HEPBURN (with whom he carried on an enduring off-screen romance) in a number of films, including *Woman of the Year* (1942), *State of the Union* (1948), *Adam's Rib* (1949) and *Pat and Mike* (1952). He also gave notable performances in *The Old Man and the Sea* (1958), *Inherit the Wind* (1960) and *Judgment at Nuremberg* (1961). Tracy was reunited with Hepburn in his last film, *Guess Who's Coming to Dinner* (1967).

Trades Union Congress [TUC]. Federation of about 160 British trade unions, founded in 1968. The TUC's basic function is to coordinate union action by annual conferences of union representatives where matters of common concern are discussed. As an umbrella organization, the TUC is somewhat analogous to the AFL-CIO in the U.S.

Trakl, Georg (1887–1914). Austrian poet. Trakl is one of the most intense and visionary poets of the 20th century. While most of his verse was published only posthumously, Trakl was recognized in his own lifetime by luminaries such as the philosopher Ludwig WITTGENSTEIN, who gave the poet a substantial sum of money to support his writing. Wittgenstein observed that Trakl's poems possessed "the tone of a man of real genius." Born in Salzburg, Trakl trained as a chemist but soon turned to poetry as his true vocation. During his short tragic lifetime, he abused drugs and alcohol and suffered from incestuous longings for his sister. Drafted by the Austrian army at the start of WORLD WAR I, he committed suicide in a military hospital in Cracow, Poland. Trakl's poems have been frequently translated into English. *Selected Poems* (1968), edited by the British poet Christopher Middleton, contains a good bilingual sampling of Trakl's verse.

Spencer Tracy in the title role of the film adaptation of Ernest Hemingway's The Old Man and the Sea *(1958).*

transistor. Miniature device that permits a very small signal (in the form of electrical current) in one circuit to control a relatively large current in another circuit. Invented in 1947 by John BARDEEN, Walter H. BRATTAIN and William SHOCKLEY at Bell Laboratories in New Jersey, the transistor revolutionized the electronics industry. Further research and work on transistors and transistor theory led to astonishing breakthroughs in the field of superconductivity. Technological advances have made it possible to install millions of transistors on a single **silicon chip** (also known as a microchip). The transistor has had an immense effect on everyday life. It replaced bulky vacuum tubes and made possible the development of a myriad of products taken for granted in the late 20th century, ranging from the transistor radio to the home computer. The cheap cost of the transistor has also made these products available to a mass market of consumers. Communications satellites, modern telephone equipment, videocassette cameras and recorders—all would be impossible without the transistor.

Trans-Jordan. See JORDAN.

Trans-Siberian Railway. Railway, running from Chelyabinsk in the Urals to Vladivostok on the Pacific, constructed between 1891 and 1915. It is 4,388 miles long and is the world's longest railway. Its construction greatly aided Russian colonization of SIBERIA and the Far East.

Traubel, Helen (1903–1972). American opera singer. One of the great Wagnerian sopranos of her time, Traubel made her concert debut in 1924 with the St. Louis Symphony. In 1937 she sang the only female role in the world premiere of Walter Damrosch's opera *The Man Without a Country.* She made her debut as a member of the New York Metropolitan Opera as Sieglinde in *Die Walkure* in 1939. During her 14 years with the Met, Traubel's most famous roles were Isolde in *Tristan und Isolde* and Brunnhilde in *Die Walkure.* From 1953 she gave concerts, appeared in nightclubs and on television, and in two films, and also authored a mystery set at the Met.

Traven, B. [pen name of Ret Marut, Otto Feige or Traven Torsvan?]. B. Traven is one of the most mysterious figures in 20th-century literature; his exact identity and place and date of birth are still subject to much doubt. Some investigators believe that B. Traven was the pen name of Otto Feige, a German who traveled widely and worked variously as a manual laborer, an actor and as the editor of an anarchist journal. He was also rumored to be the illegitimate son of Kaiser Wilhelm I. Traven's widow announced in 1990 that he had been Ret Marut, a left-wing revolutionary in Germany during WORLD WAR I; he may have been born in Chicago. Sometime between 1914 and 1924 Traven arrived in Mexico, where he lived for the bulk of his remaining years. His novels and stories were written in German and first published in Germany in the 1920s. They have since been translated into more than 30 languages and sold more than 25 million copies, and are now required reading in Mexican schools. Traven wrote about serious issues of social justice, cruelty and greed while employing a taut, suspenseful style. His most notable books include *The Death Ship* (1926), *The Treasure of the Sierra Madre* (1927, made into a classic film by director John HUSTON in 1948), *Stories By The Man Nobody Knows* (1961) and *The Night Visitor* (1966).

For further reading:

Guthke, Karl S., *Traven: Biography of an Enigma*. Chicago: Chicago Review Press, 1991.

Traynor, Harold Joseph "Pie" (1899–1972). American baseball player. Considered one of the finest third-basemen in the game, Traynor played for 17 years with the Pittsburgh Pirates (1920–37). He was also team manager (1934–39) and for several years a player-manager. He compiled a lifetime batting average of .320. He was elected to the Baseball Hall of Fame in 1987.

Treblinka. Nazi CONCENTRATION CAMP. In June 1941, Hitler proposed the FINAL SOLUTION in his attempt to destroy people he considered "non-aryan." In June 1942 Treblinka was established in central Poland as an extermination/death camp. Many of its victims were JEWS from the Warsaw ghetto. At its peak as many as 25,000 were killed daily—over 870,000 in all. One survivor later testified, "Treblinka has no beginning and no end, whoever was in Treblinka will never get out of it."

Trend, Lord (Burke St. John) (1914–1987). British civil servant. Trend was secretary of the cabinet (1963–1973) during the governments of British Prime Ministers Harold MACMILLAN and Harold WILSON. After a fifty-year career in civil service, he was made a life peer upon his retirement in 1974. In 1974–75 he undertook an Inquiry to determine whether or not Sir Roger Hollis, former director general of MI5, the counterintelligence unit of the British intelligence service, was a Soviet spy.

Trepov, General Dmitry Fedorovich (1855–1906). Russian military official. From 1896 to 1905 Trepov was the much disliked chief of police in Moscow, and from 1905 he served as governor-general of St. Petersburg. He was the instigator of the pogroms carried out by the BLACK HUNDRED antirevolutionary group, and in 1905, he was made commandant of the Winter Palace.

Trepper, Leopold (1904–1982). Polish-born anti-fascist. As leader of the so-called "Red Orchestra" network in NAZI Europe, Trepper was one of the most successful spymasters of WORLD WAR II. The network was largely responsible for supplying intelligence that helped the Soviets defeat Hitler's forces at STALINGRAD (1942–43). Later arrested by the GESTAPO, Trepper escaped and became active in the RESISTANCE. However, on his return to the U.S.S.R. in 1945 he was arrested by the Soviets on charges of having collaborated with the Germans—a common fate for many Russians and Poles in similar circumstances. Repatriated to Poland under house arrest after STALIN's death in 1955, he was allowed to emigrate to Israel in 1973 after a worldwide campaign for his release.

Tretyakov, Sergei Mikhailovich (1892–1939). Soviet author and journalist. Tretyakov's poetry includes the collection *Iron Pause* (1919), but it was as a playwright that he achieved fame. His grotesque anticolonial *Road China* (1926) was widely successful. He proclaimed the death of fiction and a new empirical writing that would be the true expression of Marxist-Leninist materialism, and suggested the creation of literary workshops. He was arrested and executed during the Purges as an alleged Chinese spy.

Trevelyan, George M(acauley) (1876–1962). English historian. Trevelyan was one of the most widely read and influential English historians of his generation. His approach was marked by a deeply humanistic belief in political and societal progress. Educated at Harrow and at Trinity College, Cambridge, Trevelyan served as Regius Professor of Modern History at Cambridge (1927–1940) and as Master of Trinity College (1940–51). While Trevelyan wrote numerous volumes on English history from the Elizabethan period to the modern era, he remains best known for his three volume *History of England* (1926).

Trevelyan, John (1904–1986). British film censor. As secretary of the British Board of Film Censors from 1958 to 1971, Trevelyan became as well-known a figure in Britain as any non-acting member of the film industry. Though opposed to censorship in principle, he argued that safeguards for children were needed by society.

Trevino, Lee Buck (1939–). U.S. golfer. Although his personality sometimes overshadowed his achievements, the charismatic Trevino was one of the leading golfers of the 1970s. He won two U.S. Opens, the second in a memorable 1971 playoff with Jack NICKLAUS, two PGA championships and two British Opens. He represented the United States on six Ryder Cup teams and five World Cup teams. After 27 tour victories, he went on to combine play on the Senior Tour with a career as a broadcaster.

Trevor, William [William Trevor Cox] (1928–). Anglo-Irish novelist and short story writer. Trevor is notable for his poignant, closely drawn fiction that focuses on Ireland. His first, *A Standard of Behavior* (1958) was well received, but he achieved greater recognition with *The Old Boys* (1964), which he would later adapt into a play. While his work is often sad, Trevor is able to infuse it with an ironic wit. For example, one of his finest novels, *Mrs. Eckdorf at O'Neill's Hotel* (1973), borrows from the absurd vision of Flann O'BRIEN and the realism and sympathy of James JOYCE. His many short story collections include *The Day We Got Drunk on Cake, and Other Stories* (1967), *Angels at the Ritz and Other Stories* (1975) and *Family Sins and Other Stories* (1990). Other novels are *Other People's Worlds* (1980) and *The Silence in the Garden* (1988). Trevor has also written plays and adapted his fiction for British television.

For further reading:

Schirmer, Gregory A., *William Trevor: A Study of His Fiction*. London: Routledge, 1990.

Trevor-Roper, Hugh (Redwald) [Baron Dacre of Glanton] (1914–). British historian. Trevor-Roper attended Oxford, where he was Regius professor of modern history from 1957 to 1980. Also involved in contemporary affairs, he was director of the *Times* newspapers from 1974. He was created a baron in 1979. Trevor-Roper is a prolific writer with enormous range. His books include *Archbishop Laud* (1940), *The Last Days of Hitler* (1947), *The Gentry, 1540–1640* (1953), *The Rise of Christian Europe* (1966), *Renaissance Essays* (1985) and *Catholics, Anglicans and Puritans* (1987).

Trial, The. Classic novel (1937) by Czechoslovakian author Franz KAFKA. *The Trial* stands as one of the paradigmatic novels of the 20th century. Its basic plot concerns the travails and anguish of one Joseph K., who is summoned to appear before a tribunal at a vague future date for an unspecified offense. While Joseph K. regards himself, at first, as innocent, his own underlying sense of guilt and of spiritual confusion lead him, in essence, to inwardly try the merits of his own soul while continuing to yearn for outward official absolution. Numerous critics have interpreted *The Trial* as a masterful parable on the absurdly tangled relationship between government bureaucracy and individual citizens, as well as a commentary on the absence of a clearly revealed moral or spiritual law for humankind. A film version of the novel was directed by Orson WELLES in 1962. (See also THE CASTLE.)

Triangle Shirtwaist fire. Deadly fire that occurred in a women's clothing workshop in a loft building in New York City on March 25, 1911. Blocked exits and inadequate fire escapes caused many to be trapped inside the burning building and resulted in the death of 146 workers, mainly young Jewish and Italian women, many of them poor immigrants. The fire drew the public's attention to the terrible conditions in America's urban sweatshops. This aroused consciousness ultimately resulted in legislation that improved fire, health and sanitary regulations and upgraded factory working conditions.

"trickle-down" theory. See SUPPLY-SIDE ECONOMICS.

Triennale. Design exhibition held every three years at Milan, Italy. The first Milan Triennale was held in 1933, showing the work of many of Europe's pioneer modern designers, including Walter GROPIUS, LE CORBUSIER, Adolf LOOS and Ludwig MIES VAN DER ROHE. The sequence of exhibitions was interrupted during World War II, but resumed in 1947 and continues as a showcase of modern, mostly Italian, design achievements.

Trifonov, Yuri Valentinovich (1925–1981). Soviet novelist. Trifonov was best known for works that explored the Stalinist era and the moral conflicts of Moscow intellectuals (see also STALIN, STALINISM). His first novel, *Students* (1950), won a Stalin Prize, but his later books were more original. Although he was not among the more outspoken dissident writers, he wrote with great allusive artistry that tested the limits of Soviet censorship. Among his major literary works were *The Old Man* (1984), *The Exchange* (1978), *Taking Stock* (1978), and *The Long Goodbye* (1978).

Trilling, Lionel (1905–1975). American literary critic, novelist, and educator. Trilling was one of the most influential literary critics of his generation. Educated at Columbia University, he taught at that institution for over four decades. His first book, *Matthew Arnold* (1939), was an intensive study of the 19th century English critic who strongly influenced Trilling as to the importance of culture as a formative aspect of personality. *The Middle of the Journey* (1947), Trilling's only novel, concerns a one-time political liberal who finds that all political ideologies have begun to fail him. *The Opposing Self* (1955) is a collection of essays on the importance of an ongoing struggle between self and society. Trilling's later works include *Sincerity and Authenticity* (1972) and *Mind in the Modern World* (1973).

Trinidad and Tobago. Southernmost of the Caribbean islands, Trinidad is seven miles north of Venezuela and covers an area of 1,863 square miles; Tobago (116 sq. mi.) is 20 miles northeast of Trinidad. British possessions since 1787 and 1814, respectively, Trinidad and Tobago were linked together in 1888. They became part of the Federation of the West Indies in 1958 and achieved full independence in 1962. In 1976 the Republic of Trinidad and Tobago was formed and joined the COMMONWEALTH OF NATIONS. Since the 1980s various opposition political groups have jockeyed for power.

Triple Alliance. Alliance among GERMANY, the AUSTRO-HUNGARIAN EMPIRE and ITALY in the years leading up to WORLD WAR I. These nations pledged to help defend one another if any one of them was attacked. The formation of the Triple Alliance stirred distrust among other European nations; Britain, France and Russia formed the TRIPLE ENTENTE in response. During World War I Italy fought against her former allies.

Triple Entente. Alliance among the UNITED KINGDOM, FRANCE and RUSSIA that made these nations partners in WORLD WAR I. The Triple Entente was formed in response to the perceived threat posed by the TRIPLE ALLIANCE. In 1904 Britain and France formed the ENTENTE CORDIALE. Three years later, Britain and Russia signed the ANGLO-RUSSIAN CONVENTION.

Trippe, Juan Terry (1899–1981). American airline pioneer. In 1927 Trippe founded PAN AMERICAN WORLD AIRWAYS, which he headed for the next 41 years. An aggressive entrepreneur, he seized every opportunity to extend international airline service, eventually expanding Pan Am's original 90–mile route into a worldwide network connecting the U.S. with 85 countries. Under his leadership Pan Am established a number of firsts in air passenger transportation. He established the first international airmail service (1927), the first scheduled service between the U.S. and Asia (1935) and the first scheduled service between the U.S. and Europe (1939). Trippe's success made long-distance air travel an everyday reality and also spelled the end of the era of the great OCEAN LINERS. Ironically, in the decade after Trippe's death, Pan Am experienced serious financial difficulties, and the airline's existence was in jeopardy.

Tropic of Cancer. Autobiographical novel published in 1934 by American writer Henry MILLER. *Tropic of Cancer,* which is today widely regarded as a classic work of 20th-century American literature, drew a great deal of controversy in the first three decades after its publication. The book initially appeared in PARIS in 1934. Miller, an expatriate American living in the French capital during the worldwide GREAT DEPRESSION, wrote an uninhibited and joyous account of his bohemian life and appetites. Those appetites included great books and art, fine wines, the observation of Parisian street life and frequent sex with all manner of women. It was Miller's frank accounts of sexual pleasure that led to *Tropic of Cancer* being banned in numerous countries, including the U.S. In 1964 the U.S. Supreme Court ruled that *Tropic of Cancer* was a significant work of artistic expression and hence not obscene.

Trotsky, Lev Davidovich (Bronshteyn) (1879–1940). Soviet politician. Trotsky joined the Social Democrats in 1896. He was banished to SIBERIA but escaped and became a member of *Iskra.* When the party split in 1903, he became

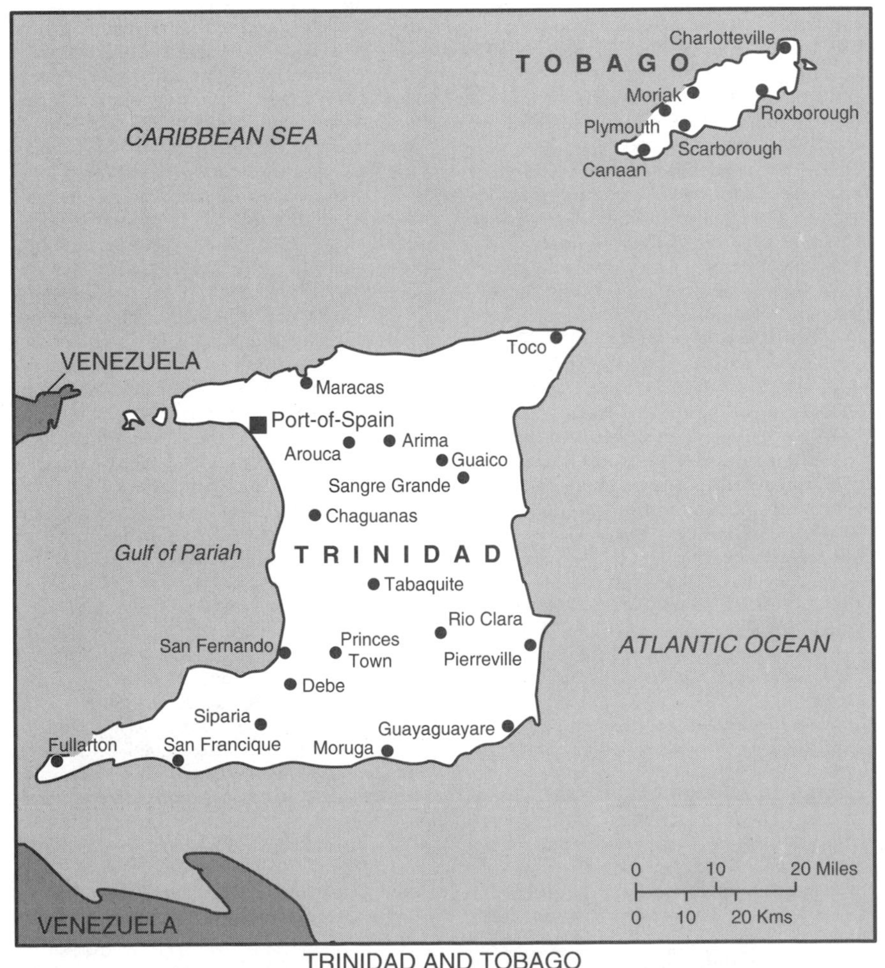

TRINIDAD AND TOBAGO

Leon Trotsky, Russian revolutionary.

a MENSHEVIK, prophesying that Leninist theory would result in a one-man dictatorship. He was again banished as a result of his role in the 1905 Revolution, when he held the position of chairman of the St. Petersburg Soviet. While trying to reunite the factions of the Russian Social Democrats, he led the internationalist wing of the Mensheviks during WORLD WAR I. Expelled from FRANCE as a result of his pacifist propaganda, Trotsky settled in the United States. Back in Russia following the FEBRUARY REVOLUTION, Trotsky became a BOLSHEVIK and the chief supporter of LENIN, and played a leading role in organizing and carrying out the OCTOBER REVOLUTION. Trotsky was head of the St. Petersburg Soviet and its military revolutionary committee, commissar for foreign affairs (1917–18), commissar for war (1918–25), leader of the RED ARMY during the RUSSIAN CIVIL WAR, and from 1919 to 1927 was a member of the Politburo. A frequent opponent of STALIN, Trotsky was expelled from the party in 1927. The "combined opposition" of Trotsky, Grigory ZINOVIEV and Lev KAMENEV was unsuccessful, and in 1929 he was expelled from the Soviet Union. He was accused of espionage during the GREAT PURGE and was murdered in Mexico City by Soviet agents. In 1930 he wrote *My Life: An Attempt at an Autobiography.*

For further reading:

Deutscher, Isaac, *The Prophet Armed: Trotsky, 1879–1921.* New York: Oxford University Press, 1980.

——, *The Prophet Outcast: Trotsky, 1929–1940.* New York: Oxford University Press, 1980.

———, *The Prophet Unarmed: Trotsky, 1921–1929.* New York: Oxford University Press, 1980.

Trudeau, Garry (1948–). American cartoonist. Trudeau attended Yale University, where he edited the campus humor magazine and published a cartoon strip in the school's *Daily News.* In 1970, he created for the Universal Press Syndicate the topical cartoon strip *Doonesbury,* which lampoons public figures and satirizes contemporary American life. The strip, which won a wide readership, is syndicated in about 500 newspapers and collected into several paperback books. In 1975 Trudeau was awarded the PULITZER PRIZE.

Trudeau, Pierre Elliott (1919–). Canadian prime minister. Born in Montreal, Trudeau studied at the University of Montreal, Harvard, the Ecole des Sciences Politiques (Paris) and the London School of Economics. He worked as a labor and civil rights lawyer and taught law at the University of Montreal before being elected a Liberal member of the Canadian parliament government of Lester Pearson. Trudeau became prime minister in 1968, a post he held until 1979 and then from 1980 to 1984. As prime minister, Trudeau successfully opposed Quebec separation, and in 1981 he gained approval of the new Canadian constitution. In the international arena, Trudeau supported arms reductions and argued for enhanced participation of developing nations in the world economy.

Truesdell, Karl, Jr. (1882–1955). American Air Force general. Truesdell led the first Air Force daylight bombing raid on BERLIN in WORLD WAR II. He also led the mission that dropped supplies to Polish patriots fighting against the NAZIS in the streets of Warsaw in 1944. He retired with the rank of major general.

Truffaut, Francois (1932–1984). French film director and critic, a leader (with Jean-Luc GODARD, Claude CHABROL and Jacques Rivette) of the NOUVELLE VAGUE of the late 1950s. From the circumstances of his lonely childhood—neglect at home, time in a reform school, a prison sentence for deserting the army—he retreated into the dream world of the movies. An association with the most important critic of the day, Andre Bazin (who became his unofficial adopted father), led to a staff position as film critic on CAHIERS DU CINEMA. He soon achieved notoriety as one of the fiercest polemicists in a small circle of young contributors, including Godard. Like them he had a love-hate relationship with the HOLLYWOOD cinema—detesting its commercial priorities but admiring its formulas and energies. More importantly, cinema for Truffaut was a "first-person" medium, like a confession or an intimate diary; and through the alter-ego of "Antoine Doinel" (played by actor Jean-Pierre Leaud), Truffaut enacts in film after film all the pain, uncertain joys and sexual arousals of his own life. In *Les Quatre Cents Coups* (*The 400 Blows,* 1959), Doinel runs away from home and is put in a reform school. In successive films—*L'Amour a Vingt Ans* (*Love at Twenty,* 1962), *Baisers voles* (*Stolen Kisses,* 1968) and *Domicile conjugal* (*Bed and Board,* 1970)—Doinel endures first love, rejection and eventual courtship and marriage. In other films Truffaut indulges his affection for American genres, like the gangster film (*Tirez sur le pianiste/Shoot the Piano Player,* 1960), the thriller (*La Mariee etait en Noir/The Bride Wore Black,* 1968) and science fiction (*Fahrenheit 451,* 1966).

Pierre Trudeau, Canadian prime minister (1979).

Many critics regard the ACADEMY AWARD-winning *La Nuit americaine* (*Day for Night,* 1973), the story of a filmmaker, as Truffaut's most telling achievement; others find his most touching personal statement in *La Chambre verte* (*The Green Room,* 1978), where he appears as a man who preserves in photographs the memory of the dead. It invites us to remember the words of the narrator in an earlier film, *Les Mistons* (*Mischief-Makers,* 1957): "Some moments are so precious we become slaves to them." The frozen moments of the celluloid film strip both bound—and liberated—Truffaut.

For further reading:

Truffaut by Truffaut. New York: Harry N. Abrams, 1987.

Trujillo, Rafael (Molina) (1891–1961). Dominican political leader, president of the DOMINICAN REPUBLIC (1930–38, 1942–52). A career military man, Trujillo joined the army in 1919 and was trained in a country occupied by U.S. Marines; he rose to the rank of general in 1927, three years after American forces left his country. He led a coup against President Horacio Vasquez in 1930, ran unopposed for the presidency and was elected later that year. In the years that followed, Trujillo ruled the nation as dictator, even when he was officially out of office. He was a wily and ruthless ruler, wielding terror to repress any opposition to his government. Trujillo was in a constant state of difficulty with neighboring Caribbean states, and he was eventually censured by the ORGANIZATION OF AMERICAN STATES. He was assassinated by army officers on May 30, 1961.

Truly, Richard (1937–). U.S. astronaut; logged over eight days in space during his two U.S. SPACE SHUTTLE missions, STS-2 (November 12–14, 1981) and STS-8 (August 30–September 5, 1983). STS-8 was the first U.S. Space Shuttle mission to be launched and to land at night. Truly succeeded James FLETCHER (in his second term) as administrator of NASA in April 1989, after serving as associate administrator for space transportation systems since February 1986.

Truman, Harry S (1884–1972). Senator from Missouri and 33rd president of the UNITED STATES. Following graduation from public high school in Independence, Harry Truman went to work on his father's farm and pursued a series of odd-job occupations. During WORLD WAR I he served in the Meuse-Argonne theater, and after the armistice he returned to Missouri to open a haberdashery business that proved unsuccessful. Truman never received a formal college education and used this fact to garner the support of the common man, but he did attend Kansas City School of Law from 1923 to 1925.

Truman began his political career as an adherent of the Democratic Party machine of Kansas City's Thomas J. PENDERGAST but without acquiring any of the unsavory reputation of the machine. After serving in local offices and judgeships, he was elected to the U.S. Senate in 1934 and reelected in 1940. As senator, he established a national reputation, heading a committee formed to investigate defense department contracts awarded to private industry.

Picked by President Franklin D. ROOSEVELT to be his running mate in the 1944 election, Truman became president when Roosevelt died on April 12, 1945. His immediate concern was to end WORLD WAR II in the Pacific, which he managed by authorizing the world's first ATOMIC BOMB drops (1945), on the Japanese cities of HIROSHIMA and NAGASAKI. Despite most predictions, he was reelected to a full term by defeating Thomas E. DEWEY in 1948.

During his two terms, Truman continued the domestic policies of Roosevelt, but his most important achievements were in foreign policy. At first an advocate of cooperation with Russia, he then formulated the TRUMAN DOCTRINE (May 15, 1947) to protect GREECE and TURKEY from communist domination. With UNITED NATIONS approval he sent U.S. military forces to protect SOUTH KOREA from invasion by communist NORTH KOREA. The first U.S. ground troops arrived there on June 1, 1950. One of his most controversial acts was the removal of General Douglas MACARTHUR (April 11, 1951) from his Far Eastern command, because Truman contended that MacArthur had failed to heed a presidential directive. This raised a great furor among MacArthur's many supporters. Truman also established the MARSHALL PLAN to assist European recovery from World War II, beginning April 2, 1948. On September 25, 1949, the president signed the NATO pact, forming the NORTH ATLANTIC TREATY ORGANIZATION for the defense of North Atlantic countries.

In domestic matters, he proposed the far-reaching reforms that he called the FAIR DEAL. Some of his proposals were intended to complete Roosevelt NEW DEAL programs. The Fair Deal called for measures dealing with civil rights, improvement of schools nationwide and assistance for the disadvantaged and the elderly. The Fair Deal was blocked by conservatives of both parties, and Truman failed to overcome this obstacle. However, much of the Truman plan for the Fair Deal was carried out during the Lyndon Baines JOHNSON period. Although eligible for a second full term, Truman chose to retire in 1952 to his home in Independence.

For further reading:

Collins, David R., *Harry S Truman: The People's President*. New York: Chelsea House, 1991.

President Harry S Truman, 33rd president of the United States (Dec. 16, 1950).

Truman Doctrine. Policy promulgated by President Harry S TRUMAN in 1947. It began with Truman's request of March 1947 for massive military and economic aid to GREECE and TURKEY. Aimed at containing the spread of international communism, the doctrine provided for assistance to countries resisting "attempted subjugation by armed minorities or by outside pressures" and clearly spelled out an American COLD WAR ideology that would prevail for over four decades.

Trump, Donald (1946–). American entrepreneur known for his brash deal-making and glitzy lifestyle during the 1980s, when he amassed a giant real estate empire. His company built the elaborate Trump Tower skyscraper in New York City and casino-hotels in ATLANTIC CITY, New Jersey. In 1989 Trump financed the purchase of the bankrupt Eastern Airlines shuttle with junk bonds through the investment firm Drexel Burnham Lambert. In 1990 his empire suddenly began to collapse. The Trump Shuttle and the newly-opened Taj Mahal hotel lost millions. Unable to make his debt payments, Trump was forced into near bankruptcy.

Tsander, Fridrikh (1887–1933). Among Russia's foremost early rocket pioneers, Tsander began working on liquid-propelled rocket engines in the 1920s. Static tests of his rockets—the OR-1 powered by gasoline and air and the OR-2 propelled by gasoline and oxygen—had begun by the 1930s. He also pioneered the idea of a space station, along with several of his contemporaries, including K.E. TSIOLKOVSKY and Y.V. Kondratyuk, Hermann OBERTH, Walter Hohmann, Guido von Pirquet and Hermann NOORDUNG. Tsander's book, *Problems of Flight by Means of Reactive Devices* (or, *Problems of Jet Propulsion*), published in 1934, made a significant contribution in that field. In November 1933, the same year Tsander died, the first fully liquid-propelled Soviet rocket, GIRD X, was successfully tested. It was powered by Tsander's OR-2 engine.

Ts'ao K'un (1862–1938). Chinese military and political figure, president of the Republic of CHINA (1923–1924). Ts'ao was a soldier in Korea and Manchuria during the SINO-JAPANESE WAR (1894–95), rising to the rank of division commander. When revolution broke out in China in 1911, his division was sent as a peace-keeping force to Peking by his mentor Yuan Shih-k'ai. After Yuan's death in 1916, his supporters split, and Ts'ao eventually headed the Chihl Clique, which bested the Anhwei Clique in 1920. After defeating the Manchurian warlord Chang Tso-Lin in 1922, Ts'ao attempted to unify China, and served as its president for two years. He was forced to resign by the warlord Feng Yuhsiang.

Tsatsos, Constantine (1899–1987). Greek scholar and politician. An author and law professor, Tsatsos combined academic activity with politics for much of his life. He held several cabinet posts in liberal governments in the 1950s and 1960s. He became president after the collapse of the 1967–1974 military dictatorship and the December 1974 referendum that abolished the Greek monarchy. From 1975 to 1980 he served as the first elected president of the republic of GREECE.

Tshombe, Moise (Kapenda) (1919–1969). Congolese political leader. Born in the BELGIAN CONGO, Tshombe was educated at an American mission school. A businessman, he served on the Provincial Council of Katanga (now Shaba) province from 1951 to 1953. In 1959 he founded the CONAKAT (Confederation des Associations Tribales du Katanga), a Belgian-supported political party advocating an independent but loosely federated Congo. In 1960 he attended the Brussels Congo Conference, where he pressed the CONAKAT program, which was rejected later that year when the Congo became independent as a centralized republic. After independence, Tshombe, the provincial president, led the mineral-rich Katanga's secession from the republic, thus creating the Congo Crisis. For the next two-and-a-half years he and his army of Katangese and white mercenaries fought for Katangan independence. During this period the controversial Tshombe was implicated in the murder (1961) of Patrice LUMUMBA. In 1963 Tshombe's forces were defeated by troops of the central government supported by UN forces. He fled to Spain but returned in 1964 when President Joseph KASAVUBU named him prime minister in a reconciliation government. The following year, he was dismissed from the office, and in 1966 he was accused of treason. Again going into exile, he was sentenced to death in absentia in 1967. Later that year he was kidnapped and brought to Algeria, where he died under house arrest two years later.

Tsiolkovsky, Konstantin (1857–1935). Pioneer Russian space theorist, sometimes called "the grandfather of the space age." Tsiolkovsky is seen by many as the prophet of today's modern space programs, both Soviet and American. Born to a poor family, he was a self-educated schoolteacher who had been practically deaf from childhood. Taking an early interest in the problems of space and space flight, he wrote a remarkable series of technical papers and articles dealing with all aspects of his subject from astronautics to space suits and colonization of the solar system, including the problems of building and operating future space stations. "The Earth is the cradle of mankind, but mankind cannot stay in the cradle forever," Tsiolkovsky once wrote. In a fitting tribute the inscription on his gravesite reads "Mankind will not remain tied to the Earth forever." Well-informed opinion is that the Soviet government planned to launch their first artificial satellite, SPUTNIK, on the hundredth anniversary of Tsiolkovsky's birth, but delays put off the launch by several days.

Tsiranana, Philibert (1910–1978). President of MADAGASCAR (1959–72). He was appointed head of a provisional government in 1958. He became the country's first elected president in 1959 and declared the island's full independence from French colonial rule in 1960. He was reelected twice, but in 1972 was deposed in a bloodless military coup.

Tsvetaeva, Marina (1892–1941). Russian poet. Regarded as one of the major Russian poets of the 20th century, Tsvetaeva was born the daughter of a Moscow University professor. By the age of 18 she had won acclaim for her poetic gifts; *Evening Album* (1910) was her first book. She married Sergei Efron in 1912. During the RUSSIAN CIVIL WAR he joined the White Army, and they were separated for five years, throughout which she endured grinding poverty. In 1922 she followed Efron into exile in Prague, then to Paris from 1925 to 1939. Tragedy shadowed much of her life. One daughter died of starvation in 1919 and another was sent to the labor camps. Her husband, after operating as a Soviet agent abroad, was arrested and executed when they returned to the U.S.S.R. in 1939. Tsvetaeva hanged herself in 1941 in the provincial town of Yelabuga.

For further reading:

Feinstein, Elaine, *A Captive Lion.* New York: Dutton, 1987.

Tuan, Pham (1947–). The first Asian in space, the Vietnamese Pham Tuan served as cosmonaut-researcher, with Viktor Gorbatko, aboard the Soviet SOYUZ 37 (July 1980), spending eight days in space as Soyuz linked up with the SALYUT space station and its occupants Leonid POPOV and Valery Ryumin.

Tuchman, Barbara (Wertheim) (1912–1989). American historian whose best-selling books focused on war and the lives of men involved in war. Tuchman became well known in 1962 with the publication of *The Guns of August*, a classic study of the events leading up to WORLD WAR I. The book won Tuchman her first PULITZER PRIZE the following year. Her second Pulitzer Prize was won for the biography of U.S. General Joseph STILWELL, *Stillwell and the American Experience in China, 1911–1945* (1971). Among her other best-selling works were *A Distant Mirror: The Calamitous Fourteenth Century* (1978), *The March of Folly: From Troy to Vietnam* (1984) and *The First Salute* (1988). Although professional historians occasionally found fault with her accuracy on minor facts, she was universally praised for her lucid style and dramatic narrative ability.

Tucker, Preston Thomas (1903–1956). Flamboyant but unsuccessful American automobile designer and manufacturer. Following an early career as an auto salesman and a manufacturer of war materiel, Tucker founded a company to produce his own automobile. However, after the car's highly publicized premiere in Chicago on June 19, 1947, the firm collapsed due to financial and management problems; only 51 of the autos were produced. Tucker filed for bankruptcy in 1949 and was subsequently indicted on, but acquitted of, mail fraud and securities violations. He died of cancer on December 26, 1956.

Tucker, Richard (1913–1975). American opera singer. Noted for his large, rich voice, Tucker was an outstanding tenor of the 1950s and 1960s. In 1945 he made his debut at the New York Metropolitan Opera as Enzo in *La Gioconda*. International recognition came with his performance as Radames in *Aida* in 1949. Specializing in the Italian and, to a lesser degree, the French repertories, Tucker excelled as Alfredo in *La Traviata* and Manrico in *Il Trovatore*, among other roles.

Tudor, Antony [born William Cook] (1909–1987). British-born choreographer. Tudor revolutionized ballet through the introduction of psychologically revealing gestures reflecting the influence of Freudian thought. He created his first ballet in London in 1931 and five years later produced his early masterpiece *Jardin aux Lilas* (*Lilac Garden*). In 1939 he came to the U.S. at the invitation of the AMERICAN BALLET THEATER and was closely associated with that company for much of the rest of his career. Perhaps the most popular of his works was *Pillar of Fire* (1942), which catapulted American dancer Nora Kaye to stardom. Other notable Tudor ballets were his personal favorite *Dark Elegies* (1937), *Undertow* (1945) and *Echoing of Trumpets*.

Tugendhat House. Major early work of Ludwig MIES VAN DER ROHE built in Brno, Czechoslovakia, in 1930. In it, the space concepts first demonstrated in the BARCELONA PAVILION, are introduced in a large and luxurious residence. The main living space of the house is an open area, not divided into conventional rooms, but partially divided by screen walls of rich materials. The outside walls are of floor-to-ceiling glass, arranged to retract into the basement so as to leave the house entirely open to the out-of-doors. Structural support is provided by slim steel columns encased in chromium. Bedrooms and service spaces are of more conventional design. A number of special furniture designs were developed for the house, some of them once more in production. The Tugendhat house, widely known through publication, became an influential classic of the INTERNATIONAL STYLE.

Tugwell, Rexford Guy (1895–1979). American economist and government official, a member of President Franklin D. ROOSEVELT'S BRAIN TRUST. Tugwell became undersecretary of agriculture in 1934, and later headed the Rural Resettlement Administration (1935–36). He was one of Roosevelt's top advisers on NEW DEAL programs, including tax reform, relief and public works. During WORLD WAR II he was governor of Puerto Rico. A strong believer in national economic planning, he was considered a brilliant and controversial figure.

Tukhachevsky, Michael Nikolayevich (1893–1937). Marshal of the Soviet Union. Of a noble family, Tukhachevsky served as an officer in WORLD WAR I, but in 1918 he joined the BOLSHEVIKS and the RED ARMY. He was commander in 1918–19 and was commander of all the Red forces in the Caucasus in 1920. In 1921 he was commander of the government forces against the KRONSTADT REBELLION. He was head of the military academy, commander of the western and Leningrad military districts and the Red Army's chief of staff (1925–28). Deputy commissar for military and naval affairs in 1931, in 1935 Tukhachevsky was appointed one of the first five marshals. He was accused of leading a military conspiracy and was tried and shot during the GREAT PURGE. His reputation was rehabilitated in 1958.

Tung, C(hao) Y(ung) (1911–1982). Chinese shipping magnate. Born in mainland China, Tung fled to Hong Kong in 1949 during the Communist takeover (see also CHINESE CIVIL WAR OF 1945–49). He founded his own shipping empire, the C.Y. Tung Group, building it into the second largest independent merchant fleet in the world, with about 150 ships totaling some 11 million deadweight tons.

Tunisia. Tunisia covers an area of 63,153 square miles on the Mediterranean coast of North Africa. A French protectorate from 1883 to 1956, Tunisia was occupied by the Axis powers during WORLD WAR II, until liberated by British and American forces in 1943. Independence from FRANCE was granted in 1956, with the leader of the nationalist movement, Habib BOURGUIBA, becoming president. Elected president for life in 1974, he established a government that survived labor unrest in 1968 and 1978 and rioting in 1984, as well as a coup attempt in 1980. He was deposed in 1987 in a bloodless coup. Dis-

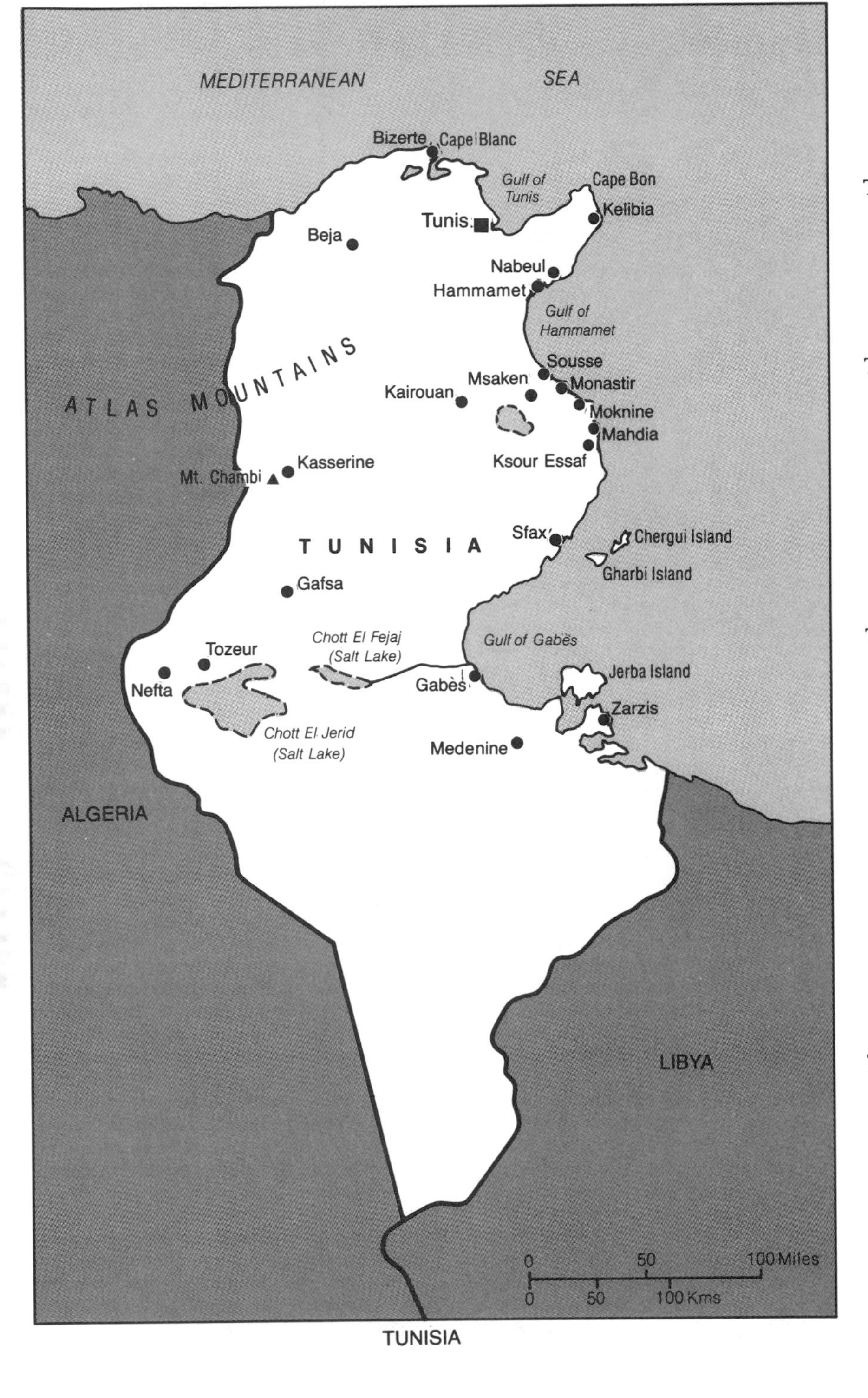

TUNISIA

putes with Algeria and Libya were resolved in 1983 and 1987, respectively.

Tunner, William H. (1906–1983). American Air Force general who directed the BERLIN AIRLIFT in 1948–1949. During his military career, he was considered the leading authority on airlifts. A veteran of WORLD WAR II, during the 1950s he served as commander of U.S. air forces in Europe, deputy chief of staff for operations (1957) and was named commander of the Military Air Transport Service in 1958.

Tunney, Gene [James Joseph Tunney] (1898–1978). American boxer. As a Marine stationed in Paris, Tunney won his first championship, that of the American Expeditionary Forces. After the war, he turned to professional boxing and won the light heavyweight title in 1922. A skillful, rather than overpowering fighter, he moved up through the heavyweight ranks and won a chance at that title in 1926. Tunney faced Jack DEMPSEY, whom he completely outboxed before a crowd of more than 130,000. The duo met again in 1927, where Tunney won a much-debated decision in 10 rounds. Tunney fought only once more and then retired with his heavyweight crown intact. A popular public figure, he married an heiress and went on to a successful business career.

Tupamaros. Marxist urban guerrillas in URUGUAY, about 1,000 in number, including many professional men. They were effective in creating unrest before 1972 when police and right-wing paramilitary groups carried out actions against them. Since then they have been relatively inactive.

Tupolev, Andrei Nikolayevich (1888–1972). Aircraft designer and lieutenant general of the Soviet air force. Having studied under N.Y. Zhukovsky at the Moscow Higher Technical School, in 1916 Tupolev established the Aerodynamic Aircraft Design Bureau. He has designed and directed work on both civil and military aircraft, including the ANT25 and the TU104 and TU114. Arrested during the GREAT PURGE in 1938, he was released and rehabilitated in 1943.

Tupper, Earl S. (1907–1983). American businessman who in 1942 created **Tupperware,** an elaborate line of plastic food and drink containers that revolutionized the American kitchen and led to the acceptance of plastics in the household. Tupperware was manufactured by the Tupperware Corporation and was originally sold primarily at "Tupperware parties," neighborhood gatherings where the products' uses were demonstrated. The company claimed that an average of 75,000 such parties took place daily around the world. In 1958 Tupper sold the company to the Rexall Drug Co. for $9 million, but the products continued to bear his name. More than $800,000 worth of Tupperware was sold in 1982, the year before Tupper's death.

Turing, Alan (Mathison) (1912–1954). British mathematician. Turing studied at Cambridge University, where he gained a fellowship in 1935. From 1936 to 1938 he worked at Princeton. He was at the National Physical Laboratory from 1945 to 1948 and subsequently became reader in mathematics at Manchester University.

His most important work consisted in giving a precise mathematical characterization of the intuitive concept of computability. Turing developed a precise formal characterization of an idealized computer—the Turing machine—and equated the formal notion of effective decidability with computability by such a machine. Turing was thus able to show that a number of important mathematical problems could have no effective decision procedure. In 1937 he showed the undecidability of first-order predicate calculus and in 1950 that of the word problem for semigroups with cancellation.

He was able to put his theoretical work on computability into practice during his time at the National Physical Laboratory when the ACE computer was built under his supervision, and later when he became assistant director of the Manchester automatic digital machine.

Turing had the misfortune to be a homosexual at a time when this was still a criminal offense in England. He committed suicide as a direct result of a prosecution for alleged indecency.

Turkey. Situated partly in southeastern Europe and partly in western Asia, Turkey covers an area of 300,868 square miles—a lot less than it covered at the beginning of this century. The OTTOMAN EMPIRE, decrepit heir of an empire that had once stretched from the Plains of Hungary to the Gulf of Aden, was dominated from 1908 to 1920 by reformers known as the YOUNG TURKS, who aligned Turkey with the Central Powers during WORLD WAR I. The Central Powers lost the war and Turkey lost the few remnants of its once-glorious empire. In the GRECO-TURKISH WAR OF 1921–22, Turks resisted Allied occupation by the Greek army, decisively defeated the Greeks at the Sakarya River and drove them 250 miles westward, into the Aegean Sea, slaughtering Greeks by the thousands at Smyrna. Sultan Mohammed VI was deposed in 1922 and the sultanate abolished. The Turkish Republic was declared in 1923, and Mustapha Kemal (later surnamed ATATURK), hero of Turkey's victory on the GALLIPOLI PENINSULA in 1915, became the first president (1923–38). The capital was moved from Constantinople to ANKARA; in 1924 a new constitution abolished the caliphate and made Turkey a secular state.

Neutral during most of WORLD WAR II, Turkey finally declared war on Germany and Japan in 1945. Turkey joined NATO in 1952. Political instability during the 1950s and 1960s culminated in the imposition of martial law in 1971. Turkey's invasion of northern CYPRUS in 1974 created a crisis with Greece that remains unresolved (see CYPRIOT WAR OF 1974). In 1980 the military under General Kenan EVREN seized power after several years of ineffective coalition governments, a worsening economy and intense violence. A new constitution was approved in 1982, with Evren acting as head of state until 1989. Turkey and its president, Turgut OZAL, supported UNITED NATIONS sanctions against Iraq for its invasion of Ku-

TURKEY

1908	Young Turks force sultan to restore constitutional rule and convene a parliament.
1911	War with Italy results in loss of Libya.
1920	Turkey accepts loss of Arab territories in the Middle East with the signing of the Treaty of Sevres.
1922	(October) Sultan Mohammed VI is deposed and the sultanate abolished.
1923	(Oct. 29) A Turkish republic is declared with Ankara as its capital and Ataturk as president.
1952	Turkey joins NATO.
1971	(March) Suleyman Demirel is forced from the premiership by the army and martial law is imposed.
1974	(July) Turkey invades northern Cyprus, creating an ongoing crisis with Greece.
1982	(November) New constitution reaffirms Turkey's democratic, secular and parliamentary identity.
1987	(March) Martial law lifted except in the four Kurdish provinces.
1989	(October) Turgut Ozal is elected president.
1991	Hundreds of thousands of Iraqi Kurds fleeing from Saddam Hussein attempt to cross into Turkey.

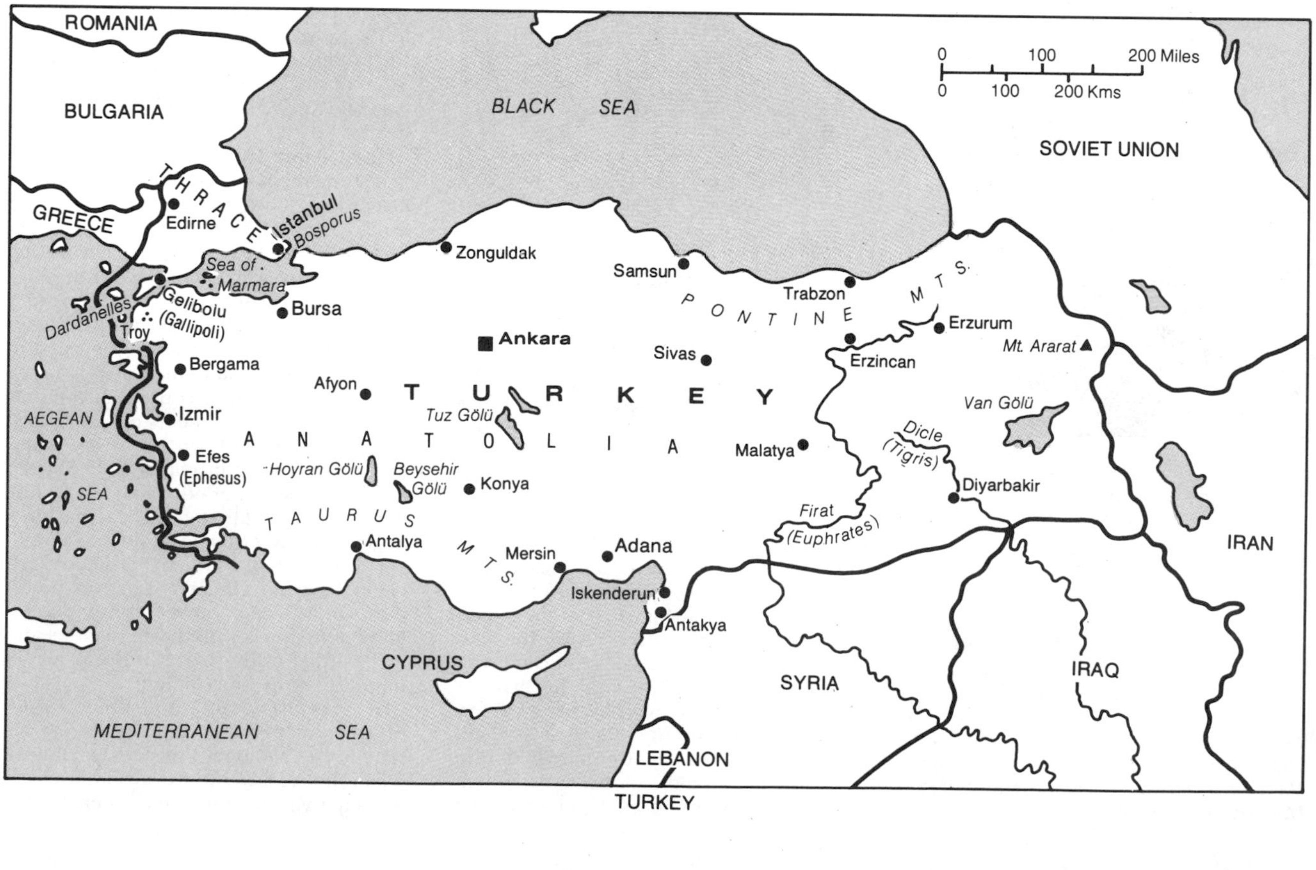

TURKEY

wait in 1990. (See also CYPRIOT WAR OF 1963–64.)

Turkish War of Independence. Movement of 1919–23 led by Mustapha Kemal (later called ATATURK) to prevent the Allied powers from dismembering the Turkish heartland of the OTTOMAN EMPIRE after World War I. When Sultan Mohammed VI refused to resist the Allies, Kemal, a prominent Turkish general, led his forces from Asiatic Turkey against both the sultan and the Allies. By 1920 Kemal had forced the government in Constantinople (now Istanbul) to refuse territorial concessions. The Allies occupied Constantinople and Kemal declared an independent government to be established in Ankara. In 1922 Kemal's forces occupied Constantinople and moved toward establishing a republic. The war ended with Greece's defeat in the GREEK-TURKISH WAR (1921–22). At the Conference of Lausanne (1923) Turkey's present boundaries were drawn, and the sultanate and caliphate were abolished.

Turks and Caicos Islands. The Turks and Caicos Islands are a group of 30 islands (eight of which are inhabited) in the Atlantic Ocean, just north of the island of Hispaniola; the capital is Grand Turk. In 1873 the islands became a dependency of Jamaica, some 400 miles to the southwest, and remained so until 1959, when they received their own governor. On Jamaica's independence from Britain in August 1962, the islands again became a British crown colony. The Turks and Caicos received their own governor again in 1972 and greater internal autonomy in 1976. In 1980 the ruling pro-independence People's Democratic Movement (PDM) agreed with the British government that independence would be achieved if the PDM won the 1980 general election. The PDM lost the election to the Progressive National Party (PNP), which supported continued dependent status. The leader of the PNP, Norman Saunders, became chief minister. In 1985 Saunders and two of his associates were arrested and convicted in the U.S. on drug charges. The PNP maintained itself in power by winning the by-elections held as a result; but on July 24, 1986, the governor dissolved the government and replaced it with an advisory council after a report found that Chief Minister Nathaniel Francis, two other ministers and two PDM members of the legislative council were unfit to hold office. A constitutional commission was created to suggest possible revisions to the constitution and electoral process. A general election under the provisions of the new constitution, with voting in multi-member constituencies, was held on March 3, 1988. It was won convincingly by the PDM, whose leader, Oswald Skippings, became prime minister.

Turner, Dame Eva (1892–1990). British opera singer. She was one of the first British divas to achieve international fame. Noted for a dramatic soprano voice of extraordinary range and power, she was best known for her performances in the title role of Puccini's *Turandot*. After her retirement in 1949, she became a teacher at the University of Oklahoma and at the Royal Academy of Music in London.

Turner, Frederick Jackson (1861–1932). American historian. Born in Portage, Wisconsin, Turner taught at the University of Wisconsin from 1885 to 1910 and at Harvard from 1910 to 1924. Although not a prolific writer, Turner had a major influence on American historical writing. In 1893 he delivered an address, "The Significance of the Frontier in American History," which brilliantly outlined the effect of the frontier on American democracy. Turner emphasized the importance of abundant, free land in reinforcing democratic beliefs and saw the close of the frontier as a turning point in American political history.

Turner, John Napier (1929–). Prime minister of CANADA (1984). Turner graduated from the University of British Columbia (1945) and studied law at Oxford. First elected to the House of Commons in 1962, he held various cabinet posts in the Pearson and Trudeau governments but left politics in 1975. He returned in 1984 and became prime minister after Trudeau's resignation. A few months later the Liberals were defeated in a general election and Brian MULRONEY became prime minister.

Turner, Joseph Vernon "Big Joe" (1911–1985). American singer. A Kansas City BLUES "shouter," Turner was widely known as the "Boss of the Blues." He was perhaps the most recorded and imitated blues singer in U.S. history, and was the first to perform and popularize such seminal rock and roll songs as "Shake, Rattle-and-Roll" and "Corrina, Corrina."

Turner, Ted (Robert E. III) (1938–). American entrepreneur. Turner began working in his father's advertising business in Georgia in 1960. After his father shot himself over business losses in 1963, Turner brought the firm out of debt and made a success of it. He became known for his cable television empire, and also as the winner of the 1977 America's Cup, and owner of the Atlanta Braves baseball team and Atlanta Hawks basketball team. He began by buying small television stations and making their programming available nationwide by satellite. In 1980 he launched Cable News Network (CNN), which was enormously successful, and by 1990 was available and watched worldwide. Turner Broadcasting Inc. later began expanding its media holdings. Turner formed alliances with the networks: ABC became involved with Turner's ESPN sports channel in 1987, and CBS and Turner negotiated an alliance for joint presentation of the 1992 and 1994 Winter Olympics in 1990, although his threatened takeover of CBS in 1985 had caused serious management problems for the network. He acquired the rights to 1,000 Columbia films in 1989 and also bought MGM-United Artists film company that year. Turner also aroused controversy in 1990 when he announced that his cable station, TBS, would present *Abortion for Survival*, a program advocating the right to abortion.

Turner, Thomas Wyatt (1877–1978). American CIVIL RIGHTS pioneer and educator. Turner founded the Federation of Colored Catholics and was a charter member of the NATIONAL ASSOCIATION FOR THE ADVANCEMENT OF COLORED PEOPLE. A friend of Booker T. WASHINGTON, he taught biology at Tuskegee Institute in 1901. He was a professor for 10 years at Howard University and for over 20 years at the Hampton Institute.

Tutu, Desmond (1931–). South African Anglican archbishop. Tutu, who won the NOBEL PRIZE for peace in 1984, is one of the leading black spokespersons for a nonviolent end to APARTHEID. Tutu is a strong advocate of black unity and of the policies of the AFRICAN NATIONAL CONGRESS. Because of his status as the spiritual leader of the Anglican Church in SOUTH AFRICA, he is also a voice that can be heard by the white minority of that country. Born in South Africa, Tutu attended King's College, London. In 1976 he was named bishop of Lesotho, South Africa. In 1978 he became secretary-general of the South African Council of Churches, an ecumenical group that has been a key force against apartheid. Tutu has been an outspoken opponent of the Afrikaner-dominated National Party and has been subjected to much government harassment.

Tuvalu. Covering a total land area of 9.2 square miles, the nine atolls formerly known as the Ellice Islands lie in the west

Bishop Desmond Tutu, flanked by Reverend Jesse Jackson (left) and Mayor Harold Washington at a prayer breakfast in Chicago (Jan. 24, 1986).

central Pacific, 652 miles north of Fiji and 2,496 miles northeast of Sydney, Australia. The coral chain is 360 miles long. Britain annexed the islands in 1892 and formed the Gilbert and Ellice Islands Protectorate; in 1916 these became a crown colony. In 1942, during WORLD WAR II, American forces occupied the Ellice Islands to counter the advance of the Japanese, who had invaded the Gilberts. The period from 1963 to 1977 saw steady constitutional development toward the present system of government in Tuvalu. In 1974 the Ellice Islanders voted in a referendum to separate from the Micronesian Gilbertese. Tuvalu achieved independence on October 1, 1978, as a constitutional monarchy within the COMMONWEALTH, with the governor general as the queen's representative. In March 1984 Tuvalu established diplomatic relations with Kiribati, and in 1987 the Tuvalu Trust Fund was set up by Britain, New Zealand, Australia and South Korea to provide development aid. Dr. Tomasi Puapua, who became prime minister following the general election of 1981, was reelected in 1985.

Tuve, Merle A. (1901–1982). American physicist. He was educated at the University of Minnesota (B.S., 1922) and Johns Hopkins University (Ph.D., 1926) and taught mainly at the Carnegie Institute in Washington, D.C. (1926–42, 1946–66). His discoveries opened the door for the development of RADAR and nculear energy. His studies in atomic structure led to his confirmation (1933) of the existence of the neutron. His observation that short-pulse radio waves reflected off the upper atmosphere was the theoretical basis for the development of radar. During WORLD WAR II he worked for the U.S. Office of Scientific Research and Development; here he oversaw the development of the **proximity fuse,** a device that set off artillery or anti-aircraft shells as they neared their target. The proximity fuse also stopped the German Buzz bomb attacks on Britain.

Tvardovsky, Alexander Trifonovich (1910–1971). Soviet writer. In 1936 Tvardovsky published *The Land of Muravia* and in 1942 the famous portrait of the Soviet soldier, *Vasily Terkin.* He edited the literary journal *Novy mir,* was dismissed from the post in 1954 but reinstated in the 1960s. Tvardovsky was responsible for publishing SOLZHENITSYN'S *A Day in the Life of Ivan Denisovich* in the Soviet Union, where it appeared in *Novy mir.*

20th Century-Fox. One of the Hollywood "Big Five" production/exhibition motion picture studios (along with METRO-GOLDWYN-MAYER, WARNER BROS., RKO, and PARAMOUNT). It was formed in 1935, a merger between an established studio fallen on hard times, the Fox Film Corp., and a new studio, Twentieth Century. The origins of the Fox Film Corp. go back to the nickelodeon days when entrepreneur William Fox formed the Greater New York Film Rental Company to distribute motion pictures. In 1915 he moved the operation to Los Angeles and changed the name to the Fox Film Corp. By the late 1920s, Fox had acquired numerous theaters, produced successful features with top stars and directors and made important experiments with synchronized sound. However, he ran afoul of government antitrust actions and was forced out of the company in 1930. Meanwhile, Darryl F. ZANUCK, a successful production chief at Warner Bros., was growing dissatisfied with his relationship with Jack Warner. He resigned in 1933 and with former United Artists executive Joseph Schenck formed Twentieth Century Pictures. The next two years saw releases like *The Affairs of Cellini* (1934), *The House of Rothschild* (1935) and *Les Miserables* (1935). After the merger with Fox in 1935, Zanuck assumed complete control. For the next 20 years a diverse roster of stars, filmmakers and pictures were developed. Little Shirley TEMPLE, the most famous child star of her day, virtually kept the studio afloat in the 1935–39 period, with hits like *Captain January* (1936) and *Wee Willie Winkie* (1937). Director John FORD was in his prime, scoring with *Drums Along the Mohawk* (1939), *The Grapes of Wrath* (1940), *Young Mr. Lincoln* (1940) and many others. Some of the greatest of all Technicolor musicals from the 1940s exploited the so-called Fox Blondes, Betty Grable, June Haver and Alice Faye (Marilyn Monroe came along in the 1950s). Outside of Warner Bros., the studio developed the most important series of "social consciousness" films in the 1940s with pictures like *Wilson* (1943), *Gentleman's Agreement* (1947) and *The Snake Pit* (1947). In 1956 Zanuck left the company. After the debacle of *Cleopatra* (1961), he returned as chairman of the board with son Richard as Hollywood production chief. Although some smash successes followed, like *The Sound of Music* (1965) and the first *Star Wars* film in 1977, both Zanucks were eventually forced out. Since 1985 Australian magnate Rupert MURDOCH has been the studio's owner. Ironically, in 1989 the studio's moviemaking division assumed the name of William Fox's original silent-era studio,the Fox Film Corp.

For further reading:
Mosley, Leonard, *Zanuck.* Boston: Little, Brown, 1984.

20th Party Congress. Meeting of the Communist Party of the Soviet Union held in February 1956; presided over by Premier Nikita KHRUSHCHEV and attended by Soviet party members and representatives of other national parties. During the meeting, the first since the death of Joseph STALIN (1953), Khrushchev gave a secret speech in which he denounced Stalin for his destructive and dictatorial policies and in which he condemned the "cult of personality" that had grown up around the former Soviet strongman. This speech was made public several months later. At the same conference, Khrushchev also announced that war with capitalist forces was no longer inevitable and he pressed for "peaceful coexistence" between the world's two ideological camps. The conference was important in easing COLD WAR tensions and in providing the U.S.S.R. with the philosophical revisions necessary for eventual reform.

Twenty-one Demands. A number of demands presented by JAPAN to CHINA in 1915 by which Japan attempted to make China a virtual protectorate. Declaring war against GERMANY in August 1914, Japan made its participation in WORLD WAR I a pretext for invading Kiaochow, Germany's leased territory in Shantung province. Japan then presented its Twenty-one Demands to president YUAN SHIH-K'AI, threatening war if they were not met. Divided into five groups, the demands stipulated that Japan would assume Germany's role in Shantung; that it would have special commercial and colonial rights in Manchuria and Mongolia; that Japan would have exclusive coal-mining privileges in China; that China would exclude further coastal development to any power but Japan; and that Japan would serve as adviser in China's political, military, commercial and financial affairs. The demands were intended to realize Japan's imperialistic aims in China and to undermine the influences of Russia and Great Britain. They were presented in secret, but were leaked to the American minister in Peking, and soon became known worldwide. Ultimately, the demand for control over every aspect of Chinese life was dropped, but China was forced to accede to other provisions of the ultimatum. The demands provoked enormous suspicion and resentment of Japan by the Chinese public, ultimately providing impetus for the MAY FOURTH MOVEMENT and for the whole national unification movement.

"Twilight Zone, The". Television's most famous anthology series of fantasy and science fiction. Prestigious playwright Rod Serling (*Patterns, Requiem for a Heavyweight*) had written a time travel fantasy called "Time Element" for the "Desilu Playhouse" in 1958. Enthusiastic response led to a pilot for a weekly CBS series to be called "The Twilight Zone." Serling, who thought he invented the term, found out later that it had been in common use among Air Force pilots to describe a lack of visibility of the horizon. Serling wrote the first story, "Where Is Everybody?" and narrated and hosted the show, which premiered on October 2, 1959. He remained with the program, narrating and furnishing many of the scripts, until the series' demise in September 1965. The half-hour format predominated, except for the fourth season, when shows were expanded to an hour. Everything about the series became famous: Serling's beetle-browed appearance and stentorian narration ("You're travelling through another dimension"); the oscillating monotony of the musical theme (written by Marius Constant); and the weird characters arrayed against the ordinary world—"the witches and the warlocks, the elves and the gnomes, the odd ones and the not-quite-right ones," as Serling described them. Original stories and scripts came from some of Serling's favorite writers: Richard Matheson, Charles Beaumont, Ray BRADBURY, Jerome Bixby and Jerry Sohl. And prestigious directors worked here, like Jacques Tourneur, Norman Z. McLeod, John Brahm and Richard Donner. Pound for pound, there were more memorable moments than in any television series this side of Owl Creek Bridge: the transformation of an old man into the Devil in "The Howling Man"; the creature on the airplane wing in "Nightmare at 20,000 Feet"; the slapstick homage to the legendary Buster KEATON in "Once Upon a Time"; the switcheroo ending of "To Serve Man." And everybody remembers the meek little bookworm (Burgess Meredith) in "Time Enough at Last"; he plans to catch up on his reading after the Bomb has destroyed the world—until he breaks his glasses.

For further reading:

Zicree, Marc Scott, *The Twilight Zone Companion*. New York: Bantam Books, 1982.

Twining, Nathan F. (1897–1982). American Air Force officer. During WORLD WAR II Twining commanded allied aerial campaigns in Europe and in the South Pacific and won several decorations. Later, during the COLD WAR, he played an important role in the development of U.S. nuclear air weapons and the supersonic missiles and jets designed to deliver them. He was Air Force chief of staff (1953–57) and chairman of the joint chiefs of staff (1957–60) during the EISENHOWER administration.

Twomey, Seamus (1919–1989). One of the Irish founders of the Provisional branch of the IRISH REPUBLICAN ARMY (IRA), which was set up in the wake of renewed sectarian strife in NORTHERN IRELAND in 1969. Twomey was arrested in the Irish Republic in 1973 and later escaped by helicopter from a Dublin prison, but was recaptured in 1977 and sentenced to a five-year prison term.

Tynan, Kenneth (1920–1980). British theater critic, playwright and essayist. Tynan was a highly influential force in theater and in popular culture during his lifetime. In addition to his writings, he expressed his forceful and controversial views in frequent radio and television appearances. Tynan first came to prominence in the 1950s as a drama critic for the *London Observer* who championed the new realism of British drama. He went on to serve for ten years as the literary manager of Britain's National Theater and to author an erotic musical, *Oh Calcutta*, that began a lengthy Broadway run in the 1960s. Tynan's reviews and profiles of theatrical and Hollywood figures appeared frequently in *The New Yorker*.

Typhoid Mary (1868–1938). Name given to Irish immigrant Mary Mallon, who was probably the first known carrier of the typhoid fever bacillus in the U.S. Infected by a bout of the disease, she knowingly spread it by working as a cook in New York City-area homes and institutions. During 1906–1907 she is thought to have been involved in at least 25 cases of the highly infectious disease. Identified and detained in a city hospital, she refused treatment and was released in 1910. In 1915, after an outbreak of typhoid fever at New York's Sloane Hospital, she was found to have worked in its kitchen. Arrested and hospitalized, she continued to refuse treatment. She eventually became a laboratory technician and was confined to the grounds of the hospital, where she died.

Tyson, Michael Gerard (1966–). American boxer. "Iron Mike" Tyson rose from his background as a street fighter in Brooklyn to the heavyweight championship of the world. Discovered while in reform school by noted trainer Cus D'Amato, he went on to an amateur record of 24–3 before turning professional in 1985. The following year, Tyson became the youngest heavyweight champion in history. A devastating puncher, he defended his title successfully for three years, amassing a professional record of 37–0 before being upset by underdog Buster Douglas in 1990. Tyson's career has been marked by scandal, including erratic behavior and a well-publicized divorce from actress Robin Givens.

Tyuratam. The Soviet spacecraft launch site, on the broad, flat steppes of Central Asia, about 200 miles from the town of Baikonur (the name often used by the Soviets for the launch site).

Tzara, Tristan [Sami Rosenstock] (1896–1953). Romanian-born poet, aesthetic theorist and playwright. Tzara is not widely read, but he remains one of the most influential thinkers of this century by virtue of his seminal role in the founding of the DADA movement in Zurich, Switzerland in 1916. According to fellow Dadaist Hans ARP, it was Tzara himself who coined the word Dada. In any event, it was Tzara who wrote its first Manifestoes and became its leader in attacking the accepted conventions of bourgeois culture and the pretensions of human reason. Tzara, born into a Jewish family, published his first poems in Romanian in 1912. Shortly thereafter, he switched to French as his literary language. Tzara moved to Zurich in 1915 and then to Paris in 1919. There he became involved with SURREALISM and ultimately clashed with its leader, Andre BRETON. Tzara's major works include *Twenty-five Poems* (1918) and the play *The Gas Operated Heart* (1923).

Udaltsova, Nadezhda (1886–1961). Painter and one of the chief representatives of the Cubist school in RUSSIA. Udaltsova studied with Lyubov Popova at Arseneva's gymnasium (1907–10), and they then took a studio together in Moscow. They went to PARIS in 1912, but Udaltsova returned to Russia in 1914. One of her best-known paintings is *At the Piano.*

UDI [Unilateral Declaration of Independence]. Declared by the Rhodesian Front government of Ian SMITH on November 11, 1965, it was rejected by Britain and condemned by the UNITED NATIONS, which saw it as a rebellion consequent upon RHODESIA's refusal to introduce black majority rule. (See also ZIMBABWE.)

Uganda [Republic of Uganda]. Located on the equator in East Africa, Uganda is a landlocked country covering an area of 91,111 square miles—a protectorate of the British Empire from 1895 until granted independence in 1962. Resistance to Prime Minister Milton OBOTE's leftist policies and suspension of the constitution resulted in Idi AMIN and the army seizing power in 1971. During Amin's eight-year rule thousands of Ugandans were killed, foreigners were expelled and the economy collapsed. Uganda was accused of collusion with terrorists when passengers from a highjacked Air France plane were held hostage at Entebbe Airport until Israeli commandos rescued them (see raid on ENTEBBE). In 1979 Amin was overthrown, and in 1980 Obote was elected president. Opposition from the National Resistance Army (NRA) led by Yoweri Museveni resulted in intense guerrilla warfare and tremendous loss of life. The NRA gained control of most of Uganda by 1986, and Museveni became president, forming a coalition government. The Museveni government has brought some stability to the country in spite of continued resistance in some areas and an attempted coup in 1988. At the same time, AIDS has spread through a large percentage of the population, causing a major health crisis in the country.

Ukraine. European region in the western Soviet Union, contiguous with the Ukrainian Soviet Socialist Republic (established 1922). The inhabitants, the Ukrainians, are a Slavic people. Throughout much of its long history, the Ukraine has been dominated by either Poland or Russia. It entered the 20th century as part of the Russian empire under Czar NICHOLAS II. At the outbreak of the RUSSIAN REVOLUTION in 1917, the Ukraine declared independence from Russia and formed its own government. During the ensuing RUSSIAN CIVIL WAR, the Ukraine was fought over by the Red Army of the BOLSHEVIKS and the anti-Bolshevik WHITES and was also claimed by POLAND, while the Ukrainians vainly attempted to maintain their independence. With their victory in the civil war, the Bolsheviks incorporated the Ukraine into the new UNION OF SOVIET SOCIALIST REPUBLICS in 1922, although

UGANDA

1962	Becomes independent member of Commonwealth with Milton Obote as prime minister.
1966	Obote suspends constitution, declares himself executive president.
1971	Obote is overthrown in military coup led by Major General Idi Amin; suspension of Political Activities Decree abolishes all constitutional rights; Armed Forces (Power of Arrest) Decree places the armed forces above the law; Detention (Presumption of Time Limit) Decree grants army wide powers of detention without trial and the power to shoot on sight; an estimated 300,000 Ugandans are killed over the next eight years.
1973	Foreign businesses are expropriated without compensation and distributed among the military and police.
1979	Amin overthrown by Ugandan exiles with help of Tanzanian army; after year of political chaos, Obote returns to power; opposition leader Yoweri Museveni forms National Resistance Army (NRA) and starts guerrilla war against Obote; civilian casualties from government anti-guerrilla activity exceed those of Amin's rule.
1985	Obote overthrown in tribal coup that brings General Tito Okello to power; Okello unable to defeat NRA, which occupies Kampala and takes control of country by next year.
1986	Yoweri Museveni sworn in as president and creates National Resistance Council government, which includes 68 ministers with broad range of political interests; rival political parties banned.
1990	Led by Major General Fred Rwigyema, who fought in NRA with President Museveni, a rebel army of refugee Rwandan Tutsi tribesmen, many of whom had been in Ugandan army, invade Rwanda in attempt to seize government that is dominated by rival Hutu tribe; Ugandan government condemns attack and declares no prior knowledge of invasion.

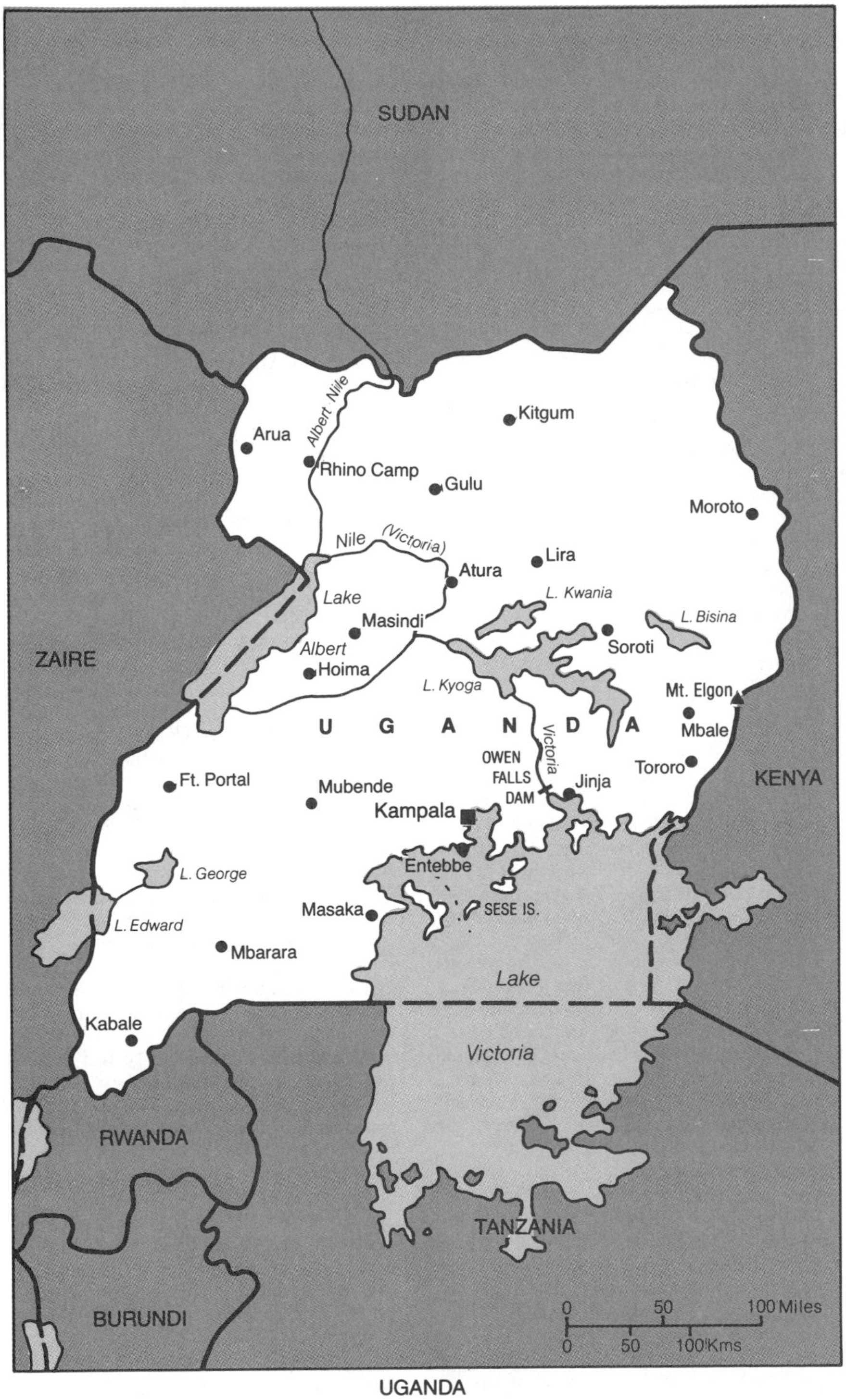

UGANDA

Ukrainian nationalism was not subdued. During the reign of Joseph STALIN, the Ukraine suffered from a disastrous famine caused largely by Stalin's policy of forced collectivization of the Ukrainian farms and his confiscation of Ukrainian grain for export. When GERMANY invaded the Soviet Union during WORLD WAR II, the Ukrainians at first welcomed the Germans as liberators. However, the Nazis regarded them not as potential allies against Stalin but as an inferior race fit only for slavery, and the brutal German occupation caused much death and suffering. In the mid-1980s the region again suffered, this time from radioactive contamination resulting from the CHERNOBYL DISASTER.

Ulam, Stanislaw Marcin (1909–1984). Polish-born mathematician. Considered one of the greatest figures in 20th-century mathematics, Ulam was a key figure in the development of the HYDROGEN BOMB. In 1935 Ulam joined the Institute for Advanced Study in Princeton, New Jersey at the invitation of mathematician John von NEUMANN. In 1943 he was recruited to work on the MANHATTAN PROJECT in Los Alamos, New Mexico, where he remained until 1967. With physicist Edward TELLER he devised the "Teller-Ulam" solution, which made the H-bomb possible. Ulam served as professor and chairman of the mathematics department at the University of Colorado. His books include *Adventures of a Mathematician*.

Ulanova, Galina Sergeyevna (1910–). Prima ballerina. She made her debut in 1928 at the Kirov Theater, Leningrad, in *Les Sylphides*. Her dancing represented a survival of the best of the prerevolutionary Russian school. She was taught by Agrippina VAGANOVA, who was in turn taught by Nicholas Legat; her parents were dancers at the Imperial Theater in St. Petersburg, the Maryinsky. Although comparatively unknown outside the Soviet Union until her visit to London in 1956, she established herself as one of the world's greatest dancers. In addition to her stage performances, she appeared in the films *Giselle* (1957) and *Romeo and Juliet* (1954). On retiring in 1963, she joined the Bolshoi Theater as ballet mistress.

Ulbricht, Walter (1893–1973). East German political leader. Born in Leipzig, Ulbricht was a Social Democrat and trade unionist through World War I but joined the German Communist Party on its founding in 1918 and remained a lifelong Marxist. He was a member of the Reichstag from 1928 to 1933, fleeing HITLER to settle in Moscow in 1933. Ulbricht returned to GERMANY with conquering Russian troops in 1945, becoming deputy premier of the newly created German Democratic Republic in 1949 and secretary general of the Socialist Unity Party (successor to the Communist Party) in 1950. As the autocratic leader of EAST GERMANY, he molded his nation into a strict Stalinist state and helped to make it the world's eighth-ranked economic power. Opposed to the policies of West Germany and angered by the exodus of East Germans to the West, Ulbricht was responsible for the 1961 construction of the BERLIN WALL. He gave up his post as party secretary to Erich HONECKER in 1971 but remained in the figurehead position of chairman of the Council of State until his death.

Ultra. Code name for the material gained from Britain's successful effort to break the codes produced by Germany's **Enigma** cipher machine during WORLD WAR II. The first Enigma machine was produced in Germany in 1926, and it was modified in 1937. The most important characteristic of the machine was that codes produced by it could not be deciphered without the use of another Enigma device. With Polish help, England and France were able to reconstruct Enigma, and by 1939 two replicas of the machine were in Allied hands. In 1940 cryptanalysts (including mathematician Alan TURING) working for the British War Office at Bletchley Park, England, broke Germany's Enigma cipher. From then on the Allies were able to eavesdrop on virtually all of Germany's most important coded messages and get vital German intelligence. Information obtained included data on the activity and location of German U-boats that enabled the Allies to sink about 30 enemy SUBMARINES, as well as vital intelligence on the Italian campaign, the Mediterranean and Middle East theaters and the activities of ROMMEL's Afrika Corps.

For further reading:

Bennett, Ralph, *Ultra and Mediterranean Strategy*. New York: William Morrow, 1989.

Kozaczuk, Waldyslaw, *Enigma: How the German Machine Cipher Was Broken, and How It Was Read by the Allies in World War II*. Westport, Conn.: Greenwood, 1984.

Winterbortham, F.W., *The Ultra Secret*. New York: Dell, 1975 (reissue).

Winton, John, *Ultra at Sea: How Breaking the Nazi Code Affected Allied Naval Strategy During World War II*. New York: William Morrow, 1989.

Ulysses (1922). Classic novel by the Irish writer James JOYCE. *Ulysses* is perhaps the single most acclaimed novel of this century. Since its independent publication in Paris in 1922 by the bookseller Sylvia BEACH, who believed in *Ulysses* as a work of genius while commercial publishers shied away from its experimental language and sexual frankness, the novel has earned the highest praise from each successive generation of writers and literary critics. The basic plot concerns the strangely intertwined wanderings of two men, the young artist Stephen Dedalus and the cuckolded husband Leopold Bloom, through a June day and night in Dublin. Each chapter of the novel derives thematic inspiration from episodes of the *Odyssey* by the Greek epic poet Homer, and Bloom and Dedalus bear a resemblance to Odysseus and his son Telemachus. *Ulysses* was the first major work to make use of the STREAM OF CONSCIOUSNESS technique—precise linguistic rendering of the random thought flows and fantasies of its individual characters. While *Ulysses* was at first banned in the U.S. for obscenity, a famous 1933 ruling by federal judge John M. Woolsey stirringly affirmed its literary greatness.

Under the Volcano (1947). Acclaimed novel by British author Malcolm LOWRY. *Under the Volcano* is widely regarded as one of the most intense and poignant works of fiction of the 20th century. The novel was the final product of numerous drafts worked and reworked by Lowry in a squatter's shack he built for himself in Dollarton, British Columbia. *Under the Volcano* draws heavily upon Lowry's own life, notably his visit to MEXICO in the 1930s, his two difficult marriages and his longtime battle with alcoholism. The setting is the Mexican town of Quauhnahuac (Cuernavaca). The year is 1939, and the town is celebrating the Day of the Dead, a Mexican festival with ominous emotional overtones. Geoffrey Firmin, a onetime consul of the British foreign service, is drinking himself into oblivion. Neither his half-brother nor his ex-wife can reach him emotionally. Firmin cannot tolerate the callous values of the world, and alcohol is his means of suicide. Written in a STREAM-OF-CONSCIOUSNESS style, *Under the Volcano* is a tour de force filled with incisive psychological portrayals and showing the influence of esoteric philosophies, including kabbalah.

Underwood, Oscar Wilder (1862–1929). American politician. A member from Alabama of the U.S. HOUSE OF REPRESENTATIVES (1897–1915) and Senate (1915–27), Underwood was a strong supporter of President Woodrow WILSON's foreign policies. He was a contender for the presidential nomination in 1912, and in 1913 wrote the Underwood Tariff Act, which severely reduced tariff rates until it was nullified by WORLD WAR II.

Undset, Sigrid (1882–1949). Norwegian novelist. Undset was the daughter of a noted archeologist and antiquarian whose interests would later influence her work. Her first works were *Fru Marta Oulie* (1907, *Mrs. Marta Oulie*), the short story collection *Den lykkelige alder* (1908, *The Happiest Years*), and *Fortellingen om Viga-Ljot og Vigdis* (1909, translated as *Gunnar's Daughter*). It was with *Jenny: Roman* (1911, *Jenny: A Novel*) that she first achieved acclaim. The novel is a roman a clef portraying her affair with an older married man, Anders Castus Svarstad, whom she would later marry. Undset is most celebrated for the medieval fiction she wrote later in life. This includes the trilogy, *Kristin Lavransdatter*, which consists of the novels *Kransen* (1920, translated in the U.K. as *The Garland* and in the U.S. as *The Bridal Wreath*), *Husfrue* (1922) translated as *The Mistress of Husaby*), and *Korset* (1922, *The Cross*). This was followed by the related novels *Olav Audunsson i Hestviken* (1925, *The Master of Hestviken*) and *Olav Audunsson og hans born* (1927, *Olav Audunsson and His Children*), which were published as a tetralogy in English consisting of *The Axe, The Snake Pit, In the Wilderness* and *The Son Avenger*, referred to as a whole as *The Master of Hestviken*. Undset was awarded the NOBEL PRIZE for literature in 1928.

Ungar, Frederick (1898–1988). Austrian-born publisher who fled Nazi Austria in 1938 and founded Frederick Ungar Publishing Co. in New York City in 1940. The firm published works of literature, criticism, history, philosophy, science and the arts, as well as translations of Goethe, Thomas MANN and Erich FROMM.

Ungaretti, Giuseppe (1888–1970). Italian poet and essayist. Ungaretti was born of Italian emigrants living in Alexandria, Egypt. He was educated in Egypt but left in 1912 to study law at the Sorbonne in Paris. While in Paris Ungaretti became active in artistic circles, forming friendships with the poet Guillaume APOLLINAIRE and the Cubist painters Georges BRAQUE and Pablo PICASSO, as well as with members of the Italian Futurist circle (see FUTURISM). Ungaretti fought in the Italian infantry during WORLD WAR I, during which time he published his first book of poems, *Il Porto Sepolto* (1916). In the 1920s, Ungaretti was for a time a supporter of Benito MUSSOLINI. In 1936 Ungaretti became Professor of Italian Literature at the University of Sao Paolo, Brazil. His international reputation as a poet was consolidated with a series of volumes he published late in his life—*Poesie disperse* (1945), *Il Dolore* (1947), *Un Grido e Paesaggi* (1952) and *Vita d'un Uomo* (1969), which contained his collected poems.

unidentified flying object. Also known as a UFO—an airborne object whose appearance or behavior cannot be readily identified or explained. Anecdotal evidence suggests that the people of the ancient world saw "flying objects" they could not identify. Modern sightings began in the U.S. in 1878 and continued during 1896–97. In the 20th century, UFOs were reported by flyers in World War II and by citizens of Scandinavia and, to a lesser degree, other European countries in 1946. UFOs came to wide public attention after June 24, 1947, when Kenneth Arnold, an American pilot flying over the Cascade Mountains in the state of Washington sighted nine shining and weaving disks that, he said, moved "like a saucer skipping across water." From this description came the popular term "flying saucer." As interest mounted, so did the other reported sightings, some by ordinary citizens, some by trained military observers. Since then UFO sightings have reoccurred in clusters, peaking in southern Europe in 1954, in New Guinea in 1958, in the Soviet Union in 1967 and in the U.S. in 1947, 1952, 1957, 1965–67 and 1973. Most sightings have eventually been explained as such things as weather balloons, planets, fireballs and other meteorological phenomena, the sun's rays bouncing off airplanes, and even mass hysteria and outright hoax. A U.S. Air Force investigation, Project Blue Book, which studied UFO reports from 1948–69, concluded that the "objects" posed no threat to national security and that no evidence could be found for any extraterrestrial origin for them. The report notwithstanding, people continue to see objects in the sky that they cannot identify, and some 10% of all those objects seem to remain a 20th century mystery.

Union of South Africa. Name of the southernmost nation in Africa from 1910 until 1961, when it became the Republic of South Africa. (See also SOUTH AFRICA.)

Union of Soviet Socialist Republics [U.S.S.R.]. The Union of Soviet Socialist Republics is the largest country in the world: it covers a total area of 8,647,172 square miles, nearly 1/6th of the total global land surface, and extends eastwest across northern Eurasia for nearly 6,210 miles from the Pacific Ocean to the Baltic Sea, and for nearly 3,105 miles north-south at its widest point. The U.S.S.R. consists of 15 Union (constituent) Republics, occupying (with a few exceptions) the area that before 1918 was imperial RUSSIA. The RUSSIAN REVOLUTION of 1917 forced the abdication of Czar NICHOLAS and installed a provisional government (see FEBRUARY REVOLUTION) to rule Russia; the subsequent OCTOBER REVOLUTION brought a Marxist (Bolshevik) govern-

UNION OF SOVIET SOCIALIST REPUBLICS

ment to power, led by V.I. LENIN, which sought to eliminate all vestiges of the old regime and to radically transform Russian society. In the course of the 20th century, this transformation brought about periods of intense human suffering but also made the U.S.S.R. into a world superpower.

The BOLSHEVIKS renamed Russia the Russian Soviet Federated Socialist Republic in 1918 (with Moscow reinstated as the capital), and in December 1922 this became part of the Union of Soviet Socialist Republics following the consolidation of Soviet power in the UKRAINE, Transcaucasia and Central Asia. The Bolshevik party became the Russian Communist Party (Bolsheviks) in 1918, the All-Union Communist Party (Bolsheviks) in 1925, and the COMMUNIST PARTY OF THE SOVIET UNION (CPSU) in 1952.

During the RUSSIAN CIVIL WAR the Bolsheviks pursued a policy of WAR COMMUNISM, involving highly centralized economic administration, conscription of all private and public wealth and manpower, a ban on private trade, and forcible requisitioning of grain and other foodstuffs from the peasantry. "War communism" gradually alienated the regime from the workers and peasants and prompted manifestations of discontent culminating in the KRONSTADT REBELLION, a mutiny in March 1921 at the Kronstadt naval garrison near Petrograd. Shortly afterwards, recognizing the need to recoup popular support for the regime as well as to restore the war-ravaged industrial base, Lenin announced the NEW ECONOMIC POLICY (NEP). Originally limited to replacing forcible requisitioning of peasants' produce with a tax-in-kind on surpluses, the NEP became a general retreat from principles of a socially owned economy towards what Lenin termed "state capitalism," combining state ownership of the "commanding heights" of the economy (heavy industry, public utilities and the financial system) with a free market and private ownership of small-scale industry and agriculture. When Lenin died in January 1924, the party leadership was split into four factions led by Leon TROTSKY; Joseph STALIN; Grigory ZINOVIEV and Lev KAMENEV; and Nikolai BUKHARIN, Alexei RYKOV and Mikhail Tomsky. Zinoviev and Kamenev allied with Stalin to ensure that Trotsky did not succeed Lenin as leader, and were instrumental in convincing the party central committee to ignore Lenin's recommendation (made shortly before his death) that Stalin should be ousted as party general secretary (an office he had assumed in 1922) because he was accumulating unlimited authority. However, fear of Stalin's growing power prompted Zinoviev and Kamenev to break with him in 1925, and in the following year they allied with Trotsky, while Stalin allied with Bukharin's group. Stalin's opponents were expelled from the party in 1927; Zinoviev and Kamenev were subsequently readmitted, but Trotsky was forced into exile in 1929. Economic policy was a key issue in the factional struggle: Trotsky advocated accelerated industrialization, financed at the peasants' expense, whereas Bukharin favored conciliation of the peasantry. In this he was supported initially by Stalin, but once the LEFT OPPOSITION was defeated in 1927 Stalin turned against the RIGHT OPPOSITION and in 1929 secured the expulsion of Bukharin, Rykov and Tomsky from the politburo. At the beginning of 1928 Stalin launched a policy of rapid industrialization under the first five-year plan, signaling the end of the NEP. Meanwhile, in the countryside a growing crisis over the withholding of grain supplies by the KULAKS (well-off peasant farmers who were generally hostile to government agricultural policy) prompted a government terror campaign in 1929–30, during which the kulaks were liquidated. These measures met with fierce resistance and caused massive disruption to agriculture, leading to widespread famine in 1932–33. During the 17th party congress in January 1934 there were suggestions that Stalin should be replaced by Sergei KIROV (the party leader in Leningrad). In December 1934 Kirov was assassinated (probably on Stalin's orders) and his death was made the pretext for a reign of terror which reached its height in 1936–38 (see GREAT PURGE). An estimated half a million people were executed and millions more were imprisoned (mostly without trial) in forced labor camps, while at show trials Stalin's former opponents in the party leadership (including Zinoviev, Kamenev, Bukharin and Rykov) were condemned to death after making obviously false confessions of treason and terrorism. Trotsky was also sentenced to death in absentia, and was murdered by a Soviet agent in Mexico in 1940. Severe political repressions lasted until Stalin's death in March 1953.

Unsuccessful Soviet attempts to form an alliance with Great Britain and France were followed by the signing in August 1939 of a non-aggression pact with Nazi Germany (see GERMAN–SOVIET NON-AGGRESSION PACT). On June 22, 1941, Germany violated the pact and invaded the Soviet Union, capturing vast territories and inflicting massive human and material damage in the European part of the country. The German armies were finally expelled in 1944 after a struggle in which about 20 million Soviet citizens lost their lives (see WORLD WAR II ON THE RUSSIAN FRONT). Soviet troops went on to liberate the nations of Eastern Europe, where Soviet-backed communist regimes took power; in 1955 the WARSAW PACT created a formal military alliance of the Soviet Union and these nations (except YUGOSLAVIA, which had broken with the Soviet Union in 1948). Meanwhile the wartime alliance with Great Britain, France and the U.S. was supplanted by the COLD WAR of mutual suspicion, hostility and a contest to achieve military supremacy.

On his death in 1953, Stalin was succeeded by a triumvirate comprising Georgi MALENKOV (Stalin's successor as prime minister and party leader), Vyacheslav MOLOTOV (the foreign minister) and Lavrenti BERIA (the notorious head of the SECRET POLICE). However, after little more than a week Malenkov was forced to relinquish the party leadership to Nikita KHRUSHCHEV, while Beria was expelled from the party in July 1953 and was later executed for treason. At the 20TH PARTY CONGRESS in February 1956, Khrushchev launched a bitter attack on Stalin's dictatorship and cult of personality. Later that year the U.S.S.R. sent troops into HUNGARY to crush the HUNGARIAN UPRISING. In the following year Malenkov, Molotov and Lazar KAGANOVICH attempted to depose Khrushchev, whereupon they were expelled from the party central committee (see ANTI-PARTY GROUP CRISIS). By the early 1960s Khrushchev's erratic domestic policies (including unworkable overhauls of regional administration and economic planning) and his unpredictable conduct of international relations (see CUBAN MISSILE CRISIS) were arousing strong opposition. In October 1964 his critics in the leadership engineered his replacement as party first secretary (later general secretary) by Leonid BREZHNEV, under whom Khrushchev's comparatively liberal policies were largely reversed and a limited degree of STALINISM was reimposed. After the Soviet invasion of CZECHOSLOVAKIA in 1968, the so-called BREZHNEV DOCTRINE enunciated the right of the Soviet Union to intervene in socialist countries where socialism was threatened; this doctrine was put into practice when Soviet troops entered AFGHANISTAN in 1979. Upon his death in November 1982, Brezhnev was succeeded by Yuri ANDROPOV both as party general secretary and president of the presidium of the Supreme Soviet (ceremonial head of state). Andropov introduced cautious economic reforms and a major anti-corruption campaign, and began to remove leading officials associated with Brezhnev, but he fell seriously ill after less than a year in office and died in February 1984. He was succeeded in both posts by Konstantin CHERNENKO, a conservative former Brezhnev protege. In the 13 months until Chernenko's death in March 1985, Andropov's limited reforms were continued, albeit at a more cautious pace and without any major new initiatives.

Mikhail GORBACHEV (at 54 the youngest member of the party politburo) was elected by the party central committee as Chernenko's successor on March 11, 1985. Formerly an Andropov protege, he immediately resumed the campaign to remove "Brezhnevite" officials and to root out corruption, leading to a massive turnover in the government and party leadership. Complaining that the economy had been stagnating since the 1970s, he announced a policy of complete PERESTROIKA ("restructuring"), to involve technical innovation, more efficient use of labor and materials, and managerial autonomy; subsequent initiatives introduced limited private enterprise, including private farming, and a reduction in central planning. However, by the end of 1990 this had failed significantly to improve economic performance. Perestroika in the economy was accomplished in the political and cultural spheres by the policy of GLASNOST ("openness"). Glasnost led to a freer press, official willingness to acknowledge unwelcome developments, a frequently damning reappraisal of Soviet history and greater tolerance of individual expression: by the end of 1988 virtually all political prisoners had been freed. However, the loosening of fetters on Soviet political life led to the unleashing of pent-up ethnic tensions. In February 1988 a dispute flared between Armenians and Azerbaijanis. Massive demonstrations and strikes gripped Armenia and Azerbaijan intermittently throughout 1988–89. Dur-

In the age of glasnost, Soviet citizens demonstrate for democratic reforms (Feb. 25, 1990).

UNION OF SOVIET SOCIALIST REPUBLICS

1917 Lenin and Bolsheviks seize power in October Revolution.

1918-21 Russian Civil War and period of War Communism.

1924 Death of Lenin.

1925-29 Stalin consolidates his power, expels key opponents from the Communist Party.

1928 Stalin launches first five-year plan for rapid industrialization.

1929 Trotsky forced into exile; Stalin begins campaign against the Kulaks.

1934 Assassination of Sergei Kirov.

1936-38 Stalin's Great Purge; millions executed or imprisoned.

1939 Soviet Foreign Minister Molotov and German Foreign Minister von Ribbentrop sign German–Soviet Non-Aggression Pact.

1940 U.S.S.R. annexes Latvia, Lithuania, Estonia.

1941 Germany invades the Soviet Union in World War II.

1941-44 Siege of Leningrad.

1942 Soviets stop Germans at battle of Stalingrad.

1943 Soviets defeat Germans in massive tank battle at Kursk.

1945 Soviets drive Germans out of Eastern Europe, occupy several Eastern European nations, including Poland, Czechoslovakia, Hungary; (April) Soviet troops link up with Americans on the Elbe River; (April-May) Soviets enter Berlin; end of World War II in Europe.

1948-49 Soviets close off West Berlin, precipitating Berlin Crisis; Allies respond with Berlin Airlift.

1953 Death of Stalin.

1955 Formation of Warsaw Pact, military alliance of communist Eastern bloc nations under U.S.S.R.

1956 Khrushchev condemns Stalin for "cult of personality" at 20th Party Congress; Soviets and Warsaw Pact troops invade Hungary to put down anticommunist uprising.

1957 (Oct. 4) U.S.S.R. becomes first nation to put artifical satellite into orbit with launch of *Sputnik 1*; (Nov. 3) Soviets launch the dog Laika into Earth orbit aboard *Sputnik 2*—first Earth creature in space.

1958 Boris Pasternak forced to repudiate Nobel Prize for literature.

1959 Soviet *Lunik III* spacecraft passes behind the moon, sends back first pictures of moon's far side.

1961 (Apr. 12) Soviet cosmonaut Yuri Gagarin becomes first human in space, making single Earth orbit aboard *Vostok 1*.

1962 (October) Cuban Missile Crisis—U.S.S.R. and U.S. on brink of nuclear war before U.S.S.R. backs down and removes ballistic missiles from Cuba.

1963 Nuclear Test Ban Treaty among the U.S., U.S.S.R. and Britain.

1964 Khrushchev removed from office, replaced by Brezhnev and Kosygin.

1968 (April) Soviet invasion of Czechoslovakia ends Prague Spring reforms; Brezhnev Doctrine signals that the U.S.S.R. will not tolerate deviation from hard-line communism among the Warsaw Pact nations.

1974 Novelist-historian Alexander Solzhenitsyn expelled from U.S.S.R. after publication of *The Gulag Archipelago*.

1975 Soviet Soyuz spacecraft links up with U.S. Apollo spacecraft, first joint U.S.-U.S.S.R. space venture.

1979 Brezhnev signs SALT II agreement with U.S. President Carter; Soviet invasion of Afghanistan.

1980 U.S. boycotts summer Olympic Games in Moscow in protest of Afghanistan invasion.

1982 (November) Brezhnev dies; succeeded by Yuri Andropov.

1984 (February) Andropov dies; succeeded by Konstantin Chernenko.

1985 (March) Chernenko dies; succeeded by Mikhail Gorbachev; beginning of glasnost and perestroika reforms.

1986 (April) Chernobyl nuclear power plant disaster.

1990-91 Gorbachev's economic reforms in trouble; secessionist movements in Lithuania, Georgia and elsewhere threaten to break apart the U.S.S.R.; Boris Yeltsin calls for Gorbachev's resignation; U.S.S.R. supports UN and U.S. action against Iraq; Warsaw Pact dissolved after Eastern European nations oust communist governments and restore democracy.

ing 1989 intercommunal violence and nationalist unrest erupted in other southern republics, notably Uzbekistan and Georgia. Also in 1988–89 ESTONIA, LATVIA and LITHUANIA witnessed a coalescence of the goals of unofficial nationalist agitation with official initiatives for greater autonomy: in all three republics the authorities permitted the establishment in October 1988 of independent movements which combined support for Gorbachev's reforms with radical autonomy programs and proposals for political pluralism, while the official initiatives featured unilateral declarations of the republics' "sovereignty" and open condemnation of their 1940 annexation by the Soviet Union.

Soviet foreign policy also changed under Gorbachev as he began a global diplomatic offensive. Four summit meetings between Gorbachev and U.S. president Ronald REAGAN culminated in May 1988 in the Treaty on Intermediate Nuclear Forces, providing for the elimination over a three-year period of all intermediate-range land-based nuclear weapons held by the Soviet Union and the U.S. Soviet

UNION OF SOVIET SOCIALIST REPUBLICS: LEADERS

1917-1924	V.I. Lenin
1924-1927	Collective leadership, with Joseph Stalin as central figure
1927-1953	Joseph Stalin
1953	Interim government led by Georgi Malenkov, Vyacheslav Molotov, Lavrenti Beria, Nikita Khrushchev
1953-1964	Nikita Khrushchev
1964-1982	Leonid Brezhnev, with Alexei Kosygin initially as joint leader
1982-1984	Yuri Andropov
1984-1985	Konstantin Chernenko
1985-	Mikhail Gorbachev

troops were withdrawn in full from Afghanistan by February 1989.

In accordance with constitutional amendments passed on December 1, 1988 elections were held in early 1989 for a new supreme representative body, the 2,250–member Congress of People's political groups and Baltic nationalists, and a rout of conservative party figures. When the Congress convened on May 25, 1989 it overwhelmingly elected Gorbachev to a new executive presidency. The work of the Congress and of a restyled Supreme Soviet, notably the freedom and contentiousness of debate, demonstrated a radical change in the conduct of Soviet politics. However, with increasing ethnic unrest, calls for greater economic reforms and new challenges to Gorbachev's authority (notably by popular communist reform politician Boris YELTSIN), Gorbachev seemed to retreat from his earlier emphasis on glasnost and perestroika and side with hard-line elements in the politburo. When Gorbachev demanded stronger powers, his foreign secretary, Edvard SCHEVARDNADZE (a leading figure in the reform wing of the party and widely respected in the West) resigned in protest. Early in 1991, in moves reminiscent of the earlier crackdowns on Hungary and Czechoslovakia, the U.S.S.R. used force to quell independence movements in LITHUANIA and ESTONIA. Soviet Georgia declared independence from the U.S.S.R. in April 1991, and a wave of strikes swept the republic despite Gorbachev's call for a one-year moratorium on strikes.

For further reading:

Dziewanowski, M. Kamil, *A History of Soviet Russia*, 3rd. ed. New York: Prentice Hall, 1989.

Hosking, Geoffrey A., *The Awakening of the Soviet Union*. Cambridge, Mass.: Harvard University Press, 1990.

Mantin, Peter, *From Romanov to Gorbachev: Russia in the 20th Century*. Chester Springs, Penn.: Dufour Editions, 1989.

Westwood, J.N., *Endurance and Endeavour: Russian History 1812–1986*. Oxford: Oxford University Press, 1987.

UNITA [National Union for the Total Independence of Angola]. A group fighting alongside the MPLA and FNLA between 1961 and 1975 to achieve Angolan independence (see ANGOLAN WAR OF INDEPENDENCE). Following independence in 1975, MPLA and UNITA set up rival governments. In the subsequent ANGOLAN CIVIL WAR, the South African-backed UNITA (led by Jonas SAVIMBI) and FNLA were defeated. In the late 1980s UNITA forces still controlled some areas of southern Angola. In 1989 there was evidence that UNITA forces had slaughtered thousands of elephants, using their ivory tusks to finance a continuation of the war.

Unitas, John Constantine (1933–). American football player. During a college career with a mediocre team, his personal numbers as quarterback were good enough for him to be drafted by the Pittsburgh Steelers. Let go by that team, Unitas turned to semi-pro ball until he

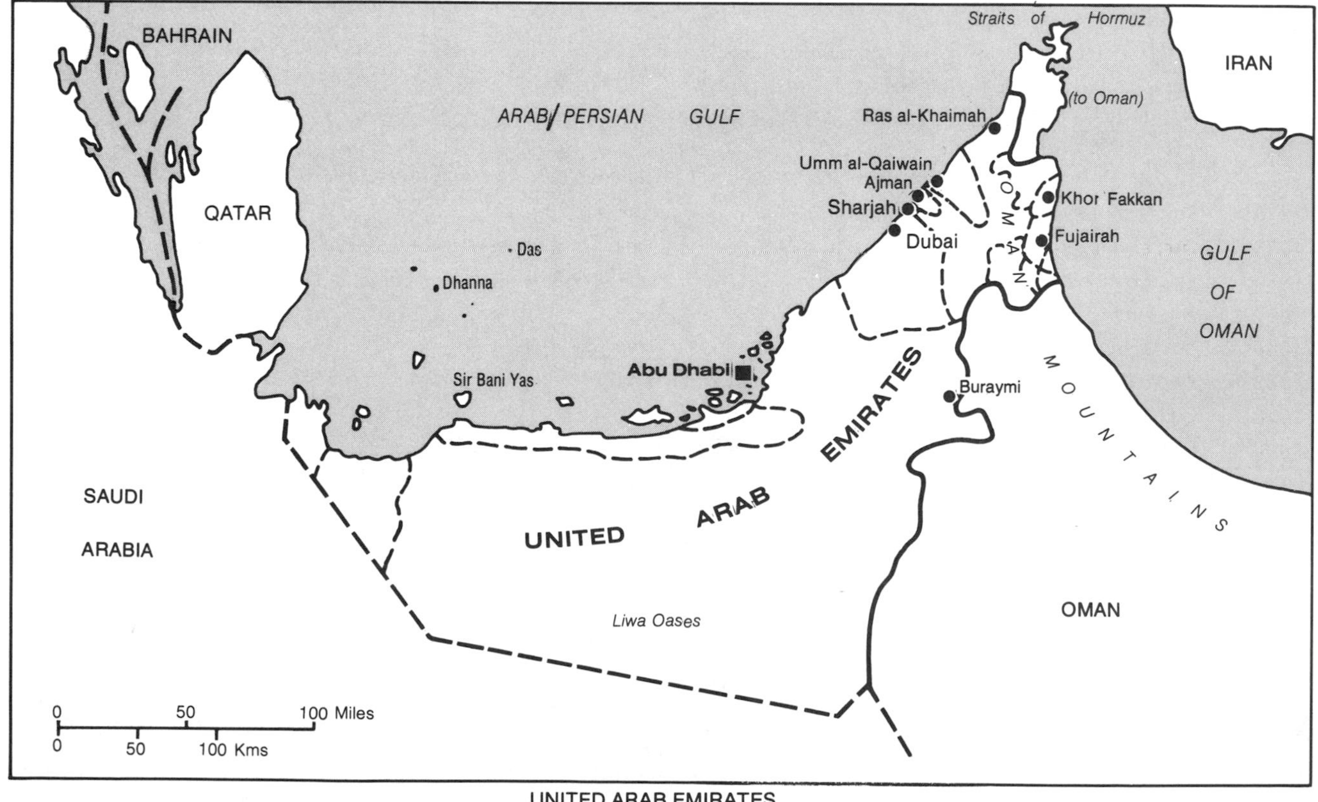

UNITED ARAB EMIRATES

was offered a slot on the roster of the Baltimore Colts in 1956. The following year, he was named the NFL's most valuable player. In 1958 he led the Colts to the league championship over the New York Giants. He finished his career with the San Diego Chargers, holding most passing records, including most consecutive games throwing for a touchdown, 47.

United Arab Emirates. A federation of seven emirates located along the east-central coast of the Arabian Peninsula; total area of 32,270 square miles. Until 1971 the emirates were British protectorates and were called the Trucial States. With independence in that year Abu Dhabi, Dubai, Sharjah, Ajman, Umn al-Qaiwain and Fugairah formed the United Arab Emirates. Ras al-Khaimah joined the federation in 1972. Territorial disputes with Saudi Arabia and Iran, with the latter country entering into armed conflict with Ras al-Khaimah for a period, were settled by 1974. The petroleum-rich sheikdoms of Abu Dhabi and Dubai have political predominance, causing some tensions with the other emirates.

United Artists. One of Hollywood's "Little Three" motion picture companies (along with COLUMBIA PICTURES and UNIVERSAL PICTURES). Founded in 1919 by four of the greatest names in the movies—Mary PICKFORD, Douglas FAIRBANKS Sr., Charles CHAPLIN and D.W. GRIFFITH—United Artists was the first company in which motion picture performers acquired complete autonomy over their work. As heads of their own respective production companies, they controlled all artistic, financial and promotional activities. They insisted each picture be sold and promoted individually, not as part of a package of films, which was the standard practice at the time. Some of the best known work of each member came from the first decade of the studio. Fairbanks turned exclusively to costume epics like *The Mark of Zorro* (1920) and *Robin Hood* (1923). Chaplin discontinued short comedies and turned to features like *The Gold Rush* (1925) and *The Circus* (1927). Mary Pickford turned from the "little girl" roles of *Pollyanna* (1920) to more mature roles in *Dorothy Vernon of Haddon Hall* (1925) and *The Taming of the Shrew* (1929). And Griffith, before his departure in 1924, made two of his most successful films, *Way Down East* (1920) and *Orphans of the Storm* (1922). In 1925 Joseph Schenck became the board chairman and an influx of new talent began releasing through the studio—Buster KEATON, Gloria SWANSON, and William S. Hart. A chain of theaters was organized in 1926, the United Artists Theatre Circuit, Inc., which gave the company guaranteed screenings. In the 1930s the company became increasingly a packager for the films of independent producers, Walter Wanger and David O. SELZNICK and, in London, Alexander KORDA. After some difficult times in the 1940s the studio went through a series of reorganizations. Then in retirement, Chaplin and Pickford sold off their stock in 1950. A syndicate took over until 1967 when TransAmerican Corporation bought the company. A merger with METRO-GOLDWYN-MAYER began in 1981. And five years later the conglomerate's film library was purchased for television by entrepreneur Ted TURNER. Notable films from the 1950 to 1990 period include *The African Queen* (1952), *High Noon* (1952), *Some Like It Hot* (1959), the James Bond films of the 1960s and *Rain Man* (1988).

For further reading:

Bergan, Ron, *The United Artists Story*. New York: Crown Publishers, 1986.

United Kingdom. The death of Queen Victoria (Jan. 22, 1901) and the accession of EDWARD VII ended an era in which Britain had projected self-confidence both at home and abroad. The foundation of the Labour Movement (Feb. 27, 1900) signaled that a new force, the urban proletariat, would be demanding a voice in Parliament. The budget was strained by foreign wars. The BOER WAR (1899–1902) in SOUTH AFRICA was controversial for the British use of mass internment in CONCENTRATION CAMPS to cut off the Boer soldiers from their support among the Afrikaner population.

As the LABOUR PARTY's strength grew at the polls, the Liberal government of Prime Minister Henry CAMPBELL-BANNERMAN introduced the first old-age pensions in 1908, unemployment insurance and labor exchanges in 1909, medical and limited unemployment insurance in 1911 and a limited working week in the same year, and a minimum wage for coal-miners in 1912. In 1905, after a bill to allow women the vote was defeated in Parliament, suffragettes were imprisoned for assaulting police. It was not until the Representation of People Act in 1917 that wives over 30 could vote—as well as all men over 21. In 1918 Parliament allowed for women MPs.

The Liberal Herbert ASQUITH, who succeeded Campbell-Bannerman as prime minister in 1908, attacked the power of the House of Lords. Asquith emerged in 1910 with a Liberal government dependent on Labour and Irish Nationalist support. The House of Lords accepted (by passing the Parliament Act in August 1911) strict limitations on its power to hold up the passage of legislation.

British governments began to accept the idea of Irish HOME RULE but faced a dilemma over Ulster, a largely Protestant province (see IRELAND; NORTHERN IRELAND). A Home Rule Bill was amended to exclude Ulster; it became law in September 1913. With world war impending, the government shelved the Irish issue. When Germany invaded Belgium, Britain declared war in response (Aug. 4, 1914). An all-party coalition government was formed under Asquith (May 1915), who was succeeded by David LLOYD GEORGE in December 1916. Parliament voted for conscription in January 1916. WORLD WAR I proved to be an exercise in futility and despair. Although Britain and her allies ultimately won the war, the human cost was staggering. Some 750,000 British troops died, along with 200,000 other soldiers from the BRITISH EMPIRE, a third of them Indian. The war cost Britain US $35 billion—more than any nation except Germany.

Lloyd George's postwar coalition faced a rising unemployment that reached 2.2 million by June 1921. The unemployment benefit was increased, and food and coal rationing was reintroduced. During the 1920s Britain faced a challenge in INDIA (where GANDHI launched massive campaigns of passive resistance); particularly volatile was the Middle East, where Britain and France had been awarded LEAGUE OF NATIONS mandates. The imperial conference of 1926 agreed that CANADA, AUSTRALIA, NEW ZEALAND, South Africa and NEWFOUNDLAND would be self-governing dominions, equal in status to Britain. In Ireland, the Free State compromise offered to the south in December 1921 extricated Britain from its attempt to sustain rule by martial law.

The wartime coalition ended when the CONSERVATIVE PARTY won the election of November 1922, and Labour, under Ramsay MACDONALD, became the official opposition. Prime Minister Andrew Bonar LAW was followed (May 1923) by Stanley BALDWIN, who lost an election (November 1923) over his pro-tariff policy. The first Labour government, with Liberal support, lasted just one year. Britain's first GENERAL STRIKE (May 3–12, 1926) rekindled class animosities. Ramsay MacDonald's second minority Labour government (June 1929–August 1931) maintained fiscal conservatism despite the international GREAT DEPRESSION. Unemployment topped 2,000,000. MacDonald backed draconian spending cuts, losing the support of his own party but surviving in 1931 as prime minister of an all-party NATIONAL GOVERNMENT. The austerity measures precipitated nationwide strikes and hunger marches. Faced with belligerent NAZISM in Germany and FASCISM in Italy, the government reversed its policy of cutting arms spending in November 1933. Stanley Baldwin led the Conservatives to a huge general election victory in November 1935, but his new government faced public outrage at appeasement of Italy over Abyssinia (see ITALO-ETHIOPIAN WAR OF 1935–36).

1936 began with the death of King GEORGE V and ended with a constitutional crisis that saw the abdication (Dec. 11, 1936) of his successor, EDWARD VIII, compelled to step down because he intended to marry divorcee Wallis Simpson (see Duchess of WINDSOR). In May 1937 GEORGE VI was crowned king, and Neville CHAMBERLAIN succeeded Baldwin as prime minister. The House of Commons in April 1938 approved a deal with France to defend CZECHOSLOVAKIA against a threatened German invasion. Chamberlain, however, clung to the belief that APPEASEMENT would avert war, and described as "peace in our time" his MUNICH PACT with HITLER (Sept. 30, 1938), allowing Germany to take over the SUDETENLAND.

COUNTIES OF ENGLAND
1. AVON
2. BEDFORDSHIRE
3. BERKSHIRE
4. BUCKINGHAMSHIRE
5. CAMBRIDGESHIRE
6. CHESHIRE
7. CLEVELAND
8. CORNWALL
9. CUMBRIA
10. DERBYSHIRE
11. DEVON
12. DORSET
13. DURHAM
14. EAST SUSSEX
15. ESSEX
16. GLOUCESTERSHIRE
17. GREATER LONDON
18. GREATER MANCHESTER
19. HAMPSHIRE
20. HEREFORD AND WORCESTER
21. HERTFORDSHIRE
22. HUMBERSIDE
23. ISLE OF WIGHT
24. ISLES OF SCILLY
25. KENT
26. LANCASHIRE
27. LEICESTERSHIRE
28. LINCOLNSHIRE
29. MERSEYSIDE
30. NORFOLK
31. NORTHAMPTONSHIRE
32. NORTHUMBERLAND
33. NORTH YORKSHIRE
34. NOTTINGHAMSHIRE
35. OXFORDSHIRE
36. SALOP
37. SOMERSET
38. SOUTH YORKSHIRE
39. STAFFORDSHIRE
40. SUFFOLK
41. SURREY
42. TYNE AND WEAR
43. WARWICKSHIRE
44. WEST MIDLANDS
45. WEST SUSSEX
46. WEST YORKSHIRE
47. WILTSHIRE

DISTRICTS OF NORTHERN IRELAND
1. ANTRIM
2. ARDS
3. ARMAGH
4. BALLYMENA
5. BALLYMONEY
6. BAINBRIDGE
7. BELFAST
8. CARRICKFERGUS
9. CASTLEREAGH
10. COLERAINE
11. COOKSTOWN
12. CRAIGAVON
13. DOWN
14. DUNGANNON
15. FERMANAGH
16. LARNE
17. LIMAVADY
18. LISBURN
19. LONDONDERRY
20. MAGHERAFELT
21. MOURNE
22. MOYLE
23. NEWTOWNABBEY
24. NORTH DOWN
25. OMAGH
26. STRABANE

REGIONS OF SCOTLAND
1. BORDERS
2. CENTRAL
3. DUMFRIES AND GALLOWAY
4. FIFE
5. GRAMPIAN
6. HIGHLAND
7. LOTHIAN
8. ORKNEY ISLANDS
9. SHETLAND ISLANDS
10. STRATHCLYDE
11. TAYSIDE
12. WESTERN ISLES

COUNTIES OF WALES
1. CLWYD
2. DYFED
3. GWENT
4. GWYNEDD
5. MID GLAMORGAN
6. POWYS
7. SOUTH GLAMORGAN
8. WEST GLAMORGAN

UNITED KINGDOM

When Hitler broke his promise by invading the rest of Czechoslovakia within six months, Britain formed a military pact with Poland and France (April 1939) and introduced conscription. When Germany and the U.S.S.R. signed a surprise nonaggression pact in August, Britain began evacuating children from her cities. Germany invaded Poland on September 1, and Britain entered WORLD WAR II on September 3.

Britain introduced food rationing, censorship and an Emergency Powers Act, banning strikes and commandeering goods. After failing to halt Germany's invasion of NORWAY, Chamberlain resigned in May 1940. Winston S. CHURCHILL became prime minister at the head of an all-party coalition government, offering "nothing but blood, toil, tears and sweat." After the evacuation of DUNKIRK, Britain stood alone against German aerial bombing of London, Coventry and other major cities. The RAF won what became known as the BATTLE OF BRITAIN, but the raids continued. By mid-1941 bombs were falling at a rate of up to 100,000 a night, and in two months 20,000 Londoners died. Women joined war work (compulsory for all in 1943). In 1944 German V-1 buzz-bombs began falling on England, but by then the tide had turned. In North Africa, General MONTGOMERY's Eighth Army had ended ROMMEL's German advance at EL ALAMEIN (see NORTH AFRICAN CAMPAIGN). The U.S. entered the war on the Allied side in December 1941, having already leased bases and lent arms to Britain; they had cemented their "special relationship" with the ATLANTIC CHARTER in August 1941. Britain became a virtual armed camp for Allied troops, preparing for the June 1944 invasion of Germany's FORTRESS EUROPE. The war cost half a million lives from Britain and the empire and Commonwealth.

Churchill called the first election since 1935, which he lost to Clement ATTLEE's Labour Party in a landslide victory (July 5, 1945). By 1946 the new Parliament had voted to nationalize the Bank of England, railways, ports, road haulage, civil aviation, coal, electricity, gas, atomic energy and finally steel. The NATIONAL HEALTH SERVICE (NHS) opened, along with National Insurance offices, in July 1948. The 1940s also saw Britain grant independence to India/Pakistan.

Pauperized by the war and the loss of its merchant fleet, in 1946 Britain accepted a 936-million-pound loan from the U.S., and reintroduced wartime rationing, some of which continued until the early 1950s. Britain was also helped by the U.S. MARSHALL PLAN. Britain began lifting manufacturing restrictions in 1948 but devalued the pound by 30% in September 1949. In October 1951 Churchill and the Tories returned to power, and in February 1952 King George VI died and was succeeded by his elder daughter, Queen ELIZABETH II. That same month Churchill revealed that Britain had the atom bomb. British troops enforced a defense pact and SUEZ CANAL agreement in

1952 and flew into KENYA in response to MAU MAU unrest.

Churchill handed over the leadership in April 1955 to Sir Anthony EDEN, who won a snap election. In 1956 Chancellor Harold MACMILLAN launched the tightest credit squeeze since 1931 to stifle inflation. When Nasser nationalized the Suez Canal in July 1956, Britain froze her Egyptian assets and arranged for a joint Anglo-French force to bombard Suez while Israel attacked from the north—but had to withdraw under U.S. pressure and the threat of a run on sterling (see SUEZ CRISIS). Eden resigned and handed the premiership to Macmillan in January 1957. Macmillan emphasized the U.K.-U.S. special relationship, accepting U.S. nuclear missiles in Britain. He introduced cheaper home loans and luxury taxes and opened the first motorway (1958). Overseas, he welcomed peaceful independence for Malaya (see MALAYSIA) but sent troops to quell unrest in CYPRUS and JORDAN. Macmillan promised independence to NIGERIA and Cyprus, and in February 1960 he delivered his WIND OF CHANGE speech, heralding a decade of decolonization on the African continent. Macmillan favored membership in a EUROPEAN FREE TRADE ASSOCIATION and continued preferential trade with the British COMMONWEALTH; in 1961 Britain applied to join the EUROPEAN ECONOMIC COMMUNITY, but France's President DE GAULLE vetoed the idea of British membership on special terms.

The government passed a stricter Commonwealth Immigrants Act in July 1962, to stem immigration from the Caribbean and Indian sub-continent. Following the

St. Paul's Cathedral shines gloriously amid the rubble of London during the Battle of Britain (1940).

UNITED KINGDOM

1899-1902	Boer War.
1900	Labour Party formed.
1901	Death of Queen Victoria.
1909	Liberal government introduces unemployment insurance.
1911	Reformation of the House of Lords.
1914-18	Nearly one million soldiers from the United Kingdom and British Empire killed in World War I; over two million wounded.
1916	(April) Easter Rebellion in Ireland put down by British troops.
1926	First nationwide general strike in Britain.
1936	Death of King George V; abdication crisis; Edward VIII gives up the throne to marry Wallis Warfield Simpson.
1938	Neville Chamberlain signs Munich Pact with Adolf Hitler, proclaims "peace in our time."
1939-45	World War II.
1940	(May 10) Winston Churchill becomes prime minister, pledges to fight until Nazi Germany is defeated; (May-June) 340,000 British troops evacuated from Dunkirk, France, as Germans advance; Royal Air Force (RAF) wins strategic victory over German Luftwaffe in Battle of Britain.
1945	Clement Attlee's Labour government begins to institute "Welfare State" and nationalize key industries.
1947	India granted independence.
1948	National Health Service begins operation.
1956	Suez Crisis—United Kingdom and France intervene in Arab-Israeli War, rebuffed by United States; Prime Minister Eden resigns.
1963	Profumo scandal leads to resignation of Prime Minister Harold Macmillan.
1969	British troops sent to Northern Ireland to restore order between Catholic and Protestant communities.
1972	Britain joins European Economic Community.
1978-79	"Winter of Discontent"—widespread labor strikes lead to defeat of Callaghan's Labour government in general election (May 3, 1979); Margaret Thatcher becomes Britain's first woman prime minister, initiates radical conservative policies.
1981	Four leading politicians leave Labour Party to found moderate Social Democratic Party.
1982	Argentina seizes Falkland Islands; British convoy sails to Falklands, defeats Argentinians.
1983	Prime Minister Thatcher reelected.
1984	IRA bombs Brighton hotel in attempt to kill Thatcher and cabinet members.
1985	Britain and Ireland sign Anglo-Irish Accord ("Hillsborough Agreement") as framework for solution to Northern Ireland problem.
1987	Liberal Party and Social Democratic Party merge, forming Liberal Democrats; Thatcher wins reelection.
1990	Unpopular community charge (poll tax) replaces local rates (property taxes) in England and Wales, leading to protests and rioting; Thatcher forced to resign over European issue; British forces sent to Saudi Arabia as part of UN coalition against Saddam Hussein.
1991	British air and ground forces participate in Operation Desert Storm to oust Iran from Kuwait in Persian Gulf War;

UNITED KINGDOM: MONARCHS

1837-1901	Victoria
1901-1910	Edward VII
1910-1936	George V
1936	Edward VIII
1936-1952	George VI
1952-	Elizabeth II

PROFUMO AFFAIR, Macmillan resigned in favor of Sir Alec DOUGLAS-HOME. Labour under Harold WILSON narrowly won the general election in October 1964. Committed to a national economic plan, Wilson faced immediate crises; he raised income tax, set an import tax and borrowed more than a billion pounds. Labour greatly increased its majority in the 1966 election, and a huge majority of MPs supported Wilson's new application for EEC membership, but De Gaulle dismissed it (May 16, 1967). After an influx of East African Asians with British passports in 1968, Enoch POWELL's "rivers of blood" speech (April 21, 1968) condemned immigration. In August 1969, British troops were sent to Northern Ireland to restore order after sectarian rioting broke out between Catholics and Protestants.

The Conservatives under Edward HEATH were elected in June 1970. After a year of Heath's leadership, strikes were at their highest level since 1926, with 8.8 million working days lost. In 1971 the first British soldier died in Northern Ireland. The new radical "provisional" wing of the IRA started a terror campaign against British troops. IRA members were interned and all marches banned. The IRA began a series of bombings in Britain itself. Conversion to decimal currency (Feb. 15, 1971) came amid rising unemployment and inflation. Britain joined the EEC (Jan. 22, 1972) after getting special terms for certain Commonwealth products. After the IRA bombed a British Army base at Aldershot, England, Heath imposed direct rule on Ulster (March-April 1972). In November 1973 new Arab oil price increases forced petrol rationing. An election, called for March 1974, returned Harold Wilson to office. He conceded almost all the demands of striking miners. As 1974 ended, inflation stood at 26%; a budget raised the VAT and initiated defense spending cuts. In February 1975 Margaret THATCHER ousted Heath as Tory leader, becoming the first woman to head a British political party. A North Sea oil pipeline came into operation. By March 1977 Labour needed Liberal support to stave off a no-confidence vote and formed the so-called "Lib-Lab Pact." The **social contract** between unions and government collapsed as unions condemned the incomes policy and sought higher wage deals. Fresh strikes hit Britain in the **winter of discontent** of early 1979. A general election in May 1979 was won by the Tories with a majority of 43 seats.

New Prime Minister Thatcher vowed to take a tougher line with the IRA after the assassination of Lord MOUNTBATTEN (Aug. 27, 1979). RHODESIA's 14 years of unilaterally declared independence ended in the Lancaster House peace deal signed in London (Dec. 21, 1979). The stationing of American CRUISE MISSILES in Britain prompted the biggest nuclear disarmament protests in 20 years. Oil price rises fueled inflation, and, by squeezing the money supply, Thatcher caused industrial retrenchment. By August 1980 two million were out of work. Thatcher outlined her PRIVATIZATION policy: selling off nationalized industries, starting with British Aerospace and proceeding over the next decade with British Gas, Electricity, British Telecommunications, British Steel and the water boards. A new share-owning democracy would at one stroke break class barriers and boost government revenue. In January 1981, four senior politicians resigned from the Labour Party and started the SOCIAL DEMOCRATIC PARTY, which subsequently formed an electoral alliance with the Liberal Party. In Ulster in May 1981 there were riots in Belfast in protest at the death by hunger strike of IRA member Bobby Sands. But most eyes were fixed on the wedding of Prince CHARLES to Lady Diana Spencer (July 29, 1981).

By January 1982 unemployment topped three million. The government recovered its popularity with the British victory in the FALKLAND ISLANDS WAR. On June 10, 1983, the electorate returned Thatcher with a 144–seat majority. A bitter one-year miners' strike (March 1984–March 1985) saw half the pits shut down, police clashing with pickets, and union funds sequestrated by the courts. In October 1984 an IRA bomb intended to kill the whole cabinet exploded in a Brighton hotel (see BRIGHTON BOMBING). In May 1985 two football disasters, the Bradford fire (over 40 dead) and the Heysel stadium rampage (38 dead), shocked the nation. The November 1985 Anglo-Irish accord gave

UNITED KINGDOM: PRIME MINISTERS

1895-1902	Robert Gascoyne-Cecil, Lord Salisbury (Conservative)
1902-1905	Arthur James Balfour (Conservative)
1905-1908	Henry Campbell-Bannerman (Liberal)
1908-1916	Herbert Asquith (Liberal; wartime coalition 1915-16)
1916-1922	David Lloyd George (Liberal; wartime coalition 1916-18)
1922-1923	Andrew Bonar Law (Conservative)
1923-1924	Stanley Baldwin (Conservative)
1924	Ramsay MacDonald (Labour; coalition with Liberals)
1924-1929	Stanley Baldwin (Conservative)
1929-1935	Ramsay MacDonald (Labour; national coalition 1931-35)
1935-1937	Stanley Baldwin (Conservative; national coalition 1935)
1937-1940	Neville Chamberlain (Conservative)
1940-1945	Winston Churchill (Conservative; wartime coalition)
1945-1951	Clement Attlee (Labour)
1951-1955	Winston Churchill (Conservative)
1955-1957	Anthony Eden (Conservative)
1957-1963	Harold Macmillan (Conservative)
1963-1964	Alec Douglas-Home (Conservative)
1964-1970	Harold Wilson (Labour)
1970-1974	Edward Heath (Conservative)
1974-1976	Harold Wilson (Labour)
1976-1979	James Callaghan (Labour)
1979-1990	Margaret Thatcher (Conservative)
1990-	John Major (Conservative)

Eire a role in Northern Ireland (see HILLSBOROUGH ACCORD).

The Anglo-French ENGLISH CHANNEL TUNNEL got the go-ahead in 1986. In June 1987 the Tories were elected for a third time, and the SDP-Liberal Alliance broke down in failure; the SDP and Liberals subsequently merged as the Liberal Democrats. In 1988 the trade deficit deepened while house prices soared. An airliner (PAN AM 103) crashed over Lockerbie in Scotland on Dec. 21, the victim of international terrorism. During 1990 protests, sometimes violent, occurred throughout England in response to the introduction of a controversial "community charge" or poll tax to fund local government. In autumn 1990, Mrs. Thatcher was forced to resign after disagreements with her cabinet over the proposed European Monetary Union (see EUROPEAN MONETARY SYSTEM); she claimed that the new European integration scheduled for 1992 could threaten parliamentary sovereignty. Thatcher was replaced by Chancellor of the Exchequer John MAJOR, who promised to review the poll tax. Britain strongly supported the allied coalition in the PERSIAN GULF WAR, and British forces played a significant role in the fighting.

For further reading:

Havighurst, Alfred F., *Britain in Transition: The Twentieth Century*, 4th ed. Chicago, Ill.: University of Chicago Press, 1985.

Lloyd, T.O., *Empire to Welfare State: English History, 1906–1985*, 3rd ed., rev. Oxford: Oxford University Press, 1986.

Oxbury, Harold, ed., *Great Britons: Twentieth-Century Lives*. Oxford: Oxford University Press, 1985.

Taylor, A.J.P., *English History, 1914–1945*, reissue. Oxford: Oxford University Press, 1985.

United Nations (UN). International organization formed after WORLD WAR II as a successor to the largely discredited LEAGUE OF NATIONS. It was officially founded on October 24, 1945, when the UN charter was ratified by its 51 original members meeting in San Francisco. In general, the organization aims at the elimination of war and the promotion of international cooperation, human rights and freedom. By the beginning of the 1990s, the UN had 160 member states. The principal organizational components of the United Nations are six: the Security Council, General Assembly, Economic and Social Council, Trusteeship Council, International Court of Justice, and the Secretariat. In addition, there are a number of specialized agencies that deal with a multitude of social, economic and political issues.

All the principal organs of the UN have their headquarters in New York, with the exception of the International Court, which is situated in The Hague. The Security Council has a membership of 15: the permanent "Big Five" (China, France, U.K., U.S.S.R., U.S.) and ten others chosen by the General Assembly for two-year terms. The Security Council has the main responsibility for maintaining international peace through its recommendations and actions that include economic sanctions and military efforts. Important decisions require a nine-vote majority, and vetoes by the Big Five are permitted. The General Assembly is made up of all UN member states and is the organization's main deliberative body. It can make recommendations but cannot compel any actions. Important decisions require a two-thirds majority. The Economic and Social Council has 54 members, elected to three-year terms by the General Assembly. It deals with economic and social questions and reports to the assembly and other organs. The council also coordinates specialized agencies and initiates activities relating to such issues as trade, human rights, population control, the status of women and social welfare.

The Trusteeship Council oversees non-self-governing territories that were previously governed under League of Nations mandates and others formed since then. It includes representatives of the administering states, representatives from the Security Council and other elected members. The International Court of Justice, which superseded the World Court, consists of 15 judges selected by the General Assembly and Security Council who serve nine-year terms. The court renders judgments on disputes between member nations but has only a limited jurisdiction. It also issues advisory opinions. The Secretariat is the UN's administrative body; with a large staff, it is headed by a secretary-general. These have been: Trygve LIE (1945–53), Dag HAMMARSKJOLD (1953–61), U THANT (1961–72), Kurt WALDHEIM (1972–81) and Javier PEREZ DE CUELLAR (1982–). The Secretariat's varied work includes studying and reporting on international trends in politics and economics, mediating international disputes, administering UN peacekeeping activities, organizing conferences, compiling statistics and bringing appropriate international situations to the attention of the UN's many specialized agencies. These agencies include the Food and Agriculture Organization, General Agreement on Tariffs and Trades, International Atomic Energy Agency, International Development Association, International Monetary Fund and WORLD HEALTH ORGANIZATION. Among the UN's many other agencies are the UNITED NATION'S CHILDREN'S FUND (UNICEF), the Conference on Trade and Development, and the High Commission for Refugees.

Early hopes for international accord were largely shattered by the coming of the COLD WAR, which split the international community and the UN into two warring camps and rendered many of the organization's efforts ineffective. With the waning of the Cold War and the increase in the UN's THIRD WORLD membership, the balance of power in the organization has also tended to shift away from the U.S. and the U.S.S.R., which dominated the organization's first decades.

United Nations Children's Fund [UNICEF]. Children's relief arm of the UNITED NATIONS. The United Nations Children's Fund was originally established in 1946 as the United Nations International Children's Emergency Fund by the UN General Assembly to aid the approximately 20 million European children suffering in the aftermath of WORLD WAR II. Under its first executive director, the American, Maurice Pate, UNICEF spent some $112 million distributing clothing, food and medical care, and rebuilding food production and distribution facilities. In 1950 UNICEF began to turn its attention toward long-term programs for children's welfare in developing countries as well, and in 1953 was reorganized and renamed, though the well-known acronym was maintained. It has continued to provide nutritional, medical and educational materials to children and their mothers worldwide. UNICEF is funded by voluntary contributions, mostly from member nations. Additional funds come from charitable organizations and the sale of UNICEF holiday cards. UNICEF has its headquarters in the UN complex in New York City, and some thirty regional offices in Europe, North and South American, Asia and Africa.

United Nations Educational, Scientific and Cultural Organization [UNESCO]. UNESCO was established by the United Nations General Assembly in 1946 to promote cultural contact and understanding between member countries, and to encourage scientific and educational collaboration among them. Due to a perceived anti-Western bias, the U.S. withdrew from UNESCO in 1984. The BUSH administration upheld the U.S. withdrawal in 1990, citing UNESCO's poor management and refusal to defend freedom of the press. UNESCO is headquartered in Paris, FRANCE.

United Nations Relief and Rehabilitation Administration [U.N.R.R.A.]. The United Nations Relief and Rehabilitation Administration was formed in 1943, during the WORLD WAR II, when the term "United Nations" referred to the anti-Axis Allies. It was established to assist in reconstruction and rehabilitating refugees at the end of the war. Between 1943 and 1949, U.N.R.R.A. spent approximately 600 million pounds on relief work worldwide, three-quarters of which funding came from the U.S. Following the implementation of the MARSHALL PLAN, U.N.R.R.A.'s diversified programs were taken up by other specialized agencies, such as UNICEF, the WORLD HEALTH ORGANIZATION and OXFAM, and it was dissolved in 1949.

United Press International (UPI). American news agency; formed in 1958 by the merger of the United Press, begun in 1907, and International News Service, founded in 1909. In 1907, E.W. Scripps established United Press by merging the Scripps-McRae Press Association, Scripps News Association and Publishers' Press Association. Unlike AP, its competition, UPI was a profitmaking service that anyone could buy. In its early days, telegraphers transcribed Morse code coming over the wire on typewriters. UP established many foreign bureaus, and by 1914 some 200 newspapers subscribed to the service. In 1982, the E.W. Scripps Co. sold UPI to the Media News Corporation of Nashville, Tennessee. UPI has almost 6,500 subscribers worldwide, and its staff of over 10,000 in 235 news bureaus transmits about 4.5 million words of copy a day.

United States of America. By the end of the 19th century, the U.S. had become a leading economic power. The Spanish-American War of 1898 catapulted the U.S. out of its isolationism and into European-dominated international affairs. The war left it a major power in the Caribbean and in the Pacific, with the acquisition of Puerto Rico, Guam and the Philippines and effective control of the island of Cuba. America's expansion outside the continental U.S. continued with the opening of the PANAMA CANAL in 1914 and the purchase of the Danish Virgin Islands in 1916. During the same period, the U.S. formulated its Open Door policy toward China, which was designed to force Europeans to accept American businessmen on an equal footing.

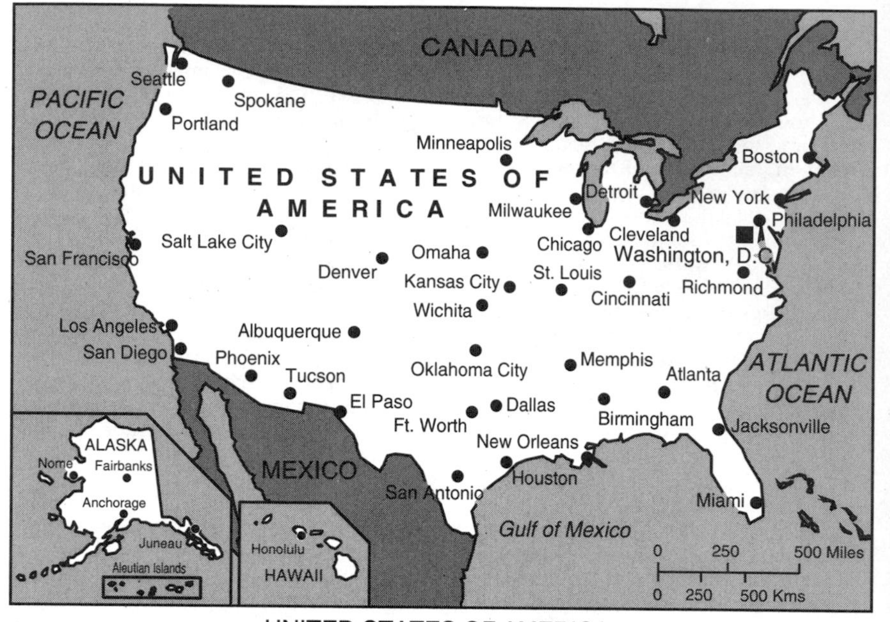

UNITED STATES OF AMERICA

When WORLD WAR I broke out in Europe in 1914, the vast majority of Americans were in favor of staying neutral. President Woodrow WILSON reflected these sentiments and spent the first three years of the war trying to mediate between Britain and Germany and keep America out of the war. But the German decision in January 1917 to launch an out-out submarine attack against neutral shipping led to the U.S. entering the war on the Allied side. The infusion of 1,250,000 American soldiers was an important factor in defeating the German Western Offensive that began in March 1918, after which Germany was forced to accept an armistice. At the subsequent PARIS PEACE CONFERENCE, Wilson dominated the negotiations with his FOURTEEN POINTS. The idealism of Wilson's position was undermined by the Allies' desire to exact vengeance upon their defeated enemies and by the failure of the U.S. Senate to ratify the treaty (and so join the LEAGUE OF NATIONS).

The immediate postwar years saw a short depression, but by 1925 the economy was booming. Throughout the 1920s industrial production increased by 50%. The growth was stimulated by the laissez-faire economic policies of the administrations of Presidents Warren HARDING (1921–23) and Calvin COOLIDGE (1923–29). But this unbridled growth also encouraged rampant speculation, and in October 1929 the New York stock market collapsed (see STOCK MARKET CRASH OF 1929; GREAT DEPRESSION). Republican President HOOVER attempted some remedial action but was hampered by his commitment to laissez-faire economics. In 1932, Democrat Franklin D. ROOSEVELT, who promised a NEW DEAL of unprecedented government intervention to bring the U.S. out of the Depression, was elected president. In his first HUNDRED DAYS in office, Roosevelt sent Congress bills that created the TENNESSEE VALLEY AUTHORITY, unemployment relief, banking reforms, an agricultural recovery program, federal supervision of investment securities and prevented the foreclosure of mortgages on private homes. This legislation was later followed by the SOCIAL SECURITY ACT and the Fair Labor Standards Act, which established a minimum wage. The New Deal did much to alleviate the personal hardships of the Depression but failed to correct the structural weaknesses that had created it and were eventually to be eliminated only by the outbreak of WORLD WAR II in Europe.

Renewed hostilities between Britain and Germany forced Britain to turn again to the U.S. for capital and defense material, which was made available on generous terms under the LEND-LEASE Act (1941). The U.S. entered the war on Dec. 7, 1941, after the Japanese bombed the U.S. Pacific fleet at PEARL HARBOR. The U.S. played a much larger role in World War II than it had in World War I. An estimated 16 million men and women went into uniform. They fought in North Africa, Western Europe, Asia and the Pacific. Factory output doubled, with the result that the U.S. produced 196,400 aeroplanes, 6,500 naval vessels and 86,300 tanks. World War II also saw the American development of the ATOMIC BOMB, which would come to dominate international relations in the postwar period.

Roosevelt died on Apr. 12, 1945, and was succeeded by Vice President Harry S TRUMAN, who ordered the dropping of atomic bombs on HIROSHIMA and NAGASAKI to end the war in the Pacific. The relationship between the Western Allies and the Soviet Union had been deteriorating; efforts to find common ground, such as the YALTA CONFERENCE (1945), were only partially successful. Disputes broke out in Eastern Europe and in Korea over the political complexion of governments to be installed in the liberated territories. This antipathy developed into the COLD WAR as the U.S. and the Soviet Union each sought to prevent the other from extending its influence. The MARSHALL PLAN revitalized Western European economies with American aid. The 1949 formation of the NORTH ATLANTIC TREATY ORGANIZATION (NATO) committed the U.S. to the defense of Western Europe and eventually led to over 300,000 American troops being permanently based in Europe.

In Asia, the Chinese communists led by MAO TSE-TUNG drove CHIANG KAI-SHEK off the mainland of China to the island of Taiwan, where he established a government-in-exile. On the advice of his diplomats, President Truman refused to throw full American military support behind Chiang. This led to later accusations that Truman and various American diplomats had "lost" China.

In the charged anticommunist atmosphere of the late 1940s and early 1950s, Americans were prepared to believe that the success of the Chinese communists was part of a global strategy orchestrated by the Soviet Union with the aid of disloyal Americans. The loss of China also encouraged Truman and successive presidents to take an increasingly interventionist line in Asian affairs. This led to the KOREAN WAR (1950–53), support for the French in their Indochina War (1946–54) and, finally, the VIETNAM WAR (1964–75). In Europe, some of the major Cold War crises were the Berlin Blockade of 1948 and the Berlin crises of 1953 and 1961, the year of the erection of the BERLIN WALL. Fear of the Soviet Union spilled over into domestic politics with the rise of demagogic Senator Joseph MCCARTHY. In September 1949, the Soviet Union exploded its first atomic bomb. The U.S.

UNITED STATES

1901 McKinley assassinated; Cuba made U.S. protectorate.

1905 Theodore Roosevelt makes first trip outside U.S. by a sitting president—to Panama Canal Zone.

1908 Ford Motor Co. builds first Model T.

1914 Wilson proclaims neutrality in Europe; Marines enter Vera Cruz, Mexico.

1915 First transcontinental phone call.

1917 War declared on Germany.

1918 Battle of the Meuse-Argonne; Wilson issues 14 points for world peace; armistice signed.

1919 Prohibition ratified.

1920 Harding defeats Cox; *Main Street* by Sinclair Lewis published.

1923 Teapot Dome scandal begins to unfold.

1929 Stock market crash begins Great Depression.

1932 Franklin D. Roosevelt elected to first of four terms.

1933 Prohibition repealed; Roosevelt sets up New Deal programs for economic recovery.

1936 Boulder Dam completed; auto workers gain power through sit-down strikes.

1938 Self-propelled combine introduced; leads to massive grain harvests.

1940 Lend-Lease program sends war materiel to Britain; first peacetime draft.

1941 Pearl Harbor attacked; war declared on Axis powers; war industries boost economy.

1942 Battle of Midway turns tide of war in Pacific.

1944 D-day; invasion of Normandy signals coming defeat for Germany.

1945 Atomic bombs used against Japan; Axis powers surrender; Roosevelt dies and is succeeded by Truman.

1948 Marshall Plan and Berlin Airlift aid postwar Europe.

1949 NATO founded to confront Soviets.

1950 U.S. troops oppose North Korean invasion of South Korea; Senator Joseph McCarthy begins investigation of communists in government.

1952 Eisenhower elected.

1953 Armistice in Korea; Julius and Ethel Rosenberg executed as Soviet spies.

1954 First private nuclear power plant begins construction; Elvis Presley records "Don't Be Cruel."

1960 Kennedy elected; U-2 spy plane shot down over U.S.S.R.

1962 Nation faces nuclear war in Cuban missile crisis; John Glenn orbits Earth.

1963 Kennedy assassinated; Johnson assumes presidency.

1964 Gulf of Tonkin Resolution passed; Vietnam buildup begins; Civil Rights Act passed; Martin Luther King Jr. wins Nobel Prize for peace.

1968 Nixon elected; riots destroy inner cities after Martin Luther King Jr. assassinated; Robert F. Kennedy assassinated.

1969 Apollo 11 makes first moon landing; Woodstock music festival celebrates the "counterculture."

1970 Student protesters killed by troops at Jackson State and Kent State.

1972 Nixon reelected in landslide; visits China; Watergate break-in.

1973 Vice President Agnew indicted; oil prices skyrocket.

1974 Nixon resigns to avoid impeachment; Patty Hearst kidnapped by Symbionese Liberation Army.

1975 Fall of Saigon ends Vietnam War.

1976 Jimmy Carter upsets Gerald Ford in presidential election.

1978 Carter mediates Camp David Accord between Israel and Egypt.

1981 American hostages in Teheran released minutes after Reagan inaugurated.

1983 Two hundred forty-one marines killed in Lebanon bombing; AIDS epidemic sweeps nation; invasion of Grenada.

1987 Congressional hearings on sale of arms to Iran and illegal aid to Contra rebels; "Just Say No" campaign against drugs.

1988 George Bush elected; power of Soviet Union reduced by internal disorder.

1990 Massive scandal in savings and loan industry unfolds; Michael Milken imprisoned for illegal stock trading; Bush gives ultimatum to Iraqi invaders of Kuwait; begins huge troop buildup.

1991 U.S.-led forces invade Iraq; create new balance of power in Middle East.

UNITED STATES: PRESIDENTS

1897-1901	William McKinley (Republican)
1901-1909	Theodore Roosevelt (Republican)
1909-1913	William Howard Taft (Republican)
1913-1921	Woodrow Wilson (Democrat)
1921-1923	Warren G. Harding (Republican)
1923-1929	Calvin Coolidge (Republican)
1929-1933	Herbert Hoover (Republican)
1933-1945	Franklin D. Roosevelt (Democrat)
1945-1953	Harry S. Truman (Democrat)
1953-1961	Dwight D. Eisenhower (Republican)
1961-1963	John F. Kennedy (Democrat)
1963-1969	Lyndon Baines Johnson (Democrat)
1969-1974	Richard M. Nixon (Republican)
1974-1977	Gerald R. Ford (Republican)
1977-1981	James Earl Carter (Democrat)
1981-1989	Ronald Reagan (Republican)
1989-	George Bush (Republican)

responded with the development of the HYDROGEN BOMB, which the U.S.S.R. quickly matched. The two countries then competed in developing the quantity and quality of nuclear weapons and delivery systems as well as increasingly expensive conventional forces.

Truman was succeeded by Republican Dwight D. EISENHOWER (1953–61), who adopted a laissez-faire policy toward the economy. Government intervention increased under the successive Democratic administrations of John F. KENNEDY (1961–63) and Lyndon B. JOHNSON (1963–69). By the time of the Johnson administration, the economy was beginning to feel the strain of heavy defense expenditures and expanded social spending. Another source of concern was the lack of CIVIL RIGHTS for American blacks. In 1954, the U.S. Supreme Court ruled that racial segregation in public schools was unconstitutional. The black community embarked on a campaign of civil disobedience to secure its constitutional rights. The civil disobedience erupted into race riots in the 1960s and eventually led to passage of the CIVIL RIGHTS ACT (1964). But the deep-seated prejudices of some white Americans were underscored by the assassination of Martin Luther KING Jr. in April 1968.

Throughout the first 20 years of the postwar period, the U.S. based its claim to world leadership on a superior New World morality. President Kennedy's assassination in November 1963 shocked the world and to some extent marked the end of these illusions. The death of Kennedy was quickly followed by the VIETNAM WAR, which seriously split American society (see ANTIWAR MOVEMENT). In 1964 Congress passed the TONKIN GULF RESOLUTION authorizing the president to take whatever steps were necessary to prosecute the war, which the U.S. had been supporting in a limited capacity. Over 541,000 U.S. troops saw combat. Under President NIXON, the troops were gradually withdrawn. Although it was the South Vietnamese who lost Saigon and the war in 1975, official casualty figures revealed that 46,079 Americans had earlier been killed and 303,640 wounded. Public opposition to the war was fueled by reports of atrocities such as the MY LAI MASSACRE of Vietnamese civilians (1969).

In 1972 the Democratic Party's Washington, D.C., campaign headquarters was burgled by a team hired by the campaign committee of President Nixon. The subsequent investigation led to the WATERGATE scandal and Nixon's resignation in August 1974. While Nixon's handling of Watergate was deemed reprehensible, his foreign policy marked America's coming of age as a superpower. Under the direction of Henry KISSINGER, the U.S. adopted a realpolitik approach to foreign affairs. Nixon paid a historic visit to China (1972) and developed a working relationship with the Soviet Union, which became known as detente. Diplomatic relations with China were eventually established in 1979. At the same time, suspicion grew of U.S. covert involvement in attempts to destablize or overthrow left-wing regimes, notably in CHILE and in ANGOLA. Part of the reason for improved relations with the communist bloc was a more complex, multipolar system of conflicting national aspirations. U.S. dominance of the world's economy was challenged by the growing power of the EUROPEAN ECONOMIC COMMUNITY and Japan, and the emerging nations of Asia and Africa were establishing governments and pursuing policies that failed to fit into the capitalist-versus-communist formula. Nixon was succeeded by Vice President Gerald FORD (1974–77), who retained Kissinger as secretary of state and maintained his predecessor's foreign and domestic policies. In 1976 Jimmy CARTER was elected president. Carter offered a fresh face and unblemished past to an American electorate seeking a politician untainted by Vietnam or the discredited Washington power circles. Although he scored a notable foreign-policy success with the conclusion of the U.S.-sponsored Egyptian-Israeli CAMP DAVID agreement (1978), he was humiliated by the seizure of American hostages in Teheran in 1979 (see IRAN HOSTAGE CRISIS).

In 1980, former film actor Ronald REAGAN was elected president. For many Americans, Reagan and his policies typified basic national values that predated the Roosevelt years. On domestic issues, he stressed the importance of family, thrift and industriousness. In foreign affairs, he took a tough anti-Soviet position and backed this up with increased defense spending. Reagan secured public support for these policies with a relaxed manner and a series of televised homespun homilies that struck a basic chord with the American public. Toward the end of his term, the administration held summit meetings between Reagan and Mikhail GORBACHEV at Geneva (1985), Reykjavik (1986) and Washington (1987). Congress had become unwilling to fund Reagan's proxy crusade against NICARAGUA's left-wing Sandinista government. The upshot was the uncovering of what became known as the IRAN-CONTRA SCANDAL (November 1986), implicating several National Security Agency officials. Less convoluted was U.S. hostility toward LIBYA, whose leader, Col. QADAFFI, the administration held responsible for supporting acts of terrorism in the Middle East.

Reagan was succeeded by Vice President George BUSH, who defeated Democratic contender Michael DUKAKIS in the 1988 elections. Bush was faced with the continuing American budget deficit, international financial instability, and the lack of a clear response to the wave of liberalization within communist regimes. After IRAQ invaded KUWAIT (Aug. 2, 1990), Bush sent several hundred thousand U.S. troops to protect Saudi Arabia in **Operation Desert Shield**. He mobilized world opinion and persuaded the UN to support joint international action to drive Iraq from Kuwait. American forces launched **Operation Desert Storm,** the largest U.S. military operation since the Vietnam War, on January 16, 1991, bombing numerous military targets in Iraq. A wave of patriotism swept the U.S.; Iraq was handily defeated in February. However, the U.S. recession continued and other international problems followed in the wake of the war.

For further reading:

Contosta, David R., *America in the Twentieth Century: Coming of Age.* New York: HarperCollins, 1987.

Evans, Harold, *The American Century: 1890–1990.* New York: Bantam, 1990.

Freidel, Frank, *America in the Twentieth Century*, 5th, rev. ed. New York: Knopf, 1982.

United States v. Butler (1936). U.S. Supreme Court decision ruling that the New Deal's AGRICULTURAL ADJUSTMENT ACT was unconstitutional. President Franklin D. ROOSEVELT'S NEW DEAL program attempted to have the federal government regulate agriculture through a system of subsidies and production quotas. Farmers would be paid subsidies if they reduced their production—with the goal of stabilizing production and commodity prices. The farm subsidies were to be financed out of a tax on food processors.

The Supreme Court struck down the act as unconstitutional because the federal government had no power to regulate agriculture, a purely local activity. Additionally, the Court reasoned that the tax was unlawful because its purpose was regulation rather than revenue-raising. The decision was a major blow to the New Deal program. The Supreme Court later reversed itself and upheld federal price supports and regulation of agriculture, even when the farm products were raised and sold within one state.

United States v. Curtiss-Wright Export Corp. (1936). U.S. Supreme Court decision granting the president almost unlimited power in the field of foreign affairs. Congress had granted the president the right to embargo arms shipments to countries at war in South America. The statute was attacked as an illegal delegation of congressional power to the president. However, the Supreme Court upheld the delegation, holding that Congress had the power to vest a great deal of power in the president to conduct the nation's foreign affairs.

United States v. Darby (1941). U.S. Supreme Court decision outlawing the sale of goods produced by child labor. In 1918 the Supreme Court had struck down an earlier law that attempted to ban child labor, reasoning that manufacturing was not "commerce" and was outside the scope of Congress' regulatory authority. In 1937 Congress again attempted to discourage child labor by passing the Fair Labor Standards Act, which severely limited the use of child labor in factories and also established a federal minimum wage and the 40–hour work week. Although the law was challenged, the Supreme Court upheld both the wage and hour provisions and the ban on the sale of products manufactured by child labor. The act was an important milestone in employee rights.

United States v. Nixon (1974). Unanimous U.S. Supreme Court decision holding that President Richard M. NIXON could not claim an executive privilege to protect tape recordings of conversations made in the White House. During the 1972 election, in which Nixon was reelected president, the DEMOCRATIC PARTY headquarters at the WATERGATE Apartments was burglarized. When the president and his staff later tried to hide the details of the burglary, the entire administration was rocked and the president was forced to resign.

During the scandal it was revealed that Nixon had taped his White House conversations, and he refused to comply with a subpoena to turn these over to investigators, claiming they were protected by an executive privilege similar to an attorney-client privilege. The Court rejected the contention that any privilege protected the president's conversations with his aides and ordered the tapes to be turned over.

UNIVAC. Acronym for *U*niversal *A*utomatic Computer—a COMPUTER invented by J. Presper Eckert and John Mauchley in 1951; it was the successor to their ENIAC. While more advanced than the ENIAC, UNIVAC was still huge, bulky and slow by the standards of the late 20th century. It was the first computer to be used commercially, and its first customer was the U.S. Census Bureau. On election night in 1952, UNIVAC became the first computer ever used to tally votes.

Universal Pictures. One of HOLLYWOOD'S "Little Three" production companies (along with UNITED ARTISTS and COLUMBIA PICTURES). Its formative years were presided over by the formidable Carl LAEMMLE. Having established by 1909 one of the largest film exchanges in America, he turned to production that same year in defiance of the monopoly, the Motion Picture Patents Company, and established his own Independent Motion Picture Company. In 1912 he combined it with several other companies to form "The Universal" (a name he allegedly borrowed from the sign on a Universal Pipe Fittings truck). Three years later he opened the largest motion picture production facility in the world, Universal City, located in the San Fernando Valley. It remains the oldest continuously operating studio in America. The silent era was marked by the emerging talents of director John FORD, production chief Irving THALBERG, and actor Lon CHANEY. Future studio chief at Columbia, Harry COHN, got his start as one of Laemmle's secretaries. With the TALKING PICTURE revolution, Carl Laemmle Jr. was appointed head of production and several prestige pictures appeared, including ALL QUIET ON THE WESTERN FRONT (1929) and SHOW BOAT (1936). He also initiated one of the studio's most famous series of pictures, their horror films, including *Dracula* (1931), FRANKENSTEIN (1931) and *The Invisible Man* (1933). However, by the mid-1930s the studio was on the verge of financial collapse and after Carl, Jr. was replaced by a series of other producers, the roster of releases reverted to the low-budget. These included the popular Deanna Durbin musicals and, later in the 1940s, the Basil RATHBONE SHERLOCK HOLMES movies and the ABBOTT AND COSTELLO comedies. In 1946 Universal merged with International Pictures. Decca Records bought the company in 1952 and subsequently was absorbed in 1962 by MCA, the former talent agency. By now, their movie output had been upgraded, ranging from a glossy series of Doris Day vehicles to blockbusters like *Airport* (1970), *The Sting* (1973), *Jaws* (1975), and E.T. (1982). In 1964 the Universal City Tours began. In 1989 Universal opened a second studio in Florida.

For further reading:

Hirschhorn, Clive, *The Universal Story*. New York: Crown Publishers, 1983.

University of California v. Bakke. See BAKKE CASE.

Unknown Soldier. Name given to an unidentified member of the armed forces who has died in the service of his or her country. Since the end of WORLD WAR I, a number of nations have memorialized their unidentified war dead with a tomb in which a symbolic one of their number is buried. In the U.S., a soldier who had been killed in France was buried in a temporary crypt at Arlington National Cemetery on Armistice Day, Nov. 11, 1921. Exactly eleven years later, the completed Tomb of the Unknown Soldier was dedicated. On Memorial Day of 1958, the memorial came to include the unidentified dead of other wars when the remains of a soldier from WORLD WAR II and another from the KOREAN WAR were also buried in the tomb, which was officially renamed the Tomb of the Unknowns. An unknown soldier from the VIETNAM WAR was interred in the crypt on Memorial Day in 1984. The tomb is provided with a military honor guard at all times, and services are held there each Memorial Day. Other such memorials are located under the Arc de Triomphe in Paris; in Westminster Abbey in London; in front of the Victor Emmanuel monument in Rome; and at the base of the Colonnade of the Congress in Brussels.

Untermeyer, Louis (1885–1977). American poet and editor. While working in a New York City jewelry company, Untermeyer began writing at night, publishing his first volume of poetry in 1911. He left his job to write full time in 1923, and he produced some 20 collections of traditional poetry, two novels, and many volumes of criticism. His varied works include *This Singing World* (1926), *Blue Rhine, Black Forest: A Hand and Day-Book* (1930) and *A Treasury of Laughter* (1946). He is best known in his capacity as an editor, and his many anthologies include *Modern American Poetry* (first edition, 1919), Modern British poetry (1920) and *A Treasury of Great Poems, English and American* (1942). Untermeyer was English poetry consultant to the Library of Congress from 1961 to 1963, and wrote two volumes of autobiography, *From Another World* (1939) and *Bygones* (1965).

Updike, John (Hoyer) (1932–). American author. Updike, who was born in Pennsylvania and educated at Harvard University, published his early short stories in THE NEW YORKER, where he served as staff writer from 1955 to 1957. He is best known for his fictional tetralogy, *Rabbit, Run* (1960), *Rabbit Redux* (1971), *Rabbit is Rich* (1981), which won the 1982 PULITZER PRIZE for fiction, and *Rabbit at Rest* (1990), which follows the life of Harry Angstrom through four decades of sexual

American author John Updike, whose fiction chronicles contemporary middle-class suburban life.

and social upheaval. Updike's fiction generally presents middle-class Americans, whom he depicts as self-obsessed and materialistic, diverting and sedating themselves with marital infidelity and alcohol. Other fiction includes the novels *Couples* (1968), *The Witches of Eastwick* (1984) and *Roger's Version* (1988); and the short story collections *Pigeon Feathers and other stories* (1962) and *Problems and other stories* (1979). In 1991 Updike received a second Pulitzer Prize, for *Rabbit at Rest*.

Upper Volta. See BURKINA FASO.

Urban League. American CIVIL RIGHTS organization; its full name is the National Urban League. Founded in 1910, its aims are the end of racial discrimination and the increase of economic status and political power for blacks and other racial minorities in the U.S. Under the direction of Whitney YOUNG (1961–71), the League broadened its programs and adopted a more aggressive approach to problems, while maintaining a basically moderate and nonviolent stance. Beginning in 1968, it shifted from mainly social service work to grass-roots organizing in the ghetto. Led by Vernon Jordan since 1972, it has focused on such aspects of urban poverty as police relations, welfare, tenants' rights and employment. With headquarters in New York City, it had a membership of some 50,000 in the early 1990s.

urban renewal. American movement aimed at eliminating inadequate housing and business properties in city areas and replacing them with improved facilities. Urban renewal began with the slum clearance projects of the 1930s and was a particular priority in the 1950s, due to the Housing Acts of 1949 and 1954. These provided federal funds to cities earmarked for the destruction of slums in the inner cities and for new construction. Cities purchased blighted areas, cleared the land by demolishing the old buildings and resold the tracts to developers. These developers were to submit competitive bids and follow city plans for redevelopment, whether for private or public housing, institutions or commercial use. In the course of urban renewal, many cities used the power of eminent domain, forcing the sale of private property to the government. During the 1950s, more than 2,000 of these projects were initiated, and many successes achieved. Urban renewal has produced housing as well as such public facilities as parks, schools, hospitals and museums, and cities such as Chicago, New York City, St. Louis and San Francisco have profited from such projects. Their main drawback, however, has been the displacement of families caused by the destruction of their homes, and the lack of sufficient new lower- and middle-income housing to fill their needs. Urban renewal efforts were revived by President Jimmy CARTER in the late 1970s in a program that attempted to deal with urban recovery. In the 1980s, however, the federal government sharply curtailed its housing efforts, and urban renewal was left to city and state governments, many of which lacked the funds to pursue the task with vigor.

Urey, Harold C(layton) (1893–1981). American chemist. Born in Walkerton, Indiana, he attended Montana State University (B.S., 1917), the University of California, Berkeley (Ph.D., 1923) and the Institute for Theoretical Physics at the University of Copenhagen, where he studied under Niels BOHR. He taught chemistry at Johns Hopkins University from 1924 to 1929 before joining the faculty at Columbia University, where he taught until 1945. In 1931 he was successful in isolating deuterium (heavy hydrogen), a landmark discovery that earned him the NOBEL PRIZE for chemistry in 1934. Urey later did research on a diffusion process for separating uranium isotopes and on heavy water, work that he continued in the wartime MANHATTAN PROJECT that produced the ATOM BOMB. After the war, Urey was a professor at the University of Chicago (1945–58) and later served as a professor-at-large at the University of California. He was also involved in a campaign to warn the public about the dangers posed by atomic energy. Urey later worked in geochemistry and astrophysics, on the nature of climate change and the origins of life on earth.

Urrutia, Manuel Lleo (1901–1981). Cuban political leader. A judge, he became the first president of revolutionary CUBA when Fidel CASTRO overthrew the government of Fulgencio BATISTA in 1959. Six months later, however, he denounced COMMUNISM and was forced to resign his largely symbolic post. He then spent four years of house arrest and asylum in the Venezuelan and Mexican embassies in Havana. In 1963 he was granted a safe-conduct pass to the U.S., where he published a book criticizing Castro's Cuba as a "Red hell." Settling in Florida, he headed a league of 22 anti-Castro exile groups known as the **Democratic Revolutionary Alliance,** which condoned violence directed at government authorities in Cuba. (See also BAY OF PIGS.)

Uruguay [Eastern Republic of Uruguay]. Uruguay covers an area of 68,021 square miles on the Atlantic coast of eastern South America. Political and economic problems created during the 19th century were alleviated during the presidency of Jose Batlle y Ordonez (1903–07; 1911–15), who promoted economic growth and class harmony. His successors chose a different course, which led to a coup in 1933, followed by a a period of prosperity and stability under Luis Batlle Berres (1947–56). The late 1950s and 1960s brought severe economic problems and political repression, which led to the brutal suppression of Tupamaros guerrilla groups in 1971–72 and the military seizure of power in 1973. Mass emigration and the continuing economic and social crises brought a return to democracy in 1984. In 1989 the first free elections in 18 years resulted in Luis Alberto Lacalle Herrera becoming president.

Uruguayan Revolution of 1933. URUGUAY suffered from the depression in 1931 when Gabriel Terra (1873–1942) of the liberal Colorado party was elected president. Facing opposition from radicals and conservatives and checked by the national council of administration, Terra dissolved both council and congress March 30, 1933, and abolished the constitution. A new constitution promulgated in 1934 concentrated power in the presidency, and provided proportional representation in the cabinet and senate. Reelected, Terra ruled dictatorially, suppressed a small revolt (1935), restricted freedom of press and speech, but Uruguay's economy improved. In 1938 Terra was succeeded by his brother-in-law General Alfredo Baldomir (1884–1948) in a fairly free election. Baldomir restored democratic government.

U.S.S.R. See UNION OF SOVIET SOCIALIST REPUBLICS.

Ustase. Name of a secret Croatian terrorist group formed in 1929 by nationalist Ante Pavelic (1889–1959); originally, a term applied to Croatian rebel bands. Operating during the 1930s from bases in HUNGARY, AUSTRIA and ITALY, the Ustase fought the Yugoslav monarchy and was implicated in the murder of King ALEXANDER in 1934. In collaboration with German and Italian forces, it established an independent Croatian government in 1941 and was responsible for the slaughter of many Serbians. After the war, Pavelic fled to SPAIN and ARGENTINA, but his movement lived on as an anticommunist Croatian separatist group. As such, it carried out assassinations and bombings in SWEDEN, WEST GERMANY and AUSTRALIA during the 1960s and 1970s.

Ustinov, Dimitri Fedorovich (1908–1984). Soviet party official. Ustinov joined the COMMUNIST PARTY of the Soviet Union in 1927. In 1934 he graduated from the Institute of Military Mechanical Engineering and worked as a fitter and machine operator. From 1934 until 1941, Ustinov was U.S.S.R. people's commissar. He climbed up the ranks of party posts, being made a member of the central committee in 1952. He was the U.S.S.R. minister of the defense industry (1953–57), chairman of the U.S.S.R. supreme economic coun-

URUGUAY

cil (1963–65) and a member of the Presidium and Politburo central committee. From 1976 Ustinov has been minister of defense, general of the army and marshal of the Soviet army.

Ustinov, Peter (Alexander) (1921–). English film and theater actor, playwright, director. Ustinov is one of the more versatile talents in show business, having scored successes both on the stage and in films, as well as through his writings. He began his career on the London stage in the 1930s, and in the 1940s his first plays were produced, including *House of Regrets* (1942) and *The Banbury Nose* (1944). Since the 1950s, Ustinov has been active as a film actor, with notable roles in *Beat the Devil* (1954), *Lola Montez* (1955), *Spartacus* (1960), *Topkapi* (1964), for which he won an Oscar as best supporting actor, and as Agatha CHRISTIE's Hercule Poirot in several films based on the fictional detective's exploits. His later plays include *Romanoff and Juliet* (1956) and *Beethoven's Tenth* (1983).

U Thant (1909–1974). Burmese diplomat. Educated at University College, Rangoon, he was a teacher and headmaster before entering the diplomatic service in 1948. He served in the Burmese ministry of information from 1949 to 1957, becoming Burma's permanent representative to the UNITED NATIONS in 1957. After the death of Dag HAMMARSKJOLD in 1961, Thant was named acting secretary general and was elected to the post the following year, serving until his retirement in 1971. During his early years in office, Thant helped to resolve the CUBAN MISSILE CRISIS (1962), the civil wars in the CONGO (1963) and CYPRUS (1964) and the INDO-PAKISTANI WAR (1965). Later crises proved more difficult to end, and Thant struggled with the VIETNAM WAR, the SIX-DAY WAR of 1967 (which he helped to mediate) and the 1971 Indo-Pakistan War. Thant helped to steer the UN toward a greater role in the economic, social and political development of THIRD WORLD nations and was influential in the organization's decision to recognize the People's Republic of CHINA in 1971.

Utley, Freda (1898–1978). British-born author, lecturer and journalist. Utley began her career as a correspondent for the *Manchester Guardian* (1926–28). From 1930 to 1936 she served as a senior scientific worker at Moscow's Institute of World Economy and Politics, part of the ACADEMY OF SCIENCES OF THE U.S.S.R. She was subsequently a war correspondent in CHINA, covering the SINO-JAPANESE WAR. She emigrated to the U.S. in 1939 after her husband's arrest and death in a Soviet prison camp. Utley became a U.S. citizen in 1950. She testified at the McCarthy hearings on Communist influence over U.S. Far Eastern policy in the early 1950s. (See also Joseph MCCARTHY.)

U-2 Incident (1960). Downing of an American Lockheed U-2, a high-altitude photographic reconnaissance airplane, by a Soviet surface-to-air missile over Sverdlovsk, Russia, on May 1, 1960. Days later, at a summit meeting between U.S. President EISENHOWER and U.S.S.R. Chairman KHRUSHCHEV in Paris, the Soviet leader demanded an apology for the incident. The U.S. at first denied any spying activities but—confronted with the wrecked plane and the admissions of the pilot, Francis Gary Powers—was forced to admit to its spy overflights. After the incident, a major embarrassment to U.S. intelligence, U-2 flights over the U.S.S.R. ceased. Powers was returned to the U.S. in an exchange for Soviet spy Rudolf Abel in February 1962.

American pilot Francis Gary Powers testifies before the U.S. Senate Armed Forces Committee after his release from the U.S.S.R.

V

Vaganova, Agrippina (1879–1951). Russian ballerina and teacher. She published *Fundamentals of the Classic Dance* (1934) and was an influential teacher who stressed that technique is grounded in developing bodily strength, balance and coordination. Her pupils included Natalya DUDINSKAYA and Galina ULANOVA.

Vakhtangov, Yevgeny Bagrationovich (1833–1927). Russian actor and director. He was a pupil of Konstantin STANISLAVSKY. Vakhtangov joined the MOSCOW ART THEATER in 1911 as an actor and producer in its First Studio, and in his own Third Studio from 1920. In 1926 the Third Studio was renamed the Vakhtangov Theater. He experimented with the concept of the modern mystery play.

Valachi, Joseph M. (1903–1971). American gangster. A minor member of the American MAFIA, he was a soldier in the New York ranks of Salvatore Maranzano and "Lucky" LUCIANO until sentenced to prison on a narcotics charge in 1959. After murdering a fellow prisoner, he turned informer and became one of the few members of the criminal organization to break its code of silence. Valachi was a main witness in the widely-televised Senate investigation of organized crime that took place in September-October, 1963, describing in detail the murderous inner workings of the New York Mafia. His testimony was supplemented by his memoirs, *The Valachi Papers*, published in 1969. A protected inmate, Valachi died in prison of natural causes.

Valentine, Kid Thomas (1896–1987). American jazz musician. A jazz trumpeter and long-time leader of the Preservation Hall dance band, he was a legend among New Orleans jazz musicians. Known just as Kid Thomas, he and his band members played all over the world.

Valentino, Rudolph [Rodolfo di Valentino d'Antonguolla] (1895–1926). Italian-born silent film actor; a legendary figure from the silent film era of the 1920s. As a romantic lead, Valentino became the exotic symbol of male sexual allure for millions of women around the world. While critics dismissed him as an actor, his dark looks and flamboyant style made him a box-office star. Valentino emigrated from ITALY to America as a young man and worked as an exhibition dancer on the New York club scene before moving to Hollywood in 1918. His major film successes were *The Four Horsemen of the Apocalypse* (1921), *The Sheik* (1921), *Blood and Sand* (1922), *The Eagle* (1925) and *The Son of the Sheik* (1926). At the height of his fame he died of a perforated ulcer.

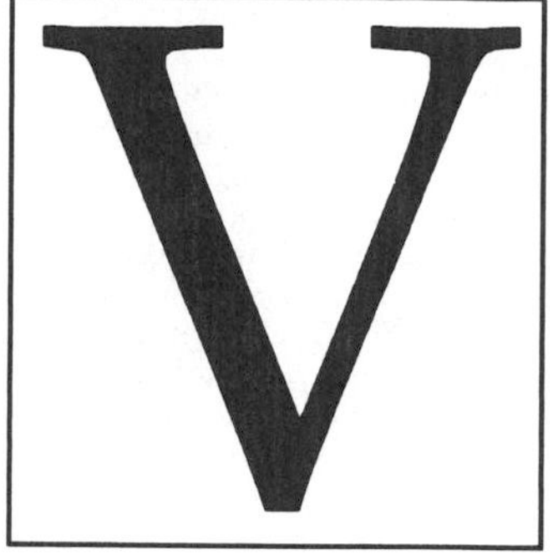
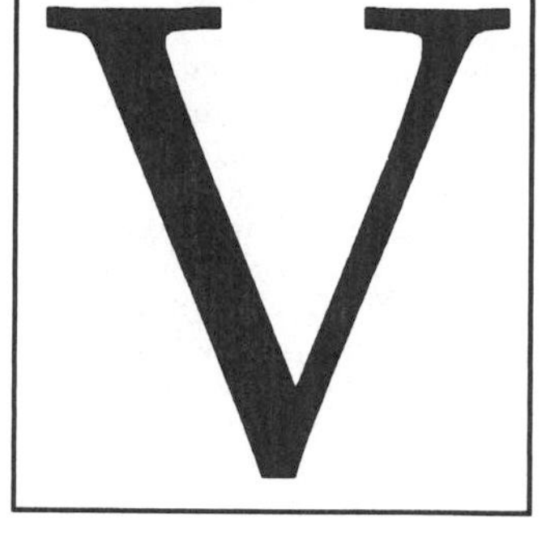

Rudolph Valentino, a matinee idol of the silent film era, in The Son of the Sheik *(1926).*

Valeriano, Napoleon D. (1917–1975). Philippine military leader and specialist in international affairs. Valeriano resisted the Japanese invasion of the PHILIPPINES early in WORLD WAR II IN THE PACIFIC and survived the BATAAN death march. In the late 1940s and early 1950s he helped suppress the Hukbalahap Rebellion. A strong supporter of U.S.-Philippine cooperation, he held the rank of colonel in both the Philippine and U.S. armies.

Valery, Paul (1871–1945). French poet and essayist. Valery is one of the most unique and esteemed figures in 20th-century French literature. In one sense, he was the last great representative of the 19th-century poetic school of Symbolism. Valery was an ardent disciple of Symbolist poet Stephane Mallarme, and Valery's own poems—most notably his verse masterpiece *La Jeune Parque* (1917)—show the influence of Mallarme's oblique imagery and precisely toned language. But Valery was also a modernist in terms of his fascination with the nature of consciousness itself. In essays such as *Introduction to the Method of Leonardo da Vinci* (1894), Valery explored the means by which the human mind perceived the world and sought to attain self-knowledge. Valery also wrote frequently on aesthetic subjects such as painting, architecture and the dance. He was elected to the French Academy in 1927 and to the Chair of Poetry at the College de France in 1937.

Valium. Trade name for diazepam, a tranquilizer and sedative hypnotic drug. In the late-20th century, Valium was one of the most widely prescribed drugs in the Western world. It is used to relieve anxiety and stress. It also is prescribed in treating recovering alcoholics. Patients who take diazepam can develop physical and psychological dependence and may come to rely on the drug as a cure-all.

Vallee, Rudy [born Hubert Prior Vallee] (1901–1986). American singer. A singing idol of the late 1920s and '30s, he personified the term "crooner," and foreshadowed such entertainers as Frank SINATRA in his ability to generate mass hysteria among female fans. His show business career took off in 1928 at the Heigh Ho Club in New York City. The club was the inspiration for his "heigh-ho, everybody" greeting, as well as for his singing through a megaphone to amplify his nasal voice. In 1929, he made his first film, *The Vagabond Lover*, and went on to make many more over the next two decades. He enjoyed a resurgence in the 1960s for his Broadway portrayal of a tycoon in *How to Succeed in Business Without Really Trying*.

Vallejo, Cesar (Abraham) (1892–1938). Peruvian poet. Vallejo grew up in a poor mestizo family but nonetheless attended university (1913–17), studying literature and law. His first book, *Los heraldos negros* (1918), was virtually ignored. *Trilce* (1922) included more radical, experimental poetry, some of it written in prison where he was detained unjustly for inciting to riot. Embittered by the repressive regime in PERU, he left for PARIS in 1923; except for trips to RUSSIA in 1928, 1929 and 1931 and to SPAIN in 1936 and 1937, he remained there till his death. He joined the communist party in 1931. His ultra-modern, emotionally powerful poems represent a cry for justice in a world of suffering and chaos. *Poemas humanos* (1939) and *Espana, aparta de mi este caliz* (1940) were published posthumously by his wife.

Valois, Ninette de [Edris Stannus] (1898–). British dancer, choreographer and ballet director. One of the pioneers of British ballet, Valois first gained notice as a *demi-caractere* dancer, primarily with Serge DIAGHILEV'S BALLETS RUSSES (1923–25). She founded the Academy of Choreographic Art in London in 1926, then established the Vic-Wells Ballet (with Lilian Baylis) in 1931 and served as its director until 1963, guiding the company through its transformation into the SADLER'S WELLS BALLET and finally the ROYAL BALLET (1956). She was an adviser to the Royal Ballet School and became a Life Governor in 1971. Recipient of many awards, including Dame Commander of the British Empire (D.B.E.) in 1951, she retired at age 73. Her many choreographic works include *Job* (1931) and *Checkmate* (1937).

Van Allen, James Alfred (1914–). American physicist. Van Allen's intensive work in terrestrial magnetism and applied physics was instrumental in the experiments launched in 1958 by America's first satellite—EXPLORER I—which measured cosmic rays and other energy particles. The discovery of unexpectedly high radiation levels in certain regions of the Earth's atmosphere contradicted the observations cited five months earlier by the Russians' first satellite, SPUTNIK I, and led to further space exploration. Subsequent breakthroughs included locating where the Earth's magnetic field traps high-speed charged particles. These zones were christened Van Allen belts, in honor of the man whose entire life's work has greatly advanced our knowledge of the cosmos.

Van Damm, Sheila (1922–1987). British race car driver; the top British woman in auto racing during the 1950s. In 1960, Van Damm inherited the Windmill Theater from her father, who had kept it open at the height of the Blitz in September 1940. Forced to close it in 1964, Van Damm retired afterwards.

Vandenberg, Arthur Hendrick (1884–1951). U.S. senator. Vandenberg was born in Grand Rapids, Michigan. He was editor and publisher of the Grand Rapids *Herald* from 1906 to 1928 when he was appointed to the U.S. Senate. An influential Republican who became president pro tem in 1947, he served in the upper house until his death. Vandenberg opposed most NEW DEAL legislation. Prior to WORLD WAR II he was an isolationist, but in the postwar period, he became a leading proponent of bipartisan support for President Harry S TRUMAN'S foreign policy. Vandenberg served as chairman of the Senate Committee on Foreign Affairs (1946–51) and was instrumental in securing Senate approval of the MARSHALL PLAN and the NORTH ATLANTIC TREATY ORGANIZATION. He served as a delegate to the UN Conference on International Organization in San Francisco (1945) and to the Paris Peace Conference in 1947.

Vandergrift, Alexander Archer (1887–1973). American Marine Corps officer. Vandergrift commanded the First Marine Division in the capture of GUADALCANAL (1942), which was the first full-scale U.S. offensive against the Japanese during World War II. Promoted that year to major general, he held the island against repeated attempts to retake it. Vandergrift also commanded the First Marine Amphibious Corps at the Bougainville Invasion (1943). He was appointed the 18th commandant of the Marine Corps in 1944.

Vander Meer, Johnny (1914–). Known as "Double No-Hit" Johnny, Vander Meer spent his professional baseball career in Ohio, first as a pitcher with the Cincinnati Reds from 1937 to 1950. He gained his greatest fame as the only pitcher in the history of professional baseball to hurl two consecutive no-hitters, first against the Boston Braves and second against the Brooklyn Dodgers. After his career in Cincinnati, he went to Cleveland in 1951.

Van Deventer, Mills (1862–1942). Associate justice, U.S. Supreme Court (1910–37). A graduate of DePauw University and the University of Cincinnati Law School, Van Deventer practiced law with his father in Marion, Indiana, but soon moved to Wyoming Territory, where he briefly served as territory chief justice. Active in Republican politics, he was brought to Washington, D.C., as an assistant attorney general. President Theodore ROOSEVELT appointed him a judge of the U.S. Court of Appeals for the Eighth Circuit in 1903. President William Howard TAFT appointed Van Deventer to the Supreme Court in 1910. He proved a conservative on the bench, generally opposed to government regulation of business.

Van Druten, John (1901–1957). British-born playwright and novelist. Van Druten remains best known for his play I AM A CAMERA (1951), which was adapted from *Goodbye to Berlin*, a collection of sketches and stories on 1930s BERLIN by Christopher ISHERWOOD. *I Am A Camera* later became the basis for the hit musical CABARET (1966). Van Druten immigrated to the U.S. after the banning of his early play *Young Woodley* (1925) in Britain due to its controversial handling of the theme of adolescence. In the U.S., Van Druten earned a reputation as an adroit writer of light comedies, most notably *Bell, Book and Candle* (1950).

Vanguard. The U.S. Naval Research Laboratories had already begun Project Vanguard to design a rocket capable of launching satellites into space when the Soviets launched their SPUTNIK satellite in October 1957. On December 6, 1957, at CAPE CANAVERAL, a Vanguard rocket bearing a 6–inch satellite was ignited and exploded a few seconds later. A second Vanguard broke up in flight in February 1958. At last, in March 1958, the three-pound Vanguard 1 soared into space, equipped with a radio transmitter that would continue to send signals for nearly six years. Between December 1957 and September 1959, 11 Vanguard launch attempts were made, with only three successes.

Van Heusen, Jimmy [born Edward Chester Babcock] (1913–1990). American composer. Along with his lyricist partners Johnny Burke and Sammy CAHN, he wrote such popular songs as "Moonlight Becomes You" and "My Kind of Town." Many of his biggest hits were performed by Frank SINATRA, who recorded 76 Van Heusen songs, and Bing CROSBY. Four of his songs—"Swingin' On a Star" from the film *Going My Way* (1944), "All the Way" from *The Joker is Wild* (1957), "High Hopes" from *A Hole in the Head* (1959) and "Call Me Irresponsible" from *Papa's Delicate Condition* (1963)—won ACADEMY AWARDS. He was one of 10 songwriters inducted into the Songwriters Hall of Fame when it was founded in 1971.

Van Niel, Cornelius Bernardus (1897–1985). Dutch-born microbiologist. In the 1930s Van Niel became the first scientist to explain the chemical basis for photosynthesis. He arrived at the correct formula while working with bacteria; in the 1940s, his formula was shown to be correct for green plants as well. For many years he taught at Stanford University's Hopkins Marine Station in Southern California.

Vanuatu. Located in the South Pacific Ocean, 621 miles west of Fiji and 249 miles northeast of New Caledonia, Vanuatu has a total area of 5,697 square miles. The archipelago consists of 13 large islands and 70 islets. Joint British and French rule of the islands was formalized in 1906. On July 30, 1980 the islands achieved independence as the Republic of Vanuatu, which became a member of the COMMONWEALTH. In September of the same year a secession movement in Espiritu Santo, the largest island, was put down with help from PAPUA NEW GUINEA. In 1983 Vanuatu became a member of the Non-Aligned Movement, and the ruling left-wing Vanuaaku Party, under the leadership of Prime Minister Walter Lini, was returned to government. The party won a further election in November 1987 but was subject to increasing internal dissension as Barak Sope attempted to wrest the leadership from Lini. Following Sope's expulsion from the Vanuaaku Party, his uncle, George Sokomanu—the country's president—tried to dismiss Lini's agreement and swear in Sope as prime minister. Both Sope and Sokomanu were imprisoned for mutiny, although the latter was later released on appeal. In 1989 Fred Timakata, a former member of Lini's cabinet, was elected president of Vanuatu.

Vare, Glenna Collett (1903–1989). American golfer. She was a pioneer of women's golf in the U.S. She won six national women's titles between the years 1922 and 1935 and was named a charter member of the Women's Golf Hall of Fame in 1950. The Vare Trophy, given annually by the Ladies Professional Golfers Association (LPGA) to the player with the lowest average on the tour, was named for her.

Varese, Edgar (Edgard) (1883–1965). American composer. An experimentalist whose music often elicited controversy, Varese exerted considerable influence on the development of modern music with his concept of "organized sound." He spent his early career in Paris and Berlin among the avant-garde artists. In 1915 he came to the U.S.; then in 1922 he and Carlos Salzedo cofounded the International Composers' Guild. Many of his compositions use electronic devices and taped sounds. His most important works include *Deserts* (1954) and *Ionisation* (1931).

Vargas Llosa, Mario (1936–). Peruvian novelist, intellectual and political figure. Vargas Llosa attended military school and university in Lima and obtained a doctorate in Madrid (1958); thereafter he lived in Paris until 1966. He has also resided in London, Barcelona and the U.S. He first achieved renown and notoriety with *La ciudad y los perros* (1963; tr. 1966 as *The Time of the Hero*). A thousand copies of the book, which described his military school experience, were burned on the school's patio. Subsequent novels include *La casa verde* (1966; tr. 1968 as *The Green House*), *Conversacion en la catedral* (1969; tr. 1975 as *The Conversation in the Cathedral*), *Pantaleon y las visitadoros* (1973; tr. 1978 as *Captain Pantoja and the Special Service*), *La tia Julia y el escribidor* (1977; tr. 1982 as *Aunt Julia and the Scriptwriter*), *La Guerra del fin del Mondo* (1981; tr. 1984 as *The War of the End of the World*) and *Historia de Mayta* (1985; tr. 1986 as *The Real Life of Alejandro Mayta*). He has also written studies of GARCIA MARQUEZ (1971) and Flaubert (1975). A one-time leftist and supporter of communist CUBA, Vargas Llosa later changed his views, becoming an advocate of democracy who vigorously opposes tyrannies of the right or left. In 1990 he ran unsuccessfully for the office of president of PERU.

For further reading:

Castro-Klaren, Sara, *Understanding Mario Vargas Llosa*. Columbia: University of South Carolina Press, 1989.

Illanes, Julia U., *My Life with Mario Vargas Llosa*. New York: Peter Lang, 1988.

Williams, Raymond L., *Mario Vargas Llosa*. New York: Ungar Publishing, 1987.

Vasiliev and Maximova. Soviet dancers, Vladimir Victorovich Vasiliev (1940–) and Yekaterina Sergeyevna Maximova (1934–). This husband and wife have forged a popular partnership, appearing together in such ballets as *Sleeping Beauty* and *Spartacus* to much acclaim. In 1964 each won a gold medal at the International Ballet Competition in Varna, Italy. As stars of the BOLSHOI BALLET they have gained an international reputation, Vasiliev for his virtuosity and dynamic stage presence and Maximova for her beautiful technique. Individually, he has excelled in such ballets as *Ivan the Terrible* (1975) while his wife is admired for her roles in *The Stone Flower* and *Don Quixote*.

Vatican [Vatican City]. The ecclesiastical state of Vatican City, seat of the Holy See, lies within the city of Rome, ITALY, on the western bank of the Tiber River. Its total area of 0.17 square mile makes it the world's smallest state: In the 19th-century, the Papal States were incorporated by force into the emerging Italian state, culminating in the seizure of Rome in 1870 by King Victor Emmanuel II. In protest, successive Popes refused to leave the Vatican until February 1929, when Pope PIUS XI and MUSSOLINI concluded the Lateran Treaties, which recognized the Holy See's sovereignty in Vatican City and incorporated a concordat by which Catholicism became Italy's state religion. During WORLD WAR II Pope PIUS XII incurred much international criticism by adhering to a strict neutrality. In the postwar era, the Vatican combined its spiritual role with active diplomacy as a neutral sovereign state, signing the Final Act of the Conference on Security and Cooperation in Europe (1975) and establishing diplomatic relations with over 100 countries, including Britain (1982) and the U.S. (1984). In 1978 Cardinal Karol Wojtyla of Poland became, as Pope JOHN PAUL II, the first non-Italian pontiff since the 16th century. He undertook an unprecedented number of papal visits abroad and survived two assassination attempts, one in Rome in 1981 and another in Portugal a year later.

The privileged status of the Catholic Church in Italy was ended under a revised concordat signed in February 1984. In a major reorganization of Vatican administration, the Pope delegated most of his temporal duties to Secretary of State Cardinal Agostino Casaroli, amid concern over the alleged involvement of the Vatican Bank in the 1982 fraudulent bankruptcy of Milan's Banco Ambrosiano. Ambrosiano's collapse was precipitated by the death of its chairman, Roberto Calvi, who was found hanging beneath Blackfriars Bridge in London on June 18, 1982. Calvi's death was first found to be suicide; at a second inquest in June 1983 an open verdict was returned; in February 1989 a Milan court ruled that his death had been murder. Under a financial settlement agreed upon in May 1984 the Vatican Bank agreed to pay 109 creditor banks $250 million of the $406 million it owed following the liquidation of Banco Ambrosiano.

Vatican II (1962–63). Council summoned by Pope JOHN XXIII to promulgate reforms within the Roman Catholic Church. Proceedings began on October 11, 1962, in the presence of over 8,000 Catholic bishops and observers from Anglican and Orthodox churches. The 16 decrees that emerged encouraged greater tolerance toward non-Catholic Christians and provided for the use of the vernacular rather than Latin in Catholic liturgy. Vatican II was a watershed in the history of the Catholic Church in the 20th century, with far-reaching consequences for Catholics and non-Catholics alike. Many of the council's decrees continued to stir controversy decades after they were issued. Traditionalists have argued that the council contradicted many of the long-accepted practices and beliefs of the church, while liberals have complained that the reforms did not go far enough in making the church responsive to the contemporary world.

vaudeville. A term used to describe popular variety entertainment in the U.S. during the early part of the 20th century. Similar to the music halls in Britain, a vaudeville program contained a dozen or so variety acts: singers and comedy sketches; dance, magic and animal acts; and even swimmers and acrobats. Many well known performers—BURNS AND ALLEN, Bob HOPE, Jimmy DURANTE, the MARX BROTHERS, Eddie CANTOR, Al JOLSON, Jack BENNY and many more—got their start in show business on the vaudeville stage. Vaudeville was at its peak during the 1910s and early 1920s. During the 1920s the popularity of SILENT FILM and RADIO soared, causing vaudeville's decline.

Vaughan, Harry H(awkins) (1893–1981). American military officer and aide to Harry S TRUMAN. He served with fellow Missourian Truman during WORLD WAR I and earned a number of decorations as an artillery captain in France. He also established a long-lasting friendship with the future president. He worked for Truman's Senate reelection campaign (1939–40). After service in Australia in WORLD WAR II, he became Vice President Truman's military aide (1944), remaining in that position throughout Truman's vice presidency and presidency. A plain-spoken individualist like his mentor, Vaughan's remarks often caused controversy, and he was reprimanded by the Senate (1949) for misuse of influence.

Vaughan, Sarah (Lois) (1924–1990). American jazz vocalist. Vaughan was noted for the remarkable three-octave range of her voice and her mastery of such vocal techniques as vibrato, vocal leaps, skat singing and improvisation. Her career spanned nearly 50 years, beginning in the 1940s, and included such popular recordings as "Make Yourself Comfortable" (1954), "Mr. Wonderful" (1956) and "Broken-Hearted Melody" (1959). Although she began by singing be-bop with such performers as Dizzy GILLESPIE, Charlie PARKER and Billy ECKSTINE, she later branched out into pop music as well. She remained a popular performer throughout her career, and appeared at nightclubs, jazz festivals and with symphony orchestras until shortly before her death.

Vaughan, Stevie (Stephen Ray) (1954–1990). American musician. He was one of the U.S.'s top blues and rock guitar players. Together with his band, Double Trouble, he won the 1984 Grammy for best traditional blues recording for "Texas Flood." In 1989, he won the Grammy for best contemporary blues recording for "In Step." He performed with such rock artists as David BOWIE, Joe Cocker and Eric CLAPTON. The younger brother of guitarist Jimmie Vaughan, he died in a helicopter crash while touring with Clapton.

Vaughan-Thomas, (Lewis John) Wynford (1908–1987). Welsh-born British radio and television commentator. Wynford Vaughan-Thomas guided listeners and viewers through events ranging from the coronation of King GEORGE VI to the weddings of the present generation of young royalty. After working for the BRITISH BROADCASTING CORPORATION for more than three decades, he returned to Wales to work with Harlech Television, where he was director of programs until 1972 and remained a director and broadcaster thereafter.

Vaughan Williams, Ralph (1872–1958). British composer. A prolific composer whose work spans more than half of the 20th century, Vaughan Williams is best known for his nine symphonies, the *Fantasia on a Theme by Thomas Tallis* (1910), *The Lark Ascending* (1920, for orchestra and violin solo) and his setting of the traditional folksong *Greensleeves* (1929). He also composed operas, ballet music, film scores and songs. He studied with Sir Charles Stanford and Hubert Parry at the Royal College of Music in London, as well as with Max Bruch in Berlin and Maurice RAVEL in Paris. However, the major influences on his style were English folk song and the polyphonic English church music of the 16th century. Slow to mature as a composer, he did not complete his First Symphony (*A Sea Symphony*, a massive choral work set to poems by Walt Whitman) until 1910. Although he occasionally experimented with dissonance (notably in the Fourth Symphony, 1931–34), his music is generally evocative and melodically and harmonically rich. Other important compositions include the Second Symphony (*A London Symphony*, 1913), the Fifth Symphony (1943), *Five Variants on Dives and Lazarus* (1939) and *The Pilgrim's Progress* (1951). His second wife was the poet Ursula Wood.

For further reading:

Kennedy, Michael, *The Works of Ralph Vaughan Williams*. New York: Oxford University Press, 1971.

Lunn, John E., *Ralph Vaughan Williams: A Pictorial Biography*. New York: Oxford University Press, 1971.

Vavilov, Nicholas Ivanovich (1887–1943). Russian botanist and chemist. He held many important posts, including that of director of the All-Union Institute of Plant Breeding (1924–40), and enjoyed an international reputation as one of the greatest contributors to the study of botanical populations. Although he had supported some of the experiments of Trofim D. LYSENKO, he opposed many of the latter's more outrageous scientific claims. As a result he was arrested (1940) and died in a concentration camp. After the death of STALIN his reputation was rehabilitated.

Veblen, Thorstein B. (1857–1929). American economist. Veblen is considered one of the most creative thinkers in American economic history. He studied at Carleton College and took a Ph.D. in philosophy from Yale in 1884, but could not find a teaching place and so returned home to farm work. Eventually he was accepted at the University of CHICAGO to teach political economy (1892–1906). His scholarly and satiric book, *The Theory of the Leisure Class* (1899), attacked false values and social waste and brought him almost instant fame. He advocated a planned economic society in which scientists and engineers would play a significant role. His ideas were so controversial that he was forced to leave the university and spent many years at other schools.

V-E Day. Victory in Europe—May 8, 1945. On this day, Germany's unconditional surrender (signed the day before) was ratified, ending WORLD WAR II IN EUROPE.

Veeck, Bill (1914–1986). American sports executive. During his various stints as the owner of three major league baseball teams, the Cleveland Indians, the St. Louis Browns and the Chicago White Sox, he became known as the "Barnum of Baseball." He installed the first exploding scoreboard, invented season tickets and bat days, and introduced the practice of printing players' names on the back of their uniforms. In 1951, he perpetrated one of the most memorable stunts in baseball when he sent a midget to bat. More than a brilliant promoter, he twice led unimpressive teams to pennants in a short time, the Indians in 1948 and the White Sox in 1959. In 1948, he signed the first black player to play in the American League, Larry Doby. Veeck was named to the Baseball Hall of Fame in 1991.

British composer Ralph Vaughan Williams meets with conductors G. Wallace Woodworth and Sir Adrian Boult (London, July 3, 1956).

Velasco Ibarra, Jose Maria (1893–1979). President of ECUADOR (1934–35; 1944–47; 1952–56; 1960–61; 1968–72). One of Ecuador's leading politicians, Velasco was elected president five times but completed only one term (1952–56). Each of his other four terms ended when he was overthrown by the military.

Velcro. The Swiss inventor Georges de Mestral was reportedly inspired to create Velcro after wondering why burrs stuck to his trousers. He discovered that the burrs were made up of thousands of tiny hooks, and he went on to develop Velcro (a combination of "velvet" and "crochet," the French word for hook). Its strips of tiny loops and tiny nylon hooks made it suitable for use in everything from clothing to spacecraft and artificial hearts.

Velikovsky, Immanuel (1895–1979). Russian-born psychoanalyst, astronomer-theorist and author. Velikovsky was known mainly for his unorthodox theories of cosmic evolution. A controversial and iconoclastic figure, in his writings he combined a vast knowledge of Biblical and mythological lore with Freudian psychology. In his book *Worlds in Collision* (1950), he claimed that a comet had collided with the Earth in 1500 B.C., causing tumultuous changes on the planet. While many readers considered Velikovsky a great visionary, his ideas never won acceptance from the scientific establishment.

Venezuela [Republic of Venezuela]. Venezuela covers an area of 352,051 square miles on the Caribbean Sea coast of northern South America, stretching to mountainous inlands and the northern edge of the Amazon Basin. Dictator Juan Vicente GOMEZ ruled the country from 1908 to 1935. In the 1920s oil was discovered, changing the country's economy from predominantly agricultural to industrial. Subsequent social change led to the formation of opposition groups among students, intellectuals and labor unions, which demanded an end to dictatorship and repression. Under the leadership of Romulo BETANCOURT (1945–48, 1958–63) a new constitution was created and economic and social reforms enacted. The corrupt military government of Marcos Perez, which seized power in 1948 and had U.S. support, was ousted in 1958 and Betancourt returned as president. After 1963 the presidency changed hands several times amid growing economic problems and student and union demonstrations. Current President Carlos Andrez

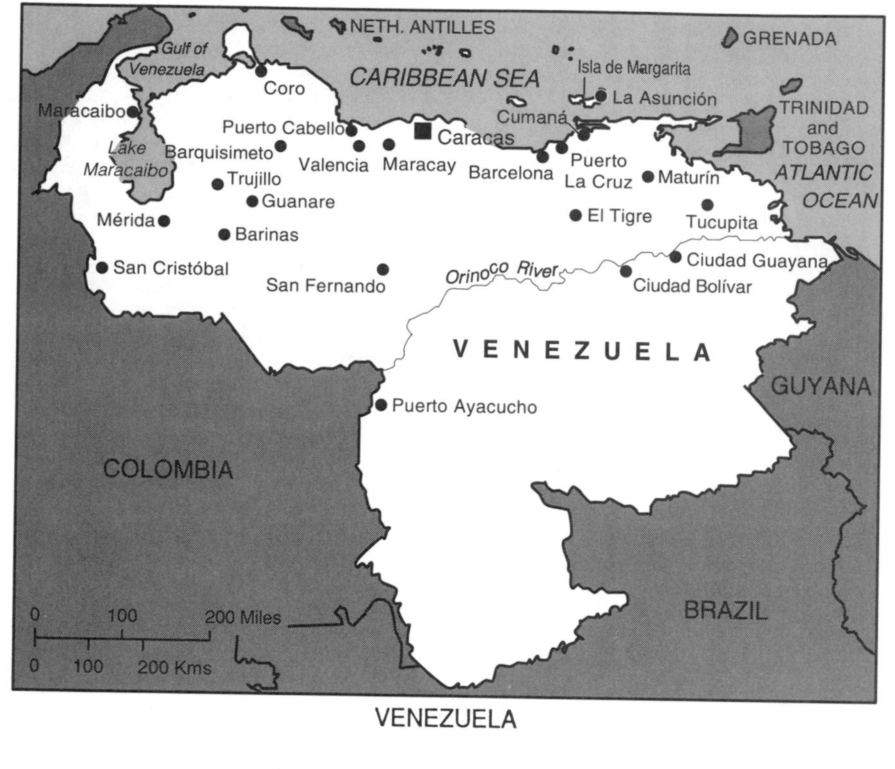

VENEZUELA

Perez was elected in 1988, but the economic recession and social unrest continued.

For further reading:

Ewell, Judith, *Venezuela: A Century of Change.* Stanford, California: Stanford University Press, 1984.

Venizelos, Eleutherios (1864–1936). Greek statesman, six-time premier (1910–15, 1915, 1917–20, 1924, 1928–32, 1933). Born on Crete, he played an important part in the 1897 revolt against the Turks. In 1905, he announced the union of GREECE and Crete, a goal that was not to be achieved until 1913. In 1909 he went to Greece at the behest of the Military League, which was pressing for political reforms. Becoming premier in 1910, he led Greece during the BALKAN WARS (1912–13) and greatly increased the nation's territory. He was a strong proponent of the Allied cause in WORLD WAR I, causing conflicts with the pro-German king CONSTANTINE I, who forced his resignation in 1915. Elected premier again that year, he was again forced from office by the king. He formed a provisional government at Salonika the following year and after the king was compelled to step down, became premier again in 1917 and brought Greece into the war on the Allied side. Venizelos lost the elections in 1920 and Constantine was restored. After the defeat of TURKEY and Constantine's abdication (1922), Venizelos served briefly as premier in 1924 and retired from office. An elder statesman, he won the elections in 1928, was forced to resign by royalist pressure and the trials of economic depression in 1932 and was premier again for a short period in 1933. Fearing that the monarchy would be reinstated, he was involved in the unsuccessful armed insurrection of 1935 and forced into exile in Paris, where he died the following year.

VENEZUELA

1908	Juan Vicente Gomez seizes power and becomes a virtual dictator.
1920s	Oil is discovered.
1935	General Eleazar Lopez Contreras becomes president on Gomez's death and initiates political and economic reform.
1945	Romulo Betancourt elected president, begins constitutional reforms.
1948	Marcos Perez overthrows Betancourt and begins dictatorial rule.
1958	Perez overthrown by military; Betancourt returns to office.
1960	Venezuela takes the lead in forming OPEC.
1976	All foreign mining companies are nationalized.
1988	(December) Running as a populist, Carlos Andrez Perez wins the 1988 presidential elections.

Verdun, Battle of (1916). Verdun, the major French fortress on the Meuse River, became the object of a German offensive in February 1916, during WORLD WAR I. After a heavy artillery bombardment, German troops advanced and captured several of the smaller forts surrounding Verdun. French forces counterattacked and stopped the German drive. The battle raged on for months. Areas were taken and retaken by both sides; there were strong attacks and counterattacks. "They shall not pass" became the cry of French resistance, and indeed Verdun did stand resolute against relentless German shelling. By August 1916, the Germans realized they could not capture the fortress and ceased their attacks. About a million Frenchmen lost their lives in this struggle, which was one of the most destructive of the war.

Veresayev, Vikenty Vikentevich (Smidovich) (1867–1946). Russian writer. A physician by profession, he explored the minds of perplexed intellectuals in many of his novels. His early works included *Without Road* (1895) and *At the Turning Point* (1902). In 1901 he published *A Doctor's Sketches;* other nonfiction includes essays on Dostoyevsky, Tolstoy and Pushkin. His two best-known books since the Revolution are *In a Blind Alley* (1922) and *The Sisters* (1933).

Vernadsky, Vladimir Ivanovich (1863–1945). Russian geochemist and mineralogist. He was considered a founder of geochemistry. Although he was active in the ZEMSTVA movement and opposed the BOLSHEVIKS, he returned to his work after the Civil War and was founder of the biogeochemical laboratory of the Academy of Sciences in Leningrad, becoming its director in 1928.

Versailles, Treaty of. Several treaties negotiated and signed at the French palace of Versailles. In the 20th century, the term applies to the treaty of 1919, the most important of the five peace treaties that officially ended WORLD WAR I because it fixed the terms of the peace with GERMANY. The Treaty of Versailles was the result of negotiations at the lengthy and often rancorous PARIS PEACE CONFERENCE. It was signed on June 28, 1919 by the defeated Germany on one side and the victorious FRANCE, ITALY, UNITED KINGDOM and UNITED STATES on the other. The treaty forced Germany to admit war guilt and placed stringent limitations on its ability to rearm. Largely through the insistence of the French, Germany was obliged to pay heavy war reparations. It was also compelled to give up certain territories. The most significant of these were: the restoration of Alsace and Lorraine to France, the awarding of much of Prussia to Poland and the creation of Danzig as a free city. The treaty largely rejected President WILSON'S FOURTEEN POINTS but did establish the LEAGUE OF NATIONS. It placed Germany's colonies under League mandates, forced Germany to accept French administration of the Saar and demanded plebiscites that gave the residents of territories previously held by the Central Powers the right of self-determination. While Germany protested that the treaty was overly severe, the nation had no choice but to sign it, and the Treaty of Versailles became effective in January 1920. The treaty's harsh terms are often cited as a contributing cause for the rise of NAZISM in post-World War I Germany.

Vertov, Dziga (1896–1954). Russian filmmaker and theoretician, father of the Russian newsreel and documentary film. He was born Denis Kaufman in Russian-held Poland. During the early years of World War I he studied medicine and psychology; but soon his interest in FUTURISM and its preoccupation with machines and technology led him to poetry and the adoption of a new name, "Dziga Vertov" (which means "turning," or "revolving"). With the Bolshevik seizure of power in October 1917 he became editor of the newsreel, *Film Weekly*. To his editing bench in Moscow came raw film actualities from across RUSSIA. His assembled film strips went by "agit-train" to villages and soldiers at the fronts with information and propaganda about the "revolutionary struggles." After the war, he continued to champion the documentary film at the expense of the fiction, HOLLYWOOD-style, film, which he called "a scabby substitute" for life. His monthly newsreel, *Kino-Pravda* (*Film-Truth*) appeared from 1922–25; and his studio, Kultkino, produced information films after 1925. Numerous pamphlets and manifestoes hailed the "Kino-Eye," or "Camera-Eye," as the new means to "decipher in a new way a world unknown to you," to assemble and record actualities ("life facts") into new cinematic structures ("film things"). His masterpiece, *Cheloveks Kinoapparatom* (*Man with a Movie Camera*, 1929) was a free-wheeling kaleidoscope of special effects and actualities—life in Moscow captured and reassembled by the camera eye and film editor. But, like his colleagues, PUDOVKIN, KULESHOV, and EISENSTEIN, such experiments ran Vertov afoul of the STALIN regime. After two sound films, *Entusiazm*, (*Enthusiasm*, 1931) and *Tri Pesni O Leninye* (*Three Songs of Lenin*, 1934) Vertov fell out of favor and spent the remainder of his life editing newsreels. A revival of interest in his work came in the 1960s, a decade after his death.

For further reading:

Leyda, Jay, *A History of the Russian and Soviet Film*. London: George, Allen and Unwin, 1960.

Verwoerd, Hendrik (Frensch) (1901–1966). South African politician and prime minister (1958–66). Born in Holland, he was brought to SOUTH AFRICA as a baby by his missionary parents. He was educated in GERMANY and at Stellenbosch University, where he taught psychology and sociology from 1927–37. In 1928 he became editor of the Afrikaans nationalist newspaper *Die Transvaaler*, following an editorial policy of opposition to the nation's entry into WORLD WAR II, to Jan SMUTS and to black Africans, Jews and the British. After becoming a senator in 1948, he held a number of positions in the nationalist government, notably minister of native affairs (1950–58). In 1958, he became the leader of the National party and prime minister. He was a harsh proponent of white supremacy and racial separation, upholding APARTHEID and aiding in the establishment of "Bantu homelands." Instrumental in making South Africa a republic in 1961, he severed the nation's ties with the British Commonwealth. He was stabbed to death by a fanatic parliamentary messenger during a session of parliament in 1966.

Vesely, Artem [Nicholas Ivanovich Kochkurov] (1899–1939). Russian novelist. He wrote several novels about the Revolution, including *The Fiery Rivers* (1942), *Land of My Birth* (1926) and *Russia Washed with Blood* (1929–31). His historical novel about Yermak, a 17th-century adventurer and conqueror of Siberia, *The Sporting Volga*, was published in 1933. He was detained in 1939 in the GREAT PURGE, and nothing was heard of him again.

Vichy France. Government that controlled unoccupied France and its colonies for much of WORLD WAR II after the German invasion in 1940. Authorized by a vote of the French National Assembly meeting in the resort town of Vichy in July, 1940 and headed by Premier Henri Philippe PETAIN, it succeeded France's Third Republic. A new constitution was promulgated that established a corporate state, and a new government controlled by right-wing politicians and stressing the virtues of order and authority was put in place. The Vichy regime collaborated with the Nazis to a greater or lesser extent during its existence depending on who held the real power in the government, with collaboration strong under Pierre LAVAL and strongest under Admiral Jean Francois DARLAN. After German troops entered unoccuppied France in November, 1942, the Vichy regime lost virtually all of its real automomy and increasingly became a tool of Germany. The regime fled to Germany as the Allies advanced and ceased to exist on German surrender in 1945.

Vickers, Jon(athan Stewart) (1926–). Canadian singer. An internationally acclaimed dramatic tenor, Vickers made his opera debut in *Rigoletto* at the Toronto Opera Festival in 1952. From 1957 to 1960 he sang with the opera at Covent Garden and first performed one of his most celebrated roles, Aeneas in *Les Troyens*. He debuted at the New York Metropolitan Opera in 1960 as Canio in *I Pagliacci*. His most famous roles include the title role in *Peter Grimes*, Samson in *Samson and Delilah* and the title role in *Parsifal*. In addition, he appeared in the film versions of *Carmen*, *Otello* and *I Pagliacci*.

Victor Emmanuel III (1869–1947). King of ITALY (1900–46). The son of Humbert I, Victor Emmanuel married Princess Helena of Montenegro in 1896 and succeeded to the throne upon the assassination of his father. At first a proponent of neutrality, he entered WORLD WAR I on the Allied side in 1915. Unable to cope with the postwar turmoil in Italian politics, in 1922 he invited Benito MUSSOLINI to become premier and thus brought the Fascists to power (see FASCISM). During the Fascist era, Victor Emmanuel gained the titles of Emperor of Ethiopia (1936) and King of Albania (1936), but he was virtually a figurehead throughout his reign. After the Fascist grand council withdrew support from Mussolini in 1943, the king dismissed the premier, had him arrested and replaced him with Pietro BADOGLIO. When Italy surrendered to the Allies seven weeks later, Germany occupied Rome and Victor Emmanuel fled to Brindisi. In 1946, the unpopular monarch abdicated in favor of his son, Humbert II. A year later, Victor Emmanuel died in exile in EGYPT.

Vidal, Gore (Eugene Luther) (1925–). American writer. An eclectic writer who has produced novels, plays, poetry, song lyrics and critical essays, Vidal usually focuses on social, political and historical themes in his works. His first novel, *Williwaw* (1946), was a critical and popular success, but his 1968 novel *Myra Breckinridge* stirred controversy because of its transsexual main character. Vidal is best known for his television plays *Visit to a Small Planet* (1955) and *The Best Man* (1960), which were later adapted to film and the stage, and for his historical fiction, including *Burr* (1973) and *Lincoln* (1984). He has also written two science fiction novels, *Messiah* (1954) and *Kalki* (1978). Collections of his political essays include *The Second American Revolution* (1982).

For further reading:

Kiernan, Robert, *Gore Vidal*. New York: Ungar, 1982.

Vidor, King (1894–1982). American film director. Vidor began working in HOLLYWOOD in the 1920s, setting out to make films about the lives of ordinary people at a time when he thought movies were overacted and bore little resemblance to the real world. His directed the classic silent films *The Big Parade* (1925) and *The Crowd* (1928), for METRO-GOLDWYN-MAYER, and went on to direct some 50 films over the next 30 years. Many of his early sound films challenged Hollywood notions of movies as commercial, escapist entertainment. Notable among his early sound films are *Hallelujah* (1929), with an all-black cast; *The Champ* (1931), and the erotic *Bird of Paradise* (1932). Vidor nearly went broke when he used his own money to write, direct, and produce *Our Daily Bread* (1934), about farm life during the Great Depression. Other Vidor films include *Stella Dallas* (1937), *The Citadel* (1938), and *The Fountainhead* (1949), an adaptation of Ayn RAND's novel. His adaptation of Tolstoy's *War and Peace* (1955) featured a fine performance by Henry FONDA, among others, but failed to capture the historical vitality and complexity of the novel. Perhaps his best and most popular later film was the epic western, *Duel in the Sun* (1946). He retired from movie-making after *Solomon and Sheba* (1959).

Viet Cong. Viet Cong was a derogatory term for Vietnamese communists in South VIETNAM during the VIETNAM WAR. At the end of the war between the French and the VIET MINH (1946–54) 90,000 Viet Minh troops in what was to become South Vietnam were to be repatriated to the north. But the Viet Minh left behind an estimated 5,000 to 10,000 soldiers as a fifth column in the south. Instructed by Hanoi to lie low until 1959, they were then activated by the North Vietnamese Politburo to begin a guerrilla war in the south in an attempt to subvert and overthrow the standing government. Viet Cong forces included "main force" units organized into companies and battalions (and later into regiments and divisions) and after 1964 reinforced by North Vietnamese regular Army units. There was also what was called the Viet Cong infrastructure, or VCI, which consisted of a party secretary, a finance and supply unit, and information and cultural, social welfare, and proselytizing sections to gain recruits both from the civilian population and the South Vietnamese military. SEARCH-AND-DESTROY operations by both U.S. and South Vietnamese units were designed to neutralize the Viet Cong and North Vietnamese Army main force units while clear-and-hold operations, and after 1968 the Phoenix program, were designed to root out the VCI with interdependent operations. The Viet Cong were effectively destroyed by the TET OFFENSIVE of 1968, when believing their propaganda that such an attack would provoke a "general uprising," the Viet Cong led an assault on cities throughout South Vietnam. Thereafter the Viet Cong remnants were cadred and controlled by North Vietnamese regulars.

Viet Minh [contraction of "Vietnam Doc Lap Dong Minh," League for Vietnamese Independence]. The Viet Minh was founded at the Eighth Plenum of the Indochina Communist Party in 1941. It was the overall title of the Vietnamese—nationalists as well as communists—who fought the French from 1946 to 1954.

Vietnam [The Socialist Republic of Vietnam]. Vietnam is a part of the Indochina Peninsula on the coast of Southeast Asia and comprises an area of 127,210 square miles. At the beginning of the century Vietnam was under French control, but covert nationalist organizations proliferated, including the Indochina Communist Party, founded by HO CHI MINH in 1930. During WORLD WAR II JAPAN occupied the country. After the war the Democratic Republic of Vietnam was formed with Ho as president, but the POTSDAM Agreement (1945) temporarily divided the country into the Chinese-occupied North, which recognized Ho's government, and the British-occupied South, which did not. The French seized SAIGON, then bombed Haiphong in 1946, starting a war with Ho's communist regime. The French surrendered in 1954, and Vietnam remained divided, with Ho's government in the North and the U.S.-supported regime of Ngo Dinh DIEM in the South. Diem's oppressive rule led to the formation of the National Liberation Front (VIET CONG) and his overthrow in 1963. The military regime of General Nguyen Van THIEU came to power in the South in 1965.

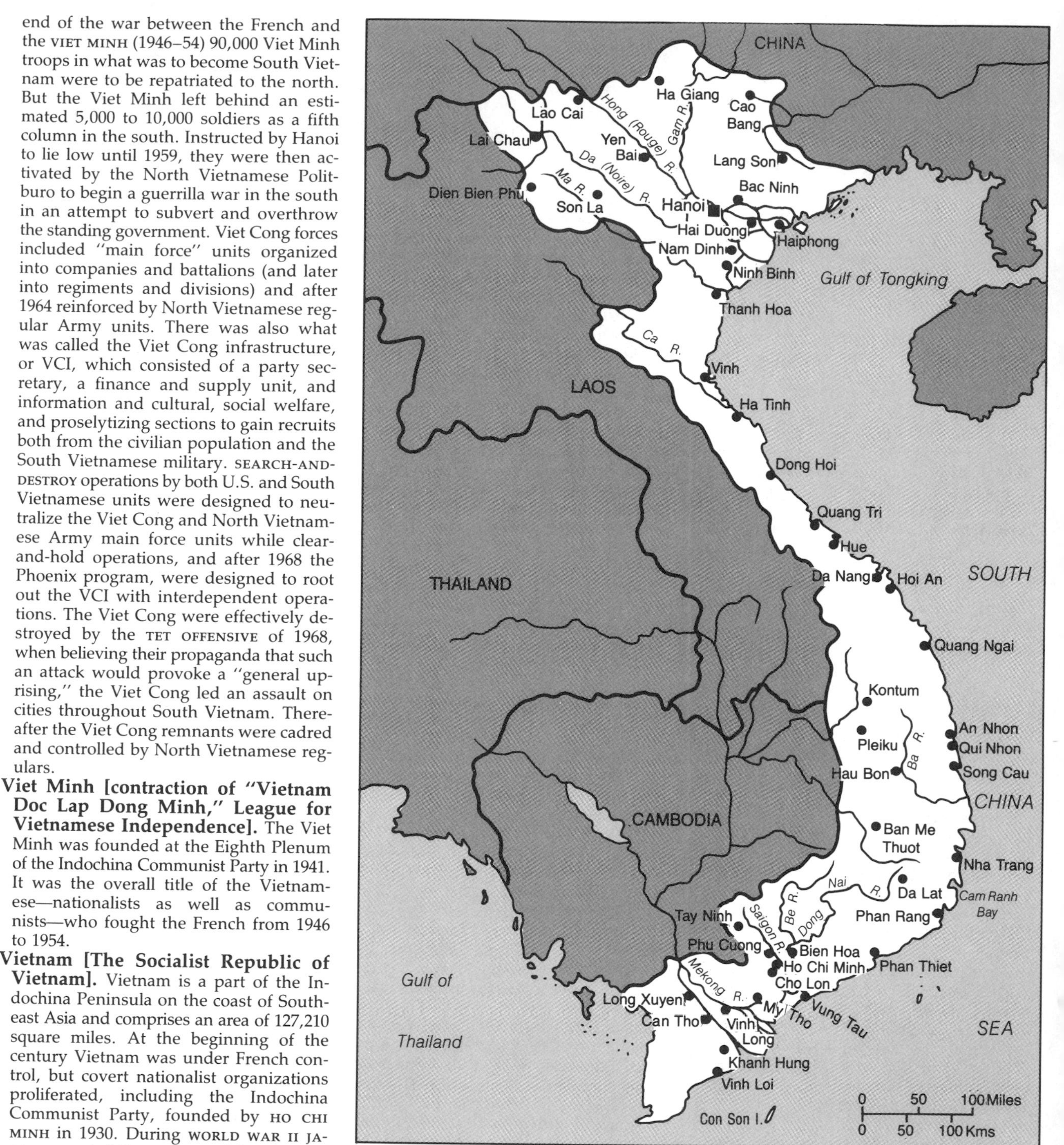

VIETNAM

U.S involvement in the VIETNAM WAR escalated when U.S. patrol boats were attacked in the Gulf of Tonkin in 1964 (see TONKIN GULF RESOLUTION). The southern-based Viet Cong joined the war against the U.S. Peace negotiations began in 1969 among all warring groups; the final PARIS PEACE ACCORD was signed in 1973. The Saigon regime fell in 1975, and the country was reunified as the Socialist Republic of Vietnam in 1976, with Pham Van Dong as premier. Vietnam invaded CAMBODIA in 1978, overthrowing a murderous Khmer Rouge regime that had been killing its own people by the hundreds of thousands and making border raids into Vietnam. From the mid-1980s the government of NGUYEN VAN LINH focused on rebuilding the country's economy.

VIETNAM

1930	Ho Chi Minh founds Indochinese Community Party; nationalist uprising in Tonkin, followed by a communist-led peasant revolt.
1940	Japanese forces occupy Vietnam in World War II.
1941	Ho establishes Viet Minh as alliance of communist and nationalist interests; Viet Minh carries on guerrilla resistance to Japanese with some assistance from U.S. military.
1945	After Japanese surrender, Viet Minh takes over Hanoi and Saigon; Emperor Bao Dai abdicates; Democratic Republic of Vietnam (DRV) declared with Ho as president and Hanoi as capital; Potsdam agreement, concluded among U.S., Britain and Soviet Union, temporarily divides Vietnam into North zone, occupied by Chinese, and South zone, occupied by British troops.
1946	Compromise signed by French and Vietnamese governments recognizing DRV as "free state" within French Union; repeated clashes follow and finally French navy bombards Haiphong.
1954	French forces capitulate following 56-day siege of French stronghold, Dien Bien Phu, by Viet Minh forces; Geneva Ceasefire Agreement provisionally partitions country along 17th parallel.
1955	French forces leave country; in South Ngo Dinh Diem becomes chief of state in popular referendum, replacing Emperor Bao Dai; Republic of Vietnam (RVN) proclaimed with capital at Saigon.
1960	National Liberation Front (NLF), South Vietnamese guerrillas supported by Hanoi, launch insurrection.
1961	U.S. and RVN sign treaty of amity; U.S. military presence in country increases 10-fold.
1963	Military junta led by General Duong Van Minh assassinates Diem in coup, allegedly with U.S. cooperation.
1964	U.S. destroyer *Maddox* attacked in Tonkin Gulf by Hanoi torpedo boats; U.S. Congress passes Tonkin Gulf resolution sanctioning use of U.S. armed forces in Vietnam; 185,000 U.S. troops land by year end.
1965	U.S. President Lyndon Johnson orders continuous bombing raids on North Vietnam below 20th parallel.
1967	In national elections, army chief of staff Nguyen Van Thieu is elected president with Ky as vice president.
1968	NLF and DRV launch Tet offensive, attacking Saigon and 30 provincial capitals; Johnson orders bombing halt.
1969	President Richard Nixon announces Vietnamization policy under which U.S. begins phased pull-out of troops; Ho Chi Minh dies.
1972	U.S. resumes intensive bombing of the North.
1973	Paris Peace Agreement ending U.S. involvement in the Vietnam War is signed by Secretary of State Henry Kissinger and NLF representative Le Duc Tho; last U.S. forces leave Vietnam.
1975	NLF sweeps across South to Saigon; General Duong Van Minh announces unconditional surrender of the Republic of Vietnam.
1976	Vietnam's reunification officially proclaimed under the name Socialist Republic of Vietnam.
1979	In support of Kampuchean National United Front for National Salvation fighting Pol Pot's Khmer Rouge regime, Vietnamese troops overrun Cambodia, seize Phnom Penh, oust Pol Pot government.
1989	Vietnam continues scheduled withdrawal of troops from Cambodia and participates in peace negotiations among the rival interests dividing Cambodia.
1991	Vietnam agrees to resolve cases of American soldiers missing since the Vietnam War.

For further reading:

Harrison, James P., *The Endless War: Vietnam's Struggle for Independence,* 2nd ed. New York: Columbia University Press, 1989.

Taylor, Keith W., *The Birth of Vietnam.* Berkeley, Calif.: University of California Press, 1983.

Vietnamese Civil War of 1955–65. With American military advisory assistance, Premier Ngo Dinh DIEM of South Vietnam (proclaimed an independent republic after the FRENCH INDOCHINA WAR OF 1946–54) gained control of the army and used it to fight three rebellious, well-equipped religious groups (the Binh Xuyen, Hoa Hao and Caodaist sects). In 1955, Binh Xuyen rebels in Saigon (Ho Chi Minh City), South Vietnam's capital, battled government troops until being driven out of the city; the rebels' continued harassment forced Diem to attack them at Can Tho and Vinh Long and in the Seven Mountains. When Diem refused to hold general elections in 1956 as promised, North Vietnam directed VIET CONG rebels to begin a campaign of guerrilla warfare and terrorism to overthrow South Vietnam's regime. Diem suppressed a military revolt against him (1960), but his U.S.-trained army proved generally ineffective against the tactics of the Viet Cong, who established the National Front for the Liberation of South Vietnam. U.S. military aid increased in an effort to wipe out the Viet Cong; South Vietnam's "strategic hamlet program" was started in 1962 to resettle peasants in towns defended against the Viet Cong. The Diem government's harassment of opposing Buddhist priests led to riots and self-immolations. On November 1–2, 1963, a military coup toppled the South Vietnamese government; Diem was killed, and a military-controlled provisional regime was established. A period of political instability ensued, with South Vietnam trying to strengthen its anticommunist military effort. By 1965, the Armed Forces Council, headed by Generals Nguyen Cao KY and Nguyen Van THIEU was running the country. (See also VIETNAM WAR.)

Vietnamese Uprisings of 1930–31. Failure to gain concessions from the French led the Vietnamese to form revolutionary organizations; the Viet Nam Quoc Dan Dang (VNQDD), led by Nguyen Thai Hoc (1904–1930), hoped to achieve an independent democratic government. A planned military uprising began February 9–10, 1930, when native troops at Yen Bai garrison in Tonkin (north Vietnam) mutinied, killing the French officers. The French crushed the uprising before it could spread, and Hoc and other leaders were beheaded. Afterwards many VNQDD members joined the Indochina Communist Party (ICP) formed in 1930 by Nguyen That Thanh, later known as HO CHI MINH

Dedicated in 1982, the Vietnam Veterans Memorial is inscribed with the names of all Americans missing or killed in the Vietnam War.

(1890–1969). The ICP fomented uprisings in Tonkin and central Vietnam which were harshly suppressed by the French, but the disturbances continued, gaining in vehemence.

Vietnam Veterans Memorial. The Vietnam Veterans Memorial in Washington, D.C., was the dream of Vietnam veteran Jan Skruggs, whose Vietnam Veterans Memorial Fund collected $7 million and conducted a design contest for the memorial. It was won by a 21–year-old architecture student at Yale, Maya Ying Lin, in 1981. Her design consisted of a 594–foot chevron-shaped wall of polished black granite cut into a hillside, with the names of servicemen and women killed or missing in Vietnam engraved into the surface. Dedicated in 1982, the memorial was the object of some controversy because many veterans felt that its stark modernistic design failed to properly commemorate the sacrifice of the men and women who fought and died in Vietnam. In an effort to accommodate those who felt this way, a more traditional statue of four fighting men was placed near the wall. That statue, by sculptor Frederick E. Hart, was dedicated on Memorial Day, 1984. The wall, the most visited memorial in Washington in 1984, now contains the names of 58,022 service members who died or are missing in action in Vietnam.

Vietnam War (1956–75). The country of VIETNAM had been divided at the 17th parallel into the Republic of Vietnam (South Vietnam) and the Democratic Republic of Vietnam (North Vietnam) after the FRENCH INDOCHINA WAR OF 1946–54. In 1956, a civil war broke out between the communist government of the north, supported by the VIET MINH, and the nominally democratic, U.S.-backed government of the south. At first the fighting was a mainly bloody guerrilla warfare carried out by Viet Minh soldiers—the so-called VIET CONG—who had returned to their homes in the south and fought there against the Army of the Republic of Vietnam (ARVN). The U.S. provided military advisers to the ARVN and, in 1961, authorized them to fight with the South Vietnamese units they were training.

On August 23, 1964, North Vietnamese patrol boats reportedly attacked two U.S. destroyers in the Gulf of TONKIN. U.S. President Lyndon B. JOHNSON was given congressional authorization to repel any armed attack, and U.S. warplanes began bombing raids over North Vietnam. American troops were sent to South Vietnam to participate as allies of the South Vietnamese. North Vietnamese army units marched continuously down the HO CHI MINH TRAIL in Cambodia to fight alongside the Viet Cong. In an attempt to clear the countryside, U.S. forces and the ARVN initiated the tactics called "SEARCH AND DESTROY," "free fire zones" and "pacification." They also regularly bombed military and civilian targets in the north and supply dumps in Cambodia.

At the end of January 1968, the communist-formed NATIONAL LIBERATION FRONT (NLF) and the Viet Cong launched their great TET OFFENSIVE against 36 provincial cities and wreaked wide destruction in South Vietnam before they withdrew with heavy losses. Their fighting ability, however, amazed the world. Meanwhile, protests and demonstrations occurred frequently in the U.S. against this undeclared war. At that time, 1968–69, about 500,000 American troops were in Vietnam. In July 1968, the U.S. announced a new policy of "Vietnamization," in which the South Vietnamese themselves would gradually do all the fighting. In May of the next year, American Army units began to leave, but air support units remained. In 1972, the communist forces of the NLF crossed the demilitarized zone (DMZ) around the 17th parallel and seized a northern South Vietnamese province. The U.S. retaliated by mining the harbors of Haiphong and other North Vietnamese ports. When the peace talks between the U.S. and North Vietnam, which had been going on sporadically since 1968, broke down entirely in December 1972, U.S. President Richard M. NIXON ordered 11 days of intensive "Christmas bombing" of North Vietnamese cities. Later, talks resumed and led to a ceasefire agreement among the U.S., Viet Cong and North and South Vietnam on January 27, 1973.

But the fighting continued as before, with both sides accusing the other of violations. In 1974, the ARVN began withdrawing troops from distant outposts, and the NLF seized several provincial capitals. The long-expected communist offensive started in January 1975; NLF forces gained control of Vietnam's central high-

A young American lieutenant awaits medical aid after being burned by a Vietcong white phosphorus booby trap.

lands. When the South Vietnamese government decided to evacuate its northern cities of Quang Tri and Hue, its collapse and defeat were in sight. Southern coastal cities were abandoned, civilians and army troops took flight, and the remaining U.S. personnel escaped from the country by sea and air. On April 30, 1975, South Vietnam surrendered unconditionally to the communists, who occupied its capital, SAIGON (Ho Chi Minh City), without a fight. North and South Vietnam were formally united as the Socialist Republic of Vietnam on July 2, 1976.

For further reading:

Young, Marilyn B., *The Vietnam Wars 1945–1990*. New York: HarperCollins, 1991.

Olson, James S. and Randy Roberts, *Where the Domino Fell: America and Vietnam, 1945 to 1990*. New York: St. Martin's Press, 1991.

Mexican rebel leader Pancho Villa (third from right) became a national hero for his role in Mexico's political struggles (1910–1920).

Villa, Pancho (1878?-1923). Mexican rebel leader. One of the larger-than-life figures of the early 20th century, Pancho Villa was considered a patriot and hero by his followers and a bandit by his enemies. Of peasant origin, he became involved in Mexican national politics when he joined Francisco Madero in the MEXICAN CIVIL WAR OF 1911 and helped overthrow dictator Porfirio DIAZ. He was also a leading figure in the MEXICAN REVOLT OF 1914–15. He incurred the wrath of the U.S. government when his forces crossed the border and raided the town of Columbus, New Mexico in 1916 (see VILLA'S RAIDS). For all his involvement in contemporary Mexican affairs, Villa never held any official position. He withdrew from public life in 1920 and was assassinated in 1923.

Villa-Lobos, Heitor (1887–1959). Brazilian composer. A champion of Brazilian nationalism, Villa-Lobos is one of the most original and prolific composers of the 20th century. He has written over 1,300 compositions, including several ballets, operas, oratorios, symphonies and string quartets. He recreated the melodies and rhythms of folk songs and Indian songs in his works, developing an eclectic compositional technique. His most important works include the 15 *Chords* (composed 1920–29) with their vigorous dance rhythms, and the nine suites, *Bachianas Brasileiras* (composed 1932–44). In 1932 he became director of music education in Brazil, introducing bold new approaches that emphasized native resources. He established the Brazilian Academy of Music in Rio de Janeiro in 1945.

Villa's Raids (1916–17). The 1911 overthrow of Mexico's dictator-president Porfirio DIAZ (1830–1915), set off a struggle for power. Francisco "Pancho" VILLA (1877–1923), with American support, was winning until 1915 when Alvaro Obregon (1880–1928) defeated him, elevating Venustiano Carranza (1859–1920), Villa's enemy, as Mexico's chief. The U.S. recognized Carranza. In response, Villa's forces attacked Americans in Mexico, and raided across the border in Columbus, N. Mexico, March 9, 1916, killing about a dozen. U.S. President Woodrow WILSON (1859–1924) ordered General John J. PERSHING (1860–1948) on a punitive expedition in pursuit of Villa in Mexico. Pershing withdrew after 11 months, unable to capture Villa. The invasion so angered Mexicans that Villa became a national hero, despite leading rebels until 1920.

Villella, Edward (1936–). American dancer and company director, primarily responsible for changing the image of the male ballet dancer through his athletic prowess and virility in performance. Villella danced with the NEW YORK CITY BALLET (1957–78), quickly becoming one of the company's stars and creating roles in such ballets as BALANCHINE's *A Midsummer Night's Dream* (1962). His most famous role was as Balanchine's *Prodigal Son*. After retiring from performing, Villella served as artistic coordinator of the Eglevsky Ballet (1979–84), director of Ballet Oklahoma (1983–85) and founder-director of the Miami City Ballet (1986–present).

Vilna Dispute. Conflict between POLAND and LITHUANIA over the city of Vilna, Lithuania's medieval capital. Beginning in 1918, the city was claimed by Poland. It was seized by Polish forces in October, 1920 and was incorporated into Poland in 1922. The dispute over the nationality of the city prevented relations between Poland and Lithuania in the period between the two world wars. Vilna was returned to Lithuania by the U.S.S.R. in October, 1939. Under its Lithuanian name, Vilnius, it is now the capital of Lithuania.

Vincent, Francis T. "Fay" (1938–). American lawyer, business executive and commissioner of baseball. When Bart GIAMATTI became baseball commissioner in 1989 he chose his friend Fay Vincent as deputy commissioner. Unanimously elected as commissioner following Giamatti's sudden death later that year, Vincent was thrust into the public limelight. The soft-spoken attorney quickly won the respect of citizens, fans and players for his sensitive handling of the 1989 World Series after the deadly 1989 San Francisco earthquake. In July 1990 he took firm action to remove George Steinbrenner as principal owner of the New York Yankees. Before entering baseball, Vincent served as director of the Securities and Exchange Commission's (SEC) Division of Corporation Finance and as chief executive of COLUMBIA PICTURES.

Vinson, Carl (1883–1981). American politician. A Democrat from Georgia, he served in the U.S. House of Representatives for a record 50 years (1914–65). For 14 of those years (1950–64) he was chairman of the powerful House Armed Services Committee; before that, he headed the Naval Affairs Committee (1931–47) and was largely responsible for building up the U.S. Navy during WORLD WAR II. Known as the "Swamp Fox" for his mastery of parliamentary procedure and virtually unchallenged rule over military matters, he was considered a potential secretary of defense in 1950. He ended all speculation about his possible appointment to that post by saying "Shucks, I'd rather go on running the Pentagon from up here." His major role in strengthening the nation's defense was saluted in 1980 when a new nuclear aircraft carrier was named in his honor—the first U.S. Navy warship to be named after a person still living.

Vinson, Fred(erick) M(oore) (1890–1953). American politician, public servant and chief justice of the Supreme Court (1946–53). A graduate of Centre College and its law school in Kentucky, Vinson was a successful local businessman and lawyer before his election to Congress in 1924. He became a member of the Ways and Means Committee, which initiates tax legislation, and a prominent supporter of President Franklin D. ROOSEVELT'S NEW DEAL In 1938 Roosevelt appointed him to the U.S. Court of Appeals for the District of Columbia. Five years later, Vinson undertook a new career as Roosevelt's director of the Office of Economic Stabilization. In 1945 he briefly headed the Office of War Mobilization and Reconversion. Shortly after Roosevelt's death (1945), President Harry S TRUMAN named Vinson secretary of the treasury. Vinson quickly became one of Truman's closest and most trusted advisors. In 1946 Truman appointed him chief justice of the Supreme Court. On the Court, the pragmatic Vinson continued to work closely with Truman. He supported increased governmental regulation and executive power. He dissented in the case of *Youngstown Sheet and Tube Co. v. Sawyer* (1952), in which the majority decided that President Truman had exceeded his authority in seizing steel mills to prevent a steel strike. He wrote several significant opinions in racial discrimination cases and cautiously extended CIVIL RIGHTS for blacks. Truman unsuccessfully tried to persuade Vinson to enter the 1952 presidential race. He died unexpectedly in 1953 while still on the Court, and was succeeded by California Governor Earl WARREN.

Virgin Islands, British. The British Virgin Islands are on the northwestern edge of the Caribbean and cover a total area of 58 square miles; the capital is Road Town. Between 1872 and 1956 they were administered as part of the Federal Colony of the Leeward Islands. A new constitution granting greater internal self-government was introduced in 1977. Elections in 1975 had the Virgin Islands Party (VIP) and the United Party (UP) each winning three seats. An independent member, former Chief Minister Willard Wheatley, held the balance of power. He formed a government with the VIP, with himself as chief minister. In 1979 Wheatley's deputy H. Lavitty Stoutt was able to secure enough support after elections in that year to become chief minister. Another tied election result in 1983 allowed the one independent member, Cyril Romney, to form a government with the UP, with Romney as chief minister. In 1986 Romney faced allegations over illegal conduct and he called an early general election rather than face a vote of "no confidence." In the elections, the VIP won a majority of the seats and Stoutt returned to power as chief minister.

Virgin Islands, United States. The U.S. Virgin Islands are on the northwestern edge of the Caribbean and cover a total area of 136 square miles; the capital is Charlotte Amalie. The terrain is mostly hilly or rugged and mountainous. Denmark, which had held the islands since the 17th century, sold them to the U.S. in 1916 for $25,000,000, and they were transferred to U.S. military administration in 1917. U.S. citizenship was granted in 1927. In 1931 a civil administration replaced control by the Navy Department, and the islands came under the control of the Department of the Interior. Revisions to the Organic Act in 1954, which created an elected senate, prompted the development of political parties, the principal parties being affiliates of the U.S. Republican and Democratic parties. The Virgin Islands were given the right to elect their own governor in 1968, and the first election in 1970 was won by Melvin Evans of the Republicans. In 1974 Cyril King, the leader of a breakaway faction of the Democratic Party known as the Independent Citizen's Movement, was elected governor. King died in 1978 and was succeeded by his deputy, Juan Luis, who was re-elected in 1982. The elections in 1986 were won convincingly by the Democrats and Alexander Farrelly became governor. The last referendum on a constitution giving greater autonomy to the islands failed to achieve a sufficient majority in favor when it was held in November 1981.

Virgin Land Campaign. In 1953, Soviet Premier KHRUSHCHEV ordered the reclamation of virgin and waste land in Central Asia. Within three years nearly 90 million acres (36.4 million hectares) had been cultivated in Kazakhstan, Siberia and the southern Urals. The aim was self-sufficiency in cereals. After the initial stage of the campaign, intensive rather than extensive cultivation was practiced. The campaign was interpreted by some as an attempt to russify minor nationalities.

Visconti, Luchino (1906–1976). Italian stage and film director. Visconti won international fame both for his directorial work in the theater, and for his controversial films that often focused on the decadent state of European culture and politics. He began his career as a stage director in Paris, then moved to the Teatro Eliseo in Rome where he presented an innovative repertoire of modern classic plays by Anton CHEKHOV, Jean COCTEAU, and Tennessee WILLIAMS, among others. Visconti took up film directing in the postwar era and became renowned for his lush visual style and settings that highlighted the moral decay of his characters. Among his best known films are *The Damned* (1969) and *Death in Venice* (1971), an adaptation of the famous novella by Thomas MANN.

Vishnevskaya, Galina (1926–). Russian soprano. Born in Leningrad, Vishnevskaya spent her childhood in Kronstadt where she began her singing career during World War II. Returning to Leningrad in 1943, she received vocal training and became a member of the Leningrad Light Opera Company. She joined the Bolshoi Opera in 1952, rising steadily to stardom in such roles as Cio-Cio-San in *Madama Butterfly*, Violetta in *La Traviata*, Mimi in *La Boheme*, *Tosca* and *Aida*. In 1955, while at the Prague Festival, she met the Soviet cellist, Mstislav ROSTROPOVICH, and days later the two were married. From 1955 to 1960 she made appearances throughout Europe, making her debut in the U.S. in 1960. Starring in *Aida* in 1961, Visnevskaya became the first Soviet prima donna to appear with the Metropolitan Opera. After she and her husband sheltered Aleksandr SOLZHENITSYN in 1970, both musicians fell from favor with the Soviet authorities and their musical activities were severely curtailed. In 1974 they left the U.S.S.R., and in 1978 they were stripped of Soviet citizenship. Dividing her time among London, Paris, New York and Washington, Vishnevskaya has since made numerous appearances in the U.S. and Europe.

Vishnevsky, Vsevolod (1900–1951). Soviet novelist and playwright. He was basically a propagandist, and in the screenplay *The Unforgettable Year 1919* (1949) he flatters STALIN by the sheer exaggeration of his involvement in the CIVIL WAR. His plays included *Trial of the Kronstadt Mutineers* (1921) and *The Optimistic Tragedy* (1932).

Vishniac, Roman (1897–1990). Russian-born biologist and photographer. His best-known works were the series of photographs he had taken of Jewish life in Eastern Europe in the 1930s. The photographs depicted the lives of ordinary JEWS in GERMANY, POLAND, LITHUANIA, LATVIA, HUNGARY, ROMANIA and CZECHOSLOVAKIA on the eve of the HOLOCAUST. He later concentrated on scientific microphotography, and emigrated to the U.S. in 1940. He became a professor at Pratt Institute and Yeshiva University.

Vitria, Emmanuel (1920–1987). French transplant recipient. He lived a record 18 years with a transplanted heart. He became the world's longest surviving heart transplant patient in 1977 upon the death of a U.S. woman who had been operated on one month earlier than he had been. After his transplant, he ignored medical advice and continued to smoke, drink and eat rich foods, apparently with little ill effect.

Vize, Vladimir Yulyevich (1888–1954). Russian geographer and explorer. He was part of the team led by G.Y. Sedov that attempted to reach the NORTH POLE (1912–14). He helped organize the North Polar Drift Expedition in 1937, and between 1910 and 1937 he participated in 14 Arctic expeditions.

V-J Day. Victory in JAPAN—August 14, 1945. On this day, Emperor HIROHITO formally announced JAPAN'S surrender to the Allies, ending WORLD WAR II.

Vlasov, Andrei Andreyevich (1900–1946). Russian general and leader of the anticommunist movement among Soviet PRISONERS OF WAR during WORLD WAR II in Germany. He enlisted in the Red Army in 1919 and played a prominent part in the defense of Kiev and Moscow (1941–42). After capturing him in 1942, German officers persuaded him to assist with the Russian anticommunist movement. He was chairman of the Committee for the Liberation of the Peoples of Russia in 1944. He surrendered to the Americans in 1945 and was returned to the Soviets, who executed him.

V-1 and V-2 rockets. Rockets developed by Germany and used as flying bombs during WORLD WAR II. The **V-1** was basically a winged airplane with an automatic pilot. Also known as the **buzz bomb,** it was the first of Germany's *Vergeltungswaffen* (vengeance weapons), so named because they were used to retaliate against Allied air attacks. First proposed in 1939, it made its maiden flight two years later. The V-1 was powered by gasoline and driven by a pulse-jet engine; it measured about 25 feet long, weighed five tons and contained some 1,100 pounds of explosives. Maximum altitude was 3,000 feet, range, under 200 miles, speed, 400 mph. Upon reaching its target, it was directed into a steep dive, its engines cut and its warhead electrically detonated upon contact with the ground. It arrived with a whine and then an abrupt silence, during which those attacked had only seconds to seek shelter. Because the V-1 could not be directed with any precision to a specific target but fell at random within a general area, it had limited military usefulness; rather, it was a terror weapon, designed to demoralize Britain's civilian population. More than 8,000 V-1s were used to bomb London in attacks launched near Calais, France, beginning in 1944.

The much more advanced **V-2** was developed from 1938 to 1942 at PEENEMUNDE, Germany, under the direction of Wernher von BRAUN. It, too, had a liquid-propelled jet engine; however, the fuel was methyl alcohol and it carried its own liquid oxygen, which was used as a combustion booster. This feature enabled the V-2 to cruise at oxygen-depleted high altitudes. The cigar-shaped rocket was 45 feet long and 66 inches in diameter; it weighed 13 tons, with a one-ton warhead, and its range was over 200 miles. The V-2 was fired vertically to an altitude of some 15–18 miles. It then went into an inclined trajectory, guided by graphite flaps controlled by a preset gyroscope and directed by radio. Its maximum speed was some 3,600 mph. The V-2 was successfully test-launched for the first time in October 1942. From September 6, 1944, to March 27, 1945, over 4,000 V-2 rockets were launched against London, Antwerp and other targets. The V-2 was the precursor of many modern intercontinental ballistic missiles and spacecraft; several of the project's engineers were brought to the U.S. after the war and became leading figures in the U.S. space program. (See also OPERATION PAPERCLIP.)

Vodopyanov, Mikhail V. (1900–1980). Soviet flier and Artic adventurer. He gained prominence in the mid-1930s when he pioneered new polar air routes and took part in the rescue of a marooned scientific expedition along the north coast of Siberia. He is believed to have been the first person to land a plane at the NORTH POLE.

Voice of America [VOA]. Radio broadcasting arm of the International Communication Agency. Established in 1942, the VOA began broadcasting in English to Germany during WORLD WAR II. It now broadcasts radio programming in English and 41 other languages for overseas audiences. Its intent is to promote the American viewpoint worldwide, and its programming includes news, analysis of events from Washington, feature programs and music. Its traditional function as an organ of propaganda has aroused controversy and endangered the integrity of its news programming.

Voinovich, Vladimir (1932–). Exiled Russian writer who lives in Paris. After serving in the Soviet army in Poland, Voinovich worked as a carpenter and started to write. In 1963 he published *I Want to Be Honest* in *Novy Mir*. In 1966 he signed a letter defending Yuri DANIEL and Andrei SINYAVSKY and in 1968 signed one protesting the arrest of Alexander GINZBERG and Yuri Galakovsk. In 1973 Voinovich refused to attack Andrei SAKHAROV, although pressure was put on him to do so. In 1974 he was expelled from the Writer's Union and in 1980 went into exile. His satirical novel *The Life and Extraordinary Adventures of Private Ivan Chonkin* has won him much support abroad as well as in Russia, among those who have managed to read it in *Samizdat*.

Volkov, Vladislav (1935–1971). Soviet cosmonaut, flight engineer aboard the ill-fated Soyuz 11 flight that initially met with enormous success, including an unprecedented 23–day stay aboard a space station. Headed for home, as the crew jettisoned the docking module a pressure equalization valve blew open prematurely. Volkov and fellow cosmonauts Georgy DOBROVOLKSY and Viktor PATSAYEV were not wearing pressurized suits and all three died instantly.

Volkswagen. German automobile manufacturer; in German the word means "people's car," a name given to an automobile design proposal of Ferdinand PORSCHE in 1933. The encouragement of the HITLER regime lead to actual production beginning in 1936. The body design for the rear-engined car was developed by Erwin KOMENDA. In time it became widely popular and was sold in vast numbers worldwide after World War II. The design is regarded as either ugly or as a model of simple functionalism. In English the name "beetle" or "bug" came to describe its rounded, streamlined shape. As increasing prosperity made the original VW seem too spartan in quality and as concerns developed about its safety record, Volkswagen turned to development of a replacement design, with front wheel drive and more comfort. The resulting car, variously named Golf, Polo and Rabbit in different versions and markets, has largely taken the place of the original VW.

Voloshin, Maximilian Alexandrovich (1877–1931). Russian symbolist poet. Born in southern Russia, he traveled extensively in Central Asia and around the Mediterranean. He also lived in Paris, studying painting there. Voloshin's poetry reflects the influence that Catholic mysticism, the occult, the Aegean and ancient Greek culture had on him. He wrote a series of historical poems on the subject of the destiny of Russia, as a result of the Revolution, in which he developed the concept of a "Holy Russia." He felt that a country of Christian mysticism was being oppressed by the state.

von Bulow case (1982). Criminal trial of socialite Claus von Bulow, a noted Danish-born aristocrat alleged to have poisoned his wife Sunny, who had previously inherited $75 million. A few years after their marriage, Sunny twice fell into a mysterious coma. She never emerged from the second coma but remained at a hospital in a persistent vegetative state. The couples' maid suspected foul play and alerted Sunny's children from a prior marriage of her suspicions. Claus von Bulow stood to gain millions on his wife's death. He was ultimately tried for attempted murder and convicted based on circumstantial evidence, including a black bag that contained a hypodermic syringe. During the trial it was revealed that he maintained a mistress while his wife was in a coma. The conviction was thrown out because the black bag was illegally seized evidence. A retrial followed, but after a hard-fought trial, the jury acquitted von Bulow.

Von Euler, Ulf Svante. See Hans EULER-CHELPIN.

Vo Nguyen Giap (1912–). North Vietnamese general and minister of defense. Giap was born in 1912 in the French protectorate of Annam, which later became part of North Vietnam. Active in the communist underground, he was recruited into the VIET MINH movement in the early 1940s. During the FRENCH INDOCHINA WAR OF 1946–54, Giap was the Viet Minh's leading military commander, and he directed the stunning victory over the French at DIEN BIEN PHU. With independence, he became North Vietnam's minister of defense. During the war with South Vietnam, Giap advocated direct clashes with American forces, a strategy that cost North Vietnam more than half a million soldiers from 1964 to 1969 (see VIETNAM WAR). In 1972, Giap convinced the government that, with the heavy withdrawals of U.S. forces, the time had finally come to launch a massive invasion of the South, which again proved disastrous. Thereafter, Giap was replaced as commander by Van Tien Dung, who planned and executed the final offensive that brought North Vietnam ultimate victory in 1975. In 1980, Van Tien Dung also replaced Giap as minister of defense.

Von Manteuffel, Hasso (1897–1978). German general who was commander of the Nazi attack during the BATTLE OF THE BULGE in WORLD WAR II.

Prior to the 30th anniversary of the battle of Dien Bien Phu, victorious General Vo Nguyen Giap revisits the battlefield (May 7, 1984).

Vonnegut, Kurt, Jr. (1922–). American author. Although his works were generally ignored by mainstream critics until the publication of his novel *Cat's Cradle* (1963), Vonnegut is now regarded as a master of contemporary fiction. His dominant themes of the dehumanizing effects of technology, the need for kindness, and the struggle of man against a hostile universe are presented in a style that blends irony, satire, fantasy, the tragicomic, and a colloquial speech that contains many coined words. His first novel, *Player Piano* was published in 1952. In 1969 he published his best known work, *Slaughterhouse Five,* which recreates his experiences as a prisoner of war in Dresden during the Allied firebombing in WORLD WAR II. Other major works include the novels *Breakfast of Champions* (1973) and *Slapstick* (1976), the play *Happy Birthday, Wanda June* (1970), and the story collection *Welcome to the Monkey House* (1968). He has also taught at several schools, including Harvard University.

For further reading:

Klinkowitz, Jerome, *Kurt Vonnegut.* London: Methuen, 1982.

Von Neumann, John (1903–1957). German mathematician who studied at the University of Berlin, the Berlin Institute of Technology and the University of Budapest, from which he obtained his doctorate in 1926. Von Neumann was Privatdozent at Berlin (1927–29) and taught at Hamburg (1929–30). He left Europe in 1930 to work in Princeton, first at the university and later at the Institute for Advanced Study. From 1943 he was a consultant on the ATOMIC BOMB project. Von Neumann may have been one of the last men able to span the fields of pure and applied mathematics. His first work was in set theory (the subject of his doctoral thesis), but in 1928 he published his first paper in the field for which he is best known, the mathematical theory of games. This work culminated in 1944 with the publication of *The Theory of Games and Economic Behavior,* which von Neumann had coauthored with Oskar Morgenstern. Not all the results in this work were novel, but it was the first time the field had been treated in such a large-scale and systematic way. Apart from the theory of games von Neumann did important work in the theory of operators. Dissatisfied with the resources then available for solving the complex computational problems that arose in hydrodynamics, von Neumann developed a broad knowledge of the design of COMPUTERS and, with his interest in the general theory of automata, became one of the founders of a whole new discipline. He was much interested in the general role of science and technology in society, and this led to his increasing involvement with high-level government scientific committees.

von Schlabrendorff, Fabian (1907–1980). German army officer involved in plots against Adolf HITLER during WORLD WAR II. In 1943 von Schlabrendorff smuggled a bomb disguised as a case of brandy aboard Hitler's plane, but the bomb failed to explode. The following year, with Count Claus von Stauffenberg, he took part in the famous failed assassination attempt on Hitler on July 20, 1944. Von Schlabrendorff was arrested, tortured by the GESTAPO, and spent the remainder of the war in a CONCENTRATION CAMP. After the war he was a lawyer and judge in West Germany.

Von Stade, Frederica (1945–). American singer. An outstanding mezzo-soprano, she gained international renown as Cherubino in *The Marriage of Figaro.* She made her Metropolitan Opera debut in a small role in *The Magic Flute* in 1970 and her European debut as Cherubino at the Royal Theater at Versailles in 1973. She has performed at the Glyndebourne and Salzburg Festivals and with opera companies throughout the world. Her many roles include Rosina in *The Barber of Seville* and Melisande in *Pelleas and Melisande.*

Von Trapp, Baroness Maria [born Maria Augusta Kutschera] (1905–1987). Austrian singer. She was the guiding force behind a family of singers who became known throughout the world when their story was told in the play and film *The Sound of Music.* The family's tale of flight from Austria in 1938 to avoid complicity with Nazi rule was transformed, in 1965, into one of Hollywood's greatest success stories. Julie Andrews portrayed Baroness Von Trapp in the film.

Voorhees, Donald (1903–1989). American conductor. He was best known as the musical director of the "Bell Telephone Hour," a show that ran on radio from 1940 to 1959 and on television from 1959 to 1968. The show was one of the most popular musical programs in U.S. broadcasting history.

Voronsky, Alexander Konstantinovich (1884–1935). Russian critic and editor of *Krasnaya Nov,* the main journal for FELLOW TRAVELERS. Voronsky and the Pass group were the targets for official attack in 1927, and Voronskyism became synonymous with nonconformity, since Voronsky was accused of being a Bergsonian, a Freudian and a Trotskyist. His theory of "shedding the veils" involved a rejection of political propaganda in literature. This met with the party's disapproval, although Voronsky was a Marxist. He produced essays, memoirs and short stories.

Voroshilov, Kliment Efremovich (1881–1969). Soviet military and political leader, and a close friend of STALIN. He joined the Bolsheviks in 1903, organized the workers of Lugansk in the 1905 revolution and was subsequently deported. After returning to RUSSIA in 1917, Voroshilov earned an outstanding military reputation as a Red Army commander during the Civil War. He was a member of the central committee of the Communist Party and entered the Politburo in 1926. Following Stalin's death in 1953, he was appointed chairman of the Presidium of the Supreme Soviet. In 1960, however, he was dropped from the Presidium and in 1961 was expelled from the central committee; he was later restored to full membership. (See also REVOLUTION OF 1905.)

Vorster, B(althazar) J(ohannes) "John" (1915–1983). Prime minister of SOUTH AFRICA (1966–78). He was interned during World War II because of his pro-Nazi sympathies. A member of South Africa's Nationalist party, he was elected to the South African parliament in 1953. In the early 1960s he served as minister of justice and police. During this time he created a repressive security apparatus, banned multiracial organizations, arrested thousands who opposed APARTHEID, and crushed South Africa's Communist Party. As prime minister, he staunchly upheld apartheid. Implementing a program conceived by his predecessor, Hendrik VERWOERD, Vorster established nominally independent "homelands" or mini-states for the nation's blacks; in reality, these states, which occupied the poorest land, were economically and politically dependent on South Africa. Toward the end of his tenure as prime minister, Vorster eased some discriminatory policies, opening more theaters, hotels, and parks to blacks and allowing racially mixed sports competitions. In 1978 he stepped down because of ill health, accepting the ceremonial post of president. However, he resigned the presidency in 1979 after a government report concluded that he had been involved in the so-called **Muldergate Scandal,** the illegal state funding of a multimillion-dollar propaganda program while he was prime minister.

Voskhod. A modified Soviet VOSTOK spacecraft, used for two manned missions in 1964–65. Its name means "ascent."

Vostok. The first manned Soviet spacecraft. Its name means "east." (See also Yuri GAGARIN.)

Voting Rights Act of 1965. Landmark U.S. CIVIL RIGHTS legislation that enforced voting rights for blacks throughout the U.S. Although the post-Civil War Fifteenth Amendment to the Constitution and three 20th-century civil rights laws guaranteed equal political rights to blacks, this promise remained largely unfulfilled for nearly 100 years after the war. Various devices, including poll taxes, literacy tests and outright harassment and intimidation, were used to prevent blacks from voting. The Voting Rights Act was passed to eliminate these injustices. The act basically gave the federal government the power to supervise local registration procedures and elections wherever voting participation was below 50%. In practice, the law applied only in the South, where blacks were being systematically excluded. Under the law local voting laws would be valid only on federal court approval. Federal law would control voter requirements and stiff fines were imposed for violation of the act. Once the federal government became involved, universal suffrage became more than an empty promise.

Voyager 1. Voyager 1 was actually the second-launched of the two ambitious U.S. Voyager space probes. However, it was designated 1 because its path enabled it to reach its destination before VOYAGER 2. Launched September 5, 1977, it was designed to fly past the largest planets of the solar system, Jupiter and Saturn, as well as the outer planets, Uranus and Neptune. It passed Jupiter in March 1979 and reached Saturn more than a year and a half later, in November 1980, sending back the first close-up pictures of those giants.

Voyager 2. The U.S. *Voyager 2* spacecraft, launched on August 20, 1977, passed within 3,000 miles of the planet Neptune August 24–25, 1989. The fly-by produced a multitude of striking images and startling discoveries about the distant planet, climaxing a 12–year interplanetary mission. The mission earlier also yielded revelations about Jupiter, Saturn and Uranus. The mission's success dramatically exceeded the initial expectations of its planners. Covering four of the five outer planets of the solar system, it was the most far-ranging exploration of the planets since the space age began with the launch of SPUTNIK in 1957. With the completion of the mission, only Pluto, the outermost planet, remained unexplored by spacecraft. The mission was directed by scientists at NASA's JET PROPULSION LABORATORY in Pasadena, California. The mission's chief project scientist since 1972, Edward C. Stone, called it "a journey of a lifetime."

Voznesensky, Andrei A. (1933–). Russian poet. After studying architecture Voznesensky embarked on a full-time career as poet. His first work was published in 1958, and he has traveled abroad on reading tours, which have included several visits to the U.S. He has enjoyed the approval of the regime apart from a short time in 1963. His first book, *Mosaica* (1960), consists mostly of lyrical poems; later collections of his work, such as *The Triangular Pear* (1962), show greater subtlety and irony.

Voznesensky, Nicholas Alekseyevich (1903–1950). Soviet Communist politician. Having joined the party in 1919, Voznesensky studied at Sverdlov Communist University and at the Economic Institute of Red Professorship, and in 1934 he was appointed a member of the committee of party control. From 1935 he worked with Andrei ZHDANOV in Leningrad and rose to the posts of chairman of Gosplan (1938), deputy prime minister (1939) and a member of the state defense committee during World War II. In 1947, Voznesensky was made a full member of the Politburo. As a result of Georgy MALENKOV's persecution of Zhdanovites, he was arrested and shot.

Vreeland, Diana Dalziel (1903?-1989). Legendary fashion arbiter and editor. She was editor of *Harper's Bazaar* (1939–62) and of *Vogue* (1962–71). Under her editorship, the magazines chronicled the most extreme examples of glamour and the newest fashions. She was fired as editor of *Vogue* in 1971 for promoting fashions that were considered too avant-garde to be marketable. In 1973, she began a new career mounting historical fashion exhibits for the Metropolitan Museum of Art's costume institute.

Vyborg, Battle of. See FINNISH WAR OF INDEPENDENCE.

Vyborg Manifesto. About 180 deputies met in Vyborg to protest the dissolution of the first DUMA by NICHOLAS II in July 1906. The largest majority were Kadets, and the manifesto urged the people not to pay taxes or undertake military service when conscripted. The plan failed and the deputies were arrested, given three months' imprisonment and, probably more important for Russia, deprived of their right to stand for election to the second duma.

Vyshinsky, Andrei Yanuaryevich (1883–1954). Soviet lawyer and politician. He became public prosecutor in 1931 and was soon notorious for the rancor and vindictiveness with which he conducted state trials, notably in the Metropolitan-Vickers trial (1933) and the GREAT PURGES of 1936–37. After 1940 he became active in foreign affairs and was MOLOTOV's successor as foreign minister (1949–53), having been deputy minister (1940–49). As a delegate to the UNITED NATIONS he often attacked Western policies with the same venom that he had shown in the Soviet courts.

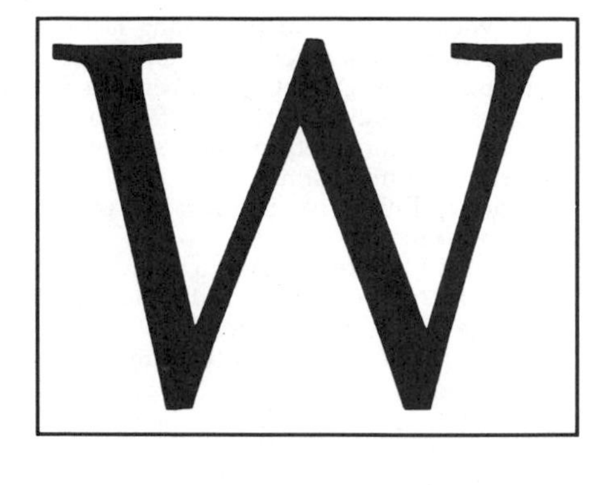

Wafd [Arab., "delegation"]. Main nationalist party of inter-war EGYPT. It was discredited by wartime cooperation with the British, and considered corrupt by NASSER and SADAT. Following its 1950 election victory, FREE OFFICERS encouraged civil unrest, and Wafd was dismissed by King FAROUK before he himself was deposed in 1952. Wafd and all other Egyptian parties were dissolved in 1953.

Wagner, John Peter "Honus" ["The Flying Dutchman"] (1874–1955). American baseball player. Wagner spent 56 years with the Pittsburgh organization, the first 17 years (1900–17) as a player, the remainder as a coach. One of the greatest shortstops of all time, his long arms and huge hands added to his legendary fielding skill. Over the course of his career, he played every position except catcher. He led the league in hitting eight times and topped the .300 mark 17 times. A Honus Wagner baseball card is now worth over $100,000, or 10 times more than Wagner was ever paid in any year of his career. He was named to the Hall of Fame in 1936.

Wailers, The. See Bob MARLEY.

Wainwright, Jonathan (Mayhew) (1883–1953). American general who commanded the U.S. and Filipino forces on BATAAN and CORREGIDOR after General MACARTHUR was ordered to leave in March 1942. Outnumbered and desperately short of supplies, Wainwright's forces held out until May 6, 1942, when they surrendered to the Japanese. Wainwright was mistreated as a PRISONER OF WAR for more than three years. He was freed after the liberation of the Philippines and was present on the battleship U.S.S. MISSOURI when the Japanese formally surrendered to General MacArthur in Tokyo Harbor. Wainwright was awarded the Congressional Medal of Honor.

Waite, Terry (1940–). Lay official of the Church of England. In the 1980s, as a special representative of Archbishop of Canterbury Robert RUNCIE, Waite held a number of meetings with terrorists in LEBANON to win the release of several Western hostages. On January 20, 1987, Waite disappeared in Beirut and was presumed to have been taken hostage himself. As of early 1991 he was still missing.

Waiting for Godot (1952). Two-act play by Irish-born author Samuel BECKETT; perhaps the classic work of the school of playwriting known as THEATER OF THE ABSURD. Written by Beckett in 1952, *Waiting for Godot* received its first public performance in 1953 and has since become a standard part of the theater repertoire around the world. The plot concerns two down and out men, Vladimir and Estragon, failed suicides who are waiting in vain for a man named Godot—whose identity and purpose are never clarified—to meet them as agreed upon. Vladimir and Estragon display an oddly British music-hall style of humor as they bide their time on the roadside. Passing them by are two strange vagabonds, Pozzo and Lucky, who in act one behave as ringmaster and slave but find their roles reversed in act two, when a blinded Pozzo is now led along by Lucky. Interpretations of *Waiting for Godot* abound, ranging from a depiction of existential nihilism to a modernist religious parable on the nature of faith.

Wake Island. Atoll in the central Pacific, between Hawaii and Guam; Japanese outpost during WORLD WAR II. Japanese forces overran Wake's small garrison of U.S. Marines on December 23, 1941; the island was retaken by U.S. forces in September 1945.

Waksman, Selman Abraham (1888–1973). Ukranian-American microbiologist. Waksman immigrated to the U.S. in 1910 and received his Ph.D. from the University of California at Berkeley in 1918. For the next four decades, he taught at Rutgers, where he had done his undergraduate work. In 1939 Waksman began a systematic search among soil microbes for germ-destroying compounds he called "antibiotics." In 1943 he isolated the antibiotic streptomycin from the mold *Streptomyces griseus* and discovered that it was successful in treating a type of tuberculosis as well as other diseases. In 1952 he was awarded the NOBEL PRIZE for physiology or medicine for this work.

Walcott, Derek (1930–). West Indian poet and playwright, widely considered one of the finest English-language poets of his generation. Born in St. Lucia of English and black West Indian parentage, Walcott was educated at St. Mary's College (class of 1953), St. Lucia, and the University of the West Indies, where he taught comparative literature. He began his writing career in Trinidad as a book reviewer, art critic and playwright and in 1959 he founded the Trinidad Theater Workshop. His first work, *Twenty-five Poems,* was published in 1948. He has since written more than 20 volumes of poetry and plays, combining lush imagery and Caribbean dialect with traditional English literary forms. Selections from his nine books of poetry, including the entire text of his autobiographical *Another Life,* are gathered in his *Collected Poems 1948–1984* (1986); his plays are collected in *Dreams on Monkey Mountain and Other Plays* (1970). Later work includes *The Arkansas Testament* (1987) and *Omeros* (1990), a Homerian epic embedded in the history and contemporary rhythm of Caribbean life. Walcott has taught at various universities in the U.S., including Harvard and Boston University. In 1981 he was awarded a MacArthur fellowship.

Waldheim, Kurt (1918–). Austrian diplomat and president (1986–). Waldheim entered the Austrian diplomatic service immediately after World War II. He was Austria's foreign minister from 1968 to 1970 and was an unsuccessful presidential candidate in 1971. He succeeded U THANT as secretary-general of the UNITED NATIONS in 1971. Regional conflicts and mutual suspicion between the power blocs hampered Waldheim's efforts, especially in the Middle East, while he lacked any practical means of overcoming the procrastinating tactics of the South Africans

Kurt Waldheim, who has served as UN secretary general (1972–82) and Austrian president (1986–), denied allegations that he was a Nazi officer during World War II.

over NAMIBIA. He retired from the UN in 1982. In 1986 Waldheim was elected president of Austria amid controversy surrounding his alleged Nazi activities during World War II. He was subsequently barred from entering the U.S. on a state visit.

Walesa, Lech (1943–). Polish labor leader and statesman, president of POLAND (1990–). Born in a village near Warsaw, the son of a carpenter, Walesa attended a state vocational school and became an electrician. After military service, he began work (1967) in the Lenin Shipyard at Gdansk. There he became a shop steward and was active in the movement to promote workers' rights. In 1976, after joining protests against the economic policies of Edward GIEREK, Walesa was fired from his shipyard post. Supporting himself with odd jobs, he became more active in Poland's labor movement, and in 1979 signed a charter demanding independent trade unions and the right to strike. When strikers seized the Lenin Shipyard in 1980, Walesa was reinstated and became head of a strike coordinating committee. Later that year he was named chairman of the newly approved SOLIDARITY union and soon became known for his moderate and even-handed approach, his ability to win concessions from the government and his willingness to compromise with authorities in order to solidify union gains. When Prime Minister JARUZELSKI imposed martial law and outlawed Solidarity in Dec. 1981, Walesa and other union leaders were imprisoned. He was released after nearly a year of solitary confinement. For his activities on behalf of Poland's workers, Walesa was awarded the 1983 NOBEL PRIZE for peace, and he was widely hailed as a national hero. Throughout the 1980s Walesa trod a careful path but continued to press the government for reforms, often in direct dialog with communist leaders. By the late 1980s, Walesa had achieved many of his goals, including the re-legalization of Solidarity and the promise of free elections. In the 1990 presidential elections, Walesa defeated Premier Tadeusz MAZOWIECKI, a Solidarity intellectual, but was forced into a runoff with expatriate businessman Stanislaw Tyminski, whom he bested in a landslide.

Lech Walesa, leader of Poland's Solidarity union, was awarded the Nobel Prize for peace in 1983 and elected the nation's president in 1990.

Walker, Alice (1944–). Black American writer. Born in Georgia and educated at Sarah Lawrence College, Walker is a prolific writer of fiction, essays and poetry. Walker's work is marked by a keen interest in African-American history and culture and a strong spiritual sensibility. She is perhaps best known for her novel, *The Color Purple*. The book was a great commercial success and was made into a film, but was also controversial for its use of dialect, which some critics thought stereotypical, and its negative portrayal of black men. Walker is the author of several other novels (including *Meridian*, about the CIVIL RIGHTS struggle of the 1950s and '60s) poetry collections (including *Goodnight, Willie Lee* and *Ill See You in the Morning*), volumes of short stories and essays, and a biography of Langston HUGHES for children. Walker founded a small publishing house as well. She is also the editor of an anthology of work by Zora Neale HURSTON, and is largely responsible for a renewed interest in Hurston, an important figure in the HARLEM RENAISSANCE.

Walker, Fred "Dixie" (1910–1982). American baseball player. A hard-hitting outfielder, he suffered a multitude of injuries during his first years in the major leagues in the 1930s. However, he came back as a star player for the Brooklyn Dodgers from 1939 to 1947. Known to Brooklyn fans as "the Peepul's Cherce," he took the National League batting crown in 1944 with an average of .357; during the next season he led the league in runs batted in, with 124. When Jackie ROBINSON, the first black player in the majors, joined the Dodgers (1947), Walker was traded at his own request.

Walker, James "Jimmy" (1881–1946). Mayor of NEW YORK CITY (1925–32). Dubbed "Beau James" by the tabloid press because of his sartorial splendor, Jimmy Walker was a handsome and popular mayor known to frequent fashionable night-spots during the prosperous 1920s. Walker was known for his quick wit; in a debate over a censorship law while he was in the state legislature, Walker commented that he had never seen a girl ruined by a book. Walker, the son of Irish immigrants, was a loyal member of Tammany Hall—the New York Democratic club—served in the state legislature for sixteen years and was ultimately rewarded with the mayoralty. He had previously worked for ten years as a songwriter on New York's Tin Pan Alley. Walker's luck ran out shortly after the STOCK MARKET CRASH OF 1929. Although previous city administrations had been characterized by graft and corruption, the level of wrongdoing escalated under Walker and was ultimately exposed in a series of public investigations. One commissioner explained that his ill-gotten gains appeared magically in a tin box under his mattress. Walker resigned in 1932 and fled to Europe to seek his girlfriend, Betty Compton, whom he later married. He was succeeded by the reform mayor, Fiorello LAGUARDIA.

For further reading:

Fowler, Gene, *Beau James*. Fairfield, N.J.: Augustus M. Kelley, 1973.

Walker, Joseph (1892–1985). American cameraman and cinematographer. Walker was best known for his collaborations with Frank CAPRA on a series of classic comedies including *It Happened One Night* and *It's a Wonderful Life*. A prolific inventor, he made numerous contributions to motion picture technology which were recognized in a special Academy Award in 1982.

Walker, Joseph (1921–1966). U.S. test pilot. Between March 1960 and August 1963, Walker made 25 flights in the X-15 experimental rocket plane at Edward Air Force Base. He set world record in both speed and altitude, taking the feisty plane to 4,104 miles per hour and to an altitude, on August 22, 1963, of almost 67 miles (354,300 feet). Walker made two X-15 flights to altitudes higher than 62 miles, which is the International Aeronautical Federation (FAI) standard for qualifying space flights. He died in a mid-air crash.

Wall, Max [born Maxwell George Lorimer] (1908–1990). British comedian, best known for his music hall performances in the 1920s and 1930s. Wall's most famous creation was the character Professor Wallofski. The character's bizarre walk was said to have inspired John Cleese of MONTY PYTHON'S FLYING CIRCUS. Wall won renewed popularity late in life in the late 1960s, appearing in a number of serious theater works, including Samuel BECKETT'S WAITING FOR GODOT and *Krapp's Last Tape*.

Wallace, George Corley (1919–). American politician. Born into a lower-middle-class family in Clio, Alabama, Wallace earned a law degree from the University of Alabama (1942), served in World War II and was later a circuit court judge (1953–59). He began his political career as a Democrat and a committed segregationist. Elected governor in 1962, during his first inaugural speech he vowed that he would fight for "segregation now, segregation tomorrow, and segregation forever." He gained national attention in 1963 when, defying a desegregation order from President John F. KENNEDY, he stood in a doorway of the University of Alabama to block the admission of two black students; he yielded after the state National Guard was federalized. He also opposed the integration of local schools, but again backed down after receiving a federal court order.

In 1965 he tried to prevent Martin Luther KING Jr.'s march from SELMA to MONTGOMERY. Capitalizing on disaffection with both major parties and stressing STATES' RIGHTS, populist views and a hawkish position on the VIETNAM WAR (see HAWKS), Wallace campaigned for the U.S. presidency as an independent in 1968; he won 45 electoral votes and nearly 10 million popular votes. While campaigning for the Democratic presidential nomination in 1972, he was shot and partially paralyzed. During the late 1970s and the 1980s, Wallace reversed many of his earlier positions on race relations and gained new credibility among black voters. Wallace served longer than any other governor of Alabama (1963–67, 1971–75, 1975–79, 1983–87); he was also the behind-the-scenes power while his first wife, Lurleen Wallace, was governor (1967–71). (See also CIVIL RIGHTS MOVEMENT.)

For further reading:
Kurland, George, *George Wallace: Southern Governor & Presidential Candidate.* Charlottesville, N.C.: Samhar Press, 1972.

George Wallace, longtime governor of Alabama and contender for the U.S. presidency, was for many years a strong advocate of racial segregation.

Henry A. Wallace was vice president of the United States during Franklin D. Roosevelt's third term as president (1941–1945).

Wallace, Henry A(gard) (1888–1965). American politician, presidential candiate and Vice President (1941–45). Born and raised in Iowa, Wallace was the son of a noted agriculturist who served as U.S. Secretary of Agriculture in the administration of President Warren G. HARDING. Wallace himself soon earned his own reputation as an agricultural expert and a champion of farmers. During the 1920s he changed his party affiliation from Republican to Democrat. Chosen as Secretary of Agriculture by President Franklin D. ROOSEVELT in 1933, Wallace helped shape the active federal farm policy under the NEW DEAL. Most notably, he reorganized the Department of Agriculture and helped draft the Agricultural Adjustment Act of 1933. He also spoke out in support of labor reform, CIVIL RIGHTS and welfare legislation. Roosevelt chose Wallace as his vice presidential running mate in 1940. Wallace served one term as vice president, but proved too liberal for many in the party, and Roosevelt was persuaded to replace him with Harry S TRUMAN as his running mate in 1944. Named Secretary of Commerce by Roosevelt, Wallace continued to serve in that post under Truman, but became increasingly critical of Truman's anti-communist foreign policy. Wallace took a naive view of Joseph STALIN's repressive domestic and expansive foreign policies, and pushed for U.S. cooperation with the U.S.S.R. Forced to resign in September 1946, Wallace continued to attack Truman's foreign policy, criticizing not only U.S. intervention in GREECE but also the MARSHALL PLAN. In 1948 Wallace and the Progressive Citizens of America (PCA), which included many Communist Party members, launched a third-party presidential campaign. Although at first a credible candidate, Wallace soon lost support from liberals because of his refusal to repudiate Communists within the PCA. He won 1.2 million votes in the election but failed to carry any states. Although he continued to make controversial statements, Wallace's political influence declined thereafter.

For further reading:
Walker, J. Samuel, *Henry A. Wallace and American Foreign Policy.* Westport, Conn.: Greenwood, 1976.

Wallace, Irving (1916–1990). American author. His books were frequently panned by the critics, but they were read by millions of people. His 16 novels and 17 nonfiction works were reported to have sold a total of more than 120 millon copies around the world. Among these were *The Chapman Report* (1960), *The Prize* (1962) and *The Fan Club* (1974). With his son, David Wallechinsky, he wrote *The People's Almanac* (1975) and *The Book of Lists* (1977).

Wallenberg, Raoul (1912–19?). Swedish diplomat. Posted as an envoy to Hungary in 1944, Wallenberg is credited with rescuing some 20,000 Hungarian JEWS from the Nazi HOLOCAUST. He used a number of methods to secure their escape, often issuing them Swedish passports. He disappeared into the Soviet sector in 1945. It is known that he was arrested, and the U.S.S.R. reported his death in 1947. However, a number of reliable witnesses have reported seeing him after that date, alive in Soviet prison camps. Wallenberg was awarded an honorary American citizenship in 1981.

Wallenstein, Alfred (1898–1983). American conductor and cellist, believed to be the first native-born American ever to conduct a major symphony orchestra. He was principal cellist with the Chicago Symphony Orchestra and the New York Philharmonic before becoming music director of the Los Angeles Philharmonic from 1943 to 1956. As music director of WOR radio in New York City from 1935 to 1945, he also pioneered the programming of classical music on radio.

Waller, Thomas "Fats" (1904–1943). During the 1920s and 1930s, Thomas "Fats" Waller won enormous success as a songwriter, entertainment "personality" and gifted jazz pianist. His unique keyboard style was marked by a strong rhythmic pulse, springhtly right-hand improvisations and strong left-hand harmonic underpinnings reconfigured from the "stride" tradition that Waller had learned as a youth in his native New York City from stride piano greats Russell Brooks and James P. Johnson. His lithe virtuosity was further refined through piano studies with Leopold Godowsky. In 1922, Waller made his first solo recordings; greater recognition came with his effervescent accompaniments for BLUES singers Bessie SMITH and Alberta Hunter. Waller gained widespread prominence as a radio personality where his satiric reframings of popular songs made his singing and pianistic talents nationally known. However, Waller is best remembered as the composer of such ingenious and witty

Best known as an entertainer, Fats Waller was one of the most influential piano stylists in the history of jazz.

songs as "Ain't Misbehavin'," "Honeysuckle Rose," "Squeeze Me," "Jitterbug Waltz" and "Keepin' Out of Mischief Now," all standards in the repertory of the American popular song; many of these were written for such successful and pioneering all-black Broadway shows as *Keep Shufflin'* (1928) and *Hot Chocolates* (1929). Waller also is credited as being the first keyboardist to successfully exploit the jazz possibilities of the pipe organ and electric Hammond organ.

For further reading:
Balliett, Whitney, "Fats," in *Jelly Roll, Jabbo and Fats*. New York: Oxford University Press, 1983.

Wallis, Sir Barnes Neville (1887–1979). British aircraft designer who invented the "bouncing bombs" used to destroy German dams along the RUHR River in WORLD WAR II. Wallis's invention and the bombing mission were the subjects of a postwar book and film, *The Dam Busters* (1954). Working for Vickers, he also designed the World War II Wellington bomber. As chief of aeronautical research for the British Aircraft Corporation (1945–71), he designed the first successful swing-wing airplane. Wallis was knighted in 1968.

Wallis, Hal B. (1899–1986). American film producer. From his early career with WARNER BROS. through his later days as an independent, he was associated with some of HOLLYWOOD's best known films, including *Little Caesar* (1930), *The Maltese Falcon* (1941), *Casablanca* (1942), *Come Back, Little Sheba (1952), and True Grit* (1969). He was credited with the discovery of many actors, including Burt LANCASTER and Kirk DOUGLAS. He helped make stars out of an array of others, including Edward G. ROBINSON, Humphrey BOGART and Bette DAVIS. *Rooster Cogburn* (1975) was his last film.

Wallis and Futuna Islands. The Wallis and Futuna Islands are volcanic islands in the South Pacific Ocean, north of New Zealand and northeast of New Caledonia. They cover a total area of 106 square miles; the capital is Mata-Utu. The Wallis and Futuna Islands were first settled over 2,000 years ago. Dutch navigators arrived at Futuna in 1616. Wallis takes its name from the English sea captain who was the first European to land there in 1767. In 1886 Wallis became a French protectorate, Futuna following in 1887. The islands assumed the official status of a colony of France in 1924. During WORLD WAR II Wallis was an important American military base and the runway at Hihifo remains of strategic value to the French.

Wall Street Journal, The. American newspaper founded in 1889. Established by Charles H. Dow and Edward D. Jones, *The Wall Street Journal* is now owned and published by Dow Jones & Co. The *Journal* has a circulation of approximately 1,839,000 daily, the largest of any American paper, and is published in four regional editions. Its main emphasis is business, financial and economic news, but it also contains general news and features. Its editorial policy is conservative, supporting a free market economy and corporate America.

Walpole, Sir Hugh (Seymour) (1884–1941). British novelist. Born in New Zealand, Walpole was raised and educated in Great Britain. His first successful novel was his third, *Perrin and Mr. Traill* (1911) which reflected his brief experiences as a schoolmaster. *The Dark Forest* (1916), drew on his experiences in the Russian Red Cross during World War I, and also dealt with homosexuality. A friend of Virginia WOOLF, Walpole admired literary MODERNISM, and worried that his own popular fiction was too traditional. Other works include *Jeremy* (1919), *The Cathedral* (1922), and a series of historical novels beginning with *Rogue Herris* (1930), which are set in the Lake District where Walpole lived. Walpole was unattractively portrayed as Alroy Dear in Somerset MAUGHAM's *Cakes and Ale* (1930). Walpole was knighted in 1937.

Walser, Robert (1878–1956). Swiss novelist and poet. Walser was a haunting and evocative literary visionary whose German language stories and novels were greatly admired by contemporaries, including Hermann HESSE and Franz KAFKA. Born in Biel, in central Switzerland, Walser left school at age fourteen and worked at a series of odd jobs to support both his fondness for lengthy walking tours and his nascent writing. His first poems and stories appeared in 1898, and Walser continued to write in those genres over the next three decades. The best known of his eight novels, only four of which survive, is *Jakob von Gunten* (1908). Walser's writings were never commercially successful, and he endured fierce poverty. In 1929, he committed himself to the Waldau Sanatorium near Berne, Switzerland, where he was diagnosed as schizophrenic. After an involuntary transfer in 1933 to a sanitorium in eastern Switzerland, Walser never wrote again. He died on Christmas Day, 1956, while taking a walk on the sanitorium grounds. His *Selected Stories* (1982) appeared in English with a foreword by Susan Sontag.

Walsh, Raoul (1887–1980). American film director. In a career that spanned nearly 50 years, he directed more than 100 films. His movies, characterized by swift-paced action, included adventure dramas, gangster films, and westerns. He won early acclaim for such silent films as *The Thief of Bagdad* (1924), *What Price Glory?* (1926), and *Sadie Thompson* (1928). However, he achieved his best work directing Errol FLYNN, Humphrey BOGART, and James CAGNEY in the 1940s. Among his films of this period were *The Roaring Twenties* (1939), *They Drive By Night (1940), Strawberry Blonde* (1941), *High Sierra* (1941), *Objective Burma* (1945), and *White Heat* (1949).

Walter, Bruno [born Bruno Schlesinger] (1876–1962). German-born orchestra and opera conductor. Walter was born in Berlin. Although trained as a piano prodigy, he was inspired by Hans von Bulow to become a conductor. At age seventeen he had his first engagement with the Cologne Opera. A year later, in 1894, he met the man who was so profoundly to affect his life and music, the composer Gustav MAHLER. After a succession of appointments in Breslau (1896), Pressburgh (1897), and Berlin (1900), he was invited by Mahler to work as his assistant at the Vienna Court Opera, where he remained until 1913. After Mahler's death he gave the premieres of *Das Lied von der Erde* in Munich in 1911 and of the *Ninth Symphony* in 1910. An indefatigable traveller, Walter toured the U.S. several times, performed throughout Europe and Russia, and distinguished himself at Covent Garden in London for a cycle of Mozart operas. In 1933 he fell victim to ANTI-SEMITISM and was forced to abandon his post at the Leipzig Gewandhaus Orchestra (where he was succeeded by Richard STRAUSS). During the war years he led many American orchestras in the standard Austrian-German repertoire and, of course, he continued to champion the music of Mahler. Many of his last recordings were made with the Columbia Symphony Orchestra, a magnificent ensemble culled from the Hollywood studios and the Los Angeles Philharmonic. Music was, for Walter, a religious experience. The musician was its high priest. The conductor, he wrote in his autobiographies, *Theme and Variations* (1947) and *Of Music and Music Making* (1957), must be able to fulfill the "spiritual demands of the works he performs." Music, he insisted, was witness to man's "divinely creative and ruling character." Like MONTEUX and TOSCANINI, he conducted until well into his eighties.

For further reading:
Schonberg, Harold C., *The Great Conductors*. New York: Simon & Schuster, 1967.

Walters, Barbara (1931–). American journalist. Walters established herself during her 12–year stint as cohost of NBC's "Today" television show, where she was noted for her personal interviewing technique. In 1976, she became the first woman to co-anchor a network news show and the highest-paid newscaster in television, with a $1–million-a-year contract. Walters shared the anchor spot on the "ABC Evening News" with Harry Reasoner, but the two failed to get along, and Walters was criticized for having no hard news experience. Both were removed from the show within a year. Walters went on to cohost the news magazine "20/20" and to do celebrity interviews.

Walton, Sir William (Turner) (1902–1983). One of the major British composers of the 20th century, Walton wrote orchestral music, ballets, film scores and operas as well as coronation marches for King GEORGE VI and Queen ELIZABETH II. He achieved fame in 1923 with the first performance of his *Facade,* musical parodies accompanying satirical poems by Edith SITWELL. Among his other compositions are the Viola Concerto (1929), *Belshazzar's Feast* (1931), the Violin Concerto (1939), and the scores for Laurence OLIVIER's film classics *Henry V* (1945) and *Richard III* (1955).

Wang, An (1920–1990). Chinese-born physicist, computer engineer and entrepreneur. Wang emigrated to the U.S. in 1945, and three years later invented the computer memory core, which was the most common device used for storing computer data before the invention of the microchip. In 1951, he founded Wang Laboratories, which went on to become one of the world's largest producers of office word-processing systems. The company experienced a slump in the late 1980s, and posted a loss of some $400 million in 1989. In response, Wang sold off some of the company's assets and eased out his son, who had been named president in 1986, in favor of an outsider.

Wang Ching-wei (1883–1944). Chinese nationalist leader. While still a student, he became a friend and disciple of SUN YAT-SEN. After an attempt on the life of the Chinese regent in 1910, he was sentenced to life imprisonment, but was released with the outbreak of revolution in 1912. He subsequently studied in France, returned to China in 1917, and became a leader of the left wing of the KUOMINTANG and an opponent of CHIANG KAI-SHEK. He was China's premier from 1932–35. Opposed to the policies of Chiang, wary of the communists and convinced of the futility of war with Japan, Wang served as head of a Japanese puppet government in Nanking throughout World War II, from 1940 until his death.

Wang Hongwen. See GANG OF FOUR.

Wankel, Felix (1902–1988). German inventor. Wankel developed the Wankel rotary engine in a private workshop in the period between the two world wars. His invention required fewer moving parts than a conventional engine and produced more power in less space with less noise and vibration. The first Wankel-powered car did not appear until 1964, and only the Mazda Motor Corporation of Japan adopted the design for many of its models. The Wankel engine's perceived fuel inefficiency caused it to lose popularity following the 1973 oil crisis.

War Admiral (1934–1959). Thoroughbred racehorse. Undefeated as a three-year-old, this son of MAN O'WAR captured the Triple Crown in 1937 and was named Horse of the Year. He went on to win the Jockey Club Gold Cup in 1938, but his most notable race was one he lost in 1939. War Admiral's 1-1/8 mile match race against Sea Biscuit at Pimlico is regarded as one of the greatest races of all time, the horses and jockeys dueling every stride of the way, with Sea Biscuit the eventual winner by three lengths in the record time of 1:56:6. War Admiral retired after his four-year-old season to a successful stud career.

War Communism. Name given to the Bolshevik government's social and economic policies of 1918–21. In order to support the BOLSHEVIKS in the RUSSIAN CIVIL WAR fully, and to build communism in general, War Communism was characterized by the nationalization of industry and trade, wages in kind for workers and enforced labor service. These measures were unpopular, and in 1921 there occurred several uprisings. War Communism was replaced by the NEW ECONOMIC POLICY in 1921.

Ward, Dame Barbara (Mary) [Baroness Jackson of Lodsworth] (1914–1981). British economist, journalist, and author. Ward was foreign editor of the *Economist* during World War II, as well as a popular public speaker and radio personality. In the postwar years she was a strong advocate of foreign aid to underdeveloped nations. While serving on UNITED NATIONS and VATICAN special commissions, she urged the transfer of wealth from rich to poor nations. Her belief in the interdependence of nations extended to world environmental policies.

Warhol, Andy [born Andrew Warhola] (1927–1987). American artist, film maker, and celebrity, the best known figure to emerge from the POP ART movement of the 1960s. He won fame early in the 1960s with his images of Campbell's soup cans. Later works included images of Marilyn MONROE and other celebrities. His New York City art studio, "the Factory," was a legendary hangout for artists and social dropouts, whose lives he portrayed in his unconventional films. A constant presence on the New York social scene, he remained elusive as he went about photographing and tape-recording celebrities for his *Interview* magazine. Warhol had a flair for attracting publicity and for coming up with memorable quotes, such as "In the future, everybody will be famous for 15 minutes."

American artist Andy Warhol first gained recognition for his paintings of commercial products like these of steel wool pads.

Warner, Jack L. (1892–1978). American film producer. Jack Warner was the youngest of the four brothers who founded WARNER BROTHERS Studios in 1923. He was production director, president or chairman of the board for over 50 years. A pioneer in talking pictures, he produced over 5,000 movies. These included several with dog-star RIN-TIN-TIN in the 1920s, the gangster cycle's *Little Caesar* and *Public Enemy,* as well as the Busby BERKELEY musicals in the 1930s, and *Casablanca, The Treasure of the Sierra Madre, My Fair Lady* and *Bonnie and Clyde.*

Warner Bros. One of HOLLYWOOD's "Big Five" production/exhibition motion picture studios (along with METRO-GOLDWYN-MAYER, 20TH CENTURY-FOX, RKO, and PARAMOUNT) and the only one operated by a family. Harry, Albert, Sam, and Jack Warner were the sons of a Polish immigrant who had come to American in the early 1880s by cattleboat. After dabbling in various nickelodeon projects, the brothers moved to Los Angeles and in 1918 produced their first important feature film, *My Four Years in Germany.* The studio moved into high gear in the 1920s with its most popular stars John BARRYMORE and the legendary canine, RIN-TIN-TIN. An important acquisition came in 1925 when the brothers bought the Vitagraph Company, a Brooklyn-based studio from the early days of the silent film. Experiments began in 1926 with Western Electric to develop a sound-on-disc synchronized-sound system for TALKING PICTURES. Numerous sound short films and features like *Don Juan* (1926) and *The Jazz Singer* (1927) stimulated industry-wide the talkie revolution. The four brothers at this time had the following responsibilities: Sam was the technological experimenter, but he died before *The Jazz Singer* realized his dreams. Jack oversaw all production at the Burbank studio, Albert was in charge of overseas distribution, and Harry acted as president from his New York office. An energetic policy of theater acquisition was consolidated in 1929 with the purchase of the First National chain. More than most studios, Warner Bros. in the 1930s established its own "look" and style, largely due to its efficient factory system and the supervision until 1933 of all production by Darryl F. ZANUCK. "Social consciousness" films and contemporary dramas included gangster films like *The Public Enemy* (1930) and *Little Caesar* (1930); problem dramas like *Five-Star Final* (1931) and *I Am a Fugitive from a Chain Gang* (1932); biographies like *The Story of Louis Pasteur* (1936); musicals like *42nd Street* (1932) and *Gold Diggers of 1933.* Directors known for their fast, lean style included Mervyn LeRoy and William Wellman. Stars famous for their fast-talking, cynical manner included James CAGNEY, Edward G. ROBINSON, and Bette DAVIS. The bizarre hallucinations of musical wizard

Busby BERKELEY revolutionized the art of the form. Apart from the Walt DISNEY studio, no other Hollywood studio contributed more to the World War II effort than Warners'. First to release an anti-Nazi film, *Confessions of a Nazi Spy* (1939), the studio went on to make numerous short subjects, documentaries, and features promoting the Allies (*Casablanca*, 1943; *Air Force*, 1943; *Mission to Moscow*, 1944; etc.). In 1956, after divesting itself of its theaters due to anti-trust government activities, the studio sold rights to its films to Associated Artists, which in turn sold them to UNITED ARTISTS. In 1967 Jack, by now the only brother left in the business, sold out to Seven Arts; and two years later the company was renamed Warner Communications. Time, Inc., merged with Warner in 1989 to form Time-Warner, Inc., which now supervises film production.

For further reading:

Hirschhorn, Clive, *The Warner Bros. Story*. New York: Crown Publishers, 1979.

"War of the Worlds" broadcast (October 30, 1938). Famous radio broadcast that inadvertently convinced millions of American citizens that a Martian invasion had occurred. The CBS "Mercury Theatre of the Air," produced by John HOUSEMAN and Orson WELLES, performed on a Sunday night its adaptation of H.G. WELLS' science-fiction novel *The War of the Worlds*. Although an announcer periodically stressed that listeners were hearing a dramatization, the excellence of the performances (notably Welles himself as an eyewitness broadcaster of the Martian landings in New Jersey) coupled with a realistic and cleverly constructed script created panic across the United States. An estimated four million listeners believed that the invasion had occurred. Reactions included heart attacks and attempted suicides. CBS and Welles ultimately apologized, while the FCC took steps to see that such an incident could not recur. Social scientists still ponder why the broadcast was so widely believed, attributing public credulity in part to the atmosphere of crisis—HITLER and the GREAT DEPRESSION—that dominated the news in the late 1930s.

Warren, Earl (1891–1974). American politician, chief justice of the U.S. Supreme Court (1953–69). A judicial activist, Warren was leader of the influential "Warren Court" of the 1950s and 1960s that issued many landmark CIVIL RIGHTS and individual liberties cases. A graduate of the University of California, the Republican Warren was elected state attorney general and gained a reputation as a crime fighter. He capitalized on this reputation and was elected governor of California, a post he held from 1942 until his appointment to the Supreme Court (1953). At the time in California, a candidate could enter any party's primary elections; Warren was so popular that he once won both the Republican and Democratic primaries for attorney general and then repeated the feat as governor. In 1948 he was the unsuccessful candidate for vice president on the

Under Chief Justice Earl Warren, the U.S. Supreme Court issued a number of far-reaching rulings (1953–69).

Republican ticket with Thomas DEWEY. Although he sought the Republican presidential nomination in 1952, he withdrew and endorsed Dwight D. EISENHOWER.

After the death of Chief Justice Fred VINSON, President Eisenhower nominated Warren as chief justice. Eisenhower later reportedly called Warren's appointment "the biggest damn-fool mistake I ever made." Although Warren was a Republican and, at least during his early years in office, a conservative governor, he proved a liberal once on the high court. The Warren majority was known as an activist Court and established many landmark decisions. Warren himself wrote many of the opinions, including BROWN V. BOARD OF EDUCATION (school desegregation), MIRANDA V. ARIZONA (right against self-incrimination) and *Cooper v. Aaron*. This case, heard by itself in a highly unusual special summer session, refused to grant further delays for school desegregation in LITTLE ROCK, Arkansas, after the Brown decision. Warren also headed the WARREN COMMISSION that investigated the assassination of President John F. KENNEDY. He retired from the Court in 1969.

Warren remains perhaps the most controversial chief justice of the 20th century. Libertarians continue to regard him as a champion of civil liberties, while conservatives charge that the Warren Court overstepped the proper role of the judiciary and favored the rights of criminals at the expense of law enforcement officials.

For further reading:

Schwartz, Bernard, *Super Chief: Earl Warren & His Supreme Court, A Judicial Biography*. New York: New York University Press, 1983.

White, G. Edward, *Earl Warren: A Public Life*. New York: Oxford University Press, 1982.

Warren, Harry [born Salvatore Guaragno] (1893–1981). American Hollywood composer who wrote over 300 songs. In collaboration with lyricist Al Dubin in the 1930s, he was a major force in the success of the early screen musical. During his 59 years as a songwriter he won three Academy Awards, for *Lullabye of Broadway* (1935), *You'll Never Know* (1940), and *On the Atchison, Topeka and the Santa Fe* (1946). He also wrote the music for *42nd Street* (1933).

Warren, Lingan A. (1889–1984). American retail executive. Warren was president of Safeway Stores from 1930 to 1955. He helped turn a group of loosely organized food stores into one of the largest retail supermarket chains in the U.S. He invented such supermarket practices as cutting prices to meet those of any competitor and selling produce by weight rather than by the dozen.

Warren, Robert Penn (1905–1989). American author. One of the most versatile American men of letters of the 20th century, Warren was a poet, novelist, teacher and critic. He won the PULITZER PRIZE three times—in 1946 for his novel ALL THE KING'S MEN, the tale of a populist southern politician (inspired by Huey LONG) who becomes corrupted by power; in 1957 for *Promises: Poems, 1954–1956;* and in 1978 for *Now and Then: Poems 1976–1978*. Warren was also the first poet laureate of the U.S. from 1986–88. His other honors include the National Medal for Literature in 1970 and the Presidential Medal of Freedom in 1980. Besides his achievements in fiction and poetry, Warren was coauthor (with Cleanth BROOKS) of two seminal works of literary criticism, *Understanding Poetry* (1938) and *Understanding Fiction* (1943), which helped introduce the NEW CRITICISM into American colleges.

Warren was born in Guthrie, Kentucky and attended Vanderbilt University, graduating in 1925. He pursued graduate studies at Berkeley, Yale and Oxford, where he was a Rhodes Scholar. He taught at Louisiana State University in the 1930s (where he edited *The Southern Review*), at the University of Minnesota in the 1940s, and at Yale from 1950 until retirement.

Warren Commission. Government investigation of the 1963 assassination of President John F. KENNEDY. The events surrounding the assassination had aroused suspicion. Lee Harvey OSWALD, the alleged assassin, had been shot while in police custody by Jack RUBY. Although he appeared to have acted alone, Oswald had a Russian wife, and many suspected a conspiracy. Some suggested Russia or Cuba was to blame, while others pointed a finger at organized crime. The matter was investigated by a commission headed by Supreme Court Chief Justice Earl WARREN. Other members of the eight-member panel were Representative Gerald FORD, who later became president, two senators and former CIA chief Allen DULLES. After a massive investigation the commission concluded that Oswald had acted alone. Critics refused to believe that the assassination was not the result of a conspiracy, and the Warren Commission report remains controversial.

Warsaw Pact. A military alliance, formally known as the Warsaw Treaty Organization (WTO); established on May 14, 1955, as a Soviet-bloc counterpart to the NORTH ATLANTIC TREATY ORGANIZATION (NATO). Formed a week after a remilitarized WEST GERMANY entered NATO, it included ALBANIA, BULGARIA, CZECHOSLOVAKIA, EAST GERMANY, HUNGARY, POLAND, ROMANIA and the U.S.S.R. It provided for a unified military command headquartered in Moscow, with Soviet or Soviet-trained divisions stationed in member nations to provide a common defense in case of attack on any one or more of the signatories. Albania formally withdrew from the pact in 1968. The one action in which Warsaw Pact nations collaborated was the armed occupation of Czechoslovakia that destroyed the democracy movement of 1968. Following the fall of communist governments in Eastern Europe in 1989–90 and the reunification of GERMANY in October 1990, the Warsaw Pact effectively unravelled. Early in 1991 the U.S.S.R. announced that the Warsaw Pact would be formally dissolved in April 1991.

Warsaw Uprising (August–October 1944). Revolt against Nazi occupation forces in Warsaw by the Polish underground, a RESISTANCE group known as the Home Army and commanded by General Count Tadeusz Komorowski (1895–1966). As Germany's fortunes were on the wane and the Soviet army reached the Vistula, underground forces attempted to take the Polish capital from the Germans. During the first four days of August, the Home Army was successful in gaining control of over half of the city. However, oncoming Soviet troops halted for resupply, and the Polish forces soon ran short of food and ammunition. Although some supplies were flown in by Allied airmen, it was not enough to sustain the Poles. ss reinforcements coupled with German troops in Warsaw quelled the rebellion in fierce fighting and, after a futile Soviet assault in September, the Home Army was forced to capitulate in October. In reprisal for the uprising, the Germans razed much of the city.

Washington, Booker T. (1856–1915). American educator; the preeminent African-American figure of his time. Born a slave on a Virginia farm, he was freed at the age of nine and from 1872 to 1875 was enrolled at Hampton Institute. After teaching for some years, in 1881 Washington became head of the Tuskegee Normal and Industrial Institute, in Alabama, which he built into a major institution for black students. In 1895, he delivered his famous Atlanta Exposition Address, arguing "In all things that are purely social we can be as separate as the fingers, yet one as the hand in mutual progress." While he then quickly became the black spokesman most acceptable to whites, other black leaders, most notably W.E.B. DUBOIS, rejected his segregationist position and railed against Jim Crow laws and other forms of discrimination. Washington wrote four books about his experiences, most notably *Up From Slavery*, published to much acclaim in 1901 and translated into over 15 languages. Washington was tireless in his efforts to find Northern patrons for Tuskegee (receiving more than $600,000 worth of bonds from Andrew Carnegie) and was invited to the White House by President Theodore ROOSEVELT in 1901.

Washington Conference. Held from November 21, 1921, to February 6, 1922, this post-World War I conference was intended to provide for naval disarmament and to ease tensions in the Far East. Convened in Washington, D.C., it was attended by representatives of BELGIUM, CHINA, FRANCE, the UNITED KINGDOM, ITALY, JAPAN, the NETHERLANDS, PORTUGAL and the U.S. Three main treaties resulted. In the Four Power Treaty of December 1921, the U.K., France, Japan and the U.S. agreed to respect one another's Pacific possessions. These nations plus Italy were signatories of the Five Power Naval Armaments Treaty of February 1922, which provided for a 10–year moratorium on the building of warships and established a ratio controlling the number of such ships each could maintain. In another agreement, China's independence was collectively guaranteed, and Japan was pledged to return Shantung to China. The Washington Conference treaties remained in effect until the mid-1930s.

Washington Post, The. American newspaper established in 1877. Founded as a Democratic paper, the *Post* was acquired by John R. McLean in 1905. The paper went into receivership after the stock market crash and was bought by Eugene Meyer in 1933. Meyer rejuvenated the *Post* and in 1948 transferred his voting stock to his daughter and son-in-law, Katharine and Philip GRAHAM. When Philip committed suicide in 1963, Katharine Graham became president, and she and her sons continue to oversee the paper and its holdings. One of the most influential newspapers in the nation, the *Post* championed civil liberties and civil rights in the postwar years and supported the United Nations. It was assailed for its attack on MCCARTHYISM in the 1950s. In 1954, the *Post* acquired and absorbed its competition, the *Washington Times-Herald*, and in 1961 it acquired NEWSWEEK magazine. The next year it set up the Los Angeles Times-Washington Post News Service.

Graham hired Benjamin C. BRADLEE as managing editor in 1965; three years later he became executive editor. The *Post*, which had already aroused the enmity of the NIXON administration for its criticism of Vice President Spiro AGNEW, broke the story of WATERGATE, to which Bradlee had assigned reporters Bob WOODWARD and Carl BERNSTEIN. In 1973, the paper received a PULITZER PRIZE for its investigation of Watergate. The paper continues to be noted for its investigative reporting and maintains its standing as the nation's leading political paper. The Washington Post Company's holdings include additional newspapers, magazines and four television stations. Bradlee retired in 1991.

Wasserman, August von (1866–1925). German bacteriologist. Wasserman was educated at the Universities of Erlangen, Vienna, Munich and Strasbourg, where he graduated in 1888. From 1890 he worked under Robert Koch at the Institute for Infectious Diseases in Berlin, becoming head of the department of therapeutics and serum research in 1907. In 1913 he moved to the Kaiser Wilhelm Institute, where he served as director of experimental therapeutics until his death. Wasserman is best remembered for the **Wasserman test,** which he introduced in 1906 for the diagnosis of syphilis. The test is still widely used as a diagnostic tool.

Waste Land, The (1922). Written by T.S. ELIOT while he was recovering from a nervous breakdown in 1921–22, this long poem in five sections is generally regarded as the most important work of Eliot's early period. Using a complex structure and symbolism inspired in part by the mythic archetypes of Jessie L. Weston's *From Ritual to Romance* and Sir James Frazer's *The Golden Bough*, *The Waste Land* contrasts the sterility of modern life to the richness of traditional spiritual and mythological forces. In a remarkable collaboration, the original text (over 1,000 lines) was radically altered and condensed by Ezra POUND to produce a more concentrated and ambiguous work of just over 400 lines. Many readers and critics were initially baffled by the poem's jux-

Civilians taken prisoner during the destruction of the Warsaw Ghetto (1943).

taposition of topical images and colloquial language with obscure literary allusions. However, it was soon widely recognized as a revelation of modern sensibility. The publication of *The Waste Land* is often considered as the birth of literary MODERNISM.

Wat, Aleksander (1900–1967). Polish poet and intellectual. Jewish by birth, Wat was involved in various European intellectual movements in the 1920s, including DADA and FUTURISM. During this time he lived in Warsaw, Berlin and Paris, associating with some of the leading modernist writers of the time (see MODERNISM). In 1929 he became editor of an influential Polish Communist journal. However, after HITLER and STALIN partitioned POLAND in 1939, Wat was arrested by the Soviets on charges of being a Trotskyite, Zionist, and agent of the VATICAN. He spent WORLD WAR II in various Soviet prisons and converted to Christianity in 1941. He returned to Poland in 1946. Although he remained out of official favor because he refused to adhere to the doctrine of SOCIALIST REALISM, he continued to write. A writer of wide culture, although little known outside intellectual circles, Wat was one of the leading European thinkers of his generation.

For further reading:

Wat, Aleksander. *My Century: The Odyssey of a Polish Intellectual.* Edited and translated by Richard Lourie. Berkley: University of California Press, 1988.

Watergate. The name given to a series of scandals in the administration of President Richard M. NIXON leading to Nixon's resignation on August 9, 1974. Watergate refers to the burglarizing of the Democratic Party national headquarters in Washington, D.C., on June 17, 1972. Five men arrested in the break-in and two of their accomplices were tried and convicted. James McCord, one of the convicted burglars, charged that there had been a cover-up of the burglary. In the wake of the McCord accusation, and the investigative reporting of Carl Bernstein and Bob WOODWARD of the WASHINGTON POST, a special Senate committee chaired by Senator Sam ERVIN (Democrat-North Carolina) held nationally televised hearings into the Watergate affair in the spring and summer of 1973. Former White House Counsel John DEAN charged that the Watergate break-in was approved by Attorney General John MITCHELL and that White House aides H.R. "Bob" Haldeman and John Ehrlichman were involved in the cover-up. In May 1973, then Attorney General Elliot Richardson appointed Archibald COX as a special prosecutor to investigate the entire "Watergate affair." Cox began to uncover evidence of improper conduct in the Nixon reelection committee, and illegal wiretapping by the administration. In July 1973, it became known that presidential conversations in the White House had been taped since 1971. In October 1973, when Cox tried to obtain these tapes from the President, Nixon fired him. This touched off calls for Nixon's impeachment from the press and from some in government. The House Judiciary Committee began an impeachment inquiry, which ended in the adoption of three articles of impeachment against Nixon in July 1974. On August 5, 1974, Nixon released the transcripts of three of the recorded conversations that Special Prosecutor Leon JAWORSKI (who Nixon had appointed to replace Cox) had sought from him. Nixon admitted that he had known about the Watergate cover-up shortly after the burglary had occurred and that he had tried to stop the Federal Bureau of Investigation's inquiry into the break-in. On August 9, 1974 Nixon resigned and Vice President Gerald R. FORD was sworn in as president. The next month, Ford pardoned Nixon for any crimes he might have committed as president; however, Mitchell, Haldeman, Ehrlichman and Dean were among those who were convicted for their part in the Watergate scandals.

For further reading:

Kutler, Stanley I., *The Wars of Watergate: The Last Crisis of Richard Nixon.* New York: Knopf, 1990.

McQuaid, Kim, *The Anxious Years: America in the Vietnam-Watergate Era.* New York: Basic Books, 1989.

Schell, Jonathan, *The Time of Illusion.* New York: Knopf, 1975.

Woodward, Bob, and Carl Bernstein, *All the President's Men.* New York: Simon & Schuster, 1974.

Watkins v. United States (1957). U.S. Supreme Court McCarthy-era decision involving the power of congressional investigations. A congressional committee, the HOUSE UN-AMERICAN ACTIVITIES COMMITTEE, questioned a union leader about his membership in and relations with the U.S. Communist Party. When he refused to implicate others, he was prosecuted for contempt and convicted. On appeal he protested that the committee's questioning constituted a fishing expedition with no particular goal. The Supreme Court held that the investigating committee had exceeded its power and the defendant had the right to refuse to answer questions that were not relevant to its investigation. The decision was controversial at the time because anti-communist sentiment was still strong in the U.S.

Watson, James Dewey (1928–). American biochemist. In 1951 James began to pursue in earnest the structure of DNA, at the Cavendish Laboratory in Cambridge, England. By 1953 he and Francis CRICK published *General Implications of the Structure of Deoxyribonucleic Acid,* which showed how genetic information can be expressed in the form of a chemical code. For this work, Watson and Crick shared the 1962 NOBEL PRIZE for physiology or medicine with Maurice Wilkins. He continued to study the genetic code at the California Institute of Technology and, later, at Harvard. He concentrated on cancer research at the Cold Spring Harbor Laboratory in New York, where he became director in 1968. Also in 1968, he published his controversial account of the discovery of the structure of DNA, *The Double Helix.*

Watson, John Broadus (1878–1958). American psychologist and advertising agent. A graduate of Furman University (1900), Watson promoted a comprehensive understanding of behaviorist theory, thus altering the course of U.S. psychological thinking by focusing on observed responses to external stimuli rather than introspective analysis. He was president of the American Psychological Association (1915), a noted educator and the author of several influential works, including *Behaviorism* (1925).

Watson, Tom (1949–). American golfer. The first player to earn a half-million dollars in a single year, he was the first to win the PGA championship six times. The dominant player of the 1970s and early 1980s, he won five British Opens, two Masters titles and one U.S. Open. He has represented the United States on the Ryder Cup team four times.

Watts riots (August 11–16, 1965). The attempted arrest of a drunk driver in Los Angeles' predominantly black Watts district flared into six days of rioting, looting, arson and sniping by an estimated 7,000 to 10,000 blacks. The National Guard was called out. Thirty-five people were killed, 864 treated in hospital for injuries, and 4,170 arrested. The riots were later ascribed to poverty, unemployment, racism and general disrespect for law and order.

Waugh, Evelyn Arthur St. John (1903–1966). British novelist. An indifferent student at Hertford College, Oxford, Waugh became a schoolmaster, and his experiences as such inspired the acclaimed and enormously popular, *Decline and Fall* (1928), his first novel. Waugh's subsequent witty and intelligent social satires, such as *Vile Bodies* (1930) and *A Handful of Dust* (1934), chronicled the cynical "Bright Young Things" of the 1920s and 1930s. Waugh was also an inspired journalist and travel writer. After a short-lived marriage in the late 1920s, he was received into the Catholic Church. In 1937 he married Laura Herbert, a cousin of his first wife. Waugh served in the Royal Marines during World War II. There is a profound sense of desolation and regret for the vanished pre-war world in *Brideshead Revisited* (1945), perhaps his best known novel. Other works include the wartime trilogy consisting of *Men at Arms* (1952), *Officers and Gentlemen* (1955) and *Unconditional Surrender* (1961). His *Diaries* were published in 1976. Waugh was a champion of "high Tory" values and has been much criticized for snobbery. Waugh's brother, **Alec Waugh** (1898–1981) was also a novelist and noted travel author whose works include *The Loom of Youth* (1917), and Waugh's son, **Auberon Waugh,** is a journalist.

Wavell, Archibald Percival [1st Earl Wavell] (1883–1950). British soldier and colonial administrator. Born and educated at Winchester and a graduate of Sandhurst, he entered the military as an officer in the Black Watch regiment in

1901. His early service was in the BOER WAR and in India. During WORLD WAR I, he served in Belgium and on ALLENBY'S staff in Palestine. He returned there as head of the British forces, assigned to deal with the Arab-Jewish conflicts of 1937–39. During WORLD WAR II, he was appointed commander in chief of the Middle East (1939), defeated the Italians in North Africa (1940–41), but was routed by German forces late in 1941. Exchanging commands with General AUCHINLECK, he commanded British troops in India in 1941, and in Southeast Asia in 1942. Hit by losses to the Japanese in Singapore and Burma, the Asian command was abolished and Wavell again assumed command in India. In 1943, he became the Indian viceroy and governor general and was made a field marshall. Thereafter, until his resignation in 1947, Wavell attempted to prepare India for independence and to ease the tensions between Hindus and Moslems.

Wayne, John [Marion Michael Morrison] (1907–1979). American film star. An actor of limited range, Wayne nonetheless transcended his limitations to become a cultural icon, a larger-than-life figure who represented American rugged individualism. In a 50-year career he appeared in more than 200 films, nearly half of which were Westerns. His films grossed over $800 million, and he was among the top-10 box office stars for a record 25 consecutive years. Wayne began acting in HOLLYWOOD in 1928, appearing mainly in low-budget action films and serials that brought him little popular or critical attention. He made his breakthrough in the 1939 classic Western, *Stagecoach*, directed by his friend John FORD; Wayne went on to star in 14 pictures by Ford, notably *She Wore a Yellow Ribbon* (1949), *The Quiet Man* (1952), and *The Searchers* (1956).

Nicknamed "the Duke," Wayne was idolized by moviegoers, especially during the 1940s, 1950s and early 1960s. He projected an image of brave, rugged, sincere and sometimes stubborn masculinity. Best known for his portrayal of the quintessential hero of the American West, Wayne also made his mark in war movies, in which he usually portrayed what many believed was the ideal Army, Navy or Marine Corps officer. Among his best WORLD WAR II movies were *They Were Expendable* (1945) and *Sands of Iwo Jima* (1949). In his later years, Wayne's screen persona was transferred to the realm of politics. He became a prominent spokesman for conservative causes, and his support of America's involvement in the VIETNAM WAR led many to dismiss him as a simpleminded patriot. Many of his films of this time were critical failures, although he gave fine performances in *True Grit* (1969), for which he won his only ACADEMY AWARD, and *The Shootist* (1976), his last movie.

Weathermen. Radical left-wing group whose aim was to overthrow the American political system. The group's name was drawn from the lyrics of songwriter Bob DYLAN. The membership was drawn from a well-educated social strata. The Weathermen committed specific and well-planned acts of violence, including bombings, robberies and murders, in the U.S. in the 1970s. (See also SDS.)

Weather Report. Jazz-rock ensemble cofounded in 1970 by keyboardist Joe Zawinul and saxophonist Wayne Shorter. Weather Report epitomized and influenced the artistic evolution and popular success of the FUSION approach, where freewheeling improvisations float above ostinato-like ROCK, funk and Latin rhythmic patterns. In contrast to the various BEBOP-oriented styles from the 1950s and 1960s, which emphasized virtuosic soloing, jazz-rock fusion exploited popular dance rhythms (like the swing bands of the 1930s and 1940s) and collective improvisation (similar in concept to the Dixieland tradition of New Orleans). Weather Report also capitalized on the availability of a new generation of electronic instruments and processors, unlike the jazz "mainstream" which did not swerve from its devotion to acoustic instruments. The band appealed to a wide and largely youthful audience that had grown up with rock and roll; in the process, it brought notoriety to its two leaders, Zawinul and Shorter, as well to such prominent musicians of the 1970s-1980s as electric bassist Jaco Pastorius and drummer Peter Erskine. The band's greatest hit was "Birdland" (1976). The group broke up in 1985.

For further reading:

Kernfield, Barry, ed., "Weather Report," in *The New Grove Dictionary of Music*. New York: Macmillan, 1988.

Weaver, Robert Clifton (1907–). American statesman. The great-grandson of a slave, Weaver put himself through Harvard by working as an electrician. He received a B.S. in economics (1929), an M.A. two years later and a Ph.D. in 1934, after which he took a position with the Department of Interior. Under President Franklin ROOSEVELT he was an adviser on housing and unemployment, moving into war mobilization in the 1940s. Weaver was president of the NATIONAL ASSOCIATION FOR THE ADVANCEMENT OF COLORED PEOPLE, and in 1961 he was appointed by President John KENNEDY to run the Housing and Home Finance Agency. In 1966 President Lyndon JOHNSON recommended him to head the newly-formed Department of Housing and Urban Development.

Weavers, The. American folk music quartet founded in 1949 by Pete SEEGER, Ronnie Gilbert, Lee Hays, and Fred Hellerman. Influenced by Woody GUTHRIE, the group helped spark the folk music boom of the 1950s. The members had left-wing backgrounds and specialised in union songs and songs of social protest. In the 1950s, they were investigated by anticommunist groups and the HOUSE UN-AMERICAN ACTIVITIES COMMITTEE (HUAC) and were blacklisted for a time. Their songs included "If I Had a Hammer" and "Where Have All the Flowers Gone?" After the Weavers officially disbanded in 1963, the members went their separate ways but occasionally regrouped to give reunion concerts.

Webb, Chick [William Webb] (1909–1939). American jazz drummer and big band leader. Webb was an accomplished jazz drummer of great verve and timing, best remembered as the leader of one of the preeminent JAZZ big bands of the 1920s and 1930s. Among the featured vocalists who performed with the Webb big band was Ella FITZGERALD, who joined the band in 1935 and sang one of the band's biggest hits, "A-Tisket A-Tasket" (1938). Webb was a cocomposer of numerous jazz and pop songs, including "Stompin' at the Savoy," "Lonesome Moments," "Holiday in Harlem," "You Showed Me The Way" and "Heart of Mine." Webb died prematurely due to tuberculosis of the spine.

Webb, Clifton [Webb Parmalee Hollenbeck] (1891–1966). American stage and film actor. Webb, who began his acting career as a teenager, enjoyed a long and successful career in which he triumphed both on Broadway and in Hollywood. From the 1910s through the 1930s, Webb starred in numerous Broadway musicals—most notably *Listen Lester* (1919) and *Sunny* (1925)—in which his singing and dancing talents were featured. From the mid-1940s through the 1950s, Webb shifted his focus to Hollywood, where he became a successful character actor who specialized in dignified upper-class roles. His best known films are *Laura* (1944), *Sitting Pretty* (1948) and *Titanic* (1953).

Webb, James E. (1906–). NASA's second administrator, from February 1961 until October 1968. During his tenure, the MERCURY, GEMINI, and APOLLO programs were developed.

Webb, Sidney and Beatrice. British authors and social reformers, Sidney James Webb (1859–1947) and (Martha) Beatrice Webb (nee Potter, 1858–1943). The Webbs, who were married in 1892, were committed socialists. Before their marriage, Beatrice, who came from a wealthy family, had written *The Co-operative Movement in Great Britain* (1891). Sidney Webb had been a civil servant, but turned to politics as a member of the London County Council in 1892. Both helped found the Fabian Society in 1884 and the London School of Economics in 1895. They sat on many Royal Commissions, for one of which Beatrice wrote a Minority Report in 1909 which influenced the Poor Law, and they were active in the trade union movement. In 1913, they were instrumental in starting *The New Statesman*, a weekly socialist paper. Following World War I, Sidney sat on the executive committee of the LABOUR PARTY, and in 1922 was elected to Parliament. In 1924 and from 1929 to 1931, he held various ministerial posts in the Labour government. The Webb's works of social history include *The History of Trade Unionism* (1894), the ten-volume *English Local Government* (1906–1929), *The Decay of Capitalist Civilization* (1921) and *Soviet Communism* (1935). Beatrice's diaries provided the fodder for her works, *My Ap-*

prenticeship (1926) and *Our Partnership* (1948).

Weber, Max (1864–1920). German social scientist. Weber studied at a number of German universities and later taught at the universities of Freiburg, Munich and Heidelberg. His interests and writings in the social sciences were wide-ranging and extremely influential. A founder of modern sociology, he sought to create systematized concepts of the social sciences, and was the author of the influential volume *Methodology of the Social Sciences* (1922, tr. 1949). He rejected the idea that any one factor determines social dynamics, and stressed a multi-faceted understanding of society. Deeply interested in religion and its impact on society, he developed an analysis that linked the self-denying asceticism of Calvinism with the genesis of capitalism in *The Protestant Ethic and the Spirit of Capitalism* (1904–05, tr. 1930). Prefiguring much of later sociological thought, Weber was deft in his analysis of politics and class, and he stressed the importance of the development of bureaucracy in the economic and political life of Western society. Among his other books are *General Economic History* (1924, tr. 1927) and *Economy and Society* (4th ed. 1956, tr. 1968).

Weber, Max (1881–1961). American painter. Born in Russia, Weber and his family immigrated to the U.S. in 1891 and settled in Brooklyn, New York. He attended Pratt Institute (1898–1900) and traveled abroad in 1905, studying in Paris with Arthur Dow and Jean Paul Laurens and traveling throughout Europe. Weber became thoroughly familiar with the tenets of European modernism and also became personally acquainted with many of the European avant garde painters of the era. Returning to New York in 1909, his own work first reflected the brilliant coloristic experiments of FAUVISM, then the spatial innovations of CUBISM and later the swirling movement of FUTURISM. One of the best known of his cubist paintings is the lively and colorful *Chinese Restaurant* (Whitney Museum, New York City). Weber's post-1917 work tends to be more figurative and to deal often with specifically Jewish subject matter. The social concerns of the 1930s are reflected in his works of that period, while his post-World War II paintings are increasingly linear and range from the abstract to the figurative.

Weber & Fields. American vaudeville comedy team of Joe Weber (born Morris Weber; 1867–1942) and Lew Fields (born Moses Schanfield; 1867–1941). Both born in New York City, they became a song-and-dance team at the age of ten, at first performing on the street and later playing small theaters in New York City and boardwalk shows in Coney Island. Opposites in physical appearance—Weber was short and chubby, Fields tall and angular—they began playing burlesque in 1884 and became famous for their broad comedy routines, slapstick turns, parodies of current hit plays and dialect sketches. In 1896 they leased their own Broadway theater, producing and starring in shows there for the next eight years and presenting some of the leading performers of their era in their shows. Weber & Fields became the prototypes for much of 20th-century comedy. Separated after a quarrel in 1904, they were reunited seven years later and retired in 1930.

Webern, Anton von (1883–1945). Viennese composer and influential disciple of the modern 12-tone techniques of Arnold SCHOENBERG. He was born in Vienna and with colleague and friend Alan BERG studied with Schoenberg from 1904 to 1910. His first works, like the *Passacaglia for Orchestra* (1908) clung to tonal implications; while later works, beginning with the song cycles on texts by Stefan GEORGE (1909) and the *Six Pieces for Orchestra* (1910) experiment with atonality. Adopting some of the so-called "12-tone" techniques pioneered by Schoenberg—basing compositions on the rigorous use of patterns of the 12 chromatic intervals—he composed the important *Symphony* (1928) and the *Variations for Orchestra* (1940). During this time Webern made a living conducting in Vienna, generously filling his programs with the music of his idols—Brahms, Wagner, MAHLER, and—of course—Arnold Schoenberg. There are striking distinctions that may distinguish Webern's music from that of his colleagues. He was noted for the clear—even simple—textures of his polyphony and instrumentation. Without compromising the modernity of his work, he achieved a direct and immediate response from his listeners that makes his work increasingly popular today. And, above all, he strove for an amazing brevity and conciseness to many of his pieces. He is the great aphorist of the serial composers (the fourth of the *Five Pieces for Orchestra*, 1913, requires only 19 seconds for performance). Describing this aspect of the work, Schoenberg said: "Each glance may be extended to a poem, each sigh to a novel." Webern's death came suddenly in 1945 while staying with his daughter in Mittersill, Austria. Unaware of a curfew imposed on all Austrians by the occupying American forces, he was shot while taking a stroll.

For further reading:

Ewen, David, *Composers Since 1900*. New York: The H.W. Wilson Co., 1969.

Webster, Paul F. (1907–1984). HOLLYWOOD lyricist who wrote over 500 songs. He started his Hollywood career writing for Shirley TEMPLE and wrote his first hit song, "Rainbow on the River," in 1936. He won ACADEMY AWARDS for "Secret Love," from the film *Calamity Jane* (1953); "Love is a Many-Splendored Thing," the title song to a 1955 film; and "The Shadow of Your Smile," from *The Sandpiper* (1965). His lyrics were sung by Doris Day, Sammy Fain, Duke ELLINGTON and Hoagy CARMICHAEL, among others. Webster also wrote the title songs for such television shows as "Maverick" and "Spider Man."

Webster v. Reproductive Health Services (1989). U.S. Supreme Court case regarding ABORTION. The case involved a Missouri law prohibiting abortions in public hospitals and clinics, barring the use of public funds to inform women of/or counsel women to have abortions, and requiring doctors to test to determine whether a fetus 19 weeks old was viable. The law was challenged as unconstitutional by those in favor of legal abortions. Missouri officials were joined by the REAGAN administration asking the court to rule in favor of the Missouri law and to overturn ROE V. WADE, the controversial 1973 decision allowing abortions. The *Webster* case was highly charged politically. On July 3, 1989, the court ruled to uphold the Missouri law by a 5 to 4 decision. However, it did not overturn *Roe v. Wade*. The majority opinion was written by Chief Justice William REHNQUIST and joined by justices Byron R. WHITE and Anthony M. KENNEDY. Justice Antonin SCALIA voted with the majority but strongly criticized his colleagues for not overturning *Roe* outright. Justice Sandra Day O'CONNOR also voted with the majority but asserted that the case did not necessitate a new ruling on *Roe*. Justice Harry A. BLACKMUN, the author of *Roe v. Wade*, wrote a critical dissent. He was joined by justices William J. BRENNAN, Jr. and Thurgood MARSHALL. A separate dissent was presented by Justice John Paul STEVENS. Essentially, the decision neither reaffirmed nor overturned *Roe v. Wade*, but turned the issue back to the individual states until a more decisive test case could be brought before the court. Thus, abortion again became a major and issue in state and local politics and was the focus of the 1989 elections throughout the U.S.

Wedemeyer, Albert Coady (1897–1989). American Army general who helped plan the grand allied strategy for winning WORLD WAR II. Toward the end of the war he served as U.S. commander in China.

Wedtech Scandal. Procurement fraud scandal in the mid-1980s involving government contracts that resulted in the conviction of Representative Mario Biaggi for influence-peddling, and also ensnarled several local politicians from the Bronx, New York. Wedtech was a small Bronx machine shop that landed a number of large federal government contracts thanks to the help of Biaggi. The scheme unravelled when Wedtech was unable to deliver on the contracts. Investigations revealed that Biaggi had in effect extorted $1.8 million in Wedtech stock and $50,000 in cash for his help in getting the contracts. Biaggi was convicted, as were his son Richard, Stanley Simon, the former Bronx Borough president, and John Mariotta, the founder and chairman of Wedtech.

Wegener, Alfred Lothar (1880–1930). German meteorologist and geologist. Wegener distinguished himself with his 1915 hypothesis of continental drift, published as *Origin of Continents and Oceans.* His proposal—that the continents were once contiguous—at first was met with outrage. To support his premise, Wegener used four main arguments, which in part were corroborated in 1929 by Arthur Holmes, who was able to account for the continental movement as suggested by Wegener. Advances in geomagnetism and oceanography led to full acceptance of Wegener's theory, and to a new geophysical discipline of plate tectonics after World War II.

Weil, Simone (1909–1943). French philosopher and theologian. Weil, all of whose works were published posthumously, earned a reputation as one of the most incisive and original thinkers of her era. Albert CAMUS, for one, referred to her has "the only great spirit of our time." Weil, whose brother Andre was a distinguished mathematician, was raised in an agnostic Jewish family. As a youth, she studied under the noted French philosopher Alain. In 1928, she finished first in the entrance examination for the Ecole Normale Superieure; Simone DE BEAUVOIR finished second. In the 1930s, Weil alternated stints of teaching philosophy with manual labor in factories and fields in order to understand the real needs of the workers. In the mid-1930s, Weil became increasingly drawn to Christianity but refused baptism into the Catholic Church. Her political philosophy, which cannot be categorized as left- or right-wing, is best expressed in *The Need for Roots* (1953), which she wrote in 1943 at the request of the FREE FRENCH organization as a guide to the reconstruction of postwar FRANCE. That same year Weil, who was living in London, fell ill but frequently refused food and medical treatment out of sympathy for the plight of the people of Occupied France. Those refusals hastened her death. Other major works by Weil include *Waiting for God* (1951) and *Gravity and Grace* (1952).

For further reading:

Coles, Robert, *Simone Weil: A Modern Pilgrimage.* Reading, Massachusetts: Addison-Wesley, 1987.

Fiori, Gabriella, *Simone Weil: An Intellectual Biography.* Athens: University of Georgia Press, 1989.

Little, Pat, *Simone Weil.* New York: St. Martin's Press, 1988.

Weill, Kurt (1900–1950). German-born opera and BROADWAY musical show composer who was best known for *Die Dreigroschenoper* (*The Threepenny Opera*). Dissatisfied with his early training in Berlin under Ferruccio BUSONI and with the limited appeal of sophisticated, abstract music in general, Weill embraced the German aesthetic *Zeitkunst* movement and wrote a kind of "song-play," or "musical theater," as he put it, that infused classical forms with contemporary jazz, cabaret songs, popular dances, and topical references. A mocking, sarcastic satire of decadent, bourgeois post-war German life hovered over collaborations with dramatists Georg KAISER, *Der Zar laesst sich photographieren (The Czar Has Himself Photographed,* 1927); and with Bertolt BRECHT, *Aufstieg und Fall der Stadt Mahagonny (The Rise and Fall of the City of Mahagonny,* 1927–1929) and *Die Dreigroschenoper* (1928). Despite the popularity of the latter opera—songs like "Moritat" ("Mack the Knife") made it the most successful musical production in Germany between the two World Wars—Weill and his wife, the actress Lotte LENYA, fled Nazi persecution in 1933 and, after two years in PARIS, came to their permanent home in the U.S. Weill's subsequent Broadway musical shows continued the pattern of broad eclecticism that marked most of his work. With Maxwell ANDERSON he satirized President ROOSEVELT in *Knickerbocker Holiday* (1938). (Its most popular song, "September Song," has become a standard.) With Moss HART he explored themes concerning psychoanalysis in *Lady in the Dark* (1941). With Elmer RICE he depicted tenement life in New York in *Street Scene.* And in *Huckleberry Finn,* unfinished at the time of his death in 1950, he quoted the songs of the Missouri Ozarks. In HOLLYWOOD he reunited with Brecht and scored the Fritz LANG film *You and Me* (1938). Weill's music was frequently pungent, spare, lyric, and brutal by turns—and profoundly divided between its serious motivations and sometimes brittle, artificial effects.

For further reading:

Ewen, David, *Composers Since 1900.* New York: The H.W. Wilson Co., 1969.

Weimar Republic. Name generally used to refer to GERMANY, and its democratic government, during the period from just after the nation's defeat in WORLD WAR I (1918) to shortly after the appointment of Adolf HITLER as chancellor (1933). In February 1919 a national assembly gathered in the German town of Weimar to create a new form of government for the nation. On July 31, 1919 it officially adopted a constitution that provided for a president, a chancellor (prime minister), a two-house legislature and proportional representation. Despite the good intentions of the Weimar constitution, the government was handicapped by complex economic and political problems: heavy war reparations; runaway inflation during the 1920s and the GREAT DEPRESSION during the 1930s; and the proliferation of political parties, including several anti-democratic extremist groups. The democratic socialist Friedrich Ebert served as president from 1919 to 1925; he was succeeded by Field Marshal Paul von HINDENBURG, who held the office until his death in 1933. Gustav STRESEMANN and Heinrich BRUNING were among the prominent statesmen of the Weimar Republic. The strain of social and political turmoil in the early 1930s finally tore the fabric of the republic. In 1932 Hitler's Nazi Party became the single largest party in the legislature, and Hitler demanded to be appointed chancellor. On March 23, 1933—two months after President Hindenburg had appointed him chancellor (Jan. 30)—Hitler suspended the Weimar constitution and thereafter made himself the personal master of Germany.

For further reading:

Phelan, Anthony, *The Weimar Dilemma: Intellectuals in the Weimar Republic.* New York: St. Martin's Press, 198‘.

Weinberg, Steven (1933–). American physicist. In 1979, Weinberg shared the NOBEL PRIZE for physics with Sheldon Glashow and Abdus SALAM for work developed independently that concerned two of the four fundamental forces of physics—electromagnetic interaction (which occurs between charged particles) and weak interaction (which explains certain radioactive decay processes). Weinberg, along with his colleagues, formulated a single theory that unified these two forces. Their formulation led the way toward a single theory of strong, electromagnetic, weak and gravitational interactions, as sought by EINSTEIN and Erwin SCHRODINGER, among others.

Weingartner, Felix (1863–1942). Yugoslavian-born orchestra conductor. He was the first and most important transitional figure between traditions in 19th century conducting and the modern attitudes of the new century. He was born at Zara (modern Zadar, Yugoslavia) and was influenced early in his career by composers Johannes Brahms and Franz Liszt. He conducted extensively throughout the rest of the century in Danzig (1885–1887), Hamburg (1887–1889) and at the Vienna Opera in 1908 (succeeding MAHLER). He came to the U.S. for the first time in 1905, later conducting the Boston Opera Company. A prolific composer of six symphonies and eight operas (including a trilogy from Aeschylus), he regarded it as the tragedy of his life that his eclectic style of music was never generally accepted. Although originally in the great 19th century romantic tradition, he broke with one of its chief exponents, Hans von Bulow, and attacked prevalent excesses in interpretation and performance. He abandoned his former histrionic podium style and adopted a quiet, restrained, dignified manner. The cause of the composer's music, and not the egotism of the conductor, he wrote in his book, *On Conducting* (1895) should be the chief priority. Weingartner, a handsome and personable figure, was also an indefatigable editor and writer, pioneering a modern revival of Hector Berlioz, and classic editions of the symphonies of Schubert, Beethoven, and Schumann. Critic Harold C. Schonberg has written that to many "he remains the most rounded and satisfactory of all conductors in his chosen repertoire."

For further reading:

Schonberg, Harold C., *The Great Conductors.* New York: Simon & Schuster, 1967.

Weir, Peter (1944–). Australian film director; a leading figure in the so-called new wave of Australian motion pictures that began in the 1970s. Weir's movies often have a mystical atmosphere; they examine the conflict between social mores and personal values with sympathy for the underdog. Among his films are *The Last Wave* (1977), *Gallipoli* (1981), *The Year of Living Dangerously* (1983), *Dead Poets Society* (1989) and *Green Card* (1990).

Weiss, George M. (1895–1972). American baseball executive. Weiss was general manager of the New York Yankees from 1947 to 1960. During this time the Yankees were virtually a dynasty, winning 10 American League pennants and seven World Series. Weiss was later the first president of the New York Mets (1961–66). He was elected to the Baseball Hall of Fame in 1971.

Weiss, Paul Alfred (1898–1989). Austrian-born U.S. biologist who won the National Medal of Science for his pioneering work in the theory of cellular development. Among other findings, he established the principle of cellular self-organization and helped prove that nerve cells could replenish themselves in all parts of the body. He taught at the University of CHICAGO for 21 years and was a professor emeritus at Rockefeller University.

Weiss, Peter (1916–1982). German-born playwright and novelist. He fled Nazi Germany as a teenager in 1934 and later became a naturalized Swedish citizen. His plays were considered profounding disturbing. Centering on historical events and taking a Marxist outlook, they were essentially dialogues between representatives of opposing ideas. Weiss was best known for his prize-winning play *Marat/Sade* (1964), set in an insane asylum where inmates depict the 1793 assassination of the French Revolutionary leader Jean Marat. The play shocked audiences with its graphic violence and helped establish a new genre, **theater of cruelty**.

Weissmuller, Johnny (1904–1984). American swimmer and actor. Weissmuller set 67 swimming records during the 1920s. He won five gold medals in the 100–meter and 400–meter individual, and 800–meter relay, freestyle events in the 1924 and 1928 OLYMPIC GAMES. He then went on to play the role of TARZAN in some 18 movies. Of the many actors who played the Edgar Rice BURROUGHS hero during the 20th century, Weissmuller was probably the most closely identified with the role.

Weizmann, Chaim (1874–1952). Chemist, Zionist leader, first president of Israel (1948–52). Born in Russia, he studied at the University of Freiburg, where he obtained his Ph.D. in 1900. He taught chemistry at the University of Geneva (1901–3) and moved to the faculty of the University of Manchester in 1904. Already a committed Zionist, he soon became a leader of British ZIONISM, visited PALESTINE in 1907 and became a British subject in 1910. During WORLD WAR I, he was director of the Admiralty Laboratories (1916–19). In 1917, Weizmann was instrumental in the creation of the BALFOUR DECLARATION, and the following year he headed the Zionist Commission to Palestine and cofounded the Hebrew University in Jerusalem. He was twice (1920–31, 1935–46) the president of the World Zionist Organization. In that office, he stressed the need for settlement in Palestine as well as for British support of a Jewish homeland. In 1934, he established a research institute at Rehoboth, which later became the world-renowned Weizmann Institute of Science. He returned to British service at the outbreak of WORLD WAR II, serving as advisor to the ministry of supply. When ISRAEL became independent in 1948, Weizmann was elected president, serving in that office until his death.

Welensky, Roy (1907–). Rhodesian statesman. Born in Salisbury (now Harare), he became a railway engineer and trade union leader. In 1938 he founded the Labour Party in Northern Rhodesia (now ZAMBIA) and in 1953 aided in the union of Northern Rhodesia, Southern Rhodesia (now ZIMBABWE) and Nyasaland (now MALAWI) into the Federation of Rhodesia and Nyasaland. He served in a number of Federation posts before becoming prime minister in 1956. As head of the government, Welensky advocated interracial cooperation. However, he was unsuccessful in preventing the dissolution of the Federation late in 1963. Opposed to Ian SMITH's declaration of Southern Rhodesian independence from Britain, he retired from politics in 1965.

welfare state. Term for the state that guarantees its citizens' economic and social well-being. This policy has applied to democratic governments particularly in the post-World War II period and has addressed such problems as unemployment, illness, disability, old age, housing and social services. The concept of the welfare state is highly developed in the Scandinavian nations and the Netherlands, and was taken for granted in the UNITED KINGDOM from the time of Clement ATTLEE'S LABOUR PARTY government until the government of Margaret THATCHER. Manifestations of this approach to social policy include Great Britain's NATIONAL HEALTH SERVICE and unemployment insurance in the U.S. and the U.K. American adaptations of welfare state policies include SOCIAL SECURITY, workers compensation, MEDICAID and MEDICARE.

Welk, Lawrence (1903–). American band leader. An accordionist, Welk led a six-man band that played on radio in North Dakota in 1925. Welk moved to Chicago during the 1930s to develop his sound, known as "Champagne Music." After 1953 his musicians were heard on radio and seen on television, becoming one of the most popular programs on the air. As musical tastes and social mores changed in the 1960s and later, Welk was the object of many good-natured jokes and satires concerning his "square" music and his Central European accent.

Welles, (George) Orson (1915–1985). Legendary American actor and director. In his long, spectacular but uneven career, Welles was active in the theater, radio and film. However, his successes all came before he reached the age of 30. He starred on Broadway during his 20s, and also became known to millions as the voice of Lamont Cranston on the radio mystery series "The Shadow." In 1938, he presented a radio dramatization of H.G. WELLS's *War of the Worlds* that frightened tens of thousands of listeners into thinking that Martians were truly invading Earth. His first film, CITIZEN KANE, was released in 1941. The film, which he directed, coauthored and starred in, was in 1962 selected as the "best film in motion picture history." In later life, he lived and worked in Europe, taking roles in second rate films and commercials to allow him to finance his own projects.

American actor and director Orson Welles convinced the American public that Martians had landed when he broadcast H.G. Wells' War of the Worlds *(Oct. 30, 1938).*

Wells, Dickie (William) (1909–1985). Jazz trombonist and composer. Wells was one of the leading jazz trombonists of the 1930s and 1940s. He was especially well-known for his rhythmic intensity and inventive solos. Wells was raised in Louisville, Kentucky, and first came to New York in the mid-1920s. Over the next two decades, he played with numerous big bands, most notably those led by Fletcher HENDERSON and Count BASIE. Wells remained active as a jazz performer through the 1970s. His compositions include the jazz songs "Sugar Hip" and "Kansas City Strike." He wrote an autobiography, *The Night People* (1971).

Wells, Edward C. (1910–1986). American engineer. His work on the 1935 design for the flap system of the wing of the B-17 Flying Fortress bomber was adopted for use on nearly all U.S.-made jet aircraft. He held 20 patents, including the one for the landing-gear system on the last plane he helped design, Boeing's 767 medium-range passenger jet. He was Boeing's chief engineer when he retired.

Wells, H(erbert) G(eorge) (1866–1946). British social prophet, novelist, pioneer in science fiction, and, in the words of Bertrand RUSSELL, "an important liberator of thought and action." The son of a shopkeeper, Wells' early education and experience ranged from jobs as a draper's assistant, school teacher, and text-book writer to study under T.H. Huxley in biology. His first novel, the brilliant *The Time Machine* (1895) was the first literary work in history to suggest the possibility of time travel by means of a *machine.* Integral to the story of a man who travels to the year 30,000,000 (by which time man has become extinct) are the sciences of physics, biology, astronomy, and chemistry. In this and succeeding novels and stories in the next five years—including

Many of the predictions of British science fiction author and social critic H.G. Wells were realized during the 20th century.

The Island of Dr. Moreau, The Invisible Man, The War of the Worlds, and *The First Men in the Moon*—he produced his best work. As if echoing the words of the Time Traveller, Wells could say: "With a kind of madness growing upon me, I flung myself into futurity." He kicked away the traces of the 19th century art and ideas and looked to the 20th century and beyond, tackling issues of politics, nuclear war, evolution, interplanetary space travel, mind-altering drugs, and new communications technologies. His tendency to sermonize about the ills of man and society came to the fore after the turn of the century in "realistic" novels like *The History of Mr. Polly* and *Ann Veronica* (both 1909) and *The Shape of Things to Come* (1933). His later years were preoccupied with causes like the FABIAN SOCIETY and the LEAGUE OF NATIONS. Many of Wells' stories have been adapted for motion pictures, radio, and television, beginning in 1918 with an adaptation for the British Gaumont Film Company of *The First Men in the Moon.* That his early optimism about man's progress was replaced late in life by a darker pessimism can be seen in his first and last works. In *The Island of Dr. Moreau* the narrator, Prendrick, concludes that "whatever is more than animal within us" must remain our solace and hope. However, in his last essay, "Mind at the End of Its Tether" (1945), Wells declares that Man is doomed because he cannot and will not adapt himself to his technological circumstances. After a long illness, Wells died of cancer in 1946.

For further reading:

West, Anthony, *H.G. Wells: Aspects of a Life.* New York: Random House, 1984.

Welsh nationalism. Political and cultural movement starting among Welsh intellectuals in 1886; favored Welsh language rights, religious equality and local autonomy. The movement, led by Tom Ellis (1859–99) and David LLOYD GEORGE, secured disestablishment of the Church of England (1920) in Wales. Weakened by the challenge of the Labour Party, the movement formed PLAID CYMRU—a political party favoring dominion status for Wales. The party was split between socialists and cultural nationalists, and it turned to violence in the late 1930s. Several of its leaders were imprisoned in 1938. The party gained parliamentary seats only in 1966, and it has held at least two seats in all subsequent elections. Despite failure in the 1979 Devolution Referendum, the movement continued non-violent action in favor of Welsh-language signs, and opposed English immigration into Welsh-speaking areas.

Welty, Eudora (1909–). American author. Educated at Mississippi State College for Women and the University of Wisconsin, Welty studied advertising at Columbia University in New York City and originally planned to become a commercial artist. She began writing short stories; her first collection, *A Curtain of Green* (1941), was such a popular success that it enabled her to write full-time in her hometown. A regional writer, she is noted for the colloquial accuracy of her dialogue and for her comically understated presentation of absurd rural events. She is the author of the novels *Delta Wedding* (1946) and *The Optimist's Daughter* (1972), as well as collections of short stories, including *The Wide Net* (1943), *The Golden Apples* (1949) and *Thirteen Stories* (1965), *One Time, One Place: Mississippi in the Depression: a Snapshot Album* (1971), *One Writer's Biginnings* (1984), and *Eudora Welty: Photographs* (1989).

For further reading:

Trouard, Dawn, ed., *The Eye of the Storyteller.* Kent, Oh.: Kent State University Press, 1989.

Bloom, Harold, ed., *Eudora Welty.* New York: Chelsea House Publishers, 1986.

Werfel, Franz (1890–1945). Czech-born Jewish novelist and playwright. Werfel, who spent most of his writing career in Austria, was a highly popular novelist and playwright in the era between the two world wars. Werfel served in the Austrian army during World War I, an experience that left him with a deeply held antimilitarist viewpoint. Influenced by EXPRESSIONISM in German drama, Werfel wrote plays including *The Goat Song* (1921) and *Juarez and Maximilian* (1924). Werfel achieved international fame with his novel *The Forty Days of Musa Dagh* (1934), a classic historical novel that portrays Armenian resistance to the Turks in 1915. A subsequent novel, *The Song of Bernadette* (1942), also achieved great popularity for its exploration of inspirational religious themes. Werfel was forced to flee Austria in 1938 to escape the Nazi terror. He settled in the U.S. His final play, *Jacobowsky and the Colonel* (1940), was sucessfully staged in New York in 1944.

Wertheimer, Max (1880–1943). German psychologist. Wertheimer, along with Kurt KOFFKA and Wolfgang KOHLER, was a key figure in the development of Gestalt theory as a field of psychological research. Wertheimer's researches helped to demonstrate that humans perceive in terms of immediately structured patterns—termed gestalts—as opposed to continual piecemeal assemblages of the outside world. Wertheimer earned his doctorate in psychology at the University of Wurzberg in 1904. He taught for several decades at the Universities of Frankfurt and Bonn before leaving GERMANY in 1937 to escape Nazi rule. Emigrating to New York, he taught at the New School for Social Research in his final years, applying gestalt theory to social issues. *Productive Thinking* (1945) is his major work.

West, Jerome Alan "Jerry" (1938–). American basketball player. West was drafted by the Minneapolis Lakers out of West Virginia University, where he was twice an All-American and 1959 NCAA most valuable player. The team moved before his rookie year, so West spent his entire career with the Los Angeles Lakers. In 1970, he led the league in scoring with 2,309 points and a 31.2 points per game average. An outstanding play making guard, his 2,435 assists place him sixth on the all-time list. A 10–time all-star, he finished his career in 1974 with 25,192 points. Two years after his retirement from active play, West was named coach of the Lakers, a post he held until 1979. That same year, he was named to the Basketball Hall of Fame.

West, Mae (1892–1980). American stage, film, and nightclub comedienne known for her sex appeal and saucy, suggestive wit. West's trademarks were her tight gowns, blond hair, sultry voice, suggestive manner, and racy double-entendres. Her line, "Why don't you come up and see me sometime?" became one of the most often repeated phrases of its day. Mae West's career spanned more than 60 years, but her heyday was in the 1920s and '30s. She was born in Brooklyn, New York and performed in VAUDEVILLE while still a child. She acted in several Broadway musicals before starring in *Sex* (1926), which she also wrote, produced and directed. The play caused an uproar; when West was arrested and jailed on obscenity charges, she became an instant celebrity and enjoyed great success in several more plays over the next few years. West made her film debut in HOLLYWOOD in *Night After Night* (1932) with George RAFT and Constance Cummings, and emerged as a bona fide movie star in *She Done Him Wrong* (1933, with Cary GRANT) and *I'm No Angel* (1933), for which she wrote her own dialogue. Her suggestive performances in these films led the film industry to strengthen the HAYS CODE in 1934. Among her other films were *Belle of the Nineties* (1934); her popularity peaked with *My Little Chickadee* (1940, with W.C. FIELDS). She later appeared in the movie *Myra Breckenridge* (1970). Her autobiography is *Goodness Had Nothing to Do with It* (1959).

West, Nathanael [Nathan Weinstein] (1903–1940). American writer. West graduated from Brown University in 1924. His experience as a night manager in a New York City hotel led to the novel *Miss Lonelyhearts* (1933). During the 1930s West worked as a HOLLYWOOD screenwriter and

British author and journalist Rebecca West, an early feminist spokeswoman.

gained inspiration for *The Day of the Locust* (1939). The juxtaposition of disillusion and despair for society with compassion and humor for humanity characterizes his work. His *Complete Works* were published in 1957.

West, Rebecca [Cecily Isabel Fairfield] (1892–1983). British novelist, critic and journalist. Born and educated in Edinburgh, West was briefly an actress in London before turning to journalism. She adopted her pseudonym when she was 19 after the heroine in Ibsen's *Rosmersholm.* West was a committed feminist and her first works appeared in such periodicals as *The Freewoman* and *The Clarion.* Her review of H.G. WELLS' *Marriage* (1912) brought about their meeting and a stormy ten-year relationship during which their son Anthony West (1914–87) was born. Many of her early pieces have been collected into *The Young Rebecca* (1982). West's incisive works of nonfiction include *Henry James* (1916); *Black Lamb and Grey Falcon* (1941), which details a trip she took through YUGOSLAVIA in 1937; *The Meaning of Treason* (1947), which evolved from articles on the NUREMBERG TRIALS commissioned by *The New Yorker;* and *1900* (1982). West's novels include *The Return of Soldier* (1918), *The Thinking Reed* (1936), *The Fountain Overflows* (1956), which is the first of three semi-autobiographical novels; and *The Birds Fall Down* (1966). The unfinished *Sunflower,* which draws upon her experiences with Wells and with Lord BEAVERBROOK, was published posthumously in 1986. Her fiction intelligently explores her character's motivations and feelings. West, who had married Henry Maxwell Andrews in 1930, remained active and pugnacious to the end of her life, continuing to write and even appearing briefly in the 1981 film *Reds.* In 1959 she was made Dame Commander in the Order of the British Empire.

West Bank. An area of west of the Jordan river, formerly Jordanian territory. Captured by ISRAEL in the 1967 SIX DAY WAR, it has been occupied and administered by Israel ever since. JORDAN's King HUSSEIN renounced Jordanian claims to the West Bank in 1988. However, the Palestinian Liberation Organization has demanded an end to the Israeli occupation and the establishment of a Palestinian homeland in the West Bank region. The INTIFADA (Palestinian uprising) against Israeli rule that began in the late 1980s has been centered in the West Bank.

Western Sahara. Located on the Atlantic coast of northwestern Africa, Western Sahara covers an area of 102,676 square miles. SPAIN, which ruled Western Sahara from 1926 to 1976, crushed a revolt (1957–58), stopped a liberation movement (1967–70), rejected a UNITED NATIONS-proposed self-determination referendum for the country (1966) and dismissed claims to the country by MOROCCO and MAURITANIA. In 1976 Spain formally ended its control and partitioned the country between Morocco and Mauritania. Morocco occupied the entire country when Mauritania withdrew its claim in 1979. A Western Sahara nationalist movement declared independence as the "Saharan Arab Democratic Republic" in 1976 and fought Morocco for control during the 1980s. Although both sides accepted a UN peace plan in 1988, fighting erupted again in 1989.

Western Samoa [Independent State of Western Samoa]. Located in the southwestern Pacific Ocean, approximately 1,600 miles northeast of New Zealand, Western Samoa is comprised of two main islands (Upolu and Savai'i) and a number of smaller islands, and has a total land area of 1,093 square miles. New Zealand annexed Western Samoa in 1914 and administered it (1920–62) on behalf of the LEAGUE OF NATIONS and the UNITED NATIONS. A constitution was drafted and independence achieved in 1962. The island state became a full member of the British Commonwealth in 1970 and joined the UN in 1976.

West Germany [Bundesrepublik Deutschland—BRD, or Federal Republic of Germany—FRG]. Located in north-central Europe, West Germany had an area of 96,001 square miles, with West Berlin as a separate entity within the territory of EAST GERMANY. The Federal Republic of Germany (FRG) was established in May 1949 and granted partial sovereignty by Western occupation forces. Konrad ADENAUER became the first federal chancellor (1949–63), guiding the country to full sovereignty on May 5, 1955. During the 1950s and 1960s rapid economic recovery from postwar devastation occurred, and West Germany became a member of the EUROPEAN ECONOMIC COMMUNITY and NATO. An influx of East Germans, coupled with Adenauer's refusal to recognize the East German government and its desire to absorb all of BERLIN, led to the erection of the BERLIN WALL (1961) by East Germany. From 1966 to the late 1970s the country experienced social unrest, with protests and terrorism sponsored by the leftist BAADER-MEINHOF GROUP; its offshoot, the Red Army Faction; and the German Socialist Students' Union (SDS). In 1972 Arab BLACK SEPTEMBER guerrillas attacked Israeli quarters at the Munich Olympics, resulting in tragedy (see MUNICH OLYMPICS MASSACRE). The chancellorship of Willy BRANDT (1969–74) and his OSTPOLI-

WEST GERMANY

1949	Federal Republic of Germany created from three Western occupation zones.
1961	(August) Construction of Berlin Wall.
1963	(January) FRG signs friendship treaty with France.
1968	Baader-Meinhof terrorist group formed.
1972	(September) "Black September" massacre of Israeli athletes at Munich Olympics.
1989	Mass exodus of East Germans into FRG; Berlin Wall opened; Chancellor Kohl proposes reunification of Germany.
1990	Reunification of Germany (Oct. 3); Kohl elected chancellor in first nationwide election since 1933 (Dec. 2).

WEST GERMANY: CHANCELLORS

1949-1963	Konrad Adenauer (Christian Democrat)
1963-1966	Ludwig Erhard (Christian Democrat)
1966-1969	Kurt Kiesinger (Christian Democrat)
1969-1974	Willy Brandt (Social Democrat)
1974-1982	Helmut Schmidt (Social Democrat)
1982-	Helmut Kohl (Christian Democrat)

WEST GERMANY

TIK policy brought treaties with the Soviet Union and East Germany and membership in the UN (1973). Controversy erupted during the chancellorship of Helmut SCHMIDT (1974–82) over the deployment of U.S. nuclear (INF) missiles in the country, leading to huge peace marches in 1982–83. Christian Democrat Helmut KOHL, who became chancellor in 1982, orchestrated the unification of East and West Germany in Oct. 1990. The new nation kept the official name Federal Republic of Germany.

For further reading:

Bark, Dennis L., *A History of West Germany*. Oxford: Basil Blackwell, 1989.

Turner, Henry A., Jr., *The Two Germanies Since 1945: East and West*. New Haven, Conn.: Yale University Press, 1987.

West Indies Federation. A union of ten British Colonies—ANTIGUA, BARBADOS, DOMINICA, GRENADA, JAMAICA, MONSERRAT, ST. CHRISTOPHER-NEVIS and Anguilla, St. Lucia, ST. VINCENT and TRINIDAD and TOBAGO—established in 1958. The idea for a federation comprised of Barbados, Jamaica, Trinidad and Tobago, and the Leeward and Windward Islands arose in 1947, and finally came to fruition in 1958 with its parliament at Port-of-Spain, Trinidad. In Jamaica, particularly, it was felt that the British were attempting to saddle the wealthier areas of the Caribbean with the poorer ones; and led by Jamaican Prime Minister Sir Alexander BUSTAMENTE, opposition to the federation grew. Following Jamaica's and then Trinidad and Tobago's secession and subsequent independence, the Federation ended in 1962. Barbados became independent in 1966. The lesser islands banded together loosely as the West Indies Associate States, but by the 1980's, all had achieved independence except St. Christopher-Nevis, from which Anguilla separated itself in 1980.

Westland Affair. Internal British government arguments over the fate of Britain's failing Westland Helicopter Co. broke into the open in January 1986 with the leak of sensitive cabinet letters. The letters suggested that the government had decided to sell the firm to an American company rather than to a European consortium that had made a higher bid. This revelation prompted the resignation of Defense Minister Michael HESELTINE and of the industry minister; it also compromised the traditional neutrality of the civil service and undermined the reputation of Prime Minister Margaret THATCHER, who was accused of deeper involvement than she admitted.

Westmoreland, William C(hilds) (1914–). American general, commander of U.S. forces during the VIETNAM WAR. Born in Spartanburg County, S.C., Westmoreland graduated from West Point in 1936. He was a combat officer in World War II and the Korean War. Returning to the U.S., he was promoted to the rank of general, commanded an airborne division and served as superintendent of West Point (1960–63). After the outbreak of the Vietnam War, he was appointed head of the Military Assistance Command (MACV) (1964), commanding U.S. forces in the field in South Vietnam. Continuing to direct U.S. efforts until 1968, and presiding over American involvement as it grew from several thousand advisers to over

General William Westmoreland, commander of the U.S. forces in Vietnam from 1964 to 1968.

500,000 soldiers, Westmoreland became the focus of much public animosity toward the war. Returned to Washington, D.C., in 1968, he served as Army chief of staff until 1972, when he retired from active duty. He later criticized the JOHNSON administration's handling of the war, claiming that he could have defeated North Vietnam after the TET OFFENSIVE if the administration had let him attack communist sanctuaries in Laos, Cambodia and North Vietnam. He brought a libel suit against CBS after a 1982 CBS documentary charged that he had manipulated intelligence data during the war. The suit was settled out of court in 1985. Westmoreland is the author of *A Soldier Reports* (1976).

Weston, Edward (1886–1958). American photographer. Weston is widely regarded as one of the greatest American photographers of the century. A master craftsman with a superb aesthetic eye, Weston became famous for his photographic studies of natural forms such as shells, cacti, peppers, clouds and human nudes. In the 1930s, he founded a school of photography known as "f64," after the smallest camera lens opening—thus signifying the school's emphasis on fine technique. Major published collections of photographs by Weston include the two-volume *Daybooks of Edward Weston* (1961, 1966) and *Edward Weston: Fifty Years* (1979).

West Pakistan. See PAKISTAN.

West Side Story. A landmark in the American musical theater; arguably, with SHOW BOAT (1927), PORGY AND BESS (1935) and OKLAHOMA! (1943), among the greatest of all American music-dramas. It premiered in New York at the Winter Garden Theater on September 26, 1957, and ran for 732 performances. Leonard BERNSTEIN and Stephen SONDHEIM wrote the songs, Arthur Laurents wrote the book and Jerome ROBBINS choreographed the dancing. Basically, it was a variant of *Romeo and Juliet:* Verona was replaced by New York's West Side; the lovers were Maria and Tony; and the feuding families of the Montagues and the Capulets were transformed into rival juvenile gangs—Puerto Rican "Sharks" and American "Jets." Despite its impressive achievement, many critics and audiences at the time were annoyed at its violence, bitter humor and unhappy ending. ("Although the material is horrifying," wrote Brooks ATKINSON, "the workmanship is admirable.") The songs were, by turns, crude ("Gee, Officer Krupke"), raucous ("America") and sentimental ("Tonight" and "Maria"). The tender "Wedding Song" remains one of its most effective moments. The dances had an edgy, finger-snapping pulse reflective of the frenetic rhythms of city streets. After several successful revivals, a film adaptation was made in 1961, directed by Robert Wise and Jerome Robbins, starring Natalie Wood and Richard Beymer as Maria and Tony. It won 10 ACADEMY AWARDS, including one as best picture. In 1969 *West Side Story* entered the regular repertory of the distinguished Vienna opera house, the Volksoper.

For further reading:
Ewen, David, *The Complete Book of the American Musical Theater*. New York: Holt, Rinehart and Winston, 1970.

"Wetbacks". Derogatory term applied to illegal immigrants entering the U.S. from MEXICO. They are so-called because they originally arrived in the U.S. by swimming across the Rio Grande. Such immigrants provide cheap labor for California landowners and others, who encourage them to immigrate illegally. (See also MIGRANT LABOR.)

Wets. Derogatory term applied to members of the British CONSERVATIVE PARTY who did not support the radical free-market policies of former Prime Minister Margaret THATCHER. (See also DRIES.)

Weygand, Maxime (1867–1965). French general. Born in Brussels, he attended the military college at St. Cyr and became a career army officer. During WORLD WAR I and until 1923, he was chief of staff to Marshal FOCH, and in 1920 he reorganized the Polish army and successfully repelled Soviet attacks. His distinguished career included posts as high commissioner of Syria (1923–24), military educator (1924–29) and chief of the French general staff (1930–35). Early in WORLD WAR II he was commander of Middle Eastern forces (1939–40), and was recalled to France to serve as supreme French commander in May, 1940. Unable to prevent the fall of France, Weygand served the VICHY government as commander in North Africa (1940) and governor general of Algeria (1941). Suspected of RESISTANCE sympathies, he was imprisoned by the Germans from 1942 to 1945. Returning to France, he was tried and acquitted of charges of collaboration with Germany.

Weyland, Otto P(aul) (1902–1979). American Air Force officer. During WORLD WAR II Weyland commanded the 84th Fighter Wing of the U.S. Army Air Force in England. In February 1944 he became head of the XIX Tactical Air Command. In this capacity, after the INVASION OF NORMANDY he provided the air support for General George S. PATTON's Third Army in Europe. During the KOREAN WAR he was commander of the Far East Air Forces and won the Silver Star for leading a bombing raid on North Korea. He later headed the Tactical Air Command (1954–59), a position he had also held briefly (1950–51) before the Korean War.

Whale, James (1896–1957). British-born film and theatrical director. Whale began his career as a cartoonist before becoming drawn to the theater while serving in a German prisoner of war camp during WORLD WAR I. After a successful stint as a theater director in London in the 1920s, Whale was invited to HOLLYWOOD to make a film adaptation of the play *Journey's End* (1930). Whale's most memorable films were in the horror genre—FRANKENSTEIN (1931), *The Old Dark House* (1932), *The Invisible Man* (1933), and *The Bride of Frankenstein* (1935). Whale gave up his Hollywood career in 1941 to devote himself to painting.

Wharton, Edith [born Edith Newbold Jones] (1862–1937). American novelist of society and manners, whose *The Age of Innocence* won a PULITZER PRIZE in 1920. Born into a socially prominent New York family, she grew up in the social milieu of many of her works—a world of "first families" whose wealth and position were declining under the impact of modern industrial democracy. She married Edward Wharton in 1885 and began a writing career that scored its first big success with *The House of Mirth* in 1905. Two years later she moved to France, where she spent the rest of her life, although many of her subsequent works continued to have American settings. Her wide range of tone and subject was impressive. In *The House of Mirth* and *The Custom of the Country* (1913) she explored with cool, detached prose the tragedy that threatened the pleasure-loving society of the idle rich. "A frivolous society can acquire dramatic significance only through what its frivolity destroys," she wrote. "Its tragic implication lies in its power of debasing people and ideals." In two of her finest works, *Ethan Frome* (1911) and *Summer* (1917), she wielded a more severe prose style to illuminate the stunted lives of New England farmers and villagers. And she used her magnificent horror stories as vehicles for her strongest feminist concerns. The stock devices of vampire ("Bewitched"), ghost ("The Lady Maid's Bell") and witch cult ("All Souls") represent the sexual repression and social injustice endured by women. In the opinion of biographer R.W.B. Lewis, Wharton was without peer in her generation in the ability to depict "the modes of entrapment, betrayal, and exclusion devised for women in the first decades of the American and European twentieth century."

For further reading:
Lewis, R.W.B., *Edith Wharton*. New York: Harper and Row, 1975.

Wheat, Zach(ariah) (1888–1972). American baseball player. Wheat had a 19–year career (1909–1927) as a left fielder, first with the Brooklyn Dodgers and then with the Philadelphia Athletics. He posted a .317 lifetime batting average and was elected to the Baseball Hall of Fame in 1959.

Wheldon, Sir Huw Prys (1916–1986). BRITISH BROADCASTING CORPORATION executive. Wheldon joined the BBC in 1952 as a television publicity officer, but later worked on many chidren's shows and documentaries. Deeply committed to the arts, he was responsible for "Monitor," the first arts program on British TV. As managing director of BBC television (1968–75), he was a major influence on British television programming. His assumption of that post marked the first time that a programmer was given overall control of British television.

Whirlaway (1938–1953). American race horse; one of the standard-bearers of the great Calumet era, during which seven Calumet horses in less than two decades won the Kentucky Derby. Known for his long, elegant tail, Whirlaway was ridden by Eddie ARCARO to victories in the Kentucky Derby, Preakness and Belmont, becoming only the fifth horse in history to win racing's Triple Crown.

White, Byron R(aymond) (1917–). Associate justice, U.S. Supreme Court (1962–). A graduate of the University of Colorado and Yale Law School, and a Rhodes Scholar at Oxford University, White gained the nickname of "Whizzer" for his exploits on the football field and played professional football for one year after college before enrolling at Oxford. He continued to play professional football while attending Yale Law School before a Navy career in World War II. White worked as a law clerk for Supreme Court Chief Justice Frederick VINSON before joining a large Denver law firm. A Democrat, he worked in the presidential campaign of John F. KENNEDY, who appointed him to the Supreme Court in 1962. Although initially perceived as member of the liberal majority of the WARREN Court, White's views seemed to grow more conservative, until he was perceived as a member of the conservative block in the later part of his career on the REHNQUIST Court.

White, Eartha Mary Magdalene (1876–1974). American social and community activist. After schooling in New York City, she returned south and started several successful businesses (1905–30). In 1900 she joined Booker T. WASHINGTON to found the National Negro Business League. In 1928 she founded the Clara White Mission, a community house that became the focus of black relief work and a WPA headquarters during the GREAT DEPRESSION. Her work in organizing the proposed 1941 march on Washington led to Presidential Order 8802 banning discrimination in federal hiring for defense and government. In 1967 White founded the Eartha M. White Nursing Home.

White, Edward (1930–1967). U.S. astronaut. With Gemini 4 White became the first American to walk in space on June 3, 1965. Attached to his spacecraft by a long tether, White floated out into the vast vacuum of space while fellow crewmember James MCDIVITT took some of the most stunning photographs of the space program. White tested a small gas handgun to propel himself for part of his 10-minute extravehicular activity (EVA), gaining better control than just pushing off could do. The two returned to Earth after four days in orbit. With Gus GRISSOM and Roger CHAFFEE, White was scheduled to make the first flight in the APOLLO series that would ultimately land human beings on the moon. But as the three sat sealed and strapped inside the Apollo 1 cabin during a dry-run test, a sudden spark from an electrical short resulted in an instant inferno, raging through the pure-oxygen atmosphere. Grissom, Chaffee and White never had a chance to get out. White was buried at West Point.

White, Edward Douglass (1845–1921). American politician and jurist. White received a Roman Catholic Jesuit education before fighting briefly with the Confederate Army during the Civil War. He was then trained in a New Orleans law office, elected Democratic state senator (1874–78), was appointed to the state supreme court (1879–80) and was elected to the U.S. Senate (1891–94). President Grover Cleveland appointed him to the U.S. Supreme Court in 1894, and President William Howard TAFT appointed him the ninth chief justice in 1910. He served until his death. His major contribution to U.S. jurisprudence was his establishment of the idea that restraint of trade by a monopolistic business must be "unreasonable" to be illegal under the Sherman Anti-Trust Act of 1890 (1911). His failure to adequately define "reasonable" restraint laid many antitrust decisions open to wide interpretation.

White, E(lwyn) B(rooks) (1899–1985). American author and essayist. White was widely regarded as one of the most engaging prose stylists in 20th Century American literature; for most of his writing career he was associated with THE NEW YORKER. White—along with James THURBER—was principal in shaping the magazine's tone and direction. Among the best known of his many books was *The Elements of Style* (first edition, 1959), a guide to correct English usage that drew upon the privately printed notes of Cornell English Professor William Strunk. In its various editions, the book became a staple of the curriculum in high school and college English classes. White was also the author of three books for children that came to be regarded as classics: *Stuart Little, Charlotte's Web* (1952) and *The Trumpet of the Swan* (1970). White was awarded a special PULITZER PRIZE in 1978.

White, Patrick (Victor Martindale) (1912–1990). Anglo-Australian author. Born in London of Australian parents, White grew up in Australia, but was educated in England at Cheltenham and King's College, Cambridge. After serving in the RAF in WORLD WAR II, he returned permanently to Australia in 1947. His first published work was a collection of verse written before 1930, *The Ploughman and Other Poems* (1935), and his first novel was *Happy Valley* (published in London, 1939; in the U.S., 1940). *The Aunt's Story* (1948) was acclaimed in the U.K. and the U.S., but was generally ignored in Australia. It was *The Tree of Man* (1955), a realistic family saga of a couple establishing a farm in the Australian outback, which established his reputation and drew comparisons to the work of Leo Tolstoy and D.H. LAWRENCE. Subsequent celebrated works include, *Voss* (1957), *The Vivisectors* (1970), and the *Eye of the Storm* (1973). White was awarded the NOBEL PRIZE for literature in 1973. Later works include the self-portrait, *Flaws in the Glass* (1981) and the novel *Memoirs of Many in One* (1986). White was also a playwright.

White, Robert (1924–). American test pilot. The first person to fly a plane to an altitude higher than 50 miles, X-15 pilot White qualified for Air Force astronaut wings on July 17, 1962, reaching an altitude of 314,750 feet, more than 59 miles. He didn't, however, meet the test of "flying in space," that was later established by the Federation Aeronautique Internationale (FAI) at 62 miles (100 km). In November 1961 he also became the first to fly at Mach 6, six times the speed of sound.

White, Ryan (1971–1990). American AIDS activist. An Indiana teenager who was a hemophiliac, Ryan White was diagnosed with AIDS in 1984. He was shunned by his classmates and banned from classes. He sued the Kokomo, Indiana school system and was readmitted. Later, his family moved to Cicero, Indiana, where he found greater acceptance. His story was made into a television movie, and Ryan became an articulate and important spokesman for PWAs (people with AIDS). His funeral was attended by more than 1,500 people, including First Lady Barbara BUSH and singers Michael JACKSON and Elton JOHN.

White, Theodore H(arold) (1915–1986). American political writer. One of the most influential journalists of his time, he won early recognition while reporting from China for such publications as the Manchester Guardian, the Boston Globe and Time magazine. His book *The Making of the President 1960*, was one of the seminal works of modern political reporting. The book became a huge best-seller for which White won a PULITZER PRIZE. He wrote three further *Making of the President* books in 1964, 1968, and 1972. He had planned to write about the 1976 election, but the WATERGATE scandal led him to write *Breach of Faith: The Fall of Richard Nixon*. He later wrote a personal memoir entitled *In Search of History*.

White, Walter Francis (1893–1955). Black American leader and author. White was a strong force in the promotion of racial justice in the U.S., as described in his autobiography *A Man Called White* (1948). His other books include *Fire in the Flint* (1924), *Flight* (1926), *A Rising Wind* (1945) and *How Far the Promised Land* (1955). He was secretary of the NATIONAL ASSOCIATION FOR THE ADVANCEMENT OF COLORED PEOPLE (1931–55).

Whitehead, Alfred North (1861–1947). British mathematician and philosopher. A graduate of Trinity College, Cambridge, and teacher at Cambridge (until 1922), the University of London (1911–24) and Harvard University (1924–1937), Whitehead is known primarily for his contributions to the fields of mathematics, logic metaphysics and the philosophy of science. His three-volume work *Principia Mathematica* (1910–13), written with his protege Bertrand RUSSELL, remains a milestone inthe field of logic. In *Process and Reality* (1929), Whitehead created a complex vocabulary to formulate his concept of reality, which he termed the "philosophy of organism."

For further reading:

Lowe, Victor, *Alfred North Whitehead: The Man and His Work*, 2 vols. Baltimore, Md.: Johns Hopkins University Press, 1985, 1990.

White Hotel, The (1981). Novel by British author D.M. THOMAS. *The White Hotel* became an international bestseller upon its publication and remains the most famous work by Thomas. In highly charged, poetic prose it recounts the life of its Russian-Jewish protagonist, Lisa Erdman, an actual patient of Sigmund FREUD. Thomas invented a fictionalized but highly detailed case history replete with erotic dreams and tortured emotional conflicts. Erdman, an opera singer, undergoes a Freudian cure but meets her death—as she foresaw in her dreams—during the 1941 mass murder of Jews at BABI YAR in the U.S.S.R. The novel occasioned much criticism, including charges that Thomas had plagiarized many passages from other sources.

Whiteman, Paul (1891–1967). American musician. A highly successful leader of JAZZ orchestras and bands, Whiteman conducted two transcontinental symphonic jazz concert tours of the United States between 1924 and 1926, the year his musicians toured the major capitals of Europe. With his work in symphonic music, he became a highly regarded link between classical and jazz forms. He was one of George GERSHWIN's most effective supporters, and conducted the first performance of Gershwin's RHAPSODY IN BLUE, which was composed for Whiteman's band.

Whites. Name given to the anti-Bolshevik forces at the time of the RUSSIAN CIVIL WAR. The majority of Whites were Social Revolutionaries, right-wing Social Democrats who disagreed with the MENSHEVIK party, and other rightists. The White Army was first formed among the Don Cossacks and was led by General Lavr KORNILOV and the former czarist chief of staff, Anton DENIKIN. In 1919 General Nicholas YUDENICH, advised by the British, marched from Estonia to take Petrograd. This was unsuccessful; once back in Estonia, his forces disintegrated. As a result, Denikin withdrew and handed over his position to General Peter WRANGEL. Wrangel was defeated, and his forces evacuated from the south of Russia in 1920. By 1922 the Reds had taken Vladivostok, the last stronghold of the Whites. The Whites were unsuccessful because they lacked any leadership of the caliber mustered by the Reds, had no sense of a common purpose, and were unable to generate peasant support.

Whiting, Margaret (1924–). American popular singer. The daughter of composer Richard WHITING and singer-actress Barbara Whiting, she began her singing career while still in high school, performing in 1941 with Johnny MERCER. Gifted with fine vocal quality and a lively interpretive style, Whiting had her greatest successes during the 1940s. Her first hit, "That Old Black Magic," was followed in 1943 by "My Ideal" and in 1944 by one of her most outstanding records, "Moonlight in Vermont." Her career continued to flourish in the early 1950s, but waned later in the decade. She continued to perform throughout the years that followed, touring with other figures from the 1940s into the 1990s.

Whiting, Richard (1891–1938). American composer. A native of Los Angeles, he was mainly self-taught as a pianist and composer. He first gained notice as a composer of scores for Broadway musicals, beginning with *George White's Scandals of 1919* and *Toot Sweet* (both, 1919). Other stage scores included *Take a Chance* (1932), which contained such memorable songs as "Eadie Was a Lady" and "You're an Old Smoothie." His many movie musical scores include *Close Harmony* (1929), *Ready, Willing and Able* (1937) and *Hollwood Hotel* (1938), for which he composed the famous "Hooray for Hollywood." Among his other well-known songs are "Japanese Sandman," "Ain't We Got Fun," "My Ideal" (later a hit record by his daughter, Margaret WHITING) and "Too Marvelous for Words."

Whitlam, (Edward) Gough (1916–). Prime minister of AUSTRALIA (1972–75). Whitlam was born and educated in Sydney, and served in the Royal Australian Air Force before becoming a barrister. He was elected a Labour M.P. in 1952, and established his reputation as a moderate. Whitlam served as deputy leader of the Australian Labour Party from 1960 to 1967, when he succeeded A.A. Calwell as party leader. Labour won the 1972 elections, though without a majority in the Senate, and Whitlam became prime minister, serving until 1975. His tenure was a difficult one. He was unable to enact any Labour measures due to the LIBERAL-dominated senate, and there was dissention in his party over the inflation and high unemployment of the time. Whitlam was forced to discharge his Deputy Prime Minister and his Energy Minister. In 1975, Sir John Kerr, the Governor-General, dismissed the government and called for a general election. The Australian Labour party lost the 1976 election, but Whitlam remained party leader. In the following year, Labour lost again and Whitlam stepped down from the leadership. He became Australia's ambassador to UNESCO in 1983.

Whittaker, Charles E(vans) (1901–1973). Associate justice, U.S. Supreme Court (1957–62). A native of Kansas, Whittaker attended the Kansas City Law School. A Republican, he was appointed a U.S. District Court judge in 1954 and was elevated to the U.S. Court of Appeals for the Eighth Circuit by President EISENHOWER in 1956. In 1957, Eisenhower nominated Whittaker to the Supreme Court. Whittaker generally aligned himself with the conservative minority of the WARREN Court, but was not always consistent in his opinions. He resigned after five years for health reasons and maintained an active public life until his death in 1973.

Who, The. British ROCK AND ROLL band, founded in 1964. The Who ranked just behind the BEATLES and the ROLLING STONES as one of the three major bands to emerge from the "British Invasion" that swept rock and roll audiences around the world in the 1960s. The original personnel of the Who were Roger Daltrey, vocals; John Entwhistle, bass; Pete Townshend, guitar; and Keith Moon, bass. Moon died in 1978 and was replaced by drummer Kenney Jones; the remaining three musicians have continued on as members of the Who to the present day, although Townshend and Daltrey have also pursued solo musical projects. The Who is best known for its driving, slashing rock style featuring the powerful guitar solos of Townshend and the melodramatic vocals of Daltrey. Its biggest hit singles include "My Generation" (1965), "I Can See For Miles" (1967), "Pinball Wizard" (1969), "See Me, Feel Me" (1970) and "Won't Get Fooled Again" (1971). *Tommy* (1969), a rock opera, remains the band's most successful album. *Quadrophenia* (1979) was the soundtrack to a feature film of the same name; *The Kids are Alright* (1979) was the soundtrack to a film documentary of the band. The Who continues to record and mount major live tours.

Who's Afraid of Virginia Woolf? (1962). Acclaimed play by American playwright Edward ALBEE. *Who's Afraid of Virginia Woolf* was a dramatic hit on Broadway in 1962 and earned widespread fame for its author. The play is a biting portrayal of a long-time marriage between a professor and his vitriolic and seductive wife that has decayed into mutual hatred between the spouses. A younger married couple that witnesses this hatred—during the course of an evening's visit—is thereby compelled to face the hypocrisy and fear that governs their own union as well. *Who's Afraid of Virginia Woolf* was adapted into a 1966 film directed by Mike NICHOLS and starring Richard BURTON and Elizabeth TAYLOR, who won a Best Actress Award for her role as Martha, the professor's wife.

Wiener, Norbert (1894–1964). American mathematician. Wiener is considered one of the most extraordinary mathematicians to be born in the U.S. A child prodigy, his diverse interests included studying mathematical logic with Bertrand RUSSELL. In 1919 Wiener accepted a post at the Massachusetts Institute of Technology, where he remained throughout his stellar career. Among his vast body of singular achievements is his theory of stochastic (random) processes and Brownian motion. He also delved into the work of Fourier, such as the Fourier transforms. He also developed the subject he dubbed "cybernetics." This involves the mathematical analysis of the flow of information in such systems as mechanics and biology, and the analogies between them. Also of import was his work on quantum mechanics.

Wiesel, Elie [Eliezer Wiesel] (1928–). Romanian-born Jewish author who won the 1986 NOBEL PRIZE for peace. Wiesel is a remarkable writer who has earned both literary acclaim and an international following for his role as a spokesman for peace and justice. Raised in a pious Hasidic family, Wiesel's world was shattered by the HOLOCAUST, which claimed his father, mother and sister among the six

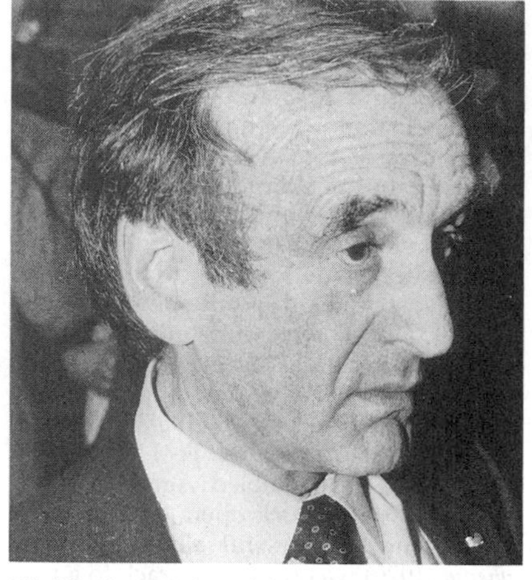

Elie Wiesel, a survivor of the Holocaust and a spokesman for humanity.

million JEWS murdered by the Nazis during WORLD WAR II. Wiesel, a young boy, survived internment in the death camps and came to Paris as a refugee after the war. He worked for over a decade as a journalist before publishing *Night* (1958), his only autobiographical work, which told movingly of the Holocaust horrors. Since then, Wiesel's writing output has been prodigious, including novels such as *Dawn* (1962), *The Gates of the Forest* (1964), *A Beggar in Jerusalem* (1968), and *The Fifth Son* (1983), as well as plays, essays, Biblical interpretations, and studies of the rabbinical Hasidic masters. In 1978, Wiesel was named by President Jimmy CARTER as chairman of the President's Commission on the Holocaust, on which he served through 1987. Wiesel has been an outspoken opponent of prejudice and injustice in the U.S.S.R., South Africa, and other areas of the world. He also stirred political controversy by opposing the visit of President Ronald REAGAN to the German army cemetary at Bitburg in 1985.

For further reading:

Wiesel, Elie, *From the Kingdom of Memory: Reminiscences*. New York: Summit Books, 1990.

Wiesenthal, Simon (1908–). Born in Russia, Wiesenthal trained as an architect and engineer. Most of his family died in Nazi CONCENTRATION CAMPS during WORLD WAR II. Wiesenthal survived and vowed to dedicate his life to bringing Nazi war criminals to justice. In 1961 he founded the Jewish Documentation Center in Vienna. The center documents HOLOCAUST deaths and gathers information on Nazis still at large. He has been instrumental in the capture of many Nazis, including Adolf EICHMANN.

Wigner, Eugene Paul (1902–). Hungarian-American physicist. After receiving his doctorate in engineering in 1925, at the Berlin Institute of Technology, Wigner moved to the U.S. in 1930 and took a post at Princeton, where he was appointed chair of theoretical physics. He remained there until his retirement in 1971. Among his many fundamental contributions to quantum and nuclear physics is his early work on chemical reactions and the spectra of compounds. In the 1930s Wigner shed light on the nuclear force that binds neutrons and protons. He was later involved in the early stages of nuclear reactors, which led to the first controlled nuclear chain reaction. In 1963, Wigner shared the NOBEL PRIZE for physics with Maria Goeppert Mayer and J. Hans Jensen.

Wilder, (Samuel) Billy (1906–). American film writer, director and producer. Born in Vienna, Wilder briefly studied law, became a reporter for a Berlin newspaper and began screenwriting in GERMANY in 1929. Wilder fled Hitler's Germany, moved to France where he directed his first film in 1933, and emigrated to the U.S. later that year. He soon developed a reputation for cynical, sophisticated and sharply comedic scripts. Among his early Hollywood works were *Bluebeard's Eighth Wife* (1938), *Ninotchka* (1939) and *The Major and the Minor* (1942), a popular farce that marked his American directorial debut. He established his ability with the *film noir* genre in *Double Indemnity* (1944), which was followed by the fiercely brilliant ACADEMY AWARD-winning drama *The Lost Weekend* (1945). Wilder won his second best director Oscar for the melodrama *Sunset Boulevard* (1950). Among his later works are the comedies *The Seven Year Itch* (1955), *Some Like It Hot* (1959), *The Apartment* (1960; Academy Award), *Irma La Douce* (1963), *The Fortune Cookie* (1966) and *Buddy, Buddy* (1981).

Wilder, Thornton (1897–1975). American playwright and novelist. A teacher by profession, Wilder first gained recognition as a writer with his philosophical novel *The Bridge of San Luis Rey*, which won the 1927 PULITZER PRIZE. In 1938 he made theatrical history and received his second Pulitzer with the non-realistically constructed play *Our Town*, which used a narrator and improvised staging. His next prize-winning play, *The Skin of Our Teeth* (1942), combined allegory and farce to present human history through the story of a suburban New Jersey family. All of his major writing reflects his concern with man's place in the universe. Other novels include *The Ides of March* (1948), and other dramas include *Three Plays for Bleecker Street* (1962). His last work, *Theophilus North* (1973), is a semi-autobiographical story of a retired teacher.

For further reading:

Burbank, Rex J., *Thornton Wilder*. Boston: Twayne, 1978.

Wilhelm II (1859–1941). King of Prussia and kaiser (emperor) of GERMANY, reigned 1888–1918. Wilhelm, who was later to be known as Kaiser Wilhelm, was born in Berlin, the son of Emperor Frederick III and Princess Victoria of England. Frederick III had ruled only three months when he died of cancer and Wilhelm succeeded. Wilhelm was intent on building up the Prussian army and the Prussian profile in the world. Although he had been a childhood admirer of Chancellor Bismarck (1815–1898), Wilhelm dismissed Bismarck in 1890, preferring to surround himself with more malleable advisors. Wilhelm's arrogance and provocative behavior alienated Britain, France and Russia, and the kaiser began to gear up for what he thought would be a short, preventative war. When Archduke FRANZ FERDINAND was assassinated in 1914 and WORLD WAR I began, even Italy, the third member of the Triple Alliance, fought against Germany and Austria. Wilhelm was eclipsed by his generals as the war continued, and on their advice he fled to

Kaiser Wilhelm II, the last emperor of Germany (1888–1918).

Holland in 1918. At the 1919 PARIS PEACE CONFERENCE, it was requested of Queen Wilhelmina of Holland that he be returned. She refused, and Wilhelm remained in Doorn with his second wife, Princess Hermine of Reuss. At the advent of the Second World War, Winston CHURCHILL offered him asylum in England, and Adolph HITLER had offered to allow him to return to one of his estates in Germany, but Wilhelm died in Holland.

Wilkins, Roy (1901–1981). American campaigner for CIVIL RIGHTS, head of the NATIONAL ASSOCIATION FOR THE ADVANCEMENT OF COLORED PEOPLE (NAACP) from 1931 to 1977. A diplomatic but indefatigable crusader for racial integration and social justice through constitutional means, he fought the doctrines of black separatism and white supremacy alike. The grandson of a Mississippi slave, Wilkins joined the NAACP while a student at the University of Minnesota. After graduating in 1923, he worked as a journalist for a black newspaper in Kansas City, Missouri, while rising through the ranks of the NAACP. He became leader of the organization in 1931 and guided it through its strongest years. During the 1930s he successfully campaigned for antilynching laws in the South. He was the chief architect of the legal onslaught on school segregation that resulted in the 1954 BROWN V. BOARD OF EDUCATION decision outlawing "separate but equal" public schools. He was also a moving force behind the passage of the CIVIL RIGHTS ACT OF 1964.

Will, George F. (1941–). American political columnist, commentator and author. A thoughtful and eloquent spokesman for traditional CONSERVATISM, Will began his career on the staff of Senator Gordon Allott (R., Colo.) before joining the NATIONAL REVIEW as Washington editor in 1973. In 1974, Will began a regular column for the WASHINGTON POST and two years later was named a contributing editor to *Newsweek*. Will also acted as an informal campaign advisor to President Ronald REAGAN in 1980. Will promotes conservative viewpoints in his journalism; since the 1980s he has been featured on the weekly news analysis program, *This Week With David Brinkley*. He is the author of several books, including *The Pursuit of Happiness and Other Sobering Thoughts* (1978); *Suddenly: The American Idea Abroad and At Home, 1986–1990* (1990) and *Political Essays* (1990). He has also revealed his passion for and knowledge of baseball in *Men at Work: The Craft of Baseball* (1990).

Williams, Betty (1943–). Northern Irish peace activist. (See Mairead CORRIGAN.)

Williams, Edward Bennett (1920–1988). American trial lawyer; a Washington, D.C., insider whose clients included many controversial and even notorious figures. Among Williams' best known clients were Teamsters leaders Jimmy HOFFA and Dave BECK, Senator Joseph MCCARTHY, mobster Frank Costello, fugitive financier Robert Vesco and U.S. Representative Adam Clayton POWELL. Politically active, Williams was a liberal Republican until 1964. That year, he became a Democrat because of the Republicans' treatment of Nelson A. ROCKEFELLER and their nomination of Barry GOLDWATER. He was on good terms with all presidents in the years that followed, except Jimmy CARTER; he led the "Dump Carter" movement in 1980. At the time of his death he headed the law firm of Williams & Connolly and was owner of the Baltimore Orioles baseball team.

Williams, Eric (Eustace) (1911–1981). Historian, politician, Prime Minister of TRINIDAD AND TOBAGO (1962–81). He was widely regarded as the father of British West Indian independence. A graduate of Oxford University, he received his Ph.D. (1938) for a thesis later published as *Capitalism and Slavery* (1944), which became a classic in the field. After teaching history at Howard University in Washington (1939–53), he returned to Trinidad and Tobago, where he quickly became a leader in the independence movement. He founded the People's National Movement (PNM) in 1955, and the following year became chief minister in the colonial government. He was elected prime minister of the newly independent nation of Trinidad and Tobago in 1962. As prime minister, he helped transform the islands from a chain of poverty-stricken sugar colonies into a modern industrialized state.

For further reading:

Trifonov, Yuri V. *The Exchange*. Cambridge, Mass.: Basil Blackwell, 1989.

Williams, Garth (1912–). American children's book illustrator. Williams studied art at the Westminster School of Art and the Royal Academy of Art in London, winning the 1936 Prix de Rome. After WORLD WAR II he returned to New York and began working as a magazine artist, primarily for the NEW YORKER. He achieved fame for his pencil drawings in E.B. WHITE's children's book, *Stuart Little* (1945). The 70 books he has illustrated include 11 by Margaret Wise Brown and all of Laura Ingalls Wilder's *Little House* series, as well as many others by prominent children's writers. His pencil drawings and paintings are by turns delicately realistic and whimsical.

American country music legend Hank Williams performs in Columbus, Ohio, in 1951, two years before his tragic death at 29.

Williams, Hank (1923–1953). American country music composer, vocalist, guitarist. Williams is widely acknowledged as the greatest star—and most influential composer—in the history of American country music. The story of his life, which saw his rise from small-time musician in Montgomery, Alabama, to star of Nashville's Grand Ole Opry in the early 1950s, has become the stuff of legend, not to mention a biographical Hollywood film, *Your Cheatin' Heart* (1964). In the final years of his meteoric career, Williams was plagued by a failed marriage coupled with alcohol and drug abuse. He died of a heart attack at age 29. His classic songs include "Your Cheatin' Heart," "Honky Tonkin'," "I'm So Lonesome I Could Cry," "Jambalaya," "Hey, Good Lookin'," "Cold, Cold Heart" and "I'll Never Get Out Of This World Alive." His son, Hank Williams Jr., is also a major country music star. (See also COUNTRY AND WESTERN MUSIC.)

Williams, John (Towner) (1932–). American film score composer. Commercially one of the most successful HOLLYWOOD composers ever, Williams has written the music for eight of Hollywood's top-fifteen biggest-grossing movies: *Jaws* (1975), *Star Wars* (1977), *Close Encounters of the Third Kind* (1977), *The Empire Strikes Back* (1980), *Raiders of the Lost Ark* (1981), E.T. (1982), *Return of the Jedi* (1983) and *Home Alone* (1990). Born in Flushing, New York, Williams studied music at Juilliard and then at UCLA. His first Hollywood project was for a film titled *Because They're Young* (1960); he has since scored more than 40 movies, including *The Killers*, *Valley of the Dolls* and *The Poseidon Adventure*. By the mid-1970s he had become one of the most sought-after composers in Hollywood. His notable collaborations with producer George LUCAS and director Steven SPIELBERG subsequently earned him five ACADEMY AWARDS for best original score. In 1980 he was named conductor of the Boston Pops Orchestra, although his tenure there was not without controversy.

Williams, Mary Lou [born Mary Elfrieda Scruggs] (1910–1981). American JAZZ pianist, arranger, and composer. During her 50–year career she was associated with most of the well-known jazz musicians of the time. Versatile and influential, she was regarded almost as a barometer of musical style, playing and excelling in RAGTIME, DIXIELAND, SWING, BEBOP, and sacred jazz music. She made a number of recordings, including such numbers as *Walkin' but Swingin'* and *Froggy Bottom*. She wrote such songs as *Roll 'Em* and *Camel Hop* for Benny GOODMAN.

Williams, Paul Revere (1895–1980). American architect. The first African-American member and fellow of the American Institute of Architects, he practiced in Los Angeles from 1915–73. He is known for the sumptuous southern California homes he designed for important figures in the film industry, beautifully-detailed structures executed in a number of period styles including Georgian, Colonial, Tudor, Mediterranean and Norman. One of his most significant designs is the Litton Industries Building (originally the M.C.A. Building), an award-winning Beverly Hills landmark built in the mid-1930s. Among Williams' other designs are the Grave of the Unknown Sailor in Pearl Harbor, the Polo Lounge at the Beverly Hills Hotel and elements of the Los Angeles International Airport.

Williams, Raymond (1921–1988). British cultural historian. In such works as *Culture and Society* (1958) and *The Country and the City* (1973) Williams examined the relationship between literature and society from a leftist perspective. His books also included novels and a major critical biography of author George ORWELL (1971). Williams was professor of drama at Cambridge University from 1974 to 1983.

Williams, Roger J. (1893–1988). U.S. biochemist and nutritionist; discovered the growth-promoting vitamin pantothenic acid. For more than four decades Williams directed the University of Texas laboratory that was credited with the discovery of more vitamins and their variants than any other lab in the world. His older brother, Robert R. Williams, was the scientist who isolated vitamin B-1.

Williams, Shirley Vivien Teresa Brittain (1930–). British politician. The daughter of the author Vera BRITTAIN, Williams served as secretary to the FA-

American playwright Tennessee Williams celebrates his 69th birthday (March 21, 1980).

BIAN SOCIETY from 1960 to 1964, when she was elected to Parliament. She held various junior ministerial posts, and served as Secretary of State for prices and consumer protection from 1974 to 1976, and for education and science from 1976 to 1979, when she lost her seat. In 1981, along with Roy JENKINS, William RODGERS and David OWEN, she left the LABOUR PARTY and formed the SOCIAL DEMOCRATIC PARTY, serving as its president in 1982. She was considered the most left-wing of the moderate "GANG OF FOUR." Williams was re-elected to parliament in a by-election in 1981, but was unseated in the general election of 1983.

Williams, Tennessee [Thomas Lanier Williams] (1911–1983). American playwright, generally considered one of the greatest of all 20th century American writers for the stage. Raised in Mississippi, he was catapulted to fame in 1945 with the performance of his first successful play, *The Glass Managerie*. His plays, usually set in his native South and often partly autobiographical, frequently dealt with the loss of beauty, the harshness of reality, and the appeal of illusion. In addition to *The Glass Menagerie*, the most notable of his 24 plays were *A Streetcar Named Desire* (1947) and *Cat on a Hot Tin Roof* (1955), both of which won PULITZER PRIZES. Williams also won four Drama Critics Circle Awards. His plays after *The Night of the Iguana* (1961), however, were received less favorably by both critics and audiences, and his career declined. In his later years, Williams suffered from alcoholism, drug addiction, and mental illness, but he continued to write. He died by choking on a bottle cap. In its decadent atmosphere and dark intensity, his work is often compared to that of William FAULKNER and Eugene O'NEILL. Among leading American actors who gained distinction in his plays or in screen adaptations of them were Marlon BRANDO, Burl IVES, Paul NEWMAN, and Elizabeth TAYLOR.

Williams, Theodore Samuel "Ted" (1918–). American baseball player. Obsessed by the art of hitting, Williams translated his studies into six American League batting championships, a total surpassed only by Ty COBB. He spent 20 seasons with the Boston Red Sox, twice interrupted for military service, and amassed a total of 521 home runs and a batting average of .344. His left-handed swing is regarded as one of the most classic in the history of the game. Williams' temper was as legendary as his stance, as he had little patience for writers, fans or most other ballplayers. He retired in 1960 and was named to the Hall of Fame in 1966. From 1969 to 1972, he was manager of the Washington Senators/Texas Rangers.

Williams, Tom (1886–1985). Canadian aviator. A WORLD WAR I flying ace, Williams was a founding member of the Royal Canadian Air Force. His original commercial pilot's certificate was signed by one of the fathers of aviation, Orville WRIGHT. In 1972, the GUINNESS BOOK OF WORLD RECORDS listed Williams as the world's oldest active pilot in recognition of a solo flight he had made in 1971 at age 86.

Williams, William B. [born William Breitbard] (1923–1986). American radio personality. A program host on New York City's WNEW-AM for more than four decades, his *Make Believe Ballroom* showcased standard tunes by such performers as Frank SINATRA, Perry Como and Lena HORNE. He nicknamed Sinatra "Chairman of the Board," and was credited by the singer with resurrecting his career by continuing to play his music after it had gone out of fashion.

Williams, William Carlos (1883–1963). American poet and novelist. Williams was born in Rutherford, New Jersey, and received an M.D. from the University of Pennsylvania Medical School in 1906. While practicing medicine in Rutherford, he published poetry in Ezra POUND's anthology *Des Imagistes* (1914) and in the periodicals *Poetry*, *The Egotist* and *The Little Review*. He also coedited *Contact* (1920–23). Influenced by IMAGISM as well as CUBISM and SURREALISM, Williams used consciously plain language to reveal the beauty of everyday objects and surroundings. His well-known poems include "January Morning" (1917), "The Great Figure" (1921), "The Red Wheelbarrow" (1923); his long poem "Paterson" is considered his masterwork. His short stories were collected in *The Farmer's Daughters* (1961), and his novels include *White Mule* (1937), *In the Money* (1940) and *The Build-up* (1952). Although retiring from medicine in 1951, following a stroke, Williams wrote copiously until his death. In 1963 he won the PULITZER PRIZE and the Gold Medal of the National Institute of Arts and Letters.

For further reading:

Mariani, Paul J., *William Carlos Williams: A New World Naked*. New York: W.W. Norton, 1990.

Willis, Frances E. (1899–1983). The first woman career officer in the U.S. Foreign Service to serve as a U.S. ambassador. Commissioned in the Foreign Service in 1927, she was named by President Dwight D. EISENHOWER to head the U.S. embassy in SWITZERLAND in 1953. In 1957, Eisenhower appointed her ambassador to NORWAY. In 1961, President John F. KENNEDY appointed her ambassador to Ceylon (now SRI LANKA), where she served until her retirement in 1964.

Willkie, Wendell (Lewis) (1892–1944). American lawyer and presidential candidate. Willkie attracted national attention during the GREAT DEPRESSION as president and chief executive officer of the Commonwealth and Southern Corporation, a giant utility holding company, and as a crusader for the LEAGUE OF NATIONS and against the KU KLUX KLAN and two policies of the NEW DEAL: the Public Utility Holding Company Act and the TENNESSEE VALLEY AUTHORITY. While acknowledging past abuses in the management of utilities, Willkie opposed public ownership and excessive federal control. His winning of the Republican presidential nomination in 1940 over better known candidates such as Thomas E. DEWEY and Robert A. TAFT was remarkable, considering that many of his best friends never knew that he had changed party affiliation and that he did not actively campaign until May, too late to enter many primaries. His victory was due to his reputation in the business community, his support from several key Republicans, his personal charisma and his strong stand for aid to England after Germany's easy conquest of the continent. In the election Willkie polled a larger popular vote than any other Republican candidate before Eisenhower, but lost to F.D. ROOSEVELT by a wide margin.

Following the election, Willkie worked to unite the country behind aid to Britain. He supported Roosevelt's LEND-LEASE proposal and became the president's goodwill ambassador to the Middle East, the Soviet Union and China. His "Report to the People" radio broadcast upon his return to the United States was estimated to have had a larger audience than any speech except Roosevelt's following the attack on PEARL HARBOR. His theme became one of encouraging colonial peoples to join the West in a global partnership based on economic, racial and political justice. Willkie campaigned for the 1944 Republican presidential nomination, but lost in the Wisconsin primary and with-

Wendell Willkie, Republican candidate for the U.S. presidency in 1940.

drew from the race. Excluded by Dewey from an active role, Willkie attempted to influence the party with a series of newspaper articles entitled a "Proposed Platform" in which he called for anti-lynching laws, an extension of social security, and a world organization in which the small states would have real power. Campaigning weakened him, and he died after a series of heart attacks.

For further reading:
Neal, Steve, *Dark Horse: A Biography of Wendell Willkie.* Lawrence, Kan.: University Press of Kansas, 1989.

Wills, Garry (1934–). American journalist, educator and author. Wills is a conservative commentator who has occasionally embraced liberal issues. While writing for the *National Review,* he adopted an anti-Vietnam War, pro-civil rights stance and moved on to write for *Esquire.* Wills developed the theory of "the convenient state," which posits that a confluence of interests rather than an enforcing authority holds things together. He writes a nationally syndicated column, "The Outrider," and is a professor of American culture and public policy at Northwestern University. His books include *Confessions of a Conservative* (1979), *Explaining America* (1981) and *The Kennedy Imprisonment* (1982).

Wilson, Charles Thomson Rees (1869–1959). Scottish physicist. The son of a sheep farmer, Wilson studied physics at Cambridge University. There he began experiments to duplicate cloud formation in the laboratory. He observed the effect of X-rays on cloud formation. In 1911 he perfected the cloud chamber, for which he won the NOBEL PRIZE for physics in 1927. The cloud chamber became an indispensable aid to research into subatomic particles and, with the addition of a magnetic field, made different particles distinguishable by the curvature of their tracks. Returning to the study of real clouds, Wilson also investigated atmospheric electricity and developed a sensitive electrometer to measure it. He was able to determine the electric structure of thunderclouds.

Wilson, Colin (1931–). English novelist, philosopher and literary critic. Wilson is a prolific writer whose central interests—as expressed in both his fiction and his nonfictional works—revolve around the evolutionary potential of humankind and the unique and startling capacities of the brain. Wilson won international acclaim for his first book, *The Outsider* (1956), an analysis of existential alienation and its role in 20th-century philosophy and literature. He has since written over 40 more books, including the novel *The Philosopher's Stone* (1968), the scholarly compendium *The Occult: A History* (1971) and a biographical study, *Aleister Crowley: The Nature of the Beast* (1987).

Wilson, Sir David Clive (1935–). British diplomat. Educated at Keble College, Oxford, Wilson was knighted and named governor of HONG KONG on January 16, 1987; he assumed office formally as the 27th governor in April 1987, succeeding Sir Edward Youde, who died while on a visit to Beijing in December 1986. Formerly assistant undersecretary of state at the British Foreign and Commonwealth Office, Wilson was a long-time China scholar. He was deeply involved in the negotiations with China over the future of Hong Kong, and headed the British delegation of the Sino-British liaison group appointed to oversee the transition to Chinese sovereignty.

Wilson, Edmund (1895–1972). American social and literary critic, widely considered the foremost critic of his time. Wilson was the son of an affluent lawyer and one-time attorney general in Red Bank, New Jersey. Early on he was exposed to the literary life, contributing to Princeton University's *Nassau Literary Magazine* and befriending F. Scott FITZGERALD. In 1920 Wilson became managing editor of *Vanity Fair* (1920–1921). A year later he was hired as the drama critic for *The New Republic,* and in 1926 he was named associate editor of the magazine. During this decade his influential essays helped determine the literary fate of some of the 20th century's greatest writers, including Henry JAMES, Ernest HEMINGWAY, Eugene O'NEILL and Willa CATHER. In the 1930s he became a political activist of sorts, writing articles condemning LIBERALISM and hailing the principles of COMMUNISM. But his reputation as a leading critic and man of letters continued into the 1940s when he became book critic for THE NEW YORKER (1944–48). Over the years his pieces were collected in volumes such as *Axel's Castle* (1931), *The American Jitters: A Year of the Slump* (1932), *The Wound and the Bow* (1941) and *The Shores of Light* (1952). In spite of his controversial political status and opposition to paying taxes, Wilson was awarded the Presidential Medal of Freedom in 1953.

For further reading:
Groth, Janet, *Edmund Wilson: A Critic for Our Time.* Athens, Ohio: Ohio University Press, 1989.

Wilson, Edward Osborne (1929–). American entomologist, ecologist and sociobiologist. Wilson emerged as a controversial household name in 1975, when he argued that "a single strong thread does indeed run from the conduct of termite colonies and turkey brotherhoods to the social behavior of man." In his earlier work as an entomologist, he restricted his theories to the organization of social insects such as ants, which was comprehensively outlined in the 1971 publication of his *Insect Societies.* However, when he extrapolated to include human behavior in his sociobiological belief system, his viewpoint was dismissed by many.

Wilson, Harold Albert (1874–1964). British-born physicist and educator. Educated in England, Wilson taught in London, Montreal and Glasgow before taking a professorship at Rice Institute in Houston (1912–47). He achieved fame for his verification of the electromagnetic equations of such forebears as Albert EINSTEIN. His books include *The Mysteries of the Atom: Electricity* (1934).

Wilson, (James) Harold (1916–). British politician, prime minister of the UNITED KINGDOM (1964–70, 1974–76). Born in Yorkshire, Wilson was educated at Wirral Grammar School and Jesus College, Oxford, where he later lectured in economics. During WORLD WAR II, Wilson was a civil servant in the Ministry of Fuel, and was elected to Parliament as a Labour member in 1945. He served as president of the Board of Trade from 1947 to 1951, and in 1954 joined the LABOUR PARTY's parliamentary committee. During Hugh GAITSKELL's party leadership, Wilson was the party's mouthpiece on economic matters, and was considered the leader of Labour's left wing. Wilson succeeded Gaitskell as party leader in 1963, and became prime minister following the 1964 elections, which Labour won by a narrow margin. By the following year, his majority in parliament had increased nearly 100 percent. Wilson balanced the budget and heightened the role of prime minister in global affairs, but he was castigated by the press and in the 1970 elections the Conservatives were voted into power. Wilson became prime minister again in 1974, following Edward HEATH's inability to cope with economic strife and labor strikes. Wilson placated labor with the "social compact" agreement with trade unions, which gained him a sufficient majority in the elections later in the year; he also devalued the pound, froze prices and wages and raised taxes in an attempt to bolster the economy. He resigned unexpectedly in 1976, and was succeeded

British Prime Minister Harold Wilson (second from left) and Foreign Secretary James Callaghan (center) meet with Soviet leader Leonid Brezhnev in Moscow (Feb. 13, 1975).

by James CALLAGHAN. Wilson was knighted that year, and named a baron in 1983, thus entering the House of Lords.

Wilson, Lanford Eugene (1937–). Pulitzer-Prize-winning American playwright, product of the off-off-Broadway theater scene in the 1960s. He was born in Lebanon, Missouri (subsequent location for several plays) and grew up in the towns of Springfield and Ozark, Missouri, where he finished high school. Early plans to be a painter and illustrator were abandoned when he discovered that he could write. He migrated to New York in the summer of 1962 and soon had a number of short plays produced at the Caffe Cino, an important independent theater in the growing "off-off-Broadway" movement in GREENWICH VILLAGE. He found there an atmosphere of theatrical experimentation denied writers on Broadway—or even on off-Broadway. An early play, *Home Free*! (1964) was directed by Marshall W. Mason, with whom Wilson formed a productive professional relationship. Subsequent plays of this period included *Balm in Gilead* (1965), *Rimers of Eldritch* (1966), and *The Gingham Dog* (1968). They forged the Wilson style—disparate groups of people peopling late-night diners, town squares, and hotel rooms, each character representing a counterpoint of dreams, false hopes and crippling reality. Numerous plots and dialogues unfold simultaneously and the action seems to repeat and double back up on itself. Realism and a more poetic symbolism become a shifting figure-ground relationship. In 1968 Wilson and Mason co-founded the Circle Repertory Company, which he has described as "sort of a loose collective of writers and designers and actors and directors, presently located in Greenwich Village." It has premiered many of his subsequent plays, *The Hot L Baltimore* (1973), *The Mound Builders* (1975), *Burn This* (1986), and the so-called "Talley Trilogy"—*Fifth of July* (1978), *Talley's Folly* (1980), and *A Tale Told* (1981). The trilogy tells the story of the Talley family over several generations and is set in Lebanon, Missouri. The second play won Wilson a PULITZER PRIZE in 1980. Although many of his plays have been staged on television, to date none of them have been adapted for motion pictures. He cites playwrights Tennessee WILLIAMS and Brendan BEHAN as important influences on his work; in turn, younger playwrights like David Mamet acknowledge Wilson's impact upon them.

For further reading:

Tibbetts, John C., "Lanford Wilson: A Portrait." *Journal of Dramatic Theory and Criticism*, Spring 1991.

Wilson, Margaret (1882–1976). American author. Wilson was educated at the University of Chicago and went to India as a Presbyterian missionary. She wrote many articles and gave numerous lectures on life in India, especially on the treatment of Indian women. In India she met Douglas Turner, a British criminologist, and they were married. Wilson continued her writing, and in 1924 won the PULITZER PRIZE for fiction for her novel *The Able McLaughlins*, which she claimed was a true account of life in the Traer, Iowa, community where she grew up. Her writing continued with other novels and the non-fiction *The Crime of Punishment*. This was based on her study of the British criminal system which her husband headed. The book was widely hailed and as widely criticized for its sharp denunciation of the system.

Wilson, Teddy (1912–1986). American jazz pianist and arranger. Wilson is one of the most popular—and critically acclaimed—JAZZ pianists of the century. His style is marked by restraint, elegance and depth of feeling. Wilson was raised in Alabama and first won renown for his playing in the Chicago area in the early 1930s, including a stint with a band led by Louis ARMSTRONG. Wilson then moved to New York where he achieved national fame through his work with various bands led by Benny GOODMAN. Wilson also led his own small jazz combos and became a favored accompanist for jazz vocalists, including Ella FITZGERALD and Billie HOLIDAY. Wilson remained active on the New York jazz scene through the 1970s and participated in several reunion concerts by the Benny Goodman band.

Wilson, Woodrow (1856–1924). American educator, author, governor of New Jersey and 28th president of the U.S. The son of a Presbyterian minister, the future president was named Thomas Woodrow Wilson at birth. He moved with his family from Virginia to Georgia, South Carolina and North Carolina in his youth, and first attended college at Davidson in North Carolina in 1873. The bulk of his undergraduate education, however, took place at Princeton, where he graduated with a B.A. in 1879. Wilson returned to the South to study law at the University of Virginia and practice law in Atlanta, Georgia, then studied history and political science at Johns Hopkins University in Baltimore, where he was awarded his Ph.D. in 1886. After brief teaching appointments at Bryn Mawr College in Pennsylvania and Wesleyan University in Connecticut, he accepted a full professorship of jurisprudence and political science at Princeton, where he remained until 1910.

An influential writer in his field and on education subjects, Wilson became president of Princeton in 1902. His knowledge of political theory led to ambitions for practical political influence, and in 1910 he resigned from the university and successfully ran for the governorship of New Jersey as a Democrat. Only two years later, in 1912, he became the Democratic nominee for president on the basis of support from William Jennings BRYAN; he won the general election when dissension between supporters of Theodore ROOSEVELT and William Howard TAFT split the REPUBLICAN PARTY.

Re-elected by a slight margin in 1916, Wilson oversaw the American involvement in WORLD WAR I. On April 2, 1917, he reluctantly asked Congress to declare war on Germany, which it did on April 6. In 1918 Wilson formulated the famous FOURTEEN POINTS that he thought would make the world "safe for democracy." Peace came with the TREATY OF VERSAILLES on January 18, 1919, and because this was negotiated according to Wilson's formulations he was awarded the NOBEL PRIZE for peace in that year. The treaty included establishment of a LEAGUE OF NATIONS, but for lack of a clause to guarantee U.S. supremacy on war votes it was not ratified in the U.S. Senate. Wilson launched a concentrated campaign to secure ratification of the League of Nations idea, but it failed to sway the Senate. Bitterly disappointed, and taxed by overwork, in October 1919 he suffered a stroke from which he never fully recovered.

For further reading:

Link, Arthur S., *Woodrow Wilson: Revolution, War & Peace*. Arlington Heights, Ill.: Davidson, Harlan, Inc., 1979.

Burton, David Henry, *The Learned Presidency: Theodore Roosevelt, William Howard Taft, Woodrow Wilson*. Rutherford, New Jersey: Fairleigh Dickinson University Press, 1988.

Clements, Kendrick A., *Woodrow Wilson, World Statesman*. Boston: Twyane, 1987.

Winchell, Walter (1897–1972). American columnist and radio commentator. During the 1930s and 1940s Winchell had the most popular radio show and newspaper column in the country. He is regarded as the creator of the modern gossip column. Originally a vaudeville performer, he began writing columns for *The Vaudeville News* and *Billboard* in the early 1920s. Then, after five years as entertainment editor for the *Evening Graphic*, he joined the staff of *The Mirror* (1929) in New York City. His melodramatic, slang-filled items on show-business people and politicians reflected his personal views. His column and popularity had faded by 1960.

For further reading:

Herr, Michael, *Walter Winchell*. New York: Knopf, 1990.

Windgassen, Wolfgang (1914–1974). German singer. Windgassen is most often associated with his regular performances in the Wagnerian heldentenor roles at the BAYREUTH FESTIVAL. He made his operatic debut in Verdi's *La Forza del Destino* in 1941 and achieved widespread fame with his performance in the title role of *Parsifal* at Bayreuth in 1951. His major roles include Tristan in *Tristan und Isolde* and title roles in *Tannhauser* and *Lohengrin*.

"Wind of Change". Phrase used by British Prime Minister Harold MACMILLAN in a speech to the South African parliament in 1960 to describe the growth of black national consciousness in Africa. Macmillan acknowledged that the time had come to grant independence to Britain's colonies, and believed that Britain should work to make the transition to independence as orderly as possible.

Windscale accident (October 7–10, 1957). A fire in Great Britain's Windscale Pile No. 1 plutonium production plant (later renamed SELLAFIELD) caused the escape of as much as 20,000 curies of radioactive

The Duke and Duchess of Windsor. King Edward VIII renounced the British throne to marry American divorcee Wallis Warfield Simpson.

iodine, the largest known release of radioactive gases. More than 30 cancer cases were eventually linked to the incident, but the British government did not acknowledge the accident's scope until 1978. Along with CHERNOBYL and THREE MILE ISLAND, Windscale has entered the lexicon of the late 20th century as a symbol of the potential for disaster in nuclear power.

Windsor, Duchess of [Wallis Warfield Simpson] (1896–1986). An American divorcee, she was at the heart of a British constitutional crisis in 1936, when it became known that King EDWARD VIII, a 41-year-old bachelor, wished to marry her and have her crowned queen. His family, the government, and the Church of England were violently opposed, leading to his abdication in December 1936. He was given the title Duke of Windsor, and she became Duchess when they married in 1937. The couple lived outside England the rest of their lives as international socialites. She and the duke returned to England in 1976 to attend a ceremony commemorating the duke's mother, and upon their deaths, both were buried there.

Windsor, Duke of. See Edward VIII.

Wingate, Orde (Charles) (1903–1944). British general. A colorful career army officer, famous for his brilliantly unorthodox style, Wingate was commissioned in the Royal Artillery in 1922. From 1928 to 1933 he served in the Sudan. On special duty in PALESTINE (1936–39), he organized Jewish guerrilla squads against Arab sabotage. During WORLD WAR II, he again called on his tactical cunning in leading the "Gideon's Force" guerrillas against the Italians in Ethiopia in 1940–41. He is best known for his subsequent guerilla activities in Burma. In 1942–43, Wingate trained and led an Anglo-Indian force known as the "Chindits," harassing Japanese forces from behind their own lines. Promoted to the rank of major general in command of airborne strikes into Burma in 1944, he was killed in an airplane crash shortly thereafter.

Winston, Henry (1911–1986). American Communist party chairman. Born into a family of Mississippi sharecroppers, he was active in the Southern Youth Negro Congress before joining the U.S. Communist Party in 1933. Convicted in 1949 under the Smith Act of conspiring to teach and advocate forcible overthrow of the U.S. government, he was jailed upon his surrender in 1956. He went blind before winning his release in 1961. He served as chairman of the Communist Party, U.S.A. from 1966 until his death.

Winter War. See RUSSO-FINNISH WAR OF 1939–40.

Witte, Count Sergei Yulyevich (1849–1915). Russian statesman. In 1892 Witte was appointed minister of transport and from 1892 to 1903 was minister of finance. He encouraged industrial growth in RUSSIA by protectionist tariffs, large foreign loans and the large-scale building of railways. From 1903 to 1906 Witte was prime minister. He was in charge of negotiating the peace treaty with Japan at Portsmouth, New Hampshire. As a moderate conservative, Witte was attacked by both liberals and the extreme right. After his dismissal by the czar, he continued as an independent member of the council of state.

Wittgenstein, Ludwig J(osef) J(ohann) (1889–1951). Austrian-born philosopher. Wittgenstein was one of the most influential philosophers of the 20th century. Born in Vienna, he trained as an engineer in his native land and at the University of Manchester in Britain before switching to the study of philosophy at Cambridge University in 1912. At Cambridge, his major mentor was Bertrand RUSSELL, whose interests in mathematics and the foundations of logic were shared by Wittgenstein. Wittgenstein's interest in language as an expression of experience was evidenced by the patronage he provided during this period—out of his inherited family funds—to poets Rainer Maria RILKE and George TRAKL. During WORLD WAR I, he served in the Austrian army. His first major work was the *Tractatus Logico-Philosophicus* (1922), which argued that logical truth was no more than tautology, that language functions as a "picture" of reality and that certain aspects of reality cannot be said, only shown. Yet, Wittgenstein asserted, "the world is everything that is the case." Other works by Wittgenstein include *Philosophical Investigations* (1935) and *Remarks on the Foundations of Mathematics* (1956). Wittgenstein taught at Cambridge University for most of the final decades of his life. Wittgenstein's brother **Paul Wittgenstein** was a noted concert pianist who lost his right arm in World War I. Several composers subsequently wrote new works for Paul Wittgenstein; among these is Maurice RAVEL's Concerto for the Left Hand.

For further reading:

Monk, Ray, *Ludwig Wittgenstein: The Duty of Genius*. New York: Free Press, 1990.

Wodehouse, P(elham) G(renville) ["Plum"] (1881–1975). British-born comic author. Most of Wodehouse's works are parodies of life among the British aristocracy of the 1920s and '30s. Dubbed "the Master" by Evelyn WAUGH, he is best known for his novels featuring Bertie Wooster, a bumbling but likeable aristocrat, and Jeeves, his discreet and capable valet. His work is rich in simile, as well as fractured fragments of schoolboy knowledge. During WORLD WAR II Wodehouse made several humorous broadcasts that some officials considered treasonous. He was exonerated in later years. After the war he moved to the U.S. and became a citizen, settling on Long Island, where he continued to turn out his popular books for an appreciative trans-Atlantic readership. The England that he depicted in fact bore little relation to the actual place, but evolved in his work into a land where time stood still. Wodehouse also wrote numerous articles, essays, plays, screenplays and lyrics. He was knighted in 1975, shortly before his death.

Wolf, Christa (1929–). East German novelist and literary critic. Wolf is one of the leading novelists to have been published in communist EAST GERMANY prior to the 1990 German reunification. Born in Landsberg an der Warthe, Wolf was educated at the Universities of Jena and Leipzig. She won immediate critical praise for her first novel, *Divided Heaven* (1963), which explored the psychological and social effects caused by the division of the German nation. This theme was again successfully pursued in Wolf's next novel, *The Quest for Crista T.* (1968). *The Reader and the Writer* (1972) is a collection of critical essays. Wolf's more recent works include *No Place on Earth* (1979) and *Cassandra: A Novel and Four Essays* (1983). She publically expressed her skepticism and criticism of German reunification.

Wolfe, Bernard (1915–1985). Author; perhaps best known for his 1959 novel *The Great Prince Died*, based on the events leading to the 1940 assassination of Leon TROTSKY in Mexico. Wolfe had served as Trotsky's personal secretary and bodyguard in 1937. His other works included *Memoirs of a Not Altogether Shy Pornographer*, which told of his literary apprenticeship as a producer of pornography for a New York City rare book dealer. Another of his books, *Limbo*, was hailed in 1952 as one of the first postwar antinuclear novels.

Wolfe, Thomas Clayton (1900–1938). One of the most important of modern

American novelists. In his fiction Wolfe described at length his hometown of Asheville under the name Altamont. His father was a stonecutter and his mother the proprietor of a boarding house, as are the Gants in *Look Homeward, Angel* (1929). Like Eugene Gant in that novel, young Thomas Wolfe worked at odd jobs, absorbed his father's love of poetry and was attentive to the stories told by his mother's boarders. In 1916 Wolfe enrolled at the University of North Carolina, where his creative energies were devoted to the theater until his graduation in 1920. Wolfe benefited from the presence there of the Carolina Playmakers and the lectures of the group's founder, Frederick Koch. After graduation he completed an M.A. program at Harvard before heading to New York City with a play under his arm in 1922.

During the late 1920s he was deeply influenced by Aline Bernstein, the Esther Jack of his novels. Wolfe's plays were never professionally produced, a fact that he rued for the rest of his life. While subsisting on a teaching job at New York University, he began to spin out the expansive novels on which his reputation now rests. *Look Homeward, Angel* appeared in 1929 after substantial editorial trimming by Maxwell PERKINS. Presented with a long and chaotic manuscript, Perkins helped Wolfe set aside independent episodes and sometimes revise them into short stories. The novel that resulted was a great success, and it was followed by an important second novel, *Of Time and the River* (1935), *The Web and the Rock* (1939), *You Can't Go Home Again* (1940) and distinguished collections of short stories.

Wolfe never indulged in the experiments with style common in the work of his contemporaries, such as William FAULKNER. His fame rests instead on a panoramic vision of the South, an enthusiasm for travel and appetite for life, and a continuing interest in relations between different social classes and the members of extended families.

For further reading:

Donald, David H. *Look Homeward: A Life of Thomas Wolfe*. New York: Fawcett Book Group, 1988.

Nowell, Elizabeth, *Thomas Wolfe: A Biography*. Westport, Conn.: Greenwood Publishing Group, 1973.

Wolfe, (Thomas Kenerly) Tom (1931–). American journalist, social critic and novelist. Wolfe achieved a rare blending of critical acclaim and popular acceptance in his writing career. He first won fame in the 1960s as a primary proponent of the NEW JOURNALISM, as a frequent contributor to *Esquire* and other magazines and as the author of books such as *The Kandy-Kolored Tangerine-Flake Streamline Baby* (1965), a collection of pieces on pop culture, and *The Electric Kool-Aid Acid Test* (1968), an account of Ken KESEY and the Merry Pranksters. Wolfe has continued as a prolific writer, with works including *From Bauhaus to Our House* (1981), a study of modern architectural trends, and the novel *The Bonfire of the Vanities* (1987), a bitter satire on greed and ambition in Manhattan.

Wolff, Karl Friedrich Otto (1900–1984). Nazi SS General, head of the personal staff of SS Reichsfuhrer Heinrich HIMMLER. During 1943–44 Wolff commanded the German forces in ITALY, and in 1945 he negotiated the surrender of German troops in Italy to the Allies. Wolff escaped prosecution in the NUREMBERG TRIAL after the war. However, in 1962 he was arrested and charged by the Munich state prosecutor with complicity in the deaths of 300,000 JEWS at the Treblinka death camp. He was convicted and sentenced to 15 years' imprisonment but was released after six years because of poor health.

women's movements. Women's, or feminist, movements are, generally speaking, political organizations initiated by women to expand their rights and role in society. In the United States, women began campaigning for suffrage, or the right to vote, in the early 1800s. In 1890, the two major U.S. organizations seeking the vote and women's equality joined to form the National American Woman Suffrage Association (NAWSA). At the beginning of the 20th century, suffragists (sometimes called suffragettes) in the United States and Great Britain intensified their efforts, planning marches and distributing literature in support of their cause. Many women were ridiculed, arrested and jailed. Important figures in the struggle for suffrage include Susan B. Anthony (1820–1906) and the Englishwoman Emmeline PANKHURST (1857–1928). In the United States, the 19th Amendment to the Constitution, granting women the right to vote, was adopted in 1920. In Great Britain, women were granted the vote in 1928. In many other countries, such as France, the fight for suffrage continued into the 1940s. NAWSA evolved into the League of Women Voters, which continues to disseminate information on political issues.

Other social issues that motivated women to action in the early 20th century were birth control and temperance. Women who supported temperance, or the abolition of alcoholic beverages, were frequently scorned as puritanical fanatics, but their involvement in the issue often began after they had suffered domestic violence at the hands of drunken husbands. The movement was later taken up by religious organizations and became less a women's issue than a moral one. In the early 1900s the dissemination of birth control, or even related, information was illegal. Believing that uncontrolled pregnancies contributed to poverty, Margaret SANGER led a movement to provide contraceptive information to women, and organized the National Birth Control League, which later became Planned Parenthood. She was jailed in 1916 when she attempted to open a clinic in Brooklyn, New York, but by 1923 she had successfully sponsored several clinics in the United States.

Although many feminists continued their efforts on behalf of increased rights for women, the next wave of society-wide

American women demonstrate outside the White House for the right to vote (1916).

feminist activity did not occur until the 1960s. Important catalysts at this time were *The Feminine Mystique* (1963) by Betty FRIEDAN and *The* SECOND SEX (1949) by Simone DE BEAUVOIR. Both books analyzed women's roles as determined by society. Among the spokeswomen who emerged at the time are Gloria STEINEM, author and founder of *MS.* Magazine, and Germaine GREER, who wrote about women's issues. Women began forming "consciousness raising groups," informal gatherings in which they discussed their problems, and also political organizations to fight for equal rights.

In 1961, President KENNEDY established the Commission on the Status of Women, which exposed the barriers to women in many fields, the disparity between women's and men's salaries, and women's lesser civil rights. Many organizations were formed to address these issues, including the National Organization for Women (NOW) in 1966, the Women's Equity Action League in 1968 and the National Women's Political Caucus in 1971. These groups were able to effect many legal gains for women, including the Equal Pay Act of 1963; Title VII of the CIVIL RIGHTS ACT OF 1964, which outlawed job discrimination on the basis of sex as well as race; Title IX of the Education Amendments of 1972, which prohibited federally-funded colleges and universities from discriminating against women; and the Equal Credit Opportunity Act of 1975. The EQUAL RIGHTS AMENDMENT (ERA) to the Constitution was passed by Congress in 1972 and sent to states for passage, but only 35 of the necessary 38 states approved the ERA by the 1982 deadline.

The impact of the women's movement is evident in the United States, most particularly in the American work force. In 1989, 57% of American women worked outside of the home; yet as recently as 1987, women's salaries were still 70% of those earned by men. Women continue to struggle for equal salaries and for access to fields of employment from which they are still barred. (See also FEMINISM.)

Wonder, Stevie [Steveland Judkins Morris] (1950–). American singer-composer. Born in Detroit's black ghetto, Wonder was discovered playing the harmonica and dancing at age 10 and had his first gold hit at age 13. He then learned other instruments—piano, drums, organ and synthesizer. A consummate musician, he composed, performed and arranged his own albums. Hit singles include "You Are the Sunshine of My Life" (1972), "Living for the City (1973) and "I Wish" (1977). He has also composed film scores and championed the movement against APARTHEID in South Africa.

Wood, Grant (1891–1942). American painter. He attended the Art Institute of Chicago and traveled to Europe, where he studied in Paris. During his European travels in the late 1920s, Wood was struck by the meticulous realism of such Northern Renaissance painters as the Van Eycks. Returning to the U.S., he adopted this almost magical Flemish realism to portray quintessentially American subjects such as the famous *American Gothic* (1930, Art Institute of Chicago) and *Daughters of Revolution* (1932, Cincinnati Art Museum). His brilliantly incisive portraits and simplified, stylized landscapes put Wood in the forefront of regionalist painting in the U.S.

Wood, Sir Henry J(oseph) (1869–1944). British conductor. Born in London, Wood studied the organ and conducting at the Royal Academy of Music. He began conducting in 1888 and served in a number of minor conducting posts before being appointed conductor of the newly-formed Promenade concerts in 1895. For the next 49 years, Wood directed the popular nightly performances in London each fall, playing the standard repertoire, British composers and many modern composers. Wood also conducted the Queen's Hall Orchestra in Saturday concerts that began in 1897. He later developed an interest in Russian music as well. Wood was knighted in 1911 and became a professor at the Royal Academy of Music in 1923. A thoroughly British conductor, he performed in the U.S. but turned down the post of director of the Boston Symphony in 1918. He was one of the most beloved and influential figures on the British classical music scene.

Woodcock, George (1904–1979). British labor leader, secretary of the TRADES UNION CONGRESS (TUC) (1960–69). As head of Britain's labor movement, Woodcock attempted to steer unions toward a broader role in the making of national economic policy. He also stressed the need for Britain to be more competitive in world markets.

Woodcock, Leonard (Freel) (1911–). American labor leader and diplomat. Born in Providence, R.I., Woodcock grew up in Europe and returned to the U.S. where he attended Wayne State University, Detroit. He began work at a Detroit auto parts factory in 1933, joined the United Automobile Workers (UAW) and became active in the union. Appointed administrative assistant to union president Walter REUTHER in 1946, he rose in the union hierarchy and was elected an international vice president in 1955. Upon Reuther's death in 1970, Woodcock succeeded to the UAW's presidency. A skilled negotiator, he helped to negotiate a number of important auto industry contracts before leaving the UAW (union rules made him ineligible for a third term) in 1977. Closely allied with the Democratic Party, Woodcock was appointed head of the U.S. Liaison Office in Peking by President Jimmy CARTER in 1979. When diplomatic relations between the U.S. and CHINA were established later that year, Woodcock became ambassador. After leaving that post in 1981, he took up a teaching post at the University of Michigan.

Woodhouse, Barbara (1910–1988). British dog trainer. Woodhouse publicized her training techniques in the BBC's "Training Dogs the Woodhouse Way" and became an international celebrity in the late 1970s and early 1980s.

Woodruff, Robert Winship (1889–1985). Atlanta businessman. As head of the COCA-COLA Co. from 1923 to 1955, he transformed it from a debt-ridden, one-product soda fountain business into an international financial empire. A dynamic promoter and salesman, he created a network of independent bottlers and distributors that eventually made Coke available almost everywhere in the world. During World War II he turned millions of American servicemen into Coke drinkers by making the product available to them at a nickel a bottle. After he retired, he remained influential as a director until 1984. Enormously wealthy, he was a prominent philanthropist and donated an estimated $350 million to Emory University and other Atlanta institutions.

Woodson, Carter Godwin (1875–1950). Black American historian, editor and educator. Soon after receiving his Ph.D. from Harvard in 1912, Woodson founded the Association for the Study of Afro-American Life and History. One of the association's primary goals was to train black historians; its *The Journal of Negro History* flourished for 30 years under Woodson's direction. His educational posts included dean of the College of Liberal Arts at Howard University in Washington, D.C., and dean of West Virginia State College. He also founded a black-oriented publishing concern, Associated Publishers, and authored *The Negro in Our History* (1922) and *A Century of Negro Migration* (1918).

Woodstock (1969). Legendary ROCK music festival during the summer of 1969. Promoters put together a concert featuring such groups as JEFFERSON AIRPLANE; the WHO; CROSBY, STILLS AND NASH; Arlo GUTHRIE and others—expecting a turnout of 10,000 to 20,000. In fact, some 300,000 to 400,000 people converged on a farm near Woodstock, New York, on the wet, rainy weekend of August 15–17. Although facilities were completely overburdened and attendees shared food, liquor and drugs, no violence was reported. The Woodstock weekend is remembered as the ultimate BE-IN, the high point of the HIPPIE era and the culmination of the 1960s COUNTERCULTURE movement.

Woodward and Bernstein. American journalists Robert Woodward (1943–) and Carl Bernstein (1944–). While working as reporters for the *Washington Post,* this pair of award-winning journalists investigated and exposed the WATERGATE scandal. They coauthored *All the President's Men* (1974) and *The Final Days* (1976), which dealt with the scandal and its aftermath. Woodward became the *Post*'s metropolitan editor in 1979 and assistant managing editor in 1981. His other books include *The Brethren* (1979), *Wired* (1984) and *Veil: the Secret Wars of the CIA* (1987). Bernstein served as Washington bureau chief for ABC from 1979 to 1981, and as an ABC New York City correspondent from 1981 to 1984.

Woolcott, Alexander (1887–1943). American drama critic, columnist, radio commentator, actor and renowned wit. Woolcott was one of the best known

American journalists of the 1920s and 1930s and emerged as an oft-quoted member of the group of New York-based celebrity raconteurs known as the Algonquin Round Table (due to their frequent social meetings at the Algonquin Hotel). Woolcott, who was born in New Jersey and attended Hamilton College, became the drama critic of the *New York Times* in 1914. He later contributed to numerous other newspapers and also wrote a column, "Shouts and Murmurs," for the NEW YORKER. Woolcott acted the role of Sheridan Whiteside (based on Woolcott himself) in a road company production of the George S. KAUFMAN and Moss HART classic comedy, *The Man Who Came to Dinner* (1937). He also was a commentator on the CBS radio network in the 1930s.

Woolf, Virginia (1882–1941). English novelist, essayist, diarist, literary critic and feminist; one of the premier figures in all of 20th-century British literature. The daughter of prominent 19th-century literary critic Leslie Stephen, Woolf never received a formal university education but easily took her part as a key member of the BLOOMSBURY GROUP of British intellectuals that flourished from the 1910s to the 1930s. In the 1920s, Woolf became one of the foremost practitioners of the fictional technique known as STREAM OF CONSCIOUSNESS. Her major works include the novels *Mrs. Dalloway* (1925), *To the Lighthouse* (1927) and *The Waves* (1931), the feminist study *A Room of One's Own* (1929) and the posthumous *A Writer's Diary* (1953). With husband, the economist **Leonard Woolf,** she founded the **Hogarth Press,** a small but influential literary publishing house that published many of her own works. Woolf suffered from bouts of depression and mental instability throughout her life. She took her life by drowning herself in the River Ouse near her home in Sussex.

For further reading:

Gordon, Lyndall, *Virginia Woolf: A Writer's Life*. New York: W.W. Norton, 1986.

Rose, Phyllis, *Woman of Letters: A Life of Virginia Woolf*. San Diego, Calif.: Harcourt Brace Jovanovich, 1987.

Wootton, Barbara (Frances) [Baroness Wootton of Abinger] (1897–1988). British social scientist. Wooton challenged conventional wisdom in fields ranging from economics to sociology to criminology. Her experiences as a lay magistrate for nearly half a century and as chairman of juvenile courts in London for 16 years formed the basis for her seminal work *Social Science and Social Pathology* (1959). She was a member of four royal commissions and was one of four women among the first life peers created in 1958.

Workers' Opposition. Opposition, mainly from trade unionists with the Bolshevik Party, that in 1920 criticized the bureaucratic control of industry by the government and the central party organs and advocated the establishment of an All-Russian Congress of Producers to run the country's economy. At the 10th Party Congress (1921) the opposition was condemned and a resolution was carried forbidding "factionalism." The Workers' Opposition was alleged to have continued during the following year. Most of the Workers' Opposition leaders were expelled from the party, and all the known leaders, except Alexandra KOLLONTAY, disappeared during the GREAT PURGE.

Works Progress Administration. NEW DEAL agency that employed thousands of unemployed Americans during the GREAT DEPRESSION. When President Franklin D. ROOSEVELT took office in 1933 the U.S. was in the midst of its worst economic downturn, with one-quarter of the workforce unemployed. FDR took the then-radical step of creating government agencies to employ thousands, paying their salaries with borrowed money. Established in 1935, the Works Progress Administration (later called the Work Projects Administration) employed thousands in public construction jobs. The federal government helped localities build bridges, highways, courthouses. Artists, musicians and writers were also employed by the government, which established programs to assist artists, the theater and symphony orchestras. The WPA's FEDERAL WRITERS' PROJECT is best known for its series of guidebooks for each of the U.S. states.

World Bank. International bank that encourages investment in developing nations. The Bank, formally known as the **International Bank for Reconstruction and Development,** was established along with the International Monetary Fund at the BRETTON WOODS CONFERENCE in 1944, during World War II. Although the initial purpose of the bank was the reconstruction of war-torn member nations, it later shifted its emphasis toward making loans to the governments of developing nations. The bank's funds are supplied by contributions from the 44 member nations and also from the proceeds of bond sales. The bank makes loans to developing nations who are facing hardships because of balance of payment problems or trade problems. The bank has encountered controversy in the third world by requiring borrowers to adopt austerity budgets as a condition for receiving these loans.

World Council of Churches. International organization of some 300 Protestant and Orthodox churches. With headquarters in Geneva, Switzerland, the group fosters interchurch cooperation and Christian unity and attempts to relate church activities to worldwide problems. While the WCC constitution was drafted in 1937, the group was not formed until after World War II, at the Amsterdam Conference of 1948. Among the areas in which the WCC is active are education, missionary activities, aid to the poor, help for refugees, study of religio-social issues, promotion of world peace, work for social justice and promotion of ecumenicism. Its views are stated in recommendations to its member churches, which are not legally obliged to follow its lead, but which are given the opportunity to act in concert regarding matters of common concern. The WCC's activities and interests are bound up with nearly every part of Christian service on an international scale. The organization is administered by six presidents and a 145–member central committee, the members of which are elected by the WCC's diverse member churches. The group meets annually, and assemblies of representatives from member churches are held once every six or seven years.

World Health Organization [WHO]. Agency of the UNITED NATIONS. Founded in 1948, WHO has the mission of improving health care throughout the world, particularly in developing countries. WHO's activities include the prevention of disease, the establishment of standards for food and medicine, the identification and classification of diseases, and the sponsoring of medical research. The agency's main headquarters are in Geneva, Switzerland.

World of Art, The. In 1870 Savva Marmantov, a businessman, established an artists' colony at Abramtsevo near Moscow. The setup was similar to that of William Morris. The World of Art group was devoted to art for art's sake, in contrast with the social aims of the Wanderers. In 1904 DIAGHILEV founded a magazine called *The World of Art,* which became the organ of the group. Leon BAKST was probably the colony's best known member.

World War I (1914–18). Although the assassination in SERBIA of the heir to the Austro-Hungarian throne was the event that sparked the beginning of the so-called "Great War," international tensions and competition had been mounting for many years (see BALKAN WARS). On July 28, 1914, the AUSTRO-HUNGARIAN EMPIRE declared war on Serbia. RUSSIA began mobilizing troops along the German border, and GERMANY declared war on Russia and its ally, FRANCE. Immediately German armies went into action against France, planning to conquer it in a few months and then to turn the powerful German military machine against Russia. When German troops disregarded the neutrality of LUXEMBOURG and BELGIUM by invading these countries to sweep through France from the northeast, Great Britain joined France to repel the invaders. The Central Powers of Austria-Hungary and Germany, later joined by the OTTOMAN EMPIRE (Turkey) and BULGARIA, were aligned against the Allies of France, Great Britain, Serbia, Russia, and Belgium, which were later joined by ITALY, ROMANIA, PORTUGAL, Montenegro, JAPAN, AUSTRALIA, the U.S., and 20 other countries. Within a month German divisions reached the outskirts of Paris, but the retreating French rallied and counterattacked (see MARNE, FIRST BATTLE OF THE), driving the Germans back to the north. For the next four years the opposing armies faced each other, sometimes only a few hundred feet apart, in a long line extending from the North Sea to Switzerland (see WORLD WAR I ON THE WESTERN FRONT). Bloody battles were fought at YPRES, Artois, on the

The German high command: Field Marshal Hindenburg, Kaiser Wilhelm II and General Ludendorff plan for war.

World War I battlefield—a charred, barren landscape (1918).

SOMME, in the Meuse Valley and the Argonne Forest, and elsewhere (see VERDUN, BATTLE OF) with staggering losses on both sides, but basically the line remained stationary until the fall of 1918. Austro-Hungarian troops had to face the Russians on their eastern border (see WORLD WAR I ON THE EASTERN FRONT) and Italians in the south (see WORLD WAR I ON THE ITALIAN FRONT), while they subdued Serbia and Montenegro (see WORLD WAR I IN THE BALKANS). When its navy could no longer operate from the North Sea (see JUTLAND, BATTLE OF), Germany resorted to unrestricted submarine warfare. This so angered the Americans that they declared war on Germany on April 6, 1917; although it was some time before they could send large numbers of men and material, their entry into the conflict gave the Allies a great moral boost. Despite a defeat at Gallipoli (see DARDANELLES CAMPAIGN), Britain remained master of the seas by protecting the Suez Canal (see WORLD WAR I IN EGYPT), and this enabled it to seize German colonies in Africa, to supply its armies in the Middle East (see WORLD WAR I IN MESOPOTAMIA; WORLD WAR I IN PALESTINE), and to transport troops from its COMMONWEALTH countries. When Russia dropped out of the war in 1917 (see BOLSHEVIK REVOLUTION), the Germans were able to transfer troops from the Eastern Front to help the Austro-Hungarians and the Turks, whose empires were crumbling, but even fresh troops could not break the stalemate on the Western Front. As the French, British, and Americans slowly, doggedly drove the Germans back to the "Hindenburg Line," Bulgaria fell, the Ottoman Empire sued for peace, and Austria-Hungary collapsed. The war-weary Germans revolted, and their kaiser and generals were forced to sign an armistice on November 11, 1918. The ensuing Treaty of VERSAILLES and other treaties changed the geographical face of Europe and the Middle East and brought about numerous political, economic, and social changes. The war had seen the introduction of tanks, airplanes, and poison gas and had caused enormous suffering and destruction wherever it was fought. More than 10 million persons had died, and many more were injured. (See also RUSSO-POLISH WAR OF 1919–20; TURKISH WAR OF INDEPENDENCE; ZEEBRUGGE RAID.)

World War I in Egypt (1914–17). As soon as the OTTOMAN EMPIRE (Turkey) announced that it was entering World War I against the Allies, Great Britain declared Egypt a British protectorate and deposed the pro-German ruler. Egypt's SUEZ CANAL was an essential lifeline and had to be protected at all costs; both the Turks and the Germans were anxious to gain control of the canal. In February 1915, three Turkish forces approached the canal by different routes, but the British had already fortified the western bank; the Turks were driven away with heavy losses. A year later the British began to fortify the eastern bank of the canal along an 80–mile stretch and to secure the Sinai Desert. As they slowly made their way north toward El Arish on the border with PALESTINE, they laid railroad tracks and a water pipeline. In July 1916, they were attacked by a sizable Turkish force, but again the Turks were severely beaten, and many prisoners were taken. By December that year, the British were within 20 miles of their destination, which was garrisoned by Turkish troops, who withdrew without a fight. Two Turkish contingents still remained in Egypt, but they were dispatched by surprise attacks by the British Camel Corps. By 1917, the last Turkish forces were gone from Egypt, and the Suez Canal was no longer in danger.

World War I in Mesopotamia (1914–18). Shortly after the OTTOMAN EMPIRE (Turkey) entered World War I in November 1914, on the side of the Central Powers, the British sent a small force from India to the head of the PERSIAN GULF to establish a British sphere of influence in Mesopotamia to protect INDIA and EGYPT. The troops were ordered to move northward up the gulf to seize BAGHDAD eventually. At first the British forces were successful against the Turkish forces, but when the Anglo-French armies failed on the Gallipoli peninsula (see DARDANELLES CAMPAIGN), Turkish divisions were rushed to Mesopotamia. The British were driven

A Yorkshire regiment advancing at dusk, somewhere in France.

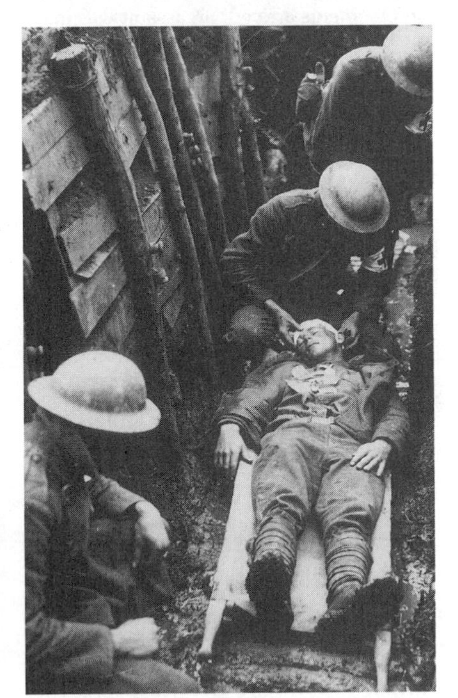

Life and death in the trenches (March 22, 1918).

back to Kut-el-Amara, which was surrounded and besieged. Several relief expeditions were dispatched, but they were unable to break through the Turkish lines. After a 143–day siege, the British surrendered in April 1916. The following year Allied reinforcements and gunboats were sent to the Persian Gulf, and the British quickly established themselves on both sides of the Tigris River as they proceeded north. After heavy fighting, Kut-el-Amara was captured, and the retreating Turks were pursued up the river to Baghdad. To prevent any counterattacks, the British continued their pursuit of the fleeing Turks and so gained control of most of Mesopotamia, including the Baghdad-Samara Railroad. Although all this action did not have great strategic significance for the war as a whole, it did boost the sagging morale of the Allies and dealt the Ottoman Empire a blow from which it never recovered.

World War I in Palestine (1917–18). Once the British had driven the Turks from EGYPT (see WORLD WAR I IN EGYPT), they continued to pursue their enemy north into Palestine. Their first two efforts to capture the stronghold of Gaza failed, but the third under the command of Edmund H.H. ALLENBY succeeded. Earlier he had captured Beersheba to the east, and after the victory at Gaza his men proceeded northward, meeting little resistance until they reached Lydda, a junction point on the railroad between Jaffa and Jerusalem. After fierce fighting they dislodged the Turks and effectively cut their forces in two. The British next took Jaffa on the coast and then turned east toward Jerusalem, which was strongly fortified. Allenby devised a plan to surround the city and take all the outposts. This involved much hard fighting in difficult terrain and bad weather. After reinforcements arrived, an assault was made on the Holy City on December 8, 1917, and the next day the Turks surrendered. However, they regrouped and attempted to retake Jerusalem two weeks later, but to no avail. Gradually the British drove them from the hills and into what was then called Syria. Palestine became a British protectorate after centuries of Turkish rule.

World War I in the Balkans (1915–18). The Balkan peninsula in southeastern Europe had long been seething with nationalistic rivalries and competing territorial desires (see BALKAN WARS). Although the AUSTRO-HUNGARIAN EMPIRE declared war on the Balkan state of SERBIA on July 28, 1914 (see WORLD WAR I), it was not until after combined Austro-Hungarian and German forces had driven the Russians from Galacia (see WORLD WAR I ON THE EASTERN FRONT) that the Austrians turned their attention to Serbia and invaded it from the north. In October 1915, BULGARIA joined the Central Powers (GERMANY, Austro-Hungary, and the OTTOMAN EMPIRE) and promptly launched an invasion of Serbia from the south; Bulgarian troops were crushed by superior numbers and firepower. The Austrians then moved against Serbia's neighbor, Montenegro, and captured its capital in January 1916. Bulgarian and Austrian armies next invaded ALBANIA from the north and east, but failed to drive an Italian force from the southern region. ROMANIA wavered for two years, debating which side was most apt to win the war; in August 1916, it decided to join the Allies and declared war on the Central Powers. Romanian troops invaded Transylvania in Hungary with initial success, but were soon pushed back by two German armies. Soon Rumania itself was overrun by Bulgarians and Germans. In Greece, the Allies seized control of the telegraph and postal systems, the Greek navy, and large stores of munitions from the army and blockaded the coast. A French and British expeditionary force in Salonica, in northern Greece, made sure that Greece maintained its neutrality in the war, but it made no move against the Bulgarians in Macedonia until September 1918. Reinforced by exiled Serbian soldiers and Greek troops, the Allies attacked on three fronts and, within two weeks, captured the major Bulgarian strong points. Bulgaria soon sued for peace and agreed to an unconditional surrender. The Allies continued their advance northward as they liberated both Serbia and Montenegro. Rumanian forces reentered the Balkan war arena and helped drive the Austro-Hungarian and German soldiers from its borders and southern Russia. The pro-German rulers of the Balkan states (present day Albania, Greece, Romania, Bulgaria, YUGOSLAVIA, and the European part of Turkey) were deposed, and the fate of the states was decided at the forthcoming peace conference. (See also HUNGARIAN REVOLUTION OF 1918.)

World War I on the Eastern Front (1914–17). When Austria-Hungary declared war on SERBIA on July 28, 1914 (see WORLD WAR I), Russia began to mobilize its armies despite Germany's protests; on August 1, 1914 the two countries were at war. Russian troops invaded East Prussia but were badly defeated at the Battle of Tannenberg (August 29–30, 1914), where many prisoners and materiel were seized by the Germans, and at the Battle of Masurian Lakes (September 9–14, 1914). The Russians were more successful in Galacia (southeast Poland and western Ukraine) against the Austro-Hungarian forces, from whom they wrested key passes in the Carpathian Mountains and captured the capital city, Lemberg (Lvov), and the fortress city of Przemysl in early 1915. During the previous fall German armies had twice invaded Russian Poland and had twice failed to capture Warsaw, although they did control western Poland. By the winter of 1915, the opposing forces were facing each other from trenches along a 900–mile front. In May that year combined Austro-Hungarian and German armies struck in Galicia; their heavy artillery routed the Russians from their mountain strongholds; Lemberg and Przemysl were retaken. Then the Germans launched a major offensive, called "Hindenburg's Drive" after the brilliant strategist General Paul von HINDENBURG (1847–1934), to drive the Russians out of Poland. By encircling maneuvers, they threatened to trap the Russians, who hastily retreated, leaving Warsaw, Brest-Litovsk, Vilna, and part of Lithuania to the enemy. A year later, in June 1916, the Russians began an offensive against Austria-Hungary in the area of the Styr and Sereth (Siretul) rivers and succeeded in advancing 20 to 50 miles along a 250–mile front; they were halted only when their supplies gave out. Meanwhile, discontent over the corrupt government of the czar was increasing in Russia; in March 1917, the czar's regime was toppled (see BOLSHEVIK REVOLUTION; FEBRUARY REVOLUTION). The new Russian government quickly made peace with GERMANY, and the war on the Eastern Front ended.

World War I on the Italian Front (1915–18). Italy remained neutral until May 23, 1915, when it decided to join the Allies and fight its traditional enemy, Austro-Hungary (see WORLD WAR I). The Italian army took the offensive in the Isonzo River valley, but the Austrians had already fortified the peaks in that mountainous area, and the Italians were unable to make any tangible headway, although they made assault after assault. They did manage to cross the river in the Caporetto area in the fall of 1915 and in 1916 captured Gorizia. The following year the Italians pushed forward again in several places, and the Germans, fearing their Austrian allies might withdraw, sent reinforcements. This turned the tide. After a heavy bombardment, the demoralized Italian troops began to retreat from Caporetto, and the retreat soon became a rout that stopped only when the army reached the Piave River. The other large-scale action on the Italian front occurred in the Trentino alpine area to the west where the Austrians launched an offensive in 1916 against ill-prepared Italian outposts. The Austrians swept across the border, and it seemed possible that they might sieze Venice and cut off the armies on the Isonzo. However, an Italian force holding a commanding position on Monte Ciove held firm against overwhelming odds and stopped the Austrian advance. This offensive weakened Austria's eastern front and permitted the Russians to invade its territory in the Styr and Sereth (Siretul) rivers region (see WORLD WAR I ON THE EASTERN FRONT). In November 1918, the Austrians surrendered to an Italian general whose troops had beaten them at Vittoria Veneto, and under the peace terms Italy regained Trieste and other territory the Austrians had seized in previous wars.

World War I on the Western Front (1914–18). At the beginning of World War I, the rapid and powerful German advance through Belgium and northeastern France was stopped by the French and British in September 1914 (see MARNE, FIRST BATTLE OF THE), and the German armies were forced back beyond the Aisne River. In the north the Allies contended

A French citizen weeps as the Nazis march into Paris (June 1940).

with the Germans for control of Ypres in southwestern Belgium and the English Channel ports, while in the southeast the Germans were driven back to the mountains. By December 1914, both sides had dug into a series of fortified trenches almost 600 miles long and stretching from Ostend (Oostende, Belgium) to Douai, Saint-Quentin, Rheims, Verdun, Saint-Mihiel, and Luneville (northeastern French towns) and then south to the Swiss border. This battle line remained almost stationary for the next four years; although there were frequent bombardments and waves of soldiers sent out of the trenches ("over the top") against the enemy, the gains in territory were insignificant, but the losses in lives were very high. Life in the trenches was miserable for all; many novels and memoirs have described the horror, mud, cold and filth of that trench warfare. In 1916, the Germans launched a major offensive against the strongest Allied fortress (see VERDUN, BATTLE OF); there the French held fast. Another German offensive was repulsed by the Allies in July 1918, and was followed by a massive counterattack in which the Allies under Marshal Ferdinand FOCH drove the Germans out of most of France and Belgium; a counteroffensive by American troops pushed the Germans from the Argonne Forest and Saint-Mihiel. The Western Front moved eastward as the war drew to a close.

World War II (1939–45). The principal Axis power—GERMANY—felt cheated by the harsh terms of the Treaty of VERSAILLES (see WORLD WAR I) and was eager to regain or expand its territories. Germany had become fascist, and was ruled by a military dictatorship—under Adolf HITLER it began to disregard treaties and commit acts of aggression. It remilitarized the RHINELAND in 1935, annexed AUSTRIA and subsequently CZECHOSLOVAKIA'S SUDETENLAND in 1938, occupied Czechoslovakia in 1939 (see MEMEL, INSURRECTION AT). Also fascist, Italy under Benito MUSSOLINI conquered Ethiopia (see ITALO-ETHIOPIAN WAR OF 1935–36) and seized Albania in 1939. Japan invaded Manchuria in 1931 and began an undeclared war against China (see SINO-JAPANESE WAR OF 1937–45). Most of the world wanted peace and watched these warlike acts with apprehension. When Hitler's troops invaded Poland (see BLITZKRIEG), Great Britain and France had to honor their agreement to protect the Poles, although it was too late to save them. At first Russia sided with the Axis powers and seized the Baltic states and Finland (see RUSSO-FINNISH WAR OF 1939–40), but in 1941 Hitler turned on his former ally and invaded Russian territory (see WORLD WAR II ON THE RUSSIAN FRONT). After conquering Poland (September 1939), Hitler turned his energies westward; Britain and France had declared war on Germany on September 3, 1939. Hitler's mechanized, powerful armies swept through Denmark and invaded Norway (see NORWAY, GERMAN INVASION OF). A month later, May of 1940, German Nazi troops marched on Holland, Belgium, and Luxembourg, broke through France's defensive MAGINOT LINE (see FRANCE, BATTLE OF), and seized ports on the English Channel while dislodging a British expeditionary force (see DUNKIRK, EVACUATION OF). After occupying northern France and setting up the puppet VICHY government in the south, the Germans used their Luftwaffe (air force) to attempt to bomb Great Britain into submission, but without success (see BATTLE OF BRITAIN). By the end of 1939, the war had expanded into the Balkan peninsula (see WORLD WAR II IN THE BALKANS) and to North Africa, where the Italians invaded Egypt. Although the U.S. remained neutral, it did set up a lend-lease agreement with Britain, whereby food and supplies were shipped across the Atlantic in armed convoys to protect them from German U-boats or submarines (see ATLANTIC, BATTLE OF THE). The year 1941 was grim for Britain as it faced the Axis powers alone until Russia was invaded by the Germans and the U.S. naval base at PEARL HARBOR was attacked by the Japanese. In early 1942, Japan rapidly expanded its "Great East Asia Co-prosperity Sphere," but the Americans recovered

Hundreds of cities in Europe and Asia suffered damage like this inflicted on a German city.

quickly from their initial defeat and began to demolish the Japanese naval strength (see WORLD WAR II IN THE PACIFIC). Germany's Afrika Korps was beaten at EL ALAMEIN in northern Egypt (see NORTH AFRICAN CAMPAIGN), and the lifeline of the SUEZ CANAL was preserved. The British, joined by FREE FRENCH and American forces, which landed in Algeria and French Morocco, drove the Axis troops out of Africa by May 1943. The supposed German victory in Russia turned into defeat at STALINGRAD (Volgograd) in early 1943, and the Allies invaded SICILY and Italy from their North African bases (see WORLD WAR II ON THE ITALIAN FRONT). The leaders of the Allies (chiefly Britain, France, Canada, Australia, Russia, Belgium, the Netherlands, China and the U.S.) met at a number of conferences to decide future strategy and objectives and to sign the United Nations declaration. In the east, the Japanese fought doggedly against Chinese, American, British, and Australian forces in Burma (see BURMA CAMPAIGN) and the Pacific islands, but only in China were they successful (see WORLD WAR II IN CHINA). German-occupied Europe was severely bombed by the Allies before they landed troops to liberate the area (see NORMANDY, INVASION OF; WORLD WAR II ON THE WESTERN FRONT). By the end of 1944, an Allied victory was assured and, with some grievous setbacks (see BULGE, BATTLE OF THE), the Russians, Americans and British advanced steadily on BERLIN, Germany's capital, from the east and the west. Their forces met at Torgau in Saxony (later part of East Germany) on April 25, 1945, and a few days later Hitler and his mistress-turned-wife presumably killed themselves in a bunker in Berlin. Germany surrendered unconditionally on May 7, 1945. After U.S. ATOMIC BOMBS devastated two of its large cities, HIROSHIMA and NAGASAKI, Japan surrendered on August 14, 1945. The U.S. and the U.S.S.R. emerged as superpowers after this most terrible of wars, in which millions of soldiers, sailors, airmen, marines and civilians died in air raids, U-boat sinkings, rocket attacks, concentration camps, death marches and bloody battles, and from disease, starvation, torture and forced labor.

World War II in China (1941–45). CHINA, which had been at war with JAPAN for many years (see SINO-JAPANESE WAR OF 1937–45), entered World War II on the side of the Allies in late 1941. Most of the Chinese coast was in the hands of the Japanese, and the Chinese armies in the interior were supplied by material trucked in over the BURMA ROAD. When the road was sealed off in 1942 (see BURMA CAMPAIGN), supplies were flown into China over the Himalayan "hump" by expert British and American fliers. The U.S. Fourteenth Air Force set up bases in southeastern China, from which it effectively carried out bombing raids on Japanese shipping: U.S. General Joseph "Vinegar Joe" STILWELL served as chief of staff of American forces for CHIANG KAI-SHEK, supreme Allied commander of air and land forces in the Chinese war theater. In the spring of 1944, the Japanese mounted a new large offensive. First they occupied Honan province, whose armies had fled, and then moved south along the rail line from Hankow to Canton. The Japanese forces traveled by night to try to avoid the FLYING TIGERS, P-40 fighter planes flown by the U.S. Volunteer Group in China, which unremittingly bombed and strafed their lines of march. Each time a Chinese force opposed the Japanese, it was overcome. By November 1944, the Japanese had fulfilled their objective of controlling the railroad from Indochina north to Peking and had taken eight Chinese provinces. In the north, however, they did not fare so well, for the Chinese Communist Eighth Route Army and peasant militia used guerrilla tactics to harass their garrisons and strongholds. Later, when the war ended, the Chinese Communists would demand the surrender of the Japanese and take over their arms. Despite large amounts of British and American aid, the corrupt and strife-ridden Chinese Nationalist government at Chungking never took an initiative against the Japanese, preferring instead to reserve its best troops for possible use against the Communists.

World War II in the Balkans (1939–41). Benito MUSSOLINI, ITALY'S dictator, dreamed of a glorious Italian empire obtained with the help of his Fascist ally in GERMANY, Adolf HITLER. In April 1939, Italian troops invaded and soon conquered Albania, and from there they invaded GREECE in October 1940. The Greeks, however, were far better soldiers than the Italians, who were soon chased back to Albania. In August 1940, Russia demanded two provinces from ROMANIA, and HUNGARY demanded control of Transylvania; both demands were met reluctantly by the pro-German dictators of Romania and Transylvania. To make sure of his allies on the Balkan peninsula, Hitler sent German troops into Hungary and Romania in January 1941 and into Bulgaria shortly afterward. YUGOSLAVIA'S leaders signed a pact making them Nazi puppets, but its army objected and resolved to fight. On April 6, 1941, the Luftwaffe (German air force), accompanied by troops, attacked both Yugoslavia and Greece, neither of which could counter the superior German arms and forces. Yugoslavia was overrun in 11 days; its capital, Belgrade, was bombed mercilessly in "Operation Punishment"; and the remnants of the Yugoslavian army fled to the mountains, from which they waged damaging guerrilla warfare against the Nazis during the next three years. A British expeditionary force had been sent to aid the Greeks, but the most it could do was fight delaying actions. Greek forces surrendered in Albania on April 20, 1941, and in Greece proper four days later. The British were evacuated to Crete, but the Germans pursued them, and the Luftwaffe pounded this island into submission after a ten-day aerial and naval battle. TURKEY signed a friendship treaty with Germany and granted the Germans passage through the DARDANELLES. The loss of the Balkans was a severe blow to Britain as it struggled alone against the Nazi war machine.

World War II in the Middle East (1941). Britain sought to prevent the Middle East from falling into the hands of the Axis powers in World War II. In IRAQ, whose government had become pro-German, the British landed forces at BASRA and Habbaniyah, their air base west of BAGHDAD. The Iraqis flooded the land between the Tigris and Euphrates rivers to thwart the British advance on Baghdad. After three weeks of scattered fighting, Iraqi resistance collapsed, and the British secured Baghdad. About a week later, on June 8, 1941, FREE FRENCH forces, supported by British COMMONWEALTH troops, invaded SYRIA and LEBANON from PALESTINE and Trans-Jordan; British forces from Iraq invaded Syria soon afterward. At the Lebanese city of Sidon, VICHY French forces resisted the invaders until British bombardments drove them out. Westward-moving Allied armies captured the Syrian cities of Aleppo and Latakia. The Germans made air strikes against the Allies without much success. An armistice was signed at Acre (Akko, Israel) on July 14, 1941; the Free French and British occupied Syria and Lebanon for the remainder of the war. In Iran, German technicians helped operate the oil fields, which the British wanted to control. In late summer of 1941, the Allies carried out an invasion of Iran with remarkable speed; Soviet troops moved down both sides of the Caspian Sea and seized major ports, while Soviet planes bombed Tehran; British forces invaded from Iraq and seized oil fields; the minuscule Iranian naval force was sunk. The Allied campaign ended successfully about four days after it began; Britain had gained its objectives with little loss of life and materiel.

World War II in the Pacific (1941–45). Hours after their surprise attack on PEARL HARBOR, Japanese bombers destroyed most of the U.S. planes on the ground at a field outside Manila in the Philippines; three days later they sank three British battleships in the Gulf of Siam. With little to stop them, the Japanese then seized WAKE and GUAM islands and the British base at HONG KONG and invaded the PHILIPPINES in full force. BATAAN and CORREGIDOR in the Philippines held out for almost five months before they fell. In February 1942, after the surrender of THAILAND, the Japanese moved down the Malay Peninsula and seized the British port of SINGAPORE, where they took 70,000 troops captive. Java, Borneo, Bali, Sumatra, Timor and BURMA fell in turn until the Japanese occupied all East Asia. PORT MORESBY on New Guinea was their next target; from there they planned to attack AUSTRALIA. But the indecisive **Battle of the Coral Sea** (May 7–8, 1942) between the Japanese and American fleets prevented this from happening. Then the tide turned in the **Battle of Midway** (June 4, 1942), which was fought almost en-

The Japanese delegation arrives aboard the U.S.S. Missouri *for the official surrender ceremonies ending World War II in the Pacific (September 2, 1945).*

tirely by planes that tried to sink each other's warships; the Japanese suffered heavy losses. Afterward the Americans took the offensive; they won GUADALCANAL after a bloody six-month fight in the jungles there (August 7, 1942–February 9, 1943) and Papua in New Guinea. In 1943, the Japanese were cleared out of the Aleutian Islands off Alaska. The SOLOMON, Gilbert (Kiribati) and Marshall islands were seized next by the Allies in large-scale amphibious operations supported by air and naval bombardments. Saipan, Tinian and Guam in the Marianas were taken in August 1944. The Americans were now within flying distance of Japan, which they bombed repeatedly. On October 20, 1944, American forces landed on LEYTE in the Philippines, and U.S. General Douglas MACARTHUR, supreme Allied commander in the Southwest Pacific, announced "I have returned." One of the greatest naval engagements of all times was fought in the Gulf of Leyte on October 23–26, 1944; the Japanese were defeated, but the fighting on land continued for four months before the Philippines were completely liberated. IWO JIMA was captured by U.S. Marines in March 1945, and Okinawa was invaded the next month; there the Japanese resisted for over two months. In July 1945, the Allies sent Japan an ultimatum with terms that had been determined at the POTSDAM CONFERENCE, but the Japanese ignored it. The agonizing American decision was then made to use the newly developed ATOMIC BOMB. On August 6, 1945, one such bomb was dropped on the Japanese city of HIROSHIMA, 90 percent of which was leveled, with about 130,000 persons killed or injured. A second bomb fell on NAGASAKI on August 9, 1945, ruining a third of this Japanese city and killing or wounding about 75,000 persons. Five days later Japan's Emperor HIROHITO overruled his military advisers and accepted the peace terms of Potsdam.

World War II on the Italian Front (1943–45). After defeating the Axis forces in the NORTH AFRICAN CAMPAIGN (q.v.), the Allies turned their attention to Italy. On July 10, 1943, thousands of American and British soldiers landed under the cover of darkness on the shores of southern SICILY. They took the Germans and Italians garrisoned there by complete surprise and, within hours, gained control of 150 miles of the coast. After one battle at the Gela beachhead, Allied troops swept across the island, captured Palermo, and by August 17, 1943, secured all of Sicily. Meanwhile, the Italian dictator, Benito MUSSOLINI had been deposed, and his successor had sued for peace, which was granted on September 3, 1943, the same day the British landed on the toe of the Italian peninsula. Six days later U.S. forces made a large amphibious landing at Salerno, expecting little resistance. Adolf HITLER, Germany's dictator, had sent German troops to occupy strategic places in Italy, and they fought the Allied invaders ruthlessly. Slowly the Allies moved up the peninsula, seized Naples, and by December 1943, reached CASSINO Pass, south of Rome, which the Germans had fortified. Some of the toughest fighting of the war occurred in this mountainous terrain. In an effort to outflank the Germans, another Allied force was sent ashore at the Anzio beachhead, but German reinforcements arrived, and the Allies had to struggle to maintain their foothold. Finally, in May 1944, they overcame the Germans at Anzio and Cassino Pass and advanced northward again. Rome was liberated on June 4, 1944, and Florence two months later. The Allies, however, were stopped at the German Gothic Line stretching across the Alps in northern Italy. A stalemate developed during which time Italian partisans harassed the Germans wherever they were stationed. In April 1945, Allied forces crossed the Po River and partisan forces seized Milan, Genoa, and Venice. Mussolini was captured by partisans as he tried to flee the country and was summarily shot to death with his mistress. On April 29, 1945, the Germans in Italy surrendered; shortly after the partisans handed over their arms and dissolved their resistance movement.

World War II on the Russian Front (1941–45). Although the U.S.S.R. had entered World War II as an Axis power and had defeated FINLAND (see RUSSO-FINNISH WAR OF 1939–40) and absorbed the Baltic states, its Soviet leaders realized that Adolf HITLER, the German fuhrer (leader), was not to be trusted. There was worldwide surprise when three German armies, supported by Rumanian, Hungarian, Italian, Finnish, Solvak, and Spanish troops, invaded Russia on June 22, 1941. Even more surprise was shown at the valiant resistance displayed by Soviet soldiers and civilians. Hitler had expected to overrun Russia in four to six weeks, but he had underrated his opponents, the vast distances to be covered in Russia and the scarcity of good roads and railroads there. At first the Germans were successful as they swept eastward in their tanks and armored vehicles against the retreating Russians. The city of LENINGRAD was surrounded and besieged for two harrowing years; KIEV fell and half a million Soviet soldiers were killed or taken prisoner; the rich agricultural and industrial region of the Ukraine fell into German hands; Nazi troops were within sight of Moscow. But then winter set in, and the war bogged down. In the spring of 1942, the Germans resumed their offensive, intending to conquer the Caucasus region and its oil fields, but they were stopped at STALINGRAD (Volgograd). The city was bombed to rubble, but the Russians fought stubbornly from house to house, factory to factory. In mid-November 1942, the Russian military high command assembled its remaining troops, which began to advance upon Stalingrad from the north and south. The two Russian forces met behind the German lines, trapping the enemy's army in the smoldering city. All efforts to break out failed, and on February 2, 1943, the Germans surrendered.

Field Marshal Wilhelm Keitel signs surrender terms for the German Army at Russian headquarters in Berlin (May 7, 1945).

The victory at Stalingrad was the turning point of the war; thereafter the Russians took the offensive and drove the retreating Nazis, who slaughtered and destroyed as they withdrew, from their country. By 1944, Russian troops had control of the Baltic states, eastern Poland, the Ukraine, Romania, Bulgaria, and Finland. Early in 1945, they conquered East Prussia, Czechoslovakia and eastern Germany, and in April that year they took BERLIN, Germany's capital. As Napoleon I (1769–1821) had done before him, Hitler had underestimated the will of the Russian people and the severity of the Russian winters.

World War II on the Western Front (1944–45). Although British and American bombers had struck the principal industrial centers of Germany during 1942 and 1943 in World War II, it was not until the successful Allied landing on France's Normandy beaches in June 1944 (see NORMANDY, INVASION OF) that a Western Front was established on European soil. The mechanized U.S. Third Army moved southward into the Loire River valley and then proceeded east toward German-occupied Paris, which was liberated on August 25, 1944. A month later the American forces had advanced eastward to the Moselle River, had captured the fortress city of Liege, and were at the German border near Aachen, while the British had recaptured Brussels and Antwerp in Belgium and another Allied force had landed in southern France and was making its way north. But lack of supplies, especially fuel, slowed the Allied advance to a standstill until the continental harbors and ports could be reopened. An attempt to seize the RHINE bridge at Arnhem in the Netherlands failed in September 1944. Three months later the Germans launched a surprise offensive against the weak American line at the Ardennes Forest (see BULGE, BATTLE OF THE), hoping to divide and conquer the Allied forces, but this last strike failed. In February 1945, the Allies again went on the offensive, cleared the retreating Germans from the west banks of the Rhine River, crossed the river at REMAGEN and later other places, and trapped some 300,000 German troops in the RUHR Valley. Thereafter the Western Front moved rapidly eastward toward Berlin.

Worth, Irene (1916–). One of the great actresses of the 20th century, Worth has excelled in a wide range of drama from Greek tragedy and Shakespeare to works by modern masters (ALBEE, COWARD, SHAW, Ibsen and CHEKHOV). She made her New York debut in 1943 and in 1951 joined the Old Vic Company in London. In 1960 she starred on BROADWAY in Lillian Hellman's *Toys in the Attic.* She then returned to London and the Royal Shakespeare Company for acclaimed portrayals of Lady Macbeth and Goneril in *King Lear.* More recent roles have included performances in Samuel BECKETT's *Happy Days* (1979) and David HARE's *Wrecked Eggs* (1986).

Wortman, Sterling (1923–1981). American plant geneticist and a leading figure in the so-called GREEN REVOLUTION. Wortman experimented with grain production and developed high-yielding grains. He was also a vice president and president of the influential Rockefeller Foundation.

Wozzeck. Landmark modern opera by Viennese composer Alban BERG (1925). With Claude DEBUSSY's *Pelleas et Melisande* it is regarded as the greatest opera of the 20th century. It was adapted from a play by Georg Buechner, *Woyzeck* (1836). Based on the real-life trial and beheading of a Leipzig murderer, Buechner's play depicted the doomed love of a downtrodden soldier for his mistress, Marie. With the appearance of a rival, a drum-major, Woyzeck kills Marie and drowns himself in a pool. Berg's opera employed the musical device of the "Sprechstimme," a kind of song-speech devised by mentor Arnold SCHOENBERG in his song-cycle, *Pierrot Lunaire* (1912). The brooding atmosphere of terror and derangement, the swooping vocal lines against stark, atonal harmonies, the bewildering profusions of all manner of instrumental ensembles—military bands, restaurant orchestras, chamber orchestras, and strange instruments like an out-of-tune piano and an accordion—confused and outraged audiences and critics at the first performances in Berlin and Prague in 1925 and 1926. Venomous attacks called the stage action "an insane asylum" and the music "a capital offense." However, by the time Leopold STOKOWSKI introduced it to America in 1931 its cause-celebre status was changing into that of a bona-fide modern classic. By the mid-1950s it had entered the repertory of the Metropolitan Opera. Despite its potential cacophony it has exerted a strange fascination for audiences. "Even the non-technical listener," critic Ernest Newman has said, "finds himself, perhaps for the first time in his life, taking a vast amount of non-tonal music and not merely not wincing at it but being engrossed by it." Philosophically, it expresses Buechner's and Berg's acceptance of life on its own terms. "One must love mankind in order to penetrate the particular existence of each thing," Buechner wrote. "There must be nothing too common or too ugly. The most insignificant of faces can make a deeper impression than the mere sensation of beauty."

For further reading:

Monson, Karen, *Wozzeck—Alban Berg.* Boston: Houghton Mifflin Co., 1979.

WPA. See WORKS PROGRESS ADMINISTRATION.

Wragg, Harry (1902–1985). British jockey. Wragg rode from the end of World War I until 1946. During his career as a trainer, from 1947 until 1983, he won six English classics, with only the Oaks eluding him.

Wrangel, Baron Peter Nikolayevich (1878–1928). General. Following service in the RUSSO-JAPANESE WAR and WORLD WAR I, he joined the anti-Bolshevik forces of General Anton DENIKIN. After Denikin's defeat in November 1919 he was left in command of the disorganized White army. He advanced against the BOLSHEVIKS but was forced to retreat, and the remnants of his troops were evacuated from Sevastopol to Turkey in 1920. He spent the rest of his life in Belgium.

Wrathall, John James (1913–1978). British-born president of RHODESIA (1976–78). A leading figure in the rebel colony after UDI (UNILATERAL DECLARATION OF INDEPENDENCE, 1964), Wrathall served as finance minister under Ian SMITH from 1964 to 1975.

Wright Brothers. Orville (1871–1948) and Wilbur (1867–1912) Wright, pioneers in powered aircraft. They first became interested in the possibility of powered flight in the 1890s, after hearing about the glider flights of the German aviation pioneer Otto Lilienthal. In their Dayton, Ohio, bicycle repair shop and factory, the Wrights, very able mechanics, were experimenting (most called it tinkering) with kites and gliders and every other aspect of aerodynamics. In their efforts to learn about every discovery having to do with flight, it was said they read every book in the Dayton public library pertaining to

The Wright Brothers make the first powered airplane flight at Kitty Hawk, North Carolina (Dec. 17, 1903).

aerodynamics. They built a wind tunnel, the world's first, and developed their own science of flying, drawing up valuable tables of wind current and drift and noting other discoveries. They discovered the use of the aileron, probably the single most important discovery they made in preparation for the world's first flight of a heavier-than-air craft at Kitty Hawk, North Carolina (December 17, 1903). They chose Kitty Hawk because their investigations showed that its air currents were probably the best for their purposes. They continued their experiments at Dayton.

The record-breaking flights of Wilbur in the United States and Orville in France brought them world fame, as well as orders from government and private organizations. They formed the American Wright Company in 1909. After Wilbur's death, Orville retired from the business to engage in private research. In 1948, the year of Orville's death, their historic Kitty Hawk plane was installed at the Smithsonian Institution. The house where Orville was born, and their bicycle shop laboratory, were bought by Henry FORD and moved to his Greenfield Village in Michigan, where they were restored and put on public display.

For further reading:

Crouch, Tom, *The Bishop's Boys: A Life of Wilbur and Orville Wright*. New York: W. W. Norton, 1990.

Howard, Fred, *Wilbur and Orville: A Biography of the Wright Brothers*. New York: Alfred A. Knopf, 1987.

Wright, Frank Lloyd (1867–1959). American architect. Wright, considered by some as one of America's most imaginative architects, left a wealth of striking architectural forms. He studied civil engineering at the University of Wisconsin from 1884 to 1888, when he was apprenticed to CHICAGO architects Louis Sullivan and Dankmar Adler and soon became their chief draftsman. He left in 1893 to build his own practice, but continued to show Sullivan's influence in attempts to bring harmony to a building's function, form and location.

Wright's unique style soon brought him the extremes in praise and scorn usually reserved for politicians. The Unity Temple in Oak Park, Illinois, was the first public building in the United States to show its concrete construction. Wright planned many "Prairie-style" houses in and around Chicago. Prairie-style buildings permit the open spaces inside to expand into the outdoors through the use of terraces and porches. The Willitts house in Highland Park, Illinois, is shaped like a cross, with rooms arranged so that they seem to flow into each other. The Robie house in Chicago appears to be a series of horizontal layers floating in the air. The Johnson Wax building in Racine, Wisconsin, gave the same impression of streamlined style as Wright's other products of the late 1930s. The building featured a smooth, curved exterior of glass and brick. One of his most famous buildings was Fallingwater at Mill Run, Pennsylvania. Another was the Imperial hotel in Tokyo completed in 1922, one of the major buildings to survive the terrible earthquake of the next year.

Pioneering American architect Frank Lloyd Wright with his model for the Guggenheim Museum in New York City (1959).

While Wright's influence was felt internationally, he remained a Midwesterner at heart. In 1932 Wright established the Taliesin Fellowship where architectural students were paid to live and work with Wright in the summer at TALIESIN, Wright's home in Spring Green, Wisconsin, and in the winter at Taliesin West, his home in Scottsdale, Arizona. He continued to design controversial buildings such as the Guggenheim Museum in New York City, a daring spiral structure (1959).

For further reading:

Murphy, Wendy, *Frank Lloyd Wright*. Morristown, N.J.: Silver Burdett Press, 1990.

Wright, J. Skelly (1911–1988). U.S. judge; an enemy of segregation whose landmark 1960 desegregation order integrated public schools and public transportation in New Orleans. Reviled by many Southerners as a traitor to his race, Wright later served as a judge on the U.S. Court of Appeals for the District of Columbia, where he championed the cause of the poor, particularly those of the inner cities.

Wright, Peter (1916–). British counterintelligence agent, author of *Spycatcher*. Wright joined MI5 in 1955 as a scientific advisor in electronics. Following the defection of Kim PHILBY (1963), Wright headed the seven-man committee that investigated Soviet infiltration of British intelligence. He retired from MI5 in 1976 and later moved to Australia. His controversial book *Spycatcher* (1985), a purported expose of the British intelligence services, was banned in Britain for several years under the Official Secrets Act and was the subject of fierce legal battles in Britain and Australia (1986–87). Among other things, Wright claimed that Sir Roger Hollis had been a Soviet agent—the so-called "Fifth Man."

Wright, Richard (1908–1960). American novelist and social critic. The son of black sharecroppers, Wright was an errand boy in Memphis when he borrowed his white employer's library card and steeped himself in the work of such socially-conscious writers as Theodore DREISER and Sinclair LEWIS. During the Depression of the 1930s he joined the FEDERAL WRITERS PROJECT and directed the Federal Negro Theater. His collection of stories *Uncle Tom's Children* (1938) won a prize as best book submitted by anyone in the project. As Harlem editor of the *Daily Worker* (1940), he displeased fellow communists, which led to a troubled disaffiliation from the party and eventually to expatriation from America. Considered by many the most important black writer of his time, he also wrote his autobiography *Black Boy* (1945) and several books about the lives of blacks around the world.

For further reading:

Miller, Eugene E., *Voice of a Native Son: The Poetics of Richard Wright*. Jackson, Miss.: University Press of Mississippi, 1990.

Gayle, Addison, *Ordeal of a Native Son*. New York: Peter Smith, 1983.

Wright, Sewall (1889–1988). American geneticist who is widely regarded as the foremost U.S. evolutionary theorist of the 20th century. Together with R.A. Fisher and J.B.S. HALDANE of Great Britain, he founded the field of population genetics, thus providing a mathematical underpinning for the 19th-century theories of Charles Darwin and Gregor Mendel. The fourth and final volume of his magnum opus, *Evolution and the Genetics of Populations*, was published in 1968.

Wright, Willard Huntington [S.S. Van Dine] (1883–1939). New York art and literary critic whose detective novels in the 1920s and 1930s (written under the pseudonym S.S. Van Dine) were among the most famous and influential works in modern American crime fiction. Wright was born in Charlottesville, Virginia, educated at Harvard, and, worked from 1907 to 1923 as a critic for magazines like *Smart Set* and *Town Topics*. His first book, *Europe After 8:15*, was a series of witty social and artistic observations written in collaboration with H. L. MENCKEN and George Jean Nathan. He suffered a nervous breakdown in 1923 and, for the next few years, turned his interests to the "recreational pursuits" of the detective story. From 1926 to 1939 under the "Van Dine" name, he wrote the twelve "Philo Vance" detective novels that secured his fame. Vance was Wright's alter-ego, a curious mixture of incisive intellect, great artistic erudition, exotic, eclectic tastes and a haughty, pretentious manner. In the preface to his groundbreaking anthology, *The Great Detective Stories* (1927), Wright formulated a series of "rules" for the genre, demanding the same kind of consistency and craft commonly applied to classical literary forms. Although at the time of his death from thrombosis in 1939, he had grown tired of Vance and had outlived his popularity, he was, for a few years at least, according to scholar Howard Haycraft, "the best known American writer of the detective story since Poe."

For further reading:

Haycraft, Howard, *Murder for Pleasure: The Life and Times of the Detective Story*. New York: Appleton, Century Co., 1941.

Wu, John C. H. (1899–1986). Chinese statesman. A leading cultural figure in the Chinese Nationalist government, he was the principal author of the Nationalist Constitution in 1946. He later served as a judge of the Permanent Court of Arbitration at the Hague.

Wunderlich, Fritz (1930–1966). German lyric tenor, known for his sensitive singing in the operas of Mozart, Rossini and Donizetti and the operettas of Nicolai and Lehar. Wunderlich, whose professional career lasted a brief 11 years, is widely acknowledged as possessing one of the most beautiful voices of any singer of his generation. His first professional appearance was in 1955, at the Wurttemberg State Opera in Stuttgart, in a supporting role in Wagner's *Die Meistersinger;* soon after, he gained acclaim when he substituted for another singer as Tamino in Mozart's *The Magic Flute*. Wunderlich sang in Germany, Austria (at the SALZBURG FESTIVAL) and Britain. He died at age 36 when he fell down a staircase in Heidelberg, just one month before his scheduled American debut. His voice has been preserved in numerous recordings.

Wyeth, Andrew (1917–). American painter; the son of renowned American artist, muralist and children's book illustrator Newell Convers WYETH (1882–1944). The vast majority of Andrew's canvases depict people and landscapes from his native Pennsylvania or from Maine, where the painter had a summer home. His paintings are generally simple in form and subject matter but exhibit technical virtuosity and convey an emotional impact. Wyeth's most famous work is *Christina's World* (1948). In the 1980s, nude studies completed by Wyeth in the latter decades of his life were exhibited for the first time.

Wyeth, Nathaniel Convers [born Newell Convers Wyeth] (1920–1990). U.S. engineer. In the 1970s, while working for E.I. du Pont de Nemours & Co., he invented the plastic soda bottle. The bottle, made from polyethylene terephthalate (PET), quickly became the industry standard as it did not contaminate its contents as earlier plastic bottles had. By 1990, 15 billion of the PET bottles were being produced annually. He was also a brother of artist Andrew Wyeth and son of the late illustrator N.C. Wyeth.

For further reading:

Allen, Douglas and Douglas Allen, Jr., *N.C. Wyeth*. New York: Bonanza Books, 1972.

Wyeth, N(ewell) C(onvers) (1882–1944). American painter noted for his book and magazine illustrations. Influenced by the picturesque, colonial flavor of his native Needham, Massachusetts, Wyeth began his art training at the Massachusetts Normal Art School and later studied with illustrator Howard Pyle in Wilmington, Delaware. Wyeth sold his first *Saturday Evening Post* cover in 1903. After a trip West that produced a notable series of Western paintings (1906–07), Wyeth settled in Chadds Ford, Pennsylvania. Generations of Wyeths and a number of other painters, notably Frank Schoonover, lived and worked there. From 1903 until his death, Wyeth produced nearly 4,000 works, including important murals such as the "Pilgrim" series for the Metropolitan Life Insurance Company in New York (1939), numerous magazine and newspaper illustrations, and magnificent work for the Scribner's Classics series, beginning with *Treasure Island* (1911)—arguably the most famous book illustrations by any American artist in this century. Wyeth was elected to the National Academy in 1941.

Wyler, William (1902–1981). Hollywood film director whose career spanned nearly 50 years. Born in Alsace (then part of Germany, now in France) to a Swiss family, he immigrated to the U.S. to work for UNIVERSAL PICTURES (1922). He held a number of jobs in the movie business before directing his first feature film in 1925. His career took off when he left Universal to work for Samuel GOLDWYN (1936). Wyler was most successful in filming adaptations of the works of well-known novelists and playwrights. A notoriously demanding director, he insisted on the best performances possible from his actors and actresses, 14 of whom won ACADEMY AWARDS for their roles in his films. He himself received twelve best-director nominations, winning the award three times. Among his most notable films were *Dodsworth* (1936), *Wuthering Heights* (1939), *The Little Foxes, Mrs. Miniver* (1942), *The Best Years of Our Lives* (1946), *The Big Country* (1958), *Ben-Hur* (1959) and *Funny Girl* (1968).

Wyndham-White, Eric (1913–1980). British economist. He was an expert in world trade and commerce. For 20 years (1948–69) he was the executive secretary and director-general of the General Agreement on Tariffs and Trade (GATT), the Swiss-based international agency set up after World War II to establish rules for world trade. He was considered one of the main architects of post-war cooperation among governments to promote international trade and economic growth, and also played an important role in the **Kennedy round** of trade negotiations that led to reductions in import tariffs (1967).

Wynn, Early "Gus" (1920–). American baseball pitcher. A hard-throwing right hander for the Washington Senators, Cleveland Indians and Chicago White Sox, Wynn had 300 victories in a 22–year season (1939–63). He won 20 games or more in five seasons. He was elected to the Baseball Hall of Fame in 1972.

Wynne, Greville Maynard (1944–1990). British businessman and spy. Wynne worked for the British secret intelligence service MI6 during the height of the COLD WAR in the 1960s. He spent 18 months in a Soviet prison after being arrested on espionage charges in Budapest in 1962. Although he was sentenced to eight years in prison, he was released in 1964 in exchange for a Soviet spy being held by the British. He detailed his experiences in two books, *The Man from Moscow* (1967) and *The Man from Odessa*.

Wyszynski, Stefan (1901–1981). Roman Catholic cardinal, primate of POLAND (1949–81). Ordained a priest in 1924, Wyszynski was a distinguished scholar, receiving a doctorate in sociology and canon law from Lublin's Catholic University in 1929. He took an active part in the RESISTANCE during WORLD WAR II, and after the war (1946) he was named bishop of Lublin. In 1949 he was appointed archbishop of Gniezno and Warsaw and primate of Poland, and in 1953 he was elevated to the office of cardinal. He was imprisoned by the pro-Soviet Polish regime from 1953 to 1956. After his release, he worked to achieve reconciliation between the church and the communist government, thus strengthening the church's position within Poland. With the rise of the SOLIDARITY movement, he met often with Lech WALESA and government officials, becoming an active force in mediating disputes between the unions and the Polish authorities.

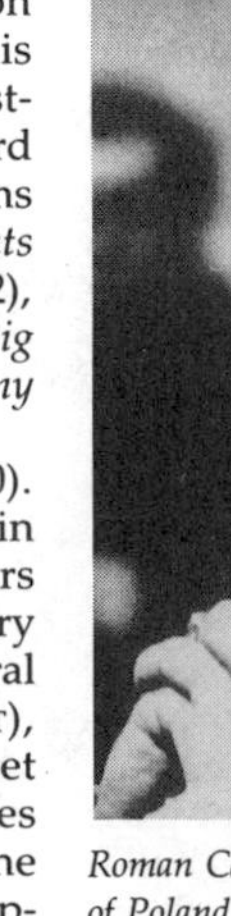

Roman Catholic Cardinal Stefan Wyszynski, primate of Poland from 1949 to 1981.

Xian. Capital of China's SHENSI province, on the Wei River about 80 miles upstream from the confluence of the Wei and the Yellow River. In 1900 it was besieged by the Boxers (see BOXER UPRISING), and in 1902 the Emperor and Dowager Empress took refuge here. In the 20th century, however, it is best known as the site of the XIAN INCIDENT.

Xian Incident. Kidnapping of CHIANG KAI-SHEK by ZHANG XUELIANG in the city of XIAN in 1936. At the time, Chiang was planning to attack and destroy Chinese communist forces in northwestern China and had traveled to Xian to announce the offensive. The powerful warlord Zhang feared a split in China that would jeopardize the country's opposition to Japanese aggression. The bold kidnapping forced Chiang to agree to cooperate with the communists. After announcing this agreement, Chiang was released in December 1936, and the period of uneasy cooperation between communist and Nationalist forces lasted until the end of WORLD WAR II. The truce also allowed the communists to regroup, gather strength and position themselves to take over the government of China in 1949.

X ray. A form of energy—electromagnetic radiation—with an extremely short wavelengths. X rays are produced naturally by the sun, but were only discovered in 1895 by German physicist Wilhelm Roentgen. Because of its short wavelength, X rays can penetrate all but the densest materials. Artificially-generated X rays have a myriad of medical, scientific and industrial applications. They have become indispensable in the diagnosis of injury and disease. They are also used to shrink and destroy cancerous tumors. However, overexposure to X rays can cause cancers.

X series aircraft. Experimental rocket-powered aircraft. Developed by the U.S. to test and expand the limits of aircraft, the single-seat planes set records for speed and altitude. The prototype **X-1** was designed to reach supersonic speeds. The sleek winged craft was launched from the belly of a B-29. Powered by a liquid oxygen and ethyl-alcohol engine, it first went beyond the speed of sound (Mach 1) on October 14, 1947, piloted by Colonel Charles E. (Chuck) YEAGER. The next in the series was the **X-2,** taken aloft by a B-50 bomber. The first of these aluminum-steel planes with stainless steel wings exploded on its maiden test flight, killing pilot Skip Ziegler and a member of the B-50 crew. In subsequent flights, the aircraft achieved speeds of Mach 2.93 and a height of 126,200 ft. On its last flight on September 27, 1956, pilot Milburn Apt flew the plane at Mach 3.196 (2,094 mph) before crashing. The **X-15,** the last in the series, was a joint project of the Air Force, the Navy and the National Advisory Committee for Aeronautics (later the NATIONAL AERONAUTICS AND SPACE ADMINISTRATION). It had a wingspan of 22 ft. and was crafted of stainless steel and titanium covered by a chrome-nickel alloy and coated with a silicon-based substance to reduce the temperature of its skin at supersonic speeds. Its seat was capable of ejecting at speeds up to Mach 4 and altitudes to 120,000 ft. With a rocket engine producing 57,300 lbs. of thrust, powered by a liquid oxygen and anhydrous ammonia fuel, the X-15 was launched from the underside of a Boeing B-52 wing. The first flight, on June 8, 1959, was piloted by A. Scott CROSSFIELD, who had also acted as a project adviser. After two other 1959 flights using older engines, the first flight to employ the full one-million horsepower XLR-99 engine was made by Crossfield on November 15, 1960. Flights continued until 1967, pushing the X-15 to higher altitudes and greater speeds. On August 22, 1963, a NASA pilot set the aircraft's altitude record at 67 miles (353,760 ft). The speed record of Mach 6.7 (4,520 mph) was set by Air Force pilot William J. (Pete) Knight on October 3, 1967.

Xu Jiatun (1916–). Chinese political figure. Born in Jiangsu province, Xu became director of the HONG KONG branch of China's official Xinhua news agency in 1983 and is China's chief representative in Hong Kong. Prior to his arrival in Hong Kong in 1983 he held a variety of party and government posts in Jiangsu. He served as a member of the 11th (1977–82) and 12th (1982–85) central committees and in 1985 became a member of the Central Advisory Committee. As head of the local branch of the Chinese Communist Party (the Hong Kong and Macau Work Committee), he revamped the party and recruited local businesspeople and professionals. He has served as vice chairman of the committee drafting the basic law for the Hong Kong special administrative region since 1985 and has been an outspoken critic of local demands for democratic reform.

Xu Xiangqian [Hsu Hsiang-chien] (1901–1990). Chinese military leader. He joined the COMMUNIST PARTY in the 1920s and participated in the epic LONG MARCH from southeast to northwest CHINA in 1934 and 1935. After the founding of the People's Republic of CHINA in 1949, he was named army chief of staff. In 1955, Chairman MAO named him as one of 10 marshals of China's Red Army. He later served as defense minister (1978–81).

Yablonski, Joseph (1910–1969). American labor leader. Born in Pittsburgh, he began working in the mines at the age of 15. Joining the United Mine Workers (UMW), he rose to be president of the Pittsburgh district (1958), but in 1966 was forced to resign by union president "Tony" BOYLE. While acting as the union's head lobbyist in Washington, Yablonski became increasingly enraged at abuses in the union, and in 1969 he announced his candidacy for the union's presidency. After Boyle's reelection, Yablonski charged fraud and on December 30, 1969 he, his wife and daughter were murdered in a gangland-style execution. In 1975 Boyle was convicted as a co-conspirator in the Yablonski family killing.

Yacoub, Talaat (1943?-1988). Palestinian leader; head of the PALESTINE Liberation Front, a small hardline guerrilla faction. In 1981 the group split in half, with one group remaining loyal to Yacoub and the other to Abul Abbas. The Abbas group was responsible for the 1985 hijacking of the Italian cruise ship ACHILLE LAURO. Yacoub denounced the hijackers as "pirates."

Yadin, Yigael (1917–1984). Israeli archaeologist, military hero and politician. Yadin used his knowledge of biblical history and ancient fortifications to outwit an Egyptian force in the ARAB-ISRAELI WAR OF 1948–49. He subsequently played a major role in organizing the Israeli army in its formative years. As an archaeologist, he obtained the Dead Sea Scrolls and other ancient manuscripts and led the excavations at the fortress of Masada. He served as deputy prime minister under Menachem BEGIN from 1977 to 1981.

Yagoda, Genrikh Grigorevich (1891–1937). Soviet political official. He became deputy chairman of the GPU in 1924 and chief of the security police in 1934. He was responsible for the first purge. In 1936 he was dismissed, having been accused of slackness by STALIN. He was a defendant at the show trial of the "Anti-Soviet bloc of Rightists and Trotskyites" and in 1937 was executed.

Yahya Khan, Agha Muhammad (1917–1980). Military ruler of PAKISTAN (1969–71). A career army officer, he became commanding general of the Pakistani army in 1966. In 1969 he was appointed to lead the country under martial law; he became president later that year. His presidency was marked by civil war (see BANGLADESH) and the simultaneous INDO-PAKISTANI WAR OF 1971; Pakistan lost both wars. Yahya Khan was forced out of office in 1971 and spent five years under house arrest.

Yakovlev, Aleksandr Sergeyevich (1906–1989). Leading Soviet designer of WORLD WAR II fighter planes and postwar military and civilian aircraft. Among the best-known Yakovlev planes in service at the time of his death were the vertical takeoff YAK-38, known by Western military experts as the Forger, and the 120-seat YAK-38 short-haul passenger jet.

Yalow, Rosalyn Sussman (1921–). American physicist. Since 1947 Yalow has worked as a physicist at the Bronx Veterans Administration Hospital in New York City. Together with Solomon A. Berson in the 1950s, she developed the technique of radioimmunoassay (RIA), which enables the detection of minute substances in plasma and other bodily tissues. This duo's collaborative efforts, which lasted 22 years, began by using radioisotopes to measure blood volume, assess the distribution of serum protein in bodily tissues, and diagnose thyroid disease. Their subsequent investigations into diabetes led to their published description of RIA in 1959. The many uses for RIA include detecting drugs in bodily fluids or tissues, screening blood for the hepatitis virus, early cancer detection, and measuring levels of neurotransmitters and hormones. In 1977 she shared the 1977 NOBEL PRIZE for physiology or medicine.

Yalta Conference. World War II summit meeting held by Great Britain's Winston CHURCHILL, the U.S.S.R.'s Joseph STALIN and the U.S.'s Franklin D. ROOSEVELT and their staffs at the Black Sea resort town of Yalta, February 4–11, 1945. Among the agreements arrived at was the Soviet promise to declare war against JAPAN 30 days after the surrender of GERMANY. In return, the U.S. agreed to grant the U.S.S.R. southern SAKHALIN Island and the Kuril Islands, lost in the RUSSO-JAPANESE WAR, and a zone of occupation in

The "Big Three" at Yalta: Winston S. Churchill, Franklin D. Roosevelt and Josef Stalin (February 1945).

Korea. Germany's unconditional surrender was again demanded and its postwar occupation by the "Big Three" and France was settled. The leaders also agreed to convene a conference later that year to make plans for the UNITED NATIONS. In addition, the three powers endorsed the reorganization of an independent Poland, the establishment of free elections in Poland and the fixing of Polish boundaries. Most of the Yalta Conference agreements were arrived at in secret, and a complete text was not published until 1947. This secrecy, together with what some considered excessive concessions to the Soviets by Roosevelt, later brought the American president a great deal of criticism at home and abroad.

For further reading:
Laloy, Jean, *Yalta: Yesterday, Today, Tomorrow.* New York: HarperCollins, 1990.

Yamamoto, Isoruko (1884–1943). Japanese admiral. Born at Nagaoka, he was educated in Japan and in the U.S. at Harvard University. Naval attache to Washington from 1925 to 1927, he was made assistant naval minister in 1936. Appointed commander in chief of the navy in 1939, he maintained that only quick destruction of the U.S. fleet could assure JAPAN's wartime success, and he was the force behind the 1941 attack on PEARL HARBOR. An advocate of strong naval air power, he achieved early victories in WORLD WAR II, but was halted in 1942 at the battle of the CORAL SEA and at MIDWAY. Yamamoto was chief of Japan's Pacific operations until his plane was shot down by American fighters on April 18, 1943.

Yamasaki, Minoru (1912–1986). Japanese-American architect. He designed more than 300 structures, among them the Federal Science Pavilion at the 1962 Seattle World's Fair. He was perhaps best-known as the designer of New York's colossal twin towers, the World Trade Center.

Yamashita, Tomoyuki (188?-1946). Japanese general. A career officer, he served in the RUSSO-JAPANESE WAR, WORLD WAR I and the SINO-JAPANESE WAR OF 1937–45. A leading Japanese commander during WORLD WAR II, he led troops in northern CHINA in 1939 and headed the successful Malayan campaign in 1941 that resulted in the surrender of SINGAPORE in February, 1942. Commanding Japanese forces in the PHILIPPINES, he took BATAAN and CORREGIDOR in 1944, but was overwhelmed by the Allied invasion under General Douglas MACARTHUR. He surrendered in 1945, was tried for atrocities committed by his troops, found guilty and hanged in 1946.

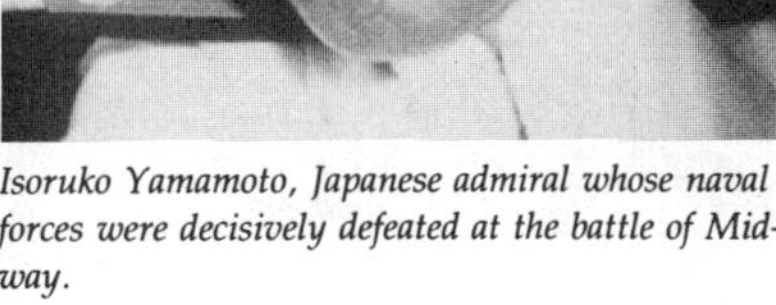

Isoruko Yamamoto, Japanese admiral whose naval forces were decisively defeated at the battle of Midway.

Yao Wenyuan. See GANG OF FOUR.

Yardley, Norman (1915–1989). English cricketer. He played for Cambridge and for Yorkshire, and captained the England eleven 14 times, beginning in 1947. During his career he scored a total of 18,173 runs. He served as chairman of the selectors committee for England in 1951 and 1952; he also remained active as president of the Yorkshire Cricket Club from 1981 through 1984.

Yardumian, Richard (1917–1985). American composer. Largely self-taught, many of his pieces drew on his Armenian heritage. His music was often conducted by Eugene ORMANDY, who premiered a number of his works with the Philadelphia Orchestra. His best known piece was the 1954 *Armenian Suite.*

Yaroslavsky, Yemelyan Mikhailovich [Miney Izrailevich Gubelman] (1878–1943). Jewish politician active in the Social Democratic Labor Party from 1898, for which he was imprisoned and exiled. As a supporter of LENIN he was involved in the BOLSHEVIK REVOLUTION of 1917, but in 1918 he became critical of Lenin's policies and joined the Left Communists. He became a supporter of STALIN and the official historian of the COMMUNIST PARTY in the U.S.S.R. and was instrumental in falsifying the history of the party. He was also a militant atheist. He wrote *Twenty-five Years of Soviet Power,* which was published in 1943.

Yastrzemski, Michael "Carl" [Yaz] (1939–). American baseball player. In his 23 years with the Boston Red Sox, Yastrzemski became the only American League player to reach both the 3,000 hit and 400 homer plateau. An 18–time All Star, he was an outstanding fielder, with seven Gold Gloves, and was the winner of three batting titles. His most memorable season was 1967, when he was the league's Most Valuable Player as he led the Red Sox through a four-team pennant race in the final weeks of the season, to their first title in 21 seasons. Although he hit .400 in the series, the Sox fell short of the championship. He retired at the age of 43, in 1982. Yaz was named to the Hall of Fame in 1989.

Ydigoras Fuentes, Miguel (1895–1982). President of GUATEMALA (1958–63). A right-wing general, he was overthrown in a coup by junior army officers.

Yeager, Charles Elwood "Chuck" (1923–). American test pilot. Yeager was the first pilot to break the sound barrier, flying at a speed of 700 miles per hour in his Bell X-1 aircraft in 1947. He had served as a fighter pilot in WORLD WAR II. As a test pilot after the war, he first broke the sound barrier, then a speed record, flying at 1,650 miles per hour in 1953. His accomplishments contributed to the training of the first astronauts in the U.S. space program.

For further reading:
Wolfe, Tom, *The Right Stuff.* New York: Farrar, Straus & Giroux, 1973.

Yeats, Jack Butler (1871–1957). Irish painter. The son of painter John Butler YEATS and younger brother of poet William Butler YEATS, he was born in London. He lived in Dublin from 1880–87, when the family moved back to London, where he attended several different art schools. During his early career, he illustrated books, created posters and wrote children's stories. Returning to Ireland in 1910, he began to paint in oils, and his work was exhibited in the American Armory Show of 1913. He is noted for his expressionistic portrayals of Irish landscapes and seascapes.

Yeats, John Butler (1839–1922). Irish portrait painter. The father of William Butler YEATS and Jack Butler YEATS, he began his career as a barrister. Turning to painting in 1867, he studied art in London. Yeats returned to Ireland in 1902 and from then until 1907, he painted many portraits of literary figures involved in the IRISH LITERARY REVIVAL. He journeyed to New York in 1907 and stayed for the rest of his life, while his famous sons remained in Ireland.

Yeats, William Butler (1865–1939). Irish poet, dramatist, essayist, memoirist and national figure. Yeats, who won the NOBEL PRIZE for literature in 1923, is universally regarded as one of the greatest poets of the 20th century. His poetic output, which began in the 1880s and continued until his death, spanned the schools of Symbolism and MODERNISM but ultimately transcended them all. Yeats possessed not only great lyric gifts but also a remarkably unique vision that encom-

William Butler Yeats, Ireland's greatest poet.

passed Celtic myth and romance, Western and Eastern occult and mystical traditions, and the political aspirations of the Irish people. Major poetic works by Yeats include *The Wanderings of Oisin and Other Poems* (1889), *Last Poems* (1939) and *Collected Poems* (1950). In addition, Yeats was a gifted poetic dramatist who, with Lady Augusta GREGORY and John SYNGE, helped found the ABBEY THEATRE in Dublin. Plays by Yeats include *The Countess Cathleen* (1899) and *Deirdre* (1906). He also collected and wrote numerous fictional adaptations of Celtic legends. From 1922 to 1928, Yeats served by appointment as a senator of the Irish Free State. *A Vision* (1937) is a highly fascinating and idiosyncratic account of Yeats' mystical beliefs, while *Autobiographies* (1955) contains much revelatory material on his life. (See also IRELAND, IRISH LITERARY REVIVAL.)

For further reading:

Ellmann, Richard, *The Identity of Yeats* (2nd edition, reissue). New York: Oxford University Press, 1985.

Jeffares, A. Norman, *W.B. Yeats: A New Biography*. New York: Farrar, Straus & Giroux, 1989.

MacLiammoir, Micheal, *W.B. Yeats and His World*. New York: Macmillan, 1978.

Yefimov, Michael Nikiforovich (1881–1920). Russian pilot. In 1910 he won first prize in aviation competitions at Nice and at St. Petersburg and was appointed the first Russian pilot instructor of military aviation. In 1920 he was shot by White Guards in Sevastopol.

Yegorov, Boris (1937–). Soviet cosmonaut; made a one-day flight aboard the Soviet Voskhod 1 mission (October 12, 1964). The first physician to fly in space, he observed the effects of weightlessness on fellow cosmonauts Vladimir Komarov and Konstantin Feoktistov.

Ye Jianying (1897–1986). Chinese army officer. A survivor of the LONG MARCH OF 1934–35, he was CHINA's defense minister from 1975 to 1978. He also held the ceremonial post of head of state from 1978 to 1983. His retirement as head of state, purportedly due to ill health, was widely seen as buttressing the faction led by DENG XIAOPING. As the most renowned survivor of the military old guard, Ye had come to symbolize the entrenched conservatism that Deng was trying to eliminate.

Yeltsin, Boris Nikolayevich (1931–). Russian political figure. Born in the Ural Mountains, the son of peasants, Yeltsin was educated as a civil engineer. He joined the COMMUNIST PARTY and quickly rose in its ranks, becoming party leader in his home region of Sverdlovsk. In the mid-1980s, new Soviet leader Mikhail GORBACHEV chose Yeltsin to head the Moscow party organization; Yeltsin also became a member of the ruling Politburo. Yeltsin was one of the first Soviet politicians to take advantage of Gorbachev's new policy of GLASNOST, and he publically criticized Gorbachev for what he saw as the sluggish pace of economic reform in Soviet society. Yeltsin's attacks went too far for Gorbachev's liking, and in 1988 Gorbachev publicly chastised Yeltsin and dismissed him from the party leadership. In 1989 Yeltsin's political career was resurrected as popular disaffection with political leadership swept him into the Soviet parliament as a deputy from Moscow. A fiery populist and passionate spokesman for reform, Yeltsin became the leader of the opposition, the Interregional Deputies Group. In 1990 he was elected to the powerful position of president of the Russian Republic and soon resigned from the Communist Party. Yeltsin constantly chided Gorbachev for slowness in reform while strongly advocating decentralization, privatization and the promotion of a free market economy. Some Kremlin-watchers have criticized Yeltsin's Communist background and questioned his intellectual ability, but by 1990 he was widely viewed as a formidable rival and potential successor to Gorbachev.

Boris Yeltsin, Soviet politician (May 24, 1990).

Yemen. Located at the mouth of the Red Sea, on the southwestern tip of the Arabian Peninsula, Yemen covers an area of about 207,000 square miles; until recently, the area was divided into the two separate countries of **North Yemen** (pro-Western) and **South Yemen** (pro-Soviet). Gaining its independence from the OTTOMAN EMPIRE in 1918, North Yemen's absolute monarch Muhammad al-Badr was overthrown in 1962 and the Yemen Arab Republic proclaimed. Civil war erupted (1962–68), followed by governments influenced by Saudi Arabia in the 1970s. An independent South Yemen was formed by joining the British colony of ADEN and the British protectorate of South Arabia in 1967. When the country became a Marxist state (the People's Republic of Yemen) in 1970, thousands fled to North Yemen, thereby precipitating conflict between the two Yemens that lasted for years. War erupted twice during the 1970s. The two countries united as the Republic of Yemen in May 1990, with General Ali Abdullah Saleh of North Yemen as the first president.

Yerkes, Robert Mearns (1876–1956). American psychobiologist. An expert on ape psychology, Yerkes was responsible for Army psychological testing during WORLD WAR I. After earning his Ph.D. at Harvard, he developed the Department of Comparative Animal Psychology there. Following the war he joined the Yale faculty (1924–56) developing the Yale Laboratories of Primate Biology at Orange Park, Florida (1929), renamed the Yerkes Laboratories in 1942.

Yevtushenko, Yevgeny Aleksandrovich (1933–). Russian poet. The poem *Babi Yar* (1961), in which he denounced Nazi and Russian ANTI-SEMITISM, made Yevtushenko internationally famous. Encompassing both personal and social-political themes, his poetry is characterized by a concern for human suffering and oppression. Although a loyal communist, his attacks on STALINISM have caused government censure. Nevertheless, he has been allowed to travel widely in the West.

Yezhov, Nicholas Ivanovich (1895–1939?). Soviet Communist Party official. He joined the COMMUNIST PARTY after the RUSSIAN REVOLUTION but was not well known until 1934, when he became a member of the central committee. He was appointed chairman of the commission of party control and from 1936 to 1938 was chief of security police (NKVD), directing

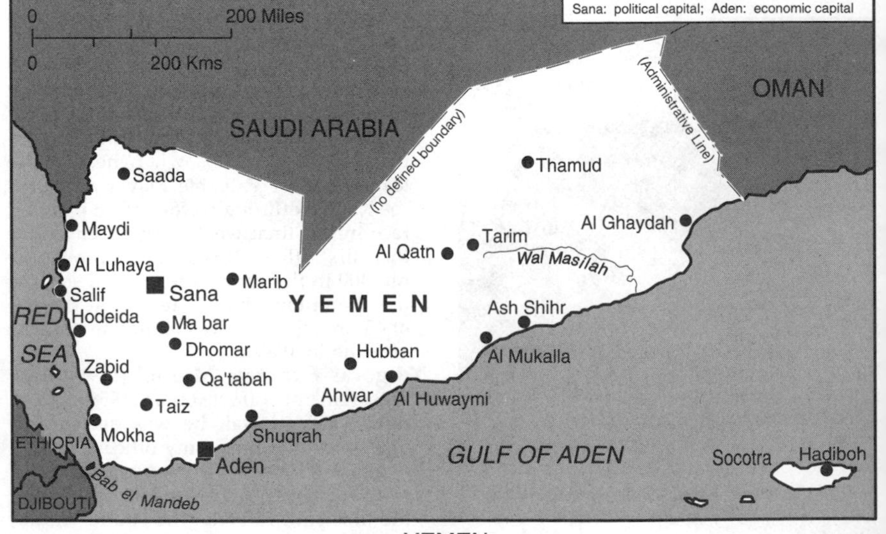

YEMEN

the GREAT PURGE (*Yezhovshchina*). He was succeeded by Lavrenti BERIA in 1938 and disappeared in 1939.

Yom Kippur War. See ARAB-ISRAELI WAR OF 1973.

Yonai, Mitsumasa (1880–1948). Japanese naval official. An admiral, he was naval minister at various times from 1937–45. He vainly attempted to stop the warfare in CHINA in 1937 and later opposed Japanese ties with the AXIS powers and JAPAN's plans for war with the Allies (see SINO-JAPANESE WAR OF 1937–45). As premier during the first half of 1940, he fostered expansionist pressures in French INDOCHINA and the Dutch East Indies. Serving as naval minister during the last year of WORLD WAR II, he pressed his nation to sue for peace.

Yorkshire Ripper case. Case involving the serial murder of 13 young women in Yorkshire in the north of England in the late 1970s. In 1981, following a lengthy and controversial search, Peter B. Sutcliffe, a 35–year-old truck driver from Bradford in West Yorkshire, was arrested and charged with the murders. He was found in a car with a prostitute; and was armed with a hammer and a knife, items that had been used to brutalize previous victims. Sutcliffe confessed to the 13 murders and to seven other attempted murders, but pleaded not guilty by reason of "diminished responsibility." His defense claimed that he had heard voices telling him to kill prostitutes, which eight of his victims had been. Sutcliffe was found guilty and sentenced to life in prison.

Yoshida, Shigeru (1878–1967). Japanese statesman. A career diplomat, Yoshida received a law degree from Tokyo Imperial University in 1906, entered the foreign service and served as ambassador to Italy (1930–32) and Great Britain (1936–39). An advocate of conciliation, he was imprisoned in 1945 for attempting to negotiate peace. After JAPAN's surrender, he headed the Liberal party, becoming premier in 1946 and holding the post for the majority of time until 1954. Probably the most important figure in postwar Japanese politics, he was supported by the occupying American forces in his administration of the constitution of 1947, his implementation of land reform and his revamping of Japan's shattered economy. As premier, he also negotiated the end of occupation and promulgated treaties with the U.S. and other Allied powers.

Youlou, Fulbert (1917–1972). First president of the People's Republic of the CONGO (1960–63). Before independence, he served as premier and minister of agriculture of the French Congo. Strongly pro-Western, he spent three years in office as president of the newly independent nation. He was deposed amid charges of corruption and later went into exile in Spain.

Youmans, Vincent (1898–1946). American composer. Born in New York City, he began composing and producing musicals while in the navy during World War I. After the war he worked as a pianist and song-plugger. He scored his first Broadway hit with *Two Little Girls in Blue* (1921), with lyrics by Ira GERSHWIN. After that, many stage successes followed, making him one of the most important Broadway composers of the 1920s and 1930s. These included *No, No, Nanette* (1925), *Hit the Deck* (1927), *Great Day!* (1929) and *Take a Chance* (1932). His movie credits include the classic *Flying Down to Rio* (1933). Among his best-known songs are *Tea for Two, I Want to Be Happy, More Than You Know*, and *Time on My Hands*. The successful early 1970s revival of *No, No, Nanette* helped to again focus attention on Youmans' music.

Young, Cy [Denton True Young] (1867–1955). American baseball pitcher for whom the Best Pitcher of the Year award is named. Young began his career in the National League with Cleveland in 1890 and continued with St. Louis from 1899 to 1900. He went to the American League with Boston, from 1901 to 1908, and ended his playing career with the Cleveland Indians from 1909 to 1911 and the Boston Braves (of the National League) in 1912. His record of 511 wins still stands. He pitched a perfect game in 1904, and was a 20–game winner 16 times and 30–game winner 15 times. He was inducted into the Baseball Hall of Fame in 1937.

Young, John (1930–). U.S. astronaut; as a veteran of six space flights, Young has logged over 835 hours in space. His first mission was as pilot for Gemini 3 (March 23, 1965); with fellow astronaut Gus GRISSOM he tested the first manned spacecraft to maneuver in orbit. Young's second space mission was Gemini 10 (July 18–21, 1966), during which he served as commander with pilot Michael Collins. The GEMINI missions had been in preparation for America's APOLLO moon series, and in May 1969 Young served as command module pilot for Apollo 10 (May 18–26, 1969), a mission that took its crew of Young and fellow astronauts Thomas STAFFORD and Eugene CERNAN into lunar orbit with Young waiting aboard the command module. Stafford and Cernan approached to within 10 miles of the lunar surface but the mission was only an elaborate dress rehearsal for a lunar landing and no touchdown on the moon was made.

Young finally made it to the moon as commander of Apollo 16 (April 16–27, 1972) when he and fellow astronaut Charles Duke spent three days on the lunar surface while command module pilot Thomas Mattingly orbited overhead. Moving over to the U.S. SPACE SHUTTLE program, Young's next command was aboard America's first Space Shuttle flight STS-1 (April 12–14, 1981), with Robert Crippen as pilot. His last space flight to date was Shuttle mission STS-9 (November 28–December 8, 1983), the first flight to carry the European-built Spacelab. Young had also been scheduled to command the Shuttle launch of the Hubble Space Telescope in 1986 when the CHALLENGER tragedy forced a postponement of the mission.

Young, Lester (1909–1959). American tenor saxophonist. Young, one of jazzdom's great stylists, coined a uniquely light, lyrical sound and improvisational approach. Until Young appeared in the late 1930s as a featured soloist with the Count BASIE Band, virtually all horn players sought an extroverted, bravura style best epitomized in the exuberant work of Young's contemporary and fellow tenor saxophonist, Coleman HAWKINS; indeed, Young's flowing melodism can be thought of as the *yin* contrasting to the *yang* of Hawkins' muscular assertiveness. Young attributed his unique sound to his efforts to replicate the melodious sound of Paul WHITEMAN saxophonist Frankie Trumbauer, who played "C melody saxophone," an instrument slightly smaller than Young's tenor saxophone. In addition to productive stints with Basie, Young achieved success in a number of small group recordings, including seminal collaborations with singer Billie HOLIDAY, who dubbed Young "The President" or "Prez," a tribute to Young's preeminence as an instrumental soloist. Young's beautiful sound and ethereal yet bluesy improvisations have been pivotal influences on such prominent yet varied saxophonists as Stan GETZ, Zoot SIMS and Sonny Rollins. Sadly, Young's playing deteriorated in his later years, which were marred by personal and legal problems.

For further reading:

Buchmann-Moller, Frank, *You Just Fight for Your Life: The Story of Lester Young*. New York: Prager, 1990.

Young, Victor (1900–1956). American popular music composer, bandleader, film composer. Young began his career as a classically trained violinist in the 1910s and 1920s, switched his focus to popular music in the mid-1920s and became one of the finest songwriters of the Tin Pan Alley era that extended through the 1930s. Notable songs by Young include the classic "Sweet Sue" as well as "Can't We Talk It Over?" and "My Love." He led various bands in the 1930s and 1940s but gradually shifted his focus to Hollywood movie scores. The film *Love Letters* (1946) featured two well-known Young songs—the eponymous "Love Letters" and "Stella by Starlight." Young won a posthumous ACADEMY AWARD for his score for the film *Around the World in Eighty Days* (1956).

Young, Whitney M(oore, Jr.) (1921–1971). American civil rights leader. Born in Lincoln Ridge, Kentucky, Young studied at the University of Minnesota, obtained an M.A. and embarked upon a career in social work. Young held a variety of positions with the URBAN LEAGUE from 1947 to 1954. He was dean of Atlanta University's School of Social Work from 1954 to 1961, leaving to become the Urban League's executive director. As the group's leader throughout the tumultuous 1960s he turned the organization from a social services agency into an activist group. He sponsored anti-poverty and job-training programs, but was widely criticized by militants for his cooperative rather than confrontational style. Under his leadership, the Urban League grew into a large and effective organization that was favored by the nonviolent wing of the CIVIL RIGHTS MOVEMENT and well funded by liberal individuals and corporations. Young drowned while at a beach resort in Lagos, Nigeria; he had been there for a conference.

Young Guard [Molodaya Gvardiya]. Organization of about 100 KOMSOMOL members that existed from September to December 1942 in Krasnodon, UKRAINE, during WORLD WAR II ON THE RUSSIAN FRONT. The group showed much heroism against the occupying Germans but was betrayed by an informer; most of its members were arrested, tortured, and murdered. The novelist Alexander A. FADEYEV describes the group in *The Young Guard* (1946, rev. 1951).

Young Plan (1929). A plan for revising GERMANY'S WORLD WAR I reparations payments. The DAWES PLAN (1924) had revised the payment schedule set up by the 1919 VERSAILLES Treaty, but by 1929 Germany was unable to meet its payments under the Dawes Plan. Conceived by an international committee headed by Owen D. Young, the Young Plan reduced Germany's debts and made them payable over a 58.5–year period. It took effect in 1930, but the GREAT DEPRESSION soon made it impossible for Germany to comply. Adolf HITLER abrogated the Young Plan after he became chancellor in 1933.

Young Turks. Coalition of various reform groups in the OTTOMAN EMPIRE opposed to the reactionary regime of Sultan ABDUL HAMID II. In July 1908 army officers belonging to this group revolted in Salonika (now Thessaloniki, Greece), demanding liberal reforms. In 1908 the influential Young Turk organization, the Committee of Union and Progress (CUP), forced Abdul Hamid to restore the 1876 constitution and recall the parliament. In 1909 the CUP overthrew the sultan after an attempted counterrevolution, and set up Mohammed V (1844–1918) as sultan. Some of the CUP leaders, including ENVER BEY, Mehmed TALAAT and Ahmed DJEMAL, took a more nationalistic position than some liberal members, who had returned from exile in 1908, and favored alliance with Germany. Enver and Talaat continued to dominate Turkish politics until late 1918.

Yourcenar, Marguerite [born Marguerite de Crayencour] (1907–1987). Belgian-born author. She was a novelist, playwright, poet, classicist and translator. She grew up in France, but moved to the U.S. in the 1940s and became a citizen. In 1980, she became the first woman to be elected to the French Academy. She was best known to English-speaking readers for her 1951 novel *Memoirs of Hadrian.*

Ypres, battles of. Three important WORLD WAR I military encounters, fought in and around the medieval Belgian city of Ypres. The first battle occurred from October 12 to November 11, 1914, and formed the last of the "race to the sea" engagements in which Germany attempted to turn the flank of the Allies. The German move toward the Channel ports of Dunkirk and Calais in northern France was halted by the British Expeditionary Force, with aid from Belgium and France. A costly battle, it resulted in about 100,000 casualties on each side. The second engagement took place from April 22 to May 24, 1915. In the course of this unsuccessful assault against the British line, the Germans won an unenviable place in history by using poison gas for the first time. The Allies suffered about 65,000 casualties, the Germans some 35,000. The third battle of Ypres, also known as PASSCHENDAELE, lasted from July 31 to November 10, 1917. The British, seeking to break the German line, were hampered by mud and rain; their troops advanced only five miles during all this time, capturing a ridge and the town of Passchendaele. This dirty, hard-fought campaign consumed some 310,000 Allied and about 260,000 German lives. Fighting continued in and around the city of Ypres throughout 1918.

For further reading:

Brice, Beatrice, *The Battle Book of Ypres: A Reference to Military Options.* New York: St. Martin's, 1988.

Macdonald, Lyn, *They Called It Passchendaele.* New York: Macmillan, 1989.

Warner, Philip, *Passchendaele: The Story Behind the Tragic Victory of 1917.* New York: Macmillan, 1988.

Yuan Shih-k'ai (1859–1916). Chinese political figure, president of China (1912–16). He began his career in the military in 1880, and served as the Chinese resident in Korea from 1885–94. Yuan served in the Sino-Japanese War, and thereafter was in charge of creating a modern military force for CHINA. A protege of the dowager empress Tz'u-hsi, he was her viceroy in Pechili province from 1901–07 and was forced to resign from the army at her death in 1908. At the outbreak of revolution in 1911, he returned to the Ch'ing court, where he was called upon to defend the empire. However, he quickly moved to consolidate his own power, encouraging the abdication of the emperor Pu Yi (see Henry PU-YI) in February, 1912 and the resignation of SUN YAT-SEN, first president of the Republic of China, in his favor a few months later. Yuan assumed dictatorial powers, dissolved the parliament in 1914 and attempted to restore the monarchy with himself as emperor in 1916. His plans were thwarted almost immediately when rebellion at home and opposition abroad forced him to restore the republic, and he died shortly thereafter.

Yudenich, Nicholas Nikolayevich (1862–1933). General commanding a Russian force in the war against Japan (1905) and during World War I. In 1919 he led a White Russian army (based on the Baltic) against Petrograd but was defeated and driven back. He died in exile. (See also WHITES.)

Yugoslavia [Socialist Federal Republic of Yugoslavia]. Yugoslavia covers an area of 98,739 square miles in south-

YUGOSLAVIA

YUGOSLAVIA

1918	(Dec. 1) Kingdom of Serbs, Croats and Slovenes proclaimed.
1919	Communist Party of Yugoslavia (CPY) is formed.
1929	Kingdom renamed Yugoslavia; King Alexander imposes dictatorship.
1934	(Oct. 9) King Alexander is assassinated by Croat separatists.
1937	Josip Broz Tito becomes head of the CPY.
1941	(April) Yugoslavia is overrun by the Nazis.
1945	(Nov. 29) Monarchy is abolished and the Federative People's Republic of Yugoslavia is established, modeled along Soviet lines.
1948	(June) Tito breaks with the U.S.S.R.
1961	Yugoslavia becomes a founding member of the Non-Aligned Movement.
1980	(May 4) Tito dies and power is assumed by a collective leadership.
1981	(May) Albanian population in Serbia's province of Kosovo stages uprising in protest of the Serbian administration.
1989	(Jan. 19) Amid growing ethnic unrest, Yugoslavia's collective presidency chooses Ante Markovic to be prime minister.
1991	Slovenia declares independence; European Community intervenes in attempt to prevent civil war.

central Europe. After World War I disparate regions were carved from the ruins of the OTTOMAN and AUSTRO-HUNGARIAN empires and united to form the Kingdom of Serbs, Croats, and Slovenes (1918). In 1929 the kingdom was renamed Yugoslavia, and Serbian King Alexander became dictator, igniting Croat-Serb hostilities. The king was assassinated by Croat separatists in 1934, and Prince Paul governed the country as regent until Germany invaded and partitioned Yugoslavia in 1941. Resistance was carried out by the mainly Serbian, anti-communist CHETNIKS under Draza MIHAILOVIC and by the left-wing PARTISANS under Josip Broz TITO. The Allies supported the formation of a provisional government under Tito in 1943, and the monarchy was abolished in 1945. Tito introduced a socialist system patterned after the Soviet Union, but followed an independent policy and did not join the WARSAW PACT. The country was named the Socialist Federal Republic of Yugoslavia in 1974. After Tito's death in 1980 the country was governed by a Serbian-dominated collective leadership that curbed provincial autonomy. As a result, ethnic rivalries intensified. The country moved closer to collapse and civil war in Feburary 1991 when Slovenia declared its intention to secede and Croatia boycotted a meeting of the presidents of Yugoslavia's six republics, convened to avert the breakup of the country.

For further reading:

Pavlowitch, Stevan, *The Improbable Survivor: Yugoslavia and Its Problems, 1918–1988.* Athens, Ohio: University of Ohio Press, 1989.

Shingleton, Fred, *A Short History of the Yugoslav Peoples.* Cambridge: Cambridge University Press, 1985.

Yukawa, Hideki (1907–1981). Japanese physicist. He was educated at Kyoto and Osaka universities, receiving his doctorate in 1938. He also taught at both universities. Yukawa's work involved the structure of the atom and subatomic particles. He was puzzled by the fact that electrons and protons could exist together in the same atom; normally, charged particles like these repel one another. In 1935, Yukawa predicted the existence of mesons, subatomic particles intermediate in mass between electrons and protons. These mesons were the "glue" that held the atom together. Over the next twelve years, his hypothesis was confirmed by other scientists. In 1949, Yukawa was awarded the NOBEL PRIZE for physics—the first Japanese to win a Nobel Prize. He was director of Kyoto University's Research Institute for Fundamental Physics from 1954 until his retirement in 1970. In his later years he opposed atomic energy research because he believed that it would not be used for peaceful purposes.

Yun Po Sun (1898–1990). South Korean politician. He served as president of SOUTH KOREA from 1960 to 1962, resigning following a military coup by Major General PARK CHUNG HEE. He retired from politics in 1967 after losing two elections to Park, and became a strong critic of Park's government. He was tried in 1979 for supporting dissident organizations. His two-year sentence was forgiven because of his age.

Yuon, Konstantin (1875–1958). Russian painter. A pupil of Mstislav Dobrzhinsky, Yuon was later a member of the WORLD OF ART society. One of his best-known paintings is *A Sunny Spring Day*, executed in a neoclassical style. Yuon was first chairman of the Union of Soviet Artists.

Yutkevich, Sergei (1904–1985). Soviet film director. He won two Cannes Film Festival prizes, including the 1956 best director for his version of Shakespeare's *Othello*. Best known in his own country for a series of films dealing with the life of LENIN, he was honored with the title Hero of Socialist Labor in 1974.

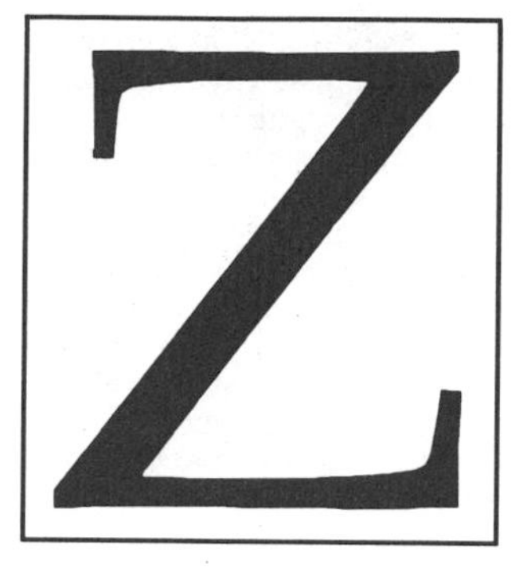

Zabern Incident (1913). International incident that occurred in the town of Zabern (now Saverne) in Alsace, then under German rule. A German officer made insulting public remarks about Alsatians. This led to rioting and the arrest of 29 civilians. The German Reichstag voted 293 to 55 to censure the army for its conduct. However, Chancellor BETHMANN-HOLLWEG and Kaiser WILHELM II chose to ignore the vote—an ominous indication of the army's political influence on the eve of WORLD WAR I.

Zabolotsky, Nicholas Alekseyevich (1903–). Russian poet. A member of the short-lived Leningrad literary group *Oberyu,* Zabolotsky was exiled and sent to prison camps between 1938 and 1946. Prior to this, it is considered that his poetry displayed genuine talent and potential. After Zabolotsky's political rehabilitation, publication of his work resumed in 1948. Something of a puppet in the hands of the government, he has won much critical esteem in the Soviet Union.

Zaccagnini, Benigno (1912–1989). Italian politician. From 1975 to 1980 he was the secretary of ITALY's dominant Christian Democratic party. He played a key role in forging a "historic compromise" that resulted in a brief alliance with the Italian Communist party. Known as "the upright man" of the scandal-plagued Christian Democrats, he remained influential after his resignation, heading a leftist faction of the party.

Zacharias, Jerrold R(elnach) (1905–1986). American nuclear physicist. He directed the engineering division of the MANHATTAN PROJECT, which developed the first atomic bomb during WORLD WAR II. After the war, while director of the Massachusetts Institute of Technology's Laboratory of Nuclear Science, he designed the world's first atomic clock. In 1956, he formed the Physical Science Study Committee, which revolutionized the teaching of high school physics in the U.S.

Zaharias, Babe. See Babe DIDRIKSON.

Zaire [Republic of Zaire]. Located in central equatorial Africa, Zaire occupies an area of 905,328 square miles. First known as the Congo Free State (1885–1908) and ruled directly by King Leopold II of Belgium; subsequently called the BELGIAN CONGO (1908–1959) and ruled by the Belgian government, the country achieved independence in 1960 and became the Republic of the Congo. Almost immediately, Katanga province, under its governor Moise TSHOMBE, seceded, and UNITED NATIONS troops arrived to help restore order. Intense fighting and controversy surround the events of the next few years. In 1965 General Joseph MOBUTU took control of the Republic, changing the country's name to Zaire and Africanizing all place names. From neighboring ANGOLA, exiled Katangese rebels invaded Zaire in 1977 and 1978, and Western and African countries sent troops to help quell the rebellion. The Katanga secession ended in 1983. During the 1980s Zaire experienced student protests and riots (1988–89) and charges of human-rights violations by its military.

For further reading:

Young, Crawford, *The Rise and Decline of the Zairian State.* Madison: University of Wisconsin Press, 1985.

Zaleski, August (1883–1972). Polish statesman. Zaleski was POLAND's foreign minister from 1926 to 1932. He served as chairman of the Council of the LEAGUE OF NATIONS in 1930. Two weeks after the German invasion of POLAND (1939) he was again named foreign minister, and subsequently went to London with the Polish government in exile. A strong anti-communist, he remained in London after WORLD WAR II, and was president of the Polish Republic in Exile from 1947 until his death in 1972.

Zambia [Republic of Zambia]. Zambia is a landlocked country in southern Africa, covering an area of 290,507 square miles. Known during the colonial era as

ZAIRE

1960	Belgium grants independence to the Congo; (May) Patrice Lumumba becomes first prime minister; (July 11) Province of Katanga, led by Moise Tshombe, breaks away, receiving support from Belgium; (July) Lumumba government receives help from the UN to restore order.
1961	(August) UN forces become involved in the fighting at Elisabethville to help end the Katanga secession, four months before they are given UN authority to use force.
1965	After renouncing the secession of Katanga and having gone into exile, Tshombe is invited to return and become prime minister.
1965	General Joseph Mobutu seizes power.
1971	Congo renamed Zaire.
1982	Attempt to form second political party is crushed.
1983	(January) Katanga secession ends.
1990	(May 11) At least 12 are murdered by a masked commando unit during a raid on student dissidents; Belgian foreign aid is subsequently frozen.

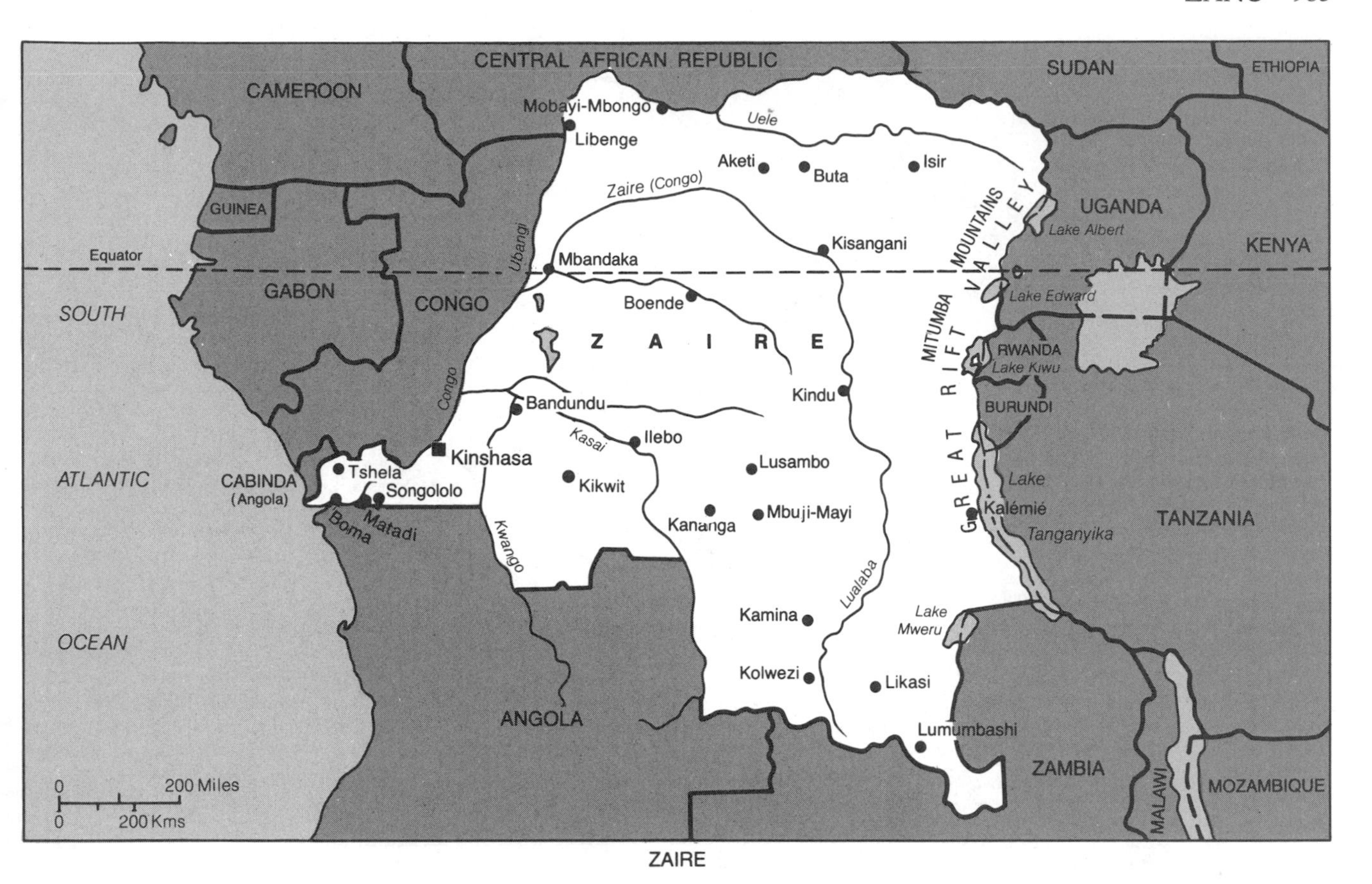

ZAIRE

Northern Rhodesia, the area was administered by the British South Africa Company until 1924, then by the British government (until 1953), which developed its mining industry (primarily copper) during the 1920s-40s. The country was part of the Central African Federation from 1953 to 1963. With the formation of the AFRICAN NATIONAL CONGRESS (1951), nationalistic feelings strengthened. Zambia became an independent republic in 1964, with Kenneth KAUNDA as its only president. Zambia has played a major foreign policy role in Africa by supporting independence movements in several countries as well as through its attempts to settle the SOUTH AFRICA conflict. Kaunda's one-party rule was challenged in the early 1990s and there were calls for him to step down.

ZAMBIA

1911	Northern Rhodesia formed by merger of two British protectorates.
1951	African National Congress (ANC) founded to resist white settler domination of Central African Federation.
1964	Northern Rhodesia becomes independent Republic of Zambia, with David Kaunda as first president.
1968	Kaunda issues Mulungushi Declaration announcing state takeover of 51% ownership in 25 major companies through the Industrial Development Corporation.
1969	Kaunda sponsors Lusaka Manifesto condemning South Africa and Rhodesia but calling for peaceful change instead of confrontation to eliminate racism.
1973	Kaunda signs into law new constitution establishing Zambia as a "one party participating democracy"; Rhodesia closes border with Zambia.
1974	Kaunda nationalizes country's two major mining companies.
1975	Tan Zam rail link between Dar es Salaam and Kapiri Mposhi opens.
1976	State of emergency declared as depressed copper prices cause severe economic difficulties.
1986	South African planes raid Lusaka and other targets in pursuit of ANC rebels.
1990	Food riots erupt over doubled price of cornmeal; Kaunda announces national referendum on multi-party political system; after 27 years in prison, newly-released Nelson Mandela visits Zambia to attend strategy meeting of ANC.

Zamora, Ricardo (1901–1978). Legendary Spanish soccer player. Zamora was goalie on the Spanish national team from 1920 to 1936. In 20 of his 46 international matches, he allowed no goals by the opposing team. This feat prompted a newspaper reporter to write, "There are only two gatekeepers—St. Peter in heaven and Ricardo Zamora on earth."

Zamyatin, Yevgeny Ivanovich (1884–1937). Russian neo-realist writer. A Bolshevik in his early life, Zamytatin became critical of the regime after the revolution. His 20th-century novel *My* (*We;* tr. 1925) anticipated HUXLEY's *Brave New World* and Orwell's *1984*, and also prophesied the reign of STALIN, which estranged him from the authorities. He lived in France from 1931.

ZANU [Zimbabwe African National Union]. Organization founded in 1963 by former ZAPU members to force the Rhodesian government to grant black majority rule (see ZIMBABWE). It was immediately banned. The failure of the Geneva talks on RHODESIA's future (1976) led to increased guerrilla activity up to 1979, when the ban was lifted. In the 1980 elections, ZANU won 57 seats and 63

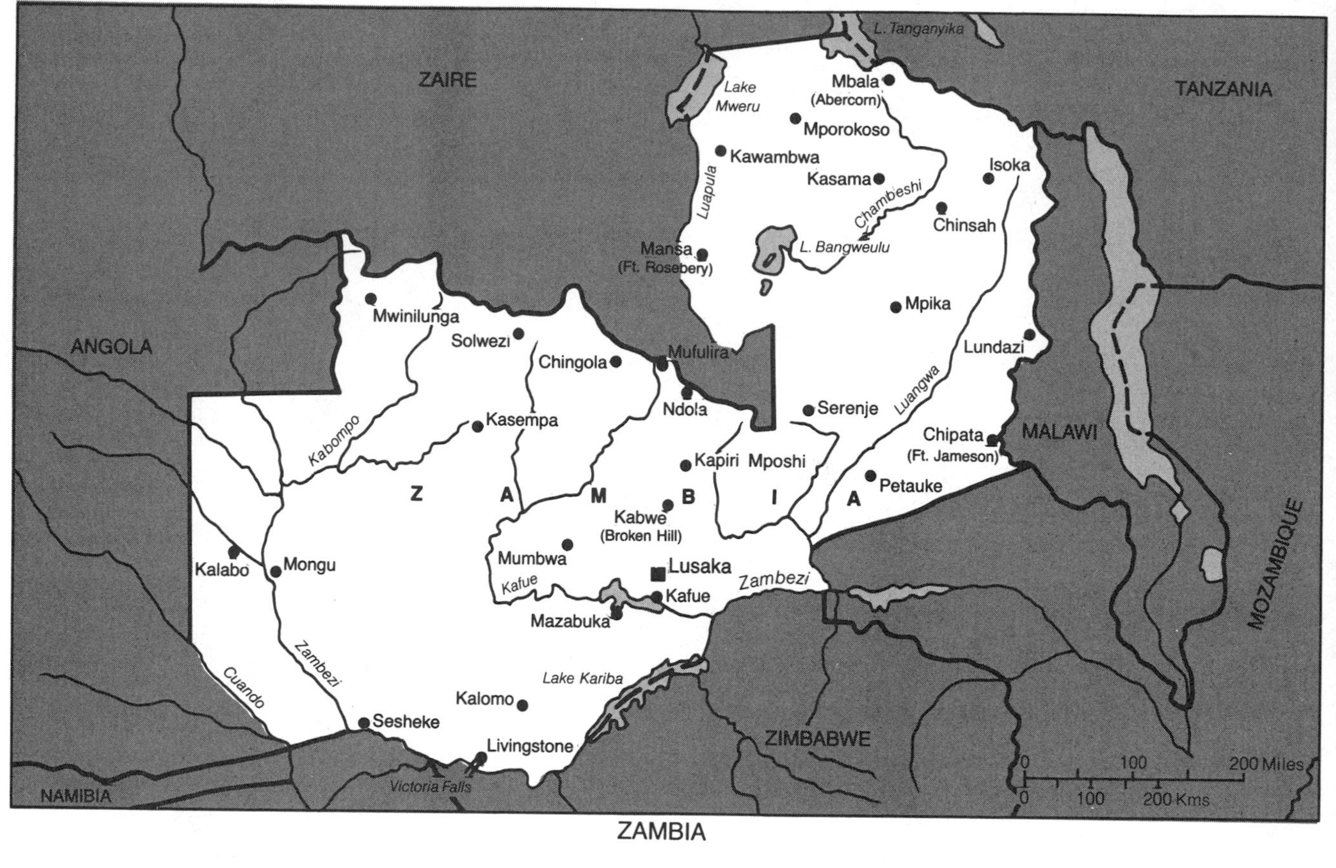

ZAMBIA

percent of the vote. Its leader, Robert MUGABE, became leader of a coalition government that included ZAPU members.

Zanuck, Darryl F(rancis) (1902–1979). American motion picture producer. After service in World War I, Zanuck worked as a scriptwriter for WARNER BROTHERS in HOLLYWOOD. He rose to head of production for Warners and played a key role in the talking picture revolution of the late 1920s and early 1930s. In 1933 he left Warner Brothers, founded his own Twentieth Century Pictures, with Joseph M. Schenck, and in 1935 he combined with the ailing Fox Films to establish TWENTIETH CENTURY-FOX, serving as vice president in charge of production until 1956. He spent several years as an independent producer but returned to the studio in the mid-1960s, retiring in 1971. In a career of some 40 years, he created screen stars and made many popular film classics from gangster movies to musicals, social-problem melodramas and historical epics. Notable films that he produced included *Little Caesar* (1931), *Forty-Second Street* (1933), *The Grapes of Wrath* (1940), *All About Eve* (1950) and *The Longest Day* (1962). He won ACADEMY AWARDS for *How Green Was My Valley* (1941) and *Gentleman's Agreement* (1947).

Zanzibar. Island off the coast of East Africa; now part of the nation of TANZANIA. In 1890 the United Kingdom established a protectorate over Zanzibar. At the time, the population consisted of Muslims (descended from Arab traders), who formed the ruling class; Indians; and black Africans. Zanzibar gained independence in 1963; its first prime minister and head of state were both Arabs. The following year they were overthrown by left-wing black revolutionaries. The revolutionaries established a one-party state, nationalized the Arab holdings and declared a republic. As a result, most of the Arab and Indian population left the country. Zanzibar merged with Tanganyika to form the new nation of Tanzania in 1964.

Zanzibar Rebellion of 1964. In 1963, Britain granted independence to the island of **Zanzibar,** whose governmental power was in the hands of two Arab-dominated political parties and whose head of state was an Arab sultan. On January 12, 1964, the government was overthrown in a violent leftist rebellion by black African nationalists, some of whom had been trained in Communist China. A people's republic was declared; the Arab parties were banned; thousands of Arabs were arrested and imprisoned, and their property was confiscated; and the sultan was sent into exile. The new government, directed by the Afro-Shirazi party (whose supporters were black Africans), initiated land reforms and measures to abolish class privileges. To stabilize and strengthen its economy, Zanzibar merged (1964) with TANGANYIKA to form the United Republic of TANZANIA under the leadership of President Julius NYERERE.

Zapata, Emiliano (1879–1919). Mexican revolutionary and peasant leader in the MEXICAN REVOLT OF 1914–15. An Indian, Zapata championed land reform. He raised arms against dictator Porfirio DIAZ in the MEXICAN CIVIL WAR OF 1911 and then, with Pancho VILLA, rebelled against Diaz's successors, Francisco Madero, Victoriano Huerta and Venustiano Carranza. He was eventually assassinated on Carranza's orders.

Zappa, Frank [Francis Vincent Zappa, Jr.] (1940–). American ROCK and roll songwriter, intrumental composer, guitarist, and vocalist. Zappa became a widely known COUNTERCULTURE figure in the 1960s after forming the satiric and innovative rock band *The Mothers of Invention.* Notable albums by this band include *Freak Out* (1966), *Burnt Weenie Sandwich* (1969), and *Weasels Ripped My Flesh* (1970). Since 1970, Zappa has issued a large number of albums—such as *Bongo Fury* (1975), *Sheik Yerbouti* (1979), and *Does Humor Belong In Music* (1986)—that have featured constantly shifting musical personnel and have explored JAZZ, electronic music, 1950s rock and roll, and PUNK ROCK. Zappa, who in interviews displays a caustic wit directed at all social and artistic pretensions, has become a leading spokesman against censorship of rock music. His two children, daughter Moon Unit and son Dweezil, have also made pop recordings.

ZAPU [Zimbabwe African People's Union]. Organization founded in 1961 by Joshua NKOMO with the aim of achieving black majority rule in RHODESIA (later ZIMBABWE). It was banned and undertook guerrilla activities with ZANU in a Patriotic Front alliance. In the 1980 elections, against the hopes and expectations of Western governments, it won only 20 seats. In 1982 and after, ZANU alleged that ZAPU sought to overthrow the government. ZAPU claimed that ZANU committed atrocities in order to intimidate ZAPU. Nkomo fled Zimbabwe in 1983.

Zeebrugge Raid (1918). After German forces invaded Belgium in 1914 at the start of WORLD WAR I, the Germans converted the Belgian port of Zeebrugge into a U-boat (submarine) base for preying upon Allied shipping in the North Sea and Atlantic Ocean. On the night of April 22–23, 1918, a daring British naval force under the command of Sir Roger J.B. Keyes raided the port, sank three old cruisers filled with cement in the harbor channel, and knocked out some of the submarine operations, although three U-boats did manage to make their way out the next day. At the same time a British raid on the Belgian port of Ostend (Oostende) was unsuccessful. On May 9–10, 1918, however, a similar raid by Keyes and his men closed Ostend's harbor, whose entrance was blocked with a sunken cruiser.

Zeffirelli, Franco (1923–). Italian-born opera and motion picture director. After a troubled childhood—he was born illegitimate and could not take his father's name, Corsi (the name "Zeffirelli" is a reference to Mozart's opera, *Cosi fan tutte*)—he studied architecture and fought in the RESISTANCE in the hills around Florence during WORLD WAR II. A screening of Laurence OLIVIER's *Henry V* and an association with Italian opera and film director, Luchino VISCONTI, confirmed his ambitions to work on stage and screen. In the late 1940s he designed stage productions for Visconti. By the mid-1950s he was a successful opera director, guiding the careers of such luminaries as Maria CALLAS and Joan SUTHERLAND. He is most famous for his theatrically-oriented movies, including the Shakespearean films—*The Taming of the Shrew* (1967), *Romeo and Juliet* (1968), and *Hamlet* (1990)—such opera films as *Otello* (1987) and *La Traviata*. He has been critized for a style he describes in his autobiography, *Zeffirelli* (1986), as "lavish in scale and unashamedly theatrical." He defended this theatricality in an interview: "From my childhood I remember the little troupes of players who would perform with lamps on the floor before them, throwing diabolical shadows on the walls. These performers were the true descendants of the world of Boccaccio. I've always believed more in their fantasies than in anything else. I am always irritated by those who say 'art' must be difficult and only for an elite few. I think culture—especially opera and Shakespeare—must be available to as many people as possible. All my training has been a preparation for the one medium that can do that—the motion picture."

Zeller, Andre (1898–1979). French army officer. Zeller was one of four retired generals who tried to take over ALGERIA by military force in 1961, in an abortive attempt to prevent Algerian independence. He was arrested, stripped of his rank and sentenced to 15 years in prison for treason. Five years later he was pardoned by President Charles DE GAULLE as part of an amnesty.

zemstva. Name for institutions of local self-government for European Russia and the Ukraine, established in 1864 during the period of the Great Reforms. The aim of the *zemstva* was to provide social and economic services. Although they were limited from time to time in their authority and revenues and were dominated by the nobility, their existence and liberal influence achieved much in the fields of education, communications, agriculture and health. The authority of the *zemstva* was increased after the FEBRUARY REVOLUTION of 1917, but they were replaced by Soviets after the Bolshevik seizure of power. (See also ZEMSTVO UNION.)

Zemstvo Union. The union or association of *zemstva* and their professional employees, which acted as a body campaigning for social reform and supported revolutionary activity in 1904–05 and 1917. The *zemstva* were introduced in 1864 as elected local government assemblies at the provincial and county level. They were elected by all classes, from the peasants upward; they had power to levy taxes and to spend on schools, roads and public health. Much of their effort at social amelioration was obstructed by the central government. They were abolished in 1918. (See also ZEMSTVA.)

Zeppelin. A rigid cigar-shaped dirigible invented by Ferdinand, Graf von Zeppelin (1838–1917) and first flown by him on July 2, 1900. His original airship was a 419–foot-long vehicle of aluminum filled with hydrogen gas, covered with fabric and powered by twin 16–hp engines. The invention was met with great enthusiasm in Germany, where passenger-carrying airships flew some 100,000 miles from 1909 to 1914. During WORLD WAR I, German zeppelins made extensive bombing raids, and some 40 of the slow-flying dirigibles were brought down by Allied fire. At war's end, they resumed commercial

The German zeppelin Hindenburg *becomes an inferno when its hydrogen-filled cigar-shaped superstructure ignites (May 6, 1937).*

service. The zeppelin program was virtually eliminated after the HINDENBURG DISASTER in 1937.

Zhang Chungqiao. See GANG OF FOUR.

Zhang Xueliang (1902–). Chinese military and political figure. Born in northeastern CHINA, he was the son of Zhang Zuolin, a powerful warlord popularly known as the Old Marshal. When his father was assassinated by the Japanese in 1928, Zhang, also known as the Young Marshal, inherited his father's army of 200,000 and his status as one of China's most influential warlords. In 1936, Zhang precipitated the XIAN INCIDENT by briefly kidnapping CHIANG KAI-SHEK. Zhang thus played the leading role in preventing a Chinese civil war and in presenting a united front to Japan. Given the opportunity to flee with MAO TSE-TUNG, Zhang instead chose to abandon his wealth and power and to stay with his old friend Chiang, who had him arrested and tried by a military court. Sentenced to house arrest, he remained under surveillance on the mainland and later on TAIWAN. In his 80s, Zhang was finally granted a measure of freedom. He is widely viewed as an example of selfless patriotism and heroism to the Chinese people.

Zhao Ziyang (1918–). Chinese political leader. Zhao was in the forefront of liberalization and modernization efforts in the 1980s. Purged during the CULTURAL REVOLUTION, in the mid-1970s he distinguished himself by his bold economic modernization in Sichuan province. He was called to Beijing in the 1980s by DENG XIAOPING and quickly became Deng's foremost associate. Zhao has also vigorously promoted an open-door position to the West and a conciliatory foreign policy. In June 1989, following the military suppression of the pro-democracy student demonstrations, Zhao was demoted from all his positions and denounced for "counterrevolutionary" activities. (See also TIANANMEN SQUARE MASSACRE.)

Zhdanov, Andrei Alexandrovich (1896–1948). Soviet politician. From 1934 to 1944, he was first secretary of the Leningrad Party, holding also the secretaryship of the central committee. As secretary he was in charge of ideological affairs. He introduced strict political control and extreme nationalism into the arts and opposed Western cultural influences. *Decisions of the Central Committee . . . on Literature and Art*, published by the Communist Party of the Soviet Union in 1951, is an English text of the decrees initiated by Zhdanov. He wrote *Essays on Literature, Philosophy, and Music* (1905). He participated in the defense of Leningrad (see LENINGRAD, SIEGE OF) during World War II, and organized the establishment of the COMINFORM in 1947. He died in 1948, and in 1953 a group of Jewish doctors was accused of his murder, but the charges were dropped after Stalin's death.

Zhivkov, Todor (1911–). Bulgarian political leader. A member of the Communist Party from 1932, he was a PARTISAN leader during WORLD WAR II. Elected to the national assembly in 1945, he became a candidate member of the central committee of the party that same year and a full member three years later. He was named to the central committee secretariat in 1950 and to the politburo in 1951. In a steady rise to power, Zhivkov became first secretary of the central committee in 1954, premier in 1961 and chairman of the council of state (president) in 1971. Maintaining close ties with the Soviet Union, he built the Bulgarian economy by stimulating the industrial sector and provided the country with stability for about two decades. In late 1989, however, amid worsening economic conditions and a wave of anti-communist feeling that swept Eastern Europe, he and his fellow hardliners were ousted from office. The disgraced Zhivkov, once the most pro-Moscow leader in the Soviet bloc, soon renounced communism and apologized for his long-time policies.

Marshal Zhukov (center) decorates Field Marshal Montgomery (left) with the Russian Order of Victory at General Eisenhower's headquarters at Frankfurt (1945).

Zhordnia, Noah Nikolayevich (1870–1953). Georgian revolutionary and MENSHEVIK leader. He served as head of the government of the Georgian independent republic (1918–21) and stated, "We prefer the imperialists of the west to the fanatics of the east." He immigrated to Paris when the BOLSHEVIKS took over Georgia in 1921.

Zhou Yang [Chou Yang] (1907–1989). Chinese Communist official. One of the Communist Party's leading arbiters of literature in CHINA for nearly 60 years, he held several influential posts in the 1950s and 1960s, including vice minister of culture. He was purged along with many other intellectuals during the CULTURAL REVOLUTION but was rehabilitated in 1977. Although he had initially supported strong party control of literature and had participated in the purges of other intellectuals, later in his life he became a champion of artistic freedom.

Zhukov, Georgi Konstantinovich (1896–1974). Marshal of the Soviet Union. He joined the Red Army in 1918 and the COMMUNIST PARTY in 1919. During WORLD WAR II he was at first chief of the general staff and subsequently deputy commissar of defense and deputy supreme commander in chief of the Soviet armed forces. He was prominent in the planning of Soviet operations and is particularly remembered in the defense of Moscow (1941), the SIEGE OF STALINGRAD (1942), the relief of LENINGRAD (1943) and the advance toward GERMANY (1943–44). On May 8, 1945, he received the surrender of the German High Command in Berlin, but in 1946 he was removed from the post by STALIN, and after a brief period as commander in chief, land forces, and deputy minister of the armed forces he was sent into semi-retirement.

He again became a first deputy minister of defense upon Stalin's death in 1953 and in 1955 was appointed minister of defense. He took KHRUSHCHEV's side against MALENKOV, KAGANOVICH and MOLOTOV, and he became a full member of the Presidium upon their expulsion in 1957. However, he was himself expelled from the Presidium and the central committee and was dismissed as minister of defense later that year. In 1964 he was partially rehabilitated after the fall of Khrushchev and was awarded the Order of Lenin (1966).

Zia ul-Haq, Muhammad (1924–1988). Pakistani politician. A career army officer, Zia overthrew prime minister Zulfikar Ali BHUTTO in a bloodless coup in 1979. Zia soon reinstated Islamic penal laws, imposed martial law and postponed elections indefinitely. A referendum in 1985 supported Zia for president. Buoyed by this result, Zia lifted martial law and allowed opposition parties to form and elections to take place. Three years of political unrest followed. On August 17, 1988, a transport plane carrying Zia, the U.S. ambassador and Pakastani officials mysteriously crashed; all were killed.

Ziaur Rahman (1936–1981). President of BANGLADESH (1975–81). In November 1975, Bangladesh's army chief of staff, General Ziaur Rahman, assumed control of the country after the assassination of President Mujibur RAHMAN; Ziaur was sworn in as president in April 1977. He was credited with bringing some stability to Bangladesh, but on May 30, 1981, Ziaur was assassinated in an attempted coup

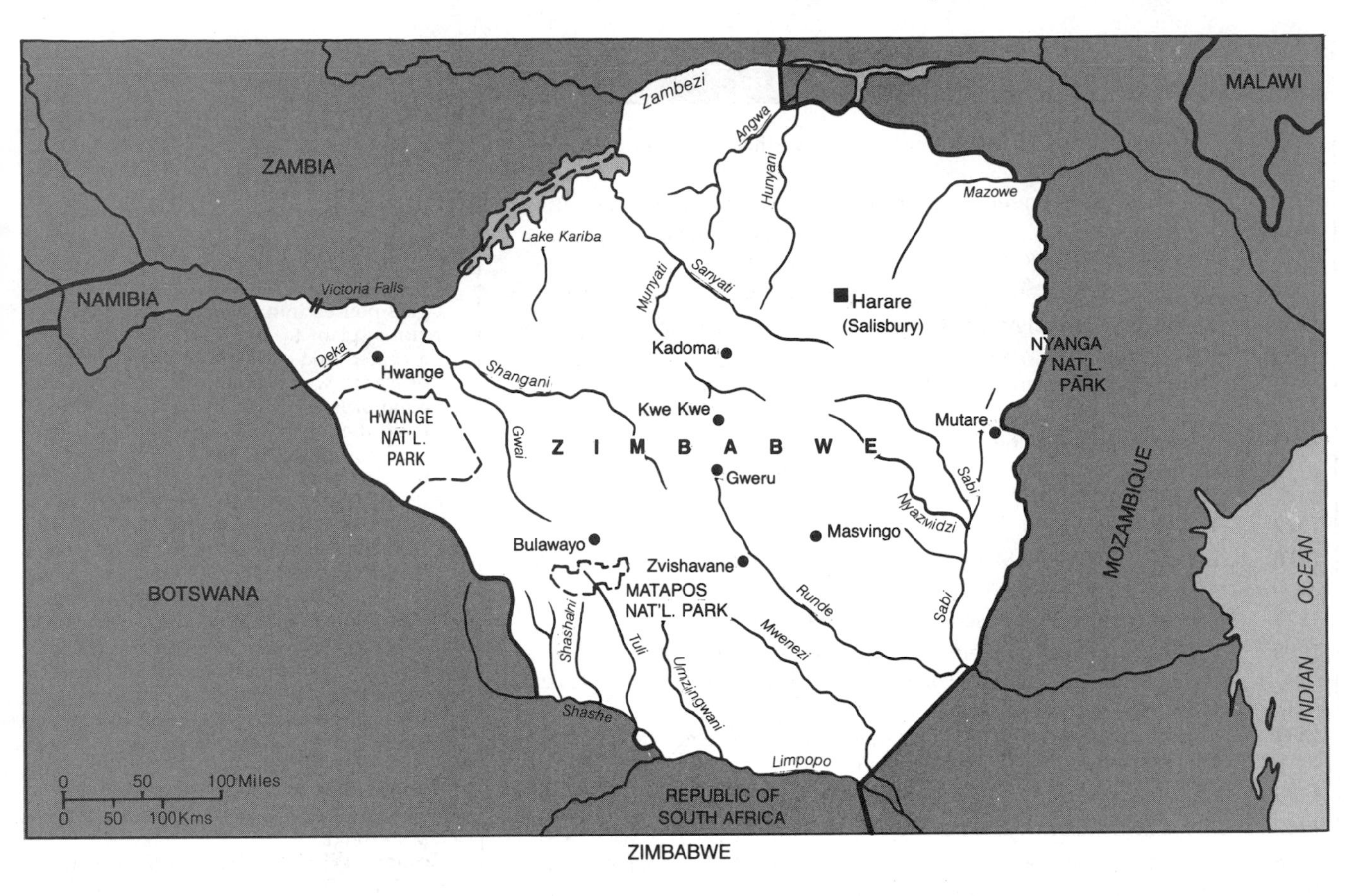

ZIMBABWE

by a group of army officers led by Major General Manzur Ahmed. The rebellion was quelled, and on June 2 the government announced that Manzur had been killed by enraged guards.

Ziegfeld Follies. Musical comedy extravaganzas staged in New York City by the American showman Florenz Ziegfeld beginning in 1907. Modeled on the Parisian revues at the Folies-Bergere, the *Follies* featured lavish musical numbers, top-flight comedians, gorgeous showgirls dubbed the "Ziegfeld Girls," opulent sets and spectacular costumes. These immensely popular shows were produced annually until Ziegfeld's death in 1932 and were staged on an irregular basis until 1957. Often imitated, the *Follies* provided a model for the variety shows that were among television's earliest hits.

Zimbabwe. Zimbabwe, a landlocked republic located in southern Africa, covers an area of 150,764 square miles; known successively as **Southern Rhodesia** (1911–64), **Rhodesia** (1964–79) and **Zimbabwe Rhodesia** (1979–80). The country was administered by the British South Africa Company until 1923, when it was granted self-government and annexed by the British Crown. Led by Prime Minister Ian SMITH, the country declared its independence as Rhodesia in 1965. African nationalist organizations ZANU and ZAPU, banned by the white minority government, went underground and pursued guerrilla warfare during the 1960s and 1970s. In 1979 an agreement between the white government and African nationalists was reached at the British-organized Lancaster House Conference, which provided for a transition to independence based on majority rule. In 1980 Zimbabwe became an independent republic within the British COMMONWEALTH, with Robert MUGABE as prime minister. In 1987 he became the country's first elected executive president. Internationally, Zimbabwe has worked toward the stabilization of Africa and an end to APARTHEID in neighboring SOUTH AFRICA.

For further reading:
Charlton, Michael, *The Last Colony in Africa: Diplomacy and the Independence of Rhodesia*. Oxford: Basil Blackwell, 1990.

Zimbalist, Efrem, Sr. (1890–1985). Russian-born violin virtuoso. Zimbalist was one of the major concert violinists of the 20th century. He made his American debut with the Boston Symphony Orchestra in 1911 and continued to play in public for more than 40 years. In 1928 he joined the faculty of the newly formed Curtis Institute of Music in Philadelphia, and was the institute's director from 1941 to 1968. He also composed. His son, Efrem Zimbalist Jr., was a television actor, as was his granddaughter, Stephanie Zimbalist.

Zimmerman telegram. Secret telegram sent from Berlin by Arthur Zimmerman, GERMANY's foreign secretary, to Count Johann von Bernstorff, Germany's ambassador to the U.S., on January 16, 1917. Composed in a numerical code, it was intercepted and deciphered by the British, who turned it over to the U.S. Its text indicated that if Germany and the U.S. were to go to war, Germany would seek to gain Mexico as an ally by promising the return of Texas, New Mexico and Arizona after a German victory. Released to the press by President Woodrow WILSON on March 1, 1917, the Zimmerman telegram caused a public outcry and helped to convince many to favor America's entry into WORLD WAR I.

Zinn, Walter Henry (1906–). Canadian-American physicist. Zinn moved to the U.S. in 1930 and received a Ph.D. from Columbia University in 1934. He continued research there in collaboration with Leo SZILARD, investigating atomic fission. In 1938 he became a U.S. citizen. A year later, Zinn and Szilard demonstrated that uranium underwent fission when bombarded with neutrons and that part of the mass was converted into energy according to Albert EINSTEIN's famous formula, "$E = mc^2$." This work led Zinn into research during the construction of the ATOMIC BOMB in WORLD WAR II (see MANHATTAN PROJECT). After the war, Zinn worked on the design of an atomic reactor and, in 1951, built the first breeder reactor.

Zinoviev, Grigori Yevseyevich (Radomyslsky) (1883–1936). Soviet politician. He joined the Social Democratic Labor Party in 1901 and its BOLSHEVIK faction in 1903. He emigrated after the 1905 Revolution and accompanied Lenin on his return to Russia after the February 1917 Revolution, but he was not in agreement with the APRIL THESES, the OCTOBER REV-

ZIMBABWE

1897	Final defeat of Shona and Ndebele tribes by British South Africa Company under Cecil Rhodes.
1922	Settlers vote to form self-governing British colony named Rhodesia.
1931	Land Apportionment Act reserves all mining rights and 50% of total land area for whites, who are under 5% of population.
1934	Original African National Congress founded in South Africa and Rhodesia.
1953	British form Central African Federation from Rhodesia and other colonies.
1963	CAF broken up as Zambia and Malawi move toward independence; nationalist movement in Rhodesia splits along tribal lines—ZANU represents majority Shona; ZAPU the less populous Ndebele.
1965	White government under Ian Smith unilaterally declares independence; British impose economic embargo; ZANU and ZAPU wage limited guerrilla war.
1972	Full-scale war begins.
1976	ZANU under Robert Mugabe and ZAPU under Joshua Nkomo form Patriotic Front to negotiate with Smith government and British.
1979	Lancaster House Agreement paves way for majority rule.
1980	Zimbabwe created as a republic within the Commonwealth; Mugabe elected prime minister; huge independence celebration features Western pop stars.
1982	Nkomo and ZAPU members expelled from government; inter-tribal violence breaks out.
1985	Mugabe reelected; South Africa raids ANC bases inside Zimbabwe.
1987	Zimbabwe clashes with rebels from Mozambique.
1988	Nkomo and Mugabe reach agreement; ZANU and ZAPU merged.
1990	Mugabe reelected again; calls for one-party system; white South African businessmen meet with ANC leaders in Harare.

OLUTION or the Treaty of BREST-LITOVSK. He was chairman of the Petrograd Soviet after the October Revolution, became a candidate member of the Politburo in 1919, was a full member from 1921 to 1926 and was chairman of the executive committee of the Communist International from 1919 to 1926. After Lenin's death he first opposed TROTSKY and then joined him against STALIN. He was falsely accused of complicity in the murder of Sergei KIROV and in 1935 was sentenced to 10 years' imprisonment. He was retried in the great treason trial (1936) and executed. He became notorious in British politics with the publication (1924) of a letter, allegedly by him, urging supporters in Great Britain to prepare for violent insurrection. This contributed materially to Ramsay MACDONALD's electoral defeat and the deterioration of British-Soviet relations.

Zinoviev letter. Letter allegedly written by Grigori Yevseyevich (Radomyslsky) ZINOVIEV, the head of the Soviet Comintern, to the British Communist party. It called for revolution in Great Britain provoked by acts of sedition. The letter was published in the English press in 1924 and was the cause of a great deal of antileftist feeling. The letter was quite possibly a forgery. In any event, it was certainly a factor in the defeat of Ramsay MACDONALD's Labour government and the victory of the Conservatives in the 1924 British elections and in the deterioration of British-Soviet relations.

Zionism. Movement for the return of a Jewish nation to PALESTINE. It dates back to the 6th-century B.C. beginning of the Diaspora and, later, to the Roman destruction of Jerusalem in 70 A.D. Zionism was mainly a cultural movement until the very end of the 20th century, when it became a worldwide political cause. Its modern manifestation was largely prompted by the widespread ANTISEMITISM of 19th-century Europe. In 1897 Theodore HERZL convened the first World Jewish Congress in Basel, Switzerland to promote the idea of a Jewish home in Palestine guaranteed by public law, and modern Zionism was born. While there was some opposition from assimilated JEWS, who feared for their status, from fundamentalists, who believed only the Messiah could create such a state, and from those who favored an immediate Jewish homeland in some other part of the world, the Zionist movement gathered strength in the early part of this century. Chaim WEIZMANN assumed leadership of the movement and was a key figure in securing the BALFOUR DECLARATION OF 1917, which assured British support. The LEAGUE OF NATIONS followed with its mandate for Palestine in 1922. During the period of the British mandate, increasing tensions and violence between Jews and Arabs and Britain's shifting interpretation of the Declaration led to splits among Zionists. Vladimir Jabotinsky's Revisionists demanded large and immediate Jewish immigration, while the General Zionists continued to favor compromise. After WORLD WAR II the horrors of the HOLOCAUST caused an intensification of Zionist activities and Jewish refugees poured into Palestine. A UNITED NATIONS plan to partition Palestine was accepted and on May 14, 1948 the state of ISRAEL was proclaimed. Since the creation of Israel, Zionists have largely centered their activities on promoting immigration, education, cultural matters and fund-raising.

Zita [Zita Maria Grazia Adelgonda Michela Raffaella Gabriella Giuseppina Antonia Luisa Agnese of Bourbon-Parma] (1892–1989). Last empress of the Hapsburg empire of AUSTRIA-HUNGARY. In 1911 she married Archduke Karl, who was crowned emperor of Austria-Hungary following the death of his uncle, Franz Josef, in 1916. Karl was forced to relinquish his imperial rights following the Allied victory in WORLD WAR I, and died in 1922. Thereafter, Zita lived an austere life in a Franciscan convent in Switzerland. (See also AUSTRO-HUNGARIAN EMPIRE.)

Zorach, William (1887–1966). American sculptor. Born in Lithuania, he and his family immigrated to the U.S. in 1891 and settled near Cleveland. He studied at the Cleveland Institute of Art (1902–05) and New York's National Academy of Design (1908–10) before traveling to Paris, where he studied from 1910 to 1911. At first a painter, his work in Paris showed the influence of FAUVISM, and the pictures he painted after his return to the U.S. have many of the characteristics of CUBISM. In 1922 Zorach turned to sculpture, in which he had no formal training. Working directly in carved stone or wood and sometimes in cast metal, he created figures that are noted for their simplified monumentality. Zorach created a number of important sculptural commissions, among them, for the RADIO CITY MUSIC HALL, New York City (*Spirit of the Dance*, 1932), the NEW YORK WORLD'S FAIR (*Builders of the Future*, 1939) and the MAYO CLINIC, Rochester, Minnesota (1954). His best known works include *Mother and Child* (Metropolitan Museum, New York City) and *Pegasus* (Whitney Museum, New York City). A popular teacher at New York's Art Students League, he was the author of *Zorach Explains Sculpture* (1947).

Zoshchenko, Mikhail Mikhailovich (1895–1958). Ukrainian satirical writer. From 1921 he began to gain popularity with his short stories depicting the bewilderment and disbelief of the ordinary citizen in Soviet Russia. In 1946 he was the main target of Andrei ZHDANOV's attacks when the latter began his campaign to impose absolute party control over cultural life. He was expelled from the Union of Soviet Writers and his works were banned. His books include *Youth Restored* (1933), *Russia Laughs* (tr. 1935), *The Woman Who Could Not Read* (tr. 1940) and *The Wonderful Dog* (tr. 1942).

Zubatov, Sergei Vasilyevich (1864–1917). Chief of the Moscow Okhrana (1890–1903) (see SECRET POLICE). In 1901 he founded, with others, a society of mutual help for workers in mechanical production. Under police protection this society flourished and legal trade unions were established in Minsk, Odessa and St. Petersburg. He was able to maintain control of the movement in Moscow, but elsewhere the unions got out of control and were used for revolutionary purposes. In 1903 the government withdrew its protection and Zubatov was dismissed.

Zuckerman, Yitzhak (1915?-1981). Leader of the Polish RESISTANCE movement during WORLD WAR II. Zuckerman was the last commander of the Jewish uprising against the Nazis in the Warsaw ghetto in 1943–44 (see WARSAW UPRISING). He led the ghetto's survivors to safety through the city's sewer system. He was later part of an underground network that transported Jewish survivors to the Mediterranean coast and thence to PALESTINE. He settled in Palestine (now ISRAEL) after the war, and later helped establish a Tel Aviv museum memorializing the HOLOCAUST.

Zukor, Adolph (1873–1976). Zukor was perhaps the most ambitious, most powerful and most successful of all the HOLLYWOOD movie studio moguls. Born in Risce, Hungary, he immigrated to New York's Lower East Side at the age of 15 in 1888. By 1912 he had worked his way up from store sweeper, fur salesman and theater owner to successful film distributor. With Daniel Frohman he formed one of the first important production studios, Famous Players, with the express intent of bringing famous stage stars to feature-length movies. After several mergers and an active campaign to acquire theaters, Zukor transformed the studio into PARAMOUNT PICTURES, serving as its president until 1936. His policy of integrating production, distribution and exhibition under one corporate roof revolutionized a chaotic system. Zukor helped put the industry on a sound economic footing by creating a reliable supply and constant demand, at the same time making it a respectable, legitimate business. Zukor eventually became chairman of the board and for the remainder of his days was the gray eminence of the corporation, downplaying to the very end his status as the greatest of all the moguls—but attesting to that in his autobiography *The Public Is Never Wrong* (1953). In 1949 his "contributions to the industry" earned Zukor a special ACADEMY AWARD. Having once sworn to outlive his enemies, he lived to the age of 103.

For further reading:

Zukor, Adolph, *The Public Is Never Wrong*. New York: G.P. Putnam's Sons, 1953.

Zweig, Stefan (1881–1942). Austrian-born Jewish novelist, story writer, poet, playwright and biographer. Zweig was a gifted and versatile writer who was one of the most popular German-language writers in the decades between the two world wars. His works for the theater include the pacifist play *Jeremias* (1917) and an adaptation of *Volpone* (1926), from the Elizabethan playwright Ben Jonson. As a popular biographer, he romanticized subjects ranging from the Renaissance humanist Erasmus of Rotterdam (1934) to the Spanish explorer Ferdinand Magellan (1938). His best-known work of fiction is the novella *The Royal Game* (1944). *The World of Yesterday* (1943) is his autobiography. Zweig's lyric adaptations of Jewish folktales were collected in *Legends* (1945). Due to his Jewish background, Zweig was compelled to flee Austria. In despair over the Nazi conquests, Zweig committed suicide in Brazil in 1942.

Zworykin, Vladimir Kosma (1889–1982). Russian-American physicist who made a number of contributions to electron optics and invented the first electronic scanning television camera—the iconoscope. Zworykin studied electrical engineering at St. Petersburg (now Leningrad), graduated in 1912 and served in WORLD WAR I as a radio officer in the Russian army. He moved to America in 1919 and joined the Westinghouse Electric Corporation in 1920 and the Radio Corporation of America (RCA) in 1929; that year he successfully transmitted a picture from a television camera onto a cathode-ray tube.

INDEX

Boldface numbers indicate main headings. Italic numbers and asterisks indicate illustrations.

A

B

C

E

G

K

L

N

O

P

Q

R

T

U

Walker, Joseph (1921-1966), **943**
Walker, Margaret, 374
Wall, Max (1908-1990), **943**
Wallace, Chris, 611
Wallace, De Witt, 756
Wallace, George Corley (1919-), 450, 548, **944***
Wallace, Henry A. (1888-1965), 661, 881, **944**, *944*
Wallace, Irving (1916-1990), **944**
Wallace, Mike, 833
Wallenberg, Raoul (1912-?), **944**
Wallenstein, Alfred (1898-1983), **944**
Waller, Thomas "Fats" (1904-1943), **944–945**, *945*
Wallis, Sir Barnes Neville (1887-1979), **945**
Wallis, Hal B. (1899-1986), **945**
Wallis and Futuna Islands, **945**
Wall Street Journal, The (newspaper), **945**
Walpole, Sir Hugh (1884-1941), **945**
Walser, Martin, 398
Walser, Robert (1878-1956), **945**
Walsh, Raoul (1887-1980), **945**
Walter, Bruno (1876-1962), 376, 548, 581, **945**
Walters, Barbara (1931-), 437, **945–946**
Walton, E. T. S., 208
Walton, Sir William (Turner) (1902-1983), 555, **946**
Wandrei, Donald
Lovecraft, 569
Wang, An (1920-1990), **946**
Wang Ching-wei (1883-1944), **946**
Wangchuk, Sir Ugyen, 102
Wanger, Walter, 916
Wang Hongwen, 359
Wankel, Felix (1902-1988), **946**
Wannsee Conference, 297, 328, 439
War Admiral (racehorse) (1934-1959), **946**
Warburg, E.M.M., 518
Warburg, H., 275
War Communism, **946**
Lavrenyov, 540
war criminals
Rauff, 755
Ward, Dame Barbara (1914-1981), **946**
Ward, Joseph, 556
Warhol, Andy (1927-1987), *238*, **946***
Warner, Jack L. (1892-1978), 908, **946**
Warner Bros., **946–947**
"War of the Worlds" broadcast, **947**
War Relocation Authority, 646
Warren, Earl (1891-1974), 140, 264, 341, 624, **947***
Warren, Harry (1893-1981), **947**
Warren, Lingan A. (1889-1984), **947**
Warren, Robert Penn (1905-1989), 24, 137, 264, 351, 512, **947**
Warren Commission, 509, **947**
wars—*See specific wars and battles (e.g., Pork Chop Hill)*
Warsaw Pact, 37, 209, 243, 529, **948**
Warsaw Uprising, 63, **948***, 991
Washington, Booker T. (1856-1915), 281, 361, **948**
Washington, Harold, *907*
Washington Conference, 279, **948**
Washington Post, The (newspaper), **948**
Washkansky, Louis, 75
Wasserman, August von (1866-1925), 118, **948**
Wasserman test, 948
Waste Land, The (Eliot), **948–949**
Waston, Tom (1949-), **949**
Wat, Aleksander (1900-1967), **949**
Watchguard International, Ltd., 858
Water, Roger, 725
Watergate, **949**
Jack Anderson, 30
Bradlee, 126
Conservatism, 219
Archibald Cox, 230
John Dean, 253–254
Ervin, 310
executive privilege, 315
Goldwater, 382
Haig, 406
Hufnagel, 449
Jaworski, 486
John Mitchell, 625
Nixon, 670
Sirica, 832
Woodward and Bernstein, 967
Waters, Muddy, 480
waterways—*See rivers*
Watkins v. United States (1957), **949**
Watson, James Dewey (1928-), 60, 232, 346, 358, *672*, **949**
Watson, John Broadus (1878-1958), **949**
Watson, Thomas J., 458–459
Watson, Thomas J., Jr., 458–459
Watt, Charlie, 776
Watts, Alan, 659
Watts riots, **949**
Waugh, Alec, 949
Waugh, Auberon, 949
Waugh, Evelyn Arthur St. John (1903-1966), 392, **949**
Wavell, Archibald Percival (1883-1950), **949–950**
Wayne, John (1907-1979), **950**
Hathaway, 417
L'Amour, 534
Nathan Levine, 553
Weathermen, **950**
Weather Report, 411, **950**
Weaver, Robert Clifton (1907-), **950**
Weaver, Sylvester, 897
Weavers, The, **950**
Webb, Chick (1909-1939), 411, **950**
Webb, Clifton (1891-1966), **950**
Webb, James E. (1906-), 377, **950**
Webb, Sidney and Beatrice, 317, **950–951**
Weber, Joe, 951
Weber, Max (1864-1920), **951**
Weber, Max (1881-1961), **951**
Weber & Fields, **951**
Webern, Anton von (1883-1945), **951**
Leinsdorf, 548
serial music, 817
Webster, Paul F. (1907-1984), **951**
Webster v. Reproductive Health Services (1989), **951**
abortion, 4
Weckl, Dave
Corea, 223
Wedekind, Frank, 488
Wedemeyer, Albert Croady (1897-1989), **951**
Wedtech scandal, **951**
Wegener, Alfred Lothar (1880-1930), **951**–**952**
Wegner, Hans, 247
Weidman, Charles, 186, 560
Weil, George, 54
Weil, Simone (1909-1943), 430, **952**
Weill, Kurt (1900-1950), **952**
Ira Gershwin, 368
Jacobi, 480
Gertrude Lawrence, 541
Lenya, 550
Weimar Republic, **952**—*See also Germany*
Wein, George, 660
Weinberg, Steven (1933-), **952**
Weinberger, Caspar, 84, 736
Weingartner, Felix (1863-1942), 527, **952**
Weir, Alden, 417
Weir, Bob, 389
Weir, Peter (1944-), **952**
Weiss, George M. (1895-1972), **952–953**
Weiss, Paul Alfred (1898-1989), **953**
Weiss, Peter (1916-1982), 479, **953**
Weissmuller, Johnny (1904-1984), 552, *880*, **953**
Weizmann, Chaim (1874-1952), 474, **953**
Welch, Joseph, 46
Welch, Robert H.W., Jr., 490
Welensky, Roy (1907-), **953**
welfare state, 156, 220, 556, 564, **953**
Welk, Lawrence (1903-), **953**
Wellek, Rene, 137
Welles, Orson (1915-1985), 202, 372, 420, 427, 429, 446, 589, 692, **953***
"War of the Worlds" broadcast, 947
Wells, Dickie (1909-1985), **953**
Wells, Edward C. (1910-1986), **953**
Wells, H(erbert) G(eorge) (1866-1946), 89, 151, **953–954**, *954*, 955
Wells, Mary Ann, 48
Wells, Sumner, 237
Welsh nationalism, **954**
Welty, Eudora (1909-), **954**
Wentworth, Charles, 231
Werfel, Franz (1890-1945), **954**
Werker, Alfred, 328
Wertheimer, Max (1880-1943), 369, 520, 521, **954**
West, Anthony, 955
West, Jerome Alan "Jerry" (1938-), **954**
West, Mae (1892-1980), 388, 420, **954**
West, Nathanial (Nathan Weinstein) (1903-1940), **954–955**
West, Rebecca (1892-1983), **955***
West Bank, 24, 714, 750, **955**
West Cork Flying Columns, 76
Westerman, Clayton, 849
Western European Union, 141
Western Sahara, **955**
Western Samoa, **955**
West Germany, **955–956***—*For specific places, people and events, see proper names and subjects in this index*
West Indies Federation, 73, 274, **956**
Westland Affair, 428, **956**
Westmoreland, William C(hilds) (1914-), 5, 8, **956*–957**
Weston, Edward (1886-1958), **957**
Weston, Jessie L., 948
West Side Story (musical), **957**
Wet, Christiaan de, 812
"Wetbacks," **957**
Wets, **957**
Weybright, Victor, 713
Weygand, Maxime (1867-1965), **957**
Weyland, Otto P(aul) (1902-1979), **957**
Whale, James (1896-1957), **957**
Whalen, Philip, 83
WHA (radio station), 751
Wharton, Edith (Edith Newbold Jones) (1862-1937), 393, 482, **957**
Wheat, Zach (1888-1972), **957**
Wheatley, Willard, 938
Wheeler, John
black hole, 107
Wheldon, Sir Huw Prys (1916-1986), **957**
Whirlaway (1938-1958), **957–958**
White, Byron R(aymond) (1917-), **958**
White, Clarence H., 723
White, Eartha Mary Magdalene (1876-1974), **958**
White, Edward (1930-1967), 184, 363, 395, **958**
White, Edward Douglass (1845-1921), **958**
White, E(lwyn) B(rooks) (1899-1985), **958**
Charlotte's Web, 190
White, Patrick (Victor Martindale) (1912-1990), **958**
White, Robert (1924-), **958**
White, Ryan (1971-1990), **958**
White, Stanford, 888
White, Theodore H(arold) (1915-1986), **958**
White, Walter Francis (1893-1955), **958**
Whitehead, Alfred North (1861-1947), 536, 785–786, **958**
Whitehead, Mary Beth, 63
White Hotel, The (Thomas), **959**
Whiteman, Paul (1891-1967), 396, **959**
Whites (anti-Bolshevik forces), **959**
White Sands Missile Range, 16
Whiting, Margaret (1924-), **959**
Whiting, Richard (1891-1938), **959**
Whitlam, (Edward) Gough (1916-), 57–58, 346, 556, **959**
Whitman, Walt, 374
Whitmore, Hugh, 479
Whitney, Dorothy, 661
Whitney, John Hay, 662
Whittaker, Charles E(vans) (1901-1973), **959**
Whittle, Frank, 60, 488
Who, the, **959**
Who's Afraid of Virginia Woolf? (Albee), 18, **959**
Wiener, Norbert (1894-1964), **959**
Wiener Werkstatte, 243, 637
Wiesel, Elie (Eliezer Wiesel) (1928-), **959–960***
Wiesenthal, Simon (1908-), **960**
Wigman, Mary, 439
Wigner, Eugene Paul (1902-), **960**
Wilcox, Harvey, 438
Wilcox, Herbert, 655
Wilde, Oscar, 303, 372, 415, 481
Wilder, (Samuel) Billy (1906-), 265, 548, **960**
Wilder, Thornton (1897-1975), 419, 577, **960**
Wilfert, Karl, 615
Wilhelm II (1859-1941) (King of Prussia) (Kaiser of Germany), 366, 431, 513, **960***, *969*
Wilkins, Hurbert, 37
Wilkins, Maurice, 232, 346, *672*
Wilkins, Roy (1901-1981), 652, **960**
Wilkinson, Geoffrey, 331
Will, George F. (1941-), 220, **961**
Willard, Jess, 491
Williams, Andy, 897
Williams, Betty (1943-), 225, *225*, 675, **961**
Williams, Edward Bennett (1920-1988), **961**
Williams, Eric (Eustace) (1911-1981), 482, **961**
Williams, Garth (1912-), **961**
Williams, Hank (1912-1953), **961***
Williams, Harrison
ABSCAM, 5
Williams, John (Towner) (1932-), **961**
Williams, Mary Lou (Mary Elfrieda Scruggs) (1910-1981), 502, **961**
Williams, Paul Revere (1895-1980), **961**
Williams, Raymond (1921-1988), **961**
Williams, Robert R., 961
Williams, Robin
"Laugh-In," 539
Williams, Roger J. (1893-1988), **961**
Williams, Shirley Vivien Teresa Brittain (1930-), 135, 317, 359, 488, **961–962**
Williams, Spencer, 29
Williams, Tennessee (Thomas Lanier Williams) (1911-1983), 419, 477, 548, 687, **962***
azan, 506
Williams, Theodore Samuel "Ted" (1918-), **962**
Williams, Tom (1886-1985), **962**
Williams, Tony, 353, 411
Williams, Wayne B., 53
Williams, William B. (William Breitbard) (1923-1986), **962**
Williams, William Carlos (1883-1963), 460
Williams, W.J.
Country Party, 228
Williamson, Nicol, 766
Willis, Francis E. (1899-1983), **962**
Willis, Gordon, 379
Willkie, Wendell (Lewis) (1892-1944), 264, 555, **962*–963**
Wills, Garry (1934-), **963**
Wils, Jan, 273
Wilson, Bill, 18
Wilson, Charles E., 172
Wilson, Charles Thomson Rees (1869-1959), 215, **963**
Wilson, Colin (1931-), **963**
Wilson, Colin St. John, 135
Wilson, Sir David Clive (1935-) **963**
Wilson, Edmund (1895-1972), **9**
Agnon, 13
Wilson, Edward Osborne (1929- **963**
Wilson, Eleanor, 606
Wilson, (James) Harold (1916-), 161, 360, 366, 420, 532, 546, 82 **963*–964**
Wilson, Harold Albert (1874-19 **963**
Wilson, Lanford Eugene (1937- **964**
Wilson, Margaret (1882-1976), **9**
Wilson, Robert, 25, 376
Wilson, Teddy (1912-1966), 384, 437, **964**
Wilson, Woodrow (1856-1924), *704*, **964**
Ballinger-Pinochet Controver 70
Birth of a Nation, 106
Cecil, 180
James Cox, 230
Democratic Party, 259
Edward House, 446
R.La Follette, 533
Lansing, 537
League of Nations, 542
H.C.Lodge, 565
Lusitania, 572
Mayakovsky, 604
McReynolds, 610
Mexican Revolt of 1914-15, 61
Orlando, 691
Walter Page, 696
Paris Peace Conference, 704
Zimmerman telegram, 989
Wimsatt, William K., 137
Winchell, Walter (1897-1972), **9**
Windaus, Adolf, 155
Windgassen, Wolfgang (1914-1974), **964**
"Wind of Change," **964**
Window, The (Albright), 18
Windscale accident, **964–965**
Windsor, Duchess of [Wallis W field Simpson] (1896-1986), 2 **965***
Abduction Crisis (1936), 3
Wingate, Orde (1903-1944), **965**
Winnie the Pooh, 623
Winogradsky, Lewis—*See Grad Baron Lew*
Winston, Henry (1911-1986), **96**
Witte, Count Sergei Yulyevich (1849-1915), 102, **965**
Nicholas II, 665
Wittgenstein, Ludwig J.J. (1889-1951), 412, **965**
Logical Positivism, 566
Wittgenstein, Paul, 965
Wizard of Oz, The (film), 361
Wodehouse, P. G., 116
Wodehouse, P(elham) G(renvill (1881-1975), **965**
Wojtyla, Karol Jozef—*See John P II, Pope*
Wolf, Blanche, 520
Wolf, Christa (1929-), **965**
"Wolf Boy"—*See Ramu*
Wolfe, Bernard (1915-1985), **965**
Wolfe, Thomas Clayton (1900-1938), **965–966**
Wolfe, Tom (1931-), 99, **966**
Wolff, Karl Friedrich Otto (1900 1984), **966**
Wolfflin, Heinrich, 354, 372
Women's Action Alliance, 854
women's movement
Nineteenth Amendment, 669
women's movements, *966*, **966–**
abortion, 4
Jane Addams, 8–9
gay rights movement, 362–36

X

Y

Z